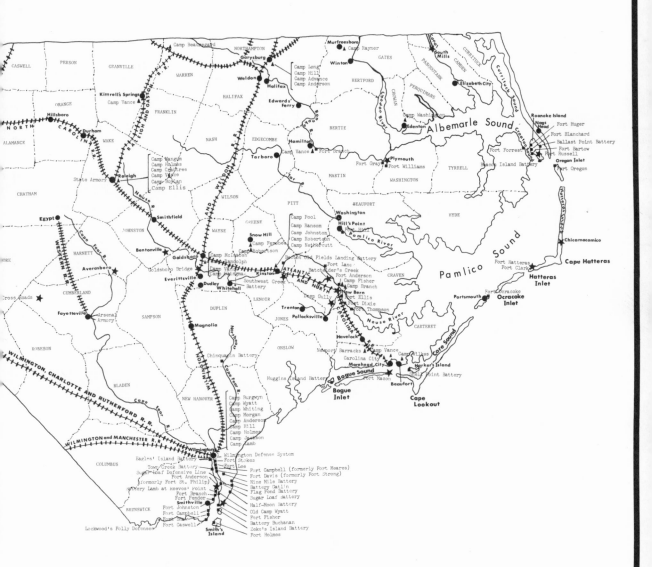

NORTH CAROLINA TROOPS

1861-1865

A ROSTER

Pvt. (later Cpl.) Andrew Jackson Daniel was born in Greene County and was a twenty-year-old farmer when he enlisted in the 61st North Carolina on May 16, 1862. He was wounded in the hand at Morris Island, Charleston Harbor, South Carolina, August 26, 1863; returned to duty in November-December, 1863; and was retired to the Invalid Corps on July 22, 1864, presumably because of disability from his wound. Daniel's image presents a splendid example of an armed North Carolina Confederate. Seven-button shell jackets and M1853 Enfield rifle-muskets (caliber .577) were in common use among the state's troops, as were the style of roller buckle on his waist belt and the type of cartridge box (perhaps a Confederate copy of the Enfield model) barely visible on his left side. Daniel's service record appears on page 707. Image provided by the Iconographic Collection, North Carolina Division of Archives and History.

North Carolina Troops
1861-1865
A Roster

WEYMOUTH T. JORDAN JR.

VOL. XIV
INFANTRY

57TH–58TH, 60TH–61ST
REGIMENTS

RALEIGH, NORTH CAROLINA
NORTH CAROLINA OFFICE OF ARCHIVES AND HISTORY

First printing, 1998
Second printing, 2004

Reprinted by
Broadfoot Publishing Company, Wilmington, North Carolina

ISBN 0-86526-280-2 (Volume XIV)
ISBN 0-86526-005-2 (Set)

PREFACE

North Carolina Troops, 1861-1865: A Roster commemorates, through the publication of their military service records and the histories of the units in which they served, more than 125,000 North Carolinians—African Americans, Native Americans, and whites—who fought for the Confederacy and the Union during the Civil War. The project to publish this series was inaugurated in 1961 under the auspices of the North Carolina Confederate Centennial Commission and was transferred to the Department of Archives and History (now the Division of Archives and History of the Department of Cultural Resources) when the commission concluded its work in 1965. Through the years, thousands of records and manuscripts have been abstracted, and approximately 300 cubic feet of service record data on North Carolina's Civil War personnel have been accumulated. The publication of these data in the fourteen volumes that have appeared to date provides a vivid portrait of the men who served and an invaluable source of genealogical, sociological, and statistical information.

North Carolina Troops has received an enthusiastic reception from scholars, two of whom have described it as a "magnificent achievement" and "the finest state roster ever produced." In this volume, which covers the Fifty-seventh, Fifty-eighth, Sixtieth, and Sixty-first Regiments, readers will enjoy the detailed and comprehensive regimental histories, which are based on extensive research in Confederate records, on letters, diaries, newspapers, and reminiscences, and on a wide range of published works. Of particular interest are the Fifty-seventh Regiment's valiant performances at Fredericksburg, Gettysburg, and Third Winchester; the Sixty-first's equally laudable fights at Charleston Harbor, Petersburg, and The Crater; and the Fifty-eighth and Sixtieth Regiments' service in the Army of Tennessee under Genls. Braxton Bragg, Joseph E. Johnston, and John Bell Hood. Amid the march of events and the turmoil and terror of war, the individuality, humanity, heroism, non-heroism, and personal tragedy of these North Carolinians emerges in kaleidoscopic diversity. There is Pvt. John P. Morgan, whose chronic absence from duty was attributed in part by a Confederate surgeon to "terrori Yankeebus"; Pvt. Robert D. Stedman, who alone and under heavy fire loaded, sighted, and fired an abandoned cannon at Battery Wagner, striking a Federal gunboat; Cpl. Aaron T. Croom, who died of typhoid fever in August 1862, leaving a wife and "five small children . . . in distress"; and Pvt. Benjamin C. Gibson, whose record of sequential Confederate-Federal-Confederate-Federal service, and nimble avoidance of firing squads, is probably unique.

North Carolina Troops is a fitting memorial to the devotion and sacrifice of the Tar Heel soldiers who fought and died for the Confederacy and the Union, for their principles, freedom, or way of life, and for their state. I am pleased to commend it to historians and students of the Civil War, to bibliophiles and genealogists, and—as a compendium of their Civil War heritage—to the people of North Carolina.

JAMES B. HUNT JR.
Governor of North Carolina
March 10, 1998

CONTENTS

MAPS

Illustrations appear on pages ii, xxv, xxvi, and following pages 211, 422, and 592.

* For an explanation of the use of asterisks in service records, see page xii of the introduction.

INTRODUCTION

The service records published in this volume are derived primarily from materials in the North Carolina section of National Archives Record Group 109. That collection, entitled the "Compiled Service Records of Confederate Solders Who Served in Organizations from the State of North Carolina," consists of approximately 125,000 envelopes, each of which contains service record information for a soldier who served in a North Carolina unit. Some envelopes contain original documents such as pay vouchers, requisitions, court-martial proceedings, enlistment and discharge certificates, and letters of recommendation or resignation. However, most of the material consists of abstracts from company muster rolls, regimental returns, hospital and prison registers, parole ledgers, appointment books, promotion lists, general and special orders, inspection reports, the North Carolina adjutant general's "Roll of Honor," and other records. The entire North Carolina collection has been reproduced in a 580-reel microfilm edition (M270) that is available in the state archives in Raleigh. That copy has been utilized in preparing this volume.

A second National Archives source utilized in this volume is the Unfiled Papers and Slips Belonging in Confederate Compiled Service Records (M347). That collection consists of documents and data cards collected or abstracted for inclusion in the Compiled Service Records but, for various reasons, not filed therein. Other National Archives collections of which some use was made are the Compiled Records Showing Service of Military Units in Confederate Organizations (M861); Records Relating to Confederate Naval and Marine Personnel (M260); Compiled Service Records of Confederate Soldiers Who Served in Organizations Raised Directly by the Confederate Government (M258); Selected Records of the War Department Relating to Confederate Prisoners of War, 1861-1865 (M598); Register of Confederate Soldiers, Sailors, and Citizens Who Died in Federal Prisons and Military Hospitals in the North, 1861-1865 (M918); Confederate States Army Casualties: Lists and Narrative Reports, 1861-1865 (M836); Orders and Circulars Issued by the Army of the Potomac and the Army and Department of Northern Virginia, C.S.A., 1861-1865 (M921); and the Compiled Service Records of Confederate Soldiers Who Served in Organizations from the States of Alabama (M311), Arkansas (M317), Georgia (M266), Mississippi (M269), South Carolina (M267), Tennessee (M268), and Virginia (M324).

Material obtained from the National Archives was supplemented by records in the North Carolina state archives. Those include muster rolls, bounty payrolls, militia records, wartime claims for bounty pay and allowances, postwar registers of claims for artificial limbs, Confederate Soldiers' Home records, and postwar pension applications filed by Confederate veterans and their widows. Information was obtained also from the 1860 and 1870 federal censuses of North Carolina; casualty lists and obituaries in Civil War newspapers; *The War of the Rebellion: A Compilation of the Official Records of the Union and Confederate Armies*; the North Carolina volume of the extended edition of *Confederate Military History*; Walter Clark's *Histories of the Several Regiments and Battalions from North Carolina in the Great War, 1861-'65*; the *Confederate Veteran*; the North Carolina *County Heritage Book* series; pension applications filed with the states of Tennessee and Florida by North Carolina veterans and their widows; published and unpublished genealogies; gravestone indexes; biographical dictionaries; records of the North Carolina division of the United Daughters of the Confederacy; and published registers of Hollywood Cemetery (Richmond, Virginia), Stonewall Cemetery (Winchester, Virginia), and the cemeteries at

Sharpsburg, Maryland; Gettysburg, Pennsylvania; and Elmira, New York. Relevant letters, diaries, reminiscences, and other manuscripts in the North Carolina state archives, the Southern Historical Collection (University of North Carolina-Chapel Hill), and the Duke University Library Special Collections Department were abstracted, and useful information was received from professional and lay historians, from descendants of Civil War veterans, and from other private individuals. John W. Moore's *Roster of North Carolina Troops in the War Between the States*, although a commendable effort for its day (1882), is now outdated and was utilized only for cross-checking and comparison purposes.

The regimental rosters in this volume are organized as follows:

—Field officers (colonels, lieutenant colonels, and majors), staff officers (adjutants, assistant quartermasters, assistant commissaries of subsistence, surgeons, chaplains, and ensigns), and regimental noncommissioned officers and other ranks (sergeants major, quartermaster sergeants, commissary sergeants, ordnance sergeants, and hospital stewards) are grouped together by rank under a major heading entitled "Field and Staff." Each soldier is listed in the chronological sequence in which he served. Members of regimental bands are listed alphabetically at the end of the Field and Staff section.

—Rosters of the ten or more companies of which each regiment was composed follow the Field and Staff section and are divided into two major sections entitled "Officers" and "Noncommissioned Officers and Privates." Within the Officers section are separate subsections for Captains and Lieutenants. Captains are listed in chronological order; lieutenants are listed alphabetically. Sergeants, corporals, and privates are grouped together alphabetically in the Noncommissioned Officers and Privates section.

—Following the last company roster is a Miscellaneous section listing soldiers who were members of the regiment but whose records do not indicate the company to which they belonged.

The procedures adopted in composing the service records in this volume are as follows:

—Spelling of surnames and given names is determined by comparing information in the Compiled Service Records with information from other sources such as descendants, Confederate pension applications, the 1860 and 1870 federal censuses of North Carolina, the North Carolina *County Heritage Book* series, and gravestone indexes. Such sources have been utilized heavily. Even so, errors are inevitable, and the volume's index has been extensively cross-referenced to facilitate the location of names that may appear in corrupted form.

—References to counties are as of 1861-1865 boundaries. When primary records indicate that a soldier was born in a county that was not extant at the time of his birth, an asterisk has been placed after the county citation; for example, Born in Alamance County*. Presumably, the individual was born at a locality that became part of the specified county when the county was formed.

—Prewar occupations are derived primarily from the Compiled Service Records; however, the 1860 federal census, the *County Heritage Book* series, and other sources have been utilized also.

—Age-at-date-of-enlistment information is derived primarily from the Compiled Service Records, which are frequently contradictory on the subject. In the absence of a more reliable source or a reason to favor one Compiled Service Records age over another, the youngest age among those reported is cited. It must be candidly admitted that if a service record contains any single item of misinformation, it is in all probability the soldier's age.

—Enlistment dates and places of enlistment are derived, with a few exceptions, from company muster-in rolls or from the first company muster roll on which a soldier's name appears.

—Cities and towns are cited under the names by which they where known in 1861-1865; however, in instances where a name change has occurred, the 1861-1865 designation is followed by the current name in parentheses—for example, Smithville (Southport). North Carolina counties, cities, and towns are not followed by a reference to the state except for clarity (Asheville; but Washington, North Carolina). Counties and localities in other states are followed by the name of the state only in the first instance that they are mentioned in a service record. West Virginia place names are cited as being in "West Virginia" if the date of the reference is on or subsequent to June 20, 1863, the date that the state was admitted to the Union. If the reference is prior to that date, the locality is cited as being in "[West] Virginia." In a few cases, it proved impossible to determine the state or county in which a town or geographical feature was located, either because no such place could be identified or because two or more places with the same name were located and no evidence was available as to the one intended. Such place names appear in quotation marks ("Table Knob," "Warrenton").

—Causes of death, reasons for discharge or execution, and other potentially unsavory, unheroic, or unwelcome information is presented in quotation marks to emphasize authenticity and channel the dismay of descendants toward the documentary source (the malignancy of which the editor joins in deprecating; there is no need to write). Information that is ambiguous, contradictory, unverifiable, or of doubtful accuracy also appears in quotation marks.

—"On or about" indicates that dates derived from primary records are historically improbable or otherwise dubious: "Wounded at Gettysburg, Pennsylvania, on or about July 6, 1863." That phrase is used also when an event that is not a verified or verifiable historical fact is cited in primary records as having occurred on two or more dates that are more or less consecutive, the date cited being the one that seems most probably correct on the basis of available evidence: "Died at Raleigh on or about May 8, 1864." When there is no reason to favor one date over another, hyphenated dates are cited if the dates are consecutive: "Died at Raleigh, May 8-9, 1864." When such dates are not consecutive they are rendered with a virgule or cited individually: "Died at Raleigh on May 8/11, 1864"; "Died at Raleigh on May 8 or June 5, 1864." Hyphenated dates preceded by "during" indicate a condition that prevailed throughout the period in question: "Hospitalized at Raleigh during March-April, 1864." Dates preceded by "in" indicate a single event that occurred during the specified time frame; for example, "Hospitalized at Raleigh in March-April, 1864," indicates that a soldier was admitted to a Raleigh hospital on an unknown date during March-April, 1864. This system was found necessary because in many instances the exact date of an event could not be determined.

—"Present or accounted for" indicates that a soldier was either present for duty or absent for reasons other than desertion or absence without leave. Desertion and absence without leave are terms that were often employed without distinction by company clerks; hence, a soldier who absented himself without authorization but returned of his own accord sixty days later could be listed during his absence either as a deserter or as absent without leave. The editor has judged it best not to arbitrarily standardize those terms, and references to desertion or absence without leave are, in the overwhelming majority of cases, quoted directly from primary sources. In most instances, unauthorized absences of twenty days or less have been excluded.

—"No further records" appears at the end of a service record when there is doubt as to the manner in which the soldier's military career terminated: "Company muster rolls indicate that he was discharged at Weldon on May 9, 1864; however, medical records indicate that he died in hospital at Weldon on May 30, 1864. No further records." Use of that phrase does not preclude the existence of additional military records of any description but of those relative to the important aspects of a soldier's service. Additional records pertaining to furloughs, special assignments, issuance of clothing, and other relatively insignificant matters exist, sometimes in quantity, for many of the soldiers whose service records appear in this volume.

—Brackets are utilized at the end of service records to convey information that could not be readily incorporated in the main text. They also enclose interpolations, source citations, cross-references, and editorial comments.

During the thirty-seven years since the inception of the roster project, rules of capitalization, punctuation, and other matters of style have changed considerably; for example, it is no longer considered good form to capitalize an individual's title or rank unless it appears before his name. However, except in those few instances where a new methodology provided greater clarity or otherwise seemed distinctly advantageous, stylistic usages employed in earlier volumes have been retained. One particularly noticeable punctuation oddity that should be mentioned involves the use in the possessive case of singular nouns ending in "s." Personal names are rendered "s's" (Jones's brigade), but, on the theory that the historic spelling of a community or geographical feature should not be altered by modern rules of punctuation, place-names ending in the possessive are rendered without the final "s" (Jones' Mill, Virginia).

I would like to express my appreciation to those persons who have contributed to the publication of this volume:

—Joe A. Mobley, administrator of the Historical Publications Section, read the 60th Regiment history in page proof.

—Matthew M. Brown, assistant editor of the Civil War Roster Project (February 1994-to date), typed approximately 4,000 service record cards, computerized the 61st Regiment roster, undertook numerous research assignments and special projects, checked the histories and rosters for factual accuracy, made valuable contributions to the readability of both, proofread the histories and rosters in manuscript and page proof, standardized and verified footnote citations, and prepared the index.

—Trudy M. Rayfield, acting secretary and editorial assistant (September 1989-June 1995), typed approximately 2,000 service record cards, computerized the rosters of the 57th, 58th, and 60th Regiments, and undertook a number of special projects.

—William A. Owens Jr. and Susan M. Trimble of the Historical Publications Section provided vital expertise in computer typesetting.

—Lisa Bailey, proofreader of the Historical Publications Section, proofread the four regimental histories in manuscript.

—Henry Mintz of Shelby, the North Carolina Civil War Roster Project's indispensable man, assisted in locating and obtaining Civil War images and manuscripts in private hands and public repositories; Greg Mast of Roxboro, North Carolina's most knowledgeable Civil War historian, provided valuable tips on source materials; cartographer Blake Magner drew the maps and demonstrated exceptional professionalism and patience in going the extra mile to achieve accuracy; Donald Taylor of Kinston furnished information for the Kinston map; Mickey Black of Salisbury shared his impressive knowledge of Civil War weapons, uniforms, and accouterments by analyzing the photographic illustrations and providing information for their captions; A. S. Perry of Raleigh contributed valuable information concerning North Carolina soldiers who were executed for desertion; and Bob High of Whiteville, the roster project's oldest friend, provided valuable information abstracted from North Carolina Civil War newspapers. I am grateful to each of them for giving so graciously and generously of their time, expertise, and friendship.

—Librarians, archivists, and officials at a number of institutions, organizations, and historic sites contributed immeasurably to this book. They include Judy Bolton of the Hill Memorial Library, Louisiana State University; Conley L. Edwards and Minor T. Weisiger of the Virginia State Library and Archives; William R. Erwin Jr., of the Special Collections Library, Duke University; Barbara Fagen of the Cleveland Public Library, Cleveland, Tennessee; Henry G. Fulmer of the South Caroliniana Library, University of South Carolina; Linda H. Jones of the Virginia Historical Society; Donald R. Lennon of the East Carolina Manuscript Collection, East Carolina University; Leon C. Miller of the Howard-Tilton Memorial Library, Tulane University; Michael Musick and Michael Pilgrim of the National Archives; William H. Richter of the University of Texas at Austin; Michael R. Ridderbusch of West Virginia University; Richard A. Shrader and John E. White of the Southern Historical Collection, University of North Carolina-Chapel Hill; Charles Sherrill of the Tennessee State Library and Archives; Richard J. Sommers of the U.S. Army Military History Institute; Guy R. Swanson of The Museum of the Confederacy; and John R. Woodard of the Z. Smith Reynolds Library, Wake Forest University. The assistance provided by these able and knowledgeable professionals is acknowledged with gratitude.

—In addition, I received photocopies of letters, diaries, reminiscences, and other manuscripts from the following private individuals: Larry E. Beason of King, North Carolina; Mrs. C. Knox Council of Jacksonville, North Carolina; James L. Douthat of Signal Mountain, Tennessee; Minnie W. Hall of Mouth of Wilson, Virginia; John Silver Harris of Boca Raton, Florida; Helen S. Keever of Hiddenite, North Carolina; Nancy McDaniel of Roanoke, Virginia; Ann Walker Peninger of Mt. Pleasant, North Carolina; O. A. Pickett of Pensacola, Florida; Trula Fay Parks Purkey of Alexandria, Virginia; Betty Ann Phillips Rice of Roanoke, Virginia; Professor James I. Robertson of Virginia Polytechnic Institute; Al G. Taylor of Greensboro, North Carolina; Donald B. Taylor of Kinston, North Carolina; James C. Taylor of Mars Hill, North Carolina; Rouse Vallotton of Valdosta, Georgia; Raymond W. Watkins of Falls Church, Virginia; and Jeffrey C. Weaver of Arlington, Virginia. To each I express my sincere thanks.

Weymouth T. Jordan Jr.
Editor
March 8, 1998

NORTH CAROLINA TROOPS

1861-1865

A ROSTER

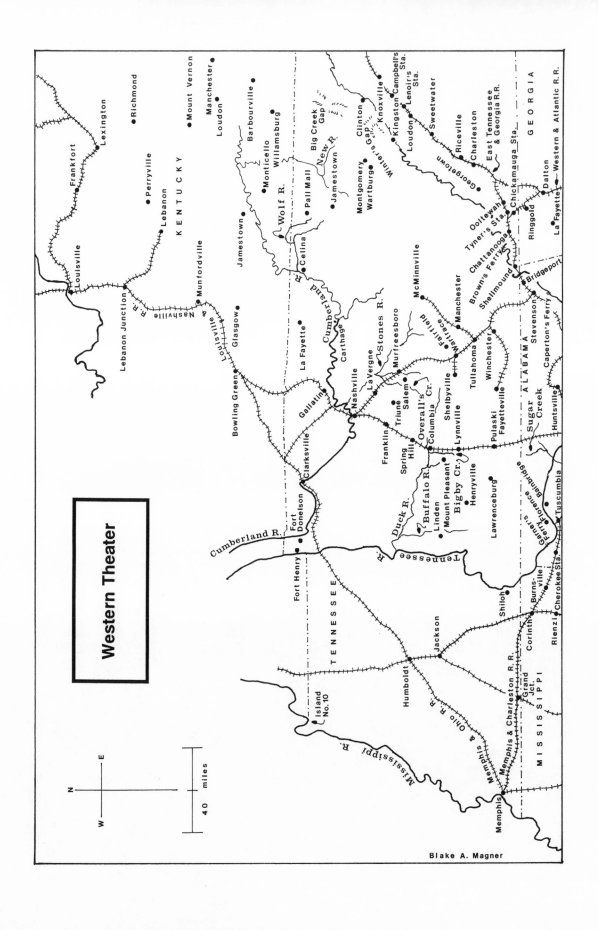

Western Theater

Blake A. Magner

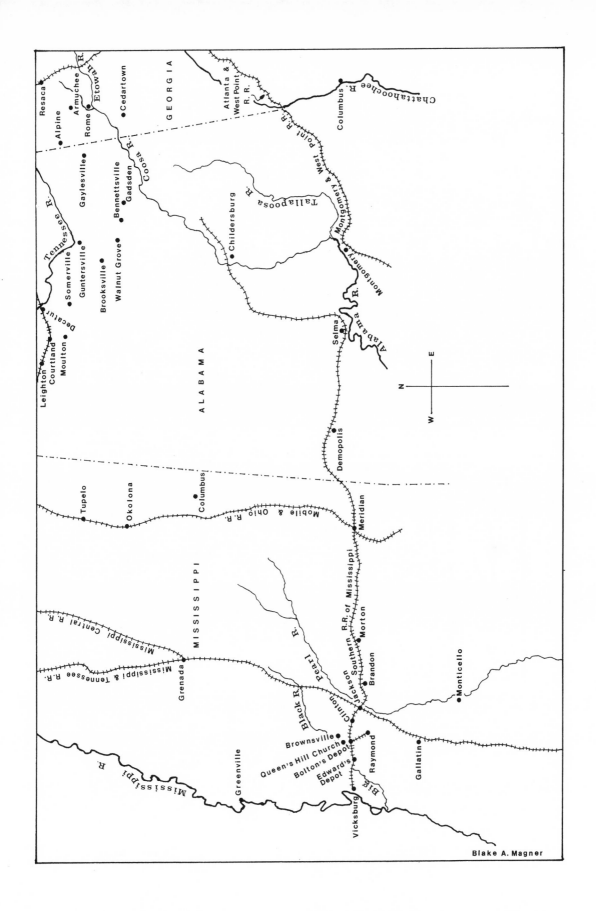

Blake A. Magner

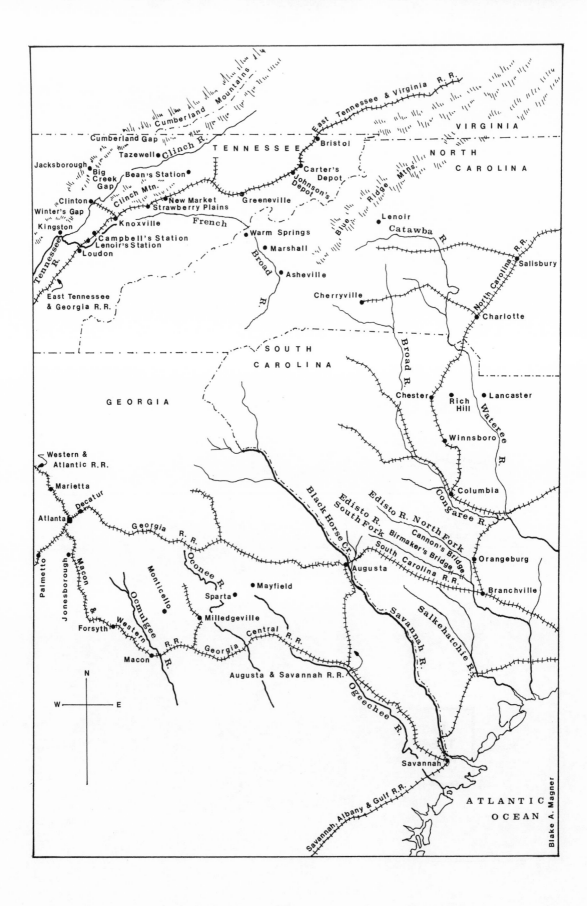

CUMBERLAND MOUNTAINS

East Tennessee & Virginia R.R.

VIRGINIA

NORTH CAROLINA

Cumberland Gap
Tazewell
Clinch R.
TENNESSEE
Bristol

Jacksborough
Big Creek Gap
Bean's Station
Carter's Depot
Johnson's Depot

Clinton
Clinch Mtn.
New Market
Strawberry Plains
Greeneville

Blue Ridge Mtns.

Winter's Gap
Knoxville
French
Lenoir
Catawba R.

Kingston
Campbell's Station
Lenoir's Station
Loudon
Warm Springs

Marshall

Salisbury

Tennessee R.
East Tennessee & Georgia R.R.
Broad R.
Asheville

North Carolina R.R.

Cherryville

Charlotte

SOUTH CAROLINA

Broad R.

GEORGIA

Chester
Rich Hill
Lancaster

Wateree R.

Winnsboro

Western & Atlantic R.R.
Marietta
Decatur
Columbia

Atlanta

Georgia R.R.

Black Horse Cr.
South Fork
Edisto R. South Fork
Edisto R. North Fork
Congaree R.

Cannon's Bridge
Birmaker's Bridge

Palmetto
Macon
Oconee R.
Monticello
Mayfield
Augusta
South Carolina R.R.
Orangeburg

Jonesborough
Sparta
Branchville

&
Forsyth
Western
Ocmulgee R.
Milledgeville
Central R.R.
Savannah R.
Salkehatchie R.

Macon
R.R.
Georgia
Augusta & Savannah R.R.

N

W — E

Ogeechee R.

Savannah

Savannah, Albany & Gulf R.R.

ATLANTIC OCEAN

Blake A. Magner

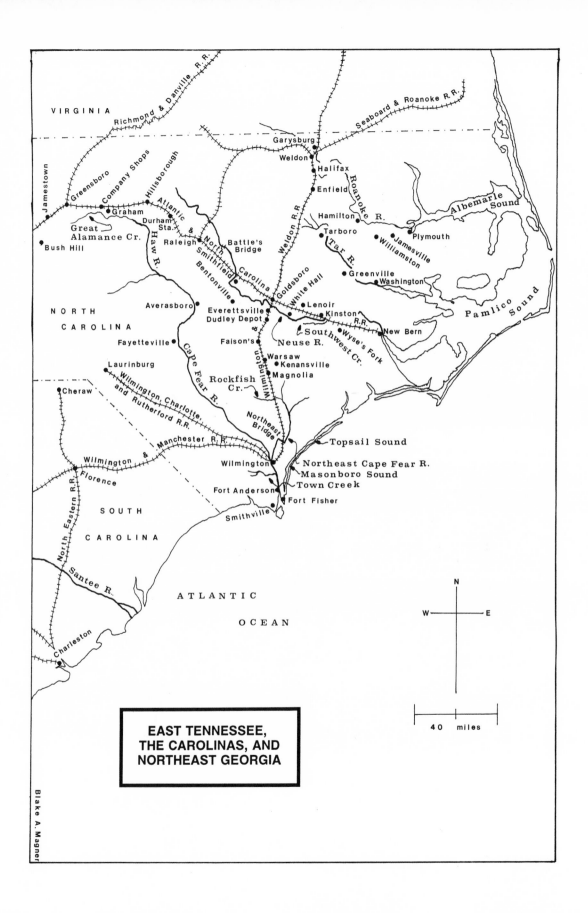

VIRGINIA

Richmond & Danville R.R.

Seaboard & Roanoke R.R.

Jamestown

Greensboro

Company Shops

Hillsborough

Atlantic

Graham

Durham Sta.

Great Alamance Cr.

Bush Hill

Haw R.

Raleigh

Battle's Bridge

North

Smithfield

Bentonville

Carolina

Averasboro

Everettsville
Dudley Depot

&

NORTH CAROLINA

Fayetteville

Faison's

Wilmington

Laurinburg

Cape Fear R.

Rockfish Cr.

Cheraw

Wilmington, Charlotte, and Rutherford R.R.

Manchester R.R.

Wilmington &

Florence

North Eastern R.R.

SOUTH CAROLINA

Santee R.

ATLANTIC

OCEAN

Charleston

Garysburg

Weldon

Halifax

Enfield

Weldon R.R.

Roanoke R.

Albemarle Sound

Hamilton

Tarboro

Plymouth

Jamesville

Williamston

Tar R.

Greenville

Washington

Goldsboro

White Hall

Lenoir

Kinston

R.R.

New Bern

Pamlico Sound

Southwest Cr.

Wyse's Fork

Neuse R.

Warsaw

Kenansville

Magnolia

Northeast Bridge

Topsail Sound

Wilmington

Northeast Cape Fear R.

Masonboro Sound

Fort Anderson

Town Creek

Fort Fisher

Smithville

N

W   E

40 miles

**EAST TENNESSEE,
THE CAROLINAS, AND
NORTHEAST GEORGIA**

Blake A. Magner

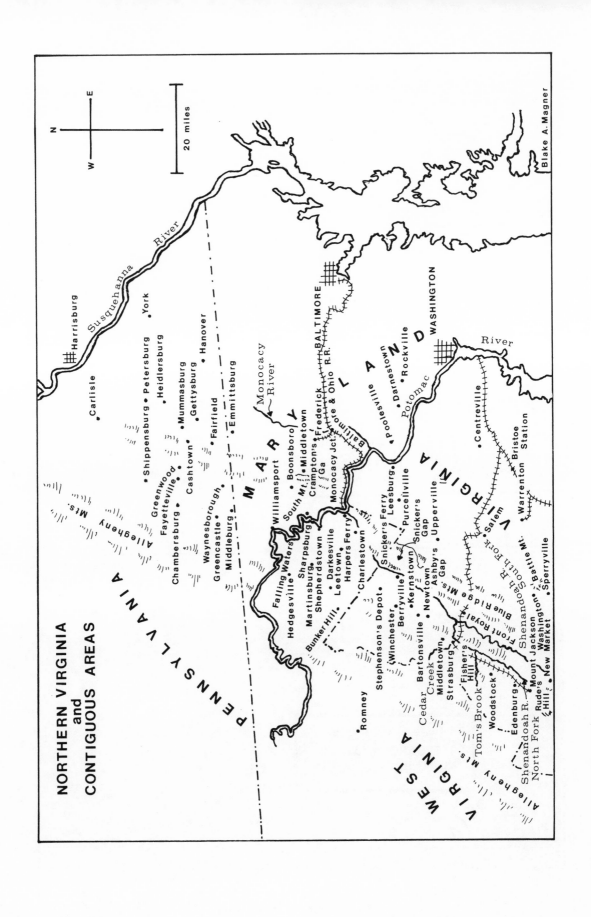

NORTHERN VIRGINIA
and
CONTIGUOUS AREAS

Blake A. Magner

20 miles

PENNSYLVANIA

M A R Y L A N D

WEST VIRGINIA

VIRGINIA

BALTIMORE

WASHINGTON

Harrisburg

Susquehanna River

Carlisle

Shippensburg   Petersburg

Heidlersburg

York

Greenwood

Fayetteville   Mummasburg

Cashtown   Gettysburg

Chambersburg   Hanover

Waynesborough   Fairfield

Greencastle   Emmittsburg

Middleburg

Allegheny Mts.

Williamsport

Boonsboro

Middletown

Crampton's   Frederick
Ga

South Mt.   Monocacy Jct.

Monocacy River

Baltimore & Ohio R.R.

Poolesville

Darnestown

Rockville

Potomac River

Falling Waters

Hedgesville

Sharpsburg

Martinsburg

Shepherdstown

Darkesville

Leetown

Harpers Ferry

Charlestown

Bunker Hill

Snicker's Ferry

Leesburg

Snicker's Gap

Purcellville

Upperville

Ashby's
Gap

Newtown

Kernstown

Berryville

Centreville

Warrenton

Bristoe
Station

Salem

Stephenson's Depot

Winchester

Bartonsville

Romney

Cedar
Creek

Middletown

Strasburg

Front Royal

Blue Ridge Mts.

Shenandoah
R.

South Fork

Battle Mt.

Washington

Sperryville

Fishers
Hill

Tom's Brook

Woodstock

Edenburg

Mount Jackson

Rude's
Hill

New Market

Shenandoah R.

North Fork

Allegheny Mts.

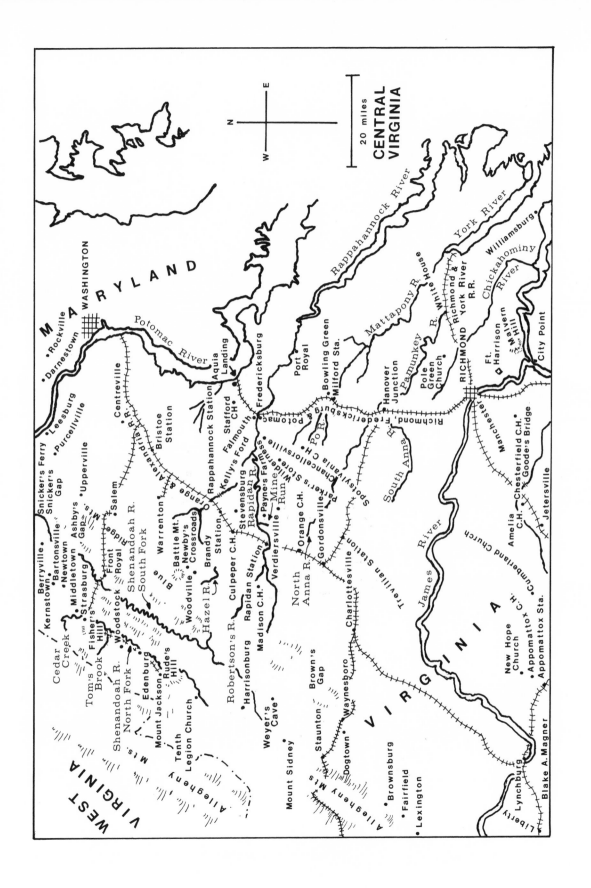

CENTRAL VIRGINIA

20 miles

MARYLAND

WASHINGTON

Rockville
Darnestown

Potomac River

Rappahannock River

York River

Williamsburg

Chickahominy River

RICHMOND

Ft. Harrison
Malvern Hill
City Point

Mattapony R.

Pamunkey R.
White House R.

Richmond York River R.R.

Bowling Green
Milford Sta.

Hanover Junction

Pole Green Church

Port Royal

Aquia Landing
Fredericksburg
Stafford C.H.
Falmouth
Kelly's Ford

Richmond, Fredericksburg & Potomac

Po R.
South Anna R.

Manchester

Chesterfield C.H.
Goode's Bridge

Snicker's Ferry
Snicker's Gap
Leesburg
Purcellville
Upperville

Centreville

Bristoe Station

Rappahannock Station

Stevensburg
Rapidan R.
Paynes Farms
Mine Run
Wilderness
Parker's Store
Chancellorsville
Spotsylvania C.H.

James River

Cumberland Church

Amelia C.H.

Jetersville

Berryville
Bartonsville
Newtown
Middletown
Strasburg
Ashby's Gap
Salem
Warrenton

Front Royal
Shenandoah R. South Fork
Blue Ridge Mts.
Battle Mt.
Woodville
Newby's Crossroads
Brandy Station
Hazel R.
Culpeper C.H.
Robertson's R.
Rapidan Station
Madison C.H.

Verdiersville

North Anna R.
Orange C.H.
Gordonsville

Trevilian Station

Charlottesville

New Hope Church
Appomattox C.H.
Appomattox Sta.

Kernstown
Cedar Creek
Fisher's Hill
Woodstock
Rude's Hill
Edenburg
Mount Jackson
Shenandoah R. North Fork
Tom's Brook
Harrisonburg

Weyer's Cave

Brown's Gap
Staunton
Waynesboro
Dogtown

Mount Sidney

Tenth Legion Church

Allegheny Mts.

WEST VIRGINIA

Allegheny Mts.

VIRGINIA

Brownsburg
Fairfield
Lexington

Liberty
Lynchburg

Blake A. Magner

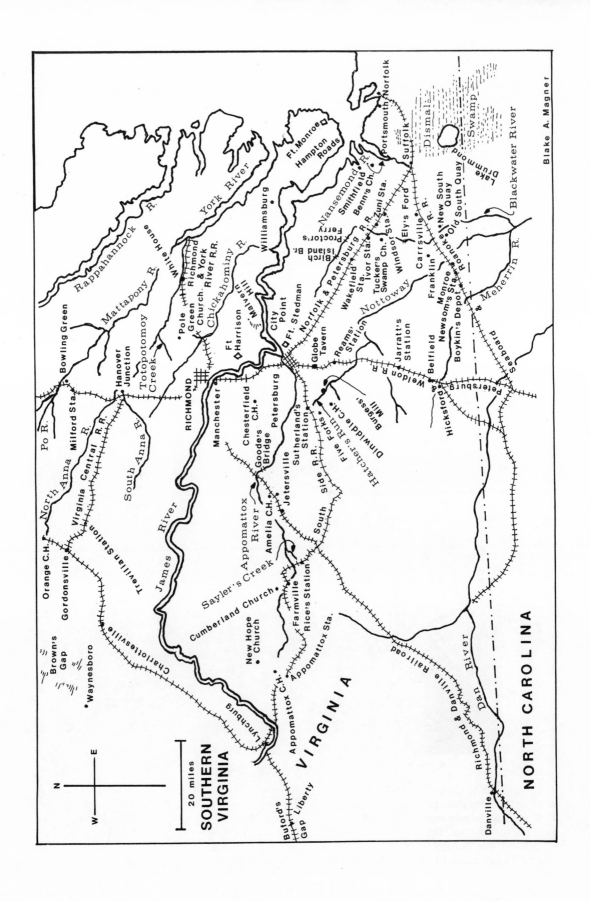

Blake A. Magner

SOUTHERN VIRGINIA

20 miles

NORTH CAROLINA

VIRGINIA

This ambrotype of Capt. Alfred Alexander Miller of Company K, 57th North Carolina, was almost certainly taken by the same photographer who took the ambrotype of Sgt. G. A. J. Sechler on the following page. The chair in which the men are seated and the sword they hold appear to be identical. Very possibly, they visited the photographer together. The book in Miller's lap is probably a Bible. Miller, a former Rowan County militia officer, was shot through the head and killed on December 13, 1862, at Fredericksburg, Virginia—the 57th Regiment's first battle. His service record appears on page 202. Image provided by J. A. L. Miller.

The chevrons on the sleeves of his shell jacket identify G. A. J. Sechler of Company K, 57th North Carolina, as a sergeant. He holds an M1842 U.S. musket (caliber .69) in his right hand and an officer's sword (probably lent to him by Capt. A. A. Miller; see preceding image) in his left. A bayonet and scabbard are on his left hip. On his right hip, barely visible, is a cartridge box, and there is a leather cap box beside his belt buckle. Sechler was promoted captain of Company K on May 20, 1863; was captured at Rappahannock Station, Virginia, November 7, 1863; and survived nineteen months of imprisonment at Johnson's Island, Ohio. His service record appears on page 202. Image provided by Mrs. Ruby Stirewalt.

57TH REGIMENT N.C. TROOPS

The 57th Regiment N.C. Troops was organized at Salisbury, in Rowan County, on July 6, 1862, and was composed of men primarily from Alamance, Cabarrus, Catawba, Forsyth, Lincoln, and Rowan Counties.[1] Archibald Campbell Godwin, a Virginian and former California gold prospector who had been sent to Salisbury to establish a military prison, was elected colonel.[2] Hamilton Chamberlain Jones Jr., a 24-year-old Rowan County native, University of North Carolina graduate, attorney, and former captain in the 5th Regiment N.C. State Troops, was elected lieutenant colonel. Twenty-year-old James Alexander Craige, a Rowan County resident and former United States Military Academy cadet, was elected major. In a letter to his wife dated July 8, Pvt. Morgan A. Walker of Company F pronounced himself "well satisfied" with military life but disappointed that, unlike "about one third of our men [who] got furlouws . . . right off," he would not be able to go home for four days. Pvt. George Rhyne of Company G informed his wife on the same date that he had "seen a thousand yankies [at the military prison] and . . . bin in a mong them. . . . [S]ome of them looks like sheep killing dogs and some . . . as brave as a lion. . . ." After two days in the Confederate army, he too was "well satisfied."[3]

For the next month the regiment remained at Salisbury drilling and performing tedious duty as commissary and prison guards. The latter assignment, according to Pvt. James C. Zimmerman of Company D, was singularly unpleasant. "[I]f you was here," he assured his wife on July 12, "you would think [the prison] the stinkines place in the world[.] [I]t is enough to make a ded man heeve. . . ." Occasionally the routine was broken by incidents between the prisoners and guards or escape attempts. Such an attempt occurred during the wee hours of July 18 when "6 or 8 Deserters broke oute [causing] a great alarm . . . and firing of guns." For the most part, all remained quiet. "[W]e dril twice A day [and] the gards go on gard mountain [mount guard duty] once A day," Pvt. John Marcus Hefner of Company E wrote a few weeks later. The heavy dose of drill seemingly produced beneficial results. "I believe," Hefner added, "that we have the best Company in north carolina. . . ."[4]

1. The ten companies comprising the 57th North Carolina were raised primarily in the following counties: Company A–Rowan; Company B–Rowan; Company C–Rowan; Company D–Forsyth; Company E–Catawba; Company F–Cabarrus; Company G–Lincoln; Company H–Rowan; Company I–Alamance; and Company K–Rowan.

2. Godwin was born in 1831. The month and day of his birth are unknown.

3. Morgan A. Walker to Margaret C. Walker (his wife), July 8, 1862, Morgan A. Walker Letters, Roster Document No. 1087, Civil War Roster Project (CWRP), North Carolina Division of Archives and History (NCDAH), Raleigh, hereafter cited as M. A. Walker Letters; George Rhyne to Mary Ann Rhyne, July 8, 1862, Rhyne, Houser, and Huss Letters, Roster Document No. 1097, CWRP, NCDAH, hereafter cited as Rhyne, Houser, and Huss Letters. See also William F. Wagner to Nancy M. Wagner (his wife), July 10, 1862, in Joe M. Hatley and Linda B. Huffman, eds., *Letters of William F. Wagner: Confederate Soldier* (Wendell, N.C.: Broadfoot's Bookmark, 1983), 5-6, hereafter cited as Hatley and Huffman, *Letters of William F. Wagner*.

4. James C. Zimmerman to Martha A. Zimmerman (his wife), July 12, 1862, James C. Zimmerman Papers, Special Collections Department, Duke University Library (SCD-DU), Durham, hereafter cited as Zimmerman Letters; John Marcus Hefner to Kizia Hefner (his wife), July 18 and "August" 1862, John Marcus Hefner Papers, Private Collections, NCDAH, hereafter cited as Hefner Papers. "[W]e take a march to the Crick once a day to wash and drill," Hefner wrote in his July 18 letter. "I am very well satisfied."

On the morning of August 11 three companies of the 57th North Carolina departed for Virginia as escorts for a group of Federal prisoners being transferred for exchange. Two more companies, also escorting prisoners, left on August 15. In the meantime, a decision was made by the Confederate high command to transfer the entire regiment to Drewry's Bluff, on the James River between Richmond and Petersburg. However, before those orders could be fully implemented the regiment was ordered to Richmond—probably in response to a Federal advance in northern Virginia that resulted two weeks later in the Battle of Second Manassas. After a lengthy delay caused by a shortage of railroad cars, two more companies departed Salisbury on August 25.[5]

We left Salisbury last monday a week was a weak ago [Private Zimmerman wrote on September 4] and started to Richmond we had a fine ride on the cares to Petersburg there we stoped and stayed all night next morning [August 26] we was ordered to march three miles out of town and strike up camp we fixed up our tents three times [moved camp three times] as soon as we got fixt up and thought to stay awhile we was ordered to go to Richmond last Sunday morning [August 31] so Sunday all day we was cooking our rashins till in the night it a raining as hard as it could so on monday morning we started back to Petersburg . . . [where] we was to have transportition on the cares [to Richmond] but we had to take it a foot to Richmond with all our nopsacks and lugage Twenty five miles we marched about seventeen miles the first day started from our camps at nine oclock . . . [and] marched in the night [until after nightfall] the swet pored off two or three dropp at every step a cloud come up just at dark and rained hard we just had to take it ruff shod through the rain it was eleven oclock when we come to camp we kindled up a little fire about half of us could get to it so we had to lay on the wet groung in our wet clothes I nearly frose towards day we reached Richmon the next day from there we went six miles north of that place and staid all night in the edge of the old field with tents next morning we came back one mile to where we are now we received our new guns this morning our company got Rifles only seven companies are togeather[.][6]

5. See W. F. Wagner to N. M. Wagner, August 10, 1862, in Hatley and Huffman, *Letters of William F. Wagner*, 10; J. C. Zimmerman to M. A. Zimmerman, August 14 and 23 and September 4, 1862, Zimmerman Letters; M. A. Walker to M. C. Walker, August 16, 26, and 28, 1862, M. A. Walker Letters; R. N. Scott and others, eds., *The War of the Rebellion: A Compilation of the Official Records of the Union and Confederate Armies*, 70 vols. (Washington, D.C.: Government Printing Office, 1880-1901), ser. 1, 11 (pt. 3):675-676, 12 (pt. 3):922, 929, 15:794, hereafter cited as *Official Records (Army)*. The first group of companies to depart Salisbury and possibly the second were in the vicinity of Drewry's Bluff for eight or nine days and at several other locations as well. "[A]t first we went to Richmond," Private Wagner informed his wife on August 26, "and then to [the] Bell Island [prison camp] and thene to Richmond and then a bout Twelve Miles Below Richmn nd near drures Bluff about Two Miles Below the Bluff in an ole pine field and stade 2 or 3 days and then we cleaned off a camp in the woods about foure or 5 hundred yards from the ole field and mooved thare and stade 6 days and yesterday Evining we mooved a gain. . . ." Wagner's letter was written from "Camp CamBell," Proctor's Creek, Chesterfield County. W. F. Wagner to N. M. Wagner, August 26, 1862, in Hatley and Huffman, *Letters of William F. Wagner*, 11.

6. J. C. Zimmerman to M. A. Zimmerman, September 4, 1862, Zimmerman Letters. See also M. A. Walker to M. C. Walker, September 4, 1862, M. A. Walker Letters. On August 28, according to Walker's letter of that date, the regiment was at Camp Stonewall, near Petersburg. "We are . . . right behind the brest works," Walker wrote. "[T]he best works is seven miles long[.] [T]here is fifteen hundred negroes at work on the fortification[.] [T]he yankeys are fifteen miles from here[.] [T]here is fighting to day about city po[i]nt[.] I herd the cannons rore. . . ." M. A. Walker to M. C. Walker, August 28, 1862, M. A. Walker Letters.

According to Private Walker, the men were given "nothing to eat hardly for three days" and arrived at Richmond "about half mad." No doubt their tempers did not improve when they found that their new camp, Camp Salisbury, was "a sickly place . . . right in the bottom of brook Creek." On September 4 Walker reported that "about fifteen" members of Company F were sick with "something like the chils and feaver." New cases of measles and mumps, which had plagued the regiment since at least mid-August, also broke out. "We are in a flat level country," Zimmerman wrote. "[Y]ou can see for miles and the watter is the worst kind and no [fire]wood atall."[7]

For the next two weeks the 57th North Carolina remained near Brook Creek—"five miles north of richmon on the [Brook] turn pike"—under the command of Maj. Gen. Gustavus W. Smith.[8] The regiment's bout with ill health continued, and on September 10 Sgt. Alexander ("Sandy") Patton informed his sister that "only a bout 36 privates [in Company I were] able for duty." Private Zimmerman noted four days later that "about thirty" members of Company D were sick. Fortunately, mortality remained low. "We have a great Deal of sickness in the Regiment," Private Walker observed on September 18, "but non bad off."[9] Men who were fit for duty spent most of their time constructing fortifications. "[W]e are working on brest workes in a half a mile of our camp," Zimmerman wrote, "two hunred of this Ridgment and two of an other. . . . [W]e have hard times. . . ."[10]

On about September 17, while Robert E. Lee's Army of Northern Virginia and G. B. McClellan's Army of the Potomac were locked in bloody combat near Sharpsburg, Maryland, the 57th North Carolina marched southeast toward Williamsburg.[11] "I hope we wont

---

7. M. A. Walker to M. C. Walker, September 4, 1862, M. A. Walker Letters; J. C. Zimmerman to M. A. Zimmerman, September 4, 1862, Zimmerman Letters. See also M. A. Walker to M. C. Walker, August 16, 1862, M. A. Walker Letters; Alexander ("Sandy") Patton to Ellen Patton (his sister), August 29 and September 10, 1862, Patton Family Papers, SCD-DU, hereafter cited as Patton Papers.

8. Alexander Patton to Ellen Patton, September 10, 1862, Patton Papers. During September and October the 57th was not permanently assigned to a brigade but may have served briefly in those of Brig. Gens. James Johnston Pettigrew and Henry A. Wise. According to Private Walker in a letter dated August 28, the 57th was commanded by Pettigrew during its brief stay at Petersburg. Subsequently, according to Privates Wagner and Zimmerman in letters dated September 21 and September 27 respectively, the regiment was in Wise's Brigade. An accurate if obscure description of the regiment's brigade-affiliation status during September and October appears in an undated letter written by an unidentified member of the 57th and quoted in the October 13 issue of the *Carolina Watchman*. According to the writer, the 57th was "not yet [permanently] attached to any Brigade. . . . [It] could enter a North Carolina Brigade if the Colonel desired it; but [he] fears they will be thrown into a Virginia Brigade, and believes it will result in mischief." *Carolina Watchman* (Salisbury), October 13, 1862. See also M. A. Walker to M. C. Walker, August 28, 1862, M. A. Walker Letters; W. F. Wagner to N. M. Wagner, September 21, 1862, in Hatley and Huffman, *Letters of William F. Wagner*, 15; J. C. Zimmerman to M. A. Zimmerman, September 27, 1862, Zimmerman Letters.

9. Alexander Patton to Ellen Patton, September 10, 1862, Patton Papers; J. C. Zimmerman to M. A. Zimmerman, September 14, 1862, Zimmerman Letters; M. A. Walker to M. C. Walker, [September] 18, 1862, M. A. Walker Letters. According to figures compiled from service records in this volume, only three deaths occurred in the 57th North Carolina during September.

10. J. C. Zimmerman to M. A. Zimmerman, September 14, 1862, Zimmerman Letters. "[W]e have Corn bread and beef to eat and not very plenty at that," Zimmerman added. Private Walker was more positive on the subject of rations, at least from a quantitative standpoint. "We g[e]t plenty to eat," he wrote on September 18, "such as it is." M. A. Walker to M. C. Walker, [September] 18, 1862, M. A. Walker Letters.

11. According to Private Wagner, that movement took place on September 16; Private Zimmerman says Septem-

see as hard a times [again] as we have saw [on our march down the James River]," Pvt. John Houser of Company G grumbled ten days later after the regiment returned to Camp Salisbury. "I tell you marching is hard. . . . [W]e started to go to Williamsburg but . . . went [only] as far as a place called Charles City Court house and stade their a cuply days an then we got or ders to come back. . . . [W]e got to our camp last knight about dusk[.] [T]he distance going an coming is about 80 miles and I tell you the[re] was a heap sot down beside of the road[.] [T]he[y] jist give out. . . . I made the trip but it went mity hard." "[W]e had . . . to throw a great many of our clothes away," Private Zimmerman related. "[A]t one place we throwed away over two hundred garments pants coats shirts drawers allmost all right new. . . . One shirt and drawers and a blanket is as much as one can carry with his gun and amunition."[12]

Following their return from Charles City Court House, the bedraggled 57th neophytes again settled down in their swampy camp near Brook Creek. An improvement in rations took place almost immediately, but that happy development was offset by a new bout of illness. "[I]f we stay here we will all get down sick and die," Zimmerman wailed on October 5. "[W]hen we was here before we all took sick nerly[.] [S]ince we came back the rest of us are getting sick[.] I think any man of sence could see that this is a unhelthy place and if he cared for his men he would move some where els. . . . About two therds of our regiment is sick. There is 30 in our company able to do duty."[13]

On October 10 the regiment moved to a new camp, called Camp Vance, in a "stuble field" about "2 1/2 miles north from Richmond on the gordonsvile Road."[14] That relocation produced no immediate improvement in the men's health. On October 24 only sixteen members of Company E were able to drill, and three days later Zimmerman informed his wife that he was just recovering from a succession of "chills and feavor," "Mumps," and "yellow Janders [jaundice]."[15] Nevertheless, it seems evident that the regiment was better

---

ber 17. The purpose of the expedition is unclear but was probably connected with a skirmish at Williamsburg on September 9 that sparked temporary Confederate hopes of recapturing the town. See J. C. Zimmerman to M. A. Zimmerman, September 27, 1862, Zimmerman Letters; W. F. Wagner to N. M. Wagner, September 21, 1862, in Hatley and Huffman, *Letters of William F. Wagner*, 14; *Official Records (Army)*, ser. 1, 18:11-13, 387-391.

12. John Houser to D. H. Dellinger (his uncle), September 27, 1862, Rhyne, Houser, and Huss Letters; J. C. Zimmerman to M. A. Zimmerman, September 27, 1862, Zimmerman Letters. See also W. F. Wagner to N. M. Wagner, September 21, 1862, in Hatley and Huffman, *Letters of William F. Wagner*, 14-15.

13. J. C. Zimmerman to M. A. Zimmerman, October 5, 1862, Zimmerman Letters. See also W. F. Wagner to N. M. Wagner, October 3, 1862, in Hatley and Huffman, *Letters of William F. Wagner*, 17. On October 1 General Smith reported that 621 officers and men of the 57th were present for duty; on October 20 he reported 587 officers and men present. By October 31 the figure was down to 570. *Official Records (Army)*, ser. 1, 18:751, 759, 764.

14. W. F. Wagner to N. M. Wagner, October 10, 1862, in Hatley and Huffman, *Letters of William F. Wagner*, 18; M. A. Walker to M. C. Walker, "October 1862," M. A. Walker Letters. "We are two miles nearer Richmond thand we was last week," Private Zimmerman wrote. J. C. Zimmerman to M. A. Zimmerman, October 16, 1862, Zimmerman Letters.

15. J. C. Zimmerman to M. A. Zimmerman, October 27, 1862, Zimmerman Letters. See also J. M. Hefner to Kizia Hefner, October 26, 1862, Hefner Papers. According to an unidentified 57th North Carolina soldier whose undated letter was paraphrased in the *Carolina Watchman*, "About 400" members of the regiment were "on the sick list." In a letter written on November 2, Zimmerman estimated that "only about two [hundred] and fifty men" were "able for duty out of Eleven hundred sixty in the Ridgment." The latter figure is probably too high

situated than at Camp Salisbury. Complaints about bad water and lack of firewood disappeared from the men's letters, and their rations continued to improve. By October 26 Private Hefner was reporting "plenty to eate at this time[.] [W]e get beef and baken and flower and shoogar and sometimes sheld beans and peas." Numerous prayer meetings, baptisms, and confirmations helped divert the men's attention from their troubles and, perhaps, raised their spirits.[16] However, six consecutive days of rain together with the arrival of "very cold" weather in mid-October caused severe discomfort and probably suffering among the "many" who were shoeless. Considerably more serious from the standpoint of regimental morale were reports of distress at home among soldiers' families. "I have been troubled . . . more than ever before in my life," a 57th soldier wrote to a Salisbury newspaper, "on reading accounts of robberies in Rowan. There is great excitement among the men who have left their wives and children behind to come here to defend the country. The practices of the extortioners and robbers are unnerving us, and making us indifferent as to our duties here, and careless of life itself. If our friends at home fail to protect our families and they send to us their cries for help, who shall say what will be the consequences! I beg you as a friend to look after the welfare of my family, and encourage them all you can."[17]

On about November 6 the 57th North Carolina and a sister unit, the 54th North Carolina, were assigned to Brig. Gen. Joseph R. Davis's Brigade of Maj. Gen. Samuel G. French's Department of North Carolina and Southern Virginia. However, within a day or so the two regiments were transferred in exchange for two Mississippi infantry regiments (the 2nd and 11th) and ordered to report to General Lee for duty with the Army of Northern Virginia. The 54th and 57th left Camp Vance to join Lee near Culpeper Court House on November 7.[18] "[W]e left our ole camp last friday and it was a snowing as hard as it could

---

by at least several hundred, but there seems no reason to doubt that 400 men were sick. Mortality figures compiled for this volume indicate that seventeen members of the 57th North Carolina died of disease during October. During November and December the figures were thirteen and nineteen respectively. *Carolina Watchman* (Salisbury), October 13, 1862; J. C. Zimmerman to M. A. Zimmerman, November 2, 1862, Zimmerman Letters. See also W. F. Wagner to N. M. Wagner, October 10, 1862, in Hatley and Huffman, *Letters of William F. Wagner*, 18.

16. J. M. Hefner to Kizia Hefner, October 26, 1862, Hefner Papers. Regimental prayer meetings, according to the unidentified soldier whose letter was quoted in the foregoing footnote, were "regularly kept up, and well attended." Private Wagner wrote on October 16 that he "heard P. C. Henkle [a visiting Lutheran minister from Catawba County] preach last nite which done me good to my heart. . . . [T]hare was 2 Baptised and 15 confermed[.] [H]e all so preached to day at Elevin oclock. . . . [H]is tex . . . is found in st John the 5 chapt 25 vers." *Carolina Watchman* (Salisbury), October 13, 1862; W. F. Wagner to N. M. Wagner, October 16, 1862, in Hatley and Huffman, *Letters of William F. Wagner*, 22. See also J. M. Hefner to Kizia Hefner, October 17, 1862, Hefner Papers; George Rhyne to D. H. Dellinger (his "father"), October 20, 1862, Rhyne, Houser, and Huss Letters.

17. J. M. Hefner to Kizia Hefner, October 17, 1862, Hefner Papers; *Carolina Watchman* (Salisbury), October 13, 1862.

18. See M. A. Walker to M. C. Walker, November 9 and 24, 1862, M. A. Walker Letters; *Official Records (Army)*, ser. 1, 19 (pt. 2):694-695, 697, 699, 705, 709-710, 715. Lieutenant Colonel Jones's postwar history of the 57th can be interpreted to imply that the regiment was in Brig. Gen. Joseph R. Davis's Brigade during part of the period from late August to early November; however, that was not the case. See Hamilton C. Jones, "Fifty-seventh Regiment," in Walter Clark, ed., *Histories of the Several Regiments and Battalions from North Carolina in the Great War, 1861-'65*, 5 vols. (Raleigh and Goldsboro: State of North Carolina, 1901), 3:406,

from morneing till nearly 12 o clock," Private Wagner informed his wife on November 9. "[T]he snow was about 4 inches deep and we marched to Richmond and such a mud and water I never traveled in and we got [there] too late for the morning trane and then we had to ly [over] in Richmond til 8 o clock in the Evining and I never in all my days was as near frose as I was that day[.] [W]e ditent git to a bit of fire from that morning till next and [it] snowed alitle all day. . . ." The 57th then moved by rail to Mitchell's Station and went into camp "about five miles" from Culpeper Court House.[19] There the 54th and 57th were assigned to Brig. Gen. Evander M. Law's Brigade, Maj. Gen. John B. Hood's Division, Lt. Gen. James Longstreet's Corps. In addition to the 54th and 57th North Carolina, the brigade was composed of the 6th Regiment N.C. State Troops and the 4th and 44th Regiments Alabama Infantry. Under orders from Hood to drill the 57th until it was "fit to go in[to] battle," Colonel Godwin kept the men marching and maneuvering six hours a day: "three in the fore noon," Zimmerman groaned, "and three in the after noon and [we] never stop till the time is out. . . . [T]hey keep us busy all the time . . . and if we dont obey we are punished severley and have to do wors than a negro under a mean master."[20]

Two weeks prior to the 57th North Carolina's move to Culpeper Court House, General McClellan, following up at last on his narrow victory at Sharpsburg, crossed the Potomac River and began a snail-like advance into northern Virginia. On November 7 an exasperated President Lincoln sacked the self-assured but slow-footed McClellan and replaced him with the self-doubting and equally slow-footed Maj. Gen. Ambrose E. Burnside. Acting with unwonted decisiveness, Burnside promptly produced a plan to win the war: he would concentrate his army south of Warrenton as if to attack Longstreet at Culpeper Court House, then lunge suddenly southeast toward Fredericksburg, on the south bank of the Rappahannock River. Before Lee could react, Burnside would cross the Rappahannock, occupy Fredericksburg, and seize Marye's Heights, a formidable but virtually undefended ridge overlooking the town. After establishing a base at Fredericksburg, where a navigable river guaranteed a secure supply line, he would "move . . . upon Richmond."[21]

On November 15 the Army of the Potomac advanced, and on the seventeenth it reached Falmouth, across and slightly upriver from Fredericksburg. Fearful that his army would be divided into two isolated parts if he began fording the frigid, rising Rappahannock, Burnside reluctantly halted to await the arrival of pontoons. Three days later the vanguard of Longstreet's Corps reached Fredericksburg after an arduous march in cold, rainy weather. The 57th North Carolina, which spent three days slogging through "any amount" of mud "shoe mouth to [a] half leg deep," began straggling in on November 22. Wet, exhausted, mud-caked members of the regiment were still arriving, some without their

---

hereafter cited as Jones, "Fifty-seventh Regiment," in Clark, *Histories of the North Carolina Regiments*.

19. W. F. Wagner to N. M. Wagner, November 9, 1862, in Hatley and Huffman, *Letters of William F. Wagner*, 23; M. A. Walker to M. C. Walker, November 9, 1862, M. A. Walker Letters. See also J. C. Zimmerman to M. A. Zimmerman, November 7 and 9, 1862, Zimmerman Letters; M. A. Walker to M. C. Walker, November 24 and 29, 1862, M. A. Walker Letters.

20. J. C. Zimmerman to M. A. Zimmerman, November 16, 1862, Zimmerman Letters. See also *Official Records (Army)*, ser. 1, 51 (pt. 2):643.

21. *Official Records (Army)*, ser. 1, 19 (pt. 2):552.

knapsacks and other discarded impedimenta, the next morning.[22] "I can inform [you] that I never saw as many broke down men in my life," Private Hefner wrote on November 23. "It was the Mudest time and the slickest time I ever saw. . . . I have saw some part of the elephant."[23]

As his five divisions came up, Longstreet positioned them on Marye's Heights. Hood's Division, including Law's Brigade and the 57th North Carolina, was on the far right of Longstreet's line at Hamilton's Crossing. Lt. Gen. Thomas J. ("Stonewall") Jackson's Corps, which reached the scene on November 29, was deployed downstream to guard Lee's vulnerable right flank. Four days earlier Burnside's pontoons finally began arriving, but by then he was apprehensively watching the growing Confederate force across the river and having second thoughts about attacking Marye's Heights. Another week went by while Burnside assessed the possibility of a flanking movement downstream at Skinker's Neck. By that time Jackson was in position. Forced to think again, Burnside convinced himself that Marye's Heights had been weakened to bolster the Confederate right. He therefore reverted to his original strategy: he would bridge the Rappahannock at Fredericksburg and launch a frontal assault.

At two o'clock on the morning of December 11, Federal engineers set to work assembling three pontoon bridges opposite Fredericksburg and two more a mile downstream, where a second Federal force under Maj. Gen. William B. Franklin was to cross. As the sun rose and the morning mist burned off, Brig. Gen. William Barksdale's Mississippi brigade, inside Fredericksburg, opened fire on the bridge builders from a distance of eighty yards, killing or wounding several and sending the rest scrambling for cover. A Federal artillery barrage temporarily suppressed Barksdale's riflemen, but when the fire lifted they opened up again. A second bombardment, this time by approximately 100 guns, set parts of Fredericksburg ablaze but failed to subdue the stubborn Barksdale. Federal infantry then crossed the river in boats, setting off a vicious little battle in the streets and propelling the Mississippians back to a stone wall at the foot of Marye's Heights. The pontoniers then completed their work. Downstream, near the mouth of Deep Run, Franklin's bridges were also laid despite the best efforts of 100 sharpshooters.

22. M. A. Walker to M. C. Walker, November 24, 1862, M. A. Walker Letters; J. C. Zimmerman to M. A. Zimmerman, November 24, 1862, Zimmerman Letters. Walker wrote that "The boys are all in good spirit [and] the[ir] health is generly good all though we have tolerable hard times[.] [W]e have to eat our bread and meat with out salt half of the time . . . and no tents to sleep in[.] [W]e havent got anything with us but what we caried on our backs. . . . [Y]ou may juge for your self what por times we have." See also "Record of Events," abstracts of November-December 1862 muster rolls for Companies A and C, 57th Regiment N.C. Troops, Record Group 109: Records of Confederate Soldiers Who Served During the Civil War, Compiled Service Records of Confederate Soldiers Who Served in Organizations from the State of North Carolina, M270, reel 526, National Archives and Records Administration (NARA), Washington, D.C., hereafter cited as Compiled Confederate Service Records (North Carolina).

23. J. M. Hefner to Kizia Hefner, November 23, 1862, Hefner Papers. See also John Frazier to Dorothy F. Frazier (his wife), November 24, 1862, Roster Document No. 1098, CWRP, NCDAH, hereafter cited as Frazier Letters. Private Zimmerman reported that "a great many gave out and some died[.] I hel[d] out though it was a bargin[.] [T]he officers told the gard if the men did not come to stick the bayonet in them." J. C. Zimmerman to M. A. Zimmerman, November 24, 1862, Zimmerman Letters.

That evening Burnside began crossing the Rappahannock. The next morning, when a dense fog shrouding the valley lifted, the Confederates beheld an astonishing sight. "The ground next to the river," one of Hood's men marveled, "which the day before was yellow with the stubble of grass and grain, was now blue with Yankee uniforms, the monotony relieved only by the glistening of burnished arms and the bright colors of a hundred flags. Massed between railroad and river, division behind division, artillery in front, cavalry in rear and infantry in the center, and protected by the heavy siege guns planted on the low range of hills crowning the north bank of the stream, Burnside's army was an imposing, awe-inspiring spectacle."[24] At Deep Run, Hood reinforced his skirmish line along the Bowling Green road but, believing correctly that his right flank was dangerously exposed, then withdrew most of the skirmishers to Hamilton's Crossing. Meanwhile, Lee recalled Jackson's scattered divisions from below Fredericksburg and positioned them on Longstreet's right. Hood's Division was relieved by Maj. Gen. A. P. Hill's Division of Jackson's Corps and moved about a mile to its left but returned to its original position at nightfall. There Law's Brigade was placed in "the second or reserve line, extending along the range of hills from the vicinity of Hamilton's Crossing to Dr. Reynolds' house." "[O]ur regiment lay there all day," Private Zimmerman related, "[with] the bums and shells flying over our heads doing us no injury though some fell verry close. . . ."[25]

At 10:00 A.M. on December 13 Franklin's command launched a frontal assault against Jackson. Shortly thereafter the Federal right wing advanced into a storm of musketry and cannon fire at Marye's Heights. As the Federals were scythed down near the stone wall, the suicidal nature of Burnside's plan seemingly became apparent to everyone on the field except Burnside, who continued to hammer away. By the time darkness fell, seven ill-coordinated, division-strength attacks were methodically shot to pieces by the incredulous and increasingly sickened Confederates. Meanwhile, on the Federal left, Franklin's attack was stalled by Confederate battery fire but, after a furious artillery duel of three hours' duration, was followed at 1:00 P.M. by a new effort. This time the Unionists penetrated a boggy, undefended woods thought by the Confederates to be impassable. Bursting out of the trees, a Pennsylvania division under Maj. Gen. George G. Meade surprised a brigade of South Carolinians, most of whom, thinking that Confederates were in their front, were idling about with their arms stacked. Many of the Carolinians were shot down as they leaped for their weapons or fled, and their commander, Brig. Gen. Maxcy Gregg, was mortally wounded. Two reserve divisions of Jackson's Corps then crashed into the Federals, and Confederate units on both sides of the breach joined the fray. Under fire from three sides and inadequately supported by Franklin, Meade withdrew.

At about 3:00 P.M. Franklin tried again. Just north of the woods Brig. Gen. A. T. A. Torbert's New Jersey brigade, reinforced by two regiments from another brigade and concealed by a "skirt of timber," moved up the ravine of Deep Run toward Law's position.

24. "Incidents at Fredericksburg [transcript of letter dated December 20, 1862; author anonymous]," *Confederate Veteran* 4 (September 1896): 305, hereafter cited as "Incidents at Fredericksburg." The Federals were in fact massed between the river and the Bowling Green road.

25. *Official Records (Army)*, ser. 1, 21:623; J. C. Zimmerman to M. A. Zimmerman, December 22, 1862, Zimmerman Letters.

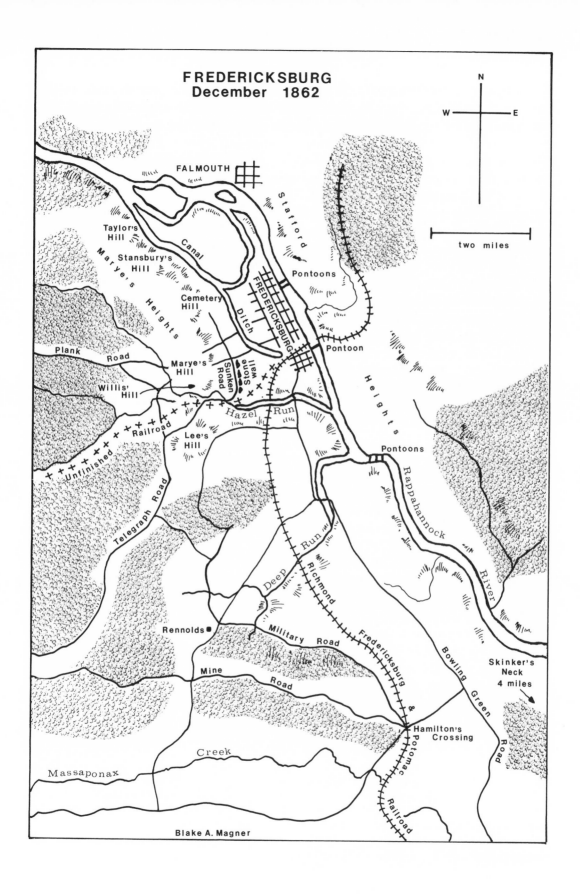

FREDERICKSBURG
December 1862

N
W — E
S

two miles

FALMOUTH

Taylor's Hill

Stafford

Canal

Stansbury's Hill

Pontoons

Marye's Heights

Cemetery Hill

FREDERICKSBURG

Ditch

Pontoon

Plank Road

Marye's Hill

Sunken Road

Stone wall

Willis' Hill

Hazel Run

Heights

Railroad

Lee's Hill

Unfinished

Pontoons

Telegraph Road

Rappahannock River

Deep Run

Richmond

Rennolds

Military Road

Fredericksburg

Mine Road

Bowling Green Road

Skinker's Neck 4 miles

Creek

Hamilton's Crossing

Massaponax

Fredericksburg & Potomac Railroad

Blake A. Magner

Shortly thereafter Torbert's men defiled from the woods about 500 yards from the Confederate works, drove a line of skirmishers from the tracks of the Richmond, Fredericksburg and Potomac Railroad, and prepared to attack a Confederate battery. The 54th and 57th North Carolina—"all dressed in homespun" and presenting to the "fastidious eyes" of Hood's veterans "a very unsoldierly appearance"—were then ordered forward.[26] "In order to get into line of battle," Confederate staff officer Clarence R. Hatton recalled, the two regiments "had to go over a corduroy road through [a] swamp with front of fours under heavy artillery fire as well as the sharp rifle fire of the enemy. . . ." With Federal shells "singing and exploding" over and around them, the men formed a line of battle and, accompanied by the 16th North Carolina of Brig. Gen. William D. Pender's Brigade, charged the enemy line "with fixed bayonets."[27] "Soon the rifle fire from the cut became terrific," Hatton continued; "then double-quick, and with the Rebel yell, a sudden rush . . . [and the three regiments were] at the railway cut with loaded guns. The enemy was driven out, killed or captured, and over the cut . . . [the North Carolinians] rushed. . . ." After routing the Federals at the railroad, the three regiments came under fire from a woods to their left, forcing the 54th North Carolina to change front to cover the left flank of the 57th. The latter, "dealing death by the bushel," continued its "magnificent charge . . . across the plain . . . under the concentrated fire of a battalion of artillery" and drove the Federals "without intermission or let up" about a half mile to a point near the Bowling Green road. There Hood recalled the badly overextended regiment to save it from "certain capture." The men then took shelter in the railroad cut where, Private Hefner wrote, the Federals "shot at us some three ours [sic]."[28]

With the failure of the attack at Deep Run, Franklin ceased offensive action against the Confederate right, permitting Lee to reinforce his left. There the slaughter continued until nightfall, leaving "dead yankeys lying in piles." "It was awful and hard fighting truly," Lt. Samuel W. Gray of Company D stated in summary of the 57th's role in the battle, "and . . . We suffered severely."[29]

---

26. *Official Records (Army)*, ser. 1, 21:623 (see also 527-529, 624); "Incidents at Fredericksburg," 305. The unknown author of the "dressed in homespun" comment erroneously believed that the two regiments were "composed [entirely] of conscripts—young men under twenty and old men."

27. Clarence R. Hatton, "Gen. Archibald Campbell Godwin," *Confederate Veteran* 28 (April 1920): 134 (first quotation), hereafter cited as Hatton, "Gen. Archibald Godwin"; *Biblical Recorder* (Raleigh), January 14, 1863 (second and third quotations). "[T]he Bum shells was a fliing and bursting over our heads," Private Wagner wrote. "I hope to God I will never git in a nother such a [s]crape[.]" W. F. Wagner to N. M. Wagner, December 18, 1862, in Hatley and Huffman, *Letters of William F. Wagner*, 27. See also "Incidents at Fredericksburg," 305.

28. Hatton, "Gen. Archibald Godwin," 134 (first quotation); *Daily Progress* (Raleigh), December 20 (second quotation) and 27 (third quotation), 1862; "Incidents at Fredericksburg," 305 (fourth and fifth quotations); J. M. Hefner to Kizia Hefner, December 18, 1862 (sixth quotation), Hefner Papers. See also *People's Press* (Salem), December 25, 1862. It is unclear whether the 16th North Carolina joined the 57th in the pursuit of the Federals to the Bowling Green road. Comparative casualty figures suggest that it did not.

29. J. M. Hefner to Kizia Hefner, December 18, 1862, Hefner Papers; *Daily Progress* (Raleigh), December 29, 1862.

[T]hat eavining we retired back to a thick woods [Private Zimmerman wrote]. The next morning we was drawn up in line of battle and lay under the bums of the enemy all day[.] [I]n the eavning we commensed throwing up brestworks and worked all night[.] [W]e got them ready by light that day being Monday [December 15]. . . . [T]hey shell[ed] us a while in the morning doing no harm[.] [T]hat night we lay back of our works in the open air with out much fire and it was very cool. Next morning I was glad the enemy had cross[ed] over the river[.] [T]hey fought a little that day and quit so it has been very still sience. . . . Tuesday we buryed our dead[.] [W]ensday I was over a part of the battle field. . . . I saw any amount of horse[s] killed laying on the field. . . . [S]ome places you could count thirty. . . . I always wanted to be in one battle to see how it did go but I never want to be in another one.[30]

By the morning of December 16 the badly mauled Army of the Potomac, as Zimmerman stated, was back across the Rappahannock. Federal casualties totaled more than 12,000 men killed, wounded, and missing. Confederate casualties, most of which were sustained by Jackson's Corps, numbered about 5,000. Losses in the 57th North Carolina, according to General Law's report, were 32 killed, 90 wounded, and 2 or 3 missing. A report by the medical director of the Army of Northern Virginia dated January 10, 1863, revised the figures to 32 killed and "192" wounded (the figure intended was undoubtedly 92).[31] According to information compiled from the rosters in this volume, the 57th lost 55 men killed or mortally wounded and 89 wounded at Fredericksburg.

General Law was delighted by the performance of the 54th and 57th North Carolina, describing the conduct of the inexperienced Tar Heels as "admirable. I cannot speak in too high terms," he wrote "of their steady courage in advancing, and the coolness with which they retired to the line of railroad when ordered. Colonel Godwin, commanding the Fifty-seventh, and Colonel [J. C. S.] McDowell, commanding the Fifty-fourth, ably assisted by Lieutenant Colonels Jones [57th] and [Kenneth M.] Murchison [54th], handled their commands with great skill and coolness." In a personal message to Godwin and his men, General Hood also extended his "congratulations upon the gallant and brilliant manner in which you charged the enemy in the battle of Saturday, 13th December—a charge which elicited the admiration of every one who witnessed it." He had "no fears," Hood continued, "of the conduct of such troops in any future encounter," and he relied "confidently" upon them to sustain "the reputation . . . gained in this their maiden effort."[32]

30. J. C. Zimmerman to M. A. Zimmerman, December 22, 1862, Zimmerman Letters.

31. *Official Records (Army)*, ser. 1, 21:559. See also J. C. Zimmerman to M. A. Zimmerman, December 14, 1862, Zimmerman Letters; *Official Records (Army)*, ser. 1, 21:623-624. A casualty list compiled by 57th North Carolina adjutant Edward A. Semple gives the regiment's losses as 32 killed, 90 wounded, and 3 missing. See *State Journal* (Raleigh), January 7, 1863.

32. *Official Records (Army)*, ser. 1, 21:624; *Daily Progress* (Raleigh), December 27, 1862. See also *Official Records (Army)*, ser. 1, 21:622; *Spirit of the Age* (Raleigh), January 5, 1863. In later years Hood recalled this episode somewhat differently (and no doubt with some embellishment): "They [the 16th, 54th, and 57th regiments] pursued the broken enemy across the railroad for a mile into the plains. Although scourged by a galling flank fire, it was not until repeated messengers had been sent to repress their ardor that they were recalled. I verily believe the mad fellows would have gone on in spite of me and the enemy together; and as they returned, some of them were seen weeping with vexation because they had been dragged from the bleeding haunches of the foe, and exclaiming: 'It is because he has no confidence in Carolinians! If we had been some of his Texans he would have let us go on and got [*sic*] some glory.'" Quoted in John Marshall Williams, "Fifty-fourth

The 57th North Carolina remained in camp near Fredericksburg until late January. Guard and picket duty became routine, and inspections were frequent. Several reviews took place in early January, including one of Hood's entire division on the ninth. Drill was presumably conducted when the weather permitted, but there is little evidence to support that assumption. Perhaps the glutinous mud was prohibitive. A few of the more deserving men received furloughs. Construction of winter quarters probably began during the week following the Battle of Fredericksburg but was abandoned when the regiment moved to a new camp prior to December 22. On January 10, 1863, Private Zimmerman informed his wife that he and his companions were "farring verry badly": tents were "leeky," firewood was "geting scarse," there was "verry much" suffering from the "coal," and the men were on "half rashens." "I could eat all that is allowed me for a day at one meal," Zimmerman grumbled, "and there is no chance to buy any thing. . . . If I only had some good meat or sosags [sausages] and butter. I wish you could send me a box with something if it was only a pone of cornbread. . . ."[33]

On January 19 the 6th, 54th, and 57th North Carolina were transferred, probably against their will, from Law's Brigade, Hood's Division, Longstreet's Corps, to Isaac R. Trimble's Brigade, Richard S. Ewell's Division, "Stonewall" Jackson's Corps. At about the same time Trimble was promoted to major general and replaced by newly promoted Brig. Gen. Robert F. Hoke, formerly colonel of the 21st North Carolina. The 21st became the fourth member of the brigade. The 1st Battalion N.C. Sharpshooters was also assigned to Hoke's Brigade at about that time. Ewell was still absent because of wounds received the previous August, and his division was commanded temporarily by Maj. Gen. Jubal A. Early. Thus the 57th North Carolina was in Hoke's Brigade, Early's Division, Jackson's Corps.[34]

Regiment," in Clark, *Histories of the North Carolina Regiments*, 3:268-269, hereafter cited as Williams, "Fifty-fourth Regiment," in Clark, *Histories of the North Carolina Regiments*. See also *Official Records (Army)*, ser. 1, 21:554, 634.

33. J. C. Zimmerman to M. A. Zimmerman, January 10, 1863, Zimmerman Letters. See also John Frazier to D. F. Frazier, January 7, 1863, Frazier Letters.

34. See *Official Records (Army)*, ser. 1, 21:1099. The transfer of the three North Carolina regiments was not welcomed by Law and Hood or, apparently, by the units themselves. Law expressed his "sorrow" and "deep regret" over their loss, complimented the 54th and 57th again for their "brilliant debut" at Fredericksburg, and bid them a "reluctant farewell." Hood expressed his "regrets," praising the two regiments for their "gallantry" at Fredericksburg as well as their "courtesy, soldier[l]y bearing and strict attention to every duty. . . ." And Cpl. John K. Walker of the 6th North Carolina wrote that "we all hated to leave the old 3rd Brigade very much." There was unhappiness in Trimble's old brigade as well. Capt. William J. Pfohl of the 21st North Carolina noted that "The old Regts [21st Georgia and 15th Alabama] were very averse to leaving us, as an attachment had been formed cemented by the many bloody fields on which we had stood up to each other side by side, & an effort was made to keep them here with us but without success. . . . We hope, however, the change in the Brigade has been none for the worse. The 6th is said to be a good Regt, the 57th we know has done good service on one field; of the other [the 54th] I know nothing either good or bad." *State Journal* (Raleigh), February 11, 1863; John Kerr Walker to his aunt and uncle, February 14, 1863, John Kerr Walker Papers, SCD-DU, hereafter cited as J. K. Walker Papers; William J. Pfohl to Christian Thomas Pfohl, February 5, 1863, Christian Thomas Pfohl Papers, Southern Historical Collection (SHC), University of North Carolina Library, Chapel Hill, hereafter cited as Pfohl Papers.

On January 24, the conclusion date of Burnside's so-called "Mud March"—a farcical six-day attempt by the Federal commander to conduct a winter campaign—the 6th, 54th, and 57th North Carolina departed Fredericksburg to join Hoke's Brigade near Port Royal, sixteen miles downstream on the south bank of the Rappahannock. Whatever their feelings about their transfer to a new brigade, the men were probably unhappy to leave Fredericksburg, where construction of winter quarters had resumed after a brief spell of unseasonably warm weather. Morale and dispositions were not improved by intermittent rain and muddy roads. Some members of the 57th, including Pvt. John Houser of Company G, were "mity nigh giving out" when the regiment arrived near Port Royal on January 25. Most were still wearily constructing chimneys for their tents or building shelters when snow began falling on the night of the twenty-seventh. It continued throughout the twenty-eighth and, by the next day, was "about [a] half leg deep."[35] "We have tolerable hard times," Houser complained. "I hope to god the day of peace hant far off. . . . I would give a[l]most anything . . . if I was at home to knight with my wife an children. . . . [T]he snow is deep and it is cold and us pore soldiers haf to ly on the damp ground [with] not much to ly on nor to civer [us]. [G]od bles you Dear granmaw," he concluded mournfully. "[I]f I never see you on earth I pray to god I will [meet] you in heaven."[36]

Hoke's Brigade remained near Port Royal until early March. The 57th North Carolina performed two-day stints of picket duty at six-day intervals; otherwise, the weeks passed with few diversions and little cheer. "[W]e hav just lan[d]ed [come] back to camp from on picket," Sergeant Patton wrote on March 1. "[T]he yankes stand on one side an hour men on the other side of the river[.] [W]e ar knot loud to talk to the yankes[.] [T]hey hollar to us but we make no ancer[.] [W]e ar knot loud to far [fire] on them unless thay Come over half way acros. . . ." Prospects for battles and furloughs were primary topics of discussion, but few of the latter were granted. "[O]ur Regt has a poore chance to git furlows," Private Wagner grumbled on February 25. "[T]here was 4 furlowed in our camp in a bout 2 month." As for combat, at least one member of the 57th was ready and confident. "Gen Hooker [who replaced Burnside as commander of the Army of the Potomac on January 26] says [mistakenly] that Gen Longstreet has gon to Tenissee," Private Zimmerman wrote on February 15, "and the most of the other soldiers are gon to North Carolina [also incorrect] and it will be a easy job to thrash what fiew that is left here[.] But if every [ever] he crosses the river he will find out who is here in time to get his hook broke. . . ."[37]

---

35. John Houser to D. H. Dellinger, January 29, 1863, Rhyne, Houser, and Huss Letters. See also "Record of Events," abstract of January-February 1863 muster roll for Company A, 57th Regiment N.C. Troops, Compiled Confederate Service Records (North Carolina), M270, reel 526. The 6th North Carolina's camp and probably those of Hoke's other regiments were "within 4 miles" of Port Royal. J. K. Walker to his father and mother, February 14, 1863, J. K. Walker Papers.

36. John Houser to D. H. Dellinger and Houser's grandmother, January 29, 1863, Rhyne, Houser, and Huss Letters. By February 14 Cpl. J. K. Walker of the 6th was reporting that the men were "in very good log Cabins and very comfortably situated, a great deal better than where we come from but wood is very scarce. . . ." J. K. Walker to his father and mother, February 14, 1863, J. K. Walker Papers.

37. Alexander Patton to Ellen Patton, March 1, 1863, Patton Papers; W. F. Wagner to N. M. Wagner, February 25, 1863, in Hatley and Huffman, *Letters of William F. Wagner*, 37; J. C. Zimmerman to M. A. Zimmerman, February 15, 1863, Zimmerman Letters. See also J. K. Walker to his father and mother, February 14, 1863, J. K. Walker Papers.

Interludes of springlike weather provided relief from the rigors of winter, but snow fell on February 5, 10, 11, 17, 22, and 23. Possibly because he was tired of seeing his men lounging and moping about, General Hoke ordered and led a snowball attack on Lawton's Georgia brigade on the twenty-fourth. During the ensuing free-for-all involving some 2,500 combatants, the Georgians were "run . . . through their camp" but finally repulsed Hoke's men with the aid of reinforcements and a barrage of "brick[s] bones [and] durt." Driven back to their own camp and in danger of losing their precious "pots and skillets," the North Carolinians rallied on a knoll, attacked the Georgians as they charged through a "hollow" below, and "run them about a mile." "Therty or fourty" mounted cavalrymen assisted Hoke in the counterattack, riding down and reportedly breaking the legs of two Georgians. "[S]ome of them got their eyes put out [black eyes?] and a good many got their noses mashed," Private Zimmerman wrote with apparent satisfaction. At the height of the battle, Zimmerman continued, the flying snowballs were "like a swarm of bees over our heads . . . and such howlowing I never herd."[38]

Although not exactly underfed, the men were poorly nourished. "We dont get more then anuff to eat," Pvt. M. A. Walker wrote on February 17. "[W]e get a quarter of a pound of bacon . . . and a pound and one eight[h] of flour a day to the m[a]n."[39] Although many were lost or stolen en route, boxes from home sometimes proved a godsend. Cpl. J. K. Walker of the 6th North Carolina informed his parents on February 14 that his six-man mess had received four hams, three chicken pies, and an unspecified quantity of "Loaf bread." "[Y]ou had better know," Walker exulted in another letter, "that we have been living high. . . ." Probably because of a combination of undernourishment and exposure, the health of the 57th, which rarely had been good, deteriorated further. Private Wagner reported on February 25 that members of the regiment were dying "tolerable fast" and desertion was increasing.[40] There is no evidence of a significant desertion problem in the

38. J. C. Zimmerman to M. A. Zimmerman, February 26, 1863, Zimmerman Letters. In the history of the 54th North Carolina in volume 13 of *North Carolina Troops*, the editor of this series, relying on a lengthy and very detailed letter published in the *North Carolina [Semiweekly] Standard* (Raleigh) of March 13, 1863, described a small and "hitherto unknown" engagement on February 24, 1863, between Hoke's Brigade and an unidentified Federal unit. The author of the letter, a 6th North Carolina soldier who signed himself "Caroline," was in fact presenting a tongue-in-cheek account of the aforementioned snowball fight between Hoke's and Lawton's Brigades. "Caroline" disguised his spoof very adroitly, even naming two 6th North Carolina captains who were "wounded," but he also inserted several clues that should have aroused suspicion. One was the fact that the camps of both combatants were on the south bank of the Rappahannock! Mortifyingly, my suspicions were not aroused until I discovered, while doing research for the 57th North Carolina history, five letters written by members of that regiment in the aftermath of the events of February 24. None contains references to a skirmish with Yankees on that date, but several contain accounts of a snowball fight. Readers who own copies of volume 13 should make charitable emendations on page 180.

39. M. A. Walker to M. C. Walker, February 17, 1863, M. A. Walker Letters. According to Pvt. John Wesley Armsworthy of the 54th North Carolina, the area around Port Royal was "eat out" and there was "no chance of getting anything . . . more than we draw from the government, bacon & flour." John Wesley Armsworthy to Edna Jane Armsworthy, February 26, 1863, John Wesley Armsworthy Letters (typescript; transcribed by W. R. Horton and quoted by permission of Robert G. Furches), Roster Document No. 0602, CWRP, NCDAH, hereafter cited as Armsworthy Letters.

40. J. K. Walker to his father and mother, February 14, 1863, and J. K. Walker to his uncle and aunt, February 14, 1863, J. K. Walker Papers; W. F. Wagner to N. M. Wagner, February 25, 1863, in Hatley and Huffman,

57th during the winter of 1862-1863, but between December 14 and April 14 eighty-four members of the regiment died of disease.[41]

On March 3 the 57th North Carolina marched upriver to its "same old camp" near Fredericksburg.[42] There the familiar routines, duties, and amusements of winter stand-down resumed.

We are in the midst of a splendid snowstorm this morning [a member of the regiment who identified himself as "57th" wrote on March 10]. . . . Snow, however, has been no uncommon thing for the past two months in this vicinity, and the soldiers being comfortably settled and provided for, seem to enjoy it, as it exempts them from drill, and gives occasion for reading, writing or the more active sport of snowballing. . . . Our Regiment is now camped on an elevation overlooking the valley of the Rappahannock and the city of Fredericksburg, but how changed is the prospect!—The axe of the soldier has been busy, and the dense forests that covered the hills for miles last December, have been leveled[.] [N]ow it is difficult to get wood even for our comfort. The valley, the city, the hills beyond, and the Yankee camps, are spread out before our unobstructed view. . . . The enemy seem very busy beyond the river, and if we were to judge of their numbers by their camps, we would conclude that there was still a great army of them. . . . We frequently see a monster balloon rise out of the woods and ascend fifteen hundred or two thousand feet. After remaining up for half an hour and fulfilling its mission, it as slowly descends to its hiding place.[43]

As "57th" indicated, there was some improvement during March in the regiment's material circumstances. Sergeant Patton noted on March 19 that the men had "plenty to eat" and were paid and issued clothing on the previous day. "[W]e ar doing very well now," he added, "if we onley co[u]ld stay in hour cabens." However, by April 5 Private Houser was complaining that "we live scant out here [and] if we diden buy we coulden stand it." "[P]ervishens is geting very scarce," Private Hefner lamented a week later. "We get one half pound of baken for two days[.] [W]e get good flower and some shooger . . . [and] some rice and some times we get Molasses."[44] Bad health continued to afflict the men, but

---

Letters of William F. Wagner, 37. "The 57th Regt is campt close to us," Pvt. Levi A. Fesperman of the 6th North Carolina wrote on February 11. "[T]here is A grate meny of them dying. . . ." Levi A. Fesperman to David A. Hampton, February 11, 1863, Caleb Hampton Papers, SCD-DU.

41. Most of the fatalities occurred in January (31) and February (23). Causes of death varied widely, but the primary killers were pneumonia (21), typhoid fever (14), and smallpox (11). No figures are available on absence without leave during the same period; however, only eight men have been identified as deserters. (Quarterly desertion figures for the 57th regiment during the war appear in footnote 265 below.) Pvt. Samuel Stone, a deserter belonging to Company K, was shot by a firing squad on March 16. Another deserter in Hoke's command, Pvt. Portland Bailey of the 6th North Carolina, was executed in the presence of the entire brigade on February 28. See J. C. Zimmerman to M. A. Zimmerman, February 28, 1863, Zimmerman Letters; Alexander Patton to Ellen Patton, March 1 and 19, 1863, Patton Papers; M. A. Walker to M. C. Walker, February 27 and March 8, 1863, M. A. Walker Letters; Carolina Watchman (Salisbury), March 16, 1863; Henry Huss to D. H. Dellinger (his uncle), March 21, 1863, Rhyne, Houser, and Huss Letters.

42. Alexander Patton to [Ellen Patton], March 4, 1863, Patton Papers. "[W]e all stood the march very well," Patton wrote. See also W. F. Wagner to N. M. Wagner, March 8, 1863, in Hatley and Huffman, Letters of William F. Wagner, 38; W. J. Pfohl to C. T. Pfohl, March 7, 1863, Pfohl Papers; M. A. Walker to M. C. Walker, March 8, 1863, M. A. Walker Letters.

43. Carolina Watchman (Salisbury), March 16, 1863.

44. Alexander Patton to Ellen Patton, March 19, 1863, Patton Papers; John Houser to D. H. Dellinger, April 5,

a significant decline in the mortality rate was evident. "We have a great deal of sickness in our regiment," Pvt. M. A. Walker accurately observed, "but not many Deaths."[45] Weather permitting, the men were drilled twice daily, but rain, lingering cold, and more snow (on March 19-21, on about March 28, and on April 5) kept them under shelter a good part of the time. Picket and guard duty were stood in all conditions. "I was on gard yesterday and last night," Private Zimmerman wrote on April 5, "and I had a time of it sure[.] [T]he wind blew all day yestardy as hard and as regulor as I ever saw it and as cold[.] [T]owards night I thought the wind would lay, but, insted . . . It clowded up and commensed snowing and such a storm of snow I hardly ever saw. [I]t snowed and blowed all night[.] It is about eleven oclock in the day [and] it has quit snowing but the wind keeps blowing hard. . . . [A] fine Rock house where our pickets stay caught on fire and burnt down . . . [and] several tents burned up in the camps. . . . [O]urs nearly blowed away and toor all to pieces[.]"[46]

During March and April apprehensions among the men about the coming spring campaign were increased by the cancellation of furloughs, the issuance and cancellation of marching orders on several occasions, the shipment of excess baggage to Richmond (on about April 1), and the periodic and distant (but by April 12 almost daily) sound of cannon fire.[47] On the evening of April 23 orders were issued to cook two days' rations, litter bearers were detailed, and the men were instructed to be ready to march the next day at a moment's notice. Rain on the twenty-fourth put an end to whatever movement was afoot, but it was evident that the regiment's winter sabbatical was almost over. "We are a looking fur a nother fite hare at fredricks Burg," Pvt. Henry Huss of Company G informed his uncle a

---

1863, Rhyne, Houser, and Huss Letters; J. M. Hefner to Kizia Hefner, April 13, 1863, Hefner Papers. "I had 7 eggs for my easter," Houser wrote, "but I had to pay mity high for them." Private Zimmerman returned from furlough on March 25 bearing a rare treat that he shared with his messmates: a keg of spirits (probably brandy). "I made them sassy when I tap[p]ed the ceg," he assured his wife. J. C. Zimmerman to M. A. Zimmerman, March 27, 1863, Zimmerman Letters.

45. M. A. Walker to M. C. Walker, April 12, 1863, M. A. Walker Letters. See also J. M. Hefner to Kizia Hefner, March 27, 1863, Hefner Papers; Henry Huss to D. H. Dellinger, March 21, 1863, Rhyne, Houser, and Huss Letters. Eleven men died of disease in March and fourteen in April.

46. J. C. Zimmerman to M. A. Zimmerman, April 5, 1863, Zimmerman Letters. See also John Houser to D. H. Dellinger, April 5, 1863, Rhyne, Houser, and Huss Letters. Pickets from the two armies, according to Zimmerman, were "in allmost throwing distance" across the Rappahannock. Both sides held their fire and exchanged newspapers, coffee, tobacco, and good-natured insults. Private Wagner wrote that one Yankee outfit had "a little Boot [boat] a bout as large as a water Buckit" that they sent over when they wished to engage in commerce. "[W]e had a fine time with the yanks," Sgt. J. K. Walker of the 6th North Carolina wrote after a stint of picket duty, "talking and exchanging Papers and sending over Tobacco for Pipes and Coffee and Canteens &c[.] [T]hey seem to be very friendly." J. C. Zimmerman to M. A. Zimmerman, April 13, 1863, Zimmerman Letters; W. F. Wagner to N. M. Wagner, March 25, 1863, in Hatley and Huffman, *Letters of William F. Wagner*, 41; J. K. Walker to his father, April 19, 1863, J. K. Walker Papers. See also J. M. Hefner to Kizia Hefner, March 27, 1863, Hefner Papers.

47. For a time, brief furloughs were granted by lottery at the rate of "too at a time out of a company." Henry Huss to Margaret Dellinger (his cousin), March 21, 1863, Rhyne, Houser, and Huss Letters. See also Alexander Patton to Ellen Patton, March 19, 1863, Patton Papers; W. F. Wagner to N. M. Wagner, March 25 and 26, 1863, in Hatley and Huffman, *Letters of William F. Wagner*, 41, 43; J. M. Hefner to Kizia Hefner, March 27, 1863, Hefner Papers; John Frazier to D. F. Frazier, March 30, 1863, Frazier Letters; J. C. Zimmerman to M. A. Zimmerman, April 5 and 13, 1863, Zimmerman Letters; M. A. Walker to M. C. Walker, April 12, 1863, M. A. Walker Letters.

few weeks earlier, "but i hope to god thay will soon quit fiten and make peace. . . . [I] dont mutch ceare how [just] so thay make peace fur we are all a giting tird of staying out heare[.] [I] wood give all i have got or ever will git if it wood help to make peace[.] [D]ear uncle," he concluded lugubriously, "you dont know how bad we want to get home."[48]

On April 27, 1863, Maj. Gen. "Fighting Joe" Hooker began moving his battle-ready, 134,000-man army out of its camps across the river from Fredericksburg. Possessing a better than two-to-one advantage over Lee (whose army was reduced to 60,000 men by the absence of part of Longstreet's Corps in southeastern Virginia), Hooker was convinced that he could destroy the Army of Northern Virginia, capture Richmond, and crush the rebellion. Another frontal assault on Marye's Heights being manifestly out of the question, Hooker planned to turn Lee's left flank by crossing the Rappahannock with Maj. Gens. Meade's, Oliver O. Howard's, and Henry Slocum's Corps twenty miles upstream at lightly defended Kelly's Ford. Howard and Slocum would then move south, cross the Rapidan River, and head directly for Chancellorsville—a one-house crossroads "village" located in a forest of stunted hardwoods and dense undergrowth known as the Wilderness. Meade would march down the south bank of the Rappahannock and drive the Confederate defenders from United States Ford and then Banks' Ford, where two divisions of Maj. Gen. Darius Couch's Corps would be waiting to cross. After crossing the Rappahannock, Couch would remain south of the river awaiting developments and orders. Meanwhile, Meade would join Howard and Slocum at Chancellorsville. To hold Lee in place at Fredericksburg, Maj. Gen. Dan Sickles's Corps and Couch's third division, commanded by Brig. Gen. John Gibbon, would remain on the north bank of the Rappahannock in clear view of the Confederates. Two additional corps, under Maj. Gens. John Sedgwick and John Reynolds, would cross the river at Fredericksburg as if preparing to attack Marye's Heights. Meantime, 10,000 cavalrymen under Maj. Gen. George Stoneman would attempt to get in Lee's rear and disrupt his communications.

Hooker's complex plan, although running behind schedule, otherwise worked almost perfectly during its early stages. Concealed by a heavy, sound-muffling fog that blanketed the Rappahannock before dawn on April 29, one of Sedgwick's brigades crossed the river in boats just below the mouth of Deep Run and surprised the 54th North Carolina, which was on picket. "The movement had been conducted with so much secrecy," General Early recalled, "the boats being brought to the river by hand, that the first intimation of it . . . was the landing of the force." In the camp of the 57th North Carolina the "long rool was beet" and the men hurried to their "brest work towards the river. [T]here we lay in the road (being the advanced line) all day and night," Private Zimmerman wrote. "[I]t rained in the eavning considerable and was very cool[.] [W]e had no fire and I like to frooze[.] I never was chilled worse[.] [W]e was relivd next morning. . . ."[49] Assisted by the lingering fog and a

48. Henry Huss to D. H. Dellinger, March 21, 1863, Rhyne, Houser, and Huss Letters. "[A]s for hard times," Huss added, "no tonge can tell." See also J. C. Zimmerman to M. A. Zimmerman, April 24, 1863, Zimmerman Letters.

49. Jubal A. Early, *Lieutenant General Jubal Anderson Early, C.S.A.: Autobiographical Sketch and Narrative of the War between the States* (Philadelphia: J. B. Lippincott Company, 1912; Wilmington, N.C.: Broadfoot Publishing Company, 1989), 193, hereafter cited as Early, *Autobiographical Sketch*; J. C. Zimmerman to M. A. Zimmerman, May 7, 1863, Zimmerman Letters. "[O]ur reg. [the 57th] was thrown out as skirmishers and went

light rain that began that evening and continued the next day, Sedgwick laid pontoon bridges and began crossing his troops. Upriver, Meade, Howard, and Slocum were also on the move. By midafternoon on April 30, all three had reached Chancellorsville. Couch's two divisions, which crossed at United States Ford rather than Banks' Ford as planned, were not far behind. Hooker then paused to bring up Sickles's Corps from Fredericksburg. Pending Sickles's arrival, Meade, Howard, and Slocum held their ground on orders from Hooker, thereby squandering an opportunity to get clear of the Wilderness's constricting thickets, uncover Banks' Ford, and substantially reduce the distance between the two halves of the Federal army.

By the evening of April 29 Lee was thoroughly alert to the growing danger on his left but still uncertain of Hooker's intentions. He therefore sent Maj. Gen. Richard H. Anderson's Division toward Chancellorsville to provide a trip wire in the event of an attack. Anderson's men marched westward on the evening of April 29 and arrived at Chancellorsville about midnight. There they found William Mahone's Virginia brigade, which had been flanked out of its position at United States Ford. Learning that the Federals had crossed the Rapidan in strong force at Ely's and Germanna Fords and were approaching Chancellorsville, Anderson retired eastward and entrenched on open ground near Tabernacle Church. Lee, convinced by Anderson's reports and Sedgwick's passivity that the main Federal effort was directed at his left flank, moved the bulk of his army west at midnight on the thirtieth. Early's Division, including the 57th North Carolina, remained behind with a Mississippi brigade and an artillery contingent to confront Sedgwick and Reynolds.

On May 1 heavy but inconclusive fighting broke out west of Tabernacle Church as the Federals emerged from the Wilderness and Lee advanced to meet them. Beyond the Confederate right, Meade's Corps moved toward Banks' Ford, menacing Lee's rear. By early afternoon Hooker seemed poised for the decisive victory that he longed to present to President Lincoln and the nation. At that juncture, for reasons that remain unclear, he lost his nerve: over the vehement protests of his lieutenants, Hooker withdrew into the Wilderness, assumed a defensive posture, and began fortifying his lines. On the morning of May 2 Lee discovered that Hooker's right was "in the air" and dispatched Jackson with 26,000 men on one of history's most famous flank marches. That movement was detected by the Federals but, thanks largely to the carelessness of General Howard, achieved tactical surprise and devastating results. Darkness and Reynolds's newly arrived corps finally combined to bring the attack to a halt, and the fighting ended a few hours later with an unsuccessful night counterattack by Hooker and the mortal wounding of Jackson.

---

as fare as the turnpike road nearly opposite deep run not very fare from the river," Pvt. Samuel W. Eaton of Company B recorded in his diary. "[O]ur reg. deployed out along the road. Some few went about 100 yds. beyond the road." "The morning of the 28 [29th] befour I got up," Pvt. B. Y. Malone of the 6th stated, "I herd a horse come threw the camp in a full lope and it was not meney minutes untell the man come back and sais Boys you had better get up we will have a fight hear to reckly and I comenced geting up and befour I got my close on they comenced beating the long roal and it was not but a minnet or too untill I herd the Adgertent hollow fall in with armes the Reg: then [we] was formed and marched to the Battel field. . . ." Samuel W. Eaton Diary (typescript), April 29, 1863, Samuel W. Eaton Papers, SHC, hereafter cited as Eaton Diary; William Whatley Pierson Jr., ed., *Whipt 'em Everytime: The Diary of Bartlett Yancey Malone, Co. H, 6th N.C. Regiment* (Jackson, Tenn.: McCowat-Mercer Press, 1960; Wilmington, N.C.: Broadfoot Publishing Company, 1987), 76 (April 28 [29], 1863), hereafter cited as Pierson, *Diary of Bartlett Yancey Malone.*

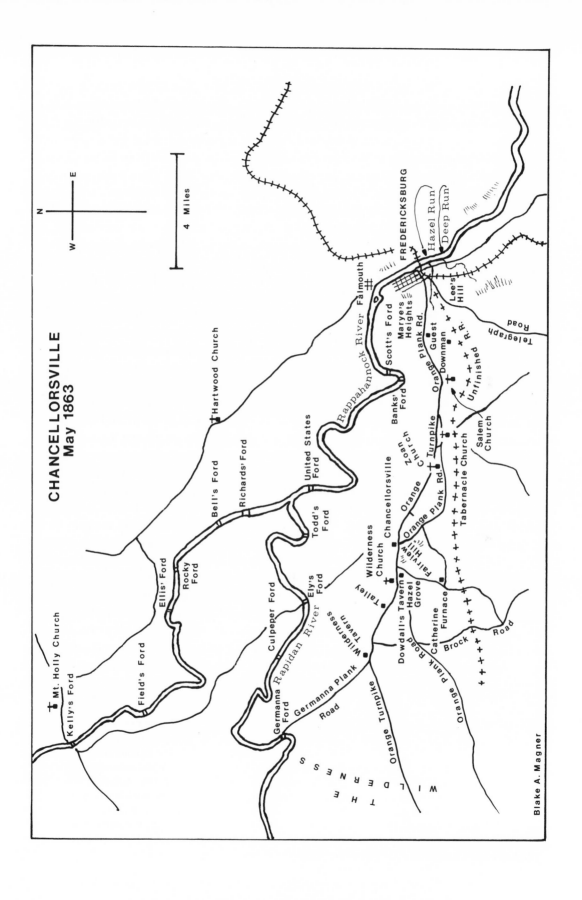

CHANCELLORSVILLE
May 1863

N / E / W / S

4 Miles

Blake A. Magner

Mt. Holly Church

Kelly's Ford

Field's Ford

Ellis' Ford

Rocky Ford

Culpeper Ford

Germanna Rapidan River Ford

Germanna Plank Road

Ely's Ford

Wilderness Tavern

Orange Turnpike

THE WILDERNESS

Dowdall's Tavern

Hazel Grove

Catherine Furnace

Orange Plank Road

Brock Road

Talley

Wilderness Church

Fairview Hill

Chancellorsville

Orange Plank Rd.

Tabernacle Church

Zoan Church

Turnpike

Salem Church

Unfinished R. R.

Downman

Guest

Orange Plank Rd.

Lee's Hill

Telegraph Road

Todd's Ford

United States Ford

Richards' Ford

Bell's Ford

Hartwood Church

Rappahannock River

Banks' Ford

Scott's Ford

Falmouth

Marye's Heights

FREDERICKSBURG

Hazel Run

Deep Run

Shaken by the day's events and hoping to disrupt further offensive operations by Lee, Hooker ordered Sedgwick to attack Early at Fredericksburg on the morning of May 3.

While Lee and Hooker grappled in the Wilderness, Hoke's men, in line of battle behind their breastworks near Fredericksburg, enjoyed a surprisingly tranquil two days. Pvt. Samuel W. Eaton of the 57th North Carolina noted in his diary on May 1 that although "right smart" cannonading was audible downriver, he "had a fine time frying and eating herine [herring]." The troops "seemed to be in good spirits that night," he wrote, "[and] there was a great deal of holering along the lines."[50] More cannonading was heard on May 2, but the day was notable mainly for a misinterpretation of orders that sent most of Early's force on an unnecessary six-mile march in the direction of Chancellorsville. The men returned to Fredericksburg after the mistake was discovered and before the Federals could seize Marye's Heights.

At 5:00 A.M. on May 3 Sedgwick, in obedience to Hooker's orders, brushed aside light Confederate opposition and advanced into Fredericksburg. Gibbon's Division crossed the Rappahannock on a newly constructed pontoon bridge, and at daybreak the Federals attacked. "The enemy was then in frunt in large force," Zimmerman informed his wife. "[T]hey advanced up the creek [Deep Run] that run from our lines towards the river. . . . [W]e fired a voley and they fell back[.] [O]ur canon killed a good many where they could bee seen above the banks and our sharp shooters took down several. . . . They soon found it two hot a place for them and they had to retire[.]" Along other parts of the six-mile-long Fredericksburg line matters did not go as well for the Confederates. Early's badly outnumbered command fended off three Federal assaults, but a fourth overpowered Barksdale's Mississippians and captured Marye's Heights. That evening, fearing that Federal artillery on Marye's Heights would be "ranged upon us," Hoke withdrew his men "double quick across the bottom" and then south along the Telegraph Road. With the rest of Early's command, they then formed a line about two miles below Lee's Hill.[51]

Around 2:00 P.M. Sedgwick began advancing toward Chancellorsville. Gibbon's Division remained behind to hold Marye's Heights. Two hours later Sedgwick reached Salem Church, six miles west of Fredericksburg, and collided with Cadmus M. Wilcox's Alabama brigade and four others commanded by Lafayette McLaws, which had been sent from Chancellorsville to reinforce Early. Sedgwick's leading division, anticipating only slight opposition, was unexpectedly thrown back by the superior Confederate force. McLaws then went over to the attack but was rebuffed by Sedgwick's second division. Meantime, at Chancellorsville, Jackson's Corps, commanded by Maj. Gen. J. E. B. Stuart, renewed its assault during the morning. Jackson's flank march had in effect split the already divided Army of Northern Virginia into a third segment, presenting Hooker with yet another opportunity for victory. Nevertheless, he continued to fall back toward the Rappahannock, enabling Stuart

---

50. Eaton Diary, May 1, 1863.

51. J. C. Zimmerman to M. A. Zimmerman, May 7, 1863, Zimmerman Letters; Eaton Diary, May 3, 1863. According to its chaplain, John Paris, the 54th North Carolina "was under a heavy fire of shell and cannon shot nearly all day . . . on the plateau below the city, but being compelled to lie down for safety, few casualties occurred." Presumably for the same reason, casualties in the 57th North Carolina were also minimal (two men reported wounded). *Spirit of the Age* (Raleigh), May 25, 1863.

to rejoin Lee. Lee was preparing a new attack when word came of the Federal success at Fredericksburg. McLaws was then dispatched to reinforce Early, as stated above, and was followed the next day by three brigades of Anderson's Division. Stuart remained behind at Chancellorsville to watch the quiescent Hooker.

On the morning of May 4, while Anderson's brigades marched toward Fredericksburg, Early moved to recapture Marye's Heights. Hoke's and Hays's Brigades, on Early's right, crossed Hazel Run to flank Gibbon; Early advanced directly against Marye's Heights with the brigades of Barksdale and Brig. Gens. John B. Gordon and William Smith. Badly outnumbered, Gibbon retired into Fredericksburg without offering resistance. Leaving Barksdale to hold Marye's Heights and Smith in reserve, Early then advanced "through the bushes, & over hills and hollows" against Sedgwick, linking up en route with the newly arrived Anderson. Sedgwick fell back to the north, anchoring his flanks on the Rappahannock, protecting his pontoon bridge at Scott's Ford, and holding a portion of the Orange Plank Road so as to hinder Lee's deployments.[52]

At about 6:00 P.M. Early attacked, and Hoke's men, along with those of Brig. Gen. Ambrose R. Wright on their left, found themselves charging up a low ridge near the home of a farmer named Downman.[53] The Federal position, according to Wright's report, consisted of "a strong line of sharpshooters occupying the crest of the ridge and the house and fencing around Downman's yard, with heavy batteries on the hills in their rear." After moving through a sheltering ravine, Wright's Georgians stormed "across the fields, swept by the house, and reached the woods opposite, driving the enemy before [them] like chaff." Fearful of colliding with one of McLaws's brigades, Wright then called a halt along the edge of the woods, where he remained under a "murderous" fire until dark.[54]

In the meantime, Hoke's Brigade advanced "with a rush over rough ground and under terrific fire of rifle and canister."[55] According to Early's postwar account, Hoke charged

across the plateau . . . between Downman's house and Hazel Run, then down the slope, across the valley, and up the steep ascent of the next ridge towards the Plank road . . . while the guns at Guest's house played upon his advancing line without disturbing his beautiful order. Hays [on Hoke's right] rapidly ascended the hill in front, immediately encountering the right[?] of the enemy's front line, which he swept before him, and continued his advance without a halt. It was a splendid sight to see the rapid and orderly advance of these two brigades, with the enemy flying before them. The officers and men manning the artillery[,] which had been posted on eminences along the Telegraph road and on the right bank of Hazel Run so as to protect the infantry retreat in case of disaster [and was thus] debarred from . . . active participation in the action, could not refrain from enthusiastically cheering the infantry, as it so handsomely swept everything in front.[56]

52. Eaton Diary, May 4, 1863.

53. Early's combined force outnumbered Sedgwick's about 21,000 to 19,000. McLaws's Division was on the Confederate left, Anderson's in the center, and Early's on the right. Hays was on Hoke's right and Gordon to the right of Hays. The left-to-right alignment of Hoke's command is unclear, but it appears that the 1st Battalion N.C. Sharpshooters was on the extreme left with the 57th North Carolina on its right.

54. *Official Records (Army)*, ser. 1, 25 (pt. 1):869.

55. Hatton, "Gen. Archibald Godwin," 134.

56. Early, *Autobiographical Sketch*, 228-229.

At that juncture, as the two brigades neared the woods below the Guest house, they began to converge.

The artillery at Guest's house had been compelled to fly in order to prevent capture [Early continued], and the enemy was retiring in confusion on all parts of the line confronting them and Gordon, but just then Hoke fell from his horse, with his arm badly shattered by a ball near the shoulder joint.

The brigade thus losing its commander, to whom alone the instruction [plan of attack] had been given, and without any one to direct its movement at that particular crisis, pushed on across the Plank road, encountered Hays' brigade in the woods still advancing, and the two commingling together were thrown into confusion. They crossed each other's paths in this condition, but still continued to advance, getting far into the woods. Hays' brigade pressed on in its proper direction, but Hoke's . . . had got to its right. The regiments of both brigades had lost their organization, and in the woods it was impossible to restore it. Portions of both brigades penetrated a considerable distance into the woods, still driving the enemy before them, but . . . [finally] were compelled to retire themselves, leaving some prisoners in the enemy's hands. . . .[57]

In a letter to his wife dated May 7, 1863, Private Wagner was less specific than Early but more graphic: "Dear Wife I was in a fite . . . last Monday [May 4] but I got spaird by the hand of the almity Father once more a gain[.] Dear we aut all to pray Everyday[.] Dear I never saw such a time since God made me[.] I hope and pray to God they soone will quit it[.] [W]e routted them compleatly[.] Dear we lost a good many men on Boothe sides. . . . I hope to God they will serrendered so we neatin to fite any more now for the way I went through the Balls and Bum shells and grape shot and canisters is a nough to mak any mans hare crall on his head. . . ."[58] Private Zimmerman also left a lively account of the May 4 fight:

[W]e . . . marched two miles in line of battle through brush and fallen timber until we taken a position undder a hill in some small groth[.] [T]here we lay till most night then order come that we had to charge the enemy[.] [W]hen all was ready two canons fired as a signal for the charg[.] [T]hen the holl line mooved off at a double quick[.] Our line was over five miles long and we had to go two miles before we got to the enemy[.] [O]ur men was almost broak down before they got there but when they got there they mad[e] the yankeys run and leave every thing they had[.] I never saw the like of knapsack[s] blankets overcoats and just any thing you could name[.] [W]e took a lot of canon and

57. Early, *Autobiographical Sketch*, 229-230. In his battle report, Early wrote that "Hays' and Hoke's brigades were thrown into some confusion by coming in contact after they crossed the Plank road below Guest's house, and it becoming difficult to distinguish our troops from those of the enemy, on account of the growing darkness, they had, therefore, to fall back to reform. . . ." Brig. Gen. William N. Pendleton, chief of artillery of the Army of Northern Virginia, described the charge of Hoke's Brigade (perhaps inadvertently omitting Hays) as "brilliant." *Official Records (Army)*, ser. 1, 25 (pt. 1):1002, 817. See also *Spirit of the Age* (Raleigh), May 25, 1863; Jones, "Fifty-seventh Regiment," in Clark, *Histories of the North Carolina Regiments*, 3:410.

58. W. F. Wagner to N. M. Wagner, May 7, 1863, in Hatley and Huffman, *Letters of William F. Wagner*, 50. Pvt. J. W. Armsworthy of the 54th North Carolina described the enemy's fire as so heavy that it seemed "impossible for any of us to be missed. . . ." J. W. Armsworthy to E. J. Armsworthy, May 28, 1863, Armsworthy Letters. See also "[Report on the Battle of Chancellorsville by Maj. Rufus W. Wharton]," May 13, 1863, Perry Family Papers, SHC; *Spirit of the Age* (Raleigh), May 25, 1863; Early, *Autobiographical Sketch*, 227-228.

prisners[.] I got two large yankey blankets and could of picked up hundrids more if I could a crryed them. . . . We lost a good many killed wounded and missen[.][59]

While Hoke and Hays triumphed on the left, Gordon's attack on the right turned the enemy flank. Hoke's men then re-formed on the Plank road "just below Guest's house" and were sent to reinforce Gordon's left. There they spent the night of May 4. During the night Sedgwick moved back across the Rappahannock at Scott's Ford, and the next morning Gibbon crossed to the north bank at Fredericksburg. Determined to crush Hooker's forces near Chancellorsville despite their heavy field fortifications, Lee recalled McLaws and Anderson from Fredericksburg. However, his attack preparations were delayed by a violent rainstorm, and on the night of May 5 Hooker abandoned his works and began retreating. Before the Confederates could get into position for an assault the next day, he was gone. Casualties in Hoke's Brigade at the Battle of Chancellorsville were officially reported as 35 men killed and 195 wounded. In the 57th North Carolina, 9 men were reported killed or mortally wounded, 73 wounded, and 51 missing. Figures compiled for this volume indicate that the regiment lost 27 men killed or mortally wounded, 59 wounded, and 50 captured.[60]

Following the Battle of Chancellorsville, the 57th North Carolina remained at Fredericksburg and resumed its two-day picket details on the banks of the Rappahannock.

Our [picket] post [Captain Pfohl wrote] is a very pleasant one in a good house with fine shady grounds around it, & it is quite a relief to get there occasionally, to change the sultry tents for . . . pleasant shade & blooming flowers. . . . Our duties there are not very arduous. We have about 10 sentries on the river bank during the day, extending up & down about one mile. At night we double the numbers, & to make matters more secure, send down some 2 companies who sleep in the rifle pits which are on the bluff, a short distance from the edge of the water. . . . The enemys' pickets are very numerous on the opposite bank, which, as the river is not more than from 75 to 100 yds wide, brings them in close proximity to us. . . . Our orders are very strict . . . allowing no communication with them in word or otherwise. Yesterday morning [May 28] they were jubilating over the down fall of Vicksburg, but later in the day they were not quite so sanguine of success, having probably heard later [and more accurate] news not quite so favorable. . . . They were very anxious to know what our papers said of the affair, but of course we made them no reply.[61]

On May 27 Early's Division was reviewed by Generals Lee, Early, A. P. Hill, and Henry Heth. "[E]ach Regt. was divided into two divisions & drawn up in line one in rear of

59. J. C. Zimmerman to M. A. Zimmerman, May 7, 1863, Zimmerman Letters. See also Alexander Patton to [Ellen Patton], May 7, 1863, Patton Papers; J. M. Hefner to Kizia Hefner, May 7, 1863, Hefner Papers; Eaton Diary, May 4, 1863; M. A. Walker to M. C. Walker, May 8, 1863, M. A. Walker Letters; Pierson, *Diary of Bartlett Yancey Malone*, 79 (May 4, 1863).

60. Early, *Autobiographical Sketch*, 230. See also *Official Records (Army)*, ser. 1, 25 (pt. 1):808; "List of casualties of the 57th N.C. Regt in the 2d battle near Fredericksburg, Va. May 3 & 4, 1863," *Confederate States Army Casualties: Lists and Narrative Reports, 1861-1865*, NARA, M836, reel 6; *Carolina Watchman* (Salisbury), May 25, 1863. Total Confederate casualties at Chancellorsville were 1,665 killed, 9,081 wounded, and 2,018 missing; Federal losses were 1,606 killed, 9,762 wounded, and 5,919 missing. See Patricia L. Faust, ed., *Historical Times Encyclopedia of the Civil War* (New York: Harper and Row, 1986), 127.

61. W. J. Pfohl to C. T. Pfohl, May 29, 1863, Pfohl Papers. See also *Spirit of the Age* (Raleigh), June 1, 1863.

the other about half wheeling distance," a 6th North Carolina soldier recalled. "[I]t formed a line of Regimental divisions about one mile long each Regiment marching one after the other. . . . [I]t was a grand thing to a spectator. . . . I had a tolerable chance to see the whole Division[;] the most men I ever saw at one time before."[62] Aside from the minimal diversions provided by picket duty and the May 27 review, times were "dul." Rations improved somewhat, but that development was perceived in some quarters as ominous: "they are fatning us to cross the river," Private Zimmerman predicted with characteristic gloom. Prospects for a new offensive indeed became a primary topic of discussion in the 57th but, the victory at Chancellorsville notwithstanding, were viewed dimly. Zimmerman feared a "thrashen," and Private Hefner, taking the long view, was even more pessimistic: "we may Whip them hear," he wrote, "and at some other point they whip us[,] and after a while we ar ruint for ever."[63]

Shortly before midnight on June 4, Hoke's Brigade, commanded by Col. Isaac E. Avery of the 6th North Carolina in the absence of the wounded Hoke, marched with the rest of Ewell's Corps (formerly Jackson's) to begin the campaign that would end at Gettysburg. Ewell's column was followed immediately by Longstreet's Corps; A. P. Hill's newly organized corps remained temporarily at Fredericksburg to watch Federal forces opposite the town. The brigade arrived at Spotsylvania Court House a little after sunrise and rested for an hour and a half before moving another six miles and camping for the night. On June 6 the men advanced eight miles through a "very hard" rain.[64] Marching by way of Verdiersville, they crossed the Rapidan River at Somerville Ford about noon on the seventh, reached Culpeper Court House the next day, and bivouacked two miles west of the town (see map on page 61). On June 9 the brigade was dispatched with the rest of Ewell's Corps to assist "Jeb" Stuart in a closely fought cavalry battle at Brandy Station. The Federal horsemen, content with their near victory over the redoubtable Stuart and averse to challenging Confederate infantry, withdrew before Ewell could get into position.

Early's men resumed their march on June 10 and reached the Hazel River that evening. On the eleventh they passed through Woodville, Sperryville, and Washington (in Rappahannock County), where Sgt. Bartlett Y. Malone saw "meney pritty and kind Ladies [who] . . . had water all along the streets for the Soldiers to drink[.]" About sunup on June 12 the men set out again. "After a toilsome march," Chaplain John Paris of the 54th North Carolina wrote, "we crossed the Blue Ridge [at Chester Gap that afternoon] . . . passed the village of Front Royal at its base, forded the beautiful Shenandoah, and bivouacked on its northern bank." "We . . . took up camp at sun set," Private Eaton recorded in

62. Quoted in Richard W. Iobst, *The Bloody Sixth: The Sixth North Carolina Regiment Confederate States of America* (Raleigh: Confederate Centennial Commission, 1965; Gaithersburg, Md.: Butternut Press, 1987), 121-122, hereafter cited as Iobst, *Bloody Sixth*.

63. J. M. Hefner to Kizia Hefner, May 31 (first quotation) and June 2, 1863 (third quotation), Hefner Papers; J. C. Zimmerman to M. A. Zimmerman, May 17, 1863 (second quotation), Zimmerman Letters. There was a good deal of sickness in the regiment during May and fifteen deaths. See J. C. Zimmerman to M. A. Zimmerman, May 23, 1863, Zimmerman Letters; M. A. Walker to M. C. Walker, May 28, 1863, M. A. Walker Letters.

64. Pierson, *Diary of Bartlett Yancey Malone*, 80 (June 6, 1863). See also Eaton Diary, June 4-6, 1863.

his diary, and "cooked one days rations, which keep [*sic*] us up till after midnight after having marched 20 m[ile]s and was very tired indeed."[65]

On the morning of June 13, Early received orders from Ewell to cooperate with Maj. Gen. Edward Johnson's Division in an attack on Winchester, defended by 6,000 men under the inept command of Maj. Gen. Robert H. Milroy. At the same time, Maj. Gen. Robert Rodes's Division would attack a smaller Federal force ten miles to the east at Berryville. Upon reaching Winchester a few hours later, Early's men skirmished briskly with Milroy's troops, driving them back to their fortifications. Avery's Brigade took "no active part" in the fighting and was ordered to nearby Kernstown that evening to protect the ambulances, wagons, and artillery. The next day, following a night of "violent" storms and "drenching" rain, Avery's men moved back to Winchester and participated in Early's flank march west of the town. During the late afternoon Early attacked and overran part of Milroy's works. Badly outnumbered and threatened with encirclement, Milroy retreated that night but was intercepted by Johnson. Four thousand Federals were captured along with 23 pieces of artillery, 300 loaded wagons, more than 300 horses, and "quite a large amount" of commissary and quartermaster stores. During the fighting the 57th North Carolina supported "batteries on the left" and later took a supporting position behind Hays. There it was exposed to Federal battery fire and lost one man killed and four wounded.[66]

The 57th remained near Winchester for four days guarding prisoners and helping itself to the cornucopia of Federal provisions and equipment. "Our boys got a great many pants, haversacks, canteens and a quantity of shugar, coffee, rice, beans &c," Private Eaton wrote.[67] "[A] little after daylight" on June 19 the regiment was "again on the tramp." The roads were "quite muddy," Eaton noted in his diary, "[but] We marched very hard for . . . about 20 ms. [and] arived within 3 miles of Shepardstown, on the Potomac river [and] took up camp about 3 o'clk[.]" Avery's Brigade, minus the 54th North Carolina, which was detailed to escort Federal prisoners to Staunton and did not rejoin its sister units until July 10, remained on the banks of the Potomac for two days waiting for high water to subside. "We started early [on June 22] on our march for Maryeland," Eaton continued, "[and] passed through Shepardstown. The town appeared to be quite loyal [to the Confederacy]. The ladies waved their flags and white handkerchiefs at us, and with their cheering countannances bid us good luck & glorious victories[.] We crossed the Potomac between 8 & 9 o'clk. We was about 25 minutes crossing. [I]t was about 175 [or] 200 yds wide[.] [M]arched through

65. Pierson, *Diary of Bartlett Yancey Malone*, 81 (June 11, 1863); *Spirit of the Age* (Raleigh), June 29, 1863; Eaton Diary, June 12, 1863 (see also June 11, 1863).

66. *Official Records (Army)*, ser. 1, 27 (pt. 2):487 (first quotation), 442 (fourth quotation), 483 (fifth quotation); Early, *Autobiographical Sketch*, 243 (second and third quotations). See also Eaton Diary, June 13-14, 1863; *Greensborough Patriot*, July 2, 1863; *Official Records (Army)*, ser. 1, 27 (pt. 2):462-463. Casualty figures are derived from service records in this volume. The regiment's losses were officially reported as one man killed and one wounded. See *Official Records (Army)*, ser. 1, 27 (pt. 2):335.

67. Eaton Diary, June 16, 1863. "I never saw as many things at one plase in my life," Private Wagner exulted. "[C]loathing and Rashins and waggons and sugar and coffey Reddy ground up[.] I got a litle pocket fool of coffey and a new haver sack and a shirt[.] [O]ur boys some of them got new sutes all over and some got lots of writeing paper[.] [W]e got Thousands of Dollars worth of things[:] canonons and horses[,] infact nearly Ever thing a man can name I think we got[.]" W. F. Wagner to N. M. Wagner, June 17, 1863, in Hatley and Huffman, *Letters of William F. Wagner*, 54.

Sharpsburg 3 ms. from [the] Po[tomac] and through Boonsborough 6 ms. from Sharpsburg[.] [T]ook up camp near the cave town road, marched about 16 miles."[68]

During the next eight days the 57th North Carolina continued its northward advance with the rest of Lee's army. It bivouacked near Waynesborough, just over the Pennsylvania line, on June 23, reached the vicinity of Fayetteville on the twenty-fourth, and, after a day of rest, moved on through an all-day rain to Mummasburg on the twenty-sixth. On June 27 the regiment arrived at East Berlin, and on the twenty-eighth it reached York. There, along with Avery's other two regiments, it was "put into quarters in some extensive buildings put up for hospitals." Following two nights of comparative luxury at York, the men retraced their route westward on June 30, passing through East Berlin and bivouacking that night about three miles east of Heidlersburg. Cashtown, Early's destination, was about sixteen miles to the southwest. Gettysburg, the town to which he would in fact march the next day, was in a somewhat more southerly direction, thirteen miles distant.[69]

On the night of June 28, while Avery's men were sleeping under a roof at York, Lee learned that the Army of the Potomac was at Frederick, thirty-five miles south of Fayetteville. Fearing for the safety of his communication lines, Lee issued orders to concentrate the scattered Army of Northern Virginia. Hill's Corps was instructed to move from Fayetteville to Cashtown on the twenty-ninth, and Longstreet's Corps, a few miles to the west of Fayetteville at Chambersburg, was ordered to follow the next day. Early was recalled from York, as indicated above, and Ewell's other two divisions, under Rodes and Johnson, were ordered south from Carlisle. Hill arrived at Cashtown during the evening of June 30 and learned that Federal troops (believed to be "principally cavalry") were present at Gettysburg, eight miles southeast. With characteristic aggressiveness, he decided to advance at daylight the next morning and "discover," as he later reported, "what was in my front." Maj. Gen. Henry Heth's Division would take the lead, followed by that of Maj. Gen. William D. Pender.[70]

Approaching Gettysburg from the west via the Chambersburg Pike on the sultry morning of July 1, Heth topped a height known as Herr Ridge to find himself confronted by a strong line of dismounted troopers. Pitching into the Federals with the brigades of Brig. Gens. James J. Archer and Joseph R. Davis, Heth made slow and costly progress against the cavalrymen's rapid-firing breechloaders until Federal infantry arrived. A furious fight then erupted with the Federal "Iron Brigade," sending Archer reeling back across a creek known as Willoughby Run. North of the pike, Davis flanked the Federals and forced them to

68. Eaton Diary, June 19 and 22, 1863.

69. *Official Records (Army)*, ser. 1, 27 (pt. 2):466. The foregoing itinerary is based primarily on the Eaton Diary, June 23-30, 1863; Pierson, *Diary of Bartlett Yancey Malone*, 83-84 (June 23-30, 1863); "Record of Events," abstracts of April 30 (or May 1 or May 11)-August 31 (or September 1), 1863, muster rolls for Companies A-G and I-K, 57th Regiment N.C. Troops, Compiled Confederate Service Records (North Carolina), M270, reel 526. Those sources do not agree in all particulars.

Private Eaton, like almost all of Lee's Confederates, was impressed by the well-ordered prosperity of Pennsylvania. "The country is very fine indeed," he wrote admiringly. "[The] wheat, corn, & meadow wheat looks very fine. . . . People live [h]ear on an equality [that is, there was not much variation in individual wealth], have beautiful farms, and comfortable houses to live in[.] [T]hey are generally dutch." Eaton Diary, June 24, 1863.

70. *Official Records (Army)*, ser. 1, 27 (pt. 2):607.

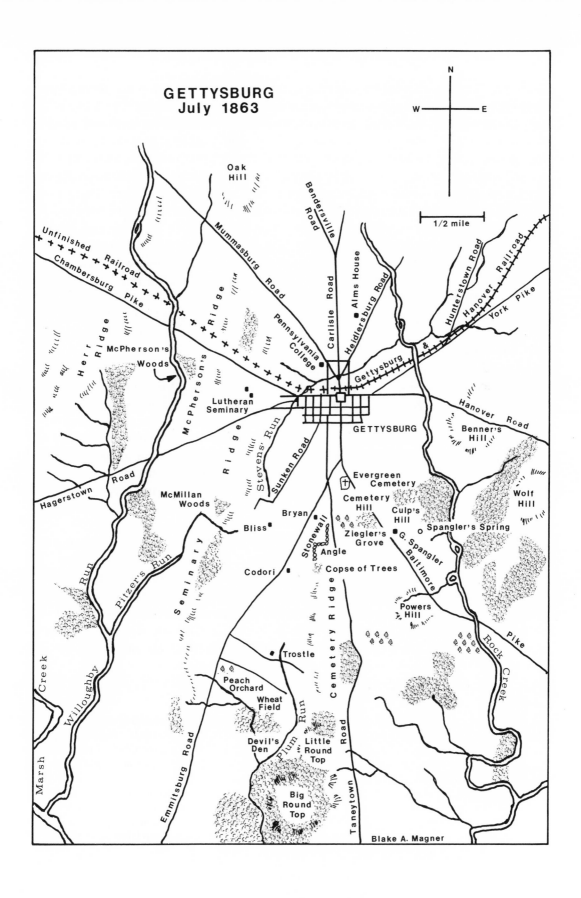

retreat precipitately to Seminary Ridge, just west of Gettysburg. However, Davis's men were flanked in turn and driven into a deep railroad cut, where many surrendered. The focus of the fighting then shifted to Heth's left as Rodes, arriving on the field with his division, found to his astonishment that "the enemy . . . had no troops facing me at all." That opportunity swiftly disappeared: in the time that it took Rodes to deploy, the frantically improvising Federals established a line south of a height known as Oak Hill. Shortly thereafter, they inflicted a bloody repulse on Rodes's charging infantrymen.[71]

While Heth and Rodes engaged the enemy on the morning and early afternoon of July 1, Early's Division marched toward Gettysburg on the Heidlersburg road.

As the head of the column reached a point some three or four miles from Gettysburg [Lieutenant Colonel Jones of the 57th wrote], somewhere about mid-day, two reports of field guns were heard in the direction of Gettysburg. . . . Owing to a peculiar atmospheric condition, the sound seemed farther off than it really was, and it was supposed by all to be a cavalry engagement some twenty miles away. . . . While officers were still discussing the matter . . . [a staff officer] was seen approaching the head of the column at full speed. He brought an order from General Early saying General A. P. Hill was hard pressed at Gettysburg, and for the division to make all haste to his assistance. Men disengaged themselves of their blankets and whatever else encumbered them, leaving them to be gathered by the rear guard and wagon train, and took the quick step for Gettysburg. The last mile was made at double-quick, for they could already see a cloud of white smoke floating over Gettysburg and could hear the noise of the great conflict.[72]

Early's Division arrived at Gettysburg shortly after 2:00 P.M. during Rodes's fight with elements of the Federal I and XI Corps near Oak Hill and the Mummasburg road. Early then went into position on Rodes's left, northeast of the town. Avery's Brigade was placed just to the left (east) of the Heidlersburg road. "The division went into line and halted ten minutes to rest the men," Jones continued. "From our position we could see the Confederate and Federal lines arrayed one against the other in open ground, no breastworks, no fortifications, but they stood apart in battle array . . . in plain view for two miles except where the line was lost in the depressions of the hills." At 3:00 P.M. Lee launched a combined assault by Heth's, Pender's, Rodes's, and Early's Divisions. "[A] Confederate brigade away on our extreme right moved forward," Jones remembered. "[Then] came a jet of white smoke from along the enemy's line and a scarcely audible roar of musketry . . . [and] artillery; then . . . the expected yell, a rush, and the enemy's line broke. As this first brigade moved, a second was moving in echelon [sequentially]; there was the same yell, the same rush, and the same flight of the enemy. Still another brigade; the sound of the conflict and yell of men becoming more distinct; a rush forward and the Stars and Stripes were seen in full retreat. As the conflict neared our position . . . the men were wild with excitement, and when their time came they went in with the wildest enthusiasm, for from where they stood they could see two miles of the enemy's line in full retreat. It looked indeed as if the end of the war had come."[73]

71. *Official Records (Army)*, ser. 1, 27 (pt. 2):552.

72. Jones, "Fifty-seventh Regiment," in Clark, *Histories of the North Carolina Regiments*, 3:412-413.

73. Jones, "Fifty-seventh Regiment," in Clark, *Histories of the North Carolina Regiments*, 3:413-414.

"The enemy had formed line of battle on the hillside [Barlow Knoll] in front of the town," Colonel Godwin of the 57th North Carolina reported, "under cover of a strong fence, portions of which were made of stone. Our advance was made with great deliberation until we approached a sluggish stream [Rock Creek] . . . about 200 yards in front of the enemy's lines, when the batteries opened upon us with grape and canister, seconded by a very destructive fire from the infantry." The brigade then charged across the creek and up the hill. "[T]he enemy stubbornly . . . [held] their position until we had climbed over into their midst," Godwin continued. "[A] large number of prisoners [were] taken . . . [and] sent to the rear. The enemy now fled into the town, many of them being killed in the retreat." "[B]roken" and, it appeared to Lieutenant Colonel Jones, "utterly routed," the Federals recoiled through the streets of Gettysburg to Cemetery Hill. "There was not an officer . . . [or] man [in the 57th]," he added, "that did not expect that the war would be closed upon the hill that evening. . . ." However, no further Confederate attacks occurred. "[S]ome one," Jones wrote sadly thirty-eight years later (referring no doubt to General Ewell), "made a blunder that lost the battle of Gettysburg, and, humanly speaking, the Confederate cause."[74]

After assisting in the rout of the XI Corps, Avery moved his three regiments under artillery fire to a field east of Gettysburg, across the tracks of the Gettysburg and Hanover Railroad. There he sheltered them behind a low ridge and bivouacked "near a spring house" for the night. "The night passed quietly," Jones recalled, "except that we could hear the picks and shovels of the enemy engaged in fortifying their line, and the rumble of guns and the tramp of infantry, as at intervals . . . their reinforcements arrived. When morning came, they had worked wonders in fortifying that hill in so short a time."[75] During most of the day the men "layed in line of battle" under sharpshooter fire while Longstreet's powerful attack on the Round Tops was narrowly beaten back in heavy fighting. Shortly before dusk, Johnson's Division of Ewell's Corps assaulted Culp's Hill, on the extreme right of the Federal line. At about 8:00 P.M., Avery's and Harry T. Hays's Brigades launched an attack on Cemetery Hill in support of Johnson. Avery's line of battle, in left-to-right order, consisted of the 57th, 21st, and 6th North Carolina. Hays's Louisianians were on the right of the 6th. "The sun was low when the order came," Jones continued. "[W]hen the bugle sounded . . . the line advanced in beautiful order, and as it pointed to the southwest there was a glint all along the line of bayonets that was very striking and marked how beautifully they were aligned. In an instant after becoming visible the enemy opened fire with artillery, but the brigades went forward in the same beautiful order across the interposing valley lying between the town and Cemetery Hill. Not only from the front but from away out toward Culp's Hill, on the enemy's extreme right, artillery had opened on us. Before the hill was reached, the musketry fire had become very heavy, and the Fifty-seventh Regiment . . . suffered heavily from both artillery and infantry."[76]

74. *Official Records (Army)*, ser. 1, 27 (pt. 2):484; Jones, "Fifty-seventh Regiment," in Clark, *Histories of the North Carolina Regiments*, 3:414.

75. Eaton Diary, July 2, 1863; Jones, "Fifty-seventh Regiment," in Clark, *Histories of the North Carolina Regiments*, 3:414.

76. Eaton Diary, July 2, 1863; Jones, "Fifty-seventh Regiment," in Clark, *Histories of the North Carolina Regiments*, 3:415.

Avery's men "advanced in gallant style to the attack, passing over the ridge in front of them under a heavy artillery fire. . . ." They then crossed a hollow and a "high plank fence," obliqued to the right under "a furious shower of shot and shell," climbed "a very strong, high, morticed fence," and, obliqueing again to the right, at last reached their jumping off point.[77] During those intricate maneuvers—executed not only under fire but in gathering darkness, over rugged terrain, and in part without the leadership of Colonel Avery, who had been mortally wounded—the brigade became divided into two groups: the 57th North Carolina and part of the 21st diverging to the left; the remainder of the 21st, the 6th, and Hays's Brigade angling to the right. Elements of the 6th and 21st, together with some of Hays's Louisianians, broke through the main Federal line at a stone wall, captured two batteries in hand-to-hand fighting, and briefly penetrated to the summit of Cemetery Hill. The 57th and the left battalion of the 21st also attacked the stone wall but twice failed to dislodge the enemy. Federal reinforcements rushed to the scene, but calls for help by Maj. Samuel McD. Tate, commanding the 6th and the right battalion of the 21st, went unheeded. Enfiladed on both flanks and with enemy troops filtering into their rear, Tate and Hays were forced to retreat, taking the 57th and the left battalion of the 21st with them. "The moon was just rising over the trees on Culp's wooded hill to our left," a 6th North Carolina officer wrote, "and it shone through the battle smoke, with an enfeebled, sicklied light into the pale faces of our dead, as we quietly made our way . . . down. . . ." "[W]e attempted to drive them from the hills but found it too hard a job," Pvt. John Frazier summed up matters succinctly. "The loss on both sides was very great."[78]

Shortly before daylight on July 3, Avery's Brigade, now commanded by Colonel Godwin, was ordered to a position in the railroad cut on the outskirts of Gettysburg. On the afternoon of July 3 it formed on the left of Hays's Brigade in one of the upper streets of the town. The 57th and its two sister regiments remained there throughout the day, listening to the roar of battle while Pickett's, Pettigrew's, and Trimble's troops fought bravely but futilely on the slopes of Cemetery Ridge. "I never herd the like be fore of cannading and musckry," Frazier marveled in a letter to his wife two weeks later, "and never imagined anything like it."[79]

Following the failure of the Pickett-Pettigrew Charge, the Army of Northern Virginia remained in position on July 4 to receive an expected but nonforthcoming attack. The next morning the army began its retreat, cautiously followed by the Federals. "Started on our

77. *Official Records (Army)*, ser. 1, 27 (pt. 2):470 (first quotation only); *North Carolina [Semi-weekly] Standard* (Raleigh), August 11, 1863.

78. Neil W. Ray, "Capture of Cemetery Hill: The Second Day at Gettysburg," in Clark, *Histories of the North Carolina Regiments*, 5:607-608; John Frazier to D. F. Frazier, July 17, 1863, Frazier Letters. "There was harder fighting today than I ever knew of before," Private Eaton noted in his diary that night. "Our reg. lost about 71, killed, wd. & missing." Eaton Diary, July 2, 1863. See also W. F. Wagner to N. M. Wagner, July 16 and 18, 1863, in Hatley and Huffman, *Letters of William F. Wagner*, 55-56; J. M. Hefner to Kizia Hefner, July 10[?], 1863, Hefner Papers.

79. John Frazier to D. F. Frazier, July 17, 1863, Frazier Letters. Casualties in the 57th North Carolina at Gettysburg were officially reported as 4 men killed and 15 wounded on July 1; 2 killed, 5 wounded, and 36 missing on July 2; and none killed, wounded, or missing on July 3. Figures compiled for this volume indicate that the 57th lost a total of 16 men killed or mortally wounded, 20 wounded, and 50 captured (of whom 9 were wounded). See *Official Records (Army)*, ser. 1, 27 (pt. 2):474-475 (see also 340).

retreat before day," Private Eaton wrote, "the morning very rainy, the enemy pursued us a short distance and threw a few shells at us in the evening. We formed a line of battle about 8 ms. from Gayttersburg at a little villige but the enemy did not attack us, marched about 9 ms. today[.] Stood picket at night in a wheat field. . . . [The next morning we] Started on our march early, was marching over the mountains more than half the day. Our Boys being very hungary, shot hogs and sheep down on the way to eat and baked bread out of brand, crossed the mountains at South Gap at a little villige on South side called Waterloo, then marched through Waynesborough & camped 1 m. from town[.]"[80] On July 7 the army reached Hagerstown, where a line of battle was established to wait for the rain-swollen Potomac to subside. Construction of a pontoon bridge began near Falling Waters. Skirmishing broke out on the afternoon of July 10 and continued all day on the eleventh and twelfth. Around midnight on the twelfth Godwin's troops marched "two miles to the right" to the support of A. P. Hill's Corps. On July 13 "very brisk" picket firing began early and, a hard rain notwithstanding, continued until midmorning. "At 6 oclock," Chaplain Paris wrote, "orders came to pack and march for Virginia. Without rations we marched at dusk amid darkness rain and mud. Marched all night." About sunup the next morning the brigade waded the Potomac at Williamsport. "[T]he water came nearley under my armes," Private Wagner informed his wife, "but it never hurt me. . . ."[81]

Godwin's Brigade marched about six miles before halting for the night. On July 15 the brigade moved to a point about two miles beyond Martinsburg, and on the sixteenth it reached the vicinity of Darkesville. There, much to the gratification of Private Frazier, who was "nearly broke down," it remained in camp for three days. On the evening of July 20 the brigade moved with the rest of Early's Division toward Hedgesville, where an enemy column was advancing. After bivouacking for the night at Gerrardstown, Early reached Hedgesville on July 21 to find that the Federals had retreated. "We had a hard days march," Private Eaton noted in his diary. "[S]tarted early and marched in a peart gate all the way and over the mountains." On July 22 Early moved south to Bunker Hill. "The day intensely hot," Chaplain Paris recorded in his diary. "The forced march of 17 miles on Yesterday, and the heat to day greatly affected our troops. . . . A vast amount of robbing done. . . . Hundreds have straggled on the road. Reached Camp at Bunkerhill at 6 oclock." More hard marching followed during the next week. On July 23 the 57th North Carolina, with the rest of Early's command, moved through Winchester, and on the twenty-fourth—a day on which "Many" members of the regiment "gave out"—it passed through Middletown and Strasburg. The next morning the frazzled troops were on the move before sunrise. "The heat . . . was intensely great," Paris wrote. "Many fainted on the march. Passed Woodstock and Edinburgh [sic]. Marched seventeen miles. . . . The dust was very severe. Halted about

80. Eaton Diary, July 5-6, 1863. The 57th North Carolina was in "the rear of the army" during the march to Hagerstown but apparently saw no significant action. Jones, "Fifty-seventh Regiment," in Clark, *Histories of the North Carolina Regiments*, 3:416.

81. Diary of John Paris, July 12-13, 1863, John Paris Papers, SHC, hereafter cited as Paris Diary; W. F. Wagner to N. M. Wagner, July 30, 1863, in Hatley and Huffman, *Letters of William F. Wagner*, 59. "[W]e all got over safe without being pursued," a member of the 54th North Carolina wrote. "[B]eing rather low in stature, it came very near swimming me." *Spirit of the Age* (Raleigh), August 10, 1863.

4 oclock P.M. Thunder and some rain."[82] New afflictions befell the men that night when their camp was struck by a rainstorm. "My tent blew down," Paris noted irritably, "and every thing got wet." The division pressed on toward New Market in more clement weather on July 26, crossed the Shenandoah River on a pontoon bridge the next day, and reached the foot of the Blue Ridge, which it crossed in a heavy rain by a "dreadful bad" road on July 28. On the afternoon of the twenty-ninth Godwin's Brigade passed through Madison Court House and camped three miles beyond the town. There it was joined by General Hoke, whose return and resumption of command were received with "wild" cheers—"the spontaneous, heartfelt welcome of brave men to a brave commander."[83] A much-needed day of "Washing and sleeping" followed on July 30. "[W]e are as near worn out," an exhausted 54th North Carolina soldier complained, "as we can well be."[84]

On July 31 Hoke's Brigade marched again, this time heading southeast toward Orange Court House. During that day and the next the men "Suffered much . . . for Want of Water, and on account of bad roads." "Severely hot" weather continued on August 1. When they halted near Rapidan Station that night they "threw themselves down upon the grass in a few moments," Chaplain Paris recorded in his diary, "and went to sleep." The next day the good chaplain, along with many other members of Hoke's Brigade, was in a state of near collapse: "I am broken down by overmarching," he wrote, "and badly used up. Hardly able to go. . . . The Weather to day is intensely hot. Continued in bivouack all night. . . . But little to eat. Times hard."[85]

Hoke's men remained near Rapidan Station for more than a month performing picket duty, resting, and recovering their strength. According to Q.M. Sgt. Henry W. Barrow of the 21st North Carolina, the health of the troops was "tolerable good" and their campsite, which they moved one mile on August 6, "tolerable pleasant." However, "rashens," in Sergeant Patton's disgruntled estimation, were "light." "[W]e get flower meal bacon & beef," Patton wrote on August 18, "[and] we make out with what we by[.] I bought a peck of irish potatees yesterday . . . & a dosen of rosen years [a dozen roasting ears]. . . ."[86] As was

82. John Frazier to D. F. Frazier, July 17, 1863, Frazier Letters; Eaton Diary, July 21, 1863; Paris Diary, July 22 and 24-25, 1863. See also *Official Records (Army)*, ser. 1, 27 (pt. 2):472; "Record of Events," abstract of May 11-August 31, 1863, muster roll for Company E, 57th Regiment N.C. Troops, Compiled Confederate Service Records (North Carolina), M270, reel 526.

83. Paris Diary, July 26 (first quotation) and 28, 1863 (second quotation); *Daily Progress* (Raleigh), August 15, 1863 (third quotation). See also *Spirit of the Age* (Raleigh), August 10, 1863. The occasion was further improved after tattoo with "patriotic airs" by the 6th North Carolina band, three cheers for "the Hero of Fredericksburg," and speeches by Hoke, Colonel Godwin, Lieutenant Colonel Jones, and Col. William W. Kirkland (21st North Carolina). *Daily Progress* (Raleigh), August 15, 1863.

84. Paris Diary, July 30, 1863; *Spirit of the Age* (Raleigh), August 10, 1863. See also W. F. Wagner to N. M. Wagner, July 30, 1863, in Hatley and Huffman, *Letters of William F. Wagner*, 58.

85. Paris Diary, July 31 and August 1-2, 1863. See also Eaton Diary, July 31 and August 1, 1863; "Record of Events," abstract of April 30-August 31, 1863, muster roll for Company A, 57th Regiment N.C. Troops, Compiled Confederate Service Records (North Carolina), M270, reel 526.

86. Henry W. Barrow to C. T. Pfohl, August 9, 1863, Pfohl Papers; Alexander Patton to Ellen Patton, August 18, 1863, Patton Papers. "[W]e git . . . Beefe and Bacon some times," Private Wagner wrote on August 28, "[and] we git a pound and a quarter of corne meal a day to a man and when we draw flower we git a pound and a Eighth a day . . . and some times [we get] a fiew peese. . . . [T]hat is our fare onley [not counting] what we buy

common throughout the Army of Northern Virginia after Gettysburg, morale was low and absenteeism increased. "I am the worst out of heart I Ever was yet," the woebegone Private Wagner moaned to his wife. "I got out of heart as sone as we got in Pensilvania to see the men they have thare that never bin in the war[.] [T]hey have more men that never bin in the war then we Ever had in the war. . . . I Believe in my heart that we are whiped [and will] git all our poor men kiled up and that is a bout all the good we Ever done. . . ." "Dear the way the solegers Runs a way," Wagner wrote in another letter, "the [Confederacy will] have to quit . . . or fite with out men[.] [S]ome Runs a way nearly Ever nite[.] [T]hare was 4 run a way out of our Regt last nite[.] [A]ll I wish I wish the last man would Run a way and then I Recken they will stop . . . [the war] for I dont Believe we Ever can whip the north. . . ."[87] Not everyone was as gloomy as Wagner. In fact, in a letter to the *Carolina Watchman* dated August 22, 1863, a member of the regiment who identified himself as "57th" painted a positively idyllic picture: "The mellow days of autumn are at hand. Nature's verdue [sic] is already fading, and the cool dews of moonlight evenings refresh us as we lay aside the cares and duties of camp to sing the songs we've sung before when other friends were 'round us. We are enjoying army life as well as we ever did. Step in and see us, you will find us merry, cheerful, full of fun, and though not eager for a fight, yet fully recovered from the weariness and disheartening effects of the Pennsylvania campaign." It is probable that morale did indeed begin recovering in late August and September. With that exception, it is likely that "57th's" affirmations bear a tenuous relation to reality.[88]

Autumn blustered in with a heavy rain during the night of August 24 and "Very cool and chilly" weather on the night of the twenty-sixth. The brigade was reviewed by Hoke on August 29 and September 2 and by General Lee on about September 7. On September 8 or thereabouts Hoke was ordered to western North Carolina with a small force to suppress the "vast number of deserters" who, according to Gov. Zebulon B. Vance, were "set[ting] the local militia at defiance. . . ." In Hoke's absence, Colonel Godwin again assumed command of the brigade.[89]

On September 13 the Army of the Potomac, commanded by General Meade, advanced toward the Rapidan River and occupied Culpeper Court House. Lee's Army of Northern Virginia moved forward to meet the Federals along the Rapidan, and Godwin's Brigade was sent to Somerville Ford at daylight on September 14. The Yankees "began to

---

and that haint much for we cant git it and if we could git it we couldent buy for it is too high. . . ." W. F. Wagner to N. M. Wagner, August 28, 1863, in Hatley and Huffman, *Letters of William F. Wagner*, 73-74.

87. W. F. Wagner to N. M. Wagner, August 2 and 4 and July 30, 1863, in Hatley and Huffman, *Letters of William F. Wagner*, 61, 63, 60. See also Alexander Patton to Ellen Patton, August 18, 1863, Patton Papers. There was a high instance of absence without leave during August, but all of the absentees with one exception eventually returned to duty.

88. *Carolina Watchman* (Salisbury), September 7, 1863. Civil War letters-to-the-editor were commonly written by educated officers or enlisted men and often contain excellent information about battles, troop movements, and other factual matters. However, they typically present images of indomitability and good cheer calculated to bolster civilian spirits, and on topics such as morale and living conditions they are less reliable than private letters. That appears to be the case in this instance.

89. Paris Diary, August 26, 1863 (see also August 24-25, 1863); *Official Records (Army)*, ser. 1, 29 (pt. 2):676 (see also 729). Hoke's force consisted of the 21st North Carolina (from his own brigade), the 56th North Carolina (Brig. Gen. Matt W. Ransom's Brigade), and a cavalry squadron.

throw bom shells among us," Sgt. J. K. Walker of the 6th North Carolina wrote, "but as soon as our Artilerry come up you joist ought to have seen the[m] run."[90] After a brief flurry of firing on the morning of September 15, the day passed quietly. "[W]e laid in the woods all day," Sergeant Malone reported. Sporadic firing resumed on September 16 but diminished on the seventeenth to "a few picket shots evry now an then."[91] Showers and cool temperatures were succeeded by a cold rain on the morning of the eighteenth, and inclement weather continued for the next four days. On September 19 Godwin's Brigade was ordered to cook two days' rations and load wagons with foodstuffs for an additional four days, raising expectations of a new advance by Lee; however, no movement occurred. On September 24 Godwin's Brigade began constructing rifle pits on the brow of a hill over-looking the Rapidan at Somerville Ford. Beginning the next day and continuing through October 7, the 6th, 54th, and 57th regiments were assigned two-day stints of picket duty in the new pits. The enemy, according to Chaplain Paris, remained "perfectly quiet" during most of that period, but deserters arrived "daily." On October 4, while Godwin's men were attending Sunday services, the "roar of artillery . . . Scattered the congregation." However, it was quickly discovered that mischievous Confederate gunners were "firing . . . at Yanks stealing corn in a field over the river." The men then returned to their devotions. More alarums followed the next day when Godwin's Brigade was ordered to march to the ford to repulse an apparent Federal attack. Amid "Great excitement and Confusion" the men hurried to their posts but, Chaplain Paris wrote, "no Signs of a hostile move" were evident. "I ditent see no yankees and I dont Believe any boddy Els did," a disgusted Private Wagner complained to his wife, "onley what we can see Every day." Presently, it developed that the Federals were moving their camp. At dark Godwin's men, minus a regiment detailed for picket duty (probably the 57th), returned to camp near Rapidan Station.[92]

    On October 8 General Lee, after learning of the dispatch to Chattanooga of two of Meade's corps, set his army in motion to turn the Federal right flank and advance on Washington. At dusk the long roll sounded in Godwin's camp near Somerville Ford. "Surprise overwhelmed us," Chaplain Paris noted in his diary. "The order to 'fall in' was repeated on all sides. The regiment being formed, marched off to the rear with the brigade. Orders were given for the baggage train to follow as soon as tents could be pulled down and packed. In less than an hour our camp was entirely abandoned, and we were plodding our way through

---

90. J. K. Walker to his father and mother, September 17, 1863, Walker Papers. See also *Official Records (Army)*, ser. 1, 29 (pt. 2):175. "[O]ur enemy comenced throwing bumbs amung us," Sergeant Malone wrote, "but as soon as our Batterys got position and fired a few shots the yanks all left the field." According to Walker, that action took place at Raccoon Ford (about two miles downstream from Somerville Ford), but he was almost certainly mistaken. Although fighting occurred at both fords on September 14, the Paris and Malone diaries and several reports by Federal officers all point to Somerville Ford as the scene of the 57th's engagement. Pierson, *Diary of Bartlett Yancey Malone*, 89 (September 14, 1863). See also Paris Diary, September 14, 1863; *Official Records (Army)*, ser. 1, 29 (pt. 1):119, 124.

91. Pierson, *Diary of Bartlett Yancey Malone*, 89-90 (September 15 and 17, 1863). An account of the September 16 skirmish appears in J. K. Walker to his father and mother, September 17, 1863, Walker Papers. It seems probable that only the 6th North Carolina was involved.

92. Paris Diary, October 2 (first and second quotations), 4 (third and fourth quotations), and 5 (fifth and sixth quotations), 1863; W. F. Wagner to N. M. Wagner, October 7, 1863, in Hatley and Huffman, *Letters of William F. Wagner*, 76.

the fields, sometimes falling over stumps or rocks, and anon, plunging into a mudhole or a ditch, and doing only the best we could in the way of travel on one of the darkest of nights. Marching about three miles we bivouacked for the night. . . ." On October 9 the 57th North Carolina marched at daylight with the rest of the division, reached Orange Court House at noon, and crossed the Rapidan. Keeping Robertson's River on its right, it then moved toward Madison Court House, confining its line of advance "as much as possible" to the "valleys, plantations and country roads . . . to escape observation." On October 10 the regiment passed through Madison Court House and crossed Robertson's River. Heavy artillery firing in the brigade's front announced that Meade had discovered the Confederate maneuver and was conducting a fighting withdrawal. The next day the 57th reached a point about five miles north of Culpeper Court House, and on October 12 it crossed the Hazel River. Hearing artillery fire in its front that afternoon, it camped for the night about a mile from the Rappahannock. Meade retreated up the tracks of the Orange and Alexandria Railroad, fighting a series of rearguard actions.[93]

At "early dawn" on the morning of October 13, Godwin's Brigade crossed the Rappahannock at Warrenton Springs, where "sad and sickening" evidence of a skirmish the previous day "met the eye at every turn." The brigade moved forward at daylight the next morning and immediately encountered elements of the Federal rear guard. A "heavy artillery duel" erupted at sunrise, followed by another "furious" thirty-minute exchange around 10:00 A.M. In the interim, "brisk skirmishing with sharpshooters prevailed."[94] While A. P. Hill's Corps circled to the north to fall upon the retreating Federals at Bristoe Station, Ewell's Corps, including the 57th North Carolina, moved eastward by a more direct route. "[On] [t]he 14th we left for Bristol [Bristoe Station]," Sergeant Malone wrote, "but had to drive our enemey befour us[.] [O]ur Cavalry was fiting them allday and some times the Infantry[.] [O]ur Divishion don a great deal of hard marchen [and] had to dubbelquick nearly one third of our time."[95]

Two North Carolina brigades of A. P. Hill's Corps arrived first at Bristoe Station and found a Federal corps crossing Broad Run. Without reconnoitering, Hill ordered the Carolinians forward. Immediately, a "murderous" fire erupted from behind a railroad embankment to their right, where another Federal corps was lying concealed. The two brigades changed direction and made a forlorn-hope charge against the embankment, only to be sent reeling back with the loss of 1,300 men. "Indeed it seemed like being marched into a slaughter pen," Chaplain Paris wrote somberly after walking over the field the next day.[96] During the night the Federals completed their withdrawal across Broad Run, and Lee halted his pursuit. Leaving his cavalry to harass the enemy, he began tearing up the tracks of the Orange and Alexandria Railroad all the way south to the Rappahannock. On October 18 the

93. *Watchman & Harbinger* (Greensboro), November 6, 1863, hereafter cited as *Watchman & Harbinger*.

94. *Watchman & Harbinger*, November 6, 1863 (first, second, third, and sixth quotations); Paris Diary, October 14, 1863 (fourth and fifth quotations).

95. Pierson, *Diary of Bartlett Yancey Malone*, 91 (October 14, 1863).

96. *Watchman & Harbinger*, November 6, 1863. Concerning the 1,300-man casualty estimate, which unnamed officers quoted to Paris and which modern historians generally accept, Paris stated after his "walk of observation" that he "discover[ed] no reason to doubt it."

army fell back. Godwin's Brigade spent that night four miles north of the river. The next day it marched through "the severest storm of wind and rain we have encountered in Virginia," crossed the Rappahannock on a pontoon bridge at noon, and took up position "near the river . . . at the crossing of the railroad."[97] On October 20 the brigade moved to Brandy Station, where it remained for the next three days. On October 24 it marched northeast for a brief picket assignment across the Rappahannock but returned—"having Suffered much from exposure in the rain and mud"—on the twenty-fifth. On October 26 the brigade was sent back to the river in response to a heavy Federal cannonade lasting almost six hours. When an attack failed to materialize, the men returned to their Brandy Station camp that evening. The next day they moved to a new camp nearby. On October 28 and 29 the 57th was assigned to picket duty on the Rappahannock. "[B]regaid drill" was conducted on October 30 and "muster inspection" on the thirty-first. The brigade moved again on November 1, this time to a point "two miles west of Brandy Station on the Rail Road." Prompted by a spell of cold weather and the hope that they were at the site of their winter camp, the men began constructing cabins on November 2. That work was still going briskly forward on November 7 when Meade attacked at Rappahannock Station and Kelly's Ford.[98]

Meade's attacks did not come as a surprise to Lee, who planned to defend a bridgehead on the north bank of the river at Rappahannock Station but allow the Federals to cross at Kelly's Ford. He would then defeat the divided Federal army at Kelly's Ford before Meade could consolidate his lodgment. That plan fell apart quickly when Meade crossed the Rappahannock at some unguarded rapids near Kelly's Ford, wrecked two isolated North Carolina regiments of Brig. Gen. Stephen D. Ramseur's Brigade, and, before Lee could react, firmly established himself on the south bank. At Rappahannock Station the result was even more disastrous. The Confederate bridgehead, or tête-de-pont as it was known in contemporary parlance, was located just upstream from a burned railroad bridge and was tenuously connected to the south bank by a pontoon bridge. The Confederate defenses consisted of two artillery redoubts linked by a line of rifle pits anchored on the river at both extremities. One of the redoubts was an old Federal work that, for Confederate purposes, faced the wrong way. By closing in its open northern face the Confederates in effect had turned it around or, more accurately, converted it into a small fort. The second redoubt, built by the Confederates in the spring of 1862, was open on the side facing the river. The rifle pits, in Early's opinion, were "slight," affording little protection to their defenders and little obstacle to the enemy. Rising ground to the front commanded the entire position and, on the left, enabled an attacker to advance under cover to within "a few yards" of the Confederate works.[99] On the right, the embankment of the Orange and Alexandria Railroad afforded the Federals a similar advantage. The pontoon bridge, located near the right center of the

97. *Watchman & Harbinger*, November 6, 1863. See also "Record of Events," abstract of September-October 1863 muster roll for Company B, 57th Regiment N.C. Troops, Compiled Confederate Service Records (North Carolina), M270, reel 526.

98. Paris Diary, October 25 (first quotation) and November 1 (fourth quotation), 1863 (see also November 2-3 and 6, 1863); Pierson, *Diary of Bartlett Yancey Malone*, 91 (October 30 [second quotation] and 31 [third quotation], 1863).

99. Early, *Autobiographical Sketch*, 308; Jeffry D. Wert, "Rappahannock Station," *Civil War Times Illustrated* 15 (December 1976): 42.

Confederate line and laid across a deep pond created by a mill dam, was the only escape route to the south bank. Moreover, the bridge was already within range of Federal artillery and would be swept by musketry if any portion of the Confederate line fell into enemy hands.

Well aware of the vulnerability of their position, the Confederates had constructed supporting works on the south bank consisting of an artillery redoubt for a four-gun battery, pits designed for six additional cannons, and connecting trenches. Those guns would theoretically provide cover for the entire Confederate line; however, the artillery lacked the range to perform its mission. Furthermore, the ground on the south bank was generally lower than that on the north, making it difficult for the cannoneers to fire over the heads of the infantry if the latter were compelled to withdraw. In short, the artillery could neither repel an attack nor cover a retreat.

When Lee and Early reached Rappahannock Station on the afternoon of November 7, they found the north bank held by a four-gun battery (two guns in each redoubt) and the 800 men of Hays's Louisiana brigade. On the south bank, two more batteries, totaling eight guns, were in position. As soon as Hoke's Brigade (still commanded by Godwin) reached the scene, it was dispatched across the pontoon bridge "under a heavy fire of artillery" to reinforce Hays. The men were then placed in position somewhat to the left of the bridge to plug a gap in Hays's line. Two of Hays's regiments (the 7th and 5th Louisiana) were on Godwin's left somewhat in advance of the main line, where they were attempting to hold a knoll that commanded part of the Confederate works. Hays's other three regiments, the 8th, 9th, and 6th Louisiana, were on Godwin's right. The alignment of Godwin's units was 54th North Carolina on the left, 6th North Carolina in the center, and the 57th North Carolina on the right.[100]

Reluctant to give up his tête-de-pont, which threatened the Federal rear, and also convinced that Meade's advance at Rappahannock Station was a feint, Lee concluded that no further reinforcements were required. When Early's other two brigades (Gordon's and Brig. Gen. John Pegram's) arrived, they were ordered to take positions on the south bank. Meantime, the Federals slowly developed their attack, driving in Confederate skirmishers, enveloping Hays's and Godwin's line, and bringing the defenders under artillery fire from several angles. On the Confederate left, the 5th and 7th Louisiana were dislodged from their high ground and went into position on Godwin's left. A cautious Federal advance then took

100. *Spirit of the Age* (Raleigh), November 23, 1863. The 21st North Carolina was still on assignment with Hoke in North Carolina. The whereabouts of the 1st Battalion N.C. Sharpshooters is uncertain, but the battalion was detached for special duty several times during the war and was probably so on this occasion. There is no evidence, contrary to one recent scholar, that the 1st Battalion was with Hoke in North Carolina at the time or during operations along Mine Run in late November. The battalion fought at Mine Run, and it remained in Virginia until it was transferred to Kinston in late January 1864. See Everard H. Smith, "The Civil War Diary of Peter W. Hairston, Volunteer Aide to Maj. Gen. Jubal A. Early, November 7-December 4, 1863," *North Carolina Historical Review* 67 (January 1990): 62-63, hereafter cited as Smith, "Diary of Peter W. Hairston"; "Record of Events," abstracts of muster rolls for Company A (January-February 1864) and Company B (November-December 1863), 9th (1st) Battalion N.C. Sharpshooters, Compiled Confederate Service Records (North Carolina), M270, reel 189.

place along the entire front. Across the river, the Confederates attempted to place a gun in an empty pit near the railroad embankment but were driven off by enemy sharpshooters.[101]

At dark the Federals advanced on both sides of the railroad and made a bayonet charge against the 6th, 8th, and 9th Louisiana. Unable to aid their comrades because of the darkness and their poor angles of fire, the Confederate cannoneers on the south bank stood by helplessly while the three Louisiana units, joined during the latter stages of the seesaw contest by the 57th North Carolina, were overpowered after a brave resistance. Many of the defenders were captured; others fled across the pontoon bridge or attempted to swim the frigid river. Meantime, the 6th and 54th North Carolina and the 5th and 7th Louisiana, unaware of the disaster on their right because of the darkness and a strong, sound-muffling wind, waited apprehensively for orders and developments. A few gun flashes from the vicinity of the redoubts, crisscrossing in ominous proximity, finally aroused alarm. Capt. Benjamin F. White of the 6th North Carolina recalled what happened next:

Sam Brown [of Company E] said I am going to see if the Yankees are in the Fort. In a short while Lt. Brown came back, saying "boys damned if the yankees haint got the Fort, less go and drive em out". Lt. Col. H. C. Jones came to us calling for aid, his Reg. [the 57th North Carolina] was on our right. I right faced my men and started down the trench at a trail arms. Soon the way was blocked. They were still calling for help on my right. I called to my men ["]will you foll ow your Capt." The reply was Capt we will foll ow wherever you lead. I called my Co. out of the ditch or trench and started for the right when I was wounded in the shoulder. We however kept on and formed a line without order of Co or men or banks [ranks]. Col. [Robert F.] Webb [of the 6th North Carolina] gave the order–Charge. At that ins[t]ant a volley from the Fort greeted us, and with it the remains of the Louisianians and the 57th N.C. came down on us in rout and confusion and we fled across the pontoon bridge[.] [T]he rest of us [went] back when [to where] we started on our last move.[102]

Almost immediately the 54th and probably some elements of the 6th and 57th were hit by a bayonet attack by two Federal regiments. "[T]he line advanced at quick time to within 30 yards of the works," wrote Col. Emory Upton, commanding the 121st New York and 5th Maine, "when the order to charge was given. The work was carried at the point of the bayonet, and without firing a shot. The enemy fought stubbornly over their colors, but being overpowered soon surrendered."[103] "Under cover of the night," Col. Clark S. Edwards of the 5th Maine reported, "we approached to within 25 yards of the enemy in his

101. Peter W. Hairston wrote in his diary entry for November 7 that "When Genl. Early was sending Hoke's Brigade across, Genl. Lee remarked he was sending too many men . . . but as they had begun to go over he might let them go. If our artillery had been up in time the position might have been held. Genl. Early wanted a piece sent into the pits before the ford. Genl. Lee consented & requested me to present his compliments to . . . Capt. [Willis J. Dance, commander of the Powhatan Artillery] & ask him to carry it there. But the enemy's sharp shooters commencing, he [Lee] said it was too late they would pick off the horses & had the order counter manded [sic]. The enemy had their batteries on the range of the hills to the left & finally carried one round to the right." Smith, "Diary of Peter W. Hairston," 70.

102. "B. F. White Reminiscences," volume 2 of notes for a history of the 6th North Carolina, 16, in Alphonso Calhoun Avery Papers, SHC, hereafter cited as "B. F. White Reminiscences."

103. *Official Records (Army)*, ser. 1, 29 (pt. 1):592. Among the captured colors were those of the 57th North Carolina, which were taken by Cpl. Emery P. Blondell of Company D, 5th Regiment Maine Infantry. See *Official Records (Army)*, ser. 1, 29 (pt. 1):595.

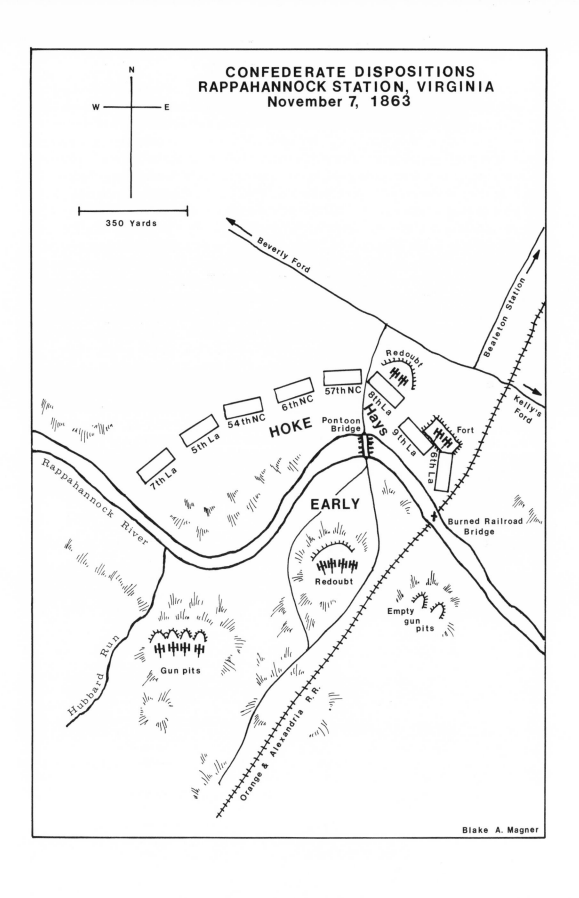

CONFEDERATE DISPOSITIONS
RAPPAHANNOCK STATION, VIRGINIA
November 7, 1863

350 Yards

N
W E

Beverly Ford

Bealeton Station

Redoubt

Kelly's Ford

57th NC

6th NC

54th NC

5th La

HOKE

7th La

8th La

Hays

Pontoon Bridge

9th La

Fort

6th La

EARLY

Redoubt

Rappahannock River

Burned Railroad Bridge

Empty gun pits

Hubbard Run

Gun pits

Orange & Alexandria R.R.

Blake A. Magner

pits, when I gave the order to 'charge.' At this moment we received a terrific volley from the enemy's infantry, and the next our boys had sprung into the rifle-pits, sweeping everything before them. These intrenchments [sic] were occupied by more than double the men that my own front presented, but so sudden and unexpected was our movement upon them that the enemy seemed paralyzed. After disarming them, by a rapid movement to the right we succeeded in capturing nearly the whole force in the pits, who were then ignorant of the fate of those on the left." While the Confederate line imploded, Godwin rallied a disorganized group of North Carolinians and Louisianians and attempted to cut his way to the bridge. "[W]hen his [Godwin's] men had dwindled to 60 or 70," Early reported, "the rest having been captured, killed, wounded, or lost in the darkness, and he was completely surrounded by the enemy, who were, in fact, mixed up with his men . . . [h]e was literally overpowered by mere force of numbers and was taken with his arms in his hands."[104] In the darkness and confusion, a number of men were able to escape across the pontoon bridge, which was not yet closely guarded by the Federals. Others attempted to swim the river. Of the latter, a few crossed safely, more were turned back by the icy water, and "some others," according to Chaplain Paris, were drowned.[105]

Casualties in the 57th North Carolina were officially reported as 4 wounded and 292 missing. Figures compiled from service records in this volume indicate that the regiment lost 6 men killed or mortally wounded, 4 wounded, and 281 captured (of whom 3 were wounded). According to Chaplain Paris in a letter written on November 10, Hoke's Brigade was "almost annihilated." The survivors, estimated by Paris as "about 275 men," were organized under the command of Lieutenant Colonel Tate of the 6th North Carolina and

104. *Official Records (Army)*, ser. 1, 29 (pt. 1):594, 623-624 (see also 629-630). According to the November 7 diary entry of Peter W. Hairston, Godwin "acted with distinguished gallantry. The last heard of him some one cried out Col. Godwin says 'Surrender'. He told them 'it was a d___d lie & if he repeated it he would kill him yet before the Yankees get you.'" Quoting a conversation with General Hays on the same date, Hairston wrote that Hays "had no idea of making his escape but he had his sword drawn & could not sheathe it—his horse continued to plunge so much & the enemy were constantly firing—so he gave his horse the reins & he plunged across the bridge & altho' a storm of bullets were fired at him he fortunately escaped uninjured." According to Hairston, Hays stated also that "he never saw men behave better than his did in his life. They covered the ground litterally [sic] from one hundred & fifty yards up to the entrenchments with the Yankee dead & in some places piled them up one upon another. He thinks he killed over one thousand of them dead upon the field. The first line which came said I surrender & threw down their arms & came inside of the entrenchments but on came the other columns firing but little & steadily advancing & their ranks were thinned by our men, they closed them up again & came on until they finally reached the entrenchments & even then some of them were actually thrown back by the fire there. But their force was so large they completely overpowered us and took them prisoners." That account may reflect Hays's shock at losing a sizable part of his command and his confusion about what happened on the dark battlefield. Whatever the case, it greatly overstates the number of Federal attackers and casualties. Smith, "Diary of Peter W. Hairston," 69-70.

105. *Spirit of the Age* (Raleigh), November 23, 1863. Lieutenant Colonel Tate stated that attempts to swim the river resulted, he "regret[ted] to believe," in the loss of "many valuable lives." Captain White wrote that "I attempted to swim the river but failed to do so and was captured. This ended my military career. . . ." *Official Records (Army)*, ser. 1, 29 (pt. 1):630; "B. F. White Reminiscences," 2:16. See also Jones, "Fifty-seventh Regiment," in Clark, *Histories of the North Carolina Regiments*, 3:417-418.

temporarily attached to the Louisiana brigade.[106] In his report dated November 11, Early estimated that Hoke's Brigade lost "very nearly three-fourths" of its numbers and that only "between 100 and 150" men escaped.[107] Total Confederate losses in the battle were officially reported as 6 killed, 39 wounded, and 1,629 missing; Federal casualties numbered 83 killed, 330 wounded, and 6 missing or captured.[108]

During the night Lee began falling back, and on November 8 he formed a line of battle near Culpeper Court House. That night he retreated to his former position on the south side of the Rapidan. Several weeks of relative quiet followed. The remnants of the 57th and Hoke's other regiments remained in camp about two and one-half miles from Raccoon Ford. Snow fell on November 9, prompting the men to resume building winter quarters.[109] On November 22 Hoke returned from his assignment in North Carolina and was "Serenaded by the band of the 6th . . . and cheered by the crowd." There was "Some excitement," Paris wrote on November 24, caused by a "rumour" that Hoke planned "to obtain leave to carry back the fragments of his Brigade to N.C. to recruit his wasted ranks." On the twenty-sixth Hoke did indeed start alone for Raleigh to obtain Gov. Zebulon B. Vance's approval for the anticipated recruiting project.[110]

On the same day that Hoke departed for North Carolina, General Meade, galvanized by an intelligence report that his army was now approximately twice the size of Lee's, advanced across the Rapidan at Germanna, Ely's, and Jacob's Fords. Meade's plan was to hold Lee in place by feinting crossings at Raccoon Ford and other points upriver, then destroy the right wing of the Army of Northern Virginia before the left wing could come to its aid. That plan miscarried when his lead corps, which was to cross at Jacob's Ford, failed to set off on schedule and then took the wrong road. Bad weather further slowed Federal progress. By the time all five of Meade's corps were across the Rapidan on November 27, Lee had concentrated most of his army.

For the men of Hoke's Brigade, this unwelcome winter campaign began when Federal shells exploded in their camp about nine o'clock on the morning of November 26. Rousted

106. *Spirit of the Age* (Raleigh), November 23, 1863. See also *Official Records (Army)*, ser. 1, 29 (pt. 1):630. Casualties in the 6th North Carolina were officially reported as 3 men killed, 13 wounded, and 307 missing; in the 54th North Carolina the official figures were none killed, 2 wounded, and 306 missing. See *Official Records (Army)*, ser. 1, 29 (pt. 1):630.

107. *Official Records (Army)*, ser. 1, 29 (pt. 1):625. Lt. William James Kincheloe of the 49th Virginia Infantry (Pegram's Brigade) stated in his diary entry for November 8 that he "witnessed with my own eyes the extent of our loss by the capture of the works at the bridge. . . . Hoke's Brigade had about 120 men left with a Captain and Lieut." Quoted in Laura Virginia Hale and Stanley S. Phillips, eds., *History of the Forty-ninth Virginia Infantry C.S.A.: "Extra Billy Smith's Boys"* (Lanham, Md.: S. S. Phillips and Associates, 1981), 99 (November 8, 1863), hereafter cited as Hale and Phillips, *Forty-ninth Virginia Infantry*. Early estimated that Hays's Brigade lost "less than one-half" of the men present for duty and that "Nearly 300" escaped. Total casualties in the five Louisiana regiments were reported as 2 men killed, 16 wounded, and 684 missing. *Official Records (Army)*, ser. 1, 29 (pt. 1):625 (see also 629).

108. See *Official Records (Army)*, ser. 1, 29 (pt. 1):616, 560.

109. They began work again when the brigade moved to a new camp about three-quarters of a mile from the ford on November 17.

110. Paris Diary, November 22 and 24, 1863 (see also November 26, 1863). Hoke probably returned on or about December 15, 1863. See H. W. Barrow to C. T. Pfohl, December 14, 1863, Pfohl Papers.

out "in a great hurry," the startled Carolinians were rushed to Raccoon Ford, where a two-hour exchange of gunfire followed. At two o'clock on the "very cold" morning of November 27, Hoke's troops, still attached to the Louisiana Brigade (temporarily commanded by Col. William Monaghan of the 6th Regiment Louisiana Infantry), set off downriver with the rest of Early's Division. (Early's Division was temporarily commanded by Brigadier General Hays; Early was in temporary command of Ewell's Corps.) After passing through Verdiersville and crossing Mine Run, Hays encountered Federal infantry atop a timbered ridge known as Locust Grove. As Early's other two divisions, under Rodes and Johnson, came up, they took position on Hays's left. Unable to see the enemy dispositions because of the wooded terrain, Early held his ground during a day of severe skirmishing. Meantime, Johnson's Division became involved in heavy fighting that brought the Federal advance to a halt.[111]

During the "Freezing" night of November 27 Lee withdrew across Mine Run. Skirmishing resumed early the next morning and, notwithstanding a "very heavy" rain that began at 9:00 A.M. and lasted nearly all day, swelled into an artillery duel around noon.[112] During the night of the twenty-eighth the Confederates fell back another half mile to a ridge and began entrenching by torch light. By "an early hour in the forenoon" of November 29 they had constructed "a formidable line of breast-works of logs and earth with strong abatis in front."[113] More skirmishing and artillery exchanges occurred on that day and the thirtieth. The weather cleared somewhat, but the "terrible" cold continued and a gusty wind blew choking, blinding smoke in the faces of those men fortunate enough to have fires. By the night of December 1 the frigid temperatures and Meade's reluctance to attack the forbidding Confederate works reduced military activity to an occasional sharpshooter's potshot.[114] The next morning Lee attempted to turn the Federal left, only to find that during the night Meade had withdrawn. After participating in an abortive pursuit, the 57th North Carolina returned to its camp near Raccoon Ford on December 3. Casualties in the 57th during the Mine Run campaign were officially reported by General Hays as one man wounded.[115] According to service records compiled for this volume, Pvt. James L. Stowe of Company F was wounded mortally.

111. Paris Diary, November 26-27, 1863. See also *Official Records (Army)*, ser. 1, 29 (pt. 1):832.

112. Quoted in Hale and Phillips, *Forty-ninth Virginia Infantry*, 101 (November 27-28, 1863). See also Paris Diary, November 28, 1863. Kincheloe is quoted in *Forty-ninth Virginia Infantry* as stating that the rain "put . . . a stop to all military operations"; however, that is clearly an exaggeration. See Archie P. McDonald, ed., *Jedediah Hotchkiss, Make Me a Map of the Valley: The Civil War Journal of Stonewall Jackson's Topographer* (Dallas: Southern Methodist University Press, 1973), 213 (November 28, 1863), hereafter cited as McDonald, *Make Me a Map: Hotchkiss Journal*.

113. *Official Records (Army)*, ser. 1, 29 (pt. 1):839. "When iron shovels could not be had," Lt. W. J. Kincheloe noted, "the men made wooden ones." Quoted in Hale and Phillips, *Forty-ninth Virginia Infantry*, 102 (November 29, 1863).

114. Quoted in Hale and Phillips, *Forty-ninth Virginia Infantry*, 102 (November 29, 1863). See also Paris Diary, November 29-30 and December 1, 1863.

115. See *Official Records (Army)*, ser. 1, 29 (pt. 1):841 (see also 836). According to Sgt. J. K. Walker of the 6th North Carolina, Hoke's Brigade lost two men killed and eight wounded, not counting "1 or 2" members of the 6th who were "slightly wounded." Walker added that "we had little or no fighting to do excepting Skirmishing and Artillery fighting." J. K. Walker to his mother, December 4, 1863, Walker Papers.

At Raccoon Ford, Hoke's men resumed their picket duties. Freezing temperatures, after moderating briefly, returned with a vengeance on December 6. "This night was the Coldest of the Season thus far," Paris wrote. "Ice very thick." On December 8 the half-frozen Paris "kept about the fireside principally." Brigade morale, never at its best during severe weather, may have hit a low point on December 12. "Weather dark, damp and Cloudy," Paris wrote. "The hope of the Brigade being removed to Carolina has become faint, and men are gloomy." The next day Paris received a furlough. The 57th North Carolina's activities during the month that followed, if indeed there were any of importance, are unknown.[116]

On January 9, 1864, Paris rejoined Hoke's Brigade, arriving in the midst of a new cold wave to find the ground covered with four inches of snow. In spite of the icy weather, most of the men probably managed to stay reasonably warm when they were under shelter. "I am comfortably situated," Lt. Joseph S. Ragsdale of the 54th wrote on January 8. "I have a good tent and good chimney." Both Ragsdale and Paris commented on the tedium of winter camp. "Every thing is quite dull," Ragsdale wrote in the letter cited above, and Paris complained of "dull monotony" in his diary entry for January 11. Wiser heads, including Sgt. J. K. Walker and no doubt many other veterans of Chancellorsville and Rappahannock Station, sensibly preferred boredom to combat: "we are fairing very well," Walker wrote contentedly, "[and have] nothing to do but to sit around the fire."[117]

On January 20 Hoke's Brigade received orders for its long-awaited transfer to North Carolina. Although instructed to recruit his regiments up to strength if possible, Hoke's primary mission was to assist Maj. Gen. George E. Pickett in recapturing New Bern. At four o'clock on the morning of January 21, Hoke's "highly elated" troops marched toward Orange Court House. At dusk they boarded railroad cars for Richmond but were detained for six hours en route when their engine ran off the tracks.[118] Upon reaching Richmond the next morning they marched to Manchester and bivouacked for the night. At 11:00 A.M. on January 23 they left by rail for Petersburg, which they reached around two o'clock that afternoon. At 9:00 P.M. they departed by train and arrived at Weldon at seven o'clock on the morning of the twenty-fourth. Following a five-day layover, they boarded a train on January 29, traveled all night "at a slow pace," passed through Goldsboro at daybreak on January 30, and reached Kinston at ten o'clock the same morning. They then marched about five

---

116. Paris Diary, December 6, 8, and 12, 1863. Most of the 57th North Carolina soldiers whose letters have contributed to this narrative were captured at Rappahannock Station. Private Wagner died in a Federal prison, and Private Zimmerman was not exchanged until the last weeks of the war. Sergeant Patton and Private Frazier were exchanged in March 1864, but both were captured again in September. No further Frazier letters and only two written by Patton survive. Pvt. M. A. Walker, another excellent 57th source, was mortally wounded four months earlier at Gettysburg. Thus only Private Hefner, who was captured at Fisher's Hill on September 22, 1864, and whose last letter is dated June 1 of that year, remains. The last 57th North Carolina letter located of *any* description is dated September 20, 1864—more than six months before the war's end. The pages that follow consequently reflect a regrettable degree of dependence on "sister unit" diaries and letters written by members of the 6th, 21st, and 54th North Carolina and the 1st Battalion N.C. Sharpshooters.

117. Joseph S. Ragsdale to his mother, January 8, 1864, Military Collection: Civil War Collection, box 44, folder 27, NCDAH; Paris Diary, January 11, 1864; J. K. Walker to his mother, January 19, 1864, Walker Papers.

118. W. J. Pfohl to C. T. Pfohl, February 9, 1864, Pfohl Papers. See also *Official Records (Army)*, ser. 1, 33:1103-1104; Paris Diary, January 21, 1864. "Night awfully Cold," Paris wrote.

miles down the Dover road in the direction of New Bern and went into camp to await the start of the campaign.[119]

Located at the confluence of the Neuse and Trent Rivers, New Bern was the most important Federal base in North Carolina and a jumping-off point for Federal raiders whose depredations in the eastern part of the state had destroyed large quantities of property and foodstuffs and devastated civilian morale. Pickett, commanding a force of 13,000 men concentrated at Kinston, planned a three-column attack. One column, under Hoke, would advance between the Neuse and Trent, endeavor to surprise a small Federal force at the Batchelder's Creek bridge, silence the guns of the star fort and the batteries west of New Bern, and "penetrate the town."[120] A second column, commanded by Brig. Gen. Seth M. Barton, would move down the south bank of the Trent and capture three forts defending New Bern's southern approaches. If practicable, Barton was to cross the Atlantic and North Carolina Railroad bridge into the town; if not, he was to prevent reinforcements from arriving by land or water from Beaufort or Morehead City. The third column, under Col. James Dearing, would advance down the north bank of the Neuse, neutralize or capture Fort Anderson (across the Neuse from New Bern), and situate itself so as to enfilade New Bern's western works (that is, those confronting Hoke). At the same time, a naval force of fourteen cutters would descend the Neuse and attack any Federal gunboats that were encountered.

On the afternoon of January 30 Hoke's column, led by his own brigade, advanced five miles down the New Bern road before bivouacking for the night.[121] After marching fifteen miles the next day through what Chaplain Paris described as "the most dreary part of Carolina I ever saw," the men crossed Core Creek at 3:00 P.M., put out flank guards, and bivouacked about two miles from the Batchelder's Creek bridge. In order not to alert the garrison, fires were prohibited, and any civilians encountered were arrested. In the wee hours of

---

119. Paris Diary, January 29, 1864. See also S. C. James to C. T. Pfohl, January 30, 1864, Pfohl Papers.

120. *Official Records (Army)*, ser. 1, 33:1102.

121. Hoke's depleted brigade was reinforced by the 43rd North Carolina of Brig. Gen. Junius Daniel's Brigade. The date that the 43rd joined Hoke is uncertain but was apparently between January 20 and 24. See Joseph Robert Peele Ellis (43rd North Carolina) to Betsy Ellis, January 26, 1864, Joseph Robert Peele Ellis Papers, Special Collections, East Carolina University Library (SC-ECU), Greenville, North Carolina, hereafter cited as Ellis Papers.

The 57th North Carolina was commanded during the New Bern campaign by Maj. James A. Craige. Craige assumed command of the 57th after the Battle of Rappahannock Station and held it until he was wounded and permanently disabled at Winchester on July 20, 1864. He was replaced by the senior captain of the regiment, John Beard of Company C. (Colonel Godwin was exchanged on April 30, 1864, but apparently never resumed command of the 57th. He was promoted to brigadier general and placed in command of Hoke's former brigade in August 1864.) Capt. Miles H. Hunter of Company B was reported in command of the 57th on September 30, 1864; otherwise, Captain Beard seems to have remained in command until Lieutenant Colonel Jones, who was captured at Rappahannock Station, was exchanged and returned to duty in late February 1865. Beard took over the regiment again when Jones was wounded at Fort Stedman on March 25, 1865. When Lt. Col. (later Brig. Gen.) William G. Lewis—who command the brigade from approximately April 20 through August 14, 1864, and who resumed command after Godwin was killed on September 19—was wounded and captured on April 7, 1865, Beard, the senior officer of any description present for duty, was given command of the brigade. See *Official Records (Army)*, ser. 1, 42 (pt. 3):1194, 1365, and 43 (pt. 2):883, 912; Jones, "Fifty-seventh Regiment," in Clark, *Histories of the North Carolina Regiments*, 3:418-422, 426; "Paroles of the Army of Northern Virginia," *Southern Historical Society Papers* 15: 202-203.

the morning of February 1, Hoke moved out again. "It Was very dark," Paris recorded in his diary. "At 15 minutes before 3, the van guard fell in With the enemy's pickets and firing began. Our Troops pushed the enemy back to Batchelor's [sic] creek. The Yanks had taken up the bridge. The enemy had two redoubts and a block House on the Other bank and fought stubbornly. One battery of Our Artillery Was brought up and the battle Was furious in the darkness. Col. [Henry M.] Shaw of the 8th N.C.T. fell."[122]

Having suffered "a number" of casualties in attempting to seize the bridge, Hoke cast about for a means of driving off the Federals without assaulting their "very formidable" blockhouse. About 9:00 A.M. two regiments crossed the creek below the bridge on trees felled on Hoke's orders.[123] Shortly thereafter the "Yanks," under flank and frontal attack, "gave way in confusion. . . ." Federal reinforcements reached the scene about the same time but were "completely routed" and pursued in the direction of New Bern, losing "a good many prisoners & [much] property."[124] After failing by five minutes to capture an armored train upon which he had hoped to load his command and steam into town with guns blazing, Hoke halted a mile from New Bern to await Barton's attack from the south.[125] Barton, in the meantime, reached his objective to find a maze of breastworks, blockhouses, gun emplacements, forts, and felled trees bristling in terrain that was dangerously open in some places and impassably marshy in others. He therefore decided not to attack and sent a request to Pickett, who was with Hoke's column, for instructions.

Scanning the field as he impatiently awaited the sound of Barton's guns, Hoke suddenly saw to his "amazement" two trains roll into New Bern from Morehead City, establishing that Barton had failed to disrupt the garrison's communications. An exasperated Pickett, after receiving Barton's request for instructions the next morning, ordered him to join Hoke immediately for a "coup de main." That command the hapless Barton was unable to execute with the requisite promptness, forcing the cancellation (so Pickett claimed) of the entire operation. The Confederates then withdrew to Kinston.[126]

Casualties in the 57th North Carolina during the disappointing New Bern campaign were not officially reported. According to Pickett, total Confederate losses were "about" forty-five men killed and wounded, none of whom appears to have been a member of the 57th. The achievements of the campaign, as itemized by Pickett, were as follows: "[Federal] Killed and wounded, about 100; captured, 13 officers, 284 privates, 14 negroes,

122. Paris Diary, January 31 and February 1, 1864.

123. *Official Records (Army)*, ser. 1, 33:96; W. J. Pfohl to C. T. Pfohl, February 9, 1864, Pfohl Papers. The two regiments were the 21st North Carolina and 21st Georgia.

124. Paris Diary, February 1, 1864; *Official Records (Army)*, ser. 1, 33:96; W. J. Pfohl to C. T. Pfohl, February 9, 1864, Pfohl Papers. "We followed them up," Major Pfohl commented, "but as usual on a retreat they were too fast for us, & most of them succeeded in getting into Newbern." Sgt. J. K. Walker of the 6th North Carolina wrote that "our Brigade had a fierce engagement . . . but Succeeded in routing them and driving them on into Town, capturing the most of them." A substantial number of prisoners were indeed taken, but "the most" of the Federals escaped. J. K. Walker to his mother, February 7[?], 1864, Walker Papers. See also J. R. P. Ellis to Betsy Ellis, February 6, 1864, Ellis Papers.

125. The train, according to Major Pfohl, consisted of a "mounted battery of 3 guns" and "cars containing stores [mostly food and ammunition]." W. J. Pfohl to C. T. Pfohl, February 9, 1864, Pfohl Papers.

126. *Official Records (Army)*, ser. 1, 33:96 (see also 94).

2 rifled pieces and caissons, 300 stands of small-arms, 4 ambulances, 3 wagons, 103 animals, a quantity of clothing, camp and garrison equipage, and 2 flags."[127] With a trace of sarcasm, Chaplain Paris noted also the liberation of "aplenty of forage and chickens."[128]

On February 5 Hoke arrived with his brigade at Kinston and began recruiting to replace the men captured at Rappahannock Station. In a report dated February 8 he stated that he had already recruited his brigade somewhat and was "sanguine" about increasing it "a good deal."[129] Those expectations may have been justified. By the end of February, at least 1,665 officers and men were present for duty: a figure that included, however, the 43rd North Carolina and the 21st Georgia (both on loan from other brigades). Also, the 21st North Carolina, which had not been present at Rappahannock Station, undoubtedly remained considerably larger than the 6th, 54th, and 57th. Nevertheless, it is known that the 6th, and probably the 54th and 57th as well, received "a large number of recruits." Among them were many "principles of substitutes"—men who hired substitutes early in the war to serve in their place but, because of the recent repeal of the substitution law, were required to report for duty. Those men were "beginning to arrive freely in camp" by March 9. Of even greater concern to Hoke than recruitment was completion of the ironclad ram *Neuse*, which was under construction at Kinston. "I have but [put] 95 carpenters and mechanics and 50 laborers . . . to work on the gun-boat," Hoke wrote to Lee on February 8, "and they will soon have it completed. . . . In the mean time I will remain here, where I have already made my men comfortable, and push forward the work, and at the same time give the boat protection, which is absolutely necessary."[130] Hoke hoped that the *Neuse* and her sister ram, the *Albemarle* (under construction at Edwards Ferry on the Roanoke River), would spearhead a new Confederate effort to evict the Federals from the eastern part of the state. Although disappointed in the New Bern campaign and anxious for Hoke's Brigade to rejoin the Army of Northern Virginia, Lee allowed his aggressive young paladin to remain in North Carolina "under the expectation that the object of his visit . . . may yet be accomplished."[131]

---

127. *Official Records (Army)*, ser. 1, 33:94. The U.S. Navy gunboat *Underwriter* was destroyed also.

128. Paris Diary, February 2, 1864. Sergeant Walker's inventory of men and materiel captured included "the rise of 400 Prisoners 2 pieces of Artillery 40 horses 300 Small arms and Equipments Some few negros an amount of Commissary and Quarters [*sic*] Masters Stores Clothing &c." J. K. Walker to his mother, February 5[?], 1864, Walker Papers.

129. *Official Records (Army)*, ser. 1, 33:96. "My men are in good health and fine spirits," Hoke continued. "The troops do not look upon our campaign as a failure, as the real object was not known to them and the capture of several rich camps pleased them wonderfully." *Official Records (Army)*, ser. 1, 33:96-97.

130. House of Representatives, *Murder of Union Soldiers in North Carolina*, 39th Cong., 1st sess., 1865, H. Doc. 98, 69 (first quotation), hereafter cited as House, *Murder of Union Soldiers in North Carolina*; W. J. Pfohl to C. T. Pfohl, March 9, 1864 (second and third quotations), Pfohl Papers; *Official Records (Army)*, ser. 1, 33:97 (fourth quotation). See also *Official Records (Army)*, ser. 1, 33:1201-1202. "The work on the gunboat, building at this place, has been redoubled," Maj. W. J. Pfohl of the 21st North Carolina noted on February 9. "All the carpenters & black smiths from our Brigade being engaged in it." On March 9 Pfohl wrote that "The work on our gunboat is progressing finely; they put in the guns a few days ago. I expect to have it done in the course of several weeks. . . ." W. J. Pfohl to C. T. Pfohl, February 9 and March 9, 1864, Pfohl Papers.

131. *Official Records (Army)*, ser. 1, 33:1245. In preparation for the *Neuse*'s projected voyage to New Bern, Lt. Col. W. G. Lewis of the 43rd North Carolina was placed in charge of "cleaning out obstructions" in the

While work on the two rams went forward, the 57th remained quietly in the vicinity of Kinston. On February 6 the regiment accompanied the brigade to a new camp about a mile north of the town, and two days later it moved to another campsite on the south side of the Neuse. Pvt. Jesse Hill, a 21st North Carolina veteran of emphatic and often profane opinions, denounced Kinston as "the damdis plase that I ever was at. . . . [W]e ar smoked as black as negros and as lousy as hogs and I dont . . . like the plase one dam bit." Q.M. Sgt. Henry W. Barrow, also of the 21st, was marginally less critical: "This is a very low Swampy Country," he wrote. "The water is not good & fire wood is very Scarce . . . [but] I dont think we will be troubled with mud . . . for it is rather sandy. . . ." The weather was unusually mild for the season, Barrow continued, but on about February 15 springlike conditions disappeared abruptly with the arrival of a "very cold Rain." According to Barrow, the men, "thinking the cold weather was over," had "neglected Building Chimneys" during a ten-day period of "fine & pleasant" weather and were caught unprepared by the sudden return of winter.[132]

February was notable for the hanging at Kinston of twenty-two Confederate deserters— none from the 57th North Carolina—who had fallen into Pickett's hands after enlisting in the Federal army. Two were hanged on the fifth, five on the twelfth, thirteen on the fifteenth, and two on the twenty-second. Hoke's Brigade and other units were forced to witness the executions as an "example" to the "weak-kneed." Although fully persuaded that they deserved their fate, Chaplain Paris provided the condemned with spiritual consolation during their final hours.[133]

During March Paris's intermittent diary reveals little of the brigade's activities except an effort to supplement rations by "operations in fishing" in the Neuse. Rations in Hoke's Brigade following its return from New Bern may have needed a lot of supplementing. Lt. George W. Wills, whose regiment (the 43rd North Carolina) was still temporarily assigned to Hoke, pronounced himself ready to receive "provisions . . . every time anyone [from his family] comes, because we are living mostly from home now. . . ." "When my Horse comes," Quartermaster Sergeant Barrow wrote, "I want to Ride out some distance to look for Forage & to try to purchase some Potatoes & Eatables for our Mess."[134] Early in the

---

river. Lewis made a survey on February 20 and pronounced the task "considerably difficult." Whether the 57th North Carolina was involved in that work is unclear. See House, *Murder of Union Soldiers in North Carolina*, 75; William Gaston Lewis to Mittie Pender, February 21, 1864, William Gaston Lewis Papers, SHC, hereafter cited as Lewis Papers.

132. Jesse Hill to Emoline Hill (his wife), February 7, 1864, in Chris Ripple, ed., *The Letters of Private Jesse Hill, a farmer from Davidson County* (n.p., 1992), hereafter cited as Ripple, *Jesse Hill Letters*; H. W. Barrow to C. T. Pfohl, February 17, 1864, Pfohl Papers. "There is some sickness here," Barrow added. "Some of the men have measles."

133. House, *Murder of Union Soldiers in North Carolina*, 69. See also Paris Diary, February 5, 11-12, 14-15, and 21-22, 1864. Paris's account of the hangings appears in the *North Carolina Presbyterian* (Fayetteville), April 13, 1864. See also W. J. Pfohl to C. T. Pfohl, February 9, 1864, Pfohl Papers. Pfohl stated that the first two "buffaloes" hanged had deserted "quite recently" and were captured "with arms in their hands." According to Pfohl, their execution took place on "last Saturday [February 6]," but that date is almost certainly erroneous.

134. Paris Diary, March 17, 1864; George Whitaker Wills to his sister, March 16, 1864, George Whitaker Wills Letters, SHC, hereafter cited as George W. Wills Letters; H. W. Barrow to C. T. Pfohl, February 17, 1864, Pfohl Papers. Corse's Virginia brigade, which had enjoyed "relative plenty" at Tarboro during the last half of March,

month a reconnaissance force, led by a captain and two lieutenants and composed of "about 65 of the stoutes" members of the 21st North Carolina, was sent in the direction of New Bern. Similar scouting expeditions involving members of the 57th North Carolina may have been dispatched during the following weeks. An attack by Federal cavalry on a picket post at about that time led to a flurry of excitement and the issuance of marching orders, but nothing came of the affair. There is no evidence that the 57th was involved.[135]

During the night of March 15 winter weather, which had moderated earlier in the month, returned with a "Considerable" snow. That melted during the following day, and by the nineteenth the temperature rose sufficiently to resume fishing.[136] However, on the morning of March 22 snow fell again, accompanied this time by sleet. "Weather distressingly Severe," Paris wrote. "Sleet very deep at night." An all-day fall of sleet and snow followed on March 23, precipitating a major snowball battle similar to the one that took place on February 24, 1863. "Gen. Hoke at the head of his Brigade Attacked Gen. [Montgomery D.] Corse's Brigade of Virginians . . . and Was Whipt," Paris wrote. "Corse attacked us in camp and got whipt in turn."[137] By March 27 the weather was

found itself reduced at Kinston, where it arrived on April 7, to "'a little meat & a little meal" and "occasionally some peas." So many troops had been stationed in the Kinston area, one of Corse's men complained, that "everything has been swept." Robert K. Krick, *30th Virginia Infantry* (Lynchburg, Va.: H. E. Howard, 1983), 46-47 (second and fourth quotations quoted in), hereafter cited as Krick, *30th Virginia Infantry*.

135. Jesse Hill to Emoline Hill, March 16, 1864, in Jesse Hill Papers, SC-ECU, hereafter cited as Hill Papers. "[W]e thought we could get to catch som yankeys," Hill wrote, "but we did not get to see any and our men Just robed the poor wimen and children[.] [I]t was a site[.] [T]ha went to the houses and takeing any thing tha wanted[.] I hope the army will never hav to com thrugh wher you liv for tha wuld steal every thing you hav[.] [T]he Soldiers is the rogishist people that livs[.] [W]e kild hogs Chickens and any thing we wanted[.]" See also W. J. Pfohl to C. T. Pfohl, March 9, 1864, Pfohl Papers; Henry William Barrow to John W. Fries, March 10, 1864, in Marian H. Blair, ed., "Civil War Letters of Henry W. Barrow Written to John W. Fries, Salem," *North Carolina Historical Review* 34 (January 1957): 80, hereafter cited as Blair, "Letters of Henry W. Barrow"; J. K. Walker to Lucinda Walker, March 14, 1864, Walker Papers.

136. Paris Diary, March 16, 1864. It is doubtful that the men's fishing expeditions were more than intermittently successful. In a letter dated February 17, 1864, H. W. Barrow of the 21st North Carolina reported that "Some of the Boys are catching very fine Fish out of the River"; however, on April 9 he wrote that "The Neuse River has been very high. . . . There has been very few fish caught here for some time. . . ." In Corse's Brigade, fish were selling during the same month for the "exorbitant" price of $5.00 each. Private Hefner's letter of April 16 suggests he would have gladly eaten fish or almost anything except cornbread: "[I]f there is any Chance I want you to Send me Something to eat," he instructed his wife. "I can tel you that corn bread for breakfast and corn bread for diner and [corn bread] for super dont take so well." H. W. Barrow to C. T. Pfohl, February 17, 1864, Pfohl Papers; H. W. Barrow to J. W. Fries, April 9, 1864, in Blair, "Letters of Henry W. Barrow," 81; Krick, *30th Virginia Infantry*, 47; J. M. Hefner to Kizia Hefner, April 16, 1864, Hefner Papers.

137. Paris Diary, March 22-23, 1864. Pvt. George Leitz of the 17th Virginia (Corse's Brigade) confirmed Paris's report that Hoke "got whipt": "Gen'l Hoek's Brigade came over to drive us out of our Camp with Snow balls[.] [T]he[y] came with there Band playing and halted in front of our Camp[.] [B]efore we knew what the[y] were after the[y] charged us and drove in our camp where we kept them in chek for some time[.] [I]n the meantime word where send to the 29th Va Regt of our Brigade to come to our asistance which the[y] did very promptly[.] [W]e made a yell and charged them and drove them back over the ground the[y] had gained in to a Swamp where we kept them[.] [O]n there retreat we took Gen'l Hoek & 3 other field officers prisoners[.] Gen'l Hoek acknowledged that he was fairly wipped, after which he returned to his camp. If you had seen how we Pepperd those officers with snow balls you would [have] laught to your hearts content." George Leitz to O. Woody [Aurelia] Hooper, March 27, 1864, Aurelia Hooper Papers, SCD-DU, hereafter cited as Hooper Papers.

"Clear, Warm and very Windy." "Monotonous" times, accompanied by a "vast deal of Rain," continued into the first half of April. When conditions permitted, drilling was "the chief order of the day."[138] According to Lieutenant Wills, "The officers of this Brig. are generally so loose, that they had to go to drilling to keep the men from plundering the country[.] [A]wful state of affairs, not so in Daniels Brig [of which Wills's regiment was a part]."[139] Another reason for the heavy dose of drill was the arrival of more recruits. Lieutenant Colonel Tate traveled as far west as Morganton recruiting for the 6th North Carolina, and a soldier in that regiment reported on March 14 that his company had received fourteen enlistees.[140] Sixty more conscripts joined the 6th on March 23. Most of the new arrivals, in the opinion of Sergeant Walker of the 6th, were "very good looking men" who seemed to be "getting along fine." The 57th North Carolina also received recruits, and many of the regiment's Rappahannock Station captives were paroled on March 20. It is not clear exactly when those men returned to duty, but it appears that most of them were back with the regiment by the time it returned to Virginia in early May. According to Lieutenant Colonel Jones of the 57th, the regiment "in the course of time . . . again filled up to respectable proportions."[141]

On April 14 a 7,000-man Confederate "army" commanded by Hoke—General Pickett, Hoke's department commander, was by then back at his headquarters in Petersburg—set out from Kinston and Weldon to begin a campaign to recapture Plymouth, "Little Washington," and New Bern. The 54th and 57th regiments, along with Corse's Brigade, were left behind at Kinston "to guard against a movement [against the town] from New Bern" and discourage the Federals from sending reinforcements from New Bern to Plymouth. At

138. Paris Diary, March 27 and April 6, 1864; H. W. Barrow to J. W. Fries, April 9, 1864, in Blair, "Letters of Henry W. Barrow," 81; G. W. Wills to his sister, April 2, 1864, George W. Wills Letters. "I do not like the place [Kinston] at all," Pvt. George Leitz of the 17th Virginia wrote. "[W]e have only two things to relieve the monotony of Camp life, rain & drill[;] when it is not raining we are drilling constantly from morning till night & on the contrary, when we are not drilling it is raining all the time." George Leitz to O. W. [Aurelia] Hooper, March 27, 1864, Hooper Papers.

139. G. W. Wills to his sister, April 2, 1864, George W. Wills Letters. Lt. William Beavans, another member of the 43rd, wrote in his diary on April 6: "Busy drilling: all day nothing but drilling." Five days later he complained again of "nothing but drilling 3 times per diem." Like Wills, Beavans did not think much of Hoke as a disciplinarian, describing him as "not very strict." Short rations probably had a good deal to do with the "plundering" problem. Corse's men, too, were called to account for indiscipline and accused by their commander of "lawlessness," "straggling," "thieving," and "disgraces and outrages." William Beavans Books, SHC (2 volumes), 2: April 6, 11, and 5, 1864, hereafter cited as Beavans Books; quoted in Krick, *30th Virginia Infantry*, 47.

140. See Iobst, *Bloody Sixth*, 181; J. K. Walker to Lucinda Walker, March 14, 1864, Walker Papers. In the 54th North Carolina conscripts were coming in "daily" according to Lt. J. Marshall Williams of Company C. Williams, "Fifty-fourth Regiment," in Clark, *Histories of the North Carolina Regiments*, 3:274.

141. J. K. Walker to his father, April 7, 1864, Walker Papers; Jones, "Fifty-seventh Regiment," in Clark, *Histories of the North Carolina Regiments*, 3:418. See also Hatton, "Gen. Archibald Godwin," 135. According to a postwar statement by Lieutenant Colonel Tate, the 6th North Carolina was assigned some men "from the reserves [the recently organized North Carolina Junior Reserves]" at that time. Whether any reservists were assigned to the 57th North Carolina is uncertain. House, *Murder of Union Soldiers in North Carolina*, 70.

Of the fifteen company officers captured at Rappahannock Station, only one subsequently returned to duty. Regiments had a complement of forty company officers, and the permanent loss of fourteen in one battle constituted a very serious blow to the 57th's leadership and combat effectiveness.

sunrise on April 15 the two regiments moved east down the Dover road, presumably as a feint against New Bern or in response to a report of Federal activity. That night they returned to Kinston. On the morning of the sixteenth Corse's Brigade marched southeast toward Batchelder's Creek, about twenty-five miles down the tracks of the Atlantic and North Carolina Railroad.[142] The next day the 54th was sent off at midnight to Free Bridge, near Trenton. As far as can be determined, the 57th North Carolina remained at Kinston on April 17 and throughout the Plymouth and Washington campaigns.[143] Meantime, at New Bern on the afternoon of April 18, Maj. Gen. John J. Peck, commander of the Federal District of North Carolina, received "advices by deserters that General Corse was in front of the outposts at Batchelder's Creek with a large force of all arms, and that General Pickett would attack Little Washington on Tuesday [April 19]." That report was probably a ruse by two phony "deserters" supplied by Hoke (although it may have been a major muddling of the facts by two genuine deserters or by the Federal officer who questioned them). In any case, unbeknown to Peck, Corse (commanding his own brigade; not "a large force") was on his way back to Kinston, and Plymouth (not Washington) had been under attack by Hoke (not Pickett) since the previous afternoon. On the basis of the deserters' misinformation, Peck immediately dispatched a gunboat and two steamers "loaded with troops" to "Little Washington."[144]

Early on the morning of the nineteenth Peck received a dispatch dated April 17 from Brig. Gen. Henry W. Wessells, the commanding officer at Plymouth, stating that his badly outnumbered garrison was besieged and the *Albemarle* was moving down the Roanoke. By the time Peck learned of the situation at Plymouth, the Confederates had captured Fort Wessells, an important component of General Wessells's fortifications, and the entire garrison was in jeopardy. On April 19 the *Albemarle* reached Plymouth, sank two Federal gunboats, and drove two others downriver. Too late, Peck dispatched reinforcements and ammunition by steamers. Those vessels were intercepted and diverted in Albemarle Sound by Federal gunboats that survived the fight with the *Albemarle*. On the morning of April 20, Peck received word that the fall of Plymouth was imminent, a forecast that was fulfilled before the end of the day. At a cost of a few hundred casualties, Hoke had captured the town and 2,600 prisoners, seemingly paving the way for the reconquest of eastern North Carolina. As a reward for his "brilliant" victory, he received a resolution of thanks from the Confederate Congress and, by order of Pres. Jefferson Davis, was promoted to major general to rank from April 20, 1864, the date of Wessells's surrender. Lt. Col. William G. Lewis of the 43rd North Carolina was placed in command of Hoke's former brigade.[145]

---

142. Jones, "Fifty-seventh Regiment," in Clark, *Histories of the North Carolina Regiments*, 3:419. Corse halted at Deep Creek, several miles above Batchelder's Creek, and returned to Kinston on the evening of April 18. His movement was a feint intended to prevent the dispatch of reinforcements from New Bern to Plymouth. See Krick, *30th Virginia Infantry*, 48.

143. See Paris Diary, April 17, 1864; J. M. Hefner to Kizia Hefner, April 16 and 29, 1864, Hefner Papers. There is no evidence of Federal operations in the Free Bridge area, and the purpose of the movement is unknown. Possibly the 54th's mission (if not a feint) was to guard against an enemy thrust south of Dover Swamp that would turn Corse's right flank at Deep Creek or result in a surprise attack on Kinston and the destruction of the *Neuse*.

144. *Official Records (Army)*, ser. 1, 33:288.

145. *Official Records (Army)*, ser. 1, 33:305, and 51 (pt. 2):874. See also W. T. Jordan Jr. and Gerald W. Thomas,

On April 25 the confident Confederates advanced on Washington, which they reached on April 26.[146] Finding the Federals in the midst of a hurried evacuation, Hoke settled down to wait for the town to fall bloodlessly into his hands. After three days of pillage, the last of the Federals boarded ship for New Bern on April 30. Fires broke out at the same time, reducing at least half of Washington to a smoking ruin. Hoke then moved south via Greenville to Deep Gully (eight miles west of New Bern), where a Federal force was driven from its redoubts by Lewis's Brigade on May 4.[147] On May 5 Hoke crossed the Trent at Pollocksville and began making preparations for a full-scale assault on New Bern. Lewis's Brigade, excluding the 6th North Carolina, which remained at Washington and did not re-join the brigade until May 26, was at Pollocksville that day and, according to Chaplain Paris, "in fine Spirits." At eight o'clock the next morning a Confederate "Mosquito fleet" bound for New Bern passed Pollocksville on its way down the Trent. Two hours later Lewis was instructed to be ready to march at a moment's notice. At 11:00 A.M. his men moved out—not northeast toward New Bern, as they expected, but northwest toward Kinston.[148] By order of Gen. P. G. T. Beauregard, Hoke's new department commander, Hoke was instructed to "repair forthwith to Petersburg, no matter how far his operations might have advanced. . . ." Those orders, issued by authority of President Davis, were prompted by a massive attack at the Wilderness by the new general-in-chief of Federal armies, Lt. Gen. Ulysses S. Grant. Although resigned to the necessity of his recall to Virginia, Hoke later pronounced Beauregard's order "one of the greatest disappointments I ever had."[149]

The 57th North Carolina reached Kinston at one o'clock the next afternoon and left by rail for Goldsboro at sunset with the rest of the brigade. At Goldsboro the engine "ran off the road," but at seven o'clock on the morning of May 8 the men boarded the cars again and departed for Weldon. From Weldon they moved by rail about twenty-two miles up the line to a point below Jarratt's Station, where raiding Federal cavalrymen had torn up the tracks. They then marched to Jarratt's Station (which they found burned except for one small house), crossed the Nottoway River on the remains of a burned bridge, and marched to Stony Creek. After fording the creek near the charred ruins of another bridge, they boarded a train and proceeded to Petersburg. They arrived at dark on the evening of the

"Massacre at Plymouth: April 20, 1864," *North Carolina Historical Review* 72 (April 1995): 133; John W. Graham, "The Capture of Plymouth: 20 April, 1864," in Clark, *Histories of the North Carolina Regiments*, 5:175, 193-194. Some modern writers have placed the 57th North Carolina at the Battle of Plymouth, but such was not the case.

146. Some reports indicate that Hoke reached Washington on the twenty-seventh.

147. The Federals were "strongly entrenched," Capt. Samuel C. James of the 21st North Carolina wrote, "but the works were carried without much resistance as they [had] only a small force there." S. C. James to C. T. Pfohl, May 5, 1864, Pfohl Papers.

148. Paris Diary, May 5-6, 1864. See also J. K. Walker to his father, May 3 and [June] 4, 1864, Walker Papers.

149. Alfred Roman, *The Military Operations of General Beauregard in the War between the States, 1861 to 1865, Including a Brief Personal Sketch and a Narrative of His Services in the War with Mexico, 1846-8,* 2 vols. (New York: Harper and Brothers, 1884), 2:199, hereafter cited as Roman, *General Beauregard*; Robert D. Graham, "Fifty-sixth Regiment," in Clark, *Histories of the North Carolina Regiments*, 3:350.

ninth, marched to a point four miles "below town" near the Jordan house, and bivouacked for the night.[150]

During the week of May 5-11, 1864, while the Army of Northern Virginia was locked in combat with the Army of the Potomac at the Wilderness and Spotsylvania Court House, Maj. Gen. Benjamin F. Butler's 40,000-man Federal army disembarked from transports at City Point (at the confluence of the James and Appomattox Rivers a few miles northeast of Petersburg) and at nearby Bermuda Hundred (a neck of land between the James and Appomattox). At the same time, 12,000 Federal cavalrymen under Maj. Gen. Philip H. Sheridan set out from the vicinity of Spotsylvania Court House on a raid to disrupt Lee's communications, threaten Richmond, and "whip ['Jeb'] Stuart." In response to those thrusts, Lewis's Brigade moved on May 10 to the vicinity of Swift Creek, just north of Petersburg, where an inconclusive engagement between Butler and Brig. Gen. Bushrod R. Johnson's command had been fought the previous day.[151] After a bumbling advance southwest in the direction of Petersburg and its vital railroad junctions, Butler began falling back round noon on the tenth. Lewis's Brigade and the rest of Hoke's Division were then ordered to Drewry's Bluff, a bastion on the south bank of the James defending the southern approaches to Richmond. The 57th North Carolina bivouacked that night two miles south of Drewry's Bluff and about eleven miles north of Petersburg.[152]

On the morning of May 12, as Butler began edging his way up the south bank of the James toward Richmond, the 57th took position "behind the out works" just south of Drewry's Bluff. Three hours later the regiment crossed the James on a pontoon bridge in a heavy rain and moved to Chaffin's Bluff. That evening Confederate authorities, reacting to what appeared to be an imminent attack on Richmond by Sheridan, ordered reinforcements sent from the James River defenses. At 6:00 P.M. the 57th boarded steamers with the rest of the brigade and was transported upriver to the Confederate capital. The men arrived at dark and "marched out in the rain to the Breastworks 4 miles East of the city." It was probably on the same date, May 12, that Lewis's Brigade was transferred from Hoke's Division to that of Maj. Gen. Robert Ransom.[153] On May 13, after the Federal cavalry alarum subsided, Lewis's Brigade was ordered to "take the cars on the Fredericksburg R. Road" and join the hard-pressed Army of Northern Virginia near Spotsylvania Court House. Those orders were countermanded almost immediately because of the developing threat posed by

---

150. Paris Diary, May 7 and 9, 1864. "I was uneasy all the time," Capt. Cary W. Whitaker of the 43rd North Carolina acknowledged in his diary on May 9, "as I knew how easy it would be for the Enemy to throw the train off the track and attack us and throw us in confusion and probably kill a good many of us." Diary of Cary W. Whitaker, May 9, 1864, Cary Whitaker Papers, SHC, hereafter cited as Whitaker Diary.

151. Gordon C. Rhea, *The Battles for Spotsylvania Court House and the Road to Yellow Tavern, May 7-12, 1864* (Baton Rouge: Louisiana State University Press, 1997), 68. Johnson reported that "parts" of Lewis's Brigade arrived on the morning of May 10, but it is uncertain whether the 57th was among them. The 6th North Carolina was protecting railroad bridges in the vicinity of Belfield and Hicksford and is one (perhaps the only one) of Lewis's regiments that was not at Swift Creek. *Official Records (Army)*, ser. 1, 36 (pt. 2):244. See also Iobst, *Bloody Sixth*, 203.

152. See Paris Diary, May 11, 1864; *Official Records (Army)*, ser. 1, 36 (pt. 2):991.

153. Paris Diary, May 12, 1864. See also *Official Records (Army)*, ser. 1, 36 (pt. 2):212, 987, 995. It is certain that the brigade was still under Hoke on May 10 but had been transferred to Ransom by May 16.

Butler's advance, and the brigade was "sent over the James on Coalfield Road in the night." The next day the weary men returned to Drewry's Bluff and were involved in "Heavy" skirmishing that continued into the evening.[154] After another day of skirmishing—"but at times," according to Chaplain Paris, "very slight"—Beauregard took the offensive on the foggy morning of May 16. At 4:45 A.M. Ransom's Division advanced in two lines toward Federal entrenchments south of Drewry's Bluff. Lewis's Brigade was on the right of Ransom's first line, with Hoke's Division on its right.[155] Beauregard's plan called for Ransom to drive back and turn Butler's right flank, thereby cutting off the Federals from Bermuda Hundred. Hoke would demonstrate against Butler's left to hold it in place and prevent the dispatch of reinforcements to oppose Ransom. As soon as Ransom turned Butler's right, Hoke would attack. A third division, under Brig. Gen. Alfred H. Colquitt, would remain in reserve, and the Petersburg garrison, under Maj. Gen. W. H. C. Whiting, would fall upon Butler's rear as he retreated.

Ransom's initial attack carried the first line of Federal breastworks, but Confederate casualties were high, ammunition ran short, and the assault lost cohesion as units became disoriented and intermixed in the fog.[156] Ransom therefore halted to reorganize. Unable to judge Ransom's progress because of the poor visibility, Hoke skirmished with the enemy as ordered. After waiting an hour for Ransom to accomplish his turning movement, Hoke attacked with the brigades of Brig. Gens. Johnson Hagood and Bushrod Johnson and easily carried the Federals' lightly defended outer line. Rather than launch an unauthorized frontal assault against the heavily manned Federal second line, Hoke then halted. The wisdom of that decision was confirmed shortly thereafter when one of Hagood's regiments stumbled into a force of entrenched Federals while attempting to make contact with Lewis's Brigade and suffered severe losses. Two counterattacks against Hoke were then "handsomely repulsed," but another enemy thrust threatened to turn his right and resulted in heavy fighting. Ransom, meantime, discovered that Lewis's Brigade and several of Colquitt's Georgia regiments, which had been sent to Hoke's assistance, had overlapped Hoke's left. Another delay ensued while Ransom moved his "whole line" to the left to give Lewis and the Georgians a clear field of fire. At that juncture a frustrated Beauregard ordered a temporary cessation to offensive operations to await an assault by Whiting from the south. However, despite repeated telegraphic urging, Whiting failed to move.[157] Night and a heavy rainfall brought the bungled battle to an end.

Although hardly a tactical credit to any Confederate general, the battle at Drewry's Bluff halted Butler's advance on Richmond. Moreover, Beauregard triumphed despite a

154. Paris Diary, May 13-14, 1864.

155. Paris Diary, May 15, 1864. The 6th North Carolina was on detail near Petersburg, and the 1st Battalion N.C. Sharpshooters was on assignment in North Carolina. The 43rd North Carolina was still on temporary duty with Lewis's Brigade. Thus the units present were the 21st, 43rd, 54th, and 57th regiments.

156. "One could hardly see anything," a 43rd North Carolina officer wrote. "[C]ould only fire in the direction from which the balls came." Whitaker Diary, May 16, 1864.

157. *Official Records (Army)*, ser. 1, 36 (pt. 2):237, 213. In one of his telegrams, Beauregard exhorted Whiting to "Remember Dessaix at Marengo and Blucher at Waterloo." Those two generals, it will be recalled, saved Napoleon Bonaparte and the Duke of Wellington respectively from disaster during the Napoleonic Wars. Roman, *General Beauregard*, 2:561.

numerical disadvantage of almost two to one. That night Butler, having reconfirmed his well-earned reputation for incompetence, fell back to Bermuda Hundred. By the twentieth he was "firmly corked" in the Bermuda Hundred "bottle" and, at least for the moment, out of the war. In a letter to his wife, Pvt. Jesse Hill of the 21st North Carolina described Drewry's Bluff as "the hardis fight we hav had. . . ." "I dont see how any of us ever got out a live," he wrote in another letter. "[T]he men lay as thick as the whete bundles in a harvist field[.]" Chaplain Paris reported that Confederate losses were "very heavy," and Capt. Cary W. Whitaker of the 43rd North Carolina estimated that they "equalled if not exceeded the enemys." According to figures compiled for this volume, the 57th North Carolina lost 3 men killed or mortally wounded, 2 wounded, and 2 captured.[158]

The 57th remained in the vicinity of Drewry's Bluff on May 17. On May 18 the regiment erected breastworks near the north bank of the Appomattox River and was under fire from Federal gunboats. "The Enemy have been shelling us a good deal," Captain Whitaker wrote, "[and] have managed to get our range pretty well although our works are entirely hid from them."[159] "Lively" picket firing and another gunboat shelling occurred on the morning of May 19. About sunset orders arrived transferring Lewis's Brigade to the Army of Northern Virginia. The men returned immediately to Drewry's Bluff, boarded steamers, and were transported to Richmond, where they arrived around midnight. After marching across town to the Fredericksburg station, they "lay down on the pavements" at 1:00 A.M. and "slept until light." At 6:00 A.M. on May 20 Lewis's troops left by rail for Milford Station, near Bowling Green, where they arrived in the early afternoon. They then marched six miles in the direction of Spotsylvania Court House and bivouacked for the night. "Weary and broken down" after a march of "over twenty miles," they reached the front on May 21 about an hour before sunset and were assigned to Early's Division of Ewell's Corps. They were then informed that "the whole army was falling back" and they "must act as the rear guard." At dusk they set out again, this time on a twelve-mile march that lasted until midnight.[160] The next day Lewis's troops moved to Hanover Junction. Chaplain Paris reported "Great Straggling" in the brigade "owing to the broken down Condition of the men. . . . Yesterday's forced march told heavily upon our Command. My feet are dreadfully blistered. Every step I make is with pain."[161] On May 23 the Federal army crossed the

---

158. Jesse Hill to Emoline Hill, May 22 and 19, 1864, in Ripple, *Jesse Hill Letters*; Paris Diary, May 16, 1864; Whitaker Diary, May 16, 1864. Several of those casualties probably occurred on May 15 and 17. Losses in Lewis's Brigade as a whole were officially reported as 25 men killed, 137 wounded, and 25 missing. See *Official Records (Army)*, ser. 1, 36 (pt. 2):205. Beauregard's postwar account of the battle, entitled "The Defense of Drewry's Bluff," appears in Robert Underwood Johnson and Clarence Clough Buel, eds., *Battles and Leaders of the Civil War . . . Being for the Most Part Contributions by Union and Confederate Officers, Based Upon "The Century War Series,"* 4 vols. (New York: Century Company, 1887-1888; New York: Castle Books, 1956), 4:195-205.

159. Whitaker Diary, May 18, 1864. Whitaker described the brigade's location as "one or two miles East of the turnpike about ten miles West of Bermuda hundreds."

160. Paris Diary, May 19 and 21, 1864. "[W]e dont get half enough to ete and what we do get hant fit for dogs," Private Hill wrote on May 22. "[M]y hounds wood not ete such bread as I hav to ete." Jesse Hill to Emoline Hill, May 22, 1864, in Ripple, *Jesse Hill Letters*.

161. Paris Diary, May 22, 1864. Early found Lewis's Brigade "very much reduced in strength" at the time of its arrival. Early, *Autobiographical Sketch*, 359. The 43rd North Carolina rejoined Daniel's (Grimes's) Brigade on

North Anna River at Jericho Ford. Several days of inconclusive fighting, in which Lewis's Brigade, on the Confederate right, was not directly involved, convinced Grant of the tactical inferiority of his North Anna position. On the night of May 26 he recrossed the river and moved southeastward toward the Pamunkey.

On May 27 Ewell's Corps, temporarily commanded by General Early (Brig. Gen. Stephen D. Ramseur assumed temporary command of Early's Division), marched twenty-four miles and entrenched between Beaver Dam Creek and Pole Green Church. Longstreet's Corps, under temporary command of Maj. Gen. Richard H. Anderson, came up on Early's right; Hill's Corps went into position on Early's left. On May 30 Lee attempted to halt Grant's flanking sidle toward the Chickahominy River by attacking that portion of the Federal army that had crossed Totopotomoy Creek. Rodes's Division of Early's Corps drove a Federal brigade back near Bethesda Church that afternoon, and shortly thereafter Ramseur ordered an attack by John Pegram's Virginia brigade. The unfortunate Virginians quickly blundered into a line of massed artillery, suffering murderous casualties. The 57th North Carolina was "in line of battle 3 miles east of Mechanicsville" but took no significant part in the fighting.[162]

On May 31, after failing to arrest Grant's movement toward the Chickahominy, Early fell back to a position just west of Bethesda Church on the Mechanicsville road. "Lively Cannonading" occurred in the vicinity of the 57th North Carolina until 11:00 A.M., and picket firing continued throughout the "intensely hot" day. In the meantime, Grant dispatched cavalry units under Sheridan a few miles further south to occupy Cold Harbor, a strategic road junction whose capture would afford the Federals a shorter route to their supply base at White House Landing, on the Pamunkey, and open a new avenue of advance on Richmond. Finding Cold Harbor occupied that same morning by Rebel cavalry under Maj. Gen. Fitzhugh Lee, Sheridan began a day-long struggle for possession of the dismal hamlet. The arrival of a brigade of Hoke's Division failed to swing the battle against the Federal troopers and their seven-shot Spencer carbines, and Sheridan seized Cold Harbor in the late afternoon. An attempt by one of Anderson's divisions to retake the place the next day was turned back by murderous blasts of grape and canister and sheets of fire from the deadly Spencers. Stymied, the Confederates began entrenching. That afternoon, following the arrival of reinforcements on both sides, the Federals attacked. A near breakthrough was achieved at one point, but withering Confederate fire sent the Yankees reeling back, as one Tar Heel noted with satisfaction, "faster than they come."[163] On the same day, June 1, Private Hefner penned a letter to his wife that provides a cameo view of conditions and morale among the men of the 57th: "I am on picket post at this time[.] I have bin on picket and on skermish for the last week[.] I would rather do that than to bild brestworks[.] [W]e bild brestworks every day[.] I can inform you that We fare very well since we left kinston[.] [W]e get plenty [of] meat and bread [and] we can forage something sometimes on skermish. . . . [T]here is two much fiting on hand [at this time.] [I]t hasant stopt since the third

May 22. See Whitaker Diary, May 22, 1864.

162. Paris Diary, May 30, 1864.

163. Paris Diary, May 31, 1864; diary of John A. Foster (52nd North Carolina), June 1, 1864, Alfred M. and John A. Foster Papers, SCD-DU.

day of May[.] [T]her is skermish fiting and charging in hearing every day and I expect the worst aint come yet[.] I dont look for this fite to stop til peace is Made[.] [L]ee has fell back from Rapadan ten mile from or near Richmond[.] [T]his is the bludest time that . . . ever was nown[.] [T]hey ar fiting now on the rite as hard as they can tare[.] [T]he cry of the woonded is herd now almost evry whare[.]"[164]

Convinced that the Confederate infantry were too weakened and demoralized by a month of bloody fighting to withstand another blow, Grant planned a massive assault on the entire Confederate line for the morning of June 2. However, one of his corps missed its way during the night and arrived in such a state of exhaustion that the attack had to be delayed. An afternoon probe by Early's Corps further disrupted the timetable. When a heavy rain began falling, the assault was postponed until the next day. Meanwhile, Lee's entire army arrived on the field and busied itself constructing a virtually impregnable line of fortifications between Totopotomoy Creek and the Chickahominy River.

At 4:30 on the cool, misty morning of June 3, approximately 40,000 Federals, many of whom correctly sensed that they had seen their last sunrise, advanced through the mud into a curtain of fire whose thunderous roar was clearly audible in Richmond eight miles away. Staggered by the hailstorm of musketry, case shot, and double-shotted canister that raked them from several angles, the Federals milled about in confusion and agony, unable to advance or (because of their comrades charging up behind them) retreat. In a matter of minutes the attack was over. At least 7,000 Federals were dead or wounded. During the battle Early's Corps, on the Confederate left, was targeted for attack by the Federal V and IX Corps, under Maj. Gens. Gouverneur K. Warren and A. E. Burnside. However, Warren failed to move at all, and Burnside succeeded only in taking a few trenches well forward of the main Confederate works. Along Ramseur's front, skirmishing was so heavy that Ramseur called in his sharpshooters from their exposed positions. Some members of the 57th North Carolina were probably involved in the fighting, but the regiment's casualties, if any, were very light.[165]

For over a week following the battle of June 3 the two battered armies remained in position observing and skirmishing. Along some segments of Early's front, particularly on the left where Robert Rodes's Division was stationed, an uneasy quiet prevailed. On Ramseur's portion of the line there was considerably more activity. A member of the 6th North Carolina, Sgt. John K. Walker, wrote on June 4 that "We are now in our Breast works near [the] Mechanicksville road 9 mile[s] below Richmond. . . . There is fighting going on every Day on some portion of the line. Our works and the Yankees are about 600 yds apart and heavy Cannonading and Sharp skirmishing is going on incessantly from daylight until dark, and an occasional assault of the enemy upon our Breast works, but generally repulsed with hea[v]y loss. . . . [W]e have not been in no regular engagement yet but are skirmishing heavy evry day. . . . [T]he cannon[a]ding and skirmishing is raging furiously while I write."[166]

---

164. J. M. Hefner to Kizia Hefner, June 1, 1864, Hefner Papers.

165. Chaplain Paris's diary entry for that day refers to a "furious" battle in the center and a "heavy artillery duel all along the line." Paris Diary, June 3, 1864.

166. J. K. Walker to his father, [June] 4, 1864, Walker Papers. "[O]ur Troops are in good Breastworks and in

Fighting tailed off somewhat on June 5—"as if," Chaplain Paris wryly observed, "each army had some reverence left for the Sabbath." On the sixth General Early, after discovering that the enemy had fallen back slightly on his front, launched an attack but quickly bogged down in a swamp. Heavier fighting took place the next day as Early again attempted to get at the Federals. Lewis's Brigade "skirmished all day with vigor," Chaplain Paris wrote. "Charged and took the rifle pits of the enemy's sharpshooters. . . . Our Brigade was relieved at night by Pegram's." According to Major Pfohl of the 21st North Carolina, "The Brigade was highly complimented by both Ewell & Early for the manner in which they performed their work. . . ."[167] June 8 featured more sharpshooting and an artillery duel at dusk. "We are having a disagreeable, dirty life at present in the trenches," Major Pfohl wrote on that day. "Our works & those of the enemy are on parallel lines scarcely a mile apart, the balls from the skirmishers, who are between the lines, reaching into the works, & causing the men to keep low." A "strange and unaccountable calm" followed on June 9, a member of Hoke's Brigade who signed himself "SIGMA" informed the editor of the Raleigh *Daily Confederate*. "The crack of the sharp shooter's rifle were [*sic*] but seldom heard, and the roar of artillery, as if by common consent, was hushed." That evening Ramseur's Division moved two miles to the right and bivouacked. "Slow and lazy cannonading all day extending into the night" occurred on June 10 and "dull" cannon fire on the eleventh and twelfth.[168] "We are getting plenty of rations, Such as meal, flour, Sugar, coffee, rice, peas, Onions &c," Paris wrote on June 12. "Weather very dry, and remarkably cool for the Season. . . ."[169]

At 3:00 A.M. on the morning of June 13, Lewis's troops were awakened in their camp near Gaines' Mill and ordered to "pack up and . . . be ready to march at a moment's notice." Shortly thereafter the men "struck off" with the rest of Early's Corps for Lynchburg, an important railroad junction, supply depot, and medical center about ninety miles west of Richmond. There an attack was anticipated by Maj. Gen. David Hunter, whose Yankee army of about 18,000 men had just sacked Staunton, burned the military institute at Lexington, and completed a heavy-handed conquest of the Confederacy's Shenandoah Valley breadbasket. Opposing Hunter were the cavalry command of Brig. Gen. John D. Imboden and two small infantry brigades under Maj. Gen. John C. Breckinridge. The 57th North Carolina set off at 4:00 A.M. on a twenty-five mile march, made another twenty miles the next day, passed through Trevilian Station on the afternoon of June 15, and was within four miles of Charlottesville by the evening of the sixteenth. "The troops [are] in fine Spirits," Chaplain Paris

---

fine Spirits Just waiting for the yankees to come on us," Walker continued, "and we whip them every time they attack us. . . . [We are] getting plenty of every thing to eat."

167. Paris Diary, June 5 and 7, 1864; W. J. Pfohl to C. T. Pfohl, June 8, 1864, Pfohl Papers. See also *Daily Confederate* (Raleigh), June 17, 1864.

168. W. J. Pfohl to C. T. Pfohl, June 8, 1864, Pfohl Papers; *Daily Confederate* (Raleigh), June 17, 1864; Paris Diary, June 10-12, 1864. "In Some places our line of breastworks is Within 150 Yards of the enemy," Paris wrote on June 11. See also diary (typescript) of John Walton (6th North Carolina), June 9, 1864, SHC, hereafter cited as Walton Diary. The *Daily Confederate* letter referred to above indicates that "within the last ten days [June 1-10]" the 57th North Carolina lost 1 man killed, 6 wounded, and 1 missing.

169. Paris Diary, June 12, 1864.

observed that night, "thinking We are on the Way to Pennsylvania."[170] The next morning the men marched at first light for Charlottesville. There Ramseur's Division and part of John B. Gordon's boarded railroad cars and moved over the rickety tracks of the Orange and Alexandria Railroad to Lynchburg. They arrived around two o'clock that afternoon, having covered about sixty miles in seven hours, and were placed in line of battle.[171]

In the meantime Hunter, whose leisurely advance was further slowed by skirmishing with Breckinridge's command, reached the outskirts of Lynchburg on the evening of June 17. During the night Early ordered that "a yard engine, with box cars attached [be] . . . run up and down the Southside Railroad, making as much noise as possible" to a cacophony of cheers and drums. Convinced by the hullabaloo that "large bodies of troops" were arriving, Hunter bivouacked for the night and prepared to advance cautiously the next day. By the morning of June 18 Early was partially entrenched west of Lynchburg astride the Salem road. Gordon was on the left, Ramseur in the center, and Breckinridge on the right. In the absence of part of Gordon's Division and all of Rodes's, Early adopted a defensive posture. Hunter, uncertain of the size of the Confederate force, launched several probing attacks. According to Early, the enemy's loss was "considerable." That afternoon Rodes's Division and the rest of Gordon's arrived by rail and were sent into the line by Early. Early then began making plans to attack the next day.[172]

During the night Hunter arrived at the remarkable conclusion that Early's force was "at least double" the size of his own and withdrew toward Liberty.[173] Early set off in a "hotly pressed" pursuit at daylight. In the late afternoon Ramseur's Division, after a "terrible" march over "very rough" roads, overtook the Federal rear guard. A sharp skirmish ensued in the midst of which the Federals broke and fled through Liberty, leaving, according to Chaplain Paris, nineteen dead on the field.[174] For the next two days the chase continued in "very disagreeable" heat and dust as Hunter retreated precipitately westward. On June 20 he crossed the Blue Ridge Mountains at Buford's Gap, and on the

---

170. *Daily Confederate* (Raleigh), July 13, 1864; Paris Diary, June 16, 1864. Most of Early's army appears to have reached Charlottesville on the afternoon of June 16, and it is unclear why Lewis's Brigade would have been four miles down the road from the town that night. See footnote 171 below for information concerning the 57th Regiment's time of departure for Charlottesville the next morning and its time of departure by rail from Charlottesville to Lynchburg.

171. Paris states that the 54th North Carolina "marched at light for the R. Road and took the Cars at 7 Oclock for Lynchburg. Reached the latter place at 2 Oclock." However, John Walton, a diarist belonging to the 6th North Carolina, wrote that his regiment "Arrived at Lynchburg at 12 o'clock on the 17th." Paris Diary, June 17, 1864; Walton Diary, June 16[17], 1864.

172. Charles M. Blackford, "The Campaign and Battle of Lynchburg," *Southern Historical Society Papers* 30: 289; *Official Records (Army)*, ser. 1, 37 (pt. 1):99; Early, *Autobiographical Sketch*, 375. Paris's diary entry for June 18 indicates picket and artillery firing (apparently in the morning) and a "furious artillery duel" of an hour's duration beginning at 2:00 P.M. Paris Diary, June 18, 1864. According to figures compiled for this volume, the 57th North Carolina lost five men wounded on June 18.

173. *Official Records (Army)*, ser. 1, 37 (pt. 1):100. Hunter claimed also that his troops "had scarcely enough . . . ammunition left to sustain another well contested battle."

174. *Daily Confederate* (Raleigh), July 13, 1864 (first quotation); Early, *Autobiographical Sketch*, 376 (second and third quotations). See also Paris Diary, June 19, 1864. In his advance on Lynchburg, Hunter came down the north-south roads leading from Staunton to Lexington to Liberty and then turned east; however, in his retreat he was forced to continue west from Liberty because the Confederates held an interior railroad line to Staunton.

morning of the twenty-first he passed through Salem. Harried by Confederate cavalry, he then disappeared into the Allegheny Mountains, conceding the Shenandoah Valley to the Confederates, taking his army out of the war for a month, and leaving open the Valley route to Washington. According to Chaplain Paris, the Confederates captured "about 150" prisoners, thirteen pieces of artillery, fifteen wagons, thirty beeves, 150 horses, and reduced the Federals to the indignity of "beg[inning] to burn their own [wagon] trains."[175]

On June 22 Early rested his weary troops near Salem. Baths in Botetourt Springs revived the men, some of whom partook of the spring's curative sulfur water. That night there was an officers' dance at Hollins Institute, the nearby academy for women. The next day the army moved northeast to Buchanan, where most of Ramseur's Division, in the van, crossed the James River on planks laid across the stringers of a burned bridge. On the twenty-fourth—an "intensely hot" day—the 57th North Carolina moved out with the van at daylight and marched about twenty miles, crossing Natural Bridge.[176] On June 25 Early's force, now styled the Army of the Valley, passed through Lexington, detouring slightly to march "in silence with arms reversed" past the grave—"covered with beautiful fresh flowers"—of "Stonewall" Jackson. The men then crossed the North River on the ruins of another burned bridge and arrived at Fairfield around 2:00 P.M.[177]

On June 26, in deference to a week of "intense" heat during which the troops had "Suffered greatly," the army moved out at 3:00 A.M., halting around noon after making about fourteen miles. The next morning the 57th marched about half that distance to a point two miles below Staunton, where it spent the rest of the day "cooking and washing." Lieutenant Walton of the 6th North Carolina apparently found plenty to cook. "I'm very much

175. Walton Diary, June 20, 1864; Paris Diary, June 21, 1864. For Hunter's account of the cavalry fight, see *Official Records (Army)*, ser. 1, 37 (pt. 1):101. SIGMA wrote that "In the advance and retreat of the Yankee army upon Lynchburg . . . they certainly afforded to the world unmistakable evidence . . . that in baseness and villany [sic], their claims to a distinguished position in the scale of infamy, were not to be disputed by either Goths or Vandals. Numbers of horses and milk cows were shot down by them along the road and in the grass lots. Every bushel of corn or wheat, meal or flour, and every piece of bacon that could be found, was carried off by them; ladies' drawers and trunks [were] broken open, their fine clothes carried off or torn up before their faces; their table ware and looking glasses smashed up and destroyed in their presence; and they [were] cursed and abused by the degenerate and debased yankees." *Daily Confederate* (Raleigh), July 13, 1864.

176. Paris Diary, June 24, 1864. The previous day, according to Paris, was also one of "intense" heat. Paris Diary, June 23, 1864. "Went down and looked at . . . [Natural Bridge]," Lieutenant Walton of the 6th North Carolina wrote. "Thought it was a grand site. Band was ordered down there to play. Music sounded splendidly. Reverberation was excellent." Maj. Kyd Douglas of Early's staff recalled the same occasion many years later with a lyrical touch: "I took several bands and have never forgotten the solemn effect of their music as it rose and swelled in volume, and filled the great arch and seemed to press against the sides of that cathedral dome, and then rolled along the high rocks that walled the ravine and died away in the widening wood." Walton Diary, June 24, 1864; Henry Kyd Douglas, *I Rode with Stonewall* (Chapel Hill: University of North Carolina Press, 1940; New York: Ballantine Books, 1974), 280, hereafter cited as Douglas, *I Rode with Stonewall*.

177. Paris Diary, June 25, 1864; W. G. Lewis to Mittie Lewis, June 27, 1864, Lewis Papers. "Here lay the great christian patriot & soldier," Lewis wrote, "the unsurpassed warrior of his time, cold in death, & as harmless as the flowers that covered his grave. . . . I believe some of Jacksons [sic] spirit was instilled into the breasts of those hardy veterans who had followed him in so many hard marches, & fought with him on so many stubborn but victorious fields."

pleased with the Valley and community," he wrote. "Find them very hospitable and kind. Have been faring sumptiously [*sic*] for three or four days. . . ." According to General Lewis, the march was an "ovation" whose primary celebrants, he teasingly assured his new bride, were "the prettiest ladies you ever saw." Indeed, Lewis continued with evident relish, "The roads were decked with them, who came from the surrounding country, to give a welcome & wave a nice white handkerchief, & smile sweetly at the 'boys' who had rid them of the Yankee plunderers & thieves."[178]

On June 28 the 57th North Carolina marched through Staunton. There, in preparation for serious campaigning, it left most of its nonessential baggage. Taking the Valley Pike to the northeast, the troops passed through country whose fields of wheat, grass, and clover impressed Chaplain Paris as "grand" and "the best I have ever Seen." Plentiful rations, shorter marches, and "Somewhat Cooler" weather kept morale and spirits high. Lieutenant Walton reported on June 29 that he was "Still getting butter and milk." As a result of a successful foraging expedition, he also enjoyed apple butter and "lightbread" that day.[179] On June 30 the army passed through New Market and bivouacked near Mount Jackson. A brief shower laid the dust a bit, and some of the troops bathed in the North Fork of the Shenandoah River that evening. On July 1—an "exceedingly Sultry" day—they marched through Edenburg and Woodstock, and on the second they passed through Strasburg, Middletown, and Newtown and bivouacked in the vicinity of Winchester. After pausing briefly to inflict damage on the Winchester and Potomac Railroad, the army continued on through Winchester early on the morning of July 3 and split into two columns: one, under Breckinridge, advanced on Martinsburg; the other, consisting of Rodes's and Ramseur's Divisions, moved through Smithfield and Charlestown to Harpers Ferry. Martinsburg was captured by Breckinridge on July 3 after a meager resistance. Rodes and Ramseur seized Bolivar Heights, overlooking Harpers Ferry, on the fourth. Skirmishing and artillery exchanges began there at midmorning and lasted until after nightfall. Finding Harpers Ferry within range of Federal artillery atop Maryland Heights, on the opposite side of the Potomac, Early contented himself with "demonstrating" with Rodes's and Ramseur's Divisions on the fifth and briefly occupying the town.[180]

While Early was engaged at Harpers Ferry on July 5, Breckinridge crossed the Potomac at Shepherdstown. Rodes's Division and most of Ramseur's followed on July 6. Lewis's Brigade remained at Harpers Ferry to watch the Federals on Maryland Heights and was subjected to "occasional" shelling on the sixth and seventh.[181] Late on the afternoon of July 7 the brigade was ordered to rejoin Ramseur. During a thirty-mile march

178. Paris Diary, June 26-27, 1864; Walton Diary, June 27, 1864 (see also June 26, 1864); W. G. Lewis to Mittie Lewis, June 27, 1864, Lewis Papers. Lewis's promotion to brigadier general dated from May 31, 1864.

179. Paris Diary, June 28, 1864; Walton Diary, June 29, 1864. Cartographer Jedediah Hotchkiss noted happily in his diary that "Cherries are in their prime." McDonald, *Make Me a Map: Hotchkiss Journal*, 213 (June 23, 1864).

180. Paris Diary, July 1, 1864; Early, *Autobiographical Sketch*, 384. It seems improbable that Lewis's Brigade was involved in any fighting on July 5.

181. Walton Diary, July 7, 1864 (see also July 6, 1864). Paris states that at 11:00 A.M. on the sixth "the enemy showed a disposition to cross over in force to attack us, and created some degree of alarm"; however, no attack took place. Paris Diary, July 6, 1864.

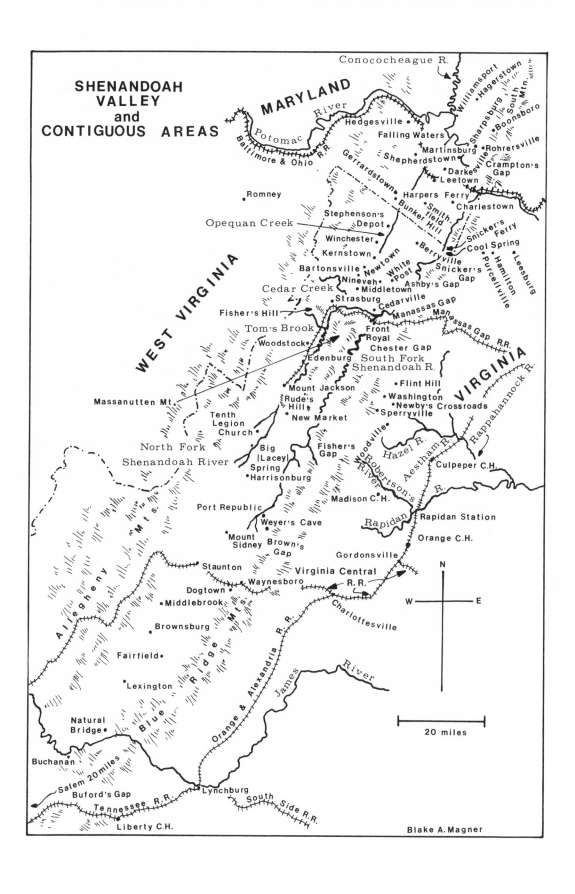

SHENANDOAH
VALLEY
and
CONTIGUOUS AREAS

Conococheague R.

MARYLAND

Potomac River

Baltimore & Ohio R.R.

Williamsport
Hagerstown
Sharpsburg
South Mt.
Boonsboro
Hedgesville
Falling Waters
Martinsburg
Rohrersville
Shepherdstown
Crampton's Gap
Darkesville
Leetown
Harpers Ferry
Charlestown
Gerrardstown

Romney

WEST VIRGINIA

Opequan Creek

Stephenson's Depot
Bunker Hill
Smith-field
Winchester
Snicker's Ferry
Cool Spring
Kernstown
Berryville
Leesburg
Bartonsville
Newtown
White Post
Snicker's Gap
Hamilton
Nineveh
Ashby's Gap
Purcellville
Cedar Creek
Middletown
Strasburg
Cedarville
Manassas Gap
Fisher's Hill
Manassas Gap R.R.
Tom's Brook
Front Royal
Woodstock
Chester Gap
Edenburg
South Fork Shenandoah R.
Flint Hill
Mount Jackson
Washington
Rude's Hill
Newby's Crossroads
Sperryville
New Market

VIRGINIA

Tenth Legion Church
North Fork Shenandoah River
Big (Lacey) Spring
Fisher's Gap
Woodville
Hazel R.
Rappahannock R.
Harrisonburg
Robertson's River
Aestham R.
Culpeper C.H.
Port Republic
Madison C.H.
Weyer's Cave
Rapidan
Rapidan Station
Mount Sidney
Brown's Gap
Orange C.H.
Staunton
Gordonsville
Waynesboro
Virginia Central R.R.
Dogtown
Middlebrook
Charlottesville

Allegheny Mts.

Blue Ridge Mts.

Brownsburg

Fairfield

Lexington

Orange & Alexandria R.R.

James River

Natural Bridge

Buchanan

Salem 20 miles

Buford's Gap

Tennessee R.R.

Lynchburg

South Side R.R.

Liberty C.H.

N
W — E
S

20 miles

Blake A. Magner

that lasted all night and into the next day, the men forded the Potomac at Shepherds-town, overtook Ramseur "near Boonsborough," crossed South Mountain that afternoon, and bivouacked for the night eight miles from Frederick.[182] On July 9 the little army moved on and, after a "leasurely [*sic*]" but "very hard" march led by Ramseur, reached Frederick.[183] Just south of the town, in position on both sides of the Monocacy River, about 5,000 Federal militiamen and Army of the Potomac veterans blocked the road to Washington. Their commander, Maj. Gen. "Lew" Wallace, knew that his makeshift force had little chance of defeating Early. He hoped, however, to buy time for reinforcements to reach the nation's virtually undefended and highly apprehensive capital, scarcely thirty-five miles away.

At midmorning on July 9 Rodes's Division attacked—without notable success—a contingent of Baltimore militiamen on the Federal right. Ramseur, confronted by two blockhouses in the Federal center, was rebuffed in a gingerly probing attack on a railroad bridge. Gordon's Division, opposite Wallace's vulnerable left flank, then crossed the Monocacy in the wake of a hard-fighting but outgunned cavalry unit and charged across fields crisscrossed by fences and studded with haystacks. A change of front by most of the Federals confronting Ramseur brought Gordon's men to a temporary halt, but a new effort by Gordon, in combination with an attack by Brig. Gen. Thomas F. Toon's Brigade of Ramseur's Division, routed the Federals and sent them hot-footing toward Baltimore. Federal casualties have been variously estimated but probably numbered about 1,500 men; Confederate losses were about 700. Lewis's Brigade was left at Frederick to protect Early's rear during the battle and was involved in a skirmish with Federal cavalry. No casualties were reported in the 57th North Carolina.[184]

On the morning of July 10 Early set out with most of his army for Washington. Ramseur's Division remained behind to destroy the iron railroad bridge over the Monocacy, a structure that proved perfectly invulnerable to flames, solid shot, and gunpowder alike. Presently, Ramseur gave up and set off on Early's trail, skirmishing with Federal cavalry as he went. "[I]ntense" heat and clouds of dust—the day, in the words of Chaplain Paris, was "the most dusty one I ever saw"—caused "Vast numbers" of men to break down on the road. Around midnight, after a march of perhaps seventeen miles, the army halted a few miles from Rockville. At daylight the next morning Early resumed his advance. Stifling heat blanketed the parched countryside "even at a very early hour in the morning,"

182. *Daily Confederate* (Raleigh), July 28, 1864. According to a postwar statement by Lieutenant Walton, the men crossed the Potomac wading "three abreast, a short man between two taller ones." Walton Diary, footnote to entry for July 7, 1864.

183. G. W. Wills to his sister, July 17, 1864, William Henry Wills Papers, SHC; Beavans Books, 2: July 9, 1864. "[W]hat a change!" SIGMA wrote, from the cool reception the army received at Sharpsburg, Boonsborough, and Middletown. "Both doors and hearts stood wide open. . . . The ladies appeared everywhere waving their handkerchiefs, the men were busy in bringing to the side-walks buckets of cool water to refresh the weary soldier, [and] the hungry were invited into the rooms of private families, to partake of a friendly breakfast. . . ." *Daily Confederate* (Raleigh), July 28, 1864.

184. "It fell to the lot of the brigade to care for the wounded of that battle," Lieutenant Colonel Jones later wrote, "and to have them removed to Frederick[,] and while so doing, [we] had quite a spirited action with some Federal cavalry." Jones, "Fifty-seventh Regiment," in Clark, *Histories of the North Carolina Regiments*, 3:419. See also *Daily Confederate* (Raleigh), July 28, 1864.

and some units of Ramseur's Division (and probably the entire army) stopped to rest at Rockville for an hour or two.[185] "The heat & dust were terrible," Ramseur wrote, "water scarce & Everything conspired to make the march a terrible one." In the early afternoon the Capitol dome loomed in the distance, and by 3:00 P.M. the army was in line of battle. Lewis's exhausted brigade, minus hundreds of stragglers, formed up near Silver Spring in the backyard of Postmaster General Montgomery Blair. According to Major Pfohl, the number of men present for duty in Lewis's command "did not exceed 350 out of 1600."[186] Meantime, consternation reigned in the streets and halls of Washington, where sketchy information concerning Early's strength, whereabouts, and probable intentions had produced a sluggish response. Now the implications of Early's march down the Shenandoah Valley were dawning, and reinforcements were on the way. Nevertheless, when the Confederate army arrived before Washington's northern defenses on July 11, the city, though formidably fortified, was defended by scarcely 10,000 men.

Quickly sizing up the situation, Early ordered Rodes to "move into the works if he could." Unfortunately, Rodes's men, after their suffocating march, were in a state of near collapse. While Rodes struggled to organize an attack, Early watched in dismay as a large enemy column emerged from a cloud of dust behind the imposing fortifications and "filed into them on the right and left. . . ." In short order, Early wrote gloomily, enemy skirmishers were "thrown out in front" and "artillery fire was opened on us from a number of batteries." Stymied, Early contented himself with reconnoitering and probing the "impregnable" earthworks now bristling with men and weaponry. Skirmishing continued during the remainder of the day and on the morning of July 12. By then, Ramseur wrote, "the Yanks had more men behind the strongest field works I ever saw than we had in front of them." During the afternoon the fighting increased in intensity as the Federals, who were still receiving heavy reinforcements, began to lash out at Rodes. Ramseur's Division, near Silver Spring but in range of the enemy's heavy guns, took some fire but suffered little damage.[187]

At dusk, Early, fearing entrapment by the increasingly active Federal army, withdrew toward Rockville, where he arrived at daylight the next morning. Ramseur's Division brought up the rear and at one point was deployed in line of battle in the vicinity of the Georgetown road. At Rockville the army turned west, passed through Darnestown, and halted for a rest at about 2:00 P.M. At sunset the men set off on an all-night march, and on the morning of July 14 they crossed the Potomac at White's Ford, near Leesburg. After spending the fifteenth resting, bathing, and washing clothes—Chaplain Paris pronounced himself "quite prostrated" and "Wrote an application . . . for a transfer"—the army moved

185. Paris Diary, July 10, 1864 (see also July 11, 1864); *Official Records (Army)*, ser. 1, 37 (pt. 1):348. Some historians place Early's army south of Rockville on the night of July 10; however, it is this author's opinion that such was not the case. For a discussion, see Jordan, *North Carolina Troops*, 13:219 (footnote 213).

186. Stephen Dodson Ramseur to David Schenck, August 1, 1864, Stephen Dodson Ramseur Papers, folder 17, SHC, hereafter cited as Ramseur Papers (quoted by permission of Paul W. Schenck Jr.); W. J. Pfohl to C. T. Pfohl, July 23, [1864], Pfohl Papers. "All the Boys are worn out marching," Sergeant Walker wrote. "[O]ur aggregate in the Co. is 78 and only 37 men are present." J. K. Walker to his brother, July 12, 1864, Walker Papers.

187. Early, *Autobiographical Sketch*, 390; S. D. Ramseur to David Schenck, August 1, 1864, Ramseur Papers. The 57th North Carolina lost seven men captured during the fighting at Washington on July 12.

west through Leesburg, Hamilton, and Purcellville on July 16.[188] Near Purcellville, Early's "immense" baggage train was attacked by Federal cavalry and lost a number of wagons and ambulances. One regiment of Lewis's Brigade immediately counterattacked with other Confederate units, driving off the Federals and recapturing a considerable number of vehicles. It is unknown whether the 57th North Carolina was involved in the fighting.[189]

On the morning of July 17, Ramseur's Division crossed the Blue Ridge Mountains at Snicker's Gap and forded the Shenandoah River at Snicker's (Castleman's) Ferry, near Cool Spring. The men then marched west to Berryville, where they turned northeast and moved four or five miles up the Charlestown road.[190] Gordon's Division and that of Brig. Gen. John Echols (formerly Breckinridge's) remained at Snicker's Ferry to guard the crossing; Rodes's Division was nearby. In the meantime, Maj. Gen. Horatio Wright's Federal corps forded the Potomac and trailed cautiously behind Early's army. Hunter's troops, having rediscovered the war with the aid of their new commander, Brig. Gen. George Crook, moved toward a junction with Wright. Late on the afternoon of July 18 elements of Wright's and Crook's united commands were driven back across the Shenandoah in a sharp fight at Snicker's Ferry. Ramseur's Division moved from its position north of Berryville and deployed about one mile east of the town but took no part in the battle.[191]

At six o'clock on the evening of July 19 Ramseur received orders to march to Winchester (about seventeen miles distant), which was reportedly menaced by an enemy force. There, with the assistance of a small cavalry brigade under Brig. Gen. John C. Vaughn, he was to repel the enemy, evacuate patients in the military hospital, remove stores, and protect a Confederate wagon train that was moving south toward Newtown (about seven miles south of Winchester).[192] Ramseur reached a point near Stephenson's Depot, four miles northeast of Winchester, at daylight. His men being "very tired" from their all-night march

---

188. Paris Diary, July 15, 1864. Sergeant Walker of the 6th North Carolina confirmed that the men were "nearly worn out marching." However, he clearly regarded the Washington raid as a success. "[W]e have marched over 600 mile[s] Since the 13th of June and did that [which] no other Troops have ever done[:] went in 2 mile[s] of Washington City, near enough to throw Shells in the city[.] [W]e got to Washington on monday and old abe left good and Soon on [the] Sunday morning before [in fact, Lincoln remained in Washington.] I tell you we took them by surpze[.] [W]e wh[i]pped out old Wallace on the 9th & on the 11th we were at Washington[.] [Y]ou better know the name of Ewells Corps is enough for them." J. K. Walker to his father, July 18, 1864, Walker Papers. See also *Daily Confederate* (Raleigh), July 28, 1864.

189. Paris Diary, July 16, 1864. General Lewis wrote that "I had a fight a day or two ago with some cavalry who had captured some of our wagons. I had a regiment against them, whipped them easily, recaptured some of the wagons & took a piece of artillery from them, & would have taken another if I had not been ordered very peremptorily to go no farther." W. G. Lewis to Mittie Lewis, July 18, 1864, Lewis Papers. See also *Daily Confederate* (Raleigh), August 2, 1864; *Official Records (Army)*, ser. 1, 37 (pt. 1):320.

190. Chaplain Paris states that the 54th North Carolina camped that night "Within 8 miles of Charles town." Paris Diary, July 17, 1864.

191. "Never since the sound of the rifle was first heard in this beautiful Valley," SIGMA wrote, "have the 'sea green' waters of the Shenandoah been so reddened with human gore. . . ." *Daily Confederate* (Raleigh), August 2, 1864. For a good account of this engagement, see Peter J. Meaney, *The Civil War Engagement at Cool Spring, July 18, 1864* (Morristown, N.J.: privately printed, 1980).

192. The evacuation of the sick and wounded began at two o'clock on the morning of July 19. Chaplain Paris, "broken down with Sore feet" from "long, Weary and Toilsome Marches," was in one of the ambulances. Paris Diary, July 18, 1864 (see also July 19-20, 1864).

and the cumulative fatigue of a long campaign, Ramseur called a halt but sent Vaughn ahead to "meet the En[em]y & if possible to drive him back."[193] As the day progressed, several reports came in from Vaughn indicating that the Federals were not present in strength. Around 2:00 P.M. a courier brought word from Vaughn that the enemy force consisted of four cavalry regiments. If Ramseur wished to lay an ambush, Vaughn stated, he would attempt to draw the troopers south. Unable to locate a suitable ambush site and considering his division physically unfit for battle, Ramseur rejected Vaughn's proposal and allowed his men to continue resting.

Around 4:00 P.M. Ramseur heard rifle fire, got his command under arms, and moved a short distance up the road. There he met Vaughn's troopers falling back before an enemy force of, Vaughn now reported, one infantry regiment, one cavalry regiment, and four guns. Hoping to lure the supposedly weaker Federals into a rash assault, Ramseur ordered Lewis's Brigade forward, a decision that initiated the 57th North Carolina's worst combat performance of the war. As the men moved into position, some of Vaughn's cavalry "rushed back through the ranks" of the 57th and "threw them into confusion."[194] The shaken regiment apparently held its ground for a moment, but at about the same time, Ramseur informed his brother-in-law a month later,

I discovered three large Regts advancing rapidly on . . . [Lewis's] Right. I sent [Brig. Gen. R. D.] Johnston['s Brigade (formerly Toon's)] to meet them. About five minutes after the firing commenced the Yanks in front of Johnston & the right of Lewis were broken to pieces. I had discovered just as the firing commenced that the Yankee line over lapped Lewis['s] left about 200 yds. I immediately ordered [Brig.] Genl [Robert D.] Lilley who was in line behind Lewis to form on Lewis' left. Lilley was slow about moving & before he got in position the 57th & 54th re[gts] broke & ran like Sheep. I was on the right with Johnston's Brigade at this time. I immediately galloped [sic] to the left & by every means endeavoured to check the flying panic stricken men. All the regts took up the panic from left to right. The woods were of such a nature that the men on the right could not see the cause of the running on the left, they only knew that every thing on the left was routed & they imagined there was sufficient cause for it & joined in.[195]

It was "the most perfect rout I ever saw," the "deeply mortified" Ramseur stated, "a perfect & unaccountable panic." "[A]fter a fight of five minutes [my men] ran off the field in wild disorder." "I did every thing that mortal man could to stop the run aways. By appealing to the 'Brave men (if any were there)' to follow me I succeeded finally in stopping a few." Fortunately, most of the Federals withdrew fifteen minutes later. Ramseur then fell back to Kernstown, where he arrived around midnight. Losses in his division, according to Ramseur, were 24 men killed, 52 wounded, 16 wounded and captured, and 142 captured. Losses in the 57th North Carolina, according to figures compiled for this volume, were 4 men killed or mortally wounded, 17 wounded, and 40 captured (of whom 8 were wounded).[196]

193. S. D. Ramseur to David Schenck, August 20, 1864, Ramseur Papers.

194. *Daily Confederate* (Raleigh), August 2, 1864. See also S. D. Ramseur to David Schenck, August 1, 1864, Ramseur Papers.

195. S. D. Ramseur to David Schenck, August 20, 1864, Ramseur Papers.

196. S. D. Ramseur to Ellen Ramseur, July 23, 1864 (two letters of same date), and S. D. Ramseur to David

On July 21 Ramseur's Division fell back with the rest of the army through Newtown and Middletown and bivouacked for the night about five miles northeast of Strasburg. The next day the men moved to Strasburg, formed a line of battle, and rested on the twenty-third.[197] In the meantime General Wright, concluding that his assignment to speed Early's retreat was accomplished, headed back to Washington on July 20, leaving Crook to maintain the Federal position in the Shenandoah Valley. On July 23 Early learned of Wright's departure. The next morning he marched northeast toward Kernstown, where Crook's Army of West Virginia was concentrated. Preceded by a screen of cavalry, three of Early's divisions, under Gordon, Rodes, and Brig. Gen. Gabriel C. Wharton (who had assumed command of Echols's Division), reached Kernstown shortly before noon. Ramseur's Division advanced by a more westerly route to attempt to turn the Federal right. Thinking he was confronting only a Confederate reconnaissance force, Crook immediately launched one of his three divisions in an assault against three-quarters of Early's army. While the attackers recoiled before a blistering fire from Gordon's Division, Wharton moved around Crook's dangling left flank, precipitating a rout. With Rodes in pursuit, the Federals stampeded through Winchester and down the road to Stephenson's Depot. So abrupt and disastrous was their collapse that they were gone before Ramseur could launch his flanking attack. By the time Lewis's Brigade reached its assigned position, Lieutenant Walton wrote, they found only stragglers, abandoned equipment, and a trail of "burning ordinance [*sic*] trains." By July 26 Crook was back across the Potomac, leaving the Shenandoah Valley once more—if briefly and for the last time—in Confederate hands.[198]

Schenck, August 1 and 20, 1864, Ramseur Papers. Ramseur's chagrin and humiliation over the "disgraceful retreat" and "shameful" behavior of his men at Stephenson's Depot were profound. "The Yankees whipped me the other day," he wrote despondently to his wife on July 28. "'Twas mighty hard to bear. . . ." "After my disaster of the 20th ultimo," he stated in a report to General Ewell, "I need all the encouragement you can give me." S. D. Ramseur to Ellen Ramseur, July 23 and 28, 1864, Ramseur Papers; *Official Records (Army)*, ser. 1, 36 (pt. 1):1081.

Lewis was "unhesitatingly" censured by Ramseur for the poor performance of his brigade. In response, Lewis was "widely quoted as believing that Ramseur failed to take proper precautions before advancing." (After the war Lewis conceded that, because of the faulty intelligence supplied by Vaughn, "Ramseur was not altogether responsible for the mistake that occurred. . . .") Ramseur, however, was not without defenders. From Early and Gordon he received assurances of continued esteem, and Rodes even defended his friend in a letter to Ewell. That did not prevent criticism—much of which was unfair—in the press and other quarters; for example, see *Daily Confederate* (Raleigh), July 30, 1864. Some members of Lewis's Brigade, including Chaplain Paris, were also critical of Ramseur's generalship. Paris, who obviously knew nothing of Vaughn's role in the affair, wrote that Ramseur had been "routed" after becoming "incautiously involved With a very superior force. . . ." S. D. Ramseur to Ellen Ramseur, August 3, 1864, Ramseur Papers; Gary W. Gallagher, *Stephen Dodson Ramseur: Lee's Gallant General* (Chapel Hill: University of North Carolina Press, 1985), 198 (footnote 55), hereafter cited as Gallagher, *Stephen Dodson Ramseur*; William R. Cox, *Address on the Life and Character of Maj. Gen. Stephen D. Ramseur Before the Ladies' Memorial Association of Raleigh, N.C., May 10th, 1891* (Raleigh: n.p., 1891), 36; Paris Diary, July 20, 1864. See also *Official Records (Army)*, ser. 1, 37 (pt. 1):353-354.

197. Ramseur seems to have had no particular trouble rounding up and reorganizing the July 20 fugitives, and there is no evidence that Lewis's Brigade was permanently affected by the events of that day. In a letter dated August 20, Ramseur wrote that "In the subsequent fight [at Kernstown] the men behaved well. They are doing well now. They are much ashamed of their former conduct & I think I'm getting up a good spirit among them." S. D. Ramseur to David Schenck, August 20, 1864, Ramseur Papers.

198. Walton Diary, July 24, 1864. Sergeant Walker wrote that Crook and his "Demoralized crew . . . got one of

Early remained in camp for most of the day on July 25 but marched northeast in the direction of Martinsburg at about 5:00 P.M. and bivouacked for the night near Darkesville. Around noon on the twenty-sixth the army reached Martinsburg, which it found abandoned by the enemy. Early then renewed his destructive attentions to the much-abused Baltimore and Ohio Railroad and prepared to send his cavalry across the Potomac on a raid into Pennsylvania. After escorting the troopers to Williamsport and sending Lewis's Brigade briefly across the river to collect commissary stores, Early fell back to Martinsburg on July 30.[199] The next day the army moved south to Bunker Hill, where it remained through August 3. At 3:30 A.M. on the fourth Lewis's Brigade marched for the Potomac with the rest of Early's command to assist the returning cavalrymen. Lewis's men bivouacked that night at Hedgesville, just north of Martinsburg. The next morning Ramseur's and Rodes's Divisions crossed the river at Williamsport and pushed on to St. James College (about six miles from Boonsborough), where they camped for the night. On August 6 Early learned of a Federal concentration at Harpers Ferry and recrossed the Potomac. By August 7 the army was back at Bunker Hill. Three days later it retreated to the vicinity of Winchester.

On August 10 the reinforced Federal army, now officially designated the Army of the Shenandoah and led by its aggressive new commander, Maj. Gen. Phil Sheridan, began moving southwest from Harpers Ferry. Early skirmished with the advancing Federals near Winchester that day and the next. On August 12 he fell back through Kernstown to a position just north of Strasburg and began throwing up fortifications along Cedar Creek. That evening the Confederates moved south through Strasburg to Fisher's Hill and resumed digging. Sheridan halted for the night at Cedar Creek. A quiet day on August 13 was followed by skirmishing on the fourteenth and fifteenth. During that period (August 13-15) Archibald C. Godwin, former colonel of the 57th North Carolina and newly promoted to brigadier general, arrived and assumed command of Hoke's old brigade. (Lewis was reassigned to duty in eastern North Carolina.) On August 16 Sheridan, under the mistaken impression that an entire corps rather than a single division (Maj. Gen. Joseph B. Kershaw's) was en route from the Army of Northern Virginia to reinforce Early, decided to withdraw. Fighting occurred at Winchester the next day as Wharton's Division, supported by Ramseur's sharpshooters, overtook the retreating Yankees. Pillars of smoke arose in the wake of the Federal army as barns, mills, hayricks, and anything combustible that might contribute to the Confederate war effort went up in flames. Another fight, in which Ramseur's Division took part, occurred on August 21 near Charlestown, and skirmishing continued there for the next three days. Leaving Kershaw's Division (temporarily commanded by Richard H. Anderson)

the worst whippings ever. . . . [H]is loss was terrible in killed, wounded & Prisoners. . . . [Y]ou just ought to [have] Seen the yankees run and burn their wagons &c. I guess they wont follow us any more Soon." Walker confirms that Lewis's Brigade was not "generally engaged" except for skirmishing. The 57th North Carolina apparently suffered no casualties at Kernstown. J. K. Walker to his father, July 29, 1864, Walker Papers.

199. Early states in his memoirs that "One of Rodes' brigades was crossed over at Williamsport [on July 29] and subsequently withdrawn"; however, in a letter dated August 1, 1864, Sergeant Walker of the 6th North Carolina (Lewis's Brigade, Ramseur's Division) wrote that "we went from Martinsburg down to Williamsport on the other side of the Potomac and stayed one night and got commissary Stores that were there and then marched back toward Winchester and are in 6 [16?] mile[s] of Winchester at a little place called Bunker Hill." Early, *Autobiographical Sketch*, 402; J. K. Walker to his father, August 1, 1864, Walker Papers.

in the vicinity of Charlestown to "amuse" Sheridan, Early lunged toward Shepherdstown on August 25 as if to cross the Potomac.[200] Undeceived by Anderson's diversions, Sheridan sent two cavalry divisions toward Shepherdstown, where they blundered into Wharton's infantry. Heavy fighting ensued, and the Federals were repulsed. Casualties on both sides were severe, but Ramseur's Division, which brought up the rear during the advance toward the Potomac, was not involved.

On the afternoon of August 26 the Army of the Valley marched to Leetown, and the next day it moved toward Bunker Hill, which it reached late that afternoon.[201] On August 28 cavalry skirmishing broke out on the Smithfield road and escalated into an infantry fight the next day as Ramseur and Rodes drove the Federals through Smithfield. After three relatively quiet days in camp, the army (minus Rodes's Division, which was at Stephenson's Depot) marched toward Charlestown in response to a reported enemy advance. While en route, word came that a Confederate wagon train was under attack by Federal cavalry near Bunker Hill. The men then returned to Bunker Hill, but by the time they arrived the Federals had been repulsed by Rodes. More skirmishing with Federal cavalry occurred near Bunker Hill on September 3. On the evening of the same day, Kershaw's Division (which had been recalled by Lee and was on its way out of the Shenandoah Valley) was suddenly confronted by a large Federal force at Berryville. A sharp fight during which Kershaw's troops were driven back toward Winchester brought Early to the scene the next day with Ramseur's Division and other reinforcements, but a planned attack was canceled when Early discovered that Sheridan's entire army was in his front. After warily probing the Federal lines on September 4 and 5, Early withdrew to Stephenson's Depot. Ramseur's Division, serving as rear guard, fell back in a hard rain the same evening.

Two weeks of relative quiet punctuated by intermittent skirmishing followed.[202] Rainy weather kept the men close to camp during part of the period and allowed them some much needed rest. On September 10 Rodes's and Ramseur's Divisions marched in a light rain to the vicinity of Bunker Hill. There Rodes assisted Confederate cavalry in driving off a force of Federal horsemen. On the morning of September 11, following a night of heavy rain, thunder, and "vivid" lightning, the men marched back to their camp near Stephenson's Depot. "[W]et disagreeable weather" continued on the twelfth. On September 13 Ramseur's and Gordon's Divisions were sent to nearby Opequon Creek, where a force of enemy cavalry and infantry was advancing. A "fierce" artillery duel was followed by a Confederate advance across the creek, after which the Federals withdrew. Ramseur's men returned to their camp at sunset. At sunrise on September 15 Kershaw's Division started again for Richmond to rejoin the Army of Northern Virginia. At the same time Ramseur's Division moved south to Winchester to occupy the position vacated by Kershaw.[203]

200. Early, *Autobiographical Sketch*, 409.

201. Writing from Bunker Hill on August 28, Q.M. Sgt. Henry W. Barrow of the 21st North Carolina reported that the army was in "a healthy section of Country where we have very good Water to drink. We Draw tolerable good Rations of Beef & Flour here." H. W. Barrow to C. T. Pfohl, August 28, 1864, Pfohl Papers.

202. Godwin's Brigade was located during that period, Chaplain Paris reported, "on the Martinsville [Martinsburg] Turnpike Six miles from [north of] Winchester." Paris Diary, September 7, 1864.

203. McDonald, *Make Me a Map: Hotchkiss Journal*, 228 (September 11, 1864); Walton Diary, September 12, 1864; Paris Diary, September 13, 1864. According to Paris, the division's new position on September 15 was

In the meantime Sheridan, after waiting impatiently at Berryville for almost two weeks for news of Kershaw's departure, learned of that event on September 16 from a Federal sympathizer. He then made preparations to march on Newtown, cut Early's line of retreat, and force a battle. Those plans were revised abruptly on September 17 when Early, intent upon wrecking the Baltimore and Ohio Railroad and feinting a new incursion across the Potomac, marched toward Martinsburg with the divisions of Gordon and Rodes. Ramseur's Division, which was still at Winchester, and Wharton's Division, at Stephenson's Depot, were thus exposed to a Federal advance from Berryville. Sheridan, well apprised of Early's movements and dispositions by his cavalry, which now heavily outnumbered that of the Confederates, determined to strike Ramseur during Early's absence. On September 18 Early became suspicious of Sheridan's intentions while reading a batch of captured telegrams at Martinsburg. A forced march brought Rodes's Division to the side of Wharton at Stephenson's Depot the same evening. Gordon, however, was eight miles or so up the road at Bunker Hill, and Ramseur, at Winchester, was still alone.

The Army of the Shenandoah, numbering about 35,000 infantry and 5,000 cavalry, advanced on Winchester on the clear, bright morning of September 19. Early's battle-tested Army of the Valley numbered about 12,000 men, but for the moment only Ramseur's 1,700-man division barred the way. Fortunately for Ramseur, the Federals chose to approach the field through a narrow, wooded, two-mile-long canyon and got into such a tangle that it was after 11:00 A.M. before they were fully deployed. That did not prevent them from bringing severe pressure to bear on Robert D. Johnston's Brigade, which conducted a skillful fighting withdrawal from a point near the mouth of the canyon. Another of Ramseur's brigades, under John Pegram, was sent to Johnston's support but was flanked and routed. Johnston gave way a few moments later. Presently, Ramseur found himself confronting another Stephenson's Depot-like debacle as Godwin's Brigade, after moving to the assistance of Johnston and Pegram, fell back "in confusion." In Ramseur's words, the division then "did some tall running" for the rear. "I tried by Exhortation & Example to stop them," Ramseur continued. "It wouldn't do. So I took a musket and rode to the foremost and Knocked him down. I then Knocked Every man on the head who refused to halt and by this means and the Exertions of my Staff and some gallant off[ice]rs of the Brig[ade]s I got the div[isio]n again in line."[204]

After rallying his division on the 57th North Carolina, Ramseur charged and drove the Federals back some 400 yards. At 10:00 A.M. his men retreated to higher ground, where they were joined by the divisions of Rodes, who held the Confederate center, and Gordon, on the left. In general, the Confederate line ran along a plateau that sloped gently down to the area held by the Federals. Cornfields, pastures, woods, steep-sided ravines, and several barns and houses dotted the landscape, and undulations created swales and hollows here and there. Rodes's and Gordon's men were sheltered by a belt of timber that largely concealed them from their opponents; Ramseur's troops were visible, appearing to one Federal

---

"one mile South of Winchester." Paris Diary, September 15, 1864.

204. Jones, "Fifty-seventh Regiment," in Clark, *Histories of the North Carolina Regiments*, 3:420; S. D. Ramseur to David Schenck, October 10, 1864, Ramseur Papers. "I can say that I made Early's old Div[isio]n do splendid fighting at Winchester," Ramseur wrote with justifiable pride.

like "white specks on the cornfield, and clustered in groups around barns and houses."[205] Both ends of the Confederate line were anchored on watercourses: the left on boggy Red Bud Run, the right on a less formidable stream called Abraham's Creek. To the northeast, Wharton's infantry division and a 2,000-man cavalry contingent, both commanded by Breckinridge, remained at Stephenson's Depot protecting Early's exposed left flank from two divisions of Federal cavalry.

With his army in position at last, Sheridan ordered an attack at 11:40 A.M. While the XIX Corps (commanded by Maj. Gen. William H. Emory) plowed into Gordon's line, two of Horatio Wright's VI Corps divisions (under Brig. Gens. George W. Getty and James B. Ricketts) stormed forward against Rodes and Ramseur. Meantime, the cavalry divisions of Brig. Gens. Wesley Merritt and William W. Averell prepared to advance against Breckinridge. A third cavalry division under Brig. Gen. James H. Wilson was ordered to turn the Confederate right.

Raked by a murderous fire from Gordon, Emory's men made slow progress until a gap developed between their left and Ricketts's Division, which instead of attacking Rodes had veered off into Ramseur's left. Gordon and Rodes, acting on their own initiative, then launched a spoiling attack into the resulting vacuum, sending one Federal division and part of another reeling back. At that point Brig. Gen. David A. Russell's Division of Wright's Corps charged into the melee, cutting off and capturing some of the Confederates and forcing the others to retreat. On the Confederate right, Ramseur managed to fend off Ricketts and Getty until the counterattack by Rodes and Gordon relieved the pressure on his front. A paucity of Confederate reports makes it difficult to reconstruct events on Ramseur's part of the line, but reports by Federal officers in Getty's and Ricketts's Divisions suggest that the attack by Gordon and Rodes saved Ramseur from a severe drubbing. Pegram, in Ramseur's center, seemingly fared the worst, giving way "precipitately" and "in great confusion" as the Federals "carr[ied] everything before them."[206] On Johnston's front, to the left of Pegram, the Federals were subjected to heavy musketry and a "terrible fire of shot and shell" but were pressing ahead until the counterattack by Gordon and Rodes forced them to halt.[207] Godwin's Brigade, on Pegram's right, probably remained the steadiest of Ramseur's three, partially because Brig. Gen. Daniel D. Bidwell's attacking brigade was more exposed to artillery fire than some of its sister units. After a 300-yard advance during which he "lost considerably," Bidwell discovered that a skirmish line he had established south of Abraham's Creek was under attack. Fearing that he was about to be flanked, he called a

---

205. Quoted in Jeffry D. Wert, *From Winchester to Cedar Creek: The Shenandoah Campaign of 1864* (New York: Simon and Schuster, 1987), 54, hereafter cited as Wert, *From Winchester to Cedar Creek.*

206. *Official Records (Army)*, ser. 1, 43 (pt. 1):204, 207, 197. See also Hale and Phillips, *Forty-ninth Virginia Infantry*, 163 (September 19, 1864). Pegram was probably opposed by the brigades of Brig. Gen. Frank Wheaton and Col. James M. Warner (Getty's Division); Johnston by those of Cols. Joseph W. Keifer and William Emerson (Ricketts's Division); and Godwin by that of Brig. Gen. Daniel D. Bidwell (Getty's Division). No doubt there was some overlapping; for example, some elements of Wheaton's Brigade may have attacked Godwin's left.

207. *Official Records (Army)*, ser. 1, 43 (pt. 1):236. The report of one Federal colonel who fought on that part of the line describes Johnston as "in full and speedy retreat toward Winchester." *Official Records (Army)*, ser. 1, 43 (pt. 1):260.

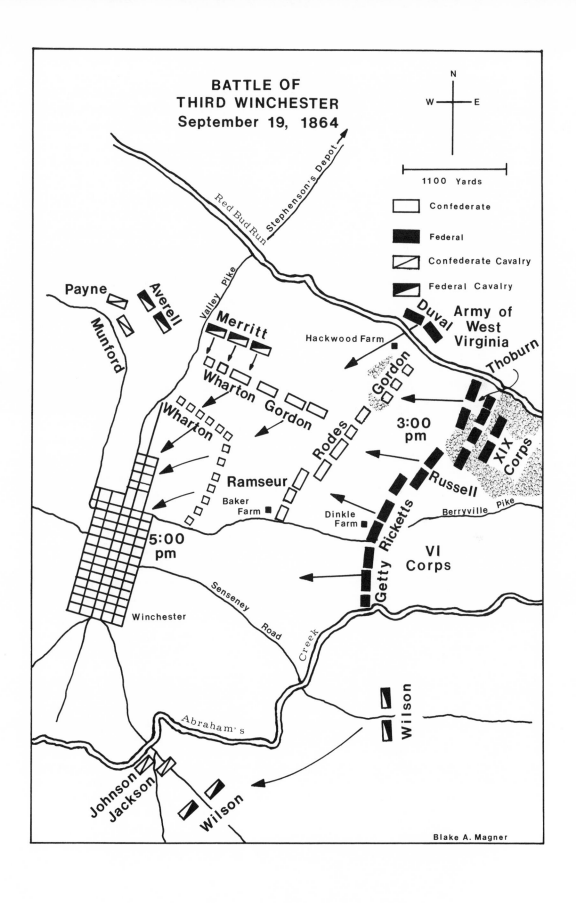

BATTLE OF
THIRD WINCHESTER
September 19, 1864

N
W   E
S

1100 Yards

Confederate

Federal

Confederate Cavalry

Federal Cavalry

Payne

Averell

Munford

Merritt

Valley Pike

Red Bud Run

Stephenson's Depot

Hackwood Farm

Duval

Army of West Virginia

Thoburn

Gordon

Wharton

Gordon

Wharton

Rodes

3:00 pm

XIX Corps

Russell

Ramseur

Baker Farm

Dinkle Farm

Berryville Pike

Getty Ricketts

5:00 pm

Winchester

Senseney Road

Creek

VI Corps

Wilson

Abraham's

Johnson

Jackson

Wilson

Blake A. Magner

halt.[208] Brig. Gen. Frank Wheaton's Brigade, on Bidwell's right, was halted in turn by enfilading fire from a battery that Bidwell had failed to suppress.[209] After Wheaton and Bidwell began falling back, some units of Ramseur's Division (possibly Pegram's men but more likely Godwin's) charged Wheaton's left and were repulsed by Bidwell's artillery. That attack, and the absence of any complaint by Ramseur about his men's conduct during that stage of the battle, suggests that Ramseur's difficulties were somewhat exaggerated by the Federals and necessitated no further resort to musket butts. Nevertheless, there seems little doubt that Ramseur's Division was in serious danger. Gordon states that Ramseur was "nearly overwhelmed" when he (Gordon) and Rodes launched their counterattack, and Early clearly implies in his official report that the assault was made to save Ramseur.[210]

After a lull during which Wharton's Division was summoned from Stephenson's Depot and placed on Gordon's left, George Crook's two divisions (commanded by Cols. Joseph Thoburn and Isaac H. Duval) launched an assault on Wharton and Gordon. Fighting desperately, the two Confederate generals wheeled their lines to the left to prevent Crook from flanking them. That maneuver created a Confederate front in the shape of an inverted L with Wharton and Gordon at the top and Rodes and Ramseur, who came under renewed attack, on the side. Slowly the Confederate lines were compressed toward Winchester. Crook was finally fought to a bloody standstill, but at about the same time the Confederate cavalry near Stephenson's Depot, deprived of its infantry support, buckled under a massive attack by Merritt and Averell. The Federal horsemen then roared down on Wharton and Gordon, "burst[ing] like a storm of case-shot in their midst," Merritt wrote, "showering saber blows on their heads and shoulders, trampling them . . . and routing them in droves. . . . Many of them threw down their arms and cried for mercy; others hung tenaciously to their muskets, using them with their muzzles against our soldiers' breasts; a number took refuge in a house and fought through the doors and windows. . . . Four stand[s] of colors were here taken and over 500 prisoners. . . ." Chaplain Paris, who spent the day bringing off the dead and wounded, described the rout of the cavalry and the mob scene that followed in the streets of Winchester: "[Our cavalry,] Without being pressed, broke and fled through Winchester in the Wildest disorder and Confusion, Crying the Yankees are Coming. A panic spread all around. Skulkers, teamsters[,] drivers, negroes, boys and fools all fled in Wild

---

208. *Official Records (Army)*, ser. 1, 43 (pt. 1):191 (see also 212). The attack on Bidwell's skirmish line was almost certainly made by a weak line of dismounted cavalrymen from Brig. Gen. Bradley T. Johnson's command; however, there is evidence that some of Godwin's skirmishers were across the creek. In any case, Sheridan had an ample cavalry force on the south bank, and it is highly unlikely that Bidwell's left flank was in serious danger. See *Official Records (Army)*, ser. 1, 43 (pt. 1):610.

209. See *Official Records (Army)*, ser. 1, 43 (pt. 1):197. Bidwell's claim of an advance of "about 300 yards" was considerably less than the 800 yards claimed by one Federal regimental commander on Pegram's front and the mile claimed by another. George W. Getty, Bidwell's division commander, stated that Warner, Wheaton, and Bidwell "drove back the enemy's lines in confusion [an average of?] 500 yards beyond his original position." *Official Records (Army)*, ser. 1, 43 (pt. 1):212, 192 (see also 202, 204).

210. John B. Gordon, *Reminiscences of the Civil War* (New York: Charles Scribner's Sons, 1903), 321. See also *Official Records (Army)*, ser. 1, 43 (pt. 1):212, 554-555. Wert states that Ramseur's men "streamed toward Winchester" at that juncture; Gallagher writes that they "absorbed the shock of Sheridan's attack, recoiled slightly, then, as Rodes and Gordon hit the Union flank, inched their way forward." Gallagher seems closer to the mark. Wert, *From Winchester to Cedar Creek*, 65; Gallagher, *Stephen Dodson Ramseur*, 143.

dismay. Some of our Brigades Were shaken."[211] Ramseur's Division, its "organization unbroken" and with Godwin's Brigade "bringing up the rear in good order," fell back through Winchester. During the retreat down the Strasburg pike, the division acted as rear guard, repulsing several attacks and saving the wagons and artillery. "[W]e had a hard fight at Winchester," Pvt. William Patton of the 57th summed up matters. "[It] commenc[e]d at daylight an continued unto nine in the evning[.] [I]t was the hardist fight i bleleve that i ever was in. . . . [T]he yankeeys was to hard for us. . . . [O]ur force was to small. . . ."[212]

Federal casualties in the battle numbered 5,018; Confederate losses, as reported by Early, were 226 killed, 1,567 wounded, and 1,818 missing.[213] Among the Confederate dead were Generals Rodes and Godwin. Losses in the 57th North Carolina, according to service records compiled for this volume, were 7 killed or mortally wounded, 23 wounded, and 11 captured (of whom 3 were wounded). Although the specific actions of the 57th North Carolina cannot be determined, the regiment played an important role, as indicated above, in rallying Ramseur's Division at a critical moment early in the battle. Clarence R. Hatton, adjutant general of Godwin's Brigade, wrote many years later that "Godwin extended his line over to Pegram's support and managed to rally the men after falling back to a better position on his old regiment, the 57th North Carolina, whose steadiness saved the day. . . ." Hatton's account is by no means implausible: "part" of Godwin's Brigade—perhaps the 57th North Carolina—was positioned at that time just north of Abraham's Creek on a country road that could have been used to turn Ramseur's right flank. Those men were not under attack but were undoubtedly ordered to withdraw when the rest of the division was routed. Presumably they retained their organization and could have served as a rallying point. However, there is another version of the regiment's role in rallying the division. Lieutenant Colonel Jones of the 57th, who would hardly have slighted a stalwart performance by his own men, wrote somewhat ambiguously in his postwar account that "Pegram, overwhelmed, was retreating when Godwin came up. This for a time threw Godwin's Brigade in confusion, and here again the Fifty-seventh Regiment exhibited its old-time steadiness. *It rallied first in the retreat* [emphasis added] and upon it the rest of the brigade soon rallied and opposed the advance of the enemy." That account suggests that the 57th provided a rallying point because the skulls of some of its members were the first to make contact with Ramseur's musket butt. The musket-butt scenario is perhaps the more likely of the two if only because Ramseur, in the letter quoted above, says nothing about any heroics by the 57th North Carolina or Godwin's Brigade during that stage of the battle.[214]

Whatever the precise role of the 57th North Carolina at the Battle of Winchester, it clearly redeemed itself, as did Godwin's Brigade as a whole, for its poor performance at Stephenson's Depot. Ramseur felt that after he quelled the incipient panic on the morning

211. *Official Records (Army)*, ser. 1, 43 (pt. 1):444-445; Paris Diary, September 19, 1864.

212. S. D. Ramseur to David Schenck, October 10, 1864, Ramseur Papers; Hatton, "Gen. Archibald Godwin," 136; William Patton to Ellen Patton (his sister), September 20, 1864, Patton Papers. According to Ramseur, Rodes's Division came off the field "in tolerable order."

213. See *Official Records (Army)*, ser. 1, 43 (pt. 1):118, 555, 557.

214. Hatton, "Gen. Archibald Godwin," 136; Wert, *From Winchester to Cedar Creek*, 51; Jones, "Fifty-seventh Regiment," in Clark, *Histories of the North Carolina Regiments*, 3:420.

of September 19 the men "fought splendidly."[215] Capt. James F. Beall, speaking of the 21st North Carolina (one of the 57th's sister units in Godwin's Brigade), wrote that "At no time during the war was the courage, endurance and discipline of the regiment put to a greater test than in this battle. Amid great confusion, it fought with a desperation rarely equaled, and by its steadiness, contributed largely in preventing a disastrous rout. At no time was its line broken." And in his postwar history, Lieutenant Colonel Jones wrote proudly of the "desperate and bloody" fight by the 57th and Godwin's Brigade: "Time and again the enemy assailed the line and time and again they were repulsed with great loss. This continued until sundown, the fight having lasted nearly all day, when the Federal troops again turned our flank and compelled our somewhat precipitate retreat. From this battlefield and under these circumstances Godwin's Brigade, after an all-day's desperate fight, and with the enemy threatening and pressing its flank, came back in perfect order and without the slightest sign of confusion."[216]

"[W]orn out, whipped and hungry," the Confederates limped into Newtown, seven miles south of Winchester, where they bivouacked on the night of September 19.[217] The next day they moved another twelve miles south to Fisher's Hill, a high, steep, boulder-strewn bluff cleaved by gullies and ravines. Anchored by Three Top Mountain on its densely wooded eastern end but slightly detached from Little North Mountain on its less formidable and partly cleared western extremity, Fisher's Hill was a four-mile-long "plug" in the Shenandoah Valley. If defended by an adequate force, it would be virtually impregnable. It was also, in Early's opinion, the only position short of the upper reaches of the Valley where he had a chance to stop Sheridan.

By the afternoon of September 20, Early was in position to receive a Federal attack. Wharton's Division was on the eastern end of Fisher's Hill with Gordon's Division on its left. On Gordon's left was Ramseur's former division, commanded by Brig. Gen. John Pegram. Rodes's former division was assigned to Ramseur and was positioned on Pegram's left. To Ramseur's left, holding the sloping ground leading down to the foot of Little North Mountain, was Brig. Gen. Lunsford L. Lomax's dismounted cavalry division. Godwin's

---

215. S. D. Ramseur to Ellen Ramseur, September 25, 1864, Ramseur Papers. It is not clear whether Ramseur was referring to his division alone or to the Confederate infantry as a whole, which had indeed put up one of the war's more remarkable fights against very long odds. Whatever the case, he meant to include his own men in his encomiums.

216. James Franklin Beall, "Twenty-first Regiment," in Clark, *Histories of the North Carolina Regiments*, 2:141-142, hereafter cited as Beall, "Twenty-first Regiment," in Clark, *Histories of the North Carolina Regiments*; Jones, "Fifty-seventh Regiment," in Clark, *Histories of the North Carolina Regiments*, 3:420. Staff officer Henry Kyd Douglas, presumably a disinterested observer, wrote that during the early stages of the battle Ramseur, "With determination and tenacity . . . stopped the way. Never did that division or any other do better work. . . . Ramseur's division, the first on the field, was the last to leave it; it had held its own during the long day, and when the army was defeated it was thrown across the rear and, that night, covered the retreat. The censure Ramseur had received for the battle of July 20th and the reflections which had been cast upon his division were splendidly retrieved. . . . The Confederate troops, in the disasters which soon followed, failed to gain the credit which their heroic fight on the 19th September deserved; but Ramseur was unquestionably the hero of the day." Douglas, *I Rode with Stonewall*, 296-297.

217. Quoted in David F. Riggs, *13th Virginia Infantry* (Lynchburg, Va.: H. E. Howard, 1988), 57.

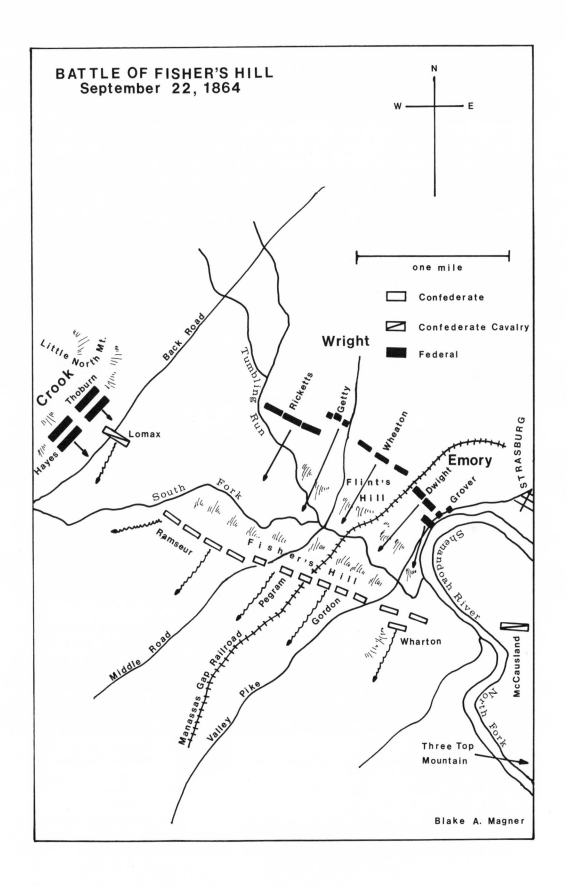

BATTLE OF FISHER'S HILL
September 22, 1864

N
W   E

one mile

Confederate

Confederate Cavalry

Federal

Little North Mt.

Crook

Thoburn

Hayes

Lomax

Back Road

Tumbling Run

Wright

Ricketts

Getty

Wheaton

STRASBURG

Emory

Flint's Hill

Dwight

Grover

South Fork

Ramseur

Fisher's Hill

Shenandoah River

Middle Road

Manassas Gap Railroad

Pegram

Gordon

Valley Pike

Wharton

McCausland

North Fork

Three Top Mountain

Blake A. Magner

Brigade was under temporary command of Lt. Col. William S. Davis, 12th Regiment N.C. Troops. Thus the 57th North Carolina was in Davis's Brigade of Pegram's Division.

Sheridan reached Strasburg, just north of Fisher's Hill, on the afternoon of September 20. Heavy skirmishing broke out the next day as the Federals drove Confederate sharpshooters from a house where they had established a nest. The Federals then attempted to wrest Flint's Hill, a strongpoint somewhat in advance of the Confederate center, from a heavy line of skirmishers. The latter, probably members of Pegram's Division, fought from skirmish pits reinforced by rail breastworks. Although "sorely pressed," the Confederates, according to Chaplain Paris, "manfully" held their ground until an attack at dusk by four Federal regiments drove them back "about 200 y[ar]ds."[218]

By the morning of September 22, Sheridan had his army in position for an assault on Fisher's Hill. Crook's two divisions (commanded by Thoburn and Col. Rutherford B. Hayes) were concealed in a woods, where their departure on a march around Early's left would not be observed. They now set off silently through the timber toward the western slopes of Little North Mountain. Wright's three divisions (commanded by Ricketts, Getty, and Wheaton) and Emory's two (under Brig. Gens. William Dwight and Cuvier Grover) prepared to storm Fisher's Hill when Crook struck and, in the interim, skirmished briskly with the Confederates to divert their attention. Two cavalry divisions, under Brig. Gen. A. T. A. Torbert, had been dispatched the previous day around Three Top Mountain and down the east side of fifty-mile-long Massanutten Mountain. Torbert's mission was to cross Massanutten at New Market Gap, get behind Early's army, and cut off its retreat. Fighting intensified about midday when the Federals launched a probing attack on Ramseur's front. Feeling increasingly uneasy about his position, Early made preparations to withdraw that night. Meanwhile, Crook's self-styled "Mountain Creepers," having rearranged, muffled, or discarded accoutrements that might clank or rattle and with their general himself in the lead, wound their way through woods, ravines, and underbrush. Confederate pickets and vedettes, detecting movement on the slopes of Little North Mountain, fired an occasional shot at the Federals, prompting a few exploratory rounds from Rebel cannoneers on Fisher's Hill. At least one Confederate officer in the vicinity, Brig. Gen. Bryan Grimes of Ramseur's Division, became suspicious and then alarmed at the threat that seemed to be developing beyond his left. However, nothing was done.

By 4:00 P.M. Crook had his men in position and in line of battle. As Confederate artillery opened up again, the Federals charged down the mountainside, losing their alignment and organization among the trees and thickets but smashing into Lomax "like an avalanche" and sending his demoralized cavalrymen flying.[219] At about the same time, Wright and

218. Paris Diary, September 21, 1864. See also *Official Records (Army)*, ser. 1, 43 (pt. 1):199. A Federal officer involved in the action claimed that the Confederates were on Flint's Hill "in force." *Official Records (Army)*, ser. 1, 43 (pt. 1):206 (see also 205, 254, 264). Chaplain Paris, in his diary entry for September 21, wrote that "To day we have sharp skirmishing all along in front of our Works. . . . About dark the enemy's line of battle attacked this position of skirmishers and were twice driven back, but on the 3rd attack [our men] fell back. . . ." See also Gallagher, *Stephen Dodson Ramseur*, 147.

219. Pulaski Cowper, ed., *Extracts of Letters of Major-General Bryan Grimes, to His Wife, Written While in Active Service in the Army of Northern Virginia, Together with Some Personal Recollections of the War, Written by Him after Its Close, Etc.* (Raleigh: Alfred Williams and Company, 1884; Wilmington, N.C.: Broadfoot

Emory surged forward against the Confederate front. Brig. Gen. Cullen A. Battle's Brigade, ordered to the left by Ramseur, stalled Crook for a moment with the aid of battery fire but gave way before a renewed Federal assault. Another of Ramseur's brigades, under Brig. Gen. William R. Cox, was also sent to the Confederate left but lost its way in rugged terrain and marched out of the battle. Ramseur's third brigade (on Davis's left), commanded by Brig. Gen. Philip Cook, was apparently driven back by Wright at about the same time that Crook's men flanked Battle and stormed into the Confederate rear. Grimes's regiments remained in action a few minutes longer but then, virtually surrounded and facing imminent capture, beat a hasty retreat.

Meantime, Pegram's troops, who apparently did not have a clear view of what was taking place on Ramseur's part of the field, "nervous[ly]" held their ground despite the uproar on their left, the "considerable [enemy] activity" in their front, and at least one report that they were flanked. Davis's men were on the left of Pegram's Division with Johnston's North Carolina brigade on their right and Col. John S. Hoffman's (formerly Pegram's) Virginia brigade on the right of Johnston. As at Winchester, Getty's Division of the VI Corps provided the opposition with Bidwell's, Col. James M. Warner's (formerly Wheaton's), and Col. George P. Foster's (formerly Warner's) Brigades in left-to-right order. Thus the brigade match-ups should have been, with some overlapping, Bidwell versus Hoffman, Warner versus Johnston, and Foster versus Davis. However, when the collapse occurred on Ramseur's front, Pegram moved Hoffman's Brigade from his right flank to his left, where Hoffman probably assumed a perpendicular position to Davis.[220] Elsewhere along the disintegrating line, similar troop movements and realignments, mostly frantic and impromptu, took place amid "roaring confusion" as Early and his lieutenants desperately fought to stave off defeat. Somewhere in the debacle, no doubt attempting for the most part to do their duty, were the men of the 57th North Carolina. However, in the absence of detailed reports and memoirs, the regiment's location and activities cannot be determined. Probably it remained about where it was at the time of Crook's assault.[221]

Around 4:30 P.M. Crook, supported by Ricketts's Division of Wright's Corps, thundered into Pegram's left and rear. At about the same time, Getty's men charged up the slopes of Fisher's Hill. "The enemy poured in one tremendous volley as the troops were struggling across the defile," Getty reported concisely, "then broke and fled in the wildest

---

Publishing Company, 1986), 69 (September 26, 1864), hereafter cited as Cowper, *Letters and Recollections of Bryan Grimes.*

220. Samuel D. Buck, "Battle of Fisher's Hill," *Confederate Veteran* 2 (November 1894): 338, hereafter cited as Buck, "Battle of Fisher's Hill." See also *Official Records (Army),* ser. 1, 43 (pt. 1):199, 208, 212. The only evidence located for Hoffman's move, which was almost imperative under the circumstances, is a postwar reminiscence by Samuel D. Buck, an officer of the 13th Regiment Virginia Infantry (Hoffman's Brigade). If Buck's information is accurate, the works vacated by Hoffman were probably occupied either by Gordon, who would have extended his left, or by Davis and Johnston, who shifted to the right. See Buck, "Battle of Fisher's Hill," 338.

221. Wert, *From Winchester to Cedar Creek,* 123. Bidwell's Brigade, which was driven back during its first assault, was probably too far to Davis's right to be involved in any fighting with the 57th. Warner's Brigade, in the center, seemingly made slow progress while Bidwell regrouped. Foster, Davis's most likely opponent, was held up by rugged terrain and the fire of Confederate sharpshooters.

disorder."[222] Lieutenant Walton of the 6th North Carolina categorized the retreat as a "great panic" in which everyone fled "in the greatest confusion, leaving the most of our artillery. *After running two miles* we succeeded in rallying the men. Many of the men went to the mountains." Chaplain Paris's diary entry for September 22 is perhaps one of the better accounts of the day's misfortunes by a member of Davis's Brigade: "Skirmishing Sharpe [*sic*] and Severe began early in the day and continued [until late afternoon]. At 5 Oclock P.M. [probably somewhat earlier] The Yanks attacked our extreme left. One of 'Imboden's regiments [Brig. Gen. John D. Imboden commanded one of Lomax's cavalry brigades]' being posted at this, the weakest point of the line, broke and fled without making More than the show of a fight. The Yanks fell upon our rear and took 12 guns and a large number of prisoners. We began the retreat at Sunset. I marched nearly all night on foot. At nine next morning I was in New Market, 31 miles off. The baggage Trains came off safely; not more than 5 or 6 [wagons] broke down and had to be abandoned. Gen. Early is greatly blamed for our defeat."[223] Only the failure of the Federal cavalry to reach its assigned postion in Early's rear and effectively pursue the "badly whipped" Confederates marred Sheridan's triumph. Federal casualties of all descriptions numbered 528. On the Confederate side, Early reported 30 men killed, 210 wounded, and 995 missing.[224] No members of the 57th North Carolina were killed or wounded, but twenty-five were captured.

222. *Official Records (Army)*, ser. 1, 43 (pt. 1):192. Samuel D. Buck, the 13th Virginia officer referred to in footnote 220 above, published the following Fisher's Hill recollection in 1894: "[Shortly after Crook's attack] a cavalryman from our left came down our line, walking on top of our works, reporting to each command that 'we are flanked!' This did much for Sheridan, and the worthless soldier should have been shot then and there. I shall always regret not having arrested him, as I believe it would have saved our right from the disgraceful scene that followed. Immediately on our left was a North Carolina brigade, and I could see that this report demoralized them. I took it upon myself to force some of the men to remain in the works. As the firing drew nearer on our left Gen. Pegram rode up to our brigade and told us he wanted us 'to file out of the works, and drive the enemy back.' The brigade moved out in perfect order and formed a line of battle facing the advancing enemy, who were not in sight, and would have saved the day, but the North Carolina brigade on our left, already referred to, broke without firing a gun or seeing a yankee. [Presumably Buck means the North Carolina brigade (Johnston's) *originally* on his *immediate* left; by that point Hoffman had moved to the left of Pegram's line and the left-to-right sequence, which had been Davis-Johnston-Hoffman, was now, as stated above, Hoffman-Davis-Johnston, with Hoffman at a right angle to the other two. In short, both North Carolina units were now on Hoffman's right.] Those men [the North Carolinians] claimed that Gen. Pegram was trying to save his old brigade and let them [the North Carolinians] be captured. While the Carolinians—usually excellent soldiers—were breaking over us Gen. Early rode up and ordered our regiment to fire into them if they would not stop. His order was not obeyed. Gen. Pegram, and the officers generally, made every effort to rally the men, but commands and entreaties had no effect. One grand rush was made for the valley pike." Proceeding on the doubtful assumption that Buck's account is entirely reliable, the "demoralized" North Carolina brigade on the "left" of the 13th Virginia was probably Johnston's. It seems probable also that if Hoffman's new position was indeed perpendicular to that of Johnston and Davis, as the evidence strongly suggests, credit for firing the "tremendous volley" referred to in Getty's report goes to one or both of the North Carolina brigades. In any event, the certainty is that all three brigades were routed. Buck, "Battle of Fisher's Hill," 338.

223. Walton Diary, September 22, 1864; Paris Diary, September 22, 1864. Paris probably overestimated the distance to New Market by at least three or four miles.

224. W. J. Pfohl to C. T. Pfohl, October 4, 1864, Pfohl Papers. "The position at Fishers Hill could have been held," Pfohl wrote, "if Early had used any precaution, but here again [as at Winchester] he suffered himself to be flanked, & another stampede was the consequence." See also *Official Records (Army)*, ser. 1, 43 (pt. 1):124, 556.

On September 23 Early retreated in the rain and mud to Mount Jackson, where a heavy skirmish with Federal cavalrymen occurred that evening.[225] After dark the army crossed the North Fork of the Shenandoah River and formed a line of battle at Rude's Hill. When the enemy began maneuvering the next day as though to turn the Confederate left, Early fell back, skirmishing most of the way, to the vicinity of Tenth Legion Church. There he formed another line of battle.[226] That night he pulled back again, crossed the South Fork of the Shenandoah River near Port Republic, and reached Brown's Gap in the Blue Ridge Mountains by the evening of September 25. Sheridan moved to Harrisonburg, about eighteen miles northwest of Brown's Gap. On September 26 Kershaw's Division rejoined Early, adding approximately 2,000 muskets to his command and bringing his strength up to about 10,000 men. Davis's Brigade was involved in a skirmish with Federal cavalry on the road to Weyer's Cave. On September 27 Early marched in the direction of Weyer's Cave and drove the Federal cavalrymen toward Harrisonburg. The next day the Army of the Valley moved south to the vicinity of Waynesboro. Pegram's Division encountered more Federal troopers near Dogtown and drove them in the direction of Staunton. Two quiet days in camp near Waynesboro followed as Early sought to rebuild his "exhausted" and "very much shattered" army.[227] A number of soldiers who fled into the mountains after Fisher's Hill returned to their units, new clothing was issued, shoes were supplied to the "many" men who were without them, and morale began to improve. By October 9 Early was informing Lee that "my infantry is now in good heart and condition."[228]

In the meantime, Sheridan began a slow withdrawal down the Shenandoah Valley, killing livestock and burning farm buildings, crops, and mills. Early trailed in Sheridan's wake but was unable to effectively hamper the Federal incendiaries. On October 1 Early marched north in a heavy rain to Mount Sidney, on October 6 he moved to Harrisonburg, and on the seventh he reached New Market. Cold weather, including frost, hail, and snow, made its seasonal debut on October 8. On the twelfth the army set off in the direction of Strasburg, where it arrived on the morning of October 13. A heavy skirmish at Stickley's farm, near Cedar Creek, took place later that day as the opposing commanders probed each others' lines. Pegram's Division was on the field but took no part in the fighting. At dark Early disengaged and moved south to Fisher's Hill. Two days of relative quiet followed while Sheridan and Grant debated strategy by telegraph. Determined to reach an understanding about future operations in the Valley, Sheridan departed on the evening of October 15 for a conference in Washington, leaving his army under the command of General Wright. The Federals, scattered over a large area in their camp at Cedar Creek, threw up a few light fortifications but seemingly felt no apprehension of danger. Early, still badly outnumbered, strengthened his lines and sought an advantageous way to get at his opponent.

---

225. The 6th North Carolina and possibly other units of Davis's Brigade were involved in that fighting.

226. The enemy "Shell[ed] us furiously all day," Lieutenant Walton wrote. Walton Diary, September 24, 1864.

227. *Official Records (Army)*, ser. 1, 43 (pt. 1):558. "[T]ha hant meny of my company here any more," Pvt. Jesse Hill of the 21st North Carolina wrote on September 30 after returning from an extended absence without leave. "[T]ha has ben lots of our men taken [prisoner] and a heape Kild and our men ses tha was badly whiped [at Winchester and Fisher's Hill.]" Jesse Hill to Emoline Hill, September 30, 1864, Hill Papers.

228. *Official Records (Army)*, ser. 1, 43 (pt. 1):558, 560.

Pegram's Division was dispatched on a reconnaissance mission toward Cedar Creek on October 17, but no serious fighting resulted.

On the foggy night of October 18 the divisions of Gordon, Ramseur, and Pegram, under the overall command of Gordon and with Brig. Gen. Clement A. Evans in temporary command of Gordon's Division, were sent by Early on a wide circuit around the Federal left with orders to attack the enemy camp at daylight. At the same time, Kershaw's Division was to attack Col. Joseph Thoburn's isolated division of Crook's Corps in the Federal center, and Wharton's Division would press up the pike toward the village of Middletown to cut the Federals' line of retreat. Brig. Gen. Thomas L. Rosser's cavalry would attack the Federal right flank while Lomax's troopers cut the pike further north in the vicinity of Newtown or Winchester. In addition to surprise, the Confederates would enjoy another important advantage: Sheridan, although en route from Washington, was still twenty miles away at Winchester.

Marching single file along a "pig path" that meandered through dense woods and up and down steep ridges, Gordon's flanking force waded the North Fork of the Shenandoah River twice as it struggled toward its objective during the wee hours of October 19. "We would sometimes lose our foot-hold and fall down the mountain side," Lt. J. Marshall Williams of the 54th North Carolina wrote, "and would have literally to pull ourselves up by bushes, roots or anything projecting. . . ." So "steep or slanting" was the path that it appeared at times to Capt. Clarence R. Hatton, adjutant general of Davis's Brigade, to be "right over the river."[229] At about 5:40 A.M. Gordon's men, wet and cold from their river crossings, stormed out of the fog and darkness. Dozens of Federals were shot down as they emerged from tents, leaped up from breakfast fires, or lunged for weapons; most took to their heels at the sound of gunshots and rebel yells. So complete was the surprise that the first Federals encountered, according to Captain Hatton, "did not have a chance to, or anyway they did not, form any regular line against us, but with a few shots fled. . . ." Here and there pockets of bluecoated infantrymen made a show of resistance, but in a matter of minutes Hayes's Division of Crook's Corps and a provisional division under Col. John H. Kitching were stampeded. "[I]t was the most complete rout I ever saw," Captain Hatton wrote.[230]

While Hayes's and Kitching's men were fleeing their camps, Thoburn's Division (Crook's Corps) was suffering a similar embarrassment at the hands of Kershaw. With the

---

229. Samuel D. Buck, *With the Old Confeds: Actual Experiences of a Captain in the Line* (Baltimore: H. E. Houck and Company, 1925), 123; Williams, "Fifty-fourth Regiment," in Clark, *Histories of the North Carolina Regiments*, 3:280; Clarence R. Hatton, "The Great Battle at Cedar Creek," *Southern Historical Society Papers* 34 (1906): 197, hereafter cited as Hatton, "Battle at Cedar Creek."

230. Hatton, "Battle at Cedar Creek," 198. "Every now and then we struck some fresh troops," Hatton recalled. "Each succeeding body, having more time to make formation, gave us harder fighting, but none stood against our charges, but broke and fled." Lieutenant Williams, in his history of the 54th North Carolina, remembered the attack (with somewhat doubtful accuracy) as follows: "We . . . dashed into their camp without firing a gun[?], capturing 1,500 prisoners and 18 pieces of artillery, while a good many were in bed and asleep. We then fell upon another corps immediately in front of our cavalry[?], which was soon panic stricken, and fled in dismay, leaving all their artillery behind, which was turned upon them. Our infantry followed on closely for four miles, when General Early gave over the pursuit." Williams, "Fifty-fourth Regiment," in Clark, *Histories of the North Carolina Regiments*, 3:280.

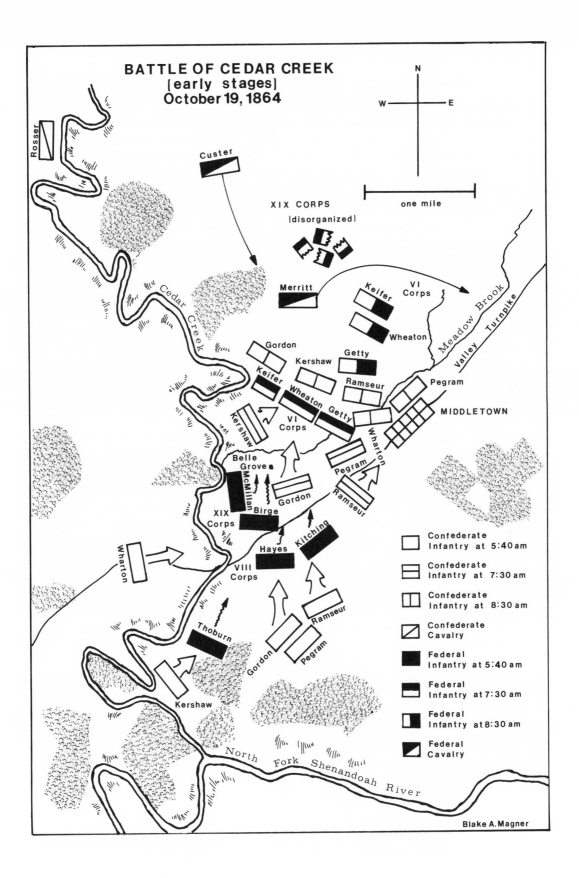

BATTLE OF CEDAR CREEK
(early stages)
October 19, 1864

N
W — E

one mile

Rosser

Custer

XIX CORPS
(disorganized)

Merritt

Keifer

VI
Corps

Meadow Brook

Valley Turnpike

Wheaton

Cedar Creek

Gordon

Kershaw

Getty

Keifer

Ramseur

Pegram

Wheaton
Getty

Kershaw

VI
Corps

Wharton

MIDDLETOWN

Belle
Grove

McMillan

Pegram

Gordon

Ramseur

XIX
Corps

Birge

Wharton

Kitching

Hayes

VIII
Corps

Ramseur

Thoburn

Gordon

Pegram

Kershaw

North Fork Shenandoah River

| | Confederate Infantry at 5:40 am |
| Confederate Infantry at 7:30 am |
| Confederate Infantry at 8:30 am |
| Confederate Cavalry |
| Federal Infantry at 5:40 am |
| Federal Infantry at 7:30 am |
| Federal Infantry at 8:30 am |
| Federal Cavalry |

Blake A. Magner

assistance of Evans and Wharton, Kershaw then overran Emory's XIX Corps. Wheaton's and Col. Joseph W. Keifer's (formerly Ricketts's) Divisions of the VI Corps, after a brief stand, were wrecked in turn by Kershaw and Evans. With the exception of its cavalry units and the ubiquitous VI Corps division of Getty, which fell back in good order to a low ridge, the entire Army of the Shenandoah was in rapid and, in some cases, panic-stricken retreat.

During the initial attack on Hayes and Kitching, Pegram's Division was in a second line behind the divisions of Gordon and Ramseur and was not engaged. Likewise, it took no part in the defeat of the XIX Corps or in the attack that routed Keifer and Wheaton. Pegram's men, supported on the right by Battle's Brigade (commanded by Lt. Col. Edwin L. Hobson) of Ramseur's Division, were then ordered forward to tackle the redoubtable Getty. Pegram's attack focused on the brigades of Warner (on the Federal right) and Brig. Gen. Lewis A. Grant (in the center); Hobson probably advanced against Bidwell. "[O]ur men moved as on parade," Captain Hatton wrote. "I never saw them in better line. I was on the right of the brigade . . . and in front of our lines. I could see the whole movement. . . ."[231]

Sheltered to some extent by scattered woods and slight breastworks of earth and rails, the Federals opened fire on Pegram's men from a distance of thirty yards, blistering their line "with terrible effect."[232] The Confederates returned the fire for a few moments, then, in the face of a Federal counterattack, fell back, according to Warner, "in confusion" and "with heavy loss."[233] Lieutenant Colonel Davis was wounded at about that time, and Lieutenant Colonel Tate of the 6th North Carolina assumed command of the brigade. For the next hour Getty stubbornly held his ground, fending off a gallant but unsupported attack by Grimes's North Carolina brigade as well as an assault by Wharton's Division. Massed Confederate cannon then rained down a furious fire on the dogged Federals. Around 9:00 A.M. Getty, seeing the divisions of Kershaw and Gordon (who had taken over from Evans) overlapping his right flank, withdrew, first to a position north of Middletown and then to a line somewhat farther north. There he was reinforced on the left by most of the 7,500 cavalrymen belonging to the divisions of Brig. Gens. Merritt and George A. Custer. The Confederates advanced through Middletown, forming a staggered line of (from left to right) Gordon, Kershaw, Ramseur, Pegram, and Wharton. Wharton, confronting Merritt's troopers, launched an attack shortly after 10:00 A.M. but was repulsed by the latter's Spencer repeaters. Pegram's Division joined the fighting shortly thereafter. Sheltered by woods on each flank and by the houses and fences of Middletown, Wharton and Pegram skirmished

231. Hatton, "Battle at Cedar Creek," 198.

232. Quoted in Wert, *From Winchester to Cedar Creek*, 208. According to some reports, the Federals were under orders not to fire until the Confederates were within thirty yards; however, Col. Thomas W. Hyde of the 1st Maine Veteran Infantry, who took command of Bidwell's Brigade after Bidwell was mortally wounded, gives a different version that seemingly has the ring of truth: "During all this time the fog had been very dense, and the smoke from the guns of our skirmishers, who were warmly engaged with the foe, rendered the atmosphere still more dense, so that it was almost impossible to see through it a short distance, when suddenly the enemy appeared in two lines, within thirty yards of our line of battle. The density of the fog had allowed them to rush over our vedettes without their being able to warn the line, and under cover of the steepness of the hill they approached thus near unobserved." *Official Records (Army)*, ser. 1, 43 (pt. 1):215. See also Wert, *From Winchester to Cedar Creek*, 207.

233. *Official Records (Army)*, ser. 1, 43 (pt. 1):201.

with the dismounted Yankee horsemen for the next five hours. Several probing attacks were launched by both sides during the fighting, and the Confederates came close to flanking their opponents on at least one occasion. Early, however, considered the day won and was primarily concerned with preventing a repetition of the disastrous cavalry attack he had suffered at Winchester. His men had also become somewhat disorganized by their rapid advance and by their scavenging activities among the cornucopian riches of the Federal camp. Few units, including Davis's Brigade, resisted that temptation. "A good number of our men," Lieutenant Williams wrote, "thinking the enemy had fled to Winchester, took advantage of this heavy fog and fell out of ranks and returned to plunder the camp, so rich in spoils."[234] "[S]harp skirmish[ing]" continued, but both sides were compelled to hold their ground: Wharton and Pegram were constrained by Early's orders and the superior numbers and weaponry of the Federal cavalry; Merritt and Custer were largely neutralized by the "truly terrific" Confederate artillery fire.[235]

A lull then descended over the field while both sides regrouped. The Federals, their confidence and organization restored by the return of Sheridan at about 10:00 A.M., dug in. At 1:00 P.M. Early ordered Evans, Kershaw, and Ramseur, under the collective command of Gordon, to probe the enemy lines and launch an attack if prospects seemed promising. Speedily convinced by the sharp Federal reaction that he was overmatched, Gordon fell back to a point somewhat south of his previous position. Another lull followed as the pugnacious Sheridan prepared to take the offensive. At 4:00 P.M. the Federals struck. Some progress was made against the Confederate left, where Gordon's flank was essentially in the air, but the Federal infantry paid a heavy price and soon halted to await help. Along the Confederate center Kershaw's and Ramseur's men, crouching behind stone walls and breastworks of fence rails and earth, fought the Federals to a bloody standstill. Pegram's troops, still holed up among the houses, fences, and gardens of Middletown, repulsed two charges by Col. Thomas C. Devin's cavalry brigade with a "terrible" fire.[236] Wharton's

234. Williams, "Fifty-fourth Regiment," in Clark, *Histories of the North Carolina Regiments*, 3:280. As is typical in Williams's history of the 54th North Carolina, it is not entirely certain whether he is writing in this instance about his regiment, his brigade, his division, or about battlefield events in general. However, it is clear that there was misbehavior by Davis's Brigade. In a letter to his wife dated October 21, Private Hill of the 21st North Carolina stated that he had "capturd . . . a pocket book with 44 dollars of green back[s] and a nap sack and ablanket and a good oil chloth and pare of boots and severl other little tricks and [a] little pocket knife." Hill managed to keep all of his booty even though, he said, the Yankees "run me" for "a bout 5 mils" and "through the river twise." Jesse Hill to Emoline Hill, October 21, 1864, Hill Papers.

235. *Official Records (Army)*, ser. 1, 43 (pt. 1):450. The Confederate artillery fire, according to Merritt, had "seldom been equaled for accuracy of aim and excellence of ammunition. The batteries attached to this division did nobly, but were overpowered at times by weight of metal and superior ammunition. So excellent was the practice of the enemy that it was utterly impossible to cover a cavalry command from the artillery fire. . . ." Federal cavalry general Thomas C. Devin reported that the enemy made "several determined efforts" to drive his men from their position during the period in question, but that is probably an exaggeration. *Official Records (Army)*, ser. 1, 43 (pt. 1):450, 479.

236. Hazard Stevens, "The Battle of Cedar Creek," *Papers of the Military Historical Society of Massachusetts*, 16 vols., *The Shenandoah Campaigns of 1862 and 1864 and the Appomattox Campaign 1865* (Boston: Published by the Society, 1907; Wilmington, N.C.: Broadfoot Publishing Company, 1989), 6:137. "[I]t was impossible from the nature of the ground to reach the enemy's infantry," Devin wrote. *Official Records (Army)*, ser. 1, 43 (pt. 1):479.

Division and William T. Wofford's Brigade of Kershaw's Division, on Pegram's right, also managed to fend off the Federal troopers. At that juncture, Custer's cavalry crashed into the Confederate left, routing Gordon's Division and producing a sequential, left-to-right collapse by Kershaw's men. "We ran [with such single-minded enthusiasm]," one of the latter facetiously recollected, that "we struck the ground in high places only." On the right, Merritt's cavalry drove a wedge through Wharton's right flank, and Pegram and Wofford began to buckle. Ramseur, in the center, held most of his division together with a magnificent display of combat leadership before going down with a fatal ball through the lungs. Meantime, Pegram, Wharton, and Wofford's troops retreated under orders from Early, initially retaining some degree of cohesion but losing most of it while crossing Cedar Creek under fire. Once again, as at Winchester and Fisher's Hill, the Army of the Valley fell back in defeat and confusion in the twilight. The battle, in the rueful words of Jesse Hill, was "the worst whiping we ever had[.]"[237]

Details of the part played by Davis's Brigade at Cedar Creek are scant. "Just after daybreak," Chaplain Paris wrote, "the roar of artillery and Small arms [was heard]. In less than an hour the whole line of the enemy's breastworks had been carried, Several flags taken, and his entire camp taken as it stood. The Slaughter among the Yanks was great, ours Small. They retreated one mile beyond Middletown, fighting. At 3 1/2 Oclock P.M. our left took a panic, and fled in disorder; the right followed in a regular stampede. We had captured 36 pieces of artillery, 2000 prisoners. We lost some guns. Gen. Ramseur was killed [mortally wounded.] Our troops scattered to the mountains and [are] greatly demoralized." Predictably, Private Hill's account of the last stage of the battle, if exaggerated and inexplicit, was graphic: "I [am] glad . . . [to] say I com out safe for tha was lots of our men kild[.] I dont see how I ever com out safe for the bullets and grape and Shel com so thick and tore up the men[.] [T]he pecs [pieces] of flesh flew all over me and the men fel all a round me thek[.] [T]he dead lay thick for bout 4 miles long and 2 miles wide[.] I [can't] tel how many thousand was kild but tha was a site. . . ."[238] To these glimmers of enlightenment can be added Lieutenant Walton's diary entry for October 19 and a postwar account of the battle by Lieutenant Colonel Jones. "Late in the evening," Walton wrote, "Col. Tate's extreme left was broken and everything commenced falling back in the greatest confusion. [We] lost all the artillery we had captured and a great many wagons and ambulances also. Col. Tate was wounded in the retreat. Capt. [James F.] Beale [Beall, of the 21st North Carolina] took command of the brigade. We marched all night." According to Jones, the 57th North Carolina's performance at Cedar Creek was superior, as it had been at Winchester, to that of the rest of the brigade. "It has been many times recorded," he asserted, "that General Robert D. Johnston's Brigade of North Carolinians was the largest body of Confederate troops that retired . . . in good order. Beside this noble brigade stood the

237. [Sanders W.] Benson, "Battle of Cedar Creek, Va.," *Confederate Veteran* 27 (October 1919): 390; Jesse Hill to Emoline Hill, October 21, 1864, Hill Papers.

238. Paris Diary, October 19, 1864; Jesse Hill to Emoline Hill, October 21, 1864, Hill Papers. Lieutenant Williams of the 54th North Carolina wrote that after the counterattack by Sheridan's cavalry, "Our line was . . . thrown in disorder, and soon retreated in much confusion, and the fruits of this brilliant victory [were] lost. Many of us were soon ridden down by the cavalry and captured, killed or wounded, while our cavalry was of little assistance." Williams, "Fifty-fourth Regiment," in Clark, *Histories of the North Carolina Regiments*, 3:280.

Fifty-seventh Regiment, which was next in line, and this regiment came off with Johnston's Brigade in like good order and with great steadiness."[239]

Early's battered army reassembled as best it could that night at Fisher's Hill. At three o'clock the next morning it began a thirty-five-mile retreat to New Market. Confederate losses at Cedar Creek numbered about 1,860 killed or wounded and 1,200 captured. Federal losses were 644 killed, 3,430 wounded, and 1,591 missing or captured.[240] Service records compiled for this volume indicate that the 57th North Carolina lost 9 killed, 18 wounded, and 7 captured (of whom 4 were wounded).

The organized remnants of the Army of the Valley reached New Market on the afternoon of October 20, and hundreds of stragglers and fugitives drifted into camp during the next week. On October 21 Pegram, intent upon rebuilding morale and discipline, delivered an inspirational "lecture" to the officers of Davis's Brigade. On about the same date he "had Johnston's Brigade drawn out in the open field and complimented the men in the presence of other troops for their splendid conduct during the panic at Belle Grove [Cedar Creek]." Col. Hamilton A. Brown of the 1st Regiment N.C. State Troops assumed temporary command of Davis's Brigade by October 31. Details of the brigade's activities during late October and early November are lacking because of a gap in the Paris diary, but it seems evident that Pegram was busy training and re-equipping his command. Twice-a-day drills began in Johnston's Brigade on October 24 and were probably instituted in Brown's Brigade as well.[241] On November 6 Johnston began holding dress parade on a daily basis. Parades and inspections in Brown's Brigade were apparently frequent also. By November 5 cartographer Jed Hotchkiss was reporting that the army was "filling up rapidly" but was "Much in want of small arms."[242]

On the morning of November 10 the Army of the Valley marched north in the direction of Woodstock. The next day it moved to the vicinity of Newtown, where it found Sheridan entrenching. After a day of skirmishing on November 12, the Confederates fell back to Fisher's Hill. Unable to feed his men and seeing no disposition on Sheridan's part to offer

239. Walton Diary, October 19, 1864; Jones, "Fifty-seventh Regiment," in Clark, *Histories of the North Carolina Regiments*, 3:422.

240. See Thomas A. Lewis, *The Guns of Cedar Creek* (New York: Dell Publishing, 1988; New York: Harper and Row, 1990), 309; *Official Records (Army)*, ser. 1, 43 (pt. 1):137.

241. Walton Diary, October 21, 1864; Walter Alexander Montgomery, "Twelfth Regiment," in Clark, *Histories of the North Carolina Regiments*, 1:649. See also diary of James Benjamin Jones (1st Battalion N.C. Sharpshooters) in Jones Family Papers, SHC, October 24, 1864, hereafter cited as Jones Diary. On October 27 Johnston's Brigade began holding roll call four times a day, and on the thirtieth a guard was posted around its camp: measures that indicate a serious desertion problem. There is no evidence that similar steps were taken in Brown's Brigade, but desertion was very much on the minds of some of Brown's men, including the incorrigible Private Hill. "[T]ha say we will move camp to marrow," he wrote from the vicinity of New Market on November 16. "[T]ha say we will go up to wards *Stanton* and that *soots* me for that is nearer towards home. . . . [I]f I get up about *linchburg* I think I will slip the hatter and try to come home for here we hav the hardis times I ever saw. . . ." Jesse Hill to Emoline Hill, November 16, 1864, in Ripple, *Jesse Hill Letters*. See also Jones Diary, October 27 and 30, 1864.

242. McDonald, *Make Me a Map: Hotchkiss Journal*, 242 (November 5, 1864). See also Walton Diary, October 24-November 8, 1864 (individual entries).

battle, Early continued his retreat at sunup on November 13.[243] The raw and windy conditions that had prevailed on the twelfth intensified when "*extraordinarily* cold" weather arrived accompanied by "some little snow." On November 14 the army returned to New Market, and two days later it moved to a camp "nine miles nearer" Strasburg. Clothing was issued to "all the troops" the same day, and Pvt. James B. Jones of the 1st Battalion N.C. Sharpshooters reported that the men were "All now well shod & clad." On November 17 Pegram's Division marched south to a new camp at Big Spring (Lacey Spring), northeast of Harrisonburg, and began putting up temporary winter quarters.[244]

Pegram's troops remained in camp in the vicinity of Big Spring for the next three weeks. Rain on November 18 was followed the next morning by snow—"flakes as large as hen eggs"—and a "dreadful" rain that evening. Once again the men began constructing temporary winter quarters, which in this instance meant adding chimneys to their tents. More rain fell on November 20 and 21, followed by snow on the night of the twenty-first and "very cold" weather on the twenty-third.[245] On November 24 conditions began to moderate, inaugurating eleven welcome days of mostly "Clear & beautiful" and occasionally "warm" and "summer-like" weather. As usual when the army was in camp for extended periods, life became "very monotonous," relieved only by unwelcome interruptions such as inspections and twice-daily drills.[246] However, somewhat unexpectedly considering the season and the devastation wrought by Sheridan, the food situation began improving during the last week of November. As late as November 19 the chronically ravenous Private Hill complained that "we hant had any thing [to eat] in two days" and forecast that the men could not "stand it much longer on the rashions we get now." But by December 2 Sergeant Walker and his messmates were "fairing tolerable well, get enough to eat twice a day, and the Boys does some foraging once and a while." Private Jones reported on November 30 that "apples [are] abundant in camp," and, after a successful hunting trip on November 22, some members of the 6th North Carolina enjoyed a turkey dinner on Thanksgiving Day (November 24).[247] Unfortunately, by mid-December matters were back to normal and possibly worse than before. "I hav to suffer vary bad for som thing to ete," Hill moaned to his wife on December 20. "I could ete dog now if I had it. . . . [S]end me somthing . . . as quick

243. "[W]e had to march two days with out one mouth full to eat," Private Hill wrote, "and then when we got something we did not get half enough." Jesse Hill to Emoline Hill, November 16, 1864, in Ripple, *Jesse Hill Letters*.

244. Jones Diary, November 13 (first and second quotations) and 16 (fourth and fifth quotations), 1864; Walton Diary, November 16, 1864 (third quotation). The new camp was named Camp Ramseur.

245. Jones Diary, November 19 and 23, 1864; Walton Diary, November 19, 1864. A skirmish between a contingent of Federal cavalry and three divisions of Early's army took place at Rude's Hill on November 22, but Pegram's Division was not involved.

246. Jones Diary, November 25, 1864; McDonald, *Make Me a Map: Hotchkiss Journal*, 246 (November 29 and December 4, 1864); Walton Diary, November 24, 1864. "[O]rders are very strict," Sergeant Walker wrote on December 2. J. K. Walker to his brother, December 2, 1864, Walker Papers.

247. Jesse Hill to Emoline Hill, November 19, 1864, in Ripple, *Jesse Hill Letters*; J. K. Walker to his brother, December 2, 1864, Walker Papers; Jones Diary, November 30, 1864. See also Walton Diary, November 19, 22, and 24, 1864; H. W. Barrow to J. W. Fries, November 23, 1864, in Blair, "Letters of Henry W. Barrow," 82. On December 4 Hill wrote a letter devoid of comments about victuals, positive proof that for the moment they were adequate. Jesse Hill to Emoline Hill, December 4, 1864, in Ripple, *Jesse Hill Letters*.

as you can[.]" "[I]f I was thar and could far[e] as good as your dogs," Hill added four days later, "I would think I was buly."[248]

Concurrent with the temporary improvement in rations, the division's strength slowly increased as detailed men were recalled, convalescents returned, and conscripts arrived. A "good many" of the latter deserted at the first opportunity; nevertheless, Pegram's Division reported 2,479 men "effective present" on November 30.[249] Another positive development was the return from assignment in North Carolina of Brigadier General Lewis. The date on which he replaced Brown as brigade commander is uncertain but was probably during the first two weeks of November.[250]

On December 6 Gordon's and Pegram's Divisions received orders to rejoin the Army of Northern Virginia near Petersburg. Lewis's Brigade marched in the direction of Staunton at 11:00 A.M., "Moved rapidly all day," and bivouacked near Mount Sidney that night. The men arrived at Waynesboro on December 7, reached Richmond by rail at noon the next day, and arrived at Petersburg during a snowstorm the same night.[251] On December 10 they "Moved to the right about 10 miles in the direction of Stony Creek. . . ." "[W]e had to take a tramp after the yankeys," Private Hill wrote, "and it snod and rained and sleted. . . . [W]e sufferd a site . . . [from the] cold and a hep for somthing to eat[.]" The men formed a line of battle and advanced but, finding no Yankees, returned to Petersburg. They then went into camp "about three miles" from town in cabins previously occupied by Brig. Gen. James H. Lane's Brigade.[252] Three days later they moved to a "pretty" location "about a mile & a half below Burgess Mills on the Plank road" and began constructing shanties for the winter.[253] Two quiet weeks followed during which Lewis's troops completed work on their

248. Jesse Hill to Emoline Hill, December 20, 1864, and Jesse Hill to his father and mother, December 24, 1864, in Ripple, *Jesse Hill Letters*.

249. *Official Records (Army)*, ser. 1, 43 (pt. 1):587. See also *Official Records (Army)*, ser. 1, 42 (pt. 3):1237. The strength of the division on September 30 was 1,630 men present and effective for field duty; on October 31 the figure was 1,818. *Official Records (Army)*, ser. 1, 43 (pt. 2):882, 911.

250. See W. G. Lewis to Mittie Lewis, November 16, 1864, Lewis Papers; *Official Records (Army)*, ser. 1, 42 (pt. 3):1194, 1365. The *Official Records* indicate that Lieutenant Colonel Jones, who was captured at Rappahannock Station in November, 1863, was in command of the 57th on November 30, 1864; however, that is incorrect. Capt. John Beard of Company C was in command of the 57th on that date. Jones was still in a Federal prison and was not exchanged until February 20, 1865. He rejoined the regiment prior to March 25, 1865. See *Official Records (Army)*, ser. 1, 42 (pt. 3):1245.

251. Walton Diary, December 6, 1864. "[A] terrible night for the poor soldiers in the field!" wrote Confederate War Department clerk John B. Jones. John Beauchamp Jones, *A Rebel War Clerk's Diary*, ed. Earl Schenck Miers (Philadelphia: J. B. Lippincott, 1866; New York: A. S. Barnes, 1961), 458 (December 9, 1864).

252. Walton Diary, December 10, 1864; Jesse Hill to Emoline Hill, December 11, 1864, in Ripple, *Jesse Hill Letters*; W. G. Lewis to Mittie Lewis, December 11, 1864, Lewis Papers. See also Williams, "Fifty-fourth Regiment," in Clark, *Histories of the North Carolina Regiments*, 3:281. According to Private Hill, the camp was five miles southeast of Petersburg.

253. Walton Diary, December 14, 1864 (see also December 13, 1864); W. G. Lewis to Mittie Lewis, December 16, 1864, Lewis Papers. Lewis described his position as "about fifteen miles from Stony Creek on the Weldon & Petersburg Railroad. . . ." In a letter dated December 20, Private Hill stated that he was camped "9 miles south west of Petersburg." On February 4, 1865, when Chaplain Paris returned from a furlough, Lewis's Brigade was camped "On the Boydton Plank Road, nine miles West of Petersburg." Jesse Hill to Emoline Hill, December 20, 1864, Hill Papers; Paris Diary, February 4, 1865.

quarters, stood inspection, policed their camp, and in some lucky cases were granted furloughs. Orders requiring daily company and brigade drill came down on December 26.[254]
At about that time, Early's old corps (the 2nd) of the Army of Northern Virginia was
assigned to Gordon.[255] Thus the 57th North Carolina was in Lewis's Brigade, Pegram's
Division, Gordon's Corps.[256]

Lewis's Brigade remained in position southwest of Petersburg through January 1865.
Brigade morale, if Jesse Hill's account is any indication, was poor.

[I]t is though[t] that tha will be pese be fore long and I think tha had better try and make pese
be fore spring for the men is runing away ever day or night more or les and some goes home and som
to the yankeys tha avredg a bout one houndred a night and in the Spring tha will all leve or nearly all
I think tha is a talk here in the army that old N C is going back in the union and I hope it will I think
this war will hav to stop before long for the rashions is nearly giv out tha ar put up to it the hardist
sort to get anough to keep us a live we suffer for som thing to ete I wold like to get a little somthing
to ete from home if you see any chance to send me any any time in [the] next month for a bout
Spring I am a going to try to get home or go some where elce tha cant cock crow over me any longer
than then[.][257]

"I think," Hill wrote in another estimation of the Confederacy's prospects, "the thing is
about gone up the spout and fel out at the little end."[258]

On February 2 a review of Pegram's Division was held, ostensibly for Lee and Gordon but unofficially, one suspects, in honor of Pegram's wife of two weeks, the former
Hetty Cary of Baltimore. Generals James Longstreet, A. P. Hill, Richard Anderson, and
Henry Heth also attended.[259] The next day the Federals attacked southwest of Petersburg
near Hatcher's Run to interdict Confederate supply wagon traffic on the Boydton Plank
Road. Pegram's pickets were driven in by Yankee cavalry shortly after sunrise on the icy
morning of February 5, provoking an all-day skirmish with enemy sharpshooters. Evans's
Division of Gordon's Corps and Heth's Division of A. P. Hill's Corps clashed with the
intruders that afternoon but were unable to dislodge them from their rifle pits and log

254. Walton Diary, December 15-28, 1864. Lieutenant Walton reported with satisfaction and probable amazement that he celebrated Christmas Day with eggnog.

255. Early remained behind in the Shenandoah as commander of the Army of the Valley, but his "army" consisted only of Wharton's Division and some cavalry and artillery units.

256. The present-for-duty strength of Pegram's Division on December 31, 1864, was 2,447 men. *Official Records (Army)*, ser. 1, 42 (pt. 3):1362.

257. Jesse Hill to Emoline Hill, January 19, 1865, Hill Papers.

258. Jesse Hill to Emoline Hill, December 27, 1864, in Ripple, *Jesse Hill Letters*.

259. One veteran still remembered the occasion with pleasure more than fifty years later: "I have frequently
recalled," he wrote, "the superb picture of Mrs. Pegram . . . handsomely mounted, and General Lee, on foot,
with his hand resting on her horse's neck, engaged in conversation while awaiting the coming of the division to
be reviewed. . . . You can imagine the splendor of the group: a beautiful woman, a noble man in appearance and
every other respect, and a handsome horse." Kyd Douglas recalled that during the review a Tar Heel soldier was
"nearly knocked down" by Mrs. Pegram's horse. The soldier "quickly sprang up and, as she reined up her horse
and began to apologize, he broke in as he seized his old hat from his head. 'Never mind, Miss. You might have
rid all over me, indeed you might.'" Randolph Barton, "The Battle of Hatcher's Run," *Confederate Veteran* 25
(March 1917): 119; Douglas, *I Rode With Stonewall Jackson*, 311.

breastworks. Skirmishing resumed on Pegram's front the next morning and continued until early afternoon when the Federals launched a probing attack along Hatcher's Run. Pegram lashed back and routed a regiment of dismounted troopers but was repulsed by other cavalry and infantry units.[260] Unable to maneuver properly or even to see their opponents consistently in the marshy, rolling, heavily wooded terrain, many exhausted, half-frozen soldiers in both armies bolted at virtually the first sign of opposition. On the Federal side, infantry units fired blindly into each other, were thrown into confusion when panic-stricken cavalrymen stampeded through their ranks, or withdrew because of alleged ammunition shortages. Pegram's reinforced division attacked again around 4:00 P.M., routing some Federal regiments and pushing others back for more than a mile through the frigid woods. At that point the Confederates collided with a charging Federal brigade. "The enemy broke at the first volley from our men," a Federal officer wrote, "and left the field in great disorder, leaving their killed and wounded in our hands, together with several prisoners." Pegram went down with a mortal wound, and cries of "Pegram is killed" and "we're flanked" echoed up and down the line. The fleeing Confederates were rallied shortly thereafter by Gordon, who counterattacked with Maj. Gen. William Mahone's newly arrived division and "drove the enemy in confusion to his works."[261]

As though sickened by the day's pathetic proceedings, the gods of war conjured up a blizzard that night, putting an end to the fighting and to any wounded men lying in the woods. Sleet and rain continued the next day. The Federals launched one tentative probe, then fell back. The net results of the battle were a three-mile extension of the Federal lines to the southwest, about 1,500 Federal dead and wounded, and 1,000 Confederate casualties. According to Lieutenant Williams of the 54th North Carolina, the fighting at Hatcher's Run was "unprecedented in its fury" and "protracted beyond all expectations." Other members of Lewis's and Johnston's Brigades reported that their commands were "heavily engaged" in "very fierce" combat and "lost heavily."[262] However, casualties in the 57th North Carolina were light. According to information compiled for this volume, the regiment lost one man wounded and six captured. The fallen Pegram was replaced temporarily by General Lewis and then by General Johnston. Brig. Gen. James A. Walker was assigned to permanent command of the division on or about February 27. Thus the 57th North Carolina was in Lewis's Brigade, Walker's Division, Gordon's Corps.

260. See *Official Records (Army)*, ser. 1, 46 (pt. 1):369.

261. *Official Records (Army)*, ser. 1, 46 (pt. 1):266 (first quotation), 390 (fourth quotation); H. C. Wall, *Historical Sketch of the Pee Dee Guards* (Raleigh: Edwards, Broughton and Company, 1876), 92 (second and third quotations).

262. Williams, "Fifty-fourth Regiment," in Clark, *Histories of the North Carolina Regiments*, 3:281; Neill W. Ray, "Sixth Regiment," in Clark, *Histories of the North Carolina Regiments*, 1:328, hereafter cited as Ray, "Sixth Regiment," in Clark, *Histories of the North Carolina Regiments*; Beall, "Twenty-first Regiment," in Clark, *Histories of the North Carolina Regiments*, 2:143; Veines Edmunds Turner and Henry Clay Wall, "Twenty-third Regiment," in Clark, *Histories of the North Carolina Regiments*, 2:262. A return for Lewis's Brigade dated February 27 indicates that 905 men were present for duty. The strength of Walker's Division was 2,326 on about the same date. On January 10 and January 31 the division reported 2,574 and 2,472 men present for duty. *Official Records (Army)*, ser. 1, 46 (pt. 1):388, 383, 385.

After moving to a new camp "one mile on the road towards Petersburg" on the night of February 7, the 57th North Carolina returned to its previous quarters the next afternoon. A week of "very roof" weather brought fighting to a virtual halt.[263] On February 15 temperatures began to moderate, but an extended rainy spell turned the roads to quagmires. "Clear and Warm" weather on February 27 provided momentary relief, but rain returned on the twenty-eighth.[264] Desertion seemingly continued to be a serious problem in Lewis's Brigade. "Som time ago I was in hops tha would mak pese," Private Hill admitted, "but I see no chance now wuntil the yankes whips us out. . . . [O]ur men is out of hart again and a runing away like every thing[.] [T]ha was 5 left the Reg last night and tha is houndreds a going to the yankeys every week and as soon as warm wether coms nearly all our Brigade say tha will go home or som where elce[.] [T]ha say it hant of any use to stay here and be kild for nothing[.] [T]ha all say we ar whiped and tha all no it[.]"[265]

On March 15, following several days of "warm and pleasant" weather, Lewis's Brigade marched from its winter camp to a position near Fort Stedman (east of Petersburg), exchanging places with Matt Ransom's North Carolina brigade. That part of the line was considerably more active than the position vacated by Lewis's men: "our brest works and the yanketsy brest works is about 1 houndred yards apart and [we] keep fireing at ech other all the time," Private Hill wrote.[266] "[E]very time a man show[s] his head," Pvt. W. J. Walker of the 6th North Carolina observed, "he is shot." Instead of their comfortable shanties, the troops found themselves inhabiting pits with "little tents" stretched over them. "[O]ur fare is ruff," Walker continued, "but a soldier dont exspect anything else. I am sorry

---

263. Paris Diary, February 7, 1865 (see also February 8, 1865); J. K. Walker to his brother, February 15, 1865, Walker Papers. Little is known concerning the 57th North Carolina or Lewis's Brigade during February, but it is likely that military activity other than picket duty was minimal. Sergeant Walker wrote on February 15 that "There is a Detachment sent on Picket from our Brigade every three days." Rations and the health of the brigade, if not necessarily its morale, were seemingly adequate: "[W]e are fairing very well at this time," Walker stated. On February 26 Walker wrote that the men were "busily engaged in throwing up Breastworks and building our Quarters to move in, but I am doubtful of us remaining in them long. We are still in our old cabins yet and will remain in them until we get our new ones done." J. K. Walker to his brother, February 26, 1865, Walker Papers.

264. Paris Diary, February 27, 1865. The roads, according to Paris, continued to be "dreadful bad." Paris Diary, March 2, 1865.

265. Jesse Hill to Emoline Hill, February 25, 1865, Hill Papers. Quarterly desertion figures in the 57th North Carolina during the war, as derived from service records in this volume, were as follows: third quarter 1862–16; fourth quarter 1862–9; first quarter 1863–6; second quarter 1863–3; third quarter 1863–2; fourth quarter 1863–3; first quarter 1864–2; second quarter 1864–7; third quarter 1864–5; fourth quarter 1864–10; first quarter 1865–6. In the *North Carolina Troops* series, desertion is defined for statistical purposes as *ultimate* failure to return to duty from an unauthorized absence of whatever length. The foregoing figures are therefore an inadequate reflection of absenteeism without leave, a problem that, in terms of the number of men involved, was undoubtedly more serious.

266. Paris Diary, March 14, 1865; Jesse Hill to Emoline Hill, March 17, 1865, in Ripple, *Jesse Hill Letters*. Pvt. William J. Walker of the 6th North Carolina estimated that the two lines were "about 50 yards" apart. Sgt. J. K. Walker, William's brother, put the distance at "about 60 yards." W. J. Walker to his father and mother, March 16, 1865, and J. K. Walker to his brother, March 21, 1865, Walker Papers. See also Williams, "Fifty-fourth Regiment," in Clark, *Histories of the North Carolina Regiments*, 3:282.

to inform you that a great many of the boys have got discouraged and worn out of the war."[267]

Hoping to puncture the Federal siege lines and escape with part of his army to North Carolina, where the seemingly invincible army of William T. Sherman had just won another victory at Bentonville, Lee planned an attack on Fort Stedman for the morning of March 25. Fifty axmen would clear a pathway through the Federals' chevaux-de-frise (barricades of wooden spikes) for three 100-man assault squads that would bypass Fort Stedman and seize three small auxiliary forts in its rear. Almost half of Lee's army would then pour through the gap in three columns. While the center column (including Lewis's Brigade) captured Battery Number 10 and Fort Stedman, the left column would veer northward against Battery Number 9 and the right column would move south to capture Battery Number 11. Other Confederate units, still en route, would assist in exploiting the breakthrough; meantime, a division of cavalry would move through the fractured Federal line and drive in the direction of Grant's supply base at City Point. Given the disparity of forces, the chances of success were minuscule. However, desperate circumstances called for desperate measures, and Lee believed that a forlorn-hope gamble was preferable to passively awaiting an enemy blow that might prove lethal.

In its initial stages the assault proceeded with clock-like precision. The axmen quickly cleared a way for the infantry, and Battery Number 10 was seized almost before the drowsy Federals realized they were under attack. An assault on Fort Stedman was then spearheaded by the 6th and 57th North Carolina. "[T]he command was given to go forward," Pvt. W. J. Walker of the 6th wrote, "and we leaped over the breast works and gave a yell and made one mighty rush and in lest [sic] time than it would take to mention, we were inside of the enemy works."[268] With Fort Stedman in Confederate hands, some elements of the center column, including Lewis's and Lt. Col. John G. Kasey's (formerly Hoffman's) Brigades, advanced beyond the fort, driving the disorganized Federals from four successive positions. The right column, with help from some of the Fort Stedman victors, overran Batteries Number 11 and 12. However, at that juncture the plan began to unravel. Reports arrived that the three 100-man squads were unable to locate their objectives and were wandering aimlessly about the field. The left column, moving along the Federal works, was halted by heavy artillery fire and determined resistance at Battery Number 9. On the right, the Confederates were repulsed in three separate attacks on Fort Haskell, the next fortification down the line. Beyond Fort Stedman, Lewis's and Kasey's troops encountered Federal

267. W. J. Walker to his father and mother, March 16, 1865, Walker Papers. "We keep up a regular Sharpshooting every night all the time," Sgt. J. K. Walker wrote on March 21, "but remain quiet in the day time. We can talk to each other from one breastwork to the other and have exchanged some newspapers but that is stopped[.] [O]ur fair is about like it has been and our quarters very common made of Tents and Bomb Proofs. . . . The most of the Boys are very well contented I believe." Pvt. George G. Dailey of the 6th North Carolina succinctly summed up matters as follows: "This is the worst place I ever was at for we have so much hard duty to doe hear we cant rest day nor inght [sic]. . . ." J. K. Walker to his brother, March 21, 1865, and George Graham Dailey to Garrison Walker, March 28, 1865, Walker Papers.

268. W. J. Walker to his father and mother, March 28, 1865, Walker Papers. See also Jones, "Fifty-seventh Regiment," in Clark, *Histories of the North Carolina Regiments*, 3:423-424; J. D. Barrier, "Breaking Grant's Line," *Confederate Veteran* 33 (November 1925): 417-418.

artillery and infantry on a crest and fell back to a point about 200 yards east of the fort. Gordon called for reinforcements, but they failed to arrive. Meanwhile, Federal reinforcements began reaching the scene, adding their musketry to the increasing barrage of shells.

Around 7:30 A.M. Confederate units near Fort Haskell, demoralized by the ferocious bombardment, began falling back toward Fort Stedman with Union infantrymen on their heels. In the absence of orders to retreat, some of Kasey's Virginians held their positions beyond Fort Stedman and were cut off. Most of Lewis's troops made it back to the fort, where they were subjected to a "tirrible fire of both Musketry and Artillery." Lee then canceled the operation and ordered all units to withdraw. By that time, "a hurricane of shells" swept the no-man's-land between Fort Stedman and the Confederate line. "[I]t look[ed] almost impossible for any of us to escape," Pvt. W. J. Walker wrote. "[T]he grape and shell was comeing so thik that several laid down and was taken Prisoners but when I thought of Point Look[out] you better know I come out. . . ."[269] Five members of the 57th North Carolina were killed or mortally wounded, 11 wounded, and 63 captured (of whom 4 were wounded). Among the wounded was Lieutenant Colonel Jones, who was replaced as regimental commander by Capt. John Beard of Company C. The regiment also lost its battleflag, which was captured by Sgt. Maj. Charles H. Pinkham of the 57th Regiment Massachusetts Volunteer Infantry. Casualties in Lewis's Brigade, according to one report, numbered 271 killed, wounded, and missing.[270] Total Confederate losses were around 3,500, of whom the Federals claimed 1,949 were taken prisoner and "about 200" killed. Federal losses were officially reported as 72 killed, 450 wounded, and 522 captured or missing.[271]

An afternoon of sharp skirmishing on March 25 was followed by a quiet day on the twenty-sixth while the two sides buried their dead.[272] At 4:00 A.M. on March 27 Lewis's men retook their picket line, which had been lost to the Federals two days earlier. Picket firing and occasional cannonading continued through the twenty-eighth. A sudden attack by the Federals on the night of March 29 produced, in the words of Chaplain Paris, an "awfully grand" fireworks display lasting more than two hours. According to Paris, Lewis's Brigade lost three men killed and thirteen wounded. No ground was gained or lost by either side.[273]

In the meantime Phil Sheridan's victorious Army of the Shenandoah, having all but destroyed the remnants of Early's army at Waynesboro, Virginia, on March 2, joined Grant.

---

269. J. K. Walker to _____, [March 27], 1865 (first quotation), and W. J. Walker to his father and mother, March 28, 1865 (third quotation), Walker Papers; Williams, "Fifty-fourth Regiment," in Clark, *Histories of the North Carolina Regiments*, 3:282 (second quotation). See also R. D. Funkhouser, "Fort Stedman–'So Near and Yet So Far,'" *Confederate Veteran* 19 (May 1911): 217-218. "It did not luok much like giting back [alive]," Pvt. G. G. Dailey of the 6th North Carolina wrote, "but I thank God I got out with out ben hurt whiel the men fell all around me. . . ." G. G. Dailey to Garrison Walker, March 28, 1865, Walker Papers.

270. See *Official Records (Army)*, ser. 1, 46 (pt. 1):335, 340, 1032. Casualty statistics for the 57th North Carolina are derived from service record data compiled for this volume. The casualty figure for Lewis's Brigade is quoted in Iobst, *The Bloody Sixth*, 252.

271. *Official Records (Army)*, ser. 1, 46 (pt. 1):321 (see also 71).

272. See Paris Diary, March 25, 1865. The mayhem wrought by the Federal artillery was particularly ghastly. "[O]ur Dead was brought in and put in a pit," Pvt. W. J. Walker wrote, "and sutch a sight I never saw before[:] some with there heads arms [and] legs off. . . ." W. J. Walker to his father and mother, March 28, 1865, Walker Papers. See also Jesse Hill to Emoline Hill, March 6[26?], 1865, in Ripple, *Jesse Hill Letters*.

273. Paris Diary, March 29, 1865 (see also March 26-28, 1865).

Anticipating an immediate attack on his remaining supply routes to the south, Lee concentrated most of his cavalry west of Petersburg and, on the evening of March 29, ordered Confederate infantry units to join them. Maj. Gen. George E. Pickett assumed command of the force. On March 29 the Federal movement began with Sheridan's cavalrymen making a wide detour to the east and south of Petersburg before turning northwest. At the same time, a powerful Federal infantry force under Maj. Gen. G. K. Warren advanced slowly westward through rain and mud and crossed the Boydton Plank Road. Warren continued to inch westward through torrential rain on March 30, and Sheridan reached the road junction at Five Forks before falling back in the face of Pickett's infantry. Severe fighting occurred on March 31 as Pickett drove Sheridan back to Dinwiddie Court House and Warren came under attack by troops commanded by Bushrod Johnson. At Five Forks the next day Pickett's force of about 19,000 men was subjected to a late-afternoon surprise attack by the 50,000-man army of Sheridan and Warren and driven from the field in disorder. That calamity uncovered the western flank of the entire Confederate defense system and opened an avenue to the rear of the Petersburg fortifications. Grant then gave orders for an assault on the Confederate lines south of Petersburg.

Walker's Division was still in position near Fort Stedman at eleven o'clock on the night of April 1 when, Chaplain Paris wrote, "the enemy opened . . . a most terrible bombardment, from all his guns, and a furious attack of his sharp Shooters which lasted until after One Oclock, when it lulled. I had to fly from the house in which I am lodging and Seek safety behind a brick Wall. . . ." Around 3:00 A.M. another "hideous" bombardment rocked Lewis's lines.[274] From Fort Mahone (at the junction of Petersburg's eastern and southern defenses) westward, Federal units formed up for an attack scheduled for 4:00 A.M. North of Fort Mahone, where the Confederate works were older and more formidable, Federal units prepared to demonstrate to prevent the dispatch of reinforcements south of the city. At the appointed hour, the Federals surged forward. On Gordon's right, the Confederates lost and then recaptured Fort Mahone in heavy fighting. Lewis's Brigade, still in the vicinity of Fort Stedman, lost parts of its line to weak Federal probes but then struck back hard, throwing the Federals out and forcing them to call for reinforcements. Southwest of Petersburg, along A. P. Hill's front, a debacle of Five Forks dimensions occurred as the Federals swept forward in waves and stormed into the Confederate rear. Only the heroic defense of Fort Gregg prevented the isolation and destruction of Confederate units east and southeast of Petersburg. Left with no choice except a hasty withdrawal to the west, Lee issued orders to evacuate Richmond and Petersburg that night. Lee planned to march to Amelia Court House, about forty miles southwest of Richmond, where a stock of badly needed rations supposedly awaited. The army would then attempt to retreat over the Richmond and Danville Railroad to Danville and unite with Gen. Joseph E. Johnston's army moving up from North Carolina.

That night the survivors of the 57th North Carolina, probably numbering no more than 125 men, fell back with the rest of Gordon's Corps through Petersburg, crossed to the north bank of the Appomattox River over one of the Petersburg bridges, and took the road to Chesterfield Court House. After an exhausting, all-night march—"I never laid down,"

274. Paris Diary, April 1-2, 1865.

Chaplain Paris wrote—the men were "well away" down the Chesterfield road by morning.[275] The next day Gordon's men crossed the winding Appomattox at Goode's Bridge and marched toward Amelia Court House, which they reached on the morning of April 5. Unfortunately, the vital rations requisitioned by Lee had failed to arrive, necessitating a twenty-four hour delay while foraging parties scoured the countryside for food and fodder. Meantime, Federal cavalry and infantry, paralleling Lee's line of retreat, slipped ahead of the Confederates, occupied Jetersville, and cut the Richmond and Danville Railroad. Abandoning the railroad, Lee's army moved out of Amelia Court House about noon on the fifth, looping to the northwest to avoid Jetersville. After marching all night in a driving rain, the head of the column, under Longstreet, reached Rice's Station on the South Side Railroad around noon the next day.

Walker's Division, acting with the rest of Gordon's Corps as the rear guard of the army, left Amelia Court House around 5:00 P.M. on April 5. "[V]ery much impeded" by the "miserable management" of the wagon train, the troops marched all night. Presently, Gordon became separated from the center of the Confederate column, under Generals Ewell and Anderson, who in turn lost contact with the van. In what were in effect three separate battles, the commands of Ewell, Anderson, and Gordon were brought to bay on April 6 in the vicinity of Sayler's Creek. Ewell's 3,000-man force was overwhelmed and captured after a brave but brief resistance; Anderson was flanked and routed with the loss of another 3,000. Gordon's Corps attempted to defend the wagon train in a running fight that lasted from about eleven o'clock that morning until about four in the afternoon. When the train became snarled while crossing Sayler's Creek, Gordon took position on a ridge in front of the creek and, with the help of several cannons, momentarily repulsed the Federals in heavy fighting. Gordon was then flanked on both sides and driven across the creek, whereupon his men "broke" and retreated "in confusion." Most of the wagon train and 1,700 prisoners fell into Federal hands. One member of the 57th North Carolina was killed and four captured (of whom one was wounded). Gordon retired with what remained of his command toward Farmville.[276]

Harassed by Federal cavalry, the Army of Northern Virginia moved on, marching all night to reach Farmville, where boxcars loaded with provisions waited. In the midst of a hurried, half-cooked breakfast, word was received that Federal cavalry and infantry were approaching, forcing a hasty retreat over the Farmville bridges to the north side of the rain-swollen Appomattox. There, about three miles north of Farmville, the rear guard, now under General Mahone, was assaulted near Cumberland Church by two divisions of Maj. Gen. Andrew A. Humphreys's II Corps on the morning of April 7. At about the same time, another Federal division attacked what was left of the Confederate wagon train and was beaten back by Gordon.[277] Gordon then moved to the support of Mahone and was followed

275. Paris Diary, April 3, 1865; Ray, "Sixth Regiment," in Clark, *Histories of the North Carolina Regiments*, 1:330.

276. Bryan Grimes to John W. Moore, November 5, 1879, in Cowper, *Letters and Recollections of Bryan Grimes*, 110-111. See also Williams, "Fifty-fourth Regiment," in Clark, *Histories of the North Carolina Regiments*, 3:283. "[A] large portion of the brigade [was] captured," Chaplain Paris wrote. Paris Diary, April 6, 1865.

277. General Lewis was wounded and captured in the fighting near Farmville, and Capt. John Beard of the 57th

shortly thereafter by Longstreet. Unaware that he was beyond the reach of prompt rein-forcement, Humphreys launched a heavy attack and succeeded in turning Mahone's left and seizing several cannons. Grimes's Division of Gordon's Corps then charged the Federals, driving them back and capturing a considerable number of prisoners. Although lacking the strength to overwhelm the Confederates, Humphreys delayed Lee's retreat for the rest of the day.

During the night of April 7 Lee's bone-weary men were on the move again, this time headed for Appomattox Station, on the South Side Railroad, where supplies sent from Lynchburg waited. The army continued its march the next day in a welcome if ominous absence of serious harassment: enemy units in Lee's rear failed to overtake their quarry, while to the south the Federals hurried forward to get across Lee's line of march at Appo-mattox Station. Gordon now took the lead, with Longstreet in the rear. Three miles from Appomattox Station the army bivouacked. At about 9:00 P.M. a short burst of cannon fire was heard from the southwest, followed by silence. Presently, Lee's worst fears were con-firmed: Federal forces had captured the vital supplies at Appomattox Station and blocked his line of retreat.

Later that evening Lee and his generals held their last council of war. The essential questions were: how strong was the Federal force at Appomattox Station, and did it include infantry? Cavalry might be brushed aside, but if infantry units were present in strength it would be impossible for Lee to break through with his haggard, starving, disintegrating army, now reduced to an organized force of perhaps 12,000 men. In that case, surrender would be the only rational option.

Upon hearing the cannon fire at Appomattox Station on the night of April 8, General Grimes, on orders from Gordon, began making preparations for battle the next morning. Before daylight his command, augmented by the 57th North Carolina and other units of Walker's Division, marched through Appomattox Station and, on the opposite side, found the enemy waiting. Shortly thereafter Gordon's entire corps, led by Grimes and supported by the cavalry of Maj. Gen. Fitzhugh Lee, advanced in an attempt to cut a path through the Federals. Sheridan's troopers, expecting infantry support momentarily, slowly fell back, allowing a gap to open in their center that was soon filled by Maj. Gen. Edward O. C. Ord's Army of the James. Grimes then withdrew under orders from Gordon. Presently, Gordon found himself cut off from Fitz Lee and threatened with assault from three directions. In the Confederate rear, Longstreet braced for an attack by a newly arrived Federal corps. Trapped and hopelessly outnumbered, Lee surrendered the Army of Northern Virginia at the nearby hamlet of Appomattox Court House that afternoon.

Chaplain Paris's diary for April 9, written in brief entries as the historic day pro-gressed, is worth quoting in full:

North Carolina assumed command of the brigade. Chaplain Paris wrote in his diary that an "immense amount of our waggons [sic] had to be abandoned and burnt [on April 7], with many Caisons [sic], and much ammunition and baggage destroyed. The very bad condition of the roads and the weak state of our horses and mules ren-dered this step necessary." Paris Diary, April 8, 1865.

Marched at daybreak. At Sunrise the enemy opened fire upon our advance at Appomattox C. House. Line of battle was soon formed, and Sharp shooters thrown forward. The fighting Was animated, and the Yankees driven back; two batteries of artillery of four pieces each were Captured and brought in at half past eight oclock. A flag of truce followed them into our lines immediately with propositions of Surrender to Gen. Lee. Hostilities Soon Ceased, and flags have continued to pass and repass up to this hour, four oclock P.M. Excitement among the officers and men is intense. Many propose to fight on to the bitter end, rather than to Surrender. Others are determined to take to the bushes and then take Care of themselves. I made my Arrangements to take to the woods [and] Reach my family, If possible. I went to my Brigade Commander and he advised against it as an act incompatible [with] my Relationship to my regiment. I Yielded to his Suggestions. At 4:20 P.M. the army was marched up in a dense Column in the field, and addressed by Major Gen. Gordon in the best speech to which I have ever listened. He was followed by Brig. Gens. Walker and [Henry A.] Wise. Governor Wise predicted Our Ultimate triumph. The evening was cloudy and glo[o]my, and sadness pervaded our feelings. The terms of the Surrender were stated to us by Gen. Gordon, and a better feeling [began] to prevail.[278]

On April 12, seventy-nine members of the 57th North Carolina, of whom thirty-one were "bearing arms," were paroled.[279]

---

278. Paris Diary, April 9, 1865. Wise was a former governor of Virginia.

279. "Paroles of the Army of Northern Virginia," Southern Historical Society Papers 15: 196, 202-203. Capt. John H. Miller of Company A, 21st North Carolina, was in command of the 21st, 54th, and 57th North Carolina at Appomattox.

FIELD AND STAFF

COLONELS

GODWIN, ARCHIBALD CAMPBELL

Born in Nansemond County, Virginia, in 1831. Appointed Colonel of this regiment on July 17, 1862. Hospitalized at Richmond, Virginia, October 13, 1862, with icterus. Furloughed for twenty days on October 22, 1862. Returned to duty in November, 1862. Wounded in the knee at Chancellorsville, Virginia, May 4, 1863. Returned to duty prior to May 11, 1863. Captured at Rappahannock Station, Virginia, November 7, 1863. Confined at Old Capitol Prison, Washington, D.C., November 8, 1863. Transferred to Johnson's Island, Ohio, where he arrived on November 14, 1863. Transferred to Point Lookout, Maryland, April 22, 1864. Paroled at Point Lookout on April 27, 1864. Received at City Point, Virginia, April 30, 1864, for exchange. Returned to duty on an unspecified date. Appointed Brigadier General to rank from August 5, 1864. "He was in every sense a magnificent gentleman. He was of commanding presence, being about six feet high and symmetrically formed. He was a man of intelligence, possessed a high order of courage and very great self-reliance, all of which combined to make him the [ideal] type of the Confederate soldier." [Clark's *Regiments* 3:406.]

BEARD, JOHN

Served as Captain of Company C of this regiment. Reported in command of this regiment for most of the period from July 20, 1864, through late February, 1865, and again from March 25 through April 7, 1865. On the latter date he was appointed acting commander of Brig. Gen. William G. Lewis's Brigade.

LIEUTENANT COLONEL

JONES, HAMILTON CHAMBERLAIN, JR.

Previously served as Captain of Company K, 5th Regiment N.C. State Troops. Appointed Lieutenant Colonel of this regiment on July 17, 1862. Reported present on surviving regimental muster rolls through October 31, 1863. Captured at Rappahannock Station, Virginia, November 7, 1863. Confined at Old Capitol Prison, Washington, D.C., November 8, 1863. Transferred to Johnson's Island, Ohio, where he arrived on November 14, 1863. Transferred to Fort Monroe, Virginia, February 8, 1865. Exchanged on February 20, 1865. Returned to duty prior to March 1, 1865. Wounded in the left arm at Fort Stedman, Virginia, March 25, 1865. Paroled at Salisbury on May 12, 1865.

MAJOR

CRAIGE, JAMES ALEXANDER

Previously served as Captain of Company G, 6th Regiment N.C. State Troops. Appointed Major of this regiment on July 17, 1862. Hospitalized at Richmond, Virginia, November 1, 1862, with intermittent fever. Furloughed for sixty days on November 5, 1862. Returned to duty on an unspecified date. Reported present or accounted for in January-April and September-October, 1863. Reported in command of the regiment from November 7 through December 31, 1863. Wounded in the knee at Winchester, Virginia,

July 20, 1864. Hospitalized at Richmond. Furloughed on August 25, 1864. Paroled at Salisbury on May 3, 1865.

ADJUTANTS

SEMPLE, EDWARD A.

Resided in Alabama. Appointed Adjutant (Captain) of this regiment on August 1, 1862. Reported present in November, 1862-February, 1863. Wounded in the groin at Salem Church, Virginia, May 4, 1863. Hospitalized at Richmond, Virginia. Furloughed on May 16, 1863. Appointed Captain of Company A of this regiment to rank from May 20, 1863.

MORRISON, JOSEPH GRAHAM

Previously served as an Aide-de-Camp (Lieutenant) to Lt. Gen. Thomas J. ("Stonewall") Jackson and as a staff officer to Brig. Gen. Robert F. Hoke. Appointed Adjutant (Captain) of this regiment on August 1, 1863. Reported present in September-December, 1863. Appointed Captain of Company F of this regiment in January-April, 1864.

ASSISTANT QUARTERMASTER

McNEELY, WILLIAM G.

Resided in Rowan County. Appointed Assistant Quartermaster (Captain) on July 17, 1862. Reported present or accounted for on surviving company muster rolls through December 31, 1863. "Reassigned" on September 15, 1864.

ASSISTANT COMMISSARIES OF SUBSISTENCE

RIGHTON, STARK A. W.

Resided in Bertie County. Appointed Assistant Commissary of Subsistence (Captain) on August 5, 1862, to rank from August 1, 1862. Hospitalized at Richmond, Virginia, October 14, 1862, with hemiplegia. Furloughed for sixty days on or about November 1, 1862. Captured in Chowan County on February 1, 1863. Confined at Old Capitol Prison, Washington, D.C. Paroled and transferred to City Point, Virginia, where he was received on March 29, 1863, for exchange. Retroactively dropped from the rolls of the regiment on February 5, 1863.

EMERSON, JOHN

Previously served as Sergeant in the Signal Corps. Appointed Assistant Commissary of Subsistence (Captain) of this regiment on April 11, 1863, to rank from February 4, 1863. Relieved from duty with this regiment on July 24, 1863, and appointed post commissary at Buchanan, Virginia.

SURGEONS

CALDWELL, JULIUS A.

Previously served as Assistant Surgeon of the 6th Regiment N.C. State Troops. Appointed Surgeon of this regiment on an unspecified date. Reported present in October, 1862. No further records.

[May have served briefly as Surgeon of the 54th Regiment N.C. Troops and as Assistant Surgeon of the 13th Regiment N.C. Troops (3rd Regiment N.C. Volunteers).]

MORTON, CHARLES S.

Resided in Virginia. Appointed Surgeon of this regiment on November 10, 1862. Reported present or accounted for on surviving company muster rolls through February 29, 1864. Probably served with the 57th Regiment until the end of the war. He was an "able, cool and very efficient" officer who was "universally beloved in the command." [Clark's *Regiments*, 3:428.]

ASSISTANT SURGEON

BINION, ALBIGON H.

Resided in Mississippi. Appointed Assistant Surgeon of this regiment on or about November 9, 1862. Reported present in January-April, 1863. Reported absent on sick furlough of thirty days on October 30, 1863. Reported absent without leave in November-December, 1863. Returned to duty on an unspecified date. Reported present in January-February, 1865. Surrendered at Appomattox Court House, Virginia, April 9, 1865. He was an "able, cool and very efficient" officer who was "universally beloved in the command." [Clark's *Regiments*, 3:428.]

CHAPLAINS

MANN, JAMES E.

Methodist-Episcopalian. Previously served as Captain of Company D of this regiment. Appointed Chaplain of this regiment on February 12, 1863, to rank from January 13, 1863. Resigned on September 18, 1863. Reason he resigned not reported.

ALFORD, JOHN B.

Methodist-Episcopalian. Dates of service with this regiment not reported. Served also as Chaplain of the 51st Regiment N.C. Troops.

MILLER, _____

Presbyterian. Dates of service with this regiment not reported. May have been an itinerant preacher rather than Chaplain of the 57th Regiment. [See John Marcus Hefner to Kizia Hefner, October 17, 1862, in John Marcus Hefner Papers, Private Collections, N.C. Division of Archives and History, Raleigh.]

SERGEANTS MAJOR

GRAY, AUGUSTUS H.

Previously served as Sergeant in Company B of this regiment. Appointed Sergeant Major on November 10, 1862, and transferred to the Field and Staff. Wounded in the leg at Fredericksburg, Virginia, December 13, 1862. Appointed 3d Lieutenant of Company

B of this regiment on December 21, 1862, while absent wounded. [See the Lieutenants' section in the roster for Company B of this regiment.]

EARNHEART, WILLIAM P.

Previously served as Corporal in Company B of this regiment. Appointed Sergeant Major on December 22, 1862, and transferred to the Field and Staff. Reported present through May 11, 1863. Appointed 2nd Lieutenant of Company K of this regiment on May 22, 1863.

TUNSTALL, WILLIAM H.

Previously served as Private in Company H of this regiment. Detailed as acting Sergeant Major of this regiment and transferred to the Field and Staff in May-August, 1863. Captured at Rappahannock Station, Virginia, November 7, 1863. Confined at Point Lookout, Maryland, November 11, 1863. Paroled at Point Lookout on March 16, 1864. Received at City Point, Virginia, March 20, 1864, for exchange. Returned to duty on an unspecified date. Appointed Sergeant Major subsequent to March 20 but prior to July 20, 1864, and assigned to permanent duty with the Field and Staff. Wounded in the abdomen and captured at Winchester, Virginia, July 20, 1864. Hospitalized at Cumberland, Maryland. Transferred to Atheneum Prison, Wheeling, West Virginia, on or about December 1, 1864. Transferred to Camp Chase, Ohio, where he arrived on December 6, 1864. Released at Camp Chase on June 12, 1865, after taking the Oath of Allegiance.

QUARTERMASTER SERGEANTS

FARRIS, JOSEPH B.

Previously served as Private in Company B of this regiment. Appointed Quartermaster Sergeant prior to September 1, 1862, and transferred to the Field and Staff. Discharged at Richmond, Virginia, November 8, 1862, by reason of "double hernia."

McCRAY, WILLIAM JAMES

Previously served as Private in Company I of this regiment and as acting regimental Ordnance Sergeant. Reported on duty as acting Quartermaster Sergeant in March-April, 1863; September-December, 1863; and September-October, 1864.

COMMISSARY SERGEANTS

WILSON, HENRY A.

Previously served as Sergeant in Company H of this regiment. Reported on detail as acting Commissary Sergeant in November-December, 1862, and May-August, 1863. Promoted to the permanent rank of Commissary Sergeant in September-October, 1863. Deserted to the enemy at or near Culpeper, Virginia, on or about November 10, 1863. Confined at Old Capitol Prison, Washington, D.C., November 14, 1863. "Re[leased] on Parole for 10 days per order [of the] Sec[retary] of War" on or about the same date. No further records.

HESTER, JAMES R.

Served as Private in Company I of this regiment. Reported on duty as acting regimental Commissary Sergeant in September-October, 1864.

OGBURN, SIHON ALEXANDER

Previously served as Sergeant in Company D of this regiment. Promoted to Commissary Sergeant in January-February, 1865, and transferred to the Field and Staff. Surrendered at Appomattox Court House, Virginia, April 9, 1865.

ORDNANCE SERGEANTS

McCRAY, WILLIAM JAMES

Served as Private in Company I of this regiment. Reported on duty as acting Ordnance Sergeant in January-February, 1863. Served also as acting regimental Quartermaster Sergeant.

WRIGHT, MINTON AUGUSTUS

Previously served as Private in Company B of this regiment. Appointed Ordnance Sergeant in April-May, 1863, and transferred to the Field and Staff. Appointed 3rd Lieutenant of Company K of this regiment on May 22, 1863.

CHESHIRE, JONATHAN WESLEY

Served as Sergeant in Company K of this regiment. Appointed acting Ordnance Sergeant on or about May 22, 1863, and transferred to the Field and Staff. Reported on duty as acting Ordnance Sergeant through December 31, 1863. Died of disease. Place and date of death not reported.

COMPANY A

This company was raised in Rowan County on July 4, 1862. It was mustered into service at Salisbury on July 17, 1862, and assigned to the 57th Regiment N.C. Troops as Company A. After joining the regiment the company functioned as a part of the regiment, and its history for the remainder of the war is reported as a part of the regimental history.

The following roster was compiled primarily from information in the microfilm edition of the Compiled Service Records of Soldiers Who Served in Organizations from the State of North Carolina (Record Group 109, M270), National Archives and Records Administration, Washington, D.C. Record Group 109 includes enlistment papers, pay vouchers, requisitions, letters of resignation, discharge certificates, and abstracts of medical and prisoner of war returns. Materials relating specifically to this company include a muster-in and descriptive roll dated July 17, 1862, and muster rolls dated July, 1862-December, 1863, and March, 1864-February, 1865.

Also utilized in this roster were *The War of the Rebellion: A Compilation of the Official Records of the Union and Confederate Armies*, the North Carolina Adjutant General's *Roll of Honor*, state militia records, newspaper casualty lists and obituaries, wartime claims for bounty pay and allowances, postwar registers of claims for artificial limbs, Confederate pension applications filed with the states of North Carolina, Tennessee, and Florida, Confederate Soldiers' Home records, and the 1860 and 1870 federal censuses of North Carolina.

A search was made also for relevant letters, diaries, reminiscences, and other manuscripts in the Southern Historical Collection (University of North Carolina-Chapel Hill), the Duke University Library Special Collections Department, and the North Carolina Division of Archives and History.

Among the secondary sources consulted were records of the North Carolina division of the United Daughters of the Confederacy, postwar rosters, regimental and county histories, marriage bond, will, and cemetery indexes, published and unpublished genealogies, biographical dictionaries, the North Carolina *County Heritage Book* series, the *Confederate Veteran*, Walter Clark's *Histories of the Several Regiments and Battalions from North Carolina in the Great War, 1861-'65*, and the North Carolina volume of the extended edition of *Confederate Military History*.

OFFICERS

CAPTAINS

HOWARD, WILLIAM H.

Previously served as Captain of William H. Howard's Company, N.C. Prison Guards. Transferred to this company on July 4, 1862. Resigned on or about August 1, 1862. Reason he resigned not reported.

SLOAN, JAMES H. S.

Born in Rowan County where he resided as a farmer prior to enlisting in Rowan County at age 23. Appointed 2nd Lieutenant on July 17, 1862. Elected Captain on August 8, 1862. Reported present through December 31, 1862. Died in hospital at Richmond, Virginia, January 8, 1863, of "pneumonia."

LORD, WILLIAM CAMPBELL

Previously served as 1st Lieutenant of Company G, 7th Regiment N.C. State Troops. Appointed Captain of this company on March 20, 1863. Wounded in the left lung at Chancellorsville, Virginia, May 4, 1863. Died "in his mother's arms" near Hamilton's Crossing, Virginia, May 20, 1863, of wounds. He was "a gallant and gifted gentleman" and "a model of goodness and excellence." [*Carolina (Weekly) Watchman* (Salisbury), June 1, 1863; Clark's *Regiments*, 3:410.]

MILLER, JESSE W.

Served as 2nd Lieutenant of Company C of this regiment. Reported in command of this company from May 27 through July 31, 1863.

SEMPLE, EDWARD A.

Previously served as Adjutant of this regiment. Appointed Captain of this company to rank from May 20, 1863. Reported absent on wounded furlough through October 31, 1863. Reported on detail at Richmond, Virginia, from November 21, 1863, through September 6, 1864. Reported on detached service at Columbia, South Carolina, in September-October, 1864. Retired from service on December 13, 1864. He was a "gallant and very efficient officer." [Clark's *Regiments*, 3:427.]

BEARD, JOHN

Served as Captain of Company C of this regiment. Reported in command of this company in November-December, 1863.

GRAHAM, FURGERSON M.

Served as 1st Lieutenant of Company C of this regiment. Reported in command of this company in March-April, 1864.

HUNTER, MILES H.

Served as Captain of Company B of this regiment. Reported in command of this company in November-December, 1864.

LIEUTENANTS

CRANFORD, ABNER LOCKE, 1st Lieutenant

Previously served as 1st Lieutenant of Captain William H. Howard's Company, N.C. Prison Guards. Transferred to this company on July 4, 1862. Reported present through October 31, 1862. Wounded at Fredericksburg, Virginia, December 13, 1862. Hospitalized at Richmond, Virginia, where he died on January 2, 1863, of "pneumonia." "He cheerfully performed all the duties appertaining to a soldier's life, and was warmly beloved by the officers and men of his company. . . ." [Carolina (Weekly) Watchman (Salisbury), January 19, 1863.]

EARNHEART, WILLIAM P., 2nd Lieutenant

Previously served as 2nd Lieutenant of Company K of this regiment. Transferred to this company on September 29, 1863. Captured at Rappahannock Station, Virginia, November 7, 1863. Confined at Old Capitol Prison, Washington, D.C., November 8, 1863. Transferred to Johnson's Island, Ohio, where he arrived on November 14, 1863. Transferred to Point Lookout, Maryland, April 22, 1864. Hospitalized at Point Lookout on April 26, 1864, with chronic diarrhoea. Died at Point Lookout on June 9, 1864. Cause of death not reported.

HALL, JOHN ANDERSON, 3rd Lieutenant

Previously served as Private in Capt. William H. Howard's Company, N.C. Prison Guards. Appointed 3rd Lieutenant of this company on July 4, 1862. Resigned on or about December 20, 1862. Reason he resigned not reported; however, his letter of resignation is annotated by Col. Archibald C. Godwin of the 57th Regiment as follows: "[He] resigns to avoid having charges preferred against him by his Company Officers for bad conduct in the battle of the 13th Dec [at Fredericksburg, Virginia]. Being wholly unfit for the position he now holds, I respectfully recommend that his resignation be accepted." Resignation accepted on January 20, 1863.

LESLIE, THOMAS B., 1st Lieutenant

Resided in Iredell County and was by occupation a carriage maker prior to enlisting in Rowan County at age 30, July 4, 1862, for the war. Mustered in as Corporal. Reduced to ranks prior to September 2, 1862. Hospitalized at Richmond, Virginia, October 28, 1862, with intermittent fever. Returned to duty on January 15, 1863. Promoted to Sergeant on June 18, 1863. Reported present through August 31, 1863. Promoted to 1st Sergeant prior to November 1, 1863. Reported present on surviving company muster rolls from September 1, 1863, through February 28, 1865. Appointed 1st Lieutenant on March 19, 1864. Captured at Fort Stedman, Virginia, March 25, 1865. Confined at Old Capitol Prison, Washington, D.C., March 27, 1865. Transferred to Fort Delaware, Delaware, where he arrived on March 31, 1865. Released at Fort Delaware on June 17, 1865, after taking the Oath of Allegiance.

OWEN, J. A., 1st Lieutenant

Enlisted in Rowan County on July 4, 1862, for the war. Mustered in as Corporal. Promoted to 1st Sergeant prior to September 2, 1862. Reported present through December 31, 1862. Elected 3rd Lieutenant on January 24, 1863. Reported present in January-February, 1863. Reported present and in command of the company in March-April, 1863. Wounded in the side and arm at Chancellorsville, Virginia, May 4, 1863. Returned to duty prior to May 11, 1863. Promoted to 2nd Lieutenant on May 20, 1863. Reported in command of the company in May-October, 1863. Promoted to 1st Lieutenant on August 1, 1863. Captured at Rappahannock Station, Virginia, November 7, 1863. Confined at Old Capitol Prison, Washington, D.C., November 8, 1863. Transferred to Johnson's Island, Ohio, where he arrived on November 14, 1863. Died at Johnson's Island on January 5, 1864, of "pneumonia."

PARNELL, BENJAMIN, 1st Lieutenant

Resided in Davie County and was by occupation a smith prior to enlisting in Rowan County at age 34. Appointed 2nd Lieutenant on July 4, 1862. Reported in command of the company in September, 1862-February, 1863. Promoted to 1st Lieutenant on January 8, 1863. Resigned on April 10, 1863, for reasons of health. Resignation accepted on or about April 25, 1863.

PEELER, DAVID D., 2nd Lieutenant

Resided in Rowan County and was by occupation a farmer. Appointed 2nd Lieutenant of this company on an unspecified date (probably subsequent to February 28, 1865). Was about 40 years of age at the time of his appointment. Paroled at Salisbury on May 30, 1865.

NONCOMMISSIONED OFFICERS AND PRIVATES

BAITY, J. W., Private

Resided in Davie County and was by occupation a tobacconist prior to enlisting in Rowan County at age 33, July 4, 1862, for the war. Hospitalized at Richmond, Virginia, on or about October 20, 1862, with remittent fever. Died in hospital at Richmond on or about December 25, 1862, of "variola conf[luen]t."

BEAVER, ALLEN A., Private

Resided in Rowan County where he enlisted at age 25, July 4, 1862, for the war. Reported present in July, 1862-October, 1863. Captured at Rappahannock Station, Virginia, November 7, 1863. Sent to Washington, D.C. Confined at Point Lookout, Maryland, November 11, 1863. Paroled at Point Lookout on March 16, 1864. Received at City Point, Virginia, March 20, 1864, for exchange. Returned to duty in May-August, 1864. Wounded in the leg at Cedar Creek, Virginia, October 19, 1864. Leg amputated. Died in hospital at Mount Jackson, Virginia, October 20, 1864, of wounds.

BEAVER, RINDHOLD E., Private

Previously served as Private in Capt. William H. Howard's Company, N.C. Prison Guards. Enlisted in this company on or about July 4, 1862. Mustered in as Private. Appointed Musician prior to September 1, 1862. Reported present through October, 1862. Wounded in the hip at Fredericksburg, Virginia, December 13,

1862. Hospitalized at Richmond, Virginia. Transferred to hospital at Salisbury on January 17, 1863. Returned to duty in March-April, 1863. Reduced to ranks in May-August, 1864. Reported present on surviving company muster rolls through August 31, 1864. Captured at Fisher's Hill, Virginia, September 22, 1864. Sent to Harpers Ferry, West Virginia. Transferred to Point Lookout, Maryland, where he arrived on October 3, 1864. Released at Point Lookout on June 23, 1865, after taking the Oath of Allegiance.

BECK, HENRY, Private

Resided in Davie County and was by occupation a tobacconist prior to enlisting in Rowan County at age 31, July 4, 1862, for the war. Reported present through October 31, 1862. Hospitalized at Richmond, Virginia, November 25, 1862, with typhoid fever. Transferred to hospital at Farmville, Virginia, December 20, 1862, with "local paralysis." Discharged from service at Farmville on January 8, 1863, by reason of "paralysis of left arm." Took the Oath of Allegiance at Salisbury on June 2, 1865.

BECK, J. W., Private

Resided in Davie County and enlisted in Rowan County at age 23, July 4, 1862, for the war. Reported present through October 31, 1863. Captured at Rappahannock Station, Virginia, November 7, 1863. Sent to Washington, D.C. Confined at Point Lookout, Maryland, November 11, 1863. Paroled at Point Lookout on March 16, 1864. Received at City Point, Virginia, March 20, 1864, for exchange. Reported absent without leave from May 20 through September 6, 1864. Reported absent on a surgeon's certificate in September, 1864-February, 1865. Paroled at Mocksville on June 9, 1865.

BOGER, GEORGE A., Sergeant

Previously served as Private in Capt. William H. Howard's Company, N.C. Prison Guards. Enlisted in this company on or about July 4, 1862. Mustered in as Private. Reported present through October 31, 1863. Promoted to Corporal on June 4, 1863. Captured at Rappahannock Station, Virginia, November 7, 1863. Sent to Washington, D.C. Confined at Point Lookout, Maryland, November 11, 1863. Paroled at Point Lookout on March 16, 1864. Received at City Point, Virginia, March 20, 1864, for exchange. Returned to duty in May-September, 1864. Promoted to Sergeant in September-October, 1864. Reported present through December 31, 1864. Furloughed home on February 18, 1865. Returned to duty on an unspecified date. Surrendered at Appomattox Court House, Virginia, April 9, 1865. Took the Oath of Allegiance at Salisbury on July 8, 1865.

BOGER, JAMES W., Private

Previously served as Private in Capt. William H. Howard's Company, N.C. Prison Guards. Enlisted in this company on or about July 4, 1862. Reported present through September 1, 1862. Sent to hospital at Richmond, Virginia, October 25, 1862. Died in hospital at Richmond on or about November 9, 1862, of "typhoid fever."

BRAWLEY, WILLIAM B., Private

Born in Iredell County and resided in Rowan County where he enlisted at age 19, July 4, 1862, for the war. Hospitalized at Richmond, Virginia, September 18, 1862, with rubeola. Returned to duty on November 24, 1862. Sent to hospital on February 20, 1863. Died in hospital at Gordonsville, Virginia, February 26, 1863, of "febris typhoides."

BROCK, J. W., Corporal

Resided in Davie County and was by occupation a farmer prior to enlisting in Rowan County at age 26, July 4, 1862, for the war. Mustered in as Private. Hospitalized at Richmond, Virginia, on or about August 31, 1862. Promoted to Corporal prior to September 1, 1862. Reported in hospital at Richmond on October 3, 1862, with rubeola. Returned to duty on November 4, 1862. Sent to hospital at Richmond on December 31, 1862. Returned to duty on or about March 13, 1863. Reported missing at Gettysburg, Pennsylvania, July 2, 1863. Captured at Gettysburg on or about July 5, 1863. Confined at Fort Delaware, Delaware. Transferred to Point Lookout, Maryland, October 20, 1863. Died at Point Lookout on July 13, 1864. Cause of death not reported.

BUCKLOW, WILLIAM, Private

Place and date of enlistment not reported. Captured and paroled at Athens, Georgia, May 8, 1865.

CASPER, DAVID, Private

Resided in Rowan County and was by occupation a blacksmith prior to enlisting in Rowan County at age 34, July 4, 1862, for the war. Reported present through December 31, 1863. Reported on detached service at Kinston on February 5, 1864. Deserted on or about July 1, 1864. Took the Oath of Allegiance at Salisbury on June 13, 1865.

CLARK, ARCHIBALD A., Private

Resided in Iredell County and enlisted in Rowan County at age 27, July 4, 1862, for the war. Hospitalized at Richmond, Virginia, September 24, 1862. Died in hospital at Richmond on October 16, 1862, of "febris typh[oides]."

COBLE, JAMES A., Private

Previously served as Private in Capt. William H. Howard's Company, N.C. Prison Guards. Enlisted in this company on or about July 4, 1862. Hospitalized at Richmond, Virginia, October 22, 1862, with remittent fever. Died in hospital at Richmond on November 21, 1862, of "typhoid fever."

COPE, FREDERICK T., Private

Resided in Davie County and was by occupation a laborer prior to enlisting in Davie County at age 26, July 4, 1862, for the war. Reported sick at home in July-September, 1862. Reported absent without leave on October 27, 1862. Returned to duty in November-December, 1862. Reported present in January-October, 1863. Captured at Rappahannock Station, Virginia, November 7, 1863. Sent to Washington, D.C. Confined at Point Lookout, Maryland, November 11, 1863. Paroled at Point Lookout on March 16, 1864. Received at City Point, Virginia, March 20, 1864, for exchange. Reported absent without leave from May 20, 1864, through February 28, 1865. Took the Oath of Allegiance at Salisbury on an unspecified date in 1865. [North Carolina pension records indicate that he was wounded at Fredericksburg, Virginia, December 13, 1862.]

CORNELIUS, WILLIAM OSBORNE, Private

Resided in Iredell County and was by occupation a farmer prior to enlisting in Rowan County at age 24, July 4, 1862, for the war. Reported present through October 31, 1862. Hospitalized at Richmond, Virginia, November 27, 1862. Returned to duty on January 7, 1863. Reported present through October 31, 1863. Captured at

Rappahannock Station, Virginia, November 7, 1863. Sent to Washington, D.C. Confined at Point Lookout, Maryland, November 11, 1863. Paroled at Point Lookout on March 16, 1864. Received at City Point, Virginia, March 20, 1864, for exchange. Returned to duty prior to July 20, 1864, when he was captured at Winchester, Virginia. Confined at Camp Chase, Ohio, July 28, 1864. Paroled and transferred to Boulware's Wharf, James River, Virginia, where he was received on March 10-12, 1865, for exchange. Survived the war.

CORRELL, WILLIAM C., Sergeant

Previously served as Corporal in Capt. William H. Howard's Company, N.C. Prison Guards. Enlisted in this company on or about July 4, 1862. Mustered in as Sergeant. Reported present through May 11, 1863. Reported missing at Gettysburg, Pennsylvania, July 2, 1863. Captured at Gettysburg on or about July 5, 1863. Confined at Fort Delaware, Delaware. Transferred to Point Lookout, Maryland, October 20, 1863. Died in hospital at Point Lookout on or about November 24, 1863, of "smallpox."

CRANFORD, HENRY G., Corporal

Resided in Rowan County where he enlisted at age 20, July 4, 1862, for the war. Mustered in as Corporal. Hospitalized at Richmond, Virginia, October 9, 1862, with typhoid fever. Furloughed on November 6, 1862. Returned to duty on February 12, 1863. Wounded in the abdomen, left hip, and left side at Chancellorsville, Virginia, May 4, 1863. Hospitalized at Richmond. Furloughed on or about June 9, 1863. Reported on detached service at Salisbury in November-December, 1863. Reported absent on surgeon's certificate in March-April, 1864. Reported absent without leave from June 15 through September 6, 1864. Rejoined the company prior to October 31, 1864, but was declared unfit for duty. Reported on detached duty at Staunton, Virginia, from November 26 through December 31, 1864. Returned to duty with the company in January-February, 1865. Surrendered at Appomattox Court House, Virginia, April 9, 1865.

CRAVER, JAMES WISEMAN, Private

Born in Davidson County on January 22, 1837. Resided in Davidson County and was by occupation a farmer prior to enlisting in Rowan County at age 25, July 4, 1862, for the war. Reported present through October 31, 1862. Wounded at Fredericksburg, Virginia, December 13, 1862. Died near Fredericksburg on December 14, 1862, of wounds.

DEAL, ANDREW A., Private

Resided in Rowan County where he enlisted at age 18, July 4, 1862, for the war. Reported present through October 31, 1862. Wounded in the foot at Fredericksburg, Virginia, December 13, 1862. Hospitalized at Richmond, Virginia. Furloughed for forty days on January 4, 1863. Returned to duty in March-May, 1863. Reported present through October 31, 1863. Captured at Rappahannock Station, Virginia, November 7, 1863. Sent to Washington, D.C. Confined at Point Lookout, Maryland, November 11, 1863. Paroled at Point Lookout on March 9, 1864. Received at City Point, Virginia, March 15, 1864, for exchange. Hospitalized at Richmond the same date with debility. Furloughed for sixty days on March 16, 1864. Hospitalized at Winchester, Virginia, July 22, 1864, with diarrhoea. Reported in hospital at Charlottesville, Virginia, August 17, 1864, with debilitas. Transferred to hospital at Lynchburg, Virginia, August 18, 1864. Returned to duty on an unspecified date. Hospitalized at Richmond on November 13, 1864, with a gunshot contusion of the right hand. Place and date wounded not reported.

Returned to duty on December 24, 1864. Captured at Hatcher's Run, Virginia, February 6, 1865. Confined at Point Lookout on February 9, 1865. Released at Point Lookout on June 12, 1865, after taking the Oath of Allegiance.

DEAL, LEVI A., Private

Resided in Rowan County where he enlisted at age 27, July 4, 1862, for the war. Reported present through October 31, 1862. Wounded slightly at Fredericksburg, Virginia, December 13, 1862. Returned to duty prior to January 1, 1863. Reported present through August 31, 1863. Hospitalized at Orange Court House, Virginia, on or about October 9, 1863, with an unspecified illness. Returned to duty in November-December, 1863. Reported present in March-October, 1864. Detailed for provost guard duty on an unspecified date. Hospitalized at Richmond, Virginia, December 10, 1864, with remittent fever. Returned to duty on December 24, 1864. Reported present with the company in January-February, 1865. Paroled at Salisbury on May 18, 1865. Took the Oath of Allegiance at Salisbury on July 10, 1865.

DEAL, WILLIAM E., Private

Resided in Rowan County and was by occupation a farmer prior to enlisting at Camp Holmes, near Raleigh, at age 33, March 9, 1864, for the war. Hospitalized at Richmond, Virginia, May 16, 1864, with a gunshot wound of the forearm. Place and date wounded not reported. Furloughed for sixty days on June 3, 1864. Reported present but disabled and on duty at division headquarters in November-December, 1864. Returned to duty with the company in January-February, 1865. Surrendered at Appomattox Court House, Virginia, April 9, 1865. Took the Oath of Allegiance at Salisbury on July 11, 1865.

ELLIOTT, J. H., Private

Enlisted at Rowan County at age 20, July 5, 1862, for the war. Transferred to Company K of this regiment on or about July 17, 1862.

EMERY, WILLIAM W., Private

Previously served as Sergeant in Capt. William H. Howard's Company, N.C. Prison Guards. Enlisted in this company on or about July 4, 1862, as a substitute. Reported present through October 31, 1863. Captured at Rappahannock Station, Virginia, November 7, 1863. Sent to Washington, D.C. Confined at Point Lookout, Maryland, November 11, 1863. Paroled at Point Lookout on March 16, 1864. Received at City Point, Virginia, March 20, 1864, for exchange. Returned to duty subsequent to April 30, 1864. Reported absent on detached service at Salisbury from July 7 through December 31, 1864. Rejoined the company in January-February, 1865. Captured near Petersburg, Virginia, April 2, 1865. Confined at Hart's Island, New York Harbor, April 7, 1865. Released at Hart's Island on June 17, 1865, after taking the Oath of Allegiance.

ETCHISON, C. H., Private

Resided in Davie County and enlisted in Rowan County at age 28, July 4, 1862, for the war. Hospitalized at Richmond, Virginia, October 10, 1862, with rubeola. Returned to duty on November 4, 1862. Hospitalized at Richmond on January 28, 1863. Returned to duty on February 21, 1863. Reported present through October 31, 1863. Captured at Rappahannock Station, Virginia, November 7, 1863. Confined at Point Lookout, Maryland, November 11, 1863. Paroled at Point Lookout on March 16, 1864. Received at City Point, Virginia, March 20, 1864, for exchange. Returned to duty subsequent to April 30, 1864. Captured at Fisher's Hill, Virginia, September 22, 1864. Sent to Harpers Ferry, West Virginia. Confined at Point Lookout, Maryland, October 3, 1864. Paroled at Point Lookout on or about February 13, 1865. Received at Cox's Wharf, James River, Virginia, February 14-15, 1865, for exchange. Reported present in camp near Richmond on February 19, 1865. No further records. Survived the war.

EVANS, OBADIAH, Private

Born in Davidson County and resided in Forsyth County where he was by occupation a farmer prior to enlisting at Camp Holmes, near Raleigh, at age 40, March 1, 1864, for the war. Deserted on May 1, 1864. Returned to duty prior to September 6, 1864. Captured at Winchester, Virginia, September 19, 1864. Sent to Harpers Ferry, West Virginia. Confined at Point Lookout, Maryland, September 26, 1864. Released at Point Lookout on October 14, 1864, after taking the Oath of Allegiance and joining the U.S. Army. Assigned to Company A, 4th Regiment U.S. Volunteer Infantry.

EVERHART, F. H., Private

Resided in Davidson County and enlisted in Rowan County at age 23, July 4, 1862, for the war. Reported present through February 28, 1863. Wounded in the chest (ribs fractured) at Chancellorsville, Virginia, May 4, 1863. Hospitalized at Richmond, Virginia. Furloughed for sixty days on June 11, 1863. Reported absent without leave from August 17 through December 31, 1863. Returned to duty prior to April 30, 1864. Reported absent without leave from May 7, 1864, through February 28, 1865. Survived the war.

EVERHART, ROBERT, Private

Enlisted at Camp Holmes, near Raleigh, March 1, 1864, for the war. Reported present through April 30, 1864. Hospitalized at Richmond, Virginia, May 29, 1864. Died in hospital at Richmond on or about July 12, 1864, of disease.

FABY, J. H., Private

Enlisted in Rowan County at age 21, July 5, 1862, for the war. Discharged on or about July 17, 1862. Reason discharged not reported.

FEEZOR, J. H., Private

Resided in Davidson County and enlisted in Rowan County at age 24, July 4, 1862, for the war. Hospitalized at Richmond, Virginia, September 26, 1862, with mumps. Returned to duty on October 6, 1862. Reported present or accounted for through October 31, 1864. Served as a teamster during much of that period. Reported absent on furlough in November-December, 1864. Returned to duty prior to February 6, 1865, when he was captured at Hatcher's Run, Virginia. Confined at Point Lookout, Maryland, February 9, 1865. Released at Point Lookout on June 27, 1865, after taking the Oath of Allegiance.

FISHER, JACOB RUFUS, Private

Resided in Rowan County and was by occupation a farmer prior to enlisting in Rowan County at age 26, July 4, 1862, for the war. Reported present through October 31, 1862. Wounded in the hip at Fredericksburg, Virginia, December 13, 1862. Returned to duty in March-April, 1863. Wounded in the leg at Chancellorsville, Virginia, May 4, 1863. Returned to duty prior to May 11, 1863. Hospitalized at Charlottesville, Virginia, August 31, 1863, with intermittent fever. Returned to duty on September 22, 1863. Captured at Rappahannock Station, Virginia, November 7, 1863. Sent to

Washington, D.C. Confined at Point Lookout, Maryland, November 11, 1863. Paroled at Point Lookout on March 16, 1864. Received at City Point, Virginia, March 20, 1864, for exchange. Returned to duty prior to July 20, 1864, when he was captured (may have been slightly wounded) at Winchester, Virginia. Confined at Camp Chase, Ohio, July 28, 1864. Released at Camp Chase on March 23, 1865, after taking the Oath of Allegiance.

FREELAND, C. A., Private

Resided in Iredell County and enlisted in Rowan County at age 17, July 4, 1862, for the war as a substitute. Mustered in as Private. Hospitalized at Richmond, Virginia, September 25, 1862, with measles. Returned to duty on October 18, 1862. Reported present in November, 1862-October, 1863. Promoted to Corporal on August 9, 1863. Captured at Rappahannock Station, Virginia, November 7, 1863. Sent to Washington, D.C. Confined at Point Lookout, Maryland, November 11, 1863. Paroled at Point Lookout on March 16, 1864. Received at City Point, Virginia, March 20, 1864, for exchange. Reduced to ranks in May-August, 1864. Wounded in the right thigh at Smithfield, West Virginia, August 29, 1864. Captured in hospital at Winchester, Virginia, September 19, 1864. Transferred to hospital at Baltimore, Maryland, December 17, 1864. Confined at Fort McHenry, Maryland, February 10, 1865. Paroled and transferred on February 20, 1865, for exchange. Exchanged on an unspecified date. Hospitalized at Richmond on March 2, 1865, with debilitas. Furloughed for thirty days on March 13, 1865.

FREELAND, SAMUEL F., Private

Resided in Iredell County and enlisted in Rowan County at age 32, July 4, 1862, for the war. Hospitalized at Richmond, Virginia, October 27, 1862, with typhoid pneumonia. Furloughed for thirty days on November 14, 1862. Returned to duty in March-May, 1863. Hospitalized at Orange Court House, Virginia, on or about October 9, 1863. Returned to duty in November-December, 1863. Reported present on surviving company muster rolls through February 28, 1865. Captured at Farmville, Virginia, April 6, 1865. Confined at Newport News, Virginia, April 14, 1865. Released at Newport News on June 26, 1865, after taking the Oath of Allegiance.

FURCHES, LEWIS ALEXANDER, Private

Resided in Davie County and enlisted in Rowan County at age 29, July 4, 1862, for the war. Reported present through October 31, 1862. Wounded in the breast at Fredericksburg, Virginia, December 13, 1862. Hospitalized at Richmond, Virginia. Furloughed for forty days on or about February 13, 1863. Reported absent wounded or absent on furlough until January 18, 1864, when he was reported absent without leave. Returned to duty in September-October, 1864. Reported present but on duty at division headquarters in November-December, 1864. Rejoined the company in January-February, 1865. Surrendered at Appomattox Court House, Virginia, April 9, 1865.

GRAHAM, JOHN W., Private

Resided in Rowan County where he enlisted at age 27, July 4, 1862, for the war. Reported present through February 28, 1863. Hospitalized at Richmond, Virginia, May 20, 1863, with chronic diarrhoea. Furloughed for thirty days (convalescent from typhoid fever) on or about July 11, 1863. Returned to duty prior to August 31, 1863. Reported present on surviving company muster rolls through December 31, 1864. Captured at Hatcher's Run, Virginia, February 6, 1865. Confined at Point Lookout, Maryland, February

9, 1865. Released at Point Lookout on June 27, 1865, after taking the Oath of Allegiance.

GRAHAM, W., Private

Resided in Rowan County where he enlisted at age 21, July 4, 1862, for the war. Reported present through October 31, 1862. Discharged on or about November 4, 1862. Reason discharged not reported.

GRANT, A. T., Private

Resided in Davie County and enlisted in Rowan County at age 24, July 4, 1862, for the war. Reported present through May 31, 1863. Served as a hospital clerk and surgeon's orderly during much of that period. Reported present on surviving company muster rolls through December 31, 1864. Captured at Hatcher's Run, Virginia, February 6, 1865. Confined at Point Lookout, Maryland, February 9, 1865. Released at Point Lookout on June 16, 1865, after taking the Oath of Allegiance.

GRAY, DAVID Z., Private

Born on May 29, 1835. Resided in Iredell County and enlisted in Rowan County at age 27, July 4, 1862, for the war. Mustered in as Sergeant. Reported present through December 31, 1862. Sent to hospital on February 20, 1863. Furloughed home on an unspecified date. Returned to duty in May-August, 1863. Reduced to ranks on June 4, 1863. Discharged on or about October 27, 1863. Reason discharged not reported.

GRAY, SAMUEL B., Private

Resided in Iredell County and enlisted in Rowan County at age 31, July 4, 1862, for the war. Reported present through October 31, 1862. Hospitalized at Lynchburg, Virginia, on or about December 12, 1862. Died in hospital at Lynchburg on December 19, 1862, of "hepatitis chron[ica]."

HARKEY, WILLIAM L., Sergeant

Previously served as Private in Capt. William H. Howard's Company, N.C. Prison Guards. Enlisted in this company on or about July 4, 1862. Mustered in as Private. Reported present through February 28, 1863. Promoted to Sergeant on February 2, 1863. Wounded at Chancellorsville, Virginia, May 4, 1863. Died on May 5, 1863, of wounds. Place of death not reported.

HARRISON, RICHARD, Sergeant

Resided in Rowan County and was by occupation a cabinetmaker prior to enlisting in Rowan County at age 32, July 4, 1862, for the war. Mustered in as Private. Promoted to Corporal in November-December, 1862. Reported present through December, 1862. Furloughed home on February 10, 1863. Returned to duty in March-May, 1863. Promoted to Sergeant on June 4, 1863. Reported present through October 31, 1863. Captured at Rappahannock Station, Virginia, November 7, 1863. Sent to Washington, D.C. Confined at Point Lookout, Maryland, November 11, 1863. Paroled at Point Lookout on March 16, 1864. Received at City Point, Virginia, March 20, 1864, for exchange. Returned to duty subsequent to April 30, 1864. Killed at Cedar Creek, Virginia, October 19, 1864. [See obituary in *Daily Carolina Watchman* (Salisbury), November 7, 1864.]

HARTSELL, JONAS, 1st Sergeant

Resided in Stanly County and enlisted in Rowan County at age 23, July 4, 1862, for the war. Mustered in as Private. Reported present through October 31, 1863. Captured at Rappahannock Station, Virginia, November 7, 1863. Confined at Point Lookout, Maryland. Paroled at Point Lookout on March 16, 1864. Received at City Point, Virginia, March 20, 1864, for exchange. Returned to duty in May-September, 1864. Promoted to Sergeant in September-October, 1864. Reported present in September, 1864-February, 1865. Promoted to 1st Sergeant on or about December 1, 1864. Captured at Farmville, Virginia, April 6, 1865. Confined at Newport News, Virginia, April 14, 1865. Released at Newport News on June 26, 1865, after taking the Oath of Allegiance. [May have served previously as Captain in the 83rd Regiment N.C. Militia.]

HELLARD, JOE, Private

Resided in Davie County and enlisted in Rowan County at age 30, July 4, 1862, for the war. Hospitalized at Richmond, Virginia, October 29, 1862, with chronic diarrhoea. Furloughed for sixty days on November 28, 1862. Died at home in Davie County on January 4, 1863, of "typhoid pneumonia & diarrhoea."

HELLARD, THOMAS, Private

Resided in Davie County and enlisted in Rowan County at age 33, July 4, 1862, for the war. Reported present through May 11, 1863. Killed at Gettysburg, Pennsylvania, July 2, 1863.

HINSON, HENRY, Private

Previously served as Corporal in Capt. William H. Howard's Company, N.C. Prison Guards. Enlisted in this company on or about July 4, 1862, as a substitute. Deserted at or near Charles City Court House, Virginia, September 24, 1862.

HINSON, JOHN D., Private

Previously served as Private in Capt. William H. Howard's Company, N.C. Prison Guards. Enlisted in this company on or about July 4, 1862. Left sick at Salisbury on or about August 25, 1862. Reported absent without leave on or about December 1, 1862. Apprehended on an unspecified date. Confined at Castle Thunder Prison, Richmond, Virginia. Hospitalized at Richmond on February 25, 1863, with variola. Transferred back to Castle Thunder Prison on May 18, 1863. Sent to hospital at Jordan's Springs, Virginia, June 16, 1863. Returned to duty on an unspecified date. Reported absent without leave from October 25 through December 31, 1863. Returned to duty prior to April 30, 1864. Reported absent without leave from May 15 through September 6, 1864. Returned to duty prior to October 31, 1864. Wounded in the left leg near Petersburg, Virginia, December 10-12, 1864. Left leg amputated. Furloughed on January 26, 1865. Survived the war.

HODGENS, J. H., Private

Resided in Rowan County where he enlisted at age 25, July 4, 1862, for the war. Sent to hospital sick on September 14, 1862. Returned to duty on October 12, 1862. Hospitalized at Richmond, Virginia, December 12, 1862, with pneumonia or debilitas. Transferred on January 16, 1863. Returned to duty on an unspecified date. Hospitalized at Richmond on May 7, 1863, with typhoid pneumonia. Returned to duty on May 28, 1863. Reported present through October 31, 1863. Captured at Rappahannock Station, Virginia, November 7, 1863. Sent to Washington, D.C. Confined at Point Lookout, Maryland, November 11, 1863. Exchanged on September 30, 1864. Reported absent without leave from December 5, 1864, through February 28, 1865. Took the Oath of Allegiance at Salisbury on June 7, 1865.

HODGENS, JORDAN C., Private

Resided in Rowan County where he enlisted at age 23, July 4, 1862, for the war. Hospitalized at Richmond, Virginia, September 25, 1862, with measles. Returned to duty on October 28, 1862. Detailed for duty as a blacksmith on January 2, 1863. Rejoined the company in March-May, 1863. Hospitalized at Charlottesville, Virginia, June 10, 1863, with acute diarrhoea and inflammation of the hip joint. Furloughed for forty days on July 29, 1863. Returned to duty in September-October, 1863. Captured at Rappahannock Station, Virginia, November 7, 1863. Sent to Washington, D.C. Confined at Point Lookout, Maryland, November 11, 1863. Released at Point Lookout on June 27, 1865, after taking the Oath of Allegiance.

HOUSTON, JAMES A., Sergeant

Resided in Rowan County where he enlisted at age 33, July 4, 1862, for the war. Mustered in as Sergeant. Reported present through October 31, 1862. Wounded at Fredericksburg, Virginia, December 13, 1862. Hospitalized at Scottsville, Virginia, where he died on or about January 1, 1863, of wounds.

HUFFMAN, D. A., Private

Previously served as Private in Capt. William H. Howard's Company, N.C. Prison Guards. Enlisted in this company on or about July 4, 1862. Discharged on or about July 17, 1862. Reason discharged not reported. Later served as Private in Company G, 66th Regiment N.C. Troops.

HURDT, JESSE C., Private

Born in Montgomery County and was by occupation a shoemaker prior to enlisting at Camp Holmes, near Raleigh, March 7, 1864, for the war. Deserted at Kinston on May 1, 1864. Later served as Private in Company A, 3rd Regiment N.C. Mounted Infantry (Union). [Was about 33 years of age at time of enlistment.]

JOHNSON, T. J., ———

North Carolina pension records indicate that he served in this company.

JOHNSTON, JOSEPH D., Private

Resided in Rowan County where he enlisted at age 18, July 4, 1862, for the war. Reported present through October 31, 1862. Sent to hospital on December 30, 1862. Admitted to hospital at Richmond, Virginia, January 19, 1863, with pneumonia. Furloughed for sixty days on March 16, 1863. Died in Rowan County on April 16, 1863, of disease.

JOSEY, LAFAYETTE, Private

Born in Rowan County on August 2, 1836. Resided in Rowan County and was by occupation a house painter or farmer prior to enlisting in Rowan County at age 25, July 4, 1862, for the war. Reported present through February 28, 1863. Wounded in the right thigh at Chancellorsville, Virginia, May 4, 1863. Hospitalized at Richmond, Virginia. Reported absent wounded or absent on furlough through December 31, 1863. Detailed for guard duty at the Confederate distillery at Macon, Georgia, April 5, 1864. Furloughed home prior to September 6, 1864. Reported absent on furlough through February 28, 1865. Paroled at Salisbury on an unspecified date. Took the Oath of Allegiance at Salisbury on June 11, 1865.

JOSEY, THEOPHILUS, Private

Born on June 2, 1834. Resided in Rowan County and was by occupation a carriage maker prior to enlisting in Rowan County at age 28, July 4, 1862, for the war. Reported present through October 31, 1863. Captured at Rappahannock Station, Virginia, November 7, 1863. Sent to Washington, D.C. Confined at Point Lookout, Maryland, November 11, 1863. Paroled at Point Lookout and transferred to City Point, Virginia, where he was received on March 20, 1864, for exchange. Returned to duty subsequent to April 30, 1864. Killed at Winchester, Virginia, September 19, 1864.

KELLER, FRALEY THOMAS, Private

Resided in Davie County and was by occupation a farmer prior to enlisting in Rowan County at age 30, July 4, 1862, for the war. Reported present through October 31, 1862. Sent to hospital at Richmond, Virginia, December 15, 1862 (apparently suffering from debilitas). Transferred to hospital at Danville, Virginia, April 23, 1863. Returned to duty in January-April, 1864. Captured near Washington, D.C., July 12, 1864. Confined at Old Capitol Prison, Washington, July 13, 1864. Transferred to Elmira, New York, where he arrived on July 25, 1864. Paroled at Elmira on March 2, 1865, and transferred for exchange. No further records.

KENNERLY, A. M., Private

Resided in Iredell County and enlisted in Rowan County at age 26, July 4, 1862, for the war. Reported present through October 31, 1863. Captured at Rappahannock Station, Virginia, November 7, 1863. Sent to Washington, D.C. Confined at Point Lookout, Maryland, November 11, 1863. Died at Point Lookout on January 15, 1864, of disease.

KEPLEY, JACOB N., Private

Enlisted in Rowan County at age 30, July 4, 1862, for the war. Transferred to Company K of this regiment prior to September 2, 1862.

KETCHEY, JOHN L., Private

Previously served as Private in Capt. William H. Howard's Company, N.C. Prison Guards. Enlisted in this company on or about July 4, 1862. Reported present through May 11, 1863. Reported absent without leave on July 21, 1863. Company muster rolls of later date indicate that he was "lost on [the] march" and presumed captured near New Market, Virginia, July 24, 1863; however, records of the Federal Provost Marshal do not substantiate the report of his capture. No further records.

KILPATRICK, NEWTON LEROY, Private

Resided in Rowan County and was by occupation a farmer prior to enlisting in Rowan County at age 19, July 4, 1862, for the war. Sent to hospital at Petersburg, Virginia, August 22, 1862. Reported absent sick or absent on furlough until February 18, 1863, when he returned to duty. Reported present until August 4, 1863, when he was sent to hospital at Orange Court House, Virginia. Returned to duty in September-October, 1863. Captured at Rappahannock Station, Virginia, November 7, 1863. Sent to Washington, D.C. Confined at Point Lookout, Maryland, November 11, 1863. Paroled at Point Lookout on March 16, 1864. Received at City Point, Virginia, March 20, 1864, for exchange. Returned to duty prior to September 6, 1864. Wounded in the thigh at Cedar Creek, Virginia, October 19, 1864. Reported absent wounded through February 28, 1865. Paroled at Staunton, Virginia, May 10, 1865.

KLUTTZ, ANDREW L., Private

Resided in Rowan County where he enlisted at age 24, July 4, 1862, for the war. Hospitalized at Richmond, Virginia, October 23, 1862, with remittent fever. Furloughed on November 6, 1862. Returned to duty on January 13, 1863. Reported present through October 31, 1863. Captured at Rappahannock Station, Virginia, November 7, 1863. Sent to Washington, D.C. Confined at Point Lookout, Maryland, November 11, 1863. Paroled at Point Lookout on March 16, 1864. Received at City Point, Virginia, March 20, 1864, for exchange. Returned to duty in May-September, 1864. Reported present through February 28, 1865. Surrendered at Appomattox Court House, Virginia, April 9, 1865. Took the Oath of Allegiance at Salisbury on June 10, 1865.

KLUTTZ, CHARLES F., Private

Previously served as Private in Capt. William H. Howard's Company, N.C. Prison Guards. Enlisted in this company on or about July 4, 1862. Reported present through October 31, 1862. Wounded at Fredericksburg, Virginia, December 13, 1862. Returned to duty on April 6, 1863. Wounded in the finger and/or left hand at Chancellorsville, Virginia, May 4, 1863. Reported absent wounded until October 25, 1863, when he was reported absent without leave. Hospitalized at Richmond, Virginia, January 29, 1864, still suffering from wounds received at Chancellorsville. Returned to duty on March 22, 1864. Reported present or accounted for through February 28, 1865. Captured at Fort Stedman, Virginia, March 25, 1865. Confined at Point Lookout, Maryland, March 28, 1865. Released at Point Lookout on June 6, 1865, after taking the Oath of Allegiance.

KLUTTZ, GREEN C., Private

Resided in Davie County and was by occupation a "smith" prior to enlisting in Rowan County at age 27, July 4, 1862, for the war. Transferred to Company K of this regiment on or about July 17, 1862.

LENTZ, HENRY G., Private

Resided in Rowan County and was by occupation a farmer prior to enlisting in Rowan County at age 28, July 5, 1862, for the war. Discharged on or about July 17, 1862. Reason discharged not reported. Died in Rowan County prior to September 25, 1862. Cause of death not reported.

LENTZ, RUFUS C., Private

Resided in Rowan County where he enlisted at age 27, July 4, 1862, for the war. Died at home in Rowan County on or about August 11, 1862. Cause of death not reported.

LEWIS, M. P., Private

Resided in Wilson County. Place and date of enlistment not reported. Paroled at Goldsboro in 1865.

LITTLE, DANIEL M., Private

Resided in Davie County and enlisted in Rowan County at age 24, July 4, 1862, for the war. Reported absent sick at Salisbury on August 12, 1862. Reported absent without leave on October 27, 1862. Returned to duty prior to November 1, 1862. Reported present or accounted for through February 28, 1863. Wounded in the abdomen at Chancellorsville, Virginia, May 4, 1863. Died on or about May 5, 1863, of wounds. Place of death not reported.

LYERLY, HENRY, Private

Resided in Rowan County where he enlisted at age 21, July 4, 1862, for the war. Reported present through December 31, 1862. Furloughed for twenty days on February 18, 1863. Returned to duty prior to May 11, 1863. Wounded in the leg at Gettysburg, Pennsylvania, July 1, 1863. Left in the hands of the enemy. Hospitalized at Gettysburg where he died on July 12, 1863, of wounds.

McKAY, ABRAHAM M., Private

Resided in Iredell County and was by occupation a farmer prior to enlisting in Rowan County at age 28, July 4, 1862, for the war. Reported present through October 31, 1862. Hospitalized at Richmond, Virginia, November 9, 1862, with an unspecified illness. Reported absent sick through May 11, 1863. Returned to duty on an unspecified date. Sent to hospital on September 12, 1863. Returned to duty in January-April, 1864. Captured (may have been wounded also) at Winchester, Virginia, on or about July 20, 1864. Confined at Camp Chase, Ohio, on or about July 28, 1864. Released at Camp Chase on May 13, 1865, after taking the Oath of Allegiance.

McKINNIS, P. H., Private

Resided in Iredell County and enlisted in Rowan County at age 27, July 4, 1862, for the war. Reported present through May 11, 1863. Captured at Gettysburg, Pennsylvania, July 2, 1863. Sent to Fort McHenry, Maryland. Confined at Fort Delaware, Delaware, on or about July 9, 1863. Died at Fort Delaware on March 15, 1864, of "intermittent fever."

McNEELY, SILAS A., Sergeant

Resided in Rowan County where he enlisted at age 29, July 4, 1862, for the war. Mustered in as Private. Hospitalized at Richmond, Virginia, November 25, 1862, with rheumatism (subsequently developed catarrhus and bronchitis). Furloughed for thirty days on January 14, 1863. Reported absent without leave in February, 1863. Returned to duty in March-May, 1863. Reported present in June-October, 1863. Captured at Rappahannock Station, Virginia, November 7, 1863. Sent to Washington, D.C. Confined at Point Lookout, Maryland, November 11, 1863. Paroled at Point Lookout on March 16, 1864. Received at City Point, Virginia, March 20, 1864, for exchange. Returned to duty in May-August, 1864. Promoted to Corporal on December 1, 1864. Reported present through February 28, 1865. Promoted to Sergeant subsequent to February 28, 1865. Wounded in the head at Fort Stedman, Virginia, March 25, 1865. Captured in hospital (probably at Petersburg, Virginia) on April 3, 1865. Hospitalized at Point of Rocks, Virginia, April 23, 1865. Transferred to hospital at Fort Monroe, Virginia, May 17, 1865. Was apparently released on or about June 21, 1865, after taking the Oath of Allegiance.

MENIUS, JOHN C., Private

Resided in Rowan County where he enlisted at age 31, July 4, 1862, for the war. Reported present through October 31, 1863. Captured at Rappahannock Station, Virginia, November 7, 1863. Sent to Washington, D.C. Confined at Point Lookout, Maryland, November 11, 1863. Paroled at Point Lookout on or about November 1, 1864. Received at Venus Point, Savannah River, Georgia, November 15, 1864, for exchange. Reported absent without leave from December 5, 1864, through February 28, 1865. Returned to duty on an unspecified date. Captured at Farmville, Virginia, April 6, 1865. Confined at Newport News, Virginia, April 14, 1865.

Released at Newport News on June 26, 1865, after taking the Oath of Allegiance.

MICHAEL, WILLIAM R., Private

Previously served as Private in Capt. William H. Howard's Company, N.C. Prison Guards. Enlisted in this company on or about July 4, 1862. Reported present through February 28, 1863. Wounded "above the knee" at Chancellorsville, Virginia, May 4, 1863. Reported absent wounded until he was reported absent without leave on or about November 19, 1863. Returned to duty in January-April, 1864. Captured near Washington, D.C., on or about July 12, 1864. Confined at Old Capitol Prison, Washington. Transferred to Elmira, New York, where he arrived on July 25, 1864. Paroled at Elmira on March 14, 1865. Received at Boulware's Wharf, James River, Virginia, March 18-21, 1865, for exchange. Paroled at Greensboro on May 5, 1865.

MILLER, AUGUSTUS L., Private

Previously served as Private in Capt. William H. Howard's Company, N.C. Prison Guards. Enlisted in this company on or about July 4, 1862. Discharged on or about July 17, 1862. Reason discharged not reported.

MILLER, DAVID A., Private

Resided in Rowan County where he enlisted at age 23, July 4, 1862, for the war. Reported present through October 31, 1862. Hospitalized at Richmond, Virginia, January 28, 1863. Returned to duty subsequent to May 11, 1863. "Lost on march" near Hagerstown, Maryland, July 10, 1863, and was captured by the enemy. Confined at Fort Mifflin, Pennsylvania. Transferred to Fort Delaware, Delaware, November 17, 1863. Released at Fort Delaware on June 19, 1865, after taking the Oath of Allegiance.

MILLER, J. A., Private

Enlisted in Rowan County at age 34 on or about July 5, 1862, for the war. No further records.

MILLER, J. R., Private

Resided in Rowan County where he enlisted at age 21, July 4, 1862, for the war. Reported present through October 31, 1862. Wounded at Fredericksburg, Virginia, December 13, 1862. Died near Fredericksburg on December 14, 1862, of wounds.

MILLER, JOHN C. CALHOUN, Private

Resided in Rowan County where he enlisted at age 19, July 4, 1862, for the war. Hospitalized at Richmond, Virginia, September 25, 1862, with measles. Returned to duty on October 25, 1862. Hospitalized at Richmond on November 8, 1862, with parotitis. Transferred on December 1, 1862, to hospital at Danville, Virginia, where he was diagnosed with pneumonia. Returned to duty on January 17, 1863. Reported present through October 31, 1863. Captured at Rappahannock Station, Virginia, November 7, 1863. Sent to Washington, D.C. Confined at Point Lookout, Maryland, November 11, 1863. Paroled at Point Lookout on March 16, 1864. Received at City Point, Virginia, March 20, 1864, for exchange. Returned to duty prior to July 12, 1864, when he was captured near Washington, D.C. Confined at Old Capitol Prison, Washington. Transferred to Elmira, New York, where he arrived on July 25, 1864. Died at Elmira on February 10, 1865, of "variola."

MILLER, JOHN W., Private

Resided in Rowan County where he enlisted at age 19, July 4, 1862, for the war. Reported present or accounted for through December 31, 1862. Sent to hospital on February 21, 1863. Died in hospital at Lynchburg, Virginia, March 4, 1863, of "phthisis pulm[onalis]."

MILLER, STEPHEN W., Sergeant

Previously served as Private in Capt. William H. Howard's Company, N.C. Prison Guards. Enlisted in this company on or about July 4, 1862. Mustered in as Sergeant. Hospitalized at Richmond, Virginia, on or about December 23, 1862. Died in hospital at Richmond on January 21, 1863, of "variola conf[luen]t."

MILLER, W. J., Private

Enlisted in Rowan County at age 29, July 5, 1862, for the war. No further records.

MILLS, WILLIE E., Private

Resided in Iredell County and enlisted in Rowan County at age 19, July 4, 1862, for the war. Hospitalized at Richmond, Virginia, on an unspecified date. Returned to duty on September 30, 1862. Reported present through October 31, 1863. Captured at Rappahannock Station, Virginia, November 7, 1863. Sent to Washington, D.C. Confined at Point Lookout, Maryland, November 11, 1863. Paroled at Point Lookout on March 16, 1864. Received at City Point, Virginia, March 20, 1864, for exchange. Returned to duty prior to June 18, 1864, when he was wounded (probably in the right thigh) at Lynchburg, Virginia. Returned to duty prior to September 22, 1864, when he was captured at Fisher's Hill, Virginia. Sent to Harpers Ferry, West Virginia. Confined at Point Lookout on October 3, 1864. Paroled at Point Lookout on January 17, 1865. Received at Boulware's Wharf, James River, Virginia, January 21, 1865, for exchange. Survived the war.

MOORE, JAMES A., Private

Previously served as Private in Capt. William H. Howard's Company, N.C. Prison Guards. Enlisted in this company on or about July 4, 1862. Hospitalized at Richmond, Virginia, October 9, 1862, with hemoptisis. Returned to duty in November-December, 1862. Reported present in January-February, 1863. Hospitalized at Richmond on May 2, 1863, with rheumatism. Transferred to hospital at Danville, Virginia, May 7, 1863. Transferred to another hospital on July 16, 1863. Returned to duty in January-April, 1864. Captured at Drewry's Bluff, Virginia, May 18, 1864. Confined at Point Lookout, Maryland, May 21, 1864. Paroled at Point Lookout on September 18, 1864. Received at Varina, Virginia, September 22, 1864, for exchange. Reported absent without leave on December 5, 1864. Returned to duty in January-February, 1865. Hospitalized at Danville, Virginia, March 18, 1865. Furloughed for thirty days on April 8, 1865. Paroled at Statesville on May 27, 1865. Took the Oath of Allegiance at Salisbury on June 6, 1865.

MOORE, JOHN H., Private

Resided in Iredell County and enlisted in Rowan County at age 21, July 4, 1862, for the war. Hospitalized at Richmond, Virginia, September 26, 1862, with mumps. Later contracted intermittent fever. Transferred to hospital at Farmville, Virginia, December 20, 1862. Furloughed for thirty days on January 15, 1863. Returned to duty prior to May 4, 1863, when he was wounded in the finger at Chancellorsville, Virginia. Finger amputated. Returned to duty prior to July 2-5, 1863, when he was captured at Gettysburg, Pennsylvania.

Confined at Fort Delaware, Delaware, on or about July 9, 1863. Died at Fort Delaware on April 10, 1864, of "bronchitis chronic."

MOORE, O. R., Private

Resided in Iredell County and was by occupation a shoemaker prior to enlisting in Rowan County at age 23, July 4, 1862, for the war. Reported present through October 31, 1863. Captured at Rappahannock Station, Virginia, November 7, 1863. Sent to Washington, D.C. Confined at Point Lookout, Maryland, November 11, 1863. Released at Point Lookout on May 14, 1865, after taking the Oath of Allegiance.

MOOSE, CHRISTOPHER, Private

Born on April 11, 1833. Resided in Rowan County where he enlisted at age 29, July 4, 1862, for the war. Hospitalized at Richmond, Virginia, September 24, 1862, with an unspecified complaint. Returned to duty in November-December, 1862. Reported present on surviving company muster rolls through April 30, 1864. Reported absent without leave on June 16, 1864. Returned to duty in September-October, 1864. Reported present through February 28, 1865. Wounded in the right hand at Petersburg, Virginia, on or about March 30, 1865. Hospitalized at Richmond. Captured in hospital at Richmond on April 3, 1865. Confined at Libby Prison, Richmond, on an unspecified date. Transferred to Newport News, Virginia, April 23, 1865. Released at Newport News on June 15, 1865, after taking the Oath of Allegiance.

MOWRY, M. J., Private

Enlisted in Rowan County at age 19, July 5, 1862, for the war. Transferred to "Capt Miller's Co" on or about July 17, 1862. [He is probably the same soldier who is listed in the roster for Company K of this regiment as Pvt. A. J. Mowery.]

MURDOCH, DAVID, Private

Resided in Rowan County and was by occupation a carpenter prior to enlisting in Rowan County at age 28, July 5, 1862, for the war. No further records.

NADING, F. S., Private

Enlisted at Camp Holmes, near Raleigh, March 12, 1864, for the war. Reported present through April 30, 1864. Captured at the North Anna River, Virginia, on or about May 23, 1864. Confined at Point Lookout, Maryland, May 30, 1864. Paroled at Point Lookout on March 14, 1865. Received at Boulware's Wharf, James River, Virginia, March 16, 1865, for exchange. No further records.

NADING, NATHANIEL WEBSTER, Private

Resided in Forsyth County and enlisted at Camp Holmes, near Raleigh, at age 27, March 12, 1864, for the war. Reported present through April 30, 1864. Hospitalized at Richmond, Virginia, May 16, 1864, with a gunshot wound of the right shoulder. Place and date wounded not reported. Furloughed for sixty days on June 7, 1864. Reported absent without leave in August, 1864. Reported absent on surgeon's certificate in September-October, 1864. Returned to duty in November-December, 1864. Reported present through February 28, 1865. Captured at Farmville, Virginia, April 6, 1865. Confined at Newport News, Virginia, April 14, 1865. Released at Newport News on June 26, 1865, after taking the Oath of Allegiance.

OVERCASH, L. A., Private

Resided in Iredell County and enlisted in Rowan County at age 25, July 4, 1862, for the war. Reported present through December 31,

1863. Reported on detached service at Kinston in March-April, 1864. Returned to duty prior to July 12, 1864, when he was captured near Washington, D.C. Confined at Old Capitol Prison, Washington. Transferred to Elmira, New York, where he arrived on July 25, 1864. Paroled at Elmira on October 11, 1864. Received at Venus Point, Savannah River, Georgia, November 15, 1864, for exchange. Reported absent without leave on December 5, 1864. Paroled at Statesville on May 28, 1865.

PATTON, JAMES M., Private

Resided in Rowan County and was by occupation a house carpenter prior to enlisting in Rowan County at age 30, July 4, 1862, for the war. Hospitalized at Richmond, Virginia, September 18, 1862, with debility and dyspepsia. Returned to duty on October 1, 1862. Sent to hospital on December 11, 1862. Returned to duty in May-August, 1863. Wounded at Rappahannock Station, Virginia, on or about November 7, 1863. Returned to duty in January-April, 1864. Reported at home on a surgeon's certificate in May-August, 1864. Reported on detached service at Salisbury from September 29, 1864, through February 28, 1865. Paroled at Salisbury on May 2, 1865.

PENNINGER, WILLIAM A., Private

Enlisted in Rowan County at age 30, July 5, 1862, for the war. Transferred to Company K of this regiment on or about July 17, 1862.

PHILLIPS, J. L., Private

Resided in Rowan County where he enlisted at age 25, July 4, 1862, for the war. Reported present through October 31, 1862. Sent to hospital on January 28, 1863. Returned to duty in March-May, 1863. Hospitalized at Charlottesville, Virginia, June 10, 1863, with chronic bronchitis. Furloughed for forty days on July 19, 1863. Returned to duty prior to September 1, 1863. Company records indicate that he was captured at Rappahannock Station, Virginia, November 7, 1863; however, records of the Federal Provost Marshal do not substantiate that report. Was probably killed at Rappahannock Station.

REICH, REUBEN V., Private

Enlisted at Camp Holmes, near Raleigh, March 12, 1864, for the war. Captured at Hanover Junction, Virginia (or near the North Anna River, Virginia), May 23-24, 1864. Confined at Point Lookout, Maryland. Transferred to Elmira, New York, where he arrived on July 26, 1864. Died at Elmira on November 8, 1864, of "chronic diarrhoea."

REYNOLDS, COLUMBUS L., 1st Sergeant

Previously served as Private in Company D, 21st Regiment N.C. Troops (11th Regiment N.C. Volunteers). Enlisted in this company on July 4, 1862, while absent without leave from the 21st North Carolina. Reported present through October 31, 1862. Wounded in the right hip at Fredericksburg, Virginia, December 13, 1862. Hospitalized at Richmond, Virginia. Furloughed for thirty days on December 23, 1862. Promoted to 1st Sergeant on February 2, 1863. Returned to duty in March-May, 1863. Transferred back to Company D, 21st North Carolina, prior to July 5, 1863.

RITCHIE, GEORGE W., Private

Resided in Rowan County where he enlisted at age 26, July 4, 1862, for the war. Hospitalized at Richmond, Virginia, October 7, 1862, with rubeola. Returned to duty in November-December, 1862. Reported present through October 31, 1863. Captured at

Rappahannock Station, Virginia, November 7, 1863. Sent to Washington, D.C. Confined at Point Lookout, Maryland, November 11, 1863. Hospitalized at Point Lookout on November 25, 1863, with "pneumonia acuta." Died in hospital at Point Lookout on December 15, 1863.

RITCHIE, JOHN A., Private

Resided in Rowan County where he enlisted at age 29, July 4, 1862, for the war. Hospitalized at Richmond, Virginia, October 7, 1862, with rubeola. Returned to duty on November 10, 1862. Wounded at Fredericksburg, Virginia, December 13, 1862. Hospitalized at Richmond on April 5, 1863, with erysipelas. Transferred to hospital at Danville, Virginia, April 22, 1863. Returned to duty prior to May 4, 1863, when he was wounded in the hand at Chancellorsville, Virginia. Returned to duty prior to August 31, 1863. Detailed as a hospital nurse at Richmond on October 12, 1863. Reported absent on detail through February 28, 1865. Took the Oath of Allegiance at Salisbury on June 10, 1865.

RITCHIE, PETER A., Private

Born in Rowan County where he resided as a stonecutter or farmer prior to enlisting in Rowan County at age 32, July 4, 1862, for the war. Hospitalized at Richmond, Virginia, September 19, 1862. Returned to duty on September 28, 1862. Discharged on or about October 8, 1862, by reason of "disability caused by ulceration of the foot." Paroled at Salisbury on May 18, 1865. Took the Oath of Allegiance at Salisbury on May 30, 1865.

ROSE, J. J., Corporal

Resided in Iredell County and enlisted in Rowan County at age 31, July 4, 1862, for the war. Mustered in as Private. Promoted to Corporal prior to September 2, 1862. Hospitalized at Richmond, Virginia, November 10, 1862, with an unspecified complaint. Returned to duty on November 17, 1862. Sent to hospital on February 20, 1863. Died at Guinea Station, Virginia, February 24, 1863, of disease.

RUFTY, WILLIAM W., Private

Resided in Rowan County where he enlisted at age 26, July 4, 1862, for the war. Hospitalized at Richmond, Virginia, October 29, 1862, with pneumonia. Transferred to hospital at Farmville, Virginia, December 16, 1862. Furloughed for sixty days from hospital at Farmville on January 22, 1863, convalescent from chronic bronchitis and ascites. Reported absent without leave from April 1, 1863, through February 28, 1865. Paroled at Salisbury on May 15, 1865. Took the Oath of Allegiance at Salisbury on June 14, 1865.

RUSHER, ALFRED WILEY, Sergeant

Resided in Rowan County and was by occupation a farmer prior to enlisting in Rowan County at age 26, July 4, 1862, for the war. Mustered in as Private. Reported present through October 31, 1862. Wounded at Fredericksburg, Virginia, December 13, 1862. Returned to duty prior to January 1, 1863. Promoted to Sergeant on February 2, 1863. Reported present until July 1, 1863, when he was wounded in the foot at Gettysburg, Pennsylvania. Hospitalized at Richmond, Virginia. Furloughed for sixty days on or about July 29, 1863. Reported on detached service at Salisbury in November-December, 1863. Returned to duty on an unspecified date. Reported present in March-April, 1864. Reported on detached service at Richmond from June 15, 1864, through February 28, 1865. Took the Oath of Allegiance at Salisbury on June 24, 1865.

SELLERS, LEMUEL, Private

Place and date of enlistment not reported (probably enlisted subsequent to February 28, 1865). Was about 45 years of age at the time of his enlistment. Paroled at Greensboro on May 14, 1865.

SHOAF, JONATHAN C., Private

Previously served as Private in Capt. William H. Howard's Company, N.C. Prison Guards. Enlisted in this company on or about July 4, 1862. Reported present through February 28, 1863. Hospitalized at Richmond, Virginia, May 1, 1863, with "int[ermittent] fever." Died in hospital at Richmond on or about May 6, 1863.

SHOAF, OTHO H., Private

Resided in Rowan County where he enlisted at age 18, July 4, 1862, for the war. Hospitalized at Richmond, Virginia, September 24, 1862, with an unspecified complaint. Returned to duty on October 15, 1862. Reported present through February 28, 1863. Wounded in the leg at Chancellorsville, Virginia, May 4, 1863. Died in hospital at Richmond on June 12, 1863, of "febris typh[oides]."

SHUPING, A. A., Private

Resided in Rowan County where he enlisted at age 28, July 4, 1862, for the war. Died in a field hospital at Taylor's Farm, Virginia, October 2, 1862, of "rubeola."

SHUPING, W. M., Private

Resided in Rowan County where he enlisted at age 26, July 4, 1862, for the war. Hospitalized at Richmond, Virginia, October 16, 1862, with measles. Furloughed for thirty days on October 24, 1862. Returned to duty in March-May, 1863. Reported present in June-October, 1863. Captured at Rappahannock Station, Virginia, November 7, 1863. Sent to Washington, D.C. Confined at Point Lookout, Maryland, November 11, 1863. Paroled at Point Lookout on March 16, 1864. Received at City Point, Virginia, March 20, 1864, for exchange. Returned to duty in May-August, 1864. Killed at Cedar Creek, Virginia, October 19, 1864.

SIDES, ELI, Private

Resided in Forsyth County and was by occupation a farmer prior to enlisting at Camp Holmes, near Raleigh, at age 40, March 12, 1864, for the war. Reported present through April 30, 1864. Captured (possibly wounded) at Winchester, Virginia, July 20, 1864. Confined at Camp Chase, Ohio, July 28, 1864. Released at Camp Chase on May 13, 1865, after taking the Oath of Allegiance.

SIDES, GEORGE M., Private

Born in Forsyth County* where he resided as a farmer or farm laborer prior to enlisting at Camp Holmes, near Raleigh, at age 28, March 12, 1864, for the war. Captured near Hanover Junction, Virginia (or at the North Anna River, Virginia), May 23-24, 1864. Confined at Point Lookout, Maryland, May 30, 1864. Released at Point Lookout on October 16, 1864, after taking the Oath of Allegiance and joining the U.S. Army. Assigned to Company A, 4th Regiment U.S. Volunteer Infantry.

SMITH, ALFRED ANDERSON, Private

Born in Davidson County on November 12, 1841. Resided in Davidson County and was by occupation a farmer prior to enlisting in Rowan County at age 20, July 4, 1862, for the war. Reported present through October 31, 1862. Wounded in the right wrist at Fredericksburg, Virginia, December 13, 1862. Hospitalized at Richmond, Virginia. Furloughed for sixty days on March 1, 1863. Reported absent without leave on October 17, 1863. Reported on detached service at Lexington, North Carolina, in March-December, 1864. Retired to the Invalid Corps on February 14, 1865, by reason of "complete anchylosis of the [right wrist] joint."

STEELE, SILAS S., Private

Resided in Iredell County and enlisted in Rowan County at age 25, July 4, 1862, for the war. Reported absent sick through December 31, 1862. Returned to duty on February 9, 1863. Wounded in the hand at Chancellorsville, Virginia, May 4, 1863. Reported absent without leave on August 21, 1863. Reported absent on detached service at Raleigh in November-December, 1863. Reported at home on furlough in March-April, 1864. Reported on detached service at Charlotte from August 22, 1864, through February 28, 1865. Survived the war.

STILLER, JULIUS M., Sergeant

Resided in Rowan County where he enlisted at age 24, July 4, 1862, for the war. Mustered in as Private. Hospitalized at Richmond, Virginia, November 1, 1862, with parotitis. Transferred to hospital at Danville, Virginia, December 19, 1862 (suffering from rheumatism). Returned to duty on March 24, 1863. Hospitalized at Richmond on May 3, 1863, with acute diarrhoea. Furloughed on June 14, 1863. Reported absent without leave on September 6, 1863. Returned to duty in November-December, 1863. Captured near Richmond on May 13, 1864. Confined at Point Lookout, Maryland, May 16, 1864. Paroled at Point Lookout on or about September 30, 1864. Reported absent without leave on December 5, 1864. Returned to duty in January-February, 1865. Promoted to Sergeant prior to April 2, 1865, when he was captured near Petersburg, Virginia. Confined at Hart's Island, New York Harbor, April 7, 1865. Released at Hart's Island on June 17, 1865, after taking the Oath of Allegiance. [May have served previously as Private in 2nd Company B, 42nd Regiment N.C. Troops.]

THOMASON, RUFUS M., Private

Resided in Rowan County where he enlisted at age 18, July 5, 1862, for the war. Transferred to Company K of this regiment on or about July 17, 1862.

THOMPSON, JAMES W., Private

Previously served as Private in Capt. William H. Howard's Company, N.C. Prison Guards. Enlisted in this company on or about July 4, 1862. Mustered in as Corporal. Reduced to ranks in November-December, 1862. Reported present through December 31, 1862. Reported absent on detached service from January 29 through February 28, 1863. Rejoined the company prior to May 4, 1863, when he was wounded in the left thigh at Chancellorsville, Virginia. Hospitalized at Richmond, Virginia. Returned to duty prior to September 1, 1863. Sent to hospital sick on October 22, 1863. Returned to duty prior to November 7, 1863, when he was captured at Rappahannock Station, Virginia. Sent to Washington, D.C. Confined at Point Lookout, Maryland, November 11, 1863. Paroled at Point Lookout on March 16, 1864. Received at City Point, Virginia, March 20, 1864, for exchange. Hospitalized at Richmond on June 11, 1864. Reported absent sick through December 31, 1864. Returned to duty in January-February, 1865. Surrendered at Appomattox Court House, Virginia, April 9, 1865.

[North Carolina pension records indicate that he was wounded in the right hand at or near Fredericksburg, Virginia, or about December 12, 186(2).]

TURRENTINE, WILLIAM F., Private

Resided in Davie County and enlisted in Rowan County at age 32, July 4, 1862, for the war. Reported present through October 31, 1862. Killed at Fredericksburg, Virginia, December 13, 1862.

VAN EATON, F. M., Private

Resided in Davie County and was by occupation a farmer prior to enlisting in Rowan County at age 24, July 4, 1862, for the war. Reported present or accounted for through October 31, 1863. Captured at Rappahannock Station, Virginia, November 7, 1863. Sent to Washington, D.C. Confined at Point Lookout, Maryland, November 11, 1863. Paroled at Point Lookout on March 16, 1864. Received at City Point, Virginia, March 20, 1864, for exchange. Returned to duty subsequent to April 30, 1864. Captured at Winchester, Virginia, July 20, 1864. Confined at Camp Chase, Ohio, July 28, 1864. Paroled at Camp Chase on or about March 2, 1865. Received at Boulware's and Cox's Wharves, James River, Virginia, March 10-12, 1865, for exchange. No further records.

WALTON, MILAS J., Private

Resided in Rowan County and was by occupation a farmer prior to enlisting in Rowan County at age 30, July 4, 1862, for the war. Reported present through October 31, 1863. Captured at Rappahannock Station, Virginia, November 7, 1863. Sent to Washington, D.C. Confined at Point Lookout, Maryland, November 11, 1863. Paroled at Point Lookout on March 16, 1864. Received at City Point, Virginia, March 20, 1864, for exchange. Hospitalized at Richmond, Virginia, March 20, 1864, with ulcus. Furloughed for thirty days on March 26, 1864. Returned to duty subsequent to April 30, 1864. Captured at Fisher's Hill, Virginia, September 22, 1864. Sent to Harpers Ferry, West Virginia. Transferred to Point Lookout where he arrived on October 3, 1864. Paroled at Point Lookout on February 13, 1865. Received at Cox's Wharf, James River, Virginia, February 14-15, 1865, for exchange. Paroled at Salisbury on May 20, 1865. Took the Oath of Allegiance at Salisbury on June 3, 1865.

WEBB, P. R., Private

Place and date of enlistment not reported (probably enlisted subsequent to February 28, 1865). Records of the Federal Provost Marshal indicate that he was captured and paroled at Athens, Georgia, on or about May 8, 1865.

WHITE, MOSES A., JR., Private

Resided in Iredell County and enlisted near Fredericksburg, Virginia, at age 18, April 22, 1863, for the war. Reported absent without leave from August 14, 1863, through April 30, 1864. Reported at home on surgeon's certificate in May-August, 1864. Reported on detached service at Salisbury from September 30, 1864, through February 28, 1865. No further records.

WHITE, W. G., Private

Resided in Iredell County and enlisted in Rowan County at age 27, July 4, 1862, for the war. Reported present through October 31, 1862. Hospitalized at Richmond, Virginia, November 25, 1862, with intermittent fever. Transferred to hospital at Danville, Virginia, December 20, 1862 (suffering from dysentery and rheumatism). Returned to duty on or about January 14, 1863. Wounded in the foot at Chancellorsville, Virginia, May 4, 1863. Hospitalized at Richmond. Furloughed on June 18, 1863. Detailed for duty at Salisbury on September 30, 1864. Reported absent on detail through February 28, 1865. No further records.

WILHELM, MUMFORD S., Private

Previously served as Private in Capt. William H. Howard's Company, N.C. Prison Guards. Enlisted in this company on or about July 4, 1862. Hospitalized at Richmond, Virginia, September 25, 1862, with anasarca. Transferred to hospital at Petersburg, Virginia, October 9, 1862 (suffering from ascites). Furloughed for forty days on October 31, 1862. Hospitalized at Richmond on February 27, 1863, with varioloid. Returned to duty on March 24, 1863. Hospitalized at Richmond on July 26, 1863. Reported absent without leave on October 22, 1863. Apparently returned to duty in January-February, 1864. Hospitalized at High Point on April 14, 1864, with anasarca. Transferred to another hospital on April 15, 1864. Hospitalized at High Point on May 17, 1864, with erysipelas. Returned to duty on May 18, 1864. Hospitalized at Richmond on August 17, 1864, with ascites. Furloughed for thirty days on September 1, 1864. Reported on detached service at Salisbury on September 30, 1864. Rejoined the company in November-December, 1864. Hospitalized at Richmond on January 8, 1865, with dropsy. Furloughed for sixty days on February 11, 1865. Paroled at Salisbury on May 11, 1865. Took the Oath of Allegiance at Salisbury on June 10, 1865.

WILSON, ROBERT FRANKLIN, Private

Born on January 23, 1829. Resided in Davidson County and enlisted in Rowan County at age 33, July 4, 1862, for the war. Reported present through December 31, 1862. Reported on duty as an ambulance driver in January-April, 1863. Hospitalized at Richmond, Virginia, July 31, 1863, with an unspecified complaint. Returned to duty prior to September 1, 1863. Hospitalized at Richmond on September 22, 1863. Reported at home on surgeon's certificate in November-December, 1863. Returned to duty prior to May 1, 1864. Hospitalized at Richmond on June 12, 1864. Reported at home on surgeon's certificate on or about October 31, 1864. Returned to duty in November-December, 1864. Captured at Hatcher's Run, Virginia, February 6, 1865. Confined at Point Lookout, Maryland, February 9, 1865. Released at Point Lookout on June 21, 1865, after taking the Oath of Allegiance.

WINDERS, JOHN H., Musician

Resided in Rowan County where he enlisted at age 26, July 4, 1862, for the war. Mustered in as Musician. Reported present through October 31, 1862. Wounded at Fredericksburg, Virginia, December 13, 1862. Hospitalized at Richmond, Virginia, where he died on December 19, 1862, of wounds.

WISE, WILLIAM A., Private

Previously served as Private in Capt. William H. Howard's Company, N.C. Prison Guards. Enlisted in this company on or about July 4, 1862. Reported present through February 28, 1863. Wounded in the right leg at Chancellorsville, Virginia, May 4, 1863. Hospitalized at Richmond, Virginia. Furloughed on June 7, 1863. Reported absent on furlough through April 30, 1864. Reported on detached duty at Salisbury from August 16, 1864, through February 28, 1865. Paroled at Salisbury on May 2, 1865. Took the Oath of Allegiance at Salisbury on June 23, 1865.

COMPANY B

This company was raised in Rowan County on July 4, 1862. It was mustered into service at Salisbury on July 17, 1862, and assigned to the 57th Regiment N.C. Troops as Company A. After joining the regiment the company functioned as a part of the regiment, and its history for the remainder of the war is reported as a part of the regimental history.

The following roster was compiled primarily from information in the microfilm edition of the Compiled Service Records of Soldiers Who Served in Organizations from the State of North Carolina (Record Group 109, M270), National Archives and Records Administration, Washington, D.C. Record Group 109 includes enlistment papers, pay vouchers, requisitions, letters of resignation, discharge certificates, and abstracts of medical and prisoner of war returns. Materials relating specifically to this company include a muster-in and descriptive roll dated July 17, 1862, and muster rolls dated July, 1862-December, 1863, and March, 1864-February, 1865.

Also utilized in this roster were *The War of the Rebellion: A Compilation of the Official Records of the Union and Confederate Armies*, the North Carolina adjutant general's *Roll of Honor*, state militia records, newspaper casualty lists and obituaries, wartime claims for bounty pay and allowances, postwar registers of claims for artificial limbs, Confederate pension applications filed with the states of North Carolina, Tennessee, and Florida, Confederate Soldiers' Home records, and the 1860 and 1870 federal censuses of North Carolina. A search was made also for relevant letters, diaries, reminiscences, and other manuscripts in the Southern Historical Collection (University of North Carolina-Chapel Hill), the Duke University Library Special Collections Department, and the North Carolina Division of Archives and History.

Among the secondary sources consulted were records of the North Carolina division of the United Daughters of the Confederacy, postwar rosters, regimental and county histories, marriage bond, will, and cemetery indexes, published and unpublished genealogies, biographical dictionaries, the *Confederate Veteran*, Walter Clark's *Histories of the Several Regiments and Battalions from North Carolina in the Great War, 1861-'65*, and the North Carolina volume of the extended edition of *Confederate Military History*.

OFFICERS

CAPTAINS

BROWN, WILLIAMS

Previously served as Private in Capt. William H. Howard's Company, N.C. Prison Guards. Appointed Captain of this company on July 4, 1862. Hospitalized at Richmond, Virginia, September 27, 1862. Furloughed on October 1, 1862. Reported absent without leave on October 29, 1862. Dropped from the company rolls on December 3, 1862, for prolonged absence without leave. Restored to the company rolls on January 2, 1863. Resigned on January 12, 1863, by reason of "stricture & chronic disease of urinary organs." Resignation accepted on or about February 1, 1863.

HUNTER, MILES H.

Resided in Mecklenburg County or in South Carolina and enlisted in Rowan County at age 27. Appointed 1st Lieutenant on July 4, 1862. Reported in command of the company in July-October, 1862. Promoted to Captain on February 1, 1863. Reported present or accounted for on surviving company muster rolls through February 28, 1865. Captured at Sayler's Creek, Virginia, April 6, 1865. Confined at Old Capitol Prison, Washington, D.C. Transferred to Johnson's Island, Ohio, where he arrived on April 19, 1865. Released at Johnson's Island on June 18, 1865, after taking the Oath of Allegiance. [At various times in 1863-1865 he was reported in command of Companies A, C, E, G, and K.]

LIEUTENANTS

CRAWFORD, JAMES A., 2nd Lieutenant

Born on October 27, 1827. Resided in Iredell County and was by occupation a farmer prior to enlisting in Rowan County at age 34, July 4, 1862, for the war. Mustered in as Sergeant. Reported present through February 28, 1863. Appointed 2nd Lieutenant on or about February 12, 1863, to rank from February 1, 1863. Reported present through October 31, 1863. Captured at Rappahannock Station, Virginia, November 7, 1863. Sent to Washington, D.C. Transferred to Johnson's Island, Ohio, where he arrived on November 14, 1863. Released at Johnson's Island on June 12, 1865, after taking the Oath of Allegiance.

FITZGERALD, JOHN BURGESS, 3rd Lieutenant

Born on February 8, 1835. Resided in Davidson County and enlisted in Rowan County at age 27. Appointed 3rd Lieutenant on July 4, 1862. Hospitalized at Richmond, Virginia, October 13, 1862, with icterus. Furloughed on October 16, 1862. Dropped from the company rolls on December 19, 1862. Reason he was dropped not reported.

GRAY, AUGUSTUS H., 1st Lieutenant

Resided in Rowan County where he enlisted at age 30, July 4, 1862, for the war. Mustered in as Private. Promoted to Corporal prior to September 1, 1862. Promoted to Sergeant on October 14, 1862. Appointed Sergeant Major on November 10, 1862, and transferred to the Field and Staff of this regiment. Appointed 3rd Lieutenant of this company on December 21, 1862, while absent wounded. Furloughed for thirty days from hospital at Richmond, Virginia, on or about December 31, 1862. Promoted to 1st Lieutenant on February 12, 1863. Reported for duty prior to March 1, 1863. Reported present until November 7, 1863, when he was captured at Rappahannock Station, Virginia. Confined at Old Capitol Prison, Washington, D.C. Transferred to Johnson's Island, Ohio, where he arrived on November 14, 1863. Released at Johnson's Island on June 1, 1864, after taking the Oath of Allegiance.

OVERCASH, JOHN O., 2nd Lieutenant

Previously served as Private in Capt. William H. Howard's Company, N.C. Prison Guards. Appointed 2nd Lieutenant of this company on July 4, 1862. Reported absent sick from August 11 through November 30, 1862. Dropped from the company rolls on or about December 3, 1862, for prolonged absence without leave. Restored to the company rolls on January 7, 1863. Died in camp near Port Royal, Virginia, February 12, 1863. Cause of death not reported.

NONCOMMISSIONED OFFICERS AND PRIVATES

BAILEY, J. W., Private

Resided in Davidson County and enlisted in Rowan County at age 31, July 4, 1862, for the war. Hospitalized at Richmond, Virginia,

December 4, 1862, with icterus. Furloughed on January 5, 1863. Returned to duty in March-April, 1864. Hospitalized at Richmond on or about August 27, 1864, with chronic diarrhoea. Arrested for desertion on or about September 7, 1864. Court-martialed on or about December 8, 1864. Reported under arrest through February 28, 1865. Hospitalized at Richmond on or about March 4, 1865, with chronic diarrhoea. Returned to duty on or about March 27, 1865. Paroled at Salisbury on May 22, 1865.

BAILEY, W. H., Private

Resided in Davidson County and enlisted in Rowan County at age 18, July 4, 1862, for the war. Hospitalized at Richmond, Virginia, September 18, 1862, with rubeola. Returned to duty on October 1, 1862. Hospitalized at Richmond on November 9, 1862, with orchitis. Returned to duty on November 14, 1862. Reported present in January-April, 1863. Hospitalized at Richmond on June 4, 1863, with scorbutus. Later contracted typhoid fever. Returned to duty on August 19, 1863. Captured at Rappahannock Station, Virginia, November 7, 1863. Sent to Washington, D.C. Confined at Point Lookout, Maryland, November 11, 1863. Paroled at Point Lookout on February 24, 1865. Received at Aiken's Landing, James River, Virginia, February 25-28 or March 2-3, 1865, for exchange. No further records.

BARBER, WILLIAM THOMAS, Private

Resided in Forsyth County and was by occupation a day laborer prior to enlisting in Forsyth County at age 39, March 12, 1864, for the war. Sent to hospital from Harpers Ferry, West Virginia, July 5, 1864. Died at Old Town (Forsyth County) on July 16, 1864. Cause of death not reported.

BILES, EBEN M., Private

Enlisted in Stanly County at age 22, March 7, 1864, for the war. Reported present through December 31, 1864. Furloughed on February 15, 1865. Survived the war.

BIRKHEAD, JAMES A., Private

Resided in Rowan County where he enlisted at age 21, July 4, 1862, for the war. Hospitalized at Richmond, Virginia, October 29, 1862, with intermittent fever. Returned to duty in January-February, 1863. Reported present through May 11, 1863. Hospitalized at Danville, Virginia, June 18, 1863, with chronic diarrhoea. Transferred to Salisbury on June 25, 1863. Returned to duty prior to September 1, 1863. Captured at Rappahannock Station, Virginia, November 7, 1863. Sent to Washington, D.C. Confined at Point Lookout, Maryland, November 11, 1863. Paroled at Point Lookout on March 16, 1864. Received at City Point, Virginia, March 20, 1864, for exchange. Reported absent without leave for one month and fourteen days. Returned to duty prior to September 1, 1864. Reported present through February 28, 1865. Surrendered at Appomattox Court House, Virginia, April 9, 1865. [The Salem *People's Press* of October 13, 1864, states that he was wounded in the hip at Winchester, Virginia, September 19, 1864.]

BOLCH, JOSEPH, Sergeant

Born in Catawba County* where he resided prior to enlisting in Rowan County at age 31, July 4, 1862, for the war. Mustered in as Sergeant. Reported present or accounted for through February 28, 1863. Hospitalized at Richmond, Virginia, March 8, 1863, with fever and/or rheumatism. Died in hospital at Richmond on March 19, 1863, of "scrofula."

BOST, DANIEL D., Private

Resided in Iredell County and enlisted in Rowan County at age 21, July 4, 1862, for the war. Accidentally wounded in the hand at Chaffin's Bluff, Virginia, September 18, 1862. Hand amputated because of gangrene. Died in hospital at Richmond, Virginia, October 2, 1862, of "shock & bronchitis."

BOST, W. W., Private

Resided in Iredell County and enlisted in Rowan County at age 23, July 4, 1862, for the war. Reported present or accounted for on surviving company muster rolls through April 30, 1864. Hospitalized at Petersburg, Virginia, May 10, 1864. Returned to duty on May 16, 1864. Reported present until September 19, 1864, when he was killed at Winchester, Virginia.

BOST, WILLIAM E., Private

Resided in Iredell County and was by occupation a farmer prior to enlisting in Rowan County at age 22, July 4, 1862, for the war. Reported present or accounted for through October 31, 1863. Captured at Rappahannock Station, Virginia, November 7, 1863. Sent to Washington, D.C. Confined at Point Lookout, Maryland, November 11, 1863. Paroled at Point Lookout and transferred to Aiken's Landing, James River, Virginia, February 24, 1865. Received at Aiken's Landing on February 25-28 or March 2-3, 1865, for exchange. Paroled at Statesville on May 26, 1865.

BROOKS, ADDISON CAUSE, Private

Born in Davie County and resided in Davidson County where he was by occupation a farmer prior to enlisting in Rowan County at age 25, July 4, 1862, for the war. Wounded in the left hand at Fredericksburg, Virginia, December 13, 1862. Two fingers amputated. Hospitalized at Richmond, Virginia. Furloughed for forty days on December 30, 1862. Reported absent without leave in February-October, 1863. Reported present but under arrest in November-December, 1863. Hospitalized at Richmond on April 19, 1864, with intermittent fever and bronchitis. Transferred to Castle Thunder Prison, Richmond, April 23, 1864. Rejoined the company prior to May 1, 1864. Reported present but under arrest for desertion in May-August, 1864. Returned to duty prior to September 20, 1864, when he was captured at or near Newtown, Virginia. Sent to Harpers Ferry, West Virginia. Transferred to Point Lookout, Maryland, where he arrived on October 3, 1864. Released at Point Lookout on May 12-14, 1865, after taking the Oath of Allegiance.

BROOKS, HENRY M., Private

Resided in Davidson County and enlisted in Rowan County at age 21, July 4, 1862, for the war. Deserted at Fredericksburg, Virginia, December 25, 1862.

BUTNER, J., Private

Place and date of enlistment not reported (probably enlisted subsequent to February 28, 1865). Hospitalized at Richmond, Virginia, April 1, 1865, with gunshot wounds of the right arm and side. Place and date wounded not reported. Died in hospital at Richmond on April 10, 1865, of wounds.

CARPENTER, JOHN, Corporal

Resided in Catawba County and enlisted in Rowan County at age 34, July 4, 1862, for the war. Mustered in as Private. Hospitalized at Richmond, Virginia, September 24, 1862. Returned to duty on October 21, 1862. Reported present through February 28, 1863.

Promoted to Corporal in January-February, 1863. Reported present until May 4, 1863, when he was wounded slightly in the hand at Chancellorsville, Virginia. Returned to duty prior to May 11, 1863. Reported present until November 7, 1863, when he was captured at Rappahannock Station, Virginia. Sent to Washington, D.C. Confined at Point Lookout, Maryland, November 11, 1863. Paroled at Point Lookout on February 24, 1865. Received at Aiken's Landing, James River, Virginia, February 25-28 or March 2-3, 1865, for exchange. Survived the war.

CAUBLE, JACOB, Private

Resided in Rowan County and was by occupation a mechanic prior to enlisting in Rowan County at age 27, July 4, 1862, for the war. Hospitalized at Richmond, Virginia, November 9, 1862, with diarrhoea. Returned to duty on November 14, 1862. Hospitalized at Richmond on December 6, 1862, with catarrh and variola. Transferred to another hospital on December 18, 1862. Returned to duty prior to January 1, 1863. Hospitalized at Richmond on March 8, 1863, with diarrhoea. Transferred to hospital at Danville, Virginia, April 25, 1863. Returned to duty on June 30, 1863. Hospitalized at Richmond on July 10, 1863, with ascites. Transferred to Salisbury on July 17, 1863. Reported absent on sick furlough through December 31, 1863. Returned to duty in January-April, 1864. Sent to hospital from Harpers Ferry, West Virginia, July 5, 1864. Hospitalized at Richmond on August 19, 1864. Furloughed for fifty days on August 20, 1864. Detailed for light duty at Salisbury prior to November 1, 1864. Rejoined the company in November-December, 1864. Reported present through February 28, 1865. Surrendered at Appomattox Court House, Virginia, April 9, 1865.

CHAMBERLAIN, MARTIN C., Private

Served during most of the war as Private in Company D, 21st Regiment N.C. Troops (11th Regiment N.C. Volunteers). Enlisted in this company (probably while still a member of the 21st North Carolina) subsequent to December 31, 1863. Deserted near Kinston on April 14, 1864. Subsequently rejoined the 21st North Carolina.

CLINE, DARIUS, Corporal

Resided in Catawba County and was by occupation a farmer prior to enlisting in Rowan County at age 27, July 4, 1862, for the war. Mustered in as Private. Reported present or accounted for through October 31, 1863. Promoted to Corporal on or about November 1, 1863. Captured at Rappahannock Station, Virginia, November 7, 1863. Sent to Washington, D.C. Confined at Point Lookout, Maryland, November 11, 1863. Paroled at Point Lookout on March 16, 1864. Received at City Point, Virginia, March 20, 1864, for exchange. Returned to duty prior to July 20, 1864, when he was captured at or near Winchester, Virginia. Confined at Camp Chase, Ohio, July 28, 1864. Paroled at Camp Chase on March 2, 1865. Received at Boulware's and Cox's Wharves, James River, Virginia, March 10-12, 1865, for exchange. Survived the war.

CLINE, L. H. G., Private

Resided in Catawba County and enlisted in Rowan County at age 32, July 4, 1862, for the war. Hospitalized at Richmond, Virginia, September 6, 1862, with diarrhoea. Returned to duty on October 24, 1862. Hospitalized at Richmond on December 30, 1862, with pneumonia. Transferred to another hospital on January 16, 1863. Returned to duty prior to February 1, 1863. Reported present until November 7, 1863, when he was captured at Rappahannock Station, Virginia. Sent to Washington, D.C. Confined at Point Lookout, Maryland, November 11, 1863. Paroled at Point Lookout and transferred to City Point, Virginia, March 16, 1864. Received at City Point on March 20, 1864, for exchange. Returned to duty on an unspecified date. Reported absent without leave on or about July 19, 1864. Returned to duty subsequent to September 1, 1864. Wounded ("leg shot off below the knee") at Winchester, Virginia, September 19, 1864. Died (probably in the hands of the enemy) on September 19-20, 1864, of wounds.

CLODFELTER, H. L., Private

Resided in Iredell County and enlisted in Rowan County at age 33, July 4, 1862, for the war. Reported present or accounted for until captured at Gettysburg, Pennsylvania, July 2-5, 1863. Confined at Fort Delaware, Delaware, on or about July 9, 1863. Died in hospital at Fort Delaware on August 20, 1863, of "pneumonia."

CLODFELTER, JACOB, Private

Resided in Davidson County and enlisted in Rowan County at age 18, July 4, 1862, for the war. Died in hospital at Lynchburg, Virginia, on or about December 6, 1862, of "tabes mesenterica."

CLODFELTER, JOSEPH L., Private

Resided in Davidson County and enlisted in Rowan County at age 30, July 4, 1862, for the war. Discharged at Salisbury on August 11, 1862, by reason of disability.

CLODFELTER, M. L., Private

Resided in Iredell County and enlisted in Rowan County at age 28, July 4, 1862, for the war. Hospitalized at Richmond, Virginia, September 24, 1862. Furloughed for thirty days on November 9, 1862. Returned to duty in March-May, 1863. Hospitalized at Richmond on May 28, 1863, with "febris typhoid." Died in hospital at Richmond on May 30, 1863.

COLLEY, D. C., Private

Resided in Rowan County and was by occupation a farmer prior to enlisting at Camp Stokes at age 36, October 26, 1864, for the war. Hospitalized at Richmond, Virginia, December 18, 1864, with acute rheumatism. Furloughed on January 29, 1865. Hospitalized at Richmond on April 2, 1865. Captured in hospital at Richmond on April 3, 1865. Escaped from hospital on April 26, 1865. Took the Oath of Allegiance at Salisbury on June 21, 1865.

CORNISH, ANDREW C., Private

Resided in Davidson County and enlisted in Rowan County at age 28, July 4, 1862, for the war. Hospitalized at Richmond, Virginia, September 24, 1862. Furloughed for twenty-five days on December 6, 1862. Reported absent without leave in January-August, 1863. Listed as a deserter in September-October, 1863. Reported in the guard house in November-December, 1863. Returned to duty prior to May 1, 1864. Reported absent without leave for two months in May-August, 1864. Reported on duty as a provost guard in September-October, 1864. Reported under arrest on December 24, 1864. Reason he was arrested not reported. Returned to duty in January-February, 1865. Captured at Chester Station, Virginia, on or about April 5, 1865. Confined at Point Lookout, Maryland, April 15, 1865. Released at Point Lookout on June 24, 1865, after taking the Oath of Allegiance.

COX, HENRY C., Private

Resided in Iredell County and was by occupation a farmer prior to enlisting in Rowan County at age 22, July 4, 1862, for the war.

Hospitalized at Richmond, Virginia, September 3, 1862, with typhoid fever. Transferred to another hospital on September 25, 1862. Returned to duty prior to November 1, 1862. Reported present through February 28, 1863. Hospitalized at Richmond on May 1, 1863, with rheumatism. Transferred to hospital at Danville, Virginia, May 7, 1863. Died in hospital at Danville on June 18, 1863, of "congestion of lungs."

CRAVER, JOHN N., Private

Resided in Davidson County and enlisted in Rowan County at age 28, July 4, 1862, for the war. Reported present or accounted for in September, 1862-February, 1863. Reported absent on detached service in March-April, 1863. Returned to duty on an unspecified date. Reported present through August 31, 1863. Reported on duty as a teamster in September, 1864-February, 1865. Survived the war.

CULVERHOUSE, WILLIAM A., 1st Sergeant

Resided in Rowan County and was by occupation a clerk prior to enlisting in Rowan County at age 21, July 4, 1862, for the war. Mustered in as Sergeant. Promoted to 1st Sergeant on October 14, 1862. Reported present through January 1, 1863. Died in hospital at Lynchburg, Virginia, on or about February 8, 1863, of "febris typhoides."

DEARMAN, H. W., Private

Born on December 15, 1833. Resided in Iredell County and enlisted in Rowan County at age 28, July 4, 1862, for the war. Hospitalized at Richmond, Virginia, September 18, 1862, convalescent from rubeola and dyspepsia. Furloughed on October 22, 1862. Reported absent without leave in January-December, 1863, and March, 1864-February, 1865. Survived the war.

EARNHEART, WILLIAM P., Corporal

Resided in Rowan County where he enlisted at age 20, July 4, 1862, for the war. Mustered in as Corporal. Appointed Sergeant Major on December 22, 1862, and transferred to the Field and Staff of this regiment.

EATON, SAMUEL W., Private

Resided in Davidson County and enlisted in Rowan County at age 22, July 4, 1862, for the war. Reported present or accounted for through October 31, 1863. Captured at Rappahannock Station, Virginia, November 7, 1863. Sent to Washington, D.C. Confined at Point Lookout, Maryland, November 11, 1863. Paroled at Point Lookout on February 18, 1865. Received at Boulware's and Cox's Wharves, James River, Virginia, February 20-21, 1865, for exchange. No further records. Survived the war.

FARRIS, JOSEPH B., Private

Born in Powhatan County, Virginia, and resided in Rowan County where he was by occupation a bookkeeper prior to enlisting in Rowan County at age 26, July 4, 1862, for the war. Appointed Quartermaster Sergeant prior to September 1, 1862, and transferred to the Field and Staff of this regiment.

FERRELL, DAVID W., Corporal

Enlisted in Rowan County at age 30, July 4, 1862, for the war. Mustered in as Corporal. Hospitalized at Richmond, Virginia, November 25, 1862, with rheumatism. Returned to duty on December 30, 1862. Died in hospital at Lynchburg, Virginia, February 28, 1863, of "laryngitis."

FERRELL, E. L., Private

Resided in Davie County and enlisted in Rowan County at age 18, July 4, 1862, for the war. Reported absent without leave in September, 1862-April, 1863. Returned to duty in May-August, 1863. Captured at Rappahannock Station, Virginia, November 7, 1863. Sent to Washington, D.C. Confined at Point Lookout, Maryland, November 11, 1863. Paroled at Point Lookout on March 16, 1864. Received at City Point, Virginia, March 20, 1864, for exchange. Returned to duty prior to August 17, 1864, when he was wounded in the right arm at Winchester, Virginia. Hospitalized at Kernstown, Virginia. Reported absent wounded through February 28, 1865. Survived the war.

FISHER, JULIUS A., Private

Resided in Iredell County and was by occupation a farmer prior to enlisting in Rowan County at age 26, July 4, 1862, for the war. Hospitalized at Richmond, Virginia, November 21, 1862, with dysentery. Returned to duty on December 2, 1862. Sent to hospital at Port Royal, Virginia, February 25, 1863. Returned to duty prior to May 11, 1863. Reported present on surviving company muster rolls until June 6, 1864, when he was wounded in the left leg near Richmond. Hospitalized at Richmond. Furloughed on August 27, 1864. Reported absent wounded through February 28, 1865. Disabled by his wounds. Survived the war.

FOX, Z. M., Private

Resided in Rowan County where he enlisted at age 28, July 4, 1862, for the war. Hospitalized at Richmond, Virginia, September 24, 1862. Returned to duty on December 2, 1862. Hospitalized at Richmond on or about June 20, 1863, with acute hepatitis. Confined at Castle Thunder Prison, Richmond, July 1, 1863. Reason he was confined not reported. Returned to duty prior to September 14, 1863, when he deserted from camp near Orange Court House, Virginia. Reported under arrest in May-October, 1864. Returned to duty on an unspecified date. Deserted on January 1, 1865. [North Carolina pension records indicate that he was "struck with a gun in the groin" at Fredericksburg, Virginia, on or about April 20, 1863, and suffered a rupture.]

FREEZE, WILLIAM F., Private

Resided in Rowan County and was by occupation a farmer prior to enlisting in Rowan County at age 32, July 4, 1862, for the war. Hospitalized at Richmond, Virginia, September 20, 1862, with typhoid pneumonia. Furloughed for thirty days on or about November 14, 1862. Returned to duty in January-February, 1863. Reported present until November 7, 1863, when he was captured at Rappahannock Station, Virginia. Sent to Washington, D.C. Confined at Point Lookout, Maryland, November 11, 1863. Paroled at Point Lookout on March 16, 1864. Received at City Point, Virginia, March 20, 1864, for exchange. Returned to duty prior to July 20, 1864, when he was captured at Winchester, Virginia. Confined at Camp Chase, Ohio, July 28, 1864. Paroled at Camp Chase on March 2, 1865. Received at Boulware's Wharf, James River, Virginia, March 10-12, 1865, for exchange. Survived the war.

GARVEY, THOMAS, Private

Resided in Duplin County and enlisted at Camp Holmes, near Raleigh, June 10, 1864, for the war. Hospitalized at Charlottesville, Virginia, July 25, 1864, with rubeola. Transferred to hospital at Lynchburg, Virginia, July 26, 1864. Hospitalized at Richmond, Virginia, October 2, 1864, with intermittent fever. Returned to duty on October 31, 1864. Reported present in November, 1864-February, 1865. Captured at Fort Stedman, Virginia, March 25,

1865. Confined at Point Lookout, Maryland, March 28, 1865. Released at Point Lookout on June 27, 1865, after taking the Oath of Allegiance. [North Carolina pension records indicate that he was about 22 years of age at the time of his enlistment.]

HAIR, JAMES A., Private

Resided in Iredell County and was by occupation a blacksmith prior to enlisting in Rowan County at age 32, July 4, 1862, for the war. Hospitalized at Richmond, Virginia, October 31, 1862, with typhoid fever. Furloughed on December 31, 1862. Hospitalized at Charlottesville, Virginia, July 27, 1863, with debilitas. Returned to duty on July 31, 1863. Reported present through October 31, 1863. Captured at Rappahannock Station, Virginia, November 7, 1863. Sent to Washington, D.C. Confined at Point Lookout, Maryland, November 11, 1863. Died at Point Lookout on or about March 4, 1864, of "chronic diarrhoea."

HASS, HARVEY F., Private

Resided in Catawba County and enlisted in Rowan County at age 30, July 4, 1862, for the war. Hospitalized at Richmond, Virginia, on or about September 1, 1862. Reported absent sick through August 31, 1863. Reported absent without leave in September, 1863-August, 1864. Returned to duty in September-October, 1864. Reported present in November-December, 1864. Died in camp on January 12, 1865. Place and cause of death not reported.

HEDRICK, DAVID, Private

Resided in Davidson County and was by occupation a farmer prior to enlisting in Rowan County at age 30, July 4, 1862, for the war. Sent to hospital (probably at Liberty, Virginia) on November 18, 1862. Furloughed on an unspecified date. Died at home in Davidson County on March 1, 1863. Cause of death not reported.

HOLBROOKS, JAMES FRANKLIN, Private

Resided in Rowan County and was by occupation a laborer prior to enlisting in Rowan County at age 29, July 4, 1862, for the war. Reported present through February 28, 1863. Wounded in the breast and left arm at Chancellorsville, Virginia, May 4, 1863. Died at or near Chancellorsville on or about May 5, 1863, of wounds.

HONEYCUTT, L. M., Private

Resided in Davidson County and enlisted in Rowan County at age 27, July 4, 1862, for the war. Hospitalized at Richmond, Virginia, September 6, 1862, with rheumatism. Reported in hospital at Richmond on April 4, 1863, with pneumonia. Returned to duty on April 6, 1863. Reported present on surviving company muster rolls through April 30, 1864. Deserted near Botetourt Springs, Virginia, June 16, 1864. Reported present but under arrest on October 28, 1864. Court-martialed on or about December 8, 1864. Returned to duty subsequent to December 31, 1864. Captured at Hatcher's Run, Virginia, February 6, 1865. Confined at Point Lookout, Maryland, February 9, 1865. Released at Point Lookout on June 27, 1865, after taking the Oath of Allegiance.

HONEYCUTT, MILES N., Private

Resided in Davidson County and enlisted in Rowan County at age 22, July 4, 1862, for the war. Hospitalized at Richmond, Virginia, September 6, 1862, with phthisis pulmonalis. Returned to duty in May-August, 1863. Captured at Rappahannock Station, Virginia, November 7, 1863. Sent to Washington, D.C. Confined at Point Lookout, Maryland, November 11, 1863. Paroled at Point Lookout on March 9, 1864. Received at City Point, Virginia, March 15, 1864, for exchange. Reported absent without leave on May 1, 1864.

Returned to duty prior to August 6-7, 1864, when he was captured at Hagerstown, Maryland. Confined at Old Capitol Prison, Washington, D.C., August 13, 1864. Transferred to Elmira, New York, October 24, 1864. Released at Elmira on May 29, 1865, after taking the Oath of Allegiance.

HONEYCUTT, ROBERT R., Private

Resided in Rowan County where he enlisted at age 32, July 4, 1862, for the war. Hospitalized at Richmond, Virginia, September 22, 1862, with debilitas. Returned to duty on December 17, 1862. Reported present in January-February, 1863. Discharged at Fredericksburg, Virginia, March 16, 1863. Reason discharged not reported.

HOUPE, J. WILSON, Private

Born on June 29, 1839. Resided in Iredell County and enlisted in Rowan County at age 23, July 4, 1862, for the war. Hospitalized at Richmond, Virginia, September 3, 1862, with parotitis. Transferred to another hospital on October 19, 1862. Returned to duty in January-February, 1863. Reported present through October 31, 1863. Captured at Rappahannock Station, Virginia, November 7, 1863. Sent to Washington, D.C. Confined at Point Lookout, Maryland, November 11, 1863. Paroled at Point Lookout and transferred to Aiken's Landing, James River, Virginia, September 18, 1864. Received at Varina, Virginia, September 22, 1864, for exchange. Returned to duty in November-December, 1864. Reported present through February 28, 1865. Captured at or near Farmville, Virginia, April 6, 1865. Confined at Newport News, Virginia, April 14, 1865. Released at Newport News on June 26, 1865, after taking the Oath of Allegiance.

HUFFMAN, JOSEPH W., Private

Resided in Catawba County and was by occupation a farmer prior to enlisting in Catawba County at age 40, March 9, 1864, for the war. Reported present through August 31, 1864. Wounded in the thigh (fracture) and captured at Winchester, Virginia, September 19, 1864. Leg amputated. Died in hospital at Winchester on October 25, 1864, of "tetanus."

IVY, JOHN R., Private

Resided in Stanly County and was by occupation a farmer prior to enlisting in Stanly County at age 41, March 7, 1864, for the war. Hospitalized at Charlottesville, Virginia, July 26, 1864, with chronic bronchitis. Transferred to Lynchburg, Virginia, the same date. Returned to duty in November-December, 1864. Reported present through February 28, 1865. No further records.

JONES, WILLIAM A., Private

Enlisted in Forsyth County on March 12, 1864, for the war. Reported present through August 31, 1864. Captured at Fisher's Hill, Virginia, September 22, 1864. Confined at Point Lookout, Maryland, October 3, 1864. Paroled at Point Lookout on November 1, 1864. Received at Venus Point, Savannah River, Georgia, November 15, 1864, for exchange. Reported absent sick from November 26, 1864, through February 28, 1865. Survived the war. [Confederate Gravestone Records indicate that he was 36 years of age at time of enlistment.]

KENNERLY, S. A., Private

Born on May 16, 1829. Resided in Rowan County where he enlisted at age 33, July 4, 1862, for the war. Reported present or accounted for through February 28, 1863. Hospitalized at

Richmond, Virginia, May 8, 1863, with debilitas. Transferred to Lynchburg, Virginia, May 9, 1863. Captured during the "raid in the rear of Lee's army" on May 24, 1863. Paroled and exchanged on an unspecified date. Failed to return to duty and was reported absent without leave on January 1, 1864. Reported absent without leave through February 28, 1865. Survived the war.

KNOX, BENJAMIN, Private

Resided in Iredell County and enlisted in Rowan County at age 27, July 4, 1862, for the war. Reported absent sick at Camp Salisbury, near Richmond, Virginia, September 22, 1862. Returned to duty prior to November 1, 1862. Reported present through October 31, 1863. Captured at Rappahannock Station, Virginia, November 7, 1863. Confined at Point Lookout, Maryland, November 11, 1863. Paroled at Point Lookout and transferred to Aiken's Landing, James River, Virginia, February 24, 1865. Received at Aiken's Landing on or about March 3, 1865, for exchange. Hospitalized at Richmond on March 4, 1865, with chronic bronchitis. Furloughed for thirty days on March 10, 1865.

KNOX, W. L., Private

Enlisted in Rowan County at age 31, July 7, 1862, for the war. No further records.

LAZENBY, R. W., Private

Resided in Iredell County and was by occupation a farmer prior to enlisting in Rowan County at age 30, July 4, 1862, for the war. Hospitalized at Richmond, Virginia, September 3, 1862, with intermittent fever. Returned to duty on September 8, 1862. Reported present or accounted for through January 1, 1863. Hospitalized at Richmond on January 12, 1863. Died in hospital at Richmond on January 18, 1863, of "typhoid fever."

LEATHERMAN, RUFUS P., Private

Resided in Catawba County and enlisted in Rowan County at age 18, July 4, 1862, for the war. Sent to hospital in September-October, 1862. Returned to duty in November-December, 1862. Hospitalized at Richmond, Virginia, January 1, 1863. Furloughed for ninety days on January 15, 1863. Died at home in Catawba County on February 10, 1863. Cause of death not reported.

LEONARD, J. H., Private

Resided in Davidson County and enlisted in Rowan County at age 23, July 4, 1862, for the war. Reported present through January 1, 1863. Sent to hospital at Fredericksburg, Virginia, January 24, 1863. Died at Farmville, Virginia, March 1, 1863, of "smallpox."

LEONARD, SOLOMON, Private

Resided in Davidson County and was by occupation a farmer prior to enlisting in Rowan County at age 28, July 4, 1862, for the war. Mustered in as Private. Promoted to Corporal in January-February, 1863. Reported present until May 4, 1863, when he was wounded slightly in the knee at Chancellorsville, Virginia. Returned to duty prior to May 11, 1863. Reduced to ranks on July 12, 1863. Reported present until November 7, 1863, when he was captured at Rappahannock Station, Virginia. Confined at Point Lookout, Maryland, November 11, 1863. Paroled at Point Lookout on March 16, 1864. Received at City Point, Virginia, March 20, 1864, for exchange. Reported absent without leave on May 1, 1864. Returned to duty prior to September 19, 1864, when he was captured at Winchester, Virginia. Confined at Point Lookout on September 26, 1864. Paroled at Point Lookout on March 15, 1865. Received at

Boulware's Wharf, James River, Virginia, March 18, 1865, for exchange. Hospitalized at Richmond, Virginia, the same date. Transferred to another hospital on March 19, 1865. No further records.

LIVINGOOD, JOHN, Private

Resided in Forsyth County where he enlisted on March 12, 1864, for the war. Reported present through August 31, 1864. Sent to hospital at New Market, Virginia, October 30, 1864. Died at home in Forsyth County prior to January 1, 1865. Cause of death not reported.

LYERLY, JOHN T., Private

Resided in Iredell County and enlisted in Rowan County at age 20, July 4, 1862, for the war. Reported present through May 11, 1863. Captured (or deserted to the enemy) in Pennsylvania on June 25 or July 5, 1863. Confined at Fort Delaware, Delaware. Transferred to Point Lookout, Maryland, in October, 1863. Hospitalized at Point Lookout on October 22, 1863, with debilitas. Died in hospital at Point Lookout on December 14, 1863, of "febris intermit[ten]s."

MASTERS, G. A., Private

Enlisted at Camp Stokes at age 28, October 26, 1864, for the war. Reported present through December 31, 1864. Captured near Hatcher's Run, Virginia, February 6, 1865. Confined at Point Lookout, Maryland, February 9, 1865. Released at Point Lookout on May 12, 1865, after taking the Oath of Allegiance.

MATTHEWS, JAMES, Private

Resided in Mecklenburg County and enlisted in Rowan County at age 17, July 4, 1862, for the war as a substitute for J. Luther Miller of Davidson County. Deserted at Salisbury on August 1, 1862.

MILLS, CLAYTON A., Private

Resided in Iredell County and enlisted in Rowan County at age 23, July 4, 1862, for the war. Sent to hospital on October 4, 1862. Reported absent sick through February 28, 1863. Reported absent without leave in March-April, 1863. Hospitalized at Richmond, Virginia, May 1, 1863, with chronic diarrhoea. Returned to duty on May 29, 1863. Captured at or near Chambersburg, Pennsylvania, July 1-5, 1863. Confined at Fort Delaware, Delaware, August 19, 1863. Paroled at Fort Delaware on September 28, 1864. Received at Varina, Virginia, October 5, 1864, for exchange. Returned to duty in November-December, 1864. Reported present through February 28, 1865. Captured at Fort Stedman, Virginia, March 25, 1865. Confined at Point Lookout, Maryland, March 28, 1865. Released at Point Lookout on June 29, 1865, after taking the Oath of Allegiance. [North Carolina pension records indicate that he was struck in the left shoulder by a shell on an unspecified date.]

MONTGOMERY, GEORGE L., Private

Enlisted at Camp Stokes on November 18, 1864, for the war. Reported present through February 28, 1865. Captured at Fort Stedman, Virginia, March 25, 1865. Confined at Point Lookout, Maryland, March 28, 1865. Died at Point Lookout on June 2, 1865, of "inf[lammation] of lungs."

MONTGOMERY, R. A., Private

Resided in Iredell County and enlisted in Rowan County at age 18, July 4, 1862, for the war. Reported present through February 28, 1863. Hospitalized at Richmond, Virginia, May 1, 1863, with intermittent fever. Returned to duty on June 9, 1863. Sent to hospital

on September 25, 1863. Returned to duty in November-December, 1863. Reported present on surviving company muster rolls through February 28, 1865. Paroled at Statesville on May 27, 1865.

MORRISON, JAMES W., Private

Resided in Iredell County and enlisted in Rowan County at age 24, July 4, 1862, for the war. Hospitalized at Richmond, Virginia, on or about September 4, 1862, with typhoid fever. Transferred to another hospital on October 1, 1862. Apparently returned to duty in March-April, 1863. Hospitalized at Richmond on May 2, 1863, with acute diarrhoea. Transferred to hospital at Danville, Virginia, May 7, 1863 (also suffering from rheumatism). Returned to duty on June 12, 1863. Sent to hospital at Shepherdstown, West Virginia, June 19, 1863. Captured at Shepherdstown on July 6, 1863. Was apparently hospitalized at Baltimore, Maryland. Transferred to Fort McHenry, Maryland, August 23, 1863. Transferred to Point Lookout, Maryland, September 15, 1863. Paroled at Point Lookout on April 27, 1864. Received at City Point, Virginia, April 30, 1864, for exchange. Hospitalized at Richmond on May 1, 1864, with acute diarrhoea. Furloughed for sixty days on May 9, 1864. Died at home in Iredell County prior to October 21, 1864. Cause of death not reported.

MORROW, JAMES W., Private

Resided in Iredell County and enlisted in Rowan County at age 24, July 4, 1862, for the war. Hospitalized at Richmond, Virginia, September 22, 1862. Returned to duty on September 26, 1862. Hospitalized at Richmond on October 25, 1862, with rubeola. Furloughed on November 12, 1862. Returned to duty on an unspecified date. Hospitalized at Richmond on April 14, 1863, with pneumonia. Transferred to hospital at Danville, Virginia, April 18, 1863. Returned to duty on July 2, 1863. Hospitalized at Richmond on July 8, 1863, with "meningitis" and died on July 12, 1863.

MURR, SAMUEL H. P., Private

Resided in Rowan County where he enlisted at age 31, July 4, 1862, for the war. Reported present or accounted for through February 28, 1863. Reported absent without leave on May 11, 1863. Returned to duty prior to September 1, 1863. Captured at Rappahannock Station, Virginia, November 7, 1863. Sent to Washington, D.C. Confined at Point Lookout, Maryland, November 11, 1863. Paroled at Point Lookout and transferred to Aiken's Landing, James River, Virginia, February 24, 1865. Received at Aiken's Landing on February 25-28 or March 2-3, 1865, for exchange. Survived the war. [Name appears on a letter dated April 10, 1865, from the captain commanding the Salisbury arsenal which requests that Private Murr be detailed at Salisbury as a harness- and shoemaker because "mechanics of his class cannot be hired."]

MYERS, DANIEL HENDERSON, Private

Born on August 8, 1835. Resided in Davidson County and enlisted in Rowan County at age 26, July 4, 1862, for the war. Mustered in as Corporal. Reduced to ranks prior to September 2, 1862. Hospitalized at Richmond, Virginia, November 1, 1862. Died in hospital at Richmond on or about December 1, 1862, of "typhoid fever."

MYERS, RICHARD BARTON, Private

Born on August 16, 1840. Resided in Davidson County and enlisted in Rowan County at age 21, July 4, 1862, for the war. Reported present until December 13, 1862, when he was wounded in the head (skull fractured) at Fredericksburg, Virginia. Reported absent wounded through October 31, 1863. Returned to duty in November-December, 1863. Reported present or accounted for on surviving company muster rolls through February 28, 1865. Captured at Farmville, Virginia, April 6, 1865. Confined at Newport News, Virginia, April 14, 1865. Released at Newport News on June 26, 1865, after taking the Oath of Allegiance.

NADING, FRANCIS A., Private

Born on October 21, 1840. Resided in Forsyth County where he enlisted at age 23, March 12, 1864, for the war. Hospitalized at Petersburg, Virginia, May 21, 1864, with gonorrhea. Returned to duty on June 3, 1864. Sent to hospital at Winchester, Virginia, July 23, 1864. Returned to duty in September-October, 1864. Reported present through February 28, 1865. Captured at Fort Stedman, Virginia, March 25, 1865. Confined at Point Lookout, Maryland, March 28, 1865. Released at Point Lookout on June 15, 1865, after taking the Oath of Allegiance.

OVERCASH, AARON J., Private

Resided in Rowan County and was by occupation a farmer prior to enlisting in Rowan County at age 30, July 4, 1862, for the war. Reported present until July 2, 1863, when he was killed at Gettysburg, Pennsylvania.

OVERCASH, ABRAHAM, Private

Born on May 6, 1829. Resided in Rowan County where he enlisted at age 33, July 4, 1862, for the war. Hospitalized at Richmond, Virginia, September 22, 1862. Furloughed for thirty days on October 16, 1862. Returned to duty in January-February, 1863. Captured at Chancellorsville, Virginia, on or about May 4, 1863. Confined at Old Capitol Prison, Washington, D.C. Transferred to Fort Delaware, Delaware, May 7, 1863. Paroled at Fort Delaware and transferred to City Point, Virginia, where he was received on May 23, 1863, for exchange. Reported absent sick on surviving company muster rolls until December 1, 1864, when he was reported absent without leave. Returned to duty in January-February, 1865. Captured at Farmville, Virginia, April 6, 1865. Confined at Newport News, Virginia, April 14, 1865. Released on June 26, 1865, after taking the Oath of Allegiance.

OVERCASH, CORNELIUS ANSMOND, Sergeant

Born in Rowan County on October 7, 1830. Resided in Rowan County where he enlisted at age 31, July 4, 1862, for the war. Mustered in as Corporal. Hospitalized at Richmond, Virginia, November 9, 1862, with debilitas. Returned to duty on November 14, 1862. Promoted to Sergeant in January-February, 1863. Reported present until May 4, 1863, when he was wounded slightly in the leg at Chancellorsville, Virginia. Returned to duty prior to May 11, 1863. Reported present through October 31, 1863. Captured at Rappahannock Station, Virginia, November 7, 1863. Sent to Washington, D.C. Confined at Point Lookout, Maryland, November 11, 1863. Paroled at Point Lookout on March 16, 1864. Received at City Point, Virginia, March 20, 1864, for exchange. Reported absent without leave for one month and fifteen days during May-August, 1864. Returned to duty prior to September 22, 1864, when he was captured at Fisher's Hill, Virginia. Confined at Point Lookout on October 3, 1864. Released at Point Lookout on June 29, 1865, after taking the Oath of Allegiance.

OVERCASH, DANIEL A., Private

Resided in Rowan County where he enlisted at age 22, July 4, 1862, for the war. Hospitalized at Richmond, Virginia, September 22, 1862. Returned to duty on or about October 1, 1862. Wounded at Fredericksburg, Virginia, December 13, 1862. Hospitalized at Richmond where he died on or about January 5-7, 1863, of wounds.

OVERCASH, HENRY W., Private

Resided in Rowan County where he enlisted at age 27, July 4, 1862, for the war. Hospitalized at Richmond, Virginia, September 22, 1862. Furloughed for twenty days on October 16, 1862. Returned to duty in January-February, 1863. Sent to hospital from camp near Port Royal, Virginia, February 25, 1863. Hospitalized at Richmond on April 25, 1863, with typhoid fever. Transferred to another hospital on May 1, 1863. Returned to duty prior to September 1, 1863. Wounded in the chest and captured at Rappahannock Station, Virginia, November 7, 1863. Hospitalized at Washington, D.C., where he died on December 10, 1863, of wounds.

OVERCASH, IRA EPHRAM, Private

Born on March 19, 1828. Resided in Rowan County and was by occupation a farmer prior to enlisting in Rowan County at age 34, July 4, 1862, for the war. Hospitalized at Richmond, Virginia, September 22, 1862, with debilitas. Furloughed for twenty-five days on October 27, 1862. Returned to duty in November-December, 1862. Reported present in January-February, 1863. Hospitalized at Richmond on May 8, 1863, with debilitas. Transferred to Lynchburg, Virginia, May 11, 1863. Captured during the "raid in the rear of Lee's army" on May 24, 1863. Paroled and exchanged on an unspecified date. Returned to duty prior to September 1, 1863. Captured at Rappahannock Station, Virginia, November 7, 1863. Sent to Washington, D.C. Confined at Point Lookout, Maryland, November 11, 1863. Paroled at Point Lookout on March 16, 1864. Received at City Point, Virginia, March 20, 1864, for exchange. Returned to duty prior to July 20, 1864, when he was captured at Winchester, Virginia. Confined at Camp Chase, Ohio, July 28, 1864. Paroled at Camp Chase on March 2, 1865. Received at Boulware's and Cox's Wharves, James River, Virginia, March 10-12, 1865, for exchange. Survived the war.

OVERCASH, P. A., Private

Resided in Rowan County where he enlisted at age 23, July 4, 1862, for the war. Hospitalized at Richmond, Virginia, October 8, 1862, with icterus. Transferred to Salisbury on October 21, 1862. Returned to duty prior to November 1, 1862. Reported present until July 2-5, 1863, when he was captured (or deserted to the enemy) at Gettysburg, Pennsylvania. Confined at Fort Delaware, Delaware, on or about July 9, 1863. Transferred to Point Lookout, Maryland, October 20, 1863. Admitted to the smallpox hospital at Point Lookout on November 17, 1863. Died at Point Lookout on November 26, 1863.

OVERCASH, P. L., Private

Resided in Rowan County where he enlisted at age 25, July 4, 1862, for the war. Sent to hospital on November 28, 1862. Hospitalized at Richmond, Virginia, January 5, 1863, with catarrhus. Returned to duty on January 12, 1863. Wounded in the leg at Chancellorsville, Virginia, May 4, 1863. Returned to duty in September-October, 1863. Captured at Rappahannock Station, Virginia, November 7, 1863. Sent to Washington, D.C. Confined at Point Lookout, Maryland, November 11, 1863. Paroled at Point Lookout on March 16, 1864. Received at City Point, Virginia, March 20, 1864, for exchange. Returned to duty prior to July 20, 1864, when he was killed at Winchester, Virginia.

OVERCASH, PAUL S., Private

Resided in Rowan County where he enlisted at age 23, July 4, 1862, for the war. Reported present through April 30, 1863. Hospitalized at Richmond, Virginia, May 2, 1863, with debilitas. Transferred to hospital at Danville, Virginia, May 7, 1863 (also suffering from rheumatism). Furloughed on or about June 23, 1863. Returned to duty prior to September 1, 1863. Captured at Rappahannock Station, Virginia, November 7, 1863. Sent to Washington, D.C. Confined at Point Lookout, Maryland, November 11, 1863. Paroled at Point Lookout on March 16, 1864. Received at City Point, Virginia, March 20, 1864, for exchange. Returned to duty on an unspecified date. Sent to hospital from Harpers Ferry, West Virginia, July 5, 1864. Returned to duty in January-February, 1865. Captured at Farmville, Virginia, April 6, 1865. Confined at Newport News, Virginia, April 14, 1865. Released at Newport News on June 26, 1865, after taking the Oath of Allegiance.

OVERCASH, PHILIP J., Private

Resided in Rowan County where he enlisted at age 30, July 4, 1862, for the war. Reported absent sick from July 25 through August 31, 1862. Returned to duty in September-October, 1862. Hospitalized at Richmond, Virginia, May 8, 1863. Transferred to hospital at Lynchburg, Virginia, May 9, 1863. Captured on May 24, 1863, during the "raid in the rear of Lee's army." Paroled on or about the same date. Hospitalized at Farmville, Virginia, July 15, 1863, with acute nephritis (apparently also valvular disease of the heart and hepatization of the lower lobes of the lungs). Furloughed for sixty days on August 14, 1863. Reported absent on sick furlough through April 30, 1864. Reported sick at home in Rowan County in September-October, 1864. Reported absent without leave from December 1, 1864, through February 28, 1865. Survived the war.

OVERCASH, REUBEN G., Private

Born in Rowan County where he resided prior to enlisting in Rowan County at age 27, July 4, 1862, for the war. Hospitalized at Richmond, Virginia, September 22, 1862. Returned to duty on or about September 30, 1862. Wounded slightly at Fredericksburg, Virginia, December 13, 1862. Hospitalized at Richmond. Transferred to hospital at Farmville, Virginia, March 9, 1863. Died in hospital at Farmville on April 7, 1863, of "smallpox."

OVERCASH, SOLOMON W., Private

Resided in Rowan County where he enlisted at age 34, July 4, 1862, for the war. Reported present or accounted for until May 4, 1863, when he was captured at Chancellorsville, Virginia. Confined at Old Capitol Prison, Washington, D.C. Transferred to Fort Delaware, Delaware, May 7, 1863. Paroled at Fort Delaware and transferred to City Point, Virginia, where he was received on May 23, 1863, for exchange. Died at Petersburg, Virginia, May 24 or July 16, 1863. Cause of death not reported.

PAYNE, W. T., Sergeant

Place and date of enlistment not reported (probably enlisted subsequent to February 28, 1865). Promotion record not reported. Paroled at Lynchburg, Virginia, April 15, 1865.

PHIFER, JOHN D., Sergeant

Resided in Mecklenburg County and was by occupation a laborer prior to enlisting in Rowan County at age 40, July 4, 1862, for the war as a substitute for S. H. Johnston of Mecklenburg County. Mustered in as Private. Hospitalized at Richmond, Virginia, October 27, 1862, with pneumonia. Furloughed for twenty days on November 14, 1862. Hospitalized at Richmond on December 29, 1862. Returned to duty in January-February, 1863. Reported on duty as color bearer on February 28, 1863. Promoted to Sergeant

in March-May, 1863. Hospitalized at Richmond on June 17, 1863, with chronic diarrhoea. Returned to duty on July 1, 1863. Sent to hospital on September 25, 1863. Returned to duty in January-April, 1864. Wounded at Winchester, Virginia, July 20, 1864. Hospitalized at Staunton, Virginia. Furloughed for sixty days from hospital at Richmond on August 20, 1864. Reported absent wounded through February 28, 1865. Paroled at Charlotte on May 15, 1865.

PHIFER, MARTIN L., Private

Resided in Iredell County and enlisted in Rowan County at age 25, July 4, 1862, for the war. Reported present until May 4, 1863, when he was wounded slightly in the hand at Chancellorsville, Virginia. Hospitalized at Charlottesville, Virginia, July 27, 1863, with debilitas. Returned to duty on July 31, 1863. Captured at Rappahannock Station, Virginia, November 7, 1863. Sent to Washington, D.C. Confined at Point Lookout, Maryland, November 11, 1863. Paroled at Point Lookout on October 30, 1864. Received at Venus Point, Savannah River, Georgia, November 15, 1864, for exchange. Reported absent without leave on December 5, 1864. Returned to duty in January-February, 1865. Captured at Farmville, Virginia, April 6, 1865. Confined at Newport News, Virginia, April 14, 1865. Released at Newport News on June 26, 1865, after taking the Oath of Allegiance.

PLUMMER, FRANK E., Private

Resided in Rowan County and was by occupation a clerk prior to enlisting in Rowan County at age 20, July 4, 1862, for the war. Reported present until December 13, 1862, when he was wounded slightly in the head at Fredericksburg, Virginia. Hospitalized at Richmond, Virginia. Transferred to hospital at Danville, Virginia, December 23, 1862. Returned to duty in January-February, 1863. Reported present through August 31, 1863. Hospitalized at Richmond on October 2, 1863, with chronic diarrhoea. Furloughed for thirty days on October 24, 1863. Reported absent on furlough through December 31, 1863. Transferred to Company K, 8th Regiment N.C. State Troops, January 21, 1864, in exchange for Cpl. William P. Rainey.

RAINEY, WILLIAM P., Private

Previously served as Corporal in Company K, 8th Regiment N.C. State Troops. Transferred to this company on January 21, 1864, in exchange for Pvt. Frank E. Plummer. Reported present in March-April, 1864. Killed at Winchester, Virginia, July 20, 1864.

REINHEART, ANDREW, Private

Enlisted in Rowan County at age 34, July 4, 1862, for the war. Reported present or accounted for through December 31, 1862. Sent to hospital at Richmond, Virginia, February 25, 1863. Returned to duty in September-October, 1863. Captured at Rappahannock Station, Virginia, November 7, 1863. Sent to Washington, D.C. Confined at Point Lookout, Maryland, November 11, 1863. Paroled at Point Lookout on March 16, 1864. Received at City Point, Virginia, March 20, 1864, for exchange. Returned to duty subsequent to April 30, 1864. Reported on detail as a teamster from November 9, 1864, through February 28, 1865. Surrendered at Appomattox Court House, Virginia, April 9, 1865.

REINHEART, JOHN, Private

Resided in Catawba County and enlisted in Rowan County at age 27, July 4, 1862, for the war. Sent to hospital on September 22, 1862. Hospitalized at Richmond, Virginia, December 24, 1862, with pneumonia. Furloughed for forty days on January 29, 1863. Returned to duty prior to May 11, 1863. Sent to hospital on June 19, 1863. Died prior to November 1, 1863. Place and cause of death not reported.

RICKARD, J. A., Private

Resided in Davidson County and enlisted in Rowan County at age 27, July 4, 1862, for the war. Reported present on surviving company muster rolls through October 31, 1864. Served as a teamster during most of that period. Furloughed on December 22, 1864. Returned to duty in January-February, 1865. Wounded in the abdomen at Fort Stedman, Virginia, March 25, 1865. Hospitalized at Richmond, Virginia. Captured in hospital at Richmond on April 3, 1865. Transferred to hospital at Point Lookout, Maryland, May 2, 1865. Released at Point Lookout on or about June 26, 1865, after taking the Oath of Allegiance.

RODGERS, LEONARD F., Private

Resided in Rowan County where he enlisted at age 29, July 4, 1862, for the war. Reported absent sick on August 4, 1862. Returned to duty in September-October, 1862. Reported present in November, 1862-February, 1863. Hospitalized at Richmond, Virginia, May 6, 1863. Transferred to Lynchburg, Virginia, May 11, 1863. Captured on or about May 24, 1863, during the "raid in the rear of Lee's army." Paroled on or about the same date. Returned to duty in November-December, 1863. Reported present on surviving company muster rolls through August 31, 1864. Captured at Fisher's Hill, Virginia, September 22, 1864. Confined at Point Lookout, Maryland, October 3, 1864. Paroled at Point Lookout and transferred to Aiken's Landing, James River, Virginia, March 17, 1865. Received at Boulware's Wharf, James River, March 19, 1865, for exchange. Survived the war.

SCOTTIE, G. B., Private

Resided in Rowan County where he enlisted at age 31, July 4, 1862, for the war. Mustered in as 1st Sergeant. Reduced to ranks on October 14, 1862. Hospitalized at Richmond, Virginia, October 27, 1862, convalescent from diarrhoea. Deserted on or about November 13, 1862. Returned to duty on November 17, 1862. Deserted at Port Royal, Virginia, February 17, 1863.

SHORES, JOHN H., Private

Resided in Forsyth County where he enlisted at age 18, March 12, 1864, for the war. Sent to hospital at Lynchburg, Virginia, June 13, 1864. Died at Lynchburg on July 2, 1864. Cause of death not reported.

SIGMOND, J. T., Private

Place and date of enlistment not reported (probably enlisted subsequent to February 28, 1865). Paroled at or near Farmville, Virginia, April 11-21, 1865.

SMITH, AMOS V., Private

Resided in Rowan County where he enlisted at age 24, July 4, 1862, for the war. Reported present until December 13, 1862, when he was wounded in the left leg at Fredericksburg, Virginia. Hospitalized at Richmond, Virginia. Transferred to another Richmond hospital on February 21, 1863, suffering from varioloid. Furloughed for thirty days on May 14, 1863. Returned to duty in January-April, 1864. Sent to hospital at Staunton, Virginia, June 21, 1864. Returned to duty in September-October, 1864. Reported

on detached duty at Staunton from November 26, 1864, through February 28, 1865. Returned to duty on an unspecified date. Surrendered at Appomattox Court House, Virginia, April 9, 1865.

SMITH, S. LOGAN, Private

Enlisted in Wake County on April 1, 1864, for the war. Hospitalized at Charlottesville, Virginia, September 1, 1864, with "sequelae of rubeola." Returned to duty on September 5, 1864. Wounded in the right foot and captured at Cedar Creek, Virginia, October 19, 1864. Hospitalized at Baltimore, Maryland. Transferred to Point Lookout, Maryland, October 25, 1864. Paroled at Point Lookout on October 29, 1864. Received at Venus Point, Savannah River, Georgia, November 15, 1864, for exchange. Furloughed on December 13, 1864. Reported absent on furlough through February 28, 1865. Survived the war. [North Carolina pension records indicate that he was about 18 years of age at time of enlistment.]

SNIDER, A. W., Private

Resided in Davie County and enlisted in Rowan County at age 18, July 4, 1862, for the war. Died in hospital at Richmond, Virginia, on or about October 11, 1862, of "brain fever."

SOSSAMAN, J. W., Corporal

Resided in Rowan County and was by occupation a buggy maker prior to enlisting in Rowan County at age 36, July 4, 1862, for the war as a substitute for W. L. Knox of Iredell County. Mustered in as Private. Hospitalized at Richmond, Virginia, on or about September 14, 1862. Transferred to hospital at Petersburg, Virginia, October 9, 1862. Returned to duty prior to January 1, 1863. Promoted to Corporal in March-May, 1863. Reported present through May 11, 1863. Captured at Gettysburg, Pennsylvania, July 1-5, 1863. Confined at Fort Delaware, Delaware, on or about July 10, 1863. Released at Fort Delaware on June 19, 1865, after taking the Oath of Allegiance.

SWICEGOOD, JESSE A., Private

Enlisted in Rowan County at age 16, July 7, 1862, for the war as a substitute for J. F. Lomax of Davidson County. Transferred to Company K of this regiment on or about July 17, 1862.

SWIFT, GEORGE W., Private

Born in Davidson County and was by occupation a farmer prior to enlisting in Rowan County at age 20, July 4, 1862, for the war. Reported present or accounted for through May 11, 1863. Hospitalized at Richmond, Virginia, May 18, 1863, with debilitas. Transferred to Salisbury on or about June 7, 1863. Returned to duty prior to September 1, 1863. Captured at Rappahannock Station, Virginia, November 7, 1863. Confined at Point Lookout, Maryland, November 11, 1863. Released at Point Lookout on January 23, 1864, after taking the Oath of Allegiance and joining the U.S. Army. Assigned to Company G, 1st Regiment U.S. Volunteer Infantry.

TATE, LEMUEL ROBERT, Private

Born on March 7, 1829. Resided in Davidson County and enlisted in Rowan County at age 33, July 4, 1862, for the war. Sent to hospital on November 13, 1862. Reported in hospital at Danville, Virginia, February 3, 1863, with otorrhea. Returned to duty on March 13, 1863. Reported present until September 28, 1863, when he was sent to hospital. Returned to duty in November-December, 1863. Reported present in March-April, 1864. Sent to hospital on July 23, 1864. Returned to duty in September-October, 1864.

Reported present through February 28, 1865. Wounded in the left foot and captured at Fort Stedman, Virginia, March 25, 1865. Hospitalized at Washington, D.C. Released on June 14, 1865, after taking the Oath of Allegiance.

TEACHEY, STEPHEN B., Private

Resided in Duplin County and was by occupation a farmer prior to enlisting in Wake County at age 18, April 1, 1864, for the war. Captured at Winchester, Virginia, July 20, 1864. Confined at Camp Chase, Ohio, July 28, 1864. Released at Camp Chase on May 15, 1865, after taking the Oath of Allegiance.

TERRELL, D. W., Corporal

Resided in Davie County and enlisted at age 30, July 4, 1862, for the war. Mustered in as Corporal. Died at Port Royal, Virginia, February 25, 1863. Cause of death not reported.

THOMPSON, J. C., Private

Resided in Iredell County and enlisted in Rowan County at age 27, July 4, 1862, for the war. Reported present or accounted for on surviving company muster rolls through August 31, 1864. Captured at Cedar Creek, Virginia, October 19, 1864. Confined at Point Lookout, Maryland, October 28, 1864. Paroled at Point Lookout on February 10, 1865. Received at Cox's Wharf, James River, Virginia, February 14-15, 1865, for exchange. Hospitalized at Lynchburg, Virginia, February 19, 1865, with aphonia and phthisis. Detailed for hospital duty at Lynchburg on an unspecified date. No further records.

TRAFFENSTEDT, JOSEPH, Private

Resided in Catawba County and was by occupation a farmer prior to enlisting in Rowan County at age 32, July 4, 1862, for the war. Died at Culpeper, Virginia, November 17, 1862, of "brain fever."

TUCKER, JOHN, Private

Resided in Davie County and enlisted in Rowan County at age 32, July 4, 1862, for the war. Hospitalized at Richmond, Virginia, October 25, 1862, with debility. Died in hospital at Richmond on January 5, 1863, of "variola & pneumonia."

TUCKER, M., Private

Enlisted in Rowan County at age 31, July 7, 1862, for the war. No further records.

TUCKER, THOMAS D., Private

Resided in Davie County and enlisted in Rowan County at age 19, July 4, 1862, for the war. Reported present through October 31, 1862. Killed at Fredericksburg, Virginia, December 13, 1862.

WADDELL, WILLIAM HENRY, Private

Resided in Iredell County and enlisted in Rowan County at age 22, July 4, 1862, for the war. Reported absent sick from August 11 through October 31, 1862. Killed at Fredericksburg, Virginia, December 13, 1862.

WALSER, BURTON, Private

Resided in Davidson County and enlisted in Rowan County at age 21, July 4, 1862, for the war. Reported present or accounted for through August 31, 1863. Reported absent on sick furlough in September-December, 1863. Returned to duty prior to May 1, 1864. Hospitalized at Richmond, Virginia, May 27, 1864, with

debility. Returned to duty subsequent to June 27, 1864. Captured at Fisher's Hill, Virginia, September 22, 1864. Confined at Point Lookout, Maryland, October 3, 1864. Paroled at Point Lookout on March 17, 1865. Received at Boulware's Wharf, James River, Virginia, March 19, 1865, for exchange. Survived the war.

WALSER, J. H., Private

Resided in Davidson County and enlisted in Rowan County at age 23, July 4, 1862, for the war. Mustered in as Private. Promoted to Corporal in November-December, 1862. Promoted to Sergeant in March-May, 1863. Reported present until June 4, 1863, when he was hospitalized at Richmond, Virginia, with diarrhoea. Returned to duty on July 3, 1863. Captured at Rappahannock Station, Virginia, November 7, 1863. Sent to Washington, D.C. Confined at Point Lookout, Maryland, November 11, 1863. Paroled at Point Lookout on March 16, 1864. Received at City Point, Virginia, March 20, 1864, for exchange. Hospitalized at Richmond on June 27, 1864, with rubeola. Reported absent without leave on an unspecified date. Returned to duty prior to September 1, 1864. Reported present through December 31, 1864. Reduced to ranks in January-February, 1865. Captured at Hatcher's Run, Virginia, February 6, 1865. Confined at Point Lookout on February 9, 1865. Released at Point Lookout on June 21, 1865, after taking the Oath of Allegiance.

WALSER, ROLAND, Corporal

Resided in Davidson County and enlisted in Rowan County at age 23, July 4, 1862, for the war. Mustered in as Private. Reported present through February 28, 1863. Hospitalized at Richmond, Virginia, May 8, 1863, with dyspepsia. Transferred to Lynchburg, Virginia, May 9, 1863. Captured at Lynchburg on or about May 24, 1863, during the "raid in the rear of Lee's army." Paroled on or about the same date. Hospitalized at Farmville, Virginia, June 16, 1863, with debilitas. Returned to duty on or about July 30, 1863. Promoted to Corporal prior to November 7, 1863, when he was captured at Rappahannock Station, Virginia. Sent to Washington, D.C. Confined at Point Lookout, Maryland, November 11, 1863. Paroled at Point Lookout and transferred to Aiken's Landing, James River, Virginia, February 24, 1865. Received at Aiken's Landing on February 25-28 or March 2-3, 1865, for exchange. Survived the war.

WALSER, W. H., Private

Resided in Davidson County and enlisted in Rowan County at age 33, July 4, 1862, for the war. Reported present or accounted for through October 31, 1862. Hospitalized at Richmond, Virginia, December 9, 1862. Died in hospital at Richmond on or about January 12, 1863, of "typhoid fever."

WARLICK, DAVID L., Sergeant

Resided in Catawba County and enlisted in Rowan County at age 18, July 4, 1862, for the war. Mustered in as Private. Promoted to Corporal in November-December, 1862. Promoted to Sergeant in January-February, 1863. Reported present through May 11, 1863. Wounded in the finger at Gettysburg, Pennsylvania, July 1-2, 1863. Finger amputated. Returned to duty prior to September 1, 1863. Captured at Rappahannock Station, Virginia, November 7, 1863. Confined at Point Lookout, Maryland, November 11, 1863. Paroled at Point Lookout on March 16, 1864. Received at City Point, Virginia, March 20, 1864, for exchange. Returned to duty prior to September 1, 1864. Reported present through February 28, 1865. Surrendered at Appomattox Court House, Virginia, April 9, 1865.

WARLICK, J. M., Private

Resided in Catawba County and enlisted in Rowan County at age 29, July 4, 1862, for the war. Sent to hospital on or about August 11, 1862. Deserted on October 20, 1862. Returned to duty on February 1, 1863. Reported present until November 10, 1863, when he was hospitalized at Richmond, Virginia. Died at home in Catawba County prior to May 1, 1864. Cause of death not reported.

WEANT, BENJAMIN FRANK, 1st Sergeant

Previously served as Private in Capt. William H. Howard's Company, N.C. Prison Guards. Enlisted in this company on or about July 4, 1862. Mustered in as Sergeant. Promoted to 1st Sergeant in January-February, 1863. Reported present until April 27, 1863, when he was hospitalized at Charlottesville, Virginia, with chronic diarrhoea. Returned to duty prior to September 1, 1863. Captured at Rappahannock Station, Virginia, November 7, 1863. Sent to Washington, D.C. Confined at Point Lookout, Maryland, November 11, 1863. Paroled at Point Lookout on February 24, 1865. Received at Aiken's Landing, James River, Virginia, February 25-28 or March 2-3, 1865, for exchange. Paroled at Salisbury on May 20, 1865. Took the Oath of Allegiance at Salisbury on June 24, 1865.

WESMORELAND, WILLIAM D., Private

Enlisted in Rowan County at age 22, July 7, 1862, for the war. No further records.

WHISENHUNT, JOHN, Private

Resided in Catawba County and enlisted in Rowan County at age 34, July 4, 1862, for the war. Sent to hospital from camp near Fredericksburg, Virginia, December 14, 1862. Died at home in Catawba County on January 14, 1863. Cause of death not reported.

WILLIAMS, ANDREW MADISON, Private

Born on December 8, 1836. Resided in Davidson County and was by occupation a farmer prior to enlisting in Rowan County at age 25, October 10, 1862, for the war. Wounded in the left hand at Fredericksburg, Virginia, December 13, 1862. Hospitalized at Richmond, Virginia. Furloughed for forty days on or about December 30, 1862. Reported absent without leave on May 11, 1863. Reported under arrest for desertion in November-December, 1863. Returned to duty prior to May 1, 1864. Captured at Winchester, Virginia, September 19, 1864. Confined at Point Lookout, Maryland, September 27, 1864. Released at Point Lookout on May 14, 1865, after taking the Oath of Allegiance. [North Carolina pension records indicate that he was wounded in the head by a piece of shell at Lynchburg, Virginia, on an unspecified date.]

WILLIAMS, HIRAM STOKES, Private

Resided in Davidson or Davie County and enlisted in Rowan County at age 31, July 4, 1862, for the war. Hospitalized at Richmond, Virginia, October 10, 1862, with remittent fever. Furloughed on November 20, 1862. Returned to duty prior to December 13, 1862, when he was wounded at Fredericksburg, Virginia. Reported absent wounded through February 28, 1863. Reported absent without leave in March-August, 1863. Returned to duty in September-October, 1863. Reported under arrest (probably at Salisbury) in November, 1863-December, 1864, for desertion. Returned to duty in January-February, 1865. Captured at Fort Stedman, Virginia, March 25, 1865. Confined at Point Lookout, Maryland, March 28, 1865. Released at Point Lookout on June 21, 1865, after taking the Oath of Allegiance.

WILLIAMS, WILLIAM A., Private

Resided in Davidson County and was by occupation a farmer prior to enlisting in Rowan County at age 34, July 4, 1862, for the war. Wounded in the finger at Fredericksburg, Virginia, December 13, 1862. Hospitalized at Richmond, Virginia. Furloughed for forty days on or about December 30, 1862. Reported absent without leave in March-October, 1863. Returned to duty in January-April, 1864. Reported under arrest for desertion in September-December, 1864. Returned to duty in January-February, 1865. Captured at Fort Stedman, Virginia, March 25, 1865. Confined at Point Lookout, Maryland, March 28, 1865. Released at Point Lookout on June 21, 1865, after taking the Oath of Allegiance.

WILLIFORD, WILLIAM H., Private

Resided in Rowan County and was by occupation a farmer prior to enlisting in Rowan County at age 27, July 4, 1862, for the war. Hospitalized at Richmond, Virginia, September 3, 1862, with hemiplegia. Furloughed for thirty days on September 5, 1862. Died in Rowan County on April 10, 1863, of "pneumonia."

WORLDS, JOHN, Private

Resided in Davidson County and enlisted in Rowan County at age 34, July 4, 1862, for the war. Hospitalized at Richmond, Virginia, September 24, 1862. Returned to duty on or about September 29, 1862. Sent to hospital on October 12, 1862. Returned to duty in January-February, 1863. Reported present through October 31, 1863. Captured at Rappahannock Station, Virginia, November 7, 1863. Sent to Washington, D.C. Confined at Point Lookout, Maryland, November 11, 1863. Paroled at Point Lookout on March 16, 1864. Received at City Point, Virginia, March 20, 1864, for exchange. Returned to duty prior to September 1, 1864, after being absent without leave for two months and eighteen days. Wounded in the neck either at Winchester, Virginia, September 19, 1864, or near Cedar Creek, Virginia, on or about October 12, 1864. Reported absent wounded through February 28, 1865. Survived the war.

WRIGHT, JAMES A., Private

Resided in Rowan County and was by occupation a farmer prior to enlisting in Rowan County at age 28, July 4, 1862, for the war. Reported absent sick at Camp Salisbury, near Richmond, Virginia, September 23, 1862. Reported absent without leave on December 1, 1862. Returned to duty subsequent to December 31, 1862. Hospitalized at Richmond on May 8, 1863, with debilitas. Transferred to hospital at Danville, Virginia, May 11, 1863. Hospitalized at Richmond on an unspecified date after being "wound[ed] in foot with an axe severing extensor tendons." Furloughed for forty days on June 4, 1863. Reported absent without leave on January 1, 1864. Returned to duty in September-October, 1864, and was detailed as an ambulance driver. Reported absent on detached service at Staunton, Virginia, from December 21, 1864, through February 28, 1865. No further records.

WRIGHT, MINTON AUGUSTUS, Private

Previously served on the North Carolina coast as an unattached engineer (acting 1st Lieutenant). Subsequently served as 3rd Lieutenant in Lt. Col. Paul F. DeGournay's Battalion Louisiana Heavy Artillery and as Private in Capt. Charles R. Grandy's Company, Norfolk Light Artillery Battalion. Transferred to this company on April 5, 1863. Appointed Ordnance Sergeant prior to May 11, 1863, and transferred to the Field and Staff of this regiment.

COMPANY C

This company was raised in Rowan County on July 4, 1862. It was mustered into service at Salisbury on July 17, 1862, and assigned to the 57th Regiment N.C. Troops as Company C. After joining the regiment the company functioned as a part of the regiment, and its history for the remainder of the war is reported as a part of the regimental history.

The following roster was compiled primarily from information in the microfilm edition of the Compiled Service Records of Soldiers Who Served in Organizations from the State of North Carolina (Record Group 109, M270), National Archives and Records Administration, Washington, D.C. Record Group 109 includes enlistment papers, pay vouchers, requisitions, letters of resignation, discharge certificates, and abstracts of medical and prisoner of war returns. Materials relating specifically to this company include a muster-in and descriptive roll dated July 17, 1862, and muster rolls dated July, 1862-December, 1863, and March, 1864-February, 1865.

Also utilized in this roster were *The War of the Rebellion: A Compilation of the Official Records of the Union and Confederate Armies*, the North Carolina adjutant general's *Roll of Honor*, state militia records, newspaper casualty lists and obituaries, wartime claims for bounty pay and allowances, postwar registers of claims for artificial limbs, Confederate pension applications filed with the states of North Carolina, Tennessee, and Florida, Confederate Soldiers' Home records, and the 1860 and 1870 federal censuses of North Carolina. A search was made also for relevant letters, diaries, reminiscences, and other manuscripts in the Southern Historical Collection (University of North Carolina-Chapel Hill), the Duke University Library Special Collections Department, and the North Carolina Division of Archives and History.

Among the secondary sources consulted were records of the North Carolina division of the United Daughters of the Confederacy, postwar rosters, regimental and county histories, marriage bond, will, and cemetery indexes, published and unpublished genealogies, biographical dictionaries, the North Carolina *County Heritage Book* series, the *Confederate Veteran*, Walter Clark's *Histories of the Several Regiments and Battalions from North Carolina in the Great War, 1861-'65*, and the North Carolina volume of the extended edition of *Confederate Military History*.

OFFICERS

CAPTAINS

BEARD, JOHN

Resided in Rowan County and was by occupation a farmer prior to enlisting at age 28. Appointed Captain on July 4, 1862. Reported present or accounted for on surviving company muster rolls through February 28, 1865. Paroled at Appomattox Court House, Virginia, April 9, 1865. Took the Oath of Allegiance at Salisbury on June 24, 1865. [Reported in command of Company A of this regiment in November-December, 1863. Reported in command of Brig. Gen. William G. Lewis's brigade on April 9, 1865.]

HUNTER, MILES H.

Served as Captain of Company B of this regiment. Reported in command of this company in November-December, 1864.

LIEUTENANTS

GRAHAM, FURGERSON M., 1st Lieutenant

Resided in Rowan County where he enlisted at age 33. Appointed 1st Lieutenant on July 4, 1862. Reported present through August 31, 1863. Hospitalized at Richmond, Virginia, October 24, 1863, with a gunshot wound of the left hip. Place and date wounded not reported. Furloughed for forty days on or about November 18, 1863. Returned to duty on an unspecified date. Reported in command of the company in March-April, 1864. Killed at Harpers Ferry, West Virginia, July 5, 1864. [Reported in command of Company A of this regiment in March-April, 1864. He was "a most excellent officer." (Clark's *Regiments*, 3:419).]

MILLER, JESSE W., 2nd Lieutenant

Resided in Rowan County and was by occupation a farmer prior to enlisting in Rowan County at age 32. Elected 2nd Lieutenant on July 4, 1862. Reported present or accounted for through July 31, 1863. Promoted to Captain on August 1, 1863, and transferred to Company E of this regiment. [Previously served as Captain of Company E, 120th Regiment N.C. Militia. Reported in command of Company A of this regiment from May 27 through July 31, 1863.]

VERBLE, HENRY DANIEL, 3rd Lieutenant

Resided in Rowan County and enlisted at age 31. Appointed 3rd Lieutenant on July 4, 1862. Reported present or accounted for through February 28, 1863. Captured at Chancellorsville, Virginia, May 4, 1863. Confined at Old Capitol Prison, Washington, D.C. Paroled on May 18, 1863. Hospitalized at Richmond, Virginia, July 2, 1863, with chronic diarrhoea. Returned to duty on July 20, 1863. Reported present through October 31, 1863. Captured at Rappahannock Station, Virginia, November 7, 1863. Confined at Old Capitol Prison. Transferred to Johnson's Island, Ohio, where he arrived on November 14, 1863. Released at Johnson's Island on June 13, 1865, after taking the Oath of Allegiance.

NONCOMMISSIONED OFFICERS AND PRIVATES

ALBRIGHT, JACOB J., Private

Resided in Rowan County where he enlisted at age 32, July 4, 1862, for the war. Mustered in as Sergeant. Hospitalized at Richmond, Virginia, November 8, 1862, with intermittent fever. Transferred to hospital at Danville, Virginia, December 19, 1862 (suffering from debilitas). Reduced to ranks in November-December, 1862. Returned to duty on March 13, 1863. Reported present until November 7, 1863, when he was captured at Rappahannock Station, Virginia. Confined at Point Lookout, Maryland. Paroled at Point Lookout on March 16, 1864. Received at City Point, Virginia, March 20, 1864, for exchange. Returned to duty prior to July 10, 1864, when he was captured at the Monocacy River, Maryland. Hospitalized at Frederick, Maryland, the same date with an unspecified complaint. Hospitalized at Baltimore, Maryland, July 25, 1864, with diarrhoea. Transferred to Point Lookout on October 25, 1864. Paroled at Point Lookout and transferred for exchange on or about October 30, 1864. Received at Venus Point, Savannah River, Georgia, November 15, 1864, for exchange. Reported absent without leave from December 18, 1864, through February 28, 1865. Paroled at Salisbury on May 18, 1865.

ALBRIGHT, JOHN J., ———

North Carolina pension records indicate that he served in this company.

ALBRIGHT, PETER, Private

Resided in Rowan County and was by occupation a farmer prior to enlisting in Rowan County at age 33, July 4, 1862, for the war. Hospitalized at Richmond, Virginia, October 19, 1862, with intermittent fever. Transferred to hospital at Danville, Virginia, December 19, 1862 (suffering from debilitas). Returned to duty on January 17, 1863. Captured at Chancellorsville, Virginia, May 3-4, 1863. Confined at Fort Delaware, Delaware, on or about May 7, 1863. Paroled and transferred to City Point, Virginia, where he was received on May 23, 1863, for exchange. Returned to duty in September-October, 1863. Captured at Rappahannock Station, Virginia, November 7, 1863. Confined at Point Lookout, Maryland, November 11, 1863. Paroled at Point Lookout and transferred to City Point where he was received on March 20, 1864, for exchange. Returned to duty prior to July 20, 1864, when he was captured at Winchester, Virginia. Confined at Camp Chase, Ohio, July 28, 1864. Released at Camp Chase on May 13, 1865, after taking the Oath of Allegiance.

ALBRIGHT, PETER R., Private

Resided in Rowan County and was by occupation a farmer prior to enlisting in Rowan County at age 30, July 4, 1862, for the war. Hospitalized at Richmond, Virginia, September 25, 1862, with diarrhoea. Transferred to hospital at Farmville, Virginia, January 15, 1863. Returned to duty on May 15, 1863. Wounded in the right leg (fracture) at Gettysburg, Pennsylvania, July 1-3, 1863. Captured at Williamsport, Maryland, July 14, 1863. Hospitalized at Harrisburg, Pennsylvania, and Philadelphia, Pennsylvania. Confined at Fort Delaware, Delaware, on an unspecified date (probably on or about November 1, 1863). Paroled at Fort Delaware on September 14, 1864. Received at Aiken's Landing, James River, Virginia, September 18, 1864, for exchange. Hospitalized at Richmond on September 21, 1864, still suffering from wounds received at Gettysburg. Furloughed for sixty days on October 5, 1864. Reported absent on furlough through December 31, 1864. Reported absent without leave in January-February, 1865. Took the Oath of Allegiance at Salisbury on June 17, 1865.

ALBRIGHT, WILLIAM M., Private

Resided in Rowan County and was by occupation a farmer prior to enlisting in Rowan County at age 32, July 4, 1862, for the war. Reported present in July-August, 1862. Wounded in the left thigh at Fredericksburg, Virginia, December 13, 1862. Hospitalized at Richmond, Virginia, where he died on or about January 30, 1863, of wounds and/or disease.

BAKER, HENRY F., Private

Resided in Rowan County where he enlisted at age 32, July 4, 1862, for the war. Hospitalized at Richmond, Virginia, November 9, 1862. Furloughed for thirty days on or about December 6, 1862. Returned to duty prior to March 1, 1863. Sent to hospital at Richmond on September 9, 1863. Returned to duty on October 27, 1863. Captured at Rappahannock Station, Virginia, November 7, 1863. Confined at Point Lookout, Maryland, November 11, 1863. Paroled at Point Lookout on March 16, 1864. Received at City

Point, Virginia, March 20, 1864, for exchange. Returned to duty in May-August, 1864. Reported present through February 28, 1865. Surrendered at Appomattox Court House, Virginia, April 9, 1865. Took the Oath of Allegiance at Salisbury on June 13, 1865.

BAKER, JOHN, Private

Resided in Rowan County and enlisted in Guilford County on October 26, 1864, for the war. Reported present through February 28, 1865. Took the Oath of Allegiance at Salisbury on June 15, 1865.

BARRINGER, E. F., Private

Resided in Rowan County and was by occupation a farmer prior to enlisting in Rowan County at age 20, July 4, 1862, for the war. Hospitalized at Richmond, Virginia, December 24, 1862, with typhoid fever. Transferred to hospital at Huguenot Springs, Virginia, January 16, 1863. Returned to duty prior to March 1, 1863. Captured at Chancellorsville, Virginia, May 3-4, 1863. Confined at Fort Delaware, Delaware, on or about May 7, 1863. Paroled at Fort Delaware and transferred to City Point, Virginia, where he was received on May 23, 1863, for exchange. Returned to duty prior to September 1, 1863. Captured at Rappahannock Station, Virginia, November 7, 1863. Confined at Point Lookout, Maryland, November 11, 1863. Paroled at Point Lookout on March 17, 1864. Received at City Point on March 20, 1864, for exchange. Returned to duty prior to July 20, 1864, when he was captured at Winchester, Virginia. Confined at Camp Chase, Ohio, July 28, 1864. Paroled at Camp Chase and transferred to City Point on March 2, 1865. Received at Boulware's and Cox's Wharves, James River, Virginia, March 10-12, 1865, for exchange. Hospitalized at Richmond on March 12, 1865, with debilitas. Furloughed for thirty days on March 22, 1865.

BARRINGER, JOHN, Private

Resided in Rowan County where he enlisted on May 20, 1864, for the war. Sent to hospital on June 22, 1864. Returned to duty on an unspecified date. Reported present in November, 1864-February, 1865. Surrendered at Appomattox Court House, Virginia, April 9, 1865. Took the Oath of Allegiance at Salisbury on June 10, 1865. [May have served previously as Private in Capt. William H. Howard's Company, N.C. Prison Guards.]

BEARD, JOHN, Private

Enlisted in Wake County on March 12, 1864, for the war. Reported present or accounted for through February 28, 1865. Surrendered at Appomattox Court House, Virginia, April 9, 1865.

BEARD, W. W., Private

Enlisted at Brown's Gap, Virginia, September 25, 1864, for the war. Reported present or accounted for through December 31, 1864. No further records.

BEARD, WILLIAM, Private

Enlisted in Guilford County on October 23, 1864, for the war. Reported present through February 28, 1865. No further records.

BEAVER, ALEXANDER, Private

Resided in Rowan County where he enlisted at age 30, July 4, 1862, for the war. Hospitalized at Richmond, Virginia, September 25, 1862. Returned to duty prior to December 13, 1862, when he was wounded in the arm at Fredericksburg, Virginia. Died in hospital at Richmond on April 10, 1863, of wounds.

BEAVER, CRAWFORD, Private

Resided in Rowan County where he enlisted at age 28, July 4, 1862, for the war. Mustered in as Private. Hospitalized at Richmond, Virginia, October 23, 1862, with typhoid fever. Furloughed for thirty days on November 25, 1862. Returned to duty prior to March 1, 1863. Promoted to Corporal in May-August, 1863. Reported present through October 31, 1863. Captured at Rappahannock Station, Virginia, November 7, 1863. Confined at Point Lookout, Maryland, November 11, 1863. Paroled at Point Lookout on March 16, 1864. Received at City Point, Virginia, March 20, 1864, for exchange. Returned to duty prior to September 1, 1864. Reduced to ranks in September-October, 1864. Wounded in the shoulder at Cedar Creek, Virginia, October 19, 1864. Returned to duty prior to January 1, 1865. Reported present in January-February, 1865. Paroled at Salisbury on May 12, 1865.

BEAVER, GEORGE M., Private

Born in Rowan County where he resided as a shoemaker or farmer prior to enlisting in Rowan County at age 32, July 4, 1862, for the war. Hospitalized at Richmond, Virginia, November 3, 1862, with intermittent fever. Furloughed for thirty days on November 18, 1862. Hospitalized at Richmond on January 15, 1863, with pneumonia. Transferred to hospital at Danville, Virginia, March 14, 1863. Returned to duty on July 3, 1863. Discharged at Farmville, Virginia, on or about August 15, 1863, by reason of "cancer of tongue." Took the Oath of Allegiance at Salisbury on June 15, 1865.

BEAVER, TOBIAS, Private

Resided in Rowan County and was by occupation an overseer prior to enlisting in Rowan County at age 29, July 4, 1862, for the war. Hospitalized at Richmond, Virginia, October 16, 1862, with typhoid fever. Furloughed for thirty days on or about December 24, 1862. Returned to duty prior to March 1, 1863. Captured at Chancellorsville, Virginia, May 4, 1863. Confined at Fort Delaware, Delaware, on or about May 7, 1863. Paroled and transferred to City Point, Virginia, where he was received on May 23, 1863, for exchange. Returned to duty prior to September 1, 1863. Wounded in the left leg (fracture) and captured at Rappahannock Station, Virginia, November 7, 1863. Hospitalized at Washington, D.C. Died in hospital at Washington on March 27, 1864, of "secondary hemorrhage."

BESCHERER, JOHN, Private

Resided in Rowan County and was by occupation a farmer prior to enlisting in Rowan County at age 33, July 4, 1862, for the war. Reported present through February 28, 1863. Hospitalized at Charlottesville, Virginia, April 27, 1863, with rheumatism. Returned to duty on August 25, 1863. Reported present in September-October, 1863. Sent to hospital on December 3, 1863. Returned to duty prior to May 1, 1864. Captured at Winchester, Virginia, July 20, 1864. Confined at Camp Chase, Ohio, July 28, 1864. Hospitalized at Camp Chase on October 12, 1864. Died in hospital at Camp Chase on November 8, 1864, of "smallpox."

BLACK, J., Private

Enlisted in Rowan County on July 4, 1862, for the war. No further records.

BLACKWELL, GEORGE, Private

Born in Rowan County where he resided as a farmer prior to enlisting in Rowan County at age 25, July 4, 1862, for the war.

Reported present or accounted for through February 28, 1863. Wounded in the left shoulder (fracture) at Chancellorsville, Virginia, on or about May 4, 1863. Hospitalized at Richmond, Virginia, where he died on May 17, 1863, of wounds.

BLACKWELL, JOHN, Private

Resided in Rowan County and was by occupation a farmer prior to enlisting in Rowan County at age 30, July 4, 1862, for the war. Reported present through April 30, 1863. Wounded in the thigh at Gettysburg, Pennsylvania, July 1, 1863. Reported absent wounded or absent on furlough through April 30, 1864. Detailed in the ordnance department at Salisbury on August 6, 1864. Rejoined the company in November-December, 1864. Reported present through February 28, 1865. Surrendered at Appomattox Court House, Virginia, April 9, 1865. Took the Oath of Allegiance at Salisbury on June 13, 1865.

BOSTIAN, DANIEL M., Private

Resided in Rowan County where he enlisted at age 23, July 4, 1862, for the war. Reported present through February 28, 1863. Captured at Chancellorsville, Virginia, on or about May 4, 1863. Confined at Fort Delaware, Delaware, on or about May 7, 1863. Paroled at Fort Delaware and transferred to City Point, Virginia, where he was received on May 23, 1863, for exchange. Hospitalized on May 23, 1863, with chronic diarrhoea. Furloughed on June 22, 1863. Returned to duty on October 24, 1863. Captured at Rappahannock Station, Virginia, November 7, 1863. Confined at Point Lookout, Maryland, November 11, 1863. Paroled at Point Lookout on February 24, 1865. Received at Aiken's Landing, James River, Virginia, February 25-28 or March 2-3, 1865, for exchange. Paroled at Salisbury on May 15, 1865. Took the Oath of Allegiance at Salisbury on June 16, 1865.

BOSTIAN, JAMES A., Private

Resided in Rowan County where he enlisted at age 26, July 4, 1862, for the war. Mustered in as Private. Reported present through August 31, 1862. Promoted to Sergeant in September-October, 1862. Hospitalized at Richmond, Virginia, November 9, 1862. Returned to duty on December 2, 1862. Reduced to ranks prior to January 1, 1863. Sent to hospital at Richmond (sick) on January 15, 1863. Furloughed on April 30, 1863. Died of disease. Place and date of death not reported. [Previously served as 2nd Lieutenant of Company G, 120th Regiment N.C. Militia.]

BROWN, ALLEN, Private

Resided in Rowan County where he enlisted at age 18, July 4, 1862, for the war as a substitute. Hospitalized at Richmond, Virginia, September 28, 1862, with rheumatism. Returned to duty on October 3, 1862. Hospitalized at Charlottesville, Virginia, November 20, 1862. Transferred to hospital at Lynchburg, Virginia, the same date. Reported absent sick through October 31, 1863. Returned to duty in November-December, 1863. Wounded in the right gluteal region and captured at Winchester, Virginia, July 20, 1864. Hospitalized at Cumberland, Maryland, where he died on October 11, 1864, of wounds and "consumption."

BROWN, NATHAN, Private

Resided in Rowan County where he enlisted at age 25, July 4, 1862, for the war. Hospitalized at Richmond, Virginia, October 19, 1862, with remittent fever. Furloughed for thirty days on November 14, 1862. Returned to duty prior to January 1, 1863. Captured at

Chancellorsville, Virginia, May 3-4, 1863. Confined at Fort Delaware, Delaware, on or about May 7, 1863. Paroled at Fort Delaware and transferred to City Point, Virginia, where he was received on May 23, 1863, for exchange. Hospitalized at Farmville, Virginia, August 3, 1863, with scorbutus. Returned to duty on September 23, 1863. Captured at Rappahannock Station, Virginia, November 7, 1863. Confined at Point Lookout, Maryland, November 11, 1863. Paroled at Point Lookout on March 17, 1864. Received at Boulware's Wharf, James River, Virginia, March 20, 1864, for exchange. Returned to duty subsequent to April 30, 1864. Captured at Fisher's Hill, Virginia, September 22, 1864. Confined at Point Lookout on October 3, 1864. Paroled at Point Lookout on or about March 17, 1865. Received at Boulware's Wharf on March 19, 1865, for exchange. Paroled at Salisbury on May 15, 1865. Took the Oath of Allegiance at Salisbury on June 10, 1865.

BURGESS, O. A., Private

Resided in Rowan County where he enlisted at age 51, September 15, 1862, for the war as a substitute. Reported present through December 31, 1862. Hospitalized at Richmond, Virginia, January 27, 1863. Died in hospital at Richmond on February 10, 1863, of "chronic diarrhoea."

CASPER, ADAM MILAS, Private

Born on June 3, 1832. Resided in Rowan County and was by occupation a farm laborer prior to enlisting in Rowan County at age 30, July 4, 1862, for the war. Reported present through December 31, 1862. Hospitalized at Richmond, Virginia, February 21, 1863, with typhoid pneumonia. Transferred to Salisbury on April 13, 1863. Returned to duty prior to September 1, 1863. Reported present through April 30, 1864. Captured at Harpers Ferry, West Virginia, July 7-8, 1864. Confined at Old Capitol Prison, Washington, D.C., July 17, 1864. Transferred to Elmira, New York, where he arrived on July 25, 1864. Paroled at Elmira on February 20, 1865, and transferred for exchange. Hospitalized at Richmond on February 28, 1865. Transferred on March 1, 1865. Took the Oath of Allegiance at Salisbury on May 31, 1865.

CASTOR, HENRY A., Private

Born on April 8, 1833. Resided in Rowan or Cabarrus County and was by occupation a farm laborer prior to enlisting in Rowan County at age 29, July 4, 1862, for the war. Reported present or accounted for through December 31, 1862. Hospitalized at Richmond, Virginia, January 5, 1863, with catarrhus. Returned to duty on January 12, 1863, and was detailed as a teamster. Reported present on surviving company muster rolls through April 30, 1864. Served as a teamster during part of that period. Wounded at Harpers Ferry, West Virginia, July 6, 1864, and sent to hospital. Furloughed for forty days from hospital at Richmond on July 23, 1864. Reported absent on surgeon's certificate through December 31, 1864. Retired to the Invalid Corps on January 13, 1865. Paroled at Salisbury on May 2, 1865.

CASTOR, JACOB F., Private

Resided in Rowan County where he enlisted at age 24, July 4, 1862, for the war. Hospitalized at Richmond, Virginia, September 25, 1862, with debility. Transferred to Salisbury on October 7, 1862. Reported absent without leave on December 31, 1862. Confined at Castle Thunder Prison, Richmond, on an unspecified date. Hospitalized at Richmond on February 25, 1863, with variola. Returned to duty on March 24, 1863. Reported present on surviving company muster rolls through December 31, 1864. Wounded in the right leg at Hatcher's Run, Virginia, February 6, 1865. Hospitalized at

Richmond. Furloughed for sixty days on March 4, 1865. Paroled at Salisbury on May 23, 1865.

CAUBLE, JOHN M., Private

Resided in Rowan County where he enlisted at age 41, July 4, 1862, for the war as a substitute for William McKneely. Hospitalized at Richmond, Virginia, November 8, 1862, with chronic bronchitis. Later contracted smallpox. Returned to duty on January 29, 1863. Wounded in the shoulder at Chancellorsville, Virginia, May 4, 1863. Hospitalized at Richmond where he died on May 21, 1863, of wounds and/or "pneumonia."

CLONTS, WILLIAM L., Private

Resided in Rowan County where he enlisted at age 30, July 4, 1862, for the war. Hospitalized at Richmond, Virginia, October 20, 1862, with rubeola. Furloughed for thirty days on November 6, 1862. Returned to duty prior to January 1, 1863. Wounded in the side at Chancellorsville, Virginia, May 4, 1863. Returned to duty prior to September 1, 1863. Transferred to Company H of this regiment prior to November 1, 1863.

COLLY, JAMES M., Sergeant

Resided in Rowan County where he enlisted at age 25, July 4, 1862, for the war. Mustered in as Private. Promoted to Sergeant in November-December, 1862. Reported present through October 31, 1863. Captured at Rappahannock Station, Virginia, November 7, 1863. Confined at Point Lookout, Maryland, November 11, 1863. Paroled at Point Lookout on March 16, 1864. Received at City Point, Virginia, March 20, 1864, for exchange. Returned to duty subsequent to April 30, 1864. Wounded in the right leg and captured at or near Mount Jackson, Virginia, on or about September 23, 1864. Hospitalized at Winchester, Virginia, October 6, 1864. Admitted to hospital at Baltimore, Maryland, October 13, 1864. Confined at Point Lookout on October 18, 1864. Paroled and transferred to Venus Point, Savannah River, Georgia, where he was received on November 15, 1864, for exchange. Reported absent without leave on December 18, 1864. Returned to duty in January-February, 1865. Wounded in the ear and neck at Fort Stedman, Virginia, March 25, 1865. Hospitalized at Richmond, Virginia. Captured in hospital at Richmond on April 3, 1865. Transferred to Newport News, Virginia, where he arrived on April 24, 1865. Released at Newport News on June 30, 1865, after taking the Oath of Allegiance.

CORRELL, SAMUEL W. J., Private

Resided in Rowan County where he enlisted at age 18, August 24, 1862, for the war. Hospitalized at Richmond, Virginia, November 3, 1862. Died in hospital at Richmond on November 16, 1862, of "typhoid dysentery."

CORRIHER, L. BENJAMIN, Private

Resided in Rowan County where he enlisted at age 18, July 4, 1862, for the war. Reported present or accounted for through December 31, 1862. Hospitalized at Richmond, Virginia, January 11, 1863, with bronchitis. Transferred to Huguenot Springs, Virginia, on or about April 1, 1863. Returned to duty prior to May 1, 1863. Reported present until November 7, 1863, when he was captured at Rappahannock Station, Virginia. Confined at Point Lookout, Maryland, November 11, 1863. Paroled at Point Lookout on March 16, 1864. Received at City Point, Virginia, March 20, 1864, for exchange. Sent to hospital on July 19, 1864. Reported absent without leave on September 25, 1864. Deserted to the enemy on an unspecified date. Released at Clarksburg, West Virginia, November 5, 1864, after taking the Oath of Allegiance.

COWEN, JOHN M., Corporal

Resided in Rowan County where he enlisted at age 20, July 4, 1862, for the war. Mustered in as Corporal. Hospitalized at Richmond, Virginia, November 8, 1862, with typhoid fever. Transferred to hospital at Danville, Virginia, December 19, 1862 (suffering from debility). Reduced to ranks in November-December, 1862. Returned to duty on March 24, 1863. Furloughed on July 11, 1863. Returned to duty in September-October, 1863. Captured at Rappahannock Station, Virginia, November 7, 1863. Confined at Point Lookout, Maryland, November 11, 1863. Paroled at Point Lookout on March 16, 1864. Received at City Point, Virginia, March 20, 1864, for exchange. Promoted to Corporal in September-October, 1864. Reported present until February 6, 1865, when he was wounded in the jaw (fracture) at Hatcher's Run, Virginia. Hospitalized at Richmond. Furloughed for sixty days on March 2, 1865. Paroled at Salisbury on May 15, 1865. Took the Oath of Allegiance at Salisbury on June 19, 1865.

CRESS, CALVIN, Private

Resided in Iredell County and was by occupation a harness maker prior to enlisting in Guilford County on October 23, 1864, for the war. Reported present through December 31, 1864. Captured at Hatcher's Run, Virginia, February 6, 1865. Confined at Point Lookout, Maryland, February 9, 1865. Released at Point Lookout on May 13, 1865, after taking the Oath of Allegiance.

CRISWELL, JACOB D., Private

Resided in Rowan County where he enlisted at age 28, July 4, 1862, for the war. Reported present or accounted for on surviving company muster rolls through April 30, 1864. Captured at Harpers Ferry, West Virginia, on the night of July 7, 1864. Confined at Old Capitol Prison, Washington, D.C., July 17, 1864. Transferred to Elmira, New York, July 23, 1864. Died at Elmira on or about August 22, 1864, of "scorbutus."

CRISWELL, W. C., Private

Resided in Rowan County where he enlisted at age 18, July 4, 1862, for the war. Hospitalized at Richmond, Virginia, November 14, 1862. Returned to duty on December 2, 1862. Reported present through August 31, 1863. Sent to Richmond on October 9, 1863, under charges of "desertion [and] cowardice in face of the enemy." Returned to duty prior to January 1, 1864. Reported at Kinston working on gunboat in March-April, 1864. Rejoined the company in May-August, 1864. Reported present through December 31, 1864. Captured at Hatcher's Run, Virginia, February 6, 1865. Confined at Point Lookout, Maryland, February 9, 1865. Released at Point Lookout on June 24, 1865, after taking the Oath of Allegiance.

DOBY, LEWIS D., Private

Resided in Rowan County where he enlisted at age 36, July 4, 1862, for the war. Deserted at Salisbury on August 30, 1862. Died at Edenboro prior to May 2, 1863. Cause of death not reported.

EARNHARDT, STEPHEN A., Private

Resided in Rowan County and enlisted in Wake County at age 18, March 5, 1864, for the war. Reported present through February 28,

1865. Captured at Fort Stedman, Virginia, March 25, 1865. Confined at Point Lookout, Maryland, March 28, 1865. Released at Point Lookout on June 11, 1865, after taking the Oath of Allegiance.

EARNHART, ALBERT S., Private

Resided in Rowan County and was by occupation a farmer prior to enlisting in Rowan County at age 24, July 4, 1862, for the war. Reported present through April 30, 1863. Wounded in the right thigh at Gettysburg, Pennsylvania, July 1-3, 1863. Hospitalized at Richmond, Virginia. Returned to duty in January-April, 1864. Hospitalized at Richmond on June 14, 1864, with an unspecified complaint. Reported at home on surgeon's certificate from October 6 through December 31, 1864. Sent to hospital on February 18, 1865. Retired from service on March 14, 1865. Reason he was retired not reported. Captured (probably while on hospital duty) at Lynchburg, Virginia, in April, 1865. Took the Oath of Allegiance at Salisbury on June 3, 1865.

EARNHART, BENJAMIN, Private

Resided in Rowan County where he enlisted at age 34, July 4, 1862, for the war. Hospitalized at Richmond, Virginia, October 28, 1862, with diarrhoea. Returned to duty on December 30, 1862. Reported present until May 4, 1863, when he was reported missing at Chancellorsville, Virginia. Was probably killed at Chancellorsville.

EARNHART, EDWARD, Private

Resided in Rowan County where he enlisted at age 25, July 4, 1862, for the war. Reported present through February 28, 1863. Hospitalized at Richmond, Virginia, May 1, 1863, with erysipelas. Transferred to hospital at Danville, Virginia, May 7, 1863. Returned to duty in November-December, 1863. Court-martialed on or about January 19, 1864. Reason he was court-martialed not reported. Reported present on surviving company muster rolls through December 31, 1864. Wounded in the fourth toe of the left foot (fracture) at Hatcher's Run, Virginia, February 6, 1865. Hospitalized at Petersburg, Virginia. Paroled at Salisbury on May 1, 1865.

EDDLEMAN, JOHN MOSES, Sergeant

Resided in Rowan County where he enlisted at age 24, July 4, 1862, for the war. Mustered in as Private. Hospitalized at Charlottesville, Virginia, November 20, 1862. Transferred to Lynchburg, Virginia, the same date. Returned to duty prior to November 28, 1862, when he was sent to hospital at Culpeper, Virginia. Returned to duty subsequent to February 28, 1863. Wounded in the left side at Chancellorsville, Virginia, on or about May 4, 1863. Hospitalized at Richmond, Virginia, July 24, 1863, with remittent fever. Returned to duty on September 2, 1863. Promoted to Sergeant in September-October, 1863. Captured at Rappahannock Station, Virginia, November 7, 1863. Confined at Point Lookout, Maryland, November 11, 1863. Reduced to ranks prior to January 1, 1864, while a prisoner of war. Paroled at Point Lookout on March 16, 1864. Received at City Point, Virginia, March 20, 1864, for exchange. Returned to duty in May-August, 1864. Promoted to Sergeant prior to September 1, 1864. Reported present through February 28, 1865. Captured at Fort Stedman, Virginia, March 25, 1865. Confined at Point Lookout on March 27, 1865. Released at Point Lookout on June 12, 1865, after taking the Oath of Allegiance.

EDDLEMAN, WILLIAM C., Private

Resided in Rowan County where he enlisted at age 19, July 4, 1862, for the war. Reported present or accounted for until May 4, 1863, when he was wounded in the hip at Chancellorsville, Virginia. Hospitalized at Richmond, Virginia, July 11, 1863, with dyspepsia. Transferred to Raleigh on July 28, 1863. Returned to duty prior to November 7, 1863, when he was captured at Rappahannock Station, Virginia. Confined at Point Lookout, Maryland, November 11, 1863. Paroled at Point Lookout on March 16, 1864. Received at City Point, Virginia, March 20, 1864, for exchange. Returned to duty in May-August, 1864. Reported present until February 6, 1865, when he was wounded in the right leg at Hatcher's Run, Virginia. Hospitalized at Richmond. Furloughed for sixty days on or about February 11, 1865. Paroled at Salisbury on an unspecified date in 1865.

EDDLEMAN, WILLIAM H. C., Private

Resided in Rowan County where he enlisted at age 19, July 4, 1862, for the war. Hospitalized at Richmond, Virginia, October 16, 1862. Returned to duty on December 13, 1862. Reported present until May 4, 1863, when he was wounded in the thigh at Chancellorsville, Virginia. Hospitalized at Richmond where he died on June 28, 1863, of wounds.

ELLER, JOHN, Private

Resided in Rowan County where he enlisted at age 28, July 4, 1862, for the war. Reported present or accounted for until November 7, 1863, when he was captured at Rappahannock Station, Virginia. Confined at Point Lookout, Maryland, November 11, 1863. Paroled at Point Lookout on March 16, 1864. Received at City Point, Virginia, March 20, 1864, for exchange. Returned to duty subsequent to April 30, 1864. Reported present or accounted for through February 28, 1865. Captured at Fort Stedman, Virginia, March 25, 1865. Confined at Point Lookout on March 28, 1865. Released at Point Lookout on June 11, 1865, after taking the Oath of Allegiance.

ELLER, JOHN M., Private

Born in Rowan County where he resided as a farmer prior to enlisting in Rowan County at age 26, July 4, 1862, for the war. Discharged on October 20, 1862, by reason of disability.

ELLER, JOSEPH, Private

Resided in Rowan County where he enlisted at age 19, July 4, 1862, for the war. Hospitalized at Richmond, Virginia, October 25, 1862, with remittent fever. Furloughed on November 6, 1862. Returned to duty prior to January 1, 1863. Sent to hospital at Richmond on March 2, 1863. Died in Rowan County on June 28, 1863, of "chronic diarrhoea."

FESPERMAN, C. R., ——

Place and date of enlistment not reported. Probably enlisted subsequent to February 28, 1865. Paroled at Salisbury on June 15, 1865.

FESPERMAN, SIMEON G., Private

Resided in Rowan County where he enlisted at age 26, July 4, 1862, for the war. Hospitalized at Richmond, Virginia, October 25, 1862, with remittent fever. Furloughed on November 6, 1862. Returned to duty in January-February, 1863. Reported present on surviving company muster rolls until February 4, 1865, when he was reported absent without leave. Hospitalized at Charlotte on February 17, 1865, with a gunshot wound of the lower left extremities. Place and date wounded not reported. No further records.

FILE, REUBEN M., Private

Resided in Rowan County where he enlisted on February 26, 1864, for the war. Reported present until October 19, 1864, when he was wounded in the right elbow (fracture) at Cedar Creek, Virginia. Hospitalized at Richmond, Virginia. Furloughed for sixty days on November 11, 1864. Returned to duty subsequent to February 28, 1865. Captured at Petersburg, Virginia, April 3, 1865. Confined at Hart's Island, New York Harbor, April 10, 1865. Released at Hart's Island on June 19, 1865, after taking the Oath of Allegiance. [Was about 18 years of age at time of enlistment.]

FREEZE, GEORGE, Private

Resided in Rowan County where he enlisted at age 26, July 4, 1862, for the war. Reported present until May 1, 1863, when he was hospitalized at Richmond, Virginia, with intermittent fever. Transferred to hospital at Lynchburg, Virginia, May 11, 1863. Returned to duty prior to September 1, 1863. Captured at Rappahannock Station, Virginia, November 7, 1863. Confined at Point Lookout, Maryland, November 11, 1863. Paroled at Point Lookout on March 16, 1864. Received at City Point, Virginia, March 20, 1864, for exchange. Returned to duty prior to September 1, 1864. Furloughed on December 23, 1864. Returned to duty in January-February, 1865. Paroled at Farmville, Virginia, April 11-21, 1865. Took the Oath of Allegiance at Salisbury on June 19, 1865.

FRY, NOAH W., Private

Resided in Rowan County and was by occupation a farmhand prior to enlisting in Rowan County at age 24, July 4, 1862, for the war. Reported present through December 31, 1862. Died in camp near Fredericksburg, Virginia, January 16-17, 1863, of "pneumonia."

GARDNER, J. W., Private

Resided in Rowan County and was by occupation a shoemaker prior to enlisting in Rowan County at age 26, July 4, 1862, for the war. Discharged on October 13, 1862, by reason of "large scrofulous ulcers [on leg] of several years standing."

GASKEY, GEORGE A., Private

Resided in Rowan County where he enlisted at age 36, December 28, 1862, for the war. Hospitalized at Richmond, Virginia, January 27, 1863. Returned to duty prior to March 1, 1863. Sent to hospital on April 21, 1863. Died at Gordonsville, Virginia, May 8, 1863, of disease.

GASKEY, JOSHUA, Private

Resided in Rowan County where he enlisted at age 23, July 4, 1862, for the war. Mustered in as Private. Reported present through December, 1862. Promoted to Corporal in November-December, 1862. Sent to hospital at Richmond, Virginia, January 26, 1863. Reported in hospital at Richmond on February 20, 1863, with varioloid. Returned to duty on March 23, 1863. Hospitalized at Richmond on May 5, 1863, with debility. Deserted on May 14, 1863. Reduced to ranks prior to September 1, 1863. Returned to duty subsequent to October 31, 1863. Sent to hospital on December 1, 1863. Returned to duty prior to May 1, 1864. Wounded in the right leg at Winchester, Virginia, September 19, 1864. Hospitalized at Charlottesville, Virginia. Returned to duty in November-December, 1864. Captured at Hatcher's Run, Virginia, February 6, 1865. Confined at Point Lookout, Maryland, February 9, 1865. Released at Point Lookout on June 27, 1865, after taking the Oath of Allegiance.

GILLESPIE, RICHARD T., Private

Enlisted in Rowan County at age 18, November 28, 1862, for the war. Hospitalized at Richmond, Virginia, December 21, 1862, with rubeola. Transferred to hospital at Danville, Virginia, January 8, 1863. Died in hospital at Danville on March 9, 1863, of "variola."

GOODMAN, ALFRED MOSES, Private

Resided in Rowan County where he enlisted at age 28, July 4, 1862, for the war. Mustered in as Private. Promoted to Corporal in November-December, 1862. Reported present on surviving company muster rolls through April 30, 1864. Hospitalized at Richmond, Virginia, May 16, 1864, with a gunshot wound of the head. Place and date wounded not reported. Returned to duty on July 8, 1864. Reported present through October 31, 1864. Reduced to ranks in late October, 1864, for "throwing away gun & accoutrements" on the battlefield at Cedar Creek, Virginia, October 19, 1864. Reported present in November, 1864-February, 1865. Wounded mortally at Fort Stedman, Virginia, March 25, 1865. Place and date of death not reported.

GRAHAM, JAMES S., 1st Sergeant

Born in Rowan County where he resided prior to enlisting in Rowan County at age 25, July 4, 1862, for the war. Mustered in as Sergeant. Promoted to 1st Sergeant in November-December, 1862. Reported present through February 28, 1863. Wounded in the leg (fracture) at Chancellorsville, Virginia, May 4, 1863. Died at or near Chancellorsville on or about May 5, 1863, of wounds. [Previously served as 2nd Lieutenant of Company K, 76th Regiment N.C. Militia, and of Company E, 120th Regiment N.C. Militia.]

GRAHAM, JOSEPH A., Sergeant

Resided in Rowan County and was by occupation a farmer prior to enlisting in Rowan County at age 27, July 4, 1862, for the war. Mustered in as Sergeant. Discharged on an unspecified date (probably in the summer of 1862) after providing Pvt. John S. Lowrance as a substitute.

GRAHAM, RICHARD F., Corporal

Resided in Rowan County and was by occupation a farmer prior to enlisting in Rowan County at age 35, July 4, 1862, for the war. Mustered in as Private. Promoted to Corporal in November-December, 1862. Reported present until November 7, 1863, when he was captured at Rappahannock Station, Virginia. Confined at Point Lookout, Maryland, November 11, 1863. Paroled at Point Lookout on March 16, 1864. Received at City Point, Virginia, March 20, 1864, for exchange. Returned to duty in May-August, 1864. Captured at Hatcher's Run, Virginia, February 6, 1865. Confined at Point Lookout on February 9, 1865. Released at Point Lookout on June 27, 1865, after taking the Oath of Allegiance.

GRAHAM, WILLIAM THOMAS, Private

Resided in Rowan County where he enlisted at age 30, July 4, 1862, for the war. Accidentally wounded in the chest on October 21, 1862. Hospitalized at Richmond, Virginia. Furloughed for thirty days on November 6, 1862. Returned to duty prior to March 1, 1863. Hospitalized at Danville, Virginia, June 18, 1863, with chronic diarrhoea. Transferred to Salisbury on June 25, 1863. Returned to duty prior to September 1, 1863. Reported present on surviving company muster rolls until May 16, 1864, when he was hospitalized at Richmond. Furloughed for thirty days on June 16, 1864. Returned to duty prior to September 1, 1864. Wounded in the breast and right arm at Cedar Creek, Virginia, October 19, 1864.

Returned to duty prior to January 1, 1865. Reported present through February 28, 1865. Captured at Hatcher's Run, Virginia, April 6, 1865. Confined at Newport News, Virginia, April 14, 1865. Released at Newport News on June 26, 1865, after taking the Oath of Allegiance.

HAMRICK, GEORGE W., Private

Born in Surry County and resided in Rowan County where he was by occupation a farmer prior to enlisting in Rowan County at age 26, July 4, 1862, for the war. Hospitalized at Richmond, Virginia, October 20, 1862, with typhus fever. Discharged on December 17, 1862, by reason of "dementia." Died in hospital at Richmond on December 28, 1862, of "variola."

HARE, JAMES M., Private

Resided in Rowan County where he enlisted at age 18, September 9, 1862, for the war. Hospitalized at Richmond, Virginia, October 16, 1862, with hemorrhage of lungs. Furloughed for thirty days on or about November 11, 1862. Returned to duty in March-April, 1863. Sent to hospital at Jordan's Springs, Virginia, on or about June 18, 1863. Returned to duty in September-October, 1863. Captured at Rappahannock Station, Virginia, November 7, 1863. Confined at Point Lookout, Maryland, on or about November 11, 1863. Paroled at Point Lookout on March 16, 1864. Received at City Point, Virginia, March 20, 1864, for exchange. Returned to duty prior to July 4, 1864, when he was sent to hospital. Returned to duty in September-October, 1864. Detailed as an ambulance driver on November 22, 1864. Rejoined the company in January-February, 1865. Captured at Farmville, Virginia, April 6, 1865. Confined at Newport News, Virginia, April 14, 1865. Released at Newport News on June 26, 1865, after taking the Oath of Allegiance.

HARTMAN, PINKNEY ALEXANDER, Musician

Previously served as Private in Capt. William H. Howard's Company, N.C. Prison Guards. Transferred to this company on or about July 4, 1862. Mustered in as Private. Appointed Musician in November-December, 1862. Reported present on surviving company muster rolls through December 31, 1864. Captured at Hatcher's Run, Virginia, February 6, 1865. Confined at Point Lookout, Maryland, February 9, 1865. Paroled at Point Lookout on February 18, 1865. Received at Boulware's and Cox's Wharves, James River, Virginia, February 20-21, 1865, for exchange. Paroled at Salisbury on May 13, 1865. Took the Oath of Allegiance at Salisbury on June 20, 1865.

HEILIG, ALLEN H., Private

Resided in Rowan County where he enlisted at age 27, July 4, 1862, for the war. Reported present through February 28, 1863. Wounded in the head at Chancellorsville, Virginia, May 4, 1863. Reported absent wounded through December 31, 1863. Reported on detached service at Salisbury in March, 1864-February, 1865. Paroled at Salisbury on May 2, 1865. Took the Oath of Allegiance at Salisbury on June 6, 1865.

HEILIG, JAMES M., Private

Resided in Rowan County where he enlisted at age 33, July 4, 1862, for the war. Reported present until November 7, 1863, when he was captured at Rappahannock Station, Virginia. Confined at Point Lookout, Maryland, November 11, 1863. Paroled at Point Lookout on March 16, 1864. Received at City Point, Virginia, March 20,

1864, for exchange. Returned to duty in May-August, 1864. Killed near Mount Jackson, Virginia, September 23, 1864.

HEILIG, RICHARD, Private

Resided in Rowan County and enlisted at age 31, July 4, 1862, for the war. Hospitalized at Richmond, Virginia, November 9, 1862. Discharged from service on or about December 5, 1862, by reason of "paralysis."

HOLSHOUSER, CALVIN, Private

Born in Rowan County where he resided prior to enlisting in Rowan County at age 21, July 4, 1862, for the war. Reported present through February 28, 1863. Died in camp near Fredericksburg, Virginia, on or about April 15, 1863, of "pneumonia."

HOLSHOUSER, CRAWFORD M., Sergeant

Resided in Rowan County where he enlisted at age 28, July 4, 1862, for the war. Mustered in as Private. Promoted to Sergeant prior to September 1, 1862. Died in hospital at Richmond, Virginia, on or about October 19, 1862, of "typhoid fever." [Previously served as 1st Lieutenant of Company E, 76th Regiment N.C. Militia.]

HOLSHOUSER, ELI, Private

Resided in Rowan County and was by occupation a house carpenter prior to enlisting in Rowan County at age 29, July 4, 1862, for the war. Reported present through February 28, 1863. Captured at Chancellorsville, Virginia, on or about May 4, 1863. Confined at Fort Delaware, Delaware, on or about May 7, 1863. Paroled and transferred to City Point, Virginia, where he was received on May 23, 1863, for exchange. Sent to hospital on June 12, 1863. Returned to duty in November-December, 1863. Reported at Kinston working on gunboat in March-April, 1864. Rejoined the company in May-August, 1864. Reported present through February 28, 1865. Captured near Farmville, Virginia, April 6, 1865. Confined at Newport News, Virginia, April 14, 1865. Released at Newport News on or about June 25, 1865, after taking the Oath of Allegiance.

HOLSHOUSER, MILAS ALEXANDER, Private

Resided in Rowan County and was by occupation a cabinet maker prior to enlisting in Rowan County at age 33, July 4, 1862, for the war. Reported present until November 7, 1863, when he was captured at Rappahannock Station, Virginia. Confined at Point Lookout, Maryland, November 11, 1863. Paroled at Point Lookout on March 16, 1864. Received at City Point, Virginia, March 20, 1864, for exchange. Returned to duty in May-August, 1864. Reported present through February 28, 1865. Surrendered at Appomattox Court House, Virginia, April 9, 1865.

HOOKER, ALLEN H., Private

Resided in Rowan County and was by occupation a miller prior to enlisting in Rowan County at age 32, July 4, 1862, for the war. Hospitalized at Richmond, Virginia, October 9, 1862, with chronic bronchitis. Transferred to hospital at Farmville, Virginia, December 20, 1862 (suffering from debilitas). Furloughed for forty days on January 9, 1863. Returned to duty prior to May 1, 1863. Hospitalized at Richmond on June 3, 1863, with pneumonia. Furloughed for sixty days on or about July 3, 1863. Returned to duty on an unspecified date. Captured at Rappahannock Station, Virginia, November 7, 1863. Confined at Point Lookout, Maryland, November 11, 1863. Released at Point Lookout on January 25, 1864, after taking the Oath of Allegiance and joining the U.S. Navy.

HOPE, W., Private

Place and date of enlistment not reported (probably enlisted subsequent to February 28, 1865). Captured and paroled at Athens, Georgia, on or about May 8, 1865.

HUGHEY, GEORGE E., Private

Resided in Rowan County and enlisted at Camp Holmes, near Raleigh, November 30, 1864, for the war. Captured at Hatcher's Run, Virginia, February 6, 1865. Confined at Point Lookout, Maryland, February 9, 1865. Released at Point Lookout on June 27, 1865, after taking the Oath of Allegiance.

KELLY, MICHAEL, Private

Resided in Rowan County where he enlisted at age 51, July 4, 1862, for the war as a substitute. Deserted on September 15, 1862.

KERR, JAMES Mc., Private

Resided in Rowan County where he enlisted at age 27, July 4, 1862, for the war. Reported present through April 30, 1863. Sent to hospital at Culpeper, Virginia, June 8, 1863. Died on October 14, 1863, of disease. Place of death not reported. [Served as a teamster during much of his military career.]

KLUTTS, A. M. A., Private

Resided in Rowan County and was by occupation a farmer prior to enlisting in Rowan County at age 26, July 4, 1862, for the war. Mustered in as 1st Sergeant. Hospitalized at Richmond, Virginia, October 30, 1862, with diarrhoea. Returned to duty on December 30, 1862. Reduced to ranks in November-December, 1862. Died in camp near Port Royal, Virginia, February 24, 1863, of "bronchitis."

KLUTTS, JULIUS A., Private

Enlisted in Rowan County on February 26, 1864, for the war. Captured at Harpers Ferry, West Virginia, on the night of July 7, 1864. Confined at Old Capitol Prison, Washington, D.C. Transferred to Elmira, New York, where he arrived on July 25, 1864. Released at Elmira on May 29, 1865, after taking the Oath of Allegiance. [Records of the Federal Provost Marshal dated September, 1864, give his age as 18.]

LINGLE, WILSON A., Private

Resided in Rowan County where he enlisted at age 31, July 4, 1862, for the war. Reported present through February 28, 1863. Captured at Chancellorsville, Virginia, on or about May 4, 1863. Confined at Fort Delaware, Delaware, on or about May 7, 1863. Paroled and transferred to City Point, Virginia, where he was received on May 23, 1863, for exchange. Returned to duty on an unspecified date. Reported present or accounted for until November 7, 1863, when he was captured at Rappahannock Station, Virginia. Confined at Point Lookout, Maryland, November 11, 1863. Paroled at Point Lookout on March 16, 1864. Received at City Point on March 20, 1864, for exchange. Returned to duty prior to August 31, 1864. Wounded at Winchester, Virginia, September 19, 1864. Survived the war.

LIPE, SIMON J., Private

Resided in Rowan County where he enlisted at age 33, July 4, 1862, for the war. Hospitalized at Richmond, Virginia, September 29, 1862. Returned to duty prior to November 1, 1862. Wounded slightly at Fredericksburg, Virginia, December 13, 1862. Returned to duty prior to January 1, 1863. Hospitalized at Richmond on May 8, 1863, with hepatitis. Transferred to hospital at Lynchburg, Virginia, May 11, 1863. Captured and paroled on or about May 24, 1863, during the "raid in the rear of Lee's army." Returned to duty prior to September 1, 1863. Captured at Rappahannock Station, Virginia, November 7, 1863. Confined at Point Lookout, Maryland, November 11, 1863. Paroled at Point Lookout on March 16, 1864. Received at City Point, Virginia, March 20, 1864, for exchange. Returned to duty prior to September 1, 1864. Reported present or accounted for through February 28, 1865. Captured at Farmville, Virginia, April 6, 1865. Confined at Newport News, Virginia, April 14, 1865. Released at Newport News on June 26, 1865, after taking the Oath of Allegiance.

LOWRANCE, JOHN S., Private

Resided in Rowan County where he enlisted at age 17, July 4, 1862, for the war as a substitute for Pvt. Joseph A. Graham. Reported present until May 4, 1863, when he was wounded in the finger at Chancellorsville, Virginia. Finger amputated. Returned to duty on October 8, 1863. Captured at Rappahannock Station, Virginia, November 7, 1863. Confined at Point Lookout, Maryland, November 11, 1863. Paroled at Point Lookout on December 24, 1863. Received at City Point, Virginia, December 28, 1863, for exchange. Returned to duty prior to May 1, 1864. Reported present through February 28, 1865. Surrendered at Appomattox Court House, Virginia, April 9, 1865. Paroled at Salisbury on May 12, 1865. Took the Oath of Allegiance at Salisbury on June 30, 1865.

LYERLY, ALEXANDER, Sergeant

Resided in Rowan County where he enlisted at age 35, July 4, 1862, for the war. Mustered in as Private. Promoted to Corporal in September-October, 1862. Promoted to Sergeant in November-December, 1862. Reported present until September 9, 1863, when he was sent to hospital at Richmond, Virginia (not clear whether he was sick or wounded). Returned to duty in November-December, 1863. Reported present or accounted for on surviving company muster rolls through April 30, 1864. Captured near Drewry's Bluff, Virginia, May 12-13, 1864. Confined at Point Lookout, Maryland, May 16, 1864. Paroled at Point Lookout and transferred to Cox's Wharf, James River, Virginia, where he was received on February 14-15, 1865, for exchange. Paroled at Salisbury on May 11, 1865. Took the Oath of Allegiance at Salisbury on June 10, 1865.

LYERLY, CHARLES, Private

Resided in Rowan County where he enlisted at age 33, July 4, 1862, for the war. Reported present or accounted for until August 3, 1863, when he was sent to hospital from camp near Rapidan Station, Virginia. Returned to duty prior to November 7, 1863, when he was captured at Rappahannock Station, Virginia. Confined at Point Lookout, Maryland, November 11, 1863. Paroled at Point Lookout on March 16, 1864. Received at City Point, Virginia, March 20, 1864, for exchange. Returned to duty in May-August, 1864. Reported present through February 28, 1865. Paroled at Farmville, Virginia, April 11-21, 1865.

LYERLY, JACOB, Private

Born in Rowan County where he resided as a farmer prior to enlisting in Rowan County at age 34, July 4, 1862, for the war. Hospitalized at Richmond, Virginia, September 25, 1862. Discharged from service on October 11, 1862, by reason of "chronic epilepsy."

McCONNAUGHEY, GEORGE C., 1st Sergeant

Resided in Rowan or Cabarrus County and was by occupation a physician prior to enlisting at Petersburg, Virginia, at age 25, September 22, 1863, for the war. Mustered in as Private. Reported present but on detached duty as a Hospital Steward through October 31, 1863. Reported present in November-December, 1863, and March-April, 1864. Appointed Hospital Steward prior to November 1, 1864. Reported present through February 28, 1865. Promoted to 1st Sergeant on an unspecified date. Took the Oath of Allegiance at Salisbury on June 21, 1865.

MALONEY, JAMES S., Private

Born in South Carolina and resided in Rowan County where he enlisted at age 28, July 4, 1862, for the war. Hospitalized at Richmond, Virginia, November 8, 1862, with rheumatism. Reported in hospital at Richmond on December 16, 1862, with intermittent fever. Transferred to hospital at Danville, Virginia, December 23, 1862. Died in hospital at Danville on or about January 8, 1863, of "smallpox."

MAXWELL, ANDREW W., Private

Resided in Rowan County where he enlisted at age 28, July 4, 1862, for the war. Hospitalized at Richmond, Virginia, October 22, 1862, with bronchitis. Furloughed for thirty days on November 14, 1862. Returned to duty prior to January 1, 1863. Reported present through April 30, 1863. Reported missing on the march near Port Royal, Virginia, June 12, 1863. Returned to duty prior to July 3-5, 1863, when he was captured at Gettysburg, Pennsylvania. Confined at Fort Delaware, Delaware, on or about July 9, 1863. Transferred to Point Lookout, Maryland, on or about October 18, 1863. Paroled at Point Lookout on February 10, 1865. Received at Cox's Wharf, James River, Virginia, February 14-15, 1865, for exchange. Paroled at Salisbury on May 23, 1865. Took the Oath of Allegiance at Salisbury on June 10, 1865.

MAXWELL, JOHN, Private

Born in Rowan County where he resided as a farmer prior to enlisting in Rowan County at age 32, July 4, 1862, for the war. Discharged on October 20, 1862, by reason of disability.

MENIUS, FRANK E., Private

Born on January 3, 1842. Resided in Rowan County where he enlisted at age 20, July 4, 1862, for the war. Sent to Gordonsville, Virginia, sick on November 19, 1862. Returned to duty subsequent to February 28, 1863. Hospitalized at Richmond, Virginia, May 7, 1863, with acute rheumatism. Transferred to Raleigh on July 25, 1863. Returned to duty prior to September 1, 1863. Captured at Rappahannock Station, Virginia, November 7, 1863. Confined at Point Lookout, Maryland, November 11, 1863. Paroled at Point Lookout on March 16, 1864. Received at City Point, Virginia, March 20, 1864, for exchange. Returned to duty prior to September 1, 1864. Reported present or accounted for through February 28, 1865. Surrendered at Appomattox Court House, Virginia, April 9, 1865. Took the Oath of Allegiance at Salisbury on June 24, 1865.

MENIUS, GEORGE MONROE, Private

Resided in Rowan County where he enlisted at age 33, July 4, 1862, for the war. Reported present through April 30, 1863. Sent to hospital from camp near Williamsport, Maryland, July 18, 1863. Returned to duty in November-December, 1863. Reported present in March-April, 1864. No further records.

MILLER, ALBERT M., Private

Resided in Rowan County where he enlisted at age 28, July 4, 1862, for the war. Mustered in as Corporal. Sent to hospital sick on or about November 7, 1862. Reduced to ranks in November-December, 1862. Hospitalized at Richmond, Virginia, February 13, 1863. Died in hospital at Richmond on February 27, 1863, of "ch[ronic] diarrhoea."

MILLER, CALVIN J., Private

Resided in Rowan County where he enlisted at age 23, July 4, 1862, for the war. Hospitalized at Richmond, Virginia, September 29, 1862, with intermittent fever. Transferred to Salisbury on October 17, 1862. Returned to duty prior to December 13, 1862, when he was wounded at Fredericksburg, Virginia. Returned to duty prior to January 1, 1863. Sent to hospital at Richmond on February 20, 1863. Returned to duty in May-August, 1863. Captured at Rappahannock Station, Virginia, November 7, 1863. Confined at Point Lookout, Maryland, November 11, 1863. Paroled at Point Lookout on March 16, 1864. Received at City Point, Virginia, March 20, 1864, for exchange. Returned to duty subsequent to April 30, 1864. Sent to hospital on August 15, 1864. Reported absent sick through February 28, 1865. Paroled at Salisbury on May 11, 1865. Took the Oath of Allegiance at Salisbury on June 2, 1865.

MILLER, JOHN M., Private

Resided in Rowan County where he enlisted at age 26, July 4, 1862, for the war. Hospitalized at Richmond, Virginia, November 9, 1862. Returned to duty on November 27, 1862. Hospitalized at Richmond on or about December 9, 1862. Died in hospital at Richmond on December 22, 1862, of "pneumonia" and/or "typhoid fever."

MILLER, JOHN R., Corporal

Resided in Rowan County where he enlisted at age 19, July 4, 1862, for the war. Mustered in as Private. Wounded in the arm at Fredericksburg, Virginia, December 13, 1862. Returned to duty in March-April, 1863. Promoted to Corporal in May-August, 1863. Reported present until November 7, 1863, when he was captured at Rappahannock Station, Virginia. Confined at Point Lookout, Maryland, November 11, 1863. Paroled at Point Lookout on March 16, 1864. Received at City Point, Virginia, March 20, 1864, for exchange. Returned to duty in May-August, 1864. Reported present through February 28, 1865. Wounded in the face and/or right hand at Fort Stedman, Virginia, March 25, 1865. Hospitalized at Richmond, Virginia. Captured in hospital at Richmond on April 3, 1865. Confined at Newport News, Virginia, April 24, 1865. Released at Newport News on June 26, 1865, after taking the Oath of Allegiance.

MILLER, JOSEPH, Private

Resided in Rowan County and was by occupation a day laborer prior to enlisting in Rowan County at age 37, April 11, 1863, for the war. Hospitalized at Charlottesville, Virginia, October 10, 1863, with acute diarrhoea. Returned to duty on November 15, 1863. Reported present on surviving company muster rolls through February 28, 1865. Wounded in the right leg and captured at Sayler's Creek, Virginia, April 6, 1865. Right leg amputated. Hospitalized at Washington, D.C., where he died on May 6, 1865, of wounds.

MINCY, WILLIAM H., Private

Resided in Rowan County where he enlisted at age 16, July 4, 1862, for the war as a substitute for J. H. (or G. H.) Heilig. Reported present or accounted for on surviving company muster rolls through December 31, 1864. Captured at Hatcher's Run, Virginia, February 6, 1865. Confined at Point Lookout, Maryland, February 9, 1865. Paroled at Point Lookout on February 18, 1865. Received at Boulware's and Cox's Wharves, James River, Virginia, February 20-21, 1865, for exchange. Survived the war.

MISENHEIMER, MORGAN, Private

Resided in Rowan County and was by occupation a miner or stage driver prior to enlisting in Rowan County at age 28, July 4, 1862, for the war as a substitute for Pvt. J. A. Rendleman. Reported present on surviving company muster rolls through December 31, 1864. Served as a teamster during much of that period. Captured at Hatcher's Run, Virginia, February 6, 1865. Confined at Point Lookout, Maryland, February 9, 1865. Released at Point Lookout on May 12, 1865, after taking the Oath of Allegiance.

NIBLOCK, ALEXANDER, Private

Resided in Rowan County and was by occupation a farmer prior to enlisting in Rowan County at age 31, July 4, 1862, for the war. Reported absent on sick furlough on September 18, 1862. Reported absent without leave on October 27, 1862. Returned to duty prior to November 1, 1862. Reported present through April 30, 1863. Hospitalized at Farmville, Virginia, June 10, 1863. Died in hospital at Farmville on June 19, 1863, of "camp fever."

NIBLOCK, BENJAMIN, Private

Resided in Rowan County where he enlisted at age 35, July 4, 1862, for the war. Reported present or accounted for through December 31, 1862. Hospitalized at Richmond, Virginia, January 13, 1863. Died in hospital at Richmond on January 25, 1863, of "pneumonia typhoides."

NIBLOCK, GEORGE, Private

Enlisted near Brandy Station, Virginia, at age 38, November 5, 1863, for the war. Captured at Rappahannock Station, Virginia, November 7, 1863. Confined at Point Lookout, Maryland, November 11, 1863. Paroled at Point Lookout on March 16, 1864. Received at City Point, Virginia, March 20, 1864, for exchange. Returned to duty in May-August, 1864. Reported present through February 28, 1865. Surrendered at Appomattox Court House, Virginia, April 9, 1865.

NIBLOCK, THOMAS, Private

Resided in Rowan County where he enlisted at age 27, July 4, 1862, for the war. Reported absent on sick furlough on or about September 15, 1862. Reported absent without leave on October 27, 1862. Returned to duty prior to November 1, 1862. Reported present through December 31, 1862. Hospitalized at Richmond, Virginia, February 13, 1863, with typhoid fever. Later reported to be suffering from variola. Furloughed for thirty days on May 14, 1863. Returned to duty prior to September 1, 1863. Captured at Rappahannock Station, Virginia, November 7, 1863. Confined at Point Lookout, Maryland, November 11, 1863. Paroled at Point Lookout on March 16, 1864. Received at City Point, Virginia, March 20, 1864, for exchange. Returned to duty on an unspecified date. Wounded in action at Lynchburg, Virginia, June 18, 1864. Returned to duty in September-October, 1864. Reported present through February 28, 1865. Captured at Farmville, Virginia, April 6, 1865. Confined at Newport News, Virginia, April 14, 1865. Released at Newport News on June 26, 1865, after taking the Oath of Allegiance.

OVERCASH, MICHAEL, Private

Born in Rowan County where he resided prior to enlisting in Rowan County at age 51, July 4, 1862, for the war as a substitute for Pvt. William L. Steele. Reported present or accounted for through December 31, 1862. Sent to Richmond, Virginia, sick on January 26, 1863. Died in hospital at Lynchburg, Virginia, on or about March 25, 1863, of "gastritis."

PACE, JOHN FLETCHER, Private

Resided in Rowan County where he enlisted at age 18, July 4, 1862, for the war. Mustered in as Private. Promoted to Sergeant in December, 1862, for "gallantry at Fred[erick]sb[ur]g," Virginia, December 13, 1862. Reported present or accounted for through October 31, 1863. Promoted to 1st Sergeant in May-August, 1863. Captured at Rappahannock Station, Virginia, November 7, 1863. Confined at Point Lookout, Maryland, November 11, 1863. Paroled at Point Lookout on March 16, 1864. Received at City Point, Virginia, March 20, 1864, for exchange. Returned to duty in May-August, 1864. Reported present and in command of the company in May-October, 1864. Reduced to ranks on November 20, 1864, for "misconduct." Reported present or accounted for through February 28, 1865. Surrendered at Appomattox Court House, Virginia, April 9, 1865. Took the Oath of Allegiance at Salisbury on June 27, 1865. "[I]n many of the later battles he commanded his company with great courage and skill." [Clark's *Regiments*, 3:428.]

PEELER, ALEXANDER, Private

Resided in Rowan County and was by occupation a farmer prior to enlisting in Rowan County at age 26, July 4, 1862, for the war. Mustered in as Corporal. Reported present through October 31, 1863. Reduced to ranks in May-August, 1863. Captured at Rappahannock Station, Virginia, November 7, 1863. Confined at Point Lookout, Maryland, November 11, 1863. Paroled at Point Lookout on March 16, 1864. Received at City Point, Virginia, March 20, 1864, for exchange. Returned to duty in May-August, 1864. Reported present through February 28, 1865. Paroled at Farmville, Virginia, April 11-21, 1865. Took the Oath of Allegiance at Salisbury on June 15, 1865.

PEELER, JACOB M., Private

Resided in Rowan County where he enlisted at age 27, July 4, 1862, for the war. Hospitalized at Richmond, Virginia, November 4, 1862, with general debility. Furloughed for twenty days on November 24, 1862. Returned to duty prior to January 1, 1863. Reported present or accounted for until November 7, 1863, when he was captured at Rappahannock Station, Virginia. Confined at Point Lookout, Maryland, November 11, 1863. Paroled at Point Lookout on March 16, 1864. Received at City Point, Virginia, March 20, 1864, for exchange. Returned to duty in May-August, 1864. Reported present through February 28, 1865. Surrendered at Appomattox Court House, Virginia, April 9, 1865. Took the Oath of Allegiance at Salisbury on June 9, 1865.

PEELER, JOHN C., Private

Born in Rowan County where he resided prior to enlisting in Rowan County at age 19, July 4, 1862, for the war. Hospitalized at Richmond, Virginia, November 1, 1862, with measles followed by typhoid fever. Furloughed for thirty days on December 31, 1862. Returned to duty prior to February 28, 1863. Hospitalized at Richmond on May 5, 1863, with "debility & fever typhoid." Died in hospital on or about May 27, 1863.

PEELER, JOSEPH A., Corporal

Resided in Rowan County where he enlisted at age 31, July 4, 1862, for the war. Mustered in as Private. Hospitalized at Richmond, Virginia, November 1, 1862, with rubeola. Transferred on February 17, 1863. Returned to duty prior to May 4, 1863, when he was wounded in the left shoulder at Chancellorsville, Virginia. Returned to duty on an unspecified date. Sent to hospital sick on September 18, 1863. Returned to duty in November-December, 1863. Reported present on surviving company muster rolls until wounded in the right leg near Drewry's Bluff, Virginia, May 15-16, 1864. Hospitalized at Richmond. Furloughed for sixty days on June 4, 1864. Returned to duty in September-October, 1864, and was promoted to Corporal. Reported present through February 28, 1865. Surrendered at Appomattox Court House, Virginia, April 9, 1865. Took the Oath of Allegiance at Salisbury on June 21, 1865.

PEELER, MOSES M., Private

Resided in Rowan County where he enlisted at age 24, July 4, 1862, for the war. Hospitalized at Richmond, Virginia, October 29, 1862, with rubeola. Died in hospital at Richmond on or about November 23, 1862, of "cystitis."

PEELER, PAUL, 1st Sergeant

Resided in Rowan County where he enlisted at age 29, July 4, 1862, for the war. Mustered in as Sergeant. Reported present through February 28, 1863. Wounded in the wrist and/or left arm at Chancellorsville, Virginia, on or about May 4, 1863. Returned to duty in September-October, 1863. Captured at Rappahannock Station, Virginia, November 7, 1863. Confined at Point Lookout, Maryland, November 11, 1863. Paroled at Point Lookout on March 16, 1864. Received at City Point, Virginia, March 20, 1864, for exchange. Returned to duty prior to July 20, 1864, when he was wounded in the foot at Winchester, Virginia. Hospitalized at Charlottesville, Virginia. Furloughed for forty days on or about August 13, 1864. Promoted to 1st Sergeant in November-December, 1864. Returned to duty in January-February, 1865. Captured near Petersburg, Virginia, April 3, 1865. Confined at Hart's Island, New York Harbor, April 11, 1865. Released at Hart's Island on June 19, 1865, after taking the Oath of Allegiance.

PEELER, SOLOMON, Private

Resided in Rowan County where he enlisted at age 30, July 4, 1862, for the war. Reported present through February 28, 1863. Captured at Chancellorsville, Virginia, May 3, 1863. Confined at Fort Delaware, Delaware, on or about May 7, 1863. Paroled and transferred to City Point, Virginia, where he was received on May 23, 1863, for exchange. Returned to duty prior to September 1, 1863. Captured at Rappahannock Station, Virginia, November 7, 1863. Confined at Point Lookout, Maryland, November 11, 1863. Paroled at Point Lookout on March 16, 1864. Received at City Point on March 20, 1864, for exchange. Returned to duty prior to September 1, 1864. Captured at Fisher's Hill, Virginia, September 22, 1864. Confined at Point Lookout on October 3, 1864. Paroled at Point Lookout on March 17, 1865. Received at Boulware's Wharf, James River, Virginia, March 19, 1865, for exchange.

PENNY, JOHN A., Private

Resided in Rowan County where he enlisted at age 26, July 4, 1862, for the war. Reported present on surviving company muster rolls through February 28, 1865. Surrendered at Appomattox Court House, Virginia, April 9, 1865. [Served briefly as a Musician in March-April, 1864.]

PHIFER, J. COWAN, Private

Resided in Rowan County where he enlisted at age 35, July 4, 1862, for the war. Hospitalized at Richmond, Virginia, November 1, 1862, with measles. Returned to duty on December 10, 1862. Hospitalized at Richmond on December 19, 1862. Died in hospital at Richmond on January 7, 1863, of "pneumonia."

PHIFER, JOHN COWAN, Private

Resided in Rowan County and was by occupation a farmer prior to enlisting in Rowan County at age 33, July 4, 1862, for the war. Hospitalized at Richmond, Virginia, November 1, 1862. Furloughed for thirty days on December 5, 1862. Returned to duty in March-April, 1863. Reported present or accounted for until November 7, 1863, when he was captured at Rappahannock Station, Virginia. Confined at Point Lookout, Maryland, November 11, 1863. Paroled at Point Lookout on March 16, 1864. Received at City Point, Virginia, March 20, 1864, for exchange. Returned to duty in May-June, 1864. Sent to hospital on June 28, 1864. Detailed for guard duty at Salisbury on September 11, 1864. Reported under arrest in the regimental guard house in November-December, 1864. Reason he was arrested not reported. Returned to duty in January-February, 1865. Captured at Farmville, Virginia, April 6, 1865. Confined at Newport News, Virginia, April 14, 1865. Released at Newport News on June 15, 1865, after taking the Oath of Allegiance. Hospitalized at Fort Monroe, Virginia, the same date with chronic diarrhoea. Released on June 20, 1865, after again taking the Oath of Allegiance.

PROPST, ADOLPHUS D. MONROE, Private

Resided in Rowan County where he enlisted at age 22, July 4, 1862, for the war. Wounded in the left hip at Fredericksburg, Virginia, December 13, 1862. Hospitalized at Richmond, Virginia. Transferred to hospital at Danville, Virginia, May 8, 1863. Furloughed on June 23, 1863. Returned to duty in September-October, 1863. Captured at Rappahannock Station, Virginia, November 7, 1863. Confined at Point Lookout, Maryland, November 11, 1863. Paroled at Point Lookout on March 16, 1864. Received at City Point, Virginia, March 20, 1864, for exchange. Returned to duty subsequent to April 30, 1864. Wounded in both legs at Charlestown, West Virginia, on or about August 22, 1864. Reported absent wounded through February 28, 1865. Took the Oath of Allegiance at Salisbury on June 2, 1865.

PROPST, THOMAS M., Private

Resided in Rowan County where he enlisted at age 26, July 4, 1862, for the war. Reported present until December 14, 1862, when he was sent to hospital. Died in hospital at Lynchburg, Virginia, on or about February 18, 1863, of "chronic diarrhoea."

RENDLEMAN, J. A., Private

Enlisted in Rowan County on July 4, 1862, for the war. Discharged prior to September 1, 1862, after providing Pvt. Morgan Misenheimer as a substitute.

RENDLEMAN, JOHN L., Private

Resided in Rowan County where he enlisted at age 20, July 4, 1862, for the war. Reported present through October 31, 1863. Captured at Rappahannock Station, Virginia, November 7, 1863. Confined at Point Lookout, Maryland, November 11, 1863. Paroled at Point Lookout on March 16, 1864. Received at City Point, Virginia, March 20, 1864, for exchange. Returned to duty prior to August 22, 1864, when he was captured at Charlestown, West Virginia. Confined at Elmira, New York, August 29, 1864.

Released at Elmira on June 21, 1865, after taking the Oath of Allegiance.

RIMER, SAMUEL M., Private

Born in Rowan County where he resided prior to enlisting in Rowan County at age 26, July 4, 1862, for the war. Reported absent sick on September 1, 1862. Reported absent without leave on October 27, 1862. Returned to duty prior to November 1, 1862. Reported present through February 28, 1863. Died in camp near Fredericksburg, Virginia, April 14-15, 1863, of "pneumonia."

ROGERS, JAMES I., Private

Place and date of enlistment not reported (probably enlisted subsequent to February 28, 1865). Paroled at Salisbury on May 23, 1865.

ROSE, J. W. A., Sergeant

Resided in Rowan County and was by occupation a farmer prior to enlisting in Rowan County at age 23, July 4, 1862, for the war. Mustered in as Private. Reported present or accounted for through April 30, 1863. Promoted to Sergeant in May-June, 1863. Captured at Gettysburg, Pennsylvania, July 1-3, 1863. Confined at Point Lookout, Maryland, where he died in the smallpox hospital on November 24, 1863. [See obituary in *Carolina (Weekly) Watchman* (Salisbury), April 18, 1864.]

SAFRIT, WILLIAM, Private

Resided in Rowan County where he enlisted at age 34, July 4, 1862, for the war. Reported present through October 31, 1863. Wounded in the back and captured at Rappahannock Station, Virginia, November 7, 1863. Hospitalized at Washington, D.C. Confined at Old Capitol Prison, Washington, on or about December 28, 1863. Transferred to Point Lookout, Maryland, February 3, 1864. Paroled at Point Lookout on March 16, 1864. Received at City Point, Virginia, March 20, 1864, for exchange. Returned to duty in May-August, 1864. Captured at Fisher's Hill, Virginia, September 22, 1864. Confined at Point Lookout on October 3, 1864. Released at Point Lookout on June 20, 1865, after taking the Oath of Allegiance.

SHULIBARINGER, JOHN L., Private

Born in Rowan County where he resided as a student prior to enlisting in Rowan County at age 18, July 4, 1862, for the war. Sent to Richmond, Virginia, sick on November 28, 1862. Discharged from service on February 21, 1863, by reason of "phthisis pulmonalis & ascites." Enlisted in Company G, 42nd Regiment N.C. Troops, August 14, 1863. Discharged from that unit on September 21, 1863. Reenlisted in this company on April 26, 1864. Reported present until February 6, 1865, when he was captured at Petersburg, Virginia. Confined at Point Lookout, Maryland, February 9, 1865. Released at Point Lookout on June 20, 1865, after taking the Oath of Allegiance.

SLOOP, MONROE, Private

Resided in Rowan County where he enlisted at age 27, July 4, 1862, for the war. Died in hospital at Charlottesville, Virginia, November 19, 1862, of "emphysema."

STEELE, WILLIAM L., Private

Resided in Rowan County and was by occupation a farmer. Conscripted on or about July 4, 1862, but was discharged after providing Pvt. Michael Overcash as a substitute. Enlisted in the company in Guilford County at age 34, October 26, 1864, for the war. Reported present through February 28, 1865. Captured at Fort Stedman, Virginia, March 25, 1865. Confined at Point Lookout, Maryland, March 28, 1865. Released at Point Lookout on June 19, 1865, after taking the Oath of Allegiance.

TREXLER, CALEB C., Private

Enlisted in Wake County on March 5, 1864, for the war. Reported present through August 31, 1864. "Shot through the head and instantly killed" at Cedar Creek, Virginia, October 19, 1864.

WADE, LUCIUS P., Private

Resided in Rowan County where he enlisted at age 21, July 4, 1862, for the war. Mustered in as Corporal. Reduced to ranks in September-October, 1862. Killed at Fredericksburg, Virginia, December 13, 1862.

WAGONER, CARMI J., Private

Resided in Rowan County where he enlisted at age 29, July 4, 1862, for the war. Reported present through February 28, 1863. Sent to Richmond, Virginia, sick on April 21, 1863. Returned to duty in November-December, 1863. Reported present in March-April, 1864. Hospitalized at Petersburg, Virginia, May 21, 1864, with acute diarrhoea and/or debility. Transferred to Raleigh on May 26, 1864. Returned to duty on an unspecified date. Reported present in September, 1864-February, 1865. Surrendered at Appomattox Court House, Virginia, April 9, 1865. Paroled at Salisbury on May 24, 1865.

WAGONER, MATHEW D., Private

Born in Rowan County where he resided as a farmer or day laborer prior to enlisting in Rowan County at age 27, July 4, 1862, for the war. Hospitalized at Richmond, Virginia, on or about November 9, 1862. Discharged from service at Richmond on February 16, 1863, by reason of "phthisis pulmonalis." Took the Oath of Allegiance at Salisbury on June 12, 1865.

WEBB, JOHN P., Private

Previously served as Private in Company H of this regiment. Transferred to this company in September-October, 1863. Captured at Rappahannock Station, Virginia, November 7, 1863. Confined at Point Lookout, Maryland, November 11, 1863. Released at Point Lookout on January 25, 1864, after taking the Oath of Allegiance and joining the U.S. service.

WEST, CYRUS M., Private

Resided in Rowan County where he enlisted at age 30, July 4, 1862, for the war. Hospitalized at Richmond, Virginia, November 23, 1862, with asthma. Transferred to Palmyra, Virginia, December 1, 1862. Reported sick in hospital through December 31, 1863. Shot by the Home Guard at his home on August 4, 1864, while trying to avoid arrest. "While the Guard was approaching the house in the rear, West broke out of the front door and ran. He was repeatedly halted [ordered to halt], but refusing to heed the summons, four of the Guard fired on him and he fell dead. . . . [H]e was a man of very low instincts before he took to the bushes, and is suspected of many offenses since. . . ." [Daily Carolina Watchman (Salisbury), August 5, 1864.]

WILHELM, JACOB B., Private

Resided in Rowan County where he enlisted at age 26, July 4, 1862, for the war. Reported present through December 31, 1862.

Hospitalized at Richmond, Virginia, January 20, 1863. Died in hospital at Richmond on or about February 8, 1863, of "typhoid pneumonia."

WILHELM, JOHN M., Private

Resided in Rowan County and was by occupation a farmer prior to enlisting in Rowan County at age 30, July 4, 1862, for the war. Reported absent sick on or about September 11, 1862. Reported absent without leave on October 27, 1862. Returned to duty prior to November 1, 1862. Reported present through December 31, 1862. Hospitalized at Richmond, Virginia, February 13, 1863, with pneumonia. Later diagnosed with bronchitis. Transferred to hospital at Huguenot Springs, Virginia, April 20, 1863. Admitted to hospital at Danville, Virginia, May 9, 1863, with debilitas. Returned to duty on June 12, 1863. Captured at Rappahannock Station, Virginia, November 7, 1863. Confined at Point Lookout, Maryland, November 11, 1863. Paroled at Point Lookout on March 16, 1864. Received at City Point, Virginia, March 20, 1864, for exchange. Returned to duty in May-August, 1864. Reported present through February 28, 1865. Captured at Farmville, Virginia, April 6, 1865. Confined at Newport News, Virginia, April 14, 1865. Released at Newport News on June 26, 1865, after taking the Oath of Allegiance.

WILHELM, LEWIS A., Private

Resided in Rowan County and was by occupation a farmer prior to enlisting in Rowan County at age 32, July 4, 1862, for the war. Hospitalized at Richmond, Virginia, November 1, 1862, with remittent fever. Furloughed for sixty days on November 26, 1862. Returned to duty in March-April, 1863. Wounded in the hand at Winchester, Virginia, June 14, 1863. Returned to duty prior to September 1, 1863. Captured at Rappahannock Station, Virginia, November 7, 1863. Confined at Point Lookout, Maryland, November 11, 1863. Paroled at Point Lookout on March 16, 1864. Received at City Point, Virginia, March 20, 1864, for exchange. Sent to hospital on May 13, 1864. Returned to duty in September-October, 1864. Reported present through February 28, 1865. Captured at Farmville, Virginia, April 6, 1865. Confined at Newport News, Virginia, April 14, 1865. Released at Newport News on June 26, 1865, after taking the Oath of Allegiance.

WINECOFF, J. M., Private

Resided in Rowan County where he enlisted at age 19, July 4, 1862, for the war. Died in camp near Culpeper Court House, Virginia, November 16, 1862, of disease.

COMPANY D

This company was raised in Forsyth County on July 4, 1862. It was mustered into service at Salisbury on July 17, 1862, and assigned to the 57th Regiment N.C. Troops as Company D. After joining the regiment the company functioned as a part of the regiment, and its history for the remainder of the war is reported as a part of the regimental history.

The following roster was compiled primarily from information in the microfilm edition of the Compiled Service Records of Soldiers Who Served in Organizations from the State of North Carolina (Record Group 109, M270), National Archives and Records Administration, Washington, D.C. Record Group 109 includes enlistment papers, pay vouchers, requisitions, letters of resignation, discharge certificates, and abstracts of medical and prisoner of war returns. Materials relating specifically to this company include a muster-in and descriptive roll dated July 17, 1862, and muster rolls dated July, 1862-December, 1863, and March, 1864-February, 1865

Also utilized in this roster were *The War of the Rebellion: A Compilation of the Official Records of the Union and Confederate Armies*, the North Carolina adjutant general's *Roll of Honor*, state militia records, newspaper casualty lists and obituaries, wartime claims for bounty pay and allowances, postwar registers of claims for artificial limbs, Confederate pension applications filed with the states of North Carolina, Tennessee, and Florida, Confederate Soldiers' Home records, and the 1860 and 1870 federal censuses of North Carolina. A search was made also for relevant letters, diaries, reminiscences, and other manuscripts in the Southern Historical Collection (University of North Carolina-Chapel Hill), the Duke University Library Special Collections Department, and the North Carolina Division of Archives and History.

Among the secondary sources consulted were records of the North Carolina division of the United Daughters of the Confederacy, postwar rosters, regimental and county histories, marriage bond, will, and cemetery indexes, published and unpublished genealogies, biographical dictionaries, the North Carolina *County Heritage Book* series, the *Confederate Veteran*, Walter Clark's *Histories of the Several Regiments and Battalions from North Carolina in the Great War, 1861-'65*, and the North Carolina volume of the extended edition of *Confederate Military History*.

OFFICERS

CAPTAINS

MANN, JAMES E.

Resided in Forsyth County and was by occupation a minister (Methodist-Episcopalian) prior to enlisting in Forsyth County at age 29. Appointed Captain on July 4, 1862. Resigned on October 6, 1862. Resignation accepted on October 18, 1862. Later served as Chaplain of this regiment (see Field and Staff section).

BUTNER, ELIAS J.

Resided in Forsyth County and was by occupation a farmer prior to enlisting in Forsyth County at age 32. Appointed 1st Lieutenant on July 4, 1862. Hospitalized at Richmond, Virginia, October 4, 1862. Furloughed for thirty days on October 16, 1862. Promoted to Captain on October 18, 1862. Returned to duty on an unspecified date. Shot through the breast and killed at Fredericksburg, Virginia, December 13, 1862.

GRAY, SAMUEL WILEY

Born on July 19, 1842. Resided in Forsyth County and was by occupation a farmer prior to enlisting in Forsyth County at age 19, July 4, 1862, for the war. Mustered in as Sergeant. Promoted to 1st Sergeant prior to September 1, 1862. Elected 1st Lieutenant on November 23, 1862. Promoted to Captain on December 13, 1862. Reported present through May 11, 1863. Killed at Gettysburg, Pennsylvania, July 2, 1863. ["While in the army, his spirit and conduct, both upon the field and in camp, were such as to win the confidence and esteem of his comrades and fellow-soldiers." *People's Press* (Salem), August 13, 1863.]

PROPST, WILLIAM M.

Served as 1st Lieutenant of Company F of this regiment. Reported in command of this company in November-December, 1864.

LIEUTENANTS

BARROW, JAMES L., 3rd Lieutenant

Resided in Forsyth County and was by occupation a farmer prior to enlisting in Forsyth County at age 25. Appointed 3rd Lieutenant on July 4, 1862. Reported present through October 31, 1862. Died in hospital at Richmond, Virginia, on or about December 26, 1862, of "typhoid fever." [May have submitted his resignation on September 5, 1862.]

CLAYTON, WILLIAM F., 2nd Lieutenant

Born on November 28, 1828. Resided in Forsyth County and was by occupation a farmer prior to enlisting at age 33. Appointed 2nd Lieutenant on July 4, 1862. Hospitalized at Richmond, Virginia, October 25, 1862, with jaundice. Furloughed for twenty days on October 30, 1862. Returned to duty in November-December, 1862. Resigned on February 20, 1863, by reason of "ch[ronic] dyspepsia & general impairment of health." Resignation accepted on February 26, 1863.

GORRELL, ALBERT BURROW, 2nd Lieutenant

Born on March 6, 1840. Resided in Forsyth County where he enlisted at age 22, July 4, 1862, for the war. Mustered in as Sergeant. Elected 2nd Lieutenant on January 23, 1863. Reported present or accounted for on surviving company muster rolls through December 31, 1864. Wounded in the right arm at Hatcher's Run, Virginia, February 6, 1865. Reported absent wounded through February 28, 1865. Paroled at Greensboro on May 24, 1865.

GORRELL, ROBERT D., 1st Lieutenant

Born on December 20, 1834. Resided in Forsyth County where he enlisted at age 27, July 4, 1862, for the war. Mustered in as Corporal. Elected 2nd Lieutenant on November 23, 1862. Elected 1st Lieutenant on December 18, 1862. Reported present through May 11, 1863. Hospitalized at Richmond, Virginia, July 30, 1863, with febris communis. Furloughed for thirty days on or about August 5, 1863. Returned to duty and was reported in command of the company in September-October, 1863. Captured at Rappahannock Station, Virginia, November 7, 1863. Confined at Old Capitol Prison, Washington, D.C., November 8, 1863. Transferred to Johnson's Island, Ohio, where he arrived on November 14, 1863. Released at Johnson's Island on June 13, 1865, after taking the Oath of Allegiance.

STANDEFOR, JAMES Y., 3rd Lieutenant

Resided in Forsyth County where he enlisted at age 28, July 4, 1862, for the war. Mustered in as Private. Reported present through May 11, 1863. Elected 3rd Lieutenant on June 1, 1863. Reported present and in command of the company in June-August, 1863. Reported present in September-October, 1863. Captured at Rappahannock Station, Virginia, November 7, 1863. Confined at Johnson's Island, Ohio, November 14, 1863. Released at Johnson's Island on June 13, 1865, after taking the Oath of Allegiance.

NONCOMMISSIONED OFFICERS
AND PRIVATES

ADAMS, EDWIN T., Private

Previously served as Private in Company H, 29th Regiment Virginia Infantry. Transferred to this company on April 1, 1864. Captured near Hanover Junction, Virginia, May 22, 1864. Confined at Point Lookout, Maryland, May 30, 1864. Released at Point Lookout on June 3, 1864, after taking the Oath of Allegiance and joining the U.S. Army. Assigned to Company G, 1st Regiment U.S. Volunteer Infantry.

BANNER, JOHN W., Private

Resided in Forsyth County and was by occupation a carpenter prior to enlisting in Forsyth County at age 28, July 4, 1862, for the war. Reported sick in hospital at Richmond, Virginia, in September, 1862. Returned to duty in November-December, 1862. Reported present through May 11, 1863. Captured at or near Hagerstown, Maryland, on or about July 14, 1863. Confined at Fort Delaware, Delaware, July 23, 1863. Died at Fort Delaware on August 10, 1863, of "pneumonia."

BARROW, JAMES E., Private

Resided in Forsyth County and was by occupation a farmer prior to enlisting in Forsyth County at age 27, July 4, 1862, for the war. Hospitalized at Richmond, Virginia, September 25, 1862, with measles. Furloughed on October 18, 1862. Returned to duty prior to November 1, 1862. Wounded in the left leg at Fredericksburg, Virginia, December 13, 1862. Left leg amputated. Hospitalized at Richmond. Retired to the Invalid Corps on November 23, 1864. Survived the war.

BECK, GEORGE LEONARD, Private

Born in Forsyth County* on August 1, 1842. Resided in Forsyth County where he enlisted at age 19, July 4, 1862, for the war. Reported present until December 13, 1862, when he was wounded at Fredericksburg, Virginia. Returned to duty prior to January 1, 1863. Reported present through October 31, 1863. Captured at Rappahannock Station, Virginia, November 7, 1863. Confined at Point Lookout, Maryland, November 11, 1863. Paroled at Point Lookout on March 16, 1864. Received at City Point, Virginia, March 20, 1864, for exchange. Returned to duty in May-August, 1864. Reported present through February 28, 1865. Wounded in the right arm on an unspecified date (probably on or about March 31, 1865). Right arm amputated. Captured in hospital at Richmond, Virginia, April 3, 1865. Paroled on May 17, 1865.

BELL, B. FRANK, Private

Resided in Forsyth County where he enlisted at age 29, July 4, 1862, for the war. Reported present through October 31, 1862. Reported missing at Fredericksburg, Virginia, December 13, 1862. Returned to duty prior to December 31, 1862. Reported on detached service with the Pioneer Corps in March-December, 1863, and March-April, 1864. Returned to duty on an unspecified date. Captured at or near Frederick, Maryland, on or about July 10, 1864. Confined at Old Capitol Prison, Washington, D.C. Transferred to Elmira, New York, July 23, 1864. Released at Elmira on May 29, 1865, after taking the Oath of Allegiance.

BENNETT, J. A., Private

Resided in Stokes County. Reportedly enlisted in Stokes County on July 16, 1862; however, he was not listed in the records of this company until November-December, 1864. Reported present in November, 1864-February, 1865. Captured at Farmville, Virginia, April 6, 1865. Confined at Newport News, Virginia, April 14, 1865. Released at Newport News on June 26, 1865, after taking the Oath of Allegiance.

BLACKBURN, EDWIN A., Private

Resided in Forsyth County and was by occupation a farmer or day laborer prior to enlisting in Forsyth County at age 27, July 4, 1862, for the war. Hospitalized at Richmond, Virginia, October 6, 1862, with parotitis. Furloughed for thirty days on October 31, 1862. Returned to duty prior to January 1, 1863. Hospitalized at Richmond on March 28, 1863, with debilitas. Transferred to hospital at Danville, Virginia, April 21, 1863. Reported "absent without proper authority" in May-October, 1863. Returned to duty in November-December, 1863. Reported present in March-April, 1864. Died at home on or about September 16, 1864, of disease.

BLACKBURN, LEWIS W., Private

Resided in Forsyth County where he enlisted at age 19, July 4, 1862, for the war. Hospitalized at Richmond, Virginia, September 27, 1862, with rubeola. Furloughed for thirty days on October 22, 1862. Returned to duty prior to January 1, 1863. Reported present through May 11, 1863. Hospitalized at Richmond on June 3, 1863. Died in hospital at Richmond on June 6, 1863, of "feb[ris] typhoides."

BLACKBURN, NEWTON W., Private

Resided in Forsyth County where he enlisted at age 21, July 4, 1862, for the war. Hospitalized at Richmond, Virginia, September 25, 1862, with measles. Furloughed on October 22, 1862. Returned to duty subsequent to February 28, 1863. Wounded in the side at Chancellorsville, Virginia, May 4, 1863. Hospitalized at Richmond. Returned to duty on June 4, 1863. Captured at Gettysburg, Pennsylvania, on or about July 2, 1863. Confined at Fort Delaware, Delaware. Transferred to Point Lookout, Maryland, October 20, 1863. Paroled at Point Lookout on February 18, 1865. Received at Boulware's and Cox's Wharves, James River, Virginia, February 20-21, 1865, for exchange. Hospitalized at Richmond on February 21, 1865, with a carbuncle. Furloughed for thirty days on March 4, 1865.

BORUM, GEORGE A. R., Private

Resided in Forsyth County where he enlisted at age 30, August 6, 1862, for the war. Reported present through October 31, 1862. Wounded in the leg at Fredericksburg, Virginia, December 13, 1862. Hospitalized at Richmond, Virginia. Transferred to hospital at Farmville, Virginia, December 20, 1862. Furloughed for thirty days on December 23, 1862. Returned to duty on November 26, 1863. Reported present through April 30, 1864. Reported at home on sick furlough from June 4, 1864, until January 1, 1865, when he was reported absent without leave. No further records.

BOYER, JOHN, Private

Resided in Forsyth County and enlisted in Forsyth or Rowan County at age 25, August 6, 1862, for the war. Reported absent sick in September-October, 1862. Returned to duty in November-December, 1862. Reported present through May 11, 1863. Reported at home on sick furlough in June-December, 1863. No further records.

BROWN, W. D., Corporal

Resided in Forsyth County where he enlisted at age 22, July 4, 1862, for the war. Mustered in as Private. Reported present through

October 31, 1863. Promoted to Corporal in May-August, 1863. Captured at Rappahannock Station, Virginia, November 7, 1863. Confined at Point Lookout, Maryland, November 11, 1863. Paroled at Point Lookout on March 16, 1864. Received at City Point, Virginia, March 20, 1864, for exchange. Returned to duty prior to September 1, 1864. Wounded in the leg at Cedar Creek, Virginia, October 19, 1864. Hospitalized at Richmond, Virginia. Furloughed for thirty days on November 13, 1864. Returned to duty in January-February, 1865. Surrendered at Appomattox Court House, Virginia, April 9, 1865.

BURKE, J. Y., Private

Resided in Forsyth County where he enlisted at age 23, July 4, 1862, for the war. Killed at Fredericksburg, Virginia, December 13, 1862.

BURKE, L. C., Private

Enlisted in Forsyth County at age 21, July 4, 1862, for the war. Reported present through October 31, 1862. Wounded in the head at Fredericksburg, Virginia, December 13, 1862. Died in hospital at Richmond, Virginia, December 18, 1862, of wounds.

CLEMMONS, H. E., Private

Enlisted in Wake County on November 14, 1863, for the war. Reported present or accounted for until August 10, 1864, when he was reported absent without leave. Returned to duty prior to October 19, 1864, when he was wounded in the left shoulder at Cedar Creek, Virginia. Hospitalized at Lynchburg, Virginia. Reported absent without leave on January 1, 1865. Survived the war. [Was about 30 years of age at time of enlistment.]

COLTRANE, JEFFREY H., Private

Resided in Forsyth County and was by occupation a farmer prior to enlisting in Forsyth County at age 31, July 4, 1862, for the war. Reported present until December 13, 1862, when he was wounded in the hand ("two or three fingers off") at Fredericksburg, Virginia. Hospitalized at Richmond, Virginia. Furloughed for forty days on January 26, 1863. Returned to duty prior to May 11, 1863. Reported at home on sick furlough on August 31, 1863. Reported absent without proper authority from October 25 through December 31, 1863. Returned to duty prior to May 1, 1864. Hospitalized at Richmond on June 27, 1864. Returned to duty in September-October, 1864. Captured near Petersburg, Virginia, February 6, 1865. Confined at Point Lookout, Maryland, February 9, 1865. Died at Point Lookout on May 23, 1865, of "chr[onic] diarrhoea."

CONRAD, JOHN L., Corporal

Born on July 7, 1832. Resided in Forsyth County and was by occupation a farmer prior to enlisting in Forsyth County at age 29, July 4, 1862, for the war. Hospitalized at Richmond, Virginia, November 8, 1862. Returned to duty on November 25, 1862. Killed at Fredericksburg, Virginia, December 13, 1862.

COX, WILLIAM H., Private

Resided in Forsyth County where he enlisted at age 23, July 4, 1862, for the war. Hospitalized at Richmond, Virginia, November 8, 1862, with bronchitis. Furloughed for thirty-five days on December 2, 1862. Returned to duty in March-May, 1863. Hospitalized at Charlottesville, Virginia, June 10, 1863, with chronic diarrhoea. Furloughed for thirty days on July 31, 1863. Returned to duty in January-April, 1864. Reported in hospital at Richmond from June 27 through September 1, 1864. Reported in hospital at

Wilson from October 20, 1864, through February 28, 1865. Returned to duty prior to March 25, 1865, when he was captured at Fort Stedman, Virginia. Confined at Point Lookout, Maryland, March 28, 1865. Released at Point Lookout on June 24, 1865, after taking the Oath of Allegiance.

CREWS, JOHN, Private

Resided in Forsyth County and was by occupation a farmer prior to enlisting in Forsyth County at age 26, July 4, 1862, for the war. Hospitalized at Richmond, Virginia, October 25, 1862, with typhoid fever. Died in hospital at Richmond on or about December 23, 1862, of "variola."

CREWS, JOSEPH H., Corporal

Born on September 15, 1843. Resided in Forsyth County where he enlisted at age 18, July 4, 1862, for the war. Mustered in as Private. Hospitalized at Richmond, Virginia, December 12, 1862, with mumps. Returned to duty on December 23, 1862. Reported present through October 31, 1863. Captured at Rappahannock Station, Virginia, November 7, 1863. Confined at Point Lookout, Maryland, November 11, 1863. Paroled at Point Lookout on March 16, 1864. Received at City Point, Virginia, March 20, 1864, for exchange. Returned to duty in May-August, 1864. Promoted to Corporal in September, 1864. Wounded in the head at Winchester, Virginia, September 19, 1864. Returned to duty in November-December, 1864. Reported present through February 28, 1865. Surrendered at Appomattox Court House, Virginia, April 9, 1865.

DAVIS, JOHN W., Private

Resided in Stokes County where he enlisted at age 32, July 4, 1862, for the war. Reported present or accounted for on surviving company muster rolls through February 28, 1865. Captured at Farmville, Virginia, April 6, 1865. Confined at Newport News, Virginia, April 14, 1865. Released at Newport News on June 26, 1865, after taking the Oath of Allegiance.

DAWSON, MILTON H., Private

Resided in Forsyth County and was by occupation a farmer prior to enlisting in Forsyth County at age 24, July 4, 1862, for the war. Hospitalized at Richmond, Virginia, on or about September 22, 1862. Furloughed on or about October 28, 1862. Returned to duty in January-February, 1863. Reported present until November 7, 1863, when he was captured at Rappahannock Station, Virginia. Confined at Point Lookout, Maryland, November 11, 1863. Paroled at Point Lookout on March 16, 1864. Received at City Point, Virginia, March 20, 1864, for exchange. Returned to duty in May-August, 1864. Captured at Fisher's Hill, Virginia, September 22, 1864. Confined at Point Lookout on October 3, 1864. Paroled at Point Lookout on November 1, 1864. Received at Venus Point, Savannah River, Georgia, November 15, 1864, for exchange. Reported absent without leave on December 5, 1864. Survived the war.

EDMONDSON, WILLIAM JAMES, 1st Sergeant

Resided in Forsyth County and was by occupation a farmer prior to enlisting in Forsyth or Rowan County at age 26, July 29, 1862, for the war. Mustered in as Private. Promoted to 1st Sergeant on November 23, 1862. Reported present until May 4, 1863, when he was captured at Chancellorsville, Virginia. Confined at Fort Delaware, Delaware, on or about May 7, 1863. Paroled at Fort Delaware and transferred to City Point, Virginia, where he was received on May 23, 1863, for exchange. Returned to duty prior to September

1, 1863. Reported present on surviving company muster rolls through August 31, 1864. Appointed 2nd Lieutenant and transferred to Company H of this regiment on October 20, 1864.

FAIR, BARNABAS, Private

Resided in Yadkin County and enlisted in Forsyth County at age 51, July 4, 1862, for the war as a substitute for Frank Miller. Hospitalized at Richmond, Virginia, October 29, 1862, with typhoid fever. Furloughed for thirty days on or about November 11, 1862. Reported absent sick without proper authority from January 1, 1863, through February 28, 1865. No further records.

FLYNT, JOHN P., Private

Born on April 27, 1829. Resided in Forsyth County and was by occupation a saddler prior to enlisting in Forsyth County at age 33, July 4, 1862, for the war. Reported present through October 31, 1862. Wounded in the left hip at Fredericksburg, Virginia, December 13, 1862. Hospitalized at Richmond, Virginia. Furloughed for thirty days on December 29, 1862. Returned to duty subsequent to February 28, 1863. Wounded in both hands at Chancellorsville, Virginia, on or about May 4, 1863. Two fingers of right hand and one finger of left hand amputated. Returned to duty in January-April, 1864. Reported at home on sick furlough from May 3, 1864, through February 28, 1865. Survived the war.

FLYNT, SAMUEL R., Private

Resided in Forsyth County where he enlisted at age 25, July 4, 1862, for the war. Hospitalized at Richmond, Virginia, September 6, 1862, with parotitis and orchitis. Transferred to Salisbury on September 24, 1862. Returned to duty in January-February, 1863. Captured at Chancellorsville, Virginia, May 3-4, 1863. Confined at Fort Delaware, Delaware, on or about May 7, 1863. Paroled and transferred to City Point, Virginia, where he was received on May 23, 1863, for exchange. Returned to duty in May-August, 1863. Killed at Rappahannock Station, Virginia, November 7, 1863.

FLYNT, SANDY L., Private

Resided in Forsyth County where he enlisted at age 18, July 4, 1862, for the war. Hospitalized at Richmond, Virginia, September 6, 1862, with parotitis. Furloughed for fifteen days on or about September 21, 1862. Returned to duty in November-December, 1862. Reported present on surviving company muster rolls through February 28, 1865. Survived the war.

FRAZIER, JOHN, Corporal

Resided in Forsyth County and was by occupation a farmer prior to enlisting in Forsyth County at age 30, July 4, 1862, for the war. Mustered in as Private. Promoted to Corporal on November 23, 1862. Reported present through February 28, 1863. Hospitalized at Richmond, Virginia, May 1, 1863, with rheumatism. Transferred to Danville, Virginia, May 7, 1863. Returned to duty on May 26, 1863. Reported present through October 31, 1863. Captured at Rappahannock Station, Virginia, November 7, 1863. Confined at Point Lookout, Maryland, November 11, 1863. Paroled at Point Lookout on March 16, 1864. Received at City Point, Virginia, March 20, 1864, for exchange. Returned to duty in May-August, 1864. Captured at Winchester, Virginia, September 19, 1864. Confined at Point Lookout on September 26, 1864. Died at Point Lookout on February 1, 1865, of "acute dysentery."

FULP, THOMAS D., Private

Resided in Stokes County and enlisted in Guilford County at age 36, March 19, 1863, for the war. Hospitalized at Richmond,

Virginia, May 24, 1863, with typhoid fever. Furloughed for forty days on or about June 14, 1863. Reported absent without proper authority in September-October, 1863. Returned to duty on December 9, 1863. Reported present in March-April, 1864. Hospitalized at Richmond on May 25, 1864, with chronic diarrhoea. Transferred on July 4, 1864. Returned to duty in September-October, 1864. Reported present through February 28, 1865. Captured at Farmville, Virginia, April 6, 1865. Confined at Newport News, Virginia, April 14, 1865. Released at Newport News on June 26, 1865, after taking the Oath of Allegiance.

FULTON, ABRAM, Sergeant

Resided in Forsyth County and was by occupation a farmer prior to enlisting in Forsyth County at age 30, July 4, 1862, for the war. Mustered in as Sergeant. Discharged on October 20, 1862, after providing Pvt. W. Sipple as a substitute. [Served also as Captain in the 121st Regiment N.C. Militia.]

FULTON, HENRY C., Private

Resided in Forsyth County and enlisted in Rowan County at age 18, August 6, 1862, for the war. Hospitalized at Richmond, Virginia, October 31, 1862, with parotitis. Returned to duty on November 10, 1862. Reported present through May 11, 1863. Reported absent sick in June-December, 1863. Returned to duty prior to May 1, 1864. Captured near Harpers Ferry, West Virginia, July 8-9, 1864. Confined at Old Capitol Prison, Washington, D.C., July 17, 1864. Transferred to Elmira, New York, July 23, 1864. Released at Elmira on July 3, 1865, after taking the Oath of Allegiance.

FULTON, JACOB, Private

Born on March 18, 1840. Resided in Forsyth County and was by occupation a farmer prior to enlisting in Forsyth County at age 22, July 4, 1862, for the war. Reported present through October 31, 1862. Wounded in the thigh at Fredericksburg, Virginia, December 13, 1862. Hospitalized at Richmond, Virginia. Transferred to hospital at Farmville, Virginia, December 20, 1862. Furloughed for thirty days on December 22, 1862. Reported absent wounded through May 11, 1863. Reported on detail as an "ag[en]t" in June-December, 1863. Returned to duty prior to May 1, 1864. Hospitalized at Richmond on May 16, 1864, apparently still suffering from the wound he received at Fredericksburg. Transferred to another hospital on June 2, 1864. Returned to duty prior to July 20, 1864, when he was captured at Winchester, Virginia. Confined at Camp Chase, Ohio, July 28, 1864. Paroled at Camp Chase and transferred on March 2, 1865. Received at Boulware's and Cox's Wharves, James River, Virginia, March 10-12, 1865, for exchange. Survived the war.

GENTRY, RALEIGH G., Private

Resided in Stokes County and enlisted in Forsyth County at age 20, July 4, 1862, for the war. Reported present through October 31, 1863. Captured at Rappahannock Station, Virginia, November 7, 1863. Confined at Point Lookout, Maryland, November 11, 1863. Paroled at Point Lookout on March 16, 1864. Received at City Point, Virginia, March 20, 1864, for exchange. Returned to duty in May-August, 1864. Wounded in the left arm at Winchester, Virginia, September 19, 1864. Returned to duty prior to November 1, 1864. Enlisted in (or was transferred to) Company G, 21st Regiment N.C. Troops (11th Regiment N.C. Volunteers), in January-February, 1865.

GIBSON, HENRY M., Private

Resided in Stokes County and enlisted in Forsyth County at age 33, July 4, 1862, for the war. Reported present through February 28, 1863. Hospitalized at Richmond, Virginia, May 4, 1863, with chronic rheumatism. Transferred to Salisbury on June 10, 1863. Reported absent without proper authority from August 25, 1863, through February 28, 1865. Survived the war. [North Carolina pension records indicate that he was wounded in the head, back, right arm, and both ankles by the explosion of a shell at Fredericksburg, Virginia, December 1, 1862.]

GIBSON, JEREMIAH, Private

Born in Stokes County in 1844. Resided in Stokes County and enlisted in Forsyth or Rowan County on July 4, 1862, for the war. Reported present or accounted for through October 31, 1863. Captured at Rappahannock Station, Virginia, November 7, 1863. Confined at Point Lookout, Maryland, November 11, 1863. Paroled at Point Lookout on March 16, 1864. Received at City Point, Virginia, March 20, 1864, for exchange. Hospitalized at Richmond, Virginia, the same date with intermittent fever. Furloughed for sixty days on March 31, 1864. Returned to duty in May-August, 1864. Captured at Fisher's Hill, Virginia, September 22, 1864. Confined at Point Lookout on October 3, 1864. Paroled at Point Lookout on March 17, 1865. Received at Boulware's Wharf, James River, Virginia, March 19, 1865, for exchange. Survived the war.

GIBSON, RAYMOND, Private

Resided in Stokes County and enlisted in Forsyth County at age 31, July 4, 1862, for the war. Hospitalized at Richmond, Virginia, October 19, 1862, with remittent fever. Furloughed for twenty days on November 8, 1862. Returned to duty in January-February, 1863. Captured (or deserted to the enemy) at or near Gettysburg, Pennsylvania, on or about July 5, 1863. Confined at Fort Delaware, Delaware, on or about July 9, 1863. Transferred to Point Lookout, Maryland, October 20, 1863. Paroled and exchanged on an unspecified date. Returned to duty prior to November 7, 1863, when he was captured at Rappahannock Station, Virginia. Confined at Point Lookout. Paroled at Point Lookout on March 16, 1864. Received at City Point, Virginia, March 20, 1864, for exchange. Returned to duty prior to August 22-23, 1864, when he was captured near Charlestown, West Virginia. Confined at Elmira, New York, August 29, 1864. Released at Elmira on June 16, 1865, after taking the Oath of Allegiance.

GRUBBS, JESSE F., Private

Resided in Forsyth County and was by occupation a farmer prior to enlisting in Forsyth or Rowan County at age 33, July 4, 1862, for the war. Mustered in as Private. Promoted to Sergeant on December 18, 1862. Reported present on surviving company muster rolls through April 30, 1864. Transferred to Company K of this regiment on June 23 or July 23, 1864. Reduced to ranks and transferred back to this company on November 26, 1864. Reported present or accounted for through February 28, 1865. Surrendered at Appomattox Court House, Virginia, April 9, 1865.

HALL, F. M., Private

Place and date of enlistment not reported. Reported sick in camp at Salisbury on September 18, 1862. No further records.

HAMPTON, WILLIAM A., Private

Resided in Forsyth County and was by occupation a day laborer prior to enlisting in Forsyth County at age 23, July 4, 1862, for the

war. Hospitalized at Richmond, Virginia, on an unspecified date. Returned to duty on October 12, 1862. Killed at Fredericksburg, Virginia, December 13, 1862.

HARKEY, WILLIAM A., Private

Place and date of enlistment not reported (probably enlisted subsequent to February 28, 1865). Paroled at Montgomery, Alabama, May 16, 1865.

HARMON, ANDREW, Private

Resided in Forsyth County where he enlisted at age 26, July 4, 1862, for the war. Reported present through February 28, 1863. Captured at Chancellorsville, Virginia, May 3-4, 1863. Confined at Fort Delaware, Delaware, on or about May 7, 1863. Paroled and transferred to City Point, Virginia, where he was received on May 23, 1863, for exchange. Hospitalized at Petersburg, Virginia, where he died on or about May 25, 1863, of disease.

HARMON, DAVID, Private

Resided in Forsyth County where he enlisted at age 28, July 4, 1862, for the war. Hospitalized at Richmond, Virginia, September 22, 1862, with diarrhoea. Furloughed for thirty days on October 29, 1862. Returned to duty in January-February, 1863. Wounded in the head and face at Chancellorsville, Virginia, May 4, 1863. Reported absent wounded or absent sick through December 31, 1863. Returned to duty in January-April, 1864. Reported sick in hospital from June 22 through August 31, 1864. Returned to duty prior to November 1, 1864. Reported present through February 28, 1865. Captured at Farmville, Virginia, April 6, 1865. Confined at Newport News, Virginia, April 14, 1865. Released at Newport News on June 26, 1865, after taking the Oath of Allegiance.

HARROLD, JOHN FRANK, Private

Resided in Forsyth County and enlisted in Wake County at age 43, November 14, 1863, for the war. Sent to hospital on December 11, 1863. Returned to duty prior to May 1, 1864. Hospitalized at Richmond, Virginia, May 16, 1864, with a gunshot wound. Place and date wounded not reported. Furloughed on October 6, 1864. Returned to duty prior to October 19, 1864, when he was wounded in the left arm (fracture) at Cedar Creek, Virginia. Hospitalized at Raleigh on November 26, 1864. Transferred to another hospital on January 1, 1865. Survived the war.

HARTMAN, JOHN T., Private

Resided in Forsyth County where he enlisted on March 1, 1864, for the war. Reported present through February 28, 1865. Captured at Farmville, Virginia, April 6, 1865. Confined at Newport News, Virginia, April 14, 1865. Released at Newport News on June 26, 1865, after taking the Oath of Allegiance.

HAYNES, JOEL H., Private

Resided in Forsyth County where he enlisted at age 18, July 4, 1862, for the war. Reported present through October 31, 1862. Wounded in both legs at Fredericksburg, Virginia, December 13, 1862. Reported absent wounded through May 11, 1863. Hospitalized at Richmond, Virginia, June 3, 1863, with typhoid fever. Died in hospital at Richmond on or about June 12, 1863.

HIRE, SALATHIEL, Private

Born on September 18, 1832. Resided in Forsyth County and was by occupation a farmer prior to enlisting in Forsyth County at age

29, July 4, 1862, for the war. Hospitalized at Richmond, Virginia, on or about September 22, 1862. Furloughed for twenty-five days on October 11, 1862. Returned to duty prior to January 1, 1863. Reported present through May 11, 1863. Wounded in the face and/or neck at Gettysburg, Pennsylvania, July 1, 1863. Returned to duty in January-March, 1864. Reported present through February 28, 1865. Captured at Farmville, Virginia, April 6, 1865. Confined at Newport News, Virginia, April 14, 1865. Released at Newport News on June 26, 1865, after taking the Oath of Allegiance.

HOOVER, JOSEPH CALVIN, Private

Resided in Forsyth County where he enlisted at age 21, July 4, 1862, for the war. Reported present or accounted for through October 31, 1862. Wounded in the left hand at Fredericksburg, Virginia, December 13, 1862. Hospitalized at Richmond, Virginia. Furloughed on December 29, 1862. Returned to duty prior to March 1, 1863. Wounded in the finger at Chancellorsville, Virginia, May 4, 1863. Returned to duty prior to November 1, 1863. Reported sick in camp with smallpox in November-December, 1863. Reported present in March-April, 1864. Hospitalized at Richmond on May 23, 1864 (apparently suffering from organic disease of the heart). Returned to duty in September-October, 1864. Captured near Petersburg, Virginia, February 6, 1865. Confined at Point Lookout, Maryland, February 9, 1865. Released at Point Lookout on May 15, 1865, after taking the Oath of Allegiance.

HOPKINS, B. N., Private

Resided in Forsyth County where he enlisted at age 36, July 4, 1862, for the war as a substitute. Mustered in as Sergeant. Hospitalized at Richmond, Virginia, October 20, 1862, with chronic diarrhoea. Furloughed for thirty days on or about November 18, 1862. Returned to duty in January-February, 1863. Reduced to ranks on January 18, 1863. Wounded in the head at Chancellorsville, Virginia, on or about May 2, 1863. Captured and paroled on or about May 24, 1863, during the "raid in the rear of Lee's army." Returned to duty prior to September 1, 1863. Reported on duty as acting Commissary Sergeant in November-December, 1863. Reported present on surviving company muster rolls through August 31, 1864. Wounded in the right thigh at Cedar Creek, Virginia, October 19, 1864. Hospitalized at Charlottesville, Virginia. Furloughed on November 21, 1864. Returned to duty subsequent to December 31, 1864. Furloughed on February 25, 1865. No further records.

HUDLER, JOHN W., Private

Resided in Forsyth County where he enlisted at age 25, July 4, 1862, for the war. Hospitalized at Richmond, Virginia, November 8, 1862, with chronic diarrhoea. Transferred to Scottsville, Virginia, November 28, 1862. Returned to duty in March-May, 1863. Hospitalized at Richmond on June 3, 1863. Died in hospital at Richmond on June 6, 1863, of "feb[ris] typhoides" and/or "super double pneumonia."

JARVIS, TENNISON, Private

Resided in Forsyth County where he enlisted at age 34, July 4, 1862, for the war. Sent to hospital at Richmond, Virginia, on or about September 18, 1862. Returned to duty in November-December, 1862. Hospitalized at Richmond on March 8, 1863. Died in hospital at Richmond on or about March 26, 1863, of "pleurisy," "typh[oid] pneumonia, and/or "measels [sic]."

JOYNER, BEN J., Private

Resided in Forsyth County where he enlisted at age 22, July 4, 1862, for the war. Hospitalized at Richmond, Virginia, on an unspecified date. Returned to duty on September 30, 1862. Hospitalized at Richmond on November 8, 1862, with intermittent fever. Transferred to hospital at Petersburg, Virginia, November 14, 1862. Returned to duty prior to January 1, 1863. Reported present through May 11, 1863. Reported absent sick in June-December, 1863. Returned to duty prior to May 1, 1864. Hospitalized at Richmond on May 26, 1864, with chronic diarrhoea. Returned to duty on June 18, 1864. Captured at Fisher's Hill, Virginia, September 22, 1864. Sent to Harpers Ferry, West Virginia. Confined at Point Lookout, Maryland, January 3, 1865. Paroled at Point Lookout on February 18, 1865. Received at Boulware's and Cox's Wharves, James River, Virginia, February 20-21, 1865, for exchange. Survived the war. [North Carolina pension records indicate that he injured his left hand and left ankle at Harpers Ferry on July 4, 1864, "by a peice (sic) of timber falling on it while we were attempting (sic) to tear the bridge down. . . ."]

KETNER, T. J., Private

Enlisted in Forsyth County on March 1, 1864, for the war. Hospitalized at Winchester, Virginia, on or about August 1, 1864. Transferred to hospital at Richmond, Virginia, on or about August 15, 1864. Returned to duty in November-December, 1864. Reported present through February 28, 1865. Surrendered at Appomattox Court House, Virginia, April 9, 1865.

KING, N. S., Private

Resided in Forsyth County where he enlisted at age 32, July 4, 1862, for the war. Sent to hospital at Richmond, Virginia, on or about September 14, 1862. Returned to duty in January-February, 1863. Wounded in the hand at Chancellorsville, Virginia, on or about May 4, 1863. Returned to duty prior to July 2, 1863, when he was captured at Gettysburg, Pennsylvania. Confined at Fort Delaware, Delaware, on or about July 9, 1863. Paroled at Fort Delaware on or about July 31, 1863. Received at City Point, Virginia, August 1, 1863, for exchange. Hospitalized at Petersburg, Virginia, where he died September 15, 1863, of "phthisis."

LASLEY, EDWARD F., Private

Resided in Forsyth County where he enlisted at age 20, July 4, 1862, for the war. Hospitalized at Richmond, Virginia, September 22, 1862, with pneumonia. Returned to duty on October 6, 1862. Wounded in the thigh at Fredericksburg, Virginia, December 13, 1862. Hospitalized at Richmond where he died on or about January 18, 1863, of wounds and/or disease.

LAWRENCE, ADDISON S., Private

Resided in Forsyth County where he enlisted at age 26, July 4, 1862, for the war. Accidentally wounded in the thigh on September 18, 1862, "while loading a wagon with guns." Died in hospital at Richmond, Virginia, on or about the same date.

LINEBACK, CALVIN C., Private

Resided in Forsyth County where he enlisted at age 21, July 4, 1862, for the war. Hospitalized at Richmond, Virginia, November 25, 1862, with typhoid fever. Furloughed for sixty days on March 16, 1863. Died on August 17, 1863, of disease. Place of death not reported.

LINEBACK, W. H., Private

Resided in Forsyth County where he enlisted at age 19, July 4, 1862, for the war. Hospitalized at Richmond, Virginia, October 9, 1862, with remittent fever. Furloughed on November 2, 1862. Returned to duty in January-February, 1863. Hospitalized at

Richmond on July 31, 1863. Returned to duty on December 11, 1863. Reported present in March-April, 1864. Hospitalized at Charlottesville, Virginia, June 17, 1864, with acute diarrhoea. Returned to duty in September-October, 1864. Detailed for duty at Richmond on or about January 5, 1865. Died in hospital at Richmond on February 2, 1865, of "pneumonia."

LIVENGOOD, ABSALOM, Private

Born on February 1, 1832. Resided in Forsyth County and was by occupation a farmer prior to enlisting in Forsyth County at age 30, July 4, 1862, for the war. Sent to hospital on or about November 10, 1862. Reported absent sick through May 11, 1863. Hospitalized at Richmond, Virginia, July 4, 1863, with chronic rheumatism. Furloughed for thirty-five days on August 12, 1863. Reported absent without proper authority in September-December, 1863. Returned to duty prior to May 1, 1864. Captured at Hanover Junction, Virginia, May 23-24, 1864. Confined at Point Lookout, Maryland, June 8, 1864. Transferred to Elmira, New York, July 8, 1864. Paroled at Elmira on October 11, 1864. Received at Venus Point, Savannah River, Georgia, November 15, 1864, for exchange. Reported absent without authority from December 5, 1864, through February 28, 1865. Survived the war.

LIVENGOOD, ALFRED B., Private

Resided in Forsyth County and was by occupation a farmer prior to enlisting in Forsyth County at age 26, July 4, 1862, for the war. Hospitalized at Richmond, Virginia, November 8, 1862, with remittent fever. Furloughed on November 20, 1862. Returned to duty on December 10, 1862. Killed at Fredericksburg, Virginia, December 13, 1862.

LIVENGOOD, HENRY W., Private

Resided in Forsyth County where he enlisted at age 19, July 4, 1862, for the war. Hospitalized at Richmond, Virginia, November 8, 1862, with chronic diarrhoea. Transferred to Scottsville, Virginia, November 28, 1862. Reported absent sick through May 11, 1863. Returned to duty prior to September 1, 1863. Captured at Rappahannock Station, Virginia, November 7, 1863. Confined at Point Lookout, Maryland, November 11, 1863. Hospitalized at Point Lookout on November 23, 1863, with scorbutus and chronic bronchitis. Paroled at Point Lookout on March 17, 1864. Received at City Point, Virginia, March 20, 1864, for exchange. Hospitalized at Richmond on March 20, 1864, with scorbutus. Furloughed for thirty days on March 26, 1864. Returned to duty prior to July 20, 1864, when he was wounded in the right leg (possibly also in the breast and knees) at Winchester, Virginia. Returned to duty prior to September 1, 1864. Reported present or accounted for through February 28, 1865. Surrendered at Appomattox Court House, Virginia, April 9, 1865. [North Carolina pension records indicate that he was wounded in the head at Gettysburg, Pennsylvania, July 3, 1863.]

LIVENGOOD, JACOB, Private

Resided in Forsyth County where he enlisted at age 24, July 4, 1862, for the war. Reported present through October 31, 1862. Killed at Fredericksburg, Virginia, December 13, 1862.

LOWRIE, JAMES A., Private

Resided in Guilford County and enlisted in Forsyth County at age 19, July 4, 1862, for the war. Reported present through October 31, 1862. Wounded in the foot at Fredericksburg, Virginia, December 13, 1862. Hospitalized at Farmville, Virginia (also suffering from pneumonia). Furloughed for thirty days on February 10,

1863. Returned to duty in May-October, 1863. Sent to hospital on November 6, 1863. Returned to duty in January-April, 1864. Reported present through August 31, 1864. Wounded in the face at Winchester, Virginia, September 19, 1864. Returned to duty prior to September 26, 1864, when he was wounded in the right leg near Weyers Cave, Virginia. Right leg amputated. Hospitalized at Charlottesville, Virginia. Furloughed on December 21, 1864. Reported absent wounded through February 28, 1865. Paroled at Greensboro on May 29, 1865.

MARSHALL, EMANUEL, Private

Resided in Forsyth County and was by occupation a day laborer prior to enlisting in Rowan County at age 31, July 29, 1862, for the war. Reported present through May 11, 1863. Company records indicate that he was captured at Hagerstown, Maryland, July 14, 1863; however, records of the Federal Provost Marshal do not substantiate that report. No further records.

MARSHALL, JAMES, Private

Resided in Forsyth County and was by occupation a farmer prior to enlisting in Forsyth County at age 27, July 4, 1862, for the war. Reported present through October 31, 1862. Wounded in the arm at Fredericksburg, Virginia, December 13, 1862. Arm amputated. Died in hospital at Richmond, Virginia, December 19, 1862, of wounds.

MARSHALL, JOSEPHUS, Private

Resided in Forsyth County where he enlisted at age 28, July 4, 1862, for the war. Hospitalized at Richmond, Virginia, September 22, 1862, with debilitas. Returned to duty on October 2, 1862. Hospitalized at Richmond on November 8, 1862, with acute diarrhoea. Transferred to another hospital on November 30, 1862. Returned to duty in January-February, 1863. Reported present until November 7, 1863, when he was captured at Rappahannock Station, Virginia. Confined at Point Lookout, Maryland, November 11, 1863. Paroled at Point Lookout on March 16, 1864. Received at City Point, Virginia, March 20, 1864, for exchange. Reported sick in hospital or absent on sick furlough from July 23 through December 31, 1864. Reported absent without proper authority in January-February, 1865. Paroled at Greensboro on May 13, 1865.

MARSHALL, TANDY, Private

Resided in Forsyth County and was by occupation a farmer prior to enlisting in Rowan County at age 34, July 29, 1862, for the war. Hospitalized at Richmond, Virginia, November 8, 1862, with acute diarrhoea. Transferred to another hospital on November 30, 1862. Returned to duty prior to January 1, 1863. Hospitalized at Richmond on March 26, 1863, with rheumatism. Detailed as a hospital nurse at Richmond on May 1, 1863. Rejoined the company on September 23, 1863. Captured at Rappahannock Station, Virginia, November 7, 1863. Confined at Point Lookout, Maryland, November 11, 1863. Paroled at Point Lookout on or about March 16, 1864. Received at City Point, Virginia, on or about March 20, 1864, for exchange. Died prior to June 23, 1864. Place, date, and cause of death not reported. [The N.C. Adjutant General's Roll of Honor states that he was "a bad egg."]

MATHEWS, HUGH M. PETIS, Private

Resided in Forsyth or Stokes County and was by occupation a farmer prior to enlisting in Forsyth County at age 23, July 4, 1862, for the war. Reported present through October 31, 1863. Captured at Rappahannock Station, Virginia, November 7, 1863. Confined at Point Lookout, Maryland, November 11, 1863. Paroled at Point Lookout on March 16, 1864. Received at City Point, Virginia, March 20, 1864, for exchange. Returned to duty prior to July 20, 1864, when he was captured at Winchester, Virginia. Confined at Camp Chase, Ohio, July 28, 1864. Paroled at Camp Chase on March 2, 1865. Received at Boulware's and Cox's Wharves, James River, Virginia, March 10-12, 1865, for exchange. Paroled at Greensboro on May 17, 1865.

MATHEWS, WILLIAM H. H., Private

Resided in Forsyth County where he enlisted at age 24, July 4, 1862, for the war. Reported present through October 31, 1863. Captured at Rappahannock Station, Virginia, November 7, 1863. Confined at Point Lookout, Maryland, November 11, 1863. Died at Point Lookout on or about August 12, 1864. Cause of death not reported.

MITCHELL, GEORGE W., Private

Resided in Forsyth County where he enlisted at age 30, July 4, 1862, for the war. Reported present through May 11, 1863. Wounded in the toe at Gettysburg, Pennsylvania, July 1, 1863. Reported absent wounded through December 31, 1863. Reported absent on detached service at Kinston in March-April, 1864. Hospitalized at Lynchburg, Virginia, June 18, 1864. Returned to duty in September-October, 1864. Reported present through February 28, 1865. Captured at Farmville, Virginia, April 6, 1865. Confined at Newport News, Virginia, April 14, 1865. Released at Newport News on June 26, 1865, after taking the Oath of Allegiance.

MOIR, ROBERT A., Private

Resided in Forsyth County and was by occupation a farmer prior to enlisting in Forsyth County at age 28, July 4, 1862, for the war. Reported present through October 31, 1863. Captured at Rappahannock Station, Virginia, November 7, 1863. Confined at Point Lookout, Maryland, November 11, 1863. Paroled at Point Lookout on March 16, 1864. Received at City Point, Virginia, March 20, 1864, for exchange. Returned to duty in May-August, 1864. Wounded in the thigh at Winchester, Virginia, September 19, 1864. Reported absent without proper authority in January-February, 1865. Survived the war.

MORGAN, GEORGE W., Private

Enlisted in Forsyth County on March 1, 1864, for the war. Reported present through August 31, 1864. Wounded in the left hand at or near Mount Jackson, Virginia, September 23, 1864. Hospitalized at Charlottesville, Virginia. Transferred to hospital at Lynchburg, Virginia, September 28, 1864. Reported absent on furlough in November-December, 1864. Returned to duty prior to February 28, 1865. Surrendered at Appomattox Court House, Virginia, April 9, 1865.

MORGAN, HENRY S., Private

Resided in Forsyth County and was by occupation a farmer prior to enlisting in Wake County at age 43, October 6, 1864, for the war. Reported present through February 28, 1865. Captured at Fort Stedman, Virginia, March 25, 1865. Confined at Point Lookout, Maryland, March 28, 1865. Released at Point Lookout on June 20, 1865, after taking the Oath of Allegiance.

NELSON, WILLIAM T., Sergeant

Resided in Forsyth County and was by occupation a farmer prior to enlisting in Forsyth County at age 30, July 4, 1862, for the war.

Mustered in as Corporal. Reported present through October 31, 1862. Wounded in the left foot at Fredericksburg, Virginia, December 13, 1862. Hospitalized at Richmond, Virginia, December 16, 1862. Furloughed for thirty days on or about December 24, 1862. Returned to duty in March-May, 1863. Reported present on surviving company muster rolls through October 31, 1864. Promoted to Sergeant in September-October, 1864. Reduced to ranks on November 15, 1864. Reported present in November, 1864-February, 1865. Promoted to Sergeant in January-February, 1865. Captured at Farmville, Virginia, April 6, 1865. Confined at Newport News, Virginia, April 14, 1865. Released at Newport News on June 26, 1865, after taking the Oath of Allegiance.

NULL, JAMES M., Private

Resided in Forsyth County where he enlisted at age 17, July 4, 1862, for the war. Hospitalized at Richmond, Virginia, November 8, 1862, with measles. Transferred to another hospital on November 30, 1862. Returned to duty in March-May, 1863. Hospitalized at Richmond on May 28, 1863, with typhoid fever. Furloughed for thirty days on or about June 30, 1863. Returned to duty prior to November 1, 1863. Captured at Rappahannock Station, Virginia, November 7, 1863. Confined at Point Lookout, Maryland, November 11, 1863. Paroled at Point Lookout on March 16, 1864. Received at City Point, Virginia, March 20, 1864, for exchange. Died on April 10, 1864. Place and cause of death not reported.

OAKES, GEORGE W., Corporal

Resided in Forsyth County and was by occupation a farmer prior to enlisting in Forsyth County at age 24, July 4, 1862, for the war. Mustered in as Private. Promoted to Corporal on December 18, 1862. Reported present through February 28, 1863. Hospitalized at Richmond, Virginia, March 23, 1863. Died in hospital at Richmond on May 1, 1863, of disease.

OGBURN, C. J., Private

Resided in Forsyth County where he enlisted at age 19, July 4, 1862, for the war. Hospitalized at Richmond, Virginia, September 22, 1862, with rubeola. Furloughed on October 13, 1862. Returned to duty on or about November 1, 1862. Reported present through February 28, 1863. Wounded in the right foot at Chancellorsville, Virginia, May 4, 1863. Right foot amputated. Reported absent wounded until November 23, 1864, when he was retired to the Invalid Corps. Paroled at Greensboro on May 9, 1865.

OGBURN, JOHN WICK, Private

Born on October 18, 1843. Resided in Forsyth County where he enlisted at age 19, February 16, 1863, for the war. Reported present through October 31, 1863. Captured at Rappahannock Station, Virginia, November 7, 1863. Confined at Point Lookout, Maryland, November 11, 1863. Paroled at Point Lookout on March 16, 1864. Received at City Point, Virginia, March 20, 1864, for exchange. Returned to duty in May-August, 1864. Reported present through December 31, 1864. Captured at Hatcher's Run, Virginia, February 6, 1865. Confined at Point Lookout on February 9, 1865. Released at Point Lookout on June 23, 1865, after taking the Oath of Allegiance.

OGBURN, SIHON ALEXANDER, Sergeant

Born on March 17, 1840. Resided in Forsyth County and was by occupation a farmer prior to enlisting in Forsyth County at age 22, July 4, 1862, for the war. Mustered in as Private. Promoted to Corporal in early November, 1862. Promoted to Sergeant on November 23, 1862. Wounded in the ribs and right elbow (fracture) at Fredericksburg, Virginia, December 13, 1862. Hospitalized at Richmond, Virginia. Furloughed for ninety days on April 2, 1863. Reported absent wounded through December 31, 1863. Detailed for duty as a yard master at Greensboro on March 20, 1864. Rejoined the company in November-December, 1864. Promoted to Commissary Sergeant in January-February, 1865, and transferred to the Field and Staff of this regiment. [Previously served as 2nd Lieutenant in the 71st Regiment N.C. Militia.]

PACE, JESSE A., Private

Resided in Forsyth County where he enlisted at age 23, July 4, 1862, for the war. Reported present or accounted for through October 31, 1863. Captured at Rappahannock Station, Virginia, November 7, 1863. Confined at Point Lookout, Maryland, November 11, 1863. Paroled at Point Lookout on March 16, 1864. Received at City Point, Virginia, March 20, 1864, for exchange. Sent to hospital on August 23, 1864. Returned to duty in November-December, 1864. Captured near Petersburg, Virginia, February 6, 1865. Confined at Point Lookout on February 9, 1865. Released at Point Lookout on June 16, 1865, after taking the Oath of Allegiance.

PARISH, JAMES, Private

Enlisted near Orange Court House, Virginia, January 16, 1864, for the war. Reported present through February 28, 1865. Wounded in the thigh at Fort Stedman, Virginia, March 25, 1865. Hospitalized at Richmond, Virginia, where he died on April 3, 1865, presumably of wounds.

PEGRAM, WILLIAM A., Private

Resided in Forsyth County where he enlisted at age 24, July 4, 1862, for the war. Hospitalized at Richmond, Virginia, October 29, 1862, with parotitis. Furloughed for thirty days on November 12, 1862. Returned to duty in January-February, 1863. Wounded in the hand, left side, and/or right leg at Chancellorsville, Virginia, May 4, 1863. Hospitalized at Richmond. Returned to duty on July 13, 1863. Detailed as a hospital nurse at Staunton, Virginia, August 25, 1863 (suffering from ascites and rheumatism). Rejoined the company in January-April, 1864. Sent to hospital on July 12, 1864. Returned to duty in September-October, 1864. Reported present through February 28, 1865. Captured at Farmville, Virginia, April 6, 1865. Confined at Newport News, Virginia, April 14, 1865. Released at Newport News on June 26, 1865, after taking the Oath of Allegiance.

PETRE, WESLEY T., Private

Resided in Forsyth County and enlisted at Petersburg, Virginia, at age 19, September 1, 1862, for the war. Sent to hospital at Richmond, Virginia, on or about October 20, 1862. Died in hospital at Richmond on February 9, 1863, of "smallpox."

PETREE, EMMANUEL, Private

Resided in Forsyth County and was by occupation a farmer prior to enlisting in Forsyth County at age 28, July 4, 1862, for the war. Reported present through October 31, 1862. Killed at Fredericksburg, Virginia, December 13, 1862.

PFAFF, VIRGIL, Private

Resided in Forsyth County where he enlisted at age 20, July 4, 1862, for the war. Hospitalized at Richmond, Virginia, September 29, 1862, with measles. Returned to duty on October 29, 1862. Wounded in the right leg and captured at Fredericksburg, Virginia, December 13, 1862. Right leg amputated. Hospitalized at Wash-

ington, D.C., where he died on or about December 29, 1862, of wounds.

PULLIAM, SIMEON L., Color Sergeant

Resided in Forsyth County and enlisted in Forsyth or Rowan County at age 29, July 4, 1862, for the war. Mustered in as Private. Reported present through October 31, 1862. Promoted to Color Sergeant in November-December, 1862. Killed at Fredericksburg, Virginia, December 13, 1862. [Previously served as 2nd Lieutenant of Company K, 72nd Regiment N.C. Militia.]

REICH, HENRY T., Private

Resided in Forsyth County where he enlisted at age 20, July 4, 1862, for the war. Reported present or accounted for through October 31, 1862. Wounded at Fredericksburg, Virginia, December 13, 1862. Hospitalized at Richmond, Virginia, where he died on December 20, 1862, of wounds.

REICH, JOHN HILARY, ———

North Carolina pension records indicate that he served in this company.

REICH, L. J., Private

Resided in Forsyth County where he enlisted at age 19, July 4, 1862, for the war. Reported present or accounted for through October 31, 1862. Wounded in the left leg at Fredericksburg, Virginia, December 13, 1862. Left Leg amputated. Hospitalized at Richmond, Virginia, where he died on December 18, 1862, of wounds.

REYNOLDS, T. H., Corporal

Resided in Forsyth County where he enlisted at age 23, July 4, 1862, for the war. Mustered in as Private. Reported present through December 31, 1862. Promoted to Corporal on January 18, 1863. Reported present in January-October, 1863. Captured at Rappahannock Station, Virginia, November 7, 1863. Confined at Point Lookout, Maryland, November 11, 1863. Paroled at Point Lookout on March 16, 1864. Received at City Point, Virginia, March 20, 1864, for exchange. Returned to duty in May-August, 1864. Captured at Fisher's Hill, Virginia, September 22, 1864. Confined at Point Lookout on October 3, 1864. Paroled at Point Lookout on February 18, 1865. Received at Boulware's and Cox's Wharves, James River, Virginia, February 20-21, 1865, for exchange. Reported at Camp Lee, near Richmond, Virginia, February 23, 1865. No further records.

RICHMOND, WILLIAM G., Private

Resided in Forsyth County and was by occupation a farmer prior to enlisting in Forsyth County at age 21, July 4, 1862, for the war. Reported present through October 31, 1862. Wounded in the left leg at Fredericksburg, Virginia, December 13, 1862. Left leg amputated. Hospitalized at Richmond, Virginia, where he died on or about January 8, 1863, of wounds.

ROBERTSON, ADAMS W., Private

Resided in Forsyth County where he enlisted at age 23, July 4, 1862, for the war. Reported present through May 11, 1863. Hospitalized at Charlottesville, Virginia, June 10, 1863, with scorbutus. Transferred to hospital at Lynchburg, Virginia, September 21, 1863. Returned to duty prior to November 1, 1863. Captured at Rappahannock Station, Virginia, November 7, 1863. Confined at Point Lookout, Maryland, November 11, 1863. Paroled at Point

Lookout on March 16, 1864. Received at City Point, Virginia, March 20, 1864, for exchange. Returned to duty prior to July 20, 1864, when he was wounded in the "left side feet" at Winchester, Virginia. Hospitalized at Charlottesville. Furloughed for sixty days on August 10, 1864. Returned to duty in November-December, 1864. Captured near Petersburg, Virginia, February 6, 1865. Confined at Point Lookout on February 9, 1865. Released at Point Lookout on June 17, 1865, after taking the Oath of Allegiance.

RUTLEDGE, B. S., Private

Resided in Stokes County and enlisted in Forsyth County at age 22, July 4, 1862, for the war. Hospitalized at Richmond, Virginia, September 25, 1862, with measles. Returned to duty on October 28, 1862. Reported present until hospitalized at Richmond on October 28, 1863. Returned to duty in January-April, 1864. Reported present or accounted for through February 28, 1865. Captured at Farmville, Virginia, April 6, 1865. Confined at Point Lookout, Maryland, April 14, 1865. Released at Point Lookout on June 26, 1865, after taking the Oath of Allegiance.

RUTLEDGE, JOSEPH M., Private

Resided in Stokes County and was by occupation a farmer prior to enlisting in Forsyth or Rowan County at age 32, July 4, 1862, for the war. Reported present or accounted for through February 28, 1863. Wounded in the left leg at Chancellorsville, Virginia, May 4, 1863. Reported absent wounded or absent without proper authority through April 30, 1864. Reported on detached service at Raleigh from May 24 through October 31, 1864. Returned to duty in November-December, 1864. Reported present through February 28, 1865. Captured at Fort Stedman, Virginia, March 25, 1865. Confined at Point Lookout, Maryland, March 31, 1865. Released at Point Lookout on May 14, 1865, after taking the Oath of Allegiance.

SAUNDERS, J. H., 1st Sergeant

Resided in Forsyth or Rockingham County and enlisted in Forsyth County at age 18, July 4, 1862, for the war. Mustered in as Corporal. Reported present through October 31, 1862. Wounded at Fredericksburg, Virginia, December 13, 1862. Returned to duty prior to January 1, 1863. Promoted to Sergeant on June 18, 1863. Reported present through October 31, 1863. Captured at Rappahannock Station, Virginia, November 7, 1863. Confined at Point Lookout, Maryland, November 11, 1863. Paroled at Point Lookout on March 16, 1864. Received at City Point, Virginia, March 20, 1864, for exchange. Returned to duty prior to September 1, 1864. Promoted to 1st Sergeant in January-February, 1865. Reported present through February 28, 1865. Captured at Farmville, Virginia, April 6, 1865. Confined at Newport News, Virginia, April 14, 1865. Released at Newport News on June 26, 1865, after taking the Oath of Allegiance.

SHAMEL, ELI E., Private

Resided in Forsyth County and was by occupation a farmer prior to enlisting in Forsyth County at age 34, July 4, 1862, for the war. Hospitalized at Richmond, Virginia, September 22, 1862, with diarrhoea. Furloughed for thirty days on October 14, 1862. Reported absent sick or absent without proper authority through August 31, 1863. Hospitalized at Richmond in October, 1863, with Bright's disease. Reported absent without leave from February 20 through October 31, 1864. Returned to duty in November-December, 1864. Reported present through February 28, 1865. Captured at Fort Stedman, Virginia, March 25, 1865. Confined at Point Lookout, Mary-

land, March 28, 1865. Released at Point Lookout on June 20, 1865, after taking the Oath of Allegiance.

SHAMEL, FRANCIS E., Private

Resided in Forsyth County and was by occupation a farmer prior to enlisting in Forsyth County at age 24, July 4, 1862, for the war. Hospitalized at Richmond, Virginia, September 22, 1862, with acute rheumatism. Returned to duty on October 17, 1862. Reported present through February 28, 1863. Hospitalized at Richmond on May 1, 1863, with intermittent fever. Transferred to hospital at Wilmington where he arrived on or about May 20, 1863. Furloughed for thirty days on May 27, 1863. Reported absent sick or absent without proper authority until November 6, 1863, when he returned to duty. Captured at Rappahannock Station, Virginia, November 7, 1863. Confined at Point Lookout, Maryland, November 11, 1863. Paroled at Point Lookout on March 16, 1864. Received at City Point, Virginia, March 20, 1864, for exchange. Returned to duty prior to July 20, 1864, when he was captured at Winchester, Virginia. Confined at Camp Chase, Ohio, July 28, 1864. Released at Camp Chase on or about February 11, 1865, after taking the Oath of Allegiance.

SHEPPARD, WILLIAM P., Private

Resided in Forsyth County and enlisted in Lenoir County on April 20, 1864, for the war. Reported in hospital on July 4, 1864. Hospitalized at Danville, Virginia, October 19, 1864, with pneumonia. Transferred to hospital at Raleigh on November 26, 1864 (also suffering from chronic bronchitis). Returned to duty on December 2, 1864. Captured near Petersburg, Virginia, February 6, 1865. Confined at Point Lookout, Maryland, February 9, 1865. Released at Point Lookout on June 20, 1865, after taking the Oath of Allegiance.

SIPPLE, W., Private

Resided in Forsyth County and enlisted at Camp Vance, near Richmond, Virginia, at age 46, October 17, 1862, for the war as a substitute for Sgt. Abram Fulton. "Deserted immediately."

SPAINHOUR, ROBERT, Private

Enlisted in Forsyth County at age 18, July 4, 1862, for the war. Reported present through October 31, 1862. Killed at Fredericksburg, Virginia, December 13, 1862.

SPEASE, AUGUSTIN J., Private

Resided in Forsyth County and was by occupation a farmer prior to enlisting in Forsyth County at age 31, July 4, 1862, for the war. Reported present through February 28, 1863. Hospitalized at Richmond, Virginia, May 7, 1863, with pneumonia. Transferred to hospital at Lynchburg, Virginia, on or about May 8, 1863. Captured on May 24, 1863, during the "raid in the rear of Lee's army." Paroled on or about the same date. Returned to duty on November 20, 1863. Reported present but under arrest in March-April, 1864. Reason he was arrested not reported. Returned to duty in May-August, 1864. Reported present through February 28, 1865. Surrendered at Appomattox Court House, Virginia, April 9, 1865.

SPEASE, JOHN W., Private

Resided in Forsyth County where he enlisted at age 25, July 4, 1862, for the war. Hospitalized at Richmond, Virginia, September 22, 1862, with diarrhoea. Returned to duty on or about September 29, 1862. Wounded in the bowels at Fredericksburg, Virginia, December 13, 1862. Hospitalized at Richmond where he died on December 17, 1862, of wounds.

STARBUCK, ISAIAH, Private

Born in Guilford County and resided in Stokes or Forsyth County where he was by occupation a day laborer prior to enlisting in Forsyth County on July 4, 1862, for the war. Reported present through August 31, 1864. Served as a teamster during much of that period. Reported absent without leave on October 20, 1864. Returned to duty prior to January 1, 1865. Reported present through February 28, 1865. Captured at Fort Stedman, Virginia, March 25, 1865. Confined at Point Lookout, Maryland, March 28, 1865. Released at Point Lookout on June 20, 1865, after taking the Oath of Allegiance. [Confederate military records give his age as 24. A Tennessee pension application gives his year of birth as 1834 and states that he was wounded in the left wrist at Fort Stedman.]

STARBUCK, SALATHIEL J., Private

Born in Forsyth County* where he resided prior to enlisting in Forsyth County at age 18, July 4, 1862, for the war. Hospitalized at Richmond, Virginia, October 2, 1862, with typhoid fever. Furloughed for thirty days on October 15, 1862. Returned to duty in November-December, 1862. Reported present until May 4, 1863, when he was killed at Chancellorsville, Virginia. "He died a true patriot and soldier." [People's Press (Salem), June 5, 1863.]

STOLTZ, DAVID, Private

Resided in Forsyth County where he enlisted at age 21, July 4, 1862, for the war. Hospitalized at Richmond, Virginia, November 8, 1862, with debility. Transferred to Farmville, Virginia, on or about December 15, 1862 (suffering from diarrhoea). Returned to duty on December 31, 1862. Discharged from service at Liberty, Virginia, on or about February 24, 1863, by reason of "phthisis pul[monalis]."

SULLIVAN, JOHN V., Private

Resided in Forsyth County where he enlisted at age 30, July 4, 1862, for the war. Reported present through October 31, 1862. Killed at Fredericksburg, Virginia, December 13, 1862.

SULLIVAN, WILLIAM T., Private

Born in Stokes County on March 28, 1844. Resided in Stokes County where he enlisted at age 18, July 4, 1862, for the war. Hospitalized at Richmond, Virginia, October 28, 1862, with measles. Returned to duty on November 20, 1862. Wounded in the leg at Fredericksburg, Virginia, December 13, 1862. Returned to duty in March-May, 1863. Captured at Rappahannock Station, Virginia, November 7, 1863. Confined at Point Lookout, Maryland, November 11, 1863. Paroled at Point Lookout on March 16, 1864. Received at City Point, Virginia, March 20, 1864, for exchange. Returned to duty in May-August, 1864. Reported present through February 28, 1865. Captured at Farmville, Virginia, April 6, 1865. Confined at Newport News, Virginia, April 14, 1865. Released at Newport News on June 26, 1865, after taking the Oath of Allegiance. [A Tennessee pension application states that, in addition to his Fredericksburg wound, he was wounded at Monocacy, Maryland, July 6, 1864, and at Fort Stedman, Virginia, March 25, 1865. He was wounded at various unspecified times in the left leg (flesh), right leg ("bone shattered"), left hand (thumb dislocated), and head (concussion).]

TAYLOR, R. H., Private

Resided in Stokes County and enlisted in Forsyth County at age 23, July 4, 1862, for the war. Hospitalized at Richmond, Virginia, November 8, 1862, with chronic bronchitis. Transferred to another hospital on November 30, 1862. Returned to duty prior to January 1, 1863. Reported present through October 31, 1863. Captured at Rappahannock Station, Virginia, November 7, 1863. Confined at Point Lookout, Maryland, November 11, 1863. Paroled at Point Lookout on March 16, 1864. Received at City Point, Virginia, March 20, 1864, for exchange. Returned to duty in May-August, 1864. Captured at Fisher's Hill, Virginia, September 22, 1864. Confined at Point Lookout on October 3, 1864. Paroled at Point Lookout on February 18, 1865. Received at Boulware's and Cox's Wharves, James River, Virginia, February 20-21, 1865, for exchange. Paroled at Greensboro on May 16, 1865.

TEAGUE, ANDREW F., Sergeant

Resided in Forsyth County and was by occupation a clerk prior to enlisting in Forsyth County at age 27, July 4, 1862, for the war. Mustered in as Sergeant. Hospitalized at Richmond, Virginia, November 8, 1862. Returned to duty on or about November 23, 1862. Reported present or accounted for through May 11, 1863. Captured at Gettysburg, Pennsylvania, July 2, 1863. Confined at Fort Delaware, Delaware. Paroled at Fort Delaware and transferred to City Point, Virginia, where he was received on August 1, 1863, for exchange. Returned to duty in January-April, 1864. Reported present through February 28, 1865. Captured at Farmville, Virginia, April 6, 1865. Confined at Newport News, Virginia, April 14, 1865. Released at Newport News on June 26, 1865, after taking the Oath of Allegiance.

TRANSOU, LEWIS B., Private

Resided in Forsyth County and was by occupation a farmer prior to enlisting in Forsyth County at age 23, July 4, 1862, for the war. Reported present or accounted for through October 31, 1862. Killed at Fredericksburg, Virginia, December 13, 1862.

VAWTER, J. C., Private

Resided in Forsyth County where he enlisted at age 32, July 4, 1862, for the war. Hospitalized at Richmond, Virginia, September 22, 1862, with debilitas. Returned to duty on or about October 2, 1862. Reported present through February 28, 1863. Killed at Chancellorsville, Virginia, May 4, 1863.

VOGLER, AUGUSTUS G., Private

Resided in Forsyth County and was by occupation a farmer prior to enlisting in Forsyth County at age 32, July 4, 1862, for the war. Hospitalized at Richmond, Virginia, September 22, 1862, with debilitas. Returned to duty on or about September 29, 1862. Hospitalized at Richmond on November 3, 1862, with typhoid fever. Returned to duty on April 6, 1863. Captured at Gettysburg, Pennsylvania, on or about July 2, 1863. Confined at Fort Delaware, Delaware, on or about July 9, 1863 . Transferred to Point Lookout, Maryland, October 20, 1863. Died at Point Lookout on March 22, 1865, of "chronic diarrhoea."

WALDRIVAN, ALEXANDER J., Private

Resided in Forsyth County where he enlisted at age 22, July 4, 1862, for the war. Reported present through May 11, 1863. Hospitalized at Richmond, Virginia, May 25, 1863, with "febris typhoid." Died in hospital at Richmond on or about June 5, 1863.

WHICKER, ALLISON G., Private

Resided in Stokes or Forsyth County and was by occupation a farmer prior to enlisting in Rowan County at age 30, July 29, 1862, for the war. Hospitalized at Richmond, Virginia, September 22, 1862, with intermittent fever. Furloughed for twenty-five days on October 27, 1862. Returned to duty in January-February, 1863. Hospitalized at Richmond on May 2, 1863, with pneumonia. Transferred to hospital at Danville, Virginia, May 7, 1863. Reported absent without proper authority in June-October, 1863. Returned to duty on or about November 22, 1863. Reported present in March-April, 1864. Hospitalized at Richmond on May 24, 1864, with a gunshot wound. Place and date wounded not reported. Furloughed for sixty days on June 13, 1864. Reported absent without leave from August 10, 1864, through February 28, 1865. Paroled at Greensboro on May 9, 1865.

WHICKER, JAMES F., Private

Resided in Forsyth County where he enlisted at age 20, July 4, 1862, for the war. Reported present through October 31, 1862. Reported absent in hospital in November, 1862-February, 1863. Returned to duty in March-May, 1863. Captured at Gettysburg, Pennsylvania, July 3, 1863. Confined at Fort Delaware, Delaware, on or about July 9, 1863. Died at Fort Delaware on September 15, 1863, of "chronic diarrhoea."

WHICKER, ROBERT Y., Private

Resided in Forsyth County and was by occupation a day laborer prior to enlisting in Forsyth County at age 22, July 4, 1862, for the war. Reported absent sick at Salisbury on August 20, 1862. Returned to duty in November-December, 1862. Hospitalized at Richmond, Virginia, May 8, 1863, with typhoid fever. Transferred to hospital at Danville, Virginia, May 14, 1863. Returned to duty on June 5, 1863. Hospitalized at Richmond on July 20, 1863, with debilitas. Transferred on August 13, 1863. Reported absent sick on surviving company muster rolls through February 28, 1865. Survived the war. [North Carolina pension records indicate that he was wounded in the left leg on an unspecified date.]

WHICKER, S. E., Private

Resided in Forsyth County where he enlisted at age 26, July 4, 1862, for the war. Reported present through May 11, 1863. Reported absent sick or absent on detached duty in hospital at Richmond, Virginia, in June-December, 1863. Returned to duty in January-April, 1864. Captured at the North Anna River, Virginia, May 23, 1864. Confined at Point Lookout, Maryland, May 30, 1864. Transferred to Elmira, New York, July 25, 1864. Died at Elmira on September 14, 1864, of "chronic diarrhoea."

WRIGHT, ISAAC B., Private

Resided in Forsyth County where he enlisted at age 23, July 4, 1862, for the war. Reported present through October 31, 1862. Wounded in the left leg at Fredericksburg, Virginia, December 13, 1862. Leg amputated. Hospitalized at Richmond, Virginia. Transferred to Farmville, Virginia, March 9, 1863. Furloughed for thirty days on May 5, 1863 (also suffering from chronic diarrhoea). Died prior to September 1, 1863. Place and cause of death not reported.

YOUNG, A. PINK, Private

Resided in Forsyth County where he enlisted at age 26, July 4, 1862, for the war. Hospitalized at Richmond, Virginia, November 8, 1862. Transferred to hospital at Scottsville, Virginia, November 28, 1862. Returned to duty in January-February, 1863. Captured at Chancellorsville, Virginia, May 3-4, 1863. Confined at Fort Delaware, Delaware, on or about May 7, 1863. Paroled and transferred to City Point, Virginia, where he was received on May 23, 1863,

for exchange. Reported absent sick through December 31, 1863. Reported absent on detached service at Salisbury in March-October, 1864. Reported absent on detached service at Graham from November 3 through December 31, 1864. Reported on detached service at Salisbury in January-February, 1865. Surrendered at Appomattox Court House, Virginia, April 9, 1865.

ZIMMERMAN, JAMES C., Private

Resided in Forsyth County and was by occupation a farmer prior to enlisting in Forsyth County at age 29, July 4, 1862, for the war. Wounded in the right hand at Fredericksburg, Virginia, December 13, 1862. Returned to duty prior to December 31, 1862. Reported present through October 31, 1863. Captured at Rappahannock Station, Virginia, November 7, 1863. Confined at Point Lookout, Maryland, November 11, 1863. Paroled at Point Lookout on March 16, 1864. Received at City Point, Virginia, March 20, 1864, for exchange. Returned to duty prior to July 20, 1864, when he was captured at Winchester, Virginia. Confined at Camp Chase, Ohio, July 28, 1864. Paroled at Camp Chase on March 2, 1865. Received at Boulware's and Cox's Wharves, James River, Virginia, March 10-12, 1865, for exchange. Survived the war.

COMPANY E

This company was raised in Catawba County on July 4, 1862. It was mustered into service at Salisbury on July 17, 1862, and assigned to the 57th Regiment N.C. Troops as Company E. After joining the regiment the company functioned as a part of the regiment, and its history for the remainder of the war is reported as a part of the regimental history.

The following roster was compiled primarily from information in the microfilm edition of the Compiled Service Records of Soldiers Who Served in Organizations from the State of North Carolina (Record Group 109, M270), National Archives and Records Administration, Washington, D.C. Record Group 109 includes enlistment papers, pay vouchers, requisitions, letters of resignation, discharge certificates, and abstracts of medical and prisoner of war returns. Materials relating specifically to this company include muster rolls dated July, 1862-December, 1863, and March, 1864-February, 1865.

Also utilized in this roster were *The War of the Rebellion: A Compilation of the Official Records of the Union and Confederate Armies*, the North Carolina adjutant general's *Roll of Honor*, state militia records, newspaper casualty lists and obituaries, wartime claims for bounty pay and allowances, postwar registers of claims for artificial limbs, Confederate pension applications filed with the states of North Carolina, Tennessee, and Florida, Confederate Soldiers' Home records, and the 1860 and 1870 federal censuses of North Carolina. A search was made also for relevant letters, diaries, reminiscences, and other manuscripts in the Southern Historical Collection (University of North Carolina-Chapel Hill), the Duke University Library Special Collections Department, and the North Carolina Division of Archives and History.

Among the secondary sources consulted were records of the North Carolina division of the United Daughters of the Confederacy, postwar rosters, regimental and county histories, marriage bond, will, and cemetery indexes, published and unpublished genealogies, biographical dictionaries, the North Carolina *County Heritage Book* series, the *Confederate Veteran*, Walter Clark's *Histories of the Several Regiments and Battalions from North Carolina in the Great War, 1861-*

'65, and the North Carolina volume of the extended edition of *Confederate Military History*.

OFFICERS

CAPTAINS

RHINE, DANIEL W.

Previously served as 2nd Lieutenant of Company B, Maj. George C. Gibbs's Battalion N.C. Prison Guards. Defeated for reelection when Gibbs's Battalion was reorganized as the 42nd Regiment N.C. Troops in April, 1862. Appointed Captain of this company on July 4, 1862. Hospitalized at Richmond, Virginia, September 30, 1862, with typhoid fever. Transferred to Salisbury on October 7, 1862. Dropped from the company rolls on or about December 3, 1862, for prolonged absence without leave. Reinstated on or about January 29, 1863, after he returned to duty. Resigned on April 7, 1863, for reasons of "health." Resignation accepted on April 18, 1863.

MILLER, JESSE W.

Previously served as 2nd Lieutenant of Company C of this regiment. Promoted to Captain on August 1, 1863, and transferred to this company. Captured at Rappahannock Station, Virginia, November 7, 1863. Confined at Old Capitol Prison, Washington, D.C., November 8, 1863. Transferred to Johnson's Island, Ohio, where he arrived on November 14, 1863. Released at Johnson's Island on June 13, 1865, after taking the Oath of Allegiance.

HUNTER, MILES H.

Served as Captain of Company B of this regiment. Reported in command of this company in November-December, 1863, and January-February, 1865.

CARPENTER, PHILIP W.

Served as Captain of Company G of this regiment. Reported in command of this company in September-October, 1864.

LIEUTENANTS

COCHRAN, L. WILLIAM, 2nd Lieutenant

Enlisted in Catawba County. Appointed 2nd Lieutenant on July 4, 1862. Reported present and in command of the company in July-October, 1862. Reported absent on sick furlough on November 7, 1862. Returned to duty in December, 1862. Resigned on January 11, 1863. Resignation accepted on January 27, 1863. Reason he resigned not reported.

GILBERT, JACOB H., 3rd Lieutenant

Previously served as 1st Lieutenant of Company C, 28th Regiment N.C. Troops. Enlisted in this company in Catawba County on July 4, 1862, for the war. Mustered in as Sergeant. Reported present through October 31, 1862. Appointed 3rd Lieutenant on December 1, 1862. Reported present but sick in November, 1862-February, 1863. Reported in command of the company in March-May, 1863. Wounded slightly at Chancellorsville, Virginia, on or about May 4, 1863. Captured at Jack's Mountain, Pennsylvania, on or about July 5, 1863. Confined at Fort McHenry, Maryland. Transferred to Johnson's Island, Ohio, where he arrived on July 20, 1863.

Transferred to Point Lookout, Maryland, April 22, 1864. Transferred to Fort Delaware, Delaware, June 23, 1864. Transferred from Fort Delaware to Hilton Head, South Carolina, August 20, 1864. Paroled at Charleston, South Carolina, December 15, 1864. Reported absent sick from December 20, 1864, through February 28, 1865. Returned to duty on an unspecified date. Surrendered at Appomattox Court House, Virginia, April 9, 1865.

RINGO, DANIEL W., 1st Lieutenant

Previously served as Lieutenant Colonel of Col. John B. Cocke's Regiment, Arkansas Infantry. Enlisted in this company on an unspecified date (probably in the spring or early summer of 1863). Mustered in with an unspecified rank. Wounded in the left thigh at Gettysburg, Pennsylvania, July 2, 1863. Appointed 1st Lieutenant on August 1, 1863. Returned to duty on December 17, 1863. Hospitalized at Richmond, Virginia, February 24, 1864, with syphilis. Returned to duty on or about March 1, 1864. Reported in command of the company in May-August, 1864. Killed at Cedar Creek, Virginia, October 19, 1864. ["He was conspicuous not only for his high courage, but for his remarkable intelligence and aptitude for the business of a soldier." After he was "disabled" at Gettysburg, he "served with the sharpshooters upon horseback. . . ." (Clark's *Regiments*, 3:427.)]

SHERRILL, WILLIAM WESLEY, 2nd Lieutenant

Resided in Catawba County and was by occupation a farmer prior to enlisting in Catawba County at age 25, July 4, 1862, for the war. Mustered in as Private. Promoted to Sergeant on December 1, 1862. Appointed 2nd Lieutenant on February 20, 1863. Captured at South Mountain, Maryland, July 5-6, 1863. Confined at Fort Delaware, Delaware, July 11, 1863. Transferred to Johnson's Island, Ohio, where he arrived on July 20, 1863. Paroled at Johnson's Island on March 14, 1865. Received at Cox's Wharf, James River, Virginia, March 22, 1865, for exchange. Survived the war.

WYCOFF, WILLIAM D., 3rd Lieutenant

Resided in Catawba or Burke County and was by occupation a farmer prior to enlisting in Catawba County at age 51. Appointed 3rd Lieutenant on July 4, 1862. Resigned on or about September 12, 1862, by reason of "physical inability." Resignation accepted on September 20, 1862. Later served as Private in Company E, 32nd Regiment N.C. Troops.

YOUNT, GEORGE DANIEL LAFAYETTE, 1st Lieutenant

Born on March 18, 1832. Resided in Catawba County and was by occupation a farmer prior to enlisting in Catawba County at age 30. Appointed 1st Lieutenant on July 4, 1862. Hospitalized at Richmond, Virginia, on or about September 22, 1862, with measles. Transferred to Salisbury on October 7, 1862. Dropped from the company rolls on or about December 3, 1862, for prolonged absence without leave. Reinstated on January 7, 1863. Resigned on February 11, 1863, by reason of "phthisis." Resignation accepted on February 17, 1863.

NONCOMMISSIONED OFFICERS AND PRIVATES

ANTHONY, JACOB, Corporal

Born on September 30, 1840. Resided in Catawba County where he enlisted at age 21, July 4, 1862, for the war. Mustered in as

Private. Reported present through February 28, 1863. Promoted to Corporal on February 28, 1863. Captured at Chancellorsville, Virginia, May 3-4, 1863. Confined at Fort Delaware, Delaware, on or about May 7, 1863. Paroled and transferred to City Point, Virginia, where he was received on May 23, 1863, for exchange. Returned to duty prior to September 1, 1863. Captured at Rappahannock Station, Virginia, November 7, 1863. Confined at Point Lookout, Maryland, November 11, 1863. Records of the Federal Provost Marshal are contradictory regarding his career as a prisoner of war. According to one set of records, he was paroled at Point Lookout on February 13, 1865; according to another set of records, he was released at Point Lookout on June 23, 1865, after taking the Oath of Allegiance. Survived the war.

BAKER, HENRY, Private

Resided in Catawba County and was by occupation a carriage maker prior to enlisting in Catawba County at age 33, July 4, 1862, for the war. Reported present through February 28, 1863. Hospitalized at Richmond, Virginia, May 2, 1863, with rheumatism. Transferred to hospital at Danville, Virginia, May 7, 1863. Returned to duty on June 2, 1863. Captured at Gettysburg, Pennsylvania, July 2-5, 1863. Confined at Fort Delaware, Delaware. Transferred to Point Lookout, Maryland, October 20, 1863. Paroled at Point Lookout on February 18, 1865. Received at Boulware's and Cox's Wharves, James River, Virginia, February 20-21, 1865, for exchange. Survived the war.

BARGER, BABEL, Private

Resided in Catawba County and was by occupation a day laborer prior to enlisting in Catawba County at age 28, July 4, 1862, for the war. Reported sick in hospital at Richmond, Virginia, in September-October, 1862. Returned to duty prior to December 31, 1862. Reported present through October 31, 1863. Captured at Rappahannock Station, Virginia, November 7, 1863. Confined at Point Lookout, Maryland, November 11, 1863. Died at Point Lookout on March 10, 1865, of "chronic dysentery."

BARGER, MAXWELL W., Private

Resided in Catawba County and was by occupation a farm laborer prior to enlisting in Catawba County at age 24, July 4, 1862, for the war. Hospitalized at Richmond, Virginia, November 2, 1862, with general debility. Transferred to another hospital on January 12, 1863. Died in hospital at Richmond on May 27, 1863, of "diarrh[oea] ch[ronica]."

BARNES, MILTON, Private

Enlisted in Catawba County at age 27, July 4, 1862, for the war. Reported present or accounted for through May 11, 1863. Sent to hospital sick on July 8, 1863. Reported absent without leave from April 1, 1864, through February 28, 1865. Survived the war. [North Carolina pension records indicate that he was wounded at Winchester, Virginia, in June, 1863.]

BARNES, MURPHY, Private

Enlisted in Catawba County on July 4, 1862, for the war. Reported present or accounted for from September 1, 1862, through October 31, 1863. Captured at Rappahannock Station, Virginia, November 7, 1863. Confined at Point Lookout, Maryland, November 11, 1863. Died in hospital at Point Lookout on January 27, 1865, of "pneumonia."

BEARD, JACOB WAITSEL, Private

Resided in Catawba County where he enlisted on July 7, 1862, for the war. Hospitalized at Richmond, Virginia, October 20, 1862,

with typhoid fever. Returned to duty on October 28, 1862. Deserted from camp at Fredericksburg, Virginia, December 25, 1862. Returned to duty in January-February, 1863. Hospitalized at Richmond on May 2, 1863, with rheumatism. Transferred to hospital at Danville, Virginia, May 7, 1863. Returned to duty on June 2, 1863. Hospitalized at Charlottesville, Virginia, June 10, 1863, with debilitas. Returned to duty on September 8, 1863. Reported present on surviving company muster rolls through April 30, 1864. Sent to hospital wounded on May 21, 1864. Place and date wounded not reported. Returned to duty in September-October, 1864. Reported present but under arrest on December 26, 1864. Reason he was arrested not reported. Returned to duty in January-February, 1865. Captured at Farmville, Virginia, April 6, 1865. Confined at Newport News, Virginia, April 14, 1865. Released at Newport News on June 26, 1865, after taking the Oath of Allegiance. [Was about 27 years of age at the time of enlistment.]

BOLICK, ABSALOM E. L., Private

Resided in Catawba County where he enlisted on July 4, 1862, for the war. Reported present or accounted for through October 31, 1863. Captured at Rappahannock Station, Virginia, November 7, 1863. Confined at Point Lookout, Maryland, November 11, 1863. Paroled on or about November 1, 1864. Received at Venus Point, Savannah River, Georgia, November 15, 1864, for exchange. Reported absent sick on December 3, 1864. Returned to duty in January-February, 1865. Wounded in the finger at Fort Stedman, Virginia, March 25, 1865. Captured at Farmville, Virginia, April 6, 1865. Confined at Newport News, Virginia, April 14, 1865. Exchanged on an unspecified date.

BOLICK, EPHRAIM, Private

Resided in Catawba County and was by occupation a farm laborer prior to enlisting in Catawba County at age 25, July 4, 1862, for the war. Hospitalized at Richmond, Virginia, September 22, 1862, with debility. Furloughed on September 29, 1862. Returned to duty in January-February, 1863. Reported present through October 31, 1863. Captured at Rappahannock Station, Virginia, November 7, 1863. Confined at Point Lookout, Maryland, November 11, 1863. Paroled at Point Lookout on March 15, 1865. Received at Boulware's Wharf, James River, Virginia, March 18, 1865, for exchange. Survived the war.

BOLICK, ISRAEL, Private

Resided in Catawba County and was by occupation a day laborer prior to enlisting in Lenoir County at age 24, May 1, 1864, for the war. Sent to hospital sick on June 20, 1864. Died on September 12, 1864, while on sick furlough. Place and cause of death not reported.

BOOVEY, WILLIAM P., Private

Resided in Catawba County and was by occupation a day laborer prior to enlisting in Catawba County at age 29, July 4, 1862, for the war. Reported present or accounted for through October 31, 1863. Reported present in March-April, 1864. Hospitalized at Richmond, Virginia, May 26, 1864, with acute bronchitis. Transferred to another hospital on June 27, 1864 (suffering from chronic diarrhoea). Returned to duty on October 1, 1864. Reported present through December 31, 1864. Company records indicate that he was captured at Hatcher's Run, Virginia, February 6, 1865; however, records of the Federal Provost Marshal do not substantiate that report. No further records.

BOST, AMZI A., Private

Resided in Catawba County and was by occupation a farmer prior to enlisting in Catawba County at age 32, July 4, 1862, for the war.

Hospitalized at Richmond, Virginia, October 22, 1862, with remittent fever. Furloughed for twenty days on November 17, 1862. Returned to duty in January-February, 1863. Captured at Chancellorsville, Virginia, May 3-4, 1863. Confined at Fort Delaware, Delaware, on or about May 7, 1863. Paroled at Fort Delaware and transferred to City Point, Virginia, where he was received on May 23, 1863, for exchange. Died in hospital at Winchester, Virginia, on or about July 29, 1863. Cause of death not reported.

BOST, JETHRO CALVIN, Private

Resided in Catawba County and was by occupation a farmer prior to enlisting in Catawba County at age 26, July 4, 1862, for the war. Hospitalized at Richmond, Virginia, November 1, 1862, with phthisis. Furloughed for thirty days on or about November 18, 1862. Returned to duty prior to January 1, 1863. Reported present through May 11, 1863. Killed at Gettysburg, Pennsylvania, on or about July 2, 1863, apparently while serving as a color bearer.

BURNS, FRANKLIN A., Private

Resided in Catawba County where he enlisted at age 32, July 4, 1862, for the war. Hospitalized at Richmond, Virginia, November 8, 1862, with chronic rheumatism. Returned to duty on December 6, 1862. Reported absent sick on December 31, 1862. Reported at home on furlough in January-April, 1863. Reported absent without leave on August 31, 1863. Returned to duty in November, 1863-April, 1864. Sent to hospital on June 19, 1864. Reported absent sick through August 31, 1864. Returned to duty in September-October, 1864. Reported present in November-December, 1864. Captured at Hatcher's Run, Virginia, February 6, 1865. Confined at Point Lookout, Maryland, February 9, 1865. Released at Point Lookout on June 23, 1865, after taking the Oath of Allegiance.

CAMPBELL, ENOS L., Private

Resided in Lincoln County and was by occupation a blacksmith prior to enlisting in Catawba County at age 29, July 4, 1862, for the war. Reported present through August 31, 1862. Wounded in the left arm and left knee at Fredericksburg, Virginia, December 13, 1862. Left arm amputated. Reported absent wounded until October 12, 1864, when he was retired to the Invalid Corps. Survived the war.

CANSLER, GEORGE W., Private

Resided in Catawba County and was by occupation a farmer prior to enlisting in Catawba County at age 30, July 4, 1862, for the war. Reported present or accounted for through February 28, 1863. Hospitalized at Richmond, Virginia, May 6, 1863, with acute hepatitis. Transferred to hospital at Lynchburg, Virginia, May 8, 1863. Returned to duty prior to September 1, 1863. Captured at Rappahannock Station, Virginia, November 7, 1863. Confined at Point Lookout, Maryland, November 11, 1863. Paroled at Point Lookout on February 10, 1865. Received at Cox's Wharf, James River, Virginia, February 14-15, 1865, for exchange. Survived the war.

CARPENTER, WILLIAM WILKIE, Sergeant

Resided in Catawba County where he enlisted at age 20, July 4, 1862, for the war. Mustered in as Private. Reported present through February 28, 1863. Hospitalized at Richmond, Virginia, March 23, 1863, with scrofula. Transferred to hospital at Danville, Virginia, April 20, 1863 (suffering from syphilis). Furloughed on August 1, 1863. Returned to duty in November-December, 1863. Reported present on surviving company muster rolls through August 31, 1864. Promoted to Sergeant on March 1, 1864. Wounded in the leg at Winchester, Virginia, September 19, 1864.

Hospitalized at Charlottesville, Virginia. Transferred to hospital at Lynchburg, Virginia, September 28, 1864. Returned to duty in January-February, 1865. Captured at Fort Stedman, Virginia, March 25, 1865. Confined at Point Lookout, Maryland, March 28, 1865. Released at Point Lookout on June 24, 1865, after taking the Oath of Allegiance.

CLINE, CICERO, Private

Born in Catawba County* where he resided as a blacksmith prior to enlisting in Catawba County at age 23, July 4,' 1862, for the war. Reported present through February 28, 1863. Wounded in the right leg at Chancellorsville, Virginia, May 3, 1863. Hospitalized at Richmond, Virginia. Furloughed for thirty-five days on August 12, 1863. Reported absent wounded through October 31, 1864. Returned to duty in January-February, 1865. Retired on March 7, 1865, by reason of wounds received at Chancellorsville "destroying the action of the gastrocnemius muscle to such an extent as to impair the power [of] locomotion."

CLINE, ELI D., Private

Resided in Catawba County and was by occupation an overseer prior to enlisting in Catawba County at age 33, July 4, 1862, for the war. Reported present through October 31, 1862. Hospitalized at Richmond, Virginia, November 9, 1862, with rheumatism. Returned to duty on November 16, 1862. Hospitalized at Richmond on January 27, 1863. Died in hospital at Richmond on or about February 1, 1863, of "pneumonia typhoides."

CLINE, EPHRAIM ELCANAH, 1st Sergeant

Previously served as 3rd Lieutenant of Company C, 28th Regiment N.C. Troops. Enlisted in this company in Catawba County on July 4, 1862, for the war. Mustered in as Sergeant. Wounded in the right hip at Fredericksburg, Virginia, December 13, 1862. Promoted to 1st Sergeant in January-February, 1863. Returned to duty in May-August, 1863. Reported present on surviving company muster rolls through February 28, 1865. Captured at Farmville, Virginia, April 6, 1865. Confined at Newport News, Virginia, April 14, 1865. Released at Newport News on June 26, 1865, after taking the Oath of Allegiance.

CLINE, JAMES CALVIN, Private

Resided in Catawba County and was by occupation a day laborer prior to enlisting in Catawba County at age 24, July 4, 1862, for the war. Reported present through October 31, 1862. Deserted from camp near Fredericksburg, Virginia, January 17, 1863. Died at Castle Thunder Prison, Richmond, Virginia, February 11, 1863. Cause of death not reported.

CONRAD, W. JAMES, Corporal

Enlisted in Catawba County on July 4, 1862, for the war as a substitute for Pvt. John Wilfong Robinson. Mustered in as Private. Reported present through May 11, 1863. Promoted to Corporal on February 28, 1863. Furloughed home for eighteen days prior to September 1, 1863. Returned to duty in September-October, 1863. Captured at Rappahannock Station, Virginia, November 7, 1863. Confined at Point Lookout, Maryland, November 11, 1863. Died in hospital at Point Lookout on March 18, 1865, of "acute diarrhoea." Was 17 years of age at the time of his death.

COULTER, PHILIP AUGUSTUS, Private

Born in Catawba County* on June 15, 1834. Resided in Catawba County and was by occupation a farm laborer prior to enlisting in Catawba County at age 28, July 4, 1862, for the war. Reported present or accounted for through February 28, 1863. Reported at home on sick furlough on April 22, 1863. Returned to duty prior to September 1, 1863. Reported present on surviving company muster rolls through April 30, 1864. Captured at or near Spotsylvania Court House, Virginia, May 22, 1864. Confined at Point Lookout, Maryland, May 30, 1864. Paroled on or about October 30, 1864. Received at Venus Point, Savannah River, Georgia, November 15, 1864, for exchange. Reported absent sick on December 2, 1864. Returned to duty in January-February, 1865. Captured at Farmville, Virginia, April 6, 1865. Confined at Newport News, Virginia, April 14, 1865. Released at Newport News on June 14, 1865, after taking the Oath of Allegiance.

CRAVER, A. J., Private

Previously served as Private in Company G of this regiment. Transferred to this company prior to July 17, 1862. Transferred to Company K of this regiment on an unspecified date (probably in the summer of 1862).

CROUSE, LEVI ROBINSON, Private

Resided in Lincoln County and was by occupation a miller prior to enlisting in Catawba County at age 32, July 4, 1862, for the war. Hospitalized at Richmond, Virginia, November 23, 1862, with debility. Returned to duty on January 7, 1863. Reported present through May 11, 1863. Hospitalized at Danville, Virginia, July 22, 1863, with debilitas. Furloughed on July 30, 1863. Returned to duty in November-December, 1863. Reported present in March-April, 1864. Sent to hospital sick on July 24, 1864. Returned to duty on an unspecified date. Captured at Winchester, Virginia, September 19, 1864, after he was left behind as a nurse for the wounded. Reported in hospitals at Frederick, Maryland, and Baltimore, Maryland, in January, 1865. Confined at Fort McHenry, Maryland, on or about February 10, 1865. Transferred to Point Lookout, Maryland, on or about February 20, 1865. Exchanged on an unspecified date. Hospitalized at Richmond on March 8, 1865, with debilitas. Furloughed for thirty days on March 13, 1865.

CURTIS, H. R., Private

Born in England and resided in Catawba County where he was by occupation a doctor prior to enlisting in Catawba County at age 34, July 4, 1862, for the war. Was reportedly appointed Assistant Surgeon on August 23, 1862; however, his appointment was apparently not confirmed and he continued to serve as a Private in this company. Reported in hospital at Richmond, Virginia, in September-October, 1862. Returned to duty in November-December, 1862. Reported present through May 11, 1863. Captured at Williamsport, Maryland, July 6, 1863, after he was left behind as a nurse for the wounded. No further records.

DRUM, JOSHUA, Private

Resided in Catawba County where he enlisted on July 1, 1862, for the war. Reported present through May 11, 1863. Captured (or deserted to the enemy) at or near Gettysburg, Pennsylvania, July 2-6, 1863. Confined at Fort Delaware, Delaware, on or about July 9, 1863. Released at Fort Delaware on May 5, 1865, after taking the Oath of Allegiance.

DRUM, MILES, Private

Resided in Catawba County and was by occupation a farmer prior to enlisting in Catawba County at age 29, July 7, 1862, for the war.

Reported present through August 31, 1862. Killed at Fredericksburg, Virginia, December 13, 1862.

FLOWERS, HENRY F., Private

Resided in Catawba County and was by occupation a day laborer prior to enlisting in Catawba County at age 34, July 4, 1862, for the war. Hospitalized at Richmond, Virginia, October 29, 1862, with hemorrhoids. Returned to duty on February 2, 1863. Reported present through October 31, 1863. Captured at Rappahannock Station, Virginia, November 7, 1863. Confined at Point Lookout, Maryland, November 11, 1863. Paroled at Point Lookout on February 24, 1865. Received at Aiken's Landing, James River, Virginia, February 25-28 or March 2-3, 1865, for exchange. Survived the war.

FRAZIER, CYRUS J., Private

Resided in Catawba County and was by occupation a farmer prior to enlisting at Brandy Station, Virginia, at age 43, November 1, 1863, for the war. Captured at Rappahannock Station, Virginia, November 7, 1863. Confined at Point Lookout, Maryland, November 11, 1863. Paroled at Point Lookout on November 1, 1864. Received at Venus Point, Savannah River, Georgia, November 15, 1864, for exchange. Returned to duty in January-February, 1865. Captured at Fort Stedman, Virginia, March 25, 1865. Confined at Point Lookout on March 28, 1865. Released at Point Lookout on June 3, 1865, after taking the Oath of Allegiance.

FRAZIER, HUGHIE YEARBY, Private

Born in Scotland in 1820. Enlisted at Fredericksburg, Virginia, at age 43, April 1, 1863, for the war. Reported present or accounted for through October 31, 1863. Captured at Rappahannock Station, Virginia, November 7, 1863. Confined at Point Lookout, Maryland, November 11, 1863. Hospitalized at Point Lookout on January 27, 1865, with "chronic bronchitis." Died in hospital at Point Lookout on February 4, 1865.

FRAZIER, WILLIAM, Private

Enlisted in Catawba County on July 4, 1862, for the war. Reported present until February 20, 1863, when he was sent to hospital. Returned to duty in May-August, 1863. Reported present in September-October, 1863. Captured at Rappahannock Station, Virginia, November 7, 1863. Confined at Point Lookout, Maryland, November 11, 1863. Died at Point Lookout on January 27, 1865, of "congestion of the brain."

FRY, ANDREW S., Private

Resided in Catawba County and was by occupation a farmer prior to enlisting in Catawba County on July 4, 1862, for the war. Hospitalized at Richmond, Virginia, November 25, 1862, with paronychia. Returned to duty on December 16, 1862. Reported present through October 31, 1863. Captured at Rappahannock Station, Virginia, November 7, 1863. Confined at Point Lookout, Maryland, November 11, 1863. Paroled at Point Lookout on February 24, 1865. Received at Aiken's Landing, James River, Virginia, February 25-28 or March 2-3, 1865, for exchange. No further records.

FRY, ELKANA E., Private

Enlisted in Catawba County on July 4, 1862, for the war. Hospitalized at Richmond, Virginia, November 9, 1862, with debilitas. Returned to duty on November 16, 1862. Reported present through

February 28, 1863. Died at Staunton, Virginia, April 2-3, 1863, of "typhoid fever."

FRY, WILLIAM, Private

Enlisted in Catawba County on July 4, 1862, for the war. Reported present through October 31, 1862. Died in camp on January 16, 1863. Cause of death not reported.

GILLELAND, HENRY A., Sergeant

Enlisted in Catawba County at age 29, July 4, 1862, for the war. Mustered in as Private. Reported present through August 31, 1862. Wounded in the head and left hand at Fredericksburg, Virginia, December 13, 1862. Hospitalized at Richmond, Virginia. Furloughed for forty days on January 1, 1863. Promoted to Sergeant on February 1, 1863. Returned to duty prior to March 1, 1863. Reported present through October 31, 1863. Captured at Rappahannock Station, Virginia, November 7, 1863. Confined at Point Lookout, Maryland, November 11, 1863. Paroled at Point Lookout on February 24, 1865. Received at Aiken's Landing, James River, Virginia, February 25-28 or March 2-3, 1865, for exchange. Survived the war.

HALLMAN, EPHRAIM, Private

Enlisted in Catawba County on July 4, 1862, for the war. Reported present or accounted for through October 31, 1863. Captured at Rappahannock Station, Virginia, November 7, 1863. Confined at Point Lookout, Maryland, November 11, 1863. Paroled at Point Lookout on or about November 1, 1864. Received at Venus Point, Savannah River, Georgia, November 15, 1864, for exchange. Reported absent sick on December 2, 1864. Returned to duty in January-February, 1865. Surrendered at Appomattox Court House, Virginia, April 9, 1865. [Went west after the war.]

HARTSOE, R. A., Private

Enlisted in Catawba County on July 4, 1862, for the war. Hospitalized at Richmond, Virginia, October 3, 1862, with rubeola. Returned to duty on November 11, 1862. Reported present through October 31, 1863. Captured at Rappahannock Station, Virginia, November 7, 1863. Confined at Point Lookout, Maryland, November 11, 1863. Paroled at Point Lookout on February 24, 1865. Received at Aiken's Landing, James River, Virginia, February 25-28 or March 2-3, 1865, for exchange. Hospitalized at Richmond on March 6, 1865. Furloughed for thirty days on March 7, 1865.

HARVESON, ABEL SHELL, Private

Resided in Catawba County and was by occupation a day laborer prior to enlisting in Catawba County at age 24, July 4, 1862, for the war. Reported present or accounted for through December 31, 1862. Hospitalized at Charlottesville, Virginia, February 8, 1863, with chronic bronchitis. Returned to duty on March 24, 1863. Wounded in the back at Chancellorsville, Virginia, May 4, 1863. Died in hospital at Richmond, Virginia, May 26, 1863, of wounds.

HARVESON, HENRY, Private

Resided in Catawba County and was by occupation a day laborer prior to enlisting in Catawba County at age 28, July 4, 1862, for the war. Reported present through February 28, 1863. Captured at Chancellorsville, Virginia, May 3-4, 1863. Confined at Fort Delaware, Delaware, on or about May 7, 1863. Paroled and transferred to City Point, Virginia, where he was received on May 23, 1863, for exchange. Sent to hospital sick on June 3 or June 30, 1863.

Reported absent without leave in Catawba County in September-October, 1863. Reported in hospital at Petersburg, Virginia, in November-December, 1863. Returned to duty prior to May 1, 1864. Sent to hospital on June 9, 1864. Reported absent without leave on October 1, 1864. Returned to duty in January-February, 1865. Captured at Fort Stedman, Virginia, March 25, 1865. Confined at Point Lookout, Maryland, March 28, 1865. Released at Point Lookout on June 27, 1865, after taking the Oath of Allegiance.

HASS, WILLIAM G., Private

Enlisted in Catawba County on July 4, 1862, for the war. Hospitalized at Richmond, Virginia, November 9, 1862, with debilitas. Returned to duty on November 16, 1862. Reported present through October 31, 1863. Captured at Rappahannock Station, Virginia, November 7, 1863. Confined at Point Lookout, Maryland, November 11, 1863. Paroled at Point Lookout on or about November 1, 1864. Received at Venus Point, Savannah River, Georgia, November 15, 1864, for exchange. Died at Savannah, Georgia, on an unspecified date (probably in December, 1864). Cause of death not reported.

HEFNER, JOHN MARCUS, Private

Enlisted in Catawba County on July 4, 1862, for the war. Reported present through May 11, 1863. Deserted prior to September 1, 1863. Reported under arrest for desertion in September-December, 1863. Court-martialed on or about January 27, 1864. Returned to duty prior to May 1, 1864. Captured near Cold Harbor, Virginia, June 6, 1864. Confined at Point Lookout, Maryland, June 15, 1864. Died at Point Lookout on July 27, 1864. Cause of death not reported.

HOKE, GEORGE ALFERD, Private

Enlisted in Catawba County on July 4, 1862, for the war. Reported present through February 28, 1863. Reported absent on detached service as a teamster in March-October, 1863, and March, 1864-February, 1865. Survived the war.

HOLBROOKS, JOHN F., Private

Born in Rowan County and resided in Lincoln County where he was by occupation a farmer prior to enlisting in Catawba County at age 22, July 4, 1862, for the war. Reported present through October 31, 1863. Captured at Rappahannock Station, Virginia, November 7, 1863. Confined at Point Lookout, Maryland, November 11, 1863. Hospitalized at Point Lookout on March 4, 1864. Died in hospital at Point Lookout on March 24, 1864, of "bronchitis."

HOLLER, GEORGE W., Private

Resided in Catawba County and was by occupation a shoemaker prior to enlisting in Catawba County at age 24, July 4, 1862, for the war. Hospitalized at Richmond, Virginia, September 22, 1862. Returned to duty on October 9, 1862. Deserted on January 17, 1863. Returned to duty prior to March 1, 1863. Reported present through October 31, 1863. Captured at Rappahannock Station, Virginia, November 7, 1863. Confined at Point Lookout, Maryland, November 11, 1863. Paroled at Point Lookout on February 13, 1865. Received at Cox's Wharf, James River, Virginia, February 14-15, 1865, for exchange. Paroled at Newton on April 19, 1865.

HUDSON, WILLIAM S., Private

Enlisted in Catawba County on July 4, 1862, for the war. Mustered in as Sergeant. Reported present through August 31, 1862.

Hospitalized at Richmond, Virginia, December 4, 1862, with icterus. Reduced to ranks on February 1, 1863. Transferred to another hospital on February 17, 1863. Returned to duty prior to March 1, 1863. Hospitalized at Richmond on May 6, 1863, with dyspepsia. Captured on May 24, 1863, during the "raid in the rear of Lee's army." Paroled on or about the same date. Transferred to hospital at Danville, Virginia, June 13, 1863. Died in hospital at Danville on July 10, 1863, of "dyspepsia."

HUFFMAN, DANIEL F., Private

Resided in Catawba County and was by occupation a farmer or day laborer prior to enlisting in Catawba County at age 24, July 4, 1862, for the war. Reported present through October 31, 1862. Wounded at Fredericksburg, Virginia, December 13, 1862. Returned to duty prior to January 1, 1863. Reported present through May 11, 1863. Deserted prior to September 1, 1863. Reported under arrest charged with desertion in September-December, 1863. Court-martialed on or about January 27, 1864. Returned to duty prior to May 1, 1864. Captured at Winchester, Virginia, July 20, 1864. Confined at Camp Chase, Ohio, July 28, 1864. Paroled and transferred to Boulware's and Cox's Wharves, James River, Virginia, where he was received on March 10-12, 1865, for exchange. Survived the war.

HUFFMAN, HOSEA P., Private

Resided in Catawba County where he enlisted at age 15, July 4, 1862, for the war as a substitute. Hospitalized at Richmond, Virginia, September 29, 1862, with intermittent fever. Returned to duty on October 30, 1862. Reported present on surviving company muster rolls through April 30, 1864. Captured (or deserted to the enemy) near Frederick, Maryland, July 9, 1864. Confined at Fort Delaware, Delaware, July 19, 1864. Released at Fort Delaware on May 5, 1865, after taking the Oath of Allegiance.

HUFFMAN, JOSEPH, Private

Enlisted in Catawba County on July 4, 1862, for the war. Mustered in as 1st Sergeant. Reported present through February 28, 1863. Reduced to ranks on February 1, 1863. Wounded in the left arm and shoulder at Chancellorsville, Virginia, May 3-4, 1863. Died on May 9, 1863, of wounds. Place of death not reported.

HUFFMAN, L. MAXWELL E., Private

Resided in Catawba County and was by occupation a day laborer prior to enlisting in Catawba County at age 25, July 4, 1862, for the war. Reported present or accounted for through February 28, 1863. Wounded in the left shoulder at Chancellorsville, Virginia, May 4, 1863. Hospitalized at Richmond, Virginia. Returned to duty on or about April 7, 1864. Sent to hospital sick on May 8, 1864. Reported absent in hospital through February 28, 1865. Survived the war.

HUFFMAN, L. T., Private

Enlisted in Catawba County on July 4, 1862, for the war. Reported present through October 31, 1862. Wounded in the knee at Fredericksburg, Virginia, December 13, 1862. Died in hospital at Richmond, Virginia, December 21, 1862, of wounds.

HUFFMAN, LAWSON T., Private

Enlisted in Catawba County on July 4, 1862, for the war. Wounded at Fredericksburg, Virginia, December 13, 1862. Returned to duty prior to January 1, 1863. Sent to hospital on February 18, 1863. Died on April 5, 1863. Place and cause of death not reported.

HUFFMAN, MARCUS M., Private

Born in Catawba County* where he resided as a shoemaker prior to enlisting in Catawba County on July 4, 1862, for the war. Reported present through May 11, 1863. Sent to hospital sick on June 1, 1863. Reported on hospital duty at Richmond, Virginia, in September-October, 1863. Discharged from service on November 16, 1863, by reason of "rheumatism which has contorted the feet producing talipes varus." Discharge certificate gives his age as 29.

HUNSUCKER, LAWSON T., Private

Enlisted in Catawba County at age 27, July 4, 1862, for the war. Reported present or accounted for through December 31, 1862. Deserted from camp near Port Royal, Virginia, February 21, 1863. Returned to duty in March-May, 1863. Reported present through October 31, 1863. Captured at Rappahannock Station, Virginia, November 7, 1863. Confined at Point Lookout, Maryland, November 11, 1863. Paroled at Point Lookout on February 24, 1865. Received at Aiken's Landing, James River, Virginia, February 25-28 or March 2-3, 1865, for exchange.

ISAAC, JOHN R., Private

Born on September 22, 1843. Enlisted in Catawba County at age 18, July 4, 1862, for the war. Hospitalized at Richmond, Virginia, December 3, 1862. Died in hospital at Richmond on December 18, 1862, of "phthisis pulmonalis."

ISAAC, LEVI, Private

Born in Catawba County* on December 3, 1834. Resided in Catawba County and was by occupation a farmer prior to enlisting in Catawba County at age 27, July 4, 1862, for the war. Reported present through February 28, 1863. Sent to hospital sick on April 10, 1863. Returned to duty in January-April, 1864. Captured at Winchester, Virginia, July 20, 1864. Confined at Camp Chase, Ohio, July 28, 1864. Paroled at Camp Chase on March 2, 1865. Received at Boulware's and Cox's Wharves, James River, Virginia, March 10-12, 1865, for exchange. Survived the war.

KILLIAN, LABEN S., Private

Resided in Catawba County and was by occupation a farmer prior to enlisting in Catawba County at age 41, April 1, 1863, for the war. Reported present through October 31, 1863. Captured at Rappahannock Station, Virginia, November 7, 1863. Confined at Point Lookout, Maryland, November 11, 1863. Paroled at Point Lookout on February 24, 1865. Received at Aiken's Landing, James River, Virginia, February 25, 1865, for exchange. Hospitalized at Richmond, Virginia, the same date. Furloughed for thirty days on March 6, 1865. Survived the war.

KILLIAN, WILLIAM G., Private

Enlisted at Brandy Station, Virginia, November 1, 1863, for the war. Captured at Rappahannock Station, Virginia, November 7, 1863. Confined at Point Lookout, Maryland, November 11, 1863. Paroled at Point Lookout on February 24, 1865. Received at Aiken's Landing, James River, Virginia, February 25-28 or March 2-3, 1865, for exchange. No further records.

LANTZ, JACOB, Private

Place and date of enlistment not reported. Records of the Federal Provost Marshal indicate that he died at Point Lookout, Maryland, April 29, 1864. No further records.

LEATHERMAN, LAWSON M., Private

Enlisted in Lenoir County on March 1, 1864, for the war. Wounded in the shoulder and finger at or near Cold Harbor, Virginia, June 1-10, 1864. Finger amputated. Returned to duty prior to September 1, 1864. Reported present or accounted for through February 28, 1865. Surrendered at Appomattox Court House, Virginia, April 9, 1865. [Was about 18 years of age at time of enlistment.]

LEFFER, H., Private

Place and date of enlistment not reported (probably enlisted subsequent to February 28, 1865). Captured and paroled at Athens, Georgia, on or about May 8, 1865.

LEONARD, DANIEL E., JR., Private

Resided in Catawba County and was by occupation a farmer prior to enlisting in Catawba County at age 24, July 4, 1862, for the war. Reported in hospital at Richmond, Virginia, in September, 1862, with bilious fever and chronic diarrhoea. Returned to duty on September 20, 1862. Reported present through October 31, 1863. Captured at Rappahannock Station, Virginia, November 7, 1863. Confined at Point Lookout, Maryland, November 11, 1863. Paroled at Point Lookout on October 11, 1864. Received at Cox's Wharf, James River, Virginia, October 15, 1864, for exchange. Hospitalized at Richmond where he died on October 19, 1864, of disease.

LEONARD, ELI, Private

Born on November 1, 1827. Resided in Catawba County and was by occupation a carriage maker prior to enlisting in Catawba County at age 34, July 4, 1862, for the war. Reported present through May 11, 1863. Sent to hospital on August 1, 1863. Returned to duty in September-October, 1863. Reported present in November-December, 1863. Sent to hospital on February 7, 1864. Returned to duty subsequent to April 30, 1864. Hospitalized at Richmond, Virginia, June 17, 1864, with rheumatism. Returned to duty in January-February, 1865. Captured at Fort Stedman, Virginia, March 25, 1865. Confined at Point Lookout, Maryland, March 28, 1865. Released at Point Lookout on June 28, 1865, after taking the Oath of Allegiance.

LEONARD, JAMES MONROE, Private

Previously served as Private in Company F, 23rd Regiment N.C. Troops (13th Regiment N.C. Volunteers). Transferred to this company in October, 1862-February, 1863. Reported present through October 31, 1863. Captured at Rappahannock Station, Virginia, November 7, 1863. Confined at Point Lookout, Maryland, November 11, 1863. Paroled at Point Lookout on February 24, 1865. Received at Aiken's Landing, James River, Virginia, February 25-28 or March 2-3, 1865, for exchange.

LOWRANCE, CARLOS ELPHONSE, Private

Was by occupation a farmer and part-time schoolteacher prior to enlisting in Catawba County at age 31, July 4, 1862, for the war. Reported present or accounted for through October 31, 1863. Wounded in the back and captured at Rappahannock Station, Virginia, November 7, 1863. Hospitalized at Washington, D.C., where he died on November 16, 1863, of "asthenia." [A detailed description of his wound and the treatment thereof, as well as an illustration of the "conoidal ball" that killed him, appears in *Medical and Surgical History of the Civil War*, 8:583.]

LUTZ, MILES C., Private

Resided in Catawba County and was by occupation a farm laborer prior to enlisting in Catawba County at age 32, July 7, 1862, for

the war. Hospitalized at Richmond, Virginia, November 8, 1862, with intermittent fever. Returned to duty December 13, 1862. Reported present through October 31, 1863. Captured at Rappahannock Station, Virginia, November 7, 1863. Confined at Point Lookout, Maryland, November 11, 1863. Paroled at Point Lookout on or about October 30, 1864. Transferred to Fort Monroe, Virginia, where he died on November 3, 1864, of "ch[ronic] diarrhoea."

McCASLIN, ALFRED C., Private

Born in Lincoln County where he resided as a house carpenter prior to enlisting in Catawba County at age 27, July 4, 1862, for the war. Hospitalized at Richmond, Virginia, September 29, 1862, with measles. Returned to duty on October 30, 1862. Reported present through October 31, 1863. Captured at Rappahannock Station, Virginia, November 7, 1863. Confined at Point Lookout, Maryland, November 11, 1863. Paroled at Point Lookout on or about February 10, 1865. Received at Cox's Wharf, James River, Virginia, February 14-15, 1865, for exchange. Survived the war.

McCASLIN, HENRY F., Corporal

Resided in Lincoln County and was by occupation a farm laborer prior to enlisting in Catawba County at age 18, July 4, 1862, for the war. Mustered in as Private. Reported present or accounted for through October 31, 1863. Promoted to Corporal in May-August, 1863. Captured at Rappahannock Station, Virginia, November 7, 1863. Confined at Point Lookout, Maryland, November 11, 1863. Paroled at Point Lookout on March 15, 1865. Received at Boulware's Wharf, James River, Virginia, March 18, 1865, for exchange. Survived the war.

McCASLIN, J. C., Private

Enlisted in Catawba County on July 4, 1862, for the war. Hospitalized at Richmond, Virginia, September 29, 1862. Furloughed on October 13, 1862. Returned to duty prior to November 1, 1862. Died at Port Royal, Virginia, on or about February 19, 1863. Cause of death not reported.

MATHESON, J. J., Private

Enlisted in Catawba County on July 4, 1862, for the war. Reported present through December 31, 1862. Deserted from camp near Port Royal, Virginia, February 21, 1863. [One of his initials is for "Jefferson."]

MEARES, WILLIAM J., ———

North Carolina pension records indicate that he served in this company.

MICHAEL, AMBROSE, Corporal

Resided in Catawba County and was by occupation a shoemaker prior to enlisting in Catawba County at age 32, July 4, 1862, for the war. Mustered in as Corporal. Reported present through October 31, 1862. Died in hospital at Richmond, Virginia, January 29, 1863, of "pneumonia typhoides." [Previously served as 2nd Lieutenant in the 89th Regiment N.C. Militia.]

MICHAEL, JACOB L., Private

Resided in Catawba County and was by occupation a farmer prior to enlisting in Catawba County at age 29, July 4, 1862, for the war. Reported present through December 31, 1862. Died at Fredericksburg, Virginia, on or about February 7, 1863. Cause of death not reported.

MILLER, DAVID A., Private

Resided in Catawba or Rowan County and was by occupation a millwright prior to enlisting in Catawba County at age 29, July 4, 1862, for the war. Reported present or accounted for through February 28, 1863. Hospitalized at Richmond, Virginia, May 1, 1863, with rheumatism. Transferred to hospital at Danville, Virginia, May 7, 1863. Deserted on May 24, 1863. Returned to duty on an unspecified date. Captured at or near Gettysburg, Pennsylvania, on or about July 2-5, 1863. Confined at Fort Delaware, Delaware, on or about July 10, 1863. Transferred to Point Lookout, Maryland, October 20, 1863. Paroled at Point Lookout on or about February 10, 1865. Received at Cox's Wharf, James River, Virginia, February 14-15, 1865, for exchange. Survived the war.

MILLER, GEORGE B., Private

Enlisted in Catawba County on July 4, 1862, for the war. Hospitalized at Richmond, Virginia, November 8, 1862, with intermittent fever. Returned to duty on December 13, 1862. Deserted from camp near Port Royal, Virginia, February 21, 1863. Died at home on April 1, 1863. Cause of death not reported.

MILLER, JOHN MONROE, Private

Born on July 30, 1832. Resided in Catawba County and was by occupation a farmer prior to enlisting in Catawba County at age 29, July 4, 1862, for the war. Reported present through February 28, 1863. Sent to hospital on March 19, 1863. Returned to duty in May-August, 1863. Reported present in September-October, 1863. Captured at Rappahannock Station, Virginia, November 7, 1863. Confined at Point Lookout, Maryland, November 11, 1863. Paroled at Point Lookout on March 14, 1865. Received at Boulware's Wharf, James River, Virginia, March 16, 1865, for exchange. Survived the war.

MILLER, PAUL, Private

Resided in Catawba County and was by occupation a farmer prior to enlisting in Catawba County at age 31, July 4, 1862, for the war. Hospitalized at Richmond, Virginia, September 18, 1862, with diarrhoea. Furloughed on September 26, 1862. Returned to duty in January-February, 1863. Hospitalized at Richmond on May 22, 1863. Died in hospital at Richmond on May 25 or June 25, 1863, of "febris typhoides."

MILLER, WESLEY, Private

Resided in Catawba County and was by occupation a farmer prior to enlisting in Catawba County at age 32, July 4, 1862, for the war. Sent to hospital sick on or about September 29, 1862. Returned to duty in November-December, 1862. No further records.

MOONEY, JOHN SIDNEY, Private

Born on May 3, 1830. Resided in Catawba County where he enlisted at age 32, July 4, 1862, for the war. Reported present through October 31, 1863. Reported on duty as a teamster in November-December, 1863, and March-August, 1864. Reported present or accounted for in September, 1864-February, 1865. Captured at Fort Stedman, Virginia, March 25, 1865. Confined at Point Lookout, Maryland, March 28, 1865. Released at Point Lookout on June 15, 1865, after taking the Oath of Allegiance.

NAUGLE, LEVI, Private

Resided in Catawba County and was by occupation a farmer prior to enlisting in Catawba County at age 33, July 4, 1862, for the war.

Reported present or accounted for through May 11, 1863. Died in hospital at Winchester, Virginia, June 16, 1863, of "fever."

NULL, JOHN, Private

Resided in Catawba County where he enlisted at age 18, July 4, 1862, for the war. Hospitalized at Richmond, Virginia, October 29, 1862, with typhoid fever. Returned to duty on November 24, 1862. Reported present or accounted for through October 31, 1863. Captured at Rappahannock Station, Virginia, November 7, 1863. Confined at Point Lookout, Maryland, November 11, 1863. Paroled at Point Lookout on May 3, 1864. Received at Aiken's Landing, James River, Virginia, May 8, 1864, for exchange. Hospitalized at Richmond on the same date with chronic diarrhoea. Furloughed on May 20 or July 20, 1864. Reported absent without leave on September 1, 1864. Returned to duty in January-February, 1865. Captured at Fort Stedman, Virginia, March 25, 1865. Confined at Point Lookout on March 28, 1865. Released at Point Lookout on June 29, 1865, after taking the Oath of Allegiance.

PATTERSON, EMANUEL ARTHUR, Private

Born at King's Mountain on May 24, 1844. Enlisted in Catawba County at age 18, July 4, 1862, for the war. Reported present or accounted for through October 31, 1863. Captured at Rappahannock Station, Virginia, November 7, 1863. Confined at Point Lookout, Maryland, November 11, 1863. Paroled at Point Lookout on May 3, 1864. Received at Aiken's Landing, James River, Virginia, May 8, 1864, for exchange. Returned to duty prior to September 1, 1864. Captured (or deserted to the enemy) at Strasburg, Virginia, or near Woodstock, Virginia, September 23, 1864. Confined at Point Lookout on October 3, 1864. Released at Point Lookout on June 3, 1865, after taking the Oath of Allegiance.

PITTS, DAVID A., Private

Resided in Catawba County and was by occupation a farmer prior to enlisting in Catawba County at age 23, July 4, 1862, for the war. Reported present through December 31, 1862. Deserted from camp near Port Royal, Virginia, February 21, 1863. Returned to duty prior to May 4, 1863, when he was wounded in the thigh at Chancellorsville, Virginia. Returned to duty in November-December, 1863. Reported present in March-April, 1864. Wounded near Cold Harbor, Virginia, on or about June 7, 1864. Hospitalized at Richmond, Virginia. Reported on detail for light duty at Charlotte from September 1, 1864, through February 28, 1865. Captured at Farmville, Virginia, April 6, 1865. Confined at Newport News, Virginia, April 14, 1865. Released at Newport News on June 26, 1865, after taking the Oath of Allegiance.

POOVY, WILLIAM PINKNEY, Private

Born on September 7, 1834. Resided in Catawba County. Place and date of enlistment not reported (probably enlisted subsequent to February 28, 1865). Captured near Petersburg, Virginia, February 6, 1865. Confined at Point Lookout, Maryland, February 9, 1865. Released at Point Lookout on June 17, 1865, after taking the Oath of Allegiance.

POPE, ALFRED, ———

North Carolina pension records indicate that he served in this company.

POPE, DANIEL, Private

Born on February 18, 1827. Resided in Catawba County and was by occupation a ditcher prior to enlisting in Catawba County at age

35, July 4, 1862, for the war. Reported present through February 28, 1863. Wounded in the thigh and/or left knee at Chancellorsville, Virginia, May 4, 1863. Hospitalized at Richmond, Virginia. Furloughed for forty days on June 11, 1863. Reported absent wounded through February 28, 1865. Survived the war.

POPE, FRANKLIN, Private

Resided in Catawba County and was by occupation a farmer prior to enlisting in Catawba County at age 27, July 4, 1862, for the war. Reported absent sick on August 11, 1862. Returned to duty subsequent to February 28, 1863. Wounded in the right hand ("finger next to little finger shot off above knuckle") at Chancellorsville, Virginia, May 4, 1863. Returned to duty prior to September 1, 1863. Captured at Rappahannock Station, Virginia, November 7, 1863. Confined at Point Lookout, Maryland, November 11, 1863. Paroled at Point Lookout on February 10, 1865. Received at Cox's Wharf, James River, Virginia, February 14, 1865, for exchange. Hospitalized at Richmond, Virginia, the same date. Survived the war.

PROPST, DAVID FRANKLIN, Corporal

Born on February 12, 1831. Resided in Catawba County and was by occupation a farmer prior to enlisting in Catawba County at age 31, July 4, 1862, for the war. Mustered in as Corporal. Reported present through October 31, 1862. Died in hospital at Richmond, Virginia, on or about January 28, 1863, of "pneumonia."

PROPST, FRANK S., Private

Enlisted in Lenoir County on March 12, 1864, for the war. Wounded at or near Globe Tavern, Virginia, August 21, 1864. Returned to duty in November-December, 1864. Reported present through February 28, 1865. Wounded in the foot at Fort Stedman, Virginia, March 25, 1865. Hospitalized at Richmond, Virginia. Captured in hospital at Richmond on April 3, 1865. Paroled on May 31, 1865, but remained in hospital until June 5, 1865. [Went west after the war.]

PROPST, GEORGE M., Private

Resided in Catawba County and was by occupation a farmer prior to enlisting in Catawba County at age 35, July 4, 1862, for the war. Reported sick at home in Catawba County from August 11, 1862, through February 28, 1863. Returned to duty on an unspecified date. Reported present in March-May, 1863. Sent to hospital sick on July 7, 1863. Returned to duty in November, 1863-April, 1864. Sent to hospital sick on June 19, 1864. Reported absent without leave in September-October, 1864. Reported under arrest on December 26, 1864. Returned to duty in January-February, 1865. Captured at Farmville, Virginia, April 6, 1865. Confined at Newport News, Virginia, April 14, 1865. Released at Newport News on June 15, 1865, after taking the Oath of Allegiance.

PROPST, WALLACE ALEXANDER, Private

Resided in Catawba County and was by occupation a farmer prior to enlisting in Catawba County at age 33, July 4, 1862, for the war. Mustered in as Corporal. Hospitalized at Richmond, Virginia, October 25, 1862, with remittent fever. Later contracted rheumatism. Reduced to ranks on February 1, 1863. Transferred to Salisbury on April 8, 1863. Returned to duty prior to September 1, 1863. Reported present or accounted for on surviving company muster rolls through April 30, 1864. Wounded in the left gluteal region and captured at Winchester, Virginia, July 20, 1864. Confined at Camp

Chase, Ohio, August 29, 1864. Transferred to Point Lookout, Maryland, March 18, 1865. Paroled at Point Lookout and transferred to Boulware's Wharf, James River, Virginia, where he was received on March 27, 1865, for exchange.

PROPST, WILLIAM HENRY, Private

Resided in Catawba County and enlisted in Lenoir County on April 1, 1864, for the war. Hospitalized at Richmond, Virginia, May 31, 1864. Returned to duty in September-October, 1864. Reported present through February 28, 1865. Captured at Farmville, Virginia, April 6, 1865. Confined at Newport News, Virginia, April 14, 1865. Released at Newport News on June 26, 1865, after taking the Oath of Allegiance. [Was about 18 years of age at time of enlistment.]

RABB, J. FRANKLIN, Sergeant

Enlisted in Catawba County on July 4, 1862, for the war. Mustered in as Private. Promoted to Sergeant on February 1, 1863. Reported present through May 11, 1863. Hospitalized at Charlottesville, Virginia, August 25, 1863, with chronic dysentery. Transferred to hospital at Lynchburg, Virginia, September 21, 1863. Returned to duty in November-December, 1863. Reported present or accounted for on surviving company muster rolls through February 28, 1865. Wounded in the shoulder at Fort Stedman, Virginia, March 25, 1865. Hospitalized at Richmond, Virginia. Captured in hospital at Richmond on April 3, 1865. Transferred to Newport News, Virginia, April 23, 1865. Released at Newport News on an unspecified date after taking the Oath of Allegiance. [May have been wounded in the side at Fredericksburg, Virginia, December 13, 1862, and in the head at Winchester, Virginia, September 19, 1864. See G. W. Hahn, *The Catawba Soldier in the Civil War*, 324-325.]

RABY, JACOB, Private

Enlisted in Catawba County on July 4, 1862, for the war. Reported present through August 31, 1862. Hospitalized at Richmond, Virginia, November 22, 1862, with chronic rheumatism. Died in hospital at Richmond on December 3, 1862, of "ple[u]ro pneumonia."

RABY, WILLIAM M., Private

Enlisted in Catawba County at age 29, July 4, 1862, for the war. Reported present or accounted for through February 28, 1863. Hospitalized at Richmond, Virginia, April 9, 1863, with typhoid fever. Transferred to hospital at Danville, Virginia, April 21, 1863. Returned to duty prior to November 1, 1863. Captured at Rappahannock Station, Virginia, November 7, 1863. Confined at Point Lookout, Maryland, November 11, 1863. Paroled at Point Lookout on February 24, 1865. Received at Aiken's Landing, James River, Virginia, February 25-28 or March 2-3, 1865, for exchange. Survived the war.

REINHARDT, JOHN JACOB, Private

Enlisted in Catawba County on July 4, 1862, for the war. Hospitalized at Richmond, Virginia, October 10, 1862, with typhoid fever. Furloughed for thirty days on November 12, 1862. Returned to duty in January-February, 1863. Reported present through October 31, 1863. Captured at Rappahannock Station, Virginia, November 7, 1863. Confined at Point Lookout, Maryland, November 11, 1863. Paroled at Point Lookout on March 14, 1865. Received at Boulware's Wharf, James River, Virginia, March 16, 1865, for exchange. Hospitalized at Richmond on March 17, 1865, with chronic diarrhoea. Furloughed for sixty days on March 24, 1865. Survived the war.

ROBINSON, ANDREW J., Sergeant

Enlisted in Catawba County on July 4, 1862, for the war. Mustered in as Private. Hospitalized at Richmond, Virginia, September 25, 1862, with dysentery and typhoid fever. Furloughed on October 22, 1862. Returned to duty prior to January 1, 1863. Promoted to Sergeant on February 1, 1863. Wounded in the jaw at Chancellorsville, Virginia, May 4, 1863. Hospitalized at Richmond. Transferred to hospital at Lynchburg, Virginia, May 7, 1863. Returned to duty prior to September 1, 1863. Captured at Rappahannock Station, Virginia, November 7, 1863. Confined at Point Lookout, Maryland, November 11, 1863. Died at Point Lookout on January 28, 1865, of "chronic dysentery."

ROBINSON, D. L., Private

Enlisted in Catawba County on July 4, 1862, for the war. Hospitalized at Richmond, Virginia, October 10, 1862, with rubeola. Returned to duty prior to November 1, 1862. Reported present or accounted for on surviving company muster rolls through February 28, 1865. Surrendered at Appomattox Court House, Virginia, April 9, 1865.

ROBINSON, JOHN WILFONG, Private

Born on April 6, 1832. Enlisted in Catawba County at age 30, July 4, 1862, for the war. Discharged on or about the same date after providing Pvt. W. James Conrad as a substitute.

RODERICK, CEPHUS, Private

Born in Lincoln County where he resided as a farmer prior to enlisting in Rowan County at age 26, July 4, 1862, for the war. Reported present through October 31, 1863. Captured at Rappahannock Station, Virginia, November 7, 1863. Confined at Point Lookout, Maryland, November 11, 1863. Paroled at Point Lookout on April 27, 1864. Received at City Point, Virginia, April 30, 1864, for exchange. Hospitalized at Richmond, Virginia, May 1, 1864, with chronic diarrhoea. Furloughed for thirty days on May 12, 1864. Returned to duty in September-October, 1864. Reported present through February 28, 1865. Captured at Fort Stedman, Virginia, March 25, 1865. Confined at Point Lookout on March 28, 1865. Released at Point Lookout on June 17, 1865, after taking the Oath of Allegiance.

SELF, WILLIAM R., Corporal

Resided in Catawba County and was by occupation a farmer prior to enlisting in Catawba County, at age 26, July 4, 1862, for the war. Mustered in as Corporal. Reported present through October 31, 1862. Wounded in the head and/or neck at Fredericksburg, Virginia, December 13, 1862. Returned to duty prior to January 1, 1863. Reported present through May 11, 1863. Wounded in the foot at Gettysburg, Pennsylvania, July 1, 1863, "while carrying the flag." Hospitalized at Richmond, Virginia. Furloughed for forty days on or about July 29, 1863. Returned to duty in November-December, 1863. Reported present in March-April, 1864. Wounded in the left thigh at Lynchburg, Virginia, on or about June 18, 1864. Captured at Winchester, Virginia, July 20, 1864. Contracted smallpox and was apparently confined in a Federal hospital at Winchester. Exchanged on an unspecified date. Reported absent sick on December 2, 1864. Survived the war.

SETZER, JACOB HARVEY, Private

Enlisted in Catawba County on July 4, 1862, for the war. Hospitalized at Richmond, Virginia, October 10, 1862, with typhoid fever. Furloughed for thirty days on or about October 18, 1862. Returned to duty in November-December, 1862. Reported present through October 31, 1863. Captured at Rappahannock Station, Virginia, November 7, 1863. Confined at Point Lookout, Maryland, November 11, 1863. Paroled at Point Lookout on February 24, 1865. Received at Aiken's Landing, James River, Virginia, February 25-28 or March 2, 1865, for exchange. Hospitalized at Richmond on March 2, 1865. Reported still in hospital at Richmond on March 18, 1865. Apparently died in hospital at Richmond. Date and cause of death not reported.

SETZER, JOHN C., Private

Born on January 11, 1837. Enlisted in Catawba County at age 25, July 4, 1862, for the war. Hospitalized at Richmond, Virginia, November 9, 1862, with rheumatism. Transferred on December 1, 1862. Returned to duty prior to January 1, 1863. Deserted from camp near Port Royal, Virginia, February 21, 1863. Returned to duty in March-May, 1863. Wounded in the left hand (lost one finger) and right shoulder and captured at Gettysburg, Pennsylvania, July 2-5, 1863. Hospitalized at Frederick, Maryland. Transferred to hospital at Baltimore, Maryland, July 14, 1863. Confined at Fort Delaware, Delaware, on an unspecified date. Paroled at Fort Delaware on July 30, 1863. Received at City Point, Virginia, August 1, 1863, for exchange. Had not returned to duty as of September 1, 1864, when he was reported absent without leave. Listed as a deserter in January-February, 1865. [Records of the Federal Provost Marshal dated July, 1863, give his age as 25.]

SETZER, MARCUS ELCANAH, Private

Born on March 10, 1830. Enlisted in Catawba County at age 32, July 4, 1862, for the war. Hospitalized at Richmond, Virginia, October 9, 1862, with chronic catarrh. Returned to duty prior to November 1, 1862. Reported present through October 31, 1863. Captured at Rappahannock Station, Virginia, November 7, 1863. Confined at Point Lookout, Maryland, November 11, 1863. Died at Point Lookout on March 21, 1865, of "scurvy."

SETZER, PATRICK SYLVANUS, Private

Born on May 11, 1843. Enlisted in Catawba County at age 19, July 4, 1862, for the war. Reported present through October 31, 1863. Captured at Rappahannock Station, Virginia, November 7, 1863. Confined at Point Lookout, Maryland, November 11, 1863. Paroled at Point Lookout on February 24, 1865. Received at Aiken's Landing, James River, Virginia, February 25-28 or March 2-3, 1865, for exchange. Survived the war.

SETZER, WILLIAM ALLO, Private

Born on December 22, 1835. Enlisted in Catawba County at age 26, July 4, 1862, for the war. Reported present through October 31, 1863. Captured at Rappahannock Station, Virginia, November 7, 1863. Confined at Point Lookout, Maryland, November 11, 1863. Paroled at Point Lookout on February 24, 1865. Received at Aiken's Landing, James River, Virginia, February 25-28 or March 2-3, 1865, for exchange. Survived the war.

SHEPARD, JOHN, Private

Resided in Catawba County and was by occupation a day laborer prior to enlisting in Catawba County at age 36, July 4, 1862, for the war. Reported present on surviving company muster rolls through April 30, 1864. Killed by a sharpshooter at Drewry's Bluff, Virginia, in May, 1864.

SIGMAN, BENJAMIN, Private

Resided in Catawba County and was by occupation a farm laborer prior to enlisting in Catawba County at age 30, July 4, 1862, for the war. Hospitalized at Richmond, Virginia, November 8, 1862, with typhoid fever. Furloughed on November 20, 1862. Returned to duty prior to January 1, 1863. Reported present through October 31, 1863. Captured at Rappahannock Station, Virginia, November 7, 1863. Confined at Point Lookout, Maryland, November 11, 1863. Died at Point Lookout on or about July 4, 1864, of disease.

SIGMAN, JOSHUA A., Private

Resided in Catawba County and was by occupation a farm laborer prior to enlisting in Catawba County at age 25, July 4, 1862, for the war. Reported present through December 31, 1862. Reported absent sick from February 25 through October 31, 1863. Returned to duty prior to May 1, 1864. Captured at or near Spotsylvania Court House, Virginia, May 22, 1864. Confined at Point Lookout, Maryland, May 30, 1864. Paroled at Point Lookout on October 31, 1864. Received at Venus Point, Savannah River, Georgia, November 15, 1864, for exchange. Returned to duty in January-February, 1865. Captured at or near the Appomattox River, Virginia, April 3, 1865. Confined at Hart's Island, New York Harbor, April 11, 1865. Released at Hart's Island on June 19, 1865, after taking the Oath of Allegiance.

SIMMONS, JOHN, Private

Resided in Catawba County where he enlisted on July 4, 1862, for the war. Hospitalized at Richmond, Virginia, November 9, 1862, with neuralgia. Transferred to hospital at Farmville, Virginia, December 20, 1862 (suffering from intermittent fever). Returned to duty on December 31, 1862. Reported present through October 31, 1863. Captured at Rappahannock Station, Virginia, November 7, 1863. Confined at Point Lookout, Maryland, November 11, 1863. Paroled at Point Lookout on or about October 31, 1864. Received at Venus Point, Savannah River, Georgia, November 15, 1864, for exchange. Reported absent sick on December 2, 1864. Returned to duty in January-February, 1865. Captured at Fort Stedman, Virginia, March 25, 1865. Confined at Point Lookout on March 28, 1865. Released at Point Lookout on June 19, 1865, after taking the Oath of Allegiance. [Was about 20 years of age at time of enlistment.]

SIPE, F. CICERO, Private

Born in Catawba County* and resided in Gaston County where he was by occupation a carpenter prior to enlisting in Catawba County at age 26, July 4, 1862, for the war. Reported present through February 28, 1863. Reported on detached service with the Pioneer Corps in March-October, 1863. Rejoined the company in November-December, 1863. Reported present or accounted for in March-August, 1864. Captured at Fisher's Hill, Virginia, September 22, 1864. Confined at Point Lookout, Maryland, October 3, 1864. Released at Point Lookout on June 3, 1865, after taking the Oath of Allegiance.

SIPE, SIDNEY, Private

Enlisted in Catawba County on July 4, 1862, for the war. Hospitalized at Richmond, Virginia, September 29, 1862, with typhoid fever. Later developed diarrhoea. Returned to duty on October 18, 1862. Wounded at Fredericksburg, Virginia, December 13, 1862. Returned to duty in January-February, 1863. Reported present through May 11, 1863. Captured at Gettysburg, Pennsylvania, on or about July 2, 1863. Confined at Fort Delaware, Delaware, on or

about July 9, 1863. Paroled at Fort Delaware on July 30, 1863. Received at City Point, Virginia, August 1, 1863, for exchange. Returned to duty subsequent to October 31, 1863. Reported present in March-April, 1864. Captured at Spotsylvania Court House, Virginia, May 22, 1864. Confined at Point Lookout, Maryland, May 30, 1864. Died at Point Lookout on May 30, 1865, of "chro[nic] diarrhoea."

SRONCE, LOGAN E., Private

Born on June 9, 1845. Resided in Lincoln County where he enlisted at age 18, March 1, 1864, for the war. Sent to hospital sick on July 20, 1864. Returned to duty in September-October, 1864. Reported present through December 31, 1864. Sent to hospital sick on January 2, 1865. Returned to duty prior to March 25, 1865, when he was captured at Fort Stedman, Virginia. Confined at Point Lookout, Maryland, March 28, 1865. Released at Point Lookout on June 20, 1865, after taking the Oath of Allegiance.

STARR, SYLVANUS MARION, Private

Resided in Catawba County and was by occupation a farmer prior to enlisting in Catawba County at age 34, July 4, 1862, for the war. Hospitalized at Richmond, Virginia, November 9, 1862, with vertigo. Transferred to hospital at Farmville, Virginia, December 20, 1862 (suffering from disease of the liver). Returned to duty on January 3, 1863. Captured at Chancellorsville, Virginia, May 3, 1863. Confined at Fort Delaware, Delaware, on or about May 7, 1863. Paroled at Fort Delaware and transferred to City Point, Virginia, where he was received on May 23, 1863, for exchange. Returned to duty prior to September 1, 1863. Captured at Rappahannock Station, Virginia, November 7, 1863. Confined at Point Lookout, Maryland, November 11, 1863. Paroled at Point Lookout on February 24, 1865. Received at Aiken's Landing, James River, Virginia, February 25-28 or March 2-3, 1865, for exchange. Survived the war.

STOWE, W. L., Private

Resided in Gaston County and enlisted in Catawba County on July 4, 1862, for the war. Reported present through October 31, 1863. Hospitalized at Richmond, Virginia, November 9, 1863, with chronic diarrhoea. Furloughed for sixty days on or about November 25, 1863. Returned to duty prior to May 1, 1864. Reported present through August 31, 1864. Captured at Fisher's Hill, Virginia, September 22, 1864. Confined at Point Lookout, Maryland, October 3, 1864. Died at Point Lookout on January 23, 1865, of "chronic diarrhoea."

SUMMEROW, JOHN F., Private

Born in Lincoln County and was by occupation a farmer prior to enlisting in Catawba County on July 4, 1862, for the war. Hospitalized at Richmond, Virginia, October 19, 1862. Died in hospital at Richmond on December 12, 1862, of "ty[phoi]d fever followed by d[iph]theria." [Was about 21 years of age at time of enlistment.]

TRAFFENSTEADT, REUBEN D., Private

Born in Catawba County* where he resided as a farmer prior to enlisting in Catawba County on July 4, 1862, for the war. Wounded in the right arm at Fredericksburg, Virginia, December 13, 1862. Right arm amputated. Hospitalized at Richmond, Virginia, where he was discharged on February 13, 1863, by reason of disability. Discharge certificate gives his age as 31.

WAGNER, PETER LEMUEL, Private

Born on March 28, 1834. Enlisted in Catawba County at age 28, July 4, 1862, for the war. Reported present or accounted for through February 28, 1863. Hospitalized at Richmond, Virginia, March 8, 1863. Died in hospital at Richmond on April 12, 1863, of "chr[onic] dysentery."

WAGNER, WILLIAM F., Private

Born on March 21, 1831. Resided in Catawba County and was by occupation a blacksmith prior to enlisting in Catawba County at age 31, July 4, 1862, for the war. Reported present through May 10, 1863. Wounded slightly in the leg at Gettysburg, Pennsylvania, on or about July 2, 1863, but remained on duty. Reported present through October 31, 1863. Captured at Rappahannock Station, Virginia, November 7, 1863. Confined at Point Lookout, Maryland, November 11, 1863. Died at Point Lookout on January 13, 1864, of "chron[ic] diarrhoea."

WALKER, T. C., Private

Place and date of enlistment not reported (probably enlisted subsequent to February 28, 1865). Paroled at Greensboro on May 13, 1865.

WEATHERS, LABAN, Private

Enlisted in Catawba County on July 4, 1862, for the war. Reported present or accounted for through May 11, 1863. Died in hospital at Richmond, Virginia, July 4, 1863, of "diarrhoea ch[ronic]."

WEAVER, DANIEL, Private

Resided in Catawba County and was by occupation a blacksmith prior to enlisting in Catawba County at age 30, July 4, 1862, for the war. Hospitalized at Richmond, Virginia, October 18, 1862. Furloughed for thirty days on December 6, 1862. Returned to duty prior to March 1, 1863. Reported present through October 31, 1863. Captured at Rappahannock Station, Virginia, November 7, 1863. Confined at Point Lookout, Maryland, November 11, 1863. Paroled at Point Lookout on February 24, 1865. Received at Aiken's Landing, James River, Virginia, February 25-28 or March 2-3, 1865, for exchange. Survived the war.

WILKIE, HOSEA J., Private

Resided in Catawba County and was by occupation a farmer or day laborer prior to enlisting in Catawba County or at Fredericksburg, Virginia, at age 38, April 1, 1863, for the war. Hospitalized at Richmond, Virginia, May 2, 1863, with acute rheumatism. Transferred to Danville, Virginia, May 7, 1863. Reported on hospital duty at Richmond in June-October, 1863. Reported absent on sick furlough in March-April, 1864. Admitted to hospital at Richmond on July 21, 1864, with dyspepsia and chronic diarrhoea. Furloughed for thirty days on or about August 4, 1864. Returned to duty in September-October, 1864. Discharged on November 2, 1864, by reason of disability.

WILKIE, WILLIAM G., Private

Enlisted in Catawba County at age 22, July 4, 1862, for the war. Reported present through May 11, 1863. Reported on detached service driving stock at Winchester, Virginia, in June-October, 1863. Rejoined the company prior to May 1, 1864. Furloughed on July 21, 1864. Returned to duty subsequent to September 1, 1864. Captured at Fisher's Hill, Virginia, September 22, 1864. Confined at Point Lookout, Maryland. Paroled at Point Lookout on March 17, 1865. Received at Boulware's Wharf, James River, Virginia, March 19, 1865, for exchange. Reported in hospital at Richmond, Virginia, March 20, 1865. No further records.

WITHERSPOON, DAVID C., Private

Enlisted in Catawba County on July 4, 1862, for the war. Hospitalized at Richmond, Virginia, October 3, 1862, with rubeola. Died in hospital at Richmond on October 19, 1862, of "typhoid pneumonia."

WITHERSPOON, JOSEPH ALEXANDER, Private

Born in Catawba County on October 1, 1843. Resided in Catawba County where he enlisted at age 18, July 4, 1862, for the war. Reported present or accounted for through October 31, 1863. Captured at Rappahannock Station, Virginia, November 7, 1863. Confined at Point Lookout, Maryland, November 11, 1863. Paroled at Point Lookout on or about December 24, 1863. Received at City Point, Virginia, December 28, 1863, for exchange. Returned to duty prior to May 1, 1864. Sent to hospital sick on July 16, 1864. Returned to duty in September-October, 1864. Reported present through February 28, 1865. Captured at Fort Stedman, Virginia, March 25, 1865. Confined at Point Lookout on March 28, 1865. Released at Point Lookout on June 22, 1865, after taking the Oath of Allegiance.

WITHERSPOON, WILLIAM C., Private

Resided in Catawba County and enlisted at Camp Godwin, Virginia, January 1, 1865, for the war. Reported present through February 28, 1865. Captured at Fort Stedman, Virginia, March 25, 1865. Confined at Point Lookout, Maryland, March 28, 1865. Released at Point Lookout on June 22, 1865, after taking the Oath of Allegiance.

YODER, JACOB M., Private

Enlisted in Catawba County at age 23, July 4, 1862, for the war. Wounded at Fredericksburg, Virginia, December 13, 1862. Hospitalized at Richmond, Virginia. Returned to duty prior to March 1, 1863. Reported present through October 31, 1863. Captured at Rappahannock Station, Virginia, November 7, 1863. Confined at Point Lookout, Maryland, November 11, 1863. Paroled at Point Lookout on February 24, 1865. Received at Aiken's Landing, James River, Virginia, February 25-28 or March 2-3, 1865, for exchange. Hospitalized at Richmond on February 26, 1865. Furloughed for thirty days on March 6, 1865. Survived the war.

YOUNT, PATRICK ALONZO, Sergeant

Born on May 1, 1843. Resided in Catawba County where he enlisted at age 19, July 4, 1862, for the war. Mustered in as Sergeant. Reported present through October 31, 1863. Wounded in the head (fractured skull) and captured at or near Rappahannock Station, Virginia, on or about November 7, 1863. Hospitalized at Washington, D.C., November 9, 1863. Died in hospital at Washington on November 20, 1863, of wounds.

ZEIZLER, J. R., Private

Place and date of enlistment not reported (probably enlisted subsequent to February 28, 1865). Captured in hospital at Richmond, Virginia, April 3, 1865. Reported in hospital at Richmond on May 28, 1865. No further records.

COMPANY F

This company was raised in Cabarrus County on July 4, 1862. It was mustered into service at Salisbury on July 17, 1862, and assigned to the 57th Regiment N.C. Troops as Company F. After joining the regiment the company functioned as a part of the regiment, and its history for the remainder of the war is reported as a part of the regimental history.

The following roster was compiled primarily from information in the microfilm edition of the Compiled Service Records of Soldiers Who Served in Organizations from the State of North Carolina (Record Group 109, M270), National Archives and Records Administration, Washington, D.C. Record Group 109 includes enlistment papers, pay vouchers, requisitions, letters of resignation, discharge certificates, and abstracts of medical and prisoner of war returns. Materials relating specifically to this company include muster rolls dated July, 1862-December, 1863, and March, 1864-February, 1865.

Also utilized in this roster were *The War of the Rebellion: A Compilation of the Official Records of the Union and Confederate Armies*, the North Carolina adjutant general's *Roll of Honor*, state militia records, newspaper casualty lists and obituaries, wartime claims for bounty pay and allowances, postwar registers of claims for artificial limbs, Confederate pension applications filed with the states of North Carolina, Tennessee, and Florida, Confederate Soldiers' Home records, and the 1860 and 1870 federal censuses of North Carolina. A search was made also for relevant letters, diaries, reminiscences, and other manuscripts in the Southern Historical Collection (University of North Carolina-Chapel Hill), the Duke University Library Special Collections Department, and the North Carolina Division of Archives and History.

Among the secondary sources consulted were records of the North Carolina division of the United Daughters of the Confederacy, postwar rosters, regimental and county histories, marriage bond, will, and cemetery indexes, published and unpublished genealogies, biographical dictionaries, the North Carolina *County Heritage Book* series, the *Confederate Veteran*, Walter Clark's *Histories of the Several Regiments and Battalions from North Carolina in the Great War, 1861-'65*, and the North Carolina volume of the extended edition of *Confederate Military History*.

OFFICERS

CAPTAINS

CANNON, JAMES C.
Resided in Cabarrus County and was by occupation a farmer prior to enlisting in Cabarrus County at age 31. Appointed Captain on July 4, 1862. Wounded in the hip at Fredericksburg, Virginia, December 13, 1862. Furloughed for ninety days on January 2, 1863. Resigned on May 30, 1863, by reason of the wound to his hip "which prevents his walking without pain & difficulty." Resignation accepted on June 11, 1863.

CARPENTER, PHILIP W.
Served as 1st Lieutenant and Captain of Company G of this regiment. Reported in command of this company in November-December, 1863, and March-August, 1864.

MORRISON, JOSEPH GRAHAM
Previously served as Adjutant (Captain) of this regiment. Appointed Captain of this company in January-April, 1864. Wounded in the leg near Petersburg, Virginia, May 16, 1864. Hospitalized at Richmond, Virginia. Furloughed on June 3, 1864. Hospitalized at Charlotte on June 8, 1864. Wounded at the headquarters of Maj. Gen. Robert F. Hoke, near Petersburg, in late August, 1864, while

en route to rejoin his company. "About three o'clock, A. M., a shell fell among the mess with whom he was staying, exploded, and tore off his left foot and severely wounded the calf of his right leg." [*Daily Carolina Watchman* (Salisbury), August 31, 1864.] Hospitalized at Chester, Virginia. Transferred to hospital at Charlotte, where he arrived on September 17, 1864. Furloughed on November 25, 1864. Reported absent sick in January-February, 1865. Survived the war. He was a brother-in-law of Lt. Gen. Thomas. J. ("Stonewall") Jackson and was known for "his coolness and alertness in the face of the enemy." [Clark's *Regiments*, 3:427.]

EDMONDSON, WILLIAM JAMES
Served as 2nd Lieutenant of Company H of this regiment. Reported in command of this company in January-February, 1865.

LIEUTENANTS

FOUTS, PETER E., 1st Lieutenant
Resided in Cabarrus County and was by occupation a farmer prior to enlisting in Cabarrus County at age 32. Appointed 1st Lieutenant on July 7, 1862. Reported present and in command of the company in November, 1862-February, 1863. Died in hospital at Richmond, Virginia, March 29, 1863, of unknown causes. Confederate medical records indicate that he was "brought into the hospital . . . in an ambulance in a dying condition and died within 1/2 an hour." [Previously served as Captain in the 84th Regiment N.C. Militia.]

KLUTTS, WILLIAM B., 2nd Lieutenant
Resided in Cabarrus County and was by occupation a farm hand prior to enlisting in Cabarrus County at age 23, July 7, 1862, for the war. Mustered in as Corporal. Reported present or accounted for through October 31, 1863. Appointed 2nd Lieutenant on June 1, 1863. Captured at Rappahannock Station, Virginia, November 7, 1863. Confined at Old Capitol Prison, Washington, D.C., November 8, 1863. Transferred to Johnson's Island, Ohio, where he arrived on November 14, 1863. Released at Johnson's Island on June 13, 1865, after taking the Oath of Allegiance. [Previously served as 2nd Lieutenant in the 84th Regiment N.C. Militia.]

LITAKER, JAMES F., 3rd Lieutenant
Resided in Cabarrus County and was by occupation a farmer prior to enlisting in Cabarrus County at age 26. Appointed 3rd Lieutenant on July 4, 1862. Reported present or accounted for through October 31, 1863. Captured at Rappahannock Station, Virginia, November 7, 1863. Confined at Old Capitol Prison, Washington, D.C., November 8, 1863. Transferred to Johnson's Island, Ohio, where he arrived on November 14, 1863. Released at Johnson's Island on June 12, 1865, after taking the Oath of Allegiance. He was "a quiet, unambitious man, but possessed of a courage rarely equaled and never excelled by anyone the writer saw on the field of battle." Another comrade wrote that he was "as brave as a lyon [*sic*]." [Clark's *Regiments*, 3:427; M. A. Walker to M. C. Walker, May 8, 1863, Civil War Roster Document No. 1087.]

PROPST, WILLIAM M., 1st Lieutenant
Born in Cabarrus County on February 17, 1831. Resided in Cabarrus County and was by occupation a farmer prior to enlisting in Cabarrus County at age 31. Appointed 2nd Lieutenant on July 17, 1862. Reported present or accounted for through February 28, 1863. Captured at Chancellorsville, Virginia, May 3-4, 1863.

Confined at Old Capitol Prison, Washington, D.C. Paroled at Washington on May 18, 1863. Returned to duty on an unspecified date. Promoted to 1st Lieutenant in May, 1863. Wounded in the side and captured at or near Gettysburg, Pennsylvania, July 1-5, 1863. Confined at Fort Delaware, Delaware, July 10, 1863. Transferred to Johnson's Island, Ohio, where he arrived on July 20, 1863. Transferred to Point Lookout, Maryland, April 22, 1864. Paroled at Point Lookout on May 3, 1864. Received at Aiken's Landing, James River, Virginia, May 8, 1864, for exchange. Furloughed on May 12, 1864. Reported absent without leave on October 9, 1864. Returned to duty in November-December, 1864. Captured at Hatcher's Run, Virginia, February 6, 1865. Confined at Old Capitol Prison. Transferred to Fort Delaware on March 1, 1865. Released at Fort Delaware on June 8, 1865, after taking the Oath of Allegiance. [Previously served as 1st Lieutenant in the 84th Regiment N.C. Militia. Reported in command of Companies D, F, and H of this regiment in November-December, 1864.]

NONCOMMISSIONED OFFICERS AND PRIVATES

ALEXANDER, PHI L., Sergeant

Enlisted in Cabarrus County on July 7, 1862, for the war. Mustered in as Sergeant. Reported present or accounted for through December 31, 1862. Reported on duty as acting Ordnance Sergeant from January 28 through September 1, 1863. Hospitalized at Richmond, Virginia, October 20, 1863. Returned to duty in November-December, 1863. Wounded at Winchester, Virginia, July 20, 1864. Returned to duty prior to September 1, 1864. Reported present in September-December, 1864. Reported at home on furlough from February 12 through February 28, 1865. Returned to duty on an unspecified date. Surrendered at Appomattox Court House, Virginia, April 9, 1865.

ARTZ, JOHN D., Private

Resided in Cabarrus County where he enlisted at age 15, July 7, 1862, for the war. Died in hospital at Richmond, Virginia, October 22, 1862, of "typhoid fever."

BARRIER, JOHN DANIEL, Corporal

Born in Cabarrus County on September 16, 1844. Resided in Cabarrus County and was by occupation a farm hand prior to enlisting in Cabarrus County at age 17, July 7, 1862, for the war. Mustered in as Private. Reported present through December 31, 1862. Hospitalized at Charlottesville, Virginia, March 7, 1863, with debility. Returned to duty on March 31, 1863. Captured at Chancellorsville, Virginia, May 3-4, 1863. Confined at Fort Delaware, Delaware. Paroled and transferred to City Point, Virginia, where he was received on May 23, 1863, for exchange. Hospitalized at Richmond, Virginia, July 1, 1863, with typhoid fever. Transferred to hospital at Danville, Virginia, on or about July 19, 1863 (suffering from chronic diarrhoea). Returned to duty on August 25, 1863. Promoted to Corporal in September-October, 1863. Received a bayonet wound and was captured at Rappahannock Station, Virginia, November 7, 1863. Confined at Point Lookout, Maryland, November 11, 1863. Paroled at Point Lookout and transferred to City Point where he was received on March 20, 1864, for exchange. Returned to duty in May-August, 1864. Wounded in the hip at Winchester, Virginia, September 19, 1864. Returned to duty prior to November 1, 1864. Reported present through February 28,

1865. Wounded in the left shoulder and/or arm at Fort Stedman, Virginia, March 25, 1865, while "most heroically" carrying the regimental colors. Captured in hospital at Richmond on April 3, 1865. Confined at Newport News, Virginia, April 24, 1865. Released at Newport News on June 26, 1865, after taking the Oath of Allegiance. He was "distinguished for his cool courage." [Clark's Regiments, 3:428.]

BARRINGER, JOHN J., 1st Sergeant

Resided in Cabarrus County and was by occupation a farmer prior to enlisting in Cabarrus County at age 27, July 7, 1862, for the war. Mustered in as Sergeant. Wounded at Fredericksburg, Virginia, December 13, 1862. Returned to duty in March-May, 1863. Promoted to 1st Sergeant in September-October, 1863. Reported present through October 31, 1863. Captured at Rappahannock Station, Virginia, November 7, 1863. Confined at Point Lookout, Maryland, November 11, 1863. Paroled at Point Lookout on March 16, 1864. Received at City Point, Virginia, March 20, 1864, for exchange. Returned to duty in May-September, 1864. Reported present through February 28, 1865. Wounded in both thighs and captured at Sayler's Creek, Virginia, April 6, 1865. Hospitalized at Annapolis, Maryland, April 15, 1865. Transferred to hospital at Baltimore, Maryland, May 10, 1865. Confined at Fort McHenry, Maryland, on or about May 17, 1865. Released at Fort McHenry on June 10, 1865, after taking the Oath of Allegiance.

BEAVER, MOSES WILSON, Private

Enlisted in Cabarrus County on July 7, 1862, for the war. Hospitalized at Richmond, Virginia, September 22, 1862, with a gunshot wound. Place and date wounded not reported. Died on September 23, 1862, of wounds.

BEAVER, WILEY, Private

Resided in Rowan County and enlisted at New Market, Virginia, at age 37, October 31, 1864, for the war. Reported present through February 28, 1865. Captured at Farmville, Virginia, April 6, 1865. Confined at Newport News, Virginia, April 14, 1865. Released at Newport News on June 26, 1865, after taking the Oath of Allegiance.

BEAVER, WILLIAM, Private

Resided in Rowan County and was by occupation a farmer prior to enlisting in Cabarrus County at age 28, July 7, 1862, for the war. Reported present through December 31, 1862. Sent to hospital on January 24, 1863. Returned to duty subsequent to February 28, 1863. Captured at Chancellorsville, Virginia, May 3-4, 1863. Confined at Fort Delaware, Delaware. Paroled at Fort Delaware and transferred to City Point, Virginia, where he was received on May 23, 1863, for exchange. Reported in hospital until September 23, 1863, when he returned to duty. Captured at Rappahannock Station, Virginia, November 7, 1863. Confined at Point Lookout, Maryland, November 11, 1863. Paroled at Point Lookout on March 16, 1864. Received at City Point on March 20, 1864, for exchange. Returned to duty in May-August, 1864. Captured at Fisher's Hill, Virginia, September 22, 1864. Confined at Point Lookout on October 3, 1864. Paroled at Point Lookout on March 17, 1865. Received at Boulware's Wharf, James River, Virginia, March 19, 1865, for exchange. Paroled at Salisbury on May 19, 1865. Took the Oath of Allegiance at Salisbury on June 25, 1865.

BIGHAM, JOSEPH HENRY, Private

Resided in Cabarrus County where he enlisted on July 7, 1862, for the war. Hospitalized on August 31, 1862, with intermittent fever.

Returned to duty on September 6, 1862. Hospitalized at Richmond, Virginia, September 24, 1862. Returned to duty on October 12, 1862. Reported present through February 28, 1863. Hospitalized at Lynchburg, Virginia, April 13, 1863, with diarrhoea. Returned to duty in November-December, 1863. Reported present in March-April, 1864. Wounded in the left arm at or near Cold Harbor, Virginia, June 5, 1864. Detailed as a hospital nurse at Salisbury on August 10, 1864. Rejoined the company in November-December, 1864. Reported present through February 28, 1865. Surrendered at Appomattox Court House, Virginia, April 9, 1865.

BLACK, CYRUS LAWSON, Private

Born on January 10, 1835. Resided in Cabarrus County and was by occupation a farmer prior to enlisting in Cabarrus County at age 27, July 7, 1862, for the war. Killed at Fredericksburg, Virginia, December 13, 1862.

BLACKWELDER, JOHN, Private

Born in Cabarrus County where he resided as a farmer prior to enlisting in Cabarrus County at age 27, July 7, 1862, for the war. Killed at Fredericksburg, Virginia, December 13, 1862.

BOGER, MONROE, Private

Resided in Cabarrus County and was by occupation a farm hand prior to enlisting in Cabarrus County at age 26, July 7, 1862, for the war. Reported present through October 31, 1863. Captured at Rappahannock Station, Virginia, November 7, 1863. Confined at Point Lookout, Maryland. Paroled at Point Lookout on February 24, 1865. Received at Aiken's Landing, James River, Virginia, on or about February 25, 1865, for exchange. Hospitalized at Richmond, Virginia, February 26, 1865. Died in hospital at Richmond on March 9, 1865, of "chron[ic] diarrhoea."

BOGER, PETER A., Private

Resided in Cabarrus County and was by occupation a farmer prior to enlisting in Cabarrus County at age 27, July 7, 1862, for the war. Reported present or accounted for through December 31, 1862. Died in camp near Port Royal, Virginia, February 4, 1863. Cause of death not reported.

BOST, JACOB W., Sergeant

Resided in Cabarrus County and was by occupation a blacksmith prior to enlisting in Cabarrus County at age 26, July 7, 1862, for the war. Mustered in as Corporal. Reported present through February 28, 1863. Promoted to Sergeant on March 10, 1863. Wounded in the face at Chancellorsville, Virginia, May 3-4, 1863. Returned to duty prior to June 14, 1863, when he was wounded in the breast at Winchester, Virginia. Returned to duty prior to July 2, 1863, when he was wounded in the left arm at Gettysburg, Pennsylvania. Captured at Gettysburg on July 2-5, 1863. Confined at Fort Delaware, Delaware. Paroled at Fort Delaware on July 30, 1863. Received at City Point, Virginia, August 1, 1863, for exchange. Hospitalized at Petersburg, Virginia, where he died on August 15-16, 1863, of "chronic diarrhoea."

BOST, RUFUS G., Private

Resided in Cabarrus County and was by occupation a farm laborer prior to enlisting in Cabarrus County at age 28, July 7, 1862, for the war. Reported present or accounted for through December 31, 1862. Sent to hospital on January 30, 1863. Died in hospital at Lynchburg, Virginia, February 5, 1863, of "pneumonia."

BROWN, JULIUS F., Private

Enlisted in Cabarrus County at age 31, July 7, 1862, for the war. Reported present through October 31, 1863. Captured at Rappahannock Station, Virginia, November 7, 1863. Confined at Point Lookout, Maryland, November 11, 1863. Paroled at Point Lookout on March 16, 1864. Received at City Point, Virginia, March 20, 1864, for exchange. Returned to duty subsequent to April 30, 1864. Captured at or near Harpers Ferry, West Virginia, July 8-9, 1864. Confined at Old Capitol Prison, Washington, D.C. Transferred to Elmira, New York, July 23, 1864. Paroled at Elmira on March 2, 1865, and transferred for exchange. Hospitalized at Richmond, Virginia, March 10, 1865, with debilitas. Captured in hospital at Richmond on April 3, 1865. Transferred on April 14, 1865. Survived the war.

BRUMLEY, WILLIAM C., Private

Enlisted in Cabarrus County on July 7, 1862, for the war. Reported present or accounted for through December 31, 1862. Hospitalized at Richmond, Virginia, January 12, 1863. Died in hospital at Richmond on January 20, 1863, of "pneumonia."

BUCKHART, ANDREW, Private

Resided in Davidson County and was by occupation a farmer prior to enlisting in Lenoir County at age 34, March 8, 1864, for the war. Reported present through October 31, 1864. Discharged on November 26, 1864, by reason of "insanity."

BUTNER, JAMES C., Private

Resided in Forsyth County and enlisted in Lenoir County at age 19, March 18, 1864, for the war. Sent to hospital sick on May 10, 1864. Returned to duty on September 9, 1864. Wounded in the left arm at Winchester, Virginia, September 19, 1864. Reported in hospital at Staunton, Virginia, October 2, 1864. Returned to duty in November-December, 1864. Captured at Hatcher's Run, Virginia, February 6, 1865. Confined at Point Lookout, Maryland, February 9, 1865. Released at Point Lookout on June 23, 1865, after taking the Oath of Allegiance.

CALDWELL, C. FRANK, Private

Resided in Cabarrus County and was by occupation a farmer prior to enlisting in Cabarrus County at age 30, July 7, 1862, for the war. Hospitalized at Richmond, Virginia, December 3, 1862. Returned to duty on December 27, 1862. Captured at Chancellorsville, Virginia, May 3-4, 1863. Confined at Fort Delaware, Delaware, May 7, 1863. Paroled at Fort Delaware and transferred to City Point, Virginia, where he was received on May 23, 1863, for exchange. Returned to duty prior to July 2, 1863, when he was reported missing in action at Gettysburg, Pennsylvania. He was presumably killed at Gettysburg.

CALDWELL, R. W., Private

Resided in Cabarrus County and was by occupation a farmer prior to enlisting in Cabarrus County at age 33, July 7, 1862, for the war. Reported present through May 11, 1863. Captured at Gettysburg, Pennsylvania, July 2-5, 1863. Confined at Fort Delaware, Delaware, on or about July 9, 1863. Died at Fort Delaware on October 12, 1863. Cause of death not reported.

CARRIKER, DANIEL M., Private

Born in Cabarrus County where he resided as a farmer prior to enlisting in Cabarrus County at age 28, July 7, 1862, for the war. Hospitalized at Richmond, Virginia, September 18, 1862, with diarrhoea. Returned to duty on September 26, 1862. Hospitalized at Richmond on October 16, 1862, with measles. Discharged from service on November 25, 1862, by reason of "pulmonary phthisis of some years standing." Died at home on May 1, 1863, of disease.

CHEEKS, JOHN W., Private
Resided in Cabarrus County where he enlisted at age 14, July 7, 1862, for the war as a substitute for James C. Johnston. Reported present through May 11, 1863. Dropped out sick on the march in West Virginia on July 12, 1863. Captured by the enemy on or about July 25, 1863. Took the Oath of Allegiance on or about July 31, 1863.

CLAY, WILLIAM H., Private
Resided in Cabarrus County and was by occupation a farmer prior to enlisting in Cabarrus County at age 28, July 7, 1862, for the war. Hospitalized at Richmond, Virginia, September 25, 1862, with typhoid fever. Returned to duty on December 4, 1862. Wounded by a "spent grape shot just above the right knee" at Fredericksburg, Virginia, December 13, 1862. Returned to duty in March-May, 1863. Reported present in May-October, 1863. Captured at Rappahannock Station, Virginia, November 7, 1863. Confined at Point Lookout, Maryland, November 11, 1863. Paroled at Point Lookout on February 24, 1865. Received at Aiken's Landing, James River, Virginia, February 25-28 or March 2-3, 1865, for exchange. Survived the war.

CLINE, JACOB A., Private
Was by occupation a farmer prior to enlisting in Cabarrus County at age 31, July 7, 1862, for the war. Sent to hospital on November 28, 1862. Returned to duty in January-February, 1863. Sent to hospital on April 1, 1863. Returned to duty subsequent to May 11, 1863. Reported present in June-October, 1863. Captured at Rappahannock Station, Virginia, November 7, 1863. Confined at Point Lookout, Maryland, November 11, 1863. Paroled at Point Lookout on March 16, 1864. Received at City Point, Virginia, March 20, 1864, for exchange. Returned to duty subsequent to April 30, 1864. Captured at Winchester, Virginia, July 20, 1864. Confined at Camp Chase, Ohio, July 28, 1864. Paroled at Camp Chase on March 2, 1865. Received at Boulware's and Cox's Wharves, James River, Virginia, March 10-12, 1865, for exchange. Survived the war. [North Carolina pension records dated 1901 indicate that he was "nearly deaf caused by concussion of shell."]

CLONTZ, JOHN A., Private
Previously served as Private in Company H, 7th Regiment N.C. State Troops. Transferred to this company on January 28, 1865. Hospitalized at Richmond, Virginia, March 25, 1865. Captured in hospital at Richmond on April 3, 1865. Transferred to Newport News, Virginia, April 23, 1865. Released at Newport News on June 30, 1865, after taking the Oath of Allegiance. [Contrary to 4:485 of this series, the correct spelling of his surname was probably Clontz rather than Clouts.]

COPE, JAMES WILLIAM, Corporal
Born on July 29, 1840. Enlisted in Cabarrus County at age 21, July 7, 1862, for the war. Mustered in as Private. Reported present through February 28, 1863. Promoted to Corporal in January-February, 1863. Captured at Chancellorsville, Virginia, May 3-4, 1863. Confined at Fort Delaware, Delaware, May 7, 1863. Paroled at Fort Delaware and transferred to City Point, Virginia, where he was received on May 23, 1863, for exchange. Died in hospital at Richmond, Virginia, July 6, 1863, of "diarrhoea acuta enteritis."

CORL, RUFUS W., Private
Enlisted in Lenoir County on March 12, 1864, for the war. Died in hospital on July 24, 1864. Place and cause of death not reported.

CORZINE, JAMES C., Private
Resided in Cabarrus County and was by occupation a farm hand prior to enlisting in Cabarrus County at age 24, July 7, 1862, for the war. Hospitalized at Richmond, Virginia, December 3, 1862. Returned to duty on December 27, 1862. Reported present in January-February, 1863. Transferred to Company C, 33rd Regiment N.C. Troops, April 11, 1863, in exchange for Pvt. William Earnhart.

CRESS, ALFRED J., Private
Resided in Cabarrus County where he enlisted at age 16, July 7, 1862, for the war. Reported present through February 28, 1863. Wounded in the right knee at Chancellorsville, Virginia, May 4, 1863. Hospitalized at Richmond, Virginia. Furloughed for fifty days on or about June 29, 1863. Detailed at Charlotte on April 10, 1864, by reason of disability. Rejoined the company in November-December, 1864. Wounded in both thighs and captured at Hatcher's Run, Virginia, February 6, 1865. Hospitalized at Baltimore, Maryland, February 11, 1865. Transferred to Fort McHenry, Maryland, May 9, 1865. Released at Fort McHenry on June 9, 1865, after taking the Oath of Allegiance.

CRESS, EDMUND, Private
Resided in Cabarrus County and was by occupation a farm laborer prior to enlisting in Cabarrus County at age 22, July 7, 1862, for the war. Reported present through May 11, 1863. Wounded in the arm and captured at Gettysburg, Pennsylvania, July 1-5, 1863. Confined at Fort Delaware, Delaware, on or about July 9, 1863. Died at Fort Delaware. Date and cause of death not reported.

CRESS, HENRY W., Private
Resided in Cabarrus County and was by occupation a farm laborer prior to enlisting in Cabarrus County at age 24, July 7, 1862, for the war. Hospitalized at Richmond, Virginia, December 12, 1862, with remittent fever. Transferred to Farmville, Virginia, December 20, 1862. Returned to duty on January 1, 1863. Wounded in the left thigh and captured at Gettysburg, Pennsylvania, on or about July 2, 1863. Hospitalized at Gettysburg. Transferred to Davids Island, New York Harbor, July 19, 1863. Paroled at Davids Island and transferred to City Point, Virginia, where he was received on September 27, 1863, for exchange. Hospitalized at Richmond. Returned to duty in January-April, 1864. Reported present through February 28, 1865. Surrendered at Appomattox Court House, Virginia, April 9, 1865.

CRESS, PHILIP A., Private
Resided in Cabarrus County where he enlisted on July 7, 1862, for the war. Reported present or accounted for through February 28, 1865. Captured at Farmville, Virginia, April 6, 1865. Confined at Newport News, Virginia, April 14, 1865. Released at Newport News on June 26, 1865, after taking the Oath of Allegiance. [Was about 26 years of age at time of enlistment.]

CRUSE, CALEB, Private
Resided in Cabarrus County and was by occupation a farm hand prior to enlisting in Cabarrus County at age 24, July 7, 1862, for the war. Reported present or accounted for through October 31, 1863. Captured at Rappahannock Station, Virginia, November 7,

1863. Confined at Point Lookout, Maryland, November 11, 1863. Paroled at Point Lookout on March 16, 1864. Received at City Point, Virginia, March 20, 1864, for exchange. Returned to duty subsequent to April 30, 1864. Captured at Charlestown, West Virginia, August 22, 1864. Confined at Old Capitol Prison, Washington, D.C. Transferred to Fort Delaware, Delaware, September 19, 1864. Released at Fort Delaware on June 19, 1865, after taking the Oath of Allegiance. [North Carolina pension records indicate that he was wounded at Winchester, Virginia, and Gettysburg, Pennsylvania.]

CRUSE, JOSEPH, Private

Enlisted in Cabarrus County on July 7, 1862, for the war. Reported present through May 11, 1863. Killed near Winchester, Virginia, June 14, 1863.

CRUSE, MOSES, Private

Resided in Cabarrus County and was by occupation a farmer or farm hand prior to enlisting in Cabarrus County at age 30, July 7, 1862, for the war. Sent to hospital at Richmond, Virginia, October 28, 1862. Returned to duty in January-February, 1863. Reported present on surviving company muster rolls through April 30, 1864. Company records indicate that he was captured near Harpers Ferry, West Virginia, July 8, 1864; however, records of the Federal Provost Marshal do not substantiate that report. Was probably killed at or near Harpers Ferry.

CRUSE, PAUL, JR., Private

Resided in Cabarrus County and was by occupation a farm laborer prior to enlisting in Cabarrus County at age 26, July 7, 1862, for the war. Reported present through December 31, 1862. Sent to hospital on February 20, 1863. Died in hospital at Lynchburg, Virginia, on or about April 10, 1863, of "fever."

DEATES, JOHN H., Private

Resided in Forsyth County and was by occupation a miller prior to enlisting in Lenoir County at age 39, March 18, 1864, for the war. Deserted near Kinston on May 2, 1864.

DEJOURNETT, CHARLES P., Private

Born in Cabarrus County on September 22, 1844. Resided in Cabarrus County where he enlisted at age 18, February 26, 1863, for the war. Reported present through October 31, 1863. Captured at Rappahannock Station, Virginia, November 7, 1863. Confined at Point Lookout, Maryland, November 11, 1863. Paroled at Point Lookout on February 24, 1865. Received at Aiken's Landing, James River, Virginia, February 25-28 or March 2-3, 1865, for exchange. Survived the war.

DORTON, DAVID M., Private

Resided in Cabarrus County and was by occupation a day laborer prior to enlisting in Cabarrus County at age 25, July 7, 1862, for the war. Hospitalized at Charlottesville, Virginia, December 7, 1862, with pneumonia. Furloughed for sixty days on January 16, 1863. Returned to duty in May-August, 1863. Hospitalized at Richmond, Virginia, November 25, 1863, with variola. Later contracted pneumonia. Furloughed on February 10, 1864. Returned to duty in March-April, 1864. Captured near Frederick, Maryland, July 10, 1864. Confined at Washington, D.C. Paroled and exchanged on an unspecified date. Reported absent without leave on November 25, 1864. Returned to duty in January-February, 1865. Hospitalized at

Richmond on or about March 22, 1865, with pneumonia. Captured in hospital at Richmond on April 3, 1865. Confined at Newport News, Virginia, April 24, 1865. Released at Newport News on June 16, 1865, after taking the Oath of Allegiance.

EARNHART, WILLIAM, Private

Previously served as Private in Company C, 33rd Regiment N.C. Troops. Transferred to this company on April 11, 1863, in exchange for Pvt. James C. Corzine. Reported present through August 31, 1863. Reported under arrest in September-October, 1863. Reason he was arrested not reported. Returned to duty in November-December, 1863. Reported present in March-October, 1864. Deserted at Woodstock, Virginia, November 10, 1864. Reported in confinement in the division guard house in January-February, 1865. Court-martialed on or about February 2, 1865, and sentenced to be shot. Sentence remitted. Returned to duty prior to March 25, 1865, when he was captured at Fort Stedman, Virginia. Confined at Point Lookout, Maryland, March 28, 1865. Released at Point Lookout on June 12, 1865, after taking the Oath of Allegiance. [Contrary to 9:150 of this series, the correct spelling of his surname was probably Earnhart rather than Earnhardt.]

ERVIN, SAMUEL P., Private

Resided in Cabarrus County and was by occupation a farmer or farm hand prior to enlisting in Cabarrus County at age 26, July 7, 1862, for the war. Hospitalized at Richmond, Virginia, October 28, 1862, with typhoid fever. Furloughed on or about December 2, 1862. Returned to duty in January-February, 1863. Hospitalized at Richmond on April 7, 1863, with pneumonia. Transferred to hospital at Danville, Virginia, April 27, 1863. Returned to duty in May-August, 1863. Captured at Rappahannock Station, Virginia, November 7, 1863. Confined at Point Lookout, Maryland, November 11, 1863. Paroled at Point Lookout on February 24, 1865. Received at Aiken's Landing, James River, Virginia, February 25-27 or March 2-3, 1865, for exchange. Survived the war.

FAGGART, JOHN M., Private

Resided in Cabarrus County where he enlisted on July 7, 1862, for the war. Reported present through February 28, 1863. Captured at Chancellorsville, Virginia, May 3-4, 1863. Confined at Fort Delaware, Delaware, on or about May 7, 1863. Paroled at Fort Delaware and transferred to City Point, Virginia, where he was received on May 23, 1863, for exchange. Returned to duty on an unspecified date. Hospitalized at Farmville, Virginia, August 3, 1863, with chronic diarrhoea. Returned to duty on or about September 22, 1863. Captured at Rappahannock Station, Virginia, November 7, 1863. Hospitalized at Old Capitol Prison, Washington, D.C., November 9, 1863, with chronic diarrhoea. Released from the hospital on December 5, 1863, and transferred to the prison compound. Transferred to Point Lookout, Maryland, February 3, 1864. Paroled at Point Lookout on March 16, 1864. Received at City Point on March 20, 1864, for exchange. Returned to duty subsequent to April 30, 1864. Wounded in the breast at Winchester, Virginia, July 20, 1864. Returned to duty in November-December, 1864. Reported on detail as a quartermaster guard in January-February, 1865. Rejoined the company prior to April 6, 1865, when he was captured at Farmville. Confined at Newport News, Virginia, April 14, 1865. Released at Newport News on June 26, 1865, after taking the Oath of Allegiance.

FILE, DANIEL S., Private

Resided in Cabarrus County and was by occupation a farmer prior to enlisting in Cabarrus County at age 26, July 7, 1862, for the war.

Reported present through October 31, 1863. Captured at Rappahannock Station, Virginia, November 7, 1863. Confined at Old Capitol Prison, Washington, D.C. Reported in hospital at Old Capitol Prison from November 9 through December 3, 1863. Transferred to Point Lookout, Maryland, February 3, 1864. Paroled at Point Lookout on February 24, 1865. Received at Aiken's Landing, James River, Virginia, February 25-28 or March 2-3, 1865, for exchange. Paroled at Salisbury on May 12, 1865.

FISHER, GEORGE M., Private

Resided in Cabarrus County and was by occupation a farm laborer prior to enlisting in Cabarrus County at age 31, July 7, 1862, for the war. Mustered in as Sergeant. Hospitalized at Richmond, Virginia, October 2, 1862, with icterus. Transferred to Salisbury on October 17, 1862. Reported absent without leave on March 1, 1863. Reduced to ranks on March 10, 1863. Listed as a deserter on July 1, 1863. Rejoined the company on September 28, 1864, and was sent to hospital. Returned to duty in January-February, 1865. Captured at Fort Stedman, Virginia, March 25, 1865. Confined at Point Lookout, Maryland, March 28, 1865. Released at Point Lookout on June 26, 1865, after taking the Oath of Allegiance. [Previously served as Captain in the 84th Regiment N.C. Militia.]

FISHER, JOHN W., Private

Resided in Cabarrus County and was by occupation a farmer prior to enlisting in Cabarrus County at age 32, July 7, 1862, for the war. Wounded in the shoulders and neck at Fredericksburg, Virginia, December 13, 1862. Returned to duty in March-May, 1863. Reported present through October 31, 1863. Captured at Rappahannock Station, Virginia, November 7, 1863. Confined at Point Lookout, Maryland, November 11, 1863. Paroled at Point Lookout on March 16, 1864. Received at City Point, Virginia, March 20, 1864, for exchange. Returned to duty subsequent to April 30, 1864. Deserted to the enemy at Martinsburg, West Virginia, or Hagerstown, Maryland, August 7, 1864. Confined at Old Capitol Prison, Washington, D.C., August 13, 1864. Transferred to Elmira, New York, August 28, 1864. Released at Elmira on May 29, 1865, after taking the Oath of Allegiance.

FURR, PAUL M., Sergeant

Resided in Cabarrus County and was by occupation a farmer prior to enlisting in Cabarrus County at age 27, July 7, 1862, for the war. Mustered in as Private. Reported present through October 31, 1863. Promoted to Sergeant in September-October, 1863. Captured at Rappahannock Station, Virginia, November 7, 1863. Confined at Point Lookout, Maryland, November 11, 1863. Paroled at Point Lookout on March 16, 1864. Received at City Point, Virginia, March 20, 1864, for exchange. Returned to duty subsequent to April 30, 1864. Captured near Harpers Ferry, West Virginia, on or about July 8, 1864. Confined at Camp Chase, Ohio, July 13, 1864. Released at Camp Chase on March 23, 1865, after taking the Oath of Allegiance.

GANT, JOHN G., Private

Enlisted in Lenoir County on March 9, 1864, for the war. Reported present through February 28, 1865. Surrendered at Appomattox Court House, Virginia, April 9, 1865. [Was about 19 years of age at time of enlistment.]

GIBSON, WILLIAM H., Private

Resided in Cabarrus County and was by occupation a farmer prior to enlisting in Cabarrus County on April 21, 1864, for the war.

Captured near Winchester, Virginia, July 20, 1864. Confined at Camp Chase, Ohio, July 28, 1864. Paroled at Camp Chase on March 2, 1865. Received at Boulware's and Cox's Wharves, James River, Virginia, March 10-12, 1865, for exchange. No further records. [Records of the Federal Provost Marshal dated July, 1864, give his age as 23.]

GOODMAN, JACOB P., Private

Resided in Cabarrus County and was by occupation a farmer prior to enlisting in Cabarrus County at age 27, July 7, 1862, for the war. Reported present through February 28, 1863. Captured at Chancellorsville, Virginia, May 3-4, 1863. Confined at Fort Delaware, Delaware, on or about May 7, 1863. Paroled at Fort Delaware and transferred to City Point, Virginia, where he was received on May 23, 1863, for exchange. Reported present in June-October, 1863. Captured at Rappahannock Station, Virginia, November 7, 1863. Confined at Point Lookout, Maryland, November 11, 1863. Paroled at Point Lookout on March 16, 1864. Received at City Point on March 20, 1864, for exchange. Returned to duty subsequent to April 30, 1864. Reported present through February 28, 1865. Surrendered at Appomattox Court House, Virginia, April 9, 1865.

HARDY, THOMAS, Private

Negro. Resided in Cabarrus County where he enlisted at age 25, July 7, 1862, as a "free man of color." Reported present on surviving company muster rolls through December, 1864. Reported "at home on permit" on February 20, 1865. His rank was reported as "Cook" in August-October, 1862; January-December, 1863; and March-August, 1864. Reported as Private in November-December, 1862, and September, 1864-February, 1865. The 1860 Cabarrus County census (page 9) indicates that he was "idiotic." No further records.

HARRIS, EDWARD M., Private

Resided in Cabarrus County where he enlisted at age 25, July 7, 1862, for the war. Mustered in as Sergeant. Hospitalized at Richmond, Virginia, November 8, 1862, with nephritis. Furloughed for thirty days on February 9, 1863. Reduced to ranks in May-June, 1863. Died at home on July 23, 1863, of disease.

HARRIS, MATHIAS LAIRD, Private

Resided in Cabarrus County and was by occupation a farmer prior to enlisting in Cabarrus County at age 24, July 7, 1862, for the war. Reported present through December 31, 1862. Hospitalized at Richmond, Virginia, February 16, 1863, with diarrhoea. Transferred to Charlotte on March 2, 1863. Returned to duty in May-August, 1863. Captured at Rappahannock Station, Virginia, November 7, 1863. Confined at Point Lookout, Maryland, November 11, 1863. Paroled at Point Lookout on April 27, 1864. Received at City Point, Virginia, April 30, 1864, for exchange. Hospitalized at Richmond on May 1, 1864, with debility. Furloughed for thirty days on May 8, 1864. Returned to duty prior to September 1, 1864. Reported present in September-December, 1864. Transferred to Company H, 7th Regiment N.C. State Troops, January 28, 1865.

HARRIS, ROBERT E. H., Private

Born in Cabarrus County where he resided as a farm hand prior to enlisting in Cabarrus County at age 26, July 7, 1862, for the war. Reported present through February 28, 1863. Wounded in the left leg at Chancellorsville, Virginia, May 4, 1863. Left leg amputated. Died in hospital at Richmond, Virginia, June 7, 1863, of "gangrene."

HARTMAN, HENRY H., Private

Born on November 1, 1823. Resided in Iredell County and was by occupation a farmer prior to enlisting at New Market, Virginia, at age 40, October 31, 1864, for the war. Reported present through February 28, 1865. Captured at Fort Stedman, Virginia, March 25, 1865. Confined at Point Lookout, Maryland, March 28, 1865. Released at Point Lookout on June 3, 1865, after taking the Oath of Allegiance.

HARTSEL, JONAH C., Private

Resided in Cabarrus County where he enlisted at age 27, July 7, 1862, for the war. Reported present or accounted for through October 31, 1863. Captured at Rappahannock Station, Virginia, November 7, 1863. Confined at Point Lookout, Maryland, November 11, 1863. Released at Point Lookout on June 27, 1865, after taking the Oath of Allegiance.

HOLMES, B., Private

Place and date of enlistment not reported. Federal medical records indicate that he was wounded in the thigh and captured at Gettysburg, Pennsylvania, July 1-3, 1863, and died in a Gettysburg hospital on July 17, 1863, following the amputation of his leg.

HOPKINS, P. N., Private

Resided in Cabarrus County and was by occupation a farm laborer prior to enlisting in Cabarrus County at age 30, July 7, 1862, for the war. Reported present through February 28, 1863. Captured at Chancellorsville, Virginia, May 3-4, 1863. Confined at Fort Delaware, Delaware, on or about May 7, 1863. Paroled at Fort Delaware and transferred to City Point, Virginia, where he was received on May 23, 1863, for exchange. Sent to hospital the same date. Furloughed for thirty days from hospital at Farmville, Virginia, September 9, 1863 (suffering from chronic diarrhoea, emaciation, and debility of six months' standing). Returned to duty prior to November 7, 1863, when he was captured at Rappahannock Station, Virginia. Confined at Point Lookout, Maryland, November 11, 1863. Paroled at Point Lookout on February 24, 1865. Received at Aiken's Landing, James River, Virginia, February 25-28 or March 2-3, 1865, for exchange. Survived the war.

HOWEL, JACKSON M., Private

Resided in Cabarrus County and was by occupation a farmer prior to enlisting in Cabarrus County at age 25, July 7, 1862, for the war. Reported absent sick at Salisbury on August 24, 1862. Reported present in November-December, 1862. Hospitalized at Richmond, Virginia, January 12, 1863. Died in hospital at Richmond on January 26, 1863, of "pneumonia."

HOWELL, DAVID S., Private

Resided in Cabarrus County and was by occupation a farmer prior to enlisting in Cabarrus County at age 37, July 7, 1862, for the war. Reported present or accounted for through December 31, 1862. Died in camp near Fredericksburg, Virginia, January 11, 1863, of "measles."

HOWELL, JOSEPH Y., Private

Resided in Cabarrus County and was by occupation a farmer prior to enlisting in Cabarrus County at age 36, July 7, 1862, for the war. Hospitalized at Richmond, Virginia, December 12, 1862. Died in hospital at Richmond on or about January 11, 1863, of "pneumonia."

ISENHOUR, RUFUS P., Private

Resided in Cabarrus County where he enlisted at age 27, July 7, 1862, for the war. Reported present through December 31, 1863. Detailed to work on gunboat at Kinston on February 7, 1864. Rejoined the company subsequent to April 30, 1864. Wounded in the leg at Charlestown, West Virginia, August 22, 1864. Captured at Harrisonburg, Virginia, on or about September 25, 1864. Confined at various Federal hospitals. Transferred to Point Lookout, Maryland, where he arrived on November 23, 1864. Released at Point Lookout on June 26, 1865, after taking the Oath of Allegiance.

JEETER, J. B., Private

Place and date of enlistment not reported. A regimental return dated September, 1862, states he was absent sick at Salisbury since August 24, 1862. Reported on duty in hospital at Richmond, Virginia, in June, 1863. Ordered to report for duty as a hospital guard at Lynchburg, Virginia, on or about July 1, 1863. A Confederate hospital record dated January 21, 1865, states that he was wounded in the leg on an unspecified date and was currently employed as a hospital nurse at Richmond. No further records.

KLUTTS, J. W., Private

Enlisted in Cabarrus County on July 7, 1862, for the war. Reported present through May 11, 1863. Killed at Gettysburg, Pennsylvania, July 1, 1863.

KLUTTS, LAWRENCE, Sergeant

Resided in Cabarrus County and was by occupation a farm laborer prior to enlisting in Cabarrus County at age 22, July 7, 1862, for the war. Mustered in as Private. Reported present through May 11, 1863. Furloughed home on August 25, 1863. Returned to duty and was promoted to Corporal in September-October, 1863. Reported present on surviving company muster rolls through December 31, 1864. Promoted to Sergeant on or about November 21, 1864. Captured at Hatcher's Run, Virginia, February 6, 1865. Confined at Point Lookout, Maryland, February 9, 1865. Released at Point Lookout on June 28, 1865, after taking the Oath of Allegiance.

KLUTTZ, ALFRED, Private

Born on November 8, 1845. Enlisted in Cabarrus County at age 16, July 7, 1862, for the war as a substitute for C. J. Klutts. Reported present or accounted for through October 31, 1863. Captured at Rappahannock Station, Virginia, November 7, 1863. Confined at Point Lookout, Maryland, November 11, 1863. Exchanged on an unspecified date. Returned to duty in May-August, 1864. Reported present through February 28, 1865. Captured at Farmville, Virginia, April 6, 1865. Confined at Newport News, Virginia, April 14, 1865. Released at Newport News on June 26, 1865, after taking the Oath of Allegiance.

LEE, GEORGE, Private

Resided in Cabarrus County and was by occupation a blacksmith prior to enlisting at New Market, Virginia, at age 34, October 26, 1864, for the war. Detailed for duty with the Pioneer Corps on November 8, 1864. Reported absent on duty with the Pioneer Corps through February 28, 1865. No further records.

LINKER, CALEB, Private

Born on November 11, 1832. Resided in Cabarrus County and was by occupation a farmer prior to enlisting in Cabarrus County at age 29, July 7, 1862, for the war. Reported present through May 11,

1863. Captured at Gettysburg, Pennsylvania, July 1-5, 1863. Confined at Davids Island, New York Harbor. Paroled at Davids Island on August 24, 1863. Received at City Point, Virginia, August 28, 1863, for exchange. Hospitalized at Richmond, Virginia, January 29, 1864, with a gunshot wound of the left hip. Place and date wounded not reported. Returned to duty prior to May 1, 1864. Wounded in the left knee and/or left thigh and captured at Cedar Creek, Virginia, October 19, 1864. Hospitalized at Baltimore, Maryland. Transferred to Fort McHenry, Maryland, May 9, 1865. Released at Fort McHenry on June 10, 1865, after taking the Oath of Allegiance.

LINN, JAMES R., Private

Resided in Cabarrus County and was by occupation a farmer or farm hand prior to enlisting in Cabarrus County at age 26, July 7, 1862, for the war. Reported present or accounted for through October 31, 1863. Captured at Rappahannock Station, Virginia, November 7, 1863. Confined at Point Lookout, Maryland, November 11, 1863. Hospitalized at Point Lookout on December 18, 1863, with smallpox. Released from hospital on January 27, 1864. Paroled at Point Lookout on March 16, 1864. Received at City Point, Virginia, March 20, 1864, for exchange. Returned to duty subsequent to April 30, 1864. Captured near Harpers Ferry, West Virginia, July 8, 1864. Confined at Camp Chase, Ohio. Released at Camp Chase on March 23, 1865, after taking the Oath of Allegiance.

LITTLE, JOHN D., Private

Resided in Cabarrus County and was by occupation a farmer prior to enlisting in Cabarrus County at age 35, July 7, 1862, for the war. Hospitalized at Richmond, Virginia, September 18, 1862, with diarrhoea. Returned to duty on September 23, 1862. Hospitalized at Richmond on October 8, 1862. Died in hospital at Richmond on October 9, 1862, of "rubeola & gangrene."

LONG, JOHN McKENDRE, Private

Born on February 26, 1846. Resided in Forsyth County and was by occupation a farmer prior to enlisting in Lenoir County at age 18, March 18, 1864, for the war. Captured at Winchester, Virginia, July 20, 1864. Confined at Camp Chase, Ohio, July 28, 1864. Released at Camp Chase on May 13, 1865, after taking the Oath of Allegiance.

McDANIEL, WILLIAM, Private

Enlisted in Cabarrus County on July 7, 1862, for the war. Hospitalized at Richmond, Virginia, October 10, 1862. Died in hospital at Richmond on October 24, 1862, of "typhoid fever."

MAHALEY, DAVID, Private

Resided in Rowan County and was by occupation a farmer prior to enlisting in Lenoir County at age 41, March 11, 1864, for the war. Discharged at Richmond, Virginia, July 1-4, 1864. Reason discharged not reported. [The *Raleigh Daily Confederate* of August 9, 1864, states that he was wounded at Winchester, Virginia, July 20, 1864.]

MELCHOR, JULIUS A., Private

Born on July 27, 1827. Resided in Cabarrus County and was by occupation a farmer prior to enlisting in Cabarrus County at age 34, July 7, 1862, for the war. Discharged on August 2, 1862, by reason of "chronic rheumatism."

MESIMER, HENRY E., Private

Born in Iredell County and resided in Rowan County where he was by occupation a farmer prior to enlisting in Cabarrus County on July 7, 1862, for the war. Discharged at Camp Vance, near Richmond, Virginia, October 9, 1862, by reason of epilepsy. Discharge certificate gives his age as 24.

MESIMER, MOSES M., Private

Resided in Cabarrus County and was by occupation a blacksmith prior to enlisting in Cabarrus County at age 45, July 7, 1862, for the war. Reported present on surviving company muster rolls through February 28, 1865. Surrendered at Appomattox Court House, Virginia, April 9, 1865. Detailed as division blacksmith during most of the war.

MILLER, TOBIAS, Corporal

Resided in Rowan County and was by occupation a farmer prior to enlisting in Cabarrus County at age 24, July 7, 1862, for the war. Mustered in as Private. Reported present through December 31, 1862. Sent to hospital on February 20, 1863. Returned to duty subsequent to May 11, 1863. Reported present in May-October, 1863. Promoted to Corporal in September-October, 1863. Captured at Rappahannock Station, Virginia, November 7, 1863. Confined at Point Lookout, Maryland, November 11, 1863. Paroled at Point Lookout on March 16, 1864. Received at City Point, Virginia, March 20, 1864, for exchange. Returned to duty prior to July 20, 1864, when he was captured at Winchester, Virginia. Confined at Camp Chase, Ohio, July 28, 1864. Released at Camp Chase on May 13, 1865, after taking the Oath of Allegiance.

MISENHEIMER, GEORGE W., Private

Resided in Cabarrus County and was by occupation a farm laborer prior to enlisting in Cabarrus County at age 29, July 7, 1862, for the war. Sent to hospital at Petersburg, Virginia, September 1, 1862. Returned to duty in January-February, 1863. Reported present or accounted for through October 31, 1863. Captured at Rappahannock Station, Virginia, November 7, 1863. Confined at Point Lookout, Maryland, November 11, 1863. Paroled at Point Lookout on April 27, 1864. Received at City Point, Virginia, April 30, 1864, for exchange. Hospitalized at Richmond, Virginia, May 1, 1864, with chronic bronchitis. Furloughed for thirty days on May 12, 1864. Returned to duty in September-October, 1864. Reported present through February 28, 1865. Captured at Fort Stedman, Virginia, March 25, 1865. Confined at Point Lookout on March 28, 1865. Released at Point Lookout on June 29, 1865, after taking the Oath of Allegiance.

MISENHIMER, ELIAS W., Private

Born in Cabarrus County where he resided as a farmer prior to enlisting in Cabarrus County at age 21, July 7, 1862, for the war. Hospitalized at Petersburg, Virginia, September 1, 1862. Discharged from service at Petersburg on December 22, 1862, by reason of "phthisis pulmonalis."

MOODY, G. L., Private

Resided in Cabarrus County and was by occupation a farm laborer prior to enlisting in Cabarrus County at age 29, July 7, 1862, for the war. Left sick at Salisbury on or about August 24, 1862. Returned to duty in January-February, 1863. Reported present through October 31, 1863. Captured at Rappahannock Station, Virginia, November 7, 1863. Confined at Point Lookout, Maryland, November 11, 1863. Paroled at Point Lookout on February 18,

1865. Received at Boulware's and Cox's Wharves, James River, Virginia, February 20-21, 1865, for exchange. Paroled at Charlotte on May 23, 1865.

MOON, MADISON, Private

Enlisted in Lenoir County on March 9, 1864, for the war. Reported sick in hospital on June 20, 1864. Reported absent without leave on October 10, 1864. No further records.

MOOSE, J. W., Private

Resided in Cabarrus County and enlisted at New Market, Virginia, October 26, 1864, for the war. Reported present through February 28, 1865. Captured at Farmville, Virginia, April 6, 1865. Confined at Newport News, Virginia, April 14, 1865. Released at Newport News on June 15, 1865, after taking the Oath of Allegiance.

MORRIS, CALVIN G., Private

Resided in Forsyth County and was by occupation a farmer prior to enlisting in Lenoir County at age 34, March 18, 1864, for the war. Reported present through September 1, 1864. Wounded in the right hip and captured at Winchester, Virginia, September 19, 1864. Hospitalized at Baltimore, Maryland, on or about October 23, 1864. Transferred to Point Lookout, Maryland, where he arrived on October 28, 1864. Paroled at Point Lookout on October 29, 1864. Received at Venus Point, Savannah River, Georgia, November 15, 1864, for exchange.

MORRISON, JOHN H., Private

Enlisted in Cabarrus County at age 28, July 7, 1862, for the war. No further records. [May have served later as Private in Company F, 9th Regiment N.C. State Troops (1st Regiment N.C. Cavalry).] Survived the war.

MORRISON, QUINCY C., 1st Sergeant

Resided in Cabarrus County and was by occupation a farmer prior to enlisting in Cabarrus County at age 33, July 7, 1862, for the war. Mustered in as 1st Sergeant. Reported present or accounted for through February 28, 1863. Wounded in the leg at Chancellorsville, Virginia, May 4, 1863. Hospitalized at Richmond, Virginia, where he died on August 8, 1863, of wounds. [Previously served as 1st Lieutenant in the 84th Regiment N.C. Militia.]

MOSER, J. MARTIN, Private

Resided in Forsyth County and was by occupation a farmer prior to enlisting in Lenoir County at age 34, March 18, 1864, for the war. Reported sick in hospital on May 3, 1864. Reported absent without leave from October 12, 1864, through February 28, 1865. Survived the war.

MURPH, ALEXANDER M., Corporal

Resided in Cabarrus County and was by occupation a farmer prior to enlisting in Cabarrus County at age 33, July 7, 1862, for the war. Mustered in as Corporal. Died in a house about ten miles from Fredericksburg, Virginia, January 13, 1863, of smallpox.

NEESE, WILEY D., Private

Resided in Alamance County and was by occupation a farmer prior to enlisting in Lenoir County at age 38, March 9, 1864, for the war. Hospitalized at Petersburg, Virginia, May 11, 1864, with enteritis. Transferred to Raleigh on May 20, 1864. Returned to duty prior to

September 1, 1864. Sent to hospital on October 19, 1864. Reported absent in hospital through February 28, 1865. No further records.

NEWELL, JAMES A., Private

Resided in Cabarrus County and was by occupation a farm hand prior to enlisting in Cabarrus County at age 30, July 7, 1862, for the war. Reported present or accounted for on surviving company muster rolls through February 28, 1865. Served as a teamster during most of the war. No further records.

OSBORNE, AARON, Private

Resided in Cabarrus County and was by occupation a day laborer prior to enlisting in Cabarrus County at age 32, July 7, 1862, for the war. Reported present or accounted for through October 31, 1863. Captured at Rappahannock Station, Virginia, November 7, 1863. Confined at Point Lookout, Maryland, November 11, 1863. Paroled at Point Lookout on March 14, 1865. Received at Boulware's Wharf, James River, Virginia, March 16, 1865, for exchange. No further records.

PHARR, CICERO H., Private

Enlisted in Cabarrus County on July 7, 1862, for the war. Reported present through May 11, 1863. Wounded in the hip at Gettysburg, Pennsylvania, July 2, 1863. Hospitalized at Richmond, Virginia. Returned to duty on September 2, 1863. Captured at Rappahannock Station, Virginia, November 7, 1863. Confined at Point Lookout, Maryland, November 11, 1863. Died at Point Lookout on February 20, 1865, of "chronic diarrhoea." [Previously served as 2nd Lieutenant in the 84th Regiment N.C. Militia.]

PHARR, JOHN E. S., Private

Resided in Cabarrus County and was by occupation a farmer prior to enlisting in Cabarrus County at age 28, July 7, 1862, for the war. Died in hospital at Richmond, Virginia, December 12, 1862, of "typhoid pneumonia" and/or "hepatitis."

PHARR, JUNIUS JAMES, Private

Born in Iredell County and was by occupation a farmer prior to enlisting in Cabarrus County on July 7, 1862, for the war. Died in camp near Fredericksburg, Virginia, January 10, 1863, of "a congestive chill." Was 23 years of age at the time of his death.

PHARR, SAMUEL E. W., Private

Resided in Cabarrus County and was by occupation a farmer prior to enlisting in Cabarrus County at age 31, July 7, 1862, for the war. Reported present through October 31, 1862. Appointed 1st Lieutenant of Company H of this regiment on December 19, 1862.

PHARR, SAMUEL K., Private

Enlisted in Cabarrus County on July 7, 1862, for the war. Hospitalized at Richmond, Virginia, November 8, 1862, with chronic diarrhoea. Returned to duty on December 30, 1862. Reported on duty as secretary to Brig. Gen. (subsequently Maj. Gen.) Robert F. Hoke from March 10 through October 31, 1863, and from March 1 through approximately July 30, 1864. Died in hospital at Petersburg, Virginia, August 19, 1864, of disease.

PHARR, WILLIAM R., Private

Resided in Cabarrus County and was by occupation a farmer prior to enlisting in Cabarrus County at age 24, July 7, 1862, for the war.

Wounded at Fredericksburg, Virginia, December 13, 1862. Returned to duty prior to January 1, 1863. Reported present through May 11, 1863. Detailed as a teamster on June 8, 1863. Died in hospital at Lynchburg, Virginia, November 29, 1863, of "febris typhoides."

READLING, SOLOMON, Private

Enlisted in Cabarrus County on July 7, 1862, for the war. Hospitalized at Richmond, Virginia, November 9, 1862. Returned to duty in January-February, 1863. Reported present through October 31, 1863. Captured at Rappahannock Station, Virginia, November 7, 1863. Confined at Point Lookout, Maryland, November 11, 1863. Paroled at Point Lookout on February 24, 1865. Received at Aiken's Landing, James River, Virginia, on or about February 25, 1865, for exchange. Hospitalized at Richmond on February 26, 1865. Furloughed for thirty days on March 20, 1865.

RICHIE, AARON, Private

Resided in Cabarrus County and was by occupation a farmer prior to enlisting at New Market, Virginia, at age 41, October 26, 1864, for the war. Reported present through February 28, 1865. Captured at Farmville, Virginia, April 6, 1865. Confined at Newport News, Virginia, April 14, 1865. Released at Newport News on June 15, 1865, after taking the Oath of Allegiance.

RIDENHOUR, JACOB W., Private

Resided in Cabarrus County where he enlisted on July 7, 1862, for the war. Hospitalized at Richmond, Virginia, September 18, 1862, with intermittent fever. Returned to duty on September 26, 1862. Detailed as a teamster on November 15, 1862. Rejoined the company in January-February, 1863. Reported present through October 31, 1863. Captured at Rappahannock Station, Virginia, November 7, 1863. Confined at Point Lookout, Maryland, November 11, 1863. Paroled at Point Lookout on March 16, 1864. Received at City Point, Virginia, March 20, 1864, for exchange. Returned to duty subsequent to April 30, 1864. Deserted to the enemy at Hagerstown, Maryland, or near Martinsburg, West Virginia, August 8, 1864. Confined at Old Capitol Prison, Washington, D.C. Transferred to Fort Delaware, Delaware, on or about September 19, 1864. Released at Fort Delaware on June 19, 1865, after taking the Oath of Allegiance.

RITCHIE, WILLIAM N., Private

Resided in Cabarrus County and was by occupation a farmer prior to enlisting in Cabarrus County at age 29, July 7, 1862, for the war. Sent to hospital at Lynchburg, Virginia, December 8, 1862. Returned to duty in January-February, 1863. Reported present through May 11, 1863. Captured at Gettysburg, Pennsylvania, July 2-3, 1863. Confined at Fort Delaware, Delaware, on or about July 9, 1863. Transferred to Point Lookout, Maryland, October 20, 1863. Died at Point Lookout on March 21, 1864. Cause of death not reported.

SAFRIT, JOHN M., Private

Resided in Cabarrus County and was by occupation a farm laborer prior to enlisting in Cabarrus County at age 26, July 7, 1862, for the war. Reported present through May 11, 1863. Left sick in Pennsylvania on June 23, 1863. Captured at Gettysburg, Pennsylvania, July 5, 1863. Confined at Fort Delaware, Delaware, on or about July 9, 1863. Died at Fort Delaware on September 18, 1863, of "chronic diarrhoea."

SCHENCK, GEORGE ALEXANDER, ———

Confederate gravestone records indicate that he was born on August 15, 1824, and served in this company.

SELL, PHILIP, Private

Enlisted in Lenoir County at age 21, March 11, 1864, for the war. Sent to hospital on June 15, 1864. Reported absent without leave on February 10, 1865. Deserted to the enemy on an unspecified date. Was furnished transportation from Washington, D.C., to Wilmington on or about April 17, 1865. [North Carolina pension records indicate that he suffered two broken ribs at Drewry's Bluff, Virginia, in April, 1864.]

SHANK, JOSEPH A., Private

Resided in Cabarrus County and was by occupation a farm hand prior to enlisting in Cabarrus County at age 18, July 7, 1862, for the war. Reported present through May 11, 1863. Furloughed home on August 25, 1863, "on account of bad health." Returned to duty in November-December, 1863. Reported present on surviving company muster rolls through April 30, 1864. Wounded in the right gluteal region and captured at Winchester, Virginia, July 20, 1864. Hospitalized at Cumberland, Maryland. Transferred to Camp Chase, Ohio, August 25, 1864. Paroled at Camp Chase on March 18, 1865. Received at Boulware's Wharf, James River, Virginia, March 27, 1865, for exchange. No further records.

SHAVER, E. C., Private

Enlisted in Lenoir County on March 11, 1864, for the war. Killed at Cold Harbor, Virginia, on or about June 10, 1864.

SHUMAKER, JOHN P., Private

Born on July 22, 1826. Resided in Iredell County and was by occupation a blacksmith prior to enlisting at New Market, Virginia, at age 38, October 31, 1864, for the war. Reported present through December 31, 1864. Wounded in the right thigh at Hatcher's Run, Virginia, February 6, 1865. Furloughed for sixty days on March 4, 1865. Paroled at Statesville on May 28, 1865.

SLOAN, JOHN G., Private

Resided in Rowan County and enlisted at New Market, Virginia, October 31, 1864, for the war. Reported present through February 28, 1865. Captured at Farmville, Virginia, April 6, 1865. Confined at Newport News, Virginia, April 14, 1865. Released at Newport News on June 14, 1865, after taking the Oath of Allegiance.

SMITH, J. NATE, Private

Enlisted in Cabarrus County on July 7, 1862, for the war. Hospitalized at Richmond, Virginia, November 9, 1862. Returned to duty on December 15, 1862. Died in camp near Port Royal, Virginia, February 27, 1863. Cause of death not reported.

SPAINHOUR, WILLIAM, Private

Enlisted in Lenoir County on March 18, 1864, for the war. Captured at Cold Harbor, Virginia, June 6, 1864. Confined at Point Lookout, Maryland, June 15, 1864. Paroled at Point Lookout on January 17, 1865. Received at Boulware's Wharf, James River, Virginia, January 21, 1865, for exchange. Hospitalized at Richmond, Virginia, January 22, 1865, with chronic bronchitis. Transferred on February 1, 1865. Survived the war. [Was about 41 years of age at time of enlistment.]

STANCIL, WILSON, Private

Resided in Cabarrus County and was by occupation a day laborer prior to enlisting in Cabarrus County at age 20, July 7, 1862, for the war. Reported present through May 11, 1863. Captured at Gettysburg, Pennsylvania, on or about July 2, 1863. Confined at Fort Delaware, Delaware, on or about July 9, 1863. Released at Fort Delaware on June 19, 1865, after taking the Oath of Allegiance.

STOWE, JAMES L., Private

Resided in Cabarrus County and was by occupation a farmer prior to enlisting in Cabarrus County at age 31, July 7, 1862, for the war. Reported present through October 31, 1863. Wounded in the head and right arm at Mine Run, Virginia, November 27-28, 1863. Right arm amputated. Hospitalized at Charlottesville, Virginia, where he died on December 6, 1863, of wounds.

SUTHER, A. L., Private

Enlisted in Cabarrus County on July 7, 1862, for the war. Hospitalized at Richmond, Virginia, January 11, 1863, with hemorrhoids. Died in hospital at Richmond on January 18, 1863, of "pneumonia."

TEETER, J. B., Private

Enlisted in Cabarrus County on July 7, 1862, for the war. Sent to hospital "with sore leg" on August 24, 1862. Returned to duty in January-February, 1863. Detailed as a hospital nurse on April 8, 1863. Reported on detail as a nurse or cook through February 28, 1865. Captured in hospital at Richmond, Virginia, April 3, 1865. Paroled on April 20, 1865.

TREXLER, JACOB, Private

Resided in Rowan County and enlisted in Lenoir County on March 12, 1864, for the war. Wounded in the shin at Winchester, Virginia, September 19, 1864. Returned to duty prior to October 19, 1864, when he was wounded in the left thigh and right ankle at Cedar Creek, Virginia. Hospitalized at Richmond, Virginia. Furloughed on January 10, 1865. Hospitalized at Richmond on an unspecified date. Captured in hospital at Richmond on April 3, 1865. Confined at Libby Prison, Richmond, on an unspecified date. Transferred to Newport News, Virginia, April 23, 1865. Released at Newport News on July 3, 1865, after taking the Oath of Allegiance. Hospitalized at Richmond on July 7, 1865. Took the Oath of Allegiance a second time on July 20, 1865, and was released. [Was about 33 years of age at time of enlistment.]

WALKER, MORGAN A., Corporal

Resided in Cabarrus County and was by occupation a farmer prior to enlisting in Cabarrus County at age 27, July 7, 1862, for the war. Mustered in as Private. Reported present through May 11, 1863. Promoted to Corporal in May-June, 1863. Wounded in the abdomen at Gettysburg, Pennsylvania, July 1, 1863. Captured at Gettysburg on July 5, 1863. Died in hospital at Gettysburg on July 30, 1863, of wounds.

WALTER, MARTIN A., Sergeant

Resided in Cabarrus County and was by occupation a farmer prior to enlisting in Cabarrus County at age 24, July 7, 1862, for the war. Mustered in as Corporal. Hospitalized at Richmond, Virginia, on or about September 1, 1862. Furloughed for thirty days on November 13, 1862. Returned to duty in January-February, 1863.

Promoted to Sergeant in September-October, 1863. Reported present through October 31, 1863. Captured at Rappahannock Station, Virginia, November 7, 1863. Confined at Point Lookout, Maryland, November 11, 1863. Paroled at Point Lookout on March 16, 1864. Received at City Point, Virginia, March 20, 1864, for exchange. Returned to duty in May-August, 1864. Captured at Charlestown, West Virginia, August 22, 1864. Confined at Elmira, New York, August 29, 1864. Released at Elmira on June 30, 1865, after taking the Oath of Allegiance.

WALTER, MARTIN VAN, Sergeant

Resided in Cabarrus County where he enlisted on July 7, 1862, for the war. Mustered in as Private. Hospitalized at Richmond, Virginia, on or about November 9, 1862. Returned to duty on or about December 6, 1862. Promoted to Corporal in May-August, 1863. Promoted to Sergeant in September-October, 1863. Reported present through October 31, 1863. Captured at Rappahannock Station, Virginia, November 7, 1863. Confined at Point Lookout, Maryland, November 11, 1863. Paroled at Point Lookout on March 16, 1864. Received at City Point, Virginia, March 20, 1864, for exchange. Reported sick in hospital on July 20, 1864. Returned to duty in November-December, 1864. Reported present through February 28, 1865. Captured at Farmville, Virginia, April 6, 1865. Confined at Newport News, Virginia, April 14, 1865. Released at Newport News on June 26, 1865, after taking the Oath of Allegiance.

WEAVER, HENRY, Private

Resided in Rowan County and enlisted in Lenoir County on March 9, 1864, for the war. Hospitalized at Richmond, Virginia, June 12, 1864, with a gunshot wound. Place and date wounded not reported. Furloughed for forty-five days on August 8, 1864. Reported absent without leave on October 8, 1864. Returned to duty in November-December, 1864. Reported present through February 28, 1865. Hospitalized at Richmond on April 2, 1865 (sick). Captured in hospital at Richmond on April 3, 1865. Transferred to Libby Prison, Richmond, on an unspecified date. Transferred to Newport News, Virginia, where he arrived on April 24, 1865. Released at Newport News on June 30, 1865, after taking the Oath of Allegiance.

WELCH, JOHN W., Private

Resided in Cabarrus County and was by occupation a farmer prior to enlisting in Cabarrus County at age 27, July 7, 1862, for the war. Reported present through December 31, 1862. Hospitalized at Richmond, Virginia, February 16, 1863, with diarrhoea. Transferred to hospital at Charlotte on March 9, 1863. Returned to duty in May-August, 1863. Captured at Rappahannock Station, Virginia, November 7, 1863. Confined at Point Lookout, Maryland, November 11, 1863. Paroled at Point Lookout on May 3, 1864. Received at Aiken's Landing, James River, Virginia, May 8, 1864, for exchange. Hospitalized at Richmond the same date with chronic diarrhoea. Furloughed for thirty days on May 12, 1864. Returned to duty in September-October, 1864. Reported present through December 31, 1864. Hospitalized at Richmond on February 9, 1865, with debilitas. Furloughed for sixty days on March 12, 1865.

WHITE, JAMES B., Private

Resided in Cabarrus County and was by occupation a farmer or farm hand prior to enlisting in Cabarrus County at age 22, July 7, 1862, for the war. Wounded in the left thigh at Fredericksburg, Virginia, December 13, 1862. Hospitalized at Richmond, Virginia. Returned to duty subsequent to January 6, 1863. Hospitalized at

Richmond on February 21, 1863, with debilitas. Transferred to hospital at Charlotte on March 5, 1863. Returned to duty in May-August, 1863. Reported present through April 30, 1864. Captured at Winchester, Virginia, July 20, 1864. Confined at Camp Chase, Ohio, July 28, 1864. Paroled and transferred on March 2, 1865. Received at Boulware's and Cox's Wharves, James River, Virginia, March 10-12, 1865, for exchange. Survived the war.

WHITE, JOHN R., Private

Resided in Cabarrus County and was by occupation a farm hand prior to enlisting in Cabarrus County at age 21, July 7, 1862, for the war. Killed at Fredericksburg, Virginia, December 13, 1862.

WHITE, JOHN W., Private

Resided in Cabarrus County and was by occupation a farm hand prior to enlisting in Cabarrus County at age 19, July 7, 1862, for the war. Reported present through February 28, 1863. Captured at Chancellorsville, Virginia, May 3, 1863. Confined at Fort Delaware, Delaware, on or about May 7, 1863. Paroled and transferred to City Point, Virginia, where he was received on May 23, 1863, for exchange. Died in hospital at Petersburg, Virginia, June 3, 1863, of "febris typhoides."

WHITE, JOSEPH A., Private

Born in Cabarrus County where he resided as a farm hand prior to enlisting in Cabarrus County at age 20, July 7, 1862, for the war. Reported present through October 31, 1863. Captured at Rappahannock Station, Virginia, November 7, 1863. Confined at Point Lookout, Maryland, November 11, 1863. Paroled at Point Lookout and transferred to Aiken's Landing, James River, Virginia, September 18, 1864. Received at Varina, Virginia, September 22, 1864, for exchange. Hospitalized at Richmond, Virginia, where he died on September 28, 1864, of a gunshot wound. Place and date wounded not reported.

WHITE, JOSEPH R., Private

Resided in Cabarrus County and was by occupation a farm hand prior to enlisting in Cabarrus County at age 26, July 7, 1862, for the war. Hospitalized at Richmond, October 8, 1862, with rubeola. Returned to duty on November 10, 1862. Sent to hospital on February 26, 1863. Hospitalized at Richmond on April 7, 1863, with acute diarrhoea. Transferred to Danville, Virginia, April 24, 1863 (suffering from debilitas). Returned to duty on May 12, 1863. Captured at Rappahannock Station, Virginia, November 7, 1863. Confined at Point Lookout, Maryland, November 11, 1863. Paroled at Point Lookout on February 24, 1865. Received at Aiken's Landing, James River, Virginia, February 25-28 or March 2-3, 1865, for exchange. Survived the war.

WHITE, THOMAS H., Private

Resided in Cabarrus County and was by occupation a farmer prior to enlisting in Cabarrus County at age 28, July 7, 1862, for the war. Wounded in the thigh at Fredericksburg, Virginia, December 13, 1862. Hospitalized at Richmond, Virginia, where he died on February 9, 1863, of "sec[on]d[ar]y hemorrhage & gangrene."

WIGGINS, ELAM A., Private

Resided in Cabarrus County and was by occupation a farmer prior to enlisting in Cabarrus County at age 37, July 7, 1862, for the war. Detailed as an ambulance driver on November 15, 1862. Rejoined

the company in January-February, 1863. Hospitalized at Richmond, Virginia, May 2, 1863, with acute rheumatism. Transferred to hospital at Lynchburg, Virginia, on or about May 8, 1863. Returned to duty on an unspecified date. Sent to hospital on October 5, 1863. Returned to duty in November-December, 1863. Reported present through April 30, 1864. Captured near Frederick, Maryland, July 10-12, 1864. Confined at Old Capitol Prison, Washington, D.C. Transferred to Elmira, New York, July 23, 1864. Paroled at Elmira on February 20, 1865, and transferred to the James River, Virginia, for exchange. Hospitalized at Richmond on March 3, 1865. Transferred on March 4, 1865. No further records.

WILSON, SPENSER, Private

Enlisted in Cabarrus County. Enlistment date reported as July 7, 1862; however, he was not listed in the records of this company until September-October, 1864. Company muster roll of that date states that he was captured on July 2, 1863; however, records of the Federal Provost Marshal do not substantiate that report. No further records.

COMPANY G

This company was raised in Lincoln County on July 4, 1862. It was mustered into service at Salisbury on July 17, 1862, and assigned to the 57th Regiment N.C. Troops as Company F. After joining the regiment the company functioned as a part of the regiment, and its history for the remainder of the war is reported as a part of the regimental history.

The following roster was compiled primarily from information in the microfilm edition of the Compiled Service Records of Soldiers Who Served in Organizations from the State of North Carolina (Record Group 109, M270), National Archives and Records Administration, Washington, D.C. Record Group 109 includes enlistment papers, pay vouchers, requisitions, letters of resignation, discharge certificates, and abstracts of medical and prisoner of war returns. Materials relating specifically to this company include muster rolls dated July, 1862-December, 1863, and March, 1864-February, 1865.

Also utilized in this roster were *The War of the Rebellion: A Compilation of the Official Records of the Union and Confederate Armies*, the North Carolina adjutant general's *Roll of Honor*, state militia records, newspaper casualty lists and obituaries, wartime claims for bounty pay and allowances, postwar registers of claims for artificial limbs, Confederate pension applications filed with the states of North Carolina, Tennessee, and Florida, Confederate Soldiers' Home records, and the 1860 and 1870 federal censuses of North Carolina. A search was made also for relevant letters, diaries, reminiscences, and other manuscripts in the Southern Historical Collection (University of North Carolina-Chapel Hill), the Duke University Library Special Collections Department, and the North Carolina Division of Archives and History.

Among the secondary sources consulted were records of the North Carolina division of the United Daughters of the Confederacy, postwar rosters, regimental and county histories, marriage bond, will, and cemetery indexes, published and unpublished genealogies, biographical dictionaries, the North Carolina *County Heritage Book* series, the *Confederate Veteran*, Walter Clark's *Histories of the Several Regiments and Battalions from North Carolina in the Great War, 1861-'65*, and the North Carolina volume of the extended edition of *Confederate Military History*.

OFFICERS

CAPTAINS

SPECK, JOHN FRANKLIN

Previously served as Sergeant in Company K, 1st Regiment N.C. Infantry (6 months, 1861). Appointed Captain of this company on July 4, 1862. Wounded in the left leg at Fredericksburg, Virginia, December 13, 1862. Left leg amputated. Resigned on July 7, 1863. Resignation accepted on August 19, 1863.

CARPENTER, PHILIP W.

Resided in Lincoln County and was by occupation a farmer prior to enlisting in Lincoln County at age 29. Appointed 3rd Lieutenant on July 4, 1862. Reported present through February 28, 1863. Captured at Chancellorsville, Virginia, May 4, 1863. Confined at Old Capitol Prison, Washington, D.C. Paroled on May 18, 1863. Promoted to 1st Lieutenant on June 2, 1863. Returned to duty on or about the same date. Reported present and in command of the company in June-December, 1863. Promoted to Captain in January, 1864, to rank from August 19, 1863. Reported present in March-December, 1864. Reported present but on daily duty in January-February, 1865. Captured at Sayler's Creek, Virginia, April 6, 1865. Confined at Old Capitol Prison. Transferred to Johnson's Island, Ohio, where he arrived on April 19, 1865. Released at Johnson's Island on June 18, 1865, after taking the Oath of Allegiance. He was "a most gallant and efficient officer." [Clark's *Regiments*, 3:424. Reported in command of Company F of this regiment in November-December, 1863, and March-August, 1864. Reported in command of Company E of this regiment in September-October, 1864.]

HUNTER, MILES H.

Served as Captain of Company B of this regiment. Reported in command of this company in January-February, 1865.

LIEUTENANTS

BOYD, JOHN H., 1st Lieutenant

Resided in Lincoln or Cabarrus County and was by occupation a "liquor seller" prior to enlisting in Lincoln County at age 30. Appointed 1st Lieutenant on July 4, 1862. Hospitalized on August 29, 1862, apparently with mumps. Returned to duty on or about November 10, 1862. Wounded in the side at Fredericksburg, Virginia, December 13, 1862. Returned to duty prior to January 1, 1863. Killed at Chancellorsville, Virginia, May 4, 1863.

CROWELL, ELI, 2nd Lieutenant

Born in Union District, South Carolina, August 2, 1829. Resided in Lincoln County and was by occupation a physician prior to enlisting in Lincoln County at age 32. Appointed 2nd Lieutenant on July 4, 1862. Reported present or accounted for through December 31, 1862. Resigned on February 5, 1863, because "the feeble condition of my health render[s] me unfit to attend to the duties of my office." Discharged the same date by reason of "chronic dysentery with tendency to dropsy." [Previously served as Captain of Company I, 88th Regiment N.C. Militia.]

ELMORE, CHARLES E., 3rd Lieutenant

Previously served as Private in Company K, 1st Regiment N.C. Infantry (6 months, 1861). Enlisted in this company in Lincoln County on July 4, 1862, for the war. Mustered in as Sergeant. Promoted to 1st Sergeant in January-February, 1863. Reported present through May 11, 1863. Appointed 3rd Lieutenant on June 2, 1863. Wounded in the face ("left eye destroyed") and captured at Gettysburg, Pennsylvania, July 2, 1863. Hospitalized at Gettysburg. Confined at Fort McHenry, Maryland, July 12, 1863. Transferred to Fort Delaware, Delaware, where he arrived on July 14, 1863. Transferred to Johnson's Island, Ohio, where he arrived on July 29, 1863. Paroled at Johnson's Island and transferred to City Point, Virginia, February 24, 1865, for exchange. Paroled at Charlotte on May 27, 1865. [Contrary to 3:53 of this series, the correct spelling of his surname is probably Elmore rather than Elmer.]

RENDLEMAN, JOHN M., 2nd Lieutenant

Resided in Lincoln County and was by occupation an overseer prior to enlisting in Lincoln County at age 24, July 4, 1862, for the war. Mustered in as Corporal. Promoted to Sergeant in September-October, 1862. Reported present through May 11, 1863. Appointed 2nd Lieutenant on June 2, 1863. Wounded in the groin at Gettysburg, Pennsylvania, July 1, 1863. Returned to duty in September-October, 1863. Captured at Rappahannock Station, Virginia, November 7, 1863. Confined at Old Capitol Prison, Washington, D.C., November 8, 1863. Transferred to Johnson's Island, Ohio, where he arrived on November 14, 1863. Released at Johnson's Island on June 13, 1865, after taking the Oath of Allegiance.

NONCOMMISSIONED OFFICERS AND PRIVATES

ABERNATHY, ROBERT A., Private

Resided in Lincoln County where he enlisted at age 26, July 4, 1862, for the war. Reported present through October 31, 1863. Captured at Rappahannock Station, Virginia, November 7, 1863. Confined at Point Lookout, Maryland, November 11, 1863. Took the Oath of Allegiance at Point Lookout on or about January 25, 1864, and joined the U.S. Army. Rejected for service and was released.

ADERHOLDT, WILLIAM MARCUS, Sergeant

Resided in Lincoln County and was by occupation a farmer prior to enlisting in Lincoln County at age 27, July 4, 1862, for the war. Mustered in as Private. Reported present or accounted for through May 11, 1863. Promoted to Sergeant on June 2, 1863. Wounded in the left foot and captured at Gettysburg, Pennsylvania, on or about July 2, 1863. Hospitalized at Gettysburg. Transferred to hospital at Chester, Pennsylvania, where he arrived on July 27, 1863. Confined at Point Lookout, Maryland, October 4, 1863. Paroled at Point Lookout on an unspecified date. Received at City Point, Virginia, on or about March 6, 1864, for exchange. Reported absent without leave on May 1, 1864. Returned to duty on May 28, 1864. Reported on duty as a provost guard in July-December, 1864. Rejoined the company in January-February, 1865. Surrendered at Appomattox Court House, Virginia, April 9, 1865. [Previously served as 2nd Lieutenant of Company A, 88th Regiment N.C. Militia. North Carolina pension records indicate that he was wounded in the left side on April 8, 1865.]

ANTHONY, DAVID, Private

Resided in Lincoln County where he enlisted at age 30, July 4, 1862, for the war. Died in camp near Fredericksburg, Virginia, January 6, 1863, of disease.

ARMSTRONG, ALLEN S., Private

Resided in Lincoln County and enlisted in Lincoln or Rowan County at age 26, July 4, 1862, for the war. Reported present through February 28, 1863. Captured at Chancellorsville, Virginia, May 3-4, 1863. Confined at Fort Delaware, Delaware, on or about May 7, 1863. Paroled at Fort Delaware and transferred to City Point, Virginia, where he was received on May 23, 1863, for exchange. Returned to duty prior to September 1, 1863. Captured at Rappahannock Station, Virginia, November 7, 1863. Confined at Point Lookout, Maryland, November 11, 1863. Paroled at Point Lookout on September 18, 1864. Received at Varina, Virginia, September 22, 1864, for exchange. Hospitalized at Richmond, Virginia, the same date with chronic diarrhoea. Furloughed for forty days on October 11, 1864. Returned to duty in January-February, 1865. Surrendered at Appomattox Court House, Virginia, April 9, 1865. [North Carolina pension records indicate that he was wounded at Fredericksburg, Virginia, December 25, 1862.]

AVERY, GEORGE, Private

Born in Lincoln County where he resided as a farmer prior to enlisting in Lincoln County at age 30, July 4, 1862, for the war. Reported present through October 31, 1863. Captured at Rappahannock Station, Virginia, November 7, 1863. Confined at Point Lookout, Maryland, November 11, 1863. Released at Point Lookout on January 25, 1864, after taking the Oath of Allegiance and joining the U.S. Army. Assigned to Company B, 1st Regiment U.S. Volunteer Infantry.

AVERY, PHILLIP, Private

Born in Lincoln County where he resided as a farmer prior to enlisting in Lincoln County at age 27, July 4, 1862, for the war. Reported present through October 31, 1863. Captured at Rappahannock Station, Virginia, November 7, 1863. Confined at Point Lookout, Maryland, November 11, 1863. Released at Point Lookout on January 25, 1864, after taking the Oath of Allegiance and joining the U.S. Army. Assigned to the 1st Regiment U.S. Volunteer Infantry.

BAGGERLY, THOMAS W., Private

Resided in Iredell County and was by occupation a wagonmaker prior to enlisting in Iredell County at age 37, October 31, 1864, for the war. Captured at Hatcher's Run, Virginia, February 6, 1865. Confined at Point Lookout, Maryland, February 9, 1865. Died at Point Lookout on February 16, 1865, of "congestive chills."

BAKER, JOHN A., Private

Resided in Lincoln County and was by occupation a farmer prior to enlisting in Lincoln County at age 28, July 4, 1862, for the war. Reported sick in hospital at Salisbury on August 7, 1862. Reported on detail as a teamster in November, 1862. Sent to hospital at Richmond, Virginia, December 9, 1862. Reported in hospital at Richmond on January 7, 1863, suffering from debilitas. Returned to duty on March 5, 1863. Hospitalized at Richmond on May 28, 1863, with typhoid fever. Returned to duty on July 3, 1863. Reported present through December 31, 1863. Reported on duty as a teamster in March-April, 1864. Captured at Winchester, Virginia,

July 20, 1864. Confined at Camp Chase, Ohio, July 28, 1864. Paroled at Camp Chase on March 2, 1865. Received at Boulware's and Cox's Wharves, James River, Virginia, March 10-12, 1865, for exchange. No further records.

BARNES, W. M., ———

North Carolina pension records indicate that he served in this company.

BEAM, JOHN F., Private

Born in Lincoln County and resided in Lincoln or Gaston County where he was by occupation a farmer prior to enlisting in Lincoln County at age 30, July 4, 1862, for the war. Hospitalized at Richmond, Virginia, November 8, 1862, with mumps. Returned to duty on December 16, 1862. Reported present through February 28, 1863. Wounded in the finger at Chancellorsville, Virginia, May 4, 1863. Finger amputated. Returned to duty prior to September 1, 1863. Captured at Rappahannock Station, Virginia, November 7, 1863. Confined at Point Lookout, Maryland, November 11, 1863. Paroled at Point Lookout on October 29, 1864. Received at Venus Point, Savannah River, Georgia, November 15, 1864, for exchange. Furloughed on December 2, 1864. Returned to duty in January-February, 1865. Captured at Fort Stedman, Virginia, March 25, 1865. Confined at Point Lookout on March 27, 1865. Released at Point Lookout on June 23, 1865, after taking the Oath of Allegiance.

BOOZER, WILLIAM, Musician

Resided in Lincoln County and enlisted in Rowan County at age 16, July 4, 1862, for the war. Mustered in as Private. Promoted to Musician (Drummer) in November-December, 1862. Reported present through May 11, 1863. Reported missing at Gettysburg, Pennsylvania, July 5, 1863. Was presumably killed at Gettysburg.

BRANCH, WILLIAM A., Private

Resided in Wake County and enlisted at Camp Holmes, near Raleigh, April 18, 1864, for the war. Reported absent without leave on September 9, 1864. Returned to duty in November-December, 1864. Reported present through February 28, 1865. Captured at Fort Stedman, Virginia, March 25, 1865. Confined at Point Lookout, Maryland, March 28, 1865. Released at Point Lookout on June 23, 1865, after taking the Oath of Allegiance.

BROWN, JACOB J., Private

Resided in Lincoln County and was by occupation a shoemaker prior to enlisting in Lincoln County at age 30, July 4, 1862, for the war. Sent to hospital at Richmond, Virginia, January 28, 1863. Died in hospital at Lynchburg, Virginia, February 17, 1863, of "pneumonia."

CANSLER, THOMAS J., 1st Sergeant

Previously served as Corporal in Company K, 1st Regiment N.C. Infantry (6 months, 1861). Enlisted in this company in Lincoln County on July 4, 1862, for the war. Mustered in as 1st Sergeant. Hospitalized at Richmond, Virginia, January 24, 1863. Died in hospital at Richmond on February 7, 1863, of "chronic diarrhoea."

CARPENTER, JOSHUA P., Sergeant

Resided in Lincoln County and was by occupation a farmer prior to enlisting in Lincoln County at age 32, July 4, 1862, for the war.

Mustered in as Private. Promoted to Sergeant on June 2, 1863. Reported present on surviving company muster rolls through February 28, 1865. Surrendered at Appomattox Court House, Virginia, April 9, 1865. [Previously served as Captain of Company H, 88th Regiment N.C. Militia.]

CLAY, J. F., Private

Resided in Lincoln County and enlisted in Rowan County at age 19, July 4, 1862, for the war. Wounded in the right thigh at Fredericksburg, Virginia, December 13, 1862. Reported absent wounded or absent sick through February 28, 1865. No further records.

CLAY, M. C., Private

Resided in Lincoln County where he enlisted at age 27, July 4, 1862, for the war. Mustered in as Sergeant. Reduced to ranks in September-October, 1862. Reported present or accounted for through May 11, 1863. Hospitalized at Richmond, Virginia, June 1, 1863, with typhoid fever. Furloughed for thirty days on or about July 3, 1863 (also suffering from chronic diarrhoea and gastritis). Returned to duty prior to September 1, 1863. Captured at Rappahannock Station, Virginia, November 7, 1863. Confined at Point Lookout, Maryland, November 11, 1863. Paroled at Point Lookout on February 24, 1865. Received at Aiken's Landing, James River, Virginia, February 25-28 or March 2-3, 1865, for exchange. Survived the war.

CORNWELL, JOHN J., Corporal

Born in Cleveland County* and resided in Lincoln County where he was by occupation a carriage maker prior to enlisting in Lincoln County on July 4, 1862, for the war. Mustered in as Private. Reported present or accounted for through February 28, 1863. Captured at Chancellorsville, Virginia, May 3-4, 1863. Confined at Fort Delaware, Delaware, on or about May 7, 1863. Paroled and transferred to City Point, Virginia, where he was received on May 23, 1863, for exchange. Returned to duty on an unspecified date. Promoted to Corporal on July 19, 1863. Captured at Rappahannock Station, Virginia, November 7, 1863. Confined at Point Lookout, Maryland, November 11, 1863. Released at Point Lookout on January 25, 1864, after taking the Oath of Allegiance and joining the U.S. Army. Assigned to Company B, 1st Regiment U.S. Volunteer Infantry. [Roll of Honor gives his age as 33 in July, 1862. Records of the Federal Provost Marshal give his age as 28 in January, 1864.]

CRAVER, A. J., Private

Enlisted in Rowan County on July 7, 1862, for the war. Transferred to Company E of this regiment prior to July 17, 1862.

CURRY, SAMUEL B. W., Private

Born in Cabarrus County and resided in Lincoln County prior to enlisting in Lincoln County at age 19, July 4, 1862, for the war. Discharged at Salisbury on August 10, 1862. Reason discharged not reported.

DEITZ, CHRISTIAN F., Private

Previously served as Private in Company K, 35th Regiment N.C. Troops. Discharged from that company on March 12, 1863, after providing a substitute. Enlisted in this company at Camp Vance on March 9, 1864, for the war. Reported present through August 31, 1864. Wounded in the left shoulder and lung and captured at Winchester, Virginia, September 19, 1864. Died in hospital at Winchester on September 25, 1864, of wounds.

DELLINGER, S. W., Sergeant

Resided in Lincoln County where he enlisted at age 23, July 4, 1862, for the war. Mustered in as Corporal. Wounded at Fredericksburg, Virginia, December 13, 1862. Hospitalized at Richmond, Virginia. Returned to duty in January-February, 1863. Reported present through May 11, 1863. Promoted to Sergeant on June 2, 1863. Captured at Gettysburg, Pennsylvania, on or about July 2, 1863. Confined at Fort Delaware, Delaware, on or about July 9, 1863. Transferred to Point Lookout, Maryland, October 15, 1863. Died at Point Lookout prior to September 1, 1864. Cause of death not reported.

DINGLER, WILLIAM D., Private

Resided in Iredell County and was by occupation a farmer prior to enlisting in Iredell County at age 37, October 31, 1864, for the war. Hospitalized at Richmond, Virginia, December 29, 1864. Returned to duty subsequent to February 28, 1865. Captured at Fort Stedman, Virginia, March 25, 1865. Confined at Point Lookout, Maryland, March 28, 1865. Released at Point Lookout on June 12, 1865, after taking the Oath of Allegiance.

ELMORE, LEWIS, Private

Resided in Lincoln County and was by occupation a farmer prior to enlisting in Lincoln County at age 26, July 4, 1862, for the war. Reported present through May 11, 1863. Injured "by fall of a tree" near Hagerstown, Maryland, July 12, 1863. Hospitalized at Richmond, Virginia. Transferred to another hospital on September 18, 1863. Returned to duty prior to November 1, 1863. Captured at Rappahannock Station, Virginia, November 7, 1863. Confined at Point Lookout, Maryland, November 11, 1863. Released at Point Lookout on March 8, 1864, after taking the Oath of Allegiance and joining the U.S. Army. Unit to which assigned not reported.

FARMER, ABSALOM, Private

Resided in Lincoln County where he enlisted at age 28, July 4, 1862, for the war. Hospitalized at Richmond, Virginia, December 9, 1862, with typhoid pneumonia. Returned to duty on January 13, 1863. Reported present through May 11, 1863. Wounded in the arm and captured at Gettysburg, Pennsylvania, July 2, 1863. Arm amputated. Died in hospital at Gettysburg on July 26, 1863, of wounds.

FARMER, CALEB A., Private

Resided in Lincoln County where he enlisted at age 27, July 4, 1862, for the war. Reported present through February 28, 1863. Hospitalized at Richmond, Virginia, April 25, 1863, with chronic diarrhoea. Died in hospital at Richmond on June 2, 1863, of "feb[ris] typhoides."

FARMER, JOHN A., JR., Private

Resided in Lincoln County where he enlisted at age 27, July 4, 1862, for the war. Hospitalized at Richmond, Virginia, October 5, 1862, with ulcus. Returned to duty on January 15, 1863. Died in camp at Port Royal, Virginia, on or about February 14, 1863, of "dysentery."

FURR, CALEB, Private

Resided in Lincoln County and was by occupation a farm hand prior to enlisting in Rowan County at age 20, July 4, 1862, for the war. Hospitalized at Richmond, Virginia, October 5, 1862, with rubeola. Furloughed on or about November 6, 1862. Returned to duty prior to January 1, 1863. Wounded in the thigh at

Chancellorsville, Virginia, May 4, 1863. Died in hospital at Richmond on May 21, 1863, of wounds.

FURR, SIRUS J., Private

Resided in Lincoln County and enlisted in Rowan County at age 27, July 4, 1862, for the war. Hospitalized at Richmond, Virginia, September 22, 1862. Reported absent sick through December 31, 1863. Returned to duty in January-April, 1864. Reported absent sick from July 15, 1864, through February 28, 1865. No further records.

GHEEN, W. HENRY, Private

Resided in Lincoln County and was by occupation a cabinetmaker prior to enlisting in Lincoln County at age 19, July 4, 1862, for the war. Killed at Fredericksburg, Virginia, December 13, 1862.

GILBERT, ALFRED, Private

Resided in Lincoln County and enlisted in Rowan County at age 24, July 4, 1862, for the war. Hospitalized at Richmond, Virginia, November 9, 1862, with rheumatism. Transferred to hospital at Danville, Virginia, December 23, 1862. Returned to duty subsequent to May 11, 1863. Sent to hospital from camp near Winchester, Virginia, June 16, 1863. Hospitalized at Richmond on September 16, 1863, with a gunshot wound. Place and date wounded not reported. Furloughed for thirty days on October 10, 1863. Returned to duty in January-April, 1864. Reported absent sick from June 20 through August 31, 1864. Reported absent without leave on October 26, 1864. Returned to duty in November-December, 1864. Reported present through February 28, 1865. Killed at Fort Stedman, Virginia, March 25, 1865.

GREENWAY, BENJAMIN, Private

Place and date of enlistment not reported (probably enlisted subsequent to February 28, 1865). A Federal Provost Marshal record filed at Nashville, Tennessee, states he was captured at Salisbury on April 13, 1865, and transferred to Louisville, Kentucky, April 29, 1865. No further records.

HALLMAN, JOSEPH D., Private

Resided in Lincoln County and enlisted in Rowan County at age 21, July 4, 1862, for the war. Hospitalized at Richmond, Virginia, November 9, 1862, with dysentery. Returned to duty prior to January 1, 1863. Reported present or accounted for through February 28, 1865. Captured at Fort Stedman, Virginia, March 25, 1865. Confined at Point Lookout, Maryland, March 28, 1865. Paroled and exchanged on an unspecified date. Survived the war. [North Carolina pension records indicate that he was "hit five times" during the war but was "not wounded bad."]

HALLMAN, LABAN, Private

Enlisted in Catawba County on February 20, 1864, for the war. Reported present through April 30, 1864. Deserted near Fairfield, Virginia, June 26, 1864. Returned to duty in September-October, 1864. Reported present through February 28, 1865. Surrendered at Appomattox Court House, Virginia, April 9, 1865. [Was about 40 years of age at time of enlistment. North Carolina pension records indicate that he was wounded in the knee at Cedar Creek, Virginia, in October, 1864.]

HALLMAN, ROBERT L., Private

Enlisted in Lenoir County at age 18, March 10, 1864, for the war. Deserted near Fairfield, Virginia, June 26, 1864. Returned to duty

in September-October, 1864. Reported present through February 28, 1865. Surrendered at Appomattox Court House, Virginia, April 9, 1865.

HANELINE, JACOB, Private

Enlisted at Camp Holmes, near Raleigh, February 18, 1864, for the war. Reported present through April 30, 1864. Reported under arrest on July 18, 1864. Reason he was arrested not reported. Returned to duty in January-February, 1865. Captured at Farmville, Virginia, April 6, 1865. Confined at Newport News, Virginia, April 14, 1865. Died in hospital at Newport News on April 26, 1865, of "diarrhoea chr[onica]."

HAUSS, ADAM A., Private

Born in Lincoln County where he resided as a farmer or farm laborer prior to enlisting in Lincoln County at age 21, July 4, 1862, for the war. Reported present through February 28, 1863. Killed at Chancellorsville, Virginia, May 4, 1863.

HAUSS, ANDREW, Private

Resided in Lincoln County where he enlisted at age 35, July 4, 1862, for the war. Reported present or accounted for through April 30, 1864. Reported absent sick on July 8, 1864. Returned to duty in September-October, 1864. Reported present through February 28, 1865. Surrendered at Appomattox Court House, Virginia, April 9, 1865.

HAUSS, CEPHUS A., Private

Born in Lincoln County where he resided as a farmer prior to enlisting in Lincoln County at age 19, July 4, 1862, for the war. Wounded at Fredericksburg, Virginia, December 13, 1862. Died in Lincoln County on March 17, 1863, of wounds.

HAUSS, JOHN R., Private

Born in Lincoln County where he resided as a carriage maker prior to enlisting in Lincoln County at age 30, July 4, 1862, for the war. Reported present through February 28, 1863. Hospitalized at Richmond, Virginia, May 1, 1863, with chronic diarrhoea. Transferred to hospital at Danville, Virginia, May 7, 1863. Died in hospital at Danville on July 16, 1863, of "febris continua."

HAVENER, GEORGE WASHINGTON, JR., Private

Born on January 27, 1833. Resided in Lincoln County and was by occupation a farmer prior to enlisting in Lincoln County at age 29, July 4, 1862, for the war. Reported sick in hospital in September-October, 1862. Apparently returned to duty in November-December, 1862. Hospitalized at Richmond, Virginia, January 9, 1863, with bronchitis. Returned to duty in May-August, 1863. Reported present through February 28, 1865. Surrendered at Appomattox Court House, Virginia, April 9, 1865.

HAVENER, HENRY P., Private

Resided in Lincoln County where he enlisted at age 23, July 4, 1862, for the war. Hospitalized at Richmond, Virginia, October 18, 1862. Furloughed on December 6, 1862. Returned to duty in January-February, 1863. Reported present through October 31, 1863. Captured at Rappahannock Station, Virginia, November 7, 1863. Confined at Point Lookout, Maryland, November 11, 1863. Paroled at Point Lookout on February 10, 1865. Received at Cox's Wharf, James River, Virginia, February 14, 1865, for exchange. Hospitalized at Richmond the same date with debilitas. Furloughed for sixty days on February 24, 1865. Captured and paroled at Athens, Georgia, May 8, 1865.

HAYNES, WILLIAM H., Private

Resided in Lincoln County where he enlisted at age 34, July 4, 1862, for the war. Hospitalized at Richmond, Virginia, October 20, 1862, with rubeola. Returned to duty on November 10, 1862. Sent to hospital from camp near Fredericksburg, Virginia, January 27, 1863. Died in hospital at Lynchburg, Virginia, February 4, 1863, of "febris typhoides" and/or "measles."

HELMS, PINKNEY A., Private

Resided in Lincoln County where he enlisted at age 34, July 4, 1862, for the war. Hospitalized at Richmond, Virginia, November 8, 1862, with mumps. Returned to duty on December 16, 1862. Sent to hospital at Richmond on January 6, 1863. Returned to duty prior to March 1, 1863. Sent to hospital from camp near Fredericksburg, Virginia, April 6, 1863. Detailed for duty as a hospital nurse at Lynchburg, Virginia, November 21, 1863. Captured at Lynchburg in April, 1865. Survived the war.

HENKLE, CICERO, Private

Resided in Catawba County and was by occupation a farmer prior to enlisting at Camp Vance at age 40, March 9, 1864, for the war. Reported present through August 31, 1864. Wounded in the right thigh at Winchester, Virginia, September 19, 1864. Hospitalized at Charlottesville, Virginia. Transferred to hospital at Lynchburg, Virginia, September 26, 1864. Reported absent wounded through February 28, 1865. Returned to duty on an unspecified date. Surrendered at Appomattox Court House, Virginia, April 9, 1865.

HENSDALE, MARTIN V., Private

Enlisted in Forsyth County on March 12, 1864, for the war. Reported present through August 31, 1864. Wounded in the lower left leg at Winchester, Virginia, September 19, 1864. Reported absent wounded through February 28, 1865. Survived the war. [Was about 28 years of age at time of enlistment.]

HOBBS, WILLIAM H., Private

Born in Lincoln County where he resided as a farmer prior to enlisting in Lincoln County at age 19, July 4, 1862, for the war. Hospitalized at Richmond, Virginia, October 4, 1862, with a wound of the right arm. Place and date wounded not reported. Discharged at Richmond on November 25, 1862, by reason of "anchylosis of right wrist joint caused by punctured [sic] wound."

HOLDER, WILLIAM H., Private

Resided in Forsyth County and was by occupation a day laborer prior to enlisting at Camp Holmes, near Raleigh, at age 42, March 12, 1864, for the war. Hospitalized at Richmond, Virginia, May 15, 1864, with a gunshot wound of the elbow joint. Place and date wounded not reported. Died in hospital at Richmond or at Farmville, Virginia, July 8, 1864, of wounds.

HOUSER, JOHN, Sergeant

Resided in Lincoln County where he enlisted at age 30, July 4, 1862, for the war. Mustered in as Corporal. Hospitalized at Richmond, Virginia, October 9, 1862, with typhoid fever. Furloughed on October 27, 1862. Hospitalized at Richmond on December 6, 1862, with debility. Returned to duty on February 2, 1863. Promoted to Sergeant in May-June, 1863. Captured at Gettysburg,

Pennsylvania, July 2, 1863. Confined at Fort Delaware, Delaware, on or about July 9, 1863. Transferred to Point Lookout, Maryland, on or about October 20, 1863. Died in hospital at Point Lookout on December 1, 1863, of "chronic diarrhoea & erysipelas."

HOUSER, JONAS, Private

Resided in Lincoln County and was by occupation a farmer prior to enlisting in Lincoln County at age 34, July 4, 1862, for the war. Hospitalized at Richmond, Virginia, October 30, 1862, with typhoid fever. Returned to duty in January-February, 1863. Reported present or accounted for on surviving company muster rolls through April 30, 1864. Captured (or deserted to the enemy) at Middletown, Maryland, on or about July 10, 1864. Confined at Fort Delaware, Delaware, July 19, 1864. Died at Fort Delaware on January 25, 1865, of "pneumonia."

HUSS, HENRY, Private

Resided in Lincoln County and was by occupation a farm laborer prior to enlisting in Lincoln County at age 28, July 4, 1862, for the war. Mustered in as Private. Promoted to Corporal in September-October, 1862. Reduced to ranks on June 13, 1863. Reported present through October 31, 1863. Captured at Rappahannock Station, Virginia, November 7, 1863. Confined at Point Lookout, Maryland, November 11, 1863. Paroled at Point Lookout on February 18, 1865. Received at Boulware's Wharf, James River, Virginia, February 20-21, 1865, for exchange. Survived the war.

JACKSON, CURTIS L., Private

Previously served as Private in Company K, 1st Regiment N.C. Infantry (6 months, 1861). Enlisted in this company in Rowan County on July 4, 1862, for the war. Reported present or accounted for through May 11, 1863. Deserted to the enemy in Pennsylvania on June 27, 1863. Confined at Fort Delaware, Delaware, on or about July 2, 1863. Transferred to Fort Mifflin, Pennsylvania, prior to November 30, 1863. Released at Fort Mifflin on January 1, 1864, "for the purpose of working for [the] government by order [of] Gen[era]l [George] Cadwalader."

JOHNSON, HENRY, Private

Resided in Lincoln County where he enlisted at age 28, July 4, 1862, for the war. Sent to hospital at Richmond, Virginia, January 27, 1863. Died in hospital at Lynchburg, Virginia, April 24 or June 8, 1863, of "pneumonia."

JOHNSON, WILLIAM H. C., Private

Resided in Forsyth County and was by occupation a farmer prior to enlisting at Camp Holmes, near Raleigh, March 12, 1864, for the war. Hospitalized at Richmond, Virginia, June 14, 1864, with a gunshot wound. Place and date wounded not reported. Furloughed for thirty days on August 4, 1864. Hospitalized at Richmond on September 1, 1864, with chronic diarrhoea. Furloughed for thirty days on September 5, 1864. Hospitalized at Richmond on October 5, 1864, with intermittent fever. Returned to duty on January 11, 1865. Captured at Fort Stedman, Virginia, March 25, 1865. Confined at Point Lookout, Maryland, March 31, 1865. Released at Point Lookout on May 12-14, 1865, after taking the Oath of Allegiance. [Was about 19 years of age at time of enlistment.]

KEEVER, HENRY, Private

Resided in Lincoln County and was by occupation a blacksmith prior to enlisting in Lincoln County at age 34, July 4, 1862, for the war. Hospitalized at Richmond, Virginia, October 8, 1862, with rubeola. Furloughed for thirty days on October 30, 1862. Returned to duty prior to January 1, 1863. Hospitalized at Richmond on May 18, 1863, with remittent fever. Transferred to Charlotte on June 27, 1863. Returned to duty in November-December, 1863. Detailed to work on gunboat at Kinston on February 5, 1864. Reported on detached service at Kinston through December 31, 1864. Reported absent without leave on February 20, 1865. Captured and paroled at Athens, Georgia, May 8, 1865.

LEONARD, WILLIAM P., Private

Resided in Lincoln County and was by occupation a farmer prior to enlisting in Lincoln County at age 35, July 4, 1862, for the war. Hospitalized at Richmond, Virginia, November 8, 1862, with intermittent fever. Apparently returned to duty but was hospitalized at Richmond on December 16, 1862, with rheumatism and/or diarrhoea. Transferred to hospital at Danville, Virginia, January 8, 1863. Returned to duty on March 24, 1863. Reported present on surviving company muster rolls through April 30, 1864. Died of disease in Lincoln County on August 19, 1864, while at home on sick furlough.

LINGERFELT, DANIEL, Private

Resided in Lincoln County where he enlisted at age 25, July 4, 1862, for the war. Reported present or accounted for through February 28, 1863. Captured at Chancellorsville, Virginia, May 3-4, 1863. Confined at Fort Delaware, Delaware, on or about May 7, 1863. Paroled and transferred to City Point, Virginia, where he was received on May 23, 1863, for exchange. Reported absent without leave on September 1, 1863. Reported at home on furlough in September-October, 1863. Returned to duty prior to December 31, 1863. Captured at Drewry's Bluff, Virginia, May 16, 1864. Confined at Point Lookout, Maryland, May 19, 1864. Transferred to Elmira, New York, August 15, 1864. Paroled at Elmira on October 11, 1864. Received at Venus Point, Savannah River, Georgia, November 15, 1864, for exchange. Reported absent on sick furlough from November 26, 1864, through February 28, 1865. Survived the war. [North Carolina pension records indicate that he was wounded at Richmond, Virginia, January 10, 1864.]

LINKER, JAMES R., Private

Resided in Lincoln County and enlisted in Rowan County at age 19, July 4, 1862, for the war. Hospitalized at Richmond, Virginia, October 22, 1862, with rubeola. Returned to duty on November 24, 1862. Sent to hospital from camp near Fredericksburg, Virginia, January 22, 1863. Died in hospital at Richmond or at Lynchburg, Virginia, February 2, 1863, of "pneumonia."

MOREFIELD, ASA W., Private

Resided in Iredell County and was by occupation a farmer prior to enlisting in Iredell County at age 42, October 31, 1864, for the war. Reported present through February 28, 1865. Surrendered at Appomattox Court House, Virginia, April 9, 1865.

MORRIS, J. M., Private

Enlisted at Camp Holmes, near Raleigh, April 18, 1864, for the war. Reported present through August 31, 1864. Captured at Fisher's Hill, Virginia, September 22, 1864. Confined at Point Lookout, Maryland, October 3, 1864. Paroled at Point Lookout on or about February 13, 1865. Received at Cox's Wharf, James River, Virginia, February 14-15, 1865, for exchange. Hospitalized at Richmond, Virginia, February 15, 1865, with gelatio. Furloughed for sixty days on March 4, 1865.

MOSER, HENRY THOMAS, Private

Resided in Forsyth County and was by occupation a farmer prior to enlisting at Camp Holmes, near Raleigh, at age 40, March 12, 1864, for the war. Reported present through August 31, 1864. Wounded in the neck and captured at Winchester, Virginia, September 19, 1864. Hospitalized at Winchester. Transferred to hospital at Baltimore, Maryland, on an unspecified date. Confined at Point Lookout, Maryland, October 18, 1864. Paroled at Point Lookout on or about October 30, 1864. Received at Venus Point, Savannah River, Georgia, November 15, 1864, for exchange. Returned to duty in January-February, 1865. Captured at Fort Stedman, Virginia, March 25, 1865. Confined at Point Lookout, Maryland, March 28, 1865. Released at Point Lookout on June 29, 1865, after taking the Oath of Allegiance.

MULLENS, JAMES H., Private

Resided in Lincoln County where he enlisted at age 26, July 4, 1862, for the war. Hospitalized at Richmond, Virginia, October 19, 1862, with intermittent fever. Furloughed on November 17, 1862. Returned to duty prior to January 1, 1863. Reported present through May 11, 1863. Wounded in the thigh and captured at Gettysburg, Pennsylvania, July 2, 1863. Leg amputated. Died in hospital at Gettysburg on July 13, 1863, of wounds.

NASH, GEORGE W., Private

Resided in Stanly County and enlisted at Camp Holmes, near Raleigh, March 7, 1864, for the war. Deserted at Goldsboro on May 7, 1864. Returned to duty in September-October, 1864. Reported present through February 28, 1865. Captured at Fort Stedman, Virginia, March 25, 1865. Confined at Point Lookout, Maryland, March 28, 1865. Released at Point Lookout on June 29, 1865, after taking the Oath of Allegiance.

PENDLETON, WILLIAM, Private

Resided in Lincoln County where he enlisted at age 21, July 4, 1862, for the war. Hospitalized at Richmond, Virginia, November 9, 1862. Returned to duty on December 3, 1862. Reported present through May 11, 1863. Sent to hospital on June 3, 1863. Reported missing at Gettysburg, Pennsylvania, July 2, 1863. Reported absent without leave in September-October, 1863. Returned to duty in January-April, 1864. Captured at Hanover Junction, Virginia, May 24, 1864. Confined at Point Lookout, Maryland, June 8, 1864. Transferred to Elmira, New York, July 8, 1864. Released at Elmira on June 16, 1865, after taking the Oath of Allegiance.

PROPST, J. C., Private

Resided in Lincoln County where he enlisted at age 28, July 4, 1862, for the war. Killed at Fredericksburg, Virginia, December 13, 1862.

PROPST, JACOB G. H., Private

Resided in Lincoln County and was by occupation a painter or mechanic prior to enlisting in Lincoln County at age 30, July 4, 1862, for the war. Reported present through February 28, 1863. Hospitalized at Richmond, Virginia, May 3, 1863, with acute diarrhoea. Transferred to hospital at Danville, Virginia, May 11, 1863. Furloughed for thirty days on or about May 25, 1863. Listed as a deserter on or about June 24, 1863. Returned to duty in January-April, 1864. Captured (or deserted to the enemy) at Middletown, Maryland, or near Chambersburg, Pennsylvania, July 9-14, 1864. Confined at Fort Delaware, Delaware, July 19, 1864. Released at

Fort Delaware on May 11, 1865, after taking the Oath of Allegiance.

PROPST, JOHN M., Private

Resided in Lincoln County where he enlisted at age 33, July 4, 1862, for the war. Hospitalized at Richmond, Virginia, October 10, 1862, with bilious fever. Furloughed for thirty days on November 12, 1862. Returned to duty in January-February, 1863. Wounded in the left arm at Chancellorsville, Virginia, May 4, 1863. Left arm amputated at the shoulder joint. Hospitalized at Richmond. Furloughed for sixty days on June 13, 1863. Reported on detail at Salisbury in November-December, 1863. Reported absent wounded from March 1, 1864, through February 28, 1865. Survived the war.

PROPST, MARCUS M., Private

Resided in Lincoln County where he enlisted at age 20, July 4, 1862, for the war. Wounded in the left arm at Fredericksburg, Virginia, December 13, 1862. Reported absent wounded through August 31, 1863. Reported on detail in the quartermaster's department in September-December, 1863. Reported absent wounded in March-August, 1864. Reported on detail at Statesville in September-October, 1864. Reported absent wounded in November-December, 1864. Retired to the Invalid Corps on January 20, 1865. Detailed for light duty on or about February 18, 1865. Survived the war.

PROPST, WILLIAM, Private

Resided in Lincoln County and was by occupation a farmer prior to enlisting in Lincoln County at age 24, July 4, 1862, for the war. Hospitalized at Richmond, Virginia, November 2, 1862, with chronic diarrhoea. Furloughed for thirty days on November 12, 1862. Returned to duty prior to December 13, 1862, when he was wounded in the arm at Fredericksburg, Virginia. Hospitalized at Richmond. Furloughed for forty days on or about December 30, 1862. Returned to duty prior to March 1, 1863. Hospitalized at Danville, Virginia, May 11, 1863. Died in hospital at Danville on June 4, 1863, of "phthisis."

RAMSEY, E. D., Private

Resided in Lincoln County and enlisted at Camp Stokes on December 6, 1864, for the war. Reported present through February 28, 1865. Captured at Fort Stedman, Virginia, March 25, 1865. Confined at Point Lookout, Maryland, March 28, 1865. Released at Point Lookout on June 17, 1865, after taking the Oath of Allegiance. [Was about 35 years of age at time of enlistment.]

RAMSEY, S. J., Private

Resided in Lincoln County where he enlisted at age 26, July 4, 1862, for the war. Wounded at Fredericksburg, Virginia, December 13, 1862. Hospitalized at Richmond, Virginia, where he died on January 25, 1863, of wounds.

RAMSEY, WILLIAM W., 1st Sergeant

Previously served as Private in Company K, 1st Regiment N.C. Infantry (6 months, 1861). Enlisted in this company in Lincoln County on July 4, 1862, for the war. Mustered in as Sergeant. Hospitalized at Richmond, Virginia, October 29, 1862, with remittent fever. Returned to duty on November 24, 1862. Reported present through February 28, 1863. Promoted to 1st Sergeant prior to May 4, 1863, when he was wounded in the thigh at Chancellorsville,

Virginia. Returned to duty in November-December, 1863. Reported present through February 28, 1865. Wounded in both legs and captured at Fort Stedman, Virginia, March 25, 1865. Hospitalized at Washington, D.C. Released at Washington on June 12, 1865, after taking the Oath of Allegiance.

RANSOM, RICHARD B., Private

Resided in Forsyth County and was by occupation a farmer prior to enlisting at Camp Holmes, near Raleigh, March 12, 1864, for the war. Captured at Winchester, Virginia, July 20, 1864. Confined at Camp Chase, Ohio, July 28, 1864. Paroled at Camp Chase on March 2, 1865. Received at Boulware's and Cox's Wharves, James River, Virginia, March 10-12, 1865, for exchange. No further records. [Records of the Federal Provost Marshal dated July, 1864, give his age as 22. May have served previously as Private in Company K, 48th Regiment N.C. Troops.]

RAWLMAN, J. D., Private

Resided in Lincoln County. Place and date of enlistment not reported (probably enlisted subsequent to February 28, 1865). Captured at Fort Stedman, Virginia, March 25, 1865. Confined at Point Lookout, Maryland, March 28, 1865. Released at Point Lookout on June 17, 1865, after taking the Oath of Allegiance.

RHYNE, GEORGE, Private

Resided in Lincoln County and was by occupation a farmer prior to enlisting in Lincoln County at age 31, July 4, 1862, for the war. Hospitalized at Richmond, Virginia, on or about November 9, 1862. Apparently returned to duty on an unspecified date. Hospitalized at Richmond on January 7, 1863. Died in hospital at Richmond on January 23, 1863, of "pneumonia."

RHYNE, JONAS C., Private

Born in Lincoln County where he resided prior to enlisting in Lincoln County at age 34, July 4, 1862, for the war. Died in camp near Fredericksburg, Virginia, December 25-26, 1862. Cause of death not reported.

ROBINSON, MARCUS L., Private

Resided in Lincoln County and was by occupation a farmer prior to enlisting in Lincoln County at age 35, July 4, 1862, for the war. Hospitalized at Richmond, Virginia, on or about November 8, 1862, with diarrhoea. Furloughed for thirty days on November 27, 1862. Reported absent sick through December, 1863. Returned to duty in January-April, 1864. Reported absent on sick furlough from June 15, 1864, through February 28, 1865. Hospitalized at Charlotte on March 20, 1865, with chronic diarrhoea. Returned to duty on March 21, 1865. No further records.

RUDISILL, DANIEL RUFUS, Private

Resided in Lincoln County and was by occupation a journeyman carpenter prior to enlisting in Lincoln County at age 32, July 4, 1862, for the war. Reported present through May 11, 1863. Died in hospital at Richmond, Virginia, July 15, 1863, of "scorbutus."

RUDISILL, H. A., Private

Resided in Lincoln County where he enlisted at age 26, July 4, 1862, for the war. Reported present through December 31, 1862. Sent to hospital from camp near Port Royal, Virginia, February 21, 1863. Died in hospital at Lynchburg, Virginia, March 3, 1863, of "febris typhoides."

RUDISILL, J. P., Private

Resided in Lincoln County where he enlisted at age 17, July 4, 1862, for the war as a substitute. Reported present through May 11, 1863. Deserted to the enemy in Pennsylvania on June 27, 1863. Confined at Fort Mifflin, Pennsylvania, July 2, 1863. Released at Fort Mifflin on January 15, 1864, after taking the Oath of Allegiance.

RUDISILL, M. C., Private

Resided in Lincoln County where he enlisted at age 18, July 4, 1862, for the war. Killed at Fredericksburg, Virginia, December 13, 1862.

SANE, ANDREW, Private

Resided in Lincoln County where he enlisted at age 31, July 4, 1862, for the war. Wounded in the left leg at Fredericksburg, Virginia, December 13, 1862. Left leg amputated below the knee. Hospitalized at Richmond, Virginia, February 16, 1863. Furloughed for ninety days on March 12, 1863. Reported absent wounded through February 28, 1865. Survived the war.

SANE, DANIEL, Private

Born in Lincoln County where he resided as a farmer prior to enlisting in Lincoln County at age 22, July 4, 1862, for the war. Hospitalized at Richmond, Virginia, on or about November 8, 1862, with rheumatism. Transferred to hospital at Danville, Virginia, January 8, 1863. Returned to duty on March 24, 1863. Captured at Chancellorsville, Virginia, May 3-4, 1863. Confined at Fort Delaware, Delaware, on or about May 7, 1863. Paroled at Fort Delaware and transferred to City Point, Virginia, where he was received on May 23, 1863, for exchange. Returned to duty in September-October, 1863. Captured at Rappahannock Station, Virginia, November 7, 1863. Confined at Point Lookout, Maryland, November 11, 1863. Released at Point Lookout on March 8, 1864, after taking the Oath of Allegiance and joining the U.S. Army. Assigned to Company D, 1st Regiment U.S. Volunteer Infantry.

SANE, JOHN, Private

Resided in Lincoln County where he enlisted at age 20, July 4, 1862, for the war. Wounded at Fredericksburg, Virginia, December 13, 1862. Returned to duty in January-February, 1863. Died in camp (probably near Fredericksburg, Virginia) on April 11, 1863. Cause of death not reported.

SANE, JOSEPH, Private

Resided in Lincoln County where he enlisted at age 28, July 4, 1862, for the war. Hospitalized at Richmond, Virginia, October 31, 1862. Died in hospital at Richmond on or about November 25, 1862, of "typhoid fever."

SANE, LEVI E., Private

Resided in Lincoln County where he enlisted at age 35, July 4, 1862, for the war. Hospitalized at Richmond, Virginia, October 30, 1862, with typhoid fever. Returned to duty in November-December, 1863. Reported absent on sick furlough from May 3 through August 31, 1864. Hospitalized at Charlotte on September 23, 1864, with chronic ulcers. Returned to duty on October 28, 1864. Reported absent without leave on November 21, 1864. Returned to duty in January-February, 1865. Wounded in the head at Fort Stedman, Virginia, March 25, 1865. Hospitalized at Petersburg, Virginia, where he was captured on April 2, 1865. Confined at Newport News, Virginia, May 17, 1865. Released at Newport News on June 26, 1865, after taking the Oath of Allegiance.

SANE, NOAH, Private

Resided in Lincoln County where he enlisted at age 30, July 4, 1862, for the war. Wounded in the lungs at Fredericksburg, Virginia, December 13, 1862. Hospitalized at Richmond, Virginia, where he died on December 19, 1862, of wounds.

SELF, BERRYMAN H., Private

Born in Lincoln County where he resided prior to enlisting in Lincoln County at age 28, July 4, 1862, for the war. Hospitalized at Richmond, Virginia, November 22, 1862, with aphonia and pneumonia. Died in hospital at Richmond on December 23, 1862, of "pneumonia."

SHELTON, DEMPSY, ———

North Carolina pension records indicate that he served in this company.

SHUFORD, ABLE A., Private

Resided in Lincoln County where he enlisted at age 33, July 4, 1862, for the war. Hospitalized at Richmond, Virginia, November 25, 1862, with parotitis. Returned to duty on December 16, 1862. Reported present on surviving company muster rolls through August 31, 1864. Wounded in the head at Winchester, Virginia, September 19, 1864. Hospitalized at Charlottesville, Virginia. Transferred to another hospital on September 26, 1864. Returned to duty in January-February, 1865. Captured at Farmville, Virginia, April 6, 1865. Confined at Newport News, Virginia, April 14, 1865. Released at Newport News on June 26, 1865, after taking the Oath of Allegiance.

SHULL, JOSEPH DAVID, Private

Resided in Lincoln County where he enlisted at age 28, July 4, 1862, for the war. Reported present or accounted for through February 28, 1863. Wounded in the ankle at Chancellorsville, Virginia, May 4, 1863. Died at Richmond, Virginia, prior to June 1, 1863, presumably of wounds.

SMITH, G. E., Corporal

Resided in Lincoln County and enlisted in Rowan County at age 24, July 4, 1862, for the war. Mustered in as Corporal. Reported present through October 31, 1862. Hospitalized at Richmond, Virginia, January 15, 1863, with pneumonia. Furloughed for thirty days on April 17, 1863. Returned to duty in November-December, 1863. Reported present in March-April, 1864. Died in hospital at Richmond on June 22, 1864, of a gunshot wound of the right knee. Place and date wounded not reported.

SMYRE, FRANCIS SHUFORD, Private

Enlisted at Camp Vance on March 9, 1864, for the war. Captured at or near Cold Harbor, Virginia, on or about June 6, 1864. Confined at Point Lookout, Maryland, on or about June 15, 1864. Paroled at Point Lookout on March 14, 1865. Received at Boulware's Wharf, James River, Virginia, March 16, 1865, for exchange. Survived the war. [Was about 18 years of age at time of enlistment.]

STEWARD, DOLPHIS L., Corporal

Resided in Lincoln County where he enlisted at age 20, July 4, 1862, for the war. Mustered in as Private. Hospitalized at Richmond, Virginia, October 4, 1862, with rubeola. Returned to duty prior to November 1, 1862. Reported present through February 28, 1863. Wounded in the leg and/or back at Chancellorsville, Virginia, May 4, 1863. Reported absent without leave in September-October,

1863. Reported absent wounded in November-December, 1863. Returned to duty in January-April, 1864. Promoted to Corporal in September-October, 1864. Reported present or accounted for through February 28, 1865. Surrendered at Appomattox Court House, Virginia, April 9, 1865.

STROUP, ISRAEL R., Private

Resided in Lincoln or Gaston County and was by occupation a farmer prior to enlisting in Lincoln County at age 35, July 4, 1862, for the war. Reported present or accounted for through October 31, 1863. Captured at Rappahannock Station, Virginia, November 7, 1863. Confined at Point Lookout, Maryland, November 11, 1863. Paroled at Point Lookout on October 30, 1864. Received at Venus Point, Savannah River, Georgia, November 15, 1864, for exchange. Reported absent without leave from December 1, 1864, through February 28, 1865. Returned to duty on an unspecified date. Captured at Farmville, Virginia, April 6, 1865. Confined at Newport News, Virginia, April 14, 1865. Released at Newport News on June 26, 1865, after taking the Oath of Allegiance.

STROUP, JAMES R., Private

Enlisted at Camp Holmes, near Raleigh, March 12, 1864, for the war. Hospitalized at Petersburg, Virginia, May 11, 1864, with rubeola. Transferred to Raleigh on June 5, 1864. Reported absent without leave from July 8, 1864, through February 28, 1865. No further records.

STROUP, PHILIP, Private

Resided in Lincoln County where he enlisted at age 31, July 4, 1862, for the war. Hospitalized at Richmond, Virginia, November 8, 1862, with diarrhoea. Died in hospital at Richmond on November 13, 1862, of "typhoid fever."

STUBBS, FRANKLIN, Private

Born in Bangor, Maine, and resided in Lincoln County where he was by occupation an apprentice machinist prior to enlisting in Lincoln County at age 19, July 4, 1862, for the war. Mustered in as Sergeant. Wounded at Fredericksburg, Virginia, December 13, 1862. Returned to duty prior to January 1, 1863. Hospitalized at Richmond, Virginia, February 16, 1863, with diarrhoea. Transferred to Charlotte on April 2, 1863. Reduced to ranks in May-October, 1863. Detailed for duty as a laborer at the Charlotte navy yard on August 8, 1863. Reported on detail at Charlotte through October 31, 1864. Deserted to the enemy on or about December 22, 1864. Released at Washington, D.C., on or about December 30, 1864, after taking the Oath of Allegiance.

SULLIVAN, EZEKIEL M., Private

Born in Lincoln County where he resided as a farmer prior to enlisting in Lincoln County at age 29, July 4, 1862, for the war. Reported present or accounted for through May 11, 1863. Died at Jordan's Springs, Virginia, on or about July 13, 1863, of "pneumonia."

SUMMEY, LUKE D., Private

Born in Lincoln County on July 4, 1841. Resided in Lincoln County and was by occupation a farm laborer prior to enlisting in Lincoln County at age 21, July 4, 1862, for the war. Hospitalized at Richmond, Virginia, September 22, 1862. Died in hospital at Richmond on October 19, 1862, of "fever."

THARP, W. D., Private

Enlisted in Iredell County on October 31, 1864, for the war. Reported present through February 28, 1865.

TREECE, DAVID, Private

Resided in Stanly County and was by occupation a farmer prior to enlisting at Camp Holmes, near Raleigh, at age 38, March 7, 1864, for the war. Captured at Winchester, Virginia, July 20, 1864. Confined at Camp Chase, Ohio, July 28, 1864. Paroled at Camp Chase on March 2, 1865. Received at Boulware's and Cox's Wharves, James River, Virginia, March 10-12, 1865, for exchange. Survived the war.

WALLACE, ANDREW F., Private

Resided in Iredell County and was by occupation a millwright prior to enlisting in Iredell County at age 41, October 31, 1864, for the war. Captured at Hatcher's Run, Virginia, February 6, 1865. Confined at Point Lookout, Maryland, February 9, 1865. Released at Point Lookout on May 14, 1865, after taking the Oath of Allegiance.

WISE, ABSALOM, Private

Resided in Lincoln County where he enlisted at age 25, July 4, 1862, for the war. Reported present through February 28, 1863. Captured at Chancellorsville, Virginia, May 3-4, 1863. Confined at Fort Delaware, Delaware, on or about May 7, 1863. Paroled at Fort Delaware and transferred to City Point, Virginia, where he was received on May 23, 1863, for exchange. Hospitalized at Richmond, Virginia, the same day with chronic diarrhoea. Later diagnosed with scurvy. Returned to duty on or about August 3, 1863. Captured at Rappahannock Station, Virginia, November 7, 1863. Confined at Point Lookout, Maryland, on or about November 11, 1863. Paroled at Point Lookout on February 24, 1865. Received at Aiken's Landing, James River, Virginia, February 25-28 or March 2-3, 1865, for exchange. Survived the war.

WISE, AMBROSE, Corporal

Resided in Lincoln County and was by occupation a carpenter prior to enlisting in Lincoln County at age 28, July 4, 1862, for the war. Mustered in as Private. Reported present through May 11, 1863. Promoted to Corporal on June 2, 1863. Wounded in the face at Gettysburg, Pennsylvania, July 1-2, 1863. Company muster rolls indicate that he was captured at Gettysburg on or about July 5, 1863; however, records of the Federal Provost Marshal do not substantiate that report. No further records.

WISE, ANDREW N., Private

Resided in Lincoln County and was by occupation a farmer prior to enlisting in Lincoln County at age 26, July 4, 1862, for the war. Reported present through October 31, 1863. Captured at Rappahannock Station, Virginia, November 7, 1863. Confined at Point Lookout, Maryland, November 11, 1863. Paroled at Point Lookout on February 24, 1865. Received at Aiken's Landing, James River, Virginia, February 25-28 or March 2-3, 1865, for exchange. Survived the war.

WISE, FRANKLIN A., Private

Resided in Lincoln County where he enlisted at age 23, July 4, 1862, for the war. Reported present through October 31, 1863. Captured at Rappahannock Station, Virginia, November 7, 1863. Confined at Point Lookout, Maryland, November 11, 1863. Paroled at Point Lookout on February 18, 1865. Received at Boulware's and Cox's Wharves, James River, Virginia, February 20-21, 1865, for exchange.

WISE, FRANKLIN M., Private

Resided in Lincoln County and was by occupation a farmer prior to enlisting in Lincoln County at age 27, July 4, 1862, for the war.

Hospitalized at Richmond, Virginia, November 25, 1862, with icterus. Returned to duty on March 13, 1863. Wounded in the right arm at Chancellorsville, Virginia, May 4, 1863. Right arm amputated. Hospitalized at Richmond on May 9, 1863. Furloughed for sixty days on June 6, 1863. No further records. Survived the war.

COMPANY H

This company was raised in Rowan County on July 4, 1862. It was mustered into service at Salisbury on July 17, 1862, and assigned to the 57th Regiment N.C. Troops as Company H. After joining the regiment the company functioned as a part of the regiment, and its history for the remainder of the war is reported as a part of the regimental history.

The following roster was compiled primarily from information in the microfilm edition of the Compiled Service Records of Soldiers Who Served in Organizations from the State of North Carolina (Record Group 109, M270), National Archives and Records Administration, Washington, D.C. Record Group 109 includes enlistment papers, pay vouchers, requisitions, letters of resignation, discharge certificates, and abstracts of medical and prisoner of war returns. Materials relating specifically to this company include muster rolls dated July 3, 1862-February 28, 1863; April 30-December 31, 1863; and March 1, 1864-February 28, 1865.

Also utilized in this roster were *The War of the Rebellion: A Compilation of the Official Records of the Union and Confederate Armies*, the North Carolina adjutant general's *Roll of Honor*, state militia records, newspaper casualty lists and obituaries, wartime claims for bounty pay and allowances, postwar registers of claims for artificial limbs, Confederate pension applications filed with the states of North Carolina, Tennessee, and Florida, Confederate Soldiers' Home records, and the 1860 and 1870 federal censuses of North Carolina. A search was made also for relevant letters, diaries, reminiscences, and other manuscripts in the Southern Historical Collection (University of North Carolina-Chapel Hill), the Duke University Library Special Collections Department, and the North Carolina Division of Archives and History.

Among the secondary sources consulted were records of the North Carolina division of the United Daughters of the Confederacy, postwar rosters, regimental and county histories, marriage bond, will, and cemetery indexes, published and unpublished genealogies, biographical dictionaries, the North Carolina *County Heritage Book* series, the *Confederate Veteran*, Walter Clark's *Histories of the Several Regiments and Battalions from North Carolina in the Great War, 1861-'65*, and the North Carolina volume of the extended edition of *Confederate Military History*.

OFFICERS

CAPTAINS

HOWERTON, WILLIAM H.

Resided in Rowan County and was by occupation a "professor of medicine" prior to enlisting at age 32. Appointed Captain on July 4, 1862. Hospitalized at Richmond, Virginia, October 13, 1862,

with rheumatism and/or lumbago. Furloughed for twenty days on October 16, 1862. Furlough extended in early November and on November 25, 1862. Dropped from the company rolls on December 3, 1862, in the mistaken belief that he was absent without leave. Reinstated on January 10, 1863. Resigned on January 12, 1863, by reason of "the feeble condition of my health" occasioned by "ch[ronic] rheumatism." Resignation accepted on or about January 16, 1863. [Records of the United Daughters of the Confederacy indicate that he served later as Surgeon of the Confederate garrison at Salisbury and held the rank of Major.]

JOHNSTON, WILLIAM

Previously served as 1st Lieutenant of Company B, 20th Regiment N.C. Troops (10th Regiment N.C. Volunteers). Appointed 2nd Lieutenant of this company on July 4, 1862. Promoted to 1st Lieutenant on December 5, 1862. Promoted to Captain on December 19, 1862. Reported present or accounted for through February 28, 1863. Wounded at Chancellorsville, Virginia, May 4, 1863. Died at or near Fredericksburg, Virginia, on or about the same date of wounds. [Born on August 2, 1834.]

MAYNARD, RICHARD L.

Served as 1st Lieutenant of Company I of this regiment. Reported in command of this company in May-August, 1864.

PROPST, WILLIAM M.

Served as 1st Lieutenant of Company F of this regiment. Reported in command of this company in November-December, 1864.

LIEUTENANTS

EDMONDSON, WILLIAM JAMES, 2nd Lieutenant

Previously served as 1st Sergeant of Company D of this regiment. Appointed 2nd Lieutenant and transferred to this company on October 20, 1864. Reported present or accounted for through February 28, 1865. Surrendered at Appomattox Court House, Virginia, April 9, 1865. [Reported in command of Company F of this regiment in January-February, 1865.]

HALL, RICHARD F., 3rd Lieutenant

Resided in Rowan County where he enlisted at age 17. Appointed 3rd Lieutenant on July 4, 1862. Killed at Fredericksburg, Virginia, December 13, 1862.

HARRIS, CHARLES F., 1st Lieutenant

Previously served as 1st Lieutenant of Company A, 20th Regiment N.C. Troops (10th Regiment N.C. Volunteers). Appointed 1st Lieutenant of this company on July 4, 1862. Hospitalized at Richmond, Virginia, October 8, 1862, with remittent fever. Transferred to another hospital on October 18, 1862. Resigned on November 25, 1862, by reason of "asthma & chronic rheumatism." Resignation accepted on December 5, 1862.

KERR, JOHN H., 2nd Lieutenant

Resided in Davidson County and enlisted in Rowan County at age 18, July 4, 1862, for the war. Mustered in as Sergeant. Appointed 3rd Lieutenant on December 19, 1862. Reported sick in hospital from January 9 through February 28, 1863. Returned to duty on an unspecified date. Appointed 2nd Lieutenant on April 24, 1863. Reported present through December 31, 1863. Reported in command of the company in March-April, 1864. Wounded in the left leg and captured at Winchester, Virginia, July 20, 1864. Leg amputated "in the middle third." Confined at various Federal hospitals until November 14, 1864, when he was hospitalized at Baltimore, Maryland, suffering from gangrene. Leg reamputated. Paroled at Baltimore on or about February 16, 1865, and transferred for exchange. Hospitalized at Richmond, Virginia, March 4, 1865, with debility and chronic diarrhoea. Furloughed for thirty days on March 25, 1865. Survived the war. [North Carolina pension records indicate that he was wounded in the right leg at Fredericksburg, Virginia, in 1863. Records of the United Daughters of the Confederacy indicate that he received a bayonet wound in the breast on an unspecified date.]

LEFLER, ROBERT FRANKLIN, 2nd Lieutenant

Born in Cabarrus County on February 25, 1836. Resided in Cabarrus County and was by occupation a blacksmith prior to enlisting in Cabarrus County at age 26, July 4, 1862, for the war. Mustered in as Sergeant. Reported present through February 28, 1863. Appointed 2nd Lieutenant on April 24, 1863. Hospitalized at Richmond, Virginia, May 5, 1863, with debilitas. Transferred on May 8, 1863. Captured on or about May 24, 1863, during the "recent raid in the rear of Lee's army." Paroled on or about the same date. Returned to duty prior to September 1, 1863. Reported present through December 31, 1863. Wounded in the head at Drewry's Bluff, Virginia, May 16, 1864. Hospitalized at Richmond where he died on May 20, 1864, of wounds.

PHARR, SAMUEL E. W., 1st Lieutenant

Previously served as Private in Company F of this regiment. Appointed 1st Lieutenant of this company on December 19, 1862. Reported present through October 31, 1863. Captured at Rappahannock Station, Virginia, November 7, 1863. Confined at Old Capitol Prison, Washington, D.C. Transferred to Johnson's Island, Ohio, November 11, 1863. Transferred from Johnson's Island to Point Lookout, Maryland, April 22, 1864. Transferred from Point Lookout to Fort Delaware, Delaware, June 23, 1864. Paroled at Fort Delaware on October 6, 1864. Received at Cox's Wharf, James River, Virginia, October 15, 1864, for exchange. Hospitalized at Richmond, Virginia, October 16, 1864, with chronic diarrhoea. Furloughed on October 20, 1864. Reported absent without leave on November 17, 1864. Returned to duty subsequent to December 31, 1864. Captured at Hatcher's Run, Virginia, February 6, 1865. Confined at Old Capitol Prison, Washington, February 9, 1865. Transferred to Fort Delaware on March 1, 1865. Released at Fort Delaware on June 17, 1865, after taking the Oath of Allegiance.

NONCOMMISSIONED OFFICERS
AND PRIVATES

BABB, ABITHA B., Private

Resided in Wake County and was by occupation a farm tenant prior to enlisting in Wake County at age 39, August 18, 1864, for the war. Reported present or accounted for through February 28, 1865. Survived the war. [North Carolina pension records indicate that "in a charge at Drew[r]y['s] B[l]uff (Virginia) a limb of a large tree was blowed off by a shell falling on me and chrushing [sic] me to the earth causing me a great deal of pain."]

BACON, HARPER G., Private

Resided in Cabarrus County where he enlisted on July 4, 1862, for the war. Discharged at Richmond, Virginia, October 20, 1862, by reason of his "tender age (16) and weak constitution."

BARNEY, WASHINGTON, Private

Enlisted in Wake County on March 7, 1864, for the war. Sent to hospital on May 13, 1864. Furloughed for sixty days from hospital at Richmond, Virginia, on or about October 28, 1864, convalescent from chronic diarrhoea and debility. Reported absent sick through February 28, 1865. No further records.

BARNHART, ADAM, Private

Born in Cabarrus County where he resided prior to enlisting in Cabarrus County at age 29, July 4, 1862, for the war. Hospitalized at Richmond, Virginia, September 30, 1862, with rubeola. Furloughed for thirty days on October 17, 1862. Returned to duty prior to December 13, 1862, when he was wounded at Fredericksburg, Virginia. Hospitalized at Richmond where he died on December 24-25, 1862, of wounds.

BARNHART, DANIEL C., Private

Resided in Cabarrus County and was by occupation a farm laborer prior to enlisting in Cabarrus County at age 27, July 4, 1862, for the war. Reported present or accounted for through October 31, 1863. Captured at Rappahannock Station, Virginia, November 7, 1863. Confined at Point Lookout, Maryland, November 11, 1863. Died at Point Lookout on or about January 30, 1865, of "pneumonia."

BARNHART, RICHARD, Private

Resided in Cabarrus County and was by occupation a farm worker prior to enlisting in Cabarrus County at age 19, July 4, 1862, for the war. Hospitalized at Richmond, Virginia, September 26, 1862. Returned to duty on October 10, 1862. Died in hospital at Richmond on October 24, 1862, of "erysipelas."

BARRIER, DANIEL M., 1st Sergeant

Born on August 6, 1831. Resided in Cabarrus County and was by occupation a farmer prior to enlisting in Cabarrus County at age 30, July 4, 1862, for the war. Mustered in as Corporal. Promoted to Sergeant in November-December, 1862. Promoted to 1st Sergeant in March-May, 1863. Reported present or accounted for through May 11, 1863. Hospitalized at Richmond, Virginia, July 19, 1863, with debility. Transferred to another hospital on August 13, 1863. Returned to duty in November-December, 1863. Reported present on surviving company muster rolls through August 31, 1864. Wounded in the arm at Winchester, Virginia, September 19, 1864. Reported absent wounded through February 28, 1865. Returned to duty on an unspecified date. Surrendered at Appomattox Court House, Virginia, April 9, 1865.

BASS, WILLIAM J., Private

Resided in Iredell County and enlisted in Rowan County at age 34, July 4, 1862, for the war. Hospitalized at Richmond, Virginia, January 24, 1863. Died in hospital at Richmond on or about January 28, 1863, of "febris typhoides."

BASS, WILLIAM P., Corporal

Resided in Union County and enlisted in Rowan County at age 32, July 4, 1862, for the war. Mustered in as Private. Hospitalized at

Richmond, Virginia, September 19, 1862, with dysentery. Returned to duty on October 17, 1862. Wounded at Fredericksburg, Virginia, December 13, 1862. Returned to duty prior to May 11, 1863. Promoted to Corporal on August 15, 1863. Hospitalized at Richmond on October 13, 1863. Returned to duty in November-December, 1863. Reported present or accounted for on surviving company muster rolls through February 28, 1865. Captured at Petersburg, Virginia, April 3, 1865. Confined at Hart's Island, New York Harbor, April 7, 1865. Released at Hart's Island on June 17, 1865, after taking the Oath of Allegiance.

BOST, GEORGE D., Private

Resided in Cabarrus County and was by occupation a farm hand prior to enlisting in Cabarrus County at age 19, February 13, 1864, for the war. Reported absent sick on July 17, 1864. Captured (possibly in hospital) at or near Winchester, Virginia, on or about September 25, 1864. Sent to Harpers Ferry, West Virginia. Transferred to Point Lookout, Maryland, October 13, 1864. Released at Point Lookout on June 23, 1865, after taking the Oath of Allegiance.

BOYD, THOMAS F., Private

Born at "Franklin Hill" and resided in Iredell County where he was by occupation a farmer prior to enlisting in Cabarrus County at age 27, July 4, 1862, for the war. Wounded at Fredericksburg, Virginia, December 13, 1862. Hospitalized at Richmond, Virginia. Returned to duty on March 18, 1863. Reported present through April 30, 1864. Wounded in the right shoulder at Winchester, Virginia, July 20, 1864. Hospitalized at Charlottesville, Virginia. Furloughed for sixty days on August 7, 1864. Returned to duty prior to November 1, 1864. Hospitalized at Petersburg, Virginia, January 22, 1865. Died in hospital at Petersburg on February 10, 1865. Cause of death not reported.

BRINKLEY, JOHN F., Sergeant

Resided in Davie County and was by occupation a laborer prior to enlisting in Davie County at age 25, July 4, 1862, for the war. Mustered in as Private. Hospitalized at Richmond, Virginia, December 17, 1862, with bronchitis. Returned to duty on February 14, 1863. Promoted to Sergeant in March-May, 1863. Reported present through October 31, 1863. Captured at Rappahannock Station, Virginia, November 7, 1863. Confined at Point Lookout, Maryland, November 11, 1863. Paroled at Point Lookout on February 24, 1865. Received at Aiken's Landing, James River, Virginia, on or about February 25-28 or March 2-3, 1865, for exchange. Hospitalized at Richmond on March 4, 1865, with "scorbutus." Died in hospital at Richmond on March 19, 1865.

BROWN, JAMES H., Private

Resided in Iredell County and enlisted in Rowan County at age 31, July 4, 1862, for the war. Reported present or accounted for through May 11, 1863. Wounded in the finger at Gettysburg, Pennsylvania, July 1, 1863. Hospitalized at Richmond, Virginia, July 20, 1863. Furloughed on August 12, 1863. Detailed for light duty at Salisbury on December 12, 1863. Rejoined the company prior to May 1, 1864. Killed near Winchester, Virginia, July 20, 1864.

CALL, HENRY G., Private

Born in Davie County where he resided prior to enlisting in Davie County at age 19, July 4, 1862, for the war. Hospitalized at Richmond, Virginia, September 25, 1862, with measles. Returned to duty on December 9, 1862. Captured at Chancellorsville, Virginia, May 3-4, 1863. Confined at Fort Delaware, Delaware, on or about May 7, 1863. Paroled at Fort Delaware and transferred to City

Point, Virginia, where he was received on May 23, 1863, for exchange. Hospitalized at Petersburg, Virginia, on or about May 23, 1863, with pneumonia. Died in hospital at Petersburg on May 30, 1863, of "feb[ris] continua communis."

CARRIKER, WILLIAM P., Private

Resided in Cabarrus County where he enlisted at age 21, July 4, 1862, for the war. Reported present through October 31, 1863. Captured at Rappahannock Station, Virginia, November 7, 1863. Confined at Point Lookout, Maryland, November 11, 1863. Died in the smallpox hospital at Point Lookout on December 23, 1863.

CASEY, JAMES, Private

Resided in Rowan County where he enlisted at age 33, July 4, 1862, for the war. Deserted at or near Richmond, Virginia, on or about August 25, 1862.

CASSELL, WESLEY, Private

Resided in Cabarrus County and was by occupation a farmer prior to enlisting in Rowan County at age 32, July 4, 1862, for the war. Reported present through February 28, 1863. Hospitalized at Richmond, Virginia, March 23, 1863, with pneumonia. Transferred to Salisbury on April 17, 1863. Returned to duty subsequent to May 11, 1863. Wounded in the right arm at Gettysburg, Pennsylvania, July 1, 1863. Right arm amputated. Captured in Maryland on July 5, 1863. Hospitalized at Chambersburg, Pennsylvania, July 18, 1863. Transferred to hospital at Harrisburg, Pennsylvania, on or about July 21, 1863. Hospitalized at Baltimore, Maryland, August 14, 1863. Paroled at Baltimore on August 23, 1863. Received at City Point, Virginia, August 24, 1863, for exchange. Reported absent wounded until November 26, 1864, when he was retired to the Invalid Corps. Survived the war.

CHAPEL, D. A., Private

Enlisted in Wake County on February 14, 1864, for the war. Hospitalized at Goldsboro on or about May 9, 1864. Returned to duty on May 30, 1864. Reported absent sick from July 20, 1864, through February 28, 1865. No further records.

CLAYTON, JOHN F., Private

Resided in Forsyth County and was by occupation a farmer prior to enlisting in Wake County at age 19, March 12, 1864, for the war. Hospitalized at Charlotte on May 15, 1864, with chronic bronchitis. Returned to duty on June 20, 1864. Captured at Winchester, Virginia, July 20, 1864. Confined at Camp Chase, Ohio, July 28, 1864. Paroled at Camp Chase on March 2, 1865. Received at Boulware's and Cox's Wharves, James River, Virginia, March 10-12, 1865, for exchange. Survived the war.

CLONTS, WILLIAM L., Private

Previously served as Private in Company C of this regiment. Transferred to this company in September-October, 1863. Captured at Rappahannock Station, Virginia, November 7, 1863. Confined at Point Lookout, Maryland, November 11, 1863. Died in the smallpox hospital at Point Lookout on February 5, 1864.

CLONTZ, JAMES, Sergeant

Resided in Union County and was by occupation a farmer prior to enlisting in Cabarrus County at age 32, July 4, 1862, for the war. Mustered in as Private. Promoted to Corporal in November-December, 1862. Hospitalized at Richmond, Virginia, December 12, 1862, with pneumonia. Furloughed for sixty days on February

19, 1863. Returned to duty prior to May 3-4, 1863, when he was captured (possibly wounded) at Chancellorsville, Virginia. Confined at Fort Delaware, Delaware, on or about May 7, 1863. Paroled at Fort Delaware and transferred to City Point, Virginia, where he was received on May 23, 1863, for exchange. Returned to duty prior to October 31, 1863. Promoted to Sergeant in May-August, 1863. Reported present on surviving company muster rolls through April 30, 1864. Hospitalized at Richmond on May 16, 1864, with a gunshot wound of the arm. Place and date wounded not reported. Transferred on June 2, 1864. Reported absent sick or absent on furlough through October 31, 1864. Returned to duty in November-December, 1864. Captured at Fort Stedman, Virginia, March 25, 1865. Confined at Point Lookout, Maryland, March 28, 1865. Released at Point Lookout on June 24, 1865, after taking the Oath of Allegiance.

COLLINS, JOHN CALVIN, Private

Enlisted in Wake County at age 18, April 18, 1864, for the war. Reported absent sick from August 20, 1864, through February 28, 1865. Survived the war.

CONROY, MARTIN, Private

Resided in Rowan County where he enlisted at age 22, July 4, 1862, for the war as a substitute for Pvt. J. F. Houpe. Deserted at Salisbury on or about August 7, 1862.

CRIDER, JOHN H., Private

Resided in Rowan County where he enlisted at age 16, July 4, 1862, for the war as a substitute. Reported present or accounted for through October 31, 1863. Captured at Rappahannock Station, Virginia, November 7, 1863. Confined at Point Lookout, Maryland, November 11, 1863. Paroled at Point Lookout on February 24, 1865. Received at Aiken's Landing, James River, Virginia, on or about February 25-28 or March 2-3, 1865, for exchange. Hospitalized at Richmond, Virginia, March 4, 1865, with scorbutus and chronic diarrhoea. Furloughed for sixty days on March 17, 1865. Paroled at Salisbury on May 22, 1865. Took the Oath of Allegiance at Salisbury on June 15, 1865.

CURLEY, JAMES A., Private

Born in Iredell County where he resided as a farmer prior to enlisting in Rowan County at age 18, July 4, 1862, for the war. Hospitalized at Richmond, Virginia, October 8, 1862, with secondary syphilis. Returned to duty on November 1, 1862. Hospitalized at Charlottesville, Virginia, February 8, 1863, with chronic bronchitis. Died in hospital at Charlottesville on March 11, 1863, of "pneumonia."

DEADMAN, JAMES ANDERSON, Private

Resided in Davie County and enlisted in Rowan County at age 28, July 4, 1862, for the war. Reported present through December, 1862. Hospitalized at Richmond, Virginia, February 27, 1863, with typhoid fever. Died in hospital at Richmond on March 3, 1863, of "pneumonia."

DEWARE, THOMAS, Private

Resided in Virginia and enlisted at Richmond, Virginia, at age 28, September 8, 1862, for the war as a substitute for P. H. Hamton. Deserted the same date.

DOWDA, JAMES MONROE, Private

Born in Iredell County where he resided as a farmer prior to enlisting in Rowan County at age 18, July 4, 1862, for the war. Wounded in the left hip at Fredericksburg, Virginia, December 13, 1862. Reported in hospital at Richmond, Virginia, February 26, 1863. Transferred to Salisbury on March 27, 1863. Reported absent without leave in May-October, 1863. Detailed for duty as a hospital nurse at Richmond on or about November 1, 1863. Reported absent on detail through February 28, 1865 (may have been absent without leave during part of that period). Retired to the Invalid Corps on March 14, 1865.

DOWDA, RICHARD J., Private

Resided in Iredell County and enlisted in Rowan County at age 16, August 15, 1862, for the war. Detailed for duty as a hospital nurse at Richmond, Virginia, in November-December, 1862. Deserted on or about December 14, 1863.

DRY, HENRY R., Private

Resided in Cabarrus County and was by occupation a day laborer prior to enlisting in Cabarrus County at age 31, July 6, 1862, for the war. Hospitalized at Richmond, Virginia, October 8, 1862. Died in hospital at Richmond on October 16, 1862, of "vesicular bronchitis."

DRY, JOHN C., Private

Resided in Cabarrus County and was by occupation a farmer prior to enlisting in Cabarrus County at age 26, July 6, 1862, for the war. Hospitalized at Richmond, Virginia, October 5, 1862, with bronchitis. Died prior to January 13, 1864. Place, date, and cause of death not reported (probably died in the winter of 1862-1863).

DRY, PHILIP W., Private

Resided in Cabarrus County and was by occupation a farmer prior to enlisting in Cabarrus County at age 36, July 3, 1862, for the war. Hospitalized at Richmond, Virginia, October 9, 1862, with typhoid fever. Furloughed for thirty days on October 30, 1862. Returned to duty in January-February, 1863. Reported present through October 31, 1863. Captured at Rappahannock Station, Virginia, November 7, 1863. Confined at Point Lookout, Maryland, November 11, 1863. Exchanged on September 30, 1864. Hospitalized at Richmond on October 6, 1864, with chronic diarrhoea. Furloughed for thirty days on October 13, 1864. Reported absent without leave on December 2, 1864. Returned to duty in January-February, 1865. Captured at Fort Stedman, Virginia, March 25, 1865. Confined at Point Lookout on March 28, 1865. Released at Point Lookout on June 26, 1865, after taking the Oath of Allegiance.

EARP, ALSEY F., Private

Enlisted in Wake County at age 19, April 18, 1864, for the war. Reported absent sick for most of the period through February 28, 1865. Survived the war. [North Carolina pension records indicate that he was wounded at Wilderness, Virginia, on an unspecified date.]

EUDY, WILLIAM M., Sergeant

Born in Cabarrus County where he resided as a farmer prior to enlisting in Cabarrus County at age 32, July 4, 1862, for the war. Mustered in as Sergeant. Wounded in the knee at Fredericksburg, Virginia, December 13, 1862. Reported in hospital at Richmond, Virginia, February 21, 1863. Transferred to Salisbury on March 5, 1863. Reported absent wounded or absent on furlough through August 31, 1863. Reduced to ranks in September-October, 1863. Detailed for hospital duty at Raleigh on October 5, 1863. Reported absent on detail through February 28, 1865. Promoted to Sergeant subsequent to February 28, 1865. Rejoined the company on an unspecified date. Surrendered at Appomattox Court House, Virginia, April 9, 1865. [Previously served as 2nd Lieutenant in the 84th Regiment N.C. Militia.]

FINK, DAVID, Private

Resided in Cabarrus County where he enlisted at age 32, July 4, 1862, for the war. Hospitalized at Richmond, Virginia, October 10, 1862, with typhoid fever. Furloughed for thirty days on October 30, 1862. Reported absent on sick furlough or absent without leave in December, 1862-February, 1863. Returned to duty prior to September 1, 1863. Captured at Rappahannock Station, Virginia, November 7, 1863. Confined at Point Lookout, Maryland, November 11, 1863. Released at Point Lookout on June 3, 1865, after taking the Oath of Allegiance.

FINK, WILLIAM, Private

Resided in Cabarrus County and was by occupation a farm laborer prior to enlisting in Cabarrus County at age 29, July 4, 1862, for the war. Reported absent sick from November 10, 1862, through February 28, 1863. Returned to duty prior to May 11, 1863. Captured at Rappahannock Station, Virginia, November 7, 1863. Confined at Point Lookout, Maryland, November 11, 1863. Paroled at Point Lookout on February 24, 1865. Received at Aiken's Landing, James River, Virginia, February 25-28 or March 2-3, 1865, for exchange. Survived the war.

FOSTER, ANDREW J., Private

Resided in Davie County where he enlisted at age 29, July 4, 1862, for the war. Hospitalized at Richmond, Virginia, October 21, 1862, with typhoid fever. Furloughed for thirty days on November 20, 1862. Reported absent without leave on February 28, 1863. Returned to duty prior to May 11, 1863. Reported on detail as a teamster through December, 1863, and in March-August, 1864. Rejoined the company in September-October, 1864. Reported present in November, 1864-February, 1865. Captured at Fort Stedman, Virginia, March 25, 1865. Confined at Point Lookout, Maryland, March 28, 1865. Released at Point Lookout on June 26, 1865, after taking the Oath of Allegiance.

GAITHER, GEORGE W., Private

Resided in Davie County where he enlisted at age 32, July 4, 1862, for the war. Hospitalized at Richmond, Virginia, October 3, 1862, with typhoid fever. Returned to duty on October 12, 1862. Hospitalized at Richmond on November 9, 1862. Returned to duty on November 27, 1862. Hospitalized at Richmond on April 28, 1863, with pleuritis. Transferred to hospital at Danville, Virginia, May 8, 1863. Returned to duty prior to September 1, 1863, and was detailed as an ambulance driver. Reported absent on detail on surviving company muster rolls through April 30, 1864. Rejoined the company in May-August, 1864. Captured at Cedar Creek, Virginia, October 19, 1864. Confined at Point Lookout, Maryland, October 25, 1864. Paroled at Point Lookout on March 28, 1865. Received at Boulware's Wharf, James River, Virginia, March 30, 1865, for exchange.

GAITHER, JAMES M., Private

Resided in Davie County where he enlisted at age 30, July 4, 1862, for the war. Reported present or accounted for through February 28, 1863. Hospitalized at Richmond, Virginia, April 25, 1863, with pneumonia. Transferred to hospital at Danville, Virginia, May 8, 1863. Returned to duty on June 12, 1863. Detailed as a teamster prior to September 1, 1863. Reported on detail on surviving company muster rolls through April 30, 1864. Rejoined the company

in May-August, 1864. Captured at Cedar Creek, Virginia, October 19, 1864. Confined at Point Lookout, Maryland, October 25, 1864. Released at Point Lookout on June 16, 1865, after taking the Oath of Allegiance.

GULLETT, JOSEPH T., Private

Resided in Davie County and enlisted in Rowan County at age 16, July 4, 1862, for the war as a substitute for William L. Carson. Reported present through February 28, 1863. Hospitalized at Richmond, Virginia, March 28, 1863, with pneumonia. Transferred to Salisbury on or about April 22, 1863. Returned to duty subsequent to May 11, 1863. Captured at Gettysburg, Pennsylvania, on or about July 5, 1863. Confined at Fort Delaware, Delaware, on or about July 10, 1863. Transferred to Point Lookout, Maryland, October 22, 1863. Hospitalized at Point Lookout on December 19, 1863, with "chronic diarrhoea." Died at Point Lookout on January 12, 1864.

HACKETT, JAMES F., Private

Resided in Rowan County where he enlisted at age 33, August 13, 1862, for the war. Deserted at Salisbury on or about August 15, 1862.

HALL, JAMES M., Private

Place and date of enlistment not reported (probably enlisted subsequent to February 28, 1865). Captured at Salisbury on April 12, 1865. Confined at Nashville, Tennessee. Transferred to Louisville, Kentucky, April 29, 1865. Transferred to Camp Chase, Ohio, where he arrived on May 4, 1865. No further records.

HAWKINS, WESLEY, Private

Born in Yadkin County and resided in Rowan County where he was by occupation a farmer prior to enlisting in Rowan County on July 4, 1862, for the war as a substitute for "Horah." Hospitalized at Richmond, Virginia, November 8, 1862, with chronic diarrhoea. Transferred to Farmville, Virginia, December 15, 1862. Discharged at Farmville on December 24, 1862, by reason of "physical disability he being 16 years old." [May have served later as Private in Company H, 21st Regiment N.C. Troops (11th Regiment N.C. Volunteers).]

HILL, GEORGE W., Private

Resided in Davie County and was by occupation a mechanic prior to enlisting in Davie County at age 28, July 4, 1862, for the war. Reported present through February 28, 1863. Hospitalized at Richmond, Virginia, May 6, 1863, with "pneumonia" and died on May 16, 1863.

HOLMAN, J. B., Private

Enlisted in Davie County on July 8, 1862, for the war. No further records.

HOUPE, J. F., Private

Enlisted in Rowan County on July 6, 1862, for the war. Discharged on or about the same date after providing Pvt. Martin Conroy as a substitute.

HOWERTON, JAMES H., Private

Resided in Rowan County where he enlisted at age 24, July 4, 1862, for the war. Hospitalized at Richmond, Virginia, November 23, 1862, with acute diarrhoea. Transferred to Salisbury on December

4, 1862. Returned to duty prior to May 11, 1863. Deserted to the enemy near Fredericksburg, Virginia, on or about May 22, 1863. Took the Oath of Allegiance at Washington, D.C., on or about June 2, 1863.

KENNERLY, ROBERT CORNELIUS, Private

Resided in Rowan County and was by occupation a farmer prior to enlisting in Rowan County at age 27, July 4, 1862, for the war. Reported present through May 11, 1863. Captured at Gettysburg, Pennsylvania, July 3-5, 1863. Hospitalized at Gettysburg (apparently sick). Admitted to hospital at Baltimore, Maryland, on or about October 15, 1863, with debility. Transferred to Fort Mc-Henry, Maryland, on or about March 2, 1864. Transferred to Point Lookout, Maryland, July 21, 1864. Paroled at Point Lookout on February 13, 1865. Received at Cox's Wharf, James River, Virginia, February 14-15, 1865, for exchange. No further records.

KEPLEY, BURGESS, Private

Resided in Davie County and was by occupation a laborer prior to enlisting in Davie County at age 29, July 4, 1862, for the war. Hospitalized at Richmond, Virginia, October 10, 1862, with typhoid fever. Furloughed on November 6, 1862. Returned to duty prior to May 11, 1863. Reported absent with leave from May 17 through October 31, 1863. Reported absent without leave on December 1, 1863. Returned to duty in May-August, 1864. Reported absent sick from October 1 through December 31, 1864. Reported present or accounted for in January-February, 1865. No further records.

KISER, MARCUS L., Private

Resided in Cabarrus County and was by occupation a farm hand prior to enlisting in Rowan County at age 18, July 4, 1862, for the war. Reported absent sick or absent on sick furlough from August 23 through December 31, 1862. Returned to duty in January-February, 1863. Captured at Chancellorsville, Virginia, May 3-4, 1863. Confined at Fort Delaware, Delaware, on or about May 7, 1863. Paroled at Fort Delaware and transferred to City Point, Virginia, where he was received on May 23, 1863, for exchange. Reported absent sick from June 16 through October 31, 1863. Returned to duty in November-December, 1863. Reported on detached duty at Kinston in March-April, 1864. Wounded in the left arm at Lynchburg, Virginia, June 18, 1864. Left arm amputated. Placed on the "retired list" on December 22, 1864. Survived the war.

LEONARD, JACOB, Private

Resided in Davie County where he enlisted at age 24, July 4, 1862, for the war. Reported present through May 11, 1863. Reported absent without leave from May 17 through October 31, 1863. Reported present but under arrest in November-December, 1863. Court-martialed on or about January 19, 1864. Hospitalized at Richmond, Virginia, April 7, 1864, with intermittent fever. Transferred to Castle Thunder Prison, Richmond, April 15, 1864. Returned to duty prior to May 1, 1864. Captured at the North Anna River, Virginia, on or about May 23, 1864. Confined at Point Lookout, Maryland, May 30, 1864. Paroled at Point Lookout on or about March 14, 1865. Received at Boulware's Wharf, James River, Virginia, March 16, 1865, for exchange. Paroled at Salisbury on May 24, 1865.

LINKER, ELI, Private

Resided in Cabarrus County and was by occupation a day laborer prior to enlisting in Cabarrus County at age 34, July 4, 1862, for

the war. Hospitalized at Richmond, Virginia, September 26, 1862, with mumps. Returned to duty on October 6, 1862. Sent to hospital on February 19, 1863. Died in hospital at Lynchburg, Virginia, April 2-3, 1863, of disease.

LONG, HENRY G., Private

Resided in Union County and was by occupation a farm laborer prior to enlisting in Cabarrus County at age 27, July 4, 1862, for the war. Died in hospital at Richmond, Virginia, October 12, 1862, of "typhoid fever."

LONG, JAMES C., Corporal

Resided in Union County and was by occupation a farmer prior to enlisting in Cabarrus County at age 18, July 4, 1862, for the war. Mustered in as Private. Reported present or accounted for through October 31, 1863. Promoted to Corporal on November 1, 1863. Reported present on surviving company muster rolls through April 30, 1864. Captured at Winchester, Virginia, July 20, 1864. Confined at Camp Chase, Ohio, July 28, 1864. Paroled at Camp Chase on March 2, 1865. Received at Boulware's and Cox's Wharves, James River, Virginia, March 10-12, 1865, for exchange.

LONG, ROBERT L., Private

Resided in Union County and was by occupation a farmer prior to enlisting in Cabarrus County at age 18, July 4, 1862, for the war. Reported absent without leave on September 10, 1862. Reported on duty as a hospital nurse in November-December, 1862. Hospitalized at Danville, Virginia, January 8, 1863. Returned to duty on February 20, 1863. Discharged on April 10, 1863, by reason of disability.

McCALISTER, J. W., Private

Enlisted in Wake County on April 18, 1864, for the war. Deserted near Kinston on May 2, 1864.

McCANLASS, AMOS L., Private

Resided in Rowan County where he enlisted at age 22, July 4, 1862, for the war. Mustered in as Corporal. Hospitalized at Richmond, Virginia, September 22, 1862, with bronchitis. Later contracted typhoid fever. Furloughed on or about October 8, 1862. Reduced to ranks in November-December, 1862. Hospitalized at Richmond on December 20, 1862, and February 20, 1863, with phthisis. Reported absent without leave in May-August, 1863. Reported absent sick in September-December, 1863. Returned to duty prior to May 1, 1864. Reported present through February 28, 1865. Captured at Farmville, Virginia, April 6, 1865. Confined at Point Lookout, Maryland, April 14, 1865. Released at Point Lookout on June 6, 1865, after taking the Oath of Allegiance.

McCLURE, DAVID A., Private

Resided in Cabarrus County and was by occupation a farm laborer prior to enlisting in Cabarrus County at age 24, July 4, 1862, for the war. Reported present through December 31, 1862. Died at Lynchburg, Virginia, February 9, 1863, of "icterus."

McCORKLE, W. A., Private

Enlisted in Wake County on April 18, 1864, for the war. Reported absent without leave on August 24, 1864. Returned to duty in November-December, 1864. Reported present through February 28, 1865. Surrendered at Appomattox Court House, Virginia, April 9, 1865.

McDANIEL, JOHN G., Private

Resided in Davie County and enlisted in Rowan County at age 16, July 4, 1862, for the war as a substitute for John Bailey of Salisbury. Hospitalized at Richmond, Virginia, on or about September 29, 1862. Returned to duty on October 10, 1862. Reported present through May 11, 1863. Reported sick in hospital from June 16 through October 31, 1863. Reported absent without leave in November-December, 1863, and March-April, 1864. Company muster rolls dated April 30, 1864-February 28, 1865, indicate that he was captured at Gettysburg, Pennsylvania, July 3, 1863; however, records of the Federal Provost Marshal do not substantiate that report. No further records.

McGEHEE, JAMES M., Private

Resided in Guilford County and was by occupation a laborer prior to enlisting in Rowan County at age 19, July 4, 1862, for the war. Died in camp near Fredericksburg, Virginia, on or about January 8, 1863, of disease.

McLAUGHLIN, JOHN H. A., Private

Born in Iredell County where he resided prior to enlisting in Rowan County at age 21, July 4, 1862, for the war. Died in camp near Port Royal, Virginia, on or about February 19, 1863, of disease.

MAYHEW, N. J., Private

Resided in Iredell County and enlisted in Cabarrus County at age 32, July 4, 1862, for the war. Died in hospital at Richmond, Virginia, on or about September 24, 1862, of "typhoid fever."

MILLS, CHARLES M., Private

Resided in Iredell County and enlisted in Rowan County at age 25, July 4, 1862, for the war. Reported absent without leave on September 10, 1862. Hospitalized at Richmond, Virginia, December 7, 1862, with pneumonia. Transferred to Farmville, Virginia, December 21, 1862. Furloughed for twenty-five days from hospital at Farmville on March 2, 1863. Returned to duty prior to May 11, 1863. Captured at Rappahannock Station, Virginia, November 7, 1863. Confined at Point Lookout, Maryland, November 11, 1863. Died at Point Lookout on December 3, 1864, of "acute dysentery."

MILLS, GEORGE F., Private

Resided in Iredell County and enlisted in Rowan County at age 28, July 4, 1862, for the war. Reported present or accounted for through February 28, 1863. Hospitalized at Richmond, Virginia, March 27, 1863, with enteric fever. Transferred to hospital at Danville, Virginia, April 27, 1863. Reported absent on sick furlough from July 24 through August 31, 1863. Reported absent without leave from October 9 through December 31, 1863. Returned to duty prior to May 1, 1864. Reported present through February 28, 1865. Captured at Farmville, Virginia, April 6, 1865. Confined at Newport News, Virginia, April 14, 1865. Released at Newport News on June 26, 1865, after taking the Oath of Allegiance. [North Carolina pension records indicate that he was wounded in the foot "by a bursting shell which has hurt him very little" at Petersburg, Virginia, March 6, 1865.]

MILLS, JAMES W., Private

Born in Iredell County where he resided as a student prior to enlisting in Rowan County at age 21, July 4, 1862, for the war. Discharged on September 6, 1862, by reason of "valvular disease of heart." [Apparently suffered also from asthma.]

MONDAY, ISAAC, Private

Resided in Davie County and enlisted in Rowan County at age 19, July 4, 1862, for the war. Reported present through February 28, 1863. Wounded in the hand at Chancellorsville, Virginia, May 4, 1863. Returned to duty prior to September 1, 1863. Captured at Rappahannock Station, Virginia, November 7, 1863. Confined at Point Lookout, Maryland, November 11, 1863. Died in the smallpox hospital at Point Lookout on or about January 25, 1864.

MOONEYHAM, WILLIAM, Private

Enlisted in Wake County on April 18, 1864, for the war. Deserted at Kinston on May 2, 1864. Returned to duty in November-December, 1864. Reported present in January-February, 1865. Hospitalized at Richmond, Virginia, March 29, 1865, with debilitas. Captured in hospital at Richmond on April 3, 1865. Transferred to Newport News, Virginia, April 23, 1865. Died at Newport News on June 19, 1865. Cause of death not reported.

MOSS, WHITSON S., Private

Resided in Union County and enlisted in Rowan County at age 32, July 4, 1862, for the war. Wounded in the left hand at Fredericksburg, Virginia, December 13, 1862. Reported in hospital at Farmville, Virginia, January 16, 1863. Was also suffering from syphilis. Died in hospital at Farmville on or about May 6, 1863, of "gastritis."

MURPH, THOMAS D., Private

Resided in Cabarrus County and was by occupation a farmer prior to enlisting in Cabarrus County at age 21, July 4, 1862, for the war. Reported present through February 28, 1863. Reported sick in hospital on April 21, 1863. Reported absent without leave on July 10, 1863. Arrested by Federal authorities at Martinsburg, West Virginia, on an unspecified date. Reported in confinement in a Federal prison at Wheeling, West Virginia, August 5, 1863. Transferred to Camp Chase, Ohio, August 6, 1863. Was apparently released at Camp Chase shortly thereafter after taking the Oath of Allegiance.

MURPHY, STEPHEN, Private

Resided in Union County and enlisted in Rowan County at age 34, August 13, 1862, for the war. Deserted at or near Richmond, Virginia, on or about September 25, 1862.

MUSE, JAMES R., Private

Resided in Union County and enlisted in Cabarrus County at age 27, July 4, 1862, for the war. Hospitalized at Richmond, Virginia, December 12, 1862. Returned to duty on December 30, 1862. Reported present on surviving company muster rolls through August 31, 1864. Killed near Mount Jackson, Virginia, September 23, 1864. He was "a most gallant soldier." [Clark's *Regiments*, 3:428.]

NANNY, WILLIAM W., Private

Resided in Iredell County and enlisted in Rowan County at age 16, July 4, 1862, for the war as a substitute. Hospitalized at Richmond, Virginia, October 13, 1862, with remittent fever. Returned to duty on November 10, 1862. Reported absent without leave from November 22, 1862, through June 8, 1863. Reported present in September-October, 1863. Captured at Rappahannock Station, Virginia, November 7, 1863. Confined at Point Lookout, Maryland, November 11, 1863. Died in the smallpox hospital at Point Lookout on or about February 13, 1864.

OLSESCA, THOMAS A., Private

Born in Duplin County and resided in Davidson County where he was by occupation a farmer prior to enlisting in Rowan County at age 16, July 4, 1862, for the war as a substitute. Reported present through February 28, 1863. Reported sick in hospital from April 3 through May 11, 1863. Returned to duty prior to September 1, 1863. Captured at Rappahannock Station, Virginia, November 7, 1863. Confined at Point Lookout, Maryland, November 11, 1863. Admitted to the smallpox hospital at Point Lookout on December 5, 1863. Returned to the prison compound on January 18, 1864. Released at Point Lookout on January 28, 1864, after taking the Oath of Allegiance and joining the U.S. Army. Assigned to Company C, 1st Regiment U.S. Volunteer Infantry.

PHILLIPS, JOHN, Private

Enlisted in Wake County on April 18, 1864, for the war. Deserted prior to May 1, 1864. Returned to duty subsequent to August 31, 1864. Killed at Cedar Creek, Virginia, October 19, 1864.

PICKLER, R. G. D., Private

Resided in Stanly County and enlisted in Wake County at age 52, March 7, 1864, for the war. Hospitalized at Goldsboro on May 7, 1864. Returned to duty on May 18, 1864. Reported absent from June 26 through September 1, 1864. Returned to duty prior to October 19, 1864, when he was wounded (probably in the groin) at Cedar Creek, Virginia. Reported absent wounded through February 28, 1865. Paroled at Salisbury on June 20, 1865.

PINION, HENRY J., Private

Resided in Guilford County and enlisted in Cabarrus County at age 30, July 4, 1862, for the war. Reported absent in hospital from August 20, 1862, through February 28, 1863. Returned to duty prior to May 4, 1863, when he was wounded in the chest at Chancellorsville, Virginia. Hospitalized at Richmond, Virginia, where he died on May 12, 1863, of wounds.

POLK, CHARLES HARRIS, Private

Born on April 23, 1828. Resided in Cabarrus County where he enlisted at age 34, July 4, 1862, for the war. Reported present through October 31, 1863. Captured at Rappahannock Station, Virginia, November 7, 1863. Confined at Point Lookout, Maryland, November 11, 1863. Hospitalized at Point Lookout on December 8, 1863, with debilitas. Paroled at Point Lookout on or about March 17, 1864. Received at City Point, Virginia, March 20, 1864, for exchange. Hospitalized at Richmond, Virginia, on the same date with debility. Furloughed for thirty days on March 26, 1864. Returned to duty in May-August, 1864. Captured at Fort Stedman, Virginia, March 25, 1865. Confined at Point Lookout on March 28, 1865. Released at Point Lookout on June 17, 1865, after taking the Oath of Allegiance.

POLK, JAMES ALLEN, Corporal

Resided in Cabarrus County where he enlisted at age 26, July 4, 1862, for the war. Mustered in as Private. Wounded in the hand at Fredericksburg, Virginia, December 13, 1862. Reported in hospital at Farmville, Virginia, January 15, 1863, suffering from his wound and bronchitis. Returned to duty in February, 1863. Reported present through October 31, 1863. Promoted to Corporal on November 1, 1863. Captured at Rappahannock Station, Virginia, November 7, 1863. Confined at Point Lookout, Maryland, November 11, 1863. Paroled at Point Lookout on November 1, 1864. Received at Venus Point, Savannah River, Georgia, November 15, 1864, for

exchange. Reported absent with leave on December 2, 1864. Returned to duty in January-February, 1865. Captured at Fort Stedman, Virginia, March 25, 1865. Confined at Point Lookout on March 28, 1865. Released at Point Lookout on June 17, 1865, after taking the Oath of Allegiance.

POOR, JEREMIAH M., Private

Resided in Guilford County and enlisted at "Jamestown" at age 29, July 4, 1862, for the war. Reported on duty as a wagoner in September-December, 1862. Rejoined the company in January-February, 1863. Hospitalized at Richmond, Virginia, April 7, 1863, with icterus. Transferred to hospital at Danville, Virginia, May 8, 1863. Returned to duty on June 2, 1863. Reported present through October 31, 1863. Captured at Rappahannock Station, Virginia, November 7, 1863. Confined at Point Lookout, Maryland, November 11, 1863. Released at Point Lookout on January 24, 1864, after taking the Oath of Allegiance and joining the U.S. Army. Assigned to Company B, 1st Regiment U.S. Volunteer Infantry.

PRESLEY, G. WILLIAM H., Private

Resided in Anson County and was by occupation a farmer prior to enlisting in Wake County on April 17, 1864, for the war. Captured (possibly wounded) at Winchester, Virginia, July 20, 1864. Confined at Camp Chase, Ohio, July 28, 1864. Paroled at Camp Chase on March 2, 1865. Received at Boulware's and Cox's Wharves, James River, Virginia, March 10-12, 1865, for exchange. No further records. [Records of the Federal Provost Marshal dated July, 1864, give his age as 28.]

PRIDDY, WILLIAM B., Private

Place and date of enlistment not reported (probably enlisted subsequent to February 28, 1865). Captured at Hatcher's Run, Virginia, April 1, 1865. Confined at Point Lookout, Maryland, April 5, 1865. Hospitalized at Point Lookout on May 4, 1865, with "diarrhoea." Died in hospital at Point Lookout on May 15, 1865.

RABON, C., Private

Enlisted in Wake County on April 19, 1864, for the war. Wounded at Winchester, Virginia, September 19, 1864. Returned to duty in January-February, 1865. Surrendered at Appomattox Court House, Virginia, April 9, 1865.

RAINEY, WILLIAM T., Private

Resided in Rowan County and enlisted in Wake County at age 18, February 9, 1864, for the war. Reported present through February 28, 1865. Captured at Farmville, Virginia, April 6, 1865. Confined at Newport News, Virginia, April 14, 1865. Released at Newport News on June 26, 1865, after taking the Oath of Allegiance.

RICE, THOMAS G., Private

Enlisted in Rowan County on July 8, 1862, for the war. "Entry canceled."

ROWLAND, JOHN G., Private

Resided in Stanly County and was by occupation a farmer prior to enlisting in Cabarrus County at age 25, July 4, 1862, for the war. Reported absent without leave on September 10, 1862. Returned to duty prior to November 1, 1862. Reported absent in hospital from January 23 through May 11, 1863. Returned to duty prior to September 1, 1863. Reported present on surviving company muster rolls through April 30, 1864. Captured at Winchester, Virginia,

July 20, 1864. Confined at Camp Chase, Ohio, July 28, 1864. Died at Camp Chase on November 9, 1864, of "smallpox."

ROWLAND, SHERWOOD P., 1st Sergeant

Resided in Cabarrus County and was by occupation a millwright prior to enlisting in Cabarrus County at age 28, July 4, 1862, for the war. Mustered in as 1st Sergeant. Hospitalized at Richmond, Virginia, December 6, 1862. Returned to duty on December 15, 1862. Died in hospital at Richmond on January 3, 1863, of "febris typhoides."

RUSSELL, ISAAC P., Private

Resided in Cabarrus County and was by occupation a farmer prior to enlisting in Rowan County at age 18, July 4, 1862, for the war. Hospitalized at Richmond, Virginia, November 22, 1862, with parotitis. Later contracted pneumonia. Transferred to hospital at Danville, Virginia, January 8, 1863. Returned to duty on February 13, 1863. Captured at Gettysburg, Pennsylvania, on or about July 3, 1863. Confined at Fort Delaware, Delaware, on or about July 9, 1863. Died at Fort Delaware on October 27, 1863, of "int[ermittent] fever."

RUSSELL, JAMES A., Private

Resided in Cabarrus County and enlisted in Rowan County at age 32, July 4, 1862, for the war. Wounded in the elbow at Fredericksburg, Virginia, December 13, 1862. Hospitalized at Richmond, Virginia. Furloughed for sixty days on January 10, 1863. Returned to duty on an unspecified date. Captured at Gettysburg, Pennsylvania, on or about July 5, 1863, after he was left behind as a nurse for the wounded. Transferred to Davids Island, New York Harbor, on or about July 21, 1863. Paroled at Davids Island on an unspecified date. Received at City Point, Virginia, September 8, 1863, for exchange. Returned to duty in January-April, 1864. Reported present through August 31, 1864. Wounded in the left leg at Cedar Creek, Virginia, October 19, 1864. Furloughed from hospital at Richmond on January 10, 1865. Survived the war.

RUSSELL, WILLIAM McKENZIE, Private

Resided in Rowan County where he enlisted at age 24, July 4, 1862, for the war. Deserted at Salisbury on August 7, 1862. Hospitalized at Richmond, Virginia, on or about December 22, 1862. Reported absent in hospital through August 31, 1863. Listed as a deserter on October 31, 1863. Reported absent without leave in May, 1864-February, 1865. No further records.

SCOTT, ABRAHAM A., Corporal

Resided in Rowan County and enlisted in Cabarrus County at age 33, July 4, 1862, for the war. Mustered in as Corporal. Wounded in the arm at Fredericksburg, Virginia, December 13, 1862. Hospitalized at Richmond, Virginia, where he died on December 30, 1862, of wounds.

SHORT, SAMUEL H., Private

Enlisted in Rowan County on July 6, 1862, for the war as a substitute for Lawrence Hart. Reported present or accounted for through December 31, 1862. Died in camp near Port Royal, Virginia, February 5, 1863, of "pneumonia."

SHULTZ, JAMES E., Private

Enlisted in Wake County on March 12, 1864, for the war. Captured at Harpers Ferry, West Virginia, July 8, 1864. Confined at Old Capitol Prison, Washington, D.C., July 21, 1864. Transferred to Elmira, New York, July 23, 1864. Released at Elmira on March 14, 1865, after taking the Oath of Allegiance.

SMITH, HENRY D., Private

Resided in Cabarrus County and was by occupation a farm hand prior to enlisting in Cabarrus County at age 19, July 4, 1862, for the war. Reported present through December 31, 1862. Hospitalized at Richmond, Virginia, March 7, 1863, with pneumonia. Returned to duty on April 16, 1863. Captured at or near Gettysburg, Pennsylvania, on or about July 3-5, 1863. Confined at Fort Delaware, Delaware, on or about July 9, 1863. Transferred to Point Lookout, Maryland, on or about October 25, 1863. Died at Point Lookout on April 5, 1864. Cause of death not reported.

SMITH, JOSHUA, Private

Resided in Rowan County where he enlisted at age 52, July 4, 1862, for the war as a substitute for "Hammershlag." Hospitalized at Richmond, Virginia, October 31, 1862, with typhoid fever. Returned to duty on December 13, 1862. Hospitalized at Richmond on January 7, 1863, with chronic diarrhoea. Transferred to Salisbury on January 23, 1863. Reported absent without leave on September 15, 1863. Returned to duty on an unspecified date. Detailed as a harness maker at Richmond on December 4, 1863. Reported sick at home from February 1 through August 31, 1864. Reported absent on sick furlough from September 15, 1864, through February 28, 1865. Died at Salisbury on an unspecified date. Cause of death not reported.

SMITH, R. M., Private

Born in Cabarrus County where he resided as a farmer prior to enlisting in Cabarrus County at age 27, July 4, 1862, for the war. Died in hospital at Richmond, Virginia, September 19, 1862, of "rubeola."

SPRY, CALVIN, Private

Resided in Davie County and was by occupation a laborer prior to enlisting in Davie County at age 26, July 4, 1862, for the war. Reported absent without leave on September 10, 1862. Returned to duty on October 26, 1862. Reported present through May 11, 1863. Wounded in the knee and captured at Gettysburg, Pennsylvania, July 2-3, 1863. Hospitalized at Chester, Pennsylvania. Paroled at Chester on or about August 17, 1863. Received at City Point, Virginia, August 20, 1863, for exchange. Reported absent without leave from December 15, 1863, through October 31, 1864. Returned to duty in November-December, 1864. Reported present in January-February, 1865. Captured at Fort Stedman, Virginia, March 25, 1865. Confined at Point Lookout, Maryland, March 28, 1865. Released at Point Lookout on June 19, 1865, after taking the Oath of Allegiance.

STARNES, E. A., Private

Enlisted in Wake County on March 7, 1864, for the war. Reported present through August 31, 1864. Captured (possibly wounded in the head) at Winchester, Virginia, September 19, 1864. No further records.

SULLIVAN, PATRICK, Private

Resided in Davie County and enlisted in Rowan County at age 28, July 4, 1862, for the war. Deserted at Richmond, Virginia, August 13, 1862.

TAYLOR, G. M., Private

Resided in Davie County and enlisted in Rowan County at age 37, July 4, 1862, for the war as a substitute. Hospitalized at Richmond, Virginia, November 9, 1862. Died in hospital at Richmond on November 27, 1862, of "febris typhoides."

TUNSTALL, WILLIAM H., Private

Born in Virginia and resided in Rowan or Granville County where he was by occupation a master mason prior to enlisting in Rowan County at age 30, July 4, 1862, for the war. Mustered in as Corporal. Reported sick in hospital on August 12, 1862. Reduced to ranks prior to September 2, 1862. Reported absent without leave on September 10, 1862. Returned to duty subsequent to February 28, 1863. Detailed as acting Sergeant Major and transferred to the Field and Staff of this regiment in May-August, 1863. Appointed Sergeant Major subsequent to March 20 but prior to July 20, 1864, and assigned to permanent duty with the Field and Staff of this regiment.

URY, DANIEL J., Private

Resided in Cabarrus County and was by occupation a farm hand prior to enlisting in Cabarrus County at age 18, July 4, 1862, for the war. Died in hospital at Richmond, Virginia, September 10, 1862, of gunshot wounds or disease.

URY, JACOB, Private

Resided in Cabarrus County and was by occupation a farmer prior to enlisting in Cabarrus County at age 31, July 4, 1862, for the war. Hospitalized at Richmond, Virginia, September 25, 1862, with dysentery. Furloughed on October 14, 1862. Returned to duty prior to December 13, 1862, when he was wounded at Fredericksburg, Virginia. Returned to duty in January-February, 1863. Captured on or about May 24, 1863, during the "recent raid in the rear of Lee's army." Paroled on or about the same date. Returned to duty prior to September 1, 1863. Captured at Rappahannock Station, Virginia, November 7, 1863. Confined at Point Lookout, Maryland, November 11, 1863. Hospitalized at Point Lookout on December 25, 1863. Died in hospital at Point Lookout on January 16, 1864, of "chronic diarrhoea."

VAN EATON, RICHARD T., Private

Resided in Davie County and was by occupation a carpenter prior to enlisting in Rowan County at age 25, July 4, 1862, for the war. Reported present or accounted for through February 28, 1865. Surrendered at Appomattox Court House, Virginia, April 9, 1865. He was "a most gallant soldier." [Clark's *Regiments*, 3:428.]

VAN ZANT, ENOCH C., Private

Resided in Davie County where he enlisted at age 27, July 4, 1862, for the war. Reported sick on August 25 and September 26, 1862. Returned to duty prior to November 1, 1862. Reported at home on sick furlough in November-December, 1862. Returned to duty in January-February, 1863. Reported absent without leave from May 17 through October 31, 1863. Returned to duty in November-December, 1863. Reported on detail at Kinston as a blacksmith in March, 1864-February, 1865. Survived the war.

VEACH, WILLIAM E., Private

Resided in Davie County where he enlisted at age 18, July 4, 1862, for the war. Hospitalized at Richmond, Virginia, November 9, 1862. Furloughed for thirty days on December 8, 1862. Returned to duty in January-February, 1863. Hospitalized at Danville, Virginia, June 18, 1863, with intermittent fever. Transferred

to Salisbury on June 25, 1863. Returned to duty prior to September 1, 1863. Captured at Rappahannock Station, Virginia, November 7, 1863. Confined at Point Lookout, Maryland, November 11, 1863. Paroled at Point Lookout on May 3, 1864. Received at Aiken's Landing, James River, Virginia, May 8, 1864, for exchange. Reported absent without leave on December 2, 1864. Paroled at Salisbury on May 19, 1865.

WALKER, JAMES H., Corporal

Resided in Rowan County and enlisted in Cabarrus County at age 32, July 4, 1862, for the war. Mustered in as Corporal. Reported absent without leave on September 10, 1862. Returned to duty prior to November 1, 1862. Reported present through May 11, 1863. Killed (or mortally wounded) at Gettysburg, Pennsylvania, July 2-3, 1863.

WALKER, WILLIAM A., Private

Resided in Davie County and was by occupation a laborer prior to enlisting in Rowan County at age 19, July 4, 1862, for the war. Reported present through May 11, 1863. Reported absent without leave on June 29 and July 2, 1863. Captured by the enemy at or near Fairfield or Chambersburg, Pennsylvania, July 5, 1863. Hospitalized at Harrisburg, Pennsylvania, August 4, 1863, with pneumonia. Transferred to hospital at Baltimore, Maryland, August 14, 1863. Confined at Fort McHenry, Maryland, September 12, 1863. Transferred to Point Lookout, Maryland, September 15, 1863. Hospitalized at Point Lookout on October 22, 1863. Died in hospital at Point Lookout on December 6, 1863, of "chronic diarrhoea."

WALTER, JOHN E., Private

Place and date of enlistment not reported (probably enlisted subsequent to February 28, 1865). Captured at Hatcher's Run, Virginia, April 1, 1865. Confined at Point Lookout, Maryland, April 5, 1865. Released at Point Lookout on June 5, 1865, after taking the Oath of Allegiance.

WEBB, JOHN P., Private

Resided in Rowan County where he enlisted at age 17, July 4, 1862, for the war as a substitute for Webb Johnston of Salisbury. Hospitalized at Richmond, Virginia, October 25, 1862, with remittent fever. Returned to duty on November 24, 1862. Reported present or accounted for through February 28, 1863. Wounded in the right hip at Chancellorsville, Virginia, May 4, 1863. Hospitalized at Richmond. Returned to duty on June 4, 1863. Transferred to Company C of this regiment in September-October, 1863.

WEESNER, WILLIAM, Private

Enlisted in Wake County on March 12, 1864, for the war. Hospitalized at Goldsboro on April 20, 1864. Discharged from hospital on May 2, 1864. Reported absent sick from June 13 through December 31, 1864. Returned to duty in January-February, 1865. No further records.

WILLIAMS, ISHMAEL W., Private

Resided in Cabarrus County and was by occupation a day laborer prior to enlisting in Cabarrus County at age 29, July 4, 1862, for the war. Reported absent sick at Salisbury on September 8, 1862. Returned to duty prior to November 1, 1862. Reported present through February 28, 1863. Reported sick in hospital from April 21 through May 11, 1863. Reported absent on sick furlough from August 19 through December 31, 1863. Returned to duty prior to May 1, 1864. Reported present through October 31, 1864. Detailed as a provost guard on December 26, 1864. Returned to duty in January-February, 1865. Surrendered at Appomattox Court House,

Virginia, April 9, 1865. [North Carolina pension records indicate that he was wounded in the right shin by a shell in 1864.]

WILSON, GEORGE M., Private

Resided in Union or Cabarrus County and enlisted in Rowan County at age 17, July 4, 1862, for the war as a substitute for F. C. McNelly. Reported present through October 31, 1863. Captured at Rappahannock Station, Virginia, November 7, 1863. Confined at Point Lookout, Maryland, on or about November 11, 1863. Hospitalized at Point Lookout on January 24, 1864, with smallpox. Released from hospital on February 24, 1864. Paroled at Point Lookout on April 27, 1864. Received at City Point, Virginia, April 30, 1864, for exchange. Hospitalized at Richmond, Virginia, May 1, 1864, with cystitis. Furloughed for thirty days on May 6, 1864. Returned to duty prior to September 1, 1864. Reported present through February 28, 1865. Captured at Farmville, Virginia, April 6, 1865. Confined at Newport News, Virginia, April 14, 1865. Released at Newport News on June 27, 1865, after taking the Oath of Allegiance.

WILSON, HENRY A., Sergeant

Resided in Iredell County where he enlisted at age 29, July 4, 1862, for the war. Mustered in as Sergeant. Reported present but on detail as acting Commissary Sergeant in November-December, 1862, and May-August, 1863. Promoted to the permanent rank of Commissary Sergeant in September-October, 1863, and transferred to the Field and Staff of this regiment.

WILSON, JOHN N., Sergeant

Resided in Union or Stanly County and enlisted in Rowan County at age 47, July 4, 1862, for the war as a substitute for "Kelly." Mustered in as Private. Promoted to Corporal in November-December, 1862. Reported present through October 31, 1863. Promoted to Sergeant on November 1, 1863. Captured at Rappahannock Station, Virginia, November 7, 1863. Confined at Point Lookout, Maryland, November 11, 1863. Died in the smallpox hospital at Point Lookout on December 31, 1863, or January 5, 1864.

WOOD, JOSHUA, Private

Enlisted in Wake County on March 7, 1864, for the war. Reported absent sick from June 20 through August 31, 1864. Reported on detail in hospital at Lynchburg, Virginia, in September, 1864-February, 1865. Paroled at Albemarle on May 19, 1865.

COMPANY I

This company was raised in Alamance County on July 4, 1862. It was mustered into service at Salisbury on July 17, 1862, and assigned to the 57th Regiment N.C. Troops as Company I. After joining the regiment the company functioned as a part of the regiment, and its history for the remainder of the war is reported as a part of the regimental history.

The following roster was compiled primarily from information in the microfilm edition of the Compiled Service Records of Soldiers Who Served in Organizations from the State of North Carolina (Record Group 109, M270), National Archives and Records Administration, Washington, D.C. Record Group 109 includes enlistment papers, pay vouchers, requisitions, letters of resignation, discharge certificates, and abstracts of medical and prisoner of war returns. Materials relating specifically to this company include muster rolls dated July

4, 1862-December 31, 1863, and February 29, 1864-February 28, 1865.

Also utilized in this roster were *The War of the Rebellion: A Compilation of the Official Records of the Union and Confederate Armies*, the North Carolina adjutant general's *Roll of Honor*, state militia records, newspaper casualty lists and obituaries, wartime claims for bounty pay and allowances, postwar registers of claims for artificial limbs, Confederate pension applications filed with the states of North Carolina, Tennessee, and Florida, Confederate Soldiers' Home records, and the 1860 and 1870 federal censuses of North Carolina. A search was made also for relevant letters, diaries, reminiscences, and other manuscripts in the Southern Historical Collection (University of North Carolina-Chapel Hill), the Duke University Library Special Collections Department, and the North Carolina Division of Archives and History.

Among the secondary sources consulted were records of the North Carolina division of the United Daughters of the Confederacy, postwar rosters, regimental and county histories, marriage bond, will, and cemetery indexes, published and unpublished genealogies, biographical dictionaries, the North Carolina *County Heritage Book* series, the *Confederate Veteran*, Walter Clark's *Histories of the Several Regiments and Battalions from North Carolina in the Great War, 1861- '65*, and the North Carolina volume of the extended edition of *Confederate Military History*.

OFFICERS

CAPTAINS

ALBRIGHT, WILLIAM ALEXANDER

Born on May 25, 1836. Resided in Alamance County and was by occupation a farmer prior to enlisting in Rowan County at age 26. Appointed Captain on July 4, 1862. Hospitalized at Richmond, Virginia, October 7, 1862, with jaundice. Furloughed on October 14, 1862. Resigned on February 16, 1863, by reason of "great emaciation from chronic hepatitis which has produced repeated attacks of haematuria inducing great physical and nervous prostration." Resignation accepted on March 5, 1863. Took the Oath of Allegiance at Raleigh on May 11, 1865. [Previously served as 2nd Lieutenant in the 84th Regiment N.C. Militia.]

DICKEY, JOSEPH H.

Born on May 30, 1844. Resided in Alamance County and enlisted at age 18. Appointed 2nd Lieutenant on July 4, 1862. Hospitalized at Richmond, Virginia, November 22, 1862, with gonorrhea. Returned to duty on December 6, 1862. Promoted to 1st Lieutenant on December 10, 1862. Promoted to Captain on March 5, 1863. Reported absent sick in March-April, 1863. Reported present in May-December, 1863, and March-April, 1864. Reported present but sick in May-August, 1864. Returned to duty in September-October, 1864. Reported present in November, 1864-February, 1865. Surrendered at Appomattox Court House, Virginia, April 9, 1865. [Reported in command of Company K of this regiment in November, 1864-February, 1865.]

LIEUTENANTS

HOWERTON, ALBERT W., 1st Lieutenant

Previously served as Private in Company F, 9th Regiment N.C. State Troops (1st Regiment N.C. Cavalry). Appointed 1st Lieutenant of this company on July 4, 1862. Resigned on November 20, 1862, by reason of "secondary syphilis which interferes with the proper motion of his left hip joint." Resignation accepted on December 10, 1862.

MAYNARD, RICHARD L., 1st Lieutenant

Previously served as Corporal in Company E, 13th Regiment N.C. Troops (3rd Regiment N.C. Volunteers). Appointed 3rd Lieutenant on July 26, 1862, to rank from July 4, 1862, and transferred to this company. Promoted to 2nd Lieutenant on December 10, 1862. Reported present through February 28, 1863. Promoted to 1st Lieutenant on March 11, 1863. Reported in command of the company in March-May and November-December, 1863. Hospitalized at Danville, Virginia, July 3, 1863, with chronic bronchitis. Returned to duty on August 14, 1863. Reported present on surviving company muster rolls through August 31, 1864. Wounded in the right leg at Winchester, Virginia, September 19, 1864. Hospitalized at Charlottesville, Virginia. Reported absent wounded or absent sick through February 28, 1865. Paroled at Greensboro on May 10, 1865. [Reported in command of Company H of this regiment in May-August, 1864.]

RONEY, L. H., 3rd Lieutenant

Resided in Alamance County where he enlisted at age 32, July 4, 1862, for the war. Mustered in as Private. Hospitalized at Richmond, Virginia, October 8, 1862, with typhoid fever and parotitis. Furloughed on October 18, 1862. Returned to duty prior to November 1, 1862. Appointed 3rd Lieutenant on December 10, 1862. Reported present through May 11, 1863. Killed "on the skirmish line" at Gettysburg, Pennsylvania, July 1, 1863. He was "distinguished . . . for great courage and efficiency." [Clark's *Regiments*, 3:427.]

NONCOMMISSIONED OFFICERS AND PRIVATES

ADAMS, JACOB E., Private

Born in Alamance County* where he resided as a farmer prior to enlisting in Alamance County at age 30, July 4, 1862, for the war. Reported present until May 4, 1863, when he was killed at Chancellorsville, Virginia.

ADAMS, WILLIAM B., Private

Resided in Alamance County where he enlisted at age 26, July 4, 1862, for the war. Hospitalized at Richmond, Virginia, January 27, 1863. Died in hospital at Richmond on February 6, 1863, of disease.

ALDRIDGE, WILLIAM H., Corporal

Resided in Alamance County and was by occupation a farmer or laborer prior to enlisting in Alamance County at age 21, July 4, 1862, for the war. Mustered in as Private. Reported present through December 31, 1862. Promoted to Corporal on January 1, 1863. Reported present until November 7, 1863, when he was captured at Rappahannock Station, Virginia. Confined at Point Lookout, Maryland, November 11, 1863. Paroled at Point Lookout on March 16, 1864. Received at City Point, Virginia, March 20, 1864, for exchange. Reported absent sick in May-October, 1864. Returned to duty in November-December, 1864. Reported present in January-February, 1865. Captured at Fort Stedman, Virginia, March 25, 1865. Confined at Point Lookout on March 28, 1865.

Released at Point Lookout on or about May 13, 1865, after taking the Oath of Allegiance.

ANDREWS, STEPHEN, Private

Born in Orange County where he resided prior to enlisting in Orange County at age 28, July 4, 1862, for the war. Hospitalized at Richmond, Virginia, October 10, 1862, with rubeola. Furloughed on November 12, 1862. Returned to duty prior to January 1, 1863. Discharged at Lynchburg, Virginia, on or about March 16, 1863, by reason of "phthisis pulmonalis."

ANDREWS, SURREN, Private

Resided in Orange County where he enlisted at age 20, July 4, 1862, for the war. Hospitalized at Richmond, Virginia, October 21, 1862, with remittent fever. Furloughed on November 12, 1862. Returned to duty prior to January 1, 1863. Wounded in the right shoulder at Chancellorsville, Virginia, May 4, 1863. Arm amputated. Hospitalized at Richmond where he died on June 24, 1863, of wounds.

ANDREWS, WILLIAM C., Private

Resided in Alamance County and was by occupation a farmer prior to enlisting in Alamance County at age 25, July 4, 1862, for the war. Hospitalized at Richmond, Virginia, on or about September 21, 1862, with intermittent fever. Returned to duty on or about September 30, 1862. Killed at Fredericksburg, Virginia, December 13, 1862.

ATKINS, WILLIAM, Private

Resided in Alamance County where he enlisted at age 26, July 4, 1862, for the war. Hospitalized at Richmond, Virginia, September 15, 1862, with intermittent fever. Furloughed for thirty days on October 30, 1862. Reported sick in hospital in January-February, 1863. Returned to duty in March-May, 1863. Captured at Rappahannock Station, Virginia, November 7, 1863. Confined at Point Lookout, Maryland, November 11, 1863. Died at Point Lookout on February 14, 1864. Cause of death not reported.

BECK, SOLOMON R., Private

Resided in Davidson County and was by occupation a farmer or farm laborer prior to enlisting in Wake County at age 35, March 8, 1864, for the war. Captured at Winchester, Virginia, July 20, 1864. Confined at Camp Chase, Ohio, July 28, 1864. Paroled at Camp Chase on March 2, 1865. Received at Boulware's and Cox's Wharves, James River, Virginia, March 10-12, 1865, for exchange. Survived the war.

BENSON, S. F., Private

Enlisted in Alamance County on March 10, 1864, for the war. Killed at Drewry's Bluff, Virginia, May 16, 1864.

BIVENS, THOMAS W., Private

Resided in Alamance County and was by occupation a laborer prior to enlisting in Alamance County at age 28, July 4, 1862, for the war. Reported present or accounted for through February 28, 1863. Captured at Chancellorsville, Virginia, May 3-4, 1863. Confined at Fort Delaware, Delaware, on or about May 7, 1863. Paroled at Fort Delaware and transferred to City Point, Virginia, where he was received on or about May 23, 1863, for exchange. Returned to duty in September-October, 1863. Captured at Rappahannock Station,

Virginia, November 7, 1863. Confined at Point Lookout, Maryland, November 11, 1863. Paroled at Point Lookout on March 16, 1864. Received at City Point on March 20, 1864, for exchange. Returned to duty prior to July 20, 1864, when he was captured at Winchester, Virginia. Confined at Camp Chase, Ohio, July 28, 1864. Paroled at Camp Chase on March 2, 1865. Received at Boulware's and Cox's Wharves, James River, Virginia, March 10-12, 1865, for exchange. Paroled at Greensboro on May 15, 1865. [North Carolina pension records indicate that he was wounded in the outer side of the left leg just above the ankle at Gettysburg, Pennsylvania, July 1, 1863.]

BLANCHARD, WILLIAM A., Private

Resided in Alamance County and was by occupation a farmer prior to enlisting in Alamance County at age 28, July 4, 1862, for the war. Mustered in as Corporal. Reduced to ranks prior to September 2, 1862. Hospitalized at Richmond, Virginia, September 25, 1862, with measles. Furloughed on October 8, 1862. Returned to duty in November-December, 1862. Reported present through May 11, 1863. Captured at Gettysburg, Pennsylvania, July 2-5, 1863. Confined at Fort Delaware, Delaware, on or about July 9, 1863. Released at Fort Delaware on June 19, 1865, after taking the Oath of Allegiance.

BRINCEFIELD, J. A., ——

North Carolina pension records indicate that he served in this company.

BRINTLE, WILLIAM, Private

Resided in Alamance County and enlisted in Rowan County at age 28, July 4, 1862, for the war. Hospitalized at Richmond, Virginia, October 28, 1862. Died in hospital at Richmond on December 10, 1862, of "typhoid fever."

CANTRELL, BENJAMIN, Private

Resided in Alamance County where he enlisted at age 18, July 4, 1862, for the war. Reported absent sick in July-August, 1862. Returned to duty in September-October, 1862. Wounded at Fredericksburg, Virginia, December 13, 1862. Hospitalized at Richmond, Virginia. Returned to duty on December 27, 1862. Reported missing at Chancellorsville, Virginia, May 4, 1863. Was presumably killed at Chancellorsville.

COBLE, GEORGE G., Private

Resided in Alamance County and was by occupation a farmer prior to enlisting in Alamance County at age 30, July 4, 1862, for the war. Hospitalized at Richmond, Virginia, September 22, 1862. Furloughed for thirty days on October 26, 1862. Returned to duty subsequent to February 28, 1863. Captured at Chancellorsville, Virginia, May 3-4, 1863. Confined at Fort Delaware, Delaware. Died in hospital at Fort Delaware on June 19, 1863. Cause of death not reported.

COBLE, P. C., Private

Resided in Alamance County where he enlisted at age 24, July 4, 1862, for the war. Reported absent sick in July-August, 1862. Returned to duty in September-October, 1862. Reported absent sick in November-December, 1862. Died in hospital at Richmond, Virginia, January 24, 1863, of "pneumonia."

COMPTON, J. F., Private

Resided in Alamance or Orange County and enlisted in Orange County at age 28, July 4, 1862, for the war. Hospitalized at

Richmond, Virginia, October 28, 1862, with bronchitis. Transferred to hospital at Farmville, Virginia, December 21, 1862 (suffering from icterus and debility). Returned to duty on March 31, 1863. Captured at Chancellorsville, Virginia, May 3-4, 1863. Confined at Fort Delaware, Delaware, on or about May 7, 1863. Paroled and transferred to City Point, Virginia, where he was received on May 23, 1863, for exchange. Returned to duty prior to September 1, 1863. Reported present through August 31, 1864. Captured at or near Fisher's Hill, Virginia, on or about September 22, 1864. Confined at Point Lookout, Maryland, on or about October 3, 1864. Released at Point Lookout on June 24, 1865, after taking the Oath of Allegiance.

COMPTON, JOHN G., Sergeant

Resided in Alamance County and enlisted in Orange County at age 28, July 4, 1862, for the war. Mustered in as Private. Promoted to Sergeant prior to July 17, 1862. Hospitalized at Richmond, Virginia, October 20, 1862, with typhoid fever. Furloughed on November 20, 1862. Reduced to ranks on December 13, 1862. Returned to duty prior to January 1, 1863. Reported sick in hospital in January-February, 1863. Hospitalized at Richmond on May 6, 1863, with typhoid pneumonia. Transferred to Lynchburg, Virginia, on or about May 8, 1863. Returned to duty prior to September 1, 1863. Promoted to Sergeant in May-August, 1863. Captured at Rappahannock Station, Virginia, November 7, 1863. Confined at Point Lookout, Maryland, November 11, 1863. Paroled at Point Lookout on March 16, 1864. Received at City Point, Virginia, March 20, 1864, for exchange. Returned to duty prior to September 1, 1864. Wounded in the lungs at Cedar Creek, Virginia, October 19, 1864. Died prior to January 1, 1865, of wounds. Place of death not reported. [Previously served as 2nd Lieutenant in the 46th Regiment N.C. Militia.]

COOK, THOMAS, Private

Resided in Alamance County where he enlisted at age 33, July 4, 1862, for the war. Hospitalized at Richmond, Virginia, September 25, 1862, with measles. Furloughed on October 14, 1862. Returned to duty in January-February, 1863. Captured at Chancellorsville, Virginia, May 3-4, 1863. Confined at Fort Delaware, Delaware, on or about May 7, 1863. Paroled and transferred to City Point, Virginia, where he was received on May 23, 1863, for exchange. Returned to duty prior to September 1, 1863. Captured at Rappahannock Station, Virginia, November 7, 1863. Confined at Point Lookout, Maryland, November 11, 1863. Paroled at Point Lookout on March 16, 1864. Received at City Point on March 20, 1864, for exchange. Returned to duty prior to September 1, 1864. Reported present through February 28, 1865. Surrendered at Appomattox Court House, Virginia, April 9, 1865.

CORBITT, B. H., Private

Resided in Alamance County and enlisted in Orange County at age 25, July 4, 1862, for the war. Died in hospital at Richmond, Virginia, October 17, 1862, of "typhoid pneumonia."

CRABTREE, PORTER A., Private

Resided in Alamance County and enlisted in Orange County at age 26, July 4, 1862, for the war. Hospitalized at Richmond, Virginia, September 21, 1862, with intermittent fever. Returned to duty on or about September 28, 1862. Reported present through February 28, 1863. Reported sick in hospital in March-August, 1863. Reported absent without leave from September 20, 1863, through February 28, 1865. Paroled at Greensboro on May 10, 1865. [May have served previously as Private in Company G, 27th Regiment N.C. Troops.]

CRAWFORD, NATHANIEL, Private

Resided in Alamance County where he enlisted at age 24, July 4, 1862, for the war. Reported absent sick in July-October, 1862. Returned to duty in November-December, 1862. Captured at Chancellorsville, Virginia, May 4, 1863. Hospitalized at Washington, D.C., May 6, 1863, with acute bronchitis. Transferred to Old Capitol Prison, Washington, June 25, 1863. Paroled and transferred to City Point, Virginia, where he was received on June 30, 1863, for exchange. Hospitalized at Petersburg, Virginia, the same date with debilitas. Furloughed for thirty days on July 15, 1863. Reported absent sick until May 21, 1864, when he died in hospital at Raleigh of "pneumonia typh[oides]."

CRUTCHFIELD, JESSE, Private

Enlisted in Wake County on April 5, 1864, for the war. Reported absent sick from June 25, 1864, through February 28, 1865. Hospitalized at Charlottesville, Virginia, on or about March 2, 1865, with debilitas and/or chronic rheumatism. Transferred to hospital at Lynchburg, Virginia, on or about April 9, 1865. No further records.

DAILY, J. W., Private

Born in Alamance County* where he resided as a farmer prior to enlisting in Alamance County at age 26, July 4, 1862, for the war. Hospitalized at Richmond, Virginia, on or about September 22, 1862, with debilitas. Returned to duty on September 29, 1862. Died at home in Alamance County on April 20, 1863. Cause of death not reported.

DANNELLY, A. J., Private

Enlisted in Wake County on March 7, 1864, for the war. Reported absent without leave in September-December, 1864. Hospitalized at Petersburg, Virginia, February 9, 1865. Died in hospital at Petersburg on February 12, 1865. Cause of death not reported. Was 32 years of age at the time of his death.

DICKEY, J. M., Private

Enlisted in Wake County on May 20, 1864, for the war. Wounded at Winchester, Virginia, July 20, 1864. Returned to duty prior to September 1, 1864. Reported present through December 31, 1864. No further records.

EARLY, J. W., Private

Place and date of enlistment not reported. Captured and paroled at Athens, Georgia, on or about May 8, 1865.

ECTOR, T. S., Private

Resided in Alamance County where he enlisted at age 32, July 4, 1862, for the war. Reported present through August 31, 1862. Died in hospital at Richmond, Virginia, November 7, 1862, of "febris typhoides."

ECTOR, WILLIAM JAMES, Private

Resided in Alamance County where he enlisted at age 29, July 4, 1862, for the war. Mustered in as Sergeant. Reported sick in hospital in September, 1862-April, 1863. Returned to duty in May-August, 1863, and was reduced to ranks. Captured at Rappahannock Station, Virginia, November 7, 1863. Confined at Point Lookout, Maryland, November 11, 1863. Paroled at Point Lookout on March 16, 1864. Received at City Point, Virginia, March 20,

1864, for exchange. Returned to duty in May-August, 1864. Reported present through February 28, 1865. Captured at Farmville, Virginia, April 6, 1865. Confined at Newport News, Virginia, April 14, 1865. Released at Newport News on June 26, 1865, after taking the Oath of Allegiance.

FAUCETTE, ALBERT AUGUSTUS PRESTON, Sergeant

Born on November 25, 1844. Resided in Alamance County where he enlisted at age 17, July 4, 1862, for the war. Mustered in as Private. Hospitalized at Richmond, Virginia, December 4, 1862, with pneumonia. Furloughed on December 20, 1862. Returned to duty in January-February, 1863. Wounded in the leg at Chancellorsville, Virginia, May 4, 1863. Hospitalized at Richmond. Returned to duty in November-December, 1863. Reported present in March-August, 1864. Wounded in the face at Cedar Creek, Virginia, October 19, 1864. Returned to duty prior to November 1, 1864. Reported present through December 31, 1864. Captured at Hatcher's Run, Virginia, February 6, 1865. Confined at Old Capitol Prison, Washington, D.C., February 9, 1865. Transferred to Fort Delaware, Delaware, March 1, 1865. Released on an unspecified date. Survived the war.

FAUCETTE, JOHN A., Private

Resided in Orange County and was by occupation a farmer prior to enlisting in Orange County at age 33, July 4, 1862, for the war. Reported sick in hospital in September, 1862-February, 1863. Returned to duty prior to May 11, 1863. Captured at Rappahannock Station, Virginia, November 7, 1863. Confined at Point Lookout, Maryland, November 11, 1863. Paroled at Point Lookout on March 16, 1864. Received at City Point, Virginia, March 20, 1864, for exchange. Hospitalized at Richmond, Virginia, the same date with chronic rheumatism. Furloughed for thirty days on March 26, 1864. Returned to duty prior to July 20, 1864, when he was captured at Winchester, Virginia. Confined at Camp Chase, Ohio, July 28, 1864. Paroled at Camp Chase on March 2, 1865. Received at Boulware's and Cox's Wharves, James River, Virginia, March 10-12, 1865, for exchange. No further records.

FAULKNER, SANDERS, Private

Resided in Orange County where he enlisted at age 22, July 4, 1862, for the war. Reported absent sick in July-August, 1862. Returned to duty in September-October, 1862. Reported present through February 28, 1863. Reported sick in hospital on March 11, 1863. Died at Hillsborough at the residence of his father-in-law, Redding Cape, June 12, 1863, of disease. "Thus has another patriot laid his life upon the altar of his country, leaving an affectionate wife and a little boy to mourn their loss." [*Hillsborough Recorder*, August 26, 1863.]

FITCH, ANDERSON N., Private

Resided in Alamance or Caswell County and was by occupation a farmer prior to enlisting in Orange County at age 30, July 4, 1862, for the war. Hospitalized at Richmond, Virginia, November 3, 1862, with jaundice. Transferred to hospital at Farmville, Virginia, December 21, 1862, convalescent. Returned to duty on March 31, 1863. Reported on detail as a teamster from October 10, 1863, through April 30, 1864. Reported absent sick in May-October, 1864. Furloughed on December 22, 1864. Returned to duty in January-February, 1865. Captured at or near Farmville on April 6, 1865. Confined at Point Lookout, Maryland, April 14, 1865. Released at Point Lookout on June 26, 1865, after taking the Oath of Allegiance.

FONVILLE, L. J., Private

Place and date of enlistment not reported (probably enlisted subsequent to February 28, 1865). Paroled at Greensboro on May 10, 1865.

FONVILLE, WILLIAM T., Private

Enlisted in Alamance County at age 18, July 13, 1863, for the war. Reported sick in hospital on or about August 31, 1863. Returned to duty in September-October, 1863. Reported present on surviving company muster rolls through April 30, 1864. Wounded in the arm at Cold Harbor, Virginia, June 1-3, 1864. Hospitalized at Danville, Virginia, June 4, 1864. Furloughed on June 16, 1864. Returned to duty prior to September 1, 1864. Wounded in the head at Cedar Creek, Virginia, October 19, 1864. Died on November 2, 1864, of wounds. Place of death not reported.

FOSTER, EDMUND A., Private

Resided in Alamance County where he enlisted at age 30, July 4, 1862, for the war. Reported absent sick through December 31, 1862. Returned to duty in January-February, 1863. Wounded in the left leg at Chancellorsville, Virginia, May 4, 1863. Reported absent wounded through August 31, 1864. Reported absent on detail at Greensboro from September 4, 1864, through February 28, 1865. Survived the war.

FOSTER, JAMES M., Private

Resided in Alamance County where he enlisted at age 25, July 4, 1862, for the war. Mustered in as Corporal. Hospitalized at Richmond, Virginia, September 22, 1862. Furloughed for twenty days on October 8, 1862. Reported absent without leave in November-December, 1862. Returned to duty in January-February, 1863. Reduced to ranks in March-May, 1863. Captured at Gettysburg, Pennsylvania, July 2-5, 1863. Confined at Fort Delaware, Delaware, on or about July 12, 1863. Transferred to Point Lookout, Maryland, October 20, 1863. Died at Point Lookout on February 7, 1864. Cause of death not reported.

FULP, JOHN W., Private

Place and date of enlistment not reported (probably enlisted in the early summer of 1864). Captured at Bellville, Maryland, July 12, 1864. Confined at Old Capitol Prison, Washington, D.C., July 14, 1864. Transferred to Elmira, New York, where he arrived on July 25, 1864. Paroled at Elmira on March 14, 1865. Received at Boulware's Wharf, James River, Virginia, March 18 or March 21, 1865, for exchange. No further records.

GARRISON, G., Private

Born in Alamance County* where he resided prior to enlisting in Alamance County at age 28, July 4, 1862, for the war. Reported present through February 28, 1863. Hospitalized at Richmond, Virginia, on an unspecified date. Furloughed on or about April 11, 1863. Died at home in Alamance County on or about May 7, 1863. Cause of death not reported.

GARRISON, JOSEPH L., Private

Resided in Alamance County and was by occupation a farmer prior to enlisting in Alamance County at age 27, July 4, 1862, for the war. Reported absent sick in July-August, 1862. Returned to duty in September-October, 1862. Reported present or accounted for through October 31, 1863. Wounded at Rappahannock Station, Virginia, November 7, 1863. Died in hospital at Lynchburg, Virginia, February 18, 1864, of "variola."

GRAGSTON, JOHN H., Private

Resided in Alamance County where he enlisted at age 20, February 10, 1863, for the war. Captured at Gettysburg, Pennsylvania, July 2-5, 1863. Confined at Fort Delaware, Delaware, on or about July 9, 1863. Paroled at Fort Delaware on July 30, 1863. Received at City Point, Virginia, August 1, 1863, for exchange. Returned to duty in January-April, 1864. Reported on detail threshing wheat in May-August, 1864. Reported absent on detached service in September-December, 1864. No further records.

GRAGSTON, WILLIAM J., Private

Resided in Alamance County where he enlisted at age 26, July 4, 1862, for the war. Reported absent sick in September-December, 1862. Returned to duty in January-February, 1863. Hospitalized at Richmond, Virginia, March 18, 1863, with pneumonia. Transferred to Raleigh on April 11, 1863. Returned to duty prior to September 1, 1863. Captured at Rappahannock Station, Virginia, November 7, 1863. Confined at Point Lookout, Maryland, November 11, 1863. Paroled at Point Lookout on March 16, 1864. Received at City Point, Virginia, March 20, 1864, for exchange. Dropped from the company rolls in May-August, 1864, apparently for absence without leave. Returned to duty and was reported present in January-February, 1865. Captured at Fort Stedman, Virginia, March 25, 1865. Confined at Point Lookout on March 28, 1865. Released at Point Lookout on June 27, 1865, after taking the Oath of Allegiance.

GRAHAM, A., Private

Enlisted at Salisbury on July 8, 1862, for the war. No further records.

GRAVES, W. M., Private

Resided in Alamance County where he enlisted at age 21, July 4, 1862, for the war. Deserted on September 25, 1862. Returned to duty on October 25, 1862. Reported present on surviving company muster rolls through April 30, 1864. Hospitalized at Richmond, Virginia, May 15, 1864, with a gunshot wound of the left arm. Place and date wounded not reported. Furloughed for sixty days on June 3, 1864. Returned to duty on August 9, 1864. Reported present through February 28, 1865. Killed at Fort Stedman, Virginia, March 25, 1865.

GREEN, ZENO H., Private

Resided in Wilson County. Place and date of enlistment not reported (probably enlisted subsequent to February 28, 1865). Was about 35 years of age at time of enlistment. Paroled at Goldsboro in 1865. [May have served also as Private in Company B, 40th Regiment N.C. Troops (3rd Regiment N.C. Artillery). Contrary to 1:390 of this series, the correct spelling of surname was probably Green rather than Greene.]

HALL, JAMES, Private

Born in Alamance County* where he resided as a farmer prior to enlisting in Alamance County at age 28, July 4, 1862, for the war. Hospitalized at Richmond, Virginia, October 9, 1862, with parotitis. Furloughed on October 18, 1862. Died in hospital at Richmond on January 14, 1863, of "pneumonia." [North Carolina pension records indicate that he was wounded by a shell at Fredericksburg, Virginia, on or about December 12, 186(2).]

HARDER, AUSTIN W., Private

Resided in Alamance County and was by occupation a farmer prior to enlisting in Alamance County at age 32, July 4, 1862, for the war. Mustered in as Private. Promoted to Corporal prior to September 1, 1862. Hospitalized at Richmond, Virginia, October 31, 1862, with typhoid fever. Transferred to hospital at Farmville, Virginia, December 20, 1862. Reduced to ranks on January 1, 1863. Returned to duty on January 29, 1863. Captured at Gettysburg, Pennsylvania, July 2-5, 1863. Confined at Fort Delaware, Delaware, on or about July 10, 1863. Transferred to Point Lookout, Maryland, October 20, 1863. Died at Point Lookout on December 22, 1863, of disease.

HARDER, JAMES M., Private

Resided in Alamance County where he enlisted at age 20, July 4, 1862, for the war. Reported present through December 31, 1862. Died near Port Royal, Virginia, February 4, 1863, of "asthma."

HARDER, JOSEPH R., Private

Resided in Alamance County where he enlisted at age 18, July 4, 1862, for the war. Reported present through December 31, 1862. Died at Port Royal, Virginia, on or about February 5, 1863, of "pneumonia."

HESTER, JAMES R., Private

Resided in Orange County where he enlisted at age 25, July 4, 1862, for the war. Hospitalized at Richmond, Virginia, October 28, 1862, with chronic diarrhoea and chronic dysentery. Furloughed on November 15, 1862. Returned to duty prior to January 1, 1863. Hospitalized at Richmond on April 9, 1863, with bronchitis. Transferred to hospital at Danville, Virginia, April 18, 1863. Returned to duty on May 12, 1863. Detailed as a hospital nurse at Richmond on or about June 6, 1863. Rejoined the company on September 23, 1863. Reported present or accounted for on surviving company muster rolls through August 31, 1864. Reported on duty as acting Commissary Sergeant in September-October, 1864. Reported present in November, 1864-February, 1865. Captured at Fort Stedman, Virginia, March 25, 1865. Confined at Point Lookout, Maryland, March 28, 1865. Released at Point Lookout on June 3, 1865, after taking the Oath of Allegiance.

HUDDLESTON, L. T., Private

Resided in Orange County where he enlisted at age 22, July 4, 1862, for the war. Hospitalized at Richmond, Virginia, September 22, 1862. Furloughed for thirty days on October 6, 1862. Returned to duty in November-December, 1862. Reported present through February 28, 1863. Reported sick in hospital from March 10 through August 31, 1863. Reported absent without leave from September 20, 1863, through April 30, 1864. Reported absent sick from July 15 through August 31, 1864. Hospitalized at Raleigh on September 15, 1864, with chronic diarrhoea. Returned to duty on November 22, 1864. Hospitalized at Petersburg, Virginia, December 10, 1864, with acute bronchitis. Captured in hospital at Petersburg on April 3, 1865. Paroled on April 18, 1865.

ISLEY, MARTIN, Private

Resided in Alamance County and was by occupation a farmer prior to enlisting in Alamance County at age 36, March 8, 1864, for the war. Reported absent sick from May 25, 1864, through February 28, 1865. Survived the war.

ISLEY, PHILLIP, Private

Resided in Alamance County and was by occupation a farmer prior to enlisting in Alamance County at age 40, March 8, 1864, for the war. Reported present through August 31, 1864. Wounded in the

knee at Cedar Creek, Virginia, October 19, 1864. Hospitalized at Richmond, Virginia. Furloughed for thirty days on November 2, 1864. Reported absent wounded through February 28, 1865. Survived the war.

ISLEY, WESLEY, Private

Resided in Alamance County where he enlisted at age 19, April 24, 1864, for the war. Reported present through December 31, 1864. Wounded in the right leg at Hatcher's Run, Virginia, February 6, 1865. Right leg amputated. Hospitalized at Farmville, Virginia. Furloughed for sixty days on March 7, 1865. Survived the war.

JEFFRIES, A. C., Corporal

Resided in Orange County where he enlisted at age 24, July 4, 1862, for the war. Mustered in as Private. Reported present on surviving company muster rolls through October 31, 1864. Promoted to Corporal in November-December, 1864. Reported absent without leave on December 29, 1864. Returned to duty prior to March 1, 1865. Reported missing at Fort Stedman, Virginia, March 25, 1865. Was probably killed at Fort Stedman.

JOHNSON, LEMUEL, Private

Born on July 20, 1842. Resided in Alamance County where he enlisted at age 19, July 4, 1862, for the war. Hospitalized at Richmond, Virginia, November 25, 1862, with parotitis. Returned to duty on December 6, 1862. Wounded in the foot at Fredericksburg, Virginia, December 13, 1862. Hospitalized at Richmond. Furloughed for forty days on or about December 31, 1862. Returned to duty in March-May, 1863. Reported present through October 31, 1863. Wounded at Rappahannock Station, Virginia, November 7, 1863. Returned to duty in January-April, 1864. Wounded in the arm at Cold Harbor, Virginia, June 1-7, 1864. Returned to duty prior to September 1, 1864. Reported present through February 28, 1865. Surrendered at Appomattox Court House, Virginia, April 9, 1865.

KILGON, J. A., Private

Place and date of enlistment not reported (probably enlisted subsequent to February 28, 1865). Captured and paroled at Athens, Georgia, on or about May 8, 1865.

KIRKPATRICK, GEORGE W., Corporal

Resided in Alamance County and was by occupation a farmer prior to enlisting in Alamance County on July 4, 1862, for the war. Mustered in as Private. Promoted to Corporal prior to September 2, 1862. Wounded in the forearm at Fredericksburg, Virginia, December 13, 1862. Hospitalized at Danville, Virginia. Returned to duty in January-February, 1863. Captured at Chancellorsville, Virginia, May 3-4, 1863. Confined at Fort Delaware, Delaware, on or about May 7, 1863. Paroled and transferred to City Point, Virginia. Received on May 23, 1863, for exchange. Returned to duty prior to September 1, 1863. Reported present in September-October, 1863. Company records indicate that he was captured at Rappahannock Station, Virginia, November 7, 1863; however, records of the Federal Provost Marshal do not substantiate that report. Dropped from the company rolls subsequent to April 30, 1864. No further records. [Was 21 years of age in January, 1863.]

KIRKPATRICK, JAMES D., Private

Born on September 24, 1829. Resided in Alamance County where he enlisted at age 32, July 4, 1862, for the war. Reported present through February 28, 1863. Reported sick in hospital from April 6 through May 11, 1863. Returned to duty prior to July 2-5, 1863, when he was captured at Gettysburg, Pennsylvania. Confined at Fort Delaware, Delaware, on or about July 9, 1863. Died at Fort Delaware on August 24, 1863, of "general debility." [See his obituary in the *North Carolina Standard* (Raleigh), January 12, 1864.]

LONG, B. N., Private

Resided in Alamance County where he enlisted at age 23, July 4, 1862, for the war. Killed at Fredericksburg, Virginia, December 13, 1862.

McADAMS, CALVIN, Private

Resided in Alamance County where he enlisted at age 25, July 4, 1862, for the war. Reported absent without leave in July-August, 1862. Reported sick in hospital in September-October, 1862. Died in hospital at Richmond, Virginia, on or about December 20, 1862, of "febris typh[oides]."

McCRAY, WILLIAM JAMES, Private

Resided in Alamance County and was by occupation a farmer prior to enlisting in Alamance County at age 17, July 4, 1862, for the war as a substitute for J. M. Hurdle of Alamance County. Reported present through May 11, 1863. Reported on duty as acting Ordnance Sergeant in January-February, 1863. Reported on duty as acting Quartermaster Sergeant in March-April, 1863. Reported sick at home in May-August, 1863. Reported on duty as acting Quartermaster Sergeant in September-December, 1863. Reported absent on detached service in March-April, 1864. Reported present in May-August, 1864. Reported on duty as acting Quartermaster Sergeant in September-October, 1864. Reported present in November, 1864-February, 1865. Captured at Fort Stedman, Virginia, March 25, 1865. Confined at Point Lookout, Maryland. Released at Point Lookout on May 12-14, 1865, after taking the Oath of Allegiance.

McCRAY, WILLIAM JOSEPH, Private

Resided in Alamance County where he enlisted at age 18, August 10, 1863, for the war. Reported present through April 30, 1864. Captured near Washington, D.C., July 12, 1864. Confined at Old Capitol Prison, Washington, July 13, 1864. Transferred to Elmira, New York, July 23, 1864. Released at Elmira on May 15, 1865, after taking the Oath of Allegiance.

McNEELY, HENRY W., Private

Resided in Rowan County and was by occupation a farmer prior to enlisting in Wake County at age 29, March 8, 1864, for the war. Wounded at Winchester, Virginia, July 20, 1864. Returned to duty prior to September 1, 1864. Reported present through February 28, 1865. Captured at Farmville, Virginia, April 6, 1865. Confined at Newport News, Virginia, April 14, 1865. Released at Newport News on June 26, 1865, after taking the Oath of Allegiance.

MAYNARD, C. G., Private

Resided in Alamance County where he enlisted at age 20, July 4, 1862, for the war. Hospitalized at Richmond, Virginia, September 22, 1862, with diarrhoea. Returned to duty on or about September 28, 1862. Hospitalized at Richmond on October 8, 1862, with syphilis. Transferred to Salisbury on October 10, 1862. Returned to duty in January-February, 1863. Reported present through October, 1863. Captured at Rappahannock Station, Virginia, November 7, 1863. Confined at Point Lookout, Maryland, November 11,

1863. Paroled at Point Lookout on March 16, 1864. Received at City Point, Virginia, March 20, 1864, for exchange. Returned to duty in May-August, 1864. Wounded in the knee at Cedar Creek, Virginia, October 19, 1864. Reported in hospital at Richmond on December 13, 1864. Returned to duty on January 4, 1865. Surrendered at Appomattox Court House, Virginia, April 9, 1865.

MITCHELL, JOHN A., Private

Previously served as Private in Company A, 43rd Regiment N.C. Troops. Transferred to this company on March 24, 1864. Reported absent wounded in April, 1864. Place and date wounded not reported. Reported absent sick from July 25 through December 31, 1864. Captured at Woodstock, Virginia, January 11-12, 1865. Confined at Fort McHenry, Maryland, January 18, 1865. Released on May 1, 1865, after taking the Oath of Allegiance. [Records of the Federal Provost Marshal dated January 16-21, 1865, indicate that he was a "guerrilla" who was not to be exchanged until the end of the war.]

MITCHELL, R. ALEX, Private

Resided in Alamance County where he enlisted at age 27, July 4, 1862, for the war. Mustered in as Sergeant. Reported present through February 28, 1863. Reduced to ranks in March-April, 1863. Killed at Chancellorsville, Virginia, May 4, 1863.

MOSER, DANIEL M., Private

Resided in Alamance County where he enlisted at age 21, July 4, 1862, for the war. Mustered in as Private. Promoted to Sergeant on December 13, 1862, for gallant conduct at Fredericksburg, Virginia. Reported present on surviving company muster rolls through August 31, 1864. Reduced to ranks "for misconduct in action" at Cedar Creek, Virginia, October 19, 1864. Reported present in September, 1864-February, 1865. Surrendered at Appomattox Court House, Virginia, April 9, 1865.

MOSER, JAMES, Private

Resided in Alamance County where he enlisted at age 18, April 24, 1864, for the war. Wounded in the leg at Winchester, Virginia, September 19, 1864. Returned to duty prior to November 1, 1864. Reported present through February 28, 1865. Captured at Farmville, Virginia, April 6, 1865. Confined at Newport News, Virginia, April 14, 1865. Released at Newport News on June 26, 1865, after taking the Oath of Allegiance.

MURPHY, HENRY J., Private

Resided in Alamance or Orange County and was by occupation a farmer prior to enlisting in Orange County at age 36, July 4, 1862, for the war. Mustered in as Corporal. Reduced to ranks prior to September 2, 1862. Hospitalized at Richmond, Virginia, October 28, 1862, with typhoid fever. Furloughed on November 5, 1862. Returned to duty prior to January 1, 1863. Wounded in the hip at Chancellorsville, Virginia, May 4, 1863. Returned to duty in September-October, 1863. Captured at Rappahannock Station, Virginia, November 7, 1863. Confined at Point Lookout, Maryland, November 11, 1863. Paroled at Point Lookout on March 16, 1864. Received at City Point, Virginia, March 20, 1864, for exchange. Returned to duty prior to July 20, 1864, when he was wounded at Winchester, Virginia. Returned to duty prior to September 1, 1864. Captured at Fisher's Hill, Virginia, September 22, 1864. Confined at Point Lookout on October 3, 1864. Released at Point Lookout on June 29, 1865, after taking the Oath of Allegiance.

MURRAY, ELI CLAY, Private

Resided in Alamance County where he enlisted at age 19, July 4, 1862, for the war. Wounded at Fredericksburg, Virginia, December 13, 1862. Returned to duty in March-May, 1863. Captured at or near Sharpsburg, Maryland, on or about June 27, 1863. Confined at Fort McHenry, Maryland, June 30, 1863. Transferred to Fort Delaware, Delaware, July 8, 1863. Released at Fort Delaware on June 19, 1865, after taking the Oath of Allegiance.

MURRAY, JAMES F., Private

Resided in Alamance County where he enlisted at age 27, July 4, 1862, for the war. Killed at Fredericksburg, Virginia, December 13, 1862.

NICHOLS, COLUMBUS, Private

Resided in Orange or Alamance County and was by occupation a painter prior to enlisting in Orange County at age 22, July 4, 1862, for the war. Reported present through May 11, 1863. Confined at Castle Thunder Prison, Richmond, Virginia, July 1, 1863. Reason he was confined not reported. Returned to duty prior to September 1, 1863. Reported present on surviving company muster rolls through April 30, 1864. Reported absent without leave on June 28, 1864. Returned to duty prior to July 20, 1864, when he was captured at Winchester, Virginia. Confined at Camp Chase, Ohio, July 28, 1864. Paroled at Camp Chase on March 2, 1865. Received at Boulware's and Cox's Wharves, James River, Virginia, March 10-12, 1865, for exchange. No further records. Survived the war.

NICKS, BENJAMIN C., Private

Resided in Alamance or Caswell County and was by occupation a farmer prior to enlisting in Alamance County at age 30, July 4, 1862, for the war. Reported present through February 28, 1863. Hospitalized at Richmond, Virginia, May 7, 1863, with typhoid pneumonia. Transferred to hospital at Lynchburg, Virginia, May 8, 1863. Returned to duty prior to September 1, 1863. Wounded in the face by a shell at Rappahannock Station, Virginia, November 7, 1863. Hospitalized at Richmond. Later contracted variola. Reported absent wounded or absent sick through February 28, 1865. No further records.

NICKS, RICHARD JAMES, Corporal

Born in Alamance County* where he resided as a carpenter prior to enlisting in Alamance County at age 26, July 4, 1862, for the war. Reported present through May 11, 1863. Captured at Gettysburg, Pennsylvania, July 4-5, 1863. Confined at Fort Delaware, Delaware, on or about July 9, 1863. Transferred to Point Lookout, Maryland, October 20, 1863. Released at Point Lookout on February 19, 1864, after taking the Oath of Allegiance and joining the U.S. Army. Assigned to Company I, 1st Regiment U.S. Volunteer Infantry.

NUTT, H. B., Private

Resided in Alamance County where he enlisted at age 26, July 4, 1862, for the war. Hospitalized at Richmond, Virginia, December 7, 1862, with chronic diarrhoea. Later developed rheumatism. Transferred to hospital at Farmville, Virginia, December 21, 1862. Furloughed for twenty-five days on March 11, 1863. Detailed for unknown duty on October 29, 1863. Rejoined the company in January-April, 1864. Hospitalized at Richmond on May 18, 1864, with a gunshot wound. Place and date wounded not reported. Furloughed for sixty days on June 11, 1864. Reported absent on detached service from November 26, 1864, through February 28,

1865. Rejoined the company on an unspecified date. Surrendered at Appomattox Court House, Virginia, April 9, 1865.

NUTT, THOMPSON R., Private

Resided in Alamance County and was by occupation a millwright prior to enlisting in Alamance County at age 26, July 4, 1862, for the war. Reported absent sick in July-August, 1862. Returned to duty in September-October, 1862. Reported sick in hospital in November, 1862-February, 1863. Died in hospital at Lynchburg, Virginia, April 12, 1863, of "typhoid fever."

PARRISH, WILLIAM, Private

Resided in Alamance County and enlisted in Orange County at age 22, July 4, 1862, for the war. Reported present in July-October, 1862. Sent to hospital sick on January 2, 1863. Reported in hospital at Lynchburg, Virginia, March 21, 1863. Died on July 24, 1863, of disease. Place of death not reported.

PATTON, ALEXANDER M. ("SANDY"), Sergeant

Resided in Alamance County and was by occupation a carpenter prior to enlisting in Alamance County at age 28, July 4, 1862, for the war. Mustered in as Private. Promoted to Sergeant prior to September 2, 1862. Hospitalized at Richmond, Virginia, October 10, 1862, with typhoid fever. Furloughed on October 18, 1862. Returned to duty prior to November 1, 1862. Reported present through October 31, 1863. Captured at Rappahannock Station, Virginia, November 7, 1863. Confined at Point Lookout, Maryland, November 11, 1863. Paroled at Point Lookout on March 16, 1864. Received at City Point, Virginia, March 20, 1864, for exchange. Returned to duty prior to May 1, 1864. Captured at Winchester, Virginia, July 20, 1864. Confined at Camp Chase, Ohio, July 28, 1864. Paroled at Camp Chase on March 2, 1865. Received at Boulware's and Cox's Wharves, James River, Virginia, March 10-12, 1865, for exchange. Paroled at Greensboro on May 15, 1865.

PATTON, J. B., Private

Enlisted in Alamance County on March 18, 1864, for the war. Hospitalized at Richmond, Virginia, June 8, 1864. Transferred to another hospital on June 9, 1864. Returned to duty in September-October, 1864. Reported present through February 28, 1865. Surrendered at Appomattox Court House, Virginia, April 9, 1865.

PATTON, WILLIAM, Private

Resided in Alamance County where he enlisted at age 30, July 4, 1862, for the war. Reported present or accounted for through February 28, 1863. Hospitalized at Richmond, Virginia, May 3, 1863, with an ulcer of the leg. Deserted on May 28, 1863. Returned to duty prior to September 1, 1863. Captured at Rappahannock Station, Virginia, November 7, 1863. Confined at Point Lookout, Maryland, November 11, 1863. Paroled at Point Lookout on March 16, 1864. Received at City Point, Virginia, March 20, 1864, for exchange. Reported absent sick from July 18 through August 31, 1864. Returned to duty prior to September 22, 1864, when he was captured at Fisher's Hill, Virginia. Confined at Point Lookout on October 3, 1864. Paroled at Point Lookout on March 17, 1865. Received at Boulware's and Cox's Wharves, James River, Virginia, March 19, 1865, for exchange. Paroled at Greensboro on May 15, 1865.

PEARSON, J. H., Private

Resided in Alamance County where he enlisted at age 27, July 4, 1862, for the war. Reported present through August 31, 1862.

Hospitalized at Richmond, Virginia, November 4, 1862, with parotitis. Returned to duty on November 10, 1862. Died in camp near Fredericksburg, Virginia, December 25, 1862, of disease.

PHILLIPS, J. J., Private

Resided in Alamance County where he enlisted at age 20, July 4, 1862, for the war. Reported sick in hospital at Salisbury in July-August, 1862. Hospitalized at Richmond, Virginia, September 21, 1862, with intermittent fever. Returned to duty on September 28, 1862. Reported present through December 31, 1862. Reported sick in hospital on February 16, 1863. Hospitalized at Richmond on May 3, 1863, with pneumonia, intermittent fever, and diarrhoea. Transferred to hospital at Danville, Virginia, May 7, 1863. Returned to duty on May 29, 1863. Captured at Gettysburg, Pennsylvania, July 2-5, 1863. Confined at Fort Delaware, Delaware, July 9, 1863. Died at Fort Delaware on September 29, 1863, of "varioloid."

PILSON, WILLIAM LEE, Private

Resided in Surry County and enlisted at Camp Vance at age 19, April 4, 1864, for the war. Captured near Washington, D.C., July 12, 1864. Confined at Old Capitol Prison, Washington. Transferred to Elmira, New York, July 23, 1864. Released at Elmira on May 15, 1865, after taking the Oath of Allegiance.

PYLES, ANDREW, Private

Enlisted in Alamance County on March 8, 1864, for the war. Died in hospital at Richmond, Virginia, June 20, 1864, of "typhoid pneumonia."

RIPPY, CALVIN, Private

Resided in Alamance County where he enlisted at age 24, July 4, 1862, for the war. Hospitalized at Richmond, Virginia, November 25, 1862, with typhoid fever. Later contracted mumps and catarrh. Transferred to hospital at Farmville, Virginia, December 21, 1862. Returned to duty on February 13, 1863. Captured near Sharpsburg, Maryland, on or about June 27, 1863. Confined at Fort Delaware, Delaware, on or about July 9, 1863. Transferred to Point Lookout, Maryland, October 20, 1863. Died in hospital at Point Lookout on December 25, 1863, of "chronic diarrhoea."

RIPPY, EDMUND, Private

Resided in Alamance County where he enlisted at age 30, July 4, 1862, for the war. Reported present through May 11, 1863. Died during "the campaign to Pennsylvania" on June 26, 1863, of disease.

RIPPY, W. K., Private

Enlisted in Alamance County on July 4, 1862, for the war. Hospitalized at Danville, Virginia, on or about December 15, 1862, with debilitas. Deserted on February 19, 1863. Hospitalized at Danville on September 2, 1863, with chronic rheumatism. Returned to duty on September 15, 1863. Hospitalized at Richmond, Virginia, December 2, 1863, and on January 29, 1864, with rheumatism. Returned to duty on March 29, 1864. Dropped from the rolls of the company prior to May 1, 1864. Reason he was dropped not reported.

ROGERS, JOHN R., Corporal

Resided in Alamance County and was by occupation a farmer prior to enlisting in Alamance County at age 21, July 4, 1862, for the war. Mustered in as Private. Hospitalized at Richmond, Virginia,

October 31, 1862, with typhoid fever. Transferred to hospital at Danville, Virginia, December 19, 1862. Furloughed on March 17, 1863. Returned to duty in November-December, 1863. Reported present through February 28, 1865. Promoted to Corporal in November-December, 1864. Captured at Fort Stedman, Virginia, March 25, 1865. Confined at Point Lookout, Maryland, March 28, 1865. Died at Point Lookout on June 8, 1865, of "rubeola."

ROGERS, WILLIAM LEE, Private

Born in Alamance County* where he resided prior to enlisting in Alamance County at age 22, July 4, 1862, for the war. Mustered in as Corporal. Reduced to ranks prior to September 2, 1862. Hospitalized at Richmond, Virginia, October 30, 1862, with intermittent fever. Returned to duty on December 16, 1862. Hospitalized at Richmond on January 9, 1863, with paralysis. Died in hospital at Richmond on January 14, 1863, of "typhoid fever."

RONEY, AMOS L., Private

Resided in Alamance County where he enlisted at age 21, July 4, 1862, for the war. Mustered in as 1st Sergeant. Hospitalized at Richmond, Virginia, October 30, 1862, with remittent fever. Furloughed on November 20, 1862. Returned to duty in March-May, 1863. Captured at Rappahannock Station, Virginia, November 7, 1863. Confined at Point Lookout, Maryland, November 11, 1863. Paroled at Point Lookout on March 16, 1864. Received at City Point, Virginia, March 20, 1864, for exchange. Returned to duty in May-August, 1864. Reduced to ranks "for throwing away his gun" at Cedar Creek, Virginia, October 19, 1864. Reported present through February 28, 1865. Wounded in the head and/or shoulder at Fort Stedman, Virginia, March 25, 1865. Hospitalized at Richmond. Captured in hospital at Richmond on April 3, 1865. Transferred to Newport News, Virginia, April 23, 1865. Released at Newport News on June 30, 1865, after taking the Oath of Allegiance.

RONEY, JOHN, Private

Resided in Alamance County and was by occupation a farmer prior to enlisting in Alamance County at age 39, March 8, 1864, for the war. Reported present through February 28, 1865. Captured at Petersburg, Virginia, April 3, 1865. Confined at Hart's Island, New York Harbor, April 7, 1865. Released at Hart's Island on June 17, 1865, after taking the Oath of Allegiance.

RONEY, WILLIAM K., Private

Born on April 24, 1843. Resided in Alamance County where he enlisted at age 19, July 4, 1862, for the war. Hospitalized at Richmond, Virginia, October 28, 1862, with intermittent fever. Furloughed on November 6, 1862. Returned to duty in January-February, 1863. Hospitalized at Richmond on May 2, 1863, with pneumonia. Transferred to hospital at Danville, Virginia, May 7, 1863 (had also contracted diarrhoea). Returned to duty on or about July 31, 1863. Wounded in the right side at Cedar Creek, Virginia, October 19, 1864. Returned to duty in January-February, 1865. Captured at Fort Stedman, Virginia, March 25, 1865. Confined at Point Lookout, Maryland, March 28, 1865. Released at Point Lookout on June 17, 1865, after taking the Oath of Allegiance.

ROSS, JOSEPH G., Private

Resided in Alamance County and was by occupation a farmer prior to enlisting in Alamance County at age 30, July 4, 1862, for the war. Hospitalized at Richmond, Virginia, September 22, 1862. Returned to duty on September 30, 1862. Reported present through February 28, 1863. Wounded at Chancellorsville, Virginia, May 4,

1863. Hospitalized at Richmond where he contracted typhoid pneumonia. Died in hospital at Richmond on or about May 30, 1863, of wounds and/or typhoid fever.

SELLERS, D. T., Private

Resided in Alamance County where he enlisted at age 22, July 4, 1862, for the war. Reported present or accounted for through May 11, 1863. Died in hospital at Lynchburg, Virginia, August 22, 1863, of "febris typhoides."

SHARPE, W. R., Private

Place and date of enlistment not reported (probably enlisted in the autumn of 1864). Wounded in the finger at Cedar Creek, Virginia, October 19, 1864. Paroled at Greensboro on May 14, 1865.

SMITH, JO L., Private

Born in Granville County where he resided as a farmer prior to enlisting in Orange County at age 23, July 4, 1862, for the war. Hospitalized at Richmond, Virginia, October 9, 1862, with typhoid fever. Furloughed on October 22, 1862. Returned to duty prior to January 1, 1863. Wounded in the jaw at Chancellorsville, Virginia, May 4, 1863. Reported absent wounded through October 31, 1864. Reported on detached service in November-December, 1864. Retired from service on February 24, 1865, by reason of "gun shot wound of the lower jaw recieved [sic] . . . May 4, 1863, fracturing that bone and destroying and displacing his teeth which renders mastication difficult."

SMITH, WILLIAM, Private

Enlisted in Orange County on July 4, 1862, for the war. Deserted on September 6, 1862.

SMITH, ZION, Private

Enlisted at Camp Vance at age 25, April 5, 1864, for the war. Reported absent without leave on August 25, 1864. Returned to duty prior to September 22, 1864, when he was captured at Fisher's Hill, Virginia. Confined at Point Lookout, Maryland, October 3, 1864. Paroled at Point Lookout on January 17, 1865. Received at Boulware's Wharf, James River, Virginia, January 21, 1865, for exchange. Hospitalized at Richmond, Virginia, the same date with chronic diarrhoea, hemorrhage from lungs, and debility. Furloughed for sixty days on January 26, 1865. Survived the war. [North Carolina pension records indicate that he was wounded in the chest by a piece of shell at Winchester, Virginia, in 1864.]

SQUIRES, JAMES, Private

Born in Alamance County where he resided as a farmer prior to enlisting in Alamance County at age 33, July 4, 1862, for the war. Hospitalized at Richmond, Virginia, November 8, 1862. Transferred to hospital at Farmville, Virginia, December 21, 1862. Discharged from service at Farmville on February 13, 1863, by reason of "rheumatism," "hypertrophy of the heart," and "ascites."

STOCKARD, WILLIAM J., Private

Resided in Alamance County where he enlisted at age 21, July 4, 1862, for the war. Hospitalized at Richmond, Virginia, October 25, 1862, with typhoid fever. Transferred to hospital at Danville, Virginia, December 19, 1862, with debilitas. Returned to duty on January 30, 1863. Reported present on surviving company muster rolls through August 31, 1864. Company records indicate that he was wounded in the back and captured at Winchester, Virginia,

September 19, 1864; however, records of the Federal Provost Marshal do not substantiate that report. Probably killed at Winchester.

TARPLEY, MASON, Private

Resided in Alamance County and was by occupation a farmer prior to enlisting in Alamance County at age 32, July 4, 1862, for the war. Hospitalized at Richmond, Virginia, October 20, 1862, with remittent fever. Died in hospital at Richmond on December 17, 1862, of "variola conf[luen]t."

TERRY, WILLIAM S., Private

Resided in Orange County where he enlisted at age 22, July 4, 1862, for the war. Reported absent sick through October 31, 1862. Reported absent without leave in November, 1862-February, 1863. Returned to duty prior to May 11, 1863. Captured at Rappahannock Station, Virginia, November 7, 1863. Confined at Point Lookout, Maryland, November 11, 1863. Paroled at Point Lookout on March 16, 1864. Received at City Point, Virginia, March 20, 1864, for exchange. Returned to duty in May-August, 1864. Wounded in the right leg and captured at Cedar Creek, Virginia, October 19, 1864. Hospitalized at Baltimore, Maryland, January 19, 1865. Transferred to hospital at Fort McHenry, Maryland, May 9, 1865. Released at Fort McHenry on June 29, 1865, after taking the Oath of Allegiance. Died in hospital at Danville, Virginia, July 9, 1865. Cause of death not reported.

THOMAS, ANDERSON R., Private

Resided in Alamance County and was by occupation a farmer prior to enlisting in Alamance County at age 28, July 4, 1862, for the war. Hospitalized at Richmond, Virginia, October 19, 1862, with parotitis. Returned to duty in January-February, 1863. Hospitalized at Richmond on May 5, 1863, with tertiary fever. Captured and paroled on or about May 24, 1863, during the "recent raid in the rear of Lee's army." Deserted from hospital on May 28, 1863. Reported in hospital on August 31, 1863. Returned to duty in January-April, 1864. Reported present through February 28, 1865. Captured at Fort Stedman, Virginia, March 25, 1865. Confined at Point Lookout, Maryland, March 28, 1865. Released at Point Lookout on June 21, 1865, after taking the Oath of Allegiance.

THOMPSON, JAMES M., Private

Born in Orange County where he resided prior to enlisting in Orange County at age 21, July 4, 1862, for the war. Hospitalized at Richmond, Virginia, October 20, 1862. Died in hospital at Richmond on or about October 31, 1862, of "typhoid fever."

THOMPSON, JOHN, Private

Resided in Orange County where he enlisted at age 31, July 4, 1862, for the war. Reported present through February 28, 1863. Sent to hospital on April 1, 1863. Reported absent without leave on September 20, 1863. Returned to duty in September-October, 1864. Wounded in the left arm and captured at Fort Stedman, Virginia, March 25, 1865. Hospitalized at Washington, D.C., March 30, 1865. Confined at Old Capitol Prison, Washington, April 24, 1865. Transferred to Elmira, New York, May 11, 1865. Released at Elmira on July 7, 1865, after taking the Oath of Allegiance. [North Carolina pension records indicate that he died, three years after the surrender, of a wound in the left lung received in battle.]

THOMPSON, WILLIAM H., Private

Resided in Orange County where he enlisted at age 34, July 4, 1862, for the war. Hospitalized at Richmond, Virginia, November 25,

1862, with icterus. Returned to duty on January 12, 1863. Reported present through May 11, 1863. Deserted prior to September 1, 1863. Returned to duty in September-October, 1863. Died at Orange Court House, Virginia, November 14, 1863, of "pneumonia."

TROLINGER, JOHN W., Private

Resided in Alamance County where he enlisted at age 22, July 4, 1862, for the war. Reported absent sick in July-August, 1862. Returned to duty in September-October, 1862. Reported present through February 28, 1863. Captured at Chancellorsville, Virginia, May 3-4, 1863. Confined at Fort Delaware, Delaware, May 7, 1863. Paroled at Fort Delaware and transferred to City Point, Virginia, where he was received on May 23, 1863, for exchange. Died at home on or about June 10, 1863, of disease.

TURNER, C. F., Corporal

Resided in Alamance County and was by occupation a carpenter prior to enlisting in Alamance County at age 28, July 4, 1862, for the war. Mustered in as Private. Promoted to Corporal prior to September 2, 1862. Wounded in the right leg at Fredericksburg, Virginia, December 13, 1862. Hospitalized at Richmond, Virginia. Furloughed for sixty days on December 29, 1862. Returned to duty subsequent to May 11, 1863. Captured at Gettysburg, Pennsylvania, July 3-5, 1863. Confined at Fort Delaware, Delaware, on or about July 9, 1863. Transferred to Point Lookout, Maryland, October 20, 1863. Paroled at Point Lookout on March 17, 1864. Received at City Point, Virginia, March 20, 1864, for exchange. Returned to duty prior to September 1, 1864. Reported present in September, 1864-February, 1865. Captured at Farmville, Virginia, April 6, 1865. Confined at Newport News, Virginia, April 14, 1865. Released at Newport News on June 26, 1865, after taking the Oath of Allegiance.

TURNER, JOHN F., Private

Enlisted in Alamance County on July 4, 1862, for the war. Hospitalized at Richmond, Virginia, on or about September 28, 1862, with diarrhoea. Furloughed for thirty days on November 12, 1862. Returned to duty in January-February, 1863. Captured at Chancellorsville, Virginia, May 4, 1863. Confined at Old Capitol Prison, Washington, D.C. Paroled and transferred to City Point, Virginia, where he was received on June 12, 1863, for exchange. Returned to duty prior to September 1, 1863. Captured at Rappahannock Station, Virginia, November 7, 1863. Confined at Point Lookout, Maryland, November 11, 1863. Paroled at Point Lookout on March 16, 1864. Received at City Point on March 20, 1864, for exchange. Returned to duty prior to September 1, 1864. Wounded in the finger at Cedar Creek, Virginia, October 19, 1864. Returned to duty prior to November 1, 1864. Reported absent without leave on December 29, 1864. Returned to duty prior to March 1, 1865. Surrendered at Appomattox Court House, Virginia, April 9, 1865.

WALKER, JEFFERSON H., Private

Resided in Alamance County and was by occupation a farmer prior to enlisting in Alamance County at age 32, July 4, 1862, for the war. Reported present through October 31, 1863. Captured at Rappahannock Station, Virginia, November 7, 1863. Confined at Point Lookout, Maryland, November 11, 1863. Died at Point Lookout on December 29, 1863, of disease.

WALLACE, J. M., Private

Resided in Alamance County where he enlisted at age 33, July 4, 1862, for the war. Wounded at Fredericksburg, Virginia, December

13, 1862. Returned to duty prior to January 1, 1863. Reported missing and presumed captured at Chancellorsville on May 4, 1863. Was probably killed at Chancellorsville.

WARD, JAMES H., Private

Enlisted at Camp Vance on April 5, 1864, for the war. Captured near Washington, D.C., July 12, 1864. Confined at Old Capitol Prison, Washington, July 13, 1864. Transferred to Elmira, New York, July 23, 1864. Died at Elmira on August 27, 1864, of "typhoid fever."

WARREN, THOMAS, Private

Resided in Orange County and was by occupation a farmer prior to enlisting in Orange County at age 35, July 4, 1862, for the war. Died in hospital at Richmond, Virginia, October 8, 1862, of "rubeola followed by meningitis."

WARREN, Y. B., Private

Resided in Orange County where he enlisted at age 23, July 4, 1862, for the war. Reported absent sick through February 28, 1863. Wounded at Chancellorsville, Virginia, May 4, 1863. Returned to duty prior to May 11, 1863. Reported present or accounted for through February 28, 1865. Paroled at Appomattox Court House, Virginia, April 9, 1865.

WEBSTER, MALBON C. A., Private

Resided in Orange County and was by occupation a mechanic prior to enlisting in Orange County at age 35, July 4, 1862, for the war. Mustered in as Sergeant. Reduced to ranks prior to September 2, 1862. Hospitalized at Richmond, Virginia, October 4, 1862, with dysentery. Transferred to Salisbury on October 7, 1862. Hospitalized at Farmville, Virginia, May 6, 1863, with rheumatism. Returned to duty on May 21, 1863. Captured at Rappahannock Station, Virginia, November 7, 1863. Confined at Point Lookout, Maryland, November 11, 1863. Paroled at Point Lookout on March 16, 1864. Received at City Point, Virginia, March 20, 1864, for exchange. Returned to duty in May-August, 1864. Captured at Fisher's Hill, Virginia, September 22, 1864. Confined at Point Lookout on October 3, 1864. Paroled at Point Lookout on February 13, 1865. Received at Cox's Wharf, James River, Virginia, February 14-15, 1865, for exchange. Survived the war.

WELDON, ELI, Private

Resided in Alamance County and enlisted in Rowan County at age 20, July 4, 1862, for the war. Hospitalized at Richmond, Virginia, November 8, 1862, with phthisis. Furloughed for forty days on or about January 3, 1863. Returned to duty prior to May 11, 1863. Killed at Gettysburg, Pennsylvania, July 2-3, 1863.

WILKERSON, J. E., Private

Resided in Orange County where he enlisted at age 32, July 4, 1862, for the war. Hospitalized at Richmond, Virginia, November 8, 1862. Transferred to hospital at Farmville, Virginia, December 21, 1862 (suffering from rheumatism). Returned to duty on February 2, 1863. Hospitalized at Richmond on May 9, 1863. Died in hospital at Richmond on May 15, 1863, of "ty[phoid] pneumonia."

WILKINS, J. J., Private

Resided in Orange County and enlisted in Alamance County at age 23, July 4, 1862, for the war. Reported present through February 28, 1863. Died in hospital at Richmond, Virginia, or at Staunton, Virginia, on or about April 18, 1863, of disease.

WILKINS, JOHN, Private

Resided in Orange County and enlisted in Alamance County at age 30, July 4, 1862, for the war. Hospitalized at Richmond, Virginia, October 31, 1862, with remittent fever. Transferred to hospital at Farmville, Virginia, December 20, 1862. Furloughed for forty days on February 2, 1863. Returned to duty in May-August, 1863. Captured at Rappahannock Station, Virginia, November 7, 1863. Confined at Point Lookout, Maryland, November 11, 1863. Paroled at Point Lookout on March 16, 1864. Received at City Point, Virginia, March 20, 1864, for exchange. Returned to duty in May-August, 1864. Reported present through February 28, 1865. Captured at Farmville on April 6, 1865. Confined at Newport News, Virginia, April 14, 1865. Released at Newport News on June 26, 1865, after taking the Oath of Allegiance.

WRIGHT, GEORGE, Private

Place and date of enlistment not reported (probably enlisted in the autumn or early winter of 1864). Reported present in November-December, 1864. No further records.

COMPANY K

This company was raised in Rowan County on July 7, 1862. It was mustered into service at Salisbury on July 17, 1862, and assigned to the 57th Regiment N.C. Troops as Company K. After joining the regiment the company functioned as a part of the regiment, and its history for the remainder of the war is reported as a part of the regimental history.

The following roster was compiled primarily from information in the microfilm edition of the Compiled Service Records of Soldiers Who Served in Organizations from the State of North Carolina (Record Group 109, M270), National Archives and Records Administration, Washington, D.C. Record Group 109 includes enlistment papers, pay vouchers, requisitions, letters of resignation, discharge certificates, and abstracts of medical and prisoner of war returns. Materials relating specifically to this company include muster rolls dated July 7, 1862-December 31, 1863, and March 1, 1864-February 28, 1865.

Also utilized in this roster were *The War of the Rebellion: A Compilation of the Official Records of the Union and Confederate Armies*, the North Carolina adjutant general's *Roll of Honor*, state militia records, newspaper casualty lists and obituaries, wartime claims for bounty pay and allowances, postwar registers of claims for artificial limbs, Confederate pension applications filed with the states of North Carolina, Tennessee, and Florida, Confederate Soldiers' Home records, and the 1860 and 1870 federal censuses of North Carolina. A search was made also for relevant letters, diaries, reminiscences, and other manuscripts in the Southern Historical Collection (University of North Carolina-Chapel Hill), the Duke University Library Special Collections Department, and the North Carolina Division of Archives and History.

Among the secondary sources consulted were records of the North Carolina division of the United Daughters of the Confederacy, postwar rosters, regimental and county histories, marriage bond, will, and cemetery indexes, published and unpublished genealogies, biographical dictionaries, the North Carolina *County Heritage Book* series, the *Confederate Veteran*, Walter Clark's *Histories of the Several Regiments and Battalions from North Carolina in the Great War, 1861-'65*, and the North Carolina volume of the extended edition of *Confederate Military History*.

OFFICERS

CAPTAINS

MILLER, ALFRED ALEXANDER

Born on June 11, 1835. Resided in Rowan County where he enlisted at age 27. Appointed Captain on July 4, 1862. Shot through the head and killed at Fredericksburg, Virginia, December 13, 1862. [Previously served as Captain of Company N, 76th Regiment N.C. Militia, and Company B, 120th Regiment N.C. Militia.]

PROPST, ELI ALEXANDER, JR.

Born on January 25, 1828. Resided in Rowan County and was by occupation a farmer prior to enlisting in Rowan County at age 34. Appointed 1st Lieutenant on July 4, 1862. Promoted to Captain on December 13, 1862. Reported present or accounted for through February 28, 1863. Resigned on March 24, 1863, by reason of "chronic dyspepsia, neuralgia, & stricture of the urethra." Resignation accepted on April 2, 1863. Later served as Private in Company F, 9th Regiment N.C. State Troops (1st Regiment N.C. Cavalry).

SECHLER, GENERAL ANDREW JACKSON

Born on March 23, 1831. Resided in Rowan County and was by occupation a farmer prior to enlisting in Rowan County at age 31, July 7, 1862, for the war. Mustered in as Sergeant. Appointed 1st Lieutenant on December 19, 1862. Reported present through February 28, 1863. Captured at Chancellorsville, Virginia, May 4, 1863. Confined at Old Capitol Prison, Washington, D.C. Paroled on May 18, 1863, and transferred for exchange. Promoted to Captain on May 20, 1863. Hospitalized at Richmond, Virginia, June 2, 1863, with febris communis. Returned to duty on July 20, 1863. Captured at Rappahannock Station, Virginia, November 7, 1863. Confined at Old Capitol Prison on November 8, 1863. Transferred to Johnson's Island, Ohio, where he arrived on November 14, 1863. Released at Johnson's Island on June 13, 1865, after taking the Oath of Allegiance. [Previously served as Captain of Company G, 120th Regiment N.C. Militia.]

MAYNARD, RICHARD L.

Served as 1st Lieutenant of Company I of this regiment. Reported in command of this company in November-December, 1863.

HUNTER, MILES H.

Served as Captain of Company B of this regiment. Reported in command of this company in September-October, 1864.

DICKEY, JOSEPH H.

Served as Captain of Company I of this regiment. Reported in command of this company in November, 1864-February, 1865.

LIEUTENANTS

BROWN, HUGH LAWSON, 2nd Lieutenant

Resided in Rowan County and was by occupation a farmer prior to enlisting in Rowan County at age 27. Appointed 2nd Lieutenant on July 4, 1862. Wounded at Fredericksburg, Virginia, December 13, 1862. Died on December 25, 1862, of wounds. Place of death not reported.

EARNHEART, WILLIAM P., 2nd Lieutenant

Previously served as Sergeant Major of this regiment. Appointed 2nd Lieutenant of this company on May 22, 1863. Transferred to Company A of this regiment on September 29, 1863.

LENTZ, JOHN C., 1st Lieutenant

Previously served as Private in Capt. William H. Howard's Company, N.C. Prison Guards. Enlisted in this company in Rowan County on July 5, 1862, for the war. Mustered in as Sergeant. Promoted to 1st Sergeant in September-October, 1862. Wounded in the head at Fredericksburg, Virginia, December 13, 1862. Hospitalized at Richmond, Virginia. Furloughed on or about January 2, 1863. Returned to duty prior to March 1, 1863. Appointed 1st Lieutenant on May 20, 1863. Wounded in the arm at Gettysburg, Pennsylvania, on or about July 2, 1863. Hospitalized at Richmond. Furloughed for thirty days on July 20, 1863. Returned to duty prior to November 1, 1863. Captured at Rappahannock Station, Virginia, November 7, 1863. Confined at Old Capitol Prison, Washington, D.C., November 8, 1863. Transferred to Johnson's Island, Ohio, where he arrived on November 14, 1863. Released at Johnson's Island on June 12, 1865, after taking the Oath of Allegiance.

PINKSTON, JESSE ROWAN, 3rd Lieutenant

Resided in Rowan County and was by occupation a carpenter prior to enlisting at age 28. Appointed 3rd Lieutenant on July 4, 1862. Killed at Fredericksburg, Virginia, December 13, 1862.

WRIGHT, MINTON AUGUSTUS, 3rd Lieutenant

Previously served as Ordnance Sergeant of this regiment. Appointed 3rd Lieutenant of this company on May 22, 1863. Reported missing at Gettysburg, Pennsylvania, July 2, 1863. Was probably killed at Gettysburg.

NONCOMMISSIONED OFFICERS AND PRIVATES

AARON, JOHN HENRY, Private

Resided in Rowan County where he enlisted at age 16, July 7, 1862, for the war as a substitute. Reported present through October 31, 1863. Captured at Rappahannock Station, Virginia, November 7, 1863. Confined at Point Lookout, Maryland, November 11, 1863. Paroled at Point Lookout on March 16, 1864. Received at City Point, Virginia, March 20, 1864, for exchange. Returned to duty subsequent to April 30, 1864. Captured at Charlestown, West Virginia, August 22, 1864. Confined at Old Capitol Prison, Washington, D.C., August 24, 1864. Transferred to Elmira, New York, where he arrived on August 29, 1864. Released at Elmira on June 19, 1865, after taking the Oath of Allegiance. [North Carolina pension records indicate that he was wounded in the left hip by a piece of shell at Gettysburg, Pennsylvania, July 1, 1863.]

ALSABROOKS, THOMAS A., Private

Resided in Rowan County where he enlisted at age 16, July 7, 1862, for the war as a substitute for C. F. Vaneatin [van Eaton?]. Killed at Fredericksburg, Virginia, December 13, 1862.

BALL, LEWIS, Private

Enlisted in Rowan County on July 7, 1862, for the war. Deserted on or about July 22, 1862.

BARGER, CALEB, Corporal

Resided in Rowan County where he enlisted at age 32, July 7, 1862, for the war. Mustered in as Corporal. Wounded at Fredericksburg, Virginia, December 13, 1862. Returned to duty prior to January 1, 1863. Reported present through October 31, 1863. Captured at Rappahannock Station, Virginia, November 7, 1863. Confined at Point Lookout, Maryland, November 11, 1863. Paroled at Point Lookout on March 16, 1864. Received at City Point, Virginia, March 20, 1864, for exchange. Returned to duty subsequent to April 30, 1864. Wounded in the hand at Winchester, Virginia, July 20, 1864. Returned to duty in September-October, 1864. Reported present through February 28, 1865. Captured at Fort Stedman, Virginia, March 25, 1865. Confined at Point Lookout on March 28, 1865. Released at Point Lookout on June 23, 1865, after taking the Oath of Allegiance.

BARGER, JOHN, Private

Resided in Rowan County where he enlisted on July 7, 1862, for the war. Hospitalized at Richmond, Virginia, September 1, 1862, with diarrhoea. Transferred to Goldsboro on November 2, 1862. Returned to duty on or about November 10, 1862, and was detailed as a teamster. Rejoined the company prior to January 1, 1863. Captured at Chancellorsville, Virginia, May 3-4, 1863. Confined at Fort Delaware, Delaware, on or about May 7, 1863. Paroled at Fort Delaware and transferred to City Point, Virginia, where he was received on May 23, 1863, for exchange. Returned to duty on an unspecified date. Sent to hospital on August 10, 1863. Returned to duty in September-October, 1863. Reported present on surviving company muster rolls through April 30, 1864. Wounded in the arm at Winchester, Virginia, July 20, 1864. Returned to duty subsequent to August 31, 1864. Wounded in the left foot and captured at Cedar Creek, Virginia, October 19, 1864. Hospitalized at Baltimore, Maryland, October 24, 1864. Transferred to Fort McHenry, Maryland, November 19, 1864. Transferred to Point Lookout, Maryland, January 2, 1865. Released at Point Lookout on June 23, 1865, after taking the Oath of Allegiance. [Federal hospital records give his age as 31 on November 19, 1864.]

BARNES, HENRY, Private

Resided in Forsyth County and was by occupation a farmer prior to enlisting in Wake County on March 8, 1864, for the war. Hospitalized at Richmond, Virginia, May 24, 1864, with rubeola. Returned to duty on June 20, 1864. Wounded in the right thigh and captured at Winchester, Virginia, July 20, 1864. Hospitalized at Cumberland, Maryland. Confined at Camp Chase, Ohio, November 4, 1864. Died at Camp Chase on April 6, 1865, of "pneumonia." [Records of the Federal Provost Marshal dated November, 1864, give his age as 19.]

BENSON, JOHN B., Private

Enlisted in Rowan County on July 7, 1862, for the war. Hospitalized at Richmond, Virginia, September 26, 1862, with debility. Returned to duty prior to November 1, 1862. Sent to hospital at Richmond on January 26, 1863. Died in hospital at Lynchburg, Virginia, March 7, 1863, of "smallpox."

BLACK, JAMES A., 1st Sergeant

Resided in Cabarrus County and was by occupation a farm hand prior to enlisting in Cabarrus or Rowan County at age 18, July 6, 1862, for the war. Mustered in as Private. Reported present through February 28, 1863. Captured at Chancellorsville, Virginia, May 3-4, 1863. Confined at Fort Delaware, Delaware, on or about May 7, 1863. Paroled at Fort Delaware and transferred to City Point,

Virginia, where he was received on May 23, 1863, for exchange. Returned to duty prior to September 1, 1863. Promoted to Sergeant in September-October, 1863. Captured at Rappahannock Station, Virginia, November 7, 1863. Confined at Point Lookout, Maryland, November 11, 1863. Paroled at Point Lookout on March 16, 1864. Received at City Point on March 20, 1864, for exchange. Returned to duty in May-August, 1864. Promoted to 1st Sergeant in November-December, 1864. Reported present through February 28, 1865. Captured at Fort Stedman, Virginia, March 25, 1865. Confined at Point Lookout on March 28, 1865. Released at Point Lookout on June 24, 1865, after taking the Oath of Allegiance.

BLACK, MONROE B., Private

Resided in Cabarrus County and was by occupation a farm hand prior to enlisting in Cabarrus or Rowan County at age 20, July 6, 1862, for the war. Wounded in the right arm at Fredericksburg, Virginia, December 13, 1862. Reported in hospital at Farmville, Virginia, January 15, 1863. Returned to duty on February 10, 1863. Captured at Gettysburg, Pennsylvania, July 3-4, 1863. Confined at Fort Delaware, Delaware, on or about July 9, 1863. Released at Fort Delaware on June 19, 1865, after taking the Oath of Allegiance.

BOSTIAN, ANDREW A., Corporal

Resided in Rowan County and was by occupation a farmer prior to enlisting in Rowan County at age 35, July 7, 1862, for the war. Mustered in as Private. Promoted to Corporal on December 20, 1862. Reported present through May 11, 1863. Hospitalized at Richmond, Virginia, July 11, 1863, with debility. Furloughed for forty days on July 19, 1863. Returned to duty prior to September 1, 1863. Wounded in the right side and captured at Rappahannock Station, Virginia, November 7, 1863. Hospitalized at Washington, D.C., where he died on or about November 13, 1863, of wounds.

BURLEYSON, JOSEPH, Private

Enlisted in Wake County on March 8, 1864, for the war. Reported present through August 31, 1864. Wounded in the right thigh and/or hip at Winchester, Virginia, September 19, 1864. Captured at Harrisonburg, Virginia, September 25, 1864. Hospitalized at Baltimore, Maryland, October 13, 1864. Transferred to Point Lookout, Maryland, October 17, 1864. Paroled at Point Lookout on or about October 31, 1864. Received at Venus Point, Savannah River, Georgia, November 15, 1864, for exchange. No further records.

BUTNER, JOHN S., Private

Enlisted in Wake County on March 8, 1864, for the war. Deserted on November 11, 1864. [The Daily Bulletin (Charlotte) of April 4, 1865, states that he was wounded severely in the shoulder near Petersburg, Virginia, March 25, 1865.]

CARROLL, JAMES, Private

Enlisted in Rowan County on October 4, 1862, for the war. Deserted the same date.

CHESHIRE, JONATHAN WESLEY, Sergeant

Enlisted in Rowan County on July 8, 1862, for the war. Mustered in as Private. Promoted to Sergeant on January 24, 1863. Reported present through May 11, 1863. Appointed acting Ordnance Sergeant on or about May 22, 1863, and transferred to the Field and Staff of this regiment. Reported on duty as acting regimental Ordnance Sergeant through December 31, 1863. Died of disease. Place and date of death not reported.

CORRELL, JOHN L., Sergeant

Resided in Rowan County where he enlisted on July 7, 1862, for the war. Mustered in as Private. Promoted to Sergeant in May-August, 1863. Reported present through October 31, 1863. Captured at Rappahannock Station, Virginia, November 7, 1863. Confined at Point Lookout, Maryland, November 11, 1863. Paroled at Point Lookout on March 16, 1864. Received at City Point, Virginia, March 20, 1864, for exchange. Returned to duty in May-August, 1864. Reported present through February 28, 1865. Captured at Farmville, Virginia, April 6, 1865. Confined at Newport News, Virginia, April 14, 1865. Released at Newport News on June 26, 1865, after taking the Oath of Allegiance.

CORRELL, WILLIAM W., Private

Resided in Rowan County and was by occupation a farmer or miller prior to enlisting in Rowan County at age 31, July 8, 1862, for the war. Reported present in November, 1862-February, 1863. Hospitalized at Richmond, Virginia, April 9, 1863, convalescent from pneumonia. Transferred to Salisbury on April 20, 1863. Returned to duty in May-August, 1863. Captured at Rappahannock Station, Virginia, November 7, 1863. Confined at Point Lookout, Maryland, November 11, 1863. Paroled at Point Lookout on March 16, 1864. Received at City Point, Virginia, March 20, 1864, for exchange. Returned to duty subsequent to April 30, 1864. Captured at Winchester, Virginia, July 20, 1864. Confined at Camp Chase, Ohio, July 28, 1864. Died at Camp Chase on or about January 28, 1865, of "pneumonia."

CORRIHER, RICHARD A., Private

Born in Rowan County where he resided as a farmer prior to enlisting in Rowan County on July 7, 1862, for the war. Wounded in the left arm at Fredericksburg, Virginia, December 13, 1862. Left arm amputated. Hospitalized at Richmond, Virginia. Retired from service on December 21, 1864, by reason of disability from wounds. Paroled at Salisbury on May 22, 1865. Took the Oath of Allegiance at Salisbury on July 8, 1865. [Was 29 years of age in December, 1864.]

COX, WILCHER, Private

Resided in Surry County and was by occupation a "tenant [farmer]" prior to enlisting in Wake County at age 29, April 5, 1864, for the war. Reported present through August 31, 1864. Reported present but under arrest from October 1, 1864, through February 28, 1865. Reason he was arrested not reported. Returned to duty prior to April 6, 1865, when he was captured at Farmville, Virginia. Confined at Newport News, Virginia, April 14, 1865. Released at Newport News on June 26, 1865, after taking the Oath of Allegiance.

CRAVER, A. J., Private

Previously served as Private in Company E of this regiment. Transferred to this company on an unspecified date (probably in the summer of 1862). Reported present through February 28, 1863. Hospitalized at Richmond, Virginia, April 28, 1863, with intermittent fever. Transferred to hospital at Danville, Virginia, May 8, 1863. Furloughed for thirty days on May 13, 1863. Reported absent without leave on July 6, 1863. No further records.

DAVIS, GEORGE D., Private

Enlisted in Rowan County on July 7, 1862, for the war. Hospitalized at Richmond, Virginia, September 8, 1862, with diarrhoea. Returned to duty on September 11, 1862. Deserted near Fredericksburg, Virginia, November 24, 1862.

DICKSON, CHARLES B., Private

Resided in Rowan County where he enlisted at age 32, July 7, 1862, for the war. Reported absent sick at Richmond, Virginia, September 8, 1862. Returned to duty on November 28, 1862. Reported present through February 28, 1863. Hospitalized at Richmond on May 2, 1863, with acute diarrhoea. Transferred to hospital at Danville, Virginia, May 7, 1863. Returned to duty on July 9, 1863. Reported in hospital at Huguenot Springs, Virginia, from July 20, 1863, through February 29, 1864. Reported sick in hospital in March-August, 1864. Returned to duty in September-October, 1864. Reported absent sick on February 8, 1865. Returned to duty subsequent to February 28, 1865. Captured at High Bridge, Virginia, April 6, 1865. Confined at Newport News, Virginia, April 16, 1865. Released at Newport News on June 30, 1865, after taking the Oath of Allegiance.

DONAHA, WILLIAM A., Private

Enlisted in Rowan County on July 7, 1862, for the war. Hospitalized at Richmond, Virginia, October 9, 1862, with typhoid fever. Died in hospital at Richmond on November 1, 1862, of "pneumonia."

DOUTHIT, J. M., Private

Resided in Davie County and enlisted in Rowan County on July 7, 1862, for the war. Died in hospital at Richmond, Virginia, October 29, 1862, of "typhoid pneumonia."

DUNIGAN, LEWIS, Private

Resided in Surry County and enlisted in Wake County at age 18, April 5, 1864, for the war. Hospitalized at Richmond, Virginia, June 3, 1864, with rubeola. Furloughed for thirty days on July 20, 1864. Reported absent without leave on October 28, 1864. No further records.

EARNHART, NATHANIEL, Private

Born in Rowan County where he resided prior to enlisting in Rowan County at age 23, July 7, 1862, for the war. Reported present through February 28, 1863. Sent to hospital on April 8, 1863. Returned to duty in May-August, 1863. Reported present through February 28, 1865. Captured at Fort Stedman, Virginia, March 25, 1865. Confined at Point Lookout, Maryland, March 28, 1865. Released at Point Lookout on June 12, 1865, after taking the Oath of Allegiance.

ELLIOTT, J. H., Private

Previously served as Private in Company A of this regiment. Transferred to this company on or about July 17, 1862. Reported present through August 31, 1863. Sent to hospital on October 10, 1863. Reported absent on detached service in March-April, 1864. Died of disease. Place and date of death not reported.

ENNIS, WILLIAM C., Private

Resided in Rowan County and was by occupation a shoemaker prior to enlisting in Rowan County on July 7, 1862, for the war. Hospitalized at Richmond, Virginia, October 15, 1862, with typhoid fever. Returned to duty on October 25, 1862. Hospitalized at Richmond on November 8, 1862, with rubeola. Transferred to hospital at Petersburg, Virginia, November 14, 1862. Returned to duty in January-February, 1863. Sent to hospital on March 3, 1863. Reported absent without leave from June 28 through October 31, 1863. Returned to duty in January-April, 1864. Hospitalized at Richmond on May 26, 1864. Hospitalized at Raleigh on August

8, 1864, with chronic diarrhoea. Returned to duty on January 12, 1865. Surrendered at Appomattox Court House, Virginia, April 9, 1865. Took the Oath of Allegiance at Salisbury on June 14, 1865. [Was about 25 years of age at time of enlistment.]

FARRIS, COLEMAN D., Corporal

Resided in Rowan or Yadkin Counties and was by occupation a farmer prior to enlisting in Rowan County at age 25, July 7, 1862, for the war. Mustered in as Private. Hospitalized at Richmond, Virginia, September 10, 1862, with remittent fever. Later contracted dysentery. Transferred to hospital at Salisbury on October 2, 1862. Returned to duty prior to November 1, 1862. Reported present through February 28, 1863. Promoted to Corporal in March-May, 1863. Wounded in the left hand (forefinger shot off) at Chancellorsville, Virginia, May 4, 1863. Hospitalized at Richmond. Transferred to hospital at Salisbury on June 4, 1863. Detailed for duty as a provost guard at Raleigh on June 29, 1863. Reported absent on detail through December 31, 1864. Took the Oath of Allegiance at Salisbury on June 20, 1865.

FESPERMAN, MONROE, Private

Resided in Rowan County and enlisted in Wake County at age 18, March 8, 1864, for the war. Deserted at Goldsboro on May 7, 1864. Returned to duty in September-October, 1864. Deserted on November 11, 1864.

GARRIAN, T., Private

Enlisted in Rowan County on October 6, 1862, for the war as a substitute. Deserted on or about the same date.

GARRICK, CHARLES, Private

Enlisted in Rowan County on October 4, 1862, for the war. Deserted on or about the same date.

GHEEN, D. L., Private

Enlisted in Rowan County on July 7, 1862, for the war. Hospitalized at Richmond, Virginia, November 8, 1862, with debility from fever. Transferred to hospital at Petersburg, Virginia, November 14, 1862. Died in hospital at Petersburg on December 1, 1862, of "typhoid fever."

GHEEN, WILLIAM H., Corporal

Resided in Rowan County and was by occupation a farmer prior to enlisting in Rowan County at age 33, July 7, 1862, for the war. Mustered in as Private. Elected Corporal on November 10, 1862. Reported absent sick in January-February, 1863. Died in hospital at Lynchburg, Virginia, April 1, 1863, of "chronic diarrhoea."

GIBBONS, R. H., Private

Enlisted in Rowan County at age 22, July 7, 1862, for the war. Hospitalized at Richmond, Virginia, January 21, 1863, with chronic rheumatism. Reported in hospital through March 6, 1863. Reported absent without leave on May 11, 1863. Listed as a deserter in September-October, 1863.

GORRELL, JAMES, Private

Place and date of enlistment not reported (probably enlisted in the summer or autumn of 1862). Deserted on October 25, 1862.

GRACY, JOHN, Private

Enlisted in Rowan County on July 7, 1862, for the war. Deserted on July 10, 1862.

GRUBBS, JESSE F., 1st Sergeant

Previously served as Sergeant in Company D of this regiment. Transferred to this company on June 23 or July 23, 1864. Promoted to 1st Sergeant on or about the same date. Reported present and in command of the company through August 31, 1864. Reported present in September-October, 1864. Reduced to ranks and transferred back to Company D of this regiment on November 26, 1864.

HAFFMAN, W. A., Private

Enlisted in Rowan County on July 7, 1862, for the war. Discharged at Salisbury prior to September 1, 1862. Reason discharged not reported.

HAIR, JOSEPH M., Private

Resided in Iredell County and enlisted in Rowan County on July 7, 1862, for the war. Reported present or accounted for through February 28, 1865. Wounded in the groin and shoulders and captured at Fort Stedman, Virginia, March 25, 1865. Confined at Point Lookout, Maryland, March 28, 1865. Released at Point Lookout on June 6, 1865, after taking the Oath of Allegiance. [Was about 17 years of age at time of enlistment.]

HARTSEL, M. E., Private

Enlisted in Rowan County on July 7, 1862, for the war. Hospitalized at Richmond, Virginia, October 19, 1862, with chronic bronchitis. Died in hospital at Richmond on January 12, 1863, of "typhoid fever."

HOWARD, BENJAMIN W., Private

Resided in Rowan County where he enlisted at age 27, July 7, 1862, for the war. Reported present or accounted for on surviving company muster rolls through April 30, 1864. Served as a teamster during much of that period. Reported sick in hospital at Lynchburg, Virginia, in May-August, 1864. Returned to duty in September-October, 1864. Reported present through February 28, 1865. Surrendered at Appomattox Court House, Virginia, April 9, 1865. Took the Oath of Allegiance at Salisbury on June 16, 1865.

HOWARD, THOMAS A., Private

Resided in Rowan County and was by occupation a farmer prior to enlisting in Rowan County at age 37, July 7, 1862, for the war. Died in hospital at Richmond, Virginia, September 16, 1862, probably of intermittent fever and/or diarrhoea.

HOWELL, TILLMON S., Private

Enlisted in Rowan County on July 7, 1862, for the war. Wounded in the left hand at Fredericksburg, Virginia, December 13, 1862. Reported in hospital at Farmville, Virginia, January 15, 1863. Returned to duty subsequent to May 11, 1863. Wounded in the left arm at Gettysburg, Pennsylvania, July 1, 1863. Hospitalized at Richmond, Virginia. Returned to duty subsequent to October 31, 1863. Captured at Rappahannock Station, Virginia, November 7, 1863. Confined at Point Lookout, Maryland, November 11, 1863. Paroled at Point Lookout on March 16, 1864. Received at City Point, Virginia, March 20, 1864, for exchange. Reported absent without leave on May 20, 1864. Returned to duty in September-October, 1864. Sent to hospital on December 8, 1864. Admitted to hospital at Petersburg, Virginia, January 11, 1865, with pneumonia. Furloughed for thirty days on March 5, 1865. Paroled at Charlotte on May 13, 1865.

HOWELL, WILLIAM R., Private

Enlisted in Rowan County on July 7, 1862, for the war as a substitute. Hospitalized at Richmond, Virginia, September 13, 1862, with

intermittent fever. Furloughed for thirty days on September 26, 1862. Hospitalized at Richmond on November 26, 1862. Died in hospital at Richmond on or about December 1, 1862, of "typhoid pneumonia."

HUDSON, WILLIAM M., ———

North Carolina pension records indicate that he served in this company.

HUTSON, WILEY, Private

Resided in Stanly County and was by occupation a farmer prior to enlisting in Wake County at age 45, March 8, 1864, for the war. Captured at or near Fisher's Hill, Virginia, on or about September 22, 1864. Confined at Point Lookout, Maryland, October 12, 1864. Paroled at Point Lookout on March 17, 1865. Received at Boulware's Wharf, James River, Virginia, March 19, 1865, for exchange.

JACOBS, GEORGE W., Private

Resided in Rowan County and was by occupation a farmer prior to enlisting in Rowan County at age 34, July 7, 1862, for the war. Mustered in as Corporal. Hospitalized at Richmond, Virginia, September 19, 1862, with diarrhoea. Returned to duty on September 24, 1862. Reduced to ranks on or about November 10, 1862. Died in camp near Fredericksburg, Virginia, December 1, 1862, of "chronic diarrhoea."

JOSEY, RICHARD, Private

Enlisted in Rowan County on July 8, 1862, for the war. Discharged at Salisbury prior to September 1, 1862. Reason discharged not reported.

KANUP, DANIEL ALEXANDER, Private

Born on October 3, 1839. Enlisted in Rowan County at age 22, July 7, 1862, for the war. Reported present or accounted for through May 11, 1863. Wounded in the hip and/or nates and captured at Gettysburg, Pennsylvania, July 1-4, 1863. Hospitalized at Gettysburg. Transferred to hospital at Davids Island, New York Harbor, where he arrived on July 19, 1863. Died in hospital at Davids Island on August 21, 1863, of "ch[ronic] diarr[hoe]a."

KENNERLEY, DANIEL C., Private

Born in Rowan County where he resided as a farmer prior to enlisting in Rowan County at age 25, July 7, 1862, for the war. Hospitalized at Richmond, Virginia, September 13, 1862, with intermittent fever. Returned to duty on September 26, 1862. Wounded in the left hand at Fredericksburg, Virginia, December 13, 1862. Reported in hospital at Farmville, Virginia, January 16, 1863. Returned to duty on June 9, 1863. Hospitalized at Charlottesville, Virginia, June 28, 1863, with ulcus. Discharged from service at Charlottesville on July 21, 1863, by reason of "chronic ulceration of left leg near the ankle joint" caused by "fracture of tibia." Place and date injured not reported. Discharge certificate gives his age as 26. Took the Oath of Allegiance at Salisbury on June 21, 1865.

KENT, ALEX, ———

Place and date of enlistment not reported (probably enlisted in July-September, 1862). Deserted on September 23, 1862.

KEPLEY, JACOB N., Private

Previously served as Private in Company A of this regiment. Transferred to this company prior to September 2, 1862. Hospitalized at

Richmond, Virginia, September 6, 1862, with intermittent fever. Transferred to Salisbury on or about September 19, 1862. Reported absent without leave in November-December, 1862. Reported at home on furlough in January-May, 1863. Returned to duty in May-August, 1863. Reported present on surviving company muster rolls through April 30, 1864. Captured at Frederick, Maryland, on or about July 9, 1864. Confined at Old Capitol Prison, Washington, D.C. Transferred to Elmira, New York, July 23, 1864. Paroled at Elmira on October 11, 1864. Received at Venus Point, Savannah River, Georgia, November 15, 1864, for exchange. Reported absent sick from December 1, 1864, through February 28, 1865. Paroled at Salisbury on May 3, 1865.

KLUTTZ, EDMUND MILAS, 1st Sergeant

Born on April 15, 1837. Enlisted in Rowan County at age 25, July 7, 1862, for the war. Mustered in as Private. Reported present through February 28, 1863. Captured at Chancellorsville, Virginia, May 3-4, 1863. Confined at Fort Delaware, Delaware, on or about May 7, 1863. Paroled at Fort Delaware and transferred to City Point, Virginia, where he was received on May 23, 1863, for exchange. Promoted to 1st Sergeant in May-June, 1863. Returned to duty prior to July 2-5, 1863, when he was captured at Gettysburg, Pennsylvania. Confined at Fort Delaware. Died in hospital at Fort Delaware on December 25, 1863, of "smallpox."

KLUTTZ, GREEN C., Private

Previously served as Private in Company A of this regiment. Transferred to this company on or about July 17, 1862. Wounded in the leg at Fredericksburg, Virginia, December 13, 1862. Hospitalized at Richmond, Virginia. Died in hospital at Richmond on January 31, 1863, of "variola" and "gangrene."

KLUTTZ, HENRY, Corporal

Resided in Rowan County and was by occupation a farmer prior to enlisting in Rowan County at age 25, July 7, 1862, for the war. Mustered in as Private. Hospitalized at Richmond, Virginia, September 13, 1862, with intermittent fever. Returned to duty on October 2, 1862. Reported on duty as a teamster in October-November, 1862. Reported present in December, 1862-December, 1863, and March-December, 1864. Promoted to Corporal in May-August, 1864. Captured at Hatcher's Run, Virginia, February 6, 1865. Confined at Point Lookout, Maryland, February 9, 1865. Released at Point Lookout on June 28, 1865, after taking the Oath of Allegiance.

KLUTTZ, JACOB ALEXANDER, Private

Born on April 27, 1830. Resided in Rowan County where he enlisted at age 32, July 7, 1862, for the war. Mustered in as Sergeant. Reported present through February 28, 1863. Hospitalized at Richmond, Virginia, May 2, 1863, with rheumatism. Transferred to hospital at Danville, Virginia, May 7, 1863 (also suffering from diarrhoea). Furloughed on June 2, 1863. Listed as a deserter on August 9, 1863. Returned to duty prior to September 1, 1863. Reduced in ranks in September-October, 1863. Captured at Rappahannock Station, Virginia, November 7, 1863. Confined at Point Lookout, Maryland, November 11, 1863. Paroled at Point Lookout on March 16, 1864. Received at City Point, Virginia, March 20, 1864, for exchange. Returned to duty in May-August, 1864. Reported present through February 28, 1865. Surrendered at Appomattox Court House, Virginia, April 9, 1865. Took the Oath of Allegiance at Salisbury on June 17, 1865.

KLUTTZ, JESSE, Private

Resided in Rowan County and was by occupation a farmer prior to enlisting in Rowan County at age 28, July 7, 1862, for the war.

Reported present through May 11, 1863. Hospitalized at Danville, Virginia, July 16, 1863, with a gunshot wound. Place and date wounded not reported. Returned to duty on August 18, 1863. Captured at Rappahannock Station, Virginia, November 7, 1863. Confined at Point Lookout, Maryland, November 11, 1863. Paroled at Point Lookout on March 16, 1864. Received at City Point, Virginia, March 20, 1864, for exchange. Returned to duty in May-August, 1864. Wounded in the arm at Winchester, Virginia, September 19, 1864. Returned to duty in November-December, 1864. Captured at Hatcher's Run, Virginia, February 6, 1865. Confined at Point Lookout on February 9, 1865. Released at Point Lookout on June 28, 1865, after taking the Oath of Allegiance.

KLUTTZ, MOSES, JR., Private

Born on January 24, 1825. Resided in Cabarrus County where he enlisted at age 39, October 22, 1864, for the war. Reported present through February 28, 1865. Captured at Fort Stedman, Virginia, March 25, 1865. Confined at Point Lookout, Maryland, March 28, 1865. Released at Point Lookout on June 28, 1865, after taking the Oath of Allegiance.

LINN, ROBERT JOHN, Private

Resided in Rowan County and was by occupation a farmer prior to enlisting in Rowan County at age 30, July 7, 1862, for the war. No further records. [According to *Heritage of Rowan County*, 437, he died in 1867 of injuries received during the war.]

LIPPARD, JOHN, Private

Born on May 29, 1822. Resided in Cabarrus County and was by occupation a wagonmaker prior to enlisting in Cabarrus County at age 42, October 22, 1864, for the war. Captured at Hatcher's Run, Virginia, February 6, 1865. Confined at Point Lookout, Maryland, February 9, 1865. Released at Point Lookout on June 28, 1865, after taking the Oath of Allegiance.

LITAKER, GEORGE E., Private

Resided in Rowan County and was by occupation a farmer prior to enlisting in Rowan County at age 34, July 7, 1862, for the war. Killed at Fredericksburg, Virginia, December 13, 1862.

LITAKER, JOHN A., Sergeant

Born in Cabarrus County and was by occupation a farmer prior to enlisting in Rowan County on July 7, 1862, for the war. Mustered in as Sergeant. Wounded in the right arm at Fredericksburg, Virginia, December 13, 1862. Right arm amputated. Hospitalized at Richmond, Virginia. Furloughed for sixty days on January 10, 1863. Reported absent wounded through December 31, 1864. Retired from service on February 24, 1865, by reason of disability from wounds. Retirement certificate gives his age as 33.

MILLER, D. W., Private

Enlisted in Rowan County on July 7, 1862, for the war. Hospitalized at Richmond, Virginia, October 8, 1862, with chronic diarrhoea. Furloughed for sixty days on October 13, 1862. Returned to duty in March-May, 1863. Sent to hospital on July 5, 1863. Furloughed on August 25, 1863. Reported absent on furlough through October 31, 1863. Reported absent without leave in March-April, 1864. Paroled at Salisbury in 1865.

MILLER, EMANUEL, Private

Enlisted in Wake County on March 8, 1864, for the war. Hospitalized at Richmond, Virginia, May 13, 1864, with acute rheumatism.

Transferred to hospital at Danville, Virginia, May 17, 1864, with acute bronchitis. Transferred to another hospital on May 23, 1864. Returned to duty prior to July 10, 1864, when he was captured at or near Harpers Ferry, West Virginia. Confined at Old Capitol Prison, Washington, D.C., July 17, 1864. Transferred to Elmira, New York, July 23, 1864. Released at Elmira on May 29, 1865, after taking the Oath of Allegiance.

MORGAN, LINDSEY, Private

Enlisted in Rowan County on July 7, 1862, for the war. Reported present or accounted for through October 31, 1862. Deserted on December 25, 1862. Reported in confinement on December 31, 1862. Reported present but under arrest in January-February, 1863. Returned to duty prior to May 3-4, 1863, when he was captured at Chancellorsville, Virginia. Confined at Fort Delaware, Delaware, where he died on May 23, 1863, of "typhoid fever."

MORGAN, SOLOMON, Private

Resided in Rowan County and was by occupation a farmer prior to enlisting in Rowan County at age 29, July 7, 1862, for the war. Reported present through October 31, 1862. Wounded in the left arm at Fredericksburg, Virginia, December 13, 1862. Left arm amputated. Hospitalized at Richmond, Virginia. Furloughed for sixty days on March 22, 1863. Reported absent wounded through October 31, 1864. Returned to duty in November-December, 1864. Retired to the Invalid Corps on January 3, 1865. Took the Oath of Allegiance at Salisbury on July 7, 1865.

MOWERY, A. J., Private

Resided in Rowan County where he enlisted on July 7, 1862, for the war. Reported present on surviving company muster rolls through February 28, 1865. Surrendered at Appomattox Court House, Virginia, April 9, 1865. [Was about 20 years of age at time of enlistment. He is probably the same soldier who is listed in the roster for Company A of this regiment as Pvt. A. J. Mowry and who was transferred to "Capt Miller's Co" on or about July 17, 1862.]

NEWELL, A., Private

Place and date of enlistment not reported (probably enlisted subsequent to February 28, 1865). Surrendered at Appomattox Court House, Virginia, April 9, 1865.

NICHOLS, JEFFERSON N., Private

Enlisted in Wake County on April 5, 1864, for the war. Reported present through August 31, 1864. Reported present but under arrest on October 27, 1864. Reason he was arrested not reported. Court-martialed on an unspecified date and sentenced to be shot. Sentence suspended on February 19, 1865. Returned to duty prior to March 1, 1865. Surrendered at Appomattox Court House, Virginia, April 9, 1865. [Was about 35 years of age at time of enlistment. North Carolina pension records indicate that he was wounded in the right shoulder at Cedar Creek, Virginia, in 1864 and was wounded in the ankle at Petersburg, Virginia, in March, 1865.]

NOBLE, JOHN, ——

Place and date of enlistment not reported (probably enlisted in the summer of 1862). Deserted on or about September 23, 1862.

NORRIS, THOMAS, Private

Enlisted in Rowan County on October 6, 1862, for the war. Deserted the same date.

PEELING, ALONZO, Private

Enlisted in Rowan County on July 7, 1862, for the war. Reported present through October 31, 1862. Wounded at Fredericksburg, Virginia, December 13, 1862. Hospitalized at Richmond, Virginia. Returned to duty on or about February 28, 1863. Reported present through December 31, 1863. Transferred to the gunboat *Neuse* prior to May 1, 1864.

PENNINGER, WILLIAM A., Corporal

Previously served as Private in Company A of this regiment. Promoted to Corporal and transferred to this company on or about July 17, 1862. Reported present through October 31, 1862. Hospitalized at Richmond, Virginia, January 23, 1863, with chronic hepatitis. Furloughed for sixty days on March 1 or May 1, 1863. Returned to duty on an unspecified date. Sent to hospital on August 17, 1863. Furloughed on September 22, 1863. Returned to duty in January-April, 1864. Hospitalized at Richmond on June 12, 1864. Reported at home on surgeon's certificate on August 31, 1864. Returned to duty in September-October, 1864. Captured at Hatcher's Run, Virginia, February 6, 1865. Confined at Point Lookout, Maryland, February 9, 1865. Died at Point Lookout on April 19, 1865, of "inf[lammation] of the lungs."

PINKSTON, WILLIAM F., Private

Resided in Rowan County and was by occupation a farmer prior to enlisting in Rowan County at age 31, July 7, 1862, for the war. Reported present or accounted for through February 28, 1863. Wounded in the hand at Chancellorsville, Virginia, May 4, 1863. Returned to duty prior to May 11, 1863. Captured at Gettysburg, Pennsylvania, July 1-5, 1863. Confined at Fort Delaware, Delaware, on or about July 9, 1863. Transferred to Point Lookout, Maryland, October 20, 1863. Paroled at Point Lookout on February 18, 1865. Received at Boulware's and Cox's Wharves, James River, Virginia, on or about February 21, 1865, for exchange. Hospitalized at Richmond, Virginia, the same date. Furloughed on or about February 25, 1865. No further records. [According to *Heritage of Rowan County*, 406, he died of disease on an unspecified date.]

POINDEXTER, DENSON F., Private

Resided in Surry County and was by occupation a farmer prior to enlisting in Wake County at age 31, April 5, 1864, for the war. Deserted at Goldsboro on May 7, 1864.

REVELS, JOHN T., Private

Enlisted in Rowan County on July 7, 1862, for the war. Hospitalized at Richmond, Virginia, October 28, 1862, with measles. Returned to duty prior to January 1, 1863. Reported present or accounted for on surviving company muster rolls through December 31, 1864. Hospitalized at Petersburg, Virginia, February 25, 1865, with hepatitis, typhoid pneumonia, and continued fever. Died in hospital at Petersburg on March 1, 1865.

RICE, THOMAS S., Sergeant

Enlisted in Rowan County on July 7, 1862, for the war. Mustered in as Corporal. Promoted to Sergeant in November-December, 1862. Reported present through February 28, 1863. Killed at Chancellorsville, Virginia, May 4, 1863.

ROGERS, J. W., Private

Born in Rowan County and was by occupation a schoolboy prior to enlisting in Rowan County on July 7, 1862, for the war. Discharged on September 10, 1862, because "he is under age being only sixteen year[s] old & has the dropsy." [May have served later as Private in Company C, 33rd Regiment N.C. Troops.]

SECHLER, BENJAMIN COLUMBUS, Private

Born on April 19, 1833. Enlisted in Rowan County at age 29, July 7, 1862, for the war. No further records. Survived the war.

SHAVER, DAVID, Private

Enlisted in Rowan County on July 7, 1862, for the war. Hospitalized at Richmond, Virginia, September 6, 1862, with intermittent fever. Later developed diarrhoea. Transferred to Salisbury on or about September 29, 1862. Returned to duty prior to November 1, 1862. Reported present through May 11, 1863. Hospitalized at Richmond on July 22, 1863, with chronic diarrhoea. Returned to duty on November 5, 1863. Hospitalized at Richmond on November 10, 1863, with a gunshot wound of the shoulder. Place and date wounded not reported (probably wounded at Rappahannock Station, Virginia, November 7, 1863). Transferred to another hospital in Richmond on January 6, 1864, suffering from varioloid. Died in hospital at Richmond on March 7, 1864, of wounds.

SHOFFNER, JACOB E., Private

Resided in Stanly County and was by occupation a farmer prior to enlisting in Wake County at age 31, March 8, 1864, for the war. Reported present through August 31, 1864. Wounded in the leg at Winchester, Virginia, September 19, 1864. Returned to duty prior to October 19, 1864, when he was wounded at Cedar Creek, Virginia. Died (probably of wounds received at Cedar Creek) prior to January 1, 1865. Place of death not reported. [May have served previously as Private in Company C, 42nd Regiment N.C. Troops.]

SIDES, JOHN, Private

Resided in Rowan County and was by occupation a laborer prior to enlisting in Rowan County at age 32, July 7, 1862, for the war. Hospitalized at Richmond, Virginia, October 29, 1862, with continued fever. Furloughed for thirty days on November 12, 1862. Reported absent without leave on December 31, 1862. Returned to duty in January-February, 1863. Reported present through October 31, 1863. Captured at Rappahannock Station, Virginia, November 7, 1863. Confined at Point Lookout, Maryland, November 11, 1863. Paroled at Point Lookout on March 16, 1864. Received at City Point, Virginia, March 20, 1864, for exchange. Returned to duty in May-August, 1864. Wounded in the breast at Cedar Creek, Virginia, October 19, 1864. Returned to duty prior to November 1, 1864. Reported present through February 28, 1865. Surrendered at Appomattox Court House, Virginia, April 9, 1865. Took the Oath of Allegiance at Salisbury on June 20, 1865.

SPAUGH, JAMES L., Private

Enlisted in Wake County on March 8, 1864, for the war. Reported present or accounted for through August 31, 1864. Reported absent without leave on October 28, 1864. No further records.

STONE, SAMUEL, Private

Enlisted in Rowan County on July 7, 1862, for the war. Deserted at Fredericksburg, Virginia, on or about November 22, 1862. Apprehended on an unspecified date. Court-martialed prior to February 14, 1863, and sentenced to be shot. Executed on March 16, 1863. [According to a member of Company F of this regiment, Stone was a Federal prisoner in the Confederate military prison at Salisbury who took an oath of allegiance to the Confederacy, enlisted in the 57th North Carolina, and deserted. See Pvt. Morgan

A. Walker to Margaret C. Walker, March 8, 1863, Civil War Roster Document No. 1087.]

SWICEGOOD, JESSE A., Private

Previously served as Private in Company B of this regiment. Transferred to this company on or about July 17, 1862. Reported absent sick in November, 1862-February, 1863. Returned to duty in March-May, 1863. Captured at Rappahannock Station, Virginia, November 7, 1863. Confined at Point Lookout, Maryland, November 11, 1863. Paroled at Point Lookout on April 27, 1864. Received at City Point, Virginia, April 30, 1864, for exchange. Hospitalized at Richmond, Virginia, May 1, 1864, with neuralgia. Furloughed for thirty days on May 8, 1864. Returned to duty prior to September 1, 1864. Captured at Winchester, Virginia, September 19, 1864. Assigned to duty as a nurse in a Federal hospital at Baltimore, Maryland, December 11, 1864. Transferred to Fort McHenry, Maryland, February 10, 1865. Transferred to Point Lookout on February 20, 1865. Exchanged on an unspecified date. Survived the war.

SWINK, GEORGE B., Private

Enlisted in Rowan County on July 7, 1862, for the war. Hospitalized at Richmond, Virginia, October 10, 1862, with paralysis of the right leg. Transferred to Salisbury on October 30, 1862. Reported at home on furlough through May 11, 1863. Returned to duty in May-August, 1863. Reported present or accounted for on surviving company muster rolls through August 31, 1864. Wounded in the right leg and captured at Winchester, Virginia, September 19, 1864. Died in a Federal field hospital at Winchester on September 28, 1864, of wounds and "erysipelas." [Was apparently acting as color bearer when he was mortally wounded at Winchester.]

SWINK, HENRY S., Private

Resided in Rowan County and was by occupation a farmer prior to enlisting in Rowan County at age 33, July 7, 1862, for the war. Reported present through October 31, 1862. Died in hospital at Richmond, Virginia, on or about February 3, 1863, of "febris typhoides."

SWINK, JAMES R., Private

Enlisted in Rowan County at age 44, July 7, 1862, for the war. Hospitalized at Richmond, Virginia, October 10, 1862, with typhoid fever. Returned to duty on October 29, 1862. Reported present through October 31, 1863. Captured at Rappahannock Station, Virginia, November 7, 1863. Confined at Point Lookout, Maryland, November 11, 1863. Paroled at Point Lookout on March 16, 1864. Received at City Point, Virginia, March 20, 1864, for exchange. Reported at home on surgeon's certificate in May-August, 1864. Reported absent without leave on October 28, 1864. Returned to duty in January-February, 1865. Took the Oath of Allegiance at Salisbury on June 1, 1865.

TEASDALE, GEORGE, Private

Enlisted in Rowan County on July 7, 1862, for the war. Deserted on or about July 10, 1862.

THOMASON, RUFUS M., Private

Previously served as Private in Company A of this regiment. Transferred to this company on or about July 17, 1862. Reported present or accounted for through December 31, 1862; however, he was sick during much of that period. Returned to duty in January-February, 1863. Reported present or accounted for through October 31, 1863.

Captured at Rappahannock Station, Virginia, November 7, 1863. Confined at Point Lookout, Maryland, November 11, 1863. Paroled at Point Lookout on March 16, 1864. Received at City Point, Virginia, March 20, 1864, for exchange. Reported at home on surgeon's certificate in May-August, 1864. Returned to duty in September-October, 1864. Reported present through February 28, 1865. Captured at Fort Stedman, Virginia, March 25, 1865. Confined at Point Lookout on March 28, 1865. Released at Point Lookout on June 21, 1865, after taking the Oath of Allegiance. [North Carolina pension records indicate that he was wounded in the left shoulder at Lynchburg, Virginia, on an unspecified date.]

THOMPSON, GEORGE, Private

Resided in Cabarrus County and enlisted in Wake County on March 8, 1864, for the war. Captured at Harpers Ferry, West Virginia, on or about July 8, 1864. Confined at Old Capitol Prison, Washington, D.C., July 17, 1864. Transferred to Elmira, New York, where he arrived on July 25, 1864. Released at Elmira on May 29, 1865, after taking the Oath of Allegiance.

THOMPSON, JAMES L., Private

Resided in Rowan County where he enlisted on July 7, 1862, for the war. Hospitalized at Richmond, Virginia, September 10, 1862, with remittent fever. Transferred to Salisbury on an unspecified date. Returned to duty in November-December, 1862. Reported present through February 28, 1863. Hospitalized at Richmond on May 8, 1863, with debilitas. Transferred to Lynchburg, Virginia, May 9, 1863. Reported absent in hospital through October 31, 1863. Detailed as a hospital nurse at Lynchburg on February 17, 1864. Reported on duty as a hospital nurse through November 30, 1864. Was reported absent sick in December, 1864-February, 1865. Paroled at Lynchburg in April, 1865. Took the Oath of Allegiance at Salisbury on June 10, 1865.

TREXLER, ALEX, Private

Resided in Rowan County and was by occupation a molder prior to enlisting in Rowan County at age 30, July 7, 1862, for the war. Discharged on or about July 17, 1862, on a surgeon's certificate of disability. Reason discharged not reported.

TREXLER, JOHN, Private

Enlisted in Rowan County on July 7, 1862, for the war. No further records.

TREXLER, WARREN, Private

Enlisted in Rowan County on July 7, 1862, for the war. Survived the war.

TROTT, JOHN HENRY, Sergeant

Previously served as Private in Capt. William H. Howard's Company, N.C. Prison Guards. Enlisted in this company in Rowan County on July 5, 1862, for the war. Mustered in as Sergeant. Wounded in the left thigh (fracture) at Fredericksburg, Virginia, December 13, 1862. Left leg amputated. Hospitalized at Richmond, Virginia, where he died on December 17, 1862, of wounds.

TROTT, WILLIS H., Private

Enlisted in Rowan County on July 7, 1862, for the war. Reported present or accounted for through February 28, 1863. Hospitalized at Richmond, Virginia, March 28, 1863, with pneumonia. Died in hospital at Richmond or at Lynchburg, Virginia, April 1, 1863, of "fever."

VANHOY, J. F., Private

Resided in Stanly County and enlisted in Wake County at age 29, March 8, 1864, for the war. Reported present or accounted for through December 31, 1864. Captured at Hatcher's Run, Virginia, February 6, 1865. Confined at Point Lookout, Maryland, February 9, 1865. Released at Point Lookout on June 21, 1865, after taking the Oath of Allegiance.

WALTON, ALBERT T., Private

Resided in Rowan County and was by occupation a farmer prior to enlisting in Rowan County at age 32, July 8, 1862, for the war. Hospitalized at Richmond, Virginia, September 13, 1862, with intermittent fever. Furloughed for sixty days on September 22, 1862. Returned to duty in November-December, 1862. Reported absent on detached service in January-December, 1863. Apparently served as a wheelwright and carpenter during most of that period. Discharged in March-April, 1864. Reason discharged not reported. Paroled at Salisbury on May 24, 1865. Took the Oath of Allegiance at Salisbury on June 6, 1865.

WHITLEY, THOMAS A., Private

Enlisted in Wake County on April 5, 1864, for the war. Wounded in the arm at Winchester, Virginia, July 20, 1864. Reported absent wounded through February 28, 1865. No further records.

WHITMAN, JOHN A., Private

Resided in Rowan County and was by occupation a farmer prior to enlisting in Wake County at age 42, March 8, 1864, for the war. Captured at Harrisonburg, Virginia, on September 24-25 or October 6, 1864. Confined at Point Lookout, Maryland, October 20, 1864. Paroled at Point Lookout on November 1, 1864. Received at Venus Point, Savannah River, Georgia, November 15, 1864, for exchange. Reported absent sick on January 28, 1865. Returned to duty subsequent to February 28, 1865. Captured at Farmville, Virginia, April 6, 1865. Confined at Newport News, Virginia, April 14, 1865. Died at Newport News on or about May 6, 1865, of "chronic dysentery."

WINDERS, THOMAS C., Private

Resided in Rowan County where he enlisted on July 7, 1862, for the war. Reported present through May 11, 1863. Hospitalized at Richmond, Virginia, June 1, 1863, with scorbutus. Later contracted chronic diarrhoea. Furloughed for forty-five days on June 22, 1863. Returned to duty in November, 1863-April, 1864. Reported present through February 28, 1865. Captured at Farmville, Virginia, April 6, 1865. Confined at Newport News, Virginia, April 14, 1865. Released at Newport News on June 26, 1865, after taking the Oath of Allegiance.

MISCELLANEOUS

BAKER, JOHN R., ____

North Carolina pension records indicate that he served in this regiment.

COODY, W. S., Private

Place and date of enlistment not reported. Captured and paroled at Athens, Georgia, on or about May 8, 1865.

EARVING, D., Private

Place and date of enlistment not reported. Captured and paroled at Athens, Georgia, on or about May 8, 1865.

HEARDEN, H. B., Private

Place and date of enlistment not reported. Captured and paroled at Athens, Georgia, on or about May 8, 1865.

HUPP, H., Private

Place and date of enlistment not reported. Captured and paroled at Athens, Georgia, on or about May 8, 1865.

LOCK, J. R., Private

Place and date of enlistment not reported. Captured and paroled at Athens, Georgia, on or about May 8, 1865.

MALESTON, N. F., Private

Place and date of enlistment not reported. Captured and paroled at Athens, Georgia, on or about May 8, 1865.

NICKS, E. P., Private

Place and date of enlistment not reported. Captured and paroled at Athens, Georgia, on or about May 8, 1865.

PATE, HYMAN, Private

Previously served as Private in Company I, 35th Regiment N.C. Troops. Enlisted in this regiment on an unspecified date (probably in January-March, 1865). Captured at Goldsboro on March 24, 1865. Sent to New Bern. Confined at Hart's Island, New York Harbor, April 10, 1865. Released at Hart's Island on June 18, 1865, after taking the Oath of Allegiance.

PERSONS, C., Private

Place and date of enlistment not reported. Captured and paroled at Athens, Georgia, on or about May 8, 1865.

WEST, A., Private

Place and date of enlistment not reported. Captured and paroled at Athens, Georgia, on or about May 8, 1865.

WIGGS, E. E., Private

Place and date of enlistment not reported. Captured and paroled at Athens, Georgia, on or about May 8, 1865.

Frederick Albert Tobey, a native of Livingston County, New York, was promoted through the ranks from sergeant to captain of Company A, 58th North Carolina. During the last six weeks of the war he was captain of Company D of the same regiment. His sword is a popular foot-officer's model and appears to have single brass-wire wrapping on the grip, indicative of Confederate manufacture. The belt over his right shoulder provides extra support for his waist belt and any accouterments suspended therefrom. Tobey survived the war and was paroled at Greensboro on May 1, 1865. His service record appears on pages 275, 312, and 343. Image provided by Leila Doughton Hinkle.

Clad in a combination shirt-coat or "battle shirt," this handsome Mitchell County youth, Pvt. Albert Johnston Franklin, enlisted in Company A, 58th North Carolina, on December 30, 1861; was transferred to Company B, 5th Battalion N.C. Cavalry, on or about June 27, 1862; reenlisted in Company A of the 58th on April 18, 1863, while absent without leave from the 5th Battalion; and failed to report for duty after he was transferred to Company K, 65th Regiment N.C. Troops (6th Regiment N.C. Cavalry). Most of the above is probably accounted for by injuries he sustained from a "stroke of lightning" at Johnson Depot, Tennessee, on or about August 15, 1862. Franklin's service record appears on page 281. Image provided by Virginia Franklin Banks.

58TH REGIMENT N.C. TROOPS

The origins of the 58th Regiment N.C. Troops date to the late winter of 1861-1862 when Capt. John B. Palmer, commander of an independent Mitchell County company known as the "Mitchell Rangers," began raising a legion.[1] "Palmer's Legion" was organized at Camp Martin in Mitchell County, and by early May 1862 comprised three companies (one infantry and two cavalry). Shortly thereafter Palmer learned that Maj. Gen. Edmund Kirby Smith, commander of the Department of East Tennessee and Palmer's prospective superior, "did not approve of legionary formation[s]." At Smith's tactful "suggestion," Palmer abolished his nascent legion on May 13 and divided its companies into infantry and cavalry contingents. The lone infantry company and others that were placed under Palmer's authority during the next two and one-half months were ultimately assigned to a new regiment that, when its organization was completed, became the 58th Regiment N.C. Troops; the cavalry companies were provisionally designated the 5th Battalion N.C. Partisan Rangers. Pending acceptance of the 58th Regiment and 5th Battalion into Confederate service, Palmer was promoted to lieutenant colonel and ordered to continue recruiting for both units. Nominally, he commanded the 5th Battalion; in reality, the two cavalry companies, which were sent over the mountains for duty in Tennessee, functioned independently.[2]

On July 29, 1862, pursuant to orders from Secretary of War George W. Randolph dated July 15, the 58th North Carolina, comprising eleven companies rather than the usual ten, was mustered into Confederate service. A twelfth company was added in late September.[3] Meantime, the 5th Battalion N.C. Partisan Rangers failed to complete its organization

1. A legion, in Civil War parlance, was a military organization with infantry, cavalry, and artillery components and was usually designated by its commander's name. Its numerical strength, like that of all Confederate units, varied considerably but was generally greater than that of a regiment and smaller than that of a brigade. The only legion successfully raised in North Carolina was "Thomas' Legion of [Cherokee] Indians and Highlanders [Mountaineers]," more commonly known as the "Thomas Legion" or "Thomas' Legion." That unit comprised an infantry regiment, an infantry battalion, an artillery battery, and some miscellaneous cavalry elements. See William Williams Stringfield, "Sixty-ninth Regiment," in Walter Clark, ed., *Histories of the Several Regiments and Battalions from North Carolina in the Great War, 1861-'65*, 5 vols. (Raleigh and Goldsboro: State of North Carolina, 1901), 3:729, hereafter cited as Clark, *Histories of the North Carolina Regiments*; Vernon H. Crow, *Storm in the Mountains: Thomas' Confederate Legion of Cherokee Indians and Mountaineers* (Cherokee, N.C.: Press of the Museum of the Cherokee Indian, 1982).

2. John B. Palmer to Samuel Cooper, July 16, 1863, in John B. Palmer service record file, 58th Regiment N.C. Troops, Record Group 109: Records of Confederate Soldiers Who Served During the Civil War, Compiled Service Records of Confederate Soldiers Who Served in Organizations from the State of North Carolina, M270, reel 537, National Archives and Records Administration, Washington, D.C., hereafter cited as Compiled Confederate Service Records (North Carolina). Smith assumed command of the Department of East Tennessee on March 8, 1862, but that part of North Carolina west of the Blue Ridge Mountains was not added to his jurisdiction until June 3. Palmer abandoned his plans for a legion three weeks earlier because Smith had been sending troops into North Carolina since the second week of April. See Robert N. Scott and others, eds., *The War of the Rebellion: A Compilation of the Official Records of the Union and Confederate Armies*, 70 vols. (Washington, D.C.: Government Printing Office, 1880-1901), ser. 1, 9:473, 10 (pt. 1):628-629, hereafter cited as *Official Records (Army)*.

3. The twelve companies comprising the 58th North Carolina were raised primarily in the following counties: Company A–Mitchell; Company B–Mitchell; Company C–Yancey; Company D–Watauga; Company E–Caldwell; Company F–McDowell; Company G–Yancey; Company H–Caldwell; Company I–Watauga;

and was redesignated the 5th Battalion N.C. Cavalry in November 1862.[4] The companies of the new battalion, by then four in number, continued to function independently under Palmer's nominal authority until Alfred H. Hunter was appointed major of the battalion on March 18, 1863.[5]

The 58th North Carolina was ordered to East Tennessee in early August 1862 and, with the exception of two companies, was reported at Johnson's Depot on the twenty-third of that month.[6] On August 25 the 58th was assigned to Brig. Gen. Carter L. Stevenson's Division of General Smith's newly organized Army of Kentucky and ordered to report to Stevenson near Cumberland Gap.[7] The regiment moved by rail to Morristown two days later. On August 28 the men marched northwest over hot and dusty roads, stopped for "fine bathing" at the Holston River, and then continued on to Bean's Station. The regiment resumed its march on the twenty-ninth, crossed the Clinch River, and reached the vicinity of Tazewell—about ten miles southeast of Cumberland Gap. Having outstripped the

---

Company K–Mitchell; Company L–Ashe; and Company M–Watauga and Ashe. Company H included a number of transferees from other North Carolina units (most prominently Company I, 26th Regiment N.C. Troops) and was originally scheduled for assignment to the Zebulon Baird Vance Legion. When the Vance Legion failed to complete its organization, the company was transferred to the 58th North Carolina. See George Washington Finley Harper, "Fifty-eighth Regiment," in Clark, *Histories of the North Carolina Regiments*, 3:433, hereafter cited as Harper, "Fifty-eighth Regiment," in Clark, *Histories of the North Carolina Regiments*.

4. On August 3, 1863, the 5th Battalion N.C. Cavalry was combined with the 7th Battalion N.C. Cavalry to form the 65th Regiment N.C. Troops (6th Regiment N.C. Cavalry).

5. The foregoing organizational history of the 58th North Carolina differs from several modern accounts in which the 58th is described as a spin-off unit from the 5th Battalion N.C. Partisan Rangers. That probable misapprehension is based on a statement, printed on company muster roll cards for the 58th in the Compiled Confederate Service Records (North Carolina), that "The 5th (Palmer's) Battalion North Carolina Partisan Rangers, consisting of seven companies, was organized under authority of the Secretary of War dated May 13, 1862. It was increased to a regiment about July 29, 1862, by the addition of other companies and designated the 58th Regiment North Carolina Infantry (State Troops)." Insofar as the organization dates of the 5th Partisan Rangers and the 58th N.C. Troops are concerned, that statement is correct. However, there are at least two reasons to believe that the five infantry companies (A, B, C, E, and H) were never part of the 5th Battalion: (1) Palmer states in a letter dated July 16, 1863, that after his legion was disbanded "I organized the Infantry into a Regt (the 58th NC) and the cavalry into a Battn (the 5th NC), both continuing to form parts of my command"; (2) In his brief history of the 58th, Capt. Isaac H. Bailey of Company B states that "There were also three companies of cavalry . . . [which] were *transferred* [emphasis added] when the idea of creating a legion was dropped." In short, five infantry companies were indeed under Palmer's *authority* during the period from May 13 until June 27, 1862, when he began organizing the 58th North Carolina. However, the evidence that they were assigned to the 5th Partisan Rangers during that period is, in this writer's opinion, inconclusive and unconvincing. J. B. Palmer to Samuel Cooper (Confederate adjutant and inspector general), July 16, 1863, John B. Palmer service record file, 58th Regiment N.C. Troops, Compiled Confederate Service Records (North Carolina), M270, reel 537; Isaac H. Bailey, "Additional Sketch Fifty-eighth Regiment," in Clark, *Histories of the North Carolina Regiments*, 3:447, hereafter cited as Bailey, "Additional Sketch Fifty-eighth Regiment," in Clark, *Histories of the North Carolina Regiments*. See also *Asheville News*, July 10, 1862; Louis H. Manarin and Weymouth T. Jordan Jr., comps., *North Carolina Troops, 1861-1865: A Roster*, 14 vols. to date (Raleigh: Division of Archives and History, Department of Cultural Resources, 1966–), 2:348, 354, 359; Lyle D. Bishop III, "The Fifty-eighth Regiment of North Carolina Infantry: A History of its Travels," *Watauga County Times Past* 22-23 (June/September 1987): 2.

6. One company was at Zollicoffer and one at Carter's Depot. Company H, the former Vance's Legion unit, reported for duty with the 58th at Camp Stokes, Haynesville, Tennessee, on August 17.

7. See *Official Records (Army)*, ser. 1, 16 (pt. 2):773, 776, 779.

wagon containing his baggage, Lt. G. W. F. Harper of Company H "fed on green corn and bacon" for supper and then slept with two other men "on and under one shawl in [the] open air."[8]

During the six months prior to the 58th North Carolina's arrival at Tazewell, Confederate fortunes in Tennessee suffered an almost unbroken string of reversals. The loss of Forts Donelson and Henry (on the Cumberland and Tennessee Rivers respectively) resulted in the capture of Nashville in February; the Confederate Army of Mississippi under Gens. Albert S. Johnston and P. G. T. Beauregard was defeated by the combined armies of Ulysses S. Grant and Don Carlos Buell in a bloody battle at Shiloh in April; and Memphis was captured in June following the loss of Island Number 10 and five other Mississippi River bastions. After Shiloh and the death of Johnston, Beauregard retreated to Corinth, Mississippi, but, pursued by the victorious Federals, he evacuated the town on May 30 and fell back to Tupelo. A few weeks later the huge Federal army, numbering about 100,000 men, was divided: Grant's 65,000-man Army of the Tennessee moved into West Tennessee to operate against Vicksburg; Buell's 35,000-man Army of the Ohio marched east across northern Alabama toward the lightly defended railroad junction city of Chattanooga. Unfortunately for Buell, his advance was subjected to what one historian has described as "a textbook exercise in the proper use of cavalry," devastating his lines of communication and bringing the Army of the Ohio to a halt forty miles southwest of Chattanooga near Stevenson, Alabama.[9] On August 20 or thereabouts Buell began retreating northward into Middle Tennessee.

Meantime, the Army of Mississippi, still at Tupelo, was heavily reinforced, and on June 27 it received a new commander in the person of Gen. Braxton Bragg. As Buell edged toward Chattanooga during July, Kirby Smith's pleas for assistance became increasingly urgent, and on July 21 Bragg decided to go to East Tennessee. After sending a sizable force to assist in the defense of Vicksburg, he proceeded by rail and steamboat via Mobile, Montgomery, and Atlanta to Chattanooga with a force of 35,000 infantry and about 5,000 cavalry and artillery.[10] On July 31 he and Smith met at Chattanooga and agreed on a strategy to secure East Tennessee and defeat Buell. Smith, bolstered by reinforcements from Bragg, would advance against Cumberland Gap, join forces with Stevenson's Division, and capture or destroy the 10,000-man Federal garrison there commanded by Brig. Gen. George W. Morgan. Once Morgan was eliminated as a threat to Knoxville and the East Tennessee and Virginia Railroad, Smith and Bragg would move into Middle Tennessee, cut off Buell, and rout his army.[11]

Smith marched north from Knoxville with about 10,000 men on August 14 but, unilaterally revoking his agreement with Bragg, bypassed Cumberland Gap and invaded Kentucky. Stevenson's 9,000-man division remained at the gap to contain Morgan. On August 30

8. Diary of G. W. F. Harper (typescript), August 29, 1862, Southern Historical Collection (SHC), University of North Carolina Library, Chapel Hill, hereafter cited as Harper Diary.

9. Thomas L. Connelly, *Civil War Tennessee: Battles and Leaders* (Knoxville: University of Tennessee Press, 1979), 54.

10. Mounted units went overland.

11. See *Official Records (Army)*, ser. 1, 16 (pt. 2):741.

Smith defeated a Federal force at Richmond, Kentucky, and on September 3 he occupied Frankfort. Bragg marched north from Chattanooga on August 28 and, conforming perforce to Smith's singular movements, advanced into Kentucky, where he captured 4,000 Federals at Munfordville on September 17. He then set off toward Louisville. Buell also moved into Kentucky and reached Bowling Green on September 14. On October 8 Bragg and Smith clashed with Buell at Perryville in an inconclusive battle that was mismanaged by the commanders on both sides. Bragg and Smith then retreated toward East Tennessee.

In the meantime General Morgan, low on rations and in danger of being cut off, blew up his ammunition dump and began withdrawing from Cumberland Gap on September 16. On September 19 the 58th North Carolina moved from Tazewell to Cumberland Gap and reported to Stevenson the next day. Most of Stevenson's Division then marched north to join Smith, leaving the 58th behind to secure captured stores, clear roads, parole 300 Federal prisoners, and chase bushwhacking unionists. According to Pvt. Langston L. Estes of Company E, fifteen or so of the latter were apprehended and hanged between September 19 and September 26. "It was awful," Estes wrote, "to see them hanging up to an apple tree."[12] On September 29 Palmer was ordered to transfer the headquarters of his "Partisan Corps" to London, Kentucky, about forty miles northwest of Cumberland Gap, where he was to "station two-thirds of his infantry and three companies of cavalry, the balance to be stationed at Barboursville [Barbourville]. . . ." Palmer's instructions were to make "Regular scouts . . . on the route from Cumberland Gap to Mount Vernon [twenty miles northwest of London], and . . . [furnish] escorts . . . [to] all trains and couriers."[13] For unknown reasons, execution of those orders was suspended until October 16, by which time Bragg and Smith were in full retreat. The 58th North Carolina set out for Barbourville on that date but was quickly recalled and returned to Cumberland Gap a few hours later.[14]

From October 17 through the twenty-third an almost "constant stream of men, horses, mules, wagons etc." passed through Cumberland Gap as Bragg and Smith fell back from Kentucky. On October 25 the 58th was ordered to Big Creek Gap, about thirty-five miles southwest of Cumberland Gap, near Jacksborough. The men set out at 1:00 P.M. and marched ten miles before nightfall. Awaking the next morning to find the ground covered with snow, they moved eighteen miles through slush and mud to Sharp's, where they "made large campfires, raised tents and slept comfortably." They spent the twenty-seventh in camp and reached Big Creek Gap the next day.[15]

12. Langston Lorenzo Estes to his father and mother, September 26, 1862, in Bud Altmayer, *The Globe Valley Revisited, 1783-1865* (Boone, N.C.: Minor's Publishing, 1987), 213, hereafter cited as Altmayer, *The Globe Valley*.

13. Harper, "Fifty-eighth Regiment," in Clark, *Histories of the North Carolina Regiments*, 3:434; *Official Records (Army)*, ser. 1, 16 (pt. 2):887. See also George W. Morgan, "Cumberland Gap," in Robert Underwood Johnson and Clarence Clough Buel, eds., *Battles and Leaders of the Civil War . . . Being for the Most Part Contributions by Union and Confederate Officers, Based Upon "The Century War Series,"* 4 vols. (New York: Century Company, 1887-1888; New York: Castle Books, 1956), 3:68; *Official Records (Army)*, 16 (pt. 2):847, 853. Barbourville was approximately equidistant between Cumberland Gap and London.

14. It is possible that Palmer's partisan ranger companies moved into Kentucky in late September or early October as ordered; however, no information concerning their whereabouts or activities has been located.

15. Harper Diary, October 17 and 26, 1862 (see also October 18-23, 1862). "Snow two to four inches deep,"

The men of the 58th North Carolina remained in the vicinity of Big Creek Gap throughout the winter of 1862-1863 performing outpost duty, picketing the gap and other Cumberland Mountains passes, "making several expeditions into Kentucky," and, it appears, diverting themselves with gambling and profanity. "[W]ell M[ary]," Pvt. William H. Horton of Company I wrote censoriously to his sister on October 23, "this . . . is the worst Co[mpany] to swear and gambol you ever Seen in your life[.] [T]hey play Cards day and nite but I hant played A game Since I played in Carry [Carolina?] and if I keep in the Same notion . . . I never will play another game while I live and I have quit Swearing prit [pretty] near [but] Some times I git out of hart and git made and I Say dam be fore I think but I am going to try to do better. . . ."[16] From about October 31 through November 20 the 58th was assigned to the Second Brigade (Brig. Gen. Archibald Gracie Jr.), Third Division (Brig. Gen. Henry Heth), Department of East Tennessee (Maj. Gen. E. K. Smith). On the latter date "Kirby Smith's Corps," as the forces commanded by Smith were known, was merged with the Army of Mississippi to form the Army of Tennessee, under Bragg.[17] By December 27 the 58th was part of an ad hoc brigade commanded by Colonel Palmer.[18] Skirmishes were fought on several occasions, apparently with Federal loyalists, and on November 12 Lieutenant Harper noted in his diary that the 58th had "bushwhacked with effect" on the New River.[19] "[D]etails for guard duty . . . were excessive," Harper later recalled, "and the command suffered greatly from privation and exposure. The loss . . . from disease was appalling, camp fever and an epidemic of measles being extremely fatal, the natural result of inexperience and a deplorable lack of hospital accommodations and facilities." The regiment was weakened also by high incidences of absence without leave and desertion.[20]

Harper added on October 26. See also L. L. Estes to his father and mother, [October 28-31, 1862], in Altmayer, *The Globe Valley*, 212.

16. Harper, "Fifty-eighth Regiment," in Clark, *Histories of the North Carolina Regiments*, 3:434; William H. Horton to Mary A. Councill (his sister), October 23, 1862, Mary A. Horton Councill Papers, Special Collections Department, Duke University Library (SCD-DU). After the Battle of Perryville, Bragg retreated to Murfreesboro, about thirty miles southeast of Nashville, where he was attacked on December 31, 1862, by Maj. Gen. William S. Rosecrans's newly organized Army of the Cumberland. The three-day Battle of Stones River (known also as Murfreesboro) was probably a tactical victory for the Confederates, but Bragg, mistakenly believing that Rosecrans had been reinforced, fell back toward Shelbyville, twenty-five miles to the south. The 58th North Carolina was not present during the battle.

17. See *Official Records (Army)*, ser. 1, 16 (pt. 2):985, 20 (pt. 2):413. The other units in Gracie's Brigade were the 62nd and 64th Regiments N.C. Troops, the 43rd Regiment Alabama Infantry, the 55th Regiment Georgia Infantry, and a Georgia artillery battery.

18. Other units in Palmer's Brigade as of December 27, 1862, were the 64th Regiment N.C. Troops, the 5th Battalion N.C. Cavalry, two battalions of Col. Henry W. Hilliard's Alabama Legion, a cavalry battalion of Col. Sumner J. Smith's Georgia Legion, and an Alabama artillery battery. See *Official Records (Army)*, ser. 1, 20 (pt. 2):466, 475. The strength of Palmer's force as of about December 31 was 3,631 men. For minor changes in the makeup of Palmer's Brigade as of February 20 and March 19, 1863, see *Official Records (Army)*, ser. 1, 23 (pt. 2):644, 711.

19. Harper Diary, November 12, 1862 (see also November 15, 1862). No further details concerning the bushwhacking episode were located.

20. Pvt. Francis Marion Wilcox, a conscript of unionist sentiments who would soon desert from the 58th and enlist in a Federal unit, arrived at Big Creek Gap on or about November 11, 1862. "While here at this gap," Wilcox wrote in a third-person, tongue-in-cheek account, "he played Rebel soldier as demanded, yet never

During the winter of 1862-1863 (November through March), at least 100 men deserted, including twenty-eight who departed, presumably as a group, on the night of January 26.[21] "[I]f we stay here two months longer I dont think Col Palmer will have a hundredd men left," Private Estes predicted.[22] On December 12 Adj. Edmund Kirby of the 58th reported that the regiment "consists of . . . 1,082 men." However, that impressive figure probably reflects the number of men listed on the regimental rolls rather than the number present for duty.[23]

On March 30 the 58th North Carolina arrived at Clinton, Tennessee, on the Clinch River about eighteen miles south of Big Creek Gap. Pleasant but intermittently cold weather prompted Harper to add a chimney to his tent, with "very comfortable" results. On April 15 the regiment marched north to the vicinity of Jacksborough to confront a Federal force advancing south from Williamsburg, Kentucky.[24] "[T]hinking it not improbable" that they would be "attacked before morning," the men passed an uneasy night in a woods on a high ridge. On the morning of the nineteenth, the Federal threat having subsided, they returned to Clinton. There they amused themselves with "boatriding, fishing, and bathing" and enjoyed several weeks of mostly springlike weather. "Our Brigade is in fine spirits," Harper wrote on April 20, "and all seem . . . anxious to have a trial at the Yankees."[25]

On May 7 the 58th North Carolina and the other units of Palmer's Brigade, reacting to Federal cavalry activity along the Tennessee-Kentucky border, marched southwest from Clinton, passed through Winters' Gap on the eighth, and reached Montgomery, Tennessee, the

---

drew [never was issued] any gun[.] [He] stood in the line of battle one night with a borrowed musket, but no Yankies came and we shed no blood. The fright was caused by an old powder house taking fire [and] blowing up. . . . We lost no men, but quite a lot of men lost their avoirdupois through fright. The line of battle remained in position all night long, not a gun was fired, yet several flashes, minus reports, occured [sic] and at sunrise next morning, when ordered to break ranks and march to quarters, I never saw such brave, good humored boys. This was my first battle in Dixies behalf." That tale, if true, relates to an incident that occurred prior to about December 20, 1862. Francis Marion Wilcox, "A Journal Written by Francis Marion Wilcox [in 1897]," Roster Document No. 1050 (typescript), Civil War Roster Project (CWRP), North Carolina Division of Archives and History (NCDAH), Raleigh.

21. Harper, "Fifty-eighth Regiment," in Clark, *Histories of the North Carolina Regiments*, 3:434. Forty-nine of the 100 deserters belonged to Company M. That unit, in whose ranks only ninety-two men served during its existence, was so depleted that it was consolidated with Company G the following month.

22. L. L. Estes to his father and mother, February 1, 1863, in Altmayer, *The Globe Valley*, 218. Desertion figures for the 58th during the third and fourth quarters of 1862 and the first quarter of 1863 were 24, 36, and 75 men respectively. For desertion figures for the rest of the war, see footnotes 79 and 168 below.

23. Edmund Kirby to David B. Kirby (his brother), December 12, 1862, Lewis Leigh Collection, United States Army Military History Institute, Carlisle Barracks, Pennsylvania.

24. Harper Diary, April 7, 1863 (see also March 29 and April 15, 1863). "[T]he weather was warm and dry," Harper wrote on April 20, "and the road was in fine order for marching." G. W. F. Harper to Ella A. Rankin Harper (his wife), April 20, 1863, G. W. F. Harper Papers, SHC, hereafter cited as Harper Papers.

25. G. W. F. Harper to Ella Harper, April 20, 1863, Harper Papers (first and third quotations); Harper Diary, May 2, 1863 (second quotation). See also Harper Diary, April 19-May 1 and May 3-5, 1863. As of April 25, 1863, the 58th North Carolina was a component of the 5th Brigade (temporarily commanded by Palmer) of the Army of East Tennessee, which by that date was commanded by Maj. Gen. Dabney H. Maury. Other units in the 5th Brigade were the 64th Regiment N.C. Troops, the 55th Regiment Georgia Infantry, and Capt. Reuben F. Kolb's Battery of the Barbour [County, Alabama] Light Artillery. During Palmer's service as commander of the 5th Brigade, the 58th was commanded by its major, John C. Keener. *Official Records (Army)*, ser. 1, 23 (pt. 2):791-792.

following day.[26] On May 10 the men moved north at 4:00 A.M. and arrived at the Wolf River (probably in the vicinity of Pall Mall) the next evening.[27] There they established Camp McGinnis and remained for a week before marching into Kentucky. After spending a week in the vicinity of Monticello, they returned to Camp McGinnis on May 25. The next afternoon they set off for Clinton, which they reached via Jamestown, Wartburg, and Winters' Gap on the thirtieth.[28] Brig. Gen. John W. Frazer assumed command of Palmer's Brigade on June 9, and Colonel Palmer returned to duty with the 58th.[29] As of April 27 the Department of East Tennessee was commanded by Maj. Gen. Simon B. Buckner.

On June 23 Maj. Gen. William S. Rosecrans's Army of the Cumberland, encamped in the vicinity of Murfreesboro, advanced south to prevent Bragg, occupying a fortified line between Shelbyville and Wartrace, from sending reinforcements from the Army of Tennessee to the besieged fortress city of Vicksburg. Outnumbered almost two-to-one, confused by

26. See Harper Diary, May 7-9, 1863; diary of Pvt. John W. Dugger (Company D, 58th North Carolina) and "Gilliam Hodges [Cpl. Gilbert W. Hodges]" (Companies D and A, 58th North Carolina), May 6-8, 1863, reprinted in the *Watauga Democrat* (Boone), May 14, 1891, hereafter cited as Dugger-Hodges Diary, in *Watauga Democrat* (dates vary). Hodges began making entries in the diary after Dugger's death on or about August 4, 1864. Some entries may have been made by Pvt. Hezekiah Thomas, who also served in Company D. It is probable that the *Watauga Democrat*'s transcription contains minor errors.

It is unclear why Palmer's men moved southwest to Winters' Gap before moving north toward Kentucky, but at least three Federal cavalry commands were active in south-central Kentucky and north-central Tennessee in late April and early May. One, under Col. Felix W. Graham, reached Celina, Tennessee, on April 19 and, after withdrawing across the Kentucky line, returned to Celina on or about April 28. Graham may have been somewhere in the vicinity of Celina as late as May 11 or thereabouts, when he sent reinforcements to yet another Federal cavalry force engaged at La Fayette (about twenty-five miles west). As a result of those raids, Confederate forces evacuated Wayne and Clinton Counties, Kentucky, and retreated in the direction of Clinton, Tennessee. Presumably the 58th North Carolina was sent to Winters' Gap to confront Graham (or some other perceived threat to Knoxville from the west) and to assist in pushing the Federals back toward the Kentucky border. See *Official Records (Army)*, ser. 1, 23 (pt. 1):263-264, 296-300, 311-312.

27. See Harper Diary, May 10-11, 1863; Dugger-Hodges Diary, May 9-10, 1863, in *Watauga Democrat*, May 14, 1891. The Dugger-Hodges Diary indicates that the regiment departed Jacksborough on May 6 rather than May 7 (the date cited in Harper's diary). Dugger's dates continue to lag one day behind Harper's through May 11. It is likely that Harper's dates are more reliable. See also G. W. F. Harper to Ella Harper, May 12, 1863, Harper Papers.

28. See Harper Diary, May 17-18, 1863; Dugger-Hodges Diary, May 30, 1863, in *Watauga Democrat*, May 14, 1891. Harper seemingly indicates that the 58th reached Clinton on the night of May 28; however, he is referring only to Colonel Palmer and his staff (including Harper), who arrived ahead of the regiment. See Harper Diary, May 28, 1863; G. W. F. Harper to Ella Harper, May 29, 1863, Harper Papers. "We all disliked to turn our backs on the Blue Grass regions of Ky after getting so near," Harper lamented. "Hope that we can get a through ticket to the Ohio river before the summer ends." G. W. F. Harper to Ella Harper, May 26, 1863, Harper Papers.

29. It appears that Colonel Palmer expected to be elevated to the rank of brigadier general and placed in permanent command of the brigade. According to Harper, Palmer's replacement by Frazer resulted "not for any want of confidence in . . . [Palmer's] ability or patriotism" but because Buckner insisted that his brigades be commanded by brigadier generals. In any case, Palmer's removal was unpopular with his men. "The officers of the 55 Ga Regt," Harper wrote, "took the initiative . . . [and wrote] a handsome note to the Col . . . expressing their regret that he has been removed from the command, their high appreceation [*sic*] of his abilities as a commander[,] and their regard for him personally. The other Regts have done the same. . . . Gen Frazer is a pleasant gentleman & I have no doubt is a good officer [but] this Brigade . . . to a man would prefer Col. P[almer]. . . ." G. W. F. Harper to Ella Harper, June 15, 1863, Harper Papers. See also John B. Palmer service record file, 58th Regiment N.C. Troops, Compiled Confederate Service Records (North Carolina), M270, reel 537.

five separate Federal columns operating against him, and fearing for his flanks and lines of communication, Bragg retreated through a drenching rain to Tullahoma and then to Bridgeport, Alabama. By July 7 he was in camp around Chattanooga. Rosecrans was approximately fifty miles to the northwest with elements of his command at Fayetteville, Winchester, Manchester, Tullahoma, and McMinnville. Meantime, a 1,500-man Federal cavalry force commanded by Col. William P. Sanders left Mount Vernon, Kentucky, on June 14 on a raid into East Tennessee. Sanders's mission was to divert Bragg's attention from Rosecrans's advance, tie down Confederate forces, and destroy Confederate stores and communication lines. On June 17 the 58th and 64th North Carolina were sent to Big Creek Gap, where a "demonstration" by Sanders's raiders was reportedly in progress.[30] The two regiments returned to Clinton on June 18 when the Federals, instead of attempting to force their way through Big Creek Gap or retreating as the Confederates expected, moved southwest, captured a small Confederate garrison at Wartburg, and advanced toward Kingston and Loudon. On June 19 Sanders's troopers burned the depot at Lenoir's Station on the East Tennessee and Georgia Railroad, and on the evening of the same day they penetrated to the outskirts of Knoxville. As part of the Confederate effort to repulse Sanders, the 58th marched to Bell's Bridge, on the railroad between Knoxville and Clinton, on June 20. The regiment continued on to Harbison's Crossroads on the twenty-first but returned to Bell's Bridge the next day. By then Sanders had moved northeast up the railroad from Knoxville. After burning bridges at Flat Creek, Strawberry Plains, New Market, and other localities, he retreated via Smith's Gap into Kentucky. On June 26 the 58th, reacting now to Rosecrans's "Tullahoma Campaign" rather than Sanders's raid, departed Bell's Bridge in a heavy rain for Lenoir's Station, and on the twenty-seventh it was ordered eight miles further southwest to Loudon.[31] On July 11, after the conclusion of the Tullahoma Campaign, the regiment was ordered back to Bell's Bridge. Three weeks of drill and inspections followed. On August 4 the regiment departed for Big Creek Gap, which it reached on the sixth.[32]

During late July and early August, General Rosecrans came under intense pressure from his superiors in Washington to move against Bragg at Chattanooga. On August 16 Rosecrans advanced southeastward along an arc north and west of the city. On the twentieth he began crossing the Tennessee River at several points between Shellmound, Tennessee, and Caperton's Ferry, Alabama. In response, Bragg ordered Buckner to leave one brigade at Cumberland Gap and another on the railroad northeast of Knoxville and move the remainder of his troops to Loudon. When the Federals began crossing the Tennessee, Buckner's

---

30. *Official Records (Army)*, ser. 1, 23 (pt. 1):390. Colonel Sanders does not mention a cavalry demonstration at Big Creek Gap in his official report, and it is possible that no such action occurred. See *Official Records (Army)*, ser. 1, 23 (pt. 1):386-389.

31. According to Harper, the men were "pleased at the idea of getting out of sight of the Cumberland Mts." G. W. F. Harper to Ella Harper, June 28, 1863, Harper Papers.

32. Cpl. James A. King of the 54th Virginia stated that the Bell's Bridge camp was "9 miles no[r]th west of Knoxville . . . [and] about one and a half mil from the creek Gap raile road in site of our old camp." King's letter is supposedly dated August 9, 1863, but that date appears to have been incorrectly transcribed. It seems clear that the brigade moved back to Big Creek Gap, as stated above, on August 4. James A. King to William Anderson King (his brother), August 9[?], 1863, Roster Document No. 1043 (typescripts), CWRP, NCDAH, hereafter cited as King Letters.

forces at Loudon were ordered to Chattanooga. Lt. Gen. James Longstreet's Corps was also sent to Bragg's support from the Army of Northern Virginia, and the divisions of Maj. Gens. W. H. T. Walker and John C. Breckinridge were dispatched from Lt. Gen. Joseph E. Johnston's Department of the West. With the arrival of those reinforcements, Bragg's army would increase to 66,000 men and outnumber Rosecrans's forces by 6,000 muskets. Rosecrans, meanwhile, completed his crossing of the Tennessee on September 4 and began making his way through the northwest Georgia mountains. On September 8 Bragg evacuated Chattanooga and fell back toward La Fayette, Georgia. Chattanooga was occupied by the Federals the next day. Thinking that the Confederates were demoralized and in precipitate retreat, Rosecrans carelessly allowed his columns to become dispersed in the rugged North Georgia terrain. By September 18 Bragg, after missing several opportunities to attack, had moved north again and was in position near Chickamauga Creek. Realizing his peril at last, Rosecrans managed to concentrate most of his army nearby at Lee and Gordon's Mills by the morning of September 19.

In obedience to Bragg's orders to Buckner to rejoin the Army of Tennessee at Chattanooga, the 58th North Carolina evacuated Big Creek Gap on August 22 and marched to Jacksborough. At ten o'clock the next night the regiment arrived at Clinton, and on the following night it reached Campbell's Station, about fifteen miles southwest of Knoxville on the East Tennessee and Georgia Railroad. After a short march on August 25, the men moved to Lenoir's Station on the twenty-sixth and Loudon on the twenty-ninth. They reached Charleston on September 1, Georgetown on the morning of the fourth, Tyner's Station on the night of the sixth, and Chickamauga Station, seven miles east of Chattanooga, on the morning of the eighth. By the evening of September 9 they were across the Georgia line and ten miles south of Ringgold. Two days later the 58th, after more than thirteen months of active service, fired its first shots-in-anger in a skirmish that probably took place between Wood's Station and Gordon's Springs. The next morning the regiment joined the Army of Tennessee at La Fayette, and on September 17 it moved north with the army toward Chickamauga Creek. "As we approached the creek [around noon on the eighteenth]," Capt. Isaac H. Bailey of Company B later wrote, "the enemy was discovered in a large corn field on the opposite side. Our regiment . . . together with the balance of the brigade, was put in position immediately in front of the enemy, and the division formed in line of battle to the left. A brisk skirmish was kept up until after dark. . . . [We] bivouacked that night . . . on the battlefield. . . ."[33]

The Confederate line of battle on the morning of September 19, 1863, ran along a north-south axis facing west and roughly parallel to the Federal line. Thick woods and underbrush, punctuated by an occasional corn or wheat field, limited visibility and kept both Bragg and Rosecrans in doubt as to the other's dispositions, movements, and intentions. Bragg's plan, which he had hoped to execute on the previous day, was to turn Rosecrans's left flank, cut his line of retreat to Chattanooga, and force him to withdraw westward through the mountains. At the same time, Rosecrans's left-most corps, commanded by Maj. Gen. Thomas L. Crittenden, would be driven into McLemore's Cove, a bowl-like swale

---

33. Bailey, "Additional Sketch Fifty-eighth Regiment," in Clark, *Histories of the North Carolina Regiments,* 3:449.

between Missionary Ridge and Pigeon Mountain, and destroyed. However, unbeknown to Bragg, Crittenden was heavily reinforced during the night. By daylight his left flank, far from being vulnerable to a turning movement, extended three and one-half miles further north.

Fortunately for the Confederates, fighting erupted on the morning of September 19 before Bragg's plan could be implemented. Maj. Gen. George H. Thomas, on Crittenden's left, mistakenly believing that an isolated Confederate brigade was in his front, advanced with two brigades and blundered into Confederate cavalry commanded by Brig. Gen. Nathan B. Forrest. Bragg and Rosecrans poured in reinforcements, and highly confused, seesaw fighting continued throughout the day. Little progress was made by either side, and casualties were heavy. The 58th North Carolina, which was now part of Col. John H. Kelly's Brigade, Brig. Gen. William Preston's Division, Buckner's Corps, crossed the Chickamauga at Dalton's Ford at daylight and formed a reserve line in a field.[34] There it was subjected to a "brisk" cannonading but sustained no casualties. About 11:00 A.M. the men moved 400 yards or so to the right and formed a new line of battle, where they remained under occasional shellfire for the rest of the day. During the night of the nineteenth the 58th and the other three regiments of Kelly's Brigade were "vigorously engaged in constructing defenses to strengthen the left."[35] Bragg took advantage of the respite to organize his army into left and right "wings" commanded respectively by Longstreet (who reached the field at 11:00 P.M.) and Lt. Gen. Leonidas Polk. Kelly's Brigade was assigned to Longstreet.

Bragg's plans for September 20 were almost identical to those he had hoped to execute on the nineteenth. His army would attack *en echelon* (sequentially) from right to left and attempt to drive at least part of the Federal army into McLemore's Cove. Rosecrans, for his part, proposed to remain on the defensive. At 9:30 A.M. the Confederate assault began (see map on page 449). Breckinridge's men succeeded in partially turning Thomas's left and briefly cutting the Chattanooga road but were narrowly halted by reinforcements from the Federal right. Maj. Gen. Patrick R. Cleburne, on Breckinridge's left, was fought to a standstill by Federals sheltered behind log breastworks, and Walker's and Maj. Gen. Benjamin F. Cheatham's Divisions received bloody repulses in assaulting the same obstacles. About 11:30 Longstreet's troops attacked the Federal right and poured through a gap created by the withdrawal of Brig. Gen. Thomas Woods's Division to close a nonexistent gap in the Federal line. The result was a spectacular rout of Rosecrans's entire right wing. Rosecrans fled the battlefield to escape capture, and approximately half of his army retreated toward Rossville, on the Chattanooga road, in varying degrees of disorder. At least three

---

34. The 58th was probably transferred from Frazer's to Kelly's Brigade when Frazer was sent with his other three regiments to Cumberland Gap in early August. Kelly was colonel of the 8th Regiment Arkansas Infantry. At the time of the Battle of Chickamauga, Kelly's Brigade comprised the 58th North Carolina, 5th Regiment Kentucky Infantry, 63rd Regiment Virginia Infantry, and 65th Regiment Georgia Infantry. See *Official Records (Army)*, ser. 1, 30 (pt. 2):16.

35. *Official Records (Army)*, ser. 1, 30 (pt. 2):440, 414 (see also 11-20). Capt. Isaac H. Bailey of Company B, who was under artillery fire for the first time, thought that "terrible" described the September 19 barrage more precisely than "brisk." Bailey, "Additional Sketch Fifty-eighth Regiment," in Clark, *Histories of the North Carolina Regiments*, 3:450.

Federal divisions temporarily ceased to exist as organized units. Only Thomas, on the left at Snodgrass Hill, held his ground. Confederate attacks on Thomas continued throughout the day, but "The Rock of Chickamauga" could not be moved. After narrowly fending off attempts by Longstreet and Cheatham to turn his flanks and cut his line of retreat, he fell back to Rossville that night. By the morning of September 22, Thomas and the battered Army of the Cumberland were back in Chattanooga.

During the Confederate assault on the morning of September 20, the 58th North Carolina remained in the rear with Kelly's Brigade supporting Maj. Austin Leyden's artillery battalion.[36] Around 3:00 P.M. the brigade, with the exception of the 65th Georgia, advanced to the support of Archibald Gracie's Brigade on the Chattanooga road.[37] It then marched with Gracie's men to the assistance of Brig. Gens. James Patton Anderson and Joseph B. Kershaw, whose brigades were among the numerous Confederate units engaged in furious combat with Thomas's bluecoats on Snodgrass Hill.

[W]e were halted near the edge of a woodland [Lt. John T. Gaines of the 5th Kentucky recalled]. Beyond the woodland and in front of us were narrow fields at the base of the ridge stretching far to the right of our position. Fences were burning along the border of the woodland . . . and at the edge of the dense undergrowth that crowned the hill behind the open fields.

Before us was a magnificent battle scene. Away to the right . . . we saw flag after flag marking the positions of regiments of our men. Couriers and aids were dashing here and there. . . . The eminence beyond the field in front of us was a spur from the main ridge which lay beyond. . . . On this hill lay the enemy and behind it their reserves.

When we were halted and looked out upon the scene I have described, a fierce fight was raging somewhere in our front. Clouds of smoke rose above the tops of the trees, and a pandemonium of sounds issued from among them. The crash of artillery, and the rattle of small arms, was mingled with the cheers of the men engaged in the death grapple.[38]

Shortly after it arrived at 4:20 Kelly's Brigade joined Gracie's troops in a new attack on Thomas's position. "The enemy occupied a range of ridges," Colonel Palmer wrote, "the approaches to . . . [which were] along spurs and through intervening depressions, all more or less wooded, but more open and exposed opposite the right of the brigade." Partially concealed by smoke from burning leaves and brush, the 58th, on the right of Kelly's line (and thus in the more open and exposed position described by Palmer), crossed a ravine and advanced "with steadiness" through a "deadly" fire until its "extreme right arrived within 10 or 12 feet of the enemy." At that point Palmer received a cease-fire order from Colonel Kelly, who was under the mistaken impression that his brigade was attacking fellow Confederates. In the ensuing confusion the right flank of the 58th was raked by a withering

---

36. Companies A and B of the 58th and five other companies of Kelly's Brigade were sent on a reconnaissance to Alexander's Bridge at about 7:00 A.M. For details, see Bailey, "Additional Sketch Fifty-eighth Regiment," in Clark, *Histories of the North Carolina Regiments*, 3:450.

37. The 65th Georgia remained with Leyden's artillery. Kelly states in his report that he moved to Gracie's assistance at 1:00 P.M., but three of his four regimental commanders say 3:00 P.M. The fourth does not cite the time. See *Official Records (Army)*, ser. 1, 30 (pt. 2):440, 442-444, 447.

38. John Thomas Gaines, "Recollections of Chickamauga," 1, Confederate Veteran Collection, SCD-DU, hereafter cited as Gaines, "Recollections of Chickamauga."

cross fire and driven back with heavy casualties. According to Maj. Arnold McMahan, whose 21st Ohio Infantry confronted Palmer, the 58th "did not retire in good order."[39]

After rallying his right wing, Palmer held his ground "for some time" until ordered by Kelly to move the 58th to the left flank of the brigade. With its two sister regiments, the 63rd Virginia and 5th Kentucky, the 58th then "cool[ly]" advanced against the enemy, Palmer wrote, "although our ammunition was nearly, and in some instances quite, exhausted. The [two] regiments on my right being forced back out of sight, the charge was abandoned and my men sought protection behind trees, such of them as had any ammunition continuing to fire vigorously. A second line was formed and another charge attempted with like results." The fighting, in the opinion of Col. Ferdinand Van Derveer, who commanded the portion of the Federal line under attack by Kelly, was of "unexampled fury, line after line . . . being hurled against our position with a heroism and persistency which almost dignified their cause."[40]

Palmer then shifted his regiment to the right to reestablish contact with the 63rd Virginia and 5th Kentucky. Led by Palmer in the temporary absence of Kelly, the brigade then launched an attack at a sharp angle to the right and inadvertently advanced over Col. Robert C. Trigg's newly arrived Florida brigade, which was in the process of launching an attack of its own.[41] Consequently, the 58th North Carolina (on Trigg's left) again became separated from its sister units (on Trigg's right) and came to a halt. Several hundred Federals, most of whom were out of ammunition, surrendered to Trigg and the 63rd Virginia and 5th Kentucky shortly thereafter. To Palmer's dismay and mortification, the 58th was excluded from the spoils of victory—prisoners, battleflags, and weapons—that were captured by its two sister units and the late-arriving Trigg. Finding himself momentarily alone with his regiment on the slopes of Snodgrass Hill, Palmer collected the Confederate dead and wounded. The 58th then rejoined the 5th Kentucky and 63rd Virginia and, in Kelly's words, "went into bivouac on the hill which the brigade had so gallantly won."[42] Preston was delighted with the performance of Kelly's Brigade, and, to commemorate "the great battle in which . . . [their commands] achieved such brilliant distinction," he presented "eight splendid Colt's Revolving Rifles" to the color guards of the 5th Kentucky, 63rd Virginia, and 58th North Carolina. Two each went to the brave Kentuckians and Virginians; four to the valiant Tar Heels.[43]

---

39. *Official Records (Army)*, ser. 1, 30 (pt. 2):445, 30 (pt. 1):389. See also Bailey, "Additional Sketch Fifty-eighth Regiment," in Clark, *Histories of the North Carolina Regiments*, 3:451; *Official Records (Army)*, ser. 1, 30 (pt. 2):305.

40. *Official Records (Army)*, ser. 1, 30 (pt. 2):445, 30 (pt. 1):430.

41. Kelly had been ordered to report to General Preston for a conference. Just before his departure, he and Trigg had agreed to make a joint attack. See *Official Records (Army)*, ser. 1, 30 (pt. 2):441-442.

42. *Official Records (Army)*, ser. 1, 30 (pt. 2):442. "It was a sleepless night for us," Lieutenant Gaines of the 5th Kentucky wrote, "spent mostly in succoring the desperately wounded men of both armies. Towards morning we built fires and brought in the sufferers. We sent details for water, and gave it to the wounded." Gaines, "Recollections of Chickamauga," 3.

43. Letter dated September 21, 1863, from an unidentified member of 58th North Carolina, published in the *Charlotte Bulletin* on an unknown date and reprinted in the *Daily Progress* (Raleigh), October 8, 1863. A typescript is in the G. W. F. Harper Papers, Southern Historical Collection, suggesting that Harper was the author.

Confederate casualties at the Battle of Chickamauga numbered 2,312 dead, 14,674 wounded, and 1,468 missing; Federal losses were reported as 1,657 killed, 9,756 wounded, and 4,757 missing. According to a casualty return for Preston's Division, Kelly's Brigade lost 62 men killed, 238 wounded, and 29 missing out of an effective strength of 876. Kelly himself reported the loss of 303 men killed and wounded and 26 missing out of 852 that he took into the fight.[44] Casualties in the 58th North Carolina, according to Colonel Palmer, included "Every field and staff officer and one-half of the balance of the regiment killed or wounded." According to a casualty list for the 58th published in the Raleigh *Daily Progress*, 161 men were killed, mortally wounded, wounded, or missing.[45] Figures compiled from the rosters in this volume indicate that the regiment lost 57 men killed or mortally wounded, 117 wounded, and 1 captured: a total of 174.

The 58th remained on the battlefield on September 21 burying the dead. The next day it marched about six miles toward Chattanooga, which it reached on the twenty-third. After lying "under the Yankee shells all night" the men fell back about one mile the next day.[46] They were on picket duty from September 27 through the twenty-ninth, and on October 5 they were bombarded by Federal batteries and forced to move their camp. On October 24 they moved camp again. Drill, inspections, and picket duty occupied much of their time during October. Colonel Palmer assumed temporary command of the brigade on or about November 1 when Colonel Kelly was promoted to brigadier general and transferred. On November 12 the 58th was brigaded with the 60th North Carolina and the 54th and 63rd Virginia under the command of Brig. Gen. Alexander W. Reynolds.[47] Reynolds's Brigade was then assigned to Buckner's Division of Lt. Gen. William J. Hardee's Corps.[48] Palmer was relieved from duty with the 58th on or about November 18, 1863, and given command of the District of Western North Carolina, leaving the regiment with no field officers present. It was therefore consolidated "temporarily" with the 60th North Carolina under the colonel of that unit, Washington M. Hardy. The arrangement lasted for almost five months.[49]

44. See Patricia L. Faust, ed., *Historical Times Encyclopedia of the Civil War* (New York: Harper and Row, Publishers, 1986), 137; *Official Records (Army)*, ser. 1, 30 (pt. 2):420, 442. Effective strength figures for Kelly's Brigade do not include the 65th Georgia, which was detached on September 20. The 65th numbered 270 officers and men and lost only four men wounded during the battle.

45. *Official Records (Army)*, ser. 1, 30 (pt. 2):446. See also *Daily Progress* (Raleigh), October 8, 1863.

46. Dugger-Hodges Diary, September 23, 1863, in *Watauga Democrat*, May 21, 1891.

47. Reynolds, a Virginian, was 47 years old and an 1838 graduate of West Point. He had served previously in Western Virginia and at Knoxville and Vicksburg. His men called him "Old Gauley," which was also the name of his horse. It is doubtful that the appellation was affectionate.

48. See *Official Records (Army)*, ser. 1, 31 (pt. 3):686. Buckner was reduced from a corps to a division commander.

49. See *Official Records (Army)*, ser. 1, 31 (pt. 3):711; G. W. F. Harper to Ella Harper, November [16] and 22, 1863, Harper Papers. Consolidations occurred also at the company level but were intra- rather than inter-regimental; that is, two companies of the 58th were consolidated rather than one company each from the 58th and 60th. Each consolidated company retained one set of officers; supernumerary officers were assigned to recruiting or other detached duty. It appears that company-level consolidations were not implemented until December 1863.

Following his Chickamauga debacle, Rosecrans assumed a defensive and somewhat quiescent posture in Chattanooga, abandoning Lookout Mountain, Missionary Ridge, and other heights controlling access to the town. The predictable and almost immediate result was a supply crisis of near-catastrophic proportions: supplies that had previously arrived by rail from Nashville via Stevenson and Bridgeport, Alabama, now had to be off-loaded at Bridgeport. They were then transported sixty miles by wagon over a steep, narrow, and slippery mountain trail that, in a matter weeks, claimed the lives of 10,000 mules. By mid-October the hungry citizens of Chattanooga were fleeing the town, and Federal soldiers, subsisting on a fraction of their normal rations, were accosting their officers in the streets with demands for "crackers [hardtack]."[50]

Meantime, Federal reinforcements were hastily sent to shore up the tottering Federal presence in East Tennessee. On October 1 two Army of the Potomac corps under Maj. Gen. Joseph Hooker arrived at Bridgeport where, since there was little to eat in Chattanooga, they were forced to remain. Four divisions of the Army of the Tennessee, under Maj. Gen. William T. Sherman, marched east from Memphis and Vicksburg, repairing the Memphis and Charleston Railroad as they came. Rosecrans, however, far from contemplating offensive operations, seemed incapable even of devising a solution to his supply predicament. Comparing Rosecrans's performance since Chickamauga to a "duck hit on the head," President Lincoln ordered Maj. Gen. U. S. Grant to Chattanooga in mid-October. As commander of the newly constituted Military Division of the Mississippi, Grant was given authority over the three armies operating within its boundaries: the Army of the Tennessee, still en route from Vicksburg and Memphis; the Army of the Ohio, at Knoxville; and the Army of the Cumberland, at Chattanooga. Sherman and Maj. Gen. Ambrose E. Burnside were retained as commanders of the Armies of the Tennessee and the Ohio respectively; Thomas replaced Rosecrans as commander of the Army of the Cumberland.

The impact of the dynamic Grant on the situation at Chattanooga was immediate if not immediately decisive. On October 27-28 a daring attack by Maj. Gen. William F. Smith drove Bragg's forces from the banks of the Tennessee River at Brown's Ferry, west of Chattanooga, opening a new supply line to the town. Pending the arrival of Sherman, Grant then began laying plans to lift the siege. Bragg, for his part, remained virtually dormant on the Chattanooga heights: Joseph Wheeler's cavalry conducted a raid against Rosecrans's tenuous supply lines in early October, and on November 5 Longstreet's Corps was dispatched to attempt, unsuccessfully as events soon proved, to recapture Knoxville. Otherwise, Bragg contented himself with lobbing shells at enemy positions, reorganizing his command, and waiting for the Federals to withdraw, starve, or attack his seemingly impregnable position. Having frittered away the fruits of his Chickamauga victory and weakened his army vis-à-vis its opponent, Bragg in effect conceded the offensive to Grant, who was soon to make use of it.

---

50. *Official Records (Army)*, ser. 1, 30 (pt. 1):221. The Confederates were not eating very well either. In a letter to his father dated October 3, 1863, Sgt. Houston Collins of the 63rd Virginia described his rations as "quite small." Lt. Alexander S. Collins, Houston's brother and also a member of the 63rd Virginia, wrote on the same date that "there is no chance to get any nourishment in . . . [this] country for it is a vast ruin. . . ." Houston Collins to his father, October 3, 1863, and Alexander Smith Collins to his father, October 3, 1863, Roster Document No. 1044, CWRP, NCDAH, hereafter cited as Collins Letters.

On November 13 Sherman arrived at Bridgeport with the Army of the Tennessee. Grant then moved quickly to dislodge Bragg from his mountaintops. As a first step he ordered troop movements designed to convince Bragg that most of Sherman's army was en route to Knoxville to reinforce Burnside. However, Sherman's men were secretly to go into position in the hills north of Chattanooga, cross the Tennessee River on the night of November 20, and attack Bragg at daybreak on November 21. Cut off from his supply depot at Chickamauga Station, Bragg would have to abandon his formidable positions on Lookout Mountain and Missionary Ridge and retreat into the North Georgia wilderness.[51]

Although slow to take the proffered bait, Bragg at length became convinced that Grant was reinforcing Burnside, and on November 22 he ordered two divisions (Buckner's, temporarily commanded by Brig. Gen. Bushrod Johnson, and Cleburne's) to Knoxville. Buckner's Division, with the exception of Reynolds's Brigade, departed by rail the same day.[52] Meantime, Grant's plans miscarried when heavy rains prevented Sherman from reaching his jump-off point by the night of November 20. Sherman was still slogging through the mud two days later when a Confederate deserter reported inaccurately that Bragg was withdrawing from Missionary Ridge. To test that report, which if true would expose Bragg to attack at a moment of high vulnerability, Grant ordered Thomas to make a reconnaissance in force against Orchard Knob on the morning of November 23 (see map on page 229). The resulting engagement, in addition to establishing that Bragg was holding his ground, unexpectedly resulted in the capture of Orchard Knob. It also alerted Bragg that a Federal offensive might be afoot. He therefore ordered Cleburne, whose men were still at Chickamauga Station awaiting transportation to Knoxville, to take position on Tunnel Hill, at the north end of Missionary Ridge. Unfortunately for Bragg, Buckner's command, except for Reynolds's Brigade, was beyond immediate recall. Thus a Confederate force of only 46,000 men was left to confront an army of nearly 80,000 Federals.

Grant's battle plan on the morning of November 24 called for Sherman, on the Federal left, to cross the Tennessee River and capture Tunnel Hill while Hooker's troops, on the right, attempted to drive the Confederates from Lookout Mountain. If Sherman accomplished his assignment, Thomas, in the center, would attack Missionary Ridge; if not, Thomas would reinforce the flanks as necessary. That plan, as was the case with the abortive attack on November 21, went awry from the outset. Sherman's river crossing over a rickety pontoon bridge proved unexpectedly difficult and time-consuming, and it was afternoon before he was in position. By then Cleburne's Division was entrenched atop Tunnel

---

51. "[W]e are stationed a bout 3 miles from Chattanooga," Sergeant Collins of the 63rd Virginia wrote. "[W]e can see the yankees in Chattanooga evry day[.] [W]e can see their fortifycation[s.] [T]hey are well forty fied[.] [O]ur forces is forty fing hear. I do not no whether our forces intend to attact them or not. I dont think they intend to attact us[.] I think if they do they will get a whipping. . . . I can hear the yankee Drums & the sound of their axes now. . . ." Houston Collins to his father, October 3, 1863, Collins Letters.

52. On November 20 the 58th North Carolina marched in the direction of Rossville and camped for the night near General Hardee's headquarters. The next day it moved eight miles through rain and mud on the La Fayette road, about faced, marched back to Rossville, and camped. On November 22 it reached Chickamauga Station. Clearly, the regiment was recalled to Chickamauga Station to join Buckner's Division in its move to Knoxville; however, the purpose of the La Fayette road mission is uncertain. Harper speculates that it was intended "to head off an advance of the Yankees towards Rome." G. W. F. Harper to Ella Harper, November 22, 1863, Harper Papers. See also Harper Diary, November 20-22, 1863.

Hill. Convinced that too little daylight remained to accomplish anything against Cleburne, Sherman bivouacked for the night. However, Hooker's men, fighting for most of the day in a thick fog, made good progress against the outnumbered Confederates on Lookout Mountain. Toward midafternoon Bragg ordered the position abandoned, and by 8:00 P.M. the last of the Confederates were gone. To the cheers of thousands of onlooking Federals, the Stars and Stripes were raised atop the summit the next day.

On the morning of November 25, Grant ordered Sherman to launch his much delayed attack on Tunnel Hill. Thomas, as previously instructed, was to attack Missionary Ridge if Sherman were successful. Hooker was ordered to advance against the Confederate left at Rossville Gap. By evening Hooker's men had reached that objective and were driving the Confederate defenders back in confusion. Sherman, however, was unable to make any progress against the redoubtable Cleburne. Hoping to assist Sherman with a diversionary attack, Grant ordered Thomas to seize a line of Confederate trenches at the foot of Missionary Ridge. As was the case at Orchard Knob, that seemingly inconsequential thrust produced spectacular results. Advancing through heavy fire from Confederate positions atop Missionary Ridge, the Federals seized the weakly defended trench line, paused a few minutes, then, without orders, charged up the slope. Some Confederate units on the heights, unable to shoot without hitting their retreating comrades or because their works were improperly sited, fled after meager resistance. Others were overwhelmed by superior numbers. The remainder fended off the Federals for a time but were then flanked and routed. At Tunnel Hill, meantime, Cleburne's men held their ground against Sherman until ordered to withdraw. With triumphant Yankee cries of "Chickamauga, Chickamauga" ringing in their ears, Bragg's discomfited legions retreated in the darkness toward Chickamauga Station.

As stated above, Reynolds's Brigade, including the 58th North Carolina, was ordered by rail to Knoxville with the rest of Buckner's Division on November 22 but was still at Chickamauga Station with Cleburne's Division awaiting transportation the next day. When Cleburne was recalled following Thomas's attack on Orchard Knob, Reynolds's men, who were on a train and about to depart, were ordered out of the cars. They then went into position in the trenches at the foot of Missionary Ridge. The 60th North Carolina was on the left of Reynolds's line adjacent to the 7th Florida Infantry of Col. Jesse J. Finley's Brigade, Breckinridge's Division (commanded by Brig. Gen. William B. Bate). The 58th North Carolina was probably to the right of the 60th.[53] In the event of a Federal attack, Reynolds's men were instructed to offer token resistance and withdraw up the slopes. However, other units in the trenches received orders to stand and fight. Those orders were later countermanded, but some units were not informed. Atop Missionary Ridge, somewhat to the right of the trench position held below by Reynolds, was a gap in the Confederate line that Reynolds was to occupy when he fell back. Brig. Gen. James Patton Anderson's Mississippi brigade, commanded by Col. William F. Tucker, was to the right of the gap; Bate's brigade of Georgians and Tennesseans, commanded by Col. Robert C. Tyler, to the left. The 1st and

53. See *Official Records (Army)*, ser. 1, 31 (pt. 1):532, 31 (pt. 2):740, 746. The 54th and 63rd Virginia were to the right of the 58th, and the 1st Florida Cavalry (Dismounted) and 4th Florida Infantry of Finley's Brigade were probably on the right of the Virginians. The 7th Florida was sent down to the trenches later than its two sister regiments and somehow became separated from them.

3rd Florida Infantry (Consolidated) and the 6th Florida Infantry, the only two regiments of Finley's Brigade that were not below in the trenches, were to the left of Tyler.

At 2:00 P.M., about an hour before Thomas launched his attack, Reynolds received orders to "fall back from the rifle pits to the crest of Missionary Ridge." That maneuver, which Reynolds carried out "by alternate Companies," was largely but not entirely completed when Thomas advanced. Exposed to heavy fire from the immense Federal force marshaling in their front, some elements of the 60th North Carolina became panicky. "All order was soon lost," Brig. Gen. Arthur M. Manigault of Maj. Gen. Thomas Hindman's Division (commanded by Anderson) wrote, "and each [man], striving to save himself, took the shortest direction for the summit." Rather than obliqueing to the left to the slot reserved for Reynolds, those men dashed in a disorderly mass into Finley's line, where they created a momentary panic. They were then taken in hand and reorganized by their major, James T. Weaver, under whose command and that of Bate they remained throughout the battle.[54] Meantime, the rest of Reynolds's Brigade reached the top of Missionary Ridge and occupied its assigned position. There, having been divested of his commanding officer by the departure of Bushrod Johnson with the rest of Buckner's Division, Reynolds was placed under the temporary authority of Anderson. According to Reynolds, whose command was later subjected to severe criticism for its alleged misconduct, the fighting on his front proceeded as follows:

A short time after I had taken my position on the crest of the Ridge, I observed the Enemy advancing to the attack in three lines of battle. There being two pieces of artillery posted on the left of my line, I directed them to open fire on the enemy, which was done with excellent effect.

The enemy having reached our abandoned rifle pits, I was directed by Gen Anderson Comd'g the Division, who was then present with my Brigade, to cause the guns to be depressed, & open on them with canister. This was instantly done, & so terrible was the effect of this fire on the dense lines of the Enemy, that it caused them to falter for an instant, but closing up their ranks, they again advanced to the charge. In a short time the enemy came within range of musketry, & my Brigade opened on them in fine Style and as they advanced rapidly up the face of the ridge my fire, & that of the troops on my right, was so severe that for a time the enemy were checked.

Unfortunately at this Juncture . . . the troops posted in the rifle pits on the right of my Brigade broke & fled in the utmost disorder. The enemy seeing the advantage that must result from this disgraceful & inexplicable panic on the part of hitherto invincible troops, at once crossed the hill on my right and opened a heavy fire on my lines, completely enfilading my position[.] This of course

54. Reynolds's Missionary Ridge report dated December 15, 1863, in John Hoffmann, ed., *The Confederate Collapse at the Battle of Missionary Ridge: The Reports of James Patton Anderson and His Brigade Commanders* (Dayton, Oh.: Morningside House, 1985), 74, hereafter cited as Reynolds, "Missionary Ridge Report," in Hoffmann, *Reports of Anderson's Division* (quoted by permission of P. K. Yonge Library of Florida History, Department of Special Collections, George A. Smathers Libraries, University of Florida, Gainesville); R. Lockwood Tower, ed., *A Carolinian Goes to War: The Civil War Narrative of Arthur Middleton Manigault, Brigadier General, C.S.A.* (Columbia: University of South Carolina Press, 1983), 138. Reynolds states that some portions of the 60th, "in moveing [*sic*] up the ridge, were obliged, on account of the peculiar topography of the ground, to oblique somewhat too far to the right and on reaching the top of the Ridge, found themselves separated from their command, & owing to the difficulty of joining their own Regt. they remained . . . with Gen. Bate's Brigade." That statement is partially true but ignores the demoralized condition in which the men reached Finley's line.

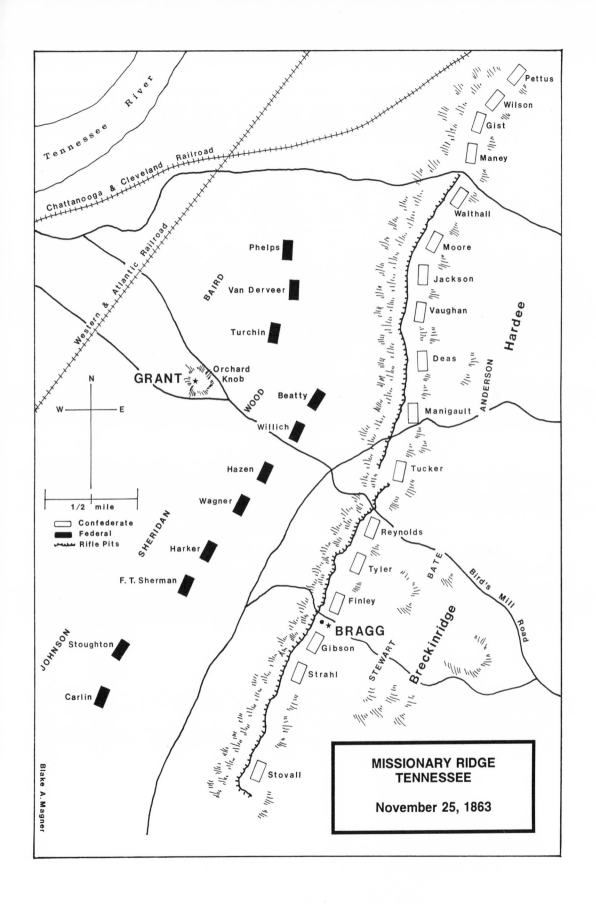

Tennessee River

Chattanooga & Cleveland Railroad

Western & Atlantic Railroad

Pettus
Wilson
Gist
Maney

Walthall

Phelps
BAIRD
Van Derveer

Moore
Jackson
Vaughan

Turchin

Deas

Hardee

N
W — E
S

GRANT
Orchard Knob

WOOD
Beatty

Manigault
ANDERSON

Willich

1/2 mile

Tucker

Confederate
Federal
Rifle Pits

Hazen

SHERIDAN

Wagner

Reynolds

BATE

Bird's Mill Road

Harker

Tyler

F. T. Sherman

Finley

BRAGG

Breckinridge

JOHNSON
Stoughton

Gibson

STEWART

Strahl

Carlin

Stovall

Blake A. Magner

**MISSIONARY RIDGE
TENNESSEE**

November 25, 1863

rendered necessary an immediate Change of position. I therefore changed front to the rear on the left Battalion. My troops perform[ed] this delicate & dangerous manoeuver under the fire of the enemy in admirable style & without the least confusion or irregularity.

As soon as my new line was formed I opened fire by Company, and continued to engage the enemy until I found that the troops on my left had also given way, and the enemy occupied the Ridge on my left & now rear. Having now no supports whatever, I considered it more prudent to withdraw my small, but gallant Brigade than to remain, with the almost certainty of capture. I therefore retired (it was now dusk) by the right flank down the ridge, sheltering my troops as much as possible from the fire of the enemy who by this time had opened our own captured guns upon me from two differ-ent & commanding points on the ridge.

Learning that Genl Bates [*sic*] & the troops on my left were proceeding towards the Pontoon bridge at Birds Mill, I moved in the direction of our extreme right, where I yet heard firing. I did this on the principle, that in the absence of orders, it was my duty to go to the support of those yet en-gaged. On reaching the road leading to "Shallow Ford" Chickamauga river, I received orders to con-duct my command to "Shallow Ford" Bridge & report to Genl Maunigault [*sic*], who would place my Command in position. I reached this point about 10 o'clock, & after remaining some two hours, took up the line of march for Chickamauga.

It is with no little pleasure & pride that I am enabled to say that both in the riflepits at the foot of the Ridge, & during the engagement on the ridge, all the officers & men of my Brigade acted with the gallantry & coolness of veterans. Throughout all the movements none left the ranks, but obeyed every order promptly & without the slightest confusion or disorder.[55]

Reynolds's report notwithstanding, his brigade was severely criticized for its perform-ance at Missionary Ridge. Those criticisms can be reduced to two basic and mutually exclu-sive charges: (1) the brigade was routed from its position at the foot of Missionary Ridge and failed to occupy its assigned position on the heights; (2) the brigade occupied its as-signed position on the heights but was the first unit to collapse during the Federal attack. The first charge is based primarily on the report of Bate, who states that "the troops of Reynolds's brigade," after offering only "slight resistance" at the foot of Missionary Ridge, "abandoned the ditches . . . and sought refuge at the top of the hill, breaking and throwing into slight confusion the left of Finley's Brigade as they passed through. Major Weaver, of the Sixtieth North Carolina Regiment, seemed to be in command. He rallied and formed these troops (who seemed to be from two or three different regiments of Reynolds' brigade) across the Crutchfield road a few paces in rear of the main line."[56] Bate was clearly under the mistaken impression that Reynolds's entire brigade rather than some elements thereof came into Finley's line. He probably believed also, since he makes no subsequent refer-ences to the presence of Reynolds's troops on his right, that with the exception of Weaver's small, ad hoc command the brigade fled up one slope of Missionary Ridge and down the other. However, the cardinal point in Reynolds's report is that his brigade, minus "some of the companies of the 60th," fought on the crest of Missionary Ridge during the Federal at-tack. That claim can be rejected only if his report is dismissed as a total fabrication. Bate's report, on the other hand, is suspect on the simple and fundamental ground that Bate

55. Reynolds, "Missionary Ridge Report," in Hoffmann, *Reports of Anderson's Division*, 74-77.

56. *Official Records (Army)*, ser. 1, 31 (pt. 2):741. The subsequent performance of Weaver's men was less than distinguished. For details, see pages 455-458 of this volume.

mistook part of Reynolds's Brigade for the whole. Moreover, it is particularly significant that Reynolds refers in his report to a consultation on the crest with Anderson, who was his commanding officer during the battle and consequently the officer to whom the report was submitted. Reynolds's reference to such a consultation, if false, would have resulted in immediate, irrefutable, and ruinous exposure.[57]

The second charge was leveled in 1873 by Bragg, who stated that Reynolds's men were the "first [that] gave way and could not be rallied."[58] It is possible that Bragg was referring to the aforementioned flight of elements of the 60th North Carolina from the trenches at the foot of Missionary Ridge, but it appears much more probable that he was speaking of the initial Federal breakthrough at the summit. If so, Bragg disbelieved, never read, completely misunderstood, willfully ignored, or totally forgot the reports of his own subordinates; namely, Anderson, Manigault, Brig. Gen. Zachariah Deas, Tucker, and Reynolds. Anderson's report contains no criticism of Reynolds, and Anderson and two of his brigade commanders (Manigault and Deas) all state that the initial breakthrough occurred along Tucker's front (on Reynolds's right).[59] Tucker himself admits as much in his own report, and the fact was substantially corroborated by Cpl. George W. Chumbley of the 54th Virginia, who wrote on December 3, eight days after the battle, that "The enemy carried the hill by some of our troops acting cowardly, running without firing a gun. The enemy broke in on our right and left and we were exposed to a cross fire. . . ."[60]

Assuming that Reynolds's Brigade was in its assigned position atop Missionary Ridge on the evening of November 25, two questions arise: why was Bate unaware of that fact, and why did Reynolds's North Carolinians and Virginians fight so well when so many other Confederate units disintegrated? In all probability, Bate was not aware of Reynolds's presence on his right because Reynolds's men were in what Bate describes as a "depression" between himself and Tucker. Peering over that depression through the twilight and the smoke and confusion of battle, his attention riveted on Tucker's travail on the height beyond, Bate either misidentified Reynolds's small brigade, which he may have mistaken for

---

57. In a letter to his wife dated December 19, 1863, Captain Harper wrote: "I send you several [news]papers. One of these . . . contains a very truthful account [by an Alabama officer] of the late battle or rather of a portion of it. . . . No doubt but little service was rendered by many that retreated from the advanced breastworks to the top of the Ridge but such was not the case with our Regt. We were on the right of the troops represented by the correspondent [as having fought badly]." G. W. F. Harper to Ella Harper, December 19, 1863, Harper Papers. See also Harper Diary, November 25, 1863.

58. Braxton Bragg to Edward Turner Sykes, February 8, 1873, in William M. Polk, *Leonidas Polk: Bishop and General*, 2 vols. (New York: Longmans, Green, and Company, 1915), 2:310.

59. Deas and then Manigault apparently gave way after Tucker. See the reports of Anderson, Manigault, Deas, Tucker, and Reynolds in Hoffmann, *Reports of Anderson's Division.*

60. George Chumbley to his father, mother, and sisters, December 3, 1863 (typescript), James I. Robertson private manuscripts collection, hereafter cited as Robertson Collection. See also the letter of Pvt. John W. Reese of the 60th North Carolina dated December 6, 1863, which confirms the accuracy of Reynolds's report and is quoted in the history of the 60th on pages 456-457 of this volume. In his official report dated November 30, 1863, Bragg does not mention Reynolds's Brigade at all but states that the collapse of Anderson's Division began "on its left, where the enemy had first crowned the ridge. . . . All to the left . . . except a portion of Bate's division, was entirely routed and in rapid flight. . . ." That criticism, although opaque, was probably directed partially (and unfairly) at Reynolds. *Official Records (Army)*, ser. 1, 31 (pt. 2):665.

a single regiment, or, possibly, failed to see it at all. For most of the same reasons, Bate was unaware that Reynolds's men were still in line on his right when, shortly thereafter, his division, which he describes as being "in much confusion," retreated.[61] The brigade's commendable combat performance is likewise attributable to its fortuitous position on the battlefield and to the "fog of war." Occupying a lower point than Bate's and Tucker's commands, Reynolds's men were in a sort of eddy between swarms of charging Federals hell-bent on reaching the top of Missionary Ridge. Subsequently, although exposed on both flanks by the collapse of Tucker and the withdrawal of Bate, they were able to retreat in good order: the light (filtered through a pall of smoke) was failing, the men were not under severe pressure, they had suffered minimal casualties, and, although under fire from "two different & commanding points on the ridge," they were "shelter[ed]" to some extent by the terrain. Under circumstances that were admittedly less difficult than those faced by other Confederate units, the 58th North Carolina and 54th and 63rd Virginia, contrary to their critics and notwithstanding some exaggerations by Reynolds, offered stout resistance, maintained their position as long as possible, and retreated with their organization intact.[62] According to figures compiled from rosters in this volume, casualties in the 58th at Missionary Ridge were 2 men killed, 10 wounded, and 42 captured (of whom 3 were wounded).[63]

Bragg's defeated army reached Chickamauga Station on the night of November 25 and continued to retreat the next day. "Tired and very sleepy[,] having slept but little for three nights," Captain Harper and his troops bivouacked near Catoosa Station, Georgia, that evening. At 5:00 P.M. on the twenty-seventh the 58th arrived at Dalton, where it remained for more than five months.[64] Under the firm hand and watchful eye of Gen. Joseph E.

---

61. *Official Records (Army)*, ser. 1, 31 (pt. 2):741-742.

62. Reynolds, "Missionary Ridge Report," in Hoffmann, *Reports of Anderson's Division*, 75. Pvt. J. W. Dugger states in his diary that "About 1 o'clock their [the Federals'] heavy columns commenced advancing on our centre, our line being deployed, so it was not more than a line of pickets were ordered to deploy as skirmishers and fall back to the end of the ridge. There we joined another line. The enemy advanced in three lines[,] Infantry and Cavalry in the rear. In quick time they charged up the Ridge. We whipped their front line but they rallied the second line and came again in desperate order. We held them in check until nearly sundown. We were [then] flanked on our right and left, and compelled to retreat[.] [W]e lost several pieces of artillery and a good many men captured." And in a letter dated December 3, 1863, Captain Harper wrote that he "would like to see what the N.C. papers say of our N.C. Regts [performance at Missionary Ridge]. [T]hey did very well and have been highly complimented. My Co[mpany] did very well." Dugger-Hodges Diary, November 25, 1863, in *Watauga Democrat*, May 28, 1891; G. W. F. Harper to Ella Harper, December 3, 1863, Harper Papers.

63. Unfair charges of a poor combat performance by Reynolds's Brigade continue to be leveled by modern historians who, unable to reconcile the conflicting accounts of Bragg, Bate, and Reynolds, seemingly conclude that Reynolds lied. Reynolds was a man of dubious morality and was clearly capable of prevarication (see footnotes 72 and 93 below). However, in this instance the evidence is ample that he spoke the truth. See James Lee McDonough, *Chattanooga: A Death Grip on the Confederacy* (Knoxville: University of Tennessee Press, 1984), 186-187; Peter Cozzens, *The Shipwreck of Their Hopes: The Battles for Chattanooga* (Urbana and Chicago: University of Illinois Press, 1994), 296-298; Jeffrey C. Weaver, *54th Virginia Infantry* (Lynchburg, Va.: H. E. Howard, 1993), 90-91, 93-94, hereafter cited as Weaver, *54th Virginia*.

64. Harper Diary, November 26, 1863. The Virginia men called their half of the Dalton encampment "Camp Extra Billy Smith" in honor of a former governor of Virginia; the North Carolinians referred to their side as "Camp Zeb Vance" in honor of their current governor. See James Miller Wysor to his father, February 10, 1864, James Miller Wysor Papers (typescripts), Virginia Historical Society, Richmond, hereafter cited as Wysor Papers.

Johnston, who replaced Bragg on December 27, the regiment was paraded, reviewed, drilled, and inspected, stood provost guard duty, and constructed shanties for the winter.[65] Supernumerary officers were detailed and furloughs were granted. Throughout December and January food supplies, at least for the long-suffering enlisted men, were quantitatively inadequate and qualitatively deplorable. However, by about mid-February, Johnston had achieved a level of gastronomic affluence for the rank and file approximating, at least for the moment, the "peace and plenty" proclaimed two months earlier by Captain Harper.[66] Even prior to that date the men's condition and morale improved markedly under Johnston. Harper pronounced a review of the entire Army of Tennessee on January 29 to be "the finest military display I have yet seen. My Company (E & H) marched beautifully and . . . was highly complimented for its appearance. The great number of men present surprised us all. . . . It was a fine looking body of men. . . ."[67] Pvt. John G. Barnes of Company I was even more enthusiastic: "[T]he hold armer [whole army] was their[.] [T]he artiller[y] was their[.] [T]he streets [of Dalton] was crouded with men as fur as you could see any way you wood look[.] Jane if [only] you could a bin hear and saw our guns and baynets glitering in the sun like silver and drumes beeting and the fifes playing and the brass bands playing and the . . . artiilery waggons runing [rumbling?] and the sound of the soldiers feet[.] [I]t roard like t[h]under of a distance[.] [I]f you could a ben hear you wood a saw the moses [most] men you ever saw in your life[.] [W]e past the in spection the nicest you ever saw[.] [E]vry mans foot struct the ground at the same time and our line was strate as a line[.] [O]ur capten said that it coud not be beet[.]"[68]

The improvements reflected in the January 29 review were accomplished by rigorous discipline as well as hard work. Johnston's disciplinary measures were neither unfair nor brutal by contemporary standards and, particularly after Johnston abolished corporal

65. "We have had more reviews in the past month than I ever saw," Capt. James Clark of the 63rd Virginia wrote disgustedly on February 15, 1864. "I can't see what good they do, [to] have us trotting round for them to look at. Every Gen. that has a wife & she comes to see him must have us paraded round. . . ." James Clark to Martha Clark (his wife), February 15, 1864, Roster Document No. 1040 (typescripts), CWRP, NCDAH, hereafter cited as Clark Letters. See also G. W. F. Harper to Ella Harper, December 15, 1863, Harper Papers.

66. Harper Diary, December 5, 1863. Pvt. James M. Wysor of the 54th Virginia wrote on February 14 that he was now getting "plenty of good rations," but not everyone agreed with that happy assessment. "[T]imes heare is mity hard," Pvt. John G. Barnes of Company I of the 58th complained on March 4. "[W]e have not had more than two mesis [messes] of meete in a weak and but litel bread[.] [I]f they have got it they dont give it to the soldiers. . . . Sumtimes we grumble about it but it [is] all of no use[.] [W]e has to put up with any thing[.]" J. M. Wysor to his father, February 14, 1864, Wysor Papers; John G. Barnes to Jane E. Barnes (his wife) and children, March 4, 1864, Roster Document No. 1099, CWRP, NCDAH, hereafter cited as Barnes Letters. See also John Howell King (54th Virginia) to Zachariah King (his father), January 2, 1864, King Letters; G. W. F. Harper to Ella Harper, December 15, 1863, Harper Papers; Thomas W. Patton letters of January 23 and 27, 1864, quoted in 60th North Carolina history on page 459 of this volume; J. G. Barnes to J. E. Barnes and children, April 11, 1864, Barnes Letters.

67. G. W. F. Harper to Ella Harper, January 30, 1864, Harper Papers.

68. J. G. Barnes to J. E. Barnes and children, February 1, 1864, Barnes Letters. Despite several discrepancies between their accounts, it seems very likely that Harper and Barnes were describing the same review. See also Thomas B. Hampton (63rd Virginia) to Jestin C. Hampton (his wife), January 31, 1864, Thomas B. Hampton Papers (typescripts), The Center for American History, The University of Texas at Austin, hereafter cited as Hampton Papers.

punishment, were accepted by most of the men with good grace. However, Private Barnes was among the dissenters. "[T]heir is meny a man [officer] that will go to hell for the way they treat men hear," he wrote on February 19, "shaveing of[f] their heads and druming them threw the camp[,] standing in the stocks[,] standing on stumps[,] walking the gard line [and] all kinds of punishment that coud be put on men[.] [W]e dont know sunday from any other day. . . ."[69] Johnston's program for restoring the Army of Tennessee to fighting trim also included a partial reorganization that, for Reynolds's Brigade, began on November 30, a month before Johnston's arrival. On that date the brigade was transferred from Buckner's Division of Breckinridge's Corps to Maj. Gen. Carter L. Stevenson's Division of Hardee's Corps. Stevenson's Division was transferred to the corps of Lt. Gen. John B. Hood on February 28, 1864. On December 14, 1863, the 58th reported 327 officers and men present for duty.[70]

Following his victory at Chattanooga and the relief of Burnside at Knoxville on December 6, Grant began planning an advance against Atlanta in the spring. In the meantime, Sherman was dispatched on a brief campaign into central and eastern Mississippi in early February. On February 22 General Thomas, on orders from Grant, advanced from Chattanooga toward Ringgold, Georgia, to prevent Johnston from sending reinforcements to confront Sherman. Heavy skirmishing broke out at Rocky Face Ridge on the twenty-third and twenty-fourth and culminated on February 25 in an attempt by Thomas to flank Johnston out of a strong position at Mill Creek Gap. At Crow Valley, east of Mill Creek Gap, Brig. Gen. Henry D. Clayton's Alabama brigade repulsed three separate Federal attacks and sustained seventy-two casualties. Reynolds's Brigade, on Clayton's right, was subjected to heavy artillery fire and took part in at least one skirmish. "[A]bout 12 o'clock," Pvt. J. W. Dugger wrote, "the enemy commenced advancing slowly and tried to flank us on the left. . . . About 2 o'clock a sharp fight took place on that wing lasting about half an hour. The 58th was not engaged except the Skirmishers, though under heavy cannonading[,] wounding 24 in the 58th and 60th . . . regiments. . . . The Yankies [sic] commenced falling back that night about 10 o'clock."[71] General Reynolds, in a brief report written on the date of the battle, stated that "My skirmishers have been engaged since early this morning, and

69. J. G. Barnes to J. E. Barnes, February 19, 1864, Barnes Letters.

70. *Official Records (Army)*, ser. 1, 31 (pt. 3):767, 823, 32 (pt. 2):812. The present-for-duty strengths for Reynolds's other three regiments on that date were 60th North Carolina 141, 54th Virginia 390, and 63rd Virginia 303, making a total of 1,161. Inasmuch as the 58th and 60th North Carolina were still consolidated under Colonel Hardy of the 60th, it is unclear why the strengths of the two units were reported separately and why Capt. Samuel M. Silver was reported as commander of the 58th. Possibly Silver's status was nominal and reflected, as did the separate troop-strength figures, the temporary nature of the consolidation. However, on January 20, 1864, Silver was reported as acting commander of *both* regiments. See *Official Records (Army)*, ser. 1, 32 (pt. 2):587.

71. Dugger-Hodges Diary, February 25, 1864, in *Watauga Democrat*, June 11, 1891. Private Barnes described the Federal artillery fire as "like the hardest thunder you ever heard . . . onley their is no ceas of it[.] [T]hey can fire the cannons three times in a minit." "They [the Federals] would stand off & shoot but wouldn't come up," Capt. James Clark of the 63rd Virginia wrote. "[Their officers] came up one time & was patting their men on the shoulders & trying to get them to charge us when we charged them. They ran like good fellows." J. G. Barnes to J. E. Barnes and children, March 4, 1864, Barnes Letters; James Clark to Martha Clark, February 28, 1864, Clark Letters.

have kept back the enemy. About 12 o'clock General Clayton sent me two regiments to extend my left to the mountain. About the time they got into position the enemy advanced in force and a fight ensued. General Clayton, with a third regiment, came up and took command of the left. The fight was entirely successful, driving the enemy back twice. My own troops have been under a heavy fire of shell and canister for several hours. All behaved well. The list of killed and wounded find below: Sixty-third Virginia, 5 wounded; Fifty-eighth and Sixtieth North Carolina Regiments, 24 wounded, 3 mortally; Fifty-fourth Virginia Regiment, 12 men wounded."[72] According to figures compiled for this volume, the 58th North Carolina lost 3 men killed or mortally wounded and 11 wounded at Rocky Face Ridge.[73]

Reynolds's Brigade remained on the battlefield at Rocky Face Ridge until February 28 and then returned to its camp near Dalton. During the late winter and early spring of 1864 the routines and diversions of camp life included inspections, reviews, "plenty [of] hard drilling," regimental band concerts, "magnificent . . . sham battle[s]," "ball play," "snipe hunting," gander pullings, chess matches, and prayer meetings.[74] A gigantic

72. *Official Records (Army)*, ser. 1, 32 (pt. 1):483. In a letter to his sister dated February 29, 1864, Reynolds penned a vainglorious account of the fighting that varies so remarkably from the one he wrote four days earlier that its veracity is in serious doubt: "The Battle of 'Stone Side' was my own fight. I was in supreme command. I selected the field and my troops *alone* gained the victory. My command consisted of My Brigade, and 3 Regts of Gen Claytons Alabama troops, in all 2500 men and opposed by [Gordon] Grangers Army Corps, Yanks, about 7000 men. The fight began about 9 O.C AM[,] our skirmishers having engaged them about 6 O.C A.M. The enemy advanced in three lines of battle with great confidence expecting to over whelm me[.] [A]t 10 O.C the battle raged furiously all along my line. The thunder of cannon and clatter of musketry was absolutely defening [*sic*], yet our boys stood fast and poured in their volleys with terrible effect. The enemy wavered and I ordered an advance. Shouts went up which rent the air and the Yankees broke. They soon reformed, and again came to the charge. We met them again and drove them, being reinforced they made their third and heaviest attack. The lines swayed to and fro for some time. I rode forward and ordered a charge, and this time entirely routed them. I never felt so glorious in my life. [I]t was a complete victory and thank God. I won it, [and] even my dear horse 'Gauley' seemed to feel and enjoy it. I am proud of my brave boys. . . ." A. W. Reynolds to S. A. Patton (his sister), February 29, 1864, West Virginia Regional History Collection, West Virginia University Libraries, Morgantown.

73. Colonel Hardy, who was still in command of the consolidated 58th and 60th North Carolina, stated that each regiment lost one man killed and eleven wounded at Rocky Face Ridge. W. M. Hardy to G. W. F. Harper, February 27, 1864, Harper Papers. Captain Clark of the 63rd Virginia wrote to his wife on February 28 that he had been "Skirmirmishing [*sic*] with the enemy for several days & have just got back to camp. Our Brigade has been in front all the time. We lost about 40 killed & wounded out of the Brigade. . . ." James Clark to Martha Clark, February 28, 1864, Clark Letters. See also T. B. Hampton to J. C. Hampton, February 29, 1864, Hampton Papers.

74. T. B. Hampton to J. C. Hampton, March 11 and April 8, 1864, Hampton Papers; Harper Diary, April 13 and 16, 1864. "Hardee's Corps had a sham fight here a few days since," Sgt. R. D. Jamison of the 45th Tennessee wrote on April 11. "It was a grand affair. Tell Henry the one he saw was nothing compared to it. I saw a cavalry Regt. charge a Regt. of infantry formed in a square four different times and were repulsed every time. It was very exciting indeed, and I might have been forced to believe there was some reality in it had there not been so many ladies, Quarter-Masters, Commissaries and their attachees present. The ridges all around were covered with these. Some of the ladies got between the lines and you may imagine their astonishment . . . when infantry and artillery were roaring all around them. . . . [T]hey did not stay there long." Robert D. Jamison to Camilla P. Jamison (his wife), April 11, 1864, in Henry Downs Jamison Jr., ed., *Letters and Recollections of a Confederate Soldier, 1860-1865* (Nashville, Tenn.: privately published, 1964), 91, hereafter cited as H. D. Jamison,

snowball battle involving thousands of men broke out on March 22. "The boys got to snow-balling individually and soon by companies and then by regiments and brigades until . . . most of the army was engaged," Sgt. Robert D. Jamison of the 45th Tennessee (Brig. Gen. John C. Brown's Brigade) wrote. "It was amusing to see the Colonels and Generals on their horses giving orders as if it was a regular battle. There was a great deal of fun in it until the snow began to melt. . . . [Then] some balls would get too hard and the infirmary corps was called into requisition to take care of the wounded. . . ."[75]

On April 6 the consolidation of the 58th and 60th North Carolina was terminated when Maj. Thomas J. Dula of the 58th, who had been wounded at Chickamauga, returned to duty. The two regiments then resumed their status as independent entities.[76] In a letter to his wife dated March 15, 1864, Captain Harper reported that "the troops here are in fine spirits and in splendid condition."[77] Rations continued to be adequate if not always of good quality. Pvt. Allen L. Bonham of the 63rd Virginia complained on April 1 about the "stuff tha [the commissary department] called . . . flour but tha was mistakin [for] it was chaf or wheat ground and was not bolted. It was nuff to take the worms out of a gaspin chickens throat." On April 19 a "Grand review" of the Army of Tennessee was held, and from April 20 through April 23 the regiment was on detail "work[ing] on fortification[s] above D[alton]."[78] On May 4, in what may have been the largest mass execution of the war, twelve members of the 58th North Carolina and two of the 60th were shot for desertion.[79] "It was

Letters and Recollections. See also J. G. Barnes to J. E. Barnes and children, April 11, 1864, Barnes Letters.

75. R. D. Jamison, "Reminiscence of a Tennessee Confederate Veteran," in H. D. Jamison, *Letters and Recollections,* 167, hereafter cited as R. D. Jamison, "Reminiscences," in H. D. Jamison, *Letters and Recollections.* According to an officer on Maj. Gen. Alexander P. Stewart's staff, "a number of soldiers had their eyes put out [received black eyes?]." Bromfield L. Ridley, *Battles and Sketches of the Army of Tennessee* (Mexico, Mo.: Missouri Printing and Publishing Company, 1906), 283, hereafter cited as Ridley, *Battles and Sketches.* See also Harper Diary, March 22, 1864; T. B. Hampton to J. C. Hampton, March 24, 1864, Hampton Papers.

76. See Harper Diary, April 6, 1864; G. W. F. Harper to Ella Harper, April 5, 1864, Harper Papers. The consolidation was probably terminated in part because of a "mutiny" that occurred in the ranks of the 58th on an unknown date between about February 15 and February 29. In response to a letter that he received from Captain Harper, Colonel Palmer of the 58th, who was still serving in Western North Carolina, wrote that he was "very sorry to hear that the 58th which has done so well on the battlefield has sullied its fame by refusing to obey orders. Insubordination, *under any circumstances,* always injures the parties engaged in it. . . . I hear that one reason was dissatisfaction with the consolidation—partiality shown to the 60th. . . . The consolidation could have been broken up without resorting to mutiny." Particulars concerning the incident and the circumstances and events that prompted it remain unclear. However, to describe the episode as a "mutiny" is perhaps an exaggeration. J. B. Palmer to G. W. F. Harper, March 4, 1864, Harper Papers.

77. G. W. F. Harper to Ella Harper, March 15, 1864, Harper Papers. Sergeant Jamison of the 45th Tennessee wrote on January 20 that "The condition of our army is better now than some time back and the men seem to be more cheerful." Harper confirmed that assessment in early April, noting that "The army is in fine health and spirits. There has not been a death in my Co[mpany] from disease for 6 mo[nth]s—last winter I lost 11 men by disease & some co[mpanie]s double that number." R. D. Jamison to C. P. Jamison, January 20, 1864, in H. D. Jamison, *Letters and Recollections,* 88; G. W. F. Harper to Ella Harper, [April 11, 1864], Harper Papers.

78. Allen L. Bonham to Joseph and Tibitha Bonham (his father and mother), April 1, 1864, in Trula Fay Parks Purkey, *Genealogy of William Bonham, Pioneer Settler of Grayson County, Virginia* (n.p.: privately published, n.d.), 60; Harper Diary, April 19 and 20, 1864. The brigade moved four miles northwest of Dalton on April 26 and began erecting fortifications on the old battlefield at Rocky Face Ridge. See Harper Diary, April 26, 1864.

79. See Harper Diary, May 4, 1864. "The recruits lately recvd into our Regt, most of them from Yadkin

the worst sight I ever saw," Capt. James Clark of the 63rd Virginia wrote, "too horrible to think about. Yet some of them was not killed the first time & some of them not touched. Their cries was horrible in the extreme. Men were ordered up one at a time to put their guns close to their hearts or heads & fired. One poor fellow told them if they were going to kill him for God sake to do it & not shoot his flesh to pieces. They all seemed very much effected about their future except one who believed there was no God & died firm in his belief. That [the execution] is old news but it is one of the scenes I shall never forget as long as life last[s]."[80]

On May 7 General Sherman, who had replaced Grant as commander of the Military Division of the Mississippi, marched toward Dalton with an army of about 100,000 men.[81] Thomas's Army of the Cumberland captured the village of Tunnel Hill the same day and advanced toward the north end of Rocky Face Ridge and the Dug and Mill Creek Gaps. The Army of the Ohio, now commanded by Maj. Gen. John M. Schofield, moved on Thomas's left around Rocky Face Ridge and into Crow Valley, east of the ridge. While Thomas and Schofield conducted demonstrations to convince Johnston that an attack was in the

---

Co[unty], turned out badly," Captain Harper wrote on November 15, 1863. "[A]bout half of them have deserted, several of them going over to the Yankees." G. W. F. Harper to Ella Harper, November 15, 1863, Harper Papers.

Quarterly desertion totals in the 58th North Carolina from April 1863 through June 1864 were as follows: second quarter 1863, 50; third quarter 1863, 83; fourth quarter 1863, 33; first quarter 1864, 60; second quarter 1864, 40. (For 58th desertion figures during other periods of the war, see footnotes 22 above and 168 below.) Desertion was a serious problem in all four regiments of the Reynolds-Palmer Brigade. Weaver estimates that 463 members of the 54th Virginia (about 25.3 percent) and 546 members of the 63rd Virginia (about 35.6 percent) deserted during the war. In the 60th North Carolina, 205 men out of the 1,116 who served deserted (about 18.4 percent); in the 58th North Carolina, 475 men out of 2,033 deserted (about 23.4 percent). It should be noted that no company muster rolls are extant for the 58th and 60th North Carolina for September 1864-April 1865, a period during which desertion was undoubtedly high. Moreover, comparative figures between the North Carolina and Virginia regiments are misleading because Weaver defines desertion as absence "for more than 30 days without proper authority, or if there was a reason to believe that the person who was absent had no intention of returning to duty regardless of the period of absence." In the *North Carolina Troops* series, a soldier who returned to duty from an unauthorized absence of whatever length is not defined for statistical purposes as a deserter. In short, desertion is defined as *ultimate* failure to return to duty. Jeffrey C. Weaver, *63rd Virginia Infantry* (Lynchburg, Va.: H. E. Howard, 1991), 100, hereafter cited as Weaver, *63rd Virginia*. See also Weaver, *54th Virginia*, 159.

80. James Clark to Martha Clark, June 16, 1864, Clark Letters. "Several men were tried as traitors who had . . . [gone home without leave] to provide for the needs of their families and had returned to their commands," Sgt. R. D. Jamison of the 45th Tennessee later recalled. "Fourteen of these were condemned to be shot. Fourteen posts were prepared and a man was secured by a rope to each post. A platoon of soldiers were given guns loaded by the officer in charge with some blank cartridges. When the volley was fired all the men seemed to have been killed but two or three. The officer took several men with loaded guns and made a critical examination, with a surgeon, of every condemned man. When one was pronounced alive a soldier was ordered to place the gun to his heart and kill him. This was repeated until all were dead. Horrible, horrible to think about. The whole army was required to be present at every execution." R. D. Jamison, "Reminiscences," in H. D. Jamison, *Letters and Recollections*, 167. See also Ridley, *Battles and Sketches*, 284-286; "Miscellaneous Information Concerning Dalton Executions," Roster Document No. 0394, CWRP, NCDAH. Additional material concerning the Dalton episode appears on pages 462-463 of this volume.

81. Sherman assumed command of the Military Division of the Mississippi on March 18. His authority, like Grant's, extended over the Armies of the Cumberland, the Tennessee, and the Ohio. Grant was promoted to lieutenant general, made general-in-chief of the Union army, and sent east to confront Lee in Virginia.

offing, the Army of the Tennessee, now commanded by Maj. Gen. James B. McPherson, edged around Johnston's left flank. McPherson's orders were to penetrate Snake Creek Gap, about eight miles southwest of Dalton, and cut Johnston's line of communications at Resaca. The Confederate army would then be caught in a vise and destroyed.[82]

The 58th North Carolina was still at the old Rocky Face Ridge battlefield performing picket duty when Sherman advanced on May 7. The regiment then moved into a reserve position with the rest of Reynolds's Brigade in Crow Valley, near the foot of Buzzard Roost. On the morning of May 8 the brigade moved to its left so that its left was on the lower slopes of Buzzard Roost and its right extended into the valley. In that position it skirmished with the enemy until dark.[83] "About 10 o'clock [on the morning of May 9]," Private Dugger wrote, "the enemy was discovered advancing and from noon until night heavy skirmishing and cannonading raged on the line from the top of Buzzard roost to the east side of the valley. The enemies skirmishers made a charge on ours and drove them back to the lines. . . . About 3 o'clock [that afternoon] three [Federal] columns charged the top of Buzzard roost but were soon repulsed by Pettess' [Pettus's] Alabama Brigade with several [severe?] losses[.] [O]ur loss exceedingly light. Fighting ceased about dark and remained quiet all night." According to Captain Harper, "Dick Col[e]man and six or seven other" members of the 58th North Carolina were wounded.[84] Light skirmishing on May 10 was followed by a "desperately hard" rain during the night. "[R]olled in a blanket I kept nearly dry," Chaplain Thomas H. Deavenport of the 3rd Tennessee wrote. "The place being very steep, I would slip down untill [*sic*] my feet got into a puddle of water, when I would pull up again. This is soldiering . . . in earnest." Sharpshooting and skirmishing commenced again on the morning of the eleventh and continued "slowly" all that day and the next.[85]

---

82. See Richard M. McMurry, "The Opening Phase of the 1864 Campaign in the West," *Atlanta Historical Journal* 27 (summer 1983): 5-24.

83. See *Official Records (Army)*, ser. 1, 38 (pt. 3):811. The exact position of Reynolds's Brigade during the fighting on May 8 and 9 is unclear. On the morning of May 8, Brig. Gen. Edmund W. Pettus's Brigade was on the crest of Buzzard Roost with Cheatham's Division on its left and Reynolds's, Brig. Gen. Alfred Cumming's, and Brown's Brigades (in left-to-right order) in Crow Valley on its right. Brown was moved to the left of Pettus during the day when the "angle" at the crest of Buzzard Roost, rightly deemed by Stevenson to be a weak point, came under attack. (The "angle" was the point where the north-south Confederate line facing west on Rocky Face Ridge turned east and faced north.) Harper states in his diary that Reynolds's Brigade moved on that date to a point "near the top" of Buzzard Roost; Dugger says that the brigade "moved to the left on the side of Buzzard roost"; and Stevenson says nothing regarding *any* movement by Reynolds. Neither Harper, Dugger, nor Stevenson report any movement by the brigade on the ninth, but Stevenson states that Brown and Pettus were on or near the crest of Buzzard Roost and Reynolds and Cumming were "in the valley." Harper to the contrary notwithstanding, the likelihood, as stated above, is that Reynolds's men were partially on the lower slopes of Buzzard Roost and partially in Crow Valley on May 8. Their location on May 9 is less certain: they either remained in the same position they occupied on the eighth or (less likely) shifted back to their right so that they were entirely in the valley. Harper Diary, May 8, 1864; Dugger-Hodges Diary, May 8, 1864, in *Watauga Democrat*, June 11, 1891; *Official Records (Army)*, ser. 1, 38 (pt. 3):811.

84. Dugger-Hodges Diary, May 9, 1864, in *Watauga Democrat*, June 11, 1891; Harper Diary, May 9, 1864.

85. Dugger-Hodges Diary, May 10 (first quotation) and 11 (third quotation), 1864, in *Watauga Democrat*, June 11, 1891; diary of Thomas Hopkins Deavenport (typescript), May 11, 1864 (page 21), Civil War Collection (Confederate), box 6, folder 5a, Tennessee State Archives, Nashville, hereafter cited as Deavenport Diary. "This is certainly the roughest place I ever saw and the rockiest," Chaplain Deavenport added. "Rocks are continually rolling down to the amusement of those highest up and annoyance of those [below]."

While most of Johnston's army confronted Sherman at Rocky Face Ridge during May 8-12, McPherson's flanking movement failed at Snake Creek Gap because of McPherson's excessive caution and the inopportune arrival at Resaca of Confederate reinforcements from Mississippi under Lt. Gen. Leonidas Polk. When Sherman began shifting the bulk of his army south to support McPherson, Johnston fell back from Rocky Face Ridge and formed a line of battle on a range of hills west and north of Resaca. Reynolds's Brigade "secretly retired" from Buzzard Roost around 9:00 P.M. on the twelfth and marched "over a very rough road" throughout the night. After halting briefly for breakfast near Tilton Station, the men continued slowly down the Resaca road on May 13. "Skirmishes out on our flanks," Harper noted dramatically, "The enemy pressing us in rear and hovering on our flank." That night Reynolds's men and the rest of Stevenson's Division went into position about two miles north of Resaca on the right center of Johnston's line: Cumming and Brown in front; Pettus and Reynolds in reserve. Hindman's Division was on Stevenson's left and Maj. Gen. Alexander P. Stewart's Division on his right.[86]

Skirmishing began at Resaca at 8:00 A.M. on May 14 and continued until shortly after noon when Schofield launched a two-division attack on Hindman and was repulsed with severe losses (see the Atlanta Campaign map on page 464). Stevenson and Stewart, reinforced by four brigades, then attacked the division of Maj. Gen. David S. Stanley, whose left flank was in the air. "About 5 o'clock that evening," Stevenson reported, "I commenced a movement to dislodge the enemy from the high point of the ridge some distance in front of General Cumming. Brown and his support (Reynolds) were directed to move out in front of their trenches and then swing around to the left. After the movement commenced General Cumming was also directed to wheel all of his brigade, which was to the right of the backbone of the ridge, to the left in front of his works. . . . I was much gratified by the gallantry with which the movement was made. . . ." Two of Stanley's brigades were overwhelmed and routed by Stevenson, but a stubborn stand by an Indiana battery and the arrival of Federal reinforcements brought the attack to a halt. Leaving numerous butternut-clad corpses strewn in front of the triumphant Indiana gunners, Stevenson withdrew.[87] Captain Harper wrote that Stevenson's men "moved out of [their] breastworks and charged the enemy[,] who ran for dear life. Magnificient [sic] charge. Advanced our lines over a mile and halted after dark. Occupied the ground until after midnight when we withdrew to our original position." Reynolds's troops played a secondary role in the fighting and escaped most of the destructive fire sustained by Brown. Their casualties, if any, were light.[88]

While most of the fighting was taking place on the Confederate right on May 14, McPherson's troops, on Johnston's left, quietly seized a lightly defended hill perilously close to the Oostanaula River bridges over which Johnston would have to retreat. Several hundred Federals belonging to Brig. Gen. Thomas W. Sweeny's Division also crossed the

86. Dugger-Hodges Diary, May 12, 1864, in *Watauga Democrat*, June 18, 1891; Deavenport Diary, May 16, 1864 (page 21); Harper Diary, May 13, 1864.

87. *Official Records (Army)*, ser. 1, 38 (pt. 3):812. See also the report of the Indiana battery commander, Capt. Peter Simonson, in *Official Records (Army)*, ser. 1, 38 (pt. 1):488-489.

88. Harper Diary, May 14, 1864. See also Dugger-Hodges Diary, May 14, 1864, in *Watauga Democrat*, June 18, 1891. Chaplain Deavenport states in his diary that "Brown's brigade . . . did all the fighting." Deavenport Diary, May 16, 1864 (page 22).

Oostanaula downriver at Lay's Ferry. Sweeny's troops quickly withdrew under the mistaken impression that they were menaced by a superior Confederate force, but the threat posed by McPherson and Sweeny to Johnston's rear was urgent. During the night Johnston dispatched a division to defend the Lay's Ferry crossing and ordered the construction of a pontoon bridge upstream from Resaca. Sherman, for his part, ordered Sweeny to recross the Oostanaula at Lay's Ferry the next morning and establish a secure bridgehead. At the same time, Maj. Gens. Joseph Hooker and Oliver O. Howard, commanding the XX and IV Corps respectively of the Army of the Cumberland, were to attack the Confederate right.

Fighting began on the morning of May 15 with cannonading and heavy musketry along most of the line. At about 1:00 P.M. Hooker and Howard advanced over broken terrain covered with underbrush and small trees and, in the face of a storm of fire from Stevenson, quickly stumbled to a halt. Around two o'clock Reynolds's men were ordered to relieve Brown in the front line, where a prolonged struggle over four abandoned Confederate cannons was raging. There they repulsed "several" enemy charges.[89] A correspondent for the Atlanta *Intelligencer* wrote that

[a]t a quarter from four o'clock, a fifth charge was made, the enemy throwing forward fresh troops every time. Th[i]s charge was very heavy, and was made with spirit. . . . [W]ith a prolonged cheer, they rushed upon our works.—A . . . terrible, death-dealing volley, was poured into their ranks, and a loud . . . yell of defiance rang out from the lips of the Virginians and North Carolinians. This was more than the men of Brown's and Pettus' Brigades [who were in reserve] could withstand, and though threatened with death by their officers . . . [they] entered the pits to assist in repelling the charge. But their services were not needed. Quickly another volley . . . [was] poured into the enemy's line of battle, and they turned and retreated in disorder to the cover of their ridge, followed by the derisive shouts of the victors. . . .

[W]ithin half an hour . . . three lines of battle, closely massed, were seen forming in front of that portion of the line held by the 58th North Carolina. There was not much time for reflection, for very soon a voice on the right of the regiment exclaimed, "they are coming!" and the first column was seen to advance. "Withhold your fire until they come close to you, and then aim low," ordered the officers. On came the enemy cheering loudly. . . . They approached within fifty yards of the line, firing rapidly upon our men—a sheet of fire was the answer, and the dead and wounded lie piled up before our works. . . . [B]ewildered by the fierceness of our fire, they scattered throughout the woods, and reached their lines, our sharp shooters killing and wounding them by dozens in their route down the ridge. . . .

This sixth column was repulsed only a few minutes when the remaining two columns of Yankees marched forward, with the hope of reaching our line before our men could fire more than one volley. But their charge was not made with the same firmness as characterized . . . the preceding one, and two or three well-aimed volleys from the fifty-eighth North Carolina, assisted by a cross fire from the fifty-fourth Virginia on the one wing, and the sixty-third [Virginia] on the other, routed the 7th attacking column of the enemy. They . . . retired to their ridge, and for a few minutes only their sharpshooters could be seen, their main body being no doubt engaged in reforming their broken columns.[90]

---

89. Harper Diary, May 15, 1864. The guns were ultimately captured by the Federals.

90. *Intelligencer* (Atlanta), unknown date, reprinted in *North Carolina [Weekly] Standard* (Raleigh), June 22, 1864.

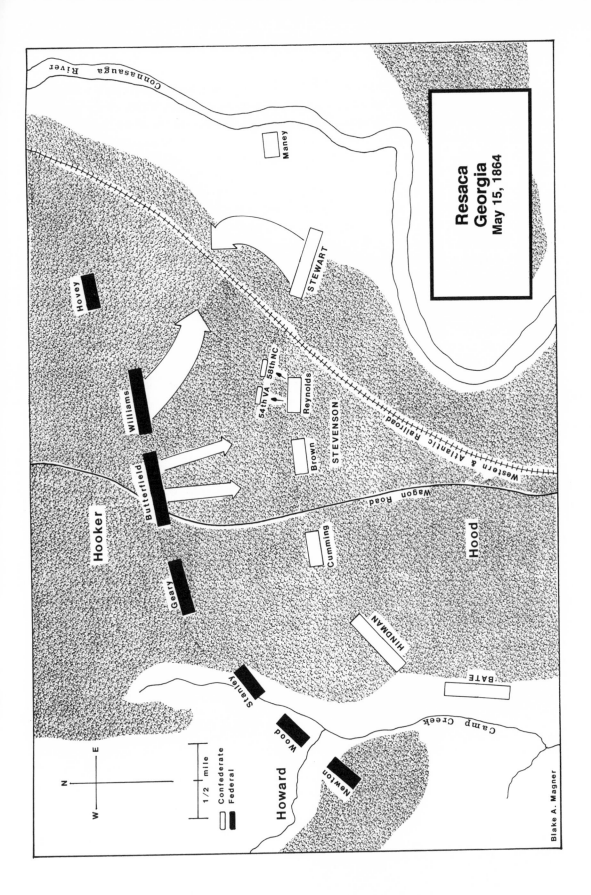

Resaca
Georgia
May 15, 1864

Connasauga River

Maney

STEWART

Hovey

Williams

54th VA 58th NC

Reynolds

STEVENSON

Butterfield

Brown

Hooker

Western & Atlantic Railroad

Wagon Road

Cumming

Geary

Hood

HINDMAN

BATE

Stanley

Camp Creek

Wood

Howard

Newton

N
W   E
S

1/2 mile

Confederate
Federal

Blake A. Magner

Encouraged by the sturdy work of Stevenson's men and hearing no reports of further Federal advances on his left, Johnston ordered Hood to attack with Stewart's, Hindman's, and Stevenson's Divisions in the late afternoon. Just as that assault was launched, Johnston learned that a powerful Federal force on his right was crossing the Oostanaula. He then attempted to cancel Hood's attack and succeeded in halting Hindman's units and some of Stevenson's but none of Stewart's. At least two of Reynolds's regiments, the 58th North Carolina and 54th Virginia, failed to receive the cancellation order. "[We] moved over the breastworks under heavy fire," Harper wrote, "and formed an advance on the Enemy, our lines not connecting with Stewart (who . . . was repulsed about or before this time). We were compelled to withdraw to the entrenchments." The 54th Virginia was the more exposed of the two regiments and "in less than fifteen minutes [according to Stevenson's report] lost above 100 officers and men."[91] Losses in the 58th North Carolina were somewhat less severe: according to a casualty list for the two-day battle prepared by acting Lt. Col. T. J. Dula and published in the *North Carolina [Weekly] Standard*, the 58th lost 5 men killed, 31 wounded, and 37 missing. "The regiment acted in the most gallant manner," Dula stated, "making several successful charges upon the enemy. As true North Carolinians, the officers and men did their whole duty. . . ."[92] According to statistics compiled for this volume, the 58th lost 8 men killed, 31 wounded, 14 captured (of whom 1 was wounded), and 2 missing during the Battle of Resaca. Total Confederate casualties were about 3,000 men; Federal losses numbered about 4,000.[93]

During the night of May 15, while most of Johnston's men crossed the Oostanaula and fell back toward Adairsville, the 58th North Carolina remained at one of the bridges covering the withdrawal of the army's wagon train. The 58th crossed the next morning and marched about six miles south. "Stopped about 11 o'clock and rested about two hours," Dugger wrote, "then moved on. Skirmishing continued on the flank all the time. Marched about three miles and took up camp. Next morning, the 17th, started before day, marched

---

91. Harper Diary, May 15, 1864; *Official Records (Army)*, ser. 1, 38 (pt. 3):813.

92. *North Carolina [Weekly] Standard* (Raleigh), June 8, 1864. Dula was promoted to the permanent rank of lieutenant colonel on July 6, 1864.

93. According to one postwar report, General Reynolds was "very much intoxicated" during the fighting on the afternoon of May 15 and ordered the 54th Virginia to attack over the protests of its commanding officer. That story may or may not be true, but it seems likely that Reynolds had a drinking problem of some description and was probably a womanizer as well. In a letter dated February 20, 1864, Capt. James Clark of the 63rd Virginia commented that "The drum beats for parade drill & that breaks my sweet reflections & I wonder if old Gen. Reynolds will be drunk this evening. . . . The boys say there are some ladies that if you could give them that name, come out to headquarters dressed in uniform with spurs on & spend the night with the Old General & his staff while the boys freeze out side standing guard." After the war Reynolds went to Egypt and served as a colonel in the army of the khedive. He died there in 1876, "lonely and broke," amid "salacious rumors," in a boardinghouse of "none-too-savory reputation." An officer who knew him in Egypt wrote that "His death was caused by *drink*. He was never sober. It was so habitual with him that people did not know that he was drunk for they had never seen him sober. He was *full* all the time. [He] had been a hard, systematic drinker for many years." Addison Jordan, *Gen. Jos. E. Johnston, A Review of His Military Career: Also, A Collection of Sketches of the Experiences of a Confederate Soldier* (Pulaski, Va.: B. D. Smith and Brothers, 1907), 60, hereafter cited as Jordan, *Gen. Jos. E. Johnston*; James Clark to Martha Clark, February 20, 1864, Clark Letters; William B. Hesseltine and Hazel C. Wolf, *The Blue and the Gray on the Nile* (Chicago: The University of Chicago Press, 1961), 217-218.

about six miles and stopped. Skirmishing commenced very soon and continued until a sharp cavalry fight took place. Our command immediately formed a line of battle. Firing ceased at night. . . ."[94]

At Adairsville, Johnston divided his army, sending Hood's and Polk's Corps southeast on the Cassville road and Hardee's south on a roughly parallel road that led to Kingston before turning due east to rejoin the main road at Cassville. Correctly reasoning that Sherman would also divide his army at the Adairsville fork, Johnston planned to reunite his forces at Cassville and defeat Sherman's eastern wing before the western wing could come to its aid. Around midnight on May 17, the 58th North Carolina, which was still part of Reynolds's Brigade, Stevenson's Division, set off for Cassville with the rest of Hood's Corps. However, by the time it arrived about 11:00 A.M., a large force of Federal cavalry on a railroad cutting mission had materialized in Hood's rear, forcing Johnston to abandon his plan and fall back to a ridge southeast of Cassville. There he hoped to entice Sherman, whose western wing arrived from Kingston that afternoon, into an attack. Reynolds's men went into position on the Confederate right, and "sharp skirmishing" and cannonading continued throughout the day. That night, after belatedly discovering that Hood's and Polk's flanks were exposed to enfilading fire by Federal artillery, Johnston ordered another retreat. At about ten o'clock the 58th North Carolina "secretly retired" with the rest of Johnston's army to Allatoona Pass, a narrow valley about twelve miles southeast of Cassville. "[We] marched until about 11 o'clock next day," Dugger wrote, "passing through Cartersville Ga. [A]rrived at the [Etowah] river [where we] made a halt and rested some hours . . . then . . . marched about three miles and took up camp. All quiet except some cannonading on the left Saturday and Saturday night the 21st until Tuesday the 24th. Marched about three miles to the railroad [on the latter date] and camped. . . ."[95]

Johnston's Allatoona Pass position, about thirty-five miles northwest of Atlanta, was if anything more formidable than the one he occupied a few weeks earlier at Rocky Face Ridge. As he had done throughout the campaign, Sherman therefore made another attempt to turn Johnston's left, sending the bulk of his army west of the Allatoona Mountains toward Dallas on May 23. That maneuver, Sherman believed, would compel Johnston to abandon his Allatoona redoubt and retreat behind the Chattahoochee River, only eight miles north of Atlanta. Quickly apprised by his scouts of Sherman's gambit, Johnston marched westward with most of his army and was waiting on a series of low, timbered ridges when Sherman arrived at Dallas on the twenty-fifth. Late that afternoon the Federals advanced through dense woods and underbrush against Stewart's Division, entrenched near New Hope Church, and were repulsed with severe casualties. Stevenson's Division, which reached the field around 1:00 P.M., was on Stewart's right with Brown's and Pettus's Brigades in front and those of Reynolds and Cumming in reserve. Several of Brown's regiments took part in the heavy fighting that followed, but the remainder of Stevenson's men were not involved. During the day General Reynolds received a "painful" wound that incapacitated him for

94. Dugger-Hodges Diary, May 16-17, 1864, in *Watauga Democrat*, June 18, 1891.
95. Dugger-Hodges Diary, May 19 [18]-24, 1864, in *Watauga Democrat*, June 18, 1891.

field service for the remainder of the war. He was succeeded as brigade commander by Colonel Trigg of the 54th Virginia.[96]

Skirmishing resumed "very soon" on the morning of May 26 and, according to Dugger, "continued all day and night[.] [S]ome cannonading going on through the day [but] no regular engagement. . . . [S]ome vollies [sic] fired on parts of the line." Heavy fighting flared at Pickett's Mill on the twenty-seventh as Sherman, varying his tactics, attempted unsuccessfully to turn Johnston's right. Cleburne's Division repulsed the Federal attackers with severe casualties; Stevenson's Division again was not involved.[97] More fighting occurred on May 28 when Johnston, shrewdly deducing that Sherman had abandoned his flanking effort and was about to move back to the Western and Atlantic Railroad, ordered an attack against McPherson's lines south of Dallas. Heavy casualties were incurred by Bate's Division and the Kentucky and Florida brigades of Brig. Gens. Joseph H. Lewis and Jesse J. Finley. Stevenson's Division took no part in the fighting.

Johnston's attack on May 28 forced Sherman to delay his withdrawal plans until McPherson could be freed from his proximate grapple with Johnston. However, another attempt to extricate McPherson on the night of the twenty-ninth was aborted when jittery Federal pickets opened fire on what they believed to be a Confederate assault column. No Confederates were on the field, but that did not prevent a thunderous exchange of fire lasting from 10:00 P.M. until daylight. On May 30 Sherman and McPherson contrived plans for a staggered withdrawal that was successfully implemented on the night of the thirty-first. Freed at last from the Confederate tar baby, Sherman sidled eastward through rain and mud, and by June 5 he was astride the railroad at Acworth, ten miles northwest of Marietta. Johnston evacuated Allatoona Pass the previous day and also fell back from his position near Dallas. Contrary to Sherman's expectations, however, Johnston did not retreat southeastward across the Chattahoochee but marched east to a line about two miles above Marietta. Private Dugger reported the activities and movements of the 58th North Carolina during the period from May 29 through June 5 as follows:

Sunday, the 29th, slow skirmishing still going on continued all day and night. Monday, the 30th, we moved to the right and formed in a pine grove. Slow skirmishing going on along the line. Tuesday, the 31st, skirmishing continued. Wednesday, June, the 1st, skirmishing still continued. Orders to be ready to move at 12 o'clock. About 1 o'clock moved about one mile and formed near the front in reserve on the right. Thursday, the 2nd, about 12 o'clock we moved farther to the right[;] slow skirmishing and some cannonading continued. An uncommon hard rain fell to-day. Friday, the 3rd, slow skirmishing continued. Our regiment moved about one-half mile to the left for the purpose of supporting a battery; arrived at 10 o'clock in the night and worked all night fortifying our line.

96. *Official Records (Army)*, ser. 1, 38 (pt. 3):814. See also Dugger-Hodges Diary, May 25, 1864, in *Watauga Democrat*, June 18, 1891. Dugger states that on the morning of May 25 the regiment "Took up line of march, marched sixteen miles and arrived at Dallas, Ga. Formed a line of battle in reserve near Dallas about 1 o'clock, some sharp shooting going on in front. Hard fighting commenced about 3 o'clock and continued until dark, then ceased and remained quiet all night."

97. Dugger-Hodges Diary, May 26, 1864, in *Watauga Democrat*, June 18, 1891. Dugger wrote that on "Friday the 27th [there was] heavy skirmishing until about 3 o'clock [when] brisk fighting commenced[.] [H]eavy cannonading going on all day[.] [S]kirmishing continued all night." Dugger-Hodges Diary, May 27, 1864, in *Watauga Democrat*, June 18, 1891.

Saturday slow skirmishing and some cannonading still continued. Cloudy and rainy. We moved off about 10 o'clock that night towards the right. After going about two hundred yards took position in the works as a skirmishing line. Remained about one hour, and then moved off again. We waded the Georgia mud at an average depth of ten inches all night and until about 9 o'clock Sunday, the 5th, completing a march of about 5 miles. We rejoined our brigade and made a halt in dense woods. Drew a ration of whiskey and rested about one hour. Our company was then ordered on picket, we went at once and found our line about half a mile in front of the brigade. Some fighting on the left.[98]

Not surprisingly, the strain of a month's virtually uninterrupted combat began to tell upon Trigg's men. "They fight some every day and very often fight some after night," Lt. David Willis of the 54th Virginia wrote on May 30. "They fought hard awhile last nite and they are picket fighting every day from morning to night, and I believe half of the night. Indeed there have been only 2 days out of 28 that we were out of hearing of musketry. You might imagine how tired I am getting. . . ."[99]

Johnston's new line in the rugged, heavily wooded country northwest of Marietta faced northwest and was anchored on Lost, Pine, and Brush Mountains. Although daunting in appearance, the line was vulnerable because Pine Mountain, between Lost Mountain (on the left) and Brush Mountain, jutted somewhat ahead of its two sister peaks, exposing its defenders to enfilading fire. Fortunately for Johnston, a much better defensive position lay only two miles to the rear, where a long, high ridge known as Kennesaw Mountain dominated the surrounding country and guarded the railroad and roads leading to Marietta. Fighting tailed off for a few days while Sherman rested his troops, repaired the railroad, and brought up supplies and reinforcements.[100] Meanwhile, Johnston improved his defenses, including those on Kennesaw Mountain. On June 11 Sherman advanced slowly through the rain: McPherson moved toward Brush Mountain, defended by Hood; Thomas toward Pine Mountain, defended by Polk; and Schofield toward Lost Mountain, defended by Hardee. On the morning of June 14, Polk was killed on Pine Mountain by Federal artillery fire, and Maj. Gen. William W. Loring assumed temporary command of his corps. Fearing that one of Hardee's divisions was about to be cut off by Thomas, Johnston withdrew from Pine Mountain that night. By June 18 threats to his flanks led Johnston to abandon Lost and Brush Mountains as well. He then took a position anchored on Kennesaw Mountain. Meantime, Schofield worked his way southwest of Lost Mountain in an attempt to turn Johnston's left. Johnston countered by moving Hood from the extreme right to the extreme left of the Confederate line. By the evening of June 21, Hood confronted Schofield southwest of Marietta. Hardee was on Hood's right, and Loring was to the right of Hardee on Kennesaw Mountain. Private Dugger's diary continues for the period from June 11 through June 21:

Saturday, the 11th, slow skirmishing continued and stormy weather. Went on picket in the evening. Sunday, the 12th, yet on picket, sharp-shooting going on all the time, raining hard[,] relieved at 4 o'clock and returned to the breast-works. Monday, the 13th, sharp-shooting continued[,] a hard rain

98. Dugger-Hodges Diary, May 29-June 5, 1864, in *Watauga Democrat*, July 2, 1891.

99. David Willis to his mother, May 30, 1864 (typescript), Robertson Collection.

100. See Dugger-Hodges Diary, June 6-10, 1864, in *Watauga Democrat*, July 2, 1891.

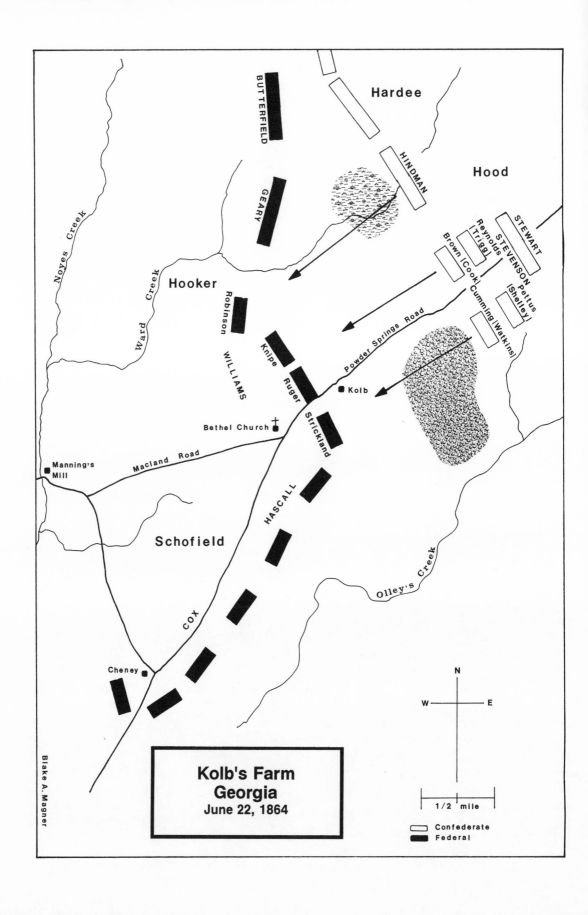

BUTTERFIELD

Hardee

HINDMAN

Hood

GEARY

STEWART

STEVENSON

Reynolds (Trigg)

Brown (Cook)

Pettus (Shelley)

Cumming (Watkins)

Hooker

Robinson

Noyes Creek

Ward Creek

WILLIAMS

Knipe

Ruger

Powder Springs Road

Kolb

Strickland

Bethel Church †

Manning's Mill

Macland Road

HASCALL

Schofield

COX

Olley's Creek

Cheney

N

W — E

Blake A. Magner

**Kolb's Farm
Georgia**
June 22, 1864

1/2 mile

☐ Confederate
■ Federal

fell to-day. Tuesday, the 14th, a short move to the right to-day . . . leaving a position where the shells were flying. . . . Wednesday the 15th some skirmishing and cannonading in front. Tuesday the 16th hard shelling commenced about 11 o'clock along the lines. A short move to the left and back again[;] commenced fortifying our position and worked until 11 o'cloc[k] that night. Friday the 17th at work again on our breastworks. At day-light some sharp shooting going on[;] heavy shelling in the evening on the left. Saturday the 18th sharp shooting continued[;] hard shelling in the evening ceased at night[.] 19th. Rallied two hours before day and moved to the extreme left. Arrived about 11 o'clock[,] some fighting going on. Rained hard all day. Moved from that position at 4 o'clock and passed through Marietta, Ga., at dark. Marched on about two miles through mud, until about 11 o'clock in the night. Halted in the woods and camped. Monday, the 20th, drew a ration of whiskey. Some cannonading in front. Moved about 10 o'clock and formed a line in reserve and went to fortify-ing our position. Rained hard to-day. About 5 o'clock we made a short move to the right and worked on a fort all night. Tuesday, the 21st, still at work on the fort. Some fighting on the left. Heavy can-nonading on Kenesaw [*sic*] mountain.[101]

Late on the afternoon of June 22, General Hood, acting entirely on his own initiative and without informing Johnston, launched an attack against the Federal right near the farm of a widow named Kolb. Stevenson's Division, supported on the right by Hindman and with Stewart's Division in reserve, advanced in two columns north and south of the Powder Springs Road. Brown's Brigade, commanded by Col. Edmund C. Cook and supported by Trigg's Brigade, was on the right; Cumming's Brigade, commanded by Col. Elihu P. Wat-kins and supported by Pettus's Brigade (under Col. Charles M. Shelley), on the left. Con-fronting Watkins and Shelley was a brigade of Brig. Gen. Milo S. Hascall's Army of the Ohio division; opposite Cook and Trigg were two brigades of Brig. Gen. Alpheus S. Wil-liams's Division, Hooker's Corps.

Contrary to Hood's professed reason for launching an unauthorized attack—namely, that the Federal right was in motion and vulnerable—Williams's men, supported by five ar-tillery batteries, were partially dug in atop a low ridge and waiting when the assault be-gan.[102] On the Confederate left, Watkins's Georgians, most of whom were inexperienced former militiamen, were halted by a single Federal regiment after two feeble thrusts. They then came under artillery fire and, in General Williams's words, "fled like scared sheep." Meanwhile, Cook and Trigg, on the right, fought somewhat better but fared considerably worse. "We had just fairly begun to pile up rails," Williams wrote, "when the heavy skir-mish line of the enemy poured out of the woods all along the open [field in our front] and advanced at a run. Three columns, massed, followed close and deployed in three and four lines."[103] Immediately, the Confederates were raked by a "murderous" crossfire of canister,

---

101. Dugger-Hodges Diary, June 11-21, 1864, in *Watauga Democrat*, July 2 and 9, 1891. Dugger's diary co-incides with ascertainable events through June 14; however, at some point between that date and June 22 the en-tries fall behind events by one day. In his entry for June 22, Dugger writes that "[we] moved at day light towards the left, passed through Marietta at 8 o'clock. Marched two miles and halted on the Powder spring road. Raining continually. . . ." Those events demonstrably occurred on the twenty-first.

102. The Federals learned from 58th and 60th North Carolina prisoners captured that day that an attack might be in the making. See Richard M. McMurry, "The Affair at Kolb's Farm," *Civil War Times Illustrated* 7 (December 1968): 21.

103. Alpheus Starkey Williams to Lewis Allen, July 17, 1864, and A. S. Williams to his children, July 10, 1864,

shell, and grape that became more enfilading and deadly as they approached the ridge.[104] "[B]efore they could get within reach of my infantry," Williams continued, "their columns were awfully plowed through [by our artillery] . . . and thrown into great confusion. Then . . . they reached a point where one brigade could reach them [with its fire]. It opened a volley of two thousand muskets! The devils, what was left of them, took refuge in a deep ravine, into which I plunged shot and shell. . . ."[105] "[A]fter enduring an hour of fruitless slaughter," another Federal officer wrote, "they were driven . . . in confusion and disorder back to their fortifications." "The[ir] numbers were formidable," Williams commented, "but the attack was indeed feeble. . . . [A]fter the first half-hour . . . [our] men considered the whole affair great sport."[106]

Private Dugger's account confirms the Federal reports quoted above: "[We] moved to the front and massed our forces about 2 o'clock, and about 4 o'clock went forward to make a charge on the enemy. We got within a hundred yards of their works, [where] we were repulsed and compelled to fall back a few steps to a huge rock at the branch [ravine] and lay under heavy fire until 9 o'clock in the night. We then fell back about one mile, suffered heavy losses; two wounded in our company." Pvt. John Fleeman of the 54th Virginia described the fight as a "terrible slaughter" and estimated that "The three brigades [presumably excluding Pettus's] lost one thousand, killed wounded and missing. Our brigade now is not as large as our regiment was when we left [the] Blackwater [River]."[107] In addition to

---

in Milo M. Quaife, ed., *From the Cannon's Mouth: The Civil War Letters of General Alpheus S. Williams* (Detroit: Wayne State University Press and the Detroit Historical Society, 1959), 333, 328, hereafter cited as Quaife, *Williams Letters*. The terrain, as described by Williams, "was an open elevated plateau with a deep gully along its front, beyond which the ground rose gently to the woods occupied by the rebel picket reserves in strong rifle-pits 500 or 600 yards distant." *Official Records (Army)*, ser. 1, 38 (pt. 2):31.

104. *Official Records (Army)*, ser. 1, 38 (pt. 2):49. "[O]ur men fell back into the clearing closely followed by the enemy's skirmishers," Samuel Toombs of the 13th New Jersey wrote, "and almost on their heels came a large body of rebel infantry, shouting and yelling. It was a splendid sight. The enemy moved forward on a run, deploying into line as they advanced and marched up steadily and in good order to attack. . . . Our skirmishers all reached the line in safety, and as the enemy ascended the hill directly in our front, a well directed volley was poured into them all along the line." Samuel Toombs, *Reminiscences of the War, Comprising a Detailed Account of the Experiences of the Thirteenth Regiment New Jersey Volunteers in Camp, On the March, and in Battle* (Orange, N.J.: printed at the *Journal* office, 1878), 141, hereafter cited as Toombs, *Reminiscences of the Thirteenth New Jersey*.

105. A. S. Williams to Lewis Allen, July 17, 1864, in Quaife, *Williams Letters*, 333. Although many of Cook's and Trigg's men took shelter in the ravine, others retreated to the woods from which they launched their attack.

106. *Official Records (Army)*, ser. 1, 38 (pt. 2):49; A. S. Williams to his children, July 10, 1864, in Quaife, *Williams Letters*, 328. "[T]he enemy . . . marched up within, perhaps, fifty yards of us," Samuel Toombs wrote, "their colors floating defiantly almost in our faces. The order [was] passed down the line to fix bayonets, and when they saw the determined faces in front of them and viewed the line of bristling steel which projected over the rail breastworks, they wavered and fell back in confusion. . . . Sixty-two dead bodies were buried in our front, and upwards of five hundred of the enemy's killed were buried along the whole line." According to the no doubt exaggerated report of a Federal artillery officer, Cook's and Trigg's troops "were completely broken and . . . utterly demoralized before they came within range of the musketry." Toombs, *Reminiscences of the Thirteenth New Jersey*, 141; *Official Records (Army)*, ser. 1, 38 (pt. 2):470.

107. Dugger-Hodges Diary, June 22, 1864, in *Watauga Democrat*, July 9, 1891; John Fleeman to his wife and children, June 23, 1864, in Jordan, *Gen. Jos. E. Johnston*, 42-43. "Our Regt lost 72 killed wounded & missing," Capt. James Clark of the 63rd Virginia wrote. "I don't believe in such charges. . . . We lost a good many men &

sustaining heavy casualties the hapless Confederates were subjected, according to General Williams, to the taunts of their tormentors as they huddled in the ravine awaiting nightfall: "They [our men] would call out, 'Come up here, Johnny Reb. Here is a weak place!' 'Come up and take this battery; we are Hooker's paper collar boys.' 'We've only got two rounds of ammunition, come and take us.' 'What do you think of Joe Hooker's Iron Clads?' and the like."[108]

Although Kolb's Farm was unarguably a defeat and a poor combat performance by Stevenson's Division, Hood made no such admission. In a brief report written on the day of the battle he said nothing about his severe casualties and implied that the Confederates were charging toward victory when "The pursuit was stopped because of . . . an enfilading [artillery] fire from a bald hill in front of Hardee. . . ." Stevenson was more forthright, admitting he was repulsed with "heavy" losses—"807 killed and wounded." However, he claimed also that "With perhaps some few exceptions the conduct of the troops was highly creditable."[109] That statement is contradicted by a number of Federal officers who described the attack with terms such as "confused mass," "utmost disorder," "confusion and disorder," "mixed up in the ravine," "completely broken," "utterly demoralized," and "retreating and disordered columns."[110] Casualties in the 58th North Carolina, according to statistics compiled from service records in this volume, were 10 men killed or mortally wounded, 48 wounded, 13 captured, and 4 missing.[111]

During the next few days fighting tailed off into skirmishing and sporadic artillery exchanges. Unable to turn Hood's flank because rain-flooded roads precluded hauling supplies more than a short distance from the railroad, Sherman lost patience and launched frontal assaults against Kennesaw Mountain and the Confederate center on June 27. Defended by Loring's Corps, Kennesaw Mountain was a long ridge with three peaks: Big Kennesaw,

gained nothing. . . . They plowed the ground in all around us, [the firing] came in [from] three directions." James Clark to Martha Clark, June 28, 1864, Clark Letters.

108. A. S. Williams to his children, July 10, 1864, in Quaife, *Williams Letters*, 328.

109. *Official Records (Army)*, ser. 1, 38 (pt. 3):760, 815. "About 5 p. m. we advanced," Stevenson wrote, "and soon struck the enemy, driving him quickly before us from his advanced works, which consisted of one line of logs and rail works complete, and one partially constructed. The fire under which this was done was exceedingly heavy, and the artillery of the enemy, which was massed in large force and admirably posted, was served with a rapidity and fatal precision which could not be surpassed. The nature of the ground over which we passed was most unfavorable to such a movement—the two right brigades moved for much of the way over open fields, the two left through dense undergrowth. The line thus became more irregular and broken every moment, and when the two right brigades had driven the enemy into their main works the line was so much broken and mixed up that, although the men were in good spirits and perfectly willing to make the attempt, it was not deemed practicable to carry the works by assault. The commands were halted and the best possible line . . . formed. Brown's [Cook's] and Trigg's . . . brigades lay in a swampy ravine within pistol-shot of the enemy's works; the other two brigades held the road on their left. The dead and wounded were all removed to the rear, and after holding our position for several hours, in compliance with the orders of General Hood, the division returned to its old position." *Official Records (Army)*, ser. 1, 38 (pt. 3):814-815.

110. *Official Records (Army)*, ser. 1, 38 (pt. 2):32 (first and second quotations), 49 (third quotation), 71 (fourth quotation), 470 (fifth and sixth quotations), 481 (seventh quotation).

111. The Battle of Kolb's Farm is known also as Zion Church and as Mount Zion Church. According to a casualty list published in the *North Carolina [Weekly] Standard* (Raleigh) of July 13, 1864, the regiment lost 6 men killed, 52 wounded, and 17 missing.

the northernmost and highest (700 feet); Little Kennesaw in the center (400 feet); and Pigeon Hill at the southern end (200 feet). South of Pigeon Hill, Hardee, still on Loring's left, defended a long, low ridge. Hood's Corps remained on the left of Hardee. Sherman planned a two pronged assault: three brigades of Maj. Gen. John A. Logan's Corps of the Army of the Tennessee would penetrate the gap between Little Kennesaw and Pigeon Hill; at the same time, two divisions of the Army of the Cumberland would break through Hardee's ridge-line position, wheel to the left, and flank Pigeon Hill. As a diversion, and in hopes of drawing reinforcements from Hardee and Loring, Schofield, on the extreme right, would demonstrate against Hood's Corps while simultaneously pushing south and threatening Johnston's left flank. If either Logan or Thomas were successful, heavy Federal reinforcements would pour into the breach, splitting Johnston's army.

On the morning of June 27, Logan's and Thomas's men, charging over steep, rock- and boulder-strewn ground into nightmarish mazes of "tanglefoot," abatis, and chevaux-de-frise, were shot to pieces by Confederate artillery and heavily entrenched infantrymen. More than 3,000 Federals were killed, wounded, and captured; Confederate casualties numbered slightly fewer than 1,000. The 58th North Carolina, still in position with the rest of Stevenson's Division near Kolb's farm, apparently took no part in the fighting. Private Dugger's laconic diary entry—"skirmishing, And cannonading all day"—reads very much the same for June 27 as for the previous two days. The regiment's casualties, if any, were very light.[112]

While Sherman's primary attacks on Kennesaw Mountain and the Confederate center were receiving bloody repulses, Schofield's diversionary movement against Johnston's flank made unexpected progress. By late afternoon one of Schofield's divisions, under Maj. Gen. Jacob D. Cox, crossed Olley's Creek and occupied a ridge overlooking Nickajack Creek, about one mile from the Chattahoochee River. If reinforced, Cox reported, he could turn Johnston's left. After pondering his options, Sherman decided to attempt such a movement, even though he would have to cut loose from the railroad north of Kennesaw Mountain. Several days elapsed while the dead were buried, supplies were accumulated, and roads dried out. On the night of July 2, Sherman began shifting his army to the right by marching the Army of the Tennessee behind the Army of the Cumberland. Johnston fell back from Kennesaw Mountain the same night and took position at Smyrna, between Nickajack and Rottenwood Creeks, about five miles below Marietta. "[H]eavy cannonading commenced at day-light," Private Dugger wrote in his diary on July 2, "lasted until 9 o'clock, skirmishing all day. At 4 o'clock P.M. our regiment went on picket and secretly

112. Dugger-Hodges Diary, June 27, 1864, in *Watauga Democrat*, July 9, 1891. Capt. Samuel M. Silver of Company K became acting commander of the 58th North Carolina on an unknown date between June 22 and June 30, 1864, and was reported as such on July 31, August 31, and September 20 of the same year. Capt. A. T. Stewart of Company E was reported as acting commander on July 10, 1864. Silver was appointed lieutenant colonel on October 29, 1864, to rank from September 1, 1864, and assumed permanent command of the regiment. His resignation, dated March 16, 1865, was accepted on April 9, 1865. Capt. Thaddeus C. Coleman, formerly an engineering officer on the staff of General Hood, was appointed lieutenant colonel of the regiment on the latter date. See *Official Records (Army)*, ser. 1, 38 (pt. 3):649, 656, 663, 672, 39 (pt. 2):853, 45 (pt. 1):1224.

retired at 12 o'clock that night. Fell back five miles toward the river, halted and commenced fortifying at 10 o'clock on Sunday the 3rd. . . ."[113]

Chastened by the bloodletting at Kennesaw Mountain, Sherman was in no mood for further frontal assaults. Johnston's new line at Smyrna was easily flanked on the left, and when McPherson and Schofield began massing their forces for such a movement Johnston retreated on the night of July 4.[114] He then took position just north of the Chattahoochee in a six-mile-long, heavily fortified line of redoubts, trenches, and stockades constructed previously by slave labor. Those formidable works, too, he was unable to hold.[115] Sherman ordered demonstrations by Thomas and McPherson to focus Johnston's attention on his left; at the same time, Schofield quietly began looking for a crossing upriver, on Johnston's right. The 58th North Carolina, on picket duty in front of Stevenson's Division on the left of Johnston's line, was involved in "a hot little skirmish fight" when "four lines of skirmish[ers] and one line of battle" charged their position on the evening of July 5. The attack was repulsed and the regiment "went back in reserve" at 9:00 P.M. Its casualties, if any, were light. At 5:30 P.M. on July 6, Trigg's Brigade crossed the Chattahoochee under shell fire and marched five miles downriver. After skirmishing near the river on the seventh, the 58th moved two miles farther downstream and camped for the night. "[S]ome sharpshooting" followed on the eighth. That same day Schofield, facing only light cavalry opposition, forced a crossing near Soap Creek, upstream from the Confederate right. By the time Johnston learned of that development on July 9, Schofield had an entire division on the south bank. During the night Johnston began withdrawing across the Chattahoochee to a position behind Peachtree Creek, five miles north of Atlanta. The 58th pulled out at midnight and reached the Peachtree Creek line at daylight on the tenth.[116]

During the next week Sherman completed his crossing of the Chattahoochee and wheeled his army in a clockwise quarter circle so as to advance on Atlanta from the east and north. On the night of July 17 Johnston received a telegram from Adjutant and Inspector General Samuel Cooper announcing that, because of his failure "to arrest the advance of the

113. Dugger-Hodges Diary, July 2-3, 1864, in *Watauga Democrat*, July 9, 1891.

114. In a dispatch sent at 8:45 P.M., McPherson informed Sherman that Maj. Gen. Grenville M. Dodge had crossed Nickajack Creek at Ruff's Mill, "r[u]n against Stevenson's division, and . . . captured a few prisoners. . . . As soon as the troops were over and in position, I directed Dodge to strengthen his skirmish line . . . and to assault the enemy's rifle-pits. The order was gallantly executed, the works taken, and some 50 prisoners captured; our loss not heavy. . . ." More detailed accounts by Federal officers who took part in the attack indicate that the fighting was fairly severe and Federal casualties fairly heavy: 140 killed and wounded according to General Dodge. It is not clear whether the 58th North Carolina was involved. Four members of the regiment were captured on that date, but they were on picket at the time. *Official Records (Army)*, ser. 1, 38 (pt. 5):47. See also *Official Records (Army)*, ser. 1, 38 (pt. 3):382.

115. For a description of those fortifications by the general who built them, see Francis A. Shoup, "Dalton Campaign–Works at Chattahoochee River–Interesting History," *Confederate Veteran* 3 (September 1895): 262-265. Sherman described the Chattahoochee works as "one of the strongest pieces of field-fortification I ever saw." William T. Sherman, *Memoirs of General William T. Sherman*, 2 vols. (New York: D. Appleton and Company, 1875; New York: Da Capo Press, 1984), 2:66.

116. Dugger-Hodges Diary, July 5 and 8, 1864, in *Watauga Democrat*, July 16, 1891. See also T. B. Hampton to J. C. Hampton, June [July] 7, 1864, Hampton Papers.

enemy to the vicinity of Atlanta," he was relieved of command of the Army of Tennessee. The new commander, who was to assume his duties immediately, was Johnston's combative subordinate, John Bell Hood. To the intense regret of most of his troops, Johnston turned over his command to Hood the next afternoon. "The change of commanders has caused a great deal of dissatisfaction among some of the men," Pvt. James M. Wysor of the 54th Virginia noted on July 19. "The whole army placed the most implicit confidence in Gen Johnston which they do not in Hood."[117]

In the meantime the Federal advance on Atlanta continued. By nightfall on July 19, McPherson, on Sherman's extreme left, had cut the Georgia Railroad and, unbeknown to Hood, occupied Decatur, six miles east of Atlanta. Schofield was advancing on a road just north of and parallel to the railroad, and Thomas, coming down from the north and separated from Schofield's right by a marshy, two-mile-wide gap, was astride Peachtree Creek. Confronting the Federals in a broad arc was Hood's 55,000-man army: Stewart's Corps (formerly Polk's and Loring's) on the left, Hardee's Corps in the center, and Hood's former corps (temporarily commanded by Maj. Gen. Benjamin F. Cheatham) on the right. Perceiving an opportunity to crush Thomas's isolated command, Hood ordered an assault for the afternoon of July 20.

Hood's plan called for Hardee and Stewart to attack *en echelon* from right to left at 1:00 P.M., trap Thomas in the wedge formed by the confluence of Peachtree Creek and the Chattahoochee, and destroy or capture his army. Cheatham would conduct a holding action against McPherson and Schofield. Execution of Hood's assault was delayed, however, by the belated discovery on the morning of the twentieth that McPherson overlapped Cheatham's right by more than two miles, had captured Decatur, and, confronted only by Joe Wheeler's cavalry, was advancing down the Georgia Railroad toward Atlanta. In an attempt to arrest that movement, Hood rotated his army slightly to the right, thereby stretching his line perilously thin in some places and creating gaps in others. That maneuver delayed his assault for three hours and failed to accomplish its object when Cheatham, for

117. *Official Records (Army)*, 38 (pt. 5):885; James M. Wysor to his father, July 19, 1864, Wysor Papers. See also James Clark to his father, July 15, 1864, and James Clark to his brother, August 10, 1864, Clark Letters. Wysor's letter is of interest also for the light it sheds on conditions and morale in Trigg's Brigade and Stevenson's Division. "Our reg't & in fact the whole brigade & division has suffered very heavy losses since the campaign opened," Wysor continued. "The brigade numbered when it left Dalton 1500 men [but] now it is reduced to one third of that number. Brown's men say that there are two 'killings' of them left. Our reg't which started with 460 muskets now reports 160 for duty. We have had the misfortune to fall on that part of the line where has been the hard fighting. We have been very much reduced in our brigade by desertion. Our Va. regiments have so disgraced themselves that I have no hopes of getting to Virginia soon. Our company however is at present trying to get a transfer to Gen [John H.] Morgan's command & I hope we will be successful for I hate to have to stay with men who have so disgraced themselves." Nevertheless, Wysor concluded, "the army is in the best of spirits & confident of whipping the Yankees whenever they have the temerity to attack us."

Wysor's reference to the Virginia regiments "disgracing themselves" was probably prompted by the mass desertion, "officers & all" (except for several absentees and three men who refused to go), of Company D, 54th Virginia, on the night of June 13, 1864. "I feel that we have disgraced the state of Va," Captain Clark wrote on July 15. "[W]e have as good men in our regt as there is in the Confederate States but a heap of them is getting tired of the war." James Clark to Martha Clark, June 16, 1864, and James Clark to his father July 15, 1864, Clark Letters. See also William Burwell Howell (54th Virginia) to Mary A. Howell (his wife), June 15 and July 13, 1864, Roster Document No. 1045 (transcripts), CWRP, NCDAH, hereafter cited as Howell Letters.

unknown reasons, halted about a mile north of the railroad. Finally, around 4:00 P.M., Hardee's troops, followed shortly thereafter by Stewart's, stormed forward through pine woods and heavy underbrush broken by networks of creeks and ravines. Taken by surprise but reacting with characteristic aplomb and sound judgment, Thomas called up artillery reinforcements and routed Bate's Division of Hardee's Corps just as it was about to capture a vital bridge over Peachtree Creek. Farther to the Federal right, two determined brigades of Loring's Division (Stewart's Corps) were repulsed by Federal reinforcements in fierce, seesaw fighting. Another of Stewart's divisions, commanded by Maj. Gen. Edward C. Walthall, flanked its opponents but was driven back by Federal artillery. Plans for an attack by Cleburne's reserve division were canceled when it developed that McPherson, still edging his way down the railroad against Wheeler's outmanned cavalry, was within a few miles of Atlanta and was directing artillery fire into the city streets. Cleburne's men were then rushed to the vicinity of Bald Hill, where they checked McPherson's advance. The 58th North Carolina, as part of Cheatham's command, was not involved in any serious fighting during the day. Dugger's diary entry for July 20 reports only "heavy skirmishing and c[a]nnonading all day and the night following."[118] Confederate casualties at the Battle of Peachtree Creek numbered about 2,500; Federal losses were approximately 1,900. No casualties were reported in the 58th North Carolina.

Fighting continued on the Confederate right on July 21 as McPherson unleashed a pulverizing bombardment of Cleburne's Division and captured Bald Hill. That night Hood withdrew Stewart's and Cheatham's Corps into the Atlanta defenses and dispatched Hardee's Corps to turn Sherman's exposed left flank (held by Maj. Gen. Frank P. Blair Jr.'s Corps) the next morning.[119] Wheeler's cavalrymen accompanied Hardee with orders to destroy McPherson's wagon train at Decatur. If Hardee's attack succeeded, Cheatham would attack McPherson from the east, driving a wedge between McPherson's right and Schofield's left.

After an exhausting march Hardee launched his assault at noon on July 22, approximately six hours late. By that time Brig. Gen. Grenville M. Dodge's Corps, which had been pinched out of Sherman's contracting line around Atlanta, was in position astride Sugar Creek, on Blair's left flank. Thus, with the exception of a quarter-mile gap between Dodge and Blair, Hardee's four divisions faced opposition along their entire front. A feeble attack on Dodge by Bate and W. H. T. Walker was easily repulsed, producing no significant result except the deaths of Walker and McPherson (who thus became the only Federal army commander killed in action during the war). Meantime, the men of Brig. Gen. Giles A. Smith's Division (Blair's Corps), on Dodge's right, leaped back and forth across their breastworks to repel uncoordinated attacks on their front and left flank by Brig. Gen. George Maney (commanding Cheatham's former division) and on their rear by Cleburne, who penetrated the gap between Dodge and Blair. Brig. Gen. Mortimer D. Leggett's troops, on Smith's

118. Dugger-Hodges Diary, July 20, 1864, in *Watauga Democrat*, July 16, 1891.

119. The 58th North Carolina "retired at 8 o'clock [P.M.]," Private Dugger wrote, "and fell back about two miles drawing in our lines around the suburbs of Atlanta, and soon fortified our position." Dugger-Hodges Diary, July 21, 1864, in *Watauga Democrat*, July 16, 1891.

right, were also rocked by Cleburne's attack and, like Smith's men, forced to fight during part of the afternoon with their backs to Atlanta.

Around 4:00 P.M., after coordinated front-and-rear attacks by two Confederate brigades drove Smith back to a line perpendicular to Leggett, Hood ordered Cheatham to launch his frontal assault. Stevenson's Division, on Cheatham's right, moved against Leggett and Brig. Gen. William Harrow's Division of Logan's Corps; in the center and on the left, Hindman's Division (commanded by John C. Brown) and Clayton's followed *en echelon*, attacking Logan's other division, commanded by Brig. Gen. Morgan L. Smith (on Harrow's right). Two of Brown's brigades punched through the Federal line at a railroad cut but then received an inexplicable order from Brown to withdraw. In the meantime, two "impetuo[u]s" but ill-sustained attacks on Leggett by Stevenson were repulsed "in handsome style" by "A few well-directed volleys."[120] A four-brigade attack by Hardee on Bald Hill was then beaten back in fighting that, at some points, was hand-to-hand. Darkness brought an end to the carnage.

The part played by Trigg's Brigade in the Battle of Atlanta (also known as the Battle of Bald Hill) is obscure. According to one recent account, all four of Stevenson's brigades were involved in Cheatham's attack: Trigg on the right, Pettus in the center, Brown's Brigade (commanded by Col. Joseph B. Palmer) on the left, and Cumming's Brigade following Pettus in support. However, Albert Castel, the leading modern authority on the Atlanta Campaign, states that the assault was made by "Stevenson's Division *or a portion thereof* [emphasis added]. . . ."[121] In the case of the 58th North Carolina, that qualification seems justified: only one member of the regiment was killed on July 22 and ten more, who may have been deserters, fell into Federal hands.[122] The likelihood is that the 58th was manning a portion of the Atlanta fortifications or in reserve during Stevenson's two assaults. That conclusion is supported by the July 22 entry in Private Dugger's diary, the only contemporary source located for the 58th's activities on that date: "heavy fighting on the right on Gen. Hardee's lines. Some success in capturing prisoners and artilery [*sic*], certain amount not known. One hundred of our regiment went on picket at night, myself in the number."[123]

120. *Official Records (Army)*, ser. 1, 38 (pt. 3):546 (first and second quotations); Albert Castel, *Decision in the West: The Atlanta Campaign of 1864* (Lawrence, Ks.: University Press of Kansas, 1992), 405 (third quotation), hereafter cited as Castel, *Decision in the West*. See also *Official Records (Army)*, ser. 1, 38 (pt. 3):565. Castel states that Stevenson's Division failed "even to dislodge the Union pickets and pioneer troops . . . occupying the former Confederate trenches west of the bald hill."

121. Castel, *Decision in the West*, 405. See also William R. Scaife, *The Campaign for Atlanta* (n.p., 1985), Plate XIV. Col. Joseph B. Palmer of the 18th Regiment Tennessee Infantry is not to be confused with Col. John B. Palmer of the 58th Regiment N.C. Troops. Joseph B. Palmer became commander of a brigade that *included* the 58th North Carolina shortly thereafter. Be it noted also that one of Sherman's division commanders during the Atlanta Campaign was Maj. Gen. John *M.* Palmer.

122. Casualty figures compiled by Jeffrey C. Weaver for his history of the 63rd Virginia indicate that 1 member of that regiment was killed, 2 wounded, and 14 captured on July 22. Weaver's history of the 54th Virginia indicates that 2 men were killed, 2 wounded, and 33 captured at Atlanta on July 20-22. Statistics compiled for this volume indicate that no casualties were sustained on July 22 by the 60th North Carolina. Weaver, *63rd Virginia*, 98; Weaver, *54th Virginia*, 157.

123. Dugger-Hodges Diary, July 22, 1864, in *Watauga Democrat*, July 16, 1891.

Total Confederate casualties during the Battle of Atlanta were approximately 5,500; Federal losses numbered about 3,700.

During the night Hood withdrew Hardee's frazzled corps to the southwest to protect the Macon and Western Railroad, his one remaining supply route. After considering his options, Sherman began shifting the Army of the Tennessee from his left wing to his right, thereby threatening the railroad—which ran south from Atlanta—from a less exposed westerly direction. By the evening of July 27 the Army of the Tennessee, advancing with great caution under its new commander, Maj. Gen. Oliver O. Howard, was just north of the Lick Skillet road near Ezra Church. Hood countered by shifting two divisions of Cheatham's former corps, now commanded by Lt. Gen. Stephen D. Lee, to the Lick Skillet road, where they arrived after nightfall. On July 28 Lee launched a series of ill-considered, uncoordinated, and bloody assaults that ultimately resulted in refusals by some units to obey orders. Subsequent attacks in the same vicinity by Loring's and Walthall's Divisions of Stewart's Corps produced "desperate fight[ing] and heavy loss" but failed to dislodge Howard.[124] Private Dugger's diary indicates that the 58th North Carolina (and, very probably, the remainder of Trigg's Brigade) was in or near the Atlanta fortifications during the battle. "At 1 o'clock p. m. [on July 27]," Dugger wrote, "we moved from that position [the one they had occupied at Atlanta since July 22] and formed behind in the . . . suburbs . . . and remained [there] until dark. We [then] moved back to the front works on the left of Kowan's [Capt. James J. Cowan's] battery and remained until 12 o'clock in the night, then rallied and went on picket. Thursday, the 28th., yet on picket, and heavy skirmishing and cannonading all day. Relieved from picket at 9 o'clo[c]k and returned to the breast works."[125]

During the next six days the 58th remained in position in the Atlanta fortifications. "Friday [July] the 29th., skirmishing and cannonading," Private Dugger wrote, "went on picket that night. Saturday the 30th., still on picket, sharp-shooting and cannonading continued. Sunday the 31st., all still to-day; raining in the evening. Monday, August the 1st., a short move to the right, skirmishing and cannonading continued. . . . [T]he brigade, except what went on picket in front of the Militia, moved to the left at dark. Tuesday, the 2nd, on picket today in front of Militia. Picket duty heavy at present. Relieved from picket ot [at] 8 o,clock [sic] P. M[.] and returned to the Brigade at the front works on the Marietta road. Wednesday, the 3rd, some sharp-shooting in front, the enemy in two hundred yards of our works. A close place for 'Rebs.'"[126]

---

124. *Official Records (Army)*, ser. 1, 38 (pt. 3):872.

125. Dugger-Hodges Diary, July 27-28, 1864, in *Watauga Democrat*, July 16, 1891. Federal casualties during the Battle of Ezra Church numbered 632; Confederate losses were probably in the neighborhood of 3,000. See Castel, *Decision in the West*, 434.

126. Dugger-Hodges Diary, July 29-August 3, 1864, in *Watauga Democrat*, July 16 and 23, 1891. In a letter dated August 2, 1864, Chaplain George T. Gray of the 63rd Virginia stated that "When we left Dalton I had 600 men in my Regiment, now I have 200. My Brigade [Trigg's] had 1600 men, now it has 600." George Thomas Gray to his wife, August 2, 1864, Robertson Collection. Pvt. James M. Wysor of the 54th Virginia noted in a letter dated August 7 that any duty "was preferable to the front where for 90 days not a day had passed in which we had not heard the boom of the cannon and but very few that we had not heard the rattle of musketry. I never was so tired of anything in my life as I was of the never ceasing boom boom of the cannon and pop pop bang bang of the skirmishers." J. M. Wysor to his father, August 7, 1864, Wysor Papers. See also T. B. Hampton to J. C. Hampton, August 7, 1864, Hampton Papers.

On August 6 Sherman made a new effort to extend his line west and south of Atlanta when Schofield's Army of the Ohio, which had taken a position on Howard's right, launched an attack at Utoy Creek, a few miles southwest of Ezra Church. There it collided with Bate's entrenched division, temporarily assigned to Lee's Corps. Bate inflicted a stinging repulse on one of Schofield's brigades, and the Confederates fell back to a new line of fortifications covering the railroad as far south as East Point. Federal losses in the Battle of Utoy Creek numbered about 300; Confederate casualties probably did not exceed twenty. Stevenson's Division, which had been temporarily detached from Lee's command and assigned to Hardee in exchange for Bate's Division, remained "immediately in front of Atlanta" during the battle and suffered no casualties. During the next three weeks the 58th North Carolina presumably continued to occupy its position on the Marietta road.[127] On about August 23, Trigg's and Brown's Brigades were consolidated under the command of Col. Joseph B. Palmer.[128]

Frustrated by his failure to outflank Hood incrementally, Sherman made tentative plans to cut loose from his railroad supply line and swing his entire army around the Confederate left. In the interim, he rested his weary men and attempted to blast Hood out of Atlanta with artillery. The bombardment began on August 9 with a barrage of 3,000 projectiles and continued at high levels of intensity for the next two weeks, producing moderate damage but only a handful of casualties. Meantime, a cavalry raid in which Sherman placed high hopes failed to seriously damage the Macon and Western Railroad. By the evening of August 23 Sherman was convinced that his new plan to flank Hood out of Atlanta would have to be implemented.

Sherman's pullback from the Atlanta fortifications began on the night of August 25. By the afternoon of August 28, two of Howard's corps had reached Fairburn, thirteen miles southwest of Atlanta and about the same distance northwest of Jonesborough, on the Macon and Western. Thomas, with two corps, was at Red Oak, three miles northeast of Fairburn. Apprehending that he would have to divide his army to defend both Atlanta and the railroad, Hood dispatched Hardee's and Lee's Corps on the evening of August 30 to intercept the advancing Federals.[129] Meanwhile, Stevenson's Division, including the 58th North

---

127. *Official Records (Army)*, ser. 1, 38 (pt. 3):763. An inspection report for Trigg's Brigade dated August 20, 1864, indicates that 270 members of the 58th North Carolina were present for duty. The condition of the men's clothing was "Bad," their military bearing "Soldierly," their military appearance "Indiff[erent]," their discipline "Good," their military instruction "Loose," and their drill "Indifferent." The 60th North Carolina, 54th Virginia, and 63rd Virginia numbered 139, 146, and 183 men respectively, giving the brigade a total strength of 738. Quoted in Weaver, *54th Virginia*, 126-127.

128. Trigg was furloughed to southwest Virginia on August 23 because of ill health and remained there on special duty for the rest of the war. Brown assumed command of Bate's Division after Bate was wounded on August 10. Palmer's newly constituted brigade comprised the 3rd, 18th, 26th, 32nd, and 45th Tennessee regiments, the 23rd Tennessee battalion, the 58th and 60th North Carolina, and the 54th and 63rd Virginia. See *Official Records (Army)*, ser. 1, 38 (pt. 3):672, 39 (pt. 2):853, 45 (pt. 1):1224. The Brown-Trigg consolidation is mistakenly thought by some historians to have taken place subsequent to the Battle of Jonesborough (August 31-September 1, 1864). For a discussion of that question, see footnote 160 on pages 480-481 of the history of the 60th North Carolina in this volume.

129. Hood believed that Sherman was trying to draw off his forces from Atlanta and launch an attack there. Consequently, he himself remained in the city.

Carolina, was relieved by Georgia militiamen in the Atlanta fortifications on the night of August 26 and began a slow march southwestward. According to the diary of Cpl. Gilbert W. Hodges of the 58th, the men "Moved to the Left at 10 o'clock, passing through Atlanta[,] marched 5 miles and halted at 12 o'clock." On the twenty-seventh the regiment "arrived on [the] extreme left" to find the "Yankees gone from their works [and apparently] falling back. . . ."[130] During the next three days the 58th moved an additional four or five miles to its left and rejoined Lee's Corps. At 11:00 on the night of August 30, in accordance with Hood's orders to Hardee and Lee, it set out for Jonesborough, which it reached at noon the next day.[131]

By midafternoon on August 31, Hardee's and Lee's troops, under the overall command of Hardee, were in position at Jonesborough and ready to attack. Hardee's plan called for his own corps (commanded by Cleburne) to move forward on the Confederate left at 3:00 with Cleburne's Division (commanded by Brig. Gen. Mark P. Lowrey) on the left, Bate's Division (commanded by John C. Brown) on the right, and Cheatham's Division (commanded by George Maney) in support. As soon as the noise of battle indicated that Cleburne was fully engaged, Lee, on Cleburne's right, would attack with Anderson's Division on the right and Stevenson's Division (bolstered by a brigade from Clayton's Division and another from Brown's) on the left. Palmer's Brigade was in Stevenson's first line between the brigades of Pettus (on its left) and Brig. Gen. William F. Brantley (of Anderson's Division).

Shortly after 3:00 P.M. Lee, mistaking the sound of heavy skirmishing on his left for Cleburne's attack, prematurely launched his assault. Most of Anderson's units advanced with middling élan but, confronted by field fortifications and raked by deadly musketry, quickly went to ground. One brigade fled. Stevenson's assault was probably even less determined and effectual. On the Confederate left, Lowrey's charging men came under flanking fire from a division of dismounted Federal cavalry, veered off in pursuit of the retreating troopers, and took themselves out of the battle. Meantime, Brown's men were driven back with heavy casualties after they stumbled into a ravine. A feeble attack by Maney's Division was repulsed amid a chorus of Federal catcalls. In forty-five minutes the farcical battle was over.

The precise activities of Palmer's Brigade at Jonesborough on August 31 are unknown. Corporal Hodges wrote that the men "reached Jonesboro, Ga., at 12 o'clock [noon] on the 31st. Came in contact with the enemy in which Hardee's and Lee's corps charged them, but inflicting but little damage. . . . Our loss [presumably Cleburne's and Lee's

---

130. Dugger-Hodges Diary, August 26-27, 1864, in *Watauga Democrat*, July 23, 1891. The last diary entry made by Private Dugger is dated August 3, 1864. Dugger's fate is unknown, but it appears that he was killed or mortally wounded in action, perhaps on August 4. A soldier identified in the *Watauga Democrat* as "Gilliam Hodges" but who was probably Cpl. Gilbert W. Hodges of Company D began making entries in Dugger's diary a few days later and continued to do so through November 30.

131. Castel writes that "At 1:30 P.M. the last of Lee's units reach Jonesboro. His troops have had little sleep for two nights, they have marched from twelve to fifteen miles over rough roads and sometimes no roads, many are shoeless and footsore, all are half-exhausted and hungry, and hundreds have dropped out along the way, unable or unwilling to keep going. Never has Major General Patton Anderson, veteran of most of the Army of Tennessee's campaigns starting with Shiloh, seen so much straggling." Castel, *Decision in the West*, 499.

combined] was considerably [*sic*]." In any case, all four regiments suffered minor casualties. The 58th North Carolina lost four men killed or mortally wounded and four wounded. Total Confederate casualties numbered at least 2,200; the Federals lost fewer than 200 men.[132]

While Hardee and Howard were locked in battle on August 31, Federal units reached the railroad near Rough and Ready and several other points north of Jonesborough. That evening Hood, unaware that most of Sherman's army was south of Atlanta and fearing an imminent assault on the city, recalled Lee's Corps from Hardee. Shortly after midnight Hood learned of Hardee's repulse at Jonesborough. Concluding that Atlanta was no longer defensible, he issued orders to evacuate the city that night and retreat toward Macon. Stewart's Corps and the Georgia militia were to march southeast on the McDonough road; Lee's Corps was halted en route to Atlanta and ordered to defend the city's southern approaches; Hardee was to remain at Jonesborough to hold open the McDonough road.

In the wee hours of the morning of September 1, Lee's men, in accordance with Hood's original order to return to Atlanta, set out and, in the words of Corporal Hodges, "marched hard all day." Six miles from their destination they were intercepted by a courier from Hood bearing new orders to "cover the evacuation of the city." That afternoon Sherman, unaware that Hood was about to abandon Atlanta and that Hardee was isolated and vulnerable, ordered an attack at Jonesborough by two of Thomas's newly arrived corps. Units of Brig. Gen. Jefferson C. Davis's Corps succeeded in punching a hole in Hardee's line, but darkness arrived before Maj. Gen. David S. Stanley's Corps could get into position to exploit the advantage. During the night the evacuation of Atlanta was completed by Hood as planned. Troops belonging to Maj. Gen. Henry W. Slocum's Corps occupied the city on the morning of September 2. By the evening of September 3, Lee was reunited with Stewart and Hardee at Lovejoy's Station. After skirmishing with Hood at Lovejoy's on the fourth and fifth, Sherman moved north to Atlanta to rest and refit his men, plan his next campaign, and claim his prize.[133]

Between September 12 and 21 a truce between the two armies remained in effect while the white civilian population of Atlanta was forcibly evacuated. In the meantime, Sherman and Hood pondered their next moves. Hood, with characteristic aggressiveness, decided to move the Army of Tennessee west and then north of Atlanta and cut Sherman's Western and Atlantic supply line to Chattanooga. He would then attack and destroy the starving Yankees as they retreated through the desolate woods and mountains of North Georgia. As an initial step toward implementing that strategy, Hood marched west from Lovejoy's Station toward Palmetto on September 18. The 60th North Carolina probably reached Palmetto on the nineteenth. During the next two days the rest of Hood's command, now reduced to approximately 40,000 men, arrived and began constructing field fortifications. On September 29, following a strategy conference with President Jefferson Davis, Hood moved six miles north to Cross Anchor. The next day he crossed the Chattahoochee on a pontoon bridge near Campbellton and reached Dark Corner, about eight miles from

132. Dugger-Hodges Diary, August 31, 1864, in *Watauga Democrat*, July 23, 1891.

133. Dugger-Hodges Diary, September 1, 1864, in *Watauga Democrat*, July 23, 1891; *Official Records (Army)*, ser. 1, 38 (pt. 3):765.

Pray's Church. Pausing briefly to tear up track in the vicinity of Marietta, he then advanced against the railroad villages of Acworth and Big Shanty, which Stewart's Corps captured with their small garrisons on October 4. After an unsuccessful attempt by Maj. Gen. Samuel G. French's Division to capture Allatoona on October 5, the men continued their northward trek, reaching Cedartown on October 8, Armuchee on October 11, and capturing Dalton on October 13. Sherman, having left Slocum's Corps behind to hold Atlanta, trailed northward in Hood's wake, trying to stay close to the elusive Confederate but evincing little interest in initiating a battle. Sherman's plans to march across central Georgia to Savannah were already made; however, Thomas, who had been sent north to defend Tennessee and was receiving reinforcements from as far afield as Missouri, was not yet strong enough to take on Hood alone. It was therefore necessary that Sherman be available to do so. When Hood appeared ready to offer battle at La Fayette on October 17, Sherman decided to jettison his passive strategy and accommodate him. However, to Hood's chagrin, his corps commanders unanimously opposed another fight with the superior Federal army. Hood therefore decided to advance into Tennessee. There, after defeating Thomas, he would invade Kentucky and, perhaps, join Robert E. Lee in Virginia.

On October 20 Hood began moving southwest down the Chattooga River valley toward Gadsden, Alabama, which he reached the next day. Sherman trailed behind as far as Gaylesville, Alabama, thirty miles northeast of Gadsden. There he abandoned the pursuit, dispatched two corps under Schofield to reinforce Thomas, and returned to Atlanta. On November 15, after destroying the war-making capacity of the city and (probably by more or less welcome accident) a good deal more of it besides, he cut his telegraph lines to the North and departed with 62,000 men and 64 cannons in the general direction of Savannah and the Atlantic Ocean. Meantime, the Army of Tennessee marched northwest from Gadsden toward Guntersville, Alabama, on October 22. There, Hood and Gen. P. G. T. Beauregard (his department commander) had agreed, the army would cross the Tennessee River. However, upon reaching Bennettsville that afternoon Hood turned west, bypassing Guntersville. During the next three days he moved northwest through Walnut Grove and Brooksville to Somerville. Captain Harper, who had returned to duty after a long convalescence from a wound received at Resaca, reported "poor and barren country," "Clear, Cool, Pleas[ant]" weather, and "badly blistered" feet. At "the shabby . . . town of Summerville [*sic*]" on October 26, Hood sent Lee's Corps west through the rain toward Moulton and marched with the rest of his troops to Decatur, on the Tennessee River.[134] On October 27 he skirmished with the Decatur garrison, and, concluding that the enemy's defenses were too strong to force a crossing, he moved west toward Courtland on the twenty-ninth.[135] Lee's

---

134. Harper Diary, October 24 (first three quotations) and 26 (fourth quotation), 1864. See also G. W. F. Harper to Ella Harper, October 26, 1864, Harper Papers.

135. "After leaving Gadsden," Asst. Q.M. George P. Erwin of the 60th North Carolina wrote, "the army went by Decatur and found the Yankees there fortified, not the Yankee army but a small garrison of some two thousand. The place was immediately surrounded & closely invested–The garrison ordered to surrender but the confounded Yanks wouldn't obey & Genl Hood left them, perfectly disgusted with their disobedience of his orders. There was a good deal of cannonading & some skirmishing, but we made no attempt to take the place." George Phifer Erwin to his sister, November 5, 1864, George Phifer Erwin Papers, SHC, hereafter cited as Erwin Papers.

Corps reached the vicinity of Courtland on the twenty-eighth and marched to a point two miles east of Leighton the next day. "High living – potatoes, apples, peaches" and "Fine farming country," Captain Harper noted amiably in his diary, but many deserted plantations and "many houses burnt by Yankees."[136]

On the evening of October 29 Hood reached Courtland with Stewart's and Cheatham's Corps. After Confederate engineers pronounced the Courtland ford unsuitable, he continued marching westward and caught up with Lee at Tuscumbia on the thirtieth. "The march was not disagreeable," Asst. Q.M. George P. Erwin of the 60th North Carolina wrote from Tuscumbia, "having good roads & beautiful weather except two days, cloudy with a little rain."[137] Two brigades of Maj. Gen. Edward Johnson's Division and one brigade of Clayton's Division, both of Lee's Corps, crossed the river on the same day and drove a small enemy force out of Florence. The remaining brigades of the two divisions were across by noon on October 31. Stevenson's Division, including the 58th North Carolina and the rest of Palmer's Brigade, crossed on the morning of November 2. The regiment probably remained near the river working on breastworks on November 3 and 4, then moved six miles north on the Lawrenceburg road with other elements of Stevenson's Division on the fifth. On November 6, after a cavalry skirmish in which the 58th took no part, the division fell back toward Florence. The next day it "moved out seven miles on the Huntsville road [east of Florence]" with the rest of Lee's Corps.[138]

On November 20 Hood, having delayed his advance for three weeks to await the arrival of Forrest's cavalry from West Tennessee and badly needed supplies from Corinth, set off through falling snow in the direction of Pulaski. Although poorly clad, shod, and fed, his men, particularly the homeward bound Tennesseans, were cheerful. Many were returning home for the first time in almost a year and, after a respite of more than two months from the almost daily battles and skirmishes of the Atlanta Campaign, their fighting spirit seemed restored. Many believed also that Hood had categorically renounced and forbidden frontal attacks against field works: a conviction in which they would soon find themselves sadly, and in many cases terminally, mistaken.

Hood's object in advancing toward Pulaski was to surprise and capture Schofield's outnumbered command, which was en route to Nashville and beyond the range of immediate help from Thomas. To accomplish that, he planned to seize Columbia, about thirty miles north of Pulaski, and trap Schofield on the south bank of the Duck River. The army would move in three columns as far as Mount Pleasant—Cheatham's Corps on the left, Lee's in the center, and Stewart's on the right. The columns would then unite for the eight-mile push to Columbia. The 58th North Carolina marched eight miles on November 20 and camped on the banks of Shoal Creek. On the twenty-first it made another ten miles through an all-day snow. "[W]e started this morning through mud from four to twenty inches deep," General French recorded in his diary, "and through snow that the keen wind blew in our faces.

136. Harper Diary, October 28 (first quotation) and 29 (second and third quotations), 1864. "Fine camping place and a big rabbit hunt," Harper added on the twenty-ninth. See also W. B. Howell to M. A. Howell, November 2, 1864, Howell Letters; W. A. King (54th Virginia) to Mary E. King (his wife), November 2, 1864, King Letters.

137. G. P. Erwin to his sister, November 5, 1864, Erwin Papers.

138. G. P. Erwin to his sister, November 7, 1864, Erwin Papers.

In the afternoon we encamped by the roadside, near a deserted habitation. The weather is bitterly cold, and the snow falling. Sleeping on the ground covered with snow."[139] The regiment passed through West Point on November 22, reached Rock Creek on the twenty-third, marched eighteen miles (passing through Henryville and crossing the Buffalo River) on the twenty-fourth, and arrived with Lee's Corps at Mount Pleasant on the twenty-fifth. Captain Harper described the march in his diary:

20th: Cold, Rain. Moved at 7 A.M. Roads exceedingly muddy. Disagreeable day. Marched on road towards West Point etc. Camped at Creek say 10 miles from T[ennessee line].

21st: A.M. Snowing and Wind. P.M. Cloudy and Cold. Marched at 7 A.M. Cold and disagreeable. Thinly settled country. Crossed State line say 17 miles for [from] F[lorence]. Camped say 5 miles beyond.

22nd: A.M. hard freeze. Blowing snow and cold. Ground frozen as hard as to bear up artillery. Moved at 8 A.M. Passed W. Springs 1 mile. West point 8 ms.– 2 ms. north of Wh. we camped. Night bitter cold. Slept well before large Hickory log fire. . . .

23rd: Clear, Cold. . . . Marched at 11 A.M. Camped at 3 P.M. having made about 5 miles.

24th: Clear, Cold. P.M. cloudy . . . [and] ground frozen hard. Marched at 7 A.M. After 10 miles struck Columbia and Waynesboro Pike and 5 miles further [we reached] Henryville. Camped 5 miles N[orth] of Henryville.

25th: Clear, Cool, Pleas[ant]. Marched at 7 A.M. on Pike. Mcadam rode [sic] at 4 miles at Bigbee Creek. . . . Foraging expedition with Doctor H.– Sumptuous dinner at Miss Griffithens [sic]. Mt. Pleasant 10 miles from last Camp. Overtook Brigade in camp 3 miles north of Mt. P. Lovely Country. Apples, Pumpkins etc.

26th: Cold. Rain all day. Marched at 7 A.M. Passed thro' beautiful country. . . . 58th and 60th [North Carolina] in advance of corps. Relieved cavalry on picket– Slight skirmishing.[140]

Lee reached Columbia on November 26. There he found Schofield, who had begun withdrawing from Pulaski on the twenty-second and won a narrow race with Forrest's cavalry to the Duck River crossings on the twenty-fourth. By the evening of November 27, Hood had the rest of his army up and in position to attack the next day; however, Schofield crossed the Duck during the night and entrenched on the north bank. Stevenson's Division entered Columbia before daylight on the twenty-eighth. "There was considerable skirmishing across the river during the day and some artillery firing," Lee reported, "resulting in nothing of importance."[141]

In a new attempt to cut Schofield's line of retreat, Hood sent Stewart's and Cheatham's Corps and Edward Johnson's Division of Lee's Corps across the Duck a few miles above Columbia on the morning of November 29 with orders to capture Spring Hill, about eight miles north of Columbia on the Nashville Pike. The remainder of Lee's Corps, including the 58th North Carolina, remained at Columbia and attempted to hold Schofield in place

139. Samuel Gibbs French, *Two Wars: An Autobiography* (Nashville: *Confederate Veteran*, 1901), 290. Assistant Quartermaster Erwin had forecast trouble with the roads as early as November 7. "It has been cloudy with occasional rain," he wrote, "enough to put the roads in very bad condition . . . for a week & last night it rained very hard all night. Terrible for army operations." G. P. Erwin to his sister, November 7, 1864, Erwin Papers.

140. Harper Diary, November 20-26, 1864.

141. *Official Records (Army)*, ser. 1, 45 (pt. 1):687.

with demonstrations. When Schofield began evacuating the town around noon, Lee made "a display of pontoons, running several of them down to the river under a heavy artillery and musketry fire."[142] Shortly thereafter, Pettus's Brigade crossed the river in boats, capturing a line of enemy rifle pits and a number of prisoners. A pontoon bridge was then laid down, and Stevenson's entire command crossed. The last of Schofield's troops pulled out around 2:30 A.M. on November 30. Leaving the 58th North Carolina behind in Columbia to guard prisoners, Lee immediately set off in pursuit.

For the men of the 58th, the order detaching them for guard duty on November 30 was the most fortunate they received during the war. As a result, they escaped the hideous slaughter inflicted upon Hood's army at the Battle of Franklin that afternoon and the less bloody but, for the Confederate cause, even more ruinous defeat sustained at Nashville on December 15-16. The extreme hardships and privations experienced by the Army of Tennessee, including short rations and marching shoeless and ill-clad through ice and snow, likewise fell to their lot in more moderate portions. Captain Harper, with his usual genius for making himself comfortable, took lodgings in Columbia at the home of a local lady, found time to take walks and tea, enjoyed an "Elegant dinner" at the home of a Mr. Gordon on December 13, and read a novel (Sir Walter Scott's *Quentin Durward*). "[W]e live on the fat of the land," Harper wrote contentedly on December 11, "having almost realized the stories of Tenn. Regts. boys that the fat hogs here walked about ready cleaned & dressed with a knife & fork sticking in their backs. . . ."[143]

On December 14 the 58th departed for Corinth with 1,600 Federal prisoners. A two-inch blanket of snow and sleet that had covered the ground since December 9 began melting the same day, but rain on December 15, 16, and 17 turned the roads into ribbons of mud. After passing through Mount Pleasant and Lawrenceburg the column reached Garner's Ferry, about twelve miles west of Florence, on the nineteenth, crossed the Tennessee River in a cold rain the next day, and moved through snow and sleet to Barton's Station on the twenty-first. Leaving the "sick and barefooted" at Barton's Station, the men of the 58th marched their prisoners seven miles west on December 22 to await rail transportation near Cherokee Station.[144] They then moved in three groups to Corinth, where the last of them arrived on Christmas Day.

The 58th North Carolina's respite at Corinth was brief. In response to a Federal cavalry raid on the Mobile and Ohio Railroad in the vicinity of Okolona, about sixty-five miles to the south, the regiment departed by rail at 10:00 A.M. on December 27. Finding the bridge near Tupelo burned by the enemy, the men detrained and marched down the tracks to Okolona, which they reached on the morning of December 29. By that time the Federals were retreating westward, and the 58th went into bivouac. The regiment remained quietly at Okolona until January 14 and then marched toward Tupelo. It rejoined Palmer's Brigade in

---

142. *Official Records (Army)*, ser. 1, 45 (pt. 1):687.

143. Harper Diary, December 13, 1864 (see also December 5-8 and 10, 1864); G. W. F. Harper to Ella Harper, December 11, 1864, Harper Papers. After finishing the Scott novel, Harper began work on *Peter Simple*, by Frederick Marryat.

144. Harper Diary, December 22, 1864. See also G. W. F. Harper to Ella Harper, December 23, 1864, Harper Papers.

camp two miles west of Tupelo the next day. There, on January 23, Hood was relieved at his own request as commander of the Army of Tennessee and replaced temporarily by Lt. Gen. Richard Taylor. Joseph E. Johnston resumed command of the remnants of his former army on February 23.[145]

In the meantime, President Jefferson Davis reached a decision in mid-January to send reinforcements from the Army of Tennessee to Georgia, where Sherman had left a smoldering trail of destruction from Atlanta to the ocean and was currently resting on his laurels in Savannah. The first units of Lee's Corps departed Tupelo by rail on January 19 and were followed three days later by the 58th North Carolina. The regiment reached Okolona on the twenty-third after a "Cold ride on Freight cars," arrived at Demopolis on the evening of the twenty-fourth, and departed for Selma at nightfall on the twenty-fifth. "Slept well on box car without fire," Captain Harper noted in his diary. After arriving at Selma at 11:00 P.M., the men were transported by steamboat up the Alabama River to Montgomery, which they reached at midnight on January 26. Following a two-day layover they moved by rail to Columbus on the twenty-ninth—"Supplied with [a] good supper by [the] ladies," Harper wrote—and reached Milledgeville on the night of the thirtieth. Finding the tracks above Milledgeville destroyed by Sherman's wrecking crews, they marched northeast the next morning, passed through Sparta on February 1, arrived at Mayfield on the second, and moved by rail to Augusta and Branchville, South Carolina, where they arrived on the morning of the fourth. From there they marched to a "count[r]y Bridge" over the Edisto River, two and one-half miles southwest of Branchville, and took up defensive positions. "I am verry dirty not having had a change of clothes in upwards of 2 weeks," Captain Hampton of the 63rd Virginia wrote, "but some of the Boys are so much worse off than I am I ought not to complain[.] I have never in [my] life seen such a dirty & filthy set of men[.] [S]omething ne[a]r half of the command has not changed shirts for 4 or 5 months & their pants are in tat[t]ers[.]"[146]

Sherman, meanwhile, marched out of Savannah on February 1 and moved north through South Carolina with two columns that he dubbed the "Left Wing" (commanded by Slocum) and the "Right Wing" (commanded by Howard). Beauregard, in overall command of Confederate forces in South Carolina, had about 22,000 men to oppose Sherman's 60,000, but those were scattered across the state. Moreover, by feinting toward Augusta with one column and Charleston with the other, Sherman confused Beauregard as to his objective, which was Columbia. Forging swiftly ahead, Sherman punched through the Confederate defenses at the Salkehatchie River on February 3 and pushed on to the Edisto, forcing Palmer to abandon his country bridge position on the night of the same day he occupied it. Palmer then fell back to Cannon's Bridge, on the South Fork of the Edisto about eleven

145. See G. W. F. Harper to Ella Harper, December 29, 1864, and January 8 and 16, 1865, Harper Papers. On January 19, 1865, the "effective" strength of the 58th North Carolina was 263 officers and men. The effective strength of Palmer's Brigade was 1,025. "[O]ur army is verry much Demoralized & nearly all Naked & barefooted," Captain Hampton wrote on January 15, "but they are Drawing clothing now [and] we get some pork corn meal & beef[.]" *Official Records (Army)*, ser. 1, 45 (pt. 2):799; T. B. Hampton to J. C. Hampton, January 15, 1865, Hampton Papers.

146. Harper Diary, January 23, 25, 29 and February 4, 1865; T. B. Hampton to J. C. Hampton, February 3, 1865, Hampton Papers.

miles northwest of Branchville. Palmer's men burned Cannon's Bridge on February 7, skirmished with an enemy probing force on the eighth, and retreated on the night of the ninth after the Federals captured Birmaker's Bridge, six miles above Cannon's Bridge. They then marched through blowing snow to Orangeburg, thirteen miles northeast. "Came near [to] being cut off," Captain Harper noted laconically in his diary.[147]

On February 10 Palmer's Brigade passed through Orangeburg and continued on to Shilling's Bridge, on the North Fork of the Edisto, which it reached on the eleventh. There the entire brigade was implausibly routed on the twelfth by, according to Captain Hampton, "a squad of about 65 Yanks [that] crossed some 300 yards to our right . . . [and] fired into [us]. . . . [O]ur Boys made the worse stampede I ever witnessed. . . . I rallied 12 men . . . all that would be ral[l]ied out of our Brigade & . . . we turned on the enemy & made them leave the field quicker than they came[.]" Palmer's troops then retreated toward Columbia, took position two miles west of the city on February 14, and began constructing breastworks in a sleet storm. The next day they fell back eastward across the Congaree River. The 58th, as the rear guard of Palmer's Brigade, fired the bridge after crossing. After spending the sixteenth "In line [of] battle in [the] streets of Columbia," Palmer evacuated the city with the rest of Lee's Corps (temporarily commanded by Stevenson) that evening, bivouacked at midnight near a bridge over the Broad River, and retreated toward Charlotte the next day.[148] The 58th reached Winnsboro at noon on February 19, passed through Rich Hill and crossed the Catawba River on the twenty-first, and camped four miles south of Charlotte on February 23.

Lee's Corps remained at Charlotte for the next nine days. Joseph Johnston arrived on February 23 and assumed command of both the Department of South Carolina, Georgia, and Florida and the Department of Tennessee and [Northwest] Georgia. Two weeks later he assumed command of "all troops" in the Department of North Carolina.[149] On February 27 he reviewed Lee's Corps, including the 58th North Carolina. The "effective strength" of Palmer's Brigade, probably not including the 54th Virginia, which was on detached duty, was 578 men.[150]

In accordance with orders from General-in-Chief Robert E. Lee to "Concentrate all available forces and drive back Sherman," Johnston ordered Lee's Corps to move by rail from Charlotte to Fayetteville on March 5.[151] Stewart's and Cheatham's Corps, at Chester, South Carolina, and Hardee's, near Cheraw, were to proceed to the same point. By March 10 the 58th North Carolina had reached Salisbury. On the twelfth it departed Salisbury by train, reached Hillsborough on the night of the thirteenth, and arrived at Smithfield at 3:00 A.M. on the fourteenth. Sherman, meanwhile, was delayed on his northward march by heavy rains but crossed the North Carolina line on March 7 and captured Fayetteville on March

---

147. Harper Diary, February 9, 1865. See also Garrett D. Gouge (Company K, 58th North Carolina) to Sarah Howell (his sister), February 8, 1865 (typescript), Roster Document No. 1057, CWRP, NCDAH.

148. T. B. Hampton to J. C. Hampton, February 3, 1865, Hampton Papers; Harper Diary, February 16, 1865. Lee was wounded at the Battle of Nashville and did not return to duty until the last days of the war.

149. *Official Records (Army)*, ser. 1, 47 (pt. 2):1320 (see also 1248, 1274, 1334).

150. *Official Records (Army)*, ser. 1, 47 (pt. 2):1285. See also Weaver, *54th Virginia*, 150.

151. *Official Records (Army)*, ser. 1, 47 (pt. 2):1247.

12. There he paused briefly before advancing again on the fifteenth. Deprived of his Fayetteville assembly point, Johnston opted to remain at Smithfield until Sherman's new destination—Goldsboro or Raleigh—could be determined. Time was growing very short. Twenty thousand Federals commanded by the ubiquitous Schofield were marching west from New Bern and had brushed aside a small Confederate force under Braxton Bragg near Kinston on March 7-10. An additional 10,000 men commanded by Maj. Gen. Alfred H. Terry moved north from Wilmington on March 15. Once Sherman, Schofield, and Terry joined forces, Johnston's faint prospects of defeating Sherman would become virtually nil. His one hope, it appeared, was to attack and destroy Sherman's Left Wing before Schofield and Terry arrived and before the Right Wing could come to its aid. In order to position himself for an ambush, however, he needed to determine Sherman's destination and to increase, if possible, the distance between Sherman's two wings. On March 15 a small battle at Averasboro between Hardee's Corps and Slocum accomplished both objects. So confident of victory was Sherman in that one-sided contest that Howard and the Right Wing continued marching and, within a few hours, passed beyond the junction of the Raleigh road. Johnston could now plan an ambush secure in the knowledge that Sherman was headed for Goldsboro, that Slocum would come to him, and that Raleigh would not be left uncovered. On March 18 he issued orders for his 20,000-man army to take position south of Bentonville.

Johnston's defensive line on the morning of March 19 began about one-half mile south of the Goldsboro road, extended northwest across the road at a point just east of the Bentonville road intersection, and then ran northeast, parallel to the Bentonville road, for another half mile. It then made a sharp angle to the west and continued about 600 yards before terminating. Most of the line south of the angle was held by Maj. Gen. Robert F. Hoke's Division (on the left) and Col. John H. Nethercutt's North Carolina Junior Reserves brigade, supported by a six-gun battery of Lt. Col. Joseph B. Starr's North Carolina artillery battalion. Both Hoke and Nethercutt were under the command of Bragg. On Nethercutt's right, in a slot reserved for Hardee's Corps, which was still en route from Averasboro, were two additional artillery batteries. West of the angle was the Army of Tennessee, commanded by Stewart and comprising Stewart's Corps (commanded by Maj. Gen. William W. Loring) on the left, Lee's Corps (commanded by Maj. Gen. D. H. Hill) in the center, and Cheatham's Corps (commanded by Maj. Gen. William B. Bate) on the right. The Army of Tennessee's portion of the line was concealed just inside the edge of a woods fronting the fields of a farmer named Cole; marshy terrain and blackjack thickets south of the angle rendered Bragg's units equally invisible. In short, Slocum would walk into a trap. His advance guard would encounter Confederate troops on the Goldsboro road, assume they were facing the usual token opposition, and, as was Sherman's patented tactic, undertake a flanking movement. Stewart's Army of Tennessee and Hardee's Corps would then deliver a hammer blow against Slocum's left, crushing his army against the anvil of Bragg's command. Slocum's strung-out, 30,000-man column would be crippled or destroyed, leaving Sherman with a choice of fighting Johnston with Howard's, Schofield's, and Terry's forces or retreating to the North Carolina coast.

On the morning of March 19 elements of Brig. Gen. William P. Carlin's Division, leading Slocum's advance, bumped into Confederate cavalry on the Goldsboro road. Carlin, as scripted, then deployed two brigades (George P. Buell's and Harrison C. Hobart's) north of the road and a third (Lt. Col. David Miles's) south of the road to turn the Confederate

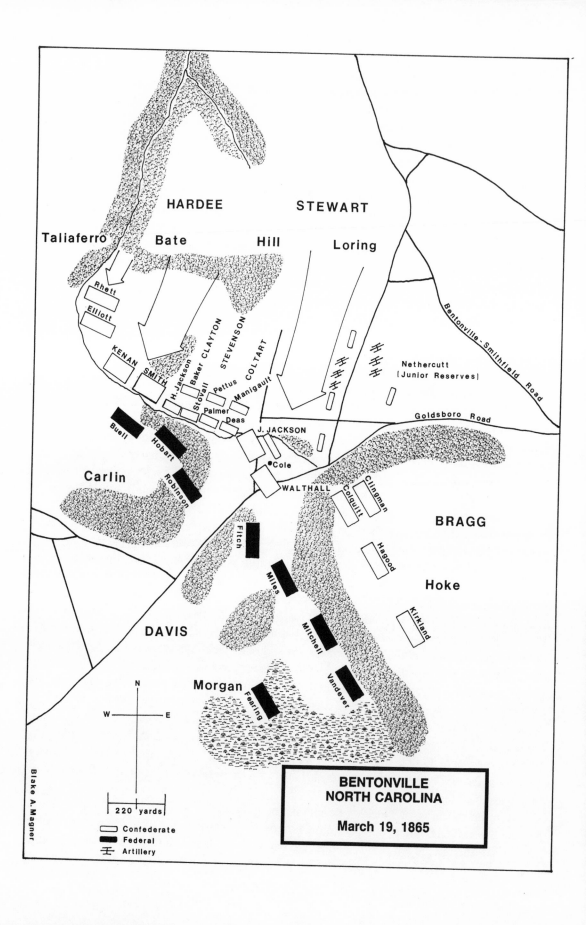

HARDEE   STEWART

Taliaferro   Bate   Hill   Loring

Rhett

Elliott

KENAN
SMITH
H. Jackson   Baker   CLAYTON
Stovall   STEVENSON
Pettus   COLTART
Palmer   Manigault
Deas

Nethercutt
(Junior Reserves)

Buell
Hobart

Carlin

Robinson

J. JACKSON

Cole

WALTHALL

Goldsboro Road

Clingman
Colquitt

BRAGG

Fitch

Hagood

Hoke

Miles

Kirkland

Mitchell

DAVIS

Vandever

Morgan
Fearing

N
W — E
S

220 yards

□ Confederate
■ Federal
Artillery

BENTONVILLE
NORTH CAROLINA

March 19, 1865

Bentonville - Smithfield Road

Blake A. Magner

flanks. Buell and Hobart quickly plowed into the Army of Tennessee, still concealed in the woods, and were ripped by "an awful volly [sic]" from a distance of fifty feet.[152] "They . . . reeled and staggered," one Confederate remembered, "while we poured volley after volley into them, and great gaps were made in their line, as brave Federals fell everywhere—their colors would rise and fall just a few feet from us, and many a gallant boy in blue is buried there in those pines who held 'Old Glory' up for a brief moment." "[We] stood as long as man can stand," a Federal officer candidly admitted, "& . . . [then] run like the deuce." Meantime, south of the road, Miles's attack bogged down in a swamp but inexplicably convinced the egregious Bragg that his position was imperiled. In a move that delayed and perhaps fatally weakened Stewart's and Hardee's counterattack, Johnston responded to Bragg's call for assistance by ordering Maj. Gen. Lafayette McLaws's Division, the first of Hardee's units to reach the field, to take position on Hoke's left.[153]

Around 1:30 P.M. Hardee's second division, commanded by Maj. Gen. William B. Taliaferro, arrived and was placed on the right of Bate's Corps. About an hour later the Army of Tennessee and Taliaferro's Division stormed out of the woods, crushing the undermanned and disorganized Federal left and precipitating, in the words of one shaken Federal, "some of the best running ever did."[154] South of the road Brig. Gen. James D. Morgan's tenacious division, which had dug in on Miles's right, hung on precariously under attacks by Bragg from the front and by Stewart and Taliaferro from the flank and rear. Battling desperately amid a "continuous and remorseless roar of musketry," Morgan's men narrowly succeeded in holding their ground until William Cogswell's Brigade of Alpheus S. Williams's XX Corps arrived and attacked the Confederates from the rear.[155] The fighting then shifted again to the Federal left, where other XX Corps units reached the field and smashed a series of Confederate assaults with a "raging leaden hailstorm of grape and canister."[156]

During the night of March 19 Sherman, who was with Howard's wing of the army, belatedly learned of the fighting at Bentonville. Preparations to go to Slocum's aid began immediately, and by the afternoon of the twentieth the army was reunited. Realizing his gambit had failed, Johnston nevertheless remained on the battlefield, allegedly to cover the evacuation of his wounded but more probably in the faint hope that a victory might somehow still be salvaged. He therefore realigned his units in a spraddled-horseshoe configuration to cover the much longer Federal line and protect his retreat route over the Mill Creek bridge. While ambulances rumbled over the bridge toward Smithfield, the Confederate commander resupplied his men as best he could and anxiously awaited developments. Sherman, however, was no more interested than Johnston in assuming the offensive. Rarely disposed to expend lives in battle if maneuver would accomplish his object, Sherman was

152. Charles S. Brown (21st Michigan Infantry) to "Mother & Etta," April 18, 1865, Charles S. Brown Papers, SCD-DU, hereafter cited as Brown Papers.

153. Lovick Pierce Thomas, "Their Last Battle," *Southern Historical Society Papers* 29 (1901): 217-218; C. S. Brown to "Etta," April 26, 1865, Brown Papers.

154. C. S. Brown to "his folks and anyone else," April 1865, Brown Papers.

155. Benson J. Lossing, *Pictorial History of the Civil War in the United States of America*, 3 vols. (Hartford, Conn.: Thomas Belknap, 1877), 3:501.

156. Samuel W. Ravenel, "Ask the Survivors of Bentonville," *Confederate Veteran* 18 (March 1910): 124.

primarily concerned with reaching the Goldsboro railhead. There he would be reinforced by Schofield and Terry, rest his army, and obtain much needed supplies and equipment. Except for several "brisk" but relatively minor Federal attacks on Hoke's front, March 20 passed quietly.[157]

The next day Johnston remained in his works and continued to evacuate his wounded. Heavy skirmishing took place all along the line, but the only action of consequence was an unauthorized attack by Maj. Gen. Joseph A. Mower's Division that broke through the Confederate left and threatened to capture the Mill Creek bridge. Against that penetration Johnston, improvising desperately, mustered just enough resistance to force the impetuous Mower to pause and call for reinforcements. Sherman then ordered him to withdraw. During the night Johnston fell back in the direction of Smithfield.

When Buell and Hobart attacked north of the Goldsboro road on the morning of March 19, the right extremity of Hobart's Brigade was confronted by the right extremity of Palmer's Brigade. Most of the damage to Carlin's two brigadiers was inflicted by Maj. Gen. Henry D. Clayton's Division, on Palmer's right, but Palmer claimed that his troops "repulsed . . . [the Federals attacking their part of the line] with ease, killing and wounding a number without any loss. . . ."[158] During Johnston's assault that afternoon, Palmer's men were in the first of D. H. Hill's two lines, between the brigades of Brig. Gens. Zachariah C. Deas and Marcellus A. Stovall.

This brigade moved steadily forward [Palmer reported] for about 400 yards in common time, preserving its alignment almost as if on parade, although for a part of that distance under considerable fire. This carried the brigade within 200 yards of the enemy's first line of works, which were at once charged and carried. This command did not halt there, but moved forward in double-quick, pursuing the enemy, flying in disorder and confusion to their second line of works, which was also charged and carried, capturing one piece of artillery near the second line. The pursuit was continued as far as the Goldsborough road, when it became necessary to halt the command, much exhausted by the two charges just made, and for the purpose of rectifying the alignment, more or less disturbed by such rapid movements through the woods thickly set with troublesome undergrowth.[159]

At that juncture Palmer's Brigade, which straddled the Goldsboro road, became separated into two "wings" by Brig. Gen. Alpheus Baker's Alabama brigade, which was moving east along the road.[160] Palmer was then ordered to remain in reserve and was still attempting to reunite his command when his right (southern) wing, consisting of the 54th Virginia, the "Tennessee Consolidation," and the 58th North Carolina, was ordered to join in the attack on Morgan.[161] That wing, Palmer reported, "immediately advanced for the distance of,

157. *Official Records (Army)*, ser. 1, 47 (pt. 1):1056.

158. *Official Records (Army)*, ser. 1, 47 (pt. 1):1099.

159. *Official Records (Army)*, ser. 1, 47 (pt. 1):1099-1100.

160. Palmer's report states that Baker "threw his line across mine, cutting nearly through the center of my brigade." *Official Records (Army)*, ser. 1, 47 (pt. 1):1100.

161. In his recent book entitled *Last Stand in the Carolinas: The Battle of Bentonville*, Mark L. Bradley states that the 54th and 63rd Virginia and the Tennessee Consolidation made the attack south of the road and the 58th and 60th North Carolina remained behind. That conclusion is seemingly deduced from a passage in Capt.

say, 300 yards beyond the Goldsborough road, taking position on Brigadier-General Baker's right. I found no works at this point in my front, but just to my left were two lines of breast-works running rather perpendicular to this road. . . . It was wholly unsafe to move farther forward or pass this force on my left, and, indeed, on discovering these works and their sin-gular direction I came to the conclusion that to carry them was in part the objective . . . of my movement. I therefore wheeled to the left, assaulted and carried the first line and part of the second. . . ."[162]

At that propitious moment Cogswell's Brigade launched its attack. "On the appear-ance of this force," Palmer wrote, "those in my front renewed their resistance, and thus my command was immediately under heavy fire both in front and rear. I at once ordered a movement as rapidly as possible by the left flank, so as to retire back on or near the Goldsborough road, but the Federals effected a junction so quickly as to capture some of my men and to cut off . . . another portion." Palmer then reunited the northern wing of his brigade with what remained of the southern and moved to a supporting position behind

---

G. W. F. Harper's history of the 58th, written approximately thirty-five years after the war, in which Harper rec-ollects orders from General Palmer to about-face his men and "look after these fellows [Federal troops]" in his right rear. However, Harper's contemporary diary contains an account of the fighting on March 19 that differs substantially from the one in his history and, because of its proximity to events, is more reliable. The relevant portion of Harper's diary entry for that date reads as follows: "Charged enemy's works at 2 P.M. and carried 3 lines and broke the 4th but not being supported [were] flanked out of last line. Enemy then charged in the open woods without defense and were repulsed. Obstinate fight until after dark without further change in position. Some artillery and prisoners captured. Firing ceased at 8 P.M. At 12 P.M. retired to the position we occupied in the morning." That account—specifically, the parts referring to a third and fourth line, to being flanked, and to "open woods"—sounds remarkably like those of fighting south of the Goldsboro road in the contemporary reports of Cogswell and one of his regimental commanders, Lt. Col. Philo B. Buckingham of the 20th Con-necticut. In an attempt to square what he believes to be the 58th's reserve position north of the Goldsboro road with Harper's recollection of a movement to the right-rear, Bradley speculates that the regiment was sent to the support of Bate. However, Palmer says nothing in his report about sending the 58th on such a mission, and Bate says nothing in his report about receiving any reinforcements until the arrival of McLaws's Division late in the day. In all probability, Palmer, advancing south of the Goldsboro road with the 54th Virginia, the Tennessee Consolidation, and the 58th North Carolina and having been "informed," as he wrote, of "a considerable Federal force not more than 100 yards to my right, and moving upon my rear," sent the 58th to "look after" it or, more precisely, to hold open a line of retreat for the rest of his command. In unsuccessfully attempting to carry out that order in the smoke-filled woods, Harper inadvertently took himself out of the direct line of Cogswell's at-tack and was able to withdraw to the Goldsboro road in some semblance of order. Thus the 58th escaped the fate of portions of the 54th Virginia and the Tennessee Consolidation, which were cut off and forced to take to the swamps. Three additional facts support the conclusion that the 60th North Carolina and the 63rd Virginia were the units that remained north of the Goldsboro road during Palmer's attack: (1) those two regiments were con-solidated during the battle under the command of Lt. Col. Connally H. Lynch of the 63rd; (2) casualties in the 60th North Carolina and 63rd Virginia were lower than those in Palmer's other regiments; and (3) in a letter dated March 23, 1865, Sgt. Houston Collins of the 63rd Virginia states that "we charged the Enemy & drove [them] out of two lines [not four, as Harper states in his diary]. . . ." Harper, "Fifty-eighth Regiment," in Clark, *Histories of the North Carolina Regiments*, 3:441-442; Harper Diary, March 19, 1865; *Official Records (Army)*, ser. 1, 47 (pt. 1):1100; Houston Collins to his father, March 23, 1865, Collins Letters. See also Mark L. Bradley, *Last Stand in the Carolinas: The Battle of Bentonville* (Campbell, Calif.: Savas Woodbury Publishers, 1996), 245, 261, 263, 294; Nathaniel Cheairs Hughes Jr., *Bentonville: The Final Battle of Sherman and Johnston* (Chapel Hill: University of North Carolina Press, 1996), 132; *Official Records (Army)*, ser. 1, 47 (pt. 1):497, 504, 826, 834, 842-843, 1095, 1099, 1101, 1105-1108.

162. *Official Records (Army)*, ser. 1, 47 (pt. 1):1100.

Pettus's Brigade.[163] His men saw no further action that day or, with the exception of skirmishing, on March 20 and 21.[164] Palmer reported the loss of 13 men killed, 113 wounded, and 55 captured plus the capture of 50 wounded and 45 unwounded Federal prisoners. Stevenson's report listed Palmer's casualties as 14 killed, 121 wounded, and 42 missing. The 58th North Carolina's losses, according to figures compiled for this volume from the scanty rec-ords available, were 3 men killed or mortally wounded and 17 wounded. Captain Harper, who commanded the 58th during the battle, recorded the loss of 3 men killed and 23 wounded in his diary.[165]

The 58th North Carolina evacuated its lines at Bentonville at 2:00 A.M. on March 22, crossed Mill Creek and probably Stone's Creek, and bivouacked for the rest of the night. "Muddy road and tiresome walk," Captain Harper wrote. On the morning of the twenty-second the regiment "Threw up breastwork[s] and waited for advance of enemy[,] who failed to make his appearance." It then marched to within six or seven miles of Smithfield and camped after dark. "Road exceedingly wet and muddy," Harper continued. "Tiresome and disagreeable march. Peach trees in bloom." After a "Smokey [sic], Windy, dusty – Disagreeable day" in camp on March 23, the regiment moved through Smithfield on the twenty-fourth and camped near the Halifax road.[166] It remained in the vicinity of Smithfield for the next two weeks with the rest of Johnston's troops. A reorganization of the army was completed on April 9, and the 58th and 60th North Carolina were consolidated under the command of Lt. Col. Thaddeus Charles Coleman, formerly of the 1st Regiment N.C. Artillery and the Engineer Corps. The new organization, variously referred to as the 58th North Carolina Regiment (Consolidated) and the 58th North Carolina Battalion, was then transferred to William F. Brantley's Brigade, D. H. Hill's Division, Lee's Corps. Other regiments in Brantley's Brigade were the 24th Mississippi and the 22nd and 37th Alabama.[167]

---

163. *Official Records (Army)*, ser. 1, 47 (pt. 1):1100. General Stevenson wrote that "My two brigades, Pettus' and Palmer's, retained their position until between 10 and 11 o'clock that night [March 19], when they withdrew under orders to the line from which we had advanced, Pettus, however, being now put in the front line in order to give Palmer's brigade, which had been compelled to move much more rapidly in the different charges which it made, and consequently was more exhausted, a better opportunity to rest. One regiment of Palmer's, the Fifty-eighth North Carolina, was, however, placed upon the front line to fill up the allotted portion of the works." *Official Records (Army)*, ser. 1, 47 (pt. 1):1095. See also *Daily Progress* (Raleigh), March 27, 1865.

164.Relevant entries in the Harper Diary for March 20-21, 1865, read as follows:

    March 20: "Clear, Pleas. 58th in front line breastworks with Petters [Pettus's] Brig. Skirmishing in front and fighting going on on our left."

    March 21: "Rain, Cool. Same as yesterday."

165. See *Official Records (Army)*, ser. 1, 47 (pt. 1):1096, 1100. Palmer complimented Harper and the other three regimental commanders in his brigade, stating that they handled their troops "with ability and bore themselves handsomely through the day. . . ." Stevenson, in an "order . . . complimenting the troops of his Division," stated that "Never was there more dash and gallantry displayed than was exhibited by Palmer's Brigade in their successful assaults upon the breastworks of the enemy." *Official Records (Army)*, ser. 1, 47 (pt. 1):1101; *Daily Progress* (Raleigh), March 27, 1865.

166. Harper Diary, March 22-23, 1865.

167. The 24th Mississippi was a consolidation of the 24th, 27th, 29th, 30th, and 34th Mississippi; the 22nd Alabama was a consolidation of the 22nd, 25th, 39th, and 50th Alabama; and the 37th Alabama was a consolidation of the 37th, 42nd, and 54th Alabama.

In the meantime, Sherman reached Goldsboro on March 23 and linked up with Schofield and Terry, who had arrived on the twenty-first. There he remained, resting and refitting his men, until April 10, when he began moving toward Smithfield. The 58th retreated with Johnston's army at 10:00 A.M. the same day, bivouacked at Battle's Bridge that evening, passed through Raleigh the following afternoon, and camped for the night three miles northwest of the city on the Hillsborough road. The retreat continued during the next five days through Hillsborough and Graham to Company Shops (present-day Burlington), where rumors of the surrender of the Army of Northern Virginia were confirmed on April 15. On April 16 the regiment reached Greensboro, and on the eighteenth it moved to Jamestown. "Paroled prisoners from Lees [sic] Army passing [through] for days past in a constant stream," Harper observed on April 20. Demoralization among Johnston's troops, a serious problem since news of the fall of Richmond arrived on April 5, increased to epidemic proportions. "Reg't melting away," Harper noted despondently on April 24.[168]

The 58th North Carolina remained at Jamestown for about a week before returning to Greensboro. In the meantime Sherman captured Raleigh on April 13. On April 17 Johnston opened surrender negotiations with Sherman. Terms were reached on April 19 but were overruled as excessively generous by the authorities in Washington. A new round of negotiations produced a quick agreement on April 26. Parole of Johnston's troops began at Greensboro the same date and continued through May 1. According to figures compiled for this volume, 27 officers and 92 men of the 58th Regiment were present to receive their paroles.[169]

168. Harper Diary, April 20 and 24, 1865. Fifty-three members of the 58th North Carolina deserted during the third quarter of 1864. No figures are available for the remainder of the war. For addition desertion statistics for the 58th, see footnotes 22 and 79 above.

169. Members of the 60th Regiment N.C. Troops who were paroled at Greensboro as part of the 58th North Carolina consolidation are counted in the parolee computation in the history of the 60th (see page 500).

FIELD AND STAFF

COLONEL

PALMER, JOHN B.

Previously served as Captain of Company A of this regiment. Appointed Lieutenant Colonel on or about May 13, 1862, and transferred to the Field and Staff. Promoted to Colonel on July 29, 1862, to rank from June 27, 1862. Reported present in March-June, 1863. Wounded at Chickamauga, Georgia, September 20, 1863. Returned to duty prior to November 1, 1863. Reported absent on detached service at Asheville from November 19, 1863, through February 28, 1865. Captured and paroled at Athens, Georgia, on or about May 8, 1865.

LIEUTENANT COLONELS

PROFFITT, WILLIAM W.

Previously served as Captain of Company C of this regiment. Elected Lieutenant Colonel on July 29, 1862, and transferred to the Field and Staff. Resigned on April 7, 1863, by reason of "phthisis pulmonalis." Resignation accepted on April 25, 1863.

KEENER, JOHN C.

Previously served as Captain of Company E of this regiment. Elected Major on July 29, 1862, and transferred to the Field and Staff. Reported present in March-June, 1863. Promoted to Lieutenant Colonel on April 25, 1863. Resigned on June 16, 1863, because "I am near fifty years of age . . . [and] now consider it my duty to retire from the [service] for the purpose of going home to attend to the wants &c. of my family." Resignation accepted on or about the same date. [A notation on his letter of resignation by Col. John B. Palmer of the 58th Regiment states that Lieutenant Colonel Keener "is not competent to perform the duties of the office he holds and the interests of the public service demand, in my opinion, that his resignation be promptly accepted."]

KIRBY, EDMUND

Served as Adjutant (1st Lieutenant) of this regiment. Was serving as acting Lieutenant Colonel when he was killed at Chickamauga, Georgia, September 20, 1863.

DULA, THOMAS JOSHUA

Previously served as Captain of Company H of this regiment. Appointed Major on April 25, 1863, and transferred to the Field and Staff. Reported absent with leave in May-June, 1863. Wounded at Chickamauga, Georgia, September 20, 1863. Returned to duty on April 6, 1864. Wounded in the thigh at Kolb's Farm, near Marietta, Georgia, June 22, 1864. Promoted Lieutenant Colonel on July 6, 1864, to rank from June 16, 1863. Resigned on August 4, 1864, "to accept the position of solicitor for the County of Caldwell . . . to which I have been elected." Reported absent on wounded furlough on August 10, 1864 (possibly still suffering from wounds received at Kolb's Farm). Resignation accepted on August 29, 1864.

SILVER, SAMUEL MARION

Previously served as Captain of Company K of this regiment. Reported in command of the regiment in March-April and July-August, 1864. Appointed Lieutenant Colonel on October 29, 1864, to rank from September 1, 1864, and transferred to the Field and

Staff. Resigned on March 16, 1865. Reason he resigned not reported. Resignation accepted on or about April 9, 1865.

COLEMAN, THADDEUS CHARLES

Previously served as 1st Lieutenant of Company C, 10th Regiment N.C. State Troops (1st Regiment N.C. Artillery), and as Engineering Officer (Captain) on the staff of Lt. Gen. John B. Hood. Appointed Lieutenant Colonel of this regiment on April 9, 1865. Paroled at Greensboro on May 1, 1865. "How tall, how brave, how handsome he was! Yet, as the king said of the prince, 'Taller he seems in death.'" [Postwar statement by Alphonso C. Avery, former Assistant Adjutant General on the staff of Maj. Gen. D. H. Hill. Roster Document No. 1085.]

MAJORS

STEWART, ALFRED THEODORE

Previously served as Captain of Company E of this regiment. Reported in command of the regiment on July 10, 1864. Appointed Major on or about August 31, 1864, and assigned to permanent duty with the Field and Staff. Killed at Jonesborough, Georgia, the same date.

HARPER, GEORGE WASHINGTON FINLEY

Previously served as Captain of Company H of this regiment. Appointed Major on April 9, 1865, and transferred to the Field and Staff. Survived the war.

ADJUTANTS

KIRBY, EDMUND

Resided in Virginia. Appointed Adjutant (1st Lieutenant) on July 29, 1862. Reported present in March-June, 1863. Appointed acting Lieutenant Colonel of the regiment on an unspecified date prior to September 20, 1863. [See Lieutenant Colonels' section above.]

HORTON, JAMES H.

Served as 2nd Lieutenant of Company I of this regiment. Reported on duty as acting Adjutant at the Battle of Chickamauga, Georgia, September 19-20, 1863. [See *Daily Progress* (Raleigh), October 8, 1863.]

PERRY, BENJAMIN L.

Resided in Mitchell County. Appointed Adjutant (1st Lieutenant) on November 5, 1863, to rank from October 13, 1863. Reported absent on detached service in March-April, 1864. Reported absent without leave in July-September, 1864. No further records.

EWING, ORVILLE, JR.

Previously served as Adjutant (1st Lieutenant) of the 60th Regiment N.C. Troops. Appointed Adjutant (1st Lieutenant) of this regiment when the 58th and 60th Regiments were consolidated on April 9, 1865. No further records.

ASSISTANT QUARTERMASTERS

BEARDEN, MARCUS J.

Resided in Buncombe County. Appointed Assistant Quartermaster (Captain) of this regiment on July 29, 1862. Reported present in

March-June, 1863. Captured at Cumberland Gap, Tennessee, September 9, 1863. Sent to Louisville, Kentucky. Transferred to Johnson's Island, Ohio, where he arrived on or about September 25, 1863. Transferred to Point Lookout, Maryland, February 9, 1864. Paroled at Point Lookout on or about March 16, 1864. Received at City Point, Virginia, March 20, 1864, for exchange. Returned to duty prior to September 1, 1864. Relieved from duty with the 58th Regiment on February 17, 1865. Served as Assistant Quartermaster (Captain) of the 60th Regiment N.C. Troops (possibly in an acting capacity) from about March 21, 1865, until April 9, 1865, when the 58th and 60th Regiments were consolidated. Survived the war.

COFFEY, THOMAS JEFFERSON

Served as 2nd Lieutenant of Company E of this regiment. Appointed acting Assistant Quartermaster on or about September 9, 1863. Returned to duty with Company E on or about June 1, 1864.

GOODWIN, J. J.

Reported on duty as acting Assistant Quartermaster (Captain) of this regiment on February 1, 1864.

ASSISTANT COMMISSARY OF SUBSISTENCE

MASON, JOSEPH P.

Previously served as Private in Company C of this regiment. Appointed Assistant Commissary of Subsistence (Captain) on July 29, 1862, and transferred to the Field and Staff. Appointed Assistant Commissary of Subsistence (Captain) of Brig. Gen. John W. Frazer's Brigade on August 19, 1863, to rank from August 3, 1863, and transferred.

SURGEONS

COLLETT, WAIGHTSTILL A.

Previously served as Assistant Surgeon of the 6th Regiment N.C. State Troops. Appointed Surgeon of this regiment on July 29, 1862. Reported absent on sick furlough in March-April, 1863. Reported present in May-June, 1863. "Dropped" (possibly resigned) on August 11, 1863.

HARRISS, WILLIAM WHITE

Previously served as Assistant Surgeon of the 61st Regiment N.C. Troops. Appointed Surgeon of this regiment on an unspecified date (probably late September or early October, 1863) to rank from August 7, 1863. Reported present in September-October, 1863; March-April, 1864; and July-August, 1864. Later served as Surgeon of the Wilmington garrison.

TOXEY, WILLIAM

Previously served as Surgeon of the 25th Regiment Alabama Infantry. Appointed Surgeon of this regiment on an unspecified date subsequent to April 3, 1865. Paroled at Greensboro on May 1, 1865. [Served at various times as a medical officer with the 39th and 50th Regiments Alabama Infantry and possibly several other Alabama units. Also served as a medical officer on the staff of Brig. Gen. Zachariah C. Deas, Army of Tennessee.]

GRIFFIN, HAMILTON

Previously served as Surgeon of the 60th Regiment N.C. Troops. Transferred to this regiment when the 58th and 60th Regiments were consolidated on April 9, 1865. Paroled at Greensboro on May 1, 1865.

ASSISTANT SURGEONS

LEWIS, OSCAR M.

Resided in Yancey County. Appointed Assistant Surgeon on August 16, 1862, to rank from July 29, 1862. Reported present in March-June, 1863. Dropped from the regimental rolls on August 11, 1863, because of "his failure to appear before a medical examining board."

PEARSON, ROBERT C.

Appointed Assistant Surgeon of this regiment to rank from October 1, 1862. No further records. [He was apparently assigned to temporary duty with the regiment as an "extra ass(istan)t."]

MITCHELL, THOMAS J.

Resided at Griffin, Georgia. Appointed Assistant Surgeon of this regiment on December 3, 1862. Reported present in September-October, 1863. Transferred to an unspecified unit or hospital in December, 1863.

WHITE, LORENZO W.

Appointed Assistant Surgeon of this regiment on November 30, 1863. Reported present in March-April and July-August, 1864. Paroled at Greensboro on May 1, 1865.

DUNN, J. F.

Previously served as Assistant Surgeon of the 60th Regiment N.C. Troops. Transferred to this regiment when the 58th and 60th Regiments were consolidated on April 9, 1865. No further records.

CHAPLAIN

RABEY, JOHN W.

Methodist-Episcopalian. Previously served as Private in Company I, 26th Regiment N.C. Troops. Appointed Chaplain of this regiment on June 9, 1864, to rank from May 4, 1864. Reported present in July-August, 1864. Resigned on September 9, 1864; however, there is no evidence that his resignation was accepted. Furloughed for thirty days on or about October 22, 1864. No further records.

ENSIGN

WOODY, GREEN B.

Previously served as Sergeant in Company C of this regiment. Appointed Ensign (1st Lieutenant) on December 30, 1864, to rank from June 15, 1864, and transferred to the Field and Staff. Survived the war.

SERGEANTS MAJOR

HERNDON, HARRISON
Born in Habersham County, Georgia, and enlisted in Mitchell County at age 36, June 23, 1862, for the war. Was apparently mustered in with the rank of Sergeant Major. Reported present in March-April, 1863. Deserted in May-June, 1863. [May have served previously as Private in Company H, 1st Regiment Georgia Regulars.]

INGLIS, JAMES
Previously served as Sergeant in Company H of this regiment. Appointed Sergeant Major in May-June, 1863, and transferred to the Field and Staff. Reported present in September-October, 1863. Killed at Rocky Face Ridge, near Dalton, Georgia, February 25, 1864.

COFFEY, DRURY D.
Previously served as Sergeant in Company E of this regiment. Appointed Sergeant Major on February 25, 1864, and transferred to the Field and Staff. Furloughed for twenty-two days on April 19, 1864. Reported present in July-August, 1864. Captured at McDonough, Georgia, September 3, 1864. Sent to Nashville, Tennessee. Transferred to Louisville, Kentucky, October 27, 1864. Transferred to Camp Douglas, Chicago, Illinois, where he arrived on November 1, 1864. Released at Camp Douglas on May 18, 1865, after taking the Oath of Allegiance.

QUARTERMASTER SERGEANTS

CONLEY, JAMES
Previously served as Private in Company B, 5th Battalion N.C. Cavalry. Appointed Quartermaster Sergeant of this regiment on an unspecified date (probably on or about July 29, 1862). Reported present in March-June, 1863. No further records.

RANKIN, J. E.
Previously served as Private in Company F of this regiment. Appointed Quartermaster Sergeant and transferred to the Field and Staff on an unspecified date (probably in July, 1863). Reduced to ranks and transferred back to Company F on an unspecified date (probably prior to August 20, 1863).

COFFEY, WILLIAM COLUMBUS
Served as Private in Company E of this regiment. Detailed for duty as regimental Quartermaster Sergeant on August 20, 1863, and transferred to the Field and Staff. Reported present or accounted for on surviving regimental muster rolls through May 30, 1864. Transferred back to Company E on June 1, 1864. Later served as 2nd Lieutenant of Company E. [North Carolina pension records indicate that he received a "severe injury in the right side by a piece of a bomb shell" at Chickamauga, Georgia, September 19-20, 1863.]

MEDARIS, JOHN E.
Previously served as Sergeant in Company E of this regiment. Appointed Quartermaster Sergeant on an unspecified date (probably in June-July, 1864) and transferred to the Field and Staff.

Reported present through August 31, 1864. Paroled at Greensboro on May 1, 1865.

COMMISSARY SERGEANTS

HALL, DAVID S.
Served as Private in Company C of this regiment. Detailed as Commissary Sergeant on August 1, 1863, and transferred to the Field and Staff. Reported present in September-October, 1863. Furloughed for forty days on February 3, 1864. Reported absent without leave on March 20, 1864. Returned to duty in May-August, 1864. No further records.

EDMISTEN, ABRAM SHUFORD
Served as Private in Company E of this regiment. Detailed as Commissary Sergeant on November 1, 1863, and transferred to the Field and Staff. Reported present in January-July, 1864. Transferred back to Company E on August 1, 1864.

ORDNANCE SERGEANT

HENSLEY, JOHN A.
Previously served as Corporal in Company A of this regiment. Appointed Ordnance Sergeant on an unspecified date (probably on or about July 29, 1862) and transferred to the Field and Staff. Reported present in March-June, 1863; September-October, 1863; and January-August, 1864. Paroled at Greensboro on May 1, 1865. [Filed a Tennessee pension application after the war.]

HOSPITAL STEWARDS

YOUNG, THOMAS S.
Previously served as Private in Company C of this regiment. Appointed Hospital Steward in July-October, 1863, and transferred to the Field and Staff. Reduced to ranks and transferred back to Company C in November, 1863-February, 1864.

THOMASON, WILLIAM J.
Previously served as Private in Company K of this regiment. Appointed Hospital Steward on December 1, 1863, and transferred to the Field and Staff. Reported present in January-April, 1864. Reduced to ranks and transferred back to Company K on July 25, 1864.

RIDDLE, JAMES MARION
Previously served as Musician (Drummer) in Company A of this regiment. Appointed Hospital Steward on August 1, 1864, and transferred to the Field and Staff. Reported absent with leave in January-February, 1865. No further records.

FOWLER, JAMES A.
Previously served as Corporal in Company L of this regiment. Appointed Hospital Steward subsequent to August 31, 1864, and transferred to the Field and Staff. Captured at Pulaski, Tennessee, December 25, 1864. Sent to Nashville, Tennessee. Transferred to Louisville, Kentucky, February 12, 1865. Transferred to Rock Is-

land, Illinois, where he arrived on February 18, 1865. Transferred to Point Lookout, Maryland, March 13, 1865. Paroled and transferred to Boulware's and Cox's Wharves, James River, Virginia, where he was received on March 23, 1865, for exchange. Survived the war. [North Carolina pension records indicate that he was wounded in the left arm at Resaca, Georgia, September 10, 186(4).]

DRUM MAJORS

ESTES, HENDERSON D.

Previously served as Drum Major of Company E of this regiment. Transferred to the Field and Staff in March-April, 1863. Reduced to ranks and transferred back to Company E on June 20, 1863.

BLAIR, JOHN CALDWELL

Previously served as Corporal in Company E of this regiment. Appointed Drum Major on October 31, 1863, and transferred to the Field and Staff. Reported present or accounted for in January-April and July-August, 1864. Paroled at Greensboro on May 1, 1865.

FORAGE MASTER

BLAIR, E. C.

Place and date of enlistment not reported. Reported absent with the wagon train at Chickamauga, Georgia, in September-October, 1863. No further records.

COMPANY A

This company, known as the "Mitchell Rangers," was raised in Mitchell County on December 31, 1861, as Capt. John B. Palmer's Company, N.C. Volunteers. It became the first company of a mixed (cavalry and infantry) unit known as "Palmer's Legion" on an unknown date (see pages 212-213 of regimental history). Palmer's Legion failed to complete its organization and was divided on or about May 13, 1862, into its cavalry and infantry components. The cavalry companies, still commanded by Palmer (who was by then a lieutenant colonel) were designated the 5th Battalion N.C. Partisan Rangers; the "Mitchell Rangers," which was apparently the only infantry company commanded by Palmer as of that date, was not assigned to the 5th Battalion but remained under Palmer's authority. On or about July 1 the company was assigned to a nascent infantry regiment, commanded by Palmer, that was mustered in as the 58th Regiment N.C. Troops on July 29, 1862. The "Mitchell Rangers" were designated Company A. The company subsequently functioned as a part of the 58th Regiment, and its history for the remainder of the war is reported as a part of the regimental history.

The following roster was compiled primarily from information in the microfilm edition of the Compiled Service Records of Soldiers Who Served in Organizations from the State of North Carolina (Record Group 109, M270), National Archives and Records Administration, Washington, D.C. Record Group 109 includes enlistment papers, pay vouchers, requisitions, letters of resignation, discharge certificates, and abstracts of medical and prisoner of war returns.

Materials relating specifically to this company include a muster-in and descriptive roll dated June 10, 1862, and muster rolls dated January-June, 1863; September-October, 1863; and January-August, 1864.

Also utilized in this roster were *The War of the Rebellion: A Compilation of the Official Records of the Union and Confederate Armies,* the North Carolina adjutant general's *Roll of Honor,* state militia records, newspaper casualty lists and obituaries, wartime claims for bounty pay and allowances, postwar registers of claims for artificial limbs, Confederate pension applications filed with the states of North Carolina, Tennessee, and Florida, Confederate Soldiers' Home records, and the 1860 and 1870 federal censuses of North Carolina. A search was made also for relevant letters, diaries, reminiscences, and other manuscripts in the Southern Historical Collection (University of North Carolina-Chapel Hill), the Duke University Library Special Collections Department, and the North Carolina Division of Archives and History.

Among the secondary sources consulted were records of the North Carolina division of the United Daughters of the Confederacy, postwar rosters, regimental and county histories, marriage bond, will, and cemetery indexes, published and unpublished genealogies, biographical dictionaries, the North Carolina *County Heritage Book* series, the *Confederate Veteran,* Walter Clark's *Histories of the Several Regiments and Battalions from North Carolina in the Great War, 1861-'65,* and the North Carolina volume of the extended edition of *Confederate Military History.*

OFFICERS

CAPTAINS

PALMER, JOHN B.

Born in Clinton County, New York, and resided in Mitchell County where he was by occupation a farmer prior to enlisting at age 36. Elected Captain on or about December 11, 1861. Appointed Lieutenant Colonel of this regiment on or about May 13, 1862, and transferred to the Field and Staff. Later served as Colonel of this regiment. [For additional information, see the first paragraph of the history of the 58th Regiment on page 212 of this volume.]

WISEMAN, MARTIN D.

Born in Burke County and resided in Mitchell County prior to enlisting at age 43. Elected 2nd Lieutenant on or about December 30, 1861. Elected 1st Lieutenant on June 10, 1862. Promoted to Captain to rank from June 27, 1862. Reported present in January-June, 1863. Resigned on July 4, 1863, because "I am over 45 years of age and my fam[i]ly is in a condition that requir[e]s my attention at home being all of the female sect [sic] and no man person on the primises [sic]; also feeling a[n] incompacency [sic] of filling the office which I now hold." Resignation accepted on July 11, 1863.

TOBEY, FREDERICK ALBERT

Born in Livingston County, New York, and enlisted at age 19, December 30, 1861. Mustered in as Sergeant. Elected 2nd Lieutenant on June 10, 1862. Reported present or accounted for in January-June, 1863. Promoted to Captain on July 11, 1863. Reported present in September-October, 1863, and January-August, 1864. Transferred to Company D of this regiment subsequent to March 15, 1865. [Reported in command of Company F of this regiment in January-February, 1864.]

BAIRD, BENJAMIN F.

Previously served as Captain of Company D of this regiment. Transferred to this company subsequent to March 15, 1865. Paroled at Greensboro on May 1, 1865. In battle he was "cool, composed, and thoughtful." He was "one of the few men that never dodged when a ball whizzed by him."

LIEUTENANTS

COFFEY, WILLIAM COLUMBUS, 1st Lieutenant

Previously served as 2nd Lieutenant of Company E of this regiment. Promoted to 1st Lieutenant and transferred to this company subsequent to March 19, 1865. Paroled at Greensboro on May 1, 1865.

DAVIS, ALBERT F., 2nd Lieutenant

Previously served as 3rd Lieutenant of Company D of this regiment. Transferred to this company subsequent to August 31, 1864. Promoted to 2nd Lieutenant on an unspecified date. Paroled at Greensboro on May 1, 1865.

OLLIS, JOHN, 1st Lieutenant

Born in Burke County and resided in Mitchell or Watauga County where he was by occupation a farmer prior to enlisting at age 43. Elected 1st Lieutenant on or about December 30, 1861. Reduced to ranks on February 11, 1862. Elected 3rd Lieutenant on June 10, 1862. Promoted to 1st Lieutenant on June 27, 1862. Reported present in January-April, 1863. Reported absent sick in May, 1863. Resigned on June 3, 1863, because "I am over fifty years of age[?] and I am too weakley constituted to perform the duties of my office. Second[,] that I do not feel myself competent and do not believe that I can acquire a sufficent knowledge of military affares to perform the duties of a lieutenant. . . ." Resignation accepted on June 17, 1863.

VANCE, WILLIAM A., 3rd Lieutenant

Previously served as Private in 2nd Company H (later consolidated into Company B), 26th Regiment Tennessee Infantry. Transferred to this company on January 22, 1863. Mustered in as Private. Reported present through June, 1863. Promoted to 1st Sergeant in July-October, 1863. Reported present in September-October, 1863. Elected 3rd Lieutenant on November 17, 1863. Furloughed for twenty-eight days on February 19, 1864. Returned to duty prior to May 1, 1864. Reported present through August 31, 1864. [Nominated for the Badge of Distinction for gallantry at Chickamauga, Georgia, September 19-20, 1863.]

WISE, JASPER J., 2nd Lieutenant

Resided in Mitchell County where he enlisted on July 10, 1862, for the war. Mustered in as Private. Reported present in January-June, 1863. Promoted to Corporal in March-April, 1863. Promoted to Sergeant in July-September, 1863. Elected 2nd Lieutenant on October 6, 1863. Reported present in September-October, 1863, and January-April, 1864. Wounded at Kolb's Farm, near Marietta, Georgia, June 22, 1864. Returned to duty prior to September 1, 1864. No further records. Survived the war. [North Carolina pension records indicate that he was wounded in the left arm at Chickamauga, Georgia, November 23, 1863. Was about 23 years of age at time of enlistment.]

WISEMAN, JOHN WESS, 3rd Lieutenant

Born in Yancey County and resided in Mitchell or Watauga County where he was by occupation a farmer prior to enlisting at age 20. Appointed 2nd Lieutenant on or about December 30, 1861. Reduced to ranks subsequent to March 1, 1862. Appointed 3rd Lieutenant on June 27, 1862. Reduced to ranks on November 24, 1862. Promoted to 1st Sergeant prior to March 1, 1863. Reported present in January-June, 1863. Appointed 3rd Lieutenant on June 17, 1863. Killed at Chickamauga, Georgia, September 20, 1863.

WISEMAN, WILLIAM HENRY, 1st Lieutenant

Previously served as Private in Company E, 6th Regiment N.C. State Troops. Elected 3rd Lieutenant of this company on or about November 24, 1862. Reported present in January-June, 1863. Promoted to 1st Lieutenant on June 17, 1863. Reported present in September-October, 1863. Reported absent on detached service on November 1, 1863. Ordered to rejoin his command on March 8, 1864. Reported absent sick from "May" through August 20, 1864. Returned to duty prior to September 1, 1864. Hospitalized at Macon, Georgia, March 25, 1865, with intermittent fever. Reported in hospital at Macon on April 21, 1865. Survived the war. [North Carolina pension records indicate that he was wounded in the right arm at Chickamauga, Georgia, September 19-20, 1863, and was "parelized [sic] for some time."]

NONCOMMISSIONED OFFICERS AND PRIVATES

ABEE, ANDREW, ———

An undated bounty pay and receipt roll indicates that he enlisted in this company.

ABEE, JAMES E., Private

Resided in Mitchell or Burke County and was by occupation a farmer prior to enlisting in Mitchell County at age 27, July 16, 1862, for the war. Furloughed for thirty days in January-February, 1863. Returned to duty in March-April, 1863. Reported present in May-June, 1863. Hospitalized at Macon, Georgia, September 26, 1863, with rheumatism. Returned to duty subsequent to October 31, 1863. Reported present in January-April, 1864. Sent to hospital on July 13, 1864. Reported in hospital through August 31, 1864. Transferred to Company D of this regiment when the 58th and 60th Regiments were consolidated on April 9, 1865.

ABEE, JOHN H., Private

Resided in Mitchell or Burke County and was by occupation a farmer prior to enlisting in Mitchell County at age 30, July 16, 1862, for the war. Reported present in January-June, 1863. Reported present but under arrest in September-October, 1863. Reason he was arrested not reported. Returned to duty prior to March 1, 1864. Reported present in March-April, 1864. Sent to hospital on July 1, 1864. Reported absent in hospital through August 31, 1864. No further records. Survived the war. [North Carolina pension records indicate that he was wounded in the right leg (fracture) and left little finger (amputated at first joint) at Missionary Ridge, Tennessee, in "June, 1863."]

ALLIS, G., ———

Place and date of enlistment not reported. Listed as a deserter on September 10, 1864.

ANDERSON, JASPER NEWTON, Private

Born in Yancey County and enlisted in Mitchell County at age 26, on or about June 10, 1862, for the war. Transferred to Company B, 5th Battalion N.C. Cavalry, on or about June 27, 1862. Later served as 1st Lieutenant of that company.

ANDERSON, JOHN P., ———

An undated bounty pay and receipt roll indicates that he enlisted in this company.

ARNETT, JOHN B., Private

Born in Burke County and resided in Mitchell or Yancey County where he was by occupation a farmer prior to enlisting at age 33, June 10, 1862, for the war. Furloughed for twenty days prior to March 1, 1863. Failed to return to duty and was listed as a deserter on March 31, 1863.

AUSBURN, JACOB, Private

Enlisted in Hamilton County, Tennessee, October 20, 1863, for the war. Reported present in January-April, 1864. Wounded at Kolb's Farm, near Marietta, Georgia, June 22, 1864. Returned to duty prior to September 1, 1864. No further records.

AUTRY, H. AVERY, Private

Born in McDowell County* and enlisted at Camp Martin (Mitchell County) at age 20, June 10, 1862, for the war. Reported present in January-June, 1863. Wounded in the left side at Chickamauga, Georgia, September 19, 1863. Hospitalized at Atlanta, Georgia. Reported absent without leave on July 2, 1864. Listed as a deserter on September 10, 1864.

AUTRY, JOSEPH P., 1st Sergeant

Born in McDowell County* and enlisted in Mitchell County at age 25, June 10, 1862, for the war. Mustered in as Private. Reported present in January-June, 1863. Promoted to Sergeant in July-October, 1863. Reported present in September-October, 1863. Promoted to 1st Sergeant in November, 1863-February, 1864. Reported present in January-April, 1864. Wounded at Kolb's Farm, near Marietta, Georgia, June 22, 1864. Returned to duty prior to September 1, 1864. No further records.

BAILEY, CHARLES, Private

Born in Yancey County and enlisted at age 19, January 21, 1862. Was reportedly transferred to Company B, 5th Battalion N.C. Cavalry, on an unspecified date; however, it is not certain that his transfer actually took place. Died prior to March 1, 1863. Place, date, and cause of death not reported.

BAKER, WILLIAM, Private

Born in Carter County, Tennessee, and enlisted at Camp Martin (Mitchell County) at age 26, June 10, 1862, for the war. No further records.

BENFIELD, ADOLPHUS L., Private

Born in Burke County and was by occupation a farmer prior to enlisting in Mitchell County at age 34, June 10, 1862, for the war. Transferred to Company K of this regiment on or about July 29, 1862.

BENFIELD, BYARD HENRY, SR., Private

Born in Burke County on January 22, 1837. Resided in Mitchell or Burke County and was by occupation a farmer prior to enlisting at

age 24, December 30, 1861. Deserted at Jacksboro, Tennessee, January 8, 1863.

BIDDIX, CHARLES, ———

An undated bounty pay and receipt roll and a pension application filed by his widow indicate that he enlisted in this company.

BIDDIX, FRANCIS A., Private

Resided in Mitchell or McDowell County and was by occupation a farmer prior to enlisting in Mitchell County at age 47, July 19, 1862, for the war. Deserted on January 25, 1863, but was "brought back" on February 5, 1863. Reported present in May-June, 1863. Wounded in the right forearm (compound fracture) and hand at Chickamauga, Georgia, September 20, 1863. Hospitalized at Atlanta, Georgia. Reported absent wounded through August 31, 1864. No further records. Survived the war.

BIDDIX, JAMES A., Private

Place and date of enlistment not reported; however, he probably enlisted subsequent to August 31, 1864. Captured at Orangeburg, South Carolina, February 12, 1865. Confined at Hart's Island, New York Harbor, April 10, 1865. Died at Hart's Island on June 8, 1865, of "dropsy from heart disease."

BLALOCK, SAMUEL W., Corporal

Enlisted on December 30, 1861. Mustered in as Private. Promoted to Corporal on February 11, 1862. No further records. Survived the war. [Was about 16 years of age at time of enlistment.]

BOLICK, JOSEPH B., Private

Born in Burke County and was by occupation a farmer prior to enlisting in Mitchell County at age 24, June 10, 1862, for the war. Transferred to Company K of this regiment on or about July 29, 1862.

BOON, JAMES, Private

An undated bounty pay and receipt roll indicates that he enlisted in this company.

BOONE, WILLIAM R., Private

Born in Rutherford County and enlisted at Camp Martin (Mitchell County) at age 25, June 10, 1862, for the war. Transferred to Company B, 5th Battalion N.C. Cavalry, on or about June 27, 1862.

BOWMAN, AMBROSE, Private

Resided in Mitchell or Burke County and was by occupation a farmer prior to enlisting in Mitchell County at age 26, July 16, 1862, for the war. Reported present in January-June, 1863. Wounded at Chickamauga, Georgia, September 20, 1863. Reported absent wounded or absent sick through February, 1864. Apparently returned to duty in March-April, 1864, but was reported absent sick on April 21, 1864. Reported absent in hospital through August 31, 1864. No further records. Survived the war.

BRIGGS, JOHN E., Private

Born in Yancey County and enlisted at age 27, February 4, 1862. Transferred to Company B, 5th Battalion N.C. Cavalry, on or about June 27, 1862.

BRINKLEY, ALEXANDER, Private

Born in Rowan County and resided in Mitchell or Yancey County where he was by occupation county registrar prior to enlisting in

Mitchell County at age 47, June 10, 1862, for the war. Reported present in January-June, 1863. Sent to hospital on August 2, 1863. No further records. Survived the war.

BROWN, ROMULUS W., Private

Born in Burke County and enlisted at age 18, December 30, 1861. Transferred to Company B, 5th Battalion N.C. Cavalry, on or about June 27, 1862.

BUCHANAN, ALLEN, Private

Resided in Mitchell or Yancey County and was by occupation a farmer prior to enlisting at age 36, April 10, 1862. No further records. Survived the war.

BURLISON, JOSEPH M., Private

Previously served as Private in Company B of this regiment. Transferred to this company on or about May 6, 1863. Deserted at Clinton, Tennessee, June 6, 1863. Later served as Private in Company C, 13th Regiment Tennessee Cavalry (Union).

BURLISON, WILLIAM, JR., Private

Born in Yancey County and enlisted at age 18, December 30, 1861. Transferred to Company B, 5th Battalion N.C. Cavalry, on or about June 27, 1862. Transferred back to this company prior to March 1, 1863. Reported present in January-June, 1863. Wounded at Chickamauga, Georgia, September 20, 1863. Hospitalized at Atlanta, Georgia. Failed to return to duty and was dropped from the company rolls on August 29, 1864.

BURLISON, WILLIAM A., Private

Enlisted at Camp Martin (Mitchell County) at age 25, June 10, 1862, for the war. Transferred to Company B, 5th Battalion N.C. Cavalry, on or about June 27, 1862.

CALLOWAY, BENJAMIN, Private

Born in Ashe County and enlisted at Camp Martin (Mitchell County) at age 22, June 10, 1862, for the war. Transferred to Company B, 5th Battalion N.C. Cavalry, on or about June 27, 1862.

CARAWAY, ELISHA, Private

Born in Yancey County where he resided as a farm laborer prior to enlisting in Mitchell County at age 23, June 10, 1862, for the war. Reported present on surviving company muster rolls through August 31, 1864. Captured at Orangeburg, South Carolina, February 12, 1865. Confined at Hart's Island, New York Harbor. Released at Hart's Island on June 19, 1865, after taking the Oath of Allegiance.

CARPENTER, ALEXANDER L., Private

Resided in Mitchell or Watauga County and was by occupation a farmer prior to enlisting at age 27, December 30, 1861. Mustered in as Sergeant. Reduced to ranks on February 11, 1862. Transferred to Company B, 5th Battalion N.C. Cavalry, on or about June 27, 1862. Transferred back to this company on or about November 1, 1862. Reported present in January-June, 1863. Deserted on August 26, 1863. [Service record omitted in volume 2 of this series. North Carolina pension records indicate that he was wounded at Jacksboro, Tennessee, December 15, 1862.]

CARPENTER, ALFRED A., Private

Born in Yancey County and resided in Mitchell or Yancey County where he was by occupation a farmer prior to enlisting at age 22,

January 7, 1862. Transferred to Company B, 5th Battalion N.C. Cavalry, on or about June 27, 1862.

CARPENTER, DAVID L., Private

Born in Yancey County and enlisted at age 22, January 14, 1862. Transferred to Company B, 5th Battalion N.C. Cavalry, on or about June 27, 1862.

CARPENTER, ERWIN L., Private

Resided in Mitchell or Yancey County and enlisted at age 15, December 30, 1861. Not reported in the records of this company subsequent to February 1, 1862. Presumably was discharged in the summer of 1862 by reason of being underage.

CARPENTER, JACOB, Private

Born in Yancey County and resided in Mitchell or Yancey County where he was by occupation a farmer prior to enlisting in Mitchell County at age 28, June 10, 1862, for the war. Reported absent on expired furlough on or about February 28, 1863. Returned to duty in March-April, 1863. Reported present in May-June, 1863. Sent to hospital at Knoxville, Tennessee, August 1, 1863. Reported absent without leave from August 20, 1863, until December 10, 1863. Reported present in January-April, 1864. Survived the war.

CARPENTER, JAMES A., Private

Born in Yancey County and resided in Mitchell or Yancey County prior to enlisting at age 20, December 30, 1861. Last reported in the records of this company on June 10, 1862. Died prior to July 14, 1863. Place, date, and cause of death not reported.

CARPENTER, JONATHAN N. M., Private

Born in Yancey County and enlisted at age 18, December 30, 1861. Transferred to Company B, 5th Battalion N.C. Cavalry, on or about June 27, 1862.

CARPENTER, JOSEPH, Private

Enlisted in Mitchell County on June 10, 1862, for the war. "Left his company without leave" on August 20, 1863. Returned to duty on October 20, 1863. Reported present in May-August, 1864.

CARPENTER, REUBEN H., Private

Born in Yancey County where he resided as a farmer prior to enlisting at age 18, December 30, 1861. Transferred to Company B, 5th Battalion N.C. Cavalry, on or about June 27, 1862.

CARPENTER, WILLIAM, Private

Enlisted at Dalton, Georgia, December 10, 1863, for the war. Reported absent sick from February 6, 1864, through August 31, 1864. Hospitalized at Jackson, Mississippi, November 8, 1864, with chronic diarrhoea. Furloughed on November 17, 1864. No further records.

CARPENTER, WILLIAM N., Private

Resided in Mitchell or Yancey County and was by occupation a farmer prior to enlisting at age 24, December 30, 1861. Last reported in the records of this company on March 1, 1862. Survived the war. [North Carolina pension records indicate that he lost his right eye as a result of typhoid fever contracted during the war.]

CARVER, WILLIAM, Private

Born in Yancey County and enlisted at Camp Martin (Mitchell County) at age 19, June 10, 1862, for the war. No further records.

CHANDLER, DAVID A., Private

Born in Yancey County and resided in Yancey or Mitchell County where he was by occupation a farmer prior to enlisting in Mitchell County at age 28, June 10, 1862, for the war. Elected 1st Lieutenant of Company K of this regiment on July 29, 1862.

CHAPMAN, NATHAN, Private

Resided in Mitchell or Burke County and enlisted in Mitchell County at age 21, July 16, 1862, for the war. Reported present in January-February, 1863. Died on March 29, 1863. Place and cause of death not reported.

CLARK, DEASTON C., Private

Born in Caldwell County and was by occupation a farmer prior to enlisting at age 20, April 3, 1862. Transferred to Company B, 5th Battalion N.C. Cavalry, on or about June 27, 1862. Transferred back to this company on an unspecified date. Transferred to Company E of this regiment on or about July 29, 1862.

CLARK, DORAN F., Private

Born in Caldwell County and was by occupation a farmer prior to enlisting at age 20, April 3, 1862. Transferred to Company B, 5th Battalion N.C. Cavalry, on or about June 27, 1862.

CLARKE, ANDREW, ———

North Carolina pension records indicate that he served in this company.

CLOUD, TERRELL C., Private

Born in Burke County and was by occupation a farmer prior to enlisting in Mitchell County on July 16, 1862, for the war. Reported present in January-June, 1863. Deserted at Lenoir Station, Tennessee, August 27, 1863. Later served as Private in Company C, 13th Regiment Tennessee Cavalry (Union).

COLLETT, ORLANDO C., Sergeant

Previously served as Sergeant in Company E of this regiment. Transferred to this company subsequent to August 31, 1864. Paroled at Morganton on May 15, 1865.

CONLEY, JAMES, Private

Born at Rochester, New York, and enlisted at age 23, December 30, 1861. Mustered in as Private. Promoted to Sergeant on February 11, 1862. Reduced to ranks subsequent to March 1, 1862. Transferred to Company B, 5th Battalion N.C. Cavalry, on or about June 27, 1862.

COOK, CALVIN HARRISON, Corporal

Born in Bradley County, Tennessee, where he resided prior to enlisting in Mitchell County at age 22, January 7, 1862. Mustered in as Private. Promoted to Corporal prior to March 1, 1863. Reported present in January-June, 1863. Deserted on September 2, 1863. Went over to the enemy on an unspecified date. Took the Oath of Allegiance at Nashville, Tennessee, on or about December 24, 1863.

COOK, ISAAC, Private

Born in Yancey County and resided in Mitchell or Yancey County where he was by occupation a farmer prior to enlisting in Mitchell County at age 28, June 10, 1862, for the war. Reported present in January-February, 1863. Deserted at Big Creek Gap, Tennessee, March 28, 1863.

COOK, JOHN, Private

Born in Yancey County and enlisted at age 18, December 30, 1861. Furloughed for thirty days at Cumberland Gap, Tennessee, on October 18, 1862. Failed to return to duty and was reported absent without leave. Dropped from the company rolls in January-February, 1864.

COOK, LEWIS D., Private

Born in Yancey County and enlisted at age 21, March 25, 1862. Transferred to Company B, 5th Battalion N.C. Cavalry, on or about June 27, 1862. Transferred back to this company on or about July 29, 1862. Reported present in January-February, 1863. Deserted at Big Creek Gap, Tennessee, March 28, 1863.

COOK, THOMAS, Private

Born in Monroe County, Tennessee, and enlisted in Mitchell County at age 34, June 10, 1862, for the war. Furloughed for twenty days at Big Creek Gap, Tennessee, November 22, 1862. Reported absent on expired furlough in January-June, 1863. Died in hospital at Atlanta, Georgia, January 27, 1864. Cause of death not reported.

CUTHBERTSON, DAVID H., Private

Born in Burke County and resided in Mitchell or Watauga County where he was by occupation a farmer prior to enlisting at age 30, February 4, 1862. Died on an unspecified date (probably subsequent to June 10, 1862, but prior to March 1, 1863). Place and cause of death not reported.

CUTHBERTSON, NATHAN M., Private

Resided in McDowell County and was by occupation a laborer prior to enlisting in Mitchell County at age 27, July 16, 1862, for the war. Reported absent on expired furlough on February 28, 1863. Returned to duty in March-April, 1863. Reported present in May-June, 1863. Sent to hospital on August 1, 1863. Reported absent without leave on August 20, 1863. Returned to duty on December 10, 1863. Reported present through April 30, 1864. Reported absent without leave on July 2, 1864. Deserted to the enemy on an unspecified date. Sent to Chattanooga, Tennessee. Transferred to Louisville, Kentucky. Released at Louisville on July 27, 1864, after taking the Oath of Allegiance.

CUTHBERTSON, SAMUEL T., Private

Resided in Mitchell or McDowell County and was by occupation a laborer prior to enlisting in Mitchell County at age 33, August 24, 1862, for the war. Was apparently mustered in with the rank of Sergeant. Reported present in January-June, 1863. Deserted from camp near Chattanooga, Tennessee, September 25, 1863. Reduced to ranks in November-December, 1864. Returned to duty on January 20, 1864. Reported present in March-August, 1864. No further records. Survived the war.

DALE, MARTIN L., Private

Resided in McDowell County and enlisted in Mitchell County on July 16, 1862, for the war. Furloughed for thirty days at Johnson's Depot, Tennessee, August 28, 1862. Reported absent on expired furlough in January-June, 1863. Returned to duty prior to November 1, 1863. Sent to hospital at Atlanta, Georgia, January 6, 1864. Had not returned to duty as of August 31, 1864. Hospitalized at Macon, Georgia, February 23, 1865, with debilitas. Returned to duty on March 28, 1865. No further records. Survived the war. [North Carolina pension records indicate that he was wounded in the right knee at Missionary Ridge, Tennessee, in November, 1863. Was about 23 years of age at time of enlistment.]

DALE, SILVANUS, ———
An undated bounty pay and receipt roll indicates that he enlisted in this company.

DANCY, SAMUEL, Private
Previously served as Private in Company E of this regiment. Enlisted in this company at Dalton, Georgia, October 17, 1863, for the war. Sent to hospital at Atlanta, Georgia, February 16, 1864, with an unspecified illness. Returned to duty in May-August, 1864. No further records.

DANIEL, MARTIN V., Private
Enlisted on December 30, 1861. Last reported in the records of this company on March 1, 1862.

DEAN, ALEXANDER C., Private
Born in Burke County and was by occupation a farmer prior to enlisting at age 24, March 18, 1862. Transferred to Company B, 5th Battalion N.C. Cavalry, on or about June 27, 1862.

DEAN, GEORGE W., Sergeant
Born in Burke County and resided in Mitchell or Yancey County where he was by occupation a farmer prior to enlisting at age 25, December 30, 1861. Mustered in as Private. Promoted to Sergeant on February 11, 1862. No further records.

DELLINGER, HENRY T., Private
Resided in Mitchell or Watauga County and was by occupation a farmer prior to enlisting at age 16, December 30, 1861. Discharged on February 1, 1862, presumably by reason of his youth.

DELLINGER, JOHN C., Private
Born in Yancey County and resided in Mitchell or Watauga County where he was by occupation a farmer prior to enlisting at age 18, December 30, 1861. Mustered in as Musician (Fifer). Reduced to ranks on February 11, 1862. Transferred to Company B, 5th Battalion N.C. Cavalry, on or about June 27, 1862. Reenlisted in this company on April 18, 1863, while absent without leave from the 5th Battalion N.C. Cavalry. Reported present in May-June, 1863. Deserted on August 20, 1863. Returned to duty on January 4, 1864. Court-martialed on an unspecified date. Reported under arrest through April, 1864. Returned to duty on an unspecified date. Wounded in the head at Resaca, Georgia, May 14-15, 1864. Reported absent without leave on July 2, 1864. Listed as a deserter on September 10, 1864.

DELLINGER, JOSEPH F., Private
Born in Lincoln County and enlisted at age 39, December 30, 1861. Reported absent on expired furlough in January-February, 1863. Returned to duty in March-April, 1863. Reported present in May-June, 1863. Sent to hospital at Loudon, Tennessee, July 1, 1863. Reported absent without leave on August 22, 1863. Returned to duty on December 10, 1863. Reported present in January-April, 1864. Wounded in the left side of the face just below the eye at Resaca, Georgia, May 14-15, 1864. Returned to duty prior to September 1, 1864. No further records. Survived the war.

DELLINGER, REUBEN A., Private
Born in Yancey County and resided in Mitchell or Watauga County where he was by occupation a farmer prior to enlisting at age 22, December 30, 1861. Transferred to Company B, 5th Battalion N.C. Cavalry, on or about June 27, 1862. Reenlisted in this company on

April 18, 1863, while absent without leave from the 5th Battalion N.C. Cavalry. Reported present in May-June, 1863. Deserted on August 20, 1863. Rejoined the company on January 4, 1864. Court-martialed on March 20, 1864, and sentenced to be shot. No further records.

EDWARDS, THOMAS, Private
Enlisted in Hamilton County, Tennessee, October 2, 1863, for the war. Sent to hospital at Atlanta, Georgia, February 16, 1864. Had not returned to duty as of August 31, 1864. No further records.

ELLIOTT, SHELLY, ———
North Carolina pension records indicate that he served in this company.

ENGLISH, ADEN, Private
Born in Burke County and resided in McDowell County where he was by occupation a farmer prior to enlisting in Mitchell County at age 33, July 13, 1862, for the war. Transferred to Company K of this regiment on or about July 29, 1862.

ENGLISH, DAVID J., Private
Enlisted on December 30, 1861. Last reported in the records of this company on March 1, 1862.

ENGLISH, JOHN MILTON, Private
Born in Burke County and resided in Mitchell or Yancey County where he was by occupation a farmer prior to enlisting at age 42, January 28, 1862. Transferred to Company B, 5th Battalion N.C. Cavalry, on or about June 27, 1862. Later served as 1st Lieutenant of that unit.

ENGLISH, JOSIAH H., Private
Enlisted on January 7, 1862. Discharged on March 10, 1862. No further records.

ENGLISH, SAMUEL W., Sergeant
Born in Burke County and resided in Mitchell or McDowell County prior to enlisting at age 35, January 14, 1862. Mustered in as Private. Promoted to Sergeant on January 21, 1862. Transferred to Company B, 5th Battalion N.C. Cavalry, June 27, 1862. Later served as Captain of that company.

ENGLISH, WILLIAM C., Private
Born in Yancey County* and resided in Madison County where he was by occupation a farmer prior to enlisting at Camp Martin (Mitchell County) at age 37, June 10, 1862, for the war. Transferred to Company B, 5th Battalion N.C. Cavalry, on or about June 27, 1862.

ERWIN, ARTHUR D., Private
Resided in Mitchell or Yancey County and was by occupation a farmer prior to enlisting at age 22, December 30, 1861. Transferred to Company B, 5th Battalion N.C. Cavalry, on or about June 27, 1862.

FAIRCLOTH, M. L., Private
Place and date of enlistment not reported. Paroled at Salisbury on May 2, 1865. Place of residence reported as Owensville (Roseboro), Sampson County.

FARECLOTH, WILLIAM, Private

Enlisted in Hamilton County, Tennessee, October 2, 1863, for the war. Sent to hospital at Atlanta, Georgia, February 16, 1864. Returned to duty in March-April, 1864. Reported present through August 31, 1864. No further records.

FINEY, FRANKLIN, Private

Enlisted at Dalton, Georgia, May 22, 1864, for the war. Reported present through August 31, 1864. No further records.

FRANKLIN, ALBERT JOHNSTON, Private

Born in Yancey County on December 8, 1843. Enlisted at age 18, December 30, 1861. Mustered in as Corporal. Reduced to ranks on February 11, 1862. Transferred to Company B, 5th Battalion N.C. Cavalry, on or about June 27, 1862. Reenlisted in this company in Mitchell County on April 18, 1863, while absent without leave from the 5th Battalion. Reported present in May-June, 1863. Was probably transferred to Company K, 65th Regiment N.C. Troops (6th Regiment N.C. Cavalry), subsequent to June 30, 1863; however, he failed to report for duty with that company. No further records. Survived the war. [North Carolina pension records indicate that he was wounded by a "stroke of lightning" at Johnson Depot, Tennessee, on or about August 15, 1862.]

FRANKLIN, DAVID S., Private

Born in Yancey County and enlisted at age 16, December 30, 1861. Reported absent on expired furlough on February 28, 1863. Returned to duty in March-April, 1863. Reported present in May-June, 1863. Deserted from camp near Chattanooga, Tennessee, September 25, 1863.

FRANKLIN, GEORGE W., Private

Born in Yancey County* and resided in Mitchell or Watauga County where he was by occupation a farmer prior to enlisting at age 34, March 25, 1862. Reported present in January-June, 1863. Reported on detached service in September-October, 1863. No further records.

FRANKLIN, J. S., ———

North Carolina pension records indicate that he served in this company.

FRANKLIN, JACOB A., Private

Born in Yancey County and resided in Mitchell County prior to enlisting at age 18, December 30, 1861. Reported present in January-February, 1863. Transferred to Company B, 5th Battalion N.C. Cavalry, April 16, 1863.

FRANKLIN, JAMES A., Private

Born in Yancey County and enlisted at Camp Martin (Mitchell County) at age 20, June 10, 1862, for the war. Transferred to Company B, 5th Battalion N.C. Cavalry, on or about June 27, 1862.

FRANKLIN, JAMES M., JR., Private

Resided in Mitchell or Watauga County and was by occupation a farmer prior to enlisting at age 39, December 30, 1861. Last reported in the records of this company on March 1, 1862. "Furloughed without pay" on an unspecified date. No further records.

FRANKLIN, LEVI A., Private

Enlisted in Mitchell County on July 16, 1862, for the war. Reported present in January-June, 1863. Wounded at Chickamauga, Geor-

gia, September 20, 1863. Deserted from camp near Chattanooga, Tennessee, September 24, 1863. Enlisted as Private in Company C, 13th Regiment Tennessee Cavalry (Union), on or about the same date. [Was 20 years of age at the time of his enlistment in the 13th Tennessee Cavalry.]

FRANKLIN, SAMUEL D., Private

Enlisted on December 30, 1861. Died at Big Creek Gap, Tennessee, prior to March 20, 1863. Date and cause of death not reported.

FREEMAN, W. LARCAN, Private

Enlisted in Mitchell County on October 15, 1863, for the war. Wounded at Kolb's Farm, near Marietta, Georgia, June 22, 1864. Returned to duty prior to September 1, 1864. Hospitalized at Augusta, Georgia, February 4, 1865. No further records.

GADDY, JAMES, Private

Born in Anson County and resided in Mitchell County where he was by occupation a farmer prior to enlisting at age 37, December 30, 1861. Transferred to Company B, 5th Battalion N.C. Cavalry, on or about June 27, 1862.

GADDY, JESSE A., Private

Resided in Mitchell County where he enlisted on August 20, 1862, for the war. Reported present or accounted for in January-June and September-October, 1863. Reported absent on detached service from November 1, 1863, through April 30, 1864. Wounded at Kolb's Farm, near Marietta, Georgia, June 22, 1864. Was reportedly captured near Atlanta, Georgia, July 20, 1864; however, that report appears to be erroneous. Hospitalized in a Confederate hospital at Macon, Georgia, July 22, 1864. Transferred on July 23, 1864. Returned to duty prior to September 17, 1864. Paroled at Greensboro on May 5, 1865. [Was about 22 years of age at time of enlistment.]

GADDY, SAMUEL H., Private

Born in Anson County and enlisted at age 19, January 17, 1862. Transferred to Company B, 5th Battalion N.C. Cavalry, on or about June 27, 1862. Transferred back to this company on an unspecified date. Reported present in January-June, 1863. Sent to hospital on August 1, 1863. Reported absent without leave on January 20, 1864. Reported present but under arrest in March-April, 1864. "Left his com[man]d" on June 30, 1864. Returned to duty on July 31, 1864. Reported present through August 31, 1864. Wounded slightly in the head at Bentonville on March 19, 1865. No further records.

GENTRY, ROBERT P., Private

Born in Buncombe County and was by occupation a farmer prior to enlisting at Camp Martin (Mitchell County) at age 23, June 10, 1862, for the war. Transferred to Company B, 5th Battalion N.C. Cavalry, on or about June 27, 1862.

GILLESPIE, HENRY, Private

Born in McDowell County* and enlisted in Mitchell County at age 24, June 10, 1862, for the war. Mustered in as Private. Reported present in January-June, 1863. Wounded at Chickamauga, Georgia, September 20, 1863. Returned to duty prior to October 31, 1863. Promoted to Corporal to rank from October 30, 1863. Reduced to ranks on January 1, 1864. Reported present in January-August, 1864. No further records. Survived the war.

GILLISPEE, FRANCIS M., Private

Resided in Mitchell or McDowell County and enlisted in Mitchell County at age 19, July 16, 1862, for the war. Reported present in January-February, 1863. Died on April 1, 1863. Place and cause of death not reported.

GREEN, JAMES M., Private

Born in Burke or Yancey County and was by occupation a farmer prior to enlisting at age 21, January 28, 1862. Transferred to Company B, 5th Battalion N.C. Cavalry, on or about June 27, 1862.

GREEN, PATERSON, Private

Enlisted in Mitchell County at age 23, March 30, 1863, for the war. Reported present through April 30, 1863. Deserted at Clinton, Tennessee, June 6, 1863. [May have served later in Company C, 13th Regiment Tennessee Cavalry (Union).]

GREEN, SAMUEL P., Private

Enlisted in Mitchell County on March 30, 186[3], for the war. Confined in an unspecified Confederate prison on an unspecified date. Reason he was confined not reported. Released from prison on July 2, 1863. Sent to hospital at Knoxville, Tennessee, August 24, 1863. No further records.

GREEN, STEPHEN M., Musician

Born in Yancey County and enlisted at age 17, December 30, 1861. Mustered in as Private. Promoted to Musician (Fifer) on February 11, 1862. Reported absent on expired furlough in January-February, 1863. Returned to duty in March-April, 1863. Reported present on surviving company muster rolls through August 31, 1864. Died at Macon, Georgia, October 17, 1864. Cause of death not reported.

GURLEY, HARVEY M., Private

Born in Burke County and enlisted at age 24, December 30, 1861. Mustered in as Private. Reported present in January-February, 1863. Promoted to Corporal prior to March 1, 1863. Reduced to ranks on an unspecified date. Died in hospital at Clinton, Tennessee, April 13, 1863. Cause of death not reported.

GUYER, ISAAC S., Private

Born in Mecklenburg County and enlisted at age 34, April 12, 1862. Transferred to Company B, 5th Battalion N.C. Cavalry, on or about June 27, 1862.

HALL, ELIJAH, Private

Resided in Mitchell or McDowell County and was by occupation a farmer prior to enlisting in Mitchell County at age 33, July 16, 1862, for the war. Reported present on surviving company muster rolls through August 31, 1864. No further records. Survived the war.

HALL, MOSES W., Private

Resided in Mitchell or McDowell County and enlisted in Mitchell County on July 16, 1862, for the war. Reported present or accounted for in January-June, 1863. Sent to hospital at Knoxville, Tennessee, July 28, 1863, suffering from measles and typhoid fever. Returned to duty on an unspecified date. Sent to hospital at Atlanta, Georgia, November 6, 1863. Returned to duty in March-April, 1864. Reported present through August 31, 1864. No further records. Survived the war. [Was about 30 years of age at time of enlistment.]

HARVEL, WILLIAM, Private

Born in Yancey County and enlisted at age 18, December 30, 1861. Transferred to Company B, 5th Battalion N.C. Cavalry, on or about June 27, 1862.

HASE, JESSE, Private

Enlisted in Hamilton or Greene County, Tennessee, October 20, 186[3], for the war. Deserted on an unspecified date. Apprehended on an unspecified date. Court-martialed on April 2, 1864, and sentenced to be shot. No further records. [His given name may have been Jake or Jacob.]

HAVENER, ALEXANDER G., Private

Enlisted on December 30, 1861. Mustered in as Corporal. Reduced to ranks on or about January 21, 1862, and "furloughed without pay." No further records.

HAVENER, JOSEPH F., Private

Born in Lincoln County and enlisted at age 23, December 30, 1861. Transferred to Company B, 5th Battalion N.C. Cavalry, on or about June 27, 1862.

HENLINE, HENRY, Private

Enlisted in Mitchell County on October 24, 1862, for the war. Reported present in January-June, 1863. Sent to hospital at Atlanta, Georgia, September 21, 1863 (was probably wounded at Chickamauga, Georgia, September 19-20, 1863). Returned to duty on an unspecified date. Reported present in January-April, 1864. Wounded at Kolb's Farm, near Marietta, Georgia, June 22, 1864. Returned to duty prior to September 1, 1864. No further records. Survived the war. [Was about 28 years of age at time of enlistment.]

HENSLEY, JOHN A., Corporal

Born in Burke County on January 8, 1827. Resided in Mitchell or Yancey County where he was by occupation a farmer prior to enlisting at age 34, December 30, 1861. Mustered in as Private. Promoted to Corporal on January 21, 1862. Appointed Ordnance Sergeant on an unspecified date (probably on or about July 29, 1862) and transferred to the Field and Staff of this regiment.

HODGES, GILBERT W., Corporal

Previously served as Corporal in Company D of this regiment. Transferred to this company subsequent to August 31, 1864. Paroled at Greensboro on May 1, 1865.

HODGES, LARKIN, Sergeant

Previously served as Sergeant in Company D of this regiment. Transferred to this company subsequent to August 31, 1864. Paroled at Greensboro on May 1, 1865. [North Carolina pension records indicate that he was wounded in the right knee (dislocated) in a skirmish at Deep Creek Gap, Tennessee, on an unspecified date.]

HOGAN, JOHN C., Private

Previously served as Private in Company B, 5th Battalion N.C. Cavalry. Transferred to this company on April 16, 1863. Reported present in May-June, 1863. Sent to hospital at Atlanta, Georgia, September 21, 1863 (was probably wounded at Chickamauga, Georgia, September 19-20, 1863). Reported absent sick through February, 1864. No further records.

HOLDSCLAW, MARION F., Private

Enlisted on December 30, 1861. Discharged on March 4, 1862. Reason discharged not reported. [May be the same man who served as Private in Company D of this regiment under the name of Francis M. Holsclaw.]

HOLIFIELD, JASPER, Private

Enlisted in Mitchell County at age 22, July 16, 1862, for the war. Reported present or accounted for in January-June, 1863. Sent to hospital at Atlanta, Georgia, September 21, 1863 (was probably wounded at Chickamauga, Georgia, September 19-20, 1863). Returned to duty prior to November 1, 1863. Reported present in January-August, 1864. Transferred to Company D of this regiment when the 58th and 60th Regiments were consolidated on April 9, 1865.

HOLIFIELD, JOSEPH, Private

Enlisted in Mitchell County at age 23, July 16, 1862, for the war. Reported present in January-June, 1863. Sent to hospital at Atlanta, Georgia, September 21, 1863 (was probably wounded at Chickamauga, Georgia, September 19-20, 1863). Returned to duty on an unspecified date. Reported present in January-August, 1864. Transferred to Company D of this regiment when the 58th and 60th Regiments were consolidated on April 9, 1865.

HOLIFIELD, MILAS, Private

Enlisted in Mitchell County on July 16, 1862, for the war. Reported present in January-February, 1863. Died on April 2, 1863. Place and cause of death not reported.

HUFFMAN, JOHN, Private

Enlisted in Mitchell County on July 16, 1862, for the war. Reported present in January-June, 1863. Wounded in the thigh at Chickamauga, Georgia, September 19-20, 1863. Hospitalized at Atlanta, Georgia. Reported absent wounded or absent sick through April, 1864. Dropped from the company rolls on August 29, 1864. Survived the war.

HUSKINS, PATTERSON, Private

Enlisted in Anderson County, Tennessee, April 18, 1863, for the war. Dropped from the company rolls ("name canceled") on or about May 1, 1863.

HUSKINS, SAMUEL P., Private

Born in Yancey County and enlisted at age 18, January 7, 1862. Transferred to Company B, 5th Battalion N.C. Cavalry, on or about June 27, 1862.

HUSKINS, WILLIAM M., Private

Born in Yancey County and resided in Mitchell or Yancey County where he was by occupation a farmer prior to enlisting at age 24, December 30, 1861. Mustered in as Private. Promoted to Corporal prior to March 1, 1863. Reported present in January-June, 1863. Hospitalized at Knoxville, Tennessee, on or about July 1, 1863. Apparently returned to duty with the company. Hospitalized at Knoxville on August 1, 1863. Reduced to ranks in July-October, 1863. Reported absent sick through October 31, 1863. No further records. [North Carolina pension records indicate that he contracted a disease in the service that caused his death about two years after the war.]

JOHNSON, ISAAC A., Private

Enlisted on December 30, 1861. Last reported in the records of this company on March 1, 1862. [May have served later in Company F, 3rd Regiment N.C. Mounted Infantry (Union).]

JOHNSON, SAMUEL, Private

Born in Wilkes County and enlisted at Camp Martin (Mitchell County) at age 31, June 10, 1862, for the war. Transferred to Company B, 5th Battalion N.C. Cavalry, on or about June 27, 1862.

KELLER, JOHN W., Private

Born in Burke County and enlisted at age 21, December 30, 1861. Mustered in as Private. Promoted to Corporal on February 11, 1862. Reduced to ranks prior to March 1, 1863. Reported absent on expired furlough in January-February, 1863. Returned to duty in March-April, 1863, and was detailed as a wagoner. Reported present in May-June, 1863. Deserted on August 25, 1863. Returned to duty on December 10, 1863. Reported present in January-April, 1864. Reported absent without leave on July 2, 1864. Listed as a deserter on September 10, 1864. Survived the war. [North Carolina pension records indicate that he received a flesh wound in the right leg in North Carolina on May 1, 1863.]

KELLER, JOSHUA, Private

Born in McDowell County* and enlisted at age 19, December 30, 1861. Reported absent on expired furlough in January-February, 1863. Returned to duty in March-April, 1863. Reported present in May-June, 1863. Killed at Chickamauga, Georgia, September 20, 1863.

KELLER, MICHAEL, Private

Enlisted on December 30, 1861. No further records.

KILPATRICK, FRANKLIN, Private

Place and date of enlistment not reported. Captured at Rough and Ready, Georgia, August 30, 1864. Sent to Nashville, Tennessee. Transferred to Louisville, Kentucky, where he arrived on October 28, 1864. Transferred to Camp Douglas, Chicago, Illinois, where he arrived on November 1, 1864. Died at Camp Douglas on December 23, 1864, of "smallpox."

KING, JOHN, Private

Enlisted in Washington County, Tennessee, August 1, 1862, for the war. Deserted at Cumberland Gap, Tennessee, on or about September 30, 1862.

KNIGHT, JOHN, Private

Enlisted in Mitchell County on December 20, 1862, for the war. Reported present in January-April, 1863. No further records.

LAIL, ALFRED, Private

Resided in Mitchell or Burke County and was by occupation a farmer prior to enlisting in Hamilton County, Tennessee, at age 42, October 20, 1863, for the war. Reported present in January-August, 1864. Died in hospital at Macon, Georgia, October 19, 1864, of disease.

LOWERY, JOHN, Private

Enlisted at Dalton, Georgia, December 10, 1863, for the war. Sent to hospital at Atlanta, Georgia, February 12, 1864. Died (presumably at Atlanta) on March 2, 1864, of disease.

LOWRIE, SAMUEL, Private

Born in McDowell County* and enlisted at age 21, April 9, 1862. Transferred to Company B, 5th Battalion N.C. Cavalry, on or about June 27, 1862. Transferred back to this company on an unspecified date. Reported absent on expired furlough in January-February, 1863. Deserted at Big Creek Gap, Tennessee, March 28, 1863. [Service record omitted in volume 2 of this series.]

LOWRIE, STEWART, Private

Born in Burke County and enlisted at age 48, December 30, 1861. Discharged on February 25, 1862. Reason discharged not reported.

McBEE, WILLIAM, Corporal

Enlisted in Mitchell County on June 10, 1862, for the war. Mustered in as Private. Reported present in January-June, 1863. Promoted to Corporal in July-September, 1863. Killed at Chickamauga, Georgia, September 20, 1863.

McCLELON, WILSON, Private

Enlisted in Mitchell County on July 16, 1862, for the war. Reported absent on expired furlough in January-February, 1863. Deserted at Big Creek Gap, Tennessee, March 28, 1863.

McCURRY, PHINEAS, Private

Born in Yancey County and enlisted at age 18, January 7, 1862. Transferred to Company B, 5th Battalion N.C. Cavalry, on or about June 27, 1862.

McCURRY, TILLMAN H., Private

Born in Yancey County and enlisted at age 19, January 7, 1862. Transferred to Company B, 5th Battalion N.C. Cavalry, on or about June 27, 1862. Transferred back to this company on an unspecified date. Reported present in March-April, 1863. Transferred back to Company B, 5th Battalion N.C. Cavalry, prior to June 19, 1863.

McCURRY, WALTER, Private

Born in Buncombe County and enlisted at age 36, December 30, 1861. Transferred to Company B, 5th Battalion N.C. Cavalry, on or about June 27, 1862.

MACE, JESSE M., Sergeant

Born in Yancey County and resided in Mitchell County where he enlisted at age 21, June 10, 1862, for the war. Mustered in as Private. Reported present in January-June and September-October, 1863. Promoted to Sergeant in November, 1863-February, 1864. Reported present in January-April, 1864. Wounded in the right wrist and left hand at Atlanta, Georgia, July 24, 1864. Hospitalized at Macon, Georgia. Admitted to hospital at Charlotte on August 28, 1864. Furloughed on August 30, 1864. Disabled by his wounds. No further records. Survived the war.

MACE, JOSEPH P., Private

Born in Yancey County and enlisted at age 18, December 30, 1861. Transferred to Company B, 5th Battalion N.C. Cavalry, on or about June 27, 1862.

McFALLS, ARTHUR, Private

Born in Burke County and resided in Mitchell or Yancey County where he was by occupation a farmer prior to enlisting in Mitchell County at age 34, June 10, 1862, for the war. Transferred to Company K of this regiment on or about July 29, 1862. Transferred back to this company prior to September 20, 1863, when he was killed at Chickamauga, Georgia.

McFALLS, DANIEL J., Private

Enlisted in Mitchell County on July 16, 1862, for the war. Reported present in January-February, 1863. Deserted on March 28, 1863.

Returned to duty on April 18, 1863. Died at Knoxville, Tennessee, May 19, 1863. Cause of death not reported.

McFALLS, GEORGE W., Private

Born in Yancey County and was by occupation a farmer prior to enlisting in Mitchell County at age 22, June 10, 1862, for the war. Transferred to Company K of this regiment on or about July 29, 1862.

McGEE, JOHN S., Private

Born in Yancey County and was by occupation a farmer prior to enlisting in Mitchell County at age 21, July 8, 1862, for the war. Transferred to Company K of this regiment on or about July 29, 1862.

McGEE, ROBERT S., Private

Born in McDowell County where he resided as a farmer prior to enlisting in Mitchell County at age 18, July 8, 1862, for the war. Transferred to Company K of this regiment on or about July 29, 1862.

McHONE, T. ZACH, Private

Enlisted in Mitchell County at age 18, October 15, 1863, for the war. Sent to hospital on July 12, 1864. Had not returned to duty as of August 31, 1864. Transferred or assigned temporarily to Company B, 1st Regiment Troops Defenses, Macon, Georgia, in September-December, 1864. No further records. Survived the war.

McKINEY, JULIUS, Private

Enlisted in Mitchell County on July 16, 1862, for the war. Reported present in January-February, 1863. Died in hospital at Knoxville, Tennessee, April 18, 1863. Cause of death not reported.

McKINNEY, JAMES, Private

Born in Yancey County and enlisted at Camp Martin (Mitchell County) at age 24, June 10, 1862, for the war. No further records. [Age discrepancies notwithstanding, it appears likely that this is the same soldier who served later as Private in Company K of this regiment.]

McKINNEY, JASON C., Private

Enlisted in Mitchell County at age 32, July 16, 1862, for the war. Reported present in January-February, 1863. Deserted on January 25, 1863. "Brought back" on February 5, 1863. Reported present in March-June, 1863. Sent to hospital on September 15, 1863. Reported present in January-August, 1864. Hospitalized at West Point, Mississippi, January 15, 1865, with rheumatism. Transferred to Company D of this regiment when the 58th and 60th Regiments were consolidated on April 9, 1865.

McKINNEY, THOMAS, Private

Resided in Mitchell or McDowell County and was by occupation a farmer prior to enlisting in Mitchell County at age 28, July 16, 1862, for the war. Reported present in January-February, 1863. Died at Big Creek Gap, Tennessee, in March, 1863, of "fever."

McVEE, WILLIAM, Private

Born in Georgia and enlisted at Camp Martin (Mitchell County) at age 19, June 10, 1862, for the war. No further records.

MARTIN, JEREMIAH, Private

Enlisted in Mitchell County on August 19, 1862, for the war. Reported present in January-June, 1863. Killed at Chickamauga, Georgia, September 20, 1863.

MILLER, MACK, Private

Resided in Mitchell or Burke County and was by occupation a farm laborer prior to enlisting in Mitchell County at age 25, July 16, 1862, for the war. Reported present on surviving company muster rolls through August 31, 1864. Wounded slightly in the arm at Bentonville on March 19, 1865. No further records.

MOSELY, SAMUEL E., Private

Born in Carter County, Tennessee, and enlisted in Mitchell County at age 17, June 10, 1862, for the war. Mustered in as Private. Reported present in January-June and September-October, 1863. Promoted to Corporal in July-October, 1863. Reduced to ranks in November, 1863-February, 1864. Reported present in January-April, 1864. Captured near Dalton, Georgia, May 12, 1864, or captured at Resaca, Georgia, May 16, 1864. Sent to Nashville, Tennessee. Transferred to Louisville, Kentucky, where he arrived on May 21, 1864. Transferred to Alton, Illinois, where he arrived on May 25, 1864. Released at Alton on June 10, 1864, after joining the U.S. Navy.

MOXLEY, WILLIAM, Private

Enlisted in Hamilton County, Tennessee, October 20, 1863, for the war. Reported present in January-August, 1864. No further records.

OLLIS, GEORGE W., Private

Born in Burke County and resided in Mitchell or Watauga County where he was by occupation a farmer prior to enlisting at age 33, December 30, 1861. Mustered in as Private. Promoted to Corporal on February 11, 1862. Reduced to ranks on an unspecified date. Transferred to Company B, 5th Battalion N.C. Cavalry, on or about June 27, 1862. Transferred back to this company on or about May 1, 1863. Reported present in May-June, 1863. Sent to hospital at Atlanta, Georgia, February 16, 1864. Returned to duty prior to April 30, 1864. Reported present but under arrest on August 24, 1864. Reason he was arrested not reported. No further records.

OLLIS, JAMES McG., Private

Born in Burke County and enlisted at age 28, March 4, 1862. Transferred to Company B, 5th Battalion N.C. Cavalry, on or about June 27, 1862.

OLLIS, LEONARD, Corporal

Enlisted in Mitchell County at age 18, August 1, 186[3], for the war. Promotion record not reported. Reported present in January-April, 1864. No further records. Survived the war.

PARKER, ALFRED T., Private

Born in Lincoln County and enlisted at Camp Martin (Mitchell County) at age 33, June 10, 1862, for the war. Transferred to Company B, 5th Battalion N.C. Cavalry, on or about June 27, 1862.

PHIFER, WILLIAM L., Private

Place and date of enlistment not reported. Killed at Chickamauga, Georgia, September 20, 1863.

PHILLIPS, JOSEPH T., Private

Enlisted on December 30, 1861. Last reported in the records of this company on March 1, 1862.

PHILLIPS, SAMUEL C., Private

Born in Yancey County* and enlisted at Camp Martin (Mitchell County) at age 34, June 10, 1862, for the war. Transferred to Company B, 5th Battalion N.C. Cavalry, on or about June 27, 1862.

PORTIA, JOHN, Private

Born in France and enlisted at Camp Martin (Mitchell County) at age 35, June 10, 1862, for the war. Transferred to Company B, 5th Battalion N.C. Cavalry, on or about June 27, 1862.

POTEET, SAMUEL A., Sergeant

Resided in Mitchell or McDowell County and was by occupation a laborer prior to enlisting in Mitchell County at age 25, July 16, 1862, for the war. Mustered in with an unspecified rank. Promoted to Sergeant prior to March 1, 1863. Reported present in January-February, 1863. Sent to Knoxville, Tennessee, sick in March-April, 1863. Reduced to ranks prior to May 1, 1863. Reported present and was promoted to Sergeant in May-June, 1863. Killed at Chickamauga, Georgia, September 20, 1863.

PRICHARD, J. C., Private

Place and date of enlistment not reported. Probably enlisted subsequent to August 31, 1864. Paroled at Morganton on May 15, 1865.

PYATT, LEANDER, Private

Resided in Mitchell or Watauga County and was by occupation a farmer prior to enlisting at Dalton, Georgia, at age 37, December 10, 1863, for the war. Died in hospital at Atlanta, Georgia, January 10, 1864. Cause of death not reported.

REED, JOHN C., Private

Enlisted in Caldwell County on May 2, 1864, for the war. Paroled at Greensboro on May 1, 1865.

RIDDLE, JAMES MARION, Musician

Born in Yancey County and resided in Mitchell County prior to enlisting at age 16, December 30, 1861. Mustered in as Private. Appointed Musician (Drummer) on February 11, 1862. Reported present on surviving company muster rolls through July 31, 1864. Appointed Hospital Steward on August 1, 1864, and transferred to the Field and Staff of this regiment.

RIDDLE, NATHAN, Private

Resided in Mitchell or Yancey County and was by occupation a farmer prior to enlisting in Mitchell County at age 39, September 4, 1862, for the war. Reported present in January-June, 1863. Wounded at Chickamauga, Georgia, September 19-20, 1863. "Sent to hospitle at Knoxville[?] Sept 21 to Atlanta." Reported absent sick in January-August, 1864. No further records. Survived the war.

ROBERTS, J. B., Corporal

Previously served as Corporal in Company B, 26th Regiment Tennessee Infantry. Transferred to this company on an unspecified date (probably in September-October, 1863). Mustered in as Private. Reported present in September-October, 1863. Promoted to Corporal in November, 1863-February, 1864. Reported present in January-February, 1864. Furloughed for twenty-eight days on April 14, 1864. Sent to hospital on July 16, 1864. Reported absent in hospital through August 31, 1864. No further records.

ROBERTS, JAMES, Private

Born in Yancey County and enlisted at age 18, December 30, 1861. Transferred to Company B, 5th Battalion N.C. Cavalry, on or about June 27, 1862.

ROSE, JOEL, Private

Born in Yancey County and enlisted at age 18, December 30, 1861. Transferred to Company B, 5th Battalion N.C. Cavalry, on or about June 27, 1862.

ROSE, SAMUEL, Private

Born in Yancey County and resided in Mitchell or Yancey County prior to enlisting in Mitchell County at age 16, June 10, 1862, for the war. Transferred to Company K of this regiment on or about July 29, 1862. Transferred back to this company on an unspecified date. Reported present in January-June and September-October, 1863. Was on detail as a wagoner during at least part of that period. Reported on extra duty from November 1, 1863, through February, 1864. Reported present in March-April, 1864. Wounded at Kolb's Farm, near Marietta, Georgia, June 22, 1864. Sent to hospital the same date. No further records.

SEALS, ALFRED, ———

Place and date of enlistment not reported; however, he probably enlisted subsequent to August 31, 1864. Died at Macon, Georgia, October 2, 1864. Cause of death not reported.

SELLERS, JOSEPH, Private

Enlisted on December 30, 1861. No further records.

SHERWOOD, THERON, Private

Enlisted in Mitchell County on April 10, 1863, for the war. Reported present in May-June, 1863. Killed at Chickamauga, Georgia, September 20, 1863.

SHOOK, STEPHEN S., Private

Born in Burke County and enlisted at Camp Martin (Mitchell County) at age 30, June 10, 1862, for the war. Transferred to Company B, 5th Battalion N.C. Cavalry, on or about June 27, 1862.

SHUFFLER, JACOB C., Private

Previously served as Private in Company E of this regiment. Transferred to this company when the 58th and 60th Regiments were consolidated on April 9, 1865. Paroled at Morganton on May 15, 1865.

SHUFFLER, POSEY C., Private

Previously served as Private in Company E of this regiment. Transferred to this company when the 58th and 60th Regiments were consolidated on April 9, 1865. Paroled at Morganton on May 15, 1865. [North Carolina pension records indicate that he "was struck on the hip by a ball but a hatchet caught the force of the ball and he was not injured except contusion which has affected hip joint ever since." Date of injury not reported.]

SHUFORD, JAMES, ———

North Carolina pension records indicate that he served in this company.

SIGMON, AMBROSE, Private

Resided in Mitchell or Burke County and was by occupation a farmer prior to enlisting in Mitchell County at age 32, July 16, 1862, for the war. Reported absent on expired furlough in January-February, 1863. Returned to duty in March-April, 1863. Reported present in May-June, 1863. Killed at Chickamauga, Georgia, September 20, 1863.

SILVER, TILMAN BLALOCK, Private

Born in Yancey County on November 26, 1839. Enlisted in Mitchell County at age 22, June 10, 1862, for the war. Reported present in January-February, 1863. Transferred to Company K of this regiment on March 1, 1863.

SIMONS, STEWART, ———

Name appears on a register of deserters dated March 11, 1864, which states that he was believed to be in Macon County.

SINGLETON, JAMES C., Private

Born in Yancey County and enlisted at age 18, December 30, 1861. Mustered in as Musician (Drummer). Reduced to ranks on February 11, 1862. Transferred to Company B, 5th Battalion N.C. Cavalry, on or about June 27, 1862. [Filed a Tennessee pension application after the war.]

SINGLETON, SAMUEL T., Private

Born in Montgomery County and enlisted at age 26, February 25, 1862. Died at Cumberland Gap, Tennessee, on an unspecified date (probably prior to March 1, 1863). Cause of death not reported.

SISEMORE, JAMES, Private

Enlisted in Mitchell County on October 4, 1862, for the war. Reported present on surviving company muster rolls through February 29, 1864. Reported present but sick in March-April, 1864. Reported present in May-July, 1864. Wounded in the left arm at Jonesborough, Georgia, August 31, 1864. Left arm amputated. Survived the war.

SISEMORE, JOHN J., Private

Enlisted in Mitchell County on October 4, 1862, for the war. Reported present on surviving company muster rolls through April 30, 1864. Sent to hospital on June 2, 1864. No further records. Survived the war.

SISEMORE, THOMAS, Corporal

Enlisted in Mitchell County on October 4, 1862, for the war. Mustered in as Private. Reported present in January-June, 1863. Promoted to Corporal in July-October, 1863. Reported present in September-October, 1863, and January-February, 1864. Furloughed for forty days on April 16, 1864. Failed to return to duty and was reported absent without leave through August 31, 1864. No further records.

SMITH, SAMUEL, ———

North Carolina pension records indicate that he served in this company.

SNIPES, MERRIT, Sergeant

Resided in Mitchell or McDowell County and was by occupation a farmer prior to enlisting in Mitchell County at age 28, July 16, 1862, for the war. Mustered in as Private. Deserted on January 25, 1863. "Brought back" on February 5, 1863. Reported present in March-June and September-October, 1863. Promoted to Sergeant in November, 1863-February, 1864. Reported present in January-April, 1864. Wounded in the face at Resaca, Georgia, May 14-15, 1864. Returned to duty and was detailed as a wagoner prior to September 1, 1864. Paroled at Charlotte on May 12, 1865.

SORRELLS, JOSHUA M., Private

Previously served as Private in Company E, 6th Regiment N.C. State Troops. Enlisted in this company on February 4, 1862. Transferred to Company B, 5th Battalion N.C. Cavalry, on or about June 27, 1862.

SPARKS, JEREMIAH P., Private

Born in Yancey County and was by occupation a farmer prior to enlisting in Mitchell County at age 18, December 30, 1861. Transferred to Company K of this regiment on or about July 29, 1862.

SPARKS, JOSEPH M., Private

Born in Yancey County and was by occupation a farmer prior to enlisting in Mitchell County at age 17, December 30, 1861. Transferred to Company K of this regiment on or about July 29, 1862.

SPARKS, MATTHEW L., Private

Enlisted on December 30, 1861. Discharged on January 14, 1862. Reason discharged not reported.

SPARKS, SAMUEL B., Private

Born in Burke County and enlisted at age 39, December 30, 1861. Transferred to Company B, 5th Battalion N.C. Cavalry, on or about June 27, 1862.

SPARKS, SAMUEL D., Private

Enlisted on December 30, 1861. Discharged on February 1, 1862. Reason discharged not reported.

SPARKS, THOMAS M., Private

Place and date of enlistment not reported. Discharged on January 14, 1862. Reason discharged not reported.

STAMEY, ELIAS A., Private

Resided in Mitchell or Burke County and was by occupation a farmer prior to enlisting in Mitchell County at age 26, July 16, 1862, for the war. Promotion record not reported. Reported as Sergeant in January-February, 1863. Reported present in January-June, 1863. Reduced to ranks in July-October, 1863. Deserted at Lenoir Station, Tennessee, August 27, 1863. [North Carolina pension records indicate that he was injured "by the falling of an old house in which we were camped while guarding prisoners(.) I was caught under a log and mashed in back and was otherwise injured."]

STAMEY, GEORGE, Private

Resided in Mitchell or Burke County and was by occupation a farmer prior to enlisting in Mitchell County at age 34, July 16, 1862, for the war. Reported absent on expired furlough in January-February, 1863. Returned to duty in March-April, 1863. Reported present in May-June, 1863. Deserted at Lenoir Station, Tennessee, August 27, 1863. [North Carolina pension records indicate he was injured near Corinth, Mississippi, on December 25, 1864, when prisoners whom he was guarding in a log house "threw the log house down and a log struck me a crows (*sic*) my head and shoulders mashing and injuring (me) badly."]

STAMEY, LOGAN, Sergeant

Resided in Mitchell or Burke County and enlisted in Mitchell County at age 27, July 16, 1862, for the war. Mustered in as Private. Reported present in January-June, 1863. Promoted to Corporal in July-October, 1863. Reported present in September-October, 1863. Promoted to Sergeant in November, 1863-February, 1864. Reported present in January-August, 1864. No further records.

STEWARD, JAMES, Private

Born in Yancey County and enlisted at age 18, January 28, 1862. Reported present in March-April, 1863. No further records.

STEWARD, JOSEPH, Private

Enlisted in Mitchell County on July 18, 1862, for the war. Reported present in January-February, 1863. Died at Jacksboro, Tennessee, March 31, 1863, of "fever."

SULLINS, ANDREW W., Private

Enlisted in Mitchell County at age 37, October 15, 1863, for the war. Reported present in May-August, 1864. No further records. Survived the war.

SWANN, JAMES M., Corporal

Born in Yancey County and resided in McDowell County prior to enlisting at age 18, December 30, 1861. Mustered in as Private. Promoted to Corporal on February 11, 1862. Transferred to Company B, 5th Battalion N.C. Cavalry, on or about June 27, 1862. [Contrary to 2:353 of this series, the correct spelling of his surname was probably Swann rather than Swan.]

TALLENT, SAMUEL, Private

Born on December 13, 1831. Enlisted in Mitchell County at age 30, July 16, 1862, for the war. Reported present in January-April, 1863. Hospitalized at Knoxville, Tennessee, in May-June, 1863. Returned to duty prior to July 1, 1863. Sent to hospital from Bell's Bridge, Tennessee, August 1, 1863. Reported present in January-August, 1864. No further records. Survived the war.

THOMAS, ABIJAH, Private

Born in Buncombe County and resided in Mitchell or Yancey County where he was by occupation a farmer prior to enlisting in Mitchell County at age 32, June 10, 1862, for the war. Furloughed for thirty days from Big Creek Gap, Tennessee, November 28, 1862. Reported absent on expired furlough in January-June, 1863. Transferred to Company K of this regiment in July-October, 1863.

THOMAS, THOMAS, Private

Born in Buncombe County and resided in Mitchell or Yancey County where he was by occupation a farmer prior to enlisting in Mitchell County at age 34, June 10, 1862, for the war. Transferred to Company K of this regiment on or about July 29, 1862.

THOMASON, PLEASANT A., Private

Born in Rutherford County and was by occupation a farmer prior to enlisting in Mitchell County at age 35, June 10, 1862, for the war. Transferred to Company K of this regiment on or about July 29, 1862.

THOMPSON, JOHN H., Private

Previously served as Private in Company D of this regiment. Transferred to this company when the 58th and 60th Regiments were consolidated on April 9, 1865. Paroled at Greensboro on May 1, 1865.

THOMPSON, JOSEPH LAFAYETTE, Private

Previously served as Private in Company E of this regiment. Transferred to this company when the 58th and 60th Regiments were consolidated on April 9, 1865. Paroled at Greensboro on May 1, 1865.

TOLLEY, JOSEPH R., Private

Resided in Mitchell or Yancey County and was by occupation a farmer prior to enlisting at age 37, December 30, 1861. Last reported in the records of this company on March 1, 1862. [May have served later as Private in Company D, 69th Regiment N.C. Troops (7th Regiment N.C. Cavalry).]

TOLLY, SANDERS, ———

Name appears on an undated bounty pay and receipt roll which does not give his place and date of enlistment.

TOLLY, SWINFIELD, Private

Resided in Mitchell or Yancey County and was by occupation a farmer prior to enlisting in Mitchell County at age 21, July 18, 1862, for the war. Deserted ("broke jail") at Jacksboro, Tennessee, February 9, 1863. Returned from desertion on an unspecified date (probably in January-April, 1864). Court-martialed on an unspecified date and was reported under arrest on April 30, 1864. Reported absent without leave on July 2, 1864. Listed as a deserter on September 10, 1864.

TOLLY, WILLIAM, Private

Enlisted on December 30, 1861. Deserted on January 25, 1863. "Brought back" on February 5, 1863. Reported present in March-June, 1863. Wounded at Chickamauga, Georgia, September 19-20, 1863. Hospitalized at Atlanta, Georgia. Died (presumably at Atlanta) prior to March 1, 1864, of wounds.

VANCE, FLEMING, Private

Born in Yancey County and resided in Mitchell or Watauga County where he was by occupation a farmer prior to enlisting at age 24, December 30, 1861. Reported absent on expired furlough in January-February, 1863. Returned to duty in March-April, 1863. Reported present in May-June, 1863. Sent to hospital at Knoxville, Tennessee, prior to September 2, 1863. Sent to hospital at Atlanta, Georgia, November 10, 1863. Reported absent sick through August 31, 1864. No further records. Survived the war.

VANCE, JOHN, Private

Enlisted in Mitchell County. Enlistment date reported as June 10, 1862; however, he was not listed in the records of this company for more than one year subsequent to that date. Reported absent without leave on August 31, 1863. Returned to duty on December 10, 1863. Reported present in January-August, 1864. No further records.

VANCE, JOHN W., Private

Born in Yancey County and enlisted at age 20, December 30, 1861. Mustered in as Sergeant. Reduced to ranks on February 11, 1862. Reported absent on expired furlough in January-February, 1863. Returned to duty prior to May 1, 1863. Reported present in May-June, 1863. Sent to hospital at Knoxville, Tennessee, July 1, 1863. Dropped from the company rolls prior to March 1, 1864. Reason he was dropped not reported. Survived the war. [North Carolina pension records indicate that he was injured in Mississippi on or about January 1, 1864, "By the falling of an house in which we camped and (were) guarding prisoners. I was caught under a large wall plate and mashed in belly (body?) and (my) bre(a)st (was) also ruptured."]

VANCE, LEWIS, Private

Born in Greenville District, South Carolina, and resided in Mitchell or Watauga County where he was by occupation a farmer prior to enlisting at age 59, December 30, 1861. No further records.

VANCE, THOMAS D., Private

Born in Yancey County in 1834. Enlisted at age 27, December 30, 1861. No further records. [His Tennessee pension application indicates that he was discharged "about" November 19, 1862, by reason of measles and kidney and lung disease. He subsequently "carried the Confederate mail" from Grassy Creek, North Carolina, to Hampton, Tennessee.]

VANCE, WILLIAM, Private

Born in Yancey County* and resided in Mitchell or Watauga County where he was by occupation a farmer prior to enlisting at age 30, December 30, 1861. Mustered in as Private. Promoted to Sergeant on an unspecified date. Reported absent on expired furlough in January-February, 1863. Returned to duty prior to May 1, 1863. Reported present in May-June, 1863. Reduced to ranks in July, 1863-February, 1864. Reported absent sick in hospital at Atlanta, Georgia, from December 20, 1863, through August 31, 1864. No further records. Survived the war. [North Carolina pension records indicate that he was ruptured at Bull's (Bell's?) Bridge, Tennessee, in 1864, "while moving Cobb's Battery."]

VANHORN, DAVID, ———

Born on May 27, 1827. Resided in Mitchell or Burke County and was by occupation a farmer. Place and date of enlistment not reported (probably enlisted between December 30, 1861, and July 1, 1862). Was about 35 years of age at time of enlistment. No further records. Survived the war.

WACASTER, JACOB HASSEL, Private

Previously served as Private in Company G of this regiment. Enlisted in this company at Dalton, Georgia, January 14, 1864. Reported absent without leave on or about February 29, 1864. Listed as a deserter on April 19, 1864. [North Carolina pension records indicate that he was injured near "Stony Face (Rocky Face Ridge)," Georgia, in February, 1864, when a bursting shell caused a tree to fall on him, breaking three ribs. The explosion also caused permanent deafness, partial loss of eyesight, and vertigo.]

WALDROPE, ELI, Private

Born in Buncombe County in 1828. Enlisted at Camp Martin (Mitchell County) at age 34, June 10, 1862, for the war. Transferred to Company B, 5th Battalion N.C. Cavalry, on or about June 27, 1862. [Filed a Tennessee pension application after the war. Contrary to 2:353 of this series, the correct spelling of his surname was probably Waldrope rather than Waldrupe.]

WALDROPE, JOSEPH, Private

Born in Yancey County* in 1826. Enlisted at Camp Martin (Mitchell County) on June 10, 1862, for the war. Transferred to Company B, 5th Battalion N.C. Cavalry, on or about June 27, 1862. [Filed a Tennessee pension application after the war. Contrary to 2:353 of this series, the correct spelling of his surname was probably Waldrope or Waldroup rather than Waldrupe.]

WALKER, JOSEPH, Private

Born in Richmond County, Georgia, and was by occupation an engineer prior to enlisting in Mitchell County at age 23, June 10,

1862, for the war. Transferred to Company K of this regiment on or about July 29, 1862.

WARD, JETHRO, ———
North Carolina pension records indicate that he served in this company.

WASHBURN, DANIEL M., Sergeant
Resided in Mitchell or McDowell County and was by occupation a farmer prior to enlisting in Mitchell County at age 29, July 16, 1862, for the war. Was apparently mustered in with the rank of Private. Deserted at Jacksboro, Tennessee, January 25, 1863. "Brought back" on February 5, 1863. Reported present in March-April, 1863. Reported under arrest at Clinton, Tennessee, June 30, 1863, for desertion. Wounded at Chickamauga, Georgia, September 20, 1863. Returned to duty prior to October 31, 1863. Promoted to Sergeant in November, 1863-February, 1864. Reported present in January-August, 1864. Transferred to Company D of this regiment when the 58th and 60th Regiments were consolidated on April 9, 1865. [Previously served as 2nd Lieutenant in the 102nd Regiment N.C. Militia.]

WEATHERMAN, SAMUEL, Private
Resided in Mitchell County where he enlisted on October 15, 1863, for the war. Reported present in May-August, 1864. Wounded in the left arm (fracture) and permanently disabled at Jonesborough, Georgia, on or about August 31, 1864. Hospitalized at Macon, Georgia, September 8, 1864. Furloughed on October 19, 1864. No further records. Survived the war. [Was about 34 years of age at time of enlistment.]

WEBB, JAMES, Private
Enlisted on April 6, 1862. Confederate medical records indicate that he died in hospital at Richmond, Virginia, April 19, 1862, of "feb[ris] typhoides"; however, the reliability of that information appears dubious. No further records.

WEBB, JOSEPH MILTON, Private
Born in Yancey County and enlisted on February 4, 1862. Transferred to Company B, 5th Battalion N.C. Cavalry, on or about June 27, 1862.

WEBB, NOAH, Private
Enlisted on February 4, 1862. Transferred to Company B, 5th Battalion N.C. Cavalry, on or about June 27, 1862.

WHITE, JOSEPH, ———
Enlisted at Camp Martin (Mitchell County) on June 10, 1862, for the war. Transferred to Company B, 5th Battalion N.C. Cavalry, on or about June 27, 1862. [Service record omitted in volume 2 of this series.]

WILLIAMS, JOHN W., Private
Enlisted at Dalton, Georgia, December 10, 1863, for the war. Sent to hospital at Atlanta, Georgia, January 1, 1864. Reported absent without leave on or about February 29, 1864. Returned to duty on an unspecified date. Sent to hospital on June 20, 1864. No further records. Survived the war. [It appears that he suffered from chronic diarrhoea. At various unspecified times he was in hospitals at

Auburn, Alabama, and La Grange, Georgia. Was about 40 years of age at time of enlistment.]

WISE, JAMES N., _____
Resided in Mitchell or Burke County and was by occupation a farmer. Place and date of enlistment not reported (probably enlisted between December 30, 1861, and July 1, 1862). Died prior to March 24, 1863. Place, date, and cause of death not reported. [Was about 26 years of age at time of enlistment.]

WISEMAN, ALEXANDER, Private
Born in Burke County and enlisted at age 40, February 11, 1862. Reported absent on expired furlough in January-February, 1863. Returned to duty prior to May 1, 1863. Reported present in May-June and September-October, 1863. Furloughed for twenty-four days on January 10, 1864. Reported present in March-August, 1864. Transferred to Company D of this regiment when the 58th and 60th Regiments were consolidated on April 9, 1865.

WISEMAN, BERRY G., Private
Enlisted on December 30, 1861. Last reported in the records of this company on March 1, 1862.

WISEMAN, ENSOR C., Sergeant
Previously served as Private in Company E, 6th Regiment N.C. State Troops. Transferred to this company on March 31, 1863. Promoted to Sergeant on an unspecified date. Reported present in April, 1863. Transferred to Company B, 5th Battalion N.C. Cavalry, in May, 1863.

WISEMAN, JAMES H., Private
Born in Yancey County* and resided in Mitchell or Yancey County where he was by occupation a farmer prior to enlisting at age 39, January 28, 1862. Transferred to Company B, 5th Battalion N.C. Cavalry, on or about June 27, 1862.

WISEMAN, JOSIAH LAFAYETTE, Private
Born in Yancey County and resided in Mitchell or Yancey County where he was by occupation a farmer prior to enlisting at age 18, December 30, 1861. Mustered in as 1st Sergeant. Reduced to ranks on an unspecified date. Transferred to Company B, 5th Battalion N.C. Cavalry, on or about June 27, 1862.

WISEMAN, THOMAS J., Private
Born in Yancey County and resided in Mitchell County where he was by occupation a farmer prior to enlisting at age 27, February 18, 1862. Transferred to Company B, 5th Battalion N.C. Cavalry, on or about June 27, 1862. Later served as 2nd Lieutenant of that company.

WISEMAN, WILSON G., Private
Enlisted at Camp Martin (Mitchell County) at age 25, June 10, 1862, for the war. Transferred to Company B, 5th Battalion N.C. Cavalry, on or about June 27, 1862.

YOUNG, JOSEPH P., ———
Born in Yancey County and enlisted at Camp Martin (Mitchell County) at age 22, June 10, 1862, for the war. Transferred to Company B, 5th Battalion N.C. Cavalry, on or about June 27, 1862.

COMPANY B

This company was raised in Mitchell County on May 17, 1862, as Capt. Jacob W. Bowman's Company, N.C. Volunteers. It was mustered into service in Mitchell County on June 16, 1862, and placed under the authority of Lt. Col. John B. Palmer. Palmer, former commander of "Palmer's Legion," a mixed (cavalry and infantry) unit that had failed to complete its organization, was by then recruiting for a cavalry unit to be known as the 5th Battalion N.C. Partisan Rangers; however, it appears that Bowman's Company was never formally assigned to the 5th Battalion. On or about July 1 Bowman's Company was designated Company B of a nascent infantry regiment, commanded by Palmer, that was mustered in as the 58th Regiment N.C. Troops on July 29, 1862. After joining the 58th Regiment the company functioned as a part of that regiment, and its history for the remainder of the war is reported as a part of the regimental history.

The following roster was compiled primarily from information in the microfilm edition of the Compiled Service Records of Soldiers Who Served in Organizations from the State of North Carolina (Record Group 109, M270), National Archives and Records Administration, Washington, D.C. Record Group 109 includes enlistment papers, pay vouchers, requisitions, letters of resignation, discharge certificates, and abstracts of medical and prisoner of war returns. Materials relating specifically to this company include a muster-in and descriptive roll dated June 16, 1862, and muster rolls dated January-June, 1863; August 31-December, 1863; and March-August, 1864.

Also utilized in this roster were *The War of the Rebellion: A Compilation of the Official Records of the Union and Confederate Armies*, the North Carolina adjutant general's *Roll of Honor*, state militia records, newspaper casualty lists and obituaries, wartime claims for bounty pay and allowances, postwar registers of claims for artificial limbs, Confederate pension applications filed with the states of North Carolina, Tennessee, and Florida, Confederate Soldiers' Home records, and the 1860 and 1870 federal censuses of North Carolina. A search was made also for relevant letters, diaries, reminiscences, and other manuscripts in the Southern Historical Collection (University of North Carolina-Chapel Hill), the Duke University Library Special Collections Department, and the North Carolina Division of Archives and History.

Among the secondary sources consulted were records of the North Carolina division of the United Daughters of the Confederacy, postwar rosters, regimental and county histories, marriage bond, will, and cemetery indexes, published and unpublished genealogies, biographical dictionaries, the North Carolina *County Heritage Book* series, the *Confederate Veteran*, Walter Clark's *Histories of the Several Regiments and Battalions from North Carolina in the Great War, 1861-'65*, and the North Carolina volume of the extended edition of *Confederate Military History*.

OFFICERS

CAPTAINS

BOWMAN, JACOB W.

Born in Mitchell County* where he resided as a farmer and state legislator prior to enlisting in Mitchell County at age 30. Appointed Captain on May 17, 1862. Resigned on March 5, 1863, because "charges having been made against me of so serious a nature as to impair my influence with the company under my command[,] I feel that the interest of the service and a proper self respect demand that

I should tender my resignation." Resignation accepted on April 16, 1863. [Previously served as Captain of Company F, 99th Regiment N.C. Militia.]

BAILEY, ISAAC H.

Born in Yancey County and resided in Mitchell County where he enlisted at age 21, May 17, 1862, for the war. Mustered in as Private. Promoted to 1st Sergeant on or about October 8, 1862. Reported present in January-June, 1863. Appointed 3rd Lieutenant on or about February 1, 1863. Promoted to 1st Lieutenant in May-June, 1863. Promoted to Captain on September 1, 1863, to rank from April 17, 1863. Wounded and permanently disabled at Chickamauga, Georgia, September 20, 1863. Reported absent wounded through August, 1864. Reported on detail for court-martial duty on September 13 and December 15, 1864. Retired on an unspecified date. Reason he retired not reported.

BRIGGS, SUEL B.

Previously served as Captain of Company C of this regiment. Transferred to this company subsequent to August 31, 1864. Paroled at Greensboro on or about May 1, 1865.

LIEUTENANTS

CONLEY, JAMES C., 1st Lieutenant

Previously served as Private in Company K, 1st Regiment N.C. Infantry (6 months, 1861). Elected 1st Lieutenant of this company on July 22, 1863. Reported present in September-December, 1863, and March-August, 1864. Reported in command of the company in September-October, 1863, and March-August, 1864. Transferred to Company D of this regiment subsequent to August 31, 1864.

DUNCAN, JONATHAN A. W., 2nd Lieutenant

Previously served as 2nd Lieutenant of Company K of this regiment. Transferred to this company subsequent to August 31, 1864. Paroled at Greensboro on or about May 1, 1865.

GARLAND, JOHN CALVIN, 3rd Lieutenant

Born in Yancey County and was by occupation a farmer prior to enlisting in Mitchell County at age 21. Appointed 3rd Lieutenant on May 17, 1862. Resigned on December 18, 1862, because "I feel myself incompetent of discharging the duties of a commissioned officer." Resignation accepted on January 20, 1863. [Previously served as 2nd Lieutenant of Company E, 99th Regiment N.C. Militia. May have served later as Captain of Company F, 3rd Regiment N.C. Mounted Infantry (Union).]

GARLAND, WILLIAM, 1st Lieutenant

Born in Burke County and was by occupation a farmer prior to enlisting in Mitchell County at age 38. Elected 2nd Lieutenant on May 17, 1862. Reported absent on sick furlough in January-February, 1863. Promoted to 1st Lieutenant on February 1, 1863. Resigned on or about April 4, 1863, because of "chronic nephritis with excessive bilious derang[e]ment." Resignation accepted on April 24, 1863.

GILBERT, LARKIN W., 1st Lieutenant

Previously served as 3rd Lieutenant of Company H of this regiment. Transferred to this company subsequent to August 31, 1864.

Promoted to 1st Lieutenant on October 12, 1864. Paroled at Greensboro on or about May 1, 1865. Took the Oath of Allegiance at Salisbury on June 7, 1865.

GREEN, JOHN C., 1st Lieutenant

Born in Burke County and resided in Mitchell or Yancey County where he was by occupation a farmer prior to enlisting in Mitchell County at age 32. Elected 1st Lieutenant on May 17, 1862. Died at Jacksboro, Tennessee, on or about January 28, 1863. Cause of death not reported.

PRITCHARD, AZOR M. C., 3rd Lieutenant

Previously served as Sergeant in Company I, 29th Regiment N.C. Troops. Transferred to this company in July, 1862. Mustered in as Sergeant. Reported present in January-June, 1863. Elected 3rd Lieutenant on July 22, 1863. Reported present or accounted for in September-December, 1863. Reported in command of the company in November-December, 1863. Furloughed home in March-April, 1864. Returned to duty on an unspecified date. Reported present in May-August, 1864. No further records.

PUTNAM, JAMES W., 2nd Lieutenant

Born in Rutherford County and resided in Mitchell County where he was by occupation a farmer prior to enlisting in Mitchell County at age 23, May 17, 1862, for the war. Mustered in as Private. Promoted to Sergeant prior to March 1, 1863. Reported present in January-June, 1863. Elected 2nd Lieutenant on July 22, 1863. Wounded in the right arm, thigh, and hip at Chickamauga, Georgia, September 20, 1863. Listed as a deserter on May 9, 1864, and was reported absent without leave on August 20, 1864; however, he was reported absent wounded on September 20, 1864. No further records. Survived the war.

STEWART, JACKSON, 2nd Lieutenant

Born in Anson County and enlisted in Mitchell County on May 17, 1862, for the war. Mustered in as Private. Transferred to Company E of this regiment on or about June 27, 1862. Transferred back to this company prior to February 2, 1863. Promoted to Sergeant on an unspecified date. Reported present in January-February, 1863. Elected 2nd Lieutenant on February 2, 1863. Resigned on April 4, 1863, because of "ill health & old age[,] having been unable for duty for the last three months." Resignation accepted on April 25, 1863. [Letter of resignation gives his age as 59.]

NONCOMMISSIONED OFFICERS
AND PRIVATES

ANDERSON, LORENZO D., Private

Born in Jefferson County, Tennessee, and resided in Mitchell or Yancey County where he was by occupation a farmer prior to enlisting in Mitchell County at age 27, May 17, 1862, for the war. Furloughed at Big Creek Gap, Tennessee, November 19, 1862. Reported absent without leave on December 9, 1862. Survived the war.

ANGLIN, RABORN B., Private

Previously served as Private in Company C of this regiment. Transferred to this company subsequent to August 31, 1864. Paroled at Greensboro on or about May 1, 1865.

ARROWOOD, ELIJAH M., Corporal

Enlisted at Camp Jackson on July 16, 1862, for the war. Mustered in as Private. Reported present in January-June and September-October, 1863. Promoted to Corporal on October 20, 1863. Reported absent without leave on or about December 1, 1863. Returned to duty on an unspecified date. Reported absent without leave on April 4, 1864. Listed as a deserter on September 10, 1864.

ARROWOOD, JAMES A., Private

Born in Yancey County and enlisted in Mitchell County at age 19, May 17, 1862, for the war. Reported absent sick in January-February, 1863. Reported present in March-April, 1863. Reported absent sick in hospital at Knoxville, Tennessee, in May-June, 1863. No further records.

ARROWOOD, JAMES P., Private

Born in Yancey County* and enlisted in Mitchell County at age 38, May 17, 1862, for the war. Deserted at Jacksboro, Tennessee, January 10, 1863. Reported in confinement in March-April, 1863. Deserted at Clinton, Tennessee, prior to July 1, 1863.

ARROWOOD, M. H., Private

Enlisted at Dalton, Georgia, January 10, 1864, for the war. Reported absent without leave from camp near Dalton on or about March 31, 1864. Dropped from the company rolls prior to September 1, 1864.

AYERS, JACOB M., Private

Previously served as Private in Company G of this regiment. Transferred to this company subsequent to June 30, 1863. Reported present in September-December, 1863, and March-April, 1864. Reported absent without leave from camp near Atlanta, Georgia, July 8, 1864. No further records. Survived the war. [North Carolina pension records indicate that he was wounded in the left thigh at Chickamauga, Georgia, in September, 1863.]

BAILEY, CURTIS, Private

Born in Yancey County and enlisted in Mitchell County at age 18, May 17, 1862, for the war. Deserted at Cumberland Gap, Tennessee, October 15, 1862.

BAILEY, JEFFERSON, Private

Born in Yancey County and was by occupation a farmer prior to enlisting in Mitchell County at age 20, May 17, 1862, for the war. Not reported in the records of this company subsequent to June 16, 1862. Later served as Private in Company F, 3rd Regiment N.C. Mounted Infantry (Union).]

BAILEY, THOMAS, Private

Born in Yancey County* and enlisted in Mitchell County at age 32, May 17, 1862, for the war. Deserted at Cumberland Gap, Tennessee, October 15, 1862.

BAILEY, THOMAS C., Private

Enlisted at Camp Jackson on July 12, 1862, for the war. Reported absent on detached service in January-February, 1863. Reported on detail in the commissary department in March-April, 1863. Reported absent on sick furlough in May-June, 1863. Died on or about July 1, 1863. Place and cause of death not reported.

BAKER, ELIJAH W., 1st Sergeant

Previously served as 2nd Lieutenant of Company I, 29th Regiment N.C. Troops. Enlisted in this company at Camp Reynolds on September 1, 1862, for the war. Mustered in as Private. Reported present or accounted for in January-June, 1863. Promoted to Corporal in May-June, 1863. Promoted to 1st Sergeant in July-October, 1863. Reported present or accounted for in September-December, 1863. Reported absent on expired furlough in March-April, 1864. Reported missing at Kolb's Farm, near Marietta, Georgia, June 22, 1864. No further records.

BAKER, NEWTON A., Private

Born in Yancey County and enlisted in Mitchell County at age 25, May 17, 1862, for the war. Mustered in as Private. Reported present in January-February, 1863. Promoted to Corporal prior to March 1, 1863. Reduced to ranks on an unspecified date. Died at Jacksboro, Tennessee, March 24, 1863. Cause of death not reported.

BAKER, ROBERT F., Private

Previously served as Corporal in Company I, 29th Regiment N.C. Troops. Transferred to this company with the rank of Private in July, 1862. Reported present in January-June, 1863. Sent to hospital from Loudon, Tennessee, in early August, 1863. Furloughed home on August 10, 1863. Reported absent on expired furlough in March-April, 1864. Returned to duty on or about May 1, 1864. Detailed for hospital duty on August 17, 1864. Discharged on January 9, 1865, by reason of "epilepsy convulsions violent and frequent with general impairment of health. . . ."

BAKER, WASH, ———

North Carolina pension records indicate that he served in this company.

BARNETT, SIMON, Private

Born in Yancey County* and enlisted in Mitchell County at age 32, May 17, 1862, for the war. Reported present in January-June, 1863. Deserted from camp near Chattanooga, Tennessee, October 5, 1863. Later served as Private in Company B, 13th Regiment Tennessee Cavalry (Union). [Previously served as 2nd Lieutenant of Company E, 99th Regiment N.C. Militia.]

BARTLETT, JOSEPH HENRY, Private

Born in Burke County and was by occupation a farmer prior to enlisting in Mitchell County at age 20, May 17, 1862, for the war. Transferred to Company K of this regiment on or about July 29, 1862.

BARTLETT, SAMUEL D., Private

Born in Buncombe County and resided in Mitchell or Yancey County where he was by occupation a farmer prior to enlisting in Mitchell County at age 30, May 17, 1862, for the war. Transferred to Company E of this regiment on or about June 27, 1862.

BEEM, JOHN, Private

Enlisted at Dalton, Georgia, December 30, 1863, for the war. Died in hospital at Dalton on April 14, 1864. Cause of death not reported.

BENNETT, ARCHIBALD, Private

Born in Buncombe County and was by occupation a farmer prior to enlisting in Mitchell County at age 29, May 17, 1862, for the

war. Deserted at Cumberland Gap, Tennessee, October 15, 1862. Later served as Private in Companies A and F, 3rd Regiment N.C. Mounted Infantry (Union).

BENNETT, JOHN, Private

Born in Yancey County and resided in Mitchell or Yancey County where he was by occupation a farmer prior to enlisting in Mitchell County at age 21, May 17, 1862, for the war. Deserted at Cumberland Gap, Tennessee, October 15, 1862. Later served as Private in Company A, 3rd Regiment N.C. Mounted Infantry (Union).

BLALOCK, JOHN, Private

Enlisted at Dalton, Georgia, December 26, 1863, for the war. Reported present in March-August, 1864. Transferred (or temporarily assigned) to Company B, 1st Regiment Troops and Defenses, Macon, Georgia, prior to January 1, 1865.

BRACKENS, JOHN, Private

Resided in Mitchell or Yancey County and was by occupation a farmer. Place and date of enlistment not reported. Deserted to the enemy on an unspecified date. Reported in confinement at Knoxville, Tennessee, May 20, 186-. Took the Oath of Allegiance on or about the same date. [Was probably about 24 years of age in 1862.]

BRADSHAW, WILLIAM F., Private

Born in Yancey County and resided in Mitchell or Yancey County where he was by occupation a farmer prior to enlisting in Mitchell County at age 18, May 17, 1862, for the war. Reported present in January-June, 1863. Killed at Chickamauga, Georgia, September 20, 1863. Nominated for the Badge of Distinction for gallantry at Chickamauga.

BROOKS, ALFRED, Private

Born in Union County* and was by occupation a farmer prior to enlisting in Mitchell County at age 21, May 17, 1862, for the war. Reported absent without leave in January-February, 1863. Returned to duty in March-April, 1863. Reported present in May-June, 1863. Wounded in the hand at Chickamauga, Georgia, September 20, 1863. Returned to duty in November-December, 1863. Reported present in March-August, 1864. Transferred to Company D of this regiment subsequent to August 31, 1864.

BROOKS, JOHN, Private

Enlisted at Camp Jackson on July 19, 1862, for the war. Reported present in January-February, 1863. Reported absent on detached service in March-April, 1863. Reported absent without leave in May-June, 1863. Returned to duty on an unspecified date. Wounded at Chickamauga, Georgia, September 20, 1863. Deserted near Chattanooga, Tennessee, October 5, 1863. [May have served later as Private in Company B, 13th Regiment Tennessee Cavalry (Union).]

BROOKS, MARTIN, Private

Born in Cleveland County and enlisted in Mitchell County at age 20, May 17, 1862, for the war. Transferred to Company E of this regiment on or about June 27, 1862.

BRYANT, BETHEL A., Private

Previously served as Private in Company G of this regiment. Transferred to this company subsequent to June 30, 1863. Left camp at

Dalton, Georgia, without leave on April 4, 1864. Dropped from the company rolls on or about August 31, 1864.

BUCHANAN, ABRAM J., Private

Born in Yancey County and enlisted in Mitchell County at age 24, May 17, 1862, for the war. Transferred to Company E of this regiment on or about June 27, 1862. Transferred from Company E to Company K of this regiment on or about July 29, 1862. Transferred back to this company prior to March 1, 1863. Reported absent without leave in January-February, 1863. Returned to duty in March-April, 1863. Deserted on May 24, 1863. Returned to duty on an unspecified date (probably subsequent to August 31, 1864). Deserted to the enemy near Columbia, South Carolina, February 19, 1865. Sent to Fort Monroe, Virginia. Transferred to Washington, D.C., April 2, 1865. Released at Washington on or about April 5, 1865, after taking the Oath of Allegiance.

BUCHANAN, ADAM, Private

Enlisted at Camp Jackson on July 19, 1862, for the war. Furloughed from Cumberland Gap, Tennessee, November 17, 1862, and failed to return. Reported absent without leave in May-June, 1863. No further records. Survived the war. [Was about 29 years of age at time of enlistment.]

BUCHANAN, ALEXANDER, Private

Born in Yancey County and was by occupation a farmer prior to enlisting in Mitchell County at age 26, May 17, 1862, for the war. Reported present in January-February, 1863. Discharged at Big Creek Gap, Tennessee, March 15, 1863, by reason of "extensive phagidenic [sic] ulcers of the leg of longstanding." [North Carolina pension records indicate that he was wounded in the right breast at Bakersville on November 1, 1864, while serving in the Home Guard.]

BUCHANAN, GREENBURY Y., Sergeant

Born in Yancey County in 1846. Was by occupation a farmer prior to enlisting in Mitchell County on May 17, 1862, for the war. Mustered in as Private. Reported present in January-June, 1863. Promoted to Corporal in May-June, 1863. Promoted to Sergeant on September 7, 1863. Reported present in September-December, 1863, and March-April, 1864. Furloughed home from hospital for sixty days on or about August 1, 1864. Name appears on a hospital muster roll datelined Montgomery, Alabama, November 15, 1864, which states that he was a patient. Later served as Private in Company E, 3rd Regiment N.C. Mounted Infantry (Union). [Filed a Tennessee pension application after the war.]

BUCHANAN, JAMES G., Private

Enlisted at Big Creek Gap, Tennessee, March 22, 1863, for the war. Reported present in April, 1863. Deserted at Clinton, Tennessee, May 20, 1863.

BUCHANAN, JAMES S., _____

North Carolina pension records indicate that he served in this company.

BUCHANAN, JAMES W., Private

Enlisted at Clinton, Tennessee, April 20, 186[3], for the war. Deserted at Clinton on May 20, 1863. [Was about 35 years of age at time of enlistment.]

BUCHANAN, JASPER N., Private

Born in Yancey County and was by occupation a farmer prior to enlisting in Mitchell County at age 19, May 17, 1862, for the war. Reported present in January-February, 1863. Reported absent sick on or about March 14, 1863. Returned to duty subsequent to June 30, 1863. Reported present in September-October, 1863. Reported absent sick in November-December, 1863. No further records.

BUCHANAN, JOSEPH M., Private

Born in Yancey County and was by occupation a farmer prior to enlisting in Mitchell County at age 20, May 17, 1862, for the war. Transferred to Company E of this regiment on or about June 27, 1862.

BUCHANAN, LEONARD M., Private

Born in Burke County and resided in Yancey County where he was by occupation a farmer and/or Baptist clergyman prior to enlisting in Mitchell County at age 52, May 17, 1862, for the war. Transferred to Company E of this regiment on or about June 27, 1862.

BUCHANAN, MARION, Private

Born in Yancey County* and resided in Mitchell or Yancey County where he was by occupation a farmer prior to enlisting in Mitchell County at age 30, May 17, 1862, for the war. No further records.

BUCHANAN, MOLTON, Private

Born in Yancey or Buncombe County and was by occupation a farmer prior to enlisting in Mitchell County at age 18, May 17, 1862, for the war. Transferred to Company E of this regiment on or about June 27, 1862.

BUCHANAN, NEWTON, Private

Previously served as Private in Company E of this regiment. Transferred to this company on an unspecified date (probably in the autumn of 1863). Furloughed home sick on November 27, 1863. Failed to return to duty and was dropped from the company rolls in May-August, 1864. [May have served also as Private in Company I, 29th Regiment N.C. Troops.]

BUCHANAN, THOMAS, Private

Born in Burke County and enlisted in Mitchell County at age 42, May 17, 1862, for the war as a substitute for Pvt. Thomas B. Young. Reported absent without leave from November 19, 1862, through June 30, 1863. Dropped from the company rolls prior to November 1, 1863.

BUCHANAN, WAIGHTSVILLE, Private

Born in Yancey County and resided in Mitchell or Yancey County where he was by occupation a farmer prior to enlisting in Mitchell County at age 27, May 17, 1862, for the war. Transferred to Company E of this regiment on or about June 27, 1862.

BUCHANAN, WILLIAM A., Private

Enlisted at Camp Reynolds on September 17, 1862, for the war. Reported present in January-June, 1863. Reported absent without leave on October 5, 1863. Reported under arrest on or about October 31, 1863. Returned to duty on or about December 1, 1863. Reported absent without leave from camp near Dalton, Georgia, April 4, 1864. Listed as a deserter on September 10, 1864. [May have served later as Private in Company E, 3rd Regiment N.C. Mounted Infantry (Union).]

BURCHFIELD, NATHAN, Private

Born in Yancey County and resided in Mitchell or Yancey County where he was by occupation a farmer prior to enlisting in Mitchell County at age 20, May 17, 1862, for the war. Deserted at Big Creek Gap, Tennessee, January 15, 1863.

BURCHFIELD, THOMAS, Private

Born in Carter County, Tennessee, and enlisted in Mitchell County at age 25, May 17, 1862, for the war. Deserted at Camp Stokes, Haynesville, Tennessee, August 16, 1862. Returned to duty in July-August, 1863. Deserted from camp near Charleston, Tennessee, September 10, 1863. Reported absent without leave through December, 1863. Listed as a deserter on September 10, 1864.

BURCHFIELD, WILSON, Private

Born in Yancey County and resided in Mitchell or Yancey County where he was by occupation a farmer prior to enlisting in Mitchell County at age 22, May 17, 1862, for the war. Deserted at Camp Stokes, Haynesville, Tennessee, August 31, 1862.

BURLESON, REUBEN P., Private

Born in Yancey County and resided in Mitchell or Yancey County where he was by occupation a farmer prior to enlisting in Mitchell County at age 21, May 17, 1862, for the war. Mustered in as Private. Promoted to Sergeant on January 20, 1863. Reported present in January-June, 1863. Deserted from camp near Charleston, Tennessee, September 5, 1863. Reduced to ranks in November-December, 1863. [Appointed Brevet Lieutenant on February 28, 1863, but the appointment was apparently canceled. May have served also in Company I, 29th Regiment N.C. Troops.]

BURLESON, WILSON M., Private

Born in Yancey County and resided in Mitchell or Yancey County where he was by occupation a farmer prior to enlisting in Mitchell County at age 28, May 17, 1862, for the war. Mustered in as Private. Promoted to Corporal on or about August 31, 1862. Reduced to ranks on or about December 31, 1862. Reported present in March-June, 1863. Deserted from camp near Charleston, Tennessee, September 10, 1863.

BURLISON, JOSEPH M., Private

Enlisted at Camp Jackson on May 17, 1862, for the war. Reported present in March-April, 1863. Transferred to Company A of this regiment on or about May 6, 1863. [Was about 20 years of age at time of enlistment.]

BUTLER, ALLEN, Private

Enlisted at Camp Jackson on July 19, 1862, for the war. Reported present in January-April, 1863. Deserted on May 24, 1863. Reported sick in hospital at Atlanta, Georgia, in September-October, 1863. Returned to duty prior to November 27, 1863, when he was captured at Ringgold, Georgia. Sent to Nashville, Tennessee. Transferred to Louisville, Kentucky, where he arrived on December 11, 1863. Transferred to Rock Island, Illinois, December 12, 1863. Released at Rock Island on January 25, 1864, after the joining the U.S. Navy.

BYRD, CARSON, Private

Born in Yancey County and enlisted in Mitchell County at age 19, May 17, 1862, for the war. Transferred to Company E of this regiment on or about June 27, 1862. Transferred back to this company prior to March 1, 1863. Reported present in January-June, 1863.

Deserted at Bell's Bridge, Tennessee, July 24, 1863. Later served as Corporal in Company B, 13th Regiment Tennessee Cavalry (Union).

BYRD, MITCHELL T., Private

Born in Yancey County and enlisted in Mitchell County at age 19, May 17, 1862, for the war. Reported present in January-June, 1863. Deserted from camp near Chattanooga, Tennessee, September 26, 1863. Returned to duty subsequent to December 31, 1863. Reported present in March-April, 1864. Wounded at Kolb's Farm, near Marietta, Georgia, June 22, 1864. Reported absent wounded through August, 1864. No further records. Survived the war. [May have been wounded also at Bald Hill, Georgia, July 22, 1864.]

BYRD, WILLIAM P., Private

Born in Yancey County and enlisted in Mitchell County at age 26, May 17, 1862, for the war. Furloughed at Big Creek Gap, Tennessee, November 19, 1862. Failed to return to duty and was reported absent without leave. Dropped from the company rolls in July-October, 1863.

CANIPE, WILLIAM, Private

Enlisted at Camp Jackson on May 17, 1862, for the war. Reported present on surviving company muster rolls through August 31, 1864. No further records. Survived the war. [Was about 26 years of age at time of enlistment.]

DEYTON, DAVID M., Private

Born in Yancey County and resided in Mitchell or Yancey County where he was by occupation a farmer prior to enlisting at Camp Jackson at age 28, May 17, 1862, for the war. Mustered in as Private. Reported absent on detached service in January-February, 1863. Promoted to Sergeant prior to March 1, 1863. Promoted to 1st Sergeant in March-April, 1863. Reported present in March-June, 1863. Deserted from camp near Charleston, Tennessee, September 5, 1863. Reported present but under arrest on or about December 31, 1863. Returned to duty on an unspecified date and was reduced to ranks. Reported present in March-April, 1864. Reported absent without leave ("left camps near Atlanta," Georgia) on July 8, 1864. Listed as a deserter on September 10, 1864.

EDWARDS, SANDERS, Private

Resided in Mitchell or Yancey County and was by occupation a farmer prior to enlisting at Camp Jackson at age 24, July 13, 1863, for the war. Wounded at Chickamauga, Georgia, September 20, 1863. Reported absent on expired furlough in March-April, 1864. Failed to return to duty and was dropped from the company rolls on or about August 31, 1864.

ELKINS, JOSEPH, Private

Enlisted at Camp Jackson on July 17, 1862, for the war. Deserted at Cumberland Gap, Tennessee, October 15, 1862. Returned to duty in March-April, 1863. Deserted on May 15, 1863. [May have served later as Private in Company B, 13th Regiment Tennessee Cavalry (Union).]

FEBRUARY, MORDECAI, Private

Born in Carter County, Tennessee, and was by occupation a farmer prior to enlisting in Mitchell County at age 27, May 17, 1862, for the war. Transferred to Company E of this regiment on or about

June 27, 1862. Transferred back to this company prior to March 1, 1863. Reported present in January-June, 1863. Killed at Chickamauga, Georgia, September 20, 1863.

FORD, THOMAS, Private

Place and date of enlistment not reported (probably enlisted subsequent to August 31, 1864). Captured at the Edisto River, South Carolina, February 10, 1865. Sent to New Bern. Transferred to Point Lookout, Maryland, where he arrived on April 3, 1865. Released at Point Lookout on May 15, 1865, after taking the Oath of Allegiance.

FRASIER, JOHN W., Private

Born in Burke County and enlisted in Mitchell County at age 41, August 12, 1862, for the war as a substitute for Pvt. Reuben M. Young, Jr. Mustered in as Private. Promoted to Corporal prior to March 1, 1863. Reported present in January-April, 1863. Reported absent on detached service in May-June, 1863. Deserted from camp near Charleston, Tennessee, September 5, 1863, and was reduced to ranks in absentia. Later served as Sergeant in Company B, 13th Regiment Tennessee Cavalry (Union).

FREEMAN, JOHN, Private

Born in Burke County and enlisted in Mitchell County at age 36, May 17, 1862, for the war. No further records. [May have served later in Company K of this regiment.]

FREEMAN, LITTLETON, Private

Born in Burke County where he resided as a farmer prior to enlisting in Mitchell County at age 45, May 17, 1862, for the war. Transferred to Company E of this regiment on or about June 27, 1862.

FREEMAN, SAMUEL, Private

Born in Burke or Yancey County and was by occupation a farmer prior to enlisting in Mitchell County at age 25, May 17, 1862, for the war. Transferred to Company E of this regiment on or about June 27, 1862.

GARDNER, ELISHA M., Private

Born in Yancey County and resided in Mitchell or Yancey County where he was by occupation a farmer prior to enlisting in Mitchell County at age 18, May 17, 1862, for the war. Reported present in January-June, 1863. Deserted at Bell's Bridge, Tennessee, July 24, 1863. Returned to duty subsequent to December 31, 1863. Reported present in March-August, 1864. Transferred to Company D of this regiment subsequent to August 31, 1864.

GARDNER, THOMAS, Private

Born in Yancey County* and resided in Mitchell or Yancey County where he was by occupation a farmer prior to enlisting in Mitchell County at age 41, May 17, 1862, for the war. Was apparently rejected for service. Reenlisted in the company on September 18, 1862, for the war. Reported present in January-June, 1863. Deserted near Bell's Bridge, Tennessee, July 24, 1863. Returned to duty subsequent to December 31, 1863. Reported present in March-April, 1864. Deserted to the enemy near Dalton, Georgia, May 11, 1864. Confined at Knoxville, Tennessee, May 25, 1864. Released on May 27, 1864, after taking the Oath of Allegiance.

GARLAND, CRISENBERY, Private

Born in Burke County and resided in Mitchell or Yancey County where he was by occupation a farmer prior to enlisting in Mitchell

County at age 37, May 17, 1862, for the war. Reported absent on sick furlough on November 19, 1862. Failed to return to duty and was reported absent without leave on February 9, 1863. Returned to duty subsequent to October 31, 1863. Reported present in March-August, 1864. Discharged on January 1, 1865, by reason of "anasarca the result of disease of mitral valves of heart with pericardial effusion producing general impairment of health."

GARLAND, EZEKIEL, Private

Resided in Mitchell or Yancey County where he was by occupation a farmer prior to enlisting at Camp Jackson at age 17, June 27, 1862, for the war. Deserted at Cumberland Gap, Tennessee, November 16, 1862. Later served as Private in Company E, 3rd Regiment N.C. Mounted Infantry (Union).

GARLAND, GIBBS, Private

Resided in Mitchell or Yancey County and was by occupation clerk of the superior court prior to enlisting at Camp Jackson at age 47, July 19, 1862, for the war. Furloughed at Cumberland Gap, Tennessee, on or about November 15, 1862. Failed to return to duty and was listed as a deserter in May-June, 1863.

GARLAND, HODGE R., Private

Born in Burke County and resided in Mitchell or Yancey County where he was by occupation a farmer prior to enlisting in Mitchell County at age 52, May 17, 1862, for the war. Died at Jacksboro, Tennessee, January 30, 1863. Cause of death not reported.

GARLAND, JOHN, Private

Born in Yancey County and resided in Mitchell or Yancey County where he was by occupation a farmer prior to enlisting in Mitchell County at age 25, May 17, 1862, for the war. Deserted at Jacksboro, Tennessee, January 10, 1863. [May have served later as Private in Company E , 3rd Regiment N.C. Mounted Infantry (Union).]

GATES, JAMES A., Private

Enlisted at Clinton, Tennessee, April 13, 1863, for the war. Company records indicate that he was captured at Clinton in August, 1863; however, records of the Federal Provost Marshal do not substantiate that report. No further records.

GHEEN, JAMES, Private

Enlisted at Dalton, Georgia, December 30, 1863, for the war. Left camp near Dalton on April 4, 1864, without leave. Reported absent without leave through August 31, 1864. Dropped from the company rolls on or about August 31, 1864.

GHEEN, THOMAS, Private

Enlisted at Dalton, Georgia, December 30, 1863, for the war. Left camp near Dalton on April 4, 1864, without leave. Listed as a deserter on September 10, 1864.

GILLILAND, JOSEPH J., Private

Previously served as Private in Company H of this regiment. Transferred to this company subsequent to November 15, 1864. Paroled at Greensboro on May 1, 1865.

GILLILAND, ROBERT, Private

Previously served as Private in Company H of this regiment. Transferred to this company subsequent to August 31, 1864. Paroled at Greensboro on or about May 1, 1865.

GREEN, JOSEPH, Private

Previously served as Private in Company D of this regiment. Transferred to this company prior to March 1, 1863. Reported present in January-June and September-October, 1863. Reported sick in hospital in November-December, 1863. Returned to duty on an unspecified date. Reported present in March-April, 1864. Furloughed from hospital for sixty days on August 16, 1864. No further records. Survived the war. [North Carolina pension records indicate that he was wounded in the left breast at Chickamauga, Georgia, September 20, 1863, when he was "struck . . . by a shell or piece of a shell knocking him down and breaking the breast bone."]

HARRELL, THOMAS C., Private

Born in Yancey County and was by occupation a farmer prior to enlisting in Mitchell County at age 18, May 17, 1862, for the war. Mustered in as Private. Reported present in January-April, 1863. Promoted to Corporal in March-April, 1863. Reduced to ranks and was reported under arrest in May-June, 1863. Promoted to Sergeant on an unspecified date. Deserted from camp near Charleston, Tennessee, September 1, 1863, and was reduced to ranks in absentia.

HERRILL, HENRY C., Private

Born in Yancey County and was by occupation a farmer prior to enlisting in Mitchell County at age 16, May 17, 1862, for the war. No further records.

HETHWOOD, M., ———

Place and date of enlistment not reported. Listed as a deserter on September 10, 1864.

HILEMAN, JACOB, Private

Born in Yancey County and enlisted in Mitchell County at age 18, May 17, 1862, for the war. Reported absent without leave in January-February, 1863. Returned to duty in March-April, 1863. Reported present in May-June, 1863. Deserted from camp near Chattanooga, Tennessee, September 26, 1863. Returned to duty subsequent to December 31, 1863. Reported present in March-August, 1864. Transferred to Company D of this regiment subsequent to August 31, 1864. [May have served also in Company E of this regiment.]

HILEMAN, JOHN, Private

Born in Burke County and was by occupation a farmer prior to enlisting in Mitchell County at age 30, May 17, 1862, for the war. Reported present in January-April, 1863. Deserted at Clinton, Tennessee, June 8, 1863. Returned to duty on an unspecified date. Reported absent without leave from Chattanooga, Tennessee, October 10, 1863. [May have served later as Private in Company E, 3rd Regiment N.C. Mounted Infantry (Union). May have served also in Company E of this regiment.]

HINSON, JOSEPH, Private

Born in Washington County, Tennessee, and resided in Mitchell or Yancey County where he was by occupation a farmer prior to enlisting in Mitchell County at age 20, May 17, 1862, for the war. Reported present in January-February, 1863. Transferred to Company A, 64th Regiment N.C. Troops, March 1, 1863, in exchange for Pvt. Reuben Proctor.

HOBSON, BENONI, JR., Private

Previously served as Private in Company E of this regiment. Transferred to this company prior to March 1, 1863. Reported present

on surviving company muster rolls from January-February, 1863, through April 30, 1864. Killed at Bald Hill, near Atlanta, Georgia, July 22, 1864.

HONEYCUTT, SAMPSON, Private

Enlisted at Camp Stokes, Haynesville, Tennessee, at age 50, August 5, 1862, for the war. Reported present in January-February, 1863. No further records. Survived the war.

HOPSON, GEORGE, Private

Born in Yancey County* and resided in Mitchell or Yancey County where he was by occupation a farmer prior to enlisting in Mitchell County at age 53, May 17, 1862, for the war. No further records.

HOPSON, JOHN, Private

Born in Yancey County and resided in Mitchell or Yancey County where he was by occupation a farmer prior to enlisting in Mitchell County at age 25, May 17, 1862, for the war. Transferred to Company K of this regiment prior to September 30, 1862.

HORN, HILLIARD, Private

Resided in Mitchell or Yancey County and was by occupation a farmer prior to enlisting in Mitchell County at age 36, May 17, 1862, for the war. Reported present in January-February, 1863. Died at Jacksboro, Tennessee, March 11, 1863. Cause of death not reported.

HOWELL, ROBERT V., Corporal

Previously served as Private in Company C of this regiment. Transferred to this company and promoted to Corporal subsequent to August 31, 1864. Paroled at Greensboro on May 1, 1865.

HUGHES, IVEN, Private

Born in Yancey County where he resided as a laborer prior to enlisting in Mitchell County at age 20, May 17, 1862, for the war. Reported present in January-April, 1863. Deserted at Clinton, Tennessee, May 24, 1863. Confined at Chattanooga, Tennessee, on or about November 12, 1864. Transferred to Louisville, Kentucky, where he arrived on November 20, 1864. Released at Louisville on November 25, 1864, after taking the Oath of Allegiance.

HUGHS, LANDON C., Private

Born in Yancey County and enlisted in Mitchell County at age 22, May 17, 1862, for the war. Deserted at Cumberland Gap, Tennessee, October 15, 1862. [May have served later as Private in Company M, 8th Regiment Tennessee Cavalry (Union).]

HUSKINS, HORACE, Private

Place and date of enlistment not reported. Paroled at Charlotte on May 6, 1865.

HUTCHINS, ALBERT, Private

Enlisted at Dalton, Georgia, December 31, 1863, for the war. Reported present but under arrest in March-April, 1864. Reason he was arrested not reported. Reported absent without leave from camp near Calhoun, Georgia, May 25, 1864. Listed as a deserter on September 10, 1864.

HUTCHINS, JAMES, Private

Born in Yancey County and was by occupation a farmer prior to enlisting in Mitchell County at age 17, May 17, 1862, for the war.

Died subsequent to September 30, 1862, but prior to February 2, 1863. Place, date, and cause of death not reported.

JARRETT, ELI, Corporal

Born in Lincoln County on March 28, 1833. Resided in Mitchell or Yancey County and was by occupation a farmer prior to enlisting at Camp Jackson at age 29, July 12, 1862, for the war. Was apparently mustered in as Private. Reported present in January-June and September-October, 1863. Promoted to Corporal in November-December, 1863. Wounded in the left leg at Missionary Ridge, Tennessee, November 25, 1863. Returned to duty subsequent to December 31, 1863. Reported present in March-April, 1864. Reported absent without leave from camp near Atlanta, Georgia, July 8, 1864. Returned to duty on an unspecified date. Transferred to Company D of this regiment subsequent to August 31, 1864.

JARRETT, LEVI, Private

Born in Lincoln County and resided in Mitchell or Yancey County where he was by occupation a farmer prior to enlisting in Mitchell County at age 32, May 17, 1862, for the war. Reported absent on sick furlough on November 19, 1862. Reported absent sick through June 30, 1863. Reported in hospital at Chickamauga, Georgia, October 30, 1863. Died in hospital at Atlanta, Georgia, November 8, 1863, of disease.

LEDFORD, WILLIAM, Private

Place and date of enlistment not reported (probably enlisted subsequent to August 31, 1864). Captured at Orangeburg, South Carolina, February 14, 1865. Confined at Hart's Island, New York Harbor, April 11, 1865. Died at Hart's Island on May 26, 1865, of "chronic diarrhoea."

LOWERY, JAMES L., Private

Enlisted at Camp Stokes, Haynesville, Tennessee, August 19, 1862, for the war. Reported present in January-June, 1863. Sent to hospital at Knoxville, Tennessee, August 4, 1863. Furloughed home on August 15, 1863. Failed to return to duty and was dropped from the company rolls on or about August 31, 1864.

McKINNEY, JAMES H., ———

North Carolina pension records indicate that he served in this company.

McKINNEY, REUBEN M., Private

Born in Yancey County and enlisted at Big Creek Gap, Tennessee, at age 23, March 22, 1863, for the war. Deserted at Clinton, Tennessee, April 2, 1863.

McKINNEY, SAMUEL B., ———

North Carolina pension records indicate that he served in this company or in Company C of this regiment. One of his pension applications states that he hired Joseph Stewart as a substitute. A man by that name served in Company A of this regiment. [May have served also in Company I, 3rd Regiment N.C. Mounted Infantry (Union).]

McVAY, WILLIAM, Private

Born in Yancey County and enlisted in Mitchell County at age 21, May 17, 1862, for the war. Reported present in January-February, 1863. Died in hospital at Jacksboro, Tennessee, March 24, 1863, of "measles."

MILLER, ANDREW, Private

Born in Yancey County and resided in Mitchell or Yancey County where he was by occupation a farmer or farm laborer prior to enlisting in Mitchell County at age 22, May 17, 1862, for the war. Transferred to Company E of this regiment on or about June 27, 1862.

MILLER, HIRAM, Private

Born in Yancey County* and enlisted in Mitchell County at age 36, May 17, 1862, for the war. No further records. Survived the war. [May have served later as Private in Companies A and F, 3rd Regiment N.C. Mounted Infantry (Union).]

MILLER, JACOB, Private

Born in Yancey County and resided in Mitchell or Yancey County where he was by occupation a farmer prior to enlisting in Mitchell County at age 25, May 17, 1862, for the war. No further records. Later served as Private in Company A, 3rd Regiment N.C. Mounted Infantry (Union).

MILLER, SAMUEL, Private

Resided in Mitchell or Yancey County and was by occupation a laborer prior to enlisting at Camp Reynolds at age 19, September 1, 1862, for the war. Reported present in January-April, 1863. Reported in confinement in the guard house in May-June, 1863. Reason he was confined not reported. Transferred to Company G of this regiment on June 30, 1863. [May have served previously as Private in Company I, 29th Regiment N.C. Troops.]

MILLER, THOMAS, Private

Born in Yancey County and enlisted in Mitchell County at age 28, May 17, 1862, for the war. No further records.

MILLER, THOMAS, Private

Born in Yancey County* and resided in Mitchell or Yancey County where he was by occupation a farmer prior to enlisting in Mitchell County at age 35, May 17, 1862, for the war. No further records.

MILLER, WILLIAM, Private

Born in Yancey County and resided in Mitchell or Yancey County where he was by occupation a farmer prior to enlisting in Mitchell County at age 24, May 17, 1862, for the war. No further records.

ODOM, ABRAHAM, Private

Born in Yancey County and resided in Mitchell or Yancey County where he was by occupation a farmer prior to enlisting in Mitchell County at age 28, May 17, 1862, for the war. Died subsequent to September 30, 1862, but prior to March 26, 1863. Place, date, and cause of death not reported.

ODOM, JOHN, Private

Born in Yancey County and resided in Mitchell or Yancey County where he was by occupation a farmer prior to enlisting in Mitchell County at age 22, May 17, 1862, for the war. Died subsequent to September 30, 1862, but prior to March 26, 1863. Place, date, and cause of death not reported.

OSBORNE, DAVID, Private

Born in Ashe County and resided in Mitchell or Yancey County where he was by occupation a farmer prior to enlisting in Mitchell

County at age 24, May 17, 1862, for the war. Deserted at Big Creek Gap, Tennessee, January 31, 1863. Later served as Corporal in Company D, 3rd Regiment N.C. Mounted Infantry (Union).

PALMER, GEORGE C., Private

Previously served as Private in Company H of this regiment. Transferred to this company subsequent to August 31, 1864. Paroled at Greensboro on or about May 2, 1865. [North Carolina pension records indicate that he was wounded at Chickamauga, Georgia, September 20, 1863.]

PHILLIPS, CRISENBERY, Musician

Enlisted at Camp Jackson on May 17, 1862, for the war. Was apparently mustered in with the rank of Musician (Drummer). Reported present in January-June, 1863. Wounded at Chickamauga, Georgia, September 20, 1863. Died on September 25, 1863, of wounds. Place of death not reported.

PRESTWOOD, SYDNEY E., Private

Born in Burke County and resided in Mitchell or Yancey County where he was by occupation a saddler prior to enlisting in Mitchell County at age 30, May 17, 1862, for the war. Was apparently mustered in with the rank of Private. Promoted to Corporal prior to March 1, 1863. Reported present in January-April, 1863. Reported absent without leave in May-June, 1863. Reduced to ranks prior to July 1, 1863. Returned to duty on an unspecified date. Deserted from camp near Charleston, Tennessee, September 5, 1863. Returned to duty subsequent to December 31, 1863. Reported present in March-April, 1864. Reported absent without leave from camp near Dalton, Georgia, May 11, 1864. Listed as a deserter on September 10, 1864.

PROCTOR, REUBEN, Private

Previously served as Private in Company A, 64th Regiment N.C. Troops. Transferred to this company on March 1, 1863, in exchange for Pvt. Joseph Hinson. Reported present in March-June, 1863. Deserted from camp near Clinton, Tennessee, August 5, 1863. Later served as Private in Companies G and K, 8th Regiment Tennessee Cavalry (Union).

RAMSEY, JOSEPH, Private

Born in Yancey County and was by occupation a farmer prior to enlisting in Mitchell County at age 19, May 17, 1862, for the war. Deserted at Cumberland Gap, Tennessee, October 15, 1862. Later served as Corporal in Company A, 3rd Regiment N.C. Mounted Infantry (Union).

RAMSEY, RILEY C., Private

Born in Yancey County and enlisted in Mitchell County at age 26, May 17, 1862, for the war. Deserted from Johnson's Depot, Tennessee, subsequent to September 30, 1862, but prior to June 30, 1863.

RIDDLE, JOHN, Private

Born in Yancey County* and resided in Mitchell or Yancey County where he was by occupation a farmer prior to enlisting in Mitchell County at age 32, May 17, 1862, for the war. Mustered in as Private. Reported absent on detached service in January-February, 1863. Appointed Musician (Fifer) prior to March 1, 1863. Reported present in March-June, 1863. Deserted from camp near Charleston, Tennessee, September 10, 1863. Reduced to ranks in November-

December, 1863. Returned to duty subsequent to December 31, 1863. Reported absent without leave from camp near Atlanta, Georgia, July 8, 1864. Listed as a deserter on September 10, 1864. [May have served later as Corporal in Company K, 3rd Regiment N.C. Mounted Infantry (Union).]

SAMS, J. F., ———

North Carolina pension records indicate that he served in this company.

SCOGGINS, JOHN B., Sergeant

Born in Rutherford County and resided in Mitchell, Yancey, or McDowell County where he was by occupation a farmer prior to enlisting in Mitchell County at age 35, May 17, 1862, for the war. Mustered in as Private. Reported present in January-February, 1863. Detailed for duty as a hospital nurse at Knoxville, Tennessee, April 16, 1863. Rejoined the company on an unspecified date. Promoted to Sergeant on September 17, 1863. Reported present in September-October, 1863. Reduced to ranks in November-December, 1863. Hospitalized at Griffin, Georgia, December 4, 1863. Returned to duty on an unspecified date and was promoted to Sergeant. Reported present in March-August, 1864. Hospitalized at Raleigh on March 15, 1865, with debilitas. Transferred to another hospital on March 21, 1865. No further records.

SCOTT, JAMES A., ———

North Carolina pension records indicate that he served in this company.

SCOTT, LORENZO D., Private

Born in Giles County, Virginia, and was by occupation a shoemaker prior to enlisting in Mitchell County at age 33, May 17, 1862, for the war. Later served as Sergeant in Company H, 13th Regiment Tennessee Cavalry (Union).

SLAGLE, A. D., Private

Enlisted at Dalton, Georgia, March 16, 1864, for the war. Reported present through April, 1864. Sent to hospital on August 1, 1864. Reported in hospital at Fort Valley, Georgia, October 21, 1864. No further records.

SLAGLE, ADOLPHUS, Private

Born in Yancey County and resided in Mitchell or Yancey County where he was by occupation a farmer prior to enlisting in Mitchell County at age 21, May 17, 1862, for the war. Transferred to Company E of this regiment on or about June 27, 1862. Transferred back to this company on an unspecified date. Discharged on October 16, 1862. Reason discharged not reported.

SLAGLE, SIMEON, Private

Born in Yancey County and was by occupation a farmer prior to enlisting in Mitchell County at age 24, May 17, 1862, for the war. Transferred to Company C of this regiment on or about June 16, 1862.

STAFFORD, WILLIAM HENRY, Private

Previously served as Private in Company H of this regiment. Transferred to this company subsequent to March 19, 1865. Paroled at Greensboro on or about May 1, 1865.

STEPHENS, JACKSON, Private

Born in Cherokee County, Georgia, and resided in Mitchell or Yancey County where he was by occupation a farmer prior to enlisting in Mitchell County at age 21, May 17, 1862, for the war. Reported present on surviving company muster rolls through April 30, 1864. Wounded at Kolb's Farm, near Marietta, Georgia, June 22, 1864. No further records.

STEPHENS, JOHN, Corporal

Born in Yancey County and resided in Mitchell or Yancey County where he was by occupation a farmer prior to enlisting in Mitchell County at age 21, May 17, 1862, for the war. Mustered in as Private. Transferred to Company E of this regiment on or about June 27, 1862. Transferred back to this company prior to March 1, 1863. Reported present in January-June, 1863. Promoted to Corporal on September 7, 1863. Wounded in the left arm at Chickamauga, Georgia, September 20, 1863. Company records indicate that he was dropped from the rolls on or about August 31, 1864, because he failed to return from wounded furlough; however, North Carolina pension records indicate that his furlough was extended until the end of the war.

STEPHENS, JOSHUA, Private

Born in Burke County and resided in Mitchell or Yancey County where he was by occupation a farmer prior to enlisting in Mitchell County at age 40, May 17, 1862, for the war. Reported present in January-June, 1863. Deserted from camp near Charleston, Tennessee, September 10, 1863. Returned to duty subsequent to December 31, 1863. Reported absent without leave from camp near Atlanta, Georgia, August 27, 1864. No further records. Survived the war. [North Carolina pension records indicate that he died on March 28, 1870, of a shell wound in the left side received at Murfreesboro, Tennessee, December 31, 1862-January 1, 1863.]

STEPHENS, SHERRED, Private

Born in Yancey County and resided in Mitchell or Yancey County where he was by occupation a farmer prior to enlisting in Mitchell County at age 26, May 17, 1862, for the war. Transferred to Company E of this regiment on or about June 27, 1862.

STEWARD, BERRY, Sergeant

Enlisted at Camp Jackson on June 1, 1862, for the war. Was apparently mustered in with the rank of Private. Reported present in January-June, 1863. Promoted to Corporal in March-April, 1863. Promoted to Sergeant on September 8, 1863. Wounded in the neck, hand, right arm, and left shoulder at Chickamauga, Georgia, September 20, 1863. Reported absent on expired furlough in March-April, 1864. Returned to duty prior to June 22, 1864, when he was wounded in the left leg at Kolb's Farm, near Marietta, Georgia. Reported absent wounded through August, 1864. No further records. Survived the war. [Was about 21 years of age at time of enlistment.]

STEWARD, JASPER, Sergeant

Previously served as Private in Company E of this regiment. Transferred to this company prior to March 1, 1863. Apparently was mustered in with the rank of Corporal. Promoted to Sergeant in March-April, 1863. Reported present in January-June, 1863. Deserted from camp on September 20, 1863. Reported present but under arrest in November-December, 1863. Furloughed for twenty-four days on April 16, 1864. Killed at Kolb's Farm, near Marietta, Georgia, June 22, 1864.

STEWARD, WILLIAM R., Private

Born in Yancey County* and resided in Mitchell or Yancey County where he was by occupation a farmer prior to enlisting in Mitchell County at age 37, May 17, 1862, for the war. No further records. Survived the war.

STEWART, BENJAMIN, ———

North Carolina pension records indicate that he served in this company.

STEWART, JAMES, Private

Born in Burke County in 1844. Enlisted at Camp Martin (Mitchell County) on May 17, 186[2], for the war. Reported present in May-June, 1863. Deserted from camp near Chattanooga, Tennessee, September 26, 1863. Reported under arrest in November-December, 1863. Returned to duty on an unspecified date. Reported present in March-April, 1864. Reported absent without leave from camp near Atlanta, Georgia, July 8, 1864. No further records. Survived the war. [His Tennessee pension application indicates that his hearing was "impaired" by "the bursting of a shell" at Chickamauga, Georgia (September 19-20, 1863).]

STREET, SAMUEL M., Private

Born in Yancey County and resided in Mitchell or Yancey County where he was by occupation a farmer prior to enlisting in Mitchell County at age 26, May 17, 1862, for the war. Transferred to Company E of this regiment on or about June 27, 1862. Transferred back to this company prior to August 16, 1862, when he deserted at Camp Stokes, Haynesville, Tennessee. [May have served later as Private in Company D, 8th Regiment Tennessee Cavalry (Union).]

TESTERMAN, FRANK M., Private

Enlisted at Dalton, Georgia, December 16, 1863, for the war. Sent to hospital on December 20, 1863. Reported absent without leave on February 10, 1864. Dropped from the company rolls on or about August 31, 1864.

TIPTON, DAVID Mc., Private

Born in Georgia or in Cherokee County, North Carolina, and was by occupation a farmer prior to enlisting in Mitchell County at age 22, May 17, 1862, for the war. Deserted at Jacksboro, Tennessee, on the night of January 10, 1863. Enlisted as Private in Company D, 3rd Regiment N.C. Mounted Infantry (Union), on or about June 4, 1864.

TIPTON, THOMAS G., Corporal

Previously served as Private in Company G of this regiment. Transferred to this company subsequent to June 30, 1863. Promoted to Corporal on an unspecified date. Killed at Chickamauga, Georgia, September 20, 1863, after saving the life of Capt. Isaac H. Bailey of this company.

TIPTON, WILLIAM, Private

Enlisted at Camp Jackson on July 12, 1862, for the war. Deserted at Cumberland Gap, Tennessee, October 15, 1862. [May have served later as Private in Company F, 3rd Regiment N.C. Mounted Infantry (Union).]

TROUTMAN, GEORGE W., Private

Enlisted at Camp Stokes, Haynesville, Tennessee, August 12, 1862, for the war. Reported present or accounted for in January-

April, 1863. Deserted at Clinton, Tennessee, May 24, 1863. Returned to duty on an unspecified date. Deserted from camp near Charleston, Tennessee, September 1, 1863.

TURBYFIELD, JAMES PICKNY, Private

Born in Lincoln County and resided in Mitchell or Yancey County prior to enlisting at Camp Jackson at age 27, July 12, 1862, for the war. Reported present in January-June and September-December, 1863. Furloughed for twenty-four days on January 29, 1864. Failed to return to duty. Reported present but under arrest in May-August, 1864. Returned to duty on an unspecified date. Hospitalized at Charlotte on February 20, 1865, with remittent fever. Returned to duty on February 26, 1865. Wounded slightly in the foot at Bentonville on March 19, 1865. No further records. Survived the war. [North Carolina and Tennessee pension records indicate that he was wounded slightly in the back and hip "by explosion of shell" near Atlanta, Georgia, September 1, 1864.]

WEBB, FRANKLIN, Private

Born in Yancey County and enlisted in Mitchell County at age 19, May 17, 1862, for the war. Reported present in January-June and September-October, 1863. Died in hospital at Marietta, Georgia, December 21, 1863. Cause of death not reported.

WHITSON, WILLIAM W., Private

Born in Tennessee and resided in Mitchell or Yancey County where he was by occupation a farmer prior to enlisting at Camp Jackson at age 26, July 12, 1862, for the war. Deserted at Big Creek Gap, Tennessee, January 31, 1863. Apprehended on an unspecified date and was probably confined at the military prison at Salisbury. Died in hospital at Salisbury on November 19, 1864, of "pneumonia."

WRIGHT, SOLOMON H., Private

Born in Burke County and enlisted in Mitchell County at age 55, May 17, 1862, for the war. Reported present in January-June, 1863. Furloughed home sick on or about July 20, 1863. Reported absent on expired furlough in March-April, 1864. Failed to return to duty and was dropped from the company rolls on or about August 31, 1864.

YELTON, JOHN L., Private

Born in Yancey County and resided in Mitchell or Yancey County where he was by occupation a farmer prior to enlisting in Mitchell County at age 26, May 17, 1862, for the war. Transferred to Company I of this regiment on or about July 24, 1862.

YOUNG, JOHN WESLEY, Private

Enlisted at Camp Jackson on July 12, 1862, for the war. Reported present in January-April, 1863. Deserted at Clinton, Tennessee, June 8, 1863. Returned to duty on an unspecified date. Deserted from camp near Charleston, Tennessee, September 10, 1863.

YOUNG, MERRITT, Private

Born in Yancey County* and was by occupation a farmer prior to enlisting in Mitchell County at age 32, May 17, 1862, for the war. Transferred to Company K of this regiment on or about July 29, 1862. Transferred back to this company prior to March 1, 1863. Reported present in January-April, 1863. Deserted at Clinton, Ten-

nessee, June 8, 1863. Later served as Sergeant in Company C, 13th Regiment Tennessee Cavalry (Union).

YOUNG, REUBEN M., JR., Private

Born in Yancey County and enlisted in Mitchell County at age 18, May 17, 1862, for the war. Discharged on August 12, 1862, after providing Pvt. John W. Frasier as a substitute.

YOUNG, THOMAS B., Private

Born in Yancey County and resided in Mitchell or Yancey County where he was by occupation a store clerk prior to enlisting in Mitchell County at age 27, May 17, 1862, for the war. Discharged on or about May 17, 1862, after providing Pvt. Thomas Buchanan as a substitute.

YOUNG, THOMAS S., Private

Previously served as Private in Company C of this regiment. Transferred to this company subsequent to August 31, 1864. Paroled at Greensboro on or about May 1, 1865.

COMPANY C

This company, known as the "Yancey Boys," was raised in Yancey County on May 29, 1862, as Capt. William W. Proffitt's Company, N.C. Volunteers. It was mustered into service at Burnsville on June 16, 1862, and placed under the authority of Lt. Col. John B. Palmer. Palmer, former commander of "Palmer's Legion," a mixed (cavalry and infantry) unit that had failed to complete its organization, was by then recruiting for a cavalry unit to be known as the 5th Battalion N.C. Partisan Rangers; however, it appears that Proffitt's Company was never formally assigned to the 5th Battalion. Shortly thereafter Proffitt's Company was designated Company C of a nascent infantry regiment, commanded by Palmer, that was mustered in as the 58th Regiment N.C. Troops on July 29, 1862. After joining 58th Regiment the company functioned as a part of that regiment, and its history for the remainder of the war is reported as a part of the regimental history.

The following roster was compiled primarily from information in the microfilm edition of the Compiled Service Records of Soldiers Who Served in Organizations from the State of North Carolina (Record Group 109, M270), National Archives and Records Administration, Washington, D.C. Record Group 109 includes enlistment papers, pay vouchers, requisitions, letters of resignation, discharge certificates, and abstracts of medical and prisoner of war returns. Materials relating specifically to this company include muster rolls dated January-June, 1863; September-October, 1863; and January-August, 1864.

Also utilized in this roster were *The War of the Rebellion: A Compilation of the Official Records of the Union and Confederate Armies*, the North Carolina adjutant general's *Roll of Honor*, state militia records, newspaper casualty lists and obituaries, wartime claims for bounty pay and allowances, postwar registers of claims for artificial limbs, Confederate pension applications filed with the states of North Carolina, Tennessee, and Florida, Confederate Soldiers' Home records, and the 1860 and 1870 federal censuses of North Carolina. A search was made also for relevant letters, diaries, reminiscences, and other manuscripts in the Southern Historical Collection (University of North Carolina-Chapel Hill), the Duke University Library Special Collections Department, and the North Carolina Division of Archives and History.

Among the secondary sources consulted were records of the North Carolina division of the United Daughters of the Confederacy, post-war rosters, regimental and county histories, marriage bond, will, and cemetery indexes, published and unpublished genealogies, biographical dictionaries, the North Carolina *County Heritage Book* series, the *Confederate Veteran*, Walter Clark's *Histories of the Several Regiments and Battalions from North Carolina in the Great War, 1861-'65*, and the North Carolina volume of the extended edition of *Confederate Military History*.

OFFICERS

CAPTAINS

PROFFITT, WILLIAM W.

Born in Buncombe County and resided in Mitchell or Yancey County where he was by occupation a sheriff prior to enlisting at age 34. Elected Captain on May 29, 1862. Elected Lieutenant Colonel on July 29, 1862, and transferred to the Field and Staff of this regiment. [Previously served as Lieutenant Colonel of the 111th Regiment N.C. Militia.]

HORTON, JONATHAN PHILMORE

Born in Yancey County and was by occupation a farmer prior to enlisting at age 22. Elected 1st Lieutenant on May 29, 1862. Promoted to Captain on July 29, 1862. Detailed for twenty days on October 27, 1862, to go home for clothing for his company. Resigned on May 16, 1863, because of "chronic bronchitis with great debility" which had rendered him "unable for duty for the last six months. . . ."

BRIGGS, SUEL B.

Born in Yancey County where he resided as a farmer prior to enlisting in Yancey County at age 25. Appointed 2nd Lieutenant on May 29, 1862. Elected 1st Lieutenant on July 29, 1862. Reported present in January-February and May-June, 1863. Promoted to Captain on May 16, 1863. Reported present in September-October, 1863, and January-August, 1864. Transferred to Company B of this regiment subsequent to August 31, 1864. [Previously served as Captain in the 111th Regiment N.C. Militia.]

CLAYTON, EDWIN M.

Previously served as Captain of Company K, 60th Regiment N.C. Troops. Appointed Captain of this company when the 58th and 60th Regiments were consolidated on April 9, 1865. Paroled at Greensboro on May 1, 1865.

LIEUTENANTS

AUSTIN, WILLIAM M., 2nd Lieutenant

Born in Buncombe County and resided in Yancey County where he was by occupation a teacher prior to enlisting in Yancey County at age 30, May 29, 1862, for the war. Mustered in as Private. Reported on detached service on February 4, 1863. Promoted to 1st Sergeant prior to March 1, 1863. Reported present in May-June, 1863. Elected 3rd Lieutenant on June 17, 1863. Promoted to 2nd Lieutenant on August 14, 1863. Wounded in the right shoulder, leg, and hip at Chickamauga, Georgia, September 20, 1863. Reported absent wounded through August 31, 1864 (was erroneously

reported absent without leave during part of that period). No further records. Survived the war.

BRIGGS, MELVIN W., 3rd Lieutenant

Previously served as Private in Company K, 29th Regiment N.C. Troops. Appointed 3rd Lieutenant and transferred to this company on November 13, 1863. Reported present in January-August, 1864. Furloughed for forty days on September 18, 1864. No further records. Survived the war.

BROOKS, STEPHEN, 2nd Lieutenant

Previously served as Private in Company H, 60th Regiment N.C. Troops. Appointed 2nd Lieutenant of this company when the 58th and 60th Regiments were consolidated on April 9, 1865. Paroled at Greensboro on May 1, 1865.

HAMPTON, MILTON P., 1st Lieutenant

Born in Yancey County where he resided as a farmer prior to enlisting in Yancey County at age 20, May 29, 1862, for the war. Mustered in as 1st Sergeant. Elected 3rd Lieutenant on July 29, 1862. Reported present in January-February, 1863. Promoted to 2nd Lieutenant on May 16, 1863. Reported under arrest on or about June 30, 1863. Reason he was arrested not reported. Returned to duty on an unspecified date. Promoted to 1st Lieutenant on August 14, 1863. Reported present in September-October, 1863. Reported absent on detached service in North Carolina on December 19, 1863. Ordered to rejoin his command on March 8, 1864. Wounded at or near Dallas, Georgia, May 28, 1864. Reported absent wounded through August 31, 1864. Reported absent without leave on an unspecified date. Dropped from the company rolls on April 2, 1865.

MOSS, BENJAMIN J., 1st Lieutenant

Born in South Carolina or in Yancey County* and resided in Yancey County where he was by occupation a carpenter prior to enlisting at age 47. Elected 3rd Lieutenant on May 29, 1862. Promoted to 2nd Lieutenant on July 29, 1862. Reported absent sick from December 25, 1862, through June 30, 1863. Promoted to 1st Lieutenant on May 16, 1863. Resigned on August 1, 1863, by reason of "enlargement of knee joint, [and] arthritis, causing locomotion to be difficult and painfull [*sic*]." Resignation accepted on August 14, 1863. [Previously served as 2nd Lieutenant in the 111th Regiment N.C. Militia.]

SALES, JOHN T., 1st Lieutenant

Previously served as 1st Lieutenant of Company K, 60th Regiment N.C. Troops. Appointed 1st Lieutenant of this company when the 58th and 60th Regiments were consolidated on April 9, 1865. Paroled at Greensboro on May 1, 1865.

NONCOMMISSIONED OFFICERS AND PRIVATES

ANGEL, JAMES G., Private

Place and date of enlistment not reported (probably enlisted in the summer of 1862). Transferred to Company B, 29th Regiment N.C. Troops, in October, 1862.

ANGLIN, JAMES, Corporal

Born in Yancey County and was by occupation a farmer prior to enlisting in Yancey County at age 18, May 29, 1862, for the war. Mustered in as Private. Promoted to Corporal prior to March 1,

1863. Reported present on surviving company muster rolls from January-February, 1863, through August 31, 1864. No further records. Survived the war.

ANGLIN, RABORN B., Private

Previously served as Sergeant in Company G of this regiment. Reduced to ranks and transferred to this company on or about June 1, 1863. Reported present in September-October, 1863, and January-February, 1864. Detailed as a gunsmith on April 18, 1864. Reported absent on detail through August 31, 1864. Transferred to Company B of this regiment subsequent to August 31, 1864.

ANGLIN, WILLIAM, Sergeant

Born in Yancey County where he resided as a farmer prior to enlisting in Yancey County at age 16, May 29, 1862, for the war. Mustered in as Private. Reported present in January-February and May-June, 1863. Promoted to Sergeant in March-June, 1863. Reported present in September-October, 1863, and January-August, 1864. Wounded in the left thigh (compound fracture) at or near Jonesborough, Georgia, August 31, 1864. Hospitalized at Macon, Georgia, September 8, 1864. Died in hospital at Macon on or about September 18, 1864, of wounds.

AYERS, WILLBURN, Private

Resided in Yancey County and was by occupation a farmer prior to enlisting in Yancey County at age 24, July 12, 1862, for the war. Reported absent on sick furlough from August 27, 1862, through February 28, 1863. Returned to duty on an unspecified date. Reported present in May-June, 1863. Furloughed for thirty days on August 25, 1863. Reported absent without leave on February 20, 1864. Listed as a deserter on April 7, 1864.

BAILEY, JAMES B., Private

Born in Yancey County where he resided as a farmer prior to enlisting at age 26, June 16, 1862, for the war. Not reported again in the records of this company until January 27, 1865, when he was hospitalized at Meridian, Mississippi, with pneumonia. Furloughed for sixty days from hospital at Meridian on or about March 7, 1865.

BAILEY, JAMES W., ———

North Carolina pension records indicate that he served in this company.

BAILEY, JESSE, Private

Previously served as Private in Company G of this regiment. Transferred to this company on or about July 15, 1862. Reported present in January-February and May-June, 1863. Deserted at Chattanooga, Tennessee, October 4, 1863. Returned to duty in March-April, 1864. Reported absent on detached service at Asheville on April 30, 1864. Rejoined the company on an unspecified date. Reported present in May-August, 1864. Hospitalized at Meridian, Mississippi, March 11, 1865, with a fracture of the right tibia. Furloughed for sixty days on or about March 7, 1865. Survived the war.

BAILEY, JESSE W., Private

Born in Yancey County and was by occupation a farmer prior to enlisting in Yancey County at age 17, May 29, 1862, for the war. Reported present in January-February and May-June, 1863. Deserted at Chattanooga, Tennessee, September 27, 1863. Returned to duty in March-April, 1864. Reported on detached service at

Asheville on April 30, 1864. Rejoined the company on an unspecified date. Reported present in May-August, 1864. No further records.

BAILEY, JOHN W., Private

Born in Yancey County where he resided as a farmer prior to enlisting in Yancey County at age 24, May 29, 1862, for the war. Mustered in as Corporal. Reported present in January-February, 1863. Reduced to ranks prior to March 1, 1863. Deserted at Clinton, Tennessee, May 21, 1863. Returned to duty on an unspecified date. Deserted at Chattanooga, Tennessee, September 27, 1863.

BAILEY, WILLIAM M., Private

Resided in Yancey County and was by occupation a farmer prior to enlisting in Yancey County at age 29, July 12, 1862, for the war. Reported absent on sick furlough from August 27, 1862, through October 31, 1863. Reported absent without leave on February 20, 1864. Listed as a deserter on April 7, 1864. Returned to duty on an unspecified date. Reported absent sick from May 25 through August 31, 1864. Hospitalized at Charlotte on March 1, 1865, with erysipelas. Returned to duty on March 12, 1865. Survived the war.

BAKER, W. B., ———

Place and date of enlistment not reported. Listed as a deserter on April 7, 1864.

BALLOW, THOMAS H., Private

Enlisted in Yancey County on July 12, 1862, for the war. Died at Jacksboro, Tennessee, January 21, 1863. Cause of death not reported.

BANKS, WILLIAM B., Private

Resided in Yancey County and was by occupation a farmer prior to enlisting in Yancey County at age 39, May 29, 1862, for the war. Mustered in as Sergeant. Reported present in January-February, 1863. Reduced to ranks prior to March 1, 1863. Reported absent on sick furlough from hospital at Knoxville, Tennessee, in May-June and September-October, 1863. Reported absent without leave from February 20 through August 31, 1864. Apprehended on an unspecified date. Court-martialed on or about April 8, 1865. No further records.

BEAVER, CHARLES R., Private

Enlisted in Yancey County on June 1, 1864, for the war. Reported present through August 31, 1864. Died prior to March 23, 1865. Place, date, and cause of death not reported.

BEAVER, J. T., ———

North Carolina pension records indicate that he served in this company.

BEAVER, WILLIAM H., Private

Born in Yancey County on June 12, 1835. Enlisted in Yancey County at age 26, May 29, 1862, for the war. Transferred to Company D of this regiment on or about June 27, 1862. Transferred back to this company on or about July 29, 1862. Reported present or accounted for on surviving company muster rolls from January-February, 1863, through August 31, 1864. Survived the war. [His Tennessee pension application states that he was "bruise(d)" on the right arm by a shell near Atlanta, Georgia, on an unspecified date (1864).]

BERLESON, WILLIAM P., Private

Place and date of enlistment not reported. Name appears on an undated bounty pay and receipt roll. No further records.

BOON, BERTON, Private

Born in Yancey County and was by occupation a farmer prior to enlisting in Yancey County at age 19, May 29, 1862, for the war. Reported present in January-February, 1863. Deserted at Clinton, Tennessee, June 5, 1863. Returned to duty on or about July 12, 1863. Reported present in September-October, 1863. Reported absent sick from February 23 through August 31, 1864. No further records.

BRIGGS, ALSON, Private

Resided in Yancey County and was by occupation a farmer prior to enlisting in Yancey County at age 29, April 1, 1864, for the war. Reported present through August 31, 1864. No further records. Survived the war.

BRIGGS, HARVEY J., Private

Resided in Yancey County and was by occupation a farmer. Place and date of enlistment not reported (probably enlisted in the summer of 1862). Died near Big Springs, Tennessee, September 29, 1862, of "measles." [Was about 32 years of age at time of enlistment.]

BRIGGS, JACKSON, Private

Resided in Yancey County and was by occupation a farmer prior to enlisting in Yancey County at age 32, July 12, 1862, for the war. Reported present in January-February, 1863. Furloughed for forty days from hospital at Knoxville, Tennessee, June 25, 1863. Returned to duty subsequent to October 31, 1863. Reported absent sick on January 27, 1864. Returned to duty subsequent to February 29, 1864. Reported present in March-April, 1864. Reported absent sick from June 25 through August 31, 1864. No further records.

BRYANT, THOMAS, Private

Born in Yancey County* where he resided as a farmer prior to enlisting in Yancey County at age 33, June 16, 1862, for the war. Transferred to Company D of this regiment on or about June 27, 1862.

BRYANT, WILLIAM, Private

Born in Yancey County and was by occupation a farmer prior to enlisting in Yancey County at age 24, June 16, 1862, for the war. Discharged on October 22, 1862. Reason discharged not reported.

BUCHANAN, ARTER T., Private

Resided in Yancey County and was by occupation a farmer prior to enlisting in Yancey County at age 43, April 19, 1864, for the war. Reported present through August 31, 1864. No further records.

BUCHANAN, JAMES C., Private

Born in Yancey County and was by occupation a farmer prior to enlisting in Yancey County at age 17, May 29, 1862, for the war. Transferred to Company E of this regiment on or about June 27, 1862. Transferred back to this company prior to March 1, 1863. Reported present on surviving company muster rolls from January-February, 1863, through October 31, 1863. Wounded in the right thigh and captured at Missionary Ridge, Tennessee, November 25, 1863. Hospitalized at Chattanooga, Tennessee. Transferred to

Dalton, Georgia, February 14, 1864, for exchange. Returned to duty subsequent to April 30, 1864. Reported present in May-August, 1864. No further records. Survived the war. [North Carolina pension records indicate that he was wounded in the left knee near Columbia, Tennessee, "about Christmas 1864."]

BURNETT, DANIEL, Private

Previously served as Private in Company K, 60th Regiment N.C. Troops. Transferred to this company when the 58th and 60th Regiments were consolidated on April 9, 1865.

BYRD, WILLIAM D., Private

Born in Yancey County and was by occupation a farmer prior to enlisting in Yancey County at age 19, May 29, 1862, for the war. Reported present in January-February, 1863. Furloughed for thirty days from hospital at Knoxville, Tennessee, June 12, 1863. Reported in hospital at Dalton, Georgia, September 6, 1863, with diarrhoea. Returned to duty prior to November 1, 1863. Wounded in the right side at Missionary Ridge, Tennessee, November 25, 1863. Returned to duty in March-April, 1864. Reported present through August 31, 1864. Hospitalized at Montgomery, Alabama, November 8, 1864. Reported in hospital at Montgomery through November 15, 1864. No further records. Survived the war.

CANNON, STEPHEN, Private

Born in Washington County, Tennessee, and was by occupation a farmer prior to enlisting in Yancey County at age 21, June 16, 1862, for the war. Transferred to Company G of this regiment on or about July 15, 1862.

CARROLL, JAMES, Private

Resided in Yancey County and was by occupation a farm laborer prior to enlisting in Yancey County at age 29, May 29, 1862, for the war. Reported present in January-February, 1863. Furloughed for sixty days from hospital at Knoxville, Tennessee, June 7, 1863. Returned to duty subsequent to October 31, 1863. Wounded at or near Rocky Face Ridge, Georgia, February 25, 1864. Hospitalized at Madison, Georgia. Reported absent wounded through August 31, 1864. No further records.

CARTWELL, JOHN, ——

Place and date of enlistment not reported. Listed as a deserter on April 7, 1864.

CAUBLE, DANIEL WEBSTER, Private

Previously served as Private in Company K, 60th Regiment N.C. Troops. Transferred to this company when the 58th and 60th Regiments where consolidated on April 9, 1865. Survived the war.

CRAWFORD, HENRY T., Private

Enlisted in Yancey County on July 12, 1862, for the war. Reported present on surviving company muster rolls from January-February, 1863, through August 31, 1864. No further records.

CRAWFORD, JAMES M., Private

Born in Yancey County and was by occupation a farmer prior to enlisting in Yancey County on July 12, 1862, for the war. Died at Jacksboro, Tennessee, January 21, 1863, of disease. Was 25 years of age at the time of his death.

CREASMON, BERRY C., Private

Born in Buncombe County and was by occupation a farmer prior to enlisting in Yancey County at age 34, June 16, 1862, for the war. Transferred to Company D of this regiment on or about June 27, 1862.

DEYTON, WILLIAM, Private

Born in Yancey County where he resided as a carpenter or farmer prior to enlisting in Yancey County at age 24, May 29, 1862, for the war. Reported present in January-February and May-June, 1863. Deserted near La Fayette, Georgia, September 19, 1863. Returned to duty on December 19, 1863. Reported present in March-April, 1864. Deserted on June 23, 1864.

DONE, MORGAN, Private

Born in Buncombe County and was by occupation a carpenter or farmer prior to enlisting in Yancey County at age 37, May 29, 1862, for the war. Transferred to Company D of this regiment on or about June 27, 1862. Transferred back to this company prior to March 1, 1863. Reported present in January-February, 1863. Reported absent on furlough in May-June, 1863. Reported present in September-October, 1863. Reported absent without leave on February 20, 1864. Listed as a deserter on April 7, 1864. Reported absent sick from June 25 through August 31, 1864. No further records. Later served as Private in Company K, 3rd Regiment N.C. Mounted Infantry (Union).

EDWARDS, JOHN R., Private

Born in Buncombe County and was by occupation a carpenter or farmer prior to enlisting in Yancey County at age 47, May 29, 1862, for the war. Reported present in January-February, 1863. Died at Knoxville, Tennessee, April 20, 1863, of "consumption."

EDWARDS, STEPHEN, Private

Born in Yancey County where he resided as a farmer or carpenter prior to enlisting in Yancey County at age 18, June 16, 1862, for the war. Transferred to Company G of this regiment on or about July 15, 1862.

ELKINS, BERTON, Private

Enlisted in Yancey County on May 29, 1862, for the war. Reported present in January-February, 1863. No further records.

FERGERSON, WILLIAM, Private

Born in Yancey County and was by occupation a carpenter prior to enlisting in Yancey County at age 20, May 29, 1862, for the war. Reported present in January-February, 1863. Deserted at Clinton, Tennessee, April 22, 1863.

FORBES, ROBERT, Private

Born in Lee County, Virginia, and was by occupation a carpenter prior to enlisting in Yancey County at age 18, May 29, 1862, for the war. Reported present in January-February, 1863. Died at Knoxville, Tennessee, June 6, 1863. Cause of death not reported.

FOX, JAMES T., Musician

Born in Wilkes County and resided in Yancey County where he was by occupation a farmer prior to enlisting in Yancey County at age 26, May 29, 1862, for the war. Mustered in as Musician (Fifer). Reported present in January-February and May-June, 1863. Wounded at Chickamauga, Georgia, September 20, 1863. Returned to duty prior to October 31, 1863. Reported present in

January-April, 1864. Deserted on August 15, 1864. [North Carolina pension records indicate that he was wounded in the right wrist on June 22, 1864.]

FOX, MOSES, Private

Born in Wilkes County and resided in Yancey County where he was by occupation a carpenter or farmer prior to enlisting in Yancey County at age 18, May 29, 1862, for the war. Reported present in January-February and May-June, 1863. Reported absent on sick furlough of thirty days on September 25, 1863. Reported absent on detached service at Asheville in January-April, 1864. Deserted on August 15, 1864.

FOX, SKELTON, Private

Born in Wilkes County on May 7, 1838. Was by occupation a carpenter prior to enlisting in Yancey County at age 24, May 29, 1862, for the war. Reported present on surviving company muster rolls from January-February, 1863, through February 29, 1864. Detailed as a wagoner on March 19, 1864. Deserted on August 15, 1864. [His Tennessee pension application indicates that he received several "slight wounds" during the war.]

GEORGE, JAMES R., Sergeant

Born in Yancey County and was by occupation a farmer prior to enlisting in Yancey County at age 25, May 29, 1862, for the war. Mustered in as Corporal. Reported present in January-February, 1863. Reduced to ranks prior to March 1, 1863. Reported present in May-June, 1863. Promoted to Sergeant prior to July 1, 1863. Deserted at Chattanooga, Tennessee, October 4, 1863. Reduced to ranks prior to November 1, 1863. Returned to duty subsequent to February 29, 1864. Promoted to Sergeant in March-June, 1864. Wounded at Kolb's Farm, near Marietta, Georgia, June 22, 1864. Reported absent wounded through August 31, 1864. No further records.

GIBBS, JOSEPH A., Private

Born in Yancey County and was by occupation a carpenter prior to enlisting in Yancey County at age 18, May 29, 1862, for the war. Transferred to Company D of this regiment on or about June 27, 1862. Transferred back to this company prior to March 1, 1863. Reported present in January-February and May-June, 1863. Deserted at Chattanooga, Tennessee, September 27, 1863. Reported absent under arrest at Atlanta, Georgia, on or about February 29, 1864. Court-martialed on April 2, 1864. "Shot to death with musketry" near Dalton, Georgia, May 4, 1864, for desertion.

GILES, JAMES B., Private

Place and date of enlistment not reported (probably enlisted subsequent to August 31, 1864). Paroled at Greensboro on May 1, 1865.

GOUGE, JOHN W., Private

Place and date of enlistment not reported. An undated bounty pay and receipt roll indicates that he served in this company.

GREGORY, ISAAC, Private

Born in Yancey County where he enlisted at age 18, May 29, 1862, for the war. Reported present in January-February, May-June, and September-October, 1863. Wounded at Missionary Ridge, Tennessee, November 25, 1863. Reported absent wounded through April 30, 1864. Reported present but under arrest in May-August, 1864. No further records.

HALCOMB, B. W., ———

Place and date of enlistment not reported. Listed as a deserter on April 7, 1864.

HALL, DAVID S., Private

Born in Yancey County and was by occupation a carpenter prior to enlisting in Yancey County at age 25, May 29, 1862, for the war. Transferred to Company D of this regiment on or about June 27, 1862. Transferred back to this company prior to March 1, 1863. Reported present in January-February and May-June, 1863. Detailed as Commissary Sergeant on August 1, 1863, and transferred to the Field and Staff of this regiment. [May have served previously as Captain in the 111th Regiment N.C. Militia.]

HAMPTON, THOMAS N., Sergeant

Born in Yancey County and was by occupation a farmer prior to enlisting in Yancey County at age 25, May 29, 1862, for the war. Mustered in as Sergeant. Reported present in January-February, 1863. No further records.

HANEY, S. C., ———

Place and date of enlistment not reported. Died at Cumberland Gap, Tennessee, on an unspecified date (probably subsequent to May 29, 1862, but prior to October 9, 1862). Cause of death not reported. Was 24 years of age at the time of his death.

HEDRICK, WILLIAM H., Corporal

Previously served as Corporal in Company H, 60th Regiment N.C. Troops. Transferred to this company when the 58th and 60th Regiments were consolidated on April 9, 1865. Paroled at Greensboro on May 1, 1865.

HENSLEY, ERWIN H., ———

North Carolina pension records indicate that he served in this company.

HENSLEY, SAMUEL F., ———

North Carolina pension records indicate that he served in this company.

HENSLY, HENDERSON, Private

Born at "Borah" and was by occupation a farmer prior to enlisting in Yancey County at age 37, June 16, 1862, for the war. No further records.

HOLCOMB, JOHN L., Private

Born in Greenville District, South Carolina, and was by occupation a carpenter prior to enlisting in Yancey County at age 20, May 29, 1862, for the war. Reported present in January-February and May-June, 1863. Wounded in the right forearm (fracture) at Chickamauga, Georgia, September 20, 1863. Furloughed on October 3, 1863. Reported absent wounded in January-August, 1864. Paroled at Morganton on June 12, 1865.

HOLCOMBE, ROBERT M., Private

Born in Wilkes County and resided in Yancey County where he was by occupation a carpenter or farmer prior to enlisting in Yancey County at age 44, May 29, 1862, for the war. Transferred to Company D of this regiment on or about June 27, 1862. Transferred back to this company prior to March 1, 1863. Reported present in January-February, 1863. Reported in hospitals at Knoxville and

Athens, Tennessee, in May-June, 1863. Furloughed for thirty days on July 25, 1863. Had not returned to duty as of October 31, 1863. Reported absent without leave on or about February 20, 1864. Returned to duty subsequent to April 30, 1864. Reported present in May-August, 1864. Paroled at Salisbury on June 12, 1865.

HONEYCUTT, DAVID D., Private

Born in Yancey County or in Washington County, Tennessee, and was by occupation a farmer prior to enlisting in Yancey County at age 19, May 29, 1862, for the war. Reported present in January-February, 1863. Died in hospital at Clinton, Tennessee, May 12 or May 19, 1863. Cause of death not reported.

HONEYCUTT, JACOB, Private

Enlisted in Yancey County on May 29, 1862, for the war. Reported present in January-February, May-June, and September-October, 1863. Furloughed for forty days on December 16, 1863, suffering from chronic diarrhoea, emaciation, and extreme debility. Returned to duty on an unspecified date. Reported on detached service at Asheville in February-April, 1864. Reported present in May-August, 1864. Reported in hospital at Augusta, Georgia, November 14, 1864. No further records.

HONEYCUTT, SAMUEL C., Private

Born in Yancey County. Place and date of enlistment not reported. Died prior to August 1, 1863. Place, date, and cause of death not reported.

HORTON, LORENZO D., Private

Born in Burke or Yancey County and was by occupation a carpenter or physician prior to enlisting at age 25, May 29, 1862, for the war. Died at Johnson's Depot, Tennessee, August 25, 1862, of "typhoid fever."

HORTON, PHINEAS, Private

Born in Burke or Yancey County and resided in Yancey County where he was by occupation a carpenter or farmer prior to enlisting in Yancey County at age 24, June 16, 1862, for the war. Died at Cumberland Gap, Tennessee, October 2, 1862. Cause of death not reported.

HOWELL, ROBERT V., Private

Born in Yancey County and was by occupation a farmer prior to enlisting in Yancey County at age 18, May 29, 1862, for the war. Mustered in as Corporal. Reported present in January-February and May-June, 1863. Deserted near La Fayette, Georgia, September 19, 1863. Reduced to ranks in November, 1863-February, 1864. Returned to duty on an unspecified date. Reported present in January-August, 1864. Transferred to Company B of this regiment subsequent to August 31, 1864.

HOWELL, SWINFIELD D., Private

Born in Yancey County* and was by occupation a carpenter prior to enlisting in Yancey County on May 29, 1862, for the war. Reported present in January-February and May-June, 1863. Deserted near La Fayette, Georgia, September 19, 1863. Rejoined the company in March-April, 1864, and was granted a pardon. Reported present in May-August, 1864. No further records. Survived the war. [North Carolina pension records indicate that he was wounded in the left leg at Lovejoy's Station, Georgia, September 30, 1863. His Tennessee pension application states he was born in 1823; however, Confederate service records give his age at time of enlistment as 49.]

HUGHES, JOHN, Sergeant

Enlisted in Yancey County on May 29, 1862, for the war. Was apparently mustered in as Sergeant. Reported present in January-February, May-June, and September-October, 1863. Nominated for the Badge of Distinction for gallantry at Chickamauga, Georgia, September 19-20, 1863. Reported present in January-August, 1864. No further records.

HUGHES, JONATHAN, Private

Enlisted in Yancey County on May 1, 1864, for the war. Reported absent sick on June 10, 1864. No further records.

HUGHS, JAMES, Private

Previously served as Private in Company G of this regiment. Enlisted in this company on May 1, 1864, for the war, apparently while absent without leave from Company G. Reported present in May-August, 1864. No further records. Survived the war. [North Carolina pension records indicate that he injured his left leg at Atlanta, Georgia, June 1, 1864.]

HUNTER, JOHN W., Private

Born in Burke County and resided in Yancey County where he was by occupation a carpenter or farmer prior to enlisting in Yancey County at age 18, May 29, 1862, for the war. Died at Jacksboro, Tennessee, January 4, 1863, of "fever."

HUNTER, SAMUEL M., ———

North Carolina pension records indicate that he served in this company.

JIMERSON, JAMES A., Private

Enlisted in Yancey County on July 12, 1862, for the war. Reported present in January-February, 1863. Deserted at Clinton, Tennessee, June 5, 1863. Returned to duty on an unspecified date. Killed at Chickamauga, Georgia, September 20, 1863.

JONES, LARKIN P., Musician

Born in Wilkes County and was by occupation a blacksmith prior to enlisting in Yancey County at age 20, May 29, 1862, for the war. Mustered in as Private. Appointed Musician (Drummer) on January 16, 1863. Reported present on surviving company muster rolls from January-February, 1863, through April 30, 1864. Reported absent sick on August 20, 1864. No further records. Survived the war.

JONES, WILLIAM J., Musician

Born in Wilkes County and was by occupation a farmer prior to enlisting in Yancey County at age 32, May 29, 1862, for the war. Mustered in as Musician (Drummer). Appointed Musician (Fifer) on an unspecified date. Died at Jacksboro, Tennessee, January 14, 1863. Cause of death not reported.

KING, GEORGE, Private

Born in Yancey County where he resided as a farmer prior to enlisting in Yancey County at age 28, July 12, 1862, for the war. Reported present in January-February and May-June, 1863. Deserted at Chattanooga, Tennessee, September 27, 1863. Rejoined the company in March-April, 1864, and was granted a pardon. Reported present in May-August, 1864. No further records. Survived the war.

LEDFORD, WILLIAM B., Private

Born in Wilkes County and resided in Yancey County where he was by occupation a farmer prior to enlisting in Yancey County at

age 28, May 29, 1862, for the war. Reported present in January-February, 1863. Deserted at Clinton, Tennessee, April 22, 1863. Returned to duty subsequent to June 30, 1863. Deserted near La Fayette, Georgia, September 19, 1863.

LETTERMAN, JOSEPH, Private

Enlisted in Yancey County. Date of enlistment not reported. Discharged on October 16, 1862. Reason discharged not reported. [May have served later as Private in Company G, 29th Regiment N.C. Troops.]

LEWIS, JACOB, Private

Born in Wilkes County and resided in Yancey County where he enlisted at age 19, May 29, 1862, for the war. Reported present in January-February, 1863. Reported absent on sick furlough of thirty days from Knoxville, Tennessee, June 12, 1863. Reported absent on sick furlough of forty days on September 21, 1863. Reported absent on detached service at Asheville in January-April, 1864. Hospitalized at Macon, Georgia, July 15, 1864, with remittent fever. Transferred on July 28, 1864. Reported absent without leave on August 25, 1864. No further records. Survived the war. [North Carolina pension records indicate that he was wounded at Asheville in May or October, 1863, when he was "thrown off the caison (sic) of an artillery (sic) wagon and dislocated his right arm at the elbow & rist (sic) joints."]

LOYD, GEORGE, Private

Born in South Carolina. Enlisted in Yancey County on July 12, 1862, for the war. Discharged at Jacksboro, Tennessee, February 7, 1863, by reason of disability from measles. [Filed a Tennessee pension application after the war.]

LOYD, THOMAS, Private

Resided in Yancey County and was by occupation a farm laborer prior to enlisting in Yancey County at age 25, July 12, 1862, for the war. Reported present in January-February and May-June, 1863. Deserted at Chattanooga, Tennessee, September 17, 1863. [May have served later as Private in Company B, 3rd Regiment N.C. Mounted Infantry (Union).]

McCANLESS, GEORGE S., Private

Resided in Yancey County and was by occupation a farmer prior to enlisting in Yancey County at age 28, July 12, 1862, for the war. Reported present in January-February, 1863. Reported in hospital at Knoxville, Tennessee, in May-June, 1863. Reported present in September-October, 1863, and January-August, 1864. No further records.

McCANLESS, JAMES E., Private

Enlisted in Yancey County on July 12, 1862, for the war. Reported present in January-February and May-June, 1863. Wounded at Chickamauga, Georgia, September 20, 1863. Hospitalized at Macon, Georgia. Furloughed on September 28, 1863. Reported absent wounded through August 31, 1864. No further records.

McCOWRY, JAMES L., Corporal

Born in Buncombe County and was by occupation a farmer prior to enlisting in Yancey County at age 31, July 16, 1862, for the war. Mustered in as Corporal. No further records.

McINTOSH, WILLIAM M., Private

Enlisted in Yancey County on July 12, 1862, for the war. Died at Jacksboro, Tennessee, January 5, 1863. Cause of death not reported.

McKINNEY, SAMUEL B., ———

North Carolina pension records indicate that he served in this company or in Company B of this regiment. One of his pension applications states that he hired Joseph Stewart as a substitute. A man by that name served in Company A of this regiment. [May have served also in Company I, 3rd Regiment N.C. Mounted Infantry (Union).]

McMAHAN, THOMAS, Private

Enlisted in Yancey County on May 29, 1862, for the war. Mustered in as Sergeant. Reported present in January-February and May-June, 1863. Reduced to ranks in March-June, 1863. Deserted at Chattanooga, Tennessee, October 4, 1863. Returned to duty on January 28, 1864. Reported present in March-April, 1864. Deserted on June 22, 1864. [Was about 28 years of age at time of enlistment.]

McMAHAN, WILLIAM B., Private

Born in Yancey County and was by occupation a farmer prior to enlisting in Yancey County at age 21, June 16, 1862, for the war. No further records. [May have served later as Private in Company A, 3rd Regiment N.C. Mounted Infantry (Union).]

MANEY, ROBERT M., Private

Born in Yancey County where he resided as a farmer prior to enlisting in Yancey County at age 18, May 29, 1862, for the war. Reported absent on sick furlough of thirty days on September 10, 1862. Failed to return to duty and was dropped from the company rolls on January 26, 1864, for desertion.

MASHBURN, WILLIAM M., Private

Enlisted in Yancey County on July 12, 1862, for the war. Reported present in January-February and May-June, 1863. Deserted on September 19, 1863. Returned to duty on October 18, 1863. Wounded at Missionary Ridge, Tennessee, November 25, 1863. Returned to duty in March-April, 1864. Reported present through August 31, 1864. No further records.

MASON, JOSEPH P., Private

Born in "Dere [presumably Londonderry]," Ireland, and was by occupation a merchant prior to enlisting in Yancey County at age 27, June 16, 1862, for the war. Appointed Assistant Commissary of Subsistence (Captain) on July 29, 1862, and transferred to the Field and Staff of this regiment.

MAUNEY, J. R., ———

North Carolina pension records indicate that he served in this company.

METCALF, HENRY C., Private

Resided in Yancey County and was by occupation a laborer prior to enlisting in Yancey County at age 17, May 29, 1862, for the war. Reported present on surviving company muster rolls from January-February, 1863, through August 31, 1864. No further records. Survived the war. [North Carolina pension records indicate that he was wounded in the head, left thigh, and left arm (fracture) at Jonesborough, Georgia, on an unspecified date.]

MILLER, CURTIS, Private

Born in Yancey County and was by occupation a farmer prior to enlisting in Yancey County at age 18, May 29, 1862, for the war. Reported present in January-February, May-June, and September-October, 1863. Reported absent sick on February 5, 1864. Died at Atlanta, Georgia, March 10, 1864. Cause of death not reported.

MOLLY, JAMES, Private

Place and date of enlistment not reported (probably enlisted in the autumn of 1863). Captured at Missionary Ridge, Tennessee, November 25, 1863. Sent to Nashville, Tennessee. Transferred to Louisville, Kentucky, where he arrived on or about December 6, 1863. Transferred to Rock Island, Illinois, where he arrived on December 9, 1863. Applied to take the Oath of Allegiance at Rock Island on March 18, 1864. No further records.

NICHOLS, JAMES W., Private

Resided in McDowell County and enlisted in Yancey County on July 12, 1862, for the war. Transferred to Company F of this regiment on December 24, 1862.

NICHOLS, JONATHAN A., Private

Enlisted in Yancey County on July 12, 1862, for the war. Transferred to Company F of this regiment in March-April, 1863.

PARKER, JAMES, Private

Resided in Yancey County and was by occupation a laborer prior to enlisting in Yancey County at age 32, July 12, 1862, for the war. Reported present in January-February and May-June, 1863. Sent to hospital in September, 1863. Reported absent without leave from September 23, 1863, until January 23, 1864; however, he was acquitted by a court-martial prior to February 29, 1864, and returned to duty. Reported present in March-August, 1864. No further records. Survived the war. [North Carolina pension records indicate that he was wounded in the left ankle by a cannon ball at Resaca, Georgia, in May, 1864. Also, his hearing was damaged during the war.]

PENLAND, CHARLES M., Private

Born in Yancey County where he resided as a farmer prior to enlisting in Yancey County at age 17, May 29, 1862, for the war. Mustered in as Private. Reported present in January-February, 1863. Promoted to Corporal prior to March 1, 1863. Reported present in May-June and September-October, 1863. Reduced to ranks in November, 1863-February, 1864. Reported present in January-August, 1864. No further records. Survived the war.

PENLAND, MILTON F., Private

Born in Yancey County where he resided as a farmer prior to enlisting in Yancey County at age 21, May 29, 1862, for the war. Reported on sick furlough of thirty days on November 19, 1862. Failed to return to duty and was dropped from the company rolls on January 26, 1864, for desertion.

PENLEY, RANSOM, ———

North Carolina pension records indicate that he served in this company.

PHILLIPS, JOHN W., Private

Born in Yancey County and was by occupation a farmer prior to enlisting in Yancey County at age 20, May 29, 1862, for the war. Died at Jacksboro, Tennessee, February 20, 1863. Cause of death not reported.

PHILLIPS, STEPHEN, Private

Born in Yancey County and was by occupation a farmer prior to enlisting in Yancey County at age 20, June 16, 1862, for the war. No further records.

PHIPPS, CONARAH D., Private

Born in Yancey County and was by occupation a farmer prior to enlisting in Yancey County at age 27, May 29, 1862, for the war. Died at Jacksboro, Tennessee, January 2, 1863. Cause of death not reported.

PRESNELL, DAVID A., Private

Resided in Yancey County and was by occupation a farmer. Place and date of enlistment not reported (probably enlisted in the summer of 1862). Transferred to Company G of this regiment on an unspecified date. [Was about 27 years of age in 1862.]

PRESNELL, HENRY, Private

Born in Iredell County and was by occupation a farmer prior to enlisting in Yancey County at age 27, June 16, 1862, for the war. No further records.

PRESNELL, JAMES BARTLEY, Private

Born in Alexander County* and was by occupation a farmer prior to enlisting in Yancey County at age 30, May 29, 1862, for the war. Reported present in January-February, 1863. Deserted at Clinton, Tennessee, June 5, 1863. Later served as Private in Company C, 13th Regiment Tennessee Cavalry (Union).

PRESNELL, JOHN C., Private

Born in Alexander County* and was by occupation a farmer prior to enlisting in Yancey County at age 21, May 29, 1862, for the war. Reported absent on sick furlough of thirty days on August 25, 1862. Failed to return to duty. Listed as a deserter and dropped from the company rolls on January 26, 1864.

RAY, GARRETT D., Private

Born in Madison County* where he resided as a farmer. An undated bounty pay and receipt roll indicates that he enlisted in this company. Place and date of enlistment not reported (probably enlisted in the summer of 1862). Later served as 3rd Lieutenant of Company A, 64th Regiment N.C. Troops. [Was about 33 years of age in 1862.]

RAY, LEANDER T., Private

Resided in Yancey County and was by occupation a farmer prior to enlisting in Yancey County at age 39, July 12, 1862, for the war. Reported present in January-February and May-June, 1863. Deserted at Chattanooga, Tennessee, September 27, 1863.

RAY, LEROY C., Private

Born in Yancey County* where he resided as a farmer prior to enlisting in Yancey County at age 35, May 29, 1862, for the war. Reported present in January-February, 1863. Reported absent on sick furlough at Knoxville, Tennessee, in May-June, 1863. Returned to duty on an unspecified date. Wounded at Chickamauga, Georgia, September 20, 1863. Returned to duty prior to October 31, 1863. Captured at Missionary Ridge, Tennessee, November 25, 1863. Sent to Nashville, Tennessee. Transferred to Louisville, Kentucky, where he arrived on December 7, 1863. Transferred to Rock Island, Illinois, where he arrived on December 9, 1863. Died at Rock Island on March 15, 1864, of "variola."

RAY, WILLIAM H., Private

Born in Yancey County where he resided as a farmer prior to enlisting in Yancey County at age 29, May 29, 1862, for the war. Transferred to Company D of this regiment on or about June 27, 1862. Transferred back to this company prior to March 1, 1863.

Reported present in January-February and May-June, 1863. Reported on duty as a provost guard at Maj. Gen. Simon B. Buckner's headquarters in September-October, 1863. Reported absent sick from February 5 through April 30, 1864. Reported absent without leave on July 15, 1864. Dropped from the company rolls on or about August 31, 1864. [May have served later as Corporal in Company K, 3rd Regiment N.C. Mounted Infantry (Union).]

RENFRO, DAVID, Private

Place and date of enlistment not reported. A company muster roll dated May-August, 1864, states that he had been absent sick since June 25, 1864.

RIDDLE, GARRETT, Private

Born in Washington County, Tennessee, and resided in Yancey County where he was by occupation a farmer prior to enlisting in Yancey County at age 33, June 16, 1862, for the war. Transferred to Company D of this regiment on or about June 27, 1862.

RIDDLE, SAMUEL, Private

Previously served as Private in Company B, 29th Regiment N.C. Troops. Transferred to this company on November 7, 1862. Reported present in January-February and May-June, 1863. Reported in hospital at Dalton, Georgia, September 6, 1863, with debilitas. Returned to duty prior to November 1, 1863. Reported present in January-April, 1864. Wounded in the left leg at Kolb's Farm, near Marietta, Georgia, June 22, 1864. Leg amputated. Reported absent wounded through August 31, 1864. No further records. Survived the war.

ROBERSON, E. EDWARD, Private

Enlisted in Yancey County on May 29, 1862, for the war. Reported present in January-February and May-June, 1863. Wounded in the right arm (fracture) and left thigh at Chickamauga, Georgia, September 20, 1863. Hospitalized at Kingston, Georgia, October 3, 1863. Reported absent wounded through August 31, 1864. No further records. Survived the war. [Was about 24 years of age at time of enlistment.]

ROBERSON, GEORGE, Private

Born in Yancey County* and was by occupation a farmer prior to enlisting in Yancey County at age 30, June 16, 1862, for the war. No further records.

ROBERSON, JAMES H., Private

Enlisted in Yancey County on July 12, 1862, for the war. Reported present in January-February, May-June, and September-October, 1863. Died at Marietta, Georgia, December 3, 1863, of "pneumonia."

ROBERSON, JOHN, Private

Place and date of enlistment not reported (probably enlisted subsequent to August 31, 1864). Reported in hospital at Macon, Georgia, November 7, 1864, with chronic diarrhoea. No further records.

ROBERSON, JOHN C., Private

Enlisted in Yancey County on July 12, 1862, for the war. Reported present in January-February and May-June, 1863. Wounded at Chickamauga, Georgia, September 20, 1863. Reported absent wounded through August 31, 1864. No further records.

ROBERSON, JULIUS, Corporal

Resided in Yancey County and was by occupation a farmer prior to enlisting in Yancey County at age 23, July 12, 1862, for the war.

Mustered in as Private. Reported present in January-February and May-June, 1863. Furloughed for fifteen days on August 21, 1863. Failed to return to duty and was listed as a deserter on January 26, 1864. Returned to duty in March-April, 1864, and was detailed for duty at Asheville. Rejoined the company on an unspecified date. Promoted to Corporal prior to August 31, 1864. Reported present in May-August, 1864. No further records. Survived the war.

ROBERSON, STEPHEN MORGAN, Private

Enlisted in Yancey County on July 9, 1863, for the war. Wounded at Chickamauga, Georgia, September 20, 1863. Returned to duty prior to October 31, 1863. Reported present in January-April, 1864. Reported absent sick from June 3 through August 31, 1864. No further records. Survived the war. [Was about 18 years of age at time of enlistment. North Carolina pension records indicate that he was wounded in the right foot at Chickamauga, Georgia, September 19-20, 1863.]

ROBERSON, WILLIAM C., Private

Enlisted in Yancey County on July 12, 1862, for the war. Reported present in January-February, 1863. Died at Knoxville, Tennessee, May 10, 1863. Cause of death not reported.

ROBERTS, GARRETT M., Private

Born in Washington County, Tennessee, and resided in Yancey County where he was by occupation a farmer prior to enlisting in Yancey County at age 24, June 16, 1862, for the war while a deserter from Company C, 5th Battalion N.C. Cavalry. No further records. Survived the war. [The correct spelling of his first name may have been Garret.]

ROWLAND, ROBERT H., Private

Born in Yancey County* where he resided as a farmer or farm laborer prior to enlisting in Yancey County at age 30, May 29, 1862, for the war. Reported present in January-February, 1863. Deserted at Clinton, Tennessee, June 5, 1863. Returned to duty on July 12, 1863. Reported present in September-October, 1863, and January-April, 1864. Shot in the breast and killed near Resaca, Georgia, on or about May 16, 1864.

ROWLAND, SILAS, Private

Born in Yancey County where he resided as a farmer prior to enlisting in Yancey County at age 26, June 16, 1862, for the war. No further records. Later served as Private in Company D, 29th Regiment N.C. Troops. [Contrary to 8:271 of this series, the correct spelling of his surname was probably Rowland rather than Roland.]

SALES, JOSEPH B., Private

Previously served as Private in Company K, 60th Regiment N.C. Troops. Transferred to this company when the 58th and 60th Regiments were consolidated on April 9, 1865. Paroled at Greensboro on May 1, 1865.

SHEHAN, JAMES E., Private

Resided in Yancey County and was by occupation a farmer prior to enlisting in Yancey County at age 19, July 12, 1862, for the war. Reported present in January-February, 1863. Reported in hospital at Knoxville, Tennessee, in May-June, 1863. Returned to duty on an unspecified date. Deserted at Chattanooga, Tennessee, September 29, 1863. Returned to duty on an unspecified date. Deserted near Dalton, Georgia, February 1, 1864. Later served as Private in Company A, 3rd Regiment N.C. Mounted Infantry (Union).

SHEPHERD, GRANDISON, Private

Born in Yancey County* where he resided as a farmer prior to enlisting in Yancey County at age 35, June 16, 1862, for the war. Died at Jacksboro, Tennessee, November 20, 1862, of "measles."

SHEPHERD, THOMAS ERWIN, Corporal

Previously enlisted as Private in Company B, 29th Regiment N.C. Troops. Rejected for service with that unit (presumably because of his extreme youth). Enlisted in this company in Yancey County at age 16, May 29, 1862, for the war. Mustered in as Private. Transferred to Company D of this regiment on or about June 27, 1862. Transferred back to this company prior to March 1, 1863. Reported present in January-February, 1863. Promoted to Corporal in March-June, 1863. Reported present on surviving company muster rolls from May-June, 1863, through April 30, 1864. Apparently deserted on an unspecified date. Later served as Private in Company K, 3rd Regiment N.C. Mounted Infantry (Union).

SHEWFORD, JAMES S., Private

Born in Yancey County and was by occupation a farmer prior to enlisting in Yancey County at age 18, June 16, 1862, for the war. Transferred to Company D of this regiment on or about June 27, 1862.

SILVER, DAVID H., 1st Sergeant

Resided in Yancey County and was by occupation a farmer prior to enlisting in Yancey County at age 24, May 29, 1862, for the war. Mustered in as Private. Reported present or accounted for in January-February and May-June, 1863. Promoted to 1st Sergeant on June 16, 1863. Reported present in September-October, 1863, and January-August, 1864. No further records. Survived the war. [North Carolina pension records indicate that he was wounded in the right ankle at New Hope Church, Georgia, June 15, 1864.]

SILVER, WILLIAM R., Private

Resided in Yancey County where he enlisted on May 29, 1862, for the war. Mustered in as Corporal. Reported present in January-February, 1863. Reduced to ranks in March-June, 1863. Reported present in May-June, 1863. Promoted to Sergeant in July-October, 1863. Reported present in September-October, 1863, and January-April, 1864. Reduced to ranks in May-August, 1864. Reported absent sick on August 10, 1864. Hospitalized at Macon, Georgia, October 23, 1864, with ulcus. Transferred on October 26, 1864. No further records.

SIMMONS, ELLIOTT, Private

Enlisted in Yancey County on July 12, 1862, for the war. Reported present on surviving company muster rolls through April 30, 1864. Wounded in the right hip at Atlanta, Georgia, July 25, 1864. No further records. Survived the war.

SLAGLE, SIMEON, Private

Previously served as Private in Company B of this regiment. Transferred to this company on or about June 16, 1862. Transferred to Company D of this regiment on or about June 27, 1862. Transferred back to this company prior to January 28, 1863, when he deserted. Returned to duty on an unspecified date. Deserted at Clinton, Tennessee, June 5, 1863.

SMITH, WILLIAM J., Private

Enlisted in Yancey County on May 1, 1864, for the war. Reported present through August 31, 1864. No further records. Survived the war. [Was about 19 years of age at time of enlistment. North

Carolina pension records indicate that he was wounded near Atlanta, Georgia, on an unspecified date.]

SNYDER, THOMAS, Private

Place and date of enlistment not reported. Captured at Missionary Ridge, Tennessee, November 25, 1863. Sent to Nashville, Tennessee. Transferred to Louisville, Kentucky, where he arrived on December 8, 1863. Transferred to Rock Island, Illinois, where he arrived on December 11, 1863. Died at Rock Island on January 9, 1864, of "bronchitis."

STEPP, ROBERT J., Sergeant

Previously served as Sergeant in Company K, 60th Regiment N.C. Troops. Transferred to this company when the 58th and 60th Regiments were consolidated on April 9, 1865. Paroled at Greensboro on May 1, 1865. [North Carolina pension records indicate that he was wounded in the shoulder at New Hope Church, Georgia, in 1864.]

STEWART, WILLIAM, Private

The service record of this soldier is unclear. It appears that he served in Company D of this regiment in September-October, 1863. He also served at various times in this company and in Companies E and K of this regiment.

STRADLEY, THOMAS, Private

North Carolina pension records indicate that he served in this company.

STYLES, JOHN WESLEY, Private

Born in Lincoln County and resided in Yancey County where he was by occupation a farmer prior to enlisting in Yancey County at age 24, May 29, 1862, for the war. Reported present in January-February and May-June, 1863. Reported on duty as a provost guard at Maj. Gen. Simon B. Buckner's headquarters in September-October, 1863. Reported present in January-February, 1864. Reported absent without leave on April 23, 1864. Returned to duty on an unspecified date. Reported present in May-August, 1864. Listed as a deserter on September 10, 1864. [North Carolina pension records indicate that he "fell from (the railroad) cars" and broke his right arm close to the shoulder on an unspecified date.]

STYLES, NOAH V., Private

Enlisted in Yancey County at age 19, May 29, 1862, for the war. Reported present on surviving company muster rolls through October 31, 1863. Captured at Missionary Ridge, Tennessee, November 25, 1863. Sent to Nashville, Tennessee. Transferred to Louisville, Kentucky, where he arrived on December 7, 1863. Transferred to Rock Island, Illinois, on or about December 8, 1863. Hospitalized at Rock Island on March 7, 1864, with variola. Returned to the prison compound on March 23, 1864. No further records. Survived the war.

THOMAS, AARON, Private

Born in Washington County, Tennessee, and was by occupation a farmer prior to enlisting in Yancey County at age 35, May 29, 1862, for the war. Transferred to Company D of this regiment on or about June 27, 1862. Transferred back to this company prior to March 1, 1863. Reported present on surviving company muster rolls through April 30, 1864. Reported absent without leave on August 25, 1864. No further records. Survived the war. [North Carolina pension records indicate that he was wounded in Alabama in 1864.]

THOMAS, JOB, Private

Born in Washington County, Tennessee, and was by occupation a farmer prior to enlisting in Yancey County at age 24, June 16, 1862, for the war. Transferred to Company D of this regiment on or about June 27, 1862.

TUCKER, ZEPHANIAH, Private

Born in Washington County, Tennessee, and was by occupation a farmer prior to enlisting in Yancey County at age 20, June 16, 1862, for the war. Transferred to Company D of this regiment on or about June 27, 1862.

WILSON, ALEXANDER, Private

Born in Washington County, Tennessee, and resided in Yancey County where he was by occupation a farmer prior to enlisting in Yancey County at age 38, June 16, 1862, for the war. No further records. Survived the war.

WILSON, DAVID R., Corporal

Born in Yancey County where he resided. Place and date of enlistment not reported (probably enlisted in the summer of 1862). Promotion record not reported. Died at Big Springs, Tennessee, September 25, 1862, of "fever."

WILSON, EDWARD, Private

Previously served as Private in Company G of this regiment. Enlisted in this company on May 1, 1864. Deserted on May 28, 1864. [Filed a Tennessee pension application after the war in which he claimed that he was absent sick with dropsy from May, 1864, until the Confederate surrender.]

WILSON, EDWARD M., Private

Enlisted in Yancey County on May 29, 1862, for the war. Died at Jacksboro, Tennessee, February 7, 1863. Cause of death not reported.

WILSON, JOHN W., Private

Resided in Yancey County and was by occupation a farmer prior to enlisting in Yancey County at age 28, May 29, 1862, for the war. Reported present in January-February, May-June, and September-October, 1863. Hospitalized at Marion on December 3, 1863. Returned to duty subsequent to February 29, 1864. Reported present in March-August, 1864. No further records. Survived the war. [North Carolina pension records indicate that he was wounded at Milledgeville, Georgia, February 1, 1865.]

WILSON, NATHANIEL, Private

Enlisted in Yancey County on May 1, 1864, for the war. Deserted on May 28, 1864.

WILSON, THOMAS F., Private

Previously served as Private in Company K, 60th Regiment N.C. Troops. Transferred to this company when the 58th and 60th Regiments were consolidated on April 9, 1865. Paroled at Greensboro on May 1, 1865. [North Carolina pension records indicate that he received flesh wounds at New Hope Church, Georgia, on an unspecified date.]

WILSON, WILLIAM H., Private

Enlisted in Yancey County on May 29, 1862, for the war. Reported present in January-February, 1863. Reported in hospital at Clinton, Tennessee, in May-June, 1863. Returned to duty on an unspecified date. Reported present in September-October, 1863. Died at La Grange, Georgia, December 18, 1863. Cause of death not reported.

WOODY, DAVID, Private

Born in Yancey County where he resided as a farmer prior to enlisting in Yancey County at age 22, June 16, 1862, for the war. Was apparently transferred to Company B, 5th Battalion N.C. Cavalry, on or about June 28, 1862.

WOODY, GREEN B., Sergeant

Born in Buncombe County and resided in Yancey County where he was by occupation a farmer prior to enlisting in Yancey County at age 33, May 29, 1862, for the war. Mustered in as Sergeant. Reported present in January-February and May-June, 1863. Sent to hospital on October 27, 1863. Reported absent without leave on March 15, 1864. Returned to duty subsequent to April 30, 1864. Wounded in the cheek at Kolb's Farm, near Marietta, Georgia, June 22, 1864. Returned to duty prior to September 1, 1864. Appointed Ensign (1st Lieutenant) on December 30, 1864, to rank from June 15, 1864, and transferred to the Field and Staff of this regiment. [Name appears on a letter of recommendation which reads in part as follows: "He is a brave soldier and is the original color bearer and has always acted very gallantly in action. He was assigned to the position of color bearer by Col. J. B. Palmer, October 1st 1863 and has acted in that capacity ever since."]

WOODY, POSEY, Private

Enlisted at Dalton, Georgia, January 24, 1864, for the war. Reported present through April 30, 1864. Wounded at Kolb's Farm, near Marietta, Georgia, June 22, 1864. Reported absent wounded through August 31, 1864. No further records.

WOODY, WYATT, Private

Born in Washington County, Tennessee, and resided in Yancey County where he was by occupation a farmer prior to enlisting in Yancey County at age 24, May 29, 1862, for the war. Reported present in January-February and May-June, 1863. Killed at Chickamauga, Georgia, September 20, 1863.

YOUNG, MELVIN H., Private

Enlisted in Yancey County at age 17, May 29, 1862, for the war. Reported present in January-February and May-June, 1863. Deserted at Chattanooga, Tennessee, September 27, 1863. Returned to duty on January 20, 1864. Reported present in March-April, 1864. Wounded in the chest and left hand at Resaca, Georgia, May 15, 1864. Reported absent wounded through August 31, 1864. No further records. Survived the war.

YOUNG, SAMUEL P., Sergeant

Previously served as Sergeant in Company K, 60th Regiment N.C. Troops. Transferred to this company when the 58th and 60th Regiments were consolidated on April 9, 1865. Paroled at Greensboro on May 1, 1865. [North Carolina pension records indicate that he was wounded at Jonesborough, Georgia, on an unspecified date.]

YOUNG, THOMAS S., Private

Born in Yancey County* where he enlisted at age 32, May 29, 1862, for the war. Reported present in January-February and May-June, 1863. Appointed Hospital Steward in July-October, 1863, and transferred to the Field and Staff of this regiment. Reduced to ranks and transferred back to this company subsequent to October 31, 1863. Reported present or accounted for in January-August, 1864. Transferred to Company B of this regiment subsequent to August 31, 1864.

COMPANY D

This company was raised in Watauga County on June 27, 1862, as Capt. Drury C. Harman's Company, N.C. Volunteers. It was placed under the authority of Lt. Col. John B. Palmer on or about the same date. Palmer, former commander of "Palmer's Legion," a mixed (cavalry and infantry) unit that had failed to complete its organization, was by then recruiting for a cavalry unit to be known as the 5th Battalion N.C. Partisan Rangers and also for a thus far undesignated infantry regiment. Harman's Company became Company D of the latter command when it was mustered in as the 58th Regiment N.C. Troops on July 29, 1862. After joining the 58th Regiment the company functioned as a part of that regiment, and its history for the remainder of the war is reported as a part of the regimental history.

The following roster was compiled primarily from information in the microfilm edition of the Compiled Service Records of Soldiers Who Served in Organizations from the State of North Carolina (Record Group 109, M270), National Archives and Records Administration, Washington, D.C. Record Group 109 includes enlistment papers, pay vouchers, requisitions, letters of resignation, discharge certificates, and abstracts of medical and prisoner of war returns. Materials relating specifically to this company include a muster-in and descriptive roll dated June 27, 1862, and muster rolls dated January-June, 1863; August 31-December, 1863; and January-August, 1864.

Also utilized in this roster were *The War of the Rebellion: A Compilation of the Official Records of the Union and Confederate Armies*, the North Carolina adjutant general's *Roll of Honor*, state militia records, newspaper casualty lists and obituaries, wartime claims for bounty pay and allowances, postwar registers of claims for artificial limbs, Confederate pension applications filed with the states of North Carolina, Tennessee, and Florida, Confederate Soldiers' Home records, and the 1860 and 1870 federal censuses of North Carolina. A search was made also for relevant letters, diaries, reminiscences, and other manuscripts in the Southern Historical Collection (University of North Carolina-Chapel Hill), the Duke University Library Special Collections Department, and the North Carolina Division of Archives and History.

Among the secondary sources consulted were records of the North Carolina division of the United Daughters of the Confederacy, postwar rosters, regimental and county histories, marriage bond, will, and cemetery indexes, published and unpublished genealogies, biographical dictionaries, the North Carolina *County Heritage Book* series, the *Confederate Veteran*, Walter Clark's *Histories of the Several Regiments and Battalions from North Carolina in the Great War, 1861-'65*, and the North Carolina volume of the extended edition of *Confederate Military History*.

OFFICERS

CAPTAINS

HARMAN, DRURY CALVIN

Resided in Watauga County and was by occupation a Baptist clergyman prior to enlisting in Watauga County at age 36. Elected Captain on June 27, 1862. Reported present in January-February, 1863. Resigned on March 12, 1863, because "I consider, having been for years a minister of the Gospel, that I am unfitted by the want of military talent and acquirements for the position which I now hold in the army. Resignation accepted on or about March 30, 1863.

BAIRD, BENJAMIN F.

Resided in Watauga County where he enlisted at age 30. Appointed 1st Lieutenant on June 27, 1862. Reported present in January-June, 1863. Promoted to Captain on April 1, 1863. Reported present but sick in camp in September-October, 1863. Returned to duty in November-December, 1863. Reported present in January-August, 1864. Transferred to Company A of this regiment subsequent to March 15, 1865.

TOBEY, FREDERICK ALBERT

Previously served as Captain of Company A of this regiment. Transferred to this company subsequent to March 15, 1865. Paroled at Greensboro on May 1, 1865.

LIEUTENANTS

BAIRD, DAVID FRANKLIN, 2nd Lieutenant

Resided in Watauga County and was by occupation a farmer prior to enlisting in Watauga County at age 27, August 20, 1862, for the war. Mustered in as Private. Reported present in January-June, 1863. Promoted to Corporal in March-April, 1863. Appointed 3rd Lieutenant on June 16, 1863. Reported present in September, 1863-February, 1864. Promoted to 2nd Lieutenant on or about March 28, 1864. Reported absent on detached service on April 8, 1864. Returned to duty on an unspecified date. Reported present in May-August, 1864. Wounded in the left breast at Lovejoy's Station, Georgia, on or about September 1, 1864. Returned to duty on an unspecified date. Wounded in the breast and left arm at Bentonville on March 19-21, 1865. Hospitalized at Greensboro. Survived the war. He was a "brave officer." [North Carolina pension records indicate that he was wounded in Georgia on an unspecified date (probably near New Hope Church in late May, 1864).]

CONLEY, JAMES C., 1st Lieutenant

Previously served as 1st Lieutenant of Company B of this regiment. Transferred to this company subsequent to August 31, 1864. Paroled at Greensboro on May 1, 1865.

DAVIS, ALBERT F., 3rd Lieutenant

Previously served as Sergeant in Company I of this regiment. Elected 3rd Lieutenant of this company on March 28, 1864. Reported present through August 31, 1864. Transferred to Company A of this regiment subsequent to August 31, 1864.

HOWINGTON, WILLIAM M., 2nd Lieutenant

Previously served as Private in Company D, 9th Regiment N.C. State Troops (1st Regiment N.C. Cavalry). Elected 3rd Lieutenant of this company on June 27, 1862. Reported present in January-June, 1863. Promoted to 2nd Lieutenant on April 1, 1863. Reported absent without leave on September 19, 1863. Listed as a deserter and dropped from the company rolls on March 23, 1864. [Born in Tennessee and was by occupation a farmer.]

MAST, WILLIAM P., 1st Lieutenant

Resided in Watauga County where he enlisted. Elected 2nd Lieutenant on June 27, 1862. Reported present in January-June, 1863. Promoted to 1st Lieutenant on April 1, 1863. Reported present but sick in camp in September-October, 1863. Reported sick in hospital in November-December, 1863. Reported absent without leave on February 12, 1864. Resigned on March 22, 1864, because "my health has been bad for the last five months and I desire to go to the Cavalry servis cincerly believing that I can be of more service to my country . . . than I can in the positon that I know hold." Dropped from the company rolls on June 28, 1864. Later served as Private in Company B, 11th Battalion N.C. Home Guard.

NONCOMMISSIONED OFFICERS AND PRIVATES

ABEE, JAMES E., Private

Previously served as Private in Company A of this regiment. Transferred to this company when the 58th and 60th Regiments were consolidated on April 9, 1865. Paroled at Greensboro on May 1, 1865.

ADAMS, DAVID, Private

Resided in Watauga County and was by occupation a farmer prior to enlisting in Watauga County at age 33, July 5, 1862, for the war. No further records. Survived the war.

ADAMS, ZACHARIAH, Private

Resided in Watauga County and was by occupation a farmer prior to enlisting in Watauga County at age 27, July 5, 1862, for the war. No further records. Survived the war.

ANGLIN, WILLIAM, ———

Enlisted on June 27, 1862, for the war. No further records.

BAIRD, ABRAM, ———

North Carolina pension records indicate that he served in this company.

BAIRD, ANDREW JACKSON, Private

Resided in Watauga County and was by occupation a day laborer prior to enlisting in Watauga County at age 20, July 7, 1862, for the war. No further records. Survived the war.

BAIRD, JOHN H., Private

Enlisted in Watauga County on June 7, 1862, for the war. Died at Jacksboro, Tennessee, prior to March 2, 1863. Date and cause of death not reported.

BEACH, JOHN W., Private

Enlisted in Watauga County on June 27, 1862, for the war. Reported "absent" in January-February, 1863. Returned to duty in March-April, 1863. Reported absent sick in May-June, 1863. Returned to duty prior to September 20, 1863, when he was wounded at Chickamauga, Georgia. Furloughed from hospital on October 9, 1863. Reported absent without leave on November 15, 1863. Returned to duty subsequent to April 30, 1864. Reported present in May-August, 1864. Captured at Atlanta, Georgia, on or about September 3, 1864. Hospitalized at Atlanta on September 20, 1864, with pneumonia. Transferred to Nashville, Tennessee, on an unspecified date. Transferred to Louisville, Kentucky, October 27, 1864. Transferred from Louisville to Camp Douglas, Chicago, Illinois, where he arrived on November 1, 1864. Paroled at Camp Douglas and transferred to Point Lookout, Maryland, February 20, 1865, for exchange. Exchanged on an unspecified date.

Hospitalized at Richmond, Virginia, February 28, 1865. Furloughed for thirty days on or about March 7, 1865.

BEAVER, WILLIAM H., Private

Previously served as Private in Company C of this regiment. Transferred to this company on or about June 27, 1862. Transferred back to Company C on or about July 29, 1862.

BISHOP, ELBERT, Private

Resided in Wilkes County and was by occupation a farm laborer prior to enlisting in Watauga County at age 29, November 7, 1862, for the war. Reported present in January-April, 1863. Reported on detached service in hospital at Clinton, Tennessee, in May-June, 1863. Deserted on August 25, 1863. Later served as Sergeant in Company I, 13th Regiment Tennessee Cavalry (Union).

BREWER, RILEY, Private

Enlisted in Watauga County on July 7, 1862, for the war. Reported absent without leave in January-February, 1863. Returned to duty on March 16, 1863. Deserted on June 25, 1863. Rejoined the company on March 7, 1864, and was placed under arrest. Reported sick in hospital in August, 1864. No further records.

BROOKS, ALFRED, Private

Previously served as Private in Company B of this regiment. Transferred to this company subsequent to August 31, 1864. Paroled at Greensboro on May 1, 1865.

BRYANT, THOMAS, Private

Previously served as Private in Company C of this regiment. Transferred to this company on or about June 27, 1862. No further records. [May have served later as Private in Company A, 3rd Regiment N.C. Mounted Infantry (Union).]

CALAWAY, WILLIAM HENDERSON, Private

Born on August 27, 1845. Enlisted in Watauga County at age 16, June 27, 1862, for the war. Reported present in January-April, 1863. Deserted on June 5, 1863. [May have served later as Private in Company F, 3rd Regiment Tennessee Cavalry (Union). After the war he had twin sons whom he named "Grant" and "Sherman."]

CLARK, JAMES W., Private

Resided in Watauga County and was by occupation a farmer prior to enlisting in Watauga County at age 37, October 25, 1862, for the war. Reported present in January-April, 1863. Deserted on June 5, 1863.

CLARK, JOHN W., Private

Resided in Watauga County and was by occupation a farmer prior to enlisting in Watauga County at age 33, June 27, 1862, for the war. Reported absent sick without leave in January-February, 1863. Reported absent without leave in September-December, 1863. Dropped from the company rolls in January-February, 1864.

CLARK, ROBERT P., Private

Enlisted in Watauga County on June 27, 1862, for the war. No further records. [May have served later as Private in Company C, 13th Regiment Tennessee Cavalry (Union).]

COFFEY, LEVI L., Private

Enlisted in Watauga County at age 28, June 27, 1862, for the war. Reported absent without leave in March-June and September-

December, 1863. Dropped from the company rolls in January-February, 1864. Survived the war.

COOK, JOHN A., Private

Enlisted in Watauga County on August 20, 1862, for the war. Reported absent sick without leave in January-February, 1863. Reported absent without leave in March-April, 1863. Listed as a deserter on June 5, 1863. Returned to duty on an unspecified date. Reported present in September-October, 1863. Reported absent without leave in November-December, 1863. Dropped from the company rolls in January-February, 1864.

CORNELL, ALFRED, Private

Resided in Watauga County and was by occupation a "domestic" prior to enlisting in Watauga County at age 22, July 7, 1862, for the war. Reported present in January-February, 1863. Sent to hospital at Knoxville, Tennessee, in March-April, 1863. Furloughed for thirty days on June 12, 1863. Returned to duty on an unspecified date. Reported present from September-October, 1863, through August 31, 1864. No further records.

CORNELL, BENJAMIN, Private

Resided in Watauga County and was by occupation a farmer or "domestic" prior to enlisting in Watauga County at age 20, June 27, 1862, for the war. Reported present in January-April, 1863. Furloughed for sixty days from hospital at Knoxville, Tennessee, June 8, 1863. Reported absent without leave from August 10, 1863, through August 31, 1864. No further records.

CORNELL, JOHN, Private

Resided in Watauga County and was by occupation a farmer prior to enlisting in Watauga County at age 23, June 27, 1862, for the war. Reported present in January-February, 1863. Sent to hospital at Knoxville, Tennessee, in March-April, 1863. Returned to duty in May-June, 1863. Deserted on or about September 20, 1863. Returned to duty on October 20, 1863. Reported present through April 30, 1864. Captured at or near Dallas, Georgia, on or about May 26, 1864. Sent to Nashville, Tennessee. Transferred to Louisville, Kentucky, where he arrived on June 3, 1864. Transferred to Rock Island, Illinois, where he arrived on June 6, 1864. Died at Rock Island on June 20, 1864, of "typh[oi]d pneumonia."

CORNELL, JOSEPH, Private

Resided in Watauga County and was by occupation a farmer or "domestic" prior to enlisting in Watauga County at age 17, June 27, 1862, for the war. Reported present in January-June, 1863. Reported absent sick with leave in September-October, 1863. Reported absent without leave in November-December, 1863. Returned to duty in January-February, 1864. Reported present through August 31, 1864. No further records.

CORNELL, THOMAS E., Private

Enlisted in Watauga County on September 16, 1862, for the war. Reported present in January-February, 1863. Reported in hospital at Knoxville, Tennessee, in March-June, 1863. Listed as a deserter on September 26, 1863.

COX, BRAXTON, Private

Resided in Watauga County where he enlisted at age 19, June 27, 1862, for the war. Reported present in January-June, 1863. Wounded at Chickamauga, Georgia, September 20, 1863. Nominated for the Badge of Distinction for gallantry at Chickamauga.

Reported absent wounded until November 20, 1863, when he was reported absent without leave. Listed as a deserter on March 15, 1864. Returned to duty subsequent to April 30, 1864. Captured at or near Dallas, Georgia, on or about May 25, 1864. Sent to Nashville, Tennessee. Transferred to Louisville, Kentucky, where he arrived on June 3, 1864. Transferred to Rock Island, Illinois, where he arrived on June 6, 1864. Released at Rock Island on June 17, 1865, after taking the Oath of Allegiance. [Died in 1919 and is buried in the Confederate cemetery at Higginsville, Missouri.]

COX, WILLIAM R., Private

Born in Yancey County and was by occupation a farmer prior to enlisting in Watauga County at age 15, July 7, 1862, for the war. Transferred to Company K of this regiment prior to March 1, 1863.

CREASMON, BERRY C., Private

Previously served as Private in Company C of this regiment. Transferred to this company on or about June 27, 1862. No further records. [May have served later as 2nd Lieutenant of Company B, 29th Regiment N.C. Troops.]

CRISENBURY, JAMES M., Private

Enlisted in Watauga County on June 27, 1862, for the war. Reported present in January-June, 1863, and September, 1863-February, 1864. Furloughed home for twenty days on April 16, 1864. Returned to duty prior to June 22, 1864, when he was wounded at Kolb's Farm, near Marietta, Georgia. Reported in hospital through August 31, 1864. No further records.

DANNER, ANDERSON A., Private

Resided in Watauga County and was by occupation a "domestic" prior to enlisting in Watauga County at age 19, June 27, 1862, for the war. Reported present in January-June, 1863. Wounded in the right thigh at Chickamauga, Georgia, September 20, 1863. Reported absent wounded until November 20, 1863, when he was reported absent without leave. Listed as a deserter on March 15, 1864. Returned to duty subsequent to April 30, 1864. Reported present in May-August, 1864. No further records. Survived the war.

DANNER, JOHN, Private

Born on June 6, 1828. Resided in Watauga County and was by occupation a shoemaker and farmer prior to enlisting in Watauga County at age 34, July 7, 1862, for the war. Reported absent without leave in January-February, 1863. Returned to duty in March-April, 1863. Reported absent on detached service in May-June, 1863. Reported sick in hospital at Griffin, Georgia, in September-November, 1863. Returned to duty in December, 1863. Reported present through August 31, 1864. No further records. Survived the war.

DAVIS, GEORGE W., Private

Enlisted in Watauga County on or about July 7, 1862, for the war. Reported present in January-April, 1863. Reported on duty as a hospital guard in May-June, 1863. Reported absent on furlough in September-October, 1863. Reported absent without leave in November-December, 1863. Dropped from the company rolls in January-February, 1864. Restored to the rolls on an unspecified date. Reported sick in hospital on August 14, 1864. No further records.

DONE, MORGAN, Private

Previously served as Private in Company C of this regiment. Transferred to this company on or about June 27, 1862. Transferred back to Company C prior to March 1, 1863.

DUGGER, B. F., ———

North Carolina pension records indicate that he served in this company.

DUGGER, JOHN W., Corporal

Enlisted in Watauga County on June 27, 1862, for the war. Was apparently mustered in with the rank of Corporal. Reported present in January-June, 1863. Wounded at Chickamauga, Georgia, September 20, 1863. Returned to duty prior to October 31, 1863. Present or accounted for through August 3, 1864. Killed at or near Atlanta, Georgia, on or about August 4, 1864.

DYER, DRURY CALVIN, Private

Born on May 14, 1841. Resided in Watauga County and was by occupation a "domestic" prior to enlisting in Watauga County at age 21, June 27, 1862, for the war. Reported present in January-June, 1863, and September, 1863-April, 1864. Reported sick in hospital from June 22 through August 31, 1864. No further records. Survived the war.

EGGERS, ADAM, Corporal

Born on July 23, 1831. Resided in Watauga County and was by occupation a farmer prior to enlisting in Watauga County at age 30, July 7, 1862, for the war. Promotion record not reported. Died at Jacksboro, Tennessee, January 2, 1863, of "fever."

FEASTER, T. P., ———

Place and date of enlistment not reported. Listed as a deserter on September 10, 1864.

FOX, NATHAN F., Private

Resided in Watauga County where he enlisted on July 7, 1862, for the war. Reported absent sick in January-June, 1863. Returned to duty on an unspecified date. Captured at Missionary Ridge, Tennessee, November 25, 1863. Sent to Nashville, Tennessee. Transferred to Louisville, Kentucky, where he arrived on or about December 22, 1863. Released on or about the same date after taking the Oath of Allegiance.

GARDNER, ELISHA M., Private

Previously served as Private in Company B of this regiment. Transferred to this company subsequent to August 31, 1864. Paroled at Greensboro on May 1, 1865.

GIBBS, JOSEPH A., Private

Previously served as Private in Company C of this regiment. Transferred to this company on or about June 27, 1862. Transferred back to Company C prior to March 1, 1863.

GLENN, DUDLEY G., Private

Resided in Watauga County and was by occupation a farmer prior to enlisting in Watauga County at age 21, June 27, 1862, for the war. Died in Tennessee in October, 1862, of "sickness."

GLENN, SIMEON, Private

Resided in Watauga County and was by occupation a farmer prior to enlisting in Watauga County at age 20, July 7, 1862, for the war. Reported present in January-June and September-December, 1863. Furloughed home for thirty-six days on February 15, 1864. Returned to duty prior to April 30, 1864. Reported present in May-August, 1864. Wounded in the head at Bentonville on March 19, 1865. Died of wounds. Place and date of death not reported.

GRAGG, ALEXANDER, Private

Enlisted in Watauga County on June 27, 1862, for the war. Mustered with an unspecified rank. Reported present in January-February, 1863. Rank reported as Corporal on March 1, 1863. Sent to hospital at Knoxville, Tennessee, in March-April, 1863. Reduced to ranks subsequent to April 30, 1863. Died at Knoxville on June 5, 1863, of "dysentery and fever."

GRAGG, EMPSEY, Private

Resided in Watauga County and was by occupation a farmer prior to enlisting in Watauga County at age 32, July 7, 1862, for the war. Reported present in January-April, 1863. Deserted on May 26, 1863. Reported present but under arrest in January-February, 1864. Reported absent without leave on April 15, 1864. Reported sick in hospital from May 17 through August 31, 1864. Deserted to the enemy on an unspecified date. Confined at Knoxville, Tennessee, June 7, 1864. Transferred to Louisville, Kentucky, where he arrived on June 14, 1864. Released on the same date after taking the Oath of Allegiance. [Previously served as Captain in the 98th Regiment N.C. Militia.]

GRAGG, HARVEY H., Private

Enlisted in Watauga County on December 27, 1863, for the war. Reported sick in hospital on January 15, 1864. Died prior to January 1, 1865. Place, date, and cause of death not reported. [Previously served as Captain in the 98th Regiment N.C. Militia.]

GRAGG, WILLIAM SMITH, _____

Previously served as Private in Company B, 37th Regiment N.C. Troops. Enlisted in this company on June 27, 1862, with an unspecified rank. Transferred to Company I of this regiment on or about July 24, 1862.

GREEN, ADAM, Private

Enlisted in Watauga County on July 7, 1862, for the war. Deserted on February 9, 1863. Died in hospital at Clinton, Tennessee, on or about March 5, 1863. Cause of death not reported.

GREEN, ALFRED, Private

Enlisted in Watauga County on June 27, 1862, for the war. No further records.

GREEN, AUGUSTUS F., Private

Born in Watauga County* where he resided as a farmer prior to enlisting in Watauga County at age 24, July 7, 1862, for the war. Transferred to Company E of this regiment on or about July 29, 1862.

GREEN, EDMUND, Private

Born in Caldwell County* and was by occupation a farmer prior to enlisting in Caldwell County at age 34, July 25, 1862, for the war. Transferred to Company E of this regiment on or about July 29, 1862.

GREEN, JACOB, Private

Resided in Watauga County and was by occupation a farmer prior to enlisting in Watauga County at age 28, July 7, 1862, for the war. Discharged on an unspecified date (probably prior to March 1, 1863). Reason discharged not reported.

GREEN, JEREMIAH, Corporal

Born in Ashe County on June 8, 1843. Resided in Watauga County and was by occupation a farmer prior to enlisting in Watauga

County at age 19, June 27, 1862, for the war. Was apparently mustered in with the rank of Private. Reported absent sick without leave in January-February, 1863. Returned to duty in March-April, 1863. Reported absent in hospital at Clinton, Tennessee, in May-June, 1863. Returned to duty in September-October, 1863. Promoted to Corporal on October 1, 1863. Reported present in November-December, 1863. Reported sick in hospital from February 23 through August 31, 1864. Reported in hospital at Vineville, Georgia, October 13, 1864. No further records. Survived the war. [North Carolina pension records indicate that he injured his ankle in a train wreck at Greensboro "shortly before the surrenender (sic)."]

GREEN, JONATHAN, Private

Resided in Caldwell County and was by occupation a farmer prior to enlisting in Caldwell County at age 30, July 8, 1862, for the war. Transferred to Company E of this regiment prior to March 1, 1863.

GREEN, JOSEPH, Private

Enlisted in Watauga County on July 7, 1862, for the war. Transferred to Company B of this regiment prior to March 1, 1863.

GREEN, LARKIN, Private

Born in Caldwell County* where he resided as a farmer prior to enlisting in Watauga County at age 23, July 7, 1862, for the war. Transferred to Company E of this regiment on or about July 29, 1862.

GREEN, LEVY, ———

Enlisted in Watauga County on June 27, 1862, for the war. No further records. [May have served later as Private in Companies D and E, 2nd Regiment N.C. Mounted Infantry (Union).]

GREENE, SOLOMON, JR., Private

Resided in Watauga County and was by occupation a farmer prior to enlisting in Watauga County at age 30, June 27, 1862, for the war. Furloughed at Big Creek Gap, Tennessee, November 20, 1862, because of illness. Reported absent without leave on surviving company muster rolls through December 31, 1863. Rejoined the company on January 27, 1864. Court-martialed and ordered to "mark time" for two hours each day for ten days. Returned to duty on an unspecified date. Wounded and captured at Resaca, Georgia, May 14-15, 1864. Sent to Nashville, Tennessee. Transferred to Louisville, Kentucky, where he arrived on May 20, 1864. Transferred to Camp Morton, Indianapolis, Indiana, where he arrived on May 22, 1864. Paroled at Camp Morton on March 15, 1865. Received at Boulware's Wharf, James River, Virginia, March 23, 1865, for exchange. Hospitalized at Richmond, Virginia, March 24, 1865, with scorbutus. Furloughed for thirty days on or about March 29, 1865. Survived the war.

GREER, DAVID, Private

Resided in Watauga County and was by occupation a farmer prior to enlisting in Watauga County on July 7, 1862, for the war. Reported present in January-February, 1863. Died on March 10, 1863. Place and cause of death not reported.

GREER, RILEY, Private

Resided in Watauga County and was by occupation a farmer prior to enlisting in Watauga County at age 21, July 7, 1862, for the war. Reported present in January-February, 1863. Sent to hospital at Knoxville, Tennessee, in March-April, 1863. Furloughed for thirty days on June 19, 1863. Reported absent without leave in

September-December, 1863. Dropped from the company rolls in January-February, 1864.

GROGAN, ANDERSON, Private

Born in South Carolina and resided in Watauga County where he was by occupation a farmer prior to enlisting in Watauga County at age 28, July 7, 1862, for the war. Deserted on February 9, 1863. Rejoined the company on March 4, 1863, and was placed under arrest. Returned to duty in May-June, 1863. Wounded at Chickamauga, Georgia, September 20, 1863. Returned to duty prior to October 31, 1863. Reported missing at Missionary Ridge, Tennessee, November 25, 1863. Returned to duty in January-February, 1864. Reported present in March-April, 1864. Captured at Resaca, Georgia, May 15, 1864. Sent to Nashville, Tennessee. Transferred to Louisville, Kentucky, where he arrived on May 19, 1864. Transferred to Camp Morton, Indianapolis, Indiana, where he arrived on May 22, 1864. Died at Camp Morton on February 12, 1865, of "chronic diarrhoea."

GRUBB, PHILLIP H., Private

Enlisted in Watauga County on November 7, 1862, for the war. Reported present in January-February, 1863. Died at "Jackson (probably Jacksboro)," Tennessee, February 27, 1863. Cause of death not reported.

GUY, JOHN C., Private

Born in Johnston County, Tennessee, and was by occupation a farmer prior to enlisting in Watauga County on August 8, 1862, for the war. Deserted on February 10, 1863. Rejoined the company on March 4, 1863, and was placed under arrest. Returned to duty on an unspecified date. Deserted on May 25, 1863. Later served as Private in Company G, 8th Regiment Tennessee Cavalry (Union). [Was 25 years of age when he enlisted in the 8th Tennessee Cavalry.]

HAGAMAN, HUGH, Private

Enlisted in Watauga County at age 25, June 27, 1862, for the war. Was apparently mustered in with the rank of Sergeant. Reported present in January-June, 1863. Deserted from hospital in July-October, 1863. Reduced to ranks in November-December, 1863. Dropped from the company rolls in January-February, 1864. [May have served also as Private in Company A, 65th Regiment N.C. Troops (6th Regiment N.C. Cavalry).]

HAGAMAN, MARTIN G., Private

Enlisted in Watauga County on July 7, 1862, for the war. No further records.

HALL, DAVID S., Private

Previously served as Private in Company C of this regiment. Transferred to this company on or about June 27, 1862. Transferred back to Company C prior to March 1, 1863.

HARMON, ANDREW J., Private

Resided in Watauga County and was by occupation a farmer prior to enlisting in Watauga County at age 27, July 7, 1862, for the war. Reported present in January-February, 1863. Reported absent without leave in March-April, 1863. Returned to duty in May-June, 1863. Deserted on September 20, 1863. Later served as Sergeant in Company E, 13th Regiment Tennessee Cavalry (Union).

HARMON, ELI G., Private

Resided in Watauga County and was by occupation a farmer prior to enlisting in Watauga County at age 27, July 7, 1862, for the war. Reported present in January-April, 1863. Deserted on an unspecified date. Returned to duty on June 14, 1863. Reported absent without leave on September 5, 1863. Dropped from the company rolls in January-February, 1864.

HARMON, EPHRAIM COUNCIL, Private

Born in 1841. Resided in Watauga County and was by occupation a "domestic" prior to enlisting in Watauga County on July 7, 1862, for the war. Reported present in January-June, 1863. Deserted on August 31, 1863. [Filed a Tennessee pension application after the war.]

HARMON, GOULDER CARROLL, Private

Resided in Watauga County and was by occupation a "domestic" prior to enlisting in Watauga County at age 24, July 7, 1862, for the war. Reported absent sick without leave in January-February, 1863. Returned to duty in March-April, 1863. Deserted on an unspecified date. Returned to duty on June 14, 1863. Reported sick in hospital in September-October, 1863. Furloughed from hospital on November 12, 1863. Dropped from the company rolls in January-February, 1864. Reason he was dropped not reported.

HARMON, JOHN WILEY, Private

Resided in Watauga County and was by occupation a "domestic" prior to enlisting in Watauga County at age 23, July 7, 1862, for the war. Reported present in January-June, 1863. Deserted on August 31, 1863.

HARMON, WILEY A., Private

Resided in Watauga County and was by occupation a farmer prior to enlisting in Watauga County at age 35, July 7, 1862, for the war. Reported absent sick in January-February, 1863. Listed as a deserter on March 13, 1863.

HATLEY, JOHN F., Private

Enlisted in Watauga County on July 7, 1862, for the war. Reported absent sick without leave in January-February, 1863. Returned to duty in March-April, 1863. Detailed as a teamster in May-June, 1863. Deserted on August 31, 1863. Later served as blacksmith in Company E, 13th Regiment Tennessee Cavalry (Union).

HATLEY, LAFAYETTE, Private

Enlisted in Watauga County on July 7, 1862, for the war. Mustered in as Private. Reported present in January-April, 1863. Reported in hospital at Knoxville, Tennessee, in May-June, 1863. Returned to duty on an unspecified date. Promoted to Corporal in July-October, 1863. Reported present in September, 1863-February, 1864. Reduced to ranks subsequent to February 29, 1864. Died at Dalton, Georgia, March 23, 1864, of "congestion of the brain."

HATLEY, RILEY B., Private

Resided in Watauga County where he enlisted on July 7, 1862, for the war. No further records. Later served as Corporal in Company E, 13th Regiment Tennessee Cavalry (Union). [Was about 24 years of age when he enlisted in the 13th Tennessee Cavalry.]

HATLEY, WILEY S., Private

Enlisted in Watauga County on July 7, 1862, for the war. Reported present in January-June, 1863. Deserted on August 31, 1863. Later served as Sergeant in Company E, 13th Regiment Tennessee Cavalry (Union). [Was 18 years of age when he enlisted in the 13th Tennessee Cavalry.]

HAYES, JACOB S., Private

Born in Watauga County where he enlisted on July 7, 1862, for the war. Died in Tennessee prior to February 4, 1863. Date and cause of death not reported.

HAYES, ROBERT, Private

Resided in Watauga County and was by occupation a farmer prior to enlisting in Watauga County at age 30, June 27, 1862, for the war. Transferred to Company I of this regiment on or about July 24, 1862.

HENSON, JORDAN, Private

Resided in Watauga County and was by occupation a farmer prior to enlisting in Watauga County at age 32, July 7, 1862, for the war. Deserted on February 10, 1863. Reported under arrest at Knoxville, Tennessee, on or about February 28, 1863. Died at Knoxville on May 10, 1863. Cause of death not reported.

HENSON, JOURDON J., Private

Enlisted in Watauga County on June 11, 1862, for the war. Deserted on February 10, 1863. Reported under arrest at Knoxville, Tennessee, on or about February 28, 1863. Returned to duty on March 4, 1863. Reported present in May-June, 1863, and September, 1863-April, 1864. Reported sick in hospital from June 16 through August 31, 1864. No further records. Survived the war. [Was about 19 years of age at time of enlistment.]

HICKS, ANDREW, Private

Born in Tennessee and resided in Watauga County where he was by occupation a farmer prior to enlisting in Watauga County at age 33, June 27, 1862, for the war. Reported absent sick with leave in January-June, 1863. Reported absent without leave in September-December, 1863. Dropped from the company rolls on or about February 29, 1864.

HICKS, CARROLL, Private

Born in Watauga County* where he resided as a farmer prior to enlisting in Watauga County at age 23, June 27, 1862, for the war. Killed at Cumberland Gap, Tennessee, on or about September 23, 1862, "by and [sic] explosion of powder."

HICKS, HARMON, Private

Born in Watauga County* where he enlisted on June 27, 1862, for the war. Died at Big Creek Gap, Tennessee, prior to March 2, 1863. Date and cause of death not reported.

HICKS, LEVI, Private

Resided in Watauga County and was by occupation a farmer prior to enlisting in Watauga County at age 30, June 27, 1862, for the war. Reported absent without leave in March-April, 1863. Listed as a deserter on June 25, 1863.

HICKS, MATHIAS, Private

Resided in Watauga County and was by occupation a farmer prior to enlisting in Watauga County at age 26, July 7, 1862, for the war. Reported present in January-June, 1863. Deserted on September

26, 1863. Returned to duty on October 20, 1863. Deserted near Dalton, Georgia, on or about January 31, 1864. Court-martialed (possibly in absentia) on or about February 18, 1864. No further records.

HICKS, PATTERSON, Private

Born in Watauga County* where he resided as a "domestic" prior to enlisting in Watauga County at age 19, June 27, 1862, for the war. Died at Cumberland Gap, Tennessee, prior to March 2, 1863. Date and cause of death not reported.

HICKS, W. W., ———

Enlisted in Watauga County on June 27, 1862, for the war. No further records.

HILEMAN, JACOB, Private

Previously served as Private in Company B of this regiment. Transferred to this company subsequent to August 31, 1864. Paroled at Greensboro on May 1, 1865. [May have served also in Company E of this regiment.]

HODGES, EDWARD, 1st Sergeant

Resided in Watauga County and was by occupation a farmer prior to enlisting in Watauga County at age 31, June 27, 1862, for the war. Was apparently mustered in as 1st Sergeant. No further records.

HODGES, GILBERT W., Corporal

Resided in Watauga County and was by occupation a "domestic" prior to enlisting in Watauga County at age 18, October 24, 1863, for the war. Mustered in as Private. Reported present through August 31, 1864. Promoted to Corporal on July 11, 1864. Transferred to Company A of this regiment subsequent to August 31, 1864.

HODGES, JOHN, Private

Place and date of enlistment not reported (probably enlisted subsequent to August 31, 1864). Captured at Boone on March 28, 1865. Sent to Chattanooga, Tennessee, April 12, 1865. No further records.

HODGES, LARKIN, Sergeant

Enlisted in Watauga County at age 20, June 27, 1862, for the war. Was apparently mustered in with the rank of Sergeant. Reported present or accounted for in January-June, 1863, and September, 1863-August, 1864. Transferred to Company A of this regiment subsequent to August 31, 1864.

HODGES, RILEY, Private

Born on March 3, 1830. Resided in Watauga County and was by occupation a farmer prior to enlisting in Watauga County at age 32, July 7, 1862, for the war. Reported absent sick with leave in January-June, 1863. Reported absent without leave in September-December, 1863. Returned to duty subsequent to February 29, 1864. Reported present in May-August, 1864. No further records. Survived the war.

HOLCOMBE, ROBERT M., Private

Previously served as Private in Company C of this regiment. Transferred to this company on or about June 27, 1862. Transferred back to Company C prior to March 1, 1863.

HOLIFIELD, JASPER, Private

Previously served as Private in Company A of this regiment. Transferred to this company when the 58th and 60th Regiments were consolidated on April 9, 1865. Paroled at Greensboro on May 1, 1865.

HOLIFIELD, JOSEPH, Private

Previously served as Private in Company A of this regiment. Transferred to this company when the 58th and 60th Regiments were consolidated on April 9, 1865. Paroled at Greensboro on May 1, 1865.

HOLLERS, WILLIAM, Private

Resided in Washington County, Tennessee, and enlisted in Watauga County on July 25, 1862, for the war. Reported present in January-June, 1863, and September, 1863-August, 1864. Captured at Atlanta, Georgia, September 5, 1864. Sent to Nashville, Tennessee. Transferred to Louisville, Kentucky, where he arrived on October 28, 1864. Transferred to Camp Douglas, Chicago, Illinois, where he arrived on November 1, 1864. Released at Camp Douglas on June 17, 1865, after taking the Oath of Allegiance. [Was about 20 years of age at time of enlistment.]

HOLLY, GEORGE, Private

Reportedly enlisted in Mitchell County on June 10, 1862, for the war; however, his name is not listed on any of the surviving muster rolls for this company. Paroled at Greensboro on May 1, 1865.

HOLSCLAW, FRANCIS M., Private

Enlisted in Watauga County on July 7, 1862, for the war. Deserted on January 14, 1863. [May be the same man who served as Private in Company A of this regiment under the name of Marion F. Holdsclaw.]

HOLSCLAW, RUFUS L., Private

Enlisted in Watauga County on July 20, 1862, for the war. No further records.

HOLSCLAW, WILEY, ———

North Carolina pension records indicate that he served in this company.

HOLSCLAW, WILLIAM L., Private

Enlisted in Watauga County on June 27, 1862, for the war. Deserted on January 14, 1863.

HOUSTON, JOHN, Private

Enlisted in Watauga County on July 7, 1862, for the war. No further records.

HOWELL, WILLIAM, ———

North Carolina pension records indicate that he served in this company.

HOWINGTON, NOEL, Private

Born in Tennessee and resided in Watauga County where he was by occupation a farmer prior to enlisting in Watauga County at age 56, September 16, 1862, for the war. Reported present in January-April, 1863. Deserted on May 26, 1863. Returned to duty on September 1, 1863. Captured at Missionary Ridge, Tennessee, November

ber 25, 1863. Sent to Nashville, Tennessee. Transferred to Louisville, Kentucky, where he arrived on December 17, 1863. Transferred to Rock Island, Illinois, where he arrived on December 23, 1863. Released at Rock Island on October 18, 1864, after taking the Oath of Allegiance.

HUFMAN, GEORGE D., Private

Resided in Washington County, Tennessee, and enlisted in Watauga County on August 20, 1862, for the war. Mustered in as Private. Reported present in January-June, 1863, and September, 1863-August, 1864. Promoted to Sergeant on July 11, 1864. Reduced to ranks subsequent to August 31, 1864. Took the Oath of Allegiance at Chattanooga, Tennessee, May 27, 1865.

HUSKINS, JACOB, Private

Enlisted in Surry County on February 20, 1865, for the war. Paroled at Greensboro on May 1, 1865.

ISAACS, HARVEY, Private

Enlisted in Watauga County on July 7, 1862, for the war. No further records. [May have served later as Private in Company D, 2nd Regiment N.C. State Troops.]

ISAACS, JAMES, Private

Place and date of enlistment not reported. Name appears on an undated bounty pay and receipt roll.

ISAACS, NOAH, Private

Born in Watauga County where he resided as a farmer prior to enlisting in Watauga County at age 24, July 7, 1862, for the war. Transferred to Company I of this regiment on or about August 5, 1862.

ISAACS, REUBEN J., Private

Resided in Watauga County where he enlisted on July 7, 1862, for the war. Reported present in January-June, 1863, and September, 1863-April, 1864. Wounded in the left hip on or about August 10, 1864. Hospitalized at Macon, Georgia. Captured at Boone on March 28, 1865. Sent to Nashville, Tennessee. Transferred to Louisville, Kentucky, where he arrived on May 14, 1865. Released at Louisville on June 17, 1865, after taking the Oath of Allegiance.

ISAACS, RICHARD, JR., Private

Enlisted in Watauga County at age 30, July 7, 1862, for the war. No further records. Survived the war. [May have served later in the 5th Regiment N.C. State Troops.]

JACKSON, JAMES R., Private

Born in Johnson County, Tennessee, and was by occupation a farmer prior to enlisting in Watauga County on June 27, 1862, for the war. Reported absent without leave in January-February, 1863. No further records. Later served as Private in Company F, 13th Regiment Tennessee Cavalry (Union). [Was about 21 years of age when he enlisted in the 13th Tennessee Cavalry.]

JAMES, ELI, Private

Born in Watauga County* where he enlisted on June 27, 1862, for the war. Died at Cumberland Gap, Tennessee, on or about September 24, 1862. Cause of death not reported (probably a gunpowder explosion).

JARRETT, ELI, Corporal

Previously served as Corporal in Company B of this regiment. Transferred to this company subsequent to August 31, 1864. Paroled at Greensboro on May 2, 1865. [Filed a Tennessee pension application after the war.]

JOHNSON, BARTLETT, Private

Resided in Watauga County and was by occupation a farmer prior to enlisting in Watauga County at age 33, June 27, 1862, for the war. Reported absent without leave in January-February, 1863. Returned to duty in March-April, 1863. Deserted on September 18, 1863. Dropped from the company rolls on or about February 29, 1864. Went over to the enemy on an unspecified date. Took the Oath of Allegiance at Chattanooga, Tennessee, August 17, 1864, and at Louisville, Kentucky, September 26, 1864.

JOHNSON, JACOB, SR., Private

Enlisted in Watauga County on June 27, 1862, for the war. Transferred to Company I of this regiment on or about July 24, 1862. Transferred back to this company prior to December 22, 1862. Died at Big Creek Gap, Tennessee, prior to March 11, 1863. Cause of death not reported.

JOHNSON, MADISON, Private

Resided in Watauga County and was by occupation a farmer prior to enlisting in Watauga County at age 44, June 27, 1862, for the war. Died at Big Creek Gap, Tennessee, prior to March 2, 1863. Date and cause of death not reported.

KILBY, ABRAHAM, ———

Place and date of enlistment not reported. An undated bounty pay and receipt roll indicates that he served in this company.

KILBY, WILLIAM E., Musician

Born in Ashe County and resided in Watauga County where he was by occupation a farmer prior to enlisting in Watauga County at age 18, July 7, 1862, for the war. Was apparently mustered in with the rank of Musician. Reported present in January-June and September-December, 1863. Sent to hospital on February 23, 1864. Reported absent without leave on or about April 17, 1864. Dropped from the company rolls on or about August 31, 1864. Later served as Private in Company I, 13th Regiment Tennessee Cavalry (Union).

LAURANCE, JAMES J., Private

Resided in Watauga County and was by occupation a farmer prior to enlisting in Watauga County at age 25, July 7, 1862, for the war. Reported present in January-June, 1863. Deserted on October 9, 1863. Returned to duty on January 27, 1864. Reported present through April 30, 1864. Deserted near Howell Ferry, Georgia, July 9, 1864.

LEWIS, DANIEL J., Private

Enlisted in Watauga County on June 27, 1862, for the war. No further records.

LUSBYFIELD, JAMES, Private

Reportedly enlisted in Mitchell County on June 10, 1862, for the war; however, his name is not listed on any muster rolls of this company. Paroled at Greensboro on May 1, 1865.

LUSK, ELKANA, Private

Resided in Watauga County where he enlisted on July 7, 1862, for the war. Reported present in January-April, 1863. Deserted on June 5, 1863. Apparently returned to duty on an unspecified date (probably in August-September, 1864). Deserted to the enemy on an unspecified date. Took the Oath of Allegiance at Atlanta, Georgia, September 27, 1864. Released at Louisville, Kentucky, on or about October 22, 1864.

McHARGUE, THOMAS L., Private

Resided in Watauga County and was by occupation a farmer prior to enlisting in Watauga County at age 30, June 27, 1862, for the war. Reported absent sick without leave in January-February, 1863. Reported absent sick with leave in March-April, 1863. Reported absent without leave in September-December, 1863. Dropped from the company rolls on or about February 29, 1864.

McKINNEY, JASON C., Private

Previously served as Private in Company A of this regiment. Transferred to this company when the 58th and 60th Regiments were consolidated on April 9, 1865. Paroled at Greensboro on May 1, 1865.

McLAIRD, JAMES W., Private

Enlisted in Watauga County on June 27, 1862, for the war. Reported present in January-April, 1863. Deserted on June 5, 1863.

McLANE, HUGH F., Private

Resided in Watauga County where he enlisted on July 7, 1862, for the war. Deserted on February 10, 1863. Hospitalized at Macon, Georgia, September 23, 1863, with debility. Returned to duty in November-December, 1863. Reported present in January-April, 1864. Deserted on an unspecified date prior to September 1, 1864.

MARCUS, SERUG, Private

Resided in Watauga County where he enlisted at age 24, June 27, 1862, for the war. Reported absent sick in January-April, 1863. Reported absent with leave in May-June, 1863. Captured (or deserted to the enemy) at Missionary Ridge, Tennessee, November 25, 1863. Sent to Nashville, Tennessee, where he took the Oath of Allegiance on December 22, 1863. Released at Louisville, Kentucky, December 25, 1863.

MAST, FINLEY PATTERSON, 1st Sergeant

Born on March 30, 1832. Resided in Watauga County and was by occupation a "domestic" prior to enlisting in Watauga County at age 30, June 27, 1862, for the war. Was apparently mustered in with the rank of 1st Sergeant. Reported present in January-June and September-December, 1863. Reported sick in hospital on January 12, 1864. Returned to duty subsequent to February 29, 1864. Reported present in March-August, 1864. Captured in Watauga County on March 28, 1865. Sent to Knoxville, Tennessee. Transferred to Chattanooga, Tennessee, April 12, 1865. Transferred to Louisville, Kentucky, where he arrived on April 26, 1865. Transferred to Camp Chase, Ohio, where he arrived on April 30, 1865. Released at Camp Chase on June 10, 1865, after taking the Oath of Allegiance.

MAST, JOHN ALLEN, Private

Resided in Watauga County and was by occupation a farmer prior to enlisting in Watauga County at age 32, July 7, 1862, for the war.

Was apparently mustered in with the rank of Sergeant. Reported present in January-June, 1863. Hospitalized at Griffin, Georgia, September 26, 1863, with an unspecified complaint. Returned to duty subsequent to October 31, 1863. Reported present in November, 1863-February, 1864. Furloughed for forty days on March 27, 1864. Deserted on July 9, 1864, and was subsequently reduced to ranks. Went over to the enemy on an unspecified date. Took the Oath of Allegiance at Chattanooga, Tennessee, on or about August 17, 1864. Released at Louisville, Kentucky, September 26, 1864.

MAST, S. J., ———
Place and date of enlistment not reported. Listed as a deserter on September 10, 1864.

MILLER, GEORGE M., Private
Resided in Watauga County and was by occupation a farmer prior to enlisting in Watauga County at age 27, on or about June 27, 1862, for the war. Transferred to Company I of this regiment on or about August 5, 1862.

MILLER, JOHN M., Private
Resided in Watauga County and was by occupation a "domestic" prior to enlisting in Watauga County at age 18, June 27, 1862, for the war. Transferred to Company I of this regiment on or about July 15, 1862.

MILLER, T. CALVIN, Private
Resided in Watauga County and was by occupation a farmer prior to enlisting in Watauga County at age 18, June 27, 1862, for the war. Transferred to Company I of this regiment on or about July 15, 1862.

MITCHELL, MICHAEL, Private
Resided in Watauga County and was by occupation a blacksmith prior to enlisting in Watauga County at age 29, July 7, 1862, for the war. Transferred to Company I of this regiment on or about August 5, 1862.

MOODY, HENRY H., Private
Resided in Watauga County where he enlisted on July 7, 1862, for the war. Reported absent sick without leave in January-February, 1863. Returned to duty in March-April, 1863. Reported present in May-June, 1863. Deserted on August 26, 1863. Returned to duty subsequent to February 29, 1864. Deserted to the enemy on an unspecified date. Took the Oath of Allegiance at Chattanooga, Tennessee, on or about August 17, 1864. Released at Louisville, Kentucky, on or about September 26, 1864.

MORE, HENRY, Private
Place and date of enlistment not reported. Reported absent without leave in March-April, 1863. No further records.

MORE, JOHN, ———
Place and date of enlistment not reported. Reported absent without leave in March-April, 1863. No further records.

NORRIS, ELIJAH JONATHAN, Sergeant
Enlisted in Watauga County at age 18, August 3, 1862, for the war. Was apparently mustered in with the rank of Private. Reported present in January-June, 1863. Promoted to Corporal in May-June, 1863. Reported present in September-October, 1863. Wounded in

both hips at Missionary Ridge, Tennessee, November 25, 1863. Reported absent wounded through February 29, 1864. Reported absent without leave on April 25, 1864. Returned to duty on an unspecified date. Promoted to Sergeant on July 11, 1864. Reported present through August 31, 1864. No further records. Survived the war.

ORRANT, JAMES C., Private
Enlisted in Watauga County on July 7, 1862, for the war. Reported present in January-February, 1863. Reported on detail as a teamster in March-June, 1863. Reported absent without leave in September-December, 1863. Returned to duty in January-February, 1864. Reported present in March-April, 1864. Reported sick in hospital (probably at La Grange, Georgia, and Auburn, Alabama) from May 22 through August 31, 1864. No further records. Survived the war. [Was about 20 years of age at time of enlistment. The correct spelling of his surname may be Arrant.]

PHILLIPS, ALFRED, Private
Previously served as Private in Company G of this regiment. Transferred to this company subsequent to August 31, 1864. Paroled at Greensboro on May 1, 1865.

POTTER, LEVI, Private
Enlisted in Watauga County on July 7, 1862, for the war. Died at Jacksboro, Tennessee, January 26, 1863. Cause of death not reported. [May have served previously as Private in Company B, 37th Regiment N.C. Troops.]

PRESNELL, BENJAMIN L., Corporal
Resided in Watauga County and was by occupation a "domestic" prior to enlisting in Watauga County at age 18, June 27, 1862, for the war. Mustered in as Private. Reported present in January-June, 1863. Reported sick in hospital in September-October, 1863. Reported present in November, 1863-August, 1864. Promoted to Corporal on April 1, 1864. Wounded mortally in the abdomen at Bentonville on March 19, 1865. Place and date of death not reported.

PRESNELL, JAMES, Private
Enlisted in Watauga County on August 11, 1862, for the war. Deserted on August 28, 1862.

PRESNELL, NATHANIEL, Private
Enlisted in Watauga County on August 11, 1862, for the war. Deserted on August 28, 1862.

PRESNELL, SQUIRE ADAMS, Private
Born in Watauga County* on August 7, 1842. Resided in Watauga County and was by occupation a "domestic" prior to enlisting in Watauga County at age 19, October 6, 1862, for the war. Reported present in January-June, 1863, and September, 1863-April, 1864. Captured at Dallas, Georgia, May 26, 1864. Sent to Nashville, Tennessee. Transferred to Louisville, Kentucky, where he arrived on June 3, 1864. Transferred to Rock Island, Illinois, where he arrived on June 6, 1864. Released at Rock Island on October 31, 1864, after taking the Oath of Allegiance. [Filed a Tennessee pension application after the war.]

PRESNELL, WESLEY WAYNE, Sergeant
Born on July 22, 1837. Resided in Watauga County and was by occupation a "domestic" prior to enlisting in Watauga County at

age 24, June 27, 1862, for the war. Was apparently mustered in with the rank of Corporal. Reported present in January-June, 1863. Wounded at Chickamauga, Georgia, September 20, 1863. Returned to duty prior to October 31, 1863. Reported present through December 31, 1863. Promoted to Sergeant on October 1, 1863. Wounded in the left arm at Rocky Face Ridge, Georgia, February 25, 1864. Left arm amputated. Hospitalized at Madison, Georgia. Reported absent wounded through August 31, 1864. No further records. Survived the war.

RAY, WILLIAM H., Private

Previously served as Private in Company C of this regiment. Transferred to this company on or about June 27, 1862. Transferred back to Company C prior to March 1, 1863.

RIDDLE, GARRETT, Private

Previously served as Private in Company C of this regiment. Transferred to this company on or about June 27, 1862. No further records. Survived the war.

ROWLAND, MICHAEL, Private

Resided in Watauga County and was by occupation a farmer prior to enlisting in Watauga County at age 25, July 7, 1862, for the war. Reported absent sick in January-February, 1863. Returned to duty in March-April, 1863. Reported present in May-June and September-December, 1863. Sent to hospital sick on January 10, 1864. Reported in hospital at Atlanta, Georgia, through April 30, 1864. Returned to duty on an unspecified date. Reported present in May-August, 1864. No further records. Survived the war. [North Carolina pension records indicate that he was wounded in the right hip at Chickamauga, Georgia (September 19-20, 1863); was wounded in the right knee at Atlanta; and suffered a broken thigh when he was kicked by a horse.]

SHELL, FRANKLIN DUGGER, Private

Born on July 3, 1832. Resided in Watauga County and was by occupation a mechanic. Place and date of enlistment not reported (probably enlisted in the summer of 1862). Was about 30 years of age at time of enlistment. No further records. Survived the war.

SHEPHERD, THOMAS ERWIN, Private

Previously served as Private in Company C of this regiment. Transferred to this company on or about June 27, 1862. Transferred back to Company C prior to March 1, 1863.

SHEWFORD, JAMES S., Private

Previously served as Private in Company C of this regiment. Transferred to this company on or about June 27, 1862. No further records. Survived the war.

SHOOK, JACOB D., Private

Resided in Watauga County and was by occupation a "domestic" prior to enlisting in Watauga County at age 17, June 27, 1862, for the war. Reported present in January-June, 1863. Reported sick in hospital in September-October, 1863. Returned to duty in November-December, 1863. Died near Dalton, Georgia, December 31, 1863. Cause of death not reported.

SHULL, JOHN F., Private

Enlisted in Watauga County on July 7, 1862, for the war. Failed to report for duty and was dropped from the company rolls on or about April 30, 1863.

SIFFORD, GEORGE H., Private

Resided in Watauga County and was by occupation a farmer prior to enlisting in Watauga County at age 33, June 27, 1862, for the war. Reported absent sick without leave in January-February, 1863. Returned to duty in March-April, 1863. Reported present in May-June, 1863, and September, 1863-August, 1864. No further records. Survived the war.

SIFFORD, JOEL, ———

Place and date of enlistment not reported. Dropped from the company rolls on or about February 29, 1864.

SIFFORD, JOHN, Private

Born in Wilkes County and resided in Watauga County where he was by occupation a farmer prior to enlisting in Watauga County on July 7, 1862, for the war. Reported absent without leave in January-February, 1863. Returned to duty in March-April, 1863. Reported in hospital at Knoxville, Tennessee, in May-June, 1863 (probably suffering from necrosis or some other disability of the left leg). Reported absent without leave in September-December, 1863. Dropped from the company rolls on or about February 29, 1864. Survived the war. [His Tennessee pension application gives his year of birth as 1836; however, his age at time of enlistment is given as 32 in the Compiled Military Service Records for North Carolina.]

SLAGLE, SIMEON, Private

Previously served as Private in Company C of this regiment. Transferred to this company on or about June 27, 1862. Transferred back to Company C prior to January 28, 1863.

SLOAN, SOLOMON, Private

Place and date of enlistment not reported. Hospitalized at Nashville, Tennessee, January 28, 1864. Died "during the month of January," 1864. Cause of death not reported.

STEWART, WILLIAM, Private

The service record of this soldier is unclear. It appears that he served in this company in September-October, 1863. He also served at various times in Companies C, E, and K of this regiment.

STRICKLAND, MOORE, Private

Born in Wilkes County in 1843. Enlisted in Watauga County on July 7, 1862, for the war. Reported present in January-June, 1863, and September, 1863-August, 1864. Wounded slightly in the right side and/or shoulder by a shell at Bentonville on March 19, 1865. Paroled at Charlotte on May 4, 1865. [Filed a Tennessee pension application after the war.]

SUTHERLAND, WILLIAM HENRY HARRISON, Private

Born in Ashe County where he resided as a farmer prior to enlisting in Watauga County at age 21, June 27, 1862, for the war. Transferred to Company I of this regiment on or about July 24, 1862.

TEASTER, FINLEY P., Private

Resided in Watauga County and was by occupation a farmer prior to enlisting in Watauga County at age 18, June 27, 1862, for the war. Reported present in January-June, 1863. Deserted on September 26, 1863. Returned to duty on January 2, 1864. Reported present through April 30, 1864. Deserted to the enemy near Atlanta, Georgia, on the evening of August 7, 1864. Transferred to Chattanooga, Tennessee, where he took the Oath of Allegiance on or about August 17, 1864. Released at Louisville, Kentucky, on or about September 26, 1864.

TEASTER, RANSOM, Private

Resided in Watauga County and was by occupation a farmer prior to enlisting in Watauga County at age 44, July 5, 1862, for the war. Deserted on February 10, 1863. Returned to duty on June 19, 1863. Reported absent without leave on September 5, 1863. Returned to duty on January 23, 1864. Died in hospital on June 10, 1864, of "typhoid fever." Place of death not reported.

THOMAS, AARON, Private

Previously served as Private in Company C of this regiment. Transferred to this company on or about June 27, 1862. Transferred back to Company C prior to March 1, 1863.

THOMAS, HEZEKIAH, Private

Born in Watauga County* in 1846. Was by occupation a farmer prior to enlisting in Watauga County on July 18, 1862, for the war. Reported present in January-June, 1863. Reported sick in hospital in September-October, 1863. Returned to duty in November-December, 1863. Reported present through August 31, 1864. Captured at Jonesborough, Georgia, September 5, 1864. Sent to Nashville, Tennessee. Transferred to Louisville, Kentucky, where he arrived on October 28, 1864. Transferred to Camp Douglas, Chicago, Illinois, where he arrived on November 1, 1864. Released at Camp Douglas on May 5, 1865, after joining the U.S. Army. Assigned to Company C, 6th Regiment U.S. Volunteer Infantry. [His Tennessee pension application states that he and "thousands more" enlisted in the Federal army at Camp Douglas because "we were all about to starve to death." After he enlisted in the Federal army he was "taken out to Fort Kerney, in Nebraska(,) and from there I was taken to Grand Island (Nebraska) to make hay for the Government and while there some of the Government horses was stolen and . . . (I was detailed with a corporal) to go . . . hunt for the horses; so we followed the horses for about 400 miles, and after we got there we decided to come home and we never went back to get our discharge."]

THOMAS, JOB, Private

Previously served as Private in Company C of this regiment. Transferred to this company on or about June 27, 1862. No further records. Survived the war.

THOMPSON, JOHN H., Private

Enlisted in Watauga County on June 27, 1862, for the war. Was apparently mustered in with the rank of Sergeant. Reported present in January-June, 1863, and September, 1863-April, 1864. Reduced to ranks on or about July 7, 1864. Reported present but under arrest on or about August 31, 1864. Reason he was arrested not reported. Transferred to Company A of this regiment when the 58th and 60th Regiments were consolidated on April 9, 1865.

TIPTUS, JOHN, ———

Enlisted in Watauga County on June 27, 1862, for the war. No further records.

TOWNSEND, JACOB, Private

Resided in Watauga County and was by occupation a farmer prior to enlisting in Watauga County at age 27, October 9, 1863, for the

war. Reported present through December 31, 1863. Reported sick in hospital on February 3, 1864. Returned to duty in March-April, 1864. Reported present through August 31, 1864. Captured (or deserted to the enemy) on an unspecified date. Took the Oath of Allegiance at Atlanta, Georgia, September 28, 1864.

TOWNSEND, JOEL, Private

Resided in Watauga County and was by occupation a "domestic" prior to enlisting in Watauga County at age 21, July 7, 1862, for the war. Reported present in January-June, 1863. Wounded at Chickamauga, Georgia, September 20, 1863. Reported absent wounded until November 20, 1863, when he was reported absent without leave. Listed as a deserter on March 15, 1864. Reported absent sick in May-August, 1864. Hospitalized at Charlotte on January 19, 1865, with intermittent fever. Captured in hospital at Charlotte and was paroled on or about May 4, 1865. Died in hospital at Charlotte on May 10, 1865. Cause of death not reported.

TOWNSEND, LARKIN, Private

Resided in Watauga County and was by occupation a farmer prior to enlisting in Watauga County at age 24, July 7, 1862, for the war. Reported present in January-June, 1863. Wounded at Chickamauga, Georgia, September 20, 1863. Returned to duty prior to October 31, 1863. Reported present through April 30, 1864. Wounded in the left arm at Resaca, Georgia, May 14-15, 1864. Returned to duty prior to September 1, 1864. Deserted to the enemy on an unspecified date. Took the Oath of Allegiance at Atlanta, Georgia, on or about September 27, 1864. Released at Louisville, Kentucky, on or about October 22, 1864.

TOWNSEND, LEVI D., Private

Resided in Watauga County and was by occupation a miller prior to enlisting in Watauga County at age 28, July 7, 1862, for the war. Reported present in January-June and September-October, 1863. Reported sick in hospital in November-December, 1863. Furloughed home from hospital for sixty days on December 22, 1863. Reported absent without leave on February 22, 1864. No further records. Survived the war.

TOWNSEND, MILES, Private

Resided in Watauga County and was by occupation a farmer prior to enlisting in Watauga County at age 25, July 7, 1862, for the war. Reported absent without leave in January-February, 1863. Returned to duty in March-April, 1863. Reported present in May-June, 1863. Wounded at Chickamauga, Georgia, September 20, 1863. Returned to duty prior to October 31, 1863. Detailed for duty as a hospital nurse at Cassville, Georgia, November 4, 1863. Returned to duty in January-February, 1864. Reported present in March-April, 1864. Wounded at Kolb's Farm, near Marietta, Georgia, June 22, 1864. Died at Atlanta, Georgia, July 8, 1864, of wounds.

TRIPLETT, WILLIAM, Private

Enlisted in Watauga County on June 27, 1862, for the war. Reported absent without leave in January-June and September-December, 1863. Dropped from the company rolls on or about February 29, 1864. [Was about 30 years of age at time of enlistment.]

TRIVETT, ELISHA, Private

Enlisted in Watauga County at age 27, July 7, 1862, for the war. Reported absent without leave in January-February, 1863. Returned to duty in March-April, 1863. Deserted on May 16, 1863.

TRIVETT, JOEL, Private

Born in Ashe County on November 16, 1840. Resided in Watauga County and was by occupation a farmer prior to enlisting in Watauga County at age 21, July 15, 1862, for the war. Reported present in January-February, 1863. Reported on detail as a teamster in March-June, 1863. Deserted on September 29, 1863. [Filed a Tennessee pension application after the war.]

TRIVETT, LAZARUS, Private

Previously served as Private in Company I of this regiment. Transferred to this company prior to March 1, 1863. Reported present in January-February, 1863. Reported present but on detail as a teamster or wagoner in March-June, 1863. Deserted on September 29, 1863.

TRIVETT, RILEY, Private

Resided in Watauga County where he enlisted on July 7, 1862, for the war. Reported present or accounted for in January-June, 1863. Reported absent without leave in September-December, 1863. Returned to duty in January-February, 1864. Reported present but under arrest on April 7, 1864. Reported sick in hospital on May 20, 1864. Deserted to the enemy on an unspecified date. Confined at Knoxville, Tennessee, June 7, 1864. Transferred to Chattanooga, Tennessee, where he took the Oath of Allegiance on or about June 11, 1864. Transferred to Louisville, Kentucky, where he was released on or about June 14, 1864.

TUCKER, ZEPHANIAH, Private

Previously served as Private in Company C of this regiment. Transferred to this company on or about June 27, 1862. No further records. [May have served also as Private in Company C, 5th Battalion N.C. Cavalry.]

VANOVER, CHARLES, Private

Born in Ashe County and was by occupation a farmer prior to enlisting in Watauga County at age 23, June 27, 1862, for the war. Transferred to Company I of this regiment on or about July 24, 1862.

WARD, DUKE B., Private

Resided in Watauga County and was by occupation a farmer prior to enlisting in Watauga County at age 19, July 7, 1862, for the war. Reported absent sick without leave in January-February, 1863. Deserted on March 1, 1863.

WARD, MICHAEL, Private

Resided in Watauga County and was by occupation a farmer prior to enlisting in Watauga County at age 25, June 27, 1862, for the war. Deserted on October 20, 1862. Returned to duty on June 19, 1863. Deserted on August 26, 1863. Returned from desertion on March 15, 1864. Court-martialed on April 4, 1864. Executed by a firing squad near Dalton, Georgia, May 4, 1864, for desertion.

WASHBURN, DANIEL M., 1st Sergeant

Previously served as Sergeant in Company A of this regiment. Transferred to this company when the 58th and 60th Regiments were consolidated on April 9, 1865. Promoted to 1st Sergeant on an unspecified date. Paroled at Greensboro on May 1, 1865.

WESLY, RYENTT, Sergeant

Reportedly enlisted in this company in Mitchell County on June 10, 1862, for the war; however, he is not listed on any company

rolls. Promotion record not reported. Paroled at Greensboro on May 1, 1865.

WHEELER, DANIEL, Private

Resided in Watauga County and was by occupation a farmer prior to enlisting in Watauga County at age 33, June 27, 1862, for the war. Reported absent sick without leave in January-February, 1863. Reported absent without leave in March-June and September-December, 1863. Dropped from the company rolls on or about February 29, 1864.

WILCOX, ALVIN, ———

North Carolina pension records indicate that he served in this company.

WILCOX, ISAIAH, ———

North Carolina pension records indicate that he served in this company.

WILSON, WILLIAM, Private

Previously served as Private in Company I of this regiment. Transferred to this company on or about August 3, 1862. Died on February 16, 1863. Place and cause of death not reported.

WISEMAN, ALEXANDER, Private

Previously served as Private in Company A of this regiment. Transferred to this company when the 58th and 60th Regiments were consolidated on April 9, 1865. Paroled at Greensboro on May 1, 1865.

YELTON, BARNETT C., Private

Resided in Watauga County and was by occupation a farmer prior to enlisting in Watauga County at age 18, June 27, 1862, for the war. Transferred to Company I of this regiment on or about July 24, 1862.

COMPANY E

This company was raised in Caldwell County on June 25, 1862, as Capt. John C. Keener's Company, N.C. Volunteers. It was placed under the authority of Lt. Col. John B. Palmer on or about the same date. Palmer, former commander of "Palmer's Legion," a mixed (cavalry and infantry) unit that had failed to complete its organization, was recruiting for a cavalry unit to be known as the 5th Battalion N.C. Partisan Rangers and also for a thus far undesignated infantry regiment. Keener's Company became Company E of the latter command when it was mustered in as the 58th Regiment N.C. Troops on July 29, 1862. After joining the 58th Regiment the company functioned as a part of that regiment, and its history for the remainder of the war is reported as a part of the regimental history.

The following roster was compiled primarily from information in the microfilm edition of the Compiled Service Records of Soldiers Who Served in Organizations from the State of North Carolina (Record Group 109, M270), National Archives and Records Administration, Washington, D.C. Record Group 109 includes enlistment papers, pay vouchers, requisitions, letters of resignation, discharge certificates, and abstracts of medical and prisoner of war returns. Materials relating specifically to this company include a muster-in and descriptive roll dated June 27, 1862; a muster-in and descriptive roll dated July 29, 1862; and muster rolls dated January-June, 1863, September-October, 1863, and January-August, 1864.

Also utilized in this roster were *The War of the Rebellion: A Compilation of the Official Records of the Union and Confederate Armies*, the North Carolina adjutant general's *Roll of Honor*, state militia records, newspaper casualty lists and obituaries, wartime claims for bounty pay and allowances, postwar registers of claims for artificial limbs, Confederate pension applications filed with the states of North Carolina, Tennessee, and Florida, Confederate Soldiers' Home records, and the 1860 and 1870 federal censuses of North Carolina. A search was made also for relevant letters, diaries, reminiscences, and other manuscripts in the Southern Historical Collection (University of North Carolina-Chapel Hill), the Duke University Library Special Collections Department, and the North Carolina Division of Archives and History.

Among the secondary sources consulted were records of the North Carolina division of the United Daughters of the Confederacy, postwar rosters, regimental and county histories, marriage bond, will, and cemetery indexes, published and unpublished genealogies, biographical dictionaries, the North Carolina *County Heritage Book* series, the *Confederate Veteran*, Walter Clark's *Histories of the Several Regiments and Battalions from North Carolina in the Great War, 1861-'65*, and the North Carolina volume of the extended edition of *Confederate Military History*.

OFFICERS

CAPTAINS

KEENER, JOHN C.

Born in Carter County, Tennessee, and resided in Yancey County where he was by occupation a farmer prior to enlisting at age 45. Elected Captain on June 25, 1862. Elected Major on July 29, 1862, and transferred to the Field and Staff of this regiment. Later served as Lieutenant Colonel of this regiment.

STEWART, ALFRED THEODORE

Previously served as 3rd Lieutenant of Company F, 26th Regiment N.C. Troops. Elected 1st Lieutenant of this company on June 25, 1862. Promoted to Captain on July 29, 1862. Reported present in January-June and September-October, 1863. Detailed for duty in the headquarters of the Army of Tennessee on December 18, 186[3]. Rejoined the company on or about March 8, 1864. Reported in command of the regiment on July 10, 1864. Appointed Major on or about August 31, 1864, and transferred to the Field and Staff.

HARPER, GEORGE WASHINGTON FINLEY

Served as Captain of Company H of this regiment. Reported in command of this company on January 30, 1864.

MARLER, JAMES B.

Born in Burke County and resided in Mitchell, Caldwell, or Watauga County where he was by occupation a farmer prior to enlisting in Caldwell County at age 31. Appointed 3rd Lieutenant on June 25, 1862. Promoted to 1st Lieutenant on July 29, 1862. Reported present or accounted for on surviving company muster rolls through April, 1864. Sent to hospital sick on June 9, 1864. Had not returned as of August 31, 1864. Promoted to Captain on August

31, 1864. Dropped from the company rolls on April 2, 1865, after being reported absent without leave for six months.

ALEXANDER, WILLIAM R.

Previously served as Captain of Company I, 60th Regiment N.C. Troops. Transferred to this company when the 58th and 60th Regiments were consolidated on April 9, 1865. Paroled at Greensboro on or about May 1, 1865.

LIEUTENANTS

CLAYTON, ROBERT M., 1st Lieutenant

Previously served as 1st Lieutenant of Company B, 60th Regiment N.C. Troops. Transferred to this company when the 58th and 60th Regiments were consolidated on April 9, 1865. Paroled at Greensboro on or about May 1, 1865.

COFFEY, THOMAS JEFFERSON, 1st Lieutenant

Born in Caldwell County* in December, 1828. Resided at Butler, Tennessee, and was by occupation a merchant prior to enlisting in Caldwell County at age 33, July 5, 1862, for the war. Mustered in as Private. Elected 2nd Lieutenant on July 29, 1862. Reported present or accounted for on surviving company muster rolls through August 31, 1864; however, he was absent on detached service as acting Assistant Quartermaster of the regiment during much of that period. Promoted to 1st Lieutenant on August 31, 1864. Hospitalized at Charlotte on March 14, 1865, with phthisis. Furloughed on the same date. Survived the war.

COFFEY, WILLIAM COLUMBUS, 2nd Lieutenant

Previously served as Corporal in Company F, 26th Regiment N.C. Troops. Transferred to this company on January 15, 1863. Mustered in as Private. Reported present through April, 1863. Detailed for duty as regimental Quartermaster Sergeant on August 20, 1863, and transferred to the Field and Staff. Transferred back to this company on June 1, 1864. Reported present through August 31, 1864. Appointed 2nd Lieutenant on October 22, 1864. Wounded slightly in the breast ("contusion shell") at Bentonville on March 19, 1865. Promoted to 1st Lieutenant of Company A of this regiment on an unspecified date.

COFFEY, WILLIAM E., 3rd Lieutenant

Born in Caldwell County* where he resided as a farmer prior to enlisting in Caldwell County at age 23, July 5, 1862, for the war. Mustered in as Private. Elected 3rd Lieutenant on July 29, 1862. Reported absent on detached service in January-February, 1863. Reported present in March-June, 1863. Reported at home on sick furlough in September-October, 1863. Returned to duty on an unspecified date. Reported present in January-February, 1864. Furloughed home for twenty days on April 18, 1864. Returned to duty on an unspecified date. Deserted to the enemy on the night of July 1, 1864. Took the Oath of Allegiance at Chattanooga, Tennessee, on or about July 16, 1864. Released at Louisville, Kentucky, on or about July 27, 1864. [May have served for a time as Brevet 2nd Lieutenant of this company.]

ESTES, DOCTOR W. T., Brevet 3rd Lieutenant

Previously served as Private in Company F, 26th Regiment N.C. Troops. Enlisted in this company in Caldwell County at age 17, June 25, 1862, for the war. Mustered in as 1st Sergeant. Reported present on surviving company muster rolls through August 31, 1864. Elected Brevet 3rd Lieutenant on July 11, 1864. No further records. [May have served for a time as Brevet 2nd Lieutenant of this company.]

LINDSEY, GEORGE WASHINGTON, 2nd Lieutenant

Previously served as Ensign (1st Lieutenant) of the 60th Regiment N.C. Troops. Transferred to this company when the 58th and 60th Regiments were consolidated on April 9, 1865. Mustered in with the rank of 2nd Lieutenant. Paroled at Greensboro on or about May 1, 1865.

SILVER, SAMUEL MARION, 2nd Lieutenant

Born in Yancey County on December 30, 1833. Resided in Mitchell County where he was by occupation a farmer prior to enlisting in Mitchell County at age 28. Elected 2nd Lieutenant on June 25, 1862. Elected Captain of Company K of this regiment on July 29, 1862.

NONCOMMISSIONED OFFICERS AND PRIVATES

ALEXANDER, BENJAMIN JULIUS, Private

Previously served as Quartermaster Sergeant of the 60th Regiment N.C. Troops. Transferred to this company when the 58th and 60th Regiments were consolidated on April 9, 1865. Mustered in as Private. Paroled at Greensboro on or about May 1, 1865.

ALEXANDER, RANDOLPH, Private

Resided in Wilkes County and was by occupation a farmer prior to enlisting in Wilkes County at age 36, December 25, 1863, for the war. Deserted near Dalton, Georgia, January 10, 1864.

ANDERSON, HOSEA PINKNEY, Corporal

Born in Caldwell County* on July 5, 1839, and was by occupation a farmer prior to enlisting in Caldwell County at age 23, July 5, 1862, for the war. Mustered in as Corporal. Reported present in January-June and September-October, 1863. Wounded in the left hand and disabled at Rocky Face Ridge, Georgia, February 25, 1864. Detailed for hospital duty at Macon, Georgia, August 15, 1864. No further records. Survived the war.

ANDERSON, JOHN MARCUS, Private

Enlisted at age 21 in the autumn of 1864 for the war. Wounded slightly in the knee at Bentonville on March 19, 1865. Survived the war.

AUSTIN, JACOB A., Private

Enlisted in Union County at age 25, December 24, 1863, for the war. Deserted near Dalton, Georgia, on or about January 20, 1864. Reported present but under arrest in March, 1864. Court-martialed on April 6, 1864. Shot at Dalton on May 4, 1864, for desertion.

BAIRD, JOSEPH C., Private

Born in Caldwell County* where he resided as a farmer prior to enlisting in Caldwell County at age 32, July 5, 1862, for the war. Reported present or accounted for in January-June, 1863. Reported absent without leave on August 26, 1863. Returned to duty on December 10, 1863. Reported present until May 15, 1864, when he

was captured at or near Resaca, Georgia. Sent to Nashville, Tennessee. Transferred to Louisville, Kentucky, where he arrived on May 19, 1864. Transferred to Camp Morton, Indianapolis, Indiana, where he arrived on May 22, 1864. Paroled at Camp Morton on March 4, 1865. Received at Boulware's and Cox's Wharves, James River, Virginia, March 10-12, 1865, for exchange. No further records. Survived the war.

BAIRD, JULIUS, Sergeant

Born in Caldwell County* where he resided as a farmer prior to enlisting in Caldwell County at age 21, July 25, 1862, for the war. Mustered in as Sergeant. Died prior to September 26, 1862, "with the fever and with cold." Place of death reported (probably erroneously) as Big Creek Gap, Tennessee.

BAIRD, WILLIAM J., Sergeant

Enlisted in Caldwell County on July 5, 1862, for the war. Promotion record not reported. Died prior to January 13, 1863. Place, date, and cause of death not reported.

BAKER, WILLIAM R., Private

Born in Caldwell County* where he resided as a farmer prior to enlisting in Caldwell County at age 33, July 5, 1862, for the war. Mustered in as Musician (Fifer). Reported present or accounted for in January-June, 1863. Reduced to ranks in July-October, 1863. Reported absent without leave in September-October, 1863. Died in hospital at Atlanta, Georgia, December 23, 1863, or February 6, 1864, of disease.

BARBER, THOMAS M., Private

Born in Caldwell County* where he resided as a farmer prior to enlisting in Mitchell or Caldwell County at age 22, June 25, 1862, for the war. Transferred to Company F, 26th Regiment N.C. Troops, October 1, 1862.

BARGER, SAMUEL, Private

Enlisted in Burke County on June 25, 1862, for the war. Reported present in January-February, 1863. Reported in hospital at Knoxville, Tennessee, in March-April, 1863. Reported sick in hospital in September-October, 1863. Reported absent on detached service from February 20 through August 31, 1864. No further records.

BARLOW, SMITH, Private

Born in Caldwell County and was by occupation a farmer prior to enlisting in Caldwell County at age 18, July 21, 1862, for the war. Reported absent on sick furlough in January-February, 1863. Returned to duty in March-April, 1863. Reported present in May-June, 1863. Reported absent without leave on October 25, 1863. Returned to duty on November 15, 1863. Reported present in January-April, 1864. Wounded in the left hand at Kolb's Farm, near Marietta, Georgia, June 22, 1864. Returned to duty prior to September 1, 1864. No further records. Survived the war.

BARNETT, THOMAS H., Private

Resided in Caldwell County where he enlisted at age 18, on or about April 4, 1864, for the war. Reported present through August 31, 1864. No further records. Survived the war.

BARRIER, SAMUEL, Private

Born in Burke County where he resided as a farmer prior to enlisting in Caldwell County at age 30, June 27, 1862, for the war.

Reported sick in hospital at Knoxville, Tennessee, in May-June, 1863. Reported sick in hospital at Rome, Georgia, in September-October, 1863. Detailed for extra duty on February 16, 1864. Reported on duty as a guard at the military prison at Atlanta, Georgia, in May-June, 1864. Hospitalized at Macon, Georgia, April 3, 1865, with ascites. Transferred on April 18, 1865. Paroled at Charlotte on May 12, 1865.

BARTLETT, SAMUEL D., Private

Previously served as Private in Company B of this regiment. Transferred to this company on or about June 27, 1862. Transferred to Company K of this regiment on or about July 29, 1862.

BELTON, PLEASANT H., Private

Resided in Rockingham County where he enlisted on December 21, 1863, for the war. Reported present in January-April, 1864. Reported on detail to guard and drive beef cattle from August 10 through August 31, 1864, and on November 15, 1864. Surrendered at Selma, Alabama, May 4, 1865.

BLAIR, JOHN CALDWELL, Corporal

Born in Caldwell County* where he resided as a farmer prior to enlisting in Caldwell County at age 22, July 5, 1862, for the war. Mustered in as Private. Reported present in January-June, 1863. Promoted to Corporal prior to March 1, 1863. Reported present in September-October, 1863. Appointed Drum Major on October 31, 1863, and transferred to the Field and Staff of this regiment.

BLANCHARD, T. C., Private

Reportedly enlisted in Buncombe County on May 16, 1862, for the war; however, he is not listed in any of the surviving records of this company. Paroled at Greensboro on or about May 1, 1865.

BOLICK, RUFUS, Private

Born in Caldwell County where he resided as a farmer prior to enlisting in Caldwell County at age 19, July 21, 1862, for the war. Reported present in January-June, 1863. Reported sick in hospital at Abingdon, Virginia, in September-October, 1863. No further records.

BRANCH, EPHRAIM, Private

Previously served as Private in Company F, 41st Regiment N.C. Troops (3rd Regiment N.C. Cavalry). Transferred to this company on February 19, 1864. Reported present in March-April, 1864. Reported sick in hospital on August 20, 1864. No further records. Survived the war.

BRAND, JOHN, Private

Enlisted in Forsyth County on November 1, 1863, for the war. Reported present in January-February, 1864. Reported under arrest charged with desertion in March-April, 1864. Returned to duty prior to June 22, 1864, when he was wounded and captured at Kolb's Farm, near Marietta, Georgia. Hospitalized at Knoxville, Tennessee, where he died on July 29, 1864 (presumably of wounds). [Federal hospital records dated July, 1864, give his age as 40.]

BRASWELL, THADDEUS, ——

Enlisted at age 27, June 27, 1862, for the war. No further records. Survived the war.

BRISTOW, SAMUEL, Private

Resided in Randolph County and was by occupation a farmer prior to enlisting in Randolph County at age 41, December 6, 1863, for the war. Reported absent sick through August 31, 1864. Hospitalized at West Point, Mississippi, January 10, 1865, with diarrhoea. Returned to duty on an unspecified date. Hospitalized at Meridian, Mississippi, February 3, 1865, with a wound. Place and date wounded not reported. No further records.

BROOKS, MARTIN, Private

Previously served as Private in Company B of this regiment. Transferred to this company on or about June 27, 1862. Last reported in the records of this company on July 23, 1862. No further records.

BUCHANAN, ABRAM J., Private

Previously served as Private in Company B of this regiment. Transferred to this company on or about June 27, 1862. Transferred to Company K of this regiment on or about July 29, 1862.

BUCHANAN, ELI, Private

Born in Burke County and resided in Mitchell or Yancey County where he was by occupation a farmer prior to enlisting in Mitchell County at age 38, June 25, 1862, for the war. Transferred to Company K of this regiment on or about July 29, 1862.

BUCHANAN, EPHRAIM, Private

Born in Yancey County and was by occupation a farmer prior to enlisting in Mitchell County at age 18, June 25, 1862, for the war. Transferred to Company K of this regiment on or about July 29, 1862.

BUCHANAN, JAMES C., Private

Previously served as Private in Company C of this regiment. Transferred to this company on or about June 27, 1862. Transferred back to Company C prior to March 1, 1863.

BUCHANAN, JAMES S., Private

Born in Yancey County and resided in Mitchell or Yancey County where he was by occupation a farmer prior to enlisting in Mitchell County at age 26, June 25, 1862, for the war. Transferred to Company K of this regiment on or about July 29, 1862.

BUCHANAN, JOEL, Private

Born in Yancey or Burke County and resided in Yancey County where he was by occupation a farmer prior to enlisting in Mitchell County at age 28, June 25, 1862, for the war. Transferred to Company K of this regiment on or about July 29, 1862.

BUCHANAN, JOHN B., Private

Born in Burke County and was by occupation a farmer prior to enlisting in Mitchell County at age 33, June 25, 1862, for the war. Transferred to Company K of this regiment on or about July 29, 1862.

BUCHANAN, JOSEPH M., Private

Previously served as Private in Company B of this regiment. Transferred to this company on or about June 27, 1862. Transferred to Company K of this regiment on or about July 29, 1862.

BUCHANAN, LEONARD M., Private

Previously served as Private in Company B of this regiment. Transferred to this company on or about June 27, 1862. Elected 2nd Lieutenant of Company K of this regiment on July 29, 1862.

BUCHANAN, MERRITT, Private

Born in Burke County and resided in Mitchell or Yancey County where he was by occupation a farmer prior to enlisting in Mitchell County at age 33, June 2, 1862, for the war. Transferred to Company K of this regiment on or about July 29, 1862.

BUCHANAN, MOLTON, Private

Previously served as Private in Company B of this regiment. Transferred to this company on or about June 27, 1862. Transferred to Company K of this regiment on or about July 29, 1862.

BUCHANAN, NEWTON, Private

Enlisted at Camp Jackson at age 18, May 17, 1862, for the war. Transferred to Company B of this regiment on an unspecified date (probably in the autumn of 1863).

BUCHANAN, ROBERT, Private

Born in Yancey County and was by occupation a farmer prior to enlisting in Mitchell County at age 27, June 28, 1862, for the war. Transferred to Company K of this regiment on or about July 29, 1862.

BUCHANAN, THOMAS, ———

Enlisted at Camp Martin (Mitchell County) on June 27, 1862, for the war. No further records.

BUCHANAN, WAIGHTSVILLE, Private

Previously served as Private in Company B of this regiment. Transferred to this company on or about June 27, 1862. Transferred to Company K of this regiment prior to January 11, 1863.

BUCHANAN, WILLIAM M., Private

Born in Yancey County* and was by occupation a farmer prior to enlisting in Mitchell County at age 29, May 19, 1862, for the war. Transferred to Company K of this regiment on or about July 29, 1862.

BUCHANAN, WILLIAM W., Private

Enlisted in Mitchell County on June 25, 1862, for the war. Transferred to Company K of this regiment prior to August 6, 1862.

BUCKNER, NIMROD, Private

Previously served as Private in Company A, 60th Regiment N.C. Troops. Transferred to this company when the 58th and 60th Regiments were consolidated on April 9, 1865. Paroled at Greensboro on or about May 1, 1865.

BURLESON, JASON C., Private

Born in Yancey County where he resided as a farmer prior to enlisting in Mitchell County at age 26, June 25, 1862, for the war. Transferred to Company K of this regiment on or about July 29, 1862.

BYRD, CARSON, Private

Previously served as Private in Company B of this regiment. Transferred to this company on or about June 27, 1862. Transferred back to Company B prior to March 1, 1863.

CAMERON, GEORGE, Private

Enlisted in Burke County on October 21, 1863, for the war. Died at Marietta, Georgia, January 10, 1864, of disease.

CARRELL, WILLIAM G., Corporal

Born in Caldwell County and was by occupation a farmer prior to enlisting in Caldwell County at age 19, July 5, 1862, for the war. Mustered in as Private. Reported present in January-June, 1863. Promoted to Corporal prior to March 1, 1863. Wounded in the face at Chickamauga, Georgia, September 20, 1863. Reported absent wounded through October 31, 1863. Returned to duty prior to March 1, 1864. Reported present through August 31, 1864. No further records. Survived the war.

CARROLL, JAMES M., Private

Previously served as Private in Company F, 26th Regiment N.C. Troops. Enlisted in this company at Camp Martin (Mitchell County) on June 25, 1862, for the war. Was apparently rejected for service. No further records.

CARROLL, JOHN P., Private

Born in Burke County and was by occupation a farmer prior to enlisting in Caldwell County at age 28, July 5, 1862, for the war. Reported present in January-June, 1863. Reported sick in hospital at Atlanta, Georgia, or at Kingston, Georgia, in September-October, 1863. Returned to duty prior to March 1, 1864. Reported present in March-April, 1864. Killed accidentally near Atlanta on August 9, 1864, by the explosion of a shell.

CHEBBS, JOSEPH R., Private

Enlisted in Caldwell County on July 5, 1862, for the war. No further records.

CLARK, CORNELIUS WASHINGTON, Private

Born in Caldwell County* and was by occupation a farmer prior to enlisting in Caldwell County at age 24, July 5, 1862, for the war. Reported present in January-June, 1863. Reported absent without leave on September 25, 1863. Returned to duty on December 10, 1863. Reported present through August 31, 1864. No further records. Survived the war.

CLARK, DEASTON C., Private

Previously served as Private in Company A of this regiment. Transferred to this company on or about July 29, 1862. Transferred to Company K of this regiment on or about the same date.

CLARK, DORAN F., Private

Previously served as Private in Company B, 5th Battalion N.C. Cavalry. Transferred to this company on or about July 29, 1862. Transferred to Company K of this regiment on or about the same date.

CLARKE, THOMAS A., Private

Born in Caldwell County where he enlisted at age 19, June 25, 1862, for the war. Reported present in January-June, 1863. Reported absent without leave on September 23, 1863. Returned to duty on December 10, 1863. Reported present through August 31, 1864. No further records. Survived the war.

COCHE, JOHN W., Private

Previously served as Private in Company A, 60th Regiment N.C. Troops. Transferred to this company when the 58th and 60th

Regiments were consolidated on April 9, 1865. Paroled at Greensboro on or about May 1, 1865.

COFFEY, BARTLETT, Private

Born in Caldwell County where he resided as a farmer prior to enlisting in Caldwell County at age 20, July 5, 1862, for the war. Reported present in January-June, 1863. Reported absent on detail as a cooper at Loudon, Tennessee, in September-October, 1863. Returned to duty on an unspecified date. Reported present in January-August, 1864. No further records. Survived the war. [North Carolina pension records indicate that he received a wound "of serious nature" on an unspecified date.]

COFFEY, CHARLES L., Private

Born in Caldwell County* where he resided as a farmer prior to enlisting in Caldwell County at age 32, July 5, 1862, for the war. No further records. Survived the war. [May have served later as Private in Company D, 9th Regiment N.C. State Troops (1st Regiment N.C. Cavalry).]

COFFEY, DRURY D., Sergeant

Born in Caldwell County* where he resided as a farmer prior to enlisting in Caldwell County at age 23, July 5, 1862, for the war. Mustered in as Private. Reported present in January-June, 1863. Promoted to Sergeant in July-September, 1863. Wounded in the hand at Chickamauga, Georgia, September 20, 1863. Reported absent wounded through October 31, 1863. Returned to duty on an unspecified date. Reported present in January-February, 1864. Wounded slightly at Rocky Face Ridge, Georgia, February 25, 1864. Appointed Sergeant Major on the same date and transferred to the Field and Staff of this regiment.

COFFEY, EDMOND, Private

Enlisted in Caldwell County on February 18, 1864, for the war. Reported present through April, 1864. Wounded in the hand at Resaca, Georgia, May 14-15, 1864. Returned to duty prior to September 1, 1864. No further records.

COFFEY, ELBERT, Private

Born in Caldwell County* and was by occupation a farmer prior to enlisting in Caldwell County at age 25, July 5, 1862, for the war. Reported present in January-April, 1863. Died at Big Creek Gap, Tennessee, May 15, 1863, of disease.

COFFEY, ELIJAH, Private

Born in Caldwell County* where he resided as a farmer prior to enlisting in Caldwell County at age 23, July 5, 1862, for the war. Reported present in January-June, 1863. Reported on duty as a cooper at Loudon, Tennessee, in September-October, 1863. Reported present in January-April, 1864. Wounded in the left hand ("loosing [sic] one finger") at Resaca, Georgia, May 14-15, 1864. Returned to duty prior to September 1, 1864. No further records. Survived the war. [Previously served as 2nd Lieutenant in the 95th Regiment N.C. Militia. North Carolina pension records indicate that he was wounded in the right hip at Chickamauga, Georgia, September 19-20, 1863.]

COFFEY, HARVEY N., ———

Previously served as Sergeant in Company F, 26th Regiment N.C. Troops. Enlisted in this company at Camp Martin (Mitchell County) on June 27, 1862, for the war. No further records.

COFFEY, ISRAEL B., Private

Enlisted in Caldwell County at age 16, June 4, 1863, for the war. Reported present in September-October, 1863. Furloughed for forty days on March 25, 1864. Returned to duty on an unspecified date. Hospitalized at Macon, Georgia, May 23, 1864, with an unspecified wound ("cuts"). Returned to duty on May 29, 1864. Reported present through August 31, 1864. No further records. Survived the war.

COFFEY, J. B., Private

North Carolina pension records indicate that he served in this company.

COFFEY, J. H., Private

Place and date of enlistment not reported. Discharged on or about July 29, 1862. Reason discharged not reported.

COFFEY, J. P., ———

North Carolina pension records indicate that he served in this company.

COFFEY, JESSE F., Private

Born in Caldwell County where he resided as a farmer prior to enlisting in Caldwell County at age 20, July 25, 1862, for the war. Reported present in January-February, 1863. Died at Big Creek Gap, Tennessee, March 7, 1863. Cause of death not reported.

COFFEY, JOHN, Private

Born in Caldwell County and was by occupation a farmer prior to enlisting in Caldwell County at age 20, July 5, 1862, for the war. Discharged on or about July 29, 1862. Reason discharged not reported.

COFFEY, JOHN BUNYON, Private

Born in Caldwell County in 1839. Enlisted in Caldwell County on July 5, 1862, for the war. Reported present on surviving company muster rolls from January 1, 1863, through February 29, 1864. Furloughed for forty days on or about March 19, 1864. Hospitalized on August 28, 1864. Reported in hospital at Greensboro in March, 1865. Survived the war. [His Tennessee pension application states that "his hands were frozen" at Cumberland Gap, Tennessee, and he was wounded "slightly in the face twice and once in the ear by spent balls" at Missionary Ridge, Tennessee, and Atlanta, Georgia.]

COFFEY, LARKIN, Private

Born in Caldwell County* where he resided as a farmer prior to enlisting in Caldwell County at age 28, July 5, 1862, for the war. Died at Cumberland Gap, Tennessee, on an unspecified date (presumably in the autumn of 1862). Cause of death not reported.

COFFEY, PATTERSON VANCE, Private

Resided in Caldwell County and was by occupation a farmer prior to enlisting in Caldwell County at age 18, February 6, 1864, for the war. Reported present through August 31, 1864. No further records. Survived the war.

COFFEY, SHUFORD, Private

Born in Caldwell County* and was by occupation a farmer prior to enlisting in Caldwell County at age 25, July 21, 1862, for the war. No further records.

COFFEY, SILAS C., 1st Sergeant

Born in Caldwell County* where he resided as a farmer prior to enlisting in Caldwell County at age 27, July 5, 1862, for the war. Mustered in as Private. Reported present in January-June and September-October, 1863. Reported on duty as a teamster from January 1 through July 1, 1864. Promoted to 1st Sergeant on July 4, 1864. Reported present in July-August, 1864. No further records. Survived the war.

COFFEY, WILLIAM C., Private

Born in Caldwell County* where he resided as a farmer prior to enlisting in Caldwell County at age 24, July 5, 1862, for the war. Reported present or accounted for on surviving company muster rolls through August 31, 1864. Hospitalized at West Point, Mississippi, January 10, 1865, with pneumonia. Returned to duty prior to March 19, 1865, when he was wounded in the "left finger & right thumb" at Bentonville. Survived the war. [North Carolina pension records indicate that he was wounded severely in the right side at Chickamauga, Georgia, September 19-20, 1863, "by a piece of a bomb shell."]

COGDILL, FIDELLA P., Private

Previously served as Private in Company B, 60th Regiment N.C. Troops. Transferred to this company when the 58th and 60th Regiments were consolidated on April 9, 1865. Paroled at Greensboro on or about May 1, 1865.

COLLETT, ORLANDO C., Sergeant

Previously served as Sergeant in Company F, 26th Regiment N.C. Troops. Transferred to this company in November, 1862-February, 1863. Mustered in as Private. Reported present in January-June, 1863. Wounded at Chickamauga, Georgia, September 20, 1863. Returned to duty prior to October 31, 1863. Promoted to Sergeant in November, 1863-February, 1864. Reported present in January-February, 1864. Furloughed for forty days on April 18, 1864. Returned to duty on an unspecified date. Reported present through August 31, 1864. Transferred to Company A of this regiment on an unspecified date.

COOK, A., Private

Place and date of enlistment not reported. Paroled at Greensboro on May 12, 1865.

COOK, WILLIAM, Private

Enlisted on November 1, 1863, for the war. Deserted near Chattanooga, Tennessee, prior to February 29, 1864. Returned to duty on an unspecified date (probably subsequent to August 31, 1864). Paroled at Greensboro on or about May 1, 1865.

CRISP, JOEL, Private

Resided in Caldwell County and was by occupation a farmer prior to enlisting at Camp Martin (Mitchell County) at age 22, June 27, 1862, for the war. No further records.

CRISP, JOHN, ———

Resided in Caldwell County and was by occupation a farmer prior to enlisting at Camp Martin (Mitchell County) at age 31, June 27, 1862, for the war. No further records. Survived the war.

CURLEE, JOHN W., Private

Resided in Union County and was by occupation a farmer prior to enlisting in Union County at age 37, December 24, 1863, for the

war. Deserted near Dalton, Georgia, on or about January 25, 1864. Apparently returned to duty on an unspecified date (probably subsequent to August 31, 1864). Furloughed on an unspecified date suffering from chronic rheumatism. Recommended for an extension of furlough on March 28, 1865.

CURTIS, WILLIAM, Private

Born in Caldwell County* where he resided as a farmer prior to enlisting in Caldwell County at age 33, July 21, 1862, for the war. Transferred to Company F, 26th Regiment N.C. Troops, in November-December, 1862.

CURTIS, WILLIAM WALTER, Private

Born in Caldwell County* on November 10, 1833. Resided in Caldwell County and was by occupation a farmer prior to enlisting in Caldwell County at age 28, July 5, 1862, for the war. Reported absent on sick furlough in January-February and September, 1863. Deserted near Chattanooga, Tennessee, October 1, 1863.

DANCY, SAMUEL, Private

Enlisted on July 7, 1862, for the war; however, his name was canceled. Later served as Private in Company A of this regiment.

DAVIDSON, WILLIAM F., Private

Previously served as Private in Company C, 60th Regiment N.C. Troops. Transferred to this company when the 58th and 60th Regiments were consolidated on April 9, 1865. Paroled at Greensboro on or about May 1, 1865.

DAVIS, JOSEPH L., Private

Enlisted in Caldwell County on July 5, 1862, for the war. Reported absent on expired furlough in January-February, 1863. Returned to duty in March-April, 1863. Reported present in May-June, 1863. Reported sick in hospital in September-October, 1863. Died at Dalton, Georgia, November 6, 1863, of disease.

DAVIS, JOSIAH, Private

Born in Burke County and was by occupation a farmer prior to enlisting in Mitchell County at age 33, June 25, 1862, for the war. Transferred to Company K of this regiment on or about July 29, 1862.

DAVIS, NICHOLAS, Private

Enlisted in Surry County on December 25, 1863, for the war. Reported present in January-April, 1864. Reported absent without leave on August 26, 1864.

DENNEY, SAMUEL, Private

Born in McDowell or Burke County and was by occupation a farmer prior to enlisting in Mitchell County at age 16, July 5, 1862, for the war. Transferred to Company K of this regiment on or about July 29, 1862.

DICKSON, JOSEPH HARVEY, Private

Enlisted in this company on or about July 29, 1862, for the war. "Name canceled." No further records. Survived the war.

DUNCAN, JONATHAN A. W., Private

Born in Yancey County* and resided in Mitchell County where he was by occupation a farmer prior to enlisting in Mitchell County at age 31, June 25, 1862, for the war. Elected 3rd Lieutenant of Company K of this regiment on July 29, 1862, and transferred.

DUNCAN, PHILIP H., Private

Born in Yancey County and was by occupation a farmer prior to enlisting in Mitchell County at age 24, June 25, 1862, for the war. Transferred to Company K of this regiment on or about July 29, 1862.

EDMISTEN, ABRAM SHUFORD, Private

Born in Caldwell County where he resided as a farmer prior to enlisting in Caldwell County at age 18, June 25, 1862, for the war. Reported present in January-June and September-October, 1863. Detailed as Commissary Sergeant and transferred to the Field and Staff of this regiment on November 1, 1863. Transferred back to this company on August 1, 1864. Reported present through August 31, 1864. No further records. Survived the war.

EDMISTEN, ALEXANDER HENDERSON, Sergeant

Born in Lincoln County where he resided as a farmer prior to enlisting in Caldwell County at age 26, June 25, 1862, for the war. Mustered in as Sergeant. Reported present in January-June, 1863. Reported sick in hospital in September-October, 1863. Returned to duty on an unspecified date. Reported present in January-April, 1864. Captured near the Chattahoochee River, Georgia, July 16, 1864. Sent to Nashville, Tennessee. Transferred to Louisville, Kentucky, where he arrived on August 5, 1864. Transferred to Camp Chase, Ohio, where he arrived on August 6, 1864. Reported in hospital at Camp Chase on October 4, 1864, with anasarca. Paroled at Camp Chase on or about March 4, 1865, and transferred to City Point, Virginia. Received at Boulware's and Cox's Wharves, James River, Virginia, March 10-12, 1865, for exchange. [May have served previously as Private in Company H of this regiment.]

EDMISTEN, JAMES M., Private

Resided in Caldwell County and was by occupation a farmer prior to enlisting in Caldwell County at age 37, March 2, 1863, for the war. Reported present or accounted for through August 31, 1864. No further records.

EDMISTEN, JOHN, Private

Resided in Caldwell County and was by occupation a farmer prior to enlisting in Caldwell County at age 35, March 2, 1863, for the war. Reported present through June 30, 1863. Reported on duty as a teamster from September 26, 1863, through February 29, 1864. Reported present in March-April, 1864. Reported present but sick in May-August, 1864. No further records.

EDMISTEN, MILAS, Private

Born in Caldwell County* where he resided as a farmer prior to enlisting in Caldwell County at age 30, July 5, 1862, for the war. Reported present in January-June, 1863. Reported absent on sick furlough in September-October, 1863. Reported present in January-February, 1864. Sent to hospital sick on May 17, 1864. Reported absent sick through August 31, 1864. No further records.

EDMISTEN, WILLIAM H., Private

Resided in Caldwell County and was by occupation a farmer prior to enlisting in Caldwell County at age 41. Enlistment date reported as October 5, 1862; however, he is not listed on company muster rolls dated January-June, 1863. Wounded at Chickamauga, Georgia, September 20, 1863. Reported absent wounded through August 31, 1864. Hospitalized at Charlotte on December 16, 1864, with a gunshot wound (fracture) of the right arm. Place and date wounded not reported (he was probably still suffering from the wound he received at Chickamauga). Furloughed on December 27, 1864. No further records.

EDMISTEN, WILLIAM HARRISON, Private

Born on January 30, 1823. Resided in Caldwell County and was by occupation a farmer prior to enlisting at age 39, October 8, 1862, for the war. Reported absent sick on expired furlough in January-February, 1863. Returned to duty in March-April, 1863. Reported present in May-June, 1863. Reported absent on wounded furlough in September-October, 1863. Place and date wounded not reported (probably wounded at Chickamauga, Georgia, September 19-20, 1863). Reported absent on sick furlough in January-February, 1864. No further records. Survived the war.

EDWARDS, ALEX, Private

Enlisted in Surry County on December 29, 1863, for the war. Reported present in January-April, 1864. Detailed to guard and drive cattle on August 10, 1864. Reported absent on detail through November 15, 1864. Transferred to Company H of this regiment on an unspecified date.

ELKINS, WILLIAM, Private

Resided in Burke County and was occupation a laborer prior to enlisting in Burke County at age 24, December 12, 1863, for the war. Deserted near Dalton, Georgia, January 7, 1864.

ENSLEY, ALFRED, Private

Previously served as Private in Company A, 60th Regiment N.C. Troops. Transferred to this company when the 58th and 60th Regiments were consolidated on April 9, 1865. Paroled at Greensboro on or about May 1, 1865.

ESTES, AMOS, Private

Born in Burke County and was by occupation a farmer prior to enlisting in Caldwell County at age 19, July 5, 1862, for the war. Name canceled. [May have enlisted previously in Company B, 37th Regiment N.C. Troops. May have served later in Company D, 9th Regiment N.C. State Troops (1st Regiment N.C. Cavalry).]

ESTES, GENERAL CORRELL, Private

Born in Caldwell County where he enlisted at age 19, July 5, 1862, for the war. Reported present in January-February, 1863. Died on March 29, 1863. Place and cause of death not reported.

ESTES, HENDERSON D., Private

Born in Caldwell County* where he resided as a farmer prior to enlisting in Caldwell County at age 24, July 5, 1862, for the war. Mustered in as Musician (Drummer). Reported present in January-February, 1863. Appointed Drum Major prior to March 1, 1863. Transferred to the Field and Staff of this regiment prior to May 1, 1863. Reduced to ranks and transferred back to this company on June 20, 1863. Reported absent without leave in September-October, 1863. Died at Cassville, Georgia, February 4, 1864. Cause of death not reported.

ESTES, JAMES MONROE, Private

Enlisted in Caldwell County at age 33, July 5, 1862, for the war. No further records. Survived the war.

ESTES, JOHN H., Private

Born in Caldwell County where he enlisted at age 19, July 5, 1862, for the war. Reported present in January-June and September-

October, 1863. Reported absent on duty as a teamster in January-February, 1864. Reported present in March-April, 1864. Killed at Kolb's Farm, near Marietta, Georgia, June 22, 1864.

ESTES, JOHN JACKSON, Private

Previously served as Private in Company F, 26th Regiment N.C. Troops. Transferred to this company on October 1, 1862. Mustered in with an unspecified rank. Reported present in January-June, 1863, and rank given as Sergeant. Reported absent sick on August 26, 1863. Reduced to ranks on an unspecified date. Returned to duty on December 10, 1863. Died at Kingston, Georgia, on or about March 11, 1864. Cause of death not reported. [Contrary to 7:539 of this series, Jackson was probably his middle name rather than his first name.]

ESTES, LANCE F., Private

Born in Caldwell County* and was by occupation a farmer prior to enlisting in Caldwell County at age 25, July 5, 1862, for the war. Discharged on or about July 29, 1862. Reason discharged not reported.

ESTES, LANGSTON LORENZO, Private

Born in Caldwell County on March 14, 1844. Enlisted in Caldwell County at age 18, July 5, 1862, for the war. Reported present in January-June, 1863. Deserted at Campbell Station, Tennessee, August 26, 1863.

ESTES, WILLIAM, Private

Previously served as Private in Company F, 26th Regiment N.C. Troops. Transferred to this company in November, 1863-February, 1864. Furloughed for forty days on April 19, 1864. Had not returned to duty as of August 31, 1864. No further records.

FEBRUARY, MORDECAI, Private

Previously served as Private in Company B of this regiment. Transferred to this company on or about June 27, 1862. Transferred back to Company B prior to March 1, 1863.

FLEMMING, WILLIAM J. B., Private

Previously served as Private in Company B, 60th Regiment N.C. Troops. Transferred to this company when the 58th and 60th Regiments were consolidated on April 9, 1865. Paroled at Greensboro on or about May 1, 1865.

FOX, ALEXANDER, Private

Born in Watauga County* and was by occupation a farmer prior to enlisting in Caldwell County at age 17, July 7, 1862, for the war. No further records.

FRANCOM, SOLOMON, Private

Born in Caldwell County* and was by occupation a farmer prior to enlisting in Caldwell County at age 25, July 21, 1862, for the war. Died "with the fever and with cold" prior to September 26, 1862. Place of death not reported.

FRANCUM, WILLIAM, Private

Born in Caldwell County* where he resided as a farmer prior to enlisting in Caldwell County at age 26, July 21, 1862, for the war. Deserted at Big Creek Gap, Tennessee, February 7, 1863. Returned to duty in March-April, 1863. Reported present in May-June and September-October, 1863. Detailed for duty as a pioneer on November 23, 1863. Furloughed for twenty days on April 19, 1864.

Captured at Bald Hill, near Atlanta, Georgia, July 21-22, 1864. Sent to Nashville, Tennessee. Transferred to Louisville, Kentucky, where he arrived on August 5, 1864. Transferred to Camp Chase, Ohio, where he arrived on August 6, 1864. Died at Camp Chase on November 27, 1864, of "typhoid fever."

FREEMAN, LITTLETON, Private

Previously served as Private in Company B of this regiment. Transferred to this company on or about June 27, 1862. Transferred to Company K of this regiment on or about July 29, 1862.

FREEMAN, SAMUEL, Private

Previously served as Private in Company B of this regiment. Transferred to this company on or about June 27, 1862. Transferred to Company K of this regiment on or about July 29, 1862.

GARLAND, ELISHA M., ———

Born in Yancey County and was by occupation a farmer prior to enlisting at Camp Martin (Mitchell County) on June 27, 1862, for the war. No further records. Later served as Corporal in Company B, 13th Regiment Tennessee Cavalry (Union). Was 18 years of age when he enlisted in the 13th Tennessee Cavalry.

GERMAN, LARKIN, Private

Born in Watauga County* and was by occupation a farmer prior to enlisting in Caldwell County at age 22, July 5, 1862, for the war. Reported present in January-June, 1863. Wounded at Chickamauga, Georgia, September 19-20, 1863. Died on October 1, 1863, of wounds. Place of death not reported.

GERMAN, WILLIAM, Private

Born in Watauga County* and was by occupation a farmer prior to enlisting in Caldwell County at age 23, July 5, 1862, for the war. Reported present in January-June, 1863. Wounded at Chickamauga, Georgia, September 19-20, 1863. Hospitalized at Kingston, Georgia, where he died on or about October 23, 1863, of wounds and/or disease.

GOFORTH, J., ———

Place and date of enlistment not reported (probably enlisted subsequent to August 31, 1864). Listed as a deserter on September 10, 1864.

GOPLIN, GEORGE J., Private

Enlisted in Caldwell County on August 24, 1863, for the war. Reported present in January-April, 1864. Captured at Cassville, Georgia, May 20, 1864. No further records.

GORENFLO, J. F., 1st Sergeant

Previously served as 1st Sergeant of Company B, 60th Regiment N.C. Troops. Transferred to this company when the 58th and 60th Regiments were consolidated on April 9, 1865. Paroled at Greensboro on or about May 1, 1865.

GOUGE, WILLIAM, Private

Born in Yancey* or Burke County and was by occupation a farmer prior to enlisting in Mitchell County at age 34, July 7, 1862, for the war. Transferred to Company K of this regiment on or about July 29, 1862.

GOURLEY, JOHN, Private

Resided at "Kalama" and enlisted in Guilford County on December 29, 1863, for the war. Reported present but on extra duty as a pioneer in January-February, 1864. Reported present in March-April, 1864. Captured at Cassville, Georgia, May 20, 1864. Sent to Nashville, Tennessee. Transferred to Louisville, Kentucky, where he arrived on May 29, 1864. Transferred to Rock Island, Illinois, where he arrived on June 1, 1864. Released at Rock Island on October 11, 1864, after taking the Oath of Allegiance. [Records of the Federal Provost Marshal dated October, 1864, give his age as 45.]

GRAGG, DANIEL, Private

Resided in Caldwell County and was by occupation a farmer prior to enlisting in Caldwell County at age 24, August 19, 1862, for the war. Reported present in January-June, 1863. Captured at Chickamauga, Georgia, September 20, 1863. Sent to Nashville, Tennessee. Transferred to Louisville, Kentucky, where he arrived on September 30, 1863. Transferred to Camp Douglas, Chicago, Illinois, where he arrived on October 4, 1863. Died at Camp Douglas on or about September 18, 1864, of "typhoid fever."

GRAGG, JAMES OSMOND, Private

Resided in Caldwell County and was by occupation a farmer prior to enlisting in Watauga County at age 29, August 29, 1862, for the war. Transferred to Company F, 26th Regiment N.C. Troops, February 1, 1863.

GREEN, ARCHIBALD B., Private

Born in Caldwell County* where he resided as a farmer prior to enlisting in Caldwell County at age 28, July 5, 1862, for the war. Reported absent on expired furlough in January-February, 1863. Returned to duty in March-April, 1863. Reported present in May-June, 1863. Reported sick in hospital in September-October, 1863. Reported present in January-April, 1864. Wounded at Kolb's Farm, near Marietta, Georgia, June 22, 1864. Returned to duty prior to September 1, 1864. No further records.

GREEN, AUGUSTUS F., Private

Previously served as Private in Company D of this regiment. Transferred to this company on or about July 29, 1862. Reported present in January-June, 1863. Deserted near Chattanooga, Tennessee, September 20, 1863. Returned to duty on February 22, 1864. Reported absent on sick furlough of sixty days from May 7 through August 31, 1864. Returned to duty on an unspecified date. Killed at Bentonville on March 19, 1865.

GREEN, BENJAMIN, Private

Born in Watauga County* and was by occupation a farmer prior to enlisting in Caldwell or Watauga County at age 18, June 25, 1862, for the war. Reported present in January-June, 1863. Reported on detail as a smith in September-October, 1863. Reported on detail as a teamster from November 20, 1863, through February 29, 1864. Reported present in May-August, 1864. No further records.

GREEN, EDMUND, Private

Previously served as Private in Company D of this regiment. Transferred to this company on or about July 29, 1862. Reported present in January-February, 1863. Sent to hospital on an unspecified date. Deserted at Big Creek Gap, Tennessee, August 26, 186[3].

GREEN, JONATHAN, Private

Previously served as Private in Company D of this regiment. Transferred to this company prior to March 1, 1863. Died at Greeneville, Tennessee, March 18, 1863. Cause of death not reported.

GREEN, JOSEPH H., Private

Born in Caldwell County and was by occupation a farmer prior to enlisting in Caldwell County at age 19, July 21, 1862, for the war. Died at Cumberland Gap, Tennessee, September 24, 1862, of "injuries caused by the explosion of a keg of powder. . . ."

GREEN, LARKIN, Private

Previously served as Private in Company D of this regiment. Transferred to this company on or about July 29, 1862. Died at Cumberland Gap, Tennessee, or Big Creek Gap, Tennessee, on or about November 18, 1862. Cause of death not reported.

GREEN, SMITH F., Private

Enlisted in Caldwell County on June 13, 1863, for the war. Reported present in June and September-October, 1863. Died in hospital at Salisbury on or about November 24, 1863, of "diarrhoea chron[ica]."

GREEN, WILEY, Private

Enlisted in Watauga County on October 10, 1862, for the war. Reported present in January-June, 1863. Reported absent without leave in September-October, 1863. Died at Asheville on November 13, 1863, of disease.

GRIFFIS, W. H., Private

Enlisted in Guilford County on December 25, 1863, for the war. Deserted near Dalton, Georgia, January 10, 1864.

GRINDSTAFF, JAKE, ———

Enlisted at Camp Martin (Mitchell County) on June 27, 1862, for the war. No further records.

GRINDSTAFF, JOBE, Private

Resided in Yancey County and was by occupation a farmer prior to enlisting in Mitchell County at age 26, June 25, 1862, for the war. Transferred to Company K of this regiment on or about July 29, 1862.

GRINDSTAFF, JOHN, Private

Born in Yancey County where he resided as a farmer prior to enlisting in Mitchell County at age 18, June 25, 1862, for the war. Transferred to Company K of this regiment on or about July 29, 1862.

HALIFIELD, ALFRED, Private

Enlisted at Camp Martin (Mitchell County) on June 27, 1862, for the war. No further records.

HAMANSAR, JACKSON, ———

Enlisted at Camp Martin (Mitchell County) on June 27, 1862, for the war. No further records.

HAREMON, CRISP, Private

Enlisted in Person County on December 24, 1863, for the war. Deserted near Dalton, Georgia, January 7, 1864.

HARREL, CLATON C., ———

Enlisted at Camp Martin (Mitchell County) on June 27, 1862, for the war. No further records.

HARRILL, D. L., Private

Enlisted in Surry County on December 24, 1863, for the war. Deserted near Dalton, Georgia, January 7, 1864.

HARRIS, JOHN P., Private

Enlisted on or about July 29, 1862; however, he was discharged on or about the same date. Reason discharged not reported. [Was about 18 years of age at time of enlistment.]

HARRISON, B. CALVIN, Private

Born in Caldwell County and was by occupation a farmer prior to enlisting in Caldwell County at age 19, March 2, 1863, for the war. Reported present through June 30, 1863. Reported sick in hospital in September-October, 1863. Returned to duty on an unspecified date. Reported sick in hospital on February 18, 1864. Returned to duty subsequent to April 30, 1864. Reported present in May-August, 1864. Captured at Orangeburg, South Carolina, February 12, 1865. Sent to New Bern. Transferred to Hart's Island, New York Harbor, where he arrived on April 10, 1865. Released at Hart's Island on June 18, 1865, after taking the Oath of Allegiance. [North Carolina pension records indicate that he was wounded in the right hip by a shell fragment near Atlanta, Georgia, August 31, 1864.]

HARTLEY, JOSEPH H., Private

Born in Caldwell County* where he resided as a farmer prior to enlisting in Caldwell County at age 33, July 21, 1862, for the war. Reported present in January-June, 1863. Wounded at Chickamauga, Georgia, September 20, 1863. Returned to duty prior to October 31, 1863. Reported present in January-August, 1864. No further records. Survived the war.

HARTLEY, NATHAN, Private

Resided in Caldwell County and was by occupation a farmer prior to enlisting at "Alexander" at age 28, July 5, 1862, for the war. Died at Big Creek Gap, Tennessee, on an unspecified date (probably in the autumn of 1862). Cause of death not reported.

HASS, JOHN, Private

Enlisted in Caldwell County on November 7, 1862, for the war. Reported present in January-June, 1863. Captured at Cumberland Gap, Tennessee, September 9, 1863. Sent to Louisville, Kentucky. Transferred to Camp Douglas, Chicago, Illinois, September 23, 1863. Arrived at Camp Douglas on September 26, 1863. Died at Camp Douglas on May 14, 1865, of "chr[onic] diarrhoea."

HAWKINS, JESSE D., Private

Born in Caldwell County* on August 1, 1831. Resided in Caldwell County and was by occupation a farmer prior to enlisting in Caldwell County at age 30, July 5, 1862, for the war. Reported present in January-June and September-October, 1863. Captured at Missionary Ridge, Tennessee, November 25, 1863. Sent to Nashville, Tennessee. Transferred to Louisville, Kentucky, where he arrived on January 8, 1864. Transferred to Rock Island, Illinois, where he arrived on January 20, 1864. Released at Rock Island on October 18, 1864, after joining the U.S. Army. Assigned to Company G, 3rd Regiment U.S. Volunteer Infantry.

HAYES, JEFFERSON M., Private

Born in Caldwell County* and was by occupation a farmer prior to enlisting in Caldwell County at age 24, July 5, 1862, for the war.

Died on an unspecified date (probably in the autumn of 1862). Place and cause of death not reported.

HAYS, HUGH, ———

Enlisted at Camp Martin (Mitchell County) on June 27, 1862, for the war. No further records.

HENDRICKS, JAMES, Private

Enlisted in Randolph County on December 3, 1863, for the war. Reported present in January-April, 1864. Captured at Resaca, Georgia, on the retreat during the night of May 15, 1864. Apparently escaped from the enemy and was hospitalized at Macon, Georgia, where he died on October 22, 1864. Cause of death not reported.

HICKS, JOHN, Private

Enlisted in Watauga County on August 26, 1862, for the war. Deserted at Big Creek Gap, Tennessee, in January, 1863. Transferred to Company H of this regiment on April 26, 1863, while listed as a deserter.

HILEMAN, JACOB, ———

Reportedly enlisted at Camp Martin (Mitchell County) on June 27, 1862, for the war. Served for most of the war in Company B of this regiment.

HILEMAN, JOHN, ———

Reportedly enlisted at Camp Martin (Mitchell County) on June 27, 1862, for the war. Served for most of the war in Company B of this regiment.

HOBBS, CALEB A., Private

Born in Lincoln County and was by occupation a farmer prior to enlisting in Caldwell County on March 16, 1864, for the war. Captured on the retreat from Dalton, Georgia, on or about May 13, 1864. Sent to Nashville, Tennessee. Transferred to Louisville, Kentucky, where he arrived on May 17, 1864. Transferred to Camp Morton, Indianapolis, Indiana, where he arrived on May 22, 1864. Released at Camp Morton on March 24, 1865, after taking the Oath of Allegiance and joining the U.S. Army. Assigned to Company G, 6th Regiment U.S. Volunteer Infantry. [Was 21 years of age at the time of his enlistment in the U.S. Army. May have served previously as Private in Company B, 23rd Regiment N.C. Troops (13th Regiment N.C. Volunteers).]

HOBBS, WALLACE, Private

Born in Lincoln County and was by occupation a farmer. Place and date of enlistment not reported (probably enlisted subsequent to April 30, 1864). Captured at Bald Hill, near Atlanta, Georgia, July 22, 1864. Sent to Nashville, Tennessee. Transferred to Louisville, Kentucky, where he arrived on August 5, 1864. Transferred to Camp Chase, Ohio, where he arrived on August 6, 1864. Took the Oath of Allegiance at Camp Chase on March 16, 1865, and joined the U.S. Army. Assigned to Company A, 6th Regiment U.S. Volunteer Infantry. [Was 20 years of age at the time of his enlistment in the U.S. Army.]

HOBSON, BENONI, JR., Private

Enlisted at Camp Martin (Mitchell County) on June 27, 1862, for the war. Transferred to Company B of this regiment prior to March 1, 1863.

HOCKINGS, JESSE D., Private

Enlisted in Caldwell County on July 5, 1862, for the war. No further records.

HOLIFIELD, JOEL A., Private

Born in Rutherford County and was by occupation a farmer prior to enlisting in Caldwell County at age 20, July 5, 1862, for the war. Reported present in January-June, 1863. Deserted at Chickamauga, Georgia, September 25, 1863. Later served as Private in Company A, 3rd Regiment N.C. Mounted Infantry (Union).

HUGHES, WILLIAM J., Private

Enlisted at Camp Martin (Mitchell County) on June 27, 1862, for the war. Was apparently rejected for service. Reason he was rejected not reported. Later served as Private in Company K of this regiment.

JASPER, WILLIAM, Private

Place and date of enlistment not reported (probably enlisted subsequent to April 30, 1864). Captured at Resaca, Georgia, May 16, 1864. Sent to Nashville, Tennessee. Transferred to Louisville, Kentucky, where he arrived on May 21, 1864. Transferred to Alton, Illinois, where he arrived on May 25, 1864. Died in hospital at Alton on June 29, 1864, of "typho[id] mal[arial] fever."

JENKINS, WILLIAM C., Private

Enlisted in Cocke County, Tennessee, December 13, 1863, for the war. Reported present through August 31, 1864. No further records.

JESTER, WILLIAM, Private

Enlisted in Yadkin County on November 1, 1863, for the war. Detailed as a pioneer on January 1, 1864. Deserted on an unspecified date. Reported under arrest on or about April 30, 1864. Died in hospital at La Grange, Georgia, May 14, 1864. Cause of death not reported.

JOPLING, GEORGE JOSHUA, Private

Previously served as Private in Company K of this regiment. Enlisted in this company in Caldwell County on August 15, 1863, for the war. Reported absent without leave in September-October, 1863. Returned to duty prior to May 14-15, 1864, when he was reported missing at Resaca, Georgia. No further records. Survived the war.

JUSTICE, HENRY, Private

Born in Burke County and was by occupation a farmer prior to enlisting in Mitchell County at age 18, July 16, 1862, for the war. Transferred to Company K of this regiment on or about July 29, 1862.

JUSTICE, WILLIAM, Private

Born in Burke County and was by occupation a farmer prior to enlisting in Mitchell County at age 25, July 16, 1862, for the war. Transferred to Company K of this regiment on or about July 29, 1862.

KEENER, JESSE, Private

Resided in Buncombe County and was by occupation a farmer prior to enlisting in Buncombe County at age 39, September 21, 1863, for the war. Reported present or accounted for in January-April, 1864. Captured at Cassville, Georgia, May 20, 1864. Sent to Nashville, Tennessee. Transferred to Louisville, Kentucky, where he arrived on May 29, 1864. Transferred to Rock Island, Illinois, where he arrived on June 1, 1864. Died at Rock Island on June 2, 1864, of "ch[ronic] diarrhoea."

KENNEY, SIMPSON, Private

Resided in Randolph County and was by occupation a farm laborer prior to enlisting in Randolph County at age 42, December 1, 1863, for the war. Deserted at Dalton, Georgia, January 10, 1864. Returned to duty subsequent to August 31, 1864. Captured at Orangeburg, South Carolina, February 14, 1865. Sent to New Bern. Confined at Hart's Island, New York Harbor, April 10, 1865. Died at Hart's Island on April 20, 1865, of "pneumonia."

LANIER, DAVID ANDERSON, Private

Born on May 24, 1842. Enlisted in McDowell County at age 20, October 20, 1862, for the war. Reported present in January-June, 1863. Reported sick in hospital in September-October, 1863. Returned to duty prior to March 1, 1864. Reported present in March-April, 1864. Sent to hospital sick on August 18, 1864. Returned to duty on an unspecified date. Hospitalized at Macon, Georgia, August 31, 1864, with a gunshot wound of the left knee. Place and date wounded not reported. Detailed as a guard in the medical purveying depot at Charlotte on November 1, 1864. No further records. Survived the war. [North Carolina pension records indicate that he was wounded in the left leg at Chickamauga, Georgia in "August, 1863," and was wounded in the same leg at Atlanta, Georgia, on an unspecified date.]

LEDFORD, JASPER, Private

Born in Yancey County and was by occupation a farmer prior to enlisting in Mitchell County at age 16, June 25, 1862, for the war. Transferred to Company K of this regiment on or about July 29, 1862.

LINDSAY, JOHN H., Private

Born in Caldwell County* and was by occupation a farmer prior to enlisting in Caldwell County at age 34, July 5, 1862, for the war. Reported present in January-February, 1863. Died on or about April 18, 1863. Place and cause of death not reported.

LINDSAY, JOSEPH ARCHIBALD, Private

Born in Caldwell County* and was by occupation a farmer prior to enlisting in Caldwell County at age 23, July 5, 1862, for the war. Reported present or accounted for in January-February and May-June, 1863. Reported absent without leave on August 26, 1863. Returned to duty on December 10, 1863. Reported present through February 29, 1864. Furloughed home for forty days on April 19, 1864. Had not returned to duty as of August 31, 1864. No further records. Survived the war.

LINDSAY, WILLIAM REID, Private

Born in Caldwell County* where he enlisted at age 21, July 5, 1862, for the war. Reported absent on sick furlough in January-February and September-October, 1863. Returned to duty on an unspecified date. Sent to hospital sick on February 18, 1864. Furloughed for forty days on April 19, 1864. Had not returned to duty as of August 31, 1864. No further records. Survived the war.

LOFTIN, DAVID M., Private

Born in Caldwell County* where he resided as a farmer prior to enlisting in Caldwell County at age 29, July 5, 1862, for the war.

Reported absent on furlough in January-February, 1863. Returned to duty in March-April, 1863. Reported present in May-June, 1863. Killed at Chickamauga, Georgia, September 20, 1863.

LOGAN, WILLIAM G., Private

Resided in Yadkin County where he enlisted on November 1, 1863, for the war. Deserted at Chickamauga, Georgia, October 6, 1863. Apparently returned to duty on an unspecified date. Deserted to the enemy on an unspecified date. Confined at Knoxville, Tennessee, June 11, 1864. Transferred to Louisville, Kentucky, where he arrived on or about June 18, 1864. Released at Louisville on or about June 19, 1864, after taking the Oath of Allegiance.

LUTHER, HILLERY, Private

Enlisted in Randolph County on December 7, 1863, for the war. Deserted near Dalton, Georgia, January 10, 1864.

McCARSON, SAMUEL, Private

Previously served as Private in Company D, 60th Regiment N.C. Troops. Transferred to this company when the 58th and 60th Regiments were consolidated on April 9, 1865. Paroled at Greensboro on or about May 1, 1865.

McKINNEY, JOHN P., Private

Born in Yancey County where he resided as a farmer prior to enlisting in Mitchell or Yancey County at age 20, June 25, 1862, for the war. Transferred to Company K of this regiment on or about July 29, 1862.

McKINNEY, JOHNSON S., Private

Born in Yancey County and was by occupation a farmer prior to enlisting in Mitchell or Yancey County at age 24, June 25, 1862, for the war. Transferred to Company K of this regiment on or about July 29, 1862.

McMILLEN, JAMES, Private

Resided in Caldwell County where he enlisted on August 27, 1863, for the war. Reported present in September-October, 1863. Sent to hospital sick on or about January 1, 1864. Reported absent sick through August 31, 1864. Was reportedly suffering from "chronic op[h]thalmia with ulceration of cornea of both eye[s]. . . ." No further records.

MARCUS, JOHN, Private

Resided in Caldwell County where he enlisted at age 19, April 7, 1864, for the war. Sent to hospital sick on June 4, 1864. Reported absent sick through August 31, 1864. No further records. Survived the war.

MARTIN, WARREN, Private

Enlisted in Randolph County on December 3, 1863, for the war. Reported present in January-April, 1864. Captured at Cassville, Georgia, May 20, 1864. Sent to Nashville, Tennessee. Transferred to Louisville, Kentucky, where he arrived on May 29, 1864. Transferred to Rock Island, Illinois, where he arrived on June 1, 1864. Died at Rock Island on June 17, 1864, of "typhoid pneumonia."

MAY, JAMES M., Private

Resided in Yadkin County and was by occupation a farm laborer prior to enlisting in Caldwell County at age 20, July 5, 1862, for

the war. Deserted at Big Creek Gap, Tennessee, December 18, 1862. Returned to duty subsequent to April 30, 1863. Deserted on August 26, 1863.

MEDARIS, JOHN E., Sergeant

Born in Caldwell County* where he resided as a merchant prior to enlisting in Caldwell County at age 25. Mustered in as Sergeant. Enlistment date reported as June 25, 1862; however, he was not listed in any of the surviving muster rolls for the company through June 30, 1864. Appointed Quartermaster Sergeant on an unspecified date (probably in June-July, 1864) and transferred to the Field and Staff of this regiment.

MEDLOCK, HENRY B., Private

Born in Alexander County* and was by occupation a farmer prior to enlisting in Alexander County on May 16, 1862, for the war. Reported present in January-February, 1863. Discharged on April 13, 1863, by reason of "phthisis pulmonalis." Discharge certificate gives his age as 34.

MILLER, ANDREW, Private

Previously served as Private in Company B of this regiment. Transferred to this company on or about June 27, 1862. Paid for service through July 23, 1862. No further records.

MOODY, ROBERT, Private

Born in Caldwell County and was by occupation a farmer prior to enlisting in Caldwell County at age 18, July 5, 1862, for the war. Reported present in January-February, 1863. Died on March 1, 1863. Place and cause of death not reported.

MOORE, ELIJAH L., Private

Enlisted in Caldwell County on July 5, 1862, for the war. Reported present on surviving company muster rolls through February 29, 1864. Reported on duty as a teamster from March 11 through August 31, 1864. No further records. Survived the war. [Was about 23 years of age at time of enlistment.]

MOORE, GEORGE WASHINGTON, Private

Born in Caldwell County* on August 8, 1830. Enlisted in Caldwell County at age 31, July 5, 1862, for the war. No further records. Survived the war.

MOORE, HIGHT C., Musician

Born in Caldwell County* and was by occupation a farmer prior to enlisting in Caldwell or Watauga County at age 27, July 5, 1862, for the war. Mustered in as Private. Reported present in January-June, 1863. Appointed Musician (Drummer) prior to March 1, 1863. Reduced to ranks in July-October, 1863. Reported sick in hospital in September-October, 1863. Reported present in January-April, 1864. Appointed Musician (Drummer) in March-April, 1864. Reported present in May-August, 1864. Died prior to January 1, 1865. Place and cause of death not reported.

MOORE, JASPER ELIJAH, Private

Born in Caldwell County* on April 10, 1841. Enlisted in Caldwell County at age 21, July 5, 1862, for the war. Reported present on surviving company muster rolls through April 30, 1864. Captured at or near Kolb's Farm, near Marietta, Georgia, June 22, 1864. Sent to Nashville, Tennessee. Transferred to Louisville, Kentucky, where he arrived on July 14, 1864. Transferred to Camp Douglas, Chicago, Illinois, where he arrived on July 16, 1864. Released at Camp Douglas on June 16, 1865, after taking the Oath of Allegiance.

MOORE, JESSE, JR., Private

Born in Caldwell County* on September 3, 1827. Resided in Caldwell County where he was by occupation a farmer prior to enlisting in Caldwell County at age 34, July 5, 1862, for the war. "Name canceled."

MOORE, JUDSON, Private

Born in Caldwell County* on June 13, 1833. Enlisted in Caldwell County at age 29, July 5, 1862, for the war. No further records. Survived the war.

MOORE, LEWIS, Private

Previously served as Private in Company B, 60th Regiment N.C. Troops. Transferred to this company when the 58th and 60th Regiments were consolidated on April 9, 1865. Paroled at Greensboro on or about May 1, 1865.

MOORE, MARTIN LUTHER, Private

Born on December 1, 1838. Enlisted in Caldwell County at age 24, June 13, 1863, for the war. Reported sick in hospital in September-October, 1863. Returned to duty on an unspecified date. Reported present in January-April, 1864. Wounded in the left arm while on picket duty near Atlanta, Georgia, on or about July 24, 1864. Reported absent wounded through August 31, 1864. Disabled by his wounds. No further records. Survived the war.

MOORE, NEWTON, Private

Born in Caldwell County* where he resided as a farmer prior to enlisting in Caldwell County at age 23, July 5, 1862, for the war. Name canceled. No further records. Survived the war.

MULWEE, JAMES O., Private

Resided in Caldwell County and was by occupation a mechanic prior to enlisting in Caldwell County at age 39, November 5, 1863, for the war. Captured at Missionary Ridge, Tennessee, November 25, 1863. Sent to Louisville, Kentucky. Transferred to Rock Island, Illinois, where he arrived on December 9, 1863. Died at Rock Island on December 21, 1863, of "pneumonia."

NELSON, GEORGE, Private

Resided in Randolph County and enlisted in Guilford County on December 22, 1863, for the war. Reported present in January-April, 1864. Accidentally wounded at Lost Mountain, Georgia, May 30, 1864. Reported absent wounded through October 31, 1864. Paroled at Greensboro on May 11, 1865.

NELSON, WILLIAM R., Sergeant

Born in Caldwell County* and was by occupation a farmer prior to enlisting in Caldwell County at age 23, July 5, 1862, for the war. Mustered in as Private. Reported present in January-June, 1863. Hospitalized at Macon, Georgia, September 23, 1863, with debility. Furloughed for thirty days on November 17, 1863. Returned to duty in March-April, 1864. Promoted to Sergeant on April 1, 1864. Wounded near Mount Zion Church, Georgia, June 25, 1864. No further records. Survived the war.

OSBORN, GEORGE, Private

Enlisted in Watauga County on August 26, 1863, for the war. Deserted at Missionary Ridge, Tennessee, October 6, 1863. [May have served later as Private in Company I, 13th Regiment Tennessee Cavalry (Union).]

OXFORD, JAMES HENRY, Private

Resided in Alexander County and was by occupation a farm laborer prior to enlisting in Alexander County at age 27, August 16, 1862, for the war. Reported present or accounted for on surviving company muster rolls through April 30, 1864. Captured at or near Kolb's Farm, near Marietta, Georgia, June 22, 1864. Sent to Nashville, Tennessee. Transferred to Louisville, Kentucky, where he arrived on July 14, 1864. Transferred to Camp Douglas, Chicago, Illinois, where he arrived on July 16, 1864. Released at Camp Douglas on June 16, 1865, after taking the Oath of Allegiance.

OXFORD, JOHN M., Private

Enlisted in Alexander County on August 16, 186[2], for the war. No further records. Survived the war. [Was about 20 years of age at time of enlistment. North Carolina pension records indicate that he was bitten by a rattlesnake at Johnson's Station, Tennessee, in October, 1862.]

OXFORD, WILLIAM C., Private

Born in Caldwell County* where he resided as a farmer prior to enlisting in Caldwell County at age 33, July 5, 1862, for the war. Reported present on surviving company muster rolls through April 30, 1864. Wounded in the jaw at Resaca, Georgia, May 14-15, 1864. Returned to duty prior to September 1, 1864. No further records. Survived the war.

PARIS, JOSIAH, ———

Enlisted on or about June 27, 1862, for the war. No further records.

PARKES, CLINTON L., Private

Resided in Burke County and was by occupation a farmer prior to enlisting in Burke County at age 31, August 29, 1862, for the war. Reported present in January-June, 1863. Reported sick in hospital in September-October, 1863. Furloughed from hospital for forty-five days on January 4, 1864. Reported absent on furlough through August 31, 1864. Hospitalized at Charlotte on February 20, 1865, with "phlegmon." No further records. Survived the war.

PARKES, SAMUEL M., Private

Born in Burke County where he resided as a farmer prior to enlisting in Caldwell County at age 19, July 5, 1862, for the war. Reported present on surviving company muster rolls through February, 1864. Sent to hospital sick on March 27, 1864. Admitted to hospital at Macon, Georgia, May 16, 1864, with pneumonia. Returned to duty on May 23, 1864. Captured at or near Kolb's Farm, near Marietta, Georgia, June 22, 1864. Sent to Nashville, Tennessee. Transferred to Louisville, Kentucky, where he arrived on July 16, 1864. Transferred to Camp Douglas, Chicago, Illinois, where he arrived on July 18, 1864. Died at Camp Douglas on October 3, 1864, of "acute diarrhoea."

PATTERSON, JOHN, ———

North Carolina pension records indicate that he served in this company.

PEARCE, ALFRED, Private

Resided in Randolph County where he enlisted on December 7, 1863, for the war. Deserted near Dalton, Georgia, February 22, 1864.

PEAREY, AARON, Private

Born in Burke County and was by occupation a farmer prior to enlisting in Mitchell County at age 25, June 25, 1862, for the war. Reported present in January-June, 1863. Reported sick in hospital in September-October, 1863. Returned to duty prior to March 1, 1864. Reported present through August 31, 1864. Wounded in the left foot and left arm at Bentonville on March 19, 1865. Hospitalized at Greensboro. Survived the war.

PENDLEY, WILLIAM N., Private

Born in Burke County where he resided as a farmer or carpenter prior to enlisting in Caldwell or Burke County at age 30, June 25, 1862, for the war. Reported present in January-June, 1863. Killed at Chickamauga, Georgia, September 20, 1863. Nominated for the Badge of Distinction for gallantry at Chickamauga.

PENNEL, JOSHUA T., Private

Born in Caldwell County and was by occupation a farmer prior to enlisting in Caldwell County at age 19, July 5, 1862, for the war. Reported present on surviving company muster rolls through April 30, 1864. Reported present but sick in May-August, 1864. No further records.

PENNELL, MILTON C., Private

Born in Wilkes County and was by occupation a farmer prior to enlisting in Caldwell County at age 34, July 5, 1862, for the war. Reported present on surviving company muster rolls through February 29, 1864. Furloughed home for 20 days on March 17, 1864. Reported present but sick in May-August, 1864. No further records. Survived the war.

PERCY, JESSE, Private

Born in Burke County and was by occupation a farmer prior to enlisting in Caldwell County at age 19, June 25, 1862, for the war. Reported present in January-June, 1863. Wounded at Chickamauga, Georgia, September 19-20, 1863. Died on September 25, 1863, of wounds. Place of death not reported.

PERCY, JOB, Private

Born in Burke County and was by occupation a farmer prior to enlisting in Caldwell County at age 32, June 25, 1862, for the war. No further records.

PERCY, JOHN, Private

Enlisted at Camp Martin (Mitchell County) on June 27, 1862, for the war. No further records.

PERCY, SIDNEY, Private

Enlisted in Burke County on November 7, 1862, for the war. Reported present in January-June, 1863. Furloughed from hospital on October 6, 1863. Reported absent on furlough through August 31, 1864. No further records. Survived the war. [Was about 37 years of age at time of enlistment.]

PETERSON, JOHN, Private

Previously served as Private in Company G of this regiment. Transferred to this company on or about November 1, 1863. Captured at

Missionary Ridge, Tennessee, November 25, 1863. Sent to Nashville, Tennessee. Transferred to Louisville, Kentucky, where he arrived on December 8, 1863. Transferred to Rock Island, Illinois, where he arrived on December 11, 1863. Released at Rock Island on May 28, 1865, after taking the Oath of Allegiance. [Records of the Federal Provost Marshal dated May, 1865, give his age as 37.]

PHILLIPS, DANIEL, Private

Resided in Burke County and was by occupation a farm laborer prior to enlisting in Burke County at age 25, August 29, 1862, for the war. Reported present in January-June, 1863. Wounded at Chickamauga, Georgia, September 19-20, 1863. Died on November 15, 1863, of wounds. Place of death not reported; however, he was buried at Myrtle Hill Cemetery, Rome, Georgia.

PHILLIPS, REUBEN O., Private

Resided in Caldwell County where he enlisted on December 13, 1863, for the war. Reported present in January-April, 1864. Captured near Cassville, Georgia, on or about May 19, 1864. Sent to Nashville, Tennessee. Transferred to Louisville, Kentucky, where he arrived on May 24, 1864. Transferred to Rock Island, Illinois, where he arrived on May 27, 1864. Released at Rock Island on June 20, 1865, after taking the Oath of Allegiance. [Records of the Federal Provost Marshal dated June, 1865, give his age as 19.]

PICKETT, WILEY, Private

Resided in Randolph County and was by occupation a farmer prior to enlisting in Randolph County at age 38, December 7, 1863, for the war. Deserted near Dalton, Georgia, January 10, 1864. Died in hospital at Atlanta, Georgia on or about January 18, 1864. Cause of death not reported.

PIPES, JOHN W., Private

Previously served as Private in Company G of this regiment. Transferred to this company subsequent to June 30, 1863. Captured (or deserted to the enemy) at Missionary Ridge, Tennessee, November 25, 1863. Died in hospital at Nashville, Tennessee, December 13, 1863, of "dysentery chronic."

POWELL, PINKNEY, Private

Enlisted on or about July 29, 1862, for the war. Discharged on an unspecified date (probably in the summer of 1862). Reason discharged not reported. [May have served later as Private in Company F, 26th Regiment N.C. Troops.]

PRATHER, GEORGE WASHINGTON, Private

Previously served as Private in Company B, 60th Regiment N.C. Troops. Transferred to this company when the 58th and 60th Regiments were consolidated on April 9, 1865. Paroled at Greensboro on or about May 1, 1865.

PRICHARD, ALEXANDER, Private

Previously served as Private in Company G of this regiment. Transferred to this company in May-June, 1863. Reported present in September-October, 1863. Captured at Missionary Ridge, Tennessee, November 25, 1863. Sent to Nashville, Tennessee. Transferred to Louisville, Kentucky, where he arrived on December 8, 1863. Transferred to Rock Island, Illinois, where he arrived on December 11, 1863. Died at Rock Island on February 13, 1864, of "pneumonia."

PRICHARD, CAMPBELL, Private

Born in Burke County and was by occupation a farmer prior to enlisting in Caldwell County at age 24, June 25, 1862, for the war.

Reported absent on sick furlough in January-February, 1863. Returned to duty on an unspecified date. Reported present on surviving company muster rolls from May-June, 1863, through August 31, 1864. No further records.

PRICHARD, RUFUS, Private

Born in Burke County and was by occupation a farmer prior to enlisting in Caldwell County at age 30, June 25, 1862, for the war. Reported present in January-June, 1863. Wounded at Chickamauga, Georgia, September 20, 1863. Returned to duty prior to October 31, 1863. Captured at Missionary Ridge, Tennessee, November 25, 1863. Sent to Nashville, Tennessee. Transferred to Louisville, Kentucky, where he arrived on December 8, 1863. Transferred to Rock Island, Illinois, where he arrived on December 11, 1863. Died at Rock Island on or about February 13, 1864, of "bronchitis."

PRICHARD, WILLIAM A., Private

Born in Burke County and was by occupation a farmer prior to enlisting in Burke County at age 21, June 25, 1862, for the war. Reported present in January-June, 1863. Deserted at Bell's Bridge, Tennessee, August 5, 1863.

PRIM, ISAAC, Private

Resided in Yadkin County and was by occupation a farmer prior to enlisting in Yadkin County at age 28, November 1, 1863, for the war. Deserted near Dalton, Georgia, February 22, 1864.

PUCKETT, JOHN, Private

Previously served as Private in Company F, 41st Regiment N.C. Troops (3rd Regiment N.C. Cavalry). Transferred to this company on February 19, 1864. Reported present through August 31, 1864. No further records.

PUETT, ELISHA, Corporal

Born in Caldwell County where he resided as a farmer prior to enlisting in Caldwell County at age 18, July 5, 1862, for the war. Mustered in as Private. Reported present in January-June, 1863. Promoted to Corporal in July-October, 1863. Reported on duty as a pioneer guard in September-October, 1863. Rejoined the company on an unspecified date. Reported present in January-April, 1864. Captured at or near Kolb's Farm, near Marietta, Georgia, June 22, 1864. Sent to Nashville, Tennessee. Transferred to Louisville, Kentucky, where he arrived on July 14, 1864. Transferred to Camp Douglas, Chicago, Illinois, where he arrived on July 18, 1864. Released at Camp Douglas on June 16, 1865, after taking the Oath of Allegiance.

PUETT, JOSEPH, Private

Born in Caldwell County where he resided as a farmer prior to enlisting in Caldwell County at age 20, July 5, 1862, for the war. Reported present in January-June, 1863. Wounded in the arm at Chickamauga, Georgia, September 20, 1863. Reported absent wounded through October 31, 1863. Returned to duty prior to February 29, 1864. Reported present in March-April, 1864. Captured at or near Kolb's Farm, near Marietta, Georgia, June 22, 1864. Sent to Nashville, Tennessee. Transferred to Louisville, Kentucky, where he arrived on July 14, 1864. Transferred to Camp Douglas, Chicago, Illinois, where he arrived on July 18, 1864. Released at Camp Douglas on June 16, 1865, after taking the Oath of Allegiance.

RABY, GEORGE W., Private

Born in Caldwell County* and was by occupation a farmer prior to enlisting in Caldwell County at age 26, July 5, 1862, for the war. Reported present in January-June, 1863. Reported absent without leave on August 26, 1863. Returned to duty on November 20, 1863. Captured near Cassville, Georgia, on or about May 19, 1864. Sent to Nashville, Tennessee. Transferred to Louisville, Kentucky, where he arrived on May 24, 1864. Transferred to Rock Island, Illinois, where he arrived on May 27, 1864. Paroled on March 20, 1865. Received at Boulware's and Cox's Wharves, James River, Virginia, March 27, 1865, for exchange. Survived the war.

REDDING, WILLIAM, Private

Resided in Randolph County and was by occupation a farmer prior to enlisting in Randolph County at age 41, December 20, 1863, for the war. Reported present in January-April, 1864. Captured at or near Resaca, Georgia, May 15-16, 1864. Sent to Nashville, Tennessee. Transferred to Louisville, Kentucky, where he arrived on May 21, 1864. Transferred to Alton, Illinois, where he arrived on May 25, 1864. Died at Alton on June 23, 1864, of "pneumonia."

REECE, AARON B., Private

Born in Lincoln County and resided in Caldwell County where he was by occupation a farmer prior to enlisting in Caldwell County at age 31, July 5, 1862, for the war. Reported present on surviving company muster rolls through April 30, 1864. Killed at Resaca, Georgia, May 13-14, 1864.

ROBBINS, JAMES B., Private

Enlisted in Watauga County on August 29, 1862, for the war. Reported present in January-June, 1863. Reported on duty as a cooper at Loudon, Tennessee, in September-October, 1863. Reported present in January-August, 1864. No further records. Survived the war. [Was about 20 years of age at time of enlistment.]

ROBBINS, JAMES LARKIN, Private

Born in Caldwell County* in February, 1827. Resided in Caldwell County and was by occupation a farmer prior to enlisting in Caldwell County at age 35, July 5, 1862, for the war. Reported present on surviving company muster rolls through February 29, 1864. Reported sick in hospital from April 10 through August 31, 1864. No further records. Survived the war.

ROBBINS, REUBEN RUFUS, Private

Born in Caldwell County* and was by occupation a farmer prior to enlisting in Caldwell County at age 33, July 5, 1862, for the war. Wounded in the thumb ("cut off") and right shoulder by "bushwhackers" near Cumberland Gap, Tennessee, September 25, 1862. Reported present in January-February, 1863. Discharged on March 8, 1863, presumably by reason of disability from wounds.

RUSH, HENRY, Private

Resided in Randolph County and was by occupation a farmer prior to enlisting in Randolph County at age 41, December 7, 1863, for the war. Deserted near Dalton, Georgia, January 10, 1864.

SANDERS, JESSIE WASHINGTON, Private

Resided in Burke County and was by occupation a farm laborer prior to enlisting in Caldwell County at age 38, August 20, 1863, for the war. Reported present in January-August, 1864. Hospitalized at West Point, Mississippi, January 10, 1865, with diarrhoea. No further records. Survived the war.

SCOTTON, JOHN, Private

Enlisted in Randolph County on December 23, 1863, for the war. Deserted near Dalton, Georgia, January 10, 1864.

SETSER, EPHRAIM D., Private

Born in Caldwell County* and was by occupation a farmer prior to enlisting in Caldwell County at age 26, July 21, 1862, for the war. No further records.

SETSER, JOSHUA, Private

Born in Caldwell County* and was by occupation a farmer prior to enlisting in Caldwell County at age 29, July 21, 1862, for the war. Reported present in January-June, 1863. Reported sick in hospital in September-October, 1863. Reported absent on sick furlough from December 30, 1863, through August 31, 1864. No further records. Survived the war.

SETSER, WILLIAM A., Private

Born in Caldwell County* where he enlisted at age 27, July 5, 1862, for the war. Reported present in January-June, 1863. Reported absent without leave on August 26, 1863. Returned to duty on December 10, 1863. Reported present in January-August, 1864. Furloughed for three days on March 12, 1865. No further records. Survived the war.

SHELL, JOHN T., Private

Resided in Caldwell County and was by occupation a farmer prior to enlisting in Caldwell County at age 36, April 7, 1864, for the war. Reported present through August 31, 1864. No further records. Survived the war.

SHELTON, DAVID, Private

Resided in Madison County and was by occupation a farmer prior to enlisting in Madison County at age 40, November 12, 1863, for the war. Deserted near Dalton, Georgia, January 10, 1864. [May have served later as Private in Company G, 3rd Regiment N.C. Mounted Infantry (Union).]

SHERRILL, ABNER R., Private

Enlisted in Caldwell County on February 18, 1864, for the war. Reported present through August 31, 1864. No further records.

SHERRILL, ADAM C., Private

Born in Caldwell County* and was by occupation a farmer prior to enlisting in Caldwell County at age 22, July 21, 1862, for the war. Reported present on surviving company muster rolls through February 29, 1864. Furloughed for twenty days on or about April 19, 1864. Returned to duty on an unspecified date. Reported present through August 31, 1864. No further records. Survived the war.

SHERRILL, ISAAC I., Private

Born in Caldwell County* where he resided as a farmer prior to enlisting in Caldwell County at age 23, July 21, 1862, for the war. Reported present in January-June, 1863. Reported absent without leave on October 25, 1863. Returned to duty on November 15, 1863. Reported present through April, 1864. Wounded accidentally near Atlanta, Georgia, August 9, 1864, by the explosion of a shell. Returned to duty subsequent to August 31, 1864. Captured

at Bentonville on or about March 22, 1865. Confined at Hart's Island, New York Harbor, April 10, 1865. Released at Hart's Island on June 19, 1865, after taking the Oath of Allegiance.

SHERRILL, WILLIAM W., Private

Born in Caldwell County* on January 23, 1828. Resided in Caldwell County and was by occupation a farmer prior to enlisting in Caldwell County at age 34, July 21, 1862, for the war. Reported present in January-February, 1863. Deserted on March 29, 1863. Returned to duty on June 10, 1863. Reported sick in hospital in September-October, 1863. Deserted to the enemy on an unspecified date. Confined at Knoxville, Tennessee, May 25, 1864. Released on or about May 27, 1864, after taking the Oath of Allegiance.

SHIPMAN, WILLIAM R., JR., Private

Previously served as Private in Company I, 60th Regiment N.C. Troops. Transferred to this company when the 58th and 60th Regiments were consolidated on April 9, 1865. Paroled at Greensboro on or about May 1, 1865.

SHUFFLER, JACOB C., Private

Born in Burke County where he resided as a farmer prior to enlisting in Burke or Caldwell County at age 28, July 5, 1862, for the war. Mustered in as Private. Promoted to Sergeant prior to March 1, 1863. Reported present in January-June, 1863. Reported absent without leave on August 26, 1863. Reduced to ranks prior to November 1, 1863. Returned to duty on November 20, 1863. Reported present in January-August, 1864. Wounded in the thigh at Bentonville on March 19, 1865. Returned to duty on an unspecified date. Transferred to Company A of this regiment when the 58th and 60th Regiments were consolidated on April 9, 1865.

SHUFFLER, POSEY C., Private

Born in Burke County and was by occupation a farmer prior to enlisting in Caldwell County at age 19, July 5, 1862, for the war. Reported present in January-June, 1863. Reported absent without leave on August 26, 1863. Returned to duty on November 20, 1863. Reported present in January-August, 1864. Transferred to Company A of this regiment when the 58th and 60th Regiments were consolidated on April 9, 1865.

SIDE, WILLIAM, Private

Enlisted in Wilkes County on December 25, 1863, for the war. Deserted near Dalton, Georgia, January 10, 1864.

SILVER, EDMUND D., Private

Born in Yancey County and resided in Mitchell County where he was by occupation a farmer prior to enlisting in Mitchell County at age 23, June 25, 1862, for the war. Transferred to Company K of this regiment on or about July 29, 1862.

SILVER, LEVI D., Private

Born in Yancey County and was by occupation a farmer prior to enlisting in Mitchell County at age 25, June 25, 1862, for the war. Transferred to Company K of this regiment on or about July 29, 1862. Later served as 3rd Lieutenant of that unit.

SLAGLE, ADOLPHUS, Private

Previously served as Private in Company B of this regiment. Transferred to this company on or about June 27, 1862. Transferred back to Company B prior to October 16, 1862.

SLAGLE, JOHN L. L., Private

Previously served as Private in Company I, 60th Regiment N.C. Troops. Transferred to this company when the 58th and 60th Regiments were consolidated on April 9, 1865. Paroled at Greensboro on or about May 1, 1865.

SMITH, MASTON D., Private

Born in Caldwell County* and was by occupation a farmer prior to enlisting in Caldwell County at age 28, July 21, 1862, for the war. Reported present on surviving company muster rolls through August 31, 1864. No further records. Survived the war.

SPENCER, ISAAC THOMAS AVERY, Corporal

Born in Lincoln County on October 23, 1829, and was by occupation a farmer prior to enlisting in Caldwell County at age 32, July 5, 1862, for the war. Mustered in as Corporal. Reported present in January-June, 1863. Wounded at Chickamauga, Georgia, September 20, 1863. Returned to duty prior to October 31, 1863. Reported present or accounted for in January-April, 1864. Wounded at Kolb's Farm, near Marietta, Georgia, June 22, 1864. Captured at the Chattahoochee River, Georgia, July 16, 1864. Sent to Nashville, Tennessee. Transferred to Louisville, Kentucky, where he arrived on August 5, 1864. Transferred to Camp Chase, Ohio, where he arrived on August 6, 1864. Paroled at Camp Chase on or about March 4, 1865, and transferred for exchange. Received at Boulware's and Cox's Wharves, James River, Virginia, March 10-12, 1865, for exchange. No further records. Survived the war.

STEELE, JOHN L., Private

Born in Caldwell County and was by occupation a farmer prior to enlisting in Caldwell County at age 20, July 21, 1862, for the war. Reported present or accounted for on surviving company muster rolls through August 31, 1864. No further records.

STEPHENS, JOHN, Private

Previously served as Private in Company B of this regiment. Transferred to this company on or about June 27, 1862. Transferred back to Company B prior to March 1, 1863.

STEPHENS, SHERRED, Private

Previously served as Private in Company B of this regiment. Transferred to this company on or about June 27, 1862. Paid for service with this company through July 23, 1862. No further records.

STEWARD, JASPER, Private

Enlisted at Camp Jackson on May 17, 1862, for the war. Transferred to Company B of this regiment prior to March 1, 1863.

STEWART, JACKSON, Private

Previously served as Private in Company B of this regiment. Transferred to this company on or about June 27, 1862. Transferred back to Company B prior to February 2, 1863.

STEWART, WILLIAM, Private

The service record of this soldier is unclear. It appears that he served in Company D of this regiment in September-October, 1863. He also served at various times in this company and in Companies C and K of this regiment. [Was about 18 years of age at time of enlistment.]

STORY, WALTER T., Private

Enlisted in Watauga County on October 28, 1863, for the war. Captured at Missionary Ridge, Tennessee, November 25, 1863. Sent to Nashville, Tennessee. Transferred to Louisville, Kentucky, where he arrived on December 5, 1863. Transferred to Rock Island, Illinois, where he arrived on December 9, 1863. Died at Rock Island on January 11, 1864. Cause of death not reported.

STREET, SAMUEL M., Private

Previously served as Private in Company B of this regiment. Transferred to this company on or about June 27, 1862. Transferred back to Company B prior to August 16, 1862.

STUART, WILLIAM H., Private

Born in Union County and was by occupation a farmer prior to enlisting in Mitchell County at age 18, June 25, 1862, for the war. Transferred to Company K of this regiment on or about July 29, 1862.

SUDDERTH, JAMES NEWTON, Private

Born in Caldwell County* where he resided as a farmer prior to enlisting in Caldwell County at age 22, July 21, 1862, for the war. Reported present or accounted for on surviving company muster rolls through June, 1863. Wounded at Chickamauga, Georgia, September 19-20, 1863. Died in hospital at Atlanta, Georgia, on or about October 6, 1863, presumably of wounds.

SUDDERTH, JOHN MARSHALL, Private

Born in Caldwell County* on September 12, 1831. Resided in Watauga County where he was by occupation a farmer prior to enlisting in Caldwell County at age 30, July 5, 1862, for the war. Transferred to Company F, 26th Regiment N.C. Troops, January 15, 1863.

SUDDERTH, NEWTON N., Private

Enlisted in Caldwell County on July 21, 1862, for the war. Reported present in January-June, 1863. No further records.

SUDDERTH, TOLIVER F., Private

Born in Caldwell County* where he resided as a farmer prior to enlisting in Caldwell County at age 22, July 5, 1862, for the war. Transferred to Company F, 26th Regiment N.C. Troops, January 15, 1863.

SUMET, ELI, ———

Enlisted at Camp Martin (Mitchell County) on June 27, 1862, for the war. No further records.

TAYLOR, JACOB, Private

Born in Burke County and was by occupation a farmer prior to enlisting in Burke or Caldwell County at age 19, June 27, 1862, for the war. Reported present in January-June, 1863. Wounded at Chickamauga, Georgia, September 20, 1863. Returned to duty prior to October 31, 1863. Reported present in January-August, 1864. No further records.

TAYLOR, JAMES E., Private

Previously served as Private in Company I of this regiment. Was apparently transferred to this company on or about November 7,

1862. Reported present in January-June, 1863. Reported sick in hospital in September-October, 1863. Returned to duty on an unspecified date. Hospitalized on February 24, 1864. Furloughed for twenty days on April 19, 1864. Returned to duty on an unspecified date. Captured at Kolb's Farm, near Marietta, Georgia, June 22, 1864. Sent to Nashville, Tennessee. Transferred to Louisville, Kentucky, where he arrived on July 14, 1864. Transferred to Camp Douglas, Chicago, Illinois, where he arrived on July 18, 1864. Died at Camp Douglas on May 7, 1865, of "pneumonia."

TAYLOR, JOHN, Private

Enlisted in Burke County on August 29, 1862, for the war. Reported present in January-June, 1863. Reported absent on detail as a provost guard in September-October, 1863. Reported present in January-April, 1864. Reported present but sick in May-August, 1864. No further records. Survived the war. [North Carolina pension records indicate that he was about 31 years of age at time of enlistment.]

TAYLOR, WEISTELL, Private

Enlisted in Burke County on August 29, 1862, for the war. Reported present in January-June, 1863. Reported sick in hospital in September-October, 1863. Died at Cassville, Georgia, January 6, 1864, of disease.

TEAGUE, JAMES, Private

Enlisted in Caldwell County on April 7, 1864, for the war. Reported present in April, 1864. Sent to hospital sick on May 15, 1864. No further records.

TEAGUE, JAMES IVERSON, Private

Born on November 2, 1846. Enlisted in Caldwell County at age 17, April 7, 1864, for the war. Hospitalized at La Grange, Georgia, on an unspecified date with pneumonia and dysentery. Furloughed on July 12, 1864, because of extreme emaciation and debility. Returned to duty prior to September 1, 1864. No further records.

TEAGUE, JOHN BLOOMINGTON, Private

Born on July 28, 1848. Enlisted in Caldwell County at age 15, April 7, 1864, for the war. Captured at Kolb's Farm, near Marietta, Georgia, June 22, 1864. Sent to Nashville, Tennessee. Transferred to Louisville, Kentucky, where he arrived on July 14, 1864. Died at Louisville on or about July 30, 1864, of "typho malarial fever."

TEAGUE, LOGAN, ———

Enlisted at Camp Martin (Mitchell County) on June 27, 1862, for the war. No further records. [May have served also as Private in Company A, 22nd Regiment N.C. Troops (12th Regiment N.C. Volunteers), and in Company F, 26th Regiment N.C. Troops.]

TEAM, ISRAEL, Private

Born in Burke County where he resided as a farmer prior to enlisting in Caldwell County at age 26, June 27, 1862, for the war. Reported present in January-June, 1863. Furloughed home sick in September-October, 1863. Returned to duty on an unspecified date. Reported present in January-August, 1864. No further records. Survived the war. [North Carolina pension records indicate that he was wounded in the right arm and received a slight wound in the head at "Missionary Ridge, in the state of Tennessee, on or about the 25th day of September (probably November), 1862."]

THOMASON, WILLIAM J., Private

Born in Rutherford County and was by occupation a farmer prior to enlisting in Mitchell or Caldwell County at age 34, June 25, 1862, for the war. Transferred to Company K of this regiment on or about July 29, 1862.

THOMPSON, JOHN W., Private

Born in Iredell County and was by occupation a farmer prior to enlisting in Caldwell County at age 30, July 5, 1862, for the war. Reported absent on sick furlough in January-February, 1863. Reported absent without leave on March 29, 1863. Furloughed home sick on an unspecified date. Returned to duty on an unspecified date. Deserted near Loudon, Tennessee, August 25, 1863.

THOMPSON, JOSEPH LAFAYETTE, Private

Born in Burke County and was by occupation a farmer prior to enlisting in Caldwell County at age 22, July 5, 1862, for the war. Reported present in January-June, 1863. Reported absent without leave on August 26, 1863. Returned to duty on November 23, 1863. Reported present through August 31, 1864. Transferred to Company A of this regiment when the 58th and 60th Regiments were consolidated on April 9, 1865.

THOMPSON, MATTHEW C., Private

Born in Caldwell County* and was by occupation a farmer prior to enlisting in Caldwell County at age 31, July 5, 1862, for the war. Reported present in January-February, 1863. Deserted on March 29, 1863. Returned to duty on June 10, 1863. Reported absent without leave in September-October, 1863. Returned to duty on February 27, 1864. Reported present in March-April, 1864. Captured near Dallas, Georgia, May 25-26, 1864. Sent to Nashville, Tennessee. Transferred to Louisville, Kentucky, where he arrived on June 3, 1864. Transferred to Rock Island, Illinois, where he arrived on June 6, 1864. Released at Rock Island on June 10, 1864, after joining the U.S. Navy.

THOMPSON, MOSES ELKANAH, Sergeant

Born in Caldwell County* on July 30, 1836, and was by occupation a farmer prior to enlisting in Caldwell County at age 25, July 5, 1862, for the war. Mustered in as Private. Reported present in January-June, 1863. Promoted to Sergeant prior to March 1, 1863. Wounded in the hip at Chickamauga, Georgia, September 20, 1863. Returned to duty prior to October 31, 1863. Furloughed for twenty days on February 13, 1864. Returned to duty on an unspecified date. Reported present in March-August, 1864. No further records. Survived the war.

TOOMS, WILLIAM F., Private

Enlisted in Guilford County on December 25, 1863, for the war. Deserted near Dalton, Georgia, January 10, 1864. Admitted to a Federal hospital at Nashville, Tennessee, February 6, 1864, with measles. Released from hospital on February 25, 1864. No further records.

TRITT, HENRY T., Private

Resided in Caldwell County where he enlisted at age 16, April 28, 1864, for the war. Reported present through August 31, 1864. No further records. Survived the war.

TRITT, J. H., ———

North Carolina pension records indicate that he served in this company.

TUCKER, BEACUM, ———
North Carolina pension records indicate that he served in this company.

VANCE, JOHN J., ———
Enlisted at Camp Martin (Mitchell County) on June 27, 1862, for the war. No further records.

WATTS, RILEY, Private
Resided in Burke County and was by occupation a farmer prior to enlisting in Burke County at age 38, November 16, 1863, for the war. Deserted near Dalton, Georgia, January 10, 1864. Admitted to a Federal hospital at Knoxville, Tennessee, February 22, 1864, with smallpox. Transferred to Camp Chase, Ohio, March 25, 1864. No further records.

WELLS, W. HENRY, Private
Previously served as Private in Company B, 60th Regiment N.C. Troops. Transferred to this company when the 58th and 60th Regiments were consolidated on April 9, 1865. Paroled at Greensboro on May 1, 1865.

WEST, ALEXANDER STEVEN COMMODORE DECATUR, Private
Born in Caldwell County* on October 30, 1836. Enlisted in Caldwell County at age 25, July 5, 1862, for the war. Transferred to Company K of this regiment on or about July 29, 1862. Transferred back to this company on an unspecified date. Discharged on February 7, 1863. Reason discharged not reported.

WHITE, ISAAC, Private
Resided in Randolph County and was by occupation a farm laborer prior to enlisting in Randolph County at age 47, December 7, 1863, for the war. Reported present through April 30, 1864. Sent to hospital sick on June 10, 1864. Reported absent sick through August 31, 1864. Paroled at Greensboro on May 9, 1865.

WHITE, JAMES A., Private
Previously served as Corporal in Company F, 26th Regiment N.C. Troops. Transferred to this company on January 15, 1863. Mustered in as Private. Reported absent on furlough on February 28, 1863. Returned to duty in March-April, 1863. Reported present in May-June, 1863. Reported absent without leave on August 26, 1863. Returned to duty on November 10, 1863. Reported present through April, 1864. Reported absent on detached duty with the "infirm corps" in May-August, 1864. No further records. Survived the war. [May have been wounded at Rocky Face Ridge, Georgia, February 25, 1864.]

WHITE, JOSEPH, Private
Resided in Caldwell County and was by occupation a farmer prior to enlisting in Caldwell County at age 38, August 27, 1863, for the war. Reported present in September-October, 1863. Hospitalized at Cassville, Georgia, in November-December, 1863. Reason he was hospitalized not reported. Reported absent sick on February 24, 1864. Furloughed home from hospital on March 31, 1864. Reported absent on sick furlough through August 31, 1864. No further records.

WHITENER, SIDNEY M., Private
Born in Lincoln County and resided in Caldwell County where he was by occupation a farmer prior to enlisting in Caldwell County at age 26, July 5, 1862, for the war. Mustered in as Corporal. Reported present in January-February, 1863. Reduced to ranks prior to March 1, 1863. Reported present in March-June, 1863. Detailed as a wagoner in September-October, 1863. Rejoined the company on an unspecified date. Reported present in January-February, 1864. Detailed as a teamster on March 1, 1864. Reported on detail through August 31, 1864. Captured at Jonesborough, Georgia, September 2, 1864. Sent to Nashville, Tennessee. Transferred to Louisville, Kentucky, where he arrived on October 28, 1864. Transferred to Camp Douglas, Chicago, Illinois, where he arrived on November 1, 1864. Released at Camp Douglas on June 17, 1865, after taking the Oath of Allegiance.

WILLIAMS, ISAKER R., Private
Enlisted in Yadkin County on November 1, 1863, for the war. Deserted near Chattanooga, Tennessee, prior to March 1, 1864. [May have served later as Private in Company C, 3rd Regiment N.C. Mounted Infantry (Union).]

WILLIAMS, JESSE FRANKLIN, Private
Enlisted in Guilford County on November 1, 1863, for the war. Reported present through August 31, 1864. No further records. Survived the war.

WILLIAMS, YANCY, Private
Resided in Randolph County and was by occupation a farmer prior to enlisting in Randolph County at age 33, November 11, 1863, for the war. Deserted near Dalton, Georgia, January 10, 1864.

WILLIS, BENJAMIN, Private
Born in Yancey County and was by occupation a farmer prior to enlisting in Mitchell County at age 19, June 25, 1862, for the war. Transferred to Company K of this regiment on or about July 29, 1862.

WILSON, BARTLETT, Corporal
Born in Buncombe or Yancey County* and was by occupation a farmer prior to enlisting in Mitchell County at age 30, June 25, 1862, for the war. Mustered in as Corporal. Transferred to Company K of this regiment on or about July 29, 1862.

WILSON, JOSEPH C., Private
Born in Caldwell County* where he enlisted at age 26, July 5, 1862, for the war. Reported absent on expired furlough in January-February, 1863. Returned to duty on an unspecified date. Deserted at Big Creek Gap, Tennessee, October 25, 1863.

WILSON, SIDNEY L., Private
Born in Yancey County and was by occupation a farmer prior to enlisting in Mitchell County at age 17, June 25, 1862, for the war. Transferred to Company K of this regiment on or about July 29, 1862.

WINTERS, STEPHEN M., Private
Born in Burke County and resided in Yancey County where he was by occupation a farmer prior to enlisting in Mitchell County at age 35, July 16, 1862, for the war. Transferred to Company K of this regiment on or about July 29, 1862.

WOOD, SPENCER, Private
Resided in Randolph County and was by occupation a farmer prior to enlisting in Randolph County at age 41, December 7, 1863, for

the war. Reported sick in hospital on February 29, 1864. Furloughed home sick for forty days on or about March 25, 1864. Returned to duty on an unspecified date. Captured at Kolb's Farm, near Marietta, Georgia, June 22, 1864. Sent to Nashville, Tennessee. Transferred to Louisville, Kentucky, where he arrived on July 14, 1864. Transferred to Camp Douglas, Chicago, Illinois, where he arrived on July 18, 1864. Released at Camp Douglas on June 16, 1865, after taking the Oath of Allegiance.

WOOD, WILLIAM, Private
Resided in Randolph County and was by occupation a farmer prior to enlisting in Randolph County at age 41, December 7, 1863, for the war. Reported present in January-February, 1864. Sent to hospital in April, 1864. Reported absent sick in hospital through August 31, 1864. No further records. Survived the war.

WOODS, GASTON, Private
Enlisted in Caldwell County on October 15, 1862, for the war. Reported present in January-June, 1863. Killed at Chickamauga, Georgia, September 20, 1863.

YOUNG, MOSES, Private
Enlisted in Mitchell County at age 39, June 27, 1862, for the war. Transferred to Company K of this regiment on or about July 29, 1862.

COMPANY F

This company, known as the "McDowell Rangers," was raised in McDowell County on July 14, 1862, as Capt. Jason Conley's Company, N.C. Volunteers. It was mustered into service at Marion on July 18, 1862, and was assigned to the 58th Regiment N.C. Troops as Company F when the regiment was organized on July 29, 1862. After joining the regiment the company functioned as a part of the regiment, and its history for the remainder of the war is reported as a part of the regimental history.

The following roster was compiled primarily from information in the microfilm edition of the Compiled Service Records of Soldiers Who Served in Organizations from the State of North Carolina (Record Group 109, M270), National Archives and Records Administration, Washington, D.C. Record Group 109 includes enlistment papers, pay vouchers, requisitions, letters of resignation, discharge certificates, and abstracts of medical and prisoner of war returns. Materials relating specifically to this company include a muster-in and descriptive roll dated July 18, 1862, and muster rolls dated January-June, 1863; September-October, 1863; and January-August, 1864.

Also utilized in this roster were *The War of the Rebellion: A Compilation of the Official Records of the Union and Confederate Armies*, the North Carolina Adjutant General's *Roll of Honor*, state militia records, newspaper casualty lists and obituaries, wartime claims for bounty pay and allowances, postwar registers of claims for artificial limbs, Confederate pension applications filed with the states of North Carolina, Tennessee, and Florida, Confederate Soldiers' Home records, and the 1860 and 1870 federal censuses of North Carolina. A search was made also for relevant letters, diaries, reminiscences, and other manuscripts in the Southern Historical Collection (University of North Carolina-Chapel Hill), the Duke University Library Special Collections Department, and the North Carolina Division of Archives and History.

Among the secondary sources consulted were records of the North Carolina division of the United Daughters of the Confederacy, postwar rosters, regimental and county histories, marriage bond, will, and cemetery indexes, published and unpublished genealogies, biographical dictionaries, the North Carolina *County Heritage Book* series, the *Confederate Veteran*, Walter Clark's *Histories of the Several Regiments and Battalions from North Carolina in the Great War, 1861-'65*, and the North Carolina volume of the extended edition of *Confederate Military History*.

OFFICERS

CAPTAINS

CONLEY, JASON
Born in Burke County and was by occupation a farmer prior to enlisting at age 30. Elected Captain on July 14, 1862. Died at Big Creek Gap, Tennessee, on or about October 31, 1862. Cause of death not reported. [Previously served as Lieutenant Colonel in the 102nd Regiment N.C. Militia.]

CONLEY, CALEB O.
Born in Burke County and was by occupation a farmer prior to enlisting in McDowell County at age 29. Appointed 1st Lieutenant on July 14, 1862. Promoted to Captain on November 1, 1862. Reported present in January-June, 1863. Wounded at Chickamauga, Georgia, September 20, 1863. Returned to duty prior to October 31, 1863. Reported absent on detached service in North Carolina from December 19, 1863, through February 29, 1864. Rejoined the company in March-April, 1864. Killed at Kolb's Farm, near Marietta, Georgia, June 22, 1864. [Previously served as 2nd Lieutenant in the 102nd Regiment N.C. Militia.]

TOBEY, FREDERICK ALBERT
Served as Captain of Company A of this regiment. Reported on duty as acting Captain of this company in January-February, 1864.

BLEVINS, POINDEXTER
Previously served as 1st Lieutenant of Company L of this regiment. Promoted to Captain of this company subsequent to August 31, 1864. Paroled at Greensboro on May 1, 1865.

LIEUTENANTS

EPPS, THOMAS P., 1st Lieutenant
Born in McDowell County* and was by occupation a clerk or farmer prior to enlisting in McDowell County at age 34, July 14, 1862, for the war. Mustered in as 1st Sergeant. Reported present in January-June, 1863. Elected 3rd Lieutenant on February 25, 1863. Reported present in September-October, 1863. Promoted to 2nd Lieutenant on September 20, 1863. Reported present but under arrest in January-February, 1864. Reason he was arrested not reported. "Suspended" for sixty days on March 15, 1864, by sentence of court-martial. Reported absent sick at the division hospital on or about August 12, 1864. Promoted to 1st Lieutenant on September 3, 1864. No further records.

FOX, JAMES AUSTIN, 1st Lieutenant

Born in Burke County and resided in McDowell County where he was by occupation a farmer prior to enlisting in McDowell County at age 25, July 14, 1862, for the war. Mustered in as Sergeant. Elected 3rd Lieutenant on November 1, 1862. Promoted to 2nd Lieutenant on February 25, 1863. Reported present in March-June and September-October, 1863. Promoted to 1st Lieutenant on September 20, 1863. Reported absent on detached service in North Carolina from December 19, 1863, through February 29, 1864. Rejoined the company on or about March 8, 1864. Reported present on April 30, 1864. Wounded at Kolb's Farm, near Marietta, Georgia, June 22, 1864. Reported absent sick at the division hospital on August 1, 1864. Resigned on August 14, 1864, because he felt unable to accept promotion to the captaincy of his company by reason of "incompetency, not feeling myself qualified to perform the duties of said office." Resignation accepted on September 3, 1864.

HURLEY, LEANDER, 1st Lieutenant

Previously served as 2nd Lieutenant of Company L of this regiment. Promoted to 1st Lieutenant of this company subsequent to August 31, 1864. Paroled at Greensboro on May 1, 1865.

MORGAN, JOHN B., 2nd Lieutenant

Resided in McDowell County where he enlisted on July 14, 1862, for the war. Mustered in as Corporal. Reported present on surviving company muster rolls through August 31, 1864. Appointed 2nd Lieutenant on June 22, 1864. Transferred to Company H of this regiment with the rank of 3rd Lieutenant subsequent to August 31, 1864.

MORRIS, JOHN H., 2nd Lieutenant

Born in McDowell County* where he resided as a farmer prior to enlisting in McDowell County at age 34. Elected 2nd Lieutenant on July 14, 1862. Resigned on January 24, 1863, by reason of "pulmonary consumption." Resignation accepted on February 25, 1863.

MORRISON, JAMES DYSART, 1st Lieutenant

Born in McDowell County* where he resided as a farmer prior to enlisting in McDowell County at age 35. Elected 3rd Lieutenant on July 14, 1862. Promoted to 1st Lieutenant on November 1, 1862. Reported present in March-June, 1863. Killed at Chickamauga, Georgia, September 20, 1863.

SILVER, LEVI D., 2nd Lieutenant

Previously served as 3rd Lieutenant of Company K of this regiment. Transferred to this company subsequent to August 31, 1864. Promoted to 2nd Lieutenant on an unspecified date. Paroled at Greensboro on May 1, 1865.

SISK, ROBERT HARRISON, 3rd Lieutenant

Born in McDowell County* where he resided as a farmer prior to enlisting in McDowell County at age 21, July 14, 1862, for the war. Mustered in as Private. Reported present in January-June, 1863. Reported absent on sick furlough in September-October, 1863. Returned to duty on an unspecified date. Promoted to Sergeant in November, 1863-February, 1864. Reported present in January-April, 1864. Appointed 3rd Lieutenant on June 22, 1864. Wounded in the right hand (fracture) near Atlanta, Georgia, August 9, 1864. Hospitalized at Macon, Georgia. Was apparently retired from service subsequent to February 6, 1865, by reason of disability from

wounds. [North Carolina pension records indicate that he was wounded also at Chickamauga, Georgia, September 20, 1863.]

NONCOMMISSIONED OFFICERS AND PRIVATES

ALEXANDER, THOMAS M., Private

Enlisted at Camp Holmes on September 8, 1863, for the war. Reported present in January-April, 1864. Wounded in the left foot near Atlanta, Georgia, August 5, 1864. Hospitalized at Macon, Georgia. Crippled by his wound. Paroled at Charlotte on May 11, 1865.

ALLEN, PASCHAL, Private

Born in Rutherford County where he resided as a farmer prior to enlisting in McDowell County at age 33, July 14, 1862, for the war. Reported absent on sick furlough in January-February, 1863. Returned to duty in March-April, 1863. Reported present in May-June, 1863. Reported absent on sick furlough in September-October, 1863. Returned to duty on an unspecified date. Reported present in January-August, 1864. Hospitalized at Charlotte on December 23, 1864, with chronic rheumatism. Transferred to hospital at Raleigh on February 19, 1865. Returned to duty on March 5, 1865. No further records. Survived the war.

ALLISON, ALEXANDER, Private

Born in McDowell County* where he enlisted at age 22, July 14, 1862, for the war. Died at Jacksboro, Tennessee, January 13, 1863. Cause of death not reported.

ALLISON, ELISHA A., Private

Born in McDowell County* where he enlisted at age 28, July 14, 1862, for the war. Died at Jacksboro, Tennessee, February 20, 1863. Cause of death not reported.

ALLRED, JOHN L., Sergeant

Born in Guilford County and resided in McDowell County where he was by occupation a laborer prior to enlisting in McDowell County at age 32, July 14, 1862, for the war. Mustered in as Private. Reported present in January-June and September-October, 1863. Promoted to Sergeant in November, 1863-February, 1864. Reported present in May-August, 1864. Captured at Orangeburg, South Carolina, February 12, 1865. Sent to New Bern. Confined at Hart's Island, New York Harbor, April 10, 1865. Released at Hart's Island on June 18, 1865, after taking the Oath of Allegiance.

ANDERSON, BURRIL, Private

Resided in Burke County and was by occupation a farmer prior to enlisting at Bell's Bridge, Tennessee, at age 53, July 28, 1863, for the war. Sent to hospital sick on September 24, 1863. No further records.

ANDERSON, GEORGE W., Private

Enlisted at Camp Vance on January 3, 1864, for the war. Reported present in March-August, 1864. No further records.

ARROWOOD, LEVI, Private

Enlisted in McDowell County at age 42, October 6, 1863, for the war. Reported absent without leave on October 21, 1863. Returned to duty on December 22, 1863. Reported present but sick on February 29, 1864. Reported present in March-August, 1864. No further records. Survived the war.

BAILEY, THOMAS L., Private

Born in McDowell County* and was by occupation a farmer prior to enlisting in McDowell County at age 21, July 14, 1862, for the war. Reported present in January-February, 1863. Discharged at Jacksboro, Tennessee, March 3, 1863, on a surgeon's certificate of disability.

BAKER, JOHN, Private

Enlisted in Mitchell County on October 15, 1864, for the war. Paroled at Greensboro on May 1, 1865.

BARKER, M., ——

Place and date of enlistment not reported. Listed as a deserter on March 15, 1864.

BENFIELD, ALFRED, Private

Born in Burke or Catawba County* and resided in Burke County where he was by occupation a farmer prior to enlisting in McDowell County at age 31, July 14, 1862, for the war. Transferred to Company C, 5th Battalion N.C. Cavalry, on or about July 29, 1862.

BENFIELD, HARRISON, Private

Born in Burke County and was by occupation a farmer prior to enlisting in McDowell County at age 21, July 14, 1862, for the war. Reported present in January-June, 1863. Reported absent without leave in September-October, 1863. No further records. Survived the war.

BENFIELD, JOHN J., Private

Born in Burke County where he resided as a farmer prior to enlisting in McDowell County at age 32, July 14, 1862, for the war. Reported present in January-February, 1863. Reported sick in hospital at Knoxville, Tennessee, in March-June, 1863. Reported absent without leave in September-October, 1863. Hospitalized at Charlotte on March 11, 1865, with pneumonia. Transferred on April 14, 1865. Paroled at Morganton on May 29, 1865.

BENFIELD, W. A., Private

Place and date of enlistment not reported (probably enlisted subsequent to August 31, 1864). Paroled at Morganton on May 16, 1865.

BENFIELD, W. JOHN, Private

Enlisted in McDowell County at age 33, October 6, 1863, for the war. Reported present in January-August, 1864; however, he was on detail as a collier ("burning coal") from January 13 through August 31, 1864. Paroled at Morganton on May 29, 1865.

BENFIELD, WEIGHSTILL, Private

Born in Burke County where he resided as a farmer or farm laborer prior to enlisting in McDowell County at age 20, July 14, 1862, for the war. Reported present in January-June, 1863. Reported absent without leave in September-October, 1863. No further records. Survived the war.

BENFIELD, WILLIAM H., Private

Resided in Burke County and was by occupation a farm laborer. Place and date of enlistment not reported (probably enlisted sub-

sequent to August 31, 1864). Paroled at Morganton on May 16, 1865. [Was about 23 years of age at time of enlistment.]

BERRY, PINKNEY, Private

Was by occupation a farmer prior to enlisting in McDowell County on or about September 13, 1863, for the war. Reported present in January-August, 1864. Paroled at Greensboro on May 1, 1865. [Records of the Federal Provost Marshal dated 1865 give his age as 21.]

BEVILL, GEORGE, Private

Resided in Yadkin County and was by occupation a farmer. Place and date of enlistment not reported. Deserted to the enemy at Chattanooga, Tennessee, November 13, 1863. Sent to Nashville, Tennessee. Transferred to Louisville, Kentucky, where he arrived on November 24, 1863. Released at Louisville on November 25, 1863, after taking the Oath of Allegiance. [Was about 32 years of age in 1863.]

BLEDSOE, J. MACON, Private

Enlisted at Camp Stokes, Haynesville, Tennessee, August 14, 1862, for the war. Reported present in January-February, 1863. Reported sick in hospital at Knoxville, Tennessee, in March-June, 1863. Reported absent on provost guard in September-October, 1863. Reported present in January-February, 1864. Furloughed for twenty days on April 10, 1864. Returned to duty on an unspecified date. Reported present in May-August, 1864. No further records.

BOWLING, JOEL, Private

Resided in Guilford County. Place and date of enlistment not reported (probably enlisted in the autumn of 1863). Deserted to the enemy at Chattanooga, Tennessee, November 13, 1863. Sent to Nashville, Tennessee. Transferred to Louisville, Kentucky, where he arrived on November 24, 1863. Released at Louisville on November 25, 1863, after taking the Oath of Allegiance.

BRADLEY, JAMES, Private

Born in Rutherford County where he resided as a day laborer prior to enlisting in McDowell County at age 24, July 14, 1862, for the war. Reported present in January-February, 1863. Reported sick in hospital at Knoxville, Tennessee, in March-April, 1863. Returned to duty in May-June, 1863. Reported absent without leave on August 16, 1863. Returned to duty on November 8, 1863. Reported present in January-April, 1864. Captured at Bald Hill, near Atlanta, Georgia, July 22, 1864. Sent to Nashville, Tennessee. Transferred to Louisville, Kentucky, where he arrived on July 30, 1864. Transferred to Camp Chase, Ohio, where he arrived on August 2, 1864. Paroled at Camp Chase and transferred to City Point, Virginia, March 4, 1865, for exchange. Received at Boulware's and Cox's Wharves, James River, Virginia, March 10-12, 1865, for exchange. No further records.

BRANCH, S. C., Private

Enlisted at Camp Stokes, Haynesville, Tennessee, August 8, 1862, for the war. Deserted at Big Creek Gap, Tennessee, November 26, 1862. Returned to duty in March-April, 1863. Reported absent under arrest at Clinton, Tennessee, in May-June, 1863. Returned to duty on an unspecified date. Reported present in September-October, 1863. Reported absent without leave on December 1, 1863. Dropped from the company rolls subsequent to February 29, 1864.

BRANCH, SIDNEY E., Private

Born in Burke County where he resided as a farmer or farm laborer prior to enlisting in McDowell County at age 22, July 14, 1862, for the war. Reported present on surviving company muster rolls through April, 1864. Wounded at Kolb's Farm, near Marietta, Georgia, June 22, 1864. Died on July 13, 1864, of wounds. Place of death not reported.

BRENDLE, LOGAN G., Private

Resided in Forsyth County. Place and date of enlistment not reported (probably enlisted in the autumn of 1863). Deserted to the enemy at Chattanooga, Tennessee, November 13, 1863. Sent to Nashville, Tennessee. Transferred to Louisville, Kentucky, where he arrived on November 24, 1863. Released at Louisville on November 25, 1863, after taking the Oath of Allegiance.

BRIGHT, ALNAY, Private

Resided in McDowell County and was by occupation a farmer prior to enlisting at Camp Stokes, Haynesville, Tennessee, at age 28, August 26, 1862, for the war. Reported present in January-June, 1863. Reported absent without leave on September 9, 1863. Returned to duty on December 16, 1863. Reported present in January-April, 1864. Received a shell wound (flesh) in the right leg at Jonesborough, Georgia, August 31, 1864. Hospitalized at Macon, Georgia, where he died on September 16, 1864, presumably of wounds.

BRIGHT, DAVIS, Private

Resided in McDowell County and was by occupation a farmer prior to enlisting at Camp Vance at age 41, October 6, 186[3], for the war. Died in hospital at Dalton, Georgia, November 20, 1863. Cause of death not reported.

BRIGHT, MERRITT, Private

Resided in McDowell County and was by occupation a farmer prior to enlisting at Camp Stokes, Haynesville, Tennessee, at age 28, August 26, 1862, for the war. Reported present in January-June, 1863. Reported absent without leave on September 9, 1863. Returned to duty on December 16, 1863. Reported present in January-August, 1864. No further records.

BROWES, JAMES W., Private

Place and date of enlistment not reported (probably enlisted subsequent to August 31, 1864). Captured by the enemy on an unspecified date. Confined at Camp Douglas, Chicago, Illinois. Paroled at Camp Douglas and transferred to Point Lookout, Maryland, February 20, 1865 ("entry canceled").

BROWN, GEORGE W., Private

Resided in Macon County and enlisted at Camp Holmes on October 6, 1863, for the war. Deserted on an unspecified date. Reported under arrest on January 6, 1864. Returned to duty in March-April, 1864. Captured near Dallas, Georgia, May 26, 1864. Sent to Nashville, Tennessee. Transferred to Louisville, Kentucky, where he arrived on June 3, 1864. Transferred to Camp Douglas, Chicago, Illinois, where he arrived on July 28, 1864. Paroled at Camp Douglas and transferred to Boulware's Wharf, James River, Virginia, where he was received on or about March 21, 1865, for exchange. Hospitalized at Richmond, Virginia, March 21, 1865, with debilitas. Furloughed for thirty days on March 28, 1865.

BURGIN, CHARLES, Private

Born in Yancey County and was by occupation a farmer prior to enlisting in McDowell County at age 18, July 14, 1862, for the war. No further records.

CALLAWAY, JACOB A., Corporal

Previously served as Corporal in Company L of this regiment. Transferred to this company subsequent to August 31, 1864. Paroled at Greensboro on May 1, 1865. [May have been promoted to Sergeant.]

CANNON, GEORGE, Private

Born in McDowell County* and was by occupation a farmer prior to enlisting in McDowell County at age 29, July 14, 1862, for the war. No further records.

CANNON, ROBERT M., Corporal

Enlisted at Big Creek Gap, Tennessee, December 2, 1862, for the war. Mustered in as Private. Reported present in January-June and September-October, 1863. Promoted to Corporal on December 31, 1863. Reported present in January-August, 1864. No further records. Survived the war. [Was about 23 years of age at time of enlistment.]

COGGINS, JAMES, Private

An undated bounty pay and receipt roll indicates that he enlisted in this company but was discharged.

CONLEY, ALFRED L., Private

Resided in Burke County and was by occupation a farmer prior to enlisting in McDowell County at age 33, July 14, 1862, for the war. Reported present in January-February, 1863. Died at Cumberland Gap, Tennessee, prior to May 9, 1863, of "fever." Date of death not reported.

CONLEY, JOHN F., Private

Born in Burke County where he resided as a farmer prior to enlisting in McDowell County at age 32, July 14, 1862, for the war. Reported present in January-June, 1863. Reported absent without leave on September 1, 1863. Returned to duty on October 1, 1863. Reported present in January-August, 1864. Paroled at Statesville on May 27, 1865.

CONLEY, JULIUS G., Private

Enlisted at Camp Reynolds on September 6, 1862, for the war. Reported present in January-June, 1863. Reported on detail in the "butcher yard" in September-October, 1863. Reported present in January-April, 1864. Captured near the Chattahoochee River, Georgia, on or about July 5, 1864. Sent to Nashville, Tennessee. Transferred to Louisville, Kentucky, where he arrived on July 24, 1864. Transferred to Camp Douglas, Chicago, Illinois, where he arrived on July 28, 1864. Died at Camp Douglas on August 19, 1864, of "dysentery." [Was about 22 years of age at time of enlistment.]

COSBY, JOSEPH, Private

Born in Burke County and was by occupation a farmer prior to enlisting in McDowell County at age 26, July 14, 1862, for the war. Reported present in January-June, 1863. Reported absent without leave on September 9, 1863. Returned to duty on November 8, 1863. Reported present in January-August, 1864. No further records.

CRAUNCH, SAMUEL, ———

An undated bounty pay and receipt roll indicates that he enlisted in this company.

CRAWLEY, ALBERT E., Sergeant

Born in Burke County and resided in McDowell County where he was by occupation a farmer prior to enlisting in McDowell County at age 32, July 14, 1862, for the war. Mustered in as Private. Reported present in January-April, 1863. Reported in hospital at Knoxville, Tennessee, in May-June, 1863. Returned to duty in September-October, 1863. Hospitalized at Griffin, Georgia, November 23, 1863, with an unspecified complaint. Returned to duty prior to February 29, 1864. Reported present in March-August, 1864. Promoted to Sergeant subsequent to August 31, 1864. Captured at Orangeburg, South Carolina, February 12, 1865. Sent to New Bern. Confined at Hart's Island, New York Harbor, April 10, 1865. Released at Hart's Island on June 18, 1865, after taking the Oath of Allegiance.

CRAWLEY, AMBROSE E., Private

Born in Burke County and was by occupation a farmer prior to enlisting in McDowell County at age 33, July 14, 1862, for the war. Reported present in January-June, 1863. Reported absent on detail as a butcher in September-October, 1863. Rejoined the company prior to February 29, 1864. Reported present in March-April, 1864. Reported absent sick in hospital from August 1 through August 31, 1864. No further records. Survived the war.

CURTIS, MERRIT B., Private

Resided in McDowell County and was by occupation a farmer prior to enlisting in McDowell County at age 33, July 14, 1862, for the war. Died in hospital at Cumberland Gap, Tennessee, October 20, 1862, of "typhoid fever."

CURTIS, STANFORD, Private

Born in Yancey County and was by occupation a farmer prior to enlisting in McDowell County at age 24, July 14, 1862, for the war. "Entry canceled." No further records. Survived the war.

DICKSON, JAMES D., Private

Previously served as Private in Company L of this regiment. Transferred to this company subsequent to February 26, 1865. Paroled at Greensboro on May 1, 1865.

DOBSON, JOHN LAFAYETTE, 1st Sergeant

Born in McDowell County* on January 13, 1833. Resided in McDowell County and was by occupation a farmer prior to enlisting in McDowell County at age 29, July 14, 1862, for the war. Mustered in as Private. Promoted to Sergeant prior to March 1, 1863. Reported present in January-June, 1863. Promoted to 1st Sergeant on September 14, 1863. Wounded at Chickamauga, Georgia, September 20, 1863. Reported absent on furlough on October 31, 1863. Returned to duty on or about August 10, 1864, and was detailed as a cattle guard. No further records. Survived the war.

DOBSON, PATRICK HENRY O'NEAL, Private

Born on October 28, 1828. Resided in Burke County and was by occupation a farmer prior to enlisting in Burke County at age 34,

March 2, 1863, for the war. Reported absent on sick furlough in March-June and September-October, 1863. Reported sick in hospital or absent on sick furlough in January-April, 1864. Reported absent without leave on July 4, 1864. No further records. Survived the war. [North Carolina pension records indicate that he was "burned up awful" on "March 1, 1862(4?)," when he was thrown by a horse and his left foot was caught in the stirrup.]

DOVER, ASA, Private

Enlisted in York District, South Carolina, at age 20, August 20, 1863, for the war. Reported absent without leave on or about February 2, 1864. Reported present but under arrest on March 8, 1864. Court-martialed on an unspecified date and sentenced to be shot. Executed at Dalton, Georgia, May 4, 1864, for desertion.

DOVER, JOHN H., Private

Resided in York District, South Carolina, where he enlisted on August 20, 186[3], for the war. Deserted to the enemy on or about February 2, 1864. Took the Oath of Allegiance at Chattanooga, Tennessee, February 14, 1864.

DOVER, ROBERT A., Private

Resided in York District, South Carolina, where he enlisted on August 20, 186[3], for the war. Deserted to the enemy on or about February 2, 1864. Took the Oath of Allegiance at Chattanooga, Tennessee, February 14, 1864.

ELLIOTT, ALNEY B., Private

Born in Burke County and was by occupation a farmer prior to enlisting in McDowell County at age 34, July 14, 1862, for the war. Reported absent on sick furlough from November 17, 1862, through April 30, 1863. Reported in hospital at Loudon, Tennessee, in May-June, 1863. Discharged on August 6, 1863. Reason discharged not reported.

ELLIOTT, CHARLES M., Private

Resided in McDowell County and was by occupation a farmer or laborer prior to enlisting in McDowell County at age 30, July 14, 1862, for the war. Reported present in January-June, 1863. Wounded at Chickamauga, Georgia, September 20, 1863. Hospitalized at Atlanta, Georgia, where he died on October 18, 1863, of wounds.

ELLIOTT, HIRAM, Private

Enlisted at Camp Holmes on November 13, 1863, for the war. Died in hospital at Kingston, Georgia, December 29, 1863. Cause of death not reported.

ELLIOTT, JASPER M., Musician

Born in McDowell County* and was by occupation a farmer prior to enlisting in McDowell County at age 28, July 14, 1862, for the war. Mustered in as Private. Reported present in January-June, 1863. Promoted to Musician (Drummer) in March-April, 1863. Reported absent without leave on August 25, 1863. Returned to duty on March 12, 1864. Reported present in May-August, 1864. No further records. Survived the war.

ELLIOTT, JOHN G., Private

Born in McDowell County* and was by occupation a farmer prior to enlisting in McDowell County at age 21, July 14, 1862, for the war. Was apparently discharged prior to March 1, 1863. Reason discharged not reported. Reenlisted in the company on October 6, 186[3]. Discharged on February 4, 1864, by reason of being a "mail contractor."

ELLIOTT, SPENCER, Private

Resided in McDowell County and was by occupation a farmer prior to enlisting in McDowell County at age 38, October 6, 186[3], for the war. Furloughed for forty days from hospital at Forsyth, Georgia, December 9, 1863. Returned to duty subsequent to April 30, 1864. Wounded near Atlanta, Georgia, on an unspecified date. Reported absent wounded on August 31, 1864. No further records. Survived the war.

ENGLISH, ADEN, Private

Previously served as Private in Company K of this regiment. Transferred to this company subsequent to November 19, 1864. Paroled at Greensboro on May 1, 1865.

ENGLISH, JAMES H., Private

Born in McDowell County* and was by occupation a farmer prior to enlisting in McDowell County at age 29, July 14, 1862, for the war. Reported present in January-June, 1863. Deserted on or about September 25, 1863. Rejoined the company on October 25, 1863. Court-martialed on November 13, 1863. Reported in confinement at Atlanta, Georgia, in January-February, 1864. Returned to duty in March-April, 1864. No further records. Survived the war.

EPLEY, DAVID, Private

Born in Burke County and was by occupation a farmer prior to enlisting in McDowell County at age 27, July 14, 1862, for the war. Reported present in January-June, 1863. Killed at Chickamauga, Georgia, September 20, 1863.

FAIRCLOTH, MICHAEL M., Private

Previously served as Private in Company L of this regiment. Transferred to this company subsequent to August 31, 1864. Wounded in the leg at Bentonville on March 19, 1865. Hospitalized at Greensboro. Survived the war.

FINLEY, JASON C., Private

Born in Rutherford County and was by occupation a farmer prior to enlisting in McDowell County at age 23, July 14, 1862, for the war. Reported present in January-June and September-October, 1863. Reported present but on duty guarding ordnance in January-February, 1864. Reported present in March-April, 1864. Wounded in the left temple near Atlanta, Georgia, on or about July 20, 1864. Hospitalized at Macon, Georgia. Reported absent wounded through August 31, 1864. No further records. Survived the war.

FLEMING, THOMAS J., Private

Born in Burke County and was by occupation a farmer prior to enlisting in McDowell County at age 29, July 14, 1862, for the war. Discharged on October 19, 1862. Reason discharged not reported.

FORNEY, JAMES ABRAM, Private

Born in Burke County on April 20, 1844, and was by occupation a farmer prior to enlisting in McDowell County at age 18, July 14, 1862, for the war. Transferred to Company C, 5th Battalion N.C. Cavalry, on or about July 29, 1862.

FOWRY, EDWARD, ———

An undated bounty pay and receipt roll indicates that he enlisted in this company. No further records.

FREEMAN, WILLIAM, Private

Born in Tennessee and resided in Haywood County where he was by occupation a hunter prior to enlisting in Haywood County at age 40, September 3, 1863, for the war. Reported present through October, 1863. Sent to hospital sick on December 15, 1863. Returned to duty in March-April, 1864. Reported present through August 31, 1864. No further records.

FRIZZLE, ALBERT, Private

Born in McDowell County* and was by occupation a farmer prior to enlisting in McDowell County at age 23, July 14, 1862, for the war. No further records.

FRIZZLE, THOMAS, Private

Born in McDowell County* where he resided as a farmer or laborer prior to enlisting in McDowell County at age 21, July 14, 1862, for the war. Reported present in January-April, 1863. Reported absent on sick furlough in May-June, 1863. Returned to duty on an unspecified date. Reported present in September-October, 1863, and January-February, 1864. Sent to hospital on April 22, 1864. Returned to duty on an unspecified date. Reported present in May-August, 1864. No further records. Survived the war.

FULLWOOD, JAMES M., Private

Born in McDowell County* where he resided as a farmer prior to enlisting in McDowell County at age 21, July 14, 1862, for the war. Mustered in as Sergeant. Reported present in January-June, 1863. Promoted to 1st Sergeant in March-April, 1863. Reduced to ranks on September 13, 1863, for absence without leave. Returned to duty prior to October 31, 1863. Reported present in January-April, 1864. Captured near Dallas, Georgia, on or about May 26, 1864. Sent to Nashville, Tennessee. Transferred to Louisville, Kentucky, where he arrived on June 3, 1864. Transferred to Rock Island, Illinois, where he arrived on June 6, 1864. Released at Rock Island on June 10, 1864, after joining the U.S. Navy.

FULLWOOD, SAMUEL B., Private

Born in Mecklenburg County and resided in Burke County where he was by occupation a farmer prior to enlisting in McDowell County at age 30, July 14, 1862, for the war. Reported present in January-June, 1863. Wounded at Chickamauga, Georgia, September 20, 1863. Died on October 18, 1863, of wounds. Place of death not reported.

GIBBS, A. N., Private

Resided in McDowell County and was by occupation a farmer prior to enlisting in McDowell County at age 43, October 6, 1863, for the war. Reported present in January-February, 1864. Sent to hospital sick on March 16, 1864. Returned to duty on an unspecified date. Reported present in May-August, 1864. No further records.

GIBBS, BRYANT C., Private

Resided in McDowell County and enlisted at Camp Vance on October 6, 1863, for the war. Reported present in October, 1863. Hospitalized on January 1, 1864. Returned to duty in March-April, 1864. Captured at or near Ruff's Mill, near Smyrna, Georgia, on or about July 4, 1864. Sent to Nashville, Tennessee. Transferred to Louisville, Kentucky, where he arrived on July 14, 1864. Transferred to Camp Douglas, Chicago, Illinois, where he arrived on July 18, 1864. Released at Camp Douglas on June 16, 1865, after taking the Oath of Allegiance.

GIBBS, JOSHUA F., Private

Born in Burke County and was by occupation a farmer prior to enlisting in McDowell County at age 32, July 14, 1862, for the war. Reported present in January-February, 1863. Reported present but on detail as a wagoner in March-June, 1863. Reported absent without leave on September 25, 1863. Returned to duty on November 8, 1863. Reported on detail as a wagoner from December 1, 1863, through August 31, 1864. No further records. Survived the war.

GIBBS, WILLIAM F., Private

Born in Burke County and enlisted in McDowell County at age 28, July 14, 1862, for the war. Reported present in January-June and September-October, 1863. Reported present but on detail guarding ordnance stores in January-February, 1864. Reported present in March-June, 1864. Paroled at Morganton on June 23, 1865. [North Carolina pension records indicate that he was wounded in the left side at Chickamauga, Georgia, and lost the index finger of his right hand as a result of wounds received at Jonesborough, Georgia.]

GIBSON, HENRY F., Private

Born in Randolph County and was by occupation a farmer prior to enlisting in McDowell County at age 33, July 14, 1862, for the war. Reported present in January-June, 1863. Killed at Chickamauga, Georgia, September 20, 1863.

GIBSON, ODOM, Private

Resided in McDowell County where he enlisted at age 43, September 13, 1863, for the war. Reported absent without leave on November 25, 1863. Returned to duty on January 26, 1864. Reported present in March-August, 1864. Captured at Shilling's Bridge, South Carolina, February 12, 1865. Sent to New Bern. Transferred to Hart's Island, New York Harbor, where he arrived on April 10, 1865. Released at Hart's Island on June 19, 1865, after taking the Oath of Allegiance. [North Carolina pension records indicate that he was wounded "between Goldsboro & Newbern" in February, 1865, when he was "struck in the rim of the belley with the musel (muzzle) of a gun."]

GILKEY, AUGUSTUS B., Private

Born in Rutherford County where he resided as a farmer prior to enlisting in McDowell County at age 29, July 14, 1862, for the war. Reported present or accounted for in January-June, 1863. Detailed as Commissary Sergeant of Brig. Gen. Joseph B. Palmer's brigade on October 1, 1863. Reported absent on detail until August 15, 1864, when he was detailed as brigade Commissary. No further records. Survived the war.

HAGEY, WILLIAM, Private

Enlisted at Camp Holmes on November 11, 1863, for the war. Reported present in January-April, 1864. Wounded in the thigh (fracture) at Resaca, Georgia, May 14-15, 1864. Died in hospital at Atlanta, Georgia, June 30, 1864, presumably of wounds.

HALL, ELIJAH Y., Corporal

Born in McDowell County* where he resided as a farmer or laborer prior to enlisting in McDowell County at age 25, July 14, 1862, for

the war. Mustered in as Private. Reported present in January-February, 1863. Detailed as a hospital nurse at Knoxville, Tennessee, April 15, 1863. Returned to duty subsequent to June 30, 1863. Wounded in the left thigh at Chickamauga, Georgia, September 20, 1863. Furloughed on September 25, 1863. Returned to duty in March-April, 1864. Promoted to Corporal prior to July 22, 1864, when he was captured at Bald Hill, near Atlanta, Georgia. Sent to Nashville, Tennessee. Transferred to Louisville, Kentucky, where he arrived on July 30, 1864. Transferred to Camp Chase, Ohio, where he arrived on August 2, 1864. Paroled at Camp Chase on March 4, 1865. Received at Boulware's and Cox's Wharves, James River, Virginia, March 10-12, 1865, for exchange. No further records. Survived the war.

HALL, JOSHUA, ———

North Carolina pension records indicate that he served in this company.

HALL, THOMAS, Private

Born in McDowell County* and was by occupation a farmer prior to enlisting in McDowell County at age 28, July 14, 1862, for the war. Died prior to April 25, 1863. Place, date, and cause of death not reported.

HANDY, F. MARION, Corporal

Previously served as Corporal in Company L of this regiment. Transferred to this company subsequent to August 31, 1864. Paroled at Greensboro on May 1, 1865.

HANEY, DANIEL W., Private

Born in McDowell County* where he resided prior to enlisting in McDowell County at age 22, July 14, 1862, for the war. Reported absent on sick furlough on September 25, 1862. Returned to duty in May-June, 1863. Reported sick in hospital in September-October, 1863. Furloughed from hospital on December 1, 1863. Reported absent sick from March 1 through August 31, 1864. Returned to duty prior to February 12, 1865, when he was captured at Shilling's Bridge, South Carolina. Sent to New Bern. Transferred to Hart's Island, New York Harbor, where he arrived on April 10, 1865. Released at Hart's Island on June 18, 1865, after taking the Oath of Allegiance.

HARVEY, GEORGE B., Private

Born in McDowell County* and was by occupation a farmer prior to enlisting in McDowell County at age 24, July 14, 1862, for the war. Reported present in January-June, 1863. Killed at Chickamauga, Georgia, September 20, 1863.

HARVEY, JOHN L., Private

Born in McDowell County* and was by occupation a farmer prior to enlisting in McDowell County at age 37, July 14, 1862, for the war. Reported absent on sick furlough from September 7, 1862, through April 30, 1863. Reported in hospital at Greenville in May-June, 1863. Reported absent sick in September-October, 1863. No further records.

HARVEY, SAMUEL S., Private

Resided in McDowell County where he enlisted at age 18, September 13, 1863, for the war. Hospitalized at La Grange, Georgia, on or about December 15, 1863. Returned to duty in March-April, 1864. Wounded in the leg at Resaca, Georgia, May 14-15, 1864.

Returned to duty prior to September 1, 1864. No further records. Survived the war.

HAYES, CALVIN, ———

Place and date of enlistment not reported. Died at or near Raleigh on March 28, 1865. Cause of death not reported.

HENSLEY, JOHN M., Private

Born in Rutherford County and was by occupation a farmer prior to enlisting in McDowell County at age 27, July 14, 1862, for the war. Reported absent on sick furlough from November 19, 1862, through April 30, 1863. Sent to hospital at Loudon, Tennessee, in May-June, 1863. Discharged on August 6, 1863, by reason of "chronic rheumatism."

HICKS, JAMES YOUNG, Private

Born on June 21, 1823. Resided in McDowell County where he enlisted at age 40, October 6, 1863, for the war. Reported present in January-August, 1864. No further records. Survived the war.

HINE, ELI, Private

Resided in Forsyth County. Place and date of enlistment not reported (probably enlisted in the autumn of 1863). Deserted to the enemy at Chattanooga, Tennessee, November 12, 1863. Sent to Nashville, Tennessee. Transferred to Louisville, Kentucky, where he arrived on November 19, 1863. Released at Louisville on November 20, 1863, after taking the Oath of Allegiance.

HOGAN, ALFRED, Private

Resided in McDowell County where he enlisted at age 40, October 6, 186[3], for the war. Reported present but under arrest in May-August, 1864. Reason he was arrested not reported. No further records. Survived the war.

HOLLIFIELD, RILEY P., Private

Born in Rutherford County and was by occupation a farmer prior to enlisting in McDowell County at age 32, July 14, 1862, for the war. Mustered in as Private. Reported present in January-April, 1863. Promoted to Sergeant in March-April, 1863. Reported absent on detached service in May-June, 1863. Reported absent on sick furlough from Knoxville, Tennessee, from August 12, 1863, through February 29, 1864. Declared unfit for field service and was ordered to report to Atlanta, Georgia, for "post duty" on April 26, 1864. Reported "absent" through August 31, 1864. Reduced to ranks in May-August, 1864. No further records. Survived the war.

HOOVER, MILAS, Private

Enlisted in McDowell County on October 6, 1863, for the war. Reported present in January-August, 1864. No further records. Survived the war. [Was about 33 years of age at time of enlistment. North Carolina pension records indicate that he was shot in the head and blinded in the left eye at Stony Side (Rocky Face Ridge), Georgia, in July or August, 186(4).]

HOYL, J. F., Private

Enlisted in McDowell County on October 6, 1863, for the war. Reported present in January-August, 1864. No further records.

HUNTER, JAMES WESLEY, Corporal

Born in Burke County where he resided as a farmer prior to enlisting in McDowell County at age 34, July 14, 1862, for the war.

Mustered in as Corporal. Transferred to Company C, 5th Battalion N.C. Cavalry, on or about July 29, 1862.

HURLEY, HARVEY, Private

Previously served as Private in Company L of this regiment. Transferred to this company subsequent to August 31, 1864. Wounded slightly in the thigh at Bentonville on March 19, 1865. Hospitalized at Greensboro. No further records.

HURLEY, THOMAS, Private

Previously served as Private in Company L of this regiment. Transferred to this company subsequent to August 31, 1864. Wounded seriously in the knee at Bentonville on March 19, 1865. Hospitalized at Greensboro. Paroled at Greensboro on May 1, 1865.

HUSIER, ALEXANDER, Private

Enlisted at Camp Holmes on October 6, 1863, for the war. Deserted on November 14, 1863. Reported under arrest on January 3, 1864. Died in "prison hospital" at Atlanta, Georgia, April 4, 1864. Cause of death not reported.

HUTCHINGS, WRIGHT, Private

Resided in Rutherford County and was by occupation a farm laborer prior to enlisting in McDowell County at age 43, October 6, 1863, for the war. Reported absent without leave on November 25, 1863. Reported under arrest on March 8, 1864. Court-martialed on April 2, 1864, and sentenced to be shot. Executed at Dalton, Georgia, May 4, 1864, for desertion.

JANES, LOSEN M., Private

Enlisted at Cumberland Gap, Tennessee, September 30, 1862, for the war. Died at Jacksboro, Tennessee, February 27, 1863. Cause of death not reported.

JARRETT, DANIEL, Private

Born in McDowell County* and was by occupation a farmer prior to enlisting in McDowell County at age 21, July 14, 1862, for the war. Reported absent on sick furlough from Big Creek Gap, Tennessee, November 15, 1862. Returned to duty in May-June, 1863. Wounded at Chickamauga, Georgia, September 20, 1863. Returned to duty on an unspecified date subsequent to October 31, 1863. Reported present in January-April, 1864. Reported present but on duty as a provost guard in May-August, 1864. No further records. Survived the war.

JARRETT, GEORGE Y., Sergeant

Resided in McDowell County where he enlisted on September 13, 1863, for the war. Mustered in as Private. Nominated for the Badge of Distinction for gallantry at Chickamauga, Georgia, September 19-20, 1863. Reported sick in hospital on February 23, 1864. Declared unfit for field service and was ordered to report for post duty at Atlanta, Georgia, on or about March 26, 1864. Reported absent on duty at Atlanta through August 31, 1864. Promoted to Sergeant subsequent to August 31, 1864. Hospitalized at Macon, Georgia, December 6, 1864, with intermittent fever. Returned to duty on February 11, 1865. No further records.

JARRETT, KILLIAN MILLS, Private

Born in McDowell County where he resided as a farmer prior to enlisting in McDowell County at age 19, July 14, 1862, for the war. Reported present on surviving company muster rolls through August 31, 1864. Captured at Orangeburg, South Carolina, February

12, 1865. Sent to New Bern. Confined at Hart's Island, New York Harbor, April 10, 1865. Released at Hart's Island on June 19, 1865, after taking the Oath of Allegiance.

JARRETT, SAMUEL C., Private

Resided in McDowell County and was by occupation a farmer prior to enlisting at Cumberland Gap, Tennessee, at age 33, September 30, 1862, for the war. Reported present in January-February, 1863. Furloughed on March 12, 1863. Returned to duty in May-June, 1863. Wounded at Chickamauga, Georgia, September 20, 1863. Apparently returned to duty briefly in January-February, 1864, but was sent to hospital by the regimental surgeon on February 24, 1864. Reported on duty at the military prison at Atlanta, Georgia, in May-June, 1864. Reported absent sick in July-August, 1864. No further records.

JEMERSON, JOHN, Private

Born in McDowell County* where he resided as a farmer prior to enlisting in McDowell County at age 24, July 14, 1862, for the war. Died at Jacksboro, Tennessee, February 11, 1863. Cause of death not reported.

JONES, JOHNSON, Private

Born in Rockingham County and was by occupation a farmer prior to enlisting in McDowell County at age 19, July 14, 1862, for the war. Reported present in January-June, 1863. Killed at Chickamauga, Georgia, September 20, 1863.

KANIPE, ELI, Private

Born in Lincoln County and was by occupation a farmer prior to enlisting in McDowell County at age 18, July 14, 1862, for the war. Reported present in January-June, 1863. Reported absent without leave on September 9, 1863. Returned to duty on November 9, 1863. Reported present through April 30, 1864. Captured at Bald Hill, near Atlanta, Georgia, July 22, 1864. Sent to Nashville, Tennessee. Transferred to Louisville, Kentucky, where he arrived on July 30, 1864. Transferred to Camp Chase, Ohio, where he arrived on August 2, 1864. Died at Camp Chase on March 7, 1865, of "variola."

KANIPE, ZEPHANIAH, Private

Enlisted at Dalton, Georgia, at age 18, January 23, 1864, for the war. Reported present in March-August, 1864. No further records. Survived the war.

KAYLER, GEORGE, Private

Born in Burke County and resided in McDowell County where he was by occupation a farmer prior to enlisting in McDowell County at age 26, July 14, 1862, for the war. Reported present in January-April, 1863. Reported in hospital at Knoxville, Tennessee, in May-June, 1863. Returned to duty on an unspecified date. Reported present in September-October, 1863. Furloughed for forty days on or about January 21, 1864. Returned to duty on an unspecified date. Reported present in March-August, 1864. Captured at Shilling's Bridge, South Carolina, February 12, 1865. Sent to New Bern. Confined at Hart's Island, New York Harbor, April 10, 1865. Released at Hart's Island on June 19, 1865, after taking the Oath of Allegiance.

KAYLOR, JOHN, ———

North Carolina pension records indicate that he served in this company.

KENNEDY, JOHN H., Private

Resided in Forsyth County. Place and date of enlistment not reported. Deserted to the enemy at Chattanooga, Tennessee, November 13, 1863. Sent to Nashville, Tennessee. Transferred to Louisville, Kentucky, where he arrived on November 24, 1863. Released at Louisville on November 25, 1863, after taking the Oath of Allegiance.

KENNER, ULRICH, Private

Enlisted at Camp Holmes on November 11, 186[3], for the war. Reported absent without leave on January 1, 1864. Listed as a deserter on March 15, 1864.

LACKEY, JAMES, Private

Born in McDowell County* and was by occupation a farmer prior to enlisting in McDowell County at age 21, July 14, 1862, for the war. Reported present in January-June, 1863. Reported absent without leave in September-October, 1863, and January-February, 1864. Listed as a deserter on April 7, 1864.

LANE, WILLIAM, Private

Enlisted at Camp Holmes on October 13, 186[3], for the war. Reported present in May-August, 1864. No further records. Survived the war. [Was about 30 years of age at time of enlistment.]

LEWIS, GEORGE, Private

Resided in McDowell County and was by occupation a laborer prior to enlisting in McDowell County at age 31, September 13, 1863, for the war. Reported sick in hospital on October 31, 1863. Returned to duty on an unspecified date. Reported present in January-April, 1864. Wounded at Kolb's Farm, near Marietta, Georgia, June 22, 1864. Died in hospital at Barnesville, Georgia, July 4, 1864, presumably of wounds.

LITTLE, J. F., Private

Resided in Mecklenburg County and enlisted at Camp Holmes on November 13, 1863, for the war. Reported present in January-February, 1864. Declared unfit for field service on April 29, 1864. Assigned to duty at the military prison at Atlanta, Georgia, in May-June, 1864. Hospitalized at Macon, Georgia, July 26, 1864, with phthisis. Furloughed on August 5, 1864. Hospitalized at Macon on September 1, 1864. Transferred on September 13, 1864. Company records do not indicate whether he returned to duty; however, he was paroled at Charlotte on May 6, 1865.

LONON, OLIVER POWELL, Corporal

Born in McDowell County* and resided in Burke County where he was by occupation a farmer prior to enlisting in McDowell County at age 29, July 14, 1862, for the war. Mustered in as Private. Reported present in January-February, 1863. Reported sick in hospital at Knoxville, Tennessee, in March-April, 1863. Promoted to Corporal in March-April, 1863. Returned to duty in May-June, 1863. Reported present or accounted for in September-October, 1863, and January-April, 1864. Captured near Dallas, Georgia, May 26, 1864. Sent to Nashville, Tennessee. Transferred to Louisville, Kentucky, where he arrived on June 3, 1864. Transferred to Rock Island, Illinois, where he arrived on June 6, 1864. Released at Rock Island on June 10, 1864, after joining the U.S. Navy.

LOVEN, ANDERSON, ———

Name appears on a muster-in roll for this company dated July 18, 1862. No further records.

McCALL, JOHN, Corporal

Born in McDowell County where he enlisted at age 18, July 14, 1862, for the war. Mustered in as Corporal. Reported present in January-April, 1863. Died in hospital at Clinton, Tennessee, May 3 or May 12, 1863. Cause of death not reported.

McGAHEY, JAMES, Private

Enlisted at Camp Stokes, Haynesville, Tennessee, August 26, 1862, for the war. Reported present in January-June, 1863. Wounded at Chickamauga, Georgia, September 20, 1863. Reported absent without leave on September 24, 1863. Returned to duty on November 8, 1863. Reported present in January-April, 1864. Captured at Bald Hill, near Atlanta, Georgia, July 22, 1864. Sent to Nashville, Tennessee. Transferred to Louisville, Kentucky, where he arrived on July 30, 1864. Transferred to Camp Chase, Ohio, where he arrived on August 2, 1864. Paroled at Camp Chase and transferred to Boulware's and Cox's Wharves, James River, Virginia, where he was received on March 10-12, 1865, for exchange. No further records.

McGALLIARD, ROBERT, Corporal

Born in McDowell County where he resided as a farmer prior to enlisting in McDowell County at age 18, July 14, 1862, for the war. Mustered in as Private. Reported present in January-June, 1863. Promoted to Musician prior to March 1, 1863. Reported absent without leave on September 13, 1863. Returned to duty on November 8, 1863. Reduced to ranks in November, 1863-February, 1864. Reported present in January-August, 1864. Promoted to Corporal on an unspecified date. Transferred to Company G of this regiment subsequent to August 31, 1864.

McGIMSEY, THEODORE CICERO, Sergeant

Born in Burke County and was by occupation a farmer prior to enlisting in McDowell County at age 26, July 14, 1862, for the war. Mustered in as Corporal. Reported present in January-June, 1863. Promoted to Sergeant in March-April, 1863. Reported present in September-October, 1863. Furloughed for forty days on January 31, 1864. Returned to duty on an unspecified date. Reported present in March-August, 1864. Transferred to Company G of this regiment subsequent to August 31, 1864. Appointed 2nd Lieutenant of Company G on an unspecified date.

MACKEY, JAMES, Private

Born in McDowell County* and was by occupation a farmer prior to enlisting in McDowell County at age 27, July 14, 1862, for the war. Furloughed for twenty days on November 19, 1862. Reported absent sick in January-February, 1863. Listed as a deserter in March-April, 1863. Reported under arrest in May-June, 1863. Reported absent without leave on August 16, 1863. Returned to duty on October 31, 1863. Reported present in January-April, 1864. Captured at Bald Hill, near Atlanta, Georgia, July 22, 1864. Sent to Nashville, Tennessee. Transferred to Louisville, Kentucky, where he arrived on July 30, 1864. Transferred to Camp Chase, Ohio, where he arrived on August 2, 1864. Paroled at Camp Chase on March 4, 1865. Received at Boulware's and Cox's Wharves, James River, Virginia, March 10-12, 1865, for exchange. No further records. Survived the war.

McKISSICK, ROBERT R., Private

Born in Iredell County and was by occupation a farmer prior to enlisting in McDowell County at age 28, July 14, 1862, for the war. Reported present in January-February, 1863. Reported in hospital at Knoxville, Tennessee, in March-June, 1863. Reported absent

without leave on August 31, 1863. Returned to duty on November 8, 1863. Reported present in January-April, 1864. Killed at Resaca, Georgia, May 14, 1864.

MANGUM, GEORGE T., Private

Born in McDowell County* and was by occupation a farmer prior to enlisting in McDowell County at age 25, July 14, 1862, for the war. Reported present in January-June, 1863. Reported absent without leave on September 9, 1863. Returned to duty on November 9, 1863. Wounded in the thumb, hand, and right arm at Rocky Face Ridge, Georgia, February 25, 1864. Hospitalized at Greensboro, Georgia. Furloughed for sixty days in March-April, 1864. Detailed for duty as a cattle guard on August 16, 1864. Declared unfit for field service on November 15, 1864, and was reported to be on detail "driving stock" at Gainesville, Alabama. Paroled at Greensboro, North Carolina, on or about May 1, 1865.

MANGUM, RICHARD G., Private

Born in Granville County and resided in McDowell County where he was by occupation a farmer prior to enlisting in McDowell County at age 33, July 14, 1862, for the war. Reported present in January-June, 1863. Reported absent without leave on September 9, 1863. Returned to duty on November 9, 1863. Reported present in January-August, 1864. Captured at Orangeburg, South Carolina, February 12, 1865. Sent to New Bern. Confined at Hart's Island, New York Harbor, April 10, 1865. Released at Hart's Island on June 19, 1865, after taking the Oath of Allegiance.

MARLIN, I. J., Sergeant

Enlisted in McDowell County. Enlistment date reported as July 14, 186-. Mustered in with an unspecified rank. Reported present in May-August, 1864, and rank reported as Corporal. Promoted to Sergeant subsequent to August 31, 1864. Wounded slightly in the arm at Bentonville on March 19, 1865. No further records.

MARLOW, ISAAC, Private

Enlisted at Big Creek Gap, Tennessee, at age 24, December 24, 1862, for the war. Reported present in January-June, 1863. Reported absent without leave on September 13, 1863. Returned to duty on December 11, 1863. Reported present in January-April, 1864. No further records. Survived the war.

MASSEY, J. H., Private

Enlisted at Cumberland Gap, Tennessee, October 1, 1862, for the war. Reported present in January-February, 1863. Died at Jacksboro, Tennessee, March 17, 1863. Cause of death not reported.

MASSEY, JOHN, Private

Enlisted at Camp Holmes on November 13, 1863, for the war. Reported absent without leave on February 25, 1864. Sent to hospital on April 27, 1864. Was later listed as a deserter.

MATHIS, MARTIN, Private

Born in South Carolina and resided in McDowell County where he was by occupation a farmer or laborer prior to enlisting in McDowell County at age 18, July 14, 1862, for the war. Reported present on surviving company muster rolls through August 31, 1864. Captured at Orangeburg, South Carolina, February 12, 1865. Sent to New Bern. Confined at Hart's Island, New York Harbor, April 10, 1865. Hospitalized at Hart's Island on May 9, 1865, with variola. Returned to the prison compound on May 30, 1865. Released at Hart's Island on June 18, 1865, after taking the Oath of Allegiance.

MOFFITT, JOHN W. L., Corporal

Born in McDowell County* where he resided as a farmer prior to enlisting in McDowell County at age 25, July 14, 1862, for the war. Mustered in as Private. Reported present in January-June, 1863. Reported absent without leave on September 23, 1863. Returned to duty on November 8, 1863. Reported present in January-August, 1864. Promoted to Corporal in May-August, 1864. Captured at Columbia, South Carolina, February 17, 1865. Sent to New Bern. Transferred to Hart's Island, New York Harbor, where he arrived on April 10, 1865. Released at Hart's Island on June 18, 1865, after taking the Oath of Allegiance.

MOFFITT, NELSON, Private

Born in McDowell County* where he resided as a farmer prior to enlisting in McDowell County at age 34, July 14, 1862, for the war. Mustered in as Private. Reported absent on sick furlough on November 19, 1862. Appointed Musician prior to March 1, 1863. Reduced to ranks in March-April, 1863. Returned to duty in May-June, 1863. Died prior to August 5, 1863. Place, date, and cause of death not reported.

MOODY, ROBERT L., Private

Born in Chattooga County, Georgia, and was by occupation a farmer prior to enlisting in McDowell County at age 22, July 14, 1862, for the war. Reported present in January-June, 1863. Reported absent without leave on August 16, 1863. Returned to duty on November 8, 1863. Reported present in January-February, 1864. Company records indicate that he was captured at Kolb's Farm, near Marietta, Georgia, June 22, 1864; however, records of the Federal Provost Marshal do not substantiate that report. No further records.

MOORE, CHARLES M., Private

Born in McDowell County* and was by occupation a farmer prior to enlisting in McDowell County at age 30, July 14, 1862, for the war. Mustered in as Private. Promoted to Sergeant prior to March 1, 1863. Reported present in January-June and September-October, 1863. Elected 2nd Lieutenant on November 20, 1863, but was rejected by the examining board. Reverted to the rank of Private on an unspecified date. Reported present in January-April, 1864. Killed at Resaca, Georgia, May 15, 1864.

MOORE, J. C., Private

Resided in McDowell County and enlisted at Camp Vance on October 6, 1863, for the war. Reported sick in hospital on February 10, 1864. Died at home in McDowell County on March 24, 1864. Cause of death not reported.

MORGAN, ELIJAH P., Private

Born in Rutherford County and was by occupation a farmer prior to enlisting in McDowell County at age 34, July 14, 1862, for the war. Reported present in January-June, 1863. Reported absent without leave in September-October, 1863. Sent to hospital sick on February 13, 1864. Died in hospital at Marietta, Georgia, February 25, 1864. Cause of death not reported.

MORGAN, J. H., Private

Enlisted at Camp Stokes, Haynesville, Tennessee. Enlistment date reported as August 16, 1862; however, he was not listed in the rolls of this company until January-February, 1864. Furloughed for forty days on January 31, 1864. Returned to duty on an unspecified date. Reported present in March-August, 1864. No further records.

MORGAN, JETHRO, Private

Born in Rutherford County and was by occupation a farmer prior to enlisting in McDowell County at age 28, July 14, 1862, for the war. Reported present in January-February, 1863. Reported on detail as a wood chopper in March-April, 1863. Reported present in May-June, 1863. Reported absent without leave on September 8, 1863. Returned to duty on December 9, 1863. Detailed as a wagoner on December 16, 1863. Reported on detail through August 31, 1864. No further records. Survived the war.

MORGAN, JETHRO C., Private

Resided in McDowell County and enlisted at Dalton, Georgia, January 23, 1864, for the war. Reported absent sick on February 29, 1864. Furloughed for sixty days from hospital on March 9, 1864. Returned to duty on an unspecified date. Reported present in May-August, 1864. Captured at Orangeburg, South Carolina, February 12, 1865. Sent to New Bern. Confined at Hart's Island, New York Harbor, April 10, 1865. Released at Hart's Island on June 18, 1865, after taking the Oath of Allegiance. [Was about 20 years of age at time of enlistment. North Carolina pension records indicate that he was wounded in the left leg at Marietta, Georgia, in November, 1864.]

MORGAN, JOHN SIMEON, Private

Born in McDowell County and was by occupation a farmer prior to enlisting in McDowell County at age 19, July 14, 1862, for the war. Reported present in January-June, 1863. Died in hospital at Clinton, Tennessee, July 7, 1863, of "fever."

MORGAN, JONATHAN, Private

Born in McDowell County* where he resided as a laborer prior to enlisting in McDowell County at age 21, July 14, 1862, for the war. Mustered in as Corporal. Reduced to ranks prior to March 1, 1863. Reported present in January-June, 1863. Reported sick in hospital in September-October, 1863. No further records.

MORGAN, PERMENTER, Private

Born in McDowell County* and was by occupation a farmer prior to enlisting in McDowell County at age 26, July 14, 1862, for the war. Reported present in January-June, 1863. Killed at Chickamauga, Georgia, September 20, 1863.

MORRISON, FRANCIS M., Private

Born in McDowell County* and was by occupation a farmer prior to enlisting in McDowell County at age 28, July 14, 1862, for the war. Reported absent on sick furlough from October 31, 1862, through April 30, 1863. Reported sick in hospital at Loudon, Tennessee, in May-June, 1863. Discharged on August 6, 1863, by reason of "incipient phthisis and the consequent . . . general debility."

MORROW, HIGGINS, Private

Enlisted in McDowell County on October 6, 186[3], for the war. Reported absent without leave on October 21, 1863. Returned to duty on January 8, 1864. Sent to hospital sick on February 23, 1864. Died in hospital at Atlanta, Georgia, February 25, 1864. Cause of death not reported.

MORROW, JOHN, Private

Resided in McDowell County and was by occupation a laborer prior to enlisting in McDowell County at age 40, October 6, 1863, for the war. Reported absent without leave on February 10, 1864. Returned to duty on an unspecified date. Captured near the

Chattahoochee River, Georgia, July 5, 1864. Sent to Nashville, Tennessee. Transferred to Louisville, Kentucky, where he arrived on July 14, 1864. Transferred to Camp Douglas, Chicago, Illinois, where he arrived on July 16, 1864. Died at Camp Douglas on August 4, 1864, of "debility."

MOSTELLER, DANIEL, Private

Born in Lincoln County and was by occupation a farmer prior to enlisting in McDowell County at age 34, July 14, 1862, for the war. Reported present in January-February, 1863. Reported absent on duty as a hospital nurse at Knoxville, Tennessee, in March-April, 1863. Rejoined the company in May-June, 1863. Reported absent without leave on September 8, 1863. Returned to duty on January 26, 1864. Reported present through April 30, 1864. Captured at Bald Hill, near Atlanta, Georgia, July 22, 1864. Sent to Nashville, Tennessee. Transferred to Louisville, Kentucky, where he arrived on July 30, 1864. Transferred to Camp Chase, Ohio, where he arrived on August 2, 1864. Released at Camp Chase on March 16, 1865, after taking the Oath of Allegiance.

MURDOCK, J. C., Private

Place and date of enlistment not reported (probably enlisted subsequent to August 31, 1864). Captured at the Edisto River, South Carolina, February 12, 1865. Sent to New Bern. Transferred to Hart's Island, New York Harbor, where he arrived on April 10, 1865. Died at Hart's Island on May 31, 1865, of "chronic diarrhoea."

MURPHY, ARCHIBALD D., Private

Resided in McDowell County and enlisted at Camp Reynolds on September 3, 1862, for the war. Mustered in as Private. Reported present in January-June, 1863. Promoted to Corporal in May-June, 1863. Wounded at Chickamauga, Georgia, September 20, 1863. Hospitalized at Atlanta, Georgia, on an unspecified date. Furloughed on October 6, 1863. Returned to duty in March-April, 1864. Reduced to ranks in May-August, 1864. Detailed for "post duty" at Atlanta on or about August 12, 1864. Captured in Itawamba County, Mississippi, January 1, 1865. Sent to Nashville, Tennessee. Transferred to Louisville, Kentucky, where he arrived on January 16, 1865. Transferred to Camp Chase, Ohio, where he arrived on January 18, 1865. Released at Camp Chase on June 13, 1865, after taking the Oath of Allegiance. [Records of the Federal Provost Marshal dated June, 1865, give his age as 30.]

NANNEY, MARTIN, Private

Born in Rutherford County where he resided as a farmer prior to enlisting in McDowell County at age 27, July 14, 1862, for the war. Dropped from the company rolls prior to March 1, 1863. Reason he was dropped not reported. Discharged on August 6, 1863, by reason of "incipient phthisis and inguinal hernia." Died in the autumn of 1863.

NICHOLS, JAMES W., Private

Previously served as Private in Company C of this regiment. Transferred to this company on December 24, 1862. Reported present in January-June, 1863. Detailed as a wagoner on an unspecified date. Captured at Cumberland Gap, Tennessee, September 9, 1863. Confined at Louisville, Kentucky. Transferred to Camp Douglas, Chicago, Illinois, where he arrived on September 26, 1863. Released at Camp Douglas on June 16, 1865, after taking the Oath of Allegiance.

NICHOLS, JONATHAN A., Private

Previously served as Private in Company C of this regiment. Transferred to this company in March-April, 1863. Reported present in May-June, 1863. Reported absent without leave on September 13, 1863. Returned to duty on October 6, 1863. Reported present in January-April, 1864. Wounded in the face near Resaca, Georgia, May 15, 1864. No further records.

NICHOLS, WILLIAM A., Private

Enlisted in Yancey County on July 12, 1862, for the war. Reported present in January-February, 1863. Died at Jacksboro, Tennessee, March 15, 1863. Cause of death not reported.

OWENSBY, AARON WHITENTON, Private

Born in McDowell County* and was by occupation a farmer prior to enlisting in McDowell County at age 26, July 14, 1862, for the war. Died at Big Creek Gap, Tennessee, January 6, 1863, of disease.

PANGLE, HENRY, Private

Enlisted at Camp Vance on October 6, 1863, for the war. Reported present in January-April, 1864. Wounded near Atlanta, Georgia, August 7, 1864. Died of wounds. Place and date of death not reported.

PARKER, WILLIAM H., Private

Enlisted in McDowell County on October 6, 1863, for the war. Reported absent without leave on February 12, 1864. Furloughed for sixty days on March 28, 1864. Reported absent without leave on May 28, 1864. Paroled at Morganton on May 27, 1865. [Was about 18 years of age at time of enlistment.]

PATTON, ROBERT V., Private

Born in McDowell County* and was by occupation a farmer prior to enlisting in McDowell County at age 32, July 14, 1862, for the war. Reported present in January-June, 1863. Wounded in the head, face, and both thighs at Chickamauga, Georgia, September 20, 1863. Hospitalized at La Grange, Georgia. Furloughed on December 10, 1863. Reported absent on expired furlough on August 31, 1864. No further records.

POWELL, A. D., Private

Enlisted in McDowell County on July 14, 1862, for the war. Reported present in January-June, 1863. Reported absent without leave in September-October, 1863. Wounded at Rocky Face Ridge, Georgia, February 25, 1864. Returned to duty in March-April, 1864. Reported present through August 31, 1864. Paroled at Morganton on May 13, 1865.

POWELL, DENNY, Private

Born in Burke County and was by occupation a farmer prior to enlisting in McDowell County at age 40, July 14, 1862, for the war as a substitute. Dropped from the company rolls prior to March 1, 1863. Reason he was dropped not reported.

QUINN, WILLIAM B., Private

Born in McDowell County* and was by occupation a farmer prior to enlisting in McDowell County at age 27, July 14, 1862, for the war. Reported present in January-April, 1863. Detailed as a wagoner in May-June, 1863. Reported on detail as a wagoner in

September-October, 1863, and January-February, 1864. Reported present in March-August, 1864. No further records. Survived the war.

RAMSEY, ALEXANDER, Private

Enlisted at Camp Vance on January 2, 1864, for the war. Reported sick in hospital from January 29 through August 31, 1864. No further records.

RANKIN, J. E., Private

Enlisted at Clinton, Tennessee, April 28, 1863, for the war. Reported present but on detail as a druggist in May-June, 1863. Appointed Quartermaster Sergeant and transferred to the Field and Staff of this regiment on an unspecified date (probably in July, 1863). Reduced to ranks and transferred back to this company on an unspecified date (probably prior to August 20, 1863). Reported "absent" in January-August, 1864. No further records. [He was captured at Cumberland Gap, Tennessee, on an unspecified date (probably in September or October, 1863) but escaped. He never rejoined his command.]

READ, SAMUEL, Private

Born in McDowell County* and was by occupation a farmer prior to enlisting in McDowell County at age 32, July 14, 1862, for the war. Reported present in January-June, 1863. Killed at Chickamauga, Georgia, September 20, 1863.

REED, ANDREW H., Private

Born in McDowell County* and was by occupation a farmer prior to enlisting in McDowell County at age 34, July 14, 1862, for the war. Reported absent on sick furlough from November 19, 1862, through April 30, 1863. Reported absent in hospital at Loudon, Tennessee, in May-June, 1863. Discharged on August 6, 1863, by reason of "incipient phthisis and consequent . . . general debility."

REEL, WILLIAM, Private

Resided in McDowell County and was by occupation a farmer prior to enlisting at Camp Vance at age 38, January 2, 1864, for the war. Sent to hospital sick on January 28, 1864. Returned to duty subsequent to April 30, 1864. Reported present in May-August, 1864. Reported in hospital at Columbus, Georgia, October 31, 1864. No further records. Survived the war.

RHODES, SAMUEL D., ———

Previously served as Private in Company G, 3rd Regiment N.C. Junior Reserves, and in Company C, 8th Battalion N.C. Junior Reserves. Transferred to this company on an unspecified date subsequent to October 31, 1864. Wounded in the left hand on an unspecified date. Hospitalized at Richmond, Virginia, December 27, 1864. Paroled on May 29, 1865.

RHODES, WILLIAM, Private

Enlisted at Charleston, Tennessee, September 8, 1863, for the war. Reported absent without leave in September-October, 1863. Returned to duty on November 8, 1863. Reported present in January-April, 1864. Reported absent sick from June 28 through August 31, 1864. Paroled at Morganton on May 29, 1865.

ROBBINS, ANDERSON, Private

Born in Randolph County and was by occupation a farmer prior to enlisting in McDowell County at age 32, July 14, 1862, for the war. Deserted at Camp Stokes, Haynesville, Tennessee, August 26,

1862. Reported in confinement in January, 1863. No further records.

ROBERSON, MILTON A., Private

Enlisted in Mitchell County at age 18, March 7, 1865, for the war. Paroled at Greensboro on May 1, 1865.

SEAGLE, JOHN A., Private

Born in McDowell County* and was by occupation a farmer prior to enlisting in McDowell County at age 26, July 14, 1862, for the war. Reported present in January-June, 1863. Reported absent without leave on September 23, 1863. Returned to duty on December 24, 1863. Reported present in January-August, 1864. No further records.

SHEHAN, ALBERT, Private

Enlisted at Camp Reynolds at age 23, September 2, 1862, for the war. Deserted at Big Creek Gap, Tennessee, November 14, 1862. Rejoined the company on March 8, 1864. Court-martialed and sentenced to wear a ball and chain for forty days. Returned to duty on an unspecified date. Reported present in May-August, 1864. No further records. Survived the war.

SHEHAN, ANDREW, Private

Enlisted in McDowell County on July 14, 1862, for the war. Reported present in January-April, 1863. Deserted at Clinton, Tennessee, May 2, 1863. Returned to duty subsequent to June 30, 1863. Reported absent without leave on February 2, 1864. Listed as a deserter on April 7, 1864. [North Carolina pension records indicate that he was "shocked by a bum shell in the left sholder and side" at Chickamauga, Georgia, September 19, 1863. Was about 36 years of age at time of enlistment.]

SHEHAN, PINKNEY, Private

Resided in Rutherford County and enlisted at Camp Reynolds at age 22, September 2, 1862, for the war. Deserted at Big Creek Gap, Tennessee, November 14, 1862. Rejoined the company on March 8, 1864, and was court-martialed. Sentenced to wear ball and chain for forty days. Returned to duty on an unspecified date. Reported present in May-August, 1864. Captured at Orangeburg, South Carolina, February 12, 1865. Sent to New Bern. Confined at Hart's Island, New York Harbor, April 10, 1865. Released at Hart's Island on June 21, 1865, after taking the Oath of Allegiance. [Probably served also as Private in Company G, 60th Regiment N.C. Troops.]

SHEHAN, WASHINGTON, Private

Resided in McDowell County and was by occupation a laborer prior to enlisting at Camp Vance at age 33, October 6, 186[3], for the war. Reported absent without leave on February 2, 1864. Listed as a deserter on April 7, 1864.

SHEPHERD, DAVID, Private

Born in Burke County and was by occupation a farmer prior to enlisting in McDowell County at age 34, July 14, 1862, for the war. Deserted at Camp Stokes, Haynesville, Tennessee, August 26, 1862. Reported in confinement on January 5, 1863. Listed as a deserter in March-June, 1863, and was subsequently dropped from the company rolls.

SHERLIN, HENRY, Private

Born in McDowell County* and was by occupation a farmer prior to enlisting in McDowell County at age 30, July 14, 1862, for the

war. Reported present in January-April, 1863. Reported under
arrest in May-June, 1863. Reason he was arrested not reported.
Returned to duty on an unspecified date. Reported absent without
leave on September 23, 1863. Returned to duty on October 24,
1863. Detailed for duty in the pioneer corps on February 10, 1864.
Returned to duty in March-April, 1864. Captured at Bald Hill, near
Atlanta, Georgia, July 22, 1864. Sent to Nashville, Tennessee.
Transferred to Louisville, Kentucky, where he arrived on August
5, 1864. Transferred to Camp Chase, Ohio, where he arrived on
August 6, 1864. Paroled at Camp Chase on or about March 4, 1865.
Received at Boulware's and Cox's Wharves, James River, Vir-
ginia, March 10-12, 1865, for exchange. No further records. Sur-
vived the war.

SHERLIN, JOHN, Private
Born in McDowell County* where he resided as a farmer or laborer
prior to enlisting in McDowell County at age 22, July 14, 1862, for
the war. Reported present in January-February, 1863. Reported
sick in hospital at Knoxville, Tennessee, in March-April, 1863.
Detailed for duty as a hospital nurse at Knoxville on April 15, 1863.
Returned to duty subsequent to June 30, 1863. Sent to hospital sick
on October 1, 1863. Died in hospital at Atlanta, Georgia, October
8, 1863. Cause of death not reported.

SILVER, TILMAN BLALOCK, Sergeant
Previously served as Corporal in Company K of this regiment.
Transferred to this company subsequent to August 31, 1864. Promoted to Sergeant on an unspecified date. Paroled at Greensboro
on May 1, 1865.

SIMMONS, JAMES M., Private
Born in McDowell County* where he resided as a farmer prior to
enlisting in McDowell County at age 30, July 14, 1862, for the war.
Reported absent on sick furlough in January-June, 1863. No further
records. Survived the war.

SISK, MARION M., Private
Born in McDowell County where he resided as a farmer prior to
enlisting in McDowell County at age 20, July 14, 1862, for the war.
Reported present in January-June, 1863. Wounded at Chickamauga, Georgia, September 20, 1863. Reported absent on sick furlough on October 31, 1863. Detailed for duty as a cattle guard on
February 15, 1864. Reported present in March-April, 1864. Captured near the Chattahoochee River, Georgia, on or about July 5,
1864. Sent to Nashville, Tennessee. Transferred to Louisville, Kentucky, where he arrived on July 14, 1864. Transferred to Camp
Douglas, Chicago, Illinois, where he arrived on July 18, 1864. Released at Camp Douglas on June 16, 1865, after taking the Oath of
Allegiance.

SMITH, G. W., Private
Enlisted at Camp Vance on August 20, 1863, for the war. Reported
present in September-October, 1863. Reported absent sick in
January-February, 1864. Returned to duty in March-April, 1864.
Reported absent without leave in May-August, 1864. No further
records.

SPARKS, GEORGE, Private
Resided in McDowell County where he enlisted at age 43, September 13, 1863, for the war. Reported present in January-April, 1864.
Reported present but under arrest in May-August, 1864. Reason he
was arrested not reported. Returned to duty on an unspecified date.

Captured at Lynch Creek, South Carolina, February 12, 1865. Sent
to New Bern. Confined at Hart's Island, New York Harbor, April
10, 1865. Released at Hart's Island on June 18, 1865, after taking
the Oath of Allegiance.

SPARKS, JOHN, Private
Born in Burke County and was by occupation a farmer prior to
enlisting in McDowell County at age 29, July 14, 1862, for the war.
Died prior to April 25, 1863. Place, date, and cause of death not
reported.

SPIVEY, JESSE, Sergeant
Previously served as Sergeant in Company L of this regiment.
Transferred to this company subsequent to August 31, 1864.
Wounded in the knee at Bentonville on March 19, 1865. Died of
wounds. Place and date of death not reported.

STEVENS, POLK, Private
Enlisted on November 12, 1863, for the war. Reported absent without leave on January 1, 1864. No further records.

STEVENS, WASH, Private
Enlisted at Gaston, Georgia, November 12, 1863, for the war. Died
in hospital at Dalton, Georgia, November 25, 1863. Cause of death
not reported.

STUARD, SIMON, Private
Enlisted in Macon County on November 15, 1863, for the war.
Reported absent without leave on January 1, 1864. No further rec-
ords.

TATE, HUGH COLUMBUS, Private
Born in Burke County on May 29, 1829, and was by occupation a
farmer prior to enlisting in McDowell County at age 33, July 14,
1862, for the war. Transferred to Company C, 5th Battalion N.C.
Cavalry, on or about the same date.

THOMASON, WILLIAM J., Private
Previously served as Private in Company K of this regiment. Trans-
ferred to this company subsequent to August 31, 1864. Paroled at
Greensboro on May 1, 1865.

TISE, CHARLES, Private
Resided in Forsyth County. Place and date of enlistment not reported. Deserted to the enemy at Chattanooga, Tennessee, November 12, 1863. Sent to Nashville, Tennessee. Transferred to Louisville, Kentucky, where he arrived on November 19, 1863. Released
at Louisville on November 24, 1863, after taking the Oath of Allegiance.

TOWERY, EDWARD, Private
Born in McDowell County* and was by occupation a farmer prior
to enlisting in McDowell County at age 32, July 14, 1862, for the
war. Died in Tennessee on November 15, 1862, of "measles."

TURNER, JOHN, Corporal
Born in McDowell County where he enlisted at age 18, July 14,
1862, for the war. Mustered in as Private. Reported present in
January-April, 1863. Promoted to Corporal prior to March 1, 1863.
Reported absent on sick furlough in May-June, 1863. Reported

absent sick in hospital in September-October, 1863. Died in hospital at Cassville, Georgia, November 22, 1863. Cause of death not reported.

WADDLE, WILLIAM, 1st Sergeant

Previously served as 1st Sergeant of Company L of this regiment. Transferred to this company subsequent to August 31, 1864. Paroled at Greensboro on May 1, 1865.

WALKER, DAVID, Private

Born in Rutherford County on September 7, 1837. Resided in McDowell County and was by occupation a farmer prior to enlisting in McDowell County at age 24, July 14, 1862, for the war. Reported present in January-February, 1863. Reported on detail as a blacksmith in March-June and September-October, 1863. Reported present in January-April, 1864. Detailed as a blacksmith at Columbus, Georgia, on or about August 12, 1864. No further records. Survived the war.

WALKER, JEREMIAH C., Private

Resided in Forsyth County. Place and date of enlistment not reported. Deserted to the enemy at Chattanooga, Tennessee, November 12, 1863. Sent to Nashville, Tennessee. Transferred to Louisville, Kentucky, where he arrived on November 19, 1863. Released at Louisville on November 25, 1863, after taking the Oath of Allegiance.

WALLS, MADISON, Private

Born in McDowell County where he resided as a farmer prior to enlisting in McDowell County at age 18, July 14, 1862, for the war. Died on September 21, 1862. Place and cause of death not reported.

WHISENHUNT, ELIAS, Private

Born in Burke County and was by occupation a farmer prior to enlisting in McDowell County at age 27, July 14, 1862, for the war. Died at Cumberland Gap, Tennessee, in October, 1862, of "measles."

WHITE, A. J., Private

Resided in Mecklenburg County. Place and date of enlistment not reported (probably enlisted subsequent to August 31, 1864). Captured at Orangeburg, South Carolina, February 12, 1865. Sent to New Bern. Confined at Hart's Island, New York Harbor, April 10, 1865. Released at Hart's Island on June 19, 1865, after taking the Oath of Allegiance.

WHITE, HARRISON T., Private

Born in McDowell County* and was by occupation a farmer prior to enlisting in McDowell County at age 23, July 14, 1862, for the war. Furloughed for twenty days on November 19, 1862. Failed to return to duty and was listed as a deserter in March-April, 1863. Returned to duty in May-June, 1863. Reported absent without leave in September-October, 1863. Listed as a deserter on April 7, 1864.

WHITE, JAMES, Private

Born in Rutherford County and enlisted in McDowell County at age 25, July 14, 1862, for the war. Reported present in January-June, 1863. Reported sick in hospital in September-October, 1863. Reported absent without leave on December 1, 1863. Returned to duty on January 1, 1864. Reported present in March-April, 1864. Captured on the march from Mount Zion Church, Georgia, on or about July 4, 1864. Sent to Nashville, Tennessee. Transferred to

Louisville, Kentucky, where he arrived on July 14, 1864. Transferred to Camp Douglas, Chicago, Illinois, where he arrived on July 18, 1864. Died at Camp Douglas on March 5, 1865, of "pneumonia."

WHITE, JAMES T., Private

Enlisted at Camp Holmes on November 13, 1863, for the war. Reported present through August 31, 1864. No further records.

WHITE, WILLIAM, Private

Born in McDowell County* where he enlisted at age 34, July 14, 1862, for the war. Died on an unspecified date (probably in the summer or fall of 1862). Place and cause of death not reported.

WILLIAMS, HEZEKIAH R., Private

Resided in Yadkin County. Place and date of enlistment not reported. Deserted to the enemy at Chattanooga, Tennessee, November 13, 1863. Sent to Nashville, Tennessee. Transferred to Louisville, Kentucky, where he arrived on November 24, 1863. Released at Louisville on November 25, 1863, after taking the Oath of Allegiance.

WILLIAMS, W. A., ———

North Carolina pension records indicate that he served in this company.

WILSON, HENRY, Private

Born in McDowell County* where he resided as a laborer prior to enlisting in McDowell County at age 29, July 14, 1862, for the war. Reported present in January-June, 1863. Killed at Chickamauga, Georgia, September 20, 1863.

WILSON, HIRAM, Private

Enlisted at Dalton, Georgia, January 23, 1864, for the war. Reported present in January-February, 1864. Sent to hospital on April 5, 1864. No further records.

WILSON, LEMUEL, Private

Born in Burke County and resided in Watauga County where he was by occupation a farmer prior to enlisting in McDowell County at age 21, July 14, 1862, for the war. Transferred to Company I of this regiment on or about July 24, 1862.

WILSON, LEMUEL L., Private

Born in Burke County and was by occupation a farmer prior to enlisting in McDowell County on July 14, 186[2], for the war. Reported absent in hospital at Loudon, Tennessee, in May-June, 1863. Discharged on July 31, 1863, by reason of "chronic rheumatism." Discharge certificate gives his age as 21.

WILSON, SAMUEL N., SR., Private

Enlisted in McDowell County on July 14, 1862, for the war. Reported present in January-February, 1863. Discharged at Jacksboro, Tennessee, March 29, 1863. Reason discharged not reported.

WILSON, SIDNEY L., Private

Previously served in Company K of this regiment. Transferred to this company on an unspecified date subsequent to July 29, 1862. Reported absent on sick furlough from November 13, 1862, through April 30, 1863. No further records. Survived the war.

WOOD, RUFUS, Private

Previously served as Private in Company L of this regiment. Transferred to this company subsequent to August 31, 1864. Paroled at Greensboro on May 1, 1865.

WOODSIDE, BENJAMIN F., Private

Born in Rowan County and was by occupation a printer prior to enlisting in McDowell County at age 23, July 14, 1862, for the war. Mustered in as Sergeant. Reported present in January-February, 1863. Reduced to ranks in March, 1863. Surviving company muster rolls for the period from March-April, 1863, through April 30, 1864, indicate that he was on detail in the commissary department. Reported absent sick from May 14 through August 31, 1864. Hospitalized at Macon, Georgia, April 23, 1865, with "nothing." Released from hospital on April 28, 1865. Paroled at Morganton on May 16, 1865.

YOUNGBLOOD, HIRAM, Private

Enlisted in Rutherford County on August 14, 1863, for the war. Reported present in September-October, 1863. Reported absent without leave on February 12, 1864. Reported under arrest on March 8, 1864. Court-martialed on April 12, 1864, and sentenced to be shot. Executed at Dalton, Georgia, May 4, 1864, for desertion.

COMPANY G

This company was raised primarily in Yancey County and enlisted at Burnsville on July 11-14, 1862, as Capt. John W. Peek's Company, N.C. Volunteers. It was mustered into service on July 15, 1862, and was assigned to the 58th Regiment N.C. Troops as Company G when the regiment was organized on July 29, 1862. After joining the regiment the company functioned as a part of the regiment, and its history for the remainder of the war is reported as a part of the regimental history.

The following roster was compiled primarily from information in the microfilm edition of the Compiled Service Records of Soldiers Who Served in Organizations from the State of North Carolina (Record Group 109, M270), National Archives and Records Administration, Washington, D.C. Record Group 109 includes enlistment papers, pay vouchers, requisitions, letters of resignation, discharge certificates, and abstracts of medical and prisoner of war returns. Materials relating specifically to this company include a muster-in and descriptive roll dated July 15, 1862, and muster rolls dated July 11, 1862-June, 1863; September-October, 1863; and January-August, 1864.

Also utilized in this roster were *The War of the Rebellion: A Compilation of the Official Records of the Union and Confederate Armies*, the North Carolina adjutant general's *Roll of Honor*, state militia records, newspaper casualty lists and obituaries, wartime claims for bounty pay and allowances, postwar registers of claims for artificial limbs, Confederate pension applications filed with the states of North Carolina, Tennessee, and Florida, Confederate Soldiers' Home records, and the 1860 and 1870 federal censuses of North Carolina. A search was made also for relevant letters, diaries, reminiscences, and other manuscripts in the Southern Historical Collection (University of North Carolina-Chapel Hill), the Duke University Library Special Collections Department, and the North Carolina Division of Archives and History.

Among the secondary sources consulted were records of the North Carolina division of the United Daughters of the Confederacy, postwar rosters, regimental and county histories, marriage bond, will, and cemetery indexes, published and unpublished genealogies, biographical dictionaries, the North Carolina *County Heritage Book* series, the *Confederate Veteran*, Walter Clark's *Histories of the Several Regiments and Battalions from North Carolina in the Great War, 1861-'65*, and the North Carolina volume of the extended edition of *Confederate Military History*.

OFFICERS

CAPTAINS

PEEK, JOHN W.

Born in Pittsylvania County, Virginia, and resided in Yancey County where he was by occupation a clerk prior to enlisting at age 51. Appointed Captain on July 14, 1862. Reported present through April 30, 1863. Resigned on May 5, 1863, by reason of "old age." Resignation accepted on or about the same date.

PHILLIPS, JONATHAN L.

Previously served as Captain of Company M of this regiment. Transferred to this company in May, 1863. Reported present on surviving company muster rolls through February, 1864. Furloughed for twenty-four days near Dalton, Georgia, April 19, 1864. Returned to duty prior to June 22, 1864, when he was wounded at Kolb's Farm, near Marietta, Georgia. Hospitalized at Barnesville, Georgia. Furloughed for thirty days on August 8, 1864. Reported absent wounded through September 20, 1864. Died on an unspecified date. Place and cause of death not reported. [Previously served as Captain in the 98th Regiment N.C. Militia.]

LONG, HAMILTON C.

Previously served as 2nd Lieutenant of Company K, 4th Regiment N.C. State Troops. Appointed Captain of this company in March, 1865, when Companies G and I of the 58th Regiment were consolidated. Paroled at Greensboro on May 1, 1865.

LIEUTENANTS

BYRD, CORNELIUS R., 3rd Lieutenant

Born in Yancey County and was by occupation a farmer prior to enlisting in Yancey County at age 20. Appointed 3rd Lieutenant on July 14, 1862. Reported present in March-June, 1863. Wounded at Chickamauga, Georgia, September 20, 1863. Hospitalized at Kingston, Georgia, where he died on November 2, 1863, of wounds.

GARDNER, JAMES W., 2nd Lieutenant

Born in Yancey County where he resided as a farmer prior to enlisting at age 19. Appointed 2nd Lieutenant on or about July 14, 1862. Reported absent with leave in March-April, 1863. No further records. [Previously served as 1st Lieutenant in the 111th Regiment N.C. Militia.]

HOPKINS, GEORGE W., 1st Lieutenant

Previously served as 1st Lieutenant of Company M of this regiment. Transferred to this company in May, 1863. Reported absent on detached service in North Carolina on June 15, 1863. Failed to rejoin the company and was dropped from the company rolls on November 16, 1863.

McGIMSEY, THEODORE CICERO, 2nd Lieutenant

Previously served as Sergeant in Company F of this regiment. Transferred to this company subsequent to August 31, 1864. Appointed 2nd Lieutenant on an unspecified date. Paroled at Greensboro on May 1, 1865.

MILLER, JONATHAN BENJAMIN, 1st Lieutenant

Previously served as 2nd Lieutenant of Company I of this regiment. Transferred to this company and promoted to 1st Lieutenant in March, 1865, when Companies G and I were consolidated. Paroled at Greensboro on May 1, 1865.

NORRIS, JOHN RILEY, 2nd Lieutenant

Previously served as 3rd Lieutenant of Company M of this regiment. Transferred to this company in May, 1863. Promoted to 2nd Lieutenant on June 15, 1863. Reported present in September-October, 1863. Furloughed for twenty-two days from camp near Dalton, Georgia, February 13, 1864. Returned to duty on an unspecified date. Reported present and in command of the company in March-April, 1864. "Shocked with shell" at Resaca, Georgia, May 14-15, 1864. Wounded at Kolb's Farm, near Marietta, Georgia, June 22, 1864. Returned to duty prior to September 1, 1864. No further records. Survived the war.

RAY, THOMAS, 2nd Lieutenant

Previously served as 2nd Lieutenant of Company M of this regiment. Transferred to this company in May, 1863. Resigned on June 5, 1863, apparently without having reported for duty. Resignation accepted on June 15, 1863.

TIPTON, JOHN, 1st Lieutenant

Born in Yancey County* and was by occupation a farmer prior to enlisting at age 40. Appointed 1st Lieutenant on July 14, 1862. Resigned on March 26, 1863, because he considered himself "wholly incompetent for the duties and responsibilities of the office [of 1st Lieutenant] through a want of education, military skill & [illegible]." Resignation accepted on or about May 15, 1863. Later served as Private in this company (see page 372 below). [Previously served as 1st Lieutenant in the 111th Regiment N.C. Militia.]

NONCOMMISSIONED OFFICERS AND PRIVATES

ANDERSON, ENOS, JR., Private

Enlisted at Camp Holmes on October 25, 1863, for the war. Reported present in January-April, 1864. Reported present but sick in May-August, 1864. No further records.

ANGLIN, RABORN B., Sergeant

Born in Yancey County* where he resided as a farmer prior to enlisting in Yancey County at age 29, July 11, 1862, for the war. Mustered in as Sergeant. Reported present through April 30, 1863. Transferred to Company C of this regiment on June 1, 1863.

ANGLIN, WILLIAM, JR., Private

Born in Yancey County* where he resided as a farmer prior to enlisting in Yancey County at age 34, July 11, 1862, for the war.

Mustered in as Musician (Fifer). Reported absent sick on company muster roll dated July 11, 1862-February 28, 1863. Returned to duty in March-April, 1863. Deserted at Clinton, Tennessee, May 26, 1863. Reduced to ranks prior to July 1, 1863. Returned to duty prior to September 20, 1863, when he was wounded at Chickamauga, Georgia. Died on October 5, 1863, of wounds. Place of death not reported.

AUTERY, JASPER, Private

Enlisted in Yancey County on July 11, 1862, for the war. Reported absent without leave on company muster roll dated July 11, 1862-February 28, 1863. Reported present in March-April, 1863. Deserted at Clinton, Tennessee, May 1, 1863. [May have served also as Private in Company D, 6th Regiment N.C. State Troops.]

AUTRY, JOHN P., Sergeant

Enlisted in Yancey County on July 11, 1862, for the war. Mustered in as Private. Reported absent without leave on company muster roll dated July 11, 1862-February 28, 1863. Returned to duty in March-April, 1863. Reported sick in hospital at Clinton, Tennessee, in May-June, 1863. Detailed as a provost guard in September-October, 1863. Rejoined the company in January-February, 1864. Promoted to Sergeant on March 1, 1864. Reported present through August 31, 1864. Wounded in the groin and right testicle "necessitating removal of gland" at or near Lovejoy's Station, Georgia, on or about September 1, 1864. Reported in hospital at Macon, Georgia, October 17, 1864. No further records. Survived the war. [Was about 27 years of age at time of enlistment.]

AYERS, JACOB M., Private

Born in Yancey County where he resided as a farmer prior to enlisting in Yancey County at age 21, July 11, 1862, for the war. Reported present through April 30, 1863. Deserted at Clinton, Tennessee, May 26, 1863. Returned to duty and was transferred to Company B of this regiment on an unspecified date (probably prior to September 19-20, 1863).

BAILEY, EZEKIEL H., Private

Born in Claiborne County, Tennessee, and resided in Yancey County where he was by occupation a farmer prior to enlisting in Yancey County at age 28, July 11, 1862, for the war. Mustered in as Corporal. Reported present through April 30, 1863. Deserted at Clinton, Tennessee, June 1, 1863. Reduced to ranks prior to July 1, 1863. Returned to duty on July 15, 1864. Reported present through August 31, 1864. No further records. Survived the war. [North Carolina pension records indicate that he was wounded in 1862. Contrary to 8:287 of this series, it appears that he did not serve previously in Company G, 29th Regiment N.C. Troops.]

BAILEY, JESSE, Private

Resided in Yancey County and was by occupation a farmer prior to enlisting in Yancey County at age 28, July 12, 1862, for the war. Transferred to Company C of this regiment on or about July 15, 1862.

BAILEY, JOHN, Private

Born in Claiborne County, Tennessee, and was by occupation a farmer prior to enlisting in Yancey County at age 26, July 11, 1862, for the war. Reported present through February 28, 1863. Sent to hospital sick at Knoxville, Tennessee, in March-April, 1863. Returned to duty prior to June 2, 1863, when he deserted at Clinton, Tennessee. Returned to duty prior to September 23, 1863, when he deserted near Chattanooga, Tennessee.

BAILEY, WILLIS, Private

Born in Claiborne County, Tennessee, and resided in Yancey County where he was by occupation a farm laborer prior to enlisting in Yancey County at age 19, July 11, 1862, for the war. Reported present through April 30, 1863. Reported sick in hospital at Clinton, Tennessee, in May-June, 1863. Returned to duty on an unspecified date. Sent to hospital sick on August 27, 1863. Reported absent sick through February 29, 1864. Reported present but under arrest in March-April, 1864. Reason he was arrested not reported. Returned to duty prior to June 22, 1864, when he was wounded at Kolb's Farm, near Marietta, Georgia. Captured (possibly deserted to the enemy) while on picket near Atlanta, Georgia, August 16, 1864. Took the Oath of Allegiance at Chattanooga, Tennessee, on or about August 22, 1864.

BALL, ALFORD T., Sergeant

Previously served as Sergeant in Company M of this regiment. Transferred to this company in May, 1863. Deserted at or near Charleston, Tennessee, September 6, 1863. Court-martialed on November 18, 1863, and sentenced to be shot. Executed at Dalton, Georgia, May 4, 1864.

BANKS, JOSEPH M., Private

Born in Buncombe County and was by occupation a farmer prior to enlisting in Yancey County at age 23, July 11, 1862, for the war. Died in Yancey County on February 7, 1863. Cause of death not reported.

BAUGUS, RICHARD, Private

Enlisted at Camp Holmes on October 25, 1863, for the war. Captured at Missionary Ridge, Tennessee, November 25, 1863. Confined at Nashville, Tennessee. Transferred to Louisville, Kentucky, where he arrived on December 5, 1863. Transferred to Rock Island, Illinois, where he arrived on December 9, 1863. No further records. Survived the war. [May have served previously as Private in Company C, 48th Regiment Tennessee Infantry (Voorhies).]

BEAVER, GEORGE L., Private

Born in Yancey County and was by occupation a farmer prior to enlisting in Yancey County at age 19, July 11, 1862, for the war. Dropped from the company rolls on an unspecified date (probably in the summer of 1862). Later served as Private in Company B, 29th Regiment N.C. Troops.

BENNET, JASON, Private

Enlisted in Yancey County on July 11, 1862, for the war. Reported absent without leave on company muster rolls dated July 11, 1862-February 28, 1863, and May-June, 1863. No further records.

BENNETT, GAINES, Private

Born in Yancey County where he enlisted on July 11, 1862, for the war. Reported present through February 28, 1863. Died in camp at Clinton, Tennessee, April 9, 1863, of "brain fever."

BENNETT, GUILDER, Private

Resided in Yancey County where he enlisted at age 31, July 11, 1862, for the war. Reported absent without leave on company muster rolls dated July 11, 1862-June 30, 1863. No further records. Survived the war.

BENNETT, JEREMIAH, Private

Born in Yancey County where he resided as a farmer prior to enlisting in Yancey County at age 21, July 11, 1862, for the war. Reported absent without leave on company muster rolls dated July 11, 1862-June 30, 1863. Later served as Private in Company D, 3rd Regiment N.C. Mounted Infantry (Union).

BENNETT, JOHN, Private

Born in Yancey County where he resided as a farmer prior to enlisting in Yancey County at age 26, July 11, 1862, for the war. Reported absent sick on company muster roll dated July 11, 1862-February 28, 1863. Reported absent without leave in March-June, 1863. No further records. Survived the war. [May have served later as Private in Company A, 3rd Regiment N.C. Mounted Infantry (Union).]

BENNETT, URIAH, Private

Born in Yancey County* where he resided as a farmer prior to enlisting in Yancey County at age 34, July 11, 1862, for the war. Reported absent without leave in March-April, 1863. No further records. Survived the war.

BENNETT, WILLIAM J., Private

Enlisted on or about July 11, 1862, for the war. Reported absent without leave in March-April, 1863. No further records. [May have served later as Private in Companies A and F, 3rd Regiment N.C. Mounted Infantry (Union).]

BISHOP, SAMUEL J., 1st Sergeant

Previously served as 1st Sergeant of Company M of this regiment. Transferred to this company in May, 1863. Reported present on surviving company muster rolls through August 31, 1864. No further records. Survived the war.

BLACKBURN, EDMOND, Private

Previously served as Private in Company M of this regiment. Transferred to this company in May, 1863. Reported present in May-June, 1863. Sent to hospital sick on June 25, 1863. Furloughed for sixty days from hospital at Kingston, Georgia, January 29, 1864. Died at home in Watauga County on May 1, 1864, of disease.

BLANKENS[H]IP, GOVAN M., Private

Born in Yancey County and was by occupation a farmer prior to enlisting in Yancey County at age 25, July 11, 1862, for the war. Discharged on July 26, 1862, on a surgeon's certificate of disability.

BLAYLOCK, ALBERT N., Private

Resided at Johnson's Depot, Tennessee, and enlisted at Camp Huston, North Carolina, October 1, 1862, for the war. Reported present in March-June, 1863. Transferred to Company K of this regiment in July-October, 1863. [Was about 18 years of age at time of enlistment.]

BREWER, JOHN A., Private

Resided in Wilkes County and was by occupation a farmer prior to enlisting at Camp Holmes on October 25, 1863, for the war. Captured at Missionary Ridge, Tennessee, November 25, 1863. Sent to Nashville, Tennessee. Transferred to Louisville, Kentucky, where he arrived on December 6, 1863. Transferred to Rock Island, Illinois, where he arrived on December 9, 1863. Released at Rock Island on June 20, 1865, after taking the Oath of Allegiance. [Records of the Federal Provost Marshal dated June, 1865, give his age as 32.]

BRYANT, BETHEL A., Private

Resided in Yancey County and was by occupation a farmer prior to enlisting in Yancey County at age 27, July 11, 1862, for the war. Reported absent without leave on company muster rolls dated July 11, 1862-June 30, 1863. Transferred to Company B of this regiment prior to April 4, 1864.

BRYANT, JOHN W., Private

Born in Yancey County and was by occupation a farmer prior to enlisting in Yancey County at age 21, July 11, 1862, for the war. Reported present through April 30, 1863. Deserted at Clinton, Tennessee, June 1, 1863. Returned to duty on an unspecified date. Deserted near Chattanooga, Tennessee, September 23, 1863. Returned to duty on an unspecified date subsequent to February 29, 1864. Reported present through August 31, 1864. No further records. Survived the war.

BYERS, WILLIAM R., Private

Resided in Rutherford County and enlisted at Camp Holmes at age 22, October 25, 1863, for the war. Court-martialed (probably for desertion) on April 2, 1864, and sentenced to be shot. It is not clear whether his execution was carried out; however, he died prior to September 1, 1864.

BYRD, CHARLES, Private

Born in Yancey County where he resided as a farmer prior to enlisting in Yancey County at age 23, July 11, 1862, for the war. Reported absent sick on company muster roll dated July 11, 1862-February 28, 1863. Reported absent without leave in March-June, 1863. No further records. Survived the war. [May have served also as 2nd Lieutenant in the 111th Regiment N.C. Militia.]

BYRD, JOSEPH Y., Corporal

Born in Yancey County where he resided as a farmer prior to enlisting in Yancey County at age 18, July 11, 1862, for the war. Mustered in as Corporal. Reported present through February 28, 1863. Reported absent on detached service in March-April, 1863. Died on an unspecified date (probably prior to July 1, 1863). Place, date, and cause of death not reported.

BYRD, MOSES J., Private

Previously served as Private in Company G, 29th Regiment N.C. Troops. Enlisted in this company on July 11, 1862, for the war. Mustered in as Sergeant. Reported present through June 30, 1863. Left the company sick on September 8, 1863, and was later furloughed for thirty days from Atlanta, Georgia. Reported absent on expired furlough on October 31, 1863. Returned to duty on December 30, 1863. Not reported present on April 30, 1864. Reduced to ranks on an unspecified date. Returned to duty prior to August 12, 1864, when he deserted near Atlanta.

BYRD, WILLIAM J. C., Private

Born in Yancey County where he resided as a farmer prior to enlisting in Yancey County at age 21, July 11, 1862, for the war. Reported absent sick on company muster roll dated July 11, 1862-February 28, 1863. Reported absent without leave on company muster rolls dated March-June, 1863. No further records.

CALLOWAY, ELIJAH, Private

Previously served as Private in Company M of this regiment. Transferred to this company in May, 1863, while listed as a deserter. No further records.

CALLOWAY, JAMES, Private

Previously served as Private in Company M of this regiment. Transferred to this company in May, 1863, while listed as a deserter. Went over to the enemy on an unspecified date. Took the Oath of Allegiance at Chattanooga, Tennessee, on or about March 26, 1864.

CALLOWAY, MARSHAL, Private

Previously served as Private in Company M of this regiment. Transferred to this company in May, 1863, while listed as a deserter. No further records.

CALLOWAY, WILLIAM, Private

Previously served as Private in Company M of this regiment. Transferred to this company in May, 1863, while listed as a deserter. No further records.

CAMPBELL, MABIN, ———

North Carolina pension records indicate that he served in this company.

CANNON, STEPHEN, Private

Previously served as Private in Company C of this regiment. Transferred to this company on or about July 15, 1862. Reported present through April 30, 1863. Discharged at Knoxville, Tennessee, May 15, 1863, by reason of "epilepsy occurring daily." Later served as Private in Company A, 3rd Regiment N.C. Mounted Infantry (Union).

CARAWAY, WILLIAM H., Private

Enlisted in Yancey County on July 11, 1862, for the war. Reported absent without leave on company muster rolls dated July 11, 1862-June, 1863. No further records. [May have served later as Private in Company C, 13th Regiment Tennessee Cavalry (Union).]

CASNER, LEVI, Private

Enlisted at Camp Holmes on October 25, 1863, for the war. Captured at Missionary Ridge, Tennessee, November 25, 1863. Sent to Nashville, Tennessee. Transferred to Louisville, Kentucky, where he arrived on December 6, 1863. Transferred to Rock Island, Illinois, where he arrived on December 9, 1863. Hospitalized at Rock Island on March 27, 1864, with chronic bronchitis. Died in hospital at Rock Island on April 11, 1864, of "pneumonia."

CAUDILL, JAMES F., Private

Enlisted at Camp Holmes on October 25, 1863, for the war. Wounded in the right thigh at Missionary Ridge, Tennessee, November 25, 1863. Hospitalized at Macon, Georgia. Furloughed for forty-five days on or about February 1, 1864. Furloughed for thirty days at Atlanta, Georgia, March 25, 1864. Had not returned to duty as of August 31, 1864. No further records. Survived the war. [Was about 18 years of age at time of enlistment.]

CHURCH, JORDAN, Private

Previously served as Private in Company M of this regiment. Transferred to this company in May, 1863, while absent without leave. Apparently failed to report for duty. Later served as Corporal in Company H, 3rd Regiment N.C. Mounted Infantry (Union).

CHURCH, MARION, Private

Previously served as Private in Company M of this regiment. Transferred to this company in May, 1863, while absent without leave. No further records.

COOK, JOHN B., ———

North Carolina pension records indicate that he served in this company.

COOK, JOHNSON, Private

Enlisted in Watauga County on September 26, 1862, for the war. Deserted at Big Creek Gap, Tennessee, on an unspecified date (probably in the autumn of 1862).

COOMBS, CALVIN, Private

Resided in Wilkes County. Place and date of enlistment not reported (probably enlisted in July-August, 1864). Deserted to the enemy on an unspecified date. Confined at Knoxville, Tennessee, September 5, 1864. Transferred to Chattanooga, Tennessee, September 12, 1864. Transferred to Louisville, Kentucky, where he arrived on September 25, 1864. Released at Louisville on September 26, 1864, after taking the Oath of Allegiance.

COOPER, JOHN, Private

Born in Yancey County and was by occupation a farmer prior to enlisting in Yancey County at age 18, July 12, 1862, for the war. Reported present on surviving company muster rolls through April 30, 1864. Reported sick in hospital from May 26 through August 31, 1864. No further records.

COX, WILLIAM R., Private

Previously served as Private in Company K of this regiment. Transferred to this company in July-September, 1863. Deserted near Chattanooga, Tennessee, September 17, 1863. Returned to duty in November, 1863-February, 1864. Reported present in March-April, 1864. Wounded at Kolb's Farm, near Marietta, Georgia, June 22, 1864. Sent to hospital sick on August 27, 1864. No further records.

CROWDER, ISAAC T., Private

Born in Yancey County* and was by occupation a farmer prior to enlisting in Yancey County at age 29, July 11, 1862, for the war. Reported present through June 30, 1863. Wounded in the left thigh and hip at Chickamauga, Georgia, September 20, 1863. Reported absent wounded through August 31, 1864. No further records. Survived the war.

DEBORDE, EZRA, Private

Resided in Wilkes County and was by occupation a farmer prior to enlisting at Camp Holmes at age 38, October 25, 1863, for the war. Killed at Missionary Ridge, Tennessee, November 25, 1863.

DOWELL, JOSHUA, Private

Resided in Wilkes County and was by occupation a farmer prior to enlisting at Camp Holmes at age 47, October 25, 1863, for the war. Reported present in January-April, 1864. Deserted from hospital at Greensboro, Georgia, June 15, 1864.

DUFF, DAVID C., Private

Previously served as Private in Company M of this regiment. Transferred to this company in May, 1863, while listed as a deserter. No further records.

DUNCAN, CALVIN, Private

Born in Ashe County and was by occupation a farmer prior to enlisting in Yancey County at age 26, June 8, 1862, for the war.

Reported present through June 30, 1863. Sent to hospital sick on October 12, 1863. Furloughed for forty days from hospital at Cassville, Georgia, February 3, 1864. Failed to return to duty and was listed as a deserter to the enemy on August 31, 1864.

DUNCAN, WILLIAM F., Sergeant

Enlisted at Camp Palmer on December 22, 1862, for the war. Mustered in as Private. Reported present on surviving company muster rolls through October, 1863. Promoted to Sergeant in November, 1863-February, 1864. Furloughed for twenty-two days near Dalton, Georgia, February 9, 1864. Failed to return to duty and was listed as a deserter to the enemy on August 31, 1864. [Previously served as 2nd Lieutenant in the 111th Regiment N.C. Militia.]

EDWARDS, JAMES N., Private

Place and date of enlistment not reported. Reported "absent at muster" on July 15, 1862. No further records.

EDWARDS, JOHN W., Private

Enlisted in Yancey County on July 11, 1862, for the war. Reported present through February 28, 1863. Deserted at Big Creek Gap, Tennessee, April 5, 1863. [May have served later as Private and Sergeant in Companies K and D, 8th Regiment Tennessee Cavalry (Union), and as Captain of Company A, 3rd Regiment N.C. Mounted Infantry (Union).]

EDWARDS, LYNVILLE, Private

Resided in Yancey County where he enlisted at age 16, June 8, 1862, for the war. Reported present through February 28, 1863. Deserted at Big Creek Gap, Tennessee, April 7, 1863.

EDWARDS, STEPHEN, Private

Previously served as Private in Company C of this regiment. Transferred to this company on or about July 15, 1862. Reported present through February 28, 1863. Died in hospital at Clinton, Tennessee, April 24, 1863. Cause of death not reported.

ELKINS, ALBERT, Private

Born in Yancey County where he resided as a farmer prior to enlisting in Yancey County at age 27, July 11, 1862, for the war. Reported absent without leave on February 28, 1863. Returned to duty in March-April, 1863. Deserted at Clinton, Tennessee, in May-June, 1863.

ELLER, PETER, Private

Resided in Wilkes County and was by occupation a farmer prior to enlisting at Camp Holmes at age 37, October 25, 1863, for the war. Reported present in January-February, 1864. Furloughed for twenty-four days from camp near Dalton, Georgia, April 18, 1864. Returned to duty on an unspecified date. Captured (or deserted to the enemy) at Bald Hill, near Atlanta, Georgia, July 22, 1864. Sent to Nashville, Tennessee. Transferred to Louisville, Kentucky, where he arrived on July 30, 1864. Transferred to Camp Chase, Ohio, where he arrived on August 2, 1864. Released at Camp Chase on or about December 14, 1864, after taking the Oath of Allegiance. [North Carolina pension records indicate that he was wounded at Atlanta on July 1, 1864, when "a shell knocked a limb from a tree and struck him on the back . . . and something hit him on the head at the same time and knocked him senseless . . . inflicting a severe wound on the head. . . ."]

ESTEPP, SAMUEL, Private

Born in Yancey County* on October 13, 1828. Was by occupation a farmer. Place and date of enlistment not reported (probably enlisted in July, 1862). Discharged prior to May 1, 1863. Reason discharged not reported. Later served as Private in Company K, 3rd Regiment N.C. Mounted Infantry (Union).

FENDER, WILLIAM, Private

Enlisted in Yancey County on July 11, 1862, for the war. Reported present on surviving company muster rolls through April, 1863. Deserted near Clinton, Tennessee, in May-June, 1863. Returned to duty on January 1, 1864. Deserted near Dalton, Georgia, March 10, 1864. [May have served later as Private in Company G, 3rd Regiment N.C. Mounted Infantry (Union).]

FORD, SQUIRE J., Private

Previously served as Private in Company M of this regiment. Transferred to this company in May, 1863, while absent without leave. No further records.

FRY, JOHN H., Private

Resided in Iredell County and enlisted at Camp Holmes on November 12, 1863, for the war. Sent to hospital from camp near Dalton, Georgia, February 24, 1864. Furloughed for forty-five days on March 11, 1864. Furlough extended through August 31, 1864. Detailed (apparently for light duty) on September 16, 1864. Detailed for light duty on November 9, 1864. Hospitalized at Charlotte on November 20, 1864, with tonsillitis. Returned to duty on December 15, 1864. Hospitalized at Charlotte on February 28, 1865, with debilitas. Returned to duty on March 25, 1865. Captured in Iredell County on April 12, 1865. Sent to Nashville, Tennessee. Transferred to Louisville, Kentucky, where he arrived on May 1, 1865. Transferred to Camp Chase, Ohio, where he arrived on May 4, 1865. Released at Camp Chase on June 13, 1865, after taking the Oath of Allegiance. [Records of the Federal Provost Marshal dated June, 1865, give his age as 20.]

FUGITT, ROBERT, Private

Resided in Wilkes County and enlisted at Camp Holmes at age 22, October 25, 1863, for the war. Captured at Missionary Ridge, Tennessee, November 25, 1863. Sent to Nashville, Tennessee. Transferred to Louisville, Kentucky, where he arrived on December 5, 1863. Transferred to Rock Island, Illinois, where he arrived on December 9, 1863. Died at Rock Island on January 30, 1864, of "diarrhoea."

GENTRY, BENJAMIN, Private

Previously served as Private in Company M of this regiment. Transferred to this company in May, 1863, while absent without leave. No further records.

GENTRY, CALLAWAY, Private

Previously served as Private in Company M of this regiment. Transferred to this company in May, 1863. Wounded at Chickamauga, Georgia, September 19-20, 1863. Nominated for the Badge of Distinction for gallantry at Chickamauga. Furloughed from hospital for forty days on October 25, 1863. Returned to duty in March-April, 1864. Deserted near Atlanta, Georgia, July 29, 1864. Captured by the enemy in Ashe County in August, 1864. Sent to Chattanooga, Tennessee. Transferred to Louisville, Kentucky, where he arrived on August 15, 1864. Released at Louisville on or about August 27, 1864, after taking the Oath of Allegiance.

GENTRY, JESSE, Corporal

Previously served as Corporal in Company M of this regiment. Transferred to this company in May, 1863. Wounded at Chickamauga, Georgia, September 20, 1863. Died on September 25, 1863, of wounds. Place of death not reported.

GENTRY, WILLIAM P., Private

Previously served as Private in Company M of this regiment. Transferred to this company in May, 1863, while listed as a deserter. No further records. Survived the war.

GOFORTH, WILLIAM, Sergeant

Resided in Iredell County and was by occupation a farmer prior to enlisting at Camp Holmes at age 40, November 12, 1863, for the war. Mustered in as Private. Reported present in January-February, 1864. "Left camp" near Dalton, Georgia, April 19, 1864. Returned to duty prior to May 1, 1864. Reported present in May-August, 1864. Promoted to Sergeant on July 9, 1864. Paroled at Macon, Georgia, April 30, 1865.

GRAGG, EDWARD P., Private

Previously served as Private in Company M of this regiment. Transferred to this company in May, 1863, while listed as a deserter. No further records.

GRAHAM, DANIEL, Private

Previously served as Private in Company M of this regiment. Transferred to this company in May, 1863, while listed as a deserter. No further records. Survived the war.

GRAY, McKINSEY M., Private

Previously served as Private in Company M of this regiment. Transferred to this company in May, 1863, while absent without leave. No further records.

GREEN, FERGERSON, Private

Previously served as Private in Company M of this regiment. Transferred to this company in May, 1863, while in hospital at Knoxville, Tennessee. Furloughed for thirty days from hospital at Knoxville on June 19, 1863. Reported absent on expired furlough in September-October, 1863. Returned to duty on an unspecified date. Reported present in January-February, 1864. Reported sick in hospital on or about April 19, 1864. Returned to duty on an unspecified date (apparently subsequent to August 31, 1864). Captured at Orangeburg, South Carolina, February 12, 1865. Sent to New Bern. Confined at Hart's Island, New York Harbor, April 10, 1865. Released at Hart's Island on June 19, 1865, after taking the Oath of Allegiance.

GREEN, ISAAC, Private

Previously served as Private in Company M of this regiment. Transferred to this company in May, 1863, while absent without leave. No further records.

GREER, ISAIAH, Private

Previously served as Private in Company M of this regiment. Transferred to this company in May, 1863, while listed as a deserter. No further records.

GREER, JEFFERSON, Private

Previously served as Private in Company M of this regiment. Transferred to this company in May, 1863, while listed as a deserter. No further records.

GREER, NOAH, Private

Previously served as Private in Company M of this regiment. Transferred to this company in May, 1863, while listed as a deserter. No further records.

GREER, PHILLIP, Private

Previously served as Private in Company M of this regiment. Transferred to this company in May, 1863, while listed as a deserter. No further records.

GREER, THOMAS, Private

Previously served as Private in Company M of this regiment. Transferred to this company in May, 1863, while listed as a deserter. No further records.

GROGAN, ELIJAH, Private

Previously served as Private in Company M of this regiment. Transferred to this company in May, 1863, while absent without leave. Apparently failed to report for duty. Later served as Private in Company I, 13th Regiment Tennessee Cavalry (Union).

GROGAN, JORDAN, Private

Previously served as Private in Company M of this regiment. Transferred to this company in May, 1863. Deserted at Clinton, Tennessee, prior to July 1, 1863. Later served as Private in Company G, 4th Regiment Tennessee Infantry (Union).

HAMLETT, OLIVER MERRITT, Private

Previously served as Private in Company M of this regiment. Transferred to this company in May, 1863, while absent without leave. Apparently failed to report for duty. Later served as Private in Company H, 4th Regiment Tennessee Infantry (Union).

HAMPTON, WILLIAM F., Private

Previously served as Private in Company M of this regiment. Transferred to this company in May, 1863. Reported present in May-June, 1863. Wounded at Chickamauga, Georgia, September 20, 1863. Returned to duty prior to October 31, 1863. Captured at Missionary Ridge, Tennessee, November 25, 1863. Sent to Nashville, Tennessee. Transferred to Louisville, Kentucky, where he arrived on December 7, 1863. Transferred to Rock Island, Illinois, where he arrived on December 9, 1863. Released at Rock Island on or about February 5, 1864, after joining the U.S. Navy.

HANES, MARION M., Private

Resided in Wilkes County and enlisted at Camp Palmer at age 16, September 25, 1862, for the war. Died on February 10, 1863. Place and cause of death not reported.

HARP, CALVIN, Private

Previously served as Private in Company M of this regiment. Transferred to this company in May, 1863, while absent without leave. No further records.

HARRISON, JOSEPH W., Private

Previously served as Private in Company M of this regiment. Transferred to this company in May, 1863, while absent without leave. Apparently failed to report for duty. Later served as Private in Company E, 13th Regiment Tennessee Cavalry (Union).

HATTON, WARREN A., Private

Previously served as Private in Company M of this regiment. Transferred to this company in May, 1863, while absent without leave. Apparently failed to report for duty. Later served as Private in Company E, 13th Regiment Tennessee Cavalry (Union).

HAWKS, JOHN, Private

Enlisted at Camp Holmes on October 25, 1863, for the war. Captured at Missionary Ridge, Tennessee, November 25, 1863. Sent to Nashville, Tennessee. Transferred to Louisville, Kentucky, where he arrived on December 7, 1863. Transferred to Rock Island, Illinois, where he arrived on December 13, 1863. Died at Rock Island on January 16, 1864, of "variola."

HAYES, JOSEPH WASHINGTON, Private

Born in Iredell County on February 27, 1825. Enlisted at Camp Holmes, near Raleigh, at age 38, October 25, 1863, for the war. Deserted from camp near Dalton, Georgia, February 6, 1864.

HENSLEY, JOHN, Private

Born in Yancey County* and was by occupation a farmer prior to enlisting in Yancey County at age 36, July 11, 1862, for the war. Reported absent without leave on company muster rolls dated July 11, 1862-April 30, 1863. No further records. [May have served later as Private in Company G, 3rd Regiment N.C. Mounted Infantry (Union).] Survived the war.

HENSLEY, JOHN E., Private

Resided in Yancey County and was by occupation a farmer prior to enlisting in Yancey County at age 25, July 11, 1862, for the war. Reported present through April 30, 1863. Reported sick in hospital at Clinton, Tennessee, in May-June, 1863. Returned to duty subsequent to October 31, 1863. Reported present in January-April, 1864. Died at home in Yancey County on August 14, 1864, of disease.

HIGGINS, CHARLES, Private

Born in Yancey County and was by occupation a farmer prior to enlisting in Yancey County at age 28, July 11, 1862, for the war. Reported present through April 30, 1863. Reported on detail at the government shoe shop at Knoxville, Tennessee, in May-June, 1863. Reported on detail in a government blacksmith shop at Atlanta, Georgia, from July 10 through October 31, 1863. Rejoined the company on an unspecified date. Reported present in January-February, 1864. Deserted near Dalton, Georgia, March 10, 1864.

HIGGINS, CURTIS, Private

Resided in Yancey County and enlisted in Buncombe County at age 18, February 5, 1864, for the war. Reported for duty on May 15, 1864. Reported present through August 31, 1864. No further records.

HIGGINS, DAVID C., Private

Born in Yancey County and was by occupation a farmer prior to enlisting in Yancey County at age 25, July 11, 1862, for the war. Reported present through April 30, 1863. Deserted at Clinton, Tennessee, prior to July 1, 1863.

HIGGINS, JAMES ERWIN, Private

Born in Yancey County* and was by occupation a farmer prior to enlisting in Yancey County at age 33, July 11, 1862, for the war.

Reported absent without leave on company muster roll dated July 11, 1862-February 28, 1863. Returned to duty in March-April, 1863. Reported absent in the guard house at Clinton, Tennessee, in May-June, 1863. Reason he was confined not reported. Returned to duty on an unspecified date. Reported present in September-October, 1863. Captured at or near Missionary Ridge, Tennessee, on or about November 25, 1863. Sent to Nashville, Tennessee. Transferred to Louisville, Kentucky, where he arrived on December 11, 1863. Transferred to Rock Island, Illinois, where he arrived on December 14, 1863. Released at Rock Island on October 13, 1864, after joining the U.S. Army. Assigned to Company I, 2nd Regiment U.S. Volunteer Infantry.

HIGGINS, JOHN, Private

Resided in Wilkes County and enlisted at Camp Holmes on November 11, 1863, for the war. Reported present in March-April, 1864. Deserted to the enemy near Dallas, Georgia, May 26, 1864. Took the Oath of Allegiance at Chattanooga, Tennessee, on or about June 3, 1864. [May have served previously as Private in Company G, 29th Regiment N.C. Troops.]

HIGGINS, THROWER, Musician

Born in Yancey County where he resided as a farmer prior to enlisting in Yancey County at age 26, July 11, 1862, for the war. Mustered in as Musician (Drummer). Reported absent sick on company muster roll dated July 11, 1862-February 28, 1863. Reported present in March-April, 1863. No further records. Survived the war.

HILL, LEVI, Private

Enlisted at Camp Holmes on October 25, 1863, for the war. Reported sick in hospital in January-February, 1864. Reported present in March-August, 1864. No further records.

HOGLER, JOHN C., ——

Place and date of enlistment not reported. Name appears on a muster-in roll dated July 15, 1862. "Column of signatures canceled." No further records.

HOLAWAY, JOHN, Private

Enlisted at Camp Holmes on October 25, 1863, for the war. Captured at Missionary Ridge, Tennessee, November 25, 1863. Sent to Nashville, Tennessee. Transferred to Louisville, Kentucky, where he arrived on December 5, 1863. Transferred to Rock Island, Illinois, where he arrived on December 9, 1863. Died at Rock Island on February 13, 1864, of "variola."

HOLEMAN, JAMES, Private

Previously served as Private in Company M of this regiment. Transferred to this company in May, 1863. Hospitalized at Knoxville, Tennessee, prior to July 1, 1863, with an unspecified complaint. Returned to duty on an unspecified date. Reported present in September-October, 1863, and January-August, 1864. No further records.

HOLEMAN, SMITH, Private

Previously served as Private in Company M of this regiment. Transferred to this company in May, 1863. Reported present through June 30, 1863. Wounded at Chickamauga, Georgia, September 20, 1863. Returned to duty prior to October 31, 1863. Reported present in January-April, 1864. Wounded at Kolb's Farm, near Marietta, Georgia, June 22, 1864. Wounded at or near the Chattahoochee River, Georgia, July 10, 1864. Died in hospital at Forsyth, Georgia, August 10, 1864, of wounds.

HOLLIFIELD, JOSEPH H., ——

Place and date of enlistment not reported. Name appears on a muster-in roll dated July 15, 1862. "Column of signatures canceled." No further records.

HONEYCUTT, GEORGE W., Private

Born in Yancey County where he resided as a farmer prior to enlisting in Yancey County at age 21, July 11, 1862, for the war. Reported present through June 30, 1863. Wounded at Chickamauga, Georgia, September 19-20, 1863. Returned from hospital subsequent to October 31, 1863. Captured at or near Missionary Ridge, Tennessee, on or about November 25, 1863. Sent to Nashville, Tennessee. Transferred to Louisville, Kentucky, where he arrived on December 11, 1863. Transferred to Rock Island, Illinois, where he arrived on December 14, 1863. Released at Rock Island on October 18, 1864, after taking the Oath of Allegiance.

HONEYCUTT, LAFAYETTE P., Private

Resided in Yancey County where he enlisted at age 22, July 11, 1862, for the war. Reported absent without leave on company muster rolls dated July 11, 1862-April 30, 1863. Returned to duty on an unspecified date. Deserted at Ooltewah Station, Tennessee, on or about September 8, 1863. Later served as Private in the 13th Regiment Tennessee Cavalry (Union).

HOWELL, HENRY, ——

North Carolina pension records indicate that he served in this company.

HOWELL, PETER, Private

Place and date of enlistment not reported. Name appears on a muster-in roll dated July 15, 1862. No further records. Survived the war.

HOWELL, THOMAS, Private

Previously served as Private in Company G, 29th Regiment N.C. Troops. Enlisted in this company in Yancey County on July 11, 1862, for the war. Reported present through April 30, 1863. Deserted at Clinton, Tennessee, in May-June, 1863. Returned to duty prior to September 20, 1863, when he deserted at Chickamauga, Georgia. Returned to duty on an unspecified date. Discharged at Marietta, Georgia, December 4, 1863, by reason of "spinal injury of 3 years standing & variola[?] & disease of the heart. . . ." Discharge certificate gives his age as 24.

HUGHES, CHARLES, Private

Enlisted at Camp Martin (Mitchell County) on June 27, 1862, for the war. Reported under arrest at Clinton, Tennessee, in March-April, 1863. Reason he was arrested not reported. Deserted at Clinton prior to July 1, 1863. [May have served later as Private in Company C, 13th Regiment Tennessee Cavalry (Union).]

HUGHS, AMOS, Private

Enlisted in Yancey County on July 10, 1862, for the war. Reported absent without leave on company muster rolls dated July 11, 1862-June, 1863. No further records.

HUGHS, DAVID, JR., Private

Enlisted in Yancey County on July 11, 1862, for the war. Reported absent without leave on company muster roll dated July 11, 1862-

February 28, 1863. Reported present in March-April, 1863. Deserted at Wolf River, Tennessee, in May-June, 1863.

HUGHS, DAVID, SR., Private

Enlisted at Camp Huston on October 1, 1862, for the war. Reported absent without leave on February 28, 1863. Reported under arrest in the guard house at Clinton, Tennessee, in March-April, 1863. Reported absent without leave in May-June, 1863. No further records.

HUGHS, JAMES, Private

Resided in Yancey County where he enlisted at age 16, July 11, 1862, for the war. Reported absent without leave on company muster rolls dated July 11, 1862-June, 1863. Enlisted in Company C of this regiment on May 1, 1864.

HUGHS, JASON, Private

Enlisted in Yancey County on June 11, 1862, for the war. Reported absent without leave on company muster rolls dated July 11, 1862-June 30, 1863.

HUTCHINS, WILLIAM B., Private

Resided in Mitchell County and enlisted at Camp Holmes on October 25, 1863, for the war. Deserted on an unspecified date. Reported present but under arrest in March-April, 1864. Deserted to the enemy on an unspecified date. Sent to Chattanooga, Tennessee. Transferred to Louisville, Kentucky, where he arrived on June 6, 1864. Released at Louisville on June 8, 1864, after taking the Oath of Allegiance.

JESSUPS, IRA, Private

Resided in Surry County and enlisted at Camp Holmes at age 34, November 11, 1863, for the war. Deserted from camp near Dalton, Georgia, January 1, 1864. Apprehended (or rejoined the company) on an unspecified date. Court-martialed on April 2, 1864, and sentenced to be shot. Died prior to September 1, 1864, probably of natural causes. Place of death not reported.

JONES, EDMOND R., Private

Previously served as Sergeant in Company M of this regiment. Transferred to this company in May, 1863. Mustered in as Sergeant. Reported present in May-June, 1863. Reduced to ranks in July-October, 1863. Reported present in September-October, 1863. Wounded at Missionary Ridge, Tennessee, November 25, 1863. Furloughed for forty days on December 7, 1863. Reported absent on expired furlough through August 31, 1864. No further records.

JONES, NELSON, Private

Born in Yancey County and was by occupation a farmer prior to enlisting in Yancey County at age 19, July 11, 1862, for the war. Reported absent sick on company muster roll dated July 11, 1862-February 28, 1863. Reported absent without leave in March-June, 1863. Deserted from hospital at Knoxville, Tennessee, September 1, 1863. Reported present but under arrest in March-April, 1864. Reported sick in hospital from May 20 through August 31, 1864. No further records.

JONES, ROBERT, Private

Previously served as Private in Company M of this regiment. Transferred to this company in May, 1863, while listed as a deserter. No further records.

KEENER, GEORGE, Private

Enlisted at Camp Holmes on October 25, 1863, for the war. Died in camp near Dalton, Georgia, January 15, 1864, of disease.

KELLER, JESSE ROBERT, Private

Previously served as Musician (Fifer) in Company M of this regiment. Transferred to this company in May, 1863. Mustered in as Private. Deserted at Clinton, Tennessee, prior to July 1, 1863. Later served as Sergeant in Company F, 3rd Regiment N.C. Mounted Infantry (Union).

KELLER, NICHOLAS, Private

Previously served as Private in Company M of this regiment. Transferred to this company in May, 1863. Deserted at Clinton, Tennessee, prior to July 1, 1863. Later served as Private in Company F, 3rd Regiment N.C. Mounted Infantry (Union).

KELLER, WILLIAM, Private

Previously served as Private in Company M of this regiment. Transferred to this company in May, 1863, while detailed as a hospital nurse at Knoxville, Tennessee. Reported for duty with the company in November, 1863-February, 1864. Reported present in March-April, 1864. Captured (or deserted to the enemy) at or near Bald Hill, near Atlanta, Georgia, on or about July 22, 1864. Sent to Nashville, Tennessee. Transferred to Louisville, Kentucky, where he arrived on July 30, 1864. Transferred to Camp Chase, Ohio, where he arrived on August 2, 1864. Released at Camp Chase on May 15, 1865, after taking the Oath of Allegiance. [Records of the Federal Provost Marshal dated May, 1865, give his age as 30.]

KILBY, THOMAS, Private

Resided in Wilkes County and was by occupation a farmer prior to enlisting at Camp Holmes at age 36, November 12, 1863, for the war. Deserted from camp near Dalton, Georgia, February 6, 1864.

LAWRENCE, JOHN W., Private

Enlisted in Yancey County on July 11, 1862, for the war. Reported present through February 28, 1863. Deserted at Big Creek Gap, Tennessee, April 5, 1863. Returned to duty subsequent to June 30, 1863. Deserted near Chattanooga, Tennessee, September 23, 1863.

LAWS, BANNESTER, Private

Place and date of enlistment not reported (probably enlisted in the autumn of 1863). Captured at Missionary Ridge, Tennessee, November 25, 1863. Sent to Nashville, Tennessee. Transferred to Louisville, Kentucky, where he arrived on December 8, 1863. Transferred to Rock Island, Illinois, where he arrived on December 11, 1863. Died at Rock Island on June 2, 1864, of "meningitis."

LAWS, JOSEPH, Private

Born in Wilkes County and resided in Yancey County where he was by occupation a farmer prior to enlisting in Yancey County at age 24, July 11, 1862, for the war. Reported present through April 30, 1863. Deserted at Clinton, Tennessee, in May-June, 1863. Returned to duty on an unspecified date. Reported sick in hospital in June-August, 1864. No further records.

LEDFORD, PETER, Private

Born in Buncombe County and was by occupation a farmer prior to enlisting in Buncombe County at age 42, July 11, 1862, for the war as a substitute for Pvt. Moses Peterson. Reported present through April 30, 1863. Deserted at Clinton, Tennessee, in May-June, 1863.

LEWIS, JAMES, Private

Previously served as Private in Company M of this regiment. Transferred to this company in May, 1863, while absent without leave. No further records. [May have served later as Private in Company G, 3rd Regiment N.C. Mounted Infantry (Union).]

LORANCE, GEORGE W., Private

Previously served as Private in Company M of this regiment. Transferred to this company in May, 1863, while listed as a deserter. No further records. Survived the war.

LYONS, JOHN, Private

Resided in Wilkes County. Place and date of enlistment not reported. Captured at Missionary Ridge, Tennessee, November 25, 1863. Sent to Nashville, Tennessee. Transferred to Louisville, Kentucky, where he arrived on December 7, 1863. Transferred to Rock Island, Illinois, where he arrived on December 11, 1863. Released at Rock Island on May 16, 1865, presumably after taking the Oath of Allegiance.

McCOURY, GEORGE W., Private

Resided in Yancey County and enlisted on July 11, 1862, for the war. Died on February 7, 1863. Place and cause of death not reported.

McCURRY, ZEPHANIAH, Private

Previously served as Private in Company K of this regiment. Transferred to this company subsequent to April 30, 1863. Deserted at Clinton, Tennessee, prior to July 1, 1863. Later served as Private in Company K, 3rd Regiment N.C. Mounted Infantry (Union).

McGALLIARD, ROBERT, Corporal

Previously served as Private in Company F of this regiment. Transferred to this company subsequent to August 31, 1864. Promoted to Corporal on an unspecified date. Paroled at Greensboro on May 1, 1865.

McINTOSH, SIDNEY, Private

Enlisted at Camp Palmer at age 35, October 10, 1862, for the war. Reported absent sick on company muster roll dated July 11, 1862-February 28, 1863. Reported absent without leave in March-April, 1863. No further records. Survived the war.

McKINEY, WILLIAM, Private

Born in Yancey County and was by occupation a farmer prior to enlisting in Yancey County at age 19, July 11, 1862, for the war. Reported present through April 30, 1863. Reported sick in hospital at Clinton, Tennessee, in May-June, 1863. Returned to duty prior to September 20, 1863, when he was wounded at Chickamauga, Georgia. Died on September 25, 1863, of wounds. Place of death not reported.

McMAHAN, JAMES, Private

Born in Yancey County and was by occupation a farmer prior to enlisting in Yancey County on July 11, 1862, for the war. Reported absent without leave on company muster rolls dated July 11, 1862-

June 30, 1863. Returned to duty on an unspecified date. Deserted near Chattanooga, Tennessee, September 23, 1863. Later served as Private in Company K, 3rd Regiment N.C. Mounted Infantry (Union).

McMAHAN, SANDERS, Private

Born in Yancey County* and was by occupation a farmer prior to enlisting in Yancey County at age 33, July 11, 1862, for the war. Deserted on October 25, 1862. Returned to duty subsequent to June 30, 1863. Sent to hospital from camp near Dalton, Georgia, January 2, 1864. Reported absent sick through August 31, 1864. No further records.

McPETERS, JONATHAN H., Corporal

Born in McDowell County* and resided in Yancey County where he was by occupation a farmer or farm laborer prior to enlisting in Yancey County at age 23, July 11, 1862, for the war. Mustered in as Private. Reported present through February 28, 1863. Promoted to Corporal prior to March 1, 1863. Sent to hospital at Knoxville, Tennessee, April 15, 1863. Returned to duty subsequent to October 31, 1863. Sent to hospital on January 18, 1864. Furloughed for thirty days from hospital at Kingston, Georgia, May 17, 1864. Reported absent on expired furlough on August 31, 1864. No further records. Survived the war.

McPETERS, SAMUEL S., Corporal

Resided in McDowell County and was by occupation a farmer prior to enlisting in Yancey County on July 11, 1862, for the war. Mustered in as Private. Reported absent without leave on company muster roll dated July 11, 1862-February 28, 1863. Returned to duty in March-April, 1863. Reported sick in hospital at Clinton, Tennessee, in May-June, 1863. Returned to duty on an unspecified date. Reported present in September-October, 1863. Reported on detail as a teamster in January-February, 1864. Rejoined the company in March-April, 1864. Promoted to Corporal on April 1, 1864. Wounded at Kolb's Farm, near Marietta, Georgia, June 22, 1864. Captured (or deserted to the enemy) on or about August 27, 1864. Sent to Atlanta, Georgia. Transferred to Louisville, Kentucky, where he arrived on October 11, 1864. Released at Louisville on or about October 14, 1864, after taking the Oath of Allegiance. [Was about 19 years of age at time of enlistment. North Carolina pension records indicate that he was wounded at Bethel Church, Georgia, in 1863. One of his wounds was a shell wound in the right leg.]

MAIN, HARRISON, Private

Previously served as Private in Company M of this regiment. Transferred to this company in May, 1863, while listed as a deserter. Prior to that date (on or about December 1-3, 1862) he enlisted as Private in Company C, 4th Regiment Tennessee Cavalry (Union).

MASON, HARRISON, Private

Born in Iredell County in 1845. Resided in Iredell County and enlisted at Camp Holmes on November 12, 1863, for the war. Reported for duty on July 10, 1864. Reported present through August 31, 1864. Paroled at Statesville on May 28, 1865. [His Tennessee pension application indicates that he was discharged in the winter of 1864-1865.]

MATHIS, JOHN, Private

Born in Sullivan County, Tennessee, and resided in Yancey County where he was by occupation a farmer or farm laborer prior to enlisting in Yancey County at age 17, July 11, 1862, for the war. Reported absent without leave on company muster roll dated July 11, 1862-February 28, 1863. Reported present in March-June, 1863. Deserted at Lenoir Station, Tennessee, September 1, 1863.

MIKEAL, ALEXANDER, Private

Previously served as Private in Company M of this regiment. Transferred to this company in May, 1863, while absent without leave. No further records.

MIKEAL, FREDERICK, Private

Previously served as Private in Company M of this regiment. Transferred to this company in May, 1863, while absent without leave. Reported for duty on an unspecified date. Deserted at Hunt's Crossroads, Tennessee, prior to July 1, 1863. Later served as Private in Company A, 3rd Regiment N.C. Mounted Infantry (Union).

MIKEAL, ISAAC, Private

Previously served as Private in Company M of this regiment. Transferred to this company in May, 1863. Mustered in as Private. Promoted to Sergeant prior to September 6, 1863, when he deserted near Charleston, Tennessee. Returned to duty subsequent to October 31, 1863. Reduced to ranks in November, 1863-February, 1864. Reported present in January-April, 1864. Captured (or deserted to the enemy) at Bald Hill, near Atlanta, Georgia, July 22, 1864. Sent to Nashville, Tennessee. Transferred to Louisville, Kentucky, where he arrived on July 30, 1864. Transferred to Camp Chase, Ohio, where he arrived on August 2, 1864. Died at Camp Chase on February 3, 1865, of "pneumonia."

MIKEAL, RILEY, Private

Born in Ohio and resided in Watauga County where he was by occupation a farmer prior to enlisting at Camp Holmes at age 39, October 25, 1863, for the war. Deserted near Chattanooga, Tennessee, November 19, 1863.

MILLER, DANIEL, Private

Resided in Yancey County and was by occupation a farmer prior to enlisting in Yancey County at age 26, July 11, 1862, for the war. Reported present through February 28, 1863. Reported in hospital at Knoxville, Tennessee, in March-April, 1863. Deserted at Clinton, Tennessee, in May-June, 1863. Reported present but under arrest (tried by court-martial) in January-February, 1864. Reported absent without leave on March 25, 1864. Captured by the enemy at Pulaski, Tennessee, December 25, 1864. Sent to Nashville, Tennessee. Transferred to Louisville, Kentucky, where he arrived on February 13, 1865. Transferred to Rock Island, Illinois, where he arrived on February 18, 1865. Released at Rock Island on May 28, 1865, presumably after taking the Oath of Allegiance.

MILLER, JOHN, Private

Resided in Mitchell County and enlisted at Camp Huston on October 1, 1862, for the war. Reported under arrest at Clinton, Tennessee, in March-April, 1863. Reason he was arrested not reported. Returned to duty in May-June, 1863. Deserted at Bell's Bridge, Tennessee, July 25, 1863. Returned to duty on December 1, 1863. Reported present in January-April, 1864. Deserted to the enemy near Dallas, Georgia, May 26, 1864. Sent to Chattanooga, Tennessee. Transferred to Louisville, Kentucky, where he arrived on June 6, 1864. Released on or about the same date after taking the Oath of Allegiance.

MILLER, MOSES, Private

Enlisted at Camp Palmer on October 10, 1862, for the war. Reported absent without leave on company muster rolls dated July 11, 1862-June, 1863. No further records.

MILLER, SAMUEL, Private

Previously served as Private in Company B of this regiment. Transferred to this company on June 30, 1863. Deserted near Chattanooga, Tennessee, September 17, 1863. Returned to duty on an unspecified date. Reported present in January-April, 1864. Deserted to the enemy near Dallas or Cassville, Georgia, on or about May 20, 1864. Sent to Nashville, Tennessee. Transferred to Louisville, Kentucky, where he arrived on May 29, 1864. Transferred to Rock Island, Illinois, where he arrived on June 1, 1864. Released at Rock Island on or about June 10, 1864, after joining the U.S. Navy.

MILLER, SOLOMON, Private

Enlisted in Yancey County on July 11, 1862, for the war. Reported present through April 30, 1863. Reported in the guardhouse at Clinton, Tennessee, in May-June, 1863. Reason he was confined not reported. Returned to duty on an unspecified date. Deserted near Chattanooga, Tennessee, September 17, 1863. Reported present in January-April, 1864 (court-martialed). Wounded in the left leg at Resaca, Georgia, May 14-15, 1864. Sent to hospital on an unspecified date. Furloughed for sixty days on June 1, 1864. Had not returned to duty as of August 31, 1864. No further records. Survived the war. [Was about 19 years of age at time of enlistment.]

MILLER, T. CALVIN, Sergeant

Previously served as Sergeant in Company I of this regiment. Transferred to this company subsequent to August 31, 1864. Paroled at Greensboro on May 1, 1865.

MITCHELL, ROBERT, Private

Previously served as Private in Company I of this regiment. Transferred to this company subsequent to August 31, 1864. Paroled at Greensboro on May 1, 1865.

MOODY, BENJAMIN, JR., Private

Previously served as Private in Company M of this regiment. Transferred to this company in May, 1863, while absent without leave. Apparently failed to report for duty. Later served as Private in Company A, 13th Regiment Tennessee Cavalry (Union).

MULKEY, ROBERT, Private

Place and date of enlistment not reported. Captured at Missionary Ridge, Tennessee, November 25, 1863. Sent to Nashville, Tennessee. Transferred to Louisville, Kentucky, where he arrived on December 7, 1863. Transferred to Rock Island, Illinois, where he arrived on December 11, 1863. Paroled at Rock Island on February 15, 1865, and transferred for exchange. Hospitalized at Richmond, Virginia, February 28, 1865, with debilitas. Furloughed for thirty days on March 7, 1865.

MULLIS, GEORGE W., Private

Resided in Iredell County and enlisted at Camp Holmes on November 12, 1863, for the war. Reported present in January-April, 1864. Reported present but sick in May-August, 1864. Captured at Stockbridge or Jonesborough, Georgia, September 4, 1864. Sent to Nashville, Tennessee. Transferred to Louisville, Kentucky, where he arrived on October 28, 1864. Transferred to Camp Douglas, Chicago, Illinois, where he arrived on November 1, 1864. Released at Camp Douglas on May 12, 1865, after taking the Oath of Allegiance. [Was about 33 years of age at time of enlistment. North Carolina pension records indicate that he was wounded in the right thigh and left arm at Missionary Ridge, Tennessee, "August 15, 1864."]

MYERS, MILTON, Private

Resided in Iredell County and was by occupation a farmer prior to enlisting at Camp Holmes at age 33, October 25, 1863, for the war. Reported present but under arrest in January-February, 1864. Reason he was arrested not reported. Reported present in March-April, 1864. Died in hospital at Newnan, Georgia, May 17, 1864, of disease.

NANEY, ISAIAH, Private

Born in Rutherford County where he resided prior to enlisting in Yancey County at age 22, July 11, 1862, for the war. Reported absent without leave on company muster rolls dated July 11, 1862-June 30, 1863. No further records.

NANEY, JORDAN, Private

Born in Rutherford County and was by occupation a farmer prior to enlisting in Yancey County at age 18, July 12, 1862, for the war. Died on February 3, 1863. Place and cause of death not reported.

NEWMAN, WILLIAM, Private

Resided in Chatham County and was by occupation a farmer prior to enlisting at Camp Holmes at age 38, October 25, 1863, for the war. Deserted from camp near Dalton, Georgia, February 22, 1864. Went over to the enemy on an unspecified date. Took the Oath of Allegiance at Chattanooga, Tennessee, on or about March 17, 1864.

NORRIS, ISAAC, Private

Previously served as Sergeant in Company M of this regiment. Transferred to this company in May, 1863, while absent without leave. Reduced to ranks prior to July 1, 1863. No further records. Survived the war.

NORRIS, WILLIAM W., Sergeant

Previously served as Corporal in Company M of this regiment. Transferred to this company in May, 1863. Wounded at Chickamauga, Georgia, September 19-20, 1863. Hospitalized at Marietta, Georgia. Furloughed on an unspecified date. Reported absent on expired furlough on October 31, 1863. Returned to duty on an unspecified date. Promoted to Sergeant prior to February 25, 1864, when he was wounded at Rocky Face Ridge, Georgia. Hospitalized at Cassville, Georgia. Furloughed for sixty days on or about April 15, 1864. No further records.

ODEER, ALBERT M., Private

Enlisted in Yancey County on July 11, 1862, for the war. Reported absent without leave on company muster roll dated July 11, 1862-February 28, 1863. Reported present in March-June, 1863. Died on or about July 31, 1863, and was buried in Bethel Cemetery, Knoxville, Tennessee. Cause of death not reported.

PATE, GEORGE W., Private

Resided in Yancey County and was by occupation a farmer prior to enlisting in Yancey County at age 37, July 11, 1862, for the war.

Reported absent without leave through June 30, 1863. No further records. [May have served later as Private in Company F, 3rd Regiment N.C. Mounted Infantry (Union).]

PATTERSON, SAMUEL F., Private

Resided in Yancey County and was by occupation a farmer prior to enlisting in Mitchell County at age 17, October 1, 1862, for the war. Reported present through April 30, 1863. Died in hospital at Clinton, Tennessee, on or about May 11, 1863. Cause of death not reported.

PERKINS, FRANKLIN, Private

Previously served as Private in Company M of this regiment. Transferred to this company in May, 1863, while absent without leave. No further records. Survived the war.

PERKINS, JOHN, Private

Previously served as Private in Company M of this regiment. Transferred to this company in May, 1863, while absent without leave. No further records. Survived the war.

PETERSON, ALLEN, Private

Born in Yancey County and was by occupation a farmer prior to enlisting in Yancey County at age 20, July 11, 1862, for the war. Reported absent without leave on company muster roll dated July 11, 1862-February 28, 1863. Returned to duty in March-April, 1863. Deserted at Wolf River, Tennessee, prior to July 1, 1863.

PETERSON, CHARLES J., Private

Born in Yancey County where he resided as a farmer prior to enlisting in Yancey County at age 26, July 11, 1862, for the war. Mustered in as Corporal. Reported absent without leave on company muster rolls dated July 11, 1862-June 30, 1863. Reduced to ranks prior to March 1, 1863. No further records.

PETERSON, JOHN, Private

Resided in Yadkin County and enlisted in Yancey County at age 34, July 11, 1862, for the war. Reported absent without leave on company muster rolls dated July 11, 1862-June 30, 1863. Transferred to Company E of this regiment on or about November 1, 1863.

PETERSON, LAWSON, Private

Born in Yancey County where he resided as a farmer prior to enlisting in Yancey County at age 21, July 11, 1862, for the war. Reported absent without leave on company muster rolls dated July 11, 1862-June 30, 1863. Later served as Private in Company A, 3rd Regiment N.C. Mounted Infantry (Union).

PETERSON, MOSES, Private

Born in Yancey County where he resided as a farmer prior to enlisting in Yancey County at age 21, July 12, 1862, for the war. Discharged on or about the same date after providing Pvt. Peter Ledford as a substitute. Later served as Private in Company F, 3rd Regiment N.C. Mounted Infantry (Union).

PETERSON, REUBEN, Private

Born in Yancey County* where he resided as a farmer prior to enlisting in Yancey County at age 31, July 11, 1862, for the war. Reported absent without leave on company muster rolls dated July

11, 1862-June 30, 1863. Later served as Private in Companies A and F, 3rd Regiment N.C. Mounted Infantry (Union).

PHILLIPS, ALFRED, Private

Born in Yancey County and was by occupation a farmer prior to enlisting in Yancey County at age 28, July 11, 1862, for the war. Reported present through February 28, 1863. Reported sick in hospital at Knoxville, Tennessee, in March-June, 1863. Returned to duty on an unspecified date. Sent to hospital sick on October 26, 1863. Reported absent sick through February, 1864. Returned to duty on an unspecified date. Reported present in March-August, 1864. Transferred to Company D of this regiment subsequent to August 31, 1864.

PHILLIPS, HAMILTON, Private

Previously served as Private in Company M of this regiment. Transferred to this company in May, 1863, while absent without leave. No further records. Survived the war.

PHILLIPS, HUGH, Private

Previously served as Private in Company M of this regiment. Transferred to this company in May, 1863, while absent without leave. Listed as a deserter on June 30, 1863. Later served as Private in Company H, 3rd Regiment N.C. Mounted Infantry (Union).

PHILLIPS, NATHAN, Private

Previously served as Private in Company M of this regiment. Transferred to this company in May, 1863, while absent without leave. Listed as a deserter on June 30, 1863. Reported for duty on an unspecified date. Captured at or near Dalton, Georgia, on or about May 13, 1864. Sent to Nashville, Tennessee. Transferred to Louisville, Kentucky, where he arrived on May 17, 1864. Hospitalized at Louisville on May 23, 1864, with varioloid. Transferred to Camp Morton, Indianapolis, Indiana, on an unspecified date. Arrived at Camp Morton on July 7, 1864. Died at Camp Morton on August 7, 1864, of "typho[id] malarial fever." [Federal hospital records dated May-June, 1864, give his age as 29.]

PHILLIPS, PAYTON, Private

Previously served as Private in Company M of this regiment. Transferred to this company in May, 1863. Reported in the guardhouse at Clinton, Tennessee, June 30, 1863. Reason he was confined not reported. Wounded at Chickamauga, Georgia, September 19-20, 1863. Hospitalized at Newnan, Georgia. Furloughed from hospital for sixty days on December 10, 1863. Reported absent on expired furlough on February 29, 1864. Had not returned to duty as of August 31, 1864. No further records. Survived the war.

PHIPPS, JOHN W., Private

Born in Yancey County and was by occupation a farmer prior to enlisting in Yancey County at age 25, July 11, 1862, for the war. Mustered in as Sergeant. Reported present through April 30, 1863. Deserted at Clinton, Tennessee, in May-June, 1863. Reduced to ranks prior to July 1, 1863. Returned to duty on an unspecified date. Wounded in the left side, right leg, and hands ("both index fingers shot off") at Chickamauga, Georgia, September 19-20, 1863. Deserted from an unspecified hospital on December 18, 1863.

PIPES, JOHN W., Private

Previously served as Private in Company M of this regiment. Transferred to this company in May, 1863, while absent without leave.

Reported for duty on an unspecified date. Transferred to Company E of this regiment subsequent to June 30, 1863.

PRESNELL, DAVID A., Private

Previously served as Private in Company C of this regiment. Transferred to this company on an unspecified date. No further records.

PRICHARD, ALEXANDER, Private

Enlisted in Yancey County on October 1, 1862, for the war. Reported present in March-April, 1863. Transferred to Company E of this regiment in May-June, 1863.

QUEEN, PETER WAITS, Private

Enlisted in Yancey County on October 1, 1862, for the war. Reported present in March-June, 1863. Deserted at Bell's Bridge, Tennessee, July 25, 1863. [Was about 18 years of age at time of enlistment.]

RANDOLPH, JAMES B., Private

Born in Yancey County* where he resided as a farmer prior to enlisting in Yancey County at age 31, July 11, 1862, for the war. Reported present through April 30, 1863. Deserted prior to June 6, 1863. Reported in the guardhouse at Clinton, Tennessee, June 30, 1863. Returned to duty on an unspecified date. Furloughed for thirty days on September 29, 1863. Reported absent on expired furlough on October 31, 1863. Returned to duty subsequent to February 29, 1864. Reported present in May-August, 1864. No further records. Survived the war. [North Carolina pension records indicate that he was wounded in the thigh on an unspecified date.]

RANDOLPH, MORGAN, Private

Enlisted at Camp Palmer on October 1, 1862, for the war. Reported absent without leave in March-April, 1863. Returned to duty on an unspecified date. Deserted near Chattanooga, Tennessee, September 6, 1863. Dropped from the company rolls on or about February 29, 1864. Hospitalized at Charlotte on February 19, 1865, with debilitas. Admitted to hospital at Greensboro on March 20, 1865. No further records. Survived the war.

RANDOLPH, THOMAS M., Private

Born in Yancey County in 1840. Resided in Mitchell County where he enlisted on October 1, 1862, for the war. Reported present through April 30, 1863. Deserted on or about June 6, 1863. Reported in the guardhouse at Clinton, Tennessee, June 30, 1863. Furloughed for forty-five days from hospital at Knoxville, Tennessee, August 26, 1863. Failed to return to duty and was listed as a deserter on February 29, 1864. Hospitalized at West Point, Mississippi, January 10, 1865, with pneumonia. Hospitalized at Raleigh on February 20, 1865, with chronic rheumatism. Transferred on March 8, 1865. No further records. Survived the war. [North Carolina pension records indicate that he received "a bad wound in the right shoulder by falling off the barracks at Columbia (Tennessee) while guarding prisoners and at the same time (and) place had hip (and left) ancle (sic) badly dislocated. . . ." Those injuries reportedly occurred on January 1, 1863. See also his Tennessee pension application.]

RANDOLPH, WILLIAM J., Private

Born in Yancey County* where he resided as a farmer prior to enlisting in Yancey County at age 35, July 11, 1862, for the war.

Reported present through February 28, 1863. Reported in hospital at Knoxville, Tennessee, in March-June, 1863. Furloughed from hospital for thirty days on July 1, 1863. Reported absent on expired furlough on October 31, 1863. Returned to duty subsequent to February 29, 1864. Sent to hospital sick on June 23, 1864. Returned to duty prior to November 22, 1864. Reported on detail as a bridge builder December 16-28, 1864. No further records. Survived the war. [North Carolina pension records indicate that he was wounded in the head at New Hope Church, Georgia, July 3, 1864.]

RASH, PAYTON, Private

Previously served as Private in Company M of this regiment. Transferred to this company in May, 1863. Deserted at Clinton, Tennessee, prior to July 1, 1863. Went over to the enemy on an unspecified date. Confined at Fort Delaware, Delaware, where he died on September 10, 1863, of "measles."

REACE, WILLIAM, Private

Previously served as Private in Company M of this regiment. Transferred to this company in May, 1863, while absent on expired furlough. Reported absent without leave on June 30, 1863. No further records.

RIDDLE, JOHN, Private

Born in Yancey County and was by occupation a farmer prior to enlisting in Yancey County at age 25, July 11, 1862, for the war. Reported absent sick on company muster rolls dated July 11, 1862-April 30, 1863. Reported absent without leave in May-June, 1863. No further records. Survived the war. [May have served later as Corporal in Company K, 3rd Regiment N.C. Mounted Infantry (Union).]

RIDDLE, ROBERT, 1st Sergeant

Born in Yancey County* and was by occupation a farmer prior to enlisting in Yancey County at age 29, July 12, 1862, for the war. Mustered in as 1st Sergeant. Reported absent sick on company muster rolls dated July 11, 1862-April 30, 1863. No further records.

RIDDLE, WILLIAM P., Private

Born in Yancey County where he resided as a farmer prior to enlisting in Yancey County at age 18, July 11, 1862, for the war. Reported present through June 30, 1863. Deserted near Chattanooga, Tennessee, September 23, 1863.

RIMER, ELI, Private

Enlisted at Camp Holmes on October 25, 1863, for the war. Sent to hospital on February 25, 1864. Returned to duty prior to May 1, 1864. Hospitalized at Griffin, Georgia, on an unspecified date. Furloughed for sixty days from hospital at Griffin on June 10, 1864. No further records. Survived the war. [Was about 38 years of age at time of enlistment. North Carolina pension records indicate that he suffered a concussion at Chattanooga, Tennessee, November 1, 1863.]

ROGERS, HIRAM DAVID, Private

Born in Wilkes County and resided in Yancey County where he was by occupation a farmer prior to enlisting in Yancey County at age 32, July 12, 1862, for the war. Sent to hospital at Knoxville, Tennessee, in March-April, 1863. Died in hospital at Knoxville on or about May 5, 1863, of "feaver" and/or "relaps of measels [sic]."

ROLAND, WILLIAM HENRY, Private

Born in Yancey County where he resided as a farmer or farm laborer prior to enlisting in Yancey County at age 21, July 12, 1862, for the war. No further records. Survived the war.

SALE, WILLIAM J., Private

Born on December 3, 1826. Enlisted at Camp Holmes at age 36, November 12, 1863, for the war. Sent to hospital sick on January 10, 1864. Returned to duty in March-April, 1864. Reported absent on duty as a litter bearer in May-August, 1864. No further records. Survived the war. [North Carolina pension records indicate that he was wounded at Atlanta, Georgia, April 15, 1863.]

SHAVER, WILLIAM LEE, Private

Resided in Iredell County and enlisted at Camp Holmes on November 12, 1863, for the war. Reported present in January-April, 1864. Wounded in both arms at Kolb's Farm, near Marietta, Georgia, June 22, 1864. Hospitalized at Macon, Georgia, where he died on July 6, 1864, of wounds.

SHAW, ALFRED, Private

Previously served as Private in Company M of this regiment. Transferred to this company in May, 1863, while absent without leave. No further records. Survived the war.

SHAW, JOHN, Private

Previously served as Private in Company M of this regiment. Transferred to this company in May, 1863. Reported in the guardhouse at Clinton, Tennessee, in May-June, 1863. Reason he was confined not reported. Returned to duty on an unspecified date. Reported present in September-October, 1863, and January-April, 1864. Deserted to the enemy near Dallas, Georgia, May 26, 1864. Sent to Chattanooga, Tennessee. Transferred to Louisville, Kentucky, where he arrived on June 6, 1864. Released on or about June 8, 1864, after taking the Oath of Allegiance.

SHAW, SOLOMON, Private

Previously served as Private in Company M of this regiment. Transferred to this company in May, 1863. Deserted at Clinton, Tennessee, prior to June 30, 1863. Returned to duty on an unspecified date (probably subsequent to April 30, 1864). Wounded in the side at Resaca, Georgia, May 14-15, 1864. Deserted to the enemy near Atlanta, Georgia, July 20, 1864. Sent to Chattanooga, Tennessee. Transferred to Louisville, Kentucky, where he arrived on August 15, 1864. Released at Louisville on or about August 29, 1864, after taking the Oath of Allegiance.

SMITH, ANDREW J., Private

Enlisted at Camp Huston on October 1, 1862, for the war. Reported present in March-April, 1863. Transferred to Company K of this regiment prior to June 15, 1863.

SPRINKLE, OBADIAH, Private

Resided in Wilkes County and was by occupation a farmer prior to enlisting at Camp Holmes at age 38, November 12, 1863, for the war. Captured at Missionary Ridge, Tennessee, November 25, 1863. Sent to Nashville, Tennessee. Transferred to Louisville, Kentucky, where he arrived on December 11, 1863. Transferred to Rock Island, Illinois, where he arrived on December 14, 1863. Released at Rock Island on May 23, 1864, after taking the Oath of Allegiance and joining the U.S. Navy.

STANBERRY, JESSE H., Private

Resided in Watauga County and was by occupation a farmer prior to enlisting at Camp Holmes at age 37, October 25, 1863, for the war. Deserted near Chattanooga, Tennessee, November 19, 1863.

STANBURY, JOSHUA S., Private

Previously served as Private in Company M of this regiment. Transferred to this company in May, 1863, while listed as a deserter. No further records.

STANBURY, NATHAN W., Private

Previously served as Private in Company M of this regiment. Transferred to this company in May, 1863, while listed as a deserter. Reported for duty on an unspecified date (probably subsequent to September 30, 1863). Reported present in March-April, 1864. Captured at Resaca, Georgia, on or about May 15, 1864. Sent to Nashville, Tennessee. Transferred to Louisville, Kentucky, where he arrived on May 20, 1864. Transferred to Camp Morton, Indianapolis, Indiana, where he arrived on May 22, 1864. Released at Camp Morton on June 12, 1865, after taking the Oath of Allegiance.

STORIE, JESSE, Private

Previously served as Private in Company M of this regiment. Transferred to this company in May, 1863, while absent without leave. Apparently failed to report for duty. Later served as Private in Company E, 13th Regiment Tennessee Cavalry (Union).

STORIE, NOAH, Private

Previously served as Private in Company M of this regiment. Transferred to this company in May, 1863, while listed as a deserter. Apparently failed to report for duty. Later served as Private in Company E, 13th Regiment Tennessee Cavalry (Union).

STRICKLIN, HENRY, Private

Enlisted at Camp Holmes on October 25, 1863, for the war. Captured at Missionary Ridge, Tennessee, November 25, 1863. Sent to Nashville, Tennessee. Transferred to Louisville, Kentucky, where he arrived on December 7, 1863. Transferred to Rock Island, Illinois, where he arrived on December 9, 1863. Died at Rock Island on September 8, 1864, of "ac[ute] dysentery."

SUITS, JAMES, Private

Resided in Wilkes County and enlisted at Camp Holmes on October 25, 1863, for the war. Reported present in January-April, 1864. Hospitalized at Macon, Georgia, June 17, 1864, with acute diarrhoea. Transferred on June 18, 1864. Reported absent sick through August 31, 1864. No further records.

TAYLOR, WILLIAM, Private

Enlisted in Yancey County on July 11, 1862, for the war. Reported present through February 28, 1863. Hospitalized at Knoxville, Tennessee, in March-April, 1863. Reported on detail as a wagoner from May 7, 1863, through February 29, 1864. Court-martialed on or about November 13, 1863. Reason he was court-martialed not reported. Reported present in March-April, 1864. Reported on detail as a wagoner in May-August, 1864. No further records.

TIPTON, JACOB, Private

Born in Yancey County and was by occupation a farmer prior to enlisting in Yancey County at age 26, July 11, 1862, for the war. Reported present through February 28, 1863. Reported absent in hospital at Knoxville, Tennessee, in March-June, 1863. Returned to duty on an unspecified date. Deserted near Charleston, Tennessee, September 6, 1863.

TIPTON, JOHN, Private

Previously served as 1st Lieutenant of this company (see page 359 above). Reenlisted in this company with the rank of Private on an unspecified date (probably subsequent to September 30, 1863). Court-martialed on or about January 12, 1864. Reason he was court-martialed not reported. No further records.

TIPTON, JOHN D., Private

Born in Yancey County and was by occupation a farmer prior to enlisting in Yancey County at age 26, July 11, 1862, for the war. Mustered in as Corporal. Reported present on company muster rolls dated July 11, 1862-June 30, 1863. Reduced to ranks in March-June, 1863. No further records. Later served as Private in Companies A and F, 3rd Regiment N.C. Mounted Infantry (Union).

TIPTON, JONATHAN, Private

Enlisted at Camp Palmer on October 10, 1862, for the war. Reported present through April 30, 1863. Reported in the guardhouse at Clinton, Tennessee, in May-June, 1863. Reason he was confined not reported. Returned to duty on an unspecified date. Deserted near Chattanooga, Tennessee, September 17, 1863. Returned to duty subsequent to February 29, 1864. Reported present in March-April, 1864. Wounded in the right arm at Resaca, Georgia, May 15, 1864. Right arm amputated. Reported absent wounded through August 31, 1864. No further records. Survived the war. [Was about 16 years of age at time of enlistment. Previously served as 1st Lieutenant in the 111th Regiment N.C. Militia.]

TIPTON, THOMAS G., Private

Enlisted at Camp Iredell on July 6, 1862, for the war. Mustered in as Private. Reported present through June 30, 1863. Transferred to Company B of this regiment in July-September, 1863.

TRIVETT, LEWIS W., Private

Previously served as Private in Company M of this regiment. Transferred to this company in May, 1863, while listed as a deserter. Reported for duty on an unspecified date (probably subsequent to September 30, 1863). Sent to hospital from camp near Dalton, Georgia, January 6, 1864. Reported present but under arrest in March-April, 1864. Returned to duty prior to May 13, 1864, when he was captured near Dalton. Sent to Nashville, Tennessee. Transferred to Louisville, Kentucky, where he arrived on May 22, 1864. Transferred to Alton, Illinois, where he arrived on May 25, 1864. Died at Alton on September 28, 1864. Cause of death not reported.

TUCKER, JAMES, Private

Previously served as Private in Company M of this regiment. Transferred to this company in May, 1863, while absent without leave. No further records.

TUGMAN, BENJAMIN F., Private

Previously served as Private in Company I of this regiment. Transferred to this company subsequent to November 19, 1864. Paroled at Greensboro on May 1, 1865. [At the time of his parole he was a patient in a Greensboro hospital.]

TURNER, A. J., Private

Previously served as Private in Company M of this regiment. Transferred to this company in May, 1863. Deserted from Ooltewah Station, Tennessee, September 8, 1863.

VANDIKE, EMANUEL, Private

Previously served as Private in Company M of this regiment. Transferred to this company in May, 1863, while absent without leave. No further records. Survived the war.

VANNOY, WILLIAM, Private

Resided in Wilkes County and was by occupation a farmer prior to enlisting at Camp Holmes at age 43, October 25, 1863, for the war. Died in hospital at Atlanta, Georgia, January 2, 1864, of "chronic diarrhoea."

VANNOY, WILLIAM H., Private

Resided in Alleghany County and enlisted at Camp Holmes on October 25, 1863, for the war. Captured at Missionary Ridge, Tennessee, November 25, 1863. Took the Oath of Allegiance at Knoxville, Tennessee, on or about December 16, 1863.

WACASTER, ELIJAH, Private

Enlisted at Camp Huston on October 1, 1862, for the war. Reported absent without leave in March-June, 1863. Returned to duty on an unspecified date. Deserted at Bell's Bridge, Tennessee, July 25, 1863. Returned to duty on an unspecified date. Court-martialed on or about February 19, 1864. Deserted prior to March 1, 1864.

WACASTER, JACOB HASSEL, Private

Enlisted at Camp Huston on October 1, 1862, for the war. Reported absent without leave in March-June, 1863. Dropped from the company rolls prior to October 1, 1863. Later served as Private in Company A of this regiment.

WALKER, JESSE F., Private

Place and date of enlistment not reported (probably enlisted subsequent to September 30, 1863). Captured at Missionary Ridge, Tennessee, November 25, 1863. Sent to Nashville, Tennessee. Transferred to Louisville, Kentucky, where he arrived on December 7, 1863. Transferred to Rock Island, Illinois, where he arrived on December 11, 1863. Died at Rock Island on February 21, 1864, of "remitt[ent] fever."

WALKER, ZEPHANIAH, Corporal

Enlisted at Camp Holmes, near Raleigh, November 12, 1863, for the war. Mustered in as Private. Reported present in January-April, 1864. Promoted to Corporal on April 1, 1864. Killed (or mortally wounded) at Kolb's Farm, near Marietta, Georgia, June 22, 1864.

WARD, JOSEPH, Private

Enlisted in Mitchell County on September 9, 1862, for the war. Reported absent without leave in March-April, 1863. No further records. [May have served later as Private in Company C, 13th Regiment Tennessee Cavalry (Union).]

WATSON, AMBROSE L. P., Private

Previously served as Private in Company M of this regiment. Transferred to this company in May, 1863, while absent without leave. No further records.

WATTS, JAMES W., Private

Born in McDowell County* and resided in Yancey County where he was by occupation a farmer prior to enlisting in Yancey County at age 34, July 12, 1862, for the war. Dropped from the company rolls prior to March 1, 1863. Reason he was dropped not reported. Deserted to the enemy on an unspecified date. Sent to Louisville, Kentucky. Released at Louisville on May 31, 1864, after taking the Oath of Allegiance.

WHITE, AMBROSE, Private

Previously served as Private in Company M of this regiment. Transferred to this company in May, 1863. Reported sick in hospital at Knoxville, Tennessee, June 30, 1863. Furloughed for thirty days from hospital at Knoxville on an unspecified date. Reported absent on expired furlough on October 31, 1863. Listed as a deserter on February 29, 1864. [May have served later as Private in Company I, 3rd Regiment N.C. Mounted Infantry (Union).]

WHITE, I. F., Private

Was by occupation a farmer prior to enlisting in October, 1863, for the war. Dropped from the company rolls on or about October 31, 1863. Paroled at Greensboro on May 1, 1865. [Records of the Federal Provost Marshal dated May, 1865, give his age as 30.]

WHITSON, CLAYTON, Private

Born in Tennessee and resided in Yancey County where he was by occupation a farmer prior to enlisting in Yancey County at age 26, September 9, 1862, for the war. Died at Camp Palmer on or about February 3, 1863. Cause of death not reported.

WILLIAMS, RANSOM H., Private

Born in Burke County and resided in Lincoln County where he was by occupation a farmer prior to enlisting in Yancey County at age 28, July 11, 1862, for the war. Reported present in March-June, 1863. Furloughed for twenty days on July 26, 1863. Deserted at Charleston, Tennessee, September 7, 1863. [North Carolina pension records indicate that he was wounded in the head near Clinton, Tennessee, November 5, 1862.]

WILLSON, WILLIAM A., Private

Born in Yancey County and was by occupation a farmer prior to enlisting in Yancey County at age 23, July 12, 1862, for the war. "Name canceled" on or about July 15, 1862. No further records.

WILSON, CALLOWAY, Private

Enlisted in Watauga County on September 26, 1862, for the war. Reported absent without leave in May-June, 1863. No further records.

WILSON, EDWARD, Private

Born in Yancey County in 1828. Enlisted in Yancey County on July 11, 1862, for the war. Reported present through February 28, 1863. Deserted at Clinton, Tennessee, April 9, 1863. Later served as Private in Company C of this regiment.

WILSON, JOHN H., Private

Previously served as Private in Company M of this regiment. Transferred to this company in May, 1863, while sick in hospital at Knoxville, Tennessee. Deserted from hospital at Montgomery Springs, Virginia, September 10, 1863.

WILSON, JONATHAN J., Private

Previously served as Private in Company M of this regiment. Transferred to this company in May, 1863, while on detail as a hospital nurse at Clinton, Tennessee. Deserted from hospital at Clinton on September 1, 1863.

WILSON, LEVI, Private

Previously served as Private in Company G, 29th Regiment N.C. Troops. Enlisted in this company in Yancey County on July 11, 1862, for the war. Reported present through June 30, 1863. Deserted near Charleston, Tennessee, September 6, 1863. Returned to duty subsequent to February 29, 1864. Captured by the enemy on August 26, 1864. Took the Oath of Allegiance at Atlanta, Georgia, September 20, 1864.

WINEBARGER, LEVI, Corporal

Previously served as Corporal in Company M of this regiment. Transferred to this company in May-June, 1863. Mustered in as Corporal. Transferred to Company I of this regiment in July-August, 1863.

WORD, JOSEPH, Private

Enlisted at Camp Huston on October 1, 1862, for the war. Reported absent without leave in May-June, 1863. No further records.

WORLEY, SAMUEL, Private

Previously served as Private in Company M of this regiment. Transferred to this company in May, 1863, while absent without leave. No further records.

YATES, THOMAS P., Private

Enlisted at Camp Palmer on October 1, 1862, for the war. Reported present through April 30, 1863. Deserted at Clinton, Tennessee, prior to July 1, 1863.

YOUNCE, ANDREW J., Private

Previously served as Sergeant in Company M of this regiment. Transferred to this company in May, 1863. Mustered in as Private. Detailed in the government shoe shop at Knoxville, Tennessee, prior to July 1, 1863. Reported absent on detail as a shoemaker at Knoxville or at Atlanta, Georgia, through February 29, 1864. Died at Atlanta on March 3, 1864, of disease.

COMPANY H

This company was raised in Caldwell County and was mustered into service on May 23, 1862, as Capt. Thomas J. Dula's Company, N.C. Volunteers. It was then placed under the authority of Lt. Col. John B. Palmer, former commander of "Palmer's Legion," a mixed (cavalry and infantry) unit that had failed to complete its organization. Palmer was by then recruiting for a cavalry unit to be known as the 5th Battalion N.C. Partisan Rangers; however, it appears that Dula's Company was never formally assigned to the 5th Battalion. Shortly thereafter Dula's Company was assigned to a nascent infantry regiment, commanded by Palmer. When the new regiment, known as the 58th Regiment N.C. Troops, was mustered in on July 29, 1862, Dula's

Company was designated Company H. After joining 58th Regiment the company functioned as a part of that regiment, and its history for the remainder of the war is reported as a part of the regimental history.

The following roster was compiled primarily from information in the microfilm edition of the Compiled Service Records of Soldiers Who Served in Organizations from the State of North Carolina (Record Group 109, M270), National Archives and Records Administration, Washington, D.C. Record Group 109 includes enlistment papers, pay vouchers, requisitions, letters of resignation, discharge certificates, and abstracts of medical and prisoner of war returns. Materials relating specifically to this company include a muster-in roll dated May 23, 1862, and muster rolls dated January-June, 1863; September-October, 1863; and January-August, 1864.

Also utilized in this roster were *The War of the Rebellion: A Compilation of the Official Records of the Union and Confederate Armies*, the North Carolina adjutant general's *Roll of Honor*, state militia records, newspaper casualty lists and obituaries, wartime claims for bounty pay and allowances, postwar registers of claims for artificial limbs, Confederate pension applications filed with the states of North Carolina, Tennessee, and Florida, Confederate Soldiers' Home records, and the 1860 and 1870 federal censuses of North Carolina. A search was made also for relevant letters, diaries, reminiscences, and other manuscripts in the Southern Historical Collection (University of North Carolina-Chapel Hill), the Duke University Library Special Collections Department, and the North Carolina Division of Archives and History.

Among the secondary sources consulted were records of the North Carolina division of the United Daughters of the Confederacy, postwar rosters, regimental and county histories, marriage bond, will, and cemetery indexes, published and unpublished genealogies, biographical dictionaries, the North Carolina *County Heritage Book* series, the *Confederate Veteran*, Walter Clark's *Histories of the Several Regiments and Battalions from North Carolina in the Great War, 1861-'65*, and the North Carolina volume of the extended edition of *Confederate Military History*.

OFFICERS

CAPTAINS

DULA, THOMAS JOSHUA

Previously served as Private in Company I, 26th Regiment N.C. Troops. Elected Captain of this company on May 23, 1862. Reported present in January-April, 1863. Appointed Major on April 25, 1863, and transferred to the Field and Staff of this regiment. [Was 31 years of age when elected Captain of this company and was by occupation a lawyer. Prior to his service in the 26th North Carolina, he served as 2nd Lieutenant in the 95th Regiment N.C. Militia.]

HARPER, GEORGE WASHINGTON FINLEY

Born in Caldwell County* on July 7, 1834. Resided in Caldwell County and was by occupation a merchant prior to enlisting in Caldwell County at age 27, May 10, 1862, for the war. Mustered in as Private. Elected 1st Lieutenant on August 19, 1862. Reported present in January-February, 1863. Promoted to Captain on April 25, 1863. Reported on extra duty as acting Assistant Adjutant General of Col. John B. Palmer's brigade on or about April 30, 1863. Rejoined the company in July-October, 1863. Reported present or accounted for in January-April, 1864. Wounded in left leg (calf) at Resaca, Georgia, May 15, 1864. Returned to duty on September

13, 1864. Appointed Major on April 9, 1865, and transferred to the Field and Staff of this regiment. [Previously served as 1st Lieutenant in the 95th Regiment N.C. Militia. Reported in command of Company E of this regiment on January 30, 1864.]

WHITE, ROBERT W.

Previously served as 2nd Lieutenant of Company F, 60th Regiment N.C. Troops. Appointed Captain and transferred to this company when the 58th and 60th Regiments were consolidated on April 9, 1865. Paroled at Greensboro on May 1, 1865.

LIEUTENANTS

FAGG, HENRY C., 2nd Lieutenant

Previously served as Corporal in Company B, 60th Regiment N.C. Troops. Appointed 2nd Lieutenant and transferred to this company when the 58th and 60th Regiments were consolidated on April 9, 1865. Paroled at Greensboro on May 1, 1865.

GILBERT, LARKIN W., 3rd Lieutenant

Resided in Caldwell County and was by occupation a clerk prior to enlisting in Caldwell County at age 26, December 20, 1862, for the war. Mustered in as Private. Reported present or accounted for on surviving company muster rolls through February 29, 1864. Was reported on duty with the commissary department during most of that period. Appointed Brevet 3rd Lieutenant on March 19, 1864. Reported present through August 31, 1864. Transferred to Company B of this regiment on an unspecified date.

HEDRICK, EMANUEL M., 1st Lieutenant

Previously served as Private in Company I, 26th Regiment N.C. Troops. Elected 2nd Lieutenant of this company on May 23, 1862. Reported present in January-June, 1863. Promoted to 1st Lieutenant on April 25, 1863. Reported present in September-October, 1863. Reported absent on detached service on February 19, 1864. Rejoined the company on or about March 8, 1864. Reported present in March-April, 1864. Deserted to the enemy from line of battle near Marietta, Georgia, July 1, 1864. Sent to Chattanooga, Tennessee. Transferred to Louisville, Kentucky, where he arrived on or about July 25, 1864. Released at Louisville on July 27, 1864, after taking the Oath of Allegiance. [Was 36 years of age at time of enlistment.]

JACKSON, ELI, 1st Lieutenant

Previously served as 2nd Lieutenant of Company G, 60th Regiment N.C. Troops. Promoted to 1st Lieutenant and transferred to this company when the 58th and 60th Regiments were consolidated on April 9, 1865. Paroled at Greensboro on May 1, 1865.

LENOIR, WALTER WAIGHTSTILL, 1st Lieutenant

Resided in Caldwell County and was by occupation a lawyer prior to enlisting in Caldwell County at age 39. Elected 1st Lieutenant on May 23, 1862. Promoted to Captain of Company A, 37th Regiment N.C. Troops, July 18, 1862, and transferred.

LINGLE, ADAM D., 2nd Lieutenant

Previously served as 3rd Lieutenant of Company I, 26th Regiment N.C. Troops. Elected 3rd Lieutenant of this company on May 23, 1862. Reported absent on detached service in January-February,

1863. Returned to duty on an unspecified date. Reported present in March-April, 1863. Promoted to 2nd Lieutenant on April 25, 1863. Reported on duty as commander of the company in May-June, 1863. Reported absent sick in September-October, 1863. Returned to duty on an unspecified date. Reported on duty as acting commander of the company in January-February, 1864. Reported present in March-April, 1864. Wounded at Kolb's Farm, near Marietta, Georgia, June 22, 1864. Returned to duty prior to September 1, 1864. Resigned on September 15, 1864, because "I have not received sufficient education to enable me to make out the reports and other papers which an officer is compelled to do when on duty." Resignation accepted on October 12, 1864. [Was about 32 years of age at time of enlistment.]

MORGAN, JOHN B., 3rd Lieutenant

Previously served as 2nd Lieutenant of Company F of this regiment. Transferred to this company with the rank of 3rd Lieutenant subsequent to August 31, 1864. Paroled at Newton on April 19, 1865.

PAGE, LAFAYETTE A., 3rd Lieutenant

Resided in Caldwell County and was by occupation a farmer prior to enlisting in Caldwell County at age 29, May 13, 1862, for the war. Mustered in as Private. Reported present in January-June, 1863. Promoted to 1st Sergeant prior to March 1, 1863. Elected 3rd Lieutenant on July 11, 1863. Reported present in September-October, 1863. Wounded at Rocky Face Ridge, Georgia, February 25, 1864. Died in hospital in Atlanta, Georgia, March 9, 1864, of wounds. [Previously served as 1st Lieutenant in the 95th Regiment N.C. Militia.]

NONCOMMISSIONED OFFICERS AND PRIVATES

ARMSTRONG, M. T., Private

Born in Surry County and was by occupation a farmer prior to enlisting in Yadkin County on October 15, 1863, for the war. Reported present in January-February, 1864. Discharged on April 17, 1864. Reason discharged not reported. Discharge certificate gives his age as 46.

AUSTIN, A. WEBB, Private

Previously served as Sergeant in Company A, 22nd Regiment N.C. Troops. Enlisted in this company in Caldwell County on June 3, 1863, for the war. Mustered in as Private. Reported present in September-October, 1863, and January-April, 1864. Reported on duty as a teamster in May-August, 1864. No further records. Survived the war.

AUSTIN, THOMAS J., Private

Born in Virginia on February 8, 1825. Resided in Caldwell County and was by occupation a farmer prior to enlisting in Caldwell County at age 38, June 3, 1863, for the war. Reported present or accounted for in September-October, 1863, and January-August, 1864. No further records. Survived the war.

BAILEY, NEAL, ———

North Carolina pension records indicate that he served in this company.

BAIRD, FINLEY P., Private

Previously served as Private in Company I, 26th Regiment N.C. Troops. Enlisted in this company in Caldwell County at age 49, May 23, 1862, for the war. Deserted from camp at Jacksboro, Tennessee, on or about February 10, 1863. Brought back to the company on March 8, 1863. Reported present through April 30, 1863. Reported on detached service in the government shoe shop at Knoxville, Tennessee, in May-June, 1863. Detailed in the government shoe shop at Atlanta, Georgia, in September-October, 1863. Hospitalized at Atlanta prior to October 31, 1863. Reported absent on detail through February 29, 1864. Was also on detail as a cooper during an unspecified period. Discharged at Dalton, Georgia, April 21, 1864, by reason of "expiration of term of enlistment & being a non conscript." [Resided in Caldwell County and was by occupation a wheelwright or miller.]

BAIRD, WILLIAM, Private

Previously served as Private in Company I, 26th Regiment N.C. Troops. Enlisted in this company in Caldwell County at age 35, May 23, 1862, for the war. Deserted from camp at Jacksboro, Tennessee, February 10, 1863. Brought back on March 8, 1863. Reported present through June 30, 1863. Reported absent on detached service in September-October, 1863. Reported present in January-April, 1864. Sent to hospital sick on August 26, 1864. No further records.

BAIRD, WILLIAM CARSON, Private

Previously served as Private in Company I, 26th Regiment N.C. Troops. Enlisted in this company in Caldwell County at age 21, May 23, 1862, for the war. Died on or about the same date. Place and cause of death not reported.

BARLOW, HAMILTON, Private

Resided in Caldwell County and was by occupation a farmer prior to enlisting in Caldwell County at age 41, August 24, 1863, for the war. Deserted from camp near Chattanooga, Tennessee, October 6, 1863. Returned to duty on November 22, 1863. Reported present in January-April, 1864. Sent to hospital sick on August 27, 1864. Hospitalized at West Point, Mississippi, January 10, 1865, with rheumatism. Admitted to hospital at Meridian, Mississippi, January 17, 1865, with a wound. Place and date wounded not reported. No further records. Survived the war.

BEAN, HENRY NEWTON, Private

Enlisted in Caldwell County on October 7, 1862, for the war. Deserted on or about December 6, 1862.

BEAN, JOHN, Private

Previously served as Private in Company I, 26th Regiment N.C. Troops. Enlisted in this company in Caldwell County at age 17, May 23, 1862, for the war. Reported present on surviving company muster rolls through August 31, 1864. Died prior to January 1, 1865. Place, date, and cause of death not reported.

BEAN, LARGENT, Private

Resided in Caldwell County and was by occupation a farmer prior to enlisting in Caldwell County at age 22, July 16, 1862, for the war. Reported present on surviving company muster rolls through April 30, 1864. Wounded in the shin (fracture) at New Hope Church, Georgia, May 29, 1864. Had not returned to duty as of August 31, 1864. No further records. Survived the war.

BEAN, MATHIAS, Private

Previously served as Private in Company I, 26th Regiment N.C. Troops. Enlisted in this company in Caldwell County at age 29, May 23, 1862, for the war. Reported present in January-February, 1863. Deserted prior to July 1, 1863.

BEAN, THOMAS, Private

Previously served as Private in Company I, 26th Regiment N.C. Troops. Enlisted in this company in Caldwell County at age 17, May 23, 1862, for the war. Deserted on December 6, 1862. [Was by occupation a farmer. May have served later as Private in Companies E and D, 2nd Regiment N.C. Mounted Infantry (Union).]

BISHOP, WILLIAM P., Private

Previously served as Private in Company G, 60th Regiment N.C. Troops. Transferred to this company when the 58th and 60th Regiments were consolidated on April 9, 1865. Paroled at Greensboro on May 1, 1865.

BOLICK, JACOB ANTHONY, Private

Born on May 6, 1845. Resided in Caldwell County where he enlisted at age 18, August 24, 1863, for the war. Reported present in September-October, 1863, and January-April, 1864. Wounded in the left arm at Resaca, Georgia, May 15, 1864. Left arm amputated. Retired to the Invalid Corps on January 26, 1865. [North Carolina pension records indicate that he was wounded in the chest (apparently also at Resaca).]

BRADSHAW, ELIJAH E., Corporal

Resided in Caldwell County where he enlisted at age 38, July 16, 1862, for the war. Mustered in as Private. Reported present in January-June, 1863. Promoted to Corporal on February 28, 1863. Reported absent sick in September-October, 1863. Returned to duty on an unspecified date. Reported present in January-April, 1864. Sent to hospital sick on or about June 5, 1864. Furloughed home. Furlough expired September 11, 1864. No further records. Survived the war.

BRADSHAW, WILLIAM, Private

Resided in Caldwell County and was by occupation a farmer prior to enlisting in Caldwell County at age 23, August 20, 1862, for the war. Wounded at Chickamauga, Georgia, September 19-20, 1863. Died in hospital near Chickamauga of wounds. Date of death not reported.

BROOKS, J. A., Private

Enlisted in Buncombe County. Place and date of enlistment not reported (probably enlisted in November, 1863). Reported absent without leave on November 24, 1863. Returned to duty subsequent to February 29, 1864. Reported absent on detached service in western North Carolina in March-April, 1864. Sent to the rear sick from the Etowah River, Georgia, May 26, 1864. No further records.

BROOKSHIRE, THOMAS PATTERSON, Corporal

Previously served as Corporal in Company E, 60th Regiment N.C. Troops. Transferred to this company when the 58th and 60th Regiments were consolidated on April 9, 1865. Paroled at Greensboro on May 1, 1865.

BROWN, ELISHA, Private

Resided in Caldwell County and was by occupation a farmer prior to enlisting in Caldwell County at age 26, May 23, 1862, for the war. Died in hospital at Jacksboro, Tennessee, on or about November 9, 1862, of disease.

BROWN, JULIUS A., Private

Enlisted in Caldwell County on April 16, 1864, for the war. Sent to hospital sick on August 27, 1864. Paroled at Morganton on May 15, 1865. [Was about 18 years of age at time of enlistment.]

BRYANT, JOHN H., Private

Resided in Caldwell County and was by occupation a farmer prior to enlisting in Caldwell County at age 26, July 16, 1862, for the war. Reported present in January-February, 1863. Reported on duty as a wagoner on surviving company muster rolls from March, 1863, through February 29, 1864. Reported present in March-August, 1864. No further records. Survived the war.

BRYANT, PETER, Private

Enlisted in Caldwell County at age 24, July 16, 1862, for the war. Reported present in January-February, 1863. Reported on detail as a wagoner on surviving company muster rolls from March, 1863, through February 29, 1864. Reported present in March-April, 1864. Reported on detail with the brigade ordnance train from May 28 through August 31, 1864. No further records. Survived the war.

BRYANT, ROBERT M., Private

Previously served as Private in Company I, 26th Regiment N.C. Troops. Enlisted in this company in Caldwell County at age 16, May 23, 1862, for the war. Reported present or accounted for on surviving company muster rolls through August 31, 1864. No further records. Survived the war.

BRYANT, TILMAN L., Private

Previously served as Private in Company I, 26th Regiment N.C. Troops. Enlisted in this company in Caldwell County at age 21, May 23, 1862, for the war. Reported present or accounted for on surviving company muster rolls through April 30, 1864. Captured on picket near Ruff's Mill, near Smyrna, Georgia, July 4, 1864. Sent to Nashville, Tennessee. Transferred to Louisville, Kentucky, where he arrived on July 14, 1864. Transferred to Camp Douglas, Chicago, Illinois, where he arrived on July 18, 1864. Paroled and transferred to Point Lookout, Maryland, February 20, 1865, for exchange. No further records. Survived the war. [North Carolina pension records indicate that he received no wounds during his military service.]

BUMGARNER, GEORGE W., Private

Enlisted in Caldwell County on July 16, 1862, for the war. Reported present or accounted for in January-June, 1863. Wounded at Chickamauga, Georgia, September 20, 1863. Died in hospital at Ringgold, Georgia, October 14, 1863, of wounds.

BUMGARNER, WILLIAM P., Musician

Previously served as Private in Company I, 26th Regiment N.C. Troops. Enlisted in this company in Caldwell County at age 24, May 23, 1862, for the war. Mustered in as Musician. Reported present on surviving company muster rolls through October 31, 1863. Nominated for the Badge of Distinction for gallantry at Chickamauga, Georgia, September 20, 1863. Reported present in January-April, 1864. Deserted to the enemy at Mount Zion Church, near Marietta, Georgia, July 1, 1864. Sent to Louisville, Kentucky. Released at Louisville on July 27, 1864, after taking the Oath of Allegiance. [Was by occupation a farmer.]

BYRD, CHARLES, JR., ———

North Carolina pension records indicate that he served in this company.

CANNON, WESLEY W., Private

Previously served as Private in Company F, 26th Regiment N.C. Troops. Transferred to this company on May 1, 1862. Reported present on October 15, 1862. No further records. [Contrary to 7:536 of this series, the correct spelling of his surname was probably Cannon rather than Canon.]

CARLYLE, JAMES H., Private

Resided in Polk County where he enlisted at age 18, October 15, 1863, for the war. Reported present in January-August, 1864. Reported in hospital at Montgomery, Alabama, November 15, 1864. No further records. Survived the war. [North Carolina pension records indicate that he was wounded in the left arm and shoulder at Egypt, Mississippi, February 1, 1865.]

CHILDS, JOHN EBIN, Private

Previously served as Private in Company B, 5th Battalion N.C. Cavalry. Transferred to this company on July 19, 1863. Killed at Chickamauga, Georgia, September 20, 1863, "while exhibiting the greatest gallantry. He was a noble youth." [Daily Progress (Raleigh), October 8, 1863. At Chickamauga "his beardless face (was) ablaze with the animation of battle, and his youthful figure (was) transformed into a hero's statue." Clark's Regiments, 3:453.]

CLAY, ANDREW, Private

Resided in Caldwell County and was by occupation a farmer prior to enlisting in Caldwell County at age 43, August 24, 1863, for the war. Reported present in September-October, 1863. Died in hospital at Atlanta, Georgia, November 9, 1863, of disease.

COBB, NEWTON, Private

Resided in Caldwell County where he enlisted at age 19, May 10, 1862, for the war. Reported present in January-June, 1863. Deserted from camp near Chickamauga, Georgia, September 23, 1863. [May have served later as Private in Company L, 11th Regiment Tennessee Cavalry (Union), and/or Company L, 9th Regiment Tennessee Cavalry (Union).]

COFFEY, ARMSTEAD N., Private

Previously served as Private in Company F, 26th Regiment N.C. Troops. Transferred to this company on or about May 1, 1862. Reported present in January-June, 1863. Deserted at Big Creek Gap, Tennessee, August 22, 1863. Returned to duty on November 8, 1863. Reported present in January-April, 1864. Wounded in the leg, right hand, and right shoulder at Resaca, Georgia, May 15, 1864. Hospitalized at Macon, Georgia. Two fingers amputated. Reported absent wounded through August 31, 1864. No further records. Survived the war. [Was by occupation a farmer.]

COFFEY, IRVIN, Private

Previously served as Private in Company F, 26th Regiment N.C. Troops. Transferred to this company on or about May 1, 1862. Deserted on December 22, 1862. Returned to duty on March 30, 1863. Reported present in May-June, 1863. Wounded at Chickamauga, Georgia, September 20, 1863. Reported absent wounded through February 29, 1864. Detailed for duty as a wagoner on April 25, 1864. Returned to duty on an unspecified date. Reported present in May-August, 1864. Wounded slightly in the hand at Bentonville on March 19, 1865. No further records. [Was by occupation a farmer.]

COLEMAN, RICHARD A., Private

Previously served as Private in Company A, 22nd Regiment N.C. Troops (12th Regiment N.C. Volunteers). Enlisted in this company in Caldwell County on October 7, 1862, for the war. Reported present on surviving company muster rolls through April 30, 1864. Wounded in the left leg or ankle at Buzzard's Roost, Georgia, May 9, 1864. Hospitalized at Macon, Georgia. Furloughed for sixty days on May 27, 1864. Reported absent on furlough through August 31, 1864. Hospitalized at Charlotte on February 22, 1865, with abscesses. Paroled at Charlotte on May 4, 1865.

CRAIG, ALFRED H., Private

Resided in Caldwell County and was by occupation a farmer prior to enlisting in Caldwell County at age 21, July 16, 1862, for the war. Reported absent without leave on expired furlough on February 28, 1863. Returned to duty in March-April, 1863. Reported present in May-June, 1863. Deserted at Big Creek Gap, Tennessee, August 16, 1863.

CRAIG, J. R., Private

Place and date of enlistment not reported. Records of the Federal Provost Marshal indicate that he was captured near Jonesborough, Georgia, September 2, 1864, and exchanged at Rough and Ready, Georgia, September 19/22, 1864.

CRAIG, JOHN S., ————

North Carolina pension records indicate that he served in this company.

CRAIGE, A. COLEMAN, Sergeant

Resided in Caldwell County and was by occupation a farmer prior to enlisting in Caldwell County at age 23, July 16, 1862, for the war. Mustered in as Private. Promoted to Corporal on February 28, 1863. Promoted to Sergeant on July 1, 1864. Reported present on surviving company muster rolls through August 31, 1864. No further records. Survived the war.

CRAIGE, ALFRED H., Private

Enlisted in Caldwell County on May 12, 1862, for the war. Reported present in January-June, 1863. Wounded in the right cheek at Chickamauga, Georgia, September 20, 1863. Reported absent wounded through August 31, 1864. Reported in hospital at Montgomery, Alabama, November 15, 1864. No further records.

CRAIGE, JOHNSON LAFAYETTE, Private

Enlisted in Caldwell County at age 20, May 23, 1862, for the war. Reported present or accounted for on surviving company muster rolls through April 30, 1864. Reported missing at Kolb's Farm, near Marietta, Georgia, June 22, 1864. Captured at Jonesborough, Georgia, on or about September 1, 1864. Sent to Nashville, Tennessee. Transferred to Louisville, Kentucky, where he arrived on October 28, 1864. Transferred to Camp Douglas, Chicago, Illinois, where he arrived on November 1, 1864. Died at Camp Douglas on December 2, 1864, of "chronic diarrhoea."

CRAIGE, SIDNEY, Sergeant

Resided in Caldwell County and was by occupation a farmer prior to enlisting in Caldwell County at age 28, May 6, 1862, for the war. Mustered in as Corporal. Reported present in January-June, 1863.

Promoted to Sergeant on February 28, 1863. Hospitalized at Macon, Georgia, September 27, 1863, with diarrhoea. Furloughed on October 10, 1863. Returned to duty on an unspecified date. Detailed for duty with the Pioneer Corps in December, 1863. Reported absent on detail through August 31, 1864. No further records. Survived the war.

CRISP, HIRAM H., Private

Resided in Caldwell County and was by occupation a farmer prior to enlisting in Caldwell County at age 17, January 4, 1863, for the war. Was unable to report for duty until May-June, 1863, because of sickness. Wounded at Chickamauga, Georgia, September 20, 1863. Died on or about the same date of wounds. Buried in the Confederate cemetery at Marietta, Georgia.

CRISP, J. P., Private

Place and date of enlistment not reported. Deserted to the enemy on an unspecified date. Took the Oath of Allegiance at Knoxville, Tennessee, June 11, 186-.

CRISP, WILLIAM L., Corporal

Resided in Caldwell County and was by occupation a farmer prior to enlisting in Caldwell County at age 36, January 4, 1863, for the war. Mustered in as Private. Reported absent without leave in January-February, 1863. Returned to duty in March-April, 1863. Reported present in May-June and September-October, 1863. Promoted to Corporal in July-October, 1863. Reported present in January-April, 1864. Wounded in the hand at Resaca, Georgia, May 14-15, 1864. Wounded in the left hand at Kolb's Farm, near Marietta, Georgia, June 22, 1864. Returned to duty prior to September 1, 1864. Captured at the Edisto River, South Carolina, February 10, 1865. Sent to New Bern. Transferred to Point Lookout, Maryland, where he arrived on April 3, 1865. Released at Point Lookout on June 26, 1865, after taking the Oath of Allegiance.

CRUMP, ELIJAH H., 1st Sergeant

Previously served as Private in Company I, 26th Regiment N.C. Troops. Enlisted in this company in Caldwell County at age 24, May 23, 1862, for the war. Mustered in as Corporal. Reported present in January-February, 1863. Reduced to ranks prior to March 1, 1863. Reported present but on detail in March-April, 1863. Reported present in May-June, 1863. Promoted to 1st Sergeant in July-October, 1863. Wounded in the right leg, right knee, right shoulder, and left foot at Chickamauga, Georgia, September 20, 1863. Reported absent wounded through August 31, 1864. No further records. Survived the war. [Resided in Caldwell County and was by occupation a farmer.]

DAVIS, ISAIAH I., Private

Apparently served previously in an unspecified unit. Transferred to this company on an unspecified date (probably subsequent to August 31, 1864). Paroled at Greensboro on May 1, 1865.

DAY, HARVEY, ————

North Carolina pension records indicate that he served in this company.

DECKER, ELISHA, Private

Previously served as Private in Company I, 26th Regiment N.C. Troops. Enlisted in this company in Caldwell County at age 31, May 23, 1862, for the war. Reported present on surviving company muster rolls through April 30, 1864. Captured on picket near Ruff's

Mill, near Smyrna, Georgia, July 4, 1864. Sent to Nashville, Tennessee. Transferred to Louisville, Kentucky, where he arrived on July 14, 1864. Transferred to Camp Douglas, Chicago, Illinois, where he arrived on July 18, 1864. Released at Camp Douglas on June 12, 1865, after taking the Oath of Allegiance. [Resided in Caldwell County and was by occupation a farmer.]

DENT, ISAIAH, Private

Previously served as Private in Company A, 31st Regiment N.C. Troops. Enlisted in this company in Robeson County on October 15, 1863, for the war. Reported sick in hospital on December 15, 1863. Furloughed for sixty days from hospital at Covington, Georgia, April 15, 1864. Reported absent without leave on June 15, 1864. Apparently returned to duty subsequent to August 31, 1864. Hospitalized at Charlotte on March 3, 1865, with chronic diarrhoea. Transferred on April 14, 1865. No further records.

EDMISTON, A. H., Private

Enlisted in Caldwell County on May 10, 1862, for the war. No further records. [May have served later as Sergeant in Company E of this regiment.]

EDMISTON, A. S., Private

Resided in Caldwell County and was by occupation a farmer prior to enlisting in Caldwell County at age 17, May 10, 1862, for the war. No further records. Survived the war.

EDWARDS, ALEX, Private

Previously served as Private in Company E of this regiment. Transferred to this company subsequent to November 15, 1864. Paroled at Greensboro on May 1, 1865.

FINCANNON, HENRY, Private

Previously served as Private in Company I, 26th Regiment N.C. Troops. Enlisted in this company in Caldwell County at age 32, May 23, 1862, for the war. Reported present in January-June, 1863. Killed at Chickamauga, Georgia, September 20, 1863.

FINCANNON, JOHN WESLEY, Private

Previously served as Private in Company I, 26th Regiment N.C. Troops. Enlisted in this company in Caldwell County at age 28, May 23, 1862, for the war. Reported present on surviving company muster rolls through August 31, 1863. Wounded "very slight[ly]" in the left leg at Chickamauga, Georgia, September 20, 1863. Returned to duty prior to March 1, 1864. Reported present through August 31, 1864. No further records. Survived the war.

FINCANNON, JAMES A., Private

Born in Burke County and resided in Caldwell County where he was by occupation a farmer prior to enlisting in Caldwell County on October 7, 1862, for the war. Reported present in January-June, 1863. Reported absent wounded in September-October, 1863. Place and date wounded not reported (was probably wounded at Chickamauga, Georgia, September 19-20, 1863). Returned to duty prior to March 1, 1864. Reported present in March-April, 1864. "Left on the field" at Cassville, Georgia, May 19-20, 1864, and was captured by the enemy. Sent to Nashville, Tennessee. Transferred to Louisville, Kentucky, where he arrived on May 29, 1864. Transferred to Rock Island, Illinois, where he arrived on June 1, 1864. Released at Rock Island on October 27, 1864, after taking the Oath of Allegiance. [Records of the Federal Provost Marshal dated October, 1864, give his age as 19.]

FINCANNON, WESLEY W., Private

Enlisted in Caldwell County on October 2, 186[2], for the war. Deserted on December 22, 1862. Arrested at Richmond, Virginia, February 8, 1863. Returned to duty prior to May 1, 1863. Reported present in May-June, 1863. Deserted at camp near Chattanooga, Tennessee, September 23, 1863.

FLEMING, DAVID, Private

Previously served as Private in Company I, 26th Regiment N.C. Troops. Enlisted in this company in Caldwell County at age 17, May 23, 1862, for the war. Reported present in January-February, 1863. Died in hospital at Clinton, Tennessee, on or about April 17, 1863. Cause of death not reported.

FLEMING, JAMES, Private

Previously served as Private in Company I, 26th Regiment N.C. Troops. Enlisted in this company in Caldwell County at age 22, May 23, 1862, for the war. Died at Johnson's Depot, Tennessee, on an unspecified date (probably prior to January 1, 1863). Cause of death not reported. [Resided in Caldwell County and was by occupation a farmer.]

FLETCHER, JAMES, Private

Resided in Caldwell County and was by occupation a blacksmith's apprentice prior to enlisting in Caldwell County at age 23, May 10, 1862, for the war. Died in hospital at Jacksboro, Tennessee, January 22, 1863. Cause of death not reported.

FOX, ELISHA CALVIN, Private

Born on February 11, 1847. Resided in Caldwell County and enlisted at age 18 in February, 1865, for the war. Wounded in the right hand (lost middle finger) at Bentonville on March 19, 1865. No further records. Survived the war.

FRISBEE, DANIEL H., Private

Previously served as Private in Company E, 60th Regiment N.C. Troops. Transferred to this company when the 58th and 60th Regiments were consolidated on April 9, 1865. Paroled at Greensboro on May 1, 1865.

GILES, JAMES B., Private

Previously served as Private in Company G, 60th Regiment N.C. Troops. Transferred to this company when the 58th and 60th Regiments were consolidated on April 9, 1865. Paroled at Greensboro on May 1, 1865.

GILLILAND, JOSEPH J., Private

Previously served as Private in Company I, 26th Regiment N.C. Troops. Enlisted in this company in Caldwell County at age 21, May 23, 1862, for the war. Reported present in January-June, 1863. Reported on extra duty as a "wood workman" in September-October, 1863. Reported present in January-April, 1864. Detailed for duty as a cattle driver on August 15, 1864. Reported on duty at Gainesville, Alabama, "driving stock" on November 15, 1864 ("unfit for field service"). Transferred to Company B of this regiment on an unspecified date.

GILLILAND, ROBERT, Private

Previously served as Private in Company I, 26th Regiment N.C. Troops. Enlisted in this company in Caldwell County at age 16, May 23, 1862, for the war. Reported present through June 30, 1863. Wounded at Chickamauga, Georgia, September 20, 1863.

Returned to duty prior to October 31, 1863. Reported present on surviving company muster rolls through August 31, 1864. Transferred to Company B of this regiment subsequent to August 31, 1864.

GLAZEBROOKS, JOHN, Private

Previously served as Private in Company I, 26th Regiment N.C. Troops. Enlisted in this company in Caldwell County at age 18, May 23, 1862, for the war. Reported present in January-June, 1863. Hospitalized at Macon, Georgia, September 26, 1863, with debility. Reported absent sick in October, 1863. Returned to duty subsequent to October 31, 1863. Reported present in January-April, 1864. "Deserted from battlefield" at Mount Zion Church, near Marietta, Georgia, July 2-3, 1864, and was captured by the enemy. Sent to Nashville, Tennessee. Transferred to Louisville, Kentucky, where he arrived on July 14, 1864. Transferred to Camp Douglas, Chicago, Illinois, where he arrived on July 18, 1864. Released at Camp Douglas on June 12, 1865, after taking the Oath of Allegiance. [Contrary to 7:578 of this series, the correct spelling of his surname was probably Glazebrooks rather than Glazebrook.]

GREEN, STEWART, Private

Previously served as Private in Company G, 60th Regiment N.C. Troops. Transferred to this company when the 58th and 60th Regiments were consolidated on April 9, 1865. Paroled at Greensboro on May 1, 1865.

GRIFFIN, DAVID AMOS, Private

Previously served as Private in Company I, 26th Regiment N.C. Troops. Enlisted in this company in Caldwell County at age 17, May 23, 1862, for the war. Reported present in January-June, 1863. Wounded in the left leg at Chickamauga, Georgia, September 20, 1863. Reported absent wounded through August 31, 1864. No further records. Survived the war. [Resided in Caldwell County and was by occupation a farmer.]

GRIFFIN, STEPHEN R., Private

Born in Stanly County* and resided in Caldwell County where he was by occupation a farmer prior to enlisting in Caldwell County on July 16, 1862, for the war. Reported present in January-February, 1863. Died in hospital at Jacksboro, Tennessee, April 1, 1863. Cause of death not reported. Was 25 years of age at the time of his death.

HAAS, EMANUEL HOSEA, Private

Resided in South Carolina and enlisted in Caldwell County on May 10, 1862, for the war. Reported present in January-February, 1863. Reported sick in hospital at Clinton, Tennessee, in March-April, 1863. Transferred to hospital at Knoxville, Tennessee, prior to May 1, 1863. Died at Kingsville, South Carolina, May 25, 1863, while on his way home on sick furlough. Cause of death not reported.

HELTON, JOHN N., Private

Previously served as Private in Company I, 26th Regiment N.C. Troops. Enlisted in this company in Caldwell County at age 23, May 23, 1862, for the war. Reported present in January-February, 1863. Reported present but on detail as a wagoner in March-June, 1863. Reported present in September-October, 1863, and January-April, 1864. Reported missing at Kolb's Farm, near Marietta, Georgia, June 22, 1864. Returned to duty prior to September 1, 1864. No further records. Survived the war. [His Tennessee pension application indicates that he was struck on the head by a piece of shell and knocked unconscious at New Hope Church, Georgia (presumably on or about May 25, 1864).]

HICKS, JOHN, Private

Previously served as Private in Company E of this regiment. Transferred to this company on April 26, 1863, while listed as a deserter. Returned to duty and was confined in the guardhouse at Clinton, Tennessee. Deserted on May 25, 1863.

HIPPS, MARCUS B., Sergeant

Previously served as Sergeant in Company E, 60th Regiment N.C. Troops. Transferred to this company when the 58th and 60th Regiments were consolidated on April 9, 1865. Paroled at Greensboro on May 1, 1865.

HOFFMAN, LEVI, Private

Enlisted in Caldwell County on July 16, 1862, for the war. Reported present in January-June, 1863. Killed at Chickamauga, Georgia, September 20, 1863.

HOWARD, ALFRED M., Private

Resided in Yadkin County. Place and date of enlistment not reported (probably enlisted in the autumn of 1863). Deserted to the enemy at Chattanooga, Tennessee, November 13, 1863. Sent to Nashville, Tennessee. Transferred to Louisville, Kentucky, where he arrived on November 24, 1863. Released at Louisville on November 25, 1863, after taking the Oath of Allegiance.

HOWELL, JAMES H., Private

Enlisted in Caldwell County on January 18, 1864, for the war. Reported present through April, 1864. Reported missing at Resaca, Georgia, May 14-15, 1864. Returned to duty prior to September 1, 1864, when he was captured at Jonesborough, Georgia. Sent to Nashville, Tennessee. Transferred to Louisville, Kentucky, where he arrived on October 28, 1864. Transferred to Camp Douglas, Chicago, Illinois, where he arrived on November 1, 1864. Took the Oath of Allegiance on an unspecified date and joined the U.S. Army. Assigned to Company F, 5th Regiment U.S. Volunteer Infantry.

HOWELL, JOHN, Private

Resided in Caldwell County and was by occupation a farmer prior to enlisting in Caldwell County at age 26, May 10, 1862, for the war. Reported present in January-June and September-October, 1863. Reported absent with leave on January 25, 1864. Returned to duty in March-April, 1864. "Deserted from battle line" at Mount Zion Church, near Marietta, Georgia, July 2-3, 1864, and was captured by the enemy. Sent to Nashville, Tennessee. Transferred to Louisville, Kentucky, where he arrived on July 18, 1864. Transferred to Camp Douglas, Chicago, Illinois, where he arrived on July 20, 1864. Died at Camp Douglas on December 12, 1864, of "smallpox."

HUFFMAN, ABLE, Private

Resided in Burke County and enlisted in Caldwell County at age 18, March 15, 1864, for the war. Reported present through August 31, 1864. No further records.

HUGHES, JEREMIAH, SR., ———

North Carolina pension records indicate that he served in this company.

INGLIS, JAMES, Sergeant

Born in Scotland and was by occupation a carpenter prior to enlisting in Caldwell County at age 30, May 10, 1862, for the war. Mustered in as Private. Reported present in January-April, 1863.

Promoted to Sergeant prior to March 1, 1863. Appointed Sergeant Major and transferred to the Field and Staff of this regiment in May-June, 1863.

JAMES, THOMAS REDDEN, Sergeant

Previously served as Sergeant in Company F, 60th Regiment N.C. Troops. Transferred to this company when the 58th and 60th Regiments were consolidated on April 9, 1865. Paroled at Greensboro on May 1, 1865.

JAMISON, NEWTON A., Private

Previously served as Private in Company E, 60th Regiment N.C. Troops. Transferred to this company when the 58th and 60th Regiments were consolidated on April 9, 1865. Paroled at Greensboro on May 1, 1865.

JONES, JOHN H., Private

Resided in Caldwell County and was by occupation a farmer prior to enlisting in Caldwell County at age 31, January 29, 1863, for the war. Reported present in March-June, 1863. Deserted at Big Creek Gap, Tennessee, August 16, 1863.

JONES, POSEY W., Private

Previously served as Private in Company E, 60th Regiment N.C. Troops. Transferred to this company when the 58th and 60th Regiments were consolidated on April 9, 1865. Paroled at Greensboro on May 1, 1865.

JOPLIN, J. WESLEY, Private

Resided in Caldwell County and was by occupation a farmer prior to enlisting in Caldwell County at age 17, January 18, 1864, for the war. Reported sick in hospital in February, 1864. Returned to duty in March-April, 1864. Hospitalized on an unspecified date. Furloughed for sixty days in August, 1864. No further records.

KAVANAUGH, PAT, Private

Resided in Mobile, Alabama. Place and date of enlistment not reported (probably enlisted in the autumn of 1863). Deserted to the enemy at or near Chattanooga, Tennessee, on or about November 13, 1863. Sent to Louisville, Kentucky, where he arrived on November 24, 1863. Released at Louisville on or about November 25, 1863, after taking the Oath of Allegiance.

KILLIAN, M. A., Private

Enlisted in Catawba County on May 22, 1864, for the war. Reported present through August 31, 1864. No further records. Survived the war. [Was about 18 years of age at time of enlistment.]

KIRBY, JOHN MARION, Private

Enlisted in Caldwell County on July 16, 1862, for the war. Reported present in January-February, 1863. Reported on detail as a hospital nurse in March-April, 1863. Reported present in May-June, 1863. Reported absent sick in September-October, 1863. Returned to duty on an unspecified date. Reported present in January-April, 1864. Captured at Resaca, Georgia, on or about May 15, 1864. Sent to Nashville, Tennessee. Transferred to Louisville, Kentucky, where he arrived on May 21, 1864. Transferred to Alton, Illinois, where he arrived on May 25, 1864. Hospitalized at Alton on August 15, 1864, with dysentery. Returned to the prison compound on August 23, 1864. Released at Alton on or about May 22, 1865, presumably after taking the Oath of Allegiance.

LEFEVERS, JOHN A., Private

Previously served as Private in Company I, 26th Regiment N.C. Troops. Enlisted in this company in Caldwell County at age 25, May 23, 1862, for the war. Deserted on December 22, 1862. Returned to duty on October 30, 1863. Reported present in January-August, 1864. No further records. Survived the war.

LINGLE, J. H., Private

Previously served as Private in Company I, 26th Regiment N.C. Troops. Enlisted in this company in Caldwell County at age 26, May 23, 1862, for the war. Died on or about the same date. Place and cause of death not reported.

LINGLE, JOHN, Private

Previously served as Private in Company I, 26th Regiment N.C. Troops. Enlisted in this company in Caldwell County at age 31, May 23, 1862, for the war. Mustered in as 1st Sergeant. Reduced to ranks prior to March 1, 1863. Reported present in January-February, 1863. Reported on duty as a blacksmith in March-June, 1863. Reported absent without leave on September 25, 1863. Returned to duty on an unspecified date. Reported present in January-April, 1864. Captured on picket near Ruff's Mill, near Smyrna, Georgia, July 4, 1864. Sent to Nashville, Tennessee. Transferred to Louisville, Kentucky, where he arrived on July 14, 1864. Transferred to Camp Douglas, Chicago, Illinois, where he arrived on July 18, 1864. Released at Camp Douglas on June 13, 1865, presumably after taking the Oath of Allegiance. [Born in Indiana and was by occupation a farmer.]

LUTHER, ROBERT J., Private

Previously served as Private in Company E, 60th Regiment N.C. Troops. Transferred to this company when the 58th and 60th Regiments were consolidated on April 9, 1865. Paroled at Greensboro on May 1, 1865.

McCALL, JACOB M., Private

Resided in Caldwell County and was by occupation a farmer prior to enlisting in Caldwell County at age 28, July 16, 1862, for the war. Reported present in January-June, 1863. Reported absent sick in September-October, 1863. Returned to duty on an unspecified date. Reported present in January-April, 1864. Reported present but under arrest on July 31, 1864. Reason he was arrested not reported. Returned to duty on an unspecified date. Wounded slightly in the breast at Bentonville on March 19, 1865. No further records. Survived the war.

McCALL, JOHN RUFUS, Corporal

Enlisted in Caldwell County on June 3, 1863, for the war. Mustered in as Private. Reported present in September-October, 1863. Sent to hospital sick on January 18, 1864. Furloughed on February 17, 1864. Returned to duty in March-April, 1864. Promoted to Corporal on July 1, 1864. Reported present through August 31, 1864. No further records.

McDOWELL, RILEY, Private

Resided in Randolph County and was by occupation a laborer prior to enlisting in Randolph County at age 25, October 15, 1863, for the war. Sent to hospital sick on February 24, 1864. Returned to duty in March-April, 1864. Captured at Resaca, Georgia, on or about May 16, 1864. Sent to Nashville, Tennessee. Transferred to Louisville, Kentucky, where he arrived on May 22, 1864.

Transferred to Alton, Illinois, where he arrived on May 25, 1864. Hospitalized at Alton on January 5, 1865, with variola. Returned to the prison compound on or about January 27, 1865. Released at Alton on February 6, 1865, after taking the Oath of Amnesty.

McLEOD, SAMUEL, Private

Resided in Caldwell County and was by occupation a farmer prior to enlisting in Caldwell County at age 43, August 20, 1863, for the war. Reported absent without leave on October 2, 1863. Returned to duty on January 1, 1864. Sent to hospital sick on February 26, 1864. Returned to duty prior to April 30, 1864. Wounded in the right arm at Resaca, Georgia, May 15, 1864. Disabled by his wounds. Reported absent wounded through August 31, 1864. No further records. Survived the war.

MARTIN, JASON CARSON, Private

Previously served as Sergeant in Company I, 26th Regiment N.C. Troops. Enlisted in this company in Caldwell County on June 3, 1863, for the war. Mustered in as Private. Reported present or accounted for on surviving company muster rolls through August 31, 1864. No further records. [Was by occupation a farmer.]

MASK, DUDLEY M., Private

Previously served as Private in Company F, 26th Regiment N.C. Troops. Transferred to this company on May 1, 1862. Mustered in as Musician. Reported present on surviving company muster rolls through October 31, 1863. Captured at Missionary Ridge, Tennessee, November 25, 1863. Sent to Nashville, Tennessee. Transferred to Louisville, Kentucky, where he arrived on December 8, 1863. Transferred to Rock Island, Illinois, where he arrived on or about December 11, 1863. Reduced to ranks on an unspecified date while a prisoner of war. Released at Rock Island on June 20, 1865, after taking the Oath of Allegiance. [Was by occupation a farmer.]

MASK, HORRY, Private

Enlisted in Caldwell County at age 23, May 13, 1862, for the war. Reported present in January-June, 1863. Furloughed from hospital on July 11, 1863. Reported absent sick or absent on furlough through August 31, 1864. No further records.

MATHESON, ELIJAH LOGAN, Private

Previously served as Private in Company I, 26th Regiment N.C. Troops. Enlisted in this company in Caldwell County at age 29, May 23, 1862, for the war. Reported present in January-February, 1863. Reported on duty as a wagon master in March-June, 1863. Reported absent without leave on September 25, 1863. Went over to the enemy on an unspecified date. Sent to Knoxville, Tennessee, where he arrived on June 11, 1864. Transferred to Louisville, Kentucky, where he arrived on or about June 16, 1864. Released on or about the same date after taking the Oath of Allegiance.

MATHESON, WESLEY GREEN, Private

Previously served as Private in Company I, 26th Regiment N.C. Troops. Enlisted in this company in Caldwell County at age 25, May 23, 1862, for the war. Reported present in January-February, 1863. Reported on detail as a wagoner in March-June, 1863. Deserted on September 25, 1863. Went over to the enemy on an unspecified date. Confined at Knoxville, Tennessee, June 11, 1864. Transferred to Louisville, Kentucky, where he arrived on or about June 16, 1864. Released at Louisville on or about the same date after taking the Oath of Allegiance.

MATHIS, ELCANNA, Private

Resided in Caldwell County and was by occupation a farmer prior to enlisting in Caldwell County on December 20, 1862, for the war. Failed to report for duty and was reported absent without leave in January, 1863. Enlisted in Company F, 26th Regiment N.C. Troops, February 4, 1863.

MEADOWS, JOHN P., Private

Previously served as Private in Company F, 60th Regiment N.C. Troops. Transferred to this company when the 58th and 60th Regiments were consolidated on April 9, 1865. Paroled at Greensboro on May 1, 1865.

MESSICK, FINLEY G., Private

Resided in Yadkin County and was by occupation a farm laborer. Place and date of enlistment not reported (probably enlisted in the autumn of 1863). Deserted to the enemy at or near Chattanooga, Tennessee, November 13, 1863. Sent to Nashville, Tennessee. Transferred to Louisville, Kentucky, where he arrived on November 24, 1863. Was apparently released on or about the same date after taking the Oath of Allegiance. [Was about 18 years of age at time of enlistment.]

MILLER, HENRY, Private

Resided in Caldwell County and was by occupation a farmer prior to enlisting in Caldwell County on August 20, 1863, for the war. Sent to hospital sick on September 19, 1863. Failed to return to duty. Dropped from the company rolls subsequent to April 30, 1864, because he was presumed dead.

MITCHUM, NATHANIEL, Private

Previously served as Private in Company I, 26th Regiment N.C. Troops. Enlisted in this company in Caldwell County at age 21, May 23, 1862, for the war. Reported present in January-June, 1863. Deserted on August 16, 1863.

MOORE, ANDREW JACKSON, Private

Resided at "Vinton [Clinton?]," Tennessee, and enlisted in Caldwell County on August 20, 1863, for the war. Reported absent without leave in September-October, 1863. Captured (or deserted to the enemy) at Missionary Ridge, Tennessee, on or about November 25, 1863. Sent to Nashville, Tennessee. Transferred to Louisville, Kentucky, where he arrived on December 10, 1863. Transferred to Rock Island, Illinois, where he arrived on December 13, 1863. Released at Rock Island on May 16, 1864, after taking the Oath of Allegiance. [Records of the Federal Provost Marshal dated May, 1864, give his age as 36.]

MORGAN, MARION H., Private

Previously served as Private in Company E, 60th Regiment N.C. Troops. Transferred to this company when the 58th and 60th Regiments were consolidated on April 9, 1865. Paroled at Greensboro on May 1, 1865.

MORROW, DANIEL, Private

Previously served as Private in Company I, 26th Regiment N.C. Troops. Enlisted in this company in Caldwell County at age 34, May 23, 1862, for the war. Reported present in January-February, 1863. Died in hospital at Clinton, Tennessee, on or about March 30, 1863. Cause of death not reported.

MORROW, GORDON, Private

Previously served as Private in Company I, 26th Regiment N.C. Troops. Enlisted in this company in Caldwell County at age 34, May 23, 1862, for the war. Deserted on October 16, 1862. Returned to the company on March 25, 1864. Court-martialed on April 4, 1864, and sentenced to be shot; however, he was pardoned on the day prior to his execution. Returned to duty on May 7, 1864. Reported present through August 31, 1864. No further records. Survived the war.

MORROW, NATHAN, Private

Previously served as Private in Company I, 26th Regiment N.C. Troops. Enlisted in this company in Caldwell County at age 22, May 23, 1862, for the war. Died at home in Caldwell County of disease on August 3, 1862, while absent on furlough. [Was by occupation a farmer.]

PALMER, DANIEL M., Private

Enlisted in Caldwell County at age 33, May 6, 1862, for the war. Reported absent sick in January-April, 1863. Returned to duty in May-June, 1863. Killed at Chickamauga, Georgia, September 20, 1863.

PALMER, GEORGE C., Private

Enlisted in Caldwell County on May 6, 1862, for the war. Reported absent sick in January-June, 1863. Returned to duty on an unspecified date. Wounded at Chickamauga, Georgia, September 20, 1863. Returned to duty prior to October 31, 1863. Reported present in January-April, 1864. Reported on detail as a teamster from May 11 through August 31, 1864. Transferred to Company B of this regiment subsequent to August 31, 1864. [Was about 30 years of age at time of enlistment.]

PEARCE, REDMOND T., Private

Born in Caldwell County* where he resided as a farmer prior to enlisting in Caldwell County at age 23, May 14, 1862, for the war. Reported absent without leave in January-February, 1863. Returned to duty in March-April, 1863. Reported present in May-June, 1863. Reported absent without leave on August 22, 1863. Returned to duty on November 23, 1863. Reported present in January-April, 1864. Captured at or near Cassville, Georgia, on or about May 20, 1864. Sent to Nashville, Tennessee. Transferred to Louisville, Kentucky, where he arrived on May 29, 1864. Transferred to Rock Island, Illinois, where he arrived on June 1, 1864. Released at Rock Island on June 18, 1864, after taking the Oath of Allegiance and joining the U.S. Army. Assigned to Company G, 3rd Regiment U.S. Volunteer Infantry.

PETERSON, M. J., ———

North Carolina pension records indicate that he served in this company.

QUEEN, CYRUS, Private

Enlisted in Wilkes County on December 24, 1863, for the war. Deserted on an unspecified date. Rejoined the company on March 15, 1864, and was placed in the guardhouse. Released from confinement on May 7, 1864, and returned to duty. Captured at Resaca, Georgia, on or about May 16, 1864. Sent to Nashville, Tennessee. Transferred to Louisville, Kentucky, where he arrived on May 21, 1864. Transferred to Alton, Illinois, where he arrived on May 25, 1864. Died at Alton on June 8, 1864, of "gastritis" and "rem[ittent] fever."

RABY, JAMES C., Private

Resided in Catawba County and enlisted in Caldwell County at age 30, May 14, 1862, for the war. Mustered in as Private. Promoted to Sergeant prior to March 1, 1863. Reported present in January-June, 1863. Reduced to ranks in July-October, 1863. Reported on extra duty as a "wood workman" in September-October, 1863. Detailed for duty as a mechanic in East Tennessee on November 22, 1863. Rejoined the company in March-April, 1864. Captured on picket near Ruff's Mill, near Smyrna, Georgia, July 4, 1864. Sent to Nashville, Tennessee. Transferred to Louisville, Kentucky, where he arrived on July 14, 1864. Transferred to Camp Douglas, Chicago, Illinois, where he arrived on July 18, 1864. Discharged at Camp Douglas on June 16, 1865, after taking the Oath of Allegiance.

RABY, WILLIAM RUFUS, Private

Enlisted in Caldwell County on July 16, 1862, for the war. Reported present in January-June, 1863. Reported absent without leave on August 22, 1863. Returned to duty on November 8, 1863. Reported present in January-April, 1864. Killed at Kolb's Farm, near Marietta, Georgia, June 22, 1864.

REID, BURGESS G., Private

Previously served as Private in Company A, 22nd Regiment N.C. Troops (12th Regiment N.C. Volunteers). Enlisted in this company at Clinton, Tennessee, April 29, 1863, for the war. Transferred to Company B, 5th Battalion N.C. Cavalry, in May-June, 1863. [Contrary to 2:352 of this series, the correct spelling of his surname was probably Reid rather than Reed.]

REID, MALAN, Private

Previously served as Private in Company A, 22nd Regiment N.C. Troops (12th Regiment N.C. Volunteers). Enlisted in this company in Caldwell County on May 14, 1863, for the war. Failed to report for duty and was reported absent sick or absent without leave through August 31, 1864. No further records.

RICE, JAMES L., Private

Enlisted in Caldwell County on February 4, 1863, for the war. Had not reported for duty as of June 30, 1863. Reported absent sick in September-October, 1863. Reported for duty on an unspecified date. Reported present in January-April, 1864. Deserted from line of battle near Dalton, Georgia, on or about May 13, 1864. Sent to Nashville, Tennessee. Transferred to Louisville, Kentucky, where he arrived on May 17, 1864. Transferred to Camp Morton, Indianapolis, Indiana, where he arrived on May 22, 1864. Died at Camp Morton on August 26, 1864, of "typho malarial fever."

RICHARDS, ISAAC M., Private

Enlisted in Caldwell County on May 23, 1862, for the war. Died in hospital at Vicksburg, Mississippi. Date and cause of death not reported.

SETTLEMIRE, SIDNEY, Private

Previously served as Private in Company I, 26th Regiment N.C. Troops. Enlisted in this company in Caldwell County on May 23, 1862, for the war. Died on an unspecified date (probably in the summer of 1862). Place and cause of death not reported. [Contrary to 7:585 of this series, the correct spelling of his surname was probably Settlemire rather than Settlemoir.]

SIDDEN, JOHN, Private

Enlisted in Surry County on December 3, 1863, for the war. Deserted from camp near Dalton, Georgia, February 22, 1864.

SMITH, AUSTIN, Private

Previously served as Private in Company I, 26th Regiment N.C. Troops. Enlisted in this company in Caldwell County at age 26, May 23, 1862, for the war. Mustered in as Sergeant. Deserted from camp at Jacksboro, Tennessee, January 25, 1863. Reduced to ranks on February 28, 1863. Returned to duty on April 1, 1863. Reported present in May-June and September-October, 1863. Reported absent without leave on January 25, 1864. Returned to duty in March-April, 1864. Killed at Resaca, Georgia, May 15, 1864.

SMITH, JAMES HENRY, Private

Previously served as Private in Company I, 26th Regiment N.C. Troops. Enlisted in this company in Caldwell County at age 21, May 23, 1862, for the war. Reported present on surviving company muster rolls through February 29, 1864. Reported on duty as a provost guard during March-August, 1864. No further records. Survived the war.

SMITH, JOAB E., Private

Previously served as Private in Company I, 26th Regiment N.C. Troops. Enlisted in this company in Caldwell County at age 35, May 23, 1862, for the war. Deserted on December 6, 1862.

SMITH, JULIUS, Corporal

Previously served as Private in Company I, 26th Regiment N.C. Troops. Enlisted in this company at age 21, May 23, 1862, for the war. Mustered in as Sergeant. Deserted on January 25, 1863. Reduced to ranks on February 28, 1863. Returned to duty on March 12, 1863. Reported present in May-June, 1863. Reported on duty as a provost guard in September-October, 1863. Reported present in January-April, 1864. Wounded in the "second finger" of the left hand and in the left shoulder at Resaca, Georgia, May 14-15, 1864. Hospitalized at Macon, Georgia. Furloughed for sixty days on or about May 23, 1864. Promoted to Corporal on July 1, 1864. Returned to duty prior to August 31, 1864. No further records. Survived the war.

SMITH, JULIUS P., Sergeant

Previously served as Private in Company I, 26th Regiment N.C. Troops. Enlisted in this company in Caldwell County at age 17, May 23, 1862, for the war. Mustered in as Corporal. Reported present in January-June and September-October, 1863. Promoted to Sergeant on February 28, 1863. Furloughed on February 15, 1864. Reported present in March-April, 1864. Captured at Kolb's Farm, near Marietta, Georgia, June 22, 1864. Sent to Nashville, Tennessee. Transferred to Louisville, Kentucky, where he arrived on July 14, 1864. Transferred to Camp Douglas, Chicago, Illinois, where he arrived on July 18, 1864. Released at Camp Douglas on June 16, 1865, after taking the Oath of Allegiance. [North Carolina pension records indicate that he was wounded by a piece of shell at Chickamauga, Georgia, September 20, 1863.]

SMITH, LAFAYETTE, ——

North Carolina pension records indicate that he served in this company.

SMITH, RICHARD W., Private

Previously served as Private in Company I, 26th Regiment N.C. Troops. Enlisted in this company in Caldwell County at age 28,

May 23, 1862, for the war. Reported present in January-February, 1863. Discharged at Clinton, Tennessee, April 5, 1863, by reason of "hydrothorax and ascites."

SMITH, ROBERT M., Corporal

Resided in Wilkes County and was by occupation a clerk prior to enlisting in Caldwell County at age 37, July 16, 1862, for the war. Mustered in as Private. Reported present in January-June, 1863. Promoted to Corporal on February 28, 1863. Killed at Chickamauga, Georgia, September 20, 1863. [May have served previously as Colonel of the 92nd Regiment N.C. Militia.]

SMITH, RUFUS, Private

Resided in Caldwell County and was by occupation a farmer prior to enlisting in Caldwell County at age 32, May 23, 1862, for the war. Reported absent with leave in January-February, 1863. Reported present in March-June and September-October, 1863. Captured at Missionary Ridge, Tennessee, November 25, 1863. Sent to Nashville, Tennessee. Transferred to Louisville, Kentucky, where he arrived on December 8, 1863. Transferred to Rock Island, Illinois, where he arrived on December 11, 1863. Released at Rock Island on June 20, 1865, after taking the Oath of Allegiance.

SMITH, WILLIAM W., Private

Previously served as Private in Company I, 26th Regiment N.C. Troops. Enlisted in this company in Caldwell County at age 39, May 23, 1862, for the war. Not listed in the records of this company until October, 1863, when he was reported sick in hospital. Admitted to hospital at Madison, Georgia, February 27, 1864, with an unspecified complaint. Returned to duty subsequent to April 30, 1864. Sent to hospital from Atlanta, Georgia, August 10, 1864. Reported on duty with Company E, 1st Regiment Troops and Defenses, Macon, Georgia, in November-December, 1864. No further records.

SPARKS, CLINGMAN, Private

Resided in Caldwell County and was by occupation a farmer prior to enlisting in Caldwell County at age 20, March 15, 1864, for the war. Sent to hospital sick on July 2, 1864. Reported absent sick through August 31, 1864. No further records. Survived the war.

SPARKS, WILLIAM M., Sergeant

Resided in Caldwell County and was by occupation a farmer prior to enlisting in Caldwell County at age 22, May 23, 1862, for the war. Mustered in as Sergeant. Reduced to the rank of Corporal prior to March 1, 1863. Reported present on surviving company muster rolls from January, 1863, through February, 1864. Furloughed on April 12, 1864. Returned to duty on an unspecified date. Promoted to Sergeant on July 1, 1864. Reported present through August 31, 1864. No further records. Survived the war. [North Carolina pension records indicate that he served as color bearer of the 58th Regiment and "rounded up (out) his more th[a]n three years of active service at the battle of Bentonville [sic] . . . in which he was distingu[i]shed for gallantry."]

STAFFORD, JOSEPH A., Private

Born in Tennessee. Resided in Caldwell County where he enlisted at age 18, April 16, 1864, for the war. Deserted to the enemy on the battlefield at Mount Zion Church, near Marietta, Georgia, July 1, 1864. Sent to Chattanooga, Tennessee. Transferred to Louisville, Kentucky, where he arrived on July 25, 1864. Released at Louisville on July 27, 1864, after taking the Oath of Allegiance.

STAFFORD, JULIUS A., Sergeant

Previously served as Private in Company I, 26th Regiment N.C. Troops. Enlisted in this company in Caldwell County on May 23, 1862, for the war. Mustered in as Private. Reported present or accounted for in January-June, 1863. Promoted to Sergeant in July-October, 1863. Reported on detail as a provost guard in September-October, 1863. Reported present in January-April, 1864. Deserted to the enemy on the battlefield at Mount Zion Church, near Marietta, Georgia, July 1, 1864. Sent to Chattanooga, Tennessee. Transferred to Louisville, Kentucky, where he arrived on July 25, 1864. Released at Louisville on July 27, 1864, after taking the Oath of Allegiance. [Was by occupation a cabinet-maker.]

STAFFORD, WILLIAM HENRY, Private

Previously served as Private in Company I, 26th Regiment N.C. Troops. Enlisted in this company in Caldwell County at age 17, May 23, 1862, for the war. Reported present in January-June, 1863. Reported absent without leave on October 2, 1863. Rejoined the company on December 21, 1863. Court-martialed on or about February 12, 1864, and was confined in the guardhouse. Returned to duty on February 24, 1864. Reported present through August 31, 1864. Wounded slightly in the arm at Bentonville on March 19, 1865. Transferred to Company B of this regiment on an unspecified date.

STALLINGS, NELSON, Private

Resided in Caldwell County and was by occupation a farmer prior to enlisting in Caldwell County at age 43, August 20, 1863, for the war. Reported absent sick in September-October, 1863. Reported present in January-February, 1864. Furloughed on or about April 12, 1864. Returned to duty prior to June 22, 1864, when he was wounded at Kolb's Farm, near Marietta, Georgia. Reported absent on wounded furlough through August 31, 1864. Returned to duty on an unspecified date. Hospitalized at West Point, Mississippi, January 10, 1865, with rheumatism. No further records. Survived the war.

STARNES, JONAS C., Private

Previously served as Private in Company I, 26th Regiment N.C. Troops. Enlisted in this company in Caldwell County at age 24, May 23, 1862, for the war. Deserted in January, 1863. Returned to duty on March 16, 1863. Reported present through June, 1863. Reported absent without leave on August 22, 1863. Returned to duty on September 27, 1863. Reported present in January-August, 1864. No further records. Survived the war. [North Carolina pension records indicate that he sprained his knee while charging breastworks in Tennessee on an unspecified date.]

STARNES, VALENTINE, Sergeant

Resided in Mecklenburg County and was by occupation a laborer prior to enlisting in Caldwell County at age 32, May 13, 1862, for the war. Mustered in as Private. Reported absent on expired furlough in January-February, 1863. Returned to duty on an unspecified date. Reported present in March-June, 1863. Promoted to Sergeant in July-October, 1863. Reported present in September-October, 1863, and January-April, 1864. Deserted from the battlefield at Mount Zion Church, near Marietta, Georgia, July 1, 1864. [Previously served as 2nd Lieutenant in the 95th Regiment N.C. Militia.]

STEVENS, MERRIT FOSTER, Private

Previously served as Private in Company F, 60th Regiment N.C. Troops. Transferred to this company when the 58th and 60th Regi-

ments were consolidated on April 9, 1865. Paroled at Greensboro on May 1, 1865. [Contrary to 5:452 of this series, the correct spelling of his first name may have been Merrit rather than Merritt.]

SWANSON, LAWSON C., Private

Enlisted in Caldwell County at age 28, July 16, 1862, for the war. Deserted on December 9, 1862. Returned from desertion on April 28, 1864, and was confined in the guardhouse. Returned to duty on May 7, 1864. Reported present through August 31, 1864. No further records. Survived the war.

TAYLOR, ANDREW J., Private

Previously served as Private in Company I, 26th Regiment N.C. Troops. Enlisted in this company in Caldwell County at age 47, May 23, 1862, for the war. Reported present in January-February, 1863. Hospitalized at Clinton, Tennessee, on an unspecified date. Transferred to hospital at Knoxville, Tennessee, prior to May 1, 1863. Reported on detached service in the government shoe shop at Knoxville in May-June, 1863. Reported on duty as a teamster in September-October, 1863, and January-February, 1864. Detailed to "finish leather" at Atlanta, Georgia, on March 18, 1864. Discharged at Dalton, Georgia, April 14, 1864. Reason discharged not reported.

TAYLOR, GEORGE W., Private

Previously served as Private in Company F, 26th Regiment N.C. Troops. Enlisted in this company in Caldwell County on June 3, 1863, for the war. Reported present in September-October, 1863, and January-April, 1864. Wounded in the hand (causing "loss of the middle finger") at Resaca, Georgia, May 15, 1864. Reported absent wounded through August 31, 1864. No further records. Survived the war.

TRIPLETT, ABNER, Private

Previously served as Private in Company I, 26th Regiment N.C. Troops. Enlisted in this company in Caldwell County at age 56, May 23, 1862, for the war. No further records. [Resided in Caldwell County and was by occupation a farmer.]

TURNMIRE, JOHN N., Private

Previously served as Private in Company I, 26th Regiment N.C. Troops. Enlisted in this company in Caldwell County at age 22, May 23, 1862, for the war. Mustered in as Corporal. Reported absent without leave on expired furlough in January-February, 1863. Returned to duty and was reduced to ranks in March-April, 1863. Reported absent on detached service at a blacksmith shop in Knoxville, Tennessee, in May-June, 1863. Rejoined the company prior to November 1, 1863. Reported present in January-August, 1864. Wounded slightly in the groin at Bentonville on March 19, 1865. No further records.

TURNMIRE, JOSEPH A., Private

Enlisted in Caldwell County at age 18, March 1, 1864, for the war. Reported present through August 31, 1864. No further records. Survived the war.

TWEED, JAMES HAMILTON, Sergeant

Previously served as Sergeant in Company F, 60th Regiment N.C. Troops. Transferred to this company when the 58th and 60th Regiments were consolidated on April 9, 1865. Paroled at Greensboro on May 1, 1865.

TWEED, THOMAS WILSON, Private

Previously served as Private in Company F, 60th Regiment N.C. Troops. Transferred to this company when the 58th and 60th Regiments were consolidated on April 9, 1865. Paroled at Greensboro on May 1, 1865.

UPCHURCH, ANSEL M., Private

Resided in Caldwell County and was by occupation a farmer prior to enlisting in Caldwell County at age 22, May 10, 1862, for the war. Reported present in January-June, 1863. Reported absent without leave on August 22, 1863. Returned to duty on October 3, 1863. Reported present in January-April, 1864. Sent to hospital sick on May 17, 1864. Furloughed home on an unspecified date. Reported absent on furlough through August 31, 1864. No further records.

UPCHURCH, WILLIAM S., Private

Resided in Caldwell County and was by occupation a farmer prior to enlisting in Caldwell County at age 29, July 16, 1862, for the war. Reported present in January-June, 1863. Reported absent without leave on August 22, 1863. Returned to duty on October 3, 1863. Reported present in January-August, 1864. No further records. Survived the war.

WAKEFIELD, RICHARD A., Private

Previously served as Private in Company A, 22nd Regiment N.C. Troops (12th Regiment N.C. Volunteers). Enlisted in this company on an unspecified date (probably subsequent to August 31, 1864). Captured in hospital at Salisbury in April, 1865. Paroled on May 2, 1865. Admitted to a Federal field hospital on May 20, 1865, with chronic diarrhoea. Released on June 25, 1865.

WATSON, HENRY ELI, Private

Previously served as Private in Company I, 26th Regiment N.C. Troops. Enlisted in this company in Caldwell County at age 23, May 23, 1862, for the war. Reported absent without leave on expired furlough in January-February, 1863. Reported in hospital at Clinton, Tennessee, in March-April, 1863. Transferred to hospital at Knoxville, Tennessee, prior to May 1, 1863. Returned to duty in May-June, 1863. Reported absent without leave on August 22, 1863. Returned to duty on October 25, 1863. Reported present in January-April, 1864. Captured at Cassville, Georgia, May 19-20, 1864. Sent to Nashville, Tennessee. Transferred to Louisville, Kentucky, May 27, 1864. Transferred from Louisville to Rock Island, Illinois, where he arrived on June 1, 1864. Released at Rock Island on October 18, 1864, after joining the U.S. Army. Assigned to Company G, 3rd Regiment U.S. Volunteer Infantry.

WATSON, NOAH, Private

Was by occupation a farmer prior to enlisting in Caldwell County at age 26, July 16, 1862, for the war. Reported absent without leave on expired furlough in January-February, 1863. Reported absent on sick furlough in March-June, 1863. Reported absent without leave on August 22, 1863. Returned to duty on November 22, 1863. Reported present in January-April, 1864. Captured at Resaca, Georgia, on or about May 15, 1864. Sent to Nashville, Tennessee. Transferred to Louisville, Kentucky, where he arrived on May 19, 1864. Transferred to Camp Morton, Indianapolis, Indiana, where he arrived on May 22, 1864. Released at Camp Morton on March 24, 1865, after taking the Oath of Allegiance and joining the U.S. Army. Assigned to Company G, 6th Regiment U.S. Volunteer Infantry.

WEBSTER, NOAH L., Private

Previously served as Private in Company I, 26th Regiment N.C. Troops. Enlisted in this company at age 23, May 23, 1862, for the war. Reported present but on detail "in work shop" in March-June, 1863. Deserted on August 24, 1863. [Resided in Caldwell County and was by occupation a wagonmaker.]

WHITE, P. HENDERSON, Private

Previously served as Private in Company I, 26th Regiment N.C. Troops. Enlisted in this company in Caldwell County at age 34, May 23, 1862, for the war. Died on June 26, 1862. Place and cause of death not reported. [Resided in Caldwell County and was by occupation a farmer.]

WILSON, H. W., Private

Resided in McDowell County. Place and date of enlistment not reported (probably enlisted subsequent to August 31, 1864). Paroled at Salisbury on May 2, 1865. Took the Oath of Allegiance at Salisbury on June 7, 1865.

WILSON, L. E., 1st Sergeant

Previously served as 1st Sergeant of Company E, 60th Regiment N.C. Troops. Transferred to this company when the 58th and 60th Regiments were consolidated on April 9, 1865. Paroled at Greensboro on May 1, 1865.

WOLF, JAMES P., Private

Previously served as Private in Company E, 60th Regiment N.C. Troops. Transferred to this company when the 58th and 60th Regiments were consolidated on April 9, 1865. Paroled at Greensboro on May 1, 1865.

YOUNTS, E. F., Private

Enlisted at Athens, Georgia, December 16, 1863, for the war. Deserted on an unspecified date. Returned from desertion on March 15, 1864. Court-martialed on April 4, 1864, and sentenced to be shot. Executed near Dalton, Georgia, May 4, 1864, for desertion.

COMPANY I

This company, known as the "Watauga Troopers," was raised in Watauga County on July 15, 1862, as Capt. William Miller's Company, N.C. Volunteers. It was mustered into service on July 25, 1862, and was assigned to the 58th Regiment N.C. Troops as Company I when the regiment was organized four days later. After joining the regiment the company functioned as a part of the regiment, and its history for the remainder of the war is reported as a part of the regimental history.

The following roster was compiled primarily from information in the microfilm edition of the Compiled Service Records of Soldiers Who Served in Organizations from the State of North Carolina (Record Group 109, M270), National Archives and Records Administration, Washington, D.C. Record Group 109 includes enlistment papers, pay vouchers, requisitions, letters of resignation, discharge certificates, and abstracts of medical and prisoner of war returns. Materials relating specifically to this company include muster rolls dated July 24, 1862; January-June, 1863; September-October, 1863; and January-August, 1864.

Also utilized in this roster were *The War of the Rebellion: A Compilation of the Official Records of the Union and Confederate Armies*; the North Carolina adjutant general's *Roll of Honor*; state militia records; newspaper casualty lists and obituaries; wartime claims for bounty pay and allowances; postwar registers of claims for artificial limbs; Confederate pension applications filed with the states of North Carolina, Tennessee, and Florida; Confederate Soldiers' Home records; and the 1860 and 1870 federal censuses of North Carolina. A search was made also for relevant letters, diaries, reminiscences, and other manuscripts in the Southern Historical Collection (University of North Carolina-Chapel Hill), the Duke University Library Special Collections Department, and the North Carolina Division of Archives and History.

Among the secondary sources consulted were records of the North Carolina division of the United Daughters of the Confederacy; postwar rosters; regimental and county histories; marriage bond, will, and cemetery indexes; published and unpublished genealogies; biographical dictionaries; the North Carolina *County Heritage Book* series, the *Confederate Veteran*; Walter Clark's *Histories of the Several Regiments and Battalions from North Carolina in the Great War, 1861-'65*; and the North Carolina volume of the extended edition of *Confederate Military History*.

OFFICERS

CAPTAINS

MILLER, WILLIAM

Previously served as Private in Company D, 9th Regiment N.C. State Troops (1st Regiment N.C. Cavalry). Elected Captain of this company on July 15, 1862. Reported present in January-June, 1863. Resigned on July 30, 1863, by reason of "old age and [also because] my hearing [is] such that I cannot understand the commands when g[i]ven at a distance." Resignation accepted on August 14, 1863.

HODGES, WILLIAM M.

Resided in Watauga County. Elected 1st Lieutenant on July 15, 1862. Reported present in January-June, 1863. Promoted to Captain on August 14, 1863. Sent to hospital at Atlanta, Georgia, in September-October, 1863. Reported present in January-February, 1864. Hospitalized at Dalton, Georgia, on an unspecified date. Furloughed for thirty days on April 19, 1864. Reported absent on furlough through September 20, 1864. Dropped from the company rolls on April 2, 1865, for prolonged absence without leave. Survived the war. [Was about 30 years of age at time of enlistment.]

LIEUTENANTS

DAVIS, WILLIAM S., 3rd Lieutenant

Resided in Watauga County and was by occupation a farmer prior to enlisting in Watauga County at age 29, August 15, 1862, for the war. Mustered in as Private. Promoted to Sergeant prior to March 1, 1863. Reported present in January-June and September-October, 1863. Promoted to 1st Sergeant in November, 1863-February, 1864. Elected 3rd Lieutenant on March 19, 1864. Reported present in January-August, 1864. Declared "supernumerary" and dropped from the company rolls in March, 1865, when Companies G and I of the 58th Regiment were consolidated. [North Carolina pension

records indicate that he was wounded in the left shoulder joint and left arm by the explosion of a bombshell near Resaca, Georgia, June 27, 186(4). Previously served as Captain in the 98th Regiment N.C. Militia.]

HORTON, JAMES H., 2nd Lieutenant

Resided in Watauga County and was by occupation a farmer prior to enlisting at age 21. Elected 3rd Lieutenant on July 15, 1862. Reported absent without leave in January-February, 1863. Reported present in March-June, 1863. Promoted to 2nd Lieutenant on August 14, 1863. Wounded slightly in the side at Chickamauga, Georgia, September 20, 1863. Rejoined the company prior to October 31, 1863, when he was reported on duty as commander of the company. Died on December 24, 1863, and was buried in the City Cemetery at Augusta, Georgia. Place and cause of death not reported. [Reported on duty as acting Adjutant at the Battle of Chickamauga on September 19-20, 1863. See *Daily Progress* (Raleigh), October 8, 1863.]

McGHEE, JORDAN C., 1st Lieutenant

Resided in Watauga County and was by occupation a brickmason prior to enlisting at age 28. Elected 2nd Lieutenant on July 15, 1862. Reported absent on detached service in January-February, 1863. Reported present in March-June, 1863. Promoted to 1st Lieutenant on August 14, 1863. Wounded slightly at Chickamauga, Georgia, September 20, 1863. Returned to duty prior to November 1, 1863. Detailed for thirty days to arrest deserters in Ashe and Watauga Counties on or about February 23, 1864. Rejoined the company prior to May 1, 1864. Wounded at Kolb's Farm, near Marietta, Georgia, June 22, 1864. Returned to duty prior to September 1, 1864. Reported in command of the company on November 1, 1864. Dropped from the company rolls as a "supernumerary" in March, 1865, when Companies G and I of the 58th Regiment were consolidated.

MILLER, JONATHAN BENJAMIN, 2nd Lieutenant

Resided in Watauga County and was by occupation a farmer prior to enlisting in Watauga County at age 18, July 15, 1862, for the war. Mustered in as Private. Reported present in January-June, 1863. Promoted to Corporal prior to March 1, 1863. Reported present in September-October, 1863. Promoted to 1st Sergeant on October 15, 1863. Elected 3rd Lieutenant on November 15/18, 1863. Promoted to 2nd Lieutenant on December 24, 1863. Reported absent with leave in January-February, 1864. Reported present in March-April, 1864. Wounded at Kolb's Farm, near Marietta, Georgia, June 22, 1864. Returned to duty prior to September 1, 1864. Transferred to Company G of this regiment and promoted to 1st Lieutenant in March, 1865, when companies G and I of the 58th Regiment were consolidated. [Probably served as acting Captain of this company in January-February, 1865.]

NONCOMMISSIONED OFFICERS AND PRIVATES

BARNES, JOHN G., Private

Resided in Alexander County and was by occupation a farmer prior to enlisting in Watauga County at age 34, November 12, 1863, for the war. Reported present in January-February, 1864. Reported present but under arrest on April 7, 1864. Reason he was arrested not reported. Died at Dalton, Georgia, May 5, 1864, of disease.

BARNES, SOLOMON, Private

Resided in Alexander County and enlisted at Camp Holmes, near Raleigh, November 12, 1863, for the war. Reported present in January-April, 1864. Sent to hospital on May 7, 1864. Captured at Resaca, Georgia, May 18, 1864. Sent to Nashville, Tennessee, where he was hospitalized on May 23, 1864. Died in hospital at Nashville on July 6, 1864, of "chronic diarrhoea." [Federal hospital records dated July, 1864, give his age as 44.]

BENTLEY, JAMES, Private

Resided in Alexander County and was by occupation a farmer prior to enlisting at Camp Holmes, near Raleigh, at age 33, November 12, 1863, for the war. Reported present in January-April, 1864. Sent to hospital from Atlanta, Georgia, August 15, 1864. No further records.

BENTLEY, WILLIAM, ———

Resided in Alexander County and was by occupation a farmer. Place and date of enlistment not reported (probably enlisted subsequent to August 31, 1864). No further records. Survived the war. [Was about 50 years of age in 1864.]

BINGHAM, WILLIAM G., 1st Sergeant

Resided in Watauga County and was by occupation a farmer prior to enlisting in Watauga County at age 27, August 15, 1862, for the war. Mustered in as 1st Sergeant. Reported present in January-June, 1863. No further records. Survived the war.

BLACKBURN, JOHN L., Private

Resided in Watauga County and was by occupation a farmer prior to enlisting in Watauga County at age 31, August 5, 1862, for the war. Mustered in as Private. Reported present in January-June, 1863. Reported absent on sick furlough from August 29 through October 31, 1863. Returned to duty on an unspecified date. Reported present in January-February, 1864. Promoted to Sergeant on March 19, 1864. Wounded in the breast and right arm at Kolb's Farm, near Marietta, Georgia, June 22, 1864. Reported absent wounded through August 31, 1864. Reduced to ranks prior to August 31, 1864. No further records. Survived the war.

BROWN, ALFORD, Private

Resided in Watauga County and was by occupation a farmer prior to enlisting in Watauga County at age 27, July 15, 1862, for the war. Reported present in January-February, 1863. Died in hospital at Clinton, Tennessee, April 17, 1863. Cause of death not reported.

BROWN, ASA, Private

Born in Ashe County and resided in Watauga County where he was by occupation a farmer prior to enlisting at age 24, on or about July 24, 1862, for the war. Transferred to Company C, 5th Battalion N.C. Cavalry, July 27, 1862.

BROWN, JOHN WESLEY, Corporal

Enlisted in Watauga County on August 5, 1862, for the war. Mustered in as Private. Reported present in January-April, 1863. Reported sick in hospital at Knoxville, Tennessee, in May-June, 1863. Reported present in September-October, 1863. Promoted to Corporal in November, 1863-February, 1864. Reported present in January-August, 1864. No further records.

BROWN, RICHARD E., Private

Resided in Watauga County and was by occupation a farmer prior to enlisting in Watauga County at age 19, August 5, 1862, for the

war. Reported present in January-June and September-October, 1863. Sent to hospital on February 4, 1864. Returned to duty subsequent to April 30, 1864. Wounded at Kolb's Farm, near Marietta, Georgia, June 22, 1864. Reported absent wounded through August 31, 1864. No further records.

BROWN, WILLIAM L., Private

Resided in Watauga County where he enlisted on August 5, 1862, for the war. Reported present in January-February, 1863. Died in hospital at Jacksboro, Tennessee, March 18, 1863, of "brain fever."

BRYAN, JOHN G., Corporal

Resided in Watauga County and was by occupation a farmer prior to enlisting in Watauga County at age 27, July 15, 1862, for the war. Mustered in as Private. Reported absent on furlough in January-February, 1863. Reported present in March-June and September-October, 1863. Promoted to Corporal on April 7, 1863. Sent to hospital on January 15, 1864. Returned to duty in March-April, 1864. Reported present through August 31, 1864. No further records. Survived the war. [North Carolina pension records indicate that he was wounded in the left arm at Boone on March 28, 1865, when he was "struck by a Union soldier . . . with a gun."]

BURLISON, WILLIAM A., Corporal

Previously served as Corporal in Company B, 5th Battalion N.C. Cavalry. Transferred to this company on June 20, 1863. Reported present in September-October, 1863. Reported absent on detached duty from November 11, 1863, through August 31, 1864. No further records.

CAMPBELL, RUFUS, Sergeant

Enlisted in Watauga County at age 18, August 5, 1862, for the war. Mustered in as Private. Reported present in January-June and September-October, 1863. Promoted to Corporal in November, 1863-February, 1864. Reported present in January-August, 1864. Promoted to Sergeant on August 1, 1864. No further records. Survived the war.

CARLTON, CORNELIUS M., Musician

Resided in Watauga County and was by occupation a "domestic" prior to enlisting in Watauga County at age 18, August 26, 1862, for the war. Was apparently mustered in with the rank of Musician. Reported present in January-February, 1863. Transferred to Company B, 37th Regiment N.C. Troops, February 28, 1863.

CEARLY, WILLIAM, Private

Enlisted at Camp Holmes, near Raleigh, November 12, 1863, for the war. Sent to hospital sick on January 5, 1864. Reported absent sick through August 31, 1864. No further records.

CHURCH, ELI M., Private

Born in Watauga County* where he resided as a farmer prior to enlisting at age 25, July 24, 1862, for the war. Transferred to Company C, 5th Battalion N.C. Cavalry, July 27, 1862.

COOK, WILLIAM S., Private

Enlisted in Watauga County at age 20, August 5, 1862, for the war. Reported present in January-June, 1863. Wounded in the right heel and left shoulder at Chickamauga, Georgia, September 20, 1863. Furloughed for forty days on November 12, 1863. Returned to duty subsequent to April 30, 1864. Captured near Atlanta, Georgia, July 28, 1864. Sent to Nashville, Tennessee. Transferred to Louisville,

Kentucky, where he arrived on August 5, 1864. Transferred to Camp Chase, Ohio, where he arrived on August 6, 1864. Paroled at Camp Chase and transferred to Boulware's and Cox's Wharves, James River, Virginia, where he was received on March 10-12, 1865, for exchange. No further records. Survived the war. [North Carolina pension records indicate that he was wounded at Atlanta in July, 1864.]

COOPER, JAMES M., Private

Resided in Watauga County where he enlisted on August 5, 1862, for the war. Mustered in as Corporal. Reduced to ranks on an unspecified date. Deserted at Big Creek Gap, Tennessee, February 17, 1863.

CORNETT, ISAAC, Private

Born in Ashe County or in Tennessee and resided in Watauga County where he was by occupation a farmer or day laborer prior to enlisting in Watauga County at age 23, July 15, 1862, for the war. Reported present in January-June, 1863. Deserted at Lenoir Station, Tennessee, August 29, 1863. Later served as Corporal in Company F, 13th Regiment Tennessee Cavalry (Union).

CORNETT, JOHN, Private

Born in Ashe County on September 22, 1835. Enlisted in Watauga County at age 26, July 15, 1862, for the war. Reported present on surviving company muster rolls through April 30, 1864. Reported absent without leave on July 20, 1864. No further records. [Filed a Tennessee pension application after the war.]

COTTRELL, CALVIN J., Sergeant

Resided in Watauga County and was by occupation a farmer prior to enlisting in Watauga County at age 19, July 15, 1862, for the war. Mustered in as Sergeant. Reduced to ranks prior to March 1, 1863. Reported present in January-June and September-October, 1863. Promoted to Sergeant on October 15, 1863. Wounded in the face ("right eye was shot out destroying also the nasal bone") at Resaca, Georgia, May 15, 1864. No further records. Survived the war.

COUNCILL, JOHN H., Private

Born in Ashe County where he resided as a farmer prior to enlisting at age 25, on or about July 24, 1862, for the war. Transferred to Company D, 5th Battalion N.C. Cavalry, July 27, 1862.

DAVENPORT, GILSON B., Private

Resided in Watauga County and was by occupation a blacksmith prior to enlisting in Watauga County at age 19, August 5, 1862, for the war. Died prior to March 1, 1863. Place and cause of death not reported.

DAVIS, ALBERT F., Sergeant

Resided in Watauga County and was by occupation a teacher prior to enlisting in Watauga County at age 27, August 15, 1862, for the war. Mustered in as Private. Promoted to Sergeant prior to March 1, 1863. Reported present in January-June and September-October, 1863. Furloughed for twenty-two days on February 5, 1864. Elected 3rd Lieutenant on March 28, 1864, and transferred to Company D of this regiment.

DAVIS, ASA, Private

Enlisted on or about July 24, 1862, for the war. Died on September 14-20, 1862, of "fever." Place of death not reported.

DAVIS, ELBERT, Private

Enlisted in Watauga County at age 28, July 15, 1862, for the war. Reported present in January-June and September-October, 1863. Reported on detail as a teamster from February 15 through August 31, 1864. No further records. Survived the war.

DAVIS, LEWIS, Private

Resided in Alexander County and was by occupation a farmer prior to enlisting at Camp Holmes, near Raleigh, November 12, 1863, for the war. Reported present in January-April, 1864. Sent to hospital on May 8, 1864. Captured by the enemy on an unspecified date. Hospitalized at Chattanooga, Tennessee, May 19, 1864. Died in hospital at Chattanooga on May 29, 1864, of "chronic diarrhoea." [Federal hospital records dated May, 1864, give his age as 29 and 32.]

DOTSON, ALLEN S., Private

Enlisted on or about July 24, 1862, for the war. No further records.

DOTSON, GEORGE W., Private

Enlisted in Watauga County on July 15, 1862, for the war. Never reported for duty. Died on March 24, 1863. Place and cause of death not reported.

DUGGER, JOEL, Private

Enlisted at Dalton, Georgia, March 1, 1864, for the war. Reported present through April 30, 1864. Reported absent without leave from Dalton on May 13, 1864. Listed as a deserter on September 10, 1864.

EGGERS, HUGH, Private

Resided in Watauga County and was by occupation a farmer prior to enlisting in Watauga County at age 33, July 15, 1862, for the war. Deserted at Big Creek Gap, Tennessee, February 17, 1863. Returned from desertion on October 30, 1863, and was placed under arrest. Returned to duty on November 29, 1863. Reported present in January-February, 1864. Sent to hospital from camp near Dalton, Georgia, April 25, 1864. No further records. Survived the war.

EGGERS, JOHN, Sergeant

Resided in Watauga County and was by occupation a farmer prior to enlisting in Watauga County at age 26, August 15, 1862, for the war. Mustered in as Corporal. Reported present in January-June, 1863. Promoted to Sergeant on April 7, 1863. Killed at Chickamauga, Georgia, September 20, 1863. Nominated for the Badge of Distinction for gallantry at Chickamauga.

EGGERS, LANDRINE, ———

Resided in Watauga County and was by occupation a farmer. Place and date of enlistment not reported (probably enlisted subsequent to August 31, 1864). No further records. Survived the war. [Was about 34 years of age at time of enlistment.]

EGGERS, RILEY, Private

Born on February 6, 1836. Resided in Watauga County and was by occupation a farmer prior to enlisting in Watauga County at age 26, August 5, 1862, for the war. Deserted at Big Creek Gap, Tennessee, February 17, 1863. Returned from desertion on October 30, 1863, and was placed under arrest. Returned to duty on November 23, 1863. Reported present in January-April, 1864. Wounded at Kolb's Farm, near Marietta, Georgia, June 22, 1864, and sent to hospital. Reported absent wounded through August 31, 1864. No further records.

EGGERS, WASHINGTON, Private
Born on August 21, 1829. Resided in Watauga County and was by occupation a farmer prior to enlisting in Watauga County at age 33, August 24, 1862, for the war. Deserted at Big Creek Gap, Tennessee, February 16, 1863.

ELLER, ALFRED P., Private
Enlisted in Watauga County on August 5, 1862, for the war. Mustered in as Private. Reported present in January-June, 1863. Promoted to Corporal in July-September, 1863. Deserted on September 20, 1863. Returned from desertion on November 12, 1863, and was reduced to ranks. Reported in confinement through February 29, 1864. Returned to duty in March-April, 1864. Captured near Marietta, Georgia, July 28, 1864. Sent to Nashville, Tennessee. Transferred to Louisville, Kentucky, where he arrived on August 5, 1864. Transferred to Camp Chase, Ohio, where he arrived on August 6, 1864. Released at Camp Chase on December 14, 1864, after taking the Oath of Allegiance.

FARTHING, ELIJAH H., Private
Enlisted in Watauga County at age 32, July 15, 1862, for the war. Reported present in January-February, 1863. Sent to hospital at Knoxville, Tennessee, on or about April 15, 1863. Reported absent sick through June, 1863. Reported sick in hospital at Abingdon, Virginia, in September-October, 1863. Reported absent sick through August 31, 1864. No further records. Survived the war.

FLETCHER, SPENCER, Private
Born in Watauga County where he resided as a farmer prior to enlisting in Watauga County at age 28, August 5, 1862, for the war. Mustered in as Sergeant. Furloughed on or about October 3, 1862. Reported absent on expired furlough in January-April, 1863. Reduced to ranks prior to March 1, 1863. Reported absent without leave in May-June, 1863. Deserted to the enemy on an unspecified date. Later served as a Private in Company A, 3rd Regiment Tennessee Mounted Infantry (Union).

FLETCHER, THOMAS BURT, Private
Born in Watauga County where he resided as a farmer or "domestic" prior to enlisting in Watauga County at age 20, July 15, 1862, for the war. Mustered in as Private. Reported present in January-June, 1863. Appointed Musician (Drummer) on April 7, 1863. Reported present in September-October, 1863, and January-August, 1864. Reduced to ranks on or about September 1, 1864. Captured at Jonesborough, Georgia, September 2, 1864. Sent to Nashville, Tennessee. Transferred to Louisville, Kentucky, where he arrived on November 22, 1864. Transferred to Camp Douglas, Chicago, Illinois, where he arrived on November 26, 1864. Released at Camp Douglas on May 5, 1865, after taking the Oath of Allegiance and joining the U.S. Army. Assigned to Company C, 6th Regiment U.S. Volunteer Infantry. [North Carolina pension records indicate that he was wounded in the right arm and left wrist at Dalton, Georgia, on or about September 30, 1864.]

GRAGG, WILLIAM SMITH, Private
Previously served in Company D of this regiment (rank not reported). Transferred to this company on or about July 24, 1862. Mustered in as Corporal. Reported present in January-February, 1863. Reduced to ranks prior to March 1, 1863. Sent to hospital at Knoxville, Tennessee, in March-April, 1863. Died in hospital at Knoxville on or about May 2, 1863, of "pneumonia."

GREEN, ALEXANDER, Private
Resided in Watauga County and was by occupation a farmer prior to enlisting in Watauga County at age 23, August 5, 1862, for the war. Furloughed on December 22, 1862. Reported absent on expired furlough in January-June, 1863. Returned to duty on an unspecified date. Hospitalized at Macon, Georgia, September 27, 1863, with debility. Furloughed for thirty days on October 6, 1863. Reported sick in camp in January-February, 1864. Furloughed for thirty days on April 19, 1864. Reported absent on sick furlough through August 31, 1864. No further records. Survived the war.

GREEN, AMOS, JR., Private
Resided in Watauga County and was by occupation a farmer prior to enlisting in Watauga County on July 15, 1862, for the war. Reported present in January-June and September-October, 1863. Reported absent on detached duty as a provost guard in January-February, 1864. Rejoined the company in March-April, 1864. Reported absent in May-August, 1864. Captured on an unspecified date in hospital at Thomasville, where he was a patient or was serving as a nurse, steward, or attendant. Paroled at Thomasville on May 1, 1865.

GREEN, DAVID, Private
Enlisted in Watauga County on July 15, 1863, for the war. Reported sick in hospital in September-October, 1863. Died in Caldwell County on December 22, 1863, of disease.

GRUBB, GEORGE W., Private
Previously served as Private in Company D, 5th Battalion N.C. Cavalry. Transferred to this company on or about July 24, 1862. Transferred back to Company D, 5th Battalion N.C. Cavalry, prior to March 1, 1863.

HAGAMAN, ISAAC, JR., Private
Resided in Watauga County and was by occupation a farmer prior to enlisting in Watauga County at age 28, August 15, 1862, for the war. Mustered in as Sergeant. Reported present in January-April, 1863. Reported sick in hospital at Knoxville, Tennessee, in May-June, 1863. Furloughed at Knoxville on July 20, 1863. Reported absent on sick furlough through October 31, 1863. Listed as a deserter on November 22, 1863. Reduced to ranks in November, 1863-February, 1864. Reported present but under arrest on April 7, 1864. Returned to duty on an unspecified date. Reported present in May-August, 1864. Captured at Orangeburg, South Carolina, February 12, 1865. Sent to New Bern. Transferred to Hart's Island, New York Harbor, where he arrived on April 10, 1865. Released at Hart's Island on June 18, 1865, after taking the Oath of Allegiance. [Previously served as 1st Lieutenant in the 98th Regiment N.C. Militia.]

HARMON, ANDREW J., Private
Resided in Watauga County where he enlisted at age 23, August 7, 1862, for the war. Furloughed on November 15, 1862. Reported absent on expired furlough in January-February, 1863. Reported absent without leave in May-June, 1863. Dropped from the company rolls on January 20, 1864. Prior to that date, he enlisted as Sergeant in Company E, 13th Regiment Tennessee Cavalry (Union).

HAYES, JOSEPH, SR., Corporal
Born in Caldwell County on October 23, 1828. Resided in Watauga County and was by occupation a farmer prior to enlisting at age 33,

on or about July 24, 1862, for the war. Mustered in as Corporal. No further records. Survived the war.

HAYES, ROBERT, Private

Previously served as Private in Company D of this regiment. Transferred to this company on or about July 24, 1862. No further records. [May have served also as Private in Company B, 5th Battalion N.C. Cavalry.]

HAYES, WILLIAM, Private

Resided in Watauga County and was by occupation a farmer prior to enlisting at age 24, on or about July 24, 1862, for the war. No further records.

HILLIARD, ALFRED, JR., Private

Resided in Watauga County and was by occupation a domestic prior to enlisting in Watauga County at age 18, July 15, 1862, for the war. Reported present in January-June, 1863. Reported sick in hospital in September-October, 1863. Reported present but under arrest on January 15, 1864. Reason he was arrested not reported. Returned to duty in March-April, 1864. Captured (or deserted to the enemy) at Resaca, Georgia, May 16, 1864. Sent to Nashville, Tennessee. Transferred to Louisville, Kentucky, where he arrived on May 21, 1864. Transferred to Alton, Illinois, where he arrived on May 25, 1864. Released at Alton on June 10, 1864, after joining the U.S. Navy.

HILLIARD, BARTLETT YOUNG, Private

Previously enlisted as Private in Company E, 37th Regiment N.C. Troops; however, he was apparently rejected for service. Enlisted in this company in Watauga County at age 29, July 15, 1862, for the war. Reported absent on furlough in January-February, 1863. Returned to duty in March-April, 1863. Reported present in May-June, 1863. Deserted at Chickamauga, Georgia, September 20, 1863. Reported present but under arrest from November 12, 1863, through February 29, 1864. Returned to duty in March-April, 1864. Captured (or deserted to the enemy) at Resaca, Georgia, May 15, 1864. Sent to Nashville, Tennessee. Transferred to Louisville, Kentucky, where he arrived on May 20, 1864. Transferred to Camp Morton, Indianapolis, Indiana, where he arrived on May 22, 1864. Paroled at Camp Morton and transferred for exchange on March 10, 1865. Received at Boulware's and Cox's Wharves, James River, Virginia, March 23, 1865, for exchange. No further records. Survived the war. [Contrary to 9:530 of this series, the correct spelling of his first name was probably Bartlett rather than Bartlet.]

HODGES, CALLAWAY, Private

Born in Watauga County* where he resided as a farmer prior to enlisting at age 18, on or about July 24, 1862, for the war. Transferred to Company C, 5th Battalion N.C. Cavalry, on or about July 27, 1862.

HODGES, WILLIAM J., Private

Enlisted in Watauga County on July 15, 1862, for the war. Reported present in January-June and September-October, 1863. No further records.

HOLDER, DAVID W., Private

Born in Watauga County* in 1845 and resided in Watauga County where he enlisted on July 15, 1862, for the war. Reported present in January-June, 1863. Reported absent on sick furlough from August 18, 1863, through February 29, 1864. Returned to duty in

March-April, 1864. Hospitalized at Macon, Georgia, August 26, 1864, with intermittent fever and acute diarrhoea. Transferred on September 11, 1864. Issued clothing on October 11, 1864. No further records. [Filed a Tennessee pension application after the war.]

HOLDER, ELIJAH THOMAS, Corporal

Born in Orange County in 1832. Resided in Watauga County where he enlisted on July 15, 1862, for the war. Mustered in as Private. Reported present in January-June and September-October, 1863. Promoted to Corporal in November, 1863-February, 1864. Reported present in January-February, 1864. Furloughed for twenty-two days from Dalton, Georgia, March 30, 1864. Returned to duty subsequent to April 30, 1864. Reported present through August 31, 1864. No further records. [His Tennessee pension application indicates that he was wounded in the left hip at Boone during the Stoneman raid in early 1865 while commanding seventy-two recruits.]

HOLMAN, THOMAS, ——

Place and date of enlistment not reported (probably enlisted subsequent to August 31, 1864). No further records.

HORTON, WILLIAM H., Private

Born in Watauga County* on February 27, 1834. Resided in Watauga County and was by occupation a farmer prior to enlisting in Watauga County at age 27, July 15, 1862, for the war. Reported present in January-June, 1863. Reported on duty "with wagon train" in September-October, 1863. Detailed as a teamster on February 16, 1864. Reported absent on detail through November 30, 1864. No further records. [Filed a Tennessee pension application after the war.]

HOWELL, AMOS, Private

Born in Ashe County and resided in Ashe or Watauga County where he was by occupation a farmer prior to enlisting at age 30, on or about July 24, 1862, for the war. Transferred to Company D, 5th Battalion N.C. Cavalry, on or about the same date.

ISAACS, HUGH M., Private

Resided in Watauga County and was by occupation a farmer prior to enlisting in Watauga County at age 23, July 15, 1862, for the war. Reported present in January-June, 1863. Reported sick in hospital in September-October, 1863. Returned to duty on an unspecified date. Reported present in January-February, 1864. Sent to hospital from camp near Dalton, Georgia, April 12, 1864. Reported absent sick through August 31, 1864. No further records. Survived the war.

ISAACS, JAMES, SR., Private

Enlisted in Watauga County on July 15, 1862, for the war. Reported present in January-June, and September-October, 1863. Furloughed for twenty days on January 22, 1864. Returned to duty in March-April, 1864. Reported present through August 31, 1864. No further records.

ISAACS, NOAH, Private

Previously served as Private in Company D of this regiment. Transferred to this company on or about August 5, 1862. Reported present in January-February, 1863. Furloughed for twenty days on or about March 14, 1863. Returned to duty on an unspecified date. Reported present in May-June, 1863. Deserted at Lenoir Station, Tennessee, August 29, 1863. Later served as Private in Company A, 3rd Regiment Tennessee Mounted Infantry (Union).

ISAACS, SOLOMON C., Private

Resided in Watauga County where he enlisted at age 18, April 1, 1864, for the war. Captured (or deserted to the enemy) at Cassville, Georgia, May 19-20, 1864. Sent to Nashville, Tennessee. Transferred to Louisville, Kentucky, where he arrived on May 29, 1864. Transferred to Rock Island, Illinois, where he arrived on June 1, 1864. Released at Rock Island on June 10, 1864, after joining the U.S. Navy.

JACKSON, ANDREW, Private

Born in Tennessee and resided in Watauga County where he was by occupation a farmer prior to enlisting in Watauga County on August 5, 1862, for the war. Furloughed for thirty days on or about October 2, 1862. Reported absent on expired furlough in January-February, 1863. Reported absent without leave in May-June, 1863. Reported under arrest on January 30, 1864. Apparently returned to duty but was again placed under arrest on April 7, 1864. Deserted to the enemy in May, 1864. Sent to Chattanooga, Tennessee. Transferred to Louisville, Kentucky, where he arrived on June 6, 1864. Released on or about the same date after taking the Oath of Allegiance.

JOHNSON, BRAXTON, ———

Born on January 16, 1823. Resided in Watauga County. Place and date of enlistment not reported (probably enlisted subsequent to August 31, 1864). No further records. Survived the war.

JOHNSON, JACOB, SR., Private

Previously served as Private in Company D of this regiment. Transferred to this company on or about July 24, 1862. Transferred back to Company D prior to December 22, 1862.

JOHNSON, JOHN T., Private

Resided in Watauga County where he enlisted on July 15, 1862, for the war. Reported present in January-June, 1863. Deserted near Chattanooga, Tennessee, October 4, 1863.

JOHNSON, WILLIAM, Private

Enlisted at Camp Holmes, near Raleigh, January 25, 1864, for the war. Reported absent without leave at Dalton, Georgia, from February 28 through August 31, 1864. No further records. Survived the war.

LEWIS, J., Private

Enlisted in this company on or about July 24, 1862, for the war. No further records.

McCULLOM, D., Sergeant

Place and date of enlistment not reported (probably enlisted subsequent to August 31, 1864). Promotion record not reported. Captured (probably in hospital) at Richmond, Virginia, April 3, 1865. Died in hospital at Richmond on May 2, 1865, of "chronic diarrhoea."

McEWIN, MAX C., Private

Enlisted in Watauga County on August 7, 1862, for the war. "Entry canceled."

MARLOW, JOHN, ———

Place and date of enlistment not reported (probably enlisted subsequent to August 31, 1864). No further records.

MATHIS, JOHN, Private

Enlisted at Camp Holmes, near Raleigh, January 14, 1864, for the war. Reported under arrest on February 29, 1864 (apparently for the loss of a musket and ammunition). Returned to duty in March-April, 1864. Reported absent without leave at Dalton, Georgia, May 13, 1864. Listed as a deserter on September 10, 1864.

MICHAEL, JOHN, Private

Enlisted in Watauga County on August 5, 1862, for the war. Reported present in January-February, 1863. Died in hospital at Jacksboro, Tennessee, March 31, 1863. Cause of death not reported.

MILLER, ALFRED HAMILTON, Private

Born on September 2, 1841. Resided in Watauga County. Place and date of enlistment not reported (probably enlisted in the spring of 1864). Deserted to the enemy on an unspecified date. Sent to Knoxville, Tennessee. Transferred to Louisville, Kentucky, where he arrived on June 29, 1864. Released at Louisville on June 30, 1864, after taking the Oath of Allegiance.

MILLER, DAVID D., Private

Resided in Watauga County and was by occupation a "domestic" prior to enlisting in Watauga County at age 18, July 15, 1862, for the war. Reported present in January-February, 1863. Died in camp at Big Creek Gap, Tennessee, March 7, 1863. Cause of death not reported.

MILLER, EPHRAIM N., Private

Resided in Watauga County and was by occupation a "domestic" prior to enlisting in Watauga County at age 15, August 5, 1862, for the war. Reported present in January-June, 1863. Reported sick in hospital from August 27, 1863, through August 31, 1864. No further records.

MILLER, FRANKLIN, Private

Born on April 8, 1840. Enlisted in Watauga County at age 22, July 15, 1862, for the war. Reported present in January-February, 1863. Reported in hospital at Knoxville, Tennessee, in March-June, 1863. Reported absent on sick furlough in September-October, 1863. Returned to duty on an unspecified date. Reported present in January-April, 1864. Sent to hospital on August 27, 1864. No further records. Survived the war.

MILLER, GEORGE M., Private

Previously served as Private in Company D of this regiment. Transferred to this company on or about August 5, 1862. Died on January 8, 1863. Place and cause of death not reported.

MILLER, JOHN H., Private

Enlisted in Watauga County on July 15, 1862, for the war. Reported present in January-June and September-October, 1863. Captured at Missionary Ridge, Tennessee, November 25, 1863. Sent to Nashville, Tennessee. Transferred to Louisville, Kentucky, where he arrived on December 17, 1863. Transferred to Rock Island, Illinois, where he arrived on December 23, 1863. Released at Rock Island on January 25, 1864, after taking the Oath of Allegiance and joining the U.S. Navy.

MILLER, JOHN M., Private

Previously served as Private in Company D of this regiment. Transferred to this company on or about July 24, 1862. Reported present in January-February, 1863. Discharged on April 25, 1863. Reason discharged not reported.

MILLER, LORENZO DOW, Musician

Born on November 9, 1843. Resided in Watauga County and was by occupation a farmer prior to enlisting in Watauga County at age 18, July 15, 1862, for the war. Mustered in as Private. Promoted to Musician (Fifer) prior to March 1, 1863. Reported present on surviving company muster rolls through August 31, 1864. No further records. Survived the war. [North Carolina pension records indicate that he was "hit with spent ball—and knocked senseless" at Lovejoy's Station, Georgia, July 1, 1863 (probably September 1, 1864).]

MILLER, T. CALVIN, Sergeant

Previously served as Private in Company D of this regiment. Transferred to this company on or about July 15, 1862. Mustered in as Private. Reported present in January-June, 1863. Wounded in the left foot at Chickamauga, Georgia, September 19-20, 1863. Returned to duty subsequent to October 31, 1863. Reported present in January-August, 1864. Promoted to Sergeant on August 1, 1864. Transferred to Company G of this regiment subsequent to August 31, 1864.

MITCHEL, GEORGE, Private

Resided in Watauga County and was by occupation a "domestic" prior to enlisting at age 30, on or about July 24, 1862, for the war. No further records.

MITCHELL, MICHAEL, Private

Previously served as Private in Company D of this regiment. Transferred to this company on or about August 5, 1862. Reported present in January-April, 1863. Detailed to work in a shop at Knoxville, Tennessee, in May-June, 1863. Returned to duty on an unspecified date. Reported present in September-October, 1863. Wounded in the left leg at Rocky Face Ridge, Georgia, February 25, 1864. Left leg amputated. Hospitalized at Atlanta, Georgia. Reported absent wounded through August 31, 1864. No further records. Survived the war.

MITCHELL, ROBERT, Private

Resided in Watauga County and was by occupation a farmer prior to enlisting in Watauga County at age 18, April 1, 1864, for the war. Reported present through August 31, 1864. Transferred to Company G of this regiment subsequent to August 31, 1864.

MITCHELL, THOMAS, Private

Resided in Watauga County and was by occupation a farmer prior to enlisting in Watauga County at age 34, July 15, 1862, for the war. Failed to report for duty and was reported absent without leave on surviving company muster rolls from March, 1863, through August 31, 1864.

MOODY, GEORGE W., Private

Resided in Watauga County and was by occupation a farmer prior to enlisting in Watauga County at age 29, July 7, 1862, for the war. Reported absent on furlough from December 15, 1862, through April 30, 1863. Reported absent without leave (furlough expired) in May-June, 1863. Reported absent on sick furlough in September-October, 1863. Listed as a deserter and dropped from the company rolls on January 20, 1864. [North Carolina pension

records indicate that he contracted a fever at Cumberland Gap, Tennessee, and was "unable to do any duty after that time."]

MORETZ, JOHN, Private

Born in Lincoln County and resided in Watauga County where he was by occupation a farmer prior to enlisting at age 31, on or about July 24, 1862, for the war. Transferred to Company C, 5th Battalion N.C. Cavalry, on or about July 27, 1862.

MORETZ, WILLIAM, Private

Born in Lincoln County and resided in Watauga County where he was by occupation a farmer prior to enlisting at age 26, on or about July 24, 1862, for the war. Transferred to Company C, 5th Battalion N.C. Cavalry, on or about July 27, 1862.

NELSON, JAMES W., Private

Enlisted in Watauga County on August 11, 1862, for the war. Reported absent on expired furlough in January-February, 1863. Returned to duty in March-April, 1863. Reported present in May-June, 1863. Sent to hospital at Knoxville, Tennessee, August 25, 1863. Reported absent sick through August 31, 1864. No further records.

NORRIS, JACOB, Private

Resided in Watauga County and was by occupation a "domestic" prior to enlisting in Watauga County at age 20, July 15, 1862, for the war. Reported present in January-June, 1863. Reported sick in hospital in September-October, 1863. Returned to duty on an unspecified date. Reported present in January-August, 1864. No further records. Survived the war.

NORRIS, JOHN, Private

Resided in Watauga County and was by occupation a "domestic" prior to enlisting in Watauga County at age 18, July 15, 1862, for the war. Reported present in January-February, 1863. Died at Jacksboro, Tennessee, March 3, 1863. Cause of death not reported.

NORRIS, THOMAS, Private

Enlisted in Watauga County on August 5, 1862, for the war. Reported present in January-June, 1863. No further records.

OLIVER, JOHN S., Private

Enlisted in Watauga County on July 15, 1862, for the war. Mustered in as Private. Reported present in January-June, 1863. Promoted to Corporal prior to March 1, 1863. Reduced to ranks in July-October, 1863. Reported present in September-October, 1863. Reported absent without leave from December 8, 1863, through February 29, 1864. Returned to duty in March-April, 1864. Reported present through August 31, 1864. No further records.

PEARCE, ALLEN, Private

Enlisted on or about July 24, 1862, for the war. No further records.

PIERCE, JOSEPH, Private

Enlisted at Bristol, Tennessee, April 9, 1864, for the war. Reported absent without leave on May 7, 1864. Captured on the "Cleveland r[ail] road" on May 9, 1864. Sent to Nashville, Tennessee. Transferred to Louisville, Kentucky, where he arrived on May 17, 1864. Transferred to Camp Morton, Indianapolis, Indiana, where he arrived on May 22, 1864. Died at Camp Morton on August 8, 1864, of "typho malarial fever."

PROFFITT, JESSE, Private

Enlisted in Watauga County at age 19, July 15, 1862, for the war. Reported present in January-February, 1863. Died at Big Creek Gap, Tennessee, March 29, 1863. Cause of death not reported.

PROFFITT, JOHN, Private

Enlisted on or about July 24, 1862, for the war. No further records.

PROFFITT, WILLIAM, Private

Born in Tennessee on January 28, 1826. Resided in Watauga County where he was by occupation a farmer prior to enlisting in Watauga County at age 36, August 5, 1862, for the war. Reported present in January-February, 1863. Reported sick in hospital at Knoxville, Tennessee, in March-June, 1863. Wounded slightly at Chickamauga, Georgia, September 20, 1863. Returned to duty prior to November 22, 1863, when he was sent to hospital. Reported in hospital through August 31, 1864. No further records. Survived the war.

RANDLES, JOSEPH, Private

Born in Ashe County where he resided as a farmer prior to enlisting at age 22, on or about July 24, 1862, for the war. Transferred to Company C, 5th Battalion N.C. Cavalry, on an unspecified date. [Contrary to 2:358 of this series, the correct spelling of his surname was probably Randles rather than Randels.]

RASH, JOSEPH, Private

Born in Wilkes County and resided in Watauga County where he was by occupation a farmer or "domestic" prior to enlisting in Watauga County at age 26, on or about July 24, 1862, for the war. Transferred to Company C, 5th Battalion N.C. Cavalry, on an unspecified date.

REVIS, T. H., ———

Place and date of enlistment not reported (probably enlisted in the summer of 1864). Listed as a deserter on September 10, 1864.

SEATS, ROBERT E., Private

Resided in Ashe County and was by occupation a day laborer prior to enlisting at age 25, on or about July 24, 1862, for the war. Died on an unspecified date (probably in the summer or autumn of 1862). Place and cause of death not reported.

SHULL, WILLIAM R., Private

Enlisted in Watauga County at age 25, July 15, 1862, for the war. Reported present in January-April, 1863. Was reportedly transferred to a cavalry unit on June 20, 1863. No further records. Survived the war.

SMITH, ANDREW, Private

Resided in Watauga County where he enlisted on August 7, 1862, for the war. Furloughed for thirty days on November 15, 1862. Reported absent on expired furlough in January-February, 1863. Reported absent without leave in May-June, 1863. Reported absent on sick furlough in September-October, 1863. Returned to duty on an unspecified date. Reported absent without leave on February 4, 1864. No further records.

SMITH, GEORGE L., Private

Resided in Watauga County where he enlisted on August 26, 1862, for the war. Reported absent on expired furlough in January-

February, 1863. Reported present in March-June, 1863. Killed at Chickamauga, Georgia, September 20, 1863. [Was about 22 years of age at time of enlistment.]

SMITH, JAMES A., Private

Enlisted in Watauga County on August 5, 1862, for the war. Reported present in January-February, 1863. Died at Big Creek Gap, Tennessee, March 19, 1863. Cause of death not reported.

SMITH, JOHN, Private

Enlisted at Camp Holmes, near Raleigh, January 25, 1864, for the war. Reported absent without leave on February 28, 1864. Listed as a deserter on April 7, 1864.

SMITH, JOHN N., 1st Sergeant

Resided in Watauga County where he enlisted on August 26, 1862, for the war. Mustered in as Private. Reported present in January-June and September-October, 1863. Promoted to Sergeant in November, 1863-February, 1864. Promoted to 1st Sergeant on May 1, 1864. Reported present in January-February, 1864. Wounded in the left shoulder and captured at Jonesborough, Georgia, September 2, 1864. Hospitalized at Atlanta, Georgia. Transferred to Nashville, Tennessee, on or about October 23, 1864. Transferred to Louisville, Kentucky, where he arrived on November 22, 1864. Transferred to Camp Douglas, Chicago, Illinois, on or about November 24, 1864. Released at Camp Douglas on June 17, 1865, after taking the Oath of Allegiance.

SMITH, NELSON, Private

Place and date of enlistment not reported (probably enlisted subsequent to August 31, 1864). Wounded slightly in the foot at Bentonville on March 19, 1865. No further records.

SMITH, SOLOMON, Private

Born in Watauga County* where he resided as a farmer or "domestic" prior to enlisting in Watauga County at age 16, August 7, 1862, for the war. Reported absent on expired furlough in January-February, 1863. Discharged at Clinton, Tennessee, April 13, 1863, by reason of "gun shot wound of the left hand which has caused a permanent contraction of the muscles and tendons. . . ." Place and date wounded not reported.

SMITH, THOMAS, Private

Resided in Watauga County where he enlisted on August 7, 1862, for the war. Reported absent on expired furlough in January-February, 1863. Returned to duty in March-April, 1863. Reported present in May-June, 1863. Deserted at Bell's Bridge, Tennessee, August 4, 1863. Returned to duty prior to March 1, 1864. Reported absent without leave on April 10, 1864. No further records.

SMITH, WILLIAM M., Private

Resided in Watauga County where he enlisted on August 7, 1862, for the war. Reported absent on expired furlough in January-February, 1863. Returned to duty in March-April, 1863. Deserted on July 5, 1863. Returned to duty subsequent to October 31, 1863. Reported absent without leave on February 28, 1864. Listed as a deserter on April 7, 1864.

SOUTH, HARRISON, Private

Resided in Watauga County and was by occupation a farmer prior to enlisting in Watauga County at age 21, July 15, 1862, for the war. Deserted on February 16, 1863. Returned to duty in March-April, 1863. Died in hospital at Clinton, Tennessee, May 13, 1863. Cause of death not reported.

SUTHERLAND, WILLIAM HENRY HARRISON, Private

Previously served as Private in Company D of this regiment. Transferred to this company on or about July 24, 1862. Transferred to Company C, 5th Battalion N.C. Cavalry, on or about July 27, 1862. [Contrary to 2:358 of this series, the correct spelling of his surname was probably Sutherland rather than Southerland.]

SWIFT, WILLBORN, Private

Resided in Watauga County and was by occupation a farmer prior to enlisting in Watauga County at age 31, July 15, 1862, for the war. Reported present in January-April, 1863. Detailed as a shoemaker at Knoxville, Tennessee, in May-June, 1863. Reported absent on detail as a shoemaker at Knoxville and Atlanta, Georgia, through June 24, 1864. Rejoined the company on or about that date. Reported present through August 31, 1864. No further records. Survived the war.

TAYLOR, JAMES E., Private

Enlisted on or about July 24, 1862, for the war. Transferred to Company E of this regiment on or about November 7, 1862.

TEAGUE, VANDAVER M., Private

Enlisted at Camp Holmes, near Raleigh, November 12, 1863, for the war. Reported present in March-August, 1864. No further records. Survived the war. [Was about 34 years of age at time of enlistment.]

TRIVETT, JESSE, Private

Enlisted in Watauga County on August 5, 1862, for the war. Died in February, 1863. Place and cause of death not reported.

TRIVETT, LAZARUS, Private

Born on November 10, 1835. Resided in Watauga County and was by occupation a farmer prior to enlisting in Watauga County at age 26, July 7, 1862, for the war. Transferred to Company D of this regiment prior to March 1, 1863.

TUGMAN, BENJAMIN F., Private

Born on December 10, 1845. Resided in Watauga County and was by occupation a farmer prior to enlisting in Watauga County at age 18, April 1, 1864, for the war. Reported present in March-August, 1864. Hospitalized at Macon, Georgia, November 6, 1864, with intermittent fever. Returned to duty on November 19, 1864. Transferred to Company G of this regiment on an unspecified date.

TUGMAN, JAMES, ———

Resided in Watauga County and was by occupation a farmer. Place and date of enlistment not reported (probably enlisted subsequent to August 31, 1864). No further records. [Was about 20 years of age in 1864.]

VANDIKE, GEORGE ELCANA, Sergeant

Resided in Watauga County and was by occupation a "domestic" prior to enlisting in Watauga County at age 19, August 5, 1862, for the war. Mustered in as Private. Reported present in January-June and September-October, 1863. Promoted to Sergeant in November,

1863-February, 1864. Reported present in January-April, 1864. Wounded in the right leg at Kolb's Farm, near Marietta, Georgia, June 22, 1864. Returned to duty prior to September 1, 1864. No further records. Survived the war.

VANOVER, CHARLES, Private

Previously served as Private in Company D of this regiment. Transferred to this company on or about July 24, 1862. Transferred to Company C, 5th Battalion N.C. Cavalry, on or about July 27, 1862.

WASHBURN, JOSEPH, ———

North Carolina pension records indicate that he served in this company.

WATSON, JOHN M., Private

Enlisted in Watauga County on August 26, 1862, for the war. Reported absent on expired furlough in January-February, 1863. Died in hospital at Jacksboro, Tennessee, March 28, 1863. Cause of death not reported.

WEISENFELD, MORETZ, Private

Born in Prussia. Resided in Watauga County and was by occupation a merchant prior to enlisting at age 28, on or about July 24, 1862, for the war. No further records. Survived the war.

WILSON, JOHN H., Private

Resided in Watauga County and was by occupation a farmer prior to enlisting in Watauga County at age 24, July 15, 1862, for the war. Reported present in January-June, 1863. Killed at Chickamauga, Georgia, September 20, 1863.

WILSON, JOSEPH, Private

Enlisted at Chickamauga, Georgia, October 30, 1863, for the war. Deserted near Chickamauga on November 12, 1863.

WILSON, LEMUEL, Private

Previously served as Private in Company F of this regiment. Transferred to this company on or about July 24, 1862. Reported present in January-June, 1863. Wounded at Chickamauga, Georgia, September 20, 1863. Deserted near Chattanooga, Tennessee, October 4, 1863. Returned to duty on an unspecified date. Wounded at Rocky Face Ridge, Georgia, February 25, 1864. Hospitalized at Atlanta, Georgia, where he died on March 18, 1864, of wounds.

WILSON, WILLIAM, Private

Enlisted on or about July 24, 1862, for the war. Transferred to Company D of this regiment on or about August 3, 1862.

WINEBARGER, ABEL, Private

Born in Catawba County and resided in Watauga County where he was by occupation a farmer prior to enlisting in Watauga County at age 22, July 15, 1862, for the war. Wounded in the left hand at Cumberland Gap, Tennessee, in October, 1862. Reported absent on expired furlough in January-February, 1863. Discharged at Clinton, Tennessee, April 13, 1863, by reason of "gun shot wound of left hand carrying away all the fingers except two, also causing contraction of the muscles and tendons."

WINEBARGER, HIRAM, Private

Resided in Watauga County and was by occupation a farmer prior to enlisting in Watauga County at age 31, July 15, 1862, for the war. Mustered in as Private. Promoted to Corporal prior to March 1, 1863. Reported present in January-June, 1863. Reported absent on sick furlough in September-October, 1863. Deserted on an unspecified date. Reduced to ranks in November, 1863-January, 1864. Dropped from the company rolls on January 20, 1864.

WINEBARGER, LEVI, Private

Previously served as Corporal in Company G of this regiment. Transferred to this company in July-August, 1863. Was apparently mustered in as Corporal. Reduced to ranks on an unspecified date. Deserted at Sweetwater, Tennessee, September 1, 1863.

WOODRING, MARCUS L., Private

Resided in Watauga County and was by occupation a farmer prior to enlisting in Watauga County at age 25, July 15, 1862, for the war. Reported present on surviving company muster rolls through August 31, 1864. No further records. Survived the war.

WOODRING, RUFUS, Private

Resided in Watauga County and was by occupation a farmer prior to enlisting in Watauga County at age 25, July 15, 1862, for the war. Reported absent on expired furlough in January-February, 1863. Reported present in March-April, 1863. Deserted on July 5, 1863. Returned to duty on September 1, 1863. Reported present in January-August, 1864. No further records. Survived the war.

YELTON, BARNETT C., Private

Previously served as Private in Company D of this regiment. Transferred to this company on or about July 24, 1862. Enlisted in Company B, 5th Battalion N.C. Cavalry, August 1, 1862.

YELTON, JOHN L., Private

Previously served as Private in Company B of this regiment. Transferred to this company on or about July 24, 1862. Enlisted in Company B, 5th Battalion N.C. Cavalry, August 1, 1862.

COMPANY K

This company was raised in Mitchell County in May-July, 1862, and was mustered in as Capt. Samuel M. Silver's Company, N.C. Volunteers, on July 29, 1862. It was assigned to the 58th Regiment N.C. Troops the same date and designated Company K. After joining the regiment the company functioned as a part of the regiment, and its history for the remainder of the war is reported as a part of the regimental history.

The following roster was compiled primarily from information in the microfilm edition of the Compiled Service Records of Soldiers Who Served in Organizations from the State of North Carolina (Record Group 109, M270), National Archives and Records Administration, Washington, D.C. Record Group 109 includes enlistment papers, pay vouchers, requisitions, letters of resignation, discharge certificates, and abstracts of medical and prisoner of war returns. Materials relating specifically to this company include a muster-in roll dated July 29, 1862, and muster rolls dated January-June, 1863; September-October, 1863; and January-August, 1864

Also utilized in this roster were *The War of the Rebellion: A Compilation of the Official Records of the Union and Confederate Armies,*

the North Carolina adjutant general's *Roll of Honor,* state militia records, newspaper casualty lists and obituaries, wartime claims for bounty pay and allowances, postwar registers of claims for artificial limbs, Confederate pension applications filed with the states of North Carolina, Tennessee, and Florida, Confederate Soldiers' Home records, and the 1860 and 1870 federal censuses of North Carolina. A search was made also for relevant letters, diaries, reminiscences, and other manuscripts in the Southern Historical Collection (University of North Carolina-Chapel Hill), the Duke University Library Special Collections Department, and the North Carolina Division of Archives and History.

Among the secondary sources consulted were records of the North Carolina division of the United Daughters of the Confederacy, postwar rosters, regimental and county histories, marriage bond, will, and cemetery indexes, published and unpublished genealogies, biographical dictionaries, the North Carolina *County Heritage Book* series, the *Confederate Veteran,* Walter Clark's *Histories of the Several Regiments and Battalions from North Carolina in the Great War, 1861- '65,* and the North Carolina volume of the extended edition of *Confederate Military History*

OFFICERS

CAPTAINS

SILVER, SAMUEL MARION

Previously served as 2nd Lieutenant of Company E of this regiment. Elected Captain of this company on July 29, 1862. Reported present in January-April, 1863. Reported absent on detached service in May-June, 1863. Reported sick in hospital in September-October, 1863. Returned to duty on an unspecified date. Reported in command of the regiment in January-April and July-August, 1864. Appointed Lieutenant Colonel on October 29, 1864, to rank from September 1, 1864, and transferred to the Field and Staff of this regiment.

SILVER, DAVID R.

Previously served as Private in Company E, 6th Regiment N.C. State Troops. Elected 1st Lieutenant of this company on July 27, 1863. Reported present in September-October, 1863. Reported absent on detached service in Mitchell County in January-February, 1864. Relieved from detached duty on April 5, 1864. Rejoined the company prior to May 1, 1864. Reported present through August 31, 1864. Promoted to Captain on September 1, 1864. Reported in hospital at West Point, Mississippi, January 15, 1865, with catarrhus. Hospitalized at Charlotte on April 9, 1865, with chronic hepatitis. Transferred to another hospital on April 14, 1865. Survived the war. [Born on February 21, 1832.]

LIEUTENANTS

BUCHANAN, LEONARD M., 2nd Lieutenant

Previously served as Private in Company E of this regiment. Elected 2nd Lieutenant of this company on July 29, 1862. Reported present in January-February, 1863. Resigned on March 5, 1863, by reason of "old age" and because he considered himself "incompetent to perform the duties of the said office." Resignation accepted on April 28, 1863.

CHANDLER, DAVID A., 1st Lieutenant

Previously served as Private in Company A of this regiment. Elected 1st Lieutenant of this company on July 29, 1862. Reported absent sick in January-February, 1863. Died at Jacksboro, Tennessee, March 31, 1863, of "sickness."

DUNCAN, JONATHAN A. W., 2nd Lieutenant

Previously served as Private in Company E of this regiment. Elected 3rd Lieutenant of this company on July 29, 1862. Reported present in January-April, 1863. Promoted to 2nd Lieutenant on April 28, 1863. Reported present but sick in May-June, 1863. Returned to duty on an unspecified date. Reported present in September-October, 1863. Reported absent on detached service in Mitchell County in January-February, 1864. Rejoined the company on or about April 5, 1864. Wounded at Resaca, Georgia, May 14-15, 1864. Returned to duty prior to September 1, 1864. Subsequently transferred to Company B of this regiment.

SILVER, LEVI D., 3rd Lieutenant

Previously served as Private of Company E of this regiment. Transferred to this company on or about July 29, 1862. Mustered in as Private. Promoted to Sergeant prior to March 1, 1863. Reported present in January-June and September-October, 1863. Elected 3rd Lieutenant on November 17, 1863. Reported present in January-February, 1864. Furloughed for twenty-six days on April 20, 1864. Returned to duty on May 16, 1864. Reported present through August 31, 1864. Transferred to Company F of this regiment on an unspecified date.

NONCOMMISSIONED OFFICERS AND PRIVATES

ANDERSON, HOLDER, Private

Enlisted in Mitchell County on November 17, 1863, for the war. Died at Atlanta, Georgia, January 1, 1864. Cause of death not reported.

BAILEY, TOM, ———

North Carolina pension records indicate that he served in this company.

BAKER, J. A., Private

Place and date of enlistment not reported (probably enlisted subsequent to August 31, 1864). Hospitalized at Charlotte on February 18, 1865, with chronic diarrhoea. Transferred to another hospital the same date. No further records.

BARTLETT, JOSEPH HENRY, Private

Previously served as Private in Company B of this regiment. Transferred to this company on or about July 29, 1862. Reported present in January-June, 1863. Wounded at Chickamauga, Georgia, September 19-20, 1863. Died at "Preston Hospital" on September 29, 1863, of wounds.

BARTLETT, SAMUEL D., Private

Previously served as Private in Company E of this regiment. Transferred to this company on or about July 29, 1862. Mustered in as Corporal. Reported present in January-June and September-October, 1863. Promoted to Sergeant prior to March 1, 1863. Reported sick in hospital on February 15, 1864. Furloughed for

thirty days on March 5, 1864. Reduced to ranks in May-July, 1864. Died at home on or about July 4, 1864, of "diarrhoea."

BENFIELD, ADOLPHUS L., Private

Previously served as Private in Company A of this regiment. Transferred to this company on or about July 29, 1862. Sent on detached service on January 12, 1863. Rejoined the company in March-April, 1863. Reported absent on detached service in May-June, 1863. Reported on detail as a blacksmith in September-October, 1863. Deserted on or about December 19, 1863. May have returned to duty subsequent to August 31, 1864 (was reportedly issued clothing on November 17, 1864). No further records.

BENNETT, SAMUEL M., ———

North Carolina pension records indicate that he served in this company. [He was reportedly the last surviving North Carolina veteran of the civil war. He died on March 9, 1951.]

BLAYLOCK, ALBERT N., Private

Previously served as Private in Company G of this regiment. Transferred to this company in July-October, 1863. Reported absent sick in September-October, 1863. Returned to duty on an unspecified date. Reported present in January-April, 1864. Captured at Kolb's Farm, near Marietta, Georgia, June 22, 1864. Sent to Nashville, Tennessee. Transferred to Louisville, Kentucky, where he arrived on July 13, 1864. Transferred to Camp Morton, Indianapolis, Indiana, where he arrived on July 14, 1864. Released at Camp Morton on May 18, 1865, after taking the Oath of Allegiance.

BOLICK, JOSEPH B., Private

Previously served as Private in Company A of this regiment. Transferred to this company on or about July 29, 1862. Reported present in January-June, 1863. Furloughed on September 10, 1863. Reported absent without leave from October 10, 1863, through August 31, 1864. No further records. Survived the war.

BUCHANAN, ABRAM J., Private

Previously served as Private in Company E of this regiment. Transferred to this company on or about July 29, 1862. Transferred to Company B of this regiment prior to March 1, 1863.

BUCHANAN, ELI, Private

Previously served as Private in Company E of this regiment. Transferred to this company on or about July 29, 1862. Furloughed for twenty days on December 19, 1862. Returned to duty on March 1, 1863. Reported present in March-June, 1863. Deserted on October 2, 1863, but was brought back under arrest on October 7, 1863. Died in hospital at Atlanta, Georgia, on or about January 1, 1864, of disease.

BUCHANAN, EPHRAIM, Private

Previously served as Private in Company E of this regiment. Transferred to this company on or about July 29, 1862. Reported present in January-June and September-October, 1863. Reported absent on detached service from November 21, 1863, through February 29, 1864. Reported present in March-August, 1864. No further records. Survived the war. [North Carolina pension records indicate that he was struck by lightning in Tennessee in August, 1864.]

BUCHANAN, JAMES S., Private

Previously served as Private in Company E of this regiment. Transferred to this company on or about July 29, 1862. Furloughed for twenty days on December 19, 1862. Returned from furlough on March 1, 1863. Reported present in March-June, 1863. Deserted near Tanner's Station, Tennessee, September 7, 1863.

BUCHANAN, JOEL, Private

Previously served as Private in Company E of this regiment. Transferred to this company on or about July 29, 1862. Reported present in January-June, 1863. Deserted from camp near Chattanooga, Tennessee, October 2, 1863. Arrested and brought back on October 7, 1863. Died in hospital at Atlanta, Georgia, October 15 or November 6, 1863. Cause of death not reported.

BUCHANAN, JOHN B., Private

Previously served as Private in Company E of this regiment. Transferred to this company on or about July 29, 1862. Reported present in January-June, 1863. Wounded at Chickamauga, Georgia, September 20, 1863. Deserted on October 2, 1863. Brought back under arrest on October 7, 1863. Sent to hospital sick from camp near Chattanooga, Tennessee, October 30, 1863. Died on an unspecified date (probably prior to March 1, 1864). Place and cause of death not reported.

BUCHANAN, JOSEPH M., Private

Previously served as Private in Company E of this regiment. Transferred to this company on or about July 29, 1862. Reported present in January-June, 1863. Wounded at Chickamauga, Georgia, September 20, 1863. Reported sick in hospital through October 31, 1863. Returned to duty on an unspecified date. Reported present in January-August, 1864. No further records.

BUCHANAN, MERRITT, Private

Previously served as Private in Company E of this regiment. Transferred to this company on or about July 29, 1862. Reported present in January-June, 1863. Deserted on October 2, 1863. Brought back under arrest on October 7, 1863. Reported in confinement through October 31, 1863. Returned to duty on an unspecified date. Reported present in January-August, 1864. No further records. Survived the war.

BUCHANAN, MOLTON, Private

Previously served as Private in Company E of this regiment. Transferred to this company on or about July 29, 1862. Mustered in as Musician (Drummer). Deserted at Big Creek Gap, Tennessee, January 11, 1863. Arrested on March 1, 1863. Reduced to ranks in March-April, 1863. Returned to duty on or about April 14, 1863. Deserted near Tanner's Station, Tennessee, September 7, 1863. Returned from desertion on March 17, 1864, and was placed under arrest. Court-martialed on an unspecified date. Returned to duty on an unspecified date. Reported present in May-August, 1864. No further records.

BUCHANAN, REUBEN, ———

North Carolina pension records indicate that he served in this company.

BUCHANAN, ROBERT, Private

Previously served as Private in Company E of this regiment. Transferred to this company on or about July 29, 1862. Furloughed for twenty days on December 15, 1862. Returned to duty on March 25, 1863. Deserted at Clinton, Tennessee, May 7, 1863.

BUCHANAN, WAIGHTSVILLE, Private

Previously served as Private in Company E of this regiment. Transferred to this company prior to January 11, 1863, when he deserted at Big Creek Gap, Tennessee. Died on March 1, 1863. Place and cause of death not reported.

BUCHANAN, WILLIAM M., Private

Previously served as Private in Company E of this regiment. Transferred to this company on or about July 29, 1862. Reported present in January-June, 1863. Wounded at Chickamauga, Georgia, September 20, 1863. Returned to duty prior to October 31, 1863. Wounded in the left hand at Rocky Face Ridge, Georgia, February 25, 1864. Hospitalized at Madison, Georgia. Furloughed for sixty days on March 8, 1864. Reported absent without leave on July 1, 1864. No further records. Survived the war.

BUCHANAN, WILLIAM W., Private

Enlisted in Mitchell County on May 19, 1862, for the war. Deserted at Big Creek Gap, Tennessee, January 11, 1863. [May have served later in the 13th Regiment Tennessee Cavalry (Union).]

BUCHANAN, WILLIAM W., Private

Previously served as Private in Company E of this regiment. Transferred to this company prior to August 6, 1862, when he deserted at Camp Stokes, Tennessee. [May have served later in the 13th Regiment Tennessee Cavalry (Union).]

BURCHFIELD, JOHN, Private

Enlisted at Clinton, Tennessee, April 20, 1863, for the war. Reported present in March-April, 1863. Deserted at Loudon, Tennessee, July 3, 1863. [May have served later as Private in Company B, 13th Regiment Tennessee Cavalry (Union).]

BURLESON, AARON, ———

North Carolina pension records indicate that he served in this company.

BURLESON, JASON C., Private

Previously served as Private in Company E of this regiment. Transferred to this company on or about July 29, 1862. Died at Jacksboro, Tennessee, February 5, 1863. Cause of death not reported.

BURLESON, MERIDA, Private

Born in Yancey County and was by occupation a farmer prior to enlisting in Mitchell County at age 28, July 11, 1862, for the war. Reported present in January-April, 1863. Deserted at Clinton, Tennessee, May 7, 1863. Returned to duty on an unspecified date. Reported present in September-October, 1863, and January-August, 1864. No further records.

BYRD, CHARLES, ———

North Carolina pension records indicate that he served in this company.

CLARK, DEASTON C., Private

Previously served as Private in Company E of this regiment. Transferred to this company on or about July 29, 1862. Reported present in January-February, 1863. Deserted at Clinton, Tennessee, April 3, 1863. Apprehended on April 11, 1863, and placed in confinement. Returned to duty on May 5, 1863. Wounded at Chickamauga,

Georgia, September 19-20, 1863. Died at "Preston Hospital" on September 23, 1863, of wounds.

CLARK, DORAN F., Private

Previously served as Private in Company E of this regiment. Transferred to this company on or about July 29, 1862. Reported present in January-February, 1863. Promoted to Corporal prior to March 1, 1863. Deserted at Clinton, Tennessee, April 3, 1863. Apprehended on April 16, 1863, and placed in confinement. Returned to duty on May 5, 1863. Reduced to ranks in May-June, 1863. Reported absent sick in September-October, 1863. Deserted near Missionary Ridge, Tennessee, September 28, 1863.

CLOER, CANEY W., Private

Born in Iredell County and was by occupation a farmer prior to enlisting in Caldwell County at age 24, July 21, 1862, for the war. No further records. Survived the war.

COFFEE, THOMAS, Private

Born in Caldwell County* and was by occupation a farmer prior to enlisting in Caldwell County at age 27, July 21, 1862, for the war. No further records. [May have served later as Private in Company B, 4th Regiment Tennessee Cavalry (Union).]

COX, JOHN, Private

Born in Yancey County and was by occupation a farmer prior to enlisting in Mitchell County at age 19, June 10, 1862, for the war. Reported present in January-June and September-October, 1863. Wounded in the left leg and captured at Missionary Ridge, Tennessee, November 25, 1863. Sent to Chattanooga, Tennessee, where his leg was amputated on November 28, 1863. Exchanged on an unspecified date. Hospitalized at Dalton, Georgia, on or about February 14, 1864. Reported in hospital at Atlanta, Georgia, in March-April, 1864. Retired to the Invalid Corps on April 30, 1864.

COX, WILLIAM R., Private

Previously served as Private in Company D of this regiment. Transferred to this company prior to March 1, 1863. Reported present in January-June, 1863. Transferred to Company G of this regiment prior to September 17, 1863.

DAVIS, JOSIAH, Private

Previously served as Private in Company E of this regiment. Transferred to this company on or about July 29, 1862. Discharged on October 16, 1862. Reason discharged not reported. [May have served later as Private in Company E, 3rd Regiment N.C. Mounted Infantry (Union).]

DEAN, GEORGE WASHINGTON, Private

Born in Yancey County and was by occupation a farmer prior to enlisting in Mitchell County at age 27, June 10, 1862, for the war. Mustered in as Private. Promoted to Corporal on an unspecified date. Furloughed for twenty days at Big Creek Gap, Tennessee, December 19, 1862. Returned to duty on March 4, 1863. Reduced to ranks on an unspecified date. Transferred to Company B, 5th Battalion N.C. Cavalry, June 11, 1863.

DEAN, NOAH, Private

Resided in Yancey County and was by occupation a farmer. Place and date of enlistment not reported (probably enlisted in the autumn of 1862). Furloughed sick for thirty days at Cumberland Gap,

Tennessee, October 16, 1862. Failed to return to duty and was listed as a deserter in May-June, 1863. [Was about 28 years of age at time of enlistment.]

DENNEY, SAMUEL, Private

Previously served as Private in Company E of this regiment. Transferred to this company on or about July 29, 1862. No further records. [Was reportedly issued clothing as a member of Company A of this regiment on May 13 and June 8, 1864; however, those reports appear to be erroneous.]

DEYTON, CHARLES P., ——

North Carolina pension records indicate that he served in this company.

DUNCAN, PHILIP H., Private

Previously served as Private in Company E of this regiment. Transferred to this company on or about July 29, 1862. Reported present in January-June, 1863. Wounded at Chickamauga, Georgia, September 19-20, 1863. Died in hospital at Dalton, Georgia, or at Ringgold, Georgia, October 10, 1863, of wounds. Nominated for the Badge of Distinction for gallantry at Chickamauga. [May have been promoted to Sergeant shortly before his death.]

ENGLISH, ADEN, Private

Previously served as Private in Company A of this regiment. Transferred to this company on or about July 29, 1862. Promoted to Corporal prior to December 19, 1862, when he was furloughed for twenty days from Big Creek Gap, Tennessee. Failed to return from furlough and was reduced to ranks prior to March 1, 1863. Returned to duty on April 18, 1863. Reported present in May-June, 1863. Reported absent sick in September-October, 1863. Returned to duty on an unspecified date. Reported present in January-August, 1864. Detailed for duty as a teamster on November 19, 1864, by reason of unfitness for field service. Transferred to Company F of this regiment on an unspecified date.

FOX, ALEXANDER, Private

Born in Caldwell County and was by occupation a farmer prior to enlisting in Caldwell or Mitchell County at age 15, July 20, 1862, for the war. Furloughed sick for thirty days at Cumberland Gap, Tennessee, October 16, 1862. Died at home on May 11, 1863. Cause of death not reported.

FOX, HENRY, Private

Born in Caldwell County and was by occupation a farmer prior to enlisting in Caldwell County at age 14, July 29, 1862, for the war. No further records. [May have served later as Private in Company F, 22nd Regiment N.C. Troops (12th Regiment N.C. Volunteers).]

FOX, NOAH, Private

Born in Caldwell County where he resided as a farmer prior to enlisting in Caldwell County at age 21, July 21, 1862, for the war. No further records. Survived the war. [May have served later as Private in Company F, 22nd Regiment N.C. Troops (12th Regiment N.C. Volunteers).]

FREEMAN, JOHN, Private

Born in Burke County and was by occupation a farmer prior to enlisting in Mitchell County at age 37, May 19, 1862, for the war. Deserted at Jacksboro, Tennessee, January 26, 1863. Arrested on an unspecified date. Released from prison on April 20, 1863.

Returned to duty in May-June, 1863. Deserted at Bell's Bridge, Tennessee, July 22, 1863. [May have served previously in Company B of this regiment.]

FREEMAN, LITTLETON, Private

Previously served as Private in Company E of this regiment. Transferred to this company on or about July 29, 1862. Deserted at Jacksboro, Tennessee, January 26, 1863. Arrested on an unspecified date. Released from prison on April 14, 1863. Returned to duty on an unspecified date. Deserted at Clinton, Tennessee, May 27, 1863.

FREEMAN, SAMUEL, Private

Previously served as Private in Company E of this regiment. Transferred to this company on or about July 29, 1862. Deserted at Big Creek Gap, Tennessee, January 11, 1863. Arrested on February 20, 1863, and placed in confinement. Returned to duty prior to May 1, 1863. Reported present in May-June, 1863. Deserted at Bell's Bridge, Tennessee, July 22, 1863. [His Tennessee pension application indicates that he ruptured himself and also injured his right hip while working on fortifications at "Deep (Big?) Creek Gap," Tennessee, presumably in the winter of 1862-1863.]

GARDNER, GEORGE, ———

North Carolina pension records indicate that he served in this company.

GOUGE, GARRETT D., Private

Resided in Mitchell County where he enlisted at age 36, December 23, 1862, for the war. Reported present in March-June, 1863. Reported absent sick in September-October, 1863. Furloughed for forty days on December 15, 1863, suffering from chronic diarrhoea, great emaciation, and debility of three months' standing. Failed to return from furlough and was reported absent without leave in January-February, 1864. Returned to duty on April 15, 1864. Reported present in May-August, 1864. No further records. Survived the war.

GOUGE, WILLIAM, Private

Previously served as Private in Company E of this regiment. Transferred to this company on or about July 29, 1862. Reported present in January-February, 1863. Reported present (name "canceled") in March-April, 1863. No further records.

GREEN, JAMES M., 1st Sergeant

Previously served as Private in Company B, 5th Battalion N.C. Cavalry. Transferred to this company on or about July 29, 1862. Mustered in as Sergeant. Reported present in January-June, 1863. Wounded in the head, hand, and shoulder at Chickamauga, Georgia, September 20, 1863. Returned to duty on March 28, 1864. Reported present in April, 1864. Promoted to 1st Sergeant on May 1, 1864. Wounded at Kolb's Farm, near Marietta, Georgia, June 22, 1864. Returned to duty prior to September 1, 1864. No further records. Survived the war.

GREEN, WILLIAM, Private

Born in Yancey County and was by occupation a farmer prior to enlisting in Mitchell County at age 25, July 15, 1862, for the war. No further records.

GRINDSTAFF, JOBE, Private

Previously served as Private in Company E of this regiment. Transferred to this company on or about July 29, 1862. Reported absent

on detached service from January 12 through February 29, 1863. Rejoined the company in March-April, 1863. Reported present on surviving company muster rolls from May-June, 1863, through April 30, 1864. Wounded at Kolb's Farm, near Marietta, Georgia, June 22, 1864. Returned to duty prior to September 1, 1864. No further records. Survived the war.

GRINDSTAFF, JOHN, Private

Previously served as Private in Company E of this regiment. Transferred to this company on or about July 29, 1862. Reported present in January-June, 1863. Deserted at Chickamauga, Georgia, September 19, 1863.

HALL, MARCUS, Private

Resided in Yancey or Mitchell County and enlisted in Mitchell County at age 18, February 4, 1864, for the war. Reported present through August 31, 1864. No further records.

HOPSON, JOHN, Private

Previously served as Private in Company B of this regiment. Transferred to this company prior to September 30, 1862, when he deserted at Camp Reynolds.

HOWELL, AARON, ———

North Carolina pension records indicate that he served in this company.

HUGHES, JEREMIAH, ———

North Carolina pension records indicate that he served in this company.

HUGHES, WILLIAM J., Private

Previously enlisted as Private in Company E of this regiment. Enlisted in this company in Mitchell County on November 19, 1863, for the war. Sent to hospital sick on February 15, 1864. Returned to duty prior to February 25, 1864, when he deserted at or near Rocky Face Ridge, Georgia. Went over to the enemy on an unspecified date. Confined at Louisville, Kentucky, November 22, 1864. Transferred to Camp Douglas, Chicago, Illinois, where he arrived on December 1, 1864. Released at Camp Douglas on or about April 1, 1865, after taking the Oath of Allegiance and joining the U.S. Army. Assigned to Company H, 6th Regiment U.S. Volunteer Infantry.

HUSKINS, JOHN S., ———

North Carolina pension records indicate that he served in this company.

HUSKINS, SAMUEL P., Sergeant

Previously served as Private in Company B, 5th Battalion N.C. Cavalry. Transferred to this company on May 1, 1863. Mustered in as Private. Reported present in May-June and September-October, 1863. Promoted to Corporal on October 2, 1863. Hospitalized at Griffin, Georgia, November 23, 1863, with an unspecified complaint. Returned to duty on an unspecified date. Reported present in January-April, 1864. Promoted to Sergeant prior to March 1, 1864. Sent to hospital sick on May 12, 1864. Reported absent sick through August 31, 1864. No further records. Survived the war. [North Carolina pension records indicate that he was wounded in the right arm at or near Atlanta, Georgia, on or about September 1 or October 1, 1864. Pension records indicate also that he received a severe wound in the back in a train collision on an unspecified date. He was guarding prisoners at the time.]

INGLE, J. J., Private

North Carolina pension records indicate that he served in this company.

JOHNSON, HENDERSON, ——

North Carolina pension records indicate that he served in this company. [See also the Tennessee pension application of Pvt. James Calhoun (Company L, 58th Regiment N.C. Troops) containing an affidavit signed by Henderson.]

JONES, L. B., ——

North Carolina pension records indicate that he served in this company.

JOPLING, GEORGE JOSHUA, Private

Born in Caldwell County* where he resided as a farmer prior to enlisting in Caldwell County at age 26, July 21, 1862, for the war. Was apparently discharged or rejected for service (probably in the autumn of 1862). Later served as Private in Company E of this regiment.

JUSTICE, HENRY, Private

Previously served as Private in Company E of this regiment. Transferred to this company on or about July 29, 1862. Reported present on surviving company muster rolls through April 30, 1864. Wounded in the breast at Resaca, Georgia, May 14-15, 1864. Company records indicate that he was also captured at Resaca, May 15, 1864; however, records of the Federal Provost Marshal do not substantiate that report. No further records.

JUSTICE, WILLIAM, Private

Previously served as Private in Company E of this regiment. Transferred to this company on or about July 29, 1862. Reported present on surviving company muster rolls through August 31, 1864. No further records.

LAWS, MESHACK F., ——

North Carolina pension records indicate that he served in this company.

LEDFORD, CURTIS, Private

Resided in Mitchell or Yancey County and was by occupation a farmer prior to enlisting in Mitchell County at age 34, November 19, 1863, for the war. Reported present in January-April, 1864. Wounded at Kolb's Farm, near Marietta, Georgia, June 22, 1864. Reported absent on furlough through August 31, 1864. No further records. Survived the war. [May have served previously as Private in Company I, 29th Regiment N.C. Troops.]

LEDFORD, JAMES H., Private

Born in Yancey County and was by occupation a farmer prior to enlisting in Mitchell County at age 19, June 10, 1862, for the war. Reported present in January-June, 1863. Reported absent on sick furlough in September-October, 1863. Returned to duty on an unspecified date. Reported present in January-April, 1864. Captured at Cassville, Georgia, May 20, 1864. Sent to Nashville, Tennessee. Transferred to Louisville, Kentucky, where he arrived on May 29,

1864. Transferred to Rock Island, Illinois, where he arrived on June 1, 1864. Released at Rock Island on June 10, 1864, after taking the Oath of Allegiance and joining the U.S. Navy.

LEDFORD, JASPER, Private

Previously served as Private in Company E of this regiment. Transferred to this company on or about July 29, 1862. Reported present in January-June, 1863. Deserted from camp near Chattanooga, Tennessee, October 2, 1863. Brought back under arrest on October 7, 1863. Reported in confinement through October 31, 1863. Returned to duty on an unspecified date. Reported present in January-August, 1864. No further records.

LETTERMAN, M. P., ——

North Carolina pension records indicate that he served in this company.

LIVINGSTON, THOMAS, Private

Born in Caldwell County where he resided as a farmer prior to enlisting in Caldwell County at age 19, July 21, 1862, for the war. No further records. Survived the war.

McCURRY, ZEPHANIAH, Private

Born in Yancey County and was by occupation a farmer prior to enlisting in Mitchell County on June 10, 1862, for the war. Reported present in January-April, 1863. Transferred to Company G of this regiment in May-June, 1863.

McFALLS, ARTHUR, Private

Previously served as Private in Company A of this regiment. Transferred to this company on or about July 29, 1862. Reported present in January-February, 1863. Deserted at Jacksboro, Tennessee, on an unspecified date. Reported in confinement in March-June, 1863. Transferred back to Company A of this regiment prior to September 20, 1863.

McFALLS, GEORGE W., Private

Previously served as Private in Company A of this regiment. Transferred to this company on or about July 29, 1862. Furloughed for twenty days on December 19, 1862. Returned to duty on April 9, 1863. Reported present in May-June, 1863. Furloughed home sick for thirty days on September 25, 1863. Reported absent without leave in January-February, 1864. Returned from desertion on March 8, 1864. Court-martialed on April 4, 1864, and sentenced to be shot. Executed at Dalton, Georgia, May 4, 1864.

McGEE, JOHN S., Private

Previously served as Private in Company A of this regiment. Transferred to this company on or about July 29, 1862. Transferred to Company E, 6th Regiment N.C. State Troops, February 16 or March 31, 1863.

McGEE, ROBERT S., Private

Previously served as Private in Company A of this regiment. Transferred to this company on or about July 29, 1862. Transferred to Company E, 6th Regiment N.C. State Troops, February 16 or March 31, 1863.

McKINEY, HENRY, Private

Resided in McDowell County and was by occupation a laborer prior to enlisting in Mitchell County at age 34, May 1, 1864, for the war. Reported present through August 31, 1864. No further records.

McKINNEY, JAMES, Private

Born in Yancey County and was by occupation a farmer prior to enlisting in Mitchell County at age 29, June 10, 1862, for the war. Reported present in January-June, 1863. Deserted from camp near Chattanooga, Tennessee, on or about October 2, 1863. Returned to duty on or about January 22, 1864. Reported present in March-August, 1864. Wounded in the head at Bentonville on March 19, 1865. No further records. Survived the war. [Age discrepancies notwithstanding, it appears likely that this is the same soldier who served previously as Private in Company A of this regiment.]

McKINNEY, JOHN P., Private

Previously served as Private in Company E of this regiment. Transferred to this company on or about July 29, 1862. Reported present in January-June, 1863. Deserted from camp near Chattanooga, Tennessee, October 2, 1863. Brought back under arrest on or about October 7, 1863. Reported in confinement through October 31, 1863. Returned to duty on an unspecified date. Reported present in January-April, 1864. Reported absent sick on August 26, 1864. No further records.

McKINNEY, JOHNSON S., Sergeant

Previously served as Private in Company E of this regiment. Transferred to this company on or about July 29, 1862. Mustered in as Sergeant. Reported present in January-June, 1863. Reported on duty as a provost guard in September-October, 1863. Reported present in January-April, 1864. Reported absent sick from July 1 through August 31, 1864. No further records. Survived the war. [North Carolina pension records indicate that he was ruptured on a march from Jacksboro, Tennessee, to Clinton, Tennessee, in 1863.]

McKINNEY, REUBEN B., Private

Born in Yancey County on June 23, 1842. Was by occupation a farmer prior to enlisting in Mitchell County at age 22, May 19, 1862, for the war. Mustered in as Private. Reported present in January-April, 1863. Appointed Musician (Drummer) in March-April, 1863. Deserted at Clinton, Tennessee, June 7, 1863. Returned to duty on an unspecified date. Reduced to ranks in July-October, 1863. Deserted from camp near Chattanooga, Tennessee, October 2, 1863. Brought back under arrest on October 7, 1863. Reported in confinement through October 31, 1863. Returned to duty on an unspecified date. Sent to hospital sick on January 15, 1864. Furloughed for forty days from hospital at Marietta, Georgia, February 23, 1864. Reported absent on sick furlough through August 31, 1864. No further records. Survived the war.

MORGAN, NATHAN, Private

Born in Moore County and was by occupation a miller prior to enlisting in Caldwell County at age 24, July 21, 1862, for the war. No further records.

MURPHY, JOHN, ———

North Carolina pension records indicate that he served in this company.

MURPHY, WESLEY, ———

North Carolina pension records indicate that he served in this company.

PHILLIPS, R. B., ———

North Carolina pension records indicate that he served in this company.

PORCHEE, JOHN, ———

North Carolina pension records indicate that he served in this company. [Possibly the same man as Pvt. John Portia of Company A.]

PRESSNELL, THOMAS S., Private

Born in Alexander County* and was by occupation a farmer prior to enlisting in Caldwell County at age 19, July 21, 1862, for the war. No further records.

RANDOLPH, REUBEN, Private

Resided in Yancey County and was by occupation a farmer prior to enlisting in Mitchell County at age 27, July 24, 1862, for the war. Reported present in January-June, 1863. Deserted at Tanner's Station, Tennessee, September 7, 1863. [May have served later as Sergeant in Company C, 13th Regiment Tennessee Cavalry (Union).]

ROBERSON, THOMAS, Private

Enlisted in Mitchell County on February 4, 1864, for the war. Sent to hospital on an unspecified date. Returned to duty on April 26, 1864. Sent to hospital sick on August 5, 1864. Reported absent sick through August 31, 1864. No further records. Survived the war. [Was about 18 years of age at time of enlistment.]

ROBERTS, JAMES, Private

Previously served as Private in Company B, 5th Battalion N.C. Cavalry. Transferred to this company on June 11, 1863. Reported present in September-October, 1863. Captured at Missionary Ridge, Tennessee, November 25, 1863. Sent to Nashville, Tennessee. Transferred to Louisville, Kentucky, where he arrived on December 7, 1863. Transferred to Rock Island, Illinois, where he arrived on December 9, 1863. Volunteered for service in the U.S. Army on October 18, 1864, but was apparently rejected. Released at Rock Island on June 22, 1865, after taking the Oath of Allegiance.

ROBERTSON, E. M., ———

North Carolina pension records indicate that he served in this company.

ROBERTSON, M. B., ———

North Carolina pension records indicate that he served in this company.

ROBINSON, NED, ———

North Carolina pension records indicate that he served in this company.

ROBINSON, THOMAS B., ———

North Carolina pension records indicate that he served in this company.

ROSE, SAMUEL, Private

Previously served as Private in Company A of this regiment. Transferred to this company on or about July 29, 1862. Transferred back to Company A prior to March 1, 1863.

ROWE, CONRADRADO, Private

Born in Burke County and resided in Caldwell County where he was by occupation a farmer prior to enlisting in Caldwell County at age 42, July 21, 1862, for the war. Discharged on October 16, 1862. Reason discharged not reported.

SELLERS, J. PINK, ——

North Carolina pension records indicate that he served in this company.

SHERRELL, JAMES M., Private

Born in Caldwell County* and was by occupation a farmer prior to enlisting in Caldwell County at age 26, July 21, 1862, for the war. No further records. Survived the war.

SILVER, ALEXANDER, Private

Enlisted in Mitchell County at age 18, April 17, 1864, for the war. Wounded in the right thigh at Resaca, Georgia, May 14-15, 1864. Returned to duty prior to September 1, 1864. Captured in hospital at Greensboro on or about April 29, 1865. Paroled at Greensboro on May 1, 1865.

SILVER, EDMUND D., 1st Sergeant

Previously served as Private in Company E of this regiment. Transferred to this company on or about July 29, 1862. Mustered in as 1st Sergeant. Reported present in January-June and September-October, 1863. Sent to hospital at Madison, Georgia, February 23, 1864. Furloughed for thirty days on March 28, 1864. Failed to return to duty and was listed as a deserter on May 8, 1864. Went over to the enemy on an unspecified date. Took the Oath of Allegiance at Knoxville, Tennessee, December 15, 1864. [Reported in command of the company in May-June, 1863. North Carolina pension records indicate that he was wounded in the left thigh at "Chickamauga, Georgia, November 22, 1863."]

SILVER, TILMAN BLALOCK, Corporal

Previously served as Private in Company A of this regiment. Transferred to this company on March 1, 1863. Mustered in as Private. Reported present in March-June and September-October, 1863. Promoted to Corporal in July-October, 1863. Reported present in January-February, 1864. Furloughed for forty days on April 24, 1864. Returned to duty on June 3, 1864. Reported present through August 31, 1864. Transferred to Company F of this regiment subsequent to August 31, 1864.

SMITH, ANDREW J., Private

Previously served as Private in Company G of this regiment. Transferred to this company in May-June, 1863. Died at Clinton, Tennessee, June 15, 1863. Cause of death not reported.

SPARKS, J. C., ——

North Carolina pension records indicate that he served in this company.

SPARKS, JEREMIAH P., Corporal

Previously served as Private in Company A of this regiment. Transferred to this company on or about July 29, 1862. Mustered in as Corporal. Died on an unspecified date (probably in the autumn of 1862). Place and cause of death not reported.

SPARKS, JOSEPH M., Corporal

Previously served as Private in Company A of this regiment. Transferred to this company on or about July 29, 1862. Mustered in as Corporal. Reported present in January-June and September-October, 1863. Reduced to ranks in July-October, 1863. Reported present in January-August, 1864. Promoted to Corporal on June 1, 1864. No further records.

STEWART, WILLIAM, Private

The service record of this soldier is unclear. It appears that he served in Company D of this regiment in September-October, 1863. He also served at various times in this company and in Companies C and E of this regiment.

STUART, WILLIAM H., Private

Previously served as Private in Company E of this regiment. Transferred to this company on or about July 29, 1862. Reported present in January-February, 1863. Reported present but on detail as a wagoner in March-June, 1863. Reported on detail as a wagoner at Clinton, Tennessee, in September-October, 1863. Reported present in January-April, 1864. Wounded at Kolb's Farm, near Marietta, Georgia, June 22, 1864. Hospitalized at Greensboro, Georgia, where he died on August 5, 1864, of wounds.

THOMAS, ABIJAH, Private

Previously served as Private in Company A of this regiment. Transferred to this company in July-October, 1863. Reported present in September-October, 1863, and January-August, 1864. Last reported in the records of this company on November 10, 1864. Survived the war.

THOMAS, JAMES H., Private

Previously served as Private in Company I, 29th Regiment N.C. Troops. Was reportedly transferred to this company on August 27, 1864. No further records. Survived the war.

THOMAS, S. F., ——

North Carolina pension records indicate that he served in this company.

THOMAS, THOMAS, Musician

Previously served as Private in Company A of this regiment. Transferred to this company on or about July 29, 1862. Mustered in as Musician (Fifer). Furloughed for twenty days on February 17, 1863. Returned to duty in March-April, 1863. Reported present on surviving company muster rolls from May 1, 1863, through April 30, 1864. Reported absent sick on August 26, 1864. No further records. Survived the war.

THOMASON, PLEASANT A., Private

Previously served as Private in Company A of this regiment. Transferred to this company on or about July 29, 1862. Reported present in January-June and September-October, 1863. Detailed for duty as a hospital orderly on December 1, 1863. Rejoined the company subsequent to April 30, 1864. Sent to hospital sick on August 11, 1864. No further records.

THOMASON, WILLIAM J., Private

Previously served as Private in Company E of this regiment. Transferred to this company on or about July 29, 1862. Mustered in as

Private. Reported present in January-June, 1863. Promoted to Corporal in March-April, 1863. Reduced to ranks on July 17, 1863. Reported present in September-October, 1863. Appointed Hospital Steward on December 1, 1863, and transferred to the Field and Staff of this regiment. Reduced to ranks on July 25, 1864, and transferred back to this company. Transferred to Company F of this regiment subsequent to August 31, 1864.

TRIPLETT, THOMAS H., Private

Resided in Watauga County and enlisted in Watauga or Caldwell County on July 26, 1862, for the war. Transferred to Company M of this regiment on or about September 26, 1862.

WALKER, JOSEPH, Private

Previously served as Private in Company A of this regiment. Transferred to this company on or about July 29, 1862. Mustered in as Sergeant. Furloughed for twenty days on November 19, 1862. Failed to return to duty and was listed as a deserter on December 11, 1862. Reduced to ranks prior to March 1, 1863. Dropped from the company rolls subsequent to June 30, 1863.

WALLACE, C. R., ———

North Carolina pension records indicate that he served in this company.

WATTS, THOMAS G., Corporal

Resided in Wilkes County and enlisted in Caldwell County on July 24, 1862, for the war. Mustered in as Private. Reported present on surviving company muster rolls from January 1, 1863, through April 30, 1864. Promoted to Corporal in November, 1863-February, 1864. Reported absent sick on June 25, 1864. Hospitalized at Macon, Georgia, July 7, 1864, with chronic diarrhoea. Transferred on July 22, 1864. Reported absent sick through August 31, 1864. No further records.

WEST, ALEXANDER STEVEN COMMODORE DECATUR, Private

Previously served as Private in Company E of this regiment. Transferred to this company on or about July 29, 1862. Transferred back to Company E prior to February 7, 1863.

WHEELING, CARSON E. C., ———

North Carolina pension records indicate that he served in this company.

WILLIS, BENJAMIN, Private

Previously served as Private in Company E of this regiment. Transferred to this company on or about July 29, 1862. Reported present in January-June, 1863. Killed at Chickamauga, Georgia, September 20, 1863.

WILSON, BARTLETT, Sergeant

Previously served as Corporal in Company E of this regiment. Transferred to this company on or about July 29, 1862. Mustered in as Sergeant. Died on an unspecified date (probably in the autumn of 1862). Place and cause of death not reported.

WILSON, P. A., ———

North Carolina pension records indicate that he served in this company.

WILSON, SIDNEY L., Private

Previously served as Private in Company E of this regiment. Transferred to this company on or about July 29, 1862. Transferred to Company F of this regiment prior to November 13, 1862.

WILSON, WILLIAM J., Private

Enlisted in Mitchell County on June 25, 1862, for the war. Was apparently mustered in with the rank of Corporal. Reported present on surviving company muster rolls from January 1, 1863, through February 29, 1864. Furloughed home for twenty-two days on April 13, 1864. Failed to return to duty and was listed as a deserter on May 15, 1864. Reduced to ranks prior to August 31, 1864. [Was about 30 years of age at time of enlistment. North Carolina pension records indicate that he was wounded at Chickamauga, Georgia, September 18-20, 1863.]

WINTERS, STEPHEN M., Private

Previously served as Private in Company E of this regiment. Transferred to this company on or about July 29, 1862. Deserted at Camp Stokes, Tennessee, August 6, 1862.

YOUNG, MERRITT, Private

Previously served as Private in Company B of this regiment. Transferred to this company on or about July 29, 1862. Transferred back to Company B prior to March 1, 1863.

YOUNG, MOSES, Corporal

Previously served as Private in Company E of this regiment. Transferred to this company on or about July 29, 1862. Reported present in January-June, 1863. Promoted to Corporal in May-June, 1863. Reported sick in hospital in September-October, 1863. Furloughed home for forty days on an unspecified date. Reported absent on expired furlough on February 29, 1864. Returned to duty on April 15, 1864. Reported present until August 27, 1864, when he was transferred to Company I, 29th Regiment N.C. Troops. [Service record omitted in volume 8 of this series.]

COMPANY L

This company was raised in Ashe County and was mustered into service at Jefferson on July 20, 1862, as Capt. William H. Gentry's Company, N.C. Volunteers. It was assigned to the 58th Regiment N.C. Troops as Company L when the regiment was organized on July 29, 1862. After joining the regiment the company functioned as a part of the regiment, and its history for the remainder of the war is reported as a part of the regimental history.

The following roster was compiled primarily from information in the microfilm edition of the Compiled Service Records of Soldiers Who Served in Organizations from the State of North Carolina (Record Group 109, M270), National Archives and Records Administration, Washington, D.C. Record Group 109 includes enlistment papers, pay vouchers, requisitions, letters of resignation, discharge certificates, and abstracts of medical and prisoner of war returns. Materials relating specifically to this company include muster rolls dated January-June, 1863; September-October, 1863; and January-August, 1864.

Also utilized in this roster were *The War of the Rebellion: A Compilation of the Official Records of the Union and Confederate Armies,* the North Carolina adjutant general's *Roll of Honor*, state militia records, newspaper casualty lists and obituaries, wartime claims for bounty pay and allowances, postwar registers of claims for artificial limbs, Confederate pension applications filed with the states of North Carolina, Tennessee, and Florida, Confederate Soldiers' Home records, and the 1860 and 1870 federal censuses of North Carolina. A search was made also for relevant letters, diaries, reminiscences, and other manuscripts in the Southern Historical Collection (University of North Carolina-Chapel Hill), the Duke University Library Special Collections Department, and the North Carolina Division of Archives and History.

Among the secondary sources consulted were records of the North Carolina division of the United Daughters of the Confederacy, postwar rosters, regimental and county histories, marriage bond, will, and cemetery indexes, published and unpublished genealogies, biographical dictionaries, the North Carolina *County Heritage Book* series, the *Confederate Veteran*, Walter Clark's *Histories of the Several Regiments and Battalions from North Carolina in the Great War, 1861-'65*, and the North Carolina volume of the extended edition of *Confederate Military History*.

OFFICERS

CAPTAINS

GENTRY, WILLIAM H.

Resided in Ashe County and was by occupation a farmer prior to enlisting in Ashe County at age 34. Elected Captain on July 20, 1862. Reported absent sick in January-May, 1863. Resigned on June 1, 1863, by reason of "pulmonary disease." Resignation accepted the same date.

ELLER, CALVIN

Resided in Ashe County and was by occupation a farmer prior to enlisting in Ashe County at age 32. Elected 1st Lieutenant on July 20, 1862. Reported absent on detached service in January-February, 1863. Reported present and in command of the company in March-April, 1863. Promoted to Captain on June 1, 1863. Reported present on surviving company muster rolls through April 30, 1864. Resigned on or about September 12, 1864, by reason of insufficient education to perform the duties of his position. Resignation accepted on October 12, 1864.

LIEUTENANTS

BLEVINS, EDWARD, 3rd Lieutenant

Resided in Ashe County and was by occupation a farmer prior to enlisting in Ashe County at age 43. Appointed 3rd Lieutenant on July 20, 1862. Resigned on January 5, 1863, under charges of "conduct unbecoming an officer and a gentleman." Reenlisted in the company with the rank of Private on April 27, 1863. [See Noncommissioned Officers and Privates' section below.]

BLEVINS, POINDEXTER, 1st Lieutenant

Resided in Ashe County where he enlisted at age 25. Appointed 2nd Lieutenant on July 20, 1862. Reported present and in command

of the company in January-February, 1863. Reported present in March-June, 1863. Promoted to 1st Lieutenant on June 1, 1863. Reported absent sick in September-October, 1863. Returned to duty on an unspecified date. Reported present in January-August, 1864. Promoted to Captain of Company F of this regiment subsequent to August 31, 1864.

HURLEY, ELISHA, 3rd Lieutenant

Resided in Ashe County and was by occupation a farmer prior to enlisting in Ashe County at age 18, July 20, 1862, for the war. Was apparently mustered in with the rank of 1st Sergeant. Reported present in January-April, 1863. Reported absent on detached service in North Carolina in May-June, 1863. Elected 3rd Lieutenant on July 11, 1863. Reported present in September-October, 1863, and January-August, 1864. Submitted his resignation on August 10, 1864; however, it is not reported whether his resignation was accepted. No further records. Survived the war. [North Carolina pension records indicate that his hearing was injured at the Battle of Chickamauga, Georgia, September 19-20, 1863.]

HURLEY, LEANDER, 2nd Lieutenant

Resided in Ashe or Mitchell County and was by occupation a weaver prior to enlisting in Ashe County at age 24, July 20, 1862, for the war. Was apparently mustered in with the rank of 1st Sergeant. Elected 3rd Lieutenant on January 28, 1863. Reported present in March-June, 1863. Promoted to 2nd Lieutenant on June 1, 1863. Hospitalized at Atlanta, Georgia, on an unspecified date. Furloughed on September 27, 1863. Reported present in January-February, 1864. Furloughed for twenty-six days on April 11, 1864. Returned to duty on an unspecified date. Reported present in May-August, 1864. Promoted to 1st Lieutenant and transferred to Company F of this regiment subsequent to August 31, 1864.

NONCOMMISSIONED OFFICERS
AND PRIVATES

BARKER, CALVIN, Corporal

Resided in Ashe County and was by occupation a farmer prior to enlisting in Ashe County at age 21, July 20, 1862, for the war. Was apparently mustered in with the rank of Corporal. Reported present in January-February, 1863. Died at Clinton, Tennessee, April 11, 1863. Cause of death not reported.

BARKER, ELI C., Private

Enlisted in Ashe County at age 39, July 20, 1862, for the war. Reported absent on sick furlough on February 10, 1863. Returned to duty in March-April, 1863. Reported present in May-June, 1863. Wounded at Chickamauga, Georgia, September 20, 1863. Hospitalized at Macon, Georgia. Furloughed on September 29, 1863. Reported absent without leave in January-April, 1864. Returned to duty on an unspecified date. Wounded at Kolb's Farm, near Marietta, Georgia, June 22, 1864. Returned to duty prior to September 1, 1864. No further records. Survived the war.

BARKER, JAMES M., Private

Born in Ashe County where he resided as a farmer prior to enlisting in Ashe County at age 20, July 20, 1862, for the war. Furloughed on November 13, 1862. Reported absent on furlough through February 28, 1863. Discharged on April 6, 1863, by reason of "otorrhea arising from caries."

BARKER, MONTGOMERY, Private

Resided in Ashe County and was by occupation a farmer prior to enlisting in Ashe County at age 24, July 20, 1862, for the war. Reported present in January-June, 1863. Wounded in the left shoulder at Chickamauga, Georgia, September 20, 1863. Hospitalized at Macon, Georgia. Furloughed for thirty days on September 27, 1863. Failed to return from furlough and was reported absent without leave in January-August, 1864. No further records. Survived the war.

BARKER, THOMAS C., Private

Resided in Ashe County and was by occupation a farmer prior to enlisting in Ashe County at age 25, July 20, 1862, for the war. Reported present in January-April, 1863. Deserted from camp near Clinton, Tennessee, May 26, 1863. Returned to duty on an unspecified date. Wounded at Chickamauga, Georgia, September 20, 1863. Returned to duty prior to October 31, 1863. Reported present in January-April, 1864. Wounded at Kolb's Farm, near Marietta, Georgia, June 22, 1864. Returned to duty prior to September 1, 1864. Captured at Stockbridge, Georgia, September 3-5, 1864. Sent to Nashville, Tennessee. Transferred to Louisville, Kentucky, where he arrived on October 28, 1864. Transferred to Camp Douglas, Chicago, Illinois, where he arrived on November 1, 1864. Released at Camp Douglas on June 17, 1865, after taking the Oath of Allegiance.

BARKER, WILLIAM POINDEXTER, Private

Resided in Ashe County and was by occupation a farmer prior to enlisting in Ashe County at age 18, July 20, 1862, for the war. Reported present on surviving company muster rolls through April 30, 1864. Reported present but on duty as a provost guard in May-August, 1864. No further records. Survived the war.

BLACK, JESSE, Private

Enlisted at Camp Holmes, near Raleigh, November 12, 1863, for the war. Reported present in January-February, 1864. Reported sick in hospital at Dalton, Georgia, from March 10 through April 30,1864. Died in hospital at Charlotte on May 10, 1864, of "diarrhoea chronic."

BLEVINS, EDWARD, Sergeant

Previously served as 3rd Lieutenant of this company. [See Lieutenants' section above.] Resignation accepted on January 5, 1863. Reenlisted in the company with the rank of Private on April 27, 1863. Reported present in May-June, 1863. Promoted to Sergeant subsequent to June 30, 1863, but prior to September 20, 1863, when he was wounded at Chickamauga, Georgia. Hospitalized at Macon, Georgia. Furloughed for thirty days on September 27, 1863. Reported present but sick in January-February, 1864. Furloughed for forty days on April 13, 1864. Returned to duty on an unspecified date. Reported present but on detail as a litter bearer in May-August, 1864. No further records.

BLEVINS, GEORGE DOUGLAS, Private

Resided in Ashe County and enlisted at Saltville, Virginia, at age 19. Enlistment date reported as May 7, 1863; however, he was not listed in the records of this company until March-April, 1864. Reported sick in hospital at Dalton, Georgia, April 11, 1864. Hospitalized at Macon, Georgia, May 16, 1864, with rubeola. Wounded in the abdomen and captured at Kolb's Farm, near Marietta, Georgia, June 22, 1864. Sent to Nashville, Tennessee. Transferred to Louisville, Kentucky, where he arrived on July 13,

1864. Transferred to Camp Morton, Indianapolis, Indiana, where he arrived on July 14, 1864. Paroled at Camp Morton on or about March 10, 1865. Received at Boulware's Wharf, James River, Virginia, March 23, 1865, for exchange. Survived the war.

BLEVINS, GEORGE W., Private

Enlisted in Ashe County on July 20, 1862, for the war. Reported present in January-April, 1863. Deserted from camp near Clinton, Tennessee, May 26, 1863. Returned to duty subsequent to June 30, 1863. Deserted at Chattanooga, Tennessee, September 23, 1863. Returned from desertion on or about December 10, 1863, and was court-martialed. Returned to duty on February 13, 1864. Reported present in March-April, 1864. Reported present but on detail as a litter bearer in May-August, 1864. No further records.

BLEVINS, JOHN, Private

Enlisted in Ashe County at age 27, July 20, 1862, for the war. Reported present in January-June, 1863. Wounded at Chickamauga, Georgia, September 20, 1863. Returned to duty prior to October 31, 1863. Reported present but on extra duty as a wagoner from December 1, 1863, through April 30, 1864. Reported present in May-August, 1864. No further records. Survived the war.

BLEVINS, MORRIS, Private

Resided in Ashe County and was by occupation a farmer prior to enlisting at Dalton, Georgia, at age 39, February 1, 1864, for the war. Reported present in February-August, 1864. Deserted to the enemy on an unspecified date (probably in September, 1864). Sent to Atlanta, Georgia. Transferred to Louisville, Kentucky, where he arrived on October 11, 1864. Released at Louisville on or about October 14, 1864, after taking the Oath of Allegiance.

BLEVINS, WILLIAM HARRISON, Sergeant

Previously served as Private in Company A, 37th Regiment N.C. Troops. Transferred to this company on or about February 14, 1863. Was apparently mustered in with the rank of Corporal. Reported present through June 30, 1863. Promoted to Sergeant in May-June, 1863. Detailed on September 21, 1863, to "wait on wounded [at Chickamauga, Georgia]." Rejoined the company subsequent to October 31, 1863. Furloughed for forty days on February 2, 1864. Reported present in March-August, 1864. Captured at Resaca, Georgia, May 14, 1864. Sent to Nashville, Tennessee. Transferred to Louisville, Kentucky, where he arrived on May 18, 1864. Transferred to Camp Morton, Indianapolis, Indiana, where he arrived on May 22, 1864. Released at Camp Morton on May 18, 1865, after taking the Oath of Allegiance.

BROOKSHIRE, BENJAMIN F., Private

Resided in Wilkes County and enlisted at Tazewell, Tennessee, October 1, 1862, for the war. Furloughed on November 15, 1862. Reported absent on expired furlough in March-April, 1863. Returned to duty in May-June, 1863. Reported absent sick in September-October, 1863. Detailed for duty as a commissary guard on February 5, 1864. Rejoined the company in March-April, 1864. Deserted to the enemy near Atlanta, Georgia, July 29, 1864. Confined at Louisville, Kentucky. Released at Louisville on or about August 27, 1864, after taking the Oath of Allegiance.

BROWN, JOHN J., Private

Born in Ashe County where he resided as a farmer prior to enlisting at Camp Holmes, near Raleigh, at age 37, November 12, 1863, for the war. Reported present in January-February, 1864. Furloughed for forty days on April 29, 1864, by reason of disability from chronic diarrhoea. Reported absent on expired furlough in May-August, 1864. No further records. Survived the war.

BUMGARNER, GEORGE W., Private

Resided in Ashe County and was by occupation a farmer prior to enlisting in Ashe County at age 30, February 20, 1863, for the war. Reported present in March-April, 1863. Detailed to work in government shops at Knoxville, Tennessee, in May-June, 1863. Deserted at Knoxville on July 20, 1863. Reported present but under arrest on February 2, 1864. Returned to duty on an unspecified date. Deserted to the enemy near Cassville, Georgia, on or about May 20, 1864. Sent to Nashville, Tennessee. Transferred to Louisville, Kentucky, where he arrived on May 29, 1864. Transferred to Rock Island, Illinois, where he arrived on June 2, 1864. Released at Rock Island on June 10, 1864, after joining the U.S. Navy.

CALHOUN, BARNABAS B., Private

Resided in Ashe County and was by occupation a farmer prior to enlisting in Ashe County at age 23, October 1, 1862, for the war. Reported present in January-April, 1863. Deserted from camp near Clinton, Tennessee, May 26, 1863.

CALHOUN, JAMES, Private

Born in Ashe County in 1833. Resided in Ashe County and was by occupation a farmer prior to enlisting in Ashe County on October 1, 1862, for the war. Reported present in January-April, 1863. Furloughed for sixty days in May-June, 1863. Reported absent on expired furlough in September-October, 1863. No further records. [Filed a Tennessee pension application after the war.]

CALLAWAY, JACOB A., Corporal

Enlisted in Ashe County on July 20, 1862, for the war. Mustered in as Private. Reported present in January-June, 1863. Promoted to Corporal in May-June, 1863. Wounded in the left breast and shoulder at Chickamauga, Georgia, September 20, 1863. Hospitalized at Macon, Georgia. Furloughed for thirty days on or about September 27, 1863. Reported absent without leave in January-April, 1864. Returned to duty on an unspecified date. Detailed for duty as a cattle guard on August 10, 1864. Transferred to Company F of this regiment subsequent to August 31, 1864. [Was about 19 years of age at time of enlistment.]

CALLAWAY, JAMES M., Sergeant

Enlisted in Ashe County on July 20, 1862, for the war. Mustered in as Private. Deserted at Big Creek Gap, Tennessee, February 10, 1863. Returned to duty on March 31, 1863. Reported present on surviving company muster rolls from May 1, 1863, through April 30, 1864. Promoted to Sergeant on March 1, 1864. Wounded in the breast at Resaca, Georgia, May 14-15, 1864. Died in hospital at Atlanta, Georgia, on or about June 5, 1864, presumably of wounds. [May have served previously as Private in Company A, 26th Regiment N.C. Troops.]

CALLAWAY, JAMES N., Private

Enlisted at Dalton, Georgia, March 10, 1864, for the war. Deserted from camp near Dalton on March 19, 1864.

CALLAWAY, MILES B., Private

Resided in Ashe County where he enlisted at age 20, July 20, 1862, for the war. Reported present in January-June and September-

October, 1863. Furloughed for twenty-two days on February 9, 1864. Furloughed for forty days on March 18, 1864. Returned to duty on an unspecified date. Reported present in May-August, 1864. No further records. Survived the war.

CHAMBERS, F. M., Private

Enlisted at Dalton, Georgia, January 28, 1864, for the war. Deserted from camp near Dalton on February 5, 1864.

COLE, DAVID F., Private

Resided in Ashe County and was by occupation a farmer prior to enlisting in Ashe County at age 22, October 1, 1862, for the war. Deserted on January 29, 1863. Brought back to his command on February 11, 1863. Returned to duty prior to May 1, 1863. Reported present in May-June, 1863. Wounded in the right shoulder at Chickamauga, Georgia, September 20, 1863. Hospitalized at Macon, Georgia. Furloughed for thirty days on September 27, 1863. Reported absent without leave in January-February, 1864. Returned to duty in March-April, 1864. Reported present in May-August, 1864. No further records. Survived the war.

COLE, JAMES, Private

Resided in Ashe County and was by occupation a farmer prior to enlisting in Ashe County at age 28, July 20, 1862, for the war. Deserted on January 29, 1863. Brought back to the company on February 11, 1863. Returned to duty prior to May 1, 1863. Reported present in May-June, 1863. Killed at Chickamauga, Georgia, September 20, 1863.

COLE, JOSEPH, Private

Resided in Ashe County and was by occupation a farmer prior to enlisting in Ashe County at age 25, July 20, 1862, for the war. Deserted at Big Creek Gap, Tennessee, January 29, 1863. Reported in hospital at Knoxville, Tennessee, April 30, 1863. Reported present but under arrest at Clinton, Tennessee, in May-June, 1863. Returned to duty on an unspecified date. Reported present in September-October, 1863. Captured at Missionary Ridge, Tennessee, November 25, 1863. Sent to Nashville, Tennessee. Transferred to Louisville, Kentucky, where he arrived on December 7, 1863. Transferred to Rock Island, Illinois, where he arrived on December 9, 1863. Died at Rock Island on February 28, 1864, of "chron[ic] diar[rhoea]."

COLE, LORENZO D., Private

Resided in Ashe County where he enlisted at age 19, on or about October 1, 1862, for the war. Reported present in January-June and September-October, 1863. Detailed for duty with the Pioneer Corps on February 12, 1864. Returned to duty on an unspecified date. Reported present in March-August, 1864. No further records. Survived the war. [North Carolina pension records indicate that he was wounded in the right breast at Jonesborough, Georgia, on or about August 31, 1864.]

COLE, WILBORN, Private

Born in Virginia and resided in Ashe County where he was by occupation a farmer prior to enlisting in Ashe County at age 30, July 20, 1862, for the war. Reported present in January-June and September-October, 1863. Furloughed for forty days on February 9, 1864. Returned to duty on an unspecified date. Reported present in May-August, 1864. No further records. Survived the war. [North Carolina pension records indicate that he was struck in the right shoulder by a spent ball near the Alabama-Georgia line on August 21, 1864.]

COMBS, MEREDITH, Private

Enlisted in Ashe County at age 23, February 20, 1863, for the war. Reported present in March-April, 1863. Deserted from camp near Clinton, Tennessee, May 20, 1863. Returned to duty on an unspecified date. Reported present in September-October, 1863, and January-August, 1864. No further records. Survived the war.

CORNUTT, WILLIAM, Private

Enlisted in Ashe County on July 20, 1862, for the war. Reported present on surviving company muster rolls through February 29, 1864. Furloughed for twenty-four days on April 13, 1864. Returned to duty on an unspecified date. Company muster rolls indicate that he was captured at Kolb's Farm, near Marietta, Georgia, June 22, 1864; however, records of the Federal Provost Marshal do not substantiate that report. No further records.

COX, NATHAN, Private

Enlisted in Ashe County on July 20, 1862, for the war. Deserted at Big Creek Gap, Tennessee, February 10, 1863.

DENNY, JAMES H., Private

Enlisted in Ashe County on July 20, 1862, for the war. Was apparently mustered in with the rank of Corporal. Reported present in January-June, 1863. Deserted at Campbell Station, Tennessee, August 26, 1863. Reduced to ranks in November, 1863-February, 1864. Reported present but under arrest on February 2, 1864. Released from the guard house on April 1, 1864, and returned to duty. Captured at Cassville, Georgia, May 19, 1864. Sent to Nashville, Tennessee. Transferred to Louisville, Kentucky, where he arrived on May 24, 1864. Transferred to Rock Island, Illinois, where he arrived on May 27, 1864. Released at Rock Island on June 10, 1864, after taking the Oath of Allegiance and joining the U.S. Navy.

DICKSON, JAMES D., Private

Resided in Ashe County where he enlisted at age 16, June 1, 1863, for the war. Reported present on surviving company muster rolls through April 30, 1864. Wounded in the right leg at Kolb's Farm, near Marietta, Georgia, June 22, 1864. Reported absent wounded through August 31, 1864. Hospitalized at Charlotte on February 20, 1865, with intermittent fever. Returned to duty on February 26, 1865. Transferred to Company F of this regiment on an unspecified date.

DOLLAR, ALEXANDER M., Private

Resided in Ashe County where he enlisted at age 28, July 20, 1862, for the war. Deserted at Big Creek Gap, Tennessee, February 9, 1863. Returned to duty on December 10, 1863. Deserted from camp near Dalton, Georgia, March 19, 1864. Went over to the enemy on an unspecified date. Took the Oath of Allegiance at Knoxville, Tennessee, October 10, 1864.

DOLLAR, WILLIAM H., Private

Enlisted in Ashe County on July 20, 1862, for the war. Deserted at Big Creek Gap, Tennessee, January 6, 1863. Returned to duty on March 31, 1863. Reported present in May-June, 1863. Deserted from hospital at Emory and Henry, Virginia, prior to October 31, 1863. Returned to duty on an unspecified date. Reported sick in hospital at Dalton, Georgia, on or about December 20, 1863.

Was apparently suffering from "ascites from chron[ic] diarrhoea." Declared unfit for field service and was assigned to duty as a hospital nurse at La Grange, Georgia, January 1, 1864. Served as a hospital nurse through August 31, 1864. No further records. Survived the war. [Confederate hospital records dated July, 1864, give his age as 25. North Carolina pension records indicate that he was wounded at La Grange in December, 1863.]

DOUGHERTY, MICHAEL, Private

Resided in Ashe County and was by occupation a farmer prior to enlisting in Ashe County at age 31, July 20, 1862, for the war. Deserted at Big Creek Gap, Tennessee, February 9, 1863. Returned to duty on February 28, 1863. Reported present in March-June, 1863. Furloughed for thirty days on September 1, 1863. Reported absent on expired furlough on October 31, 1863. Deserted to the enemy on an unspecified date. Took the Oath of Allegiance at Knoxville, Tennessee, October 10, 1864.

DUN, CALLAWAY, Private

Enlisted in Ashe County on July 20, 1862, for the war. Reported present in January-June, 1863. No further records.

EASTRIDGE, BARNABAS, Private

Born in Ashe County on April 26, 1840. Was by occupation a carpenter or farmer prior to enlisting in Ashe County at age 22, February 20, 1863, for the war. Reported present in March-June, 1863. Deserted at Campbell Station, Tennessee, August 22, 1863. Reported present but under arrest on December 10, 1863, and April 23, 1864. Returned to duty on an unspecified date. Captured at Resaca, Georgia, May 15, 1864. Sent to Nashville, Tennessee. Transferred to Louisville, Kentucky, where he arrived on May 20, 1864. Transferred to Camp Morton, Indianapolis, Indiana, where he arrived on May 22, 1864. Released at Camp Morton on March 14, 1865, after taking the Oath of Allegiance and joining the U.S. Army. Assigned to Company G, 6th Regiment U.S. Volunteer Infantry. [Filed a Tennessee pension application after the war.]

EASTRIDGE, HENRY, Private

Resided in Ashe County and was by occupation a farmer prior to enlisting in Ashe County at age 25, July 20, 1862, for the war. Deserted at Big Creek Gap, Tennessee, January 6, 1863.

EASTRIDGE, JOHN, Private

Resided in Ashe County and was by occupation a farmer prior to enlisting in Ashe County at age 29, July 20, 1862, for the war. Deserted at Big Creek Gap, Tennessee, February 9, 1863. Reported present but under arrest in March-June, 1863. Returned to duty on an unspecified date. Deserted at Campbell Station, Tennessee, August 22, 1863. Returned to duty on an unspecified date. Reported present in January-April, 1864. Deserted near the Chattahoochee River, Georgia, July 8, 1864. [May have served later as Corporal in Company E, 13th Regiment Tennessee Cavalry (Union).]

ELDREATH, JOHN, Private

Resided in Ashe County and was by occupation a farmer. Place and date of enlistment not reported (probably enlisted in the summer of 1862). Deserted in Johnson County, Tennessee, August 22, 1862.

ELDRETH, ZACHARIAH, ———

Place and date of enlistment not reported. Died prior to December 8, 1863. Place, date, and cause of death not reported.

ELLER, CALVIN, JR., Private

Resided in Ashe County where he enlisted at age 18, October 10, 1863, for the war. Reported present in January-February, 1864. Furloughed for forty days on April 11, 1864. Reported present but sick in May-August, 1864. No further records. Survived the war. [North Carolina pension records indicate that he was wounded in the left wrist at Kolb's Farm, near Marietta, Georgia, June 22, 1864.]

ELLER, JACOB, Private

Resided in Ashe County and was by occupation a farmer prior to enlisting in Ashe County at age 30, July 20, 1862, for the war. Was apparently mustered in with the rank of Sergeant. Reported present in January-April, 1863. Deserted on May 26, 1863. Returned to duty on June 19, 1863. Reduced to ranks in May-June, 1863. Reported on detail as a wood workman from August 1, 1863, through April 30, 1864. Wounded in the arm at Kolb's Farm, near Marietta, Georgia, June 22, 1864. Arm amputated. Reported absent wounded or absent sick through August 31, 1864. No further records. Survived the war.

ELLER, WILLIAM, Private

Resided in Ashe County and was by occupation a farmer prior to enlisting in Ashe County at age 26, July 20, 1862, for the war. Reported present in January-April, 1863. Deserted from camp near Clinton, Tennessee, May 26, 1863. Apparently returned to duty and deserted again at Campbell Station, Tennessee, August 26, 1863. Rejoined the company on December 10, 1863, and was court-martialed. Returned to duty on February 8, 1864. Reported present in March-April, 1864. Captured (or deserted to the enemy) near Marietta, Georgia, on or about July 2, 1864. Sent to Nashville, Tennessee. Transferred to Louisville, Kentucky, where he arrived on or about July 13, 1864. Transferred to Camp Morton, Indianapolis, Indiana, on an unspecified date. Paroled at Camp Morton on or about February 26, 1865. Received at City Point, Virginia, on an unspecified date for exchange. Hospitalized at Richmond, Virginia, March 13, 1865. Furloughed for thirty days on March 14, 1865. No further records. Survived the war.

ELLIOTT, JAMES CRAWFORD, Private

Born in Ashe County and was by occupation a farmer prior to enlisting in Ashe County on July 20, 1862, for the war. Mustered in as Musician (Drummer). Furloughed for thirty days on or about October 20, 1862. Reported absent on expired furlough in March-April, 1863. Reported present in May-June, 1863. Reduced to ranks in July-October, 1863. Deserted at Campbell Station, Tennessee, August 22, 1863. Returned to duty prior to November 25, 1863, when he was captured at Missionary Ridge, Tennessee. Sent to Nashville, Tennessee. Transferred to Louisville, Kentucky, where he arrived on December 11, 1863. Transferred to Rock Island, Illinois, where he arrived on or about December 14, 1863. Paroled at Rock Island on or about February 15, 1865. Received for exchange on an unspecified date. Hospitalized at Richmond, Virginia, March 3, 1865, with "hydrothory." Discharged on March 16, 1865, by reason of "pleuropneumonia." Discharge certificate gives his age as 23.

ELLIOTT, RUFUS, Private

Enlisted in Ashe County on July 20, 1862, for the war. Mustered in as Private. Deserted at Big Creek Gap, Tennessee, February 9, 1863. Returned to duty on March 31, 1863. Reported present in May-June and September-October, 1863. Promoted to 1st Sergeant on September 13, 1863. Captured at Missionary Ridge, Tennessee,

November 25, 1863. Sent to Nashville, Tennessee. Transferred to Louisville, Kentucky, where he arrived on December 7, 1863. Transferred to Rock Island, Illinois, where he arrived on December 9, 1863. Died at Rock Island on April 3, 1864, of "variola." [He was reduced to ranks in March-April, 1864, while a prisoner of war.]

ELLIOTT, STEPHEN, Private

Enlisted in Ashe County at age 31, July 20, 1862, for the war. Deserted at Big Creek Gap, Tennessee, February 9, 1863. Returned to duty on May 19, 1863. Reported present in September-October, 1863. Captured at Missionary Ridge, Tennessee, November 25, 1863. Sent to Nashville, Tennessee. Transferred to Louisville, Kentucky, where he arrived on December 7, 1863. Transferred to Rock Island, Illinois, where he arrived on December 9, 1863. Released at Rock Island on or about October 31, 1864, after taking the Oath of Allegiance and joining the U.S. Army. Assigned to Company H, 3rd Regiment U.S. Volunteer Infantry.

FAIRCLOTH, JOHN W., Private

Resided in Ashe County where he enlisted at age 20, February 20, 186[3], for the war. Reported present on surviving company muster rolls through August 31, 1864. No further records.

FAIRCLOTH, MICHAEL M., Private

Enlisted in Ashe County on July 20, 1862, for the war. Reported present on surviving company muster rolls through August 31, 1864. Transferred to Company F of this regiment subsequent to August 31, 1864. [Was about 18 years of age at time of enlistment.]

FARRINGTON, MUMFORD, Private

Enlisted in Ashe County on July 20, 1862, for the war. Deserted at Big Creek Gap, Tennessee, January 26, 1863. Returned to duty on March 31, 1863. Reported present in May-June and September-October, 1863. Reported on detail as a wagoner from November 20, 1863, through August 31, 1864. No further records. Survived the war. [Was about 33 years of age at time of enlistment. North Carolina pension records indicate that he was wounded in the right shoulder at Chickamauga, Georgia, September 19-20, 1863.]

FOWLER, JAMES A., Corporal

Resided in Ashe County where he enlisted at age 22, July 20, 1862, for the war. Was apparently mustered in with the rank of Corporal. Reported present in January-June and September-October, 1863. Furloughed for forty days on February 9, 1864. Returned to duty on an unspecified date. Reported present in March-April, 1864. Wounded in arm at Resaca, Georgia, May 14-15, 1864. Reported present but sick on August 31, 1864. Appointed Hospital Steward and transferred to the Field and Staff of this regiment subsequent to August 31, 1864.

FOWLER, SANDERS M., Private

Resided in Ashe County where he enlisted on July 20, 1862, for the war. Reported present in January-June, 1863. Wounded at Chickamauga, Georgia, September 20, 1863. Hospitalized at Macon, Georgia. Furloughed for thirty days on September 27, 1863. Reported present but sick in January-February, 1864. Detailed for hospital duty at Atlanta, Georgia, March 21, 1864. Returned to duty prior to July 20, 1864, when he was captured at or near Peachtree Creek, near Atlanta. Sent to Nashville, Tennessee. Transferred to Louisville, Kentucky, where he arrived on August 3, 1864. Transferred to Camp Chase, Ohio, where he arrived on August 4, 1864. Reported in hospital at Camp Chase from September 8 through October 20, 1864, with variola. Paroled at Camp Chase on or about March 4, 1865. Received at Boulware's and Cox's Wharves, James River, Virginia, on or about March 10, 1865, for exchange. Hospitalized at Richmond, Virginia, March 11, 1865, with debilitas. Captured in hospital at Richmond on April 3, 1865. Paroled on May 17, 1865. [Federal hospital records dated September-October, 1864, give his age as 21.]

GILLY, ALFRED, Private

Enlisted in Ashe County on July 20, 1862, for the war. Deserted at Big Creek Gap, Tennessee, January 26, 1863. [May have served later as Private in Company I, 13th Regiment Tennessee Cavalry (Union).]

GILLY, JAMES, ———

North Carolina pension records indicate that he served in this company.

GILLY, JOHN, Private

Resided in Ashe County and was by occupation a farmer prior to enlisting in Ashe County at age 32, July 20, 1862, for the war. Reported present in January-June, 1863. Died at home on August 6, 1863, of "diarrhoea & dropsy."

GRAYBEAL, JOHN, Private

Resided in Ashe County and was by occupation a farmer prior to enlisting in Ashe County at age 22, July 20, 1862, for the war. Reported present in January-June, 1863. Deserted near La Fayette, Georgia, September 17, 1863.

GREEN, ISAAC S., Private

Resided in Ashe County and enlisted at Dalton, Georgia, at age 18, April 4, 1864, for the war. Captured (or deserted to the enemy) near Marietta, Georgia, on or about July 2, 1864. Sent to Nashville, Tennessee. Transferred to Louisville, Kentucky, where he arrived on July 13, 1864. Transferred to Camp Morton, Indianapolis, Indiana, where he arrived on July 14, 1864. Died at Camp Morton on February 13, 1865, of "inflammation of the lungs."

GREER, JESSE, Private

Resided in Ashe County and was by occupation a farmer prior to enlisting in Ashe County on July 20, 1862, for the war. Reported present in January-June, 1863. Reported on detail as a nurse at La Fayette, Georgia, in September-October, 1863. Rejoined the company on an unspecified date. Reported present in March-April, 1864. Reported present but on duty as a litter bearer in May-August, 1864. No further records.

GREER, SOLOMON, ———

North Carolina pension records indicate that he served in this company.

HAM, ALFRED, Private

Enlisted in Ashe County at age 22, July 20, 1862, for the war. Reported present in January-June, 1863. Furloughed for thirty days at Loudon, Tennessee, July 19, 1863. Reported absent on expired furlough on October 31, 1863. Returned to duty prior to November 25, 1863, when he was captured at Missionary Ridge, Tennessee. Sent to Nashville, Tennessee. Transferred to Louisville, Kentucky, where he arrived on December 11, 1863. Transferred to Rock Island, Illinois, where he arrived on or about December 14, 1863. Transferred to New Orleans, Louisiana, May 3, 1865. Arrived at New Orleans on May 17, 1865. Exchanged at New Orleans on May 23, 1865.

HAM, GIDEON, Private

Resided in Ashe County where he enlisted at age 20, July 20, 1862, for the war. Reported present in January-June, 1863. Deserted at Knoxville, Tennessee, August 27, 1863.

HAM, JOSHUA, SR., ———

North Carolina pension records indicate that he served in this company.

HAM, THOMAS, Private

Enlisted in Ashe County at age 29, July 20, 1862, for the war. Deserted at Big Creek Gap, Tennessee, February 9, 1863. Returned to duty on March 31, 1863. Reported present in May-June, 1863. Furloughed for thirty days on September 1, 1863. Reported absent on expired furlough on October 31, 1863. Returned to duty on an unspecified date. Reported present in January-August, 1864. No further records. Survived the war.

HANDY, F. MARION, Corporal

Resided in Ashe County and was by occupation a farmer prior to enlisting in Ashe County at age 26, July 20, 1862, for the war. Mustered in as Private. Reported present in January-June and September-October, 1863. Promoted to Corporal in July-October, 1863. Furloughed for forty days on February 20, 1864. Reported present in March-April, 1864. Wounded "by explosion of shell" at Resaca, Georgia, May 14-15, 1864. Furloughed for sixty days from hospital at Griffin, Georgia, August 6, 1864. Transferred to Company F of this regiment subsequent to August 31, 1864.

HART, ANDREW, Private

Resided in Ashe County where he enlisted. Enlistment date reported as July 20, 1862; however, he was not listed in the records of this company until May, 1863. Probably enlisted in the spring of 1863. Deserted from camp near Clinton, Tennessee, May 26, 1863. Captured by the enemy in "Hocking [Hawkins?]" County, Tennessee, June 20, 1863. Sent to Lexington, Kentucky. Transferred to Camp Chase, Ohio, where he arrived on June 29, 1863. Transferred to Fort Delaware, Delaware, where he arrived on July 14, 1863. Died at Fort Delaware on September 2, 1863, of "typhoid fever." [Records of the Federal Provost Marshal dated June-July, 1863, give his age as 18.]

HART, JOSEPH, Private

Enlisted in Ashe County. Enlistment date reported as July 20, 1862; however, he was not listed in the records of this company until May-June, 1863. Probably enlisted in the spring of 1863. Deserted from camp near Clinton, Tennessee, May 26, 1863. Captured by the enemy in "Hocking [Hawkins?]" County, Tennessee, June 20, 1863. Sent to Lexington, Kentucky. Transferred to Camp Chase, Ohio, where he arrived on June 29, 1863. Transferred to Fort Delaware, Delaware, where he arrived on July 14, 1863. Died at Fort Delaware on August 26, 1863. Cause of death not reported. [Records of the Federal Provost Marshal dated June-July, 1863, give his age as 22; however, it appears probable that he was about 19 years of age at that time.]

HART, RILEY, Private

Resided in Ashe County and was by occupation a farmer prior to enlisting in Ashe County. Enlistment date reported as June 20, 1862; however, he was not listed in the records of this company until May, 1863. Probably enlisted in the spring of 1863. Was about 28 years of age at time of enlistment. Deserted from camp near Clinton, Tennessee, May 26, 1863. Captured by the enemy in

"Hocking [Hawkins?]" County, Tennessee, June 20, 1863. Sent to Lexington, Kentucky. Transferred to Camp Chase, Ohio, where he arrived on June 29, 1863. Transferred to Fort Delaware, Delaware, where he arrived on July 14, 1863. Died at Fort Delaware on or about August 26, 1863, of "rubeola."

HARTZOG, WILLIAM H., Private

Resided in Ashe County and enlisted at Dalton, Georgia, at age 18, January 28, 1864, for the war. Hospitalized at Dalton on February 25, 1864. Returned to duty prior to April 30, 1864. Died in hospital at Columbus, Georgia, June 15, 1864. Cause of death not reported.

HARVEL, MOSES ALEX, Private

Enlisted in Ashe County at age 18, July 20, 1862, for the war. Reported present in January-June, 1863. Wounded at Chickamauga, Georgia, September 19-20, 1863. Nominated for the Badge of Distinction for gallantry at Chickamauga. Returned to duty on an unspecified date. Reported present in January-February, 1864. Reported sick in hospital at Dalton, Georgia, March 26, 1864. Wounded in the breast at Resaca, Georgia, May 14-15, 1864. Reported present but on duty as a guard at Atlanta, Georgia, on August 31, 1864. Hospitalized at Macon, Georgia, November 16, 1864, with intermittent fever. Reported on duty at Macon with Company B, 2nd Battalion Troops and Defenses, December 31, 1864. Rejoined this company on an unspecified date. Paroled at Charlotte on May 23, 1865.

HILTON, JOHN W., Private

Place and date of enlistment not reported (probably enlisted in the autumn of 1863). Captured at Missionary Ridge, Tennessee, November 25, 1863. Sent to Nashville, Tennessee. Transferred to Louisville, Kentucky, where he arrived on December 11, 1863. Transferred to Rock Island, Illinois, where he arrived on or about December 14, 1863. Released at Rock Island on or about February 5, 1864, after taking the Oath of Allegiance and joining the U.S. Navy.

HOUCK, HENRY A., Private

Resided in Ashe County and was by occupation a farmer prior to enlisting in Ashe County at age 61, July 20, 1862, for the war. Reported present in January-April, 1863. Died on an unspecified date (probably in the summer of 1863). Place and cause of death not reported.

HOUCK, JOSEPH F., Private

Resided in Ashe County and was by occupation a farmer prior to enlisting in Ashe County at age 35, July 20, 1862, for the war. Was apparently mustered in with the rank of Sergeant. Reported present in January-June, 1863. Reported sick in hospital at Rome, Georgia, in September-October, 1863. Reported on detail as a hospital nurse at Covington, Georgia, and at Newnan, Georgia, from November 1, 1863, through August 31, 1864. Reduced to ranks in March-April, 1864. No further records. Survived the war. [North Carolina pension records indicate that he was wounded slightly in the left leg at Knoxville, Tennessee, July 20, 1863, and "disabled . . . from service for some time."]

HOWELL, ALVIN P., Private

Enlisted in Ashe County on July 20, 1862, for the war. Furloughed on November 15, 1862. Returned to duty in March-April, 1863. Reported present in May-June, 1863. Reported absent sick at Montgomery, Alabama, in September-October, 1863. Returned to duty

prior to November 25, 1863, when he was captured at Missionary Ridge, Tennessee. Sent to Nashville, Tennessee. Transferred to Louisville, Kentucky, where he arrived on December 7, 1863. Transferred to Rock Island, Illinois, where he arrived on December 9, 1863. Released at Rock Island on October 6, 1864, after taking the Oath of Allegiance and joining the U.S. Army. Unit to which assigned not reported.

HOWELL, GEORGE, Private

Resided in Ashe County and was by occupation a farmer prior to enlisting at Dalton, Georgia, February 1, 1864, for the war. Deserted to the enemy from camp near Dalton on March 19, 1864. Took the Oath of Allegiance at Chattanooga, Tennessee, March 24, 1864.

HOWELL, JACKSON H., Private

Resided in Ashe County and was by occupation a farmer prior to enlisting in Ashe County at age 28, July 20, 1862, for the war. Deserted at Big Creek Gap, Tennessee, February 14, 1863. Returned to duty on April 7, 1863. Reported present in May-June, 1863. Deserted at Campbell Station, Tennessee, August 20, 1863. Reported present but under arrest on March 6, 1864. Returned to duty on an unspecified date. Deserted to the enemy near Marietta, Georgia, on or about June 27, 1864.

HOWELL, JEREMIAH W., Private

Resided in Ashe County and was by occupation a farmer prior to enlisting in Ashe County at age 35, July 20, 1862, for the war. Reported present in January-June, 1863. Deserted at Campbell Station, Tennessee, August 20, 1863. Returned to duty on November 20, 1863. Reported present in January-April, 1864. Deserted to the enemy near Marietta, Georgia, on or about June 27, 1864. Took the Oath of Allegiance at Chattanooga, Tennessee, on or about July 14, 1864. Transferred to Louisville, Kentucky, where he was released on July 18, 1864.

HOWELL, SOLOMON, Private

Resided in Ashe County and was by occupation a farmer prior to enlisting at Dalton, Georgia, at age 39, April 4, 1864, for the war. Reported present but under arrest on August 23, 1864. Reason he was arrested not reported. Died in hospital in North Carolina on December 12, 1864, of disease.

HURLEY, DAVID D., Private

Resided in Ashe County where he enlisted at age 18, October 10, 1863, for the war. Reported present in January-April, 1864. Died in hospital at Oxford, Georgia, July 8, 1864. Cause of death not reported.

HURLEY, HARVEY, Private

Enlisted in Ashe County at age 29, July 20, 1862, for the war. Was apparently mustered in with the rank of Sergeant. Reported present in January-June, 1863. Promoted to 1st Sergeant subsequent to June 30, 1863. Deserted on September 23, 1863. Reduced to ranks the same date. Returned to duty subsequent to October 31, 1863. Wounded at Rocky Face Ridge, Georgia, February 25, 1864. Hospitalized at Newnan, Georgia. Furloughed for thirty days on March 5, 1864. Reported absent on expired furlough on April 30, 1864. Returned to duty prior to June 22, 1864, when he was wounded at Kolb's Farm, near Marietta, Georgia. Returned to duty prior to September 1, 1864. Transferred to Company F of this regiment subsequent to August 31, 1864.

HURLEY, JAMES F., Corporal

Resided in Ashe County and was by occupation a farmer prior to enlisting in Ashe County at age 36, October 10, 1863, for the war. Mustered in as Private. Promoted to Corporal on March 1, 1864. Reported present in January-August, 1864. Killed at Jonesborough, Georgia, August 31, 1864.

HURLEY, JASPER, Private

Resided in Ashe County and was by occupation a farmer prior to enlisting at Dalton, Georgia, at age 39, January 28, 1864, for the war. Reported present in February-April, 1864. Furloughed for thirty days from hospital at Forsyth, Georgia, August 1, 1864. No further records. Survived the war.

HURLEY, THOMAS, Private

Resided in Ashe County and was by occupation a farmer prior to enlisting in Ashe County at age 28, July 20, 1862, for the war. Reported present in January-April, 1863. Deserted from camp near Clinton, Tennessee, May 26, 1863. Returned to duty on an unspecified date. Deserted at Chattanooga, Tennessee, September 26, 1863. Returned to duty on November 20, 1863. Hospitalized at Dalton, Georgia, April 18, 1864. Returned to duty on an unspecified date. Reported present in May-August, 1864. Transferred to Company F of this regiment subsequent to August 31, 1864.

JEFFERSON, ADKINS, Private

Resided in Ashe County and was by occupation a day laborer prior to enlisting in Ashe County at age 32, July 20, 1862, for the war. Reported absent on furlough from November 15, 1862, through February 28, 1863. Returned to duty in March-April, 1863. Reported present in May-June, 1863. Deserted at Lenoir Station, Tennessee, August 28, 1863. Returned to duty subsequent to October 31, 1863. Reported present in January-April, 1864. Captured (or deserted to the enemy) near Marietta, Georgia, on or about July 2, 1864. Confined at Camp Douglas, Chicago, Illinois, where he died on October 2, 1864, of "inflammation of lungs."

JOHNSON, JAMES, Private

Resided in Ashe County where he enlisted. Enlistment date reported as July 20, 1862; however, he was not listed in the records of this company until May, 1863 (probably enlisted in the spring of 1863). Deserted from camp near Clinton, Tennessee, May 26, 1863.

JOLLY, HILE, Private

Enlisted at Chattanooga, Tennessee, at age 45, November 17, 1863, for the war. Deserted on an unspecified date. Reported under arrest on January 5, 1864. Court-martialed on an unspecified date. Released from the guard house on March 27, 1864, and returned to duty. Furloughed for thirty days from hospital at Newnan, Georgia, May 30, 1864. Failed to return to duty. No further records. Survived the war.

JONES, JASON, Private

Resided in Ashe County and was by occupation a farmer prior to enlisting in Ashe County at age 22, July 20, 1862, for the war. Deserted at Big Creek Gap, Tennessee, February 10, 1863. Returned to duty on April 23, 1863. Reported present in May-June, 1863. Detailed to guard a mill near Fincastle, Tennessee, August 10, 1863. Company muster rolls dated September-October, 1863, and January-August, 1864, state that he was supposed to have been

captured by the enemy; however, records of the Federal Provost Marshal do not substantiate that report. No further records.

JONES, JESSE F., Private

Resided in Ashe County where he enlisted at age 24, July 20, 1862, for the war. Deserted at Big Creek Gap, Tennessee, February 10, 1863. Returned to duty on March 3, 1863. Detailed as a wood workman at Clinton, Tennessee, May 1, 1863. Reported absent on detail through April 30, 1864. Died in hospital at Griffin, Georgia, August 5, 1864. Cause of death not reported.

JONES, JOHN, Private

Resided in Ashe County and was by occupation a farmer prior to enlisting at Clinton, Tennessee. Enlistment date reported as April 27, 1862; however, it appears likely that he enlisted in the summer or autumn of 1862. Deserted at Big Creek Gap, Tennessee, October 20, 1862.

JONES, MEMOCH, Private

Enlisted in Ashe County on July 20, 1862, for the war. Deserted at Big Creek Gap, Tennessee, February 10, 1863. Returned to duty subsequent to June 30, 1863. Killed at Chickamauga, Georgia, September 20, 1863.

KEMP, JOHN, Private

Enlisted in Ashe County on September 10, 1863, for the war. Died in hospital at Cassville, Georgia, January 26, 1864. Cause of death not reported.

KILBY, MILTON, Private

Born in Ashe County on October 31, 1831. Was by occupation a farmer prior to enlisting in Ashe County at age 30, July 20, 1862, for the war. Reported present in January-February, 1863. Discharged at Big Creek Gap, Tennessee, February 28, 1863, by reason of "anchilosis of the wrist joint and paralisis of the whole limb caused by the running of a team of horses."

KING, DAVID, Private

Enlisted in Ashe County on February 20, 1863, for the war. Reported present in March-June, 1863. Deserted near La Fayette, Georgia, September 17, 1863.

KING, JACOB, Private

Born in Illinois and resided in Ashe County where he was by occupation a farmer prior to enlisting in Ashe County at age 30, July 20, 1862, for the war. Deserted at Big Creek Gap, Tennessee, February 20, 1863. Went to Taylor County, Kentucky, where he "worked on farm until he found it was necessary to report [to Federal authorities] which he did at Lebanon," Kentucky. Sent to Louisville, Kentucky, where he arrived on or about May 28, 1863. Transferred to Camp Chase, Ohio, where he arrived on June 8, 1863. Released at Camp Chase on June 10, 1863, after taking the Oath of Allegiance.

KNIGHT, WILLIAM W., Private

Resided in Ashe County where he enlisted on July 20, 1862, for the war. Reported present in January-April, 1863. Detailed as a hospital nurse at Clinton, Tennessee, in May-June, 1863. Deserted at Big Creek Gap, Tennessee, August 22, 1863. Returned to duty on September 25, 1863. Captured at Missionary Ridge, Tennessee, November 25, 1863. Sent to Nashville, Tennessee. Transferred to

Louisville, Kentucky, where he arrived on December 7, 1863. Transferred to Rock Island, Illinois, where he arrived on December 9, 1863. Released at Rock Island on May 19, 1865, after taking the Oath of Allegiance. [Records of the Federal Provost Marshal dated May, 1865, give his age as 28.]

LANDRETH, WAGNER, Private
Resided in Ashe County and was by occupation a farmer prior to enlisting in Ashe County at age 27, July 20, 1862, for the war. Deserted at Big Creek Gap, Tennessee, February 23, 1863. Returned to duty on June 19, 1863. Deserted at Big Creek Gap on August 22, 1863. Returned from desertion on November 15, 1863, and was placed under arrest. Returned to duty on November 20, 1863. Reported present in January-April, 1864. Captured at Kolb's Farm, near Marietta, Georgia, June 22, 1864. Sent to Nashville, Tennessee. Transferred to Louisville, Kentucky, where he arrived on July 13, 1864. Transferred to Camp Douglas, Chicago, Illinois, where he arrived on July 16, 1864. Released at Camp Douglas on May 13, 1865, after taking the Oath of Allegiance.

LEDFORD, HENRY F., Private
Enlisted near Chattanooga, Tennessee, November 17, 1863, for the war. Captured at Missionary Ridge, Tennessee, November 25, 1863. Sent to Nashville, Tennessee. Transferred to Louisville, Kentucky, where he arrived on December 7, 1863. Transferred to Rock Island, Illinois, where he arrived on December 9, 1863. Died at Rock Island on February 14, 1864, of "diarrhoea."

LEWIS, WILLIAM, Private
Resided in Ashe County. Place and date of enlistment not reported (probably enlisted in the summer or autumn of 1862). Deserted at Big Creek Gap, Tennessee, October 15, 1862.

LOVELACE, ANDREW, Private
Resided in Ashe County and was by occupation a farmer prior to enlisting in Ashe County at age 27, July 20, 1862, for the war. Deserted at Big Creek Gap, Tennessee, February 10, 1863. Returned to duty on March 31, 1863. Reported present in May-June, 1863. Deserted at Chattanooga, Tennessee, September 23, 1863. Returned to duty on an unspecified date. Reported present in January-August, 1864. Captured at Stockbridge, Georgia, September 5, 1864. Sent to Nashville, Tennessee. Transferred to Louisville, Kentucky, where he arrived on October 28, 1864. Transferred to Camp Douglas, Chicago, Illinois, where he arrived on November 1, 1864. Released at Camp Douglas on May 17, 1865, after taking the Oath of Allegiance.

McGUIRE, GEORGE W., Private
Resided in Ashe County and was by occupation a farmer prior to enlisting in Ashe County at age 34, July 20, 1862, for the war. Deserted at Big Creek Gap, Tennessee, February 23, 1863. Returned to duty on March 31, 1863. Reported present in May-June, 1863. Deserted at Lenoir Station, Tennessee, August 28, 1863. Returned from desertion on November 15, 1863, and was placed under arrest. Returned to duty on December 1, 1863. Reported present in January-April, 1864. Captured (or deserted to the enemy) near Marietta, Georgia, on or about July 2, 1864. Sent to Nashville, Tennessee. Transferred to Louisville, Kentucky, where he arrived on July 14, 1864. Transferred to Camp Douglas, Chicago, Illinois, where he arrived on July 16, 1864. Released at Camp Douglas on May 17, 1865, after taking the Oath of Allegiance.

McLOUR, HENRY S., Private
Enlisted in Ashe County on July 20, 1862, for the war. Deserted at Big Creek Gap, Tennessee, February 14, 1863. Returned to duty subsequent to June 30, 1863. Deserted at Campbell Station, Tennessee, August 26, 1863. Reported present but under arrest on March 6, 1864. Returned to duty on an unspecified date. Deserted to the enemy near Dalton, Georgia, May 13, 1864. Sent to Knoxville, Tennessee. Released at Knoxville on or about May 23, 1864, after taking the Oath of Allegiance.

MAY, ABRAHAM, Private
Born in Arkansas and resided in Ashe County where he enlisted at age 23, July 20, 1862, for the war. Reported present on surviving company muster rolls through April 30, 1864. Furloughed for sixty days from hospital at Greensboro, Georgia, June 29, 1864. Reported absent on expired furlough on August 31, 1864. No further records.

MAY, JOHN, Private
Resided in Ashe County where he enlisted at age 18, July 20, 1862, for the war. Deserted at Big Creek Gap, Tennessee, January 29, 1863. Reported in hospital at Knoxville, Tennessee, April 30, 1863. Reported present but under arrest at Clinton, Tennessee, in May-June, 1863. Returned to duty on an unspecified date. Reported present in September-October, 1863, and January-April, 1864. Killed at Kolb's Farm, near Marietta, Georgia, June 22, 1864.

MERRILL, A. B., Private
Place and date of enlistment not reported (probably enlisted in the autumn of 1863). Captured at Missionary Ridge, Tennessee, November 25, 1863. Sent to Nashville, Tennessee. Transferred to Louisville, Kentucky, where he arrived on December 7, 1863. Transferred to Rock Island, Illinois, where he arrived on December 9, 1863. Released at Rock Island on January 25, 1864, after taking the Oath of Allegiance and joining the U.S. Navy.

NELSON, WILLIAM, Private
Enlisted at Camp Holmes, near Raleigh, November 12, 1863, for the war. Sent to hospital at Dalton, Georgia, January 15, 1864. Died in hospital at Cassville, Georgia, March 29, 1864. Cause of death not reported.

OSBORN, ALEXANDER, Private
Resided in Ashe County where he enlisted on July 20, 1862, for the war. Reported present in January-June, 1863. Reported absent sick in September-October, 1863. Returned to duty on an unspecified date. Reported present in January-April, 1864. Deserted near the Chattahoochee River, Georgia, on or about July 29, 1864. Went over to the enemy on an unspecified date. Confined at Knoxville, Tennessee, October 10, 1864. Released on or about the same date after taking the Oath of Allegiance.

OSBORN, ALFRED, Private
Resided in Ashe County and was by occupation a farmer prior to enlisting in Ashe County on July 20, 1862, for the war. Deserted at Big Creek Gap, Tennessee, January 6, 1863. [May have served later as Private in Company E, 13th Regiment Tennessee Cavalry (Union).]

OSBORN, ARIS, Private
Born in Ashe County where he resided as a farmer prior to enlisting in Ashe County at age 18, July 20, 1862, for the war. Deserted at

Big Creek Gap, Tennessee, January 26, 1863. Later served as Private in Company G, 13th Regiment Tennessee Cavalry (Union).

OSBORN, GEORGE, Private

Resided in Ashe County where he enlisted on July 20, 1862, for the war. Deserted at Big Creek Gap, Tennessee, January 26, 1863. [May have served later as Private in Company I, 13th Regiment Tennessee Cavalry (Union).]

OSBORN, JESSE, Private

Born in Ashe County in 1834. Resided in Ashe County where he enlisted on July 20, 1862, for the war. Reported present in January-June, 1863. Deserted near La Fayette, Georgia, September 17, 1863. Went over to the enemy on an unspecified date. Took the Oath of Allegiance at Knoxville, Tennessee, November 21, 1864. [Filed a Tennessee pension application after the war.]

OSBORN, JOHN, Private

Resided in Ashe County and was by occupation a farmer prior to enlisting in Ashe County on July 20, 1862, for the war. Deserted at Big Creek Gap, Tennessee, January 26, 1863.

OSBORN, WILLIAM, Private

Resided in Ashe County and was by occupation a farmer prior to enlisting in Ashe County on July 20, 1862, for the war. Deserted at Big Creek Gap, Tennessee, January 26, 1863. Returned to duty on March 31, 1863. Reported present in May-June, 1863. Deserted at Big Creek Gap on August 22, 1863. [May have served later as Private in Company G, 13th Regiment Tennessee Cavalry (Union).]

PARSONS, GEORGE W., Private

Enlisted in Ashe County at age 27, July 20, 1862, for the war. Reported present on surviving company muster rolls through April 30, 1864. Furloughed for sixty days on June 27, 1864. Captured in Currituck County or in Princess Anne County, Virginia, July 1, 1864. Confined at Fort Monroe, Virginia, July 12, 1864. Transferred to Point Lookout, Maryland, where he arrived on July 15, 1864. Transferred to Elmira, New York, where he arrived on August 6, 1864. Transferred to Norfolk, Virginia, August 14, 1864, and ordered to report to Brig. Gen. George F. Shepley. No further records.

PARSONS, WILLIAM H., Private

Resided in Ashe County where he enlisted on July 20, 1862, for the war. Reported present on surviving company muster rolls through April 30, 1864. Captured at Buzzard Roost Gap, Georgia, on or about May 8, 1864. Sent to Nashville, Tennessee. Transferred to Louisville, Kentucky, where he arrived on May 17, 1864. Transferred to Camp Morton, Indianapolis, Indiana, where he arrived on May 22, 1864. Died at Camp Morton on February 4, 1865, of "inflammation of the lungs."

PENINGTON, DOW, Private

Enlisted in Ashe County on July 20, 1862, for the war. Reported absent on furlough from October 30, 1862, through February 28, 1863. Returned to duty in March-April, 1863. Deserted from camp near Clinton, Tennessee, May 26, 1863. Returned from desertion on or about December 10, 1863, and was placed under arrest. Reported under arrest through April 30, 1864. Returned to duty on an unspecified date. Reported absent without leave on June 1, 1864. No further records.

PENINGTON, SAMUEL, Private

Enlisted at Dalton, Georgia, January 28, 1864, for the war. Reported present through February 29, 1864. No further records.

PENINGTON, THORNTON, Private

Resided in Ashe County and was by occupation a farmer prior to enlisting in Ashe County at age 23, July 20, 1862, for the war. Reported present in January-April, 1863. Deserted from camp near Clinton, Tennessee, May 26, 1863. Returned to duty prior to September 20, 1863, when he was killed at Chickamauga, Georgia.

REEDY, GEORGE WASHINGTON, Private

Resided in Ashe County where he enlisted at age 27, July 20, 1862, for the war. Deserted at Big Creek Gap, Tennessee, January 29, 1863. Returned to duty on March 31, 1863. Reported present in May-June, 1863. Deserted at Big Creek Gap on August 22, 1863. Went over to the enemy on an unspecified date. Confined at Louisville, Kentucky, October 11, 1864. Released at Louisville on or about October 16, 1864, after taking the Oath of Allegiance.

RICHARDSON, JAMES, Private

Resided in Ashe County. Place and date of enlistment not reported (probably enlisted in the summer or autumn of 1862). Deserted at Big Creek Gap, Tennessee, October 15, 1862. Died on or about November 22, 1862. Place and cause of death not reported. Buried in Bethel Cemetery, Knoxville, Tennessee.

ROARK, JOSHUA, Private

Resided in Ashe County where he enlisted at age 32, July 20, 1862, for the war. Deserted at Big Creek Gap, Tennessee, January 26, 1863. Returned to duty subsequent to June 30, 1863. Wounded in the left leg and captured at Missionary Ridge, Tennessee, November 25, 1863. Hospitalized at Bridgeport, Alabama. Transferred to hospital at Nashville, Tennessee, where he arrived on December 12, 1863. Transferred to the "pest house" in Nashville on January 28, 1864. Exchanged on an unspecified date. Deserted to the enemy on an unspecified date. Confined at Louisville, Kentucky, October 11, 1864. Released at Louisville on or about October 16, 1864, after taking the Oath of Allegiance.

ROARK, SOLOMON, Private

Resided in Ashe County and was by occupation a farmer prior to enlisting in Ashe County at age 30, July 20, 1862, for the war. Deserted at Big Creek Gap, Tennessee, February 23, 1863. Returned to duty on March 31, 1863. Reported present in May-June, 1863. Deserted at Big Creek Gap on August 22, 1863. Returned to duty on an unspecified date. Wounded at Missionary Ridge, Tennessee, November 25, 1863. Died (apparently in the hands of the enemy) of wounds. Place and date of death not reported.

ROARK, WILLIAM, Private

Enlisted at Camp Holmes, near Raleigh, November 1, 1863, for the war. Reported present on surviving company muster rolls through August 31, 1864. No further records.

ROBINSON, BENJAMIN F., Private

Resided in Ashe County where he enlisted on July 20, 1862, for the war. Deserted at Big Creek Gap, Tennessee, February 9, 1863. Went over to the enemy on an unspecified date. Confined at

Louisville, Kentucky, October 11, 1864. Released at Louisville on or about October 16, 1864, after taking the Oath of Allegiance.

ROBISON, WILBORN C., Private

Enlisted in Ashe County on July 20, 1862, for the war. Deserted at Big Creek Gap, Tennessee, February 10, 1863.

ROSE, WYATT, Private

Resided in Ashe County and was by occupation a farmer prior to enlisting in Ashe County on July 20, 1862, for the war. Deserted at Big Creek Gap, Tennessee, January 26, 1863. Returned to duty on February 28, 1863. Reported present in March-June and September-October, 1863. Captured at Missionary Ridge, Tennessee, November 25, 1863. Sent to Nashville, Tennessee. Transferred to Louisville, Kentucky, where he arrived on December 7, 1863. Transferred to Rock Island, Illinois, where he arrived on December 9, 1863. Released at Rock Island on January 25, 1864, after joining the U.S. Navy.

ROTEN, JAMES, Private

Resided in Ashe County and was by occupation a farmer prior to enlisting in Ashe County at age 25, July 20, 1862, for the war. Deserted at Big Creek Gap, Tennessee, February 9, 1863.

SHAW, DOCTOR NEWTON, Private

Born in Guilford County on August 24, 1841. Resided in Ashe County and was by occupation a farmer prior to enlisting in Ashe County at age 20, July 20, 1862, for the war. Reported present in January-June and September-October, 1863. Reported on extra duty at "Maj[or] Mason[']s quarters" from December 5, 1863, through February 29, 1864. Reported sick in hospital at Dalton, Georgia, April 21, 1864. Returned to duty on an unspecified date. Captured at or near Bald Hill, near Atlanta, Georgia, on or about July 22, 1864. Sent to Nashville, Tennessee. Transferred to Louisville, Kentucky, where he arrived on August 3, 1864. Transferred to Camp Chase, Ohio, where he arrived on August 4, 1864. Paroled at Camp Chase on or about March 4, 1865. Received at Boulware's and Cox's Wharves, James River, Virginia, March 10-12, 1865, for exchange. No further records. [Filed a Tennessee pension application after the war.]

SHEETS, LINVILL W. D., Private

Resided in Ashe County and was by occupation a farmer prior to enlisting in Ashe County at age 42, October 10, 1863, for the war. Reported present in January-February, 1864. Deserted to the enemy near Dalton, Georgia, March 19, 1864. Took the Oath of Allegiance at Chattanooga, Tennessee, March 24, 1864.

SHUMAKER, JAMES, Private

Enlisted at Chattanooga, Tennessee, November 17, 1863, for the war. Reported present but under arrest on January 1, 1864. Reason he was arrested not reported. Reported sick in hospital at Dalton, Georgia, April 7, 1864. Died in hospital at Madison, Georgia, May 23 or June 10, 1864. Cause of death not reported.

SLUDER, DAVID, Private

Resided in Ashe County where he enlisted at age 33, July 20, 1862, for the war. Reported present in January-June, 1863. Furloughed for thirty days on an unspecified date. Reported absent on expired furlough on October 31, 1863. Failed to return to duty. Deserted to the enemy on an unspecified date. Confined at Louisville,

Kentucky, October 11, 1864. Released at Louisville on or about October 16, 1864, after taking the Oath of Allegiance.

SLUDER, FELIX, Private

Resided in Ashe County and was by occupation a farmer prior to enlisting at Chattanooga, Tennessee, at age 39, November 17, 1863, for the war. Captured at Missionary Ridge, Tennessee, November 25, 1863. Sent to Nashville, Tennessee. Transferred to Louisville, Kentucky, where he arrived on December 7, 1863. Transferred to Rock Island, Illinois, where he arrived on December 9, 1863. Released at Rock Island on or about January 25, 1864, after joining the U.S. Navy.

SPIVEY, JESSE, Sergeant

Resided in Ashe County where he enlisted at age 22, July 20, 1862, for the war. Was apparently mustered in with the rank of Sergeant. Reported present in January-June and September-October, 1863. Reported sick in hospital at Dalton, Georgia, January 5, 1864. Returned to duty in March-April, 1864. Wounded at Kolb's Farm, near Marietta, Georgia, June 22, 1864. Furloughed for sixty days from hospital at Greensboro, Georgia, June 27, 1864. Returned to duty on an unspecified date. Transferred to Company F of this regiment subsequent to August 31, 1864.

STIKES, JOSEPH W., Private

Born in Ashe County on February 18, 1838. Resided in Ashe County and was by occupation a farmer prior to enlisting in Ashe County at age 24, July 20, 1862, for the war. Was apparently mustered in with the rank of Musician (Fifer). Furloughed for thirty days on October 20, 1862. Reported absent on expired furlough in March-April, 1863. Returned to duty in May-June, 1863. Reduced to ranks in July-October, 1863. Deserted at Campbell Station, Tennessee, August 26, 1863. Returned to duty on an unspecified date. Reported present in January-April, 1864. "Captured on skirmish line" (or deserted to the enemy) near Marietta, Georgia, on or about July 2, 1864. Sent to Nashville, Tennessee. Transferred to Louisville, Kentucky, where he arrived on July 14, 1864. Transferred to Camp Douglas, Chicago, Illinois, where he arrived on July 18, 1864. Released at Camp Douglas on May 13, 1865, after taking the Oath of Allegiance. [North Carolina pension records indicate that he was wounded in the foot at Lookout Mountain, Tennessee, in October, 1863. He also filed a Tennessee pension application after the war in which he states that he was wounded in the right thigh at Chickamauga, Georgia (September, 1863), and in the left thigh at Missionary Ridge, Tennessee (November, 1863).]

TESTERMAN, HUGH, Private

Resided in Ashe County where he enlisted at age 18, October 10, 1863, for the war. Sent to hospital at Dalton, Georgia, January 4, 1864. Deserted to the enemy from camp near Dalton on March 19, 1864. Took the Oath of Allegiance at Chattanooga, Tennessee, March 26, 1864.

TESTERMAN, MORGAN B., Private

Resided in Ashe County and enlisted at Dalton, Georgia, January 28, 1864, for the war. Deserted from camp near Dalton on February 5, 1864. Went over to the enemy on an unspecified date. Took the Oath of Allegiance in East Tennessee on December 14, 1864.

TREADWAY, HENRY, Private

Resided in Ashe County where he enlisted at age 21, July 20, 1862, for the war. Reported present in January-June, 1863. Detailed as a wagoner on an unspecified date. Captured at Cumberland Gap,

Tennessee, September 9, 1863. Sent to Louisville, Kentucky. Transferred to Camp Douglas, Chicago, Illinois, where he arrived on September 26, 1863. Died at Camp Douglas on November 18, 1864, of "smallpox."

TREADWAY, WILLIAM, Private

Resided in Ashe County where he enlisted on July 20, 1862, for the war. Reported present in January-February, 1863. Died at Big Creek Gap, Tennessee, March 19, 1863. Cause of death not reported.

WADDLE, WILLIAM, 1st Sergeant

Born on January 7, 1832. Resided in Ashe County and was by occupation a farmer prior to enlisting in Ashe County at age 30, July 20, 1862, for the war. Mustered in as Private. Reported present on surviving company muster rolls through February 29, 1864. Promoted to 1st Sergeant on March 1, 1864. Furloughed for forty days in March-April, 1864. Returned to duty on an unspecified date. Reported present in May-August, 1864. Transferred to Company F of this regiment subsequent to August 31, 1864.

WALLIS, WILLIAM S., Private

Enlisted in Ashe County on July 20, 1862, for the war. Deserted at Big Creek Gap, Tennessee, February 10, 1863. [May have served later as Private in Company I, 13th Regiment Tennessee Cavalry (Union).]

WILLIAMS, HUGH L., Private

Enlisted in Ashe County on July 20, 1862, for the war. Deserted at Big Creek Gap, Tennessee, February 9, 1863. Returned to duty on February 28, 1863. Reported present in May-June, 1863. Deserted near La Fayette, Georgia, September 17, 1863.

WILSON, JOHN L., Private

Enlisted in Ashe County on July 20, 1862, for the war. Deserted at Big Creek Gap, Tennessee, January 6, 1863.

WOOD, RUFUS, Private

Resided in Ashe County where he enlisted at age 19, July 20, 1862, for the war. Deserted at Big Creek Gap, Tennessee, February 23, 1863. Returned to duty on March 31, 1863. Reported present in May-June, 1863. Wounded at Chickamauga, Georgia, September 20, 1863. Hospitalized at Macon, Georgia. Furloughed for thirty days on September 27, 1863. Reported absent on expired furlough in January-February, 1864. Reported absent on furlough in March-April, 1864. Detailed for duty as a cattle guard on August 10, 1864. Transferred to Company F of this regiment subsequent to August 31, 1864.

WOOD, WILLIAM, Private

Resided in Ashe County and was by occupation a farmer prior to enlisting in Ashe County at age 24, July 20, 1862, for the war. Reported present in March-June, 1863. Deserted at Big Creek Gap, Tennessee, August 22, 1863. Returned from desertion on November 20, 1863, and was placed under arrest. Returned to duty on November 23, 1863. Reported present in January-April, 1864. Wounded at Kolb's Farm, near Marietta, Georgia, June 22, 1864. Deserted to the enemy near Atlanta, Georgia, July 29, 1864. Took the Oath of Allegiance at Chattanooga, Tennessee, on or about August 10, 1864. Transferred to Louisville, Kentucky, where he was released on or about August 29, 1864, after taking the Oath of Allegiance.

YOUNCE, WILLIAM H., Private

Born on July 26, 1842. Resided in Ashe County where he enlisted at age 19, July 20, 1862, for the war. Deserted at Big Creek Gap, Tennessee, February 10, 1863.

COMPANY M

This company was raised in Watauga and Ashe Counties. It was mustered into service at Boone on September 26, 1862, and assigned to the 58th Regiment N.C. Troops as Company M. On May 5, 1863, Company M was consolidated with Company G of the same regiment. Those members of the company who were present for duty were then transferred to Company G.

The following roster was compiled primarily from information in the microfilm edition of the Compiled Service Records of Soldiers Who Served in Organizations from the State of North Carolina (Record Group 109, M270), National Archives and Records Administration, Washington, D.C. Record Group 109 includes enlistment papers, pay vouchers, requisitions, letters of resignation, discharge certificates, and abstracts of medical and prisoner of war returns. Materials relating specifically to this company include muster rolls dated January-April, 1863.

Also utilized in this roster were *The War of the Rebellion: A Compilation of the Official Records of the Union and Confederate Armies*, the North Carolina adjutant general's *Roll of Honor*, state militia records, newspaper casualty lists and obituaries, wartime claims for bounty pay and allowances, postwar registers of claims for artificial limbs, Confederate pension applications filed with the states of North Carolina, Tennessee, and Florida, Confederate Soldiers' Home records, and the 1860 and 1870 federal censuses of North Carolina. A search was made also for relevant letters, diaries, reminiscences, and other manuscripts in the Southern Historical Collection (University of North Carolina-Chapel Hill), the Duke University Library Special Collections Department, and the North Carolina Division of Archives and History.

Among the secondary sources consulted were records of the North Carolina division of the United Daughters of the Confederacy, postwar rosters, regimental and county histories, marriage bond, will, and cemetery indexes, published and unpublished genealogies, biographical dictionaries, the North Carolina *County Heritage Book* series, the *Confederate Veteran*, Walter Clark's *Histories of the Several Regiments and Battalions from North Carolina in the Great War, 1861-'65*, and the North Carolina volume of the extended edition of *Confederate Military History*.

OFFICERS

CAPTAIN

PHILLIPS, JONATHAN L.

Elected Captain on September 26, 1862. Reported absent on detached service in Watauga County in January-February, 1863. Reported present in March-April, 1863. Transferred to Company G of this regiment in May, 1863. [Previously served as Captain in the 98th Regiment N.C. Militia.]

LIEUTENANTS

HOPKINS, GEORGE W., 1st Lieutenant

Enlisted in Watauga County. Appointed 1st Lieutenant on September 26, 1862. Reported present but sick in January-February, 1863. Reported present in March-April, 1863. Transferred to Company G of this regiment in May, 1863.

NORRIS, JOHN RILEY, 3rd Lieutenant

Previously served as Private in Company B, 37th Regiment N.C. Troops. Appointed 3rd Lieutenant of this company on September 26, 1862. Reported present in January-April, 1863. Transferred to Company G of this regiment in May, 1863.

RAY, THOMAS, 2nd Lieutenant

Resided in Ashe County and was by occupation a farmer prior to enlisting at age 29. Elected 2nd Lieutenant on September 26, 1862. Reported absent on detached service in Watauga County in January-February, 1863. Reported present in March-April, 1863. Transferred to Company G of this regiment in May, 1863.

NONCOMMISSIONED OFFICERS AND PRIVATES

BALL, ALFORD T., Sergeant

Resided in Wilkes County and enlisted in Watauga County at age 20, September 26, 1862, for the war. Was apparently mustered in with the rank of Corporal. Deserted at Big Creek Gap, Tennessee, January 27, 1863. Returned to duty on March 20, 1863. Promoted to Sergeant prior to May 1, 1863. Transferred to Company G of this regiment in May, 1863.

BISHOP, SAMUEL J., 1st Sergeant

Resided in Watauga County and was by occupation a "domestic" prior to enlisting in Watauga County at age 22, September 26, 1862, for the war. Was apparently mustered in with the rank of 1st Sergeant. Reported present in January-April, 1863. Transferred to Company G of this regiment in May, 1863.

BLACKBURN, EDMOND, Private

Resided in Watauga County where he enlisted on September 26, 1862, for the war. Reported absent without leave on December 5, 1862. Returned to duty on March 20, 1863. Transferred to Company G of this regiment in May, 1863.

CALLOWAY, ELIJAH, Private

Resided in Ashe County and enlisted in Watauga County on September 26, 1862, for the war. Deserted from camp at Big Creek Gap, Tennessee, December 21, 1862. Transferred to Company G of this regiment in May, 1863, while listed as a deserter.

CALLOWAY, JAMES, Private

Resided in Ashe County where he enlisted on September 26, 1862, for the war. Deserted at Big Creek Gap, Tennessee, December 9, 1862. Transferred to Company G of this regiment in May, 1863, while listed as a deserter.

CALLOWAY, MARSHAL, Private

Resided in Ashe County and was by occupation a farmer prior to enlisting in Watauga County at age 35, September 26, 1862, for the war. Deserted from camp at Big Creek Gap, Tennessee, December 21, 1862. Transferred to Company G of this regiment in May, 1863, while listed as a deserter.

CALLOWAY, WILLIAM, Private

Resided in Ashe County and enlisted in Watauga County on September 26, 1862, for the war. Deserted from camp at Big Creek Gap, Tennessee, December 9, 1862. Transferred to Company G of this regiment in May, 1863, while listed as a deserter.

CHURCH, JORDAN, Private

Born in Wilkes County and resided in Watauga County where he was by occupation a farmer prior to enlisting in Watauga County at age 25, September 26, 1862, for the war. Furloughed for ten days on October 25, 1862. Failed to return to duty and was reported absent without leave in January-February, 1863. Transferred to Company G of this regiment in May, 1863, while absent without leave. [May have served previously as Private in Company B, 37th Regiment N.C. Troops.]

CHURCH, MARION, Private

Resided in Watauga County and was by occupation a farmer prior to enlisting in Watauga County at age 30, September 26, 1862, for the war. Reported absent without leave on November 5, 1862. Transferred to Company G of this regiment in May, 1863, while absent without leave.

COOK, JOHN, Private

Resided in Watauga County where he enlisted on September 26, 1862, for the war. Deserted from camp at Big Creek Gap, Tennessee, January 5, 1863.

DUFF, DAVID C., Private

Resided in Johnson County, Tennessee, and enlisted in Watauga County on September 26, 1862, for the war. Deserted at Big Creek Gap, Tennessee, November 28, 1862. Transferred to Company G of this regiment in May, 1863, while listed as a deserter.

FORD, SQUIRE J., Private

Resided in Watauga County and was by occupation a day laborer prior to enlisting in Watauga County at age 22, September 26, 1862, for the war. Furloughed for fifteen days on October 25, 1862. Failed to return to duty and was reported absent without leave in January-February, 1863. Transferred to Company G of this regiment in May, 1863, while absent without leave.

GENTRY, BENJAMIN, Private

Born in Tennessee and resided in Ashe County prior to enlisting in Watauga County at age 26, September 26, 1862, for the war. Furloughed for ten days on October 25, 1862. Failed to return to duty and was reported absent without leave in January-February, 1863. Transferred to Company G of this regiment in May, 1863, while absent without leave.

GENTRY, CALLAWAY, Private

Resided in Ashe County and enlisted in Watauga County on September 26, 1862, for the war. Reported sick in hospital in January-February, 1863. Reported present in March-April, 1863. Transferred to Company G of this regiment in May, 1863.

GENTRY, JESSE, Corporal

Resided in Ashe County and enlisted in Watauga County at age 22, September 26, 1862, for the war. Mustered in as Private. Reported present in January-February, 1863. Reported sick in hospital at Clinton, Tennessee, in March-April, 1863. Promoted to Corporal in March-April, 1863. Transferred to Company G of this regiment in May, 1863.

GENTRY, JOSEPH C., ———

North Carolina pension records indicate that he served in this company.

GENTRY, WILLIAM P., Private

Resided in Ashe County and enlisted in Watauga County at age 27, September 26, 1862, for the war. Deserted at Big Creek Gap, Tennessee, December 21, 1862. Transferred to Company G of this regiment in May, 1863, while listed as a deserter.

GRAGG, EDWARD P., Private

Resided in Watauga County where he enlisted on September 26, 1862, for the war. Was apparently mustered in with the rank of Sergeant. Deserted from hospital at Jacksboro, Tennessee, February 14, 1863. Reduced to ranks prior to May 1, 1863. Transferred to Company G of this regiment in May, 1863, while listed as a deserter.

GRAHAM, DANIEL, Private

Born in Virginia and resided in Ashe County where he was by occupation a farmer prior to enlisting in Watauga County at age 35, September 26, 1862, for the war. Deserted at Big Creek Gap, Tennessee, on the night of December 19, 1862. Transferred to Company G of this regiment in May, 1863, while listed as a deserter.

GRAY, McKINSEY M., Private

Resided in Watauga County where he enlisted on September 26, 1862, for the war. Furloughed for ten days on October 25, 1862. Reported absent without leave in January-February, 1863. Transferred to Company G of this regiment in May, 1863, while absent without leave.

GREEN, FERGERSON, Private

Resided in Watauga County and was by occupation a farmer prior to enlisting in Watauga County at age 23, September 26, 1862, for the war. Reported present in January-February, 1863. Hospitalized at Knoxville, Tennessee, in March-April, 1863. Transferred to Company G of this regiment in May, 1863, while in hospital at Knoxville.

GREEN, ISAAC, Private

Resided in Watauga County and was by occupation a day laborer prior to enlisting in Watauga County at age 21, September 26, 1862, for the war. Furloughed for fifteen days on October 25, 1862. Reported absent without leave in January-February, 1863. Transferred to Company G of this regiment in May, 1863, while absent without leave.

GREEN, SMITH P., Private

Resided in Watauga County and was by occupation a blacksmith prior to enlisting in Watauga County at age 25, September 26, 1862, for the war. Reported absent without leave in January-February, 1863. Survived the war.

GREER, ISAIAH, Private

Resided in Ashe County and enlisted in Watauga County on September 26, 1862, for the war. Deserted at Big Creek Gap, Tennessee, on the night of December 19, 1862. Transferred to Company G of this regiment in May, 1863, while listed as a deserter.

GREER, JEFFERSON, Private

Resided in Ashe County and enlisted in Watauga County on September 26, 1862, for the war. Deserted at Big Creek Gap, Tennessee, on the night of December 19, 1862. Transferred to Company G of this regiment in May, 1863, while listed as a deserter.

GREER, NOAH, Private

Resided in Ashe County and enlisted in Watauga County at age 23, September 26, 1862, for the war. Deserted at Big Creek Gap, Tennessee, December 3, 1862. Transferred to Company G of this regiment in May, 1863, while listed as a deserter.

GREER, PHILLIP, Private

Resided in Watauga County where he enlisted on September 26, 1862, for the war. Deserted at Big Creek Gap, Tennessee, on the night of December 19, 1862. Transferred to Company G of this regiment in May, 1863, while listed as a deserter.

GREER, THOMAS, Private

Resided in Ashe County and enlisted in Watauga County on September 26, 1862, for the war. Deserted at Big Creek Gap, Tennessee, on the night of December 19, 1862. Transferred to Company G of this regiment in May, 1863, while listed as a deserter.

GROGAN, ELIJAH, Private

Resided in Ashe County and was by occupation a farmer prior to enlisting in Watauga County at age 25, September 26, 1862, for the war. Furloughed for twenty days on October 25, 1862. Failed to return to duty and was reported absent without leave in January-February, 1863. Transferred to Company G of this regiment in May, 1863, while absent without leave.

GROGAN, HENRY, Private

Enlisted in Watauga County on September 26, 1862, for the war. Reported absent without leave in January-February, 1863. No further records. [May have served later as Private in Company I, 13th Regiment Tennessee Cavalry (Union).]

GROGAN, JORDAN, Private

Born in Rockingham County on November 15, 1845. Resided in Ashe County and enlisted in Watauga County on September 26, 1862, for the war. Deserted at Big Creek Gap, Tennessee, January 5, 1863. Returned to duty on March 20, 1863. Transferred to Company G of this regiment in May, 1863.

HAMLETT, OLIVER MERRITT, Private

Born in Burke County and resided in Watauga County where he was by occupation a farmer or "domestic" prior to enlisting in Watauga County at age 31, September 26, 1862, for the war. Furloughed for fifteen days on October 25, 1862. Failed to return to duty and was reported absent without leave in January-February, 1863. Transferred to Company G of this regiment in May, 1863, while absent without leave.

HAMPTON, WILLIAM F., Private

Resided in Watauga County and was by occupation a farmer prior to enlisting in Watauga County at age 21, September 26, 1862, for the war. Reported absent without leave on November 5, 1862. Returned to duty on March 20, 1863. Transferred to Company G of this regiment in May, 1863.

HARP, CALVIN, Private

Resided in Watauga County where he enlisted on September 26, 1862, for the war. Furloughed for twenty days on October 25, 1862. Failed to return to duty and was reported absent without leave in January-February, 1863. Transferred to Company G of this regiment in May, 1863, while absent without leave.

HARRISON, JOSEPH W., Private

Resided in Watauga County where he enlisted on September 26, 1862, for the war. Furloughed for fifteen days on October 25, 1862. Failed to return to duty and was reported absent without leave in January-February, 1863. Transferred to Company G of this regiment in May, 1863, while absent without leave.

HATTON, WARREN A., Private

Resided in Watauga County and was by occupation a "domestic" prior to enlisting in Watauga County at age 23, September 26, 1862, for the war. Furloughed for fifteen days on October 25, 1862. Failed to return to duty and was reported absent without leave in January-February, 1863. Transferred to Company G of this regiment in May, 1863, while absent without leave.

HOLEMAN, JAMES, Private

Resided in Watauga County and was by occupation a "domestic" prior to enlisting in Watauga County at age 22, September 26, 1862, for the war. Reported present in January-April, 1863. Transferred to Company G of this regiment in May, 1863.

HOLEMAN, SMITH, Private

Resided in Watauga County and was by occupation a "domestic" prior to enlisting in Watauga County at age 20, September 26, 1862, for the war. Reported present in January-April, 1863. Transferred to Company G of this regiment in May, 1863.

JONES, EDMOND R., Sergeant

Previously served as Private in Company B, 37th Regiment N.C. Troops. Transferred to this company on February 28, 1863. Mustered in as Private. Promoted to Sergeant in March-April, 1863. Reported present in March-April, 1863. Transferred to Company G of this regiment in May, 1863.

JONES, LARKIN G., Private

Enlisted in Watauga County on September 26, 1862, for the war. Died in hospital at Jacksboro, Tennessee, March 31, 1863. Cause of death not reported.

JONES, ROBERT, Private

Resided in Ashe County and enlisted in Watauga County on September 26, 1862, for the war. Deserted at Big Creek Gap, Tennessee, on the night of December 19, 1862. Transferred to Company G of this regiment in May, 1863, while listed as a deserter.

KELLER, JESSE ROBERT, Musician

Born in Watauga County* where he resided as a farmer or "domestic" prior to enlisting in Watauga County at age 20, September 26, 1862, for the war. Mustered in as Private. Reported present in

January-April, 1863. Appointed Musician (Fifer) in March-April, 1863. Transferred to Company G of this regiment in May, 1863.

KELLER, NICHOLAS, Private

Resided in Watauga County and was by occupation a farmer or "domestic" prior to enlisting in Watauga County at age 22, September 26, 1862, for the war. Mustered in as Private. Reported absent without leave on November 5, 1862. Returned to duty on March 20, 1863. Appointed Musician (Drummer) prior to May 1, 1863. Reduced to ranks and transferred to Company G of this regiment in May, 1863.

KELLER, WILLIAM, Private

Resided in Wilkes County and was by occupation a millwright prior to enlisting in Watauga County at age 27, September 26, 1862, for the war. Reported absent without leave on November 5, 1862. Returned to duty on February 20, 1863. Detailed for duty as a hospital nurse at Knoxville, Tennessee, April 15, 1863. Transferred to Company G of this regiment in May, 1863.

LEWIS, JAMES, Private

Resided in Watauga County where he enlisted on September 26, 1862, for the war. Furloughed for five days on October 25, 1862. Failed to return to duty and was reported absent without leave in January-February, 1863. Transferred to Company G of this regiment in May, 1863, while absent without leave.

LORANCE, GEORGE W., Private

Resided in Ashe County and enlisted in Watauga County at age 21, September 26, 1862, for the war. Deserted at Big Creek Gap, Tennessee, on the night of December 19, 1862. Transferred to Company G of this regiment in May, 1863, while listed as a deserter.

MAIN, HARRISON, Private

Born in Ashe County and resided in Watauga County where he was by occupation a farmer prior to enlisting on September 26, 1862, for the war. Deserted at Big Creek Gap, Tennessee, on or about December 1-3, 1862. Transferred to Company G of this regiment in May, 1863, while listed as a deserter.

MIKEAL, ALEXANDER, Private

Resided in Ashe County and was by occupation a farmer prior to enlisting in Watauga County at age 21, September 26, 1862, for the war. Furloughed for ten days on October 25, 1862. Failed to return to duty and was reported absent without leave in January-February, 1863. Transferred to Company G of this regiment in May, 1863, while absent without leave.

MIKEAL, FREDERICK, Private

Born in Ashe County where he resided as a farmer prior to enlisting in Watauga County at age 25, September 26, 1862, for the war. Furloughed for ten days on October 25, 1862. Failed to return to duty and was reported absent without leave in January-February, 1863. Transferred to Company G of this regiment in May, 1863, while absent without leave.

MIKEAL, ISAAC, Private

Resided in Watauga County where he enlisted at age 20, September 26, 1862, for the war. Was apparently mustered in with the rank of Sergeant. Deserted from camp at Big Creek Gap, Tennessee, January 27, 1863. Returned to duty on March 20, 1863. Reduced to ranks prior to May 1, 1863. Transferred to Company G of this regiment in May, 1863.

MOODY, BENJAMIN, JR., Private

Enlisted in Watauga County at age 25, September 26, 1862, for the war. Furloughed for ten days on October 25, 1862. Failed to return to duty and was reported absent without leave in January-February, 1863. Transferred to Company G of this regiment in May, 1863, while absent without leave.

NORRIS, ISAAC, Private

Born on February 9, 1837. Resided in Watauga County where he enlisted at age 25, September 26, 1862, for the war. Was apparently mustered in with the rank of Sergeant. Deserted at Big Creek Gap, Tennessee, February 14, 1863. Returned to duty on an unspecified date. Furloughed for ten days on March 22, 1863. Transferred to Company G of this regiment in May, 1863, while absent without leave.

NORRIS, JOHN N., Private

Enlisted in Watauga County on September 26, 1862, for the war. Reported absent without leave in January-February, 1863. No further records.

NORRIS, WILLIAM W., Corporal

Resided in Watauga County and was by occupation a "domestic" prior to enlisting in Watauga County at age 21, September 26, 1862, for the war. Mustered in as Private. Deserted from camp at Big Creek Gap, Tennessee, February 14, 1863. Returned to duty on March 20, 1863. Promoted to Corporal prior to May 1, 1863. Transferred to Company G of this regiment in May, 1863.

PERKINS, FRANKLIN, Private

Resided in Ashe County and enlisted in Watauga County on September 26, 1862, for the war. Furloughed for ten days on October 25, 1862. Failed to return to duty and was reported absent without leave in January-February, 1863. Transferred to Company G of this regiment in May, 1863, while absent without leave.

PERKINS, JOHN, Private

Resided in Ashe County and was by occupation a farmer prior to enlisting in Watauga County at age 21, September 26, 1862, for the war. Furloughed for ten days on October 25, 1862. Failed to return to duty and was reported absent without leave in January-February, 1863. Transferred to Company G of this regiment in May, 1863, while absent without leave.

PHILLIPS, ELIJAH, Private

Enlisted in Watauga County on September 26, 1862, for the war. Was apparently mustered in with the rank of Corporal. Reported present but under arrest in January-February, 1863. Reason he was arrested not reported. Returned to duty and was reduced to ranks in March-April, 1863. Died at Knoxville, Tennessee, May 9, 1863. Cause of death not reported.

PHILLIPS, HAMILTON, Private

Resided in Ashe County and was by occupation a farmer prior to enlisting in Watauga County at age 30, September 26, 1862, for the war. Furloughed for ten days on October 25, 1862. Failed to return to duty and was reported absent without leave in January-February, 1863. Transferred to Company G of this regiment in May, 1863, while absent without leave.

PHILLIPS, HUGH, Private

Born in Wilkes County and resided in Ashe County where he was by occupation a farmer prior to enlisting in Watauga County at age 29, September 26, 1862, for the war. Furloughed for ten days on October 25, 1862. Failed to return to duty and was reported absent without leave in January-February, 1863. Transferred to Company G of this regiment in May, 1863, while absent without leave.

PHILLIPS, NATHAN, Private

Resided in Ashe County and enlisted in Watauga County on September 26, 1862, for the war. Furloughed for ten days on October 25, 1862. Failed to return to duty and was reported absent without leave in January-February, 1863. Transferred to Company G of this regiment in May, 1863, while absent without leave.

PHILLIPS, PAYTON, Private

Resided in Ashe County and was by occupation a farmer prior to enlisting in Watauga County at age 31, September 26, 1862, for the war. Reported present but under arrest in January-February, 1863. Reason he was arrested not reported. Returned to duty in March-April, 1863. Transferred to Company G of this regiment in May, 1863.

PIPES, JOHN W., Private

Resided in Watauga County and was by occupation a farmer prior to enlisting in Watauga County at age 34, September 26, 1862, for the war. Furloughed for ten days on October 25, 1862. Failed to return to duty and was reported absent without leave in January-February, 1863. Transferred to Company G of this regiment in May, 1863, while absent without leave.

RAINEY, WILLIAM H., Private

Resided in Johnson County, Tennessee, and enlisted in Watauga County on September 26, 1862, for the war. Deserted at Big Creek Gap, Tennessee, November 28, 1862.

RASH, PAYTON, Private

Enlisted in Watauga County on September 26, 1862, for the war. Deserted from camp at Jacksboro, Tennessee, December 29, 1862. Returned to duty on March 20, 1863. Transferred to Company G of this regiment in May, 1863.

REACE, WILLIAM, Private

Resided in Watauga County where he enlisted on September 26, 1862, for the war. Furloughed for ten days on October 25, 1862. Failed to return to duty and was reported absent without leave in January-February, 1863. Transferred to Company G of this regiment in May, 1863, while absent without leave.

SHAW, ALFRED, Private

Resided in Ashe County and was by occupation a farmer prior to enlisting in Watauga County at age 26, September 26, 1862, for the war. Furloughed for fifteen days on October 25, 1862. Failed to return to duty and was reported absent without leave in January-February, 1863. Transferred to Company G of this regiment in May, 1863, while absent without leave.

SHAW, JOHN, Private

Resided in Ashe County and enlisted in Watauga County at age 32, September 26, 1862, for the war. Reported present but under arrest in January-February, 1863. Reason he was arrested not reported.

Returned to duty in March-April, 1863. Transferred to Company G of this regiment in May, 1863.

SHAW, SOLOMON, Private

Resided in Ashe County and enlisted in Watauga County at age 27, September 26, 1862, for the war. Deserted from camp at Jacksboro, Tennessee, December 29, 1862. Returned to duty on March 20, 1863. Transferred to Company G of this regiment in May, 1863.

STANBURY, JOSHUA S., Private

Resided in Watauga County and was by occupation a farmer prior to enlisting in Watauga County at age 25, September 26, 1862, for the war. Deserted from hospital at Jacksboro, Tennessee, February 14, 1863. Transferred to Company G of this regiment in May, 1863, while listed as a deserter.

STANBURY, NATHAN W., Private

Resided in Watauga County and was by occupation a farmer prior to enlisting in Watauga County at age 28, September 26, 1862, for the war. Deserted from hospital at Jacksboro, Tennessee, February 14, 1863. Transferred to Company G of this regiment in May, 1863, while listed as a deserter.

STORIE, JESSE, Private

Enlisted in Watauga County on September 26, 1862, for the war. Furloughed for ten days on October 25, 1862. Failed to return to duty and was reported absent without leave in January-February, 1863. Transferred to Company G of this regiment in May, 1863, while absent without leave.

STORIE, NOAH, Private

Born in Ashe County and resided in Watauga County where he was by occupation a farmer prior to enlisting on September 26, 1862, for the war. Deserted from camp at Big Creek Gap, Tennessee, January 5, 1863. Transferred to Company G of this regiment in May, 1863, while listed as a deserter.

TRIPLETT, JESSE O., Corporal

Resided in Watauga County and was by occupation a farmer prior to enlisting in Watauga County at age 34, September 26, 1862, for the war. Mustered in as Private. Reported present in January-February, 1863. Promoted to Corporal in March-April, 1863. Died in hospital at Clinton, Tennessee, April 15, 1863. Cause of death not reported.

TRIPLETT, THOMAS H., Private

Previously served as Private in Company K of this regiment. Transferred to this company on or about September 26, 1862. Furloughed for ten days on October 25, 1862. Failed to return to duty and was reported absent without leave in January-February, 1863. No further records. [May have served later as Private in Companies D and E, 2nd Regiment N.C. Mounted Infantry (Union), and Company E, 13th Regiment Tennessee Cavalry (Union).]

TRIVETT, LEWIS W., Private

Resided in Ashe County and was by occupation a farmer prior to enlisting in Watauga County at age 29, September 26, 1862, for the war. Was apparently mustered in with the rank of Corporal. Deserted from camp at Big Creek Gap, Tennessee, February 14, 1863. Reduced to ranks in March-April, 1863. Transferred to Company G of this regiment in May, 1863, while listed as a deserter.

TUCKER, JAMES, Private

Resided in Watauga County and was by occupation a farmer prior to enlisting in Watauga County at age 29, September 26, 1862, for the war. Furloughed for ten days on October 26, 1862. Failed to return to duty and was reported absent without leave in January-February, 1863. Transferred to Company G of this regiment in May, 1863, while absent without leave.

TURNER, A. J., Private

Enlisted in Watauga County on September 26, 1862, for the war. Was apparently mustered in with the rank of Corporal. Deserted from hospital on February 14, 1863. Reduced to ranks in March-April, 1863. Returned to duty on April 5, 1863. Transferred to Company G of this regiment in May, 1863.

VANDIKE, EMANUEL, Private

Born in Catawba County* and resided in Watauga County where he enlisted at age 26, September 26, 1862, for the war. Furloughed for fourteen days on October 25, 1862. Failed to return to duty and was reported absent without leave in January-February, 1863. Transferred to Company G of this regiment in May, 1863, while absent without leave.

WATSON, ALFRED, Private

Enlisted in Watauga County on September 26, 1862, for the war. Died at Big Creek Gap, Tennessee, February 19, 1863, of "brain fever."

WATSON, AMBROSE L. P., Private

Resided in Watauga County and was by occupation a farmer prior to enlisting in Watauga County at age 28, September 26, 1862, for the war. Furloughed for ten days on October 25, 1862. Failed to return to duty and was reported absent without leave in January-February, 1863. Transferred to Company G of this regiment in May, 1863, while absent without leave.

WATSON, CALLAWAY, Private

Resided in Watauga County where he enlisted on September 26, 1862, for the war. Furloughed for ten days on October 25, 1862. Failed to return to duty and was reported absent without leave in January-February, 1863. No further records.

WHITE, AMBROSE, Private

Enlisted in Watauga County on September 26, 1862, for the war. Reported present in January-April, 1863. Transferred to Company G of this regiment in May, 1863.

WILCOX, FRANCIS MARION, Private

Born in Ashe County on November 13, 1843. Resided in Watauga County where he enlisted on September 26, 1862, for the war. Deserted from camp at Big Creek Gap, Tennessee, on the night of December 19, 1862. [May have served later as Private in Company D, 40th Regiment Kentucky Infantry (Union).]

WILSON, JOHN H., Private

Enlisted in Watauga County on September 26, 1862, for the war. Reported present in January-February, 1863. Reported sick in hospital at Knoxville, Tennessee, in March-April, 1863. Transferred to Company G of this regiment in May, 1863, while sick in hospital at Knoxville.

WILSON, JONATHAN J., Private

Enlisted in Watauga County on September 26, 1862, for the war. Reported present in January-February, 1863. Detailed as a hospital nurse at Clinton, Tennessee, in March-April, 1863. Transferred to Company G of this regiment in May, 1863, while on detail at Clinton.

WINEBARGER, LEVI, Corporal

Resided in Watauga County and was by occupation a farmer prior to enlisting in Watauga County at age 28, September 26, 1862, for the war. Mustered in as Sergeant. Deserted from camp at Big Creek Gap, Tennessee, February 19, 1863. Rejoined the company on or about March 3, 1863, and was reduced to the rank of Corporal. Transferred to Company G of this regiment in May-June, 1863.

WORLEY, SAMUEL, Private

Resided in Watauga County where he enlisted at age 21, September 26, 1862, for the war. Furloughed for ten days on October 25, 1862. Failed to return to duty and was reported absent without leave in January-February, 1863. Transferred to Company G of this regiment in May, 1863, while absent without leave.

YOUNCE, ANDREW J., Sergeant

Resided in Watauga County and was by occupation a mechanic prior to enlisting in Watauga County at age 31, September 26, 1862, for the war. Mustered in as Private. Deserted at Big Creek Gap, Tennessee, February 14, 1863. Returned to duty on March 20, 1863. Promoted to Sergeant prior to May 1, 1863. Transferred to Company G of this regiment in May, 1863.

MISCELLANEOUS

BROYLES, H. S., _____

Born in Huntsville, Alabama, June 25, 1847. A Tennessee pension application indicates that he served in this regiment.

BURLESON, WILLIAM P., _____

Place and date of enlistment not reported (probably enlisted in the late summer of 1862). Died at Cumberland Gap, Tennessee, September 15, 1862, of "typhoid fever." Was 18 years of age at the time of his death. "He was a pious and good boy, and leaves a father and mother to mourn his loss." [Asheville News, October 9, 1862.]

CANTRELL, THOMAS, _____

North Carolina pension records indicate that he served in this regiment.

CLONTZ, R. NELSON, _____

North Carolina pension records indicate that he served in this regiment.

CORN, N. P. M., _____

North Carolina pension records indicate that he probably served in this regiment.

DAVIS, HENRY N., Private

Resided in Adams County, Mississippi. Place and date of enlistment not reported (probably enlisted in the summer of 1864). Deserted to the enemy on an unspecified date. Confined at Atlanta, Georgia, on or about September 20, 1864. Transferred to Louisville, Kentucky, where he arrived on October 11, 1864. Released at Louisville on or about October 20, 1864, after taking the Oath of Allegiance.

FARDOW, W., Private

Place and date of enlistment not reported. Captured and paroled at Athens, Georgia, on or about May 8, 1865.

FRANKS, WILLIAM, _____

Probably resided in Madison County. Place and date of enlistment not reported. Listed as a deserter on March 15, 1864.

HAMMOND, G. C., _____

Probably resided in Watauga County. Place and date of enlistment not reported. Listed as a deserter on March 15, 1864.

HARBIN, MILTON G., Private

Served as Private in Company D, 6th Regiment N.C. State Troops. Records of the 6th Regiment indicate that he was reported absent without leave and "with" the 58th Regiment on August 1, 1862; however, records of the 58th Regiment do not indicate that he served herein. No further records.

HOWELL, JAMES J., Private

Resided in Ashe County. Place and date of enlistment not reported (probably enlisted in the summer of 1864). Deserted to the enemy on an unspecified date. Confined at Chattanooga, Tennessee, on or about July 14, 1864. Transferred to Louisville, Kentucky, July 16, 1864. Released at Louisville on or about July 18, 1864, after taking the Oath of Allegiance.

JACKSON, BILL, Cook

Died (probably at or near Big Creek Gap, Tennessee) on October 25, 1862, of measles.

PERRY, RICHARD M., Sergeant

Records of Company A, 37th Regiment N.C. Troops, indicate that he was transferred to that unit from the 58th Regiment N.C. Troops on January 13, 1863; however, records of the 58th Regiment do not indicate that he served herein.

THOMPSON, JOHN M., Private

Records of Company D, 6th Regiment N.C. State Troops, indicate that he deserted from that unit in November, 1862, and served in the 58th Regiment until he rejoined the 6th Regiment on April 3, 1863. Records of the 58th Regiment do not indicate that he served herein.

WILLIAMS, MAC, Private

Resided in Yancey County. Postwar records of the North Carolina state auditor indicate that he "lost both eyes" during the war while serving in the 58th Regiment.

James Thomas Weaver, a prosperous farmer born in Buncombe County in 1828, served as captain of a prewar militia company and subsequently as a 2nd lieutenant, 1st lieutenant, captain, major, and lieutenant colonel in the 60th North Carolina. In this ambrotype he is armed with a revolver and a militia officer's sword. The small buckle on his over-the-shoulder belt and his rectangular waist-belt plate, gold banded forage cap, and high qual- ity uniform fabric all suggest prewar militia trappings. Weaver was almost certainly the most widely respected and admired officer in the 60th Regiment. Capt. Thomas W. Patton of Company C wrote after the war that "In danger [Lieutenant Colonel Weaver] . . . was the most perfectly cool, self-possessed man I ever saw." Weaver's service record appears on pages 502 and 505. Image provided by Library of Congress.

Rutherford County native Benjamin Franklin Marlow of Company K, 60th North Carolina, was a 31-year-old McDowell County laborer when he enlisted at Asheville on May 15, 1862. He was wounded at Chickamauga, Georgia, September 20, 1863, and died at Atlanta on December 9, 1863, of disease. In this tintype Private (subsequently Corporal) Marlow wears a gray coat with spacing for six brass buttons. His revolver is an M1849 Colt (caliber 31), called the "pocket model," and his belt is an unusual type with an interlocking buckle. The cord or chain around his neck probably supports a pendant or key. Marlow's service record appears on page 588. Image provided by Mrs. Paul R. Ford.

60TH REGIMENT N.C. TROOPS

Six companies of what subsequently became the 60th Regiment N.C. Troops were organized by Joseph A. McDowell, a Madison County physician, in May 1862 as a local defense battalion for the defense of the French Broad Valley.[1] During the period that they remained part of McDowell's Battalion N.C. Infantry, known also as the 6th Battalion N.C. Infantry, the six companies were identified by the numerical designations "First" through "Sixth."[2] Subsequently, they became Companies A, B, C, E, K, and F, respectively, of the 60th N.C. Troops. The 6th Battalion was mustered into Confederate service on August 1, 1862, and redesignated the 1st Battalion N.C. Infantry.[3] A seventh company, which later became Company D of the 60th, was assigned to the 1st Battalion on the same date.[4] Two additional companies, subsequently G and H of the 60th, joined the battalion on August 29 and September 16. A tenth company, Company I, composed of "volunteers and details from [other] companies [in the regiment] unnecessarily large," was organized on September 13, 1862.[5] The 60th Regiment N.C. Troops was formally organized as such on October 8, 1862.[6]

1. McDowell, a member of the state legislature, proposed such an organization in a letter to Gov. Henry T. Clark dated February 25, 1862. Recruitment of Company A, the first company subsequently assigned to the 60th North Carolina, probably began on or about January 27, 1862, the date of Capt. Washington M. Hardy's rank as commander of that company. See Joseph A. McDowell to Henry T. Clark, February 25, 1862, Henry T. Clark, Governors Papers, State Archives, North Carolina Division of Archives and History (NCDAH), Raleigh; *Asheville News*, February 20 and May 15, 1862; James A. Ray, "Sixtieth Regiment," in Walter Clark, ed., *Histories of the Several Regiments and Battalions from North Carolina in the Great War, 1861-'65*, 5 vols. (Raleigh and Goldsboro: State of North Carolina, 1901), 3:473, hereafter cited as Ray, "Sixtieth Regiment," in Clark, *Histories of the North Carolina Regiments*.

2. McDowell's 6th Battalion N.C. Infantry is not to be confused with the following units: Lt. Col. John Thomas P. C. Cohoon's Battalion Virginia Infantry, a mixed unit of Virginians and North Carolinians that was originally known as the 6th Battalion N.C. Infantry; the 6th Battalion N.C. Junior Reserves, which later became part of the 70th Regiment N.C. Troops (1st Regiment N.C. Junior Reserves); or the unit misidentified in Clark's *Histories of the North Carolina Regiments* as the "Sixth Battalion (Armory Guards)," for which the correct designation is 2nd Battalion N.C. Local Defense Troops. See Lee A. Wallace Jr., *A Guide to Virginia Military Organizations 1861-1865*, 2nd ed. (Lynchburg: H. E. Howard, 1986), 143-144; Charles W. Broadfoot, "Seventieth Regiment (First Junior Reserves)," in Clark, *Histories of the North Carolina Regiments*, 4:9-11; Matthew P. Taylor, "Sixth Battalion (Armory Guards)," in Clark, *Histories of the North Carolina Regiments*, 4:293-300.

3. The designations of the six companies were changed from numbers to letters at that time. Those letter designations apparently differed from the ones given to the same companies after the 1st Battalion N.C. Infantry became the 60th Regiment N.C. Troops; for example, Fifth Company, McDowell's Battalion (subsequently Company K, 60th North Carolina), was designated Company B during its service in the 1st Battalion N.C. Infantry. The 1st Battalion designations of the other five companies are unknown.

4. The addition of a seventh company entitled the battalion to a commanding officer with the rank of lieutenant colonel. McDowell was therefore promoted from the rank of major.

5. Ray, "Sixtieth Regiment," in Clark, *Histories of the North Carolina Regiments*, 3:475. Company I was initially designated Company G but, apparently because it failed to complete its organization before the unit that became Company G was assigned to the 60th, it yielded its place.

6. For additional details concerning the complex organizational history of the 60th North Carolina and the background thereto, see James Carlisle Taylor III, "The Sixtieth North Carolina Regiment: A Case Study of Enlistment and Desertion in Western North Carolina During the Civil War" (master's thesis, Western Carolina

On July 17, 1862, the five Buncombe County companies belonging to the 6th Battalion N.C. Infantry marched northwest from Asheville toward Warm Springs, on the French Broad River, and rendezvoused with their sister company from Madison County (subsequently Company B, 60th North Carolina). That evening the battalion reached Alexander's "country hotel and stock stand," where some of the soldiers took shelter from the rain in a stable loft. Part of the battalion reached Warm Springs on the eighteenth after a "forced march" of twenty-seven miles. Most of the remainder arrived during the next few days.[7] On July 21 the men moved down the French Broad "some four miles" to "a beautiful island."[8] There, at Camp Smith, named for Maj. Gen. Edmund Kirby Smith, commander of the Department of East Tennessee, they remained for almost two months, drilling and learning the other skills and duties of soldiers. "The Springs are very quiet & dull," Lt. Thomas W. Patton of Company C informed his mother in a letter that was probably written during early August. "[N]othing at all to write about."[9] On or about August 26 Colonel McDowell was ordered "to hold . . . [his command] in readiness for active service," and shortly afterwards the men moved over the mountains to Greeneville, Tennessee. The date of their arrival near Greeneville is uncertain, but by September 12 they were established at Camp Martin "in a very pleasant grove."[10]

During the seven months prior to the 60th North Carolina's arrival at Greeneville, Confederate fortunes in Tennessee suffered an almost unbroken string of reversals. The loss of Forts Donelson and Henry (on the Cumberland and Tennessee Rivers respectively) resulted in the capture of Nashville in February; the Confederate Army of Mississippi under

---

University, 1997), 2-6, hereafter cited as Taylor, "Sixtieth North Carolina."

    The ten companies comprising the 60th North Carolina were raised primarily in the following counties: Company A–Buncombe; Company B–Madison; Company C–Buncombe; Company D–Henderson; Company E–Buncombe; Company F–Buncombe; Company G–Polk; Company H–Cocke, Tennessee; Company I–Buncombe; Company K–Buncombe.

7. Ray, "Sixtieth Regiment," in Clark, *Histories of the North Carolina Regiments*, 3:474; Thomas Walton Patton to Henrietta Kerr Patton (his mother), July 21, 1862, James W. Patton Papers, Southern Historical Collection (SHC), University of North Carolina at Chapel Hill, hereafter cited as Patton Papers. According to one soldier's postwar recollection, "[T]he first day's march . . . [brought] us to Captain Alexander's Boarding House, a distance of ten miles; the second day to Marshall, and on the third day we stopped two miles below Hot Springs. . . ." Daniel Webster Cauble, "Civil War Record," 1, Lowry Shuford Collection, Private Collections, NCDAH, hereafter cited as Cauble, "Civil War Record."

8. Thomas W. Patton, "Sixtieth North Carolina Regiment: Infantry," 2, Civil War Collection, box 74, folder 6, NCDAH, Raleigh, hereafter cited as Patton, "Recollections"; Ray, "Sixtieth Regiment," in Clark, *Histories of the North Carolina Regiments*, 3:474. James C. Taylor identifies the island as Bartley Island. See Taylor, "Sixtieth North Carolina," 5.

9. T. W. Patton to H. K. Patton, August [8?], 1862, Patton Papers. See also A. Matthews, "A Partial Record of the Life, Ancestry and War Experiences of W[eldon] C[ornelius] Sales [Company K, 60th North Carolina], Confederate Veteran," 2, W. C. Sales Papers, SHC, hereafter cited as Matthews, "War Experiences of W. C. Sales." General Smith's Department of East Tennessee included, as of June 3, 1862, "that part of North Carolina west of the Blue Ridge, and adjoining East Tennessee." R. N. Scott and others, eds., *The War of the Rebellion: A Compilation of the Official Records of the Union and Confederate Armies*, 70 vols. (Washington, D.C.: Government Printing Office, 1880-1901), ser. 1, 9:473, hereafter cited as *Official Records (Army)*.

10. *Official Records (Army)*, ser. 1, 16 (pt. 2):781; T. W. Patton to H. K. Patton, September 12, 1862, Patton Papers.

Gens. Albert S. Johnston and P. G. T. Beauregard was defeated by the combined armies of Ulysses S. Grant and Don Carlos Buell in a bloody battle at Shiloh in April; and Memphis was captured in June following the loss of Island Number 10 and five other Mississippi River bastions. After Shiloh and the death of Johnston, Beauregard retreated to Corinth, Mississippi, but, pursued by the victorious Federals, he evacuated the town on May 30 and fell back to Tupelo. A few weeks later the huge Federal army, numbering about 100,000 men, was divided: Grant's 65,000-man Army of the Tennessee moved into West Tennessee to operate against Vicksburg; Buell's 35,000-man Army of the Ohio marched east across northern Alabama toward the lightly defended railroad junction city of Chattanooga. Unfortunately for Buell, his advance was subjected to what historian Thomas L. Connelly described as "a textbook exercise in the proper use of cavalry," devastating his lines of communication and bringing the Army of the Ohio to a halt forty miles southwest of Chattanooga near Stevenson, Alabama.[11] On August 20 or thereabouts Buell began retreating northward into Middle Tennessee.

Meantime, the Army of Mississippi, still at Tupelo, was heavily reinforced, and on June 27 it received a new commander in the person of Gen. Braxton Bragg. As Buell edged toward Chattanooga during July, Kirby Smith's pleas for assistance became increasingly urgent, and on July 21 Bragg decided to go to East Tennessee. After sending a sizable force to assist in the defense of Vicksburg, he proceeded by rail and steamboat via Mobile, Montgomery, and Atlanta to Chattanooga with a force of 35,000 infantry and about 5,000 cavalry and artillery.[12] On July 31 he and Smith met at Chattanooga and agreed on a strategy to secure East Tennessee and defeat Buell. Smith, bolstered by reinforcements from Bragg, would advance against Cumberland Gap, join forces with Brig. Gen. Carter L. Stevenson's Division, and capture or destroy the 10,000-man Federal garrison there commanded by Brig. Gen. George W. Morgan. Once Morgan was eliminated as a threat to Knoxville and the East Tennessee and Virginia Railroad, Smith and Bragg would move into Middle Tennessee, cut off Buell, and rout his army.[13]

Smith marched north from Knoxville with about 10,000 men on August 14 but, unilaterally revoking his agreement with Bragg, bypassed Cumberland Gap and invaded Kentucky. Stevenson's 9,000-man division remained at the gap to contain Morgan. On August 30 Smith defeated a Federal force at Richmond, Kentucky, and on September 3 he occupied Frankfort. Bragg moved north from Chattanooga on August 28 and, conforming perforce to Smith's singular movements, advanced into Kentucky, where he captured 4,000 Federals at Munfordville on September 17. He then set off in the direction of Louisville. Buell also marched north into Kentucky and reached Bowling Green on September 14. On October 8 Bragg and Smith clashed with Buell at Perryville in an inconclusive battle that was mismanaged by the commanders on both sides. Bragg and Smith then retreated toward East Tennessee.

11. Thomas L. Connelly, *Civil War Tennessee: Battles and Leaders* (Knoxville: University of Tennessee Press, 1979), 54.

12. Mounted units went overland.

13. See *Official Records (Army)*, ser. 1, 16 (pt. 2):741.

While these somewhat odd and, from a Confederate standpoint, largely futile events were unfolding, the 1st Battalion remained at Greeneville guarding "stores, railroads and railroad bridges." The men were also "thoroughly drilled." On October 8 the battalion, as stated above, assumed its new regimental status as the 60th North Carolina. Conditions at Camp Martin during that period were, according to at least one 60th North Carolina soldier, less than satisfactory. "I hav the hed Ack [headache] this Eaving vary Bad," Pvt. John W. Reese of Company F complained on September 18. "[L]iving on wheat Bread dont A gree with mee." In a letter written about ten days later, Reese reported a "Rite smart of sickness hear[.] [T]hair has Binn 2 died hear . . . [and] at noxvill [at] the ganeril hoerspitle. . . . [T]ha[y] air diing 10 ten pur day. . . ."[14]

On October 9 the 60th North Carolina received orders to proceed to Murfreesboro and report to Brig. Gen. Nathan B. Forrest, commander of Confederate cavalry forces in Middle Tennessee. Forrest's current assignment was to "operate against the enemy wherever found, but especially at Nashville, Clarksville, &c., cutting off supplies, capturing trains, and harassing them in all ways practicable." That night army colporteur John Ammons led the men in a religious service. "After supper . . . Colonel [McDowell] had the signal given," Ammons wrote, "and the troops assembled in front of his quarters, squatted on the ground. . . . We sung . . . 'Amazing grace, how sweet the sound,' and many were the voices that sung out those beautiful lines. The hymn was finished, and all kneeled for prayer, and as the invocations of the minister went up . . . [a] deep-drawn sigh could be distinctly heard all around. . . . The text, 'What shall it profit a man if he shall gain the whole world and loose [sic] his own soul,' was then briefly discussed, and . . . many showed by the deep interest which they manifested, their appreciation of the subject. . . ." During the next few days the regiment moved by rail to Bridgeport, Alabama. "A better body of men, and more easily controlled, I never saw," an unidentified field officer of the regiment wrote to the *Asheville News* on October 15. "All are in fine spirits at the prospect of meeting the Yankees."[15]

On the morning of October 15, 1862, five of the 60th North Carolina's ten companies departed by rail for Murfreesboro; the remaining five probably left that evening. Maj. Gen. John C. Breckinridge succeeded Forrest in command at Murfreesboro on October 28, and the 60th North Carolina, numbering approximately 36 officers and 619 men, was assigned to Col. Francis M. Walker's Third Brigade of the Army of Middle Tennessee.[16] Walker's other three regiments were the 20th, 28th, and 45th Tennessee Infantry. The Third Brigade

14. Ray, "Sixtieth Regiment," in Clark, *Histories of the North Carolina Regiments*, 3:475; Matthews, "War Experiences of W. C. Sales," 2; John W. Reese to Christina Reese (his wife), September 18 and 29 [28?], 1862, John W. Reese Papers, Special Collections Department, Duke University (SCD–DU), Durham, hereafter cited as Reese Papers.

15. *Official Records (Army)*, ser. 1, 16 (pt. 2):877; *Biblical Recorder* (Raleigh), October 22, 1862; *Asheville News*, October 30, 1862. See also *Asheville News*, November 20, 1862. "Two of our companies have not been drilled any," the unidentified correspondent wrote, "the rest can drill pretty well. The health of the command is very good."

16. See "Morning Report" dated October 30, 1862, "Morning Reports of 60th North Carolina Troops," Record Group 109, chapter 8, volume 107, National Archives and Records Administration (NARA), Washington, D.C., hereafter cited as 60th North Carolina Morning Reports. A list of morning report strength figures for the 60th throughout the war appears on pages 500-501 below.

was ordered to encamp so "as to be able to occupy a short distance in advance of the town and upon the shortest notice the ground lying between the road leading to Nashville and the road leading to Franklin, and will form the left of the forces."[17] On November 26, following the arrival of Bragg's army at Murfreesboro, the Army of Middle Tennessee was merged with the Army of Mississippi (Bragg) and part of the Army of Kentucky (Smith) to become the Army of Tennessee, commanded by Bragg. Breckinridge's command became a division of Lt. Gen. Leonidas Polk's Corps of the newly constituted army. On December 12 Breckinridge's Division was transferred to Lt. Gen. William J. Hardee's Corps, and the 60th North Carolina was assigned to Brig. Gen. William Preston's Brigade. Other regiments in Preston's Brigade were the 20th Tennessee Infantry and the 1st, 3rd, and 4th Florida Infantry.[18]

During the period from mid-October through late December the 60th North Carolina remained in the vicinity of Murfreesboro "engaged in drilling or guard duties of one sort and another." However, as of November 3, almost a month after its formal organization, the 60th had not been drilled in regimental formation. "Our Colonel [McDowell] is becoming more & more unpopular," Lieutenant Patton wrote on that date. "[H]e has never *once* attempted to drill his Regt & I think takes very little interest in it. The officers speak of getting up a petition for him to *resign*. It would be the best thing he could do for us." "Our Colonel . . . is entirely unfit for his position," Patton wrote the next day. "Tell brother Jas [James Alfred Patton] that the other day we had a general inspection [and] the Regt was drawn up in line of battle . . . at *order* arms. The Col took his position and commanded, 'The companies will right wheel.' [W]e guessed at his meaning & wheeled into column. [A]fter the inspection we were in column of companies and at open order arms. [Our] Col comd'd 'Into line companies wheel. . . .' [H]e has been in his present position for four months, and . . . this was the very first command he had ever attempted. . . . [L]ast night the Captains or at least nine of them had a meeting to decide what to do but could come to no decission [sic] – but the Col heard of it and this morning instead of writing or acting himself he had Ed Clayton [adjutant of the 60th] to write them a letter. . . . It is very provoking

17. *Official Records (Army)*, ser. 1, 16 (pt. 2):981. See also *Biblical Recorder* (Raleigh), October 22, 1862; *Spirit of the Age* (Raleigh), October 27, 1862. Capt. James M. Ray of Company F later recalled that the regiment was camped "to the left of the railroad and very near the city." Ray, "Sixtieth Regiment," in Clark, *Histories of the North Carolina Regiments*, 3:476.

18. See *Official Records (Army)*, ser. 1, 16 (pt. 2):1003, 20 (pt. 2):419, 431, 447, 456. According to Lt. Thomas W. Patton, a "report" that Breckinridge's Division was to be transferred from Polk's Corps to Hardee's was circulating on December 21, but the transfer had not yet taken place. In a letter written on December 28, Patton confirmed that the 60th North Carolina had been transferred to Preston but identified the other regiments in Preston's Brigade as the 32nd Alabama, 20th Tennessee, and 4th Florida. Patton notwithstanding, General Preston, in his report on the Battle of Stones River or Murfreesboro, which began on December 30 (two days after the date of Patton's letter), identifies the regiments under his command as the 60th North Carolina, 20th Tennessee, 4th Florida, and 1st and 3rd Florida (Consolidated). It is uncertain whether the transfer was welcomed by the men of the 60th, but it clearly was not well received by Patton. "Our Brigade has been torn to peices [sic]," Patton wrote, "and we are put under command of Brig Genl Preston of Louisville Ky. I do not like the change much and much preferred Col Walker. Our division is annexed to Hardee's Corps. I would much rather have remained under Genl Polk." T. W. Patton to H. K. Patton, December 21, 1862, and T. W. Patton to Charlotte Kerr (his aunt), December 28, 1862, Patton Papers. See also *Official Records (Army)*, ser. 1, 20 (pt. 1):811, 814.

that after we have labored to drill our companies we should have such an officer comd'g us."[19]

During the period that the 60th remained at Murfreesboro rations were of poor quality and limited variety but otherwise adequate. "There are so many troops here now," Lieutenant Patton wrote on December 1, "that we are living 'mighty hard' on corn bread & bacon. . . . [I]f you could send any 'sausage meat' or other nice things . . . I would appreciate them very highly." On December 11 Patton complained that the "flour which they furnish us here now is the most miserable I ever saw – worse than any *shorts* you have at home and so bad that I cant eat it at all and therefore have to use corn bread entirely, and the meal is so course that it is almost like grist."[20] "[B]itter cold" in early December, including a "heavy snow storm" on the fourth, left the ground frozen "hard as a rock" and added to the men's miseries. "[I]f it were not for the chimneys which the men have built," Patton wrote, "they would suffer terribly with the cold. . . . [T]hey have good clothes and shoes, but need blankets and socks terribly." Private Reese complained that the men in his company had "But one Blankit A peace" and had been issued overcoats "fild [filled] with dog hair or goats hair[.] [M]ine is A lit tle difernt from the Rest[.] [I]t is . . . fild with hemp[.]"[21] Probably because of the severe weather, poor diet, and insufficient supplies of socks and blankets, the health of the regiment deteriorated. On October 22 Pvt. William B. Lance of Company D wrote that although the men were in "tolerable good" health there was "plenty of mumps. . . ." By November 10 Private Reese was reporting "a heep of sickness hear with the Brane feaver[.]" And on December 21 Lieutenant Patton wrote that "for the past two weeks the sickness and number of deaths has been greatly on the increase in our Regiment. [I]n four days Capt [Thomas J.] Candler lost four men out of his company [E] alone. [O]ne [member] of Co C died last Tuesday. . . . [W]e have some more very ill indeed and I fear some of them will die."[22]

As might be expected under the circumstances, regimental morale declined during the autumn and early winter months at Greeneville and Murfreesboro. In a letter written from Greeneville on October 5, Pvt. Robertson G. Freeman of Company A informed his wife that "There is one thing sure[:] if they [the 60th North Carolina] stay here, and I don't get permission to come home, I will come home anyway. I think that if this war doesn't end by

19. Ray, "Sixtieth Regiment," in Clark, *Histories of the North Carolina Regiments*, 3:476; T. W. Patton to H. K. Patton, November 3 and 4, 1862, Patton Papers.

20. T. W. Patton to H. K. Patton, December 1 and 11, 1862, Patton Papers.

21. T. W. Patton to H. K. Patton, December 7, 1862, Patton Papers; J. W. Reese to Christina Reese, undated [October-December 1862], Reese Papers. See also William A. Bryant (3rd Florida) to his mother, December 4, 1862, Stephens Family Papers, P. K. Yonge Library of Florida History, Department of Special Collections, George A. Smathers Libraries, University of Florida, Gainesville, hereafter cited as Stephens Family Papers.

22. William Burton Lance to his father and mother, October 22, 1862 (typescript), 60th Regiment N.C. Troops File, Chickamauga National Battlefield Park, Fort Oglethorpe, Georgia; J. W. Reese to Christina Reese, November 10[?], 1862, Reese Papers; T. W. Patton to H. K. Patton, December 21, 1862, Patton Papers. "[W]e hav lost thirteen men out of this Rigment since we hav Bin hear," Reese added. Patton wrote in his December 21 letter that "so much sickness is caused by us being camped so long a time on the same ground, and therefore I was very glad a day or two ago when we were ordered to move our encampment out on to the Shelbyville Turn Pike about ten miles from here, but before we could get started the order was countermanded." See also Cauble, "Civil War Record," 1.

spring that the men will come home to stay. I hear it talked by numbers and numbers of men." Private Reese wrote on or about November 10 that "[T]en [men] Run A way last nite out of this Rigment and . . . thair is sum of [the] worst home sick folks hear you Ever saw[.]" By mid-December, Reese was reporting a hemorrhage of manpower. "Thair has Bin severil left hear with out fur lows and its not A going [to] stop[.] [T]ha will go lik sheep over A fence[.] Samuel hewey and James Balenger and tobby [Hyatt] and Samuel Barrett and 8 others [left] last Sunday nite was one week A go and nite bee fore last thair was 9 nine more left[,] All out of this Rig ment[.] [T]hair has [been] A Bout fiftey I think Run A way from this Rig ment an from the way the Rest taulks I dont think thair will Be many left By the firs of march[.]"[23] Spirits were not improved by a flurry of executions authorized by General Bragg, who was thought by some to be "fond of such amusement." A private in the 28th Alabama was "fired on . . . three separate times before they killed him," Patton wrote. "I suppose from a mistaken idea of humanity they tried not to hit him." A civilian named Gray was sentenced to hang for serving the Yankees as a riverboat pilot but in effect hanged himself, Private Reese reported, by "jump[ing] off of the gales [gallows] Be fore tha could nock him off."[24] Three members of the 60th were court-martialed for desertion and condemned to be shot. Two were pardoned by Bragg, but Pvt. William Littrell of Company F was stood before a firing squad on December 26. "[H]e was shot in the presence of all the troops," Patton stated, "an awful sight. . . ." "I saw him neel down By his coffen," Private Reese wrote with scarcely concealed revulsion, "and tha was put ing A hanker Chiefe on his hed and I left."[25]

On December 26 Maj. Gen. William S. Rosecrans's 47,000-man Army of the Cumberland (formerly commanded by Buell and known as the Army of the Ohio) moved southeast from Nashville against Bragg's 38,000-man force concentrated at Murfreesboro. There Bragg massed his troops astride the shallow waters of the West Fork of Stones River with Hardee's Corps on the east bank (Bragg's right) and Polk's on the west. After waiting in

23. Robertson Gaston Freeman to Sarah Ann Buckner Freeman (his wife), October 5, 1862, in George Alexander Jones, ed., *Heritage of Henderson County*, 2 vols. (Winston-Salem: Hunter Publishing Company, 1985), 23-24, hereafter cited as Jones, *Heritage of Henderson County*; J. W. Reese to Christina Reese, November [10?] and ca. December 14, 1862, Reese Papers. During December, according to Taylor's count, sixty members of the regiment were absent without leave and "over 250" were "sick at area hospitals." Those figures represent more than 39 percent of the regiment's aggregate strength as reported on January 12, 1863. Taylor, "Sixtieth North Carolina," 6. See also *Official Records (Army)*, ser. 1, 20 (pt. 1):814. According to figures compiled for this volume, 16 members of the 60th North Carolina deserted during the third quarter of 1862 and 22 during the fourth quarter. For 60th North Carolina desertion figures during other periods of the war, see footnotes 72, 100, 167, and 215 below. Those figures do not include absentees without leave, some of whom were gone for months but ultimately returned.

24. T. W. Patton to H. K. Patton, December 21, 1862, Patton Papers; J. W. Reese to Christina Reese, December 27, 1862, Reese Papers. According to acting Surgeon Robert W. Cooper of the 60th, Gray leaped from the scaffold crying out that "no ___ rebel should hang him." Robert W. Cooper, "Some Experiences of Dr. V. W. [Robert W.] Cooper in the Confederate Army, 1861-1865," 4, Civil War Collection, box 70, folder 37, NCDAH, hereafter cited as Cooper, "Experiences in the Confederate Army."

25. T. W. Patton to Charlotte Kerr, December 28, 1862, Patton Papers; J. W. Reese to Christina Reese, December 27, 1862, Reese Papers. According to Sgt. James L. Cooper of the 20th Tennessee, Littrell's execution was "a fearful scene" that made "an indelible impression." James Litton Cooper "Memoirs" (typescript), 21, Civil War Collection (Confederate), Tennessee State Archives, Nashville, hereafter cited as Cooper, "Memoirs."

vain for an expected Federal advance on December 30, Bragg decided to attack the Federal right the next day. He therefore moved two of Hardee's divisions (commanded by Maj. Gens. John P. McCown and Patrick R. Cleburne) across the river to a position on Polk's left. Bragg's plan was to drive Rosecrans's right wing back on his left so that the two wings would be pinned against the river and cut off from their retreat route, the Nashville Turnpike. Rosecrans, for his part, planned to assault and turn the Confederate right, which was now held only by Breckinridge's Division.

Hardee struck first with McCown's and Cleburne's Divisions at dawn on the morning of December 31, catching the Federals by surprise and routing Rosecran's right-flank division under Brig. Gen. Richard W. Johnson. Brig. Gen. Jefferson C. Davis, commanding the division on Johnson's left, pulled back his right and, for a time, fended off Hardee. Polk's Corps then joined in Hardee's attack, striking Davis's left and the right of Brig. Gen. Richard B. Sheridan's Division. Under severe pressure, Davis's line buckled and fell back in confusion, forcing Rosecrans to cancel his assault on Breckinridge and call up reinforcements to save his disintegrating right flank. Maj. Gen. Lovell H. Rousseau's Division replaced Davis's battered men, and other units extended Rousseau's right flank. Meantime, Brig. Gen. James S. Negley's Division, on Sheridan's left, repulsed Polk and, after hard fighting, stabilized the Federal right along a line parallel to the Nashville Turnpike. In an effort to revitalize his flagging assault, Bragg then ordered Breckinridge, who was unaware that the Federals in his front had withdrawn, to attack the Federal left. That attack was canceled when Bragg received a false report of a large Federal force advancing down the Lebanon Turnpike, beyond Breckinridge's right flank. Meantime, Sheridan's men exhausted their ammunition and withdrew. As Hardee's troops stormed into the resulting gap, Rousseau and Negley, on Sheridan's right and left, fell back, closing the gap as they did so and forming a new line on some high ground south of the Nashville Pike. By 11:00 A.M. the Federal line was configured in a lop-sided half-circle facing west, south, and east. Concluding that the weakened Federal left and center offered his best chance for victory, Bragg ordered Breckinridge to send two brigades (Brig. Gens. Daniel W. Adams's and John K. Jackson's) across the river to join Polk in an attack. Shortly thereafter two more of Breckinridge's brigades (Preston's and Col. Joseph B. Palmer's) were ordered to Polk's support. Around 4:00 P.M. Preston and Palmer advanced on Polk's right over ground strewn with Polk's, Adams's, and Jackson's dead and wounded.

[M]y brigade, on the right [Preston reported], and that of Palmer on my left, were formed in line of battle on the ground originally occupied by Lieutenant-General Polk's command. The right of my brigade rested near the intersection of the Nashville [and Chattanooga] Railroad and turnpike, and extended nearly at right angles westwardly, about half a mile south of Cowan's, or the burnt house.

These dispositions made, the order was given to advance in the direction of the burnt house toward a cedar forest beyond [known as the "Round Forest"]. Wide and open fields intervened, through which the command passed with great animation, in fine order. As we came near the farmhouse, heavy batteries of the enemy, supported by strong lines of infantry near a railroad embankment . . . were visible obliquely to the right, on the northeast of the Nashville turnpike. The brigade advanced rapidly and steadily under a destructive fire from the artillery. The Twentieth Tennessee, passing to the right of the house, engaged the enemy with vigor on the right in some woods near the river, capturing some 25 prisoners and clearing the wood. The First and Third Florida, on the extreme left, pressed forward to the cedar forest with but little loss. The two central regiments (the

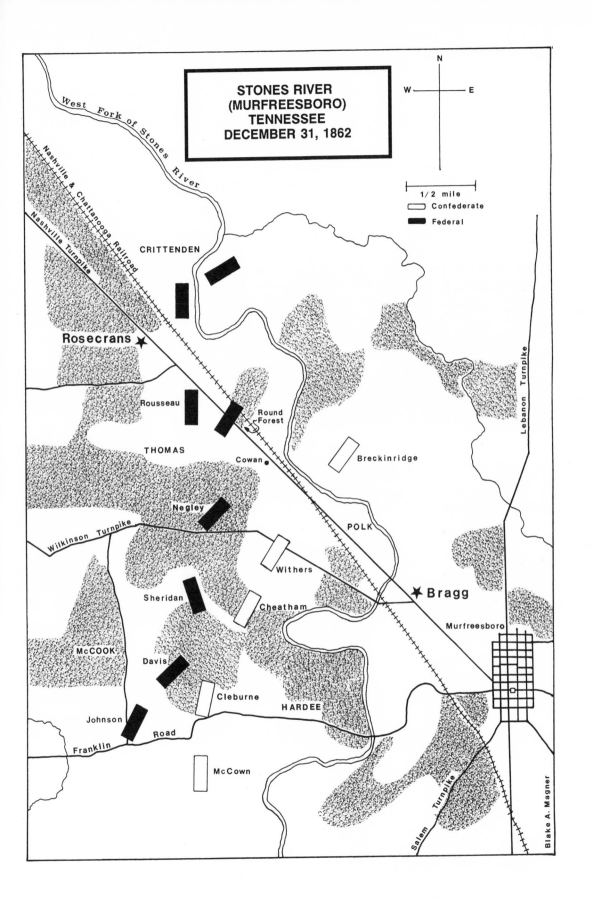

STONES RIVER
(MURFREESBORO)
TENNESSEE
DECEMBER 31, 1862

N
W — E
S

1/2 mile
☐ Confederate
■ Federal

West Fork of Stones River

Nashville & Chattanooga Railroad

Nashville Turnpike

CRITTENDEN

Rosecrans ★

Rousseau

Round
Forest

THOMAS

Cowan ●

Breckinridge

Negley

Wilkinson Turnpike

POLK

Withers

★ **Bragg**

Sheridan

Cheatham

Murfreesboro

McCOOK

Davis

Cleburne

HARDEE

Johnson

Road

Franklin

McCown

Salem Turnpike

Lebanon Turnpike

Blake A. Magner

Sixtieth North Carolina and Fourth Florida) found great difficulty in pressing through the ruins and strong inclosures [*sic*] of the farm-house, and, retarded by these obstacles and by a fire from the enemy's sharpshooters in front, and a very fierce cannonade, partially enfilading their lines, were for a moment thrown into confusion at the verge of the wood. They halted and commenced firing, but, being urged forward, they responded with loud shouts and gained the cedars. The enemy turned upon the wood a heavy fire from many pieces of artillery, across a field 400 or 500 yards distant, and, though we lost some valuable lives, the brigade maintained its position. . . .[26]

Colonel McDowell's report further explicates the 60th North Carolina's part in Polk's last attack on the afternoon of December 31:

[A]bout 2 p. m., we marched across Stone's River and formed line of battle near the Nashville pike, the Sixtieth North Carolina occupying the right-center position of the brigade. We were then marched in the direction of the enemy through an open field about three-quarters of a mile. We advanced in good order, under a heavy fire of shell, until we came upon very serious obstructions in the shape of a large brick house [the Cowan house], out-buildings, and strong picket fencing, which extended the length of our regimental line of battle. Owing to these obstructions, and the great difficulty of getting through the picket fencing, my regiment was thrown into some confusion and the line was broken. [Four companies (E, F, H, and K)] . . . succeeded in making their way through the fence, where the[ir] line was reformed . . . [and] obliqued about 200 yards through a cotton-field, taking shelter in a skirt of woods. During our march through the cotton-field we were subjected to a most terrific fire of grape and shell and musketry, losing at this point about 28 in killed and wounded. We remained for some time in this skirt of woods, our men keeping up a brisk fire.

Lieutenant [J. T.] Weaver, commanding Company A, although detached [separated] from the regiment by the obstructions above mentioned, took position on the left of the Twentieth Tennessee, and fought with that regiment until he regained his position with my regiment in the skirt of woods. At this point the general commanding [Preston] came up and seized the flag of a Florida regiment, and advanced, the brigade following him into a cedar thicket, where the enemy had been strongly posted, and from which position he had done us such serious damage; but when we reached there he had ingloriously fled, and we remained masters of the field. Night put a stop to further operations, and we slept . . . on our arms.[27]

Preston's and McDowell's reports are misleading because they seemingly suggest that the Round Forest attack captured its objective. In reality, as Polk stated in *his* report, the attack, although made with "undaunted determination," was "ineffectual." Moreover, neither Preston nor McDowell indicates the whereabouts and subsequent activities of the five 60th North Carolina companies (B, C, D, G, and I) that, owing to the fence and other obstructions encountered at the Cowan house, were "thrown into some confusion."[28]

26. *Official Records (Army)*, ser. 1, 20 (pt. 1):811-812.

27. *Official Records (Army)*, ser. 1, 20 (pt. 1):819-820.

28. *Official Records (Army)*, ser. 1, 20 (pt. 1):691, 819. See also William Preston to William Preston Johnston, January 26, 1863, Mrs. Mason Barret collection of the papers of Albert Sydney and William Preston Johnston, Howard-Tilton Memorial Library, Tulane University, New Orleans, Louisiana, hereafter cited as Johnston Papers. Pvt. Weldon Cornelius Sales of Company K recollected that the fence "was made of posts, pickets, and 2x4's of solid cedar. . . . We had to beat this fence down with our muskets. . . ." Matthews, "War Experiences of W. C. Sales," 3.

In fact, Sgt. James L. Cooper of the 20th Tennessee claimed, those companies took to their heels. "We [the 20th Tennessee] were a little confused at a Brick house on the road," Cooper wrote, "but soon got around it and swept forward in gallant style. The firing had by this time changed into a regular roar both of artillery and small arms, and . . . was so heavy that the line was ordered to lie down. We lay here close to the ground in an old cotton patch . . . for a few moments when hearing a loud cursing from our men directly, I looked around to learn the cause. I saw the cowardly North Carolina regiment who were to support us, running for dear life, every mother's son of them." Q.M. Sgt. Washington M. Ives Jr. of the 4th Florida, in a letter dated January 14, 1863, stated that "The 4th had to pass through a picket fence and in doing so we got our ranks broken and in forming the 60th N.C. crowded us so that we were all ordered out of place and the nine companies of [the] 60th turned and ran like sheep. . . ."[29]

Cooper's and Ives's statements, insofar as they apply to the five "missing" companies of the 60th, are reasonable approximations of the truth. In his "Recollections," Lieutenant Patton concedes as much when he writes that "in the hard fought battle of Murfreesborough . . . a part of . . . [the regiment] behaved with exemplary courage and bravery [but] [s]ome of the companies were thrown into confusion from which it was hard to rally them. However, if any of them failed of their duty on that occasion, it may be forgiven, for never did it happen again." And General Preston wrote that "The [four] companies of the Sixtieth North Carolina, under the immediate command of Colonel McDowell, were with me [at 'about dark' on the evening of the thirty-first]; but those separated from his regiment in passing the burnt house . . . fell back without orders to the encampment, with the exception of some of the men and officers who joined the Twentieth Tennessee Regiment, and who did not rejoin their regiment until after night."[30]

29. Cooper, "Memoirs," 23; Washington Mackey Ives Jr. to Florence and Fannie Ives (his sisters), January 14, 1863, in Jim R. Cabaniss, *Civil War Journal and Letters of Washington Ives, 4th Fla., C.S.A.* (n.p.: privately printed, 1987), 34-35, hereafter cited as Cabaniss, *Ives Journal and Letters*. See also *Official Records (Army)*, ser. 1, 20 (pt. 1):816; Alexander F. Stevenson, *The Battle of Stone's River Near Murfreesboro', Tenn.: December 30, 1862, to January 3, 1863* (Boston: James R. Osgood and Company, 1884), 116.

30. Patton, "Recollections," 8; *Official Records (Army)*, ser. 1, 20 (pt. 1):812. Capt. (subsequently Lt. Col.) James M. Ray later wrote that there "commenced [in the weeks that followed the battle] an investigation of the conduct of certain officers and companies in the fights in front of Murfreesboro, and while most, if not all, were from the peculiar state of things not greatly censurable for any neglect of duty, a pressure was brought to bear on them and several resignations were tendered. . . ." In fact, the captains of Companies B, C, and D either resigned under pressure or were removed from command: Capt. Charles M. Fletcher (Company D) was court-martialed, convicted, and dismissed from the service for, Private Reese wrote, "taking his men out of the fite at Murfrees Bo Ro with out orders"; Capt. L. A. B. Duckett (Company B) resigned rather than face a court-martial for "misbehavior before the enemy"; and Capt. F. S. H. Reynolds (Company C) resigned for what he evasively categorized as "sufficient cause." Two other officers, probably the captains of Companies G and I, whom Maj. W. W. McDowell of the 60th considered "equally as guilty" as Captain Duckett, were acquitted by courts-martial. The unpopular Colonel McDowell may have been eased out as well: complaining of hemorrhoids, he resigned on March 25, 1863. Altogether, eighteen officers, including all three field officers, resigned or otherwise left the regiment during January-May 1863 for health or family reasons or for reasons relating to their performance at Stones River. "Col McDowell starts for home in the morning on a leave of absence," the newly promoted Captain Patton wrote on April 4. "I suppose of course we will never see him here again. [H]e has not yet heard from his resignation, but no doubt it will be accepted – so all of those bothers [officers who were allegedly resigning for reasons of ill health] will be out of the war. . . . [T]o all appearances they are as healthy men as one generally

During the freezing night of December 31, Rosecrans pulled his troops out of the Round Forest and attempted to straighten his line. Preston's men "slept . . . in the cedars," Captain Ray recalled, "upon the bloody ground, in the midst of heaps upon heaps of dead men. . . . [T]hey were in arm's length . . . of almost every man, [but] [t]he horror of it was not felt in its ghastly hideousness until the morning dawned. . . ." According to Quartermaster Sergeant Ives of the 4th Florida, little sleep was had. "I like to have died of cold," Ives informed his sisters. "My teeth chattered all night, we did [not] have our blankets and the ground was hard and frozen."[31] The next day, January 1, 1863, both sides remained on the defensive. After dark Rosecrans pushed Col. Samuel Beatty's Division across the river in Breckinridge's front to seize unoccupied high ground that commanded part of the Federal line. At 4:00 P.M. on January 2, Breckinridge, on Bragg's orders, attacked Beatty's position with 4,500 men. Preston's Brigade was withdrawn from its position in the Round Forest and placed in Breckinridge's second line.

[T]he division moved forward rapidly through a wood and an open field beyond [Preston reported] . . . and our men, pressing forward with great ardor, drove the enemy over the crest of the hill and beyond the river. . . . [Beatty's] division . . . was driven down the hill-side in utter rout. . . . The enemy then rapidly concentrated large numbers of fresh troops on the other side of the river, and poured upon our dense ranks a withering fire of musketry and artillery. Our lines, originally very close in the order of advance, were commingled near the river, and this new fire from an overwhelming force from the opposite banks . . . threw them into disorder. The division recoiled over the field in the direction of the wood through which we first passed. . . . One of our batteries opened from its verge [near the woods], and I succeeded in forming my brigade for its support, and was in that position when Major-General Breckinridge arrived and ordered me to resume our original lines, about a mile in the rear, as night had come on.[32]

Although Federal musketry played a part in the repulse of Breckinridge's attack, the primary factor was the "tremendous," "murderous" fire of fifty-eight cannons massed on the west bank. "To say that the fire was terrific," Captain Ray recollected, "but mildly expresses it. How any escaped has ever been a matter of wonder. Nothing but a Divine Providence could carry men through such an ordeal." Finding their position "wholly untenable," the men, in Breckinridge's carefully chosen words, "fell back in some disorder, but

---

meets with. I think the Colonel is more sick of the war than any thing else." Ray, "Sixtieth Regiment," in Clark, *Histories of the North Carolina Regiments*, 3:483; J. W. Reese to [Christina Reese], undated [March? 1863], Reese Papers; letters of resignation in L. A. B. Duckett and F. S. H. Reynolds service record files, 60th Regiment N.C. Troops, Record Group 109: Records of Confederate Soldiers Who Served During the Civil War, Compiled Service Records of Confederate Soldiers Who Served in Organizations from the State of North Carolina, M270, reels 539, 542, NARA, Washington, D.C., hereafter cited as Compiled Confederate Service Records (North Carolina); T. W. Patton to H. K. Patton, April 4, 1863, Patton Papers. See also Joseph A. McDowell service record file, 60th Regiment N.C. Troops, Compiled Confederate Service Records (North Carolina), M270, reel 541; Taylor, "Sixtieth North Carolina," 10.

31. Ray, "Sixtieth Regiment," in Clark, *Histories of the North Carolina Regiments*, 3:479; W. M. Ives Jr. to Florence and Fannie Ives, January 14, 1863, in Cabaniss, *Ives Journal and Letters*, 35. "At daylight heavy firing began on our left," Ives added, "[and] General Preston marched us deeper into the woods so we could build small fires and [get] warm."

32. *Official Records (Army)*, ser. 1, 20 (pt. 1):812-813.

without the slightest appearance of panic."[33] Preston reported the loss of 295 men killed and wounded and another ninety missing. "I attribute the repulse on Friday [January 2]," he stated in his official report in scathing criticism of Bragg's generalship, "to the manifest hopelessness of the attempt to hurl a single division, without support, against the cardinal position of the whole hostile army. This was apparent to the least intelligent soldier." In a letter to a relative, Preston was even more caustic, skewering Bragg as a "Boomareng [Boomerang]" who "never . . . take[s] advantage of any one, especially the enemy." Preston then regaled his correspondent with a "once upon a time" fable depicting Bragg as a lion king who, inquiring of his courtiers whether reports that his breath "did stink" are true, executes flatterers and the candid alike, sparing only a fox who claims to have a cold. In the same letter, Preston inexplicably upped his Murfreesboro casualty count from 385 to 537.[34]

As was the case with the fighting on December 31, the 60th North Carolina was criticized for its performance on January 2. This time, however, the rest of Preston's Brigade was included. According to Brig. Gen. Gideon J. Pillow, the second line of Breckinridge's assault force, consisting of Preston's Brigade (on the right behind Pillow) and Col. R. L. Gibson's (on the left behind Brig. Gen. Roger W. Hanson),

advanced so rapidly that, while my line was checked for a time by the enemy's force in the thicket to my right, it overtook my line coming up ([which for] the moment . . . was lying down under my order). It likewise fell down as close in its rear as it could get, thus forming one line of four deep, and . . . commenced firing over the assaulting line in its front, which fire in the rear greatly alarmed my line, and . . . my officers expressed the opinion that my men suffered severely from this fire. . . . [W]hen the advance was again ordered, both lines went forward commingled, the whole becoming from that time forward the assaulting force, and leaving the command without any reserve. . . . I ordered the supporting line to halt, repeating the order several times, intending to move it to the right to attack the enemy's force in the thicket, but . . . no attention was paid to my orders, the supporting line rushing forward and past me. . . . [I]n conversation with General Breckinridge [afterwards, I] explained . . . the serious embarrassment occasioned to my command by the advance of the supporting line. . . . [H]is explanation was that the supporting line was ordered to keep the distance of its formation to the rear [200 yards or thereabouts], but did not obey.[35]

---

33. *Official Records (Army)*, ser. 1, 20 (pt. 1):577 (first quotation), 786-787 (fourth and fifth quotations), 833 (second quotation); Ray, "Sixtieth Regiment," in Clark, *Histories of the North Carolina Regiments*, 3:480 (third quotation). Beatty, whose retreat during the early stages of the fight was described by Preston as an "utter rout," claimed that his men put up a "determined resistance." His contention that Breckinridge's Division "fled in confusion" may therefore be doubted. Captain Ray, perhaps taking his cue from Breckinridge, recollected that the retreat of the 60th, "while not as orderly as might have been wished, was without panic. . . ." Sgt. James L. Cooper of the 20th Tennessee recollected that "Our troops were scattered in the ardour of pursuit and[,] not expecting such resistance [as was encountered at the river,] were thrown into some confusion and fell back in disorder." *Official Records (Army)*, ser. 1, 20 (pt. 1):813, 577; Ray, "Sixtieth Regiment," in Clark, *Histories of the North Carolina Regiments*, 3:481; Cooper, "Memoirs," 26.

34. *Official Records (Army)*, ser. 1, 20 (pt. 1):813; William Preston to W. P. Johnston, January 26, 1863, Johnston Papers. "Both men and officers displayed great intrepidity," Preston added. Preston's criticism of Bragg's generalship was not echoed in Breckinridge's report, but that did not prevent Bragg from subjecting Breckinridge's shaky performance to so many "disparagement[s]," "strictures," and "innuendoes" that Breckinridge demanded a court of inquiry. *Official Records (Army)*, ser. 1, 20 (pt. 1):790-791 (see also 663-672, 781-789).

35. *Official Records (Army)*, ser. 1, 20 (pt. 1):810-811. Bragg stated in his report that Breckinridge's second line

It is clear that Preston's line, being more exposed to artillery fire than Pillow's and facing a seemingly imperative choice of advancing or retreating, chose the former. Consequently, the two lines melded.[36] Pillow's charges, while accurate, were therefore somewhat less relevant and damaging than they seemed. Preston's men clearly could not stay where they were, and Preston's orders, whether explicitly issued or not, surely would not have been to abandon the field but to move forward and join the first line. Nevertheless, insofar as the 60th North Carolina is concerned, the episode was probably regarded as another instance in which Colonel McDowell and some of his subordinates lost control of their men. The primary evidence for that conclusion is a comment by Captain Ray relative to the "investigation of the conduct of certain officers and companies in the *fights* [emphasis added] in front of Murfreesboro. . . ." The results of that investigation, as was discussed in footnote 30 above, were predicated primarily on the Round Forest episode. Even so, it is probable that the regiment's performance on January 2 was a factor in the subsequent courts-martial and forced resignations.[37]

The next day, January 3, 1863, was spent, Captain Ray recalled, "in marching and countermarching, through an almost incessant rainstorm, the whole appearing to be purposeless." Erroneously convinced that the Federal army numbered almost 70,000 men and

---

"was so close to the front as to receive the enemy's fire, and, returning it, took their friends in rear." *Official Records (Army)*, ser. 1, 20 (pt. 1):668.

36. Preston wrote in his report that the two lines, "originally very close in the order of advance, were commingled near the river. . . ." Thus the primary point at issue, aside from the matter of control, is whether the commingling occurred after Federal artillery opened fire, as Preston stated, or at an earlier stage of the attack, as Pillow claimed. *Official Records (Army)*, ser. 1, 20 (pt. 1):813.

37. Ray, "Sixtieth Regiment," in Clark, *Histories of the North Carolina Regiments*, 3:483. At the behest of Breckinridge, Maj. Rice E. Graves, Breckinridge's chief of artillery, later submitted an affidavit charging that Pillow "screen[ed] himself behind a large tree whilst his Brigade was advancing on the Enemy [on January 2] and remained there until the second line had passed[,] when he was ordered to leave by the Maj Genl Commanding." Unfortunately, the aforementioned document is undated, and it is therefore unclear whether Breckinridge's charges of cowardice were a response to Pillow's charges of bungling or vice versa. Breckinridge's report dated "January 1863" contains nothing concerning Pillow's alleged skulking; on the other hand, Pillow's criticisms of the second line do not appear in his original Stones River report of January 11, 1863, but, rather suspiciously, in a supplemental report dated April 11, 1863. Breckinridge's reputation for probity, it might be added, was among the loftiest in the Confederate army. Pillow, however, was a quarrelsome and notorious prevaricator whom Winfield Scott once described as "the only person I have ever known who was wholly indifferent in the choice between truth and falsehood. . . ." Even Pillow's fair-minded biographers, N. C. Hughes and R. P. Stonesifer, describe Pillow as a "prince of pretense" who "stuffed" his battle reports with "selected evidence, basted with overstatement and understatement," "sowed distrust and discord within the leadership of the Army of Tennessee," and "tended to look upon colleagues, and certainly immediate superiors, as rivals, to be undermined . . . [and] deposed." In any case, Pillow escaped a court of inquiry or court-martial over the tree episode: possibly because Major Graves was killed at Chickamauga the following September; possibly because, as Hughes and Stonesifer tentatively suggest, Breckinridge simply decided to drop the matter. Rice E. Graves affidavit (undated), John C. Breckinridge Papers, Chicago Historical Society, Chicago, Illinois; Nathaniel Cheairs Hughes Jr. and Roy P. Stonesifer Jr., *The Life and Wars of Gideon J. Pillow* (Chapel Hill: University of North Carolina Press, 1993), 324-326 (see also 254). See also *Official Records (Army)*, ser. 1, 20 (pt. 1):781-788; William C. Davis, *Breckinridge: Statesman, Soldier, Symbol* (Baton Rouge: Louisiana State University Press, 1974), 342; James Lee McDonough, *Stones River–Bloody Winter in Tennessee* (Knoxville: University of Tennessee Press, 1980), 184-185, hereafter cited as McDonough, *Stones River*; Peter Cozzens, *No Better Place to Die: The Battle of Stones River* (Chicago: University of Illinois Press, 1990), 186.

was receiving reinforcements, Bragg began withdrawing in the direction of Shelbyville at 11:00 P.M. that night. According to Bragg, the retreat was carried out "in perfect order"; however, Lieutenant Patton described matters somewhat differently: "[U]p to last Saturday morning [January 3] we were all certain that our troops had gained a great & decided victory[,] when to our great surprise we received orders to start with our wagons in *retreat* and had to travel through the entire night and reached Manchester about 10 O'clock Sunday morning and we have been hauled about backwards & forwards every day since until yesterday [January 9] when we arrived here [at Tullahoma] & encamped. Our retreat was certainly a most shameful proceeding and I think it ought to kill Bragg. . . . [O]ur loss in the retreat must have been considerable[;] the road for thirty miles was lined with broken wagons & tents & cooking vessels thrown out."[38]

Confederate losses during the Battle of Stones River have been estimated as 1,124 men killed, 7,945 wounded, and 1,027 missing; Federal casualties were 1,730 killed, 7,802 wounded, and 3,717 missing. According to an official casualty return for the Army of Tennessee, the 60th North Carolina lost 1 man killed, 29 wounded, and 4 missing during the fighting on December 31 and 2 men killed, 29 wounded, and 10 missing on January 2. Regimental casualties were thus 3 men killed, 58 wounded, and 14 missing. According to figures compiled for this volume, the regiment lost 15 men killed or mortally wounded, 61 wounded, 32 captured (of whom 9 were wounded), and 2 missing.[39]

For the next three months the 60th North Carolina remained in the vicinity of the "miserable little muddy Rail Road station" of Tullahoma. "The weather is miserable up here," Pvt. William A. Bryant of the 3rd Florida complained on January 25, 1863, "warm, cold, rainy, & snowy, following in quick succession, & with sudden changes. . . ." "We were encamped in a low, muddy place," Sgt. James L. Cooper of the 20th Tennessee recalled, "very distant from wood, and the weather was bitter cold. . . . On the whole . . . [January] was about as disagreeable a month as I passed . . . in the army." Conditions failed to improve much during February and March. "Anybody at home has no idea about camps and how disagreeable camplife is," Pvt. R. G. Freeman of the 60th wrote on March 31. "The snow is six inches deep. . . ." "[D]__n such a climate, & state too," Bryant grumbled in two letters written in late January. "I wish we were almost anywhere else."[40]

38. Ray, "Sixtieth Regiment," in Clark, *Histories of the North Carolina Regiments*, 3:481; *Official Records (Army)*, ser. 1, 20 (pt. 1):669; T. W. Patton to H. K. Patton, January 10, 1863, Patton Papers. "Weary, hungry, and ragged," historian James Lee McDonough writes, "the soldiers straggled along the road for miles." McDonough, *Stones River*, 218.

39. See Patricia L. Faust, ed., *Historical Times Encyclopedia of the Civil War* (New York: Harper and Row, Publishers, 1986), 723, hereafter cited as Faust, *Civil War Encyclopedia*; *Official Records (Army)* ser. 1, 20 (pt. 1):679. Lieutenant Patton stated that the 60th's losses were "2 killed 70 wounded & 10 missing," and Private Reese estimated "A bout seventy wounded and kild not many kild." Taylor's figures are 16 men killed or mortally wounded, 71 wounded, and 42 captured. A morning report dated January 10, 1863, puts the regiment's losses at 6 men killed, 57 wounded, 9 missing, and 3 deserted. T. W. Patton to H. K. Patton, January 10, 1863, Patton Papers; J. W. Reese to Christina Reese, January 10, 1863, Reese Papers. See also Taylor, "Sixtieth North Carolina," 9; morning report dated January 10, 1863, in 60th North Carolina Morning Reports. In his letter of January 10, Reese described the battle as a "great slauter" but stated that "our Reg mant did not sufer like others. . . ."

40. William A. Bryant to [Davis H. Bryant (his brother)], January 25, 1863, and William A. Bryant to his

Along with bad weather, the men endured "oceans" of body lice, short rations, and poor health. "[T]he helthe of this Regmant is Bad," Private Reese wrote on February 27. "[W]e air losing A heep of men hear[.] [W]ee air in A vary un helthey place[.] [T]he lan is low [and] marshey and I think the poorest part of middle tennes see. . . . [A]s for Real good helth I hav lost it All[.] I cant Eat any thing hardley[.] [T]he corne Bread I cant Eat it to doo any good un less it is Raised[.]"[41] By March 26 the rations situation had deteriorated further. "Starvacion is A pun us," Reese wailed (with some exaggeration) on that date. "[W]e only draw [a] half pound of Bacon pur day and one pound of meal . . . or A pound of pickeld Beef . . . [and] molasses and a lit tle [illegible;] not A nuf to doo any good and our meal is so coarse that we make grits out of [it]. . . ." The men also received "A lit tle Bred. . . . I think it will gro wors in stid of Bet ter," Reese concluded gloomily. "Men is starvd out on Bred and meet so Bad," Reese wrote on April 2, "that tha will give aney price for aney kind of case[?]."[42]

As often was true when living conditions were harsh, morale declined. "[T]ha have Bin shoo[t]ing severil [soldiers] hear latly for Runing A way," Reese stated in his March 26 letter, "But I think when the woods fethers thair will Be A many A man go home."[43] The remainder of the men, or at least those who were not sick or on furlough or detail, "were kept busy when the weather would admit, fortifying, drilling, and reviewing."[44] "[W]e air well forti feid hear," Reese observed on March 26. "[T]ha never can take this place with out turbill los to them and I think tha air two smart for that." Captain Patton (newly promoted) wrote on April 4 that the 60th had been "drilling rather briskly for the past week[.] [O]n yesterday our Regiment was drilled by Gen Hardee and to-day by Breckenridge[.] [T]hey put us through rather strong[,] drilling us steadily for more than two hours on each day on a stretch."[45] "Our Regt is drilled every day," Patton added on April 8. During leisure time

---

mother, January 30, 1863, Stephens Family Papers; Cooper, "Memoirs," 27; R. G. Freeman to S. A. B. Freeman, March 31, 1863, in Jones, *Heritage of Henderson County*, 24. "I look back [on conditions during January 1863, Cooper wrote] . . . and wonder how I ever endured it." Cooper added that "There was some terrible weather [during February, March, and April], but as we had moved to a better camp and had built chimneys to our tents we did not suffer from it as much as we had before." Cooper, "Memoirs," 28.

41. R. G. Freeman to S. A. B. Freeman, March 31, 1863, in Jones, *Heritage of Henderson County*, 24; J. W. Reese to Christina Reese, February 27, 1863, Reese Papers. "[S]ickness made sad havoc with the men in our ranks [at Tullahoma]," T. W. Patton recalled, "and many good men died." According to Taylor's count, 105 men died of disease and an additional 127 were sent to area hospitals between early January and mid-May. Patton, "Recollections," 8. See also Taylor, "Sixtieth North Carolina," 10.

42. J. W. Reese to Christina Reese, March 26 and April 2, 1863, Reese Papers. As always, a food box from home could be a soldier's salvation. Lieutenant Patton, in a letter dated January 13, 1863, thanked his mother for a box containing wine, cake, apples, sugar, and books. "Rations were pretty scant [during February, March, and April]," Sergeant Cooper recollected, "but by stealing and foraging around a little we managed to keep enough on hand to sustain life." Cooper, "Memoirs," 28. See also T. W. Patton to H. K. Patton, January 13, 1863, Patton Papers.

43. J. W. Reese to Christina Reese, March 26, 1863, Reese Papers. No doubt absenteeism was high, but only ten permanent desertions appear to have occurred in the 60th North Carolina during the first four months of 1863.

44. Cooper, "Memoirs," 27-28. "We formed a complete semicircle of breastworks and redoubts around the place," Sergeant Cooper recalled, "which we were destined never to use."

45. J. W. Reese to Christina Reese, March 26, 1863, Reese Papers; T. W. Patton to H. K. Patton, April 4, 1863, Patton Papers. "Genl Breckinridge is decidedly the superior man of the two," Patton added, "and to my thinking

"the wickedness and depravity of the soldiers . . . show[ed] itself in a thousand ways," Cooper recalled. "Card playing, gambling, cock fighting and drunkenness were every day amusements." Snowball battles, foraging, band concerts, and, for the literate, reading and letter writing, were other popular pursuits. Captain Patton noted on April 4 that "The brass band of the [20th] Tennessee Regt of our Brigade has just been playing very sweetly[.] [I]t plays 'Home sweet home' almost every night. [I]t is among one of the few pleasures we have in camp life."[46]

On April 24-25 the regiment moved from Tullahoma to Wartrace, Tennessee, about thirteen miles to the northwest.[47] Captain Patton noted on May 3 that the "Regts are all quite full and altogether I think we are in a better fix for a fight than we have been for a long time." On May 6 the 60th moved from Wartrace to a new camp near Fairfield, about four miles to the northeast, where it remained for the next two and one-half weeks.[48] The general condition of the men, and presumably their morale, continued to improve. "We are drilling very heavily just now," Patton wrote on May 17, "every day except Saturday, which is given to all the men to wash thier [sic] clothes. . . . The health of the 60th is remarkably good. . . . [W]e report nearly four hundred men for duty now. [T]he whole army is in very fine condition and improving daily." Patton was also "glad to [report] . . . a great improvement in the morals of the men of this whole army," among whom there was "much less profanity . . . than formerly."[49] On May 9 General Preston was transferred to command

he is superior to any general in this army." "There were some splendid reviews near this place," Sergeant Cooper of the 20th Tennessee wrote. "Gen. Hardee drilled us twice . . . and complimented the regiment very highly upon their proficiency." Cooper, "Memoirs," 28.

46. T. W. Patton to H. K. Patton, April 4 and 8, 1863, Patton Papers; Cooper, "Memoirs," 27. As mentioned in footnote 30 above, all three of the regiment's field officers resigned during the first five months of 1863. Capt. Washington M. Hardy of Company A was appointed major on March 1, 1863, and was promoted to colonel on June 10. Capt. James M. Ray of Company F was promoted to lieutenant colonel in late June. For unknown reasons, the major's position remained vacant from Hardy's promotion to colonel until Capt. James T. Huff (Company H) was appointed major on December 23, 1863.

47. Captain Patton arrived at Wartrace on May 1 and found the regiment "camped about two miles from the Depot. I like the change of location very much. [T]his is a beautiful country, and then Lt [Samuel W.] Davidson of my company has relations living here & they keep us bountifully supplied with milk." T. W. Patton to H. K. Patton, May 2, 1863, Patton Papers.

48. T. W. Patton to H. K. Patton, May 3, 1863, Patton Papers. See also T. W. Patton to H. K. Patton, May 7, 1863. Patton says in his May 7 letter that the move was made "much to my regret. We were so comfortably fixed up and had such kind neighbors where we were. . . . I never saw such hospitallity [sic] as was shown us by the Davidsons, they kept us bountifully supplied with milk, bread & flowers [flours?]. . . ."

49. T. W. Patton to H. K. Patton, May 3 and 17, 1863, Patton Papers. Private Reese was somewhat less sanguine than Patton about the regiment's health, at least on the subject of smallpox inoculations. "[S]orey to hear that any Body ha[s] Bin vaxinated [in Buncombe County] with the vaxina cion [vaccine] thats in surk lacion now for it is not the Rite kind. . . . [T]hair has Bin a time of sore armes hear[.] A grate maney had to go to the horse pit tle and one of ouer men died from it. . . . I had it put in my arme But it did not take and it gos in my arme never no more." Reese also had nothing positive to say about the regiment's morale in general or his own in particular. "I hav not mut ch to Rite," he wrote, "onley A Bout hard times and I Expect thair is [a] janer ril [general] crop of this all over the suthern can federcy." Although he was perhaps gloomy by nature as much as by circumstance, Reese was not without a sense of humor. Commenting on the death of Maj. Gen. Earl Van Dorn, who was shot dead at his headquarters at Spring Hill, Tennessee, on May 7, 1863, by a local doctor whose wife he had allegedly seduced, Reese commented that "if All Reports is true that doctor ort to hav A grate practice in Bun Com

the Abingdon District in the Department of Southwestern Virginia and was replaced as brigade commander by Col. William S. Dilworth of the 3rd Florida. Brig. Gen. Marcellus A. Stovall was assigned to command the brigade on May 25, 1863.[50]

On May 23 Breckinridge received orders to "put the infantry of his command, except the Tennessee troops [regiments] in motion for Wartrace to-morrow morning." Dilworth's Brigade was ordered to be at the Wartrace depot by 7:00 A.M. From there the men were to move by rail to an unannounced destination that Patton, because of the growing threat to the Confederate bastion at Vicksburg, correctly guessed to be Jackson, Mississippi. On the morning of the 24th the men boarded a freight train and moved southeast. "[I]t is very hot to-day," Patton wrote from Chattanooga on May 25, "travelling very disagreable in freight cars[.] [W]e have been nearly thirty six hours coming this far. . . ."[51] Conditions deteriorated further during the next leg of the journey. "I reached here [Montgomery] in safety this morning," Patton wrote on May 28, "but after one of the most disagreable journeys I ever made – in freight cars all of the way – crowded to suffocation. [A]ll of yesterday and last night I had to ride on top of one of the cars, most of the time in a pouring rain. Sam ['Cops (Capps?),' Patton's servant] came in a train just ahead of mine. I was detained by an accident, and on reaching here found that he had gone on with most of the Regiment and taken my valise with him, so I am in a nice fix without a stitch of clothes or a blanket!"[52]

The bedraggled Patton—"positively too dirty to go courting"—reached Jackson on the evening of May 31 and rejoined his regiment, which had begun arriving the previous day.[53] The men then went into camp beside the railroad, four miles from Jackson. On June 3 the regiment moved to a new camp on the Pearl River about two miles below Jackson and, according to Capt. J. T. Weaver of Company A, "in hearing of the firing at Vicksburg." "We . . . are now located in a much pleasanter place," Patton wrote on June 4. "[W]e have a plenty of good water, which was the greatest trouble we had to contend against in the old place – having to walk two miles off & back when ever we wanted a good

[Buncombe County]." J. W. Reese to "ReBecky" Reese (his sister), May 19, 1863, Reese Papers.

50. See *Official Records (Army)*, ser. 1, 23 (pt. 2):828, 851; T. W. Patton to Fannie Patton (his sister), June 9, 1863, Patton Papers. The 20th Tennessee was transferred out of Stovall's Brigade at about this time and replaced by the 47th Georgia. That regiment probably reported to Stovall for duty between June 6, when it was listed as an unattached unit in Breckinridge's Division, and June 15. The Georgians were clearly unhappy with their new assignment. Efforts by Col. G. W. M. Williams of the 47th to have the regiment transferred began no later than June 15 when he informed Col. Claudius C. Wilson, acting commander of a Georgia brigade, that the assignment to Stovall was "entirely against the will and wishes of every man in the Regiment." Williams's efforts bore fruit on November 12, 1863, when the 47th was transferred to Brig. Gen. John K. Jackson's Georgia brigade, Maj. Gen. Benjamin F. Cheatham's Division, Hardee's Corps. Gilbert William Martin Williams to Claudius C. Wilson, June 15, 1863, Benjamin S. Williams Papers, SCD–DU, hereafter cited as Williams Papers. See also *Official Records (Army)*, ser. 1, 24 (pt. 3):952, 31 (pt. 3):686.

51. *Official Records (Army)*, ser. 1, 23 (pt. 2):849; T. W. Patton to H. K. Patton, May 25, 1863, Patton Papers. Patton described the freight cars as "chiefly cattle cars." Patton, "Recollections," 8.

52. T. W. Patton to H. K. Patton, May 28, 1863, Patton Papers.

53. T. W. Patton to H. K. Patton, June 1, 1863, Patton Papers. See also "Record of Events," Companies A-F, 60th North Carolina, May-June 1863 Muster Roll, Compiled Confederate Service Records (North Carolina), M270, reel 539; undated itinerary, Reese Papers; W. B. Lance to his wife, children, father, mother, brother, and sisters, May 31, 1863, Samuel J. Lance Papers, Louisiana and Lower Mississippi Valley Collections, Louisiana State University, Baton Rouge, Louisiana.

drink. . . . The weather was so hot that we could not carry it into camp with us, as it would become too warm to drink before we could get there. We do much better . . . now as there is a cold spring not more than a hundred yards off . . . [and we have] excellent . . . swimming and bathing. . . ." Patton's initial favorable impressions of the Pearl River camp notwithstanding, he denounced it five days later for reasons he did not explain as "the worst position for an encampment I ever saw."[54] Patton also pronounced himself "thoroughly disgusted" with what he had seen of Mississippi—"this Gomorra of a place"—and "especially" Jackson. "[I]f the Yankees could have kept it without injuring any other part of the country," he grumbled, "it would certainly be well to hire them to do so."[55]

Much to the surprise of Patton, who had thought that "reinforcements were so much needed [at Vicksburg], that we would be pushed forward immediately," the 60th North Carolina remained in camp on the Pearl for the next four weeks. Every fourth day the regiment was sent out on picket duty on the Gallatin, Monticello, and Raymond roads, south and west of Jackson.[56] "[W]e do not go more than two miles," Patton wrote, "and then bivouac in as cool a place as we can find and send out pickets on all the roads in the neighborhood a mile in advance." As Patton's letter suggests, the temperature rose to blistering levels. "I have never experienced any heat to compare with that of the past three days," he complained on June 9. "[W]e mountain men suffer with it amazingly. [W]e all go without coats and a good many minus thier [sic] nether garments. [T]he citizens here say that the hot weather has not commenced. . . . I dont [sic] know how it can get much hotter. . . ." Rations were limited, according to Patton, to "only a quarter of a pound of bacon . . . p[e]r diem and not a particle of flour," but some of the men caught "fine large *cats* [catfish] . . . in baskets [fish traps]" in the river. The trap set by Patton's mess, though "not . . . very successfull," yielded "one good dinner of 'turtle soup.'" Poor rations and excessive heat notwithstanding, the health of the regiment, Patton informed his brother on June 12, was "remarkably good."[57]

54. J. T. Weaver, in "Record of Events" section of May-June 1863 muster roll for Company A, 60th North Carolina, Compiled Confederate Service Records (North Carolina), M270, reel 539; T. W. Patton to H. K. Patton, June 1 and 4, 1863, and T. W. Patton to Fannie Patton, June 9, 1863, Patton Papers. In his "Recollections," Patton either changed his mind again about the camp or (more likely) forgot his complaints of long ago. "I do not remember a pleasanter location than our camp in the swamps," he wrote. Pvt. Daniel W. Cauble of Company K also had seemingly happy memories of camping on the Pearl: "Here we spent much of our leisure time making beautiful rings out of the shells gathered from the river, drilling and working them out with our bayonets. These souvenirs were sent back to our sisters and sweethearts." Patton, "Recollections," 8; Cauble, "Civil War Record," 1.

55. T. W. Patton to Fannie Patton, June 9, 1863, and T. W. Patton to H. K. Patton, June 12, 1863 (second quotation only), Patton Papers. Patton's animadversions upon Jackson seem to have been prompted by a *"vile proposition,"* which "came within three votes of passing" in the city council, that "no soldier should be allowed to walk on the side-walk." That proposal, Patton fumed, "is certainly the most disgraceful act of the war, only equaled by the citizens making the soldiers pay for a *drink of water*, which many of them are mean enough to do." Patton was equally unimpressed with the pallid Confederate sympathies of Mississippians, commenting that "there are as many tories [Union loyalists] here as there are in East Tennessee." T. W. Patton to Fannie Patton, June 9, 1863, Patton Papers.

56. T. W. Patton to H. K. Patton, June 4, 1863, Patton Papers. See also *Official Records (Army)*, ser. 1, 24 (pt. 3):950.

57. T. W. Patton to Fannie Patton, June 9, 1863, T. W. Patton to James Alfred Patton (his brother), June 12, 1863,

At sunrise on July 1 the 60th North Carolina moved with Gen. Joseph E. Johnston's army of approximately 31,000 men toward Vicksburg, forty miles to the west, where Maj. Gen. John C. Pemberton's starving 20,000-man garrison, surrounded by 71,000 Federals under U. S. Grant, was on the verge of capitulation. "[We marched] under the broiling sun . . . in dust shoemouth deep," Lieutenant Colonel Ray recalled, "drinking water . . . any place it could be found, and this, much of the time, being stagnant, muddy, stockponds and even . . . hog-wallows. . . ." "Suffocated with sand and dust, and burning with thirst," the regiment reached Clinton and camped for the night.[58] At 2 o'clock the next morning it marched westward toward Bolton's Depot, which it reached later that day. For the next three days Johnston remained at Bolton's searching unsuccessfully for a lightly guarded crossing of the Big Black River, defended by three corps of Grant's army commanded by Maj. Gen. William T. Sherman. Meantime, Stovall's Brigade picketed the roads leading to Brownsville and Queen's Hill. On the evening of July 5 the 60th North Carolina moved to Edward's Depot, near the east bank of the Big Black and about ten miles from Vicksburg. "[W]e remained [at Edward's Depot] till 3 O'clock the next morning," Captain Patton informed his mother, "when all of a sudden, we were ordered to retreat with all the speed possible . . . [having] heard that . . . Vicksburg had surrendered. We continued to retreat as rapidly as the hot weather would permit – and reached here [Jackson] yesterday afternoon."[59]

---

and T. W. Patton to H. K. Patton, June 15, 1863 ("turtle soup" quotation only), Patton Papers. The purchase of clothing, Patton added in his June 9 letter, was "entirely out of the question."

A Confederate soldier who possessed any mobility could usually find something to eat. "Lieutenant [John G.] Chambers rode out into the country to hunt up some of his kinfolks," Patton wrote on June 15, "and came back with a fine bag of vegetables – beans, squashes &c and butter & eggs. . . ." By June 28 Patton was informing his mother that "We [the members of his mess] have been living remarkably well for some time, as we take advantage of being out on pickett [sic] every fourth day, to forage on our own accounts[.] [D]ay before yesterday we got a fine lot of vegetables – beans, squashes, beats [sic], irish and sweet potatoes, chickens, eggs, butter, and *ripe peaches*. . . . [B]ut we have to pay the most enormous prices for every thing that you ever heard of, and I almost dread to see the day approach for settling up our mess account." T. W. Patton to H. K. Patton, June 15 and 28, 1863, Patton Papers.

58. Ray, "Sixtieth Regiment," in Clark, *Histories of the North Carolina Regiments*, 3:485; Patton, "Recollections," 8. In a letter dated July 1, Patton wrote that "the heat to-day is intense, the roads dry and dusty, marching terrible." T. W. Patton to H. K. Patton, July 1, 1863, Patton Papers. See also *Official Records (Army)*, ser. 1, 24 (pt. 3):985.

59. T. W. Patton to H. K. Patton, July 8, 1863, Patton Papers. See also *Official Records (Army)*, ser. 1, 24 (pt. 3):989, 992. "Our Regiment stood the hot & fatigueing march much better than I expected," Patton continued. "I have only heard of a very few cases of sun stroke and they, strange to say, are in the Florida Regiments." Pvt. W. C. Sales of the 60th, writing many years later, agreed that the weather was "Indescribably hot" and the march "terrible." However, contrary to Patton, Sales recalled that "many of our men died from sunstroke from the awful, overpowering heat. Just fell down by the road dead." As suggested in footnote 55 above, Mississippians put a premium on water in their torrid summer climate. "The troops fared better on the retreat than on the advance, so far as water was concerned," Lieutenant Colonel Ray wrote, "for the wells and cisterns along the route that had been stripped of buckets and drawing arrangements by the owners had been replaced after the passage of the troops and, of course, not anticipating so a speedy a return, they were found in place. . . ." Matthews, "War Experiences of W. C. Sales," 4; Ray, "Sixtieth Regiment," in Clark, *Histories of the North Carolina Regiments*, 3:485.

Ensconced with his army in the defenses of Jackson, Johnston awaited the approach of Sherman, who arrived on the afternoon of July 10 and began extending his lines before the Confederate entrenchments. On the "burning hot Sunday morning" of July 12, a Federal brigade commanded by Col. Isaac C. Pugh attempted, without a clear understanding of the location or strength of the force in its front, to move into position opposite the Confederate left. In the ensuing fight with elements of Breckinridge's Division, including portions of Stovall's Brigade, Pugh's men were "cut . . . to pieces." "Some time that morning we saw the Yankees advancing from a thick woods across an old field," Pvt. Thomas B. Ellis of the 3rd Florida wrote. "Our Company began firing as soon as [the enemy were] near enough and kept it up until we had them opposite to us, but they paid no attention to the Picket's firing, but continued the charge towards our main line and artillery. They advanced by platoons, and when well into the old field, our artillery opened up on them. . . . I never saw such slaughter as our guns made,–they were nearly all killed, captured or wounded. I never saw so many dead men in all my life."[60] Most of the damage was inflicted, as Ellis suggested, by Breckinridge's cannoneers, who mowed down their adversaries with near impunity. Some assistance was provided also by "a party of skirmishers" from the 47th Georgia and the 1st, 3rd, and 4th Florida of Stovall's Brigade. According to Captain Patton, the only casualties in Stovall's command were two artillerists who were killed. In fact, however, one infantryman in Stovall's Brigade was killed and five wounded. Two of the latter, Pvts. James Parker and Moses Hall, were members of the 60th North Carolina.[61]

The 60th North Carolina remained at Jackson with the rest of Johnston's army for the next four days. The wounded Federals from the July 12 fight were brought into Confederate lines, but, contrary to the common practice, no truce was arranged to bury the dead. Consequently, Pvt. W. C. Sales of Company K recollected, the "Union soldiers lay where they fell until late Monday afternoon [actually, late Tuesday afternoon, July 14], when our men buried them after a fashion. They had decomposed so rapidly, that they were black as Africans, and beyond recognition, many of them bursting out of their clothes. . . . Our regimental surgeon said the excessive swelling was caused from drinking beer. . . . They were buried with here a foot and there an arm stretching out. It was the best we could do."[62]

On the night of July 16 General Johnston, alarmed at the growing strength of the Federal army in his front and fearing besiegement, withdrew from Jackson.[63] "Our Regiment

60. Matthews, "War Experiences of W. C. Sales," 4; *Official Records (Army)*, ser. 1, 24 (pt. 2):575; Thomas Benton Ellis Sr., "A Short Record of Thomas Benton Ellis Sr.," 6, P. K. Yonge Library of Florida History, Department of Special Collections, George A. Smathers Libraries, University of Florida, Gainesville. "They [the dead Federals] were armed with new short Enfield Rifles," Ellis continued, "dressed in new uniforms, new knapsacks filled with clothing, etc.[,] a pair of new blankets, new rubber blankets, fine hats and shoes, and well-filled pocketbooks; had new Haversacks, loaded with good things to eat, ham, hard tack, coffee, sugar, and some of them had a bottle of wine, and some had liquor. Our soldiers at once began to appropriate their guns[,] knapsacks and Haversacks, and also their pocketbooks, and such as they wanted."

61. *Official Records (Army)*, ser. 1, 24 (pt. 1):201. See also T. W. Patton to H. K. Patton, July 15, 1863, Patton Papers. During the battle the 60th "did not fire a gun," Patton wrote, "except one company (Co K, Capt E. M. Clayton) who were deployed as skirmishers. . . ."

62. Matthews, "War Experiences of W. C. Sales," 4.

63. Jackson was also exposed to what Johnston described on July 15 as "Incessant but slight cannonading. . . ." "The Feds was throw ing shels in to Jackson last Eaving," Private Reese wrote on July 16, "and had sum of the

had been out as skirmishers all the day," Captain Patton wrote, "and at dark all the other troops were withdrawn and we [were] left until the very last to watch the Yankies [*sic*]. The evacuation was managed very well – fires were kept burning and bands . . . playing till late at night after all the troops except us had gone; we remained on the field until two o'clock and then quietly withdrew. The enemy knew nothing of it until after daylight." On the night of July 17 most of the army camped a few miles east of Brandon. Finding the water there "neither good nor sufficiently abundant," the men resumed their retreat on July 18 and reached a point three or four miles west of Morton on about July 22. There, after learning that the Federal army was falling back from Jackson to Vicksburg, Johnston called a halt. "We have marched very slowly, stopping frequently," a weary Patton wrote on July 24. "[We are camped] right in the woods, five miles south of the Rail Road. . . ."[64]

On July 28 Johnston's army moved to a new camp, "Camp Hurricane"—so called because it was "in the track of a cyclone that had [recently?] passed through that section."[65] A four-week period of, in Patton's words, "the most perfect rest and quiet . . . [with] no more sign of war than there is at home," ensued. With the exception of a brief and unseasonable but most welcome cold snap in late August, the weather continued "extremely hot." "[O]ur principal occupation," Patton wrote, "is trying to find a cool shady location; our encampment is entirely covered over with brush sheds, which are great protection from the sun and make it tollerably cool. . . ." Rations, judging from Patton's lack of complaint, were adequate, but opportunities for purchasing supplementary food or for foraging were limited. "This country is very poor and thinly settled," Patton observed on July 29, "[and] but few of the people have provisions enough for their families. . . ."[66] Furloughs and leaves of absence were granted in greater numbers than Patton had known "at any time before." Even so, desertion was a serious problem. "I have never heard so much talk of desertion," Quartermaster Sergeant Ives of the 4th Florida wrote on August 11. "I suppose over 1000 men have deserted [presumably from the army as a whole] in the last few weeks."[67]

In their quiet camp near Morton, "wickedness," in Captain Patton's censorious judgment, blossomed anew. That lamentable development, about which Patton provided no

---

town on fiar." The people of Jackson had begun to flee eastward in substantial numbers as early as July 10, when Captain Patton noted that "The citizens are leaving their homes in crowds. . . ." *Official Records (Army)*, ser. 1, 24 (pt. 1):207; J. W. Reese to Christina Reese, July 16, 1863, Reese Papers; T. W. Patton to H. K. Patton, July 10, 1863, Patton Papers.

64. T. W. Patton to H. K. Patton, July 24, 1863, Patton Papers; Joseph E. Johnston, *Narrative of Military Operations* (New York: D. Appleton and Company, 1874), 209. See also *Official Records (Army)*, ser. 1, 24 (pt. 1):208, 24 (pt. 3):1022, 1026. Johnston stated that "Desertions during the siege [of Jackson] and on the march [to Morton] were, I regret to say, frequent." *Official Records (Army)*, ser. 1, 24 (pt. 1):246.

65. Ray, "Sixtieth Regiment," in Clark, *Histories of the North Carolina Regiments*, 3:486. Patton described Camp Hurricane as being "five miles further from the Rail Road, and . . . a much better place, where we can get tolerably good water." T. W. Patton to H. K. Patton, July 29, 1863, Patton Papers. See also W. M. Ives Jr. to Washington Mackey Ives Sr. (his father), August 1, 1863, in Cabaniss, *Ives Journal and Letters*, 38; Cauble, "Civil War Record," 2.

66. T. W. Patton to H. K. Patton, August 16 and July 29, 1863, Patton Papers. Patton complained repeatedly of the extortionate prices charged by local farmers. See also *Official Records (Army)*, ser. 1, 30 (pt. 4):507.

67. T. W. Patton to H. K. Patton, August 22, 1863, Patton Papers; W. M. Ives Jr. to Florence and Fannie Ives, August 11, 1863, in Cabaniss, *Ives Journal and Letters*, 39.

specifics but which no doubt included gambling, profanity, fisticuffs, and thievery, was largely due in his opinion to the absence of moral suasion from the chaplaincy. "[W]e have but one chaplain in the Brigade," Patton wrote, "and he never seems to think it necessary to preach or have any services at all. . . . I am not sure if that may not account in a great extent, for our continued misfortunes."[68] Some of the men's iniquities might be described more aptly as horseplay, as an episode involving the regimental surgeon illustrates.

We had a little fun in camp night before last [Patton wrote on August 22], which served to enliven us up a little although I fear it will give you but a poor opinion of the discipline of our Regiment. [W]e have had for our surgeon . . . an old Scotchman named McKay . . . [who is] the most perfect *tyrant* on the sick men that I ever saw; and of course they all hate . . . him most cordially. [S]ome days ago he fixed him up a hamock [*sic*] to sleep in – suspending it from the posts of his [tent] fly. I prophesied, as soon as I saw it, that it would get the old Dr into trouble, and sure enough night before last, which was very dark and rainy, about midnight, some man with a sharp knife cut the rope, which sustained the head of the hamock, giving the old fellow a severe fall, and immediately as the noise of his fall was heard, all of the *confederates* began pouring rocks in on him as hard and fast as they could throw, and raised a tremendous shout in token of thier [*sic*] victory. In the morning the Dr had his bed tied up again and has gone on with his business exactly as heretofore, as much of a tyrant as ever; it will not be long till they try the experiment over again, and I would not be surprised if the old fellow got the worst of it next time; of course an officer cannot countenance such behavior, but none of us were much displeased at it [and] as you may imagine . . . none of the *conspirators* . . . [has] been found out. . . .[69]

During late July and early August, General Rosecrans, still in command of the Army of the Cumberland, came under intense pressure from his superiors in Washington to move against Bragg at Chattanooga. On August 16 Rosecrans advanced southeastward along an arc north and west of the city, and on the twentieth he began crossing the Tennessee River at several points between Shellmound, Tennessee, and Caperton's Ferry, Alabama. In response, Confederate authorities ordered reinforcements sent to Bragg. Most of Maj. Gen. Simon B. Buckner's command moved southwest from Knoxville; Breckinridge's and Maj. Gen. W. H. T. Walker's Divisions were sent from Mississippi by Johnston; and Lt. Gen. James Longstreet's Corps was dispatched from the Army of Northern Virginia. With the arrival of those units, Bragg's army would increase to 66,000 men and would outnumber Rosecrans's force by about 6,000 muskets.

Breckinridge's Division began moving out from Jackson by rail on August 26 and reached Chickamauga Station, seven miles east of Chattanooga, on September 1.[70] There it

---

68. T. W. Patton to H. K. Patton, August 2, 1863, Patton Papers. Quartermaster Sergeant Ives complained that "Last year there was but very little swearing done but I'm afraid now that nearly every man curses. . . ." W. M. Ives Jr. to Florence and Fannie Ives, August 15, 1863, in Cabaniss, *Ives Journal and Letters*, 40.

69. T. W. Patton to H. K. Patton, August 22, 1863, Patton Papers. See also Ray, "Sixtieth Regiment," in Clark, *Histories of the North Carolina Regiments*, 3:486.

70. "We received a very sudden order to march to Chattanooga," Quartermaster Sergeant Ives wrote. "We left old Camp Hurricane, Miss. 11 a.m. on the 26th. . . ." W. M. Ives Jr. to W. M. Ives Sr., September 4, 1863, in Cabaniss, *Ives Journal and Letters*, 41. See also *Official Records (Army)*, ser. 1, 30 (pt. 4):540; T. W. Patton to H. K. Patton, September 1 and 2, 1863, Patton Papers; Ives journal entry for August 26, 1863, in Cabaniss, *Ives Journal and Letters*, 6.

was assigned to the corps of Maj. Gen. D. H. Hill. Stovall's Brigade was posted at Sivley's Ford, on the Tennessee River northeast of Chattanooga. On September 4 the camp of the 4th Florida, and presumably the rest of Stovall's Brigade, was "1/2 mile N.E. of the crossing of the Knoxville and Chattanooga railroads 10 miles south [probably east] of Chattanooga and 2 miles north of Chickamauga, Tenn." By September 6 the brigade was in a new camp "2 miles north" of the first, "6 miles S.E. of Chattanooga[,] and 1/2 mile from [the] Tenn. River."[71]

Meantime, Rosecrans completed his crossing of the Tennessee on September 4 and began moving through the northwest Georgia mountains toward Bragg's supply and communications lines. On September 8 Bragg abandoned Chattanooga to the Federals and fell back toward La Fayette, Georgia, which he reached on the ninth. For the 60th North Carolina, that march proved almost as exhausting and demoralizing as the one to Clinton two months earlier. "[T]he dust was worse than you can possibly imagine," Captain Patton informed his mother, "and the heat almost as great as Mississippi: for some reason, our Generals chose to march in the night, which made it all the harder. I had the advantage of being mounted, but was on horse-back for two whole nights in succession, and had so much to do that I could not sleep any in the day. . . . There is a good-deal of deserting in our Regiment, we have lost over fifty men in the last week. I can hardly blame the poor fellows, for a great many of them are barefooted and the marching is terrible on them, although this is a bad excuse for them to *walk* home."[72]

During the next week Rosecrans continued edging his way into North Georgia. Reports of hardship, desertion, and poor morale in the Army of Tennessee, many of them exaggerated and some planted by Bragg's agents, convinced the Federal commander that the Confederates were unable or unwilling to offer battle. He therefore allowed his columns to become dispersed over a forty-mile front in the rugged North Georgia terrain. Aware of his opponent's vulnerability, Bragg moved north but, as a result of the ineptitude and selective obedience of several of his subordinates, failed repeatedly to attack one of Rosecran's isolated columns. By September 19 a fuming Bragg was in position near Chickamauga Creek and Rosecrans, belatedly realizing his peril, had concentrated most of his army nearby at Lee and Gordon's Mills.

The Confederate line of battle on the morning of September 19, 1863, ran along a north-south axis facing west and roughly parallel to the Federal line. Thick woods and underbrush, punctuated by an occasional corn or wheat field, limited visibility and kept

---

71. W. M. Ives Jr. to W. M. Ives Sr., September 4, 1863, and W. M. Ives Jr. to Eliza Boyd Ives (his mother), September 6, 1863, in Cabaniss, *Ives Journal and Letters*, 40-41. See also *Official Records (Army)*, ser. 1, 30 (pt. 2):137; Ives journal entry for September 5, 1863, in Cabaniss, *Ives Journal and Letters*, 6.

72. T. W. Patton to H. K. Patton, September 10, 1863, Patton Papers. "[W]e are a dirty tired and naked set," Quartermaster Sergeant Ives wrote on September 9, "for 3/4 of the men have not a single pair of shoes and no drawers, only one shirt, hat and pair of pants. . . . [I]f this army is not clothed soon it will be naked. . . . The whole army is in good spirits but it is bad to see barefoot men marching on such roads. . . . I tell you it is enough to make you shed tears to see what some of the boys are enduring. . . ." W. M. Ives Jr. to W. M. Ives Sr., September 9, 1863, in Cabaniss, *Ives Journal and Letters*, 42.

According to figures compiled for this volume, 9, 23, and 37 members of the 60th North Carolina deserted during the first, second, and third quarters of 1863 respectively. For 60th North Carolina desertion figures during other periods of the war, see footnote 23 above and footnotes 100, 167, and 215 below.

both Bragg and Rosecrans in doubt as to the other's dispositions, movements, and intentions. Bragg's plan, which he had hoped to execute on the previous day, was to turn Rosecrans's left flank, cut his line of retreat to Chattanooga, and force him to withdraw westward through the mountains. At the same time, Rosecrans's left-most corps, commanded by Maj. Gen. Thomas L. Crittenden, would be driven into McLemore's Cove, a bowl-like swale between Missionary Ridge and Pigeon Mountain, and destroyed. However, unbeknown to Bragg, Crittenden was heavily reinforced during the night. By daylight, his left flank, far from being vulnerable to a turning movement, extended three and one-half miles further north.

Fortunately for the Confederates, fighting erupted on the morning of September 19 before Bragg's plan could be implemented. Maj. Gen. George H. Thomas, on Crittenden's left, mistakenly believing that an isolated Confederate brigade was in his front, advanced with two brigades and blundered into Confederate cavalry commanded by Brig. Gen. Nathan B. Forrest. Bragg and Rosecrans poured in reinforcements, and highly confused, seesaw fighting continued through the day. Casualties were heavy, and no progress of importance was made by either side. During the fighting Breckinridge's Division, composed of brigades commanded by Brig. Gens. Stovall, Benjamin H. Helm, and Daniel W. Adams, was on the left of Bragg's line near Glass' Mill.[73] Helm's Brigade and several of Breckinridge's artillery batteries sustained a few casualties during the morning while making a reconnaissance across the Chickamauga at Glass' Ford, but Stovall's men were not engaged. During the afternoon the division took position "about 3 miles south of Lee and Gordon's Mills" on the Chattanooga-La Fayette road with orders to cover the approaches from Glass' Mill and Glass' Ford. Shortly thereafter it moved to Lee and Gordon's Mills, where it relieved Brig. Gen. James Patton Anderson's Division. "[We were] hardly in position," Breckinridge wrote, "when I received an order . . . to move to the right, cross the Chickamauga . . . and occupy a position to be indicated." The division crossed the creek at Alexander's Bridge, arrived between 10 and 11 o'clock at night at a field about a mile and a half in rear of the right of Bragg's line of battle, and bivouacked. Later that night the division was moved forward and took position on the right of Cleburne's Division, on the extreme right of the Confederate line.[74]

Bragg's plans for September 20 were almost identical to those he had hoped to execute on the nineteenth. His army would attack *en echelon* (sequentially) from right to left and attempt to drive at least part of the Federal army into McLemore's Cove. Breckinridge's Division would be the first to advance. Rosecrans, for his part, proposed to remain on the defensive. At 9:30 A.M. the Confederate assault began. Breckinridge's men succeeded in partially turning Thomas's left and briefly cutting the Chattanooga road but were narrowly halted by reinforcements from the Federal right. Cleburne, on Breckinridge's left, was fought to a standstill by Federals sheltered behind log breastworks, and Walker's and

73. Stovall's Brigade had departed its camp on the Alpine road, just west of La Fayette, on September 16 with the rest of Breckinridge's Division. It arrived at Catlett's Gap, Pigeon Mountain, about six miles to the northwest, the next day. At daylight on the eighteenth the division was sent to guard the Glass' Mill crossing of Chickamauga Creek, seven miles or so to the northeast. See Ives's journal entry for September 16, 1863, in Cabaniss, *Ives Journal and Letters*, 6; *Official Records (Army)*, ser. 1, 30 (pt. 2):139, 197.

74. *Official Records (Army)*, ser. 1, 30 (pt. 2):198.

Maj. Gen. Benjamin F. Cheatham's Divisions received bloody repulses in assaulting the same obstacles. About 11:30 Longstreet's troops attacked the Federal right and poured through a gap created by the withdrawal of Brig. Gen. Thomas Woods's Division to close a nonexistent gap in the Federal line. The result was a spectacular rout of the entire Federal right wing. Rosecrans fled the battlefield to escape capture, and approximately half of his army retreated toward Rossville, on the Chattanooga road, in varying degrees of disorder. At least three Federal divisions temporarily ceased to exist as organized units. Only Thomas, on the left at Snodgrass Hill, held his ground. Confederate attacks on Thomas continued throughout the day, but "The Rock of Chickamauga" could not be moved. After narrowly fending off attempts by Longstreet and Cheatham to turn his flanks and cut his line of retreat, he fell back to Rossville that night. By the morning of September 22, Thomas and the battered Army of the Cumberland were back in Chattanooga.

During the Confederate assault on the morning of September 20, Stovall's Brigade advanced in the center of Breckinridge's line of battle with Helm on the left and Adams on the right. The 60th North Carolina was in the center of Stovall's line between the 47th Georgia (on its left) and the 1st and 3rd Florida (Consolidated). The 4th Florida was initially in reserve but later moved into line on the left of the 47th Georgia.

Between 9 and 10 o'clock my brigade was ordered to advance [Stovall wrote]. I moved out in good order parallel to the Chattanooga road about a half mile, not without first encountering two distinct lines of the enemy's skirmishers and driving them in. Here the brigade was halted, and by a flank movement formed nearly perpendicular to its former position. Thus reformed I moved forward, and had not gone far before I encountered the enemy in heavy force and strongly intrenched [sic]. Here the battle raged fiercely. A concentrated fire of grape and canister, shot and shell of every conceivable character, was poured into us from the front, while my left suffered no less from an enfilading fire equally galling and severe. Brigadier-General Helm's brigade, having encountered the enemy's breastworks, was unable to keep up the alignment, which, taken with the fact that the reserve ordered to our support failed to come up and the further fact that my left as well as front was thus exposed[,] the brigade—in fact, the whole line—was forced to retire.[75]

In his official report, Capt. James T. Weaver, who found himself in command of the 60th North Carolina after Lieutenant Colonel Ray was wounded, reported that

[a]fter advancing about 400 yards we received a fire of musketry from the front, at which time 2 of the lieutenants . . . were so severely wounded that they had to be carried from the field. At this juncture we were ordered to charge, which was done in gallant style, and meeting but feeble resistance we crossed the Chattanooga road and advanced beyond that point about 200 yards, where we were halted. . . . Heavy firing being heard to the left, we were ordered to that point. We changed front by filing to the right, and facing by the rear rank were hurriedly marched in the direction of said fire. Having approached to within 400 yards of [the] enemy's line, we received a heavy fire from the front, and from there advanced through a brisk fire to within 200 yards of the enemy's line, where we were halted. . . . After a sharp engagement for twenty minutes, the Florida regiment on our left [the

---

75. *Official Records (Army)*, ser. 1, 30 (pt. 2):231. After the flank movement referred to by Stovall, the left-to-right alignment of his regiments was 1st and 3rd Florida (Consolidated), 4th Florida, 60th North Carolina, and 47th Georgia.

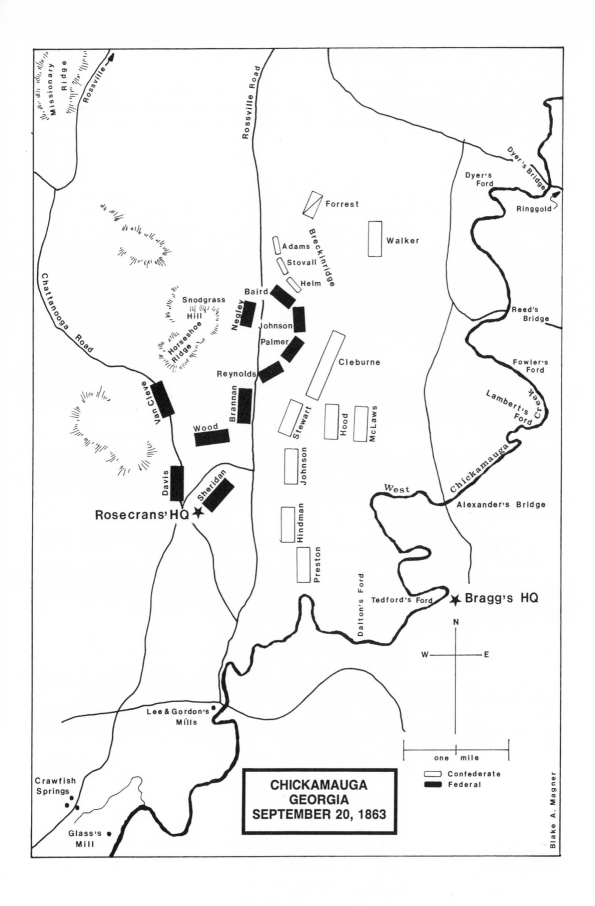

Rossville

Missionary Ridge

Dyer's Bridge

Rossville Road

Dyer's Ford

Ringgold

Forrest

Walker

Adams

Breckinridge

Stovall

Helm

Reed's Bridge

Baird

Snodgrass Hill

Negley

Johnson

Fowler's Ford

Palmer

Cleburne

Horseshoe Ridge

Chattanooga Road

Reynolds

Lambert's Ford

Chickamauga Creek

Brannan

Van Cleve

Stewart

Hood

McLaws

Wood

Johnson

West

Davis

Sheridan

Alexander's Bridge

Rosecrans' HQ ★

Hindman

Chickamauga

Preston

Dalton's Ford

Tedford's Ford

Bragg's HQ ★

N

W — E

S

one mile

Lee & Gordon's Mills

Confederate

Federal

Crawfish Springs

CHICKAMAUGA
GEORGIA
SEPTEMBER 20, 1863

Glass's Mill

Blake A. Magner

4th] was forced back by . . . a flank movement of the enemy on their left, of which movement I was ignorant, and held my men firm. However, in a short time the Forty-seventh Georgia, being hotly pressed on my right, was forced to retire, which left me no alternative but to withdraw my men or be captured.[76]

Breckinridge's Division saw no further action until "about sundown," when it was formed for another charge against Thomas's left. "[A]fter being exposed to an artillery fire for some time," Col. William S. Dilworth of the 1st and 3rd Florida wrote, "we were moved forward, and we swept through the woods and over the breastworks we had failed to take in the morning, driving the routed enemy across the Chattanooga road." Captain Weaver described that attack as "the last and final charge, which decided the fate of the day. . . ." In fact, however, Thomas was already retreating, and most of his command had passed safely up the Chattanooga road by the time it was cut by Breckinridge's men. Several Federal units that were shielding the retreat were thrown into confusion by Breckinridge's attack, but most escaped in reasonably good order and without serious losses. Breckinridge's casualties were also minimal. "[M]y regiment participated with as much enthusiasm as could be [expected]," Weaver stated, considering that "no rations [had been issued] for two days." Empty stomachs notwithstanding, the men of the 60th no doubt joined in the great victory cheer, remembered ever after by soldiers on both sides, that resounded through the dark woods as the beaten Federals trudged toward Chattanooga.[77]

Confederate casualties at the Battle of Chickamauga numbered 2,312 dead, 14,674 wounded, and 1,468 missing; Federal losses were reported as 1,657 killed, 9,756 wounded, and 4,757 missing. Losses in Stovall's Brigade, according to contemporary reports, numbered 37 killed or mortally wounded, 232 wounded, and 46 missing: a total of 315 out of 818 present for duty. Out of a startlingly low total of 150 men present for duty, the 60th North Carolina lost, Captain Weaver reported, 8 killed or mortally wounded, 36 wounded, and 16 missing. According to a casualty list for the 60th published in the Raleigh *Daily*

76. *Official Records (Army)*, ser. 1, 30 (pt. 2):238-239. A soldier in the 47th Georgia wrote that "Our Regiment stood for about 15 or 20 minutes not more than 200 yards in front of a Battery, while the guns poured grape & cannister [*sic*] shot among us & through our ranks thick & fast." Benjamin S. Williams to Gilbert and Willie Williams (his younger brothers), September 28, 1863, Williams Papers. See also Robert M. Clayton (Company B, 60th North Carolina), "Georgia at Chickamauga," in "Battles 1861-1865" folder, Confederate Veteran Collection, SCD–DU; W. M. Ives Jr. to W. M. Ives Sr. and E. B. Ives, September 27, 1863, in Cabaniss, *Ives Journal and Letters*, 42-44. The advance of the 60th North Carolina was later determined by a group of "State and United States commissioners" to be *the farthest [point] obtained by any Confederate troops in this famous charge.*" Hence the third dictum of the postwar Tar Heel boast that North Carolina was "First at Bethel, farthest at Gettysburg and Chickamauga, and last at Appomattox." Ray, "Sixtieth Regiment," in Clark, *Histories of the North Carolina Regiments*, 3:490.

77. *Official Records (Army)*, ser. 1, 30 (pt. 2):234, 239. Ives, who reached the battlefield on the night of September 20, wrote that he "found the boys [of the 4th Florida] in the best spirits I ever saw them although they had nothing to eat for a day and a half . . . [and] not a drop of water in twelve hours. . . . I tell you the Florida boys stand up like heroes and endure everything. . . ." Captain Patton wrote that "our Brigade made two noble charges on yesterday, in the first we were repulsed by superior numbers. [W]e rested a while and just at dark charged again and drove the ennemy from thier position and, held the field–the old *60th* acted bravely. . . ." W. M. Ives Jr. to W. M. Ives Sr. and E. B. Ives, September 27, 1863, in Cabaniss, *Ives Journal and Letters*, 43; T. W. Patton to H. K. Patton, September 21, 1863, Patton Papers.

Progress, 8 men were killed, 35 wounded, and 7 missing. Figures compiled from the rosters in this volume indicate that the 60th lost 18 killed or mortally wounded, 28 wounded, and 14 captured (of whom 1 was wounded).[78]

Following his Chickamauga debacle, Rosecrans assumed a defensive and somewhat quiescent posture in Chattanooga, abandoning Lookout Mountain, Missionary Ridge, and other heights controlling access to the town. The predictable and almost immediate result was a supply crisis of near-catastrophic proportions. Supplies that had previously arrived by rail from Nashville via Stevenson and Bridgeport, Alabama, now had to be off-loaded at Bridgeport. They were then transported sixty miles by wagon over a steep, narrow, and slippery mountain trail that, in a matter of weeks, claimed the lives of 10,000 mules. By mid-October the hungry citizens of Chattanooga were fleeing the town, and Federal soldiers, subsisting on a fraction of their normal rations, were accosting their officers in the streets with demands for "crackers [hardtack]."[79]

Meantime, Federal reinforcements were hastily sent to shore up the tottering Federal presence in East Tennessee. On October 1 two Army of the Potomac corps under Maj. Gen. Joseph Hooker arrived at Bridgeport where, since there was very little to eat in Chattanooga, they were forced to remain. Four divisions of the Army of the Tennessee, under General Sherman, marched east from Memphis and Vicksburg, repairing the Memphis and Charleston Railroad as they came. Rosecrans, however, far from contemplating offensive operations, seemed incapable even of devising a solution to his supply predicament. Comparing Rosecrans's performance since Chickamauga to a "duck hit on the head," President Lincoln ordered General Grant to Chattanooga in mid-October. As commander of the newly constituted Military Division of the Mississippi, Grant was given authority over the three armies operating within its boundaries: the Army of the Tennessee, still en route from Vicksburg and Memphis; the Army of the Ohio, at Knoxville; and the Army of the Cumberland, at Chattanooga. Sherman and Maj. Gen. Ambrose E. Burnside were retained as commanders of the Armies of the Tennessee and the Ohio respectively; Thomas replaced Rosecrans as commander of the Army of the Cumberland.

The impact of the dynamic Grant on the situation at Chattanooga was immediate if not immediately decisive. On October 27-28 a daring attack by Maj. Gen. William F. Smith drove Bragg's forces from the banks of the Tennessee River at Brown's Ferry, west of Chattanooga, opening a new supply line to the town. Pending the arrival of Sherman, Grant then began laying plans to lift the siege. Bragg, for his part, remained virtually dormant on the Chattanooga heights: Joseph Wheeler's cavalry conducted a raid against Rosecrans's tenuous supply lines in early October, and on November 5 Longstreet's Corps was dispatched to attempt, unsuccessfully as events soon proved, to recapture Knoxville. Otherwise, Bragg contented himself with lobbing shells at enemy positions, reorganizing his command, and waiting for the Federals to withdraw, starve, or attack his seemingly impregnable position. Having frittered away the fruits of his Chickamauga victory and weakened

---

78. See Faust, *Civil War Encyclopedia*, 137; *Official Records (Army)*, ser. 1, 30 (pt. 2):202, 232, 234-235, 238-239; *Daily Progress* (Raleigh), October 12, 1863. "[L]oss heavy in wounded," Captain Patton wrote, "not many killed. . . ." T. W. Patton to H. K. Patton, September 21, 1863, Patton Papers.

79. *Official Records (Army)*, ser. 1, 30 (pt. 1):221.

his army vis-à-vis its opponent, Bragg in effect conceded the offensive to Grant, who was soon to make use of it.[80]

The 60th North Carolina reached Chattanooga on September 23 and went into position on Missionary Ridge, east of the town. On September 28 Captain Patton, correctly divining Bragg's passive strategy but not its outcome, prophesied in a letter to his mother that "'Old Rosy' will be starved out in a short time and either forced to surrender or to fight us on our own ground, the side of this mountain, where we are fortifying and will have greatly the advantage. . . . I do not believe that this state of things can continue much longer, but that we will be in Chattanooga next week. . . ."[81]

For the 60th North Carolina, the two-month siege of Chattanooga was a period of mixed blessings, the most dubious of which related as usual to the matter of victuals. On September 28 Captain Patton noted that the "invariab[le]" menu comprised "cold boiled beef, or raw bacon, and biscuit." The rations situation probably improved somewhat in October—Patton had nothing to say on the subject; generally a sign that all was well—and by November 5 Quartermaster Sergeant Ives was celebrating the daily arrival of "Large quantities of beef cattle from Florida. . . ." However, two weeks later Private Reese complained of "the ha[r]dest times now I Ever saw in my life. [W]e dont git more than half A nuf to Eat half of the time, no meet and not [illegible]. . . . [T]ha [the Yankees] was whisiling at us all nite try ing to git us to go over to them [desert] But my mind Run Back to your Bossom and my swet lit tle chil dren [and] I cood no[t] go[.] But thair [is] A maney one going ove[r] and if tha dont feede us Better tha will All go. . . ." By that date the Confederates were undoubtedly a good deal hungrier than the Federals they had hoped to starve into submission.[82]

Shelter as well as food was a significant if temporary problem for the men of the 60th. As late as October 21 they were, Patton wrote, "still just in bivouac, without tents. . . ." On October 27 Patton and some of his comrades finally got "comfortably fixed up – had a *fly* and worked all day . . . building a nice house & beds. . . ." Unfortunately, at 3:00 A.M. that night, in response to Smith's attack at Brown's Ferry, the regiment was "waked up . . . and moved off . . . about half a mile . . . towards the left, in the direction of Lookout Mt." There, to Patton's disgust, it remained, within sight of his newly constructed "house," which, to add insult to injury, was speedily appropriated by interlopers. However, Patton says nothing further on the subject of quarters, and presumably the men proceeded with construction of shelters and huts for the winter.[83] On a more positive note, some of Bragg's "naked"

---

80. On October 8, about a week before Grant's arrival, Asst. Q.M. George P. Erwin of the 60th skewered both Bragg and Rosecrans as military Micawbers. "Both parties," he wrote, "seem to be waiting for something to turn up." George Phifer Erwin to his mother, October 8, 1863, George Phifer Erwin Papers, SHC, hereafter cited as Erwin Papers.

81. T. W. Patton to H. K. Patton, September 28, 1863, Patton Papers.

82. T. W. Patton to H. K. Patton, September 28, 1863, Patton Papers; W. M. Ives Jr. to E. B. Ives, November 5, 1863, in Cabaniss, *Ives Journal and Letters*, 49; J. W. Reese to Christina Reese, November 19, 1863, Reese Papers. Breakfast, Reese gloomily informed his wife, consisted of "A peace of Cold Corn Bread. . . ."

83. T. W. Patton to H. K. Patton, October 21 and 28, 1863, Patton Papers. Colonel Hardy returned from a lengthy furlough in late October and, in the absence of General Stovall, assumed acting command of the brigade. Captain Weaver of Company A assumed command of the regiment. See T. W. Patton to H. K. Patton, October 21, 1863, Patton Papers.

troops, probably including the 60th North Carolina, finally received significant quantities of "comfortable winter clothing." Coats, jackets, pants, shirts, caps, and underclothing were issued as well as "very excellent new blankets" of English manufacture. The pants and jackets, Quartermaster Sergeant Ives wrote, were "superior" and the blankets "large enough to cover a double bed," but the caps and underclothing were "miserable."[84] Another positive aspect of the Confederates' two month stay on the Chattanooga heights was the informal if sporadic truce that prevailed with the enemy. "Every thing is perfectly quiet," Patton informed his mother on October 24. "The pickets by agreement do not shoot at each other. [T]he yankies try to be very friendly, and are in plain view – they offered to give four pounds of coffee for a plug of Tobacco, but our men are forbiden to have any intercourse with them." "I rode around the picket lines yesterday with Col Hardy," Patton wrote two days later, "and had a fine view of yankeedom – the pickets being in full view of each other at one point, but not firing or interupting [sic] each other in any way."[85]

On November 12, 1863, as part of the reorganization of Bragg's army, the 60th North Carolina was brigaded with the 58th North Carolina and the 54th and 63rd Virginia under the command of Brig. Gen. Alexander W. Reynolds.[86] Reynolds's Brigade was then assigned to Maj. Gen. Simon B. Buckner's Division (Lt. Gen. William J. Hardee's Corps), which included the Tennessee brigade of Brig. Gen. Bushrod Johnson and the Alabama brigade of Brig. Gen. Archibald Gracie Jr. The commanding officer of the 58th, Col. John B. Palmer, was transferred to Asheville on or about November 18 to command the District of Western North Carolina, leaving the 58th with no field officers present for duty. The 58th was therefore consolidated "temporarily" with the 60th North Carolina under Colonel Hardy, an arrangement that lasted for almost five months.[87]

84. W. M. Ives Jr. to W. M. Ives Sr., September 9, 1863 (first quotation), and W. M. Ives Jr. to E. B. Ives, October 31 (second quotation) and November 11[?] (fourth, fifth, and sixth quotations), 1863, in Cabaniss, *Ives Journal and Letters*, 42, 47-48; T. W. Patton to H. K. Patton, October 26, 1863 (third quotation), Patton Papers.

85. T. W. Patton to H. K. Patton, October 24 and 26, 1863, Patton Papers. See also T. W. Patton to H. K. Patton, October 30, 1863; J. W. Reese to Christina Reese, November 19, 1863, Reese Papers. Artillery exchanges between Confederate gunners on Lookout Mountain and their Federal counterparts below increased considerably after Smith's coup at Brown's Ferry in late October. See W. M. Ives Jr. to E. B. Ives, October 31 and November 12, 1863, and W. M. Ives Jr. to W. M. Ives Sr., November 3 and 11[?], 1863, in Cabaniss, *Ives Journal and Letters*, 47-48, 50.

86. Reynolds, a Virginian, was 47 years old and an 1838 graduate of West Point. He had served previously in Western Virginia and at Knoxville and Vicksburg. His men called him "Old Gauley," which was also the name of his horse. It is doubtful that the appellation was affectionate.

87. See *Official Records (Army)*, ser. 1, 31 (pt. 3):686, 711; G. W. F. Harper (58th North Carolina) to [Ella Harper? (his wife)], November [16], 1863, George Washington Finley Harper Papers, SHC, hereafter cited as Harper Papers. See also G. W. F. Harper to Ella Harper, November 22, 1863. The temporary consolidation was also due in part to the numerical weakness of the 60th. On October 21 Captain Patton reported the regiment's strength as "a little over two hundred. . . . I do not hear any talk of consolidation, but expect something will be done in that line as soon as matters become more quiet." T. W. Patton to H. K. Patton, October 21, 1863, Patton Papers. Consolidations occurred also at the company level but were intra- rather than inter-regimental; that is, two companies of the 58th were consolidated rather than one company each from the 58th and 60th. Each consolidated company retained one set of officers; supernumerary officers were assigned to recruiting or other detached duty. It appears that company-level consolidations were not implemented until December 1863.

    It is perhaps noteworthy that as of October 21 the officers corps of the 60th included a reputed unionist, Capt. Thomas Jefferson Candler of Company E. Patton wrote on that date that "Capt Candler, who is the senior Cap-

On November 13 Sherman arrived at Bridgeport with the Army of the Tennessee. Grant then moved quickly to dislodge Bragg from his mountain tops. As a first step he ordered troop movements designed to convince Bragg that most of Sherman's army was en route to Knoxville to reinforce Burnside. However, Sherman's troops were secretly to go into position in the hills north of Chattanooga, cross the Tennessee River on the night of November 20, and attack Bragg at daybreak on November 21. Cut off from his supply depot at Chickamauga Station, Bragg would have to abandon his formidable positions on Lookout Mountain and Missionary Ridge and retreat into the North Georgia wilderness.

Although slow to take the proffered bait, Bragg at length became convinced that Grant was reinforcing Burnside, and on November 22 he ordered two divisions (Buckner's, temporarily commanded by Bushrod Johnson, and Cleburne's) to Knoxville. Buckner's Division, with the exception of Reynolds's Brigade, departed by rail the same day.[88] Meantime, Grant's plan miscarried when heavy rains prevented Sherman from reaching his jump-off point by the night of November 20. Sherman was still slogging through the mud two days later when a Confederate deserter reported inaccurately that Bragg was withdrawing from Missionary Ridge. To test that report, which if true would expose Bragg to attack at a moment of high vulnerability, Grant ordered Thomas to make a reconnaissance in force against Orchard Knob the next morning (see map on page 229). The resulting engagement, in addition to establishing that Bragg was holding his ground, unexpectedly resulted in the capture of Orchard Knob. It also alerted Bragg that a Federal offensive might be afoot. He therefore ordered Cleburne, whose men were still at Chickamauga Station awaiting transportation to Knoxville, to take position on Tunnel Hill, at the north end of Missionary Ridge. Unfortunately for Bragg, Buckner's command, except for Reynolds's Brigade, was beyond immediate recall. Thus a Confederate force of only 46,000 men was left to confront an army of nearly 80,000 Federals.

Grant's battle plan on the morning of November 24 called for Sherman, on the Federal left, to cross the Tennessee River and capture Tunnel Hill while Hooker's troops, on the right, attempted to drive the Confederates from Lookout Mountain. If Sherman accomplished his assignment, Thomas, in the center, would attack Missionary Ridge; if not, Thomas would reinforce the flanks as necessary. That plan, as was the case with the abortive attack on November 21, went awry from the outset. Sherman's river crossing over a rickety pontoon bridge proved unexpectedly difficult and time-consuming, and it was afternoon before he was in position. By then Cleburne's Division was entrenched atop Tunnel Hill. Convinced that too little daylight remained to accomplish anything against Cleburne,

tain of the Regt, has sent up his resignation, got sick and gone off to the hospital, so I suppose we will never see him again. We all hope so at all events, as he is a thourough [*sic*] tory, and a mean fellow any ways." T. W. Patton to H. K. Patton, October 21, 1863, Patton Papers.

88. On November 20 Reynolds's Brigade marched in the direction of Rossville and camped for the night near General Hardee's headquarters. The next day it moved eight miles through rain and mud on the La Fayette road, about faced, marched back to Rossville, and camped. On November 22 it reached Chickamauga Station. Clearly, the brigade was recalled to Chickamauga Station to join Buckner's Division for its move to Knoxville; however, the purpose of the La Fayette road mission is uncertain. Harper speculates that it was intended "to head off an advance of the Yankees towards Rome." G. W. F. Harper to Ella Harper, November 22, 1863, Harper Papers. See also diary of G. W. F. Harper (typescript), November 20-22, 1863, SHC, hereafter cited as Harper Diary.

Sherman bivouacked for the night. Meantime, Hooker's men, fighting for most of the day in a thick fog, made good progress against the outnumbered Confederates on Lookout Mountain. Toward mid-afternoon Bragg ordered the position abandoned, and by 8:00 P.M. the last of the Confederates were gone. To the cheers of thousands of onlooking Federals, the Stars and Stripes were raised atop the summit the next day.

On the morning of November 25, Grant ordered Sherman to launch his much delayed attack on Tunnel Hill. Thomas, as previously instructed, was to attack Missionary Ridge if Sherman was successful. Hooker was ordered to advance against the Confederate left at Rossville Gap. By evening Hooker's men had reached that objective and were driving the Confederate defenders back in confusion. Sherman, however, was unable to make any progress against the redoubtable Cleburne. Hoping to assist Sherman with a diversionary attack, Grant then ordered Thomas to seize a weakly defended trench line at the foot of Missionary Ridge. As was the case at Orchard Knob, that seemingly inconsequential thrust produced spectacular results. Advancing through heavy fire from Confederate positions atop Missionary Ridge, the Federals seized the trench line, paused a few minutes, then, without orders, charged up the slope. Some Confederate units on the heights, unable to shoot without hitting their retreating comrades or because their works were improperly sited, fled after meager resistance. Others were overpowered by superior numbers. The remainder fended off the Federals for a time but were then flanked and routed. At Tunnel Hill, meanwhile, Cleburne's men held their ground against Sherman until ordered to withdraw. With triumphant Yankee cries of "Chickamauga, Chickamauga" ringing in their ears, Bragg's discomfited legions retreated in the darkness toward Chickamauga Station.

As stated above, Reynolds's Brigade, including the 60th North Carolina, was ordered by rail to Knoxville with the rest of Buckner's Division on November 22 but was still at Chickamauga Station with Cleburne's Division awaiting transportation the next day. When Cleburne was recalled following Thomas's attack on Orchard Knob, Reynolds's men, who were on a train and about to depart, were ordered out of the cars. They then went into position in the trenches at the foot of Missionary Ridge. The 60th North Carolina was on the left of Reynolds's line adjacent to the 7th Florida Infantry of Col. Jesse J. Finley's Brigade, Breckinridge's Division (commanded by Brig. Gen. William B. Bate).[89] Two other regiments of Finley's Brigade, the 1st Florida Cavalry (Dismounted) and the 4th Florida Infantry, were probably on Reynolds's right.[90] In the event of a Federal attack, Reynolds's men were instructed to offer token resistance and withdraw up the slopes. However, other units received orders to stand and fight. Those orders were later countermanded, but some units were not informed. Atop Missionary Ridge, somewhat to the right of the trench position held below by Reynolds, was a gap in the Confederate line that Reynolds was to occupy when he fell back. Brig. Gen. James Patton Anderson's Mississippi brigade, commanded by Col. William F. Tucker, was to the right of the gap; Bate's brigade of Georgians and Tennesseans, commanded by Col. Robert C. Tyler, to the left. The 1st and 3rd Florida Infantry

89. See *Official Records (Army)*, ser. 1, 31 (pt. 1), 532, 31 (pt. 2):740, 746.

90. The 7th Florida was sent down to the trenches later than its two sister regiments and somehow became separated from them. See *Official Records (Army)*, ser. 1, 31 (pt. 2):740.

(Consolidated) and the 6th Florida Infantry, the only two regiments of Finley's Brigade that were not below in the trenches, were to the left of Tyler.

At 2:00 P.M., about an hour before Thomas launched his attack, Reynolds received orders to "fall back from the rifle pits to the crest of Missionary Ridge." That maneuver, which Reynolds carried out "by alternate Companies," was largely but not entirely completed when Thomas advanced. Exposed to heavy fire from the immense Federal force marshaling in their front, some elements of the 60th North Carolina became panicky and began scrambling up the ridge; others, refusing to brave the enemy barrage, huddled in the trenches. "All order was soon lost," Brig. Gen. Arthur M. Manigault wrote of those who fled, "and each, striving to save himself, took the shortest direction for the summit."[91] Rather than obliqueing to the left to the slot reserved for Reynolds, as Reynolds's other regiments had done, most of the 60th dashed in a disorderly mass into the left-most units of Finley's Brigade, "breaking and throwing [them] into slight confusion," General Bate wrote, "as they passed through. Major Weaver, of the Sixtieth North Carolina Regiment, seemed to be in command. He rallied and formed these troops (who seemed to be from two or three different regiments of Reynolds' brigade) across the Crutchfield road a few paces in rear of the main line."[92] Meantime, the rest of Reynolds's Brigade reached the top of Missionary Ridge and occupied its assigned position. There, having been divested of his commanding officer by the departure of Bushrod Johnson with the remainder of Buckner's Division, Reynolds was placed under the temporary authority of General Anderson (commanding Maj. Gen. Thomas Hindman's Division). A detailed account of the brigade's gallant role in the subsequent fighting, and the unjust criticism to which it was subjected, appears in the history of the 58th North Carolina on pages 228-232 of this volume. Because most of the 60th was with Weaver, that account need not be reproduced here. However, a letter written to his wife "Tena" on December 6 by the estimable Private Reese, who was with Reynolds during the battle, deserves to be quoted:

I can say to you [that] the grat Bat tle on mish nary Ridg has Bin faut and Bragg has Recieved A nother compleet whiping. . . . this fite com menct the 25 [24] of november . . . and on . . . the next day the[ir] pickets Run in ouer pickets A Bout ten o clock we was liing in ouer Brest works ouer canons was plast in our Rear on top of the mish nary Ridg and ouer Brest works was at the foot of the Ridg. . . . Ouer Battrs [batteries] cood play on the yankeys clean over us tha was shel ing Each oth er till in the Eving and the order cam up for ouer offficers to send us up to the top of the Rid[ge] just A

---

91. Reynolds's Missionary Ridge report dated December 15, 1863, in John Hoffmann, ed., *The Confederate Collapse at the Battle of Missionary Ridge: The Reports of James Patton Anderson and His Brigade Commanders* (Dayton, Ohio: Morningside House, 1985), 74, hereafter cited as Reynolds, "Missionary Ridge Report," in Hoffmann, *Reports of Anderson's Division* (quoted by permission of P. K. Yonge Library of Florida History, Department of Special Collections, George A. Smathers Libraries, University of Florida, Gainesville); R. Lockwood Tower, ed., *A Carolinian Goes to War: The Civil War Narrative of Arthur Middleton Manigault, Brigadier General, C.S.A.* (Columbia: University of South Carolina Press, 1983), 138.

92. *Official Records (Army)*, ser. 1, 31 (pt. 2):741. Reynolds states that "some of the Companies of the 60th . . . in moveing [*sic*] up the ridge, were obliged, on account of the peculiar topography of the ground, to oblique somewhat too far to the right and on reaching the top of the Ridge, found themselves separated from their command, & owing to the difficulty of joining their own Regt. they remained . . . with Gen. Bate's Brigade." That statement is true as far as it goes, but it does not reflect the demoralized condition in which the men reached Finley's line. Reynolds, "Missionary Ridge Report," 74, in Hoffmann, *Reports of Anderson's Division*.

fue at a time to keep the yankeys from dis covering the Retreat well I think I was A Bout in the third sqad that started for the top of the Ridg well the yankeys discoverd the game and hear tha cum By thousands it was A Bout half A mile from the Brest works to the top of the Ridg when I got A Bout half way . . . I loock Back over the valey the yankeys was [in] A Bout A hunered yards of ouer works and the shels was flying as thick as hale over mee Boath ways our men had to Run up to the top of the Ridg whair the in tended fite was to Cum off thair was lots of ouer men never left the Brest works at tall when the yankeys mounted the Brest works tha poored A voley down in our [illegible] poor men tha in tended I Expect to Be taken prisner But I am A frade tha lost thair livs. . . . then up the Ridg tha staretted and our men that had started for the top was caut Be twene the fiar of ouer men that had gand [gained] the top and the yankeys in the rear O what A turbill af fair ouer Bregad was in the gap of the Ridg at Braggs hed qarters we helt the top of the Ridg tell our men had giv way on Boath cides of ouer Bregade and the yankeys had gand the top of the Ridg on Boath cides of us and we had to Run out from under A croos fiar tena the Balls flue as thick as hale I cood see the durt fly up all A Round mee But thank god I got out safe. . . . tena we air A Bad whp [whipped] set of folks we lost all we had thousands of dollars worth of property went up sutch A destrocted [destructed?] armey neve[r] was Be fore[.][93]

While most of Reynolds's Brigade, including at least a small portion of the 60th North Carolina, was putting up a respectable fight on Bate's right, those elements of the 60th that retreated into Bate's lines remained under the control of Bate and, it must be admitted, performed poorly. Bate, who mistook Weaver's command for Reynolds's entire brigade, states in his report that shortly after Weaver rallied his men

scattered troops [were observed] a few hundred yards to my right, making their way, apparently without resistance, to the top of the hill. Believing them to be Confederates falling back from the trenches, I forbade my right firing upon them, and sent a staff officer to ascertain who they were. Upon receiving the answer, I directed upon them a right-oblique fire of infantry and artillery from the right of Tyler's command. It drove him to his left, but did not check his ascent of the ridge. In a few moments I saw a flag waving at the point in the line of General Anderson's division, beyond the depression in the ridge, where a section of . . . [Capt. Staunton H.] Dent's [Alabama] battery had been firing and was then located. I thought it a Confederate flag, but on nearer approach . . . I soon detected the United States colors. The [enemy] line in my front had recoiled a second time, but was rallied and was advancing up the hill in such numbers as to forbid the displacing of any of my command. I was ordered by General Bragg to withdraw a portion of my command and dislodge him [the enemy force on the right] if possible; but upon suggesting that I was without reserves, and the danger of withdrawing when so hard pressed on the front . . . he directed me to take such as could be best spared. I at once took the command under Major Weaver . . . it being disengaged, and moved it at a double-quick some 500 or 600 yards to the elevation on the right and rear of where the enemy had formed near his flag. I was unable, notwithstanding the assistance of Major Weaver, to get this command farther, and could only form it on the hill at right angles to my line, protecting that flank. . . . It was but a few moments until the second and third flags were on the ridge near the same spot, and the enemy in such numbers as to drive away the command under Major Weaver. This command, upon the advance of the enemy, broke and retired in disorder.[94]

93. J. W. Reese to Christina Reese, December 6, 1863, Reese Papers.

94. *Official Records (Army)*, ser. 1, 31 (pt. 2):741-742.

Another account of the same incident was produced in 1899 by an officer of the Washington Artillery, Lt. J. Adolph Chalaron, who even at that late date erroneously believed, like Bate, that Weaver's command was Reynolds's entire brigade. In a letter to the *National Tribune*, Chalaron stated that "The elevation to my right across [a] gap was occupied by the two guns of Dent's Battery, and this point, in my opinion, was the first one on the ridge to be carried by the Federals troops. . . . Gen. Bragg sent Reynolds's Brigade forward to retake the position. As this brigade reached my guns, coming from my left and rear, I started with a mounted Sergeant and a Corporal afoot . . . to lead the column in a charge across the gap. The troops did not respond."[95]

Contemporary and, sad to say, modern critics to the contrary, it is abundantly clear that the bulk of Reynolds's troops offered stout resistance atop Missionary Ridge, maintained their position as long as possible, and retreated in reasonably good order.[96] It is equally clear, however, that the 60th North Carolina deserves no such accolades. Once again, as at Stones River, the regiment became divided, and once again a portion of it, albeit with much company from other Confederate units, fled the field.[97]

Bragg's defeated army reached Chickamauga Station on the night of November 25 and continued to retreat the next day. "Tired and very sleepy[,] having slept but little for three nights," Reynolds's men bivouacked near Catoosa Station, Georgia, that evening. On the twenty-seventh they arrived at Dalton. Although they subsequently moved their camp several times, they remained in the vicinity of Dalton for more than five months. There the army was reorganized and its commander replaced. Bragg's resignation took effect on December 2 and, after a interim period under Hardee, Gen. Joseph E. Johnston assumed command of the Army of Tennessee on December 27. On November 30 Reynolds's Brigade was transferred from Buckner's Division to that of Maj. Gen. Carter L. Stevenson, which was transferred from Breckinridge's to Hardee's Corps. In addition to Reynolds's Brigade, Stevenson's Division contained brigades commanded by Brig. Gens. John C. Brown, Edmund W. Pettus, and Alfred Cumming. Stevenson's Division was transferred from Hardee's to Lt. Gen. John B. Hood's Corps on February 28, 1864. On December 14, 1863, it was reported that 141 members of the 60th North Carolina were present for duty.[98]

---

95. *National Tribune*, May 4, 1899.

96. See James Lee McDonough, *Chattanooga: A Death Grip on the Confederacy* (Knoxville: University of Tennessee Press, 1984), 186-187; Peter Cozzens, *The Shipwreck of Their Hopes: The Battles for Chattanooga* (Urbana and Chicago: The University of Illinois Press, 1994), 296-298; Jeffrey C. Weaver, *54th Virginia Infantry* (Lynchburg, Va.: H. E. Howard, 1993), 90-91, 93-94, hereafter cited as Weaver, *54th Virginia*.

97. According to figures compiled from the rosters in this volume, the 60th lost 2 men killed or mortally wounded, 7 wounded, and 50 captured (of whom 4 were wounded). Private Reese reported that total casualties in the consolidated 58th and 60th regiments numbered 97 men. Figures compiled for this volume indicate that the combined loss of the two regiments was 113 men.

The Battle of Missionary Ridge, in Captain Patton's sound judgment, was "miserably managed" by Bragg: "Our lines were on top of the Ridge, so situated that only a plunging Artillery shot could reach the enemy. Approaching it's [sic] foot, after reaching that point, he was entirely sheltered from our fire by the natural curvature of the mountain surface. We could not reach him with any effect until the lines were close together, and then with a rush, the Federals brought on a hand to hand conflict which was soon ended in their favor, and our forces retreated in confusion down the other side of the ridge. . . ." Patton, "Recollections," 10.

98. Harper Diary, November 26, 1863. See also *Official Records (Army)*, ser. 1, 31 (pt. 3):767, 823, 873, 32

Meantime, the 60th North Carolina settled down to an extended spell of camp life at Dalton. Shanties and log cabins were constructed for the winter, supernumerary company officers detailed, strict and very precise regulations issued for "the government of the troops . . . in camp," and a "regular system of furloughs" established.[99] The increased number of furloughs, in combination with an amnesty for deserters and prohibition of the "wooden horse" and other corporal punishment "having the character of torture," reconfirmed Johnston's popularity with men who had served under him previously and established it with those who had not. In short, morale improved and absenteeism and desertion declined. "[T]here is much less sickness in the army now than I ever knew before," Captain Patton wrote, "attributable in my opinion, to the large number of furloughs that are granted."[100]

The improvements in morale in the Army of Tennessee were all the more impressive because they were achieved despite initial food shortages, stern discipline, and an exhausting training schedule. "[T]he poor soldiers do not get more rations for all day than are sufficient for one good meal," Captain Patton informed his mother in late January, "[and] the rations of Beef that we are geting [sic] now are . . . sour and almost uneatable. . . ." "I have just eaten dinner," Patton wrote a few days later, "which consisted of poor beef boiled plain – corn bread, and rice – which articles have composed our meals for the last fortnight. . . . We [officers] can get enough, such as it is, by paying for it – which is more than the men can do – their rations being extremely short." Patton's allusion to the more favorable circumstances of officers is much to the point. In addition to superior financial resources, officers were more likely to enjoy the immeasurable blessing of food parcels from home. Patton received a parcel containing "ginger cakes, Wine, [and] molasses" in February, and two months later Assistant Quartermaster Erwin solicited, and probably received, "Pickles, vinegar, catsup, [and] molasses" from his father. Such delicacies were almost beyond the dreams of the average private. However, even for soldiers in the ranks, foodstuffs gradually increased in quantity and improved qualitatively under Johnston. Spot shortages probably

---

(pt. 2):812. The present-for-duty strengths for Reynolds's other three regiments were 58th North Carolina 327, 54th Virginia 390, and 63rd Virginia 303, making a total of 1,161. Inasmuch as the 58th and 60th North Carolina were still consolidated at that time, it is unclear why the strengths of the two units were reported separately and why Capt. Samuel M. Silver was reported as acting commander of the 58th. Possibly Silver's status was nominal and reflected, as did the separate troop-strength figures, the temporary nature of the consolidation. See *Official Records (Army)*, ser. 1, 32 (pt. 2):587.

99. *Official Records (Army)*, ser. 1, 32 (pt. 2):530; T. W. Patton to H. K. Patton, December 31, 1863, Patton Papers. Some officers were declared supernumerary because of the company consolidations mentioned in footnote 87 above. Such a consolidation was planned for Companies C and D of the 60th: "[A]s soon as Capt [Jesse R. S.] Gillilands [sic] commission arrives," Captain Patton (Company C) commented in a letter dated January 23, 1864, "I suppose I will be reported supernumerary again and will get off on some duty again." It is uncertain whether the consolidation of the two companies was effectuated. T. W. Patton to H. K. Patton, January 23, 1864, Patton Papers.

100. *Official Records (Army)*, ser. 1, 31 (pt. 3):881; T. W. Patton to Nannie Patton (his wife), January 30, 1864, Patton Papers. Thirty-seven men deserted during both the third and fourth quarters of 1863, the highest figures of the war. During the first quarter of 1864, the first under Johnston's tenure, that figure dropped by more than half (18). For 60th North Carolina desertion figures during other periods, see footnotes 23 and 72 above and 167 and 215 below. For comparative desertion figures in Reynolds's four regiments for the entire war, see footnote 79 on pages 236-237 of this volume.

persisted and quality continued to vary, but by February 14 a soldier in the 54th Virginia, a sister unit of the 60th North Carolina in Reynolds's Brigade, was commenting happily upon the issuance of "plenty of good rations."[101]

In disciplinary matters, Johnston was severe without being perceived, as was the despised Bragg, as callous, rigid, and arbitrary. "Courts martial . . . [are] the order of the day now," Captain Patton wrote on January 23. "[O]ne poor fellow is soon to be shot for desertion – and one of our Regiment was sentenced to have one side of his head shaved, and marched, with a barrell [sic] over his shoulders, all through the Brigade, each day for ten days, with the drum & fife playing the rogue's march behind him. . . ." Probably because of his genuine and self-evident concern for the welfare of his troops, such measures aroused no serious resentment or opposition. In any case, by March 27 Assistant Quartermaster Erwin was proclaiming the army's "implicit confidence" and "entire . . . devot[ion]" to Johnston, who had "worked a wonderful improvement in every respect. . . ." The men, Erwin continued, were "in better condition than even before": "better clothed, better fed, better disciplined, [and] in better spirits. It is a great blessing that Bragg was taken away. He would have ruined our cause this spring, certain."[102]

Concurrent with efforts to improve discipline, living conditions, and morale, Johnston instituted a rigorous training regimen that included inspections, reviews, battle exercises, and "a great deal of hard drilling." "We have had more reviews in the past month than I ever saw," Capt. James Clark of the 63rd Virginia groaned on February 15, 1864, and Captain Patton complained on February 6 that the men "do not have much employment except drilling. . . . [Y]esterday [there was] a grand review of the army. . . ." On January 29 Hardee's Corps was reviewed by Johnston. "[I]t was the finest Military display I have yet seen," Captain Harper of the 58th North Carolina wrote. "The great number of men present surprised us all. . . . It was a fine looking body of men. . . ."[103]

Following his victory at Chattanooga and the relief of Burnside at Knoxville on December 6, Grant began planning an advance against Atlanta in the spring. In the interim, Sherman was dispatched on a brief campaign into central and eastern Mississippi in early February. On February 22 General Thomas, on orders from Grant, advanced from Chattanooga toward Ringgold, Georgia, to prevent Johnston from sending reinforcements to

101. T. W. Patton to H. K. Patton, January 23, January 27, and February 10, 1864, Patton Papers; G. P. Erwin to his father, April 20, 1864, Erwin Papers; James Miller Wysor to his father, February 14, 1864, James Miller Wysor Papers (typescripts), Virginia Historical Society, Richmond, hereafter cited as Wysor Papers.

102. T. W. Patton to H. K. Patton, January 23, 1864, Patton Papers; G. P. Erwin to his father, March 27, 1864, Erwin Papers.

103. T. W. Patton to Nannie Patton, February 3, 1864, and T. W. Patton to H. K. Patton, February 6, 1864, Patton Papers; James Clark to Martha Clark (his wife), February 15, 1864, Roster Document No. 1040 (transcripts), Civil War Roster Project (CWRP), NCDAH, hereafter described as Clark Letters; G. W. F. Harper to Ella Harper, January 30, 1864, Harper Papers. See also G. W. F. Harper to Ella Harper, December 15, 1863. Patton grumbled that "however pleasant" the grand review on February 5 "might have been to Genl Johnston and the lady spectators, [it] was a most dreadful bore to the smaller officers and men–most of the latter having to go out without their breakfast & being kept on the feild [sic] till near three o'clock." Captain Clark was equally disgusted: "I can't see what good . . . [it does to have us] trotting round for them to look at," he wrote in the letter cited above. "Every Gen. that has a wife & she comes to see him must have us paraded round for her to look at." T. W. Patton to H. K. Patton, February 6, 1864, Patton Papers.

confront Sherman. Heavy skirmishing broke out at Rocky Face Ridge on the twenty-third and twenty-fourth and culminated in an attempt by Thomas to flank Johnston out of a strong position at Mill Creek Gap on February 25. At Crow Valley, east of Mill Creek Gap, Brig. Gen. Henry D. Clayton's Alabama brigade repulsed three separate Federal attacks and sustained seventy-two casualties. Reynolds's Brigade, on Clayton's right, was subjected to heavy artillery fire and took part in at least one skirmish. "[A]bout 12 o'clock," Pvt. John W. Dugger of the 58th North Carolina wrote, "the enemy commenced advancing slowly and tried to flank us on the left. . . . About 2 o'clock a sharp fight took place on that wing lasting about half an hour. The 58th was not engaged except the Skirmishers, though under heavy cannonading[,] wounding 24 in the 58th and 60th . . . regiments. . . . The Yankies [sic] commenced falling back that night about 10 o'clock."[104] General Reynolds, in a brief report written on the date of the battle, stated that "My skirmishers have been engaged since early this morning, and have kept back the enemy. About 12 o'clock General Clayton sent me two regiments to extend my left to the mountain. About the time they got into position the enemy advanced in force and a fight ensued. General Clayton, with a third regiment, came up and took command of the left. The fight was entirely successful, driving the enemy back twice. My own troops have been under a heavy fire of shell and canister for several hours. All behaved well. The list of killed and wounded is below: Sixty-third Virginia, 5 wounded; Fifty-eighth and Sixtieth North Carolina Regiments, 24 wounded, 3 mortally; Fifty-fourth Virginia Regiment, 12 men wounded."[105] "The action could hardly be called a battle," Captain Patton admitted, "but was decidedly a brisk skirmish where our Brigade was engaged. For a few minutes our Regiment was exposed to the hottest & most accurate shelling that I ever experienced, but fortunately for some reason this only lasted a very short time – resulting however in wounding twenty four & killing three. . . . On Sunday [February 28], the Yankees having retreated we were marched back to our old quarters." According to figures compiled for this volume, the 60th North Carolina lost 1 man killed and 11 wounded at Rocky Face Ridge.[106]

Following "the little disturbance" at Rocky Face Ridge, as Captain Patton deprecatorily described the fight, the 60th resumed its rigorous training regimen at Dalton. "At present we are having an everlasting succession of Drills, Reviews, & Inspections," Assistant

104. Diary of John W. Dugger (Company D, 58th North Carolina) and "Gilliam Hodges [Cpl. Gilbert W. Hodges]" (Companies D and A, 58th North Carolina), February 25, 1864, in *Watauga Democrat* (Boone), June 11, 1891, hereafter cited as Dugger-Hodges Diary, in *Watauga Democrat* (issue date varies). Hodges began making entries in the diary after Dugger's death on or about August 4, 1864. Some entries may have been made also by Pvt. Hezekiah Thomas (Company D). It is probable that the *Watauga Democrat*'s transcription contains minor errors. "They [the Federals] would stand off & shoot but wouldn't come up," Capt. James Clark of the 63rd Virginia wrote. "[Their officers] came up one time & was patting their men on the shoulders & trying to get them to charge us when we charged them. They ran like good fellows." James Clark to Martha Clark, February 28, 1864, Clark Letters.

105. *Official Records (Army)*, ser. 1, 32 (pt. 1):483. For a remarkably different account by Reynolds of his part in the fight at Rocky Face Ridge, see footnote 72 to the history of the 58th North Carolina on page 235 of this volume.

106. T. W. Patton to H. K. Patton, March 2, 1864, Patton Papers. For once, casualty figures compiled for a *North Carolina Troops* volume agree perfectly with a contemporary source. See W. M. Hardy to G. W. F. Harper, February 27, 1864, Harper Papers.

Quartermaster Erwin complained to his father in early April. "Genl Johns[t]on reviews the entire army this week. He keeps every body busy from his Lieut Genl down to the privates." "Sham battles" were also conducted. "Have just ret[urne]d from witnessing the grand sham battle of Hardee's Corps," Captain Harper wrote on April 7. "It was a magnificent sight. The spectators numbered thousands if not more. Many ladies from Atlanta & other places were present, adding to the beauty of the scene."[107] Amid their tedious labors, Reynolds's men found time for diversions such as band concerts, "ball play," snipe hunts, gander pullings, chess, sermons, and prayer meetings. It is likely that the 60th North Carolina took part also in a gigantic snowball fight that broke out on March 22 and involved thousands of soldiers. "The boys got to snow-balling individually and soon by companies and then by regiments and brigades until . . . most of the army was engaged," Sgt. Robert D. Jamison of the 45th Tennessee (Brown's Brigade) wrote. "It was amusing to see the Colonels and Generals on their horses giving orders as if it was a regular battle. There was a great deal of fun in it until the snow began to melt. . . . [Then] some balls would get too hard and the infirmary corps was called into requisition to take care of the wounded. . . ."[108]

On April 6 the consolidation of the 58th and 60th North Carolina, which had prompted a "mutiny" by the 58th in February, was terminated when Maj. Thomas J. Dula of that unit reported for duty.[109] The two regiments then resumed their status as independent entities. No serious punishment was meted out to the alleged mutineers, perhaps because the incident was in fact relatively innocuous. However, Johnston may have felt obliged to demonstrate that, if sufficiently provoked, he could be as iron-fisted as Bragg. Whatever the case, on May 4 fourteen deserters—twelve from the 58th and two from the 60th—were shot in a mass execution that stunned the army.

107. T. W. Patton to H. K. Patton, March 2, 1864, Patton Papers; G. P. Erwin to his father, April 10, 1864, Erwin Papers; G. W. F. Harper to Ella Harper, [April 7, 1864], Harper Papers. "Hardee's Corps had a sham fight here a few days since in the field just opposite this Hdqtrs [Brown's Brigade]," Sgt. R. D. Jamison of the 45th Tennessee wrote. "It was a grand affair. Tell Henry the one he saw was nothing compared to it. I saw a cavalry Regt. charge a Regt. of infantry formed in a square four different times and were repulsed every time. It was very exciting indeed, and I might have been forced to believe there was some reality in it had there not been so many ladies, Quarter-Masters, Commissaries and their attachees present. The ridges all around were covered with these. Some of the ladies got between the lines and you may imagine their astonishment . . . when infantry and artillery were roaring all around them. . . . [T]hey did not stay there long." Robert D. Jamison to Camilla P. Jamison (his wife), April 11, 1864, in Henry Downs Jamison Jr., ed., *Letters and Recollections of a Confederate Soldier, 1860-1865* (Nashville, Tennessee: privately published, 1964), 91, hereafter cited as H. D. Jamison, *Letters and Recollections*.

108. Harper Diary, April 13, 1864; R. D. Jamison, "Reminiscence of a Tennessee Confederate Veteran," 167, in H. D. Jamison, *Letters and Recollections*. According to an officer on Maj. Gen. Alexander P. Stewart's staff, "a number of soldiers had their eyes put out [received black eyes?]." Bromfield L. Ridley, *Battles and Sketches of the Army of Tennessee* (Mexico, Missouri: Missouri Printing and Publishing Company, 1906), 283, hereafter cited as Ridley, *Battles and Sketches*. See also Harper Diary, March 22, 1864; Weaver, *54th Virginia*, 104.

109. J. B. Palmer to G. W. F. Harper, March 4, 1864, Harper Papers. See also Harper Diary, April 6, 1864; G. W. F. Harper to Ella Harper, April 5, 1864, Harper Papers. A discussion of the mutiny appears in footnote 76 on page 236 of the history of the 58th North Carolina in this volume.

I was surgeon for this dreadful occasion [Robert W. Cooper of the 60th recalled]. All of the army there was ordered out; the Infantry formed a hollow square with cannon in the rear, while the cavalry just back of them made such a strong line it was impossible for any one to pass.

A long ditch had been prepared, and the rude coffins placed in front of it, with a stake by it, while the guard . . . marched each man to the stake & coffin prepared for him and each man bound to his stake. The senior officer ordered all in position and to make ready, and Lt Robert Clayton . . . in command, gave the order to fire. All were killed but two, as I found when I advanced to examine them. One had been shot in the side,–the other in the arm. I reported that two were alive and the guard advanced and . . . fired killing them immediately. Orders were then given to fall back to camp. Oh! What a Sunday was that! The private soldiers were all bitterly opposed to the execution of these men, and that night several hundred of them left the army and never returned.

I remained to attend the burial service of these fourteen men. Our Chaplain held service until about ten o'clock. I can never, never forget that sad scene; I was heart sick.[110]

They were shot down *"like wild beasts,"* Captain Patton wrote. "One was from . . . my Company [C]. All of that fearful night I sat beside my man in what was called 'The Bull Pen' and tried to comfort him as best I could, and I never felt more sad than when Lieutenant Clayton, to whom the duty had by lot fallen, gave the command 'Fire!' and these Confederate soldiers fell dead by the hands of their brothers."[111]

In late April, with the arrival of warmer weather, rumors began to circulating concerning the spring campaign. "It is understood," Erwin wrote on April 20, "[that] we leave our comparatively comfortable winter quarters tomorrow or next day for the front to our position in line of battle. Adieu to anything like rest till next winter." On April 26 Reynolds's Brigade did indeed move four miles northwest of Dalton and began erecting fortifications on the old battlefield at Rocky Face Ridge. Three days later Erwin, despite the impending executions of the fourteen deserters, wrote a letter reflecting optimism and good morale in the 60th North Carolina. "To human eyes it does seem as if victory was our due

110. Cooper, "Experiences in the Confederate Army," 9-10. See also pages 236-237 of this volume. Even prior to the May 4 executions, deserters were shot on a regular basis. "Nothing is stirring out here except the rather common occurrence of a deserter's being shot or a spy hung," G. P. Erwin wrote on April 20. G. P. Erwin to his father, April 20, 1864, Erwin Papers.

The fourteen men executed at Dalton on May 4, 1864, were Sgt. Alford T. Ball (G-58); Pvts. Jacob A. Austin (E-58), Asa Dover (F-58), Joseph A. Gibbs (C-58), Wright Hutchings (F-58), Christopher C. Ledford (C-60), George W. McFalls (K-58), Michael Ward (D-58), Hiram Youngblood (F-58), and E. F. Younts (H-58); and probably Pvts. William R. Byers (G-58), Reuben A. Dellinger (A-58), Jesse Hase (A-58), and James M. Randal (A-60).

111. Patton, "Recollections," 11. "Today I witnessed a sight, sad indeed," Thomas Hopkins Deavenport, chaplain of the 3rd Tennessee, Brown's Brigade, wrote in his diary on May 4. "I saw fourteen men shot for desertion. I visited them twice yesterday and attended them to the place of execution. Most of them met death manfully. Some, poor fellows, I fear were unprepared. I saw them wash and dress themselves for the grave. It was a solumn [sic] scene, they were tied to the stake, there was the coffin, there the open grave ready to receive them. . . . 'Tell my wife,' said one but a few minutes before the leaden messengers pierced his breast, 'not to grieve for me, I have no doubt of reaching a better world'. . . . I think they were objects of pity, they were ignorant, poor, and had families dependent upon them. War is a cruel thing, it heeds not the widow's tear, the orphan's moan, or the lover's anguish." Diary of Thomas Hopkins Deavenport (typescript), May 4, 1864 (pages 19-20), Civil War Collection (Confederate), box 6, folder 5a, Tennessee State Archives, Nashville, hereafter cited as Deavenport Diary.

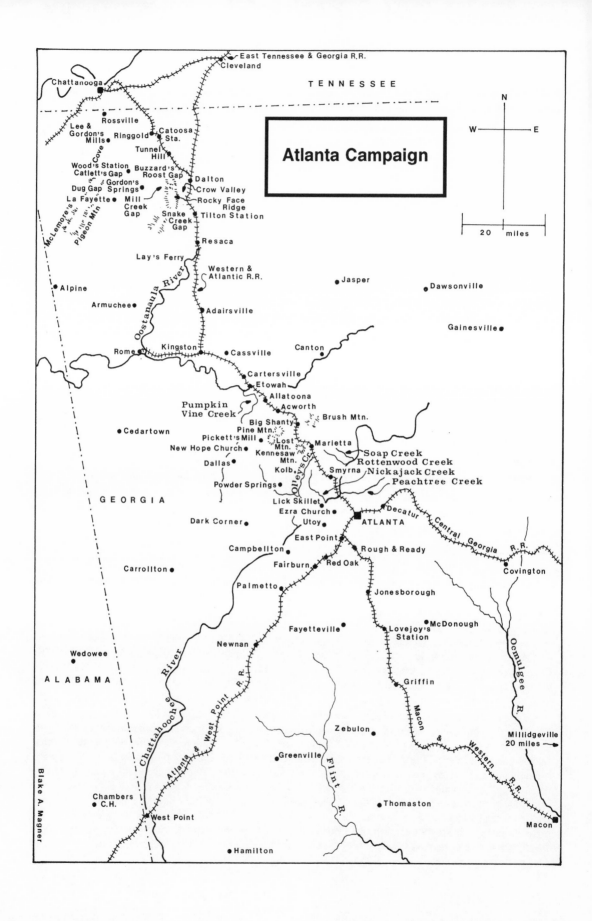

Atlanta Campaign

N
W   E

20   miles

TENNESSEE

East Tennessee & Georgia R.R.
Cleveland
Chattanooga
Rossville
Lee & Gordon's Mills
Ringgold
Catoosa Sta.
Tunnel Hill
Cove
Wood's Station
Catlett's Gap
Buzzard's Roost Gap
Dalton
Gordon's Springs
Dug Gap
Crow Valley
La Fayette
Mill Creek Gap
Rocky Face Ridge
Snake Creek Gap
Tilton Station
McLemore's
Pigeon Mtn
Resaca
Lay's Ferry
Western & Atlantic R.R.
Jasper
Dawsonville
Alpine
Armuchee
Oostanaula River
Adairsville
Gainesville
Rome
Kingston
Cassville
Canton
Cartersville
Etowah
Allatoona
Acworth
Pumpkin Vine Creek
Brush Mtn.
Cedartown
Big Shanty
Pine Mtn.
Pickett's Mill
Lost Mtn.
Marietta
Soap Creek
Rottenwood Creek
New Hope Church
Kennesaw Mtn.
Nickajack Creek
Dallas
Smyrna
Peachtree Creek
Powder Springs
Olley's Cr.
GEORGIA
Lick Skillet
Ezra Church
Dark Corner
Utoy
Decatur
ATLANTA
Central Georgia R.R.
East Point
Rough & Ready
Campbellton
Fairburn
Red Oak
Covington
Carrollton
Palmetto
Jonesborough
Fayetteville
Lovejoy's Station
McDonough
Wedowee
Newnan
Chattahoochee River
Atlanta & West Point R.R.
Griffin
Ocmulgee R.
ALABAMA
Zebulon
Millidgeville 20 miles →
Greenville
Flint R.
Macon & Western R.R.
Chambers C.H.
Thomaston
West Point
Macon
Hamilton

Blake A. Magner

now," he mused to his father. "The chances are for us, our generals skillful, our soldiers enthusiastic, [and] our numbers nearly equal to that of the enemy. . . ."[112]

On May 7 General Sherman, who had replaced Grant as commander of the Military Division of the Mississippi, marched toward Dalton with an army of about 100,000 men.[113] Thomas's Army of the Cumberland captured the village of Tunnel Hill the same day and advanced toward the north end of Rocky Face Ridge and the Dug and Mill Creek Gaps. The Army of the Ohio, now commanded by Maj. Gen. John M. Schofield, moved on Thomas's left around Rocky Face Ridge and into Crow Valley, east of the ridge. While Thomas and Schofield conducted demonstrations to convince Johnston that a frontal attack was in the offing, Maj. Gen. James B. McPherson's Army of the Tennessee, on the Federal right, marched around Johnston's left flank.[114] McPherson's orders were to penetrate Snake Creek Gap, about eight miles southwest of Dalton, and cut Johnston's line of communications at Resaca. The Confederate army would then be caught in a vise and destroyed.[115]

The 60th North Carolina was still at the old Rocky Face Ridge battlefield when Sherman advanced on May 7. The regiment then moved into a reserve position with the rest of Reynolds's Brigade in Crow Valley, near the foot of Buzzard Roost. On the morning of May 8 the brigade moved to its left so that its left was on the lower slopes of Buzzard Roost and its right extended into the valley. In that position it skirmished with the enemy until dark.[116] "About 10 o'clock [on the morning of May 9]," Private Dugger wrote, "the enemy was discovered advancing and from noon until night heavy skirmishing and cannonading raged on the line from the top of Buzzard roost to the east side of the valley. The enemies [sic] skirmishers made a charge on ours and drove them back to the lines. . . . About 3 o'clock [that afternoon] three [Federal] columns charged the top of Buzzard roost but were soon repulsed by Pettess' [Pettus's] Alabama Brigade with several [severe?] losses[.] [O]ur loss exceedingly light. Fighting ceased about dark and remained quiet all night." Light skirmishing on May 10 was followed by a "desperately hard" rain during the night. "[R]olled in a blanket I kept nearly dry," Chaplain Deavenport wrote. "The place being very steep, I would slip down untill [sic] my feet got into a puddle of water, when I would pull up again. This is soldiering it in earnest." Sharpshooting and skirmishing commenced again on the morning of the eleventh and continued "slowly" all that day and the next.[117]

112. G. P. Erwin to his father, April 20 and 29, 1864, Erwin Papers.

113. Sherman returned to Nashville from his Mississippi expedition on March 17 and assumed command of the Military Division of the Mississippi the next day. As commander of that division, his authority extended over the Armies of the Cumberland, the Tennessee, and the Ohio. Grant was promoted to lieutenant general, appointed general-in-chief of the Union army, and sent east to confront Lee in Virginia.

114. Maj. Gen. John G. Foster replaced Burnside as commander of the Army of the Ohio on December 9, 1863, and was replaced in turn by Schofield on February 9, 1864. McPherson succeeded Sherman as commander of the Army of the Tennessee on March 18, 1864.

115. See Richard M. McMurry, "The Opening Phase of the 1864 Campaign in the West," in *Atlanta Historical Journal*, 27 (1983): 5-24. As of February 29 the camp of Company D and probably the rest of the 60th was one and one-half miles southeast of Dalton. See "Record of Events" for Company D, 60th North Carolina, January-February 1864, Compiled Confederate Service Records (North Carolina), M270, reel 539.

116. See *Official Records (Army)*, ser. 1, 38 (pt. 3):811. For a detailed discussion of the location of Reynolds's Brigade on the field, see footnote 83 in the history of the 58th North Carolina on page 238 of this volume.

117. Dugger-Hodges Diary, May 9-11, 1864, in *Watauga Democrat*, June 11, 1864; Deavenport Diary, May 11,

While most of Johnston's army confronted Sherman at Rocky Face Ridge during May 8-12, McPherson's flanking movement failed at Snake Creek Gap because of McPherson's excessive caution and the inopportune arrival at Resaca of Confederate reinforcements from Mississippi under Lt. Gen. Leonidas Polk. When Sherman began shifting the bulk of his army south to support McPherson, Johnston fell back from Rocky Face Ridge and formed a line of battle on a range of hills west and north of Resaca. Reynolds's Brigade "secretly retired" from Buzzard Roost around 9:00 P.M. on the twelfth and marched "over a very rough road" throughout the night. After halting briefly for breakfast near Tilton Station, the men continued slowly down the Resaca road on May 13. "Skirmishes out on our flanks," Harper noted dramatically. "The enemy pressing us in rear and hovering on our flank." That night Reynolds's men and the rest of Stevenson's Division went into position about two miles north of Resaca on the right center of Johnston's line: Cumming and Brown in front; Pettus and Reynolds in reserve. Hindman's Division was on Stevenson's left and Maj. Gen. Alexander P. Stewart's Division on his right.[118]

Skirmishing began at Resaca at 8:00 A.M. on May 14 and continued until Schofield launched a two-division attack on Hindman shortly after noon and was repulsed with severe losses. Stevenson and Stewart, reinforced by four brigades, then attacked the division of Maj. Gen. David S. Stanley, whose left flank was in the air. "About 5 o'clock that evening," Stevenson reported, "I commenced a movement to dislodge the enemy from the high point of the ridge some distance in front of General Cumming. Brown and his support (Reynolds) were directed to move out in front of their trenches and then swing around to the left. After the movement commenced General Cumming was also directed to wheel all of his brigade, which was to the right of the backbone of the ridge, to the left in front of his works. . . . I was much gratified by the gallantry with which the movement was made. . . ." Two of Stanley's brigades were overwhelmed and routed by Stevenson, but a stubborn stand by an Indiana battery and the arrival of Federal reinforcements brought the attack to a halt. Leaving numerous butternut-clad corpses strewn in front of the triumphant Indiana gunners, Stevenson withdrew.[119] Captain Harper wrote that Stevenson's men "moved out of [their] breastworks and charged the enemy[,] who ran for dear life. Magnificient [sic] charge. Advanced our lines over a mile and halted after dark. Occupied the ground until after midnight when we withdrew to our original position." Reynolds's troops played a secondary role in the fighting and escaped most of the destructive fire sustained by Brown. Their casualties, if any, were light.[120]

While most of the fighting was taking place on the Confederate right on May 14, McPherson's troops, on Johnston's left, quietly seized a lightly defended hill perilously

---

1864 (page 21). "This is certainly the roughest place I ever saw and the rockiest," Chaplain Deavenport added. "Rocks are continually rolling down to the amusement of those highest up and annoyance of those lower down."

118. Dugger-Hodges Diary, May 12, 1864, in *Watauga Democrat*, June 18, 1891; Deavenport Diary, May 16, 1864 (page 21); Harper Diary, May 13, 1864.

119. *Official Records (Army)*, ser. 1, 38 (pt. 3):812. See also the report of the Indiana battery commander, Capt. Peter Simonson, in *Official Records (Army)*, ser. 1, 38 (pt. 1):488-489.

120. Harper Diary, May 14, 1864. See also Dugger-Hodges Diary, May 14, 1864, in *Watauga Democrat*, June 18, 1891. Chaplain Deavenport states in his diary that "Brown's brigade . . . did all the fighting." Deavenport Diary, May 16, 1864 (page 22).

close to the Oostanaula River bridges over which Johnston would have to retreat. Several hundred Federals belonging to Brig. Gen. Thomas W. Sweeny's Division also crossed the Oostanaula downriver at Lay's Ferry. Sweeny's troops quickly withdrew under the mistaken impression that they were menaced by a superior Confederate force, but the threat posed by McPherson and Sweeny to Johnston's rear was urgent. During the night Johnston dispatched a division to defend the Lay's Ferry crossing and ordered the construction of a pontoon bridge upstream from Resaca. Sherman, for his part, ordered Sweeny to recross the Oostanaula at Lay's Ferry the next morning and establish a secure bridgehead. At the same time, Maj. Gens. Joseph Hooker and Oliver O. Howard, commanding the XX and IV Corps respectively of the Army of the Cumberland, were to attack the Confederate right.

Fighting began on the morning of May 15 with cannonading and heavy musketry along most of the line. At about 1:00 P.M. Hooker and Howard advanced over broken terrain covered with underbrush and small trees and, in the face of a storm of fire from Stevenson, quickly stumbled to a halt. Around two o'clock Reynolds's men were ordered to relieve Brown in the front line, where a prolonged struggle over four abandoned Confederate cannons was raging. There they repulsed "several" enemy charges.[121] A correspondent for the Atlanta *Intelligencer* wrote that

[a]t a quarter from four o'clock, a fifth charge was made, the enemy throwing forward fresh troops every time. Th[i]s charge was very heavy, and was made with spirit. . . . [W]ith a prolonged cheer, they rushed upon our works.–A . . . terrible, death-dealing volley, was poured into their ranks, and a loud . . . yell of defiance rang out from the lips of the Virginians and North Carolinians. This was more than the men of Brown's and Pettus' brigades [who were in reserve] could withstand, and though threatened with death by their officers . . . [they] entered the pits to assist in repelling the charge. But their services were not needed. Quickly another volley . . . [was] poured into the enemy's line of battle, and they turned and retreated in disorder to the cover of their ridge, followed by the derisive shouts of the victors. . . .

[W]ithin half an hour . . . three lines of battle, closely massed, were seen forming in front of that portion of the line held by the 58th North Carolina. There was not much time for reflection, for very soon a voice on the right of the regiment exclaimed, "they are coming!" and the first column was seen to advance. "Withhold your fire until they come close to you, and then aim low," ordered the officers. On came the enemy cheering loudly. . . . They approached within fifty yards of the line, firing rapidly upon our men—a sheet of fire was the answer, and the dead and wounded lie piled up before our works. . . . [B]ewildered by the fierceness of our fire, they scattered throughout the woods, and reached their lines, our sharp shooters killing and wounding them by dozens in their route down the ridge. . . .

This sixth column was repulsed only a few minutes when the remaining two columns of Yankees marched forward, with the hope of reaching our line before our men could fire more than one volley. But their charge was not made with the same firmness as characterized . . . the preceding one, and two or three well-aimed volleys from the fifty-eighth [and probably the 60th] North Carolina, assisted by a cross fire from the fifty-fourth Virginia on the one wing, and the sixty-third [Virginia] on the other, routed the 7th attacking column of the enemy. They . . . retired to their ridge, and for

---

121. Harper Diary, May 15, 1864. The guns were ultimately captured by the Federals.

a few minutes only their sharpshooters could be seen, their main body being no doubt engaged in reforming their broken columns.[122]

Encouraged by the sturdy work of Stevenson's men and hearing no reports of further Federal advances on his left, Johnston ordered Hood to attack with Stewart's, Hindman's, and Stevenson's Divisions in the late afternoon (see map on page 241). Just as that assault was launched, Johnston learned that a powerful Federal force on his right was crossing the Oostanaula. He then attempted to cancel Hood's attack and succeeded in halting Hindman's units and some of Stevenson's but none of Stewart's. At least two of Reynolds's regiments, the 58th North Carolina and 54th Virginia, failed to receive the cancellation order, and the 54th Virginia, the more exposed of the two regiments, lost more than 100 officers and men "in less than fifteen minutes."[123] As far as can be determined, the 60th North Carolina did not take part in the attack. Its casualties during the earlier fighting on May 15, according to figures compiled for this volume, were 2 men killed, 6 wounded, and 7 captured. Total Confederate casualties were about 3,000 men; Federal losses numbered about 4,000.[124]

During the night of May 15 most of Johnston's troops crossed the Oostanaula and fell back toward Adairsville. The next day the 58th North Carolina and presumably the rest of Reynolds's Brigade marched about six miles south, "rested about two hours . . . [and] then moved on. Skirmishing continued on the flank all the time," Private Dugger wrote. "Marched about three miles and took up camp. Next morning, the 17th, started before day, marched about six miles and stopped. Skirmishing commenced very soon and continued until a sharp cavalry fight took place. Our command immediately formed a line of battle. Firing ceased at night. . . ."[125]

At Adairsville, Johnston divided his army, sending Hood's and Polk's Corps southeast on the Cassville road and Hardee's south on a roughly parallel road that led to Kingston before turning due east to rejoin the main road at Cassville. Correctly reasoning that Sherman would also divide his army at the Adairsville fork, Johnston planned to reunite his forces at Cassville and defeat Sherman's eastern wing before the western wing could come to its aid. Around midnight on May 17, Reynolds's Brigade set off for Cassville with the rest of Hood's Corps. However, by the time it arrived about 11:00 A.M. a large force of Federal cavalry on a railroad cutting mission had materialized in Hood's rear, forcing Johnston to abandon his plan and fall back to a ridge southeast of Cassville. There he hoped to entice Sherman, whose western wing arrived from Kingston that afternoon, into an attack. Reynolds's men went into position on the Confederate right, and "sharp skirmishing" and cannonading continued throughout the day. That night, after belatedly discovering that Hood's and Polk's flanks were exposed to enfilading fire by Federal artillery, Johnston

122. *Intelligencer* (Atlanta), unknown date, reprinted in *North Carolina [Weekly] Standard* (Raleigh), June 22, 1864.

123. *Official Records (Army)*, ser. 1, 38 (pt. 3):813.

124. Three additional members of the 60th were captured either on May 15 or 16. According to one postwar report, General Reynolds was "very much intoxicated" during the fighting on the afternoon of May 15 and ordered the 54th Virginia to attack over the protests of its commanding officer. For a discussion of Reynolds's drinking and womanizing propensities, see footnote 93, page 242, in the history of the 58th North Carolina.

125. Dugger-Hodges Diary, May 16-17, 1864, in *Watauga Democrat*, June 18, 1891.

ordered another retreat. At about ten o'clock Reynolds's Brigade "secretly retired" with the rest of Johnston's army to Allatoona Pass, a narrow valley about twelve miles southeast of Cassville. "[We] marched until about 11 o'clock next day," Dugger wrote, "passing through Cartersville Ga. [A]rrived at the [Etowah] river [where we] made a halt and rested some hours . . . then . . . marched about three miles and took up camp. All quiet except some cannonading on the left Saturday and Saturday night the 21st until Tuesday the 24th. Marched about three miles to the railroad [on that day] and camped. . . ."[126]

Johnston's Allatoona Pass position, about thirty-five miles northwest of Atlanta, was if anything more formidable than the one he occupied a few weeks earlier at Rocky Face Ridge. As he had done throughout the campaign, Sherman therefore made another attempt to turn Johnston's left, sending the bulk of his army west of the Allatoona Mountains toward Dallas on May 23. That maneuver, Sherman believed, would compel Johnston to abandon his Allatoona redoubt and retreat behind the Chattahoochee River, only eight miles north of Atlanta. Quickly apprised by his scouts of Sherman's gambit, Johnston marched westward with most of his army and was waiting on a series of low, timbered ridges when Sherman arrived at Dallas on the twenty-fifth. Late that afternoon the Federals advanced through dense woods and underbrush against Stewart's Division, entrenched near New Hope Church, and were repulsed with severe casualties. Stevenson's Division, which reached the field around 1:00 P.M., was on Stewart's right with Brown's and Pettus's Brigades in front and those of Reynolds and Cumming in reserve. Several of Brown's regiments took part in the heavy fighting that followed, but the remainder of Stevenson's men were not involved. During the day General Reynolds received a "painful" wound that incapacitated him for field service for the remainder of the war. He was succeeded as brigade commander by Col. Robert C. Trigg of the 54th Virginia.[127]

Skirmishing resumed "very soon" on the morning of May 26 and, according to Dugger, "continued all day and night[.] [S]ome cannonading going on through the day [but] no regular engagement. . . . [S]ome vollies [sic] fired on parts of the line." Heavy fighting flared at Pickett's Mill on the twenty-seventh as Sherman, varying his tactics, attempted unsuccessfully to turn Johnston's right. Cleburne's Division repulsed the Federal attackers with heavy casualties; Stevenson's Division again was not involved.[128] More fighting occurred on May 28 when Johnston, shrewdly deducing that Sherman had abandoned his flanking effort and was about to move back to the Western and Atlantic Railroad, ordered an attack against McPherson's lines south of Dallas. Severe casualties were incurred by

126. Dugger-Hodges Diary, May 19 [18]-24, 1864, in *Watauga Democrat*, June 18, 1891.

127. *Official Records (Army)*, ser. 1, 38 (pt. 3):814. See also Dugger-Hodges Diary, May 25, 1864, in *Watauga Democrat*, June 18, 1891. Reynolds briefly rejoined the Army of Tennessee in August 1864 but was not reinstated as commander of his former brigade. In a letter written on August 22, Captain Patton rejoiced that "Gen Reynolds has left and all of his staff, [and] I suppose, or at least hope, that our connection with him is forever disolved [sic]." T. W. Patton to Nannie Patton, August 22, 1864, Patton Papers.

128. Dugger-Hodges Diary, May 26, 1864, in *Watauga Democrat*, June 18, 1891. Dugger wrote that on "Friday the 27th [there was] heavy skirmishing until about 3 o'clock [when] brisk fighting commenced[.] [H]eavy cannonading going on all day[.] [S]kirmishing continued all night." Dugger-Hodges Diary, May 27, 1864, in *Watauga Democrat*, June 18, 1891.

Bate's Division and the Kentucky and Florida brigades of Brig. Gens. Joseph H. Lewis and Jesse J. Finley. Stevenson's Division took no part in the fighting.

Johnston's attack on May 28 forced Sherman to delay his withdrawal plans until McPherson could be freed from his proximate grapple with Johnston. However, another attempt to extricate McPherson on the night of the twenty-ninth was aborted when jittery Federal pickets opened fire on what they believed to be a Confederate assault column. No Confederates were on the field, but that did not inhibit a thunderous exchange of fire lasting from 10:00 P.M. until daylight. On May 30 Sherman and McPherson contrived plans for a staggered withdrawal that was successfully implemented on the night of the thirty-first. Freed at last from the Confederate tar baby, Sherman sidled eastward. In the meantime the orthographically challenged but ever-quotable Private Reese, who had been sick in hospital since at least May 1, rejoined the 60th on the evening of May 29. Two days later he wrote to his beloved "Tena" describing the regiment's situation and activities since his return:

I found the Regmant in fine helth. . . . I am hear in A line of Battle whair tha hav Bin fiting for sum time. . . . [T]he Regmant [is] in A Allful thicket I lay down and went to sleep and A Bout A leven oclock I was wakend By that powerful noyes of canonading we had to fall in and march out into A old field and thair we lay till day Brak then wee mooved A long the line A Bout two mils whair wee air yet thair was no fiting last nit [May 30] hardley But tha air dooing A little this morning the canons is raring how this thing will End I cant say not noing But we air A Bout 12 miles due west of maretter [Marietta]. . . . we hav lost A heep of men and kild A heep of yankeys and hear we go you all dont no any thing A Bout hard times an de struction of pro perty if you cood see the corne feelds and wheat feelds that is ful of stocks [stalks] all is de stroid thats the truth no one Escaps the hors [horrors] of this thing. . . . we hav lost But vary fue out of this Regmant. . . . the arme is fed vary well we git A half pound of Bacon pur day and plenty of Bred. . . .[129]

For the next four days Sherman slogged his way eastward through rain and mud toward the railroad. "Wednesday, June, the 1st," Private Dugger recorded in his diary, "skirmishing . . . continued. Orders to be ready to move at 12 o'clock. About 1 o'clock moved about one mile and formed near the front in reserve on the right. Thursday, the 2nd, about 12 o'clock we moved farther to the right[;] slow skirmishing and some cannonading continued. An uncommon hard rain fell to-day. Friday, the 3rd, slow skirmishing continued. Our regiment moved about one-half mile to the left for the purpose of supporting a battery; arrived at 10 o'clock in the night and worked all night fortifying our line. Saturday [June 4] slow skirmishing and some cannonading still continued. Cloudy and rainy."[130] By June 5 Sherman was astride the railroad at Acworth, ten miles or so northwest of Marietta. Johnston evacuated Allatoona Pass the previous day and simultaneously fell back from his position near Dallas. Contrary to Sherman's expectations, however, Johnston did not retreat southeastward across the Chattahoochee but marched east to a line about two miles above Marietta. "We moved off about 10 o'clock that night [June 4] towards the right," Private Dugger wrote. "After going about two hundred yards took position in the works as a skirmishing line. Remained about one hour, and then moved off again. We waded the Georgia

129. J. W. Reese to Christina Reese, May 31, 1864, Reese Papers.

130. Dugger-Hodges Diary, June 1-4, 1864, in *Watauga Democrat*, July 2, 1891.

mud at an average depth of ten inches all night and until about 9 o'clock Sunday, the 5th, completing a march of about 5 miles. We rejoined our brigade and made a halt in dense woods. Drew a ration of whiskey and rested about one hour. . . . Some fighting on the left."[131] Not surprisingly, the strain of a month's almost uninterrupted combat began to tell upon Trigg's men. "They fight some every day and very often fight some after night," Capt. David Willis of the 54th Virginia observed on May 30. "They fought hard awhile [*sic*] last nite and they are picket fighting every day from morning to night, and I believe half of the night. Indeed there have been only 2 days out of 28 that we were out of hearing of musketry. You might imagine how tired I am getting. . . ."[132]

Johnston's new line in the rugged, heavily wooded country northwest of Marietta faced northwest and was anchored on Lost, Pine, and Brush Mountains. Although daunting in appearance, the line was vulnerable because Pine Mountain, between Lost Mountain (on the left) and Brush Mountain, jutted somewhat ahead of its two sister peaks, exposing its defenders to enfilading fire. Fortunately for Johnston, a much better defensive position lay only two miles to the rear, where a long, high ridge known as Kennesaw Mountain dominated the surrounding country and guarded the railroad and roads leading to Marietta. Fighting tailed off for a few days while Sherman rested his troops, repaired the railroad, and brought up supplies and reinforcements.[133] Meanwhile, Johnston improved his defenses, including those on Kennesaw Mountain. On June 11 Sherman advance slowly through the rain: McPherson moved toward Brush Mountain, defended by Hood; Thomas toward Pine Mountain, defended by Polk; and Schofield toward Lost Mountain, defended by Hardee. On the morning of June 14, Polk was killed on Pine Mountain by Federal artillery fire, and Maj. Gen. William W. Loring assumed temporary command of his corps. Fearing that one of Hardee's divisions was about to be cut off by Thomas, Johnston withdrew from Pine Mountain that night. By June 18 threats to his flanks led Johnston to abandon Lost and Brush Mountains as well. He then took a position anchored on Kennesaw Mountain. Meantime, Schofield worked his way southwest of Lost Mountain in an attempt to turn Johnston's left. Johnston countered by moving Hood from the extreme right to the extreme left of the Confederate line. By the evening of June 21, Hood confronted Schofield southwest of Marietta. Hardee was on Hood's right, and Loring was to the right of Hardee on Kennesaw Mountain. Private Dugger's diary continues for the period from June 11 through June 21:

Saturday, the 11th, slow skirmishing continued and stormy weather. Went on picket in the evening. Sunday, the 12th, yet on picket, sharp-shooting going on all the time, raining hard[,] relieved at 4 o'clock and returned to the breast-works. Monday, the 13th, sharp-shooting continued[,] a hard rain fell to-day. Tuesday, the 14th, a short move to the right to-day . . . leaving a position where the shells were flying. . . . Wednesday the 15th some skirmishing and cannonading in front. Tuesday the 16th hard shelling commenced about 11 o'clock along the lines. A short move to the left and back again[;] commenced fortifying our position and worked until 11 o'cloc[k] that night. Friday the 17th at work again on our breastworks. At day-light some sharp shooting going on[;] heavy shelling in the evening

---

131. Dugger-Hodges Diary, June 4-5, 1864, in *Watauga Democrat*, July 2, 1891.

132. David Willis to his mother, May 30, 1864 (typescript), Robertson Collection.

133. See Dugger-Hodges Diary, June 6-10, 1864, in *Watauga Democrat*, July 2, 1891.

on the left. Saturday the 18th sharp shooting continued[;] hard shelling in the evening ceased at night[.] 19th. Rallied two hours before day and moved to the extreme left. Arrived about 11 o'clock[;] some fighting going on. Rained hard all day. Moved from that position at 4 o'clock and passed through Marietta, Ga., at dark. Marched on about two miles through mud, until about 11 o'clock in the night. Halted in the woods and camped. Monday, the 20th, drew a ration of whiskey. Some cannonading in front. Moved about 10 o'clock and formed a line in reserve and went to fortifying our position. Rained hard to-day. About 5 o'clock we made a short move to the right and worked on a fort all night. Tuesday, the 21st, still at work on the fort. Some fighting on the left. Heavy cannonading on Kenesaw mountain.[134]

Late on the afternoon of June 22, General Hood, acting entirely on his own initiative and without informing Johnston, launched an attack against the Federal right near the farm of a widow named Kolb. Stevenson's Division, supported on the right by Hindman and with Stewart's Division in reserve, advanced in two columns north and south of the Powder Springs Road. Brown's Brigade, commanded by Col. Edmund C. Cook and supported by Trigg's Brigade, was on the right; Cumming's Brigade, commanded by Col. Elihu P. Watkins and supported by Pettus's Brigade (under Col. Charles M. Shelley), on the left. Confronting Watkins and Shelley was a brigade of Brig. Gen. Milo S. Hascall's Army of the Ohio division; opposite Cook and Trigg were two brigades of Brig. Gen. Alpheus S. Williams's Division, Hooker's Corps (see map on page 246).

Contrary to Hood's professed reason for launching an unauthorized attack—namely, that the Federal right was in motion and vulnerable—Williams's men, supported by five artillery batteries, were partially dug in atop a low ridge and waiting when the assault began.[135] On the Confederate left, Watkins's Georgians, most of whom were inexperienced former militiamen, were halted by a single Federal regiment after two feeble thrusts. They then came under artillery fire and, in General Williams's words, "fled like scared sheep." Meanwhile, Cook and Trigg, on the right, fought somewhat better but fared considerably worse. "We had just fairly begun to pile up rails," Williams wrote, "when the heavy skirmish line of the enemy poured out of the woods all along the open [field in our front] and advanced at a run. Three columns, massed, followed close and deployed in three and four lines."[136] Immediately, the Confederates were raked by a "murderous" cross-fire of shell, grape, and canister that became more enfilading and deadly as they approached the

134. Dugger-Hodges Diary, June 11-21, 1864, in *Watauga Democrat*, July 2 and 9, 1891. The Dugger diary coincides with ascertainable events through June 14; however, at some point between that date and June 22 the entries fall behind events by one day. In his entry for June 22, Dugger writes that "[We] moved at day light towards the left, passed through Marietta at 8 o'clock. Marched two miles and halted on the Powder spring road. Raining continually. . . ." Those events demonstrably occurred on the twenty-first.

135. The Federals learned from 58th and 60th North Carolina prisoners captured that day that an attack might be in the making. See Richard M. McMurry, "The Affair at Kolb's Farm," *Civil War Times Illustrated*, 7 (December 1968): 21.

136. Alpheus Starkey Williams to Lewis Allen, July 17, 1864, and A. S. Williams to his children, July 10, 1864, in Milo M. Quaife, ed., *From the Cannon's Mouth: The Civil War Letters of General Alpheus S. Williams* (Detroit: Wayne State University Press and the Detroit Historical Society, 1959), 333, 328, hereafter cited as Quaife, *Williams Letters*. The terrain, as described by Williams, "was an open elevated plateau with a deep gully along its front, beyond which the ground rose gently to the woods occupied by the rebel picket reserves in strong rifle-pits 500 or 600 yards distant." *Official Records (Army)*, ser. 1, 38 (pt. 2):31.

ridge.[137] "[B]efore they could get within reach of my infantry," Williams continued, "their columns were awfully plowed through [by our artillery] . . . and thrown into great confusion. Then . . . they reached a point where one brigade could reach them [with its fire]. It opened a volley of two thousand muskets! The devils, what was left of them, took refuge in a deep ravine, into which I plunged shot and shell. . . ."[138] "[A]fter enduring an hour of fruitless slaughter," another Federal officer wrote, "they were driven . . . in confusion and disorder back to their fortifications." "The[ir] numbers were formidable," Williams commented, "but the attack was indeed feeble. . . . [A]fter the first half-hour . . . [our] men considered the whole affair great sport."[139]

Private Dugger's account confirms the Federal reports quoted above: "[We] moved to the front and massed our forces about 2 o'clock, and about 4 o'clock went forward to make a charge on the enemy. We got within a hundred yards of their works, [where] we were repulsed and compelled to fall back a few steps to a huge rock at the branch [ravine] and lay under heavy fire until 9 o'clock in the night. We then fell back about one mile, suffered heavy losses; two wounded in our company." Pvt. John Fleeman of the 54th Virginia described the fight as a "terrible slaughter" and estimated that "The three brigades [presumably excluding Pettus's] lost one thousand, killed wounded and missing. Our brigade now is not as large as our regiment was when we left [the] Blackwater [River]."[140] In addition to sustaining heavy casualties, the hapless Confederates were subjected, according to General Williams, to the taunts of their tormentors as they huddled in the ravine awaiting nightfall:

137. *Official Records (Army)*, ser. 1, 38 (pt. 2):49. "[O]ur men fell back into the clearing closely followed by the enemy's skirmishers," Samuel Toombs of the 13th New Jersey wrote, "and almost on their heels came a large body of rebel infantry, shouting and yelling. It was a splendid sight. The enemy moved forward on a run, deploying into line as they advanced and marched up steadily and in good order to attack. . . . Our skirmishers all reached the line in safety, and as the enemy ascended the hill directly in our front, a well directed volley was poured into them all along the line." Samuel Toombs, *Reminiscences of the War, Comprising a Detailed Account of the Experiences of the Thirteenth Regiment New Jersey Volunteers in Camp, On the March, and in Battle* (Orange, New Jersey: printed at the *Journal* office, 1878), 141, hereafter cited as Toombs, *Reminiscences of the Thirteenth New Jersey*.

138. A. S. Williams to Lewis Allen, July 17, 1864, in Quaife, *Williams Letters*, 333. Although many of Cook's and Trigg's men took shelter in the ravine, others retreated to the woods from which they launched their attack.

139. *Official Records (Army)*, ser. 1, 38 (pt. 2):49; A. S. Williams to his children, July 10, 1864, in Quaife, *Williams Letters*, 328. "[T]he enemy . . . marched up within, perhaps, fifty yards of us," Samuel Toombs wrote, "their colors floating defiantly almost in our faces. The order [was] passed down the line to fix bayonets, and when they saw the determined faces in front of them and viewed the line of bristling steel which projected over the rail breastworks, they wavered and fell back in confusion. . . . Sixty-two dead bodies were buried in our front, and upwards of five hundred of the enemy's killed were buried along the whole line." According to the no doubt exaggerated report of a Federal artillery officer, Cook's and Trigg's troops "were completely broken and . . . utterly demoralized before they came within range of the musketry." Toombs, *Reminiscences of the Thirteenth New Jersey*, 141; *Official Records (Army)*, ser. 1, 38 (pt. 2):470.

140. Dugger-Hodges Diary, June 22, 1864, in *Watauga Democrat*, July 9, 1891; John Fleeman to his wife and children, June 23, 1864, in Addison Jordan, *Gen. Jos. E. Johnston, A Review of His Military Career: Also, A Collection of Sketches of the Experiences of a Confederate Soldier* (Pulaski, Virginia: B. D. Smith and Brothers, 1907), 42-43. "Our Regt lost 72 killed wounded & missing," Capt. James Clark of the 63rd Virginia wrote. "I don't believe in such charges. . . . We lost a good many men & gained nothing. . . . They plowed the ground in all around us, [the firing] came in [from] three directions." James Clark to Martha Clark, June 28, 1864, Clark Letters.

"They [our men] would call out, 'Come up here, Johnny Reb. Here is a weak place!' 'Come up and take this battery; we are Hooker's paper collar boys.' 'We've only got two rounds of ammunition, come and take us.' 'What do you think of Joe Hooker's Iron Clads?' and the like."[141]

Although Kolb's Farm was unarguably a defeat and a poor combat performance by Stevenson's Division, Hood made no such admission. In a brief report written on the day of the battle he said nothing about his severe casualties and implied that the Confederates were charging toward victory when "The pursuit was stopped because of . . . an enfilading [artillery] fire from a bald hill in front of Hardee. . . ." Stevenson was more forthright, admitting he was repulsed with "heavy" losses—"807 killed and wounded." However, he claimed also that "With perhaps some few exceptions the conduct of the troops was highly creditable."[142] That statement is contradicted by a number of Federal officers who described the attack with terms such as "confused mass," "utmost disorder," "confusion and disorder," "mixed up in the ravine," "completely broken," "utterly demoralized," and "retreating and disordered columns."[143] Casualties in the 60th North Carolina, according to statistics compiled from service records in this volume, were 9 men killed or mortally wounded, 27 wounded, 9 captured, and 1 missing.[144]

During the next few days fighting tailed off into skirmishing and sporadic artillery exchanges. Unable to turn Johnston's flank because rain-flooded roads precluded hauling supplies more than a short distance from the railroad, Sherman lost patience and launched frontal assaults against Kennesaw Mountain and the Confederate center on June 27. Defended by Loring's Corps, Kennesaw Mountain was a long ridge with three peaks: Big Kennesaw, the northernmost and highest (700 feet); Little Kennesaw in the center (400 feet); and Pigeon Hill at the southern end (200 feet). South of Pigeon Hill, Hardee, still on Loring's left, defended a long, low ridge. Hood's Corps remained on the left of Hardee. Sherman planned a two pronged assault: three brigades of Maj. Gen. John A. Logan's Corps of the

141. A. S. Williams to his children, July 10, 1864, in Quaife, *Williams Letters*, 328.

142. *Official Records (Army)*, ser. 1, 38 (pt. 3):760, 815. "About 5 p. m. we advanced," Stevenson wrote, "and soon struck the enemy, driving him quickly before us from his advanced works, which consisted of one line of logs and rail works complete, and one partially constructed. The fire under which this was done was exceedingly heavy, and the artillery of the enemy, which was massed in large force and admirably posted, was served with a rapidity and fatal precision which could not be surpassed. The nature of the ground over which we passed was most unfavorable to such a movement—the two right brigades moved for much of the way over open fields, the two left through dense undergrowth. The line thus became more irregular and broken every moment, and when the two right brigades had driven the enemy into their main works the line was so much broken and mixed up that, although the men were in good spirits and perfectly willing to make the attempt, it was not deemed practicable to carry the works by assault. The commands were halted and the best possible line . . . formed. Brown's [Cook's] and Trigg's . . . Brigades lay in a swampy ravine within pistol-shot of the enemy's works; the other two brigades held the road on their left. The dead and wounded were all removed to the rear, and after holding our position for several hours, in compliance with the orders of General Hood, the division returned to its old position." *Official Records (Army)*, ser. 1, 38 (pt. 3):814-815.

143. *Official Records (Army)*, ser. 1, 38 (pt. 2):32 (first and second quotations), 49 (third quotation), 71 (fourth quotation), 470 (fifth and sixth quotations), 481 (seventh quotation).

144. The Battle of Kolb's Farm is known also as Zion Church and as Mount Zion Church. According to a casualty list published in the *North Carolina [Weekly] Standard* (Raleigh) of July 13, 1864, the regiment lost 4 men killed, 29 wounded, and 9 missing.

Army of the Tennessee would penetrate the gap between Little Kennesaw and Pigeon Hill; at the same time, two divisions of the Army of the Cumberland would break through Hardee's ridge-line position, wheel to the left, and flank Pigeon Hill. As a diversion, and in hopes of drawing reinforcements from Hardee and Loring, Schofield, on the extreme right, would demonstrate against Hood's Corps while simultaneously pushing south and threatening Johnston's left flank. If either Logan or Thomas were successful, heavy Federal reinforcements would pour into the breach, splitting Johnston's army.

On the morning of June 27, Logan's and Thomas's men, charging over steep, rock-and boulder-strewn ground into nightmarish mazes of "tanglefoot," abatis, and chevaux-de-frise, were shot to pieces by Confederate artillery and heavily entrenched infantrymen. More than 3,000 Federals were killed, wounded, and captured; Confederate casualties numbered slightly fewer than 1,000. The 60th North Carolina, still in position with the rest of Stevenson's Division near Kolb's farm, apparently took no part in the fighting. Private Dugger's laconic diary entry—"skirmishing, And cannonading all day"—reads very much the same for June 27 as for the previous two days. The regiment's casualties, if any, were very light.[145]

While Sherman's primary attacks on Kennesaw Mountain and the Confederate center were receiving bloody repulses, Schofield's diversionary movement against Johnston's flank made unexpected progress. By late afternoon one of Schofield's divisions, under Maj. Gen. Jacob D. Cox, crossed Olley's Creek and occupied a ridge overlooking Nickajack Creek, about one mile from the Chattahoochee River. If reinforced, Cox reported, he could turn Johnston's left. After pondering his options, Sherman decided to attempt such a movement, even though he would have to cut loose from the railroad north of Kennesaw Mountain. Several days elapsed while the dead were buried, supplies were accumulated, and roads dried out. On the night of July 2, Sherman began shifting his army to the right by marching the Army of the Tennessee behind the Army of the Cumberland. Johnston fell back from Kennesaw Mountain the same night and took position at Smyrna, between Nickajack and Rottenwood Creeks, about five miles below Marietta. "[H]eavy cannonading commenced at day-light," Private Dugger wrote in his diary on July 2, "lasted until 9 o'clock, skirmishing all day. . . . [A]t 12 o'clock that night [we] [f]ell back five miles toward the river, halted and commenced fortifying at 10 o'clock on Sunday the 3rd. . . ."[146]

Chastened by the bloodletting at Kennesaw Mountain, Sherman was in no mood for further frontal assaults. Johnston's new line at Smyrna was easily flanked on the left, and when McPherson and Schofield began massing their forces for such a movement Johnston retreated on the night of July 4. In a dispatch sent at 8:45 P.M., McPherson informed Sherman that Maj. Gen. Grenville M. Dodge had crossed Nickajack Creek at Ruff's Mill, "r[u]n against Stevenson's division, and . . . captured a few prisoners. . . . As soon as the troops were over and in position, I directed Dodge to strengthen his skirmish line . . . and to assault the enemy's rifle-pits. The order was gallantly executed, the works taken, and some 50 prisoners captured; our loss not heavy. . . ." More detailed accounts by Federal officers who took part in the attack indicate that the fighting was fairly severe and Federal casualties

145. Dugger-Hodges Diary, June 27, 1864, in *Watauga Democrat*, July 9, 1891.
146. Dugger-Hodges Diary, July 2-3, 1864, in *Watauga Democrat*, July 9, 1891.

fairly heavy: "about 140 killed and wounded" according to General Dodge. The Ruff's Mill affair was apparently the same one referred to by Private Reese in a letter dated July 9: "[O]ur Regmant was out on picket," Reese wrote, "an the yankeys charg them and drov them in to thair Brest work[.] [W]e lost sum in the charg. . . . [W]e air loosing A heep of men as we fall Back." Casualty figures compiled for this volume indicate that the 60th North Carolina lost at least 9 men captured at Ruff's Mill on July 4 and possibly as many as 20.[147]

Johnston now took position just north of the Chattahoochee in a six-mile-long, heavily fortified line of redoubts, trenches, and stockades constructed previously by slave labor. Those formidable works, too, he was unable to hold.[148] Sherman ordered demonstrations by Thomas and McPherson to focus Johnston's attention on his left; at the same time, Schofield quietly began looking for a crossing upriver, on Johnston's right. At 5:30 P.M. on July 6, Trigg's Brigade crossed the Chattahoochee under shell fire and marched five miles downriver. After skirmishing near the river on the seventh, the 60th moved two miles farther downstream and camped for the night. "[S]ome sharpshooting" followed on the eighth. That same day, Schofield, facing only light cavalry opposition, forced a crossing near Soap Creek, upstream from the Confederate right. By the time Johnston learned of that development on July 9, Schofield had an entire division on the south bank. During the night Johnston began withdrawing across the Chattahoochee to a position behind Peachtree Creek, five miles north of Atlanta. Trigg's Brigade pulled out at midnight and reached the Peachtree Creek line at daylight on the tenth.[149]

During the following week Sherman completed his crossing of the Chattahoochee and wheeled his army in a clockwise quarter circle in order to advance on Atlanta from the east and north.[150] On the night of July 17 Johnston received a telegram from Adjutant and

147. *Official Records (Army)*, ser. 1, 38 (pt. 5):47, 38 (pt. 3):382; J. W. Reese to Christina Reese, July 9, 1864, Reese Papers. "[W]e hav lost siveril men on marar Ches [marches]," Reese continued, "Either gon to the yankeys or home I cant say not knoing and tha all nearly talk of going[.] I for got to tell you that thair was A company out of the 54 verginia Regmant . . . one nite whil on picket the liutenant in Command of the Companey he went over an mad[e] arraing met [arrangements] with the yankey pickets and cum Back an tuck the Company over with him an sum has went sence and severil has went out of the 58 N C Regmant[.] [T]he boys calls this when on[e] Runs A way or is miss ing that the owls has cout him. . . ." For further information on the desertion of Company D, 54th Virginia, on the night of June 13, 1864, see footnote 151 below.

Sadly, Reese's July 9 letter appears to have been his last. He died at Forsyth, Georgia, August 1, 1864, of disease.

148. For a description of those fortifications by the general who built them, see Francis A. Shoup, "Dalton Campaign–Works at Chattahoochee River–Interesting History," *Confederate Veteran*, 3 (September 1895): 262-265. Sherman described the Chattahoochee works as "one of the strongest pieces of field-fortification I ever saw." William T. Sherman, *Memoirs of General William T. Sherman*, 2 vols. (New York: D. Appleton and Company, 1875; New York: Da Capo Press, 1984), 2:66.

149. Dugger-Hodges Diary, July 5 and 8, 1864, in *Watauga Democrat*, July 16, 1891. See also Thomas B. Hampton (63rd Virginia) to Jestin C. Hampton (his wife), June [July] 7, 1864, Thomas B. Hampton Papers (typescripts), The Center for American History, The University of Texas at Austin, hereafter cited as Hampton Papers.

150. "We have been the best fed army I ever saw," James Clark informed his father on July 15, 1864. "It is not of the nicest kind but plentie corn bread & bacon . . . vegetables such as potatoes, cabbage, tomatoes, onions, squashes[,] beans[,] pies [peas] . . . not as much as we can eat but mostly a good mess for all & the boys get

Inspector General Samuel Cooper announcing that, because of his failure "to arrest the advance of the enemy to the vicinity of Atlanta," he was relieved of command of the Army of Tennessee. The new commander, who was to assume his duties immediately, was Johnston's highly combative subordinate, John Bell Hood. To the intense regret of most of his troops, Johnston turned over his command to Hood the next afternoon. "The change of commanders has caused a great deal of dissatisfaction among some of the men," Pvt. James M. Wysor of the 54th Virginia noted on July 19. "The whole army placed the most implicit confidence in Gen Johnston which they do not in Hood."[151]

In the meantime the Federal advance on Atlanta continued. By nightfall on July 19, McPherson, on Sherman's extreme left, had cut the Georgia Railroad and, unbeknown to Hood, occupied Decatur, six miles east of Atlanta. Schofield was advancing on a road just north of and parallel to the railroad, and Thomas, coming down from the north and separated from Schofield's right by a marshy, two-mile-wide gap, was astride Peachtree Creek. Confronting the Federals in a broad arc was Hood's 55,000-man army: Stewart's Corps (formerly Polk's and Loring's) on the left, Hardee's Corps in the center, and Hood's former corps (temporarily commanded by Maj. Gen. Benjamin F. Cheatham) on the right. Perceiving an opportunity to crush Thomas's isolated command, Hood ordered an assault for the afternoon of July 20.

Hood's plan called for Hardee and Stewart to attack *en echelon* from right to left at 1:00 P.M., trap Thomas in the wedge formed by the confluence of Peachtree Creek and the Chattahoochee, and destroy or capture his army. Cheatham would conduct a holding action against McPherson and Schofield. Execution of Hood's assault was delayed, however, by the belated discovery on the morning of the twentieth that McPherson overlapped Cheatham's right by more than two miles, had captured Decatur, and, confronted only by Wheeler's cavalry, was advancing down the Georgia Railroad toward Atlanta. In an attempt to arrest that movement, Hood rotated his army slightly to the right, thereby stretching his

---

plentie of tobacco. . . ." James Clark to his father, July 15, 1864, Clark Letters.

151. *Official Records (Army)*, 38 (pt. 5):885; James M. Wysor to his father, July 19, 1864, Wysor Papers. See also James Clark to his father, July 15, 1864, and James Clark to his brother, August 10, 1864, Clark Letters. Wysor's letter is of interest also for the light it sheds on conditions and morale in Trigg's Brigade and Stevenson's Division. "Our reg't & in fact the whole brigade & division has suffered very heavy losses since the campaign opened," Wysor continued. "The brigade numbered when it left Dalton 1500 men [but] now it is reduced to one third of that number. Brown's men say that there are two 'killings' of them left. Our reg't which started with 460 muskets now reports 160 for duty. We have had the misfortune to fall on that part of the line where has been the hard fighting. We have been very much reduced in our brigade by desertion. Our Va. regiments have so disgraced themselves that I have no hopes of getting to Virginia soon. Our company however is at present trying to get a transfer to Gen [John H.] Morgan's command & I hope we will be successful for I hate to have to stay with men who have so disgraced themselves." Nevertheless, Wysor concluded, "the army is in the best of spirits & confident of whipping the Yankees whenever they have the temerity to attack us."

Wysor's reference to the Virginia regiments "disgracing themselves" was probably prompted by the mass desertion, "officers & all" (except for several absentees and three men who refused to go), of Company D, 54th Virginia, on the night of June 13, 1864. "I feel that we have disgraced the state of Va," Captain Clark wrote on July 15. "[W]e have as good men in our regt as there is in the Confederate States but a heap of them is getting tired of the war." James Clark to Martha Clark, June 16, 1864, and James Clark to his father July 15, 1864, Clark Letters. See also William Burwell Howell (54th Virginia) to Mary A. Howell (his wife), June 15 and July 13, 1864, Roster Document No. 1045 (transcripts), CWRP, NCDAH, hereafter cited as Howell Letters.

line perilously thin in some places and creating gaps in others. That maneuver delayed his assault for three hours and failed to accomplish its object when Cheatham, for unknown reasons, halted about a mile north of the railroad. Finally, around 4:00 P.M., Hardee's troops, followed shortly thereafter by Stewart's, stormed forward through pine woods and heavy underbrush broken by networks of creeks and ravines. Taken by surprise but reacting with characteristic aplomb and sound judgment, Thomas called up artillery reinforcements and routed Bate's Division of Hardee's Corps just as it was about to capture a vital bridge over Peachtree Creek. Farther to the Federal right, two determined brigades of Loring's Division (Stewart's Corps) were repulsed by Federal reinforcements in fierce, seesaw fighting. Another of Stewart's divisions, commanded by Maj. Gen. Edward C. Walthall, flanked its opponent but was driven back by Federal artillery. Plans for an attack by Cleburne's reserve division were canceled when it developed that McPherson, still edging his way down the railroad against Wheeler's outmanned cavalry, was within a few miles of Atlanta and was directing artillery fire into the city streets. Cleburne's men were then rushed to the vicinity of Bald Hill, where they checked McPherson's advance. The 60th North Carolina, as part of Cheatham's command, was not involved in any serious fighting during the day. Dugger's diary entry for July 20 reports only "heavy skirmishing and c[a]nnonading all day and the night following."[152] Confederate casualties at the Battle of Peachtree Creek numbered about 2,500; Federal losses were approximately 1,900. Three members of the 60th North Carolina were captured.

Fighting continued on the Confederate right on July 21 as McPherson unleashed a pulverizing bombardment of Cleburne's Division and captured Bald Hill. That night Hood withdrew Stewart's and Cheatham's Corps into the Atlanta defenses and dispatched Hardee's Corps to turn Sherman's exposed left flank (held by Maj. Gen. Frank P. Blair Jr.'s Corps) the next morning.[153] Wheeler's cavalrymen accompanied Hardee with orders to destroy McPherson's wagon train at Decatur. If Hardee's attack succeeded, Cheatham would attack McPherson from the east, driving a wedge between McPherson's right and Schofield's left.

After an exhausting march Hardee launched his assault at noon on July 22, approximately six hours late. By that time, Brig. Gen. Grenville M. Dodge's Corps, which had been pinched out of Sherman's constricting line around Atlanta, was in position astride Sugar Creek, on Blair's left flank. Thus, with the exception of a quarter-mile-wide gap between Dodge and Blair, Hardee's four divisions faced opposition along their entire front. A feeble attack on Dodge by Bate and W. H. T. Walker was easily repulsed, producing no significant result except the deaths of Walker and McPherson (who thus became the only Federal army commander killed in action during the war). Meantime, the men of Brig. Gen. Giles A. Smith's Division (Blair's Corps), on Dodge's right, leaped back and forth across their breastworks to repel uncoordinated attacks on their front and left flank by Brig. Gen. George Maney (commanding Cheatham's former division) and on their rear by Cleburne,

152. Dugger-Hodges Diary, July 20, 1864, in *Watauga Democrat*, July 16, 1891.

153. "[We] retired at 8 o'clock [P.M.]," Private Dugger wrote, "and fell back about two miles drawing in our lines around the suburbs of Atlanta, and soon fortified our position." Dugger-Hodges Diary, July 21, 1864, in *Watauga Democrat*, July 16, 1891.

who penetrated the gap between Dodge and Blair. Brig. Gen. Mortimer D. Leggett's troops, on Smith's right, were also rocked by Cleburne's attack and, like Smith's men, forced to fight during part of the afternoon with their backs to Atlanta.

Around 4:00 P.M., after coordinated front-and-rear attacks by two Confederate brigades drove Smith back to a line perpendicular to Leggett, Hood ordered Cheatham to launch his frontal assault. Stevenson's Division, on Cheatham's right, moved against Leggett and Brig. Gen. William Harrow's Division of Logan's Corps; in the center and on the left, Hindman's Division (commanded by John C. Brown) and Clayton's followed *en echelon*, attacking Logan's other division, commanded by Brig. Gen. Morgan L. Smith (on Harrow's right). Two of Brown's brigades punched through the Federal line at a railroad cut but then received an inexplicable order from Brown to withdraw. In the meantime, two "impetuo[u]s" but ill-sustained attacks on Leggett by Stevenson were repulsed "in handsome style" by "A few well-directed volleys."[154] A four-brigade attack by Hardee on Bald Hill was then beaten back in fighting that, at some points, was hand-to-hand. Darkness brought an end to the carnage.

The part played by Trigg's Brigade in the Battle of Atlanta (also known as the Battle of Bald Hill) is obscure. According to one recent account, all four of Stevenson's brigades were involved in Cheatham's attack: Trigg on the right, Pettus in the center, Brown's Brigade (commanded by Col. Joseph B. Palmer) on the left, and Cumming's Brigade following Pettus in support. However, Albert Castel, the leading modern authority on the Atlanta Campaign, states that the assault was made by "Stevenson's Division *or a portion thereof* [emphasis added]. . . ."[155] In the case of the 60th North Carolina, that qualification seems justified: no casualties of any description were reported. The likelihood is that the 60th was manning a portion of the Atlanta fortifications or in reserve during Stevenson's two assaults. That conclusion is supported by the July 22 diary entry of Private Dugger: "heavy fighting on the right on Gen. Hardee's lines. Some success in capturing prisoners, and artilery [*sic*], certain amount not known. One hundred of our regiment went on picket at night, myself in the number."[156] Total Confederate casualties during the Battle of Atlanta were approximately 5,500; Federal losses numbered about 3,700.

During the night Hood withdrew Hardee's frazzled corps to the southwest to protect the Macon and Western Railroad, his one remaining supply route. After considering his options, Sherman began shifting the Army of the Tennessee from his left wing to his right, thereby threatening the railroad—which ran south from Atlanta—from a less exposed westerly direction. By the evening of July 27 the Army of the Tennessee, advancing with great caution under its new commander, Maj. Gen. Oliver O. Howard, was just north of the Lick Skillet road near Ezra Church. Hood countered by shifting two divisions of Cheatham's

---

154. *Official Records (Army)*, ser. 1, 38 (pt. 3):546 (first and second quotations); Albert Castel, *Decision in the West: The Atlanta Campaign of 1864* (Lawrence, Ks.: University Press of Kansas, 1992), 405 (third quotation), hereafter cited as Castel, *Decision in the West*. See also *Official Records (Army)*, ser. 1, 38 (pt. 3):565. Castel states that Stevenson's Division failed "even to dislodge the Union pickets and pioneer troops . . . occupying the former Confederate trenches west of the bald hill."

155. Castel, *Decision in the West*, 405. See also William R. Scaife, *The Campaign for Atlanta* (n.p., 1985), plate XIV.

156. Dugger-Hodges Diary, July 22, 1864, in *Watauga Democrat*, July 16, 1891.

former corps, now commanded by Lt. Gen. Stephen D. Lee, to the Lick Skillet road, where they arrived after nightfall. On July 28 Lee launched a series of ill-considered, uncoordinated, and bloody assaults that ultimately resulted in a refusal by some units to obey orders. Subsequent attacks in the same vicinity by Loring's and Walthall's Divisions of Stewart's Corps produced "desperate fight[ing] and heavy loss" but failed to dislodge Howard.[157] Private Dugger's diary indicates that the 58th North Carolina (and very probably the remainder of Trigg's Brigade) was in or near the Atlanta fortifications during the battle. "At 1 o'clock p. m. [on July 27]," Dugger wrote, "we moved from that position [the one they had occupied at Atlanta since July 22] and formed behind in the . . . suburbs . . . and remained [there] until dark. We [then] moved back to the front works on the left of Kowan's [Capt. James J. Cowan's] battery and remained until 12 o'clock in the night, then rallied and went on picket. Thursday, the 28th., yet on picket, and heavy skirmishing and cannonading all day. Relieved from picket at 9 o'clo[c]k and returned to the breast works."[158]

During the next six days—a period characterized by skirmishing, sharpshooting, and cannonading—the 60th North Carolina remained in the Atlanta fortifications, probably at or near "the front works" on the Marietta road.[159] After a Federal cavalry raid to cut the Macon and Western failed during the first week of August, Sherman made a new effort to extend his line west and south of Atlanta. On August 6 Schofield's Army of the Ohio, which had taken position on Howard's right, launched an attack at Utoy Creek, a few miles southwest of Ezra Church. There it collided with Bate's entrenched division, temporarily assigned to Lee's Corps. Bate inflicted a bloody repulse on one of Schofield's brigades, but the Confederates were compelled to retreat to a new line of fortifications covering the railroad as far south as East Point. Federal losses in the Battle of Utoy Creek numbered about 300; Confederate casualties probably did not exceed twenty. Stevenson's Division, which had been temporarily detached from Lee's command and assigned to Hardee in exchange for Bate's Division, remained "immediately in front of Atlanta" during the battle and suffered no casualties. During the next three weeks the 60th North Carolina presumably continued to occupy its position on the Marietta road. On about August 23, Trigg's and Brown's Brigades were consolidated under the command of Col. Joseph B. Palmer.[160]

157. *Official Records (Army)*, ser. 1, 38 (pt. 3):872.

158. Dugger-Hodges Diary, July 27-28, 1864, in *Watauga Democrat*, July 16, 1891. Federal casualties during the Battle of Ezra Church numbered 632; Confederate losses were probably in the neighborhood of 3,000. See Castel, *Decision in the West*, 434.

159. Dugger-Hodges Diary, August 2, 1864, in *Watauga Democrat*, July 23, 1891. In a letter dated August 2, 1864, Chaplain George T. Gray of the 63rd Virginia stated that "when we left Dalton I had 600 men in my Regiment, now I have 200. My Brigade [Trigg's] had 1600 men, now it has 600." George Thomas Gray to his wife, August 2, 1864, Robertson Collection. Pvt. James M. Wysor, whose regiment, the 54th Virginia, had just returned from escorting Federal prisoners to the Andersonville prison, noted in a letter dated August 7 that any duty "was preferable to the front where for 90 days not a day had passed in which we had not heard the boom of the cannon and but very few that we had not heard the rattle of musketry. I never was so tired of anything in my life as I was of the never ceasing boom boom of the cannon and pop pop bang bang of the skirmishers." J. M. Wysor to his father, August 7, 1864, Wysor Papers.

160. *Official Records (Army)*, ser. 1, 38 (pt. 3):763. Trigg was furloughed to southwest Virginia on August 23 because of ill health and remained there on special duty for the rest of the war. Brown assumed command of Bate's Division after Bate was wounded on August 10. Palmer's newly constituted brigade comprised the 3rd,

Frustrated by his failure to flank Hood incrementally, Sherman made tentative plans to cut loose from his railroad supply line and swing his entire army around the Confederate left. In the interim, he rested his weary men and attempted to blast Hood out of Atlanta with artillery. The bombardment began on August 9 with a barrage of 3,000 projectiles and continued at high levels of intensity for the next two weeks, producing moderate damage but only a handful of casualties. Captain Patton of the 60th North Carolina, in whose informative correspondence there is a regrettable five-month gap between March and August 1864, wrote a letter to his wife on August 22 that provides insight into the regiment's circumstances during the bombardment of Atlanta:

Every thing has been going on as usual in our front. I suppose both parties are so well fortified as to make any thing like a direct attack out of the question, so both will probably stay quietly watching each other and try to operate in the rear and break communications. The Yankees keep up an almost constant shelling of the town, doing a great deal [of] damage to the houses on this side of it – especially on Marietta & Peach tree Streets (the two principal streets of the town) [where] not a single house has escaped without being struck, and many of them [are] torn all to pieces. It is wonderfull how little loss of life has occurred. I have heard of only very few casualties. I have passed through the town several times, and it does indeed present a sad spectacle. There is not so much danger to us in our fortifications as to those who have to pass about backwards & forwards [to the front] – almost all of the shells pass high over our heads and we have now moved to a part of the lines where the Yankees are not near enough to trouble us much with minnie balls. Our Brigade has been consolidated with Brown's [former brigade]. . . . We had to move along the river about a mile to the right so as to join . . . [our new command]. [W]e were obliged to make the move at night when the ennemy could not see what was going on, and unfortunately in a heavy rain. This was decidedly unpleasant, but I am very well satisfied with the change on the whole.[161]

By August 23 it was clear to Sherman that a new cavalry raid in which he had placed high hopes had failed to sever the Macon and Western Railroad permanently, that the Army of Tennessee could not be shelled out of Atlanta, and that the time had arrived to implement

---

18th, 26th, 32nd, and 45th Tennessee regiments, the 23rd Tennessee battalion, the 58th and 60th North Carolina, and the 54th and 63rd Virginia. See Weaver, *54th Virginia*, 131, 222; *Official Records (Army)*, ser. 1, 38 (pt. 3):672, 39 (pt. 2):853, 45 (pt. 1):1224.

Some historians have assumed, on the basis of orders of battle dated August 31, September 20, and November 18, 1864, in the *Official Records*, that the consolidation of Brown's and Trigg's Brigades under Palmer took place subsequent to the Battle of Jonesborough (fought on August 31) and that Col. Washington M. Hardy of the 60th North Carolina commanded Reynolds's Brigade during that battle. However, unless the consolidation mentioned in Patton's letter of August 22 had in fact not taken place, and unless Colonel Hardy did not leave for home on furlough at 4:00 P.M. on the afternoon of August 23, as Patton stated in a letter of that date that he intended to do, then the consolidation was in effect, the August 31 order of battle is incorrect, Hardy was absent on leave, and the consolidated brigade was almost certainly commanded by Palmer. See T. W. Patton to Nannie Patton, August 22, 1864, and T. W. Patton to H. K. Patton, August 23, 1864, Patton Papers.

161. T. W. Patton to Nannie Patton, August 22, 1864, Patton Papers. An inspection report for Trigg's Brigade dated August 20, 1864, indicates that 139 officers and men of the 60th North Carolina were present for duty. The condition of the men's clothing was "Poor," their military bearing "Soldierly," their military appearance "Indiff[erent]," their discipline "Good," their military instruction "Loose," and their drill "Indifferent." The 58th North Carolina, 54th Virginia, and 63rd Virginia numbered 270, 146, and 183 men respectively, giving the brigade a total strength of 738. Quoted in Weaver, *54th Virginia*, 126-127.

his plan to turn Hood's left flank. He therefore began pulling back from the Atlanta fortifications on the night of August 25. By the afternoon of August 28, two of Howard's corps had reached Fairburn, thirteen miles southwest of Atlanta and about the same distance northwest of Jonesborough, on the Macon and Western. Thomas, with two corps, was at Red Oak, three miles northeast of Fairburn. Apprehending that he would have to divide his army to defend both Atlanta and the railroad, Hood dispatched Hardee's and Lee's Corps on the evening of August 30 to intercept the advancing Federals.[162] Meanwhile, Stevenson's Division, including Palmer's Brigade, was replaced by Georgia militiamen in the Atlanta fortifications on the night of August 26 and began a slow march southwestward. According to the diary of Cpl. Gilbert W. Hodges of the 58th North Carolina, the men "Moved to the Left at 10 o'clock, passing through Atlanta[,] marched 5 miles and halted at 12 o'clock." On the twenty-seventh the brigade "arrived on [the] extreme left" to find the "Yankees gone from their works [and apparently] falling back. . . ."[163] During the next three days Palmer moved an additional four or five miles to his left and rejoined Lee's Corps with the rest of Stevenson's Division. At 11:00 on the night of August 30, in accordance with Hood's orders to Hardee and Lee, the brigade set out for Jonesborough, which it reached at noon the next day.[164]

By midafternoon on August 31, Hardee's and Lee's troops, under the overall command of Hardee, were in position at Jonesborough and ready to attack. Hardee's plan called for his own corps (commanded by Cleburne) to move forward on the Confederate left at 3:00 P.M. with Cleburne's Division (commanded by Brig. Gen. Mark Lowrey) on the left, Bate's Division (commanded by John C. Brown) on the right, and Cheatham's Division (commanded by George Maney) in support. As soon as the noise of battle indicated that Cleburne was fully engaged, Lee, on Cleburne's right, would attack with Anderson's Division on the right and Stevenson's Division (bolstered by a brigade from Clayton's Division and another from Brown's) on the left. Palmer's Brigade was in Stevenson's first line between the brigades of Pettus (on its left) and Brig. Gen. William F. Brantley (of Anderson's Division).

Shortly after 3:00 P.M. Lee, mistaking the sound of heavy skirmishing on his left for Cleburne's attack, prematurely launched his assault. Most of Anderson's units advanced with middling élan but, confronted by field fortifications and raked by deadly musketry,

---

162. Hood believed that the Federals were trying to draw off his forces from Atlanta and then launch an attack there. Consequently, he himself remained in the city.

163. Dugger-Hodges Diary, August 26-27, 1864, in *Watauga Democrat*, July 23, 1891. The last diary entry made by Private Dugger is dated August 3, 1864. Dugger's fate is unknown, but it appears that he was killed or mortally wounded in action, perhaps on August 4. A soldier identified in the *Watauga Democrat* as "Gilliam Hodges" but who was probably Cpl. Gilbert W. Hodges of Company D, 58th North Carolina, began making entries in Dugger's diary a few days later and continued to do so through November 30.

164. In his masterful study of the Atlanta Campaign, Albert Castel writes that "At 1:30 P.M. the last of Lee's units reach Jonesboro. His troops have had little sleep for two nights, they have marched from twelve to fifteen miles over rough roads and sometimes no roads, many are shoeless and footsore, all are half-exhausted and hungry, and hundreds have dropped out along the way, unable or unwilling to keep going. Never has Major General Patton Anderson, veteran of most of the Army of Tennessee's campaigns starting with Shiloh, seen so much straggling." Castel, *Decision in the West*, 499.

quickly went to ground. One brigade fled. Stevenson's assault was probably even less determined and effectual. On the Confederate left, Lowrey's charging men came under flanking fire from a division of dismounted Federal cavalry, veered off in pursuit of the retreating troopers, and took themselves out of the battle. Meantime, Brown's men were driven back with heavy casualties after they stumbled into a ravine. A feeble attack by Maney's Division was repulsed amid a chorus of Federal hoots and catcalls. In forty-five minutes the farcical battle was over.

The precise activities of the 60th North Carolina at Jonesborough on August 31 are unknown. In a diary entry that probably applied not only to his own regiment (the 58th North Carolina) but to the 60th as well, Corporal Hodges wrote that the men "reached Jonesboro, Ga., at 12 o'clock [noon] on the 31st. Came in contact with the enemy in which Hardee's and Lee's Corps charged them, but inflicting but little damage. . . . Our loss [presumably those of the two corps combined] was considerably [sic]." In any case, the 60th lost two men killed and four wounded. Total Confederate losses were at least 2,200; the Federals lost fewer than 200 men.[165]

While Hardee and Howard were locked in battle on August 31, Federal units reached the railroad near Rough and Ready and several other points north of Jonesborough. That evening Hood, unaware that most of Sherman's army was south of Atlanta and fearing an imminent assault on the city, recalled Lee's Corps from Hardee. Shortly after midnight Hood learned of Hardee's repulse at Jonesborough. Concluding that Atlanta was no longer defensible, he issued orders to evacuate the city that night and retreat toward Macon. Stewart's Corps and the Georgia militia were to march southeast on the McDonough road; Lee's Corps was halted en route to Atlanta and ordered to defend the city's southern approaches; and Hardee was to remain at Jonesborough to hold open the McDonough road.

In the wee hours of the morning on September 1, Lee's men, in accordance with Hood's original order to return to Atlanta, set out and, in the words of Corporal Hodges, "marched hard all day." Six miles from their destination they were intercepted by a courier from Hood bearing new orders to "cover the evacuation of the city." That afternoon Sherman, unaware that Hood was about to abandon Atlanta and that Hardee was isolated and vulnerable, ordered an attack at Jonesborough by two of Thomas's newly arrived corps. Units of Brig. Gen. Jefferson C. Davis's Corps succeeded in punching a hole in Hardee's line, but darkness arrived before Maj. Gen. David S. Stanley's Corps could get into position to exploit the advantage. During the night the evacuation of Atlanta was completed by Hood as planned. Troops belonging to Maj. Gen. Henry W. Slocum's Corps occupied the city on the morning of September 2. By the evening of September 3, Lee was reunited with Stewart and Hardee at Lovejoy's Station. After skirmishing with Hood at Lovejoy's on the fourth and fifth, Sherman moved north to Atlanta to rest and refit his men, plan his next campaign, and claim his prize.[166]

Between September 12 and 21 a truce between the two armies remained in effect while the white civilian population of Atlanta was forcibly evacuated. In the meantime,

---

165. Dugger-Hodges Diary, August 31, 1864, in *Watauga Democrat*, July 23, 1891.

166. Dugger-Hodges Diary, September 1, 1864, in *Watauga Democrat*, July 23, 1891; *Official Records (Army)*, ser. 1, 38 (pt. 3):765.

Sherman and Hood pondered their next moves. Hood, with characteristic aggressiveness, decided to move the Army of Tennessee west and then north of Atlanta and cut Sherman's Western and Atlantic supply line to Chattanooga. He would then attack and destroy the starving Yankees as they retreated through the desolate woods and mountains of North Georgia. As an initial step toward implementing that strategy, Hood marched west from Lovejoy's Station toward Palmetto on September 18. The 60th North Carolina probably reached Palmetto on the nineteenth. During the next two days the rest of Hood's command, now reduced to approximately 40,000 men, arrived and began constructing field fortifications.[167] On September 29, following a strategy conference with President Jefferson Davis, Hood moved six miles north to Cross Anchor. The next day he crossed the Chattahoochee on a pontoon bridge near Campbellton and reached Dark Corner, about eight miles from Pray's Church. Pausing briefly to tear up track in the vicinity of Marietta, he then advanced against the railroad villages of Acworth and Big Shanty, which Stewart's Corps captured with their small garrisons on October 4. After an unsuccessful attempt by Maj. Gen. Samuel G. French's Division to capture Allatoona on October 5, the men continued their northward trek, reaching Cedartown on October 8, Armuchee on October 11, and capturing Dalton on October 13. Sherman, having left Slocum's Corps behind to hold Atlanta, trailed northward in Hood's wake, trying to stay close to the elusive Confederate but evincing little interest in initiating a battle. Sherman's plans to march across central Georgia to Savannah were already made; however, Thomas, who had been sent north to defend Tennessee and was receiving reinforcements from as far afield as Missouri, was not yet strong enough to take on Hood alone. It was therefore necessary that Sherman be available to do so. When Hood appeared ready to offer battle at La Fayette on October 17, Sherman decided to jettison his passive strategy and accommodate him. However, to Hood's chagrin, his corps commanders unanimously opposed another fight with the superior Federal army. Hood therefore decided to advance into Tennessee. There, after defeating Thomas, he would invade Kentucky and, perhaps, join Robert E. Lee in Virginia.

On October 20 Hood began moving southwest down the Chattooga River valley toward Gadsden, Alabama, which he reached the next day. Sherman trailed behind as far as Gaylesville, Alabama, thirty miles northeast of Gadsden. There he abandoned the pursuit, dispatched two corps under Schofield to reinforce Thomas, and returned to Atlanta. On November 15, after destroying the war-making capacity of that city and (probably by more or less welcome accident) a good deal more of it besides, he cut his telegraph lines to the North and departed with 62,000 men and 64 cannons in the general direction of Savannah

---

167. A morning report for the 60th North Carolina that appears to be dated September 7, 1864, indicates that the regiment had 21 officers and 90 men present for duty: a total of 111. In short, the regiment was reduced to only slightly more than the authorized strength of a Confederate infantry company. Fifteen additional officers and men were present but sick, and another 30 were present but on extra duty. Six officers and men were absent on detached service, 5 absent with leave, 24 absent without leave, 109 absent sick, and 124 were listed as prisoners of war. Sixtieth North Carolina Morning Report, September 7[?], 1864, Harper Papers. (A list of morning report strength figures for the 60th North Carolina throughout the war appears on pages 500-501 below.)

According to figures compiled for this volume, at least 16 and 23 men deserted during the second and third quarters of 1864 respectively. For 60th North Carolina desertion figures during other periods of the war, see footnotes 23, 72, and 100 above and 215 below.

and the Atlantic Ocean. Meantime, the Army of Tennessee marched northwest from Gadsden toward Guntersville, Alabama, on October 22.[168] There, Hood and General Pierre G. T. Beauregard (his department commander) had agreed, the army would cross the Tennessee River. However, upon reaching Bennettsville that afternoon Hood turned west, bypassing Guntersville. During the next three days he moved northwest through Walnut Grove and Brooksville to Somerville. Captain Harper of the 58th North Carolina reported "poor and barren country," "Clear, Cool, Pleas[ant]" weather, and "badly blistered" feet. At "the shabby . . . town of Summerville [sic]" on October 26, Hood sent Lee's Corps west through the rain toward Moulton and marched with the rest of his troops to Decatur, on the Tennessee River.[169] On October 27 he skirmished with the Decatur garrison, and, concluding that the enemy's defenses were too strong to force a crossing, he moved west toward Courtland on the twenty-ninth.[170] Lee's Corps reached the vicinity of Courtland on the twenty-eighth and marched to a point two miles east of Leighton the next day. "High living – potatoes, apples, peaches" and "Fine farming country," Captain Harper noted in his diary, but also deserted plantations and "many houses burnt by Yankees."[171]

On the evening of October 29 Hood reached Courtland with Stewart's and Cheatham's Corps. After Confederate engineers pronounced the Courtland ford unsuitable, he continued marching westward and caught up with Lee at Tuscumbia on the thirtieth. "The march was not disagreeable," Assistant Quartermaster Erwin of the 60th wrote from Tuscumbia, "having good roads & beautiful weather except two days, cloudy with a little rain."[172] Two brigades of Maj. Gen. Edward Johnson's Division and one brigade of Clayton's Division, both of Lee's Corps, crossed the river on the same day and drove a small enemy force out of Florence. The other brigades of the two divisions were across by noon on October 31. Stevenson's Division, including the 60th North Carolina and the rest of Palmer's Brigade, crossed on the morning of November 2. The regiment probably remained near the river working on breastworks on November 3 and 4, then moved six miles north on the Lawrenceburg road with other elements of Stevenson's Division on the fifth. On November 6, after a cavalry skirmish in which the 60th took no part, the division fell back

168. Captain Patton wrote from Gadsden on October 22 that "The whole army are in the highest spirits, but especially the Tennessee troops, they are all in hopes of seeing thier [sic] homes once more after their long absence. I think the move will certainly bring about important results and perhaps will relieve all of East Tenn & Georgia of the yankees." T. W. Patton to H. K. Patton, October 22, 1864, Patton Papers.

169. Harper Diary, October 24 (first three quotations) and 26 (fourth quotation), 1864. See also G. W. F. Harper to Ella Harper, October 26, 1864, Harper Papers.

170. "After leaving Gadsden," Assistant Quartermaster Erwin wrote, "the army went by Decatur and found the Yankees there fortified, not the Yankee army but a small garrison of some two thousand. The place was immediately surrounded & closely invested–The garrison ordered to surrender but the confounded Yanks wouldn't obey & Genl Hood left them, perfectly disgusted with their disobedience of his orders. There was a good deal of cannonading & some skirmishing, but we made no attempt to take the place." G. P. Erwin to his sister, November 5, 1864, Erwin Papers.

171. Harper Diary, October 28 (first quotation) and 29 (second and third quotations), 1864. "Fine camping place and a big rabbit hunt," Harper added on the twenty-ninth. See also W. B. Howell to M. A. Howell, November 2, 1864, Howell Letters; William Anderson King (54th Virginia) to Mary E. King (his wife), November 2, 1864, Roster Document No. 1043 (typescripts), CWRP, NCDAH.

172. G. P. Erwin to his sister, November 5, 1864, Erwin Papers.

toward Florence. The next day it "moved out seven miles on the Huntsville road [east of Florence]" with the rest of Lee's Corps.[173]

On November 20 Hood, having delayed his advance for three weeks to await the arrival of Forrest's cavalry from West Tennessee and badly needed supplies from Corinth, set off through falling snow in the direction of Pulaski. Although poorly clad, shod, and fed, his men, particularly the homeward bound Tennesseans, were cheerful. Many were returning home for the first time in almost a year and, after a respite of more than two months from the almost daily battles and skirmishes of the Atlanta Campaign, their fighting spirit seemed restored.[174] Many believed also that Hood had categorically renounced and forbidden frontal attacks against field works: a conviction in which they would soon find themselves sadly, and in many case terminally, mistaken.

Hood's object in advancing toward Pulaski was to surprise and capture Schofield's outnumbered command, which was en route to Nashville and beyond the range of immediate help from Thomas. To accomplish that, he planned to seize Columbia, about thirty miles north of Pulaski, and trap Schofield on the south bank of the Duck River. The army would move in three columns as far as Mount Pleasant—Cheatham's Corps on the left, Lee's in the center, and Stewart's on the right. The columns would then unite for the eight-mile push to Columbia. The 60th North Carolina marched eight miles on November 20 and camped on the banks of Shoal Creek. On the twenty-first it made another ten miles through an all-day snow. "[W]e started this morning through mud from four to twenty inches deep," General French recorded in his diary, "and through snow that the keen wind blew in our faces. In the afternoon we encamped by the roadside, near a deserted habitation. The weather is bitterly cold, and the snow falling. Sleeping on the ground covered with snow."[175] The regiment passed through West Point on November 22, reached Rock Creek on the twenty-third, marched eighteen miles (passing through Henryville and crossing the Buffalo River) on the twenty-fourth, and arrived with Lee's Corps at Mount Pleasant on the twenty-fifth. Captain Harper of the 58th North Carolina described the difficult march in his diary:

> 20th: Cold, Rain. Moved at 7 A.M. Roads exceedingly muddy. Disagreeable day. Marched on road towards West Point etc. Camped at Creek say 5 miles from T[ennessee line].
> 21st: A.M. Snowing and Wind. P.M. Cloudy and Cold. Marched at 7 A.M. Cold and disagreeable. Thinly settled country. Crossed State line say 17 miles for [from] F[lorence]. Camped say 5 miles beyond.
> 22nd: A.M. hard freeze. Blowing snow and cold. Ground frozen as hard as to bear up artillery. Moved at 8 A.M. Passed W. Springs 1 mile. West point 8 ms.– 2 ms. north of Wh. we camped. Night bitter cold. Slept well before large Hickory log fire. . . .

---

173. G. P. Erwin to his sister, November 7, 1864, Erwin Papers.

174. "My hopes have been greatly excited by this campaign," Assistant Quartermaster Erwin had written two weeks earlier. "The campaign so far has succeeded admirably; great good has already been done. The spirit of our army is buoyant and time alone is needed before the winter rains render army movements impracticable. . . ." G. P. Erwin to his sister, November 5, 1864, Erwin Papers.

175. French, *Two Wars*, 290. Assistant Quartermaster Erwin had forecast trouble with the roads as early as November 7. "It has been cloudy with occasional rain," he wrote, "enough to put the roads in very bad condition . . . for a week & last night it rained very hard all night. Terrible for army operations." G. P. Erwin to his sister, November 7, 1864, Erwin Papers.

23rd: Clear, Cold. . . . Marched at 11 A.M. Camped at 3 P.M. having made about 5 miles.

24th: Clear, Cold. P.M. cloudy . . . [and] ground frozen hard. Marched at 7 A.M. After 10 miles struck Columbia and Waynesboro Pike and 5 miles further [we reached] Henryville. Camped 5 miles N[orth] of Henryville.

25th: Clear, Cool, Pleas[ant]. Marched at 7 A.M. on Pike. Mcadam rode [*sic*] at 4 miles at Bigbee Creek. . . . Foraging expedition with Dr. H.– Sumptuous dinner at Miss Griffithens [*sic*]. Mt. Pleasant 10 miles from last Camp. Overtook Brigade in camp 3 miles north of Mt. P. Lovely Country. Apples, Pumpkins etc.

26th: Cold. Rain all day. Marched at 7 A.M. Passed thro' beautiful country. . . . 58th and 60th [North Carolina] in advance of corps. Relieved cavalry on picket– Slight skirmishing.[176]

Lee reached Columbia on November 26. There he found Schofield, who had begun withdrawing from Pulaski on the twenty-second and won a narrow race with Forrest's cavalry to the Duck River crossings on the twenty-fourth. By the evening of November 27, Hood had the rest of his army up and in position to attack the next day; however, Schofield crossed the Duck during the night and entrenched on the north bank. Stevenson's Division entered Columbia before daylight on the twenty-eighth. "There was considerable skirmishing across the river during the day and some artillery firing," Lee reported, "resulting in nothing of importance." During the fight the 60th North Carolina was sent up stream to "obtain . . . a flanking fire upon the enemy" and "drove them back from the immediate bank of the river."[177]

In a new attempt to cut Schofield's line of retreat, Hood sent Stewart's and Cheatham's Corps and Edward Johnson's Division of Lee's Corps across the Duck a few miles above Columbia on the morning of November 29 with orders to capture Spring Hill, about eight miles north of Columbia on the Nashville Pike. The remainder of Lee's Corps, including the 60th North Carolina, would remain at Columbia and attempt to hold Schofield in place with demonstrations. When Schofield began evacuating the town around noon, Lee made "a display of pontoons, running several of them down to the river under a heavy artillery and musketry fire."[178] Shortly thereafter, Pettus's Brigade crossed the river in boats, capturing a line of enemy rifle pits and a number of prisoners. A pontoon bridge was then laid down, and Stevenson's entire command crossed. The last of Schofield's troops pulled out around 2:30 A.M. on November 30, and Lee immediately set off in pursuit. Stevenson's Division was third in Lee's line of march behind those of Edward Johnson and Henry D. Clayton. Consequently, it arrived at Franklin too late to take part in the battle of that day and escaped the hideous slaughter that cost the Army of Tennessee 6,000 men. "I went over the battle field the next morning," Lt. Samuel Robinson of the 63rd Virginia wrote, "and it [was] the turiblest sight that my eye ever beheld[.] [T]he men lay piled and crossed upon each other where . . . [they] charged. . . . I think that we had about 3 to the yankeys one kiled."[179] On December 1 Hood's bloodied army, with Lee's Corps in the van, resumed its

176. Harper Diary, November 20-26, 1864.

177. *Official Records (Army)*, ser. 1, 45 (pt. 1):687, 693.

178. *Official Records (Army)*, ser. 1, 45 (pt. 1):687.

179. Samuel Robinson to Lydia Jane Robinson (his wife) and children, January 15, 1865, Roster Document No. 1053 (typescript), CWRP, NCDAH, hereafter cited as Robinson Letter. "Never have I witnessed such a field as

advance toward Nashville. It arrived the next day and invested the city's formidable fortifications, defended by perhaps 55,000 troops under Thomas. Well aware that the 25,000-man Army of Tennessee was no match for its opponent, Hood ordered the construction of heavy defensive works and settled down to await an attack.

While Hood entrenched and, for one of the few times in his career, awaited the pleasure of the enemy, Forrest's cavalry moved southeast from Nashville on December 2. Forrest's orders were to "operat[e] upon the [Nashville and Chattanooga] railroad, blockhouses, and telegraph lines" leading to Murfreesboro and ascertain the possibilities of capturing the town and its 8,000-man garrison. General Bate, whose infantry division had also been "operating" on the railroad, was instructed to cooperate, and Palmer's and Brig. Gen. Claudius W. Sears's Brigades were sent from Nashville to provide additional support.[180] On the sixth Forrest and Bate probed the formidable works of Fortress Rosecrans, Murfreesboro's primary defensive bastion. The next morning Maj. Gen. Lovell H. Rousseau, the Federal commander, ordered seven regiments under Maj. Gen. Robert H. Milroy to "make a reconnaissance" southwest along the Salem Pike and "feel the enemy."[181] Outnumbered and fearing for his flanks, Forrest pulled back from a line west of the town and threw up breastworks of logs and rails south of and parallel to the Wilkinson Pike. His line of battle, facing south and with its right near Overall Creek, consisted of the infantry brigades of Brig. Gens. Jesse J. Finley (commanded by Maj. Jacob A. Lash), Palmer, and Sears in left-to-right order. Brig. Gens. Henry R. Jackson's and Thomas B. Smith's infantry were in reserve on the north side of the turnpike, and Forrest's cavalry was in support on both flanks.

After moving several miles along the Salem Pike, Milroy learned that Forrest had taken a new position. He therefore turned north and "presented himself" in Forrest's front. Concerned now about the security of his left flank, Forrest moved Sears's Brigade from the extreme right to the extreme left of his line and ordered Jackson to take position between Sears and Lash. Meantime, Milroy disappeared behind a ridge and some woods, causing Bate and Forrest to conclude that he had withdrawn to Fortress Rosecrans. Shortly thereafter, Milroy reappeared beyond Forrest's left astride the Wilkinson Pike and began advancing. Forrest then wheeled his entire line to the left astride the pike and, when a gap formed in his center during that maneuver, ordered Smith to fill it. Forrest and Bate were still adjusting their new line—Sears, Jackson, Smith, Lash, and Palmer in left-to-right order—and attempting to fill gaps on both sides of Smith when Milroy struck.[182]

"The enemy's line came diagonally from the left and struck Finley's [Lash's] and Palmer's brigades," Bate wrote, "crumbling and driving them from the temporary works." "[T]he infantry, with the exception of Smith's brigade . . . [then] made a shameful retreat," Forrest reported, "losing two pieces of artillery. I siezed [sic] the colors of the retreating

---

Franklin!" Captain Patton later wrote. "The carnage was awful, and literally, I thought and still think, that I could have crossed the field with each step treading on the dead body of a soldier." Patton, "Recollections," 12-13.

180. *Official Records (Army)*, ser. 1, 45 (pt. 1):754.

181. *Official Records (Army)*, ser. 1, 45 (pt. 1):617.

182. *Official Records (Army)*, ser. 1, 45 (pt. 1):746.

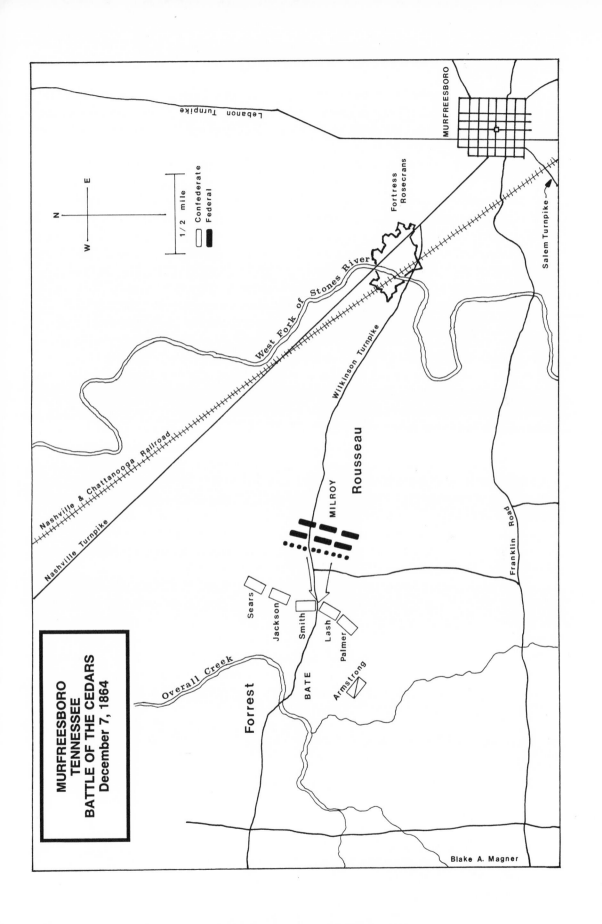

MURFREESBORO
TENNESSEE
BATTLE OF THE CEDARS
December 7, 1864

Blake A. Magner

troops and endeavored to rally them, but they could not be moved by any entreaty or appeal to their patriotism. Major-General Bate did the same thing, but was equally as unsuccessful. . . ." "The Federals came on with precision and in gallant style," Capt. John W. Morton, commander of one of Forrest's batteries recalled. "Something in their confident manner or some secret fear . . . suddenly inspired the Confederate infantry with terror, and . . . they broke in panic and fled wildly to the rear." One of the units that fled, it appears probable, was the 60th North Carolina. "[We were] enfiladed from our left," a Tennessean in Palmer's Brigade wrote. "[T]he entire line of the Confederates, including the Carolina [and Virginia] wing of Palmer's brigade, had withdrawn from the fight. . . . [O]nly Brown's old brigade [that is, the Tennessee contingent of Palmer's Brigade] was engaged."[183]

Covered by Smith's Brigade, Forrest's shattered infantry fell back to the Nashville Turnpike, near Stewart's Creek, where they bivouacked for the night. Federal losses during the battle, according to Milroy, numbered 22 men killed and 208 wounded. Milroy also claimed the capture of 197 prisoners. Bate reported that "In this day's fight there were 19 killed, 73 wounded, and 122 missing." Those figures may not include losses in Palmer's or Sears's Brigades or in cavalry units. The 60th North Carolina lost 1 man killed (Lt. Col. James T. Weaver), 1 wounded, and 2 captured.[184]

Palmer's Brigade remained in the vicinity of Stewart's Creek for at least the next three days, possibly assisting Bate's command in tearing up railroad track. Because of a heavy snow, little was accomplished by December 9, when Bate's Division departed for Nashville. On December 12 Forrest ordered Palmer's men and Col. Charles H. Olmstead's infantry brigade, which had been sent from Nashville to replace Bate's Division, to make a new effort at railroad demolition. By Forrest's account, the track between La Vergne and Murfreesboro was then "most effectually" destroyed. On the fourteenth Palmer and Olmstead were ordered to cross Stones River and move east of Murfreesboro "with a view of capturing the enemy's forage train"; however, on the evening of December 15 Forrest received word that a major battle was in progress at Nashville. Palmer and Olmstead were then recalled to Murfreesboro.[185]

On December 16 Forrest moved with his entire command to Wilkinson Crossroads, six miles northeast of Murfreesboro, where he learned that night of Hood's disastrous defeat. After dispatching part of his cavalry to cover Hood's retreat, Forrest moved to Triune, thirteen miles west of Murfreesboro, to collect his wagon train and his sick and wounded. He then headed south by "forced marches" through bitterly cold weather toward the Lillard's Mill crossing of the Duck River. "[M]y march along the almost impassable roads was unavoidably slow," Forrest reported. "Most of the infantry under my command

183. *Official Records (Army)*, ser. 1, 45 (pt. 1):746, 755; John Watson Morton, *The Artillery of Nathan Bedford Forrest's Cavalry: "The Wizard of the Saddle"* (Nashville: Publishing House of the Methodist Episcopal Church South, 1909), 282-283; Weaver, *54th Virginia*, 141. See also Edwin C. Bearss, "The History of Fortress Rosecrans," Chapter 6: "The Battle of the Cedars," 19-20, unpublished research paper, Stones River National Battlefield, Murfreesboro, Tennessee, hereafter cited as Bearss, "Battle of the Cedars." Contrary to Forrest, it appears that Jackson's Brigade, like Smith's, cannot fairly be accused of making a "shameful retreat." The conduct of Sears's Mississippians, however, is more ambiguous. See Bearss, "Battle of the Cedars," 21.

184. *Official Records (Army)*, ser. 1, 45 (pt. 1):747 (see also 619).

185. *Official Records (Army)*, ser. 1, 45 (pt. 1):756.

were barefooted and in a disabled condition. . . ." At Lillard's Mill rapidly rising water prevented Forrest from crossing more than a portion of his wagons. He therefore moved downriver toward Columbia, which he reached on the evening of the eighteenth. Hood's shattered army arrived there from Nashville earlier that day.[186]

At Columbia, Hood organized a special eight-brigade infantry force under Maj. Gen. Edward C. Walthall to cover the retreat of what remained of the Army of Tennessee. Finding all eight units severely depleted, Walthall reorganized them as four brigades. Palmer's Brigade was consolidated with that of Olmstead under the command of Palmer; the other three brigades were commanded by Brig. Gens. Daniel H. Reynolds and Winfield S. Featherston and by Col. Hume R. Feild. Altogether, Walthall's force, under overall command of Forrest, numbered only about 1,900 men, 400 of whom, according to Forrest, "were unserviceable for want of shoes."[187]

On December 20 Hood retreated toward Pulaski. Walthall followed on the twenty-second when Federal troops began crossing the Duck River two miles upriver from Columbia. Halting briefly near Lynnville to support Forrest's cavalrymen, Walthall then fell back to Richland Creek, about seven miles from Pulaski, at sunrise on the twenty-fourth. He resumed his southward march at 8:00 P.M. that evening, reached Pulaski during the night, and moved toward Bainbridge, Alabama, the next morning.

The roads now were almost impassable [Walthall wrote], and the artillery and the few wagons which made [up] our train were moved with considerable difficulty. We soon began to overhaul straggling wagons belonging to the train of the main army, and these, when practicable, were carried on with us, thus somewhat embarrassing our own movements. The enemy, with a heavy mounted force, as soon as we got on the dirt road at Pulaski, began to press us with boldness and vigor. It was determined to turn upon him, and as an advantageous position for this, a line was selected on Anthony's Hill, about seven miles from Pulaski. Here Featherston's and Palmer's commands, with a brigade of cavalry on either flank, were put in ambush to await the enemy's approach, Reynolds' and Feild's being reserved in support. So broken is the ground at that point, and so densely wooded, that there was no difficulty in effectually concealing the troops. A line no thicker than a strong line of skirmishers was exposed, which the enemy promptly engaged, and when it proved stubborn he dismounted part of his troops and made a charge. When the attacking force neared the troops lying in wait for them the latter delivered a destructive fire, and a section of artillery belonging to the cavalry,

---

186. *Official Records (Army)*, ser. 1, 45 (pt. 1):740, 756. Colonel Olmstead wrote that during the retreat to the Duck River "the sufferings of the men, who were many of them barefooted and all poorly clad, were intense." *Official Records (Army)*, ser. 1, 45 (pt. 1):740.

187. *Official Records (Army)*, ser. 1, 45 (pt. 1):757. According to a field return for Palmer's and Olmstead's Brigades dated December 21, 1864, the 60th North Carolina had an "effective total" of 46 men, a "total present" of 106, and an "aggregate present" of 122. In Palmer's Brigade—consisting of the 60th North Carolina, 54th and 63rd Virginia, 3rd and 18th Tennessee (Consolidated), and the 32nd and 45th Tennessee (but excluding the 58th North Carolina, which was absent on detail)—the effective total was 297, the total present 438, and the aggregate present of 527. Palmer's two smallest regiments, the 3rd and 18th Tennessee (Consolidated) and the 32nd Tennessee, had effective totals of twelve men each. "Effective total" figures are somewhat misleading because they do not include company and regimental officers. "Total present" figures also exclude officers but include, in addition to "effective total" men, soldiers who are present but sick, present on extra duty, or present under arrest. "Aggregate present" figures include all men counted under "total present" as well as officers who are present in whatever capacity (for duty, sick, on extra duty, or under arrest). *Official Records (Army)*, ser. 1, 45 (pt. 1):728.

concealed near by, opened upon it with considerable effect. The enemy retreated in disorder, and my command, by prompt pursuit, captured a number of prisoners and horses and one piece of artillery.[188]

Walthall withdrew about sunset and bivouacked for the night at Sugar Creek. There, in another effort to protect Hood's wagons, he again employed his Anthony's Hill tactics, with equally good results. "About sunrise [on the 26th]," Walthall reported, "Reynolds and Feild were put in position between the two crossings of the creek, and Featherston and Palmer were posted on a strong point immediately on this side of and commanding the second crossing. . . . There was a fog that morning so dense that Reynolds and Feild were enabled easily to conceal their commands, except a small force purposely exposed in advance, and this, when encountered by the enemy, fell back by previous arrangement upon the main body. The enemy, with part of his force dismounted, made vigorous pursuit, till fired on by the line in concealment, and then broke in confusion, followed by our troops. His flight being obstructed by the creek, we captured nearly all the horses of a dismounted regiment and some prisoners."[189]

Around 9:00 A.M. Walthall resumed his march toward Bainbridge. That night he bivouacked about sixteen miles from the Tennessee River, which he crossed on December 28, taking up Hood's pontoon bridge behind him. His command was then disbanded, and Palmer's Brigade rejoined Stevenson's Division.

During the whole time covered by this report [Walthall wrote in tribute to his men] the weather was excessively severe, and the troops subjected to unusual hardships. For several days the ground was covered with snow, and numbers of the men made the march without shoes, some had no blankets, and all were poorly clad for the season. What they had to endure was borne without complaint. . . . [I]t was known, of course, to them that their situation was one of extreme peril, and the serious and discouraging disasters which had but recently befallen us were well calculated to bring all commands into a state of disorganization. For their fine conduct, despite these difficulties and disadvantages and the depression which then pervaded the whole army, the officers and men of my command are entitled to no little praise.[190]

From Bainbridge the Army of Tennessee continued its grueling march west to Burnsville and Corinth, Mississippi, then moved south to Rienzi and Tupelo. The army, numbering perhaps 15,000 men, reached Tupelo on January 7, 1865, and went into winter quarters. "[W]e have retreated some too hundred miles through the wet and cold mud [a] half leg deep," Lieutenant Robinson of the 63rd Virginia wrote on January 15, "and a great many of the men was entirely barfooted and almost naked[.] [T]he men marched over the frozen ground until their feet was worn out till they could be tracked by the blood and some of them there feet was frosted and swolen till they bursted till they could not stand on there feet[.] [N]ow this is what I saw my self. . . . [T]hey was at least one third of the men left in tenn kiled wounded and captured." Robinson's comments about barefooted soldiers were

188. *Official Records (Army)*, ser. 1, 45 (pt. 1):727.

189. *Official Records (Army)*, ser. 1, 45 (pt. 1):727-728 (see also 567, 603).

190. *Official Records (Army)*, ser. 1, 45 (pt. 1):728.

no exaggeration. "I see one [member] of our regiment [the 63rd Virginia] here [in hospital at Columbus, Mississippi] with the balls of his feet frooze [*sic*] but [about?] off," Capt. James Clark informed his wife on January 22. "Many of the men have lost their toes and some their entire feet."[191]

On January 23 Hood was relieved at his own request as commander of the Army of Tennessee and replaced temporarily by Lt. Gen. Richard Taylor. Joseph E. Johnston resumed command of the remnants of his former army on February 23. On an unknown date between January 8 and January 19 the 60th North Carolina and 63rd Virginia were consolidated. It is uncertain who was initially in command of the consolidated regiment, but as of February 28 it was commanded by Lt. Col. Connally H. Lynch of the 63rd Virginia. The "effective total" of the consolidated regiment on January 19 was 275 men. The regiment remained a part of Stevenson's Division of Lee's Corps.[192]

In the meantime, President Jefferson Davis reached a decision in mid-January to send reinforcements from the Army of Tennessee to Georgia, where Sherman had left a smoldering trail of destruction from Atlanta to the ocean and was temporarily holed up in Savannah. The first units of Lee's Corps departed Tupelo by rail on January 19 and were followed three days later by the newly consolidated 60th North Carolina and 63rd Virginia regiments. The consolidated regiment, which for convenience will continue to be referred to here as the 60th North Carolina, reached Okolona on the twenty-third after a "Cold ride on Freight cars," arrived at Demopolis on the evening of the twenty-fourth, and departed for Selma at nightfall on twenty-fifth. "Slept well on box car without fire," Captain Harper noted in his diary. After arriving at Selma at 11:00 P.M., the men were transported by steamboat up the Alabama River to Montgomery, which they reached at midnight on January 26. Following a two-day layover they moved by rail to Columbus on the twenty-ninth—"Supplied with [a] good supper by the ladies," Harper wrote—and reached Milledgeville on the night of the thirtieth. Finding the tracks above Milledgeville destroyed by Sherman's wrecking crews, they marched northeast the next morning, passed through Sparta on February 1, and arrived at Mayfield on the second. They then moved by rail to Augusta and Branchville, South Carolina, where they arrived on the morning of the fourth. From there they marched to a "count[r]y Bridge" over the Edisto River, two and one-half miles southwest of Branchville, and took up defensive positions.[193] "I am verry dirty not having had a change of clothes in upwards of 2 weeks," Captain Hampton of the 63rd Virginia wrote, "but some of the Boys are so much worse off than I am I ought not to complain[.] I have never in [my] life seen such a dirty & filthy set of men[.] [S]omething ne[a]r half of the command has not changed shirts for 4 or 5 months & their pants are in tat[t]ers[.]"[194]

---

191. Samuel Robinson to L. J. Robinson and children, January 15, 1865 (typescript), Robinson Letter; James Clark to Martha Clark, January 22, 1865, Clark Letters.

192. See *Official Records (Army)*, ser. 1, 45 (pt. 2):799.

193. Harper Diary, January 23, 25, 29 and February 4, 1865. The 54th Virginia apparently did not depart from Tupelo on the same date as the rest of Palmer's Brigade. After reaching South Carolina, it was on detached duty for a time at Black Horse Creek and was subsequently detailed to guard trains. It probably rejoined Palmer's command at or near Smithfield, North Carolina, on or about March 14. See diary of William A. King, Roster Document No. 1043 (typescript), CWRP, NCDAH; Weaver, *54th Virginia*, 150.

194. T. B. Hampton to J. C. Hampton, February 3, 1865, Hampton Papers.

Sherman, meanwhile, marched out of Savannah on February 1 and moved north through South Carolina with two columns that he dubbed the "Left Wing" (commanded by Slocum) and the "Right Wing" (commanded by Howard). Beauregard, in overall command of Confederate forces in South Carolina, had about 22,000 men to oppose Sherman's 60,000, but those were scattered across the state. Moreover, by feinting toward Augusta with one column and Charleston with the other, Sherman confused Beauregard as to his objective, which was Columbia. Forging swiftly ahead, Sherman punched through the Confederate defenses at the Salkehatchie River on February 3 and pushed on to the Edisto, forcing Palmer to abandon his country bridge position on the night of the same day he occupied it. Palmer then fell back to Cannon's Bridge, on the South Fork of the Edisto about eleven miles northwest of Branchville. Palmer's men burned Cannon's Bridge on February 7, skirmished with an enemy probing force on the eighth, and retreated on the night of the ninth after the Federals captured Birmaker's Bridge, six miles above Cannon's Bridge. They then marched through blowing snow to Orangeburg, thirteen miles northeast. "Came near [to] being cut off," Captain Harper noted laconically in his diary.[195]

On February 10 Palmer's Brigade passed through Orangeburg and continued on to Shilling's Bridge, on the North Fork of the Edisto, which it reached on the eleventh. There the entire brigade was implausibly routed on the twelfth by, according to Captain Hampton, "a squad of about 65 Yanks [that] crossed some 300 yards to our right . . . [and] fired into [us]. . . . [O]ur Boys made the worse stampede I ever witnessed. . . . I rallied 12 men . . . all that would be ral[l]ied out of our Brigade & . . . we turned on the enemy & made them leave the field quicker than they came[.]" Palmer's troops then retreated toward Columbia, took position two miles west of the city on February 14, and began constructing breastworks in a sleet storm. The next day they fell back eastward across the Congaree River. After spending the sixteenth "in line [of] battle in [the] streets of Columbia," Palmer evacuated the city with the rest of Lee's Corps (temporarily commanded by Stevenson) that evening, bivouacked at midnight near a bridge over the Broad River, and retreated toward Charlotte the next day.[196] The 60th reached Winnsboro on February 19, passed through Rich Hill and crossed the Catawba River on the twenty-first, and camped four miles south of Charlotte on February 23.

Lee's Corps remained at Charlotte for the next nine days. Joseph Johnston arrived on February 23 and assumed command of both the Department of South Carolina, Georgia, and Florida and the Department of Tennessee and [Northwest] Georgia. Two weeks later he assumed command of "all troops" in the Department of North Carolina.[197] On February 27 he reviewed Lee's Corps, including the 60th North Carolina. The "effective strength" of Palmer's Brigade, probably not including the 54th Virginia, which was on detached duty, was reported as 578 men.[198]

---

195. Harper Diary, February 9, 1865. See also Garrett D. Gouge (58th North Carolina) to Sarah Howell (his sister), February 8, 1865 (typescript), Roster Document No. 1057, CWRP, NCDAH.

196. T. B. Hampton to J. C. Hampton, February 3, 1865, Hampton Papers; Harper Diary, February 16, 1865. Lee was wounded at the Battle of Nashville and did not return to duty until the last days of the war.

197. *Official Records (Army)*, ser. 1, 47 (pt. 2):1320 (see also 1248, 1274, 1334).

198. *Official Records (Army)*, ser. 1, 47 (pt. 2):1285. Lieutenant Davidson of Company C, 60th North Carolina,

In accordance with orders from General-in-Chief Robert E. Lee to "Concentrate all available forces and drive back Sherman," Johnston issued orders for Lee's Corps to move by rail from Charlotte to Fayetteville on March 5.[199] Stewart's and Cheatham's Corps, at Chester, South Carolina, and Hardee's, near Cheraw, were to proceed to the same point. By March 10 the 60th North Carolina had reached Salisbury. On the twelfth it departed Salisbury by train, reached Hillsborough on the night of the thirteenth, and arrived at Smithfield at 3:00 A.M. on the fourteenth. Sherman, meanwhile, was delayed on his northward march by heavy rains but crossed the North Carolina line on March 7 and captured Fayetteville on March 12. There he paused briefly before advancing again on the fifteenth. Deprived of his Fayetteville assembly point, Johnston opted to remain at Smithfield until Sherman's new destination—Goldsboro or Raleigh—could be determined. Time was growing very short. Twenty thousand Federals commanded by the ubiquitous Schofield were marching west from New Bern and had brushed aside a small Confederate force under Braxton Bragg near Kinston on March 7-10. An additional 10,000 men commanded by Maj. Gen. Alfred H. Terry moved north from Wilmington on March 15. Once Sherman, Schofield, and Terry joined forces, Johnston's faint prospects of defeating Sherman would become virtually nil. His one hope, it appeared, was to attack and destroy Sherman's Left Wing before Schofield and Terry arrived and before the Right Wing could come to its aid. In order to position himself for an ambush, however, he needed to determine Sherman's destination and to increase, if possible, the distance between Sherman's two wings. On March 15 a small battle at Averasboro between Hardee's Corps and Slocum accomplished both objects. So confident of victory was Sherman in that one-sided contest that Howard and the Right Wing continued marching and, within a few hours, passed beyond the junction of the Raleigh road. Johnston could now plan an ambush secure in the knowledge that Sherman was headed for Goldsboro, that Slocum would come to him, and that Raleigh would not be left uncovered. On March 18 he issued orders for his 20,000-man army to take position south of Bentonville.[200]

Johnston's defensive line on the morning of March 19 began about one-half mile south of the Goldsboro road, extended northwest across the road at a point just east of the Bentonville road intersection, and then ran northeast, parallel to the Bentonville road, for another half mile (see map on page 266). It then made a sharp angle to the west and continued about 600 yards before terminating. Most of the line south of the angle was held by Maj. Gen. Robert F. Hoke's Division (on the left) and Col. John H. Nethercutt's North

---

reported on February 22, 1865, that "on my company rolls [there are] four commissioned officers & thirty men of whom only six are present for duty." Samuel W. Davidson to Samuel Cooper, February 22, 1865, Samuel W. Davidson service record file, 60th Regiment N.C. Troops, Compiled Confederate Service Records (North Carolina), M270, reel 539.

199. *Official Records (Army)*, ser. 1, 47 (pt. 2):1247.

200. Ten officers and 72 men were present for duty in the 60th North Carolina on March 17, 1865. An additional 16 men were present but on extra duty and 4 were present but sick. According to a letter written by Lts. Samuel W. Davidson and John G. Lindsey on March 25, only 8 officers and 6 men were present for duty in Companies A and C. See Regimental Return dated March 17, 1865, Harper Papers; Samuel W. Davidson and John G. Lindsey to [Samuel Cooper], March 25, 1865, Samuel W. Davidson service record file, Compiled Confederate Service Records (North Carolina), M270, reel 539.

Carolina Junior Reserves brigade, supported by a six-gun battery of Lt. Col. Joseph B. Starr's North Carolina artillery battalion. Both Hoke and Nethercutt were under the command of Bragg. On Nethercutt's right, in a slot reserved for Hardee's Corps, which was still en route from Averasboro, were two additional artillery batteries. West of the angle was the Army of Tennessee, commanded by Stewart and comprising Stewart's Corps (commanded by Maj. Gen. William W. Loring) on the left, Lee's Corps (commanded by Maj. Gen. D. H. Hill) in the center, and Cheatham's Corps (commanded by Maj. Gen. William B. Bate) on the right. The Army of Tennessee's portion of the line was concealed just inside the edge of a woods fronting the fields of a farmer named Cole; marshy terrain and blackjack thickets south of the angle rendered Bragg's units equally invisible. In short, Slocum would walk into a trap. His advance guard would encounter Confederate troops on the Goldsboro road, assume that they were facing the usual token opposition, and, as was Sherman's patented tactic, undertake a flanking movement. Stewart's Army of Tennessee and Hardee's Corps would then deliver a hammer blow against Slocum's left, crushing his army against the anvil of Bragg's command on the right. Slocum's strung-out, 30,000-man column would be crippled or destroyed, leaving Sherman with a choice of fighting Johnston with Howard's, Schofield's, and Terry's forces or retreating to the North Carolina coast.

On the morning of March 19 elements of Brig. Gen. William P. Carlin's Division, leading Slocum's advance, bumped into Confederate cavalry on the Goldsboro road. Carlin, as scripted, then deployed two brigades (George P. Buell's and Harrison C. Hobart's) north of the road and a third (Lt. Col. David Miles's) south of the road to turn the Confederate flanks. Buell and Hobart quickly plowed into the Army of Tennessee, still concealed in the woods, and were ripped by "an awful volly [sic]" from a distance of fifty feet.[201] "They . . . reeled and staggered," one Confederate remembered, "while we poured volley after volley into them, and great gaps were made in their line, as brave Federals fell everywhere—their colors would rise and fall just a few feet from us, and many a gallant boy in blue is buried there in those pines who held 'Old Glory' up for a brief moment." "[We] stood as long as man can stand," a Federal officer candidly admitted, "& . . . [then] run like the deuce." Meantime, south of the road, Miles's attack bogged down in a swamp but inexplicably convinced the egregious Bragg that his position was imperiled. In a move that delayed and perhaps fatally weakened Stewart's and Hardee's counterattack, Johnston responded to Bragg's call for assistance by ordering Maj. Gen. Lafayette McLaws's Division, the first of Hardee's units to reach the field, to take position on Hoke's left.[202]

Around 1:30 P.M. Hardee's second division, commanded by Maj. Gen. William B. Taliaferro, arrived and was placed on the right of Bate's Corps. About an hour later the Army of Tennessee and Taliaferro's Division stormed out of the woods, crushing the undermanned and disorganized Federal left and precipitating, in the words of one shaken Federal, "some of the best running ever did."[203] South of the road Brig. Gen. James D.

201. Charles S. Brown (21st Michigan) to "Mother & Etta," April 18, 1865, Charles S. Brown Papers, SCD–DU, hereafter cited as Brown Papers.

202. Lovick Pierce Thomas, "Their Last Battle," in *Southern Historical Society Papers*, 29 (1901): 217-218; C. S. Brown to "Etta," April 26, 1865, Brown Papers.

203. C. S. Brown to "his folks and anyone else," April 1865, Brown Papers.

Morgan's tenacious division, which had dug in on Miles's right, hung on precariously under attacks by Bragg from the front and by Stewart and Taliaferro from the flank and rear. Battling desperately amid a "continuous and remorseless roar of musketry," Morgan's men narrowly succeeded in holding their ground until William Cogswell's Brigade of Alpheus S. Williams's XX Corps arrived and attacked the Confederates from the rear.[204] The fighting then shifted again to the Federal left, where other XX Corps units reached the field and smashed a series of Confederate assaults with a "raging leaden hailstorm of grape and canister."[205]

During the night of March 19, Sherman, who was with Howard's wing of the army, belatedly learned of the fighting at Bentonville. Preparations to go to Slocum's aid began immediately, and by the afternoon of the twentieth the army was reunited. Realizing his gambit had failed, Johnston nevertheless remained on the battlefield, allegedly to cover the evacuation of his wounded but more probably in the faint hope that a victory might somehow still be salvaged. He therefore realigned his units in a spraddled-horseshoe configuration to cover the much longer Federal line and protect his retreat route over the Mill Creek bridge. While ambulances rumbled over the bridge toward Smithfield, the Confederate commander resupplied his men as best he could and anxiously awaited developments. Sherman, however, was no more interested than Johnston in assuming the offensive. Rarely disposed to expend lives in battle if maneuver would accomplish his object, Sherman was primarily concerned with reaching the Goldsboro railhead. There he would be reinforced by Schofield and Terry, rest his army, and obtain much needed supplies and equipment. Except for several "brisk" but relatively minor Federal attacks on Hoke's front, March 20 passed quietly.[206]

The next day Johnston remained in his works and continued to evacuate his wounded. Heavy skirmishing took place all along the line, but the only action of consequence was an unauthorized attack by Maj. Gen. Joseph A. Mower's Division that broke through the Confederate left and threatened to capture the Mill Creek bridge. Against that penetration Johnston, improvising desperately, mustered just enough resistance to force the impetuous Mower to pause and call for reinforcements. Sherman then ordered him to withdraw. During the night, Johnston fell back in the direction of Smithfield.

When Buell and Hobart attacked north of the Goldsboro road on the morning of March 19, the right extremity of Hobart's Brigade was confronted by the right extremity of Palmer's Brigade. Most of the damage to Carlin's two brigadiers was inflicted by Maj. Gen. Henry D. Clayton's Division, on Palmer's right, but Palmer claimed that his troops "repulsed . . . [the Federals attacking their part of the line] with ease, killing and wounding a number without any loss. . . ."[207] During Johnston's assault that afternoon, Palmer's men were in the first of D. H. Hill's two lines, between the brigades of Brig. Gens. Zachariah C. Deas and Marcellus A. Stovall.

204. Benson J. Lossing, *Pictorial History of the Civil War in the United States of America*, 3 vols. (Hartford, Conn.: Thomas Belknap, 1877), 3:501.

205. Samuel W. Ravenel, "Ask the Survivors of Bentonville," in *Confederate Veteran*, 18 (March 1910): 124.

206. *Official Records (Army)*, ser. 1, 47 (pt. 1):1056.

207. *Official Records (Army)*, ser. 1, 47 (pt. 1):1099.

This brigade moved steadily forward [Palmer reported] for about 400 yards in common time, preserving its alignment almost as if on parade, although for a part of that distance under considerable fire. This carried the brigade within 200 yards of the enemy's first line of works, which were at once charged and carried. This command did not halt there, but moved forward in double-quick, pursuing the enemy, flying in disorder and confusion to their second line of works, which was also charged and carried, capturing one piece of artillery near the second line. The pursuit was continued as far as the Goldsborough road, when it became necessary to halt the command, much exhausted by the two charges just made, and for the purpose of rectifying the alignment, more or less disturbed by such rapid movements through the woods thickly set with troublesome undergrowth.[208]

At that juncture Palmer's Brigade, which straddled the Goldsboro road, became separated into two "wings" by Brig. Gen. Alpheus Baker's Alabama brigade, which was moving east along the road.[209] Palmer was then ordered to remain in reserve and was still attempting to reunite his command when his right (southern) wing, consisting of the 54th Virginia, the "Tennessee Consolidation," and the 58th North Carolina, was ordered to join in the attack on Morgan.[210] That wing, Palmer reported, "immediately advanced for the distance of, say, 300 yards beyond the Goldsborough road, taking position on Brigadier-General Baker's right. I found no works at this point in my front, but just to my left were two lines of breastworks running rather perpendicular to this road. . . . It was wholly unsafe to move farther forward or pass this force on my left, and, indeed, on discovering these works and their singular direction I came to the conclusion that to carry them was in part the objective . . . of my movement. I therefore wheeled to the left, assaulted and carried the first line and part of the second. . . ."[211]

At that propitious moment Cogswell's Brigade launched its attack. "On the appearance of this force," Palmer wrote, "those in my front renewed their resistance, and thus my command was immediately under heavy fire both in front and rear. I at once ordered a movement as rapidly as possible by the left flank, so as to retire back on or near the Goldsborough road, but the Federals effected a junction so quickly as to capture some of my men and to cut off . . . another portion." Palmer then reunited the northern wing of his brigade with what remained of the southern and moved to a supporting position behind Pettus's Brigade.[212] His men saw no further action that day or, with the exception of

208. *Official Records (Army)*, ser. 1, 47 (pt. 1):1099-1100.

209. Palmer's report states that Baker "threw his line across mine, cutting nearly through the center of my brigade." *Official Records (Army)*, ser. 1, 47 (pt. 1):1100.

210. For reasons explained elsewhere in this volume, it is this author's opinion, contrary to that of Bentonville historian Mark L. Bradley, that the 63rd Virginia, not the 58th North Carolina, remained north of the Goldsboro road with the 60th North Carolina during the attack on Morgan. For a discussion, see the history of the 58th North Carolina, page 268, footnote 161.

211. *Official Records (Army)*, ser. 1, 47 (pt. 1):1100.

212. *Official Records (Army)*, ser. 1, 47 (pt. 1):1100. General Stevenson wrote that "My two brigades, Pettus' and Palmer's, retained their position until between 10 and 11 o'clock that night [March 19], when they withdrew under orders to the line from which we had advanced, Pettus, however, being now put in the front line in order to give Palmer's brigade, which had been compelled to move much more rapidly in the different charges which it made, and consequently was more exhausted, a better opportunity to rest. One regiment of Palmer's, the Fifty-eighth North Carolina, was, however, placed upon the front line to fill up the allotted portion of the works." *Official Records (Army)*, ser. 1, 47 (pt. 1):1095. See also *Daily Progress* (Raleigh), March 27, 1865.

skirmishing, on March 20 and 21.[213] Palmer reported the loss of 13 men killed, 113 wounded, and 55 captured plus the capture of 50 wounded and 45 unwounded prisoners. Stevenson's report listed Palmer's casualties as 14 killed, 121 wounded, and 42 missing. The 60th North Carolina's losses, according to figures compiled for this volume from the scanty records available, were 4 men wounded and 1 captured.[214]

Palmer's Brigade evacuated its lines at Bentonville at 2:00 A.M. on March 22, crossed Mill Creek and probably Stone's Creek, and bivouacked for the rest of the night. "Muddy road and tiresome walk," Captain Harper wrote. On the morning of the twenty-second the brigade "Threw up breastwork[s] and waited for advance of enemy[,] who failed to make his appearance." It then marched to within six or seven miles of Smithfield and camped after dark. "Road exceedingly wet and muddy," Harper continued. "Tiresome and disagreeable march. Peach trees in bloom." After a "Smokey [sic], Windy, dusty – Disagreeable day" in camp on March 23, the brigade moved through Smithfield on the twenty-fourth and camped near the Halifax road. It remained in the vicinity of Smithfield for the next two weeks with the rest of Johnston's troops.[215] A reorganization of the army was completed on April 9, and the 58th and 60th North Carolina were consolidated under the command of Lt. Col. Thaddeus Charles Coleman, formerly of the 1st Regiment N.C. Artillery and the Engineer Corps. The new organization, variously referred to as the 58th North Carolina Regiment (Consolidated) and the 58th North Carolina Battalion, was then transferred to William F. Brantley's Brigade, Hill's Division, Lee's Corps. Other regiments in Brantley's Brigade were the 24th Mississippi and the 22nd and 37th Alabama.[216]

In the meantime, Sherman reached Goldsborough on March 23 and linked up with Schofield and Terry, who had arrived on the twenty-first. There he remained, resting and refitting his men, until April 10, when he began moving toward Smithfield. Brantley's Brigade retreated with Johnston's army at 10:00 A.M. the same day, bivouacked at Battle's Bridge that evening, passed through Raleigh the next afternoon, and camped that night three miles northwest of the city on the Hillsborough road. The retreat continued during the next five days through Hillsborough and Graham to Company Shops (present-day

---

213. Relevant entries in Harper's diary for March 20-21, 1865, read as follows:

March 20: "Clear, Pleas. 58th in front line breastworks with Petters [Pettus's] Brig. Skirmishing in front and fighting going on on our left."

March 21: "Rain, Cool. Same as yesterday."

214. See *Official Records (Army)*, ser. 1, 47 (pt. 1):1096, 1100. Palmer complimented Lieutenant Colonel Lynch and the other three regimental commanders in his brigade, stating that they handled their troops "with ability and bore themselves handsomely through the day. . . ." Stevenson, in an "order . . . complimenting the troops of his Division," stated that "Never was there more dash and gallantry displayed than was exhibited by Palmer's Brigade in their successful assaults upon the breastworks of the enemy." *Official Records (Army)*, ser. 1, 47 (pt. 1):1101; *Daily Progress* (Raleigh), March 27, 1865.

215. Harper Diary, March 22-23, 1865. According to figures compiled for this volume, four members of the 60th North Carolina deserted during the fourth quarter of 1864 and one during the first quarter of 1865. Those figures, perhaps needless to say, are based on incomplete records and are suspiciously low. For 60th North Carolina desertion figures during other periods of the war, see footnotes 23, 72, 100, and 167 above.

216. The 24th Mississippi was a consolidation of the 24th, 27th, 29th, 30th, and 34th Mississippi; the 22nd Alabama was a consolidation of the 22nd, 25th, 39th, and 50th Alabama; and the 37th Alabama was a consolidation of the 37th, 42nd, and 54th Alabama.

Burlington), where rumors of the surrender of the Army of Northern Virginia were confirmed on April 15. On April 16 the regiment reached Greensboro, and on the eighteenth it moved to Jamestown. "Paroled prisoners from Lees [*sic*] Army passing [through] for days past in a constant stream," Harper observed on April 20. Demoralization among Johnston's troops, a serious problem since news of the fall of Richmond arrived on April 5, increased to epidemic proportions. "Reg't. melting away," Harper noted despondently on April 24.[217]

The 58th North Carolina Battalion remained at Jamestown for about a week before returning to Greensboro. In the meantime Sherman captured Raleigh on April 13. On April 17 Johnston opened surrender negotiations with Sherman. Terms were reached on April 19 but were overruled as excessively generous by the authorities in Washington. A new round of negotiations produced a quick agreement on April 26. Parole of Johnston's troops began at Greensboro the same date and continued through May 1. Among the 119 members of the 58th Battalion who received their paroles, only three can be identified as former members of the 60th Regiment N.C. Troops.[218]

The following table contains present-for-duty figures in selected morning reports filed for the 60th North Carolina from October 1862 through March 1865. Reports dated prior to September 1862 are located in the chapter 8, volume 107, Record Group 109, NARA, Washington, D.C.; subsequent reports are in the Harper Papers in the Southern Historical Collection, Chapel Hill. The National Archives collection of 60th North Carolina morning reports is extensive, and those cited below have been selected primarily because of their proximity to battles in which the regiment took part. A secondary purpose was to provide a statistical picture of the regiment's gradual decline by including, when possible, at least one report for each month of the war.

Date	Officers Present	Men Present	Total Present
October 30, 1862	36	619	635
November 29, 1862	44	454	498
December 27, 1862	32	348	380
January 31, 1863	18	243	261
April 30, 1863	27	322	349
May 27-28, 1863	34	365	399
June 29, 1863	32	325	357
July 31, 1863	32	263	295
August 26, 1863	18	274	292
September 11, 1863	20	146	166

217. Harper Diary, April 20 and 24, 1865.

218. The three were Asst. Q. M. George P. Erwin, Sgt. Melville B. Roberts of Company C, and Sgt. Francis McD. Stevens of Company F. According to Captain Patton, "about seventy-five" members of the 60th North Carolina were paroled at Greensboro. However, that figure seems too high. Patton, "Recollections," 13.

October 11, 1863	19	140	159
October 31, 1863	17	168	185
November 19, 1863	18	175	193
March 17-18, 1864	22	143	165
April 20, 1864	23	184	207
May [?], 1864	27	189	216
September 7, 1864	21	90	111
November 6, 1864	25	92	117
November 17, 1864	24	104	128
December 10, 1864	18	69	87
January 7, 1865	14	67	81
March 28, 1865	14	59	73

FIELD AND STAFF

COLONELS

McDOWELL, JOSEPH A.

Previously served as Captain of Company B of this regiment. Elected Lieutenant Colonel on August 1, 1862, and transferred to the Field and Staff. Promoted to Colonel on October 1, 1862. Resigned on March 25, 1863, by reason of "hemorrhoids." Resignation accepted on April 22, 1863.

HARDY, WASHINGTON MORRIS

Previously served as Captain of Company A of this regiment. Appointed Major on March 1, 1863, to rank from February 21, 1863, and transferred to the Field and Staff. Reported present in March-April, 1863. Promoted to Colonel on June 10, 1863, to rank from May 14, 1863. Reported present or accounted for in May-June, 1863, and from November 1, 1863, until August 23, 1864, when he went home on leave. No further records. Survived the war.

LIEUTENANT COLONELS

DEAVER, WILLIAM HARRY

Previously served as 1st Lieutenant of Company A of this regiment. Elected Major on August 1, 1862, and transferred to the Field and Staff. Promoted to Lieutenant Colonel on October 1, 1862. Resigned on April 27, 1863, by reason of "general debility & prostration the result of phthisis pulmonalis of some years' standing. He is much emaciated & very feeble. . . ." Resignation accepted on May 14, 1863. ["Stunned" when he was "dashed to the ground by his frantic horse" at Murfreesboro, Tennessee, December 31, 1862-January 2, 1863. He was a "brave, gallant fellow." (Clark's *Regiments*, 3:479.)]

RAY, JAMES MITCHEL

Previously served as Captain of Company F of this regiment. Appointed Lieutenant Colonel in late June, 1863, to rank from May 14, 1863, and transferred to the Field and Staff. Wounded in the right arm (compound fracture) at Chickamauga, Georgia, September 20, 1863. Resigned on November 28, 1863, by reason of disability from wounds. Resignation accepted on December 23, 1863.

WEAVER, JAMES THOMAS

Served as Captain of Company A of this regiment. Reported on duty as acting Major of the regiment in July-October, 1863. Appointed Major on October 27, 1863, and assigned to permanent duty with the Field and Staff. Promoted to Lieutenant Colonel on December 23, 1863. Reported absent on conscription duty in North Carolina from December 18, 1863, through February 29, 1864. Rejoined the regiment in March-April, 1864. Reported present in May-June, 1864. Sent to hospital on July 18, 1864. Returned to duty subsequent to August 31, 1864. Killed at Murfreesboro, Tennessee, December 7, 1864. "How often when the balls were thickest and the shells shrieked the loudest, have we heard his voice[,] 'Steady Boys, there's no danger. . . .' [H]e was the most perfectly cool, self-possessed man I ever saw." [Capt. Thomas W. Patton (Company C), Recollections in Civil War Collection, NCDAH.]

MAJORS

McDOWELL, WILLIAM WALLACE

Previously served as Captain of Company E of this regiment. Appointed Major on October 1, 1862, and transferred to the Field and Staff. Resigned on January 24, 1863, by reason of "chronic diarrhoea." Resignation accepted on February 21, 1863.

HUFF, JAMES T.

Previously served as Captain of Company H of this regiment. Appointed Major on December 23, 1863, and transferred to the Field and Staff. Wounded slightly at Rocky Face Ridge, Georgia, February 25, 1864. Returned to duty prior to May 1, 1864. Reported present in May-June, 1864. Reported in command of the regiment in July-August, 1864. Took the Oath of Allegiance at Chattanooga, Tennessee, June 5, 1865.

ADJUTANTS

CLAYTON, EDWIN M.

Previously served as Sergeant of Company E, 1st Regiment N.C. Infantry (6 months, 1861). Appointed Adjutant (1st Lieutenant) of this regiment on November 5, 1862, to rank from August 1, 1862. Reported present or accounted for in March-April, 1863. Appointed Captain of Company K of this regiment on May 4, 1863, and transferred.

EWING, ORVILLE, JR.

Resided in Davidson County (Tennessee?). Appointed Adjutant (1st Lieutenant) of this regiment on May 4, 1863. Reported present or accounted for in May-June, 1863, and January-August, 1864. Transferred to the Field and Staff, 58th Regiment N.C. Troops, when the 58th and 60th Regiments were consolidated on April 9, 1865. [Contrary to some reports, it appears that he is not the same individual who served previously as Sergeant Major of the 20th Regiment Tennessee Infantry.]

ASSISTANT QUARTERMASTERS

PATTON, WILLIAM AUGUSTUS

Appointed Assistant Quartermaster (Captain) of this regiment on August 1, 1862. Resigned on February 24, 1863, by reason of "hypertrophy of the heart." Resignation accepted on March 11, 1863. Died at Asheville on April 5, 1863. He was 28 years of age at the time of his death and "a loss irreparable to the regiment, he being a most efficient officer and the highest type of a man in every way." [Clark's *Regiments*, 3:483. May have served previously as 2nd Lieutenant in the 106th Regiment N.C. Militia.]

ERWIN, GEORGE PHIFER

Previously served as 1st Sergeant of Company B, 11th Regiment N.C. Troops (1st Regiment N.C. Volunteers). Appointed Assistant Quartermaster (Captain) of this regiment on June 16, 1863, to rank from May 16, 1863. Reported for duty in July, 1863. Reported present or accounted for in January-June, 1864. Reported on duty as Assistant Quartermaster of Maj. Gen. Carter L. Stevenson's division on February 27, 1865. Paroled at Greensboro on April 26, 1865.

CLAYTON, EDWIN M.

Served as Adjutant (1st Lieutenant) of this regiment and as Captain of Company K. Reported on duty as acting Assistant Quartermaster of the regiment in January-February, 1864.

BEARDEN, MARCUS J.

Previously served as Assistant Quartermaster (Captain) of the 58th Regiment N.C. Troops. Served as Assistant Quartermaster (Captain) of this regiment (possibly in an acting capacity) from about March 21, 1865, until April 9, 1865, when the 58th and 60th Regiments were consolidated. Transferred back to the 58th Regiment on April 9, 1865.

ASSISTANT COMMISSARY
OF SUBSISTENCE

COLEMAN, ROBERT L.

Previously served as 1st Lieutenant of Company K, 11th Regiment N.C. Troops (1st Regiment N.C. Volunteers). Appointed Assistant Commissary of Subsistence (Captain) on November 5, 1862, to rank from September 1, 1862, and transferred to this regiment. Reported present in March-June, 1863. His office was abolished by an act of the Confederate Congress on July 31, 1863. Appointed Commissary of Subsistence (Major) on October 12, 1863, to rank from September 28, 1863, and assigned to the staff of Brig. Gen. Robert B. Vance.

SURGEONS

COOPER, ROBERT W.

Served as 1st Lieutenant in Company A of this regiment. Probably served in an unofficial capacity as Surgeon of that company and later of the entire regiment from the summer of 1862 until about January-March, 1863.

STEVENS, JAMES MITCHELL

Previously served as Captain of Company F of this regiment. Appointed Surgeon on November 5, 1862, to rank from August 1, 1862, and transferred to the Field and Staff. Resigned on March 14, 1863, because (his appointment as Surgeon notwithstanding) he was assigned the position and duties of Assistant Surgeon.

SINGLETON, _____

Was reportedly serving as Surgeon of this regiment on May 17, 1863. Departed the regiment under unknown circumstances prior to June 6, 1863. [According to Captain Thomas W. Patton of Company C of this regiment, Singleton was "a most disagreeable man" and "a dirty fellow" whom "the officers speak of getting up a petition to have . . . removed." [See Thomas W. Patton to his mother, May 17 and June 6, 1863, James W. Patton Papers, Southern Historical Collection.]

McKAY, A. L.

Served in a Scottish Highlander unit of the British Army before emigrating to America. Appointed Surgeon of this regiment to rank from May 15, 1863. Reported present through June 30, 1863.

Transferred to another command after some members of the 60th Regiment who objected to his "extra rigid regular army discipline" cut down his hammock and stoned him during the night of August 20, 1863 (see page 445 above). [Clark's *Regiments*, 3:486. See also Thomas W. Patton to his mother, August 22, 1863, James W. Patton Papers, Southern Historical Collection.]

GRIFFIN, HAMILTON

Resided in Louisville, Kentucky. Appointed Surgeon of this regiment on an unspecified date (probably in the autumn of 1863). First reported in the records of this regiment on October 24, 1863. Reported present or accounted for in January-August, 1864. Transferred to the Field and Staff, 58th Regiment N.C. Troops, when the 58th and 60th Regiments were consolidated on April 9, 1865. [May have served also as Surgeon of the 2nd Regiment Kentucky Mounted Infantry, the 14th Regiment Texas Cavalry, and/or the 50th Regiment Virginia Infantry.]

ASSISTANT SURGEONS

REYNOLDS, JOHN D.

Appointed Assistant Surgeon on August 1, 1862. Failed to report for duty and was dropped from the regimental rolls on an unspecified date (probably in the autumn of 1862).

TREADWELL, JAMES C.

Date appointed Assistant Surgeon not reported (probably the autumn of 1862). Captured at Murfreesboro, Tennessee, January 5, 1863. Confined at Louisville, Kentucky, April 26, 1863. Transferred to Baltimore, Maryland, May 6, 1863. Paroled at Fort McHenry, Maryland, May 10, 1863. Received at City Point, Virginia, May 14, 1863, for exchange. No further records.

STRAIT, JAMES L.

Resided in Mississippi. Appointed Assistant Surgeon on July 13, 1863, to rank from May 1, 1863. Reported present on surviving company muster rolls through August 31, 1864. Paroled at Macon, Mississippi, May 26, 1865.

DUNN, J. F.

Appointed Assistant Surgeon of this regiment on January 10, 1864. Furloughed for thirty days on February 4, 1864. Reported absent without leave on April 30, 1864. Hospitalized at Macon, Georgia, May 26, 1864, with secondary syphilis. Returned to duty prior to July 1, 1864. Reported present through August 31, 1864. Transferred to the Field and Staff, 58th Regiment N.C. Troops, when the 58th and 60th Regiments were consolidated on April 9, 1865.

ENSIGN

LINDSEY, GEORGE WASHINGTON

Previously served as Sergeant in Company A of this regiment. Appointed Ensign (1st Lieutenant) on May 13, 1864, to rank from April 28, 1864, and transferred to the Field and Staff. Transferred to Company E, 58th Regiment N.C. Troops, when the 58th and 60th Regiments were consolidated on April 9, 1865.

SERGEANTS MAJOR

ERWIN, STANHOPE

Resided in Burke County. Appointed Sergeant Major of this regiment on an unspecified date. Killed at Murfreesboro, Tennessee, on or about January 2, 1863.

MILLER, FRANK M.

Enlisted in Buncombe County on or about February 26, 1863, for the war. Mustered in as Sergeant Major. Reported present in March-December, 1863. Elected 3rd Lieutenant of Company A of this regiment on January 11, 1864, and transferred.

HAMBY, LEANDER S.

Previously served as Sergeant in Company I of this regiment. Appointed Sergeant Major on January 21, 1864, and transferred to the Field and Staff. Furloughed for twenty-two days on April 5, 1864. Reported absent without leave on April 30, 1864. Returned to duty on May 24, 1864. Reported absent sick on August 15, 1864. Last reported in the records of this company on December 1, 1864.

QUARTERMASTER SERGEANT

ALEXANDER, BENJAMIN JULIUS

Previously served as Quartermaster Sergeant of Company I of this regiment. Transferred to the Field and Staff in March-April, 1863. Reported present or accounted for on surviving company muster rolls from March 1, 1863, through August 31, 1864. Transferred to Company E, 58th Regiment N.C. Troops, when the 58th and 60th Regiments were consolidated on April 9, 1865. Served as Private in that company.

COMMISSARY SERGEANT

KING, MERRIDA D.

Previously served as Private in Company A of this regiment. Detailed as acting Commissary Sergeant and transferred to the Field and Staff on September 1, 1863. Reported present or accounted for on surviving company muster rolls through June 30, 1864. Transferred back to Company A in July-August, 1864.

ORDNANCE SERGEANTS

JONES, JAMES

Previously served as Private in Company B of this regiment. Appointed Ordnance Sergeant prior to May 1, 1863, and transferred to the Field and Staff. Reported present or accounted for in March-December, 1863. Furloughed for twenty days on or about January 10, 1864. Reported absent without leave on February 11, 1864. Dropped from the company rolls (presumably for desertion) in May-June, 1864.

ROBESON, THOMAS F.

Served as 1st Sergeant of Company K of this regiment. Detailed as acting Ordnance Sergeant on March 1, 1864, and transferred to the

Field and Staff. Appointed Ordnance Sergeant in May-June, 1864, to rank from February 11, 1864, and assigned to permanent duty with the Field and Staff. Reported present through August 31, 1864. No further records.

HOSPITAL STEWARD

ALEXANDER, JAMES M.

Previously served as Private in Company F of this regiment. Appointed Hospital Steward on March 20, 1863, and transferred to the Field and Staff. Reported present in November, 1863-August, 1864. Reported on duty in hospital at Atlanta, Georgia, September 17, 1864. No further records.

HENSLEY, FULTON

Place and date of enlistment not reported. Reported on duty as "Steward" in July-October, 1863. No further records. [Served also as Private in Yarbrough's Company, Smith County Texas Light Infantry Regiment, and as 1st Sergeant of Company H, 4th Regiment Kentucky Mounted Infantry.]

CHIEF MUSICIAN

RANDAL, JAMES M.

Previously served as Chief Musician (Drum Major) of Company A of this regiment. Transferred to the Field and Staff in May-June, 1863. Promoted to Sergeant prior to November 1, 1863, and transferred back to Company A.

COMPANY A

This company, known also as the "Buncombe Light Artillery," was raised in Buncombe County in the winter of 1861-1862. It was mustered into state service at Asheville on April 12, 1862, as "First Company," McDowell's Battalion N.C. Infantry (known also as the 6th Battalion N.C. Infantry). The seven-company battalion was mustered into Confederate service on August 1, 1862, and redesignated the 1st Battalion N.C. Infantry. On October 8, 1862, the 60th Regiment N.C. Troops was formally organized after three additional companies were assigned to the 1st Battalion. This company was designated Company A. After joining the regiment the company functioned as a part of the regiment, and its history for the remainder of the war is reported as a part of the regimental history.

The following roster was compiled primarily from information in the microfilm edition of the Compiled Service Records of Soldiers Who Served in Organizations from the State of North Carolina (Record Group 109, M270), National Archives and Records Administration, Washington, D.C. Record Group 109 includes enlistment papers, pay vouchers, requisitions, letters of resignation, discharge certificates, and abstracts of medical and prisoner of war returns. Materials relating specifically to this company include a muster-in and descriptive roll dated April 12, 1862, and muster rolls dated November, 1862-August, 1864.

Also utilized in this roster were *The War of the Rebellion: A Compilation of the Official Records of the Union and Confederate Armies*, the North Carolina adjutant general's *Roll of Honor*, state militia records, newspaper casualty lists and obituaries, wartime claims for bounty pay and allowances, postwar registers of claims for artificial limbs, Confederate pension applications filed with the states of North Carolina, Tennessee, and Florida, Confederate Soldiers' Home records, and the 1860 and 1870 federal censuses of North Carolina. A search was made also for relevant letters, diaries, reminiscences, and other manuscripts in the Southern Historical Collection (University of North Carolina-Chapel Hill), the Duke University Library Special Collections Department, and the North Carolina Division of Archives and History.

Among the secondary sources consulted were records of the North Carolina division of the United Daughters of the Confederacy, postwar rosters, regimental and county histories, marriage bond, will, and cemetery indexes, published and unpublished genealogies, biographical dictionaries, the North Carolina *County Heritage Book* series, the *Confederate Veteran*, Walter Clark's *Histories of the Several Regiments and Battalions from North Carolina in the Great War, 1861-'65*, and the North Carolina volume of the extended edition of *Confederate Military History*.

OFFICERS

CAPTAINS

HARDY, WASHINGTON MORRIS

Previously served as 1st Lieutenant of Company E, 1st Regiment N.C. Infantry (6 months, 1861). Appointed Captain of this company on January 27, 1862. Reported present in November-December, 1862. Appointed Major on March 1, 1863, to rank from February 21, 1863, and transferred to the Field and Staff of this regiment. Later served as Colonel of this regiment.

WEAVER, JAMES THOMAS

Born in Buncombe County on November 30, 1828. Resided in Buncombe County and was by occupation a farmer prior to enlisting in Buncombe County at age 33. Elected 2nd Lieutenant on April 12, 1862. Promoted to 1st Lieutenant on August 1, 1862. Promoted to Captain on March 1, 1863. Reported present in March-October, 1863. Reported on duty as acting Major of the regiment in July-October, 1863. Appointed Major and transferred to the Field and Staff of this regiment on October 27, 1863, because of "his cool and gallant conduct in the late Battle of Chickamauga and for his peculiar fitness for filling the position with competency and credit." Later served as Lieutenant Colonel of this regiment. [Previously served as Captain in the 108th Regiment N.C. Militia.]

TOMS, MARION C.

Previously served as Private in Company E, 1st Regiment N.C. Infantry (6 months, 1861). Enlisted in this company in Buncombe County on May 6, 1862, for the war. Mustered in as Sergeant. Promoted to 1st Sergeant on November 24, 1862. Wounded slightly in the heel at Murfreesboro, Tennessee, January 2, 1863. Returned to duty prior to March 1, 1863. Appointed 2nd Lieutenant on July 1, 1863. Reported present through October 31, 1863. Promoted to Captain on October 27, 1863. Reported present in November, 1863-February, 1864. Furloughed for twenty-five days on April 23, 1864. Returned to duty in May-June, 1864. Reported present through August 31, 1864. No further records. Survived the war. [Was reported in command of Company K of this regiment in January-February, 1864.]

LIEUTENANTS

COOPER, ROBERT W., 1st Lieutenant

Resided in Buncombe County where he enlisted on April 12, 1862. Mustered in as Private. Reported present in November, 1862-April, 1863. Elected 3rd Lieutenant on May 4, 1863. Reported present in May-December, 1863. Promoted to 2nd Lieutenant on October 27, 1863. Promoted to 1st Lieutenant on December 10, 1863. Furloughed on February 19, 1864. Reported present and in command of the company in March-April, 1864. Wounded in the right lung, right hip, and left knee at Kolb's Farm, near Marietta, Georgia, June 22, 1864. Reported absent wounded through September 20, 1864. No further records. Survived the war. [Was about 27 years of age at time of enlistment. Probably served in an unofficial capacity as Surgeon of this company and later of the 60th Regiment from the summer of 1862 until about January-March, 1863.]

DEAVER, WILLIAM HARRY, 1st Lieutenant

Born in Blount County, Tennessee, and was by occupation a farmer. Elected 1st Lieutenant of this company at age 30, April 12, 1862. Elected Major on August 1, 1862, and transferred to the Field and Staff of this regiment. Later served as Lieutenant Colonel of this regiment.

FOX, JAMES L., 3rd Lieutenant

Enlisted in this company on April 12, 1862. Mustered in as Private. Elected 3rd Lieutenant on August 1, 1862. Resigned on January 29, 1863, after charges were preferred against him for "using language unbecoming an officer and soldier." Resignation accepted on February 11, 1863.

ISRAEL, PLEASANT, 1st Lieutenant

Born in Buncombe County where he resided as a farmer prior to enlisting in Buncombe County at age 46. Elected 3rd Lieutenant on April 12, 1862. Promoted to 2nd Lieutenant on August 1, 1862. Reported present and in command of the company in January-June, 1863. Promoted to 1st Lieutenant on March 1, 1863. Detailed to "collect recruits" on July 24, 1863. Reported absent on detail through October 31, 1863. Resigned on November 17, 1863, because he was "not physically able to discharge properly and in an efficient manner active duties in [the] field." Resignation accepted on or about December 23, 1863. [A surgeon's affidavit dated November 17, 1863, states that he was suffering from "chronic irritation of the bronchial mucous membrane of 25 years' standing produced in my opinion by exposure."]

LINDSEY, JOHN GREEN, 2nd Lieutenant

Born in Spartanburg District, South Carolina, February 22, 1835. Resided in Buncombe County and was by occupation a tinner prior to enlisting in Buncombe County at age 27, April 12, 1862. Mustered in as Private. Promoted to Sergeant prior to November 24, 1862. Reported present in November, 1862-December, 1863. Promoted to 1st Sergeant on February 18, 1863. Elected 2nd Lieutenant on February 1, 1864. Wounded in the right thigh at Rocky Face Ridge, Georgia, February 25, 1864. Returned to duty prior to June 22, 1864, when he was wounded in the right breast (sixth rib fractured) at Kolb's Farm, near Marietta, Georgia. Returned to duty prior to September 1, 1864. Reported present on March 25, 1865. No further records. Survived the war. [North Carolina pension records indicate that he was wounded in the left side of the head above the ear on an unspecified date.]

MILLER, FRANK M., 3rd Lieutenant

Previously served as Sergeant Major of this regiment. Elected 3rd Lieutenant of this company on January 11, 1864. Reported on detail at Mobile, Alabama, through April 30, 1864. Reported for duty with the company prior to June 22, 1864, when he was wounded at Kolb's Farm, near Marietta, Georgia. Reported absent wounded through August 31, 1864. No further records.

NONCOMMISSIONED OFFICERS AND PRIVATES

ALEXANDER, AVERY, Private

Born in Haywood County and was by occupation a carpenter prior to enlisting in Buncombe County at age 42, April 12, 1862. Reported sick in hospital in November, 1862-April, 1863. Returned to duty in May-June, 1863. Reported present in July-October, 1863. Reported on detail "on special duty" in November-December, 1863. Rejoined the company in January-February, 1864. Reported present through June 30, 1864. Reported present but on daily duty with the medical department in July-August, 1864. No further records.

ALEXANDER, J. E., Private

Enlisted in Wake County on May 16, 1863, for the war. Reported present through June 30, 1863. Was reportedly transferred to the 28th Regiment N.C. Troops prior to November 1, 1863; however, records of the 28th Regiment do not indicate that he served therein.

ALEXANDER, JOHN L., Private

Born in Haywood County on June 10, 1845. Was by occupation a farmer prior to enlisting in Buncombe County at age 16, May 3, 1862, for the war. Captured at Murfreesboro, Tennessee, January 2, 1863. Hospitalized at St. Louis, Missouri, January 24, 1863. Died at St. Louis on January 29, 1863, of "typhoid fever."

ALLEN, WILLIAM E., ———

North Carolina pension records indicate that he served in this company.

ARROWOOD, HUGHEY G., Private

Born in Buncombe County where he resided as a farmer or farm laborer prior to enlisting in Buncombe County at age 23, April 12, 1862. Transferred to Company I of this regiment on or about August 1, 1862.

ARROWOOD, ROBERT D., Private

Born in Buncombe County and was by occupation a farmer prior to enlisting in Buncombe County at age 30, May 3, 1862, for the war. Transferred to Company I of this regiment on August 1, 1862.

ATKIN, THOMAS S., 1st Sergeant

Born in Buncombe County and was by occupation a printer prior to enlisting in Buncombe County at age 17, July 10, 1862, for the war. Mustered in as 1st Sergeant. Dropped from the company rolls subsequent to August 1, 1862. Reason he was dropped not reported. Later served as Sergeant in Company K, 11th Regiment N.C. Troops (1st Regiment N.C. Volunteers).

ATKIN, WILLIAM N., Private

Born in Buncombe County and was by occupation a blacksmith prior to enlisting in Buncombe County at age 15, April 12, 1862.

Died at Murfreesboro, Tennessee, November 19, 1862. Cause of death not reported.

BEACHBOARD, MATTHEW A., Private

Born in Buncombe County and was by occupation a farmer prior to enlisting in Buncombe County at age 26, April 12, 1862. Hospitalized at Dalton, Georgia, December 30, 1862, with dyspepsia. Returned to duty on February 2, 1863. Reported present through October 31, 1863. Reported absent "on special duty" in November-December, 1863. Rejoined the company in January-February, 1864. Reported present through April 30, 1864. Captured at Kolb's Farm, near Marietta, Georgia, June 22, 1864. Sent to Nashville, Tennessee. Transferred to Louisville, Kentucky, where he arrived on July 13, 1864. Transferred to Camp Morton, Indianapolis, Indiana, where he arrived on July 14, 1864. Paroled at Camp Morton and transferred to City Point, Virginia, March 4, 1865. Received at Boulware's and Cox's Wharves, James River, Virginia, March 10-12, 1865, for exchange. No further records.

BLACKWELL, ZACHARIAH B., Private

Born in Washington County, Tennessee, and was by occupation a farmer prior to enlisting in Buncombe County at age 23, May 7, 1862, for the war. Reported sick in hospital in November-December, 1862. Died in hospital at Tullahoma, Tennessee, January 30, 1863. Cause of death not reported.

BRADLEY, JAMES D., Private

Born in Buncombe County where he resided as a farmer or farm laborer prior to enlisting in Buncombe County at age 22, May 3, 1862, for the war. Deserted in July, 1862. Transferred to Company I of this regiment on or about August 1, 1862, while listed as a deserter. Returned to duty on an unspecified date. Transferred back to this company prior to December 12, 1862, when he deserted. Returned from desertion on February 21, 1863. Hospitalized at Dalton, Georgia, April 1, 1863, with diarrhoea. Deserted on April 14, 1863.

BRIDGES, HOUSEN NEWTON, Private

Born in South Carolina and resided in Buncombe County where he was by occupation a farmer prior to enlisting in Buncombe County at age 19, April 12, 1862. Wounded in the leg and captured at Murfreesboro, Tennessee, January 2, 1863. Died in hospital at Murfreesboro on February 22, 1863, presumably of wounds.

BRITTAIN, WILLIAM H., Private

Born in Buncombe County and was by occupation a farmer prior to enlisting in Buncombe County at age 19, April 12, 1862. Reported present through August 1, 1862. No further records.

BUCKNER, NIMROD, Private

Born in Buncombe County on February 14, 1840. Was by occupation a farmer prior to enlisting in Buncombe County at age 22, May 7, 1862, for the war. Reported present in November-December, 1862. Reported sick in hospital in January-February, 1863. Returned to duty in March-April, 1863. Reported present in May-June, 1863. Hospitalized on an unspecified date. Furloughed prior to November 1, 1863. Returned to duty prior to January 1, 1864. Reported present in January-February, 1864. Detailed as a provost guard on March 1, 1864. Sent to hospital at Atlanta, Georgia, July 1, 1864. Returned to duty prior to August 31, 1864, when he was reported on duty as a provost guard. Transferred to Company E, 58th Regiment N.C. Troops, when the 58th and 60th Regiments were consolidated on April 9, 1865.

CAPPS, JOHN E., Private

Born in Henderson County and was by occupation a farmer prior to enlisting in Buncombe County at age 18, April 12, 1862. Hospitalized at Dalton, Georgia, November 21, 1862, with chronic rheumatism. Returned to duty on December 11, 1862. Reported sick in hospital on December 31, 1862. Returned to duty in January-February, 1863. Reported sick in hospital in March-April, 1863. Died at Tullahoma, Tennessee, April 30, 1863. Cause of death not reported.

CLARK, WILLIAM M., Private

Born in Buncombe County and was by occupation a farmer prior to enlisting in Buncombe County at age 28, April 16, 1862, for the war. Hospitalized at Dalton, Georgia, November 21, 1862, with intermittent fever. Deserted on December 1, 1862. Reported absent sick in January-February, 1863. Returned to duty in March-April, 1863. Reported present through February 29, 1864. Granted a sick furlough of thirty days on April 7, 1864. Reported absent on furlough through August 31, 1864. No further records.

COCHE, JOHN W., Private

Previously served as Private in Company E, 1st Regiment N.C. Infantry (6 months, 1861). Enlisted in this company in Buncombe County on April 12, 1862. Reported present from November 1, 1862, through August 31, 1864. Transferred to Company E, 58th Regiment N.C. Troops, when the 58th and 60th Regiments were consolidated on April 9, 1865. [His Tennessee pension application indicates that he was wounded in the left hip on an unspecified date.]

COLE, FRANCIS MARION, Private

Born in Buncombe County and was by occupation a farmer prior to enlisting in Buncombe County at age 29, May 3, 1862, for the war. Hospitalized at Dalton, Georgia, December 30, 1862, with intermittent fever. Furloughed from hospital subsequent to June 30, 1863. Returned to duty prior to November 1, 1863. Captured at Missionary Ridge, Tennessee, November 25, 1863. Sent to Nashville, Tennessee. Transferred to Louisville, Kentucky, where he arrived on January 10, 1864. Transferred to Rock Island, Illinois, where he arrived on January 29, 1864. Released at Rock Island on or about October 15, 1864, after taking the Oath of Allegiance and joining the U.S. Army. Assigned to Company D, 3rd Regiment U.S. Volunteer Infantry.

COOK, WILLIAM S., Private

Born in Buncombe County and was by occupation a farmer prior to enlisting in Buncombe County at age 18, April 12, 1862. Hospitalized at Dalton, Georgia, December 30, 1862, with remittent fever. Returned to duty on January 5, 1863. Reported present through February 28, 1863. Hospitalized at Dalton on April 1, 1863, with chronic diarrhoea. Furloughed for thirty days on May 19, 1863. Returned to duty in November-December, 1863. Reported present through April 30, 1864. Detailed as a wagoner in May-June, 1864. Furloughed on surgeon's certificate of disability on August 28, 1864. No further records. Survived the war.

CURTIS, THOMAS, Private

Born in Buncombe County and was by occupation a farmer prior to enlisting in Buncombe County at age 28, May 5, 1862, for the war. Transferred to Company I of this regiment on August 1, 1862. Transferred back to this company on or about September 13, 1862. Deserted on September 14, 1862. Captured by the enemy at Warm Springs (Madison County) on October 25, 1863. Sent to Camp

Nelson, Kentucky. Transferred to Camp Chase, Ohio, where he arrived on November 14, 1863. Transferred to Rock Island, Illinois, where he arrived on January 24, 1864. Released at Rock Island on October 17, 1864, after taking the Oath of Allegiance and joining the U.S. Army. Assigned to Company F, 3rd Regiment U.S. Volunteer Infantry.

DINGLER, JOHN J., Private

Previously served as Corporal in Company E, 1st Regiment N.C. Infantry (6 months, 1861). Enlisted in this company in Buncombe County at age 39, January 1, 1863, for the war. Died in hospital at Tullahoma, Tennessee, January 6, 1863. Cause of death not reported.

EDWARDS, DANIEL G., Private

Born in Rutherford County and was by occupation a farmer prior to enlisting in Buncombe County at age 21, May 10, 1862, for the war. Reported present or accounted for from November 1, 1862, through August 31, 1864. Wounded in the left femur at Jonesborough, Georgia, August 31, 1864. Reported in hospital at Macon, Georgia, November 2, 1864. No further records. Survived the war.

EDWARDS, J. H. T., ———

North Carolina pension records indicate that he served in this company.

ELKINS, WILBURN W., Private

Born in Yancey County and was by occupation a farmer prior to enlisting in Buncombe County at age 23, May 7, 1862, for the war. Deserted on December 8, 1862. Returned to duty on May 1, 1863. Reported absent sick in hospital in July-October, 1863. Died in hospital prior to December 31, 1863. Place, date, and cause of death not reported.

ENLOE, B. M., Private

Enlisted at Tullahoma, Tennessee, February 18, 1863, for the war. Died at Ringgold, Georgia, April 22, 1863. Cause of death not reported.

ENSLEY, ALFRED, Private

Born in Buncombe County where he resided as a farmer prior to enlisting in Buncombe County at age 30, April 12, 1862. Reported sick in hospital in November, 1862-February, 1863. Returned to duty in March-April, 1863. Reported present in May-June, 1863. Reported sick in hospital at Marion, Mississippi, in July-October, 1863. Returned to duty in November-December, 1863. Reported present in January-February, 1864. Detailed as a teamster on April 30, 1864. Reported absent on detail through August 31, 1864. Transferred to Company E, 58th Regiment N.C. Troops, when the 58th and 60th Regiments were consolidated on April 9, 1865.

ENSLEY, ERWIN, Private

Resided in Buncombe County and was by occupation a farmer prior to enlisting in Buncombe County at age 31, May 13, 1862, for the war. Reported present from November 1, 1862, through June 30, 1863. Reported on duty as a teamster from January 1 through May 24, 1863. Deserted subsequent to June 30, 1863. Returned to duty on October 3, 1863. Reported present through August 31, 1864. No further records.

FORE, FIDELIO, Private

Born in Buncombe County where he resided as a farmer prior to enlisting in Buncombe County at age 33, April 12, 1862. Sent to hospital on an unspecified date. Furloughed prior to January 1, 1863. Returned to duty on an unspecified date. Reported present in March-April, 1863. Reported sick in hospital in May-June, 1863. Deserted in July-October, 1863. Returned from desertion on April 1, 1864, and was court-martialed. Reported sick in hospital in April, 1864. Returned to duty on an unspecified date. Reported present in July-August, 1864. Hospitalized at Greensboro in March, 1865. No further records. Survived the war.

FORE, PETER, Private

Born in Buncombe County where he resided as a farmer prior to enlisting in Buncombe County at age 36, April 12, 1862. Mustered in as Corporal. Hospitalized at Dalton, Georgia, November 21, 1862, with intermittent fever. Deserted on December 1, 1862. Reduced to ranks on January 1, 1863. Returned to duty prior to March 1, 1863. Reported present in March-October, 1863. Deserted on November 27, 1863. Reported under arrest in March-April, 1864. Returned to duty on May 7, 1864. Captured at or near Peachtree Creek, near Atlanta, Georgia, on or about July 20, 1864. Sent to Nashville, Tennessee. Transferred to Louisville, Kentucky, where he arrived on July 28, 1864. Transferred to Camp Douglas, Chicago, Illinois, where he arrived on August 1, 1864. Released at Camp Douglas on June 16, 1865, after taking the Oath of Allegiance.

FREEMAN, FELIX M., Private

Enlisted in Buncombe County on an unknown date (probably in March-April, 1863). Died on April 22, 1863. Place and cause of death not reported. [Previously served as Captain in the 108th Regiment N.C. Militia.]

FREEMAN, ROBERTSON GASTON, Private

Born in Rutherford County, Tennessee, March 2, 1836. Resided in Buncombe County and was by occupation a farmer prior to enlisting in Buncombe County at age 26, May 7, 1862, for the war. Mustered in as Sergeant. Deserted on December 15, 1862. Reduced to ranks prior to January 1, 1863. Returned to duty subsequent to February 28, 1863. Died at Tullahoma, Tennessee, April 22, 1863, of "fever." [Previously served as 2nd Lieutenant in the 108th Regiment N.C. Militia.]

GARRISON, JACOB M., Sergeant

Born in Buncombe County where he resided as a farmer prior to enlisting in Buncombe County at age 18, April 12, 1862. Mustered in as Private. Reported present in November, 1862-February, 1863. Reported sick in hospital in March-April, 1863. Promoted to Sergeant on May 1, 1863. Reported present in May-June, 1863. Reported sick in hospital in July-October, 1863. Returned to duty in November-December, 1863. Reported present in January-February, 1864. Furloughed for twenty-four days on April 4, 1864. Returned to duty prior to June 22, 1864, when he was killed at Kolb's Farm, near Marietta, Georgia.

GARRISON, THOMAS J., Private

Born in Buncombe County where he resided as a farmer prior to enlisting in Buncombe County at age 33, May 7, 1862, for the war. Mustered in as Corporal. Wounded in the hand at Murfreesboro, Tennessee, January 2, 1863. Hospitalized at Dalton, Georgia. Reported absent wounded through August 31, 1864. Reduced to ranks in January-February, 1864. No further records. Survived the war.

GENTRY, WILLIAM S., Private

Born in Buncombe County where he resided as a farmer prior to enlisting in Buncombe County at age 24, May 7, 1862, for the war.

Sent to hospital on an unspecified date. "Went home without leave" prior to January 1, 1863. Listed as a deserter in January-February, 1863. Returned to duty in March-April, 1863. Reported present in May-June, 1863. Reported sick in hospital at Kingston, Georgia, in July-August, 1863. Furloughed from hospital at Rome, Georgia, in September-October, 1863. Reported absent on furlough in November-December, 1863. Died in January, 1864, of "chronic diarrhoea." Place of death not reported.

GREEN, W. J., Corporal

Place and date of enlistment not reported (probably enlisted in November-December, 1862). Promotion record not reported. Wounded and captured at Murfreesboro, Tennessee, December 31, 1862-January 2, 1863. Died at Murfreesboro on January 11, 1863, of wounds.

HAIR, THOMAS, Private

Resided in Buncombe County and was by occupation a farm laborer prior to enlisting in Buncombe County at age 40, January 1, 1863, for the war. Reported present in January-February, 1863. Reported sick in hospital in March-April, 1863. Reported present in May-June, 1863. Wounded in the abdomen, hip, and thigh at Chickamauga, Georgia, September 20, 1863. Died at Atlanta, Georgia, October 16, 1863, of wounds.

HALL, ABRAHAM C., Private

Born in Haywood County where he resided as a farmer prior to enlisting in Buncombe County at age 29, April 12, 1862. Hospitalized at Dalton, Georgia, December 30, 1862, with typhoid fever. Returned to duty on February 2, 1863; however, he was reported sick in hospital through April 30, 1863. Listed as a deserter in May-June, 1863. Returned from desertion on January 13, 1864. Reported present in May-August, 1864. No further records. Survived the war.

HAREN, ARCHIBALD L., Corporal

Born in Buncombe County where he resided as a farmer prior to enlisting in Buncombe County at age 17, April 12, 1862. Mustered in as Private. Reported present in November-December, 1862. Reported sick in hospital in January-February, 1863. Reported present in March-April, 1863. Promoted to Corporal on May 1, 1863. Reported present in May-October, 1863. Captured at Missionary Ridge, Tennessee, November 25, 1863. Sent to Nashville, Tennessee. Transferred to Louisville, Kentucky, where he arrived on December 7, 1863. Transferred to Rock Island, Illinois, where he arrived on December 9, 1863. Released at Rock Island on October 17, 1864, after joining the U.S. Army. Assigned to Company F, 3rd Regiment U.S. Volunteer Infantry.

HAVNER, GEORGE F., Private

Born in Lincoln County and was by occupation a farmer prior to enlisting in Buncombe County at age 30, April 12, 1862. Hospitalized at Dalton, Georgia, December 30, 1862, with intermittent fever. Returned to duty on January 13, 1863. Reported present through June 30, 1863. Reported absent sick in July-December, 1863. Reported sick in hospital at Asheville in January-February, 1864. Returned to duty in March-April, 1864. Hospitalized on an unspecified date. Furloughed on May 16, 1864. Died prior to February 14, 1865. Place, date, and cause of death not reported.

HEMPHILL, J. T., ——

North Carolina pension records indicate that he served in this company.

HENDERSON, EZEKIEL, Private

Previously served as Private in Company E, 1st Regiment N.C. Infantry (6 months, 1861). Enlisted in this company in Buncombe County on April 12, 1862. Paid for service through August 1, 1862. No further records. [Born in Greenville District, South Carolina, and was by occupation a mechanic. May have served later as Private in Company K, 11th Regiment N.C. Troops (1st Regiment N.C. Volunteers).]

HUGHES, JOHN, Sergeant

Born in County Antrim, Ireland, and resided in Buncombe County where he was by occupation a farmer prior to enlisting in Buncombe County at age 51, April 12, 1862. Mustered in as Sergeant. Paid for service through August 1, 1862. No further records.

HUGHEY, SAMUEL, Private

Born in Buncombe County and was by occupation a farmer prior to enlisting in Buncombe County at age 32, May 1, 1862, for the war. Reported present in November-December, 1862. Died on an unspecified date in 1863. Place and cause of death not reported.

HUGHEY, WILLIAM, Private

Born in Buncombe County and was by occupation a farmer prior to enlisting in Buncombe County on April 12, 1862. Reported absent on detached service (probably as a teamster) in November, 1862-February, 1863. Reported on duty as a teamster in March-April, 1863. Reported present in May-October, 1863. Reported absent on detail "on special duty" in November-December, 1863. Reported present in January-June, 1864. Captured at or near Peachtree Creek, near Atlanta, Georgia, on or about July 20, 1864. Sent to Nashville, Tennessee. Transferred to Louisville, Kentucky, where he arrived on July 28, 1864. Transferred to Camp Douglas, Chicago, Illinois, where he arrived on August 1, 1864. Released at Camp Douglas on March 26, 1865, after taking the Oath of Allegiance and joining the U.S. Army. Assigned to Company F, 6th Regiment U.S. Volunteer Infantry. [Was 22 years of age when he joined the U.S. Army.]

HYATT, SAMUEL J., Private

Born in Buncombe County and was by occupation a farmer prior to enlisting in Buncombe County at age 33, April 12, 1862. Reported sick in hospital in November-December, 1862. Returned to duty in January-February, 1863. Reported present in March-April, 1863. Transferred to Company C of this regiment on June 1, 1863.

INGLE, LEVI, Private

Born in Rutherford County and resided in Madison County where he was by occupation a farmer prior to enlisting in Buncombe County at age 42, April 12, 1862. Reported present in November, 1862-June, 1864. Reported present but on detail in July-August, 1864. Captured at Liberty, Tennessee, December 17, 1864. Sent to Nashville, Tennessee. Transferred to Louisville, Kentucky, where he arrived on January 2, 1865. Transferred to Camp Chase, Ohio, where he arrived on January 6, 1865. Released at Camp Chase on March 21, 1865, after taking the Oath of Allegiance.

JAMES, JAMES E., Private

Born in Buncombe County and was by occupation a farmer prior to enlisting in Buncombe County at age 21, April 24, 1862, for the war. Wounded in the right heel at Murfreesboro, Tennessee, December 31, 1862. Hospitalized at Dalton, Georgia. Returned to duty on or about February 28, 1863. Reported sick in hospital in March-April, 1863. Returned to duty in May-June, 1863. Sent to hospital at Dalton on August 16, 1863. Furloughed from hospital in November-December, 1863. Transferred to Company F of this regiment on January 1, 1864.

JESTES, JAMES N., Private

Born in Buncombe County and was by occupation a farmer prior to enlisting in Buncombe County at age 23, April 12, 1862. Reported present in November, 1862-June, 1863. Deserted prior to November 1, 1863. Apprehended on an unspecified date. Court-martialed on February 12, 1864, and sentenced to be shot. No further records. [May have escaped execution and served later as Private in Company B, 2nd Regiment N.C. Mounted Infantry (Union). His correct surname may be Justice, Justus, or Jester.]

JONES, JAMES A., Private

Born in Buncombe County where he resided as a farmer prior to enlisting in Buncombe County at age 24, May 3, 1862, for the war. Reported present in November, 1862-October, 1863. Deserted on November 21, 1863. Went over to the enemy on an unspecified date. Confined at Knoxville, Tennessee, June 30, 1864. Released at Knoxville on July 1, 1864, after taking the Oath of Allegiance.

JONES, JOSEPH H., Private

Born in Buncombe County where he resided as a farmer prior to enlisting in Buncombe County at age 15, May 3, 1862, for the war. Reported present in November-December, 1862. Reported sick in hospital in January-February, 1863. Died at Ringgold, Georgia, March 23, 1863. Cause of death not reported.

KING, JOHN M., Private

Born in Buncombe County where he resided as a farmer prior to enlisting in Buncombe County at age 29, May 5, 1862, for the war. Reported present or accounted for in November, 1862-June, 1863. Deserted prior to November 1, 1863. Returned to duty on June 4, 1864. Deserted near Atlanta, Georgia, August 13, 1864.

KING, MERRIDA D., Private

Born in Stokes County and was by occupation a clerk prior to enlisting in Buncombe County at age 22, May 5, 1862, for the war. Reported present in November, 1862-June, 1863. Detailed as acting Commissary Sergeant and transferred to the Field and Staff of this regiment on September 1, 1863. Transferred back to this company in July-August, 1864. No further records.

KING, SAMUEL G., Private

Born in Stokes County and was by occupation a farmer prior to enlisting in Buncombe County at age 17, May 5, 1862, for the war. Reported present in November, 1862-October, 1863. Captured at Missionary Ridge, Tennessee, November 25, 1863. Sent to Nashville, Tennessee. Transferred to Louisville, Kentucky, where he arrived on December 7, 1863. Transferred to Rock Island, Illinois, where he arrived on December 9, 1863. Transferred to New Orleans, Louisiana, May 3, 1865. Released on May 23, 1865.

KING, WILLIAM E., Private

Born in Buncombe County and was by occupation a farmer prior to enlisting in Buncombe County at age 22, May 5, 1862, for the war. Reported present in November, 1862-June, 1863. Reported sick in hospital in July-October, 1863. Hospitalized at Griffin, Georgia, November 1, 1863, with an unspecified complaint. Returned to duty in January-February, 1864. Reported present in

March-June, 1864. Deserted near Atlanta, Georgia, August 13, 1864.

KING, WILY D., Private

Enlisted in Buncombe County at age 21, May 5, 1862, for the war. Reported present in November-December, 1862. Reported sick in hospital in January-April, 1863. Returned to duty in May-June, 1863. Reported present through December 31, 1863. Detailed as a pioneer on February 12, 1864. Rejoined the company in March-April, 1864. Reported present in May-August, 1864. No further records. Survived the war.

KNIGHT, ELIJAH P., Private

Born in Buncombe County and was by occupation a mechanic prior to enlisting in Buncombe County at age 33, May 3, 1862, for the war. Accidentally killed at Murfreesboro, Tennessee, October 21, 1862. "E. P. Knight was killed instantly, and Jno. Metcalf [Medcalf] severely wounded. The boys were both in the ordnance department cleaning guns, when a gun in the hands of another man was . . . discharged, the load passing through Knight's head and into Metcalf's shoulder. Poor fellows! Knight died without a struggle. . . . We were going to send Knight's body home, but find it impracticable–we will bury him today with the honors of war." [Letter from 1st Lt. James T. Weaver, Company A, 60th Regiment N.C. Troops, published in the *Asheville News*, November 6, 1862.]

LEMING, RUFUS, Private

Born in Haywood County and was by occupation a millwright or mechanic prior to enlisting in Buncombe County at age 32, May 5, 1862, for the war. Transferred to Company I of this regiment on August 1, 1862. Transferred back to this company on or about September 13, 1862. Hospitalized at Dalton, Georgia, December 31, 1862, with icterus. Returned to duty on January 8, 1863. Detailed as a wheelwright in March-June, 1863. Reported sick in hospital at Marion, Mississippi, in July-August, 1863. Reported sick in hospital in September, 1863-February, 1864. Died (possibly at Brandon, Mississippi) prior to July 1, 1864, of disease.

LETSINGER, THOMAS D., Private

Born in Knox County, Tennessee, and was by occupation a farmer prior to enlisting in Buncombe County at age 19, April 12, 1862. Reported present in November, 1862-April, 1863. Deserted in May-June, 1863.

LINDSEY, GEORGE WASHINGTON, Sergeant

Born in Buncombe County on January 17, 1840. Resided in Buncombe County and was by occupation a "tuner [turner?]" prior to enlisting in Buncombe County at age 22, April 12, 1862. Mustered in as Private. Reported sick in hospital in November-December, 1862. Reported present in January, 1863-April, 1864. Promoted to Sergeant in January, 1864. Appointed Ensign (1st Lieutenant) on May 13, 1864, to rank from April 28, 1864, and transferred to the Field and Staff of this regiment. [A letter of recommendation dated April 6, 1864, and signed by Colonel W. M. Hardy of the 60th Regiment states that "Sergt. Lindsey has borne the colors of this regiment with great credit on more than one bloody field."]

LINDSEY, WALTER B., Private

Born in Buncombe County and was by occupation a farmer prior to enlisting in Buncombe County at age 39, April 12, 1862. Reported present in November-December, 1862. Reported under arrest in January-February, 1863. Reason he was arrested not reported. Returned to duty in March-April, 1863. Reported present in May-June, 1863. Deserted prior to November 1, 1863.

LYNCH, FRANK A., Private

Born in Rutherford County and was by occupation a farmer prior to enlisting in Buncombe County at age 25, April 12, 1862. Reported sick in hospital in November-December, 1862. Deserted from hospital on January 19, 1863.

McCLURE, ALEXANDER, Private

Enlisted in Buncombe County on April 12, 1862. Transferred to Company C of this regiment on or about July 8, 1862.

McENTIRE, J. M., Private

Enlisted in Wake County on May 16, 1863, for the war. Reported present through June 30, 1863. Was reportedly transferred to the 28th Regiment N.C. Troops prior to November 1, 1863; however, records of the 28th Regiment do not indicate that he served therein. No further records. Survived the war.

MAXWELL, ISAAC H., Private

Born in Henderson County and was by occupation a farmer prior to enlisting in Buncombe County at age 22, April 12, 1862. Reported sick in hospital in November-December, 1862. Captured at Murfreesboro, Tennessee, December 31, 1862-January 2, 1863. Hospitalized at Murfreesboro where he died on January 16, 1863, of "typh[oid] fever."

MEDCALF, JOHN, Private

Born in Buncombe County and was by occupation a farmer prior to enlisting in Buncombe County at age 16, April 16, 1862, for the war. "Severely wounded" in an accident at Murfreesboro, Tennessee, October 21, 1862. (Pvt. Elijah P. Knight of this company was "killed instantly" at the same time.) "The boys were both in the ordnance department cleaning guns, when a gun in the hands of another man was . . . discharged, the load passing through Knight's head and Metcalf's [sic] shoulder. Poor fellows! Knight died without a struggle. Metcalf is in the hospital, well cared for. I don't think he will die." [Letter dated October 22, 1862, from 1st Lt. James T. Weaver, Company A, 60th Regiment N.C. Troops, published in the *Asheville News*, November 6, 1862.] Deserted from hospital prior to May 1, 1863.

MILLER, NATHAN A., Private

Resided in Buncombe County and was by occupation a farm laborer prior to enlisting in Buncombe County at age 27, April 12, 1862. Reported present in November, 1862-June, 1863. Deserted prior to November 1, 1863. Returned from desertion on April 1, 1864, and was court-martialed. Returned to duty prior to May 1, 1864. Wounded at Kolb's Farm, near Marietta, Georgia, June 22, 1864. Deserted near Atlanta, Georgia, August 13, 1864. [Elected 2nd Lieutenant on March 30, 1863, but was not granted a commission.]

MOONEY, GEORGE LARKIN, Private

Born in Catawba County* and was by occupation a farmer prior to enlisting in Buncombe County at age 25, May 17, 1862, for the war. Transferred to Company I of this regiment on August 1, 1862.

MORGAN, GEORGE WHITFIELD, Private

Born in Buncombe County on November 7, 1831, and was by occupation a farmer prior to enlisting in Buncombe County at age 30, May 7, 1862, for the war. Reported present in November-December, 1862. Reported absent in hospital in January-February, 1863. Detailed as a hospital nurse at Tullahoma, Tennessee, in

April, 1863. Reported on detail through June 30, 1863. Reported absent sick in July-October, 1863. Furloughed from hospital in November-December, 1863. Reported absent without leave on March 10, 1864. Appointed 1st Lieutenant of an unspecified company of the 14th Battalion N.C. Cavalry to rank from January 4, 1864. Later served as 1st Lieutenant of Company F, 69th Regiment N.C. Troops (7th Regiment N.C. Cavalry). [Previously served as 2nd Lieutenant in the 108th Regiment N.C. Militia.]

MORGAN, JOHN P., Private

Born in Buncombe County where he resided as a farmer prior to enlisting in Buncombe County at age 22, May 7, 1862, for the war. Mustered in as Corporal. Reported sick in hospital in November, 1862-April, 1863. Reduced to ranks in May-June, 1863. Detailed as a hospital nurse at Dalton, Georgia, June 1, 1863. Detailed (probably as a nurse) in hospital at La Grange, Georgia, February 4, 1864. Furloughed for twenty days on March 1, 1864. Returned to duty prior to May 1, 1864. Sent to hospital sick on May 7, 1864. Reported absent sick through August 31, 1864. No further records. [May have served briefly in 1864 as Private in Company F, 69th Regiment N.C. Troops (7th Regiment N.C. Cavalry). Records of the United Daughters of the Confederacy indicate that he was discharged on November 6, 1864, on "account of being sick." Confederate medical records indicate that he suffered during the war from chronic nephritis, chronic rheumatism, intermittent fever, extreme debility, inveterate dyspepsia, chronic gastritis, and "terrori Yankeebus."]

MORGAN, STANLEY JONES, Private

Born in Buncombe County on January 3, 1840, and was by occupation a farmer prior to enlisting in Buncombe County at age 22, May 7, 1862, for the war. Reported present in November, 1862-April, 1863. Sent to hospital sick in May-June, 1863. Listed as a deserter in July-October, 1863. Returned to duty on or about March 14, 1864. Furloughed for sixty days on April 20, 1864. Returned to duty in July-August, 1864. No further records. Survived the war.

MORGAN, WILLIAM B., Private

Resided in Henderson County. Date of enlistment not reported (probably enlisted in the late winter or early spring of 1864). Listed as a deserter on April 7, 1864. Returned to duty prior to December 5, 1864, when he deserted to the enemy. Sent to Nashville, Tennessee. Transferred to Louisville, Kentucky. Released at Louisville on or about January 29, 1865, after taking the Oath of Allegiance.

NELSON, ALEXANDER, Private

Born in Forsyth County* where he resided as a farmer prior to enlisting in Buncombe County at age 21, May 5, 1862, for the war. Reported present in November-December, 1862. Died at Tullahoma, Tennessee, prior to June 22, 1863. Date and cause of death not reported.

NORIS, JOHN F., Private

Enlisted at Dalton, Georgia, March 15, 1864, for the war. Reported present through April 30, 1864. No further records.

OWEN, DANIEL W., Sergeant

Born in Hawkins County, Tennessee, and was by occupation a carpenter prior to enlisting in Buncombe County at age 38, May 13, 1862, for the war. Mustered in as Sergeant. Reported present in November-December, 1862. Wounded slightly in the thigh at Murfreesboro, Tennessee, December 31, 1862. Returned to duty in

January-February, 1863. Reported present in March-April, 1863. Deserted prior to July 1, 1863.

PARKER, BENJAMIN F., Private

Born in Buncombe County where he resided as a farmer or farm laborer prior to enlisting in Buncombe County at age 31, May 6, 1862, for the war. Reported sick in hospital in November-December, 1862. Returned to duty in January-February, 1863. Reported present in March-April, 1863. Deserted on an unspecified date. Returned to duty on May 25, 1863. Listed as a deserter on June 30, 1863. Returned to duty on August 1, 1863. Reported present through August 31, 1864. No further records. Survived the war.

PARKER, JAMES M., Private

Born in Buncombe County where he resided as a farmer prior to enlisting in Buncombe County at age 33, July 10, 1862, for the war. Reported sick in hospital in November-December, 1862. Deserted from hospital prior to March 1, 1863. Reported sick in hospital in March-April, 1863. Deserted prior to July 1, 1863. Returned from desertion on October 20, 1863. Reported present in November, 1863-April, 1864. Captured at Kolb's Farm, near Marietta, Georgia, June 22, 1864. Sent to Nashville, Tennessee. Transferred to Louisville, Kentucky, where he arrived on July 14, 1864. Transferred to Camp Douglas, Chicago, Illinois, where he arrived on July 18, 1864. Released at Camp Douglas on May 16, 1865, after taking the Oath of Allegiance.

PARRIS, ROBERT, Private

Born in Spartanburg District, South Carolina, and was by occupation a farmer prior to enlisting in Buncombe County at age 29, April 12, 1862. Wounded severely in the hand and/or right leg at Murfreesboro, Tennessee, December 31, 1862. Hospitalized at Dalton, Georgia. Furloughed on or about February 28, 1863. Returned to duty prior to May 1, 1863. Reported present in May-October, 1863. Hospitalized on or about December 1, 1863, with chronic diarrhoea, emaciation, and debility. Furloughed for forty days on or about February 24, 1864. Reported absent on furlough through June 30, 1864. Sent to hospital sick in July-August, 1864. No further records.

PATTON, JOHN D., Corporal

Born in Haywood County and resided in Buncombe County where he was by occupation a farmer prior to enlisting in Buncombe County at age 33, May 5, 1862, for the war. Mustered in as Corporal. Reported present in November-December, 1862. No further records. Survived the war. [Previously served as 2nd Lieutenant in the 108th Regiment N.C. Militia.]

POUNDERS, WILLIAM E., Private

Previously served as Private in Company C, 39th Regiment N.C. Troops. Enlisted in this company at Jackson, Mississippi, June 15, 1863, for the war. Reported present through April 30, 1864. Wounded at Kolb's Farm, near Marietta, Georgia, June 22, 1864. Returned to duty prior to June 30, 1864. Reported present through August 31, 1864. No further records. Survived the war.

RAMSEY, JACOB E., Corporal

Born in Buncombe County and was by occupation a farmer prior to enlisting in Buncombe County at age 21, May 28, 1862, for the war. Mustered in as Private. Reported sick in hospital in November-December, 1862. Returned to duty in January-February, 1863. Promoted to Corporal on May 1, 1863. Reported present in March, 1863-February, 1864. Furloughed for thirty days on April 5, 1864. Returned to duty in May-June, 1864. Reported present through August 31, 1864. No further records.

RAMSEY, JAMES M., Private

Previously served as Private in Company F of this regiment. Transferred to this company on January 1, 1864. Reported present through February 29, 1864. Furloughed for thirty days on April 2, 1864. Returned to duty in July-August, 1864. Died at or near Augusta, Georgia, on or about September 19, 1864. Cause of death not reported.

RANDAL, JAMES M., Private

Born in Buncombe County where he resided as a farmer prior to enlisting in Buncombe County at age 21, April 16, 1862, for the war. Mustered in as Chief Musician (Drum Major). Reported present in November-December, 1862, and March-April, 1863. Transferred to the Field and Staff of this regiment in May-June, 1863. Promoted to Sergeant and transferred back to this company on an unspecified date. Deserted prior to November 1, 1863. Reduced to ranks on an unspecified date. Apprehended on an unspecified date. Court-martialed on or about April 5, 1864, and sentenced to be shot. No further records.

RANDAL, JOHN W., Private

Born in Buncombe County where he resided as a farmer prior to enlisting in Buncombe County at age 19, April 12, 1862. Reported present in November, 1862-February, 1863. Reported sick in hospital in March-April, 1863. Returned to duty in May-June, 1863. Deserted prior to November 1, 1863.

RASH, JOHN, Corporal

Born in Iredell County and was by occupation a farmer prior to enlisting in Buncombe County at age 25, May 27, 1862, for the war. Mustered in as Private. Hospitalized at Dalton, Georgia, December 31, 1862, with icterus. Returned to duty on January 8, 1863. Reported present through February 29, 1864. Promoted to Corporal on February 1, 1864. Reported present in March-August, 1864. No further records.

RASH, MUNSEY, Private

Born in Iredell County and was by occupation a farmer prior to enlisting in Buncombe County at age 20, April 12, 1862. Reported present in November, 1862-August, 1864. No further records. Survived the war. [North Carolina pension records indicate that he was wounded at "Missionary Ridge, Tennessee, April 1, 1863."]

RENO, JOHN ED., Corporal

Born in Buncombe County and was by occupation a farmer prior to enlisting in Buncombe County at age 16, April 12, 1862. Mustered in as Private. Reported sick in hospital in November, 1862-February, 1863. Returned to duty in March-April, 1863. Reported present through April 30, 1864. Promoted to Corporal on February 1, 1864. Wounded at Kolb's Farm, near Marietta, Georgia, June 22, 1864. Returned to duty in July-August, 1864. Wounded slightly at Bentonville on March 19-21, 1865. No further records.

RICE, JOHN M., Private

Previously served as Private in Company E, 1st Regiment N.C. Infantry (6 months, 1861). Enlisted in this company in Buncombe County on May 3, 1862, for the war. Reported present in November, 1862-June, 1863. Reported sick in hospital in July-August, 1863. Wounded at Chickamauga, Georgia, September 20,

1863. Furloughed from hospital in November-December, 1863. Died on January 7, 1864. Place and cause of death not reported.

RICE, WILLIAM P., Corporal

Born in Buncombe County and was by occupation a farmer prior to enlisting in Buncombe County at age 21, May 3, 1862, for the war. Mustered in as Private. Reported present in November-December, 1862. Promoted to Corporal on January 1, 1863, "for gallantry on the field [presumably at Murfreesboro, Tennessee]." Reported present in January-June, 1863. Killed at Chickamauga, Georgia, September 20, 1863. Nominated for the Badge of Distinction for gallantry at Chickamauga.

ROBERTS, ELISHA MILES, Sergeant

Previously served as Private in Company F of this regiment. Transferred to this company on July 24, 1862. Promoted to Sergeant on November 24, 1862. Died in hospital at Murfreesboro, Tennessee, December 28, 1862. Cause of death not reported.

ROBERTS, LEANDER WESLEY, Private

Born in Buncombe County and was by occupation a farmer prior to enlisting in Buncombe County at age 23, May 3, 1862, for the war. Reported present in November, 1862-April, 1863. Transferred to Company C of this regiment on June 1, 1863.

ROBERTS, WILLIAM A., Sergeant

Born in Buncombe County where he resided as a farmer prior to enlisting in Buncombe County at age 26, May 7, 1862, for the war. Mustered in as Private. Reported sick in hospital in November-December, 1862. Returned to duty in January-February, 1863. Reported sick in hospital in March-June, 1863. Returned to duty prior to November 1, 1863. Promoted to Corporal in November-December, 1863. Reported present in November, 1863-February, 1864. Promoted to Sergeant on February 1, 1864. Furloughed for twenty-four days on April 10, 1864. Reported present in May-August, 1864. No further records.

ROGERS, JASPER NICHOLAS W., Private

Born in Buncombe County and was by occupation a farmer prior to enlisting in Buncombe County on April 12, 1862. Was about 16 years of age at time of enlistment. Reported present in May-June, 1863. Deserted on an unspecified date. Returned to duty on October 3, 1863. Sent to hospital on November 25, 1863. Furloughed on December 21, 1863. Reported absent without leave on April 1, 1864. Failed to return to duty and was listed as a deserter in July-August, 1864. Later served as Private in Companies G and H, 3rd Regiment N.C. Mounted Infantry (Union).

RYMER, DAVID P., Private

Born in Buncombe County where he resided as a farmer or blacksmith prior to enlisting in Buncombe County at age 33, April 12, 1862. Hospitalized at Dalton, Georgia, December 31, 1862, with "fistula in ano." Returned to duty on January 8, 1863. Reported sick in hospital in March-October, 1863. Returned to duty in November-December, 1863. Reported present until August 31, 1864, when he died at Jonesborough, Georgia. Cause of death not reported (probably killed in battle).

SCOGGINS, JESSE, ———

North Carolina pension records indicate that he served in this company.

SLUDER, JAMES ERWIN, Private

Born in Buncombe County and was by occupation a farmer prior to enlisting in Buncombe County at age 18, April 12, 1862. Reported present in November-December, 1862. Reported sick in hospital in January-June, 1863. Furloughed on an unspecified date. Reported absent sick on or about October 31, 1863. Returned to duty in November-December, 1863. Reported present in January-April, 1864. Wounded in the left leg at Kolb's Farm, near Marietta, Georgia, June 22, 1864. Left leg amputated. Reported in hospital at Macon, Georgia, October 12, 1864. No further records. Survived the war.

SLUDER, JOSEPH, Private

Born in Buncombe County where he resided as a farmer prior to enlisting in Buncombe County at age 27, April 12, 1862. Hospitalized at Dalton, Georgia, December 31, 1862, with debilitas. Died at Dalton on February 3, 1863. Cause of death not reported.

SMITH, JAMES C., 1st Sergeant

Born in Henderson County and resided in Buncombe County where he was by occupation a farmer prior to enlisting in Buncombe County at age 19, May 3, 1862, for the war. Mustered in as Private. Reported present in November-December, 1862. Promoted to Sergeant on January 1, 1863, "for gallantry on the field [presumably at Murfreesboro, Tennessee]." Reported present in January, 1863-April, 1864. Promoted to 1st Sergeant on February 1, 1864. Killed at or near Marietta, Georgia, July 2, 1864. [May have served previously as Private in Company E, 1st Regiment N.C. Infantry (6 months, 1861).]

SNIDER, HENRY J., Private

Previously served as Private in Company I of this regiment. Transferred to this company in November-December, 1863. Deserted on an unspecified date. Returned from desertion on May 7, 1864, and was placed under arrest. Returned to duty prior to July 1, 1864. Captured at or near Peachtree Creek, near Atlanta, Georgia, July 20, 1864. Sent to Nashville, Tennessee. Transferred to Louisville, Kentucky, where he arrived on July 28, 1864. Transferred to Camp Douglas, Chicago, Illinois, where he arrived on August 1, 1864. Released at Camp Douglas on March 26, 1865, after taking the Oath of Allegiance and joining the U.S. Army. Assigned to Company F, 6th Regiment U.S. Volunteer Infantry.

SNIDER, JAMES, Private

Born in Lincoln County and was by occupation a farmer prior to enlisting in Buncombe County at age 36, May 17, 1862, for the war. Hospitalized on an unspecified date. Furloughed in November-December, 1862. Returned to duty in January-February, 1863. Reported present in March-April, 1863. Deserted in May-June, 1863. Returned to duty on July 15, 1863. Deserted on November 27, 1863. Reported present but under arrest in March-April, 1864. Returned to duty on May 7, 1864. Reported present in July-August, 1864. No further records. Survived the war. [North Carolina pension records indicate that he was wounded in the right hand (compound fracture) at Columbia, Tennessee, December 1, 1864.]

STANFORD, WILLIAM J., Sergeant

Born in Jackson County* and resided in Henderson County where he was by occupation a farmer prior to enlisting in Buncombe County at age 16, May 17, 1862, for the war. Mustered in as Private. Reported present in November, 1862-June, 1863. Promoted to Sergeant on May 1, 1863. Reported sick in hospital at Kingston, Geor-

gia, in July-August, 1863. Returned to duty subsequent to October 31, 1863. Captured at Missionary Ridge, Tennessee, November 25, 1863. Sent to Nashville, Tennessee. Transferred to Louisville, Kentucky, where he arrived on December 7, 1863. Transferred to Rock Island, Illinois, where he arrived on or about December 9, 1863. Transferred to New Orleans, Louisiana, on or about May 3, 1865. Transferred from New Orleans to Nashville on May 23, 1865. Released at Nashville on June 28, 1865, after taking the Oath of Allegiance.

STEPP, WILLIAM, Private

Born in Buncombe County and was by occupation a farmer prior to enlisting in Buncombe County at age 34, May 7, 1862, for the war. Deserted on December 12, 1862.

SURRETT, JOHN, Private

Born in South Carolina and was by occupation a farmer prior to enlisting in Buncombe County at age 33, April 12, 1862. Paid for service through August 1, 1862. No further records.

SWAN, STEPHEN, Private

Born in South Carolina and resided in Buncombe County where he was by occupation a farm laborer prior to enlisting in Buncombe County at age 44, April 12, 1862. Reported sick at home in November-December, 1862. Reported "absent at home" in January-February, 1863. Listed as a deserter in March-April, 1863. Returned to duty on an unspecified date. Deserted prior to January 1, 1864.

SWANGUM, KEMSEY A., Private

Born in Henderson County and was by occupation a farmer prior to enlisting in Buncombe County at age 20, April 12, 1862. Reported present in November, 1862-February, 1863. Reported sick in hospital in March-June, 1863. Returned to duty prior to November 1, 1863. Deserted on November 27, 1863.

TATUM, MOSES H., Private

Born in Garrard County, Kentucky, and resided in Buncombe County where he was by occupation a stonemason prior to enlisting in Buncombe County at age 44, April 12, 1862. Detailed to work in the saltworks at Saltville, Virginia, in July, 1862. Reported absent on detail through December, 1863. Deserted in January-February, 1864.

WAGGONER, DAVAULT H., Private

Born in Buncombe County and was by occupation a farmer prior to enlisting in Buncombe County at age 26, May 3, 1862, for the war. Mustered in as Private. Promoted to Sergeant on November 24, 1862. Reported present in November-December, 1862. Wounded slightly in the shoulder at Murfreesboro, Tennessee, January 2, 1863. Returned to duty prior to March 1, 1863. Reported present in March-June, 1863. Reported sick in hospital in July-October, 1863. Deserted on November 27, 1863. Reduced to ranks subsequent to December 31, 1863. Went over to the enemy on an unspecified date. Confined at Knoxville, Tennessee, June 4, 1864. Took the Oath of Allegiance at Knoxville on June 6, 1864.

WAGGONER, JESSE POWELL, Private

Born in Buncombe County and was by occupation a farmer prior to enlisting in Buncombe County at age 27, October 2, 1862, for the war. Hospitalized at Dalton, Georgia, November 21, 1862, with debilitas. Furloughed for forty days on December 5, 1862.

Returned to duty prior to March 1, 1863. Reported present in March-April, 1863. Detailed as a wagoner on June 24, 1863. Detailed as a hospital nurse at Madison, Georgia, on or about November 1, 1863. Reported on duty as a hospital nurse through August 31, 1864. No further records.

WAGGONER, WILLIAM A., Private

Born in Buncombe County where he resided as a farmer prior to enlisting in Buncombe County at age 34, July 10, 1862, for the war. Deserted in August, 1862. Returned to duty on or about September 4, 1862. Hospitalized at Dalton, Georgia, December 28, 1862, with chronic rheumatism. Reported in hospital through February 28, 1863. Returned to duty in March-April, 1863. Reported present or accounted for through August 31, 1864. No further records. Survived the war.

WEST, WILLIAM T., Private

Born in Buncombe County and was by occupation a mechanic prior to enlisting in Buncombe County at age 19, April 15, 1862. Reported absent sick in November-December, 1862. Hospitalized at Dalton, Georgia, January 25, 1863, with chronic diarrhoea. Detailed as a hospital nurse at Dalton on May 1, 1863. Reported on detail as a hospital nurse at Dalton and at La Grange, Georgia, through October 31, 1863. Rejoined the company in November-December, 1863. Reported present through April, 1864. Wounded at Kolb's Farm, near Marietta, Georgia, June 22, 1864. Reported absent wounded through August 31, 1864. No further records.

WILLIS, JOHN W., Private

Born in Buncombe County and was by occupation a farmer prior to enlisting in Buncombe County at age 23, April 12, 1862. Reported present in November-December, 1862. Reported sick in hospital in January-February, 1863. Died in hospital at Ringgold, Georgia, March 28, 1863, of "chills and fever."

WISE, DAVID THOMAS, Private

Born in Lincoln County and was by occupation a farmer prior to enlisting in Buncombe County at age 25, April 12, 1862. Reported sick in hospital in November, 1862-February, 1863. Returned to duty in March-April, 1863. Reported present in May-June, 1863. Reported sick in hospital at Marion, Mississippi, in July-October, 1863. Returned to duty in November-December, 1863. Reported present through August 31, 1864. No further records. Survived the war.

WOLF, JOSHUA E., Private

Previously served as Private in Company E, 1st Regiment N.C. Infantry. Enlisted in this company in Buncombe County on May 3, 1862, for the war. Reported sick in hospital in November-December, 1862. Returned to duty in January-February, 1863. Reported present in March-April, 1863. Reported on detail as a wagoner in May-October, 1863. Deserted on November 27, 1863. [Contrary to 3:30 of this series, it appears that the correct spelling of his surname is Wolf rather than Wolfe.]

WRIGHT, HENDERSON, Private

Resided in Buncombe County and was by occupation a farmer prior to enlisting in Wake County at age 38, May 16, 1863, for the war. Detailed as a wagoner on June 24, 1863. Transferred to Company H, 29th Regiment N.C. Troops, prior to November 1, 1863.

WRIGHT, JOSEPH, Private

Born in Buncombe County where he resided as a farmer prior to enlisting in Buncombe County at age 25, May 2, 1862, for the war. Reported sick in hospital in November, 1862-February, 1863. Returned to duty in March-April, 1863. Reported present in May-June, 1863. Wounded in the hand (two fingers amputated) at Chickamauga, Georgia, September 20, 1863. Died in hospital at Atlanta, Georgia, on or about October 19, 1863, of wounds.

WRIGHT, MARTIN B., Private

Enlisted in Buncombe County on April 12, 1862. Transferred to Company C of this regiment on or about July 8, 1862. Transferred back to this company on May 1, 1863. Reported present through June 30, 1863. No further records.

WRIGHT, THOMAS S., Private

Enlisted in Wake County on May 16, 1863, for the war. Reported present through June 30, 1863. Transferred to Company C, 29th Regiment N.C. Troops, prior to September 1, 1863.

WRIGHT, WILLIAM A., Private

Born in Buncombe County and was by occupation a mason prior to enlisting in Buncombe County on April 12, 1862. Detailed to work in the saltworks at Saltville, Virginia, in July, 1862. Reported absent on detail through December, 1863. Deserted in January-February, 1864.

COMPANY B

This company was raised in Madison County on April 5, 1862. It was mustered into state service at Marshall on that same date as "Second Company," McDowell's Battalion N.C. Infantry (known also as the 6th Battalion N.C. Infantry). The seven-company battalion was mustered into Confederate service on August 1, 1862, and redesignated the 1st Battalion N.C. Infantry. On October 8, 1862, the 60th Regiment N.C. Troops was formally organized after three additional companies were assigned to the 1st Battalion. This company was designated Company B. After joining the regiment the company functioned as a part of the regiment, and its history for the remainder of the war is reported as a part of the regimental history.

The following roster was compiled primarily from information in the microfilm edition of the Compiled Service Records of Soldiers Who Served in Organizations from the State of North Carolina (Record Group 109, M270), National Archives and Records Administration, Washington, D.C. Record Group 109 includes enlistment papers, pay vouchers, requisitions, letters of resignation, discharge certificates, and abstracts of medical and prisoner of war returns. Materials relating specifically to this company include muster rolls dated November, 1862-August, 1864.

Also utilized in this roster were *The War of the Rebellion: A Compilation of the Official Records of the Union and Confederate Armies*, the North Carolina adjutant general's *Roll of Honor*, state militia records, newspaper casualty lists and obituaries, wartime claims for bounty pay and allowances, postwar registers of claims for artificial limbs, Confederate pension applications filed with the states of North Carolina, Tennessee, and Florida, Confederate Soldiers' Home records, and the 1860 and 1870 federal censuses of North Carolina. A search was made also for relevant letters, diaries, reminiscences, and

other manuscripts in the Southern Historical Collection (University of North Carolina-Chapel Hill), the Duke University Library Special Collections Department, and the North Carolina Division of Archives and History.

Among the secondary sources consulted were records of the North Carolina division of the United Daughters of the Confederacy, post-war rosters, regimental and county histories, marriage bond, will, and cemetery indexes, published and unpublished genealogies, biographical dictionaries, the North Carolina *County Heritage Book* series, the *Confederate Veteran*, Walter Clark's *Histories of the Several Regiments and Battalions from North Carolina in the Great War, 1861-'65*, and the North Carolina volume of the extended edition of *Confederate Military History*.

OFFICERS

CAPTAINS

McDOWELL, JOSEPH A.

Resided in Madison County. Appointed Captain on April 5, 1862. Elected Lieutenant Colonel on August 1, 1862, and transferred to the Field and Staff of this regiment. Later served as Colonel of this regiment.

DUCKETT, L. A. BELTON

Resided in Madison County and was by occupation a farmer prior to enlisting at age 43. Elected 1st Lieutenant on April 5, 1862. Promoted to Captain on August 1, 1862. Resigned on February 25, 1863. A notation on his letter of resignation states that "charges were preferred against this officer for 'misbehavior before the enemy' [at Murfreesboro, Tennessee, December 31, 1862, but were withdrawn] . . . upon the tender of his resignation. Two officers of this Reg[iment] equally as guilty as this officer, having been tried by court-martial and acquitted, I am therefore of the opinion, that the good of the service will be *better* and *more promptly promoted*, by the acceptance of his resignation." Resignation accepted on March 10, 1863.

PATTON, BENJAMIN FRANKLIN

Previously served as 1st Sergeant of Company E, 1st Regiment N.C. Infantry (6 months, 1861). Elected 2nd Lieutenant of this company on April 5, 1862. Promoted to 1st Lieutenant on August 1, 1862. Promoted to Captain on March 10, 1863. Reported present in March-June, 1863. Reported absent sick in July-October, 1863. Returned to duty in November-December, 1863. Reported absent with leave for thirty days in January-February, 1864. Returned to duty in March-April, 1864. Dropped from the company rolls on May 18, 1864, for absence without leave. Reinstated on September 19, 1864. No further records. Survived the war. [His Tennessee pension application states that he was wounded in the right hip at New Hope Church, Georgia (presumably in May, 1864) and incapacitated for "near seven months."]

LIEUTENANTS

CHAMBERS, JAMES RILEY, 2nd Lieutenant

Previously served as 1st Sergeant of Company H, 2nd Battalion N.C. Infantry. Elected 2nd Lieutenant of this company on August 28, 1862. Hospitalized at Dalton, Georgia, December 30, 1862, with chronic hepatitis. Returned to duty on January 3, 1863.

Reported in command of the company in January-February, 1863. Reported absent with leave in March-April, 1863. Reported absent sick in May-June, 1863. Returned to duty on an unspecified date. Reported present in July-October, 1863. Wounded in the left thigh and captured at Missionary Ridge, Tennessee, November 25, 1863. Hospitalized at Nashville, Tennessee, December 13, 1863. Transferred to Louisville, Kentucky, where he arrived on January 24, 1864. Transferred to Camp Chase, Ohio, where he arrived on January 26, 1864. Transferred to Fort Delaware, Delaware, where he arrived on March 25, 1864. Paroled at Fort Delaware on September 14, 1864. Received at Aiken's Landing, James River, Virginia, September 22, 1864, for exchange. No further records.

CLAYTON, ROBERT M., 1st Lieutenant

Previously served as Private in Company E, 1st Regiment N.C. Infantry (6 months, 1861). Enlisted in this company in Madison County on April 5, 1862. Mustered in as Private. Promoted to 1st Sergeant in August-December, 1862. Reported absent sick in November, 1862-February, 1863. Elected 1st Lieutenant on March 10, 1863. Reported present in March-June, 1863. Reported in command of the company in July-October, 1863. Reported present in November, 1863-August, 1864. Was reported in command of the company in January-February and May-August, 1864. Detailed for fifteen days to procure clothing and blankets on January 13, 1865. Transferred to Company E, 58th Regiment N.C. Troops, when the 58th and 60th Regiments were consolidated on April 9, 1865. [Was reported in command of Company H of this regiment in March-April, 1864.]

COOK, RILEY S., 3rd Lieutenant

Resided in Madison County and was by occupation a farmer prior to enlisting at age 41. Elected 3rd Lieutenant on April 5, 1862. Resigned on December 4, 1862. Reason he resigned not reported; however, a notation on his letter of resignation suggests that he had been guilty of excessive absenteeism. Resignation accepted on January 5, 1863.

NONCOMMISSIONED OFFICERS AND PRIVATES

BALDING, ALEXANDER, Sergeant

Resided in Madison County and was by occupation a farmer prior to enlisting at Murfreesboro, Tennessee, at age 38, January 1, 1863, for the war. Mustered in as Private. Reported present in January-June, 1863. Promoted to Sergeant on March 30, 1863. Sent to hospital sick on or about November 1, 1863. Reported absent sick through August 31, 1864. No further records.

BALDING, FIDELIO A., Private

Previously served as Private in Company F of this regiment. Transferred to this company in July-September, 1863. Captured in a skirmish near Chattanooga, Tennessee, on or about September 24, 1863. Sent to Nashville, Tennessee. Transferred to Louisville, Kentucky, where he arrived on October 10, 1863. Transferred to Camp Morton, Indianapolis, Indiana, where he arrived on October 11, 1863. Died at Camp Morton on February 1, 1865, of "inflammation of the lungs."

BALDING, MARQUES D. LAFAYETTE, Private

Previously served as Private in Company F of this regiment. Transferred to this company in April-May, 1864, while listed as a deserter. Reported for duty on May 20, 1864. Captured on the retreat from Marietta, Georgia, July 2-3, 1864. Sent to Nashville, Tennessee. Transferred to Louisville, Kentucky, where he arrived on July 13, 1864. Transferred to Camp Morton, Indianapolis, Indiana, where he arrived on July 14, 1864. Paroled at Camp Morton on March 4, 1865. Received at Boulware's and Cox's Wharves, James River, Virginia, March 10-12, 1865, for exchange. [Filed a Tennessee pension application after the war.]

BRADLEY, ALFRED B., Private

Resided in Madison County and was by occupation a farmer prior to enlisting in Madison County at age 37, April 5, 1862. Reported present on surviving company muster rolls through June, 1864. Reported on detail as a hospital cook in July-August, 1864. No further records.

BRADLEY, AUGUSTUS, ———

North Carolina pension records indicate that he served in this company.

BROOKS, JOHN A., Private

Resided in Cocke County, Tennessee, and enlisted at Wartrace, Tennessee, May 1, 1863, for the war. Deserted at Dalton, Georgia, May 25, 1863. Returned to duty subsequent to August 31, 1864. Captured by the enemy near Nashville, Tennessee, December 20, 1864. Confined at Louisville, Kentucky, January 2, 1865. Transferred to Camp Chase, Ohio, where he arrived on January 6, 1865. Released at Camp Chase on March 22, 1865, after taking the Oath of Allegiance. [Records of the Federal Provost Marshal dated March, 1865, give his age as 25.]

BROOKS, TERRELL A., Sergeant

Previously served as Private in Company H, 2nd Battalion N.C. Infantry. Transferred to this company on September 1, 1862. Mustered in as Corporal. Hospitalized at Dalton, Georgia, December 31, 1862, with debilitas. Returned to duty on January 18, 1863. Promoted to Sergeant on March 30, 1863. Reported present through June 30, 1863. Wounded in the thigh at Chickamauga, Georgia, September 20, 1863. Died of wounds. Place and date of death not reported.

BROWN, JAMES V., Private

Enlisted at Chattanooga, Tennessee, October 20, 1863, for the war. Reported present through April 30, 1864. Captured on the retreat from Marietta, Georgia, July 2-3, 1864. Sent to Nashville, Tennessee. Transferred to Louisville, Kentucky, where he arrived on July 13, 1864. Transferred to Camp Morton, Indianapolis, Indiana, where he arrived on July 15, 1864. Paroled at Camp Morton on March 4, 1865. Received at Boulware's and Cox's Wharves, James River, Virginia, March 10-12, 1865, for exchange. Survived the war. [Was about 18 years of age at time of enlistment. North Carolina pension records indicate that he was injured at Missionary Ridge, Tennessee, October 31, 1863, and at Kennesaw Mountain, Georgia, on an unspecified date. According to his pension application, his skull and both of his legs were fractured and he also suffered an injury to the right hand.]

BROWN, JESSE, Private

Enlisted in Madison County on April 5, 1862. Died in hospital at Murfreesboro, Tennessee, December 18, 1862. Cause of death not reported.

BROWN, O. V., Private

Resided in Madison County and was by occupation a farmer prior to enlisting in Madison County at age 32, April 5, 1862. Reported

absent sick in November-December, 1862. Returned to duty in January-February, 1863. Reported present in March-April, 1863. Reported sick in hospital in May-June, 1863. Returned to duty in July-October, 1863. Reported present in November, 1863-February, 1864. Sent to hospital at Dalton, Georgia, in March-April, 1864. Died in hospital at Augusta, Georgia, on or about May 31, 1864, of disease.

BROWN, OBEDIAH A., Private

Previously served as Private in Company H, 2nd Battalion N.C. Infantry. Transferred to this company on September 6, 1862. Reported present on surviving company muster rolls through February, 1863. Reported sick in hospital in March-April, 1863. Reported present in May-October, 1863. Captured at Missionary Ridge, Tennessee, November 25, 1863. Sent to Nashville, Tennessee. Transferred to Louisville, Kentucky, where he arrived on December 5, 1863. Transferred to Rock Island, Illinois, where he arrived on December 7, 1863. Died at Rock Island on February 6, 1864, of "pneumonia." [Nominated for the Badge of Distinction for gallantry at Chickamauga, Georgia, September 19-20, 1863.]

BROWN, S. G., Private

Enlisted in Madison County on April 5, 1862. Reported sick in hospital in November-December, 1862. Returned to duty in January-February, 1863. Reported present through December 31, 1863. Died at Cassville, Georgia, January 18 or January 27, 1864. Cause of death not reported.

BROWN, W. G., Private

Enlisted in Madison County on April 5, 1862. Reported present in November, 1862-February, 1863. Reported sick in hospital in March-April, 1863. Returned to duty in May-June, 1863. Captured in a skirmish near Chattanooga, Tennessee, on or about September 24, 1863. Sent to Nashville, Tennessee. Transferred to Louisville, Kentucky, where he arrived on October 9, 1863. Transferred to Camp Morton, Indianapolis, Indiana, where he arrived on October 11, 1863. Died at Camp Morton on October 20, 1863. Cause of death not reported.

BROWN, WILEY B., Private

Previously served as Private in Company H, 2nd Battalion N.C. Infantry. Transferred to this company on or about September 6, 1862. Reported present on surviving company muster rolls through December 31, 1863. Reported present but on duty as a teamster in January-February, 1864. Reported present but on duty as an ambulance driver from February 1 through August 30, 1864. Wounded in the right elbow (fracture) at Jonesborough, Georgia, August 31, 1864. No further records. Survived the war.

CARTER, WILLIAM H., Private

Born in Rockingham County on November 5, 1829. Resided in Madison County and was by occupation a farmer prior to enlisting in Madison County at age 32, April 5, 1862. Reported present on surviving company muster rolls through October, 1863. Reported on detached service as a teamster at Bristol, Tennessee, in November-December, 1863. Rejoined the company in January-February, 1864. Reported present in March-April, 1864. Captured on the retreat from Marietta, Georgia, July 2-3, 1864. Sent to Nashville, Tennessee. Transferred to Louisville, Kentucky, where he arrived on July 13, 1864. Transferred to Camp Morton, Indianapolis, Indiana, where he arrived on July 14, 1864. Released at Camp Morton on May 18, 1865, after taking the Oath of Allegiance. [His Tennessee pension application states that he was wounded slightly in the leg in Calhoun, Georgia (presumably in May, 1864), but was "not off duty but 2 or 3 days."]

CLEMMONS, ALEXANDER C., Private

Enlisted in Madison County on August 1, 1862, for the war. Mustered in as Private. Hospitalized at Dalton, Georgia, on or about December 28, 1862, with chronic rheumatism. Returned to duty on January 3, 1863. Reported present or accounted for in January-June, 1863. Promoted to Corporal in January-February, 1863. Reduced to ranks on March 30, 1863. Transferred to Company H of this regiment on June 30, 1863.

COGDILL, FIDELLA P., Private

Previously served as Private in Company H, 2nd Battalion N.C. Infantry. Transferred to this company on September 1, 1862. Reported present on surviving company muster rolls through February, 1863. Reported sick in hospital in March-April, 1863. Returned to duty in May-June, 1863. Reported present through October 31, 1863. Reported absent sick in November-December, 1863. Furloughed from hospital on an unspecified date. Failed to return to duty and was listed as a deserter on March 11, 1864. Returned to duty on May 20, 1864. Reported present through August 31, 1864. Transferred to Company E, 58th Regiment N.C. Troops, when the 58th and 60th Regiments were consolidated on April 9, 1865.

COGDILL, JOSEPH, Private

Enlisted in Madison County on August 1, 1862, for the war. Reported present in January-June, 1863. Deserted near Chattanooga, Tennessee, September 7, 1863.

COOK, JAMES C., Sergeant

Resided in Madison County and was by occupation a farmer prior to enlisting in Madison County at age 23, April 5, 1862. Mustered in as Sergeant. Died in hospital at Chattanooga, Tennessee, on or about January 20, 1863. Cause of death not reported.

COOK, WILLIAM R., Private

Previously served as Private in Company H, 2nd Battalion N.C. Infantry. Transferred to this company on September 1, 1862. Wounded in the "belly" and captured at Murfreesboro, Tennessee, December 31, 1862. Sent to Nashville, Tennessee. Transferred to Louisville, Kentucky, where he arrived on an unspecified date. Transferred to Camp Butler, Illinois, where he arrived on March 23, 1863. Transferred to Fort Monroe, Virginia, on an unspecified date. Paroled at Fort Monroe on April 14, 1863. Reported absent sick or absent wounded through October 31, 1863. Deserted on December 13, 1863. Returned from desertion on May 20, 1864. Sent to hospital on June 22, 1864. Reported absent in hospital through August 31, 1864. No further records.

COPE, WILLIAM, ———

North Carolina pension records indicate that he served in this company.

CRAWFORD, JOHN KNIGHT, Sergeant

Enlisted in Madison County on April 5, 1862. Mustered in as Private. Reported present in November, 1862-June, 1863. Promoted to Sergeant on March 30, 1863. Hospitalized at Lauderdale Springs, Mississippi, July 9, 1863. Detailed as a nurse on August 1, 1863. Returned to duty on October 27, 1863. Wounded at Missionary Ridge, Tennessee, November 25, 1863. Hospitalized at

Newnan, Georgia. Furloughed for thirty days on January 30, 1864. Returned to duty in March-April, 1864. Sent to hospital on June 1, 1864. Admitted to hospital at Macon, Georgia, August 10, 1864, with nephritis and general debility. Reported in hospital through August 31, 1864. Was reportedly issued clothing on November 10, 1864. No further records.

DAVIS, DANIEL, Private

Resided in Madison County and was by occupation a farmer prior to enlisting in Madison County at age 32, April 5, 1862. Reported present on surviving company muster rolls through June 30, 1863. Wounded in the hip at Chickamauga, Georgia, September 20, 1863. Returned to duty prior to October 31, 1863. Reported absent sick in November-December, 1863. Furloughed from hospital on an unspecified date. Failed to return to duty and was listed as a deserter on March 11, 1864.

ELLISON, ISAAC, Private

Enlisted in Madison County on April 5, 1862. Hospitalized at Dalton, Georgia, December 31, 1862, with diarrhoea. Returned to duty on January 5, 1863. Reported present in January-June, 1863. Reported sick in hospital in July-December, 1863. Returned to duty in January-February, 1864. Furloughed on March 25, 1864. Died at Asheville on May 10, 1864, of disease.

EVANS, S. C., Private

Enlisted in Madison County on April 5, 1862. Reported sick in hospital in November-December, 1862. Died in hospital at Chattanooga, Tennessee, February 17, 1863. Cause of death not reported.

FAGG, HENRY C., Corporal

Enlisted in Madison County at age 16, August 1, 1862, for the war. Mustered in as Private. Reported present in November, 1862-June, 1863. Promoted to Corporal on March 30, 1863. Reported absent sick in July-October, 1863. Returned to duty in November-December, 1863. Reported present through April 30, 1864. Wounded at Kolb's Farm, near Marietta, Georgia, June 22, 1864. Returned to duty prior to June 30, 1864. Reported present through August 31, 1864. Appointed 2nd Lieutenant and transferred to Company H, 58th Regiment N.C. Troops, when the 58th and 60th Regiments were consolidated on April 9, 1865.

FLEMMING, J. G., Private

Enlisted in Madison County on April 5, 1862. Mustered in as Corporal. Reported present in November-December, 1862. Reported sick in hospital in January-February, 1863. Reduced to ranks on March 30, 1863. Discharged on April 22, 1863, by reason of disability.

FLEMMING, WILLIAM J. B., Private

Previously served as Private in Company H, 2nd Battalion N.C. Infantry. Enlisted in this company in Madison County on August 1, 1862, for the war. Mustered in as Private. Reported present in November, 1862-June, 1863. Promoted to Corporal on March 30, 1863. Reported absent sick in July-December, 1863. Furloughed on an unspecified date. Failed to return to duty and was listed as a deserter on or about February 29, 1864. Returned to duty on May 20, 1864. Reduced to ranks prior to July 1, 1864. Reported present through August 31, 1864. Transferred to Company E, 58th Regiment N.C. Troops, when the 58th and 60th Regiments were consolidated on April 9, 1865.

FRANKS, J. W., Private

Enlisted in Madison County on April 5, 1862. Reported present in November, 1862-February, 1863. Died at Tullahoma, Tennessee, April 17, 1863. Cause of death not reported.

FRANKS, JOSHUA, Private

Previously served as Private in Company H, 2nd Battalion N.C. Infantry. Transferred to this company on or about April 5, 1862. Reported present in November, 1862-April, 1863. Deserted at Dalton, Georgia, May 25, 1863. [May have served later as Private in Companies C and D, 2nd Regiment N.C. Mounted Infantry (Union).]

FRANKS, WILLIAM, Private

Resided in Cocke County, Tennessee, and enlisted at Murfrees-boro, Tennessee, December 1, 1862, for the war. Reported present through February 28, 1863. Reported absent on duty at the shoe shop at Columbus, Georgia, in March-October, 1863. Deserted on December 13, 1863. Returned to duty subsequent to August 31, 1864. Captured at Liberty, Tennessee, December 17, 1864. Sent to Nashville, Tennessee. Transferred to Louisville, Kentucky, where he arrived on January 2, 1865. Transferred to Camp Chase, Ohio, where he arrived on January 6, 1865. Released at Camp Chase on March 21, 1865, by order of President Lincoln. [Records of the Federal Provost Marshal dated March, 1865, give his age as 51.]

FRESHAUR, JOHN A., Private

Enlisted in Madison County on April 5, 1862. Reported sick in hospital in November-December, 1862. Died in hospital at Tulla-homa, Tennessee, February 20, 1863. Cause of death not reported.

FRESHAUR, JOHN C., Corporal

Enlisted in Madison County on April 5, 1862. Was apparently mustered in with the rank of Corporal. Died in hospital at Murfreesboro, Tennessee, December 29, 1862. Cause of death not reported.

GARRETT, JACOB K., Private

Resided in Madison County where he enlisted at age 25, April 5, 1862. Mustered in as Corporal. Reported present in November, 1862-June, 1863. Promoted to Sergeant on March 30, 1863. Reported absent without leave on an unspecified date. Reduced to ranks on September 10, 1863. Returned to duty prior to November 1, 1863. Sent to hospital on January 4, 1864. Reported present but sick in March-April, 1864. Furloughed home on May 3, 1864. Died at Asheville prior to September 1, 1864, of disease.

GORENFLO, J. F., 1st Sergeant

Enlisted in Madison County on April 5, 1862. Mustered in as Private. Reported present in November, 1862-April, 1863. Promoted to 1st Sergeant on March 30, 1863. Reported present in May, 1863-August, 1864. Transferred to Company E, 58th Regiment N.C. Troops, when the 58th and 60th Regiments were consolidated on April 9, 1865. [Was about 18 years of age at time of enlistment. North Carolina pension records indicate that he was wounded at Nashville, Tennessee, in December, 1864.]

GOWEN, WILLIAM, Private

Resided in Madison County and was by occupation a farmer prior to enlisting in Madison County at age 48, April 5, 1862. Reported present in November, 1862-February, 1863. Hospitalized at Dalton, Georgia, April 1, 1863, with chronic rheumatism. Returned to duty on May 25, 1863. Hospitalized at Macon, Georgia, October 19, 1863, with diarrhoea. Furloughed for thirty days on October

20, 1863. Failed to return to duty and was listed as a deserter in January-February, 1864.

GREEN, JAMES HENRY, Private

Born in Haywood County in 1846. Enlisted at the Etowah River, Georgia, May 20, 1864, for the war. Sent to hospital on June 1, 1864. Reported absent without leave on August 7, 1864. No further records. [Filed a Tennessee pension application after the war.]

HENDERSON, CANADY, Musician

Enlisted in Madison County on April 5, 1862. Mustered in as Musician (Fifer). Reported sick in hospital in November-December, 1862. Died at Tullahoma, Tennessee, February 18, 1863. Cause of death not reported.

HENDERSON, JAMES K., Private

Born in Washington County, Tennessee, March 31, 1841. Enlisted in Madison County at age 21, April 5, 1862. Reported sick in hospital in November-December, 1862. Reported sick in hospital at Dalton, Georgia, in January-February, 1863. Returned to duty in March-April, 1863. Deserted at Dalton on May 25, 1863. [Filed a Tennessee pension application after the war.]

HICKAM, JOHN J., Private

Resided in Madison County where he enlisted on April 5, 1862. Reported present in November, 1862-February, 1863. Reported sick in hospital in March-April, 1863. Reported on detached service as a wagoner in May-June, 1863. Reported in hospital at Marion, Mississippi, in July-August, 1863. Returned to duty in November-December, 1863. Reported present until June 22, 1864, when he was captured (or deserted to the enemy) at Kolb's Farm, near Marietta, Georgia. Sent to Chattanooga, Tennessee. Transferred to Louisville, Kentucky, where he arrived on July 14, 1864. Released at Louisville on July 16, 1864, after taking the Oath of Allegiance.

HICKAM, ROBERT B., Private

Born in Washington County, Tennessee, in 1842. Resided in Madison County and was by occupation a farmer prior to enlisting in Madison County at age 19, April 5, 1862. Reported sick in hospital in November, 1862-February, 1863. Reported absent sick in March-June, 1863. Returned to duty in July-October, 1863. Reported present through April 30, 1864. Wounded by a shell in the right arm, knee, and thigh at Kolb's Farm, near Marietta, Georgia, June 22, 1864. Returned to duty prior to June 30, 1864. Reported present but sick in July-August, 1864. No further records. [Filed a Tennessee pension application after the war.]

HICKS, JAMES WOODY ELCANY, Private

Enlisted in Madison County on April 5, 1862. Wounded at Murfreesboro, Tennessee, December 31, 1862. Reported absent sick in January-February, 1863. Returned to duty in March-April, 1863. Reported present in July-October, 1863. Captured at Missionary Ridge, Tennessee, November 25, 1863. Sent to Nashville, Tennessee. Transferred to Louisville, Kentucky, where he arrived on December 7, 1863. Transferred to Rock Island, Illinois, where he arrived on December 9, 1863. Died at Rock Island on April 3, 1864, of "variola."

HIPPS, JAMES A., Sergeant

Resided in Madison County and was by occupation a farmer prior to enlisting in Madison County at age 24, April 5, 1862. Mustered in as Sergeant. Captured at Murfreesboro, Tennessee, January 2, 1863. Hospitalized at St. Louis, Missouri, January 24, 1863, with bronchitis. Died in hospital at St. Louis on January 30, 1863, of "pneumonia."

HUFF, LEONARD C., Private

Resided in Cocke County, Tennessee, and enlisted in Madison County on April 5, 1862. Mustered in as Private. Transferred to Company H of this regiment on or about September 6, 1862. Later served as 2nd Lieutenant of that unit. [Was about 23 years of age at time of enlistment.]

HUFF, R. N., Corporal

Enlisted in Madison County on August 1, 1862, for the war. Mustered in as Private. Reported present in November, 1862-June, 1863. Promoted to Corporal on March 30, 1863. Reduced to ranks and transferred to Company H of this regiment on June 30, 1863.

INGRAM, JOHN, ———

North Carolina pension records indicate that he served in this company.

JONES, JAMES, Private

Enlisted at Greeneville, Tennessee, September 13, 1862, for the war. Appointed Ordnance Sergeant prior to May 1, 1863, and transferred to the Field and Staff of this regiment.

LACKEY, A. M., Private

Enlisted in Madison County on April 5, 1862. Died in hospital at Tullahoma, Tennessee, February 12, 1863. Cause of death not reported.

LACKEY, E. P., Private

Enlisted in Madison County on April 5, 1862. Reported present in November, 1862-June, 1863. Deserted at La Fayette, Georgia, September 10, 1863.

LACKEY, HENRY, Private

Resided in Madison County and was by occupation a farmer prior to enlisting in Madison County at age 30, April 5, 1862. Died in hospital at Tullahoma, Tennessee, February 11, 1863. Cause of death not reported.

LAWSON, B. FLOYD, Private

Resided in Madison County and was by occupation a farmer prior to enlisting in Madison County at age 35, April 5, 1862. Reported absent sick in November-December, 1862. Wounded in the face at Murfreesboro, Tennessee, January 2, 1863. Hospitalized at Knoxville, Tennessee. Returned to duty in March-April, 1863. Reported present in May-June, 1863. Wounded in the back at Chickamauga, Georgia, September 20, 1863. Returned to duty prior to October 31, 1863. Reported sick in hospital in November, 1863-February, 1864. Reported present but sick in March-April, 1864. Sent to hospital on May 10, 1864. Died at Greensboro, Georgia, July 21, 1864, of disease. [A pension application filed by his widow states that Private Lawson "received a wound in leg and face also from a limb of a tree top cut off by a can[n]on ball from which he afterwards went to the hospital & died."]

LAWSON, ELIJAH L., Private

Resided in Madison County and was by occupation a farmer prior to enlisting in Madison County at age 35, April 5, 1862. Reported present in November, 1862-February, 1863. Detailed in the government shoe shop at Columbus, Georgia, March 17, 1863, by reason of disability. Reported on detail at Columbus through February

29, 1864. Died at Columbus prior to May 1, 1864. Cause of death not reported.

LAWSON, G. W., Private

Resided in Madison County and was by occupation a farmer prior to enlisting in Madison County at age 37, April 5, 1862. Died at Bridgeport, Tennessee, October 19, 1862. Cause of death not reported.

MANN, JOHN, Private

Enlisted in Madison County on April 5, 1862. Reported present in November, 1862-June, 1863. Furloughed on an unspecified date. Failed to return to duty and was listed as a deserter on September 10, 1863.

MEADOWS, JOHN P., Private

Resided in Madison County and was by occupation a farmer prior to enlisting at Camp Smith (Madison County) at age 27, April 5, 1862. Transferred to Company F of this regiment on or about August 1, 1862.

MERRELL, J. W., Private

Enlisted in Buncombe County on July 8, 1862, for the war. Transferred to Company C of this regiment on August 1, 1862. [Was about 22 years of age at time of enlistment.]

MILLER, ANDERSON, Private

Enlisted in Madison County at age 26, April 5, 1862. Mustered in as Musician (Drummer). Wounded "above left eye" and "right thum[b] shot off" at Murfreesboro, Tennessee, December 31, 1862. Reported absent wounded or absent sick through April 30, 1863. Returned to duty in May-June, 1863. Reported present in July-October, 1863. Deserted on December 21, 1863. [May have served later as Private in Company H, 2nd Regiment Tennessee Mounted Infantry (Union).]

MILLER, JOHN, Private

Resided in Madison County and was by occupation a farmer prior to enlisting in Madison County at age 29, April 5, 1862. Hospitalized at Dalton, Georgia, December 31, 1862, with acute diarrhoea. Returned to duty on January 22, 1863. Reported in hospital at Ringgold, Georgia, May 14, 1863. Reported absent sick in July-December, 1863. Failed to return to duty and was listed as a deserter in January-February, 1864.

MILLER, S. F., Private

Enlisted in Madison County on August 1, 1862, for the war. Hospitalized at Dalton, Georgia, December 31, 1862, with diarrhoea. Returned to duty on January 3, 1863. Reported present through February 28, 1863. Reported sick in hospital in March-April, 1863. Returned to duty in May-June, 1863. Reported sick in hospital in July-December, 1863. Furloughed on an unspecified date. Failed to return to duty and was listed as a deserter in January-February, 1864.

MOORE, J. F., Private

Enlisted in Madison County on April 5, 1862. Reported present in November, 1862-February, 1863. Reported absent sick in March-June, 1863. Failed to return from furlough and was listed as a deserter on August 1, 1863. Returned from desertion on March 25, 1864. Captured at or near Adairsville, Georgia, on or about May 18, 1864. Sent to Nashville, Tennessee. Transferred to Louisville, Kentucky, where he arrived on May 24, 1864. Transferred to Rock Island, Illinois, where he arrived on May 27, 1864. Released at

Rock Island on June 10, 1864, after taking the Oath of Allegiance and joining the U.S. Navy.

MOORE, LEWIS, Private

Enlisted in Madison County on April 5, 1862. Hospitalized at Dalton, Georgia, December 31, 1862, with chronic rheumatism. Returned to duty on February 11, 1863. Detailed as a hospital nurse at Griffin, Georgia, April 7, 1863. Reported absent on detail at Griffin through November 30, 1863. Returned to duty in January-February, 1864. Reported present through August 31, 1864. Transferred to Company E, 58th Regiment N.C. Troops, when the 58th and 60th Regiments were consolidated on April 9, 1865.

MOORE, MADISON J., Private

Resided in Madison County where he enlisted on April 5, 1862. Reported present in November, 1862-April, 1863. Detailed as a hospital nurse at Lauderdale Springs, Mississippi, June 1, 1863. Reported on detail at Lauderdale Springs through October 31, 1863. Detailed as a hospital nurse at Montgomery, Alabama, December 17, 1863. Reported absent on detail through August 31, 1864. Deserted to the enemy on an unspecified date. Sent to Knoxville, Tennessee. Transferred to Louisville, Kentucky. Released at Louisville on or about March 10, 1865, after taking the Oath of Allegiance. [Was about 23 years of age at time of enlistment.]

PATTON, JOHN E., Private

Previously served as Private in Col. Robert C. Wood Jr.'s Regiment Confederate Cavalry (known also as Col. Wirt Adams's Regiment Mississippi Cavalry). Transferred to this company on December 6, 1862. Reported present in May-June, 1863. Reported absent sick in July, 1863-August, 1864. Retired to the Invalid Corps on October 10, 1864.

PLEMMONS, ANDREW H., JR., Private

Resided in Madison County and was by occupation a farmer prior to enlisting in Madison County at age 25, April 5, 1862. Hospitalized at Dalton, Georgia, December 31, 1862, with debilitas. Returned to duty on January 18, 1863. Reported present through June 30, 1863. Captured at Chickamauga, Georgia, on or about September 20, 1863. Sent to Nashville, Tennessee. Transferred to Louisville, Kentucky, where he arrived on September 30, 1863. Transferred to Camp Douglas, Chicago, Illinois, where he arrived on October 4, 1863. Released at Camp Douglas on an unspecified date subsequent to August 9, 1864, after taking the Oath of Allegiance.

PLEMMONS, ANDREW H., SR., Private

Enlisted in Madison County at age 50, April 5, 1862. Reported present in November, 1862-June, 1863. Reported absent sick in July-December, 1863. Listed as a deserter in January-February, 1864, after he failed to return from furlough.

PLEMMONS, BAILEY B., Private

Born in Buncombe County and was by occupation a farmer prior to enlisting in Madison County on April 5, 1862. Reported absent sick or absent on furlough from October, 1862, through June 30, 1863. Discharged on October 31, 1863, by reason of "phthisis pulmonalis." Discharge certificate gives his age as 25.

PLEMMONS, JAMES O., Private

Resided in Madison County where he enlisted on April 5, 1862. Reported absent sick or absent on furlough in November, 1862-

December, 1863. Listed as a deserter and dropped from the company rolls in January-February, 1864. [Confederate personnel records dated December, 1863, give his age as 26.]

PLEMMONS, JAMES V., Private

Enlisted at Dalton, Georgia, February 27, 1864, for the war. Reported present through April 30, 1864. Captured at Adairsville, Georgia, on or about May 18, 1864. Sent to Nashville, Tennessee. Transferred to Louisville, Kentucky, where he arrived on May 24, 1864. Transferred to Rock Island, Illinois, where he arrived on May 27, 1864. Died at Rock Island on August 4, 1864, of "ch[ronic] diarrhoea."

PLEMMONS, POSEY, Private

Enlisted in Madison County on April 5, 1862. Hospitalized at Dalton, Georgia, December 31, 1862, with debilitas. Returned to duty on an unspecified date. Hospitalized at Dalton on January 29, 1863, with debilitas. Returned to duty on February 2, 1863. Reported present through April 30, 1863. Wounded on an unspecified date (probably at Chickamauga, Georgia, September 19-20, 1863). Hospitalized at Augusta, Georgia, where he died on or about January 7, 1864, of "pyemia."

PLEMMONS, SILAS J., Private

Previously served as Private in Company F of this regiment. Transferred to this company on or about September 12, 1862. Reported present through December 31, 1863. Hospitalized on an unspecified date. Furloughed in February, 1864. Returned to duty prior to June 22, 1864, when he was wounded at Kolb's Farm, near Marietta, Georgia. Died on June 23, 1864, of wounds. Place of death not reported.

PLEMMONS, SOL F., Private

Resided in Madison County and was by occupation a farmer prior to enlisting in Madison County at age 32, April 5, 1862. Mustered in as 1st Sergeant. Reduced to ranks in August-December, 1862. Reported present in November-December, 1862. Reported sick in hospital in January-February, 1863. Returned to duty in March-April, 1863. Reported present in May, 1863-February, 1864. Furloughed for twenty-six days on April 13, 1864. Failed to return to duty and was dropped from the company rolls on or about June 30, 1864. Listed as a deserter on September 13, 1864.

PLEMMONS, WILLIAM B., Private

Resided in Madison County and was by occupation a farmer prior to enlisting in Madison County at age 18, April 5, 1862. Captured at Murfreesboro, Tennessee, January 2, 1863. Confined at Camp Douglas, Chicago, Illinois. Paroled at Camp Douglas on March 30, 1863. Received at City Point, Virginia, April 4, 1863, for exchange. Reported absent sick through June 30, 1863. Returned to duty in July-October, 1863. Wounded at Missionary Ridge, Tennessee, November 25, 1863. Reported absent wounded through April, 1864. Died in hospital at Montgomery, Alabama, prior to July 18, 1864, of disease.

PRATHER, GEORGE WASHINGTON, Private

Born in Greene County, Tennessee, in 1837. Enlisted in Madison County on April 5, 1862. Reported present on surviving company muster rolls through August 31, 1864. Transferred to Company E, 58th Regiment N.C. Troops, when the 58th and 60th Regiments were consolidated on April 9, 1865.

PRATHER, T. W., Private

Enlisted in Madison County on April 5, 1862. Died in hospital at Knoxville, Tennessee, February 2, 1863. Cause of death not reported.

PRICE, D. A., Private

Enlisted in Madison County on April 5, 1862. Died in hospital at Murfreesboro, Tennessee, December 12, 1862. Cause of death not reported.

RICE, NOAH, Private

Enlisted in Madison County on April 5, 1862. Reported present in November, 1862-February, 1863. Reported sick in hospital in March-April, 1863. Returned to duty in May-June, 1863. Deserted at La Fayette, Georgia, September 10, 1863. Died on an unspecified date and was buried in Oakhill Cemetery, Newnan, Georgia. Place and cause of death not reported.

RIDENS, JAMES, Private

Enlisted in Madison County on April 5, 1862. Deserted at Murfreesboro, Tennessee, December 18, 1862. Rejoined the company in March-April, 1863, and was court-martialed. Returned to duty on May 7, 1863. Reported present through October 31, 1863. Captured at Missionary Ridge, Tennessee, November 25, 1863. Sent to Nashville, Tennessee. Transferred to Louisville, Kentucky, where he arrived on December 5, 1863. Transferred to Rock Island, Illinois, where he arrived on December 9, 1863. Released at Rock Island on January 25, 1864, after taking the Oath of Allegiance and joining the U.S. Navy.

RINEHEART, JOHN, Private

Born in Tennessee. Enlisted in Madison County at age 26, April 5, 1862. Reported present in November, 1862-February, 1863. Reported sick in hospital in March-April, 1863. Returned to duty in May-June, 1863. Reported absent sick in July-December, 1863. Listed as a deserter in January-February, 1864, and dropped from the company rolls.

ROGERS, G. N., Private

Enlisted in Madison County on August 1, 1862, for the war. Reported present in November, 1862-June, 1863. Reported absent sick in July-December, 1863. Listed as a deserter and dropped from the company rolls in January-February, 1864, after he failed to return from furlough.

SAMS, E. BERY H., Private

Enlisted in Madison County at age 24, April 5, 1862. Detailed as a salt miner at Saltville, Virginia, September 1, 1862. Reported absent on detail through December, 1862. Reported absent without leave in March-June, 1863. Deserted at Saltville on August 1, 1863.

SAMS, REUBEN J., Sergeant

Resided in Madison County and was by occupation a farmer prior to enlisting in Madison County at age 39, April 5, 1862. Mustered in as Sergeant. Detailed as a salt miner at Saltville, Virginia, September 1, 1862. Reported absent on detail at Saltville through October 31, 1863. Deserted on December 24, 1863.

SANDERS, J. S., Private

Enlisted in Madison County on April 5, 1862. Reported absent sick in November, 1862-February, 1863. Returned to duty in March-April, 1863. Detailed as a hospital nurse at Brandon, Mississippi,

July 18, 1863. Reported on detail at Brandon through October 31, 1863. Rejoined the company prior to November 25, 1863, when he was captured at Missionary Ridge, Tennessee. Sent to Nashville, Tennessee. Transferred to Louisville, Kentucky, where he arrived on December 7, 1863. Transferred to Rock Island, Illinois, where he arrived on December 9, 1863. Released at Rock Island on January 25, 1864, after taking the Oath of Allegiance and joining the U.S. Navy.

SHELTON, JAMES, Private

Previously served as Private in Company F of this regiment. Transferred to this company subsequent to June 30, 1863. Deserted at Chattanooga, Tennessee, September 8, 1863. [May have served later as Private in Companies A and G, 3rd Regiment N.C. Mounted Infantry (Union).]

SHETLEY, JOHN S., Private

Born in Lincoln County in 1842. Resided in Madison County where he enlisted on April 5, 1862. Wounded in the "second finger" (amputated) of the left hand at Murfreesboro, Tennessee, January 2, 1863. Returned to duty in March-April, 1863. Reported present through October 31, 1863. Wounded in both hips and captured at Missionary Ridge, Tennessee, November 25, 1863. Hospitalized at Bridgeport, Alabama. Transferred to hospital at Nashville, Tennessee, where he arrived on December 13, 1863. Transferred to Louisville, Kentucky, February 14, 1864. Transferred to Fort Delaware, Delaware, February 29, 1864. Released at Fort Delaware on June 19, 1865, after taking the Oath of Allegiance. [Filed a Tennessee pension application after the war.]

SHETLEY, WILLIAM, Private

Enlisted in Madison County on April 5, 1862. Killed at Murfreesboro, Tennessee, December 31, 1862.

STOKELY, CHARLES, JR., Private

Born in Cocke County, Tennessee, in 1839. Enlisted in Madison County on April 5, 1862. Transferred to Company H of this regiment on September 6, 1862. Transferred back to this company in November-December, 1862. Wounded in the right foot and captured at Murfreesboro, Tennessee, December 31, 1862. Right foot amputated. Sent to Nashville, Tennessee. Transferred to Louisville, Kentucky. Transferred to Camp Morton, Indianapolis, Indiana, February 27, 1863. Paroled at Camp Morton and transferred to City Point, Virginia, where he was received on or about April 12, 1863, for exchange. Reported absent wounded through August 31, 1864. No further records. [Filed a Tennessee pension application after the war.]

STOKELY, JOSEPH, Private

Enlisted in Madison County on April 5, 1862. Reported absent sick in November, 1862-December, 1863. Reported absent without leave in January-February, 1864. Listed as a deserter and dropped from the company rolls on or about April 30, 1864.

STOKELY, R. E., Private

Enlisted in Madison County on August 1, 1862, for the war. Died in hospital at Tullahoma, Tennessee, November 1, 1862. Cause of death not reported.

WADDLE, GREEN, Private

Resided in Madison County and was by occupation a farmer prior to enlisting in Madison County at age 26, April 5, 1862. Reported present in November, 1862-June, 1863. Died at Morganton on September 30, 1863. Cause of death not reported.

WADDLE, J. F. M., Private

Enlisted in Madison County on April 5, 1862. Hospitalized at Dalton, Georgia, December 31, 1862, with "hepatitis chr[onic]." Died in hospital at Dalton on February 5, 1863.

WADDLE, JOHN E., Private

Born in Madison County* where he enlisted on April 5, 1862. Wounded in the hand (finger amputated) at Murfreesboro, Tennessee, January 2, 1863. Reported absent wounded or absent sick through October 31, 1863. Returned to duty prior to November 25, 1863, when he was captured at Missionary Ridge, Tennessee. Sent to Nashville, Tennessee. Transferred to Louisville, Kentucky, where he arrived on December 7, 1863. Transferred to Rock Island, Illinois, where he arrived on December 9, 1863. Transferred to New Orleans, Louisiana, May 3, 1865. Arrived at New Orleans on May 17, 1865. Exchanged at New Orleans on May 23, 1865. [Filed a Tennessee pension application after the war.]

WELLS, W. HENRY, Private

Enlisted at Tullahoma, Tennessee, April 1, 1863, for the war. Reported present through June 30, 1863. Reported sick in hospital in July-October, 1863. Returned to duty in November-December, 1863. Sent to hospital on January 20, 1864. Returned to duty in May-June, 1864. Reported present through August 31, 1864. Transferred to Company E, 58th Regiment N.C. Troops, when the 58th and 60th Regiments were consolidated on April 9, 1865.

WHITE, MARTIN W., Private

Previously served as Private in Company H, 2nd Battalion N.C. Infantry. Transferred to this company on September 1, 1863. Reported present in November, 1862-February, 1863. Reported absent on detail as a wagoner, teamster, and carpenter in March, 1863-February, 1864. Rejoined the company in March-April, 1864. Captured near Marietta, Georgia, July 2-3, 1864. Sent to Nashville, Tennessee. Transferred to Louisville, Kentucky, where he arrived on July 14, 1864. Transferred to Camp Douglas, Chicago, Illinois, where he arrived on July 18, 1864. Released at Camp Douglas on June 16, 1865, after taking the Oath of Allegiance.

WILLIAMS, N. M., Private

Enlisted in Madison County on April 5, 1862. Reported present in November, 1862-June, 1863. Reported on detail as a blacksmith in July-November, 1863. Rejoined the company in December, 1863. Detailed as a blacksmith on January 1, 1864. Reported absent on detail through August 31, 1864. No further records.

WOODSON, FRANCIS M., Private

Previously served as Private in Company H, 2nd Battalion N.C. Infantry. Records of the 2nd Battalion indicate that he was transferred to this company on September 1, 186[2]; however, records of this company do not indicate that he served herein.

WOODY, ANDREW J., Private

Resided in Madison County and was by occupation a farmer prior to enlisting in Madison County at age 30, April 5, 1862. Reported present in November-December, 1862. Reported absent sick in January-December, 1863. Listed as a deserter in January-February, 1864. Returned to duty on May 20, 1864. Captured near Marietta, Georgia, July 2-3, 1864. Sent to Nashville, Tennessee. Transferred

to Louisville, Kentucky, where he arrived on July 14, 1864. Transferred to Camp Douglas, Chicago, Illinois, where he arrived on July 18, 1864. Released at Camp Douglas on May 13, 1865, after taking the Oath of Allegiance.

WOODY, J. H., Private

Born in Texas and resided in Madison County where he was by occupation a farmer prior to enlisting in Madison County at age 43, April 5, 1862. Was apparently mustered in with the rank of Sergeant. Reported present in November, 1862-February, 1863. Reduced to ranks on March 30, 1863. Reported absent sick in March-December, 1863. Listed as a deserter and dropped from the company rolls in January-February, 1864.

WOODY, J. V., ———

North Carolina pension records indicate that he served in this company.

WOODY, JAMES, Private

Born in Madison County* where he resided as a farmer prior to enlisting in Madison County on April 5, 1862. Wounded in the head at Murfreesboro, Tennessee, December 31, 1862-January 2, 1863. Returned to duty in January-February, 1863. Reported present in March-June, 1863. Discharged on August 24, 1863, by reason of "disease of the lungs" and wounds received at Murfreesboro. Discharge certificate gives his age as 17. [His Tennessee pension application indicates that he was wounded in the foot at Chancellorsville, Virginia, and in the thigh at Missionary Ridge, Tennessee. The 60th North Carolina was not at Chancellorsville, and the Battle of Missionary Ridge took place subsequent to his discharge. However, two doctors certified in 1898 and 1903 that he had sustained gunshot wounds to the thigh and foot. His Tennessee pension application indicates also that he was born in Cocke County, Tennessee, in 1833.]

WOODY, JOHN A., Private

Resided in Madison County and was by occupation a farmer prior to enlisting in Madison County at age 32, April 5, 1862. Captured at Murfreesboro, Tennessee, January 2, 1863. Died in the hands of the enemy in late January or early February, 1863. Place and cause of death not reported.

WOODY, M. A., Private

Enlisted in Madison County on April 5, 1862. Reported present in November, 1862-June, 1863. Reported absent sick in July-December, 1863. Listed as a deserter in January-February, 1864. Returned to duty on May 20, 1864. Wounded at Kolb's Farm, near Marietta, Georgia, June 22, 1864. Reported absent wounded through August 31, 1864. No further records.

WOODY, W. M., Corporal

Born in Madison County* in 1842. Resided in Madison County and was by occupation a farmer prior to enlisting in Madison County at age 19, April 5, 1862. Mustered in as Corporal. Hospitalized at Dalton, Georgia, December 31, 1862, with general debility. Returned to duty on January 18, 1863. Reported sick in hospital in March-April, 1863. Returned to duty in May-June, 1863. Injured his left thigh and received a severe bruise on the right shoulder at Chickamauga, Georgia, September 20, 1863, when his stirrup broke and he fell from his horse. Reported absent wounded through April 30, 1864. Dropped from the company rolls on or about June 30, 1864. Listed as a deserter on September 13, 1864. [Filed a Tennessee pension application after the war in which he claimed that he served in "Capt. John Dyke's" company, 12th Regiment Tennessee Cavalry. Dyke's company has not been identified.]

COMPANY C

This company was raised in Buncombe County on July 8, 1862. It was mustered into state service at Asheville on that date as "Third Company," McDowell's Battalion N.C. Infantry (known also as the 6th Battalion N.C. Infantry). The seven-company battalion was mustered into Confederate service on August 1, 1862, and redesignated the 1st Battalion N.C. Infantry. On October 8, 1862, the 60th Regiment N.C. Troops was formally organized after three additional companies were assigned to the 1st Battalion. This company was designated Company C. After joining the regiment the company functioned as a part of the regiment, and its history for the remainder of the war is reported as a part of the regimental history.

The following roster was compiled primarily from information in the microfilm edition of the Compiled Service Records of Soldiers Who Served in Organizations from the State of North Carolina (Record Group 109, M270), National Archives and Records Administration, Washington, D.C. Record Group 109 includes enlistment papers, pay vouchers, requisitions, letters of resignation, discharge certificates, and abstracts of medical and prisoner of war returns. Materials relating specifically to this company include muster rolls dated October 29, 1862-August 31, 1864.

Also utilized in this roster were *The War of the Rebellion: A Compilation of the Official Records of the Union and Confederate Armies*, the North Carolina adjutant general's *Roll of Honor*, state militia records, newspaper casualty lists and obituaries, wartime claims for bounty pay and allowances, postwar registers of claims for artificial limbs, Confederate pension applications filed with the states of North Carolina, Tennessee, and Florida, Confederate Soldiers' Home records, and the 1860 and 1870 federal censuses of North Carolina. A search was made also for relevant letters, diaries, reminiscences, and other manuscripts in the Southern Historical Collection (University of North Carolina-Chapel Hill), the Duke University Library Special Collections Department, and the North Carolina Division of Archives and History.

Among the secondary sources consulted were records of the North Carolina division of the United Daughters of the Confederacy, postwar rosters, regimental and county histories, marriage bond, will, and cemetery indexes, published and unpublished genealogies, biographical dictionaries, the North Carolina *County Heritage Book* series, the *Confederate Veteran*, Walter Clark's *Histories of the Several Regiments and Battalions from North Carolina in the Great War, 1861-'65*, and the North Carolina volume of the extended edition of *Confederate Military History*.

OFFICERS

CAPTAINS

REYNOLDS, FLETCHER SARAH HAYNE

Born on January 30, 1834. Resided in Buncombe County and was by occupation a physician prior to enlisting at age 28. Elected Captain on July 8, 1862. Reported present in November-December,

1862. Reported present but sick in January-February, 1863. Resigned on February 23, 1863, for "sufficient cause." Resignation accepted on March 10, 1863. [His parents "had three sons already (and) desperately wanted a daughter, hence the name 'Sarah' used as a middle name. . . ." *Heritage of Buncombe County*, 2:309.]

PATTON, THOMAS WALTON

Previously served as Corporal in Company E, 1st Regiment N.C. Infantry (6 months, 1861). Elected 1st Lieutenant of this company on July 8, 1862. Promoted to Captain on March 10, 1863. Reported present in March, 1863-August, 1864. Tendered his resignation on or about August 8, 1864. No further records. Survived the war.

LIEUTENANTS

BREVARD, DAVID L., 3rd Lieutenant

Resided in Buncombe County and was by occupation a mechanic prior to enlisting at age 30. Elected 3rd Lieutenant on July 8, 1862. Resigned on or about November 23, 1862. Reason he resigned not reported. [Other Confederate personnel records indicate that he was "drpd (dropped) for absence."]

CHAMBERS, JOHN GREGG, 1st Lieutenant

Resided in Buncombe County and was by occupation a farmer prior to enlisting in Buncombe County at age 33. Elected 2nd Lieutenant on July 8, 1862. Reported present on October 29, 1862. Promoted to 1st Lieutenant on March 10, 1863. Reported present in March-October, 1863. Reported absent on detached service from December 12, 1863, through April 30, 1864. Reported present in May-July, 1864. Survived the war. [Detailed as acting Captain of Company D of this regiment in August, 1864. Capt. Thomas W. Patton later wrote of Lieutenant Chambers as follows: "Who was the bravest of them all(?) . . . Well do I know the answer which will come from the survivors of my old company. . . . *John G. Chambers* is the man. Yes, he is the one who never flinched. He is the one we would name who was ever ready to aid a comrade, always studying how to spare his men by *spending himself*. Dear old John, would that your Captain were worthy of having commanded you!" T. W. Patton, "Sixtieth North Carolina Regiment: Infantry," 3, folder 6, box 74, Civil War Collection, NCDAH.]

DAVIDSON, SAMUEL W., 3rd Lieutenant

Previously served as Private in Company E, 1st Regiment N.C. Infantry (6 months, 1861). Enlisted in this company in Buncombe County on July 8, 1862, for the war. Mustered in as Corporal. Reported present in November, 1862-June, 1863. Elected 3rd Lieutenant on January 23, 1863. Wounded in the knee at Chickamauga, Georgia, September 19-20, 1863. Returned to duty in November-December, 1863. Reported present through April 30, 1864. Wounded at Kolb's Farm, near Marietta, Georgia, June 22, 1864. Returned to duty prior to September 1, 1864. Resigned on or about September 12, 1864, but his resignation was apparently rejected. Resigned again on February 22, 1865, because of "the decrease of men in my company. . . . I certify that there is on my company rolls four commissioned officers & thirty men of whome [sic] only six are present for duty." Resignation accepted on March 22, 1865.

RHEA, HENRY KELSEY, 2nd Lieutenant

Resided in Buncombe County where he enlisted on July 8, 1862, for the war. Mustered in as Sergeant. Reported absent sick in November-December, 1862. Captured in hospital at Murfreesboro,

Tennessee, on or about January 5, 1863. Sent to Nashville, Tennessee. Transferred to Louisville, Kentucky. Transferred to Camp Butler, Illinois, where he arrived on March 23, 1863. Transferred to Fort Monroe, Virginia, on an unspecified date. Paroled at Fort Monroe on April 14, 1863. Returned to duty in May-June, 1863. Promoted to 1st Sergeant on May 15, 1863. Reported present through August 31, 1864. Appointed 2nd Lieutenant on April 30, 1864. No further records. [Served as acting Captain of Company H of this regiment in May-August, 1864. May have been wounded at Kolb's Farm, near Marietta, Georgia, June 22, 1864.]

RIDDLE, THOMAS H., 2nd Lieutenant

Resided in Henderson County and enlisted in Buncombe County on July 8, 1862, for the war. Mustered in as Sergeant. Promoted to 1st Sergeant in November-December, 1862. Reported present in November, 1862-December, 1863. Elected 2nd Lieutenant on May 15, 1863. At Rocky Face Ridge, Georgia, February 25, 1864, "he was struck on the right side by a shell & received a most horrible wound of which he died about five hours afterwards." He was "an efficient and popular young officer." [Capt. Thomas W. Patton to his mother, March 2, 1864, James W. Patton Papers, Southern Historical Collection; Clark's *Regiments*, 3:492.]

NONCOMMISSIONED OFFICERS
AND PRIVATES

ARROWOOD, STEPHEN M., Private

Resided in Buncombe County and was by occupation a farm laborer prior to enlisting in Buncombe County at age 24, July 8, 1862, for the war. Deserted at Camp Smith (Madison County) on September 1, 1862.

AYCOCK, BERRY LAWRENCE, Private

Resided in Wayne County. Place and date of enlistment not reported (probably enlisted subsequent to August 31, 1864). Paroled at Goldsboro on May 8, 1865.

BALLINGER, JAMES I., Private

Born in Buncombe County and was by occupation a farmer prior to enlisting in Buncombe County at age 20, July 8, 1862, for the war. Reported present on October 29, 1862. Deserted at Murfreesboro, Tennessee, December 8, 1862. Later served as Private in Company B, 2nd Regiment N.C. Mounted Infantry (Union).

BANKS, JACKSON, ———

North Carolina pension records indicate that he served in this company and was killed at Jonesborough, Georgia, September 15, 1864.

BANKS, JOSEPH WALTER, Private

Born on January 4, 1844. Enlisted in Buncombe County at age 18, July 8, 1862, for the war. Reported present in November, 1862-June, 1863. Deserted on October 4, 1863. Returned to duty on February 24, 1864. Reported present in March-August, 1864. No further records. Survived the war.

BARRETT, SAMUEL G., Private

Enlisted in Buncombe County on July 8, 1862, for the war. Reported present on October 29, 1862. Deserted at Murfreesboro, Tennessee, December 8, 1862. Returned to duty in March-April, 1863. Reported present in May-October, 1863. Reported "under arrest awaiting trial" in November-December, 1863. Deserted prior to March 11, 1864, and "joined the Yankees."

BARRETT, W. G., Private

Enlisted in Buncombe County on July 8, 1862, for the war. Deserted at Murfreesboro, Tennessee, October 28, 1862. Hospitalized at Dalton, Georgia, December 30, 1862, with typhoid fever. Released from hospital on January 13, 1863. Returned to duty on April 28, 1863. Reported on detail as a hospital nurse at Lauderdale Springs, Mississippi, from June 24 through December 31, 1863. Reported absent sick (suffering from epilepsy) in January-June, 1864. Dropped from the company rolls in July-August, 1864, "for prolonged absence without leave." Survived the war. [Was about 34 years of age at time of enlistment.]

BASS, WILLIAM H., Private

Resided in Wayne County. Place and date of enlistment not reported (probably enlisted subsequent to August 31, 1864). Paroled at Goldsboro in 1865. [Was about 18 years of age at time of enlistment.]

BRADLEY, A. B., Private

Enlisted in Buncombe County on July 8, 1862, for the war as a substitute for Pvt. J. M. Bradley of this company. Reported present on October 29, 1862. Deserted at Murfreesboro, Tennessee, December 18, 1862.

BRADLEY, ISAAC M., Private

Enlisted at Camp Vance on July 20, 1864, for the war. Reported present through August 31, 1864. No further records.

BRADLEY, J. M., Private

Enlisted in Buncombe County on July 8, 1862, for the war. Discharged on or about the same date after providing Pvt. A. B. Bradley of this company as a substitute.

BUCKNER, BENJAMIN F., Private

Enlisted in Buncombe County at age 25, July 8, 1862, for the war. Reported present on October 29, 1862. Deserted at Murfreesboro, Tennessee, December 18, 1862.

BUCKNER, J. M., Private

Enlisted in Buncombe County on July 8, 1862, for the war. Discharged prior to October 29, 1862. Reason discharged not reported.

BUCKNER, W. P., ———

North Carolina pension records indicate that he served in this company.

BUCKNER, WILLIAM J., Private

Enlisted in Buncombe County on July 8, 1862, for the war. Hospitalized at Dalton, Georgia, December 31, 1862, with intermittent fever. Transferred on February 12, 1863. Reported sick in hospital in March-April, 1863. Returned to duty in May-June, 1863. Hospitalized at Dalton on an unspecified date with chronic diarrhoea. Furloughed for forty days on or about October 6, 1863. Returned to duty in January-February, 1864. Reported absent sick on April 26, 1864. Returned to duty prior to June 22, 1864, when he was wounded at Kolb's Farm, near Marietta, Georgia. Died prior to July 1, 1864, of wounds. Place of death not reported.

BURLISON, J. R., Corporal

Enlisted in Buncombe County on July 8, 1862, for the war. Mustered in as Private. Promoted to Corporal in November-December, 1862. Reported present in November, 1862-October, 1863. Died at Columbia, South Carolina, December 9, 1863. Cause of death not reported.

CAPPS, JOHN D., Corporal

Resided in Buncombe County and was by occupation a farm laborer prior to enlisting in Buncombe County at age 21, July 8, 1862, for the war. Mustered in as Private. Reported present in November, 1862-June, 1863. Reported sick in hospital in July-October, 1863. Returned to duty in November-December, 1863. Promoted to Corporal on December 9, 1863. Reported present through April 30, 1864. Captured at Resaca, Georgia, on or about May 15, 1864. Sent to Nashville, Tennessee. Transferred to Louisville, Kentucky, where he arrived on May 20, 1864. Transferred to Rock Island, Illinois, where he arrived on June 1, 1864. Released at Rock Island on or about June 10, 1864, after joining the U.S. Navy.

COOK, WILLIAM N., Private

Enlisted in Buncombe County at age 32, July 8, 1862, for the war. Discharged prior to October 29, 1862. Reason discharged not reported.

COPS [CAPPS], SAM, _____

Negro. Servant to Capt. Thomas W. Patton of this company. [See T. W. Patton, "Sixtieth North Carolina Regiment: Infantry," 15, folder 6, box 74, Civil War Collection, NCDAH.]

COXEY, JONATHAN B., Private

Enlisted in Buncombe County on July 8, 1862, for the war. Reported present in November, 1862-February, 1863. Reported sick in hospital in March-October, 1863. Returned to duty in November-December, 1863. Reported present through August 31, 1864. No further records. Survived the war. [Was about 22 years of age at time of enlistment.]

DAVIDSON, WILLIAM F., Private

Resided in Buncombe County and was by occupation a farmer prior to enlisting in Buncombe County on July 8, 1862, for the war. Mustered in as 1st Sergeant. Appointed acting sutler on December 8, 1862 (apparently continued to serve with the company but drew no pay). Returned to duty with the company on November 1, 1863, and was reduced to ranks. Reported present in January-August, 1864. Transferred to Company E, 58th Regiment N.C. Troops, when the 58th and 60th Regiments were consolidated on April 9, 1865. [May have served previously as Private in Company E, 1st Regiment N.C. Infantry (6 months, 1861).]

DAVIS, M. C., Private

Born in South Carolina and was by occupation a day laborer prior to enlisting in Buncombe County at age 50, July 8, 1862, for the war. Discharged on or about the same date after providing Pvt. Joseph Justice as a substitute.

DAVIS, O. F., Private

Born in Buncombe County where he resided as a farmer prior to enlisting in Buncombe County at age 29, July 8, 1862, for the war. Transferred to Company I of this regiment on or about September 13, 1862.

DILLINGHAM, ALFRED B., Sergeant

Enlisted in Buncombe County on July 8, 1862, for the war. Mustered in as Sergeant. Reported absent sick in November-December, 1862. Died at Tullahoma, Tennessee, February 26, 1863, of "typhoid fever." [Was about 30 years of age at time of enlistment.]

DILLINGHAM, ELBERT F. S., Private

Resided in Buncombe County and enlisted at Greeneville, Tennessee, at age 16, October 11, 1862, for the war. Reported absent sick in November, 1862-October, 1863. Dropped from the company rolls in November-December, 1863, for absence without leave. [North Carolina pension records indicate that he was wounded in the right leg by a buckshot at Murfreesboro, Tennessee, January 1, 1863, and received a head injury on the same date when a brick wall was "shot down" and fell on him.]

DILLINGHAM, JOHN WASHINGTON, Private

Resided in Buncombe County and was by occupation a farmer prior to enlisting in Buncombe County at age 26, July 8, 1862, for the war. Wounded and captured at Murfreesboro, Tennessee, December 31, 1862. Hospitalized at Nashville, Tennessee, where he died on January 7 or January 21, 1863, of wounds.

DILLINGHAM, WILLIAM G., Private

Resided in Buncombe County where he enlisted at age 18, July 8, 1862, for the war. Mustered in as Private. Reported present on October 29, 1862. Promoted to Musician in November-December, 1862. Wounded in the hip and captured at Murfreesboro, Tennessee, January 2, 1863. Reported in confinement at Camp Morton, Indianapolis, Indiana, April 1, 1863. Reduced to ranks in March-April, 1863, while a prisoner of war. Paroled and transferred to City Point, Virginia, on or about March 4, 1865. Received at Boulware's and Cox's Wharves, James River, Virginia, March 10-12, 1865, for exchange. No further records. Survived the war.

DRAKE, WILLIAM, Private

Enlisted in Buncombe County on July 8, 1862, for the war. Reported absent sick on October 29, 1862. Deserted at Murfreesboro, Tennessee, December 18, 1862. [May have served later as Private in Company F, 2nd Regiment N.C. Mounted Infantry (Union).]

DULA, ELBERT SIDNEY J., Sergeant

Enlisted in Buncombe County on July 8, 1862, for the war. Mustered in as Private. Reported present in November, 1862-February, 1863. Promoted to Sergeant on December 25, 1862. Reported sick in hospital in March-April, 1863. Returned to duty in May-June, 1863. Reported sick in hospital in July-October, 1863. Captured at Missionary Ridge, Tennessee, November 25, 1863. Sent to Nashville, Tennessee. Transferred to Louisville, Kentucky, where he arrived on December 7, 1863. Transferred to Rock Island, Illinois, where he arrived on December 9, 1863. Released at Rock Island on October 17, 1864, after taking the Oath of Allegiance and joining the U.S. Army. Assigned to Company F, 3rd Regiment U.S. Volunteer Infantry.

EDMONDS, NEHEMIAH B., Private

Enlisted in Buncombe County on July 8, 1862, for the war. Reported present on October 29, 1862. Hospitalized at Dalton, Georgia, December 31, 1862, with "icterus." Died at Dalton on or about January 26, 1863.

FRADEY, H., Private

Enlisted in Buncombe County on July 8, 1862, for the war. Discharged prior to October 30, 1862. Reason discharged not reported. Reenlisted in the company at Camp Vance on October 11, 1863. Deserted on November 20, 1863. Returned from desertion in January-February, 1864, and was placed under arrest. Returned to duty on or about April 15, 1864. Reported present through June 30, 1864. Reported absent sick on August 15, 1864. No further records.

GARRISON, WILLIAM J. MITCHELL, Corporal

Born on May 5, 1831. Resided in Buncombe County and was by occupation a farmer prior to enlisting in Buncombe County at age 31, July 8, 1862, for the war. Was apparently mustered in with the rank of Corporal. Discharged prior to October 29, 1862. Reason discharged not reported. [Previously served as 2nd Lieutenant in the 108th Regiment N.C. Militia.]

GENTRY, GEORGE W., Private

Resided in Buncombe County and was by occupation a farmer prior to enlisting in Buncombe County at age 28, July 8, 1862, for the war. Mustered in as Corporal. Reported absent sick in November, 1862-April, 1863. Reduced to ranks March-April, 1863. Returned to duty in May-June, 1863. Reported present in July-October, 1863. Reported absent sick in November-December, 1863. Returned to duty in January-February, 1864. Reported present through June 30, 1864. Reported absent sick on August 10, 1864. Reported on duty as a provost guard at Macon, Georgia, in November-December, 1864. No further records. Survived the war.

GENTRY, THOMAS J., Private

Enlisted in Buncombe County at age 20, July 8, 1862, for the war. Hospitalized at Dalton, Georgia, December 31, 1862, with chronic diarrhoea. Transferred to another hospital on February 12, 1863. Reported absent sick through February 29, 1864. Dropped from the company rolls in March-April, 1864, for absence without leave. Listed as a deserter on September 13, 1864.

GRANT, JOSHUA, ———

Place and date of enlistment not reported (probably enlisted subsequent to August 31, 1864). Died at Macon, Georgia, November 9, 1864. Cause of death not reported.

HALL, GEORGE W., Private

Enlisted in Buncombe County on July 8, 1862, for the war. Reported present on October 29, 1862. Reported absent sick in November, 1862-February, 1863. Returned to duty in March-April, 1863. Reported present through October 31, 1863. Captured at Missionary Ridge, Tennessee, November 25, 1863. Sent to Nashville, Tennessee. Transferred to Louisville, Kentucky, where he arrived on December 7, 1863. Transferred to Rock Island, Illinois, where he arrived on December 9, 1863. Released at Rock Island on October 13, 1864, after taking the Oath of Allegiance and joining the U.S. Army. Assigned to Company I, 2nd Regiment U.S. Volunteer Infantry.

HARROWOOD, JASPER, Private

Resided in Buncombe County and was by occupation a farmer prior to enlisting in Buncombe County at age 24, July 8, 1862, for the war. Reported present in November-December, 1862. Hospitalized at Dalton, Georgia, January 6, 1863, with a gunshot wound. Place and date wounded not reported (was probably wounded at Murfreesboro, Tennessee, December 31, 1862-January 2, 1863). Re-

ported absent sick through April 30, 1863. Deserted on May 1, 1863. Reported under arrest awaiting trial for desertion in March-April, 1864. Reported absent sick from May 25 through August 31, 1864. Hospitalized at Macon, Georgia, December 21, 1864, with ascites. Returned to duty on March 25, 1865. No further records. Survived the war.

HARROWOOD, LEWIS H., Private

Resided in Buncombe County where he enlisted at age 21, July 8, 1862, for the war. Reported absent sick in November, 1862-February, 1864. Dropped from the company rolls in March-April, 1864, for absence without leave. Listed as a deserter on September 13, 1864.

HARROWOOD, SQUIRE H., Private

Resided in Buncombe County and was by occupation a farmer prior to enlisting in Buncombe County at age 20, July 8, 1862, for the war. Reported absent sick in November, 1862-June, 1863. Returned to duty in July-October, 1863. Reported absent sick from December 1, 1863, through April 30, 1864. Returned to duty on an unspecified date. Reported absent sick from June 25 through August 31, 1864. No further records. Survived the war.

HAWKINS, WILLIAM A., Private

Resided in Buncombe County. Place and date of enlistment not reported (probably enlisted subsequent to August 31, 1864). Captured at Salisbury on April 12, 1865. Sent to Nashville, Tennessee. Transferred to Louisville, Kentucky, where he arrived on May 1, 1865. Transferred to Camp Chase, Ohio, where he arrived on May 4, 1865. Released at Camp Chase on June 13, 1865, after taking the Oath of Allegiance. [Records of the Federal Provost Marshal dated June, 1865, give his age as 48.]

HENSLEY, THOMAS H., Private

Enlisted in Buncombe County on July 8, 1862, for the war. Reported absent sick in November, 1862-February, 1863. Returned to duty in March-April, 1863. Reported present in May-October, 1863. Captured at Missionary Ridge, Tennessee, November 25, 1863. Sent to Nashville, Tennessee. Transferred to Louisville, Kentucky, where he arrived on December 7, 1863. Transferred to Rock Island, Illinois, where he arrived on December 11, 1863. Died at Rock Island on March 4, 1864, of "variola."

HORTON, ROBERT A., Private

Resided in Rutherford County. Place and date of enlistment not reported (probably enlisted subsequent to August 31, 1864). Captured at Pulaski, Tennessee, December 26, 1864. Sent to Nashville, Tennessee. Transferred to Louisville, Kentucky, where he arrived on February 15, 1865. Transferred to Camp Chase, Ohio, where he arrived on February 18, 1865. Released at Camp Chase on June 13, 1865, after taking the Oath of Allegiance. [Records of the Federal Provost Marshal dated June, 1865, give his age as 41.]

HUDGINS, J. M., Private

Enlisted at Camp Vance on September 27, 1863, for the war. Reported present through October 31, 1863. Deserted on December 12, 1863.

HUDGINS, JOHN B., Private

Enlisted in Buncombe County on July 8, 1862, for the war. Hospitalized at Dalton, Georgia, January 29, 1863, with rheumatism. Deserted on June 2, 1863. Reported absent sick in November-

December, 1863. Died in hospital at Atlanta, Georgia, on or about January 3, 1864. Cause of death not reported.

HUDGINS, NOAH, Private

Enlisted in Buncombe County on July 8, 1862, for the war. Deserted at Camp Smith (Madison County) on September 1, 1862.

HUDGINS, STERLING, Private

Enlisted in Buncombe County at age 30, July 8, 1862, for the war. Deserted at Camp Smith (Madison County) on August 25, 1862. Returned to duty on an unspecified date. Hospitalized at Dalton, Georgia, December 31, 1862, with remittent fever. Deserted from hospital at Dalton on June 2, 1863.

HUDGINS, W. M., Private

Enlisted at Camp Vance on September 27, 1863, for the war. Reported present through October 31, 1863. Deserted on November 20, 1863.

HYATT, SAMUEL J., Corporal

Previously served as Private in Company A of this regiment. Transferred to this company on June 1, 1863. Mustered in as Corporal. Reported sick in hospital in July-October, 1863. Returned to duty in November-December, 1863. Reported present in January-February, 1864. Discharged at Dalton, Georgia, March 23, 1864, by reason of "asthma."

HYATT, SHADRICK E., Sergeant

Resided in Buncombe County where he enlisted at age 18, July 8, 1862, for the war. Mustered in as Private. Reported present in November, 1862-June, 1863. Promoted to Corporal on March 23, 1863. Promoted to Sergeant on June 1, 1863. Reported absent sick from October 11, 1863, through August 31, 1864. No further records. Survived the war.

HYATT, TOBIAS, Private

Enlisted in Buncombe County on July 8, 1862, for the war. Deserted at Murfreesboro, Tennessee, December 8, 1862. Returned from desertion on February 21, 1863. Reported present in March-April, 1863. Deserted on May 27, 1863.

JENKINS, HENRY, Private

Enlisted in Buncombe County on July 8, 1862, for the war. Discharged prior to October 29, 1862, by reason of "lung trouble." [Was about 25 years of age at time of enlistment.]

JENKINS, RUSSELL, Private

Enlisted in Buncombe County on July 8, 1862, for the war. Reported absent sick in November-December, 1862. Returned to duty in January-February, 1863. Reported present through June 30, 1863. Deserted on September 10, 1863.

JUSTICE, JOSEPH, Private

Resided in McDowell County and was by occupation a laborer prior to enlisting in Buncombe County at age 47, July 8, 1862, for the war as a substitute for Pvt. M. C. Davis of this company. Deserted at Greeneville, Tennessee, October 1, 1862.

LANKFORD, MARTIN V., Private

Resided in Buncombe County and was by occupation a carpenter prior to enlisting in Buncombe County at age 21, July 8, 1862, for the war. Reported absent sick in November, 1862-June, 1863. Died on July 20, 1863, of disease. Place of death not reported.

LANKFORD, THOMAS N., Private

Resided in Buncombe County and enlisted at age 20, July 8, 1862, for the war. Reported present in November, 1862-February, 1863. Reported absent sick in March, 1863-June, 1864. Dropped from the company rolls in July-August, 1864, for absence without leave.

LANNING, BARZILLA, Private

Resided in Buncombe County and was by occupation a farm laborer prior to enlisting in Buncombe County at age 28, July 8, 1862, for the war. Reported absent sick in November, 1862-February, 1863. Returned to duty in March-April, 1863. Reported present in May-June, 1863. Killed at Chickamauga, Georgia, September 20, 1863.

LANNING, ELLIOTT R., Private

Resided in Buncombe County and was by occupation a farmer prior to enlisting in Buncombe County at age 29, July 8, 1862, for the war. Reported absent sick on October 29, 1862. Returned to duty in November-December, 1862. Reported present in January-February, 1863. Reported sick in hospital in March-June, 1863. Returned to duty in July-October, 1863. Reported present in November, 1863-April, 1864. Captured at Resaca, Georgia, May 15, 1864. Sent to Nashville, Tennessee. Transferred to Louisville, Kentucky, where he arrived on May 21, 1864. Transferred to Alton, Illinois, where he arrived on May 25, 1864. Hospitalized at Alton on August 10, 1864, with typho-malarial fever. Released from hospital on August 13, 1864. Admitted to hospital at Alton on August 31, 1864, with hemorrhoids, diarrhoea, and scurvy. Released from hospital on October 4, 1864. Hospitalized at Alton on October 10, 1864, with diarrhoea and scorbutus. Died in hospital at Alton on November 7, 1864, of "chronic diarrhoea."

LANNING, GEORGE, Private

Enlisted in Buncombe County on July 8, 1862, for the war. Reported absent sick on October 29, 1862. Returned to duty in November-December, 1862. Reported present in January-February, 1863. Died at Chattanooga, Tennessee, April 11, 1863. Cause of death not reported.

LEDFORD, CHRISTOPHER C., Private

Resided in Buncombe County and was by occupation a farmer prior to enlisting in Buncombe County at age 28, July 8, 1862, for the war. Reported absent sick in November-December, 1862. Hospitalized at Catoosa Springs, Georgia, on an unspecified date. Deserted from hospital on February 15, 1863. Reported present in March-April, 1863. Deserted on May 26, 1863. Reported under arrest awaiting trial for desertion in March, 1864. Court-martialed on April 5, 1864. Shot at Dalton, Georgia, May 4, 1864, for desertion.

LEDFORD, MANSON C., ———

North Carolina pension records indicate that he served in this company.

LEWIS, JOSIAH, Private

Enlisted in Buncombe County on July 8, 1862, for the war. Reported present in November, 1862-June, 1863. Reported absent on detached service in July-October, 1863. Rejoined the company in November-December, 1863. Reported present but on detail as a teamster from January 1 through June 30, 1864. Reported present in July-August, 1864. No further records.

LYNCH, A. R., Private

Resided in Rutherford County and enlisted in Buncombe County on July 8, 1862, for the war. Deserted prior to September 25, 1862. Returned to duty prior to October 29, 1862. Reported absent sick in November, 1862-April, 1863. Deserted from hospital on June 1, 1863.

LYNCH, WILLIAM A., Private

Resided in Polk or Rutherford County and was by occupation a farmer prior to enlisting in Buncombe County at age 27, July 8, 1862, for the war. Deserted prior to September 25, 1862. Returned to duty prior to October 29, 1862. Reported absent sick in November, 1862-February, 1863. Returned to duty in March-April, 1863. Deserted on an unspecified date prior to July 1, 1863, but was apprehended and placed under arrest to await trial. Reported present in July-October, 1863. Captured at Missionary Ridge, Tennessee, November 25, 1863. Sent to Nashville, Tennessee. Transferred to Louisville, Kentucky, where he arrived on December 7, 1863. Transferred to Rock Island, Illinois, where he arrived on December 9, 1863. Paroled at Rock Island and transferred for exchange on March 2, 1865. No further records.

McBRAYER, RICHARD L., Private

Previously served as Private in Company K of this regiment. Transferred to this company on August 1, 1862. Reported absent sick in November-December, 1862. Furloughed from hospital for thirty days on January 24, 1863. Reported absent without leave on or about February 28, 1863. Dropped from the company rolls on March 20, 1863.

McBRAYER, WILLIAM A., Sergeant

Previously served as Private in Company K of this regiment. Transferred to this company on August 1, 1862. Mustered in as Sergeant. Wounded in the hand at Murfreesboro, Tennessee, January 2, 1863. Died on January 17, 1863, of wounds. Place of death not reported.

McCLURE, ALEXANDER, Private

Previously served as Private in Company A of this regiment. Transferred to this company on or about July 8, 1862. Hospitalized at Dalton, Georgia, December 30, 1862, with chronic dysentery. Released from hospital on January 6, 1863, but failed to rejoin his company. Listed as a deserter on March 6, 1863. Returned to duty on an unspecified date. Reported present in July, 1863-April, 1864. Wounded at Kolb's Farm, near Marietta, Georgia, June 22, 1864. Reported absent wounded or absent sick through August 31, 1864. No further records.

McCRACKIN, D. G., Private

Born in Washington County, Virginia, and was by occupation a cabinetmaker prior to enlisting in Buncombe County on July 8, 1862, for the war. Deserted at Murfreesboro, Tennessee, November 1, 1862. Discharged on February 20, 1863, by reason of "fistula which has been unsuccessfully operated upon." Discharge certificate gives his age as 49.

MERRELL, J. W., Private

Previously served as Private in Company B of this regiment. Transferred to this company on August 1, 1862. Deserted at Greeneville, Tennessee, October 1, 1862.

MOORE, C. S., Private

Enlisted in Buncombe County on July 8, 1862, for the war. Hospitalized at Dalton, Georgia, December 24, 1862, with phthisis pulmonalis. Returned to duty prior to February 28, 1863. Died at Tullahoma, Tennessee, March 4, 1863. Cause of death not reported.

MORGAN, NOAH WILLIAM, Private

Resided in Buncombe County and was by occupation a farmer prior to enlisting in Buncombe County on July 8, 1862, for the war. Died in hospital at Ringgold, Georgia, January 8, 1863. Cause of death not reported. [Was about 22 years of age at time of enlistment.]

MUNDAY, STEPHEN M., Private

Resided in Buncombe County and was by occupation a farmer prior to enlisting in Buncombe County at age 29, July 8, 1862, for the war. Reported present in November, 1862-April, 1863. Hospitalized at Dalton, Georgia, May 21, 1863, with intermittent fever. Returned to duty on June 28, 1863. Deserted on October 4, 1863.

OWENBEY, AMOS, Private

Enlisted in Buncombe County on July 8, 1862, for the war. Died in hospital at Tullahoma, Tennessee, February 13, 1863. Cause of death not reported.

OWENBEY, CALEB, Private

Enlisted in Buncombe County on July 8, 1862, for the war. Hospitalized at Dalton, Georgia, December 31, 1862, with lumbago. Returned to duty on an unspecified date. Hospitalized at Dalton on January 29, 1863, with rheumatism. Returned to duty on February 9, 1863. Reported present through June 30, 1863. Killed at Chickamauga, Georgia, September 20, 1863.

PACK, GEORGE W., Private

Enlisted in Buncombe County on July 8, 1862, for the war. Hospitalized at Dalton, Georgia, December 31, 1862, with remittent fever. Returned to duty on January 19, 1863. Reported present through February 28, 1863. Reported sick in hospital in March-April, 1863. Returned to duty in May-June, 1863. Reported present through October 31, 1863. Captured at Missionary Ridge, Tennessee, November 25, 1863. Sent to Nashville, Tennessee. Transferred to Louisville, Kentucky, where he arrived on December 7, 1863. Transferred to Rock Island, Illinois, where he arrived on December 9, 1863. Released at Rock Island on October 6, 1864, after taking the Oath of Allegiance and joining the U.S. Army. Assigned to Company B, 2nd Regiment U.S. Volunteer Infantry.

PADGETT, S., Private

Enlisted at Camp Vance on September 27, 1863, for the war. Deserted on November 1, 1863.

PARKER, B. R., Private

Previously served as Private in Company B, 18th Regiment Tennessee Volunteers. Transferred to this company on October 12, 1862. Wounded slightly in the scrotum at Murfreesboro, Tennessee, January 2, 1863. Returned to duty prior to March 1, 1863. Reported absent sick in March-April, 1863. Hospitalized at Tunnel Hill, Georgia, May 24, 1863, with toxicum. Transferred to hospital at Catoosa Springs, Georgia, June 19, 1863. Returned to duty in July-October, 1863. Reported present through April 30, 1864. Died at Atlanta, Georgia, on or about May 29, 1864, of wounds. Place and date wounded not reported.

PATTON, BENJAMIN FRANKLIN, ——

North Carolina pension records indicate that he served in this company.

PATTON, WILLIAM F., Private

Enlisted in Buncombe County on July 8, 1862, for the war. Reported absent sick in November, 1862-February, 1863. Hospitalized at Tunnel Hill, Georgia, May 18, 1863. Died in hospital at Tunnel Hill on June 28, 1863, of "pneumonia."

PENLAND, J. R., Private

Resided in Buncombe County where he enlisted on July 8, 1862, for the war. Deserted at Camp Smith (Madison County) on August 20, 1862. Returned to duty on February 21, 1863. Reported present until May 1, 1863, when he deserted. [May have served later as Private in Company B, 2nd Regiment N.C. Mounted Infantry (Union).]

PENLAND, WILLIAM S., Private

Enlisted in Buncombe County on July 8, 1862, for the war. Wounded in the hand at Murfreesboro, Tennessee, December 31, 1862-January 2, 1863. Reported absent wounded or absent sick through July 30, 1863. Reported in hospital at La Grange, Georgia, from August 1 through December 31, 1863. Detailed for light duty in hospital at La Grange on or about January 11, 1864. Reported absent on detail or absent sick through August 31, 1864. Furloughed for sixty days on January 19, 1865, suffering from "incipient phthisis following measles accompanied with frequent haemoptysis." No further records. Survived the war. [Was about 29 years of age at time of enlistment.]

RAMSEY, J. B., Private

Enlisted in Buncombe County on July 8, 1862, for the war. Discharged prior to October 29, 1862. Reason discharged not reported.

REDMON, PETER A., Corporal

Resided in Buncombe County and was by occupation a farmer prior to enlisting in Buncombe County at age 45, July 8, 1862, for the war as a substitute for Pvt. James Trentham. Mustered in as Private. Reported absent sick in November, 1862-April, 1863. Returned to duty in May-June, 1863. Reported present in July, 1863-August, 1864. Promoted to Corporal on November 1, 1863. No further records.

REED, HENRY, Corporal

Resided in Buncombe County and was by occupation a farmer prior to enlisting in Buncombe County at age 34, July 8, 1862, for the war. Mustered in as Private. Reported absent on detached service in hospital at Greeneville, Tennessee, in November, 1862-February, 1863. Rejoined the company in March-April, 1863. Promoted to Corporal on March 23, 1863. Reported present in May-June, 1863. Reported on duty as a hospital nurse at Lauderdale Springs, Mississippi, in July-October, 1863. Rejoined the company in November-December, 1863. Reported present in January-April, 1864. Reported absent sick on June 1, 1864. Furloughed for sixty days from hospital at Dalton, Georgia, on or about June 29, 1864, suffering from chronic diarrhoea, extreme emaciation, and debility. No further records. Survived the war. [North Carolina pension records indicate that he lost his left eye "by exposure" while in camp at Dalton on February 15, 186(4).]

REED, JESSE, Private

Resided in Buncombe County and was by occupation a farmer prior to enlisting in Buncombe County at age 26, July 8, 1862, for the war. Deserted on November 22, 1862. Returned to duty on January 2, 1863. Reported present in January-June, 1863. Reported absent sick from September 20, 1863, through February 29, 1864. Dropped from the company rolls in March-April, 1864, for absence without leave. Listed as a deserter on September 13, 1864.

RICE, JAMES O., Corporal

Resided in Buncombe County and was by occupation a farmer prior to enlisting in Buncombe County at age 43, July 8, 1862, for the war. Mustered in as Private. Reported absent sick in November, 1862-February, 1863. Promoted to Corporal on January 21, 1863. Died at Ringgold, Georgia, March 8, 1863. Cause of death not reported.

ROBERTS, LEANDER WESLEY, Private

Previously served as Private in Company A of this regiment. Transferred to this company on June 1, 1863. Mustered in as Corporal. Reported sick in hospital in July-October, 1863. Reduced to ranks on an unspecified date. Captured at Missionary Ridge, Tennessee, November 25, 1863. Sent to Nashville, Tennessee. Transferred to Louisville, Kentucky, where he arrived on December 7, 1863. Transferred to Rock Island, Illinois, where he arrived on December 11, 1863. Died at Rock Island on December 18, 1863. Cause of death not reported.

ROBERTS, MELVILLE B., Sergeant

Resided in Buncombe County and was by occupation a farm laborer prior to enlisting in Buncombe County at age 20, July 8, 1862, for the war. Mustered in as Private. Reported present in November, 1862-June, 1863. Promoted to Sergeant on March 25, 1863. Reported sick in hospital in July-August, 1863. Wounded at Chickamauga, Georgia, September 20, 1863. Returned to duty in November-December, 1863. Furloughed on February 23, 1864. Returned to duty in March-April, 1864. Hospitalized at Macon, Georgia, May 31, 1864, with acute dysentery. Returned to duty on June 6, 1864. Reported present in July-August, 1864. Wounded in the right thigh at Bentonville on March 19, 1865. Paroled at Greensboro on May 2, 1865. [His parole states that he was a member of Company C, 60th North Carolina; however, the 60th North Carolina was consolidated with the 58th Regiment N.C. Troops on April 9, 1865. Presumably, Sergeant Roberts was a member of the latter unit.]

ROBERTSON, A., Private

Enlisted in Buncombe County on July 8, 1862, for the war. Died in hospital at Greeneville, Tennessee, October 12, 1862. Cause of death not reported.

ROGERS, FRANCIS M., Private

Born in Buncombe County where he resided as a day laborer prior to enlisting in Buncombe County at age 34, July 8, 1862, for the war. Transferred to Company I of this regiment on August 1, 1862.

SEARCEY, A. W., Private

Resided in Rutherford County and enlisted in Buncombe County at age 35, July 8, 1862, for the war. Deserted on August 25, 1862. Returned to duty on an unspecified date. Wounded in the hand at Murfreesboro, Tennessee, on or about December 30, 1862. Furloughed for thirty days on January 24, 1863. Reported absent without leave on February 28, 1863. Returned to duty in May-June, 1863. Reported present in July-October, 1863. Deserted on December 12, 1863.

SEARCEY, REUBEN, Private

Resided in Rutherford County and enlisted in Buncombe County on July 8, 1862, for the war. Deserted at Camp Smith (Madison County) on August 27, 1862. Returned to duty on August 26, 1863. Deserted on November 20, 1863. Went over to the enemy on an unspecified date. Took the Oath of Allegiance at Chattanooga, Tennessee, April 5, 1864.

SEARCEY, WILLIAM B., Sergeant

Born in Rutherford County and was by occupation a farmer prior to enlisting in Buncombe County on July 8, 1862, for the war. Mustered in as Private. Reported present in November, 1862-October, 1863. Promoted to Sergeant in November, 1863. Captured at Missionary Ridge, Tennessee, November 25, 1863. Sent to Nashville, Tennessee. Transferred to Louisville, Kentucky, where he arrived on December 7, 1863. Transferred to Rock Island, Illinois, where he arrived on December 9, 1863. Released at Rock Island on October 17, 1864, after taking the Oath of Allegiance and joining the U.S. Army. Assigned to Company E, 3rd Regiment U.S. Volunteer Infantry. [Was about 22 years of age at time of enlistment.]

SMITH, D. L., Sergeant

Enlisted in Buncombe County on July 8, 1862, for the war. Mustered in as Private. Reported present in November, 1862-June, 1863. Promoted to Sergeant on March 23, 1863. Wounded in the head at Chickamauga, Georgia, September 20, 1863. Died in hospital at Cassville, Georgia, October 16, 1863, of wounds. Nominated for the Badge of Distinction for gallantry at Chickamauga. [Capt. Thomas W. Patton described Sergeant Smith a few days after his death as "the best man that belonged to my company." T. W. Patton to his mother, October 21, 1863, James W. Patton Papers, Southern Historical Collection.]

TAYLOR, R. W., Private

Enlisted in Buncombe County on July 8, 1862, for the war. Reported present in November, 1862-June, 1863. Reported sick in hospital in July-October, 1863. Died at home on November 10, 1863. Cause of death not reported.

TRANTHAM, JAMES, Private

Enlisted in Buncombe County on July 8, 1862, for the war. Discharged prior to October 29, 1862, after providing Pvt. Peter A. Redmon as a substitute.

VESS, ZEPHANIAH, Private

Resided in Rutherford County and enlisted in Buncombe County at age 20, July 8, 1862, for the war. Deserted at Murfreesboro, Tennessee, December 18, 1862. Later served as Private in Company B and as Corporal in Company H, 2nd Regiment N.C. Mounted Infantry (Union).

WARREN, J. E., Private

Enlisted at Camp Vance on September 27, 1863, for the war. Deserted on December 20, 1863. Reported in hospital at Raleigh on January 16, 1864. Returned to duty in March-April, 1864, and was

placed under arrest. Reported absent sick from May 23 through August 31, 1864. No further records.

WHITAKER, JOHN A., Sergeant

Born on April 30, 1838. Resided in Buncombe County and was by occupation a farmer prior to enlisting in Buncombe County at age 24, July 8, 1862, for the war. Mustered in as Sergeant. Died in hospital at Murfreesboro, Tennessee, December 15, 1862. Cause of death not reported.

WHITAKER, NOAH, Private

Resided in Buncombe County where he enlisted at age 31, July 8, 1862, for the war. Reported present in November, 1862-August, 1864. Served as teamster for approximately six months during the first half of 1864. No further records. Survived the war.

WHITAKER, RUFUS J., Private

Enlisted in Buncombe County on July 8, 1862, for the war. Reported absent sick in November, 1862-February, 1863. Hospitalized at Dalton, Georgia, March 13, 1863, with rubeola. Returned to duty subsequent to October 31, 1863. Wounded in the right foot and captured at or near Missionary Ridge, Tennessee, on or about November 25, 1863. Right foot amputated. Died in a Federal hospital at Chattanooga, Tennessee, December 20, 1863, of wounds.

WHITAKER, T. L., Corporal

Resided in Buncombe County and was by occupation a farmer prior to enlisting in Buncombe County at age 32, July 8, 1862, for the war. Mustered in as Private. Promoted to Corporal on August 1, 1862. Reported present in November, 1862-February, 1863. Reported sick in hospital in March-April, 1863. Died at Catoosa Springs, Georgia, May 5, 1863. Cause of death not reported.

WHITLOCK, JACKSON, Private

Enlisted in Buncombe County on July 8, 1862, for the war. Reported present in November-December, 1862. Wounded in the hand at Murfreesboro, Tennessee, January 2, 1863. Hospitalized at Dalton, Georgia, January 30, 1863, with chronic diarrhoea. Returned to duty in May-June, 1863. Deserted on or about September 10, 1863.

WILSON, JAMES E., Private

Resided in Buncombe County where he enlisted on July 8, 1862, for the war. Deserted at Murfreesboro, Tennessee, October 23, 1862. Returned to duty on or about May 1, 1863. Wounded in the left arm at Chickamauga, Georgia, September 20, 1863. Reported in hospital at Griffin, Georgia, November 23, 1863. Returned to duty in March-April, 1864. Reported present in May-August, 1864. Captured at Bentonville on March 22, 1865. Sent to New Bern. Transferred to Hart's Island, New York Harbor, where he arrived on April 10, 1865. Released at Hart's Island on June 19, 1865, after taking the Oath of Allegiance.

WILSON, JONATHAN A., Private

Resided in Union County, Georgia, and enlisted in Buncombe County on July 8, 1862, for the war. Reported absent sick in November-December, 1862. Deserted from hospital at Catoosa Springs, Georgia, February 15, 1863. Returned to duty in March-April, 1863. Reported present in May-June, 1863. Captured at Chickamauga, Georgia, September 20, 1863. Sent to Nashville, Tennessee. Transferred to Louisville, Kentucky, where he arrived on September 30, 1863. Transferred to Camp Douglas, Chicago, Illinois, where he arrived on October 4, 1863. Released at Camp Douglas on June 16, 1865, after taking the Oath of Allegiance.

WRIGHT, MARTIN B., Private

Previously served as Private in Company A of this regiment. Transferred to this company on or about July 8, 1862. Reported absent sick in November, 1862-February, 1863. Returned to duty in March-April, 1863. Transferred back to Company A on May 1, 1863.

WRIGHT, ROBERT FRANKLIN, Private

Born on June 3, 1829. Enlisted in Buncombe County at age 33, July 8, 1862, for the war. Reported absent sick in November-December, 1862. Returned to duty in January-February, 1863. Reported present in March-October, 1863. Reported absent sick on December 1, 1863. Reported absent sick through June 30, 1864. Dropped from the company rolls in July-August, 1864, for absence without leave.

YOUNG, JOHN G., Corporal

Born on October 13, 1837. Enlisted in Buncombe County at age 24, July 8, 1862, for the war. Was apparently mustered in with the rank of Corporal. Deserted at Murfreesboro, Tennessee, November 22, 1862.

COMPANY D

This company, known also as the "Henderson Rangers," was raised in Henderson County on July 10, 1862, as Capt. Charles M. Fletcher's [Independent] Company, N.C. Volunteers. It was mustered into Confederate service and assigned to the 1st Battalion N.C. Infantry on August 1, 1862. On October 8, 1862, it became part of the 60th Regiment N.C. Troops when three additional companies were assigned to the seven companies of the 1st Battalion. This company was designated Company D. After joining the regiment the company functioned as a part of the regiment, and its history for the remainder of the war is reported as a part of the regimental history.

The following roster was compiled primarily from information in the microfilm edition of the Compiled Service Records of Soldiers Who Served in Organizations from the State of North Carolina (Record Group 109, M270), National Archives and Records Administration, Washington, D.C. Record Group 109 includes enlistment papers, pay vouchers, requisitions, letters of resignation, discharge certificates, and abstracts of medical and prisoner of war returns. Materials relating specifically to this company include an undated muster-in and descriptive roll and muster rolls dated November, 1862-August, 1864.

Also utilized in this roster were *The War of the Rebellion: A Compilation of the Official Records of the Union and Confederate Armies*, the North Carolina adjutant general's *Roll of Honor*, state militia records, newspaper casualty lists and obituaries, wartime claims for bounty pay and allowances, postwar registers of claims for artificial limbs, Confederate pension applications filed with the states of North Carolina, Tennessee, and Florida, Confederate Soldiers' Home records, and the 1860 and 1870 federal censuses of North Carolina. A search was made also for relevant letters, diaries, reminiscences, and other manuscripts in the Southern Historical Collection (University of North Carolina-Chapel Hill), the Duke University Library Special Collections Department, and the North Carolina Division of Archives and History.

Among the secondary sources consulted were records of the North Carolina division of the United Daughters of the Confederacy, postwar rosters, regimental and county histories, marriage bond, will, and cemetery indexes, published and unpublished genealogies, biographical dictionaries, the North Carolina *County Heritage Book* series, the *Confederate Veteran*, Walter Clark's *Histories of the Several Regiments and Battalions from North Carolina in the Great War, 1861-'65*, and the North Carolina volume of the extended edition of *Confederate Military History*.

OFFICERS

CAPTAINS

FLETCHER, CHARLES M.

Born in Henderson County* and was by occupation a farmer prior to enlisting in Henderson County at age 28. Elected Captain on July 10, 1862. Reported present in November-December, 1862. Courtmartialed and dismissed from the service on or about March 12, 1863, for misconduct at the Battle of Murfreesboro, Tennessee, December 31, 1862-January 2, 1863. [Previously served as Captain in the 106th Regiment N.C. Militia. May have served later as Private in Company H, 25th Regiment N.C. Troops.]

GILLILAND, JESSE R. S.

Previously served as Private in Company A, 4th Regiment Tennessee Infantry. Appointed Captain of this company on November 17, 1863. Reported present in January-June, 1864. Wounded in the foot ("heel entirely shot away") at Ezra Church, near Atlanta, Georgia, while sleeping on the night of July 28, 1864. Reported absent wounded through August 31, 1864. "After long, lingering, and great suffering, his wound proved mortal and . . . [he] died at Asheville soon after the war ended. . . . [N]o nobler commander ever led a braver company." [Thomas W. Patton, "Sixtieth North Carolina Regiment: Infantry," 4, folder 6, box 74, Civil War Collection, NCDAH.]

CHAMBERS, JOHN GREGG

Served as 1st Lieutenant of Company C of this regiment. Detailed as acting Captain of this company in August, 1864.

LIEUTENANTS

BANNING, RUFUS P., 1st Lieutenant

Born in Henderson County* where he resided as a farmer or farm laborer prior to enlisting in Henderson County at age 25. Elected 1st Lieutenant on July 10, 1862. Reported present in November-December, 1862. Sent to hospital in March-April, 1863. Resigned on or about May 3, 1863, by reason of "chronic bronchitis" and "incipient phthis[is] pulmonalis." Resignation accepted on May 16, 1863. [Previously served as Captain in the 106th Regiment N.C. Militia.]

BRITTAIN, JAMES LAMBERT, 2nd Lieutenant

Born in Henderson County* and was by occupation a farmer prior to enlisting in Henderson County at age 32. Elected 2nd Lieutenant on July 10, 1862. Resigned on November 5, 1862, by reason of "exostosis of the bone of the leg" which rendered him "incapable of marching." Resignation accepted on November 25, 1862.

EVANS, ROBERT C., 2nd Lieutenant

Previously served as Private in Company E, 19th Battalion South Carolina Cavalry. Elected 2nd Lieutenant of this company on April 20, 1864. Reported sick in hospital on July 28, 1864 (may have been wounded at Ezra Church, near Atlanta, Georgia). Reported absent sick through September 20, 1864. No further records.

FORD, JAMES M., 2nd Lieutenant

Born in Washington County, Tennessee, and resided in Henderson County where he was by occupation a painter or carpenter prior to enlisting in Henderson County at age 29, July 10, 1862, for the war. Mustered in as Sergeant. Elected 2nd Lieutenant on December 10, 1862. Reported present in March-June, 1863 (signed roll as commander of the company). Reported absent sick in July-December, 1863. Resigned on or about January 14, 1864. Reason he resigned not reported; however, his letter is annotated by Col. W. M. Hardy of the 60th Regiment who stated that Lieutenant Ford was "so *very inefficient* that I cordially approve and respectfully forward [his resignation]." Resignation accepted on January 23, 1864.

LOWRANCE, HENRY CLAY, 1st Lieutenant

Previously served as Corporal in Company K of this regiment. Appointed 1st Lieutenant and transferred to this company on July 30, 1863. Reported present through October 31, 1863. Captured at Missionary Ridge, Tennessee, November 25, 1863. Sent to Nashville, Tennessee. Transferred to Louisville, Kentucky, where he arrived on December 4, 1863. Transferred to Johnson's Island, Ohio, where he arrived on December 7, 1863. Transferred to Point Lookout, Maryland, April 22, 1864. Hospitalized at Point Lookout on April 26, 1864, with chronic diarrhoea. Discharged from hospital on May 20, 1864. Died at Point Lookout on August 11, 1864. Cause of death not reported.

SHIPMAN, THOMAS JEFFERSON, 3rd Lieutenant

Previously served as Private in Company E, 1st Regiment N.C. Infantry (6 months, 1861). Appointed 3rd Lieutenant of this company on July 10, 1862. Reported present and in command of the company in November, 1862-February, 1863. Sent to hospital in March-April, 1863. Returned to duty in July-October, 1863. Captured at Missionary Ridge, Tennessee, November 25, 1863. Sent to Nashville, Tennessee. Transferred to Louisville, Kentucky, where he arrived on December 4, 1863. Transferred to Johnson's Island, Ohio, where he arrived on December 7, 1863. Released at Johnson's Island on June 13, 1865, after taking the Oath of Allegiance. [Born in Henderson County on November 29, 1840.]

NONCOMMISSIONED OFFICERS AND PRIVATES

ALEXANDER, JOHN W., Private

Enlisted at Camp Vance on September 7, 1863, for the war. Reported absent without leave on December 10, 1863. Rejoined the company on December 26, 1863, and was placed under arrest. Returned to duty in March-April, 1864. Reported present in May-August, 1864. No further records. Survived the war. [Was about 18 years of age at time of enlistment.]

BAILEY, W. C., Private

Enlisted at Camp Vance on September 11, 1863, for the war. Reported present through December 31, 1863. Wounded slightly at Rocky Face Ridge, Georgia, February 25, 186●. Reported in hospital in March-June, 1864. Returned to duty in July-August, 1864. Reported on detail at Macon, Georgia, in November-December, 1864. No further records.

BANNING, RICHARD B., Private

Born in Henderson County where he resided as a farmer or farm laborer prior to enlisting in Henderson County at age 18, July 10, 1862, for the war. Reported present in November, 1862-June, 1863. Captured at Chickamauga, Georgia, September 20, 1863. Sent to Nashville, Tennessee. Transferred to Louisville, Kentucky, where he arrived on September 30, 1863. Transferred to Camp Douglas, Chicago, Illinois, where he arrived on October 4, 1863. Died at Camp Douglas on or about July 5, 1864, of "dropsy."

BARNWELL, JAMES R., Private

Born in Henderson County and was by occupation a farmer prior to enlisting in Henderson County at age 21, July 10, 1862, for the war. Transferred to Company I of this regiment on August 1, 1862.

BARNWELL, RILEY M., Private

Born in Henderson County where he enlisted at age 20, July 10, 1862, for the war. Reported absent sick in November, 1862-February, 1863. Returned to duty in March-April, 1863. Sent to hospital on June 10, 1863. Reported absent on sick furlough in July-December, 1863. Returned to duty in January-February, 1864. Reported present through August 31, 1864. No further records. Survived the war.

BECK, ALLEN F., Private

Born in Haywood County and was by occupation a farmer prior to enlisting in Henderson County at age 24, July 10, 1862, for the war. Reported sick in hospital in November-December, 1862. Returned to duty in January-February, 1863. Sent to hospital on March 31, 1863. Hospitalized at Kingston, Georgia, on or about August 7, 1863. Reported absent on sick furlough in November-December, 1863. Listed as a deserter and dropped from the company rolls in March-April, 1864.

BENISON, WILLIAM P., Private

Born at Madison, South Carolina, and was by occupation a farmer prior to enlisting in Henderson County at age 34, July 10, 1862, for the war. Hospitalized at Dalton, Georgia, on or about November 21, 1862, with rheumatism and/or chronic diarrhoea. Deserted from hospital on December 14, 1862. Returned to duty in January-February, 1863. Hospitalized at Dalton on March 23, 1863, with typhoid fever. Furloughed on May 26, 1863. Returned to duty subsequent to October 31, 1863. Captured at Missionary Ridge, Tennessee, November 25, 1863. Sent to Nashville, Tennessee. Transferred to Louisville, Kentucky, where he arrived on December 7, 1863. Transferred to Rock Island, Illinois, where he arrived on December 11, 1863. No further records.

BENSON, WILSON, Private

Previously served as Private in Company G, 35th Regiment N.C. Troops. Enlisted in this company in Henderson County on July 10, 1862, for the war. Discharged on August 11, 1862. Reason discharged not reported.

BRADLEY, ABRAHAM B., Private

Born in Greenville District, South Carolina, and resided in Henderson County where he enlisted at age 23, July 10, 1862, for the war.

Deserted on November 13, 1862. Returned to duty in March-April, 1863. Reported present in May-June, 1863. Deserted on September 1, 1863. Reported sick in hospital in November-December, 1863. Died on January 4, 1864. Place and cause of death not reported.

BROILS, BRANSON, Private

Born in Randolph County and was by occupation a farmer prior to enlisting in Henderson County at age 25, July 10, 1862, for the war. Discharged prior to January 1, 1863, after providing Pvt. James A. Clark as a substitute.

BROWN, ADOLPHUS E., Private

Born in Buncombe County and was by occupation a farmer prior to enlisting in Henderson County at age 32, July 10, 1862, for the war. Deserted at Tullahoma, Tennessee, February 1, 1863. Returned to duty in March-April, 1864. Captured at Adairsville, Georgia, May 18, 1864. Sent to Nashville, Tennessee. Transferred to Louisville, Kentucky, where he arrived on May 24, 1864. Transferred to Rock Island, Illinois, where he arrived on May 27, 1864. Released at Rock Island on June 10, 1864, after taking the Oath of Allegiance and joining the U.S. Navy.

BURNETT, EDWARD P., Private

Born in Buncombe County and was by occupation a farmer prior to enlisting in Henderson County at age 18, July 10, 1862, for the war. Sent to hospital sick on December 29, 1862. Failed to return to duty and was listed as a deserter in July-October, 1863. Later served as Private in Company F, 2nd Regiment N.C. Mounted Infantry (Union).

BURNETT, OLIVER P., Sergeant

Born in Henderson County* and was by occupation a farmer prior to enlisting in Henderson County at age 33, July 10, 1862, for the war. Mustered in as Corporal. Reported present in November, 1862-February, 1863. Sent to hospital in March, 1863. Returned to duty and was promoted to Sergeant subsequent to June 30, 1863. Wounded in the right thigh at Chickamauga, Georgia, September 20, 1863. Returned to duty subsequent to February 29, 1864. Detailed for light duty on April 23, 1864, by reason of unfitness for field service. Reported absent on detail through August 31, 1864. No further records. Survived the war.

BUTLER, GEORGE WASHINGTON, Private

Born in Buncombe County and was by occupation a farmer prior to enlisting in Henderson County at age 24, July 10, 1862, for the war. Sent to hospital sick in November-December, 1862. Returned to duty in March-April, 1863. Reported present in May-June, 1863. Reported on detached duty with the Pioneer Corps in July, 1863-February, 1864. Rejoined the company in March-April, 1864. Captured at Resaca, Georgia, on or about May 15, 1864. Sent to Nashville, Tennessee. Transferred to Louisville, Kentucky, where he arrived on May 21, 1864. Transferred to Camp Morton, Indianapolis, Indiana, where he arrived on May 22, 1864. Released at Camp Morton on or about March 24, 1865, after taking the Oath of Allegiance and joining the U.S. service. Unit to which assigned not reported. [Heritage of Henderson County, 2:179, indicates that he was wound in the chin on an unspecified date.]

BUTLER, WILSON, Private

Place and date of enlistment not reported. Records of the Federal Provost Marshal indicate that he was captured at Ruff's Mill, near

Smyrna, Georgia, July 4, 1864, and was transferred to Marietta, Georgia, July 7, 1864. No further records.

CASE, JOHN L., Private

Born in Henderson County and was by occupation a farmer prior to enlisting in Henderson County at age 22, July 10, 1862, for the war. No further records. Survived the war.

CLARK, JAMES A., Private

Enlisted at Tullahoma, Tennessee, January 20, 1863, for the war as a substitute for Pvt. Branson Broils. Reported present through October 31, 1863. Died on an unspecified date in 1864. Place and cause of death not reported.

CLARK, THOMAS J., Private

Enlisted at Camp Vance on September 23, 1863, for the war. Captured at Missionary Ridge, Tennessee, November 25, 1863. Sent to Nashville, Tennessee. Transferred to Louisville, Kentucky, where he arrived on December 7, 1863. Transferred to Rock Island, Illinois, where he arrived on December 11, 1863. Died at Rock Island on January 26, 1864, of "rubeola."

CLAYTON, CALVIN C., Private

Born in Henderson County* where he resided prior to enlisting in Henderson County at age 33, July 10, 1862, for the war. Discharged on August 1, 1862. Reason discharged not reported.

CLAYTON, JOHN C., Private

Born in Henderson County where he resided as a farmer prior to enlisting in Henderson County at age 18, July 10, 1862, for the war. Died at Murfreesboro, Tennessee, November 2, 1862, of "congestive fever."

COLLINS, REUBEN E., Private

Born in Henderson County where he enlisted at age 23, July 10, 1862, for the war. Reported present in November, 1862-June, 1863. Captured at Chickamauga, Georgia, September 20, 1863. Sent to Nashville, Tennessee. Apparently died at Nashville prior to September 30, 1863. Cause of death not reported.

CORN, MATHEW D., Private

Born in Henderson County* and was by occupation a farmer prior to enlisting in Henderson County at age 29, July 10, 1862, for the war. Reported present in November, 1862-April, 1863. Deserted on May 25, 1863.

COUCH, GEORGE WASHINGTON, Private

Born in Spartanburg District, South Carolina, September 2, 1835. Resided in Henderson County and was by occupation a farmer prior to enlisting in Henderson County at age 26, July 10, 1862, for the war. Reported absent sick in November, 1862-April, 1863. Reported "present . . . by power of attorney" in May-June, 1863. Reported absent sick in July-December, 1863. Discharged on or about February 2, 1864, by reason of "great debility following cerebro spinal irritation."

DAWSON, JOSEPH S., Musician

Born in Henderson County and was by occupation a smith prior to enlisting in Henderson County at age 18, July 10, 1862, for the war. Mustered in as Musician. Sent to hospital in November-December,

1862. Died in hospital at Tullahoma, Tennessee, February 19, 1863. Cause of death not reported.

DRAKE, THOMAS B., Private

Born in Henderson County where he enlisted at age 22, July 10, 1862, for the war. Died at Murfreesboro, Tennessee, on an unspecified date (probably prior to January 1, 1863). Cause of death not reported.

DUNN, JAMES, Private

Born in South Carolina and resided in Henderson County where he was by occupation a farm laborer prior to enlisting at Camp Vance at age 33, September 10, 1863, for the war. Reported on duty as a pioneer through October 31, 1863. Captured at Missionary Ridge, Tennessee, November 25, 1863. Sent to Nashville, Tennessee. Transferred to Louisville, Kentucky, where he arrived on December 8, 1863. Transferred to Rock Island, Illinois, where he arrived on December 11, 1863. Died at Rock Island on February 27, 1864, of "variola."

EDGE, JOHN, ——

North Carolina pension records indicate that he served in this company.

EDMUNDSON, JOHN R., Private

Born in Buncombe County and was by occupation a farmer prior to enlisting in Henderson County at age 34, July 10, 1862, for the war. Hospitalized at Dalton, Georgia, November 28, 1862, with chronic diarrhoea. Returned to duty on December 13, 1862. Reported present through February 28, 1863. Reported absent sick in March, 1863-February, 1864. Returned to duty in March-April, 1864. Sent to hospital sick on June 1, 1864. Returned to duty in July-August, 1864. No further records. Survived the war.

FREEMAN, GEORGE B., Private

Born in Buncombe County and was by occupation a farmer prior to enlisting in Henderson County at age 20, July 10, 1862, for the war. Died at Murfreesboro, Tennessee, prior to January 28, 1863. Cause of death not reported.

GALLION, JOHN JACKSON, Private

Born in Cherokee County* and was by occupation a farmer prior to enlisting in Henderson County at age 24, July 10, 1862, for the war. Sent to hospital in November-December, 1862. Returned to duty in May-June, 1863. Deserted on an unspecified date. Returned to duty on October 17, 1863. Reported absent sick from November 25, 1863, through February 29, 1864. Returned to duty in March-April, 1864. Captured at or near Resaca, Georgia, on or about May 16, 1864. Sent to Nashville, Tennessee. Transferred to Louisville, Kentucky, where he arrived on May 21, 1864. Transferred to Alton, Illinois, where he arrived on May 25, 1864. Transferred to Camp Douglas, Chicago, Illinois, August 23, 1864. Released at Camp Douglas on June 20, 1865, after taking the Oath of Allegiance. [North Carolina pension records indicate that he was wounded in the left leg at "Rockyface Ridge, Tennessee, May 26, 1864." Presumably he was wounded at Rocky Face Ridge, Georgia, February 25 or May 8-12, 1864.]

GREEN, JOHN, Private

Born in Cleveland County* and was by occupation a farmer prior to enlisting in Henderson County at age 23, July 10, 1862, for the war. Died in hospital at Tullahoma, Tennessee, February 2, 1863, of disease.

GUICE, BUTLER B., Private

Born in Henderson County and was by occupation a farmer prior to enlisting in Henderson County at age 21, July 10, 1862, for the war. Reported present in November, 1862-June, 1863. Deserted on an unspecified date. Returned to duty on September 23, 1863. Reported sick in hospital in November-December, 1863. Returned to duty in January-February, 1864. Reported present in March-April, 1864. Died at or near Griffin, Georgia, June 5, 1864. Cause of death not reported.

GUICE, DAVID B., Private

Born in Henderson County on March 7, 1839, and was by occupation a farmer prior to enlisting in Henderson County at age 23, July 10, 1862, for the war. Reported present in November, 1862-June, 1863. Deserted on an unspecified date. Returned to duty on September 23, 1863. Reported present in November, 1863-August, 1864. No further records. Survived the war. [North Carolina pension records indicate that he was wounded in July, 1863.]

GUICE, PHILIP H., Musician

Born in Henderson County* on March 24, 1835. Resided in Henderson County and was by occupation a farmer or farm laborer prior to enlisting in Henderson County at age 27, July 10, 1862, for the war. Mustered in as Musician. Died at Tullahoma, Tennessee, February 11, 1863. Cause of death not reported.

HAMMIT, JAMES V., Private

Resided in Henderson County and was by occupation a miller or farm laborer prior to enlisting in Henderson County at age 31, July 10, 1862, for the war. Hospitalized at Dalton, Georgia, January 1, 1863, with chronic diarrhoea. Transferred (probably to hospital at Chattanooga, Tennessee) on February 12, 1863. Detailed as a hospital nurse at Dalton on February 28, 1863. Rejoined the company in August-October, 1863. Captured at Missionary Ridge, Tennessee, November 25, 1863. Sent to Nashville, Tennessee. Transferred to Louisville, Kentucky, where he arrived on December 8, 1863. Transferred to Rock Island, Illinois, where he arrived on December 11, 1863. Released at Rock Island on January 25, 1864, after taking the Oath of Allegiance and joining the U.S. Navy.

HESTILOW, EBER, Private

Born in Spartanburg District, South Carolina, and was by occupation a farmer prior to enlisting in Henderson County at age 17, July 10, 1862, for the war. Deserted on November 13, 1862. Returned to duty in March-April, 1863. Reported present in May-June, 1863. Deserted on an unspecified date. Returned from desertion on October 25, 1863, and was placed under arrest. Returned to duty prior to November 25, 1863, when he was captured at Missionary Ridge, Tennessee. Sent to Nashville, Tennessee. Transferred to Louisville, Kentucky, where he arrived on December 7, 1863. Transferred to Rock Island, Illinois, where he arrived on December 11, 1863. Released at Rock Island on October 6, 1864, after taking the Oath of Allegiance and joining the U.S. Army. Unit to which assigned not reported.

HILL, ALLEN L., Private

Born in Rutherford County and was by occupation a farmer prior to enlisting in Henderson County at age 34, July 10, 1862, for the war. Reported absent sick in November, 1862-February, 1864. Listed as a deserter and dropped from the company rolls on or about April 30, 1864. [May have served briefly in Company B of this regiment.]

HOOD, PERRY NEWTON, Corporal

Born in Henderson County on April 14, 1844, and was by occupation a farmer prior to enlisting in Henderson County at age 18, July 10, 1862, for the war. Mustered in as Private. Reported present in November, 1862-October, 1863. Promoted to Corporal on October 1, 1863. Captured at Missionary Ridge, Tennessee, November 25, 1863. Sent to Nashville, Tennessee. Transferred to Louisville, Kentucky, where he arrived on December 7, 1863. Transferred to Rock Island, Illinois, where he arrived on December 11, 1863. Released at Rock Island on October 6, 1864, after taking the Oath of Allegiance and joining the U.S. Army. Assigned to Company G, 2nd Regiment U.S. Volunteer Infantry.

HUDSON, NOAH, Private

Resided in Burke County and was by occupation a farmer prior to enlisting in Henderson County at age 47, July 10, 1862, for the war as a substitute for Sgt. William A. Israel. Wounded in the arm and captured at Murfreesboro, Tennessee, December 31, 1862. Confined at Louisville, Kentucky. Transferred to Camp Butler, Springfield, Illinois, where he arrived on March 23, 1863. Died at Camp Butler on or about April 18, 1863. Cause of death not reported.

ISRAEL, FREDERICK J., Private

Born in Buncombe County and resided in Henderson County where he enlisted at age 32, July 10, 1862, for the war. Wounded in the hand at Murfreesboro, Tennessee, January 2, 1863. Returned to duty prior to March 1, 1863. Reported present in March-April, 1863. Deserted on May 24, 1863. Went over to the enemy on an unspecified date. Took the Oath of Allegiance at Nashville, Tennessee, December 31, 1864.

ISRAEL, WILLIAM A., Sergeant

Born in Henderson County* and was by occupation a farmer prior to enlisting in Henderson County at age 25, July 10, 1862, for the war. Mustered in as Sergeant. Discharged on or about the same date after providing Pvt. Noah Hudson as a substitute.

JONES, LEVI, Private

Born in Henderson County* on November 15, 1836, and was by occupation a farmer prior to enlisting in Henderson County at age 25, July 10, 1862, for the war. Deserted from hospital on December 10, 1862.

JONES, SOLOMON, Private

Born in Henderson County on April 10, 1844, and was by occupation a farmer prior to enlisting in Henderson County at age 18, July 10, 1862, for the war. Deserted from hospital on December 10, 1862.

JONES, THOMAS, Private

Born in Henderson County where he enlisted at age 18, July 10, 1862, for the war. Reported present in November, 1862-June, 1863. Reported absent sick from October 9, 1863, through February 29, 1864. Reported under arrest in March-April, 1864, for absence without leave. Returned to duty on an unspecified date. Captured by the enemy on an unspecified date. Admitted to a Federal hospital at Chattanooga, Tennessee, May 25, 1864. Transferred on June 17, 1864. No further records.

KING, JASPER, Private

Born in Henderson County* where he resided as a carpenter or farmer prior to enlisting in Henderson County at age 32, July

10, 1862, for the war. Discharged on August 1, 1862. Reason discharged not reported.

KING, WILLIAM R., Private

Born in Henderson County* and was by occupation a farmer prior to enlisting in Henderson County at age 24, July 10, 1862, for the war. Sent to hospital in November-December, 1862. Reported absent sick in January-February, 1863. Died at Knoxville, Tennessee, prior to July 9, 1863. Cause of death not reported.

KITE, JOHN, Private

Resided in Burke County. Place and date of enlistment not reported (probably enlisted subsequent to August 31, 1864). Captured at Stones River, Tennessee, December 7, 1864. Sent to Nashville, Tennessee. Transferred to Louisville, Kentucky, where he arrived on January 5, 1865. Transferred to Camp Chase, Ohio, where he arrived on January 11, 1865. Released at Camp Chase on May 15, 1865, after taking the Oath of Allegiance. [Records of the Federal Provost Marshal dated May, 1865, give his age as 24.]

LANCE, CHARLES HARVEY J., Private

Born in Henderson County where he resided as a farmer or farm laborer prior to enlisting in Henderson County at age 19, July 10, 1862, for the war. Reported under arrest in November, 1862-February, 1863, for absence without leave. Court-martialed on or about March 7, 1863, and sentenced to two months' hard labor. Released from confinement on or about May 2, 1863. Reported absent in hospital in May-June, 1863. Returned to duty in July-October, 1863. Reported present through August 31, 1864. No further records. Survived the war.

LANCE, MARTIN A., Private

Born in Henderson County* and was by occupation a farmer prior to enlisting in Henderson County at age 24, July 10, 1862, for the war. No further records.

LANCE, WILLIAM BURTON, 1st Sergeant

Born in Buncombe County and was by occupation a farmer prior to enlisting in Henderson County at age 29, July 10, 1862, for the war. Mustered in as Private. Reported present in November, 1862-June, 1863. Promoted to 1st Sergeant on March 31, 1863. Captured at Chickamauga, Georgia, September 20, 1863. Sent to Nashville, Tennessee. Transferred to Louisville, Kentucky, where he arrived on September 30, 1863. Transferred to Camp Douglas, Chicago, Illinois, October 2, 1863. Died at Camp Douglas on January 8, 1864, of "diarrhoea."

LAUGHTER, JOSEPH C., Private

Born in Rutherford County and was by occupation a farmer prior to enlisting in Henderson County at age 29, July 10, 1862, for the war. Died prior to March 7, 1863. Place, date, and cause of death not reported.

LEDBETTER, JOHN W., 1st Sergeant

Born in Henderson* or Rutherford County and was by occupation a teacher prior to enlisting in Henderson County at age 30, July 10, 1862, for the war. Mustered in as 1st Sergeant. Discharged at Dalton, Georgia, January 8, 1863, by reason of "phthisis pulmonalis."

LEDBETTER, SHADRACH L., Private

Born in Polk County* where he enlisted at age 27. Enlistment date not reported; however, he probably enlisted on or about July 10,

1862. Transferred to Company G of this regiment on or about August 1, 1862.

LEWIS, GEORGE MARVILL, Private

Born in Rutherford County and was by occupation a farmer prior to enlisting in Henderson County at age 20, July 10, 1862, for the war. Died on or about December 30, 1862. Place and cause of death not reported.

LEWIS, JAMES R., Private

Born in Buncombe County and was by occupation a farmer prior to enlisting in Henderson County at age 32, July 10, 1862, for the war. Transferred to Company I of this regiment on August 1, 1862.

McCARSON, DAVID G., Private

Born in Henderson County* and was by occupation a farmer prior to enlisting in Henderson County at age 31, July 10, 1862, for the war. Died at Murfreesboro, Tennessee, on an unspecified date (probably prior to January 1, 1863). Cause of death not reported.

McCARSON, JAMES, Corporal

Born in Henderson County* on March 27, 1834. Resided in Henderson County and was by occupation a farmer or farm laborer prior to enlisting in Henderson County at age 28, July 10, 1862, for the war. Mustered in as Corporal. Died at Murfreesboro, Tennessee, December 23, 1862. Cause of death not reported.

McCARSON, SAMUEL, Private

Born in Henderson County where he resided as a farmer prior to enlisting in Henderson County at age 23, July 10, 1862, for the war. Mustered in as Private. Reported present in November, 1862-June, 1863. Promoted to Corporal on March 31, 1863. Deserted on an unspecified date. Returned to duty on October 7, 1863, and was reduced to ranks. Detailed for duty in the Pioneer Corps on October 25, 1863. Rejoined the company in March-April, 1864. Wounded in the left foot at Kolb's Farm, near Marietta, Georgia, June 22, 1864. Hospitalized at Macon, Georgia. Furloughed for thirty days on July 5, 1864. Hospitalized at Macon on August 4, 1864. Returned to duty on August 27, 1864. Transferred to Company E, 58th Regiment N.C. Troops, when the 58th and 60th Regiments were consolidated on April 9, 1865.

McCRARY, JOEL, Sergeant

Born in Buncombe County and was by occupation a farmer prior to enlisting in Henderson County at age 32, July 10, 1862, for the war. Mustered in as Sergeant. Reported sick in hospital at Murfreesboro, Tennessee, in November, 1862-February, 1863. Died at Murfreesboro on an unspecified date prior to October 5, 1863. Cause of death not reported.

McKILLOP, ARCHIBALD, Private

Born in Henderson County and was by occupation a farmer prior to enlisting in Henderson County at age 19, July 10, 1862, for the war. Reported absent sick in November, 1862-October, 1863. Returned to duty in November-December, 1863. Reported present in January-August, 1864. No further records.

McKILLOP, R. A., ———

North Carolina pension records indicate that he served in this company.

McWHORTER, JOHN B., Private

Born in Pickens District, South Carolina, and enlisted in Henderson County at age 27, July 10, 1862, for the war. Mustered in as Private. Reported absent sick in November, 1862-February, 1863. Promoted to Corporal on January 12, 1863. Returned to duty in March-April, 1863. Promoted to Sergeant on June 1, 1863. Reported present in May-June, 1863. Deserted on September 1, 1863, and was reduced to ranks.

MAXWELL, CARY, Corporal

Born in Henderson County* where he resided as a farmer prior to enlisting in Henderson County at age 33, July 10, 1862, for the war. Mustered in as Corporal. Hospitalized at Dalton, Georgia, on or about December 28, 1862, with typhoid fever. Returned to duty on January 7, 1863. Hospitalized at Dalton on January 10, 1863, with chronic diarrhoea. Returned to duty on January 26, 1863. Deserted at Tullahoma, Tennessee, March 20, 1863. Went over to the enemy on an unspecified date. Took the Oath of Allegiance at Knoxville, Tennessee, March 16, 1865.

MAXWELL, REILEY, Private

Born in Henderson County* on March 29, 1830, and was by occupation a farmer prior to enlisting in Henderson County at age 32, July 10, 1862, for the war. Reported absent on sick furlough in November, 1862-April, 1863. Returned to duty in May-June, 1863. Reported absent sick on July 8, 1863. Deserted on an unspecified date. Listed as a deserter and dropped from the company rolls on or about April 30, 1864.

MAXWELL, ROBERT H., Corporal

Born in Henderson County where he resided as a farmer or farm laborer prior to enlisting in Henderson County at age 22, July 10, 1862, for the war. Mustered in as Private. Reported present in November-December, 1862. Sent to hospital in January-February, 1863. Returned to duty in March-April, 1863. Reported present in May-October, 1863. Promoted to Corporal on October 1, 1863. Reported absent sick in November, 1863-February, 1864. Returned to duty in March-April, 1864. Killed at Resaca, Georgia, May 9, 1864.

MAXWELL, WILLIAM PINCKNEY, Corporal

Born in Henderson County* on July 21, 1833. Resided in Henderson County and was by occupation a farmer prior to enlisting in Henderson County at age 28, July 10, 1862, for the war. Mustered in as Corporal. Detailed in hospital at Murfreesboro, Tennessee, on an unspecified date. Captured at Murfreesboro on December 31, 1862-January 2, 1863. Died in a Federal hospital at Murfreesboro on January 18, 1863, of "typh[oid] fever."

MILLS, GEORGE, ———

North Carolina pension records indicate that he served in this company.

MOOR, WILLIAM H., Private

Born in Rutherford County and enlisted in Henderson County at age 29, July 10, 1862, for the war. Detailed for hospital duty at Greeneville, Tennessee, in November-December, 1862. Reported absent on detached service in January-February, 1863. Hospitalized at Dalton, Georgia, April 26, 1863. Returned to duty in July-October, 1863. Reported present in November, 1863-February, 1864. Sent to hospital sick on April 6, 1864. Reported absent sick through August 31, 1864. Hospitalized at Charlotte on January 15, 1865, with chronic diarrhoea. Returned to duty on February 6, 1865. No further records.

MOORE, GEORGE HOUGHSTON, Private

Born in Henderson County* on November 14, 1833, and was by occupation a farmer prior to enlisting in Henderson County at age 28, July 10, 1862, for the war. Reported on detail in hospital at Murfreesboro, Tennessee, November-December, 1862. Captured at Murfreesboro on December 31, 1862-January 2, 1863. Sent to Nashville, Tennessee. Transferred to Louisville, Kentucky, where he was hospitalized on February 15, 1863. Transferred to Camp Morton, Indianapolis, Indiana, February 25, 1863. Paroled and transferred to City Point, Virginia, where he was received on April 12, 1863, for exchange. Returned to duty prior to May 1, 1863. Reported present in May-June, 1863. Reported on detail as a hospital nurse and carpenter from July 7, 1863, through February 29, 1864. Rejoined the company in March-April, 1864. Reported present through August 31, 1864. Deserted to the enemy at Murfreesboro on December 6, 1864. Took the Oath of Allegiance at Chattanooga, Tennessee, December 15, 1864.

MOORE, JERRY HUSTON, ———

North Carolina pension records indicate that he served in this company.

MOORE, WILLIAM W., Private

Resided in Transylvania County and enlisted on November 15, 1864, for the war. Deserted on December 5, 1864. Went over to the enemy on an unspecified date. Sent to Nashville, Tennessee, where he took the Oath of Allegiance on January 27, 1865.

NIX, FRANCIS, Private

Born in Rutherford or Henderson* County and was by occupation a farmer prior to enlisting in Henderson County at age 25, July 10, 1862, for the war. Sent to hospital in November-December, 1862. Reported absent on detached service in January-February, 1863. Discharged at Tullahoma, Tennessee, March 29, 1863, by reason of "dropsy."

NIX, GEORGE C., Private

Born in Henderson County and was by occupation a farmer prior to enlisting in Henderson County at age 17, July 10, 1862, for the war. Sent to hospital in November-December, 1862. Died on February 17, 1863. Place and cause of death not reported.

NIX, WILLIAM H., Private

Born in Rutherford County and was by occupation a farmer prior to enlisting in Henderson County at age 22, July 10, 1862, for the war. Reported absent sick in November, 1862-February, 1863. Returned to duty in March-April, 1863. Reported present in May-June, 1863. Reported on detail as a provost guard in July-October, 1863. Rejoined the company in November-December, 1863. Reported present in January-February, 1864. Furloughed for thirty-seven days on March 24, 1864. Returned to duty in May-June, 1864. Reported present in July-August, 1864. No further records. Survived the war.

PITTILLO, JOHN L., Sergeant

Born in Buncombe County and was by occupation a farmer prior to enlisting in Henderson County at age 32, July 10, 1862, for

the war. Mustered in as Private. Sent to hospital in November-December, 1862. Captured at Murfreesboro, Tennessee, on or about January 5, 1863. Sent to Nashville, Tennessee. Transferred to Camp Morton, Indianapolis, Indiana, on an unspecified date. Paroled at Camp Morton and transferred to City Point, Virginia, where he was received on April 12, 1863, for exchange. Returned to duty and was promoted to Sergeant prior to May 1, 1863. Reported present in May-October, 1863. Wounded in the right arm and right lung and captured at Missionary Ridge, Tennessee, November 25, 1863. Right arm amputated. Hospitalized at Chattanooga, Tennessee, February 5, 1864. Exchanged on February 14, 1864. Reported absent wounded through November 1, 1864. No further records. Survived the war.

PITTILLO, MILTON Y., Private

Born in Buncombe County and resided in Henderson County where he was by occupation a farmer prior to enlisting in Henderson County at age 34, July 10, 1862, for the war. Detailed in hospital at Murfreesboro, Tennessee, in November-December, 1862. Captured at Murfreesboro on or about January 5, 1863. Sent to Nashville, Tennessee. Transferred to Camp Morton, Indianapolis, Indiana, on an unspecified date. Paroled at Camp Morton and transferred to City Point, Virginia, where he was received on April 12, 1863, for exchange. Returned to duty prior to May 1, 1863. Reported present in May-June, 1863. Deserted on September 10, 1863. Returned from desertion on an unspecified date. Reported present but under arrest in November-December, 1863. Returned to duty in January-February, 1864. Reported present in March-April, 1864. Sent to hospital on May 23, 1864, with chronic diarrhoea, extreme emaciation, and debility. Furloughed for sixty days on July 3, 1864. No further records.

PITTILLO, SAMUEL P., Private

Born in Buncombe County and was by occupation a farmer prior to enlisting in Henderson County at age 29, July 10, 1862, for the war. Sent to hospital in November-December, 1862. Captured at Murfreesboro, Tennessee, on or about January 5, 1863. Sent to Nashville, Tennessee. Transferred to Camp Morton, Indianapolis, Indiana, on an unspecified date. Paroled at Camp Morton and transferred to City Point, Virginia, where he was received on April 12, 1863, for exchange. Returned to duty prior to May 1, 1863. Reported present in May-June, 1863. Deserted on September 1, 1863. Reported under arrest in November-December, 1863. Returned to duty in January-February, 1864. Reported present through August 31, 1864. No further records. Survived the war. [North Carolina pension records indicate that he was wounded in the chest and left leg in Tennessee on an unspecified date.]

PLUMBLEE, WILLIAM P., Private

Born in Henderson County* and was by occupation a farmer prior to enlisting in Henderson County at age 32, July 10, 1862, for the war. No further records. Survived the war.

RAGAN, JOSEPH M., Private

Born in Buncombe County and was by occupation a farmer prior to enlisting in Henderson County at age 27, July 10, 1862, for the war. Reported present in November, 1862-February, 1863. Hospitalized at Dalton, Georgia, April 26, 1863, with typhoid fever. Transferred to another hospital on June 20, 1863. Hospitalized at Macon, Georgia, October 26, 1863, with diarrhoea. Furloughed for thirty days on October 31, 1863. Reported absent sick through August 31, 1864. No further records.

RAY, RILEY H., Private

Born in Henderson County* and was by occupation a farmer prior to enlisting in Henderson County at age 28, July 10, 1862, for the war. Reported present in November, 1862-June, 1863. Reported absent on sick furlough from September 4, 1863, through February 29, 1864. Returned to duty in March-April, 1864. Reported present in May-August, 1864. Reported on detail as a bridge builder December 16-28, 1864. No further records. Survived the war.

REYNOLDS, JOSEPH, Private

Resided in Buncombe County and enlisted at Camp Vance at age 25, September 10, 1863, for the war. Reported present through October 31, 1863. Captured at Missionary Ridge, Tennessee, November 25, 1863. Sent to Nashville, Tennessee. Transferred to Louisville, Kentucky, where he arrived on December 7, 1863. Transferred to Rock Island, Illinois, where he arrived on December 9, 1863. Died at Rock Island on or about January 7, 1864, of "pneumonia."

REYNOLDS, WILLIAM, Private

Resided in Burke County and was by occupation a farmer prior to enlisting at Camp Vance at age 35, September 10, 1863, for the war. Reported present through October 31, 1863. Captured at Missionary Ridge, Tennessee, November 25, 1863. Sent to Nashville, Tennessee. Transferred to Louisville, Kentucky, where he arrived on December 7, 1863. Transferred to Rock Island, Illinois, where he arrived on December 9, 1863. Died at Rock Island on December 19, 1863, of "pneumonia."

RHODES, BENJAMIN F., Private

Born in Habersham County, Georgia, and was by occupation a farmer prior to enlisting in Henderson County at age 29, July 10, 1862, for the war. Hospitalized at Dalton, Georgia, December 31, 1862, with remittent fever. Reported in hospital at Dalton on January 28, 1863, with debilitas. Returned to duty on February 9, 1863. Reported present through June 30, 1863. Hospitalized at Lockhart's Station, Mississippi, prior to August 31, 1863. Died at Lockhart's Station on September 8, 1863. Cause of death not reported.

RHODES, JESSE, Private

Born in Habersham County, Georgia, and was by occupation a farmer prior to enlisting in Henderson County at age 38, July 10, 1862, for the war. Hospitalized at Murfreesboro, Tennessee, on or about December 25, 1862. Died in hospital at Murfreesboro on January 11, 1863, of "congestive fever."

RICKMAN, DAVID W., Sergeant

Born in Henderson County* and was by occupation a farmer prior to enlisting in Henderson County at age 31, July 10, 1862, for the war. Mustered in as Sergeant. Hospitalized at Dalton, Georgia, November 21, 1862, with acute diarrhoea. Returned to duty on December 11, 1862. Reported present or accounted for through June 30, 1863. Sent to hospital sick on November 1, 1863. Returned to duty prior to January 1, 1864. Reported absent sick on February 23, 1864. Returned to duty in March-April, 1864. Reported present through August 31, 1864. [Records of the United Daughters of the Confederacy indicate that he was killed in battle on an unspecified date.]

RICKMAN, JESSE W., Corporal

Born in Henderson County* where he resided as a farmer or farm laborer prior to enlisting in Henderson County at age 31, July 10,

1862, for the war. Mustered in as Private. Reported present in November-December, 1862. Sent to hospital in January-February, 1863. Furloughed on May 5, 1863. Promoted to Corporal on October 1, 1863. Returned to duty prior to November 1, 1863. Hospitalized at Griffin, Georgia, November 23, 1863, with an unspecified complaint. Returned to duty prior to January 1, 1864. Reported present through August 31, 1864. No further records. Survived the war. [North Carolina pension records indicate that he was wounded in the left arm at Murfreesboro, Tennessee, December 7, 1864.]

RUSSELL, HARDY A., Private

Born in Henderson County* and was by occupation a farmer prior to enlisting in Henderson County at age 28, July 10, 1862, for the war. Discharged on or about the same date after providing Pvt. Samuel M. Tow as a substitute. No further records.

RUSSELL, JORDAN F., Private

Born in Henderson County and was by occupation a farmer prior to enlisting in Henderson County at age 18, July 10, 1862, for the war. Hospitalized at Murfreesboro, Tennessee, in November-December, 1862. Captured at Murfreesboro on or about January 5, 1863. Sent to Nashville, Tennessee. Hospitalized at Nashville on February 1, 1863, with debility. Transferred to Louisville, Kentucky, on an unspecified date. Was ordered transferred to Camp Chase, Ohio, February 25, 1863, but was "not able to go." Died (presumably at Louisville) on an unspecified date. Cause of death not reported.

RUSSELL, JOSEPH L., Private

Born in Henderson County and was by occupation a farmer prior to enlisting in Henderson County at age 22, July 10, 1862, for the war. Died on February 12, 1863. Place and cause of death not reported.

RUTH, WILSON A., Private

Enlisted in Henderson County at age 24, July 10, 1862, for the war. Reported under arrest for absence without leave in November, 1862-February, 1863. Court-martialed on or about March 7, 1863, and ordered to perform two months' labor at Bridgeport, Tennessee. Returned to duty on or about May 2, 1863. Deserted on May 25, 1863. Returned from desertion in March-April, 1864, and was placed under arrest. Returned to duty prior to July 4, 1864, when he was captured at Ruff's Mill, near Smyrna, Georgia. Sent to Nashville, Tennessee. Transferred to Louisville, Kentucky, where he arrived on July 14, 1864. Transferred to Camp Douglas, Chicago, Illinois, where he arrived on July 18, 1864. Died at Camp Douglas on January 24, 1865, of "pneumonia."

SHIPMAN, EDWARD J., Private

Born in Henderson County* where he resided as a farmer or farm laborer prior to enlisting in Henderson County at age 26, July 10, 1862, for the war. Discharged on August 1, 1862. Reason discharged not reported. Later served as Private in Company E, 7th Battalion N.C. Cavalry.

SHIPMAN, SIMON B., Private

Born in Henderson County* and was by occupation a farmer prior to enlisting in Henderson County at age 29, July 10, 1862, for the war. Transferred to Company I of this regiment on or about September 13, 1862.

SHIPMAN, WILLIAM R., JR., Private

Born in Henderson County and was by occupation a farmer prior to enlisting in Henderson County at age 18, July 10, 1862, for the war. Transferred to Company I of this regiment on or about September 13, 1862.

SHIPMAN, WILLIAM R., SR., Private

Born in Henderson County and was by occupation a farmer prior to enlisting in Henderson County at age 19, July 10, 1862, for the war. Sent to hospital in January-February, 1863. Returned to duty in March-April, 1863. Reported present through June 30, 1863. Reported absent sick in hospital in July-October, 1863. Returned to duty in November-December, 1863. Reported present through April 30, 1864. Captured at Ruff's Mill, near Smyrna, Georgia, July 4, 1864. Sent to Nashville, Tennessee. Transferred to Louisville, Kentucky, where he arrived on July 14, 1864. Transferred to Camp Douglas, Chicago, Illinois, where he arrived on July 18, 1864. Died at Camp Douglas on August 9, 1864, of "inflam[mation] of brain."

SHIPMAN, WILLSON, Private

Born in Henderson County* and was by occupation a farmer prior to enlisting in Henderson County at age 26, July 10, 1862, for the war. Transferred to Company I of this regiment on or about September 13, 1862.

SOLESBEE, WILLIAM WILSON, Private

Born in Spartanburg District, South Carolina, and was by occupation a farmer prior to enlisting in Henderson County at age 24, July 10, 1862, for the war. Discharged on August 1, 1862. Reason discharged not reported. Later served as Private in Company E, 18th Regiment N.C. Troops (8th Regiment N.C. Volunteers).

SOLSBEE, JOHN Q., Private

Born in Spartanburg District, South Carolina, and was by occupation a farmer prior to enlisting in Henderson County at age 27, July 10, 1862, for the war. Discharged on August 1, 1862. Reason discharged not reported.

SPAIN, JAMES N., Private

Born in Buncombe County and resided in Henderson County where he was by occupation a farmer prior to enlisting to Henderson County at age 22, July 10, 1862, for the war. Deserted on August 10, 1862, at Warm Spring. Returned from desertion (or was apprehended) on an unspecified date. Court-martialed on or about December 4, 1862, and sentenced to be shot. Sent to hospital prior to January 1, 1863. Sentence remitted on January 15, 1863. Returned to duty in May-June, 1863. Reported absent on sick furlough in July-December, 1863. Returned to duty in January-February, 1864. Reported present in March-April, 1864. Captured at or near Resaca, Georgia, May 16, 1864. Sent to Nashville, Tennessee. Transferred to Louisville, Kentucky, where he arrived on May 20, 1864. Transferred to Camp Morton, Indianapolis, Indiana, where he arrived on May 22, 1864. Released at Camp Morton on March 24, 1865, after taking the Oath of Allegiance and joining the U.S. Army. Assigned to Company G, 6th Regiment U.S. Volunteer Infantry.

SPROUCE, HOSEA M., Private

Born in Spartanburg District, South Carolina, and resided in Henderson County where he was by occupation a farmer or day laborer prior to enlisting in Henderson County at age 23, July 10, 1862, for the war. Reported on detail in hospital at Greeneville, Tennessee,

in November-December, 1862. Reported absent on detached service in January-February, 1863. Reported sick in hospital in March-April, 1863. Returned to duty in May-June, 1863. Deserted on September 1, 1863. Returned from desertion on or about December 10, 1863, and was placed under arrest. Returned to duty in January-February, 1864. Reported present in March-April, 1864. Sent to hospital sick on May 11, 1864. Returned to duty subsequent to June 30, 1864. Reported present in July-August, 1864. Deserted to the enemy on an unspecified date. Took the Oath of Allegiance at Nashville, Tennessee, on or about December 31, 1864.

STEPP, JAMES, IV, Private

Born in Henderson County* on July 19, 1829, and was by occupation a farmer prior to enlisting in Henderson County at age 32, July 10, 1862, for the war. Discharged on August 1, 1862. Reason discharged not reported. [May have served later as Private in Company A, 69th Regiment N.C. Troops (7th Regiment N.C. Cavalry).]

STEPP, STEPHEN, Sergeant

Born in Henderson County where he resided as a farmer prior to enlisting in Henderson County at age 20, July 10, 1862, for the war. Mustered in as Private. Reported present in November, 1862-October, 1863. Promoted to Corporal on June 1, 1863. Promoted to Sergeant on October 1, 1863. Reported present in November, 1863-April, 1864. Wounded at Kolb's Farm, near Marietta, Georgia, June 22, 1864. Returned to duty in July-August, 1864. Captured at Murfreesboro, Tennessee, December 7, 1864. Sent to Nashville, Tennessee. Transferred to Louisville, Kentucky, where he arrived on January 5, 1865. Transferred to Camp Chase, Ohio, where he arrived on January 11, 1865. Released at Camp Chase on June 13, 1865, after taking the Oath of Allegiance.

STUART, MELVIN M., Private

Born in Henderson County and was by occupation a farmer prior to enlisting in Henderson County at age 21, July 10, 1862, for the war. Sent to hospital in November-December, 1862. Reported absent on sick furlough in January-February, 1863. Reported absent with leave in March-April, 1863. Returned to duty in May-June, 1863. Hospitalized at Macon, Mississippi, July 12, 1863. Reported absent on sick furlough on or about October 31, 1863. Reported absent sick in November, 1863-February, 1864. Listed as a deserter and dropped from the company rolls on or about April 30, 1864. Later served as Private in Company I, 3rd Regiment N.C. Mounted Infantry (Union). [His correct surname may be Stewart or Steward.]

SUTTLES, JAMES G., Private

Born in Henderson County and was by occupation a farmer prior to enlisting in Henderson County at age 18, July 10, 1862, for the war. Died at Murfreesboro, Tennessee, on an unspecified date prior to March 9, 1863. Cause of death not reported.

SUTTLES, JOHN H., Private

Enlisted in Henderson County at age 21, July 10, 1862, for the war. Sent to hospital in November-December, 1862. Deserted on January 13, 1863. Returned to duty in May-June, 1863. Hospitalized at Lauderdale Springs, Mississippi, July 10, 1863. Detailed as a hospital nurse at Lauderdale Springs on July 18, 1863. Returned to duty on September 15, 1863. Reported, sick in hospital in November-December, 1863. Rejoined the company in January-February, 1864. Reported present in March-April, 1864. Sent to hospital sick on June 10, 1864. Reported absent sick through August 31, 1864. No further records.

SUTTLES, JOHN N., Private

Born in Anderson District, South Carolina, and was by occupation a farmer prior to enlisting in Henderson County at age 20, July 10, 1862, for the war. Sent to hospital in November-December, 1862. Reported absent on detached service or absent in hospital in January-June, 1863. Returned to duty in July-October, 1863. Sent to hospital sick in November-December, 1863. Returned to duty in March-April, 1864. Reported sick in hospital on June 10, 1864. Returned to duty prior to July 4, 1864, when he was captured at Ruff's Mill, near Smyrna, Georgia. Sent to Nashville, Tennessee. Transferred to Louisville, Kentucky, where he arrived on July 14, 1864. Transferred to Camp Douglas, Chicago, Illinois, where he arrived on July 18, 1864. Released at Camp Douglas on June 16, 1865, after taking the Oath of Allegiance.

TAYLOR, CALEB L., Sergeant

Born in Henderson County and was by occupation a farmer prior to enlisting in Henderson County at age 23, July 10, 1862, for the war. Mustered in as Private. Promoted to Sergeant prior to January 1, 1863. Died at Tullahoma, Tennessee, February 5, 1863. Cause of death not reported.

TAYLOR, DANIEL ARNOLD, Private

Born in Henderson County* and resided in Greene County, Tennessee, where he was by occupation a farmer prior to enlisting in Henderson County at age 28, July 10, 1862, for the war. Wounded in the right shoulder at Murfreesboro, Tennessee, December 31, 1862. Reported absent wounded or absent sick through April 30, 1863. Returned to duty on an unspecified date. Sent to hospital on June 24, 1863. Captured near Jackson, Mississippi, July 16-17, 1863. Sent to Snyder's Bluff, Mississippi. Transferred to Camp Morton, Indianapolis, Indiana, where he arrived on August 7, 1863. Released at Camp Morton on June 3, 1865, after taking the Oath of Allegiance.

TAYLOR, WILLIAM R., Private

Born in Henderson County* on April 28, 1830, and was by occupation a mason prior to enlisting in Henderson County at age 32, July 10, 1862, for the war. Mustered in as Musician. Apparently deserted on an unspecified date. Court-martialed on or about December 4, 1862. Reduced to ranks and sentenced to be shot. Sentence remitted on January 15, 1863. Reported present through June 30, 1863. Deserted on September 10, 1863. Returned to duty subsequent to August 31, 1864. Captured at Murfreesboro, Tennessee, December 7, 1864. Sent to Nashville, Tennessee. Transferred to Louisville, Kentucky, where he arrived on January 5, 1865. Transferred to Camp Chase, Ohio, where he arrived on January 11, 1865. Released at Camp Chase on May 13, 1865, after taking the Oath of Allegiance.

THOMAS, WILLIAM ROBERT, Private

Enlisted in Henderson County at age 24, July 10, 1862, for the war. Discharged on August 1, 1862. Reason discharged not reported. Later served as Private in Company D, 7th Battalion N.C. Cavalry.

TOW, SAMUEL M., Private

Enlisted in Henderson County on July 10, 1862, for the war as a substitute for Pvt. Hardy A. Russell. Reported present in November, 1862-April, 1863. Deserted on May 25, 1863. Returned to duty on August 21, 1863. Captured at Missionary Ridge, Tennessee, November 25, 1863. Sent to Nashville, Tennessee. Transferred to Louisville, Kentucky, where he arrived on December 25, 1863. Transferred to Rock Island, Illinois, where he arrived on

December 29, 1863. Released at Rock Island on or about January 25, 1864, after joining the U.S. Navy. [May have served previously as Private in Company H, 25th Regiment N.C. Troops.]

TOWNSEND, JEFFERSON A., Private

Born in Henderson County* where he enlisted at age 29, July 10, 1862, for the war. Reported present in November-December, 1862. Reported absent on detached service in January-February, 1863. Detailed in hospital at Tullahoma, Tennessee, March 20, 1863. Died at Jackson, Mississippi, June 27-28, 1863, of "fever."

TOWNSEND, JOSHUA B., Private

Born in Henderson County and was by occupation a farmer prior to enlisting in Henderson County at age 22, July 10, 1862, for the war. Sent to hospital in November-December, 1862. Discharged at Ringgold, Georgia, in April, 1863. Reason discharged not reported.

WARD, ALEXANDER, Private

Born in Greenville District, South Carolina, and was by occupation a farmer prior to enlisting in Henderson County at age 29, July 10, 1862, for the war. Reported present in November, 1862-February, 1863. Sent to hospital in March, 1863. Reported absent on sick furlough in July-December, 1863. Returned to duty in March-April, 1864. Captured at or near Resaca, Georgia, May 16, 1864. Sent to Nashville, Tennessee. Transferred to Louisville, Kentucky, where he arrived on May 21, 1864. Transferred to Alton, Illinois, where he arrived on May 25, 1864. Hospitalized at Alton on November 18, 1864, with "erysipela orchitis." Released from hospital on December 5, 1864. Hospitalized at Alton on December 18, 1864, and died on January 11, 1865, of "pneumonia."

WARD, BENJAMIN W., Private

Born in Henderson County and was by occupation a farmer prior to enlisting in Henderson County at age 23, July 10, 1862, for the war. Hospitalized at Dalton, Georgia, November 6, 1862, with phthisis pulmonalis and/or intermittent fever. Detailed as a hospital nurse at Dalton on an unspecified date. Deserted on December 9, 1862. Rejoined the company in March-April, 1863. Reported present in May-June, 1863. Reported on detached duty as a teamster in July-October, 1863. Died on an unspecified date (probably in November-December, 1863). Place and cause of death not reported.

WARD, J. L., Private

Enlisted at Camp Vance on September 10, 1863, for the war. Reported present through October 31, 1863. "Lost in action [probably killed]" at Missionary Ridge, Tennessee, November 25, 1863.

WARD, JAMES T., Private

Born in Greenville District, South Carolina, and was by occupation a farmer prior to enlisting in Henderson County at age 18, July 10, 1862, for the war. Deserted on October 10, 1862. Apprehended on or about April 19, 1864. No further records.

WATKINS, HENRY C., Private

Born in Stanly County* and was by occupation a farmer prior to enlisting in Henderson County at age 27, July 10, 1862, for the war. Transferred to Company I of this regiment on August 1, 1862.

WATKINS, JOEL, Private

Born in Rutherford County and was by occupation a farmer prior to enlisting in Henderson County at age 31, July 10, 1862, for the war. Transferred to Company I of this regiment on August 1, 1862.

WATKINS, JOHN S., Private

Born in Stanly County and was by occupation a farmer prior to enlisting in Henderson County at age 20, July 10, 1862, for the war. Transferred to Company I of this regiment on August 1, 1862.

WATKINS, WILLIAM, Private

Born in Rutherford County and was by occupation a farmer prior to enlisting in Henderson County at age 34, July 10, 1862, for the war. Transferred to Company I of this regiment on August 1, 1862.

WILLIAMS, GEORGE N., Private

Born in Buncombe County and enlisted in Henderson County at age 21, July 10, 1862, for the war. Deserted on November 13, 1862. Returned to duty subsequent to April 30, 1863. Sent to hospital on June 24, 1863. Reported in hospital at Marion, Mississippi, in July-October, 1863. Reported absent sick or absent on sick furlough in November, 1863-February, 1864. Listed as a deserter on or about April 30, 1864, and dropped from the company rolls.

WRIGHT, JAMES H., Private

Born in Cocke County, Tennessee, and resided in Henderson County where he was by occupation a mechanic or day laborer prior to enlisting in Henderson County at age 32, July 10, 1862, for the war. No further records.

YOUNGBLOOD, JASPER NEWTON, SR., Private

Born in Henderson County where he resided prior to enlisting in Henderson County at age 18, July 10, 1862, for the war. Reported present in November, 1862-February, 1863. Sent to hospital in March, 1863. Listed as a deserter on September 10, 1863. Went over to the enemy on an unspecified date. Confined at Knoxville, Tennessee, September 18, 1864. Transferred to Chattanooga, Tennessee, September 25, 1864. Transferred to Louisville, Kentucky, where he arrived on October 11, 1864. Released on October 22, 1864, after taking the Oath of Allegiance.

COMPANY E

This company, known also as the "Buncombe Farmers," was raised in Buncombe County on May 17, 1862. It was mustered into state service at Asheville on that date as "Fourth Company," McDowell's Battalion N.C. Infantry (known also as the 6th Battalion N.C. Infantry). The seven-company battalion was mustered into Confederate service on August 1, 1862, and redesignated the 1st Battalion N.C. Infantry. On October 8, 1862, the 60th Regiment N.C. Troops was formally organized after three additional companies were assigned to the 1st Battalion. This company was designated Company E. After joining the regiment the company functioned as a part of the regiment, and its history for the remainder of the war is reported as a part of the regimental history.

The following roster was compiled primarily from information in the microfilm edition of the Compiled Service Records of Soldiers Who Served in Organizations from the State of North Carolina (Record Group 109, M270), National Archives and Records Administration, Washington, D.C. Record Group 109 includes enlistment papers, pay vouchers, requisitions, letters of resignation, discharge certificates, and abstracts of medical and prisoner of war returns. Materials relating specifically to this company include a muster-in and descrip-

tive roll dated August 1, 1862, and muster rolls dated November, 1862-August, 1864.

Also utilized in this roster were *The War of the Rebellion: A Compilation of the Official Records of the Union and Confederate Armies*, the North Carolina adjutant general's *Roll of Honor*, state militia records, newspaper casualty lists and obituaries, wartime claims for bounty pay and allowances, postwar registers of claims for artificial limbs, Confederate pension applications filed with the states of North Carolina, Tennessee, and Florida, Confederate Soldiers' Home records, and the 1860 and 1870 federal censuses of North Carolina. A search was made also for relevant letters, diaries, reminiscences, and other manuscripts in the Southern Historical Collection (University of North Carolina-Chapel Hill), the Duke University Library Special Collections Department, and the North Carolina Division of Archives and History.

Among the secondary sources consulted were records of the North Carolina division of the United Daughters of the Confederacy, postwar rosters, regimental and county histories, marriage bond, will, and cemetery indexes, published and unpublished genealogies, biographical dictionaries, the North Carolina *County Heritage Book* series, the *Confederate Veteran*, Walter Clark's *Histories of the Several Regiments and Battalions from North Carolina in the Great War, 1861-'65*, and the North Carolina volume of the extended edition of *Confederate Military History*.

OFFICERS

CAPTAINS

McDOWELL, WILLIAM WALLACE

Previously served as Captain of Company E, 1st Regiment N.C. Infantry (6 months, 1861). Appointed Captain of this company on May 17, 1862. Appointed Major on October 1, 1862, and transferred to the Field and Staff of this regiment. [Contrary to 3:25 of this series, the correct spelling of his middle name is probably Wallace rather than Wallis.]

CANDLER, THOMAS JEFFERSON

Previously served as Private in Company F, 14th Regiment N.C. Troops (4th Regiment N.C. Volunteers). Elected 1st Lieutenant of this company on August 1, 1862. Promoted to Captain on October 1, 1862. Reported present in November, 1862-June, 1863. Resigned on or about October 2, 1863, because "I am no longer willing to retain a position in which I am not treated with the respect due my rank." Resignation accepted on October 19, 1863. Later served as Private in Company E, 69th Regiment N.C. Troops (7th Regiment N.C. Cavalry).

WRIGHT, SAMUEL C.

Born in Buncombe County where he enlisted at age 30, May 17, 1862, for the war. Mustered in as Sergeant. Elected 2nd Lieutenant on October 1, 1862. Reported present and in command of the company in March-April and July-October, 1863. Promoted to Captain on November 3, 1863. Wounded at Missionary Ridge, Tennessee, November 25, 1863. Returned to duty in January-February, 1864. Reported present in March-August, 1864. Resigned on September 7, 1864, and again on March 13, 1865; however, his resignation was disapproved on both occasions. No further records. Survived the war. [May have been wounded at Murfreesboro, Tennessee, December 31, 1862-January 2, 1863. Reported in command of Company F of this regiment in January-February, 1864.]

WHITE, ROBERT

Served as 2nd Lieutenant of Company F of this regiment. Reported on duty as acting commander of this company in November-December, 1863.

LIEUTENANTS

CANDLER, WILLIAM GASTON, 1st Lieutenant

Born in Buncombe County where he resided as a lawyer prior to enlisting in Buncombe County at age 28. Elected 1st Lieutenant on May 17, 1862. Resigned on an unspecified date. Reason he resigned not reported. Resignation accepted on August 1, 1862, after he provided Pvt. David Halford as a substitute.

COLE, JOSEPH M., 3rd Lieutenant

Born in Buncombe County where he resided as a farmer prior to enlisting in Buncombe County at age 26, May 17, 1862, for the war. Mustered in as Private. Elected 3rd Lieutenant on October 1, 1862. Reported present in March-June, 1863. Reported sick in hospital in July-October, 1863. Captured at Missionary Ridge, Tennessee, November 25, 1863. Sent to Nashville, Tennessee. Transferred to Louisville, Kentucky, where he arrived on December 4, 1863. Transferred to Johnson's Island, Ohio, where he arrived on December 7, 1863. Released at Johnson's Island on June 13, 1865, after taking the Oath of Allegiance.

HYATT, JASPER B., 1st Lieutenant

Born in Missouri or in Buncombe County and was by occupation a farmer prior to enlisting in Buncombe County at age 26. Elected 2nd Lieutenant on May 17, 1862. Promoted to 1st Lieutenant on October 1, 1862. Wounded slightly in the side at Murfreesboro, Tennessee, December 31, 1862. Returned to duty on an unspecified date. Sent to hospital on April 23, 1863. Returned to duty in May-June, 1863. Reported present in July-October, 1863. Resigned on October 22, 1863. Reason he resigned not reported; however, an annotation on the front of his letter of resignation states that he was "totally unqualif[i]ed for the proper discharge of the duties pertaining to his office." Another annotation on the letter states that his resignation was tendered at the suggestion of the brigade commander. Resignation accepted on November 3, 1863.

JONES, WILLIAM H., 3rd Lieutenant

Born in Buncombe County and was by occupation a farmer prior to enlisting at age 20. Appointed 3rd Lieutenant on or about May 17, 1862. No further records.

MANNING, FRANK, 2nd Lieutenant

Resided in Alabama. Elected 2nd Lieutenant of this company on February 16, 1864. Reported present through August 31, 1864. Paroled at Montgomery, Alabama, May 27, 1865.

NONCOMMISSIONED OFFICERS AND PRIVATES

ALEXANDER, WILLIAM P., Private

Born in Buncombe County and was by occupation a farmer prior to enlisting in Buncombe County on May 17, 1862, for the war. Transferred to Company I of this regiment on or about September 13, 1862.

BAILEY, FRANCIS M., Sergeant

Previously served as Private in Company E, 1st Regiment N.C. Infantry (6 months, 1861). Enlisted in this company in Buncombe County on May 17, 1862, for the war. Mustered in as Private. Promoted to Corporal on or about August 1, 1862. Reported present in November, 1862-June, 1863. Reduced to ranks prior to January 1, 1863. Promoted to Sergeant in May-June, 1863. Wounded in the leg at Chickamauga, Georgia, September 19-20, 1863. Died at Cassville, Georgia, October 6, 1863, presumably of wounds. [He probably served as a color bearer at the Battle of Chickamauga.]

BALL, JOHN McDOWELL, Private

Born in Buncombe County in 1845. Was by occupation a farmer prior to enlisting in Buncombe County at age 17, May 17, 1862, for the war. Transferred to Company I of this regiment on or about September 13, 1862.

BENSON, DAVID F., Private

Born in Barnwell District, South Carolina, and was by occupation a farmer prior to enlisting in Buncombe County at age 25, May 17, 1862, for the war. Reported present in November, 1862-April, 1863. Hospitalized at Tunnel Hill, Georgia, May 22, 1863, with varix of the right leg. Returned to duty on June 22, 1863. Reported present through October 31, 1863. Sent to hospital sick on or about November 24, 1863. Reported absent sick through August 31, 1864. No further records. [May have served previously as Private in Company E, 1st Regiment N.C. Infantry (6 months, 1861).]

BENSON, SOLOMON, Private

Born in Barnwell District, South Carolina, and enlisted at age 23, May 17, 1862, for the war. Died at Chattanooga, Tennessee, on an unspecified date (probably in August-December, 1862). Cause of death not reported.

BISHOP, ISAAC, Private

Born in Polk County* and was by occupation a farmer prior to enlisting in Buncombe County at age 35, May 17, 1862, for the war. Hospitalized at Dalton, Georgia, November 6, 1862, with a contusion and laceration. Returned to duty on November 9, 1862. Reported absent on detached service in November-December, 1862. Detailed as a hospital nurse at Tullahoma, Tennessee, January 12, 1863. Rejoined the company in May-June, 1863. Reported on duty as a cook in hospital at Jackson, Tennessee, in July, 1863. Rejoined the company prior to November 1, 1863. Reported present through August 31, 1864. No further records. Survived the war.

BOYD, GEORGE W., Private

Born in Buncombe County and was by occupation a carpenter prior to enlisting in Buncombe County at age 32, October 6, 1862, for the war. Died at Murfreesboro, Tennessee, on an unspecified date (probably prior to January 1, 1863). Cause of death not reported.

BROODBERY, E., Private

Place and date of enlistment not reported. Captured near Raleigh on April 12, 1865. No further records.

BROOKS, GEORGE WASHINGTON, Corporal

Born in Buncombe County and was by occupation a carpenter prior to enlisting in Buncombe County at age 18, May 17, 1862, for the war. Mustered in as Private. Reported absent sick in November, 1862-February, 1863. Returned to duty in March-April, 1863. Promoted to Corporal on May 20, 1863. Reported present in May-June, 1863. Deserted at Chickamauga, Georgia, October 4, 1863.

BROOKSHIRE, BENJAMIN F., Private

Born in Buncombe County and was by occupation a farmer prior to enlisting in Buncombe County at age 30, May 17, 1862, for the war. Last reported in the records of this company on August 1, 1862. [May have served later as Private in Company K, 24th Regiment N.C. Troops (14th Regiment N.C. Volunteers).]

BROOKSHIRE, THOMAS PATTERSON, Corporal

Born in Buncombe County where he resided as a carpenter prior to enlisting in Buncombe County at age 23, May 17, 1862, for the war. Mustered in as Private. Reported present in November, 1862-February, 1863. Hospitalized at Dalton, Georgia, April 26, 1863, with typhoid fever. Transferred to another hospital on June 20, 1863. Returned to duty prior to July 1, 1863. Reported present through December 31, 1863. Promoted to Corporal on February 1, 1864. Wounded slightly at Rocky Face Ridge, Georgia, February 25, 1864. Returned to duty in March-April, 1864. Sent to hospital sick on May 25, 1864. Reported absent sick through August 31, 1864. Transferred to Company H, 58th Regiment N.C. Troops, when the 58th and 60th Regiments were consolidated on April 9, 1865. [May have been wounded at Murfreesboro, Tennessee, December 31, 1862-January 2, 1863.]

BRYSON, JOHN W., Private

Born in Henderson County* and resided in Buncombe County where he was by occupation a farmer prior to enlisting in Buncombe County at age 29, May 17, 1862, for the war. Reported missing at Murfreesboro, Tennessee, January 2, 1863. Rejoined the company prior to January 25, 1863, when he deserted. Returned to duty in May-June, 1863. Deserted at Chickamauga, Georgia, September 5, 1863. Returned to duty on or about June 23, 1864. Captured at Ruff's Mill, near Smyrna, Georgia, July 4, 1864. Sent to Nashville, Tennessee. Transferred to Louisville, Kentucky, where he arrived on July 14, 1864. Transferred to Camp Douglas, Chicago, Illinois, where he arrived on July 18, 1864. Released at Camp Douglas on June 16, 1865, after taking the Oath of Allegiance.

CATHEY, JOHN LAFAYETTE, Corporal

Born in Macon County and was by occupation a farmer prior to enlisting Buncombe County at age 30, May 17, 1862, for the war. Mustered in as Corporal. Transferred to Company I of this regiment on or about September 13, 1862.

CLARK, WILLIAM C., Private

Born in Buncombe or Haywood County and was by occupation a farmer prior to enlisting at Camp Smith (Madison County) at age 42, May 17, 1862, for the war. Transferred to Company I of this regiment on or about September 13, 1862.

COFFEE, JOHN A., Private

Born in Watauga County* and was by occupation a farmer prior to enlisting in Buncombe County at age 26, May 17, 1862, for the war. Mustered in as Private. Reported present in November, 1862-October, 1863. Promoted to Sergeant prior to January 1, 1863. Reduced to ranks in May-October, 1863. Reported present in November, 1863-August, 1864. Served as a teamster during most of that period. No further records.

COLE, JOHN JACKSON, Private

Born in Buncombe County and was by occupation a farmer prior to enlisting in Buncombe County at age 31, May 17, 1862, for the war. Hospitalized at Dalton, Georgia, November 6, 1862, with a contusion and laceration. Returned to duty on December 13, 1862.

Reported sick in hospital in Tullahoma, Tennessee, from about January 12 through April 30, 1863. Returned to duty in May-June, 1863. Reported sick in hospital in July-October, 1863. Furloughed home in November-December, 1863. Returned to duty in May-June, 1864. Reported sick in hospital in July-August, 1864. No further records. Survived the war.

COLE, JOHN V., JR., Private

Born in Buncombe County where he resided as a farmer prior to enlisting in Buncombe County at age 21, May 17, 1862, for the war. Reported present in November, 1862-February, 1863. Sent to hospital sick on or about April 5, 1863. Reported absent sick through October 31, 1863. Furloughed in November-December, 1863. Failed to return to duty and was reported absent without leave on February 16, 1864. Listed as a deserter on April 7, 1864. Returned to duty on or about April 27, 1864. Captured at Nickajack Creek, near Smyrna, Georgia, July 5, 1864. Sent to Nashville, Tennessee. Transferred to Louisville, Kentucky, where he arrived on July 14, 1864. Transferred to Camp Douglas, Chicago, Illinois, where he arrived on July 18, 1864. Released at Camp Douglas on June 12, 1865, after taking the Oath of Allegiance.

COLE, WASHINGTON, ———

Place and date of enlistment not reported (probably enlisted in May-August, 1862). Discharged prior to November 4, 1862. Reason discharged not reported. [May have served previously as Private in Company K, 25th Regiment N.C. Troops.]

COTHRAN, JOHN CAULDWELL, Private

Born in Spartanburg District, South Carolina, and was by occupation a farmer prior to enlisting in Buncombe County at age 20, May 17, 1862, for the war. Reported absent sick in November, 1862-February, 1863. Returned to duty in March-April, 1863. Reported absent in hospital on July 1, 1863. Deserted at Ringgold, Georgia, September 4, 1863. Later served as Private in Company D, 2nd Regiment N.C. Mounted Infantry (Union).

CURTIS, GEORGE W., Private

Enlisted at Wartrace, Tennessee, May 1, 1863, for the war. Reported present in May-June, 1863. Reported in hospital at Marion, Mississippi, in July-October, 1863. Returned to duty in November-December, 1863. Reported present in January-April, 1864. Sent to hospital sick on June 10, 1864. Reported present in July-August, 1864. No further records. Survived the war.

DAVES, GEORGE W., Private

Born in Buncombe County and was by occupation a farmer prior to enlisting in Buncombe County at age 26, May 17, 1862, for the war. Reported present in November-December, 1862. Reported absent sick in January-February, 1863. Returned to duty in March-April, 1863. Reported present in May-June, 1863. Deserted at La Fayette, Georgia, in September, 1863. Later served as Private in Company D, 2nd Regiment N.C. Mounted Infantry (Union).

DAVIS, ANDREW JACKSON, Private

Born in Buncombe County and resided in Madison County where he was by occupation a farmer prior to enlisting in Buncombe County at age 23, May 17, 1862, for the war. Reported absent sick in November, 1862-February, 1863. Returned to duty in March-April, 1863. Reported present in May-June, 1863. Reported in hospital at Marion, Mississippi, in July-October, 1863. Returned to duty in November-December, 1863. Wounded slightly at Rocky Face Ridge, Georgia, February 25, 1864. Returned to duty prior to

May 1, 1864. Reported present in May-August, 1864. No further records. Survived the war. [North Carolina pension records indicate that he was wounded in the right shoulder at Missionary Ridge, Tennessee, in 1863.]

DAVIS, JOSIAH B., Private

Born in Buncombe County and was by occupation a farmer prior to enlisting in Buncombe County at age 33, May 17, 1862, for the war. Reported absent sick in November, 1862-February, 1863. Returned to duty in March-April, 1863. Reported absent in hospital from July 16 through October 31, 1863. Returned to duty in November-December, 1863. Reported absent sick in January-February, 1864. Returned to duty in March-April, 1864. Sent to hospital sick on May 15, 1864. Reported absent sick through August 31, 1864. No further records.

DAVIS, URIAH W., Private

Born in Buncombe County where he resided as a farmer prior to enlisting in Buncombe County at age 35, May 17, 1862, for the war. Mustered in as Corporal. Promoted to Sergeant prior to January 1, 1863. Hospitalized at Dalton, Georgia, January 1, 1863, with debilitas. Transferred to another hospital on February 12, 1863. Returned to duty in March-April, 1863. Reported present in May-June, 1863. Deserted at Ringgold, Georgia, September 1, 1863. Arrested on September 11, 1863. Returned to duty on June 23, 1864, and was reduced to ranks. Reported present in July-August, 1864. No further records. Survived the war.

DAVIS, WILLIAM J., Private

Born in Buncombe County where he resided as a farmer prior to enlisting in Buncombe County at age 30, May 17, 1862, for the war. Reported absent sick in November-December, 1862. Hospitalized at Dalton, Georgia, January 22, 1863, with chronic diarrhoea. Transferred to another hospital on February 12, 1863. Returned to duty in March-April, 1863. Hospitalized at Enterprise, Mississippi, July 5, 1863. Returned to duty in September-October, 1863. Captured at Missionary Ridge, Tennessee, November 25, 1863. Sent to Nashville, Tennessee. Transferred to Louisville, Kentucky, where he arrived on December 7, 1863. Transferred to Rock Island, Illinois, where he arrived on December 9, 1863. Died at Rock Island on April 10, 1864, of "variola."

DEVLIN, JAMES W., Private

Born in Edgefield District, South Carolina, and resided in Buncombe County where he was by occupation a farmer prior to enlisting in Buncombe County at age 18, May 17, 1862, for the war. Reported present in November-December, 1862. Died in hospital at Tullahoma, Tennessee, February 27, 1863. Cause of death not reported.

DEVOE, WILLIAM H., Private

Born in Edgefield District, South Carolina, and was by occupation a farmer prior to enlisting in Buncombe County at age 25, May 17, 1862, for the war. Discharged on or about August 1, 1862. Reason discharged not reported. [May have served later as Private in Company I, 25th Regiment N.C. Troops. See William Devoir.]

DOCKERY, WILLIAM B., Private

Born in Buncombe or Haywood County and was by occupation a farmer prior to enlisting in Buncombe County at age 28, May 17, 1862, for the war. Transferred to Company I of this regiment on or about September 13, 1862.

DRYMAN, A. L., Private

Born in Buncombe County where he resided as a farmer or schoolteacher prior to enlisting in Buncombe County at age 28, May 17, 1862, for the war. Discharged at Greeneville, Tennessee, on or about October 10, 1862. Reason discharged not reported.

DUPREE, THOMAS, Private

Enlisted at Tullahoma, Tennessee, February 11, 1863, for the war. Deserted at Tullahoma on March 4, 1863.

FLETCHER, ANDREW C., Private

Born in Buncombe or Anson County and was by occupation a farmer prior to enlisting in Buncombe County at age 33, May 17, 1862, for the war. Transferred to Company I of this regiment on or about September 13, 1862.

FRISBEE, DANIEL H., Private

Born in Buncombe County where he resided as a farmer prior to enlisting in Buncombe County at age 19, May 17, 1862, for the war. Reported present through June 30, 1863. Wounded in the shoulder at Chickamauga, Georgia, September 20, 1863. Returned to duty prior to October 31, 1863. Reported present through August 31, 1864. Transferred to Company H, 58th Regiment N.C. Troops, when the 58th and 60th Regiments were consolidated on April 9, 1865.

FRISBEE, FIDELIO, Corporal

Born in Buncombe County and was by occupation a farmer prior to enlisting in Buncombe County at age 24, May 17, 1862, for the war. Mustered in as Private. Hospitalized at Dalton, Georgia, December 30, 1862, with typhoid fever. Promoted to Corporal prior to January 1, 1863. Reported absent sick through February 28, 1863. Died in hospital at Tullahoma, Tennessee, April 25, 1863. Cause of death not reported. [Previously served as 2nd Lieutenant in the 109th Regiment N.C. Militia.]

GREEN, JEREMIAH, Corporal

Born in Watauga County* and was by occupation a farmer prior to enlisting in Buncombe County at age 32, May 17, 1862, for the war. Mustered in as Private. Promoted to Corporal prior to January 1, 1863. Reported absent sick in November, 1862-February, 1863. Returned to duty in March-April, 1863. Reported present in May-June, 1863. Died in hospital at Marietta, Georgia, on or about November 6, 1863. Cause of death not reported.

GREEN, JOSEPH, Private

Born in Buncombe County and was by occupation a farmer prior to enlisting in Buncombe County at age 24, May 17, 1862, for the war. Reported absent sick in November-December, 1862. Died at Chattanooga, Tennessee, prior to May 16, 1863. Date and cause of death not reported.

GREEN, WILLIAM H., Private

Resided in Buncombe County and enlisted at Tullahoma, Tennessee, January 1, 1863, for the war. Hospitalized at Dalton, Georgia, March 16, 1863, with chronic rheumatism. Furloughed for thirty days on May 11, 1863. Reported absent sick through December 31, 1863. Reported absent without leave on February 16, 1864. Returned to duty in May-June, 1864. Reported absent sick in July-August, 1864. No further records.

GREEN, WILLIAM P., Private

Born in Buncombe County and was by occupation a farmer prior to enlisting in Buncombe County at age 30, May 17, 1862, for the war. Wounded in the arm at Murfreesboro, Tennessee, January 2, 1863. Died in hospital at Murfreesboro on February 2, 1863, of wounds.

GUY, PETER, Private

Born in Macon or Henderson* County and was by occupation a farmer prior to enlisting in Buncombe County or at Camp Smith (Madison County) at age 34, May 17, 1862, for the war. Transferred to Company I of this regiment on or about September 13, 1862.

GUY, RICHARD A., Private

Born in Henderson County and was by occupation a farmer prior to enlisting at Camp Smith (Madison County) at age 16, August 1, 1862, for the war. Transferred to Company I of this regiment on or about the same date.

HALFORD, DAVID, Private

Born in Buncombe County where he resided as a farmer or house carpenter prior to enlisting in Buncombe County at age 64, August 1, 1862, for the war as a substitute for 1st Lt. William G. Candler of this company. Mustered in as Corporal. Reduced to ranks in November-December, 1862. Reported absent on sick furlough from December 29, 1862, through May 14, 1863. Detailed as a hospital nurse at Jackson, Mississippi, June 20, 1863. Hospitalized at Lauderdale Springs, Mississippi, July 17, 1863. Returned to duty as a hospital nurse subsequent to August 31, 1863. Reported absent on detail until July 12, 1864, when he was dropped from the company rolls. [Confederate medical records indicate that he was "too old" for military duty and "never a fit subject for the army. . . . Labours under diarrhoea more or less continuous(ly)."]

HALL, WILLIAM F., Private

Born in Haywood County and was by occupation a farmer prior to enlisting in Buncombe County at age 24, May 17, 1862, for the war. Reported absent sick in November, 1862-April, 1863. Returned to duty in May-June, 1863. Killed at Chickamauga, Georgia, September 20, 1863.

HAMPTON, GEORGE W., Private

Born in Buncombe County where he resided as a farmer prior to enlisting in Buncombe County at age 24, May 17, 1862, for the war. Reported present or accounted for in November, 1862-April, 1864. Captured at Nickajack Creek, near Smyrna, Georgia, July 5, 1864, after he was reported "missing on road." Sent to Nashville, Tennessee. Transferred to Louisville, Kentucky, where he arrived on July 14, 1864. Transferred to Camp Douglas, Chicago, Illinois, where he arrived on July 18, 1864. Released at Camp Douglas on June 13, 1865, after taking the Oath of Allegiance.

HAMPTON, JOHN E., Sergeant

Born in Buncombe County and was by occupation a farmer prior to enlisting in Buncombe County at age 19, May 17, 1862, for the war. Mustered in as Private. Reported present in November, 1862-October, 1863. Promoted to Sergeant in July-October, 1863. Reported present in November, 1863-April, 1864. Wounded severely at Kolb's Farm, near Marietta, Georgia, June 22, 1864. No further records.

HAMPTON, MARCUS F., Private

Previously served as Private in Company A, 56th Regiment N.C. Troops. Transferred to this company on April 15, 1864. Captured at Nickajack Creek, near Smyrna, Georgia, July 5, 1864, after he was reported "missing on road." Sent to Nashville, Tennessee. Transferred to Louisville, Kentucky, where he arrived on July 14, 1864. Transferred to Camp Douglas, Chicago, Illinois, where he arrived on July 18, 1864. Released at Camp Douglas on June 16, 1865, after taking the Oath of Allegiance.

HAMPTON, WILLIAM F., Private

Resided in Buncombe County. Place and date of enlistment not reported; however, he probably enlisted in 1864. Captured at or near Nickajack Creek, near Smyrna, Georgia, July 5, 1864. Sent to Marietta, Georgia, July 7, 1864. No further records. Survived the war. [Was about 16 years of age at time of enlistment.]

HARKINS, THOMAS J., 1st Sergeant

Born in Buncombe County and resided in McDowell County where he was by occupation a carpenter prior to enlisting in Buncombe County at age 33, May 17, 1862, for the war. Mustered in as Sergeant. Promoted to 1st Sergeant prior to January 1, 1863. Wounded slightly in the hand at Murfreesboro, Tennessee, December 31, 1862. Returned to duty in January-February, 1863. Reported absent sick at Catoosa Springs, Georgia, from March 12 through April 30, 1863. Returned to duty in May-June, 1863. Reported absent on detail in July-December, 1863. Elected 3rd Lieutenant of Company A, 14th Battalion N.C. Cavalry (later known as Company A, 69th Regiment N.C. Troops [7th Regiment N.C. Cavalry]), January 1, 1864, and transferred. [Contrary to 2:562 of this series, the correct spelling of his surname is Harkins rather than Haskins.]

HAYES, HENRY J., Private

Born in Buncombe County and was by occupation a farmer prior to enlisting in Buncombe County at age 24, May 17, 1862, for the war. Hospitalized at Dalton, Georgia, November 21, 1862, with debilitas. Deserted from hospital on or about January 20, 1863. Returned to duty on March 1, 1863. Reported present in May-October, 1863. Died in hospital at Cassville, Georgia, November 19, 1863. Cause of death not reported.

HAYES, JAMES M., Private

Born in Buncombe County and was by occupation a farmer prior to enlisting in Buncombe County at age 32, May 17, 1862, for the war. Mustered in as Corporal. Reduced to ranks prior to January 1, 1863. Deserted at Murfreesboro, Tennessee, December 31, 1862. Returned to duty on April 29, 1863. Reported present through August 31, 1864. No further records. Survived the war. [May have served previously as Captain in the 109th Regiment N.C. Militia and as Private in Company E, 1st Regiment N.C. Infantry (6 months, 1861).]

HAYES, MARCUS L., Private

Born in Buncombe County where he resided as a farmer prior to enlisting in Buncombe County at age 23, May 17, 1862, for the war. Hospitalized at Dalton, Georgia, November 6, 1862, with rheumatism. Returned to duty on December 13, 1862. Hospitalized at Dalton on December 30, 1862, with rheumatism. Returned to duty in January-February, 1863. Reported sick in hospital in March-April, 1863. No further records. Survived the war.

HAYNES, JACOB D., Corporal

Born in Haywood County where he resided prior to enlisting in Buncombe County at age 24, May 17, 1862, for the war. Mustered in as Private. Promoted to Corporal subsequent to August 1, 1862. Died in hospital at Tullahoma, Tennessee, January 31, 1863. Cause of death not reported.

HIPPS, MADISON L., Private

Born in Macon County and resided in Buncombe County where he was by occupation a farmer prior to enlisting in Buncombe County at age 23, May 17, 1862, for the war. Reported present in November-December, 1862. Reported on duty as a teamster from February 1 through March 10, 1863. Reported on detached service on June 17, 1863. Reported on detail as a wagoner in Mississippi from July 1 through October 31, 1863. Rejoined the company in November-December, 1863. Reported present in January-February, 1864. Wounded slightly at Rocky Face Ridge, Georgia, February 25, 1864. Reported on duty as a teamster in March-June, 1864. Reported present in July-August, 1864. No further records. Survived the war.

HIPPS, MARCUS B., Sergeant

Born in Macon County and resided in Buncombe County where he was by occupation a farmer prior to enlisting in Buncombe County at age 18, May 17, 1862, for the war. Mustered in as Private. Reported present in November, 1862-April, 1864. Promoted to Sergeant on February 1, 1864. Wounded at Resaca, Georgia, May 15, 1864. Returned to duty in July-August, 1864. Transferred to Company H, 58th Regiment N.C. Troops, when the 58th and 60th Regiments were consolidated on April 9, 1865.

HOWELL, E. GRADY, Private

Born in Buncombe County where he resided as a farmer prior to enlisting in Buncombe County at age 32, May 17, 1862, for the war. Wounded slightly in the hand at Murfreesboro, Tennessee, December 31, 1862. Returned to duty in January-February, 1863. Reported present in March-April, 1863. Furloughed on August 4, 1863. Returned to duty on an unspecified date. Reported present in November, 1863-August, 1864. No further records.

HUGHES, JAMES M., Private

Born in South Carolina or in Macon County and resided in Buncombe County where he was by occupation a farmer prior to enlisting in Buncombe County at age 27, May 17, 1862, for the war. Captured at Murfreesboro, Tennessee, December 31, 1862-January 2, 1863. Hospitalized at Evansville, Indiana, January 27, 1863. Died in hospital at Evansville on January 31, 1863, of "chronic diarrhoea."

ISRAEL, JOHN, Private

Resided in Buncombe County and was by occupation a farm laborer prior to enlisting in Buncombe County at age 24, December 1, 1862, for the war. Reported absent sick in January-February, 1863. Reported sick in hospital at Catoosa Springs, Georgia, in March-April, 1863. Returned to duty in May-June, 1863. Hospitalized at Jackson, Mississippi, July 13, 1863. Transferred to another hospital on July 14, 1863. Deserted at La Fayette, Georgia, or near Chattanooga, Tennessee, on or about September 9, 1863. Returned to duty on June 23, 1864. Reported present in July-August, 1864. Deserted to the enemy on or about December 27, 1864. Took the Oath of Allegiance at Nashville, Tennessee, January 10, 1865.

JAMISON, NEWTON A., Private

Born in Buncombe County and was by occupation a farmer prior to enlisting in Buncombe County at age 31, May 17, 1862, for the war. Reported present in November, 1862-June, 1863. Reported absent sick in July-October, 1863. Reported sick in hospital in November-December, 1863. Furloughed from hospital on an unspecified date. Failed to return to duty and was reported absent without leave on February 16, 1864. Listed as a deserter on April 7, 1864. Returned to duty in May-June, 1864. Reported present in July-August, 1864. Transferred to Company H, 58th Regiment N.C. Troops, when the 58th and 60th Regiments were consolidated on April 9, 1865.

JARRETT, ROBERT H., Private

Enlisted in Buncombe County at age 33, May 17, 1862, for the war. Deserted at Tullahoma, Tennessee, January 12, 1863. Returned to duty on March 31, 1863. Detailed as a hospital nurse at Point Clear, Alabama, July 24, 1863. Rejoined the company prior to November 1, 1863. No further records. Survived the war. [May have served previously as Private in Company E, 1st Regiment N.C. Infantry (6 months, 1861).]

JONES, ANDREW J., Private

Enlisted in Buncombe County at age 26, May 17, 1862, for the war. Reported absent sick in November, 1862-February, 1863. Returned to duty in March-April, 1863. Sent to hospital on August 7, 1863. Died in hospital at Lauderdale Springs, Mississippi, prior to November 1, 1863. Cause of death not reported.

JONES, POSEY W., Private

Resided in Buncombe County and was by occupation a farmer prior to enlisting in Buncombe County at age 29, May 17, 1862, for the war. Hospitalized at Dalton, Georgia, December 30, 1862, with chronic rheumatism. Returned to duty on January 19, 1863. Reported present through October 31, 1863. Detailed for duty in the Pioneer Corps on or about November 10, 1863. Reported absent on detail through August 31, 1864. Transferred to Company H, 58th Regiment N.C. Troops, when the 58th and 60th Regiments were consolidated on April 9, 1865.

JONES, THEODORE, Private

Previously served as Private in Company E, 1st Regiment N.C. Infantry (6 months, 1861). Enlisted in this company in Buncombe County on May 17, 1862, for the war. Mustered in as Sergeant. Reduced to ranks prior to January 1, 1863. Reported present in November, 1862-December, 1863. Wounded slightly at Rocky Face Ridge, Georgia, February 25, 1864. Returned to duty in March-April, 1864. Captured at Resaca, Georgia, May 15, 1864. Sent to Nashville, Tennessee. Transferred to Louisville, Kentucky, where he arrived on May 20, 1864. Transferred to Camp Morton, Indianapolis, Indiana, where he arrived on May 22, 1864. Died at Camp Morton on October 11, 1864, of "chronic diarrhoea."

JONES, WILLIAM P., Private

Born in Buncombe County and was by occupation a farmer prior to enlisting in Buncombe County at age 17, May 17, 1862, for the war. Reported absent sick in November-December, 1862. Returned to duty in January-February, 1863. Reported present in March-June, 1863. Deserted at La Fayette, Georgia, in September, 1863. Returned from desertion on October 27, 1863. Reported absent sick in November-December, 1863. Reported absent without leave in January-February, 1864. Returned to duty in March-April, 1864. Captured at Resaca, Georgia, on or about May 15, 1864. Sent to Nashville, Tennessee. Transferred to Louisville, Kentucky, where he arrived on May 20, 1864. Transferred to Camp Morton, Indianapolis, Indiana, where he arrived on May 22, 1864. Paroled at Camp Morton and transferred to City Point, Virginia, February 26, 1865, for exchange. No further records. Survived the war.

JUSTICE, WILLIAM T., Private

Enlisted in Buncombe County on May 17, 1862, for the war. Reported absent sick in November, 1862-February, 1863. No further records.

KILLIAN, DANIEL A., Private

Previously served as Private in Company E, 1st Regiment N.C. Infantry (6 months, 1861). Enlisted in this company in Buncombe County on October 1, 1862, for the war. Reported present in November-December, 1862. Reported absent sick in January-February, 1863. Transferred to Company K of this regiment on March 2, 1863. [Born in Buncombe County on April 18, 1840.]

LINDSEY, NAPHTALI FLETCHER, Private

Place and date of enlistment not reported (probably enlisted in May-July, 1862). Discharged on or about August 1, 1862. Reason discharged not reported.

LUTHER, HAMILTON A., ——

Resided in Buncombe County and was by occupation a farmer. Place and date of enlistment not reported; however, he probably enlisted in May-August, 1862. Discharged on November 4, 1862. Reason discharged not reported. Later served as Private in Company I, 25th Regiment N.C. Troops. [Was about 31 years of age at time of enlistment in this company.]

LUTHER, JOHN HUTSELL, Musician

Enlisted in Buncombe County at age 26, May 17, 1862, for the war. Mustered in as Private. Promoted to Musician prior to January 1, 1863. Reported present in November-December, 1862. Reported absent sick in hospital from February 5 through April 30, 1863. Returned to duty in May-June, 1863. Reported present through December 31, 1863. Furloughed for thirty days on February 23, 1864. Returned to duty prior to June 22, 1864, when he was wounded at Kolb's Farm, near Marietta, Georgia. Hospitalized at Barnsville, Georgia, where he died on July 5, 1864, presumably of wounds.

LUTHER, ROBERT J., Private

Born in Buncombe County and was by occupation a farmer prior to enlisting in Buncombe County at age 19, May 17, 1862, for the war. Reported absent sick in November-December, 1862. Hospitalized at Dalton, Georgia, February 14, 1863, with chronic rheumatism. Returned to duty on March 3, 1863. Reported present in May-June, 1863. Deserted at Chickamauga, Georgia, October 4, 1863. Returned from desertion on May 27, 1864. Reported present in July-August, 1864. Transferred to Company H, 58th Regiment N.C. Troops, when the 58th and 60th Regiments were consolidated on April 9, 1865.

LUTHER, SAMUEL P., Private

Born in Newberry District, South Carolina, and resided in Buncombe County where he was by occupation a farmer prior to enlisting in Buncombe County at age 34, May 17, 1862, for the war. Elected 3rd Lieutenant of Company I of this regiment on September 13, 1862, and transferred.

LUTHER, SAMUEL WAITSEL, Private

Born in Buncombe County and was by occupation a farmer prior to enlisting in Buncombe County at age 29, May 17, 1862, for the war. Transferred to Company I of this regiment on or about September 13, 1862.

McFEE, JOHN, Private

Born in Buncombe County and was by occupation a farmer prior to enlisting in Buncombe County at age 27, May 17, 1862, for the war. Reported absent sick in November, 1862-February, 1863. Reported present in March-June, 1863. Reported absent sick in July-October, 1863. Reported absent with leave in November-December, 1863. Died prior to February 29, 1864. Place, date, and cause of death not reported.

McKEE, ROBERT F., 1st Sergeant

Born in Haywood County and resided in Madison County where he was by occupation a merchant or farmer prior to enlisting in Buncombe County at age 31, May 17, 1862, for the war. Mustered in as 1st Sergeant. Last reported in the records of this company on November 18, 1862. Survived the war. [May have served previously as Assistant Commissary of Subsistence (Captain) of the 29th Regiment N.C. Troops.]

McKINNISH, WILEY, Private

Born in Buncombe County and was by occupation a farmer prior to enlisting in Buncombe County at age 33, May 17, 1862, for the war. Reported absent sick in November, 1862-February, 1863. Returned to duty in March-April, 1863. Reported absent sick from May 20 through October 31, 1863. Died in Buncombe County prior to December 15, 1863. Cause of death not reported.

MORGAN, J. G., Private

Born in Buncombe County and was by occupation a farmer prior to enlisting in Buncombe County at age 35, May 17, 1862, for the war. Reported absent sick in November, 1862-February, 1863. Returned to duty in March-April, 1863. Sent to hospital on June 30, 1863. Furloughed from hospital in January-February, 1864. Reported absent without leave on February 16, 1864. Listed as a deserter on April 7, 1864. Returned to duty in May-June, 1864. Reported present in July-August, 1864. Hospitalized at Greensboro in March, 1865. No further records.

MORGAN, JAMES H., Private

Born in Buncombe County and was by occupation a farmer prior to enlisting in Buncombe County at age 27, May 17, 1862, for the war. Discharged on September 1, 1862. Reason discharged not reported.

MORGAN, JAMES W., Private

Born in Buncombe County where he resided as a farmer prior to enlisting in Buncombe County at age 20, May 17, 1862, for the war. Reported absent sick in November, 1862-February, 1863. Returned to duty in March-April, 1863. Died at Demopolis, Alabama, June 3, 1863. Cause of death not reported.

MORGAN, JONATHAN L., Sergeant

Born in Buncombe County where he resided as a farmer prior to enlisting in Buncombe County at age 18, May 17, 1862, for the war. Mustered in as Private. Wounded slightly in the hand at Murfreesboro, Tennessee, December 31, 1862. Returned to duty in January-February, 1863. Promoted to Corporal on February 1, 1863. Reported sick in hospital at Chattanooga, Tennessee, March 27, 1863. Returned to duty in May-June, 1863. Promoted to Sergeant on December 1, 1863. Reported present through February 29, 1864. Furloughed on April 4, 1864. Returned to duty in May-June, 1864. Sent to hospital sick on July 18, 1864. Reported absent sick through August 31, 1864. No further records. [Carried the colors of his regiment at the Battle of Murfreesboro.]

MORGAN, MARION H., Private
Born in Buncombe County and was by occupation a farmer prior to enlisting in Buncombe County at age 19, May 17, 1862, for the war. Reported absent sick in November, 1862-February, 1863. Returned to duty in March-April, 1863. Hospitalized at Lauderdale Springs, Mississippi, on or about August 4, 1863. Returned to duty prior to November 1, 1863. Reported present in November, 1863-August, 1864. Transferred to Company H, 58th Regiment N.C. Troops, when the 58th and 60th Regiments were consolidated on April 9, 1865.

MORGAN, STEPHEN W., Private
Born in Buncombe County where he resided as a farmer prior to enlisting in Buncombe County at age 25, May 17, 1862, for the war. Reported present in November, 1862-June, 1863. Wounded in the "bowels" and hip at Chickamauga, Georgia, September 20, 1863. Died in hospital at Atlanta, Georgia, on or about October 14, 1863, of wounds.

OWEN, D. J. M., ———
North Carolina pension records indicate that he served in this company.

PARKER, JAMES, Private
Born in Laurens District, South Carolina, and resided in Buncombe County where he was by occupation a farmer prior to enlisting in Buncombe County at age 29, May 17, 1862, for the war. Reported present in November, 1862-April, 1863. Wounded in the right arm by a cannon ball at Jackson, Mississippi, July 12, 1863. Right arm amputated. Reported absent wounded until February 6, 1865, when he was discharged.

PARKER, JOSEPH S., Private
Born in Laurens District, South Carolina, and was by occupation a farmer prior to enlisting in Buncombe County at age 19, May 17, 1862, for the war. Reported present in November, 1862-June, 1863. Deserted at Chickamauga, Georgia, in September, 1863. Returned to duty on October 27, 1863. Reported absent sick in November, 1863-February, 1864. Returned to duty in March-April, 1864. Captured at or near Ruff's Mill, near Smyrna, Georgia, July 4, 1864. Sent to Nashville, Tennessee. Transferred to Louisville, Kentucky, where he arrived on July 15, 1864. Transferred to Camp Douglas, Chicago, Illinois, where he arrived on July 18, 1864. Died at Camp Douglas on October 3, 1864. Cause of death not reported.

PARKER, WILLIAM H., Private
Born in Laurens District, South Carolina, and was by occupation a farmer prior to enlisting in Buncombe County at age 23, May 17, 1862, for the war. Died at Murfreesboro, Tennessee, prior to February 7, 1863. Cause of death not reported.

PATTON, JOHN M., Private
Born in Buncombe County and was by occupation a farmer prior to enlisting in Buncombe County at age 16, May 17, 1862, for the war as a substitute for Pvt. Ransom S. Smith. Reported present in November, 1862-June, 1863. Wounded in the right foot at Chickamauga, Georgia, September 20, 1863. Right foot amputated. Reported absent wounded until February 7, 1865, when he was discharged.

PEEBLES, WILLIAM, Private
Born in Buncombe County where he enlisted at age 25, May 17, 1862, for the war. Deserted at Tullahoma, Tennessee, January 12, 1863.

PENLAND, CHARLES M., Private
Resided in Buncombe County and was by occupation a farmer prior to enlisting in Buncombe County at age 30, May 17, 1862, for the war. Reported present in November, 1862-June, 1863. Captured at Chickamauga, Georgia, September 20, 1863. Sent to Nashville, Tennessee. Transferred to Louisville, Kentucky, where he arrived on September 30, 1863. Transferred to Camp Douglas, Chicago, Illinois, where he arrived on October 4, 1863. Died at Camp Douglas on August 27, 1864, of "dysentery."

PENLAND, GEORGE W., Sergeant
Born in Buncombe County where he enlisted at age 29, May 17, 1862, for the war. Mustered in as Private. Promoted to Sergeant in August-December, 1862. Reported absent sick in November, 1862-April, 1863. Returned to duty in May-June, 1863. Reported present in July-October, 1863. Captured at Missionary Ridge, Tennessee, November 25, 1863. Sent to Nashville, Tennessee. Transferred to Louisville, Kentucky, where he arrived on December 7, 1863. Transferred to Rock Island, Illinois, where he arrived on December 9, 1863. Took the Oath of Allegiance at Rock Island on October 18, 1864, and joined the U.S. Army. Rejected for service in the U.S. Army (presumably because of ill health) and was released from prison on the same date.

PENLAND, HENRY C., Private
Resided in Buncombe County and enlisted at Wartrace, Tennessee, at age 19, May 1, 1863, for the war. Killed at Chickamauga, Georgia, September 20, 1863.

PENLAND, WILLIAM H., Corporal
Born in Buncombe County where he enlisted at age 34, May 17, 1862, for the war. Mustered in as Private. Reported present in November-December, 1862. Reported absent sick in January-February, 1863. Returned to duty in March-April, 1863. Promoted to Corporal on May 20, 1863. Reported sick in hospital in May-June, 1863. Returned to duty prior to September 20, 1863, when he was wounded in the hand ("finger off") at Chickamauga, Georgia. Reported absent on furlough in November-December, 1863. Reported absent without leave on February 16, 1864. Listed as a deserter on April 7, 1864.

PLEMMONS, HENRY, Private
Born in Buncombe County where he enlisted at age 19, May 17, 1862, for the war. Hospitalized at Dalton, Georgia, November 21, 1862, with lumbago. Deserted from hospital on December 1, 1862. Returned to duty prior to January 1, 1863. Reported present through February 29, 1864. Furloughed on April 11, 1864. Reported sick at home in May-June, 1864. Returned to duty in July-August, 1864. No further records.

PLEMMONS, JOHN, Private
Born in Buncombe County where he resided as a farmer prior to enlisting in Buncombe County at age 23, May 17, 1862, for the war. Died in hospital at Murfreesboro, Tennessee, December 15, 1862. Cause of death not reported.

PLEMMONS, JOSEPH J., Private

Previously served as Private in Company E, 1st Regiment N.C. Infantry (6 months, 1861). Enlisted in this company on May 17, 1862, for the war. Reported absent sick in November-December, 1862. Hospitalized at Dalton, Georgia, January 30, 1863, with chronic rheumatism. Returned to duty in March-April, 1863. Reported present in May-June, 1863. Wounded in the thigh at Chickamauga, Georgia, September 19-20, 1863. Leg amputated. Hospitalized at Atlanta, Georgia, where he died on October 11, 1863, of wounds. [Contrary to 3:28 of this series, the correct spelling of his surname was probably Plemmons rather than Plemons.]

PLEMMONS, LEVI J., Private

Previously served as Private in Company H, 2nd Battalion N.C. Infantry. Attached himself to this company on or about May 17, 1862, after most of the 2nd Battalion was captured at Roanoke Island on February 8, 1862. Transferred to Company I of this regiment on or about September 13, 1862.

RAMSEY, ALBERT G., Private

Resided in Buncombe County and was by occupation a farm laborer. Place and date of enlistment not reported; however, he probably enlisted on or about May 17, 1862. "Joined another company" prior to August 1, 1862. [Probably enlisted in Company D, 64th Regiment N.C. Troops.]

RAMSEY, W. T., Private

Place and date of enlistment not reported (probably enlisted on or about May 17, 1862). "Joined another company" prior to August 1, 1862. [Probably enlisted in Company D, 64th Regiment N.C. Troops.]

RATCLIFF, FIDELIO, Private

Resided in Buncombe County and was by occupation a farmer prior to enlisting in Buncombe County at age 22, May 17, 1862, for the war. Reported absent sick in January-December, 1863. Returned to duty in March-April, 1864. Hospitalized at Macon, Georgia, July 5, 1864, with chronic diarrhoea. Transferred on July 8, 1864. Died in hospital at Eufaula, Alabama, August 25, 1864. Cause of death not reported.

RATCLIFF, W. F., Private

Born in Buncombe County where he resided as a farmer prior to enlisting in Buncombe County at age 34, May 17, 1862, for the war. Reported absent sick in November, 1862-April, 1863. Detailed as a teamster on or about June 26, 1863. Rejoined the company in November-December, 1863. Reported present in January-April, 1864. Killed at Kolb's Farm, near Marietta, Georgia, June 22, 1864.

ROGERS, A. N., Private

Born in Buncombe County and was by occupation a farmer prior to enlisting in Buncombe County at age 34, May 17, 1862, for the war. Broke his arm "to pieces" on November 25, 1862, when he was "thrown from [a] wagon." Arm paralyzed. Reported absent sick until March 8, 1865, when he was retired to the Invalid Corps because of "double fracture of the radius & ulna near the wrist and elbow joints, with great atrophy of the arm and hand and contraction of the muscles and tendons. . . ."

ROGERS, JESSE J. S., Private

Born in Haywood County and was by occupation a farmer prior to enlisting in Buncombe County or at Camp Smith (Madison County) on August 1, 1862, for the war. Appointed Musician and transferred to Company I of this regiment on or about September 13, 1862. [Was about 18 years of age at time of enlistment.]

ROGERS, JONATHAN A., Private

Born in Haywood County and was by occupation a farmer prior to enlisting at Camp Smith (Madison County) at age 16, August 1, 1862, for the war. Transferred to Company I of this regiment on or about September 13, 1862.

SHARP, JOHN P., Private

Born in Buncombe County where he resided as a farmer prior to enlisting in Buncombe County at age 25, May 17, 1862, for the war. Mustered in as Private. Promoted to Musician prior to January 1, 1863. Detailed as a hospital nurse on January 16, 1863. Reduced to ranks in July-October, 1863. Reported absent on detail as a nurse through April 30, 1864. Dropped from the company rolls on July 12, 1864. Reason he was dropped not reported.

SLATE, WILLIAM W., Sergeant

Born in Haywood County where he resided as a "renter" prior to enlisting in Buncombe County at age 27, May 17, 1862, for the war. Mustered in as Private. Promoted to Sergeant on December 31, 1862. Wounded in the shoulder at Murfreesboro, Tennessee, January 2, 1863. Reported absent wounded or absent sick through December 31, 1863. No further records.

SLUDER, MITCHELL, Private

Born in Buncombe County where he resided as a farmer prior to enlisting in Buncombe County at age 34, May 17, 1862, for the war. Died at Murfreesboro, Tennessee, on an unspecified date (probably prior to January 1, 1863). Cause of death not reported.

SMATHERS, JOHN, Private

Born in Haywood County and resided in Haywood or Buncombe County where he was by occupation a farmer or renter prior to enlisting in Buncombe County at age 23, May 17, 1862, for the war. Transferred to Company I of this regiment on or about September 13, 1862.

SMITH, DAVID H., Private

Born in Buncombe County where he enlisted at age 28, May 17, 1862, for the war. Deserted on or about December 12, 1862. Returned to duty on April 29, 1863. Reported present in May-October, 1863. Reported absent sick in November-December, 1863. Died at Atlanta, Georgia, prior to March 1, 1864. Cause of death not reported.

SMITH, RANSOM S., Private

Previously served as Private in Company H, 29th Regiment N.C. Troops. Enlisted in this company on May 17, 1862, for the war. Discharged on or about the same date after providing Pvt. John M. Patton as a substitute. [Contrary to 8:298 of this series, it appears that he was born in 1832.]

SMITH, WILLIAM A., Private

Born in Buncombe County and was by occupation a mason prior to enlisting in Buncombe County at age 32, May 17, 1862, for the war. Reported present in November, 1862-June, 1863. Deserted at Chickamauga, Georgia, October 4, 1863. Returned from desertion and was assigned to duty at Asheville on November 1, 1863. Rejoined the company on or about April 29, 1864. Died at Thomaston,

Georgia, August 19, 1864, of wounds. Place and date wounded not reported.

SPIVY, ALEXANDER, Private

Enlisted in Buncombe County at age 27, May 17, 1862, for the war. Reported absent sick on September 1, 1862. Hospitalized at Tunnel Hill, Georgia, May 22, 1863, with acute diarrhoea. Furloughed on July 8, 1863. Reported absent sick through December 31, 1863. Reported absent without leave on February 16, 1864. Listed as a deserter on April 7, 1864.

SPIVY, JUNIUS PINKNEY, Private

Born in Buncombe County and was by occupation a farmer prior to enlisting in Buncombe County at age 33, May 17, 1862, for the war. Transferred to Company I of this regiment on or about September 13, 1862.

STARNES, FRANCIS MARION, Private

Previously served as Private in Company H, 29th Regiment N.C. Troops. Enlisted in this company in Buncombe County at age 32, May 17, 1862, for the war. Transferred to Company I of this regiment on or about September 13, 1862.

STARNES, JAMES M., Private

Born in Buncombe County where he resided as a farmer prior to enlisting in Buncombe County at age 26, May 17, 1862, for the war. Discharged prior to August 1, 1862. Reason discharged not reported.

STINES, WILLIAM A., Private

Born in Macon County and resided in Buncombe County where he was by occupation a miller prior to enlisting in Buncombe County at age 29, May 17, 1862, for the war. Reported absent sick in January-February, 1863. Returned to duty in March-April, 1863. Reported present in May-June, 1863. Deserted at La Fayette, Georgia, in September, 1863. Returned to duty in November-December, 1863. Reported present in January-April, 1864. Died in hospital at Atlanta, Georgia, June 25, 1864. Cause of death not reported.

TAYLOR, GEORGE NEWTON, Private

Born in Macon County and enlisted in Buncombe County at age 27, May 17, 1862, for the war. Reported present in November, 1862-April, 1863. Reported on detail as a blacksmith (probably at Meridian, Mississippi) from June 17, 1863, through April 30, 1864. Dropped from the company rolls on July 12, 1864. Reason he was dropped not reported.

WARREN, J. J., ———

Place and date of enlistment not reported (probably enlisted on or about May 17, 1862). Discharged prior to August 1, 1862. Reason discharged not reported.

WARREN, WASHINGTON, Private

Born in Buncombe County where he enlisted at age 18, May 17, 1862, for the war. Transferred to an unspecified unit prior to August 1, 1862.

WELLS, MARCUS B., Private

Previously served as Private in Company E, 1st Regiment N.C. Infantry (6 months, 1861). Enlisted in this company in Buncombe or Henderson County on May 17, 1862, for the war. Transferred to Company I of this regiment on or about September 13, 1862.

WELLS, R. D., Private

Enlisted at Tullahoma, Tennessee, February 11, 1863, for the war. Reported present through April 30, 1863. Deserted at Fairfield, Tennessee, May 23, 1863. [May have served later as Private in Company H, 2nd Regiment N.C. Mounted Infantry (Union).]

WELLS, S. F., Private

Born in Buncombe County and was by occupation a farmer prior to enlisting in Buncombe County at age 17, May 17, 1862, for the war. Transferred to Company I of this regiment on or about September 13, 1862.

WILSON, L. E., 1st Sergeant

Enlisted in Buncombe County at age 20, May 17, 1862, for the war. Mustered in as Private. Reported absent sick in November-December 1862. Promoted to Sergeant prior to January 1, 1863. Reported present in March-June, 1863. Reduced to ranks on June 25, 1863. Reported absent sick in July-October, 1863. Returned to duty in November-December, 1863. Promoted to 1st Sergeant on February 1, 1864. Reported present in January-August, 1864. Transferred to Company H, 58th Regiment N.C. Troops, when the 58th and 60th Regiments were consolidated on April 9, 1865.

WISE, A. M., Private

Born in Buncombe County where he enlisted at age 19, May 17, 1862, for the war. Last reported in the records of this company on October 22, 1862. No further records.

WOLF, FRANCIS M., Private

Born in Buncombe County where he resided as a brickmason prior to enlisting in Buncombe County at age 32, May 17, 1862, for the war. Reported absent on detail in the armory at Asheville in November, 1862-February, 1863. Rejoined the company prior to July 1, 1863. Reported in hospital at Kingston, Georgia, in July-August, 1863. Died in hospital at Kingston on or about September 29, 1863. Cause of death not reported.

WOLF, JAMES P., Private

Born in Buncombe County on June 10, 1832. Resided in Buncombe County where he enlisted at age 29, May 17, 1862, for the war. Mustered in as Private. Promoted to Corporal prior to January 1, 1863. Reported absent sick in November, 1862-April, 1863. Returned to duty in May-June, 1863, and was reduced to ranks. Reported absent sick in July-August, 1863. Wounded in the back at Chickamauga, Georgia, September 20, 1863. Reported absent wounded or absent sick through February 29, 1864. Returned to duty in March-April, 1864. Reported present in May-June, 1864. Reported sick in hospital in July-August, 1864. Transferred to Company H, 58th Regiment N.C. Troops, when the 58th and 60th Regiments were consolidated on April 9, 1865.

YOUNG, PLEASANT A., Private

Born in Buncombe County where he resided as a farmer prior to enlisting in Buncombe County at age 27, May 17, 1862, for the war. Deserted at Tullahoma, Tennessee, January 12, 1863. Returned to duty on March 7, 1863. Reported present in May-October, 1863. Furloughed home in November-December, 1863. Reported absent sick in January-April, 1864. Hospitalized at Griffin, Georgia, on or about June 15, 1864. Reported absent sick through August 31, 1864. Reported in hospital at Cassville, Georgia, October 31, 1864. Died on an unspecified date prior to January 1, 1865. Place and cause of death not reported.

COMPANY F

This company was raised in Buncombe County on May 16, 1862. It was mustered into state service at Asheville on that date as "Sixth Company," McDowell's Battalion N.C. Infantry (known also as the 6th Battalion N.C. Infantry). The seven-company battalion was mustered into Confederate service on August 1, 1862, and redesignated the 1st Battalion N.C. Infantry. On October 8, 1862, the 60th Regiment N.C. Troops was formally organized after three additional companies were assigned to the 1st Battalion. This company was designated Company F. After joining the regiment the company functioned as a part of the regiment, and its history for the remainder of the war is reported as a part of the regimental history.

The following roster was compiled primarily from information in the microfilm edition of the Compiled Service Records of Soldiers Who Served in Organizations from the State of North Carolina (Record Group 109, M270), National Archives and Records Administration, Washington, D.C. Record Group 109 includes enlistment papers, pay vouchers, requisitions, letters of resignation, discharge certificates, and abstracts of medical and prisoner of war returns. Materials relating specifically to this company include muster rolls dated August, 1862-August, 1864.

Also utilized in this roster were *The War of the Rebellion: A Compilation of the Official Records of the Union and Confederate Armies*, the North Carolina adjutant general's *Roll of Honor*, state militia records, newspaper casualty lists and obituaries, wartime claims for bounty pay and allowances, postwar registers of claims for artificial limbs, Confederate pension applications filed with the states of North Carolina, Tennessee, and Florida, Confederate Soldiers' Home records, and the 1860 and 1870 federal censuses of North Carolina. A search was made also for relevant letters, diaries, reminiscences, and other manuscripts in the Southern Historical Collection (University of North Carolina-Chapel Hill), the Duke University Library Special Collections Department, and the North Carolina Division of Archives and History.

Among the secondary sources consulted were records of the North Carolina division of the United Daughters of the Confederacy, postwar rosters, regimental and county histories, marriage bond, will, and cemetery indexes, published and unpublished genealogies, biographical dictionaries, the North Carolina *County Heritage Book* series, the *Confederate Veteran*, Walter Clark's *Histories of the Several Regiments and Battalions from North Carolina in the Great War, 1861-'65*, and the North Carolina volume of the extended edition of *Confederate Military History*.

OFFICERS

CAPTAINS

STEVENS, JAMES MITCHELL

Born on August 18, 1827. Enlisted in Buncombe County at age 34. Elected Captain of this company on May 16, 1862. Appointed Surgeon on November 5, 1862, to rank from August 1, 1862, and transferred to the Field and Staff of this regiment.

RAY, JAMES MITCHEL

Born in Buncombe County on November 15, 1838. Elected 1st Lieutenant of this company at age 23, May 16, 1862. Promoted to Captain on August 1, 1862. Reported present in August-October, 1862, and March-April, 1863. Appointed Lieutenant Colonel in

late June, 1863, and transferred to the Field and Staff of this regiment.

WRIGHT, SAMUEL C.

Served as Captain of Company E of this regiment. Reported on duty as acting commander of this company in January-February, 1864.

LIEUTENANTS

DAVIDSON, THOMAS FOSTER, 3rd Lieutenant

Previously served as Private in Company B, 1st Regiment N.C. Infantry (6 months, 1861). Enlisted in this company in Buncombe County on May 16, 1862, for the war. Mustered in with an unspecified rank. Reported present in August-October, 1862. Elected 3rd Lieutenant on September 27, 1862. Signed roll of as commander of the company in January-April, 1863. Reported present in May-June, 1863. Reported in command of the company in July-October, 1863. Reported present in November-December, 1863. Broke his arm while "playing ball" on or about February 1, 1864. Furloughed on an unspecified date. Reported present and in command of the company in March-June, 1864. Sent to hospital on July 28, 1864. Reported absent wounded on September 20, 1864. Place and date wounded not reported. No further records. Survived the war. [Erroneously listed as James F. Davidson in 3:10 of this series.]

REYNOLDS, JOHN HASKEW, 1st Lieutenant

Resided in Buncombe County. Enlisted at age 26. Elected 3rd Lieutenant on May 16, 1862. Promoted to 1st Lieutenant on August 1, 1862. Reported present in August-October, 1862. Reported sick in hospital at Dalton, Georgia, in March-April, 1863. Reported present but sick in May-June, 1863. Wounded in the right hand at Chickamauga, Georgia, September 20, 1863. Right hand amputated. Resigned on April 16, 1864, by reason of disability from wounds. Resignation accepted on or about August 29, 1864.

ROBERTS, GOODSON M., 2nd Lieutenant

Born in Buncombe County where he resided as a farmer or merchant prior to enlisting in Buncombe County at age 31. Elected 2nd Lieutenant on May 16, 1862. Elected Captain of Company I of this regiment on September 13, 1862, and transferred.

WEST, ERWIN, 2nd Lieutenant

Resided in Buncombe County and was by occupation a farmer prior to enlisting in Buncombe County at age 33, May 16, 1862, for the war. Mustered in as Private. Elected 2nd Lieutenant on September 27, 1862. Reported present in October, 1862. Reported present and in command of the company in November-December, 1862. Resigned on February 28, 1863. Reason he resigned not reported; however, an annotation on the back of his letter of resignation states that he was "whol[l]y incompetent to fill the office of Lieutenant." Resignation accepted on March 13, 1863.

WHITE, ROBERT W., 2nd Lieutenant

Enlisted in Buncombe County on May 16, 1862, for the war. Mustered in as 1st Sergeant. Reported present in August-October, 1862. Reported absent sick in November, 1862-February, 1863. Returned to duty in March-April, 1863, and was elected 2nd Lieutenant on March 30, 1863. Reported in command of the company in May-June, 1863. Detailed for conscript duty on August 19, 1863. Rejoined the company in November-December, 1863, and was reported in command of the company. Wounded slightly at Rocky Face Ridge, Georgia, February 25, 1864. Returned to duty in May-June, 1864. Reported present in July-August, 1864. Promoted to Captain and transferred to Company H, 58th Regiment N.C. Troops, when the 58th and 60th Regiments were consolidated on April 9, 1865. [Was about 31 years of age at time of enlistment. Was reported in command of Company E of this regiment in November-December, 1863.]

NONCOMMISSIONED OFFICERS AND PRIVATES

AIKEN, JAMES W., Private

Enlisted in Buncombe County on May 16, 1862, for the war. Reported present in August, 1862-February, 1863. Reported sick in hospital in March-April, 1863. Returned to duty in May-June, 1863. Reported present through April 30, 1864. Captured at Resaca, Georgia, May 15, 1864. Sent to Nashville, Tennessee. Transferred to Louisville, Kentucky, where he arrived on May 21, 1864. Transferred to Camp Morton, Indianapolis, Indiana, where he arrived on May 22, 1864. Paroled at Camp Morton and transferred on March 4, 1865. Received at Boulware's and Cox's Wharves, James River, Virginia, March 10-12, 1865, for exchange. Paroled at Charlotte on May 13, 1865. [Was about 27 years of age at time of enlistment.]

ALEXANDER, HENRY N., Private

Resided in Buncombe County and enlisted at Camp Smith (Madison County) on September 1, 1862, for the war. Reported present through February 28, 1863. Reported present but sick at Tullahoma, Tennessee, in March-April, 1863. Returned to duty in May-June, 1863. Reported present through April 30, 1864. Hospitalized at Macon, Georgia, May 31, 1864, with chronic bronchitis. Returned to duty on July 17, 1864. Reported present through August 31, 1864. No further records. Survived the war.

ALEXANDER, JAMES M., Private

Enlisted at Greeneville, Tennessee, September 1, 1862, for the war. Reported present through February, 1863. Appointed Hospital Steward on March 20, 1863, and transferred to the Field and Staff of this regiment.

BALDING, FIDELIO A., Private

Previously served as Private in Company H, 2nd Battalion N.C. Infantry. Transferred to this company on September 1, 1862. Reported present in September-November, 1862. Hospitalized at Dalton, Georgia, December 31, 1862, with debilitas. Returned to duty on January 18, 1863. Reported sick in hospital in March-April, 1863. Returned to duty in May-June, 1863. Transferred to Company B of this regiment in July-September, 1863.

BALDING, MARQUES D. LAFAYETTE, Private

Previously served as Sergeant in Company H, 2nd Battalion N.C. Infantry. Transferred to this company on or about September 1, 1862. Reported present in September-October, 1862. Reported absent sick in November, 1862-December, 1863. Reported absent without leave on February 16, 1864. Listed as a deserter on April 7, 1864. Transferred to Company B of this regiment prior to May 20, 1864, while listed as a deserter.

BANKS, J. M., Private

Born in Buncombe County and was by occupation a farmer prior to enlisting in Buncombe County at age 27, May 16, 1862, for the war. Transferred to Company I of this regiment on September 13, 1862.

BISHOP, WILLIAM BERRY, Private

Enlisted in Buncombe County on May 16, 1862, for the war. Reported present in August, 1862-April, 1864. Reported sick in hospital in May-June, 1864. Returned to duty in July-August, 1864. No further records. Survived the war. [Was about 24 years of age at time of enlistment.]

BLACK, FRANKLIN D., Sergeant

Resided in Buncombe County and was by occupation a Baptist preacher prior to enlisting in Buncombe County at age 33, May 16, 1862, for the war. Mustered in with an unspecified rank. Reported present in August, 1862-June, 1863. Promoted to Sergeant on September 12, 1862. Hospitalized at Lauderdale Springs, Mississippi, July 9, 1863. Detailed as a hospital nurse at Lauderdale Springs on August 1 or August 12, 1863. Rejoined the company prior to November 1, 1863. Captured at Missionary Ridge, Tennessee, November 25, 1863. Sent to Nashville, Tennessee. Transferred to Louisville, Kentucky, where he arrived on December 7, 1863. Transferred to Rock Island, Illinois, where he arrived on December 9, 1863. Died at Rock Island on February 11, 1864, of "pneumonia."

BONHAM, JOHN T., Private

Enlisted in Buncombe County on May 16, 1862, for the war. Mustered in as Musician (Fifer). Reported present in August, 1862-February, 1863. Reported absent sick in March-April, 1863. Returned to duty in May-June, 1863, and was reduced to ranks. Reported present in July, 1863-August, 1864. No further records. Survived the war. [Was about 32 years of age at time of enlistment. North Carolina pension records indicate that he was struck in the right side by a piece of shell at Chickamauga, Georgia, in "October, 1863," and ruptured.]

BROWN, CANEY, Private

Resided in Madison County and was by occupation a farmer prior to enlisting in Buncombe County at age 24, May 16, 1862, for the war. Mustered in as Sergeant. Reduced to ranks in May-July, 1862. Reported present in August, 1862-June, 1863. Reported in hospital at Marion, Mississippi, in July-August, 1863. Furloughed home prior to November 1, 1863. Reported absent without leave on February 16, 1864. Listed as a deserter and dropped from the company rolls on or about April 7, 1864.

BROWN, W. E., Private

Enlisted in Buncombe County on May 16, 1862, for the war. Reported present in August-October, 1862. Died at Ringgold, Georgia, January 25, 1863. Cause of death not reported.

CARLAND, FRANKLIN B., Private

Born in Buncombe County and resided in Henderson County where he was by occupation a farmer prior to enlisting in Buncombe County at age 24, May 16, 1862, for the war. Transferred to Company I of this regiment on September 13, 1862.

CARLAND, LABAN D., Private

Enlisted in Buncombe County on May 16, 1862, for the war. Mustered in as Private. Reported present in August-October, 1862.

Hospitalized at Dalton, Georgia, December 31, 1862, with general debility. Returned to duty on January 13, 1863. Promoted to Corporal on June 1, 1863. Reported present through June 30, 1863. Reduced to ranks prior to September 20, 1863, when he was killed at Chickamauga, Georgia.

CARSON, JOHN C., Private

Born in Blount County, Tennessee, and was by occupation a farmer prior to enlisting in Buncombe County on May 16, 1862, for the war. Reported present in August-October, 1862. Reported absent sick in November, 1862-February, 1863. Discharged on an unspecified date (probably in March-April, 1863) by reason of "spinal irritation and chronic rheumatism affecting his loins & lower extremities." Discharge certificate gives his age as 18.

COLE, HARDY, Private

Resided in Buncombe County and was by occupation a farm laborer prior to enlisting in Buncombe County at age 32, May 16, 1862, for the war. Discharged on August 15, 1862, by reason of being "incapable of duty." Reenlisted in the company on May 1, 1863. Reported present through June 30, 1863. No further records.

CORRELL, JOHN C., Private

Enlisted in Buncombe County on May 16, 1862, for the war. Reported present in August, 1862-June, 1863. Deserted on October 6, 1863. Returned from desertion on July 7, 1864. Reported present through August 31, 1864. No further records. Survived the war.

DAUER, WILLIAM M., Private

Enlisted in Buncombe County on May 16, 1862, for the war. Reported present in August, 1862-October, 1863. Reported absent sick in November, 1863-February, 1864. Returned to duty in March-April, 1864. Wounded at Kolb's Farm, near Marietta, Georgia, June 22, 1864, and sent to hospital. No further records.

DOCKERY, ALFRED, Private

Enlisted in Buncombe County on May 16, 1862, for the war. "Transferred to Richmond Sept. 13. Camp Martin." No further records.

ENSLEY, SAMUEL, Private

Resided in Buncombe County and was by occupation a farmer prior to enlisting in Buncombe County at age 32, May 16, 1862, for the war. Reported present in August-October, 1862. Detailed in hospital at Murfreesboro, Tennessee, in November-December, 1862. Captured at Murfreesboro on January 5, 1863. Sent to Nashville, Tennessee. Transferred to Louisville, Kentucky, on an unspecified date. Transferred to Camp Chase, Ohio, where he arrived on February 26, 1863. Paroled and transferred to City Point, Virginia, where he was received on April 1, 1863, for exchange. Returned to duty prior to May 1, 1863. Reported present in May, 1863-February, 1864. Reported absent without leave in March-April, 1864. Listed as a deserter and dropped from the company rolls in May-June, 1864.

FISHER, BENJAMIN H., Private

Born in Anson County and was by occupation a farmer prior to enlisting in Buncombe County at age 34, May 16, 1862, for the war. Transferred to Company I of this regiment on September 13, 1862.

FOSTER, EDWIN S., Private

Resided in Buncombe County and was by occupation a farmer prior to enlisting in Buncombe County at age 23, May 16, 1862,

for the war. Discharged on September 12, 1862, by reason of "being incapable of duty." Reenlisted in the company at Murfreesboro, Tennessee, October 12, 1862. Hospitalized at Dalton, Georgia, December 31, 1862, with dyspepsia. Returned to duty prior to January 29, 1863, when he was again hospitalized at Dalton with dyspepsia. Returned to duty on April 23, 1863. Reported present in May-June, 1863. Reported absent sick in July-October, 1863. Died at Marietta, Georgia, December 18, 1863. Cause of death not reported.

FOSTER, MICHAEL, Private

Enlisted in Buncombe County on May 16, 1862, for the war. Reported present in August-October, 1862. Wounded in the legs and captured at Murfreesboro, Tennessee, December 31, 1862. Exchanged on an unspecified date. Died at Murfreesboro subsequent to April 3, 1863. Cause of death not reported.

FOSTER, WILLIAM B., Private

Born in Buncombe County and was by occupation a farmer prior to enlisting in Buncombe County on May 16, 1862, for the war. Reported present in August-October, 1862. Discharged on November 4, 1862, by reason of "disease of the lungs, general debility, together with considerable deformity of limbs." Discharge certificate gives his age as 28.

FREEMAN, J. M., Private

Resided in Rutherford County and was by occupation a farmer prior to enlisting in Buncombe County at age 27, May 16, 1862, for the war. Transferred to Richmond, Virginia, September 13, 1862. No further records.

FRISBY, ABNER, Private

Resided in Buncombe County where he enlisted at age 19, May 16, 1862, for the war. Reported present in August, 1862-February, 1863. Reported absent sick in March-June, 1863. Reported absent on furlough in July-October, 1863. Listed as a deserter and dropped from the company rolls in November-December, 1863.

FRISBY, LEANDER, Private

Resided in Buncombe County and enlisted at "Allisona" at age 18, January 8, 1863, for the war. Died at Ringgold, Georgia, April 21, 1863, of "chr[onic] diarr[hoea]."

FRISBY, SOLOMON, Private

Resided in Madison County and enlisted in Buncombe County at age 20, May 16, 1862, for the war. Reported present in August-October, 1862. Wounded slightly in the "belly" at Murfreesboro, Tennessee, January 2, 1863. Reported absent wounded or absent sick until February 16, 1864, when he was reported absent without leave. Listed as a deserter on April 7, 1864. Returned to duty on July 7, 1864. Reported present through August 31, 1864. No further records.

GENTRY, PERMINTER M., Private

Resided in Buncombe County and was by occupation a farmer prior to enlisting at Camp McDowell at age 37, October 12, 1862, for the war. Reported absent sick in November, 1862-April, 1863. Listed as a deserter and dropped from the company rolls on June 15, 1863. Returned to duty prior to November 1, 1863. Deserted from camp near Dalton, Georgia, December 6, 1863. Later served as Private in Company C, 3rd Regiment N.C. Mounted Infantry (Union).

GOSSETT, HENRY McDONALD, ———
North Carolina pension records indicate that he served in this company.

HANEY, BRONSON, Private
Enlisted in Buncombe County on May 16, 1862, for the war. Reported present in August, 1862-February, 1863. Reported absent in hospital in March-April, 1863. Returned to duty in May-June, 1863. Reported present in July, 1863-August, 1864.

HANEY, J. BERRY, Private
Enlisted in Buncombe County on May 16, 1862, for the war. Reported present in August, 1862-February, 1863. Reported absent sick in March-April, 1863. Returned to duty in May-June, 1863. Deserted on October 6, 1863. [Was about 26 years of age at time of enlistment.]

HAWKINS, JOSEPH F., Corporal
Enlisted in Buncombe County on May 16, 1862, for the war. Mustered in as Private. Reported present in August, 1862-June, 1863. Promoted to Corporal on June 1, 1863. Reported present in July, 1863-August, 1864. No further records.

HAYNES, P. HENRY, Private
Born in Rutherford County and resided in Buncombe County where he was by occupation a farmer prior to enlisting in Buncombe County at age 32, May 16, 1862, for the war. Reported present in August-October, 1862. Reported on detail as a "steward" at Tullahoma, Tennessee, November 9-December 31, 1862. Discharged at Tullahoma on January 28, 1863, by reason of "chronic bronchitis." Took the Oath of Allegiance on September 15, 1865. [May have served later as Private in Company E, 16th Battalion N.C. Cavalry.]

HUTSON, JOHN, Private
Enlisted in Buncombe County on May 16, 1862, for the war. Reported present in August-October, 1862. Reported absent sick in November, 1862-February, 1863. Returned to duty in March-April, 1863. Reported present in May-December, 1863. Reported absent sick in January-February, 1864. Furloughed home in March-April, 1864. Returned to duty in May-June, 1864. Reported sick in hospital on August 1, 1864. No further records. Survived the war.

HUTSON, NELSON, Private
Enlisted in Buncombe County on May 16, 1862, for the war. Reported present in August-October, 1862. Wounded slightly in the foot at Murfreesboro, Tennessee, December 31, 1862. Returned to duty prior to March 1, 1863. Reported present in March, 1863-April, 1864. Killed at Kolb's Farm, near Marietta, Georgia, June 22, 1864.

HUTSON, WILLIAM, Private
Resided in Buncombe County and was by occupation a farmer prior to enlisting in Buncombe County at age 29, May 16, 1862, for the war. Reported present in August-October, 1862. Died at Tullahoma, Tennessee, February 2, 1863, of disease. He was "conspicuous for his cool bravery under fire" and was a "daring fellow." [Clark's Regiments, 3:480.]

JAMES, JAMES E., Private
Previously served as Private in Company A of this regiment. Transferred to this company on January 1, 1864. Reported sick in hospital from May 25 through August 31, 1864. Returned to duty prior to

March 19-21, 1865, when he was wounded in the head, left hand, and right arm at Bentonville. No further records. Survived the war.

JAMES, JOHN, Private
Resided in Buncombe County and was by occupation a farmer prior to enlisting in Buncombe County at age 39, May 1, 1863, for the war. Reported present through June 30, 1863. No further records.

JAMES, THOMAS REDDEN, Sergeant
Resided in Buncombe County and was by occupation a farmer prior to enlisting in Buncombe County at age 32, May 16, 1862, for the war. Mustered in as Corporal. Promoted to Sergeant on September 27, 1862. Reported present in August, 1862-August, 1864. Transferred to Company H, 58th Regiment N.C. Troops, when the 58th and 60th Regiments were consolidated on April 9, 1865.

KYLE, FRANKLIN, Private
Enlisted in Buncombe County at age 27, May 16, 1862, for the war. Reported present in August-October, 1862. Hospitalized at Dalton, Georgia, November 6, 1862, with rheumatism and/or asthma. Returned to duty on or about December 12, 1862. Reported present in January-February, 1863. Reported absent sick in March-June, 1863. Returned to duty in July-October, 1863. Reported present in November, 1863-June, 1864. Reported sick in hospital and "being sent from Pioneer Corps" in July-August, 1864. No further records.

KYLE, JOHN, JR., Private
Resided in Buncombe County and was by occupation a farm laborer prior to enlisting in Buncombe County at age 23, May 16, 1862, for the war. Hospitalized at Dalton, Georgia, November 6, 1862, with phthisis pulmonalis and/or chronic diarrhoea. Returned to duty on December 13, 1862. Reported present in January-June, 1863. Deserted on September 10, 1863.

LEDFORD, ISAAC, Private
Resided in Buncombe County and was by occupation a farmer prior to enlisting in Buncombe County at age 32, May 16, 1862, for the war. Reported present in August-October, 1862. Reported absent sick in November-December, 1862. Captured at Murfreesboro, Tennessee, January 5, 1863. Hospitalized at Nashville, Tennessee, January 21, 1863, with pneumonia. Died in hospital at Nashville on February 26, 1863, of "smallpox."

LINDSAY, THOMAS, Private
Resided in Buncombe County and was by occupation a day laborer prior to enlisting in Buncombe County at age 24, May 16, 1862, for the war. Reported present in August-October, 1862. Deserted at Murfreesboro, Tennessee, November 1, 1862. Returned to duty on February 11, 1863. Reported present in March-June, 1863. Reported absent sick in July-October, 1863. Returned to duty in November-December, 1863. Reported present in January-April, 1864. Captured at or near Smyrna, Georgia, on or about July 2-3, 1864. Sent to Nashville, Tennessee. Transferred to Louisville, Kentucky, where he arrived on July 13, 1864. Transferred to Camp Douglas, Chicago, Illinois, where he arrived on July 16, 1864. Released at Camp Douglas on April 2, 1865, after taking the Oath of Allegiance and joining the U.S. Army. Assigned to Company I, 6th Regiment U.S. Volunteer Infantry.

LINDSEY, WILLIAM E., Private
Resided in Buncombe County and was by occupation a day laborer prior to enlisting in Buncombe County at age 27, May 16, 1862,

for the war. Reported present in August-October, 1862. Hospitalized at Dalton, Georgia, November 6, 1862, with chronic diarrhoea. Returned to duty on December 13, 1862. Reported absent sick on December 31, 1862. Deserted from an unspecified hospital in January-February, 1863. Returned to duty in March-April, 1863. Reported present in May-June, 1863. Reported absent sick in July-October, 1863. Reported absent on furlough in November-December, 1863. Reported absent without leave on February 16, 1864. Listed as a deserter on April 7, 1864. Reported sick in hospital from July 1 through August 31, 1864. No further records. Survived the war.

LITTRELL, JAMES M., Private

Enlisted in Buncombe County on May 16, 1862, for the war as a substitute for Pvt. Bynum R. Phillips. Deserted on October 1, 1862. Returned to duty prior to November 1, 1862. Reported present through February 29, 1864. Reported present but under arrest awaiting trial in March-April, 1864, "for sleeping upon his post." Returned to duty in May-June, 1864. Reported present through August 31, 1864. No further records. [Was about 17 years of age at time of enlistment.]

LITTRELL, WILLIAM, Private

Resided in Buncombe County where he enlisted on May 16, 1862, for the war. Deserted on October 1, 1862. Returned from desertion (or was apprehended) on an unspecified date. Court-martialed on or about December 3, 1862, and sentenced to be shot. Executed at Murfreesboro, Tennessee, December 26, 1862. [Was about 26 years of age at time of enlistment. For additional details concerning his execution, see Civil War Collection, Miscellaneous Records, box 70, folder 37, NCDAH.]

LUNSFORD, A. W., Private

Born in Buncombe County and was by occupation a farmer prior to enlisting at Camp Smith (Madison County) at age 28, August 25, 1862, for the war. Transferred to Company I of this regiment on or about September 13, 1862.

McELRATH, JAMES, Private

Enlisted in Buncombe County on May 16, 1862, for the war. Identified as a deserter from another company and was sent back to that unit prior to November 1, 1862. [The unit from which he deserted may have been Company B, 16th Regiment N.C. Troops (6th Regiment N.C. Volunteers).]

MANN, DAVID L., Private

Enlisted in Buncombe County on May 16, 1862, for the war as a substitute for Pvt. William Mann. Reported present in August-October, 1862. Wounded in the shoulder and captured at Murfreesboro, Tennessee, January 2, 1863. Sent to Nashville, Tennessee. Transferred to Camp Morton, Indianapolis, Indiana, on an unspecified date. Died at Camp Morton on March 1, 1863, presumably of wounds.

MANN, WILLIAM, Private

Enlisted in Buncombe County on May 16, 1862, for the war. Discharged on or about the same date after providing Pvt. David L. Mann as a substitute.

MARTIN, A. J., Private

Enlisted in Buncombe County on May 16, 1862, for the war. Reported present in August-October, 1862. Reported absent sick in November, 1862-February, 1863. Returned to duty in March-April, 1863. Reported present or accounted for through June 30, 1864. Wounded on August 5, 1864, and sent to hospital. No further records.

MARTIN, JACOB, Private

Enlisted in Buncombe County on May 16, 1862, for the war. Reported present in August-October, 1862. Reported absent sick in November, 1862-February, 1863. Reported sick in hospital at Dalton, Georgia, in March-April, 1863. Returned to duty in May-June, 1863. Deserted on October 6, 1863.

MARTIN, LEANDER M., Private

Resided in Buncombe County and was by occupation a laborer prior to enlisting in Buncombe County at age 21, May 16, 1862, for the war. Reported present in August-October, 1862. Reported absent sick in November-December, 1862. Reported absent on furlough in January-February, 1863. Returned to duty in March-April, 1863. Reported present in May-June, 1863. Hospitalized at Lauderdale Springs, Mississippi, July 16, 1863. Returned to duty prior to November 1, 1863. Reported present through February 29, 1864. Hospitalized at Dalton, Georgia, April 13, 1864. Reported absent sick through August 31, 1864. No further records.

MEADOWS, JOHN P., Private

Previously served as Private in Company B of this regiment. Transferred to this company on or about August 1, 1862. Reported present through February 28, 1863. Reported absent sick in March-December, 1863. Reported absent without leave on February 16, 1864. Listed as a deserter on April 7, 1864. Returned to duty prior to June 22, 1864, when he was wounded in the left leg at Kolb's Farm, near Marietta, Georgia. Reported absent wounded through August 31, 1864. Transferred to Company H, 58th Regiment N.C. Troops, when the 58th and 60th Regiments were consolidated on April 9, 1865.

MEADOWS, ROBERT G., Private

Resided in Buncombe County and was by occupation a farmer prior to enlisting in Buncombe County at age 29, May 16, 1862, for the war. Reported present in August, 1862-June, 1863. Reported absent on furlough in July-December, 1863. Reported absent without leave on February 16, 1864. Listed as a deserter on April 7, 1864. Returned from desertion on May 25, 1864. Sent to hospital on July 1, 1864. Died at Columbus, Georgia, prior to November 18, 1864. Cause of death not reported.

MEADOWS, SAMUEL F., Private

Born in Buncombe County where he resided as a farmer prior to enlisting in Buncombe County at age 25, May 16, 1862, for the war. Transferred to Company I of this regiment on September 13, 1862.

MILLER, HENRY, Private

Born in Buncombe County in 1843. Enlisted in Buncombe County on May 16, 1862, for the war. Reported present in August, 1862-February, 1863. Reported absent sick at Catoosa Springs, Georgia, in March-April, 1863. Returned to duty in May-June, 1863. Reported present or accounted for through June 30, 1864. Deserted at Atlanta, Georgia, August 12, 1864. [His Tennessee pension application indicates that he was "hit in the breast by a piece of bomb shell" at New Hope Church, Georgia (probably in late May, 1864). He claimed also that he was wounded in the knee by a shell at Murfreesboro, Tennessee, on an unspecified date.]

PALMER, JOHN FRANK, Private

Born in Buncombe County where he resided as a farmer prior to enlisting at Murfreesboro, Tennessee, at age 34, October 21, 1862, for the war. Reported absent sick in November, 1862-February, 1863. Discharged at Tullahoma, Tennessee, April 2, 1863, by reason of "disease of the heart."

PARHAM, F. M., Private

Enlisted in Buncombe County on May 16, 1862, for the war. Reported present in August-October, 1862. Captured at Murfreesboro, Tennessee, on or about January 2, 1863. Died in hospital at St. Louis, Missouri, January 24, 1863, of "typhoid fever."

PARHAM, JOSEPH F., Private

Enlisted in Buncombe County at age 19, May 16, 1862, for the war. Reported present in August, 1862-August, 1864. No further records. Survived the war.

PARIS, D. M., Private

Enlisted in Buncombe County on May 16, 1862, for the war. Reported present in August-October, 1862. Died in hospital at Tullahoma, Tennessee, January 28, 1863. Cause of death not reported.

PARIS, JAMES ERVIN, Private

Born on September 22, 1832. Enlisted in Buncombe County at age 29, May 16, 1862, for the war. Reported present in August-October, 1862. Died in hospital at Murfreesboro, Tennessee, December 22, 1862. Cause of death not reported.

PARIS, WILLIAM FRANKLIN, Private

Enlisted in Buncombe County on May 16, 1862, for the war. Reported present in August-October, 1862. Reported absent on furlough from December 20, 1862, through December 31, 1863. Was apparently suffering from palsy. Reported absent without leave on February 16, 1864. Listed as a deserter on April 7, 1864. Dropped from the company rolls on or about April 30, 1864.

PARKER, THOMAS M., Private

Born in Laurens District, South Carolina, and resided in Buncombe County where he was by occupation a farmer prior to enlisting in Buncombe County at age 35, May 16, 1862, for the war. Reported present in August-October, 1862. Reported absent sick in November, 1862-February, 1863. Hospitalized at Dalton, Georgia, April 26, 1863, with dyspepsia. Furloughed for thirty days on May 15, 1863. Reported absent on furlough or absent sick through December 31, 1863. Reported absent without leave on February 16, 1864. Listed as a deserter on April 7, 1864. Dropped from the company rolls on or about April 30, 1864.

PENLAND, JAMES H., Corporal

Enlisted in Buncombe County on May 16, 1862, for the war. Was apparently mustered in with the rank of Corporal. Reported present in August-December, 1862. Wounded slightly in the head at Murfreesboro, Tennessee, January 2, 1863. Returned to duty prior to March 1, 1863. Reported present through June 30, 1863. Reported absent on furlough in July-December, 1863. Returned to duty in January-February, 1864. Reported present in March-June, 1864. Died at Newnan, Georgia, July 29, 1864, of wounds. Place and date wounded not reported.

PHILLIPS, BYNUM R., Private

Resided in Haywood County and was by occupation a farmer prior to enlisting in Buncombe County at age 24, May 16, 1862, for the

war. Discharged prior to November 1, 1862, after furnishing Pvt. James M. Littrell as a substitute.

PLEMMONS, JAMES E., Private

Enlisted in Buncombe County on May 16, 1862, for the war. Reported present in August, 1862-February, 1863. Hospitalized at Dalton, Georgia, April 26, 1863, with "pemphigus." Transferred to another hospital on June 20, 1863. Furloughed on an unspecified date. Returned to duty prior to September 20, 1863, when he was wounded in the hand at Chickamauga, Georgia. Returned to duty in January-February, 1864. Reported present through August 31, 1864. Hospitalized at Charlotte on January 15, 1865, with bronchitis. Transferred to another hospital on January 24, 1865. No further records. Survived the war.

PLEMMONS, JOSEPH J., Private

Enlisted in Buncombe County on May 16, 1862, for the war. Reported present in August-October, 1862. Reported absent sick in November, 1862-April, 1863. Reported absent on furlough in May-December, 1863. Returned to duty in January-February, 1864. Reported present through August 31, 1864.

PLEMMONS, SILAS J., Private

Previously served as Private in Company H, 2nd Battalion N.C. Infantry. Enlisted in this company on or about August 1, 1862. Transferred to Company B of this regiment on or about September 12, 1862.

PRESLEY, JASON, Private

Born in Buncombe County and was by occupation a farmer prior to enlisting in Buncombe County at age 32, May 16, 1862, for the war. Transferred to Company I of this regiment on September 13, 1862.

PRITCHETT, WILLIAM, Private

Enlisted at Camp McDowell on November 25, 1862, for the war. Reported missing at Murfreesboro, Tennessee, December 31, 1862. Was probably killed at Murfreesboro.

RAMSEY, JAMES M., Private

Resided in Buncombe County where he enlisted at age 25, May 16, 1862, for the war. Reported present in August-December, 1862. Hospitalized at Dalton, Georgia, January 29, 1863, with pneumonia. Returned to duty on February 2, 1863. Reported present through June 30, 1863. Hospitalized at Lauderdale Springs, Mississippi, July 17, 1863. Returned to duty in November-December, 1863. Transferred to Company A of this regiment on January 1, 1864.

RANDAL, JOHN L., Corporal

Resided in Buncombe County where he enlisted on May 16, 1862, for the war. Mustered in as Corporal. Reported present in August-December, 1862. Hospitalized at Dalton, Georgia, January 18, 1863, with chronic diarrhoea. Returned to duty on January 23, 1863. Reported present through June 30, 1863. Captured at Chickamauga, Georgia, September 20, 1863. Sent to Nashville, Tennessee. Transferred to Louisville, Kentucky, where he arrived on September 30, 1863. Transferred to Camp Douglas, Chicago, Illinois, where he arrived on October 4, 1863. Released at Camp Douglas on May 13, 1865, after taking the Oath of Allegiance.

REESE, JOHN WESLEY, Private

Resided in Buncombe County and was by occupation a miller prior to enlisting in Buncombe County at age 33, August 22, 1862, for the war. Reported present in August-October, 1862. Hospitalized at Dalton, Georgia, December 30, 1862, with continued fever. Returned to duty on January 7, 1863. Reported present through June 30, 1863. Reported absent sick in July-October, 1863. Returned to duty in November-December, 1863. Reported absent sick from February 9 through April 30, 1864. Returned to duty in May-June, 1864. Died at Forsyth, Georgia, August 1, 1864, of disease.

REVIS, F. H., Private

Born in Buncombe County and was by occupation a farmer prior to enlisting in Buncombe County at age 20, May 16, 1862, for the war. Transferred to Company I of this regiment on September 13, 1862.

REYNOLDS, THOMAS M., Sergeant

Enlisted in Buncombe County on May 16, 1862, for the war. Mustered in as Sergeant. Reported present in August-October, 1862. Reported absent sick in November, 1862-February, 1863. Died on an unspecified date and was buried in the Confederate cemetery at Chattanooga, Tennessee. Place and cause of death not reported.

RICE, MARCUS L., Private

Enlisted in Buncombe County on May 16, 1862, for the war. Reported present in August, 1862-June, 1863. Detailed as a hospital nurse at Marietta, Georgia, September 25, 1863. Rejoined the company in November-December, 1863. Reported present in January-August, 1864.

ROBERTS, ELISHA MILES, Private

Born in Buncombe County where he resided as a farmer prior to enlisting in Buncombe County at age 26, May 16, 1862, for the war. Transferred to Company A of this regiment on July 24, 1862.

ROBERTS, G. W., Private

Enlisted in Buncombe County on May 16, 1862, for the war. Reported present in August-October, 1862. Hospitalized at Dalton, Georgia, December 30, 1862, with typhoid fever. Returned to duty on February 2, 1863. Reported present in March-June, 1863. Deserted on October 6, 1863. [May have served later as Private in Company C, 2nd Regiment N.C. Mounted Infantry (Union).]

ROBERTS, PIERCE, Private

Enlisted in Buncombe County on May 16, 1862, for the war. Died at Camp Smith (Madison County) on September 2, 1862. Cause of death not reported.

ROBERTS, ROBERT M., Private

Enlisted in Buncombe County on May 16, 1862, for the war. Reported present in August-October, 1862. Deserted on December 5, 1862. Returned to duty on February 8, 1863. Reported present in March, 1863-April, 1864. Captured at or near Nickajack Creek, near Smyrna, Georgia, July 4-5, 1864. Sent to Nashville, Tennessee. Transferred to Louisville, Kentucky, where he arrived on July 14, 1864. Transferred to Camp Douglas, Chicago, Illinois, where he arrived on July 18, 1864. Released at Camp Douglas on May 16, 1865, after taking the Oath of Allegiance.

ROBERTS, THOMAS CATLETT, Sergeant

Born in July, 1831. Enlisted in Buncombe County at age 30, May 16, 1862, for the war. Was apparently mustered in with the rank of Sergeant. Discharged at Camp Martin (Mitchell County) on September 12, 1862, by reason of being "incapable for duty."

RODGERS, BENJAMIN FRANK, Corporal

Resided in Buncombe County and was by occupation a farmer prior to enlisting in Buncombe County at age 34, May 16, 1862, for the war. Mustered in as Private. Reported present in August-October, 1862. Promoted to Corporal on September 27, 1862. Reported absent sick in November, 1862-February, 1863. Deserted from hospital on March 4, 1863. Returned to duty on May 3, 1863. Reported present in May-June, 1863. Captured at Chickamauga, Georgia, September 20, 1863. Sent to Nashville, Tennessee. Transferred to Louisville, Kentucky, where he arrived on September 30, 1863. Transferred to Camp Douglas, Chicago, Illinois, where he arrived on October 4, 1863. Released at Camp Douglas on June 16, 1865, after taking the Oath of Allegiance. [Previously served as 2nd Lieutenant in the 109th Regiment N.C. Militia.]

RODGERS, MANSON W., Private

Resided in Buncombe County and was by occupation a farmer prior to enlisting in Buncombe County at age 30, May 16, 1862, for the war. Reported present in August-October, 1862. Hospitalized at Dalton, Georgia, November 6, 1862, with intermittent fever and/or phthisis pulmonalis. Detailed as a hospital nurse at Dalton on an unspecified date. Deserted at Dalton on December 16, 1862. Reported in confinement on January 20, 1863. Rejoined the company on February 8, 1863. Reported present in March-June, 1863. Died on September 6, 1863. Place and cause of death not reported.

RODGERS, WILLIAM, Private

Enlisted in Buncombe County on May 16, 1862, for the war. Mustered in as Private. Appointed Musician (Drummer) on September 27, 1862. Reported present in August-October, 1862. Reported on detail for hospital duty in November-December, 1862. Reduced to ranks prior to January 1, 1863. Rejoined the company in January-February, 1863. Died at Hurricane Springs, Tennessee, April 27, 1863. Cause of death not reported.

SHELTON, JAMES, Private

Enlisted at Camp Martin (Mitchell County) on September 12, 1862, for the war. Reported present in August-October, 1862. Deserted on December 20, 1862. Returned to duty on January 31, 1863. Reported present in March-June, 1863. Transferred to Company B of this regiment in July-August, 1863.

SHUFORD, M. L. H., Private

Enlisted at Camp McDowell on November 25, 1862, for the war. Reported present through February 28, 1863. Deserted from hospital at Dalton, Georgia, April 8, 1863. [Was about 24 years of age at time of enlistment.]

SNIDER, MILES, Private

Born in Buncombe County where he resided as a farmer or farm laborer prior to enlisting in Buncombe County at age 32, May 16, 1862, for the war. Transferred to Company I of this regiment on September 13, 1862.

SORRELLS, ALFRED ROSEVILLE, Private

Born on November 11, 1834. Resided in Buncombe County and was by occupation a farmer prior to enlisting in Buncombe County at age 27, May 16, 1862, for the war. Reported present in August-October, 1862. Reported absent sick in November, 1862-February, 1863. Returned to duty in May-June, 1863. Reported present in July-October, 1863. Captured at Missionary Ridge, Tennessee, November 25, 1863. Sent to Nashville, Tennessee. Transferred to

Louisville, Kentucky, where he arrived on December 7, 1863. Transferred to Rock Island, Illinois, where he arrived on December 9, 1863. Died at Rock Island on May 27, 1864, of "pleuro pneu-[monia]."

STEVENS, FRANCIS McDONALD, 1st Sergeant

Enlisted in Buncombe County at age 22, May 16, 1862, for the war. Mustered in as Sergeant. Reported present in August, 1862-February, 1863. Hospitalized at Dalton, Georgia, April 26, 1863, with debilitas. Returned to duty on May 25, 1863. Promoted to 1st Sergeant on June 1, 1863. Reported present through February 29, 1864. Furloughed for thirty days on April 25, 1864. Reported absent on furlough through August 31, 1864. Captured in hospital at Greensboro on an unspecified date. Paroled at Greensboro on April 28, 1865. [The 58th and 60th Regiments N.C. Troops were consolidated as the 58th North Carolina on April 9, 1865. Consequently, the 60th North Carolina was no longer extant on the date that 1st Sergeant Stevens was paroled. It is probable that he was transferred with the rest of his comrades to the 58th on April 9, 1865, but was unaware of the fact because he was in the hospital.]

STEVENS, JESSE SMITH, Sergeant

Born on January 30, 1843. Resided in Buncombe County where he enlisted at age 19, May 16, 1862, for the war. Mustered in as Private. Reported present in August-October, 1862. Reported absent sick in November, 1862-February, 1863. Returned to duty in March-April, 1863. Reported present in May-June, 1863. Promoted to Sergeant on June 1, 1863. Captured at Chickamauga, Georgia, September 20, 1863. Sent to Nashville, Tennessee. Transferred to Louisville, Kentucky, where he arrived on September 30, 1863. Transferred to Camp Douglas, Chicago, Illinois, where he arrived on October 2, 1863. Released at Camp Douglas on June 16, 1865, after taking the Oath of Allegiance.

STEVENS, MERRIT FOSTER, Private

Previously served as Private in Company F, 14th Regiment N.C. Troops (4th Regiment N.C. Volunteers). Transferred to this company on October 8, 1862. Reported present in November, 1862-June, 1863. Reported absent on detail as a teamster from July, 1863, through August 31, 1864. Transferred to Company H, 58th Regiment N.C. Troops, when the 58th and 60th Regiments were consolidated on April 9, 1865. [He was a "stalwart man" who carried Lt. Col. W. H. Deaver of this regiment from the field after he was wounded at Murfreesboro, Tennessee, January 1, 1863. Clark's *Regiments*, 3:479.]

STEVENS, ROBERT MORRIS, Private

Born in Buncombe County on August 4 or September 6, 1845. Resided in Buncombe County where he enlisted at age 16, May 16, 1862, for the war. Reported present in August, 1862-June, 1863. Hospitalized at Marietta, Georgia, September 23, 1863. Detailed in hospital at Marietta in October, 1863. Returned to duty in November-December, 1863. Reported present through August 31, 1864. No further records. Survived the war.

STEVENS, THOMAS NEWTON, Private

Previously served as Private in Company F, 14th Regiment N.C. Troops (4th Regiment N.C. Volunteers). Transferred to this company on October 8, 1862. Reported on detail as a wagoner in November, 1862-April, 1863. Returned to duty in May-June, 1863. Reported present in July-October, 1863. Reported on detached duty as a teamster in November, 1863-February, 1864. Reported present in March-August, 1864. No further records. Survived the war.

STROUP, JAMES R., Private

Resided in Buncombe County and was by occupation a farm laborer prior to enlisting in Buncombe County at age 20, May 16, 1862, for the war. Reported present in August, 1862-June, 1863. Captured at Chickamauga, Georgia, September 20, 1863. Sent to Nashville, Tennessee. Transferred to Louisville, Kentucky, where he arrived on September 30, 1863. Transferred to Camp Douglas, Chicago, Illinois, October 2, 1863. Died at Camp Douglas on January 21, 1864, of "typhoid fever."

STROUP, M. T., Private

Resided in Buncombe County and was by occupation a farmer prior to enlisting in Buncombe County at age 24, May 16, 1862, for the war. Reported present in August-October, 1862. Reported absent sick in November, 1862-February, 1863. [May have served later as Private in Company B, 69th Regiment N.C. Troops (7th Regiment N.C. Cavalry).]

SWAIM, E. P., Private

Enlisted in Asheville on May 16, 1862, for the war. Reported present in August-December, 1862. Reported absent sick in January-February, 1863. Died in hospital at Tullahoma, Tennessee, March 29, 1863. Cause of death not reported.

SWAIM, H. E., Private

Enlisted in Buncombe County on May 16, 1862, for the war. Discharged at Camp Smith (Madison County) on August 25, 1862, by reason of being "incapable for duty."

SWAIM, JAMES FLETCHER, Private

Resided in Buncombe County and was by occupation a farmer prior to enlisting at Murfreesboro, Tennessee, at age 23, October 21, 1862, for the war. Died in hospital at Murfreesboro on November 23, 1862. Cause of death not reported.

THARP, PETER, Private

Enlisted in Buncombe County on May 16, 1862, for the war. Reported present in August-October, 1862. Died in hospital at Tullahoma, Tennessee, February 9, 1863. Cause of death not reported.

TOW, ALFRED, Private

Resided in Buncombe County and was by occupation a day laborer prior to enlisting in Buncombe County at age 30, May 16, 1862, for the war. Reported present in August-October, 1862. Reported absent sick in November, 1862-February, 1863. Deserted on March 2-4, 1863. Returned to duty on April 28, 1863. Reported present in May-June, 1863. Hospitalized at Lauderdale Springs, Mississippi, July 20, 1863. Died in hospital at Lauderdale Springs on or about September 27, 1863, of "lumbago."

TOW, MATTISON, Private

Enlisted in Buncombe County on May 16, 1862, for the war. Reported present in August-October, 1862. Deserted on December 5, 1862. Returned to duty on February 5, 1863. Reported present in March-June, 1863. Wounded in the leg at Chickamauga, Georgia, September 20, 1863. Leg amputated. Died on October 2, 1863, of wounds. Place of death not reported. Nominated for the Badge of Distinction for gallantry at Chickamauga.

TWEED, JAMES HAMILTON, Sergeant

Born in Lincoln County, Tennessee, May 2, 1841. Resided in Buncombe County and was by occupation a farm laborer prior to enlisting in Buncombe County at age 21, May 16, 1862, for the war. Mustered in as Private. Promoted to Corporal on September 27, 1862. Reported present in August-October, 1862. Reported on duty as a wagoner in November-December, 1862. Wounded slightly in the leg at Murfreesboro, Tennessee, December 31, 1862. Reported absent on detached service in January-February, 1863. Rejoined the company in March-April, 1863. Reported present in May-June, 1863. Promoted to Sergeant on June 1, 1863. Reported on detail with the Pioneer Corps from October 26, 1863, through August 31, 1864. Transferred to Company H, 58th Regiment N.C. Troops, when the 58th and 60th Regiments were consolidated on April 9, 1865.

TWEED, THOMAS WILSON, Private

Enlisted at Murfreesboro, Tennessee, October 29, 1862, for the war. Reported absent sick in November, 1862-February, 1863. Returned to duty in March-April, 1863. Reported present in May-June, 1863. Reported absent sick in July-October, 1863. Returned to duty in November-December, 1863. Reported present in January-February, 1864. Sent to hospital sick on March 15, 1864. Returned to duty in May-June, 1864. Reported present in July-August, 1864. Transferred to Company H, 58th Regiment N.C. Troops, when the 58th and 60th Regiments were consolidated on April 9, 1865.

WARD, JAMES E., Private

Resided in Buncombe County and was by occupation a farm laborer prior to enlisting in Buncombe County at age 20, May 16, 1862, for the war. Died at Camp Smith (Madison County) on September 11, 1862. Cause of death not reported.

WARD, JAMES M., Private

Resided in Buncombe County and was by occupation a farmer prior to enlisting in Buncombe County at age 30, May 16, 1862, for the war. Reported present in August-October, 1862. Died at Chattanooga, Tennessee, January 8, 1863. Cause of death not reported.

WARD, JOHN D. L., Private

Resided in Buncombe or Henderson County and was by occupation a farm laborer prior to enlisting in Buncombe County at age 25, May 16, 1862, for the war. Reported present or accounted for through October 31, 1862. Reported absent sick in November, 1862-April, 1863. Listed as a deserter and dropped from the company rolls in May-June, 1863. Went over to the enemy on an unspecified date. Confined at Louisville, Kentucky, September 25, 1864. Released at Louisville on September 26, 1864, after taking the Oath of Allegiance.

WHITE, WILLIAM M., Private

Born in South Carolina and resided in Buncombe County where he was by occupation a brickmason prior to enlisting in Buncombe County at age 33, May 16, 1862, for the war. Reported present in October-November, 1862. Wounded slightly in the shoulder at Murfreesboro, Tennessee, January 2, 1863. Furloughed on January 12, 1863. Returned to duty in May-June, 1863. Reported present in July-October, 1863, and January-August, 1864. No further records.

WILSON, FRANKLIN R., Private

Enlisted in Buncombe County on May 16, 1862, for the war. Reported present in August-October, 1862. Wounded in the left foot at Murfreesboro, Tennessee, December 31, 1862. Reported absent wounded or absent sick through June 30, 1863. Returned to duty in July-August, 1863. Wounded in the back of the neck at Chickamauga, Georgia, September 20, 1863. Returned to duty prior to October 31, 1863. Reported present through April 30, 1864. Reported absent on detached service on July 1, 1864. Deserted at Atlanta, Georgia, August 12, 1864. [North Carolina pension records indicate that he was wounded in the thigh at Missionary Ridge, Tennessee. Was about 25 years of age at time of enlistment.]

WILSON, JOHN, Private

Resided in Buncombe County where he enlisted on May 16, 1862, for the war. Reported present in August-October, 1862. Wounded slightly in the thigh at Murfreesboro, Tennessee, December 31, 1862. Returned to duty in March-April, 1863. Reported present through June 30, 1864. Furloughed from hospital for sixty days on August 5, 1864. No further records. Survived the war. [North Carolina pension records indicate that his hearing was "destroyed by explosion of shell" on an unspecified date. Was about 30 years of age at time of enlistment.]

WILSON, SAMUEL M., Private

Born in Buncombe County where he resided as a farmer prior to enlisting in Buncombe County at age 26, May 16, 1862, for the war. Transferred to Company I of this regiment on September 13, 1862.

WORLEY, AMOS P., Private

Resided in Madison County and was by occupation a farmer prior to enlisting in Buncombe County at age 24, May 16, 1862, for the war. Transferred to Company H, 2nd Battalion N.C. Infantry, on or about September 1, 1862.

WORLEY, WILLIAM D., Private

Resided in Madison County and was by occupation a farmer prior to enlisting in Buncombe County at age 22, May 16, 1862, for the war. Transferred to Company H, 2nd Battalion N.C. Infantry, on or about September 1, 1862.

WRIGHT, JOHN W., Private

Born in Buncombe County where he resided as a farmer or as an apprentice brickmason prior to enlisting in Buncombe County at age 16, May 16, 1862, for the war. Transferred to Company I of this regiment on September 13, 1862.

COMPANY G

This company was raised in Polk County on August 29, 1862. It was mustered into Confederate service the same date and assigned to the 1st Battalion N.C. Infantry. On October 8, 1862, the 60th Regiment N.C. Troops was formally organized after a tenth company was assigned to the 1st Battalion. This company was designated Company G. After joining the regiment the company functioned as a part of the regiment, and its history for the remainder of the war is reported as a part of the regimental history.

The following roster was compiled primarily from information in the microfilm edition of the Compiled Service Records of Soldiers Who Served in Organizations from the State of North Carolina (Record Group 109, M270), National Archives and Records Administration, Washington, D.C. Record Group 109 includes enlistment papers, pay vouchers, requisitions, letters of resignation, discharge certificates, and abstracts of medical and prisoner of war returns. Materials relating specifically to this company include an undated muster roll and muster rolls dated January-August, 1863, and November, 1863-August, 1864.

Also utilized in this roster were *The War of the Rebellion: A Compilation of the Official Records of the Union and Confederate Armies*, the North Carolina adjutant general's *Roll of Honor*, state militia records, newspaper casualty lists and obituaries, wartime claims for bounty pay and allowances, postwar registers of claims for artificial limbs, Confederate pension applications filed with the states of North Carolina, Tennessee, and Florida, Confederate Soldiers' Home records, and the 1860 and 1870 federal censuses of North Carolina. A search was made also for relevant letters, diaries, reminiscences, and other manuscripts in the Southern Historical Collection (University of North Carolina-Chapel Hill), the Duke University Library Special Collections Department, and the North Carolina Division of Archives and History.

Among the secondary sources consulted were records of the North Carolina division of the United Daughters of the Confederacy, postwar rosters, regimental and county histories, marriage bond, will, and cemetery indexes, published and unpublished genealogies, biographical dictionaries, the North Carolina *County Heritage Book* series, the *Confederate Veteran*, Walter Clark's *Histories of the Several Regiments and Battalions from North Carolina in the Great War, 1861-'65*, and the North Carolina volume of the extended edition of *Confederate Military History*.

OFFICERS

CAPTAINS

WARD, JOHNSON L.

Resided in Polk County and was by occupation sheriff of Polk County prior to enlisting in Polk County at age 47. Elected Captain on August 29, 1862. Reported absent on detached service in January-February, 1863. Rejoined the company in March-April, 1863. Reported present in May-June, 1863. Reported absent on sick furlough in July-August, 1863. Resigned on August 19, 1863, because he was forty-eight years of age and suffering from "chronic diar[r]hoea & general debility." Resignation accepted on September 7, 1863. [Previously served as Colonel of the 105th Regiment N.C. Militia.]

SALES, JOHN T.

Served as 2nd Lieutenant in Company K of this regiment. Reported on duty as acting commander of this company in January-February, 1864.

LIEUTENANTS

DAVIS, LAWSON B., 1st Lieutenant

Previously served as Private in Company K, 16th Regiment N.C. Troops (6th Regiment N.C. Volunteers). Appointed 1st Lieutenant and transferred to this company on August 29, 1862. Reported present in January-February, 1863. Sent to hospital in March-April, 1863. Returned to duty in May-June, 1863. Reported sick in hospital in July-August, 1863. Captured at Missionary Ridge, Tennessee, November 25, 1863. Sent to Nashville, Tennessee. Transferred to Louisville, Kentucky, where he arrived on December 4, 1863. Transferred to Johnson's Island, Ohio, where he arrived on

December 7, 1863. Released at Johnson's Island on June 13, 1865, after taking the Oath of Allegiance.

JACKSON, ELI, 2nd Lieutenant

Enlisted in Polk County at age 24, August 29, 1862, for the war. Was apparently mustered in with the rank of 1st Sergeant. Reported present in January-June, 1863. Appointed 2nd Lieutenant on May 4, 1863. Reported present and in command of the company in July-August and November-December, 1863. Furloughed on February 22, 1864. Returned to duty and was reported in command of the company in March-April, 1864. Reported absent sick from May 15 through August 31, 1864. Resigned on or about September 10, 1864; however, it appears that his resignation was rejected. Promoted to 1st Lieutenant and transferred to Company H, 58th Regiment N.C. Troops, when the 58th and 60th Regiments were consolidated on April 9, 1865.

MORENO, CELESTINO S., 3rd Lieutenant

Elected 3rd Lieutenant on November 19, 1863. Reported on extra duty at brigade headquarters in January-February, 1864. Rejoined the company in March-April, 1864. Reported present and in command of the company in May-August, 1864. Resigned on August 11, 1864, because his company numbered only forty members of whom only eighteen were present for duty. His resignation was apparently accepted on September 22, 1864, but was revoked on February 15, 1865. No further records.

PONDER, GEORGE W., 2nd Lieutenant

Enlisted in Polk County. Elected 2nd Lieutenant on August 29, 1862. Sent to hospital sick in January-February, 1863. Died in hospital at Chattanooga, Tennessee, March 4, 1863. Cause of death not reported.

THOMPSON, DAVID M., 2nd Lieutenant

Enlisted in Polk County. Elected 3rd Lieutenant on August 29, 1862. Resigned on December 3, 1862, by reason of "varicocel[e]. The tumor is considerable, producing a gooddeal [sic] of pain & inconvenience." Furloughed for twenty days in January-February, 1863. Had not returned as of February 28, 1863. Promoted to 2nd Lieutenant on March 5, 1863. Submitted a new letter of resignation on April 2, 1863. Resignation accepted on April 23, 1863, by reason of "his utter incompetency for the faithful discharge of the duties of the position he holds."

NONCOMMISSIONED OFFICERS AND PRIVATES

ARMS, JAMES E., Corporal

Enlisted in Polk County on August 29, 1862, for the war. Was apparently mustered in with the rank of Corporal. Reported present in January-April, 1863. Died in hospital at Tullahoma, Tennessee, May 16 or June 9, 1863. Cause of death not reported.

BISHOP, WILLIAM P., Private

Resided in Polk County and was by occupation a laborer prior to enlisting in Polk County at age 21, August 29, 1862, for the war. Reported present in January-April, 1863. Deserted on May 26, 1863. Returned to duty on June 22, 1863. Reported present in July-August, 1863. Reported on detail as a pioneer from October 26, 1863, through August 31, 1864. Transferred to Company H, 58th

Regiment N.C. Troops, when the 58th and 60th Regiments were consolidated on April 9, 1865.

BLACKWELL, WILLIAM F., Private

Resided in Polk County and was by occupation a farmer prior to enlisting in Polk County at age 23, August 29, 1862, for the war. Reported present in January-June, 1863. Died in hospital at Shubuta, Mississippi, September 10, 1863. Cause of death not reported.

BLACKWOOD, JAMES C., Private

Enlisted in Polk County on August 29, 1862, for the war. Died in hospital at Atlanta, Georgia, January 21, 1863. Cause of death not reported.

BLACKWOOD, JOHN, 1st Sergeant

Resided in Spartanburg District, South Carolina, and enlisted in Polk County on November 5, 1862, for the war. Mustered in as Private. Reported present in January-June, 1863. Promoted to 1st Sergeant in May-June, 1863. Wounded and captured at Chickamauga, Georgia, September 20, 1863. Sent to Nashville, Tennessee. Transferred to Louisville, Kentucky, where he arrived on September 30, 1863. Transferred to Camp Douglas, Chicago, Illinois, where he arrived on October 4, 1863. Released at Camp Douglas on May 13, 1865, after taking the Oath of Allegiance.

BLACKWOOD, THOMAS, Private

Born in South Carolina and resided in Polk County where he was by occupation a farmer prior to enlisting in Polk County at age 30, August 29, 1862, for the war. Reported present in January-June, 1863. Sent to hospital sick in July-August, 1863. Reported absent on sick furlough in November-December, 1863. Wounded at Rocky Face Ridge, Georgia, February 25, 1864. Returned to duty in May-June, 1864. Deserted on August 13, 1864.

BRADLEY, NELSON, Private

Resided in Polk County and was by occupation a farmer prior to enlisting in Polk County. Enlistment date reported as October 8, 1863; however, he was not listed in the records of this company until May-June, 1864. Sent to hospital at Atlanta, Georgia, on or about June 10, 1864. No further records. [Was about 34 years of age at time of enlistment.]

BURNETT, WILLIAM, Private

Resided in Polk County and was by occupation a farmer prior to enlisting in Polk County at age 32, August 29, 1862, for the war. Hospitalized at Dalton, Georgia, December 30, 1862, with typhoid fever. Returned to duty on January 13, 1863. Reported present in March-April, 1863. Deserted on May 25, 1863. Returned to duty on June 22, 1863. Reported present or accounted for in July-August, 1863, and November, 1863-February, 1864. Reported absent sick from April 11 through August 31, 1864. No further records. Survived the war.

CARRUTH, EDWIN L., Private

Enlisted in Polk County on August 29, 1862, for the war. Reported present in January-February, 1863. Died in hospital at Union Point, Georgia, April 27, 1863. Cause of death not reported.

CARRUTH, WILLIAM P., Private

Enlisted in Polk County on August 29, 1862, for the war. Captured at Murfreesboro, Tennessee, January 2, 1863. Confined at Camp Douglas, Chicago, Illinois. Paroled and transferred to City Point, Virginia, where he was received on April 4, 1863, for exchange.

Failed to return to duty and was dropped from the company rolls on or about August 31, 1863.

CHILDERS, WILLIAM, Private

Enlisted in Polk County on August 29, 1862, for the war. Hospitalized at Dalton, Georgia, November 6, 1862, with dyspepsia and/or hepatitis. Deserted from hospital on December 16, 1862. Returned to duty on an unspecified date. Hospitalized at Dalton on June 5, 1863, with debilitas. Returned to duty on June 28, 1863. Deserted on or about August 13, 1863. Returned from desertion on November 18, 1863, and was placed under arrest. Returned to duty prior to November 25, 1863, when he was captured at Missionary Ridge, Tennessee. Sent to Nashville, Tennessee. Transferred to Louisville, Kentucky, where he arrived on December 7, 1863. Transferred to Rock Island, Illinois, where he arrived on December 11, 1863. Released at Rock Island on January 25, 1864, after joining the U.S. Navy.

COLVERT, ANDREW H., Private

Resided in Polk County where he enlisted at age 18, August 29, 1862, for the war. Reported present in January-August, 1863. Reported absent on sick furlough in November-December, 1863. Returned to duty in January-February, 1864. Reported present in March-August, 1864. No further records.

COOLEY, EDMUND, Sergeant

Enlisted in Polk County on August 29, 1862, for the war. Mustered in as Private. Reported present in January-February, 1863. Sent to hospital in March-April, 1863. Returned to duty in May-June, 1863. Promoted to Corporal on June 1, 1863. Sent to hospital sick in July-August, 1863. Reported in hospital at Rome, Georgia, in September-October, 1863. Returned to duty in November-December, 1863. Reported present in January-August, 1864. Promoted to Sergeant on May 18, 1864. No further records.

COOPER, RUFUS L., Private

Enlisted in Polk County on August 29, 1862, for the war. Hospitalized at Dalton, Georgia, December 31, 1862, with parotitis. Returned to duty on January 18, 1863. Sent to hospital sick in March-April, 1863. Returned to duty in May-June, 1863. Hospitalized at Lauderdale Springs, Mississippi, July 9, 1863. Detailed as a hospital nurse at Lauderdale Springs on or about July 10, 1863. Reported absent on sick furlough in August, 1863, and November, 1863-February, 1864. Returned to duty in March-April, 1864. Reported present in May-August, 1864. No further records.

CORN, CHARLES L., Private

Enlisted in Polk County on August 29, 1862, for the war. Reported present in January-February, 1863. Sent to hospital in March-April, 1863. Returned to duty in May-June, 1863. Reported in hospital at Marion, Mississippi, in July-August, 1863. Died in hospital at Marion on September 22, 1863, of disease.

CORN, GEORGE, Private

Enlisted in Polk County. Enlistment date reported as October 8, 1863; however, he was not listed in the records of this company until July-August, 1864. A company muster roll for that date states that he was absent sick at Atlanta, Georgia; however, the entry was canceled. No further records. [May have served previously as Private in Company D, 7th Battalion N.C. Cavalry.]

COWART, WILLIAM W., Private

Previously served as Private in Company D, 7th Battalion N.C. Cavalry. Transferred to this company on August 29, 1862.

Reported present in January-February, 1863. Detailed as a hospital nurse at Tullahoma, Tennessee, in March-April, 1863. Reported absent on detail in May-June, 1863. Reported on detail as a hospital nurse at Jackson, Mississippi, in July, 1863. Rejoined the company prior to August 31, 1863. Reported present through August 31, 1864. No further records. Survived the war. [Nominated for the Badge of Distinction for gallantry at Chickamauga, Georgia, September 19-20, 1863. North Carolina pension records indicate that he was wounded in the right shoulder and right foot at Murfreesboro, Tennessee, December 23, 1863 (probably December 31, 1862).]

CROCKER, JOHN, Private

Enlisted in Polk County on March 1, 1863, for the war. Reported present in March-June, 1863. Hospitalized at Lauderdale Springs, Mississippi, July 4, 1863. Died in hospital at Lauderdale Springs on September 20, 1863. Cause of death not reported.

DALTON, JOSEPH O., Corporal

Resided in Polk County and was by occupation a farmer prior to enlisting in Polk County at age 31, August 29, 1862, for the war. Mustered in as Private. Reported present in January-February, 1863. Sent to hospital in March-April, 1863. Returned to duty in May-June, 1863. Promoted to Corporal on June 1, 1863. Reported absent on sick furlough in July-August and November-December, 1863. Returned to duty in January-February, 1864. Died in Polk County on April 8, 1864. Cause of death not reported.

DAVIS, JESSE, Private

Resided at Charleston, West Virginia. Place and date of enlistment not reported (probably enlisted in the spring or early summer of 1864). Captured near Marietta, Georgia, July 3, 1864. Sent to Nashville, Tennessee. Transferred to Louisville, Kentucky, where he arrived on July 13, 1864. Transferred to Camp Morton, Indianapolis, Indiana, where he arrived on July 14, 1864. Released at Camp Morton on May 20, 1865, after taking the Oath of Allegiance.

EDWARDS, ALEXANDER, Private

Born on March 18, 1833. Enlisted in Polk County at age 29, August 29, 1862, for the war. Reported present in January-February, 1863. Sent to hospital in March-June, 1863. Returned to duty in July-August, 1863. Deserted on August 26 or November 25, 1863. Returned from desertion on March 24, 1864, and was placed under arrest. Returned to duty in May-June, 1864. Reported present in July-August, 1864. No further records. Survived the war. [May have been wounded at Murfreesboro, Tennessee, December 31, 1862-January 2, 1863.]

EDWARDS, DAVIDSON, Private

Resided in Polk County and was by occupation a farmer prior to enlisting in Polk County at age 24, August 29, 1862, for the war. Wounded slightly in the head at Murfreesboro, Tennessee, December 31, 1862. Returned to duty prior to March 1, 1863. Reported present in March-June, 1863. Furloughed for twenty-six days on August 30, 1863. Dropped from the company rolls on or about December 31, 1863.

EDWARDS, JOHN W., Private

Resided in Polk County where he enlisted at age 22, August 29, 1862, for the war. Reported present in January-April, 1863. Hospitalized at Tunnel Hill, Georgia, May 22, 1863, with debilitas. Transferred to hospital at Catoosa Springs, Georgia, June 29, 1863. Reported absent on sick furlough in July-August, 1863, and

November, 1863-February, 1864. Returned to duty in March-April, 1864. Reported absent sick from June 12 through August 31, 1864. No further records. Survived the war. [North Carolina pension records indicate that he was sick with typhoid fever during the war.]

EDWARDS, MALCOLM M., Private

Resided in Polk County and was by occupation a farmer prior to enlisting in Polk County at age 32, August 29, 1862, for the war. Wounded slightly in the shoulder at Murfreesboro, Tennessee, December 31, 1862. Returned to duty in January-February, 1863. Reported present in March-April, 1863. Died in hospital at Tullahoma, Tennessee, May 16 or June 9, 1863. Cause of death not reported.

EDWARDS, MARTIN F., Private

Resided in Polk County where he enlisted at age 18, March 1, 1864, for the war. Reported present in May-August, 1864. Last reported in the records of this company on November 17, 1864. Survived the war.

EGERTON, BENJAMIN F., Sergeant

Resided in Polk County and was by occupation a farmer prior to enlisting in Polk County at age 30, August 29, 1862, for the war. Was apparently mustered in with the rank of Corporal. Promoted to Sergeant on January 10, 1863. Reported present in January-February, 1863. Sent to hospital in March-April, 1863. Returned to duty in May-June, 1863. Reported present in July-August, 1863, and November, 1863-August, 1864. Wounded in the left thigh at Jonesborough, Georgia, August 31, 1864. Hospitalized at Macon, Georgia, September 24, 1864. Furloughed on September 27, 1864. No further records. Survived the war.

ELLISON, GEORGE W., Private

Resided in Polk County and was by occupation a farmer prior to enlisting in Polk County at age 24, August 29, 1862, for the war. Wounded and captured at Murfreesboro, Tennessee, December 31, 1862-January 2, 1863. Died (possibly on February 20, 1863) of wounds. Place of death not reported.

ELLISON, WILLIAM, JR., Private

Resided in Polk County and was by occupation a farmer prior to enlisting in Polk County at age 31, August 29, 1862, for the war. Reported sick in hospital in January-February, 1863. Deserted from hospital at Ringgold, Georgia, March 10, 1863. Returned to duty subsequent to October 31, 1863. Captured at Missionary Ridge, Tennessee, November 25, 1863. Sent to Nashville, Tennessee. Transferred to Louisville, Kentucky, where he arrived on December 7, 1863. Transferred to Rock Island, Illinois, where he arrived on December 9, 1863. Released at Rock Island on January 25, 1864, after taking the Oath of Allegiance and joining the U.S. Navy.

FEAGANS, EPHRAIM, Corporal

Enlisted in Polk County on August 29, 1862, for the war. Mustered in as Private. Reported present in January-June, 1863. Promoted to Corporal on June 1, 1863. Reported present in July-August, 1863, and November, 1863-August, 1864. No further records. Survived the war.

FEAGANS, HENRY J., Corporal

Resided in Polk County where he enlisted at age 22, August 29, 1862, for the war. Mustered in as Private. Hospitalized at Dalton, Georgia, December 31, 1862, with acute diarrhoea. Returned to duty on January 18, 1863. Promoted to Corporal in March-April, 1863. Died in hospital at Tullahoma, Tennessee, April 22, 1863. Cause of death not reported.

FORESTER, MARTIN O., Private

Enlisted in Polk County at age 25, August 29, 1862, for the war. Failed to report for duty and was dropped from the company rolls on or about August 31, 1863.

GILBERT, JOHN, Private

Resided in Polk County where he enlisted at age 24, August 29, 1862, for the war. Reported present in January-April, 1863. Deserted on May 25, 1863. Returned to duty on June 22, 1863. Wounded in the thigh at Chickamauga, Georgia, September 19, 1863. Died on September 30, 1863, of gangrene. Place of death not reported.

GILES, JAMES B., Private

Born in South Carolina and resided in Polk County where he was by occupation a farmer prior to enlisting in Polk County at age 23, August 29, 1862, for the war. Reported present in January-June, 1863. Detailed as a teamster on June 28, 1863, and left in Mississippi. Rejoined the company in November-December, 1863. Detailed as a guard "at slaughter pen" on February 20, 1864. Reported on detail through August 31, 1864. Transferred to Company H, 58th Regiment N.C. Troops, when the 58th and 60th Regiments were consolidated on April 9, 1865.

GOSNELL, ZIBEON, Sergeant

Born in South Carolina and resided in Polk County where he enlisted at age 18, August 29, 1862, for the war. Mustered in as Private. Reported present in January-August, 1863. Promoted to Sergeant on June 1, 1863. Captured at Missionary Ridge, Tennessee, November 25, 1863. Sent to Nashville, Tennessee. Transferred to Louisville, Kentucky, where he arrived on December 7, 1863. Transferred to Rock Island, Illinois, where he arrived on December 9, 1863. Died at Rock Island on April 8, 1864, of "rheumatism."

GREEN, JESSE, Private

Resided in Polk County and was by occupation a laborer prior to enlisting in Polk County at age 26, August 29, 1862, for the war. Hospitalized at Dalton, Georgia, December 30, 1862, with typhoid fever. Returned to duty on February 16, 1863. Reported present in March-April, 1863. Deserted on May 25, 1863. Returned to duty on June 22, 1863. Reported present in July-August and November-December, 1863. Reported sick in hospital at Dalton on February 23, 1864. Returned to duty in March-April, 1864. Wounded in the groin or "bowels" by a spent ball at Resaca, Georgia, May 15, 1864. Reported in hospital at Atlanta, Georgia, through August 31, 1864. No further records. Survived the war.

GREEN, JOHN H., Private

Resided in Polk County where he enlisted on August 29, 1862, for the war. Deserted on November 9, 1862. Returned from desertion on March 1, 1863. Reported on extra duty by sentence of court-martial in March-April, 1863. Rejoined the company on or about May 2, 1863. Deserted on or about October 4, 1863.

GREEN, STEWART, Private

Enlisted in Polk County at age 22, August 29, 1862, for the war. Deserted at Murfreesboro, Tennessee, November 9, 1862. Returned from desertion on March 1, 1863, Court-martialed on or about April 7, 1863. Reported on extra duty by sentence of court-

martial through April 30, 1863. Returned to duty on May 11, 1863. Deserted on October 4, 1863. Returned from desertion on March 8, 1864, and was placed under arrest. Sent to Dalton, Georgia, sick on or about April 7, 1864. Furloughed for sixty days on June 16, 1864, by reason of chronic diarrhoea with extreme emaciation and debility. Returned to duty on an unspecified date. Transferred to Company H, 58th Regiment N.C. Troops, when the 58th and 60th Regiments were consolidated on April 9, 1865.

GREEN, USTES B., Private

Enlisted in Polk County at age 22, August 29, 1862, for the war. Deserted on November 9, 1862. Returned from desertion on March 1, 1863. Court-martialed on or about April 7, 1863. Reported on extra duty by sentence of court-martial through April 30, 1863. Deserted from hospital at Dalton, Georgia, May 30, 1863.

GREENLEE, TILMON, Private

Resided in Polk County and was by occupation a farm laborer prior to enlisting in Polk County at age 23, August 29, 1862, for the war. No further records. [Served also in Company K, 50th Regiment N.C. Troops.]

GRIFFIN, JAMES P., Private

Previously served as Private in Company D, 7th Battalion N.C. Cavalry. Transferred to this company on August 29, 1862. Sent to hospital sick in January-April, 1863. Returned to duty in May-June, 1863. Hospitalized at Macon, Georgia, September 26, 1863, with diarrhoea. Reported absent on sick furlough in November-December, 1863. Returned to duty prior to February 25, 1864, when he was wounded in the hip by a shell at Rocky Face Ridge, Georgia. Reported absent wounded or absent sick through August 31, 1864. No further records. Survived the war.

HANNON, SAMUEL W., Private

Resided in Polk County and was by occupation a farmer prior to enlisting in Polk County at age 32, August 29, 1862, for the war. Died in hospital at Ringgold, Georgia, on or about December 28, 1862. Cause of death not reported.

HEATHERINGTON, THOMAS A., Private

Born in South Carolina and resided in Polk County where he was by occupation a farmer prior to enlisting in Polk County at age 32, August 29, 1862, for the war. Reported present in January-June, 1863. Reported absent on sick furlough in July-August and November-December, 1863. Reported sick in hospital at Columbia, South Carolina, April 7, 1864. Returned to duty in May-June, 1864. Reported present in July-August, 1864. No further records. Survived the war. [North Carolina pension records indicate that he was wounded in the head by a shell at Chattanooga, Tennessee, in 1863 and was blinded "for some time."]

HENDERSON, WILLIAM M., Private

Resided in Polk County and was by occupation a farmer prior to enlisting in Polk County at age 29, August 29, 1862, for the war. Hospitalized at Dalton, Georgia, December 31, 1862, with chronic hepatitis. Returned to duty on January 18, 1863. Sent to hospital in March-April, 1863. Reported absent on sick furlough in May-August, 1863. Failed to return to duty and was dropped from the company rolls on or about December 31, 1863.

JACKSON, ASBURY, Private

Enlisted in Polk County on August 29, 1862, for the war. Transferred to Company D, 7th Battalion N.C. Cavalry, January 30, 1863.

JACKSON, LEANDER T., Private

Enlisted in Polk County on August 29, 1862, for the war. Sent to hospital sick in January-February, 1863. Reported absent sick or absent on sick furlough in March-August, 1863, and November, 1863-April, 1864. Reported absent without leave on May 1, 1864. Listed as a deserter on September 13, 1864, and dropped from the company rolls.

JACKSON, WILLIAM R., Private

Enlisted in Polk County on August 29, 1862, for the war. Failed to report for duty and was dropped from the company rolls on or about August 31, 1863.

LEDBETTER, SHADRACH L., Sergeant

Previously served as Private in Company D of this regiment. Transferred to this company on or about August 1, 1862. Promoted to Sergeant on an unspecified date. Hospitalized at Dalton, Georgia, December 30, 1862, with "phthisis pulmonalis." Died in hospital at Dalton on February 19, 1863.

LEDBETTER, THOMAS B., Private

Resided in Rutherford County and enlisted in Polk County on March 1, 1863, for the war. Sent to hospital in March-June, 1863. Returned to duty in July-August, 1863. Deserted on November 23, 1863. Returned from desertion on March 24, 1864, and was placed under arrest. Returned to duty prior to May 15-16, 1864, when he was captured at Resaca, Georgia. Sent to Nashville, Tennessee. Transferred to Louisville, Kentucky, where he arrived on May 21, 1864. Transferred to Alton, Illinois, where he arrived on May 25, 1864. Released at Alton on January 9, 1865, after taking the Oath of Allegiance and joining the U.S. Navy. [Was about 22 years of age at time of enlistment.]

LEDFORD, ALEXANDER H., Private

Resided in Polk County and was by occupation a farmer prior to enlisting in Polk County at age 30, August 29, 1862, for the war. Reported present in January-February, 1863. Sent to hospital in March-April, 1863. Returned to duty in May-June, 1863. Died in hospital at Lauderdale Springs, Mississippi, September 17, 1863, of disease.

LEDFORD, LAWSON H., Private

Resided in Polk County and was by occupation a farmer prior to enlisting in Polk County at age 30, August 29, 1862, for the war. Reported present in January-June, 1863. Furloughed home on September 18, 1863. Died on September 30, 1863. Place and cause of death not reported.

LITTLEJOHN, WILLIAM M., Private

Previously served as Private in Company E, 7th Battalion N.C. Cavalry. Transferred to this company on August 29, 1862. Hospitalized at Dalton, Georgia, December 30, 1862, with typhoid fever. Returned to duty on February 2, 1863. Sent to hospital in March-April, 1863. Reported absent on sick furlough in May-August, 1863. Returned to duty in November-December, 1863. Reported absent sick in hospital at Dalton on February 25, 1864. Returned to duty in March-April, 1864. Sent to hospital on May 8, 1864. Returned to duty in July-August, 1864. No further records.

MACE, JAMES A., Sergeant

Enlisted in Polk County on August 29, 1862, for the war. Was apparently mustered in with the rank of Sergeant. Reported present in January-June, 1863. Fell out on the retreat from Jackson, Mississippi, and was captured by the enemy on July 17, 1863. Sent to Snyder's Bluff, Mississippi. Transferred to Camp Morton, Indianapolis, Indiana, where he arrived on August 7, 1863. Paroled at Camp Morton and transferred to City Point, Virginia, February 26, 1865, for exchange. Hospitalized at Richmond, Virginia, on or about March 7, 1865. Transferred to another hospital on March 10, 1865. No further records.

McFARLAND, JOHN W., Sergeant

Resided in Polk County where he enlisted at age 18, August 29, 1862, for the war. Was apparently mustered in with the rank of Sergeant. Hospitalized at Ringgold, Georgia, on an unspecified date. Furloughed from hospital at Ringgold for thirty days on January 8, 1863. Failed to return to duty and was dropped from the company rolls on or about June 30, 1863.

McGINNIS, JOHN, Private

Resided in Polk County and was by occupation a farmer prior to enlisting in Polk County at age 32, August 29, 1862, for the war. Died in hospital at Catoosa Springs, Georgia, February 13, 1863, of "dysentery."

McMURRAY, ANDREW W., Private

Previously served as Private in Company E, 7th Battalion N.C. Cavalry. Transferred to this company on October 21, 1862. Failed to report for duty and was transferred back to Company E, 7th Battalion N.C. Cavalry, January 30, 1863.

MILLS, JOHN S., Private

Resided in Polk County and was by occupation a farmer prior to enlisting in Polk County at age 30, August 29, 1862, for the war. Furloughed for thirty days at Murfreesboro, Tennessee, in January-February, 1863. Reported absent on furlough through April 30, 1864. Reported absent without leave on June 15, 1864. Returned to duty in July-August, 1864. Listed as a deserter on September 13, 1864.

MILLS, OTIS P., Private

Previously served as Sergeant in Company E, 7th Battalion N.C. Cavalry. Transferred to this company on August 29, 1862. Was apparently mustered in with the rank of Private. Died in hospital at Atlanta, Georgia, November 29, 1862, of "typhoid fever." [Previously served as 1st Lieutenant in the 106th Regiment N.C. Militia.]

MORROW, G. W., Private

Born in Polk County* and was by occupation a farmer prior to enlisting in Polk County on March 1, 1863, for the war. Sent to hospital in March-April, 1863. Reported absent sick or absent on sick furlough in May-August, 1863, and November, 1863-February, 1864. Reported absent without leave on April 10, 1864. Went over to the enemy on an unspecified date. Enlisted in Company B, 1st Regiment U.S. Volunteer Infantry, June 14, 1864.

NODINE, PETER, Private

Enlisted in Polk County on August 29, 1862, for the war. Reported present in January-February, 1863. Sent to hospital in March-April, 1863. Reported in hospital at Rome, Georgia, in September-October, 1863. Returned to duty in November-December, 1863. Reported present in January-February, 1864. Reported absent without leave from April 1 through August 31, 1864. Listed as a deserter on September 13, 1864.

OWENS, ROLLA T., Private

Enlisted in Polk County on August 29, 1862, for the war. Hospitalized at Dalton, Georgia, January 30, 1863, with chronic diarrhoea. Died at Dalton on March 2, 1863.

PACK, LEANDER, Private

Resided in Polk County and was by occupation a farm laborer prior to enlisting in Polk County at age 37, August 29, 1862, for the war. Wounded slightly in the foot at Murfreesboro, Tennessee, December 31, 1862. Reported absent wounded or absent sick through August 31, 1863. Returned to duty prior to November 25, 1863, when he was captured at Missionary Ridge, Tennessee. Sent to Nashville, Tennessee. Transferred to Louisville, Kentucky, where he arrived on December 7, 1863. Transferred to Rock Island, Illinois, where he arrived on December 9, 1863. Paroled at Rock Island on February 15, 1865, and transferred for exchange. No further records. Survived the war.

PACK, WILLIAM, Private

Resided in Polk County and was by occupation a farmer prior to enlisting in Polk County at age 31, August 29, 1862, for the war. Reported present in January-February, 1863. Sent to hospital in March-April, 1863. Returned to duty in May-June, 1863. Reported present in July-August, 1863, and November, 1863-August, 1864. Died prior to January 1, 1865. Place, date, and cause of death not reported. Buried at Columbus, Georgia.

PEGG, WILLIAM, Private

Resided in Polk County and was by occupation a farmer prior to enlisting in Polk County at age 20, August 29, 1862, for the war. Wounded in the foot and captured at Murfreesboro, Tennessee, December 31, 1862-January 2, 1863. Confined at Camp Morton, Indianapolis, Indiana, where he died on February 5, 1863, of wounds and disease.

PONDER, JOHN R., Private

Previously served as Private in Company K, 16th Regiment N.C. Troops (6th Regiment N.C. Volunteers). Enlisted in this company on December 28, 1862, while listed as a deserter from the 16th Regiment. Mustered in as Private. Reported present in January-June, 1863. Promoted to Sergeant on June 1, 1863. Sent to hospital sick in July-August, 1863. Reported absent on sick furlough in November-December, 1863. Returned to duty in January-February, 1864. Reported present in March-April, 1864. Reduced to ranks on May 18, 1864. Wounded at Kolb's Farm, near Marietta, Georgia, June 22, 1864. Sent to hospital at Atlanta, Georgia. Reported absent wounded or absent sick through August 31, 1864. No further records.

PRICE, JERRY, Private

Resided in Polk County and was by occupation a laborer prior to enlisting in Polk County at age 28, August 29, 1862, for the war. Reported present in January-June, 1863. Reported on duty as a wheelwright and teamster in July, 1863-February, 1864. Rejoined the company in March-April, 1864. Killed at Resaca, Georgia, May 15, 1864.

QUEEN, RICHARD A., Private

Enlisted in Polk County on August 29, 1862, for the war. Sent to hospital at Chattanooga, Tennessee, November 20, 1862. Died prior to January 1, 1864. Place, date, and cause of death not reported.

RAINS, OSBURN, Private

Resided in Polk County where he enlisted at age 20, August 29, 1862, for the war. Reported present in January-February, 1863. Sent to hospital in March-April, 1863. Died in hospital on June 25 or July 2, 1863. Place and cause of death not reported.

SHEHAN, JACKSON, Private

Resided in Polk County and was by occupation a farmer prior to enlisting in Polk County at age 32, August 29, 1862, for the war. Deserted at Murfreesboro, Tennessee, November 9, 1862. Returned to duty in March-April, 1863. Reported present in May-June, 1863. Deserted on or about October 4, 1863. Returned from desertion on March 8, 1864, and was placed under arrest. Returned to duty in May-June, 1864. Reported present in July-August, 1864. No further records. Survived the war.

SHEHAN, PINKNEY, Private

Resided in Polk County where he enlisted at age 22, March 1, 1863, for the war. Reported present in March-June, 1863. Deserted on or about October 4, 1863. [Probably served also as Private in Company F, 58th Regiment N.C. Troops.]

SPLAWN, ALEX GRAHAM, Private

Enlisted in Polk County at age 28, August 29, 1862, for the war. Reported present in January-April, 1863. Sent to hospital sick in May-June, 1863. Reported absent on sick furlough in July-August and November-December, 1863. Returned to duty in January-February, 1864. Reported present in March-April, 1864. Reported sick in hospital at Atlanta, Georgia, from June 25 through August 31, 1864. No further records. Survived the war. [North Carolina pension records indicate that he was wounded in Georgia on June 1, 1863 (probably 1864).]

SWAIN, JOHN B., Private

Enlisted in Polk County on August 29, 1862, for the war. Mustered in as Corporal. Reported present in January-February, 1863. Sent to hospital in March-April, 1863. Reduced to ranks in May-June, 1863. Served as a hospital nurse at Ringgold, Georgia, and Newnan, Georgia, during most of 1863. Rejoined the company in January-February, 1864. Reported present in March-June, 1864. Sent to Atlanta, Georgia, sick on July 12, 1864. No further records. Survived the war. [Was about 29 years of age at time of enlistment. Was probably wounded in the chest by a piece of shell at Murfreesboro, Tennessee, on or about January 1, 1863.]

TAYLOR, JAMES, Private

Resided in Polk County where he enlisted at age 21, August 29, 1862, for the war. Sent to hospital at Knoxville, Tennessee, on or about January 5, 1863. Reported absent sick through August 31, 1864. No further records.

THOMPSON, WILLIAM COLUMBUS, Private

Born in Polk County* on October 1, 1842. Enlisted in Polk County at age 19, August 29, 1862, for the war. Sent to hospital sick in January-February, 1863. Reported absent sick or absent on furlough through December 31, 1863. Failed to return to duty and was dropped from the company rolls on or about December 31, 1863. [Filed a Tennessee pension application after the war.]

TURNER, ISAAC S., Private

Previously served as Private in Company D, 7th Battalion N.C. Cavalry. Transferred to this company on August 29, 1862.

Reported present in January-December, 1863. Reported sick in hospital at Dalton, Georgia, February 23, 1864. Returned to duty in March-April, 1864. Reported present through August 31, 1864. No further records.

TURNER, ROBERT T., Private

Enlisted in Polk County on August 29, 1862, for the war. Reported for duty in March-April, 1863. Deserted on May 25, 1863. Returned to duty on June 22, 1863. Deserted on October 4, 1863.

WALDROP, ELI M., Corporal

Resided in Polk County and was by occupation a farmer prior to enlisting in Polk County at age 34, August 29, 1862, for the war. Was apparently mustered in with the rank of Corporal. Died at Murfreesboro, Tennessee, on an unspecified date. Cause of death not reported.

WALDROP, JACONIAS A., Private

Enlisted in Polk County on August 29, 1862, for the war. Hospitalized at Dalton, Georgia, December 31, 1862, with diarrhoea. Returned to duty on February 4, 1863. Reported absent on sick furlough in May-August, 1863. Captured at Missionary Ridge, Tennessee, November 25, 1863. Sent to Nashville, Tennessee. Transferred to Louisville, Kentucky, where he arrived on December 7, 1863. Transferred to Rock Island, Illinois, where he arrived on December 9, 1863. Died at Rock Island on October 30, 1864, of "apoplexy."

WALKER, JAMES D., Sergeant

Resided in Polk County and was by occupation a farmer prior to enlisting in Polk County at age 29, August 29, 1862, for the war. Was apparently mustered in with the rank of Sergeant. Hospitalized at Dalton, Georgia, December 31, 1862, with parotitis. Transferred to hospital at Atlanta, Georgia, where he died on January 10, 1863. Cause of death not reported.

WALKER, JAMES O., Corporal

Enlisted in Polk County on August 29, 1862, for the war. Mustered in as Private. Sent to hospital sick in January-February, 1863. Returned to duty in March-April, 1863. Reported present in May-August, 1863. Promoted to Corporal on June 1, 1863. Sent to hospital sick in November-December, 1863. Furloughed from hospital at Griffin, Georgia, January 9, 1864. Returned to duty in March-April, 1864. Reported present in May-August, 1864. No further records. Survived the war.

WALKER, SILAS J., Private

Enlisted in Polk County at age 32, August 29, 1862, for the war. Reported present in January-February, 1863. Detailed as a shoemaker at Columbus, Georgia, March 1, 1863. Rejoined the company in January-February, 1864. Reported present in March-June, 1864. Deserted on August 13, 1864.

WHITESIDES, WILLIAM P., Private

Resided in Polk County where he enlisted on August 29, 1862, for the war. Reported present in January-April, 1863. Deserted on May 25, 1863. Returned to duty on June 22, 1863. Wounded at Chickamauga, Georgia, September 20, 1863. Hospitalized at Rome, Georgia. Returned to duty in November-December, 1863. Reported present in January-February, 1864. Reported present but sick in March-April, 1864. Deserted to the enemy at or near Resaca, Georgia, on or about May 15, 1864. Sent to Chattanooga, Tennessee. Transferred to Louisville, Kentucky, where he arrived on May

31, 1864. Released at Louisville on or about June 1, 1864 after taking the Oath of Allegiance.

WILLIAMS, NATHAN L., Private

Resided in Polk County where he enlisted on August 29, 1862, for the war. Reported present in January-August and November-December, 1863. Furloughed on February 23, 1864. Returned to duty in March-April, 1864. Reported present in May-August, 1864. Wounded in the right leg by a cannonball at Columbia, Tennessee, November 29, 1864. Right leg amputated. Captured at Columbia on December 21, 1864. Sent to Nashville, Tennessee. Transferred to Louisville, Kentucky, where he arrived on March 8, 1865. Transferred to Camp Chase, Ohio, where he arrived on March 12, 1865. Transferred to Point Lookout, Maryland, March 26, 1865. Released at Point Lookout on June 30, 1865, after taking the Oath of Allegiance. [Records of the Federal Provost Marshal dated January-March, 1865, give his age as 28.]

WILSON, DOCTOR F., Private

Resided in Polk County and was by occupation a farmer prior to enlisting in Polk County at age 26, August 29, 1862, for the war. "Retained by civil authority" and failed to report for duty. Dropped from the company rolls on or about August 31, 1863.

WILSON, GREEN B., Private

Born in Cleveland County* and resided in Polk County where he was by occupation a farmer prior to enlisting in Polk County at age 23, August 29, 1862, for the war. Hospitalized at Dalton, Georgia, December 28, 1862, with chronic diarrhoea. Returned to duty on February 2, 1863. Discharged at Dalton on March 4, 1863, by reason of "phthisis pulmonalis."

WILSON, JAMES, Private

Resided in Polk County where he enlisted on August 29, 1862, for the war. Captured at Murfreesboro, Tennessee, January 2, 1863. Hospitalized at St. Louis, Missouri, January 24, 1863, with intermittent fever. Died in hospital at St. Louis on February 5, 1863, of "typhoid fever" and/or "chronic diarrhoea."

COMPANY H

This company was raised in Cocke County, Tennessee, on September 6, 1862. It was mustered into Confederate service on September 16, 1862, and assigned to the 1st Battalion N.C. Infantry. On October 8, 1862, the 60th Regiment N.C. Troops was formally organized after a tenth company was assigned to the 1st Battalion. This company was designated Company H. After joining the regiment the company functioned as a part of the regiment, and its history for the remainder of the war is reported as a part of the regimental history.

The following roster was compiled primarily from information in the microfilm edition of the Compiled Service Records of Soldiers Who Served in Organizations from the State of North Carolina (Record Group 109, M270), National Archives and Records Administration, Washington, D.C. Record Group 109 includes enlistment papers, pay vouchers, requisitions, letters of resignation, discharge certificates, and abstracts of medical and prisoner of war returns. Materials relating specifically to this company include muster rolls dated September 6-[October 29?], 1862, and January, 1863-August, 1864.

Also utilized in this roster were *The War of the Rebellion: A Compilation of the Official Records of the Union and Confederate Armies*, the North Carolina adjutant general's *Roll of Honor*, state militia records, newspaper casualty lists and obituaries, wartime claims for bounty pay and allowances, postwar registers of claims for artificial limbs, Confederate pension applications filed with the states of North Carolina, Tennessee, and Florida, Confederate Soldiers' Home records, and the 1860 and 1870 federal censuses of North Carolina. A search was made also for relevant letters, diaries, reminiscences, and other manuscripts in the Southern Historical Collection (University of North Carolina-Chapel Hill), the Duke University Library Special Collections Department, and the North Carolina Division of Archives and History.

Among the secondary sources consulted were records of the North Carolina division of the United Daughters of the Confederacy, postwar rosters, regimental and county histories, marriage bond, will, and cemetery indexes, published and unpublished genealogies, biographical dictionaries, the North Carolina *County Heritage Book* series, the *Confederate Veteran*, Walter Clark's *Histories of the Several Regiments and Battalions from North Carolina in the Great War, 1861-'65*, and the North Carolina volume of the extended edition of *Confederate Military History*.

OFFICERS

CAPTAIN

HUFF, JAMES T.

Resided in Cocke County, Tennessee. Elected Captain at age 22, September 6, 1862. Reported present in September-October, 1862, and January-February, 1863. Reported sick in hospital in March-April, 1863. Returned to duty in May-June, 1863. Detailed for duty as a conscription officer on or about August 19, 1863. Rejoined the company prior to December 23, 1863, when he was appointed Major and transferred to the Field and Staff of this regiment.

CLAYTON, ROBERT M.

Served as 1st Lieutenant of Company B of this regiment. Reported on duty as acting commander of this company in March-April, 1864.

RHEA, HENRY KELSEY

Served as 2nd Lieutenant of Company C of this regiment. Reported on duty as acting commander of this company in May-August, 1864.

LIEUTENANTS

BROOKS, ROYAL, 3rd Lieutenant

Enlisted in Cocke County, Tennessee, September 6, 1862, for the war. Mustered in as Private. Reported present in September-October, 1862, and January-February, 1863. Promoted to Corporal in November, 1862-February, 1863. Reported sick in hospital in March-April, 1863. Returned to duty in May-June, 1863. Elected 3rd Lieutenant on June 28, 1863. Reported absent sick in July-October, 1863. Returned to duty in November-December, 1863. Reported present in January-April, 1864. Killed at Kolb's Farm, near Marietta, Georgia, June 22, 1864.

HUFF, LEONARD C., 2nd Lieutenant

Previously served as Private in Company B of this regiment. Transferred to this company on or about September 6, 1862. Elected 2nd Lieutenant on January 20, 1863. Reported present in January-June, 1863. Wounded in the right leg at Chickamauga, Georgia, September 19-20, 1863. Returned to duty prior to November 1, 1863. Reported present in November-December, 1863. Granted a sick leave of thirty days on February 9, 1864. Failed to return to duty and was reported absent without leave in March-August, 1864. Went over to the enemy on an unspecified date. Took the Oath of Allegiance at Knoxville, Tennessee, March 4, 1865.

JONES, MARVEL M., 1st Lieutenant

Enlisted in Cocke County, Tennessee, at age 28, September 6, 1862, for the war. Mustered in as Private. Elected 3rd Lieutenant on October 5, 1862. Reported present in September-October, 1862. Wounded slightly in the knee at Murfreesboro, Tennessee, December 31, 1862. Returned to duty in March-April, 1863, when he was reported in command of the company. Promoted to 1st Lieutenant on March 20, 1863. Reported present in May-June, 1863. Reported absent sick from September 19, 1863, until February 1, 1864, when he was reported absent without leave. Dropped from the company rolls on June 27 1864, for prolonged absence without leave.

NELSON, JAMES M. P., 1st Lieutenant

Enlisted in Cocke County, Tennessee. Elected 1st Lieutenant on September 6, 1862. Reported present in September-October, 1862. Died at Murfreesboro, Tennessee, December 15, 1862. Cause of death not reported.

STOKELY, WILLIAM R., 1st Lieutenant

Enlisted in Cocke County, Tennessee. Elected 2nd Lieutenant on September 6, 1862. Reported present in September-October, 1862. Promoted to 1st Lieutenant on December 15, 1862. Reported present in January-February, 1863. Resigned on March 4, 1863. Reason he resigned not reported; however, an annotation on the front of his letter of resignation indicates that he was "*totally unqualified for the position he holds.*" Resignation accepted on March 20, 1863. Later served as Private in Company F, 5th Regiment Tennessee Cavalry (McKenzie's).

NONCOMMISSIONED OFFICERS AND PRIVATES

ANDERS, J. P., Private

Enlisted in Cocke County, Tennessee, September 6, 1862, for the war. Reported present through October 29, 1862. No further records.

BEEN, D., Private

Enlisted in Caldwell County. Enlistment date erroneously reported as July 10, 1861. Reportedly served in this company prior to November-December, 1864, when he was reported on duty as a provost guard at Macon, Georgia, serving in Company A, 1st Regiment Troops and Defenses.

BELL, WILLIAM M., Private

Enlisted in Cocke County, Tennessee, September 6, 1862, for the war. Died at Greeneville, Tennessee, October 3, 1862. Cause of death not reported.

BENSON, THOMAS, Private

Place and date of enlistment not reported. Name appears on an undated register of prisoners which states he was captured at Murfreesboro, Tennessee, on an unspecified date (probably December 31, 1862-January 2, 1863). No further records.

BERRY, SAMUEL, Private

Enlisted in Cocke County, Tennessee, September 6, 1862, for the war. Reported absent without leave on October 29, 1862. No further records.

BLACK, JESSE C., Private

Enlisted in Cocke County, Tennessee, September 6, 1862, for the war. Reported present in September-October, 1862, and January-February, 1863. Reported sick in hospital in March-April, 1863. Died at Tunnel Hill, Georgia, May 7, 1863. Cause of death not reported. Buried in the Confederate cemetery at Marietta, Georgia.

BLACK, JOHN, Private

Enlisted in Cocke County, Tennessee, September 6, 1862, for the war. Reported absent without leave on October 29, 1862. No further records.

BLACK, JOHN W., Private

Enlisted in Cocke County, Tennessee, September 6, 1862, for the war. Reported absent sick without leave on October 29, 1862. No further records.

BLACK, REUBEN, Private

Enlisted in Cocke County, Tennessee, September 6, 1862, for the war. Reported absent without leave on October 29, 1862. No further records.

BLACK, ROYAL, Private

Enlisted in Cocke County, Tennessee, at age 26, September 6, 1862, for the war. Reported absent without leave on October 29, 1862. No further records. Survived the war.

BRADFORD, ALBERT, Private

Enlisted in Cocke County, Tennessee, September 6, 1862, for the war. Reported present in September-October, 1862. Reported present but under arrest in January-February, 1863. Reason he was arrested not reported. Died in hospital on March 14, 1863. Place and cause of death not reported.

BROOKS, DAVID, Sergeant

Enlisted in Cocke County, Tennessee, September 6, 1862, for the war. Mustered in as Private. Reported present in September-October, 1862. Hospitalized at Dalton, Georgia, December 31, 1862, with acute diarrhoea. Returned to duty on January 3, 1863. Reported sick in hospital in March-April, 1863. Returned to duty in May-June, 1863. Promoted to Sergeant on June 8, 1863. Reported absent sick in July-October, 1863. Returned to duty in November-December, 1863. Reported present through August 31, 1864.

BROOKS, STEPHEN, Private

Enlisted in Cocke County, Tennessee, September 6, 1862, for the war. Hospitalized at Dalton, Georgia, December 31, 1862, with debilitas. Returned to duty on January 3, 1863. Reported sick in hospital in March-April, 1863. Reported absent on detached service in May-June, 1863. Reported absent sick in July-December, 1863.

Returned to duty in January-February, 1864. Reported absent on furlough of indulgence of forty days on April 5, 1864. Returned to duty in May-June, 1864. Reported absent sick on August 24, 1864. Appointed 2nd Lieutenant and transferred to Company C, 58th Regiment N.C. Troops, when the 58th and 60th Regiments were consolidated on April 9, 1865.

BURGIN, MERRITT, Corporal

Enlisted in Cocke County, Tennessee, September 6, 1862, for the war. Mustered in as Corporal. Hospitalized at Dalton, Georgia, December 30, 1862, with chronic diarrhoea. Returned to duty on January 3, 1863. Reported sick in hospital in March-April, 1863. Returned to duty in May-June, 1863. Deserted at Dalton on September 1, 1863.

CALDWELL, DANIEL, Private

Enlisted in Cocke County, Tennessee, September 6, 1862, for the war. Reported absent without leave on October 29, 1862. No further records.

CHAPMAN, WILEY, Corporal

Enlisted in Cocke County, Tennessee, at age 27, September 6, 1862, for the war. Mustered in as Private. Reported present in September-October, 1862. Promoted to Corporal in November, 1862-February, 1863. Wounded slightly in the back at Murfreesboro, Tennessee, December 31, 1862. Returned to duty in May-June, 1863. Deserted near Chattanooga, Tennessee, September 7, 1863.

CLARK, HUGH, Private

Enlisted in Cocke County, Tennessee, September 6, 1862, for the war. Reported absent without leave on October 29, 1862. No further records.

CLAY, ANDREW, Private

Records of the United Daughters of the Confederacy indicate that he was born in Lincoln County in 1816; resided in Caldwell County at the time of his enlistment on August 25, 1863; and died (or was discharged) on March 9, 1864. No further records.

CLEMMONS, ALEXANDER C., Private

Previously served as Private in Company B of this regiment. Transferred to this company on June 30, 1863. Died in hospital at Mobile, Alabama, on or about July 31, 1863, of "ty[phoid] fever."

COGDILL, JAMES B., Private

Born in Cocke County, Tennessee, in 1831. Enlisted in Cocke County on September 6, 1862, for the war. Reported present in September-October, 1862, and January-December, 1863. Reported on extra duty as a blacksmith in the quartermaster's department in January-June, 1864. Rejoined the company in July-August, 1864. No further records. [Filed a Tennessee pension application after the war.]

COGDILL, ROBERT, Private

Enlisted in Cocke County, Tennessee, September 6, 1862, for the war. Reported present in September-October, 1862, and January, 1863-June, 1864. Captured at or near Ruff's Mill, near Smyrna, Georgia, July 4, 1864. Sent to Nashville, Tennessee. Transferred to Louisville, Kentucky, where he arrived on July 14, 1864. Transferred to Camp Douglas, Chicago, Illinois, where he arrived on July 18, 1864. Released at Camp Douglas on June 20, 1865, after taking the Oath of Allegiance.

COGDILL, WILLIAM, Private

Enlisted in Cocke County, Tennessee, September 6, 1862, for the war. Reported present in September-October, 1862. Reported absent sick in January-February, 1863. Reported sick in hospital in March-April, 1863. Died at Chattanooga, Tennessee, March 4, 1863. Cause of death not reported.

CUMMINGS, AUGUSTUS B., Private

Enlisted in Cocke County, Tennessee, September 6, 1862, for the war. Reported present in September-October, 1862. No further records. Survived the war. [May have served later as Private in Company B, 3rd Regiment Tennessee Cavalry (Union).]

CUMMINGS, JERRY, Corporal

Enlisted in Cocke County, Tennessee, September 6, 1862, for the war. Mustered in as Corporal. Reported present in September-October, 1862. No further records. [May have served later as Private in Company B, 3rd Regiment Tennessee Cavalry (Union).]

CURRY, THOMAS, Private

Enlisted in Cocke County, Tennessee, September 6, 1862, for the war. Reported present in September-October, 1862, and January-February, 1863. Reported sick in hospital in March-April, 1863. Returned to duty in May-June, 1863. Reported present in July-October, 1863. Captured at Missionary Ridge, Tennessee, November 25, 1863. Sent to Nashville, Tennessee. Transferred to Louisville, Kentucky, where he arrived on December 7, 1863. Transferred to Rock Island, Illinois, the same date. Transferred to Fort Columbus, New York Harbor, where he arrived on February 25, 1865. Paroled and transferred to Boulware's Wharf, James River, Virginia, where he was received on March 5, 1865, for exchange. No further records. Survived the war. [Was about 27 years of age at time of enlistment. North Carolina pension records indicate that he was wounded just above the left kneecap by a shell fragment at Missionary Ridge.]

DAVIS, WILLIAM DEMPSEY, Private

Resided in Cocke or Scott County, Tennessee, and enlisted in Cocke County on September 6, 1862, for the war. Reported present in September-October, 1862, and January-February, 1863. Reported sick in hospital in March-April, 1863. Returned to duty in May-June, 1863. Deserted near Chattanooga, Tennessee, September 7, 1863. Went over to the enemy on an unspecified date. Took the Oath of Allegiance at Louisville, Kentucky, on or about June 12, 1864.

DOCKERY, ALEXANDER, Private

Enlisted in Cocke County, Tennessee, September 6, 1862, for the war. Reported present in September-October, 1862. No further records.

EISENHOWER, JOHN, Private

Enlisted in Cocke County, Tennessee, September 6, 1862, for the war. Reported present in September-October, 1862. No further records. Later served as Sergeant in Company K, 8th Regiment Tennessee Infantry (Union).

ELLIS, WILLIAM, Private

Enlisted in Cocke County, Tennessee, September 6, 1862, for the war. Reported present in September-October, 1862. Wounded and captured at Murfreesboro, Tennessee, on or about December 31, 1862. Died at Murfreesboro on January 8, 1863, of wounds.

ELLISON, GEORGE, Private

Enlisted in Cocke County, Tennessee, at age 38, September 6, 1862, for the war. Reported absent without leave in September-October, 1862. No further records. Survived the war.

ELLISON, JOHN, Sergeant

Enlisted in Cocke County, Tennessee, September 6, 1862, for the war. Mustered in as Corporal. Reported present in September-October, 1862, and January-October, 1863. Promoted to Sergeant on June 5, 1863. Reported in hospital at Griffin, Georgia, in November-December, 1863. Died in hospital at Marietta, Georgia, February 18, 1864, of "sickness."

ELLISON, NICHOLAS, Private

Enlisted in Cocke County, Tennessee, September 6, 1862, for the war. Reported present in September-October, 1862. Wounded slightly in the thigh at Murfreesboro, Tennessee, January 2, 1863. Returned to duty prior to March 1, 1863. Reported present through June 30, 1863. Deserted on September 11, 1863. Returned to duty on September 24, 1863. Sent to hospital sick on September 27, 1863. Reported in hospital at La Grange, Georgia, December 31, 1863. Furloughed for sixty days on January 8, 1864, suffering from chronic diarrhoea, extreme emaciation, and debility. Died at home on April 1, 1864. Cause of death not reported.

ELLISON, WILLIAM, Private

Enlisted in Cocke County, Tennessee, September 6, 1862, for the war. Reported absent without leave in September-October, 1862. No further records.

FORD, JOHN, Private

Enlisted in Cocke County, Tennessee, September 6, 1862, for the war. Reported absent without leave in September-October, 1862. No further records.

FOX, HENRY, Private

Enlisted in Cocke County, Tennessee, September 6, 1862, for the war. Discharged on October 7, 1862. Reason discharged not reported. [May have served later as Private in Companies C and K, 8th Regiment Tennessee Infantry (Union).]

GOWEN, DANIEL H., Private

Enlisted in Cocke County, Tennessee, September 6, 1862, for the war. Reported present in September-October, 1862, and January-February, 1863. Died in hospital on March 9, 1863. Place and cause of death not reported.

GREEN, ROBERT, Private

Enlisted in Cocke County, Tennessee, September 6, 1862, for the war. Reported present in September-October, 1862, and January-June, 1863. Deserted near Chattanooga, Tennessee, September 7, 1863.

GREEN, WILLIAM, Private

Place and date of enlistment not reported. Reported absent sick without leave in September-October, 1862. No further records.

GRIFFEY, JAMES, Private

Enlisted at Tullahoma, Tennessee, March 20, 1863, for the war. Deserted on an unspecified date. Returned to duty on or about April 1, 1863. Reported present in May-June, 1863. Deserted near Chattanooga, Tennessee, September 8, 1863.

GRIFFEY, JOHN A., Private

Enlisted at Murfreesboro, Tennessee, December 1, 1862, for the war. Reported present in January-February, 1863. Reported sick in hospital in March-April, 1863. Returned to duty in May-June, 1863. Deserted near Chattanooga, Tennessee, September 8, 1863.

GRINDSTAFF, ISAAC, Private

Place and date of enlistment not reported. Reported absent without leave in September-October, 1862. No further records. Survived the war. [Was about 19 years of age at time of enlistment. May have served later as Private in Company G, 13th Regiment Tennessee Cavalry (Union).]

HALE, KILLIS, Private

Enlisted in Cocke County, Tennessee, at age 35, September 6, 1862, for the war. Reported present in September-October, 1862. No further records. Survived the war. [May have served later as Private in Company H, 1st Regiment Tennessee Cavalry (Union).]

HARNASON, ALFRED A., Private

Enlisted in Cocke County, Tennessee, September 6, 1862, for the war. Reported present in September-October, 1862. No further records.

HEDRICK, WILLIAM H., Corporal

Enlisted in Cocke County, Tennessee, September 6, 1862, for the war. Mustered in as Private. Reported present in September-October, 1862. Wounded slightly in the hand at Murfreesboro, Tennessee, December 31, 1862. Returned to duty prior to March 1, 1863. Reported sick in hospital in March-June, 1863. Detailed as a hospital nurse at La Grange, Georgia, July 26, 1863. Rejoined the company in January-February, 1864. Promoted to Corporal on February 1, 1864. Reported present but sick in March-April, 1864. Reported present in May-August, 1864. Transferred to Company C, 58th Regiment N.C. Troops, when the 58th and 60th Regiments were consolidated on April 9, 1865.

HENDERSON, ANDREW J., Private

Place and date of enlistment not reported. Reported present in September-October, 1862. No further records.

HENDERSON, WILLIAM H., Private

Enlisted in Cocke County, Tennessee, September 6, 1862, for the war. Reported present in September-October, 1862, and January-June, 1863. Reported in hospital at Spring Hill, Alabama, in July-August, 1863. Reported absent sick from October 2, 1863, through February 29, 1864. Returned to duty in March-April, 1864. Captured at or near Ruff's Mill, near Smyrna, Georgia, July 4, 1864. Sent to Nashville, Tennessee. Transferred to Louisville, Kentucky, where he arrived on July 14, 1864. Transferred to Camp Douglas, Chicago, Illinois, where he arrived on July 18, 1864. Released at Camp Douglas on April 2, 1865, after taking the Oath of Allegiance and joining the U.S. Army. Assigned to Company I, 6th Regiment U.S. Volunteer Infantry.

HOLLAND, CHARLES, 1st Sergeant

Born in Cocke County, Tennessee, where he resided as a farmer prior to enlisting in Cocke County at age 29, September 6, 1862, for the war. Mustered in as 1st Sergeant. Reported present in September-October, 1862, and January-June, 1863. Hospitalized at Lauderdale Springs, Mississippi, July 9, 1863 (apparently suffering from "varicocele"). Detailed for duty as a hospital nurse at Lauderdale Springs on or about October 20, 1863. Rejoined the company in March-April, 1864. Deserted to the enemy (or was captured) at Kolb's Farm, near Marietta, Georgia, June 22, 1864. Sent to Chattanooga, Tennessee. Transferred to Louisville, Kentucky, where he arrived on July 14, 1864. Released at Louisville on July 16, 1864, after taking the Oath of Allegiance.

HOLLAND, JOHN, Private

Enlisted in Cocke County, Tennessee, September 6, 1862, for the war. Reported present in September-October, 1862. Hospitalized at Dalton, Georgia, December 30, 1862, with chronic diarrhoea. Returned to duty on January 3, 1863. Reported absent sick on February 28, 1863. Reported sick in hospital in March-June, 1863. Deserted near Chattanooga, Tennessee, September 7, 1863. Went over to the enemy on an unspecified date. Took the Oath of Allegiance at Knoxville, Tennessee, March 4, 1865.

HOLLAND, WILLIAM A., Sergeant

Enlisted in Cocke County, Tennessee, September 6, 1862, for the war. Mustered in as Sergeant. Reported present in September-October, 1862, and January-June, 1863. Deserted near Chattanooga, Tennessee, September 7, 1863.

HOLLAWAY, MARION H., Private

Resided in Cocke County, Tennessee, where he enlisted on September 6, 1862, for the war. Reported present in September-October, 1862. Hospitalized at Dalton, Georgia, December 30, 1862, with pneumonia. Returned to duty on January 3, 1863. Reported present through April 30, 1863. Hospitalized at Tunnel Hill, Georgia, May 25, 1863, with fever. Transferred to hospital at Catoosa Springs, Georgia, June 29, 1863. Returned to duty in July-October, 1863. Captured at Missionary Ridge, Tennessee, November 25, 1863. Sent to Nashville, Tennessee. Transferred to Louisville, Kentucky, where he arrived on December 7, 1863. Transferred to Rock Island, Illinois, where he arrived on December 9, 1863. Released at Rock Island on April 21, 1864, after taking the Oath of Allegiance. [Records of the Federal Provost Marshal dated April, 1864, give his age as 21.]

HOLT, ANDREW J., Private

Enlisted in Cocke County, Tennessee, September 6, 1862, for the war. Reported present in September-October, 1862. No further records. Survived the war.

HOLT, THOMAS, Private

Enlisted at Dalton, Georgia, April 1, 1864, for the war. Reported absent without leave on June 17, 1864. Dropped from the company rolls on or about August 31, 1864, for absence without leave.

HUFF, JOSEPH, Private

Enlisted in Cocke County, Tennessee, September 6, 1862, for the war. Reported present in September-October, 1862. Reported absent sick from December 18, 1862, through October 31, 1863. Listed as a deserter and dropped from the company rolls on or about December 31, 1863.

HUFF, R. N., Private

Previously served as Corporal in Company B of this regiment. Reduced to ranks and transferred to this company on June 30, 1863. Reported present through February 29, 1864. Furloughed for twenty-four days on April 4, 1864. Reported absent without leave in May-June, 1864. Dropped from the company rolls on or about August 31, 1864, for absence without leave.

HUFF, THOMAS B., Private

Resided in Cocke County, Tennessee. Place and date of enlistment not reported. Deserted at Dalton, Georgia, March 15, 1864. Went over to the enemy on an unspecified date. Took the Oath of Allegiance at Knoxville, Tennessee, on or about March 15, 1865.

JOHNSON, JAMES C., Private

Place and date of enlistment not reported. Reported absent without leave in September-October, 1862. No further records. Later served as Private in Company E, 2nd Regiment Tennessee Cavalry (Union).

JOHNSON, WILLIAM C., Private

Place and date of enlistment not reported. Reported absent without leave in September-October, 1862. No further records. Later served as Private in Company E, 2nd Regiment Tennessee Cavalry (Union).

JONES, CHARLES C., Sergeant

Enlisted in Cocke County, Tennessee, September 6, 1862, for the war. Mustered in as Sergeant. Reported present in September-October, 1862. Wounded slightly in the hand at Murfreesboro, Tennessee, January 2, 1863. Returned to duty in March-April, 1863. Deserted at Dalton, Georgia, May 25, 1863. Later served as Sergeant in Company F, 8th Regiment Tennessee Cavalry (Union).

JONES, ISAAC, Private

Place and date of enlistment not reported. Reported present in September-October, 1862. Died at Chattanooga, Tennessee, May 7, 1863. Cause of death not reported.

JONES, JOHN, Private

Place and date of enlistment not reported. Reported absent without leave in September-October, 1862. No further records.

JORDAN, WILLIAM, Corporal

Enlisted at Murfreesboro, Tennessee, December 1, 1862, for the war. Mustered in as Private. Reported present in January-June, 1863. Promoted to Corporal on June 5, 1863. Killed at Chickamauga, Georgia, September 20, 1863. Nominated for the Badge of Distinction for gallantry at Chickamauga.

JUSTICE, JOHN, Sergeant

Enlisted in Cocke County, Tennessee, September 6, 1862, for the war. Mustered in as Sergeant. Reported present in September-October, 1862, and January-April, 1863. Deserted at Dalton, Georgia, May 25, 1863.

KELLEY, JOSEPH, Private

Enlisted in Cocke County, Tennessee, September 6, 1862, for the war. Reported present in September-October, 1862. Died at or near Chattanooga, Tennessee. Date and cause of death not reported.

KILLIAN, DAVID, Private

Enlisted in Cocke County, Tennessee, September 6, 1862, for the war. Reported present in September-October, 1862. Reported absent sick in January-February, 1863. Returned to duty in March-April, 1863. Reported present through August 31, 1864. Took the Oath of Allegiance at Chattanooga, Tennessee, June 8, 1865.

KILLPATRICK, JAMES, Private

Place and date of enlistment not reported. Reported absent without leave in September-October, 1862. No further records.

KILLPATRICK, LEWIS, Private

Place and date of enlistment not reported. Reported absent without leave in September-October, 1862. No further records. [May have served later as Private in Company K, 8th Regiment Tennessee Cavalry (Union).]

LEDFORD, JESSE, Private

Enlisted at Jackson, Mississippi, June 26, 1863, for the war. Reported present through June 30, 1863. No further records.

McKAY, ABRAHAM B., Private

Born in Cocke County, Tennessee, October 1, 1840. Enlisted in Cocke County at age 21, September 6, 1862, for the war. Reported present in September-October, 1862, and January, 1863-August, 1864. Took the Oath of Allegiance at Chattanooga, Tennessee, on or about June 8, 1865. [Filed a Tennessee pension application after the war.]

MANTOOTH, GEORGE W., Private

Enlisted in Cocke County, Tennessee, September 6, 1862, for the war. Reported present in September-October, 1862. Captured (possibly wounded) at Murfreesboro, Tennessee, on or about December 31, 1862. Confined at Camp Douglas, Chicago, Illinois, where he died on or about February 10, 1863. Cause of death not reported.

MARROW, GEORGE M., Private

Enlisted in Cocke County, Tennessee, September 6, 1862, for the war. Reported present in September-October, 1862. Wounded slightly in the arm at Murfreesboro, Tennessee, January 2, 1863. Reported on detached service in hospital at Chattanooga, Tennessee, in March-April, 1863. Died at Ringgold, Georgia, May 6, 1863. Cause of death not reported.

MARROW, JAMES, Private

Place and date of enlistment not reported (probably enlisted on September 6, 1862). Reported absent without leave in September-October, 1862. No further records.

MESSER, THOMAS, Private

Enlisted in Cocke County, Tennessee, September 6, 1862, for the war. Reported present in September-October, 1862. Died at Murfreesboro, Tennessee, January 15, 1863, of "pneumonia."

MOONYHAM, HENRY, Private

Born in Cocke County, Tennessee, and was by occupation a farmer prior to enlisting in Cocke County on September 6, 1862, for the war. Reported present in September-October, 1862. Discharged at

Tullahoma, Tennessee, January 26, 1863, by reason of "paralysis of the right arm attended with very considerable atrophy of the muscles thereof." Discharge certificate gives his age as 18.

MOONYHAM, ISAAC C., Private

Enlisted at Camp Morton, Mississippi, at age 22, August 12, 1863, for the war. Reported present in July, 1863-February, 1864. Reported present but sick in March-April, 1864. Returned to duty in May-June, 1864. Captured at or near Ruff's Mill, near Smyrna, Georgia, July 4, 1864. Sent to Nashville, Tennessee. Transferred to Louisville, Kentucky, where he arrived on July 14, 1864. Transferred to Camp Douglas, Chicago, Illinois, where he arrived on July 18, 1864. Paroled at Camp Douglas on March 14, 1865. Received at Boulware's Wharf, James River, Virginia, March 18-21, 1865, for exchange. Hospitalized at Richmond, Virginia, March 21, 1865, with scorbutus. Furloughed for thirty days on March 28, 1865. [Filed a Tennessee pension application after the war.]

MOONYHAM, WILLIAM H., Private

Enlisted in Cocke County, Tennessee, September 6, 1862, for the war. Reported present in September-October, 1862. Reported present but under arrest in January-February, 1863. Reason he was confined not reported. Reported in prison at Tullahoma, Tennessee, in March-April, 1863. Hospitalized at Tunnel Hill, Georgia, May 25, 1863, with "vulnus contusion." Place and date injured not reported. Returned to duty on June 30, 1863. Deserted near Chattanooga, Tennessee, September 19, 1863. Hospitalized at Macon, Georgia, October 19, 1863, with debility. Returned to duty on October 31, 1863. Captured at Missionary Ridge, Tennessee, November 25, 1863. Sent to Nashville, Tennessee. Transferred to Louisville, Kentucky, where he arrived on December 7, 1863. Transferred to Rock Island, Illinois, where he arrived on December 9, 1863. Released at Rock Island on January 25, 1864, after taking the Oath of Allegiance and joining the U.S. Navy.

MOORE, WILLIAM P., Private

Enlisted in Cocke County, Tennessee, September 6, 1862, for the war. Reported present in September-October, 1862. Wounded slightly in the neck at Murfreesboro, Tennessee, January 2, 1863. Returned to duty in March-April, 1863. Reported present in May-June, 1863. Deserted near Chattanooga, Tennessee, September 7, 1863.

MORROW, JESSE, Private

Enlisted in Cocke County, Tennessee, September 6, 1862, for the war. Reported present in September-October, 1862, and January-February, 1863. Reported sick in hospital in March-June, 1863. Deserted on September 19, 1863. Returned to duty on September 27, 1863. Reported absent on detached service in November-December, 1863. Reported present in January-April, 1864. Captured at Resaca, Georgia, May 15-16, 1864. Sent to Nashville, Tennessee. Transferred to Louisville, Kentucky, where he arrived on May 21, 1864. Transferred to Alton, Illinois, where he arrived on May 25, 1864. Paroled at Alton on or about February 21, 1865. Received at Boulware's and Cox's Wharves, James River, Virginia, on or about March 6, 1865, for exchange. Hospitalized at Richmond, Virginia, March 7, 1865, with debilitas. Furloughed for thirty days on March 8, 1865.

PARKER, NICHOLAS, Private

Enlisted in Cocke County, Tennessee, September 6, 1862, for the war. Reported present in September-October, 1862. Reported absent sick in January-February, 1863. Returned to duty in March-April, 1863. Deserted at Dalton, Georgia, May 25, 1863.

PENLAND, JOHN, Private

Place and date of enlistment not reported (probably enlisted on or about September 6, 1862). Discharged on October 7, 1862. Reason discharged not reported.

PRESNELL, DAVID, Private

Enlisted at Jackson, Mississippi, June 26, 1863, for the war. Captured at Clinton, Mississippi, July 9, 1863. Confined at St. Louis, Missouri. Transferred to Camp Morton, Indianapolis, Indiana, where he arrived on August 14, 1863. Released at Camp Morton in August, 1863, after taking the Oath of Allegiance and enlisting in the 71st Regiment Indiana Volunteers.

ROBERTS, GEORGE T., Private

Enlisted at Murfreesboro, Tennessee, December 1, 1862, for the war. Hospitalized at Dalton, Georgia, December 30, 1862, with parotitis. Reported in hospital at Dalton on January 26, 1863, suffering from chronic diarrhoea. Discharged at Ringgold, Georgia, March 9, 1863, by reason of disability. [Was about 18 years of age at time of enlistment.]

ROBERTS, JESSE T., Private

Enlisted in Cocke County, Tennessee, September 6, 1862, for the war. Reported present in September-October, 1862. Reported absent sick in January-April, 1863. Returned to duty in May-June, 1863. Deserted near Chattanooga, Tennessee, September 7, 1863.

ROSE, GREEN, Private

Enlisted in Cocke County, Tennessee, September 6, 1862, for the war. Reported present in September-October, 1862, and January-June, 1863. Deserted near Chattanooga, Tennessee, September 8, 1863.

SAIN, ANDERSON, Private

Enlisted in Cocke County, Tennessee, September 6, 1862, for the war. Reported present in September-October, 1862. Reported absent sick in January-February, 1863. Died in hospital at Tullahoma, Tennessee, March 7, 1863. Cause of death not reported.

SAWYERS, ARTHUR, Private

Enlisted at Jackson, Mississippi, July 12, 1863, for the war. Deserted at Dalton, Georgia, September 1, 1863.

SAYLOR, JOHN, Corporal

Enlisted in Cocke County, Tennessee, September 6, 1862, for the war. Mustered in as Corporal. Reported present in September-October, 1862. No further records.

SEXTON, ELIJAH P., Musician

Enlisted in Cocke County, Tennessee, September 6, 1862, for the war. Mustered in as Musician (Drummer). Reported present in September-October, 1862. Died on an unspecified date (probably prior to March 1, 1863). Place and cause of death not reported.

SEXTON, GEORGE, Private

Enlisted in Cocke County, Tennessee, September 6, 1862, for the war. Mustered in as Musician (Fifer). Reported present in September-October, 1862, and January-February, 1863. Reduced to ranks prior to March 1, 1863. Reported sick in hospital in March-April, 1863. Died at Chattanooga, Tennessee, May 8, 1863. Cause of death not reported.

SEXTON, JOHN, Private

Enlisted in Cocke County, Tennessee, September 6, 1862, for the war. Reported present in September-October, 1862. Hospitalized at Dalton, Georgia, December 30, 1862, with chronic hepatitis. Returned to duty on January 3, 1863. No further records.

SEXTON, JOHN G., Private

Resided in Cocke County, Tennessee, where he enlisted on December 1, 1862, for the war. Reported absent on detached service in January-December, 1863 (probably served as a shoemaker during part of that period). Furloughed for twenty-six days on February 13, 1864. Failed to return to duty and was dropped from the company rolls on or about April 30, 1864. Went over to the enemy on an unspecified date. Took the Oath of Allegiance at Knoxville, Tennessee, March 15, 1865.

SEXTON, WILLIAM D., Private

Enlisted in Cocke County, Tennessee, at age 31, September 6, 1862, for the war. Reported present in September-October, 1862. No further records. Survived the war.

SHEPHERD, ADAM F., Private

Enlisted at Murfreesboro, Tennessee, at age 29, December 1, 1862, for the war. Reported absent on detached service in January-February, 1863. Reported absent on detached service as a miner or sapper at Wartrace, Tennessee, in March-April, 1863. Rejoined the company in May-June, 1863. Deserted at Kingston, Georgia, prior to November 1, 1863.

SMITH, JOHN, Private

Enlisted in Cocke County, Tennessee, September 6, 1862, for the war. Reported present in September-October, 1862, and January-June, 1863. Deserted near Chattanooga, Tennessee, September 7, 1863.

SMITH, WILLIAM, Private

Enlisted in Cocke County, Tennessee, September 6, 1862, for the war. Died at Chattanooga, Tennessee, on an unspecified date (probably prior to March 1, 1863). Cause of death not reported.

SNIDER, MONTREVILLE, Private

Enlisted in Cocke County, Tennessee, September 6, 1862, for the war. Reported absent sick without leave in September-October, 1862. No further records. Survived the war. [Was about 29 years of age at time of enlistment.]

SPENCER, JOSEPH H., Corporal

Enlisted in Cocke County, Tennessee, on September 6, 1862, for the war. Mustered in as Private. Reported present in September-October, 1862, and January-April, 1863. Reported sick in hospital in May-June, 1863. Reported absent sick in July-December, 1863. Returned to duty in January-February, 1864. Promoted to Corporal on February 1, 1864. Reported present in March-April, 1864. Reported absent sick from May 27 through August 31, 1864. No further records.

STOKELY, CHARLES, JR., Private

Previously served as Private in Company B of this regiment. Transferred to this company on September 6, 1862. Transferred back to Company B in November-December, 1862.

TEAGUE, SMITH, Private

Enlisted in Cocke County, Tennessee, September 6, 1862, for the war. Reported absent without leave in September-October, 1862. No further records.

TOWNSEND, PHILIP, Private

Enlisted in Cocke County, Tennessee, at age 22, September 6, 1862, for the war. Mustered in as Sergeant. Reported present in September-October, 1862. Hospitalized at Dalton, Georgia, December 30, 1862, with chronic rheumatism. Transferred to another hospital on January 7, 1863. Returned to duty in March-April, 1863. Reported present but under arrest in May-June, 1863. Reason he was arrested not reported. Court-martialed on or about July 24, 1863, and reduced to ranks. Returned to duty on an unspecified date. Deserted at Kingston, Georgia, prior to November 1, 1863.

TURNER, GEORGE, Private

Enlisted in Cocke County, Tennessee, September 6, 1862, for the war. Reported present in September-October, 1862, and January-February, 1863. Reported sick in hospital in March-April, 1863. Furloughed from hospital in May, 1863. Reported absent without leave in November-December, 1863. Listed as a deserter and dropped from the company rolls on or about February 29, 1864.

TURNER, REUBEN C., Private

Born in Cocke County, Tennessee, in 1840. Enlisted in Cocke County on September 6, 1862, for the war. Reported present in September-October, 1862. Hospitalized at Dalton, Georgia, December 31, 1862, with parotitis. Returned to duty prior to February 28, 1863. Reported present in March-June, 1863. Deserted near Chattanooga, Tennessee, September 7, 1863. [Filed a Tennessee pension application after the war.]

WILLIAMS, JOHN, Private

Enlisted in Cocke County, Tennessee, September 6, 1862, for the war. Reported present in September-October, 1862. No further records.

WILLIAMS, ROBERT D., Private

Resided in Cocke County, Tennessee, where he enlisted on September 6, 1862, for the war. Reported present in September-October, 1862, and January-October, 1863. Captured at Missionary Ridge, Tennessee, November 25, 1863. Sent to Nashville, Tennessee. Transferred to Louisville, Kentucky, where he arrived on December 5, 1863. Transferred to Rock Island, Illinois, where he arrived on December 11, 1863. Released at Rock Island on June 21, 1865, after taking the Oath of Allegiance. [Records of the Federal Provost Marshal dated June, 1865, give his age as 20.]

WILLIAMS, WILLIAM, Private

Enlisted at Jackson, Mississippi, July 17, 1863, for the war. Deserted at Dalton, Georgia, September 1, 1863.

WOODY, GEORGE, Private

Enlisted in Cocke County, Tennessee, September 6, 1862, for the war. Reported absent without leave in September-October, 1862. No further records.

YATES, SAMUEL, Private

Enlisted in Cocke County, Tennessee, September 6, 1862, for the war. Reported present in September-October, 1862, and January-April, 1863. Deserted at Dalton, Georgia, May 25, 1863.

COMPANY I

This company, known as the "French Broad Guards," was organized at Camp Smith, in Madison County, on September 13, 1862, when "volunteers and details" in "unnecessarily large" companies of the 1st Battalion N.C. Infantry were consolidated to form a new company. (Clark's *Regiments*, 3:475.) It was mustered into Confederate service on the same date. Because it was the tenth company (numerically if not alphabetically) assigned to the 1st Battalion, the battalion was formally reorganized as the 60th Regiment N.C. Troops on October 8, 1862. This company was designated Company I. (The company was initially designated Company G, but, probably because it failed to complete its organization before the unit that became Company G did so, it yielded its place.) After joining the regiment the company functioned as a part of the regiment, and its history for the remainder of the war is reported as a part of the regimental history.

The following roster was compiled primarily from information in the microfilm edition of the Compiled Service Records of Soldiers Who Served in Organizations from the State of North Carolina (Record Group 109, M270), National Archives and Records Administration, Washington, D.C. Record Group 109 includes enlistment papers, pay vouchers, requisitions, letters of resignation, discharge certificates, and abstracts of medical and prisoner of war returns. Materials relating specifically to this company include a muster-in and descriptive roll dated September 13, 1862, and muster rolls dated November, 1862-August, 1864.

Also utilized in this roster were *The War of the Rebellion: A Compilation of the Official Records of the Union and Confederate Armies*, the North Carolina adjutant general's *Roll of Honor*, state militia records, newspaper casualty lists and obituaries, wartime claims for bounty pay and allowances, postwar registers of claims for artificial limbs, Confederate pension applications filed with the states of North Carolina, Tennessee, and Florida, Confederate Soldiers' Home records, and the 1860 and 1870 federal censuses of North Carolina. A search was made also for relevant letters, diaries, reminiscences, and other manuscripts in the Southern Historical Collection (University of North Carolina-Chapel Hill), the Duke University Library Special Collections Department, and the North Carolina Division of Archives and History.

Among the secondary sources consulted were records of the North Carolina division of the United Daughters of the Confederacy, postwar rosters, regimental and county histories, marriage bond, will, and cemetery indexes, published and unpublished genealogies, biographical dictionaries, the North Carolina *County Heritage Book* series, the *Confederate Veteran*, Walter Clark's *Histories of the Several Regiments and Battalions from North Carolina in the Great War, 1861-'65*, and the North Carolina volume of the extended edition of *Confederate Military History*.

OFFICERS

CAPTAINS

ROBERTS, GOODSON M.

Previously served as 2nd Lieutenant of Company F of this regiment. Elected Captain of this company on September 13, 1862. Reported absent on detached service in February, 1863. Returned to duty in March-April, 1863. Reported sick in hospital in May-June, 1863. Returned to duty in July-October, 1863. Reported present in November, 1863-February, 1864. Furloughed on April 16, 1864. Resigned on May 9, 1864, because of "intermittent fever associated with chronic diarrhoea for the last 10 months. Said officer is feeble and conciderably [*sic*] emaciated, his general health being much impaired from the chronic character of his diseases." Resignation accepted on July 16, 1864.

ALEXANDER, WILLIAM R.

Previously served as 1st Sergeant of Company K of this regiment. Elected 1st Lieutenant of this company on September 13, 1862. Reported present in November-December, 1862. Reported absent sick in hospital in January-February, 1863. Returned to duty in March-April, 1863. Reported present in May-June, 1863. Wounded in the hand at Chickamauga, Georgia, September 20, 1863. Returned to duty prior to October 31, 1863. Reported present through August 31, 1864. Promoted to Captain on July 16, 1864. Transferred to Company E, 58th Regiment N.C. Troops, when the 58th and 60th Regiments were consolidated on April 9, 1865.

LIEUTENANTS

JONES, JOSIAH M., 2nd Lieutenant

Previously served as Corporal in Company K of this regiment. Appointed 2nd Lieutenant of this company on September 13, 1862. Reported present in November, 1862-April, 1863. Reported sick in hospital in May-June, 1863. Reported present in July, 1863-August, 1864. Resigned on August 22, 1864, because only eleven men were present in his company and only thirty-eight were on the rolls. Resignation accepted on September 8, 1864.

LUTHER, SAMUEL P., 3rd Lieutenant

Previously served as Private in Company E of this regiment. Elected 3rd Lieutenant of this company on September 13, 1862. Reported present in November, 1862-April, 1864. Wounded at Kolb's Farm, near Marietta, Georgia, June 22, 1864. Returned to duty in July-August, 1864. Resigned on September 14, 1864. Reason he resigned not reported. Resignation accepted on October 26, 1864.

NONCOMMISSIONED OFFICERS AND PRIVATES

ALEXANDER, BENJAMIN JULIUS, Quartermaster Sergeant

Previously served as Private in Company K of this regiment. Transferred to this company on or about September 13, 1862. Mustered in as Private. Appointed Quartermaster Sergeant prior to January 1, 1863. Transferred to the Field and Staff of this regiment in March-April, 1863.

ALEXANDER, GEORGE N., Sergeant

Previously served as Private in Company K of this regiment. Transferred to this company on or about September 13, 1862. Mustered in as Corporal. Promoted to Sergeant prior to January 1, 1863. Reported present in November, 1862-April, 1864. Wounded at Kolb's Farm, near Marietta, Georgia, June 22, 1864. Returned to duty prior to June 30, 1864. Reported present through August 31, 1864. No further records. Survived the war.

ALEXANDER, THOMAS F., Private

Previously served as Private in Company K of this regiment. Transferred to this company on or about September 13, 1862. Hospitalized at Dalton, Georgia, November 6, 1862, with diarrhoea and/or rheumatism. Returned to duty on December 13, 1862. Hospitalized at Dalton on December 23 or December 30, 1862, with chronic rheumatism. Returned to duty on or about January 14, 1863. Reported present in March-April, 1863. Hospitalized at Dalton on May 26, 1863, with rheumatism. Returned to duty on June 21, 1863. Died on August 20, 1863. Place and cause of death not reported.

ALEXANDER, WILLIAM P., Private

Previously served as Private in Company E of this regiment. Transferred to this company on or about September 13, 1862. Discharged at Chattanooga, Tennessee, November 18, 1862, by reason of "extreme youth & debility."

ALEXANDER, WILLIAM S., Private

Previously served as Private in Company K of this regiment. Transferred to this company on or about September 13, 1862. Captured at Murfreesboro, Tennessee, on or about January 2, 1863. Apparently died in the hands of the enemy. Place, date, and cause of death not reported.

ARROWOOD, HUGHEY G., Private

Previously served as Private in Company A of this regiment. Transferred to this company on or about August 1, 1862. Deserted from hospital at Ringgold, Georgia, on or about November 20, 1862. Returned from desertion on February 21, 1863. Returned to duty on April 23, 1863. Reported present in May-June, 1863. Sent to hospital at Marion, Mississippi, on or about August 10, 1863. Furloughed home in September, 1863. Failed to return to duty. Listed as a deserter and dropped from the company rolls on or about April 30, 1864. Later served as Sergeant in Company C, 3rd Regiment N.C. Mounted Infantry (Union).

ARROWOOD, ROBERT D., Private

Previously served as Private in Company A of this regiment. Transferred to this company on or about August 1, 1862, while listed as a deserter. Returned from desertion on February 21, 1863. Deserted from hospital at Dalton, Georgia, March 27, 1863. Later served as Private in Companies H and I, 3rd Regiment N.C. Mounted Infantry (Union).

BAIRD, GILBERT, ———

Negro. North Carolina pension records indicate that he served as a "body-servant" to Pvt. James B. Baird of this company. Survived the war.

BAIRD, JAMES B., Private

Previously served as Private in Company K of this regiment. Transferred to this company on or about September 13, 1862. Reported present in November-December, 1862. Reported absent sick in January-February, 1863. Returned to duty in March-April, 1863. Died at Tullahoma, Tennessee, May 12, 1863, of disease.

BALL, JOHN McDOWELL, Private

Previously served as Private in Company E of this regiment. Transferred to this company on or about September 13, 1862. Reported present in November-December, 1862. Reported sick in hospital in January-June, 1863. Hospitalized at Lauderdale Springs, Mississippi, July 10, 1863. Detailed as a nurse at Lauderdale Springs on August 1, 1863. Returned to duty in November, 1863. Wounded in the left arm and right hand and captured at Missionary Ridge, Tennessee, November 25, 1863. Hospitalized at

Bridgeport, Alabama. Transferred to hospital at Nashville, Tennessee, where he arrived on December 13, 1863. Transferred to Louisville, Kentucky, February 14, 1864. Transferred from Louisville to Fort Delaware, Delaware, February 29, 1864. Paroled at Fort Delaware on September 28, 1864. Received at Varina, Virginia, October 5, 1864, for exchange. Issued clothing on October 9, 1864. No further records. Survived the war.

BANKS, J. M., Private

Previously served as Private in Company F of this regiment. Transferred to this company on September 13, 1862. Reported absent sick in November-December, 1862. Died in hospital at Tullahoma, Tennessee, February 21, 1863. Cause of death not reported.

BARNWELL, JAMES R., Private

Previously served as Private in Company D of this regiment. Transferred to this company on August 1, 1862. Hospitalized at Dalton, Georgia, December 31, 1862, with debilitas. Returned to duty on January 18, 1863. Died in hospital at Ringgold, Georgia, March 11, 1863. Cause of death not reported.

BARTLETT, JAMES H., Sergeant

Previously served as Corporal in Company K of this regiment. Transferred to this company on or about September 13, 1862. Mustered in as Sergeant. Reported present in November, 1862-April, 1863. Reported absent on furlough or absent sick in May-December, 1863. Died at home on January 15, 1864, of "consumption, and chronic diarrhea."

BARTLETT, JOSHUA, Private

Born in Buncombe County and was by occupation a farmer prior to enlisting at Murfreesboro, Tennessee, at age 34, October 22, 1862, for the war. Reported present in November-December, 1862. Hospitalized at Dalton, Georgia, January 6, 1863, with chronic diarrhoea. Returned to duty on January 13, 1863. Reported present in February-June, 1863. Deserted from camp on October 5, 1863.

BRADLEY, JAMES D., Private

Previously served as Private in Company A of this regiment. Transferred to this company on or about August 1, 1862, while listed as a deserter. Reported for duty on an unspecified date. Transferred back to Company A of this regiment prior to December 12, 1862.

BRIGHT, R. W., Private

Previously served as Private in Company K of this regiment. Transferred to this company on or about September 13, 1862. Reported present in November, 1862-February, 1863. Reported sick in hospital in March-April, 1863. Furloughed for thirty days on or about May 4, 1863, convalescent from chronic diarrhoea. Returned to duty in July-October, 1863. Reported absent sick in November-December, 1863. Reported present in January-August, 1864. No further records. Survived the war.

BURNETT, DAVID, Private

Born in McDowell County. Place and date of enlistment not reported. Enlisted in this company on an unspecified date (probably in the autumn of 1862) but was apparently rejected for service. No further records.

CAGLE, FRANKLIN, Private

Enlisted at Tullahoma, Tennessee, February 12, 1863, for the war. Reported present in March-April, 1863. Deserted at Fairfield, Tennessee, May 20, 1863.

CALLAHAN, F. M., Private

Enlisted at Tullahoma, Tennessee, February 12, 1863, for the war. Reported absent sick through June 30, 1863. Returned to duty in July-October, 1863. Reported present in November, 1863-February, 1864. Reported present but sick in March-April, 1864. Wounded at Kolb's Farm, near Marietta, Georgia, June 22, 1864. Reported in hospital at Augusta, Georgia, October 12, 1864. No further records.

CANNON, HENRY C., Corporal

Previously served as Private in Company K of this regiment. Transferred to this company on or about September 13, 1862. Reported present in November, 1862-October, 1863. Promoted to Corporal in November-December, 1863. Reported present in November, 1863-February, 1864. Reported present but sick in March-April, 1864. Returned to duty in May-June, 1864. Reported present but sick in July-August, 1864. Deserted to the enemy on an unspecified date. Took the Oath of Allegiance at Nashville, Tennessee, December 31, 1864.

CANNON, JAMES H., Private

Previously served as Private in Company K of this regiment. Transferred to this company on or about September 13, 1862. Died in hospital at Chattanooga, Tennessee, November 15, 1862. Cause of death not reported.

CARLAND, FRANKLIN B., Private

Previously served as Private in Company F of this regiment. Transferred to this company on September 13, 1862. Reported absent without leave in November, 1862-February, 1863. Dropped from the company rolls in March-April, 1863. Went over to the enemy on an unspecified date. Confined at Knoxville, Tennessee, September 12, 1864. Transferred to Louisville, Kentucky, where he arrived on September 25, 1864. Released at Louisville on September 26, 1864, after taking the Oath of Allegiance. Later served as Private in Company H, 2nd Regiment N.C. Mounted Infantry (Union).

CATHEY, JOHN LAFAYETTE, Sergeant

Previously served as Corporal in Company E of this regiment. Transferred to this company on or about September 13, 1862. Mustered in as Sergeant. Reported present in November, 1862-June, 1863. Wounded in the right leg at Chickamauga, Georgia, September 20, 1863. Right leg amputated. Reported absent wounded through August 31, 1864. No further records. Survived the war. [Nominated for the Badge of Distinction for gallantry at Chickamauga.]

CLARK, J. C., Private

Enlisted in Buncombe County on September 14, 1863, for the war. Reported present through October 31, 1863. Deserted on November 21, 1863.

CLARK, W. H., Corporal

Previously served as Corporal in Company K of this regiment. Transferred to this company on or about September 13, 1862. Reported present in November, 1862-June, 1863. Reported absent sick in July-October, 1863. Died at Greenville, South Carolina, November 29, 1863. Cause of death not reported.

CLARK, WILLIAM C., Corporal

Previously served as Private in Company E of this regiment. Transferred to this company on or about September 13, 1862. Mustered in as Private. Promoted to Corporal on November 1, 1862. Reported present in November, 1862-June, 1863. Reported absent sick or absent on furlough in July-December, 1863. Reported absent without leave in January-February, 1864. Returned to duty in March-April, 1864. Reported present in July-August, 1864. No further records. Survived the war.

CLARK, WILLIAM NOAH, Private

Previously served as Private in Company B, 16th Regiment N.C. Troops (6th Regiment N.C. Volunteers). Enlisted in this company at Dalton, Georgia, March 27, 1864, while absent without leave from the 16th Regiment. Reported present through August 31, 1864. Last reported in the records of this company on October 24, 1864. Survived the war.

COLWELL, HAMILTON, Private

Born in Haywood County and was by occupation a farmer prior to enlisting at Camp Martin (Mitchell County) at age 21, October 1, 1862, for the war. No further records. Later served as Private in Company H, 3rd Regiment N.C. Mounted Infantry (Union).

COPELAND, JOSEPH P., Private

Previously served as Private in Company K of this regiment. Transferred to this company on or about September 13, 1862. Deserted from camp on November 23, 1862. Died in hospital while "returning to camp" on January 14, 1863. Place and cause of death not reported.

CREASMAN, THOMAS P., Private

Previously served as Private in Company K of this regiment. Transferred to this company on or about September 13, 1862. Reported absent sick in November-December, 1862. Died in hospital at Ringgold, Georgia, February 8, 1863. Cause of death not reported.

CURTIS, THOMAS, Private

Previously served as Private in Company A of this regiment. Transferred to this company on August 1, 1862. Transferred back to Company A on September 13, 1862.

DAVIS, O. F., Private

Previously served as Private in Company C of this regiment. Transferred to this company on or about September 13, 1862. Reported absent sick in November, 1862-February, 1863. Reported absent sick or absent on furlough in March-October, 1863. Failed to return to duty and was dropped from the company rolls on or about December 31, 1863.

DOCKERY, WILLIAM B., Private

Previously served as Private in Company E of this regiment. Transferred to this company on or about September 13, 1862. Deserted from hospital on November 20, 1862. Returned to duty on April 23, 1863. Reported sick in hospital in May-June, 1863. Died in hospital on July 30, 1863. Place and cause of death not reported.

FARMER, THOMAS S., Private

Born in Anson County and was by occupation a farmer prior to enlisting at Murfreesboro, Tennessee, at age 24, October 29, 1862, for the war. Died in hospital at Murfreesboro on November 21, 1862, of disease.

FISHER, ALFORD R., Private

Born in Madison County* and was by occupation a farmer prior to enlisting at Greeneville, Tennessee, at age 18, October 9, 1862, for the war. Wounded in the left thigh and captured at Murfreesboro, Tennessee, on or about January 2, 1863. Hospitalized at Murfreesboro. Transferred to another hospital on January 18, 1863. No further records (probably died of wounds).

FISHER, BENJAMIN H., Private

Previously served as Private in Company F of this regiment. Transferred to this company on September 13, 1862. Died in hospital at Murfreesboro, Tennessee, November 11, 1862. Cause of death not reported.

FLETCHER, ANDREW C., Private

Previously served as Private in Company E of this regiment. Transferred to this company on or about September 13, 1862. Hospitalized at Dalton, Georgia, December 30, 1862, with icterus. Returned to duty on February 2, 1863. Sent to hospital prior to March 1, 1863. Returned to duty in May-June, 1863. Reported absent sick from October 10, 1863, through February 29, 1864. Returned to duty in March-April, 1864. Reported present in May-August, 1864. No further records. Survived the war.

FLINN, J. F., Private

Place and date of enlistment not reported (probably enlisted subsequent to August 31, 1864). Paroled at Greensboro on May 19, 1865.

FLOYD, WILLIS A. B., Private

Born in Rutherford County and was by occupation a farmer prior to enlisting at Greeneville, Tennessee, at age 18, October 11, 1862, for the war. Deserted from camp on December 3, 1862. Returned from desertion on an unspecified date. Court-martialed on or about February 3, 1863. Returned to duty on March 20, 1863. Reported present in May-June, 1863. Deserted from camp on October 5, 1863. Returned from desertion on February 1, 1864, and was placed under arrest. Returned to duty on or about April 1, 1864. Wounded at Kolb's Farm, near Marietta, Georgia, June 22, 1864. Captured at or near Smyrna, Georgia, July 3, 1864. Sent to Nashville, Tennessee. Transferred to Louisville, Kentucky, where he arrived on July 13, 1864. Transferred to Camp Morton, Indianapolis, Indiana, where he arrived on July 14, 1864. Paroled at Camp Morton and transferred for exchange on March 15, 1865. Received at Boulware's and Cox's Wharves, James River, Virginia, March 23, 1865, for exchange. No further records. Survived the war. [North Carolina pension records indicate that he was wounded in the left leg at Resaca, Georgia, May 15, 1864.]

GRAGG, AMOS, Private

Born in Caldwell County and was by occupation a farmer prior to enlisting at Greeneville, Tennessee, at age 21, September 13, 1862, for the war. Reported absent sick in November-December, 1862. Wounded and captured at Murfreesboro, Tennessee, December 31, 1862-January 2, 1863. Died at Murfreesboro on or about February 6, 1863, of wounds.

GRIGGS, JAMES P., Private

Born in Buncombe County and was by occupation a farmer prior to enlisting at Murfreesboro, Tennessee, at age 22, October 29, 1862, for the war. Reported present in November, 1862-April, 1863. Reported sick in hospital in May-June, 1863. Returned to duty prior to September 20, 1863, when he was captured at Chickamauga, Georgia. Sent to Nashville, Tennessee. Transferred to Louisville, Kentucky, where he arrived on September 30, 1863. Transferred to Camp Douglas, Chicago, Illinois, where he arrived on October 4, 1863. Released at Camp Douglas on April 6, 1865,

after taking the Oath of Allegiance and joining the U.S. Army. Assigned to Company F, 5th Regiment U.S. Volunteer Infantry.

GUY, PETER, Private

Previously served as Private in Company E of this regiment. Transferred to this company on or about September 13, 1862. Wounded in the hand at Murfreesboro, Tennessee, January 2, 1863. Reported absent wounded, absent sick, or absent on furlough through December 31, 1863. Listed as a deserter on March 11, 1864. Reported absent sick from May 25 through August 31, 1864. Hospitalized at Meridian, Mississippi, January 12, 1865, with diarrhoea. Transferred to Marion, Alabama, on an unspecified date. No further records.

GUY, RICHARD A., Private

Previously served as Private in Company E of this regiment. Transferred to this company on or about August 1, 1862. Wounded slightly in the "belly" at Murfreesboro, Tennessee, December 31, 1862. Reported absent wounded or absent sick through April 30, 1863. Furloughed in May-June, 1863. Failed to return to duty and was dropped from the company rolls on or about December 31, 1863. Listed as a deserter on March 11, 1864.

HAMBY, LEANDER S., Sergeant

Previously served as Sergeant in Company K of this regiment. Transferred to this company on or about September 13, 1862. Hospitalized at Dalton, Georgia, December 31, 1862, with debilitas. Returned to duty on January 26, 1863. Reported present in March-April, 1863. Hospitalized at Tunnel Hill, Georgia, May 25, 1863, with intermittent fever. Transferred to another hospital on June 29, 1863. Returned to duty in November-December, 1863. Appointed Sergeant Major on January 21, 1864, and transferred to the Field and Staff of this regiment.

HAWKINS, F. M., Private

Born in Greenville District, South Carolina, and was by occupation a farmer prior to enlisting at Murfreesboro, Tennessee, at age 26, October 29, 1862, for the war. Died in camp at Tullahoma, Tennessee, February 13, 1863. Cause of death not reported.

HOLYFIELD, GEORGE M., Private

Previously served as Private in Company K of this regiment. Transferred to this company on or about September 13, 1862. Deserted from hospital in November, 1862.

JONES, H. C., Private

Enlisted at Marietta, Georgia, June 14, 1864, for the war. Reported absent sick on August 15, 1864. No further records.

JONES, L. W., Private

Previously served as Private in Company K of this regiment. Transferred to this company on or about September 13, 1862. Reported absent sick in November, 1862-June, 1863. Hospitalized at Lauderdale Springs, Mississippi, July 15, 1863. Died in an unspecified hospital on September 5, 1863. Cause of death not reported.

LEDBETTER, SION B., Private

Born in Transylvania County* and resided in Henderson County where he was by occupation a carpenter prior to enlisting at Murfreesboro, Tennessee, at age 26, October 29, 1862, for the war. Deserted from hospital on or about November 20, 1862. Returned from desertion on April 28, 1863. Reported under arrest in May-June, 1863. Court-martialed on or about July 24, 1863. Reported absent sick on October 31, 1863. Returned to duty in November-December, 1863. Reported present in January-February, 1864. Reported on detail as brigade carpenter from March 1 through August 31, 1864. Hospitalized at Union Springs, Alabama, on or about September 12, 1864, with intermittent fever. Returned to duty on September 18, 1864. No further records.

LEMING, RUFUS, Private

Previously served as Private in Company A of this regiment. Transferred to this company on August 1, 1862. Transferred back to Company A on or about September 13, 1862.

LEWIS, JAMES R., Private

Previously served as Private in Company D of this regiment. Transferred to this company on August 1, 1862. Deserted from hospital in November, 1862. Returned to duty on April 23, 1863. Reported sick in hospital in May-June, 1863. Died in hospital at Lauderdale Springs, Mississippi, August 26, 1863, of "chron[ic] dia[rrhoea]."

LUNSFORD, A. W., Private

Previously served as Private in Company F of this regiment. Transferred to this company on or about September 13, 1862. Reported present in November, 1862-June, 1863. Hospitalized at Marietta, Georgia, September 28, 1863. Reported absent sick through April 30, 1864. Reported on duty at the military prison at Atlanta, Georgia, in May-June, 1864. Reported absent sick in July-August, 1864. Records of the Federal Provost Marshal datelined Macon, Georgia, April 30, 1865, state that he was captured. No further records. [Presumably he was a member of the 58th Regiment N.C. Troops subsequent to April 9, 1865, the date on which the 58th and 60th Regiments were consolidated.]

LUTHER, SAMUEL WAITSEL, Private

Previously served as Private in Company E of this regiment. Transferred to this company on or about September 13, 1862. Was apparently mustered in with the rank of Musician (Drummer). Reported present in November, 1862-April, 1863. Reduced to ranks in May-June, 1863. Detailed for duty as a teamster with the supply train on June 27, 1863, and sent to Mississippi. Reported absent on detail as a teamster through August 31, 1864. No further records.

LYTLE, T. L., Private

Previously served as Private in Company K of this regiment. Transferred to this company on or about September 13, 1862. Reported present in November, 1862-April, 1863. Detailed for hospital duty at Lauderdale Springs, Mississippi, June 1, 1863. Returned to duty in September-October, 1863. Deserted on November 20, 1863. Reported under arrest near Dalton, Georgia, December 31, 1863. Returned to duty on January 11, 1864. Reported present in March-April, 1864. Wounded in the head at Resaca, Georgia, May 14, 1864. Reported absent wounded through August 31, 1864. No further records. Survived the war.

MEADOWS, SAMUEL F., Sergeant

Previously served as Private in Company F of this regiment. Transferred to this company on September 13, 1862. Mustered in as Private. Promoted to Corporal on January 1, 1863. Reported present in November, 1862-April, 1864. Promoted to Sergeant on March 1, 1864. Reported absent sick from May 18 through August 31, 1864. No further records. Survived the war.

MOONEY, GEORGE LARKIN, Private

Previously served as Private in Company A of this regiment. Transferred to this company on August 1, 1862. No further records.

NEAL, J. K., Private

Previously served as Private in Company K of this regiment. Transferred to this company on or about September 13, 1862. Mustered in as Private. Detailed for duty at Saltville, Virginia, on an unspecified date. Rejoined the company on February 1, 1863. Detailed as a wagon master or forage master on or about February 16, 1863. Detailed as a wagon master with the supply train in Mississippi on June 20, 1863. Reported absent on detail through August 31, 1864. Surrendered at Citronelle, Alabama, May 4, 1865. Paroled at Meridian, Mississippi, May 10, 1865. [Presumably he was a member of the 58th Regiment N.C. Troops subsequent to April 9, 1865, the date on which the 58th and 60th Regiments were consolidated.]

NICHOLS, JAMES, Private

Previously served as Private in Company K of this regiment. Transferred to this company on or about September 13, 1862. Reported absent without leave in November, 1862-February, 1863. Returned to duty in May-June, 1863. Reported present in July-October, 1863. Deserted on November 20, 1863. Returned to duty on June 22, 1864, and was wounded at Kolb's Farm, near Marietta, Georgia, the same date. Returned to duty in July-August, 1864. No further records.

PLEMMONS, LEVI J., Private

Previously served as Private in Company E of this regiment. Transferred to this company on or about September 13, 1862. Reported present in November, 1862-June, 1863. Reported absent sick at Griffin, Georgia, from October 10, 1863, through August 31, 1864. Returned to duty with to Company H, 2nd Battalion N.C. Infantry, in November-December, 1864.

PRESLEY, G. W., Sergeant

Born in Buncombe County and was by occupation a farmer prior to enlisting at Murfreesboro, Tennessee, at age 21, October 29, 1862, for the war. Mustered in as Private. Hospitalized at Dalton, Georgia, December 30, 1862, with intermittent fever. Returned to duty on February 2, 1863. Reported present in March-April, 1863. Reported sick in hospital in May-June, 1863. Returned to duty in July-October, 1863. Reported present in November, 1863-February, 1864. Promoted to Sergeant on March 1, 1864. Reported present in March-June, 1864. Captured at or near Smyrna, Georgia, on or about July 3, 1864. Sent to Nashville, Tennessee. Transferred to Louisville, Kentucky, October 13, 1864. Transferred to Camp Chase, Ohio, where he arrived on October 18, 1864. Released at Camp Chase on June 11, 1865, after taking the Oath of Allegiance.

PRESLEY, JAMES M., Private

Previously served as Private in Company K of this regiment. Transferred to this company on or about September 13, 1862. Reported present in November, 1862-April, 1863. Reported absent on detail in Mississippi (probably as a teamster) from June 20, 1863, through August 31, 1864. No further records. Survived the war.

PRESLEY, JASON, Private

Previously served as Private in Company F of this regiment. Transferred to this company on September 13, 1862. Reported present in November-December, 1862. Reported sick in hospital in January-February, 1863. Returned to duty in March-April, 1863. Reported present in May-June, 1863. Reported absent sick at Marietta, Georgia, from September 23, 1863, through February 29, 1864. Returned to duty in March-April, 1864. Reported present in May-August, 1864. Wounded in the right leg and captured at Franklin, Tennessee, November 30, 1864. Right leg amputated. Hospitalized at Nashville, Tennessee, April 4, 1865. Transferred to Louisville, Kentucky, where he arrived on April 7, 1865. Transferred to Camp Chase, Ohio, where he arrived on April 13, 1865. Paroled at Camp Chase on May 2, 1865. Received at Vicksburg, Mississippi, May 12, 1865, for exchange.

PRESLEY, JOHN W., Private

Born in Buncombe County where he resided as a farmer or farm laborer prior to enlisting at Murfreesboro, Tennessee, at age 21, October 29, 1862, for the war. Reported present in November, 1862-April, 1863. Reported sick in hospital in May-June, 1863. Detailed for duty as a hospital nurse at Lauderdale Springs, Mississippi, July 18, 1863. Returned to duty on September 15, 1863. Captured at Missionary Ridge, Tennessee, November 25, 1863. Died in hospital at Chattanooga, Tennessee, December 7 or December 11, 1863, of disease. [May have been wounded in the hip at Chickamauga, Georgia, September 20, 1863.]

PRESLEY, L. S., Private

Enlisted at Dalton, Georgia, February 18, 1864, for the war. Reported present through August 31, 1864. No further records. Survived the war. [Was about 23 years of age at time of enlistment.]

PRESLEY, SADANDA J., Private

Born in Buncombe County where he resided as a farmer or farm laborer prior to enlisting at Murfreesboro, Tennessee, at age 19, October 29, 1862, for the war. Died in camp at Murfreesboro on November 15, 1862. Cause of death not reported.

REVIS, F. H., Private

Previously served as Private in Company F of this regiment. Transferred to this company on September 13, 1862. Reported absent sick in November, 1862-February, 1863. Returned to duty in March-April, 1863. Reported present in May, 1863-June, 1864. Reported absent without leave on August 14, 1864. No further records.

RICE, L. H., Private

Born in Haywood County and was by occupation a farmer prior to enlisting at Greeneville, Tennessee, at age 24, September 19, 1862, for the war. Reported present in November, 1862-April, 1863. Died at Tullahoma, Tennessee, June 1 or June 9, 1863. Cause of death not reported.

ROGERS, FRANCIS M., Private

Previously served as Private in Company C of this regiment. Transferred to this company on August 1, 1862. Reported present in November, 1862-June, 1863. Deserted from camp near La Fayette, Georgia, September 10, 1863.

ROGERS, JESSE J. S., Private

Previously served as Private in Company E of this regiment. Transferred to this company on or about September 13, 1862. Mustered in as Musician (Fifer). Reported absent sick in November, 1862-April, 1863. Reduced to ranks subsequent to April 30, 1863. Discharged at Chattanooga, Tennessee, May 9, 1863, by reason of "injury of hip and general debility."

ROGERS, JONATHAN A., Private

Previously served as Private in Company E of this regiment. Transferred to this company on or about September 13, 1862. Reported absent sick in November, 1862-February, 1863. Returned to duty in March-April, 1863. Reported present in May-June, 1863.

Reported absent sick in July-October, 1863. Furloughed home in November-December, 1863. Failed to return to duty and was dropped from the company rolls on or about December 31, 1863. Survived the war. [North Carolina pension records indicate that he was "slightly wound in thigh" on an unspecified date.]

SEARCY, JOHN D., Private

Previously served as Private in Company K of this regiment. Transferred to this company on or about September 13, 1862. Died in hospital at Tullahoma, Tennessee, February 7, 1863, of disease.

SHIPMAN, SIMON B., Private

Previously served as Private in Company D of this regiment. Transferred to this company on or about September 13, 1862. Deserted from hospital on November 20, 1862. Returned to duty on April 20, 1863. Reported present in May-October, 1863. Captured at Missionary Ridge, Tennessee, November 25, 1863. Sent to Nashville, Tennessee. Transferred to Louisville, Kentucky, where he arrived on December 7, 1863. Transferred to Rock Island, Illinois, where he arrived on December 9, 1863. Died at Rock Island on January 11, 1864. Cause of death not reported.

SHIPMAN, WILLIAM R., JR., Private

Previously served as Private in Company D of this regiment. Transferred to this company on or about September 13, 1862. Reported present in November, 1862-October, 1863. Reported absent sick at Forsyth, Georgia, from December 1, 1863, through February 29, 1864. Returned to duty in March-April, 1864. Reported present in May-June, 1864. Reported absent sick on August 1, 1864. Returned to duty subsequent to August 31, 1864. Transferred to Company E, 58th Regiment N.C. Troops, when the 58th and 60th Regiments were consolidated on April 9, 1865.

SHIPMAN, WILLSON, Private

Previously served as Private in Company D of this regiment. Transferred to this company on or about September 13, 1862. Reported absent sick in November-December, 1862. Deserted on January 5, 1863. Returned to duty on April 23, 1863. Reported absent sick from July 11, 1863, through June 30, 1864. Died at Jackson, Mississippi, of disease. Date of death not reported.

SHOPE, DOCTOR VANCE, 1st Sergeant

Previously served as 1st Sergeant of Company K of this regiment. Transferred to this company on or about September 13, 1862. Hospitalized at Dalton, Georgia, December 30, 1862, with chronic rheumatism. Returned to duty on January 19, 1863. Reported present through June 30, 1864. Sent to hospital at Atlanta, Georgia, August 12, 1864. No further records. Survived the war.

SHOPE, J. MITCHELL, Private

Resided in Buncombe County and was by occupation a farmer prior to enlisting at Tullahoma, Tennessee, at age 38, January 1, 1863, for the war. Reported present in January-June, 1863. Reported absent sick in July-October, 1863. Returned to duty in November-December, 1863. Reported present in January-August, 1864. Hospitalized at Charlotte on February 20, 1865, with rheumatism. Returned to duty on February 26, 1865. No further records.

SHOPE, WILLIAM RILEY, Private

Resided in Buncombe County and was by occupation a farmer prior to enlisting in Buncombe County at age 44, September 14, 1863, for the war. Reported present through February 29, 1864.

Furloughed for twenty-two days on April 19, 1864. Reported present in May-August, 1864. Last reported in the records of this company on October 18, 1864. Survived the war.

SLAGLE, JOHN L. L., Private

Previously served as Private in Company K of this regiment. Transferred to this company on or about September 13, 1862. Reported present in November, 1862-February, 1863. Reported absent on duty as a shoemaker at Atlanta, Georgia, in March, 1863-August, 1864. Rejoined the company on an unspecified date. Transferred to Company E, 58th Regiment N.C. Troops, when the 58th and 60th Regiments were consolidated on April 9, 1865.

SMATHERS, JOHN, Private

Previously served as Private in Company E of this regiment. Transferred to this company on or about September 13, 1862. Reported absent sick in November, 1862-February, 1863. Returned to duty in March-April, 1863. Reported absent sick in May-June, 1863. Returned to duty in July-October, 1863. Deserted on November 20, 1863. Returned from desertion in January-February, 1864, and was court-martialed. Returned to duty prior to March 1, 1864. Captured at or near Nickajack Creek, near Smyrna, Georgia, July 4-5, 1864. Sent to Nashville, Tennessee. Transferred to Louisville, Kentucky, where he arrived on July 14, 1864. Transferred to Camp Douglas, Chicago, Illinois, where he arrived on July 18, 1864. Released at Camp Douglas on June 12, 1865, after taking the Oath of Allegiance.

SMITH, J. FRANK, Corporal

Born in Rutherford County and was by occupation a farmer prior to enlisting at Greeneville, Tennessee, at age 27, October 11, 1862, for the war. Mustered in as Private. Reported present in November, 1862-June, 1863. Promoted to Corporal on June 21, 1863. Deserted from camp near Chattanooga, Tennessee, September 6, 1863. Returned to duty on October 26, 1863, and was reduced to ranks. Reported present in November, 1863-April, 1864. Promoted to Corporal on March 1, 1864. Reported absent sick from May 20 through August 31, 1864. No further records. Survived the war. [North Carolina pension records indicate that he was wounded in the left hand "near Atlanta, Georgia, March 1, 1865."]

SNIDER, HENRY J., Private

Previously served as Private in Company E, 1st Regiment N.C. Infantry (6 months, 1861). Enlisted in this company at Greeneville, Tennessee, September 15, 1862, for the war. Deserted from camp on January 31, 1863. Returned from desertion on an unspecified date. Court-martialed on or about April 7, 1863. Returned to duty on May 2, 1863. Reported present through June 30, 1863. Reported absent sick in July-August, 1863. Wounded in the leg at Chickamauga, Georgia, September 20, 1863. Transferred to Company A of this regiment in November-December, 1863.

SNIDER, MILES, Private

Previously served as Private in Company F of this regiment. Transferred to this company on September 13, 1862. Died in hospital at Murfreesboro, Tennessee, November 9, 1862. Cause of death not reported.

SPIVY, JUNIUS PINKNEY, Private

Previously served as Private in Company E of this regiment. Transferred to this company on or about September 13, 1862. Reported absent sick in November, 1862-February, 1863. Returned to duty in March-April, 1863. Reported present in May-June, 1863.

Deserted from camp near La Fayette, Georgia, September 10, 1863. Died prior to February 14, 1865. Place, date, and cause of death not reported.

STARNES, FRANCIS MARION, Private

Previously served as Private in Company E of this regiment. Transferred to this company on or about September 13, 1862. Died in hospital at Murfreesboro, Tennessee, November 3, 1862, of "pneumonia."

STRINGER, T. J., Private

Enlisted at Tullahoma, Tennessee, February 12, 1863, for the war. Reported sick in hospital in January-February, 1863. Deserted from hospital on March 25, 1863.

VAUGHN, A. B., Private

Previously served as Private in Company K of this regiment. Transferred to this company on or about September 13, 1862. Furloughed from hospital at Knoxville, Tennessee, January 31, 1863. Died at home on February 10, 1863. Cause of death not reported.

WATKINS, HENRY C., Private

Previously served as Private in Company D of this regiment. Transferred to this company on August 1, 1862. Reported present in November-December, 1862. Reported sick in hospital in January-February, 1863. Returned to duty in March-April, 1863. Deserted at Dalton, Georgia, May 25, 1863. Returned to duty on August 10, 1863. Deserted on November 23, 1863. Later served as Corporal in Company C, 7th Regiment Tennessee Mounted Infantry (Union).

WATKINS, ISAAC, Private

Born in Stanly County and was by occupation a farmer prior to enlisting at Murfreesboro, Tennessee, at age 19, October 25, 1862, for the war. Reported absent sick in November-December, 1862. Died in hospital at Chattanooga, Tennessee, or Ringgold, Georgia, February 5, 1863, of disease.

WATKINS, JOEL, Private

Previously served as Private in Company D of this regiment. Transferred to this company on August 1, 1862. Reported absent sick in November, 1862-October, 1863. Rejoined the company on or about December 11, 1863, and was placed under arrest at Dalton, Georgia (probably for absence without leave). Returned to duty in January-February, 1864. Reported present in March-April, 1864. Captured at Resaca, Georgia, May 15, 1864. Sent to Nashville, Tennessee. Transferred to Louisville, Kentucky, where he arrived on May 21, 1864. Transferred to Alton, Illinois, where he arrived on May 25, 1864. Died at Alton on February 20, 1865, of "pneumonia."

WATKINS, JOHN S., Private

Previously served as Private in Company D of this regiment. Transferred to this company on August 1, 1862. Died in hospital at Murfreesboro, Tennessee, November 18, 1862. Cause of death not reported.

WATKINS, WILLIAM, Private

Previously served as Private in Company D of this regiment. Transferred to this company on August 1, 1862. Reported absent sick in November-December, 1862. Died in hospital on January 8, 1863. Place and cause of death not reported.

WEBB, JAMES ALEXANDER, Private

Previously served as Sergeant in Company K of this regiment. Transferred to this company on or about September 13, 1862. Mustered in as Sergeant. Reduced to ranks on November 1, 1862. Hospitalized at Dalton, Georgia, December 31, 1862, with intermittent fever. Returned to duty on January 19, 1863. Reported present through April 30, 1863. Reported sick in hospital or absent on detail in May-June, 1863. Returned to duty in July-October, 1863. Reported present in November, 1863-February, 1864. Reported on detail as brigade wagon master in March-June, 1864. Rejoined the company in July-August, 1864. Captured at McDonough, Georgia, September 4, 1864. Sent to Nashville, Tennessee. Transferred to Louisville, Kentucky, October 27, 1864. Transferred to Camp Douglas, Chicago, Illinois, where he arrived on November 1, 1864. Paroled at Camp Douglas and transferred on February 21, 1865, for exchange. Exchanged on an unspecified date. Hospitalized at Richmond, Virginia, February 28, 1865. Furloughed for thirty days on March 3, 1865. No further records. Survived the war.

WELLS, MARCUS B., Private

Previously served as Private in Company E of this regiment. Transferred to this company on or about September 13, 1862. Deserted from camp on November 23, 1862. Returned to duty on January 8, 1863. Reported in hospital on February 28, 1863. Deserted from camp near Tullahoma, Tennessee, April 15, 1863.

WELLS, S. F., Private

Previously served as Private in Company E of this regiment. Transferred to this company on or about September 13, 1862. Died in hospital at Murfreesboro, Tennessee, November 8, 1862. Cause of death not reported.

WILSON, SAMUEL M., Private

Previously served as Private in Company F of this regiment. Transferred to this company on September 13, 1862. Mustered in as Corporal. Wounded in the thigh at Murfreesboro, Tennessee, December 31, 1862. Captured at Murfreesboro on or about January 5, 1863. Sent to Louisville, Kentucky. Paroled at Louisville on April 4, 1863. Received at City Point, Virginia, April 11, 1863, for exchange. Hospitalized on the same date with remittent fever. Transferred to hospital at Farmville, Virginia, where he was admitted on May 8, 1863, with debilitas. Returned to duty on June 2, 1863. Reduced to ranks on June 21, 1863. Captured at Chickamauga, Georgia, September 20, 1863. Sent to Nashville, Tennessee. Transferred to Louisville, Kentucky, where he arrived on October 5, 1863. Transferred to Camp Douglas, Chicago, Illinois, October 7, 1863. Released at Camp Douglas on June 16, 1865, after taking the Oath of Allegiance.

WRIGHT, JOHN W., Private

Previously served as Private in Company F of this regiment. Transferred to this company on September 13, 1862. Reported present in November-December, 1862. Hospitalized at Dalton, Georgia, January 30, 1863, with chronic rheumatism. Returned to duty on February 4, 1863. Reported present in March-April, 1863. Reported sick in hospital in May-June, 1863. Captured at Chickamauga, Georgia, September 20, 1863. Sent to Nashville, Tennessee. Transferred to Louisville, Kentucky, where he arrived on September 30, 1863. Transferred to Camp Douglas, Chicago, Illinois, where he arrived on October 4, 1863. Released at Camp Douglas on March 26, 1865, after taking the Oath of Allegiance and joining the U.S. Army. Assigned to Company F, 6th Regiment U.S. Volunteer Infantry.

COMPANY K

This company was raised in Buncombe County on May 15, 1862. It was mustered into state service (presumably on or about the same date) as "Fifth Company," McDowell's Battalion N.C. Infantry (known also as the 6th Battalion N.C. Infantry). The seven-company battalion was mustered into Confederate service on August 1, 1862, and redesignated the 1st Battalion N.C. Infantry. This company was designated Company B. On October 8, 1862, the 60th Regiment N.C. Troops was formally organized after three additional companies were assigned to the 1st Battalion. This company was designated Company K. After joining the regiment the company functioned as a part of the regiment, and its history for the remainder of the war is reported as a part of the regimental history.

The following roster was compiled primarily from information in the microfilm edition of the Compiled Service Records of Soldiers Who Served in Organizations from the State of North Carolina (Record Group 109, M270), National Archives and Records Administration, Washington, D.C. Record Group 109 includes enlistment papers, pay vouchers, requisitions, letters of resignation, discharge certificates, and abstracts of medical and prisoner of war returns. Materials relating specifically to this company include a muster-in and descriptive roll dated August 1, 1862, and muster rolls dated November, 1862-August, 1864.

Also utilized in this roster were *The War of the Rebellion: A Compilation of the Official Records of the Union and Confederate Armies*, the North Carolina adjutant general's *Roll of Honor*, state militia records, newspaper casualty lists and obituaries, wartime claims for bounty pay and allowances, postwar registers of claims for artificial limbs, Confederate pension applications filed with the states of North Carolina, Tennessee, and Florida, Confederate Soldiers' Home records, and the 1860 and 1870 federal censuses of North Carolina. A search was made also for relevant letters, diaries, reminiscences, and other manuscripts in the Southern Historical Collection (University of North Carolina-Chapel Hill), the Duke University Library Special Collections Department, and the North Carolina Division of Archives and History.

Among the secondary sources consulted were records of the North Carolina division of the United Daughters of the Confederacy, postwar rosters, regimental and county histories, marriage bond, will, and cemetery indexes, published and unpublished genealogies, biographical dictionaries, the North Carolina *County Heritage Book* series, the *Confederate Veteran*, Walter Clark's *Histories of the Several Regiments and Battalions from North Carolina in the Great War, 1861-'65*, and the North Carolina volume of the extended edition of *Confederate Military History*.

OFFICERS

CAPTAINS

WEST, WILLIAM RILEY

Born on July 5, 1823. Enlisted in Buncombe County at age 38. Elected Captain on May 15, 1862. Resigned on February 11, 1863, by reason of "advanced age" and because "my family absolutely requires my services at home." Resignation accepted on March 2, 1863.

CLAYTON, EDWIN M.

Previously served as Adjutant (1st Lieutenant) of this regiment. Appointed Captain of this company on May 4, 1863. Reported present or accounted for through December 31, 1863. Reported on duty as acting Assistant Quartermaster of the regiment in January-February, 1864. Rejoined this company in March-April, 1864. Wounded at Resaca, Georgia, May 15, 1864. Returned to duty on or about August 8, 1864, and was appointed acting Brigade Commissary of Reynolds's Brigade. Transferred to Company C, 58th Regiment N.C. Troops, when the 58th and 60th Regiments were consolidated on April 9, 1865.

TOMS, MARION C.

Served as Captain of Company A of this regiment. Reported on duty as acting Captain of this company in January-February, 1864.

LIEUTENANTS

BAIRD, JAMES SAMUEL TASEWELL, 3rd Lieutenant

Previously served as Private in Company G, 9th Regiment N.C. Troops (1st Regiment N.C. Cavalry). Appointed 3rd Lieutenant of this company on May 15, 1862. Resigned on January 3, 1863. Reason he resigned not reported. Resignation accepted on or about February 18, 1863. Later served as a member of the medical examining board of the 10th Congressional District of North Carolina.

SALES, JOHN T., 1st Lieutenant

Previously served as Private in Company E, 1st Regiment N.C. Infantry (6 months, 1861). Elected 2nd Lieutenant of this company on May 15, 1862. Reported in command of the company in November, 1862-February, 1863. Hospitalized at Dalton, Georgia, December 30, 1862, with remittent fever. Returned to duty on or about January 3, 1863. Reported present in March, 1863-April, 1864. Wounded at Kolb's Farm, near Marietta, Georgia, June 22, 1864. Returned to duty prior to June 30, 1864. Promoted to 1st Lieutenant subsequent to August 31, 1864. Transferred to Company C, 58th Regiment N.C. Troops, when the 58th and 60th Regiments were consolidated on April 9, 1865. [Was reported in command of Company G of this regiment in January-February, 1864.]

SHACKELFORD, PLEASANT CALVIN, 3rd Lieutenant

Born in Tennessee and resided in Buncombe County where he was by occupation a brickmason prior to enlisting in Buncombe County at age 29, May 15, 1862, for the war. Mustered in as Private. Promoted to Corporal subsequent to July 31, 1862. Hospitalized at Dalton, Georgia, December 31, 1862, with debilitas. Subsequently contracted typhoid fever. Returned to duty on March 12, 1863. Promoted to Sergeant on May 1, 1863. Reported present in May-October, 1863. Reported absent on furlough in November-December, 1863. Promoted to 1st Sergeant on an unspecified date. Elected 3rd Lieutenant on December 27, 1863. Returned to duty in January-February, 1864. Reported present in May-August, 1864. No further records.

WEST, ALEXANDER, 1st Lieutenant

Born on April 16, 1830. Resided in Buncombe County and was by occupation a farm laborer prior to enlisting in Buncombe County at age 32. Elected 1st Lieutenant on May 15, 1862. Reported present in March-June, 1863. Was reported in command of the company in July-October, 1863. Reported present in November-December, 1863. Reported absent sick without leave in January-February, 1864. Listed as a deserter on April 7, 1864. Returned to duty prior to May 1, 1864. Reported in command of the company in May-August, 1864. Wounded at Kolb's Farm, near Marietta, Georgia, June 22, 1864. Returned to duty prior to June 30, 1864. Reported present in July-August, 1864. Captured at La Vergne,

Tennessee, December 8, 1864. Sent to Nashville, Tennessee. Transferred to Louisville, Kentucky, where he arrived on January 2, 1865. Transferred to Fort Delaware, Delaware, where he arrived on January 16, 1865. Released at Fort Delaware on June 17, 1865, after taking the Oath of Allegiance. [Previously served as 2nd Lieutenant in the 108th Regiment N.C. Militia.]

WHITE, WILLIAM T., 3rd Lieutenant

Born in South Carolina and resided in Buncombe County where he was by occupation a brickmason prior to enlisting in Buncombe County at age 33, May 15, 1862, for the war. Mustered in as Private. Reported present in November, 1862-June, 1863. Appointed 3rd Lieutenant on March 6, 1863. Wounded in the leg at Chickamauga, Georgia, September 20, 1863. Leg amputated. Died at Alexander's Bridge on October 13, 1863, of wounds. "A braver and truer man never lived." [*Asheville News*, October 22, 1863. May have been wounded at Murfreesboro, Tennessee, December 31, 1862-January 2, 1863.]

NONCOMMISSIONED OFFICERS AND PRIVATES

ALEXANDER, ALBERTUS NEWTON, Private

Previously served as Private in Company E, 1st Regiment N.C. Infantry (6 months, 1861). Enlisted in this company on or about May 15, 1862, for the war. Last reported in the records of this company on December 22, 1862. Later served as Private in Company C, 69th Regiment N.C. Troops (7th Regiment N.C. Cavalry). [Born on December 20, 1835. Contrary to 3:25 of this series, the correct spelling of his first name was probably Albertus rather than Albertes.]

ALEXANDER, BENJAMIN JULIUS, Private

Born in Buncombe County on January 10, 1831. Resided in Buncombe County and was by occupation a merchant or farmer prior to enlisting in Buncombe County at age 31, May 15, 1862, for the war. Transferred to Company I of this regiment on or about September 13, 1862.

ALEXANDER, GEORGE N., Private

Previously served as Private in Company E, 1st Regiment N.C. Infantry (6 months, 1861). Enlisted in this company in Buncombe County on May 15, 1862, for the war. Transferred to Company I of this regiment on or about September 13, 1862.

ALEXANDER, JAMES M., Sergeant

Previously served as Private in Company F, 14th Regiment N.C. Troops (4th Regiment N.C. Volunteers). Transferred to this company on or about September 25, 1862. Mustered in as Private. Reported present in November, 1862-June, 1863. Reported absent sick in July-October, 1863. Returned to duty in November-December, 1863. Reported present in January-February, 1864. Promoted to Sergeant on February 1, 1864. Furloughed for forty days on April 22, 1864. Reported present in May-June, 1864. Reported present but on daily duty from July 20 through August 31, 1864. Reported in hospital at Columbus, Georgia, in October, 1864. Paroled at Salisbury on May 1, 1865.

ALEXANDER, PHILETUS B., Sergeant

Enlisted in Buncombe County on May 15, 1862, for the war. Mustered in as Private. Reported sick in hospital in November-

December, 1862. Returned to duty in January-February, 1863. Reported present in March-June, 1863. Reported absent sick in July-October, 1863. Returned to duty in November-December, 1863. Promoted to Sergeant on February 1, 1864. Reported present in January-August, 1864. No further records.

ALEXANDER, ROBERT W., Private

Enlisted in Buncombe County on May 15, 1862, for the war. Wounded in the thigh and captured at Murfreesboro, Tennessee, December 31, 1862. Died in hospital at Murfreesboro on January 19, 1863, of wounds. Was 34 years of age at the time of his death.

ALEXANDER, THOMAS F., Private

Born in Buncombe County where he resided as a farmer prior to enlisting in Buncombe County at age 34, May 15, 1862, for the war. Transferred to Company I of this regiment on or about September 13, 1862.

ALEXANDER, WILLIAM R., 1st Sergeant

Previously served as Private in Company C, 1st Regiment N.C. Infantry (6 months, 1861). Enlisted in this company in Buncombe County on May 15, 1862, for the war. Mustered in as 1st Sergeant. Elected 1st Lieutenant of Company I of this regiment on September 13, 1862, and transferred.

ALEXANDER, WILLIAM S., Private

Born in Buncombe County and was by occupation a farmer prior to enlisting in Buncombe County at age 23, May 15, 1862, for the war. Transferred to Company I of this regiment on or about September 13, 1862.

ALLISON, BENJAMIN POSEY, Private

Enlisted in Buncombe County at age 27, May 15, 1862, for the war. Deserted on an unspecified date (probably prior to March 1, 1863). Returned to duty on February 22, 1864. Court-martialed for desertion but was granted a pardon. Reported present in March-June, 1864. Sent to hospital sick on August 28, 1864. No further records. Survived the war.

ALLISON, J. E., Private

Enlisted in Buncombe County on September 14, 1863, for the war. Deserted on November 29, 1863. [May have served previously as Private in Company E, 1st Regiment N.C. Infantry (6 months, 1861). May have served later as Private in Company C, 65th Regiment N.C. Troops (6th Regiment N.C. Cavalry).]

ALLISON, JAMES, Private

Enlisted in Buncombe County on May 15, 1862, for the war. Hospitalized at Dalton, Georgia, December 31, 1862, with acute diarrhoea. Returned to duty on January 31, 1863. Died in hospital at Ringgold, Georgia, March 10, 1863, of disease.

ALLISON, JONATHAN, Private

Enlisted in Buncombe County on May 15, 1862, for the war. Wounded slightly in the hip at Murfreesboro, Tennessee, January 2, 1863. Returned to duty in March-April, 1863. Reported absent in hospital in May-June, 1863. Died at Cherokee Springs, Georgia, June 5, 1863. Cause of death not reported.

ALLISON, RICHARD, Private

Enlisted in Buncombe County on May 15, 1862, for the war. Reported sick in hospital in November-December, 1862. Hospital-

ized at Dalton, Georgia, February 12, 1863, with typhoid fever. Returned to duty on February 23, 1863. Died in hospital at Tullahoma, Tennessee, April 17, 1863. Cause of death not reported.

BAIRD, JAMES B., Private

Born in Buncombe County where he resided as a farmer prior to enlisting in Buncombe County at age 19, May 15, 1862, for the war. Transferred to Company I of this regiment on or about September 13, 1862.

BAKER, W. R., Private

Enlisted in Buncombe County on November 24, 1863, for the war. Deserted near Dallas, Georgia, December 20, 1863.

BALLEW, FRANCIS M., Private

Resided in Buncombe County and was by occupation a renter prior to enlisting in Buncombe County at age 32, May 15, 1862, for the war. Died in hospital at Chattanooga, Tennessee, January 16, 1863. Cause of death not reported.

BARTLETT, JAMES H., Corporal

Born in Buncombe County where he resided as a farmer prior to enlisting in Buncombe County at age 23, May 15, 1862, for the war. Mustered in as Corporal. Transferred to Company I of this regiment on or about September 13, 1862.

BARTLETT, JOHN H., Private

Resided in Buncombe County and was by occupation a farm laborer prior to enlisting in Buncombe County at age 29, May 15, 1862, for the war. Hospitalized at Dalton, Georgia, December 31, 1862, with cystitis. Returned to duty on January 22, 1863. Reported sick in hospital in March-April, 1863. Died at Cherokee Springs, Georgia, June 15, 1863, of disease.

BARTLETT, WILLIAM R., Private

Enlisted in Buncombe County on May 15, 1862, for the war. Wounded in the back, knee, and/or hip at Murfreesboro, Tennessee, December 31, 1862. Hospitalized at Dalton, Georgia. Returned to duty on or about January 22, 1863. Reported present through June 30, 1863. Reported absent sick in July, 1863-August, 1864. No further records. Survived the war. [Was about 32 years of age at time of enlistment.]

BIRD, ALBERT LYTLE, Private

Born on April 11, 1837. Enlisted in Buncombe County at age 25, May 15, 1862, for the war. Wounded in the left arm at Murfreesboro, Tennessee, January 2, 1863. Reported absent wounded and disabled through August 31, 1864. No further records. Survived the war.

BIRD, J. W., Private

Enlisted in Burke County on October 6, 1863, for the war. Reported present in July-October, 1863. Sent to hospital at Dalton, Georgia, November 22, 1863. Reported absent sick (whereabouts unknown) through August 31, 1864. No further records. Survived the war. [Was about 25 years of age at time of enlistment.]

BIRD, THOMAS J., ———

Resided in Buncombe County and was by occupation a farmer. Place and date of enlistment not reported (probably enlisted on or about May 15, 1862). No further records. Survived the war. [Was about 33 years of age at time of enlistment. May have served later as Private in Company K, 11th Regiment N.C. Troops (1st Regiment N.C. Volunteers).]

BRADLEY, GEORGE WILLIS, Private

Resided in McDowell County and enlisted in Buncombe County on May 15, 1862, for the war. Reported sick in hospital in November, 1862-June, 1863. Failed to return to duty and was listed as a deserter on August 23, 1863. [Was about 20 years of age at time of enlistment. North Carolina pension records indicate that he was wounded slightly in the hand at Murfreesboro, Tennessee, "December 24, 1862." May have served later as Private in Companies B and H, 2nd Regiment N.C. Mounted Infantry (Union).]

BRADLEY, HAMPTON, Corporal

Resided in McDowell County and was by occupation a laborer prior to enlisting in Buncombe County at age 30, May 15, 1862, for the war. Mustered in as Private. Reported sick in hospital in November-December, 1862. Reported present in January-June, 1863. Promoted to Corporal on May 1, 1863. Deserted near Chattanooga, Tennessee, September 8, 1863.

BRIGHT, R. W., Private

Born in McDowell County* and was by occupation a farmer prior to enlisting at Camp McDowell at age 32, May 15, 1862, for the war. Transferred to Company I of this regiment on or about September 13, 1862.

BROWN, GEORGE W., Private

Born in Wilkes County where he resided as a farmer prior to enlisting in Wake County at age 36, October 17, 1863, for the war. Captured at Missionary Ridge, Tennessee, November 25, 1863. Sent to Nashville, Tennessee. Transferred to Louisville, Kentucky, where he arrived on December 7, 1863. Transferred to Rock Island, Illinois, January 27, 1864. Released at Rock Island on October 6, 1864, after joining the U.S. Army. Assigned to Company B, 2nd Regiment U.S. Volunteer Infantry.

BRYSON, J. W., ———

North Carolina pension records indicate that he served in this company.

BURNETT, DANIEL, Private

Resided in Buncombe County and was by occupation a day laborer prior to enlisting in Buncombe County at age 24, May 15, 1862, for the war. Reported present in November, 1862-June, 1863. Deserted on an unspecified date. Returned from desertion on October 20, 1863. Reported on detached service as a teamster in East Tennessee in November, 1863-February, 1864. Rejoined the company on an unspecified date. Reported present in March-August, 1864. Transferred to Company C, 58th Regiment N.C. Troops, when the 58th and 60th Regiments were consolidated on April 9, 1865.

BURNETT, WILLIAM H., Private

Born in McDowell County* and resided in Buncombe County where he was by occupation a farmer prior to enlisting in Buncombe County at age 33, May 15, 1862, for the war. Hospitalized at Dalton, Georgia, December 31, 1862, with dyspepsia. Returned to duty on January 13, 1863. Sent to hospital at Tullahoma, Tennessee, April 10, 1863. Reported absent sick until February 15, 1864, when he was reported absent without leave. Dropped from the company rolls on or about August 31, 1864.

CANNON, HENRY C., Private

Born in South Carolina or Buncombe County and resided in Buncombe County where he was by occupation a farmer prior to enlisting in Buncombe County at age 18, May 15, 1862, for the war. Transferred to Company I of this regiment on or about September 13, 1862.

CANNON, JAMES H., Private

Born in Buncombe County where he resided as a farmer or day laborer prior to enlisting in Buncombe County at age 22, May 15, 1862, for the war. Transferred to Company I of this regiment on or about September 13, 1862.

CAUBLE, ADAM L., Private

Enlisted in Buncombe County at age 18, April 1, 1864, for the war. Reported present in May-June, 1864. Sent to hospital sick on July 15, 1864. Reported absent sick through August 31, 1864. Returned to duty on an unspecified date. Wounded in the left hip at Bentonville on March 19, 1865. Paroled at Asheville on May 11, 1865.

CAUBLE, DANIEL WEBSTER, Private

Enlisted in Buncombe County at age 19, May 15, 1862, for the war. Reported present in November-December, 1862. Reported sick in hospital in January-February, 1863. Returned to duty on an unspecified date. Reported present in March, 1863-August, 1864. Transferred to Company C, 58th Regiment N.C. Troops, when the 58th and 60th Regiments were consolidated on April 9, 1865.

CHAMBERS, ROBERT C., Private

Enlisted in Burke County on September 24, 1863, for the war. Reported sick in hospital in November-December, 1863. Reported absent sick at Dalton, Georgia, January 7, 1864. Returned to duty in March-April, 1864. Reported present in May-August, 1864. Reported in hospital at Montgomery, Alabama, November 10, 1864. Reported in hospital at West Point, Mississippi, January 13, 1865, with rheumatism. No further records.

CLARK, GEORGE H., Private

Born in Buncombe County where he resided prior to enlisting in Buncombe County at age 19, May 15, 1862, for the war. Hospitalized at Dalton, Georgia, December 30, 1862, with intermittent fever. Returned to duty on February 2, 1863. Died in hospital at Catoosa Springs, Georgia, on or about April 18, 1863. Cause of death not reported.

CLARK, JOHN A., Private

Born in Haywood County and was by occupation a farmer prior to enlisting in Buncombe County at age 30, May 15, 1862, for the war. Reported present in November-December, 1862. Reported sick in hospital in January-February, 1863. Died in hospital at Ringgold, Georgia, on or about March 14, 1863. Cause of death not reported. [May have been wounded at Murfreesboro, Tennessee, December 31, 1862-January 2, 1863.]

CLARK, JOHN W., Private

Enlisted in Buncombe County on May 15, 1862, for the war. Reported present in November-December, 1862. Wounded slightly in the back at Murfreesboro, Tennessee, January 2, 1863. Returned to duty prior to March 1, 1863. Reported present through February 29, 1864. Furloughed for twenty days on April 4, 1864. Sent to hospital sick on June 12, 1864. Reported absent sick through

August 31, 1864. No further records. Survived the war. [Was about 31 years of age at time of enlistment. North Carolina pension records indicate that he was wounded in the abdomen and disabled at Kennesaw Mountain, Georgia, June 2, 1864.]

CLARK, W. H., Corporal

Born in Buncombe County and was by occupation a farmer prior to enlisting in Buncombe County at age 21, May 15, 1862, for the war. Mustered in as Private. Promoted to Corporal on an unspecified date. Transferred to Company I of this regiment on or about September 13, 1862.

CLEMMONS, ROBERT, Private

Resided in McDowell County and was by occupation a farmer prior to enlisting in Buncombe County at age 31, May 15, 1862, for the war. Died in hospital on January 17, 1863, of disease. Place of death not reported.

COGGINS, CASWELL M., Corporal

Enlisted in Buncombe County on May 15, 1862, for the war. Mustered in as Private. Promoted to Corporal in August, 1862. Reported present in November, 1862-June, 1863. Reported absent sick in July-October, 1863. Reported absent on furlough in November-December, 1863. Reported absent without leave on February 15, 1864 ("he is at home in western N. C. in enemies country sick [and] has no opportunity to report"). Listed as a deserter on April 7, 1864. [May have served previously as Private in Company E, 1st Regiment N.C. Infantry (6 months, 1861).]

COGGINS, JOHN WESLEY, Sergeant

Previously served as Private in Company E, 1st Regiment N.C. Infantry (6 months, 1861). Enlisted in this company in Buncombe County on May 15, 1862, for the war. Mustered in as Sergeant. Discharged on or about January 26, 1863, by reason of "dislocated hip of long standing."

COPELAND, JOSEPH P., Private

Born in McDowell County* and was by occupation a farmer prior to enlisting in Buncombe County at age 26, May 15, 1862, for the war. Transferred to Company I of this regiment on or about September 13, 1862.

CORDELL, ALSY, Private

Resided in Buncombe County where he enlisted at age 18, May 15, 1862, for the war. Hospitalized at Dalton, Georgia, December 31, 1862, with rubeola. Returned to duty on January 19, 1863. Reported present in March-June, 1863. Wounded in the back and/or hip at Chickamauga, Georgia, September 20, 1863. Returned to duty prior to October 31, 1863. Reported present through April 30, 1864. Reported sick in hospital from May 12 through August 31, 1864. No further records. Survived the war. [North Carolina pension records indicate that he was wounded at Chickamauga "by a tree falling that had been shot off by a cannon."]

COWAN, JAMES STEWART, Private

Born on May 12, 1831. Resided in Buncombe County and was by occupation a farmer prior to enlisting in Buncombe County at age 31, May 15, 1862, for the war. Deserted on December 30, 1862. Returned from desertion on April 28, 1863. Reported present in May-June, 1863. Deserted at Chattanooga, Tennessee, September 8, 1863.

CRAIG, JAMES T. B., Private

Enlisted in Buncombe County on May 15, 1862, for the war. Reported absent sick in November-December, 1862. Captured at Murfreesboro, Tennessee, on or about December 31, 1862-January 2, 1863. Sent to Nashville, Tennessee, where he died in hospital on March 16, 1863, of "pneumonia." Was 19 years of age at the time of his death.

CREASEMAN, WILLIAM, Private

Resided in Buncombe County and was by occupation a farmer prior to enlisting in Buncombe County at age 31, May 15, 1862, for the war. Reported sick in hospital in November-December, 1862. Returned to duty in January-February, 1863. Reported present in March-June, 1863. Wounded in the left leg at Chickamauga, Georgia, on or about September 20, 1863. Reported absent wounded through August 31, 1864. No further records. Survived the war.

CREASMAN, THOMAS P., Private

Born in Buncombe County where he resided prior to enlisting in Buncombe County at age 24, May 15, 1862, for the war. Transferred to Company I of this regiment on or about September 13, 1862.

CURRY, JAMES W., Private

Enlisted in Buncombe County on May 15, 1862, for the war. Hospitalized at Dalton, Georgia, December 31, 1862, with typhoid fever. Returned to duty on February 9, 1863. Died in hospital at Ringgold, Georgia, March 21 or March 31, 1863. Cause of death not reported.

DEBOARD, JOHN W., Private

Resided in Buncombe County where he enlisted at age 24, May 15, 1862, for the war. Hospitalized at Dalton, Georgia, December 31, 1862, with chronic diarrhoea. Furloughed for thirty days on May 11, 1863. Returned to duty in July-October, 1863. Reported sick in hospital in November-December, 1863. Reported absent sick at Dalton on February 1, 1864. Returned to duty in March-April, 1864. Reported present in May-June, 1864. Sent to hospital sick on August 20, 1864. Died in hospital at Augusta, Georgia, on or about September 8, 1864. Cause of death not reported.

DOTSON, J. G., Private

Enlisted in Buncombe County on May 15, 1862, for the war. Reported on duty as a teamster from November 12, 1862, through April 30, 1863. Rejoined the company in May-June, 1863. Deserted near Chattanooga, Tennessee, September 8, 1863.

EDMONDSON, W. R., Sergeant

Resided in Buncombe County and was by occupation a farm laborer prior to enlisting in Buncombe County at age 26, May 15, 1862, for the war. Mustered in as Private. Promoted to Sergeant in July-December, 1862. Reported present in November, 1862-April, 1863. Reported sick in hospital in May-June, 1863. Hospitalized at Lauderdale Springs, Mississippi, September 4, 1863. Died in hospital at Lauderdale Springs on October 21, 1863. Cause of death not reported.

FREEMAN, F. M., Private

Resided in Buncombe County and was by occupation a farmer prior to enlisting in Buncombe County at age 44, May 15, 1862, for the war. Reported sick at home in November-December, 1862. Reported sick at home without leave in January-February, 1863.

Reported sick in hospital in March-April, 1863. Furloughed on an unspecified date. Failed to return to duty and was listed as a deserter on May 1, 1863.

FREEMAN, GEORGE W., Corporal

Born in Anson County and was by occupation a farmer prior to enlisting in Buncombe County at age 16, May 15, 1862, for the war. Mustered in as Private. Reported present in November, 1862-April, 1863. Reported absent on detail as a wagoner and ambulance driver in May-October, 1863. Rejoined the company in November-December, 1863. Reported present in January-April, 1864. Promoted to Corporal on February 1, 1864. Wounded at Kolb's Farm, near Marietta, Georgia, June 22, 1864. Died in hospital at Marietta or at Atlanta, Georgia, June 27-28, 1864, presumably of wounds. Buried in Oakland Cemetery, Atlanta.

GILLIAM, A. W., ———

Place and date of enlistment not reported (probably enlisted on or about May 15, 1862). No further records.

GLASS, EPHRAIM, Private

Resided in Buncombe County where he enlisted at age 23, May 15, 1862, for the war. Wounded in the foot and captured at Murfreesboro, Tennessee, December 31, 1862. Died in hospital at Murfreesboro in February, 1863, presumably of wounds.

GLASS, JOSEPH A., Private

Resided in Buncombe County where he enlisted at age 18, May 15, 1862, for the war. Reported absent sick in November-December, 1862. Reported absent sick without leave in January-February, 1863. No further records. Survived the war.

GOODSON, LARKIN, Private

Resided in Buncombe County and was by occupation a farm laborer prior to enlisting in Buncombe County at age 38, May 15, 1862, for the war. Died in hospital at Tullahoma, Tennessee, February 6, 1863. Cause of death not reported.

GOODSON, WESLEY, Private

Resided in Buncombe County and was by occupation a farm laborer prior to enlisting in Buncombe County at age 30, May 15, 1862, for the war. Mustered in as Corporal. Promoted to Sergeant prior to December 31, 1862, when he was hospitalized at Dalton, Georgia, with debilitas. Returned to duty on January 22, 1863. Reported present in March-June, 1863. Deserted on October 8, 1863. Returned to duty on October 20, 1863. Reduced to ranks on October 30, 1863. Reported present in November, 1863-February, 1864. Furloughed for thirty days on April 5, 1864. Returned to duty subsequent to June 30, 1864. Sent to hospital sick on August 28, 1864. No further records.

GOODSON, WILLIAM, ———

Resided in Buncombe County and was by occupation a day laborer. Place and date of enlistment not reported (probably enlisted on or about May 15, 1862). No further records. [Was about 33 years of age at time of enlistment.]

GOSSETT, M. C., Private

Born in Tennessee and resided in Buncombe County where he was by occupation a farmer prior to enlisting in Buncombe County at age 29, May 15, 1862, for the war. Captured at Murfreesboro, Tennessee, January 2, 1863. No further records.

GRAGG, AVERY, Private

Enlisted in Buncombe County on May 15, 1862, for the war. Reported absent sick in November-December, 1862. Reported absent sick without leave in January-February, 1863. Reported sick in hospital in March-April, 1863. Returned to duty in May-June, 1863. Reported absent sick in July-October, 1863. Died in Buncombe County on December 7, 1863. Cause of death not reported.

GRAGG, WILLIAM A., Private

Enlisted in Buncombe County on May 15, 1862, for the war. Reported present in November, 1862-December, 1863. Reported absent sick at Dalton, Georgia, February 25, 1864. Returned to duty in May-June, 1864. Reported present in July-August, 1864. No further records. Survived the war. [Was about 32 years of age at time of enlistment.]

HALL, MOSES, Private

Resided in McDowell County and enlisted in Buncombe County on May 15, 1862, for the war. Wounded slightly in the head at Murfreesboro, Tennessee, December 31, 1862. Returned to duty in January-February, 1863. Reported present in March-June, 1863. Wounded in the left hand at Jackson, Mississippi, on or about July 12, 1863. Left hand amputated. Hospitalized at Lauderdale Springs, Mississippi. Reported absent wounded through August 31, 1864. No further records. Survived the war. [Was about 29 years of age at time of enlistment.]

HAMBY, LEANDER S., Sergeant

Born in Buncombe County where he resided as a farmer prior to enlisting in Buncombe County at age 24, May 15, 1862, for the war. Mustered in as Private. Promoted to Sergeant on September 1, 1862. Transferred to Company I of this regiment on or about September 13, 1862.

HARDEN, DANIEL, Private

Born in Ireland and resided in McDowell County where he was by occupation a laborer prior to enlisting in Buncombe County at age 30, May 15, 1862, for the war. Reported present in November, 1862-June, 1863. Deserted near Chattanooga, Tennessee, September 8, 1863.

HILL, D. F., Private

Enlisted in Buncombe County on May 15, 1862, for the war. Died in hospital at Chattanooga, Tennessee, on or about January 19, 1863. Cause of death not reported.

HOLYFIELD, GEORGE M., Private

Born in Buncombe County and was by occupation a farmer prior to enlisting in Buncombe County at age 28, May 15, 1862, for the war. Transferred to Company I of this regiment on or about September 13, 1862.

HUGHES, ROBERT Y., Private

Born in South Carolina and resided in Buncombe County where he was by occupation a farmer. Place and date of enlistment not reported (probably enlisted on or about May 15, 1862). No further records. Survived the war. [Was about 25 years of age at time of enlistment.]

HUGHES, WARREN C., Private

Enlisted in Buncombe County on May 15, 1862, for the war. Deserted on an unspecified date. Returned from desertion on January

5, 1863. Died in hospital at Tullahoma, Tennessee, April 11, 1863, of "typhoid fever."

INGLE, J. H., Private

Enlisted in Buncombe County on January 12, 1864, for the war. Reported present through April 30, 1864. Wounded at Kolb's Farm, near Marietta, Georgia, June 22, 1864. Died in hospital at Atlanta, Georgia, June 30, 1864, of wounds.

JONES, F. J., Private

Enlisted in Buncombe County on May 15, 1862, for the war. Reported sick in hospital in November-December, 1862. Reported absent on detached service in January-April, 1863 (served as a cook in hospital at Tullahoma, Tennessee, in March, 1863). Reported on duty as a hospital nurse in May-June, 1863. Deserted near Chattanooga, Tennessee, September 8, 1863.

JONES, JOSIAH M., Corporal

Born in Buncombe County where he resided as a farmer prior to enlisting in Buncombe County at age 28, May 15, 1862, for the war. Mustered in as Corporal. Appointed 2nd Lieutenant of Company I of this regiment on September 13, 1862, and transferred. [May have served previously as Adjutant of the 109th Regiment N.C. Militia.]

JONES, L. W., Private

Was by occupation a farmer prior to enlisting at Camp Smith (Madison County) at age 30, August 27, 1862, for the war. Transferred to Company I of this regiment on or about September 13, 1862.

JONES, LOUIS A., Private

Resided in Buncombe County and was by occupation a farmer. Place and date of enlistment not reported (probably enlisted on or about May 15, 1862). Died at Greeneville, Tennessee, September 17, 1862. Cause of death not reported. [Was about 27 years of age at time of enlistment.]

KILLIAN, CHARLES M., Private

Resided in Buncombe County and was by occupation a farm laborer prior to enlisting in Buncombe County at age 18, May 15, 1862, for the war. Reported absent sick from November, 1862, through December, 1863. Reported absent without leave on February 25, 1864. Listed as a deserter on April 7, 1864. Returned from desertion and was sent to hospital at Dalton, Georgia, April 29, 1864. Returned to duty in May-June, 1864. Reported present in July-August, 1864. No further records. Survived the war.

KILLIAN, DANIEL A., Private

Previously served as Private in Company E of this regiment. Transferred to this company on March 2, 1863. Reported present in May-June, 1863. Sent to hospital in November-December, 1863. Returned to duty in March-April, 1864. Reported sick in hospital from June 25 through August 31, 1864. No further records. Survived the war.

KING, A. J., Private

Enlisted in Buncombe County on May 7, 1863, for the war. Deserted at La Fayette, Georgia, September 11, 1863.

KING, GEORGE L., Private

Enlisted in Buncombe County on May 15, 1862, for the war. Died in hospital at Chattanooga, Tennessee, December 25, 1862. Cause of death not reported.

KING, JOSEPH H., Private

Enlisted in Buncombe County on May 7, 1863, for the war. Transferred to Company C, 29th Regiment N.C. Troops, August 1, 1863.

LEDBETTER, J. G., Private

Resided in McDowell County and was by occupation a farmer prior to enlisting in Buncombe County at age 25, May 15, 1862, for the war. Killed at Murfreesboro, Tennessee, January 2, 1863.

LEDBETTER, JAMES, Private

Enlisted in Buncombe County on May 15, 1862, for the war. Hospitalized at Dalton, Georgia, on or about January 20, 1863, with acute diarrhoea and/or pneumonia. Died in hospital at Dalton on February 16, 1863.

LEDBETTER, T. E., Private

Enlisted in Buncombe County on May 15, 1862, for the war. Reported present in November, 1862-April, 1863. Hospitalized at Lauderdale Springs, Mississippi, June 17, 1863. Died in hospital at Lauderdale Springs on September 12, 1863, of disease.

LOWRANCE, HENRY CLAY, 1st Sergeant

Previously served as Private in Company E, 1st Regiment N.C. Infantry (6 months, 1861). Enlisted in this company in Buncombe County on May 15, 1862, for the war. Mustered in as Corporal. Reported present and in command of the company in November-December, 1862. Promoted to 1st Sergeant prior to January 1, 1863. Reported present in January-June, 1863. Appointed 1st Lieutenant of Company D of this regiment on July 30, 1863, and transferred.

LYTLE, GEORGE B., Corporal

Enlisted in Buncombe County on May 15, 1862, for the war. Mustered in as Private. Hospitalized at Dalton, Georgia, December 31, 1862, with debilitas. Returned to duty on January 22, 1863. Promoted to Corporal on February 1, 1864. Reported present through April 30, 1864. Killed at Kolb's Farm, near Marietta, Georgia, June 22, 1864.

LYTLE, T. L., Private

Born in Buncombe County and was by occupation a farmer prior to enlisting in Buncombe County at age 24, May 15, 1862, for the war. Transferred to Company I of this regiment on or about September 13, 1862.

McBRAYER, BAILEY M., Corporal

Resided in Buncombe County and was by occupation a farm laborer prior to enlisting in Buncombe County at age 16, May 15, 1862, for the war. Mustered in as Private. Reported present in November, 1862-August, 1864. Promoted to Corporal on February 1, 1864. No further records.

McBRAYER, JAMES H., Private

Resided in Buncombe County and was by occupation a farm laborer prior to enlisting in Buncombe County at age 18, May 15, 1862, for the war. Died at Murfreesboro, Tennessee, December 27, 1862. Cause of death not reported.

McBRAYER, RICHARD L., Private

Resided in Buncombe County and was by occupation a farm laborer prior to enlisting in Buncombe County at age 27, July 8, 1862, for the war. Transferred to Company C of this regiment on August 1, 1862.

McBRAYER, WILLIAM A., Private

Enlisted in Buncombe County on July 8, 1862, for the war. Transferred to Company C of this regiment on August 1, 1862.

MARLOW, BENJAMIN FRANKLIN, Corporal

Born in Rutherford County on March 3, 1831. Resided in McDowell County and was by occupation a laborer prior to enlisting in Buncombe County at age 31, May 15, 1862, for the war. Mustered in as Private. Promoted to Corporal prior to January 1, 1863. Reported present in November, 1862-June, 1863. Wounded at Chickamauga, Georgia, September 20, 1863. Returned to duty prior to October 31, 1863. Died in hospital at Atlanta, Georgia, December 9, 1863, of disease.

MELTON, J. D., Corporal

Enlisted in Buncombe County on May 15, 1862, for the war. Mustered in as Private. Promoted to Corporal prior to January 1, 1863. Reported present in November, 1862-June, 1863. Died in hospital at Atlanta, Georgia, October 18, 1863, of disease.

MELTON, WILLIAM MAC, Private

Enlisted in Buncombe County on May 15, 1862, for the war. Reported sick in hospital in November-December, 1862. Died in hospital at Atlanta, Georgia, on or about February 13, 1863.

MERRIMAN, ERASMUS H., Private

Resided in Buncombe County where he enlisted at age 22, May 15, 1862, for the war. Reported absent on detached service in November-December, 1862. Returned to duty in January-February, 1863. Reported present in March, 1863-August, 1864. No further records. Survived the war.

MORGAN, A. W., Private

Resided in McDowell County and was by occupation a farmer prior to enlisting in Buncombe County at age 28, May 15, 1862, for the war. Reported present in November, 1862-October, 1863. Deserted on November 20, 1863. Returned to duty on or about May 15, 1864. Sent to hospital sick on August 23, 1864. Hospitalized at Charlotte on February 23, 1865, with rheumatism. Returned to duty on March 13, 1865. No further records.

NEAL, J. K., Private

Born in McDowell County* where he resided as a farmer prior to enlisting at Camp Smith (Madison County) at age 29, July 17, 1862, for the war. Mustered in as Sergeant. Reduced to ranks on an unspecified date. Transferred to Company I of this regiment on or about September 13, 1862.

NICHOLS, JAMES, Private

Born in Abbeville District, South Carolina, and resided in Buncombe County where he was by occupation a farmer prior to enlisting in Buncombe County at age 33, May 15, 1862, for the war. Transferred to Company I of this regiment on or about September 13, 1862.

PATTON, J. B., Private

Enlisted in Buncombe County on May 15, 1862, for the war. Reported present in November, 1862-April, 1863. Died in hospital at Brandon, Mississippi, June 8, 1863. Cause of death not reported.

PATTY, ELBERT S., Musician

Resided in Buncombe County and was by occupation a farmer prior to enlisting in Buncombe County at age 21, May 15, 1862, for the war. Mustered in as Private. Promoted to Musician (Drummer) in August-December, 1862. Died in hospital at Murfreesboro, Tennessee, December 22, 1862. Cause of death not reported.

PENLAND, JOHN M., Private

Enlisted in Buncombe County at age 20, May 15, 1862, for the war. Hospitalized at Dalton, Georgia, January 29, 1863, with morbilli. Returned to duty on February 2, 1863. Reported present in March-June, 1863. Killed at Chickamauga, Georgia, September 20, 1863. Nominated for the Badge of Distinction for gallantry at Chickamauga.

PENLAND, NOBLE ALEXANDER, Private

Born on June 2, 1847. Enlisted in Buncombe County at age 16, April 1, 1864, for the war. Captured at or near Smyrna, Georgia, on or about July 3, 1864. Sent to Nashville, Tennessee. Transferred to Louisville, Kentucky, where he arrived on July 14, 1864. Transferred to Camp Douglas, Chicago, Illinois, where he arrived on July 18, 1864. Released at Camp Douglas on June 16, 1865, after taking the Oath of Allegiance.

PINKERTON, JOHN, Private

Place and date of enlistment not reported (probably enlisted on or about May 15, 1862). Last reported in the records of this company on July 31, 1862.

POWERS, JOHN, Private

Born in Buncombe County where he resided prior to enlisting in Buncombe County at age 19, May 15, 1862, for the war. Reported sick in hospital in November, 1862-February, 1863. Reported present in March-June, 1863. Furloughed on an unspecified date. Returned to duty in January-February, 1864. Reported present in March-April, 1864. Captured at or near Smyrna, Georgia, on or about July 3, 1864. Sent to Nashville, Tennessee. Transferred to Louisville, Kentucky, where he arrived on July 14, 1864. Transferred to Camp Douglas, Chicago, Illinois, where he arrived on July 18, 1864. Released at Camp Douglas on April 6, 1865, after taking the Oath of Allegiance and joining the U.S. Army. Assigned to Company F, 5th Regiment U.S. Volunteer Infantry.

PRESLEY, JAMES M., Private

Born in Buncombe County where he resided as a farmer prior to enlisting in Buncombe County at age 19, May 15, 1862, for the war. Transferred to Company I of this regiment on or about September 13, 1862.

PRESLEY, PETER, Private

Place and date of enlistment not reported (probably enlisted on or about May 15, 1862). Last reported in the records of this company on July 31, 1862. Survived the war. [Was about 26 years of age at time of enlistment.]

REDMAN, JAMES P., Private

Resided in Buncombe County and was by occupation a farmer prior to enlisting at Fairfield, Tennessee, at age 38, May 14, 1863, for the war. Reported present through October 31, 1863. Reported in hospital at Kingston, Georgia, in November-December, 1863. Sent to hospital at Dalton, Georgia, February 10, 1864. Reported absent in hospital through August 31, 1864. No further records. Survived the war. [North Carolina pension records indicate that he received a bayonet wound in the left arm at Chickamauga, Georgia, in 1863.]

REDMAN, LEANDER H., Private

Resided in Buncombe County and was by occupation a farmer prior to enlisting in Buncombe County at age 33, May 15, 1862, for the war. Hospitalized at Dalton, Georgia, December 30, 1862, with typhoid fever. Returned to duty on January 3, 1863. Reported sick in hospital in March-April, 1863. Deserted from hospital at Catoosa Springs, Georgia, May 24, 1863. Returned from desertion on September 22, 1863. Reported present in November, 1863-April, 1864. Captured at Kolb's Farm, near Marietta, Georgia, June 22, 1864. Sent to Nashville, Tennessee. Transferred to Louisville, Kentucky, where he arrived on July 14, 1864. Transferred to Camp Douglas, Chicago, Illinois, where he arrived on July 18, 1864. Died at Camp Douglas on January 20, 1865, of "gen[eral] debility."

RICKMAN, WILLIAM, Private

Resided in Buncombe County where he enlisted at age 33, May 15, 1862, for the war. Reported sick at home in November-December, 1862. Reported on detail attending the sick at Greeneville, Tennessee, in January-February, 1863. Rejoined the company in March-April, 1863. Reported present in May-June, 1863. Reported absent sick in July-October, 1863. Deserted on an unspecified date. Returned to duty on November 27, 1863. Reported present in January-April, 1864. Captured at Kolb's Farm, near Marietta, Georgia, June 22, 1864. Sent to Nashville, Tennessee. Transferred to Louisville, Kentucky, where he arrived on July 14, 1864. Transferred to Camp Douglas, Chicago, Illinois, where he arrived on July 18, 1864. Released at Camp Douglas on May 15, 1865, after taking the Oath of Allegiance.

ROBESON, JAMES P., Private

Enlisted in Buncombe County on May 15, 1862, for the war. Reported present in November, 1862-February, 1863. Hospitalized at Dalton, Georgia, March 25, 1863, with scorbutus. Returned to duty on April 23, 1863. Reported present in May-June, 1863. Briefly listed as a deserter in October, 1863. Reported present in November, 1863-August, 1864.

ROBESON, M. A., Private

Born in Buncombe County in 1833. Enlisted in Buncombe County on May 15, 1862, for the war. Reported present in November, 1862-June, 1863. Deserted near Chattanooga, Tennessee, September 8, 1863. Returned to duty on November 21, 1863. Reported present in January-April, 1864. Wounded near Resaca, Georgia, May 15, 1864. Returned to duty prior to July 1, 1864. Reported present in July-August, 1864. Wounded in the left hand at Bentonville on March 19-21, 1865. No further records. [May have been wounded at Murfreesboro, Tennessee, December 31, 1862-January 2, 1863. Filed a Tennessee pension application after the war.]

ROBESON, MONTVILLE W., Private

Resided in Chattooga County, Georgia, and enlisted in Buncombe County at age 34, May 15, 1862, for the war. Reported sick in hospital at Knoxville, Tennessee, in November, 1862-February, 1863. Reported present in March, 1863-April, 1864. Hospitalized at Macon, Georgia, May 23, 1864, with chronic diarrhoea. Transferred on May 28, 1864. Returned to duty prior to July 1, 1864. Reported present in July-August, 1864. No further records. Survived the war.

ROBESON, THOMAS F., 1st Sergeant

Enlisted in Buncombe County on May 15, 1862, for the war. Mustered in as Sergeant. Reported present in November, 1862-February, 1863. Reported absent in hospital in March-April, 1863.

Returned to duty in May-June, 1863. Promoted to 1st Sergeant on June 30, 1863. Reported present in July, 1863-February, 1864. Detailed as Ordnance Sergeant on March 1, 1864, and transferred to the Field and Staff of this regiment. Appointed Ordnance Sergeant in May-June, 1864, to rank from February 11, 1864, and assigned to permanent duty with the Field and Staff.

RYMER, THOMAS B., Private

Resided in Buncombe County and was by occupation a renter prior to enlisting in Buncombe County on May 15, 1862, for the war. Reported on duty as a teamster from November 12, 1862, through June 30, 1863. Rejoined the company in July-October, 1863. Deserted on November 20, 1863. Returned to duty on July 30, 1864. Captured at La Vergne, Tennessee, December 8, 1864. Sent to Nashville, Tennessee. Transferred to Louisville, Kentucky, December 31, 1864. Transferred to Camp Chase, Ohio, where he arrived on January 6, 1865. Released at Camp Chase on June 12, 1865, after taking the Oath of Allegiance. [Was about 32 years of age at time of enlistment.]

SAFLEY, T. F., Private

Enlisted in Buncombe County on May 15, 1862, for the war. Reported present in November, 1862-June, 1863. Deserted at La Fayette, Georgia, September 11, 1863. [May have served later as Private in Company L, 8th Regiment Tennessee Cavalry (Union).]

SALES, JOSEPH B., Private

Previously served as Private in Company E, 1st Regiment N.C. Infantry (6 months, 1861). Enlisted in this company in Buncombe County on May 15, 1862, for the war. Reported present in November, 1862-October, 1863. Reported absent on detached duty as a teamster in November-December, 1863. Rejoined the company in January-February, 1864. Reported on duty as a teamster in March-August, 1864. Transferred to Company C, 58th Regiment N.C. Troops, when the 58th and 60th Regiments were consolidated on April 9, 1865.

SALES, ROBERT FLETCHER, Private

Enlisted in Buncombe County at age 26, May 15, 1862, for the war. Reported present in November, 1862-June, 1863. Reported absent sick in July-October, 1863. Reported absent on furlough (arm broken) in November-December, 1863. Place and date injured not reported. Returned to duty in January-February, 1864. Detailed for hospital duty (probably as a cook) on or about March 1, 1864. Reported on detail through August 31, 1864. No further records. Survived the war.

SALES, WELDON CORNELIUS, Private

Resided in Buncombe County where he enlisted at age 20, May 15, 1862, for the war. Reported present in November, 1862-October, 1863. Furloughed on December 25, 1863. Returned to duty in March-April, 1864. Captured at Kolb's Farm, near Marietta, Georgia, June 22, 1864. Sent to Nashville, Tennessee. Transferred to Louisville, Kentucky, where he arrived on July 14, 1864. Transferred to Camp Douglas, Chicago, Illinois, where he arrived on July 18, 1864. Released at Camp Douglas on June 16, 1865, after taking the Oath of Allegiance.

SALES, WILLIAM H., Private

Enlisted in Buncombe County at age 28, May 15, 1862, for the war. Hospitalized at Dalton, Georgia, December 30, 1862, with continued fever. Returned to duty on January 3, 1863. Discharged on February 26, 1863. Reason discharged not reported.

SEARCY, JOHN D., Private

Born in Buncombe County and was by occupation a farmer prior to enlisting in Buncombe County at age 32, May 15, 1862, for the war. Transferred to Company I of this regiment on or about September 13, 1862.

SHOPE, DOCTOR VANCE, 1st Sergeant

Born in Buncombe County where he resided as a farmer prior to enlisting in Buncombe County at age 34, May 15, 1862, for the war. Mustered in as Private. Appointed Musician (Fifer) subsequent to July 31, 1862. Promoted to 1st Sergeant on September 1, 1862. Transferred to Company I of this regiment on or about September 13, 1862.

SIMONS, B. H., Private

Previously served as Private in the 62nd Regiment N.C. Troops. Transferred to this company on July 30, 1864. Reported present through August 31, 1864. No further records.

SIMONS, JAMES, Private

Previously served as Private in Company I, 62nd Regiment N.C. Troops. Transferred to this company on July 30, 1864. Reported present through August 31, 1864. No further records.

SLAGLE, JOHN L. L., Private

Born in Yancey County* and was by occupation a farmer prior to enlisting in Buncombe County at age 33, May 15, 1862, for the war. Transferred to Company I of this regiment on or about September 13, 1862.

SORRELS, W. F., Private

Enlisted in Buncombe County on May 15, 1862, for the war. Reported sick in hospital in November, 1862-February, 1863. Died in hospital at Atlanta, Georgia, February 10, 1863. Cause of death not reported.

STEPP, JOSEPH M., ——

Resided in Buncombe County and was by occupation a merchant. Place and date of enlistment not reported (probably enlisted on or about May 15, 1862). No further records. Survived the war. [Was about 31 years of age at time of enlistment. May have served later as Private in Company K, 11th Regiment N.C. Troops (1st Regiment N.C. Volunteers).]

STEPP, ROBERT, Private

Resided in Buncombe County and was by occupation a farmer prior to enlisting in Buncombe County at age 27, May 15, 1862, for the war. Reported present in November, 1862-February, 1863. Hospitalized at Dalton, Georgia, May 21, 1863, with intermittent fever. Furloughed from hospital on November 20, 1863. Returned to duty in March-April, 1864. Captured at Kolb's Farm, near Marietta, Georgia, June 22, 1864. Sent to Nashville, Tennessee. Transferred to Louisville, Kentucky, where he arrived on July 14, 1864. Transferred to Camp Douglas, Chicago, Illinois, where he arrived on July 18, 1864. Released at Camp Douglas on June 12, 1865, after taking the Oath of Allegiance.

STEPP, ROBERT J., Sergeant

Enlisted in Buncombe County on May 15, 1862, for the war. Mustered in as Private. Reported present in November, 1862-June, 1863. Reported absent sick in July-October, 1863. Reported absent on furlough in November-December, 1863. Returned to duty in January-February, 1864. Promoted to Sergeant on February 1,

1864. Reported present in March-August, 1864. Transferred to Company C, 58th Regiment N.C. Troops, when the 58th and 60th Regiments were consolidated on April 9, 1865. [Confederate medical records dated June, 1863, give his age as 25. North Carolina pension records indicate that he was wounded in the shoulder at New Hope Church, Georgia, in 1864.]

STEPP, WILLIAM P., Private

Enlisted in Buncombe County on May 15, 1862, for the war. Reported present in November, 1862-October, 1863. Reported sick in hospital in November-December, 1863. Returned to duty in January-February, 1864. Reported present in March-April, 1864. Captured at Kolb's Farm, near Marietta, Georgia, June 22, 1864. Sent to Nashville, Tennessee. Transferred to Louisville, Kentucky, where he arrived on July 14, 1864. Transferred to Camp Douglas, Chicago, Illinois, where he arrived on July 18, 1864. Died at Camp Douglas on January 3, 1865, of "chronic diarrhoea."

THOMAS, JOHN W., Private

Enlisted in Buncombe County on May 15, 1862, for the war. Reported sick in hospital in November-December, 1862. Hospitalized at Dalton, Georgia, January 29, 1863, with chronic diarrhoea and typhoid fever. Died in hospital at Dalton on or about February 27, 1863.

VAUGHN, A. B., Private

Born in McDowell County* where he resided as a farmer prior to enlisting at Camp Smith (Madison County) at age 22, July 17, 1862, for the war. Transferred to Company I of this regiment on or about September 13, 1862.

WARD, WILLIAM, Private

Enlisted in Burke County on October 6, 1863, for the war. Deserted near Dalton, Georgia, December 20, 1863.

WATKINS, ARNEL, Private

Enlisted in Burke County on October 6, 1863, for the war. Deserted on November 1, 1863. Died in hospital at Raleigh on January 10, 1864, of "pneumonia."

WEBB, JAMES ALEXANDER, Sergeant

Born in Buncombe County and was by occupation a farmer prior to enlisting in Buncombe County at age 33, May 15, 1862, for the war. Mustered in as Sergeant. Transferred to Company I of this regiment on or about September 13, 1862.

WELLS, DAVID M., Private

Enlisted in Buncombe County at age 19, May 15, 1862, for the war. Reported present in November, 1862-February, 1863. Reported absent in hospital in March-April, 1863. Returned to duty in May-June, 1863. Sent to hospital subsequent to October 31, 1863. Returned to duty on an unspecified date. Furloughed from hospital on December 26, 1863. Returned to duty in May-June, 1864. Reported present in July-August, 1864. No further records. Survived the war. [May have been wounded at Murfreesboro, Tennessee, December 31, 1862-January 2, 1863.]

WHITE, JOSEPH R., Private

Enlisted in Buncombe County on May 15, 1862, for the war. Reported present in November, 1862-June, 1863. Hospitalized at Macon, Mississippi, July 16, 1863. Returned to duty in November-December, 1863. Reported present in January-August, 1864. No further records. [A casualty list in the *North Carolina (Weekly)*

Standard (Raleigh), July 13, 1864, indicates that he was missing at Kolb's Farm, near Marietta, Georgia, June 22, 1864.]

WHITE, PHARAOH, Private

Enlisted in Buncombe County on May 15, 1862, for the war. Reported present in November, 1862-February, 1863. Reported absent sick in March-October, 1863. Hospitalized at Griffin, Georgia, November 2, 1863. Returned to duty in December, 1863. Reported absent sick from January 12 through February 29, 1864. Returned to duty in March-April, 1864. Captured at Resaca, Georgia, May 15-16, 1864. Sent to Nashville, Tennessee. Transferred to Louisville, Kentucky, where he arrived on May 21, 1864. Transferred to Alton, Illinois, where he arrived on May 25, 1864. Released at Alton on or about June 10, 1864, after taking the Oath of Allegiance and joining the U.S. Navy. [Was about 27 years of age at time of enlistment.]

WHITE, SIMON T., Private

Resided in Buncombe County and was by occupation a farm laborer prior to enlisting in Buncombe County at age 28, May 15, 1862, for the war. Hospitalized at Dalton, Georgia, December 31, 1862, with typhoid fever. Returned to duty on February 4, 1863. Reported present through June 30, 1863. Reported absent sick in July-October, 1863. Returned to duty in November-December, 1863. Reported present in January-August, 1864. No further records. Survived the war.

WHITESIDES, HENRY C., Private

Born in Buncombe County where he resided as a mechanic or farm laborer prior to enlisting in Buncombe County at age 24, May 15, 1862, for the war. Reported sick at home in November-December, 1862. Reported present in January-February, 1863. Died in hospital at Tullahoma, Tennessee, on or about April 5, 1863. Cause of death not reported.

WILSON, THOMAS F., Private

Enlisted in Buncombe County on November 24, 1863, for the war. Reported present through August 31, 1864. Transferred to Company C, 58th Regiment N.C. Troops, when the 58th and 60th Regiments were consolidated on April 9, 1865. [Was about 18 years of age at time of enlistment. North Carolina pension records indicate that he received flesh wounds at New Hope Church, Georgia, on an unspecified date.]

WILSON, THOMAS H., Private

Previously served as Private in Company E, 1st Regiment N.C. Infantry (6 months, 1861). Enlisted in this company on May 15, 1862, for the war. Wounded slightly in the hand and captured at Murfreesboro, Tennessee, January 2, 1863. Confined at St. Louis, Missouri. Released at St. Louis on February 14, 1863, after taking the Oath of Allegiance.

YORK, WILLIAM, Private

Enlisted in Buncombe County on May 15, 1862, for the war. Died in hospital at Chattanooga, Tennessee, on or about December 22, 1862, of "pneumonia."

YOUNG, SAMUEL P., Sergeant

Enlisted in Buncombe County at age 23, May 15, 1862, for the war. Mustered in as Private. Wounded in the right hand and/or hip at Murfreesboro, Tennessee, January 2, 1863. Two fingers amputated. Hospitalized at Dalton, Georgia. Reported absent on furlough from February 28 through April 30, 1863. Reported on detail

as a wagon master and teamster in May-October, 1863. Rejoined the company in November-December, 1863. Reported present in January-August, 1864. Promoted to Sergeant on February 1, 1864. Transferred to Company C, 58th Regiment N.C. Troops, when the 58th and 60th Regiments were consolidated on April 9, 1865. [North Carolina pension records indicate that he was wounded at Jonesborough, Georgia, on an unspecified date.]

MISCELLANEOUS

ALEXANDER, JOSEPH B., _____

Place and date of enlistment not reported (probably enlisted in late 1864 or early 1865). Wounded slightly at Bentonville on March 19-21, 1865. [Clark's *Regiments*, 3:496.]

ALFRED, TOM, Private

Place and date of enlistment not reported. Paid on or about October 22, 1862, for service from May 16 through August 1, 1862. No further records.

BARBER, WILLIAM F., Private

Resided in Paulding County, Georgia. Place and date of enlistment not reported (probably enlisted in the spring of 1864). Deserted to the enemy on an unspecified date. Sent to Louisville, Kentucky. Released at Louisville on or about June 10, 1864, after taking the Oath of Allegiance.

CLAYTON, D. M., _____

North Carolina pension records indicate that he served in this regiment.

DALTON, BRADLEY

Resided in Henderson County and enlisted on November 13, 1864, for the war. Deserted to the enemy on December 5, 1864. Sent to Nashville, Tennessee. Took the Oath of Allegiance at Nashville on January 27, 1865.

GENTRY, JOSEPH R., 3rd Lieutenant

Served as 3rd Lieutenant of Company K, 25th Regiment N.C. Troops. Resigned from that unit on January 6, 1864, in order to transfer to the 60th Regiment, in which his brother and "a large number of relatives & acquaintances" were serving. Records of the 60th Regiment do not indicate that he served herein.

MOODY, JAMES, _____

Tennessee pension records indicate that he served in this regiment.

MORGAN, JONATHAN, Private

Place and date of enlistment not reported (probably enlisted late in 1864). Deserted to the enemy at Savannah, Georgia, on or about December 22, 1864. Sent to Hilton Head, South Carolina. Transferred to New York City on or about January 9, 1865. No further records.

WHITMORE, PLEASANT, Private

Resided in Greene County, Tennessee, and enlisted on November 1, 1864, for the war. Deserted on December 15, 1864. Took the Oath of Allegiance at Nashville, Tennessee, May 8, 1865.

WILLIAMS, MORGAN N., _____
North Carolina pension records indicate that he served in this regiment.

The two stripes on his collar and narrow piping on his sleeves clearly identify Henry Clay Koonce as a 1st lieutenant in the Confederate States Army. Koonce, a Jones County farmer, was nineteen years old when he was appointed 1st lieutenant of Company K, 61st North Carolina, on April 29, 1862. He served until September 30, 1864, when he lost the lower part of his left leg in action at Fort Harrison, Virginia. After the war he was issued a prosthesis by the state of North Carolina. The device was manufactured by Jewett's Patent Leg Company and valued at $70. According to the 1870 federal census of Jones County, Koonce, his disability notwithstanding, supported himself, his wife Susan, and his two daughters (five-year-old Nettie and one-year-old Fanny), by farming. His service record appears on page 749. Image provided by Lucien M. Koonce.

First Sgt. Allen Whitfield Wooten, his rank clearly identified by his three chevrons and the partially visible loz-
enge on his left sleeve, enlisted in Company E, 61st North Carolina, on December 19, 1863, his eighteenth
birthday. In this ambrotype Wooten wears a double-breasted frock coat and a black or dark blue forage cap,
both of which were unusual by the date of his enlistment. Perhaps he had not yet learned the benefits of a slouch
hat. His method of turning back and buttoning down his lapels was widely practiced by Confederate officers.
Wooten was wounded slightly in the knee at Cold Harbor, Virginia, May 31-June 3, 1864, and was killed at the
Crater on July 30, 1864. His service record appears on page 704. Image provided by Dan M. Busby.

61ST REGIMENT N.C. TROOPS

The regiment that became the 61st N.C. Troops was organized at Wilmington on or about September 5, 1862, but was initially designated the 59th N.C. Troops.[1] The number 59 was also assigned to a cavalry regiment organized at Garysburg on August 20, 1862, and for more than two months there were two 59th North Carolina regiments. That confusing anomaly was corrected on an unknown date between October 30 and November 22, 1862, when the infantry regiment whose history is recounted below was redesignated the 61st Regiment N.C. Troops.[2] The company designations in effect while the regiment was known as the 59th were changed as well.[3] The regiment's commanding officer as of September 5 was Col. James D. Radcliffe, former colonel of the 18th Regiment N.C. Troops.

The 61st North Carolina was stationed at Camp Radcliffe, in Wilmington, until about September 13 when, because of a yellow fever epidemic in the town, it was ordered twenty-five miles south to Smithville. It remained there, at a camp described by Lt. Joseph Kinsey of Company E as "one of the most dreary looking out of the way places in the world," for more than three weeks. At 3:00 A.M. on October 7 the regiment departed by steamer for Northeast Bridge, on the Northeast Cape Fear River about ten miles above Wilmington. By October 15 the men were "encamped upon a hill" one mile from the river. "This is quite a sickly place," Capt. Andrew J. Moore of Company F wrote, "& several are labouring under diseases contracted here."[4] On October 17 the 61st moved by rail to Everettsville, about five or six miles south of Goldsboro. Its new camp, christened Camp Collier, was in a "very sandy" place with "tol[erable]" water. "Very much pleased with the camp," Captain Moore

---

1. With the exception of Company C, the ten companies that comprised the 61st North Carolina served previously as independent units. Company C served previously as 1st Company K, 40th Regiment N.C. Troops (3rd Regiment N.C. Artillery). Company A was assigned to the 20th Regiment N.C. Troops in June 1861 but, because that regiment already had ten companies, did not report for duty. Company H was assigned to the 42nd Regiment N.C. Troops as 1st Company B in April 1862 but, for unknown reasons, was never mustered in. Company I reported for duty with the "Vance Legion" on May 9, 1862, but reverted to independent status when that unit failed to complete its organization. For further details concerning the histories of 61st North Carolina companies, see the history sections preceding the company rosters beginning on page 653 below.

   The ten companies comprising the 61st North Carolina were raised primarily in the following counties: Company A–Sampson; Company B–Beaufort; Company C–Craven; Company D–Chatham; Company E–Lenoir; Company F–Greene; Company G–New Hanover; Company H–Martin; Company I–Alleghany; Company K–Jones.

2. In a letter dated October 30, 1862, Capt. Andrew Jackson Moore identified his regiment as the 59th North Carolina. His first reference to the regiment's new number appears in a letter dated November 22, the wording of which suggests that the change had been in effect for some time. Andrew Jackson Moore to Elizabeth ("Bettie") Farmer (who became his wife in January 1864), October 30 and November 22, 1862, Andrew Jackson Moore Letters, Roster Document No. 1072, Civil War Roster Project (CWRP), North Carolina Division of Archives and History (NCDAH), Raleigh, hereafter cited as Moore Letters.

3. Companies A and G of the 59th became Companies C and I of the 61st. The 59th Regiment designations of the other eight companies are unknown.

4. Joseph Kinsey to his sister, October 5, 1862, Roster Document No. 1016, CWRP, NCDAH; A. J. Moore to Bettie Farmer, October 15, 1862, Moore Letters. "The yellow fever keeps our Regt. moving," Kinsey added. See also Samuel Simpson Biddle Jr. (61st North Carolina) to Samuel Simpson Biddle Sr., October 20, 1862, Samuel Simpson Biddle Papers, Special Collections Department, Duke University (SCD-DU), Durham, hereafter cited as Biddle Papers.

wrote. On October 21 the men moved further up the tracks of the Wilmington and Weldon Railroad to Tarboro, where they arrived at 9:00 P.M. After bivouacking for the night, they went into camp "not far from the Depot" the next day.[5]

On or about October 22 the 61st North Carolina received orders to move against the Federally occupied town of Plymouth and, in conjunction with the 17th North Carolina, "drive out the enemy and give the people of Martin, Washington, and Tyrrell Counties an opportunity to bring out their provisions &c." At twilight on the evening of the twenty-third the regiment marched ten miles eastward and bivouacked for the night. It continued its march the next day and reached Williamston by noon on the twenty-fifth. "Leaving Williamston in the evening of Saturday, October 25," Captain Moore wrote, "we reached Jamesville . . . on Sunday last. Rained all day, but . . . at dark we marched along the worst road almost I ever saw & in quick time. Encumbered with the darkness . . . & heedless of the mud, water & falling rain we moved _____ [illegible] causways [sic] & upon uneven ground[.] [M]an after man would fall & with considerable effort rise again. . . . Marching about eight miles from there along that awful road, we put up for the night. . . . We expected to leave there & rush into Plymouth before day . . . but it was not undertaken. . . ." In Moore's opinion, the 61st North Carolina's only accomplishment as of October 30 was the capture of "a good many Buffaloes [Union loyalists] & some conscripts. . . ." That assessment is, in fact, a fairly accurate summation of the expedition's achievements.[6]

By November 2 it became apparent that the 61st must retreat or be cut off by a 5,000-man Federal force under Maj. Gen. John G. Foster advancing on Williamston from Washington and New Bern. The regiment began a "forced march" westward at 2:30 that afternoon.[7] "[W]e was on a ma[r]ch fifteen or sixteen days," Pvt. Elbert Carpenter of Company D informed his father after reaching the safety of Tarboro on November 7, "and sometimes marched of a night[.] [W]e marched four or five days through the rain mud snow and water without tents or any thing at all to ly under[.] [W]e had to ly down on the ground to sleep[.] [W]e ly on our guns expecting a fight every moment[.] [S]ome of our boys ran and in fact the most of them ran and some of them lost their guns and their knapsacks[.]"[8]

5. A. J. Moore to Bettie Farmer, October 17 and 23, 1862, Moore Letters. In his October 17 letter, Moore described the camp as "upon the top of a hill just west of the road." According to one 61st North Carolina soldier, Camp Collier was named for "a very wealthy old farmer upon whose land we are encamped." S. S. Biddle Jr. to S. S. Biddle Sr., October 20, 1862, Biddle Papers.

6. R. N. Scott and others, eds., *The War of the Rebellion: A Compilation of the Official Records of the Union and Confederate Armies*, 70 vols. (Washington, D.C.: Government Printing Office, 1880-1901), ser. 1, 18:760, hereafter cited as *Official Records (Army)*; A. J. Moore to Bettie Farmer, October 30, 1862, Moore Letters.

7. Nathan Alexander Ramsey, "Sixty-first Regiment," in Walter Clark, ed., *Histories of the Several Regiments and Battalions from North Carolina in the Great War, 1861-'65*, 5 vols. (Raleigh and Goldsboro: State of North Carolina, 1901), 3:506, hereafter cited as Ramsey, "Sixty-first Regiment," in Clark, *Histories of the North Carolina Regiments*. See also *Official Records (Army)*, ser. 1, 18:768. According to Capt. Edward Mallett of Company C, the 61st North Carolina was at one point "within four miles" of Plymouth. "We have arrested a good many disloyal people and conscripts," Mallett added, "and afford[ed] protection to citizens while moving out their property." Edward Mallett to S. S. Biddle Sr., November 1, 1862, Simpson and Biddle Family Papers, Private Collections, NCDAH, hereafter cited as Simpson and Biddle Papers.

8. Elbert Carpenter to Solomon Carpenter (his father), November 22, 1862, in Zeb D. and Martha Harrington, eds., *To Bear Arms* (n.p., 1984), 243, hereafter cited as Harrington, *To Bear Arms*. "A deep snow fell on the 6th,"

On November 10 the 61st North Carolina departed Tarboro for Greenville. It arrived the next day to find that an attempt by Foster's men to burn the Tar River bridge had resulted in only "trivial" and "easily remided [*sic*]" damage. According to the best evidence available, the 61st was at Craddock's Crossroads on the fourteenth, at Black Jack Meeting House on the fifteenth, Taft's Store on the sixteenth, Nelson's Crossroads (about thirteen miles "below" Greenville) on the twenty-second, and Greenville again on the twenty-third. On December 7 the regiment marched toward Kinston, which it reached on the ninth. Captain Moore arrived there from a furlough on the tenth to find his men under rude "brush shelters" but otherwise, as he wryly observed, "rolling principally upon the ground."[9]

On December 11 Foster advanced from New Bern with 10,000 men on a raid to destroy the railroad bridge at Goldsboro and prevent the Confederates from reinforcing the Army of Northern Virginia at Fredericksburg, where Robert E. Lee faced a 120,000-man Federal army commanded by Ambrose E. Burnside. On the morning of the thirteenth Foster reached Southwest Creek, seven miles or so south of Kinston, where he found Colonel Radcliffe's 61st North Carolina waiting on the opposite bank in the vicinity of a partially destroyed bridge near Hine's Mill. An hour or so of skirmishing ensued during which Brig. Gen. Nathan G. Evans arrived with his South Carolina brigade and assumed command. Colonel Radcliffe was dispatched with three 61st North Carolina companies (C, F, and H), four 17th South Carolina companies (B, E, G, and H), and an artillery section to take command of the Confederate left wing at the Southwest Creek crossing of the Upper Trent Road. The other seven companies of the 61st, under Lt. Col. William S. Devane, took position on Evans's right at Hine's Mill. Shortly thereafter, Foster's men forced a crossing near Devane's position by edging across the Hine's Mill dam.[10]

[T]he firing seemed to be rapid and terrific [Captain Ramsey recalled]. Mini balls whistled through the air by front and cross fires from the enemy. . . . For some time we held our ground, but were forced to fall back by the enemy advancing upon us in overwhelming numbers. We retreated . . . and halted about one mile to the rear. Here we formed a line of battle and a company of skirmishers moved forward to feel for the enemy. They advanced only about a hundred yards when they met with

---

Captain Ramsey recalled, "yet, with one hundred barefooted men in the regiment, we weathered the storm. . . ." For a further discussion of the 61st's brush with the enemy on November 2, see Endnote A on page 646.

9. A. J. Moore to Bettie Farmer, November 12 and 24 and December 12, 1862, Moore Letters. See also Ramsey, "Sixty-first Regiment," in Clark, *Histories of the North Carolina Regiments*, 3:507. Ramsey states that the 61st "bivouacked at Greenville" on the thirteenth; however, unless Captain Moore's letter of November 12 is misdated, the regiment arrived there on the eleventh.

10. See *Official Records (Army)*, ser. 1, 18:112-113; John G. Barrett, *The Civil War in North Carolina* (Chapel Hill: The University of North Carolina Press, 1963), 139-140, hereafter cited as Barrett, *Civil War in North Carolina*; Ramsey, "Sixty-first Regiment," in Clark, *Histories of the North Carolina Regiments*, 3:507; deposition of Lt. Franklin Alexander Rhodes (Company H, 61st North Carolina) in "[Investigation of] the charges and specifications preferred against Colonel James D. Radcliffe [for alleged misconduct at the Battle of Kinston]," April 11, 1863, hereafter cited as "Radcliffe Charges and Specifications," and Col. Fitz William McMaster (17th South Carolina) to J. D. Radcliffe, March 2, 1863, both in J. D. Radcliffe service record file, 61st Regiment N.C. Troops, Record Group 109: Records of Confederate Soldiers Who Served During the Civil War, Compiled Confederate Service Records (North Carolina), M270, reel 548, National Archives and Records Administration, Washington, D.C., hereafter cited as Compiled Confederate Service Records (North Carolina).

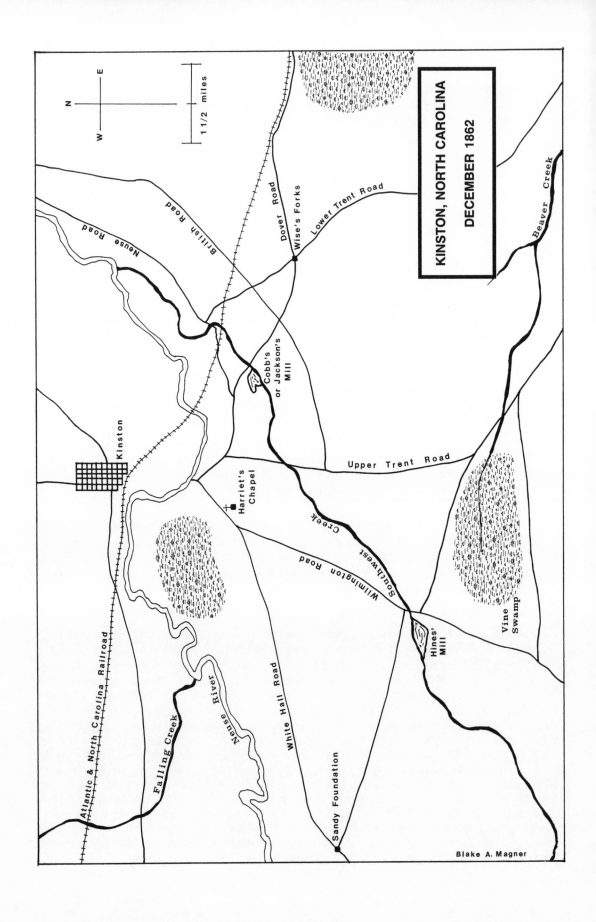

KINSTON, NORTH CAROLINA
DECEMBER 1862

N
E
W
S

1 1/2 miles

Dover Road
British Road
Neuse Road
Wise's Forks
Lower Trent Road
Beaver Creek
Cobb's or Jackson's Mill
Upper Trent Road
Kinston
Harriet's Chapel
Southwest Creek
Wilmington Road
Vine Swamp
Atlantic & North Carolina Railroad
Falling Creek
Neuse River
White Hall Road
Hines' Mill
Sandy Foundation

Blake A. Magner

what they were looking for, fired one round and had the compliment promptly acknowledged. . . . They retired as best they could, bringing the intelligence that the woods were full of blue coats, and that several regiments were flanking us on our left. Just then we had orders from General Evans to retreat under fire in good order. We did our best. We fired and fell back, and fell back and fired.[11]

At "[t]he next big field" the badly outnumbered regiment attempted to make another stand, with indifferent results. "[W]e had a pretty lively artillery duel for about an hour," Captain Ramsey continued, "and an equally lively fusillade from the small arms of the enemy. We . . . laid mighty low and did not return the fire, because our guns were inferior and we could not reach them." At about 8:00 P.M. Devane's companies "quietly stole away through swamp, mud and water toward Harriet's Chapel," about a mile from the Neuse River road bridge at Kinston. There five of them linked up with Evans's command. "It was a bitter cold night," Ramsey wrote, "and all the boys were wet, half-frozen, hungry and worn out. . . . When we bivouacked we were in hearing of the enemy, and we had no camp fires till past midnight." Meantime, Devane's other two companies (Company I and another company that has not been identified) were cut off from Kinston. "[W]e made our escape," Capt. William Thomas Choate of Company I stated in a letter to his wife, "by Retreating threw a large Swamp and makin up newse River about 9 miles above Kinston[.] [W]e thar Cross[ed] the River and taken up till morning[.] [W]e then [recrossed the river] and Starte[d] back for Kinston."[12]

On the morning of the fourteenth—a "bright, beautiful Sabbath"—Foster, who had reached the approaches of Kinston, resumed the offensive, attacking Evans's right, held by Devane and by Col. Peter Mallett's North Carolina Infantry Battalion. Although outnumbered by a margin of five-to-one, Evans was in a strong position on the south bank of the Neuse with his right protected by a swamp, his left anchored on the river, and most of his troops concealed in a woods. He therefore responded with an assault on the Federal right. During the ensuing three-hour fight Devane's two lost companies arrived from upriver.[13] "We herd the cannons commence which roared like constant thunder and the small arms was poping like green brush a fire," Captain Choate related. "[W]e pushed on . . . and a bout the edge of town we met our commisary waggon. . . . Our boys went in to it in a hurry as they had not had but 4 sweet potatoes apeace from friday. . . . [A]bout the time we got in a good way of eating the corier came with orders for us to report at the bridge which was about 1/2 mile distant[.] I told the Boys to take ther hands full and fall in which they did[.] So we pushed off in much hast for the bridge and soon found whare our Ridge ment was Stationed[.]" Shortly thereafter, Choate continued, "we was orderd to fall back a cross the Bridge" and "ly down till the enemy came up in Sight." It is not clear who issued that order or why, but before it could be executed the bridge was fired, trapping Mallett's Battalion,

11. Ramsey, "Sixty-first Regiment," in Clark, *Histories of the North Carolina Regiments*, 3:507-508.

12. Ramsey, "Sixty-first Regiment," in Clark, *Histories of the North Carolina Regiments*, 3:508; William Thomas Choate to Martha Choate, December 21, 1862, William Thomas Choate Letters, Virginia Polytechnic Institute, Blacksburg, Virginia, hereafter cited as Choate Letters.

13. Ramsey, "Sixty-first Regiment," in Clark, *Histories of the North Carolina Regiments*, 3:508. For a time after its arrival at Kinston, Devane's detachment was under the command of Colonel Mallett. See *Official Records (Army)*, ser. 1, 18:115-116; *Wilmington [Weekly] Journal*, April 16, 1863.

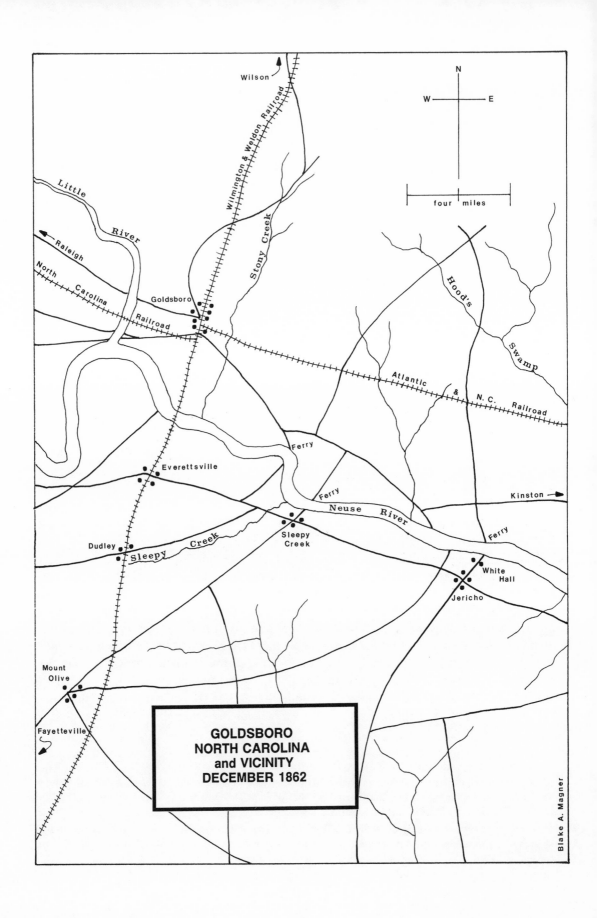

N
W   E
S

four miles

Little

River

Wilson

Wilmington & Weldon Railroad

Stony Creek

Raleigh

North Carolina

Railroad

Goldsboro

Hood's

Swamp

Atlantic

&   N. C.   Railroad

Ferry

Everettsville

Ferry

Kinston

Neuse   River

Ferry

Dudley

Sleepy   Creek

Sleepy
Creek

White
Hall

Jericho

Mount
Olive

Fayetteville

**GOLDSBORO
NORTH CAROLINA
and VICINITY
DECEMBER 1862**

Blake A. Magner

most of the 61st North Carolina, and some of Evans's South Carolinians on the south bank.[14]

"When we reached the bridge," Captain Ramsey recollected, "it was on fire, and in addition to the trying ordeal of passing over the blazing bridge, we were subjected to a terrible cross-fire from the enemy who were drawn up in line of battle 250 yards below. Here we lost several of our men and it is truly miraculous that half of them at least were not killed or burned to death." "[We] fell back in good order till we came in sight of the bridge," a South Carolina soldier wrote, "when to our amazement we saw it in flames. Every man then broke ranks and rushed to the bridge. A N.C. regiment on our right [the 61st, Mallett's Battalion, or both] started at the same time and we reached the bridge together. It was an awful scene. I . . . tried to rush across. I could feel my hair singe as I passed through the fire. About the middle of the bridge the man ahead of me stumbled and fell. I fell over him, and the men, unable to resist the pressure from behind, were piled on me. I never came so near being mashed to death and suffocated in my life. I thought my time had come and that I had passed through the balls only to perish miserably on that burning bridge, but at last I dragged myself out and tottered across. . . . When I got over I dropped perfectly exhausted." "Many could not get a cross," Captain Choate noted sadly, "so the yanks captured severell. . . . I saw some men who run through the bridge that ther hides was powerfully scourged and many of our Brave Boys fell. . . . [I]t is said that our loss was very light till the Bridge was fired."[15] During its "firey [sic] ordeal" the 61st lost, according to figures compiled for this volume, 3 men killed, 13 wounded, and 69 captured. Among the latter was Colonel Radcliffe, who was on Evans's left with his three detached companies. Eight of the captured men were wounded, two mortally. Mallett's Battalion fared even worse, losing 7 men killed, 22 wounded, 8 missing, and 175 captured.[16]

14. W. T. Choate to Martha Choate, December 21, 1862, Choate Letters. It is very likely that Evans ordered the bridge fired even though he knew that many of his men were not across. One South Carolinian at the scene wrote that "Any private in [the] ranks could have carried out things better than Genl. Evans. It was disgraceful the way he acted and sacrificed his men. He was drunk as usual, and it seems he did not know what he was about. He was not too drunk however to keep in a safe place, and he did not show himself once on the battle field. He kept on this side [of] the bridge. . . . Every commissioned officer in the Brigade has signed a petition to the War Department to have Genl Evans removed. It is a shame that the lives of men should be in the hands of such an imbecile." W. Henry Sullivan to "My dear friend," December 27, 1862, Lalla Pelot Papers, SCD-DU, hereafter cited as Pelot Papers. See also *Wilmington [Weekly] Journal*, April 16, 1863.

15. Ramsey, "Sixty-first Regiment," in Clark, *Histories of the North Carolina Regiments*, 3:509; W. H. Sullivan to "My dear friend," December 27, 1862, Pelot Papers; W. T. Choate to Martha Choate, December 21, 1862, Choate Letters. "[A] great many of our boys lost all ther Blankits and close," Choate added. Confederate artillery units north of the river, believing that Devane's and Mallett's men were on the north bank, probably contributed to the casualties and panic by firing, reportedly on orders from Evans, into positions occupied by the North Carolinians just prior to their retreat. Nevertheless, Captain Moore claimed that his men "were fighting fiercely [sic]" until "they saw the Bridge . . . in flames." A. J. Moore to Bettie Farmer, December 17, 1862, Moore Letters. See also *Official Records (Army)*, ser. 1, 18:116; W. H. Sullivan to "My dear friend," December 27, 1862, Pelot Papers; *Wilmington [Weekly] Journal*, April 16, 1863. For a further discussion of the Kinston Bridge episode, see Endnote B on page 647.

16. A. J. Moore to Bettie Farmer, December 17, 1862, Moore Letters. Colonel Radcliffe's performance at Kinston bridge led to formal allegations by Capt. Edward Mallett (Company C) and several other regimental officers of "Drunkenness on Duty," "neglect of duty on the Battle field," and "Cowardice." There is evidence that Radcliffe had been drinking, but the charges were dismissed after an investigation by a court of inquiry

Evans's shaken troops fell back from the burning bridge to a position about two miles beyond Kinston but abandoned it several hours later, retreated to Falling Creek, and bivouacked for the night.[17] Foster, after ransacking Kinston, advanced toward White Hall, where a sharp skirmish was fought with a Confederate force commanded by Brig. Gen. Beverly H. Robertson on the sixteenth. On the seventeenth Foster reached Goldsboro and advanced with five regiments, supported by six others, against the railroad bridge. There he encountered the 52nd North Carolina supported by the 8th North Carolina (which was guarding a road bridge about 500 yards upstream) and the 51st North Carolina (equidistant between the two), all under the command of Brig. Gen. Thomas L. Clingman.[18] Raked by volleys of musketry and a barrage of shells, the overmatched 51st and 52nd broke and retreated across the railroad bridge, then rallied and returned to their line only to give way again. They were then concentrated at the road bridge with orders to hold it at all hazards. Meantime, the Federals fired the railroad bridge and, to prevent any Confederate effort to save it, opened up on the structure with their field guns. Convinced that the flames were doing their work, Foster began withdrawing toward New Bern, leaving Col. Horace C. Lee's Brigade to follow as rear guard.[19]

In the meantime Clingman, bolstered by the arrival of the 61st North Carolina (which had been assigned to his brigade in November and was now joining it for the first time), was ordered to cross the river with his four regiments and the "remnant" of Mallett's Battalion and attack Lee.[20] Finding Lee's troops "posted from the river for 1 1/2 miles along the

composed of a single officer. Mallett then took his case directly to Maj. Gen. D. H. Hill, commander of the District of North Carolina. When Hill rejected Mallett's appeal, Radcliffe placed Mallett under arrest and, when forced to release him on Hill's orders, swore that he would "call M[allett] to a personal account" after the war. Bad relations between the two men continued to fester until Mallett was appointed major of the regiment on August 10, 1864. Less than a month later Radcliffe resigned. His ostensible reason, as stated in his letter of resignation, was certainly true as far as it went; namely, that "disagreements and unpleasant differences of long standing between myself and Field officers _____ [have destroyed?] the harmony of my command." A postwar duel was presumably avoided when Mallett, who by then had been promoted to lieutenant colonel of the regiment, was killed at Bentonville in March 1865. "Radcliffe Charges and Specifications," April 11, 1863, and J. D. Radcliffe to Samuel Cooper (Confederate adjutant and inspector general), September 5, 1864, both in J. D. Radcliffe service record file, 61st Regiment N.C. Troops, Compiled Confederate Service Records (North Carolina), M270, reel 548; S. S. Biddle Jr. to S. S. Biddle Sr., May 23, 1863, Biddle Papers (see also June 12, 1863). The foregoing accounts of the 61st North Carolina's complex role in the fights at Southwest Creek and Kinston are based on incomplete and somewhat contradictory evidence and are offered with some reservation. Contributions are invited from readers and researchers who have additional documentation.

17. A staff officer who arrived at the Confederate line with a surrender demand from Foster was rebuffed by Evans with "[T]ell your Genl to go to h-ll." W. H. Sullivan to "My dear friend," December 27, 1862, Pelot Papers.

18. The 8th and 51st were members of Clingman's recently formed brigade, as was, indeed, the 61st North Carolina. The 52nd was detached from Brig. Gen. James Johnston Pettigrew's Brigade. Further details concerning the organizational history of Clingman's Brigade appear in footnote 20 below.

19. In fact, the bridge was not seriously damaged and was repaired in less than three weeks.

20. *Daily Progress* (Raleigh), December 30, 1862. Clingman was appointed commander of "the troops at Wilmington" on August 18, 1862, and the 61st North Carolina temporarily came under his authority when it was organized there on or about September 5. However, Clingman's Brigade was not organized as such until the latter part of November and early December when, in accordance with a November 11 order from the secretary of war, the 8th, 31st, and 51st North Carolina were ordered to Wilmington. The 51st arrived on the evening of

railroad in line of battle, well protected by the high embankment of the road in front of them," Clingman sent the 8th and 61st North Carolina and Colonel Mallett's contingent, supported by two guns, to turn Lee's right. Shortly thereafter, a 61st officer wrote, the three units "charge[d] with fixed bayonets across an open field a half mile in width, in the direction of a strip of woods, in the rear of which was the railroad embankment. . . . On reaching this position we found it evacuated, having evidently been very recently occupied by the enemy. They fell back a distance of four hundred yards and opened on us with their artillery, giving us a most heavy shelling and graping until night. We returned the fire with only one gun. . . . [T]he other . . . was disabled while crossing the field by being driven accidentally into a large ditch. . . . Instead of falling back on account of superior numbers against us, we held our position until we ascertained through our skirmishers that the enemy had retired and left us the field."[21] The day ended with an unsupported frontal assault on Lee by the 51st and 52nd North Carolina, which were ordered forward by Evans without Clingman's knowledge and repulsed with substantial losses. Lee then retreated down the Kinston road without further molestation. The 61st North Carolina suffered no casualties during the day's fighting.[22]

The 61st remained in camp near Goldsboro for about ten days and, it seems, passed a dreary Christmas. "I . . . [t]hought of you all on Christmas Day," Lt. Samuel S. Biddle of Company C wistfully assured his sister, "sitting by a warm fire eating Cake & drinking wines of every kind, while we poor fellows were sitting under our bush shelters eating bread & pork." On or about December 28 the men marched down the tracks of the

---

November 21; the 8th on November 23; and the 31st on December 8. Clingman, who had been replaced by Brig. Gen. W. H. C. Whiting as commander of what was now styled the "defenses of [the] Cape Fear River," reached the city on November 20. The 61st North Carolina was also assigned to Clingman, but for the time being it received no orders to report. Clingman's Brigade, minus the 61st, was ordered to Goldsboro on or about December 14 in response to the Foster raid, but the first regiment to arrive, the 31st North Carolina, was diverted on the night of December 15 to reinforce Robertson at White Hall. Thus Clingman had only the 8th and 51st North Carolina during the initial fighting at Goldsboro on December 17. All four regiments were finally united under Clingman for the first time during the next few days, but the 31st did not rejoin the brigade in time for the fight at Goldsboro on December 19. *Official Records (Army)*, ser. 1, 9:480, 18:770. See also *Official Records (Army)*, ser. 1, 14:782, 785, 791; "Record of Events," Company B, 51st Regiment N.C. Troops, November-December 1862, and Company I, 8th Regiment N.C. State Troops, November 1862-February 1863, Compiled Confederate Service Records (North Carolina), M270, reels 486, 181; James H. Foote, "Historical Memorandum" dated January 4, 1864, in "North Carolina Adjutant General's Roll of Honor," NCDAH.

21. *Official Records (Army)*, ser. 1, 18:118; *Daily Progress* (Raleigh), December 30, 1862.

22. "The enemy cannot be found to-day," one observer wrote from Goldsboro on December 18. "During the night he pulled up stakes and left for parts unknown. His track, however, may be traced in the direction of Wilmington. Dense columns of smoke are to be seen on the line of the railroad, and apparently much farther off than the burning of yesterday. The whole line of railroad from the bridge over [the] Neuse, as far as Faison's, that being the point last heard from, has been torn up and destroyed. Only one small building is left standing at Dudley Depot, and wherever a farm house falls in his track, it shares the fate of the railroad. Never did an army, professing civilization, commit such wanton destruction of property. They have entered the richest portion of our State, before them is the garden of Eden, with the graneries [*sic*] of the farmer well stored, behind is a desolate waste. It is impossible to form any estimate of the amount of property destroyed, but to give some idea of their doings, the whole heavens have been blackened with smoke since early yesterday morning, extending from Lenoir up to the line of the road, embracing one-eighth of the circle of the horizon." *Daily Progress* (Raleigh), December 19, 1862.

Wilmington and Weldon Railroad toward Wilmington. After a five-and-one-half-day "tramp" though "continuous mud & water," exposed to "the most severe weather," they went into camp at Camp Lamb, at Wilmington, on or about January 2.[23] On a date subsequent to January 22 but prior to February 11, they moved to Camp Davis, "a pretty place" on Masonboro Sound about nine miles below Wilmington. There they pitched their tents "by the sea" or, more accurately, within hearing of the "roaring . . . Atlantic."[24]

January was primarily notable in the 61st North Carolina for a period of ill health. Although some of the men received smallpox vaccinations, others did not, and several deaths occurred from that disease. There were outbreaks also of mumps and measles. By February 1, however, a general recovery, perhaps prompted by the move to Camp Davis, was underway. Captain Choate wrote on that date that "The health of our Company is generally good and I am thankful I can say the smallpox has not spread. . . ." On February 11 Sgt. Parrott F. M. Daniel of Company F noted that there were no smallpox cases in the regiment "as I know of."[25]

At Masonboro Sound the tedious routines of camp life such as drill, inspections, and guard duty, punctuated by "a good deal" of breastwork construction, resumed. However, life by the sea afforded an important eatable perquisite: "We . . . get a plenty of oysters," a contented Sergeant Daniel informed his mother. "[W]hen the tide goes out we can get thousands of them."[26] Captain Moore, too, was "living pretty well." Writing to his lady love on the evening of February 15, Moore waxed picturesque about the regiment's new encampment, inviting her to "behold" in her mind's eye "blazing fires, while hearkning to the monotonous confuzion of simultanious voices, commingled with the slapping and poping of tents [in the wind], disturbed only occasionly by the . . . neighing of a steed & the unpleasant croaking of frogs, all of which go up with the heated air from the top of a beautiful hill, dotted with old-field-pines, by the sea." Pleasant vistas and "an Ocean of luxuries"

23. S. S. Biddle Jr. to Rosa Biddle (his sister), January 5, 1863, Biddle Letters, New Hanover County Museum of the Lower Cape Fear, Wilmington, hereafter cited as Biddle Letters; A. J. Moore to Bettie Farmer, January 3, 1863, Moore Letters. Some elements of the regiment appear to have arrived on the previous day. See Major (given name) Uzzell (Company C, 61st North Carolina) to his mother and father, January 1, 1863, Major Uzzell Letters, Private Collections, NCDAH.

24. Parrott F. M. Daniel to his mother, February 11, 1863 (first quotation), Asa J. Daniel Papers, Private Collections, NCDAH, hereafter cited as Daniel Papers; A. J. Moore to Bettie Farmer, February 11, 1863 (second and third quotations), Moore Letters. During a later stay at Camp Davis, Lt. S. S. Biddle of Company C described its location as "about one and a half miles from the ocean." Possibly the cite of the second Camp Davis was not identical to that of the first. S. S. Biddle Jr. to S. S. Biddle Sr., June 7, 1863, Simpson and Biddle Papers. See also A. J. Moore to Bettie Farmer, January 22, 1863.

25. W. T. Choate to Martha Choate, February 1, 1863, in *Alleghany County Heritage* (Winston-Salem: Hunter Publishing Company, 1983), 132, hereafter cited as *Alleghany County Heritage*; P. F. M. Daniel to his mother, February 11, 1863, Daniel Papers. An organizational chart for Whiting's "District of the Cape Fear" dated January 31, 1863, indicates that Company B of the 61st was on detached duty serving as part of the "City Garrison" of Wilmington. *Official Records (Army)*, ser. 1, 18:866.

26. P. F. M. Daniel to his mother, February 11, 1863, Daniel Papers. "I get oysters to eat whenever I want them," Captain Moore wrote. A. J. Moore to Bettie Farmer, February 15, 1863, Moore Letters.

were inadequate recompense, however, for the protracted separation from Bettie to which he was "doomed." "Write soon," he concluded plaintively, "to unfortunate Andrew."[27]

During the early weeks of 1863 an increase in Federal naval activity along the South Carolina and Georgia coasts necessitated the dispatch of reinforcements to that area, and on the evening of the fifteenth the 61st North Carolina and the rest of Clingman's Brigade were ordered to Charleston. On the seventeenth the regiment departed Wilmington by train. "[It was raining] when we left," a 61st North Carolina soldier who wrote under the pseudonym of "J" informed the editors of the *Wilmington Journal*, "and it kept raining all the time we were on the railroad [thirty-six hours]. . . ."[28] On February 20, the day after it arrived at Charleston, the regiment was "marched out to . . . [a] camp, near James Island & somewhat between it & [the] City. On one side," Captain Moore wrote, "is the Ashland [Ashley] River & on the other what is called the Warpoo [Wappoo] cut [Creek], in full view of the Forts & Islands around, were it not for the trees in our immediate nabourhood." "We are again without tents," "J" commented, "but the weather [is] comparatively pleasant."[29]

At 4:00 P.M. on March 2 the 61st North Carolina and two other regiments of Clingman's Brigade (the 8th and 31st) were ordered to Savannah, where Federal gunboats had destroyed the blockade-runner *Rattlesnake*, lying under the guns of Fort McAllister in the Ogeechee River, on February 28. The three regiments departed by train at about 7:30 P.M. and rolled into Savannah at nine o'clock the next morning to the reverberations of a "thundering" exchange of fire between Fort McAllister and the enemy squadron.[30] That engagement, however, was merely a Federal training exercise in preparation for an attack on Charleston. On March 8 the regiment was ordered back to that city and "hurried away" by rail around 7:00 P.M. It arrived the next day and resumed its former camp.[31] On March 12 the

27. A. J. Moore to Bettie Farmer, February 15, 1863, Moore Letters. "The roaring of the surf," Moore continued, "as it whirles in circular sheets with mighty power to expire upon the beach seizes the soul of the wayward soldier boy from the jovial customs & onerous tasks of camp to view with astonishment & deep felt admyration the sublime and powerful works of Nature's God." Such effusions were well received: Andrew and Bettie were married in January 1864. Their "wonderful" love endured, a descendant wrote, until Bettie's death fifty-four years later. See undated statement by Ruth Moore Mincher in Moore Papers.

28. "J" to "Messrs. Editors," *Wilmington [Weekly] Journal*, February 26, 1863. "[O]ur regiment . . . is now some two hundred stronger than it was some months past," "J" continued. "Governor Vance's [amnesty] proclamation has brought in a great many stragglers, deserters or other absentees that never would have otherwise come in. . . . The general health of [the] camp is good." See also A. J. Moore to Bettie Farmer, February 19, 1863, Moore Letters. The headquarters of the 61st North Carolina on that date was the American Hotel, Charleston.

29. A. J. Moore to Bettie Farmer, February 20, 1863, Moore Letters; "J" to "Messrs. Editors," *Wilmington [Weekly] Journal*, February 26, 1863. Moore added that from the roof of the city orphanage "the finest prospect I have ever seen . . . met my view; besides the City itself, there was the flags of [Fort] Sumpter [*sic*], [Fort] Moultrie, Castle Pinkney [*sic*], Morrison [Morris] & Sulivan [*sic*] Islands floating in the breeze, while still farther was the enimy's flags from four gun boats."

30. A. J. Moore to Bettie Farmer, March 3, 1863, Moore Letters. The 51st North Carolina arrived on March 4.

31. A. J. Moore to Bettie Farmer, March 10, 1863, Moore Letters. "Every recollection and association of our sojourn in Savannah is of the most pleasant and delightful character," Captain Ramsey later wrote. "We were welcomed most heartily by the noble men and women of that most beautiful of cities and royally entertained." Captain Moore was also impressed by the "beautiful" and "seemingly antique City . . . whose constructure is so happily releaved by intervening & circular Parks." Ramsey, "Sixty-first Regiment," in Clark, *Histories of the North Carolina Regiments*, 3:509; A. J. Moore to Bettie Farmer, March 10, 1863, Moore Letters.

men moved to Secessionville, on James Island. Captain Choate's initial reaction to that desolate expanse of wind-swept, gnat-infested sand was surprisingly favorable. "[W]e are campt in an Island . . . about 5 or 6 miles be low Charleston," he wrote. "[I]t is a tolerable prety plase and the water is beter than I Expected. . . . [O]ur Raotings [rations] is one lb corn meel 3/4 lb of beef and a small portion of Rise and molasses per day, so thare is no danger of our starving. . . ."[32] Captain Moore, writing four days later, offered a different view of matters. "If you could see me now," he told Bettie, "I think you perhaps would change your notions & . . . [regret] the awful mistake of Cupid, for winging his shaft in this direction, or for shooting[at] another man & striking my black & dusty [hide], for . . . [James Island] is the dustiest place I ever saw. . . . It is an unhealthy place & ten times ten thousand gnats worry ones life away. Such is James Island[,] seemingly destitute of every thing that nourishes, elates with joy, or makes one love to live."[33] Captain Ramsey was equally appalled. "Going from Savannah, Ga., to James' Island, S. C.," he recalled, "was about what I would imagine with my limited knowledge of the two localities . . . the same as dropping out of Paradise into Hell! We found James' Island a little Sahara, having plenty of wind; rolling and twisting clouds of sand; millions of black gnats (much greater pests than mosquitoes), and a very scanty supply of devilish poor beef, that a respectable Charleston buzzard would not eat. We had to sink holes here and there and everywhere to get a supply of tadpole water—at the same time there being a well of good water [nearby] at Fort Pemberton, which no Tar Heel was allowed to sample."[34]

The 61st North Carolina remained on James Island for the next eight weeks. Bad water, poor and scanty rations, insects, and sand storms took a toll on the men's health and morale, but spirits probably revived a bit on March 28 when Clingman's Brigade was reviewed by General P. G. T. Beauregard, commander of the Department of South Carolina, Georgia, and Florida. Standing in line of battle with weapons at shoulder arms and bayonets "glittering," the men heard themselves commended as "veteran[s]" and a "credit"

32. W. T. Choate to Martha Choate, March 14, 1863, Choate Letters. "The health of the co is verry good," Choate added, "infact the comp[any] is in the best health I ever saw it since we have bin in the Rigment."

33. A. J. Moore to Bettie Farmer, March 18, 1863, Moore Letters. "We do not get hardly enough to eat without buying some, but make out," Sgt. P. F. M. Daniel informed his mother. P. F. M. Daniel to his mother, April 5, 1863, Daniel Papers. Like their comrades in the 51st North Carolina, the men of the 61st probably supplemented their rations by killing rabbits, an activity pursued with such zeal and proficiency that the island's colony was reportedly almost exterminated. See Louis H. Manarin and Weymouth T. Jordan Jr., comps., North Carolina Troops, 1861-1865: A Roster, 14 vols. to date (Raleigh: Division of Archives and History, Department of Cultural Resources, 1966–), 13:261, hereafter cited as Manarin and Jordan, North Carolina Troops.

34. Ramsey, "Sixty-first Regiment," in Clark, Histories of the North Carolina Regiments, 3:510. "In Savannah," Ramsey continued, "bacon sold for 35 cents per pound; at Charleston it was 62 cents, and North Carolina money couldn't buy it at any price. Our money was refused at the postoffice, in the market, in the stores and on the streets." Pvt. William L. Burke of Company D echoed most of Moore's and Ramsey's complaints in a letter to his brother Thomas dated April 18, 1863: "I hope that you are not living as hard . . . as what we are down here where there is nothing but Sand Clouds and millions of black knats[,] our provisions Chiefly Consisting of poor bull[y] beef and Corn bread[.] [O]ur rations does not average more than 2 ounces of meat pr day[.] Some times we get a Small quantity [of] sugar but it is So Small and Seldom we get it it is not worth mentioning[.]" William L. Burke (Company D, 61st North Carolina) to Thomas T. Burke (his brother), April 8, 1863, Thomas T. Burke Papers, hereafter cited as Burke Papers, SCD-DU. See also Wilmington [Weekly] Journal, April 30 and May 7, 1863.

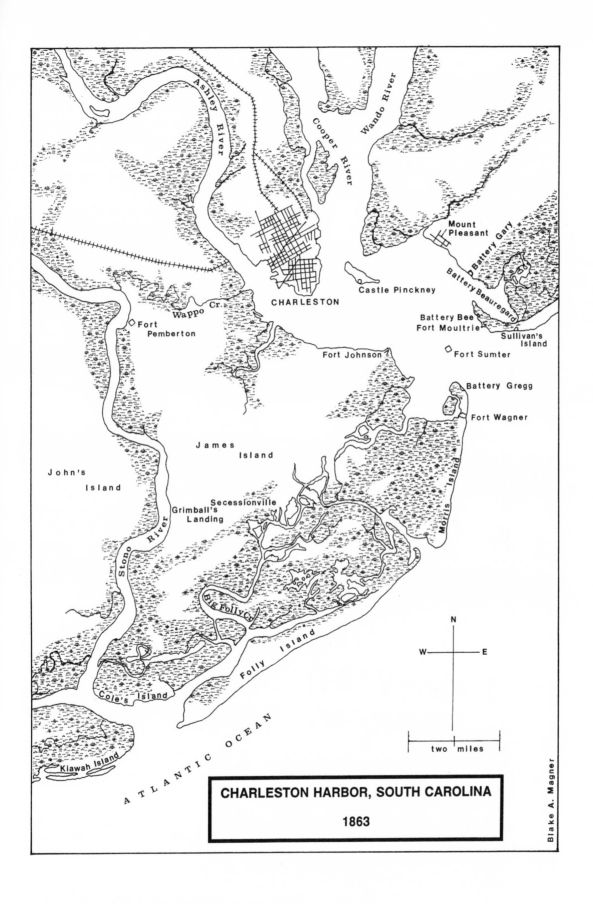

CHARLESTON HARBOR, SOUTH CAROLINA

1863

to their "noble" state.[35] However, on April 20 Beauregard returned for a "very long & fatiguing" and less successful review. "[O]f its kind," Captain Moore observed, "the review . . . was very imposing & had it not been so dry & dusty perhaps I might have enjoyed it, but you can immagine something of my delight when I tell you that the dust was awful, in marching past the Gen, & within almost ten steps I could not glimps him through the thickness of the cloud rolling be fore me. . . . [We] could not [help but] laugh at [one] another at the command halt, for such a metamorphosis in so short a period you have never seen. . . . You certainly would not have known me. . . ." Perhaps because of the austerities of James Island, the regiment experienced a religious revival. William B. Jones, the regiment's newly appointed chaplain, wrote on April 2 that the men were "more attentive at preaching and prayer meeting than the congregations at home. We have preaching twice on each Sabbath and prayer meeting every night. These prayer meetings are moved from one company to another, so that it takes me ten days to get through the Regiment. This is not the plan of most Chaplains, but I think I shall be able to do more good in this way than in any other."[36]

During a heavy attack by the Federal navy on April 7, the 61st was called to arms and "was in line ready to march at a moments warning. . . ." However, the regiment took no part in the fighting.[37] By late April it was apparent that Charleston was in no imminent danger, and Clingman's Brigade was ordered back to Wilmington. The 61st probably moved by rail with its sister unit, the 51st, which departed on the morning of May 2 and arrived after nightfall the same date.[38] By May 5 or thereabouts the 61st was encamped two miles east of Wilmington. "Our Camp is not at all a desirable one," Moore grumbled, "as it . . . is very dusty. The health of the company is not as good as desired. . . ."[39] However, by May 30 the entire brigade was back at Camp Davis, its seaside refuge of happy memory. "This [site] with some other places near [by] has been a considerable resort . . . for the people of Wilmington, in days gone," Moore wrote. "We can sport away our leisure moments in catching

35. *Wilmington [Weekly] Journal*, April 2, 1863. See also P. F. M. Daniel to his mother, April 5, 1863, Daniel Papers; Edgar Smithwick (Company H, 61st North Carolina) to his mother, April 3, 1863, Edgar Smithwick Papers, SCD-DU, hereafter cited as Smithwick Papers. Clingman's immediate superior was Brig. Gen. Roswell S. Ripley, who commanded the First Military District of South Carolina (Charleston Harbor and its defenses). See also *Wilmington [Weekly] Journal*, April 16, 1863.

36. A. J. Moore to Bettie Farmer, April 21, 1863, Moore Letters; *Biblical Recorder* (Raleigh), April 8, 1863. Chaplain Jones's righteous labor bore fruit. In a letter that was probably written in mid-May, he stated that "We have but little profanity [in the 61st] and that is saying a great deal for a regiment now. There is a good state of feeling on the subject of religion. Prayer meetings at night are well attended. I have never been so pleasantly situated." *Biblical Recorder*, May 27, 1863.

37. W. T. Choate to Martha Choate, April 7, 1863, Choate Letters. See also A. J. Moore to Bettie Farmer, April 6, 1863, Moore Letters; William M. Wright (8th North Carolina) to his father and mother, April 8, 1863, John Wright Family Papers, Private Collections, NCDAH; William L. Burke to one his brothers (either Thomas T. or Quinton R.), April 8, 1863, Burke Papers. "I am going out on picket in the morning about 5 miles from the Camp [at Secessionville]," Private Burke wrote, "and it is a verry unpleasant trip too."

38. See William James Burney (51st North Carolina) to his father, May 3, 1863, Roster Document No. 0473, CWRP, NCDAH, hereafter cited as Burney Letters.

39. A. J. Moore to Bettie Farmer, May 15, 1863, Moore Letters. The 8th North Carolina, according to Moore, was in camp one mile east of Wilmington; the 51st North Carolina was "on Topsail Sound about 12 miles a little S.E."

fish which I relish very much. . . . All conveniences taken into consideration one would call this a delightful spot. . . ."[40]

On July 11 Clingman's Brigade departed by train for Charleston, where a long-anticipated Federal amphibious assault had begun the previous day. Well protected by fortifications and natural endowments, Charleston, it seemed evident, would not be easily conquered. Guarding the city on either side and flowing into a broad harbor were the Ashley and Cooper Rivers. In the harbor's narrow mouth, formed by the channel between two large, well-fortified islands, stood Fort Sumter, a multitiered, pentagonal-shaped bastion of masonry construction. Sullivan's Island, north of the channel, was defended by venerable Fort Moultrie and Batteries Bee and Beauregard; to the south, Morris Island's defenses included Battery Gregg and Fort Wagner, a moat-ringed field work of sand, turf, and palmetto logs. Folly Island, southwest of Morris Island, was already in Federal hands, but between Folly Island and Charleston lay the expansive marshes and mud flats of James Island defended by forts, rifle pits, and battery emplacements. Mines, underwater obstructions, and floating rope mats, together with treacherous currents and shoals, further complicated the Federal task. In command of the city's defenses and ample garrison was the flamboyant but redoubtable General Beauregard, whose achievements included the capture of Fort Sumter in 1861. The Federal plan of attack called for infantry to cross the narrow inlet between Folly and Morris Islands, capture Fort Wagner and Battery Gregg, and reduce Fort Sumter with artillery from the point-blank range of scarcely more than a mile. A channel would then be cleared through the harbor obstructions, and the final advance on Charleston would begin.

On July 10, under cover of a naval barrage, Federal infantrymen advanced across Morris Island until halted abruptly by fire from Fort Wagner. An assault on the fort the next day, by which time the garrison had been reinforced, was repulsed with heavy loss. The Federal commander, Brig. Gen. Quincy A. Gillmore, then brought up forty long-range cannons and siege mortars and attempted to pound the Confederates into submission. In the meantime Clingman's Brigade, minus three companies of the 61st, arrived from Wilmington on the rainy evening of July 12.[41] The next day the 8th, 31st and 61st were sent to

40. A. J. Moore to Bettie Farmer, May 30, 1863, Moore Letters.

41. On July 5 Companies C, H, and K, with the exception of men who were on detail, were "hurried off from camp," according to Lieutenant Biddle, in response to reports of an enemy force at Warsaw, in Duplin County. Company C was apparently stationed at Kenansville (Duplin County) through October, and Company H was at Kenansville and Magnolia (Duplin County) during that period. Both companies rejoined the regiment at or near Petersburg, Virginia, on or about December 16, 1863. Company K was at Kenansville through August and rejoined the regiment at Charleston in October. The mission of the three companies, Biddle wrote, was "to prevent the enemy from making another raid upon this section." Detailed men who were not sent to Duplin County accompanied the regiment to Charleston but rejoined their companies in North Carolina on October 10. In the case of at least one company (H), the detailed contingent was relatively large: two officers and twenty-one men. S. S. Biddle Jr. to S. S. Biddle Sr., July 12, 1863, Biddle Papers. See also *Official Records (Army)*, ser. 1, 27 (pt. 3):1067, 29 (pt. 2):814, 857; "Record of Events," Companies C, H, and K, 61st Regiment N.C. Troops, July-August, September-October, and November-December, 1863, Compiled Confederate Service Records (North Carolina), M270, reel 543. (The Company H "Record of Events" for September-October 1863 is particularly valuable.) For further information concerning the whereabouts and activities of Company H, see Edgar Smithwick to his mother, July 28, August 9 and 29, October 9 and 16, November 19 and 22, and December 25, 1863, Smithwick Papers. For information concerning the whereabouts and activities of Company C, see

James Island and the 51st to Fort Wagner.[42] At about 4:00 A.M. on July 16 the 61st and four other regiments, supported by artillery and cavalry, attacked Federal troops and naval vessels near Grimball's Landing, on the Stono River. "They first brought down into the woods near Grimball's what I suppose to have been two field batteries, and opened fire upon the [gunboat] *Pawnee*," the Federal commander, Brig. Gen. Alfred H. Terry, reported. "Immediately thereafter they advanced four regiments of infantry, accompanied by artillery, upon the right of my line, drove in the outposts and supports, and commenced a severe fire from their guns. At the same time, a strong body of infantry and cavalry, with a battery, drove in our outposts on the left beyond the causeway leading to Grimball's, and attempted to debouch in front of my left. My troops were speedily under arms, and as soon as the pickets were in, I opened on the enemy from [Capt. Alfred P.] Rockwell's battery and the armed transports *Mayflower* and *John Adams*. The naval vessels [*Pawnee* and *Marblehead*] also opened a most effective fire upon my left."[43] During that attack the 61st North Carolina was on the Confederate right supporting the battery that engaged the gunboats.

At first dawn of day [Colonel Radcliffe wrote], the command was given to advance, the troops, infantry and artillery, moving up boldly and eagerly to the attack. So prompt and silent were they in taking their positions, that the whole attack proved a complete surprise, our batteries having fired about six times before the *Pawnee*, the most formidable of the two boats, could prepare for action. The rapidity and accuracy with which our batteries fired on this occasion has scarcely been equaled in artillery practice, more than one-third of the missiles discharged from our guns taking effect on the *Pawnee*, a fact easily ascertained by the crashing of her timbers and confusion and cries of her crew. Both boats finally withdrew beyond range of our guns, the *Pawnee* supposed to be very seriously crippled and the other boat more or less damaged.[44]

Contrary to Radcliffe, the *Pawnee*, although struck by more than thirty-five shells, was far from crippled. Together with the other Federal ships, she unleashed a "terrible"

S. S. Biddle Jr. to Rosa Biddle, July 27 and September 28, 1863, Sampson and Biddle Papers.

42. Clingman was initially instructed to "select [his] two strongest regiments for service on Morris Island. . . ." There, he was "given to understand," he was "to lead an attack" and "dislodge the enemy." He selected the 8th and 51st and ordered the 31st and 61st to James Island. However, the Morris Island attack was canceled the next day. The 51st was then sent to Fort Wagner, and the 8th joined the 31st and 61st on James Island. Janet B. Hewett, Noah Andre Trudeau, and Bryce A. Suderow, eds., *Supplement to the Official Records of the Union and Confederate Armies* (Wilmington, N.C.: Broadfoot Publishing Company, 1996), 5:489, hereafter cited as *Official Records Supplement*. See also A. J. Moore to Bettie Farmer, July 16, 1863, Moore Letters; *Official Records (Army)*, ser. 1, 28 (pt. 1):371.

43. *Official Records (Army)*, ser. 1, 28 (pt. 1):755. Italics added for names of naval vessels.

44. *Official Records (Army)*, ser. 1, 28 (pt. 1):590. In a letter to the *Wilmington Journal*, a 61st Regiment soldier who identified himself as "North Carolina" described Radcliffe's attack as "a perfect success. The 61st drove in the enemy's pickets and reserves, many of whom took refuge on board the *Pawnee*. The field pieces were then put in position, and opened on the gunboats at a distance of about four hundred yards. The surprise of the enemy was so great that they did not return the fire until some ten or fifteen shots had been made. The first four out of six shots struck the *Pawnee*. Both of the gunboats retired down the river shelling our artillerists and the 61st Regiment, all of whom were much exposed in an open field. . . . The artillery contest was kept up for about two hours, by which time the gunboats had retreated out of range. . . ." *Wilmington [Weekly] Journal*, July 23, 1863. (Italics added for names of naval vessels in *Official Records* report and *Wilmington Journal* letter.)

fusillade on the 61st and the other Confederate regiments, preventing them from attacking Terry.[45] After a two-hour stalemate, the Confederates withdrew. Colonel Radcliffe wrote that his men were "exposed during the entire action to a galling fire of shell and canister from the gunboats" and, although "disappointed" in not meeting the enemy infantry, "showed, both officers and men, by their proximity to danger, that they would never desert the batteries."[46] Notwithstanding the heavy fire to which it was subjected, the 61st suffered only one casualty: Cpl. Benjamin A. Davis of Company F died a few hours after his leg was shot off at the knee.

During the skirmish described above, General Gillmore's teeth-rattling, five-day bombardment of Fort Wagner continued. On the evening of July 18 Gillmore tested the fort's defenses again with an infantry attack spearheaded by a black regiment, the 54th Massachusetts. In one of the war's most famous episodes, the 54th was repulsed with murderous casualties, including its white commander, Col. Robert Gould Shaw, who was left dead on the field. Two of Clingman's regiments, the 31st and 51st North Carolina, played major roles in the battle, but the 61st was not engaged.

On the evening of July 18 the 61st and two of its sister regiments, the 8th and the shell-shocked 51st, were ordered to Sullivan's Island. The 31st followed on the nineteenth.[47] For the next seven weeks those four units alternated tours of duty between Morris Island's hellish environs and the relative tranquillity of Sullivan's Island. Meantime, Gillmore abandoned frontal assaults and instituted a siege, digging zigzag trenches (known as saps) toward Fort Wagner and moving his sharpshooters and mortars closer and closer to the embattled Confederates. That tactic, although slow to produce results, reduced conditions in the fort to new levels of intolerability. "The men were at all times exposed to the enemy's fire, both from the land and from the sea," a member of the 8th North Carolina recollected. "An attack had to be prepared for at any instant, either night or day. . . . The men had to keep under cover of the battery or in pits near by dug in the sand hills along the beach. . . . All the rations had to be prepared elsewhere and carried there. The water too, was bad."[48] Depending on the circumstances of the moment, the fort's harried defenders rushed back and forth between the maddening noise, heat, and stench of the bombproof and open areas of the fort, where enemy shells and sharpshooters were likely to bring sudden death. After firing for weeks at the same stationary target, Federal artillerymen were able to sight their pieces with almost pinpoint accuracy. Naval gunners, not to be outdone, adeptly ricocheted shells off the water, careening them into the fort at low angles and, occasionally,

45. A. J. Moore to Bettie Farmer, July 16, 1863, Moore Letters. See also Edward K. Rawson and others, eds., *The War of the Rebellion: A Compilation of the Official Records of the Union and Confederate Navies*, 31 vols. (Washington, D.C.: Government Printing Office, 1894-1927), ser. 1, 14:345, 348-349.

46. *Official Records (Army)*, ser. 1, 28 (pt. 1):590. See also *Official Records Supplement*, 5:489.

47. See *Official Records (Army)*, ser. 1, 28 (pt. 2):209, 211.

48. William Hyslop Sumner Burgwyn, "Clingman's Brigade," in Clark, *Histories of the North Carolina Regiments*, 4:485, hereafter cited as Burgwyn, "Cingman's Brigade," in Clark, *Histories of the North Carolina Regiments*.

exploding them in its deepest recesses. The establishment of a hospital in the bombproof added a new element of "loathsomeness and horror" to the men's afflictions.[49]

The 61st North Carolina's tours on Morris Island encompassed the periods July 25-31, August 6-11, and August 21-28.[50] In a letter written on August 2, Captain Moore described the July 25-31 tour:

> For the first two days there were but few casualties, the Gun-Boats not aiding the land Batteries in their attacks, but at the same time without shelter & exposed to a most scorching sun, with labour night & day, you may guess that pleasure came but seldom. . . . [T]he third day . . . was ushered into existance mid the most awful disquietude of the ossial [ostial] auditorium [the ear] I ever witnessed, all of which was caused by the attack upon Wagner by five or six gun-boats, three or four Monitors, the Ironsides [ironclads] & two Morter [mortar] Boats, in addition to their land Batteries. This was the case though not with like severity during the remainder of our stay. . . . Upon this narrow strip of land, exposed as it is to a cross fire almost, it would seem to one unacquainted with the chances of war that none but [those] who occupy the boom-proof [bombproof], of Wagner, could live, & hardly here; but it is true that [during] the five days[?] we remained, the casualties were but few. . . . Were it not for the destructiveness of war it would nearly be amusing to witness the scenes transpiring here. Those who cannot get in the Boom proof are strung along the beach upon the sand Hills [dunes] from Wagner to Battery Greg a distance of about a half mile & in full range of their Gunboats & land Batteries. During the time of my stay, two Regts occupied these Sand-Hills. Ours was one of the Regts, for I dont think a N.C. Regt. ever got the safety of the Boom-proof & in fact I prefer being killed in the open air to dying with sufication. . . . Whenever the Gunboats open fire upon these Hills, which they did often during the latter part of our stay, it was amusing to witness the rapidity with which each man sought his hole in the banks, & well it might be so, for it was almost certain death to be uncovered wholly 'mid this shower of iron hail. Whenever one of the Monitors open fire . . . you might hear several simultanious shouts of Sand fidlers [fiddler crabs] to your holes, March, double quick, &c.[51]

49. Ramsey, "Sixty-first Regiment," in Clark, *Histories of the North Carolina Regiments*, 3:511. "Battery Wagner is one of the worst dreaded places in the south," a North Carolinian serving in the 21st South Carolina assured his father. "[E]very person [would] almost as soon die as to start there. We are in danger from the time we start until we get back. [O]ur shells do us almost as much harm as the Yankees. . . . [O]ur men shell at night and loose the range very often and shell us." Henry J. Clifton to his father and mother, September 1, 1863, John L. Clifton Papers, SCD-DU, hereafter cited as Clifton Papers.

50. The 61st received orders to proceed to Morris Island on July 21; however, an identical order issued on July 25 suggests that the July 21 order was canceled or, for whatever reason, not implemented. See *Official Records (Army)*, ser. 1, 28 (pt. 2):217, 231. See also *Official Records (Army)*, ser. 1, 28 (pt. 1):375, 385, 393, 397, 407-410, 434, 443-444, 492, 499-500, 28 (pt. 2):249, 333; A. J. Moore to Bettie Farmer, August 2, 5, 13, 16, and 21, 1863, Moore Letters. Troop movements to and from Morris Island could be made safely only at night and often occurred during the wee hours, complicating the historian's task of accurately dating tours of duty. The dates cited above are those on which the 61st was at Fort Wagner during daylight hours.

51. A. J. Moore to Bettie Farmer, August 2, 1863, Moore Letters. See also *Official Records Supplement*, 5:490-497. Individual members of the 61st clearly were inside the bombproof at various times, but it seems doubtful that the unit as a whole was stationed at Fort Wagner during any of its three tours on Morris Island. During its second tour the regiment was "in the sand-hills between Batteries Gregg and Wagner," and the regiment's misadventures during its third tour (see below) also suggest a "Sand fiddler" assignment. With regard to fiddler crabs, it might be added that they were, according to Maj. John C. Gray Jr., a member of Gillmore's staff, the "only animal of importance" on the island and numbered "millions and millions." Morris Island was described by Gray as "an uncultivated sand bank in some places covered with pine trees and palmettos and a

On the night of August 6 the 61st returned to Fort Wagner for its second tour of duty. There it was subjected, in Captain Moore's words, to

one of the most severe bombardments of ancient or modern times, the result of which is yet curtained in a night of horror.

To night one week ago we took the *Chesterfield* [italics added] for Morris Island [and], having reached the Point, landed in safety, the enemy not being able to discover our Bark. For the first two days of our stay, the Gunboats fired but little & the land batteries did not regularly engage us, but on Sunday [August 9] & from Saturday night [August 8] to the time of our departure the bombardment was at times most terrific. As I had charge of the Out-Post duty for near[ly] two days & nights, I think I am able this time to tell you something in respect to the enemy. They are hard at work night & day, throwing up entrenchments [and] building Batteries, almost from one end of the Island to the other, mounting heavy guns &c., I think with a view to reduce Sumpter's [*sic*] walls. We can not now carry a Boat to sumpter, but have to carry provisions & relieve the Garrison by the aid of barges & I think they will soon put a stop to this. . . . Their Sharp-shooters can easily kill a man on the Parapets [of Fort Wagner]. . . . Those occupying the rifle Pits, as well the enemy as ourselves, dare not raise their heads. . . . Thus you see the two are too close to enjoy good health. When I visited my line of Pickets on Sunday night at 11 oclock I discovered that the Yankees had advanced their line or a part of it to within fifty yards. The two held their positions to near day when the Yanks withdrew. . . . We were relieved on Wednesday [August 12] just before day [and returned to Sullivan's Island], the casualties being . . . only one of this Regt. killed & three or four wounded slightly.[52]

During the wee hours of August 21 the 61st returned to Morris Island for what proved to be its last duty tour at Fort Wagner. By that date Federal sappers had advanced to within about 250 yards of the fort and within seventy-five of the "sand hill . . . filled with rebel rifle pits." Shortly after 6:00 P.M. on August 26 the 24th Massachusetts Infantry, supported by the 3rd New Hampshire Infantry, made a sudden rush upon the sand hill position, which was defended by a portion of the 61st North Carolina (probably Companies D, E, and G). Other elements of the regiment were nearby in support.[53]

---

dense undergrowth, in a few places more than half a mile wide and about eight miles long, a most beautiful sand beach (unfortunately abounding in sharks which have bitten some men, one fatally)." *Official Records (Army),* ser. 1, 28 (pt. 1):434; John Chipman Gray Jr. to John Codman Ropes, August 18, 1863, in John Chipman Gray Jr., *War Letters of John Chipman Gray and John Codman Ropes* (Boston and New York: Houghton Mifflin Company, 1927), 179, hereafter cited as Gray, *War Letters.*

52. A. J. Moore to Bettie Farmer, August 13, 1863, Moore Letters. Aside from the solidity and durability of the bombproof, the remarkably low Confederate casualties at Fort Wagner are explained by one soldier's laconic observation that "one shell would fill up the hole made by the last." Scarcely a week before Wagner fell, an unidentified member of the 51st North Carolina described it as "to all appearances unharmed." From a distance of "about a third of a mile," a Federal officer wrote, "Fort Wagner . . . looks like a great sand heap." A. A. McKethan, "Fifty-first Regiment," in Clark, *Histories of the North Carolina Regiments,* 3:208, hereafter cited as McKethan, "Fifty-first Regiment," in Clark, *Histories of the North Carolina Regiments; Fayetteville [Semi-weekly] Observer,* September 7, 1863; J. C. Gray Jr. to Elizabeth Gray (his sister), September 6, 1863, in Gray, *War Letters,* 192.

53. J. C. Gray Jr. to J. C. Ropes, August 30, 1863, in Gray, *War Letters,* 187. Analysis of 61st North Carolina losses during the battle suggests that the three companies cited, which accounted for more than 82 percent of the regiment's casualties, were at the focal point of the Federal attack.

An unsuccessful effort was made on the previous day to blast the Confederates out of their sand hill position

We . . . marched up and took our positions [Col. Francis A. Osborn of the 24th Massachusetts wrote], all sitting down, concealed behind the breastwork. When all was ready, I . . . cried, "All up," when every man stood up and faced the enemy. "Forward," and in an instant we were over the works and rushing upon the enemy at the top of our speed, shouting like mad. They fired but one volley, and then those who dared to take the chance of being fired at by us leaped out of their holes and ran. The rest crouched down and surrendered.

In the first pit I looked into, which was a large, deep square hole, I saw eight men sitting, one of them waving above his head an old red handkerchief in token of his having relinquished all hostile intentions. We disarmed them and sent [them] to the rear, collecting seventy in all, less than twenty having escaped. . . . Our loss, barring scratches, was only one officer and two men killed, and four men wounded.[54]

"[A]s it was necessary to reverse the works," a 3rd New Hampshire officer recalled, the "rebel prisoners were invited to take a hand at digging. Said one big fellow, 'Do you-un's make we-un's work?' The reply was a decided affirmative, coupled with the injunction: 'Dig or die!' This latter referred to . . . [artillery fire] from Wagner, which soon followed the loss of the ridge."[55] According to figures compiled for this volume, casualties in the 61st North Carolina on August 26 numbered 8 men killed or mortally wounded, 22 wounded, and 67 captured (of whom 4 were wounded). Seventy-eight of that number, including all but one of the captured men, were members of Companies D, E, and G.[56]

During the next ten days the Federal sappers continued their inexorable advance toward Fort Wagner.[57] By September 6 they had reached the moat. Under heavy artillery

---

with artillery. An infantry assault was apparently planned also but did not take place. At least four companies of the 61st (A, E, F, and I) and several companies of the 54th Georgia were under fire, and the 61st lost at least five men wounded (three mortally). Among the casualties was the doughty Captain Moore, who was wounded severely in the arm. See *Official Records (Army)*, ser. 1, 28 (pt. 1):295, 396, 444, 53:298; *Daily Bulletin* (Charlotte), August 29, 1863; Warren Ripley, ed., *Siege Train: The Journal of a Confederate Artillery Man in the Defense of Charleston* (Columbia: University of South Carolina Press, 1986), 20, hereafter cited as Ripley, *Siege Train*.

54. Alfred S. Roe, *The Twenty-fourth Regiment Massachusetts Volunteers 1861-1866 "New England Guard Regiment"* (Worcester, Mass.: Blanchard Press, 1907), 212-213 (see also 211, 214-221).

55. Daniel Eldredge, *The Third New Hampshire and All About It* (Boston: E. B. Stillings and Company, 1893), 355 (see also 354, 356). See also Ripley, *Siege Train*, 21-22; *Fayetteville Observer*, September 7, 1863. "About seventy prisoners were taken . . . in the assault on the sand hill," Major Gray wrote. "They seemed to be glad to fall into our hands, being all North Carolineans, and said they were very badly treated by the South Carolineans; they spoke of the fall of Forts Wagner and Gregg as certain." J. C. Gray Jr. to his mother, August 30, 1863, in Gray, *War Letters*, 191.

56. In a dispatch dated August 27, Gillmore reported the capture of "68 prisoners, including 2 officers" on the previous day. Beauregard stated in his campaign report that the Federals captured "76 out of 89 men of the Sixty-first North Carolina Volunteers, who formed the picket." *Official Records (Army)*, ser. 1, 28 (pt. 2):66, 28 (pt. 1):85. See also *Official Records (Army)*, ser. 1, 28 (pt. 1):407-409, 434, 492, 499, 500, 28 (pt. 2):333.

57. According to Lt. Henry J. Clifton (21st South Carolina) and at least one newspaper account, the 61st North Carolina, 20th South Carolina, and 23rd Georgia were aboard the steamer *Sumter* when it was accidentally sunk by Confederate fire on the night of August 30. The 20th South Carolina and 23rd Georgia were in fact on board, but the 61st North Carolina was not. Shallow water and a speedy rescue effort prevented serious loss of life. See H. J. Clifton to his father and mother, September 1, 1863, Clifton Papers; *Fayetteville Observer*, September 7, 1863; *Official Records (Army)*, ser. 1, 28 (pt. 1):397-398; E. Milby Burton, *The Siege of Charleston, 1861-1865* (Columbia: University of South Carolina Press, 1970), 180-182.

fire and faced with an imminent and overpowering infantry assault, the garrison withdrew that night. Meantime, Fort Sumter, which had been under bombardment by Federal batteries on Morris Island since August 17, was reduced by the twenty-third to a "pile of brick and mortar."[58] Nevertheless, its stalwart defenders, although without artillery, repulsed a Federal storming party on September 8 and continued to hold out. Unable to capture Charleston without suffering heavy casualties for a prize whose value was largely symbolic, the Federals scaled back their operations, contenting themselves with shelling the "cradle of rebellion" and pounding its most famous bastion, Fort Sumter, to rubble. Charleston remained in Confederate hands until February 18, 1865.

During September, October, and most of November, the 61st North Carolina remained at Sullivan's Island and was "Chiefly employed in doing out post duty."[59]

We are on Sullivan's Island above Fort Moultrie [a soldier who identified himself as "Sixty-first" informed a Raleigh newspaper on September 23]. . . . [T]he banks of sand . . . form our only protection against the wind, the rain and the shells of the enemy. We are on picket or fatigue duty nearly all the time. Our tents and a good many of our blankets, cooking utensils, &c. are yet in Wilmington. The wind blows cold and just before day in the morning we suffer much for want of bedding. We have been in this condition for some time, and have no hopes of being relieved as long as the siege of Charleston continues. Our men, however, are much more cheerful than you would suppose under such circumstances. It would do your heart good to attend one of our moonlight prayer-meetings on the bald pate of some of these white sand hills.[60]

On November 29 the 61st departed by rail for Goldsboro, which it reached on December 4. On December 6 Captain Choate wrote that he was "fareing sumptuously" on "Rashings" of "beef & flour plenty and some sweat potatos."[61] Eight days later the 61st moved by rail toward Petersburg, where it arrived on the sixteenth. On the seventeenth it was ordered to Joyner's Ford, on the Blackwater River about two miles south of Zuni. It remained spread out along the Blackwater guarding fords, bridges, and roads for most of the next five months. "We are faring veary Well for Someting to Eat," Edgar Smithwick wrote on Christmas Day. "We [are] under the Command of General [George E.] Picket. We are in South Hamton County[.] [I]t is a veary fine Country here[.] [T]he people are veary kind to us here[.] [T]he Weather is veary Cold . . . But We hav A plenty of good oak Wood to Burn And We hav got good Cloths And Shoes to keep us Warm."[62] On January 14,

58. H. J. Clifton to his father and mother, September 1, 1863, Clifton Papers.

59. "Record of Events," Company A, 61st Regiment N.C. Troops, September-October 1863, Compiled Confederate Service Records (North Carolina), M270, reel 543.

60. *Biblical Recorder* (Raleigh), September 30, 1863. "The men have not been paid off in about five months," "Sixty-first" added.

61. W. T. Choate to Martha Choate, December 6, 1863, Choate Letters. See also *Official Records (Army)*, ser. 1, 28 (pt. 2):527-529. Part of Clingman's Brigade was to be stationed at Goldsboro and the remainder at Weldon; however, the 51st North Carolina, which was en route to Weldon, was diverted at Enfield to guard the railroad against a Federal cavalry raid. It was then sent to Hamilton and from there to Tarboro, where it arrived on or about December 19. See *Official Records (Army)*, ser. 1, 29 (pt. 2):853, 856, 860.

62. Edgar Smithwick to his mother, December 25, 1863, Smithwick Papers. In his letter Smithwick stated that "We Will leav heire to Morrow for Petersburg." It is not certain that such a move took place, but if so the

1864, Smithwick wrote from Tucker's Swamp Church, one mile west of Zuni, complaining of snow on the ground and "veary could" weather. Fortunately, the men had "Good quarters" and, he reiterated, "A fine chance of [fire]Wood."[63] In a letter written at Joyner's Ford a week later, Lieutenant Biddle informed his father of "a little skirmish that took place near this place several days past in which several Yank's were killed."[64]

On February 17 or thereabouts the 61st North Carolina was ordered to Smithfield, Virginia, thirteen miles northeast of Zuni, where it arrived on or about the nineteenth. On the twenty-ninth the regiment marched southeast toward Federally occupied Suffolk, which it reached on March 1. There it remained for five days "annoy[ing] the yankees," as Private Smithwick described matters, so "General Randson [Matt Ransom] could go down in Gat[e]s County and get out provis[i]ons." The regiment left Suffolk about 5:00 A.M. on March 6 and reached Ivor Station on or about the eighth. It then resumed its guard duties.[65] By March 10 Captain Moore was comfortably situated in "a small Cabbin [sic]" at Proctor's Ferry "on the right bank of the Black Water River nine miles . . . above Ivor [Station] & fifteen from Smithfield."[66] A foot of snow fell on March 22 but produced no immediate problems for Moore and his men. However, when warm weather arrived two weeks later, the Blackwater flooded, and Moore and the other members of Company F found their campground transformed into "a kind of little island. . . . The water swept furiously over this little elivation," Moore complained on April 12, "& poured in its onward course knee deep through our little habitations. All have evacuated, but myself & Lt [William A.] Darden & brother [Cpl. Abram L. Darden], & we had to raise our bunk three feet from the

---

regiment was back on the Blackwater line within a few weeks. For the names and locations of some of the fords, bridges, and roads guarded by the 61st, see Herbert M. Schiller, ed., *A Captain's War: The Letters and Diaries of William H. S. Burgwyn, 1861-1865* (Shippensburg, Pa.: White Mane Publishing Company, 1994), 138 (April 28-30, 1864), hereafter cited as Schiller, *Burgwyn Letters and Diaries*.

63. Edgar Smithwick to his mother, January 14, 1864, Smithwick Papers. There was also, according to Smithwick in another letter, "plenty of Meat and flour to Eat. We are faring the Best not [now] that we hav in Sone time." Edgar Smithwick to his mother, February 7, 1864, Smithwick Papers. Tucker's Swamp Church was the regiment's headquarters as of March 10, 1864, and may have been so throughout its stay on the Blackwater. See A. J. Moore to Bettie Farmer Moore, March 10, 1864, Moore Letters.

64. S. S. Biddle Jr. to S. S. Biddle Sr., January 21, 1864, Simpson and Biddle Papers. The skirmish referred to probably occurred on January 17 at Ely's Ford, on the Blackwater about eight miles south of Zuni. See *Official Records (Army)*, ser. 1, 33:20. "The difficulty between Capt M[allett] & Col R[adcliffe] is still unsettled," Biddle added in his January 21 letter, "and it is impossible to tell when it will end." On February 1 Mallett wrote from Joyner's Ford to former North Carolina governor David L. Swain asking Swain to use his influence with the current governor, Zebulon B. Vance, to obtain Mallett's transfer to another unit. "My position in the Reg is not only very unpleasant to me," Mallett stated, "and my chances for distinction entirely cut-off, but my opportunities for doing what I might for the good of the service are greatly impaired." Swain passed Mallett's letter on to Vance, but nothing came of his request. Edward Mallett to David L. Swain, February 1, 1864, Zebulon Baird Vance Papers, 4:411, Private Collections (15.4), NCDAH.

65. Edgar Smithwick to his mother, March 9, 1864, Smithwick Papers. "We cept [kept] picket in 100 yards of the yankees," Smithwick continued. "[O]ur Company was on advance picket one Moning and the yankees Cavalry came upt within fifty yards of us. But We had orders not to fire on them Without they fired on us first." According to Captain Moore, "Nothing of consequence transpired down there, the picketts were fired into, but no dammage." A. J. Moore to Bettie Farmer Moore, March 10, 1864, Moore Letters. See also Edgar Smithwick to his mother, March 3, 1864, Smithwick Papers.

66. A. J. Moore to Bettie Farmer Moore, March 10, 1864, Moore Letters.

floor[.] [I]t has now left the floor, so that we can have fires but when we breakfast or dine, we employ the canoe. . . ."[67] At Joyner's Ford on April 14 a "considerable force" of the enemy appeared on the river bank opposite Company C. "I made arrangements with my command to give them a lively reception," Lieutenant Biddle wrote, "but they thinking that they would be severely dealt with returned to Suffolk without firing a gun. . . ."[68] Other elements of the 61st were engaged on that date near Benn's Church, about five miles south of Smithfield.[69]

On May 5, 1864, the Army of the Potomac, numbering 120,000 men under the direction of the Union's newly appointed general-in-chief, Ulysses S. Grant, marched into the Wilderness near Chancellorsville, Virginia, and began a protracted, grinding, and unprecedentedly lethal campaign to destroy Robert E. Lee's 65,000-man Army of Northern Virginia. On the same date a Federal force of 40,000 men under Maj. Gen. Benjamin F. Butler began landing at City Point, on the James River, to cut the vital Richmond and Petersburg Railroad and threaten the Confederate capital from the south. During the next five days, while Grant and Lee were locked in combat at the Wilderness and Spotsylvania Court House, Butler moved slowly toward Petersburg. There he was stymied by a heavily outnumbered Confederate force commanded by Maj. Gen. George E. Pickett, and on the tenth he fell back toward Bermuda Hundred. Two days of indecision and hesitation followed. Butler then began edging his way up the west bank of the James toward Richmond. Leaving a small garrison behind at Petersburg, Beauregard, who had assumed command from

67. A. J. Moore to Bettie Farmer Moore, April 12, 1864, Moore Letters. "The company is very healthy at this time," Moore added. See also A. J. Moore to Bettie Farmer Moore, March 22, 1864. As of April 3 the 61st North Carolina was the only unit of Clingman's Brigade on the Blackwater. "All quiet here," Moore wrote. "Our Brigade, but [except for] our Regt, is at Petersburg. We still guard this line." It appears, however, that the 51st North Carolina was sent to Ivor Station on April 14. A. J. Moore to Bettie Farmer Moore, April 3, 1864. See also *Official Records (Army)*, ser. 1, 51 (pt. 2):861; S. S. Biddle Jr. to Rosa Biddle, March 27, 1864, and S. S. Biddle Jr. to S. S. Biddle Sr., April 17, 1864, Biddle Papers; Marion Womack (Company D, 61st North Carolina) to Solomon Carpenter, April 7, 1864, in Harrington, *To Bear Arms*, 247-248; Edgar Smithwick to his mother, March 22 and April 4 and 23, 1864, Smithwick Papers. "[T]he boyes is garneley [generally] well ate this time," Private Womack observed in his April 7 letter. "[W]e Draw one thurde of Apoude [a pound] of Baken br [per] Day and one punde and Aquarte[r] of Meel br Day and Aboute Anouf Sope [soap] to washe our handes and face[.]"

68. S. S. Biddle Jr. to S. S. Biddle Sr., April 17, 1864, Biddle Papers. See also Edgar Smithwick to his mother, April 23, 1864, Smithwick Papers; *Official Records (Army)*, ser. 1, 33:272. "Two (2) regiments of our Brigade are in North Carolina," Biddle added, but that statement is incorrect: the 8th was indeed near Plymouth with Brig. Gen. Robert F. Hoke, but the 31st and 51st were in Virginia at Petersburg and Ivor Station respectively.

69. The Federals encountered at Benn's Church by elements of the 61st North Carolina on April 14 were part of a "sizable" force "searching the creeks and inlets on the south side of Hampton Roads." Their mission was to determine the strength of Confederate defenses against forthcoming James River naval operations, which were planned as part of the "Overland Campaign" (see below). In the words of historian William Glenn Robertson, the Federals, "Finding no Confederates east of their defensive positions along the Blackwater . . . soon withdrew to their bases and resumed preparations for the approaching campaign." According to an unidentified member of the 61st, the Confederate force numbered fifty-two men, of whom twenty "Scouts" were members of the 61st. William Glenn Robertson, *Back Door to Richmond: The Bermuda Hundred Campaign, April-June 1864* (Baton Rouge: Louisiana State University Press, 1987), 30, 45, hereafter cited as Robertson, *Back Door to Richmond*; *Daily Confederate* (Raleigh), April 26, 1864. See also *Official Records (Army)*, ser. 1, 33:270-276, 850-851, 51 (pt. 2):862-863.

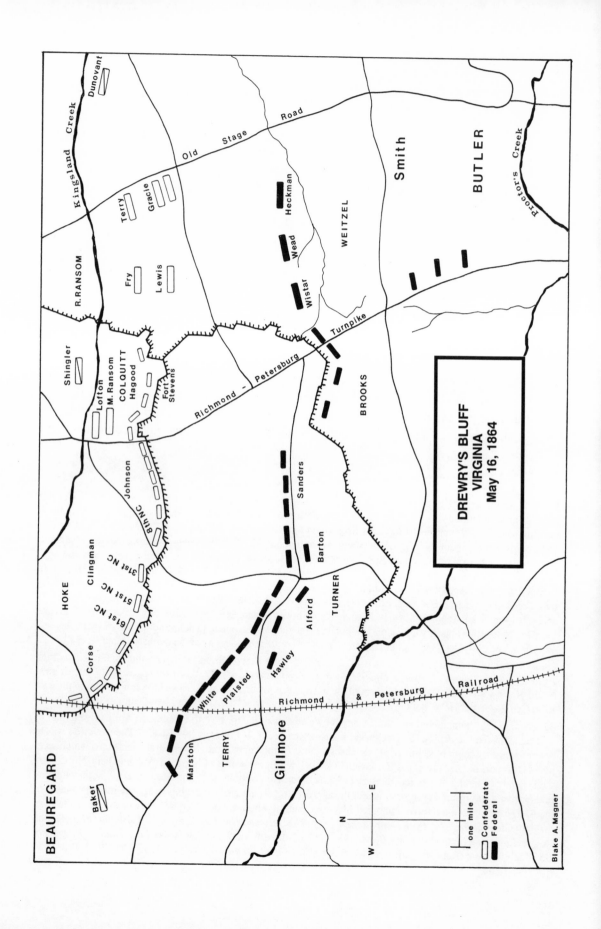

BEAUREGARD

Dunovant

Kingsland Creek

Old Stage Road

Smith

BUTLER

Proctor's Creek

Terry

Gracie

Heckman

WEITZEL

Wead

R. RANSOM

Fry

Lewis

Wistar

Turnpike

Shingler

Richmond — Petersburg

BROOKS

Lofton

M. Ransom

COLQUITT

Hagood

Fort Stevens

DREWRY'S BLUFF
VIRGINIA
May 16, 1864

Johnson

Sanders

18th NC

HOKE

Clingman

31st NC

Barton

51st NC

TURNER

61st NC

Alford

Corse

Hawley

Marston

White

Plaisted

Richmond   &   Petersburg   Railroad

TERRY

Baker

Gillmore

N

E

W

S

one mile

Confederate

Federal

Blake A. Magner

Pickett and received substantial reinforcements, moved north to block Butler at the James River bastion of Drewry's Bluff.

On May 6, while these events were unfolding on the James and north of Richmond, Brig. Gen. August V. Kautz's Federal cavalry division crossed the Blackwater at Birch Island Bridge and proceeded southwest to burn the Petersburg and Weldon Railroad bridges over the Nottoway River and Stony Creek.[70] On or about the same date, the 61st was divided into two battalions: one remained at and near Ivor Station under Colonel Radcliffe; the other established headquarters at Franklin under Maj. Henry Harding.[71] On May 7 Radcliffe was sent telegraphic orders to "move toward Petersburg," but a few hours later he was redirected to Hicksford to defend the Meherrin River railroad bridge. Either because he failed to receive his new orders or because they were canceled, Radcliffe remained at Ivor Station. On May 8 he "dr[o]ve away" an enemy cavalry unit at Broadwater Ferry, a few miles north of Zuni. Somewhat inexplicably (in view of the need for men at Drewry's Bluff), he was still at Ivor Station six days later "prepared to meet . . . [the enemy] should they come this way."[72] Harding, meanwhile, was ordered on May 7 to leave pickets on the Blackwater and retreat from Franklin to Newsom's Station, twelve miles southwest down the Seaboard and Roanoke Railroad. Those orders were amended several times during the day as Kautz's intentions and probable points of attack began to clarify themselves. By late afternoon Harding's detachment was en route to Hicksford. Whether it arrived there or took any part in the defense of the Petersburg and Weldon Railroad is unknown.[73]

On May 10 Clingman's Brigade, of which the 61st North Carolina was still a part, was ordered to reinforce the Confederate defenders at Drewry's Bluff. Three of Clingman's regiments—the 8th, 31st, and 51st North Carolina—arrived from Petersburg during the rainy night of May 10-11 and went into reserve behind the brigade of Brig. Gen. Bushrod Johnson. Harding's detachment of the 61st reached the scene by May 13 and probably saw action as skirmishers on that date and on the fourteenth and fifteenth. Radcliffe's detachment probably arrived on the fifteenth. As of May 10, Clingman's Brigade was assigned to Maj. Gen. Robert F. Hoke's Division. It served in that command for the remainder of the war.

On the foggy morning of May 16 Beauregard, still outnumbered by a margin of about two-to-one, took the offensive. Maj. Gen. Robert Ransom's Division, on the left, advanced toward Federal entrenchments south of Drewry's Bluff to turn Butler's right flank and cut him off from his base at Bermuda Hundred. Hoke's Division, on Ransom's right in a line of battle consisting of Johnson Hagood's, Bushrod Johnson's, Clingman's, and Montgomery D. Corse's Brigades in left-to-right order, demonstrated against Butler's left to hold it in place and prevent the dispatch of reinforcements to the right. When Ransom turned Butler's

70. Birch Island Bridge was defended by a five-man picket (a corporal and four privates) belonging to Captain Moore's company. According to Moore, those men "wounded a Col & Lieut & killed a horse or two . . . [before] making their escape through the swamp." A. J. Moore to Bettie Farmer Moore, May 10, 1864, Moore Letters.

71. A third detachment, including elements of Company F, believing itself cut off by Kautz, retreated to Petersburg, which it reached on May 8.

72. Robertson, *Back Door to Richmond*, 98-99; *Official Records (Army)*, ser. 1, 51 (pt. 2):896, 931. See also A. J. Moore to Bettie Farmer Moore, May 10, 1864, Moore Letters.

73. See Robertson, *Back Door to Richmond*, 98-99.

right, Hoke was to attack. A third division, under Brig. Gen. Alfred H. Colquitt, would remain in reserve, and the Petersburg garrison, commanded by Brig. Gen. W. H. C. Whiting, would fall upon Butler's rear as he retreated.

Ransom's initial assault carried the first line of Federal breastworks, but Confederate casualties were high, ammunition ran short, and the attack lost cohesion as units became disoriented and intermixed in the fog. Ransom then halted to reorganize. Unable to judge Ransom's progress because of the poor visibility, Hoke skirmished with the enemy for an hour and then moved forward with Hagood's and Johnson's Brigades. Those units easily carried the Federals' outer line but ascertained in the process that Ransom had failed to accomplish his assignment. Rather than launch an unauthorized frontal assault against the heavily manned Federal second line, Hoke halted. The wisdom of that decision was confirmed shortly thereafter when one of Hagood's regiments stumbled into a force of entrenched Federals while attempting to link up with Ransom's right and suffered heavy losses. Two Federal counterattacks were "handsomely repulsed," but another enemy thrust resulted in heavy fighting and threatened to overwhelm Hagood and Johnson. Meantime, Ransom discovered that Lt. Col. William G. Lewis's Brigade and several of Colquitt's Georgia regiments, which had been sent to Hagood's assistance, had overlapped Hagood's left. Another delay ensued while Ransom shifted his "whole line" to the left to give Lewis and the Georgians a clear field of fire. At that juncture a frustrated Beauregard suspended offensive operations to await Whiting's assault from the south. However, despite repeated telegraphic urging, Whiting dallied. Darkness and a heavy rain finally brought the bungled battle to a close. Butler, who had begun falling back hours earlier, completed his retreat to Bermuda Hundred that night.[74]

As was the case in several previous engagements, Clingman's Brigade did not fight as a unit at Drewry's Bluff on May 16. During the heavy Federal attack on Johnson and Hagood, the 8th and 61st North Carolina were sent to Johnson's support while the 31st and 51st, in an effort to relieve the pressure on Johnson, joined Corse's Brigade in an assault on Butler's left. Few details survive regarding the activities of the 8th and 61st. According to Beauregard's report, "The line of the enemy bent around his [Johnson's] right flank, subjecting his brigade for a time to fire in flank and front. With admirable firmness he repulsed frequent assaults of the enemy moving in masses against his right and rear. . . . The brigade, holding its ground nobly, lost more than a fourth of its entire number. Two regiments of the reserve [Colquitt's] were sent up to its support, but were less effective than they should have been, through a mistake of the officer posting them. Hoke also sent two regiments from Clingman [the 8th and 61st] to protect Johnson's flank. These partially partook of the same mistake, being posted in the woods where the moral and material effect of their presence was lost."[75] Casualties in the 61st North Carolina during the Battle of Drewry's Bluff

74. *Official Records (Army)*, ser. 1, 36 (pt. 2):213, 237.

75. *Official Records (Army)*, ser. 1, 36 (pt. 2):203 (see also 237). In a postwar account of the battle, Beauregard stated more pointedly that he "hurried two regiments of the reserve to . . . [Johnson's Brigade's] support, but they were not properly posted . . . and afforded but little assistance. Two regiments of Clingman's Brigade were likewise sent by General Hoke to re[i]nforce Johnson's left. They also failed to accomplish the object for which they were pressed forward." P. G. T. Beauregard, "The Defense of Drewry's Bluff," in Robert Underwood Johnson and Clarence Clough Buel, eds., *Battles and Leaders of the Civil War . . . Being for the Most Part*

cannot be determined, but statistics compiled for this volume indicate that for the period May 13-16 the regiment lost 16 men killed or mortally wounded and 58 wounded.[76]

During the next four days the two armies skirmished at Bermuda Hundred. By then Butler, as Grant pronounced with some exaggeration, was "firmly corked" in the Bermuda Hundred "bottle." "I was in front all day yesterday," Captain Moore wrote on May 20, "& there was fighting most of the day. The casualities in my Co were two wounded, one I think mortally. . . . I was relieved last night. Even now the roar of musketry in front is *awful*. The wounded are being carried by. . . . [We] [a]ttacked the Rifle pits of the enemy this morning & carried them. It was almost a regular line of battle & they continued to reinforce, so it was a servere fight. . . . Our skirmishing has been continuous for over a week besides the engagement when we drove the enimy from the Bluff & the heaviest I have ever heard of. Men who have been through all the fight nearly in Va say they never saw anything like it. . . ."[77] On May 24 Moore, who had received a disabling arm wound at Morris Island on August 26, 1863, wrote his last letter from the front before retiring to the Invalid Corps:

I am here between the James & Appomattox Rivers within one half mile of the enimy's works, which I can easily perceive are getting to be formadable. They are partially sheltered by their Gunboats, or so much so as to render it impractable to assault them. It seems to have turned into a siege, & I can hardly tell now which is the [be]sieging party. We are at work some too. . . . The[y] [the enemy] are throwing a few shell[s] occasionly, & I think mounting more guns of a heavier calibre. . . . Last night I was with my Co, ordered to the front to relieve another Co of the Regt. Every Regt has to keep enough men in advance to cover its front, last night being my time, I went forward & here received an order from Gen Cling[man] to advance the line of picketts fifty yards. [N]ow I was sattisfyed that this would bring on a fight between my line of skirmishers & the enemy, but the work must be done & straight-way I go. I succeeded before moon up in making the advance, & had the men at work digging pits as [we] were in an open field. Every-thing being all right without alarm, I thought I would ly down near one of the pits . . . & take a short knap. I knew the Yankees were close by & would fire into us as soon as the moon showed what had been done. . . . [Shortly thereafter] I am precipitately torn . . . [from sleep] by the roar & rattle of muskettry, the moon is beaming with silvery ray . . . [and] the enimy are attempting to charge our pitts the most of which are now completed. He is however soon repulsed & driven back to his original position. [T]he fight lasted about one hour, nobody hurt in my Co. He makes a seccond attempt just before day & meets a like repulse. . . .[78]

On May 21, while Federal and Confederate pickets fraternized at Bermuda Hundred, the Spotsylvania Court House blood bath (18,000 Federal and 10,000 Confederate casualties) concluded north of Richmond. Grant then began moving his army around Lee's right,

---

Contributions by Union and Confederate Officers, Based Upon "The Century War Series," 4 vols. (New York: The Century Company, 1887-1888; New York: Castle Books, 1956), 4:203, hereafter cited as Johnson and Buel, *Battles and Leaders.*

76. In a letter dated May 19, 1864, Lt. Edward F. Story of Company C estimated the regiment's casualties since the opening of the campaign as "about 75" killed and wounded. "The skirmishing," he added, "[has been] the hardest I have ever seen or heard of." *Wilmington [Weekly] Journal,* May 26, 1864. See also *Daily Confederate* (Raleigh), May 21, 1864.

77. A. J. Moore to Bettie Farmer Moore, May 20, 1864, Moore Letters.

78. A. J. Moore to Bettie Farmer Moore, May 24, 1864, Moore Letters.

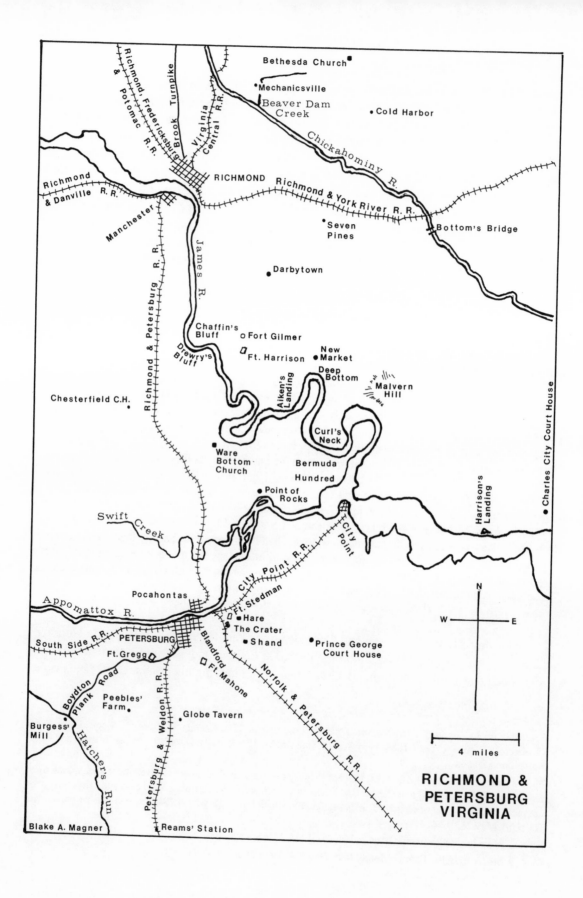

RICHMOND &
PETERSBURG
VIRGINIA

Bethesda Church

Mechanicsville

Beaver Dam Creek

Cold Harbor

Chickahominy R.

Richmond, Fredericksburg & Potomac R.R.

Brook Turnpike

Virginia Central R.R.

RICHMOND

Richmond & York River R.R.

Richmond & Danville R.R.

Manchester

Bottom's Bridge

Seven Pines

James R.

Darbytown

Richmond & Petersburg R.R.

Chaffin's Bluff

Fort Gilmer

Ft. Harrison

New Market

Deep Bottom

Drewry's Bluff

Aiken's Landing

Malvern Hill

Chesterfield C.H.

Curl's Neck

Charles City Court House

Ware Bottom Church

Bermuda Hundred

Point of Rocks

Harrison's Landing

Swift Creek

City Point R.R.

City Point

N
W E

Pocahontas

Appomattox R.

Ft. Stedman

Hare
The Crater

South Side R.R.

PETERSBURG

Blandford

Shand

Prince George Court House

Ft. Gregg

Ft. Mahone

Boydton Plank Road

Petersburg & Weldon R.R.

Norfolk & Petersburg R.R.

4 miles

Peebles' Farm

Globe Tavern

Burgess' Mill

Hatcher's Run

Blake A. Magner

Reams' Station

compelling the Confederate commander to fall back to the North Anna River. After several days of inconclusive fighting along the North Anna, Grant bypassed the Confederate right again and moved southeast toward the Pamunkey. Lee withdrew to Totopotomoy Creek. Grant then dispatched Maj. Gen. Phil Sheridan's cavalry beyond the Totopotomoy to seize Cold Harbor, a road junction nine miles northeast of Richmond. He also ordered Maj. Gen. William F. Smith to move by ship with 16,000 men from Bermuda Hundred to White House Landing, fourteen miles east of Cold Harbor on the Pamunkey. On the morning of May 31 Sheridan reached Cold Harbor, which he found occupied by Confederate cavalry. Well aware that Smith was en route, Lee, fearing a "disaster" on his right flank, called desperately for reinforcements. Hoke's Division was sent northward by Beauregard on the evening of May 30, and three of Clingman's regiments arrived in time the next day to take part in Maj. Gen. Fitzhugh Lee's unsuccessful defense of the Cold Harbor junction. The 61st North Carolina, which remained behind briefly to hold the Bermuda Hundred trenches, reached the field "about dark." Most of Hoke's remaining units and Maj. Gen. Joseph B. Kershaw's Division of Richard H. Anderson's Corps arrived during the night.[79]

On the morning of June 1 Kershaw's command attempted to recapture Cold Harbor and was shot to pieces by the seven-shot Spencer carbines of Sheridan's cavalrymen and murderous blasts of grape and canister. Hoke was under orders to join in the charge but failed to do so. Anticipating a Federal counterattack, the Confederates, many working with their bayonets and bare hands, hastily threw up breastworks. In the afternoon Federal infantry units launched a furious assault and drove a wedge through a ravine where Clingman's left and Kershaw's right intersected. Clingman's regiments (the 8th, 51st, 31st, and 61st in left-to-right order) suffered severe casualties and were forced to give ground until reinforcements restored the situation. "The Yankees charged us about three or four oclock in the evening," Pvt. John G. Hall of the 51st North Carolina wrote, "and we ran them back[.] [A]bout a half an hour [later] they flanked our men on the left and came up in our rear[.] [T]hey killed and took a good many of our men prisoners[.] [T]hey came up in ten steps of us before we knew any thing about them[.] [T]hey ordered us to lay down our arms and some did but we dident[.] [T]he 61rst Regt reinforced us and we charged them back[,] killing and wounding a great many. . . ."[80] Compared to several of its sister units, the 61st escaped relatively unscathed. The regiment's position on Clingman's right was not turned, and it benefited also from "more open" ground in its front. Thus the Federals, as Clingman later wrote, were unable to "approach nearer than either eighty or one hundred yards" and "left large numbers of dead on that part of the field." Clingman's statement seemingly implies a solid combat performance by the 61st, but that was not entirely the case. According to Clingman, Colonel Radcliffe was ordered at one point "to file his regiment out of the trenches so as to aid us [the other three regiments] in the next attack. As I afterwards learned, he himself, with the larger part of his command, did not obey this order but stayed

79. Clifford Dowdey and Louis H. Manarin, *The Wartime Papers of Robert E. Lee* (New York: Da Capo Press, 1961), 759, hereafter cited as Dowdey and Manarin, *Lee Wartime Papers*; Thomas L. Clingman, "Second Cold Harbor," in Clark, *Histories of the North Carolina Regiments*, 5:199, hereafter cited as Clingman, "Second Cold Harbor," in Clark, *Histories of the North Carolina Regiments*. See also *Official Records (Army)*, ser. 1, 51 (pt. 2):975.

80. John G. Hall to his father, June 3, 1864, William P. Hall Collection, Private Collections, NCDAH.

NORTH CAROLINA TROOPS: 1861-1865

in the trench. Being busied with forming the line under the heavy fire of the enemy, I observed soon, however, the delay of this regiment in getting into position, and going up to its left, I ordered them to file out to the rear, so as to form the right of our new line of battle. Lieutenant-Colonel Devane took out a portion of the regiment, and I thus supposed they were all following."[81]

Convinced that the Confederate infantry were too battered and demoralized by the events of the last month to withstand another blow, Grant planned a massive assault at Cold Harbor for the morning of June 2. However, one of his corps missed its way during the night and arrived so exhausted that the attack had to be delayed. A Confederate probe further disrupted the timetable. Late in the afternoon a heavy rain began falling, forcing postponement of the assault until the next day. Meantime, Lee received additional reinforcements and his men perfected their defenses, folding them into the landscape with a practiced skill that partially concealed their deadly, interlocking fields of fire. Early on the morning of the third of June, 50,000 Federals, many of whom accurately sensed that they were going to their deaths, advanced through a curtain of fire whose thunderous roar was audible eight miles away in Richmond. Staggered by a hailstorm of musketry, case shot, and double-shotted canister raking them from several angles, the Federals milled about in agony and confusion, unable to advance or (because of their comrades charging up behind them) retreat. In a matter of minutes the attack was over, with at least 7,000 maimed and mangled Unionists lying wounded or dead on the field. The 61st North Carolina's role in the fighting is obscure but was almost certainly minimal. Clingman subsequently wrote that the attack on his front was "not heav[y]" and engaged only "the right of my line." Reports by several high-ranking Federal officers whose commands faced Clingman are missing, but

81. Clingman, "Second Cold Harbor," in Clark, *Histories of the North Carolina Regiments*, 5:202-203. Writing in his diary in reference to the same incident, Captain Burgwyn, Clingman's assistant adjutant general, stated that "I rallied the men somewhat about one hundred yards in rear and about the center of the 61st which regiment still kept in the trenches, though I had ordered its Colonel James D. Radcliffe by permission of General Clingman to file also to the left front and stop the advancing enemy and act as a nucleus for our men to form on but which order as it was not obeyed I imagine he did not understand." Schiller, *Burgwyn Letters and Diaries*, 148 (June 1, 1864).

Clingman's Brigade was unjustly accused of "giving way" during the battle, thereby causing Brig. Gen. William T. Wofford's Brigade, on Clingman's left, to be flanked and routed. Clingman immediately and categorically denied that allegation and continued to do so for the rest of his life: Wofford's Brigade, not Clingman's, had broken, Clingman charged, with the result that Clingman's men were flanked and attacked from the rear. In a letter dated June 5, 1864, and quoted in the Raleigh *Daily Confederate* of June 8, Clingman asserted that the Federal attack "was repeatedly and signally repulsed with great loss to the enemy in my entire front. Near our left, where they came in columns, their dead were much thicker than I have ever seen them on any battle field. . . . There was, however, in the beginning of the engagement, a brigade from another State than my own, stationed on our left. This brigade did give way, and while the contest was going on in our front, the enemy, in large force, occupied the ground on our left flank and rear. After we had repelled the last attack in front, and the men were cheering along the line, the 8th regiment, which formed my left, was suddenly attacked on its left flank and rear. The woods there being thick, and the smoke dense, the enemy had approached within a few yards and opened a heavy fire. . . . [I]t [the 8th], by facing in two directions, attempted to hold its position, and thus lost about two thirds of its numbers." The letter goes on to say that the 31st and 61st regiments came to the aid of the 8th, and the brigade, assisted by the 27th Georgia, drove back the Federals and reoccupied its position. See also Clingman, "Second Cold Harbor," in Clark, *Histories of the North Carolina Regiments*, 5:197-205; *Official Records (Army)*, ser. 1, 36 (pt. 1):1059.

one Yankee brigadier reported dryly that the "assault . . . being deemed impracticable along our front, was not made." Casualties in the 61st cannot be determined for June 3 alone, but for the period May 31-June 3 the regiment lost, according to figures compiled for this volume, 13 men killed or mortally wounded and 39 wounded.[82]

The two armies remained in their steaming, muddy, malodorous trenches for the next nine days. "We are in 900 hunard yards of the yankees," Private Smithwick informed his mother on June 8. "We are faring Well for Something to Eat . . . and I hope that you are doing the Same." "[W]e have escape[d] death untill the presnt time while meney others has bin sleain," Pvt. John M. Lewis of Company D wrote on June 10. "[W]e have lost near aleven hundurd . . . out of our bridgade kild an wonded sence the 7 of may. . . . The yeankes an our men are veary close to geather but no fighten agoin on at present near [here and] heant bin in too or three days[,] onley the picketts[.] [W]e have lost aheap of men an the yeankes has lost aheap to[.] [T]hay have lost more thean we have. . . . I will seay to you all that we ar fearing veary well for somenting to eat[.] [W]e git aplenty[.] [W]e git corn meal an flour an aplenty of meet[.] [W]e git coffee an shuger. . . ."[83]

On the night of June 12 Grant quietly pulled his men back from Cold Harbor and began a long southward sidle to the east of Richmond. Aware of Grant's departure but forced to cover Richmond until he was certain the Federal army was crossing the James, Lee moved slowly south. On June 14 Grant began crossing the river; in the meantime, General Smith's command returned by water to Bermuda Hundred to reinforce Butler. With Lee still north of the James, a vigorous attack the next day on Beauregard's ragtag force of 3,000 men manning the Petersburg defenses would almost certainly have resulted in the capture of the town, isolating Richmond and changing the course of the war. However, the opportunity was bungled through delays, the physical exhaustion of many Federal units, a reluctance to test the formidable Petersburg defenses after the Cold Harbor butchery, and a series of tragicomic staff-work blunders. An attack late in day, although feeble, easily drove the Confederates from a mile-long section of their outer works. During the night Beauregard ordered Bushrod Johnson's Division, which was "corking" Butler at Bermuda Hundred, to march to Petersburg. Hoke's Division, including Clingman's Brigade, also arrived, bringing Beauregard's strength up to about 14,000 men. Major units of the Army of the Potomac reached the field as well, and by mid-morning on the sixteenth well over 30,000 Federals were present.

Presented with their second opportunity in two days to win what might have been the decisive battle of the war, the Federals again failed to press their advantage. A series of disjointed attacks resulted in the capture of a redan and some trenches; however, those breakthroughs were not exploited, and Federal casualties were high. Expertly shifting his limited resources, Beauregard left whole sections of the ten-mile-long fortifications and the entire Bermuda Hundred line undefended, gambling that a coordinated assault would not be forthcoming. Skirmishers from Hoke's Division and William F. Smith's XVIII Corps "pushed

82. Clingman, "Second Cold Harbor," in Clark, *Histories of the North Carolina Regiments*, 5:205; *Official Records (Army)*, ser. 1, 36 (pt. 1):671.

83. Edgar Smithwick to his mother, June 8, 1864, Smithwick Papers; John Manly Lewis to Susannah Camelia Lewis (his wife), June 10, 1864, in John Manly Lewis Confederate pension application file, NCDAH.

each other back and forth," in the words of historian Thomas J. Howe, throughout the morning.[84]

Around 6:00 P.M. on the evening on the sixteenth, elements of Winfield S. Hancock's II Corps, supported by two brigades each from the XVIII and IX Corps (Ambrose E. Burnside's), attacked the Petersburg line south of the Hare farm. Hancock's attack fell primarily on Bushrod Johnson's left and Hoke's right, which were held by Brig. Gen. James G. Martin's and Clingman's Brigades respectively. Three more redans and some additional trenches were seized by Hancock's men, but Federal casualties were again heavy. According to historian Howe, Clingman's troops "took the brunt" of the Union assault but "repelled the attack with little difficulty." Nevertheless, "desperate fighting occurred at some points along the line." A paucity of Federal and Confederate battle reports makes it difficult to determine exactly what befell Clingman's command, but its casualties were light. According to figures compiled for this volume, the 61st North Carolina lost one man mortally wounded and seventeen captured.[85]

At dawn on June 17 Brig. Gen. Robert B. Potter's IX Corps division charged a portion of Bushrod Johnson's line near the Shand house and captured 600 Tennesseans asleep on their weapons. However, Federal efforts to exploit that breakthrough failed. Around 2:00 P.M. an attack by three Federal brigades was shot to pieces by Clingman's and Henry A. Wise's Brigades when one of the Federal units became disoriented and began advancing almost parallel to Clingman's line. Unaware of the circumstances that spared his command a frontal assault, Clingman categorized that effort as a "feeble demonstration" that was "repulsed at once." Around 6:00 P.M. Brig. Gen. James H. Ledlie's IX Corps division attacked Wise's Brigade and the 23rd South Carolina (a regiment of Brig. Gen. Stephen Elliott's Brigade occupying a position between Wise and Clingman). Ledlie's initial thrust was beaten back, but a second effort punched through the Confederate defenses when the 23rd South Carolina, in the words of one of Wise's men, "ran like sheep."[86] Clingman then moved his entire brigade "somewhat to the right along the trenches" to partially seal the gap. Four companies of the 61st North Carolina, commanded by Lieutenant Colonel Devane, took a position at a right angle to the rest of the brigade's line to protect its rear.[87] Shortly thereafter, half of the 51st North Carolina was brought over from Clingman's left to extend the right of Devane's detachment.

84. Thomas J. Howe, *The Petersburg Campaign: Wasted Valor, June 15-18, 1864*, 2nd ed. (Lynchburg, Va.: H. E. Howard, 1988), 47, hereafter cited as Howe, *The Petersburg Campaign*.

85. Howe, *The Petersburg Campaign*, 55. A June 16 battlefield map in the same source seemingly indicates that Clingman's left but not his right was struck head-on by one of Hancock's assault columns. If such was the case, casualty figures for Clingman's four regiments suggest that the 51st North Carolina (which lost at least 1 man mortally wounded, 6 wounded, and 21 captured) was on the brigade's extreme left. The 61st was probably next in line with the 8th and 31st (which appear to have lost a combined total of three men captured) on the right. See Howe, *The Petersburg Campaign*, 54.

86. *Daily Confederate* (Raleigh), July 18, 1864; diary (typescript) of William Russell (26th Virginia), June 17, 1864, Petersburg National Military Park, Petersburg, Virginia.

87. *Daily Confederate* (Raleigh), July 18, 1864.

They [the 51st detachment] swept around from the rear [Clingman wrote], and driving back the enemy entered the trenches to the right of the line held by Col. Devane, with the assistance of Captain Preston [34th Virginia, Wise's Brigade]. This occurred a little before dark, and from that time the enemy were kept out of the trenches entirely, as far up as our line of fire extended. . . . The enemy for a period of two hours made repeated advances in heavy force against my entire front, but especially against the right. They did not however at any time approach nearer than twenty yards of the right . . . but were always driven back . . . chiefly by the oblique enfilading fire of my entire brigade, which could reach them as soon as they came up the hill into the field, and cut them to pieces so that after two or three volleys they invariably broke and ran to the rear. These movements, with attacks occasionally along my whole front, were kept up until nearly 10 o'clock. . . .[88]

Two hours later a moonlight charge by Archibald Gracie's and Matt Ransom's Brigades drove Ledlie's men back and reestablished the broken Petersburg lines. Casualties were heavy on both sides, and both armies were near exhaustion. During the fighting the 61st North Carolina lost at least nine men killed and ten wounded.[89]

That night Beauregard's troops fell back to a shorter line closer to Petersburg, and major elements of the Army of Northern Virginia began arriving from north of the James. Uncoordinated Federal attacks the next day resulted in no significant gains. Beauregard's abandoned line was overrun, but many Federal units simply declined to repeat the bloody fiasco at Cold Harbor by attacking Confederate fieldworks. Thus the all-out assaults planned for the day disintegrated, sometimes with the acquiescence of high-ranking officers, into demonstrations. Even so, Federal casualties were heavy. One of the few units to obey orders to attack, the inexperienced 1st Maine Heavy Artillery Regiment (fighting as infantry), lost 632 of 850 men in a matter of minutes. Clingman's Brigade was in position east of Blandford Cemetery but somewhat south of the point attacked by the 1st Maine.

The enemy appeared in heavy force, advancing with three lines of battle in our front [Drummer H. T. J. Ludwig of the 8th North Carolina recalled many years later]. It was in the forenoon, in the light of a brilliant June sun, that the lines advanced in a clear open field. If there had not been

88. *Daily Confederate* (Raleigh), July 18, 1864.

89. Although there is evidence that at least one of Wise's regiments (the 34th Virginia) did not perform well during the June 17 fight, it is clearly untrue that, as Capt. W. H. S. Burgwyn, one of Clingman's staff officers later alleged, "Wise's Brigade abandoned its position in a panic, without firing a gun." Most of Wise's men fell back under orders and for good reason, and most of them seem to have fought well thereafter. Burgwyn's contention that Clingman's "unaided" brigade "held Grant's army in check" until the arrival of Ransom's Brigade and thereby "saved the city of Petersburg" is also an exaggeration. Clingman was correct, however, in objecting to the claim of Col. John Thomas Goode, who commanded Wise's Brigade during the battle, that *his* brigade, aided by Ransom's, saved Petersburg. "As your brigade left the works before sunset," Clingman wrote to Goode in a letter published in the Raleigh *Daily Confederate*, "and as Gen. Ransom's did not advance up to them until about 11 o'clock, did it not occur to you that some [other] troops were engaged during these four hours?" Once again, Clingman's Brigade was involved in a controversy involving either a poor battlefield performance or failure to receive credit for a good one. Moreover, the 61st North Carolina again fought in detachments. The most likely explanation for that recurring circumstance, one suspects, is that Clingman was considerably more confident in the combat leadership of Lieutenant Colonel Devane than that of the somewhat dubious Colonel Radcliffe. Burgwyn, "Clingman's Brigade," in Clark, *Histories of the North Carolina Regiments*, 4:494-495; *Daily Confederate* (Raleigh), July 18, 1864. See also Walker Burford Freeman (34th Virginia), *Memoirs of Walker Burford Freeman, 1843-1935* (Richmond: n.p., 1978), 39-40.

other and more serious things to consider, the military display might have been . . . a grand one. But . . . [t]he business [of] our men . . . was to spoil such displays. This they proceeded to do. A heavy fire was opened on the advancing lines. They made a rush for a hollow or ravine in our front, some three or four hundred yards distant, and there established their line. No assault was made on our part of the line on the 18th, but during the greater part of the day the regiment was exposed to a heavy artillery fire, but few casualties, however, happening from that cause.[90]

Casualties in the 61st North Carolina on June 18 numbered at least 2 men killed or mortally wounded, 4 wounded, and 1 captured. During the period June 16-19, the regiment lost at least 16 men killed or mortally wounded, 31 wounded, and 18 captured.

Frustrated in his attempt to seize Petersburg and perhaps end the war at a single stroke, Grant put his army to work building fortifications and reviewed his options. A westward thrust to cut the Petersburg and Weldon Railroad, one of Lee's few remaining supply arteries, was successfully parried by Lee on June 22-23, convincing Grant that a protracted siege was in the offing. Accordingly, construction of extensive siege works began in early July and continued throughout the month. During that period, Clingman's Brigade remained in the lines east of Blandford Cemetery.[91] "Here we lived practically in the ground," Drummer Ludwig wrote. "We walked in ditches, ate in ditches, and slept in pits. The enemy's main line in our front was about three hundred yards distant. The picket lines were much nearer, probably not more than sixty or seventy yards apart. No pickets could be kept out in day-time. Hardly a day passed that the enemy did not fire on us from the battery immediately in our front, or from mortar batteries to our right."[92] "We are in line of Battle in frunt of Petersburg," Private Smithwick informed his mother on July 18. "[We are] in three hunard yards of the yankees. [O]ur Pickets and the yankees Pickets talk With each outher of [a] Night. The yankees Wont charg on our Workes[.] We hav got Strong Works and I think that We Shall Wate for the yankees to come on us or Stay here untill Sept. . . . We hav had 4 Men killed and 9 Wounded and three missing [in my company] . . . Since We left Ivor. . . . [T]he Weather has [been] veary dry here. We hav not had any Raine here in 50 days." "We are Still lying in our forti[fi]cations in frunt of Petersburg," Smithwick wrote

90. Henry Thomas Jefferson Ludwig, "Eighth Regiment," in Clark, *Histories of the North Carolina Regiments*, 1:406, hereafter cited as Ludwig, "Eighth Regiment," in Clark, *Histories of the North Carolina Regiments*.

91. Drummer Ludwig states in his history of the 8th North Carolina that "On the 19th [of June] the regiment [and presumably the rest of Clingman's Brigade] was ordered to take position in the line of works next to the Appomattox River, thus forming the extreme left of the army on the south side of that river." However, the presence of Hagood's Brigade on the south bank of the Appomattox can be documented on June 18 and 24, and it was probably there on June 19 as well. Ludwig, "Eighth Regiment," in Clark, *Histories of the North Carolina Regiments*, 1:406-407. See also Howe, *The Petersburg Campaign*, 126; *Official Records (Army)*, ser. 1, 40 (pt. 1):802; Johnson Hagood, *Memoirs of the War of Secession from the Original Manuscripts of Johnson Hagood, Brigadier-General, C.S.A.* (Columbia, S.C.: The State Company, 1910), 267-269, 272, hereafter cited as Hagood, *Memoirs of the War*.

92. Ludwig, "Eighth Regiment," in Clark, *Histories of the North Carolina Regiments*, 1:407. Although Clingman's Brigade was not scheduled to take part in a June 24 attack on the Federal right by Hagood's Brigade and Patton Anderson's Brigade of Field's Division, it may have been one of the units assigned to support Hagood and Anderson if a breakthrough occurred. However, the attack was bungled from the start and was canceled after three of Hagood's regiments suffered severe casualties. See *Official Records (Army)*, ser. 1, 40 (pt. 1):796-799, 802-804, 51 (pt. 1):1250-1251, 51 (pt. 2):1028; Hagood, *Memoirs of the War*, 271-278.

eleven days later. "[T]he yankees is lying Still only they Sharpe Shootet Some and they Shell Some. [T]he most damage that they do is With theare Mortars Shell. . . . I hope and trust to God that the tine may Sone come that We can all go home. Mother, We are faring only common for Somethine to Eat, But I make out veary Well."[93]

Throughout the month of July, while Clingman's men improved their fortifications and resigned themselves to another round of siege warfare, a regiment of Pennsylvania coal miners tunneled toward Confederate lines southeast of Blandford Cemetery. By July 30 the Pennsylvanians, working in around-the-clock shifts, had gouged out a 510-foot shaft terminating in two forty-foot lateral galleries immediately beneath the works of Elliott's South Carolina brigade. By the morning of July 30 a huge mine comprising four tons of gunpowder was ready for detonation. Supported by massed cannon and the corps of Maj. Gens. E. O. C. Ord and Gouverneur K. Warren, three divisions of white troops and one of black braced to charge into the breach when the mine exploded.

At 4:40 A.M. on July 30 a private in Matt Ransom's Brigade, hearing a "disturbance," rushed out of a bombproof to find "the earth heaving up above the tops of the trees like a mountain. . . ." "[W]ith a dull heavy roar and an earthquake shock," a Massachusetts soldier marveled, "the rebel fort—earth, cannon, and garrison—was blown two hundred feet into the air. . . ." "[Q]uickly jumping to our feet," another Federal wrote, "we saw a black mountain of earth and smoke rising, carrying cannon, caissons, camp equipage and human bodies in one confused mass."[94] The infernal Yankee mine, for which the Confederates had probed for two weeks, had exploded "like a volcano," blowing up nine companies of Elliott's South Carolinians, "wounding, crushing, or burying everything within its reach," and producing a crater approximately 170 feet long, sixty to eighty feet wide, and thirty feet deep.[95] While the stunned survivors attempted to collect their wits and weapons, more than 100 Federal cannons opened fire. Poorly led and almost as badly shocked by the explosion as their Confederate counterparts, Federal infantrymen straggled forward through the dust, clambered to the top of a wall of dirt and debris, and gaped into the smoking chasm. Moving forward again, they found themselves in a ruin of broken gun carriages, protruding timbers, wrecked cannons, and bloody, half-buried Confederates, some of whom were still alive and attempting to extricate themselves. The attack then lost what little cohesion it possessed as a majority of the Federals, disoriented by the unfamiliar contours of the Crater and half-blinded by torrents of dust, milled about attempting to get their bearings and

93. Edgar Smithwick to his mother, July 18 and 29, 1864, Smithwick Papers.

94. Calvin T. Dewese (56th North Carolina) to his father, August 7[?], 1864, Dewese Family Letters, Virginia State Library, Richmond, Virginia; Charles F. Walcott, *History of the Twenty-first Regiment Massachusetts Volunteers in the War for the Preservation of the Union, 1861-1865, with Statistics of the War and of Rebel Prisons* (Boston: Houghton, Mifflin and Company, 1882), 346; John Anderson, *The Fifty-seventh Regiment of Massachusetts Volunteers in the War of the Rebellion: Army of the Potomac* (Boston: E. B. Stillings and Company, 1896), 176.

95. *Official Records (Army)*, ser. 1, 40 (pt. 1):788. "The Situation around Petersburg remains unchanged," Lieutenant Biddle of the 61st wrote on July 24, "except that it is thought the enemy are mining with the view of blowing us up & we are counter mining to prevent it." S. S. Biddle Jr. to S. S. Biddle Sr., July 24, 1864, Biddle Papers.

locate their officers. Some thoughtfully paused to dig out injured Confederates or, incredibly, to pick up souvenirs.

In the meantime the Confederate regiments adjacent to the Crater, after initially giving ground, succeeded in containing the Yankee incursion with the aid of reinforcements and a devastating barrage of mortar shells. On the opposite side of the line, Federal reinforcements sustained heavy losses as they rushed across open ground to aid their hard-pressed comrades, and flank attacks by Ord and Warren stalled in the face of stiff Confederate resistance. Around 8:30 A.M. two brigades of Brig. Gen. William Mahone's Confederate division arrived and were preparing to attack when a weak line composed primarily of African American soldiers charged their position. Although still in the process of forming their line of battle, Mahone's men stormed into the midst of the courageous but unsupported and badly outnumbered Blacks, driving them back into the warren of trenches on the Crater's periphery. A new Confederate attack around ten o'clock failed to gain any additional ground, but the Federal position was clearly hopeless. Confederate artillery continued to exact a murderous toll on the increasingly desperate men huddled in the Crater, and the 100 yards of open ground separating them from the Federal line was now swept by Rebel fire.

At almost the same time that Mahone's two brigades reached the Crater on the morning of July 30, the 61st North Carolina arrived as reinforcements. "We had to march about two miles hurriedly," wrote Capt. Edward Mallett of Company C, "which, owing to the fact of the men being so long cramped up in the trenches, greatly exhausted many of them. On reaching the ground, having gone through a heavy shelling to do so, we were held for a while in reserve in a ravine, exposed to the hot sun but with only a limited supply of water. Several of the men fainted."[96] At 1:00 P.M. another attack by Mahone's men, reinforced by the 61st and several other regiments, carried to the lip of the Crater. There the Confederates paused for a moment to fire a volley into the "surging mass" and then, wielding bayonets and rifle butts, jumped in. A "tremendous slaughter" ensued as exhausted Federal soldiers fought desperately for their lives. Some, particularly Blacks, were shot, bayoneted, or bludgeoned while trying to surrender. Presently, the survivors fled in "one great confused . . . mass."[97]

It was only intended at first [Captain Mallett continued] that we should remain in reserve, as support; but the troops of Mahone's brigade[s] failing to do all that was expected of them, we were ordered in with Wilcox's brigade [actually, Brig. Gen. John C. C. Sanders's Brigade], and the 7th N.C. [17th *South* Carolina], to charge and retake the remaining portion of works. I happened to be in command of the regiment and had the honor of leading it in this charge. We went in with only one hundred and forty men, and had forty killed and wounded.

96. *Daily Confederate* (Raleigh), August 6, 1864. See also *Official Records (Army)*, ser. 1, 40 (pt. 1):791. According to Captain Mallett, the 61st was the only regiment of Clingman's Brigade sent to the Crater as reinforcements.

97. W. A. Day, *A True History of Company I, 49th Regiment, North Carolina Troops, in the Great Civil War, Between the North and South* (Newton, N.C.: Enterprise Job Office, 1893), 84 (first quotation); T. H. Pearce and Selby A. Daniels, eds., *Diary of Captain Henry A. Chambers* (Wendell, N.C.: Broadfoot's Bookmark, 1983), 210 (July 30, 1864; second and third quotations).

I have heretofore felt that I would not be hurt, but in making this charge over about three hundred yards of open field, exposed to a hail storm of bullets, and about twenty pieces of artillery, and seeing the men cut down all around me, I must say that I never expected to reach the works; but a kind Providence protected me. After reaching the works we had a stubborn fight with the enemy for about a half hour, many times being so near together that we could almost catch hold of [each] others bayonets over the banks of earth between us. The enemy finally surrendered by hoisting a dirty Confederate shirt on a ramrod as a white flag. About one hundred surrendered at this time. I took a fine sword from an officer, but was so busy looking out in front for reinforcements from the enemy that I did not think of other plunder. The fight ended about 3 o'clock (having commenced at daylight) up to which time I had been without food. After the excitement wore off I was almost completely exhausted. The hole made by the explosion from the enemy's mine is about twenty feet deep and some thirty or forty yards across, the sides and bottom of which were completely covered with dead yankees and negroes. It was the most awful sight I ever saw. We killed all of 500, and took over 1,000 prisoners.[98]

John M. Lewis, a 61st North Carolina private, wrote that he was "thangfull to my God that we ar yeat alive for we had atrble [a terrible] time the 30 of July[.] [T]he yeankes turnnel under the ground an blode our men up an kild an wonded an tuck prisner one whole Redgment but [with the exception of] a veary few an got our brest workes an we had to charge them . . . out of our works an we all most suffeard death with heat[.] [W]e did not loose near [a] man out of our compney[.] [W]e lost about eight er nine hundeard men kild an wonded an we kild as meney er more yeakes an nigers thean thay did of our men an we tuck about one thousain prisners an the biger part of them was nigers[.] [W]e kild asite [a lot] of nigers an thay fought us till the veary last[.]"[99] Federal casualties, according to one estimate, numbered 504 killed, 1,881 wounded, and 1,413 captured. Confederate losses were "somewhat fewer" than 400 killed, more than 700 wounded, and 40 captured or missing. The 61st North Carolina, according to figures compiled from rosters in this volume, lost 13 men killed and 31 wounded.[100]

---

98. *Daily Confederate* (Raleigh), August 6, 1864. See also *Official Records (Army)*, ser. 1, 40 (pt. 1):791-792. Captain Mallett was in command of the regiment because Colonel Radcliffe reportedly suffered a concussion from a shell explosion early in the fighting. Lieutenant Colonel Devane was absent wounded. Maj. Henry Harding was on the field but, for unknown reasons, did not lead the 61st's attack. He resigned three days later. See William Lucius Faison (adjutant, 61st North Carolina) to Edward White, August 2, 1864, William Lucius Faison Papers, Southern Historical Collection, University of North Carolina Library, Chapel Hill, hereafter cited as Faison Papers.

99. J. M. Lewis to S. C. Lewis, August 4, 1864, in John Manly Lewis Confederate pension application file, NCDAH. In a letter to his parents written the day after the battle, Pvt. Creed Edwards of Company I described the fighting as "the bloodiest time anybody ever saw. The Yankees undermined our works and . . . blowed up three companies of our men and killed the most of them and then the Yankees got possession of our works. . . . [W]e had to charge on them three times before we got the works back. Our regiment was in [a] charge and it was a sight to see the men a'falling. We killed hundreds of them and taken lots of prisoners. There was a great loss on both sides. . . ." Pvt. Edgar Smithwick wrote that "We killed 400 Negros[;] the Negros fought Well. We lost ten men from our Company Wounded. . . . I could Walk from our house to Joel['s] on dead Negros and yankees." Creed Edwards to his parents, July 31, 1864, *Alleghany County Heritage*, 133; Edgar Smithwick to his mother, August 9/11, 1864, Smithwick Papers. See also *Hillsborough Recorder*, August 17, 1864; *Wilmington [Weekly] Journal*, August 18, 1864.

100. Michael A. Cavanaugh and William Marvel, *The Petersburg Campaign: The Battle of the Crater, "The*

Having failed with his mine gambit, Grant reverted to siege strategy. On August 18 Warren's V Corps lunged toward the Petersburg and Weldon Railroad, captured Globe Tavern, and moved north toward Petersburg, tearing up track as it went. A counterattack that afternoon by two brigades of Heth's Division brought the Federal advance to a halt, and both sides received reinforcements that night and the following day. Late on the afternoon of the nineteenth the Confederates advanced through a drenching rain against Warren, who was in the midst of a clumsy attempt to extend his lines to the right. While Heth attacked from the front, Mahone's, Colquitt's, and Clingman's Brigades, commanded by Mahone, succeeded in getting in the rear of a Federal division and captured more than 1,700 prisoners. A member of the 51st North Carolina described the fight as "a regular woods scramble, it being impossible to preserve anything like a line of battle on account of the density of the woods." Consequently, the Confederate force, in the words of an 8th North Carolina soldier, "became scattered in the charge and some of the men were captured; some captured and recaptured twice. It was a thorough mixture in the woods. Front and rear seemed to be on all sides. The bullets came from every direction."[101] "[W]e c[h]arge[d] the yankes in frunt an Rear," Pvt. J. M. Lewis of the 61st wrote, and "tuck about thirty five hundard[?] prisners but we didt git the Real [rail] Road back. . . ."[102] During the fighting on August 19, the 61st North Carolina lost one man wounded and twelve captured. Clingman was wounded severely in the leg and was out of action until the last days of the war. Col. Hector M. McKethan of the 51st North Carolina assumed command of the brigade.[103]

McKethan's Brigade returned to its position on the south bank of the Appomattox by August 27. There it remained until about September 15, when it was sent to the rear to rest and recuperate.

I take pleasure this evening in writing you all a short-letter [Pvt. P. F. M. Daniel wrote amiably to his "Mother Brothers & Little Sister" on September 24]. I say short, because I . . . will have to go on drill soon. . . .

We are now resting and have been for about a week. We are in rear of the front lines about a half of a mile, in the ravine, neare . . . the water-works; which places us near the edge of the city. We

---

Horrid Pit," June 25-August 6, 1864, 2nd ed. (Lynchburg, Va.: H. E. Howard, 1989), 108. For mining activities by Clingman's men, see Official Records (Army), ser. 1, 42 (pt. 2):1158-1159.

101. McKethan, "Fifty-first Regiment," in Clark, Histories of the North Carolina Regiments, 3:213; Ludwig, "Eighth Regiment," in Clark, Histories of the North Carolina Regiments, 1:407. See also Official Records (Army), ser. 1, 42 (pt. 1):940.

102. J. M. Lewis to S. C. Lewis, August 22, 1864, in John Manly Lewis's Confederate pension application file, NCDAH. See also Edgar Smithwick to his mother, August 19 [probably August 28 or 29], 1864, Smithwick Papers. Two more Confederate efforts, in which Clingman's (McKethan's) troops were not involved, failed at Globe Tavern on August 21 and at Reams' Station, south of Globe Tavern, on August 25, and the Petersburg and Weldon Railroad was permanently severed.

103. Colonel McKethan served as acting brigade commander until about January 15, 1865, when he was hospitalized at Wilmington. Colonel Devane (recently promoted from lieutenant colonel) officially assumed command on or about that date but may well have been in charge during the Second Battle of Fort Fisher (January 13-15, 1865). On February 23 Brig. Gen. Collett Leventhorpe was ordered to take command of Clingman's Brigade but for unknown reasons did not do so. See Official Records (Army), ser. 1, 47 (pt. 2):1259, 1280.

are in rear of where the mine was blown up. . . . I have no idea how long we will remain here. We may go to the front soon, or be held to reinforce any point. . . . I have no war news, nor any other kind, & must soon cease. Shelling & sharp-shooting still goes on, & the pleasant hours & sweet voices of you all that I enjoyed at home has ceased, & the noise of cannons & roar of musketry is now heard instead, but I hope such will not long be the case.[104]

On September 26 General Lee reviewed Hoke's Division. "This was the only review or other military display . . . [that I witnessed] during the campaign of '64," General Hagood wrote. "It was made a gala occasion by the citizens of the beleaguered town [Petersburg], large numbers attending. The ladies were out in full force, and many were on horseback. General A. P. Hill rode on the staff of the commanding general upon a very graceful and beautiful silver grey; and horse and rider showed gallantly. General Lee reviewed the troops rapidly and seemed bored by the ceremonial and glad to be through with it. He was in full uniform, with a quantity of yellow sash around his waist, and did not look like himself. Even his horse looked as if he thought it was all foolishness."[105]

On the evening of September 29 McKethan's Brigade was moved north of the James River to the vicinity of Fort Harrison, an important link in the Richmond defenses that the Federals seized in a surprise attack earlier that day. On the thirtieth McKethan's men took part in a complex, ill-coordinated, and, for themselves, totally disastrous attempt, supervised by Lee himself, to recapture the fort (see map on page 632). Lee's plan called for a preparatory artillery bombardment followed by an assault by Charles W. Field's and Hoke's Divisions. Field, whose command was some distance behind and to the left of Hoke's, was to advance at 1:45 P.M. at an obtuse angle to the North Carolinian and then halt briefly in a ravine while the two divisions linked up. They would then attack simultaneously at two o'clock. Unfortunately for the Confederates, one of Field's three brigades, commanded by Brig. Gen. George T. Anderson, failed to halt in the ravine as ordered but stormed ahead, followed shortly thereafter by its two sister brigades on either side. Hoke, receiving no new instructions and probably neither eager nor willing to act without them, waited until 2:00 P.M. to attack, as Lee had mandated. By that time, Field had been decisively repulsed by determined Federal infantrymen, many of whom were armed with lethal Spencer repeaters. Hoke then attacked with McKethan's, Hagood's, and Brig. Gen. William W. Kirkland's Brigades in left-to-right order—Colquitt's Brigade following McKethan in support and Alfred M. Scales's Brigade of Cadmus M. Wilcox's Division following Hagood. For whatever reason, Hagood and Kirkland either halted almost immediately or, possibly, failed to move at all. However, McKethan's "little North Carolina outfit," in the words of historian Richard J. Sommers, "surged across the 450 yards of open ground" and was "'mowed . . . down like grass.'"[106]

104. P. F. M. Daniel to his "Mother Brothers & Little Sister," September 24, 1864, Daniel Papers. "[T]imes is all quiet in frunt of Petersburg . . . except Some Shelling," Pvt. Edgar Smithwick wrote in late August. "Mother times is veary heard here now. We are oneley fareing common for Something to Eate." Edgar Smithwick to his mother, August 19 [probably August 28 or 29], 1864, Smithwick Papers.

105. Hagood, *Memoirs of the War*, 303-304.

106. Richard J. Sommers, *Richmond Redeemed: The Siege at Petersburg* (Garden City, N.Y.: Doubleday and Company, 1981), 145, hereafter cited as Sommers, *Richmond Redeemed.* Having correctly concluded that the

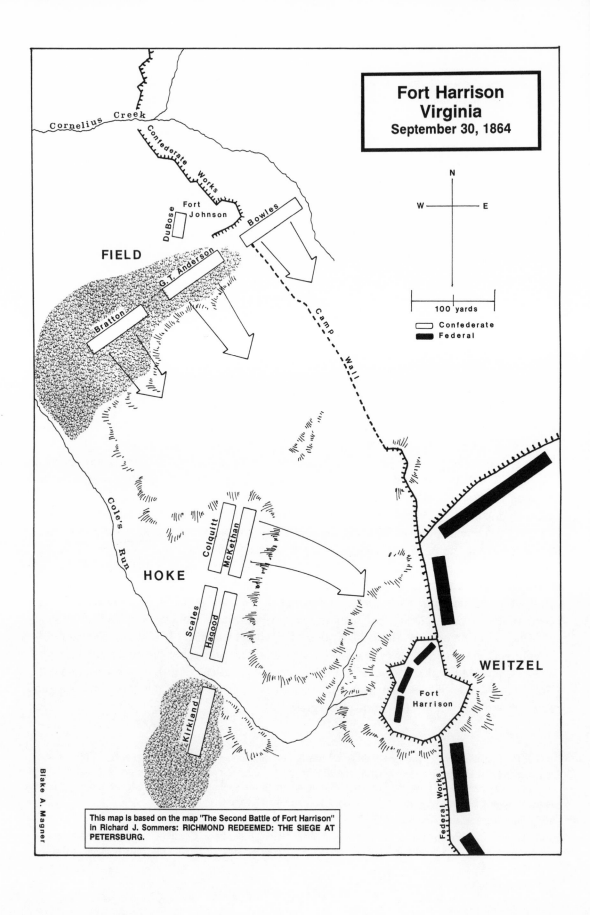

Fort Harrison
Virginia
September 30, 1864

N
W — E
S

100 yards

☐ Confederate
■ Federal

Cornelius Creek

Confederate Works

DuBose
Fort Johnson
Bowles

FIELD

G. T. Anderson

Bratton

Camp Wall

Cole's Run

HOKE

Colquitt
McKethan

Scales
Hagood

Kirkland

WEITZEL

Fort Harrison

Federal Works

Blake A. Magner

This map is based on the map "The Second Battle of Fort Harrison"
in Richard J. Sommers: RICHMOND REDEEMED: THE SIEGE AT
PETERSBURG.

As we started the whole Yankee line opened on us in plain view and about four hundred yards [distant]," Captain Burgwyn noted in his diary, "[and] as they were all armed with seven shooters the fire was awful. By the time we got [with]in about seventy yards of their works our line was entirely broken not from any falling back but literally from the men being cut down by piles . . . and [because] our support, Colquitt's Brigade . . . [had] returned behind the hill. . . ."[107] "[C]onfident of success," Colonel McKethan wrote in a seven-page letter describing the battle to General Clingman, the men rushed forward "with a chear and[,] without firing a shot[,] advanced to within 50 yds of the fort where we encountered a thick hedge of briars that was almost impassable although but a few feet high. Full[y] one third of our number having already fallen . . . it would have been folly to have advanced further . . . [and] it was impossible to extricate ourselves. . . . [O]ur only safety was in laying flat on our faces where we were and await[ing] support or the cover of night. I noticed in many cases that the least attempt to move in any direction would draw a voll[e]y from the enemy." "From . . . about 3:00 p.m. till dusk," Captain Burgwyn wrote, "we lay about seventy yards from the enemy line, some entirely exposed and some shielded from view by some weeds and grass, but all entirely at the mercy of the enemy. . . . About dark I was getting ready to run the gauntlet . . . when the enemy sent forward a line of skirmishers who captured almost without a single exception all who had not surrendered. As I got up to see if I would have to surrender or not I saw a Yankee about ten yards [away] with his gun pointed towards me calling out to surrender or he would shoot. I then took out my handkerchief and waved it and gave up my sword to a Yankee captain and was hastened to their lines. . . ."[108]

---

attack could not succeed, Hoke reportedly "importuned" Lee to cancel it and "select a new line of defence [*sic*] on ground . . . which his men were then holding." Overruled, he then requested cancellation of the preliminary bombardment, which he believed would alert the Federals that an assault was imminent and inflict, because of defective ammunition, as much damage and demoralization on his men as the enemy. Overruled again, Hoke probably felt compelled to attack precisely at 2:00 P.M. as ordered no matter what the situation warranted, which would seem to be that he assume responsibility for going forward with Field ahead of schedule. At two o'clock, having seen his worst fears confirmed by the vicious fire that greeted Field, Hoke launched what was at best a *pro forma* assault. Hagood's and Kirkland's Brigades were either ordered by Hoke to halt almost as soon as they started or, more probably, quickly halted of their own accord, after which Hoke made no further effort to get them moving. (Hagood's statement in his *Memoirs* that his brigade "was not engaged" at Fort Harrison on September 30 is revealing.) Whatever one may think about Hoke's inaction, it seems clear that his failure to attack with his entire force, which was probably nothing more than simple reluctance to sacrifice his men in a hopeless endeavor, did not cause the failure of the attack. Rather, it insured that the carnage in his division would be limited to one brigade. "Hopeless," in fact, is the operative word. Brig. Gen. E. Porter Alexander, Lee's artillery commander, used it specifically in his *Recollections*, commenting that "It was . . . almost a hopeless task to try & drive superior forces from works so strong as these now were." Brig. Gen. John Bratton of Field's Division expressed the same sentiment when he wrote that his men "failed to take the fort, but it was because the difficulties . . . were too much for human valor." Burgwyn, "Clingman's Brigade," in Clark, *Histories of the North Carolina Regiments*, 4:496; Hagood, *Memoirs of the War*, 307; Gary W. Gallagher, ed., *Fighting for the Confederacy, The Personal Recollections of General Edward Porter Alexander* (Chapel Hill: University of North Carolina Press, 1989), 478; *Official Records (Army)*, ser. 1, 42 (pt. 1):880. See also C. W. Field, "Campaign of 1864 and 1865," *Southern Historical Society Papers* 14 (1886): 556-557, hereafter cited as Field, "Campaign of 1864 and 1865," in *Southern Historical Society Papers*.

107. Schiller, *Burgwyn Letters and Diaries*, 151-153 (September 30, 1864).

108. Hector McKethan to T. L. Clingman, October 3, 1864, William Hyslop Sumner Burgwyn Papers, Private

The recently promoted Major Mallett, who commanded the 61st during the attack, was still shaken more than three weeks later, and his letter of October 24 conveys something of the trauma and terror of the regiment's experience:

We indeed had a terrible time at Fort Harrison, I trust I shall never see the like again. . . . On my way to the famous briar patch a thought would now and then occur to me that my time to fall would soon come, but on reaching the patch unhurt my faith became stronger . . . [and] I poured out my heart to God for deliverance. I had a presentiment that I would escape, though [I was] within 50 yds of the enemys works and [it was still] three hours before dark, and encouraged the men around me to have patience[,] that we would certainly escape, which all the others would have been able to do if our wounded . . . had not called so loudly on the yankees for assistance and they consequently came over to them. I remained [behind] urging the men off until the Yankees were about ten steps from me ordering me to surrender which I politely declined doing, making it convenient at same time to "change my face" [about face.] [D]uring this long afternoon I would at one moment be praying . . . when the first [thing] I would know I would be cursing and threatning to shoot some poor fellow who to save his life perhaps was obliged to go over to the enemy. . . . I visited our wounded the next day . . . [and] the sight . . . affected me more than any thing has in a long time. I could not control my self and . . . with tears in my eyes thanked our Heavenly Father for his wonderful care of me and implored him to alleviate the pains and suffering of my wounded comrades. I become a little nervous even now when I think of the trials of Fort Harrison. . . .[109]

McKethan's troops, roundly criticized for some past performances, could be proud of their work at Fort Harrison: attacking in company with the more renowned brigades of Hagood and Kirkland, they alone had attempted to carry out their orders. Moreover, their casualties were devastating. According to McKethan, of 911 men who went into the fight, only 384 returned unscathed: a net loss of 527.[110] Some recognition, albeit limited, was indeed forthcoming. "[T]he officers & men . . . have been complimented by both Genl Hoke & Genl Lee," McKethan boasted to Clingman, "who ashure me that a more gallant charge they never witnessed. . . ." And at least one modern historian also offers praise: in his fine study entitled *Richmond Redeemed*, Richard J. Sommers commends "the brave North Carolinians" for "plung[ing] unsupported into the maelstrom" and maintaining a "spattering of fire" even while hopelessly pinned down by the enemy. However, Sommers finally renders a mixed verdict on the brigade, describing its career as "inglorious," disputing McKethan's claim that his men went into action "confident of success," and stating that they "once more proved themselves incapable of storming a position."[111] For McKethan's

---

Collections, NCDAH, hereafter cited as Burgwyn Papers; Schiller, *Burgwyn Letters and Diaries*, 153 (September 30, 1864).

109. Edward Mallett to S. S. Biddle Sr., October 24, 1864, Simpson and Biddle Papers.

110. Casualties in the 61st North Carolina according to figures compiled for this volume included 22 men killed or mortally wounded, 53 wounded, and 62 captured (of whom 11 were wounded).

111. Hector McKethan to T. L. Clingman, October 3, 1864, Burgwyn Papers; Sommers, *Richmond Redeemed*, 145, 147, 445 (see also 148). According to Sommers, McKethan lost three of his four regimental commanders and twenty-seven of his forty company commanders. The 61st also lost its battleflag. See also *Daily Confederate* (Raleigh), October 11 and 12, 1864.

men, Fort Harrison was thus in one respect a new episode of an old story: a creditable combat performance for which they received, both at the time and subsequently, little credit.[112]

After the Fort Harrison calamity, McKethan's Brigade resumed its position in the lines north of the James River. On October 7 and 13 it was peripherally involved in actions on the Darbytown Road, and on October 27 it was present but played only a minor part in an engagement at Burgess' Mill. Little is known regarding the 61st North Carolina's role in those fights. It lost three men captured on October 7 and one on the twenty-seventh.[113]

Throughout most of the last three months of 1864 the 61st appears to have remained in or near its works near the Darbytown Road.[114] Only two useful letters from members of the regiment survive for that period. In the first, dated October 20, Captain Biddle wrote that he reached his command on the previous afternoon "and found it strongly intrenched. . . . The left of Hokes Division rests in this road, the right resting some where in the vicinity of Ft Gilmer. Field's Division on our left extend in the direction of Malvern Hill. Our troops are in good spirits and feel confident that they can drive back any force that the enemy may send against them. The enemy's line of works are about one mile distant in our front with thick woods intervening which prevents us from seeing them. We have so far since the late engagement on this side of [the] James [probably a reference to the fight at Fort Harrison on September 30] had a much more quiet time than on the lines around Petersburg. We are daily in expectation of some new move of Grants if he can possibly devise any for the capture of Richmond & Petersburg." In the second letter, dated November 4, Pvt. Amma F. Johnson of Company A informed W. L. Faison, the 61st North Carolina's wounded adjutant, that "Everything remains perfectly quiet down here. We are making preparations to go into winter quarters. A heavy detail is kept at work daily on the works. They are going to be thrown up from the front ditch sufficiently high to protect the men without having any ditch on the inside. The Brigade has been recruited a great deal by the order respecting extra duty men [*i.e.*, men absent on detail were required to return to

112. Lee's generalship at Fort Harrison on September 30 was, by his high standards, inferior. According to Sommers, "claims that he galloped around in the thick of the fighting at the head of Cole's Run and thrice sent Hoke's Division back to the attack may politely be termed 'inaccurate.'" If that is true, as certainly appears to be the case, the battle consisted of Field's premature assault followed by Hoke's feeble effort. Lee's failure to order a new assault by Hoke or to censure him after the fight suggests agreement, belated or otherwise, with Hoke's assessment of the attack's prospects and acquiescence in his unilateral decision not to make a suicidal charge. Indeed, the question after 2:00 P.M. was not whether to renew the attack but whether an effort should be made to rescue McKethan. It might be added that the telegram Lee sent to Secretary of War James A. Seddon that evening describing the disastrous battle seems somewhat below the peerless Confederate chieftain's customary standard of unequivocal probity: "An attempt was made this afternoon to retake Battery Harrison which, though partly successful, failed." Sommers, *Richmond Redeemed*, 146; Dowdey and Manarin, *Lee Wartime Papers*, 860.

113. During the Darbytown Road affair, General Hoke, who was instructed to advance following sequential attacks by Brig. Gen. Martin W. Gary and Field, seemingly failed to obey orders. A discussion of Hoke's controversial generalship at Darbytown Road and historian Douglas Southall Freeman's criticism thereof appears in an appendix on pages 648-650.

114. Hoke's Division, although assigned to Richard H. Anderson's newly created corps on October 19, remained on temporary duty with Longstreet's Corps until late December.

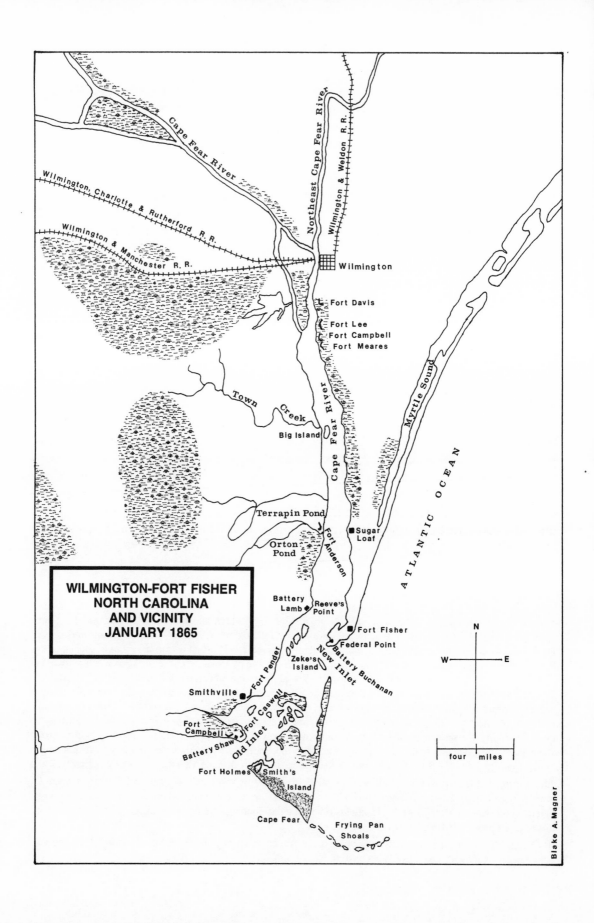

Cape Fear River

Northeast Cape Fear River

Wilmington & Weldon R.R.

Wilmington, Charlotte & Rutherford R.R.

Wilmington & Manchester R.R.

Wilmington

Fort Davis

Fort Lee
Fort Campbell
Fort Meares

Town Creek

Cape Fear River

Big Island

Myrtle Sound

ATLANTIC OCEAN

Terrapin Pond

Fort Anderson

Sugar Loaf

Orton Pond

**WILMINGTON-FORT FISHER
NORTH CAROLINA
AND VICINITY
JANUARY 1865**

Battery Lamb

Reeve's Point

Fort Fisher

Federal Point

Fort Pender

Battery Buchanan

Zeke's Island

New Inlet

N

W E

Smithville

Fort Caswell

Fort Campbell

Battery Shaw

Old Inlet

four miles

Fort Holmes

Smith's Island

Cape Fear

Frying Pan Shoals

Blake A. Magner

their regiments]. We have over 900 men present and they are coming in constantly. . . . They have sent four officers to Raleigh after conscripts for the Brigade."[115]

Biddle's and Johnson's letters seemingly reflect good morale in the regiment and, probably, tolerable health, rations, and living conditions. All of those deteriorated somewhat during November and December, but the 61st was clearly better off than Confederate units stationed closer to enemy lines. Sharpshooting casualties were minimal, and the regiment was housed in "very comfortable log cabins" rather than leaky, board-and-dirt roofed mud holes of the type occupied by many of their comrades. That suggests in turn the availability of firewood and perhaps adequate sanitation facilities, both of which were serious problems for some units. North Carolinians were also, as a rule, better clothed and shod than men from other states. Nevertheless, there is no doubt that the regiment's strength and morale, like that of other Confederate units, continued to ebb. Weakened by malnutrition and fatigue, men died of disease or spent weeks and months in hospitals trying to recover their health. During November and December, at least thirty-four members of the regiment deserted.[116]

On December 20 Hoke's Division was ordered to move by rail to Wilmington to assist in the defense of Fort Fisher (seventeen miles below the town on the ocean and the east bank of the Cape Fear River) against an anticipated amphibious assault commanded by the ubiquitous Butler. Proceeding circuitously via Danville and Greensboro, Kirkland's Brigade, the advance element of the division, reached Wilmington about midnight on the twenty-third "after a long and fatiguing ride on the cars." Learning that a naval bombardment was in progress at Fort Fisher, Kirkland marched at sunrise to Sugar Loaf Hill, four and one-half miles north of the fort. Federal infantrymen landed that afternoon but, after skirmishing briefly, withdrew incontinently to their ships on Butler's orders and sailed away. The 61st North Carolina reached Wilmington, it appears, a day or two after the Federals departed. The regiment encamped for about a week at Camp Whiting and then for about ten days at Green's Mill Pond, a mile east of the town. During that time it was occupied with "drilling and . . . other duties of camp life. . . . My company & Regiment have no shelter here except their small (Yankee) shelter tents," Captain Biddle complained, "and the consequence is that many of them express the desire to return to their winter quarters in Virginia." On January 12 Hoke's Division was mustered for a review and spent "the greater portion of the day," in the words of a 51st North Carolina officer, "marching and counter marching . . . for the benefit of a large number [of citizens] from the city."[117]

---

115. S. S. Biddle Jr. to S. S. Biddle Sr., October 20, 1864, Biddle Papers; Amma Ferdinand Johnson to W. L. Faison, November 4, 1864, Faison Papers.

116. S. S. Biddle Jr. to S. S. Biddle Sr., January 7, 1865, Biddle Letters. Quarterly desertion figures in the 61st North Carolina during the war, as derived from service records in this volume, were as follows: second quarter 1862–3; third quarter 1862–11; fourth quarter 1862–8; first quarter 1863–4; second quarter 1863–6; third quarter 1863–17; fourth quarter 1863–16; first quarter 1864–7; second quarter 1864–2; third quarter 1864–10; fourth quarter 1864–49; first quarter 1865–8. In the *North Carolina Troops* series, desertion is defined for statistical purposes as *ultimate* failure to return to duty from an unauthorized absence of whatever length. The foregoing figures are therefore an inadequate reflection of absence without leave, a problem that, in terms of the number of men involved, was undoubtedly more serious.

117. Charles G. Elliott, "Kirkland's Brigade, Hoke's Division, 1864-'65," *Southern Historical Society Papers* 23 (1895): 166, hereafter cited as Elliott, "Kirkland's Brigade," *Southern Historical Society Papers*; S. S. Biddle Jr.

Following the Christmas fiasco at Fort Fisher, General Butler was replaced by a competent officer, Brig. Gen. Alfred H. Terry, and on the night of January 12, 1865, the Federal fleet returned. The next day Terry's 9,600-man assault force landed north of the fort under cover of naval gunfire. The 61st North Carolina was dispatched from Wilmington with the rest of Hoke's 6,400-man division and arrived during the midst of the Federal landing. However, despite the Federals' apparent, or at least theoretical, vulnerability, Hoke, as Hagood recollected, "deemed it very injudicious to attack."[118] Therefore, according to Hoke's superior, Braxton Bragg, "The troops were ordered to lie upon their arms, and to move promptly and attack, should the enemy attempt to extend his lines toward the fort."[119]

After dark on the thirteenth Terry, leaving numerous campfires burning as a deception, quietly moved most of his force closer to Fort Fisher. Between 2:00 A.M. and 8:00 A.M. on January 14, Terry's men constructed "a good breast-work, reaching [three-quarters of a mile] from the river to the sea and partially covered by abatis," thereby fortifying their rear against Confederate interference.[120] Upon discovering that development the next morning,

---

to S. S. Biddle Sr., January 7, 1865, Biddle Letters; McKethan, "Fifty-first Regiment," in Clark, *Histories of the North Carolina Regiments*, 3:215. See also *Official Records (Army)*, ser. 1, 42 (pt. 3):1283.

118. Hagood, *Memoirs of the War*, 323. His implicit criticism notwithstanding, Hagood seemingly concurred with Hoke's assessment, stating that the enemy was "under cover of his fleet, which could here lie very close in shore. . . ." Rod Gragg, a modern authority of the Battle of Fort Fisher, states that Hoke's men arrived "too late, or at least Hoke felt they were too late [to attack the Federal landing party], and the Federals had come ashore unopposed. . . . His troops were a fair match for the Federal infantry, but Hoke received no new orders to attack, so he simply maintained his defensive line." Hagood, *Memoirs of the War*, 323; Rod Gragg, *Confederate Goliath: The Battle of Fort Fisher* (New York: HarperCollins Publishers, 1991), 117, hereafter cited as Gragg, *Battle of Fort Fisher*. Hoke's orders from Bragg were to "make every effort to prevent a landing of the enemy; but if that has been effected . . . you [are] to take up the position . . . agreed upon during the recent operations." Since Bragg's orders did not cover what Hoke should do if the landing were in progress, Hoke was on his own as to how to proceed. Fearing the destructive power of the Federal fleet and uncertain whether Terry intended to march directly against Wilmington or attack Fort Fisher, he assumed a defensive posture. *Official Records (Army)*, ser. 1, 46 (pt. 2):1044. See also Gragg, *Battle of Fort Fisher*, 117; Hagood, *Memoirs of the War*, 323; *Official Records (Army)*, ser. 1, 46 (pt. 1):432.

119. *Official Records (Army)*, ser. 1, 46 (pt. 1):432. Bragg wrote in his official report that when he joined Hoke's command near Sugar Loaf on the afternoon of the thirteenth he "fully approved" Hoke's dispositions. Bragg's approval clearly encompassed Hoke's decision not to attack or place all or part of his force between the fort and the enemy landing party. "Owing to the intervening swamp and sound," Bragg stated, "it was impossible for us to attack the enemy at their landing point, even if the heavy metal of the fleet had not securely covered them. . . . The command could not have been divided with any safety, and to have placed it between the enemy and Fort Fisher would have enabled them to seize our intrenched camp, and securely confine our entire force on the southern end of the peninsula, exposed without cover to the fire of the whole fleet, which reached from the sea to the river throughout the whole distance." *Official Records (Army)*, ser. 1, 46 (pt. 1):432.

120. *Official Records (Army)*, ser. 1, 46 (pt. 1):397. "During the night," Hagood wrote, "the enemy passed between or around . . . [our] cavalry [pickets], without their observing it, and when day broke Hoke discovered them on his right flank securely entrenched from the ocean beach to the river and facing Wilmington. He took position in the lines previously prepared from Sugar Loaf to the head of Masonboro Sound." That account is seemingly confirmed by Bragg, who states that "In making a reconnaissance early the next morning, the fourteenth, toward our right, whilst I was on the left, Major-General Hoke was fired upon by the enemy before reaching the line assigned his cavalry. Upon due investigation, he found a heavy force occupying an intrenched line between us and the fort, entirely across the peninsula from Battery Anderson on the sea to the river."

Bragg, according to his official report, ordered Hoke "to move upon the enemy and dislodge him if practicable." However, after a "close reconnoissance" by Hoke "and his brigadiers," Bragg "united" with Hoke for "another examination of the enemy's line" and determined, predictably, that the enemy "largely exceeded us in numbers." To that erroneous conclusion he added, on better grounds, a healthy respect for the "enormous" Federal fleet, whose firepower was being demonstrated down the beach at Fort Fisher by a blizzard of shells.[121] He therefore "concurr[ed] in the opinion already expressed [by Hoke]" and "suspended the order for the attack."[122]

At 8:00 A.M. on the fifteenth the Federal fleet opened a blistering bombardment of Fort Fisher, and around three o'clock that afternoon Terry's infantry stormed the fort. A bloody, five-and-one-half-hour, hand-to-hand fight ensued during which the badly outnumbered garrison was slowly beaten into submission. On orders from Bragg, Clingman's and Kirkland's Brigades, led in person by Hoke, advanced on Terry's breastworks shortly after the attack commenced. A line of picket posts was captured, but at that juncture part of the Federal fleet shifted its fire to Hoke's troops. Minimal damage resulted, but Bragg, believing (mistakenly) that the enemy works were defended by the bulk of Terry's force (which Bragg estimated, mistakenly, as 12,000 men), canceled the attack. As far as can be determined, the 61st North Carolina sustained no casualties in the fighting on January 15.[123]

Hagood, *Memoirs of the War*, 323-324; *Official Records (Army)*, ser. 1, 46 (pt. 1):432.

121. *Official Records (Army)*, ser. 1, 46 (pt. 1):432; Braxton Bragg to Thomas Bragg, January 20, 1865, in "Defence and Fall of Fort Fisher: Letter from General Braxton Bragg," *Southern Historical Society Papers* 10 (1882): 347 (second and third quotations only), hereafter cited as "Defence and Fall of Fort Fisher: Letter from General Braxton Bragg," *Southern Historical Society Papers*. In his excellent new book entitled *The Wilmington Campaign: Last Rays of Departing Hope*, Chris E. Fonvielle Jr. writes that the Federal fleet, comprising fifty-eight vessels mounting 594 guns–"the largest . . . assembled during the war"–maintained "a continuous bombardment for three days and two nights" during which the it fired 19,682 shells. Chris E. Fonvielle Jr., *The Wilmington Campaign: Last Rays of Departing Hope* (Campbell, Calif.: Savas Publishing Company, 1997), 308 (see also 306), hereafter cited as Fonvielle, *The Wilmington Campaign*.

122. *Official Records (Army)*, ser. 1, 46 (pt. 1):432. Bragg's contention that Hoke was reluctant to attack on January 14 appears to be accurate. According to Hagood, "Bragg . . . ordered Hoke to assail the enemy's newly entrenched line. Hoke reconnoitered it in person and, deeming it inadvisable, requested Bragg himself to examine . . . affairs on his front. This General Bragg proceeded to do, and the result was to countermand the order of assault. . . ." At 12:00 A.M. Bragg made another effort to get Hoke moving. "[T]he commanding general," one of Bragg's staff officers informed Hoke by courier or telegraph, "deems it of the highest importance to break the enemy's line, if possible, and he hopes you may be able to do it by a judicious use of artillery, they having none." Hoke's reply has not been located, but at 2:00 P.M. another of Bragg's staff officers sent a communication to Hoke stating that "Your general views, as expressed in the note by Major [James M.] Adams, will be adopted by the commanding general. He desires you will select a good line, as near the enemy as practicable, and intrench your position. . . ." Hagood, *Memoirs of the War*, 324; *Official Records (Army)*, ser. 1, 46 (pt. 2):1059 (see also 1053, 1061).

123. In a letter to his brother written five days after the battle, Bragg stated that Hoke "moved to attack . . . [the enemy] under my direction" but "found them in very strong position and heavy force ready to receive him. . . . Their line was impracticable for his small command, and I did not hesitate to recall him. *He could not have succeeded.*" Not unexpectedly, Col. William Lamb, the fort's commander, differed sharply with that opinion. In a critique of Bragg's letter published in 1882, Lamb wrote that "had General Hoke attacked the enemy resolutely at 3 P. M., he would have saved the fort, and with darkness and the cooperation of the garrison, have captured the enemy." Interestingly, the reticent and retiring Hoke, whose opinions and motives are rarely easy to determine, apparently agreed, at least in retrospect, with Bragg rather than Lamb. "[W]e all expected [Hoke to issue]

Hoke's Division, excluding Hagood's Brigade (which was stationed on the west bank of the Cape Fear River), repulsed a Federal attack at Sugar Loaf on February 11 and continued holding that position until February 19.[124] Only one letter from a member of the 61st North Carolina was located for that period. In it Private Smithwick complained to his mother of "veary heard" times and "not . . . half a nufe to Eat. . . ." "We draw tow days Rashings at a time," Smithwick stated elsewhere in the same letter, "and I Can Eate the two days Rashing of Meat and Bread at one Meal. . . . I would be glad if you could send me a quart of Brandy," "one peck of peas or Meal," "three or four pounds of dried Beef," a "quart of Molasses," "a pare of Socks," and "Some good Sewing Coton." "I Would Send you Some Monney By James Smith," Smithwick added forlornly, "But I hav not got But one Dollar in the World."[125]

On February 19, following a week of "more or less brisk" skirmishing, Hoke's Division pulled back in the face of an advance up the west bank of the Cape Fear by Maj. Gen. Jacob D. Cox's Division of Maj. Gen. John M. Schofield's XXIII Corps.[126] After a small engagement at Forks Road on February 20 in which the 61st North Carolina was probably involved, the division withdrew to Wilmington, which was captured by Schofield on the twenty-second.[127] "At daylight, on the 22nd," General Hagood recalled, "Hoke . . . marched into and through the town. The cotton, naval stores and vessels were in flames, and as the rear guard left in the early dawn a mass of black smoke had settled like a pall over the silent town; in its extent and density suggestive of the day of doom."[128] Hoke's troops, with Clingman's Brigade (commanded by Col. William S. Devane of the 61st North Carolina) covering the rear, then marched to the Wilmington and Weldon Railroad crossing of the Northeast Cape Fear River.

The enemy pushed close up to our rearguard [Drummer Ludwig of the 8th North Carolina recalled]. At the creek, about one mile from the city, he followed so closely that the bridge could not be destroyed. It was then practically a fight from the creek to the river. The enemy had to be held in check to enable our army and wagon-train to cross. . . . The last mile to the river was hotly contested. The regiment held its ground and retarded the advance of the enemy's force. As the regiment

---

the order to *charge*," Captain C. G. Elliott of Kirkland's staff wrote, but "a courier came . . . from Bragg ordering him to withdraw. . . . General Hoke since the war has told me that he concurred with Bragg." Braxton Bragg to Thomas Bragg, January 20, 1865, in "Defence and Fall of Fort Fisher: Letter from General Braxton Bragg," *Southern Historical Society Papers* 10 (1882): 348; "Defence and Fall of Fort Fisher: Account of Colonel William Lamb," *Southern Historical Society Papers* 10 (1882): 359; Charles G. Elliott, "Kirkland's Brigade," *Southern Historical Society Papers* 23 (1895): 168. See also *Official Records (Army)*, ser. 1, 46 (pt. 2):1064.

124. See Fonvielle, *The Wilmington Campaign*, 344-351.

125. Edgar Smithwick to his mother, February 1, 1865, Smithwick Papers. In one respect, Smithwick was in good shape. "I hav got a plenty of Cloth[e]s at present," he said.

126. Ludwig, "Eighth Regiment," in Clark, *Histories of the North Carolina Regiments*, 1:410. Schofield arrived on February 9 with a portion of the XXIII Corps and assumed command of the Department of North Carolina. The remainder of the corps followed subsequently. Hagood's Brigade was involved in fighting with Cox's troops at Fort Anderson on February 18 and Town Creek on February 19-20.

127. See Fonvielle, *The Wilmington Campaign*, 395-398; Ludwig, "Eighth Regiment," in Clark, *Histories of the North Carolina Regiments*, 1:410.

128. Hagood, *Memoirs of the War*, 348-349.

approached the river the enemy pressed the harder, always to be received with sharp firing. When the pontoon across the river was reached the men filed across . . . [and] the pontoon . . . was cut loose. . . .

As the regiment crossed the river the men deployed on the north bank. . . . [A] line of pickets was left along the bank, while the remaining part of the regiment moved back about two hundred yards to a small elevation and began throwing up breastworks in line with the part of the army that had preceded us.

The regiment [and the rest of Devane's Brigade] never performed finer service than it did in covering the retreat from Wilmington to Northeast River. . . . When the enemy came too close the line was formed and his progress checked. Then the march was resumed till the enemy came too close again. The men seemed to appreciate the importance of the duty they were performing. The safety of the army, and especially of the wagon-train, depended upon the steadiness with which they maintained their ground. How well the duty was performed is told above.[129]

The next day, February 23, Hoke's men moved to Rockfish Creek, in Duplin County. There they remained until March 5, when they departed by rail for Kinston to oppose a Federal column advancing on Goldsboro from New Bern under the command of Schofield.

The Battle of Southwest Creek (also known as Kinston and Wise's Forks), fought on March 7-10, 1865, was a Confederate attempt to prevent or at least delay the junction of Federal forces in eastern North Carolina with Maj. Gen. William T. Sherman's oncoming juggernaut. Mustering about 6,500 men (with an additional 2,000 en route), Bragg confronted Schofield's 10,000-man force, which increased to around 15,000 before the end of the battle. The Federal advance was halted by artillery fire on March 7, and on the morning of March 8 Hoke's Division and a smaller force under Lt. Gen. D. H. Hill attacked the Federal left and right respectively. Two isolated Federal regiments were overrun and captured by Hoke, and Hill also made good progress. However, at that critical juncture a major tactical error by Bragg, who was acting on Hoke's advice, sent Hill marching away from the fighting. By the time the mistake was discovered, the day was waning and the Confederate advantage was lost.[130] "[W]arm skirmish[ing]" and a feeble probe by Hoke occurred on March 9, followed by another attempt at a double envelopment by Hoke and Hill on the tenth. After marching through "swamps and pocosons and dense pine forests" in an unsuccessful attempt to get in the enemy's rear, Kirkland's Brigade of Hoke's Division delivered a "resolute and determined" if unauthorized and ill-advised assault that was smashed by cannon fire and a flank attack by Federal infantry.[131] Hill's "less vigorous" and

---

129. Ludwig, "Eighth Regiment," in Clark, *Histories of the North Carolina Regiments*, 1:410-411. See also Burgwyn, "Clingman's Brigade," in Clark, *Histories of the North Carolina Regiments*, 4:498.

130. See *Official Records (Army)*, ser. 1, 47 (pt. 1):1087.

131. *Official Records (Army)*, ser. 1, 47 (pt. 1):978 (first and third quotations); Elliott, "Kirkland's Brigade," *Southern Historical Society Papers* 23 (1895): 170 (second quotation). Kirkland's March 10 assault was contrary to Hoke's orders, which were, Captain Elliott was subsequently informed by Hoke, "to feel the enemy, but not to attack breastworks." Kirkland's seeming disobedience was the result of excessive zeal on the part of his men. "[T]he brigade made a charge through the woods, which were very thick, with great spirit," Elliott wrote, "and drove the skirmishers before them. . . . As soon as our line emerged from the woods we ran up against a very strongly-intrenched line of the enemy, obstructed by trees they had cut down, and supported by artillery. They poured a hot fire into us and we made our men lie down. . . . I have [since] heard that Hoke censured Kirkland for making the disastrous charge on the 10th. . . ." Elliott, "Kirkland's Brigade,"

slightly mistimed assault was called off by Bragg after the repulse of Hoke. Bragg then fell back through Goldsboro to Smithfield, where his force united with that of Gen. Joseph E. Johnston on March 17.[132]

Very little is known concerning the involvement of the 61st North Carolina and Devane's Brigade in the fighting at Southwest Creek. According to two postwar accounts, the 8th North Carolina and Devane's Brigade as a whole lost "quite a number" of men. However, that statement is seemingly contradicted by Hagood, who states in his memoirs that "Kirkland's loss . . . [on May 10] was the chief loss." Moreover, casualty figures compiled for this volume, although based on very scanty records and probably too low, indicate the loss of only 2 men mortally wounded, 2 wounded, and 11 captured (of whom 1 was wounded). Most of the regiment's casualties were probably sustained on March 8 and 9 even though Confederate losses on the eighth were, in Hagood's words, "very inconsiderable" and fighting on the ninth was, by all accounts, insignificant.[133]

On March 11 Sherman's relentless army, having completed its ruinous sweep through South Carolina, captured Fayetteville. On the fourteenth it resumed its march, advancing northeast in two 30,000-man columns. The Left Wing, commanded by Maj. Gen. Henry W. Slocum, feinted in the direction of Raleigh; the Right Wing, commanded by Maj. Gen. Oliver O. Howard, moved toward Sherman's true destination, Goldsboro. There he planned to link up with Schofield and Terry and rest and refit his men.[134] Hoping to draw Slocum and Howard farther apart and defeat them separately, Johnston ordered Lt. Gen. William J. Hardee on March 10 to "impede" Slocum's advance. At Averasboro on March 16, Hardee, outnumbered on the order of four or five to one, fought a careful defensive battle, precariously fending off Slocum's attacking bluecoats before slipping away during the night to join forces with Johnston.[135] Confident of victory in the one-sided Averasboro fight and anxious to reach the Goldsboro railhead, Sherman, far from calling on the Right Wing for assistance or ordering it to halt, allowed Howard to continue his march to the northeast while the battle raged.

Southern Historical Society Papers 23 (1895): 170-172.

132. *Official Records (Army)*, ser. 1, 47 (pt. 1):978. According to a deserter from the 51st North Carolina, Devane's Brigade was at Goldsboro on March 13 and "marched for Raleigh [Smithfield]" on the same date. *Official Records (Army)*, ser. 1, 47 (pt. 2):875.

133. Ludwig, "Eighth Regiment," in Clark, *Histories of the North Carolina Regiments*, 1:411; Burgwyn, "Clingman's Brigade," in Clark, *Histories of the North Carolina Regiments*, 4:498; Hagood, *Memoirs of the War*, 354-355; Elliott, "Kirkland's Brigade," *Southern Historical Society Papers* 23 (1895): 170. Devane's and Hagood's Brigades, according to Hagood, were side-by-side in Hoke's second line on March 10; Kirkland's and Colquitt's Brigades were in front. For further information on the Battle of Southwest Creek, see *Official Records (Army)*, ser. 1, 47 (pt. 1):912, 997-999, 1078; Barrett, *Civil War in North Carolina*, 285-290.

134. Terry moved northwest from Wilmington on March 15.

135. *Official Records (Army)*, ser. 1, 47 (pt. 2):1362. As Bentonville historian Nathaniel Cheairs Hughes Jr. observes, it was not the "calculated" Confederate "objective" at Averasboro to "stretch out the distance between Sherman's two wings and thus provide the opportunity to . . . destroy Sherman's Left Wing." Although such was Johnston's "hope" in general terms, Averasboro was neither the first step in a grand design to defeat Sherman nor evidence of Johnston's "strategic foresight." Nathaniel Cheairs Hughes Jr., *Bentonville: The Final Battle of Sherman and Johnston* (Chapel Hill: University of North Carolina Press, 1996), 34, hereafter cited as Hughes, *Bentonville*.

On March 18 Johnston began concentrating a force of 20,000 men in a woods near Bentonville, and on the morning of the nineteenth he was waiting in ambush as Slocum's strung-out column moved up the Goldsboro road.[136] Mistakenly believing that he was confronted by the usual token cavalry contingent, Slocum, without pausing for his command to close up, ordered Brig. Gen. William P. Carlin's Division to clear the way. That unsuspecting unit was received by "an awful volly [sic]" fired by massed Confederate infantry from a distance of about fifty feet. Carlin's men retreated in disarray but rebounded quickly and came on again, this time directing part of their attention at Hoke's Division, on the Confederate left. Although warmly engaged, Hoke had no difficulty holding his line. However, Bragg, unaccountably convinced that his subordinate was about to be overwhelmed, called for reinforcements. Maj. Gen. Lafayette McLaws's Division of Hardee's command, which had just reached the field from Averasboro, was then ordered by Johnston to take position on Hoke's left. That decision, in the words of Bentonville historian Nathaniel C. Hughes Jr., deprived Johnston of an "important body of troops just at the moment for [a] massive counterattack—just when the initiative passed to the Confederates. . . . This was a critical moment at Bentonville, perhaps *the* critical moment. . . ." In the judgment of Lt. Gen. Wade Hampton, Johnston's cavalry commander, that decision was Johnston's only major blunder of the day but one so irremediable that it "change[d] the fate" of the battle.[137]

Around 2:45 P.M. Confederate infantry under Hardee and Lt. Gen. Alexander P. Stewart stormed out of the brush and blackjack thickets in a devastating assault that crushed the undermanned and disorganized Federal left wing and precipitated, in the words of one candid Unionist, "some of the best running ever did." The Federal right wing then came under attack from the rear by Hardee and Stewart, and units under the command of Bragg and Hoke pitched into the beleaguered Federals from the front. Battling desperately amid a "continuous and remorseless roar of musketry," the Federal defenders narrowly succeeded in holding their position until reinforcements arrived and beat back the Confederate attack. The fighting then shifted again to the re-formed and reinforced Federal left, where five successive Confederate assaults were smashed by a "hailstorm of grape and canister." Devane's Brigade was in Hoke's second line behind Colquitt's (Col. Charles T. Zachry's) Brigade and took little or no part in Hoke's attack or the subsequent fighting.[138] The 61st North Carolina's casualties, if any, were very light.[139]

136. See Battle of Bentonville map on page 266. A considerable part of Johnston's command arrived after the battle began. Because of the paucity of documentation on the part played by Hoke's Division at Bentonville, the following account of that engagement is abbreviated. More detailed accounts appear in the histories of the 58th and 60th North Carolina, on pages 264-270 and 495-499 of this volume.

137. Charles S. Brown to "Mother & Etta," April 18, 1865, Charles S. Brown Papers, SCD-DU; Hughes, *Bentonville*, 60; Wade Hampton, "The Battle of Bentonville," in Johnson and Buel, *Battles and Leaders*, 4:703. See also *Official Records (Army)*, ser. 1, 47 (pt. 1):1056.

138. Quoted in Barrett, *Civil War in North Carolina*, 333; Benson J. Lossing, *Pictorial History of the Civil War in the United States of America*, 3 vols. (Hartford: Thomas Belknap, 1877), 3:501; Samuel W. Ravenel, "Ask the Survivors of Bentonville," *Confederate Veteran* 18 (March 1910): 124.

139. During Hoke's attack, Devane's Brigade either advanced behind Zachry's men or, more probably, was in reserve. According to Drummer Ludwig, author of the 8th North Carolina history in Clark's *Regiments*, the 8th was in fact held in reserve. Ludwig says nothing about Devane's other three regiments. Very possibly they were in reserve also. Hagood, in his memoirs, also implies that only two brigades (his own and Colquitt's) were

During the night of March 19 Sherman, who was with Howard's wing of the army, belatedly learned of the fighting at Bentonville. Preparations to go to Slocum's aid began immediately, and by the afternoon of the twentieth the army was reunited on the battlefield. Now hopelessly outnumbered, Johnston nevertheless remained at Bentonville, realigning his units in a spraddled horseshoe to cover the much longer Federal line and guard his retreat route over the Mill Creek bridge. Hoke's Division was pulled back to a position north of the Goldsboro road and formed in a line consisting of Kirkland's, Colquitt's, Devane's, and Hagood's Brigades in right-to-left order. Kirkland's Brigade was involved in a brisk skirmish during the day, but Devane's men again saw little or no action. On March 21 Johnston remained in his works and continued to evacuate his wounded. Heavy skirmishing took place all along the line, but the only action of consequence was an unauthorized attack by Maj. Gen. Joseph A. Mower's Division that broke through beyond Hoke's left flank and threatened to capture the Mill Creek bridge. Against that penetration Johnston and Hardee, improvising frantically, mustered just enough resistance to force the impetuous Mower to pause and call for reinforcements. Sherman then ordered him to withdraw.

During the desperate fight with Mower, Devane's Brigade extended its left to cover a gap created by the departure of Hagood's Brigade, which went to the assistance of Hardee. Shortly thereafter, Devane's men were involved in a sharp skirmish with a Wisconsin artillery battery and two Illinois regiments of Col. Robert F. Catterson's Brigade. After losing their forward rifle pits during an attack by the 103rd Illinois, Devane's men counterattacked through a heavy rain, regained a portion of their lost position, and were driven back again. A second counterattack, supported on the right by Colquitt's Brigade, came under flanking fire by another Illinois regiment and was repulsed in disorder. "You should have seen the Rebels run," Maj. Charles W. Wills of the 103rd Illinois wrote in his diary. "It did me a power of good."[140] Losses in Devane's Brigade during the day numbered two men killed and sixteen wounded.[141] One of the two fatalities was the brave and much-admired Edward

---

involved in the attack. The twenty casualties reportedly sustained by Devane's Brigade on March 19 were probably the result of incidental fire. One recent author's claim that the 31st North Carolina of Devane's Brigade "sustained losses of 50 per cent" on March 19 do not appear to be accurate. Daniel W. Barefoot, *General Robert F. Hoke: Lee's Modest Warrior* (Winston-Salem: John F. Blair, Publisher, 1996), 299. See also Ludwig, "Eighth Regiment," in Clark, *Histories of the North Carolina Regiments*, 1:412; Hagood, *Memoirs of the War*, 360-361; Hughes, *Bentonville*, 128; Mark L. Bradley, *Last Stand in the Carolinas: The Battle of Bentonville* (Campbell, Calif.: Savas Woodbury Publishers, 1996), 232, 495 (footnote 2).

140. Charles W. Wills, *Army Life of an Illinois Soldier* (Washington, D.C.: Globe Printing Company, 1906), 366. For somewhat different (and contradictory) accounts of this engagement, see Hagood, *Memoirs of the War*, 362, and *Official Records (Army)*, ser. 1, 47 (pt. 1):259, 261, 372. Hagood states that "Clingman's [Devane's] brigade extending behind the really good entrenchments [vacated by Hagood's men] handsomely repulsed the [enemy] assault." However, it is clear that the Federals never attempted or intended to make an attack on Devane's main line and that they retained Devane's forward rifle pits at the end of the day. Moreover, Hagood, as stated above, was not present during the events of which he speaks. Drummer Ludwig's recollection is closer to the mark: "[O]n the 21st the enemy made a heavy demonstration against our part of the line, driving in our pickets, though not assaulting the main line." Ludwig, "Eighth Regiment," in Clark, *Histories of the North Carolina Regiments*, 1:412.

141. See *Official Records (Army)*, ser. 1, 47 (pt. 1):1080. Total casualties in Devane's Brigade during the three-day fight at Bentonville were officially reported as 3 men killed, 35 wounded, and 2 missing. According to figures compiled for this volume, the 61st North Carolina lost three men killed or mortally wounded and three

Mallett, who was by now a lieutenant colonel and who commanded the 61st during the battle. Colonel Devane was wounded, and it is unclear who commanded the brigade during most of the last five weeks of its existence. It will therefore be referred to herein as Clingman's Brigade, as it is in the *Official Records*.[142]

During the night of March 21 the Confederates, with Hoke's Division acting as rear guard, retreated in the direction of Smithfield, which they reached the next day.[143] There the men enjoyed a three-week respite, and Johnston reorganized his army. The egregious Bragg was removed from field command, and Hoke's Division was placed under Hardee. Clingman's Brigade remained under Hoke but was reinforced by the 36th and 40th North Carolina, two former artillery units that had been consolidated as infantry.[144] "Drills, reviews, and inspections were the order of the day," Hagood recalled. Hardee's Corps was reviewed by Johnston on April 3 and by North Carolina governor Zebulon B. Vance on April 6.[145] Capt. W. H. S. Burgwyn, assistant adjutant general of Clingman's Brigade, wrote that "many ladies and civilians from Raleigh . . . and officers of the State and Confederate Government were present [during Vance's review]. The army presented a fine appearance and the men were in excellent spirits. . . . It was a splendid body of American soldiers; survivors of a hundred battlefields; and . . . they marched proudly in review before their General. . . ." In a letter written at Smithfield on April 4, 1865, Capt. Samuel S. Biddle paints a bleaker picture of the army's condition than did Burgwyn in his 1901 account: "I reached my command on Sunday, the 2nd inst[ant], and found it in camp about one mile north of the Central Rail Road at Smithfield depot. . . . This corps [Hardee's] is the largest, by far, in this army, and numbers about ten (10) thousand arms bearing men. The whole army is lying quietly in camp at this point, watching the movements of Sherman, who is at Goldsboro. I am fearful that this fine weather will cause active operations [to resume] before many days. I found my company numbering 5 men, which is larger than several other companies in the Regiment. . . . I regret to say that our troops are very despondent. They think that we have not men enough for us to contend with Sherman or rather to defeat him."[146]

---

wounded. Both sets of figures are probably too low; however, it is known that losses in the 8th North Carolina were "not heavy," and the same probably applies to Devane's Brigade as a whole. Ludwig, "Eighth Regiment," in Clark, *Histories of the North Carolina Regiments*, 1:412.

142. As stated above, Clingman resumed command a few days before Johnston surrendered. Capt. Nathan A. Ramsey of Company D was reported in command of the 61st on March 31, 1865; Capt. Stephen W. Noble of Company K was reported in command on April 9, 1865. See *Official Records (Army)*, ser. 1, 47 (pt. 3):732, 47 (pt. 1):1062.

143. See Hagood, *Memoirs of the War*, 363. Clingman's Brigade was probably the rear guard of Hoke's Division. See Ludwig, "Eighth Regiment," in Clark, *Histories of the North Carolina Regiments*, 1:412.

144. Hoke reported on March 31 that 769 men were present for duty in Clingman's Brigade, 885 in Colquitt's, 370 in Hagood's, 1,408 in Kirkland's, and 1,047 in Nethercutt's (Junior Reserves), making a total of 4,479. *Official Records (Army)*, ser. 1, 47 (pt. 3):745 (see also 697).

145. Hagood, *Memoirs of the War*, 364. See also *Official Records (Army)*, ser. 1, 47 (pt. 1):1062. Capt. Samuel S. Biddle's letter of April 4, 1865, confirms that Johnston's review took place on April 3 rather than April 4, as reported by some postwar sources. Vance's review, however, may have occurred on the seventh rather than the sixth. See S. S. Biddle Jr. to S. S. Biddle Sr., April 4, 1865, Biddle Papers.

146. Burgwyn, "Clingman's Brigade," in Clark, *Histories of the North Carolina Regiments*, 4:498-499; S. S.

On April 10 Sherman's inexorable advance resumed. Smithfield was captured on April 11, and Raleigh was occupied two days later. Johnston retreated westward on the eleventh with his small and, particularly after the surrender of Lee at Appomattox Court House on April 9, demoralized and rapidly shrinking army.[147] He crossed the swollen Haw River and Great Alamance Creek with "much difficulty" on April 15 and reached Greensboro the next day.[148] On April 17, with the authorization of Pres. Jefferson Davis, a fugitive from the fallen Confederate capital, Johnston opened negotiations with Sherman near Durham Station. On April 26, 1865, at the home of James Bennitt, three miles west of Durham Station, Johnston surrendered. The parole of what remained of his army began at Greensboro the same date and continued through May 1.[149] It appears that at least fourteen members of the 61st North Carolina, including two officers, were present to receive their paroles.[150]

Endnote A (see page 594, footnote 8): Carpenter's letter might imply at first glance that the 61st was involved in a running fight with Federal troops; however, a closer reading suggests that the operative phrase is "we . . . [were] *expecting* [emphasis added] a fight every moment[.]" Although there were in fact skirmishes on November 2 at Little Creek ("on the road from Washington to Williamston") and at Rawls' Mill (on Reedy Branch about one mile beyond the site of the first skirmish), the only evidence that the 61st was present is an entry in the typescript diary of Lt. Joseph Kinsey (Company E). That entry states that "On Sunday (November 2, 1862) we were in a battle at Rawles Mills near Williamston, Martin County, N.C. and in a skirmish near Tarboro, and left Tarboro for Washington, N.C." There are several problems with that statement. First, the regiment was not moving east from Tarboro to Washington on November 2 but west from Plymouth to Tarboro. It did not arrive at the latter place until about November 7, and consequently it could not have been in "a skirmish near Tarboro" on November 2. Second, there is ample evidence that the unit involved in the skirmish at Rawls' Mill was the 26th North Carolina.

Biddle Jr. to S. S. Biddle Sr., April 4, 1865, Biddle Papers.

147. Rumors concerning Lee's surrender were circulating among Johnston's men as early as April 10 but were not verified, at least in Clingman's Brigade, until April 15. On that date the brigade was at Bush Hill (present-day Archdale), in Randolph County. See Ludwig, "Eighth Regiment," in Clark, *Histories of the North Carolina Regiments*, 1:413. On the subject of desertion and demoralization in Hoke's Division, see the "memorandum diary" of Capt. William E. Stoney, Hagood's assistant adjutant general. According to Stoney's entry for April 26, desertion during "the last ten days . . . reduced Kirkland's brigade from 1,600 to 300 men; Clingman's and the brigade of junior reserves from the same cause were each no stronger; Hagood's and Colquitt's brigades had suffered, but not so much." Hagood, *Memoirs of the War*, 367, 371.

148. Captain Stoney's excellent account of the crossing of the Great Alamance Creek appears in Hagood, *Memoirs of the War*, 368. See also Ludwig, "Eighth Regiment," in Clark, *Histories of the North Carolina Regiments*, 1:412-413.

149. According to Captain Stoney, when the army was ordered to march at 11:00 A.M. on April 26, shortly before Johnston surrendered, "not more than forty men in each brigade followed Kirkland and Clingman from the ground. Officers as high as colonels, not only countenanced, but participated in the shameful conduct." Hagood, *Memoirs of the War*, 371.

150. The two officers were Capt. Augustus D. Lippitt of Company G and Lt. William H. Patrick of Company B. Lippitt was presumably in command of the regiment.

Third, all entries in Kinsey's diary prior to approximately August 26, 1863, were made from memory, and many of them are demonstrably misdated or otherwise incorrect. Finally, Captain Ramsey states that the regiment's "first battle" occurred more than a month later (on December 13 at Southwest Creek). In this author's opinion, it is probable that the 61st North Carolina was withdrawing westward near Rawls' Mill while portions of the 26th were fighting there on November 2. Thinking they were about to be cut off, some of the men then divested themselves of knapsacks, guns, and other impedimenta in their haste to escape. *Official Records (Army)*, ser. 1, 18:22 (see also 20-21, 23); diary of Joseph Kinsey, November 2, 1862, Roster Document No. 1016, CWRP, NCDAH; Ramsey, "Sixty-first Regiment," in Clark, *Histories of the North Carolina Regiments*, 3:508. See also George C. Underwood, "Twenty-sixth Regiment," in Clark, *Histories of the North Carolina Regiments*, 2:336-339; Jordan, *North Carolina Troops*, 7:458; John Washington Graham (56th North Carolina) to William Alexander Graham (his father), April 24, 1864, in J. G. de Roulhac Hamilton, Max R. Williams, and Mary Reynolds Peacock, eds., *The Papers of William Alexander Graham*, 8 vols. (Raleigh: Division of Archives and History, Department of Cultural Resources, 1957-1992), 6:71.

Endnote B (see page 599, footnote 15): Some elements of the 61st North Carolina may have contributed to their own misfortunes by withdrawing without authority on one and possibly two occasions shortly before Evans ordered a retreat. "At one time during the progress of the battle," Captain Ramsey wrote, "the Sixty-first was compelled to fall back on account of the ammunition being entirely exhausted, and on being ordered back [to the front] by General Evans, all hands without a murmur promptly obeyed and returned to within 150 yards of the enemy without a solitary cartridge and half the men without bayonets. A small supply of ammunition soon reached us, which was speedily used to the best advantage, and being entirely out again and with no hopes of a second supply, and being in a forlorn and helpless condition and being crowded so unmercifully close by such a large force of the enemy, the better part of valor was to get away from there if we could, which we did in a quiet, orderly way, or as much so as pressing circumstances permitted." During the first of those withdrawals the regiment crossed the bridge, which had not yet been fired, and, as Ramsey states, was ordered back by Evans. (Radcliffe, it appears, was also on the scene and ordered his men back into action, threatening to shoot one of them "if he ran a step.") The circumstances surrounding the regiment's supposedly unauthorized withdrawal are obscured, however, by the fact that Colonel Mallett ordered his command to cross the bridge at one point but was then ordered back to the south bank by Evans. That episode may have been the same one referred to by Ramsey. As stated above, Devane's men were under Mallett's authority during part of the battle. Ramsey, "Sixty-first Regiment," in Clark, *Histories of the North Carolina Regiments*, 3:509; McPherson Wright (22nd South Carolina) to J. D. Radcliffe, February 17, 1863, in J. D. Radcliffe service record file, 61st Regiment N.C. Troops, Compiled Confederate Service Records (North Carolina), M270, reel 548; *Wilmington [Weekly] Journal*, April 16, 1863; *Official Records (Army)*, ser. 1, 18:115-116.

APPENDIX

Critique of Douglas Southall Freeman's Charge that General Hoke "Fail[e]d to Give His Full Co-operation" in the Engagement at Darbytown Road on October 7, 1864.

In *R. E. Lee: A Biography*, distinguished Civil War historian D. S. Freeman speculated that Hoke "either misunderstood his orders [at Darbytown Road], was deterred by the obstacles in his way, or was held back by the artillery fire of the enemy." Subsequently, in *Lee's Lieutenants: A Study in Command*, Freeman rendered a harsher verdict: "Everything went in accordance with plan on October 7," he wrote, "until it came Hoke's turn to charge. For reasons never explained, he failed to assault. The result was heavy loss for the other units [Field's] and abandonment of the effort to recover the lost line. . . . Nothing was said publicly concerning Hoke's responsibility for the failure. Had his record been reviewed, it would have shown at least four and perhaps five instances in which he could have been accused of failing to give his full co-operation in [an] attack." The other instances, according to Freeman, were Cold Harbor on June 1, the attack near the Appomattox River on June 24, the attempt to recapture Fort Harrison on September 30, and perhaps the fight at Drewry's Bluff on May 16.[151]

Although Field's Darbytown Road attack was initially successful, it did not in fact go "in accordance with plan . . . until it came Hoke's turn to charge." General Hagood, in his memoirs published in 1910, wrote that Field's men encountered "parallel to . . . [their] line of advance" an "entrenched line strongly manned and being rapidly re-enforced." That line, whose existence is confirmed in Federal reports, was unsuccessfully attacked by Field. Meanwhile, Hoke's Division, which was "to follow [Field] as a reserve," moved, according to General Hagood,

from its position in the Darby Town road, where it had rested during the fight, and filing to the right followed in column behind the right of the advancing Confederate line. . . . Why General Lee did not put in his reserve [Hoke] is not known. The position in which Hoke was held during the fight . . . interposed him between the enemy and Richmond, then open to a coup de main. Possibly it was deemed important to maintain him in it. More probably the chances of success were not deemed sufficient to warrant the shattering of the whole disposable force. . . . An impression prevailed to some extent among Field's subordinate officers that Hoke was derelict in not joining in the final assault. In Colonel J[ames] R. Hagood's Memoirs of the First South Carolina Regiment, these impressions are expressed. [Colonel Hagood was General Hagood's brother.] The writer never talked with Hoke on the subject, for he gave no heed to the matter though he heard rumors of it at the time. General Lee was, however, present with the reserve during most of the day, and just before and during the last

---

151. Douglas Southall Freeman, *R. E. Lee: A Biography*, 4 vols. (New York: Charles Scribner's Sons, 1935), 3:509; D. S. Freeman, *Lee's Lieutenants: A Study in Command*, 3 vols. (New York: Charles Scribner's Sons, 1944), 3:592-593. Elsewhere in *Lee's Lieutenants*, Freeman says of Hoke that "It is unpleasant but it is the fact: subsequent to . . . [his] success at Plymouth, if he is fighting beside another Division, there nearly always is a failure of co-operation." *Lee's Lieutenants*, 3:xxviii.

assault [by Field] he was with us. This settles the fact that the part borne by Hoke was under the immediate direction of the commander-in-chief.[152]

"Immediate" is indeed the type of direction one would expect Lee to exercise over Hoke if he had any reservations concerning the latter's performance a week earlier at Fort Harrison. In short, assuming that Hoke made a unilateral albeit correct decision not to attack with his entire division at Fort Harrison, Lee, even if he agreed with that decision and thus tacitly admitted his own error, would not have wanted the episode repeated. Thus the evidence provided by General Hagood and the logic of the situation both suggest that Hoke's "failure" to attack on October 7 was attributable not to uncooperativeness but to orders from Lee. It is worth noting, incidentally, that whatever Colonel Hagood may have claimed subsequently, he neither made nor implied any criticism of Hoke in his official report written ten weeks after the battle.[153]

If Field had lived long enough to read General Hagood's memoirs, he would have learned of Lee's presence with Hoke during the critical stage of the fight at Darbytown Road. Thus he might well have deleted or revised his implied criticism of Hoke in an account of the engagement published in 1886. Be that as it may, his recollections provide a glimmer of enlightenment as to why Hoke's scheduled attack did not take place. After their initial rout by his men, Field recalled, the enemy "massed about two miles to the rear . . . a large force of infantry and artillery behind breastworks, protected in front by a line of abatis. Hoke now came up and formed in line of battle on my right, and, I understood, was to assault simultaneously with me. My gallant fellows, led by the brigade commanders on foot, rushed forward and penetrated the abattis, facing a most terrific fire, delivered, as I afterwards learned from a Yankee officer of rank . . . from those new repeating Spencer rifles. Hoke, from some unexplained cause, did not move forward. The consequence was that the whole fire was concentrated on my fellows. We were repulsed with heavy loss."[154]

Federal reports confirm the accuracy of Field's recollections regarding his severe casualties and the Spencer repeaters carried by some Federal units. Both would have been inhibitions to an attack by Hoke. However, a more critical piece of evidence appears in a report written the day after the battle by a Federal artillery officer, who stated that the fire of two of his batteries "kept, as I have since learned, Hoke's division of rebel infantry from moving forward to assist the assault of the enemy, about to commence still farther to our right." That statement provides a specific, contemporary explanation why Hoke, presumably acting on Lee's orders, did not attack as planned. Moreover, it is supported by a

152. Hagood, *Memoirs of the War*, 307-309. See also *Official Records (Army)*, ser. 1, 42 (pt. 1):731, 42 (pt. 3):116; James R. Hagood, "Memoirs of the First South Carolina Regiment of Volunteer Infantry in the Confederate War for Independence from April 12, 1861 to April 10, 1865," typescript, South Caroliniana Library, University of South Carolina, Columbia, 188-193. Colonel Hagood does in fact use the word "dereliction" to describe Hoke's failure to attack as planned. Colonel Hagood's account differs from General Hagood's in that he (Colonel Hagood) states that Hoke's Division was in line of battle on Field's right rather that in reserve behind Field. However, General Field, in an account of the battle quoted below, clearly states that Hoke did not take position on his right until *after* Field's initial success.

153. See *Official Records (Army)*, ser. 1, 42 (pt. 1):938-939.

154. Charles W. Field, "Campaign of 1864 and 1865," *Southern Historical Society Papers* 14 (1886): 557-558.

"Record of Events" entry on the September-October 1864 muster roll for Company B, 51st North Carolina, which states that the company "did not get into action" on October 7 but was "under fire of artillery." It is also consistent with the unhelpful and (as it relates to Hoke) somewhat enigmatic October 7 entry in the official war diary of the 1st Corps of the Army of Northern Virginia: "At sunrise we move down the Darbytown road with Field and Hoke. The former encounter Kautz's cavalry in the exterior trenches. With [George T.] Anderson's and [John] Bratton's brigades, and [Martin W.] Gary and [Evander McI.] Law on the Charles City Road, the cavalry is drawn off, leaving us nine pieces of artillery, ten caissons, and prisoners. Field's division is then thrown to the left on the outside of the exterior line and Hoke on the inside of it. After crossing a thick abatis and an almost impenetrable swamp, the enemy is found in position near the New Market road. Field at once attacks him, and Major [Marmaduke] Johnson has a spirited artillery combat. Field's attack fails. Hoke cannot get at the enemy out of his trenches and does not move. . . ."[155]

That account, whatever its obscure implications regarding Hoke, suggests that the decision to cancel Hoke's attack was not made because of general considerations such as the protection of Richmond against a "coup de main" and the possibility of "shattering" Lee's "whole disposable force," as General Hagood speculated. Those considerations may have been secondary, but it seems very probable that the primary concern of Lee and Hoke was the tactical situation on the battlefield; namely, Field's heavy casualties and the murderous fire of the Spencers and the two Federal batteries. In short, based on the available evidence, a strong case can be made that Lee was in close contact with Hoke at Darbytown Road and, probably after a consultation with Hoke, canceled the scheduled attack because the two agreed that it would end in a bloody failure. It is worth noting also that, whatever his disappointment in Hoke's lack of aggressiveness and overall performance at Fort Harrison and Darbytown Road, Lee did not formerly censure or criticize his lieutenant on either occasion. He surely would have done so after Darbytown Road, and perhaps relieved Hoke of command, had he considered the North Carolinian culpable in two defeats sustained by the Army of Northern Virginia one week apart.

155. *Official Records (Army)*, ser. 1, 42 (pt. 1):783-784 (first quotation), 876 (third quotation); "Record of Events," Company B, 51st Regiment N.C. Troops, September-October 1864, Compiled Confederate Service Records (North Carolina), M270, reel 486 (second quotation). See also *Official Records (Army)*, ser. 1, 42 (pt. 1):703-704, 709, 713, 716, 720-721, 727, 730-732, 759, 786-789, 791, 823-824, 881, 938-939; 42 (pt. 3):102, 107-119.

FIELD AND STAFF

COLONELS

RADCLIFFE, JAMES DILLARD

Previously served as Colonel of the 18th Regiment N.C. Troops (8th Regiment N.C. Volunteers). Elected Colonel of this regiment on August 30, 1862. Captured at Kinston on December 14, 1862. Paroled on December 15, 1862. Reported present or accounted for on surviving company muster rolls from January, 1863, through April 30, 1864. Wounded (concussion) by a shell at the Crater, near Petersburg, Virginia, July 30, 1864. Hospitalized at Petersburg. Transferred to hospital at Raleigh on August 3, 1864. Resigned on September 5, 1864, because of long standing disagreements and conflicts between himself and some of the officers of his regiment. Resignation accepted on October 11, 1864. [It is uncertain whether his middle name was Dillard or Dillon, probably the former.]

DEVANE, WILLIAM STEWART

Previously served as Captain of Company A of this regiment. Elected Lieutenant Colonel on September 5, 1862, and transferred to the Field and Staff. Reported present or accounted for on surviving company muster rolls through April 30, 1864. Wounded in the back and left shoulder near Petersburg, Virginia, June 18, 1864. Hospitalized at Richmond, Virginia. Furloughed for forty days on or about July 8, 1864. Returned to duty on an unspecified date (probably subsequent to October 15, 1864). Promoted to Colonel on December 6, 1864, to rank from October 11, 1864. Hospitalized at Wilmington on January 30, 1865, with acute diarrhoea. Returned to duty on February 9, 1865. Wounded in the neck at Bentonville on March 21, 1865, while commanding Brig. Gen. Thomas L. Clingman's Brigade. Hospitalized at Salisbury where he was paroled on May 2, 1865. He was "a competent and worthy officer."

LIEUTENANT COLONEL

MALLETT, EDWARD

Previously served as Captain of Company C of this regiment. Reported on duty as acting regimental commander in March-April, 1864. Appointed Major on August 10, 1864, and transferred to the Field and Staff. Appointed Lieutenant Colonel on December 6, 1864, to rank from October 11, 1864. Killed at Bentonville on March 21, 1865. He was a "brave man and an excellent soldier." [Johnson Hagood, *Memoirs*, 362.]

MAJOR

HARDING, HENRY

Previously served as Captain of Company B of this regiment. Appointed Major on September 5, 1862, and transferred to the Field and Staff. Reported present or accounted for in January-June, 1863. Reported in command of the regiment in July-August, 1863. Reported present or accounted for on surviving regimental muster rolls from September, 1863, through April, 1864. Resigned on August 3, 1864, "to promote the good of the service, as well as to secure my personal satisfaction and the satisfaction of those with whom I am associated. . . . I respectfully pray that I may be allowed

to join a Regt of my choice, which I promise to do within five days after this is accepted (the 41st or 50th N.C. preferred)." Resignation accepted on August 10, 1864. [There is no evidence that he served later in another unit.]

ADJUTANTS

BYRD, WILLIAM S.

Appointed acting Adjutant of the regiment on September 20, 1862, while serving as 1st Lieutenant of Company E. Served as acting Adjutant during October-December, 1862; during part of March-April, 1863; and in May-June, 1863. Promoted to Captain on July 1, 1863, and transferred back to Company E.

CHESNUTT, JULIUS M.

Appointed acting Adjutant on February 10, 1863, while serving as 3rd Lieutenant of Company A of this regiment. Reported on duty as acting Adjutant during February, 1863; during part of March-April, 1863; and in July-August, 1863. Reported on duty as acting Assistant Quartermaster of this regiment from November 30 through December 31, 1863.

FAISON, WILLIAM LUCIUS

Previously served as 1st Sergeant of Company A of this regiment. Appointed Adjutant (1st Lieutenant) on October 13, 1863, to rank from September 25, 1863, and transferred to the Field and Staff. Reported present or accounted for on surviving company muster rolls through April 30, 1864. Wounded in the abdomen and hip at Fort Harrison, Virginia, September 30, 1864. Hospitalized at Richmond, Virginia, October 1, 1864. Furloughed for thirty days on November 22, 1864. Furlough extended on December 20, 1864. Hospitalized at Wilmington on January 30, 1865, apparently still suffering from wounds. Survived the war.

MALLETT, JOHN W.

Previously served as Sergeant in Company A, 63rd Regiment N.C. Troops (5th Regiment N.C. Cavalry), and as a drillmaster assigned to the camp of instruction at Raleigh. Served as Adjutant or acting Adjutant of this regiment during November, 1864-April, 1865.

ASSISTANT QUARTERMASTERS

ANDERSON, WILLIAM S.

Resided in New Hanover County. Appointed Assistant Quartermaster (Captain) on October 7, 1862, to rank from September 17, 1862. Reported present in January-April, 1863. Resigned on May 9, 1863, because "my . . . age being above 40 and [my constitution being] feeble . . . [I] was but ill adapted to the severe exposures and cares of camp life. . . . Besides I have a large family dependent upon me for support." Resignation accepted on May 23, 1863.

MEARES, OLIVER PENDLETON

Previously served as Assistant Commissary of Subsistence (Captain) of this regiment. Appointed Assistant Quartermaster (Captain) on June 23, 1863, to rank from May 23, 1863. Reported present or accounted for on surviving company muster rolls through April 30, 1864. Appointed Quartermaster of Brig. Gen. Thomas L. Clingman's Brigade on September 20, 1864.

CHESNUTT, JULIUS M.

Served as 2nd Lieutenant of Company A of this regiment. Reported on duty as acting Assistant Quartermaster from November 30 through December 31, 1863.

ASSISTANT COMMISSARY OF SUBSISTENCE

MEARES, OLIVER PENDLETON

Previously served as Lieutenant Colonel of the 18th Regiment N.C. Troops. Appointed Assistant Commissary of Subsistence (Captain) of this regiment on April 11, 1863, to rank from September 9, 1862. Appointed Assistant Quartermaster (Captain) of this regiment on June 23, 1863, to rank from May 23, 1863. [See Assistant Quartermasters' section above.]

SURGEONS

TAYLOE, DAVID THOMAS

Born in Beaufort County on February 21, 1826. Resided in Beaufort County and was by occupation a doctor prior to enlisting at age 36. Appointed Surgeon on September 11, 1862. Resigned on November 29, 1862, because of "a sense of duty to my aged mother and to my family, now refugees from Yankee oppression." Resignation accepted on December 20, 1862.

RIVES, ALEXANDER

Date of appointment as Surgeon not reported. Paroled at Greensboro on May 1, 1865.

ASSISTANT SURGEONS

HARRISS, WILLIAM WHITE

Resided in New Hanover County. Appointed Assistant Surgeon on October 10, 1862. Reported present or accounted for on surviving company muster rolls until he resigned on August 29, 1863. Reason he resigned not reported. Resignation accepted on or about September 23, 1863. Appointed Surgeon of the 58th Regiment N.C. Troops on an unspecified date (probably late September or early October, 1863) to rank from August 7, 1863.

FRIPP, CLARENCE A.

Resided in South Carolina (probably Beaufort District) and was by occupation a physician. Appointed Assistant Surgeon of this regiment on September 23, 1863. Reported present through December 31, 1863. Transferred to an unspecified unit (probably the 24th Regiment N.C. Troops [14th Regiment N.C. Volunteers]) on April 15, 1864. [Was about 33 years of age at the time of his appointment as Assistant Surgeon of this regiment. Served also as Assistant Surgeon of the 20th Regiment South Carolina Infantry. Contrary to his 24th North Carolina Compiled Military Service Records, his surname was "Fripp" rather than "Tripp."]

BLAKENEY, JULIUS C.

Appointed Assistant Surgeon on June 1, 1864, to rank from February 9, 1864. Furloughed for thirty days on July 12, 1864, by reason of illness. Hospitalized at Richmond, Virginia, Novem-

ber 7, 1864, with cystitis. Transferred to another hospital on November 26, 1864. Relieved from duty "on account [of] ill health" on January 3, 1865.

FEW, BENJAMIN F.

Served as Assistant Surgeon of the 31st Regiment N.C. Troops. Reported on temporary duty as Assistant Surgeon of this regiment in February, 1865.

LENGELT, E. A.

Appointed Assistant Surgeon of this regiment on an unspecified date (probably subsequent to February 28, 1865). Paroled at Greensboro on May 1, 1865.

CHAPLAIN

JONES, WILLIAM BORDEN

Baptist. Appointed Chaplain of this regiment on March 11, 1863, after serving as principal of the Warsaw Baptist Seminary (Duplin County). Reported present or accounted for on surviving regimental rolls through April 30, 1864. Requested assignment to duty as Chaplain of the military hospital at Wilson on October 23, 1864, because "my labors have to a great extent exhausted my physical energies and impaired my health." Relieved from duty with this regiment on November 21, 1864.

ENSIGNS AND COLOR BEARERS

VANN, JOHN ROBERT

Served as Private in Company A of this regiment. Reported on duty as Color Bearer in November-December, 1863.

COREY, JOSHUA L.

Previously served as Sergeant in Company H of this regiment. Appointed Ensign (1st Lieutenant) on October 28, 1864, to rank from September 24, 1864, while a prisoner of war at Point Lookout, Maryland. Paroled at Point Lookout on March 17, 1865. Received at Boulware's Wharf, James River, Virginia, March 19, 1865, for exchange. No further records.

SERGEANTS MAJOR

STEVENS, DAVID

Previously served as Sergeant in Company A of this regiment. Appointed Sergeant Major on January 14, 1863, and transferred to the Field and Staff. Hospitalized at Savannah, Georgia, March 5, 1863. Died in hospital at Savannah on March 19, 1863, of "typ[hoi]d fever."

VON EBERSTEIN, WILLIAM H.

Previously served as Sergeant in Company K, 10th Regiment N.C. State Troops (1st Regiment N.C. Artillery). Appointed Sergeant Major of this regiment on July 3, 1863. Wounded in the hip at Morris Island, Charleston Harbor, South Carolina, August 26, 1863. Hospitalized at Charleston. Returned to duty on October 5, 1863. Reported present in November-December, 1863, and March-April, 1864. Wounded in the hip at Drewry's Bluff, Virginia, on or about May 16, 1864. Hospitalized at Richmond,

Virginia. Furloughed for sixty days on May 31, 1864. Discharged on October 18, 1864, presumably by reason of disability from wounds.

HINES, _____

A soldier by this name was on duty as acting Sergeant Major on October 19, 1864. He was probably either Sgt. James Hines of Company E or Pvt. William F. Hines of Company A.

QUARTERMASTER SERGEANTS

SHACKELFORD, DANIEL

Previously served as Private in Company G of this regiment. Appointed Quartermaster Sergeant on September 9, 1862, and transferred to the Field and Staff. Captured and paroled at Kinston on December 14, 1862. Returned to duty on or about January 15, 1863, when he was promoted to 1st Sergeant and transferred back to Company G. Later served as 2nd Lieutenant of Company G.

KING, CHARLES HUMPHREY

Previously served as Private in Company G, 41st Regiment N.C. Troops (3rd Regiment N.C. Cavalry). Appointed Quartermaster Sergeant of this regiment in January-February, 1863. Reported present or accounted for on surviving company muster rolls through April 30, 1864. Paroled at Greensboro on May 1, 1865.

COMMISSARY SERGEANTS

BLANKS, WILLIAM

Served as Private in Company G of this regiment. Appointed acting Commissary Sergeant on September 9, 1862, and transferred to the Field and Staff. Reported present in January-April, 1863. Transferred back to Company G prior to May 23, 1863.

ROBERTS, SAMUEL W.

Served as Private in Company G of this regiment. Reported on duty as acting Commissary Sergeant of this regiment in July, 1863-April, 1864, and September-October, 1864. No further records.

ORDNANCE SERGEANT

LANE, JOSEPH J.

Previously served as Sergeant in Company F of this regiment. Appointed Ordnance Sergeant on September 13, 1862, and transferred to the Field and Staff. Reported present or accounted for on surviving company muster rolls in November, 1862-April, 1864. No further records. Survived the war.

HOSPITAL STEWARD

OATES, JETHRO D.

Previously served as Private in Company A of this regiment. Appointed acting Hospital Steward on September 14, 1862, and assigned to temporary duty with the Field and Staff. Appointed Hospital Steward on February 26, 1863, and assigned to permanent duty with the Field and Staff. Reported present or accounted

for in surviving regimental records through August 15, 1864. Records of the Federal Provost Marshal indicate that he was paroled at Goldsboro on May 23, 1865, and give his rank as Private; however, records of the United Daughters of the Confederacy indicate that he died on March 20, 1865, of "pneumonia."

CHIEF MUSICIAN

JOHNSON, JOHN H.

Previously served as Musician in Company B of this regiment. Appointed Chief Musician (Drum Major) on September 18, 1862, and transferred to the Field and Staff. Reported present on surviving company muster rolls from January 1, 1863, through April 30, 1864. No further records.

COMPANY A

This company, nicknamed the "Sampson Confederates," was raised by Capt. Franklin J. Faison in Sampson County on April 20, 1861. It was mustered into state service on June 18, 1861, and assigned to the 20th Regiment N.C. Troops; however, that regiment already had ten companies. Faison's company was therefore transferred out of the 20th Regiment without having been assigned a letter designation. Meantime, Faison was elected lieutenant colonel of the 20th Regiment on June 18, 1861. His company was then divided into two companies commanded by Capts. James C. Holmes and William S. Devane. Holmes's command was known as Captain Holmes's Independent Company, N.C. Troops. It served as such until October 8, 1861, when it was assigned to the 30th Regiment N.C. Troops and designated Company A. Devane's command served as Captain Devane's Independent Company, N.C. Troops, until about September 5, 1862, when it was assigned to the newly organized 59th Regiment N.C. Troops. That unit was redesignated the 61st Regiment N.C. Troops on an unknown date between October 30 and November 22, 1862. Devane's Company was designated Company A. After joining the 61st Regiment the company functioned as a part of that regiment, and its history for the remainder of the war is reported as a part of the regimental history.

The following roster was compiled primarily from information in the microfilm edition of the Compiled Service Records of Soldiers Who Served in Organizations from the State of North Carolina (Record Group 109, MC 270), National Archives and Records Administration, Washington, D.C. Record Group 109 includes enlistment papers, pay vouchers, requisitions, letters of resignation, discharge certificates, and abstracts of medical and prisoner of war returns. Materials relating specifically to Company A, 61st Regiment N.C. Troops, include a company muster-in and descriptive roll dated October 6, 1862, and company muster rolls for September, 1862-April, 1864, and September-October, 1864.

Also utilized in this roster were *The War of the Rebellion: A Compilation of the Official Records of the Union and Confederate Armies*, the North Carolina adjutant general's *Roll of Honor*, state militia records, newspaper casualty lists and obituaries, wartime claims for bounty pay and allowances, postwar registers of claims for artificial limbs, Confederate pension applications filed with the states of North Carolina, Tennessee, and Florida, Confederate Soldiers' Home records, and the 1860 and 1870 federal censuses of North Carolina. A search was made also for relevant letters, diaries, reminiscences, and

other manuscripts in the Southern Historical Collection (University of North Carolina-Chapel Hill), the Duke University Library Special Collections Department, and the North Carolina Division of Archives and History.

Among the secondary sources consulted were records of the North Carolina division of the United Daughters of the Confederacy, postwar rosters, regimental and county histories, marriage bond, will, and cemetery indexes, published and unpublished genealogies, biographical dictionaries, the North Carolina *County Heritage Book* series, the *Confederate Veteran*, Walter Clark's *Histories of the Several Regiments and Battalions from North Carolina in the Great War, 1861-'65*, and the North Carolina volume of the extended edition of *Confederate Military History*.

OFFICERS

CAPTAINS

DEVANE, WILLIAM STEWART

Previously served as Captain of William S. Devane's Independent Company, N.C. Troops. Transferred to this company on September 5, 1862. Elected Lieutenant Colonel on the same date and transferred to the Field and Staff of this regiment. Later served as Colonel of the regiment.

MARSH, GEORGE WASHINGTON

Previously served as 1st Lieutenant of Capt. William S. Devane's Independent Company, N.C. Troops. Appointed Captain of this company on September 5, 1862. Reported present through April 30, 1863. Reported absent on detached duty on June 25, 1863. Reported sick in hospital at Charleston, South Carolina, in July-August, 1863. Resigned on August 14, 1863. Reason he resigned not reported. Resignation accepted on September 4, 1863.

ROBINSON, JAMES HOLMES

Previously served as 2nd Lieutenant of Capt. William S. Devane's Independent Company, N.C. Troops. Promoted to 1st Lieutenant and transferred to this company on September 5, 1862. Reported present or accounted for through August 30, 1863. Appointed Captain on September 5, 1863. Reported present or accounted for through April 30, 1864. Wounded slightly in the shoulder at or near Petersburg, Virginia, on or about June 16-19, 1864. Returned to duty on an unspecified date. Wounded in the right side and captured at Fort Harrison, Virginia, September 30, 1864. Hospitalized at Fort Monroe, Virginia. Confined at Point Lookout, Maryland, December 23, 1864. Transferred to Old Capitol Prison, Washington, D.C., January 2, 1865. Transferred to Fort Delaware, Delaware, February 3, 1865. Released at Fort Delaware on June 14, 1865, after taking the Oath of Allegiance.

STORY, EDWARD F.

Served as 3rd Lieutenant of Company C of this regiment. Reported on duty as acting commander of this company in September-October, 1864.

LIEUTENANTS

CARROLL, FRANCIS MARION, 3rd Lieutenant

Previously served as Private in Capt. William S. Devane's Independent Company, N.C. Troops. Transferred to this company on or about September 5, 1862. Mustered in as Private. Promoted to Corporal on February 7, 1863. Elected 3rd Lieutenant on September 23, 1863. Reported present through April 30, 1864. Wounded in the right side of the face at the Crater, near Petersburg, Virginia, July 30, 1864. Hospitalized at Richmond, Virginia. Furloughed on August 10, 1864. Returned to duty subsequent to October 31, 1864. Wounded in the head at Bentonville on March 19-21, 1865. Hospitalized at Raleigh. Survived the war.

CHESNUTT, JULIUS M., 2nd Lieutenant

Previously served as 1st Sergeant in Capt. William S. Devane's Independent Company, N.C. Troops. Transferred to this company on or about September 5, 1862. Mustered in as 1st Sergeant. Elected 3rd Lieutenant on September 20, 1862. Appointed acting Adjutant of this regiment on February 10, 1863, and transferred to the Field and Staff. Reported on duty as acting Adjutant during February, 1863; during part of March-April, 1863; and in July-August, 1863. Promoted to 2nd Lieutenant on September 5, 1863. Reported on duty as acting Assistant Quartermaster of this regiment from November 30 through December 31, 1863. Rejoined the company in January-February, 1864. Hospitalized on March 14, 1864, with syphilis. Transferred on May 9, 1864. Returned to duty on an unspecified date. Killed (possibly mortally wounded and captured) at Fort Harrison, Virginia, September 30, 1864.

SMITH, WILLIAM FRANKLYN, 1st Lieutenant

Previously served as 3rd Lieutenant of Capt. William S. Devane's Independent Company, N.C. Troops. Appointed 2nd Lieutenant of this company on September 5, 1862. Reported present through June 30, 1863. Hospitalized at Wilmington on July 11, 1863. Promoted to 1st Lieutenant on September 5, 1863. Furloughed on October 26, 1863. Returned to duty in November-December, 1863. Reported present through April 30, 1864. Commanded the company June 17-30, 1864. Wounded in the left thigh (fracture) at Fort Harrison, Virginia, September 30, 1864. Hospitalized at Richmond, Virginia. Furloughed for sixty days on or about November 27, 1864. No further records. [*Heritage of Sampson County*, 244, indicates that he died in 1866 as a result of his wound.]

NONCOMMISSIONED OFFICERS AND PRIVATES

ARMSTRONG, FLEET HIRAM, Private

Previously served as Private in Capt. William S. Devane's Independent Company, N.C. Troops. Transferred to this company on or about September 5, 1862. Reported sick in hospital at Goldsboro on December 24, 1862. Returned to duty prior to January 20, 1863, when he was detailed for duty as a telegraph operator. Reported on duty with the Signal Corps of the Cape Fear District from January 20, 1863, through April 30, 1864. Rejoined the company on October 19, 1864. No further records. Survived the war.

ARMSTRONG, GEORGE W., Private

Previously served as Private in Capt. William S. Devane's Independent Company, N.C. Troops. Transferred to this company on or about September 5, 1862. Reported present through June 30, 1863. Transferred to the Engineer Corps and assigned to duty at Wilmington on or about August 3, 1863.

ARMSTRONG, JAMES M., Private

Previously served as Private in Capt. William S. Devane's Independent Company, N.C. Troops. Transferred to this company on

or about September 5, 1862. Reported on detached duty with the Signal Corps through December 31, 1862. Died in hospital at Smithville (Southport) on February 20, 1863, of "small pox." He was "mourned by his associates as a kind and pleasant friend and a soldier worthy of the noble cause he sustained." [*Wilmington Journal* (Weekly), February 26, 1863.]

ARMSTRONG, JOHN O., 1st Sergeant

Previously served as Sergeant in Capt. William S. Devane's Independent Company, N.C. Troops. Transferred to this company on or about September 5, 1862. Reported present through April 30, 1864. Promoted to 1st Sergeant on March 28, 1864. Wounded in the shoulder at Drewry's Bluff, Virginia, May 13, 1864. Hospitalized at Richmond, Virginia. Returned to duty prior to September 30, 1864, when he was captured at Fort Harrison, Virginia. Confined at Point Lookout, Maryland, October 5, 1864. Paroled at Point Lookout on March 17, 1865. Received at Boulware's Wharf, James River, Virginia, March 19, 1865, for exchange. No further records. [Contrary to 8:324 of this series, this soldier did not serve in Company A, 30th Regiment N.C. Troops.]

ARMSTRONG, STEPHEN S., Private

Previously served as Private in Capt. William S. Devane's Independent Company, N.C. Troops. Transferred to this company on or about September 5, 1862. Reported present or accounted for through December 31, 1862. Detailed for duty as a telegraph operator on January 20, 1863. Reported on duty with the Signal Corps in the Cape Fear District from that date through April 30, 1864. Reported on duty with the company in September-October, 1864. No further records. Survived the war.

BENNETT, HARDY KIRVING, Private

Previously served as Private in Capt. William S. Devane's Independent Company, N.C. Troops. Transferred to this company on or about September 5, 1862. Reported present or accounted for through April, 1864. Captured at Globe Tavern, Virginia, August 19, 1864. Confined at Point Lookout, Maryland, August 24, 1864. Paroled at Point Lookout on March 17, 1865. Received at Boulware's Wharf, James River, Virginia, March 19, 1865, for exchange. No further records. Survived the war.

BLOUNT, SHERMAN J., Private

Previously served as Private in Capt. William S. Devane's Independent Company, N.C. Troops. Transferred to this company on or about September 5, 1862. Reported present or accounted for through August 31, 1863. Reported sick in hospital at Charleston, South Carolina, October 13, 1863. Returned to duty in November-December, 1863. Hospitalized on February 22, 1864, with "abscessus." Transferred on March 17, 1864. Returned to duty prior to May 1, 1864. Wounded in the side at the Crater, near Petersburg, Virginia, July 30, 1864. Reported present but on duty at regimental headquarters in September-October, 1864. Killed at Bentonville on March 19-21, 1865.

BOON, JOHN W., Private

Previously served as Private in Capt. William S. Devane's Independent Company, N.C. Troops. Transferred to this company on or about September 5, 1862. Reported present through April 30, 1863. Reported absent on fatigue duty on June 25, 1863. Returned to duty in July-August, 1863. Reported present on surviving company muster rolls through October 31, 1864. No further records. Survived the war.

BOWDEN, CALVIN JAMES, Private

Previously served as Private in Company C, 63rd Regiment N.C. Troops (5th Regiment N.C. Cavalry). Transferred to this company on October 19, 1864. Hospitalized at Greensboro on February 23, 1865, with debilitas. Returned to duty on February 25, 1865. No further records. Survived the war.

BOYKIN, ABRAHAM, Private

Previously served as Private in Capt. William S. Devane's Independent Company, N.C. Troops. Transferred to this company on or about September 5, 1862. Reported absent sick in November-December, 1862. Returned to duty in January-February, 1863. Reported on detached service as a picket guard at Hilton Ferry, near Wilmington, May 8, 1863. Rejoined the company in July-August, 1863. Transferred to Company G of this regiment on September 26, 1863.

BOYKIN, ISAAC, ———

Negro. Servant to Pvt. Abraham Boykin of this company.

BRADSHAW, THOMAS, Private

Previously served as Private in Company C, 63rd Regiment N.C. Troops (5th Regiment N.C. Cavalry). Transferred to this company on October 19, 1864. Paroled at Goldsboro on May 25, 1865.

BREWINGTON, IRELAND, ———

Negro. North Carolina pension records indicate that he served for four years as a cook in this regiment.

CARROLL, STEPHEN T., Private

Previously served as Private in Capt. William S. Devane's Independent Company, N.C. Troops. Transferred to this company on or about September 5, 1862. Reported present or accounted for through June 30, 1863. Wounded at Fort Wagner, Charleston Harbor, South Carolina, July 30, 1863. Returned to duty in September-October, 1863. Reported present through April 30, 1864. Killed near Petersburg, Virginia, June 18, 1864.

CONLIN, Q. P., ———

Resided in Greene County. Place and date of enlistment not reported (probably enlisted subsequent to October 31, 1864). Paroled at Goldsboro on May 15, 1865.

COOK, CHARLES A., Private

Born in Sampson County and resided in Duplin County where he was by occupation a carpenter prior to enlisting in Duplin County at age 37, March 5, 1863, for the war. Reported in hospital at Wilmington on May 4, 1863, with icterus. Returned to duty prior to July 1, 1863. Reported sick in hospital at Mount Pleasant, South Carolina, August 23, 1863. Returned to duty in September-October, 1863. Reported present through April 30, 1864. Reported on detached service with the Engineer Corps from August 27 through October 31, 1864. Served also as Artificer in Company G, 2nd Regiment Confederate Engineer Troops. Survived the war.

COOK, LEWIS O., Private

Previously served as Private in Capt. William S. Devane's Independent Company, N.C. Troops. Transferred to this company on or about September 5, 1862. Reported present through April 30, 1864. Wounded in the back of the head near Petersburg, Virginia, June 19, 1864. Hospitalized at Richmond, Virginia. Returned to duty prior to November 1, 1864. No further records. Survived the war.

DOWD, THOMAS, Private

Previously served as Private in 2nd Company H, 40th Regiment N.C. Troops (3rd Regiment N.C. Artillery). Transferred to this company on July 1, 1863. Wounded at Morris Island, Charleston Harbor, South Carolina, August 25, 1863. Hospitalized at Charleston where he died on or about August 28, 1863, of wounds.

DOWNING, THOMAS L., Private

Previously served as Private in Capt. William S. Devane's Independent Company, N.C. Troops. Transferred to this company on or about September 5, 1862. Reported present through February 28, 1863. Hospitalized at Wilmington on or about May 9, 1863, with diarrhoea. Reported absent sick or present but sick through October 31, 1863. Reported on detached service in camp near Petersburg, Virginia, December 16, 1863. Returned to duty in January-February, 1864. Wounded in the left hand at Cold Harbor, Virginia, on or about June 1, 1864. One finger amputated. Hospitalized at Petersburg. Transferred to hospital at Raleigh on June 5, 1864. Furloughed from hospital at High Point on June 11, 1864. Returned to duty prior to November 1, 1864. Deserted to the enemy on or about December 2, 1864. Confined at Washington, D.C., December 7, 1864. Released on or about the same date after taking the Oath of Allegiance.

DUPREE, JOHN G., Private

Resided in Stokes County and enlisted at Camp Holmes, near Raleigh, March 5, 1863, for the war. Discharged at Columbia, South Carolina, April 16, 1863, by a medical examining board. Reason discharged not reported.

EMERSON, THOMAS J., Private

Previously served as Private in Capt. William S. Devane's Independent Company, N.C. Troops. Transferred to this company on or about September 5, 1862. Reported on detached duty with the Signal Corps in the Cape Fear District from July 27, 1862, through April 30, 1864. Was on duty as a telegraph operator during part of that period and as signals officer on the steamer *Eugene* during part of that period. Rejoined the company on October 19, 1864. No further records.

EVANS, JOHN J., Private

Previously served as Private in Capt. William S. Devane's Independent Company, N.C. Troops. Transferred to this company on or about September 5, 1862. Reported present through April 30, 1863. Reported present but sick in quarters in May-June and September-October, 1863. Hospitalized at Wilmington on December 28, 1863, with remittent fever. Returned to duty on March 31, 1864. Died in hospital at Petersburg, Virginia, May 8, 1864, of "typhoid pneumonia and bronchitis." [See *Wilmington Weekly Journal*, September 1, 1864.]

FAISON, SOLOMON W., Private

Previously served as Corporal in 2nd Company A, 36th Regiment N.C. Troops (2nd Regiment N.C. Artillery). Transferred to this company on or about September 15, 1862. Mustered in as Private. Reported present through April 30, 1863. Reported present but sick in quarters in May-June, 1863. Returned to duty in July-August, 1863. Reported present through February 29, 1864. Reported on provost duty at Murphy's Station, Virginia, April 25, 1864. Killed at Drewry's Bluff, Virginia, May 13-16, 1864.

FAISON, WILLIAM LUCIUS, 1st Sergeant

Previously served as Sergeant in Capt. William S. Devane's Independent Company, N.C. Troops. Transferred to this company on or about September 5, 1862. Promoted to 1st Sergeant on October 1, 1862. Reported present or accounted for through June 30, 1863. Wounded in the knee at Morris Island, Charleston Harbor, South Carolina, on or about August 22, 1863. Hospitalized at Charleston. Returned to duty prior to August 20-September 6, 1863, when he was wounded in the thigh at Morris Island. Returned to duty on an unspecified date. Appointed Adjutant (1st Lieutenant) on October 13, 1863, to rank from September 25, 1863, and transferred to the Field and Staff of this regiment.

FREEMAN, ABSALOM C., Private

Resided in Stokes County and was by occupation a farmer prior to enlisting in Stokes County at age 36, February 23, 1863, for the war. Reported absent on sick furlough on April 21, 1863. Died at home in Stokes County on May 9, 1863. Cause of death not reported.

FRYAR, HENRY, Private

Previously served as Private in Capt. William S. Devane's Independent Company, N.C. Troops. Transferred to this company on or about September 5, 1862. Reported present or accounted for on surviving company muster rolls through October 31, 1864. Served as a mail carrier during most of that period. No further records. Survived the war.

FRYAR, OWEN, Private

Previously served as Private in Capt. William S. Devane's Independent Company, N.C. Troops. Transferred to this company on or about September 5, 1862. Reported present through April 30, 1863. Reported on duty as acting regimental mail agent in May-June, 1863. Reported sick in hospital at Mount Pleasant, South Carolina, in July-August, 1863. Returned to duty in September-October, 1863. Transferred to Company C, 63rd Regiment N.C. Troops (5th Regiment N.C. Cavalry), November 7, 1863.

FRYAR, THOMAS, 1st Sergeant

Previously served as Sergeant in Capt. William S. Devane's Independent Company, N.C. Troops. Transferred to this company on or about September 5, 1862. Reported absent sick in Sampson County from November 19, 1862, through February 28, 1863. Reported present but sick in quarters in March-April, 1863. Returned to duty in May-June, 1863. Reported at home on sick furlough from August 20 through October 31, 1863. Promoted to 1st Sergeant on September 25, 1863. Reported absent without leave on December 11, 1863. Reported absent on sick furlough in January-February, 1864. Discharged by a medical board on March 28, 1864. Reason discharged not reported.

GRAVES, THOMAS L., Sergeant

Previously served as Corporal in Capt. William S. Devane's Independent Company, N.C. Troops. Transferred to this company on or about September 5, 1862. Mustered in as Corporal. Reported present through February 28, 1863. Reported sick in hospital at Charleston, South Carolina, April 25, 1863. Returned to duty in May-June, 1863. Promoted to Sergeant on or about August 31, 1863. Reported present through February 28, 1864. Reported on extra duty as a scout on April 26, 1864. Reported on extra duty in the ordnance department in September-October, 1864. No further records. ["On 3 June, 1864, at Cold Harbor, (Virginia,) while the enemy was shelling our works, a shell fell in the trench occupied by our regiment, in a smoking condition and almost ready to burst. It was at once seized by this brave man (Sgt. Thomas L. Graves) and thrown over the parapet." (Clark's *Regiments*, 5:16.)]

GRICE, WILEY M., Private

Previously served as Private in Capt. William S. Devane's Independent Company, N.C. Troops. Transferred to this company on or about September 5, 1862. Reported present but sick in September-December, 1862. Hospitalized at Wilmington on January 13, 1863, with variola. Returned to duty on January 15, 1863. Died in hospital at Wilmington on January 24, 1863, of "smallpox."

HALL, JAMES, ———

North Carolina pension records indicate that he served in this company.

HALL, TOBIAS, Private

Previously served as Private in Capt. William S. Devane's Independent Company, N.C. Troops. Transferred to this company on or about September 5, 1862. Reported sick in camp at Tarboro on or about October 31, 1862. Detailed for duty as a teamster in the quartermaster's department in November-December, 1862. Reported on duty as a teamster on surviving company muster rolls through October 31, 1864. Deserted on an unspecified date. Reported in confinement at Faison's Depot (Duplin County) on April 8, 1865. Survived the war. [North Carolina pension records indicate that he was wounded on an unspecified date.]

HEATH, JAMES G., Private

Previously served as Private in Capt. William S. Devane's Independent Company, N.C. Troops. Transferred to this company on or about September 5, 1862. Reported present or accounted for on surviving company muster rolls through February 29, 1864. Confined at Ivor Station, Virginia, April 13, 1864. Returned to duty prior to July 30, 1864, when he was wounded in the neck and right shoulder at the Crater, near Petersburg, Virginia. Hospitalized at Petersburg. Furloughed for sixty days on August 11, 1864. Reported absent wounded through October 31, 1864. Furloughed from hospital at High Point on November 8, 1864. Paroled at Goldsboro on May 17, 1865.

HERRING, AMOS R., Private

Previously served as Private in Capt. William S. Devane's Independent Company, N.C. Troops. Transferred to this company on or about September 5, 1862. Discharged on December 6, 1862, by reason of being underage. Later served in Company G of this regiment.

HERRING, OWEN F., Corporal

Previously served as Private in Capt. William S. Devane's Independent Company, N.C. Troops. Transferred to this company on or about September 5, 1862. Mustered in as Private. Reported present or accounted for through April 30, 1864. Promoted to Corporal on or about April 13, 1864. Captured near Petersburg, Virginia, on or about August 4, 1864. Confined at Old Capitol Prison, Washington, D.C., August 10, 1864. Transferred to Fort Delaware, Delaware, where he arrived on August 12, 1864. Released at Fort Delaware on June 17, 1865, after taking the Oath of Allegiance.

HERRING, ROBERT S., Private

Previously served as Private in Capt. William S. Devane's Independent Company, N.C. Troops. Transferred to this company on or about September 5, 1862. Reported on detached duty with the Signal Corps in the Cape Fear District from September 12, 1862, through April 30, 1863. Probably served as a telegraph operator during that period. Transferred to Company F, 36th Regiment N.C. Troops (2nd Regiment N.C. Artillery), May 18, 1863.

HIGHSMITH, JAMES B., Private

Previously served as Private in Capt. William S. Devane's Independent Company, N.C. Troops. Transferred to this company on or about September 5, 1862. Reported present or accounted for through February 29, 1864. Reported absent on detached service as a scout on April 23, 1864. Returned to duty on an unspecified date. Reported present in September-October, 1864. Took the Oath of Allegiance at Raleigh on May 5, 1865.

HIGHSMITH, JOHN JAMES, Private

Previously served as Private in Capt. William S. Devane's Independent Company, N.C. Troops. Transferred to this company on or about September 5, 1862. Reported sick in hospital at Wilson in September-October, 1862. Returned to duty in November-December, 1862. Reported present but sick in quarters in January-February, 1863. Returned to duty in March-April, 1863. Reported absent on fatigue duty on June 25, 1863. Reported absent sick from July 11 through August 31, 1863. Reported on detached duty at Northeast Depot, Charleston, South Carolina, October 14, 1863. Reported on detached service in camp near Petersburg, Virginia, December 16, 1863. Hospitalized at Petersburg on February 24, 1864, with chronic rheumatism. Transferred on March 17, 1864. Reported absent sick at Ivor Station, Virginia, April 23, 1864. Discharged from hospital at Goldsboro on May 22, 1864. Returned to duty on an unspecified date. Reported present in September-October, 1864. No further records. Survived the war.

HINES, WILLIAM F., Private

Previously served as Private in Capt. William S. Devane's Independent Company, N.C. Troops. Transferred to this company on or about September 5, 1862. Reported present but on duty at the Adjutant's office in September, 1862-August, 1863. Reported at home on sick furlough from September 24 through October 31, 1863. Reported on detached service in camp near Petersburg, Virginia, from December 16, 1863, through February 29, 1864. Reported on provost duty at Murphy's Station, Virginia, April 25, 1864. Sent to the division infirmary on or about October 25, 1864. No further records. Survived the war. [A soldier named Hines was reported on duty as acting Sergeant Major of the regiment on October 19, 1864. He was probably either this man or Sgt. James Hines of Company E.]

HINES, WILLIAM S., Private

Previously served as Private in Capt. William S. Devane's Independent Company, N.C. Troops. Transferred to this company on or about September 5, 1862. Reported sick in hospital at Wilson on or about October 31, 1862. Discharged on December 6, 1862, by reason of being overage. Later served as Private in Company B, 1st Battalion N.C. Heavy Artillery.

HOBBS, H., Private

Resided in Sampson County. Place and date of enlistment not reported (probably enlisted subsequent to October 31, 1864). Paroled at Goldsboro on May 25, 1865.

HOBBS, JULIUS C., Sergeant

Previously served as Musician in Capt. William S. Devane's Independent Company, N.C. Troops. Transferred to this company on or about September 5, 1862. Mustered in as Musician. Reduced to ranks in November-December, 1862. Reported present through April 30, 1863. Reported on duty as a picket guard at Hilton Ferry, near Wilmington, from May 8 through June 30, 1863. Rejoined the company in July-August, 1863. Promoted to Corporal on September 25, 1863. Promoted to Sergeant on April 13, 1864. Reported present through April 30, 1864. Transferred to Company C, 63rd Regiment N.C. Troops (5th Regiment N.C. Cavalry), October 19, 1864.

HORN, JAMES H., Private

Previously served as Private in Capt. William S. Devane's Independent Company, N.C. Troops. Transferred to this company on or about September 5, 1862. Reported present or accounted for through April 30, 1863. Reported present but on duty as an officer's cook in May-June, 1863. Reported present in July, 1863-February, 1864. Reported present but on duty as an officer's cook in March-April, 1864. Wounded in the right arm at the Crater, near Petersburg, Virginia, July 30, 1864. Hospitalized at Richmond, Virginia. Furloughed for sixty days on October 31, 1864. No further records. Survived the war.

HUBBARD, JOSEPH HENLEY, Private

Previously served as Private in Capt. William S. Devane's Independent Company, N.C. Troops. Transferred to this company on or about September 5, 1862. Transferred to 2nd Company A, 36th Regiment N.C. Troops (2nd Regiment N.C. Artillery), September 15, 1862.

JOHNSON, AMMA FERDINAND, Private

Born in Sampson County on March 6, 1845. Resided in Sampson County and was by occupation a student at the University of North Carolina prior to enlisting in New Hanover County at age 17, February 13, 1863, for the war. Reported on detached duty as a clerk in the Assistant Adjutant General's office of Clingman's Brigade through June 30, 1863. Captured on the Wilmington and Weldon Railroad (probably near Warsaw) on or about July 4, 1863. Confined at Fort Monroe, Virginia. Paroled and transferred to City Point, Virginia, where he was received on July 17, 1863, for exchange. Reported on duty as a clerk in the Assistant Adjutant General's office of Clingman's Brigade through April 30, 1864, and in September-October, 1864. Paroled at Greensboro on May 1, 1865.

JOHNSON, EVERETT, Private

Previously served as Private in Capt. William S. Devane's Independent Company, N.C. Troops. Transferred to this company on or about September 5, 1862. Reported present through June 30, 1863. Wounded slightly in the hand at Morris Island, Charleston Harbor, South Carolina, on or about August 26, 1863. Returned to duty prior to September 1, 1863. Reported present on surviving company muster rolls through October 31, 1864. No further records. Survived the war.

JOHNSON, JAMES H., Private

Previously served as Private in Capt. William S. Devane's Independent Company, N.C. Troops. Transferred to this company on or about September 5, 1862. Reported absent sick in September-December, 1862. Returned to duty in January-February, 1863. Reported present or accounted for through April 30, 1864. Wounded in the arm and back at Drewry's Bluff, Virginia, May 13-16, 1864. Reported in hospital at Richmond, Virginia, October 2, 1864. Reported in hospital at Fayetteville from October 25, 1864, through February 28, 1865. No further records.

JOHNSON, SAMUEL, Private

Place and date of enlistment not reported (probably enlisted subsequent to October 31, 1864). Deserted to the enemy at or near Bermuda Hundred, Virginia, December 2, 1864. Took the Oath of Allegiance on December 3, 1864. Released at Washington, D.C., December 7, 1864.

JOHNSON, SYLVESTER, Private

Previously served as Private in Capt. William S. Devane's Independent Company, N.C. Troops. Transferred to this company on or about September 5, 1862. Reported present on surviving company muster rolls through October 31, 1864. Deserted to the enemy on or about November 30, 1864.

KELLY, ISAIAH J., Private

Previously served as Private in Capt. William S. Devane's Independent Company, N.C. Troops. Transferred to this company on or about September 5, 1862. Reported present through February 28, 1863. Reported present but sick in quarters in March-April, 1863. Reported in hospital at Wilmington on May 5, 1863, with typhoid fever. Returned to duty prior to July 30, 1863, when he was wounded at Fort Wagner, Charleston Harbor, South Carolina. Returned to duty prior to September 1, 1863. Reported present through April 30, 1864. Wounded in the hand at Fort Harrison, Virginia, September 30, 1864. Hospitalized at Richmond, Virginia. Returned to duty prior to November 1, 1864. No further records.

KNOWLES, JOHN J., Private

Previously served as Private in Capt. William S. Devane's Independent Company, N.C. Troops. Transferred to this company on or about September 5, 1862. Reported present through April 30, 1863. Reported on detached service arresting deserters in Robeson County from May 14 through June 30, 1863. Rejoined the company in July-August, 1863. Reported sick in hospital at Wilmington in September-October, 1863. Returned to duty in November-December, 1863. Reported present through February 29, 1864. Reported on detached service as a scout on April 26, 1864. Killed at or near Petersburg, Virginia, on or about June 16-19, 1864.

KNOWLES, JOSEPH H., Private

Previously served as Private in Capt. William S. Devane's Independent Company, N.C. Troops. Transferred to this company on or about September 5, 1862. Reported absent sick in November-December, 1862. Died at home in Sampson County on January 8, 1863, of disease.

LEWIS, RUFUS R., Private

Previously served as Private in Capt. William S. Devane's Independent Company, N.C. Troops. Transferred to this company on or about September 5, 1862. Reported present or accounted for through August 31, 1863. Served as a teamster during most of that period. Hospitalized at Wilmington on October 27, 1863, with intermittent fever. Returned to duty on December 8, 1863. Reported on duty as a teamster on surviving company muster rolls through October 31, 1864. No further records. Survived the war. [North Carolina pension records indicate that he was wounded in the arm at Fort Caswell on an unspecified date.]

LOCKAMY, JOHN O., Private

Previously served as Musician in Capt. William S. Devane's Independent Company, N.C. Troops. Transferred to this company on or about September 5, 1862. Mustered in as Musician. Reduced to ranks in November-December, 1862. Reported present through

April 30, 1864. Wounded in the head at Drewry's Bluff, Virginia, on or about May 13, 1864. Hospitalized at Richmond, Virginia, where he died on May 14, 1864, of wounds.

McARTHUR, JAMES O., Private

Previously served as Private in Capt. William S. Devane's Independent Company, N.C. Troops. Transferred to this company on or about September 5, 1862. Reported present through February 28, 1863. Reported present but sick in quarters in March-April, 1863. Reported in hospital at Wilmington on May 5, 1863, with debility. Furloughed from hospital at Wilmington on June 20, 1863, convalescent from debility and typhoid fever. Died at home in Sampson County on July 3, 1863. Cause of death not reported.

McCALOP, JAMES IRVING, Sergeant

Previously served as Corporal in Capt. William S. Devane's Independent Company, N.C. Troops. Transferred to this company on or about September 5, 1862. Mustered in as Corporal. Promoted to Sergeant on October 1, 1862. Reported present through April 30, 1863. Reported on detached service arresting deserters in Robeson County from May 14 through June 30, 1863. Returned to duty prior to August 22, 1863, when he was wounded in the side by a shell at Fort Wagner, Charleston Harbor, South Carolina. Hospitalized at Charleston and Wilmington. Furloughed for forty-five days on September 18, 1863. Returned to duty in November-December, 1863. Reported present through February 29, 1864. Detailed for provost duty at Murphy's Station, Virginia, April 25, 1864. Wounded in the right arm at or near Petersburg, Virginia, on or about June 17, 1864. Hospitalized at Petersburg. Transferred to hospital at Raleigh on June 18, 1864. Furloughed from hospital at High Point on July 19, 1864. Returned to duty prior to November 1, 1864. Paroled at Greensboro on May 1, 1865.

McKENZIE, JAMES McD., Private

Previously served as Private in Capt. William S. Devane's Independent Company, N.C. Troops. Transferred to this company on or about September 5, 1862. Reported present through April 30, 1863. Reported absent without leave on June 29, 1863. Returned to duty in July-August, 1863. Reported present but on daily duty through February 29, 1864. Hospitalized at Petersburg, Virginia, April 12, 1864. Returned to duty on an unspecified date. Reported present in September-October, 1864. No further records.

MARSHALL, JAMES, Private

Resided in Stokes County and was by occupation a farmer prior to enlisting in Stokes County at age 38, February 23, 1863, for the war. Reported present through August 31, 1863. Reported sick in hospital at Charleston, South Carolina, October 13, 1863. Reported on detached service at camp near Petersburg, Virginia, in November, 1863-February, 1864. Reported absent on sick furlough on March 30, 1864. Died at home in Stokes County in August, 1864, of "measles."

MASHBURN, JAMES M., Private

Resided in Bladen County and was by occupation a farmer prior to enlisting in New Hanover County at age 27, May 23, 1863, for the war. Reported absent sick in July-October, 1863. Returned to duty in November-December, 1863. Reported present through February 29, 1864. Reported absent on detached service escorting prisoners to Petersburg, Virginia, in March-April, 1864. Hospitalized at Wilmington on September 6, 1864, with rubeola. Returned to duty on October 5, 1864. Reported absent without leave on or about October 31, 1864. No further records. Survived the war.

MILLARD, LUTHER R., Private

Previously served as Private in Capt. William S. Devane's Independent Company, N.C. Troops. Transferred to this company on or about September 5, 1862. Reported present in November-December, 1862. Transferred to 2nd Company C, 36th Regiment N.C. Troops (2nd Regiment N.C. Artillery), in February, 1863.

MOFFITT, REUBEN E., Private

Resided in Randolph County and was by occupation a farmer prior to enlisting in Randolph County at age 31, March 5, 1863, for the war. Deserted at Camp Davis, near Wilmington, on the night of June 28, 1863. Returned from desertion on an unspecified date. Confined at Petersburg, Virginia, February 14, 1864. Rejoined the company on or about September 28, 1864. Reported present through October 31, 1864. No further records. Survived the war.

MOORE, JOHN THOMAS, Private

Resided in Sampson County and enlisted at Broad Water Ferry, Virginia, at age 17, April 13, 1864, for the war. Reported absent sick at the division infirmary in September-October, 1864. Captured in hospital at Greensboro on an unspecified date. Paroled on April 26, 1865.

MOORE, WALTER JAMES, Private

Previously served as Private in Company C, 63rd Regiment N.C. Troops (5th Regiment N.C. Cavalry). Transferred to this company on November 7, 1863. Reported present in January-February, 1864. Reported absent on furlough on April 26, 1864. Captured at Fort Harrison, Virginia September 30, 1864. Confined at Point Lookout, Maryland, October 5, 1864. Paroled at Point Lookout on March 17, 1865. Received at Boulware's Wharf, James River, Virginia, March 19, 1865, for exchange. [See his brief letter in the *Wilmington Weekly Journal*, April 7, 1864, in which he denies that he is a deserter.]

MURPHY, PATRICK H., Private

Previously served as Private in Capt. William S. Devane's Independent Company, N.C. Troops. Transferred to this company on or about September 5, 1862. Reported present or accounted for through April 30, 1864. Reported on duty in the medical department (probably as a nurse) during most of that period. Rejoined the company on an unspecified date. Reported present in September-October, 1864.

NEWTON, CHRISTOPHER COLUMBUS, Corporal

Previously served as Private in Capt. William S. Devane's Independent Company, N.C. Troops. Transferred to this company on or about September 5, 1862. Mustered in as Private. Reported present through June 30, 1863. Wounded in the arm and shoulder at Morris Island, Charleston Harbor, South Carolina, August 25, 1863. Hospitalized at Wilmington. Furloughed for thirty days on September 18, 1863. Returned to duty in November-December, 1863. Reported present through April 30, 1864. Promoted to Corporal on April 13, 1864. Wounded in the hand at or near Petersburg, Virginia, on or about June 16-19, 1864. Reported in hospital at High Point on August 17, 1864. Furloughed on August 18, 1864. Reported present in September-October, 1864. No further records. Survived the war.

OATES, JETHRO D., Private

Previously served as Private in Capt. William S. Devane's Independent Company, N.C. Troops. Transferred to this company on

or about September 5, 1862. Appointed acting Hospital Steward on September 14, 1862, and assigned to temporary duty with the Field and Staff of this regiment. Appointed Hospital Steward on February 26, 1863, and transferred to the Field and Staff of this regiment.

OATES, MARSHALL H., Corporal

Previously served as Private in Capt. William S. Devane's Independent Company, N.C. Troops. Transferred to this company on or about September 5, 1862. Reported present through April 30, 1863. Reported on detached service as a picket guard at Hilton Ferry, near Wilmington, from May 8 through June 30, 1863. Hospitalized at Wilmington on July 12, 1863, with intermittent fever. Returned to duty on July 27, 1863. Promoted to Corporal on September 25, 1863. Reported present through April 30, 1864. Captured at Fort Harrison, Virginia, September 30, 1864. Confined at Point Lookout, Maryland, October 5, 1864. Paroled at Point Lookout on March 17, 1865. Received at Boulware's Wharf, James River, Virginia, March 19, 1865, for exchange. No further records. Survived the war.

PADDISON, JOHN R., Private

Previously served as Private in Capt. William S. Devane's Independent Company, N.C. Troops. Transferred to this company on or about September 5, 1862. Discharged on December 6, 1862, by reason of being underage. Later served as Private in Capt. Abner A. Moseley's Company, Sampson Artillery.

PADDISON, RICHARD P., Private

Previously served as Private in Capt. William S. Devane's Independent Company, N.C. Troops. Transferred to this company on or about September 5, 1862. Reported on duty as acting Hospital Steward in the hospital at Fort Caswell through December 31, 1862. Appointed to the permanent rank of Hospital Steward on or about January 29, 1863, and transferred. Was apparently assigned to permanent duty in the hospital at Fort Caswell.

PARISH, ALONZO W., Private

Previously served as Private in Capt. William S. Devane's Independent Company, N.C. Troops. Transferred to this company on or about September 5, 1862. Reported present or accounted for through June 30, 1863. Reported sick in hospital at Charleston, South Carolina, in July-August, 1863. Returned to duty in September-October, 1863. Reported present through December 31, 1863. Hospitalized at Petersburg, Virginia, January 25, 1864, with a sore eye. Transferred on February 22, 1864. Returned to duty prior to May 1, 1864. Wounded in the face at Fort Harrison, Virginia, September 30, 1864. Hospitalized at Richmond, Virginia. Transferred on October 8, 1864. Paroled at Greensboro on May 1, 1865.

PEAL, JESSE, Private

Previously served as Private in Company F, 36th Regiment N.C. Troops (2nd Regiment N.C. Artillery). Transferred to this company on May 18, 1863. Reported present through April 30, 1864. Wounded in the left leg (fracture) at Cold Harbor, Virginia, June 3, 1864. Hospitalized at Richmond, Virginia. Furloughed for sixty days on or about July 19, 1864. Returned to duty in September-October, 1864. No further records.

PETERSON, JAMES, Private

Previously served as Private in Capt. William S. Devane's Independent Company, N.C. Troops. Transferred to this company on

or about September 5, 1862. Reported sick in hospital at Wilmington in September-October, 1862. Discharged on December 6, 1862, by reason of being overage.

RACKLEY, THOMAS L., Private

Previously served as Private in Capt. William S. Devane's Independent Company, N.C. Troops. Transferred to this company on or about September 5, 1862. Reported present or accounted for through April 30, 1864. Wounded at Fort Harrison, Virginia, September 30, 1864. Hospitalized at Richmond, Virginia. Furloughed on an unspecified date. No further records. Survived the war.

REGISTER, JOHN R., Private

Previously served as Private in Capt. William S. Devane's Independent Company, N.C. Troops. Transferred to this company on or about September 5, 1862. Reported present through December, 1862. Detailed for duty in the medical department (probably as an ambulance driver) on February 27, 1863. Rejoined the company on October 14, 1863. Reported present through April 30, 1864. Transferred to Company C, 63rd Regiment N.C. Troops (5th Regiment N.C. Cavalry), October 19, 1864.

RHODES, WILLIAM JAMES, Private

Previously served as Corporal in Capt. William S. Devane's Independent Company, N.C. Troops. Transferred to this company on or about September 5, 1862. Mustered in as Corporal. Reported present through October 31, 1862. Detailed for duty as acting Commissary Sergeant of Clingman's Brigade on December 18, 1862. Reduced to ranks on February 7, 1863. Reported absent on detail as acting Commissary Sergeant of Clingman's Brigade through August 31, 1863. Died in hospital at Summerville, South Carolina, September 20, 1863. Cause of death not reported.

ROBINSON, ALBERT T., Private

Previously served as Private in Capt. William S. Devane's Independent Company, N.C. Troops. Transferred to this company on or about September 5, 1862, while absent on detached duty as acting Hospital Steward of the 51st Regiment N.C. Troops. Reported on duty with the 51st Regiment through April 6, 1863. Discharged on April 6, 1863, upon appointment as Hospital Steward. Was apparently assigned to permanent duty with a military hospital. [Contrary to 12:278 of this series, his correct surname was probably Robinson rather than Robeson.]

ROBINSON, JOHN M., Sergeant

Previously served as Corporal in Capt. William S. Devane's Independent Company, N.C. Troops. Transferred to this company on or about September 5, 1862. Mustered in as Corporal. Promoted to Sergeant on February 7, 1863. Reported present through June 30, 1863. Wounded in the forehead at Morris Island, Charleston Harbor, South Carolina, August 26, 1863. Hospitalized at Charleston where he died on August 28, 1863, of wounds.

ROGERS, WILLIAM W., Corporal

Previously served as Private in Capt. William S. Devane's Independent Company, N.C. Troops. Transferred to this company on or about September 5, 1862. Mustered in as Private. Reported absent sick in Sampson County in November-December, 1862. Returned to duty in January-February, 1863. Promoted to Corporal on February 7, 1863. Reported present through April 30, 1863. Detailed for duty as a picket guard at Hilton Ferry, near Wilmington, June 28, 1863. Hospitalized at Wilmington on July 14, 1863, with diarrhoea. Returned to duty on October 8, 1863. Reported present but sick in quarters on or about October 31, 1863. Hospitalized at Charleston, South Carolina, November 29, 1863. Hospitalized at Petersburg, Virginia, February 22, 1864, with "pneumonia." Died in hospital at Petersburg on or about March 5, 1864.

SESSOMS, LOVE D., Private

Previously served as Private in Capt. William S. Devane's Independent Company, N.C. Troops. Transferred to this company on or about September 5, 1862. Reported present or accounted for through February 29, 1864. Reported on provost duty at Murphy's Station, Virginia, April 26, 1864. No further records. Survived the war.

SHURNICK, SAMUEL N., Corporal

Previously served as Private in Capt. William S. Devane's Independent Company, N.C. Troops. Transferred to this company on or about September 5, 1862. Mustered in as Private. Reported absent sick at Fayetteville from October 18, 1862, through February 28, 1863. Returned to duty in March-April, 1863. Promoted to Corporal on September 25, 1863. Reported present or accounted for on surviving company muster rolls through October 31, 1864.

SIMMONS, LOFTON B., Private

Previously served as Private in Capt. William S. Devane's Independent Company, N.C. Troops. Transferred to this company on or about September 5, 1862. Reported present or accounted for through August 31, 1863. Furloughed on October 17, 1863. Reported on detached service at camp near Petersburg, Virginia, December 16, 1863. Returned to duty in January-February, 1864. Reported present on surviving company muster rolls through October 31, 1864. No further records. [Filed a Florida pension application after the war.]

SIMMONS, WILEY, Private

Previously served as Private in Capt. William S. Devane's Independent Company, N.C. Troops. Transferred to this company on or about September 5, 1862. Reported present through December 31, 1862. Hospitalized at Wilmington on February 18, 1863, with debilitas. Returned to duty on March 9, 1863. Reported present through April 30, 1864. Killed on July 10, 1864. Place of death not reported.

SIMMONS, WILLIAM H. H., Private

Previously served as Private in Capt. William S. Devane's Independent Company, N.C. Troops. Transferred to this company on or about September 5, 1862. Reported sick in camp at Tarboro in September-October, 1862. Returned to duty in November-December, 1862. Reported present through June 30, 1863. Died in hospital at Augusta, Georgia, July 20, 1863. Cause of death not reported.

SMITH, ANDREW J., Private

Previously served as Private in Capt. William S. Devane's Independent Company, N.C. Troops. Transferred to this company on or about September 5, 1862. Deserted at Fort Caswell on September 9, 1862. Returned from desertion and was confined at Ivor Station, Virginia, April 11, 1864. Stunned (presumably by a shell) at the Crater, near Petersburg, Virginia, July 30, 1864. Reported sick in hospital in September-October, 1864. No further records. Survived the war. [North Carolina pension records indicate that he "lost sight of right eye from effect of bomb bursting near him" near Petersburg on October 1, 1864.]

SMITH, CHARLES H., Private

Previously served as Private in Capt. William S. Devane's Independent Company, N.C. Troops. Transferred to this company on or about September 5, 1862. Reported present or accounted for through June 30, 1863. Reported sick in hospital at Mount Pleasant, South Carolina, in July-August, 1863. Returned to duty in September-October, 1863. Reported present through February 29, 1864. Detailed for provost duty at Murphy's Station, Virginia, April 25, 1864. Rejoined the company prior to September 30, 1864, when he was wounded in the face at Fort Harrison, Virginia. Hospitalized at Richmond, Virginia. Returned to duty on November 1, 1864. No further records.

SMITH, JAMES M., Sergeant

Previously served as Private in Capt. William S. Devane's Independent Company, N.C. Troops. Transferred to this company on or about September 5, 1862. Mustered in as Private. Promoted to Corporal on October 1, 1862. Reported present or accounted for through August 31, 1863. Promoted to Sergeant on September 25, 1863. Reported present through April 30, 1864. Wounded in the groin at Drewry's Bluff, Virginia, May 13, 1864. Hospitalized at Richmond, Virginia. Returned to duty prior to September 30, 1864, when he was captured at Fort Harrison, Virginia. Confined at Point Lookout, Maryland, October 5, 1864. Paroled at Point Lookout on March 17, 1865. Received at Boulware's Wharf, James River, Virginia, March 19, 1865, for exchange. No further records. Survived the war.

SMITH, YANCEY B., Private

Previously served as Private in Capt. William S. Devane's Independent Company, N.C. Troops. Transferred to this company on or about September 5, 1862. Reported present through April 30, 1864. Captured on the Darbytown Road, near Richmond, Virginia, October 7, 1864. Confined at Point Lookout, Maryland, October 29, 1864. Released at Point Lookout on June 19, 1865, after taking the Oath of Allegiance.

STEVENS, DAVID, Sergeant

Previously served as Sergeant in Capt. William S. Devane's Independent Company, N.C. Troops. Transferred to this company on or about September 5, 1862. Reported present through December 31, 1862. Appointed Sergeant Major on January 14, 1863, and transferred to the Field and Staff of this regiment.

USHER, EDWIN T., Private

Previously served as Private in Capt. William S. Devane's Independent Company, N.C. Troops. Transferred to this company on or about September 5, 1862. Reported absent sick in Duplin County in November-December, 1862. Discharged on January 29, 1863, by reason of being underage.

VANN, JOHN JAMES, Private

Previously served as Private in Capt. William S. Devane's Independent Company, N.C. Troops. Transferred to this company on or about September 5, 1862. Reported present through April 30, 1864. Wounded in the right hand at Drewry's Bluff, Virginia, May 13, 1864. Hospitalized at Richmond, Virginia. Returned to duty on an unspecified date. Reported present in September-October, 1864. No further records. Survived the war.

VANN, JOHN ROBERT, Private

Previously served as Private in Capt. William S. Devane's Independent Company, N.C. Troops. Transferred to this company on

or about September 5, 1862. Reported present or accounted for through April 30, 1863. Reported on detached service in Robeson County arresting deserters on May 14, 1863. Returned to duty in July-August, 1863. Reported present but sick in quarters in September-October, 1863. Reported on duty as regimental color bearer in November-December, 1863. Rejoined the company in January-February, 1864. Reported present in March-April, 1864. Captured at Globe Tavern, Virginia, on or about August 19, 1864. Confined at Point Lookout, Maryland, August 24, 1864. Paroled at Point Lookout on November 1, 1864. Received at Venus Point, Savannah River, Georgia, November 15, 1864, for exchange. No further records. Survived the war.

WATSON, SHERMAN J., Private

Previously served as Private in Capt. William S. Devane's Independent Company, N.C. Troops. Transferred to this company on or about September 5, 1862. Reported present through December 31, 1862. Detailed for duty as a carpenter at Fort Caswell on January 5, 1863. Reported on detail as a carpenter in the Cape Fear District on surviving company muster rolls through October 31, 1864. Paroled at Greensboro on May 1, 1865.

WILSON, GEORGE FENNEL, Private

Previously served as Private in Capt. William S. Devane's Independent Company, N.C. Troops. Transferred to this company on or about September 5, 1862. Discharged on December 26, 1862, by reason of being underage. Later served as Private in Company B, 1st Battalion N.C. Heavy Artillery.

WILSON, WILLIAM W. W., Private

Previously served as Private in Capt. William S. Devane's Independent Company, N.C. Troops. Transferred to this company on or about September 5, 1862. Reported present or accounted for through April 30, 1864. Captured at Fort Harrison, Virginia, September 30, 1864. Confined at Point Lookout, Maryland, October 5, 1864. Paroled at Point Lookout on March 17, 1865. Received at Boulware's Wharf, James River, Virginia, March 19, 1865, for exchange. No further records. Survived the war.

COMPANY B

This company, known as the "Beaufort Plow Boys," was raised in Beaufort County in October, 1861, as Capt. Henry Harding's Independent Company, N.C. Troops. It was mustered into Confederate service at Washington on November 9, 1861, for twelve months. On an unknown date subsequent to April 15, 1862, its term of service was extended to three years or the duration of the war. On or about September 5, 1862, the company was assigned to the newly organized 59th Regiment N.C. Troops. That unit was redesignated the 61st Regiment N.C. Troops on an unknown date between October 30 and November 22, 1862. This company was designated Company B. After joining the 61st Regiment the company functioned as a part of that regiment, and its history for the remainder of the war is reported as a part of the regimental history.

The following roster was compiled primarily from information in the microfilm edition of the Compiled Service Records of Soldiers Who Served in Organizations from the State of North Carolina (Record Group 109, MC 270), National Archives and Records Administration, Washington, D.C. Record Group 109 includes enlistment papers, pay vouchers, requisitions, letters of resignation, discharge certificates, and abstracts of medical and prisoner of war returns. Materials relating specifically to Company B, 61st Regiment N.C. Troops, include a company muster-in and descriptive roll dated October 1, 1862, and company muster rolls for "to April 30, 1863"; May, 1863-April, 1864; and September-December, 1864.

Also utilized in this roster were *The War of the Rebellion: A Compilation of the Official Records of the Union and Confederate Armies*, the North Carolina adjutant general's *Roll of Honor*, state militia records, newspaper casualty lists and obituaries, wartime claims for bounty pay and allowances, postwar registers of claims for artificial limbs, Confederate pension applications filed with the states of North Carolina, Tennessee, and Florida, Confederate Soldiers' Home records, and the 1860 and 1870 federal censuses of North Carolina. A search was made also for relevant letters, diaries, reminiscences, and other manuscripts in the Southern Historical Collection (University of North Carolina-Chapel Hill), the Duke University Library Special Collections Department, and the North Carolina Division of Archives and History.

Among the secondary sources consulted were records of the North Carolina division of the United Daughters of the Confederacy, postwar rosters, regimental and county histories, marriage bond, will, and cemetery indexes, published and unpublished genealogies, biographical dictionaries, the North Carolina *County Heritage Book* series, the *Confederate Veteran*, Walter Clark's *Histories of the Several Regiments and Battalions from North Carolina in the Great War, 1861-'65*, and the North Carolina volume of the extended edition of *Confederate Military History*.

OFFICERS

CAPTAINS

HARDING, HENRY

Previously served as Captain of Henry Harding's Independent Company, N.C. Troops. Transferred to this company on September 5, 1862. Elected Major on September 5, 1862, and transferred to the Field and Staff.

STEVENSON, WILLIAM M.

Previously served as 2nd Lieutenant in Capt. Henry Harding's Independent Company, N.C. Troops. Appointed Captain of this company on September 5, 1862. Reported present or accounted for through April 30, 1864. Captured at Fort Harrison, Virginia, September 30, 1864. Confined at Old Capitol Prison, Washington, D.C., October 6, 1864. Transferred to Fort Delaware, Delaware, October 21, 1864. Released at Fort Delaware on June 7, 1865, after taking the Oath of Allegiance.

LANIER, JAMES C.

Served as 2nd Lieutenant of Company C of this regiment. Reported on duty as acting commander of this company in September-October, 1864.

LIEUTENANTS

PATRICK, WILLIAM H., 3rd Lieutenant

Previously served as Private in Company K, 10th Regiment N.C. State Troops (1st Regiment N.C. Artillery). Elected 3rd Lieutenant of this company on September 5, 1862. Wounded in the right arm and captured at Kinston on December 14, 1862. Paroled the same date. Reported absent wounded through December 31, 1863. Reported absent on detached service as an enrolling officer in January-April and September-December, 1864. Paroled at Greensboro on May 1, 1865.

REDDITT, DAVID F., 1st Lieutenant

Previously served as 2nd Lieutenant of Capt. Henry Harding's Independent Company, N.C. Troops. Elected 1st Lieutenant of this company on September 5, 1862. Reported present or accounted for through April 30, 1864. Captured at Fort Harrison, Virginia, September 30, 1864. Confined at Old Capitol Prison, Washington, D.C., October 6, 1864. Transferred to Fort Delaware, Delaware, October 21, 1864. Released at Fort Delaware on June 16, 1865, after taking the Oath of Allegiance.

WILKINSON, JOHN THOMAS, 2nd Lieutenant

Previously served as Sergeant in Capt. Henry Harding's Independent Company, N.C. Troops. Appointed 2nd Lieutenant of this company on September 5, 1862. Captured at Kinston on December 14, 1862. Reported present or accounted for through April 30, 1864. Hospitalized at Richmond, Virginia, September 20, 1864, with phthisis pulmonalis. Furloughed for thirty days on or about October 6, 1864. Returned to duty in November-December, 1864, and was reported in command of the company. No further records.

NONCOMMISSIONED OFFICERS AND PRIVATES

ANGEL, JOHN, Private

Previously served as Private in Capt. Henry Harding's Independent Company, N.C. Troops. Transferred to this company on or about September 5, 1862. Reported present through April 30, 1864. Captured at Fort Harrison, Virginia, September 30, 1864. Confined at Point Lookout, Maryland, October 5, 1864. Hospitalized at Point Lookout on January 27, 1865. Died at Point Lookout on February 8, 1865, of "chro[nic] diarr[hoea] & scurvy."

ANSELL, ANDREW J., SR., ———

North Carolina pension records indicate that he served in this company.

ARCHIBALD, WILLIAM, Private

Previously served as Private in Capt. Henry Harding's Independent Company, N.C. Troops. Transferred to this company on or about September 5, 1862. Reported present through April 30, 1864, and in September-December, 1864. No further records.

BAREFOOT, JOHN R., Private

Previously served as Private in Company B, 10th Battalion N.C. Heavy Artillery. Transferred to this company on May 7, 1863. Deserted at Sullivan's Island, Charleston Harbor, South Carolina, August 30, 1863.

BATES, JOHN, Private

Previously served as Private in Capt. Henry Harding's Independent Company, N.C. Troops. Transferred to this company on or about September 5, 1862. Died in hospital at Wilson on September 21, 1862, of "febris typhoides."

BEASLEY, ASHLEY, Private

Previously served (rank and company unknown) in the 10th Battalion N.C. Heavy Artillery. Transferred to this company on May 7, 1863. Wounded in the knee at Morris Island, Charleston Harbor, South Carolina, on or about August 25, 1863. Returned to duty prior to September 1, 1863. Reported present or accounted for through February 29, 1864. Deserted on March 31, 1864. Returned to duty subsequent to April 30, 1864. Captured at Bermuda Hundred, Virginia, on or about June 15, 1864. Confined at Point Lookout, Maryland, June 19, 1864. Transferred to Elmira, New York, July 9, 1864. Paroled at Elmira on March 2, 1865, and transferred to the James River, Virginia, for exchange. Hospitalized at Richmond, Virginia, March 7, 1865, with debilitas. Furloughed for thirty days on March 9, 1865. Paroled at Raleigh on May 8, 1865. [Service record omitted in volume 1 of this series.]

BELL, NOAH, Private

Previously served as Corporal in Capt. Henry Harding's Independent Company, N.C. Troops. Transferred to this company on or about September 5, 1862. Was apparently absent without leave through April 30, 1864. Returned to duty prior to June 1, 1864, when he was wounded in the knee or right thigh at Cold Harbor, Virginia. Hospitalized at Richmond, Virginia. Furloughed for forty days on or about July 11, 1864. Returned to duty prior to September 30, 1864, when he was captured at Fort Harrison, Virginia. Confined at Point Lookout, Maryland, October 5, 1864. Paroled at Point Lookout on March 17, 1865. Received at Boulware's Wharf, James River, Virginia, March 19, 1865, for exchange. No further records. Survived the war.

BISHOP, SAMUEL CALEB, Corporal

Previously served as Private in Capt. Henry Harding's Independent Company, N.C. Troops. Transferred to this company on or about September 5, 1862. Mustered in as Private. Captured and paroled at Kinston on December 14, 1862. Returned to duty prior to May 1, 1863. Hospitalized at Wilmington on May 5, 1863, with typhoid fever. Returned to duty on May 14, 1863. Reported present or accounted for through April 30, 1864. Promoted to Corporal on July 1, 1864. Captured at Fort Harrison, Virginia, September 30, 1864. Confined at Point Lookout, Maryland, October 5, 1864. Paroled at Point Lookout on March 17, 1865. Received at Boulware's Wharf, James River, Virginia, March 19, 1865, for exchange. No further records. Survived the war.

BRADDY, WILLIAM B., Private

Previously served as Musician (Drummer) in Capt. Henry Harding's Independent Company, N.C. Troops. Transferred to this company on or about September 5, 1862. Mustered in as Private. Reported present or accounted for through October 31, 1863. Deserted at Goldsboro on December 5, 1863. Returned from desertion on August 12, 1864. Reported present or accounted for through December 31, 1864. Captured near Kinston on March 10, 1865. Confined at Point Lookout, Maryland, March 16, 1865. Released at Point Lookout on or about May 12, 1865, after taking the Oath of Allegiance.

BRINN, THOMAS F., Sergeant

Previously served as Sergeant in Capt. Henry Harding's Independent Company, N.C. Troops. Transferred to this company on or about September 5, 1862. Mustered in as Sergeant. Reported present or accounted for through October 31, 1863. Deserted at Sullivan's Island, Charleston Harbor, South Carolina, November 20, 1863.

CHERRY, JOHN Q., Private

Previously served as Private in Capt. Henry Harding's Independent Company, N.C. Troops. Transferred to this company on or about September 5, 1862. Reported present or accounted for through April 30, 1864. Wounded in the head at Drewry's Bluff, Virginia, May 13-19, 1864. Reported sick in September-October, 1864. Reported present in November-December, 1864. Paroled at Greensboro on May 1, 1865.

CLARK, W. T., ———

North Carolina pension records indicate that he served in this company.

CORSON, DANIEL, Corporal

Previously served as Private in Capt. Henry Harding's Independent Company, N.C. Troops. Transferred to this company on or about September 5, 1862. Mustered in as Private. Reported present or accounted for through April 30, 1864. Promoted to Corporal in January-February, 1864. Wounded slightly in the leg at the Crater, near Petersburg, Virginia, July 30, 1864. Returned to duty on an unspecified date. Wounded at Fort Harrison, Virginia, September 30, 1864. Returned to duty prior to November 1, 1864. Reported absent without leave on December 28, 1864. No further records.

COX, WILLIAM A., Private

Born in Beaufort County. Place and date of enlistment not reported. Records of the Federal Provost Marshal indicate that he was captured near Washington, North Carolina, January 25, 1864; confined at Point Lookout, Maryland, February 27, 1864; and released at Point Lookout on April 19, 1864, after taking the Oath of Allegiance and joining the U.S. Army. Assigned to Company G, 1st Regiment U.S. Volunteer Infantry. [Records of the Federal Provost Marshal indicate that Cox was a member of Company I rather than Company B of the 61st Regiment. However, Company B was raised in Beaufort County (where Cox was born); Company I was raised in Alleghany County, which is in the western part of the state near the Tennessee border. It seems probable, therefore, that he was a member of Company B. No Confederate records establishing his service in either company were located. Cox was 17 years of age in April, 1864.]

COZZENS, WILLIAM, Private

Previously served as Private in Capt. Henry Harding's Independent Company, N.C. Troops. Transferred to this company on or about September 5, 1862. Wounded at Kinston on December 14, 1862. Returned to duty prior to May 1, 1863. Reported sick in hospital at Wilmington in July-August, 1863. Reported present but sick in camp in September-October, 1863. Returned to duty in November-December, 1863. Reported present or accounted for through April 30, 1864, and in September-December, 1864. No further records. Survived the war.

CURRY, DAVID, Corporal

Previously served as Corporal in Capt. Henry Harding's Independent Company, N.C. Troops. Transferred to this company on or about September 5, 1862. Mustered in as Corporal. Wounded in the stomach at Kinston on December 13, 1862. Discharged in January, 1863, by reason of disability from wounds.

CUTLER, ELY H., Private

Previously served as Private in Capt. Henry Harding's Independent Company, N.C. Troops. Transferred to this company on or about September 5, 1862. Reported present through June 30, 1863.

Hospitalized at Wilmington on or about July 12, 1863, with dysentery. Returned to duty on July 29, 1863. Reported sick in hospital at Charleston, South Carolina, on or about August 31, 1863. Returned to duty in September-October, 1863. Deserted at Goldsboro on December 5, 1863.

DANIELS, ANSON, Private

Previously served as Private in Capt. Henry Harding's Independent Company, N.C. Troops. Transferred to this company on or about September 5, 1862. Captured and paroled at Kinston on December 14, 1862. Hospitalized at Wilmington on February 9, 1863, with pneumonia. Returned to duty on February 19, 1863. Hospitalized at Wilmington on July 5, 1863, with rheumatism. Returned to duty on October 13, 1863. Reported on detached service at Petersburg, Virginia, in November-December, 1863. Returned to duty in January-February, 1864. Reported present in March-April and September-December, 1864. No further records. Survived the war.

DENBY, WILLIAM F., Private

Previously served as Private in Company K, 17th Regiment N.C. Troops (1st Organization). Enlisted in this company in New Hanover County on January 1, 1863, for the war as a substitute. Reported present or accounted for through December 31, 1863. Deserted to the enemy in Beaufort County on or about March 15, 1864, while on furlough. Confined at Fort Monroe, Virginia. Released at Fort Monroe on April 25, 1864, after taking the Oath of Allegiance.

EDWARDS, DAVID, Private

Previously served as Private in Capt. Henry Harding's Independent Company, N.C. Troops. Transferred to this company on or about September 5, 1862. Captured and paroled at Kinston on December 14, 1862. Returned to duty prior to May 1, 1863. Reported present or accounted for through June 30, 1863. Reported sick in hospital at Charleston, South Carolina, in July-August, 1863. Returned to duty in September-October, 1863. Reported present through April 30, 1864. Wounded in the left thigh (fracture) and captured at Fort Harrison, Virginia, September 30, 1864. Left leg amputated. Hospitalized at Fort Monroe, Virginia, October 4, 1864. Died in hospital at Fort Monroe on October 25, 1864, of "pyemia."

EDWARDS, EMANUEL, Private

Previously served as Private in Capt. Henry Harding's Independent Company, N.C. Troops. Transferred to this company on or about September 5, 1862. Deserted on an unspecified date. Returned to duty on May 1, 1863. Reported present through February 29, 1864. Wounded in the thigh, hip, and/or right arm at Drewry's Bluff, Virginia, May 16, 1864. Hospitalized at Richmond, Virginia, where he died on May 17, 1864, of wounds.

EDWARDS, JOHN, Corporal

Previously served as Private in Capt. Henry Harding's Independent Company, N.C. Troops. Transferred to this company on or about September 5, 1862. Mustered in as Private. Reported present or accounted for through December 31, 1863. Promoted to Corporal on an unspecified date (probably in early January, 1864). Deserted at the Blackwater River, Virginia, January 23, 1864.

EDWARDS, RIAL, Private

Previously served as Private in Capt. Henry Harding's Independent Company, N.C. Troops. Transferred to this company on or about September 5, 1862. Deserted on an unspecified date. Returned to duty on May 1, 1863. Reported present through April 30, 1864. Reported sick in the division infirmary in September-

October, 1864. Hospitalized at Richmond, Virginia, November 26, 1864, with remittent fever. Returned to duty on February 8, 1865. No further records. Survived the war. [North Carolina pension records indicate that he was wounded in the head by a piece of shell at Petersburg, Virginia, April 15, 1863. The *Wilmington Journal* (Weekly) of January 15, 1863, states he was reported missing at Kinston on December 14, 1862.]

EDWARDS, THOMAS, Private

Previously served as Private in Capt. Henry Harding's Independent Company, N.C. Troops. Transferred to this company on or about September 5, 1862. Deserted on an unspecified date. Returned to duty on May 1, 1863. Reported present or accounted for through April 30, 1864. Wounded slightly in the right shoulder by a piece of shell at or near Petersburg, Virginia, on or about June 16-19, 1864. Returned to duty on an unspecified date. Reported present in September-December, 1864. No further records. Survived the war.

GEER, EDWIN, JR., Sergeant

Previously served as Private in Company K, 10th Regiment N.C. State Troops (1st Regiment N.C. Artillery). Transferred to this company on September 29, 1862. Promoted to Sergeant on an unspecified date. Died at Smithville (Southport) prior to October 27, 1862, of "bilious fever." "He was acting at the time of his death as aide to Brig. Gen. [Gabriel J.] Rains." [*Fayetteville Observer* (Semiweekly), October 27, 1862.]

HARDING, WILLIAM F., Corporal

Previously served as Private in Capt. Henry Harding's Independent Company, N.C. Troops. Transferred to this company on or about September 5, 1862. Mustered in as Private. Reported present through October 31, 1863. Promoted to Corporal in November-December, 1863. Reported on detached service at Petersburg, Virginia, in November-December, 1863. Rejoined the company in January-February, 1864. Reported present in March-April and September-December, 1864. No further records. [The *Wilmington Journal* (Weekly) of January 15, 1863, states he was reported missing at Kinston on December 14, 1862.]

HARRELL, ELIJAH, Private

Previously served as Private in Capt. Henry Harding's Independent Company, N.C. Troops. Transferred to this company on or about September 5, 1862. Discharged on February 1, 1863, by reason of being overage. [The *Wilmington Journal* (Weekly) of January 15, 1863, states he was reported missing at Kinston on December 14, 1862.]

HILL, HENRY HARMON, 1st Sergeant

Previously served as Private in Capt. Henry Harding's Independent Company, N.C. Troops. Transferred to this company on or about September 5, 1862. Mustered in as Sergeant. Captured and paroled at Kinston on December 14, 1862. Reported present through December 31, 1863. Promoted to 1st Sergeant in January-February, 1864. Wounded in the head near Petersburg, Virginia, June 17, 1864. Hospitalized at Petersburg where he died on June 19, 1864, of wounds.

HILL, HILSON G. D., Private

Previously served as Private in Capt. Henry Harding's Independent Company, N.C. Troops. Transferred to this company on or about September 5, 1862. Wounded in the left wrist and/or left forearm at Kinston on December 14, 1862. Reported absent wounded through February 29, 1864. Discharged on an unspecified

date (probably in March-October, 1864) by reason of wounds received at Kinston.

HODGES, SETH V., Private

Previously served as Private in Capt. Henry Harding's Independent Company, N.C. Troops. Transferred to this company on or about September 5, 1862. Reported present through December 31, 1863. Deserted at the Blackwater River, Virginia, January 23, 1864.

HURSEY, JOSHUA, Private

Previously served as Private in Capt. Henry Harding's Independent Company, N.C. Troops. Transferred to this company on or about September 5, 1862. Discharged on April 23, 1863. Reason discharged not reported.

JENKINS, GEORGE, Cook

Enlisted at Ivor Station, Virginia, January 1, 1864, for the war. Reported present in March-April, 1864. Deserted at Chaffin's Farm, Virginia, October 5, 1864.

JOHNSON, F. H., Sergeant

Place and date of enlistment not reported (probably enlisted subsequent to February 28, 1865). Promotion record not reported. Paroled at Greensboro on or about April 28, 1865.

JOHNSON, JOHN H., Musician

Previously served as Musician in Company K, 10th Regiment N.C. State Troops (1st Regiment N.C. Artillery). Transferred to this company on September 15, 1862. Appointed Chief Musician (Drum Major) on September 18, 1862, and transferred to the Field and Staff of this regiment.

LANIER, SYLVESTER, Private

Previously served as Private in Capt. Henry Harding's Independent Company, N.C. Troops. Transferred to this company on or about September 5, 1862. Was apparently absent without leave through February 29, 1864. Reported under arrest by sentence of court-martial in March-April, 1864. Returned to duty on an unspecified date. Captured at or near Globe Tavern, Virginia, August 19-21, 1864. Confined at Point Lookout, Maryland, August 24, 1864. Paroled at Point Lookout on October 11, 1864. Received at Cox's Wharf, James River, Virginia, October 15, 1864, for exchange. Hospitalized at High Point on November 4, 1864, with chronic rheumatism. Furloughed on November 5, 1864. No further records.

LINEBACK, EMANUEL, ——

North Carolina pension records indicate that he served in this company.

McWILLIAMS, PETER, Private

Previously served as Private in Company K, 10th Regiment N.C. State Troops (1st Regiment N.C. Artillery). Transferred to this company on September 13-17, 1862. Reported present or accounted for through April 30, 1863. Reported on detail arresting deserters in Cumberland County in May-June, 1863. Reported sick in hospital at Charleston, South Carolina, in July-August, 1863. Reported present in September-October, 1863. Detailed in hospital at Petersburg, Virginia, December 16, 1863. Returned to duty in January-February, 1864. Reported present in March-April and September-December, 1864. No further records. Survived the war. [North Carolina pension records indicate that he was captured below Kinston on April 1, 1865; however, records of the Federal Provost Marshal do not substantiate that report.]

MANNING, LORENZO D., Private

Previously served as Private in Capt. Henry Harding's Independent Company, N.C. Troops. Transferred to this company on or about September 5, 1862. Deserted prior to April 30, 1863. Apprehended on an unspecified date. Court-martialed on or about April 28, 1864, and sentenced to be shot. Pardoned on an unspecified date. Wounded slightly in the head at or near Petersburg, Virginia, on or about June 16-19, 1864. Wounded slightly in the shoulder and thigh at the Crater, near Petersburg, July 30, 1864. Reported undergoing sentence of court-martial at Petersburg in September-December, 1864. Released from confinement and returned to duty on March 5, 1865. No further records. Survived the war.

MANNING, WILLIAM A., Private

Previously served as Private in Capt. Henry Harding's Independent Company, N.C. Troops. Transferred to this company on or about September 5, 1862. Deserted prior to April 30, 1863. Apprehended on an unspecified date. Court-martialed on or about April 28, 1864, and sentenced to be shot. Sentence suspended on an unspecified date. Returned to duty prior to June 12, 1864, when he was killed at Cold Harbor, Virginia. "Belonged to the sharp shooters."

MOUNT, EDGAR S., Corporal

Previously served as Private in Capt. Henry Harding's Independent Company, N.C. Troops. Transferred to this company on or about September 5, 1862. Mustered in as Corporal. Captured and paroled at Kinston on December 14, 1862. Reported present or accounted for through June 30, 1863. Killed by the explosion of a shell during the bombardment of Morris Island, Charleston Harbor, South Carolina, July 29, 1863. "A brave and gallant soldier."

MUSE, QUINCY, Private

Previously served as Private in Capt. Henry Harding's Independent Company, N.C. Troops. Transferred to this company on or about September 5, 1862. Died in hospital at Wilmington on September 25, 1862. Cause of death not reported.

NEIL, EDWARD S., Private

Previously served as Private in Capt. Henry Harding's Independent Company, N.C. Troops. Transferred to this company on or about September 5, 1862. Reported present through April 30, 1864. Wounded in the left knee and captured at Fort Harrison, Virginia, September 30, 1864. Hospitalized at Fort Monroe, on or about October 3, 1864. Transferred to the military prison at Fort Monroe on November 25, 1864. Transferred to Point Lookout, Maryland, December 23, 1864. Paroled at Point Lookout on January 17, 1865. Received at Boulware's Wharf, James River, Virginia, January 21, 1865, for exchange. No further records. Survived the war.

NEIL, WILLIAM B., Private

Previously served as Private in Capt. Henry Harding's Independent Company, N.C. Troops. Transferred to this company on or about September 5, 1862. Reported present or accounted for through February 29, 1864. Mortally wounded in the abdomen at the Crater, near Petersburg, Virginia, July 30, 1864. Place and date of death not reported.

OWENS, STEPHEN D., 1st Sergeant

Previously served as Corporal in Capt. Henry Harding's Independent Company, N.C. Troops. Transferred to this company on or about September 5, 1862. Mustered in as Corporal. Reported present through June 30, 1863. Wounded in the face and/or hand at Morris Island, Charleston Harbor, South Carolina, August 26, 1863. Returned to duty prior to November 1, 1863. Promoted to Sergeant in November-December, 1863. Reported present in November, 1863-April, 1864, and September-December, 1864. Promoted to 1st Sergeant subsequent to December 31, 1864. Captured near Kinston on March 10, 1865. Confined at Point Lookout, Maryland, March 16, 1865. Released at Point Lookout on June 29, 1865, after taking the Oath of Allegiance.

RESPESS, JAMES T., 1st Sergeant

Previously served as Sergeant in Capt. Henry Harding's Independent Company, N.C. Troops. Transferred to this company on or about September 5, 1862. Reported present through August 31, 1863. Reported absent on surgeon's certificate from October 5, 1863, through February 29, 1864. Reported absent on detached service as a scout on April 15, 1864. Returned to duty on an unspecified date. Wounded slightly in the shoulder and arm at Cold Harbor, Virginia, May 31-June 3, 1864. Promoted to 1st Sergeant on June 1, 1864. Captured near Petersburg, Virginia, August 4, 1864. Confined at Old Capitol Prison, Washington, D.C., August 10, 1864. Transferred to Fort Delaware, Delaware, where he arrived on August 12, 1864. Released at Fort Delaware on May 15, 1865, after taking the Oath of Allegiance.

RUE, HENRY, Private

Previously served as Private in Capt. Henry Harding's Independent Company, N.C. Troops. Transferred to this company on or about September 5, 1862. Apparently deserted prior to April 30, 1863. Apprehended on an unspecified date. Reported under arrest by sentence of court-martial in March-April, 1864. Returned to duty on an unspecified date. Captured at or near Globe Tavern, Virginia, August 19-21, 1864. Confined at Point Lookout, Maryland, August 24, 1864. Paroled at Point Lookout on September 18, 1864. Received at Varina, Virginia, September 22, 1864, for exchange. Hospitalized at Richmond, Virginia, September 23, 1864, with chronic diarrhoea. Furloughed for forty days on October 3, 1864. No further records.

RUSS, THOMAS D., Private

Resided in Hyde County and enlisted in New Hanover County at age 18, March 1, 1863, for the war. Wounded in the left foot (contusion) at Morris Island, Charleston Harbor, South Carolina, on or about August 26, 1863. Returned to duty prior to September 1, 1863. Reported present through December 31, 1863. Deserted at the Blackwater River, Virginia, January 23, 1864. Reported sick in hospital (under arrest) at Petersburg, Virginia, in March-April, 1864. Returned to duty prior to September 30, 1864, when he was captured at Fort Harrison, Virginia. Confined at Point Lookout, Maryland, October 5, 1864. Paroled at Point Lookout on March 17, 1865. Received at Boulware's Wharf, James River, Virginia, March 19, 1865, for exchange.

SATTERTHWAITE, HENRY D., Sergeant

Previously served as Private in Capt. Henry Harding's Independent Company, N.C. Troops. Transferred to this company on or about September 5, 1862. Mustered in as Private. Promoted to Corporal prior to May 1, 1863. Reported present through June 30, 1863. Reported sick in hospital in July-August, 1863. Returned to duty in September-October, 1863. Promoted to Sergeant in January, 1864. Reported present through April, 1864, and in September-December, 1864. No further records. Survived the war.

SATTERTHWAITE, JAMES H., Corporal

Previously served as Corporal in Capt. Henry Harding's Independent Company, N.C. Troops. Transferred to this company on or about September 5, 1862. Mustered in as Corporal. Discharged in February, 1863, under the provisions of the Conscription Act (probably because he was 40 years of age).

SATTERTHWAITE, WILLIAM A., Private

Previously served as Private in Capt. Henry Harding's Independent Company, N.C. Troops. Transferred to this company on or about September 5, 1862. Reported present or accounted for through December 31, 1863. Deserted at the Blackwater River, Virginia, January 23, 1864.

SEARLES, MARSHALL, Private

Previously served as Private in Capt. Henry Harding's Independent Company, N.C. Troops. Transferred to this company on or about September 5, 1862. Reported present through August 31, 1863. Reported present but sick in camp in September-October, 1863. Returned to duty in November-December, 1863. Reported present through April 30, 1864. Reported on detached duty at division headquarters in September-December, 1864. No further records. Survived the war.

SHAVENDER, R. THOMAS, 1st Sergeant

Previously served as 1st Sergeant in Capt. Henry Harding's Independent Company, N.C. Troops. Transferred to this company on or about September 5, 1862. Reported present or accounted for through October 31, 1863. Deserted at Sullivan's Island, Charleston Harbor, South Carolina, November 20, 1863.

SNELL, SAMUEL L., Private

Previously served as Private in Capt. Henry Harding's Independent Company, N.C. Troops. Transferred to this company on or about September 5, 1862, while in hospital at Wilmington with rubeola. Reported for duty on September 11, 1862. Reported present through June 30, 1863. Wounded at Fort Wagner, Charleston Harbor, South Carolina, July 29, 1863. Reported in hospital through October 31, 1863. Returned to duty in November-December, 1863. Reported present through April 30, 1864. Wounded in the neck and arm and captured at Fort Harrison, Virginia, September 30, 1864. Hospitalized at Fort Monroe, Virginia, October 4, 1864. Transferred to the prison camp at Fort Monroe on or about February 22, 1865. Transferred to Point Lookout, Maryland, March 1, 1865. Released at Point Lookout on May 15, 1865, after taking the Oath of Allegiance.

SPEARS, NOAH, Private

Previously served as Private in Capt. Henry Harding's Independent Company, N.C. Troops. Transferred to this company on or about September 5, 1862. Reported present through December 31, 1863. Hospitalized at Petersburg, Virginia, February 24, 1864, with morbi cutis. Transferred to another hospital on March 17, 1864. Captured near Washington, North Carolina, April 24, 1864. Confined at Point Lookout, Maryland, May 9, 1864. Exchanged on October 11, 1864. No further records. Survived the war. [North Carolina pension records indicate that he was wounded at Drewry's Bluff, Virginia, on an unspecified date.]

SWINDELL, ANANIAS, Private

Previously served as Private in Capt. Henry Harding's Independent Company, N.C. Troops. Transferred to this company on or about September 5, 1862. Reported present or accounted for through June

30, 1863. Died in hospital at Charleston, South Carolina, August 12, 1863. Cause of death not reported.

TAYLOR, RICHARD S., Private

Previously served as Private in Capt. Henry Harding's Independent Company, N.C. Troops. Transferred to this company on or about September 5, 1862. Captured and paroled at Kinston on December 14, 1862. Reported present or accounted for through April 30, 1864. Captured near Petersburg, Virginia, on or about June 15, 1864. Confined at Point Lookout, Maryland, June 19, 1864. Transferred to Elmira, New York, July 9, 1864. Released at Elmira on June 14, 1865, after taking the Oath of Allegiance.

TETTERTON, HOSEA W., Private

Previously served as Private in Capt. Henry Harding's Independent Company, N.C. Troops. Transferred to this company on or about September 5, 1862. Reported on detail as a hospital nurse at Wilson through January 31, 1863. Returned to duty prior to May 1, 1863. Hospitalized at Wilmington on July 14, 1863, with dysentery. Returned to duty on August 8, 1863. Reported present but sick in camp through October 31, 1863. Returned to duty in November-December, 1863. Reported present through April 30, 1864. Captured at Petersburg, Virginia, on or about September 10, 1864. Confined at Point Lookout, Maryland, September 23, 1864. Died in hospital at Point Lookout on November 26, 1864, of "remittent fever."

WATERFIELD, JOHN C., ———

North Carolina pension records indicate that he served in this company.

WELSH, PATRICK, Private

Previously served as Private in 2nd Company H, 40th Regiment N.C. Troops (3rd Regiment N.C. Artillery). Transferred to this company on July 7, 1863. Reported present through April 30, 1864. Killed at the Crater, near Petersburg, Virginia, July 30, 1864.

WHALEY, LEVI, ———

North Carolina pension records indicate that he served in this company.

WINDLEY, JACOB D., Private

Previously served as Private in Capt. Henry Harding's Independent Company, N.C. Troops. Transferred to this company on or about September 5, 1862. Wounded at Kinston on December 14, 1862. Returned to duty prior to May 1, 1863. Reported present through February 29, 1864. Wounded in the left arm and left hand at Cold Harbor, Virginia, June 10, 1864. Reported absent sick at the division infirmary in September-October, 1864. Reported absent sick (apparently without leave) on December 23, 1864. No further records. Survived the war.

COMPANY C

This company, originally known as the "Robinson Artillery," was raised in Craven County in January, 1862, and was mustered in at New Bern on March 5, 1862. Soon thereafter it was assigned to the 40th Regiment N.C. Troops (3rd Regiment N.C. Artillery) and designated Company K (later known as 1st Company K). On or about

September 5, 1862, it was transferred to the infantry and assigned to the newly organized 59th Regiment N.C. Troops as Company A. That regiment was redesignated the 61st Regiment N.C. Troops on an unknown date between October 30 and November 22, 1862. This company, renamed the "Neuse Guards," was designated Company C. Upon joining the 61st Regiment the company functioned as a part of that regiment, and its history for the remainder of the war is reported as a part of the regimental history.

The following roster was compiled primarily from information in the microfilm edition of the Compiled Service Records of Soldiers Who Served in Organizations from the State of North Carolina (Record Group 109, MC 270), National Archives and Records Administration, Washington, D.C. Record Group 109 includes enlistment papers, pay vouchers, requisitions, letters of resignation, discharge certificates, and abstracts of medical and prisoner of war returns. Materials relating specifically to Company A, 61st Regiment N.C. Troops, include a company muster-in and descriptive roll dated October 6, 1862, and company muster rolls for September, 1862-April, 1864, and September-October, 1864.

Also utilized in this roster were *The War of the Rebellion: A Compilation of the Official Records of the Union and Confederate Armies*, the North Carolina adjutant general's *Roll of Honor*, state militia records, newspaper casualty lists and obituaries, wartime claims for bounty pay and allowances, postwar registers of claims for artificial limbs, Confederate pension applications filed with the states of North Carolina, Tennessee, and Florida, Confederate Soldiers' Home records, and the 1860 and 1870 federal censuses of North Carolina. A search was made also for relevant letters, diaries, reminiscences, and other manuscripts in the Southern Historical Collection (University of North Carolina-Chapel Hill), the Duke University Library Special Collections Department, and the North Carolina Division of Archives and History.

Among the secondary sources consulted were records of the North Carolina division of the United Daughters of the Confederacy, postwar rosters, regimental and county histories, marriage bond, will, and cemetery indexes, published and unpublished genealogies, biographical dictionaries, the North Carolina *County Heritage Book* series, the *Confederate Veteran*, Walter Clark's *Histories of the Several Regiments and Battalions from North Carolina in the Great War, 1861-'65*, and the North Carolina volume of the extended edition of *Confederate Military History*.

Note: The following roster contains service records for twenty-two men who served in 1st Company K, 40th Regiment N.C. Troops (3rd Regiment N.C. Artillery), but who were killed in action, discharged, transferred, or otherwise left the company prior to September 5, 1862, the date it was transferred to the 59th Regiment N.C. Troops (later redesignated the 61st Regiment N.C. Troops). Because a roster for 1st Company K, 40th North Carolina, was not published in volume 1 of this series, the service records of those men appear below. However, as will be apparent, they never served in Company C, 61st Regiment N.C. Troops. All service records falling into this early-termination category conclude with a "special note" alerting readers to that fact and referring them to the information contained in this paragraph.

OFFICERS

CAPTAINS

MALLETT, EDWARD

Born in Cumberland County on February 14, 1827. Resided in Cumberland County and was by occupation a farmer prior to enlisting in Craven County at age 35. Appointed Captain on March 1, 1862. Reported present or accounted for through February 29, 1864. Reported on duty as acting regimental commander in March-April, 1864. Appointed Major on August 10, 1864, and transferred to the Field and Staff of this regiment. Later served as Lieutenant Colonel of this regiment. [Previously served as Captain in the 15th and 16th Regiments N.C. Militia.]

BIDDLE, SAMUEL SIMPSON, JR.

Born in Craven County where he resided as a student prior to enlisting in Craven County at age 18, February 25, 1862. Mustered in as 1st Sergeant. Appointed 2nd Lieutenant on July 2, 1862. Promoted to 1st Lieutenant on September 5, 1862. Reported present or accounted for through April 30, 1864. Was reported in command of the company in March-August, 1863, and March-April, 1864. Promoted to Captain on August 10, 1864. Hospitalized at Richmond, Virginia, September 29, 1864, with intermittent fever. Returned to duty on October 18, 1864. Detailed for court-martial duty on November 15, 1864. Hospitalized at Raleigh on an unspecified date. Returned to duty on April 1, 1865. No further records.

LIEUTENANTS

GUTHRIE, JOHN F., 1st Lieutenant

Born in Carteret County and resided in Craven County where he was by occupation a clerk prior to enlisting in Craven County at age 22, January 14, 1862. Mustered in as Private. Elected 3rd Lieutenant on September 5, 1862. Wounded at Kinston on December 14, 1862. Promoted to 2nd Lieutenant on February 6, 1863. Rejoined the company in March-April, 1863, but was unable to perform duty because of disability from wounds. Reported in hospital at Wilmington on June 25, 1863, suffering from a carbuncle. Reported absent at Charleston, South Carolina, in July-August, 1863. Returned to duty in September-October, 1863. Reported present or accounted for through April 30, 1864. Commanded the company at Cold Harbor, Virginia, May 31-June 3, 1864. Promoted to 1st Lieutenant on August 10, 1864. Captured at Fort Harrison, Virginia, September 30, 1864. Confined at Old Capitol Prison, Washington, D.C., October 6, 1864. Transferred to Fort Delaware, Delaware, October 21, 1864. Released at Fort Delaware on June 10, 1865, after taking the Oath of Allegiance.

JONES, THOMAS O., 1st Lieutenant

Date of appointment not reported. "Dismissed [from] the service" on September 4, 1862. Reason he was dismissed not reported. [See special note at the end of the history of Company C, 61st Regiment N.C. Troops (page 668).]

LANIER, JAMES C., 2nd Lieutenant

Born in Davidson County where he resided as a mechanic prior to enlisting in Wake County at age 22, August 27, 1862, for the war. Mustered in as Private. Promoted to Corporal on January 16, 1863. Promoted to Sergeant on October 18, 1863. Reported present or accounted for through April 30, 1864. Wounded at Drewry's Bluff, Virginia, May 13-17, 1864. Returned to duty on an unspecified date. Elected 2nd Lieutenant on September 4, 1864. Reported present and in command of Company B of this regiment in September-October, 1864. No further records. Survived the war.

STORY, EDWARD F., 3rd Lieutenant

Previously served as Private in Company I, 18th Regiment N.C. Troops (8th Regiment N.C. Volunteers). Enlisted in this company on June 28, 1862, for the war. Mustered in as Private. Promoted to

1st Sergeant on or about September 5, 1862. Elected 3rd Lieutenant on February 6, 1863. Reported present or accounted for through April 30, 1864. Wounded slightly in the thigh at Drewry's Bluff, Virginia, May 18, 1864. Returned to duty on an unspecified date. Reported sick in hospital on August 6, 1864. Returned to duty in September-October, 1864. Court-martialed on or about December 7, 1864. Reason he was court-martialed not reported. No further records. Survived the war. [Was reported on duty as acting commander of Company A of this regiment in September-October, 1864.]

TISDALE, GEORGE F., 2nd Lieutenant

Born in Craven County where he resided as a jeweler prior to enlisting in Craven County at age 23, March 3, 1862. Mustered in as Private. Promoted to Sergeant in July, 1862. Elected 2nd Lieutenant on September 5, 1862. Reported absent under arrest in November-December, 1862. Reason he was arrested not reported. Resigned on January 8, 1863. Reason he resigned not reported. Resignation accepted on or about February 4, 1863.

NONCOMMISSIONED OFFICERS AND PRIVATES

ACKROYD, WILLIAM, Private

Previously served as Private in Company B, 26th Regiment N.C. Troops. Enlisted in this company in Wake County on August 27, 1862, for the war as a substitute. Reported present through December 31, 1863. Hospitalized at Petersburg, Virginia, February 29, 1864, with meningitis. Transferred to another hospital on March 17, 1864. Returned to duty on an unspecified date. Captured at Fort Harrison, Virginia, September 30, 1864. Confined at Point Lookout, Maryland, October 5, 1864. Paroled at Point Lookout on March 17, 1865. Received at Boulware's Wharf, James River, Virginia, March 19, 1865, for exchange.

AINSWORTH, THOMAS F., Private

Resided in Craven County and enlisted in New Hanover County at age 22, March 1, 1864, for the war. Wounded in the head at Drewry's Bluff, Virginia, May 13-16, 1864. Captured (probably in hospital) at Staunton, Virginia, June 6, 1864. Confined at Camp Morton, Indianapolis, Indiana, June 21, 1864. Released at Camp Morton on May 18, 1865, after taking the Oath of Allegiance.

ANTWINE, JOHN, Corporal

Born in Jones County where he resided as a farmer prior to enlisting in Jones County at age 36, January 22, 1862. Reported present in November-December, 1862. Promoted to Corporal on February 6, 1863. Reported present through April 30, 1864. Wounded at or near the Crater, near Petersburg, Virginia, on or about August 1, 1864. Died in hospital at Richmond, Virginia, August 30, 1864, of wounds.

ARNOLD, BRYANT, Private

Born in Craven County where he resided as a farmer prior to enlisting at age 25, March 13, 1862. Discharged at Kinston on May 13 or May 20, 1862, by reason of disability. [See special note at the end of the history of Company C, 61st Regiment N.C. Troops (page 668).]

ARTHUR, WILLIAM, Private

Born in Lenoir County where he resided as a farmer prior to enlisting in Wake County at age 30, August 27, 1862, for the war.

Reported present or accounted for on surviving company muster rolls through June 30, 1863. Wounded in the head, neck, and/or back at Morris Island, Charleston Harbor, South Carolina, on or about August 26, 1863. Hospitalized at Charleston. Returned to duty in March-April, 1864. Reported present in September-October, 1864. No further records. Survived the war.

BARNES, ROBERT, Private

Born in Craven County where he resided as a farmer prior to enlisting in Craven County at age 35, March 6, 1862. Captured at Kinston on December 14, 1862. Paroled the next day. Returned to duty in March-April, 1863. Reported present or accounted for through October 31, 1863. Deserted at Kenansville on December 12, 1863.

BARNHILL, JOHN L., Private

Resided in Bladen County where he enlisted at age 21, November 16, 1862, for the war. Reported present through April 30, 1864. Wounded in the leg at Drewry's Bluff, Virginia, May 13-16, 1864. Returned to duty prior to July 30, 1864, when he was killed at the Crater, near Petersburg, Virginia.

BECK, CALVIN FULGHUM, Private

Born in Granville County where he resided as a farmer prior to enlisting in Wake County at age 22, August 27, 1862, for the war. Reported present or accounted for on surviving company muster rolls through April 30, 1864. Captured near Petersburg, Virginia, June 16, 1864. Confined at Point Lookout, Maryland, June 19, 1864. Transferred to Elmira, New York, July 25, 1864. Paroled at Elmira on October 11, 1864. Received at Venus Point, Savannah River, Georgia, November 15, 1864, for exchange. No further records. Survived the war.

BLACKLEY, WILLIAM J., Private

Born in Granville County where he resided as a farmer prior to enlisting in Wake County at age 23, August 27, 1862, for the war. Reported sick in hospital at Raleigh in November-December, 1862. Died in hospital at Raleigh on January 10, 1863, of "ty[phoid] pneu-[monia]."

BLACKWELL, THOMAS OWEN, Private

Previously served as Private in 3rd Company B, 36th Regiment N.C. Troops (2nd Regiment N.C. Artillery). Transferred to this company in March-April, 1863. Hospitalized at Wilmington on June 28, 1863. Returned to duty on August 8, 1863. Hospitalized at Wilmington on or about October 10, 1863, with "malingeria." Returned to duty on October 13, 1863. Reported absent sick in November, 1863-April, 1864. Hospitalized at Petersburg, Virginia, May 21, 1864, with lumbago. Transferred to hospital at Danville, Virginia, September 20, 1864. Hospitalized at Raleigh on October 3, 1864, with "hemeralopia." Returned to duty on December 6, 1864. No further records.

BOLT, JOHN, Corporal

Previously served as Private in Company I, 3rd Regiment N.C. State Troops, and in the C.S. Navy. Enlisted in this company in Craven County at age 36, February 9, 1862. Was apparently mustered in with the rank of Corporal. Reported present in November-December, 1862. Transferred back to the C.S. Navy on January 16, 1863.

BRATCHER, REUBEN, Private

Resided in Craven County and was by occupation a cooper prior to enlisting at age 37, January 26, 1862. Reported missing in action at New Bern on March 14, 1862. Was probably killed at New Bern. [See special note at the end of the history of Company C, 61st Regiment N.C. Troops (page 668).]

BRINKLEY, JOHN, Private

Born in Craven County and resided in Craven or Duplin County where he was by occupation a farmer prior to enlisting in Craven County at age 35, January 10, 1862. Reported missing at Kinston on December 14, 1862. Returned to duty in January-February, 1863. Reported present or accounted for through October 31, 1863. Deserted at Kenansville on December 13, 1863. Rejoined from desertion on April 11, 1864, and was placed under arrest. Returned to duty on an unspecified date. Captured at Globe Tavern, Virginia, August 19, 1864. Confined at Point Lookout, Maryland, August 24, 1864. Released at Point Lookout on June 24, 1865, after taking the Oath of Allegiance. [North Carolina pension records indicate that he was wounded in the head (fractured skull) and neck at Kinston on an unspecified date.]

BULLARD, JOHN, Private

Born in Sampson County where resided as a farmer prior to enlisting in Wake County at age 30, August 27, 1862, for the war. Mustered in as Private or Corporal. Promoted to Sergeant on or about September 5, 1862. Reported present or accounted for through June 30, 1863. Reported absent sick in July-August, 1863. Returned to duty in September-October, 1863. Reported absent sick at Petersburg, Virginia, in November-December, 1863. Reduced to ranks on January 18, 1864. Reported sick in hospital at High Point on February 27, 1864. Returned to duty in March-April, 1864. Reported present in September-October, 1864. Hospitalized at Greensboro on January 17, 1865, with acute rheumatism. Took the Oath of Allegiance at Raleigh on May 5, 1865.

BURCHETT, JOSEPH W., Private

Born in Granville County where he resided as a farmer prior to enlisting in Wake County at age 24, August 27, 1862, for the war. Reported absent sick at Moseley Hall (present-day LaGrange) in November-December, 1862. Returned to duty in January-February, 1863. Reported on detached service as a carpenter at John's Island, Charleston, South Carolina, from February 27 through April 30, 1863. Rejoined the company in May-June, 1863. Deserted on August 23, 1863.

CARMACK, THOMAS, Private

Born in Craven County where he resided as a laborer prior to enlisting in Craven County at age 32, January 20, 1862. Reported present or accounted for in November, 1862-April, 1863. Detailed for duty as a picket guard on May 6, 1863. Reported absent sick in July, 1863-February, 1864. Returned to duty in March-April, 1864. Wounded in the right arm and right side at Cold Harbor, Virginia, June 3, 1864. Hospitalized at Richmond, Virginia. Returned to duty on an unspecified date. Reported present in September-October, 1864. Hospitalized at Wilmington on January 7, 1865, with pleuritis. Transferred to hospital at Greensboro on January 15, 1865. Hospitalized at Raleigh on January 17, 1865, with debilitas. Returned to duty on February 6, 1865. Captured at Kinston on March 19, 1865. Released on an unspecified date. Survived the war.

CHAPMAN, JOHN, Corporal

Born in New York and resided in Craven County where he was by occupation a sailor prior to enlisting in Craven County at age 24, February 9, 1862. Mustered in as Private. Promoted to Corporal in November-December, 1862. Transferred to the C.S. Navy on January 16, 1863.

CIVILS, RICHARD, Private

Born in Craven County where he resided as a farmer prior to enlisting in Craven County at age 42, January 26, 1862. Died in hospital at Kinston on June 13, 1862. Cause of death not reported. [See special note at the end of the history of Company C, 61st Regiment N.C. Troops (page 668).]

CONNER, BRYAN W., Private

Born in Craven County where he resided as a farmer prior to enlisting in Craven County at age 35, January 20, 1862. Captured at Kinston on December 14, 1862. Paroled on December 15, 1862. Failed to returned to duty. Listed as a deserter and dropped from the company rolls on May 20, 1863.

CORBITT, ROBERT L., Private

Resided in Bladen County and was by occupation a farmer prior to enlisting in Bladen County at age 27, November 16, 1862, for the war. Reported present or accounted for through April 30, 1863. Hospitalized at Wilmington on June 1, 1863, with bilious fever. Returned to duty on July 1, 1863. Hospitalized at Wilmington on or about September 4, 1863, with intermittent fever. Returned to duty on September 12, 1863. Reported on guard duty at Magnolia on or about October 31, 1863. Reported absent sick at Wilson in November-December, 1863. Returned to duty in January-February, 1864. Reported present but sick in March-April, 1864. Hospitalized at Wilmington on an unspecified date with debility and chronic diarrhoea. Furloughed for thirty days on or about September 30, 1864. Hospitalized at Richmond on December 3, 1864. Furloughed for sixty days on December 19, 1864. Reported in hospital at High Point on December 27, 1864, with chronic bronchitis. No further records.

CORBITT, WILLIAM L., Private

Resided in Bladen County where he enlisted at age 22, November 16, 1862, for the war. Reported absent sick through April 30, 1863. Returned to duty in May-June, 1863. Wounded at Fort Wagner, Charleston Harbor, South Carolina, July 30, 1863. Returned to duty prior to September 1, 1863. Reported present through April 30, 1864. Captured at Globe Tavern, Virginia, August 19, 1864. Confined at Point Lookout, Maryland, August 22, 1864. Paroled at Point Lookout on or about November 1, 1864. Received at Venus Point, Savannah River, Georgia, November 15, 1864, for exchange. No further records. Survived the war.

CROSS, JAMES S., Private

Born in Beaufort County and resided in Craven County where he was by occupation a laborer prior to enlisting in Craven County at age 27, January 29, 1862. Transferred to 3rd Company G, 40th Regiment N.C. Troops (3rd Regiment N.C. Artillery), on or about September 28, 1862.

CUSTIS, PENNANT R., Private

Born in Craven County where he resided as a farmer prior to enlisting in Craven County at age 31, January 21, 1862. Reported present but sick in November, 1862-February, 1863. Returned to duty in March-April, 1863. Reported present but sick or absent sick in May-August, 1863. Returned to duty in September-October, 1863, and was detailed for duty in the Quartermaster Department at Magnolia. Reported absent on detail through April 30, 1864, and in September-October, 1864. No further records.

DAUGHERTY, JOHN H., Private

Born in Craven County where he resided as a laborer prior to enlisting in Craven County at age 17, March 8, 1862. Reported missing in action at Kinston on December 14, 1862. Returned to duty in March-April, 1863. Reported present or accounted for through October 31, 1863. Deserted at Kenansville on December 12, 1863.

DAUGHTRY, GUILFORD, Private

Previously served as Private in Company C, 63rd Regiment N.C. Troops (5th Regiment N.C. Cavalry). Transferred to this company on October 19, 1864. No further records. Survived the war.

DAVIS, JOHN M., Private

Born in Craven County where he resided as a laborer prior to enlisting in Craven County at age 50, January 27, 1862. Hospitalized at Wilmington on December 30, 1862, with acute dysentery. Returned to duty on January 9, 1863. Reported present but sick in March-April, 1863. Reported absent sick in May-August, 1863. Reported present but sick in September-October, 1863. Reported absent without leave in November-December, 1863. Reported sick in hospital at Petersburg, Virginia, in March-April, 1864. No further records.

DAWSON, JOHN, Private

Born in Craven County and resided in Lenoir County where he was by occupation a farmer or carpenter prior to enlisting in Craven County at age 34, January 14, 1862. Reported present or accounted for in November, 1862-October, 1863. Deserted at Kenansville on December 28, 1863. Returned from desertion on April 11, 1864, and was placed under arrest. Returned to duty prior to August 19, 1864, when he was captured at Globe Tavern, Virginia. Confined at Point Lookout, Maryland, August 24, 1864. Died at Point Lookout on February 22, 1865, of disease.

EBORN, WILLIAM R., Private

Resided in Craven County and enlisted at age 37, January 20, 1862. Reported missing in action at New Bern on March 14, 1862. Was probably killed at New Bern. [See special note at the end of the history of Company C, 61st Regiment N.C. Troops (page 668).]

ENGLEFIELD, CHARLES S., Private

Resided in Craven County and enlisted in New Hanover County at age 23, March 1, 1864, for the war. Wounded in the head at Drewry's Bluff, Virginia, May 13-16, 1864. Captured (probably in hospital) at Staunton, Virginia, June 7, 1864. Confined at Camp Morton, Indianapolis, Indiana, June 21, 1864. Released at Camp Morton on May 20, 1865, after taking the Oath of Allegiance.

FINE, GEORGE, Private

Born in Davidson County where he resided as a laborer prior to enlisting in Wake County at age 18, August 27, 1862, for the war. Deserted at Kinston on December 10, 1862.

FISHER, JOHN ROBERT, Private

Born in Sampson County on February 14, 1839. Resided in Sampson County and was by occupation a farmer prior to enlisting in Wake County at age 23, August 27, 1862, for the war. Reported present or accounted for in November, 1862-April, 1864. Captured at Globe Tavern, Virginia, August 19, 1864. Confined at Point Lookout, Maryland, August 22, 1864. Paroled at Point Lookout on March 14, 1865. Received at Boulware's Wharf, James River, Virginia, March 16, 1865, for exchange. No further records. Survived the war.

GASKILL, JOSEPH B., Private

Resided in Craven County where he enlisted at age 50, January 26, 1862. Reported missing in action at New Bern on March 14, 1862. Was probably killed at New Bern. [See special note at the end of the history of Company C, 61st Regiment N.C. Troops (page 668).]

GASKILL, WILLIAM A., Private

Resided in Craven County and enlisted at age 23, February 19, 1862. Reported missing in action at New Bern on March 14, 1862. Was probably killed at New Bern. [See special note at the end of the history of Company C, 61st Regiment N.C. Troops (page 668).]

GIBSON, WILLIAM A., Private

Born in Davidson County where he resided as a farmer prior to enlisting in Wake County at age 22, August 27, 1862, for the war. Reported present or accounted for in November, 1862-June, 1863. Reported on duty as a teamster in July-October, 1863. Rejoined the company in November-December, 1863. Reported present through April 30, 1864. Furloughed for sixty days from hospital at Richmond, Virginia, October 1, 1864. No further records. [Served also in the 2nd Regiment Confederate Engineer Troops.]

GRIFFIN, ISAAC, Private

Born in Wake County where he resided as a farmer prior to enlisting in Wake County at age 28, August 27, 1862, for the war. Died at Tarboro on October 24, 1862, of "disease of the heart."

GRIST, SAMUEL L., Private

Previously served as Private in Company K, 10th Regiment N.C. State Troops (1st Regiment N.C. Artillery). Transferred to this company on September 10, 1862. Mustered in as Sergeant. Promoted to 1st Sergeant on February 6, 1863. Reported present or accounted for on surviving company muster rolls through August 31, 1863. Reported absent without leave in September-October, 1863. Reduced to ranks on October 18, 1863. Transferred to Company B, 3rd Battalion N.C. Light Artillery, prior to November 1, 1863.

HALTOM, ALLISON CLARK, Private

Born in Davidson County on December 25, 1830. Resided in Davidson County and was by occupation a farmer prior to enlisting in Wake County at age 31, August 27, 1862, for the war. Reported present in November, 1862-April, 1863. Reported absent without leave on June 18, 1863. Listed as a deserter and dropped from the company rolls on October 1, 1863. Took the Oath of Allegiance at Salisbury on May 31, 1865.

HARPER, SAMUEL T., Private

Previously served as Private in Company B, 63rd Regiment N.C. Troops (5th Regiment N.C. Cavalry). Transferred to this company on October 13, 1864. No further records.

HARRIS, ASA, Private

Born in Pitt County where he resided as a laborer prior to enlisting in Craven County at age 19, March 12, 1862. Reported missing at Kinston on December 14, 1862. Returned to duty in January-February, 1863. Reported present or accounted for through April 30, 1864. Wounded slightly in the neck near Petersburg, Virginia, June 17-30, 1864. Returned to duty on an unspecified date. Hospitalized at Richmond, Virginia, September 30, 1864. Died in hospital at Richmond on October 18, 1864, of "colitis acuta." [May have served previously as Private in Company E, 27th Regiment N.C. Troops.]

HARRIS, TURNER, Private

Born in Davidson County where he resided as a farmer prior to enlisting in Wake County at age 34, August 27, 1862, for the war. Captured at Kinston on December 14, 1862. Paroled on December 15, 1862. Listed as a deserter and dropped from the company rolls on May 20, 1863. Returned to duty on August 28, 1863. Reported present through April 30, 1864. Reported on detail as a teamster in September-October, 1864. No further records. Survived the war.

HEATH, WILLIAM S., Private

Born in Craven County where he resided as a farmer prior to enlisting in Craven County on March 13, 1862. Mustered in as Corporal. Reduced to ranks on an unspecified date. Hospitalized at Wilmington on August 27, 1862. Died at Wilmington on September 1, 1862, of "catarrhus." [See special note at the end of the history of Company C, 61st Regiment N.C. Troops (page 668).]

HINES, CHARLES C., Private

Born in Lenoir County where he resided as a mechanic prior to enlisting in Craven County at age 22, February 6, 1862. Mustered in as Sergeant. Reported present or accounted for in November, 1862-October, 1863. Reduced to ranks on October 18, 1863. Reported present through April 30, 1864. Wounded in the face and/or chest at Cold Harbor, Virginia, on or about June 3, 1864. Hospitalized at Richmond, Virginia. Furloughed on June 7, 1864. Hospitalized at Goldsboro on an unspecified date. Released from hospital on July 15, 1864. Failed to return to duty and was listed as a deserter. Returned from desertion on September 10, 1864, and was arrested. Hospitalized at Petersburg, Virginia, October 11, 1864. Transferred to the provost marshal on November 5, 1864. Court-martialed on or about December 7, 1864. No further records.

HOPKINS, JAMES, Private

Born in Davidson County where he resided as a blacksmith prior to enlisting in Wake County at age 26, August 27, 1862, for the war. Reported absent sick in November, 1862-April, 1863. Listed as a deserter and dropped from the company rolls on May 20, 1863. Returned from desertion on December 16, 1863, and was placed under arrest. Returned to duty in January-February, 1864. Reported present in March-April, 1864. No further records.

HUNT, ALSTON C., Private

Born in Davidson County where he resided as a farmer prior to enlisting in Wake County at age 26, August 27, 1862, for the war. Deserted at Kinston on December 10, 1862. Returned from desertion on December 16, 1863, and was placed under arrest. Hospitalized at Petersburg, Virginia, January 18, 1864, with acute rheumatism. Later contracted hepatitis. Transferred to another hospital on March 17, 1864. Reported at home on disability furlough in September-October, 1864. No further records.

HUNT, C. W., _____

North Carolina pension records indicate that he served in this company.

JOHNSON, ABSTON G., Private

Born in Davidson County where he resided as a farmer prior to enlisting in Wake County at age 34, August 27, 1862, for the war. Reported present in November, 1862-April, 1863. Captured

at Morris Island, Charleston Harbor, South Carolina, on or about August 26, 1863. Confined at Hilton Head, South Carolina. Was apparently released at Hilton Head in September, 1863, after taking the Oath of Allegiance.

JONES, BENTON, Private

Born in Wake County where he resided as a farmer prior to enlisting in Wake County at age 20, August 27, 1862, for the war. Reported present in November-December, 1862. Reported sick in hospital at Wilmington in January-April, 1863. Reported absent without leave on June 2, 1863. Returned to duty in July-August, 1863. Reported present through February 29, 1864. Reported sick in hospital at Petersburg, Virginia, in March-April, 1864. Reported present in September-October, 1864. No further records. Survived the war.

JONES, JOHN, Private

Born in Craven County where he resided as a farmer prior to enlisting in Craven County at age 24, March 8, 1862. Discharged at Kinston on May 12 or May 20, 1862, by reason of disability. [See special note at the end of the history of Company C, 61st Regiment N.C. Troops (page 668).]

KEITH, GEORGE P., Private

Born in Wake County where he resided as a mechanic prior to enlisting in Wake County at age 34, August 27, 1862, for the war. Reported present or accounted for in November, 1862-February, 1864. Reported present but under arrest in March-April, 1864. Reason he was arrested not reported. Returned to duty on an unspecified date. Captured at Globe Tavern, Virginia, August 19, 1864. Confined at Point Lookout, Maryland, August 22, 1864. Paroled at Point Lookout on February 13, 1865. Received at Cox's Wharf, James River, Virginia, February 14-15, 1865, for exchange. No further records.

KEPLEY, GEORGE, Private

Born in Davidson County where he resided as a farmer prior to enlisting in Wake County at age 22, August 27, 1862, for the war. Deserted at Kinston on December 10, 1862. Reported in prison at Wilmington in May-June, 1863. Reported absent at Charleston, South Carolina, in July-August, 1863. Reported absent sick in September-October, 1863. Hospitalized at Petersburg, Virginia, December 23, 1863, with deafness. Furloughed for sixty days on December 24, 1863. Reported absent on furlough or absent sick in January-April and September-October, 1864. No further records. Survived the war.

KINDLEY, JAMES E., Private

Born in Davidson County where he resided as a farmer prior to enlisting in Wake County at age 22, August 27, 1862, for the war. Deserted at Kinston on December 10, 1862. Returned from desertion on December 16, 1863, and was placed under arrest. Returned to duty in January-February, 1864. Deserted on March 10, 1864. Returned from desertion on October 9, 1864. No further records. Survived the war.

KINDLEY, WILLIAM E., Private

Born in Davidson County where he resided as a farmer prior to enlisting in Wake County at age 21, August 27, 1862, for the war. Deserted at Kinston on December 10, 1862. Returned from desertion on December 16, 1863, and was placed under arrest. Returned to duty in January-February, 1864. Deserted on March 10, 1864. Returned from desertion on April 5, 1864, and was placed under arrest. Returned to duty on an unspecified date. Reported present in September-October, 1864. No further records.

KING, LEWIS J., Private

Born in Wake County where he resided as a farmer prior to enlisting in Wake County at age 33, August 27, 1862, for the war. Mustered in as Private. Reported present or accounted for in November, 1862-April, 1864. Promoted to Corporal on January 16, 1864. Reduced to ranks on March 1, 1864. Wounded in the knee at Drewry's Bluff, Virginia, May 13-16, 1864. Hospitalized at Richmond, Virginia. Died on or about July 6, 1864, of wounds and was buried in Hollywood Cemetery, Richmond.

KINNEY, EBENEZER B., Private

Born in Davidson County where he resided as a farmer prior to enlisting in Wake County at age 27, August 27, 1862, for the war. Reported present in November-December, 1862. Left sick on the road between Goldsboro and Wilmington on January 1, 1863. Listed as a deserter and dropped from the company rolls on June 1, 1863.

KOONCE, SAMUEL F., Private

Born in Craven County where he resided as a clerk prior to enlisting in Craven County at age 18, March 3, 1862. Captured at Kinston on December 14, 1862. Paroled at New Bern on December 23, 1862. Reported absent without leave in March-April, 1863. Returned to duty in May-June, 1863. Reported present through April 30, 1864. Wounded in the right leg at or near Petersburg, Virginia, on or about June 18, 1864. Hospitalized at Petersburg. Returned to duty on July 21, 1864. Killed at the Crater, near Petersburg, July 30, 1864. "Acted with great gallantry" at the Crater.

LACKEY, ALEXANDER, Private

Born in Iredell County where he resided as a mechanic or miller prior to enlisting in Wake County at age 25, August 27, 1862, for the war. Reported present or accounted for in November, 1862-August, 1863. Deserted at Sullivan's Island, Charleston Harbor, South Carolina, September 2, 1863. Hospitalized at Richmond, Virginia, December 23, 1864, with chronic bronchitis. Discharged from hospital on February 8, 1865. Paroled at Greensboro on May 5, 1865.

LAFFOON, MOSES, Private

Born in Wake County where he resided as a farmer prior to enlisting in Wake County at age 19, August 27, 1862, for the war. Reported present or accounted for in November, 1862-February, 1864. Reported present but under arrest in March-April, 1864. Reason he was arrested not reported. Captured near Petersburg, Virginia, June 16, 1864. Confined at Point Lookout, Maryland, June 19, 1864. Transferred to Elmira, New York, July 25, 1864. Arrived at Elmira on July 28, 1864. Paroled at Elmira on October 11, 1864. Received at Venus Point, Savannah River, Georgia, November 15, 1864, for exchange. No further records.

LANCASTER, JOHN R., Private

Resided in Craven County and enlisted at age 45, January 30, 1862. Reported missing in action at New Bern on March 14, 1862. Was probably killed at New Bern. [See special note at the end of the history of Company C, 61st Regiment N.C. Troops (page 668).]

LANIER, THOMAS F., Private

Born in Davidson County where he resided as a mechanic prior to enlisting in Wake County at age 29, August 27, 1862, for the

war. Reported present or accounted for in November, 1862-April, 1864. Furloughed for thirty days on October 7, 1864. No further records. [Roll of Honor indicates that he was wounded at Petersburg, Virginia, on an unspecified date.]

LAYDEN, FRANCIS, Private

Born in Beaufort County and resided in Craven County where he was by occupation a mechanic prior to enlisting in Craven County at age 31, February 20, 1862. Reported present but sick in November-December, 1862. Reported absent sick in January, 1863-April, 1864, and September-October, 1864. Hospitalized at Richmond, Virginia, December 13, 1864, with chronic diarrhoea. Returned to duty on February 1, 1865. Hospitalized at Greensboro on February 21, 1865, with catarrhus. Transferred on February 23, 1865. Paroled at Salisbury on May 2, 1865.

LEGGETT, WARREN, Private

Resided in Beaufort County and enlisted in Wake County at age 17, March 8, 1863, for the war. Reported present or accounted for through April 30, 1864. Killed near Bermuda Hundred, Virginia, May 18, 1864.

LITTLETON, AMOS C., Private

Born in Jones County where he resided as a farmer prior to enlisting in Jones County at age 35, January 22, 1862. Deserted on August 27, 1862. Returned to duty on February 26, 1863. Reported present through June 30, 1863. Wounded in the right shoulder at Morris Island, Charleston Harbor, South Carolina, on or about August 26, 1863. Reported present but sick in September-October, 1863. Deserted at Kenansville on November 23, 1863. Transferred to the C.S. Navy on December 30, 1863.

LITTLETON, ROSCOE B., Private

Born in Jones County where he resided as a farmer prior to enlisting in Jones County at age 24, January 22, 1862. Reported in hospital at Wilmington on June 29, 1862, with rubeola. Returned to duty on July 28, 1862. Hospitalized at Wilmington on August 27, 1862, with catarrh. Died in hospital at Wilmington on March 16, 1863, of "pneumonia" and/or "parotitis."

McGILL, CHARLES, Private

Previously served as Private in 2nd Company H, 40th Regiment N.C. Troops (3rd Regiment N.C. Artillery). Transferred to this company in July, 1863. Reported present in September, 1863-April, 1864. Wounded near Petersburg, Virginia, on an unspecified date. Reported absent wounded in September-October, 1864. Retired to the Invalid Corps on November 8, 1864.

McGOWN, GEORGE, Private

Resided in Craven County and enlisted at age 28, January 20, 1862. Reported missing in action at New Bern on March 14, 1862. Was probably killed at New Bern. [See special note at the end of the history of Company C, 61st Regiment N.C. Troops (page 668).]

MEEKINS, CHARLES, Private

Resided in Jones County and enlisted at age 43, January 23, 1862. Reported missing in action at New Bern on March 14, 1862. Was probably killed at New Bern. [See special note at the end of the history of Company C, 61st Regiment N.C. Troops (page 668).]

MITCHELL, FURNEY G., Private

Born in Lenoir County and resided in Jones County where he was by occupation a farmer prior to enlisting in Lenoir County at age

49, January 14, 1862. Reported present but sick in November-December, 1862. Hospitalized at Wilmington on February 18, 1863, with anemia. Returned to duty on March 16, 1863. Hospitalized at Wilmington on May 7, 1863, with rheumatism. Returned to duty on June 19, 1863. Furloughed for thirty days on June 27, 1863. Reported absent sick in July, 1863-April, 1864. Hospitalized at Richmond, Virginia, October 2, 1864. Transferred to another hospital on October 3, 1864. No further records.

MOODY, JAMES E., Private

Born in Lenoir County and resided in Jones County where he was by occupation a farmer prior to enlisting in Craven County at age 18, February 15, 1862. Reported present in November, 1862-February, 1863. Hospitalized at Columbia, South Carolina, March 12, 1863. Returned to duty in May-June, 1863. Reported present in July-October, 1863. Reported absent sick at Petersburg, Virginia, in November-December, 1863. Returned to duty in January-February, 1864. Reported present in March-April, 1864. Captured near Petersburg on or about June 16, 1864. Confined at Point Lookout, Maryland, June 19, 1864. Transferred to Elmira, New York, July 9, 1864. Arrived at Elmira on July 12, 1864. Died at Elmira on October 11, 1864, of "chronic diarrhoea."

MOORE, ALEXANDER, Sergeant

Resided in Beaufort County and enlisted in Wake County at age 22, March 8, 1863, for the war. Mustered in as Private. Promoted to Corporal on September 1, 1863. Promoted to Sergeant on October 18, 1863. Reported present through April 30, 1864. Wounded at Cold Harbor, Virginia, on or about June 1-3, 1864. Died on June 10, 1864, of wounds. Place of death not reported.

MOORE, RIGDON W., Private

Born in Lenoir County where he resided as a farmer prior to enlisting in Wake County at age 32, August 27, 1862, for the war. Reported missing in action at Kinston on December 14, 1862. Reported present but sick in January-February, 1863. Returned to duty in March-April, 1863. Reported present through August 31, 1863. Deserted at Kenansville on September 6, 1863. Returned from desertion on April 11, 1864, and was placed under arrest. Returned to duty prior to July 30, 1864, when he was wounded in the right hand and/or arm at the Crater, near Petersburg, Virginia. One finger amputated. Hospitalized at High Point on August 12, 1864. Furloughed on August 13, 1864. Reported absent wounded in September-October, 1864. No further records. Survived the war.

MOORE, SMITHSON C., Private

Born in Wayne County and resided in Jones County where he was by occupation a farmer prior to enlisting in Craven County at age 47, January 30, 1862. Detailed as a hospital nurse at Wilmington in August, 1862. Reported on detail at Wilmington through April 30, 1863. Discharged on May 9, 1863, by reason of disability.

MOORE, WILLIAM T., Private

Resided in Jones County and enlisted at age 47, January 26, 1862. Reported missing in action at New Bern on March 14, 1862. Was probably killed at New Bern. [See special note at the end of the history of Company C, 61st Regiment N.C. Troops (page 668).]

MORRIS, JOHN, Private

Born in Davidson County where he resided as a farmer prior to enlisting in Wake County at age 34, August 27, 1862, for the war. Reported sick at home in November, 1862-April, 1863. Listed as a deserter and dropped from the company rolls on May 20, 1863.

MUNDALL, JOSEPH, Private

Born in Northampton County where he resided as a farmer prior to enlisting in Wake County at age 35, August 27, 1862, for the war. Reported sick in hospital at Wilson in November-December, 1862. Returned to duty in January-February, 1863. Reported present in March-April, 1863. Reported sick in hospital at Wilmington in May-June, 1863. Returned to duty in July-August, 1863. Reported present or accounted for through April 30, 1864. Wounded in the arm at Drewry's Bluff, Virginia, May 13-16, 1864. Reported sick at the division infirmary in September-October, 1864. No further records.

NEWSOM, NICHOLAS H., Sergeant

Born in Davidson County where he resided as a farmer prior to enlisting in Wake County at age 18, August 27, 1862, for the war. Mustered in as Private. Reported present or accounted for in November, 1862-April, 1864. Promoted to Corporal on March 1, 1864. Promoted to Sergeant on October 1, 1864. Reported present in September-October, 1864. Captured near Kinston on March 10, 1865. Confined at Point Lookout, Maryland, March 16, 1865. Released at Point Lookout on June 29, 1865, after taking the Oath of Allegiance.

OGELBY, ADRIAN M. C., Private

Resided in Craven County and enlisted at age 46, February 4, 1862. Reported missing in action at New Bern on March 14, 1862. Was probably killed at New Bern. [See special note at the end of the history of Company C, 61st Regiment N.C. Troops (page 668).]

OGLESBY, JOHN N., Private

Resided in Craven County and was by occupation a carpenter prior to enlisting at age 43, February 7, 1862. Reported missing in action at New Bern on March 14, 1862. Was probably killed at New Bern. [See special note at the end of the history of Company C, 61st Regiment N.C. Troops (page 668).]

ONLY, WILLIAM D., Private

Previously served as Private in Company B, 3rd Battalion N.C. Light Artillery. Transferred to this company in September-October, 1863. Reported present in November, 1863-April, 1864, and September-October, 1864. No further records.

PARRISH, THOMAS, Private

Born in Lenoir County where he resided as a laborer prior to enlisting in Craven County at age 17, March 1, 1862. Wounded in the left arm at Kinston on December 14, 1862. Reported present but sick in January-February, 1863. Returned to duty in March-April, 1863. Reported present in May, 1863-April, 1864, and September-October, 1864. Hospitalized at Wilmington on January 10, 1865, with pneumonia. Reported in hospital at Raleigh on January 23, 1865, with debilitas. Returned to duty on an unspecified date. Deserted to the enemy at New Hope on March 17, 1865.

PASCHALL, JOSEPH P., Private

Born in Wake County where he resided as a farmer prior to enlisting in Wake County at age 24, August 27, 1862, for the war. Reported present in November, 1862-February, 1863. Reported sick in hospital at Charleston, South Carolina, April 15, 1863. Reported absent without leave on June 2, 1863. Returned to duty on August 18, 1863. Reported present in September, 1863-April, 1864. Wounded in the face at Petersburg, Virginia, June 19, 1864. Hospitalized at Farmville, Virginia, on or about June 20, 1864. Deserted from hospital on July 22, 1864. Returned to duty on an unspecified date.

Reported present in September-October, 1864. No further records. Survived the war.

PHILLIPS, MALPHUS S., Private

Born in Moore County where he resided as a shoemaker prior to enlisting in Wake County at age 27, August 27, 1862, for the war. Mustered in as Private. Reported sick in hospital at Raleigh in November-December, 1862. Promoted to Corporal on January 16, 1863. Returned to duty prior to March 1, 1863. Reported present or accounted for in March-June, 1863. Reported absent without leave in July-December, 1863. Reduced to ranks on September 1, 1863. Discharged prior to May 1, 1864, by a writ of habeas corpus.

PHILLIPS, THEODORE, Private

Born in Lenoir County where he resided as a farmer prior to enlisting in Craven County at age 18, February 25, 1862. Reported present in November, 1862-April, 1864. Wounded in the thigh, hip, and/or right arm at Drewry's Bluff, Virginia, May 16, 1864. Returned to duty prior to June 16-19, 1864, when he was wounded in the arm near Petersburg, Virginia. Hospitalized at Richmond, Virginia, where he died on July 7-8, 1864, of wounds.

PRIDGEN, CHARLES P., Private

Resided in Bladen County where he enlisted on November 16, 1862, for the war. Deserted at Wilmington on February 6, 1863. Died in hospital at Wilmington on February 28, 1863, of "pneumonia."

PRIDGEON, HENRY H., Private

Resided in Bladen County and was by occupation a farmer prior to enlisting in Bladen County at age 25, November 16, 1862, for the war. Was not listed in the records of this company until August 29, 1863, when he was hospitalized at Wilmington with dysentery. Reported in hospital at Wilmington on September 25, 1863, suffering from an inguinal hernia of the right side and debility from intermittent fever. Reported absent sick through December 31, 1863. Dropped from the company rolls prior to May 1, 1864, presumably for disability.

REEVES, JAMES S., Private

Previously served as Private in Company H, 2nd Regiment N.C. State Troops. Transferred to this company on May 31, 1862. Mustered in as Corporal. Reported present in November, 1862-February, 1863. Promoted to Sergeant on February 6, 1863. Reported present but sick in March-April, 1863. Reduced to ranks on May 13, 1863. Reported absent on detail to arrest deserters in Robeson County in May-June, 1863. Reported absent under arrest in July-August, 1863. Deserted at Sullivan's Island, Charleston Harbor, South Carolina, September 2, 1863.

RICHMOND, ROBERT, Private

Born in Pitt County and resided in Lenoir County where he was by occupation a farmer or day laborer prior to enlisting in Craven County at age 46, January 31, 1862. Deserted at Greenville on December 7, 1862. Returned from desertion on February 10, 1863. Reported present but sick in March-April, 1863. Returned to duty in May-June, 1863. Deserted subsequent to August 31, 1863. Returned from desertion on October 18, 1863, and was placed under arrest. Returned to duty in January-February, 1864. Reported present in March-April, 1864. Wounded in the shoulder and captured at Fort Harrison, Virginia, September 30, 1864. Confined at Point Lookout, Maryland, October 5, 1864. Paroled at Point Lookout on March 17, 1865. Received at Boulware's Wharf, James River,

Virginia, March 19, 1865, for exchange. No further records. Survived the war.

RILEY, WILLIAM, Private

Born in Davidson County where he resided as a farmer prior to enlisting in Wake County at age 23, August 27, 1862, for the war. Reported present in November, 1862-June, 1863. Reported absent sick in July-August, 1863. Deserted on an unspecified date. Returned from desertion on December 16, 1863, and was placed under arrest. Returned to duty in January-February, 1864. Reported present in March-April, 1864. Deserted to the enemy on or about October 9, 1864. Confined at Washington, D.C., October 12, 1864. Released on or about the same date after taking the Oath of Allegiance.

ROUARK, JOHN, Sergeant

Born in Lenoir County where he resided as a painter prior to enlisting in Wake County at age 28, August 27, 1862, for the war. Mustered in as Private. Detailed as a hospital nurse at Wilson on December 1, 1862. Rejoined the company in May-June, 1863. Reported on duty as a provost guard at Magnolia in July-October, 1863. Promoted to Corporal on October 18, 1863. Rejoined the company in November-December, 1863. Promoted to Sergeant on January 18, 1864. Reported present through April 30, 1864. Killed at Bermuda Hundred, Virginia, May 18, 1864.

SANDERFER, WILLIAM M., Private

Born in Granville County in 1843. Resided in Granville County and was by occupation a farmer prior to enlisting in Wake County at age 18, August 27, 1862, for the war. Reported absent sick in November, 1862-October, 1863. Returned to duty in November-December, 1863. Reported present in January-April and September-October, 1864. Hospitalized at Wilmington on January 30, 1865, with a gunshot wound of the right hand. Place and date wounded not reported. No further records. [Filed a Tennessee pension application after the war.]

SASSER, JOHN, Private

Born in Lenoir County where he resided as a farmer prior to enlisting in Wake County at age 39, August 27, 1862, for the war as a substitute. Reported on detail as "Col[onel]'s hostler" in November, 1862-April, 1863. Hospitalized at Wilmington on May 7, 1863, with rheumatism. Returned to duty on June 12, 1863. Reported present in July-August, 1863. Transferred to Company F, 7th Regiment Confederate Cavalry, September 1, 1863.

SHUTE, JOHN, 1st Sergeant

Born in Craven County on June 8, 1824. Resided in Lenoir County and was by occupation a farmer prior to enlisting in Craven County at age 37, January 26, 1862. Mustered in as Private. Promoted to Sergeant prior to September 5, 1862. Reported present or accounted for in November, 1862-August, 1863. Promoted to 1st Sergeant on October 18, 1863. Reported present in September, 1863-April, 1864. Hospitalized at Farmville, Virginia, June 21, 1864, with scabies. Furloughed for sixty days on August 13, 1864. Reported absent without leave on October 12, 1864. Hospitalized at High Point on October 20, 1864, with intermittent fever. Furloughed on October 21, 1864. Hospitalized at Richmond, Virginia, December 2, 1864. Furloughed for sixty days on December 29, 1864. Paroled at Thomasville on May 1, 1865.

SLAUGHTER, EZEKIEL, Private

Born in Greene County where he resided as a laborer prior to enlisting in Craven County at age 18, March 10, 1862. Reported present or accounted for in November, 1862-August, 1863. Deserted at Kenansville on December 13, 1863. Returned from desertion on February 1, 1864. Wounded in the left foot at Drewry's Bluff, Virginia, May 13-15, 1864. Hospitalized at Richmond, Virginia. Furloughed from hospital at Danville, Virginia, May 23, 1864. Returned to duty on an unspecified date. Reported present in September-October, 1864. No further records.

SMITH, CANNON, JR., Private

Born in Craven County where he resided as a farmer prior to enlisting at age 25, January 26, 1862. Deserted to the enemy at New Bern on an unspecified date (probably in March, 1862). Later served as Sergeant in Company G, 1st Regiment N.C. Infantry (Union). [See special note at the end of the history of Company C, 61st Regiment N.C. Troops (page 668).]

SMITH, NICHOL[A]S, Private

Born in Wayne County where he resided as a farmer prior to enlisting in Craven County at age 38, January 30, 1862. Captured at Kinston on December 14, 1862. Paroled at New Bern on December 23, 1862. Returned to duty in January-February, 1863. Reported present in March, 1863-April, 1864, and September-October, 1864. No further records. Survived the war.

SNYDAM, JOHN W., Private

Born in Craven County where he resided as a painter prior to enlisting in Craven County at age 38, March 5, 1862. Reported sick in hospital at Wilmington from September 5, 1862, through April 30, 1863. Listed as a deserter and dropped from the company rolls on May 20, 1863.

STEVENSON, KIMMONS, Private

Born in Johnston County where he resided as a farmer prior to enlisting in Wake County at age 34, August 27, 1862, for the war. Reported sick in hospital at Raleigh from December 20, 1862, through April 30, 1863. Reported on detail as a hospital nurse at Raleigh in May, 1863-April, 1864. Hospitalized at Raleigh on June 18, 1864, with polypus. Returned to duty on October 15, 1864. Reported absent sick at the division infirmary on or about October 31, 1864. Hospitalized at Raleigh on December 27, 1864, with nasal polypus. Captured in hospital at Raleigh on April 13, 1865. Released on an unspecified date after taking the Oath of Allegiance.

STUART, FERNIFOLD, Private

Resided in Wayne County and enlisted on January 26, 1862. Failed to report for duty and was dropped from the company rolls prior to September 5, 1862. [See special note at the end of the history of Company C, 61st Regiment N.C. Troops (page 668).]

TAYLOR, AMRIAH L., Private

Born in Lenoir County and resided in Lenoir or Duplin County where he was by occupation a farmer prior to enlisting in Wake County at age 36, August 27, 1862, for the war as a substitute. Reported absent sick in November, 1862-February, 1863. Reported present but sick in March-April, 1863. Returned to duty in May-June, 1863. Reported present in July-October, 1863. Deserted at Kenansville on December 12, 1863. [Later served as Private in Company F, 2nd Regiment N.C. Infantry (Union).]

TAYLOR, WARREN H., Private

Born in Lenoir County where he resided as a farmer or farm laborer prior to enlisting in Wake County at age 61, August 27, 1862, for

the war as a substitute. Reported absent sick in November, 1862-August, 1863. Died at home in Lenoir County on September 19, 1863. Cause of death not reported.

TIPPETT, ABNER, Private

Resided in Craven County and was by occupation a farmer prior to enlisting at age 39, January 20, 1862. Reported missing in action at New Bern on March 14, 1862. Was probably killed at New Bern. [See special note at the end of the history of Company C, 61st Regiment N.C. Troops (page 668).]

TURNER, JOHN, Private

Born in Lenoir or Wayne County and resided in Lenoir County where he was by occupation a farmer prior to enlisting in Lenoir County at age 46, January 14, 1862. Died in hospital at Fort Fisher, near Wilmington, June 2, 1862, of disease. [See special note at the end of the history of Company C, 61st Regiment N.C. Troops (page 668).]

UZZELL, JOHN, Private

Born in Lenoir or Wayne County and resided in Lenoir County where he was by occupation a farmer prior to enlisting in Lenoir County at age 20, May 15, 1862, for the war. Died in hospital at Wilmington on July 15, 1862. Cause of death not reported. [See special note at the end of the history of Company C, 61st Regiment N.C. Troops (page 668).]

UZZELL, MAJOR, Private

Born in Lenoir County and resided in Lenoir or Wayne County where he was by occupation a farmer prior to enlisting in Lenoir County at age 20, January 22, 1862. Reported absent sick in Lenoir County from December 11, 1862, through April 30, 1863. Reported present but sick in May-June, 1863. Returned to duty in July-August, 1863. Reported present in September-October, 1863. Reported absent sick in November, 1863-February, 1864. Returned to duty in March-April, 1864. Reported present in September-October, 1864. Paroled at Goldsboro on an unspecified date in 1865. [Roll of Honor indicates that he was "disabled in the loss of part of his foot by railroad accident."]

UZZELL, WILLIAM, Private

Born in Lenoir County where he resided as a farmer prior to enlisting in Lenoir County at age 23, January 22, 1862. Died at Fort Johnston, near Smithville (present-day Southport), October 9-10, 1862. Cause of death not reported.

WALTERS, JAMES, Sergeant

Born in Lenoir County where he resided as a laborer prior to enlisting in Wake County at age 29, August 27, 1862, for the war. Mustered in as Private. Reported present in November, 1862-October, 1863. Promoted to Corporal on October 18, 1863. Reported present in November, 1863-April, 1864, and September-October, 1864. Promoted to Sergeant on October 1, 1864. No further records.

WETHERINGTON, ANDREW, Private

Born in Lenoir County where he resided as a laborer prior to enlisting in Wake County at age 17, August 27, 1862, for the war as a substitute. Reported present but sick in November-December, 1862. Hospitalized at Wilmington on or about February 9, 1863, with scabies. Returned to duty on February 20, 1863. Reported sick in hospital at Summerville, South Carolina, February 27, 1863.

Detailed as a picket guard near Wilmington on June 26, 1863. Hospitalized at Wilmington on or about July 31, 1863, with bilious fever. Furloughed for thirty days on November 26, 1863. Reported absent sick through April 30, 1864, and in September-October, 1864. Hospitalized at Richmond, Virginia, December 14, 1864, with pneumonia. Furloughed for sixty days on February 3, 1865. No further records.

WHEELER, JOHN R., Private

Born in Wake County where he resided as a laborer prior to enlisting in Wake County at age 24, August 27, 1862, for the war. Reported sick in hospital at Raleigh in November-December, 1862. Reported present but sick in January-February, 1863. Discharged at Columbia, South Carolina, April 1, 1863, by reason of "organic heart trouble." [May have served later as Private in Company H, 47th Regiment N. C. Troops.]

WILKINSON, RICHARD, Private

Previously served as Private in Company F, 7th Regiment Confederate Cavalry. Transferred to this company on September 1, 1863, as a substitute. Reported present through April 30, 1864. Wounded in the shoulder at Drewry's Bluff, Virginia, May 13-16, 1864. No further records.

WILSON, JAMES D., Corporal

Born in Pitt County where he resided as a farmer prior to enlisting in Craven County at age 43, March 1, 1862. Mustered in as Private. Reported present in November, 1862-April, 1863. Promoted to Corporal in January, 1863. Reported present but sick in May-June, 1863. Returned to duty prior to November 1, 1863. Reported present through April 30, 1864. Wounded slightly in the hip at the Crater, near Petersburg, Virginia, July 30, 1864. Returned to duty on an unspecified date. Wounded in the lung and arm at Fort Harrison, Virginia, September 30, 1864. Hospitalized at Richmond, Virginia, where he died on October 23, 1864, of wounds.

WISE, MERRITT P., Private

Resided in Wayne or Lenoir County and enlisted at age 27, January 21, 1862. Transferred to Company H, 2nd Regiment N.C. State Troops, on or about June 22, 1862. [See special note at the end of the history of Company C, 61st Regiment N.C. Troops (page 668).]

WISE, RIGDON, Private

Born in Wayne County where he resided as a farmer prior to enlisting in Craven County at age 37, January 30, 1862. Reported present in November, 1862-February, 1863. Reported present but sick in March-June, 1863. Reported present in July, 1863-April, 1864, and September-October, 1864. No further records. Survived the war.

WISE, WILLIAM G., Private

Resided in Craven County and enlisted at age 26, February 4, 1862. Reported missing in action at New Bern on March 14, 1862. Was probably killed at New Bern. [See special note at the end of the history of Company C, 61st Regiment N.C. Troops (page 668).]

WOOD, EDWARD W., Private

Born in Jones County and resided in Craven County where he was by occupation a farmer prior to enlisting in Jones County at age 25, January 22, 1862. Captured at Kinston on December 14, 1862. Paroled on December 17, 1862. Reported present but sick in January-February, 1863. Returned to duty in March-April, 1863.

Reported present in May-June, 1863. Reported on duty with the Engineer Corps at Wilmington in July-December, 1863. Transferred to the Engineer Corps prior to May 1, 1864. [North Carolina pension records indicate that he was wounded in the right knee by the explosion of a shell at Fort Fisher in May, 1863.]

WOOTEN, ALLEN S., Sergeant

Previously served as Corporal in Company G, 8th Regiment N.C. State Troops. Promoted to Sergeant and transferred to this company on June 20, 1863. Reported present through April 30, 1864. Wounded in the hand at Drewry's Bluff, Virginia, May 13-19, 1864. Returned to duty on an unspecified date. Captured at Fort Harrison, Virginia, September 30, 1864. Confined at Point Lookout, Maryland, October 5, 1864. Paroled at Point Lookout on March 17, 1865. Received at Boulware's Wharf, James River, Virginia, March 19, 1865, for exchange.

WOOTTEN, JOHN B., Private

Resided in Craven County and was by occupation a farmer prior to enlisting at age 29, February 27, 1862. Mustered in as Sergeant. Detailed as a scout in April, 1862. Reduced to ranks on September 7, 1862. His name does not appear on any surviving company muster rolls and it appears that although he was assigned to duty with the 61st Regiment he was on detail as a scout throughout his career. Last reported in the records of this company on January 20, 1864. Survived the war.

COMPANY D

This company, nicknamed the "Vance Guards," was raised in Chatham County in April-September, 1862, as Capt. Nathan A. Ramsey's Independent Company. It was mustered into state service at Smithville on September 29, 1862. On the same date the company was assigned to the newly organized 59th Regiment N.C. Troops. That unit was redesignated the 61st Regiment N.C. Troops on an unknown date between October 30 and November 22, 1862. This company was designated Company D. After joining the regiment the company functioned as a part of the regiment, and its history for the remainder of the war is reported as a part of the regimental history.

The following roster was compiled primarily from information in the microfilm edition of the Compiled Service Records of Soldiers Who Served in Organizations from the State of North Carolina (Record Group 109, MC 270), National Archives and Records Administration, Washington, D.C. Record Group 109 includes enlistment papers, pay vouchers, requisitions, letters of resignation, discharge certificates, and abstracts of medical and prisoner of war returns. Materials relating specifically to Company D of the 61st Regiment include a company muster-in and descriptive roll dated September 29, 1862, and company muster rolls for November, 1862-June 30, 1864, and September-December, 1864.

Also utilized in this roster were *The War of the Rebellion: A Compilation of the Official Records of the Union and Confederate Armies*, the North Carolina adjutant general's *Roll of Honor*, state militia records, newspaper casualty lists and obituaries, wartime claims for bounty pay and allowances, postwar registers of claims for artificial limbs, Confederate pension applications filed with the states of North Carolina, Tennessee, and Florida, Confederate Soldiers' Home records, and the 1860 and 1870 federal censuses of North Carolina. A search was made also for relevant letters, diaries, reminiscences, and

other manuscripts in the Southern Historical Collection (University of North Carolina-Chapel Hill), the Duke University Library Special Collections Department, and the North Carolina Division of Archives and History.

Among the secondary sources consulted were records of the North Carolina Division of the United Daughters of the Confederacy, post-war rosters, regimental and county histories, marriage bond, will, and cemetery indexes, published and unpublished genealogies, biographical dictionaries, the North Carolina *County Heritage Book* series, the *Confederate Veteran*, Walter Clark's *Histories of the Several Regiments and Battalions from North Carolina in the Great War, 1861-'65*, and the North Carolina volume of the extended edition of *Confederate Military History*.

Note: The following roster contains service records for twenty men who enlisted in Captain Ramsey's Independent Company but whose service terminated prior to September 29, 1862, the date the company was mustered into the 59th Regiment N.C. Troops (later redesignated the 61st Regiment N.C. Troops). Those men, it will be evident, never served in the 61st Regiment. Their service records are included here because too little information survives to compile a roster for Ramsey's Independent Company. All service records falling into the early-termination category conclude with a "special note" alerting readers to that fact and referring them to the information contained in this paragraph.

OFFICERS

CAPTAIN

RAMSEY, NATHAN ALEXANDER

Previously served as Sergeant in Company M, 15th Regiment N.C. Troops (5th Regiment N.C. Volunteers). Appointed Captain of this company on March 21, 1862. Captured at Kinston on December 14, 1862. Paroled on December 15, 1862. Returned to duty in January-February, 1863. Reported present through June 30, 1864. Hospitalized at Petersburg, Virginia, August 9, 1864, with chronic diarrhoea. Returned to duty in September-October, 1864. Reported present through December 31, 1864. No further records. Survived the war.

LIEUTENANTS

COTTEN, RICHARD CLIFFORD, JR., 3rd Lieutenant

Previously served as 1st Lieutenant of Company E, 44th Regiment N.C. Troops. Appointed 3rd Lieutenant of this company on May 15, 1862. Reported present or accounted for on surviving company muster rolls through April 30, 1863. Captured at Morris Island, Charleston Harbor, South Carolina, August 26, 1863. Confined at Hilton Head, South Carolina. Transferred to Fort Columbus, New York Harbor, where he arrived on October 6, 1863. Transferred to Johnson's Island, Ohio, October 9, 1863. Transferred to Point Lookout, Maryland, March 21, 1865. Transferred to Fort Delaware, Delaware, where he arrived on April 28, 1865. Released at Fort Delaware on June 12, 1865, after taking the Oath of Allegiance. [Contrary to 10:434 of this series, the correct spelling of his surname was probably Cotten rather than Cotton.]

ELLINGTON, JAMES B., 2nd Lieutenant

Previously served as Private in Company M, 15th Regiment N.C. Troops (5th Regiment N.C. Volunteers). Appointed 2nd Lieuten-

ant of this company on March 21, 1862. Reported present on surviving company muster rolls through April 30, 1863. Wounded at Charleston, South Carolina, July 31, 1863. Reported absent wounded or absent sick through August 31, 1863. Reported on detached duty in North Carolina from November, 1863, through June, 1864. Returned to duty on an unspecified date. Killed at Fort Harrison, Virginia, September 30, 1864. [Contrary to 5:612 of this series, he did not serve in 2nd Company I, 32nd Regiment N.C. Troops, prior to his transfer to this company.]

RAMSEY, WILLIAM S., 1st Lieutenant

Previously served as Private in Company M, 15th Regiment N.C. Troops (5th Regiment N.C. Volunteers). Appointed 1st Lieutenant of this company on March 21, 1862. Reported present or accounted for on surviving company muster rolls through February 29, 1864. Hospitalized at Petersburg, Virginia, March 9, 1864, with syphilis. Returned to duty on April 4, 1864. Reported present through June 30, 1864. Wounded in the breast and left arm at Fort Harrison, Virginia, September 30, 1864. Left forearm amputated. Hospitalized at Richmond, Virginia. Furloughed on November 8, 1864. No further records. Survived the war.

NONCOMMISSIONED OFFICERS AND PRIVATES

ADCOCK, BENJAMIN F., Private

Resided in Chatham County and enlisted in Lenoir County at age 23, April 19, 1862, for the war. Roll of Honor indicates that he was transferred to the 26th Regiment N.C. Troops on an unspecified date; however, records of the 26th Regiment do not indicate that he served therein. No further records. [May have served later as Private in 2nd Company E, 2nd Regiment N.C. State Troops.]

ADCOCK, JOHN WILLIS, Private

Born on February 22, 1842. Resided in Chatham County and was by occupation a farmer prior to enlisting in Lenoir County at age 20, April 19, 1862, for the war. Transferred to Company E, 26th Regiment N.C. Troops, prior to July 1, 1862. [See special note at the end of the history of Company D, 61st Regiment N.C. Troops (page 678).]

ANDREW, A. N., Private

Resided in Chatham County where he enlisted on July 1, 1863, for the war. Reported sick at home through August 31, 1863. No further records.

ANDREWS, ALVIS, Private

Born in Orange County and resided in Chatham County where he was by occupation a farmer or laborer prior to enlisting in Chatham County at age 21, July 21, 1862, for the war. Reported present in November-December, 1862. Reported sick in hospital at Charleston, South Carolina, in January-February, 1863. Furloughed for thirty days on March 1, 1863. Reported absent sick through February 29, 1864. Returned to duty in March-June, 1864. Reported present in September-December, 1864. No further records. Survived the war.

ANDREWS, T. F., Private

Born in Chatham County where he resided as a farmer prior to enlisting in Chatham County at age 20, July 15, 1862, for the war. Reported present on surviving company muster rolls through April

30, 1863. Captured at Morris Island, Charleston Harbor, South Carolina, August 26, 1863. Sent to Hilton Head, South Carolina. Transferred to Fort Columbus, New York Harbor, where he arrived on September 22, 1863. Transferred to Point Lookout, Maryland, where he arrived on September 26, 1863. Transferred to Elmira, New York, August 16, 1864. Paroled at Elmira on October 11, 1864. Received at Venus Point, Savannah River, Georgia, November 15, 1864, for exchange. Reported absent sick on or about December 31, 1864. No further records.

AUSLEY, EDWARD ALBERT, Private

Born in Chatham County where he resided as a farmer prior to enlisting in Chatham County at age 31, July 21, 1862, for the war. Mustered in as Private. Appointed Musician on October 1, 1862. Reported present or accounted for through April 30, 1863. Reduced to ranks on July 7, 1863. Captured at Morris Island, Charleston Harbor, South Carolina, August 26, 1863. Confined at Hilton Head, South Carolina, September 1, 1863. Transferred to Fort Columbus, New York Harbor, where he arrived on September 22, 1863. Transferred to Point Lookout, Maryland, where he arrived on September 26, 1863. Transferred to Elmira, New York, August 16, 1864. Paroled at Elmira on March 10, 1865. Received at Boulware's Wharf, James River, Virginia, March 15, 1865, for exchange. No further records. Survived the war.

AUSLEY, RICHARD, Private

Born in Chatham County where he resided as a farmer prior to enlisting in Chatham County at age 22, July 21, 1862, for the war. Reported present or accounted for in November, 1862-February, 1864. Wounded in the leg and thigh at Drewry's Bluff, Virginia, May 16, 1864. Hospitalized at Richmond, Virginia. Died in hospital at Richmond on May 21, 1864, of "tetanus."

BOYD, MURPHY J., Corporal

Born in Chatham County where he resided as a farmer prior to enlisting in Chatham County at age 30, August 11, 1862, for the war. Mustered in as Private. Reported present but sick in November-December, 1862. Returned to duty in January-February, 1863. Reported present through February 29, 1864. Reported sick in hospital at Petersburg, Virginia, in March-June, 1864. Returned to duty in September-October, 1864. Reported present in November-December, 1864. Promoted to Corporal on December 31, 1864. No further records. Survived the war. [North Carolina pension records indicate that he was shot through the thigh on an unspecified date while hunting deserters.]

BRADY, JOHN, Private

Resided in Chatham County where he enlisted on July 1, 1863, for the war. Died at Charleston, South Carolina, August 24, 1863. Cause of death not reported.

BRANTLY, TYRRELL B., Private

Born in Chatham County where he resided as a farmer prior to enlisting in Chatham County at age 32, May 8, 1862, for the war. Reported present in November, 1862-April, 1863. Reported sick at home in May-August, 1863. Returned to duty prior to March 1, 1864. Reported present in March-June and September-October, 1864. Reported absent without leave in November-December, 1864. No further records. Survived the war.

BREWER, GREEN, Sergeant

Born in Chatham County where he resided as a cabinetmaker prior to enlisting in Chatham County at age 29, July 5, 1862, for the war. Mustered in as Sergeant. Reported present in November-December, 1862. Reported present but sick in quarters in January-February, 1863. Furloughed for thirty days from hospital at Charleston, South Carolina, April 9, 1863. Returned to duty in May-August, 1863. Reported present in September, 1863-June, 1864, and September-December, 1864. No further records. Survived the war.

BREWER, N., Private

Resided in Chatham County and enlisted on April 19, 1862, for the war. Transferred to an unspecified unit on an unknown date (probably prior to September 29, 1862). [May have served as Private in Company E, 26th Regiment N.C. Troops. See special note at the end of the history of Company D, 61st Regiment N.C. Troops (page 678).]

BREWER, WILLIAM HENRY, Private

Resided in Chatham County and enlisted in Lenoir County at age 20, April 19, 1862, for the war. Transferred to Company E, 26th Regiment N.C. Troops, prior to July 1, 1862. [See special note at the end of the history of Company D, 61st Regiment N.C. Troops (page 678).]

BROWN, DAVID C., Private

Born in Chatham County where he resided as a farmer prior to enlisting in Chatham County at age 28, July 21, 1862, for the war. Reported present in November, 1862-June, 1864. Hospitalized at Richmond, Virginia, October 14, 1864. Furloughed on November 8, 1864. Reported absent sick through December 31, 1864. No further records.

BROWN, J. A., Private

Resided in Chatham County where he enlisted at age 17, January 9, 1864, for the war. Wounded in the hand at or near Bermuda Hundred, Virginia, May 18, 1864. Hospitalized at Richmond, Virginia. Returned to duty subsequent to June 30, 1864. Deserted to the enemy on October 11, 1864. Released at Bermuda Hundred on October 12, 1864, after taking the Oath of Allegiance.

BROWN, J. P., Private

Resided in Chatham County where he enlisted at age 17, October 23, 1863, for the war. Reported present through February 29, 1864. Wounded in the left hand at or near Bermuda Hundred, Virginia, May 18, 1864. Reported absent wounded or absent sick through December 31, 1864. No further records.

BROWN, S. L., Private

Born in Chatham County where he resided as a farmer prior to enlisting in Chatham County at age 29, May 5, 1862, for the war. Mustered in as Sergeant. Wounded and captured at Kinston on December 14, 1862. Paroled the same date. Reported absent wounded or absent sick through August 31, 1863. Returned to duty prior to March 1, 1864. Reported sick in hospital in March-June, 1864. Returned to duty prior to November 1, 1864. Hospitalized at Richmond, Virginia, December 10, 1864. Returned to duty on December 27, 1864. Reduced to ranks on December 31, 1864. No further records.

BUCKNER, MANLY, Private

Resided in Chatham County where he enlisted at age 21, September 15, 1864, for the war. Captured on or about October 4, 1864. Released at Bermuda Hundred, Virginia, October 7, 1864, after taking the Oath of Allegiance.

BURKE, WILLIAM L., Private

Born in Chatham County where he resided as a cabinetmaker prior to enlisting in Chatham County at age 21, July 8, 1862, for the war. Captured at Kinston on December 14, 1862. Paroled the same date. Returned to duty in January-February, 1863. Reported present in March-April, 1863. Captured at Morris Island, Charleston Harbor, South Carolina, August 26, 1863. Confined at Hilton Head, South Carolina, September 1, 1863. Transferred to Point Lookout, Maryland, where he arrived on September 26, 1863. Hospitalized at Point Lookout on October 27, 1863, with chronic diarrhoea. Died in hospital at Point Lookout on December 18, 1863, of "smallpox."

CAMPBELL, THOMAS C., Private

Born in Moore County where he resided prior to enlisting in Chatham County at age 19, May 13, 1862, for the war. Reported present or accounted for in November, 1862-April, 1863. Captured at Morris Island, Charleston Harbor, South Carolina, August 26, 1863. Confined at Hilton Head, South Carolina, September 1, 1863. Transferred to Fort Columbus, New York Harbor, where he arrived on September 22, 1863. Transferred to Point Lookout, Maryland, where he arrived on September 26, 1863. Transferred to Elmira, New York, August 16, 1864. Transferred to Point Lookout on October 11, 1864. Paroled at Point Lookout on or about October 29, 1864. Received at Venus Point, Savannah River, Georgia, November 15, 1864, for exchange. Reported absent sick on or about December 31, 1864. No further records. Survived the war.

CARPENTER, ELBERT, Private

Born in Chatham County where he resided as a farmer or laborer prior to enlisting in Chatham County at age 22, August 11, 1862, for the war. Killed at Kinston on December 14, 1862.

CARPENTER, JAMES, Private

Born in Chatham County where he resided as a farmer prior to enlisting in Chatham County at age 31, August 11, 1862, for the war. Died at Tarboro on November 22, 1862, of "consumption" and "dyspepsia."

CARPENTER, NATHAN, Private

Born in Chatham County where he resided as a farmer prior to enlisting in Chatham County at age 31, July 7, 1862, for the war. Reported absent sick in November, 1862-February, 1864. Discharged on June 9, 1864, by reason of disability.

CARPENTER, THOMAS, Private

Born in Chatham County where he resided as a farmer prior to enlisting in Chatham County at age 29, August 11, 1862, for the war. Reported absent sick (phthisis pulmonalis) in November, 1862-February, 1864. Returned to duty in March-June, 1864. Furloughed for thirty days on October 3, 1864. Hospitalized at Richmond, Virginia, December 22, 1864. Returned to duty on December 30, 1864. Paroled at Greensboro on May 2, 1865.

CARPENTER, WYATT, Private

Born in Chatham County where he resided as a farmer or laborer prior to enlisting in Chatham County at age 20, August 11, 1862, for the war. Died at Tarboro on November 26, 1862. Cause of death not reported.

CARTER, JOHN A., Private

Resided in Chatham County and enlisted in Lenoir County at age 26, April 19, 1862, for the war. Transferred to Company E, 26th Regiment N.C. Troops, on or about June 19, 1862. [See special note at the end of the history of Company D, 61st Regiment N.C. Troops (page 678).]

CAUDLE, DAVID, Private

Born in Surry County and resided in Chatham County where he was by occupation an engineer prior to enlisting in Chatham County at age 36, April 15, 1862. Reported present in November, 1862-February, 1864. Wounded in the left leg at Drewry's Bluff, Virginia, May 14, 1864. Left leg amputated. Reported absent wounded in September-October, 1864. Retired to the Invalid Corps on December 5, 1864.

CAVNESS, T. H., Private

Resided in Chatham County where he enlisted at age 17, December 23, 1863, for the war. Wounded in the hand near Petersburg, Virginia, June 17-30, 1864. Returned to duty prior to July 1, 1864. Furloughed for sixty days on October 18, 1864. Hospitalized at Wilmington on December 30, 1864, with a gunshot wound. Place and date wounded not reported. Returned to duty on January 5, 1865. No further records.

CHEEK, J. T., Private

Born in Chatham County where he resided as a farmer prior to enlisting in Wayne County at age 25, September 13, 1862, for the war. Wounded in the left hand and captured at Kinston on or about December 14, 1862. Paroled on December 15, 1862. Returned to duty in January-February, 1863. Reported present in March-April, 1863. Reported absent sick in May-August, 1863. Reported absent wounded in September, 1863-June, 1864, and September-October, 1864. Reported absent sick in November-December, 1864. No further records. Survived the war.

CLARK, J. B., Private

Resided in Chatham County and enlisted at "McIvers" on September 22, 1862, for the war. Reported present in November, 1862-April, 1863. Reported sick in hospital at Wilmington in May-August, 1863. Returned to duty in September, 1863-February, 1864. Reported present in March-June and September-October, 1864. Deserted on December 24, 1864.

CLARK, MARION B., Private

Resided in Chatham County and enlisted at "McIvers" on September 22, 1862, for the war. Reported present or accounted for in November, 1862-April, 1863. Captured at Morris Island, Charleston Harbor, South Carolina, August 26, 1863. Confined at Hilton Head, South Carolina, September 1, 1863. Transferred to Fort Columbus, New York Harbor, where he arrived on September 22, 1863. Transferred to Point Lookout, Maryland, where he arrived on September 26, 1863. Released at Point Lookout on January 25, 1864, after taking the Oath of Allegiance and joining the U.S. Navy.

CLARK, NOAH A., Private

Resided in Chatham County where he enlisted at age 19, July 1, 1863, for the war. Reported present through February 29, 1864. Wounded in the left hand at Drewry's Bluff, Virginia, May 14, 1864. Hospitalized at Raleigh where he died on July 8, 1864, presumably of wounds.

CLARK, W. H., Private

Born in Chatham County where he resided as a farmer prior to enlisting in Chatham County at age 20, July 15, 1862, for the war. Reported sick at home with consumption in November-December,

1862. Hospitalized at Wilmington on January 15, 1863, with chronic rheumatism. Furloughed for sixty days on January 31, 1863. Returned to duty in September, 1863-February, 1864. Reported present in March-June, 1864. Furloughed for sixty days on October 11, 1864. Reported absent sick in November-December, 1864. No further records. Survived the war.

COBLE, J., Private

Resided in Chatham County where he enlisted on April 9, 1862. Was reportedly transferred to the 26th Regiment N.C. Troops in May, 1862; however, records of the 26th Regiment do not indicate that he served therein. [See special note at the end of the history of Company D, 61st Regiment N.C. Troops (page 678).]

COLE, STEPHEN B., Private

Born in Moore County where he resided as a farmer prior to enlisting in Chatham County at age 23, May 13, 1862, for the war. Captured and paroled at Kinston on December 14, 1862. Returned to duty in January-February, 1863. Reported present through February 29, 1864. Wounded in the thigh and shoulder at Drewry's Bluff, Virginia, May 16, 1864. Hospitalized at Richmond, Virginia, where he died on May 17, 1864, of wounds.

COOK, JOHN J., Private

Resided in Chatham County where he enlisted at age 37, July 1, 1863, for the war. Reported present through May 31, 1864. Wounded in the foot near Petersburg, Virginia, June 18, 1864. Returned to duty and was detailed for duty as a teamster on or about June 25, 1864. Reported on detail as a teamster through October 31, 1864. Deserted on December 24, 1864.

COOK, W. H., _____

North Carolina pension records indicate that he served in this company.

COTTEN, THOMAS, Private

Born in Chatham County where he resided as a farmer prior to enlisting in Chatham County at age 25, August 11, 1862, for the war. Died at Tarboro on or about November 10, 1862, of "pneumonia."

COVERT, HORATER N., Private

Resided in Chatham County where he enlisted at age 38, November 8, 1863, for the war. Reported present through June 30, 1864. Captured at Fort Harrison, Virginia, September 30, 1864. Confined at Point Lookout, Maryland, October 5, 1864. Paroled at Point Lookout on March 17, 1865. Received at Boulware's Wharf, James River, Virginia, March 19, 1865, for exchange. Hospitalized at Richmond, Virginia, the same date with dyspepsia. Furloughed for thirty days on March 24, 1865. No further records.

COVERT, NICHOLAS C., Private

Born in Chatham County where he resided as a farmer prior to enlisting in Chatham County at age 28, July 8, 1862, for the war. Died at Greenville on December 9, 1862, of "measles."

CRANFORD, E., Private

Resided in Chatham County where he enlisted on July 1, 1863, for the war. Captured at Morris Island, Charleston Harbor, South Carolina, August 26, 1863. Confined at Hilton Head, South Carolina, September 1, 1863. Transferred to Fort Columbus, New York Harbor, where he arrived on September 22, 1863. Transferred to Point Lookout, Maryland, where he arrived on September 26, 1863. Died

in hospital at Point Lookout on October 23, 1863. Cause of death not reported.

CREWS, L. B., Private

Resided in Chatham County and enlisted at "McIvers" on September 22, 1862, for the war. Reported present but sick in November-December, 1862. Returned to duty in January-February, 1863. Reported present through February 29, 1864. Detailed as a teamster on June 1, 1864. Rejoined the company in November-December, 1864. No further records.

CRUTCHFIELD, H. M., Private

Enlisted in Chatham County on October 11, 1862, for the war. Captured at Kinston on December 14, 1862. Paroled on December 15, 1862. Returned to duty in January-February, 1863. Reported present in March-April, 1863. Deserted on July 9, 1863. Returned to duty in January-February, 1864. Wounded in the back and arm (and/or side and shoulder) at Drewry's Bluff, Virginia, May 16, 1864. Hospitalized at Richmond, Virginia. Reported absent wounded through October 31, 1864. Hospitalized at Richmond on December 2, 1864. Released from hospital on December 27, 1864. Deserted on or about the same date.

CRUTCHFIELD, LEVI, Private

Born in Chatham County where he resided as a farmer prior to enlisting in Chatham County at age 30, October 21, 1862, for the war. Deserted on November 9, 1862. Returned to duty on or about September 29, 1863. Reported present through February 29, 1864. Wounded in the neck near Petersburg, Virginia, June 17, 1864. Returned to duty prior to July 1, 1864. Captured at Fort Harrison, Virginia, September 30, 1864. Confined at Point Lookout, Maryland, October 5, 1864. Released at Point Lookout on October 14, 1864, after taking the Oath of Allegiance and joining the U.S. Army. Assigned to Company B, 4th Regiment U.S. Volunteer Infantry.

CUMMINGS, DANIEL, Private

Born in Lancashire, England, and resided in Chatham County where he was by occupation a laborer prior to enlisting in Chatham County at age 47, May 12, 1862, for the war. Reported sick in hospital at Wilmington in November-December, 1862. Hospitalized at Wilmington on February 1, 1863, with pneumonia. Returned to duty on February 21, 1863. Reported sick in hospital at Wilmington in March-April, 1863. Returned to duty subsequent to April 30, 1863. Captured at Morris Island, Charleston Harbor, South Carolina, August 26, 1863. Confined at Hilton Head, South Carolina, September 1, 1863. Transferred to Fort Columbus, New York Harbor, where he arrived on September 22, 1863. Transferred to Point Lookout, Maryland, where he arrived on September 26, 1863. Transferred to Elmira, New York, August 16, 1864. Paroled at Elmira on October 11, 1864. Received at Venus Point, Savannah River, Georgia, November 15, 1864, for exchange. Died on December 27, 1864. Place and cause of death not reported; however, he was buried in Magnolia Cemetery, Charleston.

DAFFORD, JAMES, Private

Resided in Chatham County and was by occupation a day laborer prior to enlisting in Lenoir County at age 27, April 19, 1862, for the war. Was reportedly transferred to the 26th Regiment N.C. Troops on an unspecified date (probably prior to September 29, 1862); however, records of the 26th Regiment do not indicate that he served therein. [See special note at the end of the history of Company D, 61st Regiment N.C. Troops (page 678).]

DAVIS, ALLEN C., Private

Resided in Chatham County where he enlisted at age 17, February 1, 1864, for the war. Wounded in the leg at Drewry's Bluff, Virginia, May 16, 1864. Hospitalized at Richmond, Virginia. Furloughed on August 19, 1864. Reported absent sick in September-October, 1864. Returned to duty in November-December, 1864. No further records. Survived the war.

DEZERN, JOHN, Private

Born in Orange County and resided in Chatham County where he was by occupation a farm laborer prior to enlisting in Chatham County at age 27, July 5, 1862, for the war. Captured and paroled at Kinston on December 14, 1862. Returned to duty in January-February, 1863. Reported present but sick in March-April, 1863. Reported sick in hospital at Columbia, South Carolina, in May-August, 1863. Returned to duty prior to March 1, 1864. "Shocked by a shell" at Drewry's Bluff, Virginia, May 16, 1864. Hospitalized at Richmond, Virginia. Returned to duty in July-October, 1864. Reported present in November-December, 1864. No further records.

DORSETT, SAMUEL J., Private

Resided in Chatham County and was by occupation a farmer prior to enlisting in Lenoir County at age 18, April 19, 1862, for the war. Transferred to Company E, 26th Regiment N.C. Troops, prior to July 1, 1862. [See special note at the end of the history of Company D, 61st Regiment N.C. Troops (page 678).]

DORTON, ALFRED, Private

Resided in Chatham County where he enlisted on October 21, 1862, for the war. Deserted on November 9, 1862. "Killed by Lt. [Richard C.] Cotten [of this company] on 4 Dec., 1862," presumably while resisting arrest.

DOWD, THOMAS C., Private

Previously served as Sergeant in Company D, 41st Regiment N.C. Troops (3rd Regiment N.C. Cavalry). Enlisted in this company subsequent to May 12, 1862, but prior to February 1, 1864. Wounded in the hand at Cold Harbor, Virginia, May 31-June 3, 1864. No further records.

DOWDY, ELI T., Private

Born in Chatham County where he resided as a farmer prior to enlisting in Chatham County at age 29, July 7, 1862, for the war. Died on November 16, 1862, of "typhoid fever." Place of death not reported.

DOWDY, HEZEKIAH K., Private

Born in Chatham County where he resided as a farmer prior to enlisting in Chatham County at age 27, July 7, 1862, for the war. Captured and paroled at Kinston on December 14, 1862. Returned to duty in January-February, 1863. Reported present in March, 1863-June, 1864, and September-October, 1864. Reported absent with leave in November-December, 1864. No further records. Survived the war. [North Carolina pension records indicate that he was wounded on an unspecified date.]

DOWDY, R. C., Private

Resided in Chatham County where he enlisted at age 17, July 1, 1863, for the war. Captured at Morris Island, Charleston Harbor, South Carolina, August 26, 1863. Confined at Hilton Head, South Carolina, September 1, 1863. Transferred to Fort Columbus, New York Harbor, where he arrived on September 22, 1863. Transferred to Point Lookout, Maryland, where he arrived on September 26, 1863. Transferred to Elmira, New York, August 16, 1864. Died at Elmira on September 24, 1864, of "typhoid pneumonia."

DOWDY, WILLIAM T., Private

Born in Chatham County where he resided as a farmer prior to enlisting in Chatham County at age 25, May 13, 1862, for the war. Company records dated November-December, 1862, indicate that he was captured and paroled (probably at Kinston on December 14, 1862); however, records of the Federal Provost Marshal do not substantiate that report. Returned to duty in January-February, 1863. Reported present through February 29, 1864. Wounded in the leg at Drewry's Bluff, Virginia, on or about May 13, 1864. Hospitalized at Richmond, Virginia. Furloughed for sixty days on May 29, 1864. Returned to duty subsequent to June 30, 1864. Reported present in September-December, 1864. No further records. Survived the war.

DUNCAN, DAVID S., Private

Born in Chatham County where he resided as a farmer prior to enlisting in Chatham County at age 30, September 17, 1862, for the war. Reported present in November, 1862-April, 1863. Deserted on August 18, 1863.

DUNN, GEORGE W., Private

Previously served as Private in Company E, 63rd Regiment N.C. Troops (5th Regiment N.C. Cavalry). Transferred to this company on February 20, 1864. Reported present through December 31, 1864. No further records.

EARLEY, W. M., _____

Place and date of enlistment not reported. Killed at Morris Island, Charleston Harbor, South Carolina, on or about August 26, 1863. [See 61st North Carolina casualty list in *Wilmington Weekly Journal*, September 3, 1863.]

ELLINGTON, WILLIAM, Private

Born in Chatham County where he resided as a farmer prior to enlisting in Wayne County at age 22, September 13, 1862, for the war. Reported sick in hospital at Goldsboro in November-December, 1862. Died at Goldsboro on January 4, 1863, of "smallpox."

ELLIS, VANDIFORD, Private

Resided in Chatham County and was by occupation a laborer prior to enlisting in Chatham County at age 17, January 5, 1864, for the war. Reported sick in hospital at Petersburg, Virginia, in March-June, 1864. Died on July 1, 1864. Place and cause of death not reported.

ELMORE, M. G., Corporal

Born in Chatham County where he resided as a farmer prior to enlisting in Chatham County at age 23, July 7, 1862, for the war. Mustered in as Corporal. Reported present in November, 1862-April, 1863. Captured at Morris Island, Charleston Harbor, South Carolina, August 26, 1863. Confined at Hilton Head, South Carolina, September 1, 1863. Transferred to Fort Columbus, New York Harbor, where he arrived on September 22, 1863. Transferred to Point Lookout, Maryland, where he arrived on September 26, 1863. Transferred to Elmira, New York, August 16, 1864. Paroled at Elmira on March 10, 1865. Received at Boulware's Wharf, James

River, Virginia, March 15, 1865, for exchange. No further records. Survived the war.

EMERSON, JAMES K. POLK, Private

Born in Chatham County on October 19, 1845. Resided in Chatham County and enlisted in Lenoir County at age 16, April 19, 1862, for the war. Transferred to Company E, 26th Regiment N.C. Troops, on an unspecified date (probably on or about September 29, 1862). [See special note at the end of the history of Company D, 61st Regiment N.C. Troops (page 678). Filed a Florida pension application after the war.]

EUBANKS, SIDNEY, Private

Born in Chatham County where he resided as a farmer prior to enlisting in Chatham County at age 32, September 15, 1862, for the war. Reported present but sick in November-December, 1862. Returned to duty in January-February, 1863. Reported present through February 29, 1864. Wounded in the thigh at Drewry's Bluff, Virginia, May 16, 1864. Hospitalized at Richmond, Virginia. Furloughed for sixty days on May 31, 1864. Reported in hospital at Raleigh on or about June 30, 1864. Returned to duty prior to November 1, 1864. Reported present in November-December, 1864. No further records.

FIELDS, ELIAS, Private

Born in Chatham County where he resided as a farmer prior to enlisting in Chatham County at age 25, August 8, 1862, for the war. Died at Goldsboro on December 25, 1862. Cause of death not reported.

FIELDS, JAMES L., Private

Born in Chatham County where he resided as a farmer prior to enlisting in Chatham County at age 51, July 7, 1862, for the war as a substitute for Pvt. Edward Harris. Captured and paroled at Kinston on December 14, 1862. Returned to duty in January-February, 1863. Reported present through February 29, 1864. Wounded in the side at Cold Harbor, Virginia, June 1, 1864. Wounded slightly in the neck near Petersburg, Virginia, June 17-30, 1864. Returned to duty prior to July 1, 1864. Transferred to Company E, 8th Regiment N.C. State Troops, in September, 1864.

FIELDS, JOHN, Private

Born in Chatham County where he resided as a farmer prior to enlisting in Chatham County at age 28, August 8, 1862, for the war. Captured and paroled at Kinston on December 14, 1862. Returned to duty in January-February, 1863. Reported present or accounted for through June 30, 1864. Wounded in the foot at Fort Harrison, Virginia, September 30, 1864. Hospitalized at Richmond, Virginia. Returned to duty in November-December, 1864. No further records.

FOGLEMAN, WILLIAM H., Private

Resided in Chatham County and was by occupation a farmer prior to enlisting in Chatham County at age 21, April 9, 1862. Was reportedly transferred to the 26th Regiment N.C. Troops in May, 1862; however, records of the 26th Regiment do not indicate that he served therein. No further records. [See special note at the end of the history of Company D, 61st Regiment N.C. Troops (page 678).]

FOOSHEE, WILLIAM, Private

Resided in Chatham County where he enlisted at age 17, January 25, 1864, for the war. "Killed by falling shelter" at Ivor Station, Virginia, February 15, 1864.

FOWLER, MARK, Private

Resided in Chatham County and was by occupation a tailor prior to enlisting in Lenoir County at age 35, April 19, 1862, for the war. No further records. [See special note at the end of the history of Company D, 61st Regiment N.C. Troops (page 678).]

GEE, WILLIAM H., Private

Resided in Chatham County and was by occupation a farmer prior to enlisting in Chatham County at age 30, May 9, 1862, for the war. Transferred to Company E, 26th Regiment N.C. Troops, on or about June 19, 1862. [See special note at the end of the history of Company D, 61st Regiment N.C. Troops (page 678).]

GILMORE, JAMES L., Private

Born in Chatham County where he resided as a farmer prior to enlisting in Chatham County at age 26, July 17, 1862, for the war. Reported sick in hospital at Wilson in November-December, 1862. Died in hospital at Wilson on January 6, 1863, of "febris typhoides."

GUNTER, JAMES, Private

Resided in Chatham County where he enlisted at age 25, August 11, 1862, for the war. His name appears on the muster-in roll for this company dated September 29, 1862; however, he was not listed again in company records until November-December, 1864, when he was reported present. Hospitalized at Wilmington on January 11, 1865, with chronic diarrhoea. Returned to duty on January 14, 1865. Hospitalized at Wilmington on February 3, 1865, with rubeola. Transferred on February 20, 1865. No further records.

GUNTER, L. B., Sergeant

Born in Chatham County where he resided as a farmer prior to enlisting in Chatham County at age 25, September 10, 1862, for the war. Mustered in as Private. Reported present or accounted for through June 30, 1864. Promoted to Corporal on September 10, 1864. Reported present in September-December, 1864. Promoted to Sergeant on December 31, 1864. No further records.

GUNTER, WILLIAM, Private

Born in Wake County and resided in Chatham County where he was by occupation a farmer prior to enlisting in Chatham County at age 20, July 7, 1862, for the war. Died at Tarboro on December 2, 1862. Cause of death not reported.

HADLEY, ALFRED, Private

Born in Chatham County where he resided as a farmer or laborer prior to enlisting in Chatham County at age 22, August 9, 1862, for the war. Deserted near Tarboro on November 9, 1862. Returned to duty in January, 1864. Hospitalized at Richmond, Virginia, subsequent to February 29, 1864. Transferred to hospital at Raleigh in June, 1864. Furloughed home on an unspecified date. Failed to return to duty and was listed as a deserter on or about June 30, 1864. Returned to duty prior to September 30, 1864, when he was captured at Fort Harrison, Virginia. Confined at Point Lookout, Maryland, October 5, 1864. Released at Point Lookout on May 12-14, 1865, after taking the Oath of Allegiance. [North Carolina pension records indicate that he was wounded in the ankle and side on an unspecified date.]

HARMAN, G. L., Private

Born in Chatham County where he resided as a farmer prior to enlisting in Chatham County at age 27, July 17, 1862, for the war. Reported present in November, 1862-April, 1863. Captured at Morris Island, Charleston Harbor, South Carolina, August 26, 1863. Confined at Hilton Head, South Carolina, September 1, 1863. Hospitalized at Hilton Head on September 4, 1863, with dysentery. Returned to the Hilton Head prison yard on October 3, 1863. Transferred to Fort Columbus, New York Harbor, where he arrived on October 6, 1863. Transferred to Point Lookout, Maryland, October 9, 1863. Paroled at Point Lookout on March 14, 1865. Received at Boulware's Wharf, James River, Virginia, March 16, 1865, for exchange. No further records. Survived the war.

HATCH, JAMES M., Private

Born in Orange County where he resided as a wheelwright prior to enlisting in Chatham County at age 33, May 13, 1862, for the war. Mustered in as Corporal. Reported present in November, 1862-April, 1863. Promoted to Sergeant in May-August, 1863. Wounded at Morris Island, Charleston Harbor, South Carolina, on or about August 26, 1863. Reported in hospital at Petersburg, Virginia, on or about February 29, 1864. Hospitalized at Petersburg on May 21, 1864, with acute dysentery. Reduced to ranks on June 1, 1864. Reported in hospital at Raleigh on or about June 30, 1864. Returned to duty on an unspecified date. Reported present in September-October, 1864. Hospitalized at Richmond, Virginia, December 14, 1864, with chronic diarrhoea. Returned to duty on February 3, 1865. No further records.

HEADEN, WILLIAM J., Private

Previously served as 1st Lieutenant of Company E, 26th Regiment N.C. Troops. Enlisted in this company with the rank of Private subsequent to April 30, 1863. Reported present in May-August, 1863. Wounded in the hip in September, 1863-February, 1864. Place and date wounded not reported. Reported absent wounded in March-June and September-October, 1864. Reported absent sick in November-December, 1864. No further records.

HEADEN, WILLIAM P., _____

North Carolina pension records indicate that he served in this company.

HINSLEY, JAMES, Private

Previously served as Private in Company G, 48th Regiment N.C. Troops. Enlisted in this company in Chatham County on August 11, 1862, for the war. Reported present but sick in November-December, 1862. Returned to duty in January-February, 1863. Hospitalized at Charleston, South Carolina, April 9, 1863. Discharged prior to September 1, 1863, by reason of disability.

HOLT, RICHARD B., Private

Born in Chatham County where he resided as a farmer prior to enlisting in Chatham County at age 28, August 6, 1862, for the war. Died on October 3, 1862. Place and cause of death not reported.

HOLT, WILLIAM P., Private

Born in Chatham County where he resided as a farmer prior to enlisting in Chatham County at age 32, August 6, 1862, for the war. Reported sick in hospital at Raleigh in November-December, 1862. Returned to duty in January-February, 1863. Reported present in March-April, 1863. Wounded in the right thigh at Fort Wagner, Charleston Harbor, South Carolina, July 29, 1863. Reported absent wounded through February 29, 1864. Returned to duty prior to May 14, 1864, when he was wounded in the left side of the abdomen at Drewry's Bluff, Virginia. Hospitalized at Raleigh. Returned to duty prior to September 30, 1864, when he was wounded in the hand

at Fort Harrison, Virginia. Hospitalized at Richmond, Virginia. Deserted from hospital at Richmond on October 10, 1864.

HUGHES, JAMES M., Private

Resided in Chatham County where he enlisted on July 17, 1862, for the war. Reported present in November, 1862-August, 1863. Reported absent wounded in September, 1863-June, 1864, and September-October, 1864. Place and date wounded not reported. Reported absent sick in November-December, 1864. No further records.

HURLEY, WINSHIP MARSHAL, _____

Served as Private in Company G, 63rd Regiment N.C. Troops (5th Regiment N.C. Cavalry). North Carolina pension records indicate that he served also in this company.

JOHNSON, ALLEN, Private

Enlisted in Chatham County on November 6, 1862, for the war. Reported present through August 31, 1863. Wounded prior to March 1, 1864. Place and date wounded not reported. Reported absent wounded in March-June and September-October, 1864. Hospitalized at Richmond, Virginia, November 26, 1864, with a gunshot wound of the left forearm. Retired to the Invalid Corps on the same date and was ordered to report to Fayetteville for light duty.

JOHNSON, ELBERT M., Private

Enlisted in Chatham County on February 1, 1864, for the war. Reported present through June 30, 1864. Company records indicate that he was captured at Fort Harrison, Virginia, September 30, 1864; however, records of the Federal Provost Marshal do not substantiate that report. Was probably killed at Fort Harrison. No further records.

JOHNSON, G. P., Corporal

Born in Chatham County where he resided as a tanner prior to enlisting in Chatham County at age 29, June 7, 1862, for the war. Mustered in as Private. Captured at Kinston on December 14, 1862. Paroled on December 15, 1862. Returned to duty in March-April, 1863. Reported absent sick in May-August, 1863. Returned to duty prior to March 1, 1864. Reported present in March-June, 1864. Promoted to Corporal on June 1, 1864. Hospitalized at Richmond, Virginia, October 24, 1864, with a gunshot wound of the left forearm. Place and date wounded not reported. Returned to duty on December 16, 1864. Deserted on December 26, 1864.

JOHNSON, HENRY C., Private

Born in Chatham County where he resided as a blacksmith or farmer prior to enlisting in Chatham County on September 11, 1862, for the war. Captured at Kinston on December 14, 1862. Paroled on December 15, 1862. Failed to return to duty and was listed as a deserter on August 18, 1863. Returned to duty in September-October, 1864. Transferred to Company G, 26th Regiment N.C. Troops, November 30, 1864, in exchange for Pvt. Thomas S. Perry.

JOHNSON, JAMES R., Private

Born in Chatham County where he resided as a farmer or laborer prior to enlisting in Chatham County at age 25, July 7, 1862, for the war. Captured at Kinston on December 14, 1862. Paroled on December 15, 1862. Returned to duty in January-February, 1863. Reported present in March-April, 1863. Died at home in Chatham County on July 16, 1863. Cause of death not reported.

JOHNSON, JOHN W., Private

Born in Chatham County where he resided as a farmer prior to enlisting in Chatham County at age 31, July 7, 1862, for the war. Reported present but sick in November-December, 1862. Returned to duty in January-February, 1863. Reported present through February 29, 1864. Killed at Drewry's Bluff, Virginia, May 16, 1864.

JOHNSON, JOSIAH, _____

North Carolina pension records indicate that he served in this company.

JOHNSON, LUCIAN B., Private

Born in Chatham County where he resided as a farmer or farm laborer prior to enlisting in Chatham County at age 19, July 7, 1862, for the war. Died on October 11, 1862. Place and cause of death not reported.

JOHNSON, R. N., Private

Resided in Chatham County where he enlisted on September 11, 1862, for the war. Captured at Kinston on December 14, 1862. Paroled on December 15, 1862. Reported present but sick in quarters in January-February, 1863. Returned to duty in March-April, 1863. Deserted on August 22, 1863. Returned to duty in January, 1864. Reported present in February-October, 1864. Deserted on December 24, 1864.

JOHNSON, THOMAS M., Private

Born in Chatham County where he resided as a farmer prior to enlisting in Chatham County at age 31, September 11, 1862, for the war. Reported sick in hospital at Wilson in November, 1862-February, 1863. Discharged at Wilson on March 4, 1863, by reason of "phthisis pulmonalis."

JOHNSON, W. H., Private

Born in Wake County and resided in Chatham County where he was by occupation a farmer prior to enlisting in Chatham County at age 23, July 17, 1862, for the war. Reported sick in hospital at Goldsboro in November-December, 1862. Hospitalized at Wilmington on or about February 6, 1863, with pneumonia. Furloughed on March 4, 1863. Reported absent sick in May, 1863-June, 1864, and September-October, 1864. Dropped from the company rolls in November-December, 1864, for prolonged absence.

JONES, DAVID A., Private

Resided in Chatham County and was by occupation a farmer. Company records indicate that he enlisted in Chatham County at age 29, April 5, 1862; however, he was not listed on the rolls of this company until September-October, 1864. Captured at Fort Harrison, Virginia, September 30, 1864. Confined at Point Lookout, Maryland, October 5, 1864. Paroled at Point Lookout on March 17, 1865. Received at Boulware's Wharf, James River, Virginia, March 19, 1865, for exchange. Hospitalized at Richmond, Virginia, the same date with scorbutus. Furloughed for thirty days on March 24, 1865.

JONES, JOHN, Private

Resided in Chatham County where he enlisted on August 12, 1862, for the war. Was apparently discharged on or about September 29, 1862. Reason discharged not reported. Reenlisted in the company in Chatham County on September 15, 1864, for the war. Wounded in the side at Fort Harrison, Virginia, September 30, 1864. Hospitalized at Richmond, Virginia. Reported absent wounded or absent sick through December 31, 1864. No further records.

JONES, RICHARD MONROE, Private

Born in Chatham County on April 9, 1840. Resided in Chatham County where he enlisted at age 21, April 5, 1862. Transferred to Company F, 53rd Regiment N.C. Troops, in May, 1862. Reenlisted in this company on an unspecified date (probably in the summer of 1864) after deserting from the 53rd North Carolina. Wounded in the left hip at Fort Harrison, Virginia, September 30, 1864. Hospitalized at Richmond, Virginia. Furloughed for thirty days on October 14, 1864. Reported absent sick in November-December, 1864. No further records. Survived the war. [Contrary to 13:126 of this series, his first name was Richard rather than Robert.]

JONES, S. FRANKLIN, Private

Resided in Chatham County where he enlisted on April 5, 1862. Transferred to Company F, 53rd Regiment N.C. Troops, in May, 1862. Reenlisted in this company on an unspecified date (probably in the summer of 1864) after deserting from the 53rd North Carolina. Wounded in the left leg at Fort Harrison, Virginia, September 30, 1864. Hospitalized at Richmond, Virginia. Furloughed for sixty days on November 17, 1864. No further records. [Contrary to 13:126 of this series, his first initial was S rather than F.]

JONES, T. J., Private

Resided in Chatham County where he enlisted on April 7, 1862. Transferred to Company F, 53rd Regiment N.C. Troops, in May, 1862. [See special note at the end of the history of Company D, 61st Regiment N.C. Troops (page 678). Contrary to 13:126 of this series, his middle initial was J rather than G.]

JORDAN, H. E., Private

Resided in Chatham County where he enlisted on May 1, 1863, for the war. Mustered in as Sergeant. Reported present through August 31, 1863. Hospitalized at Petersburg, Virginia, February 26, 1864, with debilitas. Transferred to another hospital on March 19, 1864. Returned to duty on an unspecified date. Reduced to ranks on June 1, 1864. Wounded in the chest, neck, and/or shoulder at Cold Harbor, Virginia, June 1, 1864. Hospitalized at Richmond, Virginia, where he died on June 15, 1864, of wounds.

LEWIS, JAMES J., Private

Resided in Chatham County where he enlisted on May 25, 1863, for the war. Reported in hospital at Columbia, South Carolina, on or about August 31, 1863. Returned to duty prior to March 1, 1864. Reported present through June 30, 1864. Wounded in the hip at Fort Harrison, Virginia, September 30, 1864. Hospitalized at Richmond, Virginia. Furloughed on October 20, 1864. Deserted on December 24, 1864.

LEWIS, JOHN MANLY, Private

Resided in Chatham County where he enlisted on October 21, 1862, for the war. Reported present through April 30, 1863. Reported sick at home in May-August, 1863. Reported absent without leave for three months on an unspecified date. Returned to duty prior to March 1, 1864. Reported present through June 30, 1864. Captured at Fort Harrison, Virginia, September 30, 1864. Confined at Point Lookout, Maryland, October 5, 1864. Died at Point Lookout on April 3, 1865, of "pneumonia" and/or "measles."

LEWIS, WILLIAM M., Private

Resided in Chatham County where he enlisted on October 21, 1862, for the war. Reported present through April 30, 1863. Deserted on August 22, 1863. Returned to duty on or about January 6, 1864. Reported present through June 30, 1864. Captured at Fort Harrison, Virginia, September 30, 1864. Confined at Point Lookout,

Maryland, October 5, 1864. Released at Point Lookout on June 28, 1865, after taking the Oath of Allegiance.

LOVE, J. W., Private

Born in Moore County and resided in Chatham County where he was by occupation a farmer prior to enlisting in Chatham County at age 22, August 7, 1862, for the war. Reported present but sick in November-December, 1862. Returned to duty in January-February, 1863. Reported present through February 29, 1864. Killed near Petersburg, Virginia, June 17, 1864.

LOVE, WILLIAM A., Private

Born in Moore County where he resided as a farmer prior to enlisting in Chatham County at age 26, August 7, 1862, for the war. Captured and paroled at Kinston on December 14, 1862. Died at home in Moore County on January 15, 1863, of "typh[oid] fever."

LOYD, J. B., Private

Resided in Chatham County where he enlisted at age 17, May 27, 1863, for the war. Captured at Morris Island, Charleston Harbor, South Carolina, August 26, 1863. Confined at Hilton Head, South Carolina, September 1, 1863. Transferred to Fort Columbus, New York Harbor, where he arrived on September 22, 1863. Transferred to Point Lookout, Maryland, where he arrived on September 26, 1863. Transferred to Elmira, New York, August 16, 1864. Paroled at Elmira on October 11, 1864. Received at Venus Point, Savannah River, Georgia, November 15, 1864, for exchange. No further records.

McDANIEL, ALEXANDER, Private

Resided in Chatham County and was by occupation a farmer prior to enlisting in Chatham County at age 30, September 22, 1862, for the war. Reported present but sick in November-April, 1862. Reported present in January-April, 1863. Apparently deserted on an unspecified date. Apprehended and court-martialed prior to August 17, 1863, and sentenced to be shot. Released under the terms of a presidential proclamation and returned to duty. Captured at Morris Island, Charleston Harbor, South Carolina, August 26, 1863. Confined at Hilton Head, South Carolina, September 1, 1863. Transferred to Fort Columbus, New York Harbor, where he arrived on September 22, 1863. Transferred to Point Lookout, Maryland, where he arrived on September 26, 1863. Hospitalized at Point Lookout on November 10, 1863, with a gunshot wound of the left ankle. Was presumably shot by a guard. Died the same date of wounds.

McQUEEN, JOHN W., Private

Born in Moore County where he resided as a farmer prior to enlisting in Chatham County at age 24, August 7, 1862, for the war. Reported sick in hospital in November, 1862-February, 1863. Returned to duty in March-April, 1863. Reported present in May, 1863-June, 1864, and September-December, 1864. No further records. Survived the war.

MANESS, MATTHEW, Private

Resided in Chatham County where he enlisted on July 1, 1863, for the war. Captured at Morris Island, Charleston Harbor, South Carolina, August 26, 1863. Confined at Hilton Head, South Carolina. Transferred to Fort Columbus, New York Harbor, where he arrived on September 22, 1863. Transferred to Point Lookout, Maryland, where he arrived on September 26, 1863. Transferred to Elmira, New York, August 16, 1864. Paroled at Elmira on October 11, 1864. Received at Venus Point, Savannah River, Georgia, November 15, 1864, for exchange. No further records.

MANN, JOHNSON O., Private

Resided in Chatham County and was by occupation a farmer prior to enlisting in Chatham County at age 26, November 19, 1862, for the war. Listed as a deserter on or about January 1, 1863. Apparently reported for duty on an unspecified date but deserted on July 9, 1863. Returned to duty subsequent to June 30, 1864. Wounded in the left hip at Fort Harrison, Virginia, September 30, 1864. Hospitalized at Richmond, Virginia. Furloughed for sixty days on November 4, 1864. No further records. Survived the war.

MARTIN, LARKIN, Private

Resided in Chatham County and was by occupation a farmer prior to enlisting in Chatham County at age 22, April 9, 1862. Apparently failed to report for duty. Enlisted in Company G, 26th Regiment N.C. Troops, January 25, 1864. Deserted from that unit on April 20, 1864. Reported for duty with this company on or about September 20, 1864. Wounded in the hand and arm at Fort Harrison, Virginia, September 30, 1864. Arm amputated. Hospitalized at Richmond, Virginia, where he died on October 22, 1864, of wounds.

MARTIN, ROBERT, Private

Enlisted in Chatham County on October 11, 1862, for the war. Captured and paroled at Kinston on December 14, 1862. Returned to duty in January-February, 1863. Died in hospital at Wilmington on June 2, 1863, of "febris typhoides."

MIMS, WILLIAM H., Private

Born in Chatham County where he resided as a farmer prior to enlisting in Chatham County at age 26, August 11, 1862, for the war. Reported present but sick in November-December, 1862. Returned to duty in January-February, 1863. Captured at Morris Island, Charleston Harbor, South Carolina, August 26, 1863. Confined at Hilton Head, South Carolina, September 1, 1863. Transferred to Fort Columbus, New York Harbor, where he arrived on September 22, 1863. Transferred to Point Lookout, Maryland, where he arrived on September 26, 1863. Transferred to Elmira, New York, August 16, 1864. Paroled at Elmira on October 11, 1864. Received at Venus Point, Savannah River, Georgia, November 15, 1864, for exchange. No further records. Survived the war.

MITCHELL, EDWARD, Private

Born in Westmead, Ireland, and resided in Chatham County where he was by occupation a "sailor" prior to enlisting in Chatham County at age 36, July 7, 1862, for the war. Reported present in November, 1862-April, 1863. Captured at Morris Island, Charleston Harbor, South Carolina, August 26, 1863. Confined at Hilton Head, South Carolina, September 1, 1863. Transferred to Fort Columbus, New York Harbor, where he arrived on September 22, 1863. Transferred to Point Lookout, Maryland, where he arrived on September 26, 1863. Paroled at Point Lookout on April 27, 1864. Received at City Point, Virginia, April 30, 1864, for exchange. Hospitalized at Richmond, Virginia, May 1, 1864, with a dislocated left shoulder. Place and date injured not reported. Furloughed for thirty days on May 6, 1864. Reported sick in hospital at Raleigh on or about June 30, 1864. Retired to the Invalid Corps on December 24, 1864.

MOODY, JOHN, Private

Resided in Chatham County where he enlisted on April 9, 1862. Was reportedly transferred to the 26th Regiment N.C. Troops in May, 1862; however, records of the 26th Regiment do not indicate that he served therein. No further records. [See special note at the end of the history of Company D, 61st Regiment N.C. Troops (page 678).]

MORGAN, SPENCER P., Private

Born in Chatham County where he resided as a carpenter prior to enlisting in Chatham County at age 24, April 9, 1862. Reported present in November, 1862-April, 1863. Captured at Morris Island, Charleston Harbor, South Carolina, August 26, 1863. Confined at Hilton Head, South Carolina, September 1, 1863. Transferred to Fort Columbus, New York Harbor, where he arrived on September 22, 1863. Transferred to Point Lookout, Maryland, where he arrived on September 26, 1863. Released at Point Lookout on February 5, 1864, after taking the Oath of Allegiance and joining the U.S. Army. Assigned to Company D, 1st Regiment U.S. Volunteer Infantry.

MORGAN, WILLIAM ANDERSON, Private

Resided in Chatham County and was by occupation a shoemaker prior to enlisting in Chatham County at age 39, October 24, 1864, for the war. "Detailed in field shoe dept" in November-December, 1864. No further records.

NELSON, GEORGE, Private

Resided in Chatham County and was by occupation a day laborer prior to enlisting in Chatham County at age 40, April 9, 1862. Was reportedly transferred to the 26th Regiment N.C. Troops in May, 1862; however, records of the 26th Regiment do not indicate that he served therein. No further records. [See special note at the end of the history of Company D, 61st Regiment N.C. Troops (page 678).]

NOAH, RILEY, Private

Resided in Chatham County where he enlisted at age 37, June 1, 1863, for the war. Wounded at Morris Island, Charleston Harbor, South Carolina, on or about August 26, 1863. Hospitalized at Charleston. Returned to duty in September, 1863-February, 1864. Reported present in March-June and September-December, 1864. No further records.

OVERMAN, JACOB, Private

Resided in Chatham County and was by occupation a gem smith prior to enlisting in Chatham County at age 35, April 9, 1862. Was reportedly transferred to the 26th Regiment N.C. Troops in May, 1862; however, records of the 26th Regiment do not indicate that he served therein. No further records. Survived the war. [See special note at the end of the history of Company D, 61st Regiment N.C. Troops (page 678).]

PATTISHALL, W., Private

Resided in Chatham County and was by occupation a farmer prior to enlisting in Chatham County at age 25, August 8, 1862, for the war. No further records. [See special note at the end of the history of Company D, 61st Regiment N.C. Troops (page 678).]

PERRY, ADDISON H., Sergeant

Born in Chatham County where he resided as a farmer prior to enlisting in Chatham County at age 23, July 7, 1862, for the war. Mustered in as Private. Wounded in both hands and captured at Kinston on December 14, 1862. Paroled on December 15, 1862. Returned to duty in January-February, 1863. Reported present through February 29, 1864. Promoted to Sergeant on June 1, 1864.

Wounded in the nose and left cheek at Petersburg, Virginia, June 17, 1864. Hospitalized at Petersburg. Transferred to hospital at Raleigh on June 18, 1864. Returned to duty subsequent to June 30, 1864. Reported present in September-December, 1864. No further records. Survived the war.

PERRY, HENRY M., Private

Born in Chatham County where he resided as a farmer prior to enlisting in Chatham County at age 21, August 12, 1862, for the war. Reported present in November, 1862-April, 1863. Captured at Morris Island, Charleston Harbor, South Carolina, August 26, 1863. Confined at Hilton Head, South Carolina, September 1, 1863. No further records. Survived the war.

PERRY, J. N., Private

Resided in Chatham County where he enlisted on July 7, 1862, for the war. Deserted prior to January 1, 1863.

PERRY, JOHN J., Private

Previously served as Private in Company E, 63rd Regiment N.C. Troops (5th Regiment N.C. Cavalry). Transferred to this company on February 20, 1864. Reported absent sick on or about June 30, 1864, and in September-October, 1864. Returned to duty in November-December, 1864. Wounded in the jaw (fracture) at Kinston on March 8-10, 1865. Hospitalized at Raleigh. Transferred to another hospital on March 16, 1865. No further records.

PERRY, MARION, Private

Previously served as Private in Company E, 8th Regiment N.C. State Troops. Transferred to this company on August 29, 1864. Captured at Fort Harrison, Virginia, September 30, 1864. Confined at Point Lookout, Maryland, October 5, 1864. Paroled at Point Lookout on March 17, 1865. Received at Boulware's Wharf, James River, Virginia, March 19, 1865, for exchange. No further records. Survived the war.

PERRY, N. M., Private

Resided in Chatham County where he enlisted on July 7, 1862, for the war. Failed to report for duty. Listed as a deserter in November-December, 1862.

PERRY, ROBERT J., Private

Born in Chatham County where he resided as a farmer prior to enlisting in Chatham County at age 20, June 5, 1862, for the war. Reported present in November, 1862-April, 1863. Reported absent sick in May, 1863-June, 1864. Returned to duty prior to September 30, 1864, when he was captured at Fort Harrison, Virginia. Confined at Point Lookout, Maryland, October 5, 1864. Paroled at Point Lookout on October 30, 1864. Received at Venus Point, Savannah River, Georgia, November 15, 1864, for exchange. No further record.

PERRY, ROBERT M., Private

Born in Chatham County where he resided as a farmer prior to enlisting in Chatham County at age 24, September 11, 1862, for the war. Reported present in November, 1862-April, 1863. Reported sick at home in May, 1863-February, 1864. Hospitalized at Farmville, Virginia, on or about June 20, 1864, with hypertrophy of the heart. Furloughed for sixty days on or about July 21, 1864. Returned to duty prior to November 1, 1864. Reported absent sick at a field infirmary in November-December, 1864. No further records.

PERRY, S. J., Private

Enlisted in Chatham County on November 6, 1862, for the war. Reported present but sick in quarters in January-February, 1863. Returned to duty in March-April, 1863. Captured at Morris Island, Charleston Harbor, South Carolina, August 26, 1863. Confined at Hilton Head, South Carolina, September 1, 1863. Transferred to Fort Columbus, New York Harbor, where he arrived on September 22, 1863. Transferred to Point Lookout, Maryland, where he arrived on September 26, 1863. Died at Point Lookout on July 16, 1864, of "typh[oid] fever."

PERRY, THOMAS S., Private

Previously served as Private in Company G, 26th Regiment N.C. Troops. Transferred to this company on November 30, 1864, in exchange for Pvt. Henry C. Johnson. No further records.

PETTY, JAMES, Private

Born in Chatham County where he resided as a farmer or farm laborer prior to enlisting in Chatham County at age 27, July 12, 1862, for the war. Reported present in November-December, 1862. Hospitalized at Wilmington on or about January 10, 1863, with pneumonia. Returned to duty on January 15, 1863. Reported present through April 30, 1863. Died at home in Chatham County on June 29, 1863. Cause of death not reported.

PHILLIPS, ALBERT R., Private

Resided in Moore County and enlisted in Chatham County at age 17, January 12, 1864, for the war. Reported present through February 29, 1864. Wounded in the right forearm at Drewry's Bluff, Virginia, May 16, 1864. Hospitalized at Richmond, Virginia. Returned to duty prior to July 1, 1864. Reported present in September-December, 1864. No further records.

PHILLIPS, THOMAS J., Private

Born in Orange County and resided in Chatham County where he was by occupation a saddler prior to enlisting in Chatham County at age 49, July 8, 1862, for the war. Mustered in as Private. Reported sick in hospital at Goldsboro in November-December, 1862. Promoted to Sergeant prior to January 1, 1863. Hospitalized at Wilmington on February 6, 1863, with neuralgia. Returned to duty on February 18, 1863. Reduced to ranks in May-August, 1863. Detailed as a hospital nurse at Wilmington on July 28, 1863. Returned to duty on October 14, 1864. Reported absent in a field infirmary in November-December, 1864. Hospitalized at Wilmington on February 3, 1865, with rheumatism. No further records.

PILKENTON, ISAAC, Private

Born in Chatham County where he resided as a farmer or laborer prior to enlisting in Chatham County at age 18, September 12, 1862, for the war. Reported present in November, 1862-April, 1863. Captured at Morris Island, Charleston Harbor, South Carolina, August 26, 1863. Confined at Hilton Head, South Carolina, September 1, 1863. Transferred to Fort Columbus, New York Harbor, where he arrived on September 22, 1863. Transferred to Point Lookout, Maryland, where he arrived on September 26, 1863. Died at Point Lookout on or about January 11, 1864, of "diarrhoea."

PILKINTON, J. A., Private

Born in Chatham County where he resided as a shoemaker prior to enlisting in Chatham County at age 35, June 8, 1862, for the war. Died at Raleigh on December 29, 1862. Cause of death not reported.

POE, DAVID W., Private

Born in Chatham County where he resided as a farmer prior to enlisting in Chatham County at age 27, July 17, 1862, for the war. Reported present in November, 1862-April, 1863. Captured at Morris Island, Charleston Harbor, South Carolina, August 26, 1863. Confined at Hilton Head, South Carolina, September 1, 1863. Exchanged on an unspecified date; however, he had not rejoined the company as of December 31, 1864. No further records. Survived the war. [North Carolina pension records indicate that he lost his hearing at Charleston on an unspecified date.]

POE, TERRY, Private

Born in Chatham County where he resided as a laborer prior to enlisting in Chatham County at age 26, September 12, 1862, for the war. Died at Tarboro on or about November 25, 1862. Cause of death not reported.

RAINES, JOHN M., Private

Previously served as Private in Company E, 41st Regiment N.C. Troops (3rd Regiment N.C. Cavalry). Transferred to this company on April 4, 1864. Reported present in April-June and September-December, 1864. No further records.

RAMSEY, EDWARD B., 1st Sergeant

Previously served as Private in 2nd Company I, 32nd Regiment N.C. Troops. Transferred to this company in August, 1862. Mustered in as 1st Sergeant. Reported present or accounted for in November, 1862-February, 1864. Wounded in the breast at Petersburg, Virginia, June 17, 1864. Hospitalized at Petersburg. Reported absent on wounded furlough in September-October, 1864. Returned to duty prior to December 19, 1864, when he was hospitalized at Richmond, Virginia, with chronic diarrhoea. Deserted from hospital on or about March 11, 1865.

RIDDLE, DANIEL W., Corporal

Resided in Chatham County where he enlisted at age 23, March 1, 1863, for the war. Mustered in as Private. Reported present in March, 1863-June, 1864, and September-December, 1864. Promoted to Corporal on December 31, 1864. Captured in hospital at Raleigh on April 13, 1865. No further records. Survived the war.

RIDDLE, JAMES A., Private

Resided in Moore County and enlisted in Chatham County at age 17, December 23, 1863, for the war. Reported present through February 29, 1864. Captured near Petersburg, Virginia, June 16, 1864. Confined at Point Lookout, Maryland, June 19, 1864. Transferred to Elmira, New York, July 25, 1864. Released at Elmira on June 21, 1865, after taking the Oath of Allegiance.

ROBBINS, S., Musician

Resided in Chatham County and enlisted in Robeson County on July 1, 1863, for the war. Mustered in as Private. Appointed Musician on an unspecified date. Reported present through August 31, 1863. No further records.

ROLLINS, WYATT P., Private

Born in Chatham County where he resided as a farmer or carpenter prior to enlisting in Chatham County at age 26, August 11, 1862, for the war. Mustered in as Private. Reported present in November, 1862-April, 1863. Promoted to Corporal in May-August, 1863. Wounded in the head at Morris Island, Charleston Harbor, South Carolina, on or about August 26, 1863. Reported absent wounded or absent sick through June 30, 1864. Reduced to ranks on June 1,

1864. Reported absent sick in September-October, 1864. Hospitalized at Richmond, Virginia, December 17, 1864. Returned to duty on December 30, 1864. No further records. Survived the war.

RUSSELL, THOMAS INGRAM, Private

Resided in Chatham County where he enlisted at age 18, September 15, 1864, for the war. Wounded in the left thigh and captured at Fort Harrison, Virginia, September 30, 1864. Hospitalized at Fort Monroe, Virginia, where he died on November 5, 1864, of wounds.

SANDERS, J. W., Private

Resided in Chatham County where he enlisted at age 20, March 1, 1863, for the war. Reported present but sick in quarters in March-April, 1863. Returned to duty in May-August, 1863. Reported present through February 29, 1864. Hospitalized at Petersburg, Virginia, May 21, 1864, with acute diarrhoea. Transferred to hospital at Kittrell's Springs on June 18, 1864. Transferred to hospital at Raleigh on an unspecified date. Returned to duty on or about June 28, 1864. Hospitalized at Richmond, Virginia, October 21, 1864, with ascites. Furloughed for sixty days on November 11, 1864. No further records.

SELF, WILLIAM, Private

Born in Chatham County where he resided as a farmer prior to enlisting in Chatham County at age 21, September 17, 1862, for the war. Reported present in November, 1862-April, 1863. Captured at Morris Island, Charleston Harbor, South Carolina, August 26, 1863. Confined at Hilton Head, South Carolina, September 1, 1863. Transferred to Fort Columbus, New York Harbor, where he arrived on October 6, 1863. Transferred to Point Lookout, Maryland, where he arrived on October 11, 1863. Paroled at Point Lookout on September 18, 1864. Received at Varina, Virginia, September 22, 1864, for exchange. Reported absent sick in November-December, 1864. No further records. Survived the war.

SEYMOUR, DAVID D., Private

Resided in Chatham County where he enlisted at age 21, May 8, 1862, for the war. Transferred to 2nd Company I, 32nd Regiment N.C. Troops, September 4, 1862. [See special note at the end of the history of Company D, 61st Regiment N.C. Troops (page 678).]

SHAW, JOHN, Private

Resided in Chatham County and enlisted on April 5, 1862. Transferred to Company F, 53rd Regiment N.C. Troops, in May, 1862. Reenlisted in this company on an unspecified date (probably in the summer of 1864) after deserting from the 53rd North Carolina. Wounded in the arm at Fort Harrison, Virginia, September 30, 1864. Hospitalized at Richmond, Virginia. Transferred to hospital at Wilmington on an unspecified date. Returned to duty on January 5, 1865. Paroled at Greensboro on May 1, 1865. [Was about 23 years of age at time of enlistment.]

SHAW, WILLIAM, Private

Born in Orange County and resided in Chatham County where he was by occupation a farmer prior to enlisting Chatham County at age 24, April 5, 1862. Transferred to Company F, 53rd Regiment N.C. Troops, in May, 1862. Reenlisted in this company on an unspecified date (probably in the summer of 1864) after deserting from the 53rd North Carolina. Captured at Fort Harrison, Virginia, September 30, 1864. Confined at Point Lookout, Maryland, October 5, 1864. Released at Point Lookout on or about October 15, 1864, after taking the Oath of Allegiance and joining the U.S. Army. Assigned to Company C, 4th Regiment U.S. Volunteer Infantry.

SLOAN, ALEXANDER H., Sergeant

Born in Chatham County where he resided as a farmer prior to enlisting in Chatham County at age 22, July 17, 1862, for the war. Mustered in as Sergeant. Wounded in the right arm at Kinston on December 14, 1862. Reported absent wounded until he was discharged on or about May 1, 1863, by reason of disability from wounds.

SLOAN, DAVID, Private

Born in Chatham County where he resided as a farmer prior to enlisting in Chatham County at age 26, July 17, 1862, for the war. Reported absent sick (apparently suffering from phthisis pulmonalis) in November, 1862-August, 1863. Returned to duty prior to March 1, 1864. Wounded in the shoulder at or near Drewry's Bluff, Virginia, May 18, 1864. Returned to duty subsequent to June 30, 1864. Captured at Fort Harrison, Virginia, September 30, 1864. Confined at Point Lookout, Maryland, October 5, 1864. Paroled at Point Lookout on March 17, 1865. Received at Boulware's Wharf, James River, Virginia, March 19, 1865, for exchange. Hospitalized at Richmond, Virginia, the same date. Transferred to another hospital on March 20, 1865. No further records. Survived the war.

SMITH, GEORGE W., Private

Previously served as Private in Company E, 63rd Regiment N.C. Troops (5th Regiment N.C. Cavalry). Transferred to this company on February 20, 1864. Reported present in March-June, 1864. Hospitalized at Richmond, Virginia, on or about October 31, 1864, with chronic diarrhoea. Returned to duty on December 26, 1864. No further records.

SMITH, L., Private

Resided in Chatham County and enlisted in Lenoir County on April 19, 1862, for the war. Was reportedly transferred to the 26th Regiment N.C. Troops on an unspecified date; however, records of the 26th Regiment do not indicate that he served therein. No further records.

SMITH, SANFORD A., Private

Previously served as Private in Company E, 63rd Regiment N.C. Troops (5th Regiment N.C. Cavalry). Transferred to this company on February 20, 1864. Wounded in the thigh at Drewry's Bluff, Virginia, May 14, 1864. Hospitalized at Richmond, Virginia. Reported in hospital at Fayetteville in September-October, 1864. Returned to duty in November-December, 1864. No further records. Survived the war.

SNIPES, C. M., Private

Resided in Chatham County where he enlisted on May 28, 1863, for the war. No further records.

STANLY, ATLAS J., Private

Resided in Chatham County and was by occupation a farm laborer prior to enlisting in Lenoir County at age 18, April 19, 1862, for the war. Transferred to Company E, 26th Regiment N.C. Troops, on or about May 15, 1862. [See special note at the end of the history of Company D, 61st Regiment N.C. Troops (page 678).]

STEDMAN, ROBERT WINSHIP, Private

Previously served as Private in 2nd Company B, 36th Regiment N.C. Troops (2nd Regiment N.C. Artillery). Transferred to this company on November 29, 1862. Reported present through April 30, 1863. Reported in hospital at Charleston, South Carolina, in

May-August, 1863. Appointed 3rd Lieutenant of Company A, 44th Regiment N.C. Troops, December 1, 1863, and transferred. ["During the bombardment of Battery Wagner . . . on the 29th July, 1863, the enemy got the range of a ten-inch columbiad so completely as to render the place [one] of extreme danger, and the South Carolina troops that manned the gun left it and ran into the bomb proof for shelter. Their captain ordered them back to their post, but they refused, for a time, to obey. While the men were wrangling with their officer, a soldier named Steadman [sic] . . . by himself, loaded, sighted, and fired the abandoned gun, hitting the Yankee boat at which he shot, while a hundred balls where whistling around him." (Charlotte *Western Democrat*, August 18, 1863).]

STONE, ANDREW J., Private

Born in Chatham County where he resided as a farmer prior to enlisting in Chatham County at age 30, August 8, 1862, for the war. Reported present in November, 1862-February, 1864. Killed at Drewry's Bluff, Virginia, May 18, 1864.

STONE, JOSEPH M., Private

Resided in Chatham County where he enlisted at age 17, December 1, 1863, for the war. Reported present or accounted for through June 30, 1864. Wounded in the right leg at Fort Harrison, Virginia, September 30, 1864. Hospitalized at Richmond, Virginia. Furloughed for sixty days on November 9, 1864. No further records. Survived the war.

STRAUGHAN, ISAAC H., Corporal

Born in Chatham County where he resided as a farmer prior to enlisting in Chatham County at age 19, July 16, 1862, for the war. Mustered in as Corporal. Reported present in November, 1862-April, 1863. Captured at Morris Island, Charleston Harbor, South Carolina, August 26, 1863. Confined at Hilton Head, South Carolina, September 1, 1863. Transferred to Fort Columbus, New York Harbor, where he arrived on October 6, 1863. Transferred to Point Lookout, Maryland, where he arrived on October 11, 1863. Paroled at Point Lookout on February 10, 1865. Received at Cox's Wharf, James River, Virginia, February 14-15, 1865, for exchange. No further records. Survived the war.

TALLY, JOHN, Private

Previously served as Private in Company E, 63rd Regiment N.C. Troops (5th Regiment N.C. Cavalry). Transferred to this company on April 12, 1864. Reported for duty subsequent to June 30, 1864. Wounded in the hand at Fort Harrison, Virginia, September 30, 1864. Hospitalized at Richmond, Virginia, where he deserted on October 10, 1864.

THOMAS, JAMES M., Private

Resided in Chatham County where he enlisted at age 18, August 7, 1863, for the war. Apparently failed to report for duty and was reported absent without leave prior to February 29, 1864. Reported for duty prior to June 15-16, 1864, when he was captured near Petersburg, Virginia. Confined at Point Lookout, Maryland, June 19, 1864. Released at Point Lookout on June 20, 1865, after taking the Oath of Allegiance.

THOMAS, M. G., Private

Born in Chatham County where he resided as a farmer prior to enlisting in Chatham County at age 20, July 14, 1862, for the war. Reported present in November-December, 1862. Hospitalized at Wilmington on an unspecified date. Returned to duty on February

27, 1863. Reported present in March-April, 1863. Wounded in the head and captured at Morris Island, Charleston Harbor, South Carolina, August 26, 1863. Hospitalized at Beaufort, South Carolina, September 1, 1863. Confined in various Federal hospitals until he was exchanged at Charleston on September 23, 1864. Furloughed for sixty days on October 18, 1864. Reported absent sick in November-December, 1864. No further records. Survived the war.

THOMAS, SAMUEL, Private

Resided in Chatham County where he enlisted at age 20, April 7, 1862. Transferred to Company F, 53rd Regiment N.C. Troops, in May, 1862. Reenlisted in this company on an unspecified date (probably in the summer of 1864) after deserting from the 53rd North Carolina. Wounded in the right foot and captured at Fort Harrison, Virginia, September 30, 1864. Hospitalized at Fort Monroe, Virginia. Transferred to the prison at Fort Monroe on January 16, 1865. Transferred to Point Lookout, Maryland, February 1, 1865. Paroled at Point Lookout on February 18, 1865. Received at Boulware's and Cox's Wharves, James River, Virginia, February 20-21, 1865, for exchange. No further records. Survived the war.

THOMAS, WILLIAM, Private

Resided in Chatham County where he enlisted on or about September 15, 1864, for the war. Wounded in the foot at Fort Harrison, Virginia, September 30, 1864. Hospitalized at Richmond, Virginia. Furloughed on October 29, 1864. No further records.

THOMAS, WILLIAM M., Private

Born in Chatham County where he resided as a farmer prior to enlisting in Chatham County at age 21, July 14, 1862, for the war. Reported sick in hospital at Wilson in November, 1862-February, 1863. Returned to duty in March-April, 1863. Reported present through June 30, 1864. Wounded in the right foot at Fort Harrison, Virginia, September 30, 1864. Hospitalized at Richmond, Virginia. Furloughed for sixty days on or about October 28, 1864. Reported absent without leave on or about December 31, 1864. No further records. Survived the war.

THOMPSON, MONROE, Private

Born in Chatham County where he resided as a farmer prior to enlisting in Chatham County at age 26, September 12, 1862, for the war. Died at Tarboro on November 22, 1862. Cause of death not reported.

THROWER, S. W., Private

Resided in Richmond County and enlisted in Chatham County at age 17, October 23, 1863, for the war. Reported present through February 29, 1864. Captured near Petersburg, Virginia, June 17-18, 1864. Confined at Point Lookout, Maryland, June 24, 1864. Paroled at Point Lookout on March 14, 1865. Received at Boulware's Wharf, James River, Virginia, March 16, 1865, for exchange. No further records. Survived the war.

TOMLINSON, WILLIAM H., Private

Born in Chatham County where he resided as a farmer prior to enlisting in Chatham County at age 23, July 7, 1862, for the war. Reported present in November, 1862-April, 1863. Died at home in Chatham County in July, 1863. Cause of death not reported.

VAN DUYN, SIMON PETER, Private

Born in Somerset County, New Jersey, and resided in Chatham County where he was by occupation a carriage maker prior to enlisting in Chatham County at age 33, July 15, 1862, for the war. Mustered in as Private. Reported present or accounted for in November, 1862-April, 1863. Wounded in the cheek at Drewry's Bluff, Virginia, May 18, 1864. Hospitalized at Petersburg, Virginia. Promoted to Corporal on June 1, 1864. Returned to duty on July 17, 1864. Reduced to ranks on an unspecified date. Killed near Petersburg on September 9, 1864.

WARD, JAMES M., Private
Resided in Chatham County and enlisted on May 25, 1863, for the war. No further records. Survived the war.

WEBSTER, ALEXANDER W., Sergeant
Resided in Chatham County and enlisted at age 24, April 19, 1862, for the war. Mustered in as Sergeant. Transferred to Company E, 26th Regiment N.C. Troops, in April-June, 1862. [See special note at the end of the history of Company D, 61st Regiment N.C. Troops (page 678).]

WEBSTER, BASIL E., Sergeant
Born in Chatham County where he resided as a farmer prior to enlisting in Chatham County at age 23, July 16, 1862, for the war. Mustered in as Private. Promoted to Corporal on December 27, 1862. Reported present in November, 1862-June, 1864. Promoted to Sergeant on June 1, 1864. Reported present in September-October, 1864. Reported absent with leave in November-December, 1864. No further records. Survived the war.

WEBSTER, M. J., Private
Born in Chatham County where he resided as a shoemaker prior to enlisting in Chatham County at age 33, September 13, 1862, for the war. Reported present or accounted for in November, 1862-April, 1863. Captured at Morris Island, Charleston Harbor, South Carolina, August 26, 1863. Confined at Hilton Head, South Carolina, September 1, 1863. Transferred to Fort Columbus, New York Harbor, where he arrived on October 6, 1863. Transferred to Point Lookout, Maryland, October 9, 1863. Died in hospital at Point Lookout on November 11, 1863, of "chronic diarrhoea."

WEBSTER, NATHAN, Corporal
Born in Chatham County where he resided as a farmer prior to enlisting in Chatham County at age 27, July 16, 1862, for the war. Mustered in as Corporal. Died on December 24 or December 26, 1862. Place and cause of death not reported.

WEBSTER, NORMAN A., Private
Born in Chatham County where he resided as a farmer prior to enlisting in Chatham County at age 19, July 16, 1862, for the war. Captured at Kinston on December 14, 1862. Paroled on December 15, 1862. Returned to duty subsequent to April 30, 1863. Hospitalized at Wilmington on July 22, 1863, with a wound of the left eye. Place and date wounded not reported. Returned to duty on August 8, 1863. Reported present through February 29, 1864. Wounded in the finger (left hand) at Drewry's Bluff, Virginia, on or about May 12, 1864. Hospitalized at Richmond, Virginia. Returned to duty subsequent to June 30, 1864. Wounded in the hand at Fort Harrison, Virginia, September 30, 1864. Hospitalized at Richmond. Reported absent sick in November-December, 1864. No further records. Survived the war.

WHITEHEAD, JOHN W., Private
Born in Chatham County where he resided as a miller prior to enlisting in Chatham County at age 23, September 8, 1862, for the war. Reported present in November, 1862-April, 1863. Deserted on August 18, 1863. Returned to duty in September-October, 1864. Deserted on December 24, 1864.

WHITEHEAD, NEWTON, Private
Born in Chatham County where he resided as a farmer prior to enlisting in Chatham County at age 26, July 15, 1862, for the war. Reported present in November-December, 1862. Reported sick at home from January 25, 1863, through June 30, 1864. Dropped from the company rolls in September-October, 1864, for prolonged absence.

WHITEHEAD, OLIVER, Private
Born in Chatham County where he resided as a farmer prior to enlisting in Chatham County at age 32, September 11, 1862, for the war. Hospitalized at Wilmington on or about December 31, 1862, with chronic diarrhoea. Returned to duty on or about February 9, 1863. Reported in hospital at Columbia, South Carolina, in March-April, 1863. Reported sick at home in May-August, 1863. Returned to duty prior to March 1, 1864. Wounded in the right elbow near Petersburg, Virginia, June 17, 1864. Hospitalized at Petersburg where he died on or about July 20, 1864, of wounds.

WICKER, BENJAMIN FRANKLIN, Private
Born in Moore County and resided in Chatham County where he was by occupation a farmer prior to enlisting in Chatham County at age 21, August 7, 1862, for the war. Reported present in November, 1862-April, 1863. Right arm "shot off" at Morris Island, Charleston Harbor, South Carolina, on or about August 26, 1863. Reported absent wounded until July 13, 1864, when he was retired to the Invalid Corps.

WILLIAMS, E. W., Private
Resided in Chatham County where he enlisted at age 17, January 1, 1864, for the war. Reported absent sick in March-June and September-October, 1864. Returned to duty in November-December, 1864. No further records. Survived the war. [North Carolina pension records indicate that he was wounded in the arm and collarbone by a shell on an unspecified date.]

WILLIAMS, JOHN B., Private
Born in Chatham County where he resided as a farmer prior to enlisting in Wayne County at age 30, September 13, 1862, for the war. Captured at Kinston on December 14, 1862. Paroled on December 15, 1862. Returned to duty prior to January 1, 1863. Reported present through April 30, 1863. Captured at Morris Island, Charleston Harbor, South Carolina, August 26, 1863. Confined at Hilton Head, South Carolina, September 1, 1863. Transferred to Fort Columbus, New York Harbor, where he arrived on October 6, 1863. Transferred to Point Lookout, Maryland, October 9, 1863. Released at Point Lookout on January 25, 1864, after taking the Oath of Allegiance and joining the U.S. Navy.

WOMACK, JEFFERSON, Private
Born in Chatham County where he resided as a farmer prior to enlisting in Chatham County at age 25, August 11, 1862, for the war. Died at Raleigh on January 29, 1863, of "pneumonia."

WOMACK, JOHN R., Private
Previously served as Private in Company G, 63rd Regiment N.C. Troops (5th Regiment N.C. Cavalry). Transferred to this company on July 28, 1864. Reported absent sick on or about October 31,

1864. Returned to duty in November-December, 1864. No further records.

WOMACK, WILLIAM MARION, Private

Born in Chatham County where he resided as a farmer prior to enlisting in Chatham County at age 22, August 11, 1862, for the war. Reported present in November, 1862-June, 1864, and September-December, 1864. No further records. Survived the war.

WORKMAN, J., Private

Resided in Chatham County where he enlisted on April 9, 1862. Was reportedly transferred to the 26th Regiment N.C. Troops in April, 1862; however, records of the 26th Regiment do not indicate that he served therein. [See special note at the end of the history of Company D, 61st Regiment N.C. Troops (page 678).]

WRIGHT, THOMAS J., Private

Born in Chatham County where he resided as a farmer prior to enlisting in Chatham County at age 22, July 14, 1862, for the war. Deserted on December 17, 1862. Returned to duty subsequent to February 28, 1863. Captured at Morris Island, Charleston Harbor, South Carolina, August 26, 1863. Confined at Hilton Head, South Carolina, September 1, 1863. Transferred to Fort Columbus, New York Harbor, where he arrived on October 6, 1863. Transferred to Point Lookout, Maryland, October 9, 1863. Paroled at Point Lookout on February 10, 1865. Received at Cox's Wharf, James River, Virginia, February 14-15, 1865, for exchange. Reported present at Richmond, Virginia, February 17, 1865. No further records.

WRIGHTSMAN, ALFRED, Private

Resided in Chatham County where he enlisted at age 46, November 9, 1863, for the war. Reported present through February 29, 1864. Wounded in the back at Drewry's Bluff, Virginia, on or about May 13, 1864. Hospitalized at Richmond, Virginia. Hospitalized at Petersburg, Virginia, June 17, 1864, with dysentery. Returned to duty subsequent to June 30, 1864. Reported present in September-October, 1864. Hospitalized at Richmond on November 1, 1864, with ascites. Furloughed for sixty days on or about December 9, 1864. No further records.

WRIGHTSMAN, R., Private

Place and date of enlistment not reported (probably enlisted subsequent to December 31, 1864). Paroled at Greensboro on May 17, 1865.

COMPANY E

This company, known as the "Eastern Stars" ("Easter Star" or "Easter Stars" according to some sources), was raised in Lenoir and Greene Counties in the late winter and spring of 1862 and was known as Capt. Allen Croom's Independent Company. It was mustered into state service at Camp Mangum, near Raleigh, May 26, 1862. On or about September 29, 1862, the company was assigned to the newly organized 59th Regiment N.C. Troops. That unit was redesignated the 61st Regiment N.C. Troops on an unknown date between October 30 and November 22, 1862. This company was designated Company E. After joining the regiment the company functioned as a part of the regiment, and its history for the remainder of the war is reported as a part of the regimental history.

The following roster was compiled primarily from information in the microfilm edition of the Compiled Service Records of Soldiers Who Served in Organizations from the State of North Carolina (Record Group 109, MC 270), National Archives and Records Administration, Washington, D.C. Record Group 109 includes enlistment papers, pay vouchers, requisitions, letters of resignation, discharge certificates, and abstracts of medical and prisoner of war returns. Materials relating specifically to Company E of the 61st Regiment include a company muster-in and descriptive roll dated May 26, 1862, and company muster rolls for November, 1862-December, 1863; March-April, 1864; and September-December, 1864.

Also utilized in this roster were *The War of the Rebellion: A Compilation of the Official Records of the Union and Confederate Armies*, the North Carolina adjutant general's *Roll of Honor*, state militia records, newspaper casualty lists and obituaries, wartime claims for bounty pay and allowances, postwar registers of claims for artificial limbs, Confederate pension applications filed with the states of North Carolina, Tennessee, and Florida, Confederate Soldiers' Home records, and the 1860 and 1870 federal censuses of North Carolina. A search was made also for relevant letters, diaries, reminiscences, and other manuscripts in the Southern Historical Collection (University of North Carolina-Chapel Hill), the Duke University Library Special Collections Department, and the North Carolina Division of Archives and History.

Among the secondary sources consulted were records of the North Carolina division of the United Daughters of the Confederacy, postwar rosters, regimental and county histories, marriage bond, will, and cemetery indexes, published and unpublished genealogies, biographical dictionaries, the North Carolina *County Heritage Book* series, the *Confederate Veteran*, Walter Clark's *Histories of the Several Regiments and Battalions from North Carolina in the Great War, 1861-'65*, and the North Carolina volume of the extended edition of *Confederate Military History*.

Note: The following roster contains service records for fourteen men who enlisted in Captain Croom's Independent Company but whose service terminated prior to September 29, 1862, the date the company was mustered into the 59th Regiment N.C. Troops (later redesignated the 61st Regiment N.C. Troops). Those men, it will be evident, never served in the 61st Regiment. Their service records are included here because too little information survives to compile a roster for Croom's Independent Company (which is not to be confused with Croom's Company, N.C. Local Defense Troops). All service records falling into the early-termination category conclude with a "special note" alerting readers to that fact and referring them to the information contained in this paragraph.

OFFICERS

CAPTAINS

CROOM, ALLEN

Previously served as 2nd Lieutenant of Company K, 33rd Regiment N.C. Troops. Appointed Captain of this company on an unspecified date (probably in July-August, 1862) to rank from April 1, 1862. Company records indicate that he was captured and paroled at Kinston on December 14, 1862; however, records of the Federal Provost Marshal do not substantiate that report. Reported sick in hospital at Charleston, South Carolina, and at Wilmington in January-February, 1863. Reported absent on sick furlough from March 3 through June 30, 1863. Resigned on July 1, 1863. Reason he resigned not reported. Later served as Captain of Croom's Company, N.C. Local Defense Troops.

BIGGS, JOHN DAWSON, SR.

Served as 1st Lieutenant (later Captain) of Company H of this regiment. Reported on duty as acting commander of this company in November-December, 1862.

BYRD, WILLIAM S.

Born in Lenoir County where he resided as a lawyer prior to enlisting at age 29. Appointed 1st Lieutenant on April 1, 1862. Appointed acting Adjutant on September 20, 1862, and transferred to the Field and Staff of this regiment. Served as acting Adjutant during October-December, 1862; during part of March-April, 1863; and in May-June, 1863. Appointed Captain on July 1, 1863, and transferred back to this company. Reported absent without leave on August 10, 1863. Reported absent sick with a "severe attack of pleurisy" of two months' standing on October 7, 1863. Returned to duty in November-December, 1863. Reported present in March-April, 1864. Hospitalized at High Point on September 16, 1864, with chronic dysentery. Furloughed on September 17, 1864. Hospitalized at High Point on October 5, 1864, with pleuritis. Furloughed on October 6, 1864. Reported absent sick through December 31, 1864. Reported absent sick without leave on January 2, 1865. No further records.

LIEUTENANTS

CROOM, CHARLES SHEPPARD, 2nd Lieutenant

Previously served as Private in Company A, 40th Regiment N.C. Troops (3rd Regiment N.C. Artillery). Appointed 2nd Lieutenant of this company to rank from April 1, 1862. Resigned on August 29, 1862. Reason he resigned not reported. [See special note at the end of the history of Company E, 61st Regiment N.C. Troops (page 692).]

FIELDS, ALEXANDER, 3rd Lieutenant

Born in Lenoir County where he resided prior to enlisting at age 24. Date of appointment not reported (was probably appointed 3rd Lieutenant on or about April 1, 1862). Resigned on September 8, 186[2]. Reason he resigned not reported. [See special note at the end of the history of Company E, 61st Regiment N.C. Troops (page 692).]

JACKSON, JOHN Q., 1st Lieutenant

Born in Lenoir or Greene County in 1832. Resided in Greene County where he was by occupation a farmer prior to enlisting in Greene County at age 29, May 13, 1862, for the war. Mustered in as Sergeant. Appointed 2nd Lieutenant on August 29, 1862. Captured and paroled at Kinston on December 14, 1862. Returned to duty in January-February, 1863. Reported present and in command of the company in January-October, 1863. Promoted to 1st Lieutenant on July 1, 1863. Reported present in November-December, 1863, and March-April, 1864. Wounded in the arm at the Crater, near Petersburg, Virginia, July 30, 1864. Hospitalized at Richmond, Virginia. Furloughed for thirty days on or about August 15, 1864. Returned to duty prior to September 30, 1864, when he was captured at Fort Harrison, Virginia. Confined at Old Capitol Prison, Washington, D.C., October 6, 1864. Transferred to Fort Delaware, Delaware, October 21, 1864. Released at Fort Delaware on June 10, 1865, after taking the Oath of Allegiance.

KINSEY, JOSEPH, 2nd Lieutenant

Born in Jones County and resided in Lenoir County where he was by occupation a farmer prior to enlisting in Jones County at age 18, March 19, 1862. Mustered in as Private. Promoted to Sergeant on November 1, 1862. Reported present in November, 1862-June, 1863. Elected 3rd Lieutenant on May 16, 1863. Elected 2nd Lieutenant on July 1, 1863. Captured at Morris Island, Charleston Harbor, South Carolina, August 26, 1863. Confined at Hilton Head, South Carolina, September 1, 1863. Transferred to Fort Columbus, New York Harbor, where he arrived on October 6, 1863. Transferred to Johnson's Island, Ohio, where he arrived on October 10, 1863. Released at Johnson's Island on May 19, 1865, after taking the Oath of Allegiance.

NOBLE, STEPHEN WILLIAM, 3rd Lieutenant

Born in Lenoir County where he resided as a farmer or clerk prior to enlisting in Lenoir County at age 23, May 14, 1862, for the war. Mustered in as Sergeant. Appointed 3rd Lieutenant on September 20, 1862. Reported absent sick at Goldsboro on December 22, 1862. Appointed Captain of Company K of this regiment on April 26 or April 28, 1863. [Previously served as 2nd Lieutenant in the 20th Regiment N.C. Militia.]

RASBERRY, HENRY HOWARD, 3rd Lieutenant

Previously served as Private in Company I, 1st Regiment N.C. Infantry (6 months, 1861). Enlisted in this company in Greene County at age 24 on or about May 26, 1862, for the war. Mustered in as Corporal. Promoted to Sergeant prior to December 14, 1862, when he was captured and paroled at Kinston. Returned to duty in January-February, 1863. Promoted to 1st Sergeant on March 16, 1863. Reported present in March-June, 1863. Appointed 3rd Lieutenant on July 10, 1863. Reported sick in hospital at Mount Pleasant, South Carolina, August 30, 1863. Furloughed home on October 9, 1863. Returned to duty in November-December, 1863. Reported present in March-April and September-December, 1864. Paroled at Goldsboro on May 29, 1865. [Reported in command of the company near Petersburg, Virginia, June 17-30, 1864.]

NONCOMMISSIONED OFFICERS AND PRIVATES

ADAMS, JAMES T., Private

Resided in Greene County and was by occupation a farmer prior to enlisting in Greene County at age 32, July 15, 1862, for the war. Reported absent sick at Tarboro from October 24 through December 31, 1862. Reported absent without leave in January-February, 1863. Reported present but sick in March-April, 1863. Reported absent sick in May-August, 1863. Reported absent without leave from September 28 through October 31, 1863. Returned to duty in November-December, 1863. Reported present in March-April, 1864. Hospitalized at High Point on August 3, 1864, with phthisis pulmonalis. Furloughed on August 4, 1864. Reported absent sick in September-December, 1864. No further records. Survived the war.

BAKER, HENRY, Private

Enlisted in Greene County on July 15, 1862, for the war. Reported present or accounted for in November, 1862-April, 1864. Captured at Globe Tavern, Virginia, August 19, 1864. Confined at Point Lookout, Maryland, August 24, 1864. Hospitalized at Point Lookout on January 9, 1865. Died in hospital at Point Lookout on February 8, 1865, of "chronic diarrhoea."

BARFIELD, JAMES M., Private

Born on October 13, 1838. Enlisted in Greene County at age 23, July 15, 1862, for the war. Reported present or accounted for in

November, 1862-April, 1864. Reported sick in hospital at Richmond, Virginia, in September-October, 1864. Reported absent without leave on December 1, 1864. No further records. Survived the war.

BARFIELD, JONAS, Private

Enlisted in Greene County at age 19, July 15, 1862, for the war. Reported sick at home from August 1 through December 31, 1862. Died in camp at James Island, South Carolina, on or about February 20, 1863. Cause of death not reported.

BARFIELD, LOUIS L., Corporal

Born in Lenoir County and was by occupation a farmer prior to enlisting in Lenoir County at age 23, March 7, 1862. Mustered in as Private. Reported present or accounted for in November, 1862-December, 1863, and March-April, 1864. Promoted to Corporal in May-October, 1864. Reported present in September-December, 1864. No further records. Survived the war. [North Carolina pension records indicate that he was wounded in the left arm at Cold Harbor, Virginia, on an unspecified date.]

BARFIELD, WALTER, _____

North Carolina pension records indicate that he served in this company.

BARNETT, JAMES, Private

Resided in Lenoir County where he enlisted at age 18, January 15, 1863, for the war. Reported present or accounted for through June 30, 1863. Captured at Morris Island, Charleston Harbor, South Carolina, August 26, 1863. Confined at Hilton Head, South Carolina, September 1, 1863. Transferred to Fort Columbus, New York Harbor, where he arrived on September 22, 1863. Transferred to Point Lookout, Maryland, where he arrived on September 26, 1863. Transferred to Elmira, New York, August 16, 1864. Paroled at Elmira on March 10, 1865. Received at Boulware's Wharf, James River, Virginia, March 15, 1865, for exchange. No further records.

BEDARD, NOAH T., Private

Born in Lenoir County on September 5, 1843. Resided in Greene County prior to enlisting in Lenoir County at age 18, April 20, 1862, for the war. Failed to report for duty. Enlisted as Private in Company B, 63rd Regiment N.C. Troops (5th Regiment N.C. Cavalry), May 18, 1862. [See special note at the end of the history of Company E, 61st Regiment N.C. Troops (page 692).]

BLIZZARD, BLANY, Private

Born in Lenoir County where he resided as a farmer prior to enlisting in Lenoir County at age 21, February 16, 1862. Reported present in November, 1862-April, 1863. Furloughed on June 25, 1863. Returned to duty prior to August 26, 1863, when he was captured at Morris Island, Charleston Harbor, South Carolina. Confined at Hilton Head, South Carolina, September 1, 1863. Transferred to Fort Columbus, New York Harbor, where he arrived on September 22, 1863. Transferred to Point Lookout, Maryland, where he arrived on September 26, 1863. Transferred to Elmira, New York, August 16, 1864. Paroled at Elmira on March 10, 1865. Received at Boulware's Wharf, James River, Virginia, March 15, 1865, for exchange. No further records. Survived the war.

BLIZZARD, JOSEPH, Private

Resided in Lenoir County where he enlisted at age 18, December 19, 1863, for the war. Reported for duty on January 23, 1864. Re-

ported present in March-April and September-October, 1864. Hospitalized at Richmond, Virginia, December 12, 1864. Returned to duty on January 15, 1865. Hospitalized at Greensboro on February 22, 1865, with rubeola. Transferred to another hospital on February 23, 1865. No further records. Survived the war.

BLIZZARD, PERRY, Private

Born in Lenoir County where he resided as a farmer prior to enlisting in Lenoir County at age 19, February 16, 1862. Reported present in November, 1862-April, 1863. Furloughed home on June 25, 1863. Reported sick in hospital at Charleston, South Carolina, August 10, 1863. Reported absent without leave on October 24, 1863. Returned to duty in November-December, 1863. Reported present in March-April, 1864. Wounded in the arm and breast at Petersburg, Virginia, on or about June 17, 1864. Hospitalized at Petersburg. Furloughed on July 22, 1864. Returned to duty on an unspecified date. Killed at Fort Harrison, Virginia, September 30, 1864.

BLIZZARD, SAMUEL, Private

Born in Duplin County and resided in Lenoir County where he was by occupation a farmer prior to enlisting in Duplin County at age 22, March 11, 1862. Company records indicate that he was captured and paroled at Kinston on December 14, 1862; however, records of the Federal Provost Marshal do not substantiate that report. Reported present in January-August, 1863. Reported sick in hospital at Charleston, South Carolina, October 14, 1863. Furloughed on November 4, 1863. Returned to duty prior to May 1, 1864. Reported present in September-October, 1864. Hospitalized at Wilmington on December 29, 1864, with pneumonia. Transferred to hospital at Raleigh on January 17, 1865. Returned to duty on February 18, 1865. No further records.

BOONE, D. C., Private

Born in Lenoir County where he resided as a farmer prior to enlisting in Lenoir County at age 24, March 5, 1862. Failed to report for duty. Reported absent without leave on May 26, 1862. No further records. [See special note at the end of the history of Company E, 61st Regiment N.C. Troops (page 692).]

BRAND, ISAAC, Private

Born in Greene County where he resided as a farmer prior to enlisting in Greene County at age 25, May 8, 1862, for the war. Reported sick in hospital at Wilson on December 10, 1862. Hospitalized at Wilmington on or about February 6, 1863, with remittent fever. Returned to duty in March-April, 1863. Reported present or accounted for in May-December, 1863, and March-April, 1864. Killed near Petersburg, Virginia, June 17, 1864.

BRITT, JAMES, Private

Born in Greene County where he resided as a farmer or farm hand prior to enlisting in Greene County at age 23, May 12, 1862, for the war. Reported absent without leave on May 26, 1862. Discharged on an unspecified date (probably prior to January 1, 1863). Reason discharged not reported.

BRITT, WILLIAM H., Private

Born in Greene County where he resided as a farmer prior to enlisting in Greene County at age 24, May 8, 1862, for the war. Captured at Kinston on December 14, 1862. Paroled the same date. Returned to duty in January-February, 1863. Reported present or accounted for in March-June, 1863. Captured at Morris Island, Charleston Harbor, South Carolina, August 26, 1863. Confined at Hilton Head, South Carolina, September 1, 1863.

Transferred to Fort Columbus, New York Harbor, where he arrived on September 22, 1863. Transferred to Point Lookout, Maryland, where he arrived on September 26, 1863. Transferred to Elmira, New York, August 16, 1864. Paroled at Elmira on March 10, 1865. Received at Boulware's Wharf, James River, Virginia, March 15, 1865, for exchange. No further records.

BROWN, E. T., Private

Born in Greene County and resided in Lenoir County where he was by occupation a farmer prior to enlisting in Greene County at age 18, April 17, 1862, for the war. Rejected for service. Reason he was rejected not reported. [See special note at the end of the history of Company E, 61st Regiment N.C. Troops (page 692).]

BROWN, THOMAS, Private

Records of the United Daughters of the Confederacy indicate that he served in this company.

BUTTS, ELIAS, Private

Resided in Greene County and was by occupation a farm hand prior to enlisting in Greene County at age 29, July 15, 1862, for the war. Reported on detail as a wagoner from October 25, 1862, through December 31, 1863, and in March-April and September-December, 1864. No further records. Survived the war.

BUTTS, RICHARD F., Private

Enlisted in Greene County on July 15, 1862, for the war. Detailed for extra duty in the Quartermaster Department on October 21, 1862. Detailed as a brigade wagoner on December 20, 1862. Rejoined the company prior to July 1, 1863. Reported absent on detached service at brigade headquarters from July 5 through December 31, 1863, and in March-April and September-October, 1864. Rejoined the company in November-December, 1864. No further records.

BYRD, LEMUEL, Private

Born in Greene County where he resided as a farmer prior to enlisting in Greene County at age 28, May 13, 1862, for the war. Reported present in November, 1862-June, 1863. Captured at Morris Island, Charleston Harbor, South Carolina, August 26, 1863. Confined at Hilton Head, South Carolina, September 1, 1863. Transferred to Fort Columbus, New York Harbor, where he arrived on September 22, 1863. Transferred to Point Lookout, Maryland, where he arrived on September 26, 1863. Transferred to Elmira, New York, August 16, 1864. Paroled at Elmira on March 10, 1865. Received at Boulware's Wharf, James River, Virginia, March 15, 1865, for exchange. No further records. Survived the war.

BYRD, NATHAN, Private

Born in Lenoir County where he resided as a farmer prior to enlisting in Lenoir County at age 37, March 8, 1862. Furloughed home sick on May 25, 1862. Failed to return to duty and was reported absent without leave in November, 1862-October, 1863. Returned to duty on November 11, 1863. Reported present in March-April, 1864. Reported sick in hospital at Richmond, Virginia, in September-October, 1864. Reported absent without leave on December 1, 1864. No further records.

BYRD, WILLIAM, Corporal

Born in Greene County where he resided as a farmer prior to enlisting in Greene County on May 13, 1862, for the war. Reported

sick at home on December 15, 1862. Reported on detail working on signal stations from February 28 through April 30, 1863. Rejoined the company in May-June, 1863. Reported sick in hospital at Charleston, South Carolina, August 10, 1863. Reported absent without leave on October 20, 1863. Hospitalized at High Point on November 30, 1863, with rheumatism. Returned to duty the same date. Promoted to Corporal in May-October, 1864. Reported present on surviving company muster rolls through December 31, 1864. No further records. Survived the war. [Was about 27 years of age at time of enlistment.]

CARTER, ICABOD, _____

North Carolina pension records indicate that he served in this company.

CARTER, JOHN E., Private

Resided in Lenoir County where he enlisted at age 18, May 31, 1864, for the war. Reported sick at the division infirmary in September-December, 1864. Reported in hospital at Raleigh in January, 1865. No further records. Survived the war.

CARTER, OLIVER, Private

Resided in Lenoir County and was by occupation a farmer prior to enlisting in Lenoir County at age 43, August 19, 1863, for the war. Reported present in November-December, 1863, and March-April, 1864. Died in hospital at Richmond, Virginia, on or about September 7, 1864, of "haemoptysis." [North Carolina pension records indicate that he was mortally wounded in Virginia in May, 1864.]

CLARK, JOHN L., Private

Born in Lenoir County where he resided as a farmer prior to enlisting in Lenoir County at age 24, May 15, 1862, for the war. Reported present but on duty as colonel's orderly from September 20, 1862, through April 30, 1863. Furloughed home on June 27, 1863. Reported on duty as colonel's orderly from August 22, 1863, through April 30, 1864. Reported absent sick at the division infirmary from September 30 through December 31, 1864. No further records.

CREECH, BENJAMIN P., Private

Born in Greene County where he resided as a farmer prior to enlisting in Greene County at age 23, May 10, 1862, for the war. Reported sick in hospital at Raleigh from October 23, 1862, through April 30, 1863. Hospitalized at Wilmington on or about May 26, 1863, with dropsy. Furloughed for thirty days on May 31, 1863. Hospitalized at Wilmington on or about July 6, 1863, with intermittent fever. Reported absent sick on surviving company muster rolls through October 31, 1864. Returned to duty in November-December, 1864. Captured near Kinston on March 10, 1865. Confined at Point Lookout, Maryland, March 16, 1865. Released at Point Lookout on June 26, 1865, after taking the Oath of Allegiance.

DAIL, FRANKLIN, Sergeant

Born in Lenoir County on February 9, 1837. Resided in Lenoir County and was by occupation a farmer and turpentine maker prior to enlisting in Lenoir County at age 25, April 27, 1862, for the war. Mustered in as Private. Promoted to Corporal on December 31, 1862. Reported present in November, 1862-February, 1863. Hospitalized at Charleston, South Carolina, March 17, 1863. Returned to duty in May-June, 1863. Promoted to Sergeant on June 17, 1863. Reported present or accounted for in July-December,

1863. Hospitalized at Petersburg, Virginia, on or about February 10, 1864, with chronic bronchitis. Transferred to another hospital on March 17, 1864. Returned to duty on an unspecified date. Wounded in the head at or near Petersburg on or about June 17, 1864. Hospitalized at High Point on June 26, 1864. Furloughed the same date. Returned to duty prior to November 1, 1864. Reported present in November-December, 1864. Paroled at Goldsboro on an unspecified date in 1865.

DAIL, JESSE, Private

Resided in Greene County and was by occupation a cooper prior to enlisting in Greene County at age 39, November 1, 1864, for the war. Reported absent on duty as a brigade shoemaker in November-December, 1864. No further records. Survived the war.

DAIL, JOHN H., 1st Sergeant

Born in Lenoir County where he resided as a farmer prior to enlisting in Lenoir County at age 24, May 8, 1862, for the war. Mustered in as Private. Promoted to Corporal on September 5, 1862. Reported in hospital at Wilson from November 8 through December 31, 1862. Promoted to Sergeant on December 31, 1862. Returned to duty in January-February, 1863. Reported present through June 30, 1863. Captured at Morris Island, Charleston Harbor, South Carolina, August 26, 1863. Confined at Hilton Head, South Carolina, September 1, 1863. Transferred to Fort Columbus, New York Harbor, where he arrived on September 22, 1863. Transferred to Point Lookout, Maryland, where he arrived on September 26, 1863. Hospitalized at Point Lookout on October 12, 1863, with pneumonia. Paroled at Point Lookout on March 16, 1864. Received at City Point, Virginia, March 20, 1864, for exchange. Returned to duty on an unspecified date. Wounded in the left arm at Fort Harrison, Virginia, September 30, 1864. Hospitalized at Richmond, Virginia, October 1, 1864. Furloughed for forty days on October 14, 1864. Promoted to 1st Sergeant prior to November 1, 1864. Returned to duty in November-December, 1864. No further records. Survived the war.

DAIL, LEVI THOMAS, Private

Born in Greene County where he resided as a farmer prior to enlisting in Greene County at age 25, April 27, 1862, for the war. Reported in hospital at Wilmington from October 25 through December 31, 1862. Hospitalized at Wilmington on February 6, 1863, with dysentery. Reported absent sick through October 31, 1863. Detailed for duty in camp near Petersburg, Virginia, December 16, 1863. Reported present with the company in March-April, 1864. Reported at home on sick furlough from September 9 through December 31, 1864. No further records. Survived the war.

DAIL, THOMAS PINKNEY, Private

Born in Lenoir County on July 28, 1843. Resided in Lenoir County and was by occupation a farmer prior to enlisting in Lenoir County at age 18, May 14, 1862, for the war. Reported sick at home on December 14, 1862. Returned to duty in January-February, 1863. Reported present or accounted for on surviving company muster rolls through December 31, 1864. No further records. Survived the war.

DAVIS, JESSE T., Private

Enlisted in Greene County on July 1, 1862, for the war. Reported on detached duty working on gunboat at Wilmington from September 5, 1862, through December 31, 1864. No further records.

DAVIS, WILLIAM GEORGE, Private

Born in Lenoir County where he resided as a farmer prior to enlisting in Lenoir County at age 18, May 14, 1862, for the war. Reported absent sick at Goldsboro on December 15, 1862. Discharged on June 9, 1863. Reason discharged not reported.

DAVIS, ZACHARIAH, Private

Resided in Lenoir County and enlisted at age 55, April 20, 1862, for the war. Rejected for service (presumably by reason of being overage). [See special note at the end of the history of Company E, 61st Regiment N.C. Troops (page 692).]

DEAVER, HENRY E., Private

Enlisted in Lenoir County at age 20, July 15, 1862, for the war. Reported present or accounted for in November, 1862-June, 1863. Reported present but sick in July-October, 1863. Returned to duty in November-December, 1863. Reported present in March-April, 1864. Wounded slightly in the head at Petersburg, Virginia, June 17, 1864. Returned to duty on an unspecified date. Captured at Fort Harrison, Virginia, September 30, 1864. Confined at Point Lookout, Maryland, October 5, 1864. Paroled at Point Lookout on February 18, 1865. Received at Boulware's and Cox's Wharves, James River, Virginia, February 20-21, 1865, for exchange. No further records. Survived the war.

DENNY, WILLIAM W., _____

North Carolina pension records indicate that he served in this company.

DUNCAN, JAMES, Private

Born in Lenoir County where he resided as a farmer prior to enlisting in Lenoir County at age 25, April 20, 1862, for the war. Rejected for service. Reason he was rejected not reported. [See special note at the end of the history of Company E, 61st Regiment N.C. Troops (page 692). Later served as Private in Company B, 8th Battalion N.C. Partisan Rangers.]

FIELDS, ELIJAH, Private

Born in Lenoir County where he resided as a farmer prior to enlisting in Lenoir County at age 24, May 14, 1862, for the war. Reported present or accounted for through June 30, 1863. Reported sick in hospital at Charleston, South Carolina, August 12, 1863. Returned to duty in September-October, 1863. Reported present on surviving company muster rolls through December 31, 1864. No further records. Survived the war.

FRIZZLE, HENRY H., Sergeant

Born in Greene County where he resided as a farmer prior to enlisting in Greene County at age 21, May 13, 1862, for the war. Mustered in as Corporal. Promoted to Sergeant prior to January 1, 1863. Reported present in November, 1862-June, 1863. Captured at Morris Island, Charleston Harbor, South Carolina, August 26, 1863. Confined at Hilton Head, South Carolina, September 1, 1863. Transferred to Fort Columbus, New York Harbor, where he arrived on September 22, 1863. Transferred to Point Lookout, Maryland, where he arrived on September 26, 1863. Transferred to Elmira, New York, August 16, 1864. Paroled at Elmira on March 10, 1865. Received at Boulware's Wharf, James River, Virginia, March 15, 1865, for exchange. No further records.

FRIZZLE, JOHN J., Private

Born in Greene County where he resided as a farmer prior to enlisting in Greene County at age 27, May 13, 1862, for the war.

Reported present or accounted for through June 30, 1863. Captured at Morris Island, Charleston Harbor, South Carolina, August 26, 1863. Confined at Hilton Head, South Carolina, September 1, 1863. Transferred to Fort Columbus, New York Harbor, where he arrived on September 22, 1863. Transferred to Point Lookout, Maryland, where he arrived on September 26, 1863. Transferred to Elmira, New York, August 16, 1864. Paroled at Elmira on March 10, 1865. Received at Boulware's Wharf, James River, Virginia, March 15, 1865. No further records.

GRANT, THOMAS, Private

Born in Greene County where he resided as a farmer prior to enlisting in Greene County at age 30, May 8, 1862, for the war. Reported present in November-December, 1862. Detailed as a hospital nurse at Charleston, South Carolina, February 26, 1863. Returned to duty in March-April, 1863. Reported sick in hospital at Wilmington on July 10, 1863. Returned to duty in September-October, 1863. Reported present on surviving company muster rolls through October 31, 1864. Reported absent on furlough in November-December, 1864. No further records. Survived the war.

GRAY, JOHN P., Private

Resided in Greene County where he enlisted at age 24, July 12, 1862, for the war. Captured at Kinston on December 14, 1862. Paroled at Kinston on December 15, 1862. Returned to duty prior to March 1, 1863. Reported present or accounted for on surviving company muster rolls through April 30, 1864. Wounded in both feet at or near Fort Harrison, Virginia, on or about September 30, 1864. Hospitalized at High Point on October 8, 1864. Furloughed on October 9, 1864. Was reportedly captured at Goldsboro on April 10, 1865. No further records.

GRIMSLEY, ALLEN, Corporal

Resided in Greene County and was by occupation a carpenter prior to enlisting in Greene County at age 28, July 15, 1862, for the war. Mustered in as Private. Reported present or accounted for in November, 1862-June, 1863. Promoted to Corporal on June 17, 1863. Captured at Morris Island, Charleston Harbor, South Carolina, August 26, 1863. Confined at Hilton Head, South Carolina, September 1, 1863. Transferred to Fort Columbus, New York Harbor, where he arrived on September 22, 1863. Transferred to Point Lookout, Maryland, where he arrived on September 26, 1863. Died at Point Lookout on January 24, 1864. Cause of death not reported.

GRIMSLEY, JAMES, Private

Enlisted in Greene County on July 1, 1862, for the war. Reported present or accounted for in November, 1862-December, 1863. Reported present in March-April and September-December, 1864. No further records.

GRIMSLEY, MATTHEW, Private

Born in Greene County on September 22, 1834. Resided in Greene County and was by occupation a farmer prior to enlisting in Greene County at age 27, May 13, 1862, for the war. Reported on duty in the commissary department (probably as a teamster) from December 10, 1862, through October 31, 1864. Rejoined the company in November-December, 1864. No further records. Survived the war.

GRIMSLEY, RICHARD, Private

Born in Greene County where he resided as a farmer prior to enlisting in Greene County at age 22, May 13, 1862, for the war. Reported present or accounted for in November, 1862-June, 1863. Wounded in the leg at Morris Island, Charleston Harbor, South

Carolina, August 25, 1863. Died in hospital at Charleston on or about September 4, 1863, of wounds.

GRIMSLEY, THEOPHILUS, Private

Born in Greene County where he resided as a farmer or farm hand prior to enlisting in Greene County at age 19, May 13, 1862, for the war. Reported present in November, 1862-December, 1863, and March-April, 1864. Killed near Petersburg, Virginia, on or about June 29, 1864.

HAMILTON, WILLIAM H., Private

Enlisted in Greene County on July 3, 1862, for the war. Captured and paroled at Kinston on December 14, 1862. Returned to duty in January-February, 1863. Reported on detached service "working on signal stations" from February 28 through April 30, 1863. Reported on detached duty with the engineer department at Wilmington on June 14, 1863. Transferred to the engineer department on July 9, 1863. [Was about 31 years of age at time of enlistment.]

HARDISON, THOMAS, Private

Born in Lenoir County where he resided as an overseer prior to enlisting in Lenoir County at age 42, April 20, 1862, for the war. Rejected for service (presumably by reason of being overage). [See special note at the end of the history of Company E, 61st Regiment N.C. Troops (page 692).]

HARPER, BRIGHT, Private

Resided in Lenoir County where he enlisted at age 18, August 13, 1863, for the war. Reported present on surviving company muster rolls through April 30, 1864. Wounded slightly in the arm at or near Petersburg, Virginia, June 16-19, 1864. Returned to duty on an unspecified date. Reported present in September-December, 1864. Captured near Kinston on March 8, 1865. Confined at Point Lookout, Maryland, March 16, 1865. Released at Point Lookout on June 13, 1865, after taking the Oath of Allegiance.

HARPER, JESSE, Sergeant

Born in Lenoir County where he resided as a farmer prior to enlisting in Lenoir County at age 19, March 1, 1862. Mustered in as Private. Reported present in November, 1862-June, 1863. Promoted to Corporal on June 17, 1863. Reported sick in hospital at Mount Pleasant, South Carolina, August 23, 1863. Reported present but sick in September-October, 1863. Returned to duty in November-December, 1863. Reported present in March-April, 1864. Promoted to Sergeant in May-October, 1864. Reported present in September-October, 1864. Reported absent sick in November-December, 1864. Hospitalized at Wilmington on February 15, 1865, with rheumatism. Transferred to another hospital on February 20, 1865. No further records. Survived the war.

HEATH, BENJAMIN, Private

Born in Greene County where he resided as an overseer or farmer prior to enlisting in Greene County at age 35, May 6, 1862, for the war. Reported present or accounted for in November, 1862-August, 1863. Reported on detached duty as a hospital cook from September 1, 1863, through April 8, 1864. Rejoined the company on an unspecified date. Reported present in September-December, 1864. No further records.

HEATH, HENRY, Private

Resided in Lenoir County where he enlisted at age 29, April 20, 1862, for the war. Rejected for service. Reason he was rejected not reported. Reenlisted on July 15, 1862. Reported sick in hospital at Wilson from October 24 through December 31, 1862. Returned to duty in January-February, 1863. Reported present through June 30, 1863. Wounded in the left arm and permanently disabled at Charleston, South Carolina, August 15, 1863. Reported in hospital at Columbia, South Carolina, in September-December, 1863. Furloughed home in March-April, 1864. Reported absent wounded through December 31, 1864. No further records. Survived the war.

HEATH, JOHN B., _____

North Carolina pension records indicate that he served in this company.

HEATH, JOHN F., Private

Born in Greene County where he resided as a farmer prior to enlisting in Greene County at age 17, May 10, 1862, for the war. Reported present or accounted for in November, 1862-April, 1863. Reported absent sick without leave in May-June, 1863. Returned to duty in July-August, 1863. Reported on duty at the regimental hospital in September-October, 1863. Rejoined the company in November-December, 1863. Reported present in March-April, 1864. Wounded in the hip near Petersburg, Virginia, June 17-30, 1864. Reported absent without leave on October 10, 1864. Deserted to the enemy on or about December 1, 1864. Took the Oath of Allegiance at Bermuda Hundred, Virginia, on or about December 7, 1864.

HERRING, ENOCH K., Private

Resided in Lenoir County where he enlisted on August 13, 1863, for the war. Reported present in November-December, 1863, and March-April, 1864. Hospitalized at Richmond, Virginia, August 28, 1864, with chronic diarrhoea. Furloughed for thirty days on September 22, 1864. Returned to duty in November-December, 1864. No further records.

HERRING, STEPHEN A., Private

Born in Georgia and resided in Duplin County where he was by occupation a farmer prior to enlisting in Duplin County at age 29, July 15, 1862, for the war. Reported present or accounted for in November, 1862-June, 1863. Captured at Morris Island, Charleston Harbor, South Carolina, August 26, 1863. Confined at Hilton Head, South Carolina, September 1, 1863. Transferred to Fort Columbus, New York Harbor, where he arrived on September 22, 1863. Transferred to Point Lookout, Maryland, where he arrived on September 26, 1863. Transferred to Elmira, New York, August 16, 1864. Paroled at Elmira on October 11, 1864. Received at Venus Point, Savannah River, Georgia, November 15, 1864, for exchange. No further records. Survived the war.

HILL, JOHN, Private

Enlisted in Lenoir County on July 14, 1862, for the war. Reported present in November-December, 1862. Hospitalized at Wilmington on January 1, 1863, with catarrhus. Returned to duty the same date. Discharged from service by a medical examining board in January-February, 1863. Reason discharged not reported.

HILL, MAJOR L., Sergeant

Born in Lenoir County where he resided as a farmer prior to enlisting in Lenoir County at age 28, May 14, 1862, for the war. Mustered in as Sergeant. Killed in battle at Kinston on December 14, 1862.

HILL, PINKNEY, Private

Born in Lenoir County where he resided as a farmer prior to enlisting in Lenoir County at age 32, May 14, 1862, for the war. Reported

present or accounted for in November, 1862-June, 1863. Captured at Morris Island, Charleston Harbor, South Carolina, August 26, 1863. Confined at Hilton Head, South Carolina, September 1, 1863. Transferred to Fort Columbus, New York Harbor, where he arrived on September 22, 1863. Transferred to Point Lookout, Maryland, where he arrived on September 26, 1863. Transferred to Elmira, New York, August 16, 1864. Paroled at Elmira on March 10, 1865. Received at Boulware's Wharf, James River, Virginia, March 15, 1865, for exchange. Hospitalized at Richmond, Virginia, March 15, 1865. Transferred to another hospital on March 16, 1865. No further records.

HILL, RICHARD C., Private

Enlisted in Lenoir County at age 16, July 15, 1862, for the war. Reported present or accounted for in November, 1862-June, 1863. Captured at Morris Island, Charleston Harbor, South Carolina, August 26, 1863. Confined at Hilton Head, South Carolina, September 1, 1863. Transferred to Fort Columbus, New York Harbor, where he arrived on September 22, 1863. Transferred to Point Lookout, Maryland, where he arrived on September 26, 1863. Transferred to Elmira, New York, August 16, 1864. Paroled at Elmira on March 10, 1865. Received at Boulware's Wharf, James River, Virginia, March 15, 1865, for exchange. No further records. Survived the war.

HINES, IRA D., Private

Born in Lenoir County where he resided as a farmer prior to enlisting in Lenoir County at age 32, May 14, 1862, for the war. Reported present or accounted for in November, 1862-December, 1863, and March-April, 1864. Hospitalized at Goldsboro on an unspecified date. Returned to duty on June 11, 1864. Died in hospital at Richmond, Virginia, on or about July 25-28, 1864, of disease.

HINES, JAMES, Sergeant

Born in Greene County where he resided as a farmer or farm hand prior to enlisting in Greene County at age 23, May 13, 1862, for the war. Mustered in as Private. Reported present in November, 1862-June, 1863. Promoted to Sergeant on March 16, 1863. Captured at Morris Island, Charleston Harbor, South Carolina, August 26, 1863. Confined at Hilton Head, South Carolina, September 1, 1863. Transferred to Fort Columbus, New York Harbor, where he arrived on September 22, 1863. Transferred to Point Lookout, Maryland, on or about September 26, 1863. Hospitalized at Point Lookout on November 7, 1863. Paroled and transferred to City Point, Virginia, where he was received on March 20, 1864, for exchange. Returned to duty subsequent to April 30, 1864. Reported present in September-December, 1864. No further records. [He was the twin brother of Pvt. Sherwood Hines of this company. A soldier named Hines was reported on duty as acting Sergeant Major of the regiment on October 19, 1864. He was probably either this man or Pvt. William F. Hines of Company A.]

HINES, JOEL, Private

Born in Lenoir County where he resided as a farmer prior to enlisting in Lenoir County at age 19, March 1, 1862. Reported present or accounted for in November, 1862-August, 1863. Reported sick in hospital on October 1, 1863. Returned to duty in November-December, 1863. Reported present in March-April, 1864. Died in hospital at Richmond, Virginia, July 29, 1864, of disease.

HINES, SHERWOOD, Private

Resided in Greene County and was by occupation a farm hand prior to enlisting in Greene County at age 23, July 1, 1862, for the war. Reported present or accounted for in November, 1862-June, 1863.

Captured at Morris Island, Charleston Harbor, South Carolina, August 26, 1863. Confined at Hilton Head, South Carolina, September 1, 1863. Transferred to Fort Columbus, New York Harbor, where he arrived on September 22, 1863. Transferred to Point Lookout, Maryland, where he arrived on September 26, 1863. Died at Point Lookout on December 15 or December 22, 1863. Cause of death not reported. [He was the twin brother of Sgt. James Hines of this company.]

HINES, WILLIAM H., Private

Resided in Greene County and was by occupation a farm hand prior to enlisting in Greene County at age 25, July 15, 1862, for the war. Reported present or accounted for in November, 1862-December, 1863, and March-April, 1864. Wounded in the head or hand near Petersburg, Virginia, on or about June 17, 1864. Hospitalized at Petersburg. Transferred to hospital at Kittrell's Springs on June 18, 1864. Died in hospital at Kittrell's Springs on July 5, 1864, of "erysipelas."

HINSON, JOSHUA G., Private

Born in Lenoir County where he resided as a farmer or farm laborer prior to enlisting in Lenoir County at age 24, March 20, 1862. Reported sick in hospital at Wilson from November 10, 1862, through February 28, 1863. Returned to duty in March-April, 1863. Reported on detached service building breastworks near Northeast Bridge on June 26, 1863. Returned to duty on an unspecified date. Captured at Morris Island, Charleston Harbor, South Carolina, August 26, 1863. Confined at Hilton Head, South Carolina, September 1, 1863. Transferred to Fort Columbus, New York Harbor, where he arrived on September 22, 1863. Transferred to Point Lookout, Maryland, where he arrived on September 26, 1863. Transferred to Elmira, New York, August 16, 1864. Paroled at Elmira on March 10, 1865. Received at Boulware's Wharf, James River, Virginia, March 15, 1865, for exchange. Survived the war.

HOWARD, JAMES, Private

Resided in Lenoir County where he enlisted at age 18, August 23, 1863, for the war. Reported present in November-December, 1863, and March-April, 1864. Reported in hospital at Richmond, Virginia, from September 16 through October 31, 1864. Reported absent sick in November-December, 1864. No further records. Survived the war.

HOWARD, JOHN J., Private

Born in Lenoir County where he resided as a farmer prior to enlisting in Lenoir County at age 19, April 14, 1862. Reported present or accounted for in November, 1862-December, 1863, and March-April, 1864. Killed near Petersburg, Virginia, June 17, 1864.

HOWARD, WILLIAM, Private

Born in Lenoir County where he resided as a farmer prior to enlisting in Lenoir County at age 24, April 14, 1862. Reported present or accounted for in November, 1862-June, 1863. Captured at Morris Island, Charleston Harbor, South Carolina, August 26, 1863. Confined at Hilton Head, South Carolina, September 1, 1863. Transferred to Fort Columbus, New York Harbor, where he arrived on September 22, 1863. Transferred to Point Lookout, Maryland, where he arrived on September 26, 1863. Transferred to Elmira, New York, August 16, 1864. Died at Elmira on October 12, 1864, of "chronic diarrhoea."

HUGHES, THOMAS, Private

Born in Greene County where he resided as a farmer prior to enlisting in Greene County at age 26, May 13, 1862, for the war.

Reported absent with leave on December 14, 1862. Hospitalized at Wilmington on January 17, 1863, with hepatitis acuta. Later contracted pneumonia. Returned to duty on February 25, 1863. Reported present or accounted for in March-December, 1863, and March-April, 1864. Wounded in the left shoulder at or near Petersburg, Virginia, on or about June 18, 1864. Hospitalized at Farmville, Virginia. Furloughed for sixty days on July 19, 1864. Reported absent without leave on October 1, 1864. Returned to duty in November-December, 1864. No further records.

HUGHS, JOSIAH J., Private

Resided in Greene County where he enlisted at age 18, July 15, 1862, for the war. Reported present or accounted for in November, 1862-December, 1863, and March-April, 1864. Wounded in the side at Fort Harrison, Virginia, September 30, 1864. Hospitalized at Richmond, Virginia. Returned to duty on November 12, 1864. Reported present through December 31, 1864. No further records.

JERNIGAN, SHERWOOD, Private

Resided in Duplin County and was by occupation a laborer prior to enlisting in Duplin County at age 28, July 12, 1862, for the war. Reported present in November-December, 1862. Hospitalized at Wilmington on February 7 or February 17, 1863, with catarrhus. Returned to duty on March 1, 1863. Reported in confinement at Charleston, South Carolina, April 26, 1863. Reason he was confined not reported. Reported sick in hospital on June 15, 1863. Returned to duty in July-August, 1863. Reported present or accounted for on surviving company muster rolls through April 30, 1864. Wounded slightly in the head at or near Petersburg, Virginia, on or about June 16-19, 1864. Returned to duty on an unspecified date. Reported present in September-December, 1864. No further records.

JONES, BRYANT, Private

Born in Greene County and was by occupation a farmer prior to enlisting in Greene County on July 15, 1862, for the war. Reported absent with leave on December 14, 1862. Reported in hospital at Wilmington on January 30, 1863, with continued fever. Discharged from service on April 3, 1863, by reason of disability. [Discharge certificate gives his age as 32.]

JONES, GARDNER, Private

Resided in Greene County and was by occupation a farmer prior to enlisting in Greene County at age 32, July 1, 1862, for the war. Reported present or accounted for in November, 1862-December, 1863, and March-April, 1864. Deserted from the division infirmary on September 16, 1864.

JONES, JOHN BRYAN, Private

Resided in Greene County and was by occupation a day laborer prior to enlisting in Greene County at age 29, July 15, 1862, for the war. Captured at Kinston on December 14, 1862. Paroled at New Bern on December 23, 1862. Returned to duty in January-February, 1863. Reported present but sick in March-April, 1863. Reported sick in hospital at Wilmington on July 10, 1863. Reported on detail as a teamster at Wilmington in August-November, 1863. Reported absent on sick furlough from December 8, 1863, through April 30, 1864. Hospitalized at Richmond, Virginia, on or about October 5, 1864. Returned to duty on December 27, 1864. No further records.

JONES, THOMAS, Private

Resided in Greene County where he enlisted at age 27, July 15, 1862, for the war. Reported present in November, 1862-December,

1863, and March-April, 1864. Deserted from the division infirmary on September 6, 1864. No further records.

JONES, WRIGHT, Private
Resided in Greene County and was by occupation a farm hand prior to enlisting in Greene County at age 19, July 15, 1862, for the war. Reported present on surviving company muster rolls through December 31, 1864. No further records. Survived the war.

KENNEDY, HENRY, Private
Resided in Greene County and was by occupation a farmer prior to enlisting in Greene County at age 41, September 27, 1864, for the war. Hospitalized at Wilmington on February 16, 1865, with pneumonia. Transferred on February 20, 1865. Captured at Snow Hill on March 25, 1865. Confined at Point Lookout, Maryland, April 3, 1865. Released at Point Lookout on June 26, 1865, after taking the Oath of Allegiance.

KENNEDY, LUTHER S., Private
Previously served as Private in Company H, 2nd Regiment N.C. State Troops. Enlisted in this company in Wayne County on May 14, 1862, for the war. Reported absent without leave on or about May 26, 1862. Reported sick in hospital at Wilson on December 20, 1862. Returned to duty in January-February, 1863. Reported present on surviving company muster rolls through December 31, 1864. No further records. Survived the war.

LEE, WILLIAM R., Private
Born in Lenoir County where he resided as a farmer prior to enlisting in Lenoir County at age 28, February 26, 1862. Reported present in November, 1862-June, 1863. Transferred to the engineering department at Wilmington on or about July 9, 1863.

LITTLETON, DEXTER B., Private
Born in Onslow County and resided in Lenoir County where he was by occupation a farmer prior to enlisting in Lenoir County at age 24, May 7, 1862, for the war. Reported present in November-December, 1862. Hospitalized at Wilmington on or about February 16, 1863, with parotitis. Returned to duty on March 9, 1863. Reported present on surviving company muster rolls through October 31, 1864. Hospitalized at Wilmington on December 30, 1864, with catarrh. Returned to duty on January 3, 1865. Wounded in the neck at Kinston on or about March 10, 1865. Hospitalized at Raleigh. Reported in hospital at Charlotte on April 27, 1865. Transferred to another hospital on April 28, 1865. Survived the war.

LITTLETON, WILLIAM HENRY, Private
Born in Lenoir County where he resided as a farmer prior to enlisting in Lenoir County at age 21, May 8, 1862, for the war. Reported present in November, 1862-June, 1863. Killed by a shell at Fort Wagner, Charleston Harbor, South Carolina, August 22, 1863.

McKEEL, ELISHA, Private
Resided in Greene County and was by occupation an overseer prior to enlisting in Greene County at age 30, July 15, 1862, for the war. Captured and paroled at Kinston on December 14, 1862. Returned to duty in January-February, 1863. Reported present on surviving company muster rolls through April 30, 1864. Wounded in the arm at Fort Harrison, Virginia, September 30, 1864. Hospitalized at Richmond, Virginia. Furloughed on October 13, 1864. Returned to duty in November-December, 1864. No further records.

MALPASS, JOHN L., Private
Enlisted in Lenoir County on April 15, 1864, for the war. Wounded slightly in the thigh at or near Petersburg, Virginia, on or about June 16-19, 1864. Reported absent sick in September-December, 1864. Hospitalized at Wilmington on February 16, 1865, with rubeola. Transferred to another hospital on February 20, 1865. No further records.

MALPASS, LEWIS F., Private
Born in Lenoir County where he resided as a farmer prior to enlisting in Lenoir County at age 18, March 21, 1862. Reported present in November, 1862-December, 1863, and March-April, 1864. Wounded in the right shoulder (fracture) at Fort Harrison, Virginia, September 30, 1864. Hospitalized at Richmond, Virginia. Furloughed on January 28, 1865. No further records. Survived the war.

MALPASS, M. C., Private
Enlisted in Lenoir County on July 1, 1862, for the war. Reported present in November, 1862-February, 1863. Reported sick in hospital at Charleston, South Carolina, April 8, 1863. Furloughed home on May 15, 1863. Reported absent without leave from May 29 through August 31, 1863. Returned to duty in September-October, 1863. Reported present in November-December, 1863, and March-April, 1864. Died near Petersburg, Virginia, August 7, 1864. Cause of death not reported.

MAY, KINCHEN, Private
Enlisted in Greene County on May 12, 1862, for the war. Reported present in November, 1862-December, 1863, and March-April, 1864. Wounded in the thigh near Petersburg, Virginia, June 17-30, 1864. Hospitalized at Richmond, Virginia, July 23, 1864. Furloughed for thirty days on July 24, 1864. Reported absent without leave on October 10, 1864. Returned to duty in November-December, 1864. No further records. Survived the war.

MAY, WILLIAM L., Private
Resided in Lenoir County and enlisted in Greene County at age 26, July 15, 1862, for the war. Reported present or accounted for in November, 1862-August, 1863. Reported present but sick in September-October, 1863. Reported sick in hospital in November-December, 1863. Returned to duty prior to May 1, 1864. Reported present in September-December, 1864. No further records.

MEEKS, LEWIS W., Private
Resided in Greene County where he enlisted at age 30, July 15, 1862, for the war. Reported present or accounted for in November, 1862-December, 1863, and March-April, 1864. Deserted from the division infirmary on September 6, 1864.

MEWBORN, LEVI JESSE HARDY, Private
Born on August 31, 1842. Resided in Greene County where he enlisted at age 19, July 12, 1862, for the war. Reported present in November, 1862-December, 1863, and March-April, 1864. Wounded in the right cheek at Cold Harbor, Virginia, June 3, 1864. Hospitalized at Richmond, Virginia. Furloughed for thirty days on or about June 7, 1864. Returned to duty prior to November 1, 1864. Reported present in November-December, 1864. Was reportedly captured at Goldsboro on April 10, 1865. Survived the war.

MOODY, JOHN, Private
Born in Lenoir County where he resided as a farmer prior to enlisting in Lenoir County on May 12, 1862. Rejected for service.

Reason he was rejected not reported. [Company records give his age as 18; however, it appears probable that he was about 14 years old and was rejected for that reason. See special note at the end of the history of Company E, 61st Regiment N.C. Troops (page 692).]

MOORE, BENJAMIN R., Private

Enlisted in Pitt County on July 15, 1862, for the war. Deserted on an unspecified date. Brought back to the company on December 10, 1862. Returned to duty in January-February, 1863. Reported present in March-December, 1863, and March-April, 1864. Hospitalized at Richmond, Virginia, October 12, 1864. Returned to duty on November 12, 1864. Hospitalized at Wilmington on January 7, 1865, with pleuritis. Transferred to hospital at Greensboro on January 15, 1865. Paroled at Greensboro on May 6, 1865.

MOORE, R. M., Private

Enlisted in Pitt County on July 15, 1862, for the war. Died in hospital at Goldsboro on December 28, 1862. Cause of death not reported.

MOORE, SAMUEL G., Corporal

Enlisted in Greene County on July 15, 1862, for the war. Mustered in as Corporal. Reported sick in hospital at Wilson on December 25, 1862. Returned to duty in January-February, 1863. Reported present or accounted for through June 30, 1863. Captured at Morris Island, Charleston Harbor, South Carolina, August 26, 1863. Confined at Hilton Head, South Carolina, September 1, 1863. Transferred to Fort Columbus, New York Harbor, where he arrived on September 22, 1863. Transferred to Point Lookout, Maryland, where he arrived on September 26, 1863. Transferred to Elmira, New York, August 16, 1864. Paroled at Elmira on March 10, 1865. Received at Boulware's Wharf, James River, Virginia, March 15, 1865, for exchange. No further records.

MOORE, WILLIAM D., Private

Born in Pitt County where he resided as a farmer prior to enlisting in Greene County at age 28, May 1, 1862, for the war. Mustered in as 1st Sergeant. Captured and paroled at Kinston on December 14, 1862. Returned to duty in January-February, 1863. Appointed regimental sutler on March 16, 1863. Reported absent on furlough in May-June, 1863. Reported on duty as regimental sutler in July-December, 1863, and March-April, 1864. Reduced to ranks and rejoined the company on an unspecified date. Reported present in September-December, 1864. No further records. Survived the war. [Previously served as 2nd Lieutenant in the 17th Regiment N.C. Militia.]

MOORE, WILLIAM M., Private

Enlisted in Pitt County on July 15, 1862, for the war. Reported present in November, 1862-June, 1863. Reported sick in hospital at Charleston, South Carolina, from July 20 through August 31, 1863. Reported sick in hospital at Tarboro on October 15, 1863. Returned to duty in November-December, 1863. Reported present in March-April and September-October, 1864. Reported absent on sick furlough in November-December, 1864. Hospitalized at Wilmington on January 2, 1865, with pneumonia. Transferred to Greensboro on January 15, 1865 (suffering from nostalgia). Transferred to another hospital on January 17, 1865. No further records.

MOYE, ALFRED, Private

Born in Greene County where he resided as a farmer prior to enlisting in Greene County at age 24, May 13, 1862, for the war. Reported present in November, 1862-June, 1863. Reported miss-

ing at Morris Island, Charleston Harbor, South Carolina, on or about August 26, 1863. Was probably killed at Morris Island.

MOYE, WILLIAM, Private

Enlisted in Greene County at age 30, July 1, 1862, for the war. Reported present in November, 1862-December, 1863, and March-April, 1864. Deserted from the division infirmary on September 6, 1864.

MUND, LEVI, Private

Place and date of enlistment not reported (probably enlisted subsequent to December 31, 1864). Apparently deserted to the enemy at Moseley Hall (present-day LaGrange) on April 8, 1865. Took the Oath of Allegiance at Greensboro on or about May 9, 1865.

MURPHY, JOSEPH, Private

Born in Greene County where he resided as a farmer prior to enlisting in Greene County at age 18, March 4, 1862. Reported absent without leave on May 26, 1862. Returned to duty prior to December 28, 1862, when he was detailed for duty in the quartermaster department. Rejoined the company in March-April, 1863. Reported present in May-June, 1863. Captured at Morris Island, Charleston Harbor, South Carolina, August 26, 1863. Confined at Hilton Head, South Carolina, September 1, 1863. Transferred to Point Lookout, Maryland, on an unspecified date. Released at Point Lookout on January 25, 1864, after taking the Oath of Allegiance and joining the U.S. Navy. Rejected for service with the navy but was accepted for service in the U.S. Army. Assigned to the 1st Regiment U.S. Volunteer Infantry.

MURPHY, WILLIAM, Private

Born in Greene County and was by occupation a farmer prior to enlisting in Greene County at age 17, March 11, 1862. Reported present in November, 1862-April, 1863. Discharged on a writ of habeas corpus on May 27, 1863.

NIXON, T. A., Private

Born in Greene County where he resided as a farmer prior to enlisting in Greene County at age 40, April 10, 1862. Rejected for service (apparently by reason of being overage). [See special note at the end of the history of Company E, 61st Regiment N.C. Troops (page 692).]

NOBLE, JESSE B., Corporal

Resided in Lenoir County and was by occupation a farmer prior to enlisting in Lenoir County at age 36, April 25, 1862, for the war. Mustered in as Corporal. Captured and paroled at Kinston on December 14, 1862. Returned to duty in January-February, 1863. Reported present in March-April, 1863. Transferred to Company K of this regiment on June 1, 1863.

NOBLE, MARTIN M., Private

Born in Lenoir County where he resided as a farmer prior to enlisting in Lenoir County at age 22, May 4, 1862, for the war. Reported present or accounted for in November, 1862-April, 1863. Transferred to Company K of this regiment on June 1, 1863.

PEARCE, JOHN F., Private

Enlisted in Greene County on July 15, 1862, for the war. Reported present or accounted for in November, 1862-June, 1863. Captured at Morris Island, Charleston Harbor, South Carolina, August 26, 1863. Confined at Hilton Head, South Carolina, September 1, 1863. Transferred to Fort Columbus, New York Harbor, on an unspecified date. Transferred to Point Lookout, Maryland, October 9, 1863. Paroled at Point Lookout on November 1, 1864. Received at Venus Point, Savannah River, Georgia, November 15, 1864, for exchange. No further records.

PHILLIPS, J. A. D., Private
Resided in Greene County and was by occupation a farmer prior to enlisting in Greene County at age 33, July 15, 1862, for the war. Reported present but sick in November-December, 1862. Hospitalized at Wilmington on January 1, 1863, with catarrhus. Returned to duty on January 2, 1863. Hospitalized at Wilmington on or about February 9, 1863, with neuralgia. Returned to duty on February 22, 1863. Discharged on an unspecified date (probably in March, 1863). Reason discharged not reported.

POTTER, ABNER J., Private
Born in Duplin County and resided in Greene County where he was by occupation a farmer prior to enlisting in Lenoir County at age 22, April 20, 1862, for the war. Failed to report for duty. Enlisted in Company D, 27th Regiment N.C. Troops, April 28, 1862. [See special note at the end of the history of Company E, 61st Regiment N.C. Troops (page 692).]

POTTER, JESSE, Private
Born in Duplin County and resided in Greene County where he was by occupation a farmer prior to enlisting in Lenoir County at age 19, April 20, 1862, for the war. Failed to report for duty. Enlisted in Company D, 27th Regiment N.C. Troops, April 28, 1862. [See special note at the end of the history of Company E, 61st Regiment N.C. Troops (page 692).]

RASBERRY, JOHN R., Private
Resided in New Hanover County where he enlisted on July 26, 1862, for the war. Reported present in November, 1862-June, 1863. Captured at Morris Island, Charleston Harbor, South Carolina, August 26, 1863. Confined at Hilton Head, South Carolina, September 1, 1863. Transferred to Fort Columbus, New York Harbor, where he arrived on September 22, 1863. Transferred to Point Lookout, Maryland, where he arrived on September 26, 1863. Released at Point Lookout on January 26, 1864, after taking the Oath of Allegiance and joining the U.S. Navy.

REYNOLDS, ANDREW J., Private
Resided in Lenoir County where he enlisted on July 15, 1862, for the war. Captured and paroled at Kinston on December 14, 1862. Returned to duty in January-February, 1863. Reported present in May-June, 1863. Hospitalized at Mount Pleasant, South Carolina, August 23, 1863. Reported present but sick in September-October, 1863. Returned to duty in November-December, 1863. Reported present in March-April, 1864. Killed near Petersburg, Virginia, on or about June 19, 1864.

ROUSE, BENJAMIN, Private
Born in Lenoir County where he resided as a farmer prior to enlisting in Lenoir County at age 32, March 8, 1862. Mustered in as Corporal. Reported present or accounted for in November, 1862-December, 1863, and March-April, 1864. Reduced to ranks on April 16, 1864. Reported present in September-December, 1864. Paroled at Goldsboro on May 29, 1865.

ROUSE, JOHN W., Private
Resided in Lenoir County and was by occupation a farmer prior to enlisting in Lenoir County at age 37, July 15, 1862, for the war.

Captured at Kinston on December 14, 1862. Paroled at Kinston on December 15, 1862. Returned to duty in January-February, 1863. Reported present or accounted for in March-December, 1863, and March-April, 1864. Furloughed home sick in September, 1864. Returned to duty in November-December, 1864. No further records. Survived the war.

RUTLEDGE, EDMUND P., Private
Born in Lenoir County where he resided as a teacher prior to enlisting in Lenoir County at age 43, April 20, 1862, for the war. Reported sick in hospital at Goldsboro on December 14, 1862. Detailed for duty as a hospital nurse at Goldsboro on December 16, 1862. Died in hospital at Goldsboro on or about January 10, 1863, of "pneumonia."

SKEEN, JOHN H., Private
Resided in Lenoir County and was by occupation a laborer prior to enlisting in Lenoir County at age 20, July 4, 1862, for the war. Reported absent with leave on December 7, 1862. Reported absent without leave in January-February, 1863. Listed as a deserter on April 4, 1863. Arrested and brought back to the company on June 18, 1863. Returned to duty prior to September 1, 1863. Reported present on surviving company muster rolls through April 30, 1864. Wounded slightly in the arm at or near Petersburg, Virginia, on or about June 16-19, 1864. Returned to duty on an unspecified date. Reported present in September-October, 1864. Reported absent sick at the division infirmary in November-December, 1864. Deserted to the enemy at Kinston on March 15, 1865.

SKINNER, HERRING, Private
Enlisted in Greene County on July 1, 1862, for the war. Captured and paroled at Kinston on December 14, 1862. Returned to duty in January-February, 1863. Reported present in March-June, 1863. Captured at Morris Island, Charleston Harbor, South Carolina, August 26, 1863. Confined at Hilton Head, South Carolina, September 1, 1863. Transferred to Fort Columbus, New York Harbor, where he arrived on October 6, 1863. Transferred to Point Lookout, Maryland, October 9, 1863. Paroled at Point Lookout on February 24, 1865. Received at Boulware's Wharf, James River, Virginia, February 25-28 or March 2-3, 1865, for exchange. No further records. Survived the war.

SKINNER, JAMES, Private
Born in Greene County where he resided as a farmer or day laborer prior to enlisting in Greene County at age 20, May 13, 1862, for the war. Reported present or accounted for on surviving company muster rolls through December 31, 1864. No further records.

SKINNER, LEMUEL, Private
Born in Greene County where he resided as a farmer or farm hand prior to enlisting in Greene County at age 21, May 13, 1862, for the war. Reported present in November, 1862-June, 1863. Captured at Morris Island, Charleston Harbor, South Carolina, August 26, 1863. Confined at Hilton Head, South Carolina, September 1, 1863. Transferred to Fort Columbus, New York Harbor, where he arrived on October 6, 1863. Transferred to Point Lookout, Maryland, October 9, 1863. Paroled at Point Lookout on February 24, 1865. Received at Boulware's Wharf, James River, Virginia, February 25-28 or March 2-3, 1865, for exchange. No further records. Survived the war.

SMITH, ADAIL DUNN, Sergeant
Born in Lenoir County on January 15, 1830. Resided in Lenoir County and was by occupation a farmer prior to enlisting in Lenoir

County at age 32, May 14, 1862, for the war. Mustered in as Sergeant. Discharged on an unspecified date (probably prior to April 1, 1863). Reason discharged not reported.

SMITH, LEMMON, Private

Born in Lenoir County where he resided as a farmer or turpentine laborer prior to enlisting in Lenoir County at age 29, May 14, 1862, for the war. Failed to report for duty. Dropped from the company rolls prior to January 1, 1863.

SMITH, THOMAS W., Private

Resided in Lenoir County where he enlisted at age 19, January 15, 1863, for the war. Reported present through April 30, 1863. Transferred to Company K of this regiment on June 1, 1863.

SPEIGHT, JAMES S., Private

Born in Greene County where he resided as a farmer prior to enlisting in Greene County at age 25, May 13, 1862, for the war. Reported present on surviving company muster rolls in November, 1862-December, 1864. No further records.

SPEIGHT, WILLIAM H., Private

Born in Greene County where he resided as a farmer prior to enlisting in Greene County at age 26, May 13, 1862, for the war. Reported present or accounted for on surviving company muster rolls from November 1, 1862, through April 30, 1864. Hospitalized at Richmond, Virginia, August 8, 1864, with remittent fever. Furloughed for sixty days on August 13, 1864. Returned to duty prior to November 1, 1864. Reported present in November-December, 1864. No further records. Survived the war.

SPIVEY, MOSES, _____

Place and date of enlistment not reported (probably enlisted in the autumn or winter of 1862). The *Fayetteville Observer* of February 12, 1863, states that he died in hospital at Wilson on an unspecified date. Cause of death not reported.

STOCKS, CHARLES, Private

Enlisted in Greene County on July 15, 1862, for the war. Reported present or accounted for in November, 1862-December, 1863, and March-April, 1864. Wounded in the breast at Cold Harbor, Virginia, May 31-June 3, 1864. Returned to duty prior to June 17, 1864, when he was wounded in the left hand near Petersburg, Virginia. Hospitalized at Petersburg. Transferred to hospital at Farmville, Virginia, on or about June 21, 1864. Furloughed for forty days on July 5, 1864. Reported absent without leave on October 10, 1864. Returned to duty in November-December, 1864. No further records. Survived the war.

STOCKS, JOHN, Private

Born in Lenoir County where he resided as a farmer prior to enlisting in Lenoir County at age 26, May 14, 1862, for the war. Reported absent without leave on May 26, 1862. Reported missing at Kinston on December 14, 1862. Returned to duty in January-February, 1863. Reported present but sick in March-April, 1863. Wounded in the head at Morris Island, Charleston Harbor, South Carolina, on or about August 26, 1863. Returned to duty prior to September 1, 1863. Reported present in September-December, 1863, and March-April, 1864. Wounded in the knee at Fort Harrison, Virginia, September 30, 1864. Returned to duty prior to November 1, 1864. Reported present in November-December, 1864. No further records. Survived the war.

STOCKS, LEWIS, Private

Enlisted in Greene County on July 15, 1862, for the war. Captured and paroled at Kinston on December 14, 1862. Returned to duty in January-February, 1863. Died in hospital at Charleston, South Carolina, April 6, 1863. Cause of death not reported.

STROUD, AMOS, Private

Born on December 22, 1820. Resided in Lenoir County and was by occupation a farmer prior to enlisting in Lenoir County at age 42, August 13, 1863, for the war. Reported present on surviving company muster rolls from November 1, 1863, through December 31, 1864. Deserted to the enemy on an unspecified date. Took the Oath of Allegiance on or about March 29, 1865.

STROUD, CROOM, Private

Resided in Lenoir County where he enlisted at age 18, November 9, 1863, for the war. Reported present in November-December, 1863, and March-April, 1864. Hospitalized at Petersburg, Virginia, July 8, 1864, with diarrhoea. Hospitalized at Richmond, Virginia, August 23, 1864. Furloughed on September 3, 1864. Hospitalized at Goldsboro on an unspecified date. Released from hospital at Goldsboro on or about September 26, 1864. Returned to duty prior to November 1, 1864. Reported absent sick in November-December, 1864. No further records.

STROUD, JOB, Private

Resided in Lenoir County and was by occupation a laborer prior to enlisting at age 17, April 20, 1862, for the war. Rejected for service (probably by reason of being underage). Later served as Private in Company B, 8th Battalion N.C. Partisan Rangers. [See special note at the end of the history of Company E, 61st Regiment N.C. Troops (page 692).]

STROUD, JONAS AREATUS, Private

Resided in Lenoir or Duplin County and enlisted in Lenoir County at age 18, April 15, 1864, for the war. Hospitalized at Goldsboro on May 23, 1864. Returned to duty on May 26, 1864. Reported present in September-December, 1864. Paroled at Goldsboro on May 9, 1865.

STROUD, OWEN, Private

Resided in Lenoir County and was by occupation a farmer prior to enlisting in Lenoir County at age 42, August 13, 1863, for the war. Reported present in November-December, 1863, and March-April, 1864. Hospitalized at Petersburg, Virginia, July 8, 1864, with acute diarrhoea. Furloughed for thirty days on July 27, 1864. Reported present in September-December, 1864. No further records. Survived the war.

STROUD, RICHARD, Private

Born in Lenoir County where he resided as a farmer prior to enlisting in Lenoir County at age 28, March 1, 1862. Left sick at Greenville on December 7, 1862. Reported present but sick in March-April, 1863. Returned to duty in May-June, 1863. Reported present but sick in quarters in July-August, 1863. Returned to duty in September-October, 1863. Reported present in November-December, 1863, and March-April, 1864. Hospitalized at Richmond, Virginia, August 26, 1864, with intermittent fever and debilitas. Returned to duty on September 17, 1864. Reported sick in hospital at Richmond on or about October 31, 1864. Returned to duty in November-December, 1864. No further records. Survived the war.

STROUD, WILLIAM, Private

Resided in Lenoir County where he enlisted at age 18, May 3, 1864, for the war. Reported present in September-December, 1864. No further records.

SUGG, JOSHUA PARROTT, Corporal

Resided in Greene County where he enlisted at age 25, July 12, 1862, for the war. Mustered in as Private. Reported sick at home on December 14, 1862. Returned to duty in January-February, 1863. Reported present in March-December, 1863, and March-April, 1864. Promoted to Corporal in May-October, 1864. Wounded in the arm and leg at the Crater, near Petersburg, Virginia, July 30, 1864. Reported present in September-December, 1864. No further records.

SUGG, RICHARD LEWIS, Private

Resided in Greene County where he enlisted at age 18, July 12, 1862, for the war. Died in hospital at Raleigh on November 6, 1862, of "phthisis pul[monalis]."

SUMNER, ANDREW JACKSON, Private

Resided in Duplin County where he enlisted at age 18, July 4, 1862, for the war. Reported present on surviving company muster rolls through December 31, 1864. No further records. Survived the war.

TAYLOR, BENJAMIN F., Private

Born in Greene County where he resided as a farmer prior to enlisting in Greene County at age 27, May 13, 1862, for the war. Reported absent without leave on December 14, 1862. Returned to duty in January-February, 1863. Reported present on surviving company muster rolls through December 31, 1864. No further records.

TAYLOR, GEORGE K. P., Private

Born in Greene County where he resided as a farmer prior to enlisting in Greene County at age 24, May 13, 1862, for the war. Rejected for service. Reason he was rejected not reported. [See special note at the end of the history of Company E, 61st Regiment N.C. Troops (page 692).]

TAYLOR, JAMES S., Private

Born in Lenoir County where he resided as a farmer prior to enlisting in Lenoir County at age 21, April 14, 1862. Reported present or accounted for in November, 1862-December, 1863, and March-April, 1864. Hospitalized at Richmond, Virginia, August 28, 1864, with intermittent fever. Returned to duty on December 17, 1864. Reported present through December 31, 1864. No further records. Survived the war.

TAYLOR, LEWIS H., Private

Enlisted in Duplin County at age 23, July 1, 1862, for the war. Reported present but sick in November, 1862-February, 1863. Reported in hospital at Charleston, South Carolina, March 2, 1863. Furloughed on an unspecified date. Reported absent without leave from April 25 through August 31, 1863. Reported present but sick in September-October, 1863. Returned to duty in November-December, 1863. Reported present in March-April, 1864. Reported absent sick at Goldsboro on October 25, 1864. Returned to duty in November-December, 1864. No further records. Survived the war.

TURNAGE, JOHN FRANKLIN, Private

Resided in Greene County where he enlisted on July 15, 1862, for the war. Reported present or accounted for in November, 1862-

April, 1863. Hospitalized at Wilmington on an unspecified date with typhoid fever. Furloughed on June 20, 1863. Returned to duty prior to September 1, 1863. Reported present on surviving company muster rolls through October 31, 1864. Hospitalized at Richmond on or about December 9, 1864. No further records. Survived the war. [Was about 20 years of age at time of enlistment.]

TURNER, GEORGE, Private

Born on January 6, 1846. Enlisted in Lenoir County at age 18, January 6, 1864, for the war. Reported present in March-April, 1864. Hospitalized at High Point on October 20, 1864, with a gunshot wound of the head. Place and date wounded not reported (probably wounded at Fort Harrison, Virginia, September 30, 1864). Furloughed on October 21, 1864. Returned to duty in November-December, 1864. No further records. Survived the war.

WADSWORTH, JOHN J., Musician

Enlisted in Lenoir County on July 12, 1862, for the war. Mustered in as Musician. Died in hospital at Greenville on December 14, 1862. Cause of death not reported.

WELCH, BERNARD, Private

Previously served as Private in 2nd Company H, 40th Regiment N.C. Troops (3rd Regiment N.C. Artillery). Transferred to this company in July, 1863. Wounded in the arm and captured at Morris Island, Charleston Harbor, South Carolina, August 26, 1863. Confined at Hilton Head, South Carolina, September 1, 1863. Transferred to Fort Columbus, New York Harbor, where he arrived on October 6, 1863. Transferred to Point Lookout, Maryland, October 9, 1863. Released at Point Lookout on January 21, 1864, after taking the Oath of Allegiance and joining the U.S. Navy. [Contrary to 1:489 of this series, the correct spelling of his surname was probably Welch rather than Welsh.]

WILLIAMS, HENRY, Private

Enlisted in Greene County on July 1, 1862, for the war. Reported present in November, 1862-December, 1863, and March-April, 1864. Died in hospital at Richmond, Virginia, July 13 or July 16, 1864, of "diarrhoea ch[ronica]."

WOOTEN, ALLEN WHITFIELD, 1st Sergeant

Previously served as Corporal in Captain Croom's Company, N.C. Local Defense Troops. Enlisted in this company in Lenoir County on December 19, 1863, for the war. Mustered in with an unspecified rank. Promoted to 1st Sergeant on December 31, 1863. Reported present in March-April, 1864. Wounded "very slightly" in the knee at Cold Harbor, Virginia, May 31-June 3, 1864. Killed at the Crater, near Petersburg, Virginia, July 30, 1864.

COMPANY F

This company, nicknamed the "Trio Guards," was raised in Wilson, Greene, and Pitt Counties in March-May, 1862, as Capt. Andrew J. Moore's Independent Company. It was mustered into state service at Camp Mangum, near Raleigh, May 23, 1862. On or about September 29, 1862, the company was assigned to the newly organized 59th Regiment N.C. Troops. That unit was redesignated the 61st Regiment N.C. Troops on an unknown date between October 30 and November 22, 1862. This company was designated Company F. After joining the regiment the company functioned as a part of the regiment, and its history for the remainder of the war is reported as a part of the regimental history.

The following roster was compiled primarily from information in the microfilm edition of the Compiled Service Records of Soldiers Who Served in Organizations from the State of North Carolina (Record Group 109, MC 270), National Archives and Records Administration, Washington, D.C. Record Group 109 includes enlistment papers, pay vouchers, requisitions, letters of resignation, discharge certificates, and abstracts of medical and prisoner of war returns. Materials relating specifically to Company F of the 61st Regiment include a company muster-in and descriptive roll dated May 23, 1862, and company muster rolls for November, 1862-April, 1864, and September-December, 1864.

Also utilized in this roster were *The War of the Rebellion: A Compilation of the Official Records of the Union and Confederate Armies*, the North Carolina adjutant general's *Roll of Honor*, state militia records, newspaper casualty lists and obituaries, wartime claims for bounty pay and allowances, postwar registers of claims for artificial limbs, Confederate pension applications filed with the states of North Carolina, Tennessee, and Florida, Confederate Soldiers' Home records, and the 1860 and 1870 federal censuses of North Carolina. A search was made also for relevant letters, diaries, reminiscences, and other manuscripts in the Southern Historical Collection (University of North Carolina-Chapel Hill), the Duke University Library Special Collections Department, and the North Carolina Division of Archives and History.

Among the secondary sources consulted were records of the North Carolina division of the United Daughters of the Confederacy, postwar rosters, regimental and county histories, marriage bond, will, and cemetery indexes, published and unpublished genealogies, biographical dictionaries, the North Carolina *County Heritage Book* series, the *Confederate Veteran*, Walter Clark's *Histories of the Several Regiments and Battalions from North Carolina in the Great War, 1861-'65*, and the North Carolina volume of the extended edition of *Confederate Military History*.

Note: The following roster contains service records for thirteen men who enlisted in Captain Moore's Independent Company but whose service terminated prior to September 29, 1862, the date that it was mustered into the 59th Regiment N.C. Troops (later redesignated the 61st Regiment N.C. Troops). Those men, it will be evident, never served in the 61st Regiment. Their service records are included here because too little information survives to compile a roster for Moore's Independent Company. All service records falling into the early-termination category conclude with a "special note" alerting readers to that fact and referring them to the information contained in this paragraph.

OFFICERS

CAPTAINS

MOORE, ANDREW JACKSON

Born in Pitt County and resided in Wilson or New Hanover County where he was by occupation a farmer prior to enlisting at age 25. Appointed Captain on April 4, 1862. Reported present in November, 1862-June, 1863. Wounded in the right arm at Morris Island, Charleston Harbor, South Carolina, August 25, 1863. Hospitalized at Charleston. Reported absent on furlough in September-October, 1863. Reported in hospital at Wilson in November, 1863-February, 1864. Retired to the Invalid Corps on April 26, 1864.

DARDEN, WILLIAM ABRAM, JR.

Born in Greene County on May 15, 1836. Resided in Greene County and was by occupation a farmer prior to enlisting in Wake County at age 25. Appointed 2nd Lieutenant on April 4, 1862. Reported present or accounted for in November, 1862-April, 1864. Promoted to 1st Lieutenant on September 29, 1863. Reported in command of the company in July-October, 1863, and January-February, 1864. Promoted to Captain on April 26, 1864. Captured at Fort Harrison, Virginia, September 30, 1864. Confined at Old Capitol Prison, Washington, D.C., October 6, 1864. Transferred to Fort Delaware, Delaware, where he arrived on October 23, 1864. Released at Fort Delaware on June 10, 1865, after taking the Oath of Allegiance.

LIEUTENANTS

BARNES, JESSE D., 2nd Lieutenant

Born in Wilson County* where he resided prior to enlisting in Wilson County at age 25, April 28, 1862, for the war. Mustered in as Sergeant. Promoted to 1st Sergeant prior to January 1, 1863. Reported present in November, 1862-December, 1863. Appointed 3rd Lieutenant on October 15, 1863. Reported at home on furlough in January-February, 1864. Returned to duty in March-April, 1864. Wounded in the eye at Drewry's Bluff, Virginia, May 13-16, 1864. Promoted to 2nd Lieutenant on May 30, 1864. Returned to duty prior to July 30, 1864, when he was killed at the Crater, near Petersburg, Virginia.

BELCHER, JOHN B., 2nd Lieutenant

Born in Edgecombe County where he resided as a farmer prior to enlisting in Wilson County at age 22, April 19, 1862, for the war. Mustered in as Sergeant. Reported present in November, 1862-August, 1863. Reported on detail in the ordnance department from October 22, 1863, through April 30, 1864. Elected 3rd Lieutenant on or about June 8, 1864. Promoted to 2nd Lieutenant on July 30, 1864. Reported sick in hospital on August 2, 1864. Returned to duty in September-October, 1864. Reported present and in command of the company in September-December, 1864. No further records.

DANIEL, PARROTT F. M., 3rd Lieutenant

Born in Greene County and was by occupation a farmer prior to enlisting in Greene County at age 22, May 15, 1862, for the war. Mustered in as Sergeant. Reported present or accounted for in November, 1862-August, 1863. Furloughed home sick on September 18, 1863. Returned to duty in November-December, 1863. Reported present in January-April, 1864. Wounded slightly in the side at the Crater, near Petersburg, Virginia, July 30, 1864. Returned to duty on an unspecified date. Appointed 3rd Lieutenant on September 6, 1864. Killed at Fort Harrison, Virginia, September 30, 1864.

EXUM, JAMES H., 1st Lieutenant

Previously served as Private in Company D, 1st Regiment N.C. Infantry (6 months, 1861). Appointed 3rd Lieutenant of this company on April 4, 1862. Reported present in November, 1862-February, 1863. Reported absent on sick furlough on March 25, 1863. Returned to duty subsequent to April 30, 1863. Furloughed home on June 20, 1863. Returned to duty in July-August, 1863. Promoted to 2nd Lieutenant on October 1, 1863. Reported present and in command of the company in November-December, 1863. Reported present in January-April, 1864. Promoted to 1st

Lieutenant on May 30, 1864. Furloughed on or about October 16, 1864. Reported absent without leave on November 26, 1864. No further records.

HARRIS, HENRY, 1st Lieutenant

Born in Pitt County on September 17, 1832. Was by occupation a farmer prior to enlisting in Wake County at age 29. Appointed 1st Lieutenant on April 4, 1862. Reported present in November, 1862-April, 1863. Reported present but sick in quarters in May-June, 1863. Reported present in July-August, 1863. Resigned on September 20, 1863, by reason of "rheumatism." Resignation accepted on September 28, 1863.

NONCOMMISSIONED OFFICERS
AND PRIVATES

BAKER, BENJAMIN, Private

Resided in Wilson County and was by occupation the proprietor of (or otherwise affiliated with) a "grog shop" prior to enlisting in Wilson County at age 22, July 3, 1862, for the war. Wounded in the thigh at Kinston on December 14, 1862. Returned to duty prior to January 1, 1863. Hospitalized at Wilmington on February 13, 1863, with catarrhus. Returned to duty on February 20, 1863. Reported present but sick in March-April, 1863. Hospitalized at Wilmington on or about June 26, 1863, with rheumatism and/or anemia. Returned to duty on July 26, 1863. Reported present or accounted for in September, 1863-April, 1864, and September-December, 1864. Paroled at Goldsboro on May 9, 1865.

BAKER, BENNETT, Private

Born in Wilson County* and was by occupation a farmer prior to enlisting in Wilson County at age 21, April 12, 1862. Reported present in November-December, 1862. Discharged on February 13, 1863, by a medical examining board. Reason discharged not reported. Reenlisted in the company on an unspecified date (probably in January-April, 1864). Reported in hospital at Petersburg, Virginia, April 11, 1864. Issued clothing on May 6, 1864. No further records.

BAKER, JOHN, Private

Born in Wilson County* where he resided as a farmer prior to enlisting in Wilson at age 34, May 4, 1862, for the war. Reported present in November, 1862-February, 1863. Reported present but sick in March-April, 1863. Furloughed on June 25, 1863. Returned to duty prior to September 1, 1863. Reported present through April 30, 1864. Wounded in the face at Fort Harrison, Virginia, September 30, 1864. Returned to duty in November-December, 1864. Paroled at Goldsboro on May 15, 1865.

BAKER, RICHARD, Private

Born in Wilson County* where he resided as a shingle setter[?] prior to enlisting in Wilson County at age 25, May 4, 1862, for the war. Reported present in November, 1862-October, 1863. Reported sick in camp near Petersburg, Virginia, in November-December, 1863. Reported present in January-April, 1864. Wounded in the head at Drewry's Bluff, Virginia, May 19, 1864. Died in hospital at Bermuda Hundred, Virginia, May 20, 1864, of wounds.

BAKER, THOMAS, SR., Private

Born in Wilson County* and was by occupation a farmer prior to enlisting in Wilson County at age 28, May 8, 1862, for the war.

Reported present in November-December, 1862. Discharged on February 13, 1863, by the medical examining board of the Cape Fear District. Reason discharged not reported.

BAKER, THOMAS F., JR., Private

Born in Wilson County* where he resided as a farmer prior to enlisting in Wilson County at age 25, May 8, 1862, for the war. Reported present in November, 1862-June, 1863. Reported present but sick in quarters in July-August, 1863. Reported present in September, 1863-April, 1864, and September-December, 1864. Paroled at Goldsboro on May 15, 1865.

BARDIN, JESSE J., Private

Resided in Wilson County and enlisted in Wake County at age 23, July 16, 1862, for the war. Reported present in November-December, 1862. Discharged by the medical examining board of the Cape Fear District on February 13, 1863. Reason discharged not reported.

BOWDEN, WHITE, Private

Enlisted in Wake County on July 16, 1862, for the war. Reported present or accounted for in November, 1862-April, 1864. Killed at the Crater, near Petersburg, Virginia, July 30, 1864.

BOYCE, ZACHARIAH, Private

Resided in Wilson County and was by occupation a farm laborer prior to enlisting in New Hanover County at age 35, January 1, 1863, for the war. Reported present or accounted for in January, 1863-April, 1864. Wounded in the hip at Cold Harbor, Virginia, May 31-June 3, 1864. Reported present in September-December, 1864. Paroled at Goldsboro on May 15, 1865.

BROWN, SAMUEL H., Private

Born in Pitt County and was by occupation a farmer prior to enlisting in Pitt County at age 34, May 2, 1862, for the war. Reported present in November, 1862-June, 1863. Reported sick in hospital at Augusta, Georgia, July 14, 1863. Reported on detached service near Petersburg, Virginia, in November, 1863-February, 1864. Rejoined the company in March-April, 1864. Reported present in September-October, 1864. Hospitalized at Richmond, Virginia, December 14, 1864, with typhoid pneumonia. Returned to duty on January 24, 1865. Captured (or deserted to the enemy) near Raleigh on April 12, 1865. No further records. Survived the war.

BURRASS, BENNETT J., Private

Enlisted in Wilson County on July 3, 1862, for the war. Reported absent without leave on October 20, 1862. Returned to duty on May 27, 1863. Transferred to Company A, 2nd Regiment Confederate Engineer Troops, July 3, 1863.

BURRASS, ISAAC, Private

Born in Wilson County* and was by occupation a farmer prior to enlisting in Wilson County at age 33, May 8, 1862, for the war. Reported sick at home on December 10, 1862. Hospitalized at Wilmington on or about February 16, 1863, with parotitis. Returned to duty on March 11 or March 27, 1863. Discharged on May 1, 1863, by a medical examining board at Charleston, South Carolina. Reason discharged not reported. Reported in hospital at Wilmington on May 5, 1863, with catarrh. No further records.

CARAWAY, BENAJAH, Private

Resided in Greene County where he enlisted on June 28, 1862, for the war. Reported present or accounted for in November, 1862-

April, 1864, and September-December, 1864. No further records. [Was about 16 years of age at time of enlistment.]

CARAWAY, JESSE B., Private

Resided in Greene County and was by occupation a farm hand prior to enlisting in Greene County at age 18, June 28, 1862, for the war. Reported present or accounted for in November, 1862-April, 1864. Wounded in the shoulder at Drewry's Bluff, Virginia, on or about May 13, 1864. Hospitalized at Richmond, Virginia. Returned to duty prior to September 30, 1864, when he was captured at Fort Harrison, Virginia. Confined at Point Lookout, Maryland, October 5, 1864. Paroled at Point Lookout on March 17, 1865. Received at Boulware's Wharf, James River, Virginia, March 19, 1865, for exchange. No further records. Survived the war.

CARAWAY, JOHN H., Sergeant

Enlisted in Greene County on June 28, 1862, for the war. Mustered in as Private. Wounded at Kinston on December 14, 1862. Returned to duty prior to January 1, 1863. Promoted to Corporal on April 15, 1863. Promoted to Sergeant in November-December, 1863. Reported present through April 30, 1864. Killed at Drewry's Bluff, Virginia, May 16, 1864.

CARAWAY, WILLIAM J., Private

Born in Greene County and was by occupation a mechanic prior to enlisting in Greene County at age 27, May 15, 1862, for the war. Reported absent without leave on November 2, 1862. Returned to duty on or about March 5, 1863. Reported present but sick in quarters in May-June, 1863. Deserted on August 20, 1863.

CARAWAY, WILLIAM MARCELLUS, Private

Born on August 24, 1842. Enlisted in Greene County at age 19, July 14, 1862, for the war. Reported present in November, 1862-April, 1864, and September-October, 1864. No further records. Survived the war.

COLTRAIN, STEPHEN, Private

Enlisted in Wilson County on July 3, 1862, for the war. Reported present in November, 1862-April, 1864. Killed at Cold Harbor, Virginia, May 31-June 3, 1864.

COLTRAIN, THOMAS, Private

Enlisted in Wilson County at age 18, July 3, 1862, for the war. Reported absent sick without leave on December 14, 1862. Returned to duty in May-June, 1863. Reported present but sick in quarters in September-October, 1863. Reported absent sick in November-December, 1863. Reported absent on detached service at Petersburg, Virginia, in January-February, 1864. Rejoined the company in March-April, 1864. Reported present in September-October, 1864. Reported absent without leave on December 30, 1864. No further records. Survived the war. [North Carolina pension records indicate that he was wounded in the right thigh by a piece of shell on an unspecified date.]

CORBITT, EDMOND, Private

Born in Pitt County and was by occupation a farmer prior to enlisting in Pitt County at age 17, April 28, 1862, for the war. Discharged on or about May 24, 1862. Reason discharged not reported. [See special note at the end of the history of Company F, 61st Regiment N.C. Troops (page 705).]

CORBITT, LEESTON, Private

Born in Pitt County and enlisted in New Hanover County on January 1, 1863, for the war. Died in hospital at Charleston, South Carolina, on or about March 25, 1863. Cause of death not reported.

CORBITT, MARTIN, Private

Born in Pitt County where he resided as a farmer or laborer prior to enlisting in Pitt County at age 20, April 28, 1862, for the war. Reported present in November, 1862-April, 1864. Wounded in the thigh at Fort Harrison, Virginia, September 30, 1864. Hospitalized at Richmond, Virginia. Reported absent wounded through December 31, 1864. Paroled at Goldsboro on May 10, 1865.

CRAFT, JOHN, Private

Resided in Greene County and was by occupation a farmer prior to enlisting in Wake County at age 30, October 27, 1864, for the war. Reported present in November-December, 1864. No further records.

CRAWFORD, JAMES A., Corporal

Born in Pitt County and was by occupation a farmer prior to enlisting in Pitt County at age 18, May 6, 1862, for the war. Mustered in as Private. Reported present in November, 1862-April, 1864. Promoted to Corporal in May-October, 1864. Wounded in the hand at Fort Harrison, Virginia, September 30, 1864. Returned to duty prior to November 1, 1864. Reported absent without leave on December 16, 1864. No further records.

DANIEL, ANDREW JACKSON, Corporal

Born in Greene County and was by occupation a farmer prior to enlisting in Wayne County at age 20, May 16, 1862, for the war. Mustered in as Private. Reported present from November, 1862, until June 25, 1863, when he was detailed as an orderly. Promoted to Corporal on July 16, 1863. Wounded in the hand at Morris Island, Charleston Harbor, South Carolina, August 26, 1863. Furloughed from hospital at Charleston on September 19, 1863. Returned to duty in November-December, 1863. Reported present through April 30, 1864. Retired to the Invalid Corps on July 22, 1864, presumably by reason of wounds received at Morris Island.

DARDEN, ABRAM L., Sergeant

Resided in Greene County and was by occupation a student prior to enlisting in Greene County at age 18, March 3, 1863, for the war. Mustered in as Private. Reported present but sick in March-April, 1863. Returned to duty in May-June, 1863. Reported present in July, 1863-April, 1864. Promoted to Corporal in November-December, 1863. Wounded slightly in the wrist at the Crater, near Petersburg, Virginia, July 30, 1864. Returned to duty on an unspecified date. Promoted to Sergeant in August-October, 1864. Wounded in the neck, arm, and right foot at Fort Harrison, Virginia, September 30, 1864. Right foot amputated. Hospitalized at Richmond, Virginia. Furloughed for sixty days on or about November 10, 1864. No further records. Survived the war.

DAVIS, BENJAMIN ARCHIBALD, Corporal

Born in Pitt County where he resided as a farmer prior to enlisting in Pitt County at age 33, April 7, 1862. Mustered in as Private. Promoted to Corporal in November-December, 1862. Reported present in November, 1862-June, 1863. Mortally wounded (leg shot off at knee) at James Island, Charleston Harbor, South Carolina, July 16, 1863. Died the same date.

DeBERRY, LEMUEL J., Sergeant

Born in Pitt County where he resided as a farmer prior to enlisting in Pitt County at age 25, May 6, 1862, for the war. Mustered in as Private. Accidentally wounded in the foot by a bayonet at Kinston on December 14, 1862. Returned to duty and was promoted to Sergeant prior to January 1, 1863. Reported present in January-February, 1863. Discharged on April 14, 1863, after providing Pvt. Joseph Key as a substitute. [Previously served as 2nd Lieutenant in the 17th Regiment N.C. Militia.]

DERRING, JOHN R., Private

Born in Greene County where he resided as a student or farmer prior to enlisting in Greene County at age 18, May 15, 1862, for the war. Rejected for service. Reason he was rejected not reported. [See special note at the end of the history of Company F, 61st Regiment N.C. Troops (page 705).]

DUPREE, JAMES B., Private

Born in Pitt County where he resided as a farmer or college student prior to enlisting in Pitt County at age 18, April 7, 1862. Reported present in November-December, 1862. Died in hospital at Wilmington on January 31, 1863, of "smallpox."

EASON, CURMUDUS [MOODY], Private

Born in Wilson County* and resided in Greene County where he was by occupation a farmer or day laborer prior to enlisting in Wilson County at age 18, May 8, 1862, for the war. Rejected for service on account of "chronic derangement." [See special note at the end of the history of Company F, 61st Regiment N.C. Troops (page 705). North Carolina pension records indicate that he subsequently attempted to reenlist in the company but was rejected because of "inability to serve."]

EDWARDS, JOHN W., Private

Born in Wilson County* where he resided as a turpentiner prior to enlisting in Wilson County at age 25, April 10, 1862. Reported present or accounted for in November, 1862-April, 1864. Captured at Fort Harrison, Virginia, September 30, 1864. Confined at Point Lookout, Maryland, October 5, 1864. Died at Point Lookout on May 30, 1865, of "pneumonia."

EDWARDS, WILLIAM R., Private

Born in Greene County where he resided as a farmer prior to enlisting in Greene County at age 27, May 15, 1862, for the war. Reported present in November-December, 1862. Discharged by the medical examining board of the Cape Fear District on February 13, 1863. Reason discharged not reported.

ELLIS, JONATHAN, Private

Born in Wilson County* and was by occupation a farmer prior to enlisting in Wilson County at age 31, May 8, 1862, for the war. Reported present or accounted for in November, 1862-April, 1863. Sent home sick on June 27, 1863. Reported absent on detached service at Petersburg, Virginia, in January-February, 1864. Reported present but sick in March-April, 1864. No further records. Survived the war.

FELTON, BENJAMIN FRANK, Private

Born in Greene County where he resided as a mechanic or carpenter prior to enlisting in Greene County at age 26, May 15, 1862, for the war. Reported present or accounted for in November, 1862-April, 1864. Wounded in the elbow at Drewry's Bluff, Virginia, May 13-16, 1864. Returned to duty prior to May 31-June 3, 1864,

when he was wounded in the head at Cold Harbor, Virginia. Returned to duty prior to July 30, 1864, when he was killed at the Crater, near Petersburg, Virginia.

FELTON, JOSEPH W., Private

Born in Wilson County* where he resided as a farmer prior to enlisting in Wilson County at age 28, May 8, 1862, for the war. Reported present or accounted for in November, 1862-April, 1864. Killed at the Crater, near Petersburg, Virginia, July 30, 1864.

FLOWERS, PERRY, Private

Enlisted in Wilson County on June 3, 1863, for the war. Reported present in June, 1863-April, 1864, and September-October, 1864. Reported absent without leave on December 30, 1864. No further records. Survived the war. [Was about 48 years of age at time of enlistment. North Carolina pension records indicate that he was wounded in the forehead at New Bern on August 30, 1862, and was wounded in the leg, arm, and chin on unspecified dates.]

FRYAR, WILLIAM, Private

Born in Pitt County and was by occupation a farmer prior to enlisting in Wilson County at age 17, May 15, 1862, for the war. Discharged on or about May 24, 1862, probably by reason of being underage. Reenlisted in the company on April 15, 186[4]. Killed at Drewry's Bluff, Virginia, May 13-16, 1864. "He was a brave boy and died nobly at his post."

GARRIS, JOHN T., Private

Born in Pitt County and was by occupation a farmer prior to enlisting in Pitt County at age 34, May 6, 1862, for the war. Reported present or accounted for in November, 1862-October, 1863. Hospitalized at Wilson on December 3, 1863. Admitted to hospital at Petersburg, Virginia, February 22, 1864, with fistula in ano. Returned to duty on an unspecified date. Killed at Petersburg, Virginia, June 17, 1864.

HARRELL, JACKSON, Private

Born in Wilson County* and was by occupation a farmer prior to enlisting in Wilson County at age 21, May 15, 1862, for the war. Reported present in November-December, 1862. Hospitalized at Wilmington on February 1, 1863, with continued fever. Returned to duty on February 25, 1863. Reported sick in hospital at Wilmington in March-April, 1863. Furloughed for thirty days on June 13, 1863. Reported present but sick in quarters in September-October, 1863. Discharged by a medical examining board at Sullivan's Island, Charleston Harbor, South Carolina, on or about November 20, 1863.

HARRISON, JOHN J., Private

Born in Greene County where he resided as a farmer prior to enlisting in Greene County at age 33, May 15, 1862, for the war. Reported present in November-December, 1862. Reported sick in hospital at Wilmington from February 6 through April 30, 1863. Reported on detail as a shoemaker at Raleigh from June 10 through October 31, 1863. Reported on detached service at Petersburg, Virginia, in November, 1863-February, 1864. Reported present but sick in March-April, 1864. Reported present in September-October, 1864. Detailed in the brigade shoe shop in November-December, 1864. No further records.

HARRISON, WILLIAM H., Private

Born in Greene County where he resided as a farmer or day laborer prior to enlisting in Greene County at age 28, May 15, 1862, for the war. Reported present in November-December, 1862. Discharged by the medical examining board of the Cape Fear District on February 13, 1863. Reason discharged not reported.

HEATH, JOHN, Private

Resided in Greene County and was by occupation a farmer prior to enlisting in Greene County at age 32, June 28, 1862, for the war. Reported present in November, 1862-April, 1864, and September-December, 1864. No further records.

HOWARD, WILLIE J., Private

Resided in Wilson County where he enlisted on July 3, 1862, for the war. Reported present in November, 1862-April, 1863. Reported present but sick in quarters in May-June, 1863. Reported sick at home from August 20 through October 31, 1863. Reported sick in camp near Petersburg, Virginia, in November-December, 1863. Returned to duty in January-February, 1864. Wounded in the hand at Drewry's Bluff, Virginia, May 13-16, 1864. Hospitalized at Richmond, Virginia. Returned to duty prior to November 1, 1864. Reported present in November-December, 1864. Captured near Kinston on March 10, 1865. Confined at Point Lookout, Maryland, March 16, 1865. Released at Point Lookout on June 27, 1865, after taking the Oath of Allegiance.

JACKSON, JAMES T., Private

Enlisted in Wake County on July 16, 1862, for the war. Reported sick in hospital at Goldsboro from December 27, 1862, through April 30, 1863. Furloughed on an unspecified date. Reported sick at home through August 31, 1863. Reported sick in hospital at Goldsboro in September-December, 1863. Reported on detached service at Petersburg, Virginia, in January-February, 1864. Reported present but sick in March-April, 1864. Hospitalized at Goldsboro on an unspecified date. Returned to duty on or about October 11, 1864. Reported sick at the division infirmary on or about October 31, 1864. Hospitalized at Richmond, Virginia, December 22, 1864. Returned to duty on December 27, 1864. Hospitalized at Greensboro on January 3, 1865, with pneumonia. Furloughed on February 2, 1865. No further records.

JEFFERSON, HENRY CLAY, Private

Born in Pitt County where he resided prior to enlisting in Pitt County at age 18, April 18, 1862, for the war. Reported absent sick on May 24, 1862. No further records. Survived the war. [See special note at the end of the history of Company F, 61st Regiment N.C. Troops (page 705).]

JOHNSON, ALCUE, Private

Resided in Johnston County and enlisted in Wilson County on May 8, 1862, for the war. Reported present or accounted for in November, 1862-April, 1864, and September-December, 1864. Paroled at Goldsboro on May 12, 1865.

JONES, RODERIC, Private

Resided in Wilson County and was by occupation a farm laborer prior to enlisting in Wilson County at age 32, July 15, 1862, for the war. Reported present or accounted for in November, 1862-April, 1864. Reported on detail as a butcher from July 20 through December 31, 1864. No further records.

JOYNER, ABRAHAM, Corporal

Born in Pitt County and was by occupation a farmer prior to enlisting in Pitt County at age 17, May 16, 1862, for the war as a

substitute for J. H. Mayo. Mustered in as Corporal. Died in hospital at Richmond, Virginia, December 13, 1862, of "rheut con lungs."

KEY, JOSEPH, Private

Enlisted at James Island, Charleston Harbor, South Carolina, April 14, 1863, for the war as a substitute for Sgt. Lemuel J. DeBerry. Deserted on April 15, 1863.

LANE, JOSEPH J., Sergeant

Born in Greene County and resided in Wilson County where he was by occupation a farmer prior to enlisting in Wilson County at age 30, April 19, 1862, for the war. Mustered in as Sergeant. Appointed Ordnance Sergeant on September 13, 1862, and transferred to the Field and Staff of this regiment.

LANGLEY, JAMES, Private

Born in Edgecombe County where he resided as a farmer prior to enlisting in Pitt County at age 33, April 28, 1862, for the war. Reported present in November-December, 1862. Hospitalized at Wilmington on February 17, 1863, with abscesses of the leg. Returned to duty on March 9, 1863. Reported in hospital at Wilmington on or about April 30, 1863. Furloughed for forty days on or about July 22, 1863, suffering from extreme debility from a protracted case of rheumatism. Failed to return to duty and was reported absent without leave on or about September 1, 1863. Listed as a deserter and dropped from the company rolls in March-April, 1864.

LETCHWORTH, ELIAS, Private

Born in Greene County and was by occupation a mechanic prior to enlisting in Greene County at age 27, May 15, 1862, for the war. Reported present in November-December, 1862. Reported on detached service at Fort Caswell from January 3 through February 22, 1863. Rejoined the company in March-April, 1863. Transferred to the engineer department on July 2, 1863.

LEWIS, J. T., Private

Resided in Pitt County. Place and date of enlistment not reported (probably enlisted subsequent to February 28, 1865). Paroled at Goldsboro on an unspecified date (probably May, 1865).

LEWIS, WILLIAM T., Private

Born in England and resided in Pitt County where he was by occupation a house painter prior to enlisting in Pitt County at age 52, May 16, 1862, for the war. Wounded and captured at Kinston on December 14, 1862. Paroled on December 15, 1862. Reported absent wounded through April 30, 1864. Reported sick at the division infirmary in September-October, 1864. Reported sick in hospital in November-December, 1864. No further records.

LOTTERWHITE, L. B., _____

Resided in Wilson County. Place and date of enlistment not reported (probably enlisted subsequent to February 28, 1865). Paroled at Goldsboro on May 15, 1865.

McKEEL, JOHN D., Private

Born in Greene County and was by occupation a farmer or day laborer prior to enlisting in Greene County at age 22, May 15, 1862, for the war. Reported present in November, 1862-February, 1863. Reported present but sick in quarters in March-April, 1863.

Reported sick in hospital at Wilmington on June 27, 1863. Reported sick in hospital at Mount Pleasant, South Carolina, August 20, 1863. Furloughed home sick on October 2, 1863. Reported on detached service in camp near Petersburg, Virginia, in November-December, 1863. Returned to duty in January-February, 1864. Reported present in March-April, 1864. Wounded in the face and/or right arm at Fort Harrison, Virginia, September 30, 1864. Furloughed for forty days on October 13, 1864. Returned to duty in November-December, 1864. No further records.

McKEEL, W. R. D. SPEIGHT, Private

Born on June 15, 1845. Enlisted in Greene County at age 17, June 12, 1863, for the war. Reported present until transferred to Company F, 40th Regiment N.C. Troops (3rd Regiment N.C. Artillery), February 13, 1864.

McKEEL, WILLIAM F., Private

Born in Greene County and was by occupation a farmer prior to enlisting in Greene County at age 31, May 15, 1862, for the war. Reported present or accounted for in November, 1862-June, 1863. Deserted on August 20, 1863. Returned from desertion on October 21, 1863, and placed under arrest. Returned to duty in November-December, 1863. Reported present through April 30, 1864. Killed at Cold Harbor, Virginia, May 31-June 3, 1864.

MATTHEWS, IVEY, Private

Born in Pitt County and was by occupation a farmer prior to enlisting in Pitt County at age 34, May 10, 1862, for the war. Reported present in November, 1862-February, 1863. Died in hospital at Columbia, South Carolina, April 8, 1863. Cause of death not reported.

MATTHEWS, JOHN Q. A., Private

Born in Pitt County where he resided as a farmer prior to enlisting in Pitt County at age 26, April 7, 1862. Reported present or accounted for in November, 1862-June, 1863. Reported on detail guarding baggage at Wilmington from July 11 through December 31, 1863. Reported absent on sick furlough in January-February, 1864. Returned to duty in March-April, 1864. Wounded in the shoulder and knees and captured at Fort Harrison, Virginia, September 30, 1864. Hospitalized at Fort Monroe, Virginia, October 4, 1864. Escaped from hospital at Fort Monroe on January 6, 1865. Apprehended on an unspecified date and was confined at Fort Monroe on January 27, 1865. Transferred to Point Lookout, Maryland, February 1, 1865. Released at Point Lookout on June 29, 1865, after taking the Oath of Allegiance.

MAY, ALFRED E., 1st Sergeant

Resided in Pitt County and enlisted in New Hanover County at age 19, August 25, 1862, for the war. Mustered in as Private. Reported present in November, 1862-April, 1863. Promoted to Corporal on January 1, 1863. Promoted to Sergeant on April 15, 1863. Reported present or accounted for in May-December, 1863. Promoted to 1st Sergeant in November-December, 1863. Reported present in January-April and September-December, 1864. No further records. Survived the war.

MAY, BENJAMIN T., Private

Born in Pitt County where he resided as a farmer prior to enlisting in Pitt County at age 30, May 6, 1862, for the war. Reported present or accounted for in November, 1862-April, 1864. Wounded slightly in the head at the Crater, near Petersburg, Virginia, July

30, 1864. Reported present in September-December, 1864. No further records. Survived the war.

MAY, ROBERT S., Private

Born in Pitt County where he resided as a farmer or farm hand prior to enlisting in Pitt County at age 23, April 7, 1862. Reported present or accounted for in November, 1862-April, 1864. Died in hospital at Richmond, Virginia, October 16, 1864. Cause of death not reported. [Briefly attached to Company G, 2nd Regiment Confederate Engineer Troops, in the early autumn of 1864 as an artificer.]

MERCER, HYMAN, Private

Enlisted in Wilson County on April 15, 1864, for the war. Hospitalized at Richmond, Virginia, on an unspecified date. Furloughed on September 10, 1864. Hospitalized at High Point on October 14, 1864, with pneumonia. Furloughed on October 15, 1864. Returned to duty in November-December, 1864. Paroled at Goldsboro on May 9, 1865.

MERCER, LEVI, Private

Resided in Wilson County where he enlisted at age 40, June 1, 1863, for the war. Reported sick in hospital at Charleston, South Carolina, August 30, 1863. Reported at home on sick furlough on September 28, 1863. Returned to duty in November-December, 1863. Reported present or accounted for in January-April and September-December, 1864. Paroled at Goldsboro on May 9, 1865.

MERCER, W. JAMES, Private

Resided in Wilson County where he enlisted on April 15, 1864, for the war. Hospitalized at Petersburg, Virginia, April 30, 1864, with scrofula. Later contracted ascites. Returned to duty on May 16, 1864. Wounded in the right arm and/or left hand at or near Cold Harbor, Virginia, on or about June 1-3, 1864. Hospitalized at Danville, Virginia. Furloughed on June 6, 1864. Hospitalized at High Point on October 13, 1864, still suffering from a gunshot wound of the left hand. Furloughed on October 14, 1864. Returned to duty in November-December, 1864. Paroled at Goldsboro on May 9, 1865. [Was about 17 years of age at time of enlistment.]

MITCHELL, GEORGE W., Private

Previously served as Private in Company F, 40th Regiment N.C. Troops (3rd Regiment N.C. Artillery). Transferred to this company on February 13, 1864. Reported present in March-April, 1864. Wounded in the right arm at Cold Harbor, Virginia, May 31-June 3, 1864. Hospitalized at Richmond, Virginia, June 4, 1864. Furloughed for sixty days on June 9, 1864. Reported absent wounded through October 31, 1864. Returned to duty in November-December, 1864. No further records.

MOORE, AMOS, Private

Born in Pitt County where he resided as a farmer prior to enlisting in Pitt County at age 23, May 3, 1862, for the war. Died at home in Pitt County on December 8, 1862, of "typhoid fever."

MOORE, BENJAMIN F., Sergeant

Born in Pitt County and resided in Greene County where he was by occupation a farmer prior to enlisting in Wilson County at age 27, May 15, 1862, for the war. Mustered in as Sergeant. Dropped from the company rolls on or about May 24, 1862. Reason he was dropped not reported. [Previously served as 1st Lieutenant in the 29th Regiment N.C. Militia. See special note at the end of the history of Company F, 61st Regiment N.C. Troops (page 705).]

MOORE, DENNIS M., Private

Born in Wilson County* where he resided as a mechanic prior to enlisting in Wilson County at age 17, March 26, 1862. Reported present or accounted for in November, 1862-August, 1863. Detailed as color bearer on September 27, 1863. Died in hospital at Wilson on December 6-7, 1863, of "febris typh[oi]d[es]."

MOORE, HYMAN, Private

Born in Pitt County where he resided as a farmer or laborer prior to enlisting in Pitt County at age 30, May 15, 1862, for the war. Reported absent with leave on May 24, 1862. Dropped from the company rolls on an unspecified date (probably in the summer of 1862). [See special note at the end of the history of Company F, 61st Regiment N.C. Troops (page 705).]

MOORE, NATHAN G., Private

Born in Wilson County* and was by occupation a farmer prior to enlisting in Wilson County at age 16, March 17, 1862. Reported present or accounted for in November, 1862-October, 1863. Hospitalized at Petersburg, Virginia, December 19, 1863, with a wound of the foot. Place and date wounded not reported. Returned to duty on January 2, 1864. Reported present in January-April and September-December, 1864. No further records.

MOORE, SAMUEL L., Private

Born in Pitt County and was by occupation a farmer prior to enlisting in Jones County at age 17, May 8, 1862, for the war. Discharged on or about May 24, 1862. Reason discharged not reported. [See special note at the end of the history of Company F, 61st Regiment N.C. Troops (page 705).]

MOORE, WILLIAM J., Sergeant

Born in Pitt County where he resided as a farmer prior to enlisting in Wilson County at age 34, May 1, 1862, for the war. Mustered in as Corporal. Reported present in November-December, 1862. Promoted to Sergeant on January 1, 1863. Reported present in January, 1863-April, 1864. Hospitalized at Richmond, Virginia, October 29, 1864 (apparently suffering from chronic dysentery). Returned to duty on January 11, 1865. Hospitalized at Greensboro on February 21, 1865, with intermittent fever. Transferred to another hospital on February 23, 1865. No further records.

MOORING, BRYANT, Private

Born in Wayne County and resided in Greene County where he was by occupation a day laborer prior to enlisting in New Hanover County at age 23, August 25, 1862, for the war. Reported sick in hospital at Wilson from October 20, 1862, through June 30, 1863. Hospitalized at Wilmington on or about July 3, 1863, with catarrh. Furloughed on or about the same date. Reported absent on furlough through December 31, 1863. Discharged from service on April 2, 1864, by reason of "physical disability."

MURRAY, WILLIAM, Musician

Enlisted in Wilson County on July 15, 1862, for the war. Mustered in as Private. Reported present in November-December, 1862. Appointed Musician on February 14, 1863. Reported present in January-June, 1863. Hospitalized at Wilmington on or about August 11, 1863, with epilepsy. Furloughed for sixty days on an unspecified date. Reported absent sick at Charleston, South Carolina, October 23, 1863. Returned to duty in November-December, 1863. Reported present in January-April and September-December, 1864. No further records.

NEWTON, WILLIAM B. F., Private

Born in Pitt County where he resided as a merchant or farmer prior to enlisting in Pitt County at age 27, April 7, 1862. Reported absent with leave on May 24, 1862. Dropped from the company rolls on an unspecified date (probably in the summer of 1862). Reason he was dropped not reported. [See special note at the end of the history of Company F, 61st Regiment N.C. Troops (page 705).]

NORMAN, IRA E., Private

Born in Washington County on September 28, 1831. Resided in Greene County and was by occupation a carpenter or mechanic prior to enlisting in Wayne County at age 31, May 13, 1862, for the war. Mustered in as Musician. Reported present in November-December, 1862. Reduced to ranks in January-February, 1863. Detailed to work on the South Battery at Charleston, South Carolina, from February 22 through April 30, 1863. Rejoined the company in May-June, 1863. Reported present through October 31, 1863. Reported on detail as a regimental carpenter near Petersburg, Virginia, from November 9, 1863, through April 30, 1864. Rejoined the company on an unspecified date. Reported present in September-December, 1864. No further records. Survived the war.

OWENS, AMOS, Private

Resided in Wilson County and enlisted in Pitt County on April 7, 1862. Reported present in November-December, 1862. Detailed for duty as a teamster on January 3, 1863. Reported sick in hospital at Columbia, South Carolina, March 31, 1863. Furloughed on June 1, 1863. Reported in hospital at Wilmington on or about July 11, 1863, with typhoid fever. Reported on detached service at Petersburg, Virginia, in November, 1863-February, 1864. Reported present but sick in camp in March-April, 1864. Reported sick in hospital at Richmond in September-December, 1864. Paroled at Goldsboro on May 9, 1865.

OWENS, BENNETT M., Private

Born in Wilson County* where he resided as a farmer prior to enlisting in Wilson County at age 19, March 15, 1862. Mustered in as Corporal. Reported present or accounted for in November, 1862-April, 1864. Wounded in the head at Cold Harbor, Virginia, May 31-June 3, 1864. Hospitalized at Richmond, Virginia, June 25, 1864. Returned to duty on or about July 13, 1864. Reported sick at the division infirmary in September-October, 1864. Promoted to Sergeant prior to November 1, 1864. Reported present in November-December, 1864. Reduced to ranks on an unspecified date. Paroled at Goldsboro on May 9, 1865. [Previously served as 2nd Lieutenant in the 33rd Regiment N.C. Militia.]

OWENS, ELVERSON, Private

Born in Wilson County* where he resided as a farmer prior to enlisting in Wilson County at age 18, May 8, 1862, for the war. Rejected for service. Reason he was rejected not reported. Re-enlisted in the company on June 24, 1863. Reported present in July, 1863-April, 1864. Wounded in the head at Fort Harrison, Virginia, September 30, 1864. Returned to duty prior to November 1, 1864. Reported present in November-December, 1864. Paroled at Goldsboro on May 9, 1865.

OWENS, GEORGE R., Sergeant

Born in Wilson County* where he resided as a farmer prior to enlisting in Wilson County at age 21, May 8, 1862, for the war. Mustered in as Corporal. Reported present in November-December, 1862. Reported present or accounted for in January-October, 1863 (served as a member of the color guard during that period). Reported sick in camp near Petersburg, Virginia, in November-December, 1863. Reported on detached service at Petersburg in January-February, 1864. Reported absent on furlough in March-April, 1864. Promoted to Sergeant in May-June, 1864. Captured near Petersburg on June 16, 1864. Confined at Point Lookout, Maryland, June 19, 1864. Transferred to Elmira, New York, July 25, 1864. Paroled at Elmira on March 10, 1865. Received at Boulware's Wharf, James River, Virginia, March 15, 1865, for exchange. Paroled at Goldsboro on May 9, 1865. [Previously served as 2nd Lieutenant in the 33rd Regiment N.C. Militia.]

OWENS, JOHN T., Private

Born in Pitt County and was by occupation a farmer prior to enlisting in Wilson County at age 34, May 15, 1862, for the war. Reported present or accounted for in November, 1862-June, 1863. Wounded in the face, neck, and arm at Morris Island, Charleston Harbor, South Carolina, August 26, 1863. Hospitalized at Charleston. Furloughed from hospital on September 8, 1863. Reported on detail in the quartermaster department at Tarboro in January-April and September-December, 1864. No further records.

OWENS, JOHN W., Private

Born in Wilson County* where he resided as a farmer prior to enlisting in Wilson County at age 25, May 8, 1862, for the war. Reported present or accounted for in November, 1862-June, 1863. Wounded in the arm, neck, and/or hand at Morris Island, Charleston Harbor, South Carolina, August 26, 1863. Hospitalized at Charleston. Furloughed from hospital on September 8, 1863. Returned to duty in November-December, 1863. Reported present in January-April and September-December, 1864. Paroled at Goldsboro on an unspecified date (probably in May, 1865).

OWENS, WILLIAM Y., Private

Born in Wilson County* where he resided as a farmer prior to enlisting in Wilson County at age 24, May 8, 1862, for the war. Reported present or accounted for in November, 1862-April, 1864. Wounded in the groin at the Crater, near Petersburg, Virginia, July 30, 1864. Reported absent on wounded furlough in September-October, 1864. Hospitalized at Richmond, Virginia, November 8, 1864. Returned to duty on December 27, 1864. Paroled at Goldsboro on May 9, 1865.

PAGE, JOSEPH, Private

Born in Wilson County* and was by occupation a farmer prior to enlisting in Wilson County at age 32, May 8, 1862, for the war. Rejected for service. Reason he was rejected not reported. [See special note at the end of the history of Company F, 61st Regiment N.C. Troops (page 705).]

PEADEN, CHARLES N., Private

Born in Pitt County and was by occupation a farmer prior to enlisting in Pitt County at age 19, May 3, 1862, for the war. Reported present or accounted for in November, 1862-April, 1864, and September-December, 1864. No further records. Survived the war.

PEADEN, EDMOND, Private

Born in Pitt County where he resided as a farmer prior to enlisting in Pitt County at age 29, May 3, 1862, for the war. Reported present or accounted for in November, 1862-April, 1864. Wounded in the neck and/or groin at Drewry's Bluff, Virginia, May 13-16, 1864. Wounded in the face and neck at Cold Harbor, Virginia, May 31-June 3, 1864. Hospitalized at Richmond, Virginia.

Furloughed for sixty days on or about June 5, 1864. Returned to duty prior to November 1, 1864. Hospitalized at Richmond on December 2, 1864. Returned to duty on December 20, 1864. No further records.

PEADEN, JOHN R., Corporal

Born in Pitt County where he resided as a farmer prior to enlisting in Pitt County at age 18, May 3, 1862, for the war. Mustered in as Private. Reported present or accounted for in November, 1862-April, 1864. Promoted to Corporal in May-September, 1864. Wounded in the left heel and ankle at Fort Harrison, Virginia, September 30, 1864. Hospitalized at Richmond, Virginia, October 5, 1864. Furloughed for sixty days on October 28, 1864. Reported absent wounded through December 31, 1864. Disabled by his wounds. Survived the war.

PEADEN, WILLIAM A., Private

Born in Pitt County where he resided as a farm hand prior to enlisting in Pitt County at age 22, May 10, 1862, for the war. Reported present in November-December, 1862. Reported sick in hospital at Wilmington (probably suffering from "excessive spinal curvature") from February 6 through December 31, 1863. Detailed as a hospital nurse at Wilmington on March 9, 1864. Rejoined the company on October 14, 1864. Reported sick in hospital in November-December, 1864. Deserted near Raleigh on April 12, 1865.

PERKINS, JOHN, Private

Born in Wilson County* where he resided as a farmer or farm laborer prior to enlisting in Wilson County at age 18, April 10, 1862. Reported present in November-December, 1862. Hospitalized at Wilmington on February 18, 1863, with varicocele. Died in hospital at Wilmington on March 11, 1863, of "pneumonia."

ROGERS, ARTHUR, Private

Born in Wilson County* and resided in Pitt County where he was by occupation a farmer or laborer prior to enlisting in Wilson County at age 52, May 15, 1862, for the war. Rejected for service, probably by reason of being overage. [See special note at the end of the history of Company F, 61st Regiment N.C. Troops (page 705).]

ROGERS, HENRY, Private

Born in Pitt County where he resided as a laborer prior to enlisting in Wilson County at age 19, May 15, 1862, for the war. Rejected for service. Reason he was rejected not reported. [May have served previously as Private in Company D, 44th Regiment N.C. Troops. See special note at the end of the history of Company F, 61st Regiment N.C. Troops (page 705).]

ROGERS, NOAH, Private

Born in Wilson County* where he resided as a farmer prior to enlisting in Wilson County at age 18, May 8, 1862, for the war. Reported present or accounted for in November, 1862-April, 1864. Wounded in both legs at Drewry's Bluff, Virginia, May 19, 1864. Hospitalized at Petersburg, Virginia, May 20, 1864. Furloughed on June 3, 1864. Returned to duty prior to November 1, 1864. Reported present in November-December, 1864. Paroled at Goldsboro on May 9, 1865.

ROGERS, STEPHEN, Private

Born in Wilson County* and was by occupation a farmer prior to enlisting in Wilson County at age 22, April 29, 1862, for the war.

Reported present in November, 1862-April, 1864. Captured near Petersburg, Virginia, June 16, 1864. Confined at Point Lookout, Maryland, June 19, 1864. Transferred to Elmira, New York, July 25, 1864. Died at Elmira on October 17, 1864, of "chronic diarrhoea."

RUFF, JAMES C., Private

Born in Greene County and resided in Wilson County where he was by occupation a farmer prior to enlisting in Jones County at age 31, May 2, 1862, for the war. Mustered in as Musician. Reported present or accounted for in November, 1862-April, 1864. Reduced to ranks in January-February, 1863. Captured near Petersburg, Virginia, June 16, 1864. Confined at Point Lookout, Maryland, June 19, 1864. Transferred to Elmira, New York, July 25, 1864. Released at Elmira on June 30, 1865, after taking the Oath of Allegiance.

RUFF, WILLIAM D., Corporal

Resided in Greene County and was by occupation an overseer prior to enlisting in Greene County at age 27, June 28, 1862, for the war. Mustered in as Private. Reported present or accounted for in November, 1862-April, 1864. Wounded in the hand at Drewry's Bluff, Virginia, May 13-16, 1864. Hospitalized at Richmond, Virginia. Furloughed for sixty days on May 30, 1864. Returned to duty and was promoted to Corporal prior to November 1, 1864. Reported present in September-December, 1864. No further records. Survived the war.

RUFFIN, JOHN DAVIS, Private

Enlisted in New Hanover County on January 1, 1863, for the war. Reported present in January-February, 1863. Reported sick in hospital at Columbia, South Carolina, April 8, 1863. Reported present but sick in quarters in May-June, 1863. Returned to duty in July-August, 1863. Reported present through April 30, 1864. Wounded in the right hip and/or thigh at Drewry's Bluff, Virginia, May 13-16, 1864. Hospitalized at Richmond, Virginia. Furloughed for sixty days on July 21, 1864. Reported absent wounded through December 31, 1864. Hospitalized at Greensboro on February 22, 1865, with rubeola. Transferred to another hospital on February 23, 1865. No further records.

SAWREY, JAMES, Private

Born in Greene County where he resided as an overseer or farmer prior to enlisting in Wilson County at age 27, April 29, 1862, for the war. Died at Wilmington on October 16, 1862, of "typhoid fever."

SHACKLEFORD, WASH R., Private

Resided in Greene County and was by occupation a farmer prior to enlisting in Wake County at age 30, July 16, 1862, for the war. Reported present or accounted for in November, 1862-April, 1864. Wounded in the head at Cold Harbor, Virginia, May 31-June 3, 1864. Captured at Fort Harrison, Virginia, September 30, 1864. Confined at Point Lookout, Maryland, October 5, 1864. Released at Point Lookout on May 14, 1865, after taking the Oath of Allegiance.

SPEARES, WILLIAM H., Private

Born in Greene County and resided in Greene or Wilson County where he was by occupation a farmer or day laborer prior to enlisting in Wilson County at age 27, May 16, 1862, for the war. Reported present or accounted for in November, 1862-October, 1863. Reported on detached service at camp near Petersburg,

Virginia, in November-December, 1863. Rejoined the company in January-February, 1864. Reported present in March-April and September-December, 1864. Paroled at Goldsboro on an unspecified date (probably in May, 1865).

TAYLOR, JAMES J., Private

Born in Wilson County* and was by occupation a farmer prior to enlisting in Wilson County at age 23, May 15, 1862, for the war. Detailed as a teamster in the quartermaster department on October 23, 1862. Reported absent on duty as a teamster in November, 1862-April, 1864, and September-December, 1864. No further records. Survived the war.

TAYLOR, LAWRENCE H., Private

Born in Pitt County and was by occupation a farmer prior to enlisting in Pitt County at age 18, May 7, 1862, for the war. Reported present or accounted for in November, 1862-April, 1864. Wounded in the right arm at or near Fort Harrison, Virginia, on or about September 30, 1864. Hospitalized at Richmond, Virginia. Furloughed for forty days on October 18, 1864. Reported absent wounded through December 31, 1864. No further records.

THOMAS, H., _____

Resided in Wilson County. Place and date of enlistment not reported (probably enlisted subsequent to February 28, 1865). Paroled at Goldsboro on May 15, 1865.

VANDERFORD, JOHN B., Private

Born in Wilson County* and was by occupation a farmer prior to enlisting in Wilson County at age 18, April 10, 1862. Rejected for service. Reason he was rejected not reported. Reenlisted in the company at Wilmington on August 2, 1862, for the war. Reported present or accounted for in November, 1862-April, 1864. Hospitalized at Richmond, Virginia, October 21, 1864, with intermittent fever. Returned to duty on December 26, 1864. No further records.

VANDERFORD, STEPHEN G., Private

Resided in Johnston County and enlisted in New Hanover County at age 16, September 10, 1862, for the war. Reported present or accounted for in November, 1862-February, 1863. Reported at home on sick furlough in March-April, 1863. Returned to duty in May-June, 1863. Reported present in July, 1863-April, 1864. Hospitalized at Richmond, Virginia, October 17, 1864 (probably suffering from bronchitis). Returned to duty on December 16, 1864. Paroled at Goldsboro on May 9, 1865.

VANDERFORD, T. B., Private

Resided in Wilson County. Place and date of enlistment not reported (probably enlisted subsequent to February 28, 1865). Paroled at Goldsboro on May 9, 1865.

WALSTON, HENRY, Private

Resided in Edgecombe County where he enlisted at age 28, April 1, 1862. Reported present in November-December, 1862. Reported sick in hospital at Wilmington from February 6 through April 30, 1863. Discharged at Wilmington on or about June 10, 1863, by a medical examining board. Reason discharged not reported.

WALSTON, JOSIAH, Private

Enlisted in Greene County on March 3, 1863, for the war. Reported present or accounted for in March, 1863-April, 1864, and September-December, 1864. Hospitalized at Wilmington on

January 27, 1865, with remittent fever. Transferred to another hospital on February 20, 1865. No further records.

WALSTON, PHILIP, Private

Born in Greene County where he resided as an overseer or farmer prior to enlisting in Greene County at age 34, May 15, 1862, for the war. Dropped from the company rolls on an unspecified date (probably in the summer of 1862). Reason he was dropped not reported. Later served as Private in Company C, 1st Battalion N.C. Local Defense Troops. [See special note at the end of the history of Company F, 61st Regiment N.C. Troops (page 705).]

WALSTON, SETH, Private

Born in Greene County where he resided as a farmer or "turpentine hand" prior to enlisting in Greene County at age 31, May 15, 1862, for the war. Reported present in November-December, 1862. Hospitalized at Wilmington on February 18, 1863, with an "eruption." Returned to duty on March 9, 1863. Reported present or accounted for through April 30, 1864. Wounded in the arm at Drewry's Bluff, Virginia, May 13-16, 1864. Returned to duty prior to November 1, 1864. Reported present in November-December, 1864. No further records.

WEBB, GARRETT, Private

Resided in Edgecombe County and was by occupation a farmer prior to enlisting in Wake County at age 35, October 27, 1864, for the war. Reported present in November-December, 1864. No further records.

WEBB, GRAY, Private

Born in Wilson County* and resided in Wilson or Edgecombe County where he was by occupation a farmer or farm laborer prior to enlisting in Wilson County at age 31, May 15, 1862, for the war. Reported present in November, 1862-February, 1863. Reported present but sick in quarters in March-June, 1863. Reported in hospital at Charleston, South Carolina, August 17, 1863. Furloughed home on October 24, 1863. Returned to duty in November-December, 1863. Reported present through April 30, 1864. Wounded in the face and/or left arm at or near Petersburg, Virginia, on or about June 16-19, 1864. Reported in hospital at High Point on July 3, 1864. Furloughed on July 4, 1864. Reported absent wounded in September-December, 1864. Captured by the enemy near Raleigh on April 12, 1865. Records of the Federal Provost Marshal indicate that he was a deserter. Paroled at Goldsboro on an unspecified date (probably in May, 1865).

WHEELER, JOHN, Private

Born in Wilson County* where he resided as a farmer or shingle setter[?] prior to enlisting in Wilson County at age 25, May 9, 1862, for the war. Reported present or accounted for in November, 1862-April, 1863. Hospitalized at Wilmington on or about May 5, 1863, with catarrh. Returned to duty prior to July 1, 1863. Hospitalized at Charleston, South Carolina, August 12, 1863. Reported absent without leave on October 1, 1863. Returned to duty in November-December, 1863. Reported present in January-April, 1864. Hospitalized at Richmond, Virginia, on an unspecified date (probably suffering from chronic rheumatism). Furloughed on or about August 19, 1864. Reported absent on furlough through December 31, 1864. Paroled at Goldsboro on May 15, 1865.

WHEELER, WILLIAM H., Private

Enlisted in Wayne County on June 28, 1862, for the war. Reported present or accounted for in November, 1862-April, 1864. Captured

at Fort Harrison, Virginia, September 30, 1864. Confined at Point Lookout, Maryland, October 5, 1864. Paroled at Point Lookout on March 17, 1865. Received at Boulware's Wharf, James River, Virginia, March 19, 1865, for exchange. No further records.

WILLIAMS, JOHN, Private

Enlisted in Wayne County on June 30, 1862, for the war. Reported present in November, 1862-February, 1863. Hospitalized at Columbia, South Carolina, April 18, 1863. Transferred to hospital at Wilson on June 1, 1863. Returned to duty in July-August, 1863. Reported present through April 30, 1864. Wounded in the right hand at Drewry's Bluff, Virginia, May 13-14, 1864. Hospitalized at Richmond, Virginia. Furloughed for forty days on June 10, 1864. Reported present in September-October, 1864. Reported absent wounded in November-December, 1864. No further records. Survived the war. [Was about 30 years of age at time of enlistment.]

WOODARD, CALVIN, Private

Born in Wilson County* where he resided as a farmer prior to enlisting in Wilson County at age 34, May 8, 1862, for the war. No further records. [See special note at the end of the history of Company F, 61st Regiment N.C. Troops (page 705).]

WOOTEN, EPHRAIM, Private

Born in Edgecombe County where he resided as a farmer prior to enlisting in Wilson County at age 34, May 17, 1862, for the war. Died in Edgecombe County on October 26, 1862, of "yellow fever."

WOOTEN, WILLIAM HENRY, Private

Enlisted in Greene County on July 14, 1862, for the war. Reported present or accounted for in November, 1862-April, 1864, and September-December, 1864. No further records. Survived the war. [Was about 21 years of age at time of enlistment.]

YORKES, R., _____

Resided in Wilson County. Place and date of enlistment not reported (probably enlisted subsequent to February 28, 1865). Paroled at Goldsboro on May 15, 1865.

COMPANY G

This company was raised in New Hanover County in February-July, 1862, as Capt. John F. Moore's Independent Company. It was mustered into state service on May 12, 1862. On or about September 29, 1862, it was assigned to the newly organized 59th Regiment N.C. Troops. That unit was redesignated the 61st Regiment N.C. Troops on an unspecified date between October 30 and November 22, 1862. This company was designated Company G. After joining the regiment the company functioned as a part of the regiment, and its history for the remainder of the war is reported as a part of the regimental history.

The following roster was compiled primarily from information in the microfilm edition of the Compiled Service Records of Soldiers Who Served in Organizations from the State of North Carolina (Record Group 109, MC 270), National Archives and Records Administration, Washington, D.C. Record Group 109 includes enlistment papers, pay vouchers, requisitions, letters of resignation, discharge certificates, and abstracts of medical and prisoner of war returns. Materials relating specifically to Company G of the 61st Regiment include a company muster-in and descriptive roll dated May 12, 1862, and company muster rolls for November, 1862-April, 1864, and September-October, 1864.

Also utilized in this roster were *The War of the Rebellion: A Compilation of the Official Records of the Union and Confederate Armies*, the North Carolina adjutant general's *Roll of Honor*, state militia records, newspaper casualty lists and obituaries, wartime claims for bounty pay and allowances, postwar registers of claims for artificial limbs, Confederate pension applications filed with the states of North Carolina, Tennessee, and Florida, Confederate Soldiers' Home records, and the 1860 and 1870 federal censuses of North Carolina. A search was made also for relevant letters, diaries, reminiscences, and other manuscripts in the Southern Historical Collection (University of North Carolina-Chapel Hill), the Duke University Library Special Collections Department, and the North Carolina Division of Archives and History.

Among the secondary sources consulted were records of the North Carolina division of the United Daughters of the Confederacy, postwar rosters, regimental and county histories, marriage bond, will, and cemetery indexes, published and unpublished genealogies, biographical dictionaries, the North Carolina *County Heritage Book* series, the *Confederate Veteran*, Walter Clark's *Histories of the Several Regiments and Battalions from North Carolina in the Great War, 1861-'65*, and the North Carolina volume of the extended edition of *Confederate Military History*.

Note: The following roster contains service records for fifty-one men who enlisted in Captain Moore's Independent Company but whose service terminated prior to September 29, 1862, the date the company was mustered into the 59th Regiment N.C. Troops (later redesignated the 61st Regiment N.C. Troops). Those men, it will be evident, never served in the 61st Regiment. Their service records are included here because too little information survives to compile a roster for Moore's Independent Company. All service records falling into the early-termination category conclude with a "special note" alerting readers to that fact and referring them to the information contained in this paragraph.

OFFICERS

CAPTAINS

MOORE, JOHN F.

Born in New Hanover County where he resided as a farmer prior to enlisting at age 28. Appointed Captain on March 20, 1862. Captured and paroled at Kinston on December 14, 1862. Reported absent sick at home on February 8, 1863. Resigned on March 21, 1863, because "my wife died leaving me four little helpless children to take care of besides a large family of negroes [sic] together with other property, all of which is liable to be lost without my personal attention. In addition to the above, my arm is in a condition which renders me incapable of performing the duties of my office. . . ." Resignation accepted on April 29, 1863. [A surgeon's affidavit appended to his letter of resignation indicates that he was suffering from anchylosis of the elbow joint, the result of a fracture.]

VAN AMRINGE, STACEY

Born in New York City and resided in New Hanover County where he was by occupation a clerk prior to enlisting at age 24. Appointed 1st Lieutenant on March 20, 1862. Reported present in November-

December, 1862. Hospitalized at Charleston, South Carolina, February 19, 1863. Returned to duty in March-April, 1863. Promoted to Captain on May 1, 1863. Reported present in May-June, 1863. Resigned on August 3, 1863, by reason of "an injury of the intestines and severe contusion of the lower extremities from a fall." Resignation accepted on August 10, 1863.

KEITH, LEMUEL L.

Previously served as Private in Company C, 1st Regiment N.C. State Troops. Appointed 3rd Lieutenant of this company on March 20, 1862. Promoted to 2nd Lieutenant on May 1, 1862. Reported present or accounted for in November, 1862-April, 1863. Promoted to 1st Lieutenant on May 28, 1863. Reported present in May-August, 1863. Promoted to Captain on August 13, 1863. Wounded at Morris Island, Charleston Harbor, South Carolina, August 21-28, 1863. Reported present in September, 1863-April, 1864. Wounded in the left forearm (fracture) at Fort Harrison, Virginia, September 30, 1864. Arm amputated. Hospitalized at Richmond, Virginia, where he died on October 6, 1864, of wounds. "At last, like a brave man as he was, he . . . met death, gallantly leading his men. . . ." [*Wilmington Weekly Journal*, November 3, 1864.]

LIPPITT, AUGUSTUS D.

Born in New Hanover County where he resided as a clerk prior to enlisting at age 21. Elected 3rd Lieutenant on May 1, 1862. Reported present in November, 1862-June, 1863 (signed roll as commander of the company in January-February, 1863). Promoted to 2nd Lieutenant on May 28, 1863. Promoted to 1st Lieutenant on August 13, 1863. Reported sick in hospital at Charleston, South Carolina, August 23, 1863. Reported absent on furlough in September-December, 1863. Reported on duty at camp near Petersburg, Virginia, in January-April, 1864. Returned to duty on an unspecified date. Reported present in September-October, 1864. Promoted to Captain on October 7, 1864. Paroled at Greensboro on May 1, 1865.

LIEUTENANTS

FENNELL, NICHOLAS H., 2nd Lieutenant

Resided in New Hanover County where he enlisted at age 35, May 16, 1862, for the war. Mustered in as Private. Captured at Kinston on December 14, 1862. Paroled at Kinston on December 15, 1862. Returned to duty in January-February, 1863. Reported present in March-October, 1863. Appointed 3rd Lieutenant on September 23, 1863. Reported present or accounted for in November, 1863-April, 1864. Promoted to 2nd Lieutenant on May 16, 1864. Captured near Petersburg, Virginia, on or about June 15, 1864. Confined at Point Lookout, Maryland, June 19, 1864. Transferred to Fort Delaware, Delaware, where he arrived on June 25, 1864. Transferred to Hilton Head, South Carolina, August 20, 1864. Confined at Fort Pulaski, Georgia, October 20, 1864. Transferred to Fort Delaware subsequent to December 26, 1864. Released at Fort Delaware on June 17, 1865, after taking the Oath of Allegiance.

FOX, JOHN B., 3rd Lieutenant

Born at Culpeper, Virginia, and resided in New Hanover County where he was by occupation a merchant prior to enlisting in New Hanover County at age 24, May 15, 1862, for the war. Mustered in as Sergeant. Reported present in November-December, 1862. Hospitalized at Wilmington on or about February 9, 1863, with catarrhus. Reported absent sick at Wilmington through April 30, 1863. Hospitalized at Wilmington on May 14, 1863, with chronic diarrhoea. Returned to duty on May 26, 1863. Reported sick in hospital at Mount Pleasant, South Carolina, in July-August, 1863. Reported absent on sick furlough on October 9, 1863. Returned to duty in November-December, 1863. Reported present in January-April, 1864. Elected 3rd Lieutenant on June 9, 1864. Reported present in September-October, 1864. Resigned on January 24, 1865, under the provisions of an act of Congress dated June 14, 1864, "authorizing the formation of new commands to be composed of supernumerary officers. The co[mpany] to which I belong has not the maximum number of men to justify a full quota of officers." Resignation accepted on February 10, 1865.

SHACKELFORD, DANIEL, 2nd Lieutenant

Previously served as Private in Company I, 18th Regiment N.C. Troops (8th Regiment N.C. Volunteers). Enlisted in this company in New Hanover County on June 28, 1862, for the war. Mustered in as Private. Appointed Quartermaster Sergeant on September 9, 1862, and transferred to the Field and Staff of this regiment. Promoted to 1st Sergeant on January 15, 1863, and transferred back to this company. Reported present in January-June, 1863. Appointed 3rd Lieutenant on June 1, 1863. Promoted to 2nd Lieutenant on August 13, 1863. Reported present or accounted for in July, 1863-April, 1864. Killed at Drewry's Bluff, Virginia, May 16, 1864. "He was a brave and good boy." [*Wilmington Weekly Journal*, May 26, 1864.]

NONCOMMISSIONED OFFICERS AND PRIVATES

ARMSTRONG, THOMAS, Private

Born in Glasgow, Scotland, and resided in Columbus County where he was by occupation a farmer prior to enlisting in New Hanover County at age 41, July 10, 1862, for the war as a substitute. Captured and paroled at Kinston on December 14, 1862. Exchanged on January 13, 1863. Listed as a deserter on or about February 28, 1863. Arrested on May 15, 1863, and confined at Wilmington. Returned to duty prior to August 26, 1863, when he was captured at Morris Island, Charleston Harbor, South Carolina. Confined at Hilton Head, South Carolina, September 1, 1863. Transferred to Fort Columbus, New York Harbor, where he arrived on September 22, 1863. Transferred to Point Lookout, Maryland, where he arrived on September 26, 1863. Released at Point Lookout on February 15, 1864, after taking the Oath of Allegiance and joining the U.S. Army. Rejected for service and was released.

BATCHELOR, JAMES R., Private

Born in Duplin County and resided in New Hanover County where he was by occupation a farmer prior to enlisting in New Hanover County at age 16, May 12, 1862, for the war as a substitute. Hospitalized at Wilmington on July 18, 1862, with typhoid fever. Reported in hospital at Wilmington on July 26, 1862, with icterus. Returned to duty on August 2, 1862. Reported sick at home in New Hanover County on December 6, 1862. Hospitalized at Wilmington on February 6, 1863, with abscessus. Returned to duty on February 20, 1863. Reported present through June 30, 1863. Reported sick in hospital at Mount Pleasant, South Carolina, August 24, 1863. Furloughed on September 24, 1863. Reported absent without leave on November 26, 1863. Returned to duty on February 1, 1864. Hospitalized at Richmond, Virginia, August 12, 1864, with diarrhoea. Furloughed for thirty days on August 18, 1864. Reported absent on furlough through October 31, 1864. No further records.

BATCHELOR, JOSEPH, Private

Born in New Hanover County where he resided as a farmer prior to enlisting in New Hanover County at age 19, May 24, 1862, for the war. Hospitalized at Wilmington on July 26, 1862, with remittent fever. Returned to duty on August 2, 1862. Reported sick at home in New Hanover County from September 10 through December 31, 1862. Returned to duty in January-February, 1863. Reported present through June 30, 1863. Reported sick in hospital at Charleston, South Carolina, in July-August, 1863. Furloughed on September 24, 1863. Died at home in New Hanover County in November-December, 1863, of disease.

BEASLEY, DANIEL J., Private

Born in Duplin County and resided in Duplin or Wilson County as a farmer prior to enlisting in Duplin County at age 32, July 4, 1862, for the war. Reported sick in hospital at Wilson from October 24 through December 31, 1862. Returned to duty in January-February, 1863. Detailed as a hospital nurse at Charleston, South Carolina, March 10, 1863. Reported on detail at Charleston through December 31, 1863. Reported on detail in camp near Petersburg, Virginia, in January-April, 1864. Rejoined the company on an unspecified date. Reported present in September-October, 1864. Paroled at Goldsboro on May 17, 1865.

BENTON, JAMES B., Private

Born in Duplin County where he resided as a farmer prior to enlisting in Duplin County at age 34, July 4, 1862, for the war. Reported on detached service working on gunboat at Wilmington from December 20, 1862, through April 30, 1864. Rejoined the company on an unspecified date. Reported present in September-October, 1864. No further records.

BLANCHARD, ABRAM W., Private

Born in Duplin County where he resided as a farmer prior to enlisting in Duplin County at age 29, June 17, 1862, for the war. Reported present in November, 1862-June, 1863. Captured at Morris Island, Charleston Harbor, South Carolina, on or about August 26, 1863. Confined at Hilton Head, South Carolina, September 1, 1863. Transferred to Fort Columbus, New York Harbor, where he arrived on September 22, 1863. Transferred to Point Lookout, Maryland, where he arrived on September 26, 1863. Transferred to Elmira, New York, August 16, 1864. Paroled at Elmira on March 10, 1865. Received at Boulware's Wharf, James River, Virginia, March 15, 1865, for exchange. No further records. Survived the war.

BLANKS, WILLIAM, Private

Previously served as 1st Sergeant in Company I, 18th Regiment N.C. Troops (8th Regiment N.C. Volunteers). Enlisted in this company in New Hanover County on May 14, 1862, for the war. Appointed acting Commissary Sergeant on September 9, 1862, and transferred to the Field and Staff of this regiment. Transferred back to this company prior to May 23, 1863, when he was detailed to work on gunboat at Wilmington. Reported on duty at the Wilmington customs house in November, 1863-April, 1864, and September-October, 1864. Paroled at Charlotte on May 11, 1865.

BLANTON, JOHN T., Private

Born in Duplin County and resided in New Hanover County where he was by occupation a farmer prior to enlisting in New Hanover County at age 31, July 7, 1862, for the war. Reported present or accounted for in November, 1862-April, 1864, and September-October, 1864. No further records. Survived the war.

BLIZZARD, EZEKIEL, Private

Previously served as Private in Company E, 18th Regiment N.C. Troops (8th Regiment N.C. Volunteers). Transferred to this company in September, 1862. Killed at Kinston on December 13, 1862.

BLIZZARD, LEVIN, Private

Born in Bladen County and resided in New Hanover County where he was by occupation a farmer prior to enlisting in New Hanover County at age 20, May 15, 1862, for the war. Reported present in November-December, 1862. Reported sick in hospital at Wilmington on February 8, 1863. Returned to duty in May-June, 1863. Reported present or accounted for in July, 1863-April, 1864. Wounded in the right thigh at Petersburg, Virginia, June 17, 1864. Hospitalized at Petersburg. Transferred to hospital at Farmville, Virginia, June 20, 1864. Hospitalized at Wilmington on an unspecified date with "paralysis agitaris" of the right leg. Furloughed on an unspecified date. Hospitalized at Richmond, Virginia, December 22, 1864. Returned to duty on December 27, 1864. No further records.

BLOODWORTH, JOHN W., Sergeant

Born in New Hanover County where he resided as a farmer prior to enlisting in New Hanover County at age 40, May 15, 1862, for the war. Mustered in as Private. Reported present or accounted for in November, 1862-October, 1863. Promoted to Corporal in September-October, 1863. Reported present in November, 1863-April, 1864. Promoted to Sergeant in May-July, 1864. Reported present in September-October, 1864. No further records.

BONEY, JOHN B., Private

Born in New Hanover County where he resided as a farmer prior to enlisting at "Piney Woods" at age 30, July 6, 1862, for the war. Wounded in the arm at Kinston on December 14, 1862. Hospitalized at Wilson. Returned to duty in January-February, 1863. Reported present or accounted for in March-June, 1863. Wounded in the shoulder at Morris Island, Charleston Harbor, South Carolina, August 26, 1863. Returned to duty in September-October, 1863. Reported present or accounted for in November, 1863-April, 1864. Captured at Bermuda Hundred, Virginia, June 14-16, 1864. Confined at Point Lookout, Maryland, June 19, 1864. Transferred to Elmira, New York, July 9, 1864. Died at Elmira on January 8, 1865, of "chronic diarrhoea."

BONSOLD, JOHN, Private

Previously served as Private in Company A, 18th Regiment N.C. Troops (8th Regiment N.C. Volunteers). Enlisted in this company at Wilmington on August 20, 1862, for the war as a substitute. Reported present or accounted for in November, 1862-June, 1863. Captured at Morris Island, Charleston Harbor, South Carolina, on or about August 26, 1863. Confined at Hilton Head, South Carolina, September 1, 1863. Transferred to Fort Columbus, New York Harbor, where he arrived on September 22, 1863. Released at Fort Columbus on an unspecified date after taking the Oath of Allegiance. [He was listed as a deserter on the North Carolina adjutant general's Roll of Honor because he took the Oath of Allegiance prior to the end of the war.]

BOYKIN, ABRAHAM, 1st Sergeant

Previously served as Private in Company A of this regiment. Transferred to this company on September 26, 1863. Mustered in as 1st Sergeant. Reported present through December 31, 1863. Furloughed for thirty days on April 5, 1864. Returned to duty prior to July 16, 1864, when he was "killed . . . by a Yankee sharp shooter"

near Petersburg, Virginia. "[H]e was always in the front ranks, pressing on fearlessly to death or victory." [*Wilmington Weekly Journal*, September 22, 1864.]

BRANCH, SAMUEL W., _____

North Carolina pension records indicate that he served in this company.

BRANCH, WILLIAM, Private

Born in New Hanover County where he resided as a farmer prior to enlisting in New Hanover County at age 52, July 8, 1862, for the war as a substitute. Reported present in November-December, 1862. Hospitalized at Wilmington on or about February 6, 1863, with debility. Died in hospital at Wilmington on May 29, 1863, of "pneumonia."

BRICKHOUSE, N. A., Private

Resided in New Hanover County and enlisted on May 12, 1862, for the war. Failed to report for duty and was dropped from the company rolls (probably in the summer of 1862). [See special note at the end of the history of Company G, 61st Regiment N.C. Troops (page 715).]

BRIGMAN, LOUIS J., Private

Born in Marion District, South Carolina, and resided in New Hanover County where he was by occupation a farmer prior to enlisting in New Hanover County at age 16, March 15, 1862. Failed to report for duty and was dropped from the company rolls (probably in the summer of 1862). Later served as Private in 2nd Company D, 36th Regiment N.C. Troops (2nd Regiment N.C. Artillery). [Contrary to 1:238 of this series, his correct name was Louis J. Brigman rather than Lewis J. Bridgeman. See also special note at the end of the history of Company G, 61st Regiment N.C. Troops (page 715).]

BRYANT, JACOB, Private

Born in Robeson County and resided in Columbus County where he was by occupation a farmer prior to enlisting in New Hanover County at age 36, July 29, 1862, for the war as a substitute for I. Smith. Was reportedly issued clothing on May 25 and August 1, 1864; however, he was not listed on the rolls of this company until September-October, 1864, when he was reported present. No further records.

BURNS, JOHN, Private

Born in Dublin, Ireland, and was by occupation a mason prior to enlisting in New Hanover County at age 38, September 4, 1862, for the war. Deserted on September 7, 1862. [See special note at the end of the history of Company G, 61st Regiment N.C. Troops (page 715).]

BURTON, J. B., Private

Resided in Duplin County and enlisted at age 34, July 4, 1862, for the war. Failed to report for duty and was dropped from the company rolls (probably in the summer of 1862). [See special note at the end of the history of Company G, 61st Regiment N.C. Troops (page 715).]

BUTLER, SANDY, Private

Born in Richmond County and resided in New Hanover County where he was by occupation a farmer prior to enlisting in New Hanover County at age 20, March 14, 1862. Failed to report for duty. Dropped from the company rolls on an unspecified date (probably in the summer of 1862). [See special note at the end of the history of Company G, 61st Regiment N.C. Troops (page 715).]

CARROLL, GEORGE W., Private

Born in Chatham County and resided in New Hanover County where he was by occupation a farmer prior to enlisting at "Piney Woods" at age 49, January 30, 1862. Failed to report for duty. Dropped from the company rolls on an unspecified date (probably in the summer of 1862). [See special note at the end of the history of Company G, 61st Regiment N.C. Troops (page 715).]

CHASON, FRANKLIN, Private

Previously enlisted as Private in Company H, 36th Regiment N.C. Troops (2nd Regiment N.C. Artillery). Rejected for service in that unit. Enlisted in this company at "Piney Woods" on May 20, 1862, for the war. Failed to report for duty. Dropped from the company rolls on an unspecified date (probably in the summer of 1862). [See special note at the end of the history of Company G, 61st Regiment N.C. Troops (page 715).]

CLARENY, JOSEPH, Private

Previously served as Private in Company E, 1st Regiment N.C. State Troops. Enlisted in this company in New Hanover County on January 16, 1863, for the war as a substitute. Reported present or accounted for through June 30, 1863. Wounded in the leg and captured at Morris Island, Charleston Harbor, South Carolina, on or about August 26, 1863. Confined at Hilton Head, South Carolina, September 1, 1863. Was apparently released at Hilton Head on an unspecified date after taking the Oath of Allegiance. [Contrary to 3:193 of this series, the correct spelling of his surname was Clareny rather than Clevini.]

CLAYTON, JAMES, Private

Born in England and resided in Duplin County where he was by occupation a sailor prior to enlisting in New Hanover County at age 36, July 6, 1862, for the war as a substitute. Reported sick in hospital at Wilson on December 17, 1862. Transferred to the C.S. Navy on February 17, 1863.

CRAWFORD, MARTIN LUTHER, Private

Born in Pitt County and resided in Columbus County where he was by occupation a farmer prior to enlisting at "Piney Wood" at age 43, May 17, 1862, for the war as a substitute. Captured and paroled at Kinston on December 14, 1862. Returned to duty in January-February, 1863. Reported present or accounted for through June 30, 1863. Captured at Morris Island, Charleston Harbor, South Carolina, on or about August 26, 1863. Confined at Hilton Head, South Carolina, September 1, 1863. Transferred to Fort Columbus, New York Harbor, where he arrived on September 22, 1863. Transferred to Point Lookout, Maryland, where he arrived on September 26, 1863. Died at Point Lookout on December 11, 1863, of "smallpox."

CREWS, JOHN REUBEN, Private

Born in New Hanover County where he resided as a farmer prior to enlisting in New Hanover County at age 52, July 8, 1862, for the war. Failed to report for duty and was dropped from the company rolls (probably in the summer of 1862). [See special note at the end of the history of Company G, 61st Regiment N.C. Troops (page 715).]

CROOM, AARON T., Corporal

Born in New Hanover County where he resided as a farmer prior to enlisting in New Hanover County at age 29, April 12, 1862. Mustered in as Corporal. Hospitalized at Wilmington on July 24, 1862, with acute rheumatism. Returned to duty on July 30, 1862. Died at home in New Hanover County on August 7, 1862, of "typhoid fever," leaving a wife and five small children "in distress." [See special note at the end of the history of Company G, 61st Regiment N.C. Troops (page 715).]

DANIEL, JOHN A., Private

Resided in New Hanover County and enlisted on May 12, 1862, for the war. Failed to report for duty and was dropped from the company rolls (probably in the summer of 1862). [See special note at the end of the history of Company G, 61st Regiment N.C. Troops (page 715).]

DANIEL, NATHANIEL GREENE, Private

Born in New Hanover County and was by occupation a merchant prior to enlisting in New Hanover County at age 35, July 7, 1862, for the war. No further records. [See special note at the end of the history of Company G, 61st Regiment N.C. Troops (page 715).]

DAVIS, WILLIAM H., Private

Born in Duplin County and resided in New Hanover County where he was by occupation a farmer prior to enlisting in New Hanover County at age 17, July 14, 1862, for the war as a substitute. Reported sick in hospital at Wilson on November 7, 1862. Returned to duty in January-February, 1863. Reported present or accounted for until he was killed at Morris Island, Charleston Harbor, South Carolina, August 26, 1863.

DEXTER, M. R., Private

Born in Massachusetts and was by occupation a merchant prior to enlisting in New Hanover County at age 27, July 5, 1862, for the war. No further records. [See special note at the end of the history of Company G, 61st Regiment N.C. Troops (page 715).]

DUDLEY, ROBERT C., Private

Previously served as Corporal in Company I, 18th Regiment N.C. Troops (8th Regiment N.C. Volunteers). Enlisted in this company in New Hanover County on July 7, 1862, for the war. Mustered in as Private. Reported on detached service at the provost office in Wilmington from September 10 through December 31, 1862. Reported on duty as a hospital clerk at Wilmington in January-April, 1863. Reported on detached service with the quartermaster department in Columbia, South Carolina, in May, 1863-April, 1864, and September-October, 1864. Appointed a "bonded agent" in the quartermaster department on November 5, 1864. No further records. Survived the war.

EDWARDS, THOMAS, Private

Born in New Hanover County and was by occupation a farmer. Enlistment date not reported; however, he probably enlisted in the summer of 1863. Captured at Morris Island, Charleston Harbor, South Carolina, August 26, 1863. Confined at Point Lookout, Maryland. Released at Point Lookout on January 28, 1864, after taking the Oath of Allegiance and joining the U.S. Army. Assigned to Company D, 1st Regiment U.S. Volunteer Infantry. [Was about 18 years of age at time of enlistment.]

ENNIS, WILLIAM B., Private

Born in Duplin County where he resided as a farmer or student prior to enlisting in Duplin County at age 19, July 17, 1862, for the war. Reported present in November, 1862-June, 1863. Hospitalized at Wilmington on July 7, 1863, with debility. Returned to duty on July 12, 1863. Captured at Morris Island, Charleston Harbor, South Carolina, on or about August 26, 1863. Confined at Hilton Head, South Carolina, September 1, 1863. Transferred to Fort Columbus, New York Harbor, where he arrived on September 22, 1863. Transferred to Point Lookout, Maryland, where he arrived on September 26, 1863. Transferred to Elmira, New York, August 16, 1864. Paroled at Elmira on March 10, 1865. Received at Boulware's Wharf, James River, Virginia, March 15, 1865, for exchange. Hospitalized at Richmond, Virginia, March 15, 1865. Transferred to another hospital on March 16, 1865. Deserted to the enemy at Goldsboro on March 22, 1865. Sent to Fort Monroe, Virginia. Transferred to Washington, D.C. Released on or about April 5, 1865, after taking the Oath of Allegiance. [North Carolina pension records indicate that he received powder burns to his eyes at Morris Island on August 26, 1863.]

EZZELL, BENJAMIN P., Private

Born in Duplin County and was by occupation a farmer prior to enlisting in New Hanover County at age 56, July 23, 1862, for the war. Probably enlisted as a substitute. Reported absent without leave on an unspecified date (probably in the summer of 1862). Dropped from the company rolls on an unspecified date. Later served as Private in Company B, 1st Battalion N.C. Heavy Artillery. [See special note at the end of the history of Company G, 61st Regiment N.C. Troops (page 715).]

FENNELL, JAMES R., Sergeant

Born in New Hanover County where he resided as a farmer prior to enlisting in New Hanover County at age 29, May 16, 1862, for the war. Mustered in as 1st Sergeant. Reduced to the rank of Sergeant prior to January 1, 1863. Reported present in November, 1862-June, 1863. Killed at Morris Island, Charleston Harbor, South Carolina, August 26, 1863.

FORBES, JAMES, Private

Born in Louisiana and was by occupation a seaman prior to enlisting in New Hanover County at age 46, August 19, 186[2], for the war. Reported absent without leave on an unspecified date (probably in the late summer or autumn of 1862). No further records. [See special note at the end of the history of Company G, 61st Regiment N.C. Troops (page 715).]

GAINEY, A. J., Private

Born in Brunswick County on October 24, 1827. Resided in Brunswick County and was by occupation a farmer prior to enlisting in Duplin County at age 34, May 8, 1862, for the war. Discharged on an unspecified date (probably in the summer of 1862). Reason discharged not reported. [See special note at the end of the history of Company G, 61st Regiment N.C. Troops (page 715).]

GURGANUS, SWINSON, Private

Born in New Hanover County where he resided as a farmer prior to enlisting in Duplin County at age 35, May 7, 1862, for the war. Wounded and captured at Kinston on December 14, 1862. Paroled on December 15, 1862. Died at home in New Hanover County on January 13, 1863, of wounds.

HARRISS, JOHN H., Private

Born in Halifax County and resided in Brunswick County where he was by occupation a farmer prior to enlisting in Duplin County at age 18, May 17, 1862, for the war. Roll of Honor indicates that he "never reported for duty"; however, a company muster-in roll states that he was killed on June 30, 1862. No further records. [See

special note at the end of the history of Company G, 61st Regiment N.C. Troops (page 715).]

HERRING, ALEXANDER, Private

Born in Duplin County and resided in New Hanover County where he was by occupation a farmer prior to enlisting in Sampson County at age 31, July 4, 1862, for the war. Reported present in November, 1862-April, 1863. Reported sick in hospital at Wilmington in May-June, 1863. Returned to duty prior to August 26, 1863, when he was captured at Morris Island, Charleston Harbor, South Carolina. Confined at Hilton Head, South Carolina, September 1, 1863. Transferred to Fort Columbus, New York Harbor, where he arrived on September 22, 1863. Transferred to Point Lookout, Maryland, where he arrived on September 26, 1863. Died at Point Lookout on December 26, 1863, of "diarrhoea chronic[a]."

HERRING, AMOS R., Private

Previously served as Private in Company A of this regiment. Enlisted in this company at Ivor Station, Virginia, March 24, 1864. Captured at Fort Harrison, Virginia, September 30, 1864. Confined at Point Lookout, Maryland, October 5, 1864. Paroled at Point Lookout on March 17, 1865. Received at Boulware's Wharf, James River, Virginia, March 19, 1865, for exchange. No further records. Survived the war.

HICKS, ROBERT, Private

Born in New Hanover County where he resided as a farmer prior to enlisting in Duplin County at age 24, February 18, 1862. Reported absent without leave on an unspecified date (probably in the summer of 1862). No further records. [See special note at the end of the history of Company G, 61st Regiment N.C. Troops (page 715).]

HODGES, ISAAC FRANKLIN E., Sergeant

Born in Duplin County where he resided as a farmer prior to enlisting in Sampson County at age 30, July 15, 1862, for the war. Mustered in as Private. Promoted to Corporal prior to January 1, 1863. Reported present or accounted for in November, 1862-October, 1863. Promoted to Sergeant in November-December, 1863. Reported absent sick in camp near Petersburg, Virginia, December 16, 1863. Returned to duty prior to May 1, 1864. Wounded at or near Petersburg, Virginia, on or about June 16-19, 1864. Returned to duty on an unspecified date. Wounded in the foot at Fort Harrison, Virginia, September 30, 1864. Reported absent wounded through October 31, 1864. No further records.

HOUSTON, ROBERT M., Private

Born in New Hanover County where he resided as a merchant or clerk prior to enlisting in New Hanover County at age 23, May 10, 1862, for the war. Mustered in as Sergeant. Reported present in November-December, 1862. Promoted to 1st Sergeant prior to January 1, 1863. Reduced to ranks in January-February, 1863. Reported on detail with the engineering department at Wilmington from January 15 through June 30, 1863. Transferred to the 2nd Regiment Confederate Engineer Troops on August 3, 1863.

HUGGINS, JOHN R., Private

Born in Duplin County and resided in New Hanover County where he was by occupation a farmer prior to enlisting in Duplin County at age 34, May 15, 1862, for the war. Reported present in November, 1862-April, 1864. Court-martialed in September-October, 1864. Reason he was court-martialed not reported. No further records. Survived the war. [North Carolina pension records indicate that he was wounded on August 5, 1863.]

JOHNSON, DANIEL S., Private

Born in Brunswick County and resided in New Hanover County where he was by occupation a farmer or laborer prior to enlisting in Sampson County at age 37, March 28, 1862. Reported absent without leave on an unspecified date (probably in the summer of 1862). No further records. [See special note at the end of the history of Company G, 61st Regiment N.C. Troops (page 715).]

KEITH, GEORGE W., Private

Born in Granville County and resided in New Hanover County where he was by occupation a carpenter prior to enlisting in New Hanover County at age 34, May 15, 1862, for the war. Reported on detail working on gunboat at Wilmington from December 20, 1862, through October 31, 1864. No further records. Survived the war.

KEITH, JAMES T., Sergeant

Previously served as Private in Company C, 1st Regiment N.C. State Troops. Enlisted in this company in New Hanover County on May 12, 1862, for the war. Mustered in as Sergeant. Wounded and captured at Kinston on December 14, 1862. Hospitalized at New Bern where he died on July 27, 1863, of wounds.

KELLY, ANDREW V., Private

Enlisted in Wake County on March 5, 1863, for the war. Deserted on July 14, 1863. Went over to the enemy on an unspecified date. Confined at Bermuda Hundred, Virginia, October 13, 1864. Released the next day after taking the Oath of Allegiance.

LAMB, JOHN, Private

Born in New Hanover County where he resided as a farmer prior to enlisting at "Piney Woods" at age 32, July 8, 1862, for the war. Reported present or accounted for in November, 1862-April, 1864. Captured on the Darbytown Road, near Richmond, Virginia, October 7, 1864. Confined at Point Lookout, Maryland, October 29, 1864. Died at Point Lookout on January 12, 1865, of "chronic dysentery."

LAPASE, BLEESE, Private

Enlisted at Charleston, South Carolina, September 1, 1863, for the war. Reported sick in hospital at Charleston in September-October, 1863. Returned to duty in November-December, 1863. Reported present through April 30, 1864. Deserted to the enemy on or about August 27, 1864. Confined at Washington, D.C., August 31, 1864. Released on or about the same date after taking the Oath of Allegiance.

LARKINS, WILLIAM E., Private

Born in New Hanover County where he resided as a farmer prior to enlisting at "Piney Woods" at age 30, July 8, 1862, for the war. Discharged on an unspecified date (probably in the summer of 1862) after being reported absent without leave. [See special note at the end of the history of Company G, 61st Regiment N.C. Troops (page 715).]

LEE, GEORGE R., Private

Born in New Hanover County where he resided as a farmer prior to enlisting at "Piney Woods" on July 15, 1862, for the war. Reported present in November-December, 1862. Hospitalized at Charleston, South Carolina, February 22, 1863. Died in hospital at Summerville, South Carolina, March 20, 1863, of disease.

LEWIS, FRANCIS, Sergeant

Born in New Hanover County where he resided as a farmer prior to enlisting in New Hanover County at age 29, May 15, 1862, for the war. Mustered in as Private. Promoted to Corporal in November-December, 1862. Reported present or accounted for in November, 1862-April, 1863. Reported sick at home in New Hanover County from May 26 through August 31, 1863. Promoted to Sergeant on September 25, 1863. Reported present but under arrest in September-October, 1863 (probably for the loss of his bayonet and scabbard). Returned to duty in November-December, 1863. Reported present in January-April and September-October, 1864. No further records. Survived the war.

LEWIS, HOLDEN M., Corporal

Born in New Hanover County where he resided as a farmer or constable prior to enlisting in New Hanover County at age 36, May 17, 1862, for the war. Mustered in as Corporal. Reported present in November, 1862-June, 1863. Hospitalized at Wilmington on or about July 14, 1863, with intermittent fever. Furloughed on August 11, 1863, suffering from debility and bilious remittent fever. Reported absent without leave on September 29, 1863. Reported sick in camp near Petersburg, Virginia, December 16, 1863. Returned to duty in January-April, 1864. Reported present in September-October, 1864. No further records. Survived the war.

LEWIS, JAMES, Private

Born in New Hanover County where he resided as a farmer prior to enlisting in New Hanover County at age 18, July 14, 1862, for the war. Reported present in November, 1862-June, 1863. Hospitalized at Charleston, South Carolina, July 18, 1863. Reported absent without leave on September 3, 1863. Hospitalized at Wilmington on or about November 23, 1863, with paralysis. Returned to duty on December 30, 1863. Reported present through April 30, 1864. Captured near Petersburg, Virginia, June 16, 1864. Confined at Point Lookout, Maryland, June 19, 1864. Transferred to Elmira, New York, July 25, 1864. Paroled at Elmira on March 14, 1865. Received at Boulware's Wharf, James River, Virginia, March 18-21, 1865, for exchange. No further records.

LITCHFIELD, ORSON, Private

Born in Missouri and was by occupation an overseer prior to enlisting in New Hanover County at age 23, August 14, 1862, for the war. Reported absent without leave on an unspecified date (probably in the summer of 1862). No further records. [See special note at the end of the history of Company G, 61st Regiment N.C. Troops (page 715).]

LOEB, CHARLES, Private

Born in Germany and was by occupation a merchant prior to enlisting in New Hanover County at age 23, May 15, 1862, for the war. No further records. [See special note at the end of the history of Company G, 61st Regiment N.C. Troops (page 715).]

LOEB, MASON, Private

Previously served as Private in Company I, 18th Regiment N.C. Troops (8th Regiment N.C. Volunteers). Enlisted in this company in New Hanover County on July 10, 1862, for the war. No further records. [See special note at the end of the history of Company G, 61st Regiment N.C. Troops (page 715).]

LONG, JOHN S., Private

Resided in New Hanover County and enlisted on May 12, 1862, for the war. Never reported for duty. Dropped from the company rolls on an unspecified date (probably in the summer of 1862). [See special note at the end of the history of Company G, 61st Regiment N.C. Troops (page 715).]

McALLISTER, MALCOLM, Private

Born in New Hanover County where he resided as a farmer prior to enlisting in New Hanover County at age 45, July 9, 1862, for the war as a substitute. Hospitalized at Wilmington on August 21, 1862, with acute dysentery. Returned to duty on August 22, 1862. Died in hospital at Kinston on December 12, 1862. Cause of death not reported.

McGOWAN, DAVID G., Private

Born in Duplin County where he resided as a farmer prior to enlisting in Duplin County at age 23, July 17, 1862, for the war. Reported present or accounted for in November, 1862-April, 1864. Wounded slightly in the hand at the Crater, near Petersburg, Virginia, July 30, 1864. Wounded again (probably near Petersburg) on August 30, 1864. Hospitalized at Richmond, Virginia. Furloughed for thirty days on October 15, 1864. Hospitalized at Wilmington on December 28, 1864, with pneumonia. Returned to duty on January 14, 1865. No further records.

McGOWAN, JAMES H., Private

Born in Duplin County where he resided as a farmer prior to enlisting in Duplin County at age 26, July 15, 1862, for the war. Reported present in November, 1862-April, 1863. Reported sick at home in Duplin County from May 19 through June 30, 1863. Returned to duty in July-August, 1863. Reported present in September, 1863-April, 1864, and September-October, 1864. No further records.

McKEE, JOHN ROBERT, Private

Born in Baltimore, Maryland, and resided in New Hanover County where he was by occupation a clerk prior to enlisting in New Hanover County at age 17, July 3, 1862, for the war as a substitute. Reported sick in hospital at Goldsboro on December 7, 1862. Deserted from hospital at Goldsboro on January 20, 1863.

McPEAKE, JAMES D., Private

Previously served as 2nd Lieutenant of Company G, 18th Regiment N.C. Troops (8th Regiment N.C. Volunteers). Enlisted in this company in New Hanover County on May 15, 1862, for the war. Dropped from the company rolls on an unspecified date (probably in the summer of 1862). Later served as Private in Company C, 40th Regiment N.C. Troops (3rd Regiment N.C. Artillery). [See special note at the end of the history of Company G, 61st Regiment N.C. Troops (page 715).]

MAHN, JOHN G., Private

Born in New Hanover County where he resided as a farmer prior to enlisting in New Hanover County at age 32, May 15, 1862, for the war. Reported present in November, 1862-June, 1863. Captured at Morris Island, Charleston Harbor, South Carolina, on or about August 26, 1863. Confined at Hilton Head, South Carolina, September 1, 1863. Transferred to Point Lookout, Maryland, on an unspecified date (probably in September, 1863). Transferred to Elmira, New York, on or about August 16, 1864. Paroled at Elmira

on March 10, 1865. Received at Boulware's Wharf, James River, Virginia, March 15, 1865, for exchange. Deserted to the enemy at Goldsboro on March 24, 1865. Sent to New Bern. Confined at Washington, D.C., April 5, 1865. Hospitalized at Washington on April 6, 1865, with colic. Was apparently released on or about April 22, 1865, without taking the Oath of Allegiance.

MATTHIS, RAIL ROAD, Private

Born in Duplin County and resided in Sampson County where he was by occupation a farmer prior to enlisting in Duplin County at age 26, July 15, 1862, for the war. Reported present in November-December, 1862. Hospitalized at Wilmington on February 16, 1863, with pneumonia. Returned to duty on March 25, 1863. Reported present through April 30, 1864. Killed at Cold Harbor, Virginia, May 31-June 3, 1864.

MAYNARD, NICHOLAS A., Private

Born in Guilford County and resided in New Hanover County where he was by occupation a carpenter prior to enlisting in New Hanover County at age 26, March 13, 1862. Reported absent without leave on an unspecified date (probably in the summer of 1862). No further records. [See special note at the end of the history of Company G, 61st Regiment N.C. Troops (page 715).]

MILLER, CHARLES B., Private

Born in New Hanover County where he resided as a farmer prior to enlisting at "Piney Wood" at age 22, July 8, 1862, for the war. Died in hospital at Wilson on November 12, 1862, of disease.

MILLS, JAMES, Private

Born in New Hanover County and was by occupation a fisherman prior to enlisting in New Hanover County at age 16, July 17, 1862, for the war. Reported absent without leave on an unspecified date (probably in the summer of 1862). No further records. Survived the war. [See special note at the end of the history of Company G, 61st Regiment N.C. Troops (page 715).]

MOORE, C. PEYTON, Private

Born in New Hanover County where he resided as a farmer prior to enlisting in New Hanover County at age 32, July 7, 1862, for the war. No further records. Survived the war. [See special note at the end of the history of Company G, 61st Regiment N.C. Troops (page 715).]

MOORE, ISAAC J., Private

Born in New Hanover County where he resided as a farmer prior to enlisting in Harnett County at age 29, May 16, 1862, for the war. Captured at Kinston on December 14, 1862. Paroled at Kinston on December 15, 1862. Returned to duty in January-February, 1863. Reported sick in hospital at Charleston and Columbia, South Carolina, in March-April, 1863. Reported absent sick in May-June, 1863. Hospitalized at Wilmington on July 1, 1863, with debility. Returned to duty on October 17, 1863. Reported present through April 30, 1864. Killed in the trenches near Petersburg, Virginia, July 28, 1864.

MOORE, PETTIGREW, Private

Born in New Hanover County where he resided as a farmer prior to enlisting at "Piney Woods" at age 34, July 8, 1862, for the war. Captured and paroled at Kinston on December 14, 1862. Returned to duty in January-February, 1863. Hospitalized on

February 27, 1863. Returned to duty in May-June, 1863. Captured at Morris Island, Charleston Harbor, South Carolina, August 26, 1863. Confined at Hilton Head, South Carolina, September 1, 1863. No further records. Survived the war. [North Carolina pension records indicate that he was "injured in chest" at Kinston in 1862.]

MORGAN, BENJAMIN S., Private

Born in New Hanover County where he resided as a farmer prior to enlisting at "Piney Woods" at age 19, May 3, 1862, for the war. Reported present or accounted for in November, 1862-June, 1863. Reported present but sick in regimental hospital in July-August, 1863. Reported in hospital at Charleston, South Carolina, in September-October, 1863. Reported absent without leave on December 24, 1863. Returned to duty on March 7, 1864. Wounded in the left hip near Petersburg, Virginia, July 28, 1864. Reported absent on furlough in September-October, 1864. Hospitalized at Wilmington on or about November 1, 1864, still suffering from gunshot wounds. No further records. Survived the war.

MORSE, ANDERSON, Private

Resided in New Hanover County and enlisted on May 12, 1862, for the war. Failed to report for duty and was dropped from the company rolls on an unspecified date (probably in the summer of 1862). [See special note at the end of the history of Company G, 61st Regiment N.C. Troops (page 715).]

MORSE, WILLIS, Private

Resided in New Hanover County and enlisted on May 12, 1862, for the war. Failed to report for duty and was dropped from the company rolls on an unspecified date (probably in the summer of 1862). [See special note at the end of the history of Company G, 61st Regiment N.C. Troops (page 715).]

MOTT, ANDREW J., Private

Born in New Hanover County where he resided as a farmer prior to enlisting in New Hanover County at age 16, May 17, 1862, for the war as a substitute. Reported present in November, 1862-April, 1863. Hospitalized at Wilmington on or about May 7, 1863, with debility. Returned to duty prior to July 1, 1863. Hospitalized at Charleston, South Carolina, July 18, 1863. Returned to duty in September-October, 1863. Reported present through April 30, 1864. Hospitalized at Petersburg, Virginia, June 16, 1864, with gonorrhea. Transferred to hospital at Kittrell's Springs on June 18, 1864. Returned to duty prior to September 30, 1864, when he was wounded in the left side at Fort Harrison, Virginia. Hospitalized at Richmond, Virginia. Returned to duty on or about December 22, 1864. No further records. Survived the war.

MOTT, JOHN M., Private

Resided in New Hanover County and enlisted at age 24, July 8, 1862, for the war. Failed to report for duty and was dropped from the company rolls on an unspecified date (probably in the summer of 1862). [See special note at the end of the history of Company G, 61st Regiment N.C. Troops (page 715).]

MOTT, THOMAS G., Private

Born in New Hanover County where he resided as a farmer prior to enlisting in New Hanover County at age 56, May 16, 1862, for the war as a substitute. Hospitalized at Wilmington on or about August 11, 1862, with chronic dysentery. Returned to duty on August 19, 1862. Reported sick at home in New Hanover County

on December 20, 1862. Returned to duty in January-February, 1863. Reported present through June 30, 1863. Reported sick in hospital at Mount Pleasant, South Carolina, in July-August, 1863. Reported present but sick in quarters in September-October, 1863. Returned to duty in November-December, 1863. Reported on duty in camp near Petersburg, Virginia, in January-April, 1864. Reported present in September-October, 1864. No further records.

NEFF, JOSEPH H., Private

Born in Vermont or Connecticut and was by occupation a ship chandler and/or merchant prior to enlisting in New Hanover County at age 33, July 5, 1862, for the war. No further records. Survived the war. [See special note at the end of the history of Company G, 61st Regiment N.C. Troops (page 715).]

NEWSOM, JOAB C., Private

Born in Wayne County and resided in Columbus County where he was by occupation a farmer prior to enlisting in New Hanover County at age 33, July 10, 1862, for the war. Reported present in November, 1862-August, 1863. Reported absent without leave on October 17, 1863. Returned to duty in November-December, 1863. Reported present through April 30, 1864. Captured near Petersburg, Virginia, June 16, 1864. Confined at Point Lookout, Maryland, June 19, 1864. Transferred to Elmira, New York, July 9, 1864. Paroled at Elmira on October 11, 1864. Received at Venus Point, Savannah River, Georgia, November 15, 1864, for exchange. Hospitalized at High Point on November 22, 1864, with chronic diarrhoea. Furloughed on November 23, 1864. No further records. Survived the war.

O'BRIEN, JAMES, Private

Born in Ireland and was by occupation a farmer prior to enlisting in New Hanover County at age 45, August 25, 1862, for the war. Reported absent without leave on an unspecified date (probably in the summer of 1862). No further records. [See special note at the end of the history of Company G, 61st Regiment N.C. Troops (page 715).]

OLDHAM, CARNEY W., Private

Born in New Hanover County where he resided as a miller or merchant prior to enlisting in New Hanover County at age 23, July 5, 1862, for the war. No further records. Survived the war. [See special note at the end of the history of Company G, 61st Regiment N.C. Troops (page 715).]

ORR, TIMOTHY C., Corporal

Born in New Hanover County where he resided as a farmer prior to enlisting in New Hanover County at age 29, April 24, 1862, for the war. Mustered in as Corporal. Reported sick in hospital at Wilson on December 16, 1862. Returned to duty in January-February, 1863. Reported present through June 30, 1863. Captured at Morris Island, Charleston Harbor, South Carolina, on or about August 26, 1863. Confined at Hilton Head, South Carolina, September 1, 1863. Transferred to Fort Columbus, New York Harbor, where he arrived on September 22, 1863. Transferred to Point Lookout, Maryland, where he arrived on September 26, 1863. Transferred to Elmira, New York, August 16, 1864. Paroled at Elmira on March 10, 1865. Received at Boulware's Wharf, James River, Virginia, March 15, 1865, for exchange. Deserted to the enemy at Goldsboro on March 22, 1865. Confined at Washington, D.C., on or about April 5, 1865. Released on or about the same date after taking the Oath of Allegiance.

PENNY, WILLIAM J., Private

Born in New Hanover County where he resided as a farmer prior to enlisting in New Hanover County at age 23, May 17, 1862, for the war. Hospitalized at Wilmington on or about August 9, 1862, with continued fever. Returned to duty on an unspecified date. Reported present in November-December, 1862. Detailed to work on gunboat at Wilmington (probably as a carpenter) on January 13, 1863. Reported absent on detail at Wilmington through April, 1864, and in September-October, 1864. No further records. Survived the war.

PETERSON, ALLEN B., Private

Born in New Hanover County where he resided as a farmer prior to enlisting at "Piney Woods" at age 18, May 7, 1862, for the war. Reported present in November, 1862-February, 1863. Reported present but sick in March-April, 1863. Hospitalized at Wilmington on May 5, 1863, with debility. Returned to duty on June 13, 1863. Reported present in July, 1863-April, 1864, and September-October, 1864. No further records. Survived the war.

PETERSON, NIXON, Private

Born in Sampson County and resided in New Hanover County where he was by occupation a farmer prior to enlisting at "Piney Woods" at age 23, May 7, 1862, for the war. Hospitalized at Wilmington on August 11, 1862, with typhoid fever. Returned to duty on August 18, 1862. Reported present in November-December, 1862. Hospitalized at Wilmington on February 6, 1863, with neuralgia. Returned to duty in May-June, 1863. Reported sick in hospital at Mount Pleasant, South Carolina, in July-August, 1863. Returned to duty in September-October, 1863. Reported sick in camp near Petersburg, Virginia, December 16, 1863. Returned to duty in January-April, 1864. Reported present in September-October, 1864. No further records. Survived the war.

POPE, WILLIAM, Private

Born in Duplin County and was by occupation a farmer prior to enlisting in New Hanover County at age 34, July 5, 1862, for the war. No further records. [See special note at the end of the history of Company G, 61st Regiment N.C. Troops (page 715).]

POWELL, MILTON, Private

Born in Sampson County and resided in Sampson or Duplin County where he was by occupation a farmer prior to enlisting in New Hanover County at age 35, July 17, 1862, for the war. Reported present in November, 1862-June, 1863. Captured at Morris Island, Charleston Harbor, South Carolina, on or about August 26, 1863. Confined at Hilton Head, South Carolina, September 1, 1863. Transferred to Fort Columbus, New York Harbor, where he arrived on October 6, 1863. Transferred to Point Lookout, Maryland, October 9, 1863. Paroled at Point Lookout on January 17, 1865. Received at Boulware's Wharf, James River, Virginia, January 21, 1865, for exchange. No further records.

PRIDGEN, ALEXANDER, Private

Born in New Hanover County where he resided as a farmer prior to enlisting at "Colly Mills" at age 54, April 5, 1862. Captured and paroled at Kinston on or about December 14, 1862. Exchanged on January 13, 1863. Returned to duty on March 10, 1863. Reported present or accounted for through October 31, 1863. Deserted on November 29, 1863. Brought back from desertion on March 20, 1864. Returned to duty prior to May 1, 1864. Wounded in the left leg at Fort Harrison, Virginia, September 30, 1864. Hospitalized at Richmond, Virginia. Furloughed for sixty days on November 4,

1864. No further records. [Wounded slightly in the shoulder in May-July, 1864.]

PRIDGEN, WILLIAM L., Private

Resided in New Hanover County and enlisted on May 12, 1862, for the war. Failed to report for duty and was dropped from the company rolls (probably in the summer of 1862). [See special note at the end of the history of Company G, 61st Regiment N.C. Troops (page 715).]

PRINCE, WILLIAM R., Private

Born in Horry District, South Carolina, and resided in New Hanover County where he was by occupation a farmer prior to enlisting in New Hanover County at age 41, July 5, 1862, for the war as a substitute. Reported present in November-December, 1862. Hospitalized at Wilmington on or about February 18, 1863, with intermittent fever. Died in hospital at Wilmington on March 1, 1863, of "double pneumonia."

QUINN, DAVID, Private

Born in New Hanover County and resided in Duplin County where he was by occupation a farmer prior to enlisting in New Hanover County at age 37, July 17, 1862, for the war as a substitute. Reported present or accounted for in November, 1862-April, 1864. Killed prior to July 20, 1864. Place of death not reported.

RAY, ELI W., Private

Born in Horry District, South Carolina, and resided in New Hanover County where he was by occupation a farmer prior to enlisting in New Hanover County at age 42, July 12, 1862, for the war as a substitute. Reported present in November, 1862-June, 1863. Wounded in the head and face at Morris Island, Charleston Harbor, South Carolina, August 26, 1863. Hospitalized at Charleston. Deserted from hospital at Columbia, South Carolina, October 9, 1863. Brought back from desertion on March 20, 1864. Returned to duty prior to May 1, 1864. Reported present in September-October, 1864. No further records.

REEVES, J. S., Private

Born in New Hanover County where he resided as a farmer prior to enlisting in New Hanover County at age 18, May 15, 1862, for the war. Died in hospital at Wilmington on July 8, 1862, of disease. [See special note at the end of the history of Company G, 61st Regiment N.C. Troops (page 715).]

REEVES, THOMAS, Private

Resided in New Hanover County where he enlisted at age 20, May 15, 1862, for the war. Reported sick at home in New Hanover County from September 9 through December 31, 1862. Returned to duty on an unspecified date. Reported sick at home in New Hanover County in May-June, 1863. Died in hospital at Wilmington on July 8, 1863, of "sun stroke."

REEVES, WILLIAM C., Private

Born in New Hanover County where he resided as a farmer prior to enlisting at "Piney Woods" at age 16, May 3, 1862, for the war as a substitute. Hospitalized at Wilmington on or about August 2, 1862, with gonorrhea. Returned to duty on August 5, 1862. Reported present in November-December, 1862. Hospitalized at Wilmington on or about January 1, 1863, with chronic dysentery. Returned to duty on January 13, 1863. Hospitalized at Wilmington on February 16, 1863, with otitis. Returned to duty on March

4, 1863. Reported present or accounted for through April 30, 1864. Reported on detail as "rear guard" from May 31 through October 31, 1864. No further records. Survived the war.

RITTER, CHARLES H., Private

Born in New Hanover County where he resided as a farmer prior to enlisting in New Hanover County at age 22, May 17, 1862, for the war. Reported present in November-December, 1862. Hospitalized at Wilmington on or about February 18, 1863, with intermittent fever. Deserted from hospital on February 28, 1863. Returned to the hospital on March 3, 1863. Reported absent without leave from April 1 through August 31, 1863. Reported sick in hospital at Wilmington in September-October, 1863. Returned to duty in November-December, 1863. Reported present in January-April, 1864. Killed at Cold Harbor, Virginia, June 1-3, 1864.

RIVENBARK, A. J., Private

Born in New Hanover County where he resided as a farmer prior to enlisting in New Hanover County at age 30, July 8, 1862, for the war. Died on an unspecified date (probably in the summer of 1862). Place and cause of death not reported (probably yellow fever). [See special note at the end of the history of Company G, 61st Regiment N.C. Troops (page 715).]

RIVENBARK, HENRY D., Private

Resided in Duplin County and enlisted in New Hanover County at age 33, July 14, 1862, for the war. Reported present in November-December, 1862. Hospitalized at Wilmington on or about February 16, 1863, with pneumonia. Returned to duty on or about March 13, 1863. Reported present in May-June, 1863. Captured at Morris Island, Charleston Harbor, South Carolina, on or about August 26, 1863. Confined at Hilton Head, South Carolina, September 1, 1863. Transferred to Fort Columbus, New York Harbor, where he arrived on or about September 22, 1863. Transferred to Point Lookout, Maryland, where he arrived on or about September 26, 1863. Paroled at Point Lookout on February 24, 1865. Received at Boulware's Wharf, James River, Virginia, February 25-28 or March 2-3, 1865, for exchange. No further records. Survived the war.

RIVENBARK, JAMES M., Private

Born in Duplin County and resided in New Hanover or Sampson County where he was by occupation a farmer prior to enlisting in Sampson County at age 34, July 15, 1862, for the war. Captured and paroled at Kinston on December 14, 1862. Reported sick at home from January 13 through August 31, 1863. Reported sick in hospital at Wilson in September-December, 1863. Reported sick in hospital at Petersburg, Virginia, in January-April, 1864. Wounded in the "bowels" at Cold Harbor, Virginia, June 1-3, 1864. Hospitalized at Richmond, Virginia, where he died on June 5, 1864, of wounds.

RIVENBARK, ROBERT, Private

Born in New Hanover County where he resided as a farmer prior to enlisting in New Hanover County at age 18, May 15, 1862, for the war as a substitute. Reported present in November-December, 1862. Hospitalized at Wilmington on February 18, 1863, with intermittent fever. Died in hospital at Wilmington on March 10, 1863, of "erysipelas."

RIVENBARK, THOMAS E., Private

Born in New Hanover County where he resided as a farmer prior to enlisting in New Hanover County at age 17, July 11, 1862, for

the war. Reported present in November, 1862-June, 1863. Deserted to the enemy at Morris Island, Charleston Harbor, South Carolina, on or about August 26, 1863. Confined at Point Lookout, Maryland, September 26, 1863. Released on or about the same date after taking the Oath of Allegiance.

ROBERTS, SAMUEL W., Private

Born in Horry District, South Carolina, and resided in New Hanover County where he was by occupation a clerk prior to enlisting in New Hanover County at age 39, May 12, 1862, for the war as a substitute. Reported present or accounted for in November, 1862-June, 1863. Reported on duty as acting regimental Commissary Sergeant in July, 1863-April, 1864, and September-October, 1864. No further records. Survived the war.

RUSSELL, JOHN R., Private

Born in New Hanover County where he resided as a farmer prior to enlisting in New Hanover County at age 27, April 28, 1862, for the war. Reported sick at home in New Hanover County from October 15 through December 31, 1862. No further records.

SAVAGE, CHARLES W., Private

Born in Duplin County where he resided as a farmer prior to enlisting in New Hanover County at age 32, July 17, 1862, for the war. Deserted at Tarboro on November 7, 1862.

SELLERS, JOHN, Private

Born in Sampson County and resided in New Hanover County where he was by occupation a farmer prior to enlisting in New Hanover County at age 53, May 31, 1862, for the war. Reported absent without leave on an unspecified date (probably in the summer of 1862). No further records. [See special note at the end of the history of Company G, 61st Regiment N.C. Troops (page 715).]

SEVER, CHARLES, Private

Born in Germany and was by occupation a merchant prior to enlisting in New Hanover County at age 21, July 3, 1862, for the war. Reported absent without leave on an unspecified date (probably in the summer of 1862). No further records. [See special note at the end of the history of Company G, 61st Regiment N.C. Troops (page 715).]

SHACKELFORD, JAMES T., Sergeant

Born in Craven County and resided in New Hanover County where he was by occupation a clerk prior to enlisting in New Hanover County at age 18, July 13, 1862, for the war. Mustered in as Private. Reported present in November-December, 1862. Promoted to Sergeant on January 1, 1863. Reported present or accounted for in January-April, 1863. Furloughed for thirty days on June 29, 1863. Reported on detail in hospital at Wilmington from August 25 through October 31, 1863. Rejoined the company in November-December, 1863. Reported on duty as acting Ordnance Sergeant at Ivor Station, Virginia, in January-April, 1864. Hospitalized at Richmond, Virginia, October 7, 1864, with intermittent fever. Returned to duty on October 10, 1864. Hospitalized at Richmond on October 21, 1864, and died on or about the same date of "febris congestiva." [May have served previously as Captain in the 22nd Regiment N.C. Militia.]

SHEPPARD, JOEL H., Private

Resided in New Hanover County and enlisted on May 12, 1862, for the war. Failed to report for duty and was dropped from the company rolls on an unspecified date (probably in the summer of 1862). [See special note at the end of the history of Company G, 61st Regiment N.C. Troops (page 715).]

SHOBER, GEORGE, Private

Resided in New Hanover County and enlisted on May 12, 1862, for the war. Failed to report for duty and was dropped from the company rolls on an unspecified date (probably in the summer of 1862). [See special note at the end of the history of Company G, 61st Regiment N.C. Troops (page 715).]

SIMMONS, JAMES, Private

Born in Sampson County and was by occupation a farmer prior to enlisting in New Hanover County at age 53, September 1, 1862, for the war. Reported sick in hospital at Tarboro from October 23 through December 31, 1862. Deserted from hospital at Goldsboro on January 23, 1863. Returned to duty in May-June, 1863. Deserted on July 8, 1863. Apprehended on an unspecified date. Court-martialed on or about November 18, 1864, and sentenced to be shot on November 26, 1864. No further records.

SKIPPER, HENRY A. J., Private

Born in Brunswick County and resided in New Hanover County where he was by occupation a farmer prior to enlisting in New Hanover County at age 37, July 11, 1862, for the war as a substitute. Reported present in November, 1862-June, 1863. Captured at Morris Island, Charleston Harbor, South Carolina, on or about August 26, 1863. Confined at Hilton Head, South Carolina, September 1, 1863. Transferred to Fort Columbus, New York Harbor, where he arrived on October 6, 1863. Transferred to Point Lookout, Maryland, where he arrived on October 9, 1863. Paroled at Point Lookout on March 3, 1864. Received at City Point, Virginia, March 6, 1864, for exchange. Returned to duty subsequent to April 30, 1864. Reported present in September-October, 1864. No further records.

SMITH, JAMES M., Private

Resided in Sampson County and was by occupation a farmer prior to enlisting in Wake County at age 33, March 1, 1863, for the war. Reported present or accounted for through June 30, 1863. Reported present but sick in the regimental hospital in July-August, 1863. Returned to duty in September-October, 1863. Reported present or accounted for in November, 1863-April, 1864, and September-October, 1864. No further records. Survived the war.

SMITH, JEFFERSON, Private

Resided in Stokes County and was by occupation a farmer prior to enlisting in Wake County at age 40, March 1, 1863, for the war. Reported present or accounted for through June 30, 1863. Wounded in the right thigh and captured at Morris Island, Charleston Harbor, South Carolina, August 26, 1863. Hospitalized at Beaufort, South Carolina, September 1, 1863. Died in hospital at Beaufort on September 8, 1863, of wounds and "tetanus."

SNEED, JONATHAN B., Private

Born in Richmond County and resided in New Hanover County where he was by occupation a cooper prior to enlisting in New Hanover County at age 30, March 17, 1862. Failed to report for duty and was dropped from the company rolls on an unspecified date (probably in the summer of 1862). [See special note at the end of the history of Company G, 61st Regiment N.C. Troops (page 715).]

SPIVEY, TEMPLE, Private

Enlisted in Wake County at age 34, March 1, 1863, for the war. Reported present or accounted for through June 30, 1863. Deserted on July 14, 1863.

STATON, JAMES, Private

Born in Pitt County and was by occupation a farmer prior to enlisting in New Hanover County at age 50, August 28, 1862, for the war. Captured and paroled at Kinston on December 14, 1862. Exchanged on January 13, 1863. Failed to return to duty. Listed as a deserter and dropped from the company rolls on or about February 28, 1863.

STOKES, ROBERT J., Private

Born in Duplin County where he resided as a farmer prior to enlisting in New Hanover County at age 33, July 17, 1862, for the war. Reported present in November, 1862-April, 1864. Hospitalized at Richmond, Virginia, August 23, 1864. Transferred to another hospital on August 24, 1864. Hospitalized at Richmond on October 2, 1864. Reported sick in hospital at Richmond through October 31, 1864. No further records. Survived the war.

STOKES, SAMUEL B., Private

Born in Brunswick County and resided in Duplin County where he was by occupation a farmer prior to enlisting in New Hanover County at age 19, July 14, 1862, for the war. Reported present or accounted for in November, 1862-April, 1864. Captured at Burgess Mill, Virginia, October 27, 1864. Confined at Point Lookout, Maryland, October 31, 1864. Died at Point Lookout on January 26, 1865. Cause of death not reported.

STOKES, SYLVESTER B., Private

Resided in Duplin County where he enlisted at age 18, July 14, 1862, for the war. Captured at Kinston on or about December 13, 1862. Paroled at Kinston on December 15, 1862. Hospitalized at Wilmington on or about February 18, 1863, with intermittent fever. Returned to duty on March 1, 1863. Hospitalized at Wilmington on an unspecified date. Returned to duty in May-June, 1863. Captured at Morris Island, Charleston Harbor, South Carolina, August 26, 1863. Confined at Hilton Head, South Carolina, September 1, 1863. Transferred to Fort Columbus, New York Harbor, where he arrived on October 6, 1863. Transferred to Point Lookout, Maryland, where he arrived on October 11, 1863. Paroled at Point Lookout on March 3, 1864. Received at City Point, Virginia, March 6, 1864, for exchange. Returned to duty subsequent to April 30, 1864. Captured at Fort Harrison, Virginia, September 30, 1864. Confined at Point Lookout on October 5, 1864. Paroled at Point Lookout on October 31, 1864. Received at Venus Point, Savannah River, Georgia, November 15, 1864, for exchange. No further records.

SUTTON, WILLIAM M., Private

Resided in Sampson County and was by occupation a farm laborer prior to enlisting in New Hanover County at age 30, August 13, 1862, for the war as a substitute. Reported sick at home in Sampson County on December 20, 1862. Returned to duty in January-February, 1863. Reported present or accounted for through June 30, 1863. Reported sick in hospital at Mount Pleasant, South Carolina, in July-August, 1863. Returned to duty in September-October, 1863. Reported present through April 30, 1864. Reported on detail in the engineering department at Petersburg, Virginia, in September-October, 1864. No further records. Survived the war.

TRAINER, ARTHUR, Private

Previously served as Private in 2nd Company H, 40th Regiment N.C. Troops (3rd Regiment N.C. Artillery). Transferred to this company in July, 1863. Captured at Morris Island, Charleston Harbor, South Carolina, August 26, 1863. Confined at Point Lookout, Maryland. Died at Point Lookout prior to November 1, 1864. Date and cause of death not reported.

TREADWELL, HAYWOOD, Private

Born in Sampson County and resided in New Hanover County where he was by occupation a farmer prior to enlisting in New Hanover County at age 36, July 10, 1862, for the war as a substitute. Reported present in November, 1862-June, 1863. Wounded in the left thigh and captured at Morris Island, Charleston Harbor, South Carolina, August 26, 1863. Hospitalized at Beaufort, South Carolina, where he died on September 12, 1863, of wounds.

TURNER, A. E., Private

Resided in New Hanover County and enlisted on May 12, 1862, for the war. Failed to report for duty and was dropped from the company rolls on an unspecified date (probably in the summer of 1862). [See special note at the end of the history of Company G, 61st Regiment N.C. Troops (page 715).]

VAN AMRINGE, CYRUS STOW, Private

Born in New York City and was by occupation a merchant prior to enlisting in New Hanover County at age 25, May 12, 1862, for the war. Dropped from the company rolls on an unspecified date (probably in the summer of 1862). Reason he was dropped not reported. Died at Wilmington on October 2, 1862, of "yellow fever." [See special note at the end of the history of Company G, 61st Regiment N.C. Troops (page 715).]

VANN, VALENTINE, Private

Born in Sampson County and resided in Duplin County where he was by occupation a farmer prior to enlisting in New Hanover County at age 35, August 3, 1862, for the war. Discharged on an unspecified date (probably in the autumn of 1862) after providing a substitute. [See special note at the end of the history of Company G, 61st Regiment N.C. Troops (page 715).]

VINES, HENRY, Private

Born in Brunswick County and resided in Brunswick or New Hanover County where he was by occupation a farmer or laborer prior to enlisting in New Hanover County at age 18, March 21, 1862. Failed to report for duty and was dropped from the company rolls on an unspecified date (probably in the summer of 1862). [See special note at the end of the history of Company G, 61st Regiment N.C. Troops (page 715).]

WATKINS, R. B., Private

Born in Baltimore, Maryland, and resided in New Hanover County where he was by occupation a carpenter prior to enlisting in New Hanover County at age 24, August 12, 1862, for the war. Failed to report for duty and was dropped from the company rolls on an unspecified date (probably in the summer of 1862). [See special note at the end of the history of Company G, 61st Regiment N.C. Troops (page 715).]

WELLS, ALEXANDER, JR., Private

Resided in New Hanover County and enlisted at age 31, July 11, 1862, for the war. Failed to report for duty and was dropped from

the company rolls on an unspecified date (probably in the summer of 1862). No further records. Survived the war. [See special note at the end of the history of Company G, 61st Regiment N.C. Troops (page 715).]

WILSON, JOHN W., Private

Born in New Hanover County where he resided as a farmer prior to enlisting in New Hanover County at age 18, May 15, 1862, for the war as a substitute. Died in hospital at Wilson on December 17, 1862, of disease.

WILSON, WILLIAM, Private

Born in Columbus County and resided in New Hanover County where he was by occupation a farmer prior to enlisting in New Hanover County at age 40, June 24, 1862, for the war as a substitute. Reported present in November-December, 1862. Hospitalized at Wilmington on or about February 2, 1863, with diarrhoea. Returned to duty in May-June, 1863. Captured at Morris Island, Charleston Harbor, South Carolina, August 26, 1863. Confined at Hilton Head, South Carolina, on or about September 1, 1863. Transferred to Fort Columbus, New York Harbor, where he arrived on October 6, 1863. Transferred to Point Lookout, Maryland, October 9, 1863. Paroled at Point Lookout on September 18, 1864. Received at Varina, Virginia, on or about September 21, 1864, for exchange. Hospitalized at Richmond, Virginia, the same date. Furloughed for forty days on September 23, 1864. No further records.

WOOD, EZEKIEL, Private

Born in New Hanover County where he resided as a farmer prior to enlisting in New Hanover County at age 18, May 12, 1862, for the war as a substitute. Died in hospital at Wilson on November 5, 1862, of "typhoid pneumonia."

WOOD, JAMES O., Private

Born in New Hanover County and resided in New Hanover or Brunswick County where he was by occupation a farmer prior to enlisting in New Hanover County at age 45, July 10, 1862, for the war as a substitute. Deserted near Tarboro on November 7, 1862. Returned from desertion on June 25, 1863. Returned to duty prior to September 1, 1863. Deserted on October 7, 1863.

WOOD, JOHN S., Private

Born in New Hanover County where he resided as a student prior to enlisting in New Hanover County at age 18, May 15, 1862, for the war. Failed to report for duty and was dropped from the company rolls on an unspecified date (probably in the summer of 1862). [See special note at the end of the history of Company G, 61st Regiment N.C. Troops (page 715).]

WOODARD, JOSEPH, Private

Born in Brunswick County and resided in New Hanover County where he was by occupation a farmer prior to enlisting at age 17, February 13, 1862. Failed to report for duty and was dropped from the company rolls on an unspecified date (probably in the summer of 1862). [See special note at the end of the history of Company G, 61st Regiment N.C. Troops (page 715).]

WOODS, OWEN H., Private

Born in New Hanover County and was by occupation a farmer prior to enlisting in New Hanover County at age 16, June 29, 1862, for the war. Died in hospital at Tarboro on November 5, 1862. Cause of death not reported.

WOODS, WILLIAM R., Private

Born in New Hanover County where he resided as a farmer prior to enlisting in New Hanover County at age 19, May 12, 1862, for the war as a substitute. Hospitalized at Wilson on October 24, 1862. Died in hospital at Wilson on or about January 5, 1863, of "typhoid fever."

YOUNG, H. R., Private

Born in Brunswick County and resided in New Hanover County where he was by occupation a farmer prior to enlisting in New Hanover County at age 45, March 4, 1862. Failed to report for duty and was dropped from the company rolls on an unspecified date (probably in the summer of 1862). [See special note at the end of the history of Company G, 61st Regiment N.C. Troops (page 715).]

COMPANY H

This company, known as the "Hill Guards," was raised in Martin County after John R. Lanier was authorized to raise a company. It was mustered in on November 6, 1861, for twelve months' service. The company served as Capt. John R. Lanier's Independent Company until April, 1862, when it was assigned to the 42nd Regiment N.C. Troops and designated Company B (later known as 1st Company B). However, for unknown reasons it failed to report for duty. On or about May 1, 1862, the company was reorganized, and its term of service was extended to three years or the duration of the war. John R. Lanier was defeated for reelection, and William B. Lanier was elected captain. The company then became known as Capt. William B. Lanier's Independent Company and was mustered in as such on June 30, 1862. On or about September 29, 1862, the company was assigned to the newly organized 59th Regiment N.C. Troops That unit was redesignated the 61st Regiment N.C. Troops on an unspecified date between October 30 and November 22, 1862. This company was designated Company H. After joining the regiment the company functioned as a part of the regiment, and its history for the remainder of the war is reported as a part of the regimental history.

The following roster was compiled primarily from information in the microfilm edition of the Compiled Service Records of Soldiers Who Served in Organizations from the State of North Carolina (Record Group 109, MC 270), National Archives and Records Administration, Washington, D.C. Record Group 109 includes enlistment papers, pay vouchers, requisitions, letters of resignation, discharge certificates, and abstracts of medical and prisoner of war returns. Materials relating specifically to Company H of the 61st Regiment include an undated company muster-in and descriptive roll and company muster rolls for November, 1862-April, 1864, and September-December, 1864.

Also utilized in this roster were *The War of the Rebellion: A Compilation of the Official Records of the Union and Confederate Armies*, the North Carolina adjutant general's *Roll of Honor*, state militia records, newspaper casualty lists and obituaries, wartime claims for bounty pay and allowances, postwar registers of claims for artificial limbs, Confederate pension applications filed with the states of North Carolina, Tennessee, and Florida, Confederate Soldiers' Home records, and the 1860 and 1870 federal censuses of North Carolina. A search was made also for relevant letters, diaries, reminiscences, and other manuscripts in the Southern Historical Collection (University of North Carolina-Chapel Hill), the Duke University Library Special Collections Department, and the North Carolina Division of Archives and History.

Among the secondary sources consulted were records of the North Carolina division of the United Daughters of the Confederacy, postwar rosters, regimental and county histories, marriage bond, will, and cemetery indexes, published and unpublished genealogies, biographical dictionaries, the North Carolina *County Heritage Book* series, the *Confederate Veteran*, Walter Clark's *Histories of the Several Regiments and Battalions from North Carolina in the Great War, 1861-'65*, and the North Carolina volume of the extended edition of *Confederate Military History*.

Note: Service records of men who served in Capt. John R. Lanier's Independent Company and Capt. William B. Lanier's Independent Company but whose service terminated prior to the date that the company was transferred to the 61st Regiment will appear in a roster for Lanier's Independent Company to be published in a subsequent volume.

OFFICERS

CAPTAINS

LANIER, WILLIAM B.

Previously served as Captain of William B. Lanier's Independent Company, N.C. Troops. Transferred to this company in September, 1862. Reported present or accounted for in November, 1862-April, 1864. Wounded in the right leg at Drewry's Bluff, Virginia, May 14, 1864. Right leg amputated. Hospitalized at Richmond, Virginia, where he died on May 19, 1864, of wounds. [Previously served as Lieutenant Colonel of the 10th Regiment N.C. Militia.]

BIGGS, JOHN DAWSON, SR.

Previously served as 1st Lieutenant of Capt. William B. Lanier's Independent Company, N.C. Troops. Transferred to this company in September, 1862. Mustered in as 1st Lieutenant. Reported in command of Company E of this regiment in November-December, 1862. Reported present for duty in January-December, 1863. Reported present and in command of this company in March-April, 1864. Promoted to Captain on May 30, 1864. Reported present in September-December, 1864. Wounded in the right thigh at Bentonville on March 19-21, 1865. Hospitalized at Greensboro. No further records. Survived the war.

LIEUTENANTS

ALEXANDER, ABNER, 3rd Lieutenant

Previously served as Sergeant in Capt. William B. Lanier's Independent Company, N.C. Troops. Transferred to this company in September, 1862. Reported present in November-December, 1862. Hospitalized at Wilmington on or about February 2, 1863, with debilitas. Furloughed for thirty days on or about February 24, 1863. Returned to duty on April 18, 1863. Reported present in May, 1863-April, 1864. Wounded in the arm or right shoulder at or near Cold Harbor, Virginia, June 1, 1864. Hospitalized at Richmond, Virginia. Elected 3rd Lieutenant on June 9, 1864. Furloughed from hospital at High Point on September 29, 1864. Returned to duty prior to October 19, 1864. Applied for retirement because "his arm is of no use to him." No further records.

LANIER, HENRY H., 2nd Lieutenant

Previously served as 3rd Lieutenant of Capt. William B. Lanier's Independent Company, N.C. Troops. Transferred to this company in September, 1862. Mustered in as 3rd Lieutenant. Reported present or accounted for in November, 1862-April, 1864. Wounded in the hip at Drewry's Bluff, Virginia, May 16, 1864. Hospitalized at Richmond, Virginia. Promoted to 2nd Lieutenant on May 30, 1864. Transferred to Tarboro on May 31, 1864. Reported absent wounded in Martin County in September-October, 1864. Reported absent without leave in November-December, 1864. Dropped from the company rolls on February 23, 1865, after he "declared openly [that] he did not intend returning to his command."

RHODES, FRANKLIN ALEXANDER, 1st Lieutenant

Previously served as 2nd Lieutenant in Capt. William B. Lanier's Independent Company, N.C. Troops. Transferred to this company in September, 1862. Mustered in as 2nd Lieutenant. Reported present or accounted for in November, 1862-April, 1864. Promoted to 1st Lieutenant on May 30, 1864. Hospitalized at Richmond, Virginia, October 6, 1864, with intermittent fever. Returned to duty on October 15, 1864. Reported present through December 31, 1864. No further records. Survived the war.

NONCOMMISSIONED OFFICERS
AND PRIVATES

ANDERSON, WILLIAM, Private

Previously served as Private in Capt. William B. Lanier's Independent Company, N.C. Troops. Transferred to this company in September, 1862. Reported present in November, 1862-February, 1863. Sent to hospital at Charleston, South Carolina, April 24, 1863. Rejoined the company on June 16, 1863. Reported present through December 31, 1864. No further records.

ANGE, CHARLES H., Private

Born in Washington County and was by occupation a farmer prior to enlisting in Martin County on October 1, 1862, for the war. Deserted on November 2, 1862. Enlisted as Private in Company A, 1st Regiment N.C. Infantry (Union), December 7, 1862. Was 25 years of age at that time.

ANGE, EDWIN WILLIAMS, Private

Previously served as Private in Capt. William B. Lanier's Independent Company, N.C. Troops. Transferred to this company in September, 1862. Discharged on December 7, 1862, by reason of being underage. Enlisted as Private in Company C, 2nd Regiment N.C. Infantry (Union), February 25, 1864. Later served as Private in Companies G and L, 1st Regiment N.C. Infantry (Union).

BARNES, ABNER J., Private

Resided in Martin County and enlisted in Edgecombe County at age 18, October 1, 1862, for the war. Reported present or accounted for in November, 1862-April, 1864. Wounded slightly in the arm at or near Petersburg, Virginia, on or about June 16-19, 1864. Returned to duty on an unspecified date. Captured at Fort Harrison, Virginia, September 30, 1864. Confined at Point Lookout, Maryland, October 5, 1864. Died at Point Lookout on March 27, 1865, of "measles."

BARNHILL, ABRAM P., Private

Resided in Martin County where he enlisted at age 18, April 1, 1864, for the war. Reported present in April and September-December, 1864. No further records.

BEASLEY, JAMES A., Private

Previously served as Private in Capt. William B. Lanier's Independent Company, N.C. Troops. Transferred to this company in September, 1862. Discharged on January 29, 1863, under the provisions of the Conscription Act (presumably because he was overage).

BEST, HENRY A., Private

Born in Martin County where he resided prior to enlisting in Edgecombe County at age 24, October 1, 1862, for the war. Reported present in November, 1862-April, 1864. Died at Gaines' Farm, Virginia, June 1, 1864, of disease.

BIGGS, NOAH, Private

Previously served as Private in Company G, 41st Regiment N.C. Troops (3rd Regiment N.C Cavalry). Transferred to this company on July 17, 1863. Reported present in July, 1863-April, 1864, and September-December, 1864. No further records. Survived the war.

BOWEN, ELI H., Private

Born in Martin County where he resided as a day laborer prior to enlisting in Edgecombe County at age 18, October 1, 1862, for the war. Reported sick in hospital at Wilson on December 17, 1862. Died in hospital at Wilson on January 20, 1863, of "orchitis."

BOWEN, NATHAN, Private

Resided in Martin County and enlisted in Edgecombe County at age 18, October 1, 1862, for the war. Reported present or accounted for in November, 1862-April, 1864. Wounded in the head at or near Petersburg, Virginia, on or about June 16-19, 1864. Died on June 20, 1864, of wounds.

BULLOCK, ROBERT, Private

Resided in Martin County and enlisted in Edgecombe County at age 18, October 1, 1862, for the war. Reported present or accounted for in November, 1862-April, 1864, and September-December, 1864. Paroled at Charlotte on May 12, 1865.

BUNCH, JOHN J., Private

Previously served as Private in Company B, 3rd Battalion N.C. Light Artillery. Transferred to this company on September 1, 1863. Reported present through October 31, 1863. Deserted from camp at Lawrence Ford, Blackwater River, Virginia, December 21, 1863. Came into Federal lines at Plymouth on an unspecified date (probably on or about March 1, 1864). Confined at Fort Monroe, Virginia. Released at Fort Monroe on April 4, 1864, after taking the Oath of Allegiance.

CARRAWAY, JOSEPH G., Private

Resided in Martin County and enlisted in Edgecombe County at age 27, October 1, 1862, for the war. Furloughed home sick on December 17, 1862. Returned to duty on March 7, 1863. Reported present in May, 1863-April, 1864. Reported on duty as a provost guard in September-December, 1864. No further records. Survived the war.

CARTRETTE, LUKE R., Private

Previously served as Private in Company H, 51st Regiment N.C. Troops. Transferred to this company on March 1, 1863, in exchange for Pvt. Lucian Reynolds. Reported present or accounted for through April 30, 1864. Captured near Petersburg, Virginia, on or about June 16, 1864. Confined at Point Lookout, Maryland,

June 19, 1864. Transferred to Elmira, New York, July 9, 1864. Released at Elmira on July 11, 1865, after taking the Oath of Allegiance. Died in hospital at Wilmington on an unspecified date. Cause of death not reported. [North Carolina pension records indicate that he was wounded at Bermuda Hundred, Virginia, in June, 1864. Contrary to 12:356 of this series, the correct spelling of his surname was Cartrette rather than Cartrett, and he was transferred to this company on March 1 rather than April 1, 1863.]

CASTLE, BENJAMIN F., Private

Previously served as Private in Capt. William B. Lanier's Independent Company, N.C. Troops. Transferred to this company in September, 1862. Reported present or accounted for in November, 1862-April, 1864. Wounded slightly in the arm at Cold Harbor, Virginia, on or about June 1, 1864. Hospitalized at Richmond, Virginia. Returned to duty prior to June 18, 1864, when he was captured near Petersburg, Virginia. Confined at Point Lookout, Maryland, June 23, 1864. Paroled at Point Lookout on September 18, 1864. Received at Varina, Virginia, September 22, 1864, for exchange. Hospitalized at Richmond on September 22, 1864, with scorbutus. Furloughed for sixty days on October 5, 1864. Reported absent without leave on or about December 31, 1864. No further records. Survived the war.

CASTLE, JOHN H., Private

Previously served as Private in Company E, 17th Regiment N.C. Troops (2nd Organization). Transferred to this company on March 1, 1863. Reported present or accounted for in March, 1863-April, 1864. Reported absent sick without leave on August 26, 1864. Returned to duty on November 6, 1864. Paroled at Greensboro on an unspecified date in 1865 (probably in May).

COBB, E. T., Private

Resided in Martin County and enlisted on October 1, 1862, for the war. Died in Martin County prior to November 1, 1862, of disease.

COBURN, HENRY A., Private

Previously served as Private in Capt. William B. Lanier's Independent Company, N.C. Troops. Transferred to this company in September, 1862. Deserted on October 25, 1862. Enlisted in Company D, 17th Regiment N.C. Troops (2nd Organization), November 27, 1862, while listed as a deserter from this company.

COOPER, JAMES, Private

Resided in Martin County and enlisted in Edgecombe County at age 27, October 1, 1862, for the war. Reported sick in hospital at Raleigh on December 18, 1862. Returned to duty in January-February, 1863. Furloughed home sick from Columbia, South Carolina, April 14, 1863. Returned to duty in May-June, 1863. Reported present or accounted for in July, 1863-April, 1864. Wounded in the breast at the Crater, near Petersburg, Virginia, July 30, 1864. Reported present in September-December, 1864. No further records.

COREY, HENRY C., Private

Previously served as Private in Capt. William B. Lanier's Independent Company, N.C. Troops. Transferred to this company in September, 1862. Reported present or accounted for in November, 1862-April, 1864. Wounded in the side or right shoulder by a piece of shell at the Crater, near Petersburg, Virginia, July 30, 1864. Reported on detail as a cook at the division infirmary in September-December, 1864. No further records. Survived the war.

COREY, JOSEPH, Private

Previously served as Private in Capt. William B. Lanier's Independent Company, N.C. Troops. Transferred to this company in September, 1862. Reported present or accounted for in November, 1862-April, 1864. Wounded slightly in the arm at the Crater, near Petersburg, Virginia, July 30, 1864. Returned to duty on an unspecified date. Captured at Fort Harrison, Virginia, September 30, 1864. Confined at Point Lookout, Maryland, October 5, 1864. Released at Point Lookout on June 24, 1865, after taking the Oath of Allegiance.

COREY, JOSHUA L., Sergeant

Previously served as Sergeant in Capt. William B. Lanier's Independent Company, N.C. Troops. Transferred to this company in September, 1862. Mustered in as Sergeant. Reported present in November, 1862-April, 1864. "Volunteered his services" as color bearer on March 4, 1864. Wounded in the hand at Cold Harbor, Virginia, June 1, 1864, while "faithfully and gallantly" discharging his duties as color bearer. Returned to duty on an unspecified date. Recommended for a promotion to Ensign on September 8, 1864. Captured at Fort Harrison, Virginia, September 30, 1864. Confined at Point Lookout, Maryland, October 5, 1864. Appointed Ensign (1st Lieutenant) on October 28, 1864, to rank from September 24, 1864, while a prisoner at Point Lookout. [For his subsequent service record, see the Ensigns' section of the Field and Staff of this regiment.]

COREY, KINCHEN, Private

Previously served as Private in Capt. William B. Lanier's Independent Company, N.C. Troops. Transferred to this company in September, 1862. Reported present or accounted for in November, 1862-April, 1864, and September-December, 1864. No further records. Survived the war.

ELLIS, WILLIAM, Private

Previously served as Private in Capt. William B. Lanier's Independent Company, N.C. Troops. Transferred to this company in September, 1862. Discharged on December 7, 1862, by reason of being overage.

EVERETT, HENRY, Corporal

Resided in Martin County and enlisted in Edgecombe County at age 26, October 1, 1862, for the war. Mustered in as Private. Reported present in November, 1862-February, 1863. Promoted to Corporal on February 10, 1863. Reported present in March, 1863-April, 1864. Wounded in the right thigh near Petersburg, Virginia, June 18, 1864. Reported absent wounded in September-October, 1864. Reported absent wounded without leave in November-December, 1864. No further records. Survived the war.

FLOYD, JAMES, Private

Previously served as Private in Capt. William B. Lanier's Independent Company, N.C. Troops. Transferred to this company in September, 1862. Discharged on December 7, 1862, by reason of being overage.

GARDNER, LORTON, Private

Previously served as Private in Capt. William B. Lanier's Independent Company, N.C. Troops. Transferred to this company in September, 1862. Deserted at Greenville on December 3, 1862. Arrested in Martin County on February 14, 1863. Reported under arrest until August 1, 1863, when he was pardoned. Returned to duty prior to November 1, 1863. Deserted from camp at Lawrence

Ford, Blackwater River, Virginia, December 21, 1863. Enlisted as Private in Company B, 2nd Regiment N.C. Infantry (Union), December 30, 1863. Later served as Private in Company D, 1st Regiment N.C. Infantry (Union).

GIBSON, BENJAMIN C., Private

Previously served as Private in Capt. William B. Lanier's Independent Company, N.C. Troops. Transferred to this company in September, 1862. Placed under arrest in October, 1862, after making an unauthorized overnight visit to his family. Escaped from his guards and deserted while being taken to jail. Enlisted as Private in Company E, 2nd Regiment N.C. Infantry (Union), October 29, 1863. [Gibson was captured by Confederate forces at Plymouth on April 20, 1864, identified as a Confederate deserter, court-martialed on November 28, 1864, and sentenced to be shot. However, he escaped death, possibly because his execution was scheduled for the same date that the Federals attacked Fort Fisher (January 12, 1865). He was then allowed to rejoin Company H, 61st N.C. Troops. At the end of the war he surrendered and, on May 3, 1865, he was assigned Company C, 1st Regiment N.C. Infantry (Union). He was mustered out on June 27, 1865. Gibson's sequential service in Confederate, Federal, Confederate, and Federal units is probably unique.]

GIBSON, JOSEPH E., Private

Previously served as Private in Capt. William B. Lanier's Independent Company, N.C. Troops. Transferred to this company in September, 1862. Reported present or accounted for in November, 1862-April, 1864. Wounded in the hand at Drewry's Bluff, Virginia, May 13-16, 1864. Returned to duty on an unspecified date. Reported present in September-December, 1864. No further records. Survived the war.

GODWARD, JAMES L., 1st Sergeant

Previously served as 1st Sergeant of Capt. William B. Lanier's Independent Company, N.C. Troops. Transferred to this company in September, 1862. Reported present in November, 1862-February, 1863. Hospitalized at Charleston, South Carolina, April 18, 1863. Died in hospital at Charleston on or about May 1, 1863, of "erysipelas."

GODWARD, JOSEPH G., Corporal

Previously served as Private in Capt. William B. Lanier's Independent Company, N.C. Troops. Transferred to this company in September, 1862. Mustered in as Private. Reported present or accounted for in November, 1862-February, 1864. Reported sick at home in Martin County in March-April, 1864. Reported absent without leave on April 29, 1864. Returned to duty on an unspecified date. Promoted to Corporal prior to September 30, 1864, when he was reported missing at Fort Harrison, Virginia. Was presumably killed at Fort Harrison.

GRADLEY, E., Private

Resided in Duplin County. Place and date of enlistment not reported (probably enlisted subsequent to December 31, 1864). Paroled at Goldsboro on May 29, 1865.

GREEN, KELLY, Private

Previously served as Private in Capt. William B. Lanier's Independent Company, N.C. Troops. Transferred to this company in September, 1862. Reported present or accounted for in November, 1862-April, 1864, and September-December, 1864. No further records. Survived the war.

GRIFFIN, ASA T., 1st Sergeant

Previously served as Sergeant in Capt. William B. Lanier's Independent Company, N.C. Troops. Transferred to this company in September, 1862. Mustered in as Sergeant. Reported present in November, 1862-April, 1863. Promoted to 1st Sergeant on May 1, 1863. Reported present through April 30, 1864. Killed at Fort Harrison, Virginia, September 30, 1864.

GRIFFIN, JOHN DANIEL, Private

Previously served as Private in Capt. William B. Lanier's Independent Company, N.C. Troops. Transferred to this company in September, 1862. Reported present or accounted for in November, 1862-April, 1864, and September-December, 1864. No further records. Survived the war.

GRIFFIN, JOHN N., Private

Previously served as Private in Capt. William B. Lanier's Independent Company, N.C. Troops. Transferred to this company in September, 1862. Reported present in November-December, 1862. Hospitalized at Wilmington on February 9, 1863, with catarrhus. Returned to duty on March 2, 1863. Reported present or accounted for through April 30, 1864. Wounded in the left arm on an unspecified date. Furloughed from hospital at Richmond, Virginia, September 5, 1864. Reported absent without leave in November-December, 1864. No further records. Survived the war.

GRIMES, WILLIAM, Private

Previously served as Private in Capt. William B. Lanier's Independent Company, N.C. Troops. Transferred to this company in September, 1862. Discharged on December 7, 1862, by reason of being overage.

GURGANUS, VIRGIL A., 1st Sergeant

Previously served as Corporal in Capt. William B. Lanier's Independent Company, N.C. Troops. Transferred to this company in September, 1862. Mustered in as Corporal. Reported present or accounted for in November, 1862-April, 1864. Wounded in the thigh at Drewry's Bluff, Virginia, May 13-16, 1864. Hospitalized at Richmond, Virginia. Furloughed for thirty days on June 5, 1864. Returned to duty on an unspecified date. Reported present in September-December, 1864. Promoted to 1st Sergeant on November 1, 1864. Hospitalized at Greensboro on January 19, 1865, with pneumonia. Transferred to another hospital on January 20, 1865. No further records. Survived the war.

HAISLIP, THOMAS W., Private

Resided in Martin County and enlisted in Edgecombe County on October 1, 1862, for the war. Sent home sick on December 17, 1862. Died at home in Martin County on January 7, 1863, of disease.

HARDISON, CLAYTON, Private

Resided in Martin County and was by occupation a farmer prior to enlisting in Edgecombe County at age 30, October 1, 1862, for the war. Failed to report for duty and was reported absent without leave on November 2, 1862. Reported for duty on February 10, 1863. Reported present though April 30, 1864. Transferred to Company F, 17th Regiment N.C. Troops (2nd Organization), in July, 1864.

HARDISON, STANLY DANIEL, Private

Previously served as Private in Capt. William B. Lanier's Independent Company, N.C. Troops. Transferred to this company in

September, 1862. Reported present in November, 1862-April, 1864. Captured at Fort Harrison, Virginia, September 30, 1864. Confined at Point Lookout, Maryland, October 5, 1864. Paroled at Point Lookout on March 17, 1865. Received at Boulware's Wharf, James River, Virginia, March 19, 1865, for exchange. Hospitalized at Richmond, Virginia, the same date. Transferred to another hospital on March 20, 1865. No further records. Survived the war.

HARRIS, ARCHIBALD H., Private

Resided in Martin County and enlisted in Edgecombe County at age 20, October 1, 1862, for the war. Reported absent sick in Martin County on December 17, 1862. Reported absent sick without proper authority in January-February, 1863. Hospitalized at Charleston, South Carolina, on or about April 5, 1863. Returned to duty in May-June, 1863. Reported present through October 31, 1863. Hospitalized at Petersburg, Virginia, December 19, 1863, with intermittent fever. Returned to duty on January 4, 1864. Reported present through April 30, 1864. Wounded in the mouth at the Crater, near Petersburg, July 30, 1864. Hospitalized at Richmond, Virginia. Furloughed to Tarboro on or about August 29, 1864. Captured by the enemy at Jamesville on October 17, 1864. Sent to Norfolk, Virginia. Confined at Fort Monroe, Virginia, November 30, 1864. Transferred to Point Lookout, Maryland, December 23, 1864. Released at Point Lookout on June 27, 1865, after taking the Oath of Allegiance.

HARRISON, HENDERSON, Private

Previously served as Private in Capt. William B. Lanier's Independent Company, N.C. Troops. Transferred to this company in September, 1862. Reported present in November-December, 1862. Discharged on January 29, 1863, by reason of having completed his term of service.

HAWKINS, SAMUEL, Private

Previously served as Private in Capt. William B. Lanier's Independent Company, N.C. Troops. Transferred to this company in September, 1862. Reported present in November-December, 1862. Detailed as a ship's carpenter to work on gunboats at Wilmington on February 1, 1863. Reported on detail at Wilmington in February, 1863-April, 1864, and September-December, 1864. No further records.

HEARN, JOHN, Private

Previously served as Private in Capt. William B. Lanier's Independent Company, N.C. Troops. Transferred to this company in September, 1862. "Straggled off" during the retreat from Kinston on December 14, 1862, and was captured by the enemy. Paroled on December 15, 1862. Failed to return to duty and was reported absent without leave on or about December 31, 1862. Dropped from the company rolls prior to September 1, 1863.

HODGES, HENRY THOMAS, Private

Resided in Martin County and enlisted in Edgecombe County at age 25, October 1, 1862, for the war. Reported sick at home in Martin County on December 17, 1862. Returned to duty in January-February, 1863. Reported present or accounted for through April 30, 1864. Wounded slightly in the arm at Cold Harbor, Virginia, May 31-June 3, 1864. Wounded in the arm and hip at the Crater, near Petersburg, Virginia, July 30, 1864. Hospitalized at Richmond, Virginia, where he died on October 13, 1864, of wounds.

HODGES, JAMES R., Private

Resided in Martin County and enlisted in Edgecombe County at age 21, October 1, 1862, for the war. Reported present in November-December, 1862. Detailed as a nurse in the smallpox hospital at Wilmington on January 7, 1863. Rejoined the company on April 26, 1863. Reported present in May, 1863-April, 1864, and September-December, 1864. No further records.

HOLLIDAY, JOHN H., Private

Resided in Martin County and enlisted in Edgecombe County at age 27, October 1, 1862, for the war. "Straggled off sick" from camp near Kinston on December 13, 1862. Reported absent without leave through February 25, 1863. Returned to duty on March 7, 1863. Detailed for guard duty at Hilton Ferry, near Wilmington, in May-June, 1863. Died in hospital at Goldsboro on August 4, 1863, of "febris typhoid." [May have served previously as Private in Company G, 17th Regiment N.C. Troops (1st Organization).]

INMAN, ROBERT C., Private

Resided in Brunswick County and was by occupation a farmer prior to enlisting in Wake County at age 31, October 1, 1862, for the war. Failed to report for duty and was reported absent without leave on November 2, 1862. Listed as a deserter and dropped from the company rolls on or about April 30, 1863.

INMAN, WILLIAM A., Private

Resided in Brunswick County and enlisted in Wake County on October 1, 1862, for the war. Failed to report for duty and was reported absent without leave on November 2, 1862. Reported for duty on February 21, 1863. Reported under arrest in the guard house in March-April, 1863. Reported sick in hospital at Wilmington in May-June, 1863. Reported absent at Charleston, South Carolina, in July-August, 1863. Returned to duty in September-October, 1863. Deserted from camp near Kenansville on December 13, 1863. Reported under arrest at Petersburg, Virginia, in January-April, 1864. Returned to duty on an unspecified date. Wounded in the shoulder, back, and eyes by the bursting of a cannon at Fort Harrison, Virginia, September 30, 1864. Hospitalized at Richmond, Virginia, October 2, 1864. Returned to duty prior to November 1, 1864. Reported present in November-December, 1864. No further records. Survived the war. [Was about 25 years of age at time of enlistment.]

JAMES, AMALECK, Private

Resided in Martin County where he enlisted at age 16, October 1, 1862, for the war. Reported present or accounted for through April 30, 1864. Captured at Fort Harrison, Virginia, September 30, 1864. Confined at Point Lookout, Maryland, October 5, 1864. Paroled at Point Lookout on March 17, 1865. Received at Boulware's Wharf, James River, Virginia, March 19, 1865, for exchange. No further records. Survived the war.

JAMES, GEORGE B., Private

Enlisted in Martin County at age 16, May 1, 1864, for the war. Wounded at Fort Harrison, Virginia, September 30, 1864. Hospitalized at Richmond, Virginia. Returned to duty on December 16, 1864. Reported present through December 31, 1864. No further records.

KNOX, WILLIS, Private

Previously served as Private in Capt. William B. Lanier's Independent Company, N.C. Troops. Transferred to this company in

September, 1862. Reported present or accounted for in November, 1862-April, 1864. Hospitalized at Petersburg, Virginia, June 25, 1864, with debilitas. Died in hospital at Richmond, Virginia, June 30, 1864, of "typhoid fever."

LANIER, NOAH T., Sergeant

Previously served as Private in Company A, 17th Regiment N.C. Troops (2nd Organization). Transferred to this company on December 15, 1862. Mustered in as Private. Reported present in January-April, 1863. Promoted to Corporal on May 1, 1863. Reported present or accounted for in May, 1863-April, 1864. Stunned (presumably by a shell) at the Crater, near Petersburg, Virginia, July 30, 1864. Promoted to Sergeant in August-October, 1864. Reported present in September-December, 1864. No further records. Survived the war.

LANIER, WILLIAM J., Private

Previously served as Private in Capt. William B. Lanier's Independent Company, N.C. Troops. Transferred to this company in September, 1862. Reported present or accounted for in November, 1862-April, 1864. Hospitalized at Richmond, Virginia, August 23, 1864. Furloughed on September 10, 1864. Reported absent sick without leave on or about October 31, 1864. Returned to duty prior to December 4, 1864, when he was reported absent without leave. Returned to duty on December 14, 1864. Reported present through December 31, 1864. No further records.

LEE, JAMES G., Private

Resided in Martin County and enlisted in Edgecombe County at age 20, October 1, 1862, for the war. Reported present in November-December, 1862. Hospitalized at Charleston, South Carolina, on or about February 18, 1863. Furloughed for thirty days on March 10, 1863. Reported absent without leave on or about April 30, 1863. Hospitalized at Wilmington on or about May 7, 1863, with acute diarrhoea. Returned to duty prior to July 1, 1863. Reported absent on sick furlough in Martin County (suffering from dropsy) in July, 1863-February, 1864. Reported absent sick without leave in March-April and September-October, 1864. Returned to duty on or about December 1, 1864. Hospitalized at Greensboro on February 22, 1865, with catarrhus. Transferred to another hospital on February 23, 1865. No further records. Survived the war. [North Carolina pension records indicate that he was wounded in the left leg at Cold Harbor, Virginia, June 2, 1864.]

LEGGETT, JOHN L., Private

Born in Beaufort County and resided in Martin County where he was by occupation a farmer prior to enlisting in Edgecombe County on October 1, 1862, for the war. Sent home sick from Greenville on December 17, 1862. Reported absent without leave in January-February, 1863. Hospitalized at Charleston, South Carolina, April 24, 1863. Reported sick in hospital at Columbia, South Carolina, in May-June, 1863. Discharged at Columbia on July 4, 1863, by reason of "loss of his left eye with amanr[o]sis of the right. . . . [H]is eye was lost from the effects of a blow inflicted by a stick on the 1st April 1861. He has been in service nine months and during that period has been confined with sympathetic irritations of his left eye seven months." Discharge certificate gives his age as 27.

LEGGETT, NOAH T., Musician

Previously served as Private in Capt. William B. Lanier's Independent Company, N.C. Troops. Transferred to this company in September, 1862. Mustered in as Private. Reported present in November-December, 1862. Promoted to Musician (Drummer) in January-February, 1863. Reported present or accounted for in

January, 1863-April, 1864, and September-December, 1864. No further records. [He apparently served as a Drummer during most of the war; however, he was reported to be serving as a Fifer in July-August, 1863.]

LILLEY, NOAH T., Private

Resided in Martin County and enlisted in Edgecombe County on October 1, 1862, for the war. Reported present in November, 1862-April, 1863. Died in hospital at Wilmington on June 3, 1863, of "febris typhoides."

LILLEY, PERRY, Private

Previously served as Private in Capt. William B. Lanier's Independent Company, N.C. Troops. Transferred to this company in September, 1862. Discharged on December 7, 1862, because he was overage and his term of enlistment had expired.

LILLEY, SIMON, Private

Resided in Martin County and enlisted on October 1, 1862, for the war. Discharged in January, 1863, by reason of disability.

LILLEY, WILLIAM HENRY, Private

Resided in Martin County and enlisted in Edgecombe County at age 18, October 1, 1862, for the war. Reported present in November, 1862-June, 1863. Reported sick in hospital at Charleston, South Carolina, in July-August, 1863. Reported at home on sick furlough in September-October, 1863. Returned to duty in November-December, 1863. Reported present in January-April, 1864. Reported sick in hospital at Raleigh on June 6 and in September-October, 1864. Returned to duty in November-December, 1864. No further records. Survived the war.

LIPSCOMBE, JOHN A., Private

Previously served as Private in Capt. William B. Lanier's Independent Company, N.C. Troops. Transferred to this company in September, 1862. Deserted on or about November 4, 1862. Returned from desertion on June 12, 1863, and was confined at Wilmington. Reported "absent . . . at Charleston, S.C.," in July-August, 1863. Returned to duty in September-October, 1863. Reported present in November, 1863-April, 1864. Reported sick at home in Martin County in September-October, 1864. Reported absent without leave in November-December, 1864. No further records.

LONG, JOSEPH, Private

Resided in Brunswick County and enlisted in Wake County on October 1, 1862, for the war. Failed to report for duty and was reported absent without leave on November 2, 1862. Listed as a deserter and dropped from the company rolls in March-April, 1863.

LONG, LASPYRE, Private

Born in Brunswick County where he resided as a laborer prior to enlisting in Wake County at age 20, October 1, 1862, for the war. Failed to report for duty and was reported absent without leave on November 2, 1862. Listed as a deserter in March-April, 1863. Hospitalized at Wilmington on May 1, 1863. Detailed at Wilmington on an unspecified date. Sent back to his company on or about September 21, 1863, because he was an "idler about the streets of Wilmington." Reported sick in camp near Petersburg, Virginia, in November-December, 1863. Returned to duty in January-February, 1864. Reported on detail as a camp guard near Petersburg in March-April, 1864. Hospitalized at Raleigh on June 6, 1864. Reported sick in hospital at Raleigh in September-December, 1864. Hospitalized at Raleigh on April 10, 1865. No further records.

MANNING, ALLEN A., Private

Previously served as Private in Capt. William B. Lanier's Independent Company, N.C. Troops. Transferred to this company in September, 1862. Reported present in November, 1862-February, 1864. Reported on detail as a "scout around Suffolk, Virginia," in March-April, 1864. Reported present in September-December, 1864. No further records.

MEDFORD, JOHN W., Private

Resided in Martin County and was by occupation an overseer prior to enlisting in Edgecombe County at age 34, October 1, 1862, for the war. Straggled on the retreat from Kinston on December 14, 1862, and was reported absent without leave. Returned to duty on March 7, 1863. Reported present through April 30, 1864. Wounded in the left arm and captured at Fort Harrison, Virginia, September 30, 1864. Hospitalized at Fort Monroe, Virginia. Transferred to Point Lookout, Maryland, December 23, 1864. Paroled at Point Lookout on January 17, 1865. Received at Boulware's Wharf, James River, Virginia, January 21, 1865, for exchange. Hospitalized at Richmond, Virginia, January 21, 1865, with chilblains and chronic diarrhoea. Furloughed for sixty days on January 26, 1865. Reported in hospital at High Point on January 30, 1865. No further records. Survived the war.

MOBLEY, ALEXANDER, JR., Private

Born on February 22, 1836. Resided in Martin County and was by occupation a farmer prior to enlisting in Edgecombe County at age 26, October 1, 1862, for the war. Reported present in November, 1862-April, 1864, and September-December, 1864. No further records. Survived the war.

MOBLEY, WILLIAM J., Private

Resided in Martin County and enlisted in Edgecombe County at age 25, October 1, 1862, for the war. Reported sick at home on December 17, 1862. Returned to duty in January-February, 1863. Died in hospital at Columbia, South Carolina, on or about May 26, 1863, of disease.

MOORE, HENRY, Private

Previously served as Private in Capt. William B. Lanier's Independent Company, N.C. Troops. Transferred to this company in September, 1862. Discharged on December 7, 1862, by reason of being overage and because he had served for the term of his enlistment.

MOORE, ISAIAH, Private

Resided in Martin County and was by occupation a farmer prior to enlisting in Edgecombe County at age 30, October 1, 1862, for the war. Reported present in November-December, 1862. Hospitalized at Wilmington on or about February 18, 1863, with debilitas. Later detailed as a hospital nurse at Wilmington. Returned to duty on May 7, 1863. Reported present through April 30, 1864. Reported absent on sick furlough in September-October, 1864. Reported sick in hospital at Wilson in November-December, 1864. Wounded in the left buttock and captured near Kinston on March 9, 1865. Hospitalized at New Bern where he died on the morning of March 24, 1865, of "typhoid fever."

MYERS, JOHN W., Private

Resided in Martin County and enlisted on October 1, 1862, for the war. Transferred to Company A, 17th Regiment N.C. Troops (2nd Organization), November 10, 1862.

NICHOLSON, JAMES B., Private

Resided in Martin County and was by occupation a swamper prior to enlisting in Martin County at age 27, June 9, 1863, for the war. Reported present or accounted for through April 30, 1864. Last reported in the records of this company on August 1, 1864. Survived the war.

NICHOLSON, WILLIAM, Private

Previously served as Private in Capt. William B. Lanier's Independent Company, N.C. Troops. Transferred to this company in September, 1862. Reported present in November, 1862-April, 1864. Last reported in the records of this company on August 1, 1864.

PAGE, JAMES R., Private

Previously served as Private in Company F, 17th Regiment N.C. Troops (2nd Organization). Transferred to this company on or about May 1, 1864. Wounded in the left leg at Fort Harrison, Virginia, September 30, 1864. Left leg amputated. Hospitalized at Richmond, Virginia. Was apparently captured in hospital at Richmond on April 3, 1865. Took the Oath of Allegiance at Richmond on August 28, 1865. Reported still in hospital at Richmond on September 6, 1865.

PARKER, ROBERT B., Private

Previously served as Private in Capt. William B. Lanier's Independent Company, N.C. Troops. Transferred to this company in September, 1862. Discharged on December 7, 1862, by reason of being underage and because his term of enlistment had expired.

PEAL, ABRAM R., Sergeant

Previously served as Private in Capt. William B. Lanier's Independent Company, N.C. Troops. Transferred to this company in September, 1862. Reported present in November, 1862-June, 1863. Reported sick in hospital at Wilson in July-August, 1863. Returned to duty in September-October, 1863. Reported on detail as a camp guard near Petersburg, Virginia, in November-December, 1863. Rejoined the company in January-February, 1864. Reported present in March-April, 1864. Promoted to Sergeant in May-July, 1864. Wounded in the abdomen at the Crater, near Petersburg, July 30, 1864. Died on August 4, 1864, of wounds.

PEAL, HENRY D., Private

Born on August 10, 1846. Resided in Martin County where he enlisted at age 17, July 10, 1864, for the war. Killed at Fort Harrison, Virginia, September 30, 1864.

PEAL, HYMAN, Private

Previously served as Private in Capt. William B. Lanier's Independent Company, N.C. Troops. Transferred to this company in September, 1862. Transferred to Company A, 17th Regiment N.C. Troops (2nd Organization), December 20, 1862.

PEAL, JAMES STATON, Corporal

Previously served as Private in Capt. William B. Lanier's Independent Company, N.C. Troops. Transferred to this company in September, 1862. Mustered in as Private. Reported present in November, 1862-June, 1863. Promoted to Corporal on March 1, 1863. Reported sick in hospital at Charleston, South Carolina, in September-December, 1863. Reported absent on furlough in January-February, 1864. Returned to duty in March-April, 1864.

Wounded in the left forearm at Fort Harrison, Virginia, September 30, 1864. Hospitalized at Richmond, Virginia. Furloughed for sixty days on November 4, 1864. Captured in hospital at Raleigh on April 13, 1865. No further records. Survived the war.

PEAL, ROBERT H., Private

Previously served as Private in Capt. William B. Lanier's Independent Company, N.C. Troops. Transferred to this company in September, 1862. Reported present or accounted for in November, 1862-April, 1864. Wounded in the forehead at Drewry's Bluff, Virginia, May 13-16, 1864. Returned to duty on an unspecified date. Detailed as an engineer in order to report for duty with General Beauregard's staff in September-October, 1864. Reported on duty with the division Engineer Corps in November-December, 1864. No further records. [Served also in the 2nd Regiment Confederate Engineer Troops.]

PEAL, TURNER, Private

Previously served as Private in Capt. William B. Lanier's Independent Company, N.C. Troops. Transferred to this company in September, 1862. Reported present or accounted for in November, 1862-June, 1863. Reported sick in hospital at Wilmington in July-August, 1863. Returned to duty in September-October, 1863. Reported sick in camp near Petersburg, Virginia, in November-December, 1863. Reported on duty as a camp guard in January-April, 1864. Reported on detail as a division teamster in September-December, 1864. Transferred to Company H, 26th Regiment N.C. Troops, subsequent to December 31, 1864.

PEAL, WILLIAM J., Private

Resided in Martin County and was by occupation a farmer prior to enlisting in Martin County at age 34, May 1, 1864, for the war. Wounded in the abdomen and/or back at Drewry's Bluff, Virginia, May 13-16, 1864. Hospitalized at Richmond, Virginia, where he died on May 28, 1864, of wounds.

PERRY, WILLIAM MICAJAH, Private

Previously served as Private in Capt. William B. Lanier's Independent Company, N.C. Troops. Transferred to this company in September, 1862. Reported present or accounted for in November, 1862-February, 1863. Hospitalized at Columbia, South Carolina, in March, 1863. Furloughed for thirty days on April 1, 1863. Returned to duty in May-June, 1863. Reported present or accounted for in July, 1863-April, 1864. Stunned (presumably by a shell) at the Crater, near Petersburg, Virginia, July 30, 1864. Reported present in September-December, 1864. No further records. Survived the war.

PURVIS, JAMES G., Private

Resided in Martin County and enlisted in Edgecombe County at age 18, October 1, 1862, for the war. Reported present or accounted for in November, 1862-April, 1864. Hospitalized at Richmond, Virginia, September 27, 1864, with phthisis. Later reported to be suffering from chronic diarrhoea and emaciation. Furloughed for thirty days on or about October 6, 1864. Reported absent sick through December 31, 1864. No further records.

REASON, RILEY, Private

Previously served as Private in Capt. William B. Lanier's Independent Company, N.C. Troops. Transferred to this company in September, 1862. Discharged on December 7, 1862, by reason of being overage and because his term of enlistment had expired.

REYNOLDS, LUCIAN, Private

Resided in Brunswick County and enlisted in Wake County at age 37, October 1, 1862, for the war. Failed to report for duty and was reported absent without leave on November 2, 1862. Reported for duty on February 9, 1863. Transferred to Company H, 51st Regiment N.C. Troops, March 1, 1863, in exchange for Pvt. Luke R. Cartrette. [Contrary to 12:362 of this series, he was transferred on March 1 rather than April 1, 1863.]

ROBASON, AARON, Musician

Previously served as Private in Capt. William B. Lanier's Independent Company, N.C. Troops. Transferred to this company in September, 1862. Mustered in as Private. Reported present in November, 1862-February, 1863. Appointed Musician (Fifer) on March 1, 1863. Reported present or accounted for in March, 1863-April, 1864. Wounded slightly in the back at or near Petersburg, Virginia, on or about June 20-July 1, 1864. Returned to duty on an unspecified date. Reported present in September-December, 1864. No further records. Survived the war. [Reportedly served as a Drummer in July-August, 1863, and possibly at other times during the war.]

ROBASON, ASA T., Private

Previously served as Private in Capt. William B. Lanier's Independent Company, N.C. Troops. Transferred to this company in September, 1862. Reported present in November, 1862-April, 1864, and September-December, 1864. No further records.

ROBASON, HARMON J., Private

Resided in Martin County and enlisted in Edgecombe County at age 18, October 1, 1862, for the war. Reported present or accounted for in November, 1862-April, 1864. Hospitalized at Petersburg, Virginia, May 21, 1864, with intermittent fever. Furloughed for sixty days on June 1, 1864. Hospitalized at Richmond, Virginia, August 8, 1864, with anasarca. Furloughed for sixty days on August 18, 1864. Reported absent without leave on or about October 31, 1864. Returned to duty in November-December, 1864. Hospitalized at High Point on an unspecified date. Paroled at Greensboro on May 1, 1865.

ROBASON, HENRY, JR., Private

Previously served as Private in Capt. William B. Lanier's Independent Company, N.C. Troops. Transferred to this company in September, 1862. Reported present or accounted for in November, 1862-April, 1864. Hospitalized at High Point on August 20, 1864, with chronic diarrhoea. Furloughed on August 21, 1864. Reported on detail as a nurse in September-December, 1864. No further records. Survived the war.

ROBASON, HENRY, SR., Private

Previously served as Private in Capt. William B. Lanier's Independent Company, N.C. Troops. Enlisted in this company on October 1, 1862, for the war. Reported present in November, 1862-April, 1864. Reported absent sick without leave in September-October, 1864. Reported absent without leave in November-December, 1864. No further records.

ROBASON, JAMES BENJAMIN, Sergeant

Previously served as Corporal in Capt. William B. Lanier's Independent Company, N.C. Troops. Transferred to this company in September, 1862. Mustered in as Corporal. Reported present in November, 1862-April, 1863. Promoted to Sergeant on May 1,

1863. Reported present or accounted for in May, 1863-April, 1864. Wounded in the right foot at Drewry's Bluff, Virginia, May 13, 1864. Hospitalized at Richmond, Virginia. Furloughed for sixty days on or about June 14, 1864. Returned to duty prior to September 30, 1864, when he was captured at Fort Harrison, Virginia. Confined at Point Lookout, Maryland, October 5, 1864. Paroled at Point Lookout on March 17, 1865. Received at Boulware's Wharf, James River, Virginia, March 19, 1865, for exchange. No further records. Survived the war.

ROBASON, JAMES E., Private

Previously served as Private in Capt. William B. Lanier's Independent Company, N.C. Troops. Transferred to this company in September, 1862. Reported present or accounted for in November, 1862-April, 1864. Wounded in the arm and/or leg at Drewry's Bluff, Virginia, May 13-16, 1864. Wounded in the arm at Cold Harbor, Virginia, May 31-June 3, 1864. No further records. Survived the war.

ROBASON, JAMES THOMAS, Private

Previously served as Private in Capt. William B. Lanier's Independent Company, N.C. Troops. Transferred to this company in September, 1862. Reported present or accounted for in November, 1862-April, 1864. Wounded in the arm and/or left thigh at or near Drewry's Bluff, Virginia, on or about May 13-16, 1864. Hospitalized at Richmond, Virginia. Reported absent wounded without leave in September-October, 1864. Reported absent without leave in November-December, 1864. No further records.

ROBASON, NOAH, Private

Previously served as Corporal in Capt. William B. Lanier's Independent Company, N.C. Troops. Transferred to this company in September, 1862. Mustered in as Corporal. Reported present in November-December, 1862. Reduced to ranks on February 10, 1863, when he was detailed as a carpenter to work on gunboat at Wilmington. Reported absent on detail through April, 1864, and in September-December, 1864. No further records. Survived the war.

ROGERSON, HARRISON, Private

Previously served as Private in Capt. William B. Lanier's Independent Company, N.C. Troops. Transferred to this company in September, 1862. Reported present in November, 1862-April, 1864. Wounded in the hand at Drewry's Bluff, Virginia, May 13-16, 1864. Returned to duty on an unspecified date. Stunned (presumably by a shell) at the Crater, near Petersburg, Virginia, July 30, 1864. No further records. [May have died at Richmond, Virginia, on or about October 13, 1864.]

ROGERSON, RANSOM S., Private

Previously served as Private in Capt. William B. Lanier's Independent Company, N.C. Troops. Transferred to this company in September, 1862. Reported present or accounted for in November, 1862-April, 1864. Died at Richmond, Virginia, August 8 or August 24, 1864, of disease.

ROGERSON, RICHARD GODFREY, Private

Previously served as Private in Capt. William B. Lanier's Independent Company, N.C. Troops. Transferred to this company in September, 1862. Reported present in November, 1862-April, 1864. Wounded slightly in the shoulder at the Crater, near Petersburg, Virginia, July 30, 1864. Reported present in September-December, 1864. No further records. Survived the war.

SENATE, WILLIAM L. J., Private

Resided in Martin County and enlisted in Edgecombe County at age 19, October 1, 1862, for the war. Furloughed home sick on December 17, 1862. Later reported absent without leave. Returned from absence without leave on February 25, 1863. Returned to duty on March 7, 1863. Reported present or accounted for in May, 1863-April, 1864, and September-December, 1864. No further records. Survived the war.

SIMPSON, JAMES, Private

Previously served as Private in Capt. William B. Lanier's Independent Company, N.C. Troops. Transferred to this company in September, 1862. Discharged on December 7, 1862, by reason of being overage and because he had served for the term of his enlistment.

SMITH, JESSE A., Private

Resided in Brunswick County and enlisted in Wake County at age 33, October 1, 1862, for the war. Failed to report for duty and was reported absent without leave on November 2, 1862. Listed as a deserter and dropped from the company rolls on or about April 30, 1863.

SMITH, JOSIAH, Private

Resided in Brunswick County and enlisted in Wake County at age 33, October 1, 1862, for the war. Failed to report for duty and was reported absent without leave on November 2, 1862. Reported for duty on February 9, 1863. Furloughed for fourteen days on April 9, 1863. Reported absent without leave on April 30, 1863. Returned to duty in May-June, 1863. Reported sick in hospital at Wilmington in July-August, 1863. Reported under arrest at Wilmington in September-October, 1863. Rejoined the company on an unspecified date. Deserted from camp near Kenansville on December 13, 1863. Returned from desertion on October 1, 1864. Reported present in November-December, 1864. No further records. Survived the war. [North Carolina pension records indicate that he was wounded in the left leg by the explosion of a cannon at Charleston, South Carolina, September 20, 1863.]

SMITHWICK, EDGAR, Private

Previously served as Private in Capt. William B. Lanier's Independent Company, N.C. Troops. Transferred to this company in September, 1862. Reported present in November, 1862-April, 1864. "Stunned" (presumably by the explosion of a shell) at or near Petersburg, Virginia, on or about June 20-July 1, 1864. Returned to duty on an unspecified date. Reported present in September-December, 1864, and on February 1, 1865. No further records.

SWANNER, URIAH JAMES T., Private

Previously served as Private in Capt. William B. Lanier's Independent Company, N.C. Troops. Transferred to this company in September, 1862. Reported present or accounted for in November, 1862-April, 1864. Reported sick at home and absent without leave in September-October, 1864. Reported sick in hospital at Wilson in November-December, 1864. No further records. Survived the war.

SWINSON, J., Private

Resided in Duplin County. Place and date of enlistment not reported (probably enlisted subsequent to December 31, 1864). Paroled at Goldsboro on May 19, 1865.

SWINSON, J. L., Private

Resided in Duplin County. Place and date of enlistment not reported (probably enlisted subsequent to December 31, 1864). Paroled at Goldsboro on May 19, 1865.

TARKINTON, WILLIAM B., Private

Previously served as Private in Company G, 17th Regiment N.C. Troops (2nd Organization). Transferred to this company on or about October 1, 1862. Reported on hospital duty at Wilson from December 25, 1862, through June 30, 1863. Transferred to Company B, 3rd Battalion N.C. Light Artillery, in August, 1863.

TAYLOR, THOMAS M., Private

Resided in Edgecombe County and enlisted in Wake County at age 28, October 1, 1862, for the war. Reported present in November-December, 1862. Hospitalized at Wilmington on or about February 18, 1863, with dysentery. Detailed for duty as a hospital nurse at Wilmington on or about April 2, 1863. Rejoined the company on or about September 21, 1863. Reported present or accounted for in November, 1863-April, 1864, and September-December, 1864. No further records.

TAYLOR, WILLIAM A., Private

Previously served as Private in Capt. William B. Lanier's Independent Company, N.C. Troops. Transferred to this company in September, 1862. Reported present or accounted for in November, 1862-April, 1863. Reported sick in hospital at Wilmington in May-June, 1863. Returned to duty in July-August, 1863. Reported present in September, 1863-April, 1864. Wounded severely in the hand at or near Petersburg, Virginia, on or about June 16-19, 1864. Returned to duty on an unspecified date. Reported present in September-December, 1864. No further records.

TETTERTON, JAMES H., Private

Previously served as Private in Capt. William B. Lanier's Independent Company, N.C. Troops. Transferred to this company in September, 1862. Reported present or accounted for in November, 1862-February, 1864. Wounded in the right knee and left thigh and captured near the Nansemond River, Virginia, April 14, 1864. Hospitalized at Fort Monroe, Virginia, May 23, 1864. Transferred to the prison compound on June 29, 1864. Transferred to Point Lookout, Maryland, July 27, 1864. Died at Point Lookout on March 5, 1865, of "pneumonia."

THOMSON, NATHAN S., Private

Previously served as Private in Capt. William B. Lanier's Independent Company, N.C. Troops. Transferred to this company in September, 1862. Discharged in November-December, 1862, because he was overage and his term of enlistment had expired.

TICE, ALFRED THOMAS, Private

Previously served as Private in Capt. William B. Lanier's Independent Company, N.C. Troops. Transferred to this company in September, 1862. Furloughed for sixty days on December 17, 1862. Reported absent without leave on February 22, 1863. Returned to duty on March 20, 1863. Reported present or accounted for through April 30, 1864, and in September-December, 1864. No further records. Survived the war.

TICE, JASON, JR., Private

Previously served as Corporal in Capt. William B. Lanier's Independent Company, N.C. Troops. Transferred to this company in

September, 1862. Furloughed home sick on December 17, 1862. Returned to duty in January-February, 1863. Reduced to ranks on March 1, 1863. Reported present or accounted for in March, 1863-April, 1864. Reported absent on sick furlough in September-October, 1864. Captured at Williamston on December 10, 1864. Confined at Point Lookout, Maryland, December 27, 1864. Released a Point Lookout on June 21, 1865, after taking the Oath of Allegiance.

VAINWRIGHT, DANIEL, Private

Previously served as Private in Capt. William B. Lanier's Independent Company, N.C. Troops. Transferred to this company in September, 1862. Reported present in November, 1862-April, 1864. Killed at Cold Harbor, Virginia, June 1, 1864.

VICK, JESSE B., Private

Resided in Martin County and was by occupation a farmer prior to enlisting in Edgecombe County at age 34, October 1, 1862, for the war. Reported present in November-December, 1862. Hospitalized at Wilmington on or about February 18, 1863, with jaundice. Returned to duty on or about March 31, 1863. Reported present or accounted for through April 30, 1864. Killed at Fort Harrison, Virginia, September 30, 1864.

WARD, ANTHONY, Private

Previously served as Private in Capt. William B. Lanier's Independent Company, N.C. Troops. Transferred to this company in September, 1862. Discharged on December 7, 1862, by reason of disability.

WARD, JAMES HENRY, Private

Previously served as Private in Capt. William B. Lanier's Independent Company, N.C. Troops. Transferred to this company in September, 1862. Reported present or accounted for in November, 1862-June, 1863. Wounded in the left thigh at Morris Island, Charleston Harbor, South Carolina, August 26, 1863. Left leg amputated. Died in hospital at Charleston on November 12, 1863, of wounds.

WARD, ROBERT F., Private

Previously served as Private in Capt. William B. Lanier's Independent Company, N.C. Troops. Transferred to this company in September, 1862. Reported present or accounted for in November, 1862-April, 1864. Killed at Drewry's Bluff, Virginia, May 16, 1864.

WARD, SIMON D., Sergeant

Previously served as Sergeant in Capt. William B. Lanier's Independent Company, N.C. Troops. Transferred to this company in September, 1862. Reported present or accounted for in November, 1862-April, 1864. Wounded slightly in the right arm near Bermuda Hundred, Virginia, May 30, 1864. Wounded in the neck at Cold Harbor, Virginia, May 31-June 3, 1864. Hospitalized at Richmond, Virginia. Furloughed on August 27, 1864. Reported absent wounded through December 31, 1864. No further records. Survived the war.

WARD, WILLIAM, Private

Born on April 25, 1828. Resided in Martin County and was by occupation a farmer prior to enlisting in Edgecombe County at age 34, October 1, 1862, for the war. Furloughed home sick on December 17, 1862. Returned to duty in January-February, 1863. Reported present or accounted for through May 9, 1864. Wounded in the arm and/or head near Petersburg, Virginia, on or about June 16-19, 1864. Hospitalized at Petersburg. Transferred to hospital at Richmond, Virginia, June 29, 1864. Furloughed on August 22, 1864. Returned to duty in November-December, 1864. No further records. Survived the war.

WARD, WILLIAM H., Private

Resided in Martin County and was by occupation a farmer prior to enlisting in Edgecombe County at age 32, October 1, 1862, for the war. "Straggled in the retreat from Kinston" on December 14, 1862. Reported absent without leave on or about December 31, 1862. Returned to duty on March 7, 1863. Reported sick in hospital at Charleston, South Carolina, on April 28, 1863. Reported "at home insane" in May, 1863-April, 1864, and September-October, 1864. Reported absent without leave in November-December, 1864. No further records. Survived the war.

WARD, WILLIAM S., Private

Previously served as Musician in Capt. William B. Lanier's Independent Company, N.C. Troops. Transferred to this company in September, 1862. Was apparently mustered in with the rank of Musician. Reported present in November-December, 1862. Reduced to ranks prior to January 1, 1863. Reported on detail at Charleston, South Carolina, in January-February, 1863. Reported on detail at John's Island, Charleston Harbor, in March-April, 1863. Reported on detail clearing obstructions in the Cape Fear River, near Wilmington, in May-August, 1863. Rejoined the company in September-October, 1863. Reported present or accounted for in November, 1863-April, 1864. Wounded in the thigh at Petersburg, Virginia, June 17, 1864. Hospitalized at Petersburg where he died on July 12, 1864, of gangrene.

WHITFIELD, LOUIS A., Private

Resided in Martin County and was by occupation a day laborer prior to enlisting in Martin County at age 25, February 15, 1864, for the war. Reported present in March-April and September-December, 1864. Captured at Salisbury on April 12, 1865. Sent to Nashville, Tennessee. Transferred to Louisville, Kentucky, where he arrived on May 1, 1865. Transferred to Camp Chase, Ohio, where he arrived on May 4, 1865. Released at Camp Chase on June 13, 1865, after taking the Oath of Allegiance.

WHITFIELD, WILLIAM A., Private

Previously served as Private in Capt. William B. Lanier's Independent Company, N.C. Troops. Transferred to this company in September, 1862. Discharged on December 7, 1862, under the provisions of the Conscription Act.

WILLIAMS, H., Private

Resided in Duplin County. Place and date of enlistment not reported (probably enlisted subsequent to December 31, 1864). Paroled at Goldsboro on May 29, 1865.

WILLIAMS, LOUIS H., Private

Enlisted in Martin County on February 15, 1864, for the war. Reported present through April 30, 1864. Hospitalized at Richmond, Virginia, August 22, 1864. Furloughed on September 5, 1864. Reported absent without leave in November-December, 1864. No further records.

WINBERRY, JESSE, Private

Previously served as Private in Capt. William B. Lanier's Independent Company, N.C. Troops. Transferred to this company in September, 1862. Discharged on November 4 or December 7, 1862, because he was overage and had served out his term of enlistment.

WINBORN, HENRY, Private

Previously served as Private in Capt. William B. Lanier's Independent Company, N.C. Troops. Transferred to this company in September, 1862. Reported present or accounted for in November, 1862-April, 1864, and September-December, 1864. No further records. Survived the war.

WYNN, WILLIAM, Private

Previously served as Private in Capt. William B. Lanier's Independent Company, N.C. Troops. Transferred to this company in September, 1862. Discharged on November 4 or December 7, 1862, because he was overage and had served out his term of enlistment.

YARRELL, THOMAS, Private

Previously served as Private in Capt. William B. Lanier's Independent Company, N.C. Troops. Transferred to this company in September, 1862. Discharged on December 7, 1862, because he was underage and had served out his term of enlistment.

COMPANY I

This company, known as the "Alleghany Rangers" and the "Alleghany Home Defenders," was raised in Alleghany County on May 3, 1862, by Aras Bishop Cox. It was then assigned to Col. Zebulon B. Vance of the 26th Regiment N.C. Troops, who had been authorized by the secretary of war to raise a legion. The company was accepted by Vance on May 9, 1862, and ordered to a camp of instruction at Kittrell's Springs (in present-day Vance County). However, Vance's Legion failed to complete its organization, and on July 17, 1862, the company was mustered in at Camp Vance (Vance County) as Capt. A. B. Cox's Independent Company, N.C. Partisan Rangers. On September 29, 1862, the company was assigned to the newly organized 59th Regiment N.C. Troops and designated Company G. That regiment was redesignated the 61st Regiment N.C. Troops on an unknown date between October 30 and November 22, 1862. This company was redesignated Company I. After joining the regiment the company functioned as a part of the regiment, and its history for the remainder of the war is reported as a part of the regimental history.

The following roster was compiled primarily from information in the microfilm edition of the Compiled Service Records of Soldiers Who Served in Organizations from the State of North Carolina (Record Group 109, MC 270), National Archives and Records Administration, Washington, D.C. Record Group 109 includes enlistment papers, pay vouchers, requisitions, letters of resignation, discharge certificates, and abstracts of medical and prisoner of war returns. Materials relating specifically to Company I of the 61st Regiment include a company muster-in roll dated July 17, 1862, and company muster rolls for November, 1862-April, 1864, and September-December, 1864.

Also utilized in this roster were *The War of the Rebellion: A Compilation of the Official Records of the Union and Confederate Armies*, the North Carolina adjutant general's *Roll of Honor*, state militia records, newspaper casualty lists and obituaries, wartime claims for bounty pay and allowances, postwar registers of claims for artificial limbs, Confederate pension applications filed with the states of North

Carolina, Tennessee, and Florida, Confederate Soldiers' Home records, and the 1860 and 1870 federal censuses of North Carolina. A search was made also for relevant letters, diaries, reminiscences, and other manuscripts in the Southern Historical Collection (University of North Carolina-Chapel Hill), the Duke University Library Special Collections Department, and the North Carolina Division of Archives and History.

Among the secondary sources consulted were records of the North Carolina Division of the United Daughters of the Confederacy, postwar rosters, regimental and county histories, marriage bond, will, and cemetery indexes, published and unpublished genealogies, biographical dictionaries, the North Carolina *County Heritage Book* series, the *Confederate Veteran*, Walter Clark's *Histories of the Several Regiments and Battalions from North Carolina in the Great War, 1861-'65*, and the North Carolina volume of the extended edition of *Confederate Military History*.

Note: The following roster contains service records for six men who enlisted in Captain Cox's Independent Company, N.C. Partisan Rangers, but whose service terminated prior to September 29, 1862, the date the company was mustered into the 59th Regiment N.C. Troops (later redesignated the 61st Regiment N.C. Troops). Those men, it will be evident, never served in the 61st Regiment. Their service records are included here because too little information survives to compile a roster for Cox's Independent Company. All service records falling into the early-termination category conclude with a "special note" alerting readers to that fact and referring them to the information contained in this paragraph.

OFFICERS

CAPTAINS

COX, ARAS BISHOP
Previously served as Chaplain of the 22nd Regiment N.C. Troops. Appointed Captain of this company on May 3, 1862. Reported absent sick at Raleigh in November-December, 1862. Resigned on December 27, 1862, by reason of "pulmonary disease and general bad health." Resignation accepted on January 2, 1863.

CHOATE, WILLIAM THOMAS
Born in Ashe (present-day Alleghany) County on January 28, 1832. Appointed 2nd Lieutenant of this company on May 3, 1862. Reported present or accounted for in November, 1862-February, 1863. Promoted to 1st Lieutenant on January 3, 1863. Reported present and in command of the company in March-April, 1863. Promoted to Captain on May 28, 1863. Reported present but sick in May-June, 1863. Furloughed for thirty days on August 1, 1863. Returned to duty in September-October, 1863. Reported present through April 30, 1864. Mortally wounded at Cold Harbor, Virginia, June 2, 1864, by a minie ball that penetrated his chest "about three inches below the right nipple . . . [and] passed through and came out his backbone." Died on or about June 4, 1864.

PARKS, OLIVER CROMWELL
Enlisted at Zuni, Virginia, February 1, 1864, for the war. Mustered in as Private. Elected 3rd Lieutenant on March 19, 1864. Reported present through April 30, 1864. Promoted to Captain on June 9, 1864. Wounded in the cervical vertebra near Petersburg, Virginia, June 17, 1864. Died in hospital at Petersburg on June 19, 1864, of wounds. [Was 26 years of age at the time of his death. Contrary to 9:159 of this series, this officer did not serve as Captain of Company D, 33rd Regiment N.C. Troops.]

GRIMSLEY, GEORGE
Resided in Alleghany County and was by occupation a laborer prior to enlisting in Alleghany County at age 24, May 3, 1862, for the war. Mustered in as Corporal. Reported present in November, 1862-August, 1863. Promoted to 1st Sergeant on August 4, 1863. Sent to hospital at Charleston, South Carolina, October 18, 1863. Returned to duty in November-December, 1863. Reported present through April 30, 1864. Wounded in the face at Drewry's Bluff, Virginia, on or about May 14, 1864. Hospitalized at Richmond, Virginia. Elected 2nd Lieutenant on June 9, 1864. Furloughed for sixty days on June 10, 1864. Returned to duty prior to September 30, 1864, when he was wounded in the face at Fort Harrison, Virginia. Hospitalized at Richmond. Returned to duty prior to October 20, 1864. Reported present in November-December, 1864. Promoted to Captain on December 20, 1864. No further records. [Commanded the company in September-October, 1864, and possibly during part of March-April, 1864.]

LIEUTENANTS

COX, JOSHUA, 3rd Lieutenant
Born in Virginia and resided in Alleghany County where he was by occupation a farmer prior to enlisting in Alleghany County at age 30, May 3, 1862, for the war. Mustered in as Private. Reported present in November, 1862-April, 1863. Promoted to Corporal on April 3, 1863. Reported on detached duty as a baggage guard at Charleston, South Carolina, June 13-August 31, 1863. Rejoined the company in September-October, 1863. Reported present or accounted for through April 30, 1864. Promoted to 1st Sergeant prior to August 5, 1864. Appointed 3rd Lieutenant on September 7, 1864. Wounded in the knee at Fort Harrison, Virginia, September 30, 1864. Hospitalized at Richmond, Virginia, where he died on October 19, 1864, of wounds.

FENDER, JOHN, 2nd Lieutenant
Resided in Alleghany County and was by occupation a laborer prior to enlisting in Alleghany County at age 22, May 3, 1862, for the war. Mustered in as Sergeant. Reported present in November, 1862-April, 1864, and September-December, 1864. Appointed 2nd Lieutenant on April 8, 1865. Survived the war. [North Carolina pension records indicate that he was wounded in the left hand at Wilmington in 1864.]

GRIMSLEY, LOWRY, 2nd Lieutenant
Previously served as 1st Lieutenant of Company K, 37th Regiment N.C. Troops. Enlisted in this company in Alleghany County on May 3, 1862, for the war. Mustered in as Sergeant. Reported present in November, 1862-June, 1863. Appointed 2nd Lieutenant on June 20, 1863. Hospitalized at Wilmington on or about July 15, 1863, with debility from continued fever. Furloughed for thirty days on July 17, 1863. Returned to duty in September-October, 1863. Reported present in November-December, 1863. Resigned on January 29, 1864, because he was "so infirm as to be no longer adequate to the duties required of an officer." Resignation accepted on February 23, 1864. Took the Oath of Allegiance in Ashe County on June 7, 1865. [Contrary to 9:592 of this series, the correct spelling of his first name was probably Lowry rather than Lowrey.]

HIGGINS, ISAAC C., 1st Lieutenant
Resided in Alleghany County and was by occupation a farmer prior to enlisting in Alleghany County at age 31. Appointed 1st Lieutenant on May 3, 1862. Reported sick in hospital at Goldsboro in

November-December, 1862. Died in hospital at Goldsboro on or about December 28, 1862, of "smallpox." [Previously served as Captain in the 96th Regiment N.C. Militia.]

JOINES, JOHN W., 1st Lieutenant

Resided in Alleghany County where he enlisted at age 20. Appointed 3rd Lieutenant on May 3, 1862. Reported present in November, 1862-June, 1863. Promoted to 1st Lieutenant on May 28, 1863. Reported present in July-August, 1863. Ankle injured by "the falling of a horse [house?]" at Sullivan's Island, Charleston Harbor, South Carolina, in September, 1863. Hospitalized at Charleston. Furloughed for thirty days on October 3, 1863. Returned to duty in November-December, 1863. Resigned on January 29, 1864, because of his "inability to perform infantry service on account of lameness from a wound received on Sullivan's Island." Resignation accepted on March 18, 1864. [Previously served as Lieutenant Colonel of the 96th Regiment N.C. Militia.]

JOINES, WILLIAM H., 1st Lieutenant

Resided in Alleghany County where he enlisted at age 34, May 3, 1862, for the war. Mustered in as 1st Sergeant. Reported present in November-December, 1862. Hospitalized at Wilmington on February 6, 1863, with catarrh. Returned to duty on March 9, 1863. Reported present or accounted for through June 30, 1863. Elected 3rd Lieutenant on June 19, 1863. Reported present in July, 1863-February, 1864. Promoted to 2nd Lieutenant on February 22, 1864. Reported present in March-April, 1864. Promoted to 1st Lieutenant on June 9, 1864. Hospitalized at Richmond, Virginia, June 14, 1864, with chronic diarrhoea. Furloughed on July 2, 1864. Hospitalized at Richmond on September 20, 1864, with dysentery. Furloughed on or about October 4, 1864. Reported absent on furlough through October 31, 1864. Resigned on November 16, 1864, by reason of "disease of heart." Resignation accepted on December 22, 1864.

SPARKS, CALTON, 3rd Lieutenant

Resided in Alleghany County and was by occupation a laborer prior to enlisting in Alleghany County at age 19, May 3, 1862, for the war. Mustered in as Sergeant. Reported present in November-December, 1862. Reduced to ranks prior to January 1, 1863. Reported present in January-August, 1863. Promoted to Corporal on August 4, 1863. Promoted to Sergeant on October 22, 1863. Reported present in September, 1863-April, 1864. Elected 3rd Lieutenant on June 9, 1864. "Killed dead on the field" at the Crater, near Petersburg, Virginia, July 30, 1864.

NONCOMMISSIONED OFFICERS AND PRIVATES

ANDERS, BURRAS, Private

Resided in Alleghany County or in Wytheville, Virginia, and enlisted in Alleghany County on May 3, 1862, for the war. Wounded in the side at Kinston on December 14, 1862. Returned to duty in January-February, 1863. Reported present in March-April, 1863. Hospitalized at Wilmington on June 21, 1863. Reported in hospital at Mount Pleasant, South Carolina, August 23, 1863. Furloughed from hospital for thirty days on October 12, 1863. Returned to duty in November-December, 1863. Reported present through April 30, 1864. Wounded slightly in the breast at Cold Harbor, Virginia, May 31-June 3, 1864. Captured near Petersburg, Virginia, June 16, 1864. Confined at Point Lookout, Maryland, June 19, 1864. Transferred to Elmira, New York, July 25, 1864.

Released at Elmira on June 21, 1865, after taking the Oath of Allegiance. [Was about 18 years of age at time of enlistment.]

ANDERS, JACKSON, Private

Resided in Alleghany County and was by occupation a farmer prior to enlisting in Alleghany County at age 26, May 3, 1862, for the war. Reported on detail as a wagoner from October 24, 1862, through February 28, 1863. Rejoined the company in March-April, 1863. Reported present or accounted for through April 30, 1864. Captured at Fort Harrison, Virginia, September 30, 1864. Confined at Point Lookout, Maryland, October 5, 1864. Paroled at Point Lookout on March 17, 1865. Received at Boulware's Wharf, James River, Virginia, March 19, 1865, for exchange. No further records.

ANDERS, JAMES M., Private

Resided in Alleghany County and was by occupation a farmer prior to enlisting in Alleghany County at age 24, May 3, 1862, for the war. Reported present or accounted for in November, 1862-June, 1863. Wounded in the "privates" at Morris Island, Charleston Harbor, South Carolina, August 25, 1863. Died in hospital at Charleston on or about September 1, 1863, of wounds.

ANDERS, ROBERT, Private

Resided in Alleghany County and was by occupation a farmer prior to enlisting in Alleghany County at age 29, May 3, 1862, for the war. Reported present in November, 1862-February, 1863. Reported absent on sick furlough from April 9 through August 31, 1863. Reported absent without leave in July-October, 1863. Reported absent on detached service at Petersburg, Virginia, in November-December, 1863. Rejoined the company in January-February, 1864. Reported present in March-April, 1864. Captured at Fort Harrison, Virginia, September 30, 1864. Confined at Point Lookout, Maryland, October 5, 1864. Released at Point Lookout on May 12, 1865, after taking the Oath of Allegiance.

ATWOOD, JESSE J., Private

Resided in Alleghany County and enlisted at Zuni, Virginia, January 14, 1864, for the war. Reported on detail as a scout in March-April, 1864. Reported absent without leave on July 6, 1864. Listed as a deserter in November-December, 1864. [Was about 21 years of age at time of enlistment. North Carolina pension records indicate that he was wounded in the right hand at Loudon, Tennessee, on an unspecified date.]

AUSTIN, CALVIN, Private

Enlisted in Alleghany County on May 3, 1862, for the war. Reported present in November-December, 1862. Hospitalized at Wilmington on January 31, 1863, with epilepsy. Returned to duty on February 15, 1863. Discharged on April 10, 1863, by reason of "physical disability." [Was about 22 years of age at time of enlistment.]

BALLARD, ALEXANDER M., Private

Resided in Alleghany County where he enlisted at age 19, May 3, 1862, for the war. Died in hospital at Wilson on November 11, 1862. Cause of death not reported.

BALLARD, ROBERT FRANKLIN, Sergeant

Resided in Alleghany County and was by occupation a farmer prior to enlisting in Alleghany County at age 22, May 3, 1862, for the war. Mustered in as Private. Reported present or accounted for in November, 1862-April, 1864. Promoted to Sergeant on June 10,

1864. Captured at Fort Harrison, Virginia, September 30, 1864. Confined at Point Lookout, Maryland, October 5, 1864. Released at Point Lookout on May 12, 1865, after taking the Oath of Allegiance.

BEAMAN, WILBORN, _____

North Carolina pension records indicate that he served in this company.

BILLINGS, ELI H., Private

Resided in Alleghany County and was by occupation a farmer prior to enlisting in Alleghany County at age 27, May 3, 1862, for the war. Reported absent without leave from December 7, 1862, through February 28, 1863. Reported present but sick in March-April, 1863. Hospitalized at Wilmington on an unspecified date with debility. Returned to duty on June 25, 1863. Furloughed on August 15, 1863. Reported absent without leave from March 25 through December 31, 1864. No further records. Survived the war.

BILLINGS, SAMUEL, Private

Resided in Alleghany County where he enlisted at age 21, May 3, 1862, for the war. Reported present in November, 1862-June, 1863. Furloughed for twenty days on July 2, 1863. Reported absent without leave in November, 1863-February, 1864. Returned to duty in March-April, 1864. Captured near Petersburg, Virginia, June 16, 1864. Confined at Point Lookout, Maryland, June 19, 1864. Transferred to Elmira, New York, July 25, 1864. Released at Elmira on June 19, 1865, after taking the Oath of Allegiance.

BLEVENS, THOMAS J., Private

Resided in Alleghany County and was by occupation a laborer prior to enlisting near Richmond, Virginia, at age 18, December 22, 1864, for the war. Reported present on December 31, 1864. No further records.

BLEVINS, ISOM, Private

Born in Ashe County in 1841. Resided in Alleghany County and was by occupation a farmer or laborer prior to enlisting in Alleghany County on May 3, 1862, for the war. Reported present or accounted for in November, 1862-August, 1863. Deserted on September 1, 1863. Rejoined the company on November 23, 1863. Hospitalized at Petersburg, Virginia, prior to December 31, 1863. Returned to duty in January-February, 1864. Reported present in March-April, 1864. Wounded in the abdomen and/or right side at Drewry's Bluff, Virginia, May 14, 1864. Reported absent without leave on August 15, 1864. Returned to duty on December 19, 1864. Captured near Kinston on March 10-11, 1865. Sent to New Bern. Confined at Point Lookout, Maryland, March 16, 1865. Released at Point Lookout on May 15, 1865, after taking the Oath of Allegiance. [Filed a Tennessee pension application after the war.]

BLEVINS, JAMES, Sergeant

Resided in Alleghany County and was by occupation a laborer prior to enlisting in Alleghany County at age 22, May 3, 1862, for the war. Mustered in as Private. Reported present in November, 1862-December, 1863. Hospitalized at Petersburg, Virginia, January 1, 1864, with intermittent fever. Returned to duty on February 2, 1864. Hospitalized at Petersburg on February 17, 1864, with acute diarrhoea. Transferred to another hospital on February 22, 1864. Returned to duty prior to March 1, 1864. Reported present in March-April, 1864. Promoted to Sergeant in May-September, 1864. Killed at Fort Harrison, Virginia, September 30, 1864.

BLEVINS, JEFFERSON, Private

Resided in Alleghany County and enlisted at age 17, September 17, 1864, for the war. Wounded in the right arm at Fort Harrison, Virginia, September 30, 1864. Reported absent wounded through October 31, 1864. Reported absent without leave from November 14 through December 31, 1864. No further records. Survived the war. [Company records indicate that he was transferred from the 11th Regiment N.C. Troops (1st Regiment N.C. Volunteers) on September 17, 1864; however, records of the 11th Regiment do not indicate that he served therein.]

BLEVINS, SHUBILL, Private

Resided in Alleghany County and enlisted near Richmond, Virginia, at age 16, December 22, 1864, for the war. Reported present on December 31, 1864. No further records. Survived the war.

BOBBITT, WILLIAM, Private

Resided in Alleghany County and enlisted at Sullivan's Island, Charleston Harbor, South Carolina, at age 18, September 1, 1863, for the war. Reported present or accounted for through April 30, 1864. Wounded in the head at Fort Harrison, Virginia, September 30, 1864. Returned to duty prior to November 1, 1864. Reported present in November-December, 1864. No further records.

BRACKENS, ADAM, Private

Resided in Alleghany County and was by occupation a laborer prior to enlisting in Alleghany County at age 19, May 3, 1862, for the war. Captured and paroled at Kinston on December 14, 1862. Reported absent without leave in Alleghany County in January-February, 1863. Returned to duty in March-April, 1863. Reported present in May, 1863-April, 1864. Deserted on an unspecified date. Returned to duty in November-December, 1864. Wounded in the abdomen, right leg, and right thigh at Kinston on or about March 10, 1865. Hospitalized at Raleigh where he died on March 12, 1865, of wounds.

CARPENTER, CHRISTOPHER COLUMBUS, Private

Resided in Wilkes County and enlisted in Alleghany County at age 24, May 3, 1862, for the war. "Straggled at Battle [of] Kinston" on December 13, 1862. Reported absent without leave on January 20, 1863. Failed to return to duty and was dropped from the company rolls on or about April 30, 1864.

CARTER, JOHN WESLEY, Private

Resided in Alleghany County and was by occupation a laborer prior to enlisting in Alleghany County at age 19, May 3, 1862, for the war. Hospitalized at Wilmington on December 31, 1862, with chronic hepatitis. Returned to duty on January 3, 1863. Hospitalized at Wilmington on January 29, 1863. Died in hospital at Wilmington on February 4, 1864, of "typhoid fever" or "cont[inued] fever."

CAUDILL, DANIEL M., Private

Resided in Alleghany County and was by occupation a laborer prior to enlisting in Alleghany County at age 16, May 3, 1862, for the war. Reported present in November, 1862-February, 1863. Died at Charleston, South Carolina, on or about April 10, 1863, of "typhoid fever."

CAUDILL, DAVID DOCTOR C., Private

Resided in Alleghany County where he enlisted at age 19, May 3, 1862, for the war. Reported present in November, 1862-February,

1863. Reported sick in hospital at Charleston, South Carolina, April 10, 1863. Returned to duty in May-June, 1863. Reported present or accounted for through April 30, 1864. Wounded in the head and thigh at the Crater, near Petersburg, Virginia, July 30, 1864. Returned to duty prior to November 1, 1864. Reported present in November-December, 1864. No further records. Survived the war.

CAUDILL, JEFFERSON, Private

Resided in Alleghany County where he enlisted on May 3, 1862, for the war. Reported present or accounted for in November, 1862-June, 1863. Deserted on August 22, 1863. Returned from desertion on October 26, 1863, and was placed under arrest. Reported under arrest at Petersburg, Virginia, in November-December, 1863. Returned to duty in January-February, 1864. Reported present in March-April, 1864. Captured at Fort Harrison, Virginia, September 30, 1864. Confined at Point Lookout, Maryland, October 5, 1864. Died at Point Lookout on March 8, 1865, of "pneumonia."

CAUDILL, JESSE M. D., Private

Resided in Alleghany County where he enlisted on May 3, 1862, for the war. Furloughed home sick on November 25, 1862. Reported absent without leave in July, 1863-February, 1864. Returned to duty in March-April, 1864. Hospitalized at Farmville, Virginia, June 20, 1864, with chronic nephritis. Furloughed for thirty days on or about August 12, 1864. Reported absent without leave from September 12 through December 31, 1864. No further records.

CAUDILL, MARK, Private

Resided in Alleghany County and was by occupation a laborer prior to enlisting in Alleghany County at age 22, May 3, 1862, for the war. Detailed for duty at the smelting house at Petersburg, Virginia, on August 10, 1862. Reported absent on detail at Petersburg in November, 1862-April, 1864, and September-October, 1864. Reported absent on detail at the Greensboro lead works in November-December, 1864. Paroled at Greensboro on May 4-5, 1865.

CHEEK, ABNER, Private

Born in Ashe (present-day Alleghany) County where he resided prior to enlisting in Alleghany County at age 21, May 3, 1862, for the war. Reported present in November-December, 1862. Hospitalized at Wilmington on February 17, 1863, with catarrhus. Returned to duty on February 25, 1863. Reported present in March-April, 1863. Reported absent on detail to arrest deserters and conscripts May 12-June 30, 1863. Hospitalized at Wilmington on July 15, 1863, with intermittent fever. Returned to duty on July 27, 1863. Reported present through April 30, 1864. Wounded in the chest (left lung) near Petersburg, Virginia, on or about June 16, 1864. Hospitalized at Petersburg where he died on July 31, 1864, of wounds.

CHEEK, MERIDETH, Private

Resided in Alleghany County where he enlisted at age 20, May 3, 1862, for the war. Reported present or accounted for in November, 1862-April, 1863. Hospitalized at Wilmington on June 25, 1863, with debility. Returned to duty on July 8, 1863. Hospitalized at Wilmington on July 14, 1863, with intermittent fever. Furloughed for thirty days on or about August 11, 1863. Reported absent without leave in September-December, 1863. Furloughed for thirty days on January 29, 1864. Returned to duty in March-April, 1864. Wounded in the shoulder at Cold Harbor, Virginia, May 31-June 3, 1864. Wounded in the thigh at the Crater, near

Petersburg, Virginia, July 30, 1864. Reported absent without leave from August 1 through December 31, 1864. No further records. Survived the war.

CHEEK, RICHARD, Private

Born on September 8, 1834. Resided in Alleghany County and was by occupation a farmer prior to enlisting in Alleghany County at age 27, May 3, 1862, for the war. Reported present in November, 1862-April, 1863. Reported absent on detail to arrest deserters and conscripts May 12-June 30, 1863. Deserted on August 26, 1863. Returned from desertion on November 23, 1863, and was assigned to detached service at Petersburg, Virginia. Reported on detached service at Petersburg through April 30, 1864. Rejoined the company prior to May 14, 1864, when he was wounded in the left hand at Drewry's Bluff, Virginia. Third finger amputated. Hospitalized at Richmond, Virginia. Reported absent without leave from July 10 through December 31, 1864. No further records. Survived the war.

CHEEK, WILLIAM, JR., Private

Resided in Alleghany County where he enlisted at age 18, November 26, 1863, for the war. Reported present through April 30, 1864. Wounded in the left hip at Drewry's Bluff, Virginia, May 14, 1864. Hospitalized at Richmond, Virginia. Furloughed for sixty days on June 1, 1864. Returned to duty on an unspecified date. Reported present in September-December, 1864. No further records. Survived the war.

CHEEK, WILLIAM BRYANT, Private

Born on April 14, 1844. Resided in Alleghany County and was by occupation a laborer prior to enlisting in Alleghany County at age 18, May 3, 1862, for the war. Reported present in November, 1862-February, 1863. Furloughed for thirty days on April 9, 1863. Reported absent without leave from May 9 through December 31, 1863. Furloughed for thirty days on January 29, 1864. Returned to duty prior to May 1, 1864. Captured at Globe Tavern, Virginia, August 19, 1864. Confined at Point Lookout, Maryland, August 24, 1864. Paroled at Point Lookout on March 14, 1865. Received at Boulware's Wharf, James River, Virginia, March 16, 1865, for exchange. No further records. Survived the war.

COLLINS, JAMES A., Private

Resided in Alleghany County and was by occupation a tanner prior to enlisting in Alleghany County at age 28, May 3, 1862, for the war. Transferred to Company A, 26th Regiment N.C. Troops, November 10, 1862.

COX, WILLIAM A., Private

See roster for Company B of this regiment.

COX, WILLIAM G., 1st Sergeant

Resided in Alleghany County where he enlisted at age 28, May 3, 1862, for the war. Mustered in as 1st Sergeant. Discharged in September, 1862. Reason discharged not reported. [See special note at the end of the history of Company I, 61st Regiment N.C. Troops (page 738).]

CROUSE, BENJAMIN, Private

Born in Ashe (present-day Alleghany) County where he resided as a farmer prior to enlisting in Alleghany County at age 32, May 3, 1862, for the war. Reported present in November, 1862-April, 1863. Reported absent on detail to arrest deserters and conscripts May 12-June 30, 1863. Wounded in the face and head at Morris

Island, Charleston Harbor, South Carolina, on or about August 26, 1863. Returned to duty prior to September 1, 1863. Reported present through April 30, 1864. Shot in the head and instantly killed at Fort Harrison, Virginia, September 30, 1864.

CROUSE, HAYWOOD W., Private

Resided in Alleghany County and was by occupation a farmer prior to enlisting in Alleghany County at age 24, May 3, 1862, for the war. Captured at Kinston on December 14, 1862. Paroled at Kinston on December 15, 1862. Reported absent without leave in January-February, 1863. Returned to duty in March-April, 1863. Reported present or accounted for in May-June, 1863. Reported sick in hospital at Mount Pleasant, South Carolina, in July-August, 1863. Returned to duty in September-October, 1863. Reported present through April 30, 1864. Reported missing at Fort Harrison, Virginia, September 30, 1864. Was presumably killed at Fort Harrison.

CROUSE, HENDERSON, Private

Resided in Alleghany County and was by occupation a farmer prior to enlisting in Alleghany County at age 27, May 3, 1862, for the war. Mustered in as Corporal. Reported absent sick in November-December, 1862. Reported absent without leave in January-February, 1863. Returned to duty in March-April, 1863. Reduced to ranks on April 3, 1863. Reported present in May-June, 1863. Reported wounded and in hospital at Charleston, South Carolina, on August 8, 1863. Place and date wounded not reported. Furloughed for thirty days prior to September 1, 1863. Reported absent without leave on October 31, 1863. Returned to duty in November-December, 1863. Reported present in March-April and September-December, 1864. No further records. Survived the war.

CROUSE, HENRY McDANIEL, Private

Born in Ashe (present-day Alleghany) County on August 2, 1844. Resided in Alleghany County and was by occupation a laborer prior to enlisting in Alleghany County at age 17, May 3, 1862, for the war. Reported on detail as a regimental ambulance driver from December 10, 1862, through February 28, 1863. Hospitalized at Charleston, South Carolina, April 17, 1863. Furloughed for thirty days on June 24, 1863. Returned to duty in July-August, 1863. Deserted on September 1, 1863. Returned to duty on October 29, 1863. Reported under arrest through December 31, 1863. Returned to duty in January-February, 1864. Reported present in March-April, 1864. Hospitalized at Richmond, Virginia, July 25, 1864, with a gunshot wound of the left cheek and jaw. Place and date wounded not reported. Furloughed for thirty days on August 4, 1864. Reported absent without leave from October 1 through December 31, 1864. No further records. Survived the war.

CROUSE, MARTIN, Private

Resided in Alleghany County and was by occupation a farmer prior to enlisting in Alleghany County at age 35, May 3, 1862, for the war. Reported sick in hospital at Wilson on December 17, 1862. Returned to duty in January-February, 1863. Reported present but sick in March-April, 1863. Discharged on June 6, 1863. Reason discharged not reported.

CROUSE, REEVES, Private

Born in Ashe (present-day Alleghany) County where he resided as a farmer prior to enlisting in Alleghany County at age 32, May 3, 1862, for the war. Mustered in as Private. Reported sick in hospital on December 17, 1862. Promoted to Sergeant prior to January 1, 1863. Returned to duty prior to March 1, 1863. Reported present but sick in March-June, 1863. Reported sick in hospital at Mount

Pleasant, South Carolina, in July-August, 1863. Reduced to ranks on October 22, 1863. Furloughed from hospital for thirty days on October 23, 1863. Reported absent on furlough through April 30, 1864. Died at Richmond, Virginia, July 11, 1864, of "typhoid fever."

DILLARD, THOMAS, Private

Resided in Alleghany County and was by occupation a laborer prior to enlisting in Alleghany County at age 18, March 17, 1863, for the war. Reported sick in hospital at Charleston, South Carolina, April 15, 1863. Detailed to guard "County Bridge" on June 26, 1863. Rejoined the company prior to September 1, 1863. Reported present through April 30, 1864. Reported absent without leave on July 6, 1864. Listed as a deserter in November-December, 1864.

DILLARD, WILLIAM, Private

Resided in Alleghany County and was by occupation a laborer prior to enlisting in Alleghany County at age 23, May 3, 1862, for the war. Wounded by a shell at Kinston on December 14, 1862. Returned to duty prior to January 1, 1863. Died at Wilmington on February 20 or February 26, 1863, of "typhoid fever."

DIXON, JAMES WILEY, Private

Resided in Alleghany County where he enlisted on May 3, 1862, for the war. Reported present in November, 1862-June, 1863. Hospitalized at Wilmington on July 7, 1863, with bilious fever. Returned to duty on August 11, 1863. Reported present through April 30, 1864. No further records.

DUNCAN, HENRY ALLEN, Private

Resided in Alleghany County where he enlisted at age 18, October 20, 1862, for the war. Hospitalized at Raleigh on December 28, 1862. Reported in hospital at Wilmington on February 26, 1863, with parotitis. Returned to duty on March 9, 1863. Reported present or accounted for through June 30, 1863. Reported sick in hospital at Charleston, South Carolina, in July-August, 1863. Reported absent without leave from September 14 through October 26, 1863. Reported under arrest on October 31, 1863. Returned to duty in November-December, 1863. Reported present through April 30, 1864. Deserted to the enemy on or about October 7, 1864. Confined at Bermuda Hundred, Virginia. Released on or about October 10, 1864, after taking the Oath of Allegiance.

EDWARDS, ALLEN, Private

Resided in Alleghany County and was by occupation a farmer prior to enlisting in Alleghany County at age 28, May 3, 1862, for the war. Wounded at Kinston on December 14, 1862. Returned to duty prior to January 1, 1863. Reported present or accounted for through June 30, 1863. Deserted on August 17, 1863. Returned from desertion on October 29, 1863. Reported under arrest at Petersburg, Virginia, in November-December, 1863. Returned to duty in January-February, 1864. Reported present in March-April and September-December, 1864. No further records. Survived the war.

EDWARDS, BERRY FRANKLIN, Private

Born on February 25, 1831. Resided in Alleghany County and was by occupation a farmer prior to enlisting in Alleghany County at age 31, May 3, 1862, for the war. Reported present in November-December, 1862. Reported in hospital at Wilmington on February 6, 1863, with rheumatism. Returned to duty on February 12, 1863. Reported present but sick in March-April, 1863. Sent to hospital sick on May 15, 1863. Reported absent sick through June 30, 1863.

Deserted on August 17, 1863. Returned from desertion on October 5, 1863. Reported under arrest through December 31, 1863. Returned to duty in January-February, 1864. Reported present in March-April, 1864. Captured at Fort Harrison, Virginia, September 30, 1864. Confined at Point Lookout, Maryland, October 5, 1864. Paroled at Point Lookout on October 30, 1864. Received at Venus Point, Savannah River, Georgia, November 15, 1864, for exchange. Reported absent without leave on November 25, 1864. No further records. Survived the war.

EDWARDS, CREED, Private

Born on December 31, 1837. Enlisted in Alleghany County at age 24, May 3, 1862, for the war. Reported present in November, 1862-June, 1863. Deserted on August 22, 1863. Returned from desertion on October 29, 1863. Reported under arrest through April 30, 1864. Hospitalized on May 18, 1864, with a gunshot wound. Place and date wounded not reported (probably wounded at Drewry's Bluff, Virginia). Returned to duty on May 27, 1864. Reported present in September-December, 1864. No further records. Survived the war.

EDWARDS, DAVID, Private

Resided in Alleghany County where he enlisted at age 18, May 3, 1862, for the war. Reported present or accounted for in November, 1862-April, 1863. Hospitalized at Wilmington on June 18, 1863. Furloughed on July 24, 1863. Reported absent without leave on or about October 31, 1863. Returned to duty in November-December, 1863. Reported present through April 30, 1864. Reported sick in hospital at Richmond, Virginia, in September-October, 1864. Returned to duty in November-December, 1864. No further records. Survived the war.

EDWARDS, GEORGE W., Private

Resided in Alleghany County where he enlisted at age 30, May 3, 1862, for the war. Reported present or accounted for in November, 1862-June, 1863. Died in hospital at Charleston, South Carolina, July 30, 1863, of "diphtheria."

EDWARDS, GRANVILLE BILLING, Private

Resided in Alleghany County and was by occupation a laborer prior to enlisting in Alleghany County at age 27, October 20, 1862, for the war. Reported present in November, 1862-June, 1863. Deserted on August 17, 1863. Returned to duty on October 29, 1863. Reported under arrest through April 30, 1864. Returned to duty prior to June 2, 1864, when he was wounded in the back of the head at Cold Harbor, Virginia. Hospitalized at Richmond, Virginia. Reported absent without leave on July 20, 1864. Returned to duty on or about December 19, 1864. Wounded in the left arm (fracture) at Kinston on March 10, 1865. Captured on or about the same date. Hospitalized at New Bern where he died on April 4, 1865, of wounds.

EDWARDS, VINCENT, Private

Resided in Alleghany County where he enlisted at age 26, May 3, 1862, for the war. Reported present in November-December, 1862. Reported sick in hospital at Wilmington in January-February, 1863. Reported present but sick in March-June, 1863. Deserted on August 26, 1863.

ELLER, I. H., Private

Place and date of enlistment not reported (probably enlisted subsequent to December 31, 1864). Paroled at Greensboro on an unspecified date (probably in May, 1865).

ERVIN, ELIJAH, Private

Resided in Alleghany County where he enlisted at age 18, October 20, 1862, for the war. Reported present in November-December, 1862. Died in hospital at Wilmington on or about February 17, 1863, of "phthisis pul[monalis]."

ESTEP, HAYWOOD D., Corporal

Born on August 12, 1843. Resided in Alleghany County where he enlisted at age 18, May 3, 1862, for the war. Mustered in as Private. Reported present or accounted for in November, 1862-October, 1863. Promoted to Corporal on October 22, 1863. Reported present in November, 1863-April, 1864. Wounded in the hand and/or foot at Drewry's Bluff, Virginia, on or about May 16, 1864. Hospitalized at Richmond, Virginia. Returned to duty on an unspecified date. Reported present in September-December, 1864. No further records. Survived the war.

ESTEP, WILLIAM, Private

Place and date of enlistment not reported (probably enlisted subsequent to December 31, 1864). Hospitalized at High Point on February 24, 1865, with debilitas. Hospitalized at Raleigh on March 1, 1865, with catarrhus. Returned to duty on March 6, 1865. Captured at Kinston on March 10, 1865. Confined at Point Lookout, Maryland, March 16, 1865. Died at Point Lookout on May 15, 1865, of "ac[ute] dysentery." [Was about 17 years of age at time of enlistment.]

FAIRCHILD, JESSE F., Private

North Carolina pension records indicate that he served in this company.

FENDER, DAVID, Private

Resided in Alleghany County where he enlisted at age 24, May 3, 1862, for the war. Reported absent without leave from July 10, 1862, through February 28, 1863. Returned to duty in March-April, 1863. Detailed to construct breastworks on June 25, 1863. Deserted on August 26, 1863. Returned from desertion on November 4, 1863, and was placed under arrest. Returned to duty in January-February, 1864. Reported present through April 30, 1864. Reported absent without leave from June 20 through December 31, 1864. No further records. Survived the war. [North Carolina pension records indicate that he was wounded in the left hand near Petersburg, Virginia, in July, 1864.]

FENDER, SOLOMON, Corporal

Resided in Alleghany County and was by occupation a farmer prior to enlisting in Alleghany County at age 28, May 3, 1862, for the war. Mustered in as Corporal. Reported present or accounted for in November, 1862-June, 1863. Hospitalized at Wilmington on or about July 7, 1863, with bilious fever. Returned to duty on August 3, 1863. Sent to hospital at Charleston, South Carolina, in September-October, 1863. Furloughed on November 23, 1863. Returned to duty subsequent to April 30, 1864. Reported present in September-December, 1864. No further records.

FOWLER, W. H., _____

North Carolina pension records indicate that he served in this company.

FOWLKES, SAMUEL LANE, Sergeant

Born in Alleghany County* where he resided prior to enlisting in Alleghany County at age 18, May 3, 1862, for the war. Mustered in as Private. Reported present in November, 1862-April, 1863.

Promoted to Corporal on April 3, 1863. Reported present in May-October, 1863. Promoted to Sergeant on September 27, 1863. Reported present or accounted for in November, 1863-April, 1864. Killed at Cold Harbor, Virginia, June 2, 1864.

GILHAM, GEORGE, Private

Resided in Alleghany County and was by occupation a tanner prior to enlisting in Alleghany County at age 22, May 3, 1862, for the war. Reported present in November-December, 1862. Reported on detail as an ambulance driver from January 10 through June 30, 1863. Reported on detached service at Wilmington in July-August, 1863. Furloughed prior to November 1, 1863. Reported absent without leave from March 25 through December 31, 1864. No further records.

GODWIN, L. T., Sergeant

Place and date of enlistment not reported (probably enlisted in the autumn of 1864). Promotion record not recorded. Reported in hospital at High Point on November 22, 1864, with debilitas. Furloughed on November 23, 1864. No further records.

GOINS, SILAS A., Private

Resided in Alleghany County and was by occupation a laborer prior to enlisting in Alleghany County at age 21, May 3, 1862, for the war. Deserted on an unspecified date. Enlisted as Private in Company D, 33rd Regiment N.C. Troops, July 1, 1862, while listed as a deserter from this company. Returned to duty with this company on November 9, 1863. Reported present through April 30, 1864. Wounded in the right leg at Drewry's Bluff, Virginia, on or about May 16, 1864. Hospitalized at Richmond, Virginia. Retired to the Invalid Corps on November 4, 1864. Died in hospital at Richmond on November 24, 1864, of "pneumonia."

GRIMSLEY, DRURY, Private

Previously served as Private in Company A, 26th Regiment N.C. Troops. Transferred to this company on November 10, 1862. Reported present through February 28, 1863. Reported absent on sick furlough from April 27 through August 31, 1863. Reported absent without leave in September-October, 1863. Returned to duty on November 4, 1863. Reported absent on detail at Petersburg, Virginia, in November-December, 1863. Discharged from service at Petersburg on February 26, 1864, by reason of "epilepsy."

GRIMSLEY, JAMES K., Private

Resided in Alleghany County and enlisted at Zuni, Virginia, February 8, 1864, for the war. Reported present through April 30, 1864. Wounded in the mouth at Cold Harbor, Virginia, June 1-3, 1864. Hospitalized at Richmond, Virginia. Returned to duty on July 23, 1864. Reported present in September-December, 1864. No further records. [Was about 17 years of age at time of enlistment.]

HAWKINS, CHARLES, _____

North Carolina pension records indicate that he served in this company.

HIGGINS, CALVIN, Private

Resided in Alleghany County and was by occupation a farmer prior to enlisting in Alleghany County at age 31, May 3, 1862, for the war. Mustered in as Musician. Hospitalized at Wilson on December 17, 1862. Reduced to ranks prior to January 1, 1863.

Returned to duty in January-February, 1863. Reported present in March-April, 1863. Reported sick in hospital at Wilmington on May 25, 1863. Deserted on August 22, 1863. Returned from desertion on October 26, 1863. Reported under arrest at Petersburg, Virginia, in November-December, 1863. Died on February 21, 1864, of disease. Place of death not reported.

HIGGINS, CARTER H., Private

Resided in Alleghany County and was by occupation a laborer prior to enlisting in Alleghany County at age 28, May 3, 1862, for the war. Reported present in November-December, 1862. Died at Wilmington on January 13, 1863, of "smallpox."

HIGGINS, GRANVILLE, Private

Resided in Alleghany County and was by occupation a laborer prior to enlisting in Alleghany County at age 22, May 3, 1862, for the war. Mustered in as Private. Detailed as a wagoner on December 7, 1862. Rejoined the company in January-February, 1863. Appointed Musician on February 9, 1863. Reported present in March-April, 1863. Promoted to Sergeant on April 3, 1863. Reported present but sick in quarters in May-June, 1863. Wounded at Morris Island, Charleston Harbor, South Carolina, July 30, 1863. Returned to duty on an unspecified date. Wounded in the eye and nose at Morris Island on or about August 26, 1863. Deserted on September 1, 1863. Returned from desertion on October 29, 1863. Reduced to ranks prior to November 1, 1863. Reported under arrest at Petersburg, Virginia, in November-December, 1863. Returned to duty in January-February, 1864. Reported present in March-April, 1864. Killed near Petersburg on June 17, 1864.

HIGGINS, H. C., Private

Resided in Alleghany County where he enlisted at age 29, May 3, 1862, for the war. Died in camp near Goldsboro on January 13, 1863, of "smallpox."

HIGGINS, PLEASANT CLARK, Private

Resided in Alleghany County and was by occupation a laborer prior to enlisting in Alleghany County at age 25, May 3, 1862, for the war. Reported present in November-December, 1862. Hospitalized at Wilmington on February 6, 1863, with remittent fever. Returned to duty on February 12, 1863. Discharged on April 1, 1863, after providing Pvt. William D. Thompson as a substitute.

HILL, DAVID, Private

Resided in Alleghany County where he enlisted at age 31, August 5, 1862, for the war. Reported present in November-December, 1862. Hospitalized at Wilmington on February 6, 1863, with rheumatism. Returned to duty on February 24, 1863. Reported present or accounted for through December 31, 1863. Hospitalized at Petersburg, Virginia, January 12, 1864, with intermittent fever. Returned to duty on January 29, 1864. Reported present or accounted for through April 30, 1864. Hospitalized at Farmville, Virginia, June 20, 1864, with chronic bronchitis. Furloughed for thirty days on September 21, 1864. Reported absent without leave from October 21 through December 31, 1864. No further records.

HILL, MEREDITH, Private

Resided in Alleghany County where he enlisted at age 22, May 3, 1862, for the war. Reported present in November, 1862-April, 1864. Hospitalized at Richmond, Virginia, August 28, 1864, with acute bronchitis. Returned to duty on October 19, 1864. Reported present through December 31, 1864. No further records.

HOLLOWAY, HARDIN, Private

Born in Alleghany County* where he resided prior to enlisting at Sullivan's Island, Charleston Harbor, South Carolina, at age 21, October 29, 1863, for the war. Reported present through April 30, 1864. Killed near Petersburg, Virginia, June 18, 1864.

HOLLOWAY, MARTIN, Private

Resided in Alleghany County where he enlisted on May 3, 1862, for the war. Reported present in November, 1862-April, 1864. Reported absent without leave from October 2 through December 31, 1864. No further records.

HOLLOWAY, THOMAS, Private

Resided in Alleghany County and was by occupation a laborer prior to enlisting in Alleghany County at age 18, May 3, 1862, for the war. Reported present in November-December, 1862. Died in hospital at Wilmington on or about January 21, 1863, of "pneumonia" and/or "typhoid fever."

HOLLOWAY, WILLIAM, Private

Resided in Alleghany County where he enlisted at age 20, May 3, 1862, for the war. Reported present in November, 1862-April, 1864. Wounded in the side and/or breast at or near Petersburg, Virginia, on or about June 17, 1864. Hospitalized at Farmville, Virginia, June 20, 1864. Returned to duty on October 24, 1864. Reported present through December 31, 1864. No further records.

HOPPERS, FRANKLIN J., Private

Born in Ashe County (present-day Alleghany County) on January 16, 1834. Resided in Alleghany County and was by occupation a farmer prior to enlisting in Alleghany County at age 28, May 3, 1862, for the war. Reported present in November, 1862-February, 1863. Reported sick in hospital at Columbia, South Carolina, from March 25 through April 30, 1863. Returned to duty in May-June, 1863. Reported present in July-August, 1863. Furloughed from hospital for thirty days on October 23, 1863. Reported absent on furlough through April 30, 1864. Reported absent without leave in September-December, 1864. No further records. Survived the war. [His Tennessee pension application states that he was "crushed in body and skull cracked" at Morris or Sullivan's Island, Charleston Harbor, South Carolina, September 16, 1863.]

HUDSON, JOSEPH, Private

Resided in Alleghany County where he enlisted at age 24, May 3, 1862, for the war. Reported sick at home on November 12, 1862. Returned to duty on or about February 10, 1863. Reported present in March-June, 1863. Deserted on August 28, 1863. Returned from desertion on October 29, 1863. Reported under arrest at Petersburg, Virginia, in November-December, 1863. Returned to duty in January-February, 1864. Reported present in March-April, 1864. Wounded in the back and/or right hip at Drewry's Bluff, Virginia, on or about May 17, 1864. Hospitalized at Richmond, Virginia. Returned to duty on or about November 1, 1864. Reported present in November-December, 1864. No further records.

JENNINGS, MARTIN, Private

Resided in Alleghany County and was by occupation a farmer prior to enlisting in Alleghany County at age 33, May 3, 1862, for the war. Hospitalized at Wilmington on December 17, 1862. Returned to duty in January-February, 1863. Reported present through April 30, 1863. Hospitalized at Wilmington on June 27, 1863, with rheumatism. Reported sick in hospital at Wilmington through August 31, 1863. Hospitalized at Charleston, South Caro-

lina, in September-October, 1863. Returned to duty in November-December, 1863. Reported present in January-April, 1864. Hospitalized at Richmond, Virginia, on an unspecified date. Furloughed on August 19, 1864. Reported absent without leave in October-December, 1864. No further records. Survived the war.

JOHNSON, WILLIAM H., Private

Resided in Alleghany County where he enlisted on May 3, 1862, for the war. Hospitalized at Wilson on December 17, 1862. Returned to duty in January-February, 1863. Reported present in March-April, 1863. Hospitalized at Wilmington on June 5, 1863. Returned to duty in July-August, 1863. Reported present but sick in September-October, 1863. Furloughed for thirty days on December 4, 1863. Reported on detached service at Petersburg, Virginia, in January-April, 1864. Rejoined the company prior to November 1, 1864. Reported present but on duty as a provost guard in November-December, 1864. No further records.

JOINES, CALLOWAY, Private

Resided in Alleghany County and was by occupation a farmer prior to enlisting in Alleghany County at age 32, May 3, 1862, for the war. Reported absent on sick furlough in Alleghany County from December 26, 1862, through August 30, 1863. Failed to return to duty and was reported absent without leave in September, 1863-April, 1864. Dropped from the company rolls on or about April 30, 1864.

JOINES, EZEKIEL, Private

Born on May 9, 1824. Resided in Alleghany County where he enlisted at age 39, October 15, 1863, for the war. Reported for duty on November 15, 1863. Hospitalized at Petersburg, Virginia, January 18, 1864, with a gunshot wound of the left foot. Place and date wounded not reported. Returned to duty on February 27, 1864. Reported present through April 30, 1864. No further records. Survived the war. [North Carolina pension records indicate that he was "twice struck" by spent minie balls at Drewry's Bluff, Virginia, May 14, 1864.]

JOINES, LINVILLE, Private

Resided in Alleghany County where he enlisted at age 24, October 15, 1863, for the war. Reported present in November-December, 1863. Hospitalized at Petersburg, Virginia, January 27, 1864, with typhoid fever. Returned to duty on February 27, 1864. Reported present through April 30, 1864. Wounded slightly in the head at Cold Harbor, Virginia, May 31-June 3, 1864. Was reportedly captured (probably near Petersburg) on June 15, 1864; however, records of the Federal provost marshal do not substantiate that report. Died on August 31, 186[4], and was buried at Hampton, Virginia. Cause of death not reported.

JONES, ISRAEL L., 1st Sergeant

Resided in Alleghany County and was by occupation a farmer prior to enlisting in Alleghany County at age 29, May 3, 1862, for the war. Mustered in as Private. Reported present in November, 1862-August, 1863. Furloughed for twenty days on September 18, 1863. Reported absent without leave on or about October 31, 1863. Returned to duty in November-December, 1863. Reported present through April 30, 1864. Promoted to 1st Sergeant on September 8, 1864. Captured at Fort Harrison, Virginia, September 30, 1864. Confined at Point Lookout, Maryland, October 5, 1864. Paroled at Point Lookout on March 17, 1865. Received at Boulware's Wharf, James River, Virginia, March 19, 1865, for exchange. No further records.

LANDRETH, JOHN W., Sergeant

Resided in Alleghany County and was by occupation a laborer prior to enlisting in Alleghany County at age 24, May 3, 1862, for the war. Mustered in as Sergeant. Reported present in November, 1862-February, 1863. Died in hospital at Savannah, Georgia, March 10, 1863, of "typhoid fever" and/or "pneumonia."

MABE, JAMES, Private

Resided in Alleghany County and was by occupation a farmer prior to enlisting in Alleghany County on May 3, 1862, for the war. Reported present or accounted for through June 30, 1863. Furloughed for twenty days on July 2, 1863. Reported absent without leave on July 22, 1863. Reported under arrest on October 29, 1863. Returned to duty in November-December, 1863. Reported present through April 30, 1864. Detailed for duty with Company G, 2nd Regiment Confederate Engineer Troops, August 21, 1864. Reported absent on detail through December 31, 1864. No further records. Survived the war. [Was about 26 years of age at time of enlistment.]

MABE, JOHN, Private

Resided in Alleghany County where he enlisted at age 31, May 3, 1862, for the war. Reported present or accounted for in November, 1862-August, 1863. Deserted on September 1, 1863. Returned from desertion on October 29, 1863. Reported under arrest at Petersburg, Virginia, in November-December, 1863. Returned to duty in January-February, 1864. Reported present in March-April, 1864. Wounded in the left hand (third finger fractured) at Drewry's Bluff, Virginia, on or about May 13, 1864. Hospitalized at Richmond, Virginia. Reported absent without leave from July 25 through December 31, 1864. No further records. Survived the war.

McNEIL, JAMES O., _____

North Carolina pension records indicate that he served in this company.

MAINES, WILLIAM, Corporal

Resided in Alleghany County where he enlisted on May 3, 1862, for the war. Mustered in as Private. Reported present in November, 1862-June, 1863. Wounded at Morris Island, Charleston Harbor, South Carolina, on or about August 26, 1863. Returned to duty prior to September 1, 1863. Promoted to Corporal on October 22, 1863. Reported present through April 30, 1864. Furloughed for thirty days on September 12, 1864. Reported absent without leave from October 11 through December 31, 1864. No further records. Survived the war. [Was about 26 years of age at time of enlistment. North Carolina pension records indicate that he became ill with bilious fever in September, 1864, and was unable to perform field service thereafter.]

MALLETE, HUBERT, Sergeant

Place and date of enlistment not reported (probably enlisted subsequent to December 31, 1864). Promotion record not reported. Paroled at Greensboro on May 1, 1865.

MITCHELL, FRANCIS MARION, Sergeant

Born on May 19, 1827. Resided in Alleghany County and was by occupation a farmer prior to enlisting in Alleghany County at age 34, May 3, 1862, for the war. Mustered in as Corporal. Reported present in November-December, 1862. Hospitalized at Wilmington on January 10, 1863, with pneumonia. Returned to duty on January 19, 1863. Reduced to ranks on or about April 3, 1863. Reported in hospital at Wilmington in March-April, 1863. Returned to duty in May-June, 1863. Promoted to Sergeant on August

4, 1863. Reported present through April 30, 1864. Wounded in the right leg and/or foot at Drewry's Bluff, Virginia, on or about May 14, 1864. Lower right leg amputated. Reported absent wounded through December 31, 1864. No further records. Survived the war.

MOXLEY, JAMES, Private

Resided in Alleghany County where he enlisted at age 18, May 3, 1862, for the war. Reported absent without leave from November 15, 1862, through February 28, 1863. Returned to duty in March-April, 1863. Reported present or accounted for through December 31, 1863. Reported on detached service at Petersburg, Virginia, in January-April, 1864. Wounded in the head (believed mortally) at Drewry's Bluff, Virginia, on or about May 18, 1864. Hospitalized at Richmond, Virginia. Furloughed for sixty days on June 14, 1864. Reported absent wounded through December 31, 1864. No further records.

MOXLEY, JOHN, Private

Resided in Alleghany County and was by occupation a farmer or laborer prior to enlisting in Alleghany County at age 20, May 3, 1862, for the war. Reported present or accounted for in November, 1862-June, 1863. Reported sick in hospital at Mount Pleasant, South Carolina, in July-August, 1863. Returned to duty in September-October, 1863. Reported absent sick at Petersburg, Virginia, in November-December, 1863. Hospitalized at Petersburg on January 1, 1864, with intermittent fever. Returned to duty on February 2, 1864. Hospitalized at Petersburg on February 17, 1864, with intermittent fever. Returned to duty on February 27, 1864. Reported present through April 30, 1864. Wounded in the head and/or left shoulder at Drewry's Bluff, Virginia, May 16, 1864. Hospitalized at Richmond, Virginia. Transferred to hospital at Lynchburg, Virginia, May 22, 1864. Dropped from the company rolls prior to November 1, 1864 (probably for desertion or extended absence without leave). Deserted to the enemy on an unspecified date. Confined at Knoxville, Tennessee, January 16, 1865. Transferred to Louisville, Kentucky. Arrived at Louisville on January 27, 1865. Released at Louisville on January 31, 1865, after taking the Oath of Allegiance.

MOXLEY, NATHANIEL M., Private

Resided in Alleghany County where he enlisted on May 3, 1862, for the war. Reported present in November-December, 1862. Hospitalized at Wilmington on February 6, 1863, with diarrhoea. Returned to duty on March 9, 1863. Reported present through August 31, 1863. Deserted on September 1, 1863. Rejoined from desertion on April 7, 1864, and was placed under arrest. Reported absent sick in September-October, 1864. Hospitalized at Wilmington on December 30, 1864, with a gunshot wound. Place and date wounded not reported. Returned to duty on January 5, 1865. No further records. Survived the war. [Was about 28 years of age at time of enlistment.]

MOXLEY, THOMAS, Private

Resided in Alleghany County where he enlisted on May 3, 1862, for the war. Deserted on December 28, 1862. May have returned to duty in late 1864 or early 1865. Deserted to the enemy on an unspecified date. Confined at Knoxville, Tennessee, January 16, 1865. Transferred to Louisville, Kentucky, where he arrived on January 27, 1865. Released at Louisville on January 31, 1865, after taking the Oath of Allegiance.

MURRAY, ZACHARIAH D., Private

Resided in Alleghany County where he enlisted at age 29, May 3, 1862, for the war. Reported present or accounted for in November,

1862-April, 1864. Captured at Fort Harrison, Virginia, September 30, 1864. Confined at Point Lookout, Maryland, October 5, 1864. Paroled at Point Lookout on November 1, 1864. Received at Venus Point, Savannah River, Georgia, November 15, 1864, for exchange. Reported absent without leave on November 25, 1864. No further records.

MUSGRAVES, GEORGE, Private

Resided in Alleghany County and was by occupation a miner prior to enlisting in Alleghany County at age 24, May 3, 1862, for the war. Reported on detached duty at the lead smelting house at Petersburg, Virginia, from August 10, 1862, through October 31, 1864. Reported on detached duty at the lead works at Greensboro in November-December, 1864. Paroled at Greensboro on or about May 4, 1865.

PALMER, T. W., _____

North Carolina pension records indicate that he served in this company.

PASSMORE, COLUMBUS, Private

Resided in Alleghany County where he enlisted at age 28, May 3, 1862, for the war. Reported present in November, 1862-April, 1863. Died in hospital at Wilmington on May 27, 1863, of "febris typhoides."

PHIPPS, MORGAN, Private

Resided in Alleghany County and was by occupation a laborer prior to enlisting in Alleghany County at age 19, May 3, 1862, for the war. No further records. [See special note at the end of the history of Company I, 61st Regiment N.C. Troops (page 738).]

RICHARDSON, DANIEL, Private

Resided in Alleghany County and was by occupation a laborer prior to enlisting in Alleghany County at age 18, May 3, 1862, for the war. Reported present in November, 1862-June, 1863. Wounded at Morris Island, Charleston Harbor, South Carolina, on or about August 26, 1863. Returned to duty prior to August 31, 1863. Reported under arrest in September-October, 1863. Reason he was arrested not reported. Returned to duty in November-December, 1863. Furloughed for twenty days on February 19, 1864. Reported absent without leave from March 12 through October 31, 1864. Listed as a deserter on December 31, 1864.

RICHARDSON, DAVID, Private

Resided in Alleghany County where he enlisted at age 27, May 3, 1862, for the war. Wounded in the right leg at or near Kinston on or about December 14, 1862. Right leg amputated. Reported absent wounded through October 31, 1864. Retired from service in November-December, 1864.

RICHARDSON, ISAAC, Private

Born on March 13, 1843. Resided in Alleghany County where he enlisted at age 19, May 3, 1862, for the war. Reported present in November, 1862-April, 1863. Reported sick in hospital at Wilmington from June 27 through August 31, 1863. Returned to duty in September-October, 1863. Reported present in November-December, 1863. Hospitalized at Petersburg, Virginia, February 1, 1864, with intermittent fever. Returned to duty on February 10, 1864. Hospitalized at Petersburg on February 22, 1864, with neuralgia. Returned to duty on March 13, 1864. Wounded in the leg at Drewry's Bluff, Virginia, on or about May 16, 1864. Hospitalized at Richmond, Virginia. Furloughed for sixty days on June 11,

1864. Returned to duty on an unspecified date. Reported present in September-December, 1864. No further records.

RICHARDSON, ISOM, Private

Born on September 19, 1835. Resided in Alleghany County where he enlisted at age 26, May 3, 1862, for the war. Reported present in November, 1862-February, 1863. Hospitalized at Columbia, South Carolina, on or about April 1, 1863. Furloughed for thirty days on May 20, 1863. Reported absent without leave on June 20, 1863. Reported under arrest on October 11, 1863. Reported absent sick at Petersburg, Virginia, in November-December, 1863. Returned to duty in January-February, 1864. Reported present in March-April, 1864. Deserted on an unspecified date. Returned to duty on October 25, 1864. Reported present through December 31, 1864. No further records. Survived the war.

RICHARDSON, MEREDITH L., Private

Enlisted in Alleghany County on May 3, 1862, for the war. Reported present or accounted for in November, 1862-April, 1864. Dropped from the company rolls prior to November 1, 1864. Reason he was dropped not reported. No further records.

ROBERTS, EZRA H., Private

Resided in Alleghany County where he enlisted at age 18, May 3, 1862, for the war. Reported present in November, 1862-June, 1863. Killed by a piece of shell at Fort Wagner, Charleston Harbor, South Carolina, on or about July 30, 1863.

ROYAL, WILSON, Private

Resided in Alleghany County and was by occupation a farmer prior to enlisting at Zuni, Virginia, at age 40, January 14, 1864, for the war. Reported present through April 30, 1864. Captured near Petersburg, Virginia, June 16, 1864. Confined at Point Lookout, Maryland, June 19, 1864. Transferred to Elmira, New York, where he arrived on July 26, 1864. Died at Elmira on September 18, 1864, of "chronic diarrhoea."

SANDERS, HENRY, Private

Resided in Alleghany County and was by occupation a farmer prior to enlisting in Alleghany County at age 24, May 3, 1862, for the war. Reported present in November, 1862-April, 1863. Hospitalized at Wilmington on May 8, 1863, with dropsy. Returned to duty on June 19, 1863. Deserted on August 28, 1863. Returned from desertion on October 5, 1863. Reported under arrest at Charleston, South Carolina, October 31, 1863. Reported under arrest at Petersburg, Virginia, in November-December, 1863. Returned to duty in January-February, 1864. Reported present through April 30, 1864. Hospitalized at Richmond, Virginia, October 2, 1864. Returned to duty on November 21, 1864. Reported present through December 31, 1864. No further records. Survived the war. [North Carolina pension records indicate that his left ear was injured as a result of a shell explosion at Globe Tavern, Virginia, August 21, 1864.]

SCOTT, LARKIN, Private

Resided in Wilkes County where he enlisted at age 18, May 3, 1862, for the war. Reported present in November, 1862-April, 1863. Hospitalized at Wilmington on June 27, 1863, with continued fever. Returned to duty on August 11, 1863. Deserted on August 28, 1863.

SIMMONS, W. G., Private

Resided in Wilkes County and enlisted in Alleghany County on May 3, 1862, for the war. Died on October 10, 1862. Place and cause of death not reported.

SWINDLE, ELI, Private

Resided in Alleghany County and was by occupation a laborer prior to enlisting in Alleghany County at age 26, May 3, 1862, for the war. Discharged in September, 1862. Reason discharged not reported. [See special note at the end of the history of Company I, 61st Regiment N.C. Troops (page 738).]

TAYLOR, HENRY, Private

Resided in Alleghany County and was by occupation a farmer prior to enlisting in Alleghany County at age 26, May 3, 1862, for the war. No further records. [See special note at the end of the history of Company I, 61st Regiment N.C. Troops (page 738).]

THOMPSON, WILLIAM D., Private

Resided in Alleghany County and enlisted at James Island, Charleston Harbor, South Carolina, April 1, 1863, for the war as a substitute for Pvt. Pleasant Clark Higgins. Reported sick in hospital at Charleston on or about April 14, 1863. Hospitalized at Wilmington on or about May 7, 1863, with rheumatism. Reported absent sick through August 31, 1863. Reported absent without leave in September-October, 1863. Reported absent sick at Petersburg, Virginia, in November-December, 1863. Reported on detached service at Petersburg in January-April, 1864. Rejoined the company prior to September 30, 1864, when he was wounded in the right lung at Fort Harrison, Virginia. Hospitalized at Richmond, Virginia, where he died on or about October 4, 1864, of wounds.

TOLIVER, ALLEN, Private

Resided in Alleghany County where he enlisted at age 32, August 5, 1862, for the war. Discharged in September, 1862. Reason discharged not reported. [See special note at the end of the history of Company I, 61st Regiment N.C. Troops (page 738).]

TOLIVER, ANDREW, Private

Born in Alleghany County* where he resided as a laborer prior to enlisting in Alleghany County at age 23, May 3, 1862, for the war. Reported absent sick in Alleghany County from October 15, 1862, through April 30, 1863. Returned to duty in May-June, 1863. Hospitalized at Charleston, South Carolina, July 13, 1863. Reported absent without leave on August 29, 1863. Rejoined the company on October 16, 1863, and was placed under arrest. Returned to duty in November-December, 1863. Reported present through April 30, 1864. Died in hospital at Petersburg, Virginia, May 30, 1864, of "typhoid fever."

TOLIVER, JACOB, Private

Born in Ashe County on February 17, 1831. Resided in Alleghany County where he was by occupation a farmer prior to enlisting in Alleghany County at age 31, May 3, 1862, for the war. Hospitalized at Wilson on November 1, 1862. Returned to duty in January-February, 1863. Hospitalized at Charleston, South Carolina, April 29, 1863. Furloughed for thirty days on an unspecified date. Reported absent without leave in July, 1863-February, 1864. Returned to duty in March-April, 1864. No further records. Survived the war. [Discharged at Columbia, South Carolina, January 12, 1863, by reason of "disease of the kidney with albuminia & general debility"; however, his discharge was apparently revoked.]

TOLIVER, JESSE, Private

Resided in Alleghany County and was by occupation a farmer prior to enlisting in Alleghany County at age 32, May 3, 1862, for the war. Reported absent without leave from June 15, 1862, through February 29, 1864. Reported under arrest in March-April, 1864;

however, that report was apparently erroneous. Listed as a deserter in November-December, 1864.

TOLIVER, SOLOMON, Private

Resided in Alleghany County and was by occupation a laborer prior to enlisting in Alleghany County at age 21, May 3, 1862, for the war. Reported absent without leave from November 15, 1862, through February 28, 1863. Hospitalized at Columbia, South Carolina, April 18, 1863. Reported absent without leave on August 29, 1863. Rejoined the company on October 16, 1863, and was placed under arrest. Returned to duty in November-December, 1863. Reported present through April 30, 1864. Captured near Petersburg, Virginia, June 16, 1864. Confined at Point Lookout, Maryland, June 19, 1864. Transferred to Elmira, New York, July 25, 1864. Died at Elmira on September 11, 1864, of "chronic diarrhoea."

WILSON, DAVID I., Private

Resided in Alleghany County where he enlisted at age 21, October 20, 1862, for the war. Hospitalized at Raleigh on December 27, 1862. Furloughed for thirty days in January, 1863. Reported absent sick in Alleghany County through August 31, 1863. Reported absent without leave in September, 1863-April, 1864, and September-October, 1864. Listed as a deserter in November-December, 1864.

WILSON, JEREMIAH, Private

Resided in Alleghany County where he enlisted at age 23, May 3, 1862, for the war. Deserted on December 28, 1862. Returned from desertion on March 13, 1863. Hospitalized at Charleston, South Carolina, April 24, 1863. Returned to duty in May-June, 1863. Deserted on August 26, 1863. Went over to the enemy on an unspecified date. Confined at Knoxville, Tennessee, February 7, 1865. Transferred to Chattanooga, Tennessee, February 10, 1865. Transferred to Louisville, Kentucky, where he arrived on February 20, 1865. Released at Louisville on February 21, 1865, after taking the Oath of Allegiance.

WILSON, MARTIN, Private

Resided in Alleghany County where he enlisted at age 25, May 4, 1862, for the war. Discharged in September, 1862. Reason discharged not reported. [See special note at the end of the history of Company I, 61st Regiment N.C. Troops (page 738).]

WOOD, WILLIAM JACKSON, Private

Resided in Franklin County. Place and date of enlistment not reported (probably enlisted subsequent to December 31, 1864). Captured near Kinston on March 8, 1865. Sent to New Bern. Confined at Point Lookout, Maryland, March 16, 1865. Released at Point Lookout on June 22, 1865, after taking the Oath of Allegiance.

WOODRUFF, ROBERT, Corporal

Resided in Alleghany County and was by occupation a laborer prior to enlisting in Alleghany County at age 25, May 3, 1862, for the war. Mustered in as Private. Reported present in November-December, 1862. Hospitalized at Wilmington on February 6, 1863, with pneumonia. Returned to duty on or about March 9, 1863. Reported present through June 30, 1863. Wounded in the face and head at Morris Island, Charleston Harbor, South Carolina, on or about August 26, 1863. Returned to duty prior to September 1, 1863. Reported present or accounted for through April 30, 1864. Promoted to Corporal on June 10, 1864. Wounded (probably in the left arm) on or about July 2, 1864. Battle in which wounded not reported. Reported absent without leave on September 29, 1864.

Detailed as a guard at Charlotte on November 1, 1864. Detailed for unspecified duty on January 12, 1865. Paroled at Newton on or about April 19, 1865.

WYATT, JONATHAN, Private

Resided in Alleghany County where he enlisted at age 18, August 6, 1864, for the war. Wounded at Fort Harrison, Virginia, September 30, 1864. Hospitalized at Richmond, Virginia. Reported absent without leave on November 24, 1864. No further records.

COMPANY K

This company, known as "Koonce's State Guerrillas," was raised in Jones and Onslow Counties in late April, 1862, as Capt. Francis Duval Koonce's Independent Company. It was mustered into state service in Jones County on July 22, 1862, "to operate east of the Wilmington & Weldon Rail Road between the N[e]use and Cape Fear Rivers." On or about September 29, 1862, the company was assigned to the newly organized 59th Regiment N.C. Troops. That unit was redesignated the 61st Regiment N.C. Troops on an unknown date between October 30 and November 22, 1862. This company was designated Company K. After joining the regiment the company functioned as a part of the regiment, and its history for the remainder of the war is reported as a part of the regimental history.

The following roster was compiled primarily from information in the microfilm edition of the Compiled Service Records of Soldiers Who Served in Organizations from the State of North Carolina (Record Group 109, MC 270), National Archives and Records Administration, Washington, D.C. Record Group 109 includes enlistment papers, pay vouchers, requisitions, letters of resignation, discharge certificates, and abstracts of medical and prisoner of war returns. Materials relating specifically to Company K of the 61st Regiment include a company muster-in and descriptive roll dated July 22, 1862, and company muster rolls for November, 1862-April, 1864, and September-December, 1864.

Also utilized in this roster were *The War of the Rebellion: A Compilation of the Official Records of the Union and Confederate Armies*, the North Carolina adjutant general's *Roll of Honor*, state militia records, newspaper casualty lists and obituaries, wartime claims for bounty pay and allowances, postwar registers of claims for artificial limbs, Confederate pension applications filed with the states of North Carolina, Tennessee, and Florida, Confederate Soldiers' Home records, and the 1860 and 1870 federal censuses of North Carolina. A search was made also for relevant letters, diaries, reminiscences, and other manuscripts in the Southern Historical Collection (University of North Carolina-Chapel Hill), the Duke University Library Special Collections Department, and the North Carolina Division of Archives and History.

Among the secondary sources consulted were records of the North Carolina division of the United Daughters of the Confederacy, postwar rosters, regimental and county histories, marriage bond, will, and cemetery indexes, published and unpublished genealogies, biographical dictionaries, the North Carolina *County Heritage Book* series, the *Confederate Veteran*, Walter Clark's *Histories of the Several Regiments and Battalions from North Carolina in the Great War, 1861-'65*, and the North Carolina volume of the extended edition of *Confederate Military History*.

Note: The following roster contains service records for five men who enlisted in Captain Koonce's Independent Company but whose service terminated prior to September 29, 1862, the date the company

was mustered into the 59th Regiment N.C. Troops (later redesignated the 61st Regiment N.C. Troops). Those men, it will be evident, never served in the 61st Regiment. Their service records are included here because too little information survives to compile a roster for Koonce's Independent Company. All service records falling into the early-termination category conclude with a "special note" alerting readers to that fact and referring them to the information contained in this paragraph.

OFFICERS

CAPTAINS

KOONCE, FRANCIS DUVAL

Born in Onslow County where he resided as a law professor prior to enlisting at age 24. Appointed Captain on April 29, 1862. Reported absent sick without leave from September 12 through December 31, 1862. Resigned on an unspecified date. Resignation accepted on February 3, 1863.

NOBLE, STEPHEN WILLIAM

Previously served as 3rd Lieutenant of Company E of this regiment. Appointed Captain of this company on April 26 or April 28, 1863. Reported present through October 31, 1863. Hospitalized at Wilmington on November 30, 1863, with chronic rheumatism. Returned to duty on December 10, 1863. Reported present or accounted for through April 30, 1864, and in September-December, 1864. No further records. Survived the war.

LIEUTENANTS

GEROCK, SAMUEL L., 2nd Lieutenant

Born in Jones County where he resided as a merchant prior to enlisting in Jones County at age 24. Appointed 2nd Lieutenant on April 29, 1862. Reported absent sick without leave on November 7, 1862. Returned to duty in January-February, 1863. Reported present through June 30, 1863. Furloughed from hospital at Columbia, South Carolina, September 1, 1863. Reported absent without leave from December 1, 1863, through April 30, 1864, and in September-October, 1864. Dropped from the company rolls on or about November 24, 1864, for prolonged absence without leave. [Previously served as Captain in the 19th Regiment N.C. Militia.]

HASKINS, CALHOUN, 3rd Lieutenant

Born in Onslow County and resided in Jones County where he was by occupation an overseer or farmer prior to enlisting in Jones County at age 30. Elected 3rd Lieutenant on June 16, 1862. Reported present but sick in November-December, 1862. Resigned on December 27, 1862, by reason of "asthma." Resignation accepted on February 6, 1863.

HUMPHREY, WILLIAM, 3rd Lieutenant

Born in Onslow County. Appointed 3rd Lieutenant in this company on an unspecified date. Died at Richlands on June 17, 1862. Cause of death not reported. Was 19 years of age at the time of his death. [See special note at the end of the history of Company K, 61st Regiment N.C. Troops (page 749).]

KOONCE, HENRY CLAY, 1st Lieutenant

Born in Jones County on August 29, 1842. Resided in Jones County and was by occupation a farmer prior to enlisting at age 19. Appointed 1st Lieutenant on April 29, 1862. Reported in command of the company in November-December, 1862. Reported present or accounted for in January, 1863-April, 1864. Reported in command of the company June 17-30, 1864. Wounded in the lower left leg at Fort Harrison, Virginia, September 30, 1864. Leg amputated. Hospitalized at Richmond, Virginia. Furloughed for sixty days on November 27, 1864. No further records. Survived the war.

KOONCE, SIMON EVERETT, 3rd Lieutenant

Previously served as 1st Lieutenant of Company G, 2nd Regiment N.C. State Troops. Elected 3rd Lieutenant of this company on June 20, 1863. Reported present in September, 1863-April, 1864. Captured at Fort Harrison, Virginia, September 30, 1864. Confined at Old Capitol Prison, Washington, D.C., October 6, 1864. Transferred to Fort Delaware, Delaware, October 21, 1864. Released at Fort Delaware on June 17, 1865, after taking the Oath of Allegiance.

NONCOMMISSIONED OFFICERS AND PRIVATES

BANKS, BENJAMIN F., Private

Born in Onslow County and resided in Jones County where he was by occupation a farmer or laborer prior to enlisting in Jones County at age 23, April 28, 1862, for the war. Mustered in as Sergeant. Reported present but sick or absent sick in November, 1862-June, 1863. Reduced to ranks on July 1, 1863. Returned to duty in July-August, 1863. Reported absent on sick furlough on October 20, 1863. Reported on detached service with the enrolling officer of Jones County from November 20 through December 31, 1863. Returned to duty in January-April, 1864. Wounded in the arm at Cold Harbor, Virginia, May 31-June 3, 1864. Hospitalized at Richmond, Virginia, June 27, 1864, with chronic diarrhoea. Furloughed for sixty days on July 30, 1864. Returned to duty prior to September 30, 1864, when he was wounded in the right arm at Fort Harrison, Virginia. Returned to duty in November-December, 1864. Hospitalized at Wilmington on December 30, 1864. Returned to duty on January 5, 1865. No further records. Survived the war. [North Carolina pension records indicate that he died on November 12, 1890, of wounds received at Fort Harrison.]

BANKS, HENRY T., JR., Private

Born in Onslow County and resided in Jones County where he was by occupation a farmer prior to enlisting in Jones County at age 16, April 28, 1862, for the war. Reported present but sick in November-December, 1862. Returned to duty in January-February, 1863. Reported present or accounted for in March, 1863-April, 1864, and September-December, 1864. No further records.

BARNES, BENNETT, Private

Born in Edgecombe County and resided in Jones County where he was by occupation a farmer prior to enlisting in Jones County at age 50, May 24, 1862, for the war. Reported present or accounted for in November, 1862-April, 1864. Reported absent on sick furlough in September-October, 1864. Returned to duty in November-December, 1864. No further records.

BASDEN, HENRY GRAY, Private

Resided in Onslow County where he enlisted at age 18, March 10, 1863, for the war. Reported present or accounted for through April 30, 1864. Captured at Fort Harrison, Virginia, September 30, 1864.

Confined at Point Lookout, Maryland, October 5, 1864. Paroled at Point Lookout on March 17, 1865. Received at Boulware's Wharf, James River, Virginia, March 19, 1865, for exchange.

BASDEN, JAMES DANIEL, Private

Born in Onslow County on September 22, 1840. Resided in Onslow County and was by occupation a farmer or farm laborer prior to enlisting in Onslow County at age 21, April 29, 1862, for the war. Reported present in November-December, 1862. Hospitalized at Wilmington on February 18, 1863, with rheumatism. Returned to duty on April 20, 1863. Reported present or accounted for through April 30, 1864. Wounded in the foot and face at Cold Harbor, Virginia, May 31-June 3, 1864. Hospitalized at Richmond, Virginia. Returned to duty prior to November 1, 1864. Reported present in November-December, 1864. No further records. Survived the war.

BASDEN, JESSE, Private

Born in Onslow County where he resided as a farmer prior to enlisting in Onslow County at age 34, July 14, 1862, for the war. Reported present or accounted for in November, 1862-April, 1864. Reported absent on sick furlough in September-October, 1864. Returned to duty in November-December, 1864. Hospitalized at Raleigh on February 23, 1865, with acute diarrhoea. Returned to duty on March 1, 1865. No further records. Survived the war.

BASDEN, JOHN H., Private

Born in Onslow County where he resided as a farmer prior to enlisting in Onslow County at age 22, April 29, 1862, for the war. Reported present or accounted for in November, 1862-April, 1864. Captured at Fort Harrison, Virginia, September 30, 1864. Confined at Point Lookout, Maryland, October 5, 1864. Paroled at Point Lookout on March 17, 1865. Received at Boulware's Wharf, James River, Virginia, March 19, 1865, for exchange. No further records. Survived the war. [North Carolina pension records indicate that he was wounded slightly in the hand and shoulder at Fort Harrison.]

BASDEN, WILLIAM, Sergeant

Born in Onslow County where he resided as a farmer prior to enlisting in Onslow County at age 32, April 28, 1862, for the war. Mustered in as Sergeant. Reported present or accounted for in November, 1862-April, 1864, and September-December, 1864. No further records. Survived the war.

BASDEN, WILLIAM H., Private

Born in Onslow County where he resided as a farmer prior to enlisting in Onslow County at age 16, April 29, 1862, for the war. Hospitalized at Wilmington on or about December 31, 1862, with dyspepsia. Returned to duty on January 4, 1863. Hospitalized at Wilmington on or about January 9, 1863, with pneumonia. Returned to duty on January 19, 1863. Died in hospital at Wilmington on or about February 12, 1863, of "continued fever."

BECTON, IVY, Corporal

Born in Lenoir County where he resided as a farmer prior to enlisting in Craven County at age 40, February 13, 1862. Mustered in as Private. Reported sick at home in November-December, 1862. Hospitalized at Wilmington on February 17, 1863, with debility. Returned to duty on April 5, 1863. Reported on detail in hospital at Wilmington on April 30, 1863. Hospitalized at Wilmington on May 5, 1863, with remittent fever. Returned to duty in July-August, 1863. Reported present or accounted for through April 30, 1864.

Promoted to Corporal on February 6, 1864. Reported sick in hospital at Richmond, Virginia, in September-December, 1864. No further records. Survived the war.

BECTON, JAMES S., Sergeant

Born in Jones County and resided in Lenoir County where he was by occupation a farmer prior to enlisting in Jones County at age 23, April 28, 1862, for the war. Mustered in as Private. Reported absent without leave on December 14, 1862. Hospitalized at Wilmington on or about February 17, 1863, with debilitas. Reported absent sick at "Everettville" in March-April, 1863. Furloughed for thirty days on June 24, 1863. Returned to duty in September-October, 1863. Reported present through April 30, 1864. Promoted to Corporal on February 6, 1864. Reported present or accounted for in September-December, 1864. Hospitalized at Richmond, Virginia, on or about January 1, 1865. Returned to duty on March 16, 1865. Promoted to Sergeant on an unspecified date. Captured by the enemy on an unspecified date. Paroled at Goldsboro on an unspecified date. Survived the war.

BECTON, JARMAN, Sergeant

Born in Lenoir County on April 19, 1833. Resided in Lenoir County and was by occupation a farmer prior to enlisting in Jones County at age 29, June 30, 1862, for the war. Mustered in as Private. Reported present in November, 1862-April, 1863. Promoted to Corporal on May 1, 1863. Reported present in May, 1863-April, 1864. Promoted to Sergeant on February 6, 1864. Reported present in September-December, 1864. No further records. Survived the war.

BOWEN, EDWARD F., Private

Resided in Duplin County where he enlisted at age 18, July 11, 1863, for the war. Reported present through April 30, 1864. Died in hospital at Richmond, Virginia, October 10, 1864, of "diarr[hoea] chron[ica]."

BROWN, ZACHARIAH, Private

Born in Lenoir County where he resided as a farmer prior to enlisting in Jones County at age 29, June 30, 1862, for the war. Reported present in November, 1862-February, 1863. Reported sick in hospital at Columbia, South Carolina, in March-April, 1863. Died at Charleston, South Carolina, April 21, 1863, of disease.

BUDD, GREEN, Private

Born in Lenoir County and resided in Jones County where he was by occupation a farmer or laborer prior to enlisting in Jones County at age 37, April 29, 1862, for the war. Reported present or accounted for in November, 1862-June, 1863. Deserted on or about July 1, 1863. Enlisted as Private in Company F, 2nd Regiment N.C. Infantry (Union), November 11, 1863.

CLARK, JAMES, Private

Born in Onslow County where he resided as a farmer or farm laborer prior to enlisting in Onslow County at age 33, February 14, 1862. Reported present in November-December, 1862. Hospitalized at Wilmington on or about February 17, 1863, with anemia. Returned to duty on March 30, 1863. Reported absent without leave on April 1, 1863. Returned to duty in May-June, 1863. Reported absent in hospital in July-August, 1863. Reported sick in hospital at Goldsboro in September-December, 1863. Reported on detached service at camp near Petersburg, Virginia, in January-April, 1864. Wounded in the knee near Petersburg, Virginia, June 17-30, 1864. Leg amputated. Died in hospital at Petersburg on or about September 21, 1864, of wounds.

COLLINS, DAVID, Private

Born in Alabama and was by occupation a farmer prior to enlisting in Craven County at age 21, February 12, 1862. Failed to report for duty. Listed as a deserter and dropped from the company rolls in July-August, 1863.

CONAWAY, JAMES, Private

Resided in Onslow County and was by occupation a farm laborer prior to enlisting in Onslow County at age 35, March 10, 1863, for the war. Reported present or accounted for through October 31, 1863. Died in hospital at Charleston, South Carolina, November 6, 1863, of disease.

CONAWAY, OSCAR, Private

Resided in Onslow County and was by occupation a farm laborer prior to enlisting in Onslow County at age 30, March 10, 1863, for the war. Reported present through April 30, 1863. Reported under arrest at Wilmington in May-June, 1863. Reason he was arrested not reported. Reported on sick furlough on October 6, 1863. Reported absent without leave from November 6 through December 31, 1863. Returned to duty prior to May 1, 1864. Wounded in the thigh near Petersburg, Virginia, June 17-30, 1864. Reported absent without leave from August 28 through October 31, 1864. Reported absent on sick furlough in November-December, 1864. No further records. Survived the war. [North Carolina pension records indicate that his leg was subsequently amputated.]

COSTON, WILLIAM, Private

Resided in Onslow County and was by occupation a farm laborer prior to enlisting in Onslow County at age 30, March 10, 1863, for the war. Reported sick in hospital at Columbia, South Carolina, in March-April, 1863. Returned to duty in May-June, 1863. Reported present or accounted for through April 30, 1864. Hospitalized at Petersburg, Virginia, June 17, 1864, with intermittent fever. Transferred to hospital at Farmville, Virginia, June 20, 1864. Returned to duty on August 4, 1864. Company records indicate that he was captured at Fort Harrison, Virginia, September 30, 1864; however, records of the Federal Provost Marshal do not substantiate that report. Was probably killed at Fort Harrison.

COTTLE, JAMES D., Private

Resided in Onslow County and enlisted in Duplin County at age 18, October 13, 1863, for the war. Reported absent with leave on October 15, 1863. Returned to duty in November-December, 1863. Reported present in January-April and September-December, 1864. No further records. Survived the war.

COTTLE, JOHN W., Private

Born in Duplin County and resided in Onslow County where he was by occupation a mail carrier prior to enlisting in Onslow County at age 19, August 30, 1862, for the war. Reported present but sick or absent sick in November, 1862-June, 1863. Returned to duty in July-August, 1863. Reported present through April 30, 1864. Reported absent on sick furlough in September-October, 1864. Reported present in November-December, 1864. No further records.

COX, HARMAN, Private

Resided in Onslow County and was by occupation a farm laborer prior to enlisting in Onslow County at age 34, March 10, 1863, for the war. Reported present or accounted for through June 30, 1863. Reported sick in hospital at Summerville, South Carolina, from

August 15 through October 31, 1863. Hospitalized at Petersburg, Virginia, December 20, 1863, with intermittent fever. Died in hospital at Petersburg on January 5, 1864, of "pneumonia."

COX, WILLIAM S., Private

Born in Jones County where he resided as a farmer or farm laborer prior to enlisting in Jones County at age 18, July 16, 1862, for the war. Reported present in November, 1862-April, 1863. Transferred to Company A, 40th Regiment N.C. Troops (3rd Regiment N.C. Artillery), May 17, 1863.

CRAFT, DAVID, Private

Born in Jones County where he resided as a farmer or peddler prior to enlisting in Jones County at age 34, July 16, 1862, for the war. Reported present but sick in November-December, 1862. Hospitalized at Wilmington on February 6, 1863, with rheumatism. Returned to duty on February 14, 1863. Hospitalized at Wilmington on February 17, 1863, with continued fever. Returned to duty on March 3, 1863. Captured on the "Warsaw R[ail] R[oad]" on July 3-5, 1863. Confined at Fort Monroe, Virginia. Paroled and transferred to City Point, Virginia, where he was received on June 17, 1863, for exchange. Returned to duty in July-August, 1863. Reported present or accounted for through April 30, 1864. Wounded in the leg and right hand at or near Petersburg, Virginia, on or about June 16-19, 1864. Returned to duty on an unspecified date. Reported present in September-December, 1864. No further records. Survived the war.

CRAFTON, D., Private

Place and date of enlistment not reported. Died in hospital at Richmond, Virginia, August 9, 1863, of "chr[onic] dysentery."

CUMMINGS, LEVI B., Private

Negro. Born in Duplin County and resided in Onslow or Jones County where he was by occupation a laborer prior to enlisting in Jones County at age 26, July 14, 1862, for the war. Reported present in November, 1862-April, 1863. Reported on detail as an ambulance driver in May-June, 1863. Discharged in July-August, 1863, or on November 16, 1863, because he was "not considered white."

DAUGHERTY, BLUFORD, Private

Resided in Sampson County and was by occupation a farmer prior to enlisting in Brunswick County at age 34, October 4, 1862, for the war. Reported present through June 30, 1863. Deserted on August 22, 1863. Returned to duty on or about September 23, 1863. Reported present through April 30, 1864. Killed at Cold Harbor, Virginia, June 1, 1864.

DAVENPORT, LEVI B., Private

Resided in Lenoir County where he enlisted at age 18, June 8, 1863, for the war. Reported present or accounted for through August 31, 1863. Reported present but sick in the regimental hospital in September-October, 1863. Furloughed for sixty days on November 17, 1863. Returned to duty in January-April, 1864. Died in hospital at Goldsboro on May 22, 1864, of "pneumonia."

DAVIS, ANTHONY, Private

Resided in Lenoir County where he enlisted at age 18, August 8, 1863, for the war. Reported present through April 30, 1864, and in September-December, 1864. No further records. Survived the war.

DAVIS, JAMES T., Private

Resided in Lenoir County where he enlisted at age 21, June 13, 1863, for the war. Reported present or accounted for through April 30, 1864. Hospitalized at Richmond, Virginia, on or about August 13, 1864, with remittent fever. Died in hospital at Richmond on August 25, 1864, of disease.

DUDLEY, WILLIAM J., Private

Previously served as Private in Company G, 2nd Regiment N.C. State Troops. Enlisted in this company in Craven County on February 12, 1862. Reported sick at home from October 25, 1862, through February 28, 1863. Reported sick in hospital at Wilmington in March-April, 1863. Discharged on March 21, 1863, by reason of disability.

EUBANKS, GEORGE W., Private

Born in Jones County where he resided as a farmer prior to enlisting in Jones County at age 32, April 28, 1862, for the war. Reported present or accounted for in November, 1862-April, 1864, and September-October, 1864. No further records. Survived the war.

EUBANKS, JOHN, Private

Born in Jones County where he resided as a farmer prior to enlisting in Jones County at age 23, April 28, 1862, for the war. Reported on duty with the quartermaster department at Wilmington from October 23, 1862, through April 30, 1863. Reported present or accounted for in May, 1863-April, 1864. Hospitalized at Richmond, Virginia, August 26, 1864, with remittent fever. Furloughed for thirty days on October 14, 1864. Reported absent on sick furlough through December 31, 1864. No further records. Survived the war. [North Carolina pension records indicate that he was wounded in both legs at the Crater, near Petersburg, Virginia, July 30, 1864.]

FOY, ENOCH, Private

Born in Jones County where he resided as a farmer prior to enlisting in Jones County at age 23, August 29, 1862, for the war. Failed to report for duty. Listed as a deserter and dropped from the company rolls in July-August, 1863.

FRAZIER, ANDREW JACKSON, Private

Resided in Onslow County where he enlisted at age 17, March 10, 1863, for the war. Reported sick in hospital at Charleston, South Carolina, in March-April, 1863. Reported sick at home in May-June, 1863. Reported "absent . . . at Charleston" in July-August, 1863. Reported absent without leave in September, 1863-April, 1864. No further records. Survived the war.

GARDNER, JOHN O., Private

Born in Pitt County and resided in Lenoir County where he was by occupation a merchant or clerk prior to enlisting in Jones County at age 24, June 26, 1862, for the war. Failed to report for duty and was dropped from the company rolls on or about January 1, 1863.

GILLETT, FRANCIS COLQUITT, Private

Born in Onslow County where he resided as a farm laborer or farmer prior to enlisting in Onslow County at age 26, July 17, 1862, for the war. Reported present or accounted for in November, 1862-April, 1864. Captured at Bermuda Hundred, Virginia, June 16, 1864. Confined at Point Lookout, Maryland, June 19,

1864. Transferred to Elmira, New York, July 25, 1864. Paroled at Elmira on October 11, 1864. Received at Venus Point, Savannah River, Georgia, November 15, 1864, for exchange. No further records.

GRAY, JOHN THOMAS, Private

Born in Lenoir County and resided in Onslow County where he was by occupation a fisherman or farm laborer prior to enlisting in Onslow County at age 22, July 15, 1862, for the war. Reported sick at home in Onslow County on December 14, 1862. Hospitalized at Wilmington on February 17, 1863, with continued fever. Furloughed on March 23, 1863. Reported sick in hospital at Wilmington on or about April 30, 1863. Reported absent without leave on May 1, 1863. Reported absent in hospital in July-August, 1863. Hospitalized at Wilmington on or about September 4, 1863, with intermittent fever. Reported in hospital at Goldsboro from October 1, 1863, through April 30, 1864. Captured at Sneads Ferry on June 21, 1864. Confined at Point Lookout, Maryland, July 1, 1864. Paroled at Point Lookout on November 1, 1864. Received at Venus Point, Savannah River, Georgia, November 15, 1864, for exchange. No further records. Survived the war. [May have served previously as Private in Company B, 24th Regiment N.C. Troops (14th Regiment N.C. Volunteers).]

HALL, JOHN P., Private

Born in Jones County on June 11, 1834. Resided in Jones County and was by occupation a farmer prior to enlisting in Jones County at age 28, July 17, 1862, for the war. Captured and paroled at Kinston on December 14, 1862. Returned to duty in January-February, 1863. Reported present or accounted for through October 31, 1863. Reported on detail as colonel's orderly in November, 1863-April, 1864. Rejoined the company on an unspecified date. Reported present in September-December, 1864. No further records. Survived the war.

HARE, SIMON, Private

Resided in Sampson County and enlisted in Duplin County at age 18, September 29, 1863, for the war. Reported present in November, 1863-April, 1864. Captured at Fort Harrison, Virginia, September 30, 1864. Confined at Point Lookout, Maryland, October 5, 1864. Paroled at Point Lookout on February 13, 1865. Received at Cox's Wharf, James River, Virginia, February 14-15, 1865, for exchange. No further records. Survived the war.

HARPER, WINDAL T., Corporal

Previously served as Private in Company D, 27th Regiment N.C. Troops. Enlisted in this company in Lenoir County on June 8, 1863, for the war. Mustered in as Private. Promoted to Corporal on July 1, 1863. Reported present through April 30, 1864. Hospitalized at Richmond, Virginia, August 23, 1864. Returned to duty prior to September 30, 1864, when he was captured at Fort Harrison, Virginia. Confined at Point Lookout, Maryland, October 5, 1864. Paroled at Point Lookout on March 17, 1865. Received at Boulware's Wharf, James River, Virginia, March 19, 1865, for exchange. No further records. Survived the war.

HARRISON, DURANT H., Private

Born in Jones County where he resided as a farmer prior to enlisting in Jones County at age 24, July 16, 1862, for the war. Failed to report for duty. Enlisted in Company A, 8th Battalion N.C. Partisan Rangers, January 24, 1863, while listed as a deserter from this company.

HEATH, AMOS, Private

Born in Jones County where he resided as a farmer prior to enlisting in Jones County at age 22, July 17, 1862, for the war. Reported present but sick in November-December, 1862. Reported sick in hospital at Wilmington on February 6, 1863, with typhoid fever. Reported sick in hospital at Columbia, South Carolina, in March-April, 1863. Returned to duty in May-June, 1863. Reported present through April 30, 1864, and in September-December, 1864. No further records. Survived the war.

HEATH, JESSE W., Private

Born in Jones County where he resided as a farmer prior to enlisting in Onslow County at age 29, April 29, 1862, for the war. Reported sick at home in Onslow County on November 15, 1862. Returned to duty in January-February, 1863. Reported absent on sick furlough on April 14, 1863. Returned to duty on May 14, 1863. Reported present or accounted for through April 30, 1864. Company records indicate that he was captured at Fort Harrison, Virginia, September 30, 1864; however, records of the Federal Provost Marshal do not substantiate that report. Was probably killed at Fort Harrison.

HEATH, SAMUEL L., Private

Born in Jones County where he resided as a farmer or laborer prior to enlisting in Jones County at age 24, July 1, 1862, for the war. Reported present but sick in November-December, 1862. Hospitalized at Wilmington on or about February 18, 1863, with rheumatism. Returned to duty on March 9, 1863. Reported present or accounted for through June 30, 1863. Deserted on August 15, 1863. Returned from desertion on October 29, 1863, and was placed under arrest. Returned to duty in January-April, 1864. Wounded in the breast at Petersburg, Virginia, on or about June 20, 1864. Hospitalized at Petersburg. Transferred to hospital at Richmond, Virginia, July 1, 1864. Died of wounds. Place and date of death not reported.

HERRING, JAMES, Private

Place and date of enlistment not reported (probably enlisted subsequent to December 31, 1864). Paroled at Greensboro on May 1, 1865.

HILL, JOHN BRYANT, Private

Resided in Lenoir County where he enlisted at age 17, October 1, 1864, for the war. Reported present through December 31, 1864. No further records. Survived the war. [North Carolina pension records indicate that he was "struck by two spent balls (that) went into flesh (and) knocked me down." Place and date of injury not reported.]

HILL, WILLIAM T., Private

Resided in Lenoir County where he enlisted at age 18, June 8, 1863, for the war. Reported present or accounted for through October 31, 1863. Died in hospital at Petersburg, Virginia, December 28-29, 1863, or February 6, 1864, of "dia[rrhoea] ch[ronica]" and/or "febris typhoides."

HOWARD, HARDY H., Private

Resided in Lenoir County where he enlisted at age 21, June 8, 1863, for the war. Reported present through April 30, 1864, and in September-December, 1864. No further records. Survived the war.

HOWARD, LEWIS J., Private

Resided in Lenoir County where he enlisted at age 17, May 1, 1864, for the war. Wounded in the leg at the Crater, near Petersburg, Virginia, July 30, 1864. Returned to duty on an unspecified date. Captured at Fort Harrison, Virginia, September 30, 1864. Confined at Point Lookout, Maryland, October 5, 1864. Paroled at Point Lookout on February 18, 1865. Received at Boulware's and Cox's Wharves, James River, Virginia, February 20-21, 1865, for exchange. Hospitalized at High Point on March 3, 1865, with intermittent fever. No further records.

HOWARD, SAMUEL, Private

Previously served as Private in Company A, 40th Regiment N.C. Troops (3rd Regiment N.C. Artillery). Transferred to this company in May-June, 1863. Died on or about August 10, 1863. Place and cause of death not reported.

HOWARD, SAMUEL S., Private

Resided in Lenoir County and enlisted in Duplin County at age 42, July 27, 1863, for the war. Reported present or accounted for in November, 1863-April, 1864. Wounded slightly in the side at Cold Harbor, Virginia, May 31-June 3, 1864. Apparently returned to duty on or about the same date. Hospitalized at Petersburg, Virginia, June 17, 1864, with a gunshot wound. Place and date wounded not reported (probably wounded near Petersburg on or about the same date). Returned to duty prior to November 1, 1864. Reported present in November-December, 1864. No further records. Survived the war.

HOWARD, STEPHEN J., Private

Resided in Lenoir County where he enlisted at age 18, August 8, 1863, for the war. Reported present or accounted for in August, 1863-April, 1864. Wounded slightly in the shoulder at the Crater, near Petersburg, Virginia, July 30, 1864. Reported absent sick in September-October, 1864. Reported present in November-December, 1864. Paroled at Goldsboro on May 5, 1865.

HUFFMAN, JACOB BRIGHT, Private

Born in Onslow County where he resided as a farmer prior to enlisting in Onslow County at age 42, April 29, 1862, for the war. Reported present in November-December, 1862. Hospitalized at Wilmington on or about February 18, 1863, with bronchitis. Returned to duty on March 9, 1863. Reported absent without leave through April 30, 1863. Hospitalized at Wilmington on July 23, 1863, with continued fever. Released from hospital on August 4, 1863. Failed to return to duty and was listed as a deserter on August 31, 1863. Enlisted as Private in Company A, 2nd Regiment N.C. Infantry (Union), November 11, 1863. Later served as Private in Company I, 1st Regiment N.C. Infantry (Union).

HUFFMAN, JOHN A., Private

Born in Onslow County where he resided as a "domestic" prior to enlisting in Onslow County at age 18, April 29, 1862, for the war. Reported present in November, 1862-April, 1864. Wounded in the left thigh at Fort Harrison, Virginia, September 30, 1864. Hospitalized at Richmond, Virginia. Furloughed for sixty days on November 10, 1864. No further records. Survived the war.

HUFFMAN, WILLIAM FRANKLIN, Private

Born in Onslow County on August 9, 1844. Resided in Onslow County and was by occupation a farmer prior to enlisting in Onslow County at age 17, March 1, 1862. Reported present or accounted

for in November, 1862-August, 1863. Reported absent without leave from October 28, 1863, through April 30, 1864. Survived the war. [May have served also as Private in Company A, 2nd Regiment N.C. Infantry (Union), and Company C, 1st Regiment N.C. Infantry (Union).]

HUGGINS, EDWARD G., 1st Sergeant

Born in Jones County where he resided as a farmer prior to enlisting in Jones County at age 23, April 28, 1862, for the war. Mustered in as 1st Sergeant. Reported present in November-December, 1862. Hospitalized at Wilmington on February 18, 1863, with scurvy. Returned to duty on March 9, 1863. Reported present or accounted for through April 30, 1864. Captured at Fort Harrison, Virginia, September 30, 1864. Confined at Point Lookout, Maryland, October 5, 1864. Released at Point Lookout on June 27, 1865, after taking the Oath of Allegiance.

HUGGINS, FURNIFOLD G., Private

Born in Jones County where he resided as a schoolteacher or farmer prior to enlisting in Jones County at age 27, April 28, 1862, for the war. Reported present in November-December, 1862. Hospitalized at Wilmington on February 17, 1863, with a sore leg. Returned to duty on April 3, 1863. Reported present or accounted for through August 31, 1863. Reported sick in hospital at Wilmington or at Summerville, South Carolina, from October 20 through December 31, 1863. Returned to duty in January-April, 1864. Wounded in the head at Cold Harbor, Virginia, May 31-June 3, 1864. Hospitalized at Richmond, Virginia, where he died on June 24, 1864, of "L.C. of head & brain."

HUGGINS, WILLIAM FRANCIS, Private

Born in Jones County where he resided as a farmer prior to enlisting in Jones County at age 28, July 1, 1862, for the war. Reported present or accounted for in November, 1862-April, 1864. Reported absent without leave in September-October, 1864. Returned to duty in November-December, 1864. No further records. Survived the war. [North Carolina pension records indicate that he was wounded in the left foot at Fort Harrison, Virginia, September 30, 1864.]

HUMPHREY, LEWIS, Private

Born in Onslow County where he resided as a mail carrier and/or farmer prior to enlisting in Onslow County at age 32, April 28, 1862, for the war. Reported present or accounted for in November, 1862-April, 1864. Discharged at Petersburg, Virginia, September 9, 1864, by reason of disability.

JARMAN, JAMES, Private

Previously enlisted as Private in Company A, 35th Regiment N.C. Troops. Enlisted in this company in Onslow County on July 15, 1862, for the war. Reported present in November-December, 1862. Reported sick in hospital at Wilmington from February 16, 1863, through April 30, 1864. Returned to duty prior to November 1, 1864. Reported present in November-December, 1864. No further records.

JARMAN, LEMUEL M., Private

Resided in Onslow County and was by occupation a farmer prior to enlisting in Onslow County at age 28, April 29, 1862, for the war. Failed to report for duty. Enlisted in Company A, 35th Regiment N.C. Troops, May 2, 1862. Served with that unit throughout the war. [See special note at the end of the history of Company K, 61st Regiment N.C. Troops (page 749).]

JENKINS, AMOS, Private

Born in Edgecombe County and resided in Jones County where he was by occupation a farmer or cooper prior to enlisting in Craven County at age 38, February 13, 1862. Reported under arrest at Kinston in November-December, 1862. Returned to duty in January-February, 1863. Reported present through April 30, 1864. Hospitalized at Richmond, Virginia, October 12, 1864. Furloughed for sixty days on December 15, 1864. No further records. Survived the war.

JENKINS, JAMES, Private

Born in Edgecombe County and resided in Jones County where he was by occupation a farmer prior to enlisting in Craven County at age 50, February 13, 1862. Reported present or accounted for in November, 1862-April, 1864. Reported sick in hospital at Richmond, Virginia, in September-October, 1864. Returned to duty in November-December, 1864. No further records.

JONES, ZACHARIAH, Private

Born in Lenoir County where he resided as a farmer prior to enlisting in Jones County at age 21, July 1, 1862, for the war. Reported present or accounted for in November, 1862-June, 1863. Deserted on July 1, 1863.

KELLUM, ELIJAH, Private

Born in Jones County where he resided as a teamster or farmer prior to enlisting in Jones County at age 25, July 16, 1862, for the war. Reported present in November-December, 1862. Reported sick in hospital at Wilmington in January-April, 1863. Discharged from service at Wilmington on or about May 14, 1863, by reason of "morbi varii." Enlisted as Private in Company F, 2nd Regiment N.C. Infantry (Union), December 1, 1863. Was subsequently captured by Confederate forces and hanged for desertion.

KING, JESSE, Private

Resided in Jones County and enlisted in New Hanover County at age 19, January 20, 1863, for the war. Reported sick in hospital at Charleston, South Carolina, in January-February, 1863. Died at Columbia, South Carolina, April 11, April 21, or May 9, 1863, of disease.

KOONCE, EDWARD B., Private

Born in Onslow County where he resided as a student prior to enlisting in Jones County at age 17, April 29, 1862, for the war. Mustered in as Sergeant. Reported present but sick in November-December, 1862. Hospitalized at Wilmington on or about February 17, 1863, with pneumonia. Returned to duty prior to March 1, 1863. Reported present or accounted for through December 31, 1863. Reduced to ranks "for disorderly conduct" on February 6, 1864. Hospitalized at Richmond, Virginia, April 22, 1864, with scabies and calculus. Returned to duty on April 29, 1864. No further records.

KOONCE, GABRIEL F., Private

Born in Jones County where he resided as a farmer prior to enlisting in Jones County at age 26, April 28, 1862, for the war. Died in hospital at Wilson on December 29, 1862, or January 1, 1863, of "ty[phoid] fever."

KOONCE, ISAAC, Private

Born in Jones County where he resided as a farmer prior to enlisting in Jones County at age 27, July 1, 1862, for the war. Reported

present in November, 1862-June, 1863. Deserted on August 15, 1863. Returned from desertion on October 29, 1863, and was placed under arrest. Returned to duty in January-April, 1864. Captured at Globe Tavern, Virginia, August 19, 1864. Confined at Point Lookout, Maryland, August 24, 1864. Paroled at Point Lookout on March 14, 1865. Received at Boulware's Wharf, James River, Virginia, March 16, 1865, for exchange. No further records.

KOONCE, WILLIAM, Private

Born in Jones County where he resided as a farmer or carpenter prior to enlisting in Jones County at age 32, July 1, 1862, for the war. Reported sick at home from November 7 through December 31, 1862. Hospitalized at Wilmington on or about February 18, 1863, with rheumatism. Returned to duty on March 20, 1863. Reported present or accounted for through April 30, 1864. Reported absent sick in September-October, 1864. Reported absent wounded in November-December, 1864. Place and date wounded not reported. No further records. Survived the war.

LITTLETON, COLQUITT, _____

North Carolina pension records indicate that he served in this company.

LOFTIN, ELI N., Private

Born in Jones County and resided in Lenoir County where he was by occupation a farmer prior to enlisting in Jones County at age 34, June 30, 1862, for the war. Reported present or accounted for in November, 1862-June, 1863. Killed at Fort Wagner, Charleston Harbor, South Carolina, July 29, 1863.

LOFTIN, SAMUEL, Private

Born in Lenoir County where he resided as a farmer prior to enlisting in Jones County at age 20, June 26, 1862, for the war. Mustered in as Sergeant. Reported absent without leave on September 4, 1862. Reduced to ranks prior to January 1, 1863. Returned to duty in January-February, 1863. Reported present in March, 1863-April, 1864, and September-December, 1864. No further records.

MASHBURN, GEORGE R., Private

Born on August 27, 1843. Enlisted in Onslow County at age 18, April 29, 1862, for the war. Failed to report for duty. Later served as Private in Company A, 35th Regiment N.C. Troops. [Records of this company indicate that he enlisted in the 55th Regiment N.C. Troops; however, records of that unit do not indicate that he served therein. Contrary to 9:367 of this series, the correct spelling of his surname was probably Mashburn rather than Marshburn. See special note at the end of the history of Company K, 61st Regiment N.C. Troops (page 749).]

MASHBURN, HASKELL H., Private

Born in Onslow County where he resided as a farmer prior to enlisting in Onslow County at age 34, April 28, 1862, for the war. Reported sick at home from November 15 through December 31, 1862. Hospitalized at Wilmington on February 13, 1863, with typhoid fever. Returned to duty on February 20, 1863. Hospitalized at Wilmington on or about April 30, 1863, with acute diarrhoea. Discharged from service on or about June 2, 1863, by reason of "marasmus."

MASHBURN, JAMES E., Private

Born in Onslow County where he resided as a farmer prior to enlisting in Onslow County at age 16, June 10, 1862, for the war.

Reported present in November, 1862-April, 1864. Wounded slightly in the shoulder at Cold Harbor, Virginia, May 31-June 3, 1864. Reported present in September-December, 1864. Wounded at Petersburg, Virginia, on an unspecified date. No further records. Survived the war.

MELTON, WILLIAM M., Private

Born in Onslow County where he resided as a farmer prior to enlisting in Onslow County at age 21, July 15, 1862, for the war. Reported sick at home from December 10 through December 31, 1862. Hospitalized at Wilmington on February 17, 1863, with parotitis. Returned to duty on March 4, 1863. Hospitalized at Wilmington prior to April 30, 1863. Reported absent on sick furlough in May-August, 1863. Returned to duty in September-October, 1863. Reported present through April 30, 1864. Reported absent without leave from August 30 through October 31, 1864. Reported absent on sick furlough in November-December, 1864. No further records. Survived the war.

MERCER, GEORGE F., Private

Born in Jones County where he resided as a farmer prior to enlisting in Jones County at age 22, April 24, 1862, for the war. Reported present or accounted for in November, 1862-April, 1864. Reported on detached duty with the 2nd Regiment Confederate Engineers in September-December, 1864. No further records. Survived the war. [North Carolina pension records indicate that he was wounded in the left leg (fracture) at High Bridge, Appomattox River, Virginia, April 7, 1865.]

MILLER, LEWIS, Private

Resided in Duplin County and enlisted at Sullivan's Island, Charleston Harbor, South Carolina, at age 22, October 31, 1863, for the war. Reported present through April 30, 1864. Died at Petersburg, Virginia, July 1, 1864, of disease.

MILLS, DANIEL J., Private

Previously served as Private in Company A, 35th Regiment N.C. Troops. Enlisted in this company in Onslow County at age 19, April 28, 1862, for the war. Mustered in as Corporal. Reported present but sick in November-December, 1862. Hospitalized at Wilmington on January 10, 1863, with ambustio. Later contracted diarrhoea. Returned to duty on March 9, 1863. Reduced to ranks on May 1, 1863. Reported present or accounted for through April 30, 1864, and in September-October, 1864. Hospitalized at Wilmington on December 30, 1864, with remittent fever. Returned to duty on January 5, 1865. No further records.

MORTON, LOGAN W., Private

Born in Onslow County where he resided as a farmer prior to enlisting in Craven County at age 19, February 12, 1862. Failed to report for duty and was reported absent without leave on July 1, 1862. Dropped from the company rolls on or about August 31, 1863.

NOBLE, JESSE B., Sergeant

Previously served as Corporal in Company E of this regiment. Transferred to this company on June 1, 1863. Mustered in as Corporal. Reported present or accounted for through April 30, 1864. Promoted to Sergeant on February 6, 1864. Wounded slightly in the ear at the Crater, near Petersburg, Virginia, July 30, 1864. Reported present in September-December, 1864. No further records.

NOBLE, MARTIN M., Private

Previously served as Private in Company E of this regiment. Transferred to this company on June 1, 1863. Reported present or accounted for in June, 1863-April, 1864, and September-December, 1864. No further records. Survived the war.

OLIVER, JOHN JOSEPH, Sergeant

Born in Jones County where he resided as a farmer prior to enlisting in Jones County at age 20, July 1, 1862, for the war. Mustered in as Private. Reported present but in confinement in November-December, 1862. Reason he was confined not reported. Returned to duty in January-February, 1863. Reported present through October 31, 1863. Promoted to Sergeant on July 1, 1863. Reported on detached service at camp near Petersburg, Virginia, from December 18, 1863, through April 30, 1864. Wounded in the arm, shoulder, and leg at Fort Harrison, Virginia, September 30, 1864. Leg amputated. Hospitalized at Richmond, Virginia, where he died on October 29, 1864, of wounds.

PHILLIPS, SPENCER H., Private

Born in Lenoir County and resided in Jones County where he was by occupation a farmer prior to enlisting in Jones County at age 21, April 29, 1862, for the war. Mustered in as Private. Reported present or accounted for in November, 1862-June, 1863. Promoted to Corporal in May-June, 1863. Promoted to Sergeant in July-August, 1863. Reported present or accounted for in July, 1863-April, 1864. Reduced to ranks on February 6, 1864. Reported present in September-December, 1864. No further records. Survived the war.

PITTMAN, HEZEKIAH, Private

Born in Onslow County where he resided as a farmer prior to enlisting in Onslow County at age 24, July 15, 1862, for the war. Failed to report for duty and was reported absent without leave. Discharged in February, 1863, by reason of disability. Later served as Private in Company F, 1st Regiment N.C. Infantry (Union).

POTTER, NATHAN W., Private

Resided in Lenoir County and was by occupation a farm laborer prior to enlisting in Brunswick County at age 43, October 4, 1862, for the war. Reported present but sick in November-December, 1862. Hospitalized at Wilmington on February 18, 1863, with diarrhoea. Returned to duty on March 11, 1863. Reported present or accounted for in May, 1863-April, 1864, and September-December, 1864. No further records. Survived the war.

RIGGS, JAMES B., Private

Born in Onslow County where he resided as a farmer prior to enlisting in Onslow County at age 22, July 15, 1862, for the war. Failed to report for duty and was reported absent without leave. Reported present but on detached duty in May-June, 1863. Deserted on or about July 1, 1863. Enlisted as Private in Company A, 2nd Regiment N.C. Infantry (Union), October 3, 1863. Later served as Private in Companies E and F, 1st Regiment N.C. Infantry (Union).

RIGGS, JOHN R., Private

Born in Onslow County where he resided as a farmer prior to enlisting in Onslow County at age 18, July 15, 1862, for the war. Failed to report for duty and was dropped from the company rolls on or about December 31, 1862. Reported for duty on an unspecified date. Reported present or accounted for in May-August, 1863.

Died on or about October 1, 1863, of disease. Place of death not reported.

RIGGS, JOSEPH E., Private

Born in Onslow County where he resided as a farmer prior to enlisting in Onslow County at age 24, July 15, 1862, for the war. Failed to report for duty. Reported present but sick in July-August, 1863. Reported absent on sick furlough in October, 1863. Reported absent without leave in November, 1863-April, 1864. Listed as a deserter on an unspecified date. Returned to duty on October 29, 1864. Reported present in November-December, 1864. No further records. Survived the war.

RIGGS, ROBERT S., Private

Enlisted in Onslow County on July 15, 1862, for the war. Failed to report for duty. Reported absent without leave in January-February, 1863. Dropped from the company rolls on or about May 1, 1863.

RIGGS, WILLIAM F., Private

Born in Onslow County where he resided as a farmer prior to enlisting in Onslow County at age 30, July 15, 1862, for the war. Failed to report for duty. Reported absent without leave in January-February, 1863. Reported for duty in March-April, 1863. Reported present or accounted for in May, 1863-April, 1864, and September-December, 1864. No further records.

SANDERS, WILLIAM, Private

Born in Jones County where he resided as a farmer prior to enlisting in Jones County at age 29, April 24, 1862, for the war. Reported present in November, 1862-April, 1864. Captured at Fort Harrison, Virginia, September 30, 1864. Confined at Point Lookout, Maryland, October 5, 1864. Paroled at Point Lookout on March 17, 1865. Received at Boulware's Wharf, James River, Virginia, March 19, 1865, for exchange. No further records. Survived the war.

SIMMONS, ELZA, Private

Born in Onslow County where he resided as an overseer or farmer prior to enlisting in Onslow County at age 30, April 16, 1862, for the war. Mustered in as Sergeant. Reported present or accounted for in November, 1862-June, 1863. Reduced to ranks on July 1, 1863. Reported present or accounted for in July, 1863-April, 1864. Hospitalized at Richmond, Virginia, June 26, 1864. Returned to duty on an unspecified date. Reported absent on detached service at Richmond in September-October, 1864. Reported absent on sick furlough in November-December, 1864. Hospitalized at Richmond on February 22, 1865, with chronic diarrhoea. Returned to duty on March 28, 1865. Hospitalized at Greensboro on an unspecified date. Paroled at Greensboro on an unspecified date (probably in May, 1865). [Roll of Honor indicates that he was wounded on an unspecified date.]

SIMMONS, GEORGE H., Private

Enlisted in Onslow County on April 29, 186[3], for the war. No further records. [May have served later as Private in Company G, 7th Regiment Alabama Cavalry.]

SMITH, IRA, Private

Previously served as Private in Company D, 27th Regiment N.C. Troops. Transferred to this company on or about June 9, 1863. Reported present or accounted for in July-December, 1863. Hospitalized (probably at Petersburg, Virginia) on March 7, 1864, with

acute pneumonia. Transferred to another hospital on March 17, 1864. Reported absent sick at Ivor Station, Virginia, April 22, 1864. Returned to duty on an unspecified date. Reported present in September-December, 1864. No further records. Survived the war. [Was about 22 years of age at time of enlistment.]

SMITH, JOHN W., Private

Previously served as Private in Capt. Allen Croom's Company, N.C. Local Defense Troops. Enlisted in this company in Lenoir County on March 1, 1864, for the war. Reported present in March-April and September-December, 1864. Wounded in the back at or near Bentonville on or about March 19-21, 1865. Hospitalized at Raleigh with "paralysis of left side." Died in hospital at Raleigh on March 25, 1865, of wounds.

SMITH, LEMMON, Private

Resided in Lenoir County where he enlisted at age 34, June 8, 1863, for the war. Reported present or accounted for in July-December, 1863. Hospitalized at Petersburg, Virginia, January 12, 1864, with icterus. Returned to duty on February 12, 1864. Reported present through April 30, 1864, and in September-December, 1864. No further records. Survived the war. [May have served previously as Private in Company E of this regiment.]

SMITH, THOMAS W., Private

Previously served as Private in Company E of this regiment. Transferred to this company on June 1, 1863. Reported present or accounted for in June, 1863-April, 1864, and September-December, 1864. No further records. Survived the war. [North Carolina pension records indicate that he received "three slight skin wounds" during the war.]

STANLY, FREDERICK, Corporal

Born in Jones County where he resided as a farmer prior to enlisting in Jones County at age 27, April 28, 1862, for the war. Mustered in as Corporal. Reported present in November, 1862-April, 1864. Wounded severely in the head and neck at or near Petersburg, Virginia, on or about June 16-19, 1864. Returned to duty on an unspecified date. Captured at Fort Harrison, Virginia, September 30, 1864. Confined at Point Lookout, Maryland, October 5, 1864. Paroled at Point Lookout on June 4, 1865, and transferred to Fort Monroe, Virginia. Died at Fort Monroe on July 2, 1865, of "chronic diarrhoea."

TAYLOR, JESSE, Private

Previously served as Private in Company A, 8th Battalion N.C. Partisan Rangers. Transferred to this company in May-June, 1863. Reported absent without leave on or about August 13, 1863. Rejoined the company on or about October 29, 1863, and was placed under arrest. Hospitalized (probably at Petersburg, Virginia) on February 26, 1864, with scabies. Returned to duty on March 3, 1864. Reported present through April 30, 1864. Wounded in the abdomen at or near Petersburg on or about June 16-19, 1864. Hospitalized at Richmond, Virginia, where he died on August 18, 1864, of wounds.

TAYLOR, JOHN G., Private

Born in Lenoir County and resided in Onslow County where he was by occupation a farmer prior to enlisting in Onslow County at age 32, July 7, 1862, for the war. Failed to report for duty. Enlisted in Company E, 63rd Regiment N.C. Troops (5th Regiment N.C. Cavalry), April 7, 1863, while absent without leave from this company.

TURNER, STEPHEN, _____

North Carolina pension records indicate that he served in this company.

WALLER, WRIGHT WILLIAM, Private

Served as Private in Company H, 55th Regiment N.C. Troops. Enlisted in this company without authorization on April 29, 1862, for the war. Failed to report for duty and was dropped from the company rolls on or about January 1, 1863.

WELLS, JOSEPH F., Private

Born in Onslow County where he resided as a farmer prior to enlisting in Onslow County at age 17, July 15, 1862, for the war. Reported absent without leave through June 30, 1863. Reported for duty in July-August, 1863. Reported present and on temporary duty as a Musician (Drummer) in September-October, 1863. Reported present in November, 1863-April, 1864. Wounded in the back, thigh, and left hip at Petersburg, Virginia, June 22, 1864. Hospitalized at Petersburg. Transferred to hospital at Richmond, Virginia, July 1, 1864. Furloughed for sixty days on July 30, 1864. Reported absent without leave on or about September 28, 1864. Returned to duty in November-December, 1864. No further records. Survived the war.

WEST, JOHN B., Private

Born in New Hanover County and resided in Craven County where he was by occupation a farmer prior to enlisting in Craven County at age 31, February 12, 1862. Mustered in as Corporal. Reported present but sick in November-December, 1862. Hospitalized at Wilmington on February 6, 1863, with typhoid fever. Returned to duty on February 20, 1863. Hospitalized at Wilmington on or about April 30, 1863, with acute rheumatism. Reduced to ranks on May 1, 1863. Returned to duty in July-August, 1863. Reported sick in hospital at Goldsboro on October 1, 1863. Returned to duty in January-April, 1864. Deserted on October 9, 1864.

WESTBROOKS, JESSE E., Private

Enlisted in Jones County at age 24, April 29, 1862, for the war. Failed to report for duty. Enlisted in Company A, 43rd Regiment N.C. Troops, May 14, 1862. [See special note at the end of the history of Company K, 61st Regiment N.C. Troops (page 749).]

WHALEY, FELIX, Private

Born in Jones County and resided in Lenoir County where he was by occupation a farmer prior to enlisting in Jones County at age 17, July 1, 1862, for the war. Reported present or accounted for in November, 1862-June, 1863. Deserted on August 15, 1863. Returned from desertion on October 29, 1863, and was placed under arrest. Returned to duty in January-April, 1864. Reported present in September-December, 1864. No further records. Survived the war.

WHALEY, GEORGE, Private

Born in Jones County and resided in Lenoir County where he was by occupation a farmer prior to enlisting in Jones County at age 30, July 1, 1862, for the war. Captured and paroled at Kinston on December 14, 1862. Hospitalized at Wilmington on or about February 18, 1863, with debility. Returned to duty on April 1, 1863. Furloughed for thirty days on June 20, 1863. Reported absent without leave from August 20, 1863, through April 30, 1864. Reported sick in hospital at Raleigh in September-October, 1864. Reported absent on sick furlough in November-December, 1864. No further records. Survived the war.

WHALEY, JAMES, Private

Born in Jones County and resided in Lenoir County where he was by occupation a farmer prior to enlisting in Jones County at age 25, July 1, 1862, for the war. Reported present or accounted for in November, 1862-June, 1863. Deserted on August 15, 1863. Returned from desertion on October 29, 1863. Reported under arrest through December 31, 1863. Returned to duty in January-April, 1864. Captured at Fort Harrison, Virginia, September 30, 1864. Confined at Point Lookout, Maryland, October 5, 1864. Paroled at Point Lookout on March 17, 1865. Received at Boulware's Wharf, James River, Virginia, March 19, 1865, for exchange. No further records.

WHALEY, LOUIS J., Private

Resided in Duplin County and enlisted in Lenoir County at age 26, April 29, 1862, for the war. Failed to report for duty. Enlisted in Company A, 35th Regiment N.C. Troops, May 22, 1862. [See special note at the end of the history of Company K, 61st Regiment N.C. Troops (page 749). Contrary to 9:369 of this series, the correct spelling of his first name was probably Louis rather than Lewis.]

WHALEY, PHINEAS, Private

Born in Jones County and resided in Lenoir or Nash County where he was by occupation a farmer prior to enlisting in Jones County at age 23, July 1, 1862, for the war. Reported present or accounted for in November, 1862-April, 1864. Wounded in the right knee (fracture) and captured at Fort Harrison, Virginia, September 30, 1864. Right leg amputated. Hospitalized at Fort Monroe, Virginia. Transferred to Newport News, Virginia, on or about May 1, 1865. Released at Newport News on June 15, 1865, after taking the Oath of Allegiance.

WILLIAMS, DANIEL A., Private

Born in Onslow County where he resided as a farmer prior to enlisting in Jones County at age 22, April 29, 1862, for the war. Reported present but sick in November-December, 1862. Reported in hospital at Wilmington in February, 1863, with fever. Reported on detail in hospital at Wilmington in March-April, 1863. Rejoined the company in May-June, 1863. Reported absent in hospital in July-August, 1863. Returned to duty in September-October, 1863. Reported present through April 30, 1864. Wounded in the right arm at Fort Harrison, Virginia, September 30, 1864. Hospitalized at Richmond, Virginia. Furloughed prior to November 1, 1864. Reported absent on furlough through December 31, 1864. Hospitalized at High Point on February 9, 1865. No further records.

WILLIAMS, HENRY A., Private

Born in Onslow County where he resided as a farmer prior to enlisting in Jones County at age 17, April 29, 1862, for the war. Reported present but sick in November-December, 1862. Hospitalized at Wilmington on February 6, 1863, with intermittent fever. Returned to duty on February 20, 1863. Reported present through June 30, 1863. Hospitalized at Wilmington on July 10, 1863, with jaundice. Returned to duty on August 21, 1863. Reported present or accounted for through April 30, 1864. Reported present in September-December, 1864. Captured near Kinston on March 8, 1865. Confined at Point Lookout, Maryland, March 16, 1865. Released at Point Lookout on June 21, 1865, after taking the Oath of Allegiance.

WILLIAMS, ROBERT B., Private

Resided in Jones County where he enlisted on April 29, 1862, for the war. Reported present but sick in November-December, 1862.

Hospitalized at Wilmington on February 18, 1863, with dysentery. Returned to duty on June 11, 1863. Reported on detached service at brigade headquarters on June 30, 1863. Reported absent in hospital in July-August, 1863. Furloughed on October 9, 1863. Returned to duty in November-December, 1863. Reported present through April 30, 1864. Wounded slightly in the arm at Cold Harbor, Virginia, May 31-June 3, 1864. Reported absent without leave from June 9 through October 31, 1864. Returned to duty in November-December, 1864. No further records.

WOOD, GEORGE, Private
Born in Jones County where he resided as a farmer prior to enlisting in Jones County at age 33, April 28, 1862, for the war. Mustered in as Corporal. Reported present in November, 1862-June, 1863. Reduced to ranks on June 1, 1863. Reported present in July, 1863-April, 1864. Reported absent sick in September-October, 1864. Captured on the Darbytown Road, near Richmond, Virginia, October 7, 1864. Confined at Point Lookout, Maryland, October 29, 1864. Died at Point Lookout on February 23, 1865, of "chronic diarrhoea."

MISCELLANEOUS

AYCOCK, DAN, Private
Resided in Wilson County. Place and date of enlistment not reported (probably enlisted in late 1864 or early 1865). Paroled at Goldsboro on May 15, 1865. [May have served previously as 1st Sergeant in Capt. Allen Croom's Company, N.C. Local Defense Troops.]

BANKHEAD, _____
Place and date of enlistment not reported. Reported in hospital at Wilmington on September 28, 1863.

BARNES, WILLIAM H., Private
Reported on duty as a carpenter at Fort Caswell from December 9, 1862, until February 11, 1863.

DEWALT, JOHN, Private
Place and date of enlistment not reported. Deserted to the enemy on an unspecified date. Confined at Washington, D.C., October 6,

1864. Released on or about the same date after taking the Oath of Allegiance.

KERNEGAY, D., Private
Resided in Duplin County. Place and date of enlistment not reported. Paroled at Goldsboro on May 29, 1865.

KERNEGAY, WILLIAM, Private
Resided in Duplin County. Place and date of enlistment not reported. Paroled at Goldsboro on May 29, 1865.

KINNEY, J. M., Private
Resided in Duplin County. Place and date of enlistment not reported. Paroled at Goldsboro on May 19, 1865.

LANGLEY, ENOCH, _____
North Carolina pension records indicate that he served in this regiment.

McDONALD, J. W., _____
Place and date of enlistment not reported. Hospitalized at Wilmington on February 6, 1863, with debility. Returned to duty on March 9, 1863. Deserted to the enemy on or about December 7, 1864, and was sent to Baltimore, Maryland, after taking the Oath of Allegiance.

MARKHAM, J. G., Private
Place and date of enlistment not reported. Deserted to the enemy on an unspecified date. Received at Washington, D.C., April 22, 1865. Released on or about the same date after taking the Oath of Allegiance and was furnished transportation to Wilmington.

SHACKELFORD, JOHN F., _____
Born in Lowndes County, Alabama, August 1, 1846. Resided in New Hanover County and was educated at the Hillsborough Military Academy. Enlisted in this company on an unspecified date but was discharged (probably by reason of being underage). Later served in the C.S. Navy.

SIMS, JOHN, Private
Place and date of enlistment not reported. Deserted to the enemy on or about March 20, 1865. Confined at Washington, D.C., on or about April 6, 1865. Released on or about the same date after taking the Oath of Allegiance.

INDEX

This index contains citations for soldiers and principals of substitutes listed in the foregoing rosters and for a variety of entries, including all persons, places, regiments, and battalions, in the regimental histories. Alternate spellings of some surnames are cross-referenced. Because this index is composed primarily of personal names, a modified form of the letter-by-letter method of alphabetization has been employed whereby each entry is *initially* alphabetized to the point where the first comma appears; words that follow the first comma are alphabetized separately as a *secondary* category. That method permits the placement of entries such as "Franklin Rifles" at the end, rather than awkwardly in the middle, of the Franklin surname section. Depending on the information available concerning their initials and given names, soldiers with the same surname are divided into two individually alphabetized groups composed of (1) soldiers for whom initials (W. Franklin, W. M. Franklin) are available; (2) soldiers for whom a given name (William Franklin), a given name and an initial (William M. Franklin), or two or more given names (William Melvin Franklin) are available. Place names are placed *after* identical surnames; for example, an entry for Franklin, North Carolina, would follow an entry for all men with the surname Franklin. Regiments and battalions are listed numerically under entries in which the word "units" is preceded by the name of the state of origin.

A

Bailey, John W., 302
Bailey, Neal, 375
Bailey, Portland, 15
Bailey, Thomas, 291
Bailey, Thomas C., 291
Bailey, Thomas L., 345
Bailey, Tom, 397
Bailey, W. H., 112
Bailey, W. C., 532
Bailey, William M., 302
Bailey, Willis, 360
Baily. See Bailey, Baity
Bainbridge, Alabama, 491
Baird. See also Beard, Bird, Byrd
Baird, Abram, 312
Baird, Andrew Jackson, 312
Baird, Benjamin F., 276, 312
Baird, David Franklin, 312
Baird, Finley P., 376
Baird, Gilbert, 575
Baird, James B., 575, 583
Baird, James Samuel Tasewell, 582
Baird, John H., 312
Baird, Joseph C., 325
Baird, Julius, 325
Baird, William, 376
Baird, William Carson, 376
Baird, William J., 325
Baity, J. W., 100
Baker. See also Barker
Baker, Alpheus, 268-269, 498
Baker, Benjamin, 706
Baker, Bennett, 706
Baker, Elijah W., 292
Baker, Henry, 149, 693
Baker, Henry F., 124
Baker, J. A., 397
Baker, John, 124, 345, 706
Baker, John A., 173
Baker, John R., 210
Baker, Newton A., 292
Baker, Richard, 706
Baker, Robert F., 292
Baker, Thomas, Sr., 706
Baker, Thomas F., Jr., 706
Baker, W. B., 302
Baker, W. R., 583
Baker, Wash, 292
Baker, William, 277
Baker, William R., 325
Balch. See Bolch
Bald Hill, Georgia, 253-254,
   478-479
Balding, Alexander, 515
Balding, Fidelio A., 515, 552
Balding, Marques D. Lafayette,
   515, 552
Baley. See Bailey
Ball, Alford T., 360, 417, 463
Ball, John McDowell, 542, 575
Ball, Lewis, 203

Ballard, Alexander M., 739
Ballard, Robert Franklin, 739
Ballew. See also Ballow
Ballew, Francis M., 583
Ballinger, James I., 429, 524
Ballow. See also Ballew
Ballow, Thomas H., 302
Baltimore, Maryland, 62, 88
Baltimore and Ohio Railroad, 67,
   69
Baly. See Bailey
Bankhead, ___, 759
Banks, Benjamin F., 750
Banks, Henry T., Jr., 750
Banks, J. M., 552, 575
Banks, Jackson, 524
Banks, Joseph M., 360
Banks, Joseph Walter, 524
Banks, William B., 302
Banks' Ford (Rappahannock
   River), Virginia, 17-18
Banner, John W., 137
Banning, Richard B., 532
Banning, Rufus P., 531
Barber. See also Barger
Barber, Thomas M., 325
Barber, William F., 591
Barber, William Thomas, 112
Barbourville, Kentucky, 215
Barden. See Bardin, Basden,
   Darden
Bardin, Jesse J., 706
Barefoot, John R., 663
Barfield, James M., 693
Barfield, Jonas, 694
Barfield, Louis L., 694
Barfield, Walter, 694
Barger. See also Barber, Barker,
   Boger
Barger, Babel, 149
Barger, Caleb, 203
Barger, John, 203
Barger, Maxwell W., 149
Barger, Samuel, 325
Barham. See Parham
Baringer. See Barringer
Barker. See also Baker, Barger
Barker, Calvin, 405
Barker, Eli C., 405
Barker, James M., 405
Barker, M., 345
Barker, Montgomery, 406
Barker, Thomas C., 406
Barker, William Poindexter, 406
Barksdale, William, 7, 20-21
Barlow, Hamilton, 376
Barlow, Smith, 325
Barlow Knoll (near Gettysburg),
   Pennsylvania, 29
Barnes. See also Burns
Barnes, Abner J., 728

Barnes, Bennett, 750
Barnes, Henry, 203
Barnes, Jesse D., 705
Barnes, John G., 233-234, 387
Barnes, Milton, 149
Barnes, Murphy, 149
Barnes, Robert, 669
Barnes, Solomon, 388
Barnes, W. M., 173
Barnes, William H., 759
Barnett. See also Barrett, Bennet,
   Bennett, Burnett
Barnett, James, 694
Barnett, Simon, 292
Barnett, Thomas H., 325
Barney, Washington, 182
Barneycastle. See Barney
Barnhart, Adam, 182
Barnhart, Daniel C., 182
Barnhart, Richard, 182
Barnhill, Abram P., 728
Barnhill, John L., 669
Barns. See Barnes, Burns
Barnwell, James R., 532, 575
Barnwell, Riley M., 532
Barrett. See also Barnett
Barrett, Samuel G., 429, 524
Barrett, W. G., 524
Barrier, Daniel M., 182
Barrier, John Daniel, 161
Barrier, Samuel, 325
Barringer, E. F., 124
Barringer, John, 124
Barringer, John J., 161
Barrons. See Barnes
Barrow, Henry W., 32, 47-49, 68,
   86
Barrow, James E., 137
Barrow, James L., 136
Barry. See Berry
Bartlett, James H., 575, 583
Bartlett, John H., 583
Bartlett, Joseph Henry, 292, 397
Bartlett, Joshua, 575
Bartlett, Samuel D., 292, 326, 397
Bartlett, William R., 583
Bartley Island (French Broad
   River), North Carolina, 424
Barton, Seth Maxwell, 44-45
Barton's Station, Alabama, 262
Basden, Henry Gray, 750
Basden, James Daniel, 750
Basden, Jesse, 750
Basden, John H., 750
Basden, William, 750
Basden, William H., 750
Bass, William H., 524
Bass, William J., 182
Bass, William P., 182
Bast. See Best, Bost
Batchelder's Creek (near New

Brown, Thomas, 695
Brown, W. D., 137
Brown, W. E., 552
Brown, W. G., 516
Brown, Wiley B., 516
Brown, William L., 388
Brown, Williams, 111
Brown, Zachariah, 751
Brown's Ferry (Tennessee River, near Chattanooga), Tennessee, 225, 451-453
Brown's Gap, Virginia, 79
Brownsville, Mississippi, 442
Broyles. *See also* Broils
Broyles, H. S., 422
Brumley, William C., 162
Brush Mountain, Georgia, 245, 471
Bryan. *See also* Bryant
Bryan, John G., 388
Bryant. *See also* Bryan
Bryant, Bethel A., 292, 361
Bryant, Jacob, 717
Bryant, John H., 377
Bryant, John W., 361
Bryant, Peter, 377
Bryant, Robert M., 377
Bryant, Thomas, 303, 313
Bryant, Tilman L., 377
Bryant, William, 303
Bryant, William A., 437
Bryson, J. W., 584
Bryson, John W., 543
Buchanan, Abram J., 293, 326, 397
Buchanan, Adam, 293
Buchanan, Alexander, 293
Buchanan, Allen, 278
Buchanan, Arter T., 303
Buchanan, Eli, 326, 397
Buchanan, Ephraim, 326, 397
Buchanan, Greenbury Y., 293
Buchanan, James C., 303, 326
Buchanan, James G., 293
Buchanan, James S., 293, 326, 397
Buchanan, James W., 293
Buchanan, Jasper N., 293
Buchanan, Joel, 326, 398
Buchanan, John B., 326, 398
Buchanan, Joseph M., 293, 326, 398
Buchanan, Leonard M., 293, 327, 396
Buchanan, Marion, 293
Buchanan, Merritt, 327, 398
Buchanan, Molton, 293, 327, 398
Buchanan, Newton, 293, 327
Buchanan, Reuben, 398
Buchanan, Robert, 327, 398
Buchanan, Thomas, 293, 327
Buchanan, Waightsville, 293, 327, 398
Buchanan, William A., 293

Buchanan, William M., 327, 398
Buchanan, William W., 327, 398
Buchanan, Virginia, 59
Buck. *See also* Beck
Buck, Samuel D., 77-78
Buckingham, Philo B., 269
Buckhanan. *See* Buchanan
Buckhart, Andrew, 162
Bucklow, William, 101
Buckner. *See also* Butner
Buckner, Benjamin F., 524
Buckner, J. M., 524
Buckner, Manly, 679
Buckner, Nimrod, 327, 506
Buckner, Simon Bolivar, 218-221, 224, 226-228, 234, 445, 453-456, 458
Buckner, W. P., 524
Buckner, William J., 524
Budd, Green, 751
Buell, Don Carlos, 214-215, 425, 429
Buell, George Pearson, 265, 268, 496-497
Buffalo River (near Linden), Tennessee, 261, 486
Buford's Gap, Virginia, 58
Bullard, John, 670
Bullock, Robert, 728
Bumgarner, George W., 377, 407
Bumgarner, William P., 377
Bunch, John J., 728
Buncombe County, North Carolina, 504, 523, 541, 551, 581
Bunker Hill, West Virginia, 31, 67-68
Burchett, Joseph W., 670
Burchfield, John, 398
Burchfield, Nathan, 294
Burchfield, Thomas, 294
Burchfield, Wilson, 294
Burger. *See* Burgin
Burgess, O. A., 126
Burgess' Mill (near Petersburg), Virginia, 87, 635
Burgin, Charles, 346
Burgin, Merritt, 568
Burgis. *See* Burgess
Burgwyn, William Hyslop Sumner, 609, 622, 625, 633, 642, 645
Burke, William L., 680
Burke, J. Y., 138
Burke, L. C., 138
Burke, William L., 604, 606
Burkhead. *See* Birkhead
Burkheart. *See* Buckhart
Burleson. *See also* Berleson, Burleyson, Burlison
Burleson, Aaron, 398
Burleson, Jason C., 327, 398
Burleson, Merida, 398

Burleson, Reuben P., 294
Burleson, William P., 422
Burleson, Wilson M., 294
Burleyson. *See also* Berleson, Burleson, Burlison
Burleyson, Joseph, 204
Burlington, North Carolina, 271, 500
Burlison. *See also* Berleson, Burleson, Burleyson
Burlison, J. R., 525
Burlison, Joseph M., 278, 294
Burlison, William, Jr., 278
Burlison, William A., 278, 388
Burnett. *See also* Barnett, Bennet, Bennett
Burnett, Daniel, 303, 584
Burnett, David, 575
Burnett, Edward P., 533
Burnett, Oliver P., 533
Burnett, William, 561
Burnett, William H., 584
Burns. *See also* Barnes
Burns, Franklin A., 150
Burns, John, 717
Burnside, Ambrose Everett, 6-8, 13, 56, 225-226, 234, 451, 454, 460, 465, 595, 624
Burnsville, Mississippi, 492
Burnsville, North Carolina, 300, 358
Burrass, Bennett J., 706
Burrass, Isaac, 706
Burton, J. B., 717
Bush Hill, North Carolina, 646
Butler. *See also* Butner, Cutler
Butler, Allen, 294
Butler, Benjamin Franklin, 52-54, 615, 617-619, 623, 637-638
Butler, George Washington, 533
Butler, Sandy, 717
Butler, Wilson, 533
Butner. *See also* Buckner, Butler
Butner, J., 113
Butner, Elias J., 136
Butner, James C., 162
Butner, John S., 204
Buttler. *See* Butler, Butner
Butts, Elias, 695
Butts, Richard F., 695
Buzzard Roost, Georgia, 238-239, 465-466
Byers, William R., 361, 463
Byrd. *See also* Baird, Beard, Bird
Byrd, Carson, 294, 327
Byrd, Charles, 361, 398
Byrd, Charles, Jr., 377
Byrd, Cornelius R., 358
Byrd, Joseph Y., 361
Byrd, Lemuel, 695
Byrd, Mitchell T., 294

Halford, David, 545
Halifax, North Carolina, 270, 499
Halifield. *See also* Holifield, Hollifield, Holyfield
Halifield, Alfred, 332
Hall. *See also* Hale, Hoyl
Hall, Abraham C., 508
Hall, David S., 274, 305, 316
Hall, Elijah, 282
Hall, Elijah Y., 349
Hall, F. M., 140
Hall, George W., 526
Hall, James, 195, 657
Hall, James M., 185
Hall, John Anderson, 100
Hall, John G., 621
Hall, John P., 753
Hall, Joshua, 349
Hall, Marcus, 400
Hall, Moses, 443, 586
Hall, Moses W., 282
Hall, Richard F., 181
Hall, Thomas, 349
Hall, Tobias, 657
Hall, William F., 545
Hallifield. *See* Halifield, Holifield, Hollifield, Holyfield
Hallman. *See also* Holeman, Holman
Hallman, Ephraim, 152
Hallman, Joseph D., 175
Hallman, Laban, 175
Hallman, Robert L., 175
Halman. *See* Hallman
Haltom. *See also* Hatton, Helton
Haltom, Allison Clark, 671
Ham, Alfred, 410
Ham, Gideon, 410
Ham, Joshua, Sr., 410
Ham, Thomas, 410
Hamansar, Jackson, 332
Hamby, Leander S., 504, 577, 586
Hamilton, William H., 697
Hamilton, North Carolina, 613
Hamilton, Virginia, 64
Hamilton's Crossing, Virginia, 7-8
Hamlett, Oliver Merritt, 364, 418
Hamlin. *See* Haneline, Henline
"Hammershlag" (principal of substitute). *See* Joshua Smith
Hammit, James V., 534
Hammond. *See also* Hannon, Harman, Harmon
Hammond, G. C., 422
Hampton, George W., 545
Hampton, John E., 545
Hampton, Marcus F., 545
Hampton, Milton P., 301
Hampton, T. B., 235, 263-264, 493-494
Hampton, Thomas N., 305

Hampton, Wade, 643
Hampton, William A., 140
Hampton, William F., 364, 418, 545
Hampton Roads, Virginia, 615
Hamrick, George W., 129
Hamton, P. H. (principal of substitute). *See* Thomas Deware
Hancock, Winfield Scott, 624
Handy. *See also* Haney, Hardy
Handy, F. Marion, 349, 410
Haneline. *See also* Henline
Haneline, Jacob, 175
Hanes. *See also* Haynes, Hines
Hanes, Marion M., 364
Haney. *See also* Handy, Harvey
Haney, Bronson, 554
Haney, Daniel W., 349
Haney, J. Berry, 554
Haney, S. C., 305
Hanks. *See* Hawks
Hannon. *See also* Hammond, Harmon
Hannon, Samuel W., 563
Hanover Junction, Virginia, 54
Hansley. *See* Hensley, Hensly
Hanson. *See also* Henson, Hinson
Hanson, Roger Weightman, 435
Harbeson. *See* Harveson
Harbin. *See also* Harden
Harbin, Milton C., 422
Harbison's Crossroads, Tennessee, 219
Hardee. *See also* Hardy
Hardee, William Joseph, 224, 226, 234-235, 243, 245, 249-250, 252-258, 264-265, 267, 427, 429-430, 440, 453-454, 458, 460, 462, 468, 471, 474-475, 477-480, 482-483, 495-496, 642-645
Harden. *See also* Harbin, Harder, Harding, Hardy
Harden, Daniel, 586
Harder. *See also* Harden, Hardy
Harder, Austin W., 195
Harder, James M., 196
Harder, Joseph R., 196
Hardey. *See* Hardy
Harding. *See also* Harden, Hardy
Harding, Henry, 617, 629, 651, 662
Harding, William F., 665
Hardison. *See also* Harnason, Harrison, Harveson
Hardison, Clayton, 730
Hardison, Stanly Daniel, 730
Hardison, Thomas, 697
Hardy. *See also* Handy, Harden, Harder, Harding, Harvey
Hardy, Thomas, 165
Hardy, Washington Morris, 224, 234-235, 423, 439, 452-453, 481,

502, 505
Hare. *See also* Hair, Haren, Harp, Hart
Hare, James M., 129
Hare, Simon, 753
Hare farm (near Petersburg), Virginia, 624
Haremon. *See also* Harman, Harmon
Haremon, Crisp, 332
Haren. *See also* Hare, Herring
Haren, Archibald L., 508
Harison. *See* Harrison
Harkey. *See also* Harvey
Harkey, William A., 140
Harkey, William L., 104
Harkins, Thomas J., 545
Harman. *See also* Haremon, Harmon, Hartman
Harman, Drury Calvin, 311
Harman, G. L., 683
Harmand. *See* Harmon
Harmon. *See also* Hammond, Hannon, Haremon, Harman, Hartman
Harmon, Andrew, 140
Harmon, Andrew J., 316, 390
Harmon, David, 140
Harmon, Eli G., 316
Harmon, Ephraim Council, 316
Harmon, Goulder Carroll, 316
Harmon, John Wiley, 316
Harmon, Wiley A., 316
Harn. *See* Hearn
Harnason. *See also* Hardison, Harrison, Harveson
Harnason, Alfred A., 570
Harp. *See also* Hare, Hart
Harp, Calvin, 364, 419
Harper, Bright, 697
Harper, George Washington Finley, 214-219, 223-224, 231-233, 236-240, 242, 259-264, 269-272, 324, 374, 453-454, 458, 460, 462, 466-467, 485-487, 493-494, 499-500
Harper, Jesse, 697
Harper, Samuel T., 671
Harper, Windal T., 753
Harpers Ferry, West Virginia, 60, 67
Harrass. *See* Harris, Harriss
Harrel. *See also* Harrell, Harrill, Harrold, Herrill
Harrel, Claton C., 332
Harrell. *See also* Harrel, Harrill, Harrold, Herrill
Harrell, Elijah, 665
Harrell, Jackson, 708
Harrell, Thomas C., 296
Harrelson. *See* Harrison, Harveson

Hellard, Joe, 104
Hellard, Thomas, 104
Helm, Benjamin Hardin, 447-448
Helms, Pinkney A., 176
Helton. *See also* Haltom, Hilton
Helton, John N., 380
Hemphill, J. T., 508
Henderson, Andrew J., 570
Henderson, Canady, 518
Henderson, Ezekiel, 509
Henderson, James K., 518
Henderson, William H., 570
Henderson, William M., 563
Henderson County, North
    Carolina, 531
Hendricks, James, 333
Henkle, Cicero, 176
Henkle, P. C., 5
Henline. *See also* Haneline
Henline, Henry, 282
Henryville, Tennessee, 261,
    486-487
Hensdale, Martin V., 176
Hensley. *See also* Hensly, Hinsley
Hensley, Erwin H., 305
Hensley, Fulton, 504
Hensley, John, 364
Hensley, John A., 274, 282
Hensley, John E., 364
Hensley, John M., 350
Hensley, Samuel F., 305
Hensley, Thomas H., 526
Hensly. *See also* Hensley, Hinsley
Hensly, Henderson, 305
Henson. *See also* Hinson
Henson, Jordan, 317
Henson, Jourdon J., 317
Hern. *See* Hearn
Herndon, Harrison, 274
Heron. *See* Hearn
Herrill. *See* Harrel, Harrell, Harrill,
    Harrold
Herrill, Henry C., 296
Herring. *See also* Haren
Herring, Alexander, 719
Herring, Amos R., 657, 719
Herring, Enoch K., 698
Herring, James, 753
Herring, Owen F., 657
Herring, Robert S., 657
Herring, Stephen A., 698
Herr Ridge (near Gettysburg),
    Pennsylvania, 26
Hess. *See* Hass
Hester, James R., 99, 196
Hestilow, Eber, 534
Heth, Henry, 23, 26, 28, 88, 216,
    630
Hetherington. *See* Heatherington
Hethwood, M., 296
Hevner. *See* Havener, Havner,

Hefner
Hiatt. *See* Hyatt
Hickam, John J., 518
Hickam, Robert B., 518
Hicks, Andrew, 317
Hicks, Carroll, 317
Hicks, Harmon, 317
Hicks, James Woody Elcany, 518
Hicks, James Young, 350
Hicks, John, 333, 380
Hicks, Levi, 317
Hicks, Mathias, 317
Hicks, Patterson, 317
Hicks, Robert, 719
Hicks, W. W., 317
Hicksford, Virginia, 52, 617
Hickum. *See* Hickam
Higgins. *See also* Huggins
Higgins, Calvin, 744
Higgins, Carter H., 744
Higgins, Charles, 364
Higgins, Curtis, 364
Higgins, David C., 364
Higgins, Granville, 744
Higgins, H. C., 744
Higgins, Isaac C., 738
Higgins, James Erwin, 364
Higgins, John, 365
Higgins, Pleasant Clark, 744
Higgins, Thrower, 365
Highsmith, James B., 657
Highsmith, John James, 657
Hileman, Jacob, 296, 317, 333
Hileman, John, 296, 333
Hill, Allen L., 534
Hill, Ambrose Powell, 8, 23, 26,
    28, 31, 35, 55, 88, 93, 631
Hill, D. F., 586
Hill, Daniel Harvey, 265, 268, 270,
    446, 496-497, 499, 600, 641
Hill, David, 744
Hill, George W., 185
Hill, Henry Harmon, 665
Hill, Hilson G. D., 665
Hill, Jesse, 47-48, 54, 79, 83-88, 90
Hill, John, 698
Hill, John Bryant, 753
Hill, Levi, 365
Hill, Major L., 698
Hill, Meredith, 744
Hill, Pinkney, 698
Hill, Richard C., 698
Hill, William T., 753
Hilliard, Alfred, Jr., 391
Hilliard, Bartlett Young, 391
Hilliard, Henry Washington, 216
Hillsborough, North Carolina, 264,
    271, 495, 499
Hilman. *See* Hileman
Hilton. *See also* Helton
Hilton, John W., 411

Hindman, Thomas Carmichael,
    228, 239, 242, 247, 254, 456,
    466, 468, 472, 479
Hine, Eli, 350
Hines. *See also* Hanes, Haynes
Hines, _____, 653
Hines, Charles C., 672
Hines, Ira D., 698
Hines, James, 698
Hines, Joel, 698
Hines, Sherwood, 698
Hines, William F., 657
Hines, William H., 699
Hines, William S., 657
Hines' Mill (near Kinston), North
    Carolina, 595
Hinkle. *See* Henkle
Hinsdale. *See* Hensdale
Hinsley. *See also* Hensley, Hensly
Hinsley, James, 684
Hinson. *See also* Henson
Hinson, Henry, 104
Hinson, John D., 104
Hinson, Joseph, 296
Hinson, Joshua G., 699
Hipps, James A., 518
Hipps, Madison L., 546
Hipps, Marcus B., 380, 546
Hire, Salathiel, 140
Hix. *See* Hicks
Hobart, Harrison C., 265, 268,
    496-497
Hobbs, Caleb A., 333
Hobbs, H., 657
Hobbs, Julius C., 657
Hobbs, Wallace, 333
Hobbs, William H., 176
Hobson. *See also* Hopson
Hobson, Benoni, Jr., 296, 333
Hobson, Edwin L., 82
Hockings, Jesse D., 334
Hodgens. *See also* Hodges,
    Hudgins
Hodgens, J. H., 104
Hodgens, Jordan C., 105
Hodges. *See also* Hodgens
Hodges, Callaway, 391
Hodges, Edward, 317
Hodges, Gilbert W., 218, 257-258,
    282, 317, 461, 482-483
Hodges, Henry Thomas, 731
Hodges, Isaac Franklin E., 719
Hodges, James R., 731
Hodges, John, 317
Hodges, Larkin, 282, 317
Hodges, Riley, 317
Hodges, Seth V., 665
Hodges, William J., 391
Hodges, William M., 387
Hodgins. *See* Hodgens, Hudgins
Hoffman. *See also* Haffman,

Langford. *See* Lankford
Langley. *See also* Lasley
Langley, Enoch, 759
Langley, James, 709
Lanier. *See also* Lenoir
Lanier, David Anderson, 334
Lanier, Henry H., 727
Lanier, James C., 662, 668
Lanier, John R., 727
Lanier, Noah T., 732
Lanier, Sylvester, 665
Lanier, Thomas F., 673
Lanier, William B., 727
Lanier, William J., 732
Lankford, Martin V., 527
Lankford, Thomas N., 527
Lanning, Barzilla, 527
Lanning, Elliott R., 527
Lanning, George, 527
Lantz. *See also* Lance, Lentz
Lantz, Jacob, 153
Lapase, Bleese, 720
Larkins, William E., 720
Lash, Jacob A., 488
Lasley. *See also* Langley
Lasley, Edward F., 141
Laughter, Joseph C., 535
Laurance. *See also* Lawrence,
   Lorance, Lowrance
Laurance, James J., 319
La Vergne, Tennessee, 490
Law, Evander McIvor, 6-8, 11-12,
   650
Lawrence. *See also* Laurance,
   Lorance, Lowrance
Lawrence, Addison S., 141
Lawrence, John W., 366
Lawrenceburg, Tennessee, 260, 485
Laws, Bannester, 366
Laws, Joseph, 366
Laws, Meshack F., 401
Lawson, B. Floyd, 519
Lawson, Elijah L., 519
Lawson, G. W., 519
Lawton, Alexander Robert, 14
Layden, Francis, 673
Lay's Ferry (Oostanaula River,
   near Resaca), Georgia, 240, 467
Lazenby, R. W., 116
Leadbetter. *See* Ledbetter
Leadford. *See* Ledford
Leatherman, Lawson M., 154
Leatherman, Rufus P., 116
Lebanon Turnpike, Tennessee, 430
Ledbetter, J. G., 587
Ledbetter, James, 587
Ledbetter, John W., 535
Ledbetter, Shadrach L., 535, 564
Ledbetter, Sion B., 577
Ledbetter, T. E., 587
Ledbetter, Thomas B., 564

Ledford, Alexander H., 564
Ledford, Christopher C., 463, 527
Ledford, Curtis, 401
Ledford, Henry F., 413
Ledford, Isaac, 554
Ledford, James H., 401
Ledford, Jasper, 334, 401
Ledford, Jesse, 571
Ledford, Lawson H., 564
Ledford, Manson C., 527
Ledford, Peter, 366
Ledford, William, 297
Ledford, William B., 306
Ledlie, James Hewett, 624-625
Lee, Fitzhugh, 55, 95, 621
Lee, George, 166
Lee, George R., 720
Lee, Horace C., 600-601
Lee, James G., 732
Lee, Robert Edward, 3, 5-8, 10,
   17-18, 20-21, 23, 26, 28, 33-34,
   36-38, 41-42, 46, 52, 55-56, 68,
   79, 88, 91-96, 237, 259, 264, 271,
   465, 484, 495, 500, 595, 615, 619,
   621-623, 626, 631, 633-635, 646,
   648-650
Lee, Stephen Dill, 255-265, 270,
   480, 482-483, 485-487, 493-496
Lee, William R., 700
Lee and Gordon's Mills, Georgia,
   220, 446-447
Leesburg, Virginia, 63-64
Lee's Hill, Fredericksburg,
   Virginia, 20
Leetown, West Virginia, 68
Lefevers, John A., 381
Leffer, H., 154
Lefler, Robert Franklin, 182
Leggett, John L., 732
Leggett, Mortimer Dormer,
   253-254, 479
Leggett, Noah T., 732
Leggett, Warren, 673
Leigh. *See* Lee
Leighton, Alabama, 260, 485
Leinbach. *See* Lineback
Leitz, George, 48-49
Leming, Rufus, 510, 578
Lenard. *See* Leonard
Lengelt, E. A., 652
Lenier. *See* Lanier, Lenoir
Lenoir. *See also* Lanier
Lenoir, Walter Waightstill, 375
Lenoir County, North Carolina,
   601, 692
Lenoir's Station, Tennessee,
   219-220
Lentz. *See also* Lance, Lantz
Lentz, Henry G., 106
Lentz, John C., 203
Lentz, Rufus C., 106

Leonard, Daniel E., Jr., 154
Leonard, Eli, 154
Leonard, J. H., 116
Leonard, Jacob, 186
Leonard, James Monroe, 154
Leonard, Solomon, 116
Leonard, William P., 177
Leppard. *See* Lippard
Leslie, Thomas B., 100
Letchworth, Elias, 709
Letsinger, Thomas D., 510
Letterman, Joseph, 306
Letterman, M. P., 401
Leventhorpe, Collett, 630
Lewis, Daniel J., 319
Lewis, Francis, 720
Lewis, George, 351
Lewis, George Marvill, 536
Lewis, Holden M., 720
Lewis, J., 392
Lewis, J. T., 709
Lewis, Jacob, 306
Lewis, James, 367, 419, 720
Lewis, James J., 685
Lewis, James R., 536, 578
Lewis, John Manly, 623, 629, 685
Lewis, Joseph Horace, 244, 470
Lewis, Josiah, 527
Lewis, M. P., 106
Lewis, Oscar M., 273
Lewis, Rufus R., 658
Lewis, William, 413
Lewis, William Gaston, 44, 46-47,
   50-54, 57, 59-60, 63-67, 87-94,
   618
Lewis, William M., 685
Lewis, William T., 709
Lexington, Virginia, 57-59
Leyden, Austin, 222
Liberty, Virginia, 58
Lick Skillet, Georgia, 255, 479-480
Lienbach. *See* Lineback
Lierly. *See* Lyerly
Liggett. *See* Leggett
Lillard's Mill, Tennessee, 490-491
Lilley, Noah T., 732
Lilley, Perry, 732
Lilley, Robert Doak, 65
Lilley, Simon, 732
Lilley, William Henry, 732
Linch. *See* Lynch
Lincoln, Abraham, 6, 18, 64, 225,
   451
Lincoln County, North Carolina,
   171
Lindsay. *See also* Lindsey
Lindsay, John H., 334
Lindsay, Joseph Archibald, 334
Lindsay, Thomas, 554
Lindsay, William Reid, 334
Lindsey. *See also* Lindsay

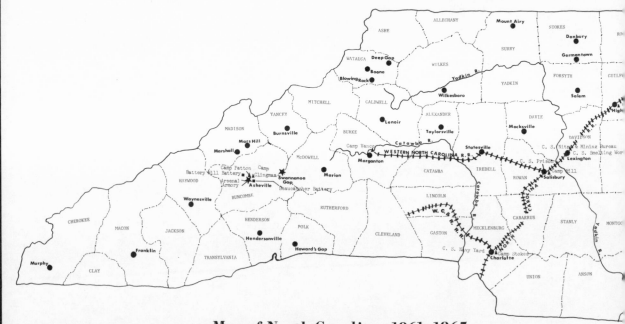

Map of North Carolina, 1861-1865

Drawn by James R. Vogt

This map locates the principal camps, forts,
towns, railroads, and engagements fought in
the State during the Civil War.

LEGEND

● – Towns
■ – Forts and batteries
▲ – Camps
✶ – Engagements
✕ – Railroads